The Poetical Works Of Robert Southey: Complete In One Volume...

Robert Southey

PRINTED BY, JULES DIDOT SENIOR,
PRINTER TO HIS MAJESTY, RUE DU PONT-DE-LODY, N° 6.

Robert Southey

THE
POETICAL WORKS

OF

ROBERT SOUTHEY.

COMPLETE IN ONE VOULME.

PARIS

PUBLISHED BY A. AND W. GALIGNANI,

N° 18, RUE VIVIENNE.

1829.

ADVERTISEMENT.

THE entire of Dr Southey's voluminous works—published in London in sixteen volumes—will be found in the present edition, in order to render which as complete as possible, it has been deemed advisable to insert, under a distinct head, the MINOR POEMS suppressed by the Author in the last collection given to the Public; to these have been added several original productions with which the Publishers have been favoured by a friend of Dr Southey. Under the same head are also given the Fugitive Pieces which have appeared in various miscellaneous publications since the last edition of his Works.

Contents.

CONTENTS.

Memoir of Robert Southey.

Mr Robert Southey is descended, both on his father's and on his mother's side, from respectable families in the county of Somerset; and at the time the subject of the present Memoir was born, on the 12th of August, 1774, his father was a linen-draper in the city of Bristol; but though a man of great integrity and habitual punctuality, he did not succeed in business. Young Southey was brought up by his mother's maiden aunt, Miss Tyler, a lady of superior mind, and great personal attractions, who lived in College-Green, Bristol. She first placed her nephew under the care of a Mr Foote, who kept a small school in Bristol; from whence, before he had reached his seventh year, he was removed to a seminary at Carston, near Bath. After continuing there about two years, he returned to his native place, where he was put under the care of a clergyman, who taught a select number of pupils for a few hours in the morning. At a very early age his friends discovered in him talents that deserved to be placed in a higher sphere than that in which his father had moved : they therefore designed him for the church. With a view to give him every advantage, Robert Southey, in the year 1787, was sent to Westminster School, having already attained, under his former instructors, such an acquaintance with the Latin and Greek languages as exempted him from the drudgery of the lower forms.

As in the infancy of nations, so in the infancy of individuals, a taste for poetry is the first fruit of cultivation. We speak of the taste for poetry as distinct from the mere sensual love of poetry, produced by the rise and fall of verse upon the ear, which can be enjoyed even by barbarians, because, as Ben Jonson says, « Nature is more strong in them than study.» According to the depth or slightness of the impression made by poetry in childhood, the tone and colour is generally given to the future life. If it be only superficial, the bustle and friction of the world soon wear it away; but in many cases the lapse of time only augments its strength, and it can never be defaced or obliterated. There are, however, few, or perhaps none, who in early youth do not exhibit, more or less, an affection for the « nurse of all knowledge and virtue.» Upon a mind like Southey's, tenderly sensible of the slightest touch of beauty, this impression could not fail to be deep, aided as it was by the individuals by whom he was surrounded, while he remained at Bristol. Miss Tyler took great pains with his education, and, by encouraging him in reading some of our best writers of the old school, converted his youthful and transitory passion into a fixed and enthusiastic attachment to the Muses. We have been told that, long before he left Carston, his productions in verse had received great applause in the little domestic circle to which his ambition was then confined; but that circle was soon enlarged, his ambition expanded in proportion, and by the time he had been only a few months at Westminster School, he became, as Randolph expresses it, an actual « graduate in the thread-bare mystery.» We have been shown two copies of verses said to have been written by Southey, when he was about fourteen years old. Deep thought, which is the offspring of experience, could not of course be expected in them; but they may be justly admired for the very easy and musical flow of the numbers : indeed they prove, from internal evidence, that the author must have been some time addicted to the « Sisters Nine » to have already attained such excellence in versification. His correct habits and amiable manners attracted the love of his companions, and by one of the Westminster masters he was treated as his own son. It happened, however, that, while he was at school there, a rebellion took place, in which he was compelled to join. Soon after, he was surprised by one of his friends, in tears; and upon being asked the reason, he replied, that his conscience had smote him for his ingratitude to his master, and that he could not refrain from weeping.

a

At the age of little more than eighteen, in November, 1792, Mr Southey entered at Baliol College, Oxford, where he was admired for his fine poetical countenance, his good nature, his singular phraseology, and the extreme punctuality with which he kept his appointments. His father was at this time in no condition, from losses in trade, to defray his expenses, which were paid, we believe, in a great measure, by his maternal uncle, the Rev. Mr Hill, and by his aunt Miss Tyler. At Easter, in 1794, Mr S. T. Coleridge, who had just abandoned Cambridge, came (with his fellow cantab Hucks) on a visit to Oxford. His fame for extraordinary powers of conversation, his stupendous talents, and eccentric manners had preceded him. He was hailed by the young Oxonians, and particularly by those who were admirers of all the extravagances of the French revolution, and of the sophisms contained in Godwin's Political Justice, which had just appeared, at that time forming a numerous and a separate class, mutually addressing each other by the title of *citizens*. A debating club upon questions of this nature was instituted: the members met in each others' rooms. Among them were the present Sir John Stoddart, then a student of Christ Church; the Rev. Dr T. F. Dibdin, then a commoner at St John's; the Rev. J. Horseman, now Rector of Heyden, then of Corpus; R. Allen, a servitor of University College, who died in Portugal, etc. etc. This jacobinical assembly created great alarm among the heads of the University, and the more so, as the exemplary moral conduct in other respects of the members prevented their taking any notice of them; so that none were or could be expelled, as has been said: two, however, were rusticated for a very trifling fault. Southey was soon induced to forsake his studies and the University, and to set off for Bristol, where he joined Coleridge, and they, in conjunction with Lovel, George Burnet, Robert Allen, and a few others, formed a plan to establish a Pantisocratical Society on the banks of the Ohio. Lovel was to supply the principal part of the funds for the infant colony, in which they were to have every thing in common, and, as the title they gave their Society implies, all were to have the same share in the administration of the public affairs of their new government. Mr Wordsworth had recently become known to Southey, through the medium of their common friend, Coleridge; but Wordsworth, though deeply infected with the same political enthusiasm, had good sense enough to decline joining in their scheme of emigration.

The excessive extravagance of their views at this distance of time, and when so many events have intervened, can scarcely be believed; and its existence is rendered certain almost solely to those who have had an opportunity of seeing the animated letters, and the high-wrought poems, of the several parties upon the subject.

When the three friends quitted college,[1] and repaired to Bristol, for the purpose of carrying their design into execution, Mr Southey's father was dead of a broken heart, in consequence of his embarrassments. It has been related by one who certainly had the best means of knowing him, that he was «a man who had been so accustomed to regulate his motions by the neighbouring clock, that the clock might at length (so punctual were his movements) have been regulated by him.» He was, also, extremely fond of the country and its employments.

Robert Southey had for some time been acquainted with a family of the name of Fricker, in which there were four daughters, three of whom were at that time of a marriageable age. To one of these young ladies (Edith) Mr Southey formed an attachment; and, as female society was necessary, in order to render the colony more extensive and flourishing, it was proposed that Mr Coleridge and Mr Lovel should marry the other two, and that the mother and her youngest daughter should accompany the expedition. In consequence of this arrangement, Lovel espoused Miss Fricker, an actress of Bristol, and Coleridge and Southey agreed to unite their destinies with her sisters, Sarah and Edith, the former being a mantua-maker, and the latter (who was very beautiful), with her youngest sister, keeping a little day-school near the church of St Mary, Radcliff. Lovel died shortly after, much regretted. Coleridge, Southey, and Burnet lived together, with great simplicity, in College-street,[2] Bristol, during 1795; but the characters of Coleridge and Southey were found to be uncongenial for so close an intimacy. Southey—all truth, sincerity, and obligingness; with (at that time) little belief in revealed religion, and affecting still less; with order in all his dealings, uprightness in all his conduct,—was but ill suited to the wild, unsettled enthusiasm, negligence, and wayward manners of Coleridge; yet admiration for his amazing powers of mind kept them together for some time. Burnet was endowed with a

---

[1] Southey's democratical opinions rendered him obnoxious to the heads of his college; but he was not expelled, as has been sometimes said by those who are no friends to his political principles.

[2] It was there he wrote his Joan of Arc, and, at the same time, a great part of Madoc, which, after more changes than any other of his poems, appeared in 1805. Coleridge gave public lectures on the French Revolution, and they jointly produced a drama, in blank verse, called the «Fall of Robespierre,» which was written and printed in the course of four days.

kind and good heart, but he wanted energy; he became a preacher at Yarmouth, and died in Marylebone workhouse, in 1811.

Mr Southey's friends, hoping that absence would wean him from his intended match, persuaded him to accompany his maternal uncle, Mr Hill (then chaplain to the English factory at Lisbon), to Portugal; but the lovers, fearing that during their separation means might be taken to prevent their union, determined on a secret marriage, which took place towards the close of the autumn of 1795, and only an hour or two ere Mr Southey's departure. They separated at the church door, and the lady continued to bear her maiden name, wearing the wedding-ring concealed and suspended from a riband round her neck!—

> How beautiful is life, in those young dreams
> Of joy and faith!—of love that never flies,
> Chain'd like the soul to truth!

When Mr Southey left England, the period fixed for his return was the end of six months; and almost to a day he kept the appointment he had made. After his arrival from Portugal, he for some years remained in Bristol and its vicinity, where he pursued his literary labours, or rather his literary pleasures, with great zeal and industry, and laid the foundation of several of the works he afterwards published. The year following that of Mr Southey's marriage, 1796, appeared his Joan of Arc: "that work," says Mr Hazlitt, "in which the love of liberty is exhaled like the breath of spring, mild, balmy, heaven-born; that is full of tears, and virgin-sighs, and yearnings of affection after truth and good, gushing warm and crimsoned from the heart." The letters which Southey wrote to his virgin-bride, during his residence in Portugal, were published in 1797, in one octavo volume, without any alterations or additions. On his return, he contributed to the Monthly Magazine, under the signatures of Joshua, T. Y., and S. In 1799-1800, conjointly with Mr C. Lamb, Mr (now Sir Humphrey) Davy, Mr Taylor, of Norwich, and Coleridge, he published two volumes of poems, called the Annual Anthology.[1]

Towards the close of the year 1801, Mr Southey was appointed Secretary to Mr Corry, then Chancellor of the Exchequer for Ireland, and this in a manner equally honourable to both parties.

Mr Corry, it appears, had an intimate friend, whom he often consulted, and whose advice he frequently took. This Gentleman, a Mr M.,[2] call-

ing on him one morning, the Chancellor informed him that, in consequence of his secretary's demise, he was in want of a person to occupy the post; "I have no doubt," said Mr Corry, "but that were I to make known the vacancy, I should have my family relations, even to my seventh cousins, tormenting me to let one of them fill it; but since it is my wish to have a young man possessed both of talents and integrity, you will oblige me by recommending such a one." Mr M. candidly acknowledged that he did not immediately recollect any person, whose character and principles he was sufficiently acquainted with as to recommend him; but added, that he would reflect upon the subject, and inform the Chancellor of the result on the following morning. A second meeting accordingly took place, when Mr M. observed, that he thought no person so well qualified for the post as a Mr Southey, with whom he had formed a strict intimacy, but of whose situation in life he was utterly ignorant; he would however write to him immediately, and inquire whether the proposed establishment would be acceptable to him. It is not to be imagined that our author deliberated for a long time on what answer he should make; he determined to be the bearer of it in person. Arrived in Dublin, he waited on Mr Corry, and having, in the course of the conversation which took place between them, convinced that gentleman of his capacity to fill the vacant post, he added, that he could by no means think of accepting it, were he required to make a sacrifice of his political principles, by actively supporting the Irish Administration. Mr Corry had, however, by this time conceived so high an idea of his talents, and was so delighted with his ingenuous eloquence, that without *making any terms*, to use the political phraseology of the day, he immediately appointed him his secretary, with a salary of 500l. sterling a year.

Mr Southey continued to hold this place until his principal quitted the office, when, we believe, Mr Southey's talents and services received a reward which they eminently merited. Before, however, he entered upon the duties of this office, he had published his poem of Thalaba, the Destroyer, which excited a strong sensation in the literary community. Much learned dust was raised in disputes respecting the pre-eminence of its merits and defects, but the decision of the public was unquestionably in its favour. Mr Southey never meant to confine himself within the rigid rules prescribed to the Greek epic, and therefore by them it was unfair to judge him. As Pope says, in his preface to Shakspeare, it would be like deciding that a man was guilty of a crime in one country when

---

[1] A third volume was published in 1802, but it was edited by Mr James Tobin, of Bristol, brother to the author of "The Honeymoon."

[2] The present Sir James Mackintosh.

he acted under the laws of another. The greater part of Thalaba was written in Portugal. In 1801 also appeared a volume of miscellaneous pieces, none of which can be read without some degree of praise; it was followed by a second volume of the same kind a few years afterwards.

In the autumn of 1802, or the spring of 1803, Mr Southey retired to Keswick, in Cumberland. His dwelling there, a very pretty house (by no means a cottage), was divided in the centre;—one half being occupied by Mr Southey, his wife, and children, and the other half by Mrs Coleridge (sister to Mrs Southey), her two daughters, and Mrs Lovel, the widowed sister of Mrs Southey, who also found a welcome asylum under the roof of her brother-in-law. Mr Southey's own family consists of one son, about ten years old, and three daughters, the eldest of whom is in her twenty-second year. He had the misfortune to lose a daughter about three years ago.

In the month of September, 1813, Mr Southey accepted the office of Poet Laureat on the death of Mr Pye.

The subjoined is a list of Mr Southey's works in verse and in prose:—Wat Tyler, a poem (afterwards suppressed).—Bion and Moschus, a Collection of Poems.—Joan of Arc, an epic Poem, 4to, 1796.—Poems, 8vo, 1797; 4th edition, 1809. — Letters written during a Short Residence in Spain and Portugal, 8vo, 1797. The Annual Anthology, a miscellaneous Collection of Poetry, of which he was the editor and principal writer, 2 vol. 12mo, 1799-1800.—Amadis de Gaul, from the Spanish Version, 4 vol. 12mo, 1803.—The Works of Chatterton, 3 vol. 8vo, 1803.—Thalaba the Destroyer, a metrical romance, 2 vol. 8vo, 1803; 2d edit. 1809.—Metrical Tales and other Poems, 8vo, 1804.—Madoc, a Poem, 4to, 1805; 2d edit. 1809.—Specimens of the late English Poets, with preliminary notes, 3 vol. 8vo, 1807.—Palmerin of England, translated from the Portuguese, 4 vol. 8vo, 1807.—Letters from England, 3 vol. 12mo, 1807; published under the fictitious name of Don Manuel Velasquez Espriella.—The Remains of Henry Kirke White, with an Account of his Life, 2 vol. 8vo, 1807; several editions. The Chronicle of Cid Rodrigo Diaz de Bivar, from the Spanish, 4to, 1808.—The History of Brazil, 4to, 1810.—The Curse of Kehama, a poem, 4to, 1810; 3d edit, 2 vol. 12mo, 1813.—Omniana, 2 vol. 12mo, 1812.—Life of Nelson, 2 vol. small 8vo, 1813.—Carmen Triumphale, 4to, 1814.—Odes to the Prince Regent, the Emperor of Russia, and the King of Prussia, 4to, 1814.—Roderick the last of the Goths, 4to, 1814; 2d edit. 2 vol. 12mo, 1815.—Minor Poems, 3 vols. 12mo, 1815.—The Poet's Pilgrimage to Waterloo, 12mo, 1816.—

The Lay of the Laureate, 12mo, 1816.—A Tale of Paraguay, 8vo, 1824.

Besides the above, Mr Southey has written the annexed works, the dates of which we are not able accurately to ascertain:—The Vision of Judgment, a Poem, 4to.—Life of Wesley.—Book of the Church.—History of the Peninsular War.—Vindiciæ Ecclesiæ Anglicanæ.

No Poet in our language, or perhaps in any other, has been more the object of contemporary criticism than Mr Southey. The frequency and boldness of his flights astonished those who could not follow him, and who, naturally enough, when they saw him enlarging the range of his art beyond their conception, solaced themselves with an opinion of his having deviated from its rules. If Poetry has any fundamental rules but those which best exhibit the feelings of the human heart, we confess that we are strangers to them. It is in proportion to his knowledge of these, and to his power of developing and delineating their action and effects, that the world in general bestow their tribute of approbation upon the Poet. Whether he lays his scene in heaven or earth, his business is with human sympathies, exalted perhaps by the grandeur of the objects which excite them, or called into existence by the circumstances which he creates, but still in their nature, progress, and ends, in every sense of the word, human. These must be the main springs and active principles of a poem; and, compared to them, the power of all other machinery is weak.

Mr Southey has shown the validity of this system in his principal poems, particularly in the metrical romance of «Thalaba,» and « the Curse of Kehama; » and whether he has drawn from the inexhaustible sources of his own imagination, and created both his personages and the world which he has given them to inhabit, or set before us pictures of elevated humanity, his principle has been true to nature, and his application of it consistent through even the wildest of his fables. Other Poets may have drawn down the gods and mingled them in their story; but he has planted a divinity in the very breasts of men, and, through the invisible agency of passion, moved them by springs at once more natural and more powerful than have ever been obtained from the inconsistent and treacherous aid of classical fictions. His march to fame has been regular, and he has made himself master of the ground over which he has passed. Indeed, it is by no means easy to mention a style of composition which Mr Southey has not attempted, and it would be still harder to point out one in which his talents might not be expected to raise him to distinguished eminence;—few authors of the present age have written so much as he has done, and still fewer have written so well. With a share of genius and fancy equalled but by few—an honesty surpassed by none—and an extent and variety of information, marked with the stamp of that industrious and almost forgotten accuracy which brings us back to the severer days of English study, he possesses a commanding knowledge of his mother-tongue, which, though the ostentation of power sometimes produces pedantry, and its attendant negligence betrays him too often into antiquated homeliness, is strongly, however, and we think, advantageously contrasted with the monotonous and unbending dignity which distinguishes the greater part of modern historians.

The severest critics on Mr Southey's poetical style allow him to be gifted with powers of fancy and of expression beyond almost any individual of his age; and that in the expression of all the tender and amiable and quiet affections, he has had but few rivals, either in past or in present times. But they accuse him of « a childish taste and an affected manner, which, if they cannot destroy genius, will infallibly deprive it of its glory.»

No Author in our days has been more the object of party criticism than Mr Southey. The charge of political inconsistency is continually reverted to and « thrown in his teeth » by his quondam friends and associates, who never can forgive what they call his apostacy from the « right cause.» In evidence of this, we give the following extracts from *Contemporary Portraits*, a well-known work by a well-known writer.

« Mr Southey,» says the critic, « as we formerly remember to have seen him, had a hectic flush upon his cheek, a roving fire in his eye, a falcon glance, a look at once aspiring and dejected—it was the look that had been impressed upon his face by the events that marked the outset of his life; it was the dawn of Liberty that still tinged his cheek, a smile betwixt hope and sadness that still played upon his quivering lip. Mr Southey's mind is essentially sanguine, even to overweeningness. It is prophetic of good; it cordially embraces it; it casts a longing, lingering look after it, even when it is gone for ever. He cannot bear to give up the thought of happiness, his confidence in his fellow-man, when all else despair. It is the very element, 'where he must live, or have no life at all.' While he supposed it possible that a better form of society could be introduced than any that had hitherto existed, while the light of the French Revolution beamed into his soul, (and long after, it was seen reflected on his brow, like the light of setting suns on the peak of some high mountain, or lonely range of clouds, floating in purer ether!) while he had this hope, this faith in man left, he cherished it with child-like simplicity, he clung to it with the fondness of a lover; he was an enthusiast, a fanatic, a leveller; he stuck at nothing that he thought would banish all pain and misery from the world; in his impatience of the smallest error or injustice, he would have sacrificed himself and the existing generation (a holocaust) to his devotion to the right cause. But when he once believed, after many staggering doubts and painful struggles, that this was no longer possible, when his chimeras and golden dreams of human perfectibility vanished from him, he turned suddenly round, and maintained that ' whatever is, is right.' Mr Southey has not fortitude of mind, has not patience to think that evil is inseparable from the nature of things. His irritable sense rejects the alternative altogether, as a weak stomach rejects the food that is distasteful to it. He hopes on against hope, he believes in all unbelief. He must either repose on actual or on imaginary good. He missed his way in Utopia, he has found it at Old Sarum.—

His generous ardour no cold medium knows:

his eagerness admits of no doubt or delay. He is ever in extremes, and ever in the wrong! The reason is, that not truth, but self-opinion, is the ruling principle of Mr Southey's mind. The charm of novelty, the applause of the multitude, the sanction of power, the venerableness of antiquity, pique, resentment, the spirit of contradiction have a good deal to do with his preferences. His inquiries are partial and hasty: his conclusions raw and unconcocted, and with a considerable infusion of whim and humour, and a monkish spleen. His opinions are like certain wines, warm and generous when new; but they will not keep, and soon turn flat or sour, for want of a stronger spirit of the understanding to give a body to them. He wooed Liberty as a youthful lover; but it was perhaps more as a mistress than a bride; and he has since wedded with an elderly lady, called Legitimacy. We must say that ' we relish Mr Southey more in the Reformer' than in his lately acquired, but by no means natural or becoming character of poet-laureat and courtier. He may rest assured that a garland of wild flowers suits him better than the laureat-wreath: that his pastoral odes and popular inscriptions were far more adapted to his genius than his presentation-poems. He is nothing akin to birth-day suits and drawing-room fopperies. ' He is nothing, if not fantastical.' In his figure, in his movements, in his sentiments, he is sharp and angular, quaint and eccentric. Mr Southey is not of the court, courtly. Every thing of him and about him is from the people. He is not classical, he is not legitimate. He is not a man cast in the mould of other men's opinions: he is not shaped on any model: he bows to no authority, he yields only to his own wayward peculiarities. He is wild, irregular, singular, extreme. He is no formalist, not he! All is crude and chaotic, self-opinionated, vain. He wants proportion, keeping, system, standard rules. He is not *teres et rotundus*. Mr Southey walks with his chin erect through the streets of London, and with an umbrella sticking out under his arm in the finest weather. He has not sacrificed to the Graces, nor studied decorum. With him every thing is projecting, starting from its place, an episode, a digression, a poetic license. He does not move in any given orbit, but, like a falling star, shoots from his sphere. He is pragmatical, restless, unfixed, full of experiments, beginning every thing anew, wiser than his betters, judging for himself, dictating to others.

« Look at Mr Southey's larger poems, his Kehama, his Thalaba, his Madoc, his Roderick. Who will deny the spirit, the scope, the splendid imagery, the hurried and startling interest that pervades them? Who will say that they are not sustained on fictions wilder than his own Glendoveer, that they are not the daring creations of a mind curbed by no law, tamed by no fear, that they are not rather like the trances than the waking dreams of genius, that they are not the very paradoxes of poetry? All this is very well, very intelligible, and very harmless, if we regard the rank excrescences of Mr Southey's poetry, like the red and blue flowers in corn, as the unweeded growth of a luxuriant and wandering fancy; or if we allow the yeasty workings of an ardent spirit to ferment and boil over—the variety, the boldness, the lively stimulus given to the mind, may then atone for the violation of rules and the offences to bed-rid authority; but not if our poetic libertine sets up for a law-giver and judge, or an apprehender of vagrants in the regions either of taste or opinion. Our motley gentleman deserves the strait-waistcoat, if he is for setting others in the stocks of servility, or condemning them to the pillory for a new mode of rhyme or reason. Or if a composer of sacred Dramas on classic models, or a translator of an old Latin author (that will hardly bear translation), or a vamper-up of vapid cantos and odes set to music, were to turn pander to prescription and palliator of every dull, incorrigible abuse, it would not be much to be wondered at or even regretted. But in Mr Southey, it was a lamentable falling off. It is indeed to be deplored, it is a stain on genius, a blow to humanity, that the author of *Joan of Arc* should ever after turn to folly, or become the advocate of a rotten cause.

After giving up his heart to that subject, he ought not (whatever others might do) ever to have set his foot within the threshold of a court. He might be sure that he would not gain forgiveness or favour by it, nor obtain a single cordial smile from greatness. All that Mr Southey is or that he does best, is independent, spontaneous, free as the vital air he draws—when he affects the courtier or the sophist, he is obliged to put a constraint upon himself, to hold in his breath; he loses his genius, and offers a violence to his nature. His characteristic faults are the excess of a lively, unguarded temperament:—Oh! let them not degenerate into cold-blooded, heartless vices! If we speak or have spoken of Mr Southey with severity, it is with ' the malice of old friends,' for we count ourselves among his sincerest and heartiest well-wishers. But while he himself is anomalous, incalculable, eccentric, from youth to age (the Wat Tyler and the Vision of Judgment are the Alpha and Omega of his disjointed career) full of sallies of humour, of ebullitions of spleen, making jets-d'eau, cascades, fountains, and water-works of his idle opinions, he would shut up the wits of others in leaden cisterns, to stagnate and corrupt, or bury them under ground—

Far from the sun and summer gale!

He would suppress the freedom of wit and humour, of which he has set the example, and claim a privilege for playing antics. He would introduce a uniformity of intellectual weights and measures of irregular metres and settled opinions, and enforce it with a high hand. This has been judged hard by some, and brought down a severity of recrimination, perhaps disproportioned to the injury done. 'Because he is virtuous' (it has been asked), ' are there to be no more cakes and ale?' Because he is loyal, are we to take all our notions from the Quarterly Review? Because he is orthodox, are we to do nothing but read the Book of the Church? We declare we think his former poetical scepticism was not only more amiable, but had more of the spirit of religion in it, implying a more heartfelt trust in nature and providence, than his present bigotry. We are at the same time free to declare that we think his articles in the Quarterly Review, notwithstanding their virulence and the talent they display, have a tendency to qualify its most pernicious effects. They have redeeming traits in them. 'A little leaven leaveneth the whole lump,' and the spirit of humanity (thanks to Mr Southey) is not quite expelled from the Quarterly Review. At the corner of his pen, ' there hangs a vaporous drop profound' of independence and liberality, which falls upon its pages, and oozes out through the pores of the public mind. There is a fortunate difference between writers whose hearts are naturally callous to truth, and whose understandings are hermetically sealed against all impressions but those of self-interest, and a man like Mr Southey. Once a philanthropist and always a philanthropist. No man can entirely baulk his nature: it breaks out in spite of him. In all those questions, where the spirit of contradiction does not interfere, on which he is not sore from old bruises, or sick from the extravagance of youthful intoxication, as from a last night's debauch, our 'laureate' is still bold, free, candid, open to conviction, a reformist without knowing it.

∗ He does not advocate the slave trade, he does not arm Mr Malthus's revolting ratios with his authority, he does not strain hard to deluge Ireland with blood. On such points, where humanity has not become obnoxious, where liberty has not passed into a by-word, Mr Southey is still liberal and humane. The elasticity of his spirit is unbroken: the bow recoils to its old position. He still stands convicted of his early passion for inquiry and improvement. Perhaps the most pleasing and striking of all Mr Southey's poems are not his triumphant taunts hurled against oppression, are not his glowing effusions to Liberty, but those in which, with a wild melancholy, he seems conscious of his own infirmities of temper, and to feel a wish to correct, by thought and time, the precocity and sharpness of his disposition. May the quaint but affecting aspiration expressed in one of these be fulfilled, that as he mellows into maturer age, all such asperities may wear off, and he himself become

Like the high leaves on the holly tree!

∗ Mr Southey's prose-style can scarcely be too much praised. It is plain, clear, pointed, familiar, perfectly modern in its texture, but with a grave and sparkling admixture of archaisms in its ornaments and occasional phraseology. He is the best and most natural prose-writer of any poet of the day. The manner is perhaps superior to the matter, that is, in his Essays and Reviews. There is rather a want of originality, and even of impetus; but there is no want of playful or biting satire, of ingenuity, of casuistry, of learning, and of information. He is 'full of wise saws and modern (as well as ancient) instances.' Mr Southey may not always convince his opponents; but he seldom fails to stagger, never to gall them. In a word we may describe his style by saying, that it has not the body or thickness of port-wine, but is like clear sherry with kernels of old authors thrown into it. He also excels as an historian and prose-translator. His histories abound in information, and exhibit proofs of the most indefatigable patience and industry. By no uncommon process of the mind, Mr Southey seems willing to steady the extreme levity of his opinions and feelings by an appeal to facts. His translations of the Spanish and French romances are also executed con amore, and with the literary fidelity and care of a mere linguist. That of the Cid, in particular, is a master-piece. Not a word could be altered for the better, in the old scriptural style which it adopts in conformity to the original. It is no less interesting in itself, or as a record of high and chivalrous feelings and manners, than it is worthy of perusal as a literary curiosity. Mr Southey's conversation has a little resemblance to a common-place book; his habitual deportment to a piece of clock-work. He is not remarkable either as a reasoner or an observer: but he is quick, unaffected, replete with anecdote, various and retentive in his reading, and extremely happy in his play upon words, as most scholars are who give their minds this sportive turn. We have chiefly seen Mr Southey in society where few people appear to advantage, we mean in that of Mr Coleridge. He has not certainly the same range of speculation, nor the same flow of sounding words; but he makes up by the details of knowledge, and by a scrupulous correctness of statement, for what he wants in originality of thought, or impetuous declamation. The tones of Mr Coleridge's voice are eloquence: those of Mr Southey are meagre, shrill, and dry. Mr Coleridge's forte is conversation, and he is conscious of this: Mr Southey evidently considers writing as his strong-hold, and, if gravelled in an argument, or at a loss for an explanation, refers to something he has written on the subject, or brings out his port-folio, doubled down in dog-ears, in confirmation of some fact.

∗ He is scholastic and professional in his ideas. He sets more value on what he writes than on what he says: he is perhaps prouder of his library than of his own productions—themselves a library!—He is more simple in his manners than his friend Mr Coleridge; but at the same time less cordial or conciliating. He is less vain, or has less hope of pleasing, and therefore lays himself less out to please. There is an air of condescension in his civility. With a tall, loose figure, a peaked austerity of countenance, and no inclination to embonpoint, you would say he has something puritanical, sometimes ascetic in his appearance. He answers to Mandeville's description of Addison, 'a parson in a tie-wig.' He is not a boon companion, nor does he indulge in the pleasures of the table, nor in any other vice; nor are we aware that Mr Southey is chargeable with any human frailty but—want of charity!

Having fewer errors to plead guilty to, he is less lenient to those of others. He was born an age too late. Had he lived a century or two ago, he would have been a happy as well as blameless character. But the distraction of the time has unsettled him, and the multiplicity of his pretensions have jostled with each other. No man in our day (at least no man of genius) has led so uniformly and entirely the life of a scholar from boyhood to the present hour, devoting himself to learning with the enthusiasm of an early love, with the sincerity and constancy of a religious vow—and well would it have been for him if he had confined himself to this, and not undertaken to pull down or to patch up the State! However irregular in his opinions, Mr Southey is constant, unremitting, mechanical in his studies, and the performance of his duties. There is nothing Pindaric or Shandean here. In all the relations and charities of private life, he is correct, exemplary, generous, just. We never heard a single impropriety laid to his charge; and if he has many enemies, few men can boast more numerous or stauncher friends.

« The variety and piquancy of his writings form a striking contrast to the mode in which they are produced. He rises early, and writes or reads till near breakfast-time. He writes or reads after breakfast till dinner, after dinner till tea, and from tea till bed-time—

> And follows so the ever-running year,
> With profitable labour to his grave—

on Derwent's banks, beneath the foot of Skiddaw. Study serves him for business, exercise, recreation. He passes from verse to prose, from history to poetry, from reading to writing, by a stop-watch. He writes a fair hand, without blots, sitting upright in his chair, leaves off when he comes to the bottom of the page, and changes the subject for another, as opposite as the antipodes. His mind is after all rather the recipient and transmitter of knowledge, than the originator of it. He has hardly grasp of thought enough to arrive at any great leading truth. His passions do not amount to more than irritability. With some gall in his pen, and coldness in his manner, he has a great deal of kindness in his heart. Rash in his opinions, he is steady in his attachments—and is a man in many particulars admirable, in all respectable—his political inconsistency alone excepted! »

Such is the homage that even a political as well as a critical opponent of Robert Southey found himself constrained to pay to his exemplary and irreproachable private character — to his good and guileless heart :—

> Incoctum generoso pectus honesto.

The inveteracy with which Lord Byron satirised Mr Southey is a matter of equal regret and notoriety : we believe that the only answer Southey ever made to these criticisms, was in a letter addressed to the Editor of the *Courier* newspaper, which, with the provocatory remarks of his Lordship, we give here :— « Mr Southey, too, in his pious preface to a poem whose blasphemy is as harmless as the sedition of Wat Tyler, because it is equally absurd with that sincere production, calls upon the 'legislature to look to it,' as the toleration of such writings led to the French Revolution : not such writings as Wat Tyler, but as those of the 'Satanic School.' This is not true, and Mr Southey knows it to be not true. Every French writer of any freedom was persecuted ; Voltaire and Rousseau were exiles ; Marmontel and Diderot were sent to the Bastille ; and a perpetual war was waged with the whole class by the existing despotism. In the next place, the French Revolution was not occasioned by any writings whatsoever, but must have occurred had no such writings ever existed. It is the fashion to attribute every thing to the French Revolution, and the French Revolution to every thing but its real cause. That cause is obvious—the government exacted too much, and the people could neither give nor bear more. Without this, the Encyclopedists might have written their fingers off without the occurrence of a single alteration. And the English Revolution (the first, I mean)—what was it occasioned by? The Puritans were surely as pious and moral as Wesley or his biographer. Acts—acts on the part of government, and not writings against them, have caused the past convulsions, and are tending to the future. I look upon such as inevitable, though no revolutionist : I wish to see the English constitution restored, and not destroyed. Born an aristocrat, and naturally one by temper, with the greater part of my present property in the funds, what have I to gain by a revolution? Perhaps I have more to lose in every way than Mr Southey, with all his places and presents for panegyrics and abuse into the bargain. But that a revolution is inevitable, I repeat. The government may exult over the repression of petty tumults ; these are the receding waves repulsed and broken for a moment on the shore, while the great tide is still rolling on and gaining with every breaker. Mr Southey accuses us of attacking the religion of the country ; and is he abetting it by writing lives of Wesley? One mode of worship is merely destroyed by another. There never was, nor ever will be, a country without a religion. We shall be told of France again, but it was only Paris and a frantic party, which for a moment upheld their dogmatic nonsense of theophilanthropy. The Church of England, if overthrown, will be swept away by the sectarians, and not by the sceptics. People are too wise, too well informed, too certain of their own immense importance in the realms of space, ever to submit to the impiety of doubt. There may be a few such diffident spec-ulators, like water in the pale sunbeam of hu-man reason, but they are very few; and their opinions, without enthusiasm or appeal to the passions, can never gain proselytes—unless, in-deed, they are persecuted—that, to be sure, will increase any thing. Mr S., with a cowardly fero-city, exults over the anticipated 'death-bed re-pentance' of the objects of his dislike; and indulges himself in a pleasant 'Vision of Judg-ment,' in prose as well as verse, full of impious impudence. What Mr S.'s sensations or ours may be in the awful moment of leaving this state of existence, neither he nor we can pretend to decide. In common, I presume, with most men of any reflection, I have not waited for a ' death-bed' to repent of many of my actions, notwith-standing the ' diabolical pride' which this pitiful renegade in his rancour would impute to those who scorn him. Whether, upon the whole, the good or evil of my deeds may preponderate, it is not for me to ascertain; but, as my means and opportunities have been greater, I shall limit my present defence to an assertion (easily proved, if necessary), that I, 'in my degree,' have done more real good in any one given year, since I was twenty, than Mr Southey in the whole course of his shifting and turncoat existence. There are several actions to which I can look back with an honest pride, not to be damped by the calumnies of a hireling. There are others to which I recur with sorrow and repentance; but the only act of my life of which Mr Southey can have any real knowledge, as it was one which brought me in contact with a near connexion of his own, did no dishonour to that connexion, nor to me. I am not ignorant of Mr Southey's calumnies on a different occasion, knowing them to be such, which he scattered abroad on his return from Switzerland against me and others: they have done him no good in this world; and if his creed be the right one, they will do him less in the next. What his ' death-bed' may be, it is not my province to predicate: let him settle it with his Maker, as I must do with mine. There is something at once ludicrous and blasphemous in this arrogant scribbler of all work sitting down to deal damnation and destruction upon his fel-low-creatures, with Wat Tyler, the Apotheosis of George the Third, and the Elegy on Marten the regicide, all shuffled together in his writing-desk. One of his consolations appears to be a Latin

note from a work of a Mr Landor, the author of ' Gebir,' whose friendship for Robert Southey will, it seems, 'be an honour to him when the ephe-meral disputes and ephemeral reputations of the day are forgotten.' I for one neither envy him ' the friendship,' nor the glory in reversion which is to accrue from it, like Mr Thelluson's fortune, in the third and fourth generation. This friend-ship will probably be as memorable as his own epics, which (as I quoted to him ten or twelve years ago in 'English Bards') Porson said ' would be remembered when Homer and Virgil are for-gotten, and not till then.' For the present, I leave him. »

MR SOUTHEY'S REPLY

« Sir,

« HAVING seen in the newspapers a note relating to myself, extracted from a recent publi-cation of Lord Byron's,[1] I request permission to reply through the medium of your journal. I come at once to his Lordship's charge against me, blowing away the abuse with which it is frothed, and evaporating a strong acid in which it is sus-pended. The residuum then appears to be, that ' Mr Southey, on his return from Switzerland (in 1817), scattered abroad calumnies, knowing them to be such, against Lord Byron and others.' To this I reply with a direct and positive denial. If I had been told in that country that Lord Byron had turned Turk, or monk of La Trappe,—that he had furnished a haram, or endowed an hospi-tal, I might have thought the account, whichever it had been, possible, and repeated it according-ly; passing it, as it had been taken in the small change of conversation, for no more than what it was worth. In this manner I might have spoken of him, as of Baron Gerambe, the Green Man, the Indian Jugglers, or any other figurante of the time being. There was no reason for any parti-cular delicacy on my part in speaking of his Lordship; and, indeed, I should have thought any thing which might be reported of him, would have injured his character as little as the story which so greatly annoyed Lord Keeper Guildford, that he had ridden a rhinoceros. He may ride a rhinoceros: and though every body would stare, no one would wonder.

« But making no inquiry concerning him when I was abroad, because I felt no curiosity, I heard nothing, and had nothing to repeat. When I spoke of wonders to my friends and acquaintance on my return, it was of the flying-tree at Alpn-acht, and the eleven thousand virgins at Cologne —not of Lord Byron. I sought for no staler sub-

[1] The Two Foscari.

ject than St Ursula. Once, and only once, in connexion with Switzerland, I have alluded to his Lordship; and as the passage was curtailed in the press, I take this opportunity of restoring it. In the Quarterly Review, speaking incidentally of the Jungfrau, I said, 'It was the scene where Lord Byron's Manfred met the Devil and bullied him—though the Devil must have won his cause before any tribunal in this world or the next, if he had not pleaded more feebly for himself, than his advocate, in a cause of canonization, ever pleaded for him.' With regard to the 'others,' whom his Lordship accuses me of calumniating, I suppose he alludes to a party of his friends, whose names I found written in the Album at Mont Auvert, with an avowal of atheism annexed in Greek, and an indignant comment in the same language underneath it. Those names, with that avowal and the comment, I transcribed in my note-book, and spoke of the circumstance on my return. If I had published it, the gentleman in question would not have thought himself slandered, by having that recorded of him which he has so often recorded of himself. The many opprobrious appellations which Lord Byron has bestowed upon me, I leave as I find them, with the praises which he has bestowed upon himself.

> How easily is a noble spirit discern'd
> From harsh and sulphurous matter, that flies out
> In contumelies, makes a noise, and stinks!
>   B. JOHNSON.

But I am accustomed to such things; and so far from irritating me are the enemies who use such weapons, that, when I hear of their attacks, it is some satisfaction to think they have thus employed the malignity which must have been employed somewhere, and could not have been directed against any person whom it could probably molest or injure less. The viper, however venomous in purpose, is harmless in effect while it is biting at the file. It is seldom, indeed, that I waste a word or a thought upon those who are perpetually assailing me. But abhorring, as I do, the personalities which disgrace our current literature, and averse from controversy as I am, both by principle and inclination, I make no profession of non-resistance. When the offence and the offender are such as to call for the whip and the branding-iron, it has been both seen and felt that I can inflict them. Lord Byron's present exacerbation is evidently produced by an infliction of this kind—not by hear-say reports of my conversation four years ago, transmitted him from England. The cause may be found in certain remarks upon the Satanic School of poetry, contained in my preface to the Vision of Judgment.

« Well would it be for Lord Byron if he could look back upon any of his writings with as much satisfaction as I shall always do upon what is there said of that flagitious school. Many persons, and parents especially, have expressed their gratitude to me for having applied the branding-iron where it was so richly deserved. The Edinburgh Reviewer, indeed, with that honourable feeling by which his criticisms are so peculiarly distinguished, suppressing the remarks themselves, has imputed them wholly to envy on my part. I give him, in this instance, full credit for sincerity: I believe he was equally incapable of comprehending a worthier motive, or of inventing a worse; and as I have never condescended to expose, in any instance, his pitiful malevolence, I thank him for having in this strip it bare himself, and exhibited it in its bald, naked, and undisguised deformity. Lord Byron, like his encomiast, has not ventured to bring the matter of those animadversions into view. He conceals the fact, that they are directed against the authors of blasphemous and lascivious books,— against men who, not content with indulging their own vices, labour to make others the slaves of sensuality like themselves,—against public panders, who, mingling impiety with lewdness, seek at once to destroy the cement of social order, and to carry profanation and pollution into private families, and into the hearts of individuals.

« His Lordship has thought it not unbecoming in him to call me a scribbler of all work. Let the word scribbler pass; it is not an appellation which will stick, like that of the Satanic School. But if a scribbler, how am I one of all work? I will tell Lord Byron what I have not scribbled,—what kind of work I have not done. I have never published libels upon my friends and acquaintance, expressed my sorrow for those libels, and called them in during a mood of better mind,—and then re-issued them, when the Evil Spirit, which for a time has been cast out, had returned and taken possession, with seven others more wicked than himself. I have never abused the power, of which every author is in some degree possessed, to wound the character of a man, or the heart of a woman. I have never sent into the world a book to which I did not dare affix my name, or which I feared to claim in a Court of Justice, if it were pirated by a knavish bookseller. I have never manufactured furniture for the brothel. None of these things have I done; none of the foul work by which literature is perverted to the injury of mankind. My hands are clean; there is no 'damned spot' upon them—no taint, which 'all the perfumes of Arabia will not sweeten.' Of the work which I have done, it becomes me not here to speak, save only as relates to the Satanic School, and its Coryphæus, the author of Don Juan. I have held up that school to public detestation, as enemies to the religion, the institutions, and the domestic morals of the country. I have given them a designation to which their founder and leader answers. I have sent a stone from my sling, which has smitten their Goliah in the forehead. I have fastened his name upon the gibbet for reproach and ignominy as long as it shall endure. Take it down who can!—One word of advice to Lord Byron before I conclude. When he attacks me again, let it be in rhyme. For one who has so little command of himself, it will be a great advantage that his temper should be obliged to keep tune. And while he may still indulge in the same rankness and virulence of insult, the metre will, in some degree, seem to lessen its vulgarity.

"ROBERT SOUTHEY.

"Keswick, Jan. 5, 1822."

We shall now conclude our brief, and, we fear, very inadequate sketch, by introducing the following interesting particulars, the accuracy and authenticity of which may be fully relied on.

After Mr Southey had left college, he devoted himself principally to poetry. The facility and rapidity with which he composes is perhaps unequalled. Southey had burnt more verses between the age of twenty and thirty than any other poet of the present day has written during the course of his whole life. Another remarkable feature in his character is the pliability and versatility of his talents. His time is strictly economized, and every part of the day has its appropriate employment. It is very seldom that he has not several literary undertakings in hand at the same time; and as soon as the hour allotted to one of them has elapsed, he transfers his attention, at pleasure, to that which succeeds it, and without any of that difficulty which men of genius generally experience in escaping from "the domination of their glorious themes," and diverting their attention from the train of imagery which their own imagination has conjured up.

Other persons read, and forget:—what Mr Southey has read may be said to belong to him, and to constitute a part of himself. This may probably arise from his habit of making extracts from books during their perusal; and we may cite his example against the assertion of Gibbon, "that what is twice read, is better remembered than what is once written." We may also add that his neat and careful handwriting may have contributed something to the adoption and utility of his practice.

In large and mixed societies Mr Southey does not often assume the place to which his talents and acquirements entitle him: he is more often a listener than a talker. In this respect he differs from Wordsworth and Coleridge, who are remarkable for the nervous and overwhelming eloquence of their language. But the character of Mr Southey can only be fully estimated by those who are intimately acquainted with him, in the domestic circle,—in those winter evenings so beautifully sketched by Cowper; then how delightful it is to hear him!

It was this love of retirement, and distaste for the hurry and fever of public life, that induced Mr Southey to refuse the unsolicited offer of a seat in the House of Commons, to which he had been previously elected. A similar feeling induced him to fix his residence in a country in which alike the Poet finds inexhaustible food for his imagination, and the Philosopher for reflection—

He, on his own green banks, in solitude,
By his soft murmuring lake, wanders along;
And to his mountains, and his forests rude,
Chaunts in sweet melody his classic song;
He makes our northern wilds a paradise,
Since spirits all sublime inhabit there ;
For at his magic call what phantoms rise,
And in his voice what music floats the air !
So heavenly soothing and so softly wild,
The peasant deems it more than mortal lay;
The grey old hermit, and the rustic child,
With beating heart, and timid footsteps stray
To catch the notes the zephyr wafts away.[1]

But though Mr Southey lives at such a distance from the theatre of public affairs, yet few, very few persons in England have had such an influence over its tastes and opinions as he has. Opinions may differ as to the tendency of the Quarterly Review, but no one will question its efficacy; and to this the pen of Mr Southey has mainly contributed. For years his articles, on an infinite variety of subjects, have instructed and amused the British nation: and he has not only proved himself a Theologian, an Historian, a Politician, and a Poet, but he has also evinced himself a master in each of these different capacities.—There is no person who collects so much from reading with so little labour as Southey. His skill in picking out the wheat from the chaff, and in arranging and digesting what is valuable, is perfectly wonderful. While others are obliged to dig and wade through a book to select what is of any value, he, without any effort, and perhaps half asleep upon his sofa, tears out the heart of a book, of which he scarcely appears to skim the surface. Hence the wonderful compass of his knowledge upon all subjects.

[1] The above lines were written, and addressed to Mr Southey, some years ago, by an English lady, of considerable taste and talent, resident in France.

Mr Southey's library, though not extensive, is very curious, which may account in some degree for his antiquarian knowledge. His acquaintance with modern languages is extensive, but not accurate, as might be inferred from his manner of reading.

It has been made matter of accusation against our author, that his opinions on political subjects were formerly very different from what they are at present.[1] While we admit the truth of the statement, we cannot acknowledge the justice of the charge. Whether he was right formerly, and wrong now,—or whether the contrary is the case,—is a question in which we have no wish to interfere. But he has a right to claim from his adversaries, that they convict him of some motive, by which he was, and ought not to have been, influenced,—some dream of ambition, some avenue to aggrandisement. Until they can do this, they may regret, but they cannot blame his determination.[2]

[1] The progress of the French revolution, with the intoxicating and visionary hopes which attended its commencement, and the violent re-action produced on his own mind by the rapid and shifting succession of events, have been powerfully sketched by Mr Wordsworth, in the third and fourth books of the « Excursion,» and in them, also, we may trace the causes which produced the change in the political principles of his friend, Mr Southey.

[2] On this subject we cannot but refer to Mr Southey's spirited and eloquent letter to William Smith, Esq., M. P. for the city of Norwich.

Mr Southey's income proceeds almost entirely from the productions of his pen. He writes both for the Quarterly Review and the Foreign Quarterly, and receives a hundred pounds for every article in each. It is a fact, which our feelings will not allow us to suppress, that Mrs Coleridge, her daughter, and Mrs Lovel rely entirely upon him for support. His kindness towards them does him the highest honour, and can only be appreciated by those who know him.—His residence is on the banks of the Greta, and about a quarter of a mile from the beautiful and picturesque Derwentwater.[1] Here he resides nearly all the year, except during the Spring, when an annual attack of asthma frequently obliges him to suspend his literary labours, and sometimes to take refuge in Holland. Mr Southey and Mr Wordsworth have continued an uninterrupted friendship since they were young men; and, as their houses are within twelve miles of each other, the intercourse between the two families is constant.

As a friend and a neighbour universally beloved; accessible and courteous to the many strangers who are attracted to Keswick by the celebrity of his name; there exists not a man who, with all the greatness of genius, has fewer of its frailties than ROBERT SOUTHEY.

[1] Here he may often be seen in his small skiff, rowed by the fair hands of his two daughters.

THE

POETICAL WORKS

OF

ROBERT SOUTHEY.

Joan of Arc,

AN EPIC POEM.

Εις οιωνος αριστος αμυνεσθαι περι παρτης.
ΟΜΗΡΟΣ.

Ut homines, ita libros, in dies seipsis meliores fieri oportet.
ERASMUS.

TO EDITH SOUTHEY.

EDITH! I brought thee late a humble gift,
The songs of earlier youth; it was a wreath
With many an unripe blossom garlanded
And many a weed, yet mingled with some flowers
Which will not wither. Dearest! now I bring
A worthier offering; thou wilt prize it well,
For well thou know'st amid what painful cares
My solace was in this; and though to me
There is no music in the hollowness
Of common praise, yet well content am I
Now to look back upon my youth's green prime,
Nor idly, nor unprofitably past,
Imping in such adventurous essay
The wing, and strengthening it for steadier flight.

1797.

PREFACE.

THE history of JOAN OF ARC is as mysterious as it is remarkable. That she believed herself inspired, few will deny; that she was inspired, no one will venture to assert; and it is difficult to believe that she was herself imposed upon by Charles and Dunois. That she discovered the King when he disguised himself among the courtiers to deceive her, and that, as a proof of her mission, she demanded a sword from a tomb in the church of St Catharine, are facts in which all historians agree. If this had been done by collusion, the Maid must have known herself an impostor, and with that knowledge could not have performed the enterprise she undertook. Enthusiasm, and that of no common kind, was necessary, to enable a young maiden at once to assume the profession of arms, to lead her troops to battle, to fight among the foremost, and to subdue with an inferior force an enemy then believed invincible. It is not possible that one who felt herself the puppet of a party, could have performed these things. The artifices of a court could not have persuaded her that she discovered Charles in disguise; nor could they have prompted her to demand the sword which they might have hidden, without discovering the deceit. The Maid, then, was not knowingly an impostor; nor could she have been the instrument of the court; and to say that she believed herself inspired, will neither account for her singling out the King, or prophetically claiming the sword. After crowning Charles, she declared that her mission was accomplished, and demanded leave to retire. Enthusiasm would not have ceased here; and if they who imposed on her could persuade her still to go with their armies, they could still have continued her delusion.

This mysteriousness renders the story of JOAN OF ARC peculiarly fit for poetry. The aid of angels and devils is not necessary to raise her above mankind; she has no gods to lackey her, and inspire her with courage, and heal her wounds : the Maid of Orleans acts wholly from the workings of her own mind, from the deep feeling of inspiration. The palpable agency of superior powers would destroy the obscurity of her character, and sink her to the mere heroine of a fairy tale.

The alterations which I have made in the history are few and trifling. The death of Salisbury is placed later, and of the Talbots earlier than they occurred. As the battle of Patay is the concluding action of the Poem, I have given it all the previous solemnity of a settled engagement. Whatever appears miraculous, is asserted in history, and my authorities will be found in the notes.

It is the common fault of Epic Poems, that we feel little interest for the heroes they celebrate. The national vanity of a Greek or a Roman might have been gratified by the renown of Achilles or Æneas; but to engage the unprejudiced, there must be more of human feelings than is generally to be found in the character of a warrior. From this objection, the Odyssey alone may be excepted. Ulysses appears as the father and the husband, and the affections are enlisted on his side.

1

The judgment must applaud the well-digested plan and splendid execution of the Iliad, but the heart always bears testimony to the merit of the Odyssey : it is the poem of nature, and its personages inspire love rather than command admiration. The good herdsman Eumæus is worth a thousand heroes ! Homer is, indeed, the best of poets, for he is at once dignified and simple; but Pope has disguised him in fop-finery, and Cowper has stripped him naked.

There are few readers who do not prefer Turnus to Æneas; a fugitive, suspected of treason, who negligently left his wife, seduced Dido, deserted her, and then forcibly took Lavinia from her betrothed husband. What avails a man's piety to the gods, if in all his dealings with men he prove himself a villain? If we represent Deity as commanding a bad action, this is not exculpating the man, but criminating the God.

The ill chosen subjects of Lucan and Statius have prevented them from acquiring the popularity they would otherwise have merited; yet in detached parts, the former of these is perhaps unequalled, certainly unexcelled. I do not scruple to prefer Statius to Virgil; with inferior taste, he appears to me to possess a richer and more powerful imagination ; his images are strongly conceived, and clearly painted, and the force of his language, while it makes the reader feel, proves that the author felt himself.

The power of story is strikingly exemplified in the Italian heroic poets. They please universally, even in translations, when little but the story remains. In proportioning his characters, Tasso has erred; Godfrey is the hero of the poem, Rinaldo of the poet, and Tancred of the reader. Secondary characters should not be introduced, like Gyas and Cloanthus, merely to fill a procession; neither should they be so prominent as to throw the principal into shade.

The lawless magic of Ariosto, and the singular theme as well as the singular excellence of Milton, render it impossible to deduce any rules of epic poetry from these authors. So likewise with Spenser, the favourite of my childhood, from whose frequent perusal I have always found increased delight.

Against the machinery of Camoens, a heavier charge must be brought than that of profaneness or incongruity. His floating island is but a floating brothel, and no beauty can make atonement for licentiousness. From this accusation, none but a translator would attempt to justify him; but Camoens had the most able of translators. The Lusiad, though excellent in parts, is uninteresting as a whole : it is read with little emotion, and remembered with little pleasure. But it was composed in the anguish of disappointed hopes, in the fatigues of war, and in a country far from all he loved; and we should not forget, that as the Poet of Portugal was among the most unfortunate of men, so he should be ranked among the most respectable. Neither his own country or Spain has yet produced his equal : his heart was broken by calamity, but the spirit of integrity and independence never forsook Camoens.

I have endeavoured to avoid what appears to me the common fault of Epic poems, and to render the Maid of Orleans interesting. With this intent I have given her, not the passion of love, but the remembrance of subdued affection, a lingering of human feelings not inconsistent with the enthusiasm and holiness of her character.

The multitude of obscure Epic writers copy with the most gross servility their ancient models. If a tempest occurs, some envious spirit procures it from the god of the winds or the god of the sea : is there a town besieged? the eyes of the hero are opened, and he beholds the powers of Heaven assisting in the attack : an angel is at hand to heal his wounds, and the leader of the enemy in his last combat is seized with the sudden cowardice of Hector. Even Tasso is too often an imitator. But notwithstanding the censure of a satirist, the name of Tasso will still be ranked among the best heroic poets. Perhaps Boileau only condemned him for the sake of an antithesis; it is with such writers, as with those who affect point in their conversation, they will always sacrifice truth to the gratification of their vanity.

I have avoided what seems useless and wearying in other poems, and my readers will find no description of armour, no muster-rolls, no geographical catalogues, lion, tiger, bull, bear and boar similes, Phœbuses or Auroras. And where in battle I have particularised the death of an individual, it is not I hope like the common lists of killed and wounded.

In Millin's National Antiquities of France, I find that M. Laverdy was in 1791 occupied in collecting whatever has been written concerning the Maid of Orleans. I have anxiously expected his work, but it is probable, considering the tumults of the intervening period, that it has not been accomplished. Of the various productions to the memory of JOAN OF ARC, I have only collected a few titles, and, if report may be trusted, need not fear a heavier condemnation than to be deemed equally bad. A regular canon of St Euverte has written *une très mauvaise poème*, entitled the Modern Amazon. There is a prose tragedy called La Pucelle d'Orléans, variously attributed to Benserade, to Boyer, and to Menardière. The abbé Daubignac published a prose tragedy with the same title in 1642. There is one under the name of Jean Baruel of 1581, and another printed anonymously at Rouen 1606. Among the manuscripts of the queen of Sweden in the Vatican, is a dramatic piece in verse called Le Mystère du Siège d'Orléans. In these modern times, says Millin, all Paris has run to the theatre of Nicolet to see a pantomime entitled *Le fameux Siège de la Pucelle d'Orléans*. I may add, that, after the publication of this Poem, a pantomime upon the same subject was brought forward at Covent-Garden Theatre, in which the heroine, like Don Juan, was carried off by devils and precipitated alive into hell. I mention it, because the feelings of the audience revolted at such a catastrophe, and after a few nights an angel was introduced to rescue her.

But among the number of worthless poems upon this subject, there are two which are unfortunately notorious,—the Pucelles of Chapelain and Voltaire. I have had patience to peruse the first, and never have been guilty of looking into the second; it is well said by Herbert the poet,

> Make not thy sport abuses, for the fly
> That feeds on dung, is coloured thereby.

On the eighth of May, the anniversary of its deliverance, an annual fête is held at Orléans ; and monuments have been erected there and at Rouen to the memory of the Maid. Her family was ennobled by

Charles; but it should not be forgotten in the history of this monarch, that, in the hour of misfortune, he abandoned to her fate the woman who had saved his kingdom.

November, 1795.

BOOK I.

THERE was high feasting held at Vaucouleur,
For old Sir Robert had a noble guest,
The Bastard Orleans; [1] and the festive hours,
Cheer'd with the Trobador's sweet minstrelsy, [2]
Pass'd lightly at his hospitable board.
But not to share the hospitable board
And hear sweet minstrelsy, Dunois had sought
Sir Robert's hall; he came to rouse Lorraine,
And glean what force the wasting war had left
For one last effort. Little had the war
Left in Lorraine, but age, and youth unripe
For slaughter yet, and widows, and young maids
Of widow'd loves. And now with his high guest
The Lord of Vaucouleur sat communing
On what might profit France, and knew no hope,
Despairing of his country, when he heard
An old man and a maid awaited him
In the castle hall. He knew the old man well,
His vassal Claude, and at his bidding Claude
Approach'd, and after meet obeisance made,
Bespake Sir Robert.

                        « Good my Lord, I come,
With a strange tale; I pray you pardon me
If it should seem impertinent, and like
An old man's weakness. But, in truth, this Maid
Hath with such boding thoughts impress'd my heart,
I think I could not longer sleep in peace
Denying what she sought. [3] She saith that God
Bids her go drive the Englishmen from France!—
Her parents mock at her and call her crazed,
And father Regnier says she is possess'd;..
But I, who know that never thought of ill
Found entrance in her heart,.. for good my Lord,
From her first birth-day she hath been to me
As mine own child,.. and I am an old man,
And have seen many moon-struck in my time,
And some who were by evil spirits vex'd,..
I, Sirs, do think that there is more in this...
And who can tell if, in these perilous times,
It should please God,.. but hear the Maid yourselves,
For if, as I believe, this is of Heaven,
My silly speech doth wrong it.»

                        While he spake
Curious they mark'd the Damsel. She appear'd
Of eighteen years; [4] there was no bloom of youth
Upon her cheek, yet had the loveliest hues
Of health with lesser fascination fix'd
The gazer's eye; for wan the Maiden was,
Of saintly paleness, and there seem'd to dwell
In the strong beauties of her countenance
Something that was not earthly.

                        « I have heard
Of this your niece's malady,» replied

The Lord of Vaucouleur, « that she frequents
The loneliest haunts and deepest solitude,
Estranged from human kind and human cares
With loathing like to madness. It were best
To place her with some pious sisterhood,
Who, duly morn and eve for her soul's health
Soliciting Heaven, may likeliest remedy
The stricken mind, or frenzied or possess'd.»

So as Sir Robert ceased, the Maiden cried,
« I am not mad. Possess'd indeed I am!
The hand of GOD is strong upon my soul,
And I have wrestled vainly with the LORD,
And stubbornly I fear me. I can save
This country, Sir! I can deliver France!
Yea..I must save the country! GOD is in me..
I speak not, think not, feel not of myself.
HE knew and sanctified me ere my birth,
HE to the nations hath ordained me,
And whither HE shall send me, I must go,
And whatso HE commands, that I must speak,
And whatso is HIS will, that I must do;
And I must cast away all fear of man
Lest HE in wrath confound me.» [5]

                        At the first
With pity or with scorn Dunois had heard
The Maid inspired; but now he in his heart
Felt that misgiving which precedes belief
In what was disbelieved and scoff'd at late
As folly. « Damsel!» said the Chief, « methinks
It would be wisely done to doubt this call,
Haply of some ill spirit prompting thee
To self-destruction.»

                        « Doubt!» the Maid exclaim'd,
« It were as easy when I gaze around
On all this fair variety of things,
Green fields and tufted woods, and the blue depth
Of heaven, and yonder glorious sun, to doubt
Creating wisdom! when in the evening gale
I breathe the mingled odours of the spring,
And hear the wild wood melody, and hear
The populous air vocal with insect life,
To doubt GOD's goodness! there are feelings, Chief,
That may not lie; and I have oftentimes
Felt in the midnight silence of my soul
The call of GOD.»

                        They listen'd to the Maid,
And they almost believed. Then spake Dunois,
« Wilt thou go with me, Maiden, to the King,
And there announce thy mission?» Thus he said,
For thoughts of politic craftiness arose
Within him, and his unconfirmed faith
Determined to prompt action. She replied,
« Therefore I sought the Lord of Vaucouleur,
That with such credence as prevents delay,
He to the King might send me. Now beseech you,
Speed our departure.»

                        Then Dunois address'd
Sir Robert: « Fare thee well, my friend and host!
It were ill done to linger here when Heaven
Hath sent such strange assistance. Let what force
Lorraine can yield to Chinon follow us;
And with the tidings of this holy Maid,
Rais'd up by GOD, fill thou the country; soon
The country shall awake as from the sleep
Of death. Now, Maid! depart we at thy will.»

« God's blessing go with thee!» exclaim'd old Claude;
« Good Angels guard my girl!» and as he spake
The tears stream'd fast adown his aged cheeks.
« And if I do not live to see thee more,
As sure I think I shall not, yet sometimes
Remember thine old Uncle.   I have loved thee
Even from thy childhood, JOAN! and I shall lose
The comfort of mine age in losing thee.
But God be with thee, Child!»
                              Nor was the Maid,
Though all subdued of soul, untroubled now
In that sad parting;—but she calm'd herself,
Painfully keeping down her heart, and said,
« Comfort thyself, my Uncle, with the thought
Of what I am, and for what enterprise
Chosen from among the people.   Oh be sure
I shall remember thee, in whom I found
A parent's love, when parents were unkind!
And when the ominous broodings of my soul
Were scoff'd and made a mock of by all else,
Thou for thy love didst hear me and believe.
Shall I forget these things?» ... By this Dunois
Had arm'd, the steeds stood ready at the gate;
But then she fell upon the old man's neck
And cried, « Pray for me! . . I shall need thy prayers!
Pray for me that I fail not in my hour!»
Thereat awhile, as if some awful thought
Had overpower'd her, on his neck she hung;
Then rising with flush'd cheek and kindling eye,
« Farewell!» quoth she, « and live in hope! anon
Thou shalt hear tidings to rejoice thy heart,
Tidings of joy for all, but most for thee!
Be this thy comfort!»   The old man received
Her last embrace, and weeping like a child
Scarcely through tears could see them on their steeds
Spring up and go their way.
                         So on they went,
And now along the mountain's winding path
Upward they journey'd slow, and now they paused
And gazed where o'er the plain the stately towers
Of Vaucouleur arose, in distance seen,
Dark and distinct; below the castled height,
Through fair and fertile pastures, the deep Meuse
Roll'd glittering on.   Domremi's cottages
Gleam'd in the sun hard by, white cottages,
That in the evening traveller's weary mind
Had waken'd thoughts of comfort and of home,
Till his heart ached for rest.   But on one spot,
One little spot, the Virgin's eye was fix'd,
Her native Arc; embower'd the hamlet lay
Upon the forest edge, whose ancient woods,
With all their infinite varieties,
Now form'd a mass of shade.   The distant plain
Rose on the horizon rich with pleasant groves,
And vineyards in the greenest hue of spring,
And streams now hidden on their winding way,
Now issuing forth in light.
                        The Maiden gazed
Till all grew dim upon her dizzy eye.
« O what a blessed world were this!» she cried,
But that the great and honourable men
Have seized the earth, and of the heritage
Which God, the Sire of all, to all had given,
Disherited their brethren! happy those
Who in the after days shall live when Time
Hath spoken, and the multitude of years

Taught wisdom to mankind![6] Unhappy France!
Fiercer than evening wolves thy bitter foes
Rush o'er the land and desolate and kill;[7]
Long has the widow's and the orphan's groan
Accused Heaven's justice;—but the hour is come;
God hath inclined his ear, hath heard the voice
Of mourning, and his anger is gone forth.»
Then said the Son of Orleans, « Holy Maid!
Fain would I know, if blameless I may seek
Such knowledge, how the heavenly call was heard
First in thy waken'd soul; nor deem in me
Aught idly curious, if of thy past days
I ask the detail.   In the hour of age,
If haply I survive to see this realm
By thee deliver'd, dear will be the thought
That I have seen the delegated Maid,
And heard from her the wonderous ways of Heaven.»

« A simple tale,» the mission'd Maid replied,
« Yet may it well employ the journeying hour,
And pleasant is the memory of the past.

« Seest thou, Sir Chief, where yonder forest skirts
The Meuse, that in its winding mazes shows
As on the farther bank the distant towers
Of Vaucouleur? there in the hamlet Arc
My father's dwelling stands; a lowly hut,
Yet nought of needful comfort did it lack,
For in Lorraine there lived no kinder Lord
Than old Sir Robert, and my father Jaques
In flocks and herds was rich.   A toiling man
Intent on worldly gains, one in whose heart
Affection had no root.   I never knew
A parent's love; for harsh my mother was,
And deem'd the cares which infancy demands
Irksome, and ill-repaid.   Severe they were,
And would have made me fear them, but my soul
Possess'd the germ of steady fortitude,
And stubbornly I bore unkind rebuke
And wrathful chatisement.   Yet was the voice
That spake in tones of tenderness most sweet
To my young heart; how have I felt it leap
With transport, when mine Uncle Claude approach'd!
For he would place me on his knee, and tell
The wonderous tales that childhood loves to hear,
Listening with eager eyes and open lips
Devoutly in attention.   Good old man!
Oh if I ever pour'd a prayer to Heaven
Unhallow'd by the grateful thought of him,
Methinks the righteous winds would scatter it!
He was a parent to me, and his home
Was mine, when in advancing years I found
No peace, no comfort in my father's house.
With him I pass'd the pleasant evening hours,
By day I drove my father's flock afield,[8]
And this was happiness.
                     Amid these wilds
Often to summer pasture have I driven
The flock; and well I know these mountain wilds,
And every bosom'd vale, and valley stream
Is dear to memory.   I have laid me down
Beside yon valley stream, that up the ascent
Scarce sends the sound of waters now, and watch'd
The Beck roll glittering to the noon-tide sun,
And listen'd to its ceaseless murmuring,
Till all was hush'd and tranquil in my soul,

Fill'd with a strange and undefined delight
That pass'd across the mind like summer clouds
Over the lake at eve, their fleeting hues
The traveller cannot trace with memory's eye,
Yet he remembers well how fair they were,
How lovely.
         Here in solitude and peace
My soul was nurst, amid the loveliest scenes
Of unpolluted nature.   Sweet it was
As the white mists of morning roll'd away·
To see the mountain's wooded heights appear
Dark in the early dawn, and mark its slope
With gorse-flowers glowing, as the rising sun
On the golden ripeness pour'd a deepening light.
Pleasant at noon beside the vocal brook
To lie me down, and watch the floating clouds,
And shape to Fancy's wild similitudes
Their ever-varying forms; and oh how sweet!
To drive my flock at evening to the fold,
And hasten to our little hut, and hear
The voice of kindness bid me welcome home.
Amid the village playmates of my youth
Was one whom riper years approved a friend.
A gentle maid was my poor Madelon,
I loved her as a sister, and long time
Her undivided tenderness possess'd,
Till that a better and a holier tie
Gave her one nearer friend; and then my heart
Partook her happiness, for never lived
A happier pair than Arnaud and his wife.

« Lorraine was call'd to arms, and with her youth
Went Arnaud to the war.   The morn was fair,
Bright shone the sun, the birds sung cheerfully,
And all the fields look'd lovely in the spring;
But to Domremi wretched was that day,
For there was lamentation, and the voice
Of anguish, and the deeper agony
That spake not.   Never will my heart forget
The feelings that shot through me, when the horn
Gave its last call, and through the castle-gate
The banner moved, and from the clinging arms
Which hung on them, as for a last embrace
Sons, brethren, husbands went.
            More frequent now
Sought I the converse of poor Madelon,
For now she needed friendship's soothing voice.
All the long summer did she live in hope
Of tidings from the war; and as at eve
She with her mother by the cottage door
Sat in the sunshine, if a traveller
Appear'd at distance coming o'er the brow,
Her eye was on him, and it might be seen
By the flush'd cheek what thoughts were in her heart,
And by the deadly paleness which ensued
How her heart died within her.   So the days
And weeks and months pass'd on, and when the leaves
Fell in the autumn, a most painful hope
That reason own'd not, that with expectation
Did never cheer her as she rose at morn,
Still linger'd in her heart, and still at night
Made disappointment dreadful.   Winter came
But Arnaud never from the war return'd,
He far away had perish'd; and when late
The tidings of his certain death arrived,
Sore with long anguish underneath that blow

She sunk.   Then would she sit and think all day
Upon the past, and talk of happiness
That never would return, as though she found
Best solace in the thoughts which minister'd
To sorrow: and she loved to see the sun
Go down, because another day was gone,
And then she might retire to solitude
And wakeful recollections, or perchance
To sleep more wearying far than wakefulness,
Dreams of his safety and return, and starts
Of agony; so neither night nor day
Could she find rest, but pin'd and pin'd away.

« DEATH! to the happy thou art terrible,
But how the wretched love to think of thee!
O thou true comforter, the friend of all
Who have no friend beside! 9 By the sick bed
Of Madelon I sate, when sure she felt
The hour of her deliverance drawing near;
I saw her eye kindle with heavenly hope,
I had her latest look of earthly love,
I felt her hand's last pressure—Son of Orleans!
I would not wish to live to know that hour,
When I could think upon a dear friend dead,
And weep not.
         I remember as her bier
Went to the grave, a lark sprung up aloft,
And soar'd amid the sunshine carolling
So full of joy, that to the mourner's ear
More mournfully than dirge or passing bell,
His joyful carol came, and made us feel
That of the multitude of beings, none
But man was wretched.
          Then my soul awoke,
For it had slumber'd long in happiness,
And never feeling misery, never thought
What others suffer.   I, as best I might,
Solaced the keen regret of Elinor;
And much my cares avail'd, and much her son's,
On whom, the only comfort of her age,
She center'd now her love.   A younger birth,
Aged nearly as myself was Theodore,
An ardent youth, who with the kindest cares
Had soothed his sister's sorrows.   We had knelt
By her death-bed together, and no bond
In closer union knits two human hearts
Than fellowship in grief.
          It chanced as once
Beside the fire of Elinor I sate,
The night was comfortless, the loud blast howl'd,
And as we drew around the social hearth,
We heard the rain beat hard: driven by the storm,
A warrior mark'd our distant taper's light;
We heapt the fire, and spread the friendly board.
' The storm beats hard,' the stranger cried: ' safe hous'd
Pleasant it is to hear the pelting rain. ·
I too were well content to dwell in peace,
Resting my head upon the lap of Love,
But that my country calls.   When the winds roar,
Remember sometimes what a soldier suffers,
And think on Conrade.'
          Theodore replied,
' Success go with thee! Something we have known
Of war, and tasted its calamity;
And I am well content to dwell in peace,
Albeit inglorious, thanking that good God

Who made me to be happy.'
          ' Did that God,'
Cried Conrade, ' form thy heart for happiness,
When Desolation royally careers
Over thy wretched country? did that God
Form thee for Peace when Slaughter is abroad,
When her brooks run with blood, and Rape, and Murder,
Stalk through her flaming towns ? live thou in peace,
Young man! my heart is human: I do feel
For what my brethren suffer.'   While he spake
Such mingled passions character'd his face
Of fierce and terrible benevolence,
That I did tremble as I listen'd to him:
And in my heart tumultuous thoughts arose
Of high achievements, indistinct, and wild,
And vast, yet such they were as made me pant
As though by some divinity possess'd.

« But is there not some duty due to those
' We love?' said Theodore; ' Is there an employ
More righteous than to cheer declining age,
And thus with filial tenderness repay
Parental care?'
          ' Hard is it,' Conrade cried,
« Aye, hard indeed, to part from those we love;
And I have suffer'd that severest pang.
I have left an aged mother; I have left
One, upon whom my heart has center'd all
Its dearest, best, affections.   Should I live
Till France shall see the blessed hour of Peace,
I shall return: my heart will be content,
My highest duties will be well discharged
And I may then be happy.   There are those
Who deem these thoughts the fancies of a mind
Strict beyond measure, and were well content,
If I should soften down my rigid nature
Even to inglorious ease, to honour me.
But pure of heart and high of self-esteem
I must be honour'd by myself: all else,
The breath of Fame, is as the unsteady wind
Worthless.'
          So saying from his belt he took
The encumbering sword.   I held it, listening to him,
And wistless what I did, half from the sheath
Drew forth its glittering blade.   I gazed upon it
And shuddering, as I touch'd its edge, exclaim'd,
How horrible it is with the keen sword
To gore the finely-fibred human frame!
I could not strike a lamb.
          He answer'd me,
'Maiden, thou hast said well. I could not strike
A lamb, . . But when the invader's savage fury
Spares not grey age, and mocks the infant's shriek
As it doth writhe upon his cursed lance,
And forces to his foul embrace, the wife
Even on her murder'd husband's gasping corse!
Almighty God! I should not be a man
If I did let one weak and pitiful feeling
Make mine arm impotent to cleave him down.
Think well of this, young Man!'[10] he cried, and seized
The hand of Theodore; ' think well of this,
As you are human, as you hope to live
In peace, amid the dearest joys of home;
Think well of this! you have a tender mother,
As you do wish that she may die in peace,
As you would even to madness agonize

To hear this maiden call on you in vain
For aid, and see her dragg'd, and hear her scream
In the blood-reeking soldier's lustful arms,
Think that there are such horrors;[11] that even now,
Some city flames, and haply as in Roan,
Some famish'd babe on his dead mother's breast
Yet hangs and pulls for food![12] . . woe be to those
By whom the evil comes! and woe to him, . .
For little less his guilt, . . who dwells in peace,
When every arm is needed for the strife!'

« When we had all betaken us to rest,
Sleepless I lay, and in my mind revolved
The high-soul'd warrior's speech.   Then Madelon
Rose in remembrance; over her the grave
Had closed; her sorrows were not register'd
In the rolls of Fame: but when the tears run down
The widow's cheek, shall not her cry be heard
In Heaven against the oppressor? will not God
In sunder smite the unmerciful, and break
The sceptre of the wicked?[13] . . thoughts like these
Possess'd my soul, till at the break of day
I slept; nor did my heated brain repose
Even then, for visions, sent, as I believe,
From the Most High, arose.   A high-tower'd town
Hemm'd in and girt with enemies, I saw,
Where Famine on a heap of carcasses,
Half envious of the unutterable feast,
Mark'd the gorged raven clog his beak with gore.
I turn'd me then to the besieger's camp.
And there was revelry: the loud lewd laugh
Burst on mine ear, and I beheld the chiefs
Sit at their feast, and plan the work of death.
My soul grew sick within me; I look'd up,
Reproaching Heaven,... lo! from the clouds an arm
As of the avenging Angel was put forth,
And from his hand a sword, like lightning, fell.

« From that night I could feel my burthen'd soul
Heaving beneath incumbent Deity.
I sate in silence, musing on the days
To come, unheeding and unseeing all
Around me, in that dreaminess of thought
When every bodily sense is as it slept,
And the mind alone is wakeful.   I have heard
Strange voices in the evening wind; strange forms
Dimly discover'd throng'd the twilight air.
The neighbours wonder'd at the sudden change,
And call'd me crazed; and my dear Uncle, too,
Would sit and gaze upon me wistfully,
A heaviness upon his aged brow,
And in his eye such trouble, that my heart
Sometimes misgave me.   I had told him all,
The mighty future labouring in my breast,
But that the hour methought not yet was come.

« At length I heard of Orleans, by the foe
Wall'd in from human succour; there all thoughts,
All hopes were turn'd; that bulwark once beat down,
All was the invaders'.   Now my troubled soul
Grew more disturb'd, and, shunning every eye,
I loved to wander where the forest shade
Frown'd deepest; there on mightiest deeds to brood
Of shadowy vastness, such as made my heart
Throb loud: anon I paused, and in a state
Of half expectance, listen'd to the wind.

« There is a fountain in the forest call'd
The Fountain of the Fairies : [14] when a child
With a delightful wonder I have heard
Tales of the Elfin tribe who on its banks
Hold midnight revelry. An ancient oak,
The goodliest of the forest, grows beside;
Alone it stands, upon a green grass plat,
By the woods bounded like some little isle.
It ever hath been deem'd their favourite tree;
They love to lie and rock upon its leaves, [15]
And bask in moonshine. Here the Woodman leads
His boy, and, showing him the green-sward mark'd
With darker circlets, says their midnight dance
Hath trac'd the ring, and bids him spare the tree.
Fancy had cast a spell upon the place,
And made it holy; and the villagers
Would say that never evil thing approach'd
Unpunish'd there. The strange and fearful pleasure
Which fill'd me by that solitary spring,
Ceased not in riper years; and now it woke
Deeper delight and more mysterious awe.

« Lonely the forest spring: a rocky hill
Rises beside it, and an aged yew
Bursts from the rifted crag that overbrows
The waters; cavern'd there unseen and slow
And silently they well. The adder's tongue,
Rich with the wrinkles of its glossy green,
Hangs down its long lank leaves, whose wavy dip
Just breaks the tranquil surface. Ancient woods
Bosom the quiet beauties of the place;
Nor ever sound profanes it, save such sounds
As Silence loves to hear, the passing wind,
Or the low murmuring of the stream scarce heard.
A blessed spot! oh how my soul enjoy'd
Its holy quietness, with what delight
Escaping from mankind I hasten'd there
To solitude and freedom! thitherward
On a spring eve I had betaken me,
And there I sate, and mark'd the deep red clouds
Gather before the wind . . the rising wind,
Whose sudden gusts, each wilder than the last,
Appear'd to rock my senses. Soon the night
Darken'd around, and the large rain drops fell
Heavy; anon tempestuously the gale
Howl'd o'er the wood. Methought the heavy rain
Fell with a grateful coolness on my head,
And the hoarse dash of waters, and the rush
Of winds that mingled with the forest roar,
Made a wild music. On a rock I sat;
The glory of the tempest fill'd my soul;
And when the thunders peal'd, and the long flash
Hung durable in heaven, and on my sight
Spread the grey forest, memory, thought, were gone, [16]
All sense of self annihilate, I seem'd
Diffus'd into the scene.
                    At length a light
Approach'd the spring; I saw my Uncle Claude:
His grey locks dripping with the midnight storm.
He came, and caught me in his arms, and cried,
'My God! my child is safe!'
                    I felt his words
Pierce in my heart; my soul was overcharged;
I fell upon his neck and told him all;
God was within me; as I felt, I spake,
And he believed.

Aye, Chieftain, and the world
Shall soon believe my mission; for the Lord
Will raise up indignation, and pour out
His wrath, and they shall perish who oppress.» [17]

BOOK II.

And now beneath the horizon westering slow
Had sunk the orb of day : o'er all the vale
A purple softness spread, save where the tree
Its giant shadow stretch'd, or winding stream
Mirror'd the light of Heaven, still traced distinct
When twilight dimly shrouded all beside.
A grateful coolness freshen'd the calm air,
And the hoarse grasshoppers their evening song
Sung shrill and ceaseless, [18] as the dews of night
Descended. On their way the travellers wend,
Cheering the road with converse, till at length
They mark a cottage lamp, whose steady light
Shone through the lattice : thitherward they turn.
There came an old man forth : his thin grey locks
Waved on the night breeze, and on his shrunk face
The characters of age were written deep.
Them, louting low with rustic courtesy,
He welcomed in; on the white-ember'd hearth
Heapt up fresh fuel, then with friendly care
Spread out the homely board, and fill'd the bowl
With the red produce of the vine that arch'd
His evening seat; they of the plain repast
Partook, and quaff'd the pure and pleasant draught.

« Strangers, your fare is homely,» said their Host;
But such it is as we poor countrymen
Earn with hard toil : in faith ye are welcome to it!
I too have borne a lance in younger days;
And would that I were young again to meet
These haughty English in the field of fight!
Such as I was when on the fatal plain
Of Agincourt I met them.»
                    « Wert thou, then,
A sharer in that dreadful day's defeat?»
Exclaim'd the Bastard : « Didst thou know the Lord
Of Orleans?»
                    « Know him!» cried the veteran,
« I saw him ere the bloody fight began
Riding from rank to rank, his beaver up,
The long lance quivering in his mighty grasp.
His eye was wrathful to an enemy,
But for his countrymen it had a smile
Would win all hearts. Looking at thee, Sir Knight,
Methinks I see him now; such was his eye,
Gentle in peace, and such his manly brow.»

« No tongue but speaketh honour of that name!»
Exclaimed Dunois. « Strangers and countrymen
Alike revered the good and gallant Chief.
His vassals like a father loved their Lord;
His gates stood open to the traveller;
The pilgrim when he saw his towers rejoiced,
For he had heard in other lands the fame
Of Orleans...And he lives a prisoner still!
Losing all hope because my arm so long
Hath fail'd to win his liberty!»
                    He turn'd

His head away to hide the burning shame
Which flush'd his face. « But he shall live, Dunois,»
Exclaim'd the mission'd Maid; « but he shall live
To hear good tidings; hear of liberty,
Of his own liberty, by his brother's arm
Achieved in hard-fought battle.   He shall live
Happy: the memory of his prison'd years [19]
Shall heighten all his joys, and his grey hairs
Go to the grave in peace.»
                                « I would fain live
To see that day,» replied their aged host:
« How would my heart leap to behold again
The gallant generous chieftain! I fought by him
When all the hopes of victory were lost,
And down his batter'd arms the blood stream'd fast
From many a wound. Like wolves they hemm'd us in,
Fierce in unhoped-for conquest: all around
Our dead and dying countrymen lay heap'd;
Yet still he strove;—I wonder'd at his valour!
There was not one who on that fatal day
Fought bravelier.»
                        « Fatal was that day to France,»
Exclaim'd the Bastard; « there Alençon fell,
Valiant in vain; there D'Albert, whose mad pride
Brought the whole ruin on.   There fell Brabant,
Vaudemont, and Marle, and Bar, and Faquenberg,
Our noblest warriors; the determin'd foe
Fought for revenge, not hoping victory,
Desperately brave; ranks fell on ranks before them;
The prisoners of that shameful day out-summ'd
Their conquerors!» [20]
                        « Yet believe not,» Bertram cried,
« That cowardice disgraced thy countrymen:
They by their leader's arrogance led on
With heedless fury, found all numbers vain,
All efforts fruitless there; and hadst thou seen,
Skilful as brave, how Henry's ready eye
Lost not a thicket, not a hillock's aid;
From his hersed bowmen how the arrows flew [21]
Thick as the snow flakes and with lightning force,
Thou wouldst have known such soldiers, such a chief,
Could never be subdued.
                                But when the field
Was won, and they who had escaped the fight
Had yielded up their arms, it was foul work
To glut on the defenceless prisoners [22]
The blunted sword of conquest. Girt around
I to their mercy had surrender'd me,
When lo! I heard the dreadful cry of death.
Not as amid the fray, when man met man
And in fair combat gave the mortal blow;
Here the poor captives, weaponless and bound,
Saw their stern victors draw again the sword,
And groan'd and strove in vain to free their hands,
And bade them think upon their plighted faith,
And pray'd for mercy in the name of God,
In vain: the King had bade them massacre,
And in their helpless prisoners' naked breasts
They drove the blade.   Then I expected death,
And at that moment death was terrible—
For the heat of fight was over; of my home
I thought, and of my wife and little ones
In bitterness of heart.   The gallant man,
To whom the chance of war had made me thrall,
Had pity, loosed my hands, and bade me fly.
It was the will of Heaven that I should live

Childless and old to think upon the past,
And wish that I had perish'd !»
                                The old man
Wept as he spake.   « Ye may perhaps have heard
Of the hard siege so long by Roan endured.
I dwelt there, strangers; I had then a wife,
And I had children tenderly beloved,
Who I did hope should cheer me in old age
And close mine eyes.   The tale of misery
May-hap were tedious, or I could relate
Much of that dreadful time.»
                                The Maid replied,
Anxious of that devoted town to learn.
Thus then the veteran:—
                                « So by Heaven preserved,
From the disastrous plain of Agincourt [23]
I speeded homewards and abode in peace.
Henry as wise as brave had back to England [24]
Led his victorious army; well aware
That France was mighty, that her warlike sons,
Impatient of a foreign victor's sway,
Might rise impetuous and with multitudes
Tread down the invaders. Wisely he return'd,
For the proud barons in their private broils
Wasted the strength of France.   I dwelt at home,
And, with the little I possessed content,
Lived happily.   A pleasant sight it was
To see my children, as at eve I sate
Beneath the vine, come clustering round my knee,
That they might hear again the oft-told tale
Of the dangers I had past: their little eyes
Did with such anxious eagerness attend
The tale of life preserved, as made me feel
Life's value.   My poor children! a hard fate
Had they! but oft and bitterly I wish
That God had to his mercy taken me
In childhood, for it is a heavy lot
To linger out old age in loneliness !

« Ah me! when war the masters of mankind,
Woe to the poor man! if he sow the field,
He shall not reap the harvest; if he see
His offspring rise around, his boding heart
Aches at the thought that they are multiplied
To the sword! Again from England the fierce foe
Rush'd on our ravaged coasts.   In battle bold,
Merciless in conquest, their victorious King
Swept like the desolating tempest round.
Dambieres submits; on Caen's subjected wall
The flag of England waved.   Roan still remain'd,
Embattled Roan, bulwark of Normandy;
Nor unresisted round her massy walls
Pitch'd they their camp.   I need not tell Sir Knight
How oft and boldly on the invading host
We burst with fierce assault impetuous forth,
For many were the warrior Sons of Roan. [25]
One gallant Citizen was famed o'er all
For daring hardihood pre-eminent,
Blanchard.   He, gathering round his countrymen,
With his own courage kindling every breast,
Had bade them vow before Almighty God [26]
Never to yield them to the usurping foe.
Before the God of Hosts we made the vow :
And we had baffled the besieging power,
Had not the patient enemy drawn round
His strong entrenchments.   From the watch-tower's top

In vain with fearful hearts along the Seine
We strain'd the eye, and every distant wave
Which in the sun-beam glitter'd fondly thought
The white sail of supply.   Alas! no more
The white sail rose upon our aching sight;
For guarded was the Seine, and that stern foe
Had made a league with Famine.[27]   How my heart
Sunk in me when at night I carried home
The scanty pittance of to-morrow's meal!
You know not, strangers! what it is to see
The asking eye of hunger.
                          Still we strove,
Expecting aid; nor longer force to force,
Valour to valour in the fight opposed,
But to the exasperate patience of the foe
Desperate endurance.[28]   Though with Christian zeal
Ursino would have pour'd the balm of peace
Into our wounds, Ambition's ear, best pleased
With the war's clamour and the groan of Death,
Was deaf to prayer.   Day after day fled on;
We heard no voice of comfort.   From the walls
Could we behold the savage Irish Kernes[29]
Ruffians half-clothed, half-human, half-baptized,[30]
Come with their spoil, mingling their hideous shouts
With moan of weary flocks, and piteous low
Of kine sore-laden, in the mirthful camp
Scattering abundance; while the loathliest food
We prized above all price; while in our streets
The dying groan of hunger, and the scream
Of famishing infants echoed,—and we heard,
With the strange selfishness of misery,
We heard and heeded not.
                       Thou would'st have deem'd
Roan must have fallen an easy sacrifice,
Young warrior, hadst thou seen our meagre limbs
And pale and shrunken cheeks, and hollow eyes;
Yet still we struggled nobly!   Blanchard still
Spake of the savage fury of the foe,
Of Harfleur's wretched race cast on the world[31]
Houseless and destitute, while that fierce King
Knelt at the altar,[32] and with impious prayer
Gave God the glory, even while the blood
That he had shed was reeking up to Heaven.
He bade us think what mercy they had found
Who yielded on the plain of Agincourt,
And what the gallant sons of Caen, by-him
In cold blood murder'd.[33]   Then his scanty food
Sharing with the most wretched, he would bid us
Bear with our miseries bravely.
                              Thus distress'd,
Lest all should perish thus, our chiefs decreed
Women and children, the infirm and old,
All who were useless in the work of war,
Should forth and take their fortune.   Age, that makes
The joys and sorrows of the distant years
Like a half-remember'd dream, yet on my heart
Leaves deep impress'd the horrors of that hour.
Then as our widow wives clung round our necks,
And the deep sob of anguish interrupted
The prayer of parting, even the pious Priest
As he implored his God to strengthen us,
And told us we should meet again in Heaven,
He groan'd and cursed in bitterness of heart[34]
That merciless man.   The wretched crowd pass'd on:
My wife—my children—through the gates they pass'd,
Then the gates closed—Would I were in my grave,

That I might lose remembrance!
                              What is man,
That he can hear the groan of wretchedness
And feel no fleshy pang?   Why did the All-Good
Create these warrior scourges of mankind,
These who delight in slaughter?   I did think
There was not on this earth a heart so hard
Could hear a famish'd woman cry for bread,
And know no pity.   As the outcast train
Drew near, relentless Henry bade his troops
Force back the miserable multitude.[35]
They drove them to the walls,—it was the depth
Of winter,—we had no relief to grant.
The aged ones groan'd to our foe in vain,
The mother pleaded for her dying child,
And they felt no remorse!»
                          The mission'd Maid
Starts from her seat—«The old and the infirm,
The mother and her babes!—and yet no lightning
Blasted this man!»
                    « Ay, Lady,» Bertram cried;
« And when we sent the herald to implore
His mercy[36] on the helpless, his stern face
Assumed a sterner smile of callous scorn,
And he replied in mockery.   On the wall
I stood and mark'd the miserable outcasts,
And every moment thought that Henry's heart,
Hard as it was, would melt.   All night I stood,—
Their deep groans came upon the midnight gale,
Fainter they grew, for the cold wintry wind
Blew bleak; fainter they grew, and at the last
All was still, save that ever and anon
Some mother shriek'd o'er her expiring child
The shriek of frenzying anguish.[37]
                              From that hour
On all the busy turmoil of the world
I gazed with strange indifference; bearing want
With the sick patience of a mind worn out.
Nor when the traitor yielded up our town[38]
Ought heeded I as through our ruin'd streets,
Through putrid heaps of famish'd carcasses,
Pass'd the long pomp of triumph.   One keen pang
I felt, when by that bloody King's command
The gallant Blanchard died.[39]   Calmly he died;
And as he bow'd beneath the axe, thank'd God
That he had done his duty.
                          I survive,
A solitary, friendless, wretched one,
Knowing no joy save in the faith I feel
That I shall soon be gather'd to my sires,
And soon repose, there where the wicked cease[40]
From troubling, and the weary are at rest.»

« And happy,» cried the delegated Maid,
« And happy they who in that holy faith
Bow meekly to the rod!   A little while
Shall they endure the proud man's contumely,
The injustice of the great.   A little while
Though shelterless they feel the wintry wind,
The wind shall whistle o'er their turf-grown grave,
And all be peace below.   But woe to those,
Woe to the Mighty Ones who send abroad
Their train'd assassins, and who give to Fury
The flaming firebrand; these indeed shall live
The heroes of the wandering minstrel's song;
But they have their reward; the innocent blood

Steams up to Heaven against them.   God shall hear
The widow's groan.»
                        « I saw him,» Bertram cried,
« Henry of Agincourt, this conqueror King,
Go to his grave.   The long procession past
Slowly from town to town, and when I heard
The deep-toned dirge, and saw the banners wave
A pompous shade,[41] and the high torches glare
In the mid-day sun a dim and gloomy light,[42]
I thought what he had been on earth who now
Was gone to his account, and blest my God
I was not such as he '»
                        So spake the old man,
And then his guests betook them to repose.

BOOK III.

Fair dawn'd the morning, and the early sun
Pour'd on the latticed cot a cheerful gleam,
And up the travellers rose, and on their way
Hastened, their dangerous way,[43] through fertile tracks
The waste of war.   They pass'd the Auxerrois;
The autumnal rains had beaten to the earth [44]
The unreap'd harvest, from the village church
No even-song bell was heard, the shepherd's dog
Prey'd on the scatter'd flock, for there was now
No hand to feed him, and upon the hearth
Where he had slumber'd at his master's feet
The rank weed flourish'd.   Did they sometimes find
A welcome, he who welcomed them was one
Who linger'd in the place where he was born,
For that alone was left him now to love.
They pass'd the Yonne, they pass'd the rapid Loire,
Still urging on their way with cautious speed,
Shunning Auxerre, and Bar's embattled wall,
And Romorantin's towers.
                        So journeying on,
Fast by a spring, which welling at his feet
With many a winding crept along the mead,
A Knight they saw, who there at his repast
Let the west wind play round his ungirt brow.
Approaching near, the Bastard recognized
The gallant friend of Orleans, the brave chief
Du Chastel; and, the mutual greeting pass'd,
They on the streamlet's mossy bank reclined
Beside him, and his frugal fare partook,
And drank the running waters.
                        « Art thou bound
For the Court, Dunois?» exclaim'd the aged Knight;
I deem'd thee far away, coop'd in the walls
Of Orleans; a hard siege her valiant sons
Right loyally endure!»
                        « I left the town,»
Dunois replied, « thinking that my prompt speed
Might seize the hostile stores, and with fresh force
Re-enter.   Fastolfe's better fate prevail'd,[45]
And from the field of shame my maddening horse
Bore me, for the barb'd arrow gored his flank.
Fatigued and faint with that day's dangerous toil,
My deep wounds bleeding, vainly with weak hand
I check'd the powerless rein.   Nor aught avail'd
When heal'd at length, defeated and alone
Again to enter Orleans.   In Lorraine
I sought to raise new powers, and now return'd

With strangest and most unexpected aid
Sent by high Heaven.   I seek the Court, and thence
To that beleaguer'd town shall lead such force,
That the proud English in their fields of blood
Shall perish.»
                        « I too,» Tanneguy replied,
« In the field of battle once again perchance
May serve my royal Master; in his cause
My youth adventured much, nor can my age
Find better close than in the clang of arms
To die for him whom I have lived to serve. [46]
Thou art for the Court; Son of the Chief I loved!
Be wise by my experience.   He who seeks
Court favour, ventures like the boy who leans
Over the brink of some high precipice
To reach the o'erhanging fruit. [47]   Thou seest me here
A banish'd man, Dunois! [48] so to appease
Richemont, [49] who, jealous of the royal ear,
With midnight murder leagues, and down the Loire
Rolls the black carcase of his strangled foe.
Now confident of strength, at the King's feet
He stabs the King's best friends, and then demands,
As with a conqueror's imperious tone,
The post of honour.   Son of that loved Chief
Whose death my arm avenged, [50] may all thy days
Be happy! serve thy country in the field,
And in the hour of peace amid thy friends
Dwell thou without ambition.»
                        So he spake.
But when the Bastard told the wonderous tale,
How interposing Heaven had its high aid
Vouchsafed to France, the old man's eyes flash'd fire,
And rising from the bank, the stately steed
That grazed beside he mounts.   « Farewell, Dunois,
Thou too the Delegate of Heaven, farewell!
I go to raise the standard! we shall meet
At Orleans.»   O'er the plain he spurr'd his steed.

They journey on their way till Chinon's towers
Rose to the distant view; imperial seat
Of Charles, for Paris with her servile sons,
A headstrong, mutable, ferocious race,
Bow'd to the invader's yoke, since that sad hour [51]
When Faction o'er her streets with giant stride
Strode terrible, and Murder and Revenge,
As by the midnight torches' lurid light
They mark'd their mangled victims writhe convulsed,
Laugh'd at the deep death groan.   Ill-fated scene!
Through many a dark age drench'd with innocent blood,
And one day doom'd to know the damning guilt
Of Brissot murder'd, and the heroic wife
Of Roland! Martyr'd patriots, spirits pure,
Wept by the good ye fell! Yet still survives,
Sown by your toil and by your blood manured,
The imperishable seed; and still its roots
Spread, and strike deep, and yet shall it become
That Tree beneath whose shade the Sons of Men
Shall pitch their tents in peace.
                        In Paris now
The invader triumph'd.   On an infant's head
Had Bedford placed the crown of Charlemagne,
And factious nobles bow'd the subject knee
In homage to their King, their baby Lord,
Their cradled mighty one!
                        « Beloved of Heaven,»
So spake the Son of Orleans as they pass'd,

« In these the walls of Chinon, this the abode
Of Charles our monarch. Here in revelry
He of his armies vanquish'd, his fair towns
Subdued, hears careless and prolongs the dance.
And little marvel I that to the cares
Of empire still he turns the unwilling ear,
For loss on loss, defeat upon defeat,
His strong holds taken, and his bravest Chiefs
Or dead or captured, and the hopes of youth
All blasted, have subdued the royal mind,
Undisciplined in Fortitude's stern school.
So may thy voice arouse his sleeping virtues!»

The mission'd Maid replied, « Go thou, Dunois,
Announce my mission to the royal ear ;
I on the river's winding banks the while
Would roam, collecting for the enterprise
My thoughts, though firm, yet troubled. Who essays
Achievements of great import will perforce
Feel the heart heave; and in my breast I feel
Such perturbation.»
                    On the banks of Vienne
Devious the Damsel turn'd. Through Chinon's gates
The Son of Orleans press'd with rapid step,
Seeking the King. Him from the public view
He found secluded with his blameless Queen,
And his partaker of the unlawful bed,
The lofty-minded Agnes.
                    « Son of Orleans!»
So as he entered cried the haughty Fair,
«Thou art well come to witness the disgrace,
The weak, unmanly, base despondency
Of this thy Sovereign Liege. He will retreat
To distant Dauphiny, [52] and fly the war!
Go then, unworthy of thy rank! retreat
To distant Dauphiny, and fly the war,
Recreant from battle; I will not partake
A fugitive's fate; when thou hast lost thy crown
Thou hast lost Agnes.—Dost not blush, Dunois!
To bleed in combat for a Prince like this,
Fit only, like the Merovingian race
On a May morning deck'd with flowers, [53] to mount
His gay-bedizen'd car, and ride abroad
And make the multitude a holiday.
Go, Charles—and hide thee in a woman's garb,
And these long locks will not disgrace thee then!» [54]

« Nay, Agnes!» Charles replied, « reproach me not,
I have enough of sorrow. Look around,
See this fair country ravaged by the foe,
My strong holds taken, and my bravest Chiefs
Fall'n in the field, or captives far away.
Dead is the Douglas ; cold thy gallant heart,
Illustrious Buchan! ye from Scotland's hills,
Not mindless of your old ally distress'd,
Rush'd to his succour : in his cause ye fought,
For him ye perish'd. Rash, impetuous Narbonne!
Thy mangled corse waves to the winds of Heaven. [55]
Cold, Graville, is thy sinewy arm in death;
Fall'n is Ventadaur ; silent in the grave
Rambouillet sleeps: Bretagne's unfaithful chief
Leagues with my foes, and Richemont, [56] or in arms
Defies my weak control, or from my side,
A friend more dreaded than the enemy,
Drives my best servants with the assassin sword.
Soon must the towers of Orleans fall !—But now

These sad thoughts boot not. Welcome to our court,
Dunois! We yet can give the friendly feast,
And from the heavy cares of empire win
One hospitable day of merriment.»

The Chief replied, « So may thy future years
Pass from misfortune free, as all these ills
Shall vanish like a vision of the night!
To thee and France I come the messenger
Of aid from Heaven. The delegated Maid
With me, whom all-wise Providence decrees
The Saviour of the realm ;—a holy Maid,
Bearing strange promise of miraculous things,
One whom it were not possible to hear
And disbelieve.»
                    Astonish'd by his speech
Stood Charles. « At one of meaner estimation
I should have smiled, Dunois. Thy well-known worth,
The loyalty of all thy noble house,
Compel me even to this, a most strange tale,
To lend a serious ear. A woman sent
From Heaven, the saviour of this wasted realm,
One whom it were not possible to hear,
And disbelieve! Dunois, ill now beseems
Aught wild and hazardous ; the throne of France
Totters upon destruction. Is my person
Known to this woman?»
                    « She has lived retired,»
The Bastard answer'd, « ignorant of courts,
And little heeding, till the spirit of God
Roused her to this great work.»
                    To him the King :
« If then she knows me not, abide thou here,
And hither, by a speedy messenger,
Summon the Maiden. On the throne meantime,
I the while mingling with the Menial throng,
Some courtier shall be seated. If the Maid
Be by the spirit of God indeed inspired,
That holy spirit will gift her with the power
To pierce deception. But if strange of mind
Enthusiast fancy fire her wilder'd brain,
She to obscurity again, thus proved,
May guiltlessly retire. Our English foes
Might well exult to see the sons of France
Led by a frenzied female.» [57] So he said;
And, with a faith half-faltering at the proof,
Dunois dispatched a messenger, to seek
Beside the banks of Vienne, the Mission'd Maid.

Soon is the court convened ; the jewell'd crown
Shines on a menial's head. Amid the throng
The Monarch stands, and anxious for the event,
His heart beats high. She comes, the Maid inspired ;
And as the Bastard led her to the throne,
Quick glancing o'er the mimic Majesty
Fix'd full her eye on Charles. [58]
                    « Thou art the King!
I come the avenging Delegate of Heaven,
To wield the fated weapon, from whose death,
Their stern hearts palsied by the arm of God,
Far, far from Orleans shall the English wolves
Speed their disastrous flight. Monarch of France!
Spread the good tidings through thy ravaged realm!
The Maid is come, the mission'd Maid, whose hand
Shall in the consecrated walls of Rheims
Crown thee the anointed King.» [59]

In wonder mute
The courtiers heard. The astonish'd King exclaimed,
« This is indeed the agency of Heaven !
Hard, Maiden, were I of belief,» he cried,
« Did I not now, with full and confirm'd faith,
Thee the redeemer of this ravaged realm
Believe. Not doubting therefore the strange will
Of all-wise Providence, delay I now
Instant to marshal the brave sons of France
Beneath thy banners; but to satisfy
Those who at distance from this most clear proof
May hear and disbelieve, or yield at best
A cold assent,—these fully to confirm
And more to manifest thy holy power,
Forthwith with all due speed I shall convene
The Doctors of Theology, 60 wise men
And skilful in the mysteries of Heaven.
By these thy mission studied and approved,
As needs it must, their sanction to all minds
Shall bring conviction, and the firm belief
Lead on thy favour'd troops to mightiest deeds,
Surpassing human credibility.»

Well pleas'd the Maiden heard. Her the King leads
From the disbanding throng, meantime to dwell
With Mary. Watchful for her Lord's return,
She sat with Agnes; Agnes, proud of heart,
Majestically fair, whose large full eye
Or flashing anger, or with scornful scowl,
Deform'd her beauteous features. Yet with her
The lawless idol of the Monarch's heart,
Mary, obedient to her husband's will,
Dwelt meekly in accord. The Maiden soon
Loved the mild Queen, and sojourning with her,
Expects the solemn summons.
                              Through the realm
Meantime the King's convoking voice was heard,
And from their palaces and monasteries
Forth came the Doctors, men acute and deep,
Grown grey in study; Priests and Bishops haste
To Chinon : teachers wise and with high names,
Seraphic, Subtile or Irrefragable,
By their admiring pupils dignified.

The Doctors met, from cloister gloom recluse,
Or from the haunts luxurious of abode
Episcopal, they met, and sought the place
Of judgment, in the ancient church assign'd.
The floor with many a monumental stone
Was spread, and brass-ensculptured effigy
Of holy abbots honour'd in their day,
Now to the grave gone down. The branching arms
Of many a ponderous pillar met aloft,
Wreath'd on the roof emboss'd. Through storied panes
Of high arch'd windows came the tinctured light.
Pure water in a font beneath reflects
The many-colour'd rays; around that font
The fathers stand, and there with rites ordain'd
And signs symbolic strew the hallowing salt,
Wherewith the limpid water, thus imbued,
So taught the church, became a spell approv'd
Against the fiends of Satan's fallen crew :
A licens'd spell of mightier potency
Than e'er the hell-hags taught in Thessaly;
Or they who sitting on the rifled grave,
By the blue tomb-fire's lurid light dim seen,

Share with the Gouls their banquet.
                              This perform'd,
The Maid is summon'd. Round the holy vase
Mark'd with the mystic tonsure and enrobed
In sacred vests, a venerable train,
They stand. The delegated Maid obeys
Their summons. As she came, a loveliest blush
O'er her fair cheek suffus'd, such as became
One mindful still of maiden modesty,
Though of her own worth conscious. Through the aisle
The cold wind moaning, as it pass'd along
Waved her dark flowing locks. Before the train
In reverent silence waiting their sage will,
With half-averted eye she stood composed.
So have I seen the simple snow-drop rise
Amid the russet leaves that hide the earth
In early spring, so seen it gently bend
In modest loveliness alone amid
The waste of winter.
                          By the Maiden's side
The Son of Orleans stood, prepared to vouch
That when on Charles the Maiden's eye had fix'd,
As led by power miraculous, no fraud,
Nor juggling artifice of secret sign
Dissembled inspiration. As he stood
Steadily viewing the mysterious rites,
Thus to the attentive Maid the Arch-Priest spake
Severe.
                  « Woman, if any fiend of hell
Lurk in thy bosom, so to prompt the vaunt
Of inspiration, and to mock the power
Of God and holy Church, thus by the virtue
Of water hallowed in the name of God
That damned spirit adjure I to depart
From his possessed prey.»
                              Slowly he spake,
And sprinkled water on the virgin's face :
Indignant at the unworthy charge, the Maid
Felt her cheek flush ; but soon the transient glow
Fading, she answer'd meek.
                              « Most holy Sires,
Ye reverend Fathers of the Christian church,
Most catholic ! I stand before you here
A poor weak woman; of the grace vouchsafed,
How far unworthy, conscious : yet though mean,
Innocent of fraud, and chosen by high Heaven
The minister of aid. Strange voices heard,
The dark and shadowing visions of the night,
And feelings which I may not dare to doubt,
These portents make me conscious of the God
Within me; he who gifted my purged eye
To know the Monarch 'mid the menial throng,
Unseen before. Thus much it boots to say.
The life of simple virgin ill deserves
To call your minds from studies wise and deep,
Not to be fathom'd by the weaker sense
Of man profane.»
                          «Thou speakest,» said the Priest,
« Of dark and shadowing visions of the night.
Canst thou remember, Maid, what vision first
Seem'd more than Fancy's shaping. From such tale,
Minutely told with accurate circumstance,
Best judgment might be formed.»
                              The Maid replied,
« Amid the mountain valleys I had driven
My father's flock. The eve was drawing on,

When by a sudden storm surprised, I sought
A chapel's neighbouring shelter; ruined now, [61]
But I remember when its vesper bell
Was heard among the hills, a pleasant sound,
That made me pause upon my homeward road,
Awakening in me comfortable thoughts
Of holiness. The unsparing soldiery
Had sack'd the hamlet near, and none was left
Duly at sacred seasons to attend
Saint Agnes' chapel. In the desolate pile
I drove my flock, with no irreverent thoughts,
Nor mindless that the place on which I trod
Was holy ground. It was a fearful night!
Devoutly to the virgin Saint I pray'd,
Then heap'd the wither'd leaves which autumn winds
Had drifted in, and laid me down upon them,
And sure I think I slept. But so it was
That, in the dead of night, Saint Agnes stood [62]
Before mine eyes, such and so beautiful
As when, amid the house of wickedness,
The Power whom with such fervent love she served
Veil'd her with glory. And she seem'd to point
To the moss-grown altar, and the crucifix
Half hid by weeds and grass;.., and then I thought
I could have wither'd armies with a look,
For from the present Saint such divine power
I felt infused..... T was but a dream perhaps.
And yet methought that when a louder peal
Burst o'er the roof, and all was left again
Utterly dark, the bodily sense was clear
And accurate in every circumstance
Of time and place.»
                        Attentive to her words
Thus the Priest answer'd.
                        « Brethren, ye have heard
The woman's tale. Beseems us now to ask
Whether of holy Church a duteous child
Before our court appears, so not unlike
Heaven might vouchsafe its gracious miracle;
Or silly heretic, whose erring thoughts,
Monstrous and vain, perchance might stray beyond
All reason, and conceit strange dreams and signs
Impossible. Say, woman, from thy youth
Hast thou, as rightly mother Church demands,
Confess'd to holy Priest each secret sin,
That, by the grace vouchsafed to him from Heaven,
He might absolve thee?»
                        « Father,» she replied,
«The forms of worship in mine earlier years
Wak'd my young mind to artificial awe,
And made me fear my God. Warm with the glow
Of health and exercise, whene'er I pass'd
The threshold of the house of prayer, I felt
A cold damp chill me ; I beheld the flame
That with a pale and feeble glimmering
Dimm'd the noon-light; I heard the solemn mass,
And with strange feelings and mysterious dread
Telling my beads, gave to the mystic prayers
Devoutest meaning. Often when I saw
The pictur'd flames writhe round a penanced soul,
Have I retired, and knelt before the cross,
And wept for grace, and trembled, and believed
A God of Terrors. But in riper years,
When as my soul grew strong in solitude,
I saw the eternal energy pervade
The boundless range of nature, with the sun

Pour life and radiance from his flamy path,
And on the lowliest flowret of the field
The kindly dew-drops shed. And then I felt
That HE who form'd this goodly frame of things
Must needs be good, and with a FATHER'S name
I call'd on HIM, and from my burthen'd heart
Pour'd out the yearnings of unmingled love.
Methinks it is not strange then, that I fled
The house of prayer, and made the lonely grove
My temple, at the foot of some old oak
Watching the little tribes that had their world
Within its mossy bark ; or laid me down
Beside the rivulet whose murmuring
Was silence to my soul, [63] and mark'd the swarm
Whose light-edged shadows on the bedded sand
Mirror'd their mazy sports; the insect hum,
The flow of waters, and the song of birds
Making a holy music to mine ear :
Oh! was it strange, if for such scenes as these,
Such deep devoutness, such intense delight
Of quiet adoration, I forsook
The house of worship? strange that when I felt
How God had made my Spirit quick to feel
And love whate'er was beautiful and good,
And from aught evil and deform'd to shrink
Even as with instinct; father! was it strange
That in my heart I had no thought of sin
And did not need forgiveness?»
                        As she spake
The Doctors stood astonish'd, and some while
They listen'd still in wonder. But at length
A Priest replied,
                        « Woman, thou seemst to scorn
The ordinances of our holy Church;
And, if I rightly understand thy words,
Thou sayst that Solitude and Nature taught
Thy feelings of religion, and that now
Masses and absolution and the use
Of mystic wafer, are to thee unknown.
How then could Nature teach thee true religion,
Deprived of these? Nature can teach to sin,
But 't is the Priest alone can teach remorse,
Can bid St Peter ope the gates of Heaven,
And from the penal fires of purgatory
Absolve the soul. Could Nature teach thee this?
Or tell thee that St Peter holds the keys,
And that his successor's unbounded power
Extends o'er either world? Although thy life
Of sin were free, if of this holy truth
Ignorant, thy soul in liquid flames must rue
Its error.»
                        Thus he spake ; the applauding look
Went round. Nor dubious to reply the Maid
Was silent.
                        « Fathers of the holy Church,
If on these points abstruse a simple maid
Like me should err, impute not you the crime
To self-will'd reason, vaunting its own strength
Above the eternal wisdom. True it is
That for long time I have not heard the sound
Of mass high-chaunted, nor with trembling lips
Partook the mystic wafer : yet the bird
Who to the matin ray prelusive pour'd
His joyous song, methought did warble forth
Sweeter thanksgiving to Religion's ear
In his wild melody of happiness,

Than ever rung along the high-arch'd roofs
Of man :... yet never from the bending vine
Pluck'd I its ripen'd clusters thanklessly,
Or of that God unmindful, who bestow'd
The bloodless banquet. Ye have told me, Sirs,
That Nature only teaches man to sin !
If it be sin to seek the wounded lamb,
To bind its wounds, and bathe them with my tears,
This is what Nature taught! No, Fathers! no,
It is not Nature that can teach to sin :
Nature is all Benevolence, all Love,
All Beauty! In the greenwood's quiet shade
There is no vice that to the indignant cheek
Bids the red current rush; no misery there;
No wretched mother, who with pallid face
And famine-fall'n, hangs o'er her hungry babes,
With such a look, so wan, so woe-begone,
As shall one day, with damning eloquence,
Against the mighty plead!... Nature teach sin !
O blasphemy against the Holy One,
Who made us in the image of Himself,
Who made us all for happiness and love,
Infinite happiness, infinite love,
Partakers of his own eternity.»

Solemn and slow the reverend Priest replied,—
« Much, woman, do I doubt that all-wise Heaven
Would thus vouchsafe its gracious miracles
On one fore-doom'd to misery; for so doom'd
Is that deluded one, who, of the mass
Unheeding, and the Church's saving power,
Deems nature sinless. Therefore, mark me well,
Brethren, I would propose this woman try
The holy ordeal. Let her, bound and stript,
Lest haply in her clothes should be conceal'd
Some holy relic so profaned, be cast
In the deep pond; there if she float, no doubt
Some fiend upholds, but if she instant sink,
Sure sign is that that Providence displays
Her free from witchcraft. This done, let her walk
Blinded and bare o'er ploughshares heated red,
And o'er these past, her naked arm plunge deep
In scalding water. If from these she pass
Unhurt, to holy father of the church,
Most blessed Pope, we then refer the cause
For judgment : and this Chief, the Son of Orleans,
Who comes to vouch the royal person known
By her miraculous power, shall pass with her
The sacred trial.»
             « Grace of God !» exclaim'd
The astonish'd Bastard; « plunge me in the pool !
O'er red-hot ploughshares make me dance to please
Your dotard fancies! Fathers of the church,
Where is your gravity? what! elder-like
Would ye this fairer than Susannah eye?
Ye call for ordeals; and I too demand
The noblest ordeal, on the English host
By victory to approve the mission sent
From favouring Heaven. To the Pope refer
For judgment! Know ye not that France even now
Stands tottering on destruction?»
                Starting wild,
With a strange look, the mission'd Maid exclaim'd.
« The sword of God is here! the grave shall speak
To manifest me!»
             Even as she spake,

A pale blue flame rose from the trophied tomb
Beside her : and within that house of death
A clash of arms was heard, as though below
The shrouded warrior shook his mailed limbs.
« Hear ye?» the Damsel cried; « these are the arms
Which shall flash terror o'er the hostile host.
These, in the presence of our Lord the King,
And of the assembled people, I will take
Here from the sepulchre, where many an age,
Incorruptible, they have lain conceal'd,
For me preserved, the delegate of Heaven »

Recovering from amaze, the Priest replied :
« Thou art indeed the delegate of Heaven !
What thou hast said surely thou shalt perform !
We ratify thy mission. Go in peace.»

BOOK IV.

The feast was spread, the sparkling bowl went round,
And to the assembled court the minstrel harp'd
The song of other days. Sudden they heard
The horn's loud blast. « This is no time for cares;
Feast ye the messenger without!» cried Charles;
« Enough is given of the wearying day
To the public weal.»
             Obedient to the King,
The guard invites the traveller to his fare.
« Nay, I will see the monarch,» he replied,
« And he shall hear my tidings; duty-urged,
I have for many a long league hasten'd on,
And will not be repell'd.» Then with strong arm
Removing him who barr'd his onward way,
The hall he enter'd.
            « King of France! I come
From Orleans, speedy and effectual aid
Demanding for her gallant garrison,
Faithful to thee, though thinn'd in many a fight,
And wither'd now by want. Thee it beseems,
For ever anxious for thy people's weal,
To succour the brave men whose honest breasts
Bulwark thy throne.»
            He said, and from the hall
With upright step departing, in amaze
At his so bold deportment left the court.
The King exclaim'd, « But little need to send
Quick succour to this gallant garrison,
If to the English half so firm a front
They bear in battle!»
            « In the field, my liege,»
Dunois replied, « yon Knight has served thee well.
Him have I seen the foremost of the fight,
Wielding so fearfully his death-red axe,
That wheresoe'er he turn'd, the affrighted foe
Let fall their palsied arms with powerless stroke,
Desperate of safety. I do marvel much
That he is here : Orleans must be hard press'd,
To send the bravest of her garrison
On such commission.»
            Swift the Maid exclaim'd,
« I tell thee, Chief, that there the English wolves
Shall never pour their yells of victory!
The will of God defends those fated walls;
And resting in full faith on that high will,

I mock their efforts. But the night draws on;
Retire we to repose. To morrow's sun,
Breaking the darkness of the sepulchre,
Shall on that armour gleam, through many an age
Kept holy and inviolate by time.»
She said, and, rising from the board, retired.

Meantime the herald's brazen voice proclaim'd
Coming solemnity, and far and wide
Spread the strange tidings. Every labour ceased;
The ploughman from the unfinish'd furrow hastes;
The armourer's anvil beats no more the din
Of future slaughter. Through the thronging streets
The buzz of asking wonder hums along.

On to St Catharine's sacred fane they go;
The holy fathers with the imaged cross
Leading the long procession. Next, as one
Suppliant for mercy to the King of Kings,
And grateful for the benefits of Heaven,
The Monarch pass'd; and by his side the Maid,
Her lovely limbs robed in a snow-white vest;
Wistless that every eye on her was fix'd,
With stately step she moved: her labouring soul
To high thoughts elevate; and gazing round
With the wild eye, that of the circling throng
And of the visible world unseeing, saw
The shapes of holy fantasy. By her
The warrior Son of Orleans strode along
Preeminent. He, nerving his young frame
With manly exercise, had scaled the cliff,
And dashing in the torrent's foaming flood,
Stemm'd with broad breast its fury; so his form,
Sinewy and firm, and fit for loftiest deeds,
Tower'd high amid the throng effeminate;
No dainty bath had from his hardy limbs
Effaced the hauberk's honourable marks; 64
His helmet bore of hostile steel the dints
Many and deep; upon his pictured shield
A Lion vainly struggled in the toils,
Whilst by his side the cub with pious rage,
His young mane floating to the desert air,
Rends the fallen huntsman. Tremouille him behind,
The worthless favourite of the slothful Prince,
Stalk'd arrogant, in shining armour clasp'd,
Emboss'd with gold and gems of richest hue,
Gaudily graceful, by no hostile blade
Defaced, and rusted by no hostile blood;
Trimly accoutred court habiliments,
Gay lady-dazzling armour, fit to adorn
In dangerless manœuvres some review,
The mockery of murder! follow'd him
The train of courtiers, summer-flies that sport
In the sun-beam of favour, insects sprung
From the court dunghill, greedy blood-suckers,
The foul corruption-gender'd swarm of state.

As o'er some flowery field the busy bees
Pour their deep music, pleasant melody
To the tired traveller, under some old oak
Stretch'd in the checquer'd shade; or as the sound
Of many waters down the far off steep
Dash'd with loud uproar, rose the murmur round
Of admiration. Every gazing eye
Dwelt on the mission'd Maid; of all beside,
The long procession and the gorgeous train,

Though glittering they with gold and sparkling gems,
And their rich plumes high waving to the air,
Heedless.
                    The consecrated dome they reach,
Rear'd to St Catharine's holy memory.
Her tale the altar told; when Maximin,
His raised lip kindled with a savage smile,
In such deep fury bade the tenter'd wheel
Tear her life piecemeal, that the very face
Of the hard executioner relax'd ·
With horror; calm she heard, no drop of blood
Forsook her cheek, her steady eye was turn'd
Heaven-ward, and Hope and meekest Piety
Beam'd in that patient look. Nor vain her trust,
For lo! the Angel of the Lord descends
And crumbles with his fiery touch the wheel!
One glance of holy triumph Catharine cast,
Then bow'd her to the sword of martyrdom. 65

Her eye averting from the storied woe,
The delegated Damsel knelt and pour'd
To Heaven the earnest prayer.
                              A trophied tomb
Close to the altar rear'd its ancient bulk.
Two pointless javelins and a broken sword,
Time-mouldering now, proclaim'd some warrior slept
The sleep of death beneath. A massy stone
And rude-ensculptured effigy o'erlaid
The sepulchre. In silent wonderment
The expectant multitude with eager eye
Gaze, listening as the mattock's heavy stroke
Invades the tomb's repose: the heavy stroke
Sounds hollow; over the high-vaulted roof
Roll the repeated echoes: soon the day
Dawns on the grave's long night, the slant sun-beam
Beams on the inshrined arms, the crested helm,
The baldrick's strength, the shield, the sacred sword.
A sound of awe-repress'd astonishment
Rose from the crowd. The delegated Maid
Over her robes the hallowed breast-plate threw,
Self-fitted to her form; on her helm'd head
The white plumes nod, majestically slow;
She lifts the buckler and the sacred sword, 66
Gleaming portentous light.
                          The wondering crowd
Raise the loud shout of transport. «God of Heaven,»
The Maid exclaimed, «Father all merciful!
Devoted to whose holy will, I wield
The sword of vengeance, go before our host!
All-just avenger of the innocent,
Be thou our Champion! God of Love, preserve
Those whom no lust of glory leads to arms.»

She ceased, and with an eager hush the crowd
Still listen'd; a brief while throughout the dome
Deep silence dwelt; then with a sudden burst
Devout and full, they rais'd the choral hymn,
« Thee, Lord, we praise, our God!» the throng without
Catch the strange tidings, join the hymn of joy,
And thundering transport peals along the heavens.

As through the parting crowd the Virgin pass'd,
He who from Orleans on the yesternight
Demanded succour, clasp'd with warmth her hand,
And with a bosom-thrilling voice exclaim'd,
« Ill-omen'd Maid! victim of thine own worth,

Devoted for the king-curst realm of France!
Ill-omen'd Maid, I pity thee!» so saying,
He turn'd into the crowd. At his strange words
Disturb'd, the warrior Virgin pass'd along,
And much revolving in her troubled mind,
Retreads the court.

       And now the horn announced
The ready banquet; they partook the feast, 67
Then' rose and in the cooling water cleans'd
Their hands; and seated at the board again
Enjoy'd the bowl, or scented high with spice,
Or flavour'd with the fragrant summer fruit,
Or luscious with metheglin mingled rich. 68
Meantime the Trouveur struck the harp; he sang
Of Lancelot du Lake, the truest Knight
That ever loved fair Lady; and the youth
Of Cornwall, 69 underneath whose maiden sword
The strength of Ireland fell, and he who struck
The dolorous stroke, 70 the blameless and the brave,
Who died beneath a brother's erring arm.
Ye have not perish'd, Chiefs of Carduel!
The songs of earlier years embalm your fame,
And haply yet some Poet shall arise,
Like that divinest Tuscan, 71 and enwreathe
The immortal garland for himself and you.

The full sound echoed o'er the arched roof,
And listening eager to the favourite lay,
The guests sat silent, when into the hall
The messenger from that besieged town
Stalk'd stately. « It is pleasant, King of France,
To feast at ease, and hear the harper's song;
Far other music hear the men of Orleans!
DEATH is among them; there the voice of Woe
Moans ceaseless.»
       « Rude unmannerly intruder!»
Exclaim'd the Monarch, « cease to interrupt
The hour of merriment; it is not thine
To instruct me in my duty.»
       Of reproof
Heedless, the stranger to the minstrel cried,
« Why harpest thou of good King Arthur's fame
Amid these walls? Virtue and Genius love
That lofty lay. Hast thou no loose lewd tale
To pamper and provoke the appetite?
Such should procure thee worthy recompense!
Or rather sing thou of that mighty one,
Who tore the ewe lamb from the poor man's bosom,
That was to him even as a daughter! Charles,
This holy tale would I tell, prophet-like,
And look at thee and cry, 'Thou art the man!'»

He said, and with a quick and troubled step
Retired. Astonish'd at his daring phrase,
The guests sat heedless of the minstrel's song,
Pondering the words mysterious. Soon the harp
Beguiled their senses of anxiety.

The court dispersed: retiring from the hall,
Charles and the delegated Damsel sought
The inner palace. There awaited them
The Queen: with her JOAN lov'd to pass the hours,
By various converse cheer'd; for she had won
The Virgin's heart by her mild melancholy,
The calm and duteous patience that deplored
A husband's cold half-love. To her she told

With what strange words the messenger from Orleans
Had roused uneasy wonder in her mind;
For on her ear yet vibrated his voice,
When lo! again he came, and at the door
Stood scowling round.
       « Why dost thou haunt me thus?»
The Monarch cried; « Is there no place secure
From thy rude insolence? Unmanner'd man!
I know thee not!»
       « Then learn to know me, Charles!»
Solemnly he replied; « read well my face,
That thou mayst know it on that dreadful day,
When at the throne of God I shall demand
His justice on thee!» Turning from the King,
To Agnes as she enter'd, in a tone
More low, more awfully severe, he cried,
« Dost thou too know me not?»
       She glanced on him,
And pale and breathless hid her head convulsed
In the Maid's bosom.
       « King of France!» he said,
« She loved me! day by day I dwelt with her,
Her voice was music, very sweet her smiles;
I left her! left her,—Charles, in evil hour,
To fight thy battles. Thou meantime didst come,
Staining most foul her spotless purity;
For she was pure :.... Alas! these courtly robes
Hide not the hideous stain of infamy.
Thou canst not with thy golden belt 72 put on
An honourable name, unhappy one!
My poor polluted Agnes!—Charles, almost
My faith in Heaven is shaken! Thou art here
Rioting in joy, while I, though innocent
Of ill, the victim of another's vice,
Drag on the loathsome burthen of existence,
And doubt Heaven's justice!»
       So he said, and frown'd
Dark as the form who at Mahommed's door
Knock'd fierce and frequent; from whose fearful look,
Bath'd with cold damps, every beholder fled.
Even the prophet, almost terrified,
Endured but half to view him, for he knew
AZRAEL, the dreadful Messenger of Fate,
And his death-day was come. Guilt-petrified
The Monarch sate, nor could endure to face
His bosom-probing frown. The mission'd Maid
Meantime had read his features, and she cried,
« I know thee, Conrade!» Rising from her seat,
She took his hand, for he stood motionless,
Gazing on Agnes now with steady eye,
Dreadful though calm: him from the court she drew,
And to the river's banks, resisting not,
Both sad and silent, led; till at the last,
As from a dream awaking, Conrade look'd
Full on the Maid, and falling on her neck,
He wept.
       « I know thee, Damsel!» he exclaim'd :
« Dost thou remember that tempestuous night,
When I, a weather-beaten traveller, sought
Your hospitable doors? ah me! I then
Was happy! you too sojourn'd then in peace.
Fool that I was, I blamed such happiness,
Arraign'd it as a guilty selfish, sloth,
Unhappily prevailing, so I fear me,
Or why art thou at Chinon?»
       Him the Maid

Answering, address'd,—« I do remember well,
That night : for then the Holy Spirit first,
Waked by thy words, possess'd me.»
                    Conrade cried,
« Poor Maiden, thou wert happy! thou hadst lived
Blessing and blest, if I had never stray'd,
Needlessly rigid from my peaceful path.
And thou hast left thine home then, and obey'd
The feverish fancies of thine ardent brain!
And hast thou left him too, the youth whose eye,
For ever glancing on thee, spake so well
Affection's eloquent tale ?»
                    So as he said,
Rush'd the warm purple to the Virgin's cheek.
« I am alone,» she answer'd, « for this realm
Devoted.» Nor to answer more the Maid
Endur'd ; for many a melancholy thought
Throng'd on her aching memory. Her mind's eye
Beheld Domremi and the fields of Arc :
Her burthen'd heart was full ; such grief she felt,
Yet such sweet solacing of self-applause
As cheers the banish'd Patriot's lonely hours
When Fancy pictures to him all he loved,
Till the big tear-drop rushes o'er its orb,
And drowns the soft enchantment.
                    With a look
That spake solicitous wonder, Conrade eyed
The silent Maid ; nor would the Maid suppress
The thoughts that swell'd within her, or from him
Hide her soul's workings. « 'T was on the last day
Before I left Domremi ; eve had closed,
I sate beside the brook, my soul was full,
As if inebriate with Divinity—
Then, Conrade! I beheld a ruffian herd
Circle a flaming pile, where at the stake
A woman stood ; the iron bruised her breast,
And round her limbs ungarmented, the fire
Curl'd its fierce flakes. I saw her countenance,
I knew MYSELF.» 73 Then, in subdued tones
Of Calmness, « There are moments when the soul
From her own impulse with strange dread recoils,
Suspicious of herself : but with a full
And perfect faith I know this vision sent
From Heaven, and feel of its unerring truth,
As that God liveth, that I live myself,
The feeling that deceives not.»
                    By the hand
Her Conrade held and cried, « Ill-fated Maid,
That I have torn thee from Affection's breast,
My soul will groan in anguish. Thou wilt serve,
Like me, the worthless Court, and having served,
In the hour of ill abandon'd, thou wilt curse
The duty that deluded. Of the world
Fatigued, and loathing at my fellow-men,
I shall be seen no more. There is a path 74—
The eagle hath not mark'd it, the young wolf
Knows not its hidden windings:—I have trod
That path, and mark'd a melancholy den,
Where one whose jaundiced soul abhors itself,
May pamper him in complete wretchedness.
There sepulchred, the ghost of what he was,
Conrade shall dwell ; and in the languid hour,
When the jarr'd senses sink to a sick calm,
Shall mourn the waste of frenzy !»
                    Then the Maid
Fix'd upon Conrade her commanding eye :

« I pass'd the fertile Auxerrois,» she cried ;
« The vines had spread their interwoven shoots
Over the unpruned vineyards, and the grape
Rotted beneath the leaves, for there was none
To tread the vintage, and the birds of heaven
Had had their fill. I saw the cattle start
As they did hear the loud alarum bell, 75
And with a piteous moaning vainly seek
To fly the coming slaughterers. I look'd back
Upon the cottage where I had partook
The peasant's meal, and saw it wrapt in flames.
And then I thank'd my God that I had burst
The stubborn ties which fetter down the soul
To selfish happiness, and on this earth
Was as a pilgrim.76—Conrade ! rouse thyself !
Cast the weak nature off! 77 a time like this
Is not for gentler feelings, for the glow
Of love, the overflowings of the heart ;
There is oppression in thy country, Conrade !
There is a cause, a holy cause, that needs
The brave man's aid. Live for it, and enjoy
Earth's noblest recompense, thine own esteem :
Or die in that good cause, and thy reward
Shall sure be found in Heaven.»
                    He answer'd not,
But clasping to his heart the Virgin's hand,
Hasten'd across the plain. She with dim eyes,
For gushing tears obscured them, follow'd him
Till lost in distance. With a weight of thought
Opprest, along the poplar-planted Vienne
Awhile she wander'd, then upon the bank
She laid her down, and watch'd the tranquil stream
Flow with a quiet murmuring, by the clouds
Of evening purpled. The perpetual flow,
The ceaseless murmuring, lull'd her to such dreams
As Memory in her melancholy mood
Loves best. The wonted scenes of Arc arose ;
She saw the forest brook, the weed that waved
Its long green tresses in the stream, the crag
Which overbrow'd the spring, and that old yew
Which through the bare and rifted rock had forced
Its twisted trunk, the berries, cheerful red
Starring its gloomy green. Her pleasant home
She saw, and those who made that home so dear,
Her loved lost friends. The mingled feelings fill'd
Her eyes, when from behind a voice was heard,
« O Lady ! canst thou tell me where to find
The Maid whom Heaven hath sent to rescue France ?»
Thrill'd by the well-known tones, she started up,
And fell upon the neck of Theodore.

« Have I then found thee !» cried the impassion'd youth ;
« Henceforth we part no more, but where thou goest,
Thither go I. Beloved ! in the front
Of battle thou shalt find me at thy side ;
And in the breach this breast shall be thy shield
And rampart. Oh, ungenerous! why from me
Conceal the inspiration ? why from me
Hide thy miraculous purpose ? Am I then
So all-unworthy that thou shouldst set forth
Beneath another's guidance ?»
                    Thus he cried,
Mingling reproach with tenderness, yet still
Clasping with warm embrace the Maid belov'd.
She, of her bidding and futurity
Awhile forgetful, patient of the embrace,

3

With silent tears of joy bedew'd his neck.
At length,—« I hope,» she cried, « thou art not come
With heavier fault and breach of nearer tie!
How did thy mother spare thee,—thou alone
The stay and comfort of her widow'd age?
Did she upon thy parting steps bestow
Her free-will blessing, or hast thou set forth,
Which Heaven forbid, unlicensed, and unblest?»

     « Oh, surely not unblest!» the youth replied:
Yet conscious of his unrepented fault,
With countenance flush'd, and faltering in reply :
« She wept at my departure, she would fain
Have turn'd me from my purpose, and my heart
Perhaps had fail'd me, if it had not glow'd
With ardour like thine own ; the sacred fire
With which thy bosom burns had kindled me :
High in prophetic hope, I bade her place
Her trust in Heaven ; I bade her look to hear
Good tidings soon of glorious victory :
I told her I should soon return,—return
With thee, and thou wouldst be to her old age
What Madelon had been.»
             As thus he spake,
Warm with the imaginary bliss, he clasp'd
The dear one closer to his yearning heart.
But the devoted Virgin in his arms
Started and shudder'd, for the flaming pile
Flash'd on remembrance now, and on her soul
The whole terrific vision rose again.
A death-like paleness at the dreadful thought
Wither'd her cheek ; the sweat suffused her brow,
And, falling on the neck of Theodore,
Feeble and faint she hung. His eager eye
Concentring all the anguish of the soul,
And strain'd in anxious love, gazed fearfully
With wondering anguish ; till the ennobling thought
Of her high mission roused her, and her soul
Collected, and she spake.
          « My Theodore,
Thou hast done ill to quit thy mother's home!
Alone and aged she will weep for thee,
Wasting the little that is left of life
In anguish. Now go back again to Arc,
And cheer her wintry hours of widowhood,
And love my memory there. »
          Swift he exclaimed,—
« Nay, Maid! the pang of parting is o'erpast,
And Elinor looks on to the glad hour
When we shall both return. Amid the war
How many an arm will seek thy single life,
How many a sword and spear—I will go with thee
And spread the guardian shield !»
          « Nay,» she replied,
« I shall not need thy succour in the war.
Me Heaven, if so seem good to its high will,
Will save. I shall be happier, Theodore,
Thinking that thou dost sojourn safe at home,
And make thy mother happy.»
          The youth's cheek
A rapid blush disorder'd. « Oh ! the court
Is pleasant, and thy soul would fain forget
A humble villager, who only boasts
The treasure of the heart !»
          She look'd at him
With the reproaching eye of tenderness:

« Injurious man ! Devoted for this realm,
I go a willing victim. The dark veil
Hath been for me withdrawn, these eyes beheld
The fearful features of Futurity.
Yes, Theodore, I shall redeem my country,
Abandoning for this the joys of life,
Yea, life itself !» Then on his neck she fell,
And with a faltering voice, « Return to Arc !
I do not tell thee there are other maids
As fair ; for thou wilt love my memory,
Hallowing to me the temple of thy heart.
Worthy a happier, [78] not a better love,
My Theodore !»—Then, pressing his pale lips,
A last and holy kiss the Virgin fix'd,
And rush'd across the plain.
          She reach'd the court
Breathless. The mingled movements of her mind
Shook every fibre. Sad and sick at heart,
Fain to her lonely chamber's solitude
The Maiden had retired ; but her the King
Met on the threshold. He of the late scene
Forgetful and his crime, as cheerful seem'd
As though there had not been a God in Heaven !
« Enter the hall,» he cried, « the masquers there
Join in the dance. Why, Maiden, art thou sad !
Has that rude madman shook thy gentle frame
With his strange frenzies ?»
          Ere the Maid replied,
The Son of Orleans came with joyful speed,
Poising his massy javelin.
          « Thou hast roused
The sleeping virtue of the sons of France ;
They crowd around the standard,» cried the Chief.
« My lance is ponderous, and my sword is sharp'd
To meet the mortal combat. Mission'd Maid,
Our brethren sieged in Orleans, every moment
Gaze from the watch-tower with the sick'ning eye
Of expectation.»
          Then the King exclaim'd,—
« O chosen by Heaven ! defer one day thy march,
That, humbled at the altar, we may join
The general prayer. Be these our holy rites
To-morrow's task ;—to-night for merriment !»

The Maid replied,—« The wretched ones in Orleans,
In fear and hunger and expiring hope,
Await my succour, and my prayers would plead
In Heaven against me, did they waste one hour
When active duty calls. For this night's mirth
Hold me excused ; in truth I am not fit
For merriment ; a heavy charge is on me,
And I must put away all mortal thoughts.» [79]
Her heart was full ; and pausing, she repress'd
The unbidden anguish. « Lo ! they crowd around
The standard ! Thou, Dunois, the chosen troops
Marshal in speed, for early with the dawn
We march to rescue Orleans from the foe.»

BOOK V.

Scarce had the early dawn from Chinon's towers
Made visible the mist that curl'd along
The river's winding way, when from her couch
The martial Maid arose. She mail'd her limbs ;

The white plumes nodded o'er her helmed head ;
She girt the sacred falchion by her side,
And, like a youth who from his mother's arms,
For his first field impatient, breaks away,
Poising the lance went forth.

          Twelve hundred men,
Rearing in order'd ranks their glittering spears,
Await her coming. Terrible in arms
Before them tower'd Dunois, his manly face
O'ershadow'd by the helmet's iron cheeks.
The assembled court gazed on the marshall'd train,
And at the gate the aged prelate stood
To pour his blessing on the chosen host.
And now a soft and solemn symphony
Was heard, and, chaunting high the hallow'd hymn,
From the near convent came the vestal maids.
A holy banner, woven by virgin hands,
Snow-white they bore. A mingled sentiment
Of awe, and eager ardour for the fight,
Thrill'd through the army, as the reverend man
Took the white standard, and with heaven-ward eye
Call'd on the God of Justice, blessing it.
The Maid, her brows in reverence unhelm'd,
Her dark hair floating on the morning gale,
Knelt to his prayer, and stretching forth her hand
Received the mystic ensign. From the host
A loud and universal shout burst forth,
As rising from the ground, on her white brow
She placed the plumed casque, and waved on high
The banner'd lilies. On their way they march,
And dim in distance, soon the towers of Chinon
Fade from the eye reverted.

          The sixth sun,
Purpling the sky with his dilated light,
Sunk westering ; when embosom'd in the depth
Of that old forest, which for many a league
Shadows the hills and vales of Orleannois,
They pitch their tents. The hum of occupation
Sounds ceaseless. Waving to the evening gale
The streamers wanton ; and, ascending slow
Beneath the foliage of the forest-trees,
With many a light hue tinged, the curling smoke
Melts in the impurpled air. Leaving her tent,
The martial Maiden wander'd through the wood ;
There, by a streamlet, on the mossy bank
Reclined, she saw a damsel ; her long locks
With willow wreathed ; upon her lap there lay
A dark-hair'd man listening as she did sing
Sad ditties, and enwreathe to bind his brow
The melancholy garland. At the sound
Of one in arms approaching, she had fled ;
But Conrade, looking upward, recognized
The Maid of Arc. « Nay, fear not, Isabel, »
Said he, « for this is one of gentle kind,
Whom even the wretched need not fear to love. »

So saying, he arose and took her hand,
And held it to his bosom. « My weak heart,
Though school'd by wrongs to loathe at human kind,
Will beat, rebellious to its own resolves.
Come hither, outcast one ! and call her friend,
And she shall be thy friend more readily,
Because thou art unhappy. »
          Isabel
Saw a tear starting in the Virgin's eye,
And glancing upon Conrade, she too wept,

Wailing his wilder'd senses.
          « Mission'd Maid ! »
The warrior cried, « be happy ! for thy power
Can make this sufferer so. From Orleans driven,
Orphan'd by war, and of her only friend
Bereft, I found her wandering in the wilds,
Worn out with want and wretchedness. Thou, *JOAN*,
Wilt his beloved to the youth restore ;
And, trust me, Maid ! the miserable feel
When they on others bestow happiness,
Their happiest consolation. »
          She replied,
Pressing the damsel's hand, in the mild tone
Of equal friendship, solacing her cares :
« Soon shall we enter Orleans, » said the Maid ;
« A few hours in her dream of victory
England shall triumph ; then to be awaked
By the loud thunder of Almighty wrath !
Irksome meantime the busy camp to me,
A solitary woman. Isabel,
Wert thou the while companion of my tent,
Lightlier the time would pass. Return with me,
I may not long be absent. »
          So she spake.
The wanderer in half-utter'd words express'd
Grateful assent. « Art thou astonish'd, Maid,
« That one though powerful is benevolent ?
In truth thou well mayest wonder ! » Conrade cried,
« But little cause to love the mighty ones
Hath the low cottager ! for with its shade
Doth Power, a barren death-dew-dropping tree,
Blast ev'ry herb beneath its baleful boughs !
Tell thou thy sufferings, Isabel ! Relate
How warr'd the chieftains, and the people died.
The mission'd Virgin hath not heard thy woes ;
And pleasant to mine ear the twice-told tale
Of sorrow. »
          Gazing on the martial Maid,
She read her wish, and spake. « A wanderer now,
Friendless and hopeless, still I love to think
Upon my native home, and call to mind
Each haunt of careless youth ; the woodbined wall,
The jessamine that round the straw-roof'd cot
Its fragrant branches wreath'd, beneath whose shade
I wont to sit and watch the setting sun,
And hear the redbreast's lay. Nor far remote,
As o'er the subject landscape round I gazed,
The towers of Yenville rose upon the view.
A foreign master holds my father's home !
I, far away, remember the past years,
And weep.

          Two brethren form'd our family ;
Humble we were, and happy. Honest toil
Procured our homely sustenance ; our herds
Duly at morn and evening to my hand
Gave their full stores ; the vineyard we had rear'd
Purpled its clusters in the southern sun,
And, plenteous produce of my father's toil,
The yellow harvest billow'd o'er the plain.
How cheerful, seated round the blazing hearth
When all the labour of the day was done,
We past the evening hours ! for they would sing
Or cheerful roundelay, or ditty sad
Of maid forsaken and the willow weed,
Or of the doughty Paladins of France,
Some warlike fit, the while my spinning wheel

Humm'd not unpleasing round !
                              Thus long we lived,
And happy.   To a neighbouring youth my hand,
In holy wedlock soon to be consign'd,
Was plighted ! my poor Francis !» Here she paused,
And here she wept awhile.

                    « We did not dream
The desolating sword of War would stoop
To us ; but soon, as with the whirlwind's speed,
Ruin rush'd round us. 80   Mehun, Clery, fell,
The banner'd Leopard waved on Gergeau's wall !
Baugenci yielded ; soon the foe approach'd
The towers of Yenville.
                    Fatal was the hour
To wretched Isabel : for from the wall
The rusty sword was taken, and the shield
Which long had moulder'd on the mouldering nail,
To meet the war repair'd.   No more was heard
The ballad, or the merry roundelay ;
The clattering hammer's clank, the grating file
Harsh sounded through the day a dismal din.
I never shall forget their mournful sound !

« My father stood encircling his old limbs
In long-forgotten arms.   ' Come, boys,' he cried,
' I did not think that this grey head again
Should bear the helmet's weight ! but in the field
Better to boldly die a soldier's death,
Than here be tamely butcher'd.   Isabel,
Go to the abbey : if we should survive
We soon shall meet again : if not, my child,
There is a better world !'
                    In broken words,
Lifting his looks to Heaven, my father breath'd
His blessing on me.   As they strode away,
My brethren gazed on me and wrung my hand
In silence, for they loved their Isabel.
From the near cottage Francis join'd the troop.
Then did I look on our forsaken home,
And almost sob my very soul away !
For all my hopes of happiness were fled,
Like a vain dream !»

                    « Perish these mighty ones,»
Cried Conrade, « these prime ministers of death,
Who stalk elated o'er their fields of fame,
And count the thousands they have massacred,
And with the bodies of the innocent, rear
Their pyramid of glory ! perish these,
The epitome of all the pestilent plagues
That Egypt knew ! who pour their locust swarms
O'er ravaged realms, and bid the brooks run blood.
FEAR and DESTRUCTION go before their path,
And FAMINE dogs their footseps.   God of Justice,
Let not the innocent blood cry out in vain !»

Thus while he spake, the murmur of the camp
Rose on their ear : first like the distant sound
When the full-foliaged forest to the storm
Shakes its hoarse head ; anon with louder din ;
And through the opening glade gleam'd many a fire.
The Virgin's tent they enter'd ; there the board
Was spread, the wanderer of the fare partook,
Then thus her tale renew'd.
                    « Slow o'er the hill
Whose rising head conceal'd our cot I past,

Yet on my journey paused awhile, and gazed
And wept ; for often had I crost the hill
With cheerful step, and seen the rising smoke
Of hospitable fire ; alas ! no smoke
Curl'd o'er its melancholy chimneys now !
Orleans I reach'd.   There in the suburbs stood
The abbey ; and ere long I learnt the fall
Of Yenville.
                    On a day, a soldier ask'd
For Isabel.   Scarce could my faltering feet
Support me—It was Francis, and alone—
The sole survivor of the fatal fight !

« And soon the foes approach'd : impending war
Soon sadden'd Orleans. 81   There the bravest chiefs
Assemble : Thouars, Coarase, Chabannes,
And the Sire Chappelle 82 in successful war
Since wounded to the death, and that good Knight
Giresme of Rhodes, who in a better cause
Can never wield the crucifix that hilts
His hallow'd sword, 83 and Xaintrailles ransom'd now,
And Fayette late released, and that young Duke 84
Who at Verneuil senseless with many a wound
Fell prisoner, and La Hire, the merriest man 85
That ever yet did win his soldiers' love,
And over all for hardihood renown'd
The Bastard Orleans.
                    These within the town
Expect the foe.   Twelve hundred chosen men
Well tried in war, uprear the guardian shield
Beneath their banners.   Dreadful was the sight
Of preparation.   The wide suburbs stretch'd
Along the pleasant borders of the Loire,
Late throng'd with multitudes, now feel the hand
Of ruin. 86   These preventive care destroys,
Lest England, shelter'd by the friendly walls,
Securely should approach.   The monasteries
Fell in the general waste.   The holy monks
Unwillingly their long-accustom'd haunts
Abandon, haunts where every gloomy nook
Call'd to awaken'd memory some trace
Of vision seen, or sound miraculous.
Trembling and terrified, their noiseless cells
For the rude uproar of a world unknown
The nuns desert : their abbess, more composed,
Collects her maids around, and tells her beads,
And pours the timid prayer of piety.
The citizens with long and ceaseless stroke
Dig up the violated earth, to impede
The foe : the hollow chambers of the dead
Echoed beneath.   The brazen-trophied tomb,
Thrown in the furnace, now prepares to give
The death it late recorded.   It was sad
To see so wide a waste ; the aged ones
Hanging their heads, and weeping as they went
O'er the fall'n dwellings of their happier years ;
The stern and sullen silence of the men
Musing on vengeance : and, but ill represt,
The mother's fears as to her breast she clasp'd
Her ill-doom'd infant.   Soon the suburbs lay
One ample ruin ; the huge stones removed,
Wait in the town to rain the storm of death.

« And now without the walls the desolate plain
Stretch'd wide, a rough and melancholy waste,
With uptorn pavements and foundations deep

Of many a ruin'd dwelling : nor within
Less dreary was the scene; at evening hour
No more the merry viol's note was heard, [87]
No more the aged matron at her door
Humm'd cheery to her spinning-wheel, and mark'd
Her children dancing to the roundelay.
The chieftains, strengthening still the massy walls,
Survey them with the prying eye of fear.
The eager youth in dreadful preparation
Strive in the mimic war.   Silent and stern,
With the hurrying restlessness of fear, they urge
Their gloomy labours.   In the city dwelt
An utter silence of all pleasant sounds,
But all day long the armourers' beat was heard,
And all the night it echoed.

     Soon the foe
Led to our walls the siege : as on they move
The clarions clangor, and the cheerful fife,
According to the thundering drum's deep sound,
Direct their measured march.   Before the ranks
Stalks the stern form of Salisbury, the scourge
Of France ; and Talbot tower'd by his side,
Talbot, at whose dread name the froward child
Clings mute and trembling to his nurse's breast.
Suffolk was there, and Hungerford, and Scales,
And Fastolffe, victor in the frequent fight.
Dark as the autumnal storm they roll'd along,
A countless host !   From the high tower I mark'd
The dreadful scene; I saw the iron blaze
Of javelins sparkling to the noontide sun,
Their banners tossing to the troubled gale,
And—fearful music—heard upon the wind
The modulated step of multitudes.

« There in the midst, shuddering with fear, I saw
The dreadful stores of death ; tremendous roll'd
Over rough roads the harsh wheels ; the brazen tubes
Flash'd in the sun their fearful splendour far,
And last the loaded waggons creak'd along.

« Nor were our chieftains, whilst their care procured
Human defence, neglectful to implore
That heavenly aid, deprived of which the strength
Of man is weakness.   Bearing through our streets
The precious relics of the holy dead,
The monks and nuns pour'd many an earnest prayer,
Devoutly join'd by all.   Saint Aignan's shrine,
Was throng'd by supplicants, the general voice
Call'd on Saint Aignan's name [88] again to save
His people, as of yore, before he past
Into the fulness of eternal rest,
When by the Spirit to the lingering camp
Of Ætius borne, he brought the timely aid,
And Attila with all his multitudes
Far off retreated to their field of shame.»

And now Dunois, for he had seen the camp
Well-order'd, enter'd.   « One night more in peace
England shall rest,» he cried, « ere yet the storm
Burst on her guilty head !   Then, their proud vaunts
Forgotten, or remember'd to their shame,
Vainly her chiefs shall curse the hour when first
They pitch'd their tents round Orleans.»
     « Of that siege,»
The Maid of Arc replied, « gladly I hear
The detail.   Isabel proceed ! for soon

Destined to rescue this devoted town,
The tale of all the ills she hath endur'd,
I listen, sorrowing for the past, and feel
High satisfaction at the saviour power
To me commission'd.»
     Thus the Virgin spake,
Nor Isabel delay'd.   « And now more near
The hostile host advancing pitch their tents.
Unnumber'd streamers wave, and clamorous shouts,
Anticipating conquest, rend the air
With universal uproar.   From their camp
A herald comes ; his garb emblazon'd o'er
With leopards and the lilies of our realm,
Foul shame to France !   The summons of the foe
He brought.»
    The Bastard interrupting cried,
« I was with Gaucour and the assembled chiefs,
When by his office privileged and proud
That herald spake, as certain of success
As he had made a league with Victory :—
'Nobles of France rebellious ! from the chief
Of yon victorious host, the mighty Earl
Of Salisbury, now there in place of him
Your Regent John of Bedford : in his name
I come, and in our sovereign Lord the King's,
Henry.   Ye know full well our Master's claim,
Incontrovertible, to this good realm,
By right descent, and solemnly confirm'd
By your great Monarch and our mighty King
Fifth Henry, in the treaty ratified
At Troyes, [89] wherein your Monarch did disclaim
All future right and title to this crown,
His own exempted, for his son and heirs
Down to the end of time.   This sign'd and seal'd
At the holy altar, and by nuptial knot
Of Henry and your princess, yields the realm,
Charles dead and Henry, to his infant son
Henry of Windsor.   Who then dares oppose
My Master's title, in the face of God
Of wilful perjury, most atrocious crime,
Stands guilty, and of flat rebellion 'gainst
The Lord's anointed.   He at Paris crown'd
With loud acclaim from duteous multitudes,
Thus speaks by me :—Deliver up your town
To Salisbury, and yield yourselves and arms,
So shall your lives be safe : and such his grace,
If of your free accord to him you pay
Due homage as your sovereign Lord and King.
Your rich estates, your houses shall be safe,
And you in favour stand, as is the Duke,
Philip of Burgundy.   But—mark me well !
If obstinately wilful, you persist
To scorn his proffer'd mercy ; not one stone
Upon another of this wretched town
Shall then be left ; and when the English host
Triumphant in the dust have trod the towers
Of Orleans, who survive the dreadful war
Shall die like traitors by the hangman's hand.
Ye men of France, remember Caen and Roan !'

« He ceased : nor Gaucour for a moment paus'd
To form reply.

     'Herald ! to all thy vaunts
Of English sovereignty let this suffice
For answer : France will only own as king
Him whom the people chuse.   On Charles's brow,

Transmitted through a long and good descent,
The crown remains. We know no homage due
To English robbers, and disclaim the peace
Inglorious made at Troyes by factious men
Hostile to France. Thy Master's proffer'd grace [94]
Meets the contempt it merits. Herald, yes,
We shall remember Meaux, and Caen, and Roan!
Go tell the mighty Earl of Salisbury,
That, as like Blanchard, Gaucour dares his power;
Like Blanchard, he can mock his cruelty,
And triumph by enduring. Speak I well,
Ye men of Orleans?'
                              Never did I hear
A shout so universal as ensued
Of approbation. The assembled host
As with one voice pour'd forth their loyalty,
And struck their sounding shields; and walls and towers
Echoed the loud uproar. The herald went.
The work of war began.»
                              «A fearful scene,»
Cried Isabel. «The iron storm of death
Clash'd in the sky; from the strong engines hurl'd
Huge rocks with tempest force convulsed the air;
Then was there heard at once the clang of arms,
The bellowing cannons, and the soldier's shout,
The female's shriek, the affrighted infant's cry,
The groan of death : discord of dreadful sounds
That jarr'd the soul!
                              Nor while the encircling foe
Leaguer'd the walls of Orleans, idly slept
Our friends : for winning down the Loire its way
The frequent vessel with provision fraught,
And men, and all the artillery of death,
Cheer'd us with welcome succour. At the bridge
These safely stranded mock'd the foeman's force.
This to prevent, Salisbury their watchful chief [90]
A mighty work prepares. Around our walls
Encircling walls he builds, surrounding thus
The city. Firm'd with massiest buttresses,
At equal distance, sixty forts protect
The pile. But chief where in the sieged town
The six great avenues meet in the midst, [91]
Six castles there he rear'd impregnable,
With deep-dug moats and bridges drawn aloft,
Where over the strong gate suspended hung
The dread portcullis. Thence the gunner's eye
From his safe shelter could with ease survey
Intended sally, or approaching aid,
And point destruction.
                              It were long to tell
And tedious, how with many a bold assault
The men of Orleans rush'd upon their foes;
How after difficult fight the enemy
Possess'd the Tournelles, [92] and the embattled tower
That shadows from the bridge the subject Loire;
Though numbering now three thousand daring men,
Frequent and fierce the garrison repell'd
Their far out-numbering foes. From every aid
Included, they in Orleans groan'd beneath
All ills accumulate. The shatter'd roofs
Gave to the dews of night free passage there,
And ever and anon the ponderous stone,
Ruining where'er it fell, with hideous crash
Came like an earthquake, startling from his sleep
The affrighted soldier. From the brazen slings
The wild-fire balls shower'd through the midnight sky; [93]

And often their huge engines cast among us
The dead and loathsome cattle of their camp,
As though our enemies, to their deadly league
Forcing the common air, would make us breathe
Poisonous pollution. [94] Through the streets were seen
The frequent fire, and heaps of dead, in haste
Piled up and steaming to infected heaven.
For ever the incessant storm of death
Pours down, and shrouded in unwholesome vaults [95]
The wretched females hide, not idle there
Wasting the hours in tears, but all employ'd,
Or to provide the hungry soldier's meal,
Or tear their garments to bind up his wounds—
A sad equality of wretchedness!

«Now came the worst of ills, for Famine came :
The provident hand deals out its scanty dole,
Yielding so little its supply to life
As but protracted death. The loathliest food
Hunted with eager eye, and dainty deem'd;
The dog is slain that at his master's feet
Howling with hunger lay; with jealous fear,
Hating a rival's look, the husband hides
His miserable meal; the famish'd babe
Clings closely to his dying mother's breast;
And...horrible to tell!...where thrown aside
There lay unburied in the open streets
Huge heaps of carcasses, the soldier stands
Eager to mark the carrion crow for food. [96]

«O peaceful scenes of childhood! pleasant fields!
Haunts of mine infancy, where I have stray'd
Tracing the brook along its winding way,
Or pluck'd the primrose, or with giddy speed
Chased the gay butterfly from flower to flower!
O days in vain remember'd! how my soul,
Sick with calamity, and the sore ills
Of hunger, dwelt upon you!... quiet home!
Thinking of you amid the waste of war,
I could in bitterness have cursed the great
Who made me what I was! a helpless one,
Orphan'd, and wanting bread!»
                              «And be they curst!»
Conrade exclaim'd, his dark eye flashing rage;
«And be they curst! O groves and woodland shades,
How blest indeed were you, if the iron rod
Should one day from Oppression's hand be wrench'd
By everlasting Justice! Come that hour,
When in the Sun the Angel of the Lord [97]
Shall stand and cry to all the fowls of heaven,
'Gather ye to the supper of your God,
That ye may eat the flesh of mighty men,
Of captains, and of kings!' Then shall be peace.»

«And now, lest all should perish,» she pursued,
«The women and the infirm must from the town
Go forth and seek their fate.
                              I will not now
Recal the moment when on my poor Francis
With a long look I hung! At dead of night
Made mute by fear, we mount the secret bark,
And glide adown the stream with silent oars:
Thus thrown upon the mercy of mankind,
I wander'd reckless where, till wearied out,
And cold at heart, I laid me down to die:
So by this warrior found. Him I had known

And loved, for all loved Conrade who had known him;
Nor did I feel so pressing the hard hand
Of want in Orleans, ere he parted thence
On perilous envoy. For of his small fare»—

«Of this enough,» said Conrade; «Holy Maid!
One duty yet awaits me to perform.
Orleans her envoy sent me, to demand
Aid from her idle Sovereign. Willingly
Did I achieve the hazardous enterprise,
For rumour had already made me fear
The ill that hath fallen on me. It remains,
Ere I do banish me from human kind,
That I re-enter Orleans, and announce
Thy march. T is night...and hark! how dead a silence!
Fit hour to tread so perilous a path!»

So saying, Conrade from the tent went forth.

BOOK VI.

The night was calm, and many a moving cloud
Shadow'd the moon. Along the forest glade
With swift foot Conrade past, and now had reach'd
The plain, where whilome by the pleasant Loire,
Cheer'd with the song, the rustics had beheld
The day go down upon their merriment:
No song of Peace now echoed on its banks,
There tents were pitch'd, and there the sentinel,
Slow pacing on his sullen rounds, beheld
The frequent corse roll down the tainted stream.
Conrade with wider sweep pursued his way,
Shunning the camp, now hush'd in sleep and still.
And now no sound was heard save of the Loire,
Murmuring along. The noise of coming feet
Alarm'd him; nearer drew the fearful sound
As of pursuit; anon...the clash of arms!
That instant rising o'er a broken cloud
The moon-beams shone, where two with force combined
Prest on a single foe; he, warding still
Their swords, retreated in the unequal fight,
As he would make the city. Conrade shook
His long lance for the war, and strode along.
Full in the breast of one with forceful arm
Plunged he the spear of death; and, as dismay'd
The other fled, «Now haste we to the gates,
Frenchman!» he cried. On to the stream they speed,
And plunging stemm'd with sinewy stroke the tide,
Soon on the opposite shore arrived and safe.

«Whence art thou?» cried the warrior; «on what charge
Commission'd!»
                «Is it not the voice of Conrade?»
Francis exclaim'd; « and dost thou bring to us
Tidings of speedy aid? Oh! had it come
A few hours earlier! Isabel is gone!»

«Nay, she is safe,» cried Conrade; «her I found
When wilder'd in the forest, and consign'd
To the protection of the holy Maid,
The delegate of Heaven. One evening more
And thou shalt see thine Isabel. Now say,
Wherefore alone? A fugitive from Orleans,
Or sent on dangerous service from the town?»

«There is no food in Orleans,» he replied,
«Scarce a meal more! the assembled chiefs resolved,
If thou shouldst bring no tidings of near aid,
To cut their way to safety, or by death
Prevent the pangs of famine. 98 One they sought
Who venturous in the English camp should spy
Where safest they might rush upon the foe.
The perilous task I chose, then desperate
Of happiness.»
                So saying, they approach'd
The gate. The sentinel, soon as he heard
Thitherward footsteps, with uplifted lance
Challenged the darkling travellers. At their voice
He draws the strong bolts back, and painful turns
The massy entrance. To the careful chiefs
They pass. At midnight of their extreme state
Counselling they sat, serious and stern. To them
Conrade:—

«Assembled warriors! sent from God,
There is a holy Maid by miracles
Made manifest. Twelve hundred chosen men
Follow her hallow'd standard. These Dunois,
The strength of France, arrays. With the next noon
Ye shall behold their march.»
                        Astonishment
Seized the assembled chiefs, and joy by doubt
Little repress'd. «Open the granaries!»
Xaintrailles exclaim'd; « give we to all the host
With hand unsparing now the plenteous meal;
To-morrow we are safe! for Heaven all just
Hath seen our sufferings and decreed their end.
Let the glad tidings echo through the town!
God is with us!»

«Rest not in too full faith,»
Graville replied, « on this miraculous aid...
Some frenzied female whose wild fantasy,
Shaping vain dreams, infects the credulous
With her own madness! That Dunois is there,
Leading in arms twelve hundred chosen men,
May give good hope, yet let not we our food
Be lavish'd, lest the warrior in the fight
Should haply fail, and Orleans be the prey
Of England!»
                «Chief! I tell thee,» Conrade cried,
« I did myself behold the sepulchre,
Fulfilling what she spake, give up those arms
Which surely for no common end the grave
Through many an age hath held inviolate.
She is the delegate of the Most High,
And shall deliver Orleans!»
                        Gaucour then:—
«Be it as thou hast said. High hope I feel,
For surely to no vulgar tale these chiefs
Would yield a light belief. Our scanty stores
Must yield us, ere another week elapse,
To death or England. Tell through all our troops
There is a holy virgin sent from God;
They in that faith invincible shall war
With more than mortal fury.»
                        Thus the Chief,
And what he said seem'd good. The men of Orleans,
Long by their foeman bay'd, a victim band
To war, and woe, and want, such transport felt,
As when the Mexicans, 99 with eager eye
Gazing to Huixachtla's distant top,
On that last night, doubtful if ever morn

Again shall cheer them, mark the mystic fire
Flame on the breast of some brave prisoner,
A dreadful altar. As they see the blaze.
Beaming on Iztapalapan's near towers,
Or on Tezcuco's calmy lake flash'd far,
Songs of thanksgiving and the shout of joy
Wake the loud echo; the glad husband tears
The mantling aloe from the female's face,
And children, now deliver'd from the dread
Of everlasting darkness, look abroad,
Hail the good omen, and expect the sun
Uninjured still to run his flaming race.

Thus while in that besieged town the night
Wan'd sleepless, silent slept the hallow'd host.
And now the morning came. From his hard couch,
Lightly upstarting and bedight in arms,
The Bastard moved along, with provident eye
Marshalling the troops. All high in hope they march;
And now the sun shot from the southern sky
His noon-tide radiance, when afar they hear
The hum of men, and mark the distant towers
Of Orleans, and the bulwarks of the foe,
And many a streamer wantoning in air.
These as they saw and thought of all the ills
Their brethren had endured, beleaguer'd there
For many a month; such ardour for the fight
Burnt in each bosom, as young Ali felt,
Then when Mohammed of the assembled tribe
Ask'd who would be his vizir. Fierce in faith,
Forth from the race of Hashem stept the youth,
« Prophet of God! lo...I will be the man!»
And well did Ali merit that high post,
Victorious upon Beder's fertile vale,
And on mount Ohud, and before the walls
Of Chaibar, when down-cleaving to the chest
His giant foe, he grasp'd the massy gate,
Shook with strong arm and tore it from the fort,
And lifted it in air, portentous shield!

« Behold the tower of Orleans!» cried Dunois.
« Lo! this the vale where on the banks of Loire,
Of yore, at close of day the rustic band
Danced to the roundelay. In younger years
As oft I glided down the silver stream,
Frequent upon the lifted oar I paused,
Listening the sound of far-off merriment.
There wave the hostile banners! martial Maid,
Give thou the signal!... let me rush upon
These ministers of murder, who have sack'd
The fruitful fields, and made the hamlet haunts
Silent, or hearing but the widow's groan.
Give thou the signal, Maiden!»
                           Her dark eye
Fix'd sadly on the foe, the holy Maid
Answer'd him. « Ere the bloody sword be drawn,
And slaughter be let loose, befits us send
Some peaceful messenger, who shall make known
The will of Heaven. So timely warn'd, our foes
Haply may yet repent, and quit in peace
Besieged Orleans, for I fain would spare
The bloody price of victory.»
                           So she said:
And as she spake, a soldier from the ranks
Came forward: « I will be thy messenger,
Maiden of God! and to the English camp

Will bear thy bidding.»
                       « Go,» the Virgin cried:
« Say to the Lord of Salisbury, and the chiefs
Of England, Suffolk, Fastolffe, Talbot, Scales,
Invaders of the country, say, thus says
THE MAID OF ORLEANS. 'With your troops retire
In peace. Of every captured town the keys
Restore to Charles; so bloodless you may seek
Your native island; for the God of Hosts
Thus hath decreed. To Charles the rightful heir,
By long descent and by the willing choice
Of duteous subjects, hath the Lord assign'd
His conquest. In his name the Virgin comes
Arm'd with his sword; yet not of mercy void.
Depart in peace: for ere the morrow dawns,
Victorious upon yonder wall shall wave
The holy banner.'» To the English camp
Fearless the warrior strode.
                           At mid-day meal
With all the dissonance of boisterous mirth,
The British chiefs caroused and quaff'd the bowl
To future conquest. By the sentinel
Conducted came the Frank.
                           « Chiefs,» he exclaim'd,
« Salisbury, and ye the representatives
Of the English king, usurper of this realm,
To ye the leaders of the invading host
I come, no welcome messenger. Thus saith
THE MAID OF ORLEANS. ' With your troops retire
In peace. Of every captured town the keys
Restore to Charles; so bloodless you may seek
Your native island; for the God of Hosts
Thus hath decreed. To Charles the rightful heir,
By long descent and by the willing choice
Of duteous subjects, hath the Lord assign'd
His conquest. In his name the Virgin comes
Arm'd with his sword; yet not of mercy void.
Depart in peace : for ere the morrow dawns,
Victorious upon yonder wall shall wave
The holy banner.' »
                       Wonder made a pause ;
To this the laugh succeeds. « What!» Fastolffe cried,
« A woman warrior hath your monarch sent
To save devoted Orleans? By the rood,
I thank His Grace. If she be young and fair,
No worthless prize, my lords! Go, tell your Maid,
Joyful we wait her coming.»
                           There was one
Among the English chiefs who had grown old
In arms, yet had not age unnerved his limbs,
But from the flexile nimbleness of youth
Braced to unyielding stiffness. One who saw
The warrior at the feast, might well have deem'd
That Talbot with his whole collected might
Wielded the sword in war, for on his neck
The veins were full,[100] and every muscle bore
The character of strength. He his stern eye
Fix'd on the herald, and before he spake,
His silence threaten'd.[101]
                           « Get thee gone!» exclaim'd
The indignant chief; «away! nor think to scare
With girlish fantasies the English host
That scorns your bravest warriors. Hie thee thence,
Insolent herald! tell this frantic girl,
This courtly minion, to avoid my wrath,
For if she dares the war, I will not stain

My good blood-rusted sword—but she shall meet
The mockery of the camp!»

        «Nay, scare her not,»
Replied their chief; «go, tell this Maid of Orleans,
That Salisbury longs to meet her in the fight.
Nor let her fear that rude and iron chains
Shall gall her tender limbs; for I myself
Will be her prison, and——»

        «Contemptuous man!
No more!» the Frank exclaim'd, as to his cheek
Rush'd the red anger. «Bearing words of peace
And timely warning came I to your camp;
Here with rude mockery and with insolence
Receiv'd. Bear witness, chieftains! that the French,
Free from blood-guiltiness, shall meet the war.»

  «And who art thou?» cried Suffolk, and his eye
Grew fierce and wrath-inflam'd: «What fool art thou,
Who at this woman's bidding comest to brave
The host of England? thou shalt have thy meed!»
Then turning to the sentinel he cried,
«Prepare a stake! and let the men of Orleans,
And let this woman who believes her name
May privilege her apostle, see the fire
Consume him. [102] Build the stake! for by my God
He shall be kalender'd of this new faith
First martyr.»

        As he spake, a sudden flush
Came o'er the herald's cheek, and his heart beat
With quicker action; but the sudden flush,
Alarmed Nature's impulse, faded soon
To such a steady hue as spake the soul
Roused up with all its powers, and unsubdued,
And glorying in endurance. Through the camp,
Soon as the tidings spread, a shout arose,
A hideous shout, more savage than the howl
Of midnight wolves; and round the Frank they throng'd,
To gaze upon their victim. He pass'd on;
And as they led him to the appointed place
Look'd round, as though forgetful of himself,
And cried aloud,—«Oh! woe it is to think
So many men shall never see the sun
Go down! ye English mothers, mourn ye now!
Daughters of England, weep! for hard of heart
Still your mad leaders urge the impious war,
And for their folly and their wickedness,
Your sons, your husbands, by the sword must fall.
Long-suffering is the Lord, and slow to wrath,
But heavy are his judgments!»

        He who spake
Was young and comely; had his cheek been pale
With dread, and had his eye look'd fearfully
Sure he had won compassion; but the blood
Gave now a livelier meaning to his cheek,
As with a prophet's look and prophet's voice
He raised his ominous warning: they who heard
Wonder'd, and they who rear'd the stake urged on
With half-unwilling hands their slacken'd toil,
And doubted what might follow.

        Not unseen
Rear'd they the stake, and piled around the wood;
In sight of Orleans and the Maiden's host, [103]
Had Suffolk's arrogant fierceness bade the work
Of death be done. The Maiden's host beheld;
At once in eager wrath they raised the loud
And general clamour,—«Lead us to the foe!»

«Not upon us, O God!» the Maid exclaim'd,
«Not upon us cry out the innocent blood!»
And bade the signal sound. In the English camp
The clarion and the trumpet's blare was heard,
In haste they seize their arms, in haste they form,
Some by bold words seeking to hide their fear
Even from themselves, some silently in prayer,
For much their hearts misgave them.

        But the rage
Of Suffolk swell'd within him. «Speed your work!»
Exclaim'd the savage earl; «kindle the pile
That France may see the fire, and in defeat
Feel aggravated shame!»

        And now they bound
The herald to the stake: he cried aloud,
And fix'd his eye on Suffolk,—«Let not him
Who girdeth on his harness boast himself
As he that puts it off![104] they come! they come!
God and the Maid!»

        The host of France approach'd,
And Suffolk, eagerly beheld the fire
Draw near the pile; sudden a fearful shout
Toward Orleans turn'd his eye, and thence he saw
A mailed man upon a mailed steed
Come thundering on.

      As when Chederles comes [105]
To aid the Moslem on his deathless steed,
Swaying his sword with such resistless arm,
Such mightiest force, as he had newly quaff'd
The hidden waters of eternal youth,
Till with the copious draught of life and strength
Inebriate; such, so fierce, so terrible,
Came Conrade through the camp. Aright, aleft,
The affrighted foemen scatter from his spear;
Onward he drives, and now the circling throng
Fly from the stake, and now he checks his course,
And cuts the herald's bonds, and bids him live,
And arm, and fight, and conquer.

        «Haste thee hence
To Orleans,» cried the warrior. «Tell the chiefs
There is confusion in the English camp.
Bid them come forth.» On Conrade's steed the youth
Leapt up, and hasten'd onward. He the while
Turn'd to the war.

      Like two conflicting clouds,
Pregnant with thunder, rush'd the hostile hosts.
Then man met man, then on the batter'd shield
Rung the loud lance, and through the darken'd sky
Fast fell the arrowy storm. Amid his foes
The Bastard's arm sway'd irresistible
The strokes of death; and by his side the Maid
Led the fierce fight,—the Maid, though all unused
To such rude conflict, now inspired by Heaven,
Flashing her flamy falchion through the troops,
That like the thunderbolt, where'er it fell,
Scatter'd the trembling ranks. The Saracen,
Though arm'd from Cashbin or Damascus, wields
A weaker sword; nor might that magic blade
Compare with this, which Oriana saw
Flame in the ruffian Ardan's robber hand,
When, sick and cold as death, she turn'd away
Her dizzy eyes, lest they should see the fall
Of her own Amadis. Nor plated shield,
Nor the strong hauberk, nor the crested casque,
Stay that descending sword. Dreadful she moved,
Like as the Angel of the Lord went forth

4

And smote his army, when the Assyrian king,
Haughty of Hamath and Sepharvaim fallen,
Blasphemed the God of Israel.
　　　　　　　　　　Yet the fight
Hung doubtful, where, exampling hardiest deeds,
Salisbury mow'd down the foe, and Fastolffe strove,
And in the hottest doings of the war
Tower'd Talbot. He, remem'bring the past day
When from his name the affrighted sons of France
Fled trembling, all astonish'd at their force
And wontless valour, rages round the field
Dreadful in fury; yet in every man
Meeting a foe fearless, and in the faith
Of Heaven's assistance firm.
　　　　　　　　　The clang of arms
Reaches the walls of Orleans. For the war
Prepared, and confident of victory,
Forth speed the troops. Not when afar exhaled
The hungry raven snuffs the steam of blood
That from some carcass-cover'd field of fame
Taints the pure air, wings he more eagerly
To riot on the gore, than rush'd the ranks;
Impatient now for many an ill endured
In the long siege, to wreak upon their foes
Due vengeance. Then more fearful grew the fray;
The swords that late flash'd to the evening sun [106]
Now quench'd in blood their radiance.
　　　　　　　　　　O'er the host
Howl'd the deep wind that, ominous of storms,
Roll'd on the lurid clouds. The blacken'd night
Frown'd, and the thunder from the troubled sky
Roar'd hollow. Javelins clash'd and bucklers rang;
Shield prest on shield; loud on the helmet jarr'd
The ponderous battle-axe; the frequent groan
Of death commingling with the storm was heard,
And the shrill shriek of fear.
　　　　　　　　　Even such a storm
Before the walls of Chartres quell'd the pride
Of the third Edward, when the heavy hail
Smote down his soldiers, and the conqueror heard
God in the tempest, and remember'd him
Of the widows he had made, and in the name
Of blessed Mary vow'd the vow of peace. [107]

Lo! where the holy banner waved aloft,
The lambent lightnings play. Irradiate round,
As with a blaze of glory, o'er the field
It stream'd miraculous splendour. Then their hearts
Sunk, and the English trembled; with such fear
Possess'd, as when the combined host beheld
The sun stand still on Gibeon, at the voice
Of that king-conquering warrior, he who smote
The country of the hills, and of the south,
From Baal-gad to Halak, and their chiefs,
Even as the Lord commanded. Swift they fled
From that portentous banner, and the sword
Of France; though Talbot with vain valiancy
Yet urged the war, and stemm'd alone the tide
Of conquest. Even their leaders felt dismay;
Fastolffe fled fast, and Salisbury in the rout
Mingles, and, all impatient of defeat,
Borne backward Talbot turns. Then echoed loud
The cry of conquest, deeper grew the storm,
And darkness, hovering o'er on raven wing,
Brooded the field of death.
　　　　　　　　　　Nor in the camp

Deem themselves safe the trembling fugitives.
On to the forts they haste. Bewilder'd there
Amid the moats by fear, and the dead gloom
Of more than midnight darkness, plunge the troops,
Crush'd by fast following numbers who partake
The death they give. As rushing from the snows
Of winter liquefied, the torrent tide
Resistless down the mountain rolls along,
Till at the brink of giddy precipice
Arrived, with deafening clamour down it falls:
Thus borne along, tumultuously the troops,
Driven by the force behind them, plunge amid
The liquid death. Then rose the dreadful cries
More dreadful, and the dash of breaking waves
That to the passing lightning as they broke
Gleam'd horrible.
　　　　　　　　Nor of the host, so late
Triumphing in the pride of victory,
And swoln with confidence, had now escaped
One wretched remnant, had not Talbot's mind,
Slow as he moved unwilling from the war,
What most might profit the defeated ranks
Ponder'd. He, reaching safe the massy fort
Named from St John, there kindled up on high
The guiding fire. Not unobserved it blazed;
The watchful guards on Tournelles, and the pile
Of that proud city in remembrance fond
Call'd London, light the beacon. Soon the fires
Flame on the summit of the circling forts
Which girt around with walls and deep-delved moats,
Included Orleans. O'er the shadowy plain
They cast a lurid splendour; to the troops
Grateful as to the way-worn traveller,
Wandering with parch'd feet o'er Arabian sands,
The far-seen cistern; he for many a league
Travelling the trackless desolate, where heaved
With tempest swell the desert billows round,
Pauses, and shudders at his perils past,
Then wild with joy speeds on to taste the wave
So long bewail'd.
　　　　　　　　Swift as the affrighted herd
Scud o'er the plain, when frequent through the sky
Flash the fierce lightnings, speed the routed host
Of England. To the sheltering forts they haste,
Though safe, of safety doubtful, still appall'd
And trembling, as the pilgrim who by night,
On his way wilder'd, to the wolf's deep howl
Hears the wood echo, when from the fell beast
Escaped, of some small tree the topmast branch
He grasps close clinging, still of that keen fang
Fearful, his teeth jar, and the big drops stand
On his cold quivering limbs.
　　　　　　　　　　Nor now the Maid
Greedy of vengeance urges the pursuit.
She bids the trumpet of retreat resound;
A pleasant music to the routed ranks
Blows the loud blast. Obedient to its voice
The French, though eager on the invaders' heads
To wreak their wrath, stay the victorious sword.

Loud is the cry of conquest as they turn
To Orleans. There what few to guard the town
Unwilling had remain'd, haste forth to meet
The triumph. Many a blazing torch they held,
Which, raised aloft amid the midnight storm,
Flash'd far a festive light. The Maid advanced;

Deep through the sky the hollow thunders roll'd; [108]
Innocuous lightnings round the hallow'd banner
Wreath'd their red radiance.
        Through the open'd gate
Slow past the laden convoy. Then was heard
The shout of exultation, and such joy
The men of Orleans at that welcome sight
Possess'd, as when, from Bactria late subdued,
The mighty Macedonian led his troops
Amid the Sogdian desert, where no stream
Wastes on the wild its fertilizing waves.
Fearful alike to pause, or to proceed;
Scorch'd by the sun that o'er their morning march
Steam'd his hot vapours, heart-subdued and faint;
Such joy as then they felt, when from the heights
Burst the soul-gladdening sound! for thence was seen
The evening sun silvering the vale below,
Where Oxus roll'd along.
        Clamours of joy
Echo along the streets of Orleans, wont
Long time to hear the infant's feeble cry,
The mother's frantic shriek, or the dread sound;
When from the cannon burst its stores of death.
Far flames the fire of joy on ruin'd piles,
And high heap'd carcasses, whence scared away
From his abhorred meal, on clattering wing
Rose the night-raven slow.
        In the English forts
Sad was the scene. There all the livelong night
Steals in the straggling fugitive; as when
Past is the storm, and o'er the azure sky
Serenely shines the sun, with every breeze
The waving branches drop their gather'd rain,
Renewing the remembrance of the storm.

BOOK VII.

Strong were the English forts, [109] by daily toil
Of thousands rear'd on high, when arrogant
With hoped-for conquest Salisbury bade rise
The mighty pile, from succour to include
Besieged Orleans. Round the city walls
Stretch'd the wide circle, massy as the fence
Erst by the fearful Roman on the bounds
Of Caledonia raised, when soul-enslaved
Her hireling plunderers fear'd the car-borne chiefs
Who rush'd from Morven down.
        Strong battlements
Crested the ample bulwark, on whose top
Secure the charioteer might wheel along.
The frequent buttress at just distance rose
Declining from its base, and sixty forts
Lifted aloft their turret-crested heads,
All firm and massy. But of these most firm,
As though of some large castle each the keep,
Stood six square fortresses with turrets flank'd,
Piles of unequall'd strength, though now deem'd weak
Gainst puissance more than mortal. Safely hence
The skilful archer, entering with his eye [110]
The city, might, himself the while unseen,
Through the long opening shower his winged deaths.
Loire's waves diverted fill'd the deep-dug moat

Circling the pile, a bulwark vast, as what
Round their dishearten'd camp and stranded ships
The Greeks uprear'd a common sepulchre
Of thousands slaughter'd, and the doom'd death-place
Of many a chief, when Priam's patriot-son
Rush'd in his wrath and scatter'd their pale tribes.

But cowering now amid their sheltering forts
Tremble the invading host. Their leader's care
In anxious vigilance prepares to ward
Assault expected. Nor the Maid's intent
Did he not rightly areed; though vain his hope
To kindle in their breasts the wonted flame
Of valour; for by prodigies unmann'd
They wait the morn. The soldiers' pride was gone,
The blood was on their swords, their bucklers lay
Unburnish'd and defiled; [111] they sharpen'd not
Their blunted spears, the affrighted archer's hand
Relax'd not his bent bow. To them, confused
With fears of unknown danger, the long night
Was dreadful, but more dreadful dawn'd the day.

The morning came. The martial Maid arose.
Lovely in arms she moved. Around the gate
Eager again for conquest throng the troops.
High tower'd the Son of Orleans, in his strength
Poising the ponderous spear. His batter'd shield,
Witnessing the fierce fray of yesternight,
Hung on his sinewy arm.
        « Maiden of Arc, »
So as he spake approaching, cried the Chief,
« Well hast thou proved thy mission, as by words
And miracles attested when dismay'd
The stern theologists forgot their doubts,
So in the field of slaughter now confirm'd.
Yon well-fenced forts protect the fugitives,
And seem as in their strength they mock'd our force.
Yet must they fall. »
        « And fall they shall! » replied
The Maid of Orleans. « Ere the sun be set,
The lily on that shatter'd wall shall wave
Triumphant.—Men of France! ye have fought well
On yon blood-reeking plain. Your humbled foes
Lurk trembling now amid their massy walls.
Wolves that have ravaged the neglected flock!
The Shepherd—the Great Shepherd is arisen!
Ye fly! yet shall not ye by flight escape
His vengeance. Men of Orleans! it were vain
By words to waken wrath within your breasts.
Look round! Your holy buildings and your homes,—
Ruins that choke the way! Your populous town,
One open sepulchre! Who is there here
That does not mourn a friend, a brother slain,
A parent famish'd—or his dear loved wife
Torn from his bosom—outcast—broken-hearted—
Cast on the mercy of mankind? »
        She ceased;
The cry of indignation from the host
Burst forth, and all impatient for the war
Demand the signal. These Dunois arrays
In four battalions. Xaintrailles, tried in war,
Commands the first; Xaintrailles, who oft subdued
By adverse fortune to the captive chain,
Still more tremendous to the enemy,
Lifted his death-fraught lance, as erst from earth

Antæus vaunting in his giant bulk,
When graspt by force Herculean, down he fell
Vanquish'd, anon uprose more fierce for war.

Gaucour o'er one presides, the steady friend
To long-imprison'd Orleans; of his town
Beloved guardian, he the dreadful siege
Firmly abiding, prudent still to plan
Irruption, and with youthful vigour swift
To lead the battle, from his soldiers' love
Prompter obedience gained, than ever fear
Forced from the heart reluctant.
                          The third band
Alençon leads: he on the fatal field
Verneuil, when Buchan and the Douglas died,
Fell senseless. Guiltless he of that day's loss,
Wore undisgraced awhile the captive chain.
The Monarch him mindful of his high rank
Had ransom'd, once again to meet the foe
With better fortune.
                          O'er the last presides
Dunois the bastard, mighty in the war.
His prowess knew the foes, and his fair fame
Confess'd, since when before his stripling arm
Fled Warwick; Warwick, he whose fair renown
Greece knew and Antioch and the holy soil
Of Palestine, since there in arms he pass'd
On gallant pilgrimage; yet by Dunois
Baffled, and yielding him the conqueror's praise.
And by his side the martial Maiden pass'd,
Lovely in arms as that Arcadian boy
Parthenopæus, when, the war of beasts [112]
Disdaining, he to murder man rush'd forth,
Bearing the bow, and those Dictæan shafts
Diana gave, when she the youth's fair form
Saw soften'd, and forgave the mother's fault.

St Loup's strong fort stood first. Here Gladdisdale [113]
Commands the fearful troops.
                          As lowering clouds
Swept by the hoarse wind o'er the blacken'd plain,
Moved on the host of France: they from the fort,
Through secret opening, shower their pointed shafts,
Or from the battlements the death-tipt spear
Hurl fierce. Nor from the strong arm only launch'd
The javelin fled, but driven by the strain'd force
Of the balista, [114] in one carcass spent
Stay'd not; through arms and men it makes its way,
And leaving death behind, still holds its course
By many a death unclogg'd. With rapid march
Right onward they advanced, and soon the shafts,
Impell'd by that strong stroke beyond the host,
Wasting their force, fell harmless. Now they reach'd
Where by the bayle's embattled wall [115] in arms
The knights of England stood. There Poynings shook
His lance, and Gladdisdale his heavy mace
For the death-blow prepared. Alençon here,
And here the Bastard strode, and by the Maid
That daring man who to the English host,
Then insolent of many a conquest gain'd,
Bore her bold bidding. A rude coat of mail [116]
Unhosed, unhooded, as of lowly line,
Arm'd him, though here amid the high-born chiefs
Pre-eminent for prowess. On his head
A black plume shadow'd the rude-featured helm. [117]
Then was the war of men, when front to front

They rear'd the hostile hand, for low the wall
Where the bold Frenchman's upward-driven spear
Might pierce the foemen.
                          As Alençon moved,
On his crown-crested helm [118] with ponderous blow
Fell Gladdisdale's huge mace. Back he recoil'd
Astounded; soon recovering, his keen lance
Thrust on the warrior's shield: there fast-infix'd,
Nor could Alençon the deep-driven spear
Recover, nor the foeman from his grasp
Wrench the contended weapon. Fierce again
He lifts the mace, that on the ashen hilt
Fell full; it shiver'd, and the Frenchman held
A pointless truncheon. Where the Bastard fought
The spear of Poynings through his plated mail
Pierced, and against the iron fence beneath [119]
Blunted its point. Again he speeds the spear;
At once Dunois on his broad buckler bears
The unharming stroke, and aims with better fate
His javelin. Through his sword-arm did it pierce,
Maugre the mail. Hot from the streaming wound
Again the weapon fell, and in his breast
Even through the hauberk drove.
                          But there the war
Raged fiercest where the martial Maiden moved,
The minister of wrath; for thither throng'd
The bravest champions of the adverse host:
And on her either side two warriors stood
Of unmatch'd prowess, still with eager eye
Shielding her form, and aiming at her foes
Their deadly weapons, of themselves the while
Little regarding. One was that bold man
Who bade defiance to the English chiefs,
Firmly he stood, untired and undismay'd,
Though on his burgonet the frequent spear
Drove fierce, and on his arm the buckler hung
Heavy, thick-bristled with the hostile shafts,
Even like the porcupine when in his rage,
Roused, he collects within him all his force,
Himself a quiver. And of loftier port
On the other hand tower'd Conrade. Firmly fenced,
A jazerent of double mail he wore,
Beneath whose weight one but of common strength
Had sunk. Untired the conflict he endured,
Wielding a battle-axe ponderous and keen,
Which gave no second stroke; for where it fell,
Not the strong buckler nor the plated mail
Might save, nor crested casque. On Molyn's head,
As at the Maid he aim'd his javelin,
Forceful it fell, and shiver'd with the blow
The iron helm, and to his brain-pan drove
The fragments. At their comrade's death amazed,
And for a moment fearful, shrunk the foes.
That instant Conrade, with an active bound, [120]
Sprung on the battlements; there firm he stood,
Guarding ascent. The herald and the Maid
Follow'd, and soon the exulting cry of France
Along the lists was heard, as waved aloft
The holy banner. Gladdisdale beheld,
And hasting from his well-defended post
Sped to the fiercer conflict. To the Maid
He strode, on her resolved to wreak his rage,
With her to end the war. Nor did not JOAN
Areed his purpose: lifting up her shield
Prepared she stood, and poised her sparkling spear.
The English Chief came on; he raised his mace;

With circling force, the iron weight swung high, [121]
As Gladdisdale with his collected might
Drove the full blow. The man of lowly line
That instant rush'd between, and rear'd his shield
And met the broken blow, and thrust his lance
Fierce through the gorget of the English knight.
A gallant man, of no ignoble line,
Was Gladdisdale. His sires had lived in peace,
They heap'd the hospitable hearth, they spread
The feast, their vassals loved them, and afar
The traveller told their fame. In peace they died;
For them the venerable fathers pour'd
A requiem when they slept, and o'er them raised
The sculptured monument. Now far away
Their offspring falls, the last of all his race,
Slain in a foreign land, and doom'd to share
The common grave.

        Then terror seized the host,
Their Chieftain dead. And lo! where on the wall,
Bulwark'd of late by Gladdisdale so well,
The Son of Orleans stood, and sway'd around
His falchion, keeping thus at bay the foe,
Till on the battlements his comrade sprang,
And raised the shout of conquest. Then appall'd
The English fled : nor fled they unpursued,
For mingling with the foremost fugitives,
The gallant Conrade rush'd ; and with the throng
The knights of France together o'er the bridge
Rush'd forward. Nor the garrison within
Durst let the ponderous portcullis fall,
For in the entrance of the fort the fight
Raged fiercely, and together through the gate
The vanquish'd English and their eager foes
Pass'd in the flying conflict.

        Well I deem
And wisely did that daring Spaniard act
At Vera-Cruz. when he, his yet sound ships
Dismantling, left no spot where treacherous fear
Might still with wild and wistful eye look back.
For knowing no retreat, his desperate troops
In conquest sought their safety; victors hence
At Tlascala, and o'er the Cholulans,
And by Otompan, on that bloody field
When Mexico her patriot thousands pour'd,
Fierce in vain valour on their dreadful foes.
There was a portal to the English fort
Which open'd on the wall; [122] a speedier path
In the hour of safety, whence the charmed eye
Might linger down the river's pleasant course.
Fierce in the gate-way raged the deadly war ;
For there the Maiden strove, and Conrade there,
And he of lowly line, bravelier than whom
Fought not in that day's battle. Of success
Desperate, for from above the garrison
Could wield no arms, so certain to bestow
Equal destruction, of the portal's aid
The foe bethought them : then with lesser force
Their weapons fell ; abandon'd was the gate ;
And soon from Orleans the glad citizens
Beheld the hallow'd banner on the tower
Triumphant. Swift along the lofty wall
The English haste to St John's neighbouring fort,
Flying with fearful speed. Nor from pursuit
The victors ceased, but with the fugitives
Mingled and waged the war : the combatants,
Lock'd in the hostile grasp, together fall

Precipitate.

        But foremost of the French,
Dealing destruction, Conrade rush'd along;
Heedless of danger, he to the near fort
Pass'd in the fight; nor did not then the Chief
What most might serve bethink him : firm he stood
In the portal, and one moment looking back
Lifted his loud voice : thrice the warrior cried,
Then to the war address'd him, now assail'd
By numerous foes, who arrogant of power
Threaten'd his single valour. He the while
Stood firm, not vainly confident, or rash,
But of his own strength conscious, and the post
Friendly; for narrow was the portal way,
To one alone fit passage, from above
O'erbrow'd by no out-jutting parapet, [123]
Whence death might crush him. He in double mail
Was arm'd; a massy burgonet, well tried
In many a hard-fought field, helming his head;
A buckler broad, and fenced with iron plates,
Bulwark'd his breast. Nor to dislodge the Chief
Could the English pour their numbers, for the way
By upward steps presented from the fort
Narrow ascent, where one alone could meet
The war. Yet were they of their numbers proud,
Though useless numbers were in that strait path,
Save by assault unceasing to out-last
A single warrior, who at length must sink
Fatigued with conquering, by long victory
Vanquish'd.

        There was amid the garrison
A fearless knight who at Verneuil had fought,
And high renown for his bold chivalry
Acquired in that day's conquest. To his fame
The thronging English yield the foremost place.
He his long javelin to transpierce the Frank
Thrust forceful : harmless in his shield it fix'd,
Advantaging the foe; for Conrade lifts
The battle-axe, and smote upon the lance,
And hurl'd its severed point [124] with mighty arm
Fierce on the foe. With wary bend the foe
Shrunk from the flying death; yet not in vain
From that strong hand the fate-fraught weapon fled :
Full on the corselet [125] of a meaner man
It fell, and pierced, there where the heaving lungs,
In vital play distended, to the heart
Roll back their brighten'd tide: from the deep wound
The red blood gush'd : prone on the steps he fell,
And in the strong convulsive grasp of death
Grasp'd his long pike. Of unrecorded name
The soldier died; yet did he leave behind
One who did never say her daily prayers
Of him forgetful; who to every tale
Of the distant war, lending an eager ear,
Grew pale and trembled. At her cottage-door
The wretched one shall sit, and with dim eye
Gaze o'er the plain, where on his parting steps
Her last look hung. Nor ever shall she know
Her husband dead, but tortured with vain hope
Gaze on... then heart-sick turn to her poor babe,
And weep it fatherless!

        The exasperate knight
Drew his keen falchion, and with dauntless step
Moved to the closer conflict. Then the Frank
Held forth his buckler, and his battle-axe
Uplifted. Where the buckler was below

Rounded, the falchion struck, but impotent
To pierce its plated folds; more forceful driven,
Fierce on his crested helm the Frenchman's stroke
Fell; the helm shiver'd; from his eyes the blood
Started; with blood the chambers of the brain
Were fill'd; his breast-plate with convulsive throes
Heaved as he fell.　Victorious, he the prize
At many a tournament had borne away
In mimic war: happy, if so content
With bloodless glory, he had never left
The mansion of his sires.

　　　　　　　　　But terrified
The English stood, nor durst adventure now
Near that death-doing man.　Amid their host
Was one who well could from the stubborn bow
Shower his sharp shafts: well skill'd in wood-craft he,
Even as the merry outlaws who their haunts
In Sherwood held, and bade their bugles rouse
The sleeping stag, ere on the web-woven grass
The dew-drops sparkled to the rising sun.
He safe in distance at the warrior aim'd
The feather'd dart; with force he drew the bow;
Loud on his bracer struck the sounding string;
And swift and strong the well-wing'd arrow flew.
Deep in his shield it hung; then Conrade raised
Again his echoing voice, and call'd for aid,
Nor was the call unheard; the troops of France,
From St Loup's captured fort along the wall
Haste to the portal; cheering was the sound
Of their near footsteps to the Chief; he drew
His falchion forth, and down the steps he rush'd.
Then terror seized the English, for their foes
Swarm'd through the open portal, and the sword
Of Conrade was among them.　Not more fierce
The injured Turnus sway'd his angry arm,
Slaughtering the robber fugitives of Troy;
Nor with more fury through the streets of Paris
Rush'd the fierce king of Sarza, Rodomont,
Clad in his dragon mail.

　　　　　　　　Like some tall rock,
Around whose billow-beaten foot the waves
Waste their wild fury, stood the unshaken man;
Though round him prest his foemen, by despair
Hearten'd.　He, mowing through the throng his path,
Call'd on the troops of France, and bade them haste
Where he should lead the way.　A daring band
Follow'd the adventurous chieftain; he moved on
Unterrified, amid the arrowy shower,
Though on his shield and helm the darts fell fast
As the sear'd leaves that from the trembling tree
The autumnal whirlwind shakes.

　　　　　　　　Nor Conrade paused;
Still through the fierce fight urging on his way,
Till to the gate he came, and with strong hand
Seized on the massy bolts.　These as he drew,
Full on his helm the weighty English sword
Descended; swift he turn'd to wreak his wrath,
When lo! the assailant gasping on the ground,
Cleft by the Maiden's falchion: she herself
To the foe opposing with that lowly man,
For they alone following the adventurous steps
Of Conrade, still had equall'd his bold course,
Shielded him as with eager hand he drew
The bolts: the gate turn'd slow: forth leapt the Chief,
And shiver'd with his battle-axe the chains

That hung on high the bridge.　The impetuous troops,
By Gaucour led, rush'd o'er to victory.

The banner'd lilies on the captured wall
Toss'd to the wind.　« On to the neighbouring fort!»
Cried Conrade; « Xaintrailles! ere the night draws on,
Once more to conquest lead the troops of France!
Force ye the lists, and fill the deep-dug moat,
And with the ram shake down their batter'd walls;
Anon I shall be with you.»　Thus he said;
Then to the Damsel: « Maid of Arc! awhile
Cease we from battle, and by short repose
Renew our strength.»　So saying he his helm
Unlaced, and in the Loire's near flowing stream
Cool'd his hot face.　The Maid her head unhelm'd,
And stooping to the stream, reflected there
Saw her white plumage stain'd with human blood!
Shuddering she saw, but soon her steady soul
Collected: on the banks she laid her down,
Freely awhile respiring, for her breath
Quick panted from the fight: silent they lay,
For gratefully the cooling breezes bath'd
Their throbbing temples.

　　　　　　　　It was now the noon:
The sun-beams on the gently-waving stream
Danced sparkling.　Lost in thought the warrior lay,
Then as his countenance relax'd he cried,—
« Maiden of Arc! at such an hour as this,
Beneath the o'er-arching forest's chequer'd shade,
With that lost woman have I wander'd on,
Talking of years of happiness to come!
Oh, hours for ever fled! delightful dreams
Of the unsuspecting heart! I do believe
If Agnes on a worthier one had fix'd
Her love, that though my heart had nurst till death
Its sorrows, I had never on her choice
Pour'd one upbraiding... but to stoop to him!
A harlot!.... an adulteress!»[126]

　　　　　　　　　In his eye
Red anger flash'd; anon of what she was
Ere yet the foul pollution of the court
Stain'd her fair fame, he thought.　« Oh, happy age!»
He cried, « when all the family of man
Freely enjoy'd their goodly heritage,
And only bow'd the knee in prayer to God!
Calm flow'd the unruffled stream of years along,
Till o'er the peaceful rustic's head the hair
Grew grey in full of time.　Then he would sit
Beneath the coetaneous oak, while round,
Sons, grandsons, and their offspring join'd to form
The blameless merriment; and learnt of him
What time to yoke the oxen to the plough,
What hollow moanings of the western wind
Foretel the storm, and in what lurid clouds
The embryo lightning lies.　Well pleased, he taught,
The heart-smile glowing on his aged cheek,
Mild as the summer sun's decaying light.
Thus quietly the stream of life flow'd on,
Till in the shoreless ocean lost at length.
Around the bed of death his numerous race
Listen'd, in no unprofitable grief,
His last advice, and caught his latest sigh:
And when he died, as he had fallen asleep,
Beneath the aged tree that grew with him
They delved the narrow house: there oft at eve

Drew round their children of the after days,
And pointing to the turf, told how he lived,
And taught by his example how to die.
Maiden ! and such the evening of my days
Fondly I hoped ; and would that I had lived [127]
In those old times, or till some better age
Slumber'd unborn ; for this is a hard race,
An evil generation : nor by day
Nor in the night have respite from their cares
And wretchedness. But I shall be at rest
Soon, in that better world of peace and love
Where evil is not : in that better world,
JOAN ! we shall meet, and he too will be there,
Thy Theodore.»

        Soothed by his words, the Maid
Had listen'd sadly, till at that loved name
She wept. « Nay, Maid!» he cried, « I did not think
To wake a tear—yet pleasant is thy grief !
Thou know'st not what it is, around thy heart
To have a false one wreathe in viper folds.
But to the battle ! in the clang of arms
We win forgetfulness.»

        Then from the bank
He sprang, and helm'd his head. The Maid arose,
Bidding awhile adieu to milder thoughts.
On to the fort they speed, whose name recall'd
England's proud capital to the English host,
Now half subdued, anticipating death,
And vainly wishing they from her white cliffs
Had never spread the sail. Cold terror creeps
Through every vein : already they turn back
Their eager eyes to meditate the flight,
Though Talbot there presided, with their Chief,
The dauntless Salisbury.

        « Soldiers tried in arms !»
Thus, in vain hope to renovate the strength
Of England, spake the Chief, « Victorious friends,
So oft victorious in the hard-fought fight,
What—shrink ye now dismay'd ? Have ye forgot
The plains of Agincourt, when vanquish'd France
Fled with her thousands from your fathers' arms ?
Have ye forgotten how our English swords,
On that illustrious day before Verneuil,
Cut down the flower of all their chivalry?
Then was that noble heart of Douglas pierced, [128]
Bold Buchan bit the earth, and Narbonne died,
And this Alençon, boaster as he is,
Cried mercy to his conqueror. Shall I speak
Of our victorious banner on the walls
Of Yenville and Baugenci triumphing :
And of that later hour of victory
When Clermont and the Bastard plied their spurs ?
Shame ! shame ! that beaten boy is here in arms,
And ye will fly before the fugitives—
Fly from a woman ! from a frantic girl !
Who with her empty mummeries tries to blast
Your courage ; or if miracles she brings,
Aid of the devil ! Who is there among you
False to his country—to his former fame—
To your old leader who so many a time
Hath led ye on to glory ?»

        From the host
A heartless shout arose ; then Talbot's cheek
Grew red with indignation. « Earl,» said he,
Addressing Salisbury, « there is no hope
From these white-liver'd dastards ; and this fort

Will fall an easy conquest : we must out
And gain the Tournelles, better fortified,
Fit to endure long siege : the hope in view
To reach a safer fortress, these our troops
Will better bide the conflict.»

        So he spake,
Wisely advising. Him the Chief replied :
« Well hast thou said : and, Talbot, if our swords
Could through the thickest ranks this sorceress reach,
The hopes of France were blasted. I have fought
In many a field, yet never to a foe
Stoop'd my proud crest : nor difficult to meet
This wizard girl, for from the battlements
I have beheld her foremost in attack,
Playing right valiantly the soldier's part ;
Yet shall not all her witcheries avail
To blunt my good sword's edge.»

        Thus communed they,
And through the host the gladdening tidings ran,
That they should seek the Tournelles. Then their hearts
Gather'd new strength, placing on those strong walls
Dependence ; empty hope ! nor the strong wall,
Nor the deep moat can save, if fear within
Palsy the soldier's arm !

        Them issuing forth,
As from the river's banks they past along,
The Maid beheld ! « Lo ! Conrade !» she exclaim'd,
« The foes advance to meet us—Look ! they lower
The bridge ! and now they rush upon the troops—
A gallant onset ! Dost thou mark the man
Who all the day has by our side endured
The hottest conflict ? I did then behold
His force, and wonder : now his deeds of death
Make all the actions of the former fight
Seem as of no account : knowest thou him?
There is not one amid the host of France
Of fairer promise.»

        « He,» the Chief replied,
« Wretched and prodigal of life, achieves
The exploits of despair : a gallant youth,
Widow'd like me of hope, and but for whom
I had been seen among mankind no more.
Maiden ! with me thy comrade in the war,
His arm is vow'd to heaven. Lo ! where he stands
Bearing the battle's brunt in unmoved strength,
Firm as the mountain, round whose misty head
The unharming tempest breaks!»

        Nor paused they now
In farther converse, to the perilous fray
Speeding, not unobserved ; for Salisbury saw
And called on Talbot. Six, the bravest knights
And sworn with them, against the Virgin's life
Bent their fierce course. She by the herald's side
Now urged the war, when on her white plumed helm
The hostile falchion fell. On high she lifts
Her hallow'd sword, the tenant of the tomb,
And drench'd it in his bosom. Conrade's blow
Fell on another, and the ponderous axe
Shatter'd his brain. With Talbot's giant force
The daring herald urged unequal fight ;
For like some oak that firm with deep-fix'd roots
Defies the storm, the undaunted earl endured
His rude assault. Warding with wary eye
The angry sword, the Frank around his foe
Wheels rapid, flashing his keen weapon fast ;
Now as he marks the earl's descending stroke

Bending anon more fierce in swift attack.
Ill-fated man! one deed of glory more
Shall with the short-lived lightning's splendour grace
This thy death-day; for SLAUGHTER even now
Stands o'er the loom of life, and lifts his sword

Upon her shield the martial Maiden bore
An English warrior's blow, and in his side
Pierced him; that instant Salisbury sped his sword,
Which glancing from her helm fell on the folds
That arm'd her neck, and making there its way,
Stain'd with her blood its edge. The herald saw,
He saw her red blood gushing from the wound,
And turn'd from Talbot heedless of himself,
And, lifting up his falchion, all his force
Concenter'd. On the breast of Salisbury
It fell, and pierced his mail, and through the plate
Beneath drove fierce, and in his heart's-blood plunged.
Lo! as he struck the strength of Talbot came:
Full on his treacherous helm he smote: it burst,
And the stern earl against his fenceless head
Drives with strong arm the murderous sword. She saw,
Nor could the Maiden save her Theodore.

Conrade beheld, and from his vanquish'd foe
Strode terrible in vengeance. Front to front
They stood, and each for the death-blow prepared
His angry might. At once their weapons fell,
The Frank's huge battle-axe, and the keen sword
Of Talbot. He, stunn'd by the weighty blow,
Sunk senseless; by his followers from the field
Convey'd with fearful speed: nor did his stroke
Fall vainly on the Frenchman's crested helm,
Though weak to wound; for from his eyes the fire
Sparkled, and back recoiling with the blow,
He in the Maiden's arms astounded fell.
But now their troops all captainless confused,
Fear seized the English. Not with more dismay
When over wild Caffraria's wooded hills,
Echoes the lion's roar, the timid herd
Fly the death-boding sound. The forts they seek,
Now reckless which, so from that battle's rage
A present refuge. On their flying ranks
The victors press, and mark their course with blood.

But loud the trumpet of retreat resounds,
For now the westering sun with many a hue
Streak'd the gay clouds. «Dunois! the Maiden cried,
Form we around yon stronger pile the siege,
There for the night encamping.» So she said.
The Chief, to Orleans for their needful food,
And enginery to batter that huge pile,
Dismiss'd a troop, and round the Tournelles led
The host beleaguering. There they pitch their tents,
And plant their engines for the morrow's war,
Then to their meal, and o'er the cheerful bowl
Recount the tale of danger; soon to rest
Betaking them, for now the night drew on.

BOOK VIII.

Now was the noon of night; and all was still,
Save where the sentinel paced on his rounds

Humming a broken song. Along the camp
High flames the frequent fire. The warrior Franks,
On the hard earth extended, rest their limbs
Fatigued, their spears lay by them, and the shield
Pillow'd the helmed head: [129] secure they slept;
And busy fancy in her dream renew'd
The fight of yesterday.
       But not to JOAN,
But not to her, most wretched, came thy aid,
Soother of sorrows, Sleep! No more her pulse,
Amid the battle's tumult throbbing fast,
Allow'd no pause for thought. With clasped hands
And fixed eye she sat, the while around
The spectres of the days departed rose,
A melancholy train! Upon the gale
The raven's croak was heard; she started up,
And passing through the camp with hasty step,
Strode to the field of blood.
       The night was calm;
Nor ever clearer welkin canopied
Chaldea, while the watchful shepherd's eye
Survey'd the host of heaven, and mark'd them rise,
Successive, and successively decay,
Lost in the stream of light, as lesser springs
Amid Euphrates' current. The high wall
Cast a deep shadow, and her faltering feet
Stumbled o'er broken arms and carcasses;
And sometimes did she hear the heavy groan
Of one yet struggling in the pangs of death.
She reach'd the spot where Theodore had fall'n,
Before fort London's gate; but vainly there
Sought she the youth, on every clay-cold face
Gazing with such a look [130] as though she fear'd
The thing she sought. Amazement seized the Maid,
For there the victim of his vengeful arm,
Known by the buckler's blazon'd heraldry,
Salisbury lay dead. So as the Virgin stood
Gazing around the plain, she mark'd a man
Pass slowly on, as burthen'd. Him to aid
She sped, and soon with unencumber'd speed
O'ertaking, thus bespake: «Stranger! this weight
Impedes thy progress. Dost thou bear away
Some slaughter'd friend? or lives the sufferer
With many a sore wound gush'd! oh! if he lives,
I will with earnest prayer petition Heaven
To shed its healing on him!»
       So she said;
And, as she spoke, stretch'd forth her careful hands
To ease the burthen. «Warrior!» he replied,
«Thanks for thy proffer'd aim; but he hath ceased
To suffer, and my strength may well suffice
To bear him to the sepulchre. Farewell!
The night is far advanced; thou to the camp
Return: it fits not darkling thus to stray.»

«Conrade!» the Maid exclaimed, for well she knew
His voice—with that she fell upon his neck
And cried, «My Theodore!—but wherefore thus
Through the dread midnight dost thou bear his corse?»

«Peace, Maiden! Conrade cried; «collect thy soul!
He is but gone before thee to that world
Whither thou soon must follow! In the morn,
Ere yet from Orleans to the war we went,
He pour'd his tale of sorrow on mine ear—
Lo, Conrade, where she moves! Beloved Maid!

Devoted for the realm of France she goes,
Abandoning for this the joys of life,
Yea—life itself! Yet on my heart her words
Vibrate. If she must perish in the war,
I will not live to bear the dreadful thought,
That I perchance had saved her. I will go,
Her unknown guardian. Conrade, if I fall...
And trust me I have little love of life...
Do thou in secret bear me from the field,
Lest haply I might meet her wandering eye
A mangled corpse. She must not know my fate.
Do this last act of friendship, and in the flood
Whelm me: so shall she think of Theodore
Without a pang. Maiden, I vow'd with him
That I would dare the battle by thy side,
And shield thee in the war. And now I hoped
Thou hadst not seen his fall.»

    As thus he spake,
He on the earth the clay-cold carcass laid.
With steady eye the wretched Maiden view'd
The life-left tenement: his batter'd arms
Were with the night-dews damp; his brown hair clung
Gore-clotted in the wound, and one loose lock
Play'd o'er his cheek's black paleness.[131] « Gallant
  youth!»
She cried, « I would to God the hour were come
When I might meet thee in the bowers of bliss!
No, Theodore! the sport of winds and waves,
Thy body shall not roll adown the stream,
The sea-wolf's banquet. Conrade, bear with me
The corpse to Orleans, there in hallow'd ground
To rest ; the priest shall say the sacred prayer,
And hymn the requiem to his parted soul.
So shall not Elinor in bitterness
Lament that no dear friend to her dead child
Paid the last office.»

    From the earth they lift
The mournful burthen, and along the plain
Pass with slow footsteps to the city gate.
The obedient sentinel at Conrade's voice
Admits the midnight travellers; on they pass,
Till, in the neighbouring abbey's porch arrived,
They rest the lifeless load.

    Loud rings the bell;
The awaken'd porter turns the heavy door.
To him the Virgin : « Father, from the slain
On yonder reeking field a dear loved friend
I bring to holy sepulture, chaunt ye
The requiem to his soul : to-morrow eve
Will I return, and in the narrow house
Behold him laid to rest.» The father knew
The mission'd Maid, and humbly bow'd assent.

Now from the city, o'er the shadowy plain,
Backward they bend their way. From silent thoughts
The Maid awakening cried...« There was a time,
When thinking on my closing hour of life,
Though with resolved mind, some natural fears
Shook the weak frame: but now the happy hour,
When my emancipated soul shall burst
The cumberous fetters of mortality,
Wishful I contemplate. Conrade! my friend,
My wounded heart would feel another pang
Shouldst thou forsake me!»

    « JOAN!» the Chief replied,
« Along the weary pilgrimage of life

Together will we journey, and beguile
The dreary road, telling with what gay hopes
We in the morning eyed the pleasant fields
Vision'd before; then wish that we had reach'd
The bower of rest!»

    Thus communing they gain'd
The camp, yet hush'd in sleep ; there separating,
Each in the post allotted, restless waits
The day-break.

    Morning came : dim through the shade
The first rays glimmer ; soon the brightening clouds
Drink the rich beam, and o'er the landscape spread
The dewy light. The soldiers from the earth
Leap up invigorate, and each his food
Receives, impatient to renew the war.
Dunois his javelin to the Tournelles points :
« Soldiers of France! behold, your foes are there !»
As when a band of hunters, round the den
Of some wood-monster, point their spears, elate
In hope of conquest and the future feast ;
When on the hospitable board their spoil
Shall smoke, and they, as the rich bowl goes round,
Tell to their guests their exploits in the chase ;
They with their shouts of exultation make
The forest ring ; so elevate of heart,
With such loud clamours for the fierce assault
The French prepare. Nor, guarding now the lists,
Durst the disheartened English man to man
Meet the close conflict. From the barbican, [132]
Or from the embattled wall, [133] they their yeugh bows
Bent forceful, and their death-fraught enginery
Discharged ; nor did the Gallic archers cease
With well-directed shafts their loftier foes
To assail : behind the guardian pavais fenced, [134]
They at the battlements their arrows aim'd,
Showering an iron storm, whilst o'er the bayle,
The bayle now levell'd by victorious France,
Pass'd the bold troops with all their mangonels ; [135]
Or tortoises, [136] beneath whose roofing safe,
They, filling the deep moat, might for the towers
Make fit foundation, or with petraries,
War-wolfs, and beugles, and that murderous sling
The matafund, from whence the ponderous stone
Fled fierce, and made one wound of whom it struck,
Shattering the frame so that no pious hand
Gathering his mangled limbs might him convey
To where his fathers slept : a dreadful train [137]
Prepared by Salisbury over the town besieged
To hurl its ruin ; but that dreadful train,
Must hurl its ruin on the invaders' head,
Such retribution righteous Heaven decreed.

Nor lie the English trembling, for the fort
Was ably garrison'd. Glacidas, the chief,
A gallant man, sped on from place to place,
Cheering the brave ; or if the archer's hand,
Palsied with fear, shot wide the ill-aim'd shaft,
Threatening the coward who betray'd himself,
He drove him from the ramparts. In his hand
The Chief a cross-bow held ; [138] an engine dread
Of such wide-wasting fury, that of yore
The assembled fathers of the Christian church
Pronounced that man accursed whose impious hand
Should point the murderous weapon. Such decrees
Befits the men of God to promulgate,
And with a warning voice, though haply vain,

         5

To cry aloud and spare not, ' Woe to them
Whose hands are full of blood!'
               An English King,
The lion-hearted Richard, their decree
First broke, and heavenly retribution doom'd
His fall by the keen quarrel ; since that day
Frequent in fields of battle, and from far
To many a good knight bearing his death-wound
From hands unknown. With such an instrument,
Arm'd on the ramparts, Glacidas his eye
Cast on the assailing host. A keener glance
Darts not the hawk when from the feather'd tribe
He marks his victim.
             On a Frank he fix'd
His gaze, who, kneeling by the Trebuchet, [39]
Charged its long sling with death. Him Glacidas,
Secure behind the battlements, beheld,
And strung his bow ; then, bending on one knee,
He in the groove the feather'd quarrel placed, [40]
And levelling with firm eye, the death-wound mark'd.
The bow-string twang'd, on its swift way the dart
Whizz'd fierce, and struck, there where the helmet's clasps
Defend the neck ; a weak protection now,
For through the tube which draws the breath of life
Pierced the keen shaft ; blood down the unwonted way
Gush'd to the lungs, prone fell the dying man
Grasping, convulsed, the earth : a hollow groan
In his throat struggled, and the dews of death
Stood on his livid cheek. The days of youth
He had pass'd peaceful, and had known what joys
Domestic love bestows, the father once
Of two fair infants ; in the city hemm'd
During the hard siege, he had seen their cheeks
Grow pale with famine, and had heard their cries
For bread! his wife, a broken-hearted one,
Sunk to the cold grave's quiet, and her babes
With hunger pined, and followed ; he survived,
A miserable man, and heard the shouts
Of joy in Orleans, when the Maid approach'd,
As o'er the corpse of his last little one
He heap'd the unhallow'd earth. To him the foe
Perform'd a friendly part, hastening the hour
Grief else had soon brought on.
             The English Chief,
Pointing again his arbalist, let loose
The string ; the quarrel, driven by that strong blow,
True to its aim, fled fatal : one it struck
Dragging a tortoise to the moat, and fix'd
Deep in his liver ; blood and mingled gall
Flow'd from the wound, and writhing with keen pangs
Headlong he fell. He for the wintry hour
Knew many a merry ballad and quaint tale,
A man in his small circle well-beloved.
None better knew with prudent hand to guide
The vine's young tendrils, or at vintage time
To press the full-swoln clusters ; he, heart-glad,
Taught his young boys the little all he knew,
Enough for happiness. The English host
Laid waste his fertile fields : he to the war,
By want compell'd, adventured, in his gore
Now weltering.
             Nor the Gallic host remit
Their eager efforts ; some the watery fence, [41]
Beneath the tortoise roof'd, with engines apt
Drain painful ; part, laden with wood, throw there
Their buoyant burthens, labouring so to gain

Firm footing : some the mangonels supply,
Or charging with huges stones the murderous sling, [42]
Or petrary, or in the espringal
Fix the brass-winged arrows. [43] Hoarse around
Rose the confused din of multitudes.
Fearless along the ramparts Gargrave moved,
Cheering the English troops. The bow he bore ;
The quiver rattled as he moved along.
He knew aright to aim the feather'd shafts,
Well-skill'd to pierce the mottled roe-buck's side,
O'ertaken in his flight. Him passing on,
From some huge martinet, [44] a ponderous stone
Struck : on his breast-plate falling, there the driving
      weight
Shatter'd the bone, and with his mangled lungs
The fragments mingled. On the sunny brow
Of a fair hill, wood-circled, stood his home,
A pleasant dwelling, whence the well-pleased eye
Gazed o'er the subject distance, and survey'd
Streams, hills, and forests, fair variety!
The traveller knew its hospitable towers,
For open were the gates, and blazed for all
The friendly fire. By glory lured, the youth
Went forth ; and he had bathed his falchion's edge
In many a Frenchman's gore ; now crush'd beneath
The ponderous fragments' force, his mangled limbs
Lie quivering.
             Lo! towards the levelled moat,
A moving tower the men of Orleans wheel [45]
Four stages elevate. Above was hung,
Equalling the walls, a bridge ; in the lower stage
The ponderous battering-ram : a troop within
Of archers, through the opening, shot their shafts. [46]
In the loftiest part was Conrade, so prepared
To mount the rampart ; for he loathed the chase,
And loved to see the dappled foresters
Browze fearless on their lair with friendly eye,
And happy in beholding happiness,
Not meditating death : the bowman's art
Therefore he little knew, nor was he wont
To aim the arrow at the distant foe,
But uprear in close conflict, front to front,
His death-red battle-axe, and break the shield,
First in the war of men. There, too, the Maid
Awaits, impatient on the wall to wield
Her falchion. Onward moves the heavy tower,
Slow o'er the moat, and steady, though the foe
Shower'd there their javelins, aim'd their engines there,
And from the arbalist the fire-tipt dart [47]
Shot lightning through the sky. In vain it flamed,
For well with many a reeking hide secured,
Pass'd on the dreadful pile, and now it reach'd
The wall. Below, with forceful impulse driven,
The iron-horned engine swings its stroke,
Then back recoils ; while they within who guide,
In backward step collecting all their strength,
Anon the massy beam with stronger arm
Drive full and fierce. So rolls the swelling sea
Its curly billows to the unmoved foot
Of some huge promontory, whose broad base
Breaks the rough wave ; the shiver'd surge rolls back,
Till, by the coming billow borne, it bursts
Again, and foams with ceaseless violence :
The wanderer, on the sunny clift outstretch'd,
Harks to the roaring surges, as they rock
His weary senses to forgetfulness.

But nearer danger threats the invaders now;
For on the ramparts, lower'd from above
The bridge reclines. [148] An universal shout
Rose from the hostile hosts.   The exultant Franks
Clamour their loud rejoicing, whilst the foe
Lift up the warning voice, and call aloud
For speedy succour there, with deafening shout
Cheering their comrades.   Not with louder din
The mountain torrent flings precipitate
Its bulk of waters, though amid the fall
Shatter'd, and dashing silvery from the rock.

Lo! on the bridge he stands, the undaunted man,
Conrade! the gather'd foes along the wall
Throng opposite, and on him point their pikes,
Cresting with armed men the battlements.
He undismay'd, though on that perilous height,
Stood firm, and hurl'd his javelin; the keen point
Pierced through the destined victim, where his arm
Join'd the broad breast: a wound which skilful care
Haply had heal'd; but, him disabled now
For farther service, the unpitying throng
Of his tumultuous comrades from the wall
Thrust headlong.   Nor did Conrade cease to hurl
His deadly javelins fast, for well within
The tower was stored with weapons, to the knight
Quickly supplied: nor did the mission'd Maid
Rest idle from the combat; she, secure,
Aim'd the keen quarrel, taught the cross-bow's use
By the willing mind that what it well desires
Gains aptly: nor amid the numerous throng,
Though haply erring from their destined mark,
Sped her sharp arrows frustrate.   From the tower
Ceaseless the bow-strings twang: the knights below,
Each by his pavais bulwark'd, thither aim'd
Their darts, and not a dart fell woundless there,
So thickly throng'd they stood; and fell as fast.
As, when the monarch of the east goes forth.
From Gemna's banks and the proud palaces
Of Delhi, the wild monsters of the wood
Die in the blameless warfare: closed within
The still-contracting circle, their brute force
Wasting in mutual rage, they perish there,
Or by each other's fury lacerate,
The archer's barbed arrow, or the lance
Of some bold youth of his first exploits vain,
Rajah or Omrah, for the war of beasts
Venturous, and learning thus the love of blood.

The shout of terror rings along the wall,
For now the French their scaling-ladders place,
And, bearing high their bucklers, to the assault
Mount fearless: from above the furious troops
Hurl down such weapons as inventive care
Or frantic rage supplies: huge stones and beams
Crush the bold foe; some, thrust adown the height,
Fall living to their death; some in keen pangs
And wildly-writhing, as the liquid lead
Gnaws through their members, leap down desperate,
Eager to cease from suffering.   Still they mount,
And, by their fellows' fate unterrified,
Still dare the perilous way.   Nor dangerless
To the English was the fight, though from above
Easy to crush the assailants: them amidst
Fast fled the arrows; the brass-wing'd darts, [149]
There driven resistless from the espringal,

Keeping their impulse even in the wound,
Whirl as they pierce the victim.   Some fall, crush'd
Beneath the ponderous fragment that descends
The heavier from its height: some the long lance,
Impetuous rushing on its viewless way,
Transfix'd.   The death-fraught cannon's thundering
    roar
Convulsing air, the soldier's eager shout,
And terror's wild shriek, echo o'er the plain
In dreadful harmony.

            Meantime the Chief,
Who equall'd on the bridge the rampart's height,
With many a well-aim'd javelin dealing death,
Made through the throng his passage: he advanced
In wary valour o'er his slaughter'd foes,
On the blood-reeking wall.   Him drawing near,
Two youths, the boldest of the English host,
Press'd on to thrust him from that perilous height;
At once they rush'd upon him: he, his axe
Dropping, the dagger drew: one through the throat
He pierced, and, swinging his broad buckler round,
Dash'd down his comrade.   Even thus unmoved,
Stood Corineus, the sire of Guendolen,
When grappling with his monstrous enemy [150].
He the brute vastness held aloft, and bore,
And headlong hurl'd, all shatter'd to the sea,
Down from the rock's high summit, since that day
Him, hugest of the giants, chronicling,
Called Langoemagog.

            The Maid of Arc
Bounds o'er the bridge, and to the wind unfurls
Her hallow'd banner.   At that welcome sight
A general shout of acclamation rose,
And loud, as when the tempest-tossing forest
Roars to the roaring wind.   Then terror seized
The garrison; and, fired anew with hope,
The fierce assailants to their prize rush on
Resistless.   Vainly do their English foes
Hurl there their beams, and stones, and javelins,
And fire-brands; fearless in the escalade,
The assailants mount, and now upon the wall.
Wage equal battle.

            Burning at the sight
With indignation, Glacidas beheld
His troops fly scatter'd; fast on every side
The foes up-rushing eager to their spoil;
The holy standard waving; and the Maid
Fierce in pursuit. « Speed but this arrow, Heaven!»
The Chief exclaim'd, « and I shall fall content.»
So saying, he his sharpest quarrel chose,
And fix'd the bow-string, and against the Maid
Levelling, let loose; her arm was raised on high
To smite a fugitive; he glanced aside,
Shunning her deadly stroke, and thus received
The Chieftain's arrow: through his ribs it pass'd,
And cleft that vessel, whence the purer blood
Through many a branching channel o'er the frame
Meanders.

      « Fool!» the exasperate knight exclaim'd,
« Would she had slain thee! thou hast lived too long.»
Again he aim'd his arbalist: the string
Struck forceful: swift the erring arrow sped
Guiltless of blood, for lightly o'er the court
Bounded the warrior Virgin.   Glacidas
Levell'd his bow again; the fated shaft
Fled true, and difficultly through the mail

Pierced to her neck, and tinged its point with blood.
« She bleeds! she bleeds!» exulting cried the Chief;
« The sorceress bleeds! nor all her hellish arts
Can charm my arrows from their destined course.»
Ill-fated man! in vain with murderous hand
Placing thy feather'd quarrel in its groove,
Dream'st thou of JOAN subdued! She from her neck
Plucking the shaft unterrified, exclaim'd,
« This is a favour! [151] Frenchmen, let us on!
Escape they cannot from the hand of God!»
But Conrade, rolling round his angry eyes,
Beheld the English Chieftain as he aim'd
Again the bow: with rapid step he strode;
Nor did not Glacidas the Frank perceive;
At him he drew the string: the powerless dart
Fell blunted from his buckler. Fierce he came,
And lifting high his ponderous battle-axe,
Full on his shoulder drove the furious stroke,
Deep buried in his bosom: prone he fell,
The cold air rush'd upon his heaving heart.
One whose low lineage gave no second name
Was Glacidas, [152] a gallant man, and still
His memory in the records of the foe
Survives.

      And now, dishearten'd at his death,
The vanquish'd English fly towards the gate,
Seeking the inner court, [153] as yet in hope
Again to dare the siege, and with their friends
Find present refuge there. Mistaken men!
The vanquish'd have no friends! Defeated thus,
Press'd by pursuit, in vain with eager voice
They call their comrades in the suppliant tones
Of pity now, now with the bitter curse
Of fruitless anger; they indeed within
Fast from the ramparts on the victor troops
Hurl their keen javelins...but the gate is barr'd...
The huge portcullis down!

          Then terror seized
Their hopeless hearts: some, furious in despair,
Turn on their foes; fear-palsied some await
The coming death; some drop the useless sword,
And cry for mercy.

         Then the Maid of Arc
Had pity on the vanquish'd; and she call'd
Aloud, and cried unto the host of France,
And bade them cease from slaughter. They obey'd
The delegated Damsel. Some there were
Apart who communed murmuring, and of those
Graville address'd her: « Mission'd Maid! our troops
Are few in number; and to well secure
These many prisoners such a force demands,
As should we spare might shortly make us need
The mercy we bestow; not mercy then,
Rather to these our soldiers, cruelty.
Justice to them, to France, and to our King,
And that regard wise Nature hath in each
Implanted of self-safety, all demand
Their deaths.»

      « Foul fall such evil policy!»
The indignant Maid exclaim'd. « I tell thee, Chief,
GOD is with us! but GOD shall hide his face
From him who sheds one drop of human blood
In calm cold-hearted wisdom; him who weighs
The *right* and the *expedient*, and resolves,
Just as the well-poised scale shall rise or fall.
These men shall live, live to be happy, Chief,

And in the latest hour of life shall bless
Us who preserved. What is the conqueror's name,
Compared to this when the death-hour shall come?
To think that we have from the murderous sword
Rescued one man, and that his heart-pour'd prayers
Already with celestial eloquence
Plead for us to the All-just?»

           Severe she spake;
Then turn'd to Conrade. « Thou from these our troops
Appoint fit escort for the prisoners:
I need not tell thee, Conrade, they are men,
Misguided men, led from their little homes,
The victims of the mighty! Thus subdued,
They are our foes no longer: hold them safe
In Orleans. From the war we may not spare
Thy valour long.»

          She said: when Conrade cast
His eyes around, and mark'd amid the court
From man to man where Francis rush'd along,
Bidding them spare the vanquish'd. Him he hail'd:
« The Maid hath bade me chuse a leader forth
To guard the captives; thou shalt be the man;
For thou wilt guard them with due diligence,
Yet not forgetting they are men, our foes
No longer!»

         Nor meantime the garrison
Ceased from the war; they, in the hour of need,
Abandoning their comrades to the sword,
A daring band, resolved to bide the siege
In desperate valour. Fast against the walls
The battering-ram drove fierce; the enginery
Plied at the ramparts fast; the catapults
Drove there their dreadful darts; the war-wolfs there
Hurl'd their huge stones; and through the kindled sky,
The engines shower'd their sheets of liquid fire. [154]

« Feel ye not, comrades, how the ramparts shake
Beneath the ponderous ram's incessant stroke?»
Exclaim'd a venturous Englishman. «Our foes,
In woman-like compassion, have dismiss'd
A powerful escort, weakening thus themselves,
And giving us fair hope, in equal field,
Of better fortune. Sorely here annoy'd
And slaughter'd by their engines from afar,
We perish. Vainly does the soldier boast
Undaunted courage and the powerful arm,
If thus pent up, like some wild beast he falls,
Mark'd for the hunter's arrows: let us out
And meet them in the battle, man to man,
Either to conquer, or, at least, to die
A soldier's death.»

         « Nay, nay...not so,» replied
One of less daring valour. « Though they point
Their engines here, our archers not in vain
Speed their death-doing shafts. Let the strong walls
First by the foe be won; 't will then be time
To meet them in the battle man to man,
When these shall fail us.»

         Scarcely had he spoke,
When full upon his breast a ponderous stone
Fell fierce impell'd, and drove him to the earth,
All shatter'd. Horror the spectators seized,
For as the dreadful weapon shiver'd him,
His blood besprinkled round, and they beheld
His mangled lungs lie quivering!

         « Such the fate

Of those who trust them to their walls' defence,»
Again exclaim'd the soldier: « thus they fall,
Betray'd by their own fears.   Courage alone
Can save us.»
        Nor to draw them from the fort
Now needed eloquence; with one accord
They bade him lead to battle.   Forth they rush'd
Impetuous.   With such fury o'er the plain,
Swoln by the autumnal tempest, Vega rolls
His rapid waters, when the gather'd storm,
On the black heights of Hatteril bursting, swells
The tide of desolation.
           Then the Maid
Spake to the Son of Orleans: « Let our troops
Fall back, so shall the English in pursuit
Leave this strong fortress, thus an easy prey.»
Time was not for long counsel.   From the court,
Obedient to Dunois, a band of Franks
Retreat, as at the irruption of their foes
Dishearten'd; they, with shouts and loud uproar,
Rush to their fancied conquest: JOAN, the while
Placing a small but gallant garrison,
Bade them secure the gates: then forth she rush'd,
With such fierce onset charging on their rear,
That terror smote the English, and they wish'd
Again that they might hide them in their walls
Rashly abandon'd, for now wheeling around
The Son of Orleans fought.   All captainless,
Ill-marshall'd, ill-directed, in vain rage
They waste their furious efforts, falling fast
Before the Maid's good falchion and the sword
Of Conrade: loud was heard the mingled sound
Of arms and men; the earth, that trampled late
By multitudes, gave to the passing wind
Its dusty clouds, now reek'd with their hot gore.

High on the fort's far summit Talbot mark'd
The fight, and call'd impatient for his arms,
Eager to rush to war; and scarce withheld,
For now, disheartened and discomfited,
The troops fled fearful.
        On the bridge there stood
A strong-built tower, commanding o'er the Loire.
The traveller sometimes linger'd on his way,
Marking the playful tenants of the stream,
Seen in its shadow, stem the sea-ward tide;
This had the invaders won in hard assault,
Before the delegate of Heaven came forth
And made them fear who never fear'd till then.
Hither the English troops with hasty steps
Retired, yet not forgetful of defence,
But waging still the war: the garrison
Them thus retreating saw, and open threw
Their guarded gates, and on the Gallic host,
Covering their vanquish'd fellows, pour'd their shafts.
Check'd in pursuit they stop.   Then Graville cried,
«Ill, Maiden, hast thou done! Those valiant troops
Thy womanish pity has dismiss'd, with us
Conjoin'd might press upon the vanquish'd foes,
Though aided thus, and plant the lilied flag
Victorious on yon tower.»
         «Dark minded man!»
The Maid of Orleans answer'd , « To act well
Brings with itself an ample recompense.
I have not rear'd the oriflamme of death, [155]
The butcher flag! the banner of the Lord

Is this, and come what will, me it behoves,
Mindful of that good power who delegates,
To spare the fallen foe: that gracious God
Sends me the minister of mercy forth,
Sends me to save this ravaged realm of France,
To England friendly as to all the world;
Foe only to the great blood-guilty ones,
The masters and the murderers of mankind.»

She said, and suddenly threw off her helm;
Her breast heaved high . . . her cheek grew red . . . her eyes
Flash'd forth a wilder lustre: «Thou dost deem
That I have illy spared so large a band,
Disabling from pursuit our weakened troops . . .
God is with us!» she cried . . . « God is with us!
Our champion manifest!»
         Even as she spake,
The tower, the bridge, and all its multitudes,
Sunk with a mighty crash.
        Astonishment
Seized on the French . . . an universal cry [156]
Of terror burst from them.   Crush'd in the fall,
Or by their armour whelm'd beneath the tide,
The sufferers sunk, or vainly plied their arms,
Caught by some sinking wretch, who grasp'd them fast,
And dragg'd them down to death: shrieking they sunk;
Huge fragments frequent dash'd with thundering roar
Amid the foaming current.   From the fort
Talbot beheld, and gnash'd his teeth, and cursed
The more than mortal Virgin; whilst the towers
Of Orleans echoed to the loud uproar,
And all who heard trembled, and cross'd their breasts,
And as they hasten'd to the city walls,
Told fearfully their beads.
        'T was now the hour
When o'er the plain the fading rays of eve
Their sober light effuse; when the lowing herd,
Slow as they stalk to shelter, draw behind
Their lengthening shades; and, seeking his high nest,
As heavily he flaps the dewy air,
The hoarse rook pours his melancholy note.
« Now then, Dunois, for Orleans !» cried the Maid,
«And give we to the flames these monuments
Of sorrow and disgrace.   The ascending flames
Shall to the dwellers of yon rescued town
Blaze with a joyful splendour, while the foe
Behold and tremble.»
        As she spake, they rush'd
To fire the forts; they shower their wild fire there,
And high amid the gloom the ascending flames
Blaze up; then joyful of their finish'd toil
The host retire.   Hush'd is the field of fight
As the calm'd ocean, when its gentle waves
Heave slow and silent, wafting tranquilly
The shatter'd fragments of the midnight wreck.

BOOK IX.

FAR through the shadowy sky the ascending flames [157]
Stream'd their fierce torrents, by the gales of night
Now curl'd, now flashing their long lightnings up
That made the stars seem pale; less frequent now
Through the red volumes briefer splendours shot,
And blacker waves roll'd o'er the darken'd heaven.

Dismay'd amid the forts which yet remain'd
The invaders saw, and clamour'd for retreat,
Deeming that aided by invisible powers
The Maid went forth to conquer.   Not a sound
Moved on the air but fill'd them with vague dread
Of unseen dangers ; if the blast arose
Sudden, through every fibre a deep fear
Crept shivering, and to their expecting minds
Silence itself was dreadful.[158]   One there was,
Who, learning wisdom in the hour of ill,
Exclaim'd, « I marvel not that the Most High
Hath hid his face from England ! Wherefore thus,
Quitting the comforts of domestic life,
Swarm we to desolate this goodly land,
Making the drench'd earth rank with human blood,
Scatter pollution on the winds of heaven?
Oh ! that the sepulchre had closed its jaws
On that foul priest,[159] on that blood-guilty man,
Who, trembling for the church's ill-got wealth,
Bade Henry look on France, ere he had drawn
The desolating sword, and sent him forth
To slaughter ! Sure that holy hermit spake [160]
The Almighty's bidding, who in his career
Of conquest met the King, and bade him cease
The work of death, before the wrath divine
Fell heavy on his head ;—and soon it fell
And sunk him to the grave ;—and soon that wrath
On us, alike in sin, alike shall fall,
For thousands and ten thousands, by the sword
Cut off, and sent before the Eternal Judge,
With all their unrepented crimes upon them,
Cry out for vengeance! For the widow's groan,
Though here she groan unpitied or unheard,
Is heard in heaven against us ! O'er this land
For hills of human slain, unsepulchred,
Steam pestilence, and cloud the blessed sun !
The wrath of God is on us—God hath call'd
This virgin forth, and gone before her path ;—
Our brethren, vainly valiant, fall beneath them,
Clogging with gore their weapons, or in the flood
Whelm'd like the Egyptian tyrant's impious host,
Mangled and swoln, their blacken'd carcasses
Toss on the tossing billows ! We remain,
For yet our rulers will pursue the war,
We still remain to perish by the sword,
Soon to appear before the throne of God,
Lost, guilty wretches, hireling murderers,
Uninjured, unprovoked, who dare to risk
The life his goodness gave us, on the chance
Of war, and in obedience to our chiefs
Durst disobey our God. »
                              Then terror seized
The troops and late repentance; and they thought
The spirits of the mothers and their babes
Famish'd at Roan sat on the clouds of night
Circling the forts, to hail with gloomy joy
The hour of vengeance.[161]
                              Nor the English chiefs
Heard their loud murmurs heedless ; counselling,
They met despondent.   Suffolk, now their chief,
Since conquer'd by the arm of Theodore
Fell Salisbury, thus began :—
                              « It now were vain
Lightly of this our more than mortal foe
To speak contemptuous.   She hath vanquish'd us,
Aided by hell's leagued powers, nor aught avails

Man unassisted 'gainst the powers of hell [162]
To dare the conflict : Were it best remain
Waiting the doubtful aid of Burgundy,
Doubtful and still delay'd? or from this scene,
Scene of our shame, retreating as we may,
Yet struggle to preserve the guarded towns
Of Orleannois ?»
                              He ceased ; and with a sigh,
Struggling with pride that heaved his gloomy breast,
Talbot replied : « Our council little boots ;
For by their numbers now made bold in fear [163]
The soldiers will not fight, they will not heed
Our vain resolves, heart-withered by the spells
Of this accursed sorceress.   Soon will come
The expected host from England : even now
Perchance the tall bark scuds across the deep
That bears my son : young Talbot comes—he comes
To find his sire disgraced ! But soon mine arm,
By vengeance nerved, and shame of such defeat,
Shall from the crest-fall'n courage of yon witch,
Regain its ancient glory.   Near the coast
Best is it to retreat, and there expect
The coming succour.»
                              Thus the warrior spake.
Joy ran through all the troops,[164] as though retreat
Were safety.   Silently in order'd ranks
They issue forth, favour'd by the deep clouds
Which mantled o'er the moon.   With throbbing hearts
Fearful they speeded on : some, thinking sad
Of distant England, and, now wise too late,
Cursing in bitterness the evil hour
That led them from her shores : some in faint hope
Calling to mind the comforts of their home :
Talbot went musing on his blasted fame
Sullen and stern, and feeding on dark thoughts,
And meditating vengeance.
                              In the walls
Of Orleans, though her habitants with joy
Humbly acknowledged the high aid of Heaven,
Of many a heavy ill and bitter loss
Mindful, such mingled sentiments they felt
As one from shipwreck saved, the first warm glow
Of transport past, who contemplates himself,
Preserved alone, a solitary wretch,
Possess'd of life indeed, but reft of all
That makes man love to live. The chieftains shared
The social bowl,[165] glad of the town relieved,
And communing of that miraculous Maid,
Who came the saviour of the realm of France,
When vanquish'd in the frequent field of shame
Her bravest warriors trembled.
                              JOAN the while
Foodless and silent to the convent pass'd :
Conrade with her, and Isabel ; both mute,
Yet gazing on her, oft with eloquent eye,
Looking the consolation that they fear'd
To give a voice to.   Now they reach'd the dome :
The glaring torches o'er the house of death
Stream'd a sad splendour.   Flowers and funeral herbs
Bedeck'd the bier of Theodore : the rue,
The dark green rosemary, and the violet,
That pluck'd like him wither'd in its first bloom.
Dissolved in sorrow Isabel her grief
Pour'd copious ; Conrade wept : the Maid alone
Was tearless, for she stood unheedingly,
Gazing the vision'd scene of her last hour,

Absorb'd in contemplation; from her eye
Intelligence was absent; nor she seem'd
To hear, though listening to the dirge of death.
Laid in his last home now was Theodore,
And now upon the coffin thrown, the earth
Fell heavy : the Maid started, for the sound
Smote on her heart; her eye one lightning glance
Shot wild; and shuddering, upon Isabel
She hung, her pale lips trembling, and her cheek
As wan as though untenanted by life.

Then in the priest arose the earnest hope,
That, weary of the world and sick with woe,
The Maid might dwell with them a vestal vow'd.
« Ah, damsel!» slow he spake, and cross'd his breast,
« Ah, damsel! favour'd as thou art of Heaven,
Let not thy soul beneath its sorrow sink
Despondent; Heaven by sorrow disciplines
The froward heart, and chastens whom it loves;
Therefore, companion of thy way of life,
Shall sorrow wean thee from this faithless world,
Where happiness provokes the traveller's chase,
And like the midnight meteor of the marsh
Allures his long and perilous pursuit,
Then leaves him dark and comfortless. O Maid!
Fix thou thine eyes upon that heavenly dawn
Beyond the night of life! thy race is run;
Thou hast delivered Orleans : now perfect
Thyself; accomplish all, and be the child
Of God. Amid these sacred haunts the groan
Of woe is never heard; these hallow'd roofs
Re-echo only to the pealing quire,
The chaunted mass, and virgin's holy hymn,
Celestial sounds! Secluded here, the soul
Receives a foretaste of her joys to come!
This is the abode of piety and peace :
Oh! be their inmate, Maiden! Come to rest,
Die to the world, and live espoused to Heaven! »

Then Conrade answer'd : « Father! Heaven has doom'd
This Maid to active virtue.»
                              « Active!» cried
The astonish'd priest : « thou dost not know the toils
This holy warfare asks; thou dost not know
How powerful the attacks that Satan makes,
By sinful nature aided! Dost thou deem
It is an easy task from the fond breast
To root affection out? to burst the cords
Which grapple to society the heart
Of social man? to rouse the unwilling spirit,
That, rebel to devotion, faintly pours
The cold lip-worship of the wearying prayer?
To fear and tremble at him, yet to love
A God of terrors! Maid, beloved of Heaven!
Come to this sacred trial! share with us
The day of penance and the night of prayer!
Humble thyself! feel thine own worthlessness,
A reptile worm! before thy birth condemn'd
To all the horrors of thy Maker's wrath,
The lot of fallen mankind! Oh, hither come!
Humble thyself in ashes; so thy name
Shall live amid the blessed host of saints,
And unborn pilgrims at thy hallow'd shrine
Pour forth their pious offerings.»
                              « Hear me, priest,»
Exclaim'd the awaken'd Maid. « Amid these tombs,

Cold as their clayey tenants, know, my heart
Must never grow to stone! Chill thou thyself,
And break thy midnight rest, and tell thy beads,
And labour through thy still repeated prayer;
Fear thou thy God of terrors; spurn the gifts
He gave, and sepulchre thyself alive!
But far more valued is the vine that bends
Beneath its swelling clusters, than the dark
And joyless ivy, round the cloister's wall
Wreathing its barren arms. For me, I know
Mine own worth, priest! that I have well perform'd
My duty, and untrembling shall appear
Before the just tribunal of that God
Whom grateful love has taught me to adore!»
Severe she spake, for sorrow in her heart
Had wrought unwonted sternness. From the dome
They past in silence, when with hasty steps,
Sent by the assembled chieftains, one they met
Seeking the mission'd Virgin, as alarm'd,
The herald of ill tidings.
                              « Holy Maid!»
He cried, « they ask thy counsel. Burgundy
Comes in the cause of England, and his troops
Scarce three leagues from our walls, a fearful power,
Rest tented for the night.»
                              « Say to the Chiefs,
At morn I will be with them,» she replied.
« Meantime their welfare well shall occupy
My nightly thoughts.»
                              So saying, on she past
Thoughtful and silent. A brief while she mused,
Brief, but sufficing to impel the soul,
As with a strange and irresistible force,
To loftiest daring. « Conrade!» she exclaim'd,
« I pray thee meet me at the eastern gate
With a swift steed prepared: for I must hence.»

Her voice was calm; nor Conrade through the gloom
Saw the faint flush that witness'd on her cheek
High thoughts conceived. She to her home repair'd,
And with a light and unplumed casquetel[166]
She helm'd her head; hung from her neck the shield,[167]
And forth she went.
                    Her Conrade by the wall
Awaited. « May I, Maiden, seek unblamed
Whither this midnight journey? may I share
The peril?» cried the warrior. She rejoin'd,
« This, Conrade, may not be. Alone I go.
That impulse of the soul which comes from God;
Hath summon'd me. Of this remain assured,
If aught of patriot enterprise required
Associate firmness, thou shouldst be the man,
Best . . . last . . . and only friend!»
                              So up she sprang,
And left him. He beheld the warden close
The gate, and listen'd to her courser's tramp,
Till soon upon his ear the far-off sound
Fell faintly, and was lost.
                              Swift o'er the vale
Sped the good courser; eagerly the Maid
Gave the loose rein, and now her speed attain'd
The dark encampment. Through the sleeping ranks
Onward she past. The trampling of the steed
Or mingled with the soldier's busy dreams,
Or with vague terrors fill'd his startled sense,
Prompting the secret prayer.

            So on she past
To where in loftier shade arose the tent
Of Burgundy: light leaping from her seat
She enter'd.
            On the earth the Chieftain slept,
His mantle scarft around him; all in arms,
Save that his shield hung near him, and his helm,
And by his side in warrior readiness
The sheathed falchion lay. Profound he slept,
Nor heard the speeding courser's sounding hoof,
Nor entering footstep. « Burgundy,» she cried,
« What, Burgundy! awake!» He started up,
And caught the gleam of arms, and to his sword
Reach'd the quick hand. But soon his upward glance
Thrill'd him, for full upon her face the lamp
Stream'd its deep glare, and in her solemn look
Was most unearthly meaning. Pale she was;
But in her eye a saintly lustre beam'd,
And that most calm and holiest confidence
That guilt knows never. « Burgundy, thou seest
THE MAID OF ORLEANS!»
            As she spake, a voice
Exclaim'd, « Die, sorceress!» and a knight rush'd in,
Whose name by her illustrated yet lives,
Franquet of Arras. With uplifted arm
Furious he came; her buckler broke the blow,
And forth she flash'd her sword, and with a stroke
Swift that no eye could ward it, and of strength
No mail might blunt, smote on his neck, his neck
Unfenced, for he in haste aroused had cast
An armet[168] on; resistless there she smote,
And to the earth prone fell the headless trunk
Of Franquet.
            Then on Burgundy she fix'd
Her eye severe: « Go, Chief, and thank thy God
That he with lighter judgments visits thee
Than fell on Sisera, or by Judith's hand
He wrought upon the Assyrian! Thank thy God,
That when his vengeance smote the invading sons
Of England, equall'd though thou wert in guilt,
Thee he has spared to work by penitence
And better deeds atonement.»
            Thus she spake;
Then issued forth, and, bounding on her steed,
Sped o'er the plain. Dark on the upland bank
The hedge-row trees distinct and colourless
Rose o'er the grey horizon, and the Loire
Form'd in its winding way islands of light
Amid the shadowy vale, when now she reach'd
The walls of Orleans.
            From the eastern clouds
The sun came forth, as to the assembled chiefs
The Maiden past. Her bending thitherwards
The Bastard met. « New perils threaten us,»
He cried, « new toils await us: Burgundy . . .»

« Fear not for Burgundy!» the Maid exclaim'd.
« Him will the Lord direct. Our earliest scouts
Shall tell his homeward march. What of the troops
Of England?»
            « They,» the Son of Orleans cried,
« By darkness favour'd, fled; yet not by flight
Shall England's robber-sons escape the arm
Of retribution. Even now our troops,
By battle unfatigued, unsatisfied
With conquest, clamour to pursue the foe.»

The delegated Damsel thus replied:
« So let them fly, Dunois! but other toils
Than those of battle these our hallow'd troops
Await. Look yonder to that carnaged plain!
Behoves us there to delve the general grave.
Then, Chieftain, for pursuit, when we have paid
The rites of burial to our fellow men,
And hymn'd our gratitude to that ALL-JUST
Who gave the conquest. Thou, meantime, dispatch
Tidings to Chinon: bid the King set forth,
That, crowning him before assembled France,
In Rheims, delivered from the enemy,
I may accomplish all.»
            So said the Maid,
Then to the gate moved on. The assembled troops
Beheld their coming Chief, and smote their shields,
Clamouring their admiration; for they thought
That she would lead them to the instant war.
She waved her hand, and silence still'd the host.
Then thus the mission'd Maid: « Fellows in arms!
We must not speed to joyful victory,
Whilst our unburied comrades, on yon plain,
Allure the carrion-bird. Give we this day
To our dead friends!»
            Nor did she speak in vain;
For as she spake, the thirst of battle dies
In every breast, such awe and love pervade
The listening troops. They o'er the corse-strewn plain
Speed to their sad employment: some dig deep
The house of death ; some bear the lifeless load;
One little troop search carefully around,
If haply they might find surviving yet
Some wounded wretches. As they labour thus,
They mark far off the iron-blaze of arms;
See distant standards waving on the air,
And hear the clarion's clang. Then spake the Maid
To Conrade, and she bade him speed to view
The coming army ; or to meet their march
With friendly greeting, or if foes they came
With such array of battle as short space
Allowed; the warrior sped across the plain,
And soon beheld the banner'd lilies wave.

Their chief was Richemont; he, when as he heard
What rites employ'd the Virgin, straightway bade
His troops assist in burial; they, though grieved
At late arrival, and the expected day
Of conquest past, yet give their willing aid:
They dig the general grave, and thither bear
English or French alike commingled now,
And heap the mound of death.
            Amid the plain
There was a little eminence, of old
Piled o'er some honoured chieftain's narrow house.
His praise the song had ceased to celebrate,
And many an unknown age had the long grass
Waved o'er the nameless mound, though barren now
Beneath the frequent tread of multitudes.
There elevate, the martial Maiden stood,
Her brow unhelm'd, and floating on the wind
Her long dark locks. The silent troops around
Stood thickly throng'd, as o'er the fertile field
Billows the ripen'd corn. The passing breeze
Bore not a murmur from the numerous host,
Such deep attention held them. She began:

« Glory to those who in their country's cause
Fall in the field of battle! Citizens,
I stand not here to mourn these gallant men,
Our comrades, nor with vain and idle phrase
Of pity and compassion, to console
The friends who loved them.   They, indeed, who fall
Beneath oppression's banner, merit well
Our pity; may the GOD OF PEACE AND LOVE
Be merciful to those blood-guilty men
Who came to desolate the realm of France,
To make us bow the knee, and crouch like slaves
Before a tyrant's footstool! Give to these,
And to their wives and orphan little-ones
That on their distant father vainly cry
For bread, give these your pity!... Wretched men,
Forced or inveigled from their homes, or driven
By need and hunger to the trade of blood;
Or, if with free and willing mind they came,
Most wretched... for before the Eternal Throne
They stand, as hireling murderers arraign'd.
But our dead comrades for their freedom fought;
No arts they needed, nor the specious bribes
Of promise, to allure them to this fight,
This holy warfare! Them their parents sent,
And as they raised their streaming eyes to heaven,
Bade them go forth, and from the ruffian's sword
Save their grey hairs: these men their wives sent out,
Fix'd their last kisses on their armed hands, [169]
And bade them in the battle think they fought
For them and for their babes. Thus roused to rage
By every milder feeling, they rush'd forth;
They fought, they conquer'd. To this high-rear'd mound
The men of Orleans in the days to come
Shall bring their boys, and tell them of the deeds
Their countrymen achieved, and bid them learn
Like them to love their country, and like them
Should wild oppression pour again its tide
Of desolation, to step forth and stem,
Fearless, the furious torrent.   Men of France!
Mourn not for these our comrades; boldly they
Fought the good fight, and that Eternal One,
Who bade the angels harbinger his word
With « peace on earth,» rewards them.   We survive,
Honouring their memories to avenge their fall
Upon the invading host; in vain the foe
Madly will drain his wealth and waste his blood
To conquer this vast realm! for, easier were it
To hurl the rooted mountain from its base,
Than force the yoke of slavery upon men
Determined to be free! Yes... let them rage,
And drain their country's wealth, and waste her blood,
And pour their hireling thousands on our coasts;
Sublime amid the storm shall France arise,
And, like the rock amid surrounding waves,
Repel the rushing ocean ... she shall wield
The thunder ... she shall blast her despot foes.»

BOOK X.

THUS to the martyrs in their country's cause
The Maiden gave their fame; and when she ceased,
Such murmur from the multitude arose,
As when at twilight hour the summer breeze
Moves o'er the elmy vale: there was not one
Who mourn'd with feeble sorrow for his friend,
Slain in the fight of freedom; or if chance
Remembrance with a tear suffused the eye,
The patriot's joy flash'd through.

                              And now the rites
Of sepulture perform'd, the hymn to Heaven
They chaunted.   To the town the Maid return'd,
Dunois with her, and Richemont, and the man,
Conrade, whose converse most the Virgin loved.
They of pursuit and of the future war
Sat communing; when loud the trumpet's voice
Proclaim'd approaching herald.

                        «To the Maid,»
Exclaim'd the messenger, « and thee, Dunois,
Son of the Chief he loved! Du Chastel sends
Greeting.   The aged warrior hath not spared
All active efforts to partake your toil,
And serve his country; and though, late arrived,
He share not in the fame your arms acquire,
His heart is glad that he is late arrived,
And France preserved thus early.   He were here
To join your host, and follow on their flight,
But Richemont is his foe.   To that high lord
Thus says my master: We though each to each
Be hostile, are alike the embattled sons
Of this our common country.   Do thou join
The conquering troops, and prosecute success:
I will the while assault what guarded towns
Bedford yet holds in Orleannois: one day,
Perhaps the Constable of France may learn
He wrong'd Du Chastel.»

                    As the herald spake,
The crimson current rush'd to Richemont's cheek:
«Tell to thy master,» eager he replied,
« I am the foe of those court parasites
Who poison the King's ear.   Him who shall serve
Our country in the field, I hold my friend:
Such may Du Chastel prove.»

                        So said the Chief,
And pausing as the herald went his way,
Gazed on the Virgin.   «Maiden! if aright
I deem, thou dost not with a friendly eye
Scan my past deeds.»

                    Then o'er the Damsel's cheek
A faint glow spread.   « True, chieftain!» she replied,
« Report bespeaks thee haughty, of thy power
Jealous, and to the shedding human blood
Revengeful.»

                « Maid of Orleans! » he exclaim'd,
« Should the wolf slaughter thy defenceless flock,
Were it a crime if thy more mighty force
Destroyed the fell destroyer? If thy hand
Had pierced the ruffian as he burst thy door
Prepared for midnight murder, wouldst thou feel
The weight of blood press heavy on thy soul?
I slew the wolves of state, the murderers
Of thousands.   JOAN! when rusted in its sheath,
The sword of justice hung, blamest thou the man
That lent his weapon for the virtuous deed? »

Conrade replied: « Nay, Richemont, it were well
To pierce the ruffian as he burst thy doors;
But if he bear the plunder safely thence,
And thou shouldst meet him on the future day,
Vengeance must not be thine: there is the law

6

To punish; and if thy impatient hand,
Unheard and uncondemn'd should execute
Death on the culprit, law will not allow
The judge in the accuser ! »
                    « Thou hast said
Right wisely, warrior;» cried the Constable ;
« But there are guilty ones above the law,
Men whose black crimes exceed the utmost bound
Of private guilt: court vermin that buzz round,
And fly-blow the King's ear, and make him waste,
In this most perilous time, his people's wealth
And blood: immersed one while in criminal sloth,
Heedless though ruin threat the realm they rule;
And now projecting some mad enterprise,
To certain slaughter send their wretched troops.
These are the men that make the King suspect
His wisest, faithfullest, hest counsellors;
And for themselves, and their dependants, seize
All places, and all profits; and they wrest
To their own ends the statutes of the land,
Or safely break them; thus, or indolent,
Or active, ruinous alike to France.
Wisely thou sayest, warrior! that the law
Should strike the guilty; but the voice of justice
Cries out, and brings conviction as it cries,
Whom the laws cannot reach the dagger should.»

The Maid replied: « I blame thee not, O Chief!
If, reasoning to thine own conviction thus,
Thou didst, well satisfied, destroy these men
Above the law: but if a meaner one,
Self-constituting him the minister
Of justice to the death of these bad men
Had wrought the deed, him would the laws have seized,
And doom'd a murderer: thee, thy power preserv'd!
And what hast thou exampled? thou hast taught
All men to execute what deeds of blood
Their will or passion sentence: right and wrong
Confounding thus, and making power, of all,
Sole arbiter. Thy acts were criminal:
Yet, Richemont, for thou didst them self-approved,
I may not blame the agent. Trust me, Chief
That when a people sorely are opprest,
The hour of violence will come too soon!
He best meanwhile performs the patriot's part,
Who, in the ear of rage and faction, breathes
The healing words of love.»
                    Thus communed they.
Meantime, all panic-struck and terrified,
The English urge their flight; by other thoughts
Possess'd than when, elate with arrogance,
They dreamt of conquest, and the crown of France
At their disposal. Of their hard-fought fields,
Of glory hardly-earn'd, and lost with shame,
Of friends and brethren slaughter'd, and the fate
Threatening themselves, they brooded sadly, now
Repentant late and vainly. They whom fear
Erst made obedient to their conquering march,
At their defeat exultant, wreak what ills
Their power allow'd. Thus many a league they fled,
Marking their path with ruin, day by day
Leaving the weak and wounded destitute
To the foe's mercy; thinking of their home,
Though to that far-off prospect scarcely Hope
Could raise her sickly eye. Oh then what joy
Inspired anew their bosoms, when like clouds

Moving in shadows down the distant hill,
They mark'd their coming succours! In each heart
Doubt raised a busy tumult; soon they knew
The friendly standard, and a general shout
Burst from the joyful ranks: yet came no joy
To Talbot: he, with dark and downward brow,
Mused sternly, till at length aroused to hope
Of vengeance, welcoming his warrior son,
He brake a sullen smile.[170]
                    « Son of my age!
Welcome, young Talbot, to thy first of fields.
Thy father bids thee welcome, though disgraced,
Baffled, and flying from a woman's arm!
Yes, by my former glories, from a woman!
The scourge of France! the conqueror of men!
Flying before a woman! Son of Talbot,
Had the winds wafted thee a few days sooner,
Thou hadst seen me high in honour, and thy name
Alone had scatter'd armies; yet, my child,
I bid thee welcome! Rest we here our flight,
And lift again the sword.»
                    So spake the Chief;
And well he counsell'd: for not yet the sun
Had reach'd meridian height, when, o'er the plain
Of Patay, they beheld the troops of France
Speed in pursuit. Soon as the troops of France
Beheld the dark battalions of the foe
Shadowing the distant plain, a general shout
Burst from the expectant host, and on they prest,
Elate of heart and eager for the fight,
With clamours ominous of victory.
Thus urging on, one from the adverse host
Advanced to meet them: they his garb of peace
Knew, and they stay'd them as the herald spake
His bidding to the chieftains: « Sirs!» he cried,
« I bear defiance to you from the earl
William of Suffolk. Here on this fit plain,
He wills to give you battle, power to power,
So please you, on the morrow.»
                    « On the morrow
We will join battle then,» replied Dunois,
« And God befriend the right!» Then on the herald
A robe rich-furr'd and broider'd he bestow'd,[171]
A costly guerdon. Through the army spread
The unwelcome tidings of delay: possess'd
With agitating hopes they felt the hours
Pass heavily; but soon the night wan'd on,
And the loud trumpets' blare from broken sleep
Roused them; a second time the thrilling blast
Bade them be arm'd, and at the third deep sound[172]
They ranged them in their ranks. From man to man
With pious haste hurried the confessor
To shrieve them,[173] lest with souls all unprepared
They to their death might go. Dunois meantime
Rode through the host; the shield of dignity[174]
Before him borne, and in his hand he held
The white wand of command. The open helm
Disclosed that eye which temper'd the strong lines
Of steady valour to obedient awe
Winning the will's assent. To some he spake
Of late earn'd glory; others, new to war,
He bade bethink them of the feats achieved
When Talbot, recreant to his former fame,
Fled from beleaguer'd Orleans. Was there one
Whom he had known in battle? By the hand
Him did he take, and bid him on that day

Summon his wonted courage, and once more
Support his chief and comrade. Happy he
Who caught his glance, or from the chieftain's lips
Heard his own name! joy more inspiriting
Fills not the Persian's soul, when sure he deems
That Mithra hears propitiously his prayer,
And o'er the scatter'd cloud of morning pours
A brighter ray responsive.
               Then the host
Partook due food, this their last meal belike
Receiving with such thoughtful doubts, as make
The soul, impatient of uncertainty,
Rush eager to the event; being thus prepared,
Upon the grass the soldiers laid themselves,
Each in his station, waiting there the sound
Of onset, that in undiminish'd strength
Strong they might meet the battle: [175] silent some
Pondering the chances of the coming day,
Some whiling with a careless gaiety
The fearful pause of action.
               Thus the French
In such array and high in confident hope
Await the signal; whilst with other thoughts,
And ominous awe, once more the invading host
Prepare them in the field of fight to meet
The Maid of God. Collected in himself
Appear'd the might of Talbot. Through the ranks
He stalks, reminds them of their former fame,
Their native land, their homes, the friends they loved,
All the rewards of this day's victory.
But awe had fill'd the English, and they struck
Faintly their shields; for they who had beheld
The hallow'd banner with celestial light
Irradiate, and the mission'd Maiden's deeds,
Felt their heart sink within them, at the thought
Of her near vengeance; and the tale they told
Roused such a tumult in the new-come troops,
As fitted them for fear. The aged Chief
Beheld their drooping valour: his stern brow,
Wrinkled with thought, bewray'd his inward doubts:
Still he was firm, though all might fly, resolved
That Talbot should retrieve his old renown,
And period life with glory. Yet some hope
Inspired the veteran, as, across the plain
Casting his eye, he mark'd the embattled strength
Of thousands; archers of unequall'd skill,
Brigans, and pikemen, from whose lifted points
A fearful radiance flash'd, and young esquires,
And high-born warriors, bright in blazon'd arms.
Nor few, nor fameless were the English chiefs:
In many a field victorious, he was there,
The garter'd Fastolffe; Hungerford, and Scales,
Men who had seen the hostile squadrons fly
Before the arms of England. Suffolk there,
The haughty chieftain, tower'd; blest had he fallen
Ere yet a courtly minion he was mark'd
By public hatred, and the murderer's name!
There too the son of Talbot, young in arms,
Moved eager; he, at many a tournament,
With matchless force, had pointed his strong lance,
O'er all opponents victor: confident
In strength, and jealous of his future fame.
His heart beat high for battle. Such array
Of marshall'd numbers fought not on the field
Of Crecy, nor at Poictiers; nor such force
Led Henry to the fight of Agincourt

When thousands fell before him.
               Onward move
The host of France. It was a goodly sight
To see the embattled pomp, as with the step
Of stateliness the barbed steeds came on;
To see the pennons rolling their long waves
Before the gale, and banners broad and bright [176]
Tossing their blazonry; and high-plumed chiefs,
Vidames [177] and Seneschalls and Chastellains,
Gay with their buckler's gorgeous heraldry,
And silken surcoats to the mid-day sun
Glittering. [178]
         And now the knights of France dismount,
For not to brutal strength they deem'd it right
To trust their fame and their dear country's weal; [179]
Rather to manly courage, and the glow
Of honourable thoughts, such as inspire
Ennobling energy. Unhorsed, unspurr'd,
Their javelins lessen'd to a wieldy length, [180]
They to the foe advanced. The Maid alone,
Conspicuous on a coal-black courser, meets
The war. They moved to battle with such sound
As rushes o'er the vaulted firmament,
When from his seat, on the utmost verge of heaven
That overhangs the void, father of winds,
Hræsvelger starting, [181] rears his giant bulk,
And from his eagle pinions shakes the storm.

High on her stately steed the martial Maid
Rode foremost of the war: her burnish'd arms
Shone like the brook that o'er its pebbled course
Runs glittering gaily to the noon-tide sun.
The foaming courser, of her guiding hand
Impatient, smote the earth, and toss'd his mane,
And rear'd aloft with many a froward bound,
Then answer'd to the rein with such a step,
As, in submission, he were proud to shew
His unsubdued strength. Slow on the air
Waved the white plumes that shadow'd o'er her helm.
Even such, so fair, so terrible in arms
Pelides moved from Scyros, where, conceal'd
He lay obedient to his mother's fears,
A seemly virgin; thus the youth appear'd
Terribly graceful, when upon his neck
Deidameia hung, and with a look
That spake the tumult of her troubled soul,
Fear, anguish, and upbraiding tenderness,
Gazed on the father of her unborn babe.

An English knight, who, eager for renown,
Late left his peaceful mansion, mark'd the Maid.
Her power miraculous, and fearful deeds,
He from the troops had heard incredulous,
And scoff'd their easy fears, and vow'd that he,
Proving the magic of this dreaded girl
In equal battle, would dissolve the spell,
Powerless opposed to valour. Forth he spurr'd
Before the ranks; she mark'd the coming foe,
And fix'd her lance in rest, and rush'd along.
Midway they met; full on her buckler driven,
Shiver'd the English spear: her better force
Drove the brave foeman senseless from his seat.
Headlong he fell, nor ever to the sense
Of shame awoke, for rushing multitudes
Soon crush'd the helpless warrior.
               Then the Maid

Rode through the thickest battle : fast they fell,
Pierced by her forceful spear.　Amid the troops
Plunged her strong war-horse, by the noise of arms
Elate and roused to rage, he tramples o'er,
Or with the lance protended from his front, [182]
Thrusts down the thronging squadrons. Where she turns
The foe tremble and die.　Such ominous fear
Seizes the traveller o'er the trackless sands,
Who marks the dread simoom across the waste
Sweep its swift pestilence: to earth he falls,
Nor dares give utterance to the inward prayer,
Deeming the genius of the desert breathes
The purple blast of death.
　　　　　　　　Such was the sound
As when the tempest, mingling air and sea,
Flies o'er the uptorn ocean : dashing high
Their foamy heads amid the incumbent clouds,
The madden'd billows, with their deafening roar,
Drown the loud thunder's peal.　In every form
Of horror, death was there.　They fall, transfix'd
By the random arrow's point, or fierce-thrust lance,
Or sink, all batter'd by the ponderous mace :
Some from their coursers thrown, lie on the earth,
Unwieldy in their arms, that, weak to save,
Protracted all the agonies of death.
But most the English fell, by their own fears
Betray'd, for fear the evil that it dreads
Increases.　Even the chiefs, who many a day
Had met the war and conquer'd, trembled now,
Appall'd before the Maid miraculous.
As the blood-nurtured monarch of the wood,
That o'er the wilds of Afric, in his strength
Resistless ranges, when the mutinous clouds
Burst, and the lightnings through the midnight sky
Dart their red fires, lies fearful in his den,
And howls in terror to the passing storm.

But Talbot, fearless where the bravest fear'd,
Mow'd down the hostile ranks.　The Chieftain stood
Like the strong oak, amid the tempest's rage,
That stands unharm'd, and while the forest falls
Uprooted round, lifts his high head aloft,
And nods majestic to the warring wind.
He fought resolved to snatch the shield of death [183]
And shelter him from shame.　The very herd
Who fought near Talbot, though the Virgin's name
Made their cheeks pale, and drove the curdling blood
Back to their hearts, caught from his daring deeds
New force, and went like eaglets to the prey
Beneath their mother's wing : to him they look'd,
Their tower of strength, [184] and follow'd where his sword
Made through the foe a way.　Nor did the son
Of Talbot shame his lineage; by his sire
Emulous he strove, like the young lionet
When first he bathes his murderous jaws in blood.
They fought intrepid, though amid their ranks
Fear and confusion triumph'd; for such dread
Possess'd the English, as the Etruscans felt,
When, self-devoted to the infernal gods,
The aweful Decius stood before the troops,
Robed in the victim garb of sacrifice,
And spake aloud, and call'd the shadowy powers
To give to Rome the conquest, and receive
Their willing prey; then rush'd amid the foe,
And died upon the hecatombs he slew.

But hope inspired the assailants.　Xaintrailles there
Spread fear and death, and Orleans' valiant son
Fought as when Warwick fled before his arm.
O'er all pre-eminent for hardiest deeds
Was Conrade.　Where he drove his battle-axe,
Weak was the buckler or the helm's defence,
Hauberk, or plated mail, through all it pierced,
Resistless as the forked flash of heaven.
The death-doom'd foe, who mark'd the coming Chief,
Felt such a chill run through his shivering frame,
As the night-traveller of the Pyrenées,
Lone and bewilder'd on his wintery way,
When from the mountains round reverberates
The hungry wolves' deep yell : on every side,
Their fierce eyes, gleaming as with meteor fires,
The famish'd troop come round : the affrighted mule
Snorts loud with terror, on his shuddering limbs
The big sweat starts, convulsive pant his sides,
Then on he rushes, wild in desperate speed.

Him dealing death an English knight beheld,
And spurr'd his steed to crush him : Conrade leap'd
Lightly aside, and through the warrior's greaves
Fix'd a deep wound : nor longer could the foe,
Tortured with anguish, guide his mettled horse,
Or his rude plunge endure ; headlong he fell,
And perish'd.　In his castle-hall was hung
On high his father's shield, with many a dint
Graced on the glorious field of Agincourt.
His deeds the son had heard ; and when a boy,
Listening delighted to the old man's tale,
His little hand would lift the weighty spear
In warlike pastime : he had left behind
An infant offspring, and did fondly deem
He too in age the exploits of his youth
Should tell, and in the stripling's bosom rouse
The fire of glory.
　　　　　　Conrade the next foe
Smote where the heaving membrane separates
The chambers of the trunk.　The dying man
In his lord's castle dwelt, for many a year,
A well-beloved servant : he could sing
Carols for Shrove-tide, or for Candlemas,
Songs for the wassel, and when the boar's head, [185]
Crown'd with gay garlands and with rosemary,
Smok'd on the Christmas board : he went to war
Following the lord he loved, and saw him fall
Beneath the arm of Conrade, and expired,
Slain on his master's body.
　　　　　　　　Nor the fight
Was doubtful long.　Fierce on the invading host
Press the French troops impetuous, as of old,
When, pouring o'er his legion slaves on Greece,
The eastern despot bridged the Hellespont,
The rushing sea against the mighty pile
Roll'd its full weight of waters ; far away
The fearful Satrap mark'd on Asia's coasts
The floating fragments, and with ominous fear
Trembled for the great king.
　　　　　　　　Still Talbot strove,
His foot firm planted, his uplifted shield
Fencing that breast which never yet had known
The throb of fear.　But when the warrior's eye,
Quick glancing round the fight, beheld the foe
Pressing to conquest, and his heartless troops

Striking with feebler force in backward step,
Then o'er his cheek he felt the patriot flush
Of shame, and loud he lifted up his voice,
And cried, « Fly, cravens ! leave your aged chief
Here in the front to perish ! his old limbs
Are not like yours so supple in the flight. [186]
Go tell your countrymen how ye escaped
When Talbot fell !»
         In vain the warrior spake,
In the uproar of the fight his voice was lost ;
And they, the nearest, who had heard, beheld
The martial Maid approach, and every thought
Was overwhelm'd in terror.   But the son
Of Talbot mark'd her thus across the plain
Careering fierce in conquest, and the hope
Of glory rose within him.   Her to meet
He spurr'd his horse, by one decisive deed
Or to retrieve the battle, or to fall
With honour.   Each beneath the other's blow
Bow'd down ; their lances shiver'd with the shock :
To earth their coursers fell : at once they rose,
He from the saddle-bow his falchion caught [187]
Rushing to closer combat, and she bared
The lightning of her sword. [188] In vain the youth
Essay'd to pierce those arms which even the power
Of time was weak to injure : she the while
Through many a wound beheld her foeman's blood
Ooze fast.   « Yet save thee, warrior !» cried the Maid,
« Me thou canst not destroy : be timely wise,
And live !»   He answer'd not, but lifting high
His weapon, drove with fierce and forceful arm
Full on the Virgin's helm : fire from her eyes
Flash'd with the stroke : one step she back recoil'd,
Then in his breast plunged deep the sword of death.

Talbot beheld his fall ; on the next foe,
With rage and anguish wild, the warrior turn'd ;
His ill-directed weapon to the earth
Drove down the unwounded Frank : he lifts the sword,
And through his all-in-vain imploring hands
Cleaves the poor suppliant.   On that dreadful day
The sword of Talbot, [189] clogg'd with hostile gore,
Made good its vaunt.   Amid the heaps his arm
Had slain, the Chieftain stood and sway'd around
His furious strokes ; nor ceased he from the fight,
Though now discomfited the English troops
Fled fast, all panic-struck and spiritless ;
And mingling with the routed, Fastolffe fled,
Fastolffe, all fierce and haughty as he was, [190]
False to his former fame ; for he beheld
The Maiden rushing onward, and such fear
Ran through his frame, as thrills the African,
When, grateful solace in the sultry hour,
He rises on the buoyant billow's breast,
If then his eye behold the monster shark
Gape eager to devour.
         But Talbot now
A moment paused, for bending thitherwards
He mark'd a warrior, such as well might ask
His utmost force.   Of strong and stately port
The onward foeman moved, and bore on high
A battle-axe, [191] in many a field of blood
Known by the English Chieftain.   Over heaps
Of slaughter'd, strode the Frank, and bade the troops
Retire from the bold Earl : then Conrade spake :
« Vain is thy valour, Talbot ! Look around,

See where thy squadrons fly ! but thou shalt lose
No glory, by their cowardice subdued,
Performing well thyself the soldier's part.»

« And let them fly !» the indignant Earl exclaim'd,
« And let them fly ! but bear thou witness, Chief !
That guiltless of this day's disgrace, I fall.
But, Frenchman ! Talbot will not tamely fall,
Nor unrevenged.»
         So saying, for the war
He stood prepared : nor now with heedless rage
The champions fought, for either knew full well
His foeman's prowess : now they aim the blow
Insidious, with quick change then drive the steel
Fierce on the side exposed.   The unfaithful arms
Yield to the strong-driven edge ; the blood streams down
Their batter'd mails.   With swift eye Conrade mark'd
The lifted buckler, and beneath impell'd
His battle-axe ; that instant on his helm
The sword of Talbot fell, and with the blow
Shiver'd.   « Yet yield thee, Englishman !» exclaim'd
The generous Frank ; « vain is this bloody strife :
Me shouldst thou conquer, little would my death
Avail thee, weak and wounded !»
         « Long enough
Talbot has lived,» replied the sullen Chief :
« His hour is come ; yet shalt not thou survive
To glory in his fall !»   So, as he spake,
He lifted from the ground a massy spear,
And rush'd again to battle.
         Now more fierce
The conflict raged, for, careless of himself,
And desperate, Talbot fought.   Collected still
Was Conrade.   Wheresoe'er his foeman aim'd
His barbed javelin, there he swung around
The guardian shield : the long and vain assault
Exhausted Talbot now ; foredone with toil,
He bare his buckler low for weariness,
His buckler now splinter'd with many a stroke [192]
Fell piecemeal ; from his riven arms the blood
Stream'd fast : and now the Frenchman's battle-axe
Drove unresisted through the shieldless mail.
Backward the Frank recoil'd.   « Urge not to death
This fruitless contest !» he exclaim'd : « Oh Chief !
Are there not those in England who would feel
Keen anguish at thy loss ? a wife perchance
Who trembles for thy safety, or a child
Needing a father's care !»
         Then Talbot's heart
Smote him.   « Warrior !» he cried, « if thou dost think
That life is worth preserving, hie thee hence,
And save thyself : I loathe this useless talk.»

So saying, he address'd him to the fight,
Impatient of existence : from their arms
Fire flash'd, and quick they panted ; but not long
Endured the deadly combat.   With full force
Down through his shoulder even to the chest,
Conrade impell'd the ponderous battle-axe ;
And at that instant underneath his shield
Received the hostile spear.   Prone fell the Earl,
Even in his death rejoicing that no foe
Should live to boast his fall.
         Then with faint hand
Conrade unlaced his helm, and from his brow
Wiping the cold dews, ominous of death,

He laid him on the earth, thence to remove,
While the long lance hung heavy in his side,
Powerless. As thus beside his lifeless foe
He lay, the herald of the English Earl
With faltering step drew near, and when he saw
His master's arms—« Alas ! and is it you,
My lord ?» he cried. « God pardon you your sins !
I have been forty years your officer,
And time it is I should surrender now
The ensigns of my office !» So he said,
And paying thus his rite of sepulture,
Threw o'er the slaughter'd Chief his blazon'd coat. 193
Then Conrade thus bespake him : « Englishman,
Do for a dying soldier one kind act !
Seek for the Maid of Orleans, bid her haste
Hither, and thou shalt gain what recompense
It pleases thee to ask.»
                        The herald soon
Meeting the mission'd Virgin, told his tale.
Trembling she hasten'd on, and when she knew
The death-pale face of Conrade, scarce could JOAN
Lift up the expiring warrior's heavy hand,
And press it to her heart.
                        « I sent for thee,
My friend !» with interrupted voice he cried,
That I might comfort this my dying hour
With one good deed. A fair domain is mine,
Let Francis and his Isabel possess
That, mine inheritance.» He paused awhile,
Struggling for utterance ; then with breathless speed,
And pale as him he mourn'd for, Francis came,
And hung in silence o'er the blameless man,
Even with a brother's sorrow : he pursued :
« This JOAN will be thy care. I have at home
An aged Mother—Francis, do thou soothe
Her childless age. Nay, weep not for me thus :
Sweet to the wretched is the tomb's repose !»

So saying Conrade drew the javelin forth,
And died without a groan.
                        By this the scouts,
Forerunning the King's march, upon the plain
Of Patay had arrived, of late so gay
With marshall'd thousands in their radiant arms,
And streamers glittering in the noon-tide sun,
And blazon'd shields and gay accoutrements,
The pageantry of slaughter... now defiled
With mingled dust and blood, and broken arms,
And mangled bodies. Soon the Monarch joins
His victor army. Round the royal flag,
Uprear'd in conquest now, the Chieftains flock
Proffering their eager service. To his arms,
Or wisely fearful, or by speedy force
Compell'd, the embattled towns submit and own
Their rightful King. Baugenci strives in vain :
Yenville and Mehun yield ; from Sully's wall
Hurl'd is the banner'd lion : on they pass,
Auxerre, and Troyes, and Chalons, ope their gates,
And by the mission'd Maiden's rumour'd deeds
Inspirited, the citizens of Rheims
Feel their own strength ; against the English troops
With patriot valour, irresistible,
They rise, they conquer, and to their liege lord
Present the city keys.
                        The morn was fair
When Rheims re-echoed to the busy hum

Of multitudes, for high solemnity
Assembled. To the holy fabric moves
The long procession, through the streets bestrewn
With flowers and laurel boughs. The courtier throng
Were there, and they in Orleans, who endured
The siege right bravely ; Gaucour, and La Hire,
The gallant Xaintrailles, Boussac, and Chabannes,
La Fayette, name that freedom still shall love,
Alençon, and the bravest of the brave,
The Bastard Orleans, now in hope elate,
Soon to release from hard captivity
A dear beloved brother ; gallant men,
And worthy of eternal memory,
For they, in the most perilous times of France,
Despair'd not of their country. By the King
The delegated Damsel pass'd along,
Clad in her batter'd arms. She bore on high
Her hallow'd banner to the sacred pile,
And fix'd it on the altar, whilst her hand
Pour'd on the Monarch's head the mystic oil, 194
Wafted of yore by milk-white dove from heaven
(So legends say) to Clovis when he stood
At Rheims for baptism ; dubious since that day,
When Tolbiac plain reek'd with his warrior's blood,
And fierce upon their flight the Almanni prest,
And rear'd the shout of triumph ; in that hour
Clovis invoked aloud the Christian God
And conquer'd : waked to wonder thus, the Chief
Became love's convert, and Clotilda led
Her husband to the font.
                        The mission'd Maid
Then placed on Charles's brow the crown of France,
And back retiring, gazed upon the King
One moment, quickly scanning all the past,
Till in a tumult of wild wonderment
She wept aloud. The assembled multitude
In awful stillness witness'd : then at once,
As with a tempest-rushing noise of winds,
Lifted their mingled clamours. Now the Maid
Stood as prepared to speak, and waved her hand,
And instant silence followed :
                        « King of France !»
She cried, « at Chinon, when my gifted eye
Knew thee disguised, what inwardly the spirit
Prompted, I spake ; arm'd with the sword of God
To drive from Orleans far the English wolves,
And crown thee in the rescued walls of Rheims.
All is accomplish'd. I have here this day
Fulfill'd my mission, and anointed thee
Chief servant of the people. Of this charge,
Or well perform'd or wickedly, high Heaven
Shall take account. If that thine heart be good,
I know no limit to the happiness
Thou mayst create. I do beseech thee, King !»
The Maid exclaim'd, and fell upon the ground
And clasp'd his knees, « I do beseech thee, King !
By all the millions that depend on thee,
For weal or woe... consider what thou art,
And know thy duty ! If thou dost oppress
Thy people, if to aggrandize thyself
Thou tear'st them from their homes, and sendest them
To slaughter, prodigal of misery !
If when the widow and the orphan groan
In want and wretchedness, thou turnest thee
To hear the music of the flatterer's tongue ;
If when thou hear'st of thousands massacred,

Thou say'st, ' I am a King! and fit it is
That these should perish for me; ... if thy realm
Should through the counsels of thy government,
Be fill'd with woe, and in thy streets be heard
The voice of mourning and the feeble cry
Of asking hunger; if at such a time
Thou dost behold thy plenty-cover'd board,
And shroud thee in thy robes of royalty,
And say that all is well,... Oh, gracious God!
Be merciful to such a monstrous man,
When the spirits of the murder'd innocent
Cry at thy throne for justice!

       King of France!
Protect the lowly, feed the hungry ones,
And be the orphan's father! thus shalt thou
Become the representative of Heaven,
And gratitude and love establish thus
Thy reign. Believe me, King! that hireling guards,
Though flesh'd in slaughter, will be weak to save
A tyrant on the blood-cemented throne
That totters underneath him.»

       Thus the Maid
Redeem'd her country. Ever may the All-Just
Give to the arms of Freedom such success.

NOTES.

Note 1, page 3, col. 1.
The Bastard Orleans.

« Lewes Duke of Orleance murthered in Paris, by
Jhon Duke of Burgoyne, was owner of the castle of
Concy, on the frontiers of Fraunce toward Arthoys,
whereof he made constable the lord of Cauney, a man
not so wise as his wife was faire, and yet she was not so
faire, but she was as well beloved of the Duke of Orle-
ance as of her husband. Betwene the duke and her
husband (I cannot tell who was father), she conceived
a child, and brought furthe a prety boye called Jhon,
whiche child beyng of the age of one yere, the duke
deceased, and not long after the mother and the lord
of Cawny ended their lives. The next of kynne to the
lord Cawny chalenged the inheritaunce, which was
worth foure thousande crounes a yere, alledgyng that
the boye was a bastard: and the kynred of the mother's
side, for to save her honesty, it plainly denied. In con-
clusion, this matter was in contencion before the pre-
sidentes of the parliament of Paris, and there hang in
controversie till the child came to the age of eight years
old. At whiche tyme it was demanded of hym openly
whose sonne he was; his frendes of his mother's side
advertised hym to require a day, to be advised of so
great an answer, which he asked, and to hym it was
granted. In the mean season, his said frendes per-
suaded him to claime his inheritance as sonne to the
lorde of Cawny, whiche was an honorable livyng, and
an auncient patrimony, affirming that if he said con-
trary, he not only slaundered his mother, shamed hym-
self. and stained his bloud, but also should have no
livyng, nor any thing to take to. The scholemaster
thinkyng that his disciple had wel learned his lesson,
and would reherse it according to his instruccion,
brought hym before the judges at the daie assigned,
and when the question was repeted to hym again, he

boldly answered, ' My harte geveth me, and my tonge
telleth me, that I am the sonne of the noble duke of
Orleaunce, more glad to be his bastarde, with a meane
livyng, than the lawful sonne of that coward cuckolde
Cawny, with his four thousand crownes.' The judges
much merveiled at his bolde answere, and his mother's
cosyns detested hym for shamyng of his mother, and his
father's supposed kinne rejoysed in gaining the patri-
mony and possessions. Charles Duke of Orleaunce
heryng of this judgment, took hym into his family, and
gave him greate offices and fees, whiche he well de-
served, for (during his captivitie) he defended his
landes, expulsed the Englishmen, and in conclusion,
procured his deliverance.»—*Hall, ff.* 104.

There can be no doubt that Shakspeare had this
anecdote in his mind when he wrote the first scene
wherein the bastard Falconbridge is introduced.

When the duke of Orleans was so villanously assas-
sinated by order of the duke of Burgundy, the murder
was thought at first to have been perpetrated by Sir
Aubert de Cauny, says Monstrellet (Johnes's translation,
vol. i. p. 198), from the great hatred he bore the duke
for having carried off his wife; but the truth was soon
known who were the guilty persons, and that sir Aubert
was perfectly innocent of the crime. Marietta d'Enguien
was the name of the adulteress.

Note 2, page 3, col. 1.
Cheer'd with the Trobador's sweet minstrelsy.

Lorraine was famous for its poets.

> There mightest thou se these flutours,
> Minstrallis and eke jogelours,
> That wel to slagin did their paine;
> Some songin songis of Loraine,
> For in Loraine there notis be
> Full swetir than in this contro.
>   *Romaunt of the Rose.*

Note 3, page 3, col. 1.
Denying what she sought.

The following account of *JOAN of ARC* is extracted
from a history of the siege of Orleans, *prise de mot à
mot, sans aucun changement de langage, d'un vieil
exemplaire escrit a la main en parchemin, et trouvé
en la maison de la dicte ville d'Orleans.* Troyes. 1621.

« Or en ce temps avoit une jeune fille au pais de
Lorraine, aagee de dix-huict ans ou environ, nommee
Janne, natifue d'un paroisse nommee Dompre, fille
d'un Laboureur nomme Jacques Tart ; qui jamais
n'avoit fait autre chose que garder les bestes aux champs,
a la quelle, ainsi qu'elle disoit, avoit estè revelè que
Dieu vouloit qu'elle allast devers le Roi Charles sep-
tiesme, pour luy aider et le conseiller a recouvrer son
royaume et ses villes et places que les Anglois avoient
conquises en ses pays. La quelle revelation elle n'osa
dire à ses pere et mere, pource qu'elle scavoit bien que
jamais n'eussent consenty qu'elle y fust allec; et te
persuada tant qu'il la mena devers un gentelhomme
nomme Messire Robert de Baudricourt, qui pour lors
estoit Cappitaine de la ville, ou chasteau de Vaucou-
leur, qui est assez prochain de la : auquel elle pria tres
instamment qu'il la fist mener devers le Roy de France,
en leur disant qu'il estoit tres necessaire qu'elle parlast
a luy pour le bien de son royaume, et que elle luy feroit
grand secours et aide a recouvrer son dict royaume, et
que Dieu le vouloit ainsi, et que il luy avoit esté revelé
par plusieurs fois. Des quelles parolles il ne faisoit que

rire et se moequer et la reputoit incensee : toutesfois elle persevera tant et si longuement qu'il luy bailla un gentelhomme, nommè Ville Robert, et quelque nombre de gens, les quels la menerent devers le Roy que pour lors estoit a Chinon. »

Note 4, page 3, col. 1.
Of eighteen years.

This agrees with the account of her age given by Holinshed, who calls her « a young wench of an eighteene years old, of favour was she counted like-some, of person stronglie made and manlie, of courage great, hardie, and stout withall; an understander of counsels though she were not at them, greet semblance of chastitie both of bodie and behaviour, the name of Jesus in hir mouth about all her businesses, humble, obedient, and fasting divers daies in the weeke.»
Holinshed, 600.

De Serres speaks thus of her :—« A young maiden named Joan of Arc, borne in a village upon the Mar-ches of Barre called Domremy, neere to Vaucouleurs, of the age of eighteene or twenty years, issued from base parents, her father was named James of Arc, and her mother Isabel, poore countrie folkes, who had brought her up to keep their cattell. She said with great boldnesse that she had a revelation how to suc-cour the king, how he might be able to chase the En-glish from Orleance, and after that to cause the king to be crowned at Rheims, and to put him fully and wholly in possession of his realme.

« After she had delivered this to her father, mother, and their neighbours, she presumed to go to the lord of Baudricourt, provost of Vaucouleurs; she boldly de-livered unto him, after an extraordinary manner, all these great mysteries, as much wished for of all men as not hoped for : especially comming from the mouth of a poore country maide, whom they might with more reason beleeve to be possessed of some melancholy humour, than divinely inspired; being the instrument of so many excellent remedies, in so desperat a season, after the vaine striving of so great and famous person-ages. At the first he mocked and reproved her, but having heard her with more patience, and judging by her temperate discourse and modest countenance that she spoke not idely, in the end he resolves to present her to the king for his discharge. So she arrives at Chinon the sixt day of May, attired like a man.

« She had a modest countenance, sweet, civill, and resolute; her discourse was temperate, reasonable and retired, her actions cold, shewing great chastity. Hav-ing spoken to the king, or noblemen with whom she was to negociate, she presently retired to her lodging with an old woman that guided her, without vanity, affectation, babling, or courtly lightnesse. These are the manners which the Original attributes to her.»
Edward Grimeston, the translator, calls her in the margin, « Joane the Virgin, or rather Witch.»

Note 5, page 3, col. 2.
Lest he in wrath confound me.

Then the word of the LORD came unto me, saying, Before I formed thee in the belly, I knew thee; and before thou camest forth out of the womb I sanctified thee, and I ordained thee a prophet unto the nations.

Then said I, Ah, LORD GOD, behold I cannot speak, for I am a child.

But the Lord said unto me, Say not, I am a child, for thou shalt go to all that I shall send thee, and what-soever I command thee, thou shalt speak.

Thou therefore gird up thy loins, and arise, and speak unto them all that I command thee : be not dismayed at their faces lest I confound thee before them.
Jeremiah, Chap. I.

Note 6, page 4, col. 2.
Taught wisdom to mankind!

But as for the mighty man he had the earth, and the honourable man dwelt in it.
Days should speak, and multitude of years should teach wisdom.   *Job.*

Note 7, page 4, col. 2.
Rush o'er the land, and desolate and kill.

« While the English and French contend for domi-nion, sovereignty, and life itself, men's goods in France were violently taken by the license of war, churches spoiled, men every where murthered or wounded, others put to death or tortured, matrons ravished, maids forcibly drawn from out their parents' arms to be de-flowered; towns daily taken, daily spoyled, daily de-faced, the riches of the inhabitants carried whether the conquerors think good; houses and villages round about set on fire, no kind of cruelty is left unpractised upon the miserable French, omitting many hundred kind of other calamities which all at once oppressed them. Add here unto that the commonwealth, being destitute of the help of laws (which for the most part are mute in times of war and mutiny), floateth up and down without any anchorage at right or justice. Neither was England herself void of these mischiefs, who every day heard the news of her valiant children's funerals, slain in perpetual skirmishes and bickerings, her general wealth continually ebbed and wained, so that the evils seemed almost equal, and the whole western world echoed the groans and sighs of either nation's quarrels, being the common argument of speech and compassion through Christendom.»—*Speed.*

Note 8, page 4, col. 2.
By day I drove my father's flock afield.

People found out a nest of miracles in her education, says old Fuller, that so lion-like a spirit should be bred among sheep like David.

Note 9, page 5, col. 2.
Death! to the happy thou art terrible,
But how the wretched love to think of thee,
O thou true comforter, the friend of all
Who have no friend beside!

O Death, how bitter is the remembrance of thee to a man that liveth at rest in his possessions, unto the man that hath nothing to vex him, and that hath pros-perity in all things! yea unto him that is yet able to receive meat!

O Death, acceptable is thy sentence unto the needy, and unto him whose strength faileth, that is now in the last age, and is vexed with all things, and to him that despaireth, and hath lost patience!—*Ecclesiasticus,* xli, 1, 2.

Note 10, page 6, col. 1.
Think well of this, young man!

Dreadful indeed must have been the miseries of the French from vulgar plunderers, when the manners of the highest classes were marked by hideous grossness and vices that may not be uttered.

Of acts so ill examples are not good.
Sir William Alexander.

The following portrait of some of these outrages I extract from the notes of Andrews's History of Great Britain :—« Agricola quilibet, sponsam juvenem acquisitus, ac in vicina alicujus viri nobilis et præpotentis habitans, crudelissime vexabatur. Nempe nonnunquam in ejus domum irruens iste optimas, magnâ comitante catervâ, pretium ingens redemptionis exigeret, ac si non protinus solveret colonus, istum miserum in magna arca protrudens, venustæ ac teneræ uxori suæ (super ipsam arcam prostratæ) vim vir nobilis adferret; voce exclamans horrrenda, ‘Audine Rustice! jamjam, super hanc arcam constupratur dilecta tua sponsa,' atque peracto hoc scelere nefando relinqueretur (hórresco referens) suffocatione expirans maritus, nisi magno pretio sponsa nuper vitiata liberationem ejus redimeret.»—*J. de Paris.*

Let us add to this the detestable history of a great commander under Charles VII of France, the bastard of Bourbon, who (after having committed the most execrable crimes during a series of years with impunity) was drowned, in 1441, by the constable Richemont (a treacherous assassin, but a mirror of justice when compared to his noble contemporaries), on its being proved against him « Quod super ipsum maritum vi prostratum, uxori frustra repugnanti, vim adtuleret.»

Ensuite il avoit fait battre et découper le mari, tant que c'étoit pitié à voir.—*Mém. de Richemont.*

Note 11, page 6, col. 2.
Think that there are such horrors.

I translate the following anecdote of the Black Prince from Froissart :—

The Prince of Wales was about a month, and not longer, before the city of Lymoges, and he did not assault it, but always continued mining. When the miners of the prince had finished their work, they said to him, « Sir, we will throw down a great part of the wall into the moat whenever it shall please you, so that you may enter into the city at your ease, without danger » These words greatly pleased the prince, who said to them, « I chuse that your work should be manifested to-morrow at the hour of day-break.» Then the miners set fire to their mines the next morning as the prince had commanded, and overthrew a great pane of the wall, which filled the moat where it had fallen. The English saw all this very willingly, and they were there all armed and ready to enter into the town; those who were on foot could enter at their ease, and they entered and ran to the gate and beat it to the earth and all the barriers also; for there was no defence, and all this was done so suddenly, that the people of the town were not upon their guard. And then you might have seen the prince, the duke of Lancaster, the count of Canterbury, the count of Pembroke, Messire Guischart Dangle, and all the other chiefs and their people who entered in, and ruffians on foot who were prepared to do mischief, and to run through the town, and to kill men and women and children, and so they had been commanded to do. There was a full pitiful sight, for men and women and children cast themselves on their knees before the prince, and cried « mercy!» but he was so

enflamed with so great rage, that he heard them not, neither man nor woman would he hear, but they were all put to the sword wherever they were found, and these people had not been guilty. I know not how they could have no pity upon poor people, who had never been powerful enough to do any treason. There was no heart so hard in the city of Lymoges which had any remembrance of God, that did not lament the great mischief that was there; for more than three thousand men and women and children had their throats cut that day; God has their souls, for indeed they were martyred. In entering the town a party of the English went to the palace of the bishop and found him there, and took him and led him before the prince, who looked at him with a murderous look (*feloneusement*), and the best word that he could say to him was that his head should be cut off, and then he made him be taken from his presence.—I, 235.

The crime which the people of Lymoges had committed was that of surrendering when they had been besieged by the duke of Berry, and in consequence *turning French.* And this crime was thus punished at a period when no versatility of conduct was thought dishonourable. The phrases tourner Anglois—tourner François—retourner Anglois, occur repeatedly in Froissart. I should add that of all the heroes of this period the Black Prince was the most generous and the most humane.

After the English had taken the town of Montereau, the seigneur de Guitery, who commanded there, retired to the castle; and Henry V threatened, unless he surrendered, to hang eleven gentlemen, taken in the town. These poor men intreated the governor to comply, for the sake of saving their lives, letting him at the same time know how impossible it was that his defence could be of any avail. He was not to be persuaded; and when they saw this, and knew that they must die, some of them requested that they might first see their wives and their friends. This was allowed : the women were sent, *la y eut de piteux regrets au prendre congé,* says Pierre de Fenin, and on the following morning they were executed as Henry had threatened. The governor held out for fifteen days, and then yielded by a capitulation which secured himself. (Coll. des Mémoires. T. v, p. 456.)

In the whole history of these dreadful times I remember but one man whom the cruelty of the age had not contaminated, and that was the Portuguese hero Nuno Alvares Pereira, a man who appears to me to have been a perfect example of patriotism, heroism, and every noble and lovely quality, above all others of any age or country.

Atrocious however as these instances are, they seem as nothing when compared to the atrocities which the French exercised upon each other. When Soissons was captured by Charles VI (1414) in person, « In regard to the destruction committed by the king's army (says Monstrelet), it cannot be estimated; for after they had plundered all the inhabitants, and their dwellings, they despoiled the churches and monasteries. They even took and robbed the most part of the sacred shrines of many bodies of saints, which they stripped of all the precious stones, gold and silver, together with many other jewels and holy things appertaining to the aforesaid churches. There is not a christian but would have shuddered at the atrocious excesses committed by the soldiery in Soissons : married women violated before their husbands ; young damsels in the presence of their parents and relatives ; holy nuns, gentlewomen of all ranks, of whom there were many in the town ; all, or the greater part, were violated against their wills by divers nobles and others, who, after having satiated their own brutal passions, delivered them over without mercy to their servants : and there is no remembrance of such disorder and havoc being done by christians, considering the many persons of high rank that were present, and who made no efforts to check them. There were also many gentlemen in the king's army who had relations in the town, as well secular as churchmen ; but the disorder was not the less on that account.»—Vol. iv, p. 31.

What a national contrast is there between the manner in which the English and French have conducted their civil wars ! Even in the wars of the Fronde, when all parties were alike thoroughly unprincipled, cruelties were committed on both sides which it might have been thought nothing but the strong feelings of a perverted religious principle could have given birth to.

Note 12, page 6, col. 2.
Yet hangs and pulls for food.

Holinshed says, speaking of the siege of Roan, « If I should rehearse how deerelie dogs, rats, mise, and cats were sold within the towne, and how greedilie they were by the poore people eaten and devoured, and how the people dailie died for fault of food, *and young infants laie sucking in the streets on their mothers breasts, being dead starved for hunger,* the reader might lament their extreme miseries.» P. 566.

Note 13, page 6, col. 2.
The sceptre of the wicked ?

« Do not the tears run down the widow's cheek ? and is not her cry against him that causeth them to fall?

« The Lord will not be slack till he have smitten in sunder the loins of the unmerciful, till he have taken away the multitude of the proud, and broken the sceptre of the unrighteous.»—*Ecclesiasticus.*

Note 14, page 7, col. 1.
The fountain of the Fairies.

In the Journal of Paris in the reigns of Charles VI. and VII. it is asserted that the Maid of Orleans, in answer to an interrogatory of the doctors, whether she had ever assisted at the assemblies held at the Fountain of the Fairies near Domprein, round which the evil spirits dance, confessed that she had often repaired to a beautiful fountain in the country of Lorraine, which she named the good Fountain of the Fairies of our Lord.—*From the notes to the English version of Le Grande Fablaux.*

Note 15, page 7, col. 1.
They love to lie and rock upon its leaves.

Being asked whether she had ever seen any fairies, she answered no : but that one of her god-mothers pretended to have seen some at the Fairy-tree, near the village of Dompre.—*Rapin.*

Note 16, page 7, col. 1.
Memory, thought, were gone.

« In this representation which I made to place myself near to Christ (says St Teresa), there would come suddenly upon me, without either expectation or any preparation on my part, such an evident feeling of the presence of God, as that I could by no means doubt, but that either he was within me, or else I all engulfed in him. This was not in the manner of a vision, but I think they call it Mistical Theology ; and it suspends the soul in such sort, that she seems to be wholly out of herself. The Will is in act of loving, the Memory seems to be in a manner lost, the Understanding, in my opinion, discourses not ; and although it be not lost, yet it works not as I was saying, but remains as it were amazed to consider how much it understands.»—*Life of St. Teresa written by herself.*

Teresa was well acquainted with the feelings of enthusiasm. I had, however, described the sensations of the Maid of Orleans before I had met with the life of the saint.

Note 17, page 7, col. 2.
—— and they shall perish who oppress.

« Raise up indignation, and pour out wrath, and let them perish who oppress the people!»—*Ecclesiasticus,* 36.

Note 18, page 7, col. 2.
Sung shrill and ceaseless.

The epithets shrill and hoarse will not appear incongruous to one who has attended to the grasshopper's chirp. Gazæus has characterised the sound by a word certainly accurate, in his tale of a grasshopper who perched upon St Francis's finger, and sung the praise of God and the wonders of his own body in his vernacular tongue, St Francis and all the grasshoppers listening with equal edification :—

> Cicada
> Canebat (ut sic efferam) cicadicè.
> *Pia Hilaria Angelini Gazei.*

St Francis seems to have laboured much in the conversion of animals. In the fine series of pictures representing his life, lately painted for the new Franciscan convent at Madrid, I recollect seeing him preach to a congregation of birds. Gazæus has a poem upon his instructing a ewe. His advice to her is somewhat curious :

> Vide ne arietes, neve in obvios ruas :
> Cave devovendos flosculos altaribus
> Vel ore laceres, vel bifurcato pede,
> Male feriatæ folis instar, proteras.

There is another upon his converting two lambs, whose prayers were more acceptable to God, Marot ! says he, than your psalms. If the nun, who took care of them in his absence, was inclined to lie a-bed—

> Frater Agnus hanc bee bed suo
> Devotus excitabat.
> O agne jam non agne sed doctor bone!

Note 19, page 8, col. 1.
The memory of his prison'd years.

The Maid declared upon her trial, that God loved the duke of Orleans, and that she had received more revelations concerning him, than any person living, except the king.—*Rapin.*

Orleans, during his long captivity, « had learnt to court the fair ladies of England in their native strains:» among the Harleian MSS. is a collection of « love poems, roundels, and songs,» composed by the French prince during his confinement.

Note 20, page 8, col. 1.

The prisoners of that shameful day outsumm'd
Their conquerors!

According to Holinshed the English army consisted of only 15,000 men, harassed with a tedious march of a month, in very bad weather, through an enemy's country, and for the most part sick of a flux. He states the number of the French at 60,000, of whom 10,000 were slain, and 1500 of the higher order taken prisoners. Some historians make the disproportion in numbers still greater. Goodwin says, that among the slain there were one archbishop, three dukes, six earls, ninety barons, fifteen hundred knights, and seven thousand esquires or gentlemen.

Note 21, page 8, col. 1.

From his hersed bowmen how the arrows flew.

This was the usual method of marshalling the bowmen. At Crecy « the archers stood in manner of an herse, about two hundred in front and but forty in depth, which is undoubtedly the best way of embattelling archers, especially when the enemy is very numerous, as at this time: for by the breadth of the front the extension of the enemies front is matched; and by reason of the thinness in flank, the arrows do more certain execution, being more likely to reach home.»— *Barnes.*

The victory at Poictiers is chiefly attributed to the herse of archers. After mentioning the conduct and courage of the English leaders in that battle, Barnes says,—« but all this courage had been thrown away to no purpose, had it not been seconded by the extraordinary gallantry of the English archers, who behaved themselves that day with wonderful constancy, alacrity, and resolution. So that by their means, in a manner, all the French battails received their first foil, being by the barbed arrows so galled and terrified, that they were easily opened to the men of arms.

« Without all question, the guns which are used now-a-days are neither so terrible in battle, nor do such execution, nor work such confusion as arrows can do: for bullets being not seen only hurt when they hit, but arrows enrage the horse, and break the array, and terrify all that behold them in the bodies of their neighbours. Not to say that every archer can shoot thrice to a gunner's once, and that whole squadrons of bows may let fly at one time, when only one or two files of musqueteers can discharge at once. Also, that whereas guns are useless when your pikes join, because they only do execution point blank, the arrows which will fall at random, may do good service even behind your men of arms. And it is notorious, that at the famous battle of Lepanto, the Turkish bows did more mischief than the Christian artillery. Besides it is not the least observable, that whereas the weakest may use guns as well as the strongest, in those days your lusty and tall yeomen were chosen for the bow, whose hose being fastened with one point, and their jackets long and easy to shoot in, they had their limbs at full liberty, so that they might easily draw bows of great strength, and shoot arrows of a yard long beside the head.»

Joshua Barnes.

Note 22, page 8, col. 1.

To glut on the defenceless prisoners.

During the heat of the combat, when the English had gained the upper hand, and made several prisoners, news was brought to king Henry that the French were attacking his rear, and had already captured the greater part of his baggage and sumpter-horses. This was indeed true, for Robinet de Bournonville, Rifflart de Clamasse, Ysambart d'Azincourt, and some other men at arms, with about six hundred peasants, had fallen upon and taken a great part of the king's baggage, and a number of horses, while the guard was occupied in the battle. This distressed the king very much, for he saw that though the French army had been routed, they were collecting on different parts of the plain in large bodies, and he was afraid they would resume the battle: he therefore caused instant proclamation to be made by some sound of trumpet, that every one should put his prisoners to death, to prevent them from aiding the enemy, should the combat be renewed. This caused an instantaneous and general massacre of the French prisoners, occasioned by the disgraceful conduct of Robinet de Bournonville, Ysambart d'Azincourt, and the others, who were afterwards punished for it, and imprisoned a very long time by duke John of Burgundy, notwithstanding they had made a present to the count de Charrolois of a most precious sword, ornamented with diamonds, that had belonged to the king of England. They had taken this sword, with other rich jewels, from king Henry's baggage, and had made this present, that in case they should at any time be called to an account for what they had done, the count might stand their friend.—*Monstrelet,* vol. iv, p. 180.

When the king of England had on this Saturday begun his march towards Calais, many of the French returned to the field of battle, where the bodies had been turned over more than once, some to seek for their lords, and carry them to their own countries for burial, others to pillage what the English had left. King Henry's army had only taken gold, silver, rich dresses, helmets, and what was of value, for which reason the greater part of the armour was untouched, and on the dead bodies; but it did not long remain thus, for it was very soon stripped off, and even the shirts and all other parts of their dress were carried away by the peasants of the adjoining villages.

The bodies were left exposed as naked as when they came into the world. On the Saturday, Sunday, Monday, Tuesday, and Wednesday, the corpses of many princes were well washed and raised, namely, the dukes of Brabant, Bar, and Alençon, the counts de Nevers, de Blaumont, de Vaudemont, de Faulquemberge, the lord de Dampierre, admiral, sir Charles d'Albreth, constable, and buried in the church of the Friars Minors at Hesdin. Others were carried by their servants, some to their own countries, and others to different churches. All who were recognized were taken away, and buried in the churches of their manors.

When Philippe count de Charrolois heard of the unfortunate and melancholy disaster of the French, he was in great grief; more especially for the death of his two uncles, the duke of Brabant and count de Nevers. Moved by compassion, he caused all that had remained exposed on the field of battle to be interred, and commissioned the abbot de Roussianville and the bailiff of Aire to have it done. They measured out a square of twenty-five yards, wherein were dug three trenches twelve feet wide, in which were buried, by an account kept, five thousand eight hundred men. It was not known how many had been carried away by their friends, nor what number of the wounded had died in hospitals, towns, villages, and even in the adjacent woods; but, as I have before said, it must have been very great.

This square was consecrated as a burying ground by the bishop of Guines, at the command and as procurator of Louis de Luxembourg, bishop of Therounne. It was surrounded by a strong hedge of thorns, to prevent wolves or dogs from entering it, and tearing up and devouring the bodies.

In consequence of this sad event, some learned clerks of the realm made the following verses :—

A chief by dolorous mischance oppress'd,
  A prince who rules by arbitrary will,
A royal house by discord sore distress'd,
  A council prejudiced and partial still,
Subjects by prodigality brought low,
Will fill the land with beggars, well we trow.

Nobles made noble in dame Nature's spite
  A timorous clergy fear, and truth conceal ;
While humble commoners forego their right,
  And the harsh yoke of proud oppression feel :
Thus, while the people mourn, the public woe
Will fill the land with beggars, well we trow.

A feeble woe! whose impotent commands
  Thy very vassals boldly dare despise :
Ah, helpless monarch! whose enervate hands
  And wavering counsels dare no high emprize,
Thy hapless reign will cause our tears to flow,
Will fill the land with beggars, well we trow.
             Johnes's Monstrelet, vol. iv. p. 195.

According to Pierre de Fenin, the English did not bury their own dead; but their loss was so small, that this is very unlikely. He says, « Après cette douloureuse journée et que toutes les deux parties se furent retirées, Louys de Luxembourg, qui estoit evesque de Teroüane, fit faire en la place où la bataille avoit esté donnée plusieurs charniers, où il fit assembler tous les morts d'un costé et d'autre; et la les fit enterrer, puis il benit la place, et la fit enclore de fortes hayes tout autour, pour la garantir du bestail. »

After the battle of Agincourt Henry lodged at Maisoncelle; « le lendemain au matin il en deslogea, et alla passer tout au milieu des morts qui avoient esté tuez en ce combat; la il s'arresta grand espace de temps, et tirèrent ses gens encor des prisonniers hors du nombre des morts, qu'ils emmenèrent avec eux.»—*Mem. de Pierre de Fenin.*

Note 23, page 8, col. 2.
From the disastrous plain of Agincourt.

Perhaps one consequence of the victory at Agincourt is not generally known. Immediately on his return, Henry sent his legates to the council of Constance : « at this councell, by the assent of all nations there present, it was authorised and ordained, that England should obtaine the name of a nation, and should be said one of the five nations that owe their devotion to the church of Rome, which thing until that time men of other nations, for envy, had delayed and letted »—*Stowe. Elmham.*

Note 24, page 8, col. 2.
Henry as wise as brave had back to England—

Henry judged, that by fomenting the troubles of France, he should procure more certain and lasting advantages than by means of his arms. The truth is, by pushing the French vigorously, he ran the risk of

uniting them all against him; in which case, his advantages, probably, would have been inconsiderable: but by granting them some respite, he gave them opportunity to destroy one another : therefore, contrary to every one's expectation, he laid aside his military affairs for near eighteen months, and betook himself entirely to negociation, which afforded him the prospect of less doubtful advantages.—*Rapin.*

Note 25, page 8, col. 2.
For many were the warrior sons of Roan.

« Yet although the armie was strong without, there lacked not within both hardie capteins and manfull soldiers, and as for people, they had more than inough : for as it is written by some that had good cause to know the truth, and no occasion to erre from the same, there were in the citie at the time of the siege 210,000 persons. Dailie were issues made out of the citie at diverse gates, sometime to the losse of the one partie and sometimes of the other, as chances of ware in such adventures happen.»—*Holinshed,* 566.

Note 26, page 8, col. 2.
Had bade them vow before Almighty God.

« The Frenchmen indeed, preferring fame before worldlie riches, and despising pleasure (the enemy to warlike prowesse), sware ech to other never to render or deliver the citie, while they might either hold sword in hand or speare in rest.»—*Holinshed,* 566.

Note 27, page 9, col. 1.
Had made a league with Famine.

« The king of England, advertised of their hautie courages, determined to conquer them by famine which would not be tamed by weapon. Wherefore he stopped all the passages, both by water and land, that no vittels could be conveied to the citie. He cast trenches round about the walls, and set them full of stakes, and defended them with archers, so that there was left neither waie for them within to issue out, nor for anie that were abroad to enter in without his license.—The king's coosine germane and alie (the king of Portugale), sent a great navie of well-appointed ships unto the mouth of the river of Seine, to stop that no French vessel should enter the river and passe up the same, to the aid of them within Rouen.

« Thus was the faire citie of Rouen compassed about with euemies, both by water and land, having neither comfort nor aid of king, dolphin, or duke.»
                        Holinshed, 566.

King Henry of England marched a most powerful army, accompanied by a large train of artillery and warlike stores, in the month of June, before the noble and potent town of Rouen, to prevent the inhabitants and garrison from being supplied with new corn. The van of his army arrived there at midnight, that the garrison might not make any sally against them. The king was lodged at the Carthusian convent; the duke of Gloster was quartered before the gate of St Hilaire; the duke of Clarence at the gate of Caen; the earl of Warwick at that of Martinville; the duke of Exeter and earl of Dorset at that of Beauvais: in front of the gate of the castle were the lord marshal and sir John de Cornwall. At the gate leading to Normandy were posted the earls of Huntingdon, Salisbury, Kyme, and the lord Neville, son to the earl of Westmoreland. On the hill fronting St Catherine's were others of the English barons. Before the English could fortify their quarters, many sallies were made on them, and several severe skirmishes passed on both sides. But the English, so soon as they could, dug deep ditches between the town and them, on the top of which they planted a thick hedge of thorns, so that they could not otherwise be annoyed than by cannon-shot and arrows. They also built a jette on the banks of the Seine, about a cannon-shot distant from the town, to which they fastened their chains, one of them half a foot under the water, another level with it, and a third two feet above the stream, so that no boats could bring provision to the town, nor could any escape from it that way. They likewise dug deep galleries of communication from one quarter to another, which completely sheltered those in them from cannon or other warlike machines.—*Monstrelet*, vol. v, p. 40.

Note 28, page 9, col 1.
Desperate endurance.

"After he had prosecuted the siege of this place for some time, the cardinal Ursino repaired to his camp, and endeavoured to persuade him to moderate his terms, and agree to an equitable peace; but the king's reply plainly evinced his determination of availing himself of the present situation of public affairs; 'Do you not see,' said he, 'that God has brought me hither, as it were by the hand? The throne of France may be said to be vacant; I have a good title to that crown; the whole kingdom is involved in the utmost disorder and confusion; few are willing, and still fewer are able, to resist me. Can I have a more convincing proof of the interposition of heaven in my favour, and that the Supreme Ruler of all things has decreed that I should ascend the throne of France?'"—*Hist. of England by Hugh Clarendon.*

Note 29, page 9, col. 1.
Could we behold the savage Irish Kernes.

"With the English sixteen hundred Irish Kernes were enrolled from the prior of Kilmainham; able men, but almost naked; their arms were targets, darts and swords, their horses little and bare no saddle, yet nevertheless nimble, on which upon every advantage they plaied with the French, in spoiling the country rifeling the houses, and carrying away children with their baggage upon their cowes backs."—*Speed*, p. 638.

The king of England had in his army numbers of Irish, the greater part of whom were on foot, having only a stocking and shoe on one leg and foot, with the other quite naked. They had targets, short javelins, and a strange sort of knives. Those who were on horseback had no saddles, but rode excellently well on small mountain horses, and were mounted on such paniers as are used by the carriers of corn in parts of France. They were, however, miserably accoutred in comparison with the English, and without any arms that could much hurt the French whenever they might meet them.

These Irish made frequent excursions during the siege over Normandy, and did infinite mischiefs, carrying back to their camp large booties. Those on foot took men, and even children from the cradle, with beds and furniture, and placing them on cows, drove all these things before them, for they were often met thus by the French.—*Monstrelet*, v, p. 42.

Note 30, page 9, col. 1.
Ruffians half-clothed, half-human, half-baptiz'd.

"In some corners of Connaught, the people leave the right armes of their infants male unchristend (as they terme it), to the end that at any time afterwards they might give a more deadly and ungracious blow when they strike; which things doe not only show how palpably they are carried away by traditious obscurities, but doe also intimate how full their hearts be of inveterate revenge."

The book from which this extract is taken wants the title. The title of the second part is, *A prospect of the most famous parts of the world. Printed for William Humble, in Pope's Head Place.* 1646.

Note 31, page 9, col. 1.
Of Harfleur's wretched race cast on the world.

"Some writing of this yeelding up of Harflue, doo in like sort make mention of the distresse whereto the people, then expelled out of their habitations, were driven: insomuch as parents with their children, yong maids and old folke went out of the towne gates with heavie harts, (God wot,) as put to their present shifts to seek them a new abode."—*Holinshed*, 550.

This act of barbarity was perpetrated by Henry that he might people the town with English inhabitants. "This doth Anglorum prælia report, saieng (not without good ground I believe), as followeth:

> Tum flentes teneră cum prole parentes
> Virgineusque chorus veteres liquere penates:
> Tum populus cunctus de portis Gallicus exit
> Mœstus, inarmatus, vacuus, miser, æger, inopsque:
> Utque novas sedes quærat migrare coactus:
> Oppidulo belli potiuntur jure Britanni."
>
> *Holinshed.*

There is a way of telling truth so as to convey falsehood. After the capture of Harfleur, Stowe says, "all the soldiers and inhabitants, both of the towne and towers, were suffered to goe freely, unharmed, whither they would," 348. Henry's conduct was the same at Caen: he "commanded all women and children to bee avoyded out of the towne, and so the towne was inhabited of new possessors."—*Stowe.*

Note 32, page 9, col. 1.
Knelt at the altar.

Before Henry took possession of Harfleur, he went bare-footed to the church to give God thanks.—*De Serres.*

Note 33, page 9, col. 1.
In cold blood murder'd.

Henry, not satisfied with the reduction of Caen, put several of the inhabitants to death, who had signalized their valour in the defence of their liberty.—*H. Clarendon.*

Note 34, page 9, col. 1.
He groan'd and cursed in bitterness of heart.

After the capture of the city "Luca Italico, the vicar generall of the archbishoprike of Rouen, for denouncing the king accursed, was delivered to him and deteined in prison till he died."—*Holinshed. Titus Livius.*

Note 35, page 9, col. 2.
Force back the miserable multitude.

"A great number of poore sillie creatures were put

out of the gates, which were by the Englishmen that
kept the trenches, beaten and driven back againe to the
same gates, which they found closed and shut against
them, and so they laie betweene the wals of the citie
and the trenches of the enemies, still crieing for help
and releefe, for lack whereof great numbers of them
dailie died.»—*Holinshed.*

Note 36, page 9, col. 2.

And when we sent the herald to implore
His mercy.

At this period, a priest of a tolerable age, and of clear
understanding, was deputed, by those besieged in Rouen,
to the king of France and his council. On his arrival
at Paris, he caused to be explained, by an Augustin
doctor, named Eustace de la Paville, in presence of
the king and his ministers, the miserable situation of
the besieged. He took for his text, « Domine quid
faciemus!» and harangued upon it very ably and
eloquently. When he had finished, the priest addressed
the king, saying, « Most excellent prince and lord, I
am enjoined by the inhabitants of Rouen to make loud
complaints against you, and against you duke of Bur-
gundy who govern the king, for the oppressions they
suffer from the English. They make known to you by
me, that if, from want of being succoured by you, they
are forced to become subjects to the king of England,
you will not have in all the world more bitter enemies;
and if they can, they will destroy you and your whole
congregation.» With these or with similar words did
this priest address the king and his council. After he
had been well received and entertained, and the duke
of Burgundy had promised to provide succours for the
town of Rouen as speedily as possible, he returned the
best way he could to carry this news to the besieged.—
Monstrelet, vol. v, p. 54.

One of the deputed citizens « shewing himself more
rash than wise, more arrogant than learned, took upon
him to shew wherein the glorie of victorie consisted;
advising the king not to shew his manhood in famish-
ing a multitude of poore simple and innocent people,
but rather suffer such miserable wretches as laie be-
twixt the wals of the citie and the trenches of his siege,
to passe through the camp, that theie might get their
living in other places; then if he durst manfullie assault
the place, and by force subdue it, he should win both
worldie fame, and merit great meed from the hands of
Almightie God, for having compassion of the poore,
needie, and indigent people. When this orator had said,
the king with a fierce countenance and bold spirit, re-
proved them for their malapert presumption in that they
should seeme to go about to teach him what belonged
to the dutie of a conqueror, and therefore since it ap-
peared that the same was unknown to them, he declared
that the goddesse of battell called Bellona had three
handmaidens, ever of necessitie attending upon her, as
Blood, Fire, and Famine, and whereas it laie in his
choice to use them all three, he had appointed onelie
the meekest maid of those three damsels to punish them
of that citie till they were brought to reason. This
answer put the French ambassador in a great studie,
musing much at his *excellent wit* and hawtinesse of
courage.»—*Holinshed.*

While the court resided at Beauvais, four gentlemen
and four citizens of Rouen were sent to lay before the
king and council their miserable state : they told them

that thousands of persons were already dead with
hunger within their town; and that from the beginning
of October, they had been forced to live on horses,
dogs, cats, mice and rats, and other things unfit for
human creatures. They had nevertheless driven full
twelve thousand poor people, men, women, and children,
out of the place, the greater part of whom had perished
wretchedly in the ditches of the town. That it had
been frequently necessary to draw up in baskets new
born children from mothers who had been brought to
bed in these ditches to have them baptized, and they
were afterwards returned to their mothers : many,
however had perished without christening—all which
things were grievous and pitiful to be related. They
then added, « To you our lord and king, and to you
noble duke of Burgundy, the loyal inhabitants of Rouen
have before made known their distress : they now
again inform you how much they are suffering for you,
to which you have not yet provided any remedy ac-
cording to your promises. We are sent to you for the
last time, to announce to you, on the part of the be-
sieged, that if within a few days they are not relieved,
they shall surrender themselves and their town to the
English king, and thenceforward renounce all allegi-
ance, faith, and service, which they have sworn to you.»
The king, duke, and council, courteously replied, that
the king's forces were not as yet adequate to raise the
siege, which they were exceedingly sorry for; but,
with God's pleasure, they should very soon be relieved.
The deputies asked by what time; the duke answered,
before the fourth day after Christmas. They then re-
turned to their town with difficulty, from the great
danger of being taken by the besiegers, and related all
that had passed.

The besieged now suffered the greatest distress; and
it is impossible to recount the miseries of the common
people from famine : it was afterward known that up-
wards of fifty thousand had perished of hunger. Some,
when they saw meat carried through the street, in de-
spair, ran to seize it, and so doing, allowed themselves
to be severely beaten, and even wounded. During the
space of three months no provisions were seen in the
markets, but every thing was sold secretly; and what
before the siege was worth a farthing, was sold for
twenty, thirty, or even forty : but those prices were too
high for the common people, and hence the great mor-
tality I have mentioned.—*Monstrelet,* vol. v, p. 61.

Note 37, page 9, col. 2.

The shriek of frenzying anguish.

The names of our Edwards and Henrys are usually
cited together, but it is disgracing the Black Prince and
his father to mention them with Henry of Monmouth.
We have seen what was the conduct of this cold-hearted
and brutal soldier to the famished fugitives from Roan.
The same circumstance occurred at the siege of Calais,
and the difference between the monarchs cannot be
better exemplified than in the difference of their con-
duct upon the same occasion. « When sir John de
Vienne perceived that king Edward intended to lie long
there, he thought to rid the town of as many useless
mouths as he could; and so on a Wednesday, being the
13th of September, he forced out of the town more than
seventeen hundred of the poorest and least necessary
people, old men, women, and children, and shut the
gates upon them : who being demanded, wherefore

they came out of the town, answered with great lamentation, that it was because they had nothing to live on. Then king Edward, who was so fierce in battle, shewed a truly royal disposition by considering the sad condition of these forlorn wretches; for he not only would not force them back again into the town, whereby they might help to consume the victuals, but he gave them all a dinner and two-pence a-piece, and leave to pass through the army without the least molestation: whereby he so wrought upon the hearts of these poor creatures, that many of them prayed to God for his prosperity.»—*Joshua Barnes.*

Note 38, page 9, col. 2.
Nor when the traitor yielded up our town.

Roan was betrayed by its Burgundian governor Bouthellier. During this siege fifty thousand men perished through fatigue, want, and the use of unwholesome provisions.

Note 39, page 9, col. 2.
The gallant Blanchard died.

«Roy d'Angleterre fist coupper la teste a Allain Blanchard cappitaine du commun.»—*Monstrelet, feuillet cxcvii.*

Note 40, page 9, col. 2.
There where the wicked cease.

«There the wicked cease from troubling, and the weary be at rest.»—*Job,* iii, 17.

Note 41, page 10, col. 1.
A pompous shade.
Cent drapeaux funebres
Etaloient en plein jour de pompeuses tenebres.
Le Moyne. St Louis, liv. xvi.

Note 42, page 10, col. 1.
In the mid-day sun a dim and gloomy light.

« When all things necessary were prepared for the conveyance of the dead king into England, his body was laid in a chariot, which was drawn by four great horses : and above the dead corpse, they laid a figure made of boiled hides, or leather representing his person, as near to the semblance of him as could be devised, painted curiously to the similitude of a living creature; upon whose head was set an imperial diademe of gold and precious stones, on his body a purple robe furred with ermine, in his right hand he held a sceptre royal, and in his left hand a ball of gold, with a cross fixed thereon. And in this manner adorned, was this figure laid in a bed in the said chariot, with his visage uncovered towards the heaven : and the couverture of his bed was red silke beaten with gold; and besides that, when the body should passe thro any good towne, a canopy of marvellous great value was borne over the chariot by men of great worship. In this manner, accompanied of the king of Scots and of all princes, lords, and knights of his house, he was brought from Roane to Abville, where the corpse was set in the church of Saint Offrane. From Abville he was brought to Hedin, and from thence to Menstreuil, so to Bulloigne, and so to Calice. In all this journey were many men about the chariot clothed all in white, which bare in their hands torches burning: after whome followed al the household servants in blacke, and after them came the princes, lords, and estates of the king's blood, adorned in vestures of mourning; and after all this, from the said

corpse the distance of two English myles, followed the queene of England right honourably accompanyed. In this manner they entered Calice.»—*Stowe.*

At about a league distant followed the queen, with a numerous attendance. From Calais they embarqued for Dover, and passing through Canterbury and Rochester, arrived at London on Martiumas-day.

When the funeral approached London, fifteen bishops dressed in pontificalibus, several mitred abbots and churchmen, with a multitude of persons of all ranks, came out to meet it. The churchmen chaunted the service for the dead as it passed over London-bridge, through Lombard-street, to St Paul's cathedral. Near the car were the relations of the late king, uttering loud lamentations. On the collar of the first horse that drew the car were emblazoned the ancient arms of England; on that of the second, the arms of France and England quartered the same as he bore during his lifetime ; on that of the third, the arms of France simply; on that of the fourth horse were painted the arms of the noble king Arthur, whom no one could conquer : they were three crowns or, on a shield azure.

When the funeral service had been royally performed in the cathedral, the body was carried to be interred at Westminster-abbey with his ancestors. At this funeral, and in regard to every thing concerning it, greater pomp and expence were made than had been done for two hundred years at the interment of any king of England; and even now as much honour and reverence is daily paid to his tomb, as if it were certain he was a saint in Paradise.

Thus ended the life of king Henry in the flower of his age, for when he died he was but forty years old. He was very wise and able in every business he undertook, and of a determined character. During the seven or eight years he ruled in France, he made greater conquests than any of his predecesors had done : it is true he was so feared by his princes and captains, that none dared to disobey his orders, however nearly related to him, more especially his English subjects. In this state of obedience were his subjects of France and England in general; and the principal cause was, that if any person transgressed his ordinances, he had him instantly punished without favour or mercy.

Monstrelet, vol. v, p. 375.

A noble knight of Picardy used a joking expression to his herald respecting king Henry, which was afterwards often repeated. Sir Sarrasin d'Arly, uncle to the vidame of Amiens, who might be about sixty years of age, resided in the castle of Acher, which he had had with his wife, sister to the lord d'Offernont, near to Pas in Artois. He was laid up with the gout, but very eager in his inquiries after news of what was going on. One day his poursuivant, named Haurenas, of the same age as himself, and who had long served him, returned from making the usual inquiries, and on sir Sarrasin questioning him and asking him if he had heard any particulars of the death of the king of England, he said that he had, and had even seen his corpse at Abville in the church of St Ulfran ; and then related how he was attired, nearly as has been before described. The knight then asked him on his faith if he had diligently observed him ? On his answering that he had, «Now, on thy oath, tell me,» added sir Sarrasin, «if he had his boots on ?» «No, my lord, by my faith he had not.» The knight then cried out, « Haurenas, my good friend, never believe me if he has not left them in France.» This expression set the company a laughing, and then they talked of other matters.

Monstrelet, vol. v, p. 377.

Note 43, page 10, col. 1.
Their dangerous way.

The governor of Vaucouleur appointed *deux gentils-hommes* to conduct the Maid to Chinon. « Ils eurent peine à se charger de cette commission, à cause qu'il falloit passer au travers du pays ennemi ; mais elle leur dit avec fermeté qu'ils ne craignissent rien, et que sûrement eux et elle arriveroient auprès du roi sans qu'il leur arrivât rien de fâcheux.

« Ils partirent, passèrent par l'Auxerrois sans obstacle, quoique les Anglois en fussent les maîtres, traversèrent plusieurs rivières à la nage, entrèrent dans les pays de la domination du roi, où les partis ennemis couroient de tous côtés, sans en rencontrer aucun : arrivèrent heureusement à Chinon, où le roi étoit, et lui donnerent avis de leur arrivée et du sujet qui les amenoit. Tout le monde fut extrêmement surpris d'un si long voyage fait avec tant de bonheur.»—*P. Daniel.*

Note 44, page 10, col. 1.
The autumnal rains had beaten to the earth.

« Nil Galliâ perturbatius, nil spoliatius, nil egentius esset. Sed neque cum milite melius agebatur, qui tametsi gaudebat prædâ, interim tamen trucidabatur passim, dum uterque rex civitates suæ factionis principes in fide retinere studeret. Igitur jam cædium satietas utrumque populum ceperat, jamque tot damna utrinque illata erant, ut quisque generatim se oppressum, laceratum, perditum ingemisceret, doloreque summo angeretur, disrumperetur, cruciaretur, ac per id animi quamvis obstinatissimi ad pacem inclinarentur. Simul urgebat ad hoc rerum omnium inopia ; passim enim agri devastati inculti manebant, cum præsertim homines provitâ tuendâ, non arva colere sed bello servire necessariò cogerentur. Ita tot urgentibus malis, neuter a pace abhorrebat, sed alter ab altero eam aut petere, vel admittere turpe putabat.»—*Polydore Virgil.*

The effect of this contest upon England was scarcely less ruinous. « In the last year of the victorious Henry V, there was not a sufficient number of gentlemen left in England to carry on the business of civil government.»

But if the victories of Henry were so fatal to the population of his country, the defeats and disasters of the succeeding reign were still more destructive. In the 25th year of this war, the instructions given to the cardinal of Winchester and other plenipotentiaries appointed to treat about a peace, authorise them to represent to those of France « that there haan been moo men slayne in these wars for the title and claime of the coroune of France, of oon nation and other, than been at this daye in both landys, and so much christine blode shed, that it is to grete a sorrow and an orrour to think or here it.»—*Henry. Rymer's Fœdera.*

Note 45, page 10, col. 1.
Fastolffe's better fate prevail'd.

Dunois was wounded in the battle of Herrings, or Rouvray Saint-Denys.

Note 46, page 10, col. 2.
To die for him whom I have lived to serve.

·Tanneguy du Châtel had saved the life of Charles when Paris was seized by the Burgundians. Lisle Adam, a man noted for ferocity even in that age, was admitted at midnight into the city with eight hundred horse. The partisans of Burgundy were under arms to assist them, and a dreadful slaughter of the Armagnacs ensued. Du Châtel, then governor of the Bastile, being unable to restrain the tumult, ran to the Louvre, and carried away the dauphin in his shirt in order to secure him in his fortress.—*Rapin.*

Note 47, page 10, col. 2.

To reach the o'erhanging fruit.
High favours like as fig-trees are
That grow upon the sides of rocks, where they
Who reach their fruit adventure must so far
As to hazard their deep downfal.

Daniel.

Note 48, page 10, col. 2.
A banish'd man, Dunois!

De Serres says, « the king was wonderfully discontented for the departure of Tanneguy of Chastel, whom he called father. A man beloved, and of amiable conditions. But there was no remedy. He had given the chief stroke to John Burgongne. So likewise he protested without any difficulty, to retire himself whithersoever his master should command him.»

Note 49, page 10, col. 2.
Richemont.

Richemont caused De Giac to be strangled in his bed, and thrown into the Loire, to punish the negligence that had occasioned him to be defeated by an inferior force at Avranches. The constable had laid siege to St James de Beuvron, a place strongly garrisoned by the English. He had been promised a convoy of money, which DeJiac, who had the management of the treasury, purposely detained to mortify the constable. Richemont openly accused the treasurer, and revenged himself thus violently. After this, he boldly declared that he would serve in the same manner any person whatsoever that should endeavour to engross the king's favour. The Camus of Beaulieu accepted De Giac's place, and was by the constable's means assassinated in the king's presence.

Note 50, page 10, col. 2.
Whose death my arm avenged.

The duke of Orleans was, on a Wednesday, the feast-day of pope St Clement, assassinated in Paris, about seven o'clock in the evening, on his return from dinner. The murder was committed by about eighteen men, who had lodged at an hotel having for sign the image of our Lady, near the Port Barbette, and who, it was afterwards discovered, had for several days intended this assassination.

On the Wednesday before mentioned, they sent one named Scas de Courteheuze, valet de chambre to the king, and one of their accomplices, to the duke of Orleans, who had gone to visit the queen of France at an hotel which she had lately purchased from Montagu, grand master of the king's household, situated very near the Port Barbette. She had lain in there of a child, which had died shortly after its birth, and had not then accomplished the days of her purification.

Scas, on his seeing the duke, said, by way of deceiving, « My lord, the king sends for you, and you must instantly hasten to him, for he has business of great importance to you and him, which he must communicate to you.» The duke, on hearing this message, was eager to obey the king's orders, although the monarch knew nothing of the matter, and immediately mounted his mule, attended by two esquires on one horse, and four or five valets on foot, who followed behind bearing torches; but his other attendants made no haste to follow him. He had made this visit in a private manner, notwithstanding at this time he had within the city of Paris six hundred knights and esquires of his retinue, and at his expence.

On his arrival at the Port Barbette, the eighteen men, all well and secretly armed, were waiting for him, and were lying in ambush under shelter of a penthouse. The night was pretty dark, and as they sallied out against him, one cried out, « Put him to death!» and gave him such a blow on the wrist with his battle-axe as severed it from his arm.

The duke, astonished at this attack, cried out, « I am the duke of Orleans!» when the assassins continuing their blows, answered, « you are the person we were looking for.» So many rushed on him that he was struck off his mule, and his skull was split that his brains were dashed on the pavement. They turned him over and over, and massacred him that he was very soon completely dead. A young esquire, a German by birth, who had been his page, was murdered with him: seeing his master struck to the ground, he threw himself on his body to protect him, but in vain, and he suffered for his generous courage. The horse which carried the two esquires that preceded the duke, seeing so many armed men advance, began to snort, and when he passed them set out on a gallop, so that it was some time before he could be checked.

When the esquires had stopped their horse, they saw their lord's mule following them full gallop: having caught him, they fancied the duke must have fallen, and were bringing it back by the bridle; but on their arrival where their lord lay, they were menaced by the assassins, that if they did not instantly depart they should share his fate. Seeing their lord had been thus basely murdered, they hastened to the hotel of the queen, crying out, Murder! Those who had killed the duke, in their turn, bawled out, Fire! and they had arranged their plan that while some were assassinating the duke, others were to set fire to their lodgings. Some, mounted on horseback, and the rest on foot, made off as they could, throwing behind them broken glass and sharp points of iron to prevent their being pursued.

Report said that many of them went the back way to the hotel d'Artois, to their master the duke of Burgundy, who had commanded them to do this deed, as he afterwards publicly confessed, to inform him of the success of their murder; when instantly afterward they withdrew to places of safety.

The chief of these assassins, and the conductor of the business, was one called Rollet d'Auctonville, a Norman, whom the duke of Orleans had a little before deprived of his office of commissioner of taxes, which the king had given to him at the request of the late duke of Burgundy: from that time the said Rollet had been considering how he could revenge himself on the duke of Orleans. His other accomplices were William Courtehouse and Seas Courteheuze, before mentioned, from the country of Guines, John de la Motte, and others to the amount of eighteen.

Within half an hour the household of the duke of Orleans, hearing of this horrid murder, made loud complaints, and with great crowds of nobles and others hastened to the fatal spot, where they found him lying dead in the street. His knight and esquires, and in general all his dependants, made grievous lamentations, seeing him thus wounded and disfigured. With many groans they raised the body and carried it to the hotel of the lord de Rieux, marshal of France, which was hard by; and shortly afterward the body was covered with a white pall, and conveyed most honourably to the Guillemins, where it lay, as being the nearest church to where the murder had been committed.

Soon afterward the king of Sicily, and many other princes, knights, and esquires, having heard of this foul murder of the only brother of the king of France, came with many tears to visit the body. It was put into a leaden coffin, and the monks of the church, with all the late duke's household, watched it all night, saying prayers, and singing psalms over it. On the morrow, his servants found the hand which had been cut off, and collected much of the brains that had been scattered over the street, all of which were inclosed in a leaden case and placed by the coffin.

The whole of the princes who were at Paris, except the king and his children, namely, the king of Sicily, the dukes of Berry, Burgundy, and Bourbon, the marquis du Pont, the counts de Nevers, de Clermont, de Vendome, de St Pol, de Dammartin, the constable of France, and several others, having assembled with a large body of the clergy and nobles, and a multitude of the citizens of Paris, went in a body to the church of the Guillemins. Then the principal officers of the late duke's household took the body and bore it out of the church, with a great number of lighted torches carried by the esquires of the defunct. On each side of the body were in due order, uttering groans and shedding tears, the king of Sicily, the dukes of Berry, Burgundy, and Bourbon, each holding a corner of the pall. After the body followed the other princes, the clergy and barons, according to their ranks, recommending his soul to his Creator; and thus they proceeded with it to the church of the Celestins. When a most solemn service had been performed, the body was interred in a beautiful chapel he himself had founded and built. After the service all the princes, and others who had attended it, returned to their homes.

Monstrelet, vol. i, p. 192.

Note 51, page 10, col. 2.
Since that sad hour.

About four o'clock on the 12th day of June, the populace of Paris rose to the amount of about sixty thousand, fearing (as they said) that the prisoners would be set at liberty, although the new provost of Paris and other lords assured them to the contrary. They were armed with old mallets, hatchets, staves, and other disorderly weapons, and paraded through the streets shouting, « Long live the king and the duke of Burgundy!» toward the different prisons in Paris, namely, the Palace, St. Magloire, St. Martin des Champs, the Chatelet, the Temple, and to other places wherein any prisoners were confined. They forced open all their doors, and killed Chepier and Chepiere, with the whole of the prisoners, to the amount of sixteen hundred or thereabouts, the principal of whom were the Count de Ar-

8

magnac, constable of France, master Henry de Maile, chancellor to the king, the bishops of Coutances, of Bayeux, of Evreux, of Senlis, of Saintes, the count de Grand-Pre, Raymonnet de la Guerre, the abbot de St Conille de Compiegne, sir Hector de Chartres, sir Enguerrand de Marcoignet, Charlot Poupart, master of the king's wardrobe, the members of the courts of justice and of the treasury, and in general all they could find : among the number were several even of the Burgundian party confined for debt.

In this massacre several women were killed, and left on the spot where they had been put to death. This cruel butchery lasted until ten o'clock in the morning of the following day. Those confined in the grand Chatelet, having arms, defending themselves valiantly, and slew many of the populace ; but on the morrow by means of fire and smoke they were conquered, and the mob made many of them leap from the battlements of the towers, when they were received on the points of the spears of those in the streets, and cruelly mangled. At this dreadful business were present the new provost of Paris, sir John de Luxembourg, the lord de Foseaux, the lord de l'Isle-Adam, the vidame of Amiens, the lord de Chevreuse, the lord de Chastellus, the Lord de Cohen, sir James de Harcourt, sir Edmond de Lombers, the lord d'Auxois, and others, to the amount of upward of a thousand combatants, armed and on horseback, ready to defend the murderers, should there be any necessity. Many were shocked and astonished at such cruel conduct; but they dared not say any thing except, « Well, my boys!» The bodies of the constable, the chancellor, and of Raymonnet de la Guerre were stripped naked, tied together with a cord, and dragged for three days by the blackguards of Paris through the streets; the body of the constable had the breadth of two fingers of his skin cut off crosswise, like to a bend in heraldry, by way of derision : and they were thus publicly exposed quite naked to the sight of all; on the fourth day they were dragged out of Paris on a hurdle, and buried with the others in a ditch called la Louviere.

Notwithstanding the great lords after this took much pains to pacify the populace, and remonstrated with them, that they ought to allow the king's justice to take its regular course against offenders; they would not desist, but went in great crowds to the houses of such as had favoured the Armagnacs, or of those whom they disliked, and killed them without mercy, carrying away all they could find. In these times it was enough if one man hated another at Paris, of whatever rank he might be, Burgundian or not, to say, « There goes an Armagnac,» and he was instantly put to death without further inquiry being made.—*Monstrelet*, vol. v, p. 22.

To add to the tribulations of these times the Parisians again assembled in great numbers, as they had before done, and went to all the prisons in Paris, broke into them, and put to death full three hundred prisoners, many of whom had been confined there since the last butchery. In the number of those murdered were sir James de Mommor, and sir Louis de Corail, chamberlain to the king, with many nobles and churchmen. They then went to the lower court of the bastille of St Anthony, and demanded that six prisoners, whom they named, should be given up to them, or they would attack the place: in fact, they began to pull down the wall of the gate, when the duke of Burgundy, who

lodged near the bastille, vexed to the heart at such proceedings, to avoid worse, ordered the prisoners to be delivered to them, if any of their leaders would promise that they should be conducted to the Chatelet prison, and suffered to be punished according to their deserts by the king's court of justice. Upon this they all departed, and by way of glossing over their promise, they led their prisoners near to the Chatelet, when they put them to death, and stripped them naked. They then divided into several large companies and paraded the streets of Paris, entering the houses of many who had been Armagnacs, plundering and murdering all without mercy. In like manner as before, when they met any person they disliked he was slain instantly; and their principal leader was Cappeluche, the hangman of the city of Paris.

The duke of Burgundy, alarmed at these insurrections, sent for some of the chief citizens, with whom he remonstrated on the consequences these disturbances might have. The citizens excused themselves from being any way concerned, and said they were much grieved to witness them: they added, they were all of the lowest rank, and had thus risen to pillage the more wealthy; and they required the duke to provide a remedy by employing these men in his wars. It was then proclaimed, in the names of the king and the duke of Burgundy, under pain of death, that no person should tumultuously assemble, nor any more murders or pillage take place; but that such as had of late risen in the insurrection should prepare themselves to march to the sieges of Montlehery and Marcoussi, now held by the king's enemies. The commonalty made reply, that they would cheerfully do so if they had proper captains appointed to lead them.

Within a few days, to avoid similar tumults in Paris, six thousand of the populace were sent to Montlehery under the command of the lord de Gohen, sir Walter de Buppes and sir Walter Raillart, with a certain number of men at arms, and store of cannon and ammunition sufficient for a siege. These knights led them to Montlehery, where they made a sharp attack on the Dauphinois within the castle.

The duke of Burgundy, after their departure, arrested several of their accomplices, and the principal movers of the late insurrection, some of whom he caused to be beheaded, others to be hanged or drowned in the Seine; even their leader Cappeluche, the hangman, was carried to the Parisians who had been sent to Montlehery, they marched back to Paris to raise another rebellion, but the gates were closed against them, so that they were forced to return to the siege.

Monstrelet, vol. v, p. 47.

To what is it owing that four centuries have made so little difference in the character of the Parisians!

Note 52, page 11, col. 1.

He will retreat
To distant Dauphiny.

Charles, in despair of collecting an army which should dare to approach the enemy's entrenchments, not only gave the city of Orleans for lost, but began to entertain a very dismal prospect with regard to the general state of his affairs. He saw that the country in which he had hitherto, with great difficulty, subsisted, would be laid entirely open to the invasion of a powerful and victorious enemy, and he already entertained thoughts of retiring with the remains of his forces into Languedoc and Dauphiny, and defending himself as long as possible in those remote provinces. But it was fortunate for this good prince, that as he lay under the dominion of the fair, the women whom he consulted had the spirit to support his sinking resolution in this desperate extremity. Mary of Anjou, his queen, a princess of great merit and prudence, vehemently opposed this measure, which she foresaw would discourage all his partizans, and serve as a general signal for deserting a prince who seemed himself to despair of success: his mistress too, the fair Agnes Sorel, who lived in entire amity with the queen, seconded all her remonstrances.—*Hume.*

« L'on fait honneur à la belle Agnès Sorel, demoiselle de Touraine, maîtresse de ce prince, d'avoir beaucoup contribué à l'encourager en cette occasion. On lui fait cet honneur principalement au sujet d'un quatrain rapporté par Saint Gelais, comme ayant été fait par le roi François Ier, à l'honneur de cette demoiselle.

> Plus de louange et d'honneur tu mérite,
> La cause étant de France recouvrer,
> Que ce que peut dedans un cloître ouvrer
> Claude nonnain, ou bien dévot hermite.»
>
> *P. Daniel.*

Note 53, page 11, col. 1.

On a May morning deck'd with flowers.

Here in this first race you shall see our kings but once a year, the first day of May, in their chariots deckt with flowres and greene, and drawn by four oxen. Whoso hath occasion to treat with them let him seeke them in their chambers, amidst their delights. Let him talk of any matters of state, he shall be sent to the Maire.—*De Serres.*

Fuller calls this race « a chain of idle kings well linked together, who gave themselves over to pleasure privately, never coming abroad, but onely on May-day they shewed themselves to the people, riding in a chariot, adorned with flowers, and drawn with oxen, *slow cattel, but good enough for so lazy luggage.*»—*Holy Warre.*

> Ces Rois hideux en longue barbe espesse,
> En longs cheveux, ornez presse sur presse,
> De chaisnes d'or et de carquans gravez,
> Hauts dans un char en triomphe elevez,
> Une fois l'an se feront voir en pompe
> Enflez d'un fard qui le vulgaire trompe.
>
> *Franciade de Ronsard.*

Note 54, page 11, col. 1.

And those long locks will not disgrace thee then.

Long hair was peculiar to the kings in the first ages of the French monarchy. When Fredegonda had murthered Clovis and thrown him into the river, the fishermen who found his body knew it by the long hair.—*Mezeray.*

At a later period the custom seems to have become general. Pasquier says, « lors de mon jeune aage nul n'estoit tondu, fors le moines. Advint par mesadventure que le roy François premier de ce nom, ayant esté fortuitement blessé à la teste d'un tizon, par le capitaine Lorges, sieur de Montgoumery, les medecins furent d'advis de le tondre. Depuis il ne porta plus longs cheveux, estant le premier de nos roys, qui par un sinistre augure degenera de ceste venerable ancienneté. Sur son exemple, les princes premierement,

puis les gentilshommes, et finalement tous les subjects se voulurent former, ill ne fut pas que les Prestres ne se meissent de ceste partie. Sur la plus grande partie du regne de François premier, et devant, chacun portoit longue chevelure, et barbe rasé, où maintenant chacun est tondu, et porte longue barbe.»

Note 55, page 11, col. 1.

Thy mangled corse waves to the winds of heaven.

« Le Vicomte de Narbonne y périt aussi, et porta la peine de sa témérité, qui avoit été une des principales causes de la perte de la bataille. Le duc de Betford ayant fait chercher son corps le fit écarteler et pendre à un gibet, parcequ'il passoit pour avoir été complice de la mort du duc de Bourgogne.»—*P. Daniel.*

Note 56, page 11, col. 1.

Leagues with my foes, and Richemont.

Richemont has left an honourable name, though he tied a prime minister up in a sack, and threw him into the river. For this he had a royal precedent in our king John, but Richemont did openly what the monarch did in the dark, and there is some difference between a murderer and an executioner, even though the executioner be a volunteer. « Il mérita sa grace (says Daniel) par les services qu'il rendit au roi contre les Anglois, malgré ce prince même. Il fut un des principaux auteurs de la réforme de la milice françoise, qui produisit la tranquillité de la France et les grandes victoires dont elle fut suivie. L'autorité qu'il avoit par sa charge de connétable, jointe à sa fermeté naturelle, lui donna moyen de tenir la main à l'observation des ordonnances publiées par le roi pour la discipline militaire; et les exemples de sévérité qu'il fit à cet égard lui firent donner le surnom de justicier. Etant devenu duc de Bretagne, quelques seigneurs de sa cour lui conseillèrent de se démettre de sa charge de connétable, comme d'une dignité qui etoit au-dessous de lui. Il ne le voulut pas, et il faisoit porter devant lui deux épées, l'une la pointe en haut, en qualité de duc de Bretagne, et l'autre dans le fourreau la pointe en bas, comme connétable de France. Son motif pour conserver la charge de connétable étoit, disoit il, d'honorer dans sa vieillesse une charge qui l'avoit honoré lui-même dans un âge moins avancé. On le peut compter au nombre des plus grands capitaines que la France ait eus à son service. Il avoit beaucoup de religion, il étoit liberal, aumônier, bienfaisant, et on ne peut guère lui reprocher que la hauteur et la violence dont il usa envers les trois ministres.» And yet this violence to the favourites may have been among the services *qu'il rendit au roi, malgré ce prince même.*

Note 57, page 11, col. 2.

Led by a frenzied female.

Yet in the preceding year, 1428, the English women had concerned themselves somewhat curiously in the affairs of their rulers. « There was one Mistris Stokes with divers others stout women of London, of good reckoning, well-apparelled, came openly to the upper parliament, and delivered letters to the duke of Glocester, and to the archbishops, and to the other lords there present, containing matter of rebuke and sharp reprehension of the duke of Glocester, because he would not deliver his wife Jaqueline out of her grievous imprisonment, being then held prisoner by the duke of Burgundy, suffering her there to remain so unkindly, and for his publick keeping by him another adultresse, contrary to the law of God, and the honourable estate of matrimony.»

Note 58, page 11, col. 2.

Fix'd full her eye on Charles.

Of this I may say with Scudery—

> O merveille estonnante, et difficile à croire!—
> Mais que nous rapportons sur la foy de l'Histoire.
>
> Alaric, l. 2.

The matter (says De Serres) was found ridiculous both by the king and his councell, yet must they make some trial. The king takes upon him the habit of a countriman to be disguised: this maid (being brought into the chamber) goes directly to the king in this attire, and salutes him *with so modest a countenance, as if she had been bred up in court all her life.* They telling her that she was mistaken, she assured them it was the king, although she had never seene him. She begins to deliver unto him this new charge, which, she sayes, she had received from the God of Heaven; so as she *turned the eyes and minds of all men upon her.*

« Ce prince prit exprès ce jour-là un habit fort simple, et se mêla sans distinction dans la foule des courtisans. La fille entra dans la chambre sans paroître aucunement étonnée; et quoiqu'elle n'eût jamais vu le roi, elle lui adressa la parole, et lui dit d'un ton ferme que Dieu l'envoyoit pour le secourir, pour faire lever le siège d'Orléans, et le conduire à Reims pour y être sacré. Elle l'assura que les Anglois seroient chassés du royaume, et que s'ils ne le quittoient au plus tôt, il leur en prendroit mal.»—*P. Daniel.*

Note 59, page 11, col. 2.

Crown thee the anointed king.

The anointing was a ceremony of much political and mystical importance. « King Henry III of England, being desirous to know what was wrought in a king by his unction, consulted by letter about it with that great scholler of the age Robert Grossetest bishop of Lincoln, who answered him in confirmation. 'Quod autem in fine literæ vestræ nobis mandastis, videlicet quod intimaremus quid unctionis sacramentum videatur adjicere regiæ dignitati, cum multi sint reges qui nullatenus unctionis munera decorentur, non est nostræ modicitatis complere hoc. Tamen non ignoramus quod regalis inunctio signum est prerogativæ susceptionis septiformis doni sacratissimi pneumatis, quod septiformi munere tenetur rex inunctus præeminentius non unctus regibus omnes regias et regiminis sui actiones dirigere; ut videlicit non communiter sed eminenter et heroicè dono *Timoris* se primò, et deinceps, quantum in ipso est, suo regimini subjectos, ab omni cohibeat illicito; dono *Pietatis* defendat subveniat et subveniri faciat viduæ, pupillo, et generaliter omni oppresso; dono *Scientiæ* leges justas ad regnum justè regendum ponat, positas observet et observari faciat, erroneas destruat; dono *Fortitudinis* omnia regno adversantia repellat et pro salute reipublicæ mortem non timeat. Ad prædicta autem præcellenter agenda dono *Concilii* decoretur, quo artificialiter et scientificè ordo hujus mundi sensibilis edocetur; deinde dono *Intellectus,* quo cœtus Angelici ordo dinoscitur. Tandem verò dono *Sapientiæ,* quo ad dilucidam cognitionem Dei pertingitur, ut ad exemplar ordinis mundi et ordinis angelici secundum leges æternas in æterna Dei ratione descriptas, quibus regit universitatem creaturæ, rempublicam sibi subjectam ordinabiliter regat tandem et ipse. Adjicit igitur regiæ dignitati unctionis sacramentum quod rex unctus præ cæteris in suo genere debet, ut prætactum est, ex septiformi spiritus munere, in omnibus suis regiminis actibus, virtutibus divinis et heroicis pollere.'

«And some other have conceived this anointing of such efficacy, that, as in baptisme all former sinnes are washt away, so also by this unction, as we see in that of Polyeuctus patriarch of Constantinople, who doubted not but that the emperor John Tzimisces was cleerd, before Heaven, of the death of Phocas, through his being anointed emperor.»—*Selden's Titles of Honour.*

The legend of the Ampulla made this ceremony peculiarly important in France. I quote the miracle from Desmarets. Clovis is on his knees waiting to be anointed by St Remigius:—

> Cependant le prélat attend les huiles saintes.
> Un diacre les porte, et fait un vain effort;
> La foule impénétrable empesche son abord.
> Du pontife sacré la douce impatience,
> Des mains et de la voix, veut en vain qu'il s'avance.
> Nul ne peut diviser, par la force des bras,
> De tant de corps pressés l'immobile ramas.
> Le prince humble, à genoux, languissoit dans l'attente,
> Alors qu'une clarté paroist plus éclatante,
> Esteint tous autres feux par sa vive splendeur,
> Et répand dans le temple une divine odeur.
> Dans un air lumineux une colombe vole,
> En son bec de corail tenant une fiole.
> Elle apporte au prélat ce vase précieux,
> Plein d'un baume sacré, rare présent des cieux.
>
> Clovis.

Guillermus Brito says that the devil brake the viol of oil which St Remigius held in his hand ready to anoint Clovis, and that the oil being so spilt, he obtained by prayer a supply of it from Heaven.—*Selden.*

Note 60, page 12, col. 1.

The doctors of theology.

Ces paroles ainsi par elle dictes, la fist le roy remener honorablement en son logis, et assemble son grand conseil, au quel furent plusieurs prelats, chevaliers, escuyers et chefs de guerre, avecques aucuns docteurs en theologie en loix et en decret, qui tous ensemble adviserent qu'elle seroit interrogue par les docteurs, pour essayer si en elle se trouveroit evidente raison de pouvoir accomplir ce qu'elle disoit. Mais les docteurs la trouverent de tant honneste contenance, et tant sage en ses paroles, que leur revelation faicte on en tent tres grand conte.

Diverses interrogations luy furent faictes par plusieurs docteurs et autres gens de grand estat, a quoy elle respondit moult bien, et par especial a un docteur Jacobin, qui luy dist, que si Dieu vouloit que les Anglois s'en allassent, qu'il ne falloit point de armes; a quoy elle respondit, qu'elle ne vouloit que peu de gens qui combattroient, et Dieu donneroit la victoire.

From the history of the siege of Orleans. Troyes. 1621.

In the *Gesta Joannæ Gallicæ of Valerandus Varanius,* one of the counsellors makes a speech of seventy lines, upon the wickedness of women, mentioning Helen, Beersheba, Semiramis, Dalilah, Messalina, etc., as examples. The council are influenced by his opinion, and the Maid, to prove her mission, challenges any one of them to a single combat.

> Quâ me stultitiâ, quâ me levitate notandam
> Credltis, o patres? armis si forsitan, inquit,

Apta minus videar, stricto procurrere ferro
Annuite; hæc nostri sint prima pericula martis,
Si cuique vis tanta animo, descendat in æquæ
Planiciem pugnæ; mihi si victoria cedat,
Credite victrici; noster si vicerit hostis,
Compede vincta abeam, et cunctis sim fabula sæclis.

Note 61, page 13, col. 1.

Ruin'd now.

Hanc virginem contigit pascendo pecora in sacello quodam vilissimo, ad declinandam pluviam obdormire; quo in tempore visa est se in somnis a Deo, qui se illi ostenderat, admoneri.

Jacobus Philippus Bergomensis de claris mulieribus.

Joanna Gallica Puella, dum oves pascit, tempestate coacta in proximum sacellum confugit, ibi obdormiens liberandæ Galliæ mandatum divinitus accepit.—*Bonfinius.*

Heroinæ nobilissimæ Joannæ Darc Lotheringæ vulgo Aurelianensis Puellæ historia. Authore Joanne Hordal serenissimi ducis Lotharingæ consiliario. Ponti-Mussi. 1612.

Note 62, page 13, col. 1.

Saint Agnes stood.

Insanus judex eam nudam ad lupanar pertrahi jussit. At ubi beata virgo vestibus exuta est, statim crine soluto, tantam capillis densitatem ejus divina gratia concessit, ut melius illorum fimbriis, quam vestibus tecta videatur. Introgressa quidem Agnes turpitudinis locum. Angelum Domini præparatum invenit: eam mox tanto lumine perfudit, ut præ magnitudine splendoris, a nemine conspici posset.

The exclamation of St Agnes at the stake should not be omitted here:—"Then Agnes in the midst of the flame, stretching out her hand, prayed unto the Lord, saying, 'I bless thee, O Almighty Father! who permittest me to come unto thee fearless even in the flames. For behold! what I have believed, I see; what I have hoped, I possess; what I have desired, I embrace with my hands. Therefore I confess thee with my lips, I desire thee with my heart, with my inmost entrails; I come to thee, the living and the true God!'" The whole passage as it stands in Acta Sanctorum is very fine: "Tunc Vicarius Aspasius nomine, jussit in conspectu omnium ignem copiosum accendi, et in medium eam præcepit jactari flammarum. Quod cum fuisset impletum, statim in duas partes divisæ sunt flammæ, et hinc atque illinc seditiosos populos exurebant, ipsam autem B. Agnen penitus in nullo contingebat incendium. Eo magis hoc non virtutibus divinis, sed maleficiis deputantes, dabant, fremitus inter se populi, et infinitos clamores ad cœlum. Tunc B. Agnes expendens manus suas in medio ignis his verbis orationem fudit ad Dominum: Omnipotens, adorande, colende, tremende, Pater Domini nostri Jesu Christi, benedico te quia per filium tuum unigenitum evasi minas hominum impiorum et spurcitias diaboli impolluta transivi. Ecce et nunc per spiritum sanctum rore cœlesti perfusa sum; focus juxta me moritur, flamma dividitur, et ardor incendii hujus ad eos a quibus ministratur, refunditur. *Benedico te pater omnipotens, qui etiam per flammas, intrepidam me ad te venire permittis. Ecce quod credidi jam video, quod speravi jam teneo, quod concupivi manibus jam complector. Te igitur labiis confi-*

teor, te corde, te totis visceribus concupisco. *Ecce ad te venio vivum et verum deum!"*

Acta Sanct. Tom. 2, p. 352. Jany. 21.

Vita S. Agnates, Auc. S. Ambrosio.

St Agnes, St Catherine, and St Margaret, were the saints more particularly reverenced by the Maid of Orleans.

Note 63, page 13, col. 2.

Was silence to my soul.

Through the scene are faintly heard
Sounds that are silence to the mind.

Charles Lloyd.

Note 64, page 15, col. 1.

Effaced the hauberk's honourable marks.

Afin d'empêcher les impressions que ce treillis de fer devoit laisser sur la peau, on avoit soin de se matelasser en dessous. Malgré ces précautions cependant il en laissoit encore; ces marques s'appeloient *camois*, et on les faisoit disparoître par le bain.—*Le Grand.*

Note 65, page 15, col. 2.

Then bow'd her to the sword of martyrdom.

Such is the legend of St Catherine, princess of Alexandria, whose story has been pictured upon sign-posts and in churches, but whose memory has been preserved in this country longer by the ale-house than by the altar. The most extravagant perhaps of Dryden's plays is upon this subject. In my former edition I had, ignorantly, represented Catherine as dying upon the wheel, and the description of her sufferings was far too minute. Dryden has committed the last fault in a far greater degree; the old martyrologies particularise no cruelties more revolting to the reader than he has detailed in the speech of Maximin when he orders her to execution.

From a passage in the *Jerusalem Conquistada* it should seem that St Catherine was miraculously betrothed to her heavenly spouse. As the crusaders approach Jerusalem, they visit the holy places on their way.

> Qual visita el lugar con llanto tierno,
> Donde la hermosa virgen Caterina
> Se desposó con el Esposo eterno,
> La Angélica Rachel siendo madrina;
> Aquel Esposo, que el nevado invierno
> Se cubrió con escarcha matutina,
> El que tiene los ojos de palomas
> Y del labio de lirio vierte aromas.
>
> *Lope de Vega.*

The marginal note adds, La Virgen fue Madrina, en los desporios de Caterina y Christo.

Of St Margaret, the other favourite saint of the Maid, I find recorded by Bergomensis, that she called the pagan præfect an impudent dog, that she was thrown into a dungeon, where a horrible dragon swallowed her, that she crossed herself, upon which the dragon immediately burst and she came out safe, and that she saw the devil standing in the corner like a black man, and seized him and threw him down.

Absurd as this legend is, it once occasioned a very extraordinary murder. A young Lombard, after hearing it, prayed so earnestly for an opportunity of fighting with the devil like St Margaret, that he went into the fields in full expectation that his desire would be gratified. A hideous old dumb woman came by; he mistook her for the tempter; her inarticulate noises confirmed him in this opinion, and he knocked her down and trampled upon her. The poor wretch died of her bruises, but a miracle was wrought to save her murderer in consideration that his madness was a pious madness, and before she died, she spoke to excuse the mistake. This tale is told in that strange collection of ludicrous stories upon religious subjects, the *Pia Hilaria.* The authority referred to is *Petr. Rausani Hist. lib.* 35.

Note 66, page 15, col. 2.
The sacred sword.

« Puella petiit gladium, quem divinitus uti aiebat, erat facta certior in templo divæ Catherinæ in Turonibus, inter antiqua donaria pendere. Miratus Carolus, gladium inquiri, ac inventum protinus Puellæ afferri jussit.»—*Polydore Virgil.*

Roland, or rather Orlando, for it is Ariosto who has immortalised him, was buried with *Durindana* at his side, and his horn *Olifant* at his feet. Charlemain also had his good sword *Joyeuse* buried with him. He was placed in his sepulchre on a golden throne, crowned and habited in his imperial robes, though a *cilicio* was next his skin ; one hand held a globe of gold, the other rested on the gospels, which were lying on his knees. His shield and sceptre were hung opposite to him, on the side of the sepulchre, which was filled with perfumes and spices, and then closed. *Tizona* was buried with the Cid, no living man being worthy to wield that sword with which Rodrigo, even after death, had triumphed ; and which had been miraculously half drawn from the scabbard to avenge the insult offered by a Jew to his corpse.

Note 67, page 16, col. 1.
They partook the feast.

« Cette cérémonie chez les grands s'annonçoit au son du cor, ou au son d'une cloche ; coutume qui subsiste encore dans les couvents et les maisons opulentes, pour annoncer le couvert et le dîné. Après le service des viandes, c'est-à-dire après ce que nous appelons entrées, rôti et entremets, on sortoit de table pour se laver les mains une seconde fois, comme chez les Romains, de qui paroit être venu cet usage. Les domestiques desservoient pendant ce tems ; ils enlevoient une des nappes et apportoient les confitures (qu'on nommait *epices*) et les vins composés. A ce moment, fait pour la gaieté, commençoient les devis plaisants et joyeux propos, car dans ce bon vieux temps on aimoit beaucoup à rire. C'étoit alors que les ménétriers venoient réciter leurs fabliaux, lorsqu'on admettoit leur présence. » —*Le Grand.*

Note 68, page 16, col. 1.
Or luscious with metheglin mingled rich.

« Il y avoit plusieurs sortes de ces vins préparés qu'on servoit après les viandes. 1. Les *vins cuits,* qui sont encore en usage dans quelques provinces, et qui ont conservé le même nom. 2. Ceux auxquels on ajoutoit le suc de quelque fruit, tels que le *Moré,* fait avec du jus de mûres. 3. Ceux qu'on assaisonnoit avec du miel, comme le *Nectar,* le *Medon,* etc. 4. Ceux où l'on faisoit infuser des plantes médicinales ou aromatiques, et qui prenoient leur nom de ces plantes, *Vins d'Absynthe, de Myrte, d'Aloès,* etc. Le *Roman de Florimont* les appelle *vins herbez.* 5. Enfin ceux dans lesquels, outre le miel, il entroit des épices. On appelloit ces derniers

du nom général de *Pimens.* C'étoient les plus estimés de tous. Nos auteurs n'en parlent qu'avec délices. Il eût manqué quelque chose à une fête ou à un repas, si on n'y eût point servi du piment : et l'on en donnoit même aux moines dans les couvents à certains jours de l'année. » —*Le Grand.*

Note 69, page 16, col. 1.
Of Cornwall.

Sir Tristram du Lyones.

Note 70, page 16, col. 1.
The dolorous stroke.

Sir Balin le Sauvage.

Note 71, page 16, col. 1.
Like that divinest Tuscan.

Ariosto.

Note 72, page 16, col. 2.
Thou canst not with thy golden belt.

Du proverbe *Bonne renommée vaut mieux que ceinture dorée.*

Lisant un arrest ancien qui est encores pour le jourd 'huy inseré aux registres du Chastelet de Paris, j'estimay qu'en ce proverbe il y avoit une notable sentence, et une longue ancienneté tout ensemble. Car par arrest qui est du 28 de Juin 1420, il est porté en termes exprés que deffenses sont faites à toutes femmes amoureuses, filles de joye, et paillardes de ne porter robbes à collets renversez, queües, ne ceintures dorees, boutonnieres à leurs chaperons, sur peine de confiscation et amende, et que les huissiers de parlement, commissaires et sergents du Chastelet qui les trouveroient, eussent à les mener prisonnieres.

Au surplus (je diray cecy en passant) à la mienne volonté que ceux qui donnerent cest urrest eussent tourné la chance, et que non seulement ces ceintures dorees, ains en toutes autres dorures, et affliquets, ils eussent fait deffenses à toutes femmes d'honneur d'emporter, sur peine d'estre declarees putains : car il n'y auroit point plus prompt moyen que cestuy, pour bannir le superfluité et bombance des dames.—*Pasquier.*

Note 73, page 17, col. 1.
I knew myself.

« Hæc igitur Janna Pulcella virgo, cum magnam gloriam in armis esset adepta, et regnum Francorum magnâ ex parte deperditum, e manibus Anglorum pugnando eripuisset, in suâ florente ætate constituta, non solum se morituram, sed et genus suæ mortis cunctis prædixit. » —*Bergomensis.*

Note 74, page 17, col. 1.
There is a path.

« There is a path which no fowl knoweth, and which the vulture's eye hath not seen : the lion's whelps have not trodden it, nor the fierce lion passed by it. » —*Job,* xxviii, 7, 8.

Note 75, page 17, col. 2.
As they did hear the loud alarum bell.

In sooth the estate of France was then most miserable. There appeared nothing but a horrible face, confusion, poverty, desolation, solitarinesse and feare. The lean and bare labourers in the country did terrifie even theeves themselves, who had nothing left them to spoile but the carkasses of these poore mise-rable creatures, wandering up and down like ghostes drawne out of their graves. The least farmes and hamlets were fortified by these robbers, English, Bour-guegnons and French, every one striving to do his worst : all men of war were well agreed to spoile the countryman and merchant. *Even the cattell, accus-omed to the larume bell, the signe of the enemy's approach, would run home of themselves without any guide by this accustomed misery.*

This is the perfect description of those times, taken out of the lamentations of our ancestors, set down in the original, says De Serres. But amidst this horrible calamity, God did comfort both the king and realme, for about the end of the yeere, he gave Charles a goodly sonne by queen Mary his wife.

Note 76, page 17, col. 1.
Was as a pilgrim.

« O my people, hear my word : make you ready to the battle, and in those evils, be even as pilgrims upon the earth. »— 2 *Esdras*, xvi, 40.

Note 77, page 17, col. 1.
Cast the weak nature off.

« Let go from thee mortal thoughts, cast away the burdens of man, put off now the weak nature.

« And set aside the thoughts that are most heavy unto thee, and haste thee to flee from these times. »— 2 *Esdras*, xiv, 14, 15.

Note 78, page 18, col. 2.
Worthy a happier.

Digna minus misero, non meliore viro.

Ovid.

Note 79, page 18, col. 2.
And I must put away all mortal thoughts.

2 *Esdras*, xiv, 14.

Note 80, page 20, col. 1.
Ruin rush'd round us.

To succeed in the siege of Orleans, the English first secured the neighbouring places, which might other-wise have annoyed the besiegers. The months of August and September were spent in this work. During that space they took Mehun, Baugenci, Gergean, Clery, Jully, Jenville, and some other small towns, and at last appeared before Orleans on the 12th of October. —*Rapin.*

Note 81, page 20, col. 2.
Soon sadden'd Orleans.

The French king used every expedient to supply the city with a garrison and provisions, and enable it to maintain a long and obstinate siege. The lord of Gau-cour, a brave and experienced captain, was appointed governor. Many officers of distinction threw them-selves into the place. The troops which they conducted were inured to war, and were determined to make the most obstinate resistance : and even the inhabitants, disciplined by the long continuance of hostilities, were well qualified in their own defence, to second the efforts of the most veteran forces. The eyes of all Europe were turned towards this scene; where, it was reason-bly supposed, the French were to make their last stand for maintaining the independence of their monarchy, and the rights of their sovereign.—*Hume.*

Note 82, page 20, col. 2.
The sire Chappelle.

This title was not discriminately used by the French. Chappelle is sometimes styled le sire, and sometimes gentilhomme de Beausse by Daniel. The same title was applied to the Almighty, and to princes ; and Selden observes from Pasquier, « these ancient barons affected rather to be stiled by the name of sire than baron, and the baron of Coucy carried to that purpose this rithme in his device :

Je ne suis roy ne prince aussi,
Je suis le sire de Coucy.

Note 83, page 20, col. 2.
Can never wield the crucifix that hilts
His hallow'd sword.

« At the creation of a knight of Rhodes a sword with a cross for the hilt was delivered to him in token that his valour must defend religion. No bastard could be a knight hospitaller, from whose order that of Rhodes was formed, except a bastard to a prince, there being honour in that dishonour, as there is light in the very spots of the moon. »—*Fuller's Historie of the Holy Warre.*

Note 84, page 20, col. 2.
And that young duke.

Alençon.

Note 85, page 20, col. 2.
La Hire, the merriest man.

« In the late warres in France between king Henry the fifth of England and Charles the seventh of France, the French armie being in distresse, one captain La Hire, a Frenchman, was sent to declare unto the said French king the estate and affaires of the warre, and how for want of victuals, money, and other necessaries, the French had lost divers townes and battailes to the English. The French king being disposed to use his captaine familiarly, shewed him such thinges as him-self was delighted in, as his buildings, his banquets, faire ladies, etc. and then asked the captaine how hee liked them : 'Trust me, sir,' quoth the captaine, speak-ing his mind freely, 'I did never know any prince that more delighted himself with his losses, than you doe with yours.'»—*Stowe.*

La Hire had just time before an engagement to make a general confession of his sins, and tell his confessor that they were all of them very soldier like ones. This done, he made this prayer :—« Dieu je te prie, que tu fasses aujourd'hui pour La Hire, autant que tu voudrois que La Hire fît pour toi, s'il etoit Dieu et tu fusses La Hire. » The epitaph of Thomas Hodmandod was evi-dently suggested by this ill-directed jest of La Hire. It is surprising how few witticisms are original.

Note 86, page 20, col. 2.
Of ruin.

« They pulled down all the most considerable build-ings in the suburbs, and among the rest twelve churches and several monasteries; that the English might not make use of them in carrying on the siege. »—*Rapin. Monstrelet.*

Note 87, page 21, col. 1.
No more the merry viol's note was heard.

The instrument which most frequently served for an accompaniment to the harp, and which disputed the pre-eminence with it in the early times of music in France, was the viol; and indeed, when reduced to four strings, and stript of the frets with which viols of all kinds seem to have been furnished till the 16th century, it still holds the first place among treble instruments under the denomination of violin.

The viol played with a bow, and wholly different from the vielle, whose tones are produced by the friction of a wheel which indeed performs the part of a bow, was very early in favour with the inhabitants of France.
Burney's History of Music.

Note 88, page 21, col. 1.
Call'd on Saint Aignan's name.

St Aignan was the tutelary saint of Orleans. He had miraculously been chosen bishop of that city when Attila besieged it. « Comme les citoyens effrayez eurent recours a leur prelat, luy, sans se soucier, pour le salut des siens, sortit de la ville et parla a Attila. Mais ne l'ayant pu flechir, il se mit en prières, fit faire des processions, et porter par les rues les reliques des saints. Un prestre s'étant mocqué, disant, que cela n'avoit de rien profité aux autres villes, tomba roide morte sur la place, portant par ce moyen la peine de son insolente temerité. Apres toutes ces choses, il commanda aux habitants de voir si le secours n'arrivoit point; ayant été répondu que non, il se remet en prieres, et puis leur fait mesme commandement : mais n'appercevant point encore de secours, pour la troisieme fois il se prosterna a terre, les yeux et l'esprit vers le Ciel. Se sentant exaucé, il fait monter a la guerite et luy rapporte-t-on que l'on ne voyoit rien si non une grosse nuée de poussiere, il assuere que c'etoit le secours d'Ætius et de Teudo Roy des Goths, lesquels tardans a se montrer a l'armee d'Attila, S. Aignan fut divinement transporte en leur champ, et les advertit que tout estoit perdu, s'ils attendoient au lendemain. Ils parurent aussi-tost, et forcerent Attila de lever si hâtivement le siege, que plusieurs des siens se noyerent dans la Loire, d'autres s'entretuerent avec regret d'avoir perdu la ville. Et non contens de cette victoire, le poursuivirent si vivement avec le Roy Merouee, que se vint joindre a eux, qu'ils le defirent en bataille rangée pres de Châlons, jonchant la campagne de 180,000 cadavres.»—*Le nouveau Parterre des fleurs des vies des Saints. Par P. Ribadeneira, André du Val, et Jean Baudoin. Lyons,* 1666.

Note 89, page 21, col. 2.
At Troyes.

« By the treaty of Troyes, Charles was to remain in quiet possession of the royal dignity and revenues. After his death the crown with all its rights and dominions, devolved to Henry and his heirs. The imbecility of Charles was so great that he could not appear in public, so that the queen and Burgundy swore for him.»—*Rapin.*

Note 90, page 22, col. 1.
Salisbury, their watchful chief.

« The besiegers received succours in the very beginning of the siege; but the earl of Salisbury, who considered this enterprise as a decisive action for the king his master, and his own reputation, omitted nothing to deprive the besieged of that advantage. He run up round the city sixty forts. How great soever this work might be, nothing could divert him from it, since the success of the siege entirely depended upon it. In vain would he have pursued his attack, if the enemies could continually introduce fresh supplies. Besides, the season, now far advanced, suggested to him, that he would be forced to pass the winter in the camp, and during that time be liable to many insults. Among the sixty forts, there were six much stronger than the rest, upon the six principal avenues of the city. The French could before with ease introduce convoys into the place, and had made frequent use of that advantage. But after these forts were built, it was with extreme difficulty that they could, now and then, give some assistance to the besieged. Upon these six redoubts the general erected batteries, which thundered against the walls.»—*Rapin.*

Note 91, page 22, col. 1.
The six great avenues meet in the midst.

Rheims had six principal streets meeting thus in one centre where the cathedral stood.

> Au centre de la ville, entre six avenues,
> S'élève un sacré temple à la hauteur des nues.
> *Chapelain.*

I know not whether towns were usually built upon this plan.

Note 92, page 22, col. 1.
Possess'd the Tournelles.

The bulwark of the Tournelles being much shaken by the besiegers' cannon, and the besieged thinking it proper to set it on fire, the English extinguished the flames, and lodged themselves in that post. At the same time they became masters of the tower on the bridge, from whence the whole city could be viewed.
Rapin.

Note 93, page 22, col. 1.
The wild-fire balls shower'd through the midnight sky.

Drayton enumerates these among the English preparations for war.

> The engineer provided the petard
> To break the strong portcullies, and the balls
> Of wild-fire devised to throw from far
> To burn to ground their palaces and halls.

And at the siege of Harfleur he says:

> Their brazen slings send in the wild-fire balls.
> Balls of consuming wild-fire
> That lickt men up like lightning, have I laught at,
> And tost 'em back again like children's trifles.
> *B. and F. The Mad Lover.*

« I do command that particular care be had, advising the gunners to have half butts with water and vinegar, as is accustomed, with bonnets and old sails, and wet mantles to defend fire, that as often is thrown.

« Every ship shall carry two boats' lading of stones, to throw to profit in the time of fight on the deck, forecastle or tops, according to his burden.

« That the wild-fire be reparted to the people most expert, that we have for the use thereof, at due time; for that if it be not overseen, giving charge thereof to those that do understand it, and such as we know can tell how to use it; otherwise it may happen to great danger.»—*Orders set down by the duke of Medina to be observed in the voyage toward England.* Harl. Misc. vol. i.

« Some were preparing to toss balls of wild-fire, as if the sea had been their tennis-court.»—*Deliverance of certain Christians from the Turks*, Harl. Misc. vol. i.

Note 94, page 22, col. 2.
Poisonous pollution.

Thus at the siege of Thin sur l'Escault :—« Ceulx de lost leur gectoient par leur engins chevaulz mors et autres bestes mortes et puantes, pour les empuantir, dont ilz estoient la dedans en moult grant destresse. Car lair estoit fort et chault ainsi comme en plein este, et de ce furent plus constraints que de nulle autre chose. Si considerent finablement entre eulx que celle messaise ilz ne pourroient longuement endurer ne souffrir, tant leur estoit la punaisie abhominable.»—*Froissart*, i. 38.

This was an evil which sometimes annoyed the besieging army. At Dan « pour la puantise des bestes que lon tuoit en lost, et des chevaulx qui estoient mors, lair estoit tout corrompu, dont moult de chevaliers et escuyers en estoient malades et merencolieux, et sey alloient les plusieurs, refreschir a Bruges et ailleurs pour éviter ce mauvais air.»—*Froissart*, i. 175.

Note 95, page 22, col. 2.
Shrouded in unwholesome vaults.

At Thin sur l'Escault, « La fist le duc charier grant foison d'engins de Cambray et de Douay, et en y eut six moult grans, le duc les fist lever devant la forteresse. Lesqlz engins gectoient nuyt et jour grosses pierres et mangonneaulx qui abatoient les combles et le hault des tours des chambres et des salles. Et en contraignoient les gens du Chastel par cest assault tresdurement. Et si nosient les compaignons qui le gardoient demourer en chambres nen sales quilz eussent, mais en caves et en celiers.»—*Froissart*, i, 38.

Note 96, page 22, col. 2.
Eager to mark the carrion crow for food.

Scudery has a most ingenious idea of the effects of famine : during the blockade of Rome by the Goths, he makes the inhabitants first eat one another, and then eat themselves.

La rage se meslant à leurs douleurs extrêmes,
Ils se mangent l'un l'autre, ils se mangent eux-mesmes.
Alaric.

Fuller expresses the want of food pithily:—« The siege grew long, and victuals short.»

Note 97, page 22, col. 2.
When in the sun the Angel of the Lord.

« And I saw an angel standing in the sun ; and he cried with a loud voice, saying to all the fowls that fly in the midst of Heaven, Come and gather yourselves together unto the supper of the great God :

« That ye may eat the flesh of kings, and the flesh of captains, and the flesh of mighty men, and the flesh of horses, and of them that sit on them.»—*Revelation*, xix. 17, 18.

The same idea occurs in Ezekiel, though not with equal sublimity.

« And thou, son of man, thus saith the Lord God, speak unto every feathered fowl, and to every beast of the field. Assemble yourselves, and come ; gather yourselves on every side to my sacrifice that I do sacrifice for you, even a great sacrifice upon the mountains of Israel, that ye may eat flesh and drink blood.

« Ye shall eat the flesh of the mighty, and drink the blood of the princes of the earth, of rams, of lambs, and of goats, of bullocks, all of them fatlings of Bashan.

« And ye shall eat fat till ye be full, and drink blood till ye be drunken, of my sacrifice which I have sacrificed for you.

« Thus ye shall be filled at my table with horses and chariots, with mighty men, and with all men of war, saith the Lord God.»—*Ezekiel*, xxxix, 17, etc.

Note 98, page 23, col. 2.
Prevent the pangs of famine.

Fuller calls this « resolving rather to lose their lives by wholesale on the point of the sword, than to retail them out by famine.»

Note 99, page 23, col. 2.
As when the Mexicans.

It was the belief of the Mexicans, that at the conclusion of one of their centuries the sun and earth would be destroyed. On the last night of every century they extinguished all their fires, covered the faces of the women and children, and expected the end of the world. The kindling of the sacred fire on the mountain of Huixachtla was believed an omen of their safety.—*Clavigero.*

Note 100, page 24, col. 2.
The veins were full.

Φαιης κεν γυιων νιν οσον σθενος ελλοπιευειν.
Αι δε οι ωδηχαντι κατ' αυχενα παχτοθεν ινες,
Και πολιω περ εοντι. το δε σθενος αξιον αβας.
ΘΕΟΚΡΙΤΟΣ.

Note 101, page 24, col. 2.
His silence threaten'd.
Son silence menace.
Le Moyne.

Note 102, page 25, col. 1.
See the fire consume him.

Reasons for burning a trumpeter.

« The letter she sent to Suffolk was received with scorn, and the trumpeter that brought it commanded to be burnt, against the law of nations, saith a French author,[1] but erroneously, for his coming was not warranted by the authority of any lawfull prince, but from a private maid, how highly soever self-pretended, who had neither estate to keep, nor commission to send a trumpeter.»—*Fuller's Profane State.*

Note 103, page 25, col. 1.
In sight of Orleans and the Maiden's host.

De Serres says, « the trumpeter was ready to be burnt in the sight of the besieged.»

Note 104, page 25, col. 2.
As he that puts it off.

« Let not him that girdeth on his harness boast himself, as he that putteth it off.»—I *Kings*, xx, 11.

Note 105, page 25, col. 2.
As when Choderlos comes.

« A ripâ fluminis Halys venimus ad Gourkurthoy ; inde Choron ; post in The Ke Thioi. Hic multa didicimus a monachis Turcicis, quos Dervis vocant, qui

[1] De Serres.

9

eo loco insignem habent ædem, de heroe quodam Chederle summâ corporis atque animi fortitudine, quem eundem fuisse cum nostro D. Georgio fabulantur; eademque illi ascribunt quæ huic nostri; nimirum vasti et horrendi draconis cæde servasse expositam virginem. Ad hæc alia adjiciunt multa, et quæ libitum est, comminiscuntur; illum per longinquas oras peregrinari solitum, ad fluvium postremo pervenisse; cujus aquæ bibentibus præstarent immortalitatem. Qui quidem fluvius, in quâ parte terrarum sit, non dicunt; nisi fortassis in Utopiâ collocari debet: tantum affirmant illum magnis tenebris, multâque caligine obductum latere; neque cuiquam mortalium post Chederlem, uti illum videret, contigisse. Chederlem vero ipsum mortis legibus solutum, huc illuc in equo præstantissimo, qui similiter ejusdem aquæ haustu mortalitatem exuerit, divagari, gaudentem præliis, adesse in bello melioribus, ant iis qui ejus opem imploraverint, cujuscunque tandem sint religionis.»—*Busbequius.*

« The Persians say, that Alexander coming to understand, that in the mountain of Kaf there was a great cave, very black and dark, wherein ran the water of immortality, would needs take a journey thither. But being afraid to lose his way in the cave, and considering with himself that he had committed a great oversight in leaving the more aged in cities and fortified places, and keeping about his person only young people, such as were not able to advise him, he ordered to be brought to him some old man, whose counsell he might follow in the adventure he was then upon. There were in the whole army but two brothers named Chidder and Elias who had brought their father along with them, and this good old man bade his sons go and tell Alexander, that to go through with the design he had undertaken, his only way were to take a mare that had a colt at her heels, and to ride upon her into the cave, and leave the colt at the entrance of it, and the mare would infallibly bring him back again to the same place without any trouble. Alexander thought the advice so good, that he would not take any other person with him in that journey but those two brothers, leaving the rest of his retinue at the entrance of the cave. He advanced so far that he came to a gate, so well polished, that notwithstanding the great darkness, it gave light enough to let him see there was a bird fastened thereto. The bird asked Alexander what he would have? He made answer that he looked for the water of immortality. The bird asked him, what was done in the world? Mischief enough, replies Alexander, since there is no vice or sin but reigns there. Whereupon the bird getting loose and flying away, the gate opened and Alexander saw an angel sitting, with a trumpet in his hand, holding it as if he were going to put it to his mouth. Alexander asked him his name. The angel made answer his name was Raphael, and that he only staid for a command from God to blow the trumpet, and to call the dead to judgement. Which having said. he asks Alexander who he was? I am Alexander, replied he, and I seek the water of immortality. The angel gave him a stone and said to him, go thy wayes, and look for another stone of the same weight with this, and then thou shalt find immortality. Whereupon Alexander asked how long he had to live? The angel said to him, till such time as the heaven and the earth which encompass thee be turned to iron. Alexander being come out of the cave, sought a long time, and

not meeting with any stone just of the same weight with the other, he put one into the balance which he thought came very near it, and finding but very little difference, he added thereto a little earth, which made the scales even; it being God's intention to shew Alexander thereby, that he was not to expect immortality till he himself were put into the earth. At last Alexander having one day a fall off his horse in the barren ground of Ghur, they laid him upon the coat he wore over his armour, and covered him with his buckler to keep off the heat of the sun. Then he began to comprehend the prophesy of the angel, and was satisfied the hour of his death was at hand; accordingly he died.

«They add to this fable, that the two brothers Chidder and Elias drunk of the water of immortality, and that they are still living but invisible, Elias upon the earth, and Chidder in the water; wherein the latter hath so great power, that those who are in danger of being destroyed by water, if they earnestly pray, vowing an offering to him, and firmly believing that he can relieve them, shall escape the danger.»—*Amb. Trav.*

« *Khidir* and *Elias* occupy a distinguished place in the legion of prophets. The name of the first signifies verdant, alluding to the power which he possessed of producing, wherever he trod, the most beautiful and enchanting verdure. These two are regarded as the protectors and tutelary gods of travellers; the former upon the sea, the latter upon the land; and they are thought to be incessantly employed in promoting these salutary objects. In their rapid and uniform courses, they are believed to meet once a year at *Mina*, in the environs of *Mecca*, the day on which the pilgrims are assembled.»—*D'Ohsson's Hist. of the Othoman Empire.*

Note 106, page 26, col. 1.

The swords that late flash'd to the evening sun.

Now does the day grow blacker than before,
The swords that glister'd late, in purple gore
Now all distain'd, their former brightnesse lose.
May's Edward III.

And again, Book 7 :

The glittering swords that shone so bright of late
Are quickly all distain'd with purple gore.

Note 107, page 26, col. 1.

Of blessed Mary vow'd the vow of peace.

« Il advint a luy et a toute sa gent, estant devant Chartres, qui moult humilia et brise son courage; car entendis que ces traicteurs Francois alloient et preschoient ledit roy et son conseil, et encores nulle response agreable nen avoient eue. Une orage une tempeste et une fouldre si grande et si horrible descendit du ciel en lost du roy Dangleterre qui sembloit proprement que le siecle deust finer. Car il cheoit si grosses pierres que elles tuoyent hommes et chevaulx, et en furent les plus hardis tous esbahis. Adoncques regarda le roy Dangleterre devers leglise de nostre dame de Chartres, et se voua et rendit devotement a nostre dame, et promist, et confissa sicomme il dist depuis quil se accorderoit a la paix »—*Froissart.*

« But while he lodged there (before Chartres), his army making a horrible spoile of the whole country, there chanced an occasion, as the work of Heaven, which suddenly quailed his ambitious design to ruin France : for behold a horrible and extraordinary tempest of haile, thunder, and lightning, fals with such violence as many horses and men in the army perished, as if that God had stretched forth his hand from heaven to stay his course.»—*De Serres.*

Note 108, page 27, col. 1.
Deep through the sky the hollow thunders roll'd.

The circumstance of the Maid's entering Orleans at midnight in a storm of thunder and lightning is historically true:—

« The Englishmen perceiving that thei within could not long continue for faute of vitaile and pouder, kepte not their watche so diligently as thei wer accustomed, nor scoured not the countrey environed as thei before had ordained. Whiche negligence the citizens shut in perceiving, sent worde thereof to the French capitaines, which with Pucelle in the dedde tyme of the nighte, and in a greate rayne and thundere, with all their vitaile and artillery entered into the citie.»—*Hall.,* *fol.* 127.

Shakspeare also notices this storm. Striking as the circumstance is, Chapelain has omitted it.

Note 109, page 27, col. 1.
Strong were the English forts.

The patience and perseverance of a besieging army in those ages appear almost incredible to us now. The camp of Ferdinand before Granada swelled into a city. Edward III made a market-town before Calais. Upon the captain's refusal to surrender, says Barnes, « he began to entrench himself strongly about the city, setting his own tent directly against the chief gates at which he intended to enter; then he placed bastions between the town and the river, and set out regular streets, and reared up decent buildings of strong timber between the trenches, which he covered with thatch, reed, broom, and skins. Thus he encompassed the whole town of Calais, from Risban on the northwest side to Courgaine on the north-east, all along by Sangate, at Port and Fort de Nicolay, commonly by the English called Newland-bridge, down by Hammes, Cologne, and Marke; so that his camp looked like a spacious city, and was usually by strangers, that came thither to market, called New Calais. For this prince's reputation for justice was so great, that to his markets (which he held in his camp twice every week, viz. on Tuesdays and Saturdays for flesh, fish, bread, wine, and ale, with cloth and all other necessaries), there came not only his friends and allies from England, Flanders, and Aquitain, but even many of king Philip's subjects and confederates conveyed thither their cattle and other commodities to be sold.»

Note 110, page 27, col. 1.
Entering with his eye.

Nunc lentus, celsis adstans in collibus, intrat
Urbem oculis, discitque locos caussasque locorum.
Silius Italicus, xii, 567.

Note 111, page 27, col. 2.
Unburnish'd and defiled.

Abjecere madentes,
Sicut erant, clypeos; nec quisquam spicula tersit,
Nec laudavit equum, nitidæ nec cassidis altam
Compsit adornavitque jubam.
Statius.

Note 112, page 28, col. 1.
When, the war of beasts.

Ipsam, Mænalià puerum cum vidit in umbrâ,
Dianam, tenero signantem gramina passu,

Ignovisse ferunt comiti, Dictæaque tela
Ipsam, et Amyclæas humeris aptasse pharetras.
—— tædet nemorum, titulumque nocentem.
Sanguinis humani pudor est nescire sagittas.
Statius, iv, 256.

Note 113, page 28, col. 1.
Hero Gladdisdale.

Gladdisdale must be the Sir William Glansdale of Shakspeare. Henry VI, Part I.—Stowe calls him William Gladesdale.

It is proper to remark that I have introduced no fictitious names among the killed. They may all be found in the various histories.

Note 114, page 28, col. 1.
The balista.

Neque enim solis excussa lacertis
Lancea, sed tenso balistæ turbine rapta,
Haud unum contenta latus transire, quiescit;
Sed pandens perque arma viam, perque ossa, relictâ
Morte fugit: superest telo post vulnera cursus.
Lucan. iii.

Vegetius says, that the balista discharged darts with such rapidity and violence, that nothing could resist their force. This engine was used particularly to discharge darts of a surprising length and weight, and often many small ones together. Its form was not unlike that of a broken bow; it had two arms, but straight and not curved like those of a cross-bow, of which the whole acting force consists in bending the bow. That of the balista as well as of the catapulta lies in its cords.—*Rollin.*

Note 115, page 28, col. 1.
Where by the bayle's embattled wall.

The bayle or lists was a space on the outside of the ditch, surrounded by strong pallisades, and sometimes by a low embattled wall In the attack of fortresses, as the range of the machines then in use did not exceed the distance of four stadia, the besiegers did not carry on their approaches by means of trenches, but began their operations above ground, with the attack of the bayle or lists, where many feats of chivalry were performed by the knights and men at arms, who considered the assault of that work as particularly belonging to them, the weight of their armour preventing them from scaling the walls. As this part was attacked by the knights and men at arms, it was also defended by those of the same rank in the place, whence many single combats were fought here. This was at the first investing of the place.—*Grose.*

Note 116, page 28, col. 1.
A rude coat of mail.

In France only persons of a certain estate, called *un fief de hauber*, were permitted to wear a hauberk, which was the armour of a knight. Esquires might only wear a simple coat of mail without the hood and hose. Had this aristocratic distinction consisted in the ornamental part of the arms alone, it would not have been objectionable. In the enlightened and free states of Greece, every soldier was well provided with defensive arms. In Rome, a civic wreath was the reward of him who should save the life of a citizen. But, to use the words of Dr Gillies, « the miserable peasants of modern Europe are exposed without defence as without remorse, by the ambition of men, whom the Greeks would have styled tyrants."

Note 117, page 28, col. 1.

The rode-featur'd helm.

The burgonet, which represented the shape of the head and features.

Note 118, page 28, col. 2.

On his crown-crested helm.

Earls and dukes frequently wore their coronets on the crest of their helmets. At the battle of Agincourt Henry wore « a bright helmet, whereupon was set a crowne of gold, repleate with pearle and precious stones, marvellous rich.»—*Stowe.*

Note 119, page 28, col. 2.

And against the iron fence beneath.

A breast-plate was sometimes worn under the hauberk.

Note 120, page 28, col. 2.

With an active bound.

The nature of this barrier has been explained in a previous note. The possibility of leaping upon it is exemplified in the following adventure, which is characteristic of the period in which it happened (1370).

« At that time there was done an extraordinary feat of arms by a Scotch knight, named sir John Assueton, being one of those men of arms of Scotland, who had now entered king Edward's pay. This man left his rank with his spear in his hand, his page riding behind him, and went towards the barriers of Noyon, where he alighted, saying, 'Here hold my horse, and stir not from hence;' and so he came to the barriers. There were there at that time sir John de Roye, and sir Lancelot de Lorris, with ten or twelve more, who all wondered what this knight designed to do. He for his part being close to the barriers said unto them, 'Gentlemen, I am come hither to visit you, and because I see you will not come forth of your barriers to me, I will come in to you, if I may, and prove my knighthood against you. Win me if you can.' And with that he leaped over the bars, and began to lay about him like a lion, he at them and they at him; so that he alone fought thus against them all for near the space of an hour, and hurt several of them. And all the while those of the town beheld with much delight from the walls and their garret windows his great activity, strength; and courage; but they offered not to do him any hurt, as they might very easily have done, if they had been minded to cast stones or darts at him: but the French knights charged them to the contrary, saying, ' How they should let them alone to deal with him.' When matters had continued thus about an hour, the Scotch page came to the barriers with his master's horse in his hand, and said in his language, ' Sir, pray come away, it is high time for you to leave off now: for the army is marched off out of sight.' The knight heard his man, and then gave two or three terrible strokes about him to clear the way, and so armed as he was, he leaped back again over the barriers and mounted his horse, having not received any hurt; and turning to the Frenchmen, said, ' Adieu, sirs! I thank you for my diversion.' And with that he rode after his man upon the spur towards the army.»—*Joshua Barnes.*

Note 121, page 29, col. 1.

The iron weight swung high.

La massue est un bâton gros comme le bras, ayant à l'un de ses bouts une forte courroie pour tenir l'arme et l'empêcher de glisser, et à l'autre trois chaînons de fer, auxquels pend un boulet pesant huit livres. Il n'y a pas d'homme aujourd'hui capable de manier une telle arme.—*Le Grand.*

The arms of the Medici family « are romantically referred to Averardo de Medici, a commander under Charlemagne, who for his valour in destroying the gigantic plunderer Mugello, by whom the surrounding country was laid waste, was honoured with the privilege of bearing for his arms six *palle* or balls, as characteristic of the iron balls that hung from the mace of his fierce antagonist, the impression of which remained on his shield.»—*Roscoe.*

Scudery enumerates the mace among the instruments of war, in a passage whose concluding line may vie with any bathos of sir Richard Blackmore:

> Là confusément frappent de toutes parts
> Pierres, piques, espieux, masses, flèches et dards,
> Lances et javelots, sabres et marteaux d'armes,
> Dangereux instruments des guerrières alarmes.
> *Alaric.*

Note 122, page 29, col. 1.

Which open'd on the wall.

Vitruvius observes, in treating upon fortified walls, that near the towers the walls should be cut within-side the breadth of the tower, and that the ways broke in this manner should only be joined and continued by beams laid upon the two extremities, without being made fast with iron; that in case the enemy should make himself master of any part of the wall, the besieged might remove this wooden bridge, and thereby prevent his passage to the other parts of the wall and into the towers.—*Rollin.*

The precaution recommended by Vitruvius had not been observed in the construction of the English walls. On each side of every tower, a small door opened upon the wall; and the garrison of one tower are represented in the poem as flying by this way from one to shelter themselves in the other. With the enterprising spirit and the defensive arms of chivalry, the subsequent events will not be found to exceed probability.

Note 123, page 29, col. 2.

O'erbrow'd by no out-jutting parapet.

The machicolation: a projection over the gate-way of a town or castle, contrived for letting fall great weights, scalding water, etc. on the heads of any assailants who might have got close to the gate. « Machecollare, or machecoulare,» says Coke, « is to make a warlike device over a gate or other passage like to a grate, through which scalding water, or ponderous or offensive things may be cast upon the assaylants.»

Note 124, page 29, col. 2.

And hurl'd its severed point.

I have met with one instance in the English history, and only one, of throwing the spear after the manner of the ancients. It is in Stowe's chronicle: « 1442. The 30th of January, a challenge was done in Smithfield within lists, before the king; the one sir Philip de Beawse of Arragon, a knight, and the other an esquire of the king's house called John Ansley or Astley. These coming to the fielde, tooke their tents, and there was the knight's sonne made knight by the king, and so brought again to his father's tent. Then the heralds of armes called them by name to doe their battell, and so they came both, all armed, with their weapons; the knight came with his sword drawn, and the esquire with his speare. The esquire cast his speare against the knight, but the knight avoiding it with his sword, cast it to the ground. Then the esquire took his axe and went against the knight suddenly, on whom he stroke many strokes, hard and sore upon his basenet, and on his hand, and made him loose and let fall his axe to the ground, and brast up his limbes three times, and caught his dagger and would have smitten him in the face, for to have slaine him in the field; and then the king cried hoo, and so they were departed and went to their tents, and the king dubbed John Astley knight for his valiant torney, and the knight of Arragon offered his armes at Windsor.»

Note 125, page 29, col. 2.

Full on the corselet.

The corselet was chiefly worn by pikemen.

Note 126, page 30, col. 2.

A harlot!... an adulteress!

This woman, who is always respectably named in French history, had her punishment both in herself and in her child.

« This fair Agnes had been five years in the service of the queen, during which she had enjoyed all the pleasures of life, in wearing rich clothes, furred robes, golden chains, and precious stones; and was commonly reported that the king often visited her, and maintained her in a state of concubinage, for the people are more inclined to speak ill than well of their superiors.

« The affection the king showed her was as much for her gaiety of temper, pleasing manners, and agreeable conversation, as for her beauty. She was so beautiful that she was called the Fairest of the Fair, and the Lady of Beaute, as well on account of her personal charms, as because the king had given her for life the castle of Beaute near Paris. She was very charitable, and most liberal in her alms, which she distributed among such churches as were out of repair, and to beggars. It is true that Agnes had a daughter who lived but a short time, which she said was the king's, and gave it to him as the proper father; but the king always excused himself as not having any claim to it. She may indeed have called in help, for the matter was variously talked of.

« At length she was seized with a bowel complaint, and was a long time ill, during which she was very contrite, and sincerely repented of her sins. She often remembered Mary Magdalin, who had been a great sinner, and devoutly invoked God and the virgin Mary to her aid like a true catholic: after she had received the sacraments, she called for her book of prayers, in which she had written with her own hand the verses of St Bernard to repeat them. She then made many gifts, (which were put down in writing, that her executors might fulfil them, with the other articles of her will,) which including alms and the payment of her servants might amount to nearly sixty thousand crowns.

« Her executors were Jacques Coeur, councellor and master of the wardrobe to the king, master Robert Poictevin physician, and master Stephen Chevalier treasurer to the king, who was to take the lead in the fulfilment of her will should it be his gracious pleasure.

« The fair Agnes, perceiving that she was daily growing weaker, said to the Lord de la Trimouille, the lady of the seneschal of Poitou, and one of the king's equeries called Gouffier, in the presence of all her damsels, that our fragile life was but a stinking ordure.

« She then required that her confessor would give her absolution, from all her sins and wickedness, conformable to an absolution, which was, as she said, at Lochés, which the confessor on her assurance complied with. After this she uttered a loud shriek, and called on the mercy of God and the support of the blessed virgin Mary, and gave up the ghost on Monday the 9th day of February, in the year 1449, about six o'clock in the afternoon. Her body was opened, and her heart interred in the church of the said abbey, to which she had been a most liberal benefactress; and her body was conveyed with many honours to Loches, where it was interred in the collegiate church of our Lady, to which also she had made many handsome donations and several foundations. May God have mercy on her soul, and admit it into Paradise!»—Monstrelet, vol. ix, p. 97.

On the 13th day of June, the seneschal of Normandy, count of Maulevrier, and son to the late sir Pierre de Breze killed at the battle of Montlehery, went to the village of Romiers, near Dourdan, which belonged to him, for the sake of hunting. He took with him his lady, the princess Charlotte of France, natural daughter of the late king Charles the VII by Agnes Sorel. After the chace, when they were returned to Romiers to sup and lodge, the seneschal retired to a single-bedded room for the night; his lady retired also to another chamber, when moved by her disorderly passions (as the husband said) she called to her a gentleman from Poitou, named Pierre de la Vergne, who was head huntsman to the seneschal, and made him lie with her. This was told to the seneschal by the master of his household, called Pierre l'Apothecaire; when he instantly arose, and taking his sword, broke open the door of the chamber where his lady and the huntsman were in bed. The huntsman started up in his shirt, and the seneschal gave him first a severe blow with his sword on the head, and then thrust it through his body, and killed him on the spot. This done, he went into an adjoining room where his children lay, and finding his wife hid under the coverlid of their bed, dragged her thence by the arm along the ground, and struck her between the shoulders with his sword. On her raising herself on her knees he ran his sword through her breast, and she fell down dead. He sent her body for interment to the abbey of Coulens, where her obsequies were performed, and he caused the huntsman to be buried in the garden of the house wherein he had been killed.—Monstrelet, vol. ii, p. 233.

Note 127, page 31, col. 1.

And would that I had lived:

Μηκετ' επειτ' ωφειλον εγω πεμπτοισι μετειναι
Ανδρασιν, αλλ' η προσθε θανειν η επειτα γενεσθαι.
Νυν γαρ δη γενος εστι σιδηρεον· ουδεποτ' ημαρ
Παυσονται καματου και οιζυος, ουδε τι νυκτωρ,
Φθειρομενοι.   ΗΣΙΟΔΟΣ.

Note 128, page 31, col. 1.

Then was that noble heart of Douglas pierced.

The heart of Bruce was, by his own dying will, intrusted to Douglas to bear it to Jerusalem. This is one of the finest stories in the whole period of chivalrous history. Douglas inshrined the heart in a golden case, and wore it round his neck; he landed in Spain on his way, and stopt to assist the Castilians against the Moors,—probably during the siege of Algeziras. There in the heat of action he took the heart from his neck and cast it into the thick of the enemy, exclaiming, as Barbour has it,

> Now pass thou forth before
> As thou wast wont in fight to be,
> And I shall follow or else die.

In this action he perished, and from that time the bloody heart has been borne by the family.

Note 129, page 32, col. 2.
Pillow'd the helmed head.

> Il n'est rien de si doux, pour des cœurs pleins de gloire,
> Que la paisible nuit qui suit une victoire ;
> Dormir sur un trophée est un charmant repos,
> Et le champ de bataille est le lit d'un héros.
> *Scudéry. Alaric.*

The night after a battle is certainly more agreeable than the night before one. A soldier may use his shield for a pillow, but he must be very ingenious to sleep upon a trophy.

Note 130, page 32, col. 2.
Gazing with such a look.

> With a dumb silence seeming that it fears
> The thing it went about to effectuate.
> *Daniel.*

Note 131, page 33, col. 1.
Play'd o'er his cheeks black paleness.

> Noire pasleur.
> *Le Moyne. St Louis,* liv. xvi.

Note 132, page 33, col. 2.
From the barbican.

Next the bayle was the ditch, foss, grass, or mote : generally where it could be a wet one, and pretty deep. The passage over it was by a draw-bridge, covered by an advance work called a barbican. The barbican was sometimes beyond the ditch that covered the draw-bridge, and in towns and large fortresses had frequently a ditch and draw-bridge of its own.—*Grose.*

Note 133, page 33, col. 2.
Or from the embattled wall.

The outermost walls enclosing towns or fortresses were commonly perpendicular, or had a very small external talus. They were flanked by semi-circular, polygonal, or square towers, commonly about forty or fifty yards distant from each other. Within were steps to mount the terre-pleine of the walls or rampart, which were always defended by an embattled or crenellated parapet.—*Grose.*

The fortifications of the middle ages differed in this respect from those of the ancients. When the besiegers had gained the summit of the wall, the descent on the other side was safe and easy. But « the ancients did not generally support their walls on the inside with earth, in the manner of the talus or slope, which made the attacks more dangerous. For though the enemy had gained some footing upon them, he could not assure himself of taking the city. It was necessary to get down, and to make use of some of the ladders by which he had mounted; and that descent exposed the soldier to very great danger.»—*Rollin.*

Note 134, page 33, col. 2.
Behind the guardian pavais fenced.

The pavais, or pavache, was a large shield, or rather a portable mantlet, capable of covering a man from head to foot, and probably of sufficient thickness to resist the missive weapons then in use. These were in sieges carried by servants, whose business it was to cover their masters with them, whilst they, with their bows and arrows, shot at the enemy on the ramparts. As this must have been a service of danger, it was that perhaps which made the office of scutifer honourable. The pavais was rectangular at the bottom, but rounded off above : it was sometimes supported by props.—*Grose.*

Note 135, page 33, col. 2.
With all their mangonels.

Mangonels is a term comprehending all the smaller engines.

Note 136, page 33, col. 2.
Or tortoises.

The tortoise was a machine composed of very strong and solid timber work. The height of it to its highest beam, which sustained the roof, was twelve feet. The base was square, and each of its fronts twenty-five feet. It was covered with a kind of quilted mattress made of raw hides, and prepared with different drugs to prevent its being set on fire by combustibles. This heavy machine was supported upon four wheels, or perhaps upon eight. It was called tortoise from its serving as a very strong covering and defence against the enormous weights thrown down on it; those under it being safe in the same manner as a tortoise under his shell. It was used both to fill up the fosse, and for sapping. It may not be improper to add, that it is believed, so enormous a weight could not be moved from place to place on wheels, and that it was pushed forward on rollers. Under these wheels or rollers, the way was laid with strong planks to facilitate its motion, and prevent its sinking into the ground, from whence it would have been very difficult to have removed it. The ancients have observed that the roof had a thicker covering, of hides, hurdles, sea-weed, etc. than the sides, as it was exposed to much greater shocks from the weights thrown upon it by the besieged. It had a door in front, which was drawn up by a chain as far as was necessary, and covered the soldiers at work in filling up the fosse with fascines.—*Rollin.*

This is the tortoise of the ancients, but that of the middle ages differed from it in nothing material.

Note 137, page 33, col. 2.
A dreadful train.

The besiegers having carried the bayle, brought up their machines and established themselves in the counterscarp, began under cover of their cats, sows, or tortoises, to drain the ditch, if a wet one, and also to fill it up with hurdles and fascines, and level it for the passage of their moveable towers. Whilst this was doing, the archers, attended by young men carrying shields (pavoises), attempted with their arrows to drive the besieged from the towers and ramparts, being themselves covered by these portable mantlets. The garrison on their part essayed by the discharge of machines, cross and long bows, to keep the enemy at a distance.—*Grose.*

Note 138, page 33, col. 2.

The chief a cross-bow held.

The cross-bow was some time laid aside in obedience to a decree of the second Lateran council held in 1139. Artem illam mortiferam et Deo odibilem ballistariorum adversus christianos et catholicos exercere de cætero sub anathemate prohibemus.» This weapon was again introduced into our armies by Richard I, who being slain with a quarrel shot from one of them, at the siege of the castle of Chaluz in Normandy, it was considered as a judgment from heaven inflicted upon him for his impiety. Guilliaume le Breton relating the death of this king, puts the following into the mouth of Atropos :

Hâc volo, non aliâ Richardum morte perire
Ut qui Francigenis ballistæ primitus usum
Tradidit, ipse, sui rem primitus experiatur,
Quemque alios docuit in se vim sentiat artis.
Grose.

Note 139, page 34, col. 1.

Who, kneeling by the trebuchet.

From the trebuchet they discharged many stones at once by a sling. It acted by means of a great weight fastened to the short arm of a lever, which being let fall, raised the end of the long arm with a great velocity. A man is represented kneeling to load one of these in an ivory carving, supposed to be of the age of Edward II.—*Grose.*

Note 140, page 34, col. 1.

He in the groove the feather'd quarrel placed.

Quarrels, or carreaux, were so called from their heads, which were square pyramids of iron.

Note 141, page 34, col. 1.

The watery fence.

The tortoises, etc. and moveable towers having reached the walls, the besiegers under them either began to mine, or batter them with the ram. They also established batteries of balistas and mangonels on the counterscarp. These were opposed by those of the enemy.

Note 142, page 34, col. 2.

Or charging with huge stones the murderous sling.

The matafunda.

Note 143, page 34, col. 2.

—— or in the espringal
Fix the brass-winged arrows.

The espringal threw large darts called muchettæ, sometimes winged with brass instead of feathers. Procopius says that because feathers could not be put to the large darts discharged from the balista, the ancients used pieces of wood six inches thick, which had the same effect.

Note 144, page 34, col. 2.

From some huge martinet.

Le lendemain viudrent deux maistres engingneurs au duc de Normandie, qui dirent que, si on leur vouloit livrer boys et ouvriers, ilz feroient quatre eschauffaulx et aulx que on meneroit aux murs du chastel, et seroient si haulz q'lz surmonteroient les murs. Le duc commanda qlz le feissent, et fist prendre tous les charpeniers du pays, et payer largement. Si furent faitz ces quatre eschauffaulx en quatre grosses nefz, mais on y mist longuement et cousterent grans deniers. Si y fist on les gens entrer q'a ceux du chastel devoient combattre. Quand ilz eurent passe la moitie de la reviere, ceulx du chastel desclinquerent quatre martinetz qlz avoient faitz nouvellement pour remedier contre lesditz eschauffaulx. Ces quatre martinetz gettoient si grosses pierres et si souvent sur ces eschauffaulx qlz furent bien tost froissez tant que les gensdarmes et ceux que les conduisoient ne se peurent dedans garantir. Si se retirerent arriere le plus tost quilz peurent. Et ainçois qlz fussent oultre la reviere lung des eschauffaulx fut enfondre au fons de leaue.—*Froissart, I, feuillet* 82.

Note 145, page 34, col. 2.

A moving tower the men of Orleans wheel.

The following extract from the history of Edward III by Joshua Barnes will convey a full idea of these moving towers:—«Now the earl of Darby had layn before Reule more than nine weeks, in which time he had made two vast belfroys or bastilles of massy timber, with three stages of floors; each of the belfroys running on four huge wheels, bound about with thick hoops of iron; and the sides and other parts that any ways respected the town were covered with raw hides, thick laid, to defend the engines from fire and shot. In every one of these stages were placed an hundred archers, and between the two bastilles there were two hundred men with pick-axes and mattocks. From these six stages six hundred archers shot so fiercely all together, that no man could appear at his defence without a sufficient punishment: so that the belfreys being brought upon wheels by the strength of men, over a part of the ditch which was purposely made plain and level by the faggots and earth and stones cast upon them, the two hundred pioneers plyed their work so well under the protection of these engines, that they made a considerable breach through the walls of the town.»

Note 146, page 34, col. 2.

Of archers, through the opening, shot their shafts.

The archers and cross-bowmen from the upper stories in the moveable towers essayed to drive away the garrison from the parapets, and on a proper opportunity to let fall a bridge, by that means to enter the town. In the bottom story was often a large ram.—*Grose.*

Note 147, page 34, col. 2.

And from the arbalist the fire-tipt dart.

Against the moveable tower there were many modes of defence. The chief was to break up the ground over which it was to pass, or by undermining it to overthrow it. Attempts were likewise made to set it on fire, to prevent which it was covered with raw hides, or coated over with alum.—*Grose.*

Note 148, page 35, col. 1.

The bridge reclines.

These bridges are described by Rollin in the account of the moving towers which he gives from Vegetius:— « The moving towers are made of an assemblage of beams and strong planks, not unlike a house. To secure them against the fires thrown by the besieged, they are covered with raw hides, or with pieces of cloth made of hair. Their height is in proportion to their base. They are sometimes thirty feet square, and sometimes forty or fifty. They are higher than the walls or even towers of the city. They are supported upon several wheels, according to mechanic principles, by the means of which the machine is easily made to move, how great soever it may be. The town is in great danger if this tower can approach the walls; for it has stairs from one story to another, and includes different methods of attack. At bottom it has a ram to batter the wall, and on the middle story a draw-bridge made of two beams with rails of basket-work, which lets down easily upon the wall of a city, when within the reach of it. The besiegers pass upon this bridge, to make themselves masters of the wall. Upon the higher stories are soldiers armed with partisans and missive weapons, who keep a perpetual discharge upon the works. When affairs are in this posture, a place seldom held out long : for what can they hope who have nothing to confide in but the height of their ramparts, when they see others suddenly appear which command them !»

The towers or belfreys of modern times rarely exceeded three or four stages or stories.

Note 149, page 35, col. 1.
The brass-winged darts.

These darts were called viretons, from their whirling about in the air.

Note 150, page 35, col. 2.
When grappling with his monstrous enemy.

« And here, with leave bespoken to recite a grand fable, though dignified by our best poets, while Brutus on a certain festival day, solemnly kept on that shore where he first landed, was with the people in great jollity and mirth, a crew of these savages breaking in among them, began on the sudden another sort of game than at such meeting was expected. But at length by many hands overcome, Goemagog the hugest, in height twelve cubits, is reserved alive, that with him Corineus, who desired nothing more, might try his strength ; whom in a wrestle the giant catching aloft with a terrible hug broke three of his ribs : nevertheless Corineus enraged heaving him up by main force and on his shoulders bearing him to the next high rock, *threw him headlong all shattered into the sea*, and left his name on the cliff, called ever since Langoemagog, which is to say, the giant's leap.»—*Milton.*

The expression *brute vastness* is taken from the same work of Milton, where he relates the death of Morindus : « Well fitted to such a beastial cruelty was his end ; for hearing of a huge monster that from the Irish sea infested the coast, and in the pride of his strength foolishly attempting to set manly valour against a brute vastness, when his weapons were all in vain, by that horrible mouth he was catched up and devoured.»

Note 151, page 36, col. 1.
This is a favour!

The tournelles adjoining to the bridge was kept by Glacidas (one of the most resolute captains among the English), having well encouraged his men to defend themselves and to fight for their lives.

« The skirmish begins at nine of the clock in the morning, and the ladders are planted. A storm of English arrows falls upon our men with such violence as they recoiled. ' How now !' saith the Virgin, ' have we begun so well to end so ill? let us charge ! they are our own, seeing God is on our side!' so every one re-

covering his forces, flocks about the Virgin. The English double the storm upon the thickest of the troops. The Virgin fighting in the foremost ranks and encouraging her men to do well was shot through the arm with an arrow ; she, nothing amazed, takes the arrow in one hand and her sword in the other, 'This is a favour!' says she, ' let us go on! they cannot escape the hand of GOD !'»

Chapelain has dilated this exclamation of the Maid into a ridiculous speech.

Quoy! valeureux Guerriers! quoy! dans vostre avantage
Un peu de sang perdu vous fait perdre courage!
Pour moy, je le repute un supreme bonheur,
Et dans ce petit mal je trouve un grand honneur :
Le succes, bien qu',heureux, n'eust eu rien d'honorable,
Si le Ciel n'eust permis un coup si favorable ;
Vous n'en verrez pas moins vos bras victorieux,
J'en verray seulement mon nom plus glorieux.

                    L. III.

Note 152, page 36, col. 1.
Was Glacidas.

I can make nothing English of this name. Monstrelet calls him Clacedas and Clasendas. Daniel says the principal leaders of the English were Suffolk, Talbot, Scales, Fastolffe, « et un nommè Glacidas ou Clacidas, dont le mérite suppléant à la naissance l'avoit fait parvenir aux prémieres charges de l'armée.»

The importance attached to a second name is well exemplified by an extract in Selden, relating to « the creation of Robert earle of Glocester natural sonne to king Henry I. The king having speech with Mabile the sole daughter and heire of Robert Fitz Hayman lord of Glocester, told her (as it is reported in an old English rithmical story attributed to one Robert of Glocester), that

— he seold his sone to her spousing avonge,
The maid was ther agen, and withsaid it long.
The king of sought her saith ynou, so that atten ende
Mabile him answered, as gode maide and hende,
Sir, hoo sede, well ichot, that your hert ope me is,
More vor mine heritage than vor my sulve iwis.
So vair eritage as ich abbe, it were me grete shame,
Vor to abbe an louerd, bote he had an toname.
Sir Roberd le Fitz Haim my faders name was,
And that he might nought be bis that of his kunne nought nas,
Therefore, sir, vor Godes love, ne let me no mon owe,
Bote he abbe an twoname war throu he be iknowe.
Damoysale, quoth the king, thou seist well in this case,
Sir Roberd de Fitz Haim thy fader twoname was ;
And as udir two name he shall abbe, gif me him may bise
Sir Roberd de Fitz Rey is name shall be.
Sire, quoth this maid tho, that is a vaire name
As who seith all his life and of greate fame
Ae wat shold his sonne hote thanne and be that of him come,
So ne might hii hote, whereof nameth gone.
The king understood that the maid ne sede no outrage,
And that Gloucestre was chief of ire heritage.
Damesseile he sede tho, thi louerd shall have a name
Vor him and vor his hairs vair without blame,
Vor Roberd earle of Gloucestre is name shall be and his,
Vor he shall be earle of Gloucestre and his heires iwis.
Sire, quoth this maid tho, well liketh me this
In this forme ichole that all my gode be his.
Thus was earle of Gloucestre first imade there
Ae his Roberd of all thulke that long bivore were,
This was end leve hundred yeare, and in the ninth yeer right
After that are louerd was in his moder a'hight.»

                Selden's Titles of Honor.

Note 153, page 36, col. 1.
Seeking the inner court.

On entering the outer gate, the next part that presented itself was the outer hallium, or bailey, separated from the inner ballium by a strong embattled wall and towered gate.

Note 154, page 36, col. 2.

The engines shower'd their sheets of liquid fire.

When the Black Prince attacked the castle of Romorantin, « there was slain hard by him an English esquire named Jacob Bernard, whereat the prince was so displeased, that he took his most solemn oath, and sware by his father's soul not to leave the siege, till he had the castle and all within at his mercy. Then the assault was renewed much hotter than ever, till at last the prince saw there was no likelihood of prevailing that way. Wherefore presently he gave order to raise certain engines, wherewith they cast combustible matter enflamed after the manner of wild fire into the base court so fast and in such quantities, that at last the whole court seemed to be one huge fire. Whereupon the excessive heat prevailed so, that it took hold of the roof of a great tower, which was covered with reed, and so began to spread over all the castle. Now therefore when these valiant captains within saw, that of necessity they must either submit entirely to the prince's courtesy, or perish by the most merciless of elements, they all together came down and yielded themselves absolutely to his grace.»—*Joshua Barnes.*

Note 155, page 37, col. 1.

I have not rear'd the oriflamme of death.

The oriflamme was a standard erected to denote that no quarter would be given. It is said to have been of red silk, adorned and beaten with very broad and fair lilies of gold, and-bordered about with gold and vermillion. Le Moyne has given it a suitable escort:

Ensuite l'oriflamme ardente et lumineuse,
Marche sur un grand char, dont la forme est affreuse.
Quatre enormes dragons d'un or ombre ecaillez,
Et de pourpre, d'azur, et de vert emaillez,
Dans quelque occasion que le besoin le porte,
Luy font une pompeuse et formidable escorte.
Dans leur terribles yeux des gneurs arrondis,
De leur feu, de leur sang, font pour aux plus hardis,
Et si ce feu paroist allumér leur audace,
Aussi paroist ce sang animer leur menace.
Le char roulant sous eux, il semble au roulement,
Qu'il les fasse voler avecque sifflement:
Et de la poudre, en l'air, il se fait des fumées
A leurs bouches du vent et du bruit animées.

Philip is said by some historians to have erected the oriflamme at Crecy, where Edward in return raised up his burning dragon, the English signal for massacre. The oriflamme was originally used only in wars against the Infidels, for it was a sacred banner, and believed to have been sent from Heaven.

Note 156, page 37, col. 2.

Seized on the French—an universal cry.

At this woman's voice amidst the sound of war, the combat grows very hot. Our men, greatly encouraged by the Virgin, run headlong to the bastion and force a point thereof; then fire and stones rain so violently, as the English being amazed, forsake their defences: some are slain upon the place, some throw themselves down headlong, and fly to the tower upon the bridge. In the end this brave Glacidas abandons this quarter, and retires into the base court upon the bridge, and after him a great number of his soldiers. The bridge greatly shaken with artillery, tried by fire, and over-

charged with the weight of this multitude, sinks into the water with a fearful cry, carrying all this multitude with it.—*De Serres.*

This circumstance has been magnified into a miracle. « The French, for the most part, draw the institution of the order of St Michael principally from a purpose that Charles had to make it, after the apparition of the archangel upon Orleans bridge, as the tutelary angell of France assisting against the English in 1428.»—*Selden's Titles of Honour.*

The expressions are somewhat curious in the patent of this, *L'ordre de Monsieur St Michael Archange.* Louis XI instituted it « à la gloire et louange de Dieu nostre createur tout puissant, et reverence de la glorieuse vierge Marie, à l'honneur et reverence de St-Michael, *premier chevalier,* qui par la querelle de Dieu, bataille contre l'ancien enemy de l'humain lignage, et le fit tresbucher de Ciel.»

Note 157, page 37, col. 2.

The ascending flames.

Les dictes bastiles et fortresses furent presentement arses et demolies jusques en terre, affin que nulles gens de guerre de quelconque pays quilz soient ne si peussent plus loger.—*Monstrelet,* ii, f. 43.

Note 158, page 38, col. 1.

Silence itself was dreadful.

Un cry, que le besoin ou la peur fait jetter,
Et les airs agités les peuvent agiter.
Une haleine, un soupir et mesme le silence
Aux chefs, comme aux soldats, font perdre l'assurance.
Chapelain, l. ix.

Note 159, page 38, col. 1.

On that foul priest.

The parliament, when Henry V demanded a supply, entreated him to seize all the ecclesiastical revenues, and convert them to the use of the crown. The clergy were alarmed, and Chichely, archbishop of Canterbury, endeavoured to divert the blow, by giving occupation to the king, and by persuading him to undertake a war against France.—*Hume.*

The Archbishop of Bourges explained to the king, in the hall of the bishop of Winchester, and in the presence of the dukes of Clarence, Bedford, and Gloucester, brothers to the king, and of the lords of the council, clergy, chivalry, and populace, the objects of his embassy. The archbishop spoke first in Latin, and then in the Walloon language, so eloquently and wisely, that both English and French who heard him were greatly surprised. At the conclusion of his harangue he made offers to the king of a large sum of ready money on his marriage with the princess Catherine, but on condition that he would disband the army he had collected at Southampton, and at the adjacent sea-ports, to invade France: and that by these means an eternal peace would be established between the two kingdoms.

The assembly broke up when the archbishop had ended his speech, and the French ambassadors were kindly entertained at dinner by the king, who then appointed a day for them to receive his answers to their propositions by the mouth of the archbishop of Canterbury.

In the course of the archbishop's speech, in which he replied, article by article, to what the archbishop of

Bourges had offered, he added to some and passed over others of them, so that he was sharply interrupted by the archbishop of Bourges, who exclaimed, « I did not say so, but such were my words.» The conclusion, however, was, that unless the king of France would give, as a marriage portion with his daughter, the duchies of Acquitaine, of Normandy, of Anjou, of Tours, the counties of Ponthieu, Maine, and Poitou, and every other part that had formerly belonged to the English monarchs, the king would not desist from his intended invasion of France, but would despoil the whole of that kingdom which had been unjustly detained from him; and that he should depend on his sword for the accomplishment of the above, and for depriving king Charles of his crown.

The king avowed what the archbishop had said, and added, that thus, with God's aid, he would act; and promised it on the word of a king. The archbishop of Bourges then, according to the custom in France, demanded permission to speak, and said, « O king! how canst thou, consistently with honour and justice, thus wish to dethrone and iniquitously destroy the most christian king of the French, our very dear lord and most excellent of all the kings in christendom? O king! with all due reverence and respect, dost thou think that he has offered by me such extent of territory, and so large a sum of money with his daughter in marriage, through any fear of thee, thy subjects or allies? By no means; but, moved by pity and his love of peace, he has made these offers to avoid the shedding of innocent blood, and that Christian people may not be overwhelmed in the miseries of war; for whenever thou shalt make thy promised attempt he will call upon God, the blessed Virgin, and on all the saints, making his appeal to them for the justice of his cause; and with their aid, and the support of his loyal subjects and faithful allies, thou wilt be driven out of his dominions, or thou wilt be made prisoner, or thou wilt there suffer death by orders of that just king whose ambassadors we are.

« We have now only to intreat of thee that thou wouldst have us safely conducted out of thy realm; and that thou wouldst write to our said king, under thy hand and seal, the answer which thou hast had given to us. »

The king kindly granted their request, and the ambassadors, having received handsome presents, returned by way of Dover to Calais, and thence to Paris.

Monstrelet, vol. iv, p. 129.

Within a few days after the expiration of the truce, king Henry, whose preparations were now completed, sent one of his heralds, called Glocester, to Paris, to deliver letters to the king, of which the contents were as ollows :—

« To the very noble prince Charles, our cousin and adversary of France, Henry by the grace of God, king of England and of France. To give to every one what is their due, is a work of inspiration and wise council, very noble prince, our cousin and adversary. The noble kingdoms of England and France were formerly united, now they are divided. At that time it was customary for each person to exalt his name by glorious victories, and by this single virtue to extol the honour of God, to whom holiness belongs, and to give peace to his church, by subjecting in battle the enemies of the public weal; but alas! good faith among kindred and brotherly love have been perverted, and Lot persecutes Abraham by

human imputation; and Dissention, the mother of Anger, has been raised from the dead.

« We, however, appeal to the sovereign Judge, who is neither swayed by prayers nor gifts from doing right, that we have, from pure affection, done every thing in our power to preserve the peace; and we must now rely on the sword for regaining what is justly our heritage, and those rights which have from old time belonged to us; and we feel such assurance in our courage, that we will fight till death in the cause of justice.

« The written law in the book of Deuteronomy ordains, that before any person commences an attack on a city he shall first offer terms of peace; and although violence has detained from us our rightful inheritances, charity, however, induces us to attempt, by fair means, their recovery; for should justice be denied us, we may then resort to arms.

« And to avoid having our conscience affected by this matter, we make our personal request to you, and exhort you, by the bowels of Jesus Christ, to follow the dictates of his evangelical doctrine. Friend, restore what thou owest; for such is the will of God to prevent the effusion of the blood of man, who was created in his likeness. Such restitution of rights, cruelly torn from us, and which we have so frequently demanded by our ambassadors, will be agreeable to the supreme God, and secure peace upon earth.

« From our love of peace we were inclined to refuse fifty thousand golden crowns lately offered us; for being more desirous of peace than riches, we have preferred enjoying the patrimony left us by our venerable ancestors, with our very dear cousin Catherine, your noble daughter, so iniquitously multiplying our treasures, and thus disgracing the honour of our crown, which God forbid!

« Given under our privy seal, in our castle of Southampton, the 5th day of the month of August.»

Monstrelet, vol. iv, p.137.

Note 160, page 38, col. 1.

Sure that holy hermit spake.

While Henry V lay at the siege of Dreux, an honest hermit, unknown to him, came and told him the great evils he brought upon christendom by his unjust ambition, who usurped the kingdom of France, against all manner of right, and contrary to the will of God; wherefore in his holy name he threatened him with a severe and sudden punishment, if he desisted not from his enterprise. Henry took this exhortation either as an idle whimsey, or a suggestion of the Dauphin's, and was but the more confirmed in his design. But the blow soon followed the threatening; for within some few months after, he was smitten in the fundament with a strange and incurable disease.—*Mexeray*.

Note 161, page 38, col. 1.

The hour of vengeance.

———— Reservaverat antrum
Tartareus Rector pallens, utque arma nefanda
Spectarent, caperentque sui solatia fati,
Invisas illuc Libyes emiserat umbras;
Undique considere arvis, nigraque corona
Infecere diem, versatilis umbra Jugurthæ,
Annibalis sævi Manes, captique Syphacis,
Qui nunc eversas secum Carthaginis arces
Ignovere Deis, postquam feralia campi
Prælia Thapsiaci, et Latios videre furores.
Supplementum Lucani, Lib. III.

I am not conscious of having imitated these lines; but I would not lose the opportunity of quoting so fine a passage from Thomas May, an author to whom I owe some obligations, and who is not remembered as his merits deserve. May himself has imitated Valerius Flaccus, though he has greatly surpassed him:

> Et pater orantes cæsorum Tartarus umbras,
> Nube cavâ, tandem ad meritæ spectacula pugnæ
> Emittit; summi nigrescunt culmina montis.

Note 162, page 38, col. 2.

Man unassisted 'gainst the powers of hell.

To some, says Speed, it may appear more honourable to our nation, that they were not to be expelled by a human power, but by a divine, extraordinarily revealing itself.

Note 163, page 38, col. 2.

For by their numbers now made bold in fear.

> Nec pavidum murmur; consensu audacia crevit,
> Tantaque turba metu pœnarum solvit ab omni.
>   Sup. Lucani.

Note 164, page 38, col. 2.

Joy ran through all the troops.

In Rymer's Fœdera are two proclamations, one « contra capitaneos et soldarios tergiversantes, incantationibus Puellæ terrificatos ;» the other, « de fugitivis ab exercitu quos terriculamenta Puellæ exanimaverant arestandis.»

Note 165, page 38, col. 2.

The social bowl.

Ronsard remarks,

> Rien n'est meilleur pour l'homme soulager
> Après le mal, que le boire et manger.
>   Franciado.

Note 166, page 39, col. 2.

Unplumed casquetel.

A lighter kind of helmet.

Note 167, page 59, col. 2.

Hung from her neck the shield.

The shield was often worn thus : — « Among the Frenchmen there was a young lusty esquire of Gascoigne, named William Marchant, who came out among the foremost into the field, well mounted, his shield about his neck, and his spear in his hand. »—Barnes.

This is frequently alluded to in romance. « Then the knight of the burning sword stept forward, and lifting up his arm as if he would strike Cynocephal on the top of his head, seized with his left hand on the shield, which he pulled to him with so much strength, that plucking it from his neck he brought him to the ground. »—Amadis de Greece.

Sometimes the shield was laced to the shoulder.

The shield of the middle ages must not be confounded with that of the ancients. The knight might easily bear his small shield around his neck; but the Grecian warrior stood *protecting his thighs, and his legs, his breast also and his shoulders with the body of his broad shield.*

> Μηρους τε κνημας τε κατω και στερνα και ωμους
> Ασπιδος ευρειης γαστρι καλυψαμενος.
>   ΤΥΡΤΑΙΟΣ.

But the most convenient shields were used by—

> Ceux qu'on voit demeurer dans les Iles Alandes,
> Qui portent pour pavois, des escailles si grandes,

> Que lors qu'il faut camper, le soldat qui s'en sert
> En fait comme une hutte, et s'y met à couvert.
>   Alaric.

Note 168, page 40, col. 1.

An armet.

The armet or chapelle de fer was an iron hat, occasionally put on by knights when they retired from the heat of the battle to take breath, and at times when they could not with propriety go unarmed.

Note 169, page 41, col. 1.

Fix'd their last kisses on their armed hands.

> Sed contra OEnotria pubes
> Non ullas voces ducis aut præcepta requirit.
> Sat matres stimulant, natique, et cara supinas
> Tendentum palmas lacrimantiaque ora parentum.
> Ostentant parvos, vagituque incita pulsant
> Corda virûm, armatis infigunt oscula dextris,
>   Silius Italicus, xli, 587.

Note 170, page 42, col. 2.

He brake a sullen smile.

> She sternly shook her dewy locks, and brake
> A melancholy smile.
>   Quarles.

Note 171, page 2, col. 2.

——— then on the herald
A robe rich-furr'd and broider'd he bestow'd.

When the armies of England and France lay in the plain between Vironfosse and Flemenguere, 1339, Edward sent to demand a day of battle of the French king. « An herald of the duke of Gueldres, being well skilled in the French tongue, was sent on this errand : he rode forth till he came to the French host, where being admitted before the king and his council, he spake aloud these words, ' Sir, the king of England is here hard by in the fields, and desires to fight you power against power ; and if you please to appoint him a day he will not fail to meet you upon the word of a king.' This message being thus delivered, king Philip yielded either to give or take battle two days after, and in token of his acceptance of the news, richly rewarded the herald with furred gowns, and other gifts bestowed on him, as well by himself as others, the princes and lords of his host, and so dismissed him again.»—Barnes.

Note 172, page 42, col. 2.

And at the third deep sound.

Every man was warned to rise from sleep at the first sound of the trumpet; at the second to arm without delay, and at the third to take horse in his due place under the colours.—Barnes.

Note 173, page 42, col. 2.

To shrive them.

Religious ceremonies seem to have preceded all settled engagements at this period. On the night before the battle of Crecy, « King Edward made a supper in his royal pavilion for all his chief barons, lords, and captains : at which he appeared wonderful chearful and pleasant, to the great encouragement of his people. But when they were all dismissed to their several quarters, the king himself retired into his private oratory, and came before the altar, and there prostrated himself to Almighty God, and devoutly prayed, ' That of his infinite goodness he would vouchsafe to look down on the justice of his cause, and remember his unfeigned endeavours for a reconcilement, altho' they had all been rendered frustrate by his enemies : that if he should be brought to a battle the next day, it would please him of his great mercy to grant him the victory, as his trust was only in him, and in the right which he had given him.' Being thus armed with faith, about midnight he laid himself upon a pallet or mattress to take a little repose : but he arose again betimes and heard mass, with his son the young prince, and received absolution, and the body and blood of his Redeemer, as did the prince also, and most of the lords and others who were so disposed.»—*Barnes.*

Thus also before the battle of Agincourt « after prayers and supplications of the king, his priests, and people, done with great devotion, the king of England in the morning very early set forth his hosts in array.» —*Stowe.*

Note 174, page 42, col. 2.
The shield of dignity.

The roundel. A shield too weak for service, which was borne before the general of an army.

Note 175, page 43, col. 1.
They might meet the battle.

The conduct of the English on the morning of the battle of Crecy is followed in the text. « All things being thus ordered, every lord and captain under his own banner and pennon, and the ranks duly settled, the valorous young king mounted on a lusty white hobby, and with a white wand in his hand, rode between his two marshals from rank to rank, and from one battalia unto another, exhorting and encouraging every man that day to defend and maintain his right and honour : and this he did with so chearful a countenance, and with such sweet and obliging words, that even the most faint-hearted of the army were sufficiently assured thereby. By that time the English were thus prepared; it was nine o'clock in the morning, and then the king commanded them all to take their refreshment of meat and drink, which being done, with small disturbance they all repaired to their colours again, and then laid themselves in their order upon the dry and warm grass, with their bows and helmets by their side, to be more fresh and vigorous upon the approach of the enemy.» —*Joshua Barnes.*

The English before the battle of Azincour « fell prostrate to the ground, and committed themselves to God, every of them tooke in his mouth a little piece of earth, in remembrance that they were mortall and made of earth, as also in remembrance of the holy communion.»— *Stowe.*

Note 176, page 43, col. 2.
To see the pennons rolling their long waves
Before the gale, and banners broad and bright.

The pennon was long, ending in two points, the banner square. « Un seigneur n'etoit banneret et ne pouvoit porter le banniere quarrée, que lors qu'il pouvoit entretenir a ses depens un certain nombre de chevaliers et d'Ecuyers, avec leur suite a la guerre : jusques-la son etendard avoit deux queues ou fanons, et, quand il devenoit plus puissant, son souverain coupoit lui-meme les fanons de son etendard, pour le rendre quarré.»—*Comte de Tressan.*

An incident before the battle of Nagera exemplifies this. « As the two armies approached near together, the prince went over a little hill, in the descending

whereof he saw plainly his enemies marching toward him : wherefore when the whole army was come over this mountain, he commanded that there they should make an halt, and so fit themselves for fight. At that instant the lord John Chandos brought his ensign folded up, and offered it to the prince, saying, 'Sir, here is my guidon : I request your highness to display it abroad, and to give me leave to raise it this day as my banner : for I thank God and your highness, I have lands and possessions sufficient to maintain it withall.' Then the prince took the pennon, and having cut off the tail, made it a square banner, and this done, both he and king Don Pedro for the greater honour, holding it between their hands displayed it abroad, it being or, a sharp pile gules : and then the prince delivered it unto the lord Chandos again, saying, 'Sir John, behold here is your banner. God send you much joy and honour with it.' And thus being made a knight banneret, the lord Chandos returned to the head of his men, and said, ' Here, gentlemen, behold my banner and yours. Take and keep it, to your honour and mine.' And so they took it with a shout, and said by the grace of God and St George they would defend it to the best of their powers. But the banner remained in the hands of a gallant English esquire named William Allestry, who bore it all that day, and acquitted himself in the service right honourably.» — *Barnes.*

Note 177, page 43, col. 2.
Vidames.

This title frequently occurs in the French Chronicles; it was peculiar to France. « the vidame or vicedominus being to the bishop in his temporals as the vicecomes or vicount anciently to the earl, in his judicials.» — *Peter Heylyn.*

Note 178, page 43, col. 2.
And silken surcoats to the mid-day sun
Glittering.

Joshua Barnes seems to have been greatly impressed with the splendour of such a spectacle. « It was a glorious and ravishing sight, no doubt,» says he, « to behold these two armies standing thus regularly embattled in the field, their banners and standards waving in the wind, their proud horses barbed, and kings, lords, knights, and esquires richly armed, and all shining in their surcoats of satin and embroidery.»

Thus also at Poictiers. « there you might have beheld a most beautiful sight of fair harness, of shining steel, feathered crests of glittering helmets, and the rich embroidery of silken surcoats of arms, together with golden standards, banners, and pennons gloriously moving in the air.»

And at Nagera « the sun being now risen, it was a ravishing sight to behold the armies, and the sun reflecting from their bright steel and shining armour. For in those days the cavalry were generally armed in mail or polished steel at all points, and besides that, the nobility wore over their armour rich surtouts of silk and satin embroidery, whereon was curiously sticht or beaten, the arms of their house, whether in colour or metal.»

Note 179, page 43, col. 2.
And their dear country's weal.

Nos ancestres, et notamment du temps de la guerre des Anglois, en combats solemnels et journées assignées,

e mettoient la plus-part du temp tous à pied ; pour ne
e fier à autre chose qu'à leur force propre et viguer
le luer courage et de luer membres, de chose si chere
jue l'honneur et la vie.—*Montaigne*, liv. i, c. 48.

In the battle of Patay, Monstrelet says, « les François
noult de pres mirent pied à terre, et descendirent la
)lus grand partie de leur chevaulx.»

In *El Cavallero Determinado*, an allegorical romance,
ranslated from the French of Olivier de la Marche by
lernando de Acuña, Barcelona, 1565, this custom is
eferred to by Understanding, when giving the knight
irections for his combat with Atropos.

> En esto es mi parecer
> Que en cavallo no te fies ;
> Por lo qual has de entender
> Que de ninguno confies
> Te lymosna y bien hazer.

Note 180, page 43, col. 2.
Their javelins lessen'd to a wieldy length.

Thus at Poictiers, « the three battails being all ready
anged in the field, and every lord in his due place
nder his own banner, command was given that all men
1ould put off their spurs, and cut their spears to five
)ot length, as most commodious for such who had left
1eir horses.»—*Barnes.*

Note 181, page 43, col. 2.
Hræsvelger starting.

> Hræsvelger vocatur
> Qui sedet in extremitate cœli,
> Gigas exuvias amictus aquilæ :
> Ex ejus alis
> Ferunt venire ventum
> Omnes super homines.
> *Vafthrudnismal.*

> Where the Heavens' remotest bound
> With darkness is encompassed round,
> There Hræsvelger sits and swings
> The tempest from his eagle wings.
> *The Edda of Sæmund, transl. by A. S. Cottle.*

At the promontory of Malea on the ruins of the
emple of Apollo, there is a chapel built to the honour
f Michael the archangel. Here we could not but laugh
t the foolish superstition of the sailors, who say, when
1e wind blows from that place, that it is occasioned by
1e violent motion of St Michael's wings, because, for-
)oth, he is painted with wings. And for that reason,
hen they sail by Michael they pray to him that he
1ay hold his wings still.—*Baumgarten.*

Note 182, page 44, col. 1.
Or with the lance protended from his front.

In a combat fought in Smithfield 1467, between the
rd Scales and the bastard of Burgoyne, « the lord
:ales' horse had on his chafron a long sharp pike of
eele, and as the two champions couped together, the
ime horse thrust his pike into the nostrils of the
1stard's horse, so that for very paine, he mounted so
igh that he fell on the one side with his master.»—
)owe.

This weapon is mentioned by Lope de Vega, and by
1 old Scotch poet.

> Unicornio el cavallo parecia
> Con la fuerte pyrámide delante,
> Que en medio del boçal resplandecia
> Como si fuera punta de diamante.
> *Jerusalem Conquistada, l. 10.*

> His horse in fine sandel was trapped to the heele,
> And, in his cheveron biforne,
> Stode as an unicorne,
> Als sharp as a thorne,
> An anlas of stele.
> *Sir Gawan and Sir Galaron.*

The Abyssinians use it at this day; Bruce says it is
a very troublesome useless piece of their armour.

Note 183, page 44, col. 1.
To snatch the shield of death.

Thus did Juba catch up the shield of death to defend
himself from ignominy.—*Cleopatra.*

Note 184, page 44, col. 1.
Their tower of strength.

> Ωσπερ γαρ μιν πυργον εν οφθαλμοισιν ορωσιν.
> ΤΥΡΤΑΙΟΣ.

Quarles has made this expression somewhat ludi-
crous by calling Sampson

> Great army of men, the wonder of whose power
> Gives thee the title of a walking tower.

Note 185, page 44, col. 2.
And when the boar's head.

Two carols for this occasion are preserved in Mr
Ritson's valuable collection of Ancient Songs. The first
of these, here alluded to, is as follows :

> Caput apri defero
> Reddens laudes domino.
> The bore's heed in hand bring I
> With garlands gay and rosemary,
> I pray you all synge merely
> Qui estis in convivio.

> The bore's heed I understande
> Is the chefe servyce in this lande,
> Looke where ever it be fande,
> Servite cum cantico.

> Be gladde lordes bothe more and lasse
> For this hath ordeyned our stewarde,
> To chere you all this christmasse
> The bore's heed with mustarde.

When Henry II had his eldest son crowned as fellow
with him in the kingdom, upon the day of coronation,
king Henry, the father, served his son at the table as
sewer, bringing up the bore's head with trumpets before
it, according to the manner; whereupon (according to
the old adage,

Immutant mores homines cum dantur honores)

the young man conceiving a pride in his heart, beheld
the standers-by with a more stately countenance than
he had been wont. The archbishop of York who sat by
him, marking his behaviour, turned unto him and said,
« Be glad, my good son, there is not another prince in
the world that hath such a sewer at his table.» To
this the new king answered as it were disdainfully thus :
« Why dost thou marvel at that? my father in doing
it thinketh it not more than becometh him, he being
born of princely blood only on the mother's side, serveth
me that am a king born, having both a king to my
father and a queen to my mother.» Thus the young
man of an evil and perverse nature, was puffed up in
pride by his father's unseemly doings.

But the king his father hearing his talk was very
sorrowful in his mind, and said to the archbishop softly
in his ear, « It repenteth me, it repenteth me, my lord,

that I have thus advanced the boy.» For he guessed hereby what a one he would prove afterward, that shewed himself so disobedient and forward already.—*Holinshed.*

Note 186, page 45, col. 1.

Are not like yours so supple in the flight.

Τους δε παλαιοτερους, ων ουκετι γουνατ' ελαρρα,
Μη καταλειποντες φευγετε τους λεραιους
Αισχρον γαρ δη τουτο μετα προμαχοισι πεσοντα.
Κεισθαι προσθε νεων ανδρα πιλαροτερον,
Ηδη λευκον εχοντα καρη, πολιον τε γενειον,
Θυμον αποπνειοντ' αλκιμον εν κονιη.

ΤΥΡΤΑΙΟΣ.

Note 187, page 45, col. 1.

He from the saddle-bow his falchion caught.

In the combat between Francus and Phouere, Ronsard says,

—— de la main leurs coutelas trouverent
Bien aiguisez qui de l'arçon pendoyent.

On this passage the commentator observes, « l'autheur arme ces deux chevaliers à la mode de nos gendarmes François, la lance en la main, la coutelace ou la mace à l'arçon, et l'espée au costé.»

Thus Desmarets says of the troops of Clovis,

A tous pend de l'arçon, à leur mode guerriere,
Et la bache tranchante, et la masee meurtriere.

And when Clovis on foot and without a weapon hears the shrieks of a woman, he sees his horse

Jette l'œil sur l'arçon, et void luire sa bache.

Lope de Vega speaks of the sword being carried in the same manner, when he describes Don Juan de Aguilar as

Desatando del arçon la espada.

Note 188, page 45, col. 1.

The lightning of her sword.

Desnudo el rayo de la ardiente espada.
Jerusalem Conquistada.

Note 189, page 45, col. 1.

The sword of Talbot.

Talbot's sword, says Camden, was found in the river of Dordon, and sold by a peasant to an armourer of Bourdeaux, with this inscription:

Sum Talboti, M. IIII. C. XLIII.
Pro vincere inimicos meos.

But pardon the Latin, for it was not his, but his camping chaplains.—A sword with bad Latin upon it, but good steel within it, says Fuller.

It was not uncommon to bear a motto upon the sword. Lope de Vega describes that of Aguilar as bearing inlaid in gold, a verse of the psalms. It was, he says,

Mas famosa que fue de hombre ceñida,
Para ocasiones del honor guardada,
Y en última defensa de la vida,
Y desde cuya guarnicion dorada
Hasta la punta la canal bruñida
Tenia escrito de David un verso.
Sellado de oro en el acero terso.
Jerusalem Conquistada.

Note 190, page 45, col. 1.

Fastolffe, all fierce and haughty as he was.

In the original letters published by Mr Fenn, Fastolffe appears in a very unfavourable light. Henry Windsor writes thus of him :—« hit is not unknown that cruelle and vengible he hath byn ever, and for the most part withoute pite and mercy. I can no more, but *vade et corripe eum,* for truly he cannot bryng about his matiers in this word (*world*), for the word is not for him. I suppose it wolnot chaunge yett be likeleness, but i besechе you sir help not to amend hym onely, but every other man yf ye kno any mo mysse disposed.»

The order of the garter was taken from Fastolffe for his conduct at Patay. He suffered a more material loss in the money he expended in the service of the state. In 1455, 4083*l*. 15. 7. were due to him for costs and charges during his services in France, « whereof the sayd Fastolffe hath had nouther payement nor assignation.» So he complains.

Note 191, page 45, col. 1.

Battle-axe.

In a battle between the Burgundians and Dauphinois near Abbeville (1421) Monstrelet especially notices the conduct of John Villain, who had that day been made a knight. He was a nobleman from Flanders, very tall, and of great bodily strength, and was mounted on a good horse, holding a battle-axe in both hands. Thus he pushed into the thickest part of the battle, and throwing the bridle on his horse's neck, gave such blows on all sides with his battle-axe, that whoever was struck was instantly unhorsed and wounded past recovery. In this way he met Poton de Xaintrailles, who, after the battle was over, declared the wonders he did, and that he got out of his reach as fast as he could.

Vol. v, p. 294.

Note 192, page 45, col. 2.

His buckler now splinter'd with many a stroke.

L'écu des chevaliers était ordinairement un bouclier de forme à peu près triangulaire, large par le haute pour couvrir le corps, et se terminant en pointe par le bas, afin d'être moins lourd. On les faisait de bois qu'on recouvrait avec du cuir bouilli, avec des nerfs ou autres matières dures, mais jamais de fer ou d'acier. Seulement il était permis, pour les empêcher d'être coupés trop aisément par les épées, d'y mettre un cercle d'or, d'argent, ou de fer, qui les entourât.—*Le Grand.*

Note 193, page 46, col. 1.

Threw o'er the slaughter'd chief his blazon'd coat.

This fact is mentioned in Andrews's History of England. I have merely versified the original expressions. « The herald of Talbot sought out his body among the slain. 'Alas my lord! and is it you! I pray God pardon you all your misdoings. I have been your officer of arms forty years and more: it is time that I should surrender to you the ensigns of my office.' Thus saying, with the tears gushing from his eyes, he threw his coat of arms over the corpse, thus performing one of the ancient rites of sepulture.»

Note 194, page 46, col. 2.

Pour'd on the monarch's head the mystic oil.

The Frenchmen wonderfully reverence this oyle; and at the coronation of their kings, fetch it from the church where it is kept, with great solemnity. For it is brought (saith Sleiden in his commentaries) by the prior sitting on a white ambling palfrey, and attended by his monkes; the archbishop of the town (Rheims) and such bishops as are present, going to the church door to meet it, and leaving for it with the prior some gage, and the king, when it is by the archbishop brought to the altar, bowing himself before it with great reverence.—*Peter Heylyn.*

The Vision of the Maid of Orleans.

Divinity hath oftentimes descended
Upon our slumbers, and the blessed troupes
Have, in the calme and quiet of the soule,
Conversed with us.
SHIRLEY. *The Grateful Servant.*

ADVERTISEMENT.

THE Vision was originally printed as the ninth book of *JOAN of ARC.* The plan and execution of that poem were equally faulty; it has been repeatedly and laboriously corrected; but as the only apology for the great and numerous faults which unavoidably remain, I request the reader to recollect that it was first written at the age of nineteen, and published at the age of one-and-twenty.   R. S.

BOOK I.

ORLEANS was hush'd in sleep.   Stretch'd on her couch
The delegated Maiden lay; with toil
Exhausted, and sore anguish, soon she closed
Her heavy eyelids; not reposing then,
For busy fantasy, in other scenes
Awaken'd: whether that superior powers,
By wise permission, prompt the midnight dream,
Instructing best the passive faculty; [1]
Or that the soul, escaped its fleshly clog,
Flies free, and soars amid the invisible world,
And all things *are* that *seem.* [2]
                              Along a moor,
Barren, and wide, and drear, and desolate,
She roam'd, a wanderer through the cheerless night.
Far through the silence of the unbroken plain
The bittern's boom was heard, hoarse, heavy, deep,
Made accordant music to the scene.
Black clouds, driven fast before the stormy wind,
Swept shadowing; through their broken folds the moon
Struggled at times with transitory ray,
And made the moving darkness visible.
And now arrived beside a fenny lake
She stands, amid whose stagnate waters, hoarse
The long reeds rustled to the gale of night.
An age-worn bark receives the Maid, impell'd
By powers unseen; then did the moon display
Where through the crazy vessel's yawning side
The muddy wave ooz'd in. A female guides,
And spreads the sail before the wind, which moan'd
As melancholy mournful to her ear,
As ever by the wretch was heard
Howling at evening round his prison towers.
Wan was the pilot's countenance, her eyes

Hollow, and her sunk cheeks were furrow'd deep,
Channell'd by tears; a few grey locks hung down
Beneath her hood, and through the Maiden's veins
Chill crept the blood, for, as the night-breeze pass'd,
Lifting her tatter'd mantle, coil'd around
She saw a serpent gnawing at her heart.

The plumeless bat with short shrill note flits by,
And the night-raven's scream came fitfully,
Borne on the hollow blast. Eager the Maid
Look'd to the shore, and now upon the bank
Leaps, joyful to escape, yet trembling still
In recollection.
                        There, a mouldering pile
Stretch'd its wide ruins, o'er the plain below
Casting a gloomy shade, save where the moon
Shone through its fretted windows: the dark yew,
Withering with age, branch'd there its naked roots,
And there the melancholy cypress rear'd
Its head; the earth was heaved with many a mound,
And here and there a half-demolish'd tomb.

And now, amid the ruin's darkest shade,
The Virgin's eye beheld where pale blue flames
Rose wavering, now just gleaming from the earth,
And now in darkness drown'd. An aged man
Sate near, seated on what in long past days
Had been some sculptured monument, now fallen
And half-obscured by moss, and gather'd heaps
Of wither'd yew-leaves and earth-mouldering bones;
His eye was large and rayless, and fix'd full
Upon the Maid; the tomb-fires on his face
Shed a blue light; his face was of the hue
Of death; his limbs were mantled in a shroud.
Then with a deep heart-terrifying voice,
Exclaim'd the spectre—« Welcome to these realms,
These regions of Despair! O thou whose steps
Sorrow hath guided to my sad abodes,
Welcome to my drear empire, to this gloom
Eternal, to this everlasting night,
Where never morning darts the enlivening ray,
Where never shines the sun, but all is dark,
Dark as the bosom of their gloomy king.»

So saying he arose, and drawing on,
Her, to the abbey's inner ruin, led
Resistless.   Through the broken roof the moon
Glimmer'd a scatter'd ray; the ivy twined
Round the dismantled column; imaged forms

Of saints and warlike chiefs, moss-canker'd now
And mutilate, lay strewn upon the ground,
With crumbled fragments, crucifixes fallen,
And rusted trophies.   Meantime over-head
Roar'd the loud blast, and from the tower the owl
Scream'd as the tempest shook her secret nest.
He, silent, led her on, and often paused,
And pointed, that her eye might contemplate
At leisure the drear scene.

      He dragg'd her on
Through a low iron door, down broken stairs;
Then a cold horror through the Maiden's frame
Crept, for she stood amid a vault, and saw,
By the sepulchral lamp's dim glaring light,
The fragments of the dead.

      « Look here!» he cried,
« Damsel, look here! survey this house of death:
O'soon to tenant it! soon to increase
These trophies of mortality! for hence
Is no return.   Gaze here! behold this skull,
These eyeless sockets, and these unflesh'd jaws,
That, with their ghastly grinning, seem to mock
Thy perishable charms; for thus thy cheek
Must moulder.   Child of grief! shrinks not thy Soul,
Viewing these horrors? trembles not thy heart
At the dread thought, that here its life's-blood soon
Shall stagnate, and the finely-fibred frame,
Now warm in life and feeling, mingle soon
With the cold clod? thing horrible to think—
Yet in thought only, for reality
Is none of suffering here; here all is peace,
No nerve will throb to anguish in the grave.
Dreadful it is to think of losing life,
But having lost, knowledge of loss is not,
Therefore no ill.   Haste, Maiden, to repose:
Probe deep the seat of life.»

      So spake Despair.
The vaulted roof echoed his hollow voice,
And all again was silence.   Quick her heart
Panted.   He drew a dagger from his breast,
And cried again, « Haste, Damsel, to repose!
One blow, and rest for ever!»   On the fiend,
Dark scowl'd the Virgin with indignant eye,
And dash'd the dagger down.   He next his heart
Replaced the murderous steel, and drew the Maid
Along the downward vault.

      The damp earth gave
A dim sound as they pass'd: the tainted air
Was cold, and heavy with unwholesome dews.
« Behold!» the fiend exclaim'd, « how gradual here
The fleshly burden of mortality
Moulders to clay!» then fixing his broad eye
Full on her face, he pointed where a corpse
Lay livid; she beheld, with loathing look,
The spectacle abhorr'd by living man.

« Look here!» Despair pursued; « this loathsome mass
Was once as lovely, and as full of life
As, Damsel! thou art now.   Those deep-sunk eyes
Once beam'd the mild light of intelligence,
And where thou seest the pamper'd flesh-worm trail,
Once the white bosom heaved.   She fondly thought
That at the hallow'd altar, soon the priest
Should bless her coming union, and the torch
Its joyful lustre o'er the hail of joy
Cast on her nuptial evening: earth to earth

That priest consign'd her, for her lover went
By glory lured to war, and perish'd there;
Nor she endured to live.   Ha! fades thy cheek?
Dost thou then, Maiden, tremble at the tale?
Look here! behold the youthful paramour!
The self-devoted hero!»

      Fearfully
The Maid look'd down, and saw the well-known face
Of Theodore! in thoughts unspeakable,
Convulsed with horror, o'er her face she clasp'd
Her cold damp hands: «Shrink not,» the phantom cried,
« Gaze on! for ever gaze!»   More firm he grasp'd
Her quivering arm: « this lifeless mouldering clay,
As well thou know'st, was warm with all the glow
Of youth and love; this is the arm that cleaved
Salisbury's proud crest, now motionless in death,
Unable to protect the ravaged frame
From the foul offspring of mortality
That feed on heroes.   Though long years were thine,
Yet never more would life reanimate
This murder'd youth; murder'd by thee! for thou
Didst lead him to the battle from his home,
Else living there in peace to good old age:
In thy defence he died: strike deep! destroy
Remorse with life.»

      The Maid stood motionless,
And, wistless what she did, with trembling hand
Received the dagger.   Starting then, she cried,
« Avaunt, Despair! Eternal Wisdom deals
Or peace to man, or misery, for his good
Alike design'd; and shall the creature cry,
' Why hast thou done this?' and with impious pride
Destroy the life God gave?»

      The fiend rejoin'd,
« And thou dost deem it impious to destroy
The life God gave? What, Maiden, is the lot
Assign'd to mortal man? born but to drag,
Through life's long pilgrimage, the wearying load
Of being; care-corroded at the heart;
Assail'd by all the numerous train of ills
That flesh inherits; till at length worn out,
This is his consummation!—think again!
What, Maiden, canst thou hope from lengthen'd life
But lengthen'd sorrow? If protracted long,
Till on the bed of death thy feeble limbs
Stretch out their languid length, oh think what thoughts,
What agonizing feelings, in that hour,
Assail the sinking heart! Slow beats the pulse,
Dim grows the eye, and clammy drops bedew
The shuddering frame; then in its mightiest force,
Mightiest in impotence, the love of life
Seizes the throbbing heart; the faltering lips
Pour out the impious prayer, that fain would change
The Unchangeable's decree; surrounding friends
Sob round the sufferer, wet his cheek with tears,
And all he loved in life embitters death!

« Such, Maiden, are the pangs that wait the hour
Of calmest dissolution! yet weak man
Dares, in his timid piety, to live;
And, veiling Fear in Superstition's garb,
He calls her Resignation!

      Coward wretch!
Fond coward; thus to make his reason war
Against his reason! Insect as he is,
This sport of chance, this being of a day,

Whose whole existence the next cloud may blast,'
Believes himself the care of heavenly powers,
That God regards man, miserable man,
And, preaching thus of power and providence,
Will crush the reptile that may cross his path!

«Fool that thou art! the Being that permits
Existence, *gives* to man the worthless boon:
A goodly gift to those who, fortune-blest,
Bask in the sunshine of prosperity;
And such do well to keep it. But to one
Sick at the heart with misery, and sore
With many a hard unmerited affliction,
It is a hair that chains to wretchedness
The slave who dares not burst it!

     Thinkest thou,
The parent, if his child should unrecall'd
Return and fall upon his neck, and cry,
' Oh! the wide world is comfortless, and full
Of vacant joys and heart-consuming cares,
I can be only happy in my home
With thee—my friend! my father!' Thinkest thou,
That he would thrust him as an outcast forth?[3]
Oh! he would clasp the truant to his heart,
And love the trespass.»

    Whilst he spake, his eye
Dwelt on the Maiden's cheek, and read her soul
Struggling within. In trembling doubt she stood,
Even as the wretch, whose famish'd entrails crave
Supply, before him sees the poison'd food
In greedy horror.

    Yet, not silent long:
« Eloquent tempter, cease!» the Maiden cried;
« What though affliction be my portion here,
Think'st thou I do not feel high thoughts of joy,
Of heart-ennobling joy, when I look back
Upon a life of duty well perform'd,
Then lift mine eyes to Heaven, and there in faith
Know my reward?—I grant, were this life all,
Was there no morning to the tomb's long night,
If man did mingle with the senseless clod,
Himself as senseless, then wert thou indeed
A wise and friendly comforter!—But, fiend,
There is a morning to the tomb's long night,
A dawn of glory, a reward in heaven,
He shall not gain who never merited.
If thou didst know the worth of one good deed
In life's last hour, thou wouldst not bid me lose
The power to benefit! if I but save
A drowning fly, I shall not live in vain.
I have great duties, fiend! me France expects,
Her heaven-doom'd champion.»

   « Maiden, thou hast done
Thy mission here,» the unbaffled fiend replied;
« The foes are fled from Orleans: thou, perchance,
Exulting in the pride of victory,
Forgettest him who perish'd! yet albeit
Thy harden'd heart forget the gallant youth,
That hour allotted canst thou not escape,
That dreadful hour, when contumely and shame
Shall sojourn in thy dungeon. Wretched Maid!
Destined to drain the cup of bitterness,
Even to its dregs! England's inhuman chiefs
Shall scoff thy sorrows, blacken thy pure fame,
Wit-wanton it with lewd barbarity,
And force such burning blushes to the cheek

Of virgin-modesty, that thou shalt wish
The earth might cover thee! In that last hour,
When thy bruis'd breast shall heave beneath the chains
That link thee to the stake; when o'er thy form
Exposed unmantled, the brute multitude
Shall gaze, and thou shalt hear the ribald taunt,
More painful than the circling flames that scorch
Each quivering member; wilt thou not in vain
Then wish my friendly aid? then wish thine ear
Had drank my words of comfort? that thy hand
Had grasp'd the dagger, and in death preserved
Insulted modesty?»

    Her glowing cheek
Blush'd crimson; her wide eye on vacancy
Was fix'd; her breath short panted. The cold fiend,
Grasping her hand, exclaim'd, « Too timid Maid,
So long repugnant to the healing aid
My friendship proffers, now shalt thou behold
The allotted length of life.»

    He stamp'd the earth,
And, dragging a huge coffin as his car,
Two Gouls came on, of form more fearful-foul
Than ever palsied in her wildest dream
Hag-ridden Superstition. Then Despair
Seized on the Maid whose curdling blood stood still,
And placed her in the seat, and on they pass'd
Adown the deep descent. A meteor light
Shot from the dæmons, as they dragg'd along
The unwelcome load, and mark'd their brethren feast
On carcasses.

    Below, the vault dilates
Its ample bulk. « Look here!»—Despair addrest
The shuddering Virgin, « see the dome of Death!»
It was a spacious cavern, hewn amid
The entrails of the earth, as though to form
The grave of all mankind: no eye could reach,
Though gifted with the eagle's ample ken,
Its distant bounds. There, throned in darkness, dwelt
The unseen power of Death.

    Here stopt the Gouls,
Reaching the destined spot. The fiend leapt out,
And from the coffin as he led the Maid,
Exclaim'd, « Where never yet stood mortal man,
Thou standest: look around this boundless vault:
Observe the dole that Nature deals to man,
And learn to know thy friend.»

    She not replied,
Observing where the Fates their several tasks
Plied ceaseless. « Mark how long the shortest web
Allow'd to man!» he cried; « observe how soon,
Twined round yon never-resting wheel, they change
Their snowy hue, darkening through many a shade,
Till Atropos relentless shuts the shears!»

Too true he spake, for of the countless threads,
Drawn from the heap, as white as unsunn'd snow,
Or as the lovely lily of the vale,
Was never one beyond the little span
Of infancy untainted: few there were
But lightly tinged; more of deep crimson hue,
Or deeper sable dyed.[4] Two genii stood,
Still at the web of being was drawn forth,
Sprinkling their powerful drops. From ebon urn,
The one unsparing dash'd the bitter wave
Of woe; and as he dash'd, his dark-brown brow
Relax'd to a hard smile. The milder form

11

Shed less profusely there his lesser store;
Sometimes with tears increasing the scant boon,
Mourning the lot of man; and happy he
Who on his thread those precious drops receives;
If it be happiness to have the pulse
Throb fast with pity, and in such a world
Of wretchedness, the generous heart that aches
With anguish at the sight of human woe.

To her the fiend, well hoping now success,
« This is thy thread! observe how short the span,
And see how copious yonder genius pours
The bitter stream of woe.» The Maiden saw
Fearless. « Now gaze!» the tempter fiend exclaim'd,
And placed again the poniard in her hand,
For Superstition, with sulphureal torch,
Stalk'd to the loom. « This, Damsel, is thy fate!
The hour draws on—now drench the dagger deep!
Now rush to happier worlds!»
                    The Maid replied,
« Or to prevent or change the will of Heaven,
Impious I strive not: let that will be done!»

BOOK II.

She spake, and lo! celestial radiance beam'd
Amid the air, such odours wafting now
As erst came blended with the evening gale,
From Eden's bowers of bliss. An angel form
Stood by the Maid; his wings, ethereal white,
Flash'd like the diamond in the noon-tide sun,
Dazzling her mortal eye: all else appear'd
Her Theodore.
                    Amazed she saw: the fiend
Was fled, and on her ear the well-known voice
Sounded, though now more musically sweet
Than ever yet had thrill'd her charmed soul,
When eloquent affection fondly told
The day-dreams of delight.
                    « Beloved Maid!
Lo! I am with thee! still thy Theodore!
Hearts in the holy bands of love combined,
Death has no power to sever. Thou art mine!
A little while and thou shalt dwell with me,
In scenes where sorrow is not. Cheerily
Tread thou the path that leads thee to the grave,
Rough though it be and painful, for the grave
Is but the threshold of eternity.

« Favour'd of Heaven; to thee is given to view
These secret realms. The bottom of the abyss
Thou treadest, Maiden! Here the dungeons are
Where bad men learn repentance! souls diseased
Must have their remedy; and where disease
Is rooted deep, the remedy is long
Perforce, and painful.»
                    Thus the spirit spake,
And led the Maid along a narrow path,
Dark gleaming to the light of far-off flames,
More dread than darkness. Soon the distant sound
Of clanking anvils, and the lengthen'd breath
Provoking fire are heard; and now they reach
A wide-expanded den, where all around
Tremendous furnaces, with hellish glare,

Flamed dreadful. At the heaving bellows stood
The meagre form of Care, and as he blew
To augment the fire, the fire augmented scorch'd
His wretched limbs: sleepless for ever thus
He toil'd and toil'd, of toil no end to know,
But endless toil and never-ending woe.

An aged man went round the infernal vault,
Urging his workmen to their ceaseless task:
White were his locks, as is the wintry snow
On hoar Plinlimmon's head. A golden staff
His steps supported; powerful talisman,
Which whoso feels shall never feel again
The tear of pity, or the throb of love.
Touch'd but by this, the massy gates give way,
The buttress trembles, and the guarded wall,
Guarded in vain, submits. Him heathens erst
Had deified, and bowed the suppliant knee
To Plutus. Nor are now his votaries few,
Even though the blessed Teacher of mankind
Hath said, that easier through the needle's eye
Shall the huge camel pass,[5] than the rich man
Enter the gates of heaven. « Ye cannot serve
Your God, and worship Mammon.»
                    « Mission'd Maid!»
So spake the angel, « know that these, whose hands
Round each white furnace ply the unceasing toil,
Were Mammon's slaves on earth. They did not spare
To wring from poverty the hard-earn'd mite,
They robb'd the orphan's pittance, they could see
Want's asking eye unmoved; and therefore these,
Ranged round the furnace, still must persevere
In Mammon's service; scorch'd by these fierce fires,
And frequent deluged by the o'erboiling ore:
Yet still so framed, that oft to quench their thirst
Unquenchable, large draughts of molten gold[6]
They drink insatiate, still with pain renew'd,
Pain to destroy.»
                    So saying, her he led
Forth from the dreadful cavern to a cell,
Brilliant with gem-born light. The rugged walls
Part gleam'd with gold, and part with silver ore
In milder radiance shone. The carbuncle
There its strong lustre like the flamy sun
Shot forth irradiate; from the earth beneath,
And from the roof there stream'd a diamond light;
Rubies and amethysts their glows commix'd
With the gay topaz, and the softer ray
Shot from the sapphire, and the emerald's hue,
And bright pyropus.
                    There on golden seats,
A numerous, sullen, melancholy train
Sat silent. « Maiden, these,» said Theodore,
« Are they who let the love of wealth absorb
All other passions; in their souls that vice
Struck deeply-rooted, like the poison-tree
That with its shade spreads barrenness around.
These, Maid! were men by no atrocious crime
Blacken'd, no fraud, nor ruffian violence:
Men of fair dealing, and respectable
On earth, but such as only for themselves
Heap'd up their treasures, deeming all their wealth
Their own, and given to them, by partial Heaven,
To bless them only: therefore here they sit,
Possess'd of gold enough, and by no pain
Tormented, save the knowledge of the bliss

They lost, and vain repentance. Here they dwell,
Loathing these useless treasures, till the hour
Of general restitution.»
                Thence they pass'd,
And now arrived at such a gorgeous dome,
As even the pomp of eastern opulence
Could never equal: wander'd through its halls
A numerous train; some with the red-swoln eye
Of riot, and intemperance-bloated cheek;
Some pale and nerveless, and with feeble step,
And eyes lack-lustre.
          « Maiden !» said her guide,
« These are the wretched slaves of Appetite,
Curst with their wish enjoy'd. The epicure
Here pampers his foul frame, till the pall'd sense
Loathes at the banquet; the voluptuous here
Plunge in the tempting torrent of delight,
And sink in misery. All they wish'd on earth,
Possessing here, whom have they to accuse
But their own folly, for the lot they chose?
Yet for that these injured themselves alone,
They to the house of Penitence may hie,
And, by a long and painful regimen,
To wearied Nature her exhausted powers
Restore, till they shall learn to form the wish
Of wisdom, and Almighty Goodness grants
That prize to him who seeks it.»
               Whilst he spake,
The board is spread. With bloated paunch, and eye
Fat swoln, and legs whose monstrous size disgraced
The human form divine, their caterer,
Hight Gluttony, set forth the smoking feast.
And by his side came on a brother form,
With fiery cheek of purple hue, and red
And scurfy-white, mix'd motley; his gross bulk,
Like some huge hogshead shapen'd, as applied.
Him had antiquity with mystic rites
Adored; to him the sons of Greece, and thine,
Imperial Rome, on many an altar pour'd
The victim blood, with godlike titles graced,
Bacchus, or Dionusus; son of Jove
Deem'd falsely, for from Folly's idiot form
He sprung, what time Madness, with furious hand,
Seized on the laughing female. At one birth
She brought the brethren, menial here below,
Though sovereigns upon earth, where oft they hold
High revels: 'mid the monastery's gloom,
Thy palace, Gluttony, and oft to thee
The sacrifice is spread, when the grave voice
Episcopal proclaims approaching day
Of visitation, or churchwardens meet
To save the wretched many from the gripe
Of poverty, or 'mid thy ample halls
Of London, mighty mayor! rich aldermen,
Of coming feast hold converse.
               Otherwhere,
For though allied in nature as in blood,
They hold divided sway, his brother lifts
His spungy sceptre. In the noble domes
Of princes, and state-wearied ministers,
Maddening he reigns; and when the affrighted mind
Casts o'er a long career of guilt and blood
Its eye reluctant, then his aid is sought
To lull the worm of conscience to repose.
He, too, the halls of country-squires frequents,
But chiefly loves the learned gloom that shades

Thy offspring, Rhedycina! and thy walls,
Granta! nightly libations there to him
Profuse are pour'd, till from the dizzy brain
Triangles, circles, parallelograms,
Moods, tenses, dialects, and demigods,
And logic, and theology, are swept
By the red deluge.
             Unmolested there
He revels; till the general feast comes round,
The sacrifice septennial, when the sons
Of England meet, with watchful care to chuse
Their delegates, wise, independent men,
Unbribing and unbribed, and chosen to guard
Their rights and charters from the encroaching grasp
Of greedy power; then all the joyful land
Join in his sacrifices, so inspired
To make the important choice.
              The observing Maid
Address'd her guide: « These, Theodore, thou say'st
Are men, who pampering their foul appetites,
Injured themselves alone. But where are they,
The worst of villains, viper-like, who coil
Around the guileless female, so to sting
The heart that loves them ?»
          « Them,» the spirit replied,
« A long and dreadful punishment awaits.
For when, the prey of want and infamy,
Lower and lower still the victim sinks,
Even to the depth of shame, not one lewd word,
One impious imprecation from her lips
Escapes, nay not a thought of evil lurks
In the polluted mind, that does not plead
Before the throne of justice, thunder-tongued
Against the foul seducer.»
             Now they reach'd
The house of Penitence. Credulity
Stood at the gate, stretching her eager head
As though to listen; on her vacant face,
A smile that promised premature assent:
Though her Regret behind, a meagre fiend,
Disciplined sorely.
           Here they enter'd in,
And now arrived where, as in study tranced,
They saw the mistress of the dome. Her face
Spake that composed severity, that knows
No angry impulse, no weak tenderness,
Resolved and calm. Before her lay that Book
Which hath the words of life; and as she read,
Sometimes a tear would trickle down her cheek,
Though heavenly joy beam'd in her eye the while.

Leaving her undisturb'd, to the first ward
Of this great lazar-house, the angel led
The favour'd Maid of Orleans. Kneeling down
On the hard stone which their bare knees had worn,
In sackcloth robed, a numerous train appear'd:
Hard-featured some, and some demurely grave;
Yet such expression stealing from the eye,
As though, that only naked, all the rest
Was one close-fitting mask. A scoffing fiend,
For fiend he was, though wisely serving here,
Mock'd at his patients, and did often pour
Ashes upon them, and then bid them say
Their prayers aloud, and then he louder laugh'd.
For these were hypocrites, on earth revered
As holy ones, who did in public tell

Their beads, and make long prayers, and cross them-
 selves,
And call themselves most miserable sinners,
That so they might be deem'd most pious saints:
And go all filth, and never let a smile
Bend their stern muscles: gloomy, sullen men,
Barren of all affection, and all this
To please their God, forsooth! and therefore Scorn
Grinn'd at his patients, making them repeat
Their solemn farce, with keenest raillery
Tormenting; but if earnest in their prayer,
They pour'd the silent sorrows of the soul
To heaven, then did they not regard his mocks
Which then came painless, and Humility
Soon rescued them, and led to Penitence,
That she might lead to heaven.
      From thence they came
Where, in the next ward, a most wretched band
Groan'd underneath the bitter tyranny
Of a fierce demon. His coarse hair was red,
Pale grey his eyes, and blood-shot: and his face
Wrinkled by such a smile as malice wears
In ecstacy. Well-pleased he went around,
Plunging his dagger in the hearts of some,
Or probing with a poison'd lance their breasts,
Or placing coals of fire within their wounds;
Or seizing some within his mighty grasp,
He fix'd them on a stake, and then drew back
And laugh'd to see them writhe.
      « These,» said the spirit,
« Are taught by Cruelty, to loathe the lives
They led themselves. Here are those wicked men
Who loved to exercise their tyrant power
On speechless brutes; bad husbands undergo
A long purgation here; the traffickers
In human flesh here too are disciplined,
Till by their suffering they have equall'd all
The miseries they inflicted, all the mass
Of wretchedness caused by the wars they waged,
The villages they burnt, the widows left
In want, the slave or led to suicide,
Or murder'd by the foul infected air
Of his close dungeon, or, more sad than all,
His virtue lost, his very soul enslaved,
And driven by woe to wickedness.
      These next,
Whom thou beholdest in this dreary room,
So sullen, and with such an eye of hate
Each on the other scowling, these have been
False friends. Tormented by their own dark thoughts,
Here they dwell: in the hollow of their hearts
There is a worm that feeds, and though thou seest
That skilful leech who willingly would heal
The ill they suffer, judging of all else
By their own evil standard, they suspect
The aid he vainly proffers, lengthening thus
By vice its punishment.»
      « But who are these,»
The Maid exclaim'd, « that, robed in flowing lawn,
And mitred, or in scarlet, and in caps,
Like cardinals, I see in every ward,
Performing menial service at the beck
Of all who bid them?»
      Theodore replied,
« These men are they who in the name of Christ
Have heap'd up wealth, and arrogating power,

Have made men bow the knee, and call'd themselves
Most reverend graces and right reverend lords.
They dwelt in palaces, in purple clothed,
And in fine linen: therefore are they here;
And though they would not minister on earth,
Here penanced they perforce must minister:
Did not the Holy One of Nazareth
Tell them, his kingdom is not of the world?»

So saying, on they pass'd, and now arrived
Where such a hideous ghastly group abode,
That the Maid gazed with half-averting eye,
And shudder'd: each one was a loathly corpse,
The worm did banquet on his putrid prey,
Yet had they life and feeling exquisite,
Though motionless and mute.
      « Most wretched men
Are these,» the angel cried. « These, JOAN, are bards
Whose loose lascivious lays perpetuated
Their own corruption. Soul-polluted slaves,
Who sate them down, deliberately lewd,
So to awake and pamper lust in minds
Unborn; and therefore foul of body now
As then they were of soul, they here abide
Long as the evil works they left on earth
Shall live to taint mankind. A dreadful doom!
Yet amply merited by that bad man
Who prostitutes the sacred gift of song!»

And now they reach'd a huge and massy pile,
Massy it seem'd, and yet in every blast
As to its ruin shook. There, porter fit,
Remorse for ever his sad vigils kept.
Pale, hollow-eyed, emaciate, sleepless wretch,
Inly he groan'd, or, starting, wildly shriek'd,
Aye as the fabric tottering from its base,
Threatened its fall, and so expectant still
Lived in the dread of danger still delay'd.
They enter'd there a large and lofty dome,
O'er whose black marble sides a dim drear light
Struggled with darkness from the unfrequent lamp.
Enthroned around, the murderers of mankind,
Monarchs, the great! the glorious! the august!
Each bearing on his brow a crown of fire,
Sat stern and silent. Nimrod, he was there,
First king, the mighty hunter; and that chief
Who did belie his mother's fame, that so
He might be called young Ammon. In this court
Cæsar was crown'd, accurst liberticide;
And he who murdered Tully, that cold villain,
Octavius, though the courtly minion's lyre
Hath hymn'd his praise, though Maro sang to him,
And when death levell'd to original clay
The royal carcass, Flattery, fawning low,
Fell at his feet, and worshipped the new god.
Titus was here,7 the conqueror of the Jews,
He the delight of human kind mis-named;
Cæsars and Soldans, emperors and kings,
Here they were all, all who for glory fought,
Here in the court of glory, reaping now
The meed they merited.
      As gazing round
The Virgin mark'd the miserable train,
A deep and hollow voice from one went forth;
« Thou who art come to view our punishment,
Maiden of Orléans! hither turn thine eye,

For I am he whose bloody victories
Thy power hath rendered vain. Lo! I am here,
The hero conqueror of Agincourt,
Henry of England!—wretched that I am,
I might have reign'd in happiness and peace,
My coffers full, my subjects undisturb'd,
And Plenty and Prosperity had loved
To dwell amongst them : but mine eye beheld
The realm of France, by faction tempest-torn,
And therefore I did think that it would fall
An easy prey. I persecuted those
Who taught new doctrines, though they taught the
truth :
And when I heard of thousands by the sword
Cut off, or blasted by the pestilence,
I calmly counted up my proper gains,
And sent new herds to slaughter. Temperate
Myself, no blood that mutinied, no vice :
Tainting my private life, I soul-brand!
Murder and rape ; and therefore am I doom'd,
Like these imperial sufferers, crown'd with fire,
Here to remain, till man's awaken'd eye
Shall see the genuine blackness of our deeds,
And warn'd by them, till the whole human race,
Equalling in bliss the aggregate we caused
Of wretchedness, shall form one brotherhood,
One universal family of love.»

BOOK III.

The Maiden, musing on the warrior's words,
Turn'd from the hall of glory. Now they reach'd
A cavern, at whose mouth a genius stood,
In front a beardless youth, whose smiling eye
Beam'd promise, but behind, wither'd and old,
And all unlovely. Underneath his feet
Lay records trampled, and the laurel-wreath
Now rent and faded : in his hand he held
An hour-glass, and as fall the restless sands,
So pass the lives of men. By him they pass'd
Along the darksome cave, and reach'd a stream,
Still rolling onward its perpetual waves,
Noiseless and undisturb'd. Here they ascend
A bark unpiloted, that down the flood,
Borne by the current, rush'd. The circling stream,
Returning to itself, an island form'd ;
Nor had the Maiden's footsteps ever reach'd
The insulated coast, eternally
Rapt round the endless course ; but Theodore
Drove with an angel's will the obedient bark.

They land ; a mighty fabric meets their eyes,
Seen by its gem-born light. Of adamant
The pile was fram'd, for ever to abide
Firm in eternal strength. Before the gate
Stood eager Expectation, as to list
The half-heard murmurs issuing from within,
Her mouth half-open'd and her head stretch'd forth
On the other side there stood an aged crone,
Listening to every breath of air ; she knew
Vague suppositions and uncertain dreams,
Of what was soon to come, for she would mark
The little glow-worm's self-created light,
And argue thence of kingdoms overthrown',

And desolated nations ; ever fill'd
With undetermined terror, as she heard
Or distant screech-owl, or the regular beat
Of evening death-watch.
                                «Maid,» the spirit cried,
« Here, robed in shadows, dwells Futurity.
There is no eye hath seen her secret form,
For round the Mother of Time eternal mists
Hover. If thou wouldst read the book of fate,
Go in!»
            The Damsel for a moment paused,
Then to the angel spake : « All-gracious Heaven!
Benignant in withholding, hath denied
To man that knowledge. I, in faith assured,
That he, my heavenly Father, for the best
Ordaineth all things, in that faith remain
Contented.»
                « Well and wisely hast thou said,»
So Theodore replied ; « and now, O Maid!
Is there amid this boundless universe
One whom thy soul would visit? Is there place
To memory dear, or vision'd out by hope,
Where thou wouldst now be present? Form the wish,
And I am with thee, there.»
                                His closing speech
Yet sounded on her ear, and lo! they stood
Swift as the sudden thought that guided them,
Within the little cottage that she loved.
« He sleeps! the good man sleeps!» enrapt she cried,
As bending o'er her uncle's lowly bed
Her eye retraced his features. « See the beads
Which never morn nor night he fails to tell,
Remembering me, his child, in every prayer.
Oh! quiet be thy sleep, thou dear old man!
Good angels guard thy rest! and when thine hour
Is come, as gently mayest thou wake to life,
As when through yonder lattice the next sun
Shall bid thee to thy morning orisons!»

« Thy voice is heard,» the angel guide rejoin'd,
« He sees thee in his dreams, he hears thee breathe
Blessings, and happy is the good man's rest.
Thy fame has reach'd him, for who has not heard
Thy wondrous exploits? and his aged heart
Hath felt the deepest joy that ever yet
Made his glad blood flow fast. Sleep on, old Claude!
Peaceful, pure spirit, be thy sojourn here,
And short and soon thy passage to that world
Where friends shall part no more !
                                Does thy soul own
No other wish? or sleeps poor Madelon
Forgotten in her grave? . . . Seest thou yon star,»
The spirit pursued, regardless of her eye
That look'd reproach ; « seest thou that evening star
Whose lovely light so often we beheld
From yonder woodbine porch? how have we gazed
Into the dark deep sky, till the baffled soul,
Lost in the infinite, return'd, and felt
The burthen of her bodily load, and yearn'd
For freedom! Maid, in yonder evening star
Lives thy departed friend. I read that glance,
And we are there!»
                        He said, and they had past
The immeasurable space.
                                Then on her ear
The lonely song of adoration rose,

Sweet as the cloister'd virgin's vesper hymn,
Whose spirit, happily dead to earthly hopes,
Already lives in heaven. Abrupt the song
Ceased, tremulous and quick a cry
Of joyful wonder roused the astonish'd Maid,
And instant Madelon was in her arms;
No airy form, no unsubstantial shape:
She felt her friend, she prest her to her heart,
Their tears of rapture mingled.

     She drew back,
And eagerly she gazed on Madelon,
Then fell upon her neck again and wept.
No more she saw the long-drawn lines of grief,
The emaciate form, the hue of sickliness,
The languid eye: youth's loveliest freshness now
Mantled her cheek, whose every lineament
Bespake the soul at rest, a holy calm,
A deep and full tranquillity of bliss.

« Thou then art come, my first and dearest friend!»
The well known voice of Madelon began;
« Thou then art come! and was thy pilgrimage
So short on earth? and was it painful too,
Painful and short as mine? But blessed they
Who from the crimes and miseries of the world
Early escape!»

    « Nay,» Theodore replied,
« She hath not yet fulfill'd her mortal work.
Permitted visitant from earth she comes
To see the seat of rest, and oftentimes
In sorrow shall her soul remember this,
And, patient of her transitory woe,
Partake the anticipated peace again.»
« Soon be that work perform'd!» the Maid exclaim'd:
« O Madelon! O Theodore! my soul,
Spurning the cold communion of the world,
Will dwell with you! but I shall patiently,
Yea even with joy, endure the allotted ills
Of which the memory in this better state
Shall heighten bliss. That hour of agony,
When, Madelon, I felt thy dying grasp,
And from thy forehead wiped the dews of death,
The very horrors of that hour assume
A shape that now delights.»

     « O earliest friend!
I too remember,» Madelon replied,
« That hour, thy looks of watchful agony,
The suppress'd grief that struggled in thine eye
Endearing love's last kindness. Thou didst know
With what a deep and melancholy joy
I felt the hour draw on: but who can speak
The unutterable transport, when mine eyes,
As from a long and dreary dream, unclosed
Amid this peaceful vale, unclosed upon
My Arnaud; he had built me up a bower,
A bower of rest.—See, Maiden, where he comes,
His manly lineaments, his beaming eye
The same, but now a holier innocence
Sits on his cheek, and loftier thoughts illume
The enlighten'd glance.»

     They met: what joy was theirs
He best can feel, who for a dear friend dead
Hath wet the midnight pillow with his tears.

Fair was the scene around; an ample vale
Whose mountain circle at the distant verge
Lay soften'd on the sight; the near ascent

Rose bolder up, in part abrupt and bare,
Part with the ancient majesty of woods
Adorn'd, or lifting high its rocks sublime.
The river's liquid radiance roll'd beneath,
Beside the bower of Madelon it wound
A broken stream, whose shallows, though the waves
Roll'd on their way with rapid melody,
A child might tread. Behind, an orange-grove,
Its gay green foliage starr'd with golden fruit;
But with what odours did their blossoms load
The passing gale of eve! less thrilling sweet
Rose from the marble's perforated floor,
Where kneeling at her prayers, the Moorish queen
Inhaled the cool delight, [8] and whilst she ask'd
The prophet for his promised paradise,
Shaped from the present scene its utmost joys.
A goodly scene! fair as that faery land
Where Arthur lives, by ministering spirits borne
From Camlan's bloody banks: or as the groves
Of earliest Eden, where, so legends say,
Enoch abides, and he who, rapt away
By fiery steeds, and chariotted in fire,
Pass'd in his mortal form the eternal ways;
And John, beloved of Christ, enjoying there
The beatific vision, sometimes seen
The distant dawning of eternal day,
Till all things be fulfilled.

     « Survey this scene!»
So Theodore address'd the Maid of Arc;
« There is no evil here, no wretchedness,
It is the heaven of those who nurst on earth
Their nature's gentlest feelings. Yet not here
Centering their joys, but with a patient hope,
Waiting the allotted hour when capable
Of loftier callings, to a better state
They pass; and hither from that better state
Frequent they come, preserving so those ties
Which through the infinite progressiveness
Complete our perfect bliss.

     « Even such, so bless'd,
Save that the memory of no sorrows past
Heighten'd the present joy, our world was once,
In the first æra of its innocence,
Ere man had learnt to bow the knee to man.
Was there a youth whom warm affection fill'd,
He spake his honest heart; the earliest fruits
His toil produced, the sweetest flowers that deck'd
The sunny bank, he gather'd for the maid,
Nor she disdain'd the gift: for Vice not yet
Had burst the dungeons of her hell, and rear'd
Those artificial boundaries that divide
Man from his species. State of blessedness!
Till that ill-omen'd hour when Cain's stern son
Delv'd in the bowels of the earth for gold,
Accursed bane of virtue,.... of such force
As poets feign dwelt in the Gorgon's locks,
Which whoso saw, felt instant the life-blood
Cold curdle in his veins, the creeping flesh
Grew stiff with horror, and the heart forgot
To beat. Accursed hour! for man no more
To Justice paid his homage, but forsook
Her altars, and bow'd down before the shrine
Of Wealth and Power, the idols he had made.
Then hell enlarged herself, her gates flew wide,
Her legion fiends rush'd forth. Oppression came,
Whose frown is desolation, and whose breath

Blasts like the pestilence; and Poverty,
A meagre monster, who with withering touch
Makes barren all the better part of man,
Mother of Miseries.   Then the goodly earth
Which God had framed for happiness, became
One theatre of woe, and all that God
Had given to bless free men, these tyrant fiends
His bitterest curses made.   Yet for the best
Hath he ordained all things, the All-wise!
For by experience roused shall man at length
Dash down his Moloch-idols, Samson-like,
And burst his fetters, only strong while he
Fears for their strength.   Then in the deep abyss
Oppression shall be chain'd, and Poverty
Die, and with her her brood of miseries;
And Virtue and Equality preserve
The reign of Love, and earth shall once again
Be paradise, where Wisdom shall secure
The state of bliss which Ignorance betray'd »

« Oh age of happiness!» the Maid exclaim'd,
«Roll fast thy current, Time, till that bless'd age
Arrive! and happy thou, my Theodore,
Permitted thus to see the sacred depths
Of Wisdom!»

                    « Such,» the blessed spirit replied,
« Beloved! such our lot: allowed to range
The vast infinity, progressive still
In knowledge and increasing blessedness,
This our united portion.   Thou hast yet
A little while to sojourn amongst men:
I will be with thee! there shall not a breeze
Wanton around thy temples, on whose wing
I will not hover near! and at that hour
When from its fleshly sepulchre let loose,
Thy phœnix soul shall soar, O best-beloved!
I will be with thee in thine agonies,
And welcome thee to life and happiness,
Eternal infinite beatitude!»

He spake, and led her near a straw-roof'd cot,
Love's palace.   By the virtues circled there,
The cherub listen'd to such melodies,
As aye, when one good deed is register'd
Above, re-echo in the halls of heaven.
Labour was there, his crisp locks floating loose,
Clear was his cheek, and beaming his full eye,
And strong his arm robust; the wood-nymph Health
Still follow'd on his path, and where he trod
Fresh flowers and fruits arose.   And there was Hope,
The general friend; and Pity, whose mild eye
Wept o'er the widow'd dove: and loveliest form,
Majestic Chastity, whose sober smile
Delights and awes the soul; a laurel-wreath
Restrain'd her tresses, and upon her breast
The snow-drop hung its head. 9 that seem'd to grow
Spontaneous cold and fair: still by the maid
Love went submiss, with eye more dangerous
Than fancied basilisk to wound whoe'er
Too bold approach'd; yet anxious would he read
Her every rising wish, then only pleased
When pleasing. Hymning him the song was raised.

« Glory to thee whose vivifying power
Pervades all Nature's universal frame!
Glory to thee, Creator Love! to thee,
Parent of all the smiling Charities,

That strew the thorny path of life with flowers!
Glory to thee, Preserver! To thy praise
The awakened woodlands echo all the day
Their living melody; and warbling forth
To thee her twilight song, the nightingale
Holds the lone traveller from his way, or charms
The listening poet's ear. Where Love shall deign
To fix his seat, there blameless Pleasure sheds
Her roseate dews; Content will sojourn there,
And Happiness behold affection's eye
Gleam with the mother's smile.   Thrice happy he
Who feels thy holy power! He shall not drag,
Forlorn and friendless, along life's long path
To age's drear abode; he shall not waste
The bitter evening of his days unsoothed;
But Hope shall cheer his hours of solitude,
And Vice shall vainly strive to wound his breast,
That bears that talisman; and when he meets
The eloquent eye of Tenderness, and hears
The bosom-thrilling music of her voice,
The joy he feels shall purify his soul,
And imp it for anticipated heaven.»

NOTES.

Note 1, page 79, col. 1.

Passive faculty.

MAY says of Serapis,

Erudit at placide humanam per somnia mentem,
Nocturnâque quiete docet; nulloque labore
Hic tantum parta est pretiosa scientia, nullo
Excutitur studio rerum.   Mortalia corda
Tunc Deus iste docet, cum sunt minus apta doceri,
Cum nullum obsequium præstant, meritisque fatentur
Nil sese debere suis; tunc recta scientes
Cum nil scire valent.   Non illo tempore sensus
Humanos forsan dignatur numen inire,
Cum propriis possunt per se discursibus uti,
Ne forte humanâ ratio divina coiret.
                                        Sup. Lucani.

Note 2, page 79, col. 1.

And all things are that seem.

I have met with a singular tale to illustrate this spiritual theory of dreams:—Guntrum, king of the Franks, was liberal to the poor, and he himself experienced the wonderful effects of divine liberality. One day as he was hunting in a forest he was separated from his companions, and arrived at a little stream of water with only one comrade. Here he found himself oppressed by drowsiness, and reclining his head upon the servant's lap went to sleep.   The servant saw a little beast creep out of the mouth of his sleeping master, and go immediately to the streamlet, which it vainly attempted to cross; he drew his sword and laid it across the water, over which the little beast past and crept into a hole of a mountain on the opposite side; from whence it made its appearance again in an hour, and returned by the same means into the king's mouth.   The king then awakened, and told his companion he had dreamt that he was arrived upon the bank of an immense river, which he had crossed by a bridge of iron, and from thence came to a mountain in which a great quantity of gold was concealed. The servant then related what he had beheld, and they both went to examine the mountain, where upon digging they discovered an immense weight of gold.—I stumbled upon this tale in a book entitled SPHINX, Theo-

logico-Philosophica. Autore Johanne Hiedfeldio, Ecclesiaste Ebersbachiano. 1621.

The same story is in Matthew of Westminster; it is added that Guntrum applied the treasures thus found to pious uses. For the truth of this theory there is the evidence of a monkish miracle. When Thurcillus was about to follow St Julian and visit the world of souls, his guide said to him, «Let thy body rest in the bed, for thy spirit only is about to depart with me; and lest the body should appear dead, I will send into it a vital breath.» The body, however, by a strange sympathy, was affected like the spirit; for when the foul and fetid smoke which arose from the tithes withheld on earth had nearly suffocated Thurcillus, and made him cough twice, those who were near his body said that it coughed twice about the same time.—*Matthew Paris.*

Note 3, page 81, col. 1.
An outcast forth.

Werter.

Note 4, page 81, col. 2.
Or deeper sable dyed.

These lines strongly resemble a passage in the Pharonnida of William Chamberlayne, who has told an interesting story in uncouth rhymes, and mingled sublimity of thought and beauty of expression with the quaintest conceits, and most awkward inversions.

> On a rock more high
> Than Nature's common surface, she beholds
> The mansion house of Fate, which thus unfolds
> Its sacred mysteries. A trine within
> A quadrate placed, both these encompast in
> A perfect circle was its form; but what
> Its matter was, for us to wonder at,
> Is undiscover'd left. A tower there stands
> At every angle, where Time's fatal hands
> The impartial Parcœ dwell; i' the first she sees
> Clotho the kindest of the Destinies,
> From immaterial essences to cull
> The seeds of life, and of them frame the wool
> For Lachesis to spin; about her flie
> Myriads of souls, that yet want flesh to lie
> Warm'd with their functions in, whose strength bestows
> That power by which man ripe for misery grows.
>
> Her next of objects was that glorious tower
> Where that swift-finger'd nymph that spares no hour
> From mortals' service, draws the various threads
> Of life in several lengths; to weary beds
> Of age extending some, whilst others in
> Their infancy are broke: *some blackt in sin,
> Others, the favourites of Heaven, from whence
> Their origin, candid with innocence;
> Some purpled in afflictions, others dyed
> In sanguine pleasures:* some in glittering pride
> Spun to adorn the earth, whilst others wear
> Rags of deformity, but knots of care
> No thread was wholly free from. Next to this
> Fair glorious tower, was placed that black abyss
> Of dreadful Atropos, the baleful seat
> Of death and horrour, in each room repleat
> With lazy damps, loud groans, and the sad sight
> Of pale grim ghosts, those terrours of the night,
> To this, the last stage that the winding clew
> Of life can lead mortality unto,
> Fear was the dreadful porter, which let in
> All guests sent thither by destructive sin.

It is possible that I may have written from the recollection of this passage. The conceit is the same, and I willingly attribute it to Chamberlayne, a poet to whom I am indebted for many hours of delight.

Note 5, page 82, col. 2.
Shall the huge camel pass.

I had originally written *cable* instead of *camel.* The alteration would not be worth noticing were it not for the circumstance which occasioned it. *Facilius elephas per foramen acus,* is among the Hebrew adages collected by Drusius; the same metaphor is found in two other Jewish proverbs, and this appears to determine the signification of καμηλος, Matt. xix, 24.

Note 6, page 82, col. 2.
Large draughts of molten gold.

The same idea, and almost the same words, are in one of Ford's plays. The passage is a very fine one:

> There is a place,
> (List, daughter!) in a black and hollow vault,
> Where day is never seen; there shines no sun,
> But flaming horror of consuming fires;
> A lightless sulphur, choak'd with smoaky foggs
> Of an infected darkness. In this place
> Dwell many thousand thousand sundry sorts
> Of never-dying deaths: there damned souls
> Roar without pity, there are gluttons fed
> With toads and adders: there is burning oil
> Pour'd down the drunkard's throat, *the usurer
> Is forced to sup whole draughts of molten gold;*
> There is the murderer for ever stabb'd,
> Yet he can never die; there lies the wanton
> On racks of burning steel, whilst in his soul
> He feels the torment of his raging lust.
> 'T is pity she 's a Whore.

I wrote this passage when very young, and the idea, trite as it is, was new to me. It occurs I believe in most descriptions of hell, and perhaps owes its origin to the fate of Crassus.

Note 7, page 84, col. 2.
Titus was here.

During the siege of Jerusalem, «the Roman commander, *with a generous clemency, that inseparable attendant on true heroism,* laboured incessantly, and to the very last moment, to preserve the place. With this view, he again and again intreated the tyrants to surrender and save their lives. With the same view also, after carrying the second wall, the siege was intermitted four days: to rouse their fears, *prisoners to the number of five hundred or more, were crucified daily before the walls; till space,* Josephus says, *was wanting for the crosses, and crosses for the captives.»—Churton's Bampton Lectures.*

If any of my readers should enquire why Titus Vespasian, the delight of mankind, is placed in such a situation — I answer, for this instance of «*his generous clemency, that inseparable attendant on true heroism!* »

Note 8, page 86, col. 2.
Inhaled the cool delight.

In the cabinet of the Alhambra where the queen used to dress and say her prayers, and which is still an enchanting sight, there is a slab of marble full of small holes, through which perfumes exhaled that were kept constantly burning beneath. The doors and windows are disposed so as to afford the most agreeable prospects, and to throw a soft yet lively light upon the eyes. Fresh currents of air too renew every instant the delicious coolness of this apartment.—*From the sketch of the History of the Spanish Moors, prefixed to Florian's Gonsalvo of Cordova.*

Note 9, page 87, col. 1.
The snow-drop hung its head.

The grave matron does not perceive how time has impaired her charms, but decks her faded bosom with the same snow-drop that seems to grow on the breast of the virgin.—P. H.

Thalaba the Destroyer.

A RHYTHMICAL ROMANCE.

Ποιημάτων ακρατης η ελευθερια, και νομος εις, το δοξαν τω ποιητη.

LUCIAN, *Quomodo Hist. Scribenda.*

PREFACE.

In the continuation of the Arabian Tales, the Dom-daniel is mentioned; a Seminary for evil Magicians, under the Roots of the Sea. From this seed the present Romance has grown. Let me not be supposed to prefer the rhythm in which it is written, abstractedly considered, to the regular blank verse; the noblest measure, in my judgment, of which our admirable language is capable. For the following Poem I have preferred it, because it suits the varied subject; it is the *Arabesque* ornament of an Arabian tale.

The dramatic sketches of Dr Sayers, a volume which no lover of poetry will recollect without pleasure, induced me, when a young versifier, to practise in this rhythm. I felt that while it gave the poet a wider range of expression, it satisfied the ear of the reader. It were easy to make a parade of learning, by enumerating the various feet which it admits; it is only needful to observe, that no two lines are employed in *sequence* which can be read into one. Two six-syllable lines, it will perhaps be answered, compose an Alexandrine: the truth is, that the Alexandrine, when harmonious, is composed of two six-syllable lines.

One advantage this metre assuredly possesses, ... the dullest reader cannot distort it into discord: he may read it prosaically, but its flow and fall will still be perceptible. Verse is not enough favoured by the English reader: perhaps this is owing to the obtrusiveness, the regular Jews'-harp *twing-twang*, of what has been foolishly called heroic measure. I do not wish the *improvisatore* tune;.. but something that denotes the sense of harmony, something like the accent of feeling,... like the tone which every Poet necessarily gives to Poetry.

Cintra, October, 1800.

BOOK I.

—— Worse and worse, young Orphane, be thy payne,
If * * thou due vengeance doe forbeare,
Till guiltie blood her guerdon do obtayne.
Faery Queen, B. 2. Can. 1.

I.

How beautiful is night!
A dewy freshness fills the silent air,
No mist obscures, nor cloud, nor speck, nor stain,
Breaks the serene of heaven:
In full-orb'd glory yonder Moon divine
Rolls through the dark blue depths.
Beneath her steady ray
The desert-circle spreads,
Like the round ocean, girdled with the sky.[1]
How beautiful is night!

II.

Who at this untimely hour
Wanders o'er the desert sands?
No station is in view,
Nor palm-grove islanded amid the waste.
The mother and her child,
The widowed mother and the fatherless boy,
They at this untimely hour
Wander o'er the desert sands.

III.

Alas! the setting sun
Saw Zeinab in her bliss,[2]
Hodeirah's wife belov'd,
Alas! the wife belov'd,
The fruitful mother late,
Whom when the daughters of Arabia nam'd,
They wished their lot like her's:
She wanders o'er the desert sands
A wretched widow now,
The fruitful mother of so fair a race,
With only one preserv'd,
She wanders o'er the wilderness.

IV.

No tear reliev'd the burthen of her heart;
Stunn'd with the heavy woe, she felt like one
Half-waken'd from a midnight dream of blood.
But sometimes when the boy
Would wet her hand with tears,
And, looking up to her fix'd countenance,
Sob out the name of MOTHER, then did she
Utter a feeble groan,
At length collecting, Zeinab turn'd her eyes
To heaven, exclaiming, « Praised be the Lord!
He gave, he takes away![3]
The Lord our God is good!»

I 2

V.

« Good is he?» cried the boy,
« Why are my brethren and my sisters slain?
Why is my father kill'd?
Did ever we neglect our prayers,
Or ever lift à hand unclean to heaven?
Did ever stranger from our tent
Unwelcom'd turn away?
Mother, he is not good!»

VI.

Then Zeinab beat her breast in agony,
« O God, forgive my child!
He knows not what he says!
Thou know'st I did not teach him thoughts like these:
O Prophet, pardon him!»

VII.

She had not wept till that assuaging prayer, ..
The fountains of her eyes were open'd then,
And tears reliev'd her heart.
She rais'd her swimming eyes to heaven,
« Allah, thy will be done!
Beneath the dispensation of thy wrath
I groan, but murmur not.
A day will come, when all things that are dark
Will be made clear;.. then shall I know, O Lord,
Why in thy mercy thou hast stricken me!
Then see and understand what now
My heart believes and feels!»

VIII.

Young Thalaba in silence heard reproof,
His brow in manly frowns was knit,
With manly thoughts his heart was full.
« Tell me who slew my father?» cried the boy.
Zeinab replied and said,
« I knew not that there liv'd thy father's foe.
The blessings of the poor for him
Went daily up to Heaven,
In distant lands the traveller told his praise;..
I did not think there liv'd
Hodeirah's enemy.»

IX.

« But I will hunt him through the earth!»
Young Thalaba exclaim'd.
« Already I can bend my father's bow,
Soon will my arm have strength
To drive the arrow-feathers to his heart.»

X.

Zeinab replied, « O Thalaba, my child,
Thou lookest on to distant days,
And we are in the desert, far from men!»

XI.

Not till that moment her afflicted heart
Had leisure for the thought.
She cast her eyes around:
Alas! no tents were there
Beside the bending sands;
No palm-tree rose to spot the wilderness.
The dark blue sky clos'd round,
And rested like a dome[4]
Upon the circling waste.

She cast her eyes around,
Famine and Thirst were there ..
And then the wretched Mother bowed her head,
And wept upon her child.

XII.

A sudden cry of wonder
From Thalaba arous'd her;
She rais'd her head, and saw
Where high in air a stately palace rose.
Amid a grove embower'd
Stood the prodigious pile;
Trees of such ancient majesty
Tower'd not on Yemen's happy hills,
Nor crown'd the stately brow of Lebanon.
Fabric so vast, so lavishly enrich'd,
For Idol, or for Tyrant, never yet
Rais'd the slave race of man,
In Rome, nor in the elder Babylon,
Nor old Persepolis,
Nor where the family of Greece
Hymn'd Eleutherian Jove.
Here studding azure tabletures [5]
And ray'd with feeble light,
Star-like the ruby and the diamond shone:
Here on the golden towers
The yellow moon-beam lay,
Here with white splendour floods the silver wall.
Less wonderous pile and less magnificent
Sennamar built at Hirah,[6] though his art
Seal'd with one stone the ample edifice,
And made its colours, like the serpent's skin,
Play with a changeful beauty: him, its Lord,
Jealous lest after effort might surpass
The now unequall'd palace, from its height
Dash'd on the pavement down.

XIII.

They enter'd, and through aromatic paths
Wondering they went along.
At length, upon a mossy bank,
Beneath a tall mimosa's shade,
Which o'er him bent its living canopy,
They saw a man reclin'd.
Young he appear'd, for on his cheek there shone
The morning glow of health,
And the brown beard curl'd close around his chin.
He slept, but at the sound
Of coming feet awaking, fix'd his eyes
In wonder, on the wanderer and her child.
« Forgive us,» Zeinab cried,
« Distress hath made us bold.
Relieve the widow and the fatherless!
Blessed are they who succour the distrest;
For them hath God appointed Paradise.»

XIV.

He heard, and he look'd up to heaven,
And tears ran down his cheeks:
« It is a human voice!
I thank thee, O my God!..
How many an age hath past
Since the sweet sounds have visited my ear!
I thank thee, O my God.
It is a human voice!»

XV.

To Zeinab turning then, he cried,
« O mortal, who art thou,
Whose gifted eyes have pierced
The shadow of concealment that hath wrapt
These bowers, so many an age,
From eye of mortal man?
For countless years have past,
And never foot of man
The bowers of Irem trod, . .
Save only I, a miserable wretch
From Heaven and Earth shut out!»

XVI.

Fearless, and scarce surpris'd
For grief in Zeinab's soul
All other feelings overpower'd,
She answer'd, « Yesterday
I was a wife belov'd,
The fruitful mother of a numerous race.
I am a widow now,
Of all my offspring this alone is left.
Praise to the Lord our God,
He gave, he takes away!»

XVII.

Then said the stranger, « Not by Heaven unseen,
Nor in unguided wanderings, hast thou reach'd.
This secret place, be sure !
Nor for light purpose is the Veil,
That from the Universe hath long shut out
These ancient bowers, withdrawn.
Hear thou my words, O mortal, in thy heart
Treasure what I shall tell;
And when amid the world
Thou shalt emerge again,
Repeat the warning tale.
Why have the Fathers suffer'd, but to make
The Children wisely safe?

XVIII.

« The Paradise of Irem7 this,
And that the palace pile
Which Shedad built, the King.
Alas! in the days of my youth,
The hum of the populous world
Was heard in yon wilderness waste!
O'er all the winding sands8
The tents of Ad were pitch'd!
Happy Al-Ahkaf then,
For many and brave were her sons,
Her daughters were many and fair.

XIX.

« My name was Aswad then . .
Alas! alas ! how strange
The sound so long unheard!
Of noble race I came,
One of the wealthy of the earth my sire.
An hundred horses in my father's stalls
Stood ready for his will :
Numerous his robes of silk,
The number of his camels was not known.
These were my heritance,
O God! thy gifts were these;
But better had it been for Aswad's soul

Had he ask'd alms on earth,
And begg'd the crumbs which from his table fell,
So he had known thy word.

XX.

« Boy, who hast reach'd my solitude,
Fear the Lord in the days of thy youth!
My knee was never taught
To bend before my God;
My voice was never taught
To shape one holy prayer.
We worshipp'd Idols, wood and stone,
The work of our own foolish hands;
We worshipp'd in our foolishness.
Vainly the Prophet's voice
Its frequent warning rais'd,
'REPENT AND BE FORGIVEN!' . . .
We mock'd the messenger of God,
We mock'd the Lord, long-suffering, slow to wrath.

XXI.

«A mighty work the pride of Shedad plann'd,
Here in the wilderness to form
A garden more surpassing fair
Than that before whose gate
The lightning of the Cherub's fiery sword
Waves wide to bar access,
Since Adam, the transgressor, thence was driven.
Here, too, would Shedad build
A kingly pile sublime,
The palace of his pride.
For this exhausted mines
Supplied their golden store,
For this the central caverns gave their gems;
For this the woodman's axe
Open'd the cedar forest to the sun;
The silkworm of the East
Spun her sepulchral egg;
The hunter African
Provok'd the danger of the elephant's wrath;
The Ethiop, keen of scent,
Detects the ebony,9
That deep-inearth'd, and hating light,
A leafless tree and barren of all fruit,
With darkness feeds her boughs of raven grain.
Such were the treasures lavished in yon pile;
Ages have past away,
And never mortal eye
Gazed on their vanity.

XXII.

« The garden,—copious springs
Blest that delightful spot,
And every flower was planted there
That makes the gale of evening sweet.
He spake, and bade the full-grown forest rise,
His own creation ; should the King
Wait for slow Nature's work?
All trees that bend with luscious fruit,
Or wave with feathery boughs,
Or point their spiring heads to heaven,
Or spreading wide their shadowy arms,
Invite the traveller to repose at noon,
Hither, uprooted with their native soil,
The labour and the pain of multitudes,
Mature in beauty, bore them.

Here, frequent in the walks,
The marble statue stood
Of heroes and of chiefs.
The trees and flowers remain,
By Nature's care perpetuate and self-sown.
The marble statues long have lost all trace
Of heroes and of chiefs;
Huge shapeless stones they lie,
O'ergrown with many a flower.

XXIII.

«The work of pride went on—
Often the Prophet's voice
Denounced impending woe—
We mock'd at the words of the Seer.
We mock'd at the wrath of the Lord.
A long-continued drought first troubled us;
Three years no cloud had form'd,
Three years no rain had fallen;
The wholesome herb was dry,
The corn matur'd not for the food of man,
The wells and fountains fail'd.
O hard of heart, in whom the punishment
Awoke no sense of guilt!
Headstrong to ruin, obstinately blind,
We to our Idols still applied for aid; [10]
Sakia we invok'd for rain,
We called on Razeka for food—
They did not hear our prayers, they could not hear!
No cloud appear'd in Heaven,
No nightly dews came down.

XXIV.

« Then to the place of concourse [11] messengers
Were sent, to Mecca, where the nations came,
Round the Red Hillock kneeling, to implore
God in his favour'd place.
We sent to call on God;
Ah fools! unthinking that from all the earth
The heart ascends to him.
We sent to call on God;
Ah fools! to think the Lord
Would hear their prayers abroad,
Who made no prayers at home!

XXV.

« Meantime the work of pride went on,
And still before our Idols, wood and stone,
We bow'd the impious knee.
'Turn, men of Ad, and call upon the Lord,'
The Prophet Houd exclaim'd;
'Turn men of Ad, and look to Heaven,
And fly the wrath to come.' —
We mock'd the Prophet's words; —
'Now dost thou dream, old man,
Or art thou drunk with wine?
Future woe and wrath to come,
Still thy prudent voice forebodes;
When it comes will we believe,
Till it comes will we go on
In the way our fathers went.
Now are thy words from God?
Or dost thou dream, old man,
Or art thou drunk with wine?'

XXVI.

« So spake the stubborn race,
The unbelieving ones.
I too, of stubborn unbelieving heart,
Heard him, and heeded not.
It chanced my father went the way of man,
He perish'd in his sins.
The funeral rites were duly paid,
We bound a camel to his grave,
And left it there to die,
So if the resurrection came [12]
Together they might rise.
I past my father's grave,
I heard the Camel moan.
She was his favourite beast,
One who had carried me in infancy,
The first that by myself I learnt to mount.
Her limbs were lean with famine, and her eyes
Look'd ghastlily with want.
She knew me as I past,
She stared me in the face. [13]
My heart was touch'd, had it been human else?
I thought no eye was near, and broke her bonds,
And drove her forth to liberty and life.
The Prophet Houd beheld,
He lifted up his voice,
Blessed art thou, young man,
Blessed art thou, O Aswad, for the deed!
In the day of visitation,
In the fearful hour of judgement,
God will remember thee!

XXVII.

« The day of visitation was at hand,
The fearful hour of judgment hastened on.
Lo Shedad's mighty pile complete,
The palace of his pride.
Would ye behold its wonders, enter in!
I have no heart to visit it.
Time hath not harm'd the eternal monument;
Time is not here, nor days, nor months, nor years,
An everlasting now of misery!—
Ye must have heard their fame,
Or likely ye have seen
The mighty Pyramids,—
For sure those mighty piles have overlived
The feeble generations of mankind.
What, though unmov'd they bore the deluge weight, [14]
Survivors of the ruined world?
What though their founder fill'd with miracles
And wealth miraculous their ample vaults?
Compar'd with yonder fabric, and they shrink
The baby wonders of a woman's work!
Here emerald columns o'er the marble courts
Fling their green rays, as when amid a shower
The sun shines loveliest on the vernal corn.
Here Shedad bade the sapphire floor be laid,
As though with feet divine
To trample azure light,
Like the blue pavement of the firmament.
Here self-suspended hangs in air,
As its pure substance loath'd material touch,
The living carbuncle; [15]
Sun of the lofty dome,
Darkness hath no dominion o'er its beams;
Intense it glows, an ever-flowing tide

Of glory, like the day-flood in its source.
Impious! the Trees of vegetable gold
Such as in Eden's groves
Yet innocent it grew;[16]
Impious! he made his boast, though heaven had hid
So deep the baneful ore,
That they should branch and bud for him,
That art should force their blossoms and their fruit,
And re-create for him whate'er
Was lost in Paradise.
Therefore at Shedad's voice
Here towered the palm, a silver trunk,
The fine gold net-work [17] growing out
Loose from its rugged boughs.
Tall as the Cedar of the mountain, here
Rose the gold branches, hung with emerald leaves,
Blossom'd with pearls, and rich with ruby fruit.
O Ad! my country! evil was the day
That thy unhappy sons
Crouch'd at this Nimrod's throne,[18]
And placed on him the pedestal of power,
And laid their liberties beneath his feet,
Robbing their children of the heritance
Their fathers handed down.
What was to him the squander'd wealth?
What was to him the burthen of the land,
The lavish'd misery?
He did but speak his will,
And, like the blasting Siroc of the East,
The ruin of the royal voice
Found its way every-where.
I marvel not that he, whose power
No earthly law, no human feeling curb'd,
Mock'd at the living God!

XXVIII.

« And now the King's command went forth
Among the people, bidding old and young,
Husband and wife, the master and the slave,
All the collected multitudes of Ad,
Here to repair, and hold high festival,
That he might see his people, they behold
Their King's magnificence and power.
The day of festival arriv'd;
Hither they came, the old man and the boy,
Husband and wife, the master and the slave,
Hither they came.   From yonder high tower top,
The loftiest of the Palace, Shedad look'd
Down on his tribe : their tents on yonder sands
Rose like the countless billows of the sea;
Their tread and voices like the ocean roar,
One deep confusion of tumultuous sounds.
They saw their King's magnificence; beheld
His palace sparkling like the Angel domes
Of Paradise; his garden like the bowers
Of early Eden, and they shouted out,
'Great is the King! a God upon the earth !'

XXIX.

« Intoxicate with joy and pride,
He heard their blasphemies;
And in his wantonness of heart he bade
The Prophet Houd be brought;
And o'er the marble courts,
And o'er the gorgeous rooms
Glittering with gems and gold,

He led the Man of God.
' Is not this a stately pile?'
Cried the Monarch in his joy.
'Hath ever eye beheld,
Hath ever thought conceiv'd,
Place more magnificent?
Houd, they say that Heaven imparted
To thy lips the words of wisdom!
Look at the riches round,
And value them aright,
If so thy wisdom can.'

XXX.

« The Prophet heard his vaunt,
And, with an awful smile, he answer'd him,
'O Shedad! only in the hour of death [19]
We learn to value things like these aright.'

XXXI.

« ' Hast thou a fault to find
In all thine eyes have seen?'
Again the King exclaim'd.
'Yea!' said the man of God;
' The walls are weak, the building ill secur'd,
Azrael can enter in !
The Sarsar can pierce through,
The Icy Wind of Death.'

XXXII.

« I was beside the Monarch when he spake—
Gentle the Prophet spake,
But in his eye there dwelt
A sorrow that disturb'd me while I gaz'd.
The countenance of Shedad fell,
And anger sat upon his paler lips.
He to the high tower-top the Prophet led,
And pointed to the multitude;
And as again they shouted out,
'Great is the King! a God upon the Earth !'
With dark and threatful smile to Houd he turn'd, —
'Say they aright, O Prophet? is the King
Great upon earth, a God among mankind?'
The Prophet answer'd not;
Over that infinite multitude
He roll'd his ominous eyes,
And tears which could not be supprest gush'd forth.

XXXIII.

« Sudden an uproar rose,
A cry of joy below,
'The Messenger is come!
Kail from Mecca comes,
He brings the boon obtain'd !'

XXXIV.

« Forth as we went we saw where overhead
There hung a deep black cloud,
On which the multitude
With joyful eyes look'd up,
And blest the coming rain.
The Messenger addrest the King
And told his tale of joy.

XXXV.

« ' To Mecca I repair'd,
By the Red Hillock knelt,

And called on God for rain.
My prayer ascended, and was heard;
Three clouds appear'd in heaven.
One white, and like the flying cloud of noon,
One red, as it had drunk the evening beams,
One black and heavy with its load of rain.
A voice went forth from heaven,
'Chuse, Kail, of the three!'
I thank'd the gracious Power,
And chose the black cloud, heavy with its wealth.'
'Right! right!' a thousand tongues exclaim'd,
And all was merriment and joy.

XXXVI.

« Then stood the Prophet up, and cried aloud,
'Woe, woe to Irem! woe to Ad!
DEATH is gone up into her palaces!
Woe! woe! a day of guilt and punishment,
A day of desolation!'—As he spake,
His large eye roll'd in horror, and so deep
His tone, it seem'd some Spirit from within
Breath'd through his moveless lips[20] the unearthly voice.
All looks were turn'd to him. 'O Ad!' he cried,
'Dear native land, by all remembrances
Of childhood, by all joys of manhood dear;
O Vale of many Waters; morn and night
My age must groan for you, and to the grave
Go down in sorrow. Thou wilt give thy fruits,
But who shall gather them? thy grapes will ripen,
But who shall tread the wine-press? Fly the wrath,
Ye who would live and save your souls alive!
For strong is his right hand that bends the Bow,
The arrows that he shoots are sharp,
And err not from their aim!'[21]

XXXVII.

« With that a faithful few
Prest through the throng to join him. Then arose
Mockery and mirth; 'Go, bald head!' and they mix d
Curses with laughter. He set forth, yet once
Look'd back :—his eye fell on me, and he call'd
'Aswad!'— it startled me—it terrified,—
'Aswad!' again he call'd,—and I almost
Had followed him—O moment fled too soon!
O moment irrecoverably lost!
The shouts of mockery made a coward of me;
He went, and I remained, in fear of MAN!

XXXVIII.

« He went, and darker grew
The deepening cloud above.
At length it open'd, and—O God! O God!
There were no waters there!
There fell no kindly rain!
The Sarsar from its womb went forth,
The Icy Wind of Death.

XXXIX.

« They fell around me, thousands fell around,
The King and all his People fell.
All! all! they perish'd all!
I—only I—was left.
There came a voice to me and said,
'In the Day of Visitation,
In the fearful hour of Judgment,
God hath remember'd thee.'

XL.

« When from an agony of prayer I rose,
And from the scene of death
Attempted to go forth,
The way was open, I beheld
No barrier to my steps.
But round these bowers the Arm of God
Had drawn a mighty chain,
A barrier that no human force might break.
Twice I essay'd to pass.
With that a voice was heard,
'O Aswad, be content, and bless the Lord!
One righteous deed hath sav'd
Thy soul from utter death.
O Aswad, sinful man!
When by long penitence
Thou feel'st thy soul prepar'd,
Breathe up the wish to die,
And Azrael comes, obedient to the prayer.'

XLI.

« A miserable man,
From Earth and Heaven shut out,
I heard the dreadful voice,
I look'd around my prison place;
The bodies of the dead were there,
Where'er I look'd they lay.
They moulder'd, moulder'd here,—
Their very bones have crumbled into dust,
So many years have past!
So many weary ages have gone by!
And still I linger here!
Still groaning with the burthen of my sins,
Have never dar'd to breathe
The prayer to be releas'd.

XLII.

« O! who can tell the unspeakable misery
Of solitude like this!
No sound hath ever reach'd my ear
Save of the passing wind—
The fountain's everlasting flow,
The forest in the gale,
The pattering of the shower,
Sounds dead and mournful all.
No bird hath ever clos'd her wing
Upon these solitary bowers;
No insect sweetly buzz'd amid these groves,
From all things that have life,
Save only me, conceal'd.
This Tree alone, that o'er my head
Hangs down its hospitable boughs,
And bends its whispering leaves
As though to welcome me,
Seems to partake of life;[22]
I love it as my friend, my only friend!

XLIII.

« I know not for what ages I have dragg'd
This miserable life;
How often I have seen
These ancient trees renew'd,
What countless generations of mankind
Have risen and fallen asleep,
And I remain the same!

My garment hath not waxed old,
Nor the sole of my shoe hath worn.

XLIV.

« I dare not breathe the prayer to die,
O merciful Lord God!—
But when it is thy will,
But when I have aton'd
For mine iniquities,
And sufferings have made pure
My soul with sin defil'd,
Release me in thine own good time,—
I will not cease to praise thee, O my God!»

XLV.

Silence ensued awhile,
Then Zeinab answer'd him;
« Blessed art thou, O Aswad! for the Lord,
Who sav'd thy soul from Hell,
Will call thee to him in his own good time.
And would that when my heart
Breath'd up the wish to die,
Azrael might visit me!
Then would I follow where my babes are gone,
And join Hodeirah now!»

XLVI.

She ceas'd, and the rushing of wings
Was heard in the stillness of night,
And Azrael, the Death-Angel, stood before them.
His countenance was dark,
Solemn, but not severe,
It awed, but struck no terror to the heart.
« Zeinab, thy wish is heard!
Aswad, thy hour is come!»
They fell upon the ground and blest the voice,
And Azrael from his sword
Let fall the drops of bitterness and death. ²³

XLVII.

« Me too! me too!» young Thalaba exclaim'd,
As wild with grief he kiss'd
His Mother's livid hand,
His Mother's quivering lips,
« Oh Angel! take me too!»

XLVIII.

« Son of Hodeirah!» the Death-Angel said,
« It is not yet the hour.
Son of Hodeirah, thou art chosen forth
To do the will of Heaven;
To avenge thy Father's death,
The murder of thy race;
To work the mightiest enterprise
That mortal man hath wrought.
Live! and REMEMBER DESTINY
HATH MARK'D THEE FROM MANKIND!»

XLIX.

He ceas'd, and he was gone.
Young Thalaba look'd round,—
The palace and the groves were seen no more,
He stood amid the Wilderness, alone.

BOOK II.

Sint licet expertes vitæ sensusque, capessunt
Jussa tamen superum venti.
MAMBRUNI CONSTANTINUS.

I.

NOT in the desert,
Son of Hodeirah,
Thou art abandon'd!
The coexistent fire,
Which in the Dens of Darkness burnt for thee,
Burns yet, and yet shall burn.

II.

In the Domdaniel caverns,
Under the Roots of the Ocean,
Met the Masters of the Spell.
Before them in the vault,
Blazing unfuell'd from the floor of rock,
Ten magic flames arose.
« Burn, mystic fires!» Abdaldar cried;
« Burn while Hodeirah's dreaded race exist.
This is the appointed hour,
The hour that shall secure these dens of night.»

III.

« Dim they burn!» exclaim'd Lobaba;
« Dim they burn, and now they waver;
Okba lifts the arm of death,
They waver,—they go out!»

IV.

« Curse on his hasty hand!»
Khawla exclaim'd in wrath;
The woman-fiend exclaim'd,
« Curse on his hasty hand, the fool hath fail'd!
Eight only are gone out.»

V.

A Teraph stood against the cavern side,
A new-born infant's head,
Which Khawla at his hour of birth had seiz'd,
And from the shoulders wrung.
It stood upon a plate of gold,
An unclean Spirit's name inscrib'd beneath.
The cheeks were deathy dark,
Dark the dead skin upon the hairless skull;
The lips were bluey pale;
Only the eyes had life,
They gleam'd with demon light.

VI.

« Tell me!» quoth Khawla, « is the Fire gone out
That threats the Masters of the Spell?»
The dead lips mov'd and spake,
« The fire still burns that threats
The Masters of the Spell.»

VII.

« Curse on thee, Okba!» Khawla cried,
As to the den the Sorcerer came;
He bore the dagger in his hand,
Hot from the murder of Hodeirah's race.

« Behold those unextinguish'd flames!
The fire still burns that threats
The Masters of the Spell!
Okba, wert thou weak of heart?
Okba, wert thou blind of eye?
Thy fate and ours were on the lot,
And we believ'd the lying stars,
That said thy hand might seize the auspicious hour!
Thou hast let slip the reins of Destiny,—
Curse thee, curse thee, Okba!»

VIII.

The Murderer, answering, said,
« O vers'd in all enchanted lore,
Thou better knowest Okba's soul!
Eight blows I struck, eight home-driven blows,
Needed no second stroke
From this envenom'd blade.
Ye frown at me as if the will had fail'd,
As if ye did not know
My double danger from Hodeirah's race,
The deeper hate I feel,
The stronger motive that inspir'd my arm!
Ye frown as if my hasty fault,
My ill-directed blow;
Had spar'd the enemy;
And not the stars that would not give,
And not your feeble spells
That could not force, the sign
Which of the whole was he!
Did ye not bid me strike them all?
Said ye not root and branch should be destroy'd?
I heard Hodeirah's dying groan,
I heard his Children's shriek of death,
And sought to consummate the work;
But o'er the two remaining lives
A cloud unpierceable had risen,
A cloud that mock'd my searching eyes.
I would have prob'd it with the dagger-point,
The dagger was repell'd;
A Voice came forth and cried,
'Son of Perdition, cease! thou canst not change
What in the Book of Destiny is written.'»

IX.

Khawla to the Teraph turn'd,
« Tell me where the Prophet's hand
Hides our destin'd enemy?»
The dead lips spake again,
« I view the seas, I view the land,
I search the ocean and the earth!
Not on Ocean is the Boy,
Not on Earth his steps are seen.»

X.

« A mightier power than we,» Lobaba cried,
« Protects our destin'd foe!
Look! look! one fire burns dim!
It quivers! it goes out!»

XI.

It quivered, it was quench'd.
One flame alone was left,
A pale blue flame that trembled on the earth,
A hovering light, upon whose shrinking edge
The darkness seemed to press.

Stronger it grew, and spread
Its lucid swell around,
Extending now where all the ten had stood,
With lustre more than all.
At that portentous sight,
The children of Evil trembled,
And Terror smote their souls.
Over the den the fire
Its fearful splendour cast,
The broad base rolling up in wavy streams,
Bright as the summer lightning when it spreads
Its glory o'er the midnight heaven.
The Teraph's eyes were dimm'd,
Which like two twinkling stars
Shone in the darkness late.
The Sorcerers on each other gaz'd,
And every face, all pale with fear,
And ghastly, in that light was seen
Like a dead man's by the sepulchral lamp.

XII.

Even Khawla, fiercest of the enchanter brood,
Not without effort drew
Her fear-suspended breath.
Anon a deeper rage
Inflam'd her reddening eye.
« Mighty is thy power, Mahommed!»
Loud in blasphemy she cried;
« But Eblis² would not stoop to man,
When Man, fair statured as the stately palm,
From his Creator's hand
Was undefil'd and pure.
Thou art mighty, O Son of Abdallah!
But who is he of woman born
That shall vie with the might of Eblis?
That shall rival the Prince of the Morning?»

XIII.

She said, and rais'd her skinny hand
As in defiance to high Heaven,
And stretch'd her long lean finger forth,
And spake aloud the words of power.
The Spirits heard her call,
And lo! before her stands
Her Demon Minister.
« Spirit!» the Enchantress cried,
« Where lives the Boy, coeval with whose life
Yon magic fire must burn?»

XIV.
Demon.

Mistress of the mighty spell,
Not on Ocean, not on earth.
Only eyes that view
Allah's glory-throne,
See his hiding-place.
From some believing Spirit, ask and learn.

XV.

« Bring the dead Hodeirah here,»
Khawla cried, « and he shall tell!»
The Demon heard her bidding, and was gone.
A moment pass'd, and at her feet
Hodeirah's corpse was laid.
His hand still held the sword he grasp'd in death,
The blood not yet had clotted on his wound.

XVI.

The Sorceress look'd, and with a smile
That kindled to more fiendishness
Her hideous features, cried,
Where art thou, Hodeirah, now? [3]
« Is thy soul in Zemzem-well? [4]
Is it in the Eden groves?
Waits it for the judgment-blast
In the trump of Israfil!
Is it plum'd with silver wings
Underneath the throne of God?
Even though beneath his throne,
Hodeirah, thou shalt hear,
Thou shalt obey my voice!»

XVII.

She said, and muttered charms which Hell in fear
And Heaven in horror heard.
Soon the stiff eye-balls roll'd,
The muscles with convulsive motion shook,
The white lips quiver'd.   Khawla saw, her soul
Exulted, and she cried,
« Prophet! behold my power!
Not even death secures
Thy slaves from Khawla's spell!
Where, Hodeirah, is thy child?»

XVIII.

Hodeirah groan'd and closed his eyes,
As if in the night and the blindness of death
He would have hid himself.

XIX.

« Speak to my question!» she exclaim'd,
« Or in that mangled body thou shalt live
Ages of torture! answer me!
Where can we find the boy?»

XX.

« God! God!» Hodeirah cried,
« Release me from this life,
From this intolerable agony!»

XXI.

« Speak!» cried the Sorceress, and she snatch'd
A Viper from the floor,
And with the living reptile lash'd his neck. [5]
Wreath'd round him with the blow,
The reptile tighter drew her folds,
And rais'd her wrathful head,
And fix'd into his face
Her deadly teeth, and shed
Poison in every wound.
In vain! for Allah heard Hodeirah's prayer,
And Khawla on a corpse
Had wreak'd her baffled rage.
The fated fire mov'd on,
And round the Body wrapt its funeral flames.
The flesh and bones in that portentous pile
Consum'd; the Sword alone
Circled with fire, was left.

XXII.

Where is the Boy for whose hand it is destin'd?
Where the Destroyer who one day shall wield
The Sword that is circled with fire?

Race accursed, try your charms!
Masters of the mighty Spell,
Mutter o'er your words of power!
Ye can shatter the dwellings of man,
Ye can open the womb of the rock,
Ye can shake the foundations of earth,
But not the word of God:
But not one letter can ye change
Of what his Will hath written!

XXIII.

Who shall seek through Araby
Hodeirah's dreaded son?
They mingle the arrows of Chance, [6]
The lot of Abdaldar is drawn.
Thirteen moons must wex and wane
Ere the Sorcerer quit his quest.
He must visit every tribe
That roam the desert wilderness,
Or dwell beside perennial streams;
Nor leave a solitary tent unsearch'd,
Till he hath found the Boy,...
The hated Boy, whose blood alone
Can quench that dreaded fire.

XXIV.

A crystal ring Abdaldar bore;
The powerful gem [7] condens'd
Primeval dews, that upon Caucasus
Felt the first winter's frost.
Ripening there it lay beneath
Rock above rock, and mountain ice up-pil'd
On mountain, till the incumbent mass assum'd,
So huge its bulk, the Ocean's azure hue.

XXV.

With this he sought the inner den
Where burnt the eternal fire.
Like waters gushing from some channell'd rock
Full through a narrow opening, from a chasm
The eternal fire stream'd up.
No eye beheld the fount
Of that up flowing flame,
Which blazed self-nurtur'd, and for ever, there.
It was no mortal element: the Abyss
Supplied it, from the fountains at the first
Prepar'd.   In the heart of earth it lives and glows
Her vital heat, till, at the day decreed,
The voice of God shall let its billows loose,
To deluge o'er with no abating flood
The consummated World;
That thenceforth through the air must roll,
The penal Orb of Fire.

XXVI.

Unturban'd and unsandall'd there,
Abdaldar stood before the flame,
And held the Ring beside, and spake
The language that the Elements obey.
The obedient flame detach'd a portion forth,
Which, in the crystal entering, was condens'd,
Gem of the gem, [8] its living Eye of fire.
When the hand that wears the spell
Shall touch the destin'd Boy,
Then shall that Eye be quench'd,

13

And the freed Element
Fly to its sacred and remember'd Spring.

XXVII.

Now go thy way Abdaldar,
Servant of Eblis,
Over Arabia
Seek the Destroyer!
Over the sands of the scorching Tehama
Over the waterless mountains of Nayd;
In Arud pursue him, and Yemen the happy,
And Hejaz, the country belov'd by believers.
Over Arabia,
Servant of Eblis,
Seek the Destroyer!

XXVIII.

From tribe to tribe, from town to town,
From tent to tent, Abdaldar past.
Him every morn the all-beholding Eye
Saw from his couch, unhallowed by a prayer,
Rise to the scent of blood;
And every night lie down,
That rankling hope within him, that by day
Goaded his steps, still stinging him in sleep,
And startling him with vain accomplishment
From visions still the same.
Many a time his wary hand
To many a youth applied the Ring,
And still the imprison'd fire
Within its crystal socket lay comprest,
Impatient to be free.

XXIX.

At length to the cords of a tent,
That were stretch'd by an Island of Palms,
In the desolate sea of the sands,
The seemly traveller came.
Under a shapely palm,
Herself as shapely, there a Damsel stood;
She held her ready robe,
And look'd towards a Boy,
Who from the tree above,
With one hand clinging to its trunk,
Cast with the other down the cluster'd dates.

XXX.

The Wizard approach'd the Tree,
He lean'd on his staff, like a way-faring man,
And the sweat of his travel was seen on his brow.
He ask'd for food, and lo!
The Damsel proffers him her lap of dates;
And the Stripling descends, and runs to the tent,
And brings him forth water, the draught of delight.

XXXI.

Anon the Master of the tent,
The Father of the family,
Came forth, a man in years, of aspect mild.
To the stranger approaching he gave
The friendly saluting of peace,
And bade the skin be spread.
Before the tent they spread the skin,9
Under a Tamarind's shade,
That, bending forward, stretch'd
Its boughs of beauty far.

They brought the Traveller rice,
With no false colours [10] tinged to tempt the eye,
But white as the new-fallen snow,
When never yet the sullying Sun
Hath seen its purity,
Nor the warm Zephyr touch'd and tainted it.
The dates of the grove before their guest
They laid, and the luscious fig,
And water from the well.
The Damsel from the Tamarind tree
Had pluck'd its acid fruit,
And steep'd it in water long;
And whoso drank of the cooling draught, [11]
He would not wish for wine.
This to the guest the Damsel brought,
And a modest pleasure kindled her cheek,
When raising from the cup his moisten'd lips,
The Stranger smil'd, and prais'd, and drank again.

XXXII.

Whither is gone the Boy?
He had pierced the Melon's pulp,
And clos'd with wax the wound,
And he had duly gone at morn
And watch'd its ripening rind,
And now all joyfully he brings
The treasure now matur'd.
His dark eyes sparkle with a boy's delight,
As out he pours its liquid [12] lusciousness,
And proffers to the guest.

XXXIII.

Abdaldar ate, and he was satisfied:
And now his tongue discours'd
Of regions far remote,
As one whose busy feet had travell'd long.
The father of the family,
With a calm eye and quiet smile,
Sate pleas'd to hearken him.
The Damsel who remov'd the meal
She loitered on the way,
And listen'd with full hands [13]
A moment motionless.
All eagerly the Boy
Watches the Traveller's lips;
And still the wily man
With seemly kindness, to the eager Boy
Directs his winning tale.
Ah, cursed one! if this be he,
If thou hast found the object of thy search,
Thy hate, thy bloody aim,...
Into what deep damnation wilt thou plunge
Thy miserable soul!...
Look! how his eye delighted watches thine!...
Look! how his open lips
Gasp at the winning tale!..
And nearer now he comes,
To lose no word of that delightful talk.
Then, as in familiar mood,
Upon the stripling's arm
The Sorcerer laid his hand,
And the fire of the Crystal fled.

XXXIV.

While the sudden shoot of joy
Made pale Abdaldar's cheek,

The Master's voice was heard :
« It is the hour of prayer,..¹⁴
My children, let us purify ourselves,
And praise the Lord our God!»
The Boy the water brought;
After the law¹⁵ they purified themselves,
And bent their faces to the earth in prayer.

XXXV.

All, save Abdaldar; over Thalaba
He stands, and lifts the dagger to destroy.
Before his lifted arm receiv'd
Its impulse to descend,
The Blast of the Desert came.
Prostrate in prayer, the pious family
Felt not the Simoom pass.¹⁶
They rose, and lo! the Sorcerer lying dead,
Holding the dagger in his blasted hand.

BOOK III.

Time will produce events of which thou canst have no idea; and
he to whom thou gavest no commission, will bring thee unexpected
news.　　　　　MOALLAKAT, *Poem of Tarafa.*

I.

THALABA.

Oneiza, look! the dead man has a ring,..
Should it be buried with him?

ONEIZA.

Oh yes.. yes!
A wicked man! whate'er is his must needs
Be wicked too!

THALABA.

But see,.. the sparkling stone!
How it hath caught the glory of the Sun,
And streams it back again in lines of light!

ONEIZA.

Why do you take it from him, Thalaba?..
And look at it so near?.. it may have charms
To blind, or poison;.. throw it in the grave!
I would not touch it!

THALABA.

And round its rim
Strange letters...

ONEIZA.

Bury it.. Oh! bury it!

THALABA.

It is not written as the Koran is;
Some other tongue perchance,.. the accursed man
Said he had been a traveller.

MOATH, *coming from the Tent.*
Thalaba,
What hast thou there?

THALABA.

A ring the dead man wore;
Perhaps, my father, you can read its meaning.

MOATH.

No, Boy,.. the letters are not such as ours.
Heap the sand over it! a wicked man
Wears nothing holy.

THALABA.

Nay! not bury it!
It may be that some traveller, who shall enter

Our tent, may read them : or if we approach
Cities where strangers dwell and learned men,
They may interpret.

MOATH.

It were better hid
Under the desert sands. This wretched man,
Whom God hath smitten in the very purpose
And impulse of his unpermitted crime,
Belike was some Magician, and these lines
Are of the language that the Demons use.

ONEIZA.

Bury it! bury it.. dear Thalaba!

MOATH.

Such cursed men there are upon the earth,
In league and treaty with the Evil powers,
The covenanted enemies of God
And of all good; dear purchase have they made
Of rule, and riches, and their life-long sway,
Masters, yet slaves of Hell. Beneath the Roots
Of Ocean, the Domdaniel caverns lie,¹
Their impious meeting; there they learn the words
Unutterable by man who holds his hope
Of Heaven; there brood the Pestilence, and let
The Earthquake loose.

THALABA.

And he who would have kill'd me
Was one of these?

MOATH.

I know not;.. but it may be
That on the Table of Destiny, thy name
Is written their Destroyer, and for this
Thy life by yonder miserable man
So sought; so saved by interfering Heaven.

THALABA.

His ring has some strange power then?

MOATH.

Every gem,¹
So sages say, has virtue; but the science
Of difficult attainment; some grow pale,
Conscious of poison,² or with sudden shade
Of darkness, warn the wearer; some preserve
From spells, or blunt the hostile weapon's edge;³
Some open rocks and mountains, and lay bare
Their buried treasures; others make the sight
Strong to perceive the presence of all Beings
Through whose pure substance the unaided eye
Passes, like empty air;.. and in yon stone
I deem some such mysterious quality.

THALABA.

My father, I will wear it.

MOATH.

Thalaba!

THALABA.

In God's name, and the prophet's! be its power
Good, let it serve the righteous; if for evil,
God, and my trust in Him, shall hallow it.

II.

So Thalaba drew on
The written ring of gold.
Then in the hollow grave
They laid Abdaldar's corpse,
And levell'd over him the desert dust.

III.

The Sun arose, ascending from beneath
The horizon's circling line.

As Thalaba to his ablutions went,
Lo! the grave open, and the corpse expos'd!
It was not that the winds of night
Had swept away the sands which covered it,
For heavy with the undried dew
The desert dust was dark and close around;
And the night air had been so calm and still,
It had not from the grove
Shaken a ripe date down.

Amaz'd to hear the tale,
Forth from the tent came Moath and his child.
Awhile the thoughtful man survey'd the corpse
Silent with downward eyes;
Then turning, spake to Thalaba, and said,
« I have heard that there are places by the abode
Of holy men, so holily possess'd,
That should a corpse be buried there, the ground
With a convulsive effort shakes it out,[4]
Impatient of pollution. Have the feet
Of Prophet or Apostle blest this place?
Ishmael, or Houd, or Saleh, or than all,
Mahommed, holier name? Or is the man
So foul with magic and all blasphemy,
That Earth,[5] like Heaven, rejects him? It is best
Forsake the station. Let us strike our tent.
The place is tainted.. and behold
The Vulture hovers yonder,[6] and his scream
Chides us that still we scare him from his banquet.
So let the accursed one
Find fitting sepulchre.»

V.

Then from the pollution of death
With water they made themselves pure;
And Thalaba drew up
The fastening of the cords;
And Moath furl'd the tent;
And from the grove of palms Oneiza led
The Camels, ready to receive their load.

VI.

The dews had ceased to steam
Towards the climbing Sun,
When from the Isle of Palms they went their way.
And when the Sun had reach'd his southern height,
As back they turn'd their eyes,
The distant Palms arose
Like to the top-sails of some far-off fleet
Distinctly seen, where else
The Ocean bounds had blended with the sky.
And when the eve came on,
The sight returning reach'd the grove no more.
They planted the pole of their tent,
And they laid them down to repose.

VII.

At midnight Thalaba started up,
For he felt that the ring on his finger was mov'd;
He call'd on Allah aloud,
And he call'd on the Prophet's name.
Moath arose in alarm,
« What ails thee, Thalaba?» he cried,
« Is the robber of night at hand?»
« Dost thou not see,» the youth exclaim'd,

« A Spirit in the Tent!»
Moath look'd round and said,
« The moon-beam shines in the Tent,
I see thee stand in the light,
And thy shadow is black on the ground.»

VIII.

Thalaba answered not.
« Spirit!» he cried, « what brings thee here?
In the name of the Prophet speak,
In the name of Allah, obey!»

IX.

He ceas'd, and there was silence in the Tent.
« Dost thou not hear?» quoth Thalaba.
The listening man replied,
« I hear the wind, that flaps
The curtain of the Tent.»

X.

« The Ring! the Ring!» the youth exclaim'd.
« For that the Spirit of Evil comes;
By that I see, by that I hear.
In the name of God, I ask thee,
Who was he that slew my Father?»

DEMON.

Master of the powerful Ring!
Okba, the wise Magician, did the deed.

THALABA.

Where does the Murderer dwell?

DEMON.

In the Domdaniel caverns,
Under the Roots of the Ocean.

THALABA.

Why were my Father and my brethren slain?

DEMON.

We knew from the race of Hodeirah
The destin'd Destroyer would come.

THALABA.

Bring me my father's sword.

DEMON.

A fire surrounds the fatal sword,
No Spirit or Magician's hand
Can pierce that guardian flame.

THALABA.

Bring me his bow and his arrows.

XI.

Distinctly Moath heard his voice, and She,
Who, through the Veil of Separation, watch'd
All sounds in listening terror, whose suspense
Forbade the aid of prayer.
They heard the voice of Thalaba;
But when the Spirit spake, the motionless air
Felt not the subtile sounds,
Too fine for mortal sense.

XII.

On a sudden the rattle of arrows was heard,
And the quiver was laid at the feet of the youth,
And in his hand they saw Hodeirah's bow.
He eyed the bow, he twang'd the string,
And his heart bounded to the joyous tone.
Anon he rais'd his voice and cried,
« Go thy way, and never more,
Evil Spirit, haunt our tent!

By the virtue of the Ring,
By Mahommed's holier might,
By the holiest name of God,
Thee, and all the Powers of Hell,
I adjure and I command
Never more to trouble us!»

XIII.

Nor ever from that hour
Did rebel Spirit on the Tent intrude,
Such virtue had the Spell.

XIV.

Thus peacefully the vernal years
Of Thalaba past on,
Till now, without an effort, he could bend
Hodeirah's stubborn bow.
Black were his eyes and bright,
The sunny hue of health
Glow'd on his tawny cheek,
His lip was darken'd by maturing life;
Strong were his shapely limbs, his stature tall;
Peerless among Arabian youths was he.

XV.

Compassion for the child
Had first old Moath's kindly heart possess'd,
An orphan, wailing in the wilderness.
But when he heard his tale, his wonderous tale,
Told by the Boy with such eye-speaking truth,
Now with sudden bursts of anger,
Now in the agony of tears,
And now with flashes of prophetic joy,
What had been pity became reverence then,
And, like a sacred trust from Heaven,
The Old Man cherish'd him.
Now, with a father's love,
Child of his choice, he lov'd the Boy,
And, like a father, to the Boy was dear.
Oneiza call'd him brother; and the youth,
More fondly than a brother, lov'd the maid;
The loveliest of Arabian maidens she.
How happily the years
Of Thalaba went by!

XVI.

It was the wisdom and the will of Heaven,
That, in a lonely tent, had cast
The lot of Thalaba.
There might his soul develop best
Its strengthening energies;
There might he from the world
Keep his heart pure and uncontaminate,
Till at the written hour he should be found
Fit servant of the Lord, without a spot.

XVII.

Years of his youth, how rapidly ye fled
In that beloved solitude!
Is the morn fair, and doth the freshening breeze
Flow with cool current o'er his cheek?
Lo! underneath the broad-leav'd sycamore
With lids half-clos'd he lies,
Dreaming of days to come.
His dog beside him,7 in mute blandishment,
Now licks his listless hand;

Now lifts an anxious and expectant eye,
Courting the wonted caress.

XVIII.

Or comes the Father8 of the Rains
From his caves in the uttermost West,
Comes he in darkness and storms?
When the blast is loud,
When the waters fill
The Traveller's tread in the sands,
When the pouring shower
Streams adown the roof,
When the door-curtain hangs in heavier folds,
When the out-strain'd tent flags loosely,
Within there is the embers' cheerful glow,
The sound of the familiar voice,
The song that lightens toil, ..
Domestic Peace and Comfort are within.
Under the common shelter, on dry sand,
The quiet Camels ruminate their food;
From Moath falls the lengthening cord,
As patiently the Old Man
Entwines the strong palm-fibres;9 by the hearth
The Damsel shakes the coffee-grains,
That with warm fragrance fill the tent;
And while, with dexterous fingers, Thalaba
Shapes the green basket,10 haply at his feet
Her favourite kidling gnaws the twig,
Forgiven plunderer, for Oneiza's sake!

XIX.

Or when the winter torrent rolls
Down the deep-channell'd rain-course, foamingly,
Dark with its mountain spoils,
With bare feet pressing the wet sand,
There wanders Thalaba,
The rushing flow, the flowing roar,
Filling his yielded faculties;
A vague, a dizzy, a tumultuous joy.
Or lingers it a vernal brook11
Gleaming o'er yellow sands?
Beneath the lofty bank reclin'd,
With idle eye he views its little waves,
Quietly listening to the quiet flow;
While, in the breathings of the stirring gale,
The tall canes bend above,
Floating like streamers on the wind
Their lank uplifted leaves.

XX.

Nor rich, nor poor,12 was Moath; God hath given
Enough, and blest him with a mind content.
No hoarded gold13 disquieted his dreams;
But ever round his station he beheld
Camels that knew his voice,
And home birds, grouping at Oneiza's call,
And goats that, morn and eve,
Came with full udders to the Damsel's hand.
Dear child! the Tent beneath whose shade they dwelt
It was her work; and she had twin'd
His girdle's many hues;
And he had seen his robe
Grow in Oneiza's loom. 14
How often, with a memory-mingled joy
Which made her Mother live before his sight,
He watch'd her nimble fingers thread the woof!

Or at the hand-mill, [15] when she knelt and toil'd,
Tost the thin cake on spreading palm,
Or fix'd it on the glowing oven's side
With bare wet arm, [16] and safe dexterity.

XXI.

'T is the cool evening hour:
The Tamarind from the dew
Sheathes its young fruit, yet green. [17]
Before their Tent the mat is spread,
The Old Man's awful voice
Intones the holy Book. [18]
What if beneath no lamp-illumin'd dome,
Its marble walls [19] bedeck'd with flourish'd truth,
Azure and gold adornment! sinks the word
With deeper influence from the Imam's voice,
Where in the day of congregation, crowds
Perform the duty-task?
Their Father is their Priest,
The Stars of Heaven their point of prayer, [20]
And the blue Firmament
The glorious Temple, where they feel
The present Deity!

XXII.

Yet through the purple glow of eve
Shines dimly the white moon.
The slacken'd bow, the quiver, the long lance,
Rest on the pillar of the Tent. [21]
Knitting light palm-leaves for her brother's brow, [22]
The dark-eyed damsel sits;
The Old Man tranquilly
Up his curl'd pipe inhales
The tranquillizing herb.
So listen they the reed [23] of Thalaba,
While his skill'd fingers modulate
The low, sweet, soothing, melancholy tones.
Or if he strung the pearls of Poesy, [24]
Singing with agitated face
And eloquent arms, and sobs that reach the heart,
A tale of love and woe; [25]
Then, if the brightening Moon, that lit his face,
In darkness favoured her's,
Oh! even with such a look, as fables say,
The mother Ostrich fixes on her egg, [26]
Till that intense affection
Kindle its light of life,
Even in such deep and breathless tenderness
Oneiza's soul is center'd on the youth,
So motionless, with such an ardent gaze,..
Save when from her full eyes
Quickly she wipes away the swelling tears
That dim his image there.

XXIII.

She call'd him Brother! was it sister-love
Which made the silver rings
Round her smooth ankles and her tawny arms, [27]
Shine daily brighten'd? for a brother's eye
Were her long fingers tinged, [28]
As when she trimm'd the lamp,
And through the veins and delicate skin
The light shone rosy? that the darken'd lids [29]
Gave yet a softer lustre to her eye?
That with such pride she trick'd
Her glossy tresses, and on holy-day

Wreath'd the red flower-crown round [30]
Their waves of glossy jet?
How happily the years
Of Thalaba went by!

XXIV.

Yet was the heart of Thalaba
Impatient of repose;
Restless he pondered still
The task for him decreed,
The mighty and mysterious work announced.
Day by day, with youthful ardour,
He the call of Heaven awaits,
And oft in visions, o'er the Murderer's head,
He lifts the avenging arm;
And oft, in dreams, he sees
The Sword that is circled with fire.

XXV.

One morn, as was their wont, in sportive mood,
The youth and damsel bent Hodeirah's bow;
For with no feeble hand, nor erring aim,
Oneiza could let loose the obedient shaft.
With head back-bending, Thalaba
Shot up the aimless arrow high in air,
Whose line in vain the aching sight pursued,
Lost in the depth of Heaven.
« When will the hour arrive,» exclaim'd the youth,
« That I shall aim these fated shafts
To vengeance long delay'd?
Have I not strength, my father, for the deed?
Or can the will of Providence
Be mutable like man?
Shall I never be call'd to the task?»

XXVI.

« Impatient boy!» quoth Moath, with a smile:
« Impatient Thalaba!» Oneiza cried,
And she too smil'd; but in her smile
A mild reproachful melancholy mix'd.

XXVII.

Then Moath pointed where a cloud
Of Locusts, from the desolated fields
Of Syria, wing'd their way.
« Lo! how created things
Obey the written doom!»

XXVIII.

Onward they came, a dark continuous cloud
Of congregated myriads numberless,
The rushing of whose wings was as the sound
Of a broad river, headlong in its course
Plunged from a mountain summit; or the roar
Of a wild ocean in the autumn storm,
Shattering its billows on a shore of rocks.
Onward they came, the winds impell'd them on,
Their work was done, their path of ruin past, [31]
Their graves were ready in the wilderness.

XXIX.

« Behold the mighty army!» Moath cried,
« Blindly they move, impell'd
By the blind Element.
And yonder birds, our welcome visitants,
Lo! where they soar above the embodied host,
Pursue their way, and hang upon their rear,

And thin their spreading flanks,
Rejoicing o'er their banquet! Deemest thou
The scent of water on some Syrian mosque
Placed with priest-mummery, and the jargon-rites
Which fool the multitude, hath led them here
From far Khorassan? [32] Allah, who decreed
Yon tribe the plague and punishment of man,
These also hath he doom'd to meet their way:
Both passive instruments
Of his all-acting will,
Sole mover he, and only spring of all.»

XXX.

While thus he spake, Oneiza's eye looks up
Where one towards her flew,
Satiate, for so it seem'd, with sport and food.
The Bird flew over her,
And as he past above,
From his relaxing grasp a Locust fell;..
It fell upon the Maiden's robe,
And feebly there it stood, recovering slow.

XXXI.

The admiring girl survey'd
His out-spread sails of green;
His gauzy underwings,
One closely to the grass-green body furl'd,
One ruffled in the fall, and half unclos'd.
She view'd his jet-orb'd eyes;
His glossy gorget bright,
Green glittering in the sun;
His plumy pliant horns,
That, nearer as she gaz'd,
Bent tremblingly before her breath.
She view'd his yellow-circled front
With lines mysterious vein'd;
« And know'st thou what is written here,
My father?» said the Maid.
« Look, Thalaba! perchance these lines
Are in the letters of the Ring,
Nature's own language, written here.»

XXXII.

The youth bent down, and suddenly
He started, and his heart
Sprung, and his cheek grew red,
For these mysterious lines were legible,.. [33]
WHEN THE SUN SHALL BE DARKENED AT NOON,
SON OF HODEIRAH, DEPART.
And Moath look'd, and read the lines aloud;
The Locust shook his wings and fled,
And they were silent all.

XXXIII.

Who then rejoiced but Thalaba?
Who then was troubled but the Arabian Maid?
And Moath sad of heart,
Though with a grief supprest, beheld the youth
Sharpen his arrows now,
And now new-plume their shafts,
Now, to beguile impatient hope,
Feel every sharpen'd point.

XXXIV.

« Why is that anxious look,» Oneiza cried,
« Still upward cast at noon?

Is Thalaba aweary of our tent?»
« I would be gone,» the youth replied,
« That I might do my task,
And full of glory to the tent return,
Whence I should part no more.»

XXXV.

But on the noontide sun,
As anxious and as oft Oneiza's eye
Was upward glanced in fear.
And now, as Thalaba replied, her cheek
Lost its fresh and lively hue;
For in the Sun's bright edge
She saw, or thought she saw, a little speck...
The sage Astronomer
Who, with the love of science full,
Trembled that day at every passing cloud,..
He had not seen it, 't was a speck so small.

XXXVI.

Alas! Oneiza sees the spot increase!
And lo! the ready Youth
Over his shoulder the full quiver slings,
And grasps the slacken'd bow.
It spreads, and spreads, and now
Hath shadowed half the Sun,
Whose crescent-pointed horns
Now momently decrease.

XXXVII.

The day grows dark, the Birds retire to rest;
Forth from her shadowy haunt
Flies the large-headed Screamer of the night. [34]
Far off the affrighted African,
Deeming his God deceas'd,
Falls on his knees in prayer,
And trembles as he sees
The fierce Hyena's eyes
Glare in the darkness of that dreadful noon. [35]

XXXVIII.

Then Thalaba exclaim'd, « Farewell,
My father! my Oneiza!» the Old Man
Felt his throat swell with grief.
« Where wilt thou go, my Child?» he cried,
« Wilt thou not wait a sign
To point thy destin'd way?»
« God will conduct me!» said the noble youth.
He said, and from the Tent,
In the depth of the darkness, departed.
They heard his parting steps,
The quiver rattling as he past away.

BOOK IV.

Fas est quoque brutæ
Telluri docilem monitis cœlestibus esse.
MANDROSI CONSTANTINUS.

I.

WHOSE is yon dawning form,
That in the darkness meets
The delegated youth?
Dim as the shadow of a fire at noon,
Or pale reflection on the evening brook

Of Glow-worm on the bank,
Kindled to guide her winged paramour.

II.

A moment, and the brightening image shaped
His Mother's form and features.   « Go,» she cried,
« To Babylon, and from the Angels learn
What talisman thy task requires.»

III.

The Spirit hung towards him when she ceas'd,
As though with actual lips she would have given
A mother's kiss.   His arms outstretch'd,
His body bending on,
His mouth unclos'd, and trembling into speech,
He prest to meet the blessing,... but the wind
Played on his cheek : he look'd, and he beheld
The darkness close.   « Again! again!» he cried,
« Let me again behold thee!» from the darkness
His Mother's voice went forth ;
« Thou shalt behold me in the hour of death.»

IV.

Day dawns, the twilight gleam dilates,
The Sun comes forth, and, like a god,
Rides through rejoicing heaven.
Old Moath and his daughter, from their tent,
Beheld the adventurous youth
Dark moving o'er the sands,
A lessening image, trembling through their tears.
Visions of high emprize
Beguil'd his lonely road ;
And if sometimes to Moath's tent
The involuntary mind recurr'd,
Fancy, impatient of all painful thoughts,
Pictur'd the bliss should welcome his return.
In dreams like these he went,
And still of every dream
Oneiza form'd a part,
And Hope and Memory made a mingled joy.

V.

In the eve he arriv'd at a Well ; ·
The Acacia bent over its side,
Under whose long light-hanging boughs
He chose his night's abode.
There, due ablutions made, and prayers perform'd,
· The youth his mantle spread,
And silently produced
His solitary meal.
The silence and the solitude recall'd
Dear recollections ; and with folded arms,
Thinking of other days, he sate, till thought
Had left him, and the Acacia's moving shade,
Upon the sunny sand,
Had caught his idle eye ;
And his awaken'd ear
Heard the grey Lizard's chirp,
The only sound of life.

VI.

As thus in vacant quietness he sate,
A Traveller on a Camel reach'd the Well,
And courteous greeting gave.
The mutual salutation past,
He by the cistern, too, his garment spread,
And friendly converse cheer'd the social meal.

VII.

The stranger was an ancient man,
Yet one whose green old age
Bore the fair characters of temperate youth.
So much of manhood's strength his limbs retain'd,
It seem'd he needed not the staff he bore.
His beard was long, and grey, and crisp ;
Lively his eyes and quick,
And reaching over them
The large broad eye-brow curl'd.
His speech was copious, and his winning words
Enrich'd with knowledge, that the attentive youth
Sate listening with a thirsty joy.

VIII.

So, in the course of talk,
The adventurer youth inquir'd
Whither his course was bent ?
The Old Man answered. « To Bagdad I go.»
At that so welcome sound, a flash of joy
Kindled the eye of Thalaba,
« And I too,» he replied,
« Am journeying thitherward ;
Let me become companion of thy way !»
Courteous the Old Man smil'd,
And willing in assent.

IX.

OLD MAN.
Son, thou art young for travel.
THALABA.
Until now
I never past the desert boundary.
OLD MAN.
It is a noble city that we seek,
Thou wilt behold magnificent palaces,
And lofty obelisks, and high-dom'd Mosques,
And rich Bazars, whither from all the world
Industrious merchants meet, and market there
The World's collected wealth.
THALABA.
Stands not Bagdad
Near to the site of ancient Babylon,
And Nimrod's impious temple ?
OLD MAN.
From the walls　.
'T is but a long day's distance.
THALABA.
And the ruins ?
OLD MAN.
A mighty mass remains ; enough to tell us
How great our fathers were, how little we. [1]
Men are not what they were ; their crimes and follies
Have dwarf'd them down from the old hero race
To such poor things as we !
THALABA.
At Babylon
I have heard the Angels expiate their guilt,
Haruth and Maruth.
OLD MAN.
'T is a history
Handed from ages down : a nurse's tale—
Which children, open-ey'd and mouth'd, devour ;
And thus as garrulous ignorance relates,
We learn it and believe—But all things feel
The power of Time and Change ! thistles and grass

Usurp the desolate palace, and the weeds
Of Falsehood root in the aged pile of Truth.
How have you heard the tale?

THALABA.

Thus—on a time
The Angels at the wickedness of man
Express'd indignant wonder; that in vain
Tokens and signs were given, and Prophets sent,—
Strange obstinacy this! a stubbornness
Of sin, they said, that should for ever bar
The gates of mercy on them.   Allah heard
Their unforgiving pride, and bade that two
Of these untempted Spirits should descend,
Judges on Earth. Haruth and Maruth went,
The chosen Sentencers; they fairly heard
The appeals of men to their tribunal brought,
And rightfully decided.   At the length
A Woman came before them; beautiful
Zohara was as yonder Evening star,
In the mild lustre [2] of whose lovely light
Even now her beauty shines.   They gaz'd on her
With fleshly eyes, they tempted her to sin.
The wily woman listen'd, and requir'd
A previous price, the knowledge of the name
Of God. [3]   She learnt the wonder-working name,
And gave it utterance, and its virtue bore her
Up to the glorious Presence, and she told
Before the awful Judgment-Seat her tale.

OLD MAN.

I know the rest.   The accused Spirits were called:
Unable of defence, and penitent,
They own'd their crime, and heard the doom deserv'd.
Then they besought the Lord, that not for ever
His wrath might be upon them; and implor'd
That penal ages might at length restore them
Clean from offence; since then by Babylon,
In the cavern of their punishment they dwell.
Runs the conclusion so?

THALABA.

So I am taught.

OLD MAN.

The common tale! and likely thou hast heard
How that the bold and bad, with impious rites
Intrude upon their penitence, and force,
Albeit from loathing and reluctant lips,
The sorcery-secret?

THALABA.

Is it not the truth?

OLD MAN.

Son, thou hast seen the Traveller in the sands
Move through the dizzy light of hot noon-day,
Huge as the giant race of elder times, [4]
And his Camel, than the monstrous Elephant,
Seem of a vaster bulk.

THALABA.

A frequent sight.

OLD MAN.

And hast thou never, in the twilight, fancied
Familiar object into some strange shape
And form uncouth?

THALABA.

Aye! many a time.

OLD MAN.

Even so
Things view'd at distance through the mist of fear,
By their distortion terrify and shock
The abused sight.

THALABA.

But of these Angels' fate
Thus in the uncreated book is written—

OLD MAN.

Wisely, from legendary fables, Heaven
Inculcates wisdom.

THALABA.

How then is the truth?
Is not the dungeon of their punishment
By ruin'd Babylon?

OLD MAN.

By Babylon
Haruth and Maruth may be found.

THALABA.

And there
Magicians learn their impious sorcery?

OLD MAN.

Son, what thou sayest is true, and it is false.
But night approaches fast; I have travelled far,
And my old lids are heavy;—on our way
We shall have hours for converse;—let us now
Turn to our due repose. Son, peace be with thee!

X.

So in his loosen'd cloak
The Old Man wrapt himself, [5]
And laid his limbs at length:
And Thalaba in silence laid him down.
Awhile he lay, and watch'd the lovely Moon,
O'er whose broad orb the boughs
A mazy fretting fram'd,
Or with a pale transparent green
Lighting the restless leaves,
The thin Acacia leaves that play'd above.
The murmuring wind, the moving leaves,
Lull'd him at length to sleep,
With mingled lullabies of sight and sound.

XI.

Not so the dark Magician by his side,
Lobaba, who from the Domdaniel caves
Had sought the dreaded youth.
Silent he lay, and simulating sleep,
Till by the long and regular breath he knew
The youth beside him slept.
Carefully then he rose,
And, bending over him survey'd him near;
And secretly he curs'd
The dead Abdaldar's ring,
Arm'd by whose amulet
He slept from danger safe.

XII.

Wrapt in his mantle Thalaba repos'd,
His loose right arm pillowing his easy head.
The Moon was on the Ring,
Whose crystal gem return'd
A quiet, moveless light.
Vainly the Wizard vile put forth his hand,
And strove to reach the gem,
Charms, strong as hell could make them, made it safe.
He called his servant-fiends,
He bade the genii rob the sleeping youth.
By the virtue of the Ring,
By Mahommed's holier power,

14

By the holiest name of God,
Had Thalaba disarm'd the evil race.

XIII.

Baffled and weary, and convinced at length,
Anger, and fear, and rancour gnawing him,
The accursed Sorcerer ceas'd his vain attempts,
Content perforce to wait
Temptation's likelier aid.
Restless he lay, and brooding many a wile,
And tortur'd with impatient hope,
And envying with the bitterness of hate
The innocent youth, who slept so sweetly by.

XIV.

The ray of morning on his eye-lids fell,
And Thalaba awoke,
And folded his mantle around him,
And girded his loins for the day ;
Then the due rites of holiness observ'd.
His comrade too arose,
And with the outward forms
Of righteousness and prayer insulted God.
They filled their water skin, they gave
The Camel his full draught.
Then on the road, while yet the morn was young,
And the air was fresh with dew,
Forward the travellers went,
With various talk beguiling the long way.
But soon the youth, whose busy mind
Dwelt on Lobaba's wonder-stirring words,
Renew'd the unfinish'd converse of the night.

XV.

THALABA.

Thou said'st that it is true, and yet is false,
That men accurst attain at Babylon
Forbidden knowledge from the Angel pair :—
How mean you?

LOBABA.

All things have a double power,
Alike for good and evil. The same fire
That on the comfortable hearth at eve
Warm'd the good man, flames o'er the house at night:
Should we for this forego
The needful element?
Because the scorching summer Sun
Darts fever, wouldst thou quench the orb of day?
Or deemest thou that Heaven in anger form'd
Iron to till the field, because when man
Had tipt his arrows for the chase, he rush'd
A murderer to the war?

THALABA.

What follows hence?

LOBABA.

That nothing in itself is good or evil,
But only in its use. Think you the man
Praiseworthy, who by painful study learns
The knowledge of all simples, and their power,
Healing or harmful?

THALABA.

All men hold in honour
The skilful Leech. From land to land he goes
Safe in his privilege ; the sword of war
Spares him ; Kings welcome him with costly gifts ;
And he who late had from the couch of pain

Lifted a languid look to him for aid,
Views him with brighten'd eyes, and blesses him
In his first thankful prayer.

LOBABA.

Yet some there are
Who to the purposes of wickedness
Apply this knowledge, and from herbs distil
Poison, to mix it in the trusted draught.

THALABA.

Allah shall cast them in the fire
Whose fuel is the cursed ! there shall they
Endure the ever-burning agony
Consuming still in flames, and still renew'd. [6]

LOBABA.

But is their knowledge therefore in itself
Unlawful?

THALABA.

That were foolishness to think.

LOBABA.

O what a glorious animal were Man,
Knew he but his own powers, and, knowing, gave them
Room for their growth and spread ! The Horse obeys
His guiding will ; the patient Camel bears him
Over these wastes of sand ; the Pigeon wafts
His bidding through the sky :—and with these triumphs
He rests contented !—with these ministers, —
When he might awe the Elements, and make
Myriads of Spirits serve him !

THALABA.

But as how ?
By a league with Hell, a covenant that binds
The soul to utter death !

LOBABA.

Was Solomon
Accurst of God ? yet to his talismans
Obedient, o'er his throne the birds of Heaven,
Their waving wings his sun-shield,[7] fann'd around him
The motionless air of noon ; from place to place,
As his will rein'd the viewless Element,
He rode the Wind ; [8] the Genii reared his temple,
And ceaselessly in fear while his dead eye
O'erlook'd them, day and night pursued their toil,
So dreadful was his power.

THALABA.

But 't was from Heaven
His wisdom came ; God's special gift,—the guerdon
Of early virtue.

LOBABA.

Learn thou, O young man !
God hath appointed Wisdom the reward
Of study ! 'T is a well of living waters,
Whose inexhaustible bounties all might drink,
But few dig deep enough.   Son ! thou art silent,—
Perhaps I say too much,—perhaps offend thee.

THALABA.

Nay, I am young, and willingly, as becomes me,
Hear the wise words of age.

LOBABA.

Is it a crime
To mount the horse, because forsooth thy feet
Can serve thee for the journey ?—is it sin,
Because the Hern soars upward in the sky
Above the arrow's flight, to train the Falcon
Whose beak shall pierce him there ? The powers which
Allah
Granted to man, were granted for his use,

All knowledge that befits not human weakness
Is placed beyond its reach—They who repair
To Babylon, and from the Angels learn
Mysterious wisdom, sin not in the deed.

THALABA.

Know you these secrets?

LOBABA.

I? alas! my Son,
My age just knows enough to understand
How little all its knowledge! Later years,
Sacred to study, teach me to regret
Youth's unforeseeing indolence, and hours
That cannot be recall'd! Something I know
The properties of herbs, and have sometimes
Brought to the afflicted comfort and relief
By the secrets of my art; under His blessing
Without whom all had failed! Also of Gems
I have some knowledge, and the characters
That tell beneath what aspect they were set.

THALABA.

Belike you can interpret then the graving
Around this Ring?

LOBABA.

My sight is feeble, Son,
And I must view it closer; let me try!

XVI.

The unsuspecting Youth
Held forth his finger to draw off the spell.
Even whilst he held it forth,
There settled there a Wasp,
And just above the Gem infix'd its dart;
All purple-swoln the hot and painful flesh
Rose round the tighten'd Ring.
The baffled Sorcerer knew the hand of Heaven,
And inwardly blasphem'd.

XVII.

Ere long Lobaba's heart,
Fruitful in wiles, devis'd new stratagem.
A mist arose at noon,
Like the loose hanging skirts
Of some low cloud that, by the breeze impell'd,
Sweeps o'er the mountain side.
With joy the thoughtless youth
That grateful shadowing hail'd;
For grateful was the shade,
While through the silver-lighted haze,
Guiding their way, appear'd the beamless Sun:
But soon that beacon fail'd;
A heavier mass of cloud,
Impenetrably deep,
Hung o'er the wilderness.
« Knowest thou the track?» quoth Thalaba,
« Or should we pause, and wait the wind
To scatter this bewildering fog?»
The Sorcerer answer'd him,
« Now let us hold right on, .. for if we stray
The Sun to-morrow will direct our course.»
So saying, he toward the desert depths
Misleads the youth deceiv'd.

XVIII.

Earlier the night came on,
Nor moon, nor stars, were visible in Heaven;
And when at morn the youth unclos'd his eyes,

He knew not where to turn his face in prayer.
« What shall we do?» Lobaba cried,
« The lights of Heaven have ceas'd
To guide us on our way:
Should we remain and wait
More favourable skies,
Soon would our food and water fail us here!
And if we venture on,
There are the dangers of the wilderness!»
« Sure it were best proceed!»
The chosen youth replies,
« So haply we may reach some tent, or grove
Of dates, or station'd tribe;
But idly to remain,
Were yielding effortless, and waiting death.»
The wily sorcerer willingly assents,
And farther in the sands,
Elate of heart, he leads the credulous youth.

XIX.

Still o'er the wilderness
Settled the moveless mist.
The timid Antelope, that heard their steps,
Stood doubtful where to turn in that dim light;
The Ostrich, blindly hastening, met them full.
At night, again in hope,
Young Thalaba laid down;
The morning came, and not one guiding ray
Through the thick mist was visible,
The same deep moveless mist that mantled all.
Oh for the Vulture's scream,
Who haunts for prey the abode of humankind!
Oh for the Plover's pleasant cry?
To tell of water near!
Oh for the Camel-driver's song!¹⁰
For now the water-skin grows light,
Though of the draught, more eagerly desir'd,
Imperious prudence took with sparing thirst.
Oft from the third night's broken sleep,
As in his dreams he heard
The sound of rushing winds,
Started the anxious youth, and look'd abroad,
In vain! for still the deadly calm endur'd.
Another day pass'd on;
The water skin was drain'd;
But then one hope arriv'd,
For there was motion in the air!
The sound of the wind arose anon,
That scatter'd the thick mist,
And lo! at length the lovely face of Heaven!

XX.

Alas .. a wretched scene
Was open'd on their view.
They look'd around, no wells were near,
No tent, no human aid!
Flat on the Camel lay the water-skin,
And their dumb servant difficultly now,
Over hot sands and under the hot sun,
Dragg'd on with patient pain.
But oh the joy! the blessed sight!
When in that burning waste the Travellers
Saw a green meadow, fair with flowers besprent
Azure and yellow, like the beautiful fields
Of England, when amid the growing grass
The blue-bell bends, the golden king-cup shines,

In the merry month of May!
    Oh joy! the Travellers
Gaze on each other with hope-brighten'd eyes,
For sure through that green meadow flows
The living stream! and lo! their famish'd beast
    Sees the restoring sight!
Hope gives his feeble limbs a sudden strength,
    He hurries on! ... The herbs so fair to eye
Were Senna, and the Gentian's blossom blue;
And kindred plants, that with unwater'd root
Fed in the burning sand, whose bitter leaves
    Even frantic Famine loath'd.[11]

XXI.

    In uncommunicating misery
Silent they stood.   At length Lobaba cried,
« Son, we must slay the Camel, or we die
For lack of water! thy young hand is firm, ..
Draw forth the knife and pierce him! » Wretch accurst!
    Who that beheld thy venerable face,
Thy features fix'd with suffering, the dry lips,
    The feverish eyes, could deem that all within
Was magic ease, and fearlessness secure,
And wiles of hellish import? The young man
Paus'd with reluctant pity: but he saw
His comrade's red and painful countenance,
And his own burning breath came short and quick,
    And at his feet the gasping beast
    Lies, over-worn with want.
Then from his girdle Thalaba took the knife[12]
With stern compassion, and from side to side
    Across the Camel's throat,[13]
    Drew deep the crooked blade.
Servant of man, that merciful deed
For ever ends thy suffering: but what doom
Waits thy deliverer! « Little will thy death
    Avail us!» thought the youth,
    As in the water-skin he pour'd
    The Camel's hoarded draught:
    It gave a scant supply,
The poor allowance of one prudent day.

XXII.

Son of Hodeirah, though thy steady soul
    Despair'd not, firm in faith,
Yet not the less did suffering nature feel
Her pangs and trials. Long their craving thirst
Struggled with fear, by fear itself inflam'd;
    But drop by drop, that poor,
    That last supply is drain'd!
Still the same burning sun! no cloud in heaven!
The hot air quivers, and the sultry mist
Floats o'er the desert, with a show
Of distant waters,[14] mocking their distress!

XXIII.

    The youth's parch'd lips were black,
His tongue was dry and rough,[15]
    His eye-balls red with heat.
His comrade gaz'd on him with looks
That seem'd to speak of pity, and he said
    Let me behold thy Ring;
« It may have virtue that can save us yet!»
    With that he took his hand
    And view'd the writing close,
    Then cried with sudden joy,

« It is a stone that whoso bears,
    The Genii must obey!
    Now raise thy voice, my Son,
And bid them in his name that here is written
    Preserve us in our need.»

XXIV.

    « Nay!» answer'd Thalaba,
« Shall I distrust the providence of God?
    Is it not he must save?
    If Allah wills it not,
    Vain were the Genii's aid.»

XXV.

    Whilst he spake, Lobaba's eye,
    Full on the distance fix'd,
    Attended not his speech.
    Its fearful meaning drew
    The looks of Thalaba.
Columns of sand came moving on,
    Red in the burning ray,
    Like obelisks of fire,
They rush'd before the driving wind.
    Vain were all thoughts of flight!
    They had not hop'd escape,
Could they have backed the Dromedary[16] then,
    Who in his rapid race
Gives to the tranquil air a drowning force.

XXVI.

High .. high in heaven upcurl'd
The dreadful sand-spouts mov'd,[17]
Swift as the whirlwind that impell'd their way,
They rush'd toward the travellers!
    The old Magician shriek'd,
    And lo! the foremost bursts,
    Before the whirlwind's force,
Scattering afar a burning shower of sand.
    « Now by the virtue of the Ring,
        Save us!» Lobaba cried.
    « While yet thou hast the power,
        Save us! O save us! now!»
    The youth made no reply,
Gazing in awful wonder on the scene.

XXVII.

« Why dost thou wait?» the Old Man exclaim'd
« If Allah and the Prophet will not save,
    Call on the Powers that will!»

XXVIII.

« Ha! do I know thee, Infidel accurst?»
    Exclaim'd the awaken'd youth.
« And thou hast led me hither, Child of Sin!
    That fear might make me sell
    My soul to endless death!»

XXIX.

« Fool that thou art!» Lobaba cried,
    «Call upon him whose name
    Thy charmed signet bears,
Or die the death thy foolishness deserves!»

XXX.

« Servant of Hell! die thou!» quoth Thalaba,
    And leaning on his bow

He fitted the loose string,
And laid the arrow in its resting-place.
« Bow of my Father, do thy duty now!»
He drew the arrow to its point,
True to his eye it fled,
And full upon the breast
It smote the wizard man.
Astonished Thalaba beheld
The blunted point recoil.

XXXI.

A proud and bitter smile
Wrinkled Lobaba's cheek.
« Try once again thine earthly arms!» he cried.
« Rash Boy! the Power I serve
Abandons not his votaries.
It is for Allah's wretched slaves, like thou,
To serve a master, who in the hour of need
Forsakes them to their fate!
I leave thee!» .. and he shook his staff, and called
The Chariot of his charms.

XXXII.

Swift as the viewless wind
Self-moved, the Chariot came;
The Sorcerer mounts the seat.
« Yet once more weigh thy danger!» he exclaim'd,
« Ascend the car with me,
And with the speed of thought
We pass the desert bounds.»
The indignant youth vouchsaf'd not to reply,
And lo! the magic car begins its course!
Hark! hark! .. he screams .. Lobaba screams!
What, wretch, and hast thou rais'd
The rushing terrors of the Wilderness
To fall on thine own head?
Death! death! inevitable death!
Driven by the breath of God,
A column of the Desert met his way.

BOOK V.

Thou hast girded me with strength unto the battle; thou hast
subdued under me those that rose up against me.
Psalm xviii, 39.

I.

WHEN Thalaba from adoration rose,
The air was cool, the sky
With welcome clouds o'ercast,
Which soon came down in rain.
He lifted up his fever'd face to heaven,
And bar'd his head, and stretch'd his hands
To that delightful shower,
And felt the coolness flow through every limb,
Freshening his powers of life.

II.

A loud quick panting! Thalaba looks up,
He starts, and his instinctive hand
Grasps the knife hilt; for close beside
A Tiger passes him.
An indolent and languid eye

The passing Tiger turn'd;
His head was hanging down,
His dry tongue lolling low,
And the short panting of his fever'd breath
Came through his hot parch'd nostrils painfully.
The young Arabian knew
The purport of his hurried pace,
And following him in hope,
Saw joyful from afar
The Tiger stoop and drink.

III.

The desert Pelican had built her nest
In that deep solitude,
And now, return'd from distant flight,
Fraught with the river-stream,
Her load of water had disburthen'd there.
Her young in the refreshing bath
Dipt down their callow heads,
Fill'd the swoln membrane from their plumeless throat
Pendant, and bills yet soft;
And buoyant with arch'd breast,
Plied in unpractis'd stroke
The oars of their broad feet.
They, as the spotted prowler of the wild
Laps the cool wave, ' around their mother crowd,
And nestle underneath her outspread wings.
The spotted prowler of the wild
Lapt the cool wave, and satiate, from the nest,
Guiltless of blood, withdrew

IV.

The mother bird had mov'd not,
But cowering o'er her nestlings,
Sate confident and fearless,
And watch'd the wonted guest.
But when the human visitant approach'd,
The alarmed Pelican
Retiring from that hostile shape
Gathers her young, and menaces with wings,
And forward thrusts her threatening neck,
Its feathers ruffling in her wrath,
Bold with maternal fear.
Thalaba drank, and in the water-skin
Hoarded the precious element.
Not all he took, but in the large nest left
Store that sufficed for life;
And journeying onward, blest the Carrier Bird,
And blest, in thankfulness,
Their common Father, provident for all.

V.

With strength renew'd, and confident in faith,
The son of Hodeirah proceeds;
Till after the long toil of many a day,
At length Bagdad appear'd,
The City of his search.
He hastening to the gate,
Roams o'er the city with insatiate eyes;
Its thousand dwellings, o'er whose level roofs
Fair cupolas appear'd, and high-domed mosques,
And pointed minarets, and cypress groves,
Every where scatter'd ² in unwithering green.

VI.

Thou too art fallen, Bagdad! City of Peace,³
Thou too hast had thy day,

And loathsome Ignorance, and brute Servitude,
Pollute thy dwellings now,
Erst for the Mighty and the Wise renown'd.
O yet illustrious for remember'd fame,
Thy founder the Victorious,[4] and the pomp
Of Haroun, for whose name by blood defil'd,
Yahia's, and the blameless Barmecides',
Genius hath wrought salvation; and the years
When Science with the good Al-Maimon dwelt;
So one day may the Crescent from thy Mosques
Be pluck'd by Wisdom, when the enlighten'd arm
Of Europe conquers to redeem the East!

VII.

Then Pomp and Pleasure dwelt within her walls;
The Merchants of the East and of the West
Met in her arch'd Bazars,[5]
All day the active poor
Shower'd a cool comfort o'er her thronging streets;
Labour was busy in her looms;
Through all her open gates
Long troops of laden Camels lin'd her roads,
And Tigris on his tameless current bore[6]
Armenian harvests to her multitudes.

VIII.

But not in sumptuous Caravansery
The adventurer idles there,
Nor satiates wonder with her pomp and wealth;
A long day's distance from the walls
Stands ruined Babylon!
The time of action is at hand;
The hope that for so many a year
Hath been his daily thought, his nightly dream,
Stings to more restlessness.
He loaths all lingering that delays the hour
When, full of glory, from his quest return'd,
He on the pillar of the Tent belov'd
Shall hang Hodeirah's sword.

IX.

The many-colour'd domes[7]
Yet wore one dusky hue;
The Cranes upon the Mosque
Kept their night-clatter still;[8]
When through the gate the early Traveller past.
And when at evening o'er the swampy plain
The Bittern's boom came far,[9]
Distinct in darkness seen,
Above the low horizon's lingering light
Rose the near ruins of old Babylon.

X.

Once from her lofty walls the Charioteer,[10]
Look'd down on swarming myriads; once she flung
Her arches o'er Euphrates' conquer'd tide,
And through her brazen portals when she pour'd
Her armies forth, the distant nations look'd
As men who watch the thunder-cloud in fear
Lest it should burst above them.   She was fallen,
The Queen of Cities, Babylon, was fallen,
Low lay her bulwark; the black Scorpion bask'd
In the palace courts; within the sanctuary
The She-Wolf hid her whelps.
Is yonder huge and shapeless heap, what once
Hath been the aërial Gardens,[11] height on height

Rising like Media's mountains crown'd with wood,
Work of imperial dotage? where the fane
Of Belus?[12] where the Golden Image now,
Which at the sound of dulcimer and lute,
Cornet and sackbut, harp and psaltery,
The Assyrian slaves ador'd?
A labyrinth of ruins, Babylon,
Spreads o'er the blasted plain:
The wandering Arab never sets his tent
Within her walls;[13] the Shepherd eyes afar
Her evil towers, and devious drives his flock.
Alone unchanged, a free and bridgeless tide,
Euphrates rolls along,
Eternal Nature's work.

XI.

Through the broken portal,
Over weedy fragments,
Thalaba went his way.
Cautious he trod, and felt
The dangerous ground before him with his bow.
The Jackal started at his steps;
The Stork, alarm'd at sound of man,
From her broad nest upon the old pillar top,
Affrighted fled on flapping wings;
The Adder, in her haunts disturb'd,
Lanced at the intruding staff her arrowy tongue.

XII.

Twilight and moonshine dimly mingling gave
An awful light obscure,
Evening not wholly clos'd,
The Moon still pale and faint.
An awful light obscure,
Broken by many a mass of blackest shade;
Long column stretching dark through weeds and moss,
Broad length of lofty wall,
Whose windows lay in light,
And of their former shape, low arch'd or square,
Rude outline on the earth
Figur'd, with long grass fringed.

XIII.

Reclin'd against a column's broken shaft,
Unknowing whitherward to bend his way,
He stood, and gaz'd around.
The Ruins clos'd him in;
It seem'd as if no foot of man
For ages had intruded there.
Soon at approaching step
Starting, he turn'd and saw
A Warrior in the moon-beam drawing near.
Forward the Stranger came,
And with a curious eye
Perus'd the Arab youth.
« And who art thou,» he cried,
« That at an hour like this
Wanderest in Babylon?
A way-bewilder'd traveller, seekest thou
The ruinous shelter here?
Or comest thou to hide
The plunder of the night?
Or hast thou spells to make
These ruins, yawning from their rooted base,
Disclose their secret wealth?»[14]

XIV.

The youth replied, « Nor wandering traveller,
Nor robber of the night,
Nor skill'd in spells am I.
I seek the Angels here,
Haruth and Maruth. Stranger, in thy turn,
Why wander'st thou in Babylon,
And who art thou, the questioner ?»

XV.

The man was fearless, and the temper'd pride
Which toned the voice of Thalaba
Displeas'd not him, himself of haughty heart.
Heedless he answer'd, « Knowest thou
Their cave of punishment ?»

XVI.

THALABA.
Vainly I seek it.
STRANGER.
Art thou firm of foot
To tread the ways of danger?
THALABA.
Point the path !
STRANGER.
Young Arab ! if thou hast a heart can beat
Evenly in danger ; if thy bowels yearn not
With human fears, at scenes where undisgraced
The soldier, tried in battle, might look back
And tremble, follow me !—for I am bound
Into that cave of horrors.

XVII.

Thalaba
Gazed on his comrade : he was young, of port
Stately and strong ; belike his face had pleas'd
A woman's eye, but the youth read in it
Unrestrain'd passions, the obdurate soul
Bold in all evil daring ; and it taught,
By Nature's irresistible instinct, doubt
Well-tim'd and wary. Of himself assur'd,
Fearless of man, and confident in faith,
« Lead on !» cried Thalaba.
Mohareb led the way !
And through the ruin'd streets,
And through the farther gate,
They pass'd in silence on.

XVIII.

What sound is borne on the wind?
Is it the storm that shakes
The thousand oaks of the forest?
But Thalaba's long locks
Flow down his shoulders moveless, and the wind
In his loose mantle raises not one fold.
Is it the river's roar
Dash'd down some rocky descent?
Along the level plain
Euphrates glides unheard.
What sound disturbs the night,
Loud as the summer forest in the storm,
As the river that roars among rocks?

XIX.

And what the heavy cloud
That hangs upon the vale,

Thick as the mist o'er a well-water'd plain
Settling at evening when the cooler air
Lets its day-vapours fall ;
Black as the sulphur-cloud,
That through Vesuvius, or from Hecla's mouth,
Rolls up, ascending from the infernal fires.

XX.

From Ait's bitumen lake [15]
That heavy cloud asbends;
That everlasting roar
From where its gushing springs
Boil their black billows up.
Silent the Arab youth,
Along the verge of that wide lake,
Follow'd Mohareb's way,
Toward a ridge of rocks that bank'd its side.
There from a cave, with torrent force,
And everlasting roar,
The black bitumen roll'd.
The moon-light lay upon the rocks;
Their crags were visible,
The shade of jutting cliffs,
And where broad lichens whiten'd some smooth spot,
And where the ivy hung
Its flowing tresses down.
A little way within the cave
The moonlight fell, glossing the sable tide
That gush'd tumultuous out.
A little way it entered, then the rock
Arching its entrance, and the winding way,
Darken'd the unseen depths.

XXI.

No eye of mortal man,
If unenabled by enchanted spell,
Had pierc'd those fearful depths ;
For mingling with the roar
Of the portentous torrent, oft were heard
Shrieks, and wild yells that scar'd
The brooding Eagle from her midnight nest.
The affrighted countrymen
Call it the Mouth of Hell;
And ever when their way leads near,
They hurry with averted eyes,
And dropping their beads fast, [16]
Pronounce the Holy Name.

XXII.

There pausing at the cavern mouth,
Mohareb turn'd to Thalaba,
« Now darest thou enter in ?»
« Behold !» the youth replied,
And leading in his turn the dangerous way,
Set foot within the cave.

XXIII.

« Stay, Madman !» cried his comrade ; « wouldst thou rush
Headlong to certain death?
Where are thine arms to meet
The Guardian of the Passage ?» A loud shriek,
That shook along the windings of the cave,
Scatter'd the youth's reply.

XXIV.

Mohareb, when the long re-echoing ceas'd,
Exclaim'd, « Fate favour'd thee,

Young Arab! when she wrote upon thy brow [17]
The meeting of to-night;
Else surely had thy name
This hour been blotted from the Book of Life!»

XXV.

So saying, from beneath
His cloak a bag he drew:
« Young Arab! thou art brave,» he cried,
« But thus to rush on danger unprepar'd,
As lions spring upon the hunter's spear,
Is blind, brute courage. Zohak keeps the cave, [18]
Giantly tyrant of primeval days.
Force cannot win the passage.» Thus he said,
And from his wallet drew a human hand,
Shrivell'd, and dry, and black,
And fitting as he spake
A taper in its hold,
Pursued: « A murderer on the stake had died;
I drove the Vulture from his limbs, and lopt
The hand that did the murder, and drew up
The tendon-strings to close its grasp,
And in the sun and wind
Parch'd it, nine weeks expos'd.
The Taper,—but not here the place to impart,
Nor hast thou done the rites,
That fit thee to partake the mystery.
Look! it burns clear, but with the air around,
Its dead ingredients mingle deathiness.
This when the Keeper of the Cave shall feel,
Maugre the doom of Heaven,
The salutary spell [19]
Shall lull his penal agony to sleep,
And leave the passage free.»

XXVI.

Thalaba answer'd not.
Nor was there time for answer now,
For lo! Mohareb leads,
And o'er the vaulted cave,
Trembles the accursed taper's feeble light.
There where the narrowing chasm
Rose loftier in the hill,
Stood Zohak, wretched man, condemn'd to keep
His Cave of punishment.
His was the frequent scream
Which far away the prowling Jackal heard,
And howl'd in terror back:
For from his shoulders grew
Two snakes of monster size,
Which ever at his head
Aim'd eager their keen teeth
To satiate raving hunger with his brain.
He, in the eternal conflict, oft would seize
Their swelling necks, and in his giant grasp
Bruise them, and rend their flesh with bloody nails,
And howl for agony,
Feeling the pangs he gave, for of himself
Inseparable parts, his torturers grew.

XXVII.

To him approaching now,
Mohareb held the wither'd arm,
The taper of enchanted power.
The unhallow'd spell in hand unholy held
Now minister'd to mercy; heavily

The wretch's eyelids clos'd;
And welcome and unfelt
Like the release of death,
A sudden sleep fell on his vital powers.

XXVIII.

Yet though along the cave
Lay Zohak's giant limbs,
The twin-born serpents kept the narrow pass,
Kindled their fiery eyes,
Darted their tongues of terror, and roll'd out
Their undulating length,
Like the long streamers of some gallant ship
Buoy'd on the wavy air,
Still struggling to flow on, and still withheld
The scent of living flesh
Inflam'd their appetite.

XXIX.

Prepar'd for all the perils of the cave,
Mohareb came. He from his wallet drew
Two human heads, yet warm.
O hard of heart! whom not the visible power
Of retributive Justice, and the doom
Of Zohak in his sight,
Deterr'd from equal crime!
Two human heads, yet warm, he laid
Before the scaly guardians of the pass.
They to their wonted banquet of old years
Turn'd eager, and the narrow pass was free.

XXX.

And now before their path
The opening cave dilates;
They reach a spacious vault,
Where the black river fountains burst their way.
Now as a whirlwind's force
Had center'd on the spring,
The gushing flood roll'd up;
And now the deaden'd roar
Echoed beneath them, as its sudden pause
Left wide a dark abyss,
Adown whose fathomless gulphs the eye was lost.

XXXI.

Blue flames that hover'd o'er the springs
Flung through the cavern their uncertain light;
Now waving on the waves they lay,
And now their fiery curls
Flow'd in long tresses up.
And now contracting, glow'd with whiter heat.
Then up they shot again,
Darting pale flashes through the tremulous air;
The flames, the red and yellow sulphur-smoke,
And the black darkness of the vault,
Commingling indivisibly.

XXXII.

« Here,» quoth Mohareb, « do the Angels dwell,
The Teachers of Enchantment.» Thalaba
Then raised his voice, and cried,
« Haruth and Maruth, hear me! not with rites
Accursed, to disturb your penitence,
And learn forbidden lore,
Repentant Angels, seek I your abode.
Me Allah and the Prophet mission here,
Their chosen servant I.
Tell me the Talisman.»

XXXIII.

« And dost thou think,»
Mohareb cried, as with a scornful smile
He glanced upon his comrade, « dost thou think
To trick them of their secret? for the dupes
Of human kind keep this lip-righteousness!
'T will serve thee in the Mosque
And in the Market-place,
But Spirits view the heart.
Only by strong and torturing spells enforced,
Those stubborn Angels teach the charm
By which we must descend.»

XXXIV.

« Descend!» said Thalaba.
But then the wrinkling smile
Forsook Mohareb's cheek,
And darker feelings settled on his brow.
« Now by my soul,» quoth he, « and I believe,
Idiot! that I have led
Some camel-kneed prayer-monger through the cave! »[20]
What brings thee hither? thou shouldst have a hut
By some Saint's grave beside the public way,[21]
There to less-knowing fools
Retail thy Koran scraps,[22]
And in thy turn, die civet-like at last
In the dung-perfume of thy sanctity!—
Ye whom I seek! that, led by me,
Feet unimitiate tread
Your threshold, this atones!
Fit sacrifice he falls!»
And forth he flash'd his scimetar,
And rais'd the murderous blow.

XXXV.

There ceas'd his power; his lifted arm,
Suspended by the spell,
Hung impotent to strike.
« Poor Hypocrite!» cried he,
« And this then is thy faith
In Allah and the Prophet! they had fail'd
To save thee, but for Magic's stolen aid;
Yea, they had left thee yonder Serpents' meal,
But that, in prudent cowardice,
The chosen Servant of the Lord came in
Safe follower of my path!»

XXXVI.

« Blasphemer! dost thou boast of guiding me?»
Kindling with pride, quoth Thalaba,
« Blindly the wicked work
The righteous will of Heaven!
Sayest thou, that, diffident of God,
In magic spells I trust?
Liar! let witness this!»
And he drew off Abdaldar's Ring,
And cast it in the gulph,
A skinny hand came up,
And caught it as it fell,
And peals of devilish laughter shook the Cave.

XXXVII.

Then joy suffus'd Mohareb's cheek,
And Thalaba beheld
The blue blade gleam, descending to destroy.

XXXVIII.

The undefended youth
Sprung forward, and he seiz'd
Mohareb in his grasp,
And grappled with him breast to breast.
Sinewy and large of limb Mohareb was,
Broad-shoulder'd, and his joints
Knit firm, and in the strife
Of danger practis'd well.
Time had not thus matur'd young Thalaba:
But now the enthusiast mind,
The inspiration of his soul,
Pour'd vigour like the strength
Of madness through his frame.
Mohareb reels before him! he right on,
With knee, with breast, with arm,
Presses the staggering foe!
And now upon the brink
Of that tremendous spring,—
There with fresh impulse, and a rush of force,
He thrust him from his hold.
The upwhirling flood receiv'd
Mohareb, then, absorb'd,
Engulph'd him in the abyss.

XXXIX.

Thalaba's breath came fast,
And, panting, he breath'd out
A broken prayer of thankfulness.
At length he spake and said,
« Haruth and Maruth! are ye here?
Or has that evil guide misled my search?
I, Thalaba, the Servant of the Lord,
Invoke you. Hear me, Angels! so may Heaven
Accept and mitigate your penitence.
I go to root from earth the Sorcerer brood,
Tell me the needful Talisman!»

XL.

Thus as he spake, recumbent on the rock
Beyond the black abyss,
Their forms grew visible.
A settled sorrow sate upon their brows,
Sorrow alone, for trace of guilt and shame
Now nought remained; and gradual as by prayer
The sin was purged away,
Their robe of glory, purified of stain,[23]
Resum'd the lustre of its native light.

XLI.

In awe the youth receiv'd the answering voice,
« Son of Hodeirah! thou hast prov'd it here;
The Talisman is Faith.»

BOOK VI.

Then did I see a pleasant Paradise,
Full of sweet flowers and daintiest delights,
Such as on earth man could not more devise
With pleasures choice to feed his cheerful sprights;
Not that which Merlin by his magic slights
Made for the gentle squire to entertain
His fair Belphœbe, could this garden stain.
Spenser. *Ruins of Time.*

I.

So from the inmost cavern, Thalaba
Retrod the windings of the rock.
Still on the ground the giant limbs
Of Zohak were outstretch'd;

The spell of sleep had ceased,
And his broad eyes were glaring on the youth:
Yet raised he not his arm to bar the way,
Fearful to rouse the snakes
Now lingering o'er their meal.

II.

Oh then, emerging from the dreadful cave,
How grateful did the gale of night
Salute his freshen'd sense!
How full of lightsome joy,
Thankful to Heaven, he hastens by the verge
Of that bitumen lake,
Whose black and heavy fumes,
Surge heaving after surge,
Roll'd like the billowy and tumultuous sea.

III.

The song of many a bird at morn
Aroused him from his rest.
Lo! by his side a courser stood!
More animate of eye,
Of form more faultless never had he seen,
More light of limbs and beautiful in strength,
Among the race whose blood,
Pure and unmingled, from the royal steed.
Of Solomon came down.

IV.

The chosen Arab's eye
Glanced o'er his graceful shape,
His rich caparisons,
His crimson trappings gay.
But when he saw the mouth
Uncurb'd, the unbridled neck,
Then flush'd his cheek, and leap'd his heart;
For sure he deem'd that Heaven had sent
The courser, whom no erring hand should guide.
And lo! the eager Steed
Throws his head, and paws the ground,
Impatient of delay!
Then up leap'd Thalaba,
And away went the self-govern'd steed.

V.

Far over the plain
Away went the bridleless steed;
With the dew of the morning his fetlocks were wet,
The foam froth'd his limbs in the journey of noon,
Nor stay'd he till over the westerly heaven
The shadows of evening had spread.
Then on a shelter'd bank
The appointed youth reposed,
And by him laid the docile courser down.
Again in the grey of the morning
Thalaba bounded up;
Over hill, over dale,
Away goes the bridleless steed.
Again at eve he stops,
Again the youth descends:
His load discharged, his errand done,
Then bounded the courser away.

VL

Heavy and dark the eve:
The Moon was hid on high,

A dim light only tinged the mist
That cross'd her in the path of Heaven.
All living sounds had ceased,
Only the flow of waters near was heard,
A low and lulling melody.

VII.

Fasting, yet not of want
Percipient, he on that mysterious steed
Had reach'd his resting place,
For expectation kept his nature up.
Now as the flow of waters near
Awoke a feverish thirst,
Led by the sound, he moved
To seek the grateful wave.

VIII.

A meteor in the hazy air
Play'd before his path;
Before him now it roll'd
A globe of living fire;
And now contracted to a steady light,
As when the solitary hermit prunes
His lamp's long undulating flame:
And now its wavy point
Up-blazing rose, like a young cypress tree
Sway'd by the heavy wind;
Anon to Thalaba it moved
And wrapp'd him in its pale innocuous fire:
Now, in the darkness drown'd,
Left him with eyes bedimm'd
And now, emerging,[2] spread the scene to sight.

IX.

Led by the sound and meteor-flame,
Advanced the Arab youth.
Now to the nearest of the many rills
He stoops; ascending steam
Timely repels his hand;
For from its source it sprung, a boiling tide.
A second course with better hap he tries,
The wave intensely cold
Tempts to a copious draught.
There was a virtue in the wave;
His limbs, that, stiff with toil,
Dragg'd heavy, from the copious draught received
Lightness and supple strength.
O'erjoy'd, and deeming the benignant Power,
Who sent the reinless steed,
Had bless'd the healing waters to his use,
He laid him down to sleep;
Lull'd by the soothing and incessant sound,
The flow of many waters, blending oft
With shriller tones, and deep low murmurings,
Which from the fountain caves
In mingled melody
Like faery music, heard at midnight, came.

X.

The sounds which last he heard at night
Awoke his sense at morn.
A scene of wonders lay before his eyes.
In mazy windings o'er the vale
Wander'd a thousand streams;
They in their endless flow[3] had channell'd deep
The rocky soil o'er which they ran,

Veining its thousand islet stones,
Like clouds that freckle o'er the summer sky;
The blue ethereal ocean circling each,
And insulating all.

XI.

A thousand shapes they wore, those islet stones,
And nature with her various tints,
Varied anew their thousand forms:
For some were green with moss,
Some rich with yellow lichen's gold,
Or ruddier tinged, or grey, or silver-white,
Or sparkling sparry radiance to the sun.
Here gush'd the fountains up,
Alternate light and blackness, like the play
Of sunbeams on the warrior's burnish'd arms.
Yonder the river roll'd, whose bed,
Their labyrinthine lingerings o'er,
Received the confluent rills.

XII.

This was a wild and wondrous scene,
Strange and beautiful as where
By Oton-tala, like a sea of stars,⁴
The hundred sources of Hoangho burst.
High mountains closed the vale,
Bare rocky mountains, to all living things
Inhospitable; on whose sides no herb
Rooted, no insect fed, no bird awoke
Their echoes, save the Eagle, strong of wing;
A lonely plunderer, that afar
Sought in the vales his prey.

XIII.

Thither towards those mountains Thalaba
Advanced, for well he ween'd that there had Fate
Destined the adventure's end.
Up a wide vale, winding amid their depths,
A stony vale between receding heights
Of stone, he wound his way.
A cheerless place! the solitary Bee,
Whose buzzing was the only sound of life,
Flew there on restless wing,
Seeking in vain one blossom, where to fix.

XIV.

Still Thalaba holds on;
The winding vale now narrows on his way,
And steeper of ascent,
Rightward and leftward rise the rocks,
And now they meet across the vale.
Was it the toil of human hands
Had hewn a passage in the rock,
Through whose rude portal way
The light of heaven was seen?
Rude and low the portal-way
Beyond the same ascending straits,⁵
Went winding up the wilds.

XV.

Still a bare, silent, solitary glen,
A fearful silence, and a solitude
That made itself be felt;
And steeper now the ascent,
A rugged path, that tired

The straining muscles, toiling slowly up.
At length again, a rock
Stretch'd o'er the narrow vale.
There also was a portal hewn,
But gates of massy iron barr'd the way,
Huge, solid, heavy-hinged.

XVI.

There hung a horn beside the gate,
Ivory-tipt and brazen-mouth'd;
He took the ivory tip,
And through the brazen mouth he breathed;
From rock to rock rebounding rung the blast;
Like a long thunder-peal!
The gates of iron, by no human arm
Unfolded, turning on their hinges slow,
Disclosed the passage of the rock.
He enter'd, and the iron gates
Fell to, and closed him in.

XVII.

It was a narrow winding way:
Dim lamps suspended from the vault,
Lent to the gloom an agitated light.
Winding it pierced the rock,
A long descending path
By gates of iron closed;
There also hung the horn beside
Of ivory tip and brazen mouth.
Again he took the ivory tip,
And gave the brazen mouth his voice again.
Not now in thunder spake the horn,
But pour'd a sweet and thrilling melody:
The gates flew open, and a flood of light
Rush'd on his dazzled eyes.

XVIII.

Was it to earthly Eden, lost so long,
The Youth had found the wondrous way?
But earthly Eden boasts
No terraced palaces,
No rich pavilions, bright with woven gold,⁶
Like these that in the vale
Rise amid odorous groves.
The astonish'd Thalaba,
Doubting as though an unsubstantial dream
Beguiled his passive sense,
A moment closed his eyes;
Still they were there,—the palaces and groves,
And rich pavilions glittering golden light.

XIX.

And lo! a man, reverend in comely age,
Advancing, meets the youth.
« Favour'd of Fortune, » he exclaim'd, « go taste
The joys of Paradise!
The reinless steed that ranges o'er the world,
Brings hither those alone for lofty deeds
Mark'd by their horoscope: permitted here
A foretaste of the full beatitude,
That in heroic acts they may go on
More ardent, eager to return and reap
Endless enjoyment here, their destined meed.
Favour'd of Fortune thou, go taste
The joys of Paradise!»

XX.

This said, he turn'd away, and left
The Youth in wonder mute;
For Thalaba stood mute,
And passively receiv'd
The mingled joy which flow'd on every sense.
Where'er his eye could reach,
Fair structures, rainbow-hued, arose;
And rich pavilions through the opening woods
Gleam'd from their waving curtains sunny gold;
And winding through the verdant vale,
Flow'd streams of liquid light;
And fluted cypresses rear'd up
Their living obelisks;
And broad-leav'd plane-trees in long colonnades [7]
O'er-arch'd delightful walks,
Where round their trunks the thousand-tendril'd vine
Wound up and hung the boughs with greener wreaths,
And clusters not their own.
Wearied with endless beauty, did his eyes
Return for rest? beside him teems the earth
With tulips, like the ruddy evening streak'd; [8]
And here the lily hangs her head of snow;
And here amid her sable cup [9]
Shines the red eye-spot, like one brightest star,
The solitary twinkler of the night;
And here the rose expands
Her paradise of leaves. [10]

XXI.

Then on his ear what sounds
Of harmony arose!
Far music and the distance-mellow'd song
From bowers of merriment;
The waterfall remote;
The murmuring of the leafy groves;
The single nightingale
Perch'd in the rosier by, so richly ton'd,
That never from that most melodious bird,
Singing a love-song to his brooding mate,
Did Thracian shepherd by the grave
Of Orpheus hear a sweeter melody, [11]
Though there the Spirit of the Sepulchre
All his own power infuse, to swell
The incense that he loves.

XXII.

And oh! what odours the voluptuous vale
Scatters from jasmine bowers,
From yon rose wilderness,
From cluster'd henna, and from orange groves,
That with such perfumes fill the breeze
As Peris to their Sister bear,
When from the summit of some lofty tree
She hangs encaged, the captive of the Dives.
They from their pinions shake
The sweetness of celestial flowers,
And, as her enemies impure
From that impervious poison far away
Fly groaning with the torment, she the while
Inhales her fragrant food. [12]
Such odours flow'd upon the world,
When at Mahommed's nuptials, word
Went forth in Heaven, to roll
The everlasting gates of Paradise

Back on their living hinges, that its gales
Might visit all below; the general bliss
Thrill'd every bosom, and the family
Of man, for once, partook one common joy. [13]

XXIII.

Full of the joy, yet still awake
To wonder, on went Thalaba;
On every side the song of mirth,
The music of festivity,
Invite the passing youth.
Wearied at length with hunger and with heat,
He enters in a banquet room,
Where round a fountain brink,
On silken carpets sate the festive train. [14]
Instant through all his frame
Delightful coolness spread;
The playing fount refresh'd
The agitated air;
The very light came cool'd through silvering panes
Of pearly shell, [15] like the pale moon-beam tinged;
Or where the wine-vase [16] fill'd the aperture,
Rosy as rising morn, or softer gleam
Of saffron, like the sunny evening mist:
Through every hue, and streak'd by all,
The flowing fountain play'd.
Around the water-edge
Vessels of wine, alternate placed,
Ruby and amber, tinged its little waves.
From golden goblets there [17]
The guests sate quaffing the delicious juice
Of Shiraz' golden grape.

XXIV.

But Thalaba took not the draught;
For rightly he knew had the Prophet forbidden
That beverage, the mother of sins. [18]
Nor did the urgent guests
Proffer a second time the liquid fire;
For in the youth's strong eye they saw
No moveable resolve.
Yet not uncourteous, Thalaba
Drank the cool draught of innocence,
That fragrant from its dewy vase [19]
Came purer than it left its native bed.
And he partook the odorous fruits,
For all rich fruits were there.
Water-melons rough of rind,
Whose pulp the thirsty lip
Dissolved into a draught:
Pistachios from the heavy-cluster'd trees
Of Malavert, or Haleb's fertile soil,
And Casbin's luscious grapes of amber hue, [20]
That many a week endure
The summer sun intense,
Till by its powerful fire
All watery particles exhal'd, alone
The strong essential sweetness ripens there.
Here cased in ice, the apricot, [21]
A topaz, crystal-set:
Here, on a plate of snow,
The sunny orange rests;
And still the aloes and the sandal-wood,
From golden censors, o'er the banquet room
Diffuse their dying sweets.

XXV.

Anon a troop of females form'd the dance,
Their ancles bound with bracelet-bells, [22]
That made the modulating harmony.
Transparent garments to the greedy eye [23]
Gave all their harlot limbs,
Which writhed, in each immodest gesture skill'd.

XXVI.

With earnest eyes the banqueters
Fed on the sight impure;
And Thalaba, he gazed,
But in his heart he bore a talisman,
Whose blessed alchemy
To virtuous thoughts refined
The loose suggestions of the scene impure.
Oneiza's image swam before his sight,
His own Arabian Maid.
He rose, and from the banquet room he rush'd,
And tears ran down his burning cheek;
And nature for a moment woke the thought,
And murmured, that, from all domestic joys
Estranged, he wandered o'er the world
A lonely being, far from all he lov'd.
Son of Hodeirah, not among thy crimes
That momentary murmur shall be written!

XXVII.

From tents of revelry,
From festal bowers, to solitude he ran;
And now he reach'd where all the rills
Of that well-watered garden in one tide
Roll'd their collected waves.
A straight and stately bridge
Stretch'd its long arches o'er the ample stream.
Strong in the evening, and distinct its shade
Lay on the watery mirror, and his eye
Saw it united with its parent pile,
One huge fantastic fabric. Drawing near,
Loud from the chambers of the bridge below, [24]
Sounds of carousal came and song;
And unveil'd women bade the advancing youth
Come merry-make with them!
Unhearing, or unheeding, Thalaba
Past o'er with hurried pace,
And plunged amid the forest solitude.

XXVIII.

Deserts of Araby!
His soul return'd to you.
He cast himself upon the earth,
And clos'd his eyes, and call'd
The voluntary vision up.
A cry, as of distress,
Arous'd him; loud it came and near!
He started up, he strung his bow,
He pluck'd the arrow forth.
Again a shriek ..a woman's shriek!
And lo! she rushes through the trees,
Her veil all rent, her garments torn!
He follows close, the ravisher...
Even on the unechoing grass
She hears his tread, so near!
« Prophet, save me! save me, God!
Help! help!» she cried to Thalaba;
Thalaba drew the bow:

The unerring arrow did its work of death.
He turn'd him to the woman, and beheld
His own Oneiza, his Arabian Maid.

BOOK VII.

Now all is done; bring home the Bride again.
Bring home the triumph of our victory!
Bring home with you the glory of her gain,
With joyance bring her, and with jollity.
Never had man more joyful day than this,
Whom Heaven would heap with bliss.
SPENSER's *Epithalamium.*

I.

FROM fear, and from amazement, and from joy,
At length the Arabian Maid recovering speech,
Threw around Thalaba her arms, and cried,
« My father! O my father!».... Thalaba
In wonder lost, yet fearful to inquire,
Bent down his cheek on hers,
And their tears met, and mingled as they fell.

II.

ONEIZA.
At night they seiz'd me, Thalaba! in my sleep,...
Thou wert not near,.. and yet when in their grasp
I woke, my shriek of terror called on thee.
My father could not save me,—an old man!
And they were strong and many,—O my God,
The hearts they must have had to hear his prayers,
And yet to leave him childless!
THALABA.
We will seek him:
We will return to Araby.
ONEIZA.
Alas!
We should not find him, Thalaba! our tent
Is desolate! the wind hath heaped the sands
Within its door, the lizard's track is left [1]
Fresh on the untrodden dust; prowling by night
The tiger, as he passes, hears no breath
Of man, and turns to search its solitude.
Alas! he strays a wretched wanderer
Seeking his child! old man, he will not rest,—
He cannot rest,—his sleep is misery,—
His dreams are of my wretchedness, my wrongs,—
O Thalaba! this is a wicked place!
Let us be gone!
THALABA.
But how to pass again
The iron doors that opening at a breath
Gave easy entrance! armies in their strength
Would fail to move those hinges for return!
ONEIZA.
But we can climb the mountains that shut in
This dreadful garden.
THALABA.
Are Oneiza's limbs
. Equal to that long toil?
ONEIZA.
Oh I am strong,
Dear Thalaba! for this—fear gives me force,
And you are with me!
So she took his hand,

And gently drew him forward, and they went
  Towards the mountain chain.

III.

It was broad moonlight, and obscure or lost
  The garden beauties lay,
But the great boundary rose, distinctly marked.
  These were no little hills,
No sloping uplands lifting to the sun
Their vineyards, with fresh verdure, and the shade
Of ancient woods, courting the loiterer
To win the easy ascent : stone mountains these,
  Desolate rock on rock,
  The burthens of the earth
Whose snowy summits met the morning beam
When night was in the vale, whose feet were fix'd
In the world's foundations.²   Thalaba survey'd
  The heights precipitous,
Impending crags, rocks unascendible,
And summits that had tir'd the eagle's wing;
  « There is no way!» he cried.
  Paler Oneiza grew,
And hung upon his arm a feebler weight.

IV.

  But soon again to hope
  Revives the Arabian maid,
As Thalaba imparts the sudden thought.
  « I past a river,» cried the youth,
  « A full and copious stream.
The flowing waters cannot be restrained,
  And where they find or force their way,
There we perchance may follow; thitherward
  The current rolled along.»
  So saying, yet again in hope
  Quickening their eager steps,
  They turned them thitherward.

V.

Silent and calm the river rolled along,
  And at the verge arriv'd
  Of that fair garden, o'er a rocky bed
  Towards the mountain-base,
Still full and silent, held its even way.
But farther as they went its deepening sound
Louder and louder in the distance rose,
  As if it forced its stream
Struggling with crags along a narrow pass.
And lo! where raving o'er a hollow course
  The ever-flowing tide
Foams in a thousand whirlpools! there adown
  The perforated rock
Plunge the whole waters; so precipitous,
  So fathomless a fall,
That their earth-shaking roar came deadened up
  Like subterranean thunders.

VI.

  « Allah save us!»
Oneiza cried, « there is no path for man
  From this accursed place!»
  And as she spake, her joints
Were loosen'd, and her knees sunk under her.
  « Cheer up, Oneiza!» Thalaba replied,
  « Be of good heart. We cannot fly
  The dangers of the place,
  But we can conquer them!»

VII.

  And the young Arab's soul
Arose within him; « What is he,» he cried,
« Who hath prepar'd this garden of delight,
  And wherefore are its snares?»

VIII.

  The Arabian Maid replied,
« The Women, when I entered, welcom'd me
To Paradise, by Aloadin's will
Chosen, like themselves, a Houri of the Earth.
They told me, credulous of his blasphemies,
That Aloadin placed them to reward
His faithful servants with the joys of Heaven.
O Thalaba, and all are ready here
To wreak his wicked will, and work all crimes!
  How then shall we escape?»

IX.

« Woe to him!» cried the Appointed, a stern smile
Darkening with stronger shades his countenance ;
  « Woe to him! he hath laid his toils
  To take the Antelope,
  The Lion is come in!»
She shook her head : « A Sorcerer he,
And guarded by so many! Thalaba,—
  And thou but one!»

X.

  He raised his hand to Heaven,
  « Is there not God, Oneiza?
I have a Talisman, that, whoso bears,
Him, nor the Earthly, nor the Infernal Powers
  Of Evil, can cast down.
  Remember, Destiny
Hath mark'd me from mankind!
Now rest in faith, and I will guard thy sleep!»

XI.

  So on a violet bank
  The Arabian Maid laid down,
Her soft cheek pillow'd upon moss and flowers.
  She lay in silent prayer,
  Till prayer had tranquilliz'd her fears,
And sleep fell on her.   By her side
  Silent sate Thalaba,
  And gaz'd upon the Maid,
  And as he gaz'd, drew in
  New courage and intenser faith,
And waited calmly for the eventful day.

XII.

Loud sung the Lark, the awaken'd Maid
Beheld him twinkling in the morning light,
And wish'd for wings and liberty like his.
The flush of fear inflam'd her cheek,
  But Thalaba was calm of soul,
  Collected for the work.
  He ponder'd in his mind
  How from Lobaba's breast
  His blunted arrow fell.
  Aloadin too might wear
  Spell perchance of equal power
  To blunt the weapon's edge!
  Beside the river-brink
Rose a young poplar, whose unsteady leaves

Varying their verdure to the gale,
With silver glitter caught
His meditating eye.
Then to Oneiza turn'd the youth,
And gave his father's bow,
And o'er her shoulders slung
The quiver arrow-stor'd.
«Me other weapon suits;» said he,
«Bear thou the Bow: dear Maid,
The days return upon me, when these shafts,
True to thy guidance, from the lofty palm
Brought down the cluster, and thy gladden'd eye,
Exulting, turn'd to seek the voice of praise.
Oh! yet again, Oneiza, we shall share
Our desert-joys!» So saying, to the bank
He mov'd, and stooping low,
With double grasp, hand below hand, he clench'd,
And from its watery soil
Uptore the poplar trunk.
Then off he shook the clotted earth,
And broke away the head
And boughs, and lesser roots;
And lifting it aloft,
Wielded with able sway the massy club.
«Now for this child of Hell!» quoth Thalaba;
«Belike he shall exchange to-day
His dainty Paradise
For other dwelling, and the fruit
Of Zaccoum, cursed tree.» [3]

XIII.

With that the youth and Arab Maid
Toward the centre of the garden past.
It chanced that Aloadin had convok'd
The garden habitants,
And with the assembled throng
Oneiza mingled, and the Appointed Youth.
Unmark'd they mingled, or if one
With busier finger to his neighbour notes
The quiver'd Maid, «haply,» he says,
«Some daughter of the Homerites, [4]
Or one who yet remembers with delight
Her native tents of Himiar!» «Nay!» rejoins
His comrade, «a love-pageant! for the man
Mimics with that fierce eye and knotty club
Some savage lion-tamer, she forsooth
Must play the heroine of the years of old!»

XIV.

Radiant with gems upon his throne of gold
Sate Aloadin; o'er the Sorcerer's head
Hovered a Bird, and in the fragrant air
Waved his wide winnowing wings,
A living canopy.
Large as the hairy Cassowar
Was that o'ershadowing Bird;
So huge his talons, in their grasp
The Eagle would have hung a helpless prey.
His beak was iron, and his plumes
Glittered like burnish'd gold,
And his eyes glow'd, as though an inward fire
Shone through a diamond orb.

XV.

The blinded multitude
Ador'd the Sorcerer,
And bent the knee before him,
And shouted out his praise:
«Mighty art thou, the Bestower of joy,
The Lord of Paradise!»
Then Aloadin rose and waved his hand,
And they stood mute, and moveless,
In idolizing awe.

XVI.

«Children of Earth,» he cried,
«Whom I have guided here
By easier passage than the gate of Death;
The infidel Sultan, to whose lands
My mountains reach their roots,
Blasphemes and threatens me.
Strong are his armies, many are his guards,
Yet may a dagger find him.
Children of Earth, I tempt ye not
With the vain promise of a bliss unseen,
With tales of a hereafter heaven
Whence never Traveller hath returned!
Have ye not tasted of the cup of joy,
That in these groves of happiness
For ever over-mantling tempts
The ever-thirsty lip?
Who is there here that by a deed
Of danger will deserve
The eternal joys of actual paradise?».

XVII.

«I!» Thalaba exclaim'd,
And springing forward, on the Sorcerer's head
He dash'd the knotty club.

XVIII.

He fell not, though the force
Shatter'd his skull; nor flow'd the blood,
For by some hellish talisman
His life imprison'd still
Dwelt in the body. The astonish'd crowd
Stand motionless with fear, and wait
Immediate vengeance from the wrath of Heaven.
And lo! the Bird — the monster Bird,
Soars up — then pounces down
To seize on Thalaba!
Now, Oneiza, bend the bow,
Now draw the arrow home!—
True fled the arrow from Oneiza's hand;
It pierced the monster Bird,
It broke the Talisman,—
Then darkness cover'd all,
Earth shook, Heaven thunder'd, and amid the yells
Of Spirits accurs'd, destroy'd
The Paradise of Sin. [5]

XIX.

At last the earth was still;
The yelling of the Demons ceased;
Opening the wreck and ruin to their sight,
The darkness roll'd away. Alone in life,
Amid the desolation and the dead,
Stood the Destroyer and the Arabian Maid.
They look'd around, the rocks were rent,
The path was open, late by magic clos'd.
Awe-struck and silent down the stony glen
They wound their thoughtful way.

XX.

Amid the vale below
Tents rose, and streamers play'd,
And javelins sparkled in the sun,
And multitudes encamp'd,
Swarm'd, far as eye could follow, o'er the plain.
There in his war-pavilion sate
In council with his Chiefs
The Sultan of the Land.
Before his presence there a Captain led
Oneiza and the Appointed Youth.

XXI.

« Obedient to our Lord's command,» said he,
« We past toward the mountains, and began
The ascending strait; when suddenly Earth shook,
And darkness, like the midnight, fell around,
And fire and thunder came from Heaven
As though the Retribution day were come.
After the terror ceas'd, and when with hearts
Somewhat assur'd, again we ventur'd on,
This youth and woman met us on the way.
They told us, that from Aloadin's haunt
They came, on whom the judgment-stroke hath fallen,
He and his sinful Paradise at once
Destroy'd by them, the agents they of Heaven.
Therefore I brought them hither to repeat
The tale before thy presence; that as search
Shall prove it false or faithful, to their merit
Thou mayest reward them.»
« Be it done to us,»
Thalaba answer'd, « as the truth shall prove! »

XXII.

The Sultan while he spake
Fix'd on him the proud eye of sovereignty;
« If thou hast play'd with us,
By Allah and by Ali, Death shall seal
The lying lips for ever! if the thing
Be as thou sayest it, Arab, thou shalt stand
Next to ourself! »
Hark! while he speaks, the cry,
The lengthening cry, the increasing shout
Of joyful multitudes!
Breathless and panting to the tent
The bearer of good tidings comes,
« O Sultan, live for ever! be thy foes
Like Aloadin all!
The wrath of God hath smitten him.»

XXIII.

Joy at the welcome tale
Shone in the Sultan's cheek;
« Array the Arab in the robe
Of honour,» he exclaim'd,
« And place a chain of gold around his neck,
And bind around his brow the diadem,
And mount him on my steed of state,
And lead him through the camp,
And let the Heralds go before and cry,
Thus shall the Sultan reward
The man who serves him well! »

XXIV.

Then in the purple robe
They vested Thalaba,
And hung around his neck the golden chain,
And bound his forehead with the diadem,
And on the royal steed
They led him through the camp,
And heralds went before and cried,
« Thus shall the Sultan reward
The man who serves him well! »[6]

XXV.

When from the pomp of triumph
And presence of the King
Thalaba sought the tent allotted him,
Thoughtful the Arabian Maid beheld
His animated eye,
His cheek inflam'd with pride.
« Oneiza!» cried the youth,
« The King hath done according to his word,
And made me in the land
Next to himself be nam'd!—
But why that serious melancholy smile?—
Oneiza, when I heard the voice that gave me
Honour, and wealth, and fame, the instant thought
Arose to fill my joy, that thou wouldst hear
The tidings, and be happy.»

ONEIZA.

Thalaba,
Thou wouldst not have me mirthful! am I not
An orphan,—among strangers?

THALABA.

But with me!

ONEIZA.

My Father,—

THALABA.

Nay, be comforted! last night
To what wert thou expos'd! in what a peril
The morning found us!—safety, honour, wealth,
These now are ours. This instant who thou wert
The Sultan ask'd. I told him from our childhood
We had been plighted;—was I wrong, Oneiza?
And when he said with bounties he would heap
Our nuptials,—wilt thou blame me if I blest
His will, that bade me fix the marriage day?—
In tears, my love?—

ONEIZA.

REMEMBER, DESTINY
HATH MARK'D THEE FROM MANKIND!

THALABA.

Perhaps when Aloadin was destroy'd
The mission ceas'd; else would wise Providence
With its rewards and blessings strew my path
Thus for accomplish'd service?

ONEIZA.

Thalaba!

THALABA.

Or if haply not, yet whither should I go?
Is it not prudent to abide in peace
Till I am summon'd?

ONEIZA.

Take me to the Deserts!

THALABA.

But Moath is not there; and wouldst thou dwell
In a Stranger's tent? thy father then might seek
In long and fruitless wandering for his child.

ONEIZA.

Take me then to Mecca! 7
There let me dwell a servant of the Temple.
Bind thou thyself my veil,—to human eye
It never shall be lifted.   There, whilst thou
Shalt go upon thine enterprise, my prayers,
Dear Thalaba! shall rise to succour thee,
And I shall live,—if not in happiness,
        Surely in hope.

THALABA.

Oh think of better things!
The will of Heaven is plain: by wonderous ways
It led us here, and soon the common voice
Will tell what we have done, and how we dwell
Under the Shadow of the Sultan's wing;
So shall thy father hear the fame, and find us
What he hath wish'd us ever—Still in tears!
Still that unwilling eye! nay—nay—Oneiza—
I dare not leave thee other than my own,—
My wedded wife.   Honour and gratitude
As yet preserve the Sultan from all thoughts
That sin against thee; but so sure as Heaven
Hath gifted thee above all other maids
With loveliness, so surely would those thoughts
Of wrong arise within the heart of Power.
If thou art mine, Oneiza, we are safe,
But else, there is no sanctuary could save.

ONEIZA.

Thalaba! Thalaba!

XXVI.

With song, with music, and with dance,
    The bridal pomp proceeds.
Following on the veiled Bride
    Fifty female slaves attend
    In costly robes, that gleam
        With interwoven gold,
    And sparkle far with gems.
An hundred slaves behind them bear
Vessels of silver and vessels of gold,
And many a gorgeous garment gay,
    The presents that the Sultan gave.
    On either hand the pages go
With torches flaring through the gloom,
    And trump and timbrel merriment
        Accompanies their way;
    And multitudes with loud acclaim
        Shout blessings on the Bride.
And now they reach the palace pile,
    The palace home of Thalaba,
And now the marriage feast is spread,
And from the finish'd banquet now
    The wedding guests are gone.

XXVII.

Who comes from the bridal chamber?—
It is Azrael, the Angel of Death.

BOOK VIII.

Quas potius decuit nostro te inferre sepulchro
    Petronilla, tibi spargimus has lacrimas,
Spargimus has lacrimas mœsti monumenta parentis, —
    Et tibi pro thalamo sternimus hunc tumulum.
Sperabam genitor tædas præferre jugales,
    Et titulo patris jungere nomen avi;
Heu! gener est Orcus; quique O dulcissima! per te
    Se sperabat avum, desinit esse pater.
                            JOACH. BELLAIUS.

I.

WOMAN.

Go not among the Tombs, Old Man!
    There is a madman there.

OLD MAN.

Will he harm me if I go?

WOMAN.

Not he, poor miserable man!
But 't is a wretched sight to see
    His utter wretchedness.
For all day long he lies on a grave,
    And never is he seen to weep,
    And never is he heard to groan;
    Nor ever at the hour of prayer
Bends his knee nor moves his lips.
I have taken him food for charity,
    And never a word he spake;
    But yet so ghastly he look'd,
That I have awaken'd at night
With the dream of his ghastly eyes.
Now, go not among the Tombs, Old Man!

OLD MAN.

Wherefore has the wrath of God
    So sorely stricken him?

WOMAN.

He came a stranger to the land,
And did good service to the Sultan,
And well his service was rewarded.
The Sultan nam'd him next himself,
    And gave a palace for his dwelling,
And dower'd his bride with rich domains.
    But on his wedding night
There came the Angel of Death.
Since that hour, a man distracted
Among the sepulchres he wanders.
The Sultan, when he heard the tale,
Said, that for some untold crime
Judgment thus had stricken him,
    And, asking Heaven forgiveness
That he had shown him favour,
    Abandon'd him to want.

OLD MAN.

A Stranger did you say?

WOMAN.

An Arab born, like you.
But go not among the Tombs,
For the sight of his wretchedness
Might make a hard heart ache!

OLD MAN.

Nay, nay, I never yet have shunn'd
    A countryman in distress:
And the sound of his dear native tongue
May be like the voice of a friend.

16

II.
Then to the Sepulchre
The woman pointed out,
Old Moath bent his way.
By the tomb lay Thalaba,
In the light of the setting eve;
The sun, and the wind, and the rain,
Had rusted his raven locks;
His cheeks were fallen in,
His face-bones prominent;
By the tomb he lay along,
And his lean fingers play'd,
Unwitting, with the grass that grew beside.

III.
The Old Man knew him not,
And drawing near him, cried,
« Countryman, peace be with thee!»
The sound of his dear native tongue
Awaken'd Thalaba;
He raised his countenance,
And saw the good Old Man,
And he arose and fell upon his neck,
And groan'd in bitterness.
Then Moath knew the youth,
And fear'd that he was childless; and he turn'd
His eyes, and pointed to the tomb.
« Old Man!» cried Thalaba,
« Thy search is ended there!»

IV.
The father's cheek grew white,
And his lip quivered with the misery;
Howbeit, collecting, with a painful voice
He answered, « God is good! his will be done!»

V.
The woe in which he spake,
The resignation that inspir'd his speech,
They soften'd Thalaba.
« Thou hast a solace in thy grief,» he cried,
« A comforter within!
Moath! thou seest me here,
Deliver'd to the Evil Powers,
A God-abandon'd wretch.»

VI.
The Old Man look'd at him incredulous.
« Nightly,» the youth pursued,
« Thy daughter comes to drive me to despair.
Moath, thou thinkst me mad;
But when the Cryer from the Minaret [1]
Proclaims the midnight hour,
Hast thou a heart to see her?»

VII.
In the Meidan now [2]
The clang of clarions and of drums
Accompanied the Sun's descent.
« Dost thou not pray, my son?»
Said Moath, as he saw
The white flag waving on the neighbouring Mosque:
Then Thalaba's eye grew wild,
« Pray!» echoed he; « I must not pray!»
And the hollow groan he gave
Went to the Old Man's heart,

And, bowing down his face to earth,
In fervent agony he call'd on God.

VIII.
A night of darkness and of storms!
Into the Chamber of the Tomb [3]
Thalaba led the Old Man,
To roof him from the rain.
A night of storms! the wind
Swept through the moonless sky,
And moan'd among the pillar'd sepulchres;
And, in the pauses of its sweep,
They heard the heavy rain
Beat on the monument above.
In silence on Oneiza's grave
The Father and the Husband sate.

IX.
The Cryer from the Minaret
Proclaim'd the midnight hour:
« Now, now!» cried Thalaba;
And o'er the chamber of the tomb
There spread a lurid gleam,
Like the reflection of a sulphur fire;
And in that hideous light
Oneiza stood before them. It was She,..
Her very lineaments,.. and such as death
Had changed them, livid cheeks, and lips of blue;
But in her eyes there dwelt
Brightness more terrible
Than all the loathsomeness of death.
« Still art thou living, wretch?»
In hollow tones she cried to Thalaba;
« And must I nightly leave my grave
To tell thee, still in vain,
God hath abandon'd thee!»

X.
« This is not she!» the Old Man exclaim'd;
« A Fiend; a manifest Fiend!»
And to the youth he held his lance;
« Strike and deliver thyself!»
« Strike HER!» cried Thalaba,
And, palsied of all powers,
Gaz'd fixedly upon the dreadful form.
« Yea, strike her!» cried a voice, whose tones
Flow'd with such sudden healing through his soul,
As when the desert shower
From death deliver'd him;
But, unobedient to that well-known voice,
His eye was seeking it,
When Moath, firm of heart,
Perform'd the bidding: through the vampire corpse [4]
He thrust his lance: it fell,
And, howling with the wound,
Its demon tenant fled.
A sapphire light fell on them,
And, garmented with glory, in their sight
Oneiza's Spirit stood.

XI.
« O Thalaba!» she cried,
« Abandon not thyself!
Wouldst thou for ever lose me?.. go, fulfil
Thy quest, that in the Bowers of Paradise
In vain I may not wait thee, O my Husband!»

To Moath then the Spirit
Turn'd the dark lustre of her Angel eyes;
« Short is thy destin'd path,
O my dear Father! to the abode of bliss.
Return to Araby,
There with the thought of death
Comfort thy lonely age,
And Azrael, the Deliverer, soon
Shall visit thee in peace.»

XII.
They stood with earnest eyes,
And arms out-reaching, when again
The darkness clos'd around them.
The soul of Thalaba reviv'd;
He from the floor the quiver took,
And, as he bent the bow, exclaim'd,
« Was it the over-ruling Providence
That in the hour of frenzy led my hands
Instinctively to this?
To-morrow, and the sun shall brace anew
The slacken'd cord, that now sounds loose and damp;
To-morrow, and its livelier tone will sing,
In tort vibration, to the arrow's flight.
I.. but I also, with recovered health
Of heart, shall do my duty.
My Father! here I leave thee then!» he cried,
« And not to meet again,
Till at the gate of Paradise
The eternal union of our joys commence.
We parted last in darkness!»... and the youth
Thought with what other hopes;
But now his heart was calm,
For on his soul a heavenly hope had dawn'd.

XIII.
The Old Man answered nothing, but he held
His garment, and to the door
Of the Tomb Chamber followed him.
The rain had ceased, the sky was wild,
Its black clouds broken by the storm.
And, lo! it chanced, that in the chasm
Of Heaven between, a star,
Leaving along its path continuous light,
Shot eastward.   « See my guide!» quoth Thalaba;
And turning, he receiv'd
Old Moath's last embrace,
And the last blessing of the good Old Man.

XIV.
Evening was drawing nigh,
When an old Dervise, sitting in the sun
At his cell door, invited for the night
The traveller; in the sun
He spread the plain repast,
Rice and fresh grapes, and at their feet there flow'd
The brook of which they drank.

XV.
So as they sate at meal,
With song, with music, and with dance,
A wedding train went by;
The veiled bride, the female slaves,
The torches of festivity,
And trump and timbrel merriment
Accompanied their way.

The good old Dervise gave
A blessing as they past;
But Thalaba look'd on,
And breath'd a low deep groan, and hid his face.
The Dervise had known sorrow, and he felt
Compassion; and his words
Of pity and of piety
Open'd the young man's heart,
And he told all his tale.

XVI.
« Repine not, O my Son!» the Old Man replied,
« That Heaven hath chasten'd thee. Behold this vine, [5]
I found it a wild tree, whose wanton strength
Had swoln into irregular twigs
And bold excrescences,
And spent itself in leaves and little rings,
So in the flourish of its outwardness
Wasting the sap and strength
That should have given forth fruit;
But when I prun'd the Tree,
Then it grew temperate in its vain expense
Of useless leaves, and knotted, as thou seest,
Into these full, clear clusters, to'repay
The hand that wisely wounded it.
Repine not, O my Son!
In wisdom and in mercy Heaven inflicts,
Like a wise Leech, its painful remedies.»

XVII.
Then pausing,.. « Whither goest thou now?» he ask'd.
« I know not;» answered Thalaba;
« Straight on, with Destiny my guide.»
Quoth the Old Man,.. « I will not blame thy trust,
And yet methinks thy feet
Should tread with certainty.
In Kaf the Simorg hath his dwelling place,
The all-knowing Bird of Ages, who hath seen
The World, with all her children, thrice destroy'd.
Long is the thither path,
And difficult the way, of danger full; [6]
But his unerring voice
Could point to certain end thy weary search.»

XVIII.
Easy assent the youth
Gave to the words of wisdom; and behold
At dawn, the adventurer on his way to Kaf.
And he hath travelled many a day,
And many a river swum over,
And many a mountain ridge hath crost,
And many a measureless plain;
And now amid the wilds advanced,
Long is it since his eyes
Have seen the trace of man.

XIX.
Cold! cold! 't is a chilly clime
That the toil of the youth has reach'd,
And he is aweary now,
And faint for the lack of food.
Cold! cold! there is no Sun in heaven,
But a heavy and uniform cloud,
And the snows begin to fall.
Dost thou wish for thy deserts, O Son of Hodeirah?
Dost thou long for the gales of Arabia?

Cold! cold! his blood flows languidly,
His hands are red, his lips are blue,
His feet are sore with the frost.
Cheer thee! cheer thee! Thalaba!
A little yet bear up!

XX.

All waste! no sign of life
But the track of the wolf and the bear!
No sound but the wild, wild wind,
And the snow crunching under his feet!
Night is come; no moon, no stars,
Only the light of the snow!
But behold a fire in the cave of the hill,
A heart-reviving fire;
And thither with strength renew'd
Thalaba presses on.

XXI.

He found a Woman in the cave,
A solitary Woman,
Who by the fire was spinning,
And singing as she spun.
The pine boughs they blazed cheerfully,
And her face was bright with the flame;
Her face was as a Damsel's face;
And yet her hair was grey.
She bade him welcome with a smile,
And still continued spinning,
And singing as she spun.
The thread the Woman drew
Was finer than the silkworm's,
Was finer than the gossamer;
The song she sung was low and sweet,
And Thalaba knew not the words.

XXII.

He laid his bow before the hearth,
For the string was frozen stiff;
He took the quiver from his neck,
For the arrow plumes were iced.
Then as the cheerful fire
Revived his languid limbs,
The adventurer ask'd for food.
The Woman answered him,
And still her speech was song:
" The She Bear she dwells near to me,
And she hath cubs, one, two, and three;
She hunts the deer, and brings him here,
And then with her I make good cheer,
And she to the chase is gone,
And she will be here anon."

XXIII.

She ceased her spinning while she spake,
And when she had answered him,
Again her fingers twirl'd the thread,
And again the Woman began,
In low, sweet tones to sing
The unintelligible song.

XXIV.

The thread she spun it gleam'd like gold
In the light of the odorous fire,
Yet was it so wonderously thin,
That, save when it shone in the light,

You might pry for it closely in vain.
The youth sate watching it,
And she beheld his wonder,
And then again she spake,
And still her speech was song:
" Now twine it round thy hands I say,
Now twine it round thy hands I pray,
My thread is small, my thread is fine,
But he must be
A stronger than thee,
Who can break this thread of mine!"

XXV.

And up she rais'd her bright blue eyes,
And sweetly she smil'd on him,
And he conceiv'd no ill;
And round and round his right hand,
And round and round his left,
He wound the thread so fine.
And then again the Woman spake,
And still her speech was song;
" Now thy strength, O Stranger, strain!
Now then break the slender chain."

XXVI.

Thalaba strove, but the thread
Was woven by magic hands,
And in his cheek the flush of shame
Arose, commixt with fear.
She beheld and laugh'd at him,
And then again she sung,
" My thread is small, my thread is fine,
But he must be
A stronger than thee,
Who can break this thread of mine!"

XXVII.

And up she rais'd her bright blue eyes,
And fiercely she smil'd on him,
" I thank thee, I thank thee, Hodeirah's son!
I thank thee for doing what can't be undone,
For binding thyself in the chain I have spun!"
Then from his head she wrench'd
A lock of his raven hair,
And cast it in the fire,
And cried aloud as it burnt,
" Sister! Sister! hear my voice!
Sister! Sister! come and rejoice!
The web is spun,
The prize is won,
The work is done,
For I have made captive Hodeirah's Son."

XXVIII.

Borne in her magic car
The Sister Sorceress came,
Khawla, the fiercest of the Sorcerer brood.
She gaz'd upon the youth,
She bade him break the slender thread,
She laugh'd aloud for scorn,
She clapt her hands for joy.

XXIX.

The She Bear from the chase came in,
She bore the prey in her bloody mouth,
She laid it at Maimuna's feet,

And she look'd up with wistful eyes
As if to ask her share.
« There! there!» quoth Maimuna,
And pointing to the prisoner-youth,
She spurn'd him with her foot,
And bade her make her meal.
But soon their mockery fail'd them,
And anger and shame arose ;
For the She Bear fawn'd on Thalaba,
And quietly lick'd his hand.

XXX.

The grey-haired Sorceress stampt the ground,
And call'd a Spirit up ;
« Shall we bear the Enemy
To the dungeon dens below?»
SPIRIT.
Woe! woe! to our Empire woe!
If ever he tread the caverns below.
MAIMUNA.
Shall we leave him fetter'd here
With hunger and cold to die?
SPIRIT.
Away from thy lonely dwelling fly!
Here I see a danger nigh,
That he should live, and thou shouldst die.
MAIMUNA.
Whither must we bear the foe?
SPIRIT.
To Mohareb's island go,
There shalt thou secure the foe,
There prevent thy future woe.

XXXI.

Then in the Car they threw
The fetter'd Thalaba,
And took their seats, and set
Their feet upon his neck ;
Maimuna held the reins,
And Khawla shook the scourge,
And away! away! away!7

XXXII.

They were no steeds of mortal race
That drew the magic car
With the swiftness of feet and of wings.
The snow-dust rises behind them,
The ice-rock's splinters fly,
And hark in the valley below
The sound of their chariot wheels,...
And they are far over the mountains!
Away! away! away!
The Demons of the air
Shout their joy as the Sisters pass;
The Ghosts of the Wicked that wander by night
Flit over the magic car.

XXXIII.

Away! away! away!
Over the hills and the plains,
Over the rivers and rocks,
Over the sands of the shore ;
The waves of ocean heave
Under the magic steeds ;
With unwet hoofs they trample the deep,
And now they reach the Island coast,

And away to the city the Monarch's abode.
Open fly the city gates,
Open fly the iron doors,
The doors of the palace-court.
Then stopt the charmed car.
The Monarch heard the chariot wheels,
And forth he came to greet
The Mistress whom he serv'd.
He knew the captive youth,
And Thalaba beheld
Mohareb in the robes of royalty, 8
Whom erst his arm had thrust
Down the bitumen pit.

BOOK IX.

Conscience!....
Poor plodding Priests and preaching Friars may make
Their hollow pulpits, and the empty aisles
Of churches ring, with that round word: but we,
That draw the subtile and more piercing air
In that sublimed region of a court,
Know all is good we make so, and go on
Secured by the prosperity of our crimes.
B. JONSON. *Mortimer's Fall.*

I.

« Go up, my Sister Maimuna,
Go up, and read the stars!»

II.

Lo! on the terrace of the topmost tower
She stands ; her darkening eyes,
Her fine face rais'd to heaven ;
Her white hair flowing like the silver streams
That streak the northern night.

III.

They hear her coming tread,
They lift their asking eyes,
Her face is serious, her unwilling lips
Slow to the tale of ill.
« What hast thou read? what hast thou read?»
Quoth Khawla in alarm.
« Danger...death...judgment!» Maimuna replied.

IV.

« Is that the language of the lights of Heaven!»
Exclaim'd the sterner Witch.
« Creatures of Allah, they perform his will,
And with their lying menaces would daunt
Our credulous folly...Maimuna,
I never lik'd this uncongenial lore!
Better befits to make the sacrifice
Of Divination ; so shall I
Be mine own Oracle.
Command the victims thou, O King!
Male and female they must be,
Thou knowest the needful rites.
Meanwhile I purify the place.»

V.

The Sultan went ; the Sorceress rose,
And North, and South, and East, and West,
She fac'd the points of Heaven ;

And ever where she turn'd
She laid her hand upon the wall ;
And up she look'd, and smote the air,
And down she stoopt, and smote the floor.
« To Eblis and his servants
I consecrate the place,
Let none intrude but they !
Whatever hath the breath of life,
Whatever hath the sap of life,
Let it be blasted and die !»

VI.

Now all is prepar'd ;
Mohareb returns,
The Circle is drawn,
The Victims have bled,
The Youth and the Maid.
She in the circle holds in either hand,
Clench'd by the hair, a head,
The heads of the Youth and the Maid.
« Go out, ye lights !» quoth Khawla,
And in darkness began the spell.

VII.

With spreading arms she whirls around
Rapidly, rapidly,
Ever around and around ;
And loudly she calls the while,
« Eblis ! Eblis !»
Loudly, incessantly,
Still she calls, « Eblis ! Eblis !»
Giddily, giddily, still she whirls,
Loudly, incessantly, still she calls ;
The motion is ever the same,
Ever around and around ;
The calling is still the same,
Still it is, « Eblis ! Eblis !»
And her voice is a shapeless yell,
And dizzily rolls her brain,
And now she is full of the Fiend.
She stops, she rocks, she reels !
Look ! look ! she appears in the darkness !
Her flamy hairs curl up
All living, like the Meteor's locks of light !
Her eyes are like the sickly Moon !

VIII.

It is her lips that move,
Her tongue that shapes the sound,
But whose is the Voice that proceeds !...
« Ye may hope and ye may fear,
The danger of his stars is near.
Sultan ! if he perish, woe !
Fate hath written one death-blow
For Mohareb and the Foe !
Triumph ! triumph ! only she
That knit his bonds can set him free. »

IX.

She spake the Oracle,
And senselessly she fell.
They knelt in care beside her,..
Her Sister and the King ;
They sprinkled her palms with water,
They wetted her nostrils with blood.

X.

She wakes as from a dream,
She asks the uttered Voice ;
But when she heard, an anger and a grief
Darken'd her wrinkling brow.
« Then let him live in long captivity !»
She answer'd : but Mohareb's quicken'd eye
Perus'd her sullen countenance,
That lied not with the lips.
A miserable man !
What boots it, that, in central caves,
The Powers of Evil at his Baptism pledg'd
The Sacrament of Hell?
His death secures them now.
What boots it that they gave
Abdaldar's guardian ring,
When, through another's life,
The blow may reach his own ?

XI.

He sought the dungeon cell
Where Thalaba was laid.
'T was the grey morning twilight, and the voice
Of Thalaba in prayer,
With words of hallow'd import, smote
The King's alarmed sense.
The grating of the heavy hinge
Rous'd not the Arabian youth ;
Nor lifted he his earthward face,
At sound of coming feet.
Nor did Mohareb with unholy voice
Disturb the duty : silent, spirit-aw'd,
Envious, heart-humbled, he beheld
The dungeon-peace of piety ;
Till Thalaba, the perfect rite performed,
Rais'd his calm eye ; then spake the Island-Chief,
« Arab ! my guidance through the dangerous Cave,
Thy service overpaid,
An unintended friend in enmity.
The hand, that caught thy ring,
Receiv'd, and bore me to the scene I sought,
Now know me grateful. I return
That amulet, thy only safety here.»

XII.

Artful he spake, with show of gratitude
Veiling the selfish deed.
Lock'd in his magic chain,
The powerless hand of Thalaba
Receiv'd again the Spell.
Remembering then with what an ominous faith
First he drew on the gem,
The Youth repeats his words of augury ;
« In God's name and the Prophet's ! be its power
Good, let it serve the holy ! if for evil,
God and my faith shall hallow it.
Blindly the wicked work
The righteous will of Heaven !»
So Thalaba receiv'd again
The written ring of gold.

XIII.

Thoughtful awhile Mohareb stood,
And eyed the captive youth.
Then, building skilfully the sophist speech,

Thus he began. « Brave art thou, Thalaba !
And wherefore are we foes?..for I would buy
Thy friendship at a princely price, and make thee
　　To thine own welfare wise.
　Hear me ! in Nature are two hostile Gods,
　Makers and Masters of existing things,
Equal in power :.. nay, hear me patiently !..
Equal.. for look around thee ! the same Earth
Bears fruit and poison; where the Camel finds
　His fragrant food, the horned Viper there
Sucks in the juice of death : the Elements
Now serve the use of man, and now assert
Dominion o'er his weakness: dost thou hear
The sound of merriment and nuptial song?
From the next house proceeds the mourner's cry,
Lamenting o'er the dead. Sayest thou that sin
　Enter'd the world of Allah? that the Fiend,
　Permitted for a season, prowls for prey?
When to thy tent the venomous serpent creeps,
Dost thou not crush the reptile? even so,
Be sure, had Allah crush'd his Enemy,
But that the power was wanting. From the first,
　Eternal as themselves their warfare is;
To the end it must endure. Evil and Good..
What are they, Thalaba, but words? in the strife
Of Angels, as of men, the weak are guilty;
Power must decide. The Spirits of the Dead
Quitting their mortal mansion, enter not,
As falsely ye are preach'd, their final seat
Of bliss, or bale; nor in the sepulchre
Sleep they the long long sleep : each joins the host
Of his great Leader, aiding in the war
　Whose fate involves his own,
　　Woe to the vanquish'd then !
Woe to the sons of man who followed him!
They, with their Leader, through eternity,
　　Must howl in central fires.
　Thou, Thalaba, hast chosen ill thy part,
If choice it may be call'd, where will was not,
Nor searching doubt, nor judgment wise to weigh.
Hard is the service of the Power, beneath
Whose banners thou wert born; his discipline
Severe, yea cruel; and his wages, rich
Only in promise; who hath seen the pay?
For us.. the pleasures of the world are ours,
Riches and rule, the kingdoms of the Earth.
We met in Babylon adventurers both,
Each zealous for the hostile Power he serv'd:
We meet again; thou feelest what thou art,
　Thou seest what I am, the Sultan here,
　　The Lord of Life and Death.
Abandon him who has abandon'd thee,
And be, as I am, great among mankind!»

XIV.

The Captive did not, hasty to confute,
　Break off that subtle speech;
But when the expectant silence of the King
Look'd for his answer, then spake Thalaba.
« And this then is thy faith ! this monstrous creed!
This lie against the Sun, and Moon, and Stars,
And Earth, and Heaven ! blind man, who canst not see
How all things work the best ! who wilt not know,
That in the Manhood of the World, whate'er
Of folly mark'd its Infancy, of vice
Sullied its Youth, ripe Wisdom shall cast off,

'Stablish'd in good, and, knowing evil, safe.
Sultan Mohareb, yes, ye have me here
In chains; but not forsaken though opprest;
Cast down, but not destroy'd. Shall danger daunt,
Shall death dismay his soul, whose life is given
For God, and for his brethren of mankind?
Alike rewarded, in that noble cause,
The Conqueror's and the Martyr's palm above
Beam with one glory. Hope ye that my blood
Can quench the dreaded flame! and know ye not,
That leagued against ye are the Just and Wise,
　And all Good Actions of all ages past,
Yea, your own Crimes, and Truth, and God in Heaven.»

XV.

　« Slave !» quoth Mohareb, and his lips
　　Quivered with eager wrath,
　« I have thee ! thou shalt feel my power,
　　And in thy dungeon loathsomeness
　Rot piece-meal, limb from limb !»
　　And out the Tyrant rushes,
　And all impatient of the thoughts
　　That canker'd in his heart,
Seeks in the giddiness of boisterous sport
Short respite from the avenging power within.

XVI.

　　What woman is she
　　So wrinkled and old,
　That goes to the wood ?
　　She leans on her staff
　　With a tottering step,
　She tells her bead-string slow
　Through fingers dull'd by age.
　The wanton boys bemock her;
　The babe in arms that meets her
　Turns round with quick affright,
And clings to his nurse's neck.

XVII.

　Hark! hark! the hunter's cry,
　Mohareb is gone to the chase!
　　The dogs, with eager yelp,
　　Are struggling to be free;
　The hawks in frequent stoop
　Token their haste for flight;
　And couchant on the saddle-bow,
With tranquil eyes, and talons sheath'd,
　The ounce expects his liberty.

XVIII.

　Propt on the staff that shakes
　Beneath her trembling weight,
The Old Woman sees them pass.
　　Halloa! halloa!
　　The game is up!
　　The dogs are loos'd,
The deer bounds over the plain :
　　The lagging dogs behind
　　Follow from afar!
But lo! the Falcon o'er his head
　Hovers with hostile wings, [2]
And buffets him with blinding strokes!
　Dizzy with the deafening strokes
　In blind and interrupted course,
　Poor beast, he struggles on;

And now the dogs are nigh!
How his heart pants! you see
The panting of his heart;
And tears like human tears
Roll down, along the big veins, fever-swoln;
And now the death-sweat darkens his dun hide; [3]
His fears, his groans, his agony, his death,
Are the sport, and the joy, and the triumph!

XIX.

Halloa! another prey,
The nimble Antelope!
The ounce is freed; one spring, [4]
And his talons are sheath'd in her shoulders,
And his teeth are red in her gore.
There came a sound from the wood,
Like the howl of the winter wind at night,
Around a lonely dwelling;
The ounce, whose gums were warm in his prey,
He hears the summoning sound.
In vain his master's voice,
No longer dreaded now,
Calls and recalls with threatful tone.
Away to the forest he goes,
For that Old Woman had laid
Her shrivell'd finger on her shrivell'd lips,
And whistled with a long, long breath;
And that long breath was the sound
Like the howl of the winter wind at night,
Around a lonely dwelling.

XX.

Mohareb knew her not,
As to the chase he went,
The glance of his proud eye
Passing in scorn o'er age and wretchedness.
She stands in the depth of the wood,
And panting to her feet,
Fawning and fearful, creeps the charmed ounce.
Well mayst thou fear, and vainly dost thou fawn:
Her form is changed, her visage new,
Her power, her heart the same!
It is Khawla that stands in the wood.

XXI.

She knew the place where the mandrake grew,
And round the neck of the ounce,
And round the mandrake's head,
She tightens the ends of her cord.
Her ears are clos'd with wax,
And her prest finger fastens them,
Deaf as the Adder, when, with grounded head,
And circled form, her avenues of sound
Barr'd safely, one slant eye
Watches the charmer's lips
Waste on the wind his baffled witchery. [5]
The spotted ounce so beautiful,
Springs forceful from the scourge:
The dying plant all agony,
Feeling its life-strings crack,
Uttered the unimaginable groan
That none can hear and live.

XXII.

Then from her victim servant Khawla loos'd
The precious poison. Next with naked hand,
She pluck'd the boughs of the manchineel.
Then of the wormy wax she took,
That, from the perforated tree forced out, [6]
Bewray'd its insect-parent's work within.

XXIII.

In a cavern of the wood she sits,
And moulds the wax to human form;
And, as her fingers kneaded it,
By magic accents, to the mystic shape
Imparted with the life of Thalaba,
In all its passive powers,
Mysterious sympathy.
With the mandrake and the manchineel
She builds her pile accurst.
She lays her finger to the pile,
And blue and green, the flesh
Glows with emitted fire,
A fire to kindle that strange fuel meet. [7]

XXIV.

Before the fire she placed the imaged wax:
« There, waste away!» the Enchantress cried, [8]
« And with thee waste Hodeirah's Son!»

XXV.

Fool! fool! go thaw the everlasting ice
Whose polar mountains bound the human reign.
Blindly the wicked work
The righteous will of Heaven!
The doom'd Destroyer wears Abdaldar's ring!
Against the danger of his horoscope
Yourselves have shielded him!
And on the sympathizing wax,
The unadmitted flames play powerlessly,
As the cold moon-beam on a plain of snow.

XXVI.

« Curse thee! curse thee!» cried the fiendly woman,
« Hast thou yet a spell of safety?»
And in the raging flames
She cast the imaged wax.
It lay amid the flames, [9]
Like Polycarp of old,
When, by the glories of the burning stake
O'er-vaulted, his grey hairs
Curl'd, life-like, to the fire
That haloed round his saintly brow.

XXVII.

« Wherefore is this!» cried Khawla, and she stampt
Thrice on the cavern floor,
« Maimuna! Maimuna!»
Thrice on the floor she stampt,
Then to the rocky gateway glanced
Her eager eyes, and Maimuna was there.
« Nay, Sister, nay!» quoth she, « Mohareb's life
Is link'd with Thalaba's!
Nay, Sister, nay! the plighted oath!
The common Sacrament!»

XXVIII.

« Idiot!» said Khawla, « one must die, or all!
Faith kept with him were treason to the rest.
Why lies the wax like marble in the fire?
What powerful amulet
Protects Hodeirah's son?»

XXIX.

Cold, marble-cold, the wax
Lay on the raging pile,
Cold in that white intensity of fire.
The Bat, that with her hook'd and leathery wings
Clung to the cave-roof, loos'd her hold,
Death-sickening with the heat;
The Toad, who to the darkest nook had crawl'd,
Panted fast with fever-pain;
The Viper from her nest came forth,
Leading her quicken'd brood,
Who, sportive with the warm delight, roll'd out
Their thin curls, tender as the tendril rings,
Ere the green beauty of their brittle youth
Grows brown, and toughens in the summer sun.
Cold, marble-cold, the wax
Lay on the raging pile,
The silver quivering of the element
O'er its pale surface shedding a dim gloss.

XXX.

Amid the red and fiery smoke,
Watching the strange portent,
The blue-eyed Sorceress and her Sister stood,
Seeming a ruined Angel by the side
Of Spirit born in hell.
Maimuna rais'd at length her thoughtful eyes,
« Whence Sister was the wax,
The work of the worm, or the bee?
Nay then I marvel not!
It were as wise to bring from Ararat
The fore-world's wood to build the magic pile, [10]
And feed it from the balm bower, through whose veins
The Martyr's blood sends such a virtue out,
That the fond mother from beneath its shade,
Wreathes the Cerastes round her playful child. [11]
This is the eternal, universal strife!
There is a Grave-wax,—I have seen the Gouls [12]
Fight for the dainty at their banquetting.»—

XXXI.

« Excellent witch!» quoth Khawla! and she went
To the cave-arch of entrance, and scowl'd up,
Mocking the blessed Sun,
« Shine thou in Heaven, but I will shadow Earth!
Thou wilt not shorten day,
But I will hasten darkness!» Then the Witch
Began a magic song,
One long low tone, through teeth half-clos'd,
Through lips slow-moving, muttered slow,
One long-continued breath,
Till to her eyes a darker yellowness
Was driven, and fuller-swoln the prominent veins
On her loose throat grew black.
Then looking upward, thrice she breath'd
Into the face of Heaven;
The baneful breath infected Heaven;
A mildewing mist, it spread
Darker and darker; so the evening sun
Pour'd his unentering glory on the mist,
And it was night below.

XXXII.

« Bring now the wax,» quoth Khawla, « for thou know'st
The mine that yields it;» forth went Maimuna,
In mist and darkness went the Sorceress forth.

And she hath reach'd the place of Tombs,
And in their sepulchres the dead
Feel feet unholy trampling over them. [13]

XXXIII.

Thou startest, Maimuna,
Because the breeze is in thy lifted locks!
Is Khawla's spell so weak?
Sudden came the breeze, and strong;
The mist that in the labouring lungs was felt
So heavy late, flies now before the gale,
Thin as an infant's breath,
Seen in the sunshine of an autumn frost.
Sudden it came, and soon its work was done,
And suddenly it ceas'd;
Cloudless and calm it left the firmament,
And beautiful in the blue sky
Arose the summer Moon.

XXXIV.

She heard the quicken'd action of her blood,
She felt the fever in her cheeks.
Daunted, yet desperate, in a tomb
Entering, with impious hand she traced
Circles, and squares, and trines,
And magic characters,
Till, riven by her charms, the grave
Yawn'd and disclos'd its dead;
Maimuna's eyes were open'd, and she saw
The secrets of the grave.

XXXV.

There sate a Spirit in the vault,
In shape, in hue, in lineaments, like life.
And by him couch'd, as if intranced,
The hundred-headed Worm that never dies.

XXXVI.

« Nay, Sorceress! not to-night!» the Spirit cried,
« The flesh in which I sinn'd may rest to-night
From suffering; all things, even I, to-night,
Even the Damn'd, repose!»

XXXVII.

The flesh of Maimuna
Crept on her bones with terror, and her knees
Trembled with their trembling weight.
« Only this Sabbath! and at dawn the Worm
Will wake, and this poor flesh must grow to meet
The gnawing of his hundred poison-mouths! [14]
God! God! is there no mercy after death?»

XXXVIII.

Soul-struck, she rush'd away,
She fled the place of Tombs,
She cast herself upon the earth,
All agony, and tumult, and despair.
And, in that wild and desperate agony,
Sure Maimuna had died the utter death,
If aught of evil had been possible
On this mysterious night;
For this was that most holy night [15]
When all Created Things know and adore
The Power that made them; Insects, Beasts, and Birds,
The Water-Dwellers, Herbs, and Trees, and Stones,
Yea, Earth and Ocean, and the infinite Heaven,

17

With all its Worlds. Man only does not know
The universal Sabbath, does not join
With Nature in her homage. Yet the prayer
Flows from the righteous with intenser love;
A holier calm succeeds, and sweeter dreams
Visit the slumbers of the penitent.

XXXIX.

Therefore, on Maimuna, the Elements
Shed healing; every breath she breath'd was balm.
Was not a flower but sent in incense up
Its richest odours, and the song of birds
Now, like the music of the Seraphim,
Enter'd her soul, and now
Made silence awful by their sudden pause.
It seem'd as if the quiet moon
Pour'd quietness, its lovely light
Was like the smile of reconciling Heaven.

XL.

Is it the dew of night
That down her glowing cheek
Shines in the moon-beam? oh! she weeps—she weeps!
And the Good Angel that abandon'd her [6]
At her hell-baptism, by her tears drawn down,
Resumes his charge.   Then Maimuna
Recall'd to mind the double oracle;
Quick as the lightning flash
Its import glanced upon her, and the hope
Of pardon and salvation rose,
As now she understood
The lying prophecy of truth.
She pauses not, she ponders not;
The driven air before her fann'd the face
Of Thalaba, and he awoke and saw
The Sorceress of the silver locks.

XLI.

One more permitted spell!
She takes the magic thread.
With the wide eye of wonder, Thalaba
Watches her snowy fingers round and round,
Unwind the loosening chain.
Again he hears the low sweet voice,
The low sweet voice so musical,
That sure it was not strange,
If, in those unintelligible tones,
Was more than human potency,
That with such deep and undefin'd delight,
Filled the surrendered soul.
The work is done, the song hath ceas'd;
He wakes as from a dream of Paradise,
And feels his fetters gone, and with the burst
Of wondering adoration, praises God.

XLII.

Her charm hath loosed the chain it bound,
But massy walls, and iron gates,
Confine Hodeirah's son.
Heard ye not, Genii of the Air, her spell,
That o'er her face there flits
The sudden flush of fear?
Again her louder lips repeat the charm,
Her eye is anxious, her cheek pale,
Her pulse plays fast and feeble.

Nay, Maimuna! thy power hath ceas'd,
And the wind scatters now
The voice which rul'd it late.

XLIII.

« Be comforted, my soul!» she cried, her eye
Brightening with sudden joy; « be comforted!
We have burst through the bonds which bound us down
To utter death; our covenant with Hell
Is blotted out! The Lord hath given me strength!
Great is the Lord, and merciful!
Hear me, ye rebel Spirits! in the name
Of Allah and the Prophet, hear the spell!»

XLIV.

Groans then were heard, the prison-walls were rent,
The whirlwind wrapt them round, and forth they flew,
Borne in the chariot of the winds abroad.

BOOK X.

And the Angel that was sent unto me said, Thinkest thou to com_
prehend the way of the Most High!... Then said I, Yea, my Lord.
And he answered me, and said, I am sent to shew thee three ways and
to set forth three similitudes before thee; whereof, if thou canst de-
clare me one, I will shew thee also the way that thou desirest to see,
and I shall shew thee from whence the wicked heart cometh. And
I said, Tell on, my Lord. Then said he unto me, Go thy way, weigh
me the weight of the fire, or measure me the blast of the wind, or
call me again the day that is past.

ESDRAS ii. 4.

I.

Ere there was time for wonder or for fear,
The way was past, and lo! again
Amid surrounding snows,
Within the cavern of the witch they stand.

II.

Then came the weakness of her natural age
At once on Maimuna;
The burthen of her years
Fell on her, and she knew
That her repentance in the sight of God
Had now found favour, and her hour was come.
Her death was like the righteous; « Turn my face
To Mecca!» in her languid eyes
The joy of certain hope
Lit a last lustre, and in death
The smile was on her cheek.

III.

No faithful crowded round her bier, [1]
No tongue reported her good deeds,
For her no mourners wail'd and wept,
No Iman o'er her perfum'd corpse,
For her soul's health inton'd the prayer;
No column rais'd by the way-side [2]
Implor'd the passing traveller
To say a requiem for the dead.
Thalaba laid her in the snow,
And took his weapons from the hearth,
And then once more the youth began
His weary way of solitude.

IV.

The breath of the East is in his face,
And it drives the sleet and the snow.
The air is keen, the wind is keen,
His limbs are aching with the cold,
His eyes are aching with the snow,[3]
His very heart is cold,
His spirit chill'd within him. He looks on
If aught of life be near,
But all is sky, and the white wilderness,
And here and there a solitary pine,
Its branches broken by the weight of snow.
His pains abate, his senses, dull
With suffering, cease to suffer.
Languidly, languidly,
Thalaba drags along,
A heavy weight is on his lids,
His limbs move slow with heaviness,
And he full fain would sleep.
Not yet, not yet, O Thalaba!
Thy hour of rest is come!
Not yet may the Destroyer sleep
The comfortable sleep;
His journey is not over yet,
His course not yet fulfill'd! . .
Run thou thy race, O Thalaba!
The prize is at the goal.

V.

It was a Cedar-tree
Which woke him from that deadly drowsiness;
Its broad round-spreading branches, when they felt[4]
The snow, rose upward in a point to heaven,
And, standing in their strength erect,
Defied the baffled storm.
He knew the lesson Nature gave,
And he shook off his heaviness,
And hope reviv'd within him.

VI.

Now sunk the evening sun,
A broad, red, beamless orb,
Adown the glowing sky;
Through the red light the snow-flakes fell like fire.
Louder grows the biting wind,
And it drifts the dust of the snow.
The snow is clotted in his hair,
The breath of Thalaba
Is iced upon his lips.
He looks around, the darkness,
The dizzy floating of the feathery sky
Close in his narrow view.

VII.

At length, through the thick atmosphere, a light
Not distant far appears.
He, doubting other wiles of enmity,
With mingled joy, and quicker step,
Bends thitherward his way.

VIII.

It was a little, lowly dwelling-place,
Amid a garden, whose delightful air
Was mild and fragrant, as the evening wind
Passing in summer o'er the coffee-groves[5]

Of Yemen, and its blessed bowers of balm.
A Fount of Fire, that in the centre play'd,
Roll'd all around its wonderous rivulets,
And fed the garden with the heat of life.
Every where magic ! the Arabian's heart
Yearn'd after human intercourse.
A light ! . . the door unclos'd ! . .
All silent . . he goes in.

IX.

There lay a Damsel, sleeping on a couch,
His step awoke her, and she gazed at him
With pleas'd and wondering look,
Fearlessly, like a yearling child,
Too ignorant to fear,
With words of courtesy,
The young intruder spake.
At the sound of his voice, a joy
Kindled her bright black eyes;
She rose, and took his hand,
But, at the touch, the joy forsook her cheek,
« Oh! it is cold!» she cried,
« I thought I should have felt it warm, like mine,
But thou art like the rest!»

X.

Thalaba stood mute awhile,
And wondering at her words:
« Cold? Lady!» then he said; « I have travelled long
In this cold wilderness,
Till life is almost spent!»

XI.

LAILA.
Art thou a Man, then?
THALABA.
Nay . . I did not think
Sorrow and toil could so have altered me,
That I seem otherwise.
LAILA.
And thou canst be warm
Sometimes? life-warm as I am?
THALABA.
Surely, Lady,
As others are, I am, to heat and cold
Subject like all.   You see a Traveller,
Bound upon hard adventure, who requests
Only to rest him here to-night, . . to-morrow
He will pursue his way.
LAILA.
Oh , . not to-morrow!
Not like a dream of joy, depart so soon!
And whither wouldst thou go? for all around
Is everlasting winter, ice, and snow,
Deserts unpassable of endless frost.
THALABA.
He who has led me here, will still sustain me
Through cold and hunger.

XII.

« Hunger?» Laila cried;
She clapt her lily hands,
And whether from above, or from below,
It came, sight could not see,
So suddenly the floor was spread with food.

XIII.

LAILA.

Why dost thou watch with hesitating eyes
The banquet! 't is for thee! I bade it come.

THALABA.

Whence came it?

LAILA.

Matters it from whence it came?
My father sent it: when I call, he hears.
Nay, .. thou hast fabled with me! and art like
The forms that wait upon my solitude,
Human to eye alone; .. thy hunger would not
Question so idly else.

THALABA.

I will not eat!
It came by magic! fool, to think that aught
But fraud and danger could await me here!
Let loose my cloak! ..

LAILA.

Begone then, insolent!
Why dost thou stand and gaze upon me thus?
Aye! watch the features well that threaten thee
With fraud and danger! in the wilderness
They shall avenge me, .. in the hour of want,
Rise on thy view, and make thee feel
How innocent I am:
And this remember'd cowardice and insult,
With a more painful shame will burn thy cheek,
Than now heats mine in anger!

THALABA.

Mark me, Lady!
Many and restless are my enemies:
My daily paths have been beset with snares
Till I have learnt suspicion, bitter sufferings
Teaching the needful vice. If I have wrong'd you, ..
And that should be the face of innocence, ..
I pray you pardon me! In the name of God, ..
And of his Prophet, I partake your food.

LAILA.

Lo, now! thou wert afraid of sorcery,
And yet hast said a charm.

THALABA.

A charm?

LAILA.

And wherefore? ..
Is it not delicate food? . . . what mean thy words?
I have heard many spells, and many names,
That rule the Genii and the Elements,
But never these.

THALABA.

How! never heard the names
Of God and of the Prophet?

LAILA.

Never . . . nay, now,
Again that troubled eye? .. thou art a strange man,
And wonderous fearful . . . but I must not twice
Be charged with fraud! if thou suspectest still,
Depart and leave me!

THALABA.

And you do not know
The God that made you?

LAILA.

Made me, man! .. my Father
Made me. He made this dwelling, and the grove,
And yonder fountain-fire; and every morn
He visits me, and takes the snow, and moulds

Women and men, like thee; and breathes into them
Motion, and life, and sense, .. but, to the touch,
They are chilling cold; and ever when night closes
They melt away again, and leave me here
Alone and sad. Oh then how I rejoice
When it is day, and my dear father comes
And cheers me with kind words, and kinder looks!
My dear, dear father! . . . Were it not for him,
I am so weary of this loneliness
That I should wish I also were of snow,
That I might melt away, and cease to be.

THALABA.

And have you always had your dwelling here,
Amid this solitude of snow?

LAILA.

I think so.
I can remember, with unsteady feet
Tottering from room to room, and finding pleasure
In flowers, and toys, and sweetmeats, things which long
Have lost their power to please; which, when I see them,
Raise only now a melancholy wish
I were the little trifler once again
Who could be pleased so lightly!

THALABA.

Then you know not
Your father's art?

LAILA.

No. I besought him once
To give me power like his, that where he went
I might go with him: but he shook his head,
And said, it was a power too dearly bought,
And kiss'd me with the tenderness of tears.

THALABA.

And wherefore hath he hidden you thus far
From all the ways of humankind?

LAILA.

'T was fear,
Fatherly fear and love. He read the stars,[6]
And saw a danger in my destiny,
And therefore placed me here amid the snows,
And laid a spell that never human eye,
If foot of man by chance should reach the depth
Of this wide waste, shall see one trace of grove,
Garden, or dwelling-place, or yonder fire,
That thaws and mitigates the frozen sky.
And, more than this, even if the enemy
Should come, I have a guardian here.

THALABA.

A guardian?

LAILA.

'T was well, that when my sight unclos'd upon thee,
There was no dark suspicion in thy face,
Else I had called his succour! wilt thou see him?
But, if a woman can have terrified thee,
How wilt thou bear his unrelaxing brow,
And lifted lightnings?

THALABA.

Lead me to him, Lady!

XIV.

She took him by the hand,
And through the porch they past.
Over the garden and the grove,
The fountain-streams of fire
Poured a broad light like noon;
A broad unnatural light,

Which made the rose's blush of beauty pale,
And dimm'd the rich geranium's scarlet blaze.
The various verdure of the grove
Now wore one undistinguishable grey,
Chequered with blacker shade.
Suddenly Laila stopt,
« I do not think thou art the enemy,»
She said, « but he will know!
If thou hast meditated wrong,
Stranger, depart in time...
I would not lead thee to thy death.»

XV.
The glance of Laila's eye
Turn'd anxiously toward the Arabian youth.
« So let him pierce my heart,» cried Thalaba,
« If it hide thought to harm you!»
LAILA.
'T is a figure,
Almost I fear to look at!.. yet come on.
'Twill ease me of a heaviness that seems
To sink my heart; and thou may'st dwell here then
In safety;.. for thou shalt not go to-morrow
Nor on the after, nor the after day,
Nor ever! It was only solitude
Which made my misery here,..
And now, that I can see a human face,
And hear a human voice...
Oh no! thou wilt not leave me!
THALABA.
Alas, I must not rest!
The star that ruled at my nativity,
Shone with a strange and blasting influence:
O gentle Lady! I should draw upon you
A killing curse!
LAILA.
But I will ask my father
To save you from all danger, and you know not
The wonders he can work; and when I ask,
It is not in his power to say me nay.
Perhaps thou knowest the happiness it is
To have a tender father?
THALABA.
He was one,
Whom, like a loathsome leper, I have tainted
With my contagious destiny. At evening
He kiss'd me as he wont, and laid his hands
Upon my head, and blest me ere I slept.
His dying groan awoke me, for the Murderer
Had stolen upon our sleep!... For me was meant
The midnight blow of death; my father died;
The brother play-mates of my infancy,
The baby at the breast, they perished all,..
All in that dreadful hour!... but I was sav'd
To remember and revenge.

XVI.
She answered not, for now,
Emerging from the o'er-arch'd avenue,
The finger of her uprais'd hand
Mark'd where the Guardian of the garden stood.
It was a brazen Image, every limb7
And swelling vein and muscle, true to life:
The left knee bending on,
The other straight, firm planted, and his hand

Lifted on high to hurl
The lightning that it grasp'd.

XVII.
When Thalaba approach'd,
The charmed image knew Hodeirah's son,
And hurl'd the lightning at the dreaded foe.
The Ring! the saviour Ring!
Full in his face the lightning-bolt was driven,
The scattered fire recoil'd.
Like the flowing of a summer gale he felt
Its ineffectual force,
His countenance was not changed,
Not a hair of his head was singed.

XVIII.
He started, and his glance
Turn'd angrily upon the Maid.
The sight disarm'd suspicion;.. breathless, pale,
Against a tree she stood;
Her wan lips quivering, and her eye
Uprais'd, in silent supplicating fear.

XIX.
She started with a scream of joy,
Seeing her father there,
And ran and threw her arms around his neck.
« Save me!» she cried, « the enemy is come!
Save me! save me! Okba!»

XX.
« Okba!» repeats the youth,
For never since that hour,
When in the Tent the Spirit told his name,
Had Thalaba let slip
The memory of his Father's murderer;
« Okba!».. and in his hand
He grasped an arrow-shaft,
And he rush'd on to strike him.

XXI.
« Son of Hodeirah!» the Old Man replied,
« My hour is not yet come;»
And putting forth his hand
Gently he repell'd the Youth.
« My hour is not yet come!
But thou mayst shed this innocent Maiden's blood,
That vengeance God allows thee!»

XXII.
Around her Father's neck
Still Laila's hands were clasp'd.
Her face was turn'd to Thalaba,
A broad light floated o'er its marble paleness,
As the wind wav'd the fountain fire.
Her large dilated eye, in horror rais'd,
Watch'd every look and movement of the youth.
« Not upon her,» said he,
« Not upon her, Hodeirah's blood cries out
For vengeance!» and again his lifted arm
Threaten'd the Sorcerer;
Again withheld, it felt
The barrier that no human strength could burst.

XXIII.
« Thou dost not aim the blow more eagerly,»
Okba replied, « than I would rush to meet it!

But that were poor revenge.
O Thalaba, thy God
Wreaks on the innocent head
His vengeance;.. I must suffer in my child!
Why dost thou pause to strike thy victim? Allah
Permits, commands the deed.»

XXIV.

« Liar!» quoth Thalaba.
And Laila's wondering eye
Looked up, all anguish, to her father's face.
« By Allah and the Prophet,» he replied,
« I speak the words of truth.
Misery, misery,
That I must beg mine enemy to speed
The inevitable vengeance now so near!
I read it in her horoscope,
Her birth-star warn'd me of Hodeirah's race.
I laid a spell, and call'd a Spirit up.
He answered, one must die,
Laila or Thalaba...
Accursed Spirit! even in Truth
Giving a lying hope!
Last, I ascended the seventh Heaven,
And, on the everlasting Table there,[8]
In characters of light,
I read her written doom.
The years that it has gnawn me! and the load
Of sin that it has laid upon my soul!
Curse on this hand, that in the only hour
The favouring stars allow'd,
Reek'd with other blood than thine.
Still dost thou stand and gaze incredulous?
Young man, be merciful, and keep her not
Longer in agony!».

XXV.

Thalaba's unbelieving frown
Scowl'd on the Sorcerer,
When in the air the rush of wings was heard,
And Azrael stood among them.
In equal terror, at the sight,
The Enchanter, the Destroyer stood,
And Laila, the victim maid.

XXVI.

« Son of Hodeirah!» said the Angel of Death,
« The accursed fables not.
When, from the Eternal Hand, I took
The yearly scroll of fate,[9]
Her name was written there;..
Her leaf hath withered on the Tree of Life.[10]
This is the hour, and from thy hands
Commission'd to receive the Maid I come.»

XXVII.

« Hear me, O Angel!» Thalaba replied;
« To avenge my father's death,
To work the will of Heaven,
To root from earth the accursed sorcerer race,
I have dared danger undismay'd,
I have lost all my soul held dear,
I am cut off from all the ties of life,
Unmurmuring. For whate'er awaits me still,
Pursuing to the end the enterprise,
Peril or pain, I bear a ready heart.

But strike this Maid! this innocent!...
Angel, I dare not do it.»

XXVIII.

« Remember,» answered Azrael, « all thou say'st
Is written down for judgment! every word
In the balance of thy trial must be weigh'd!»[11]

XXIX.

« So be it!» said the Youth,
He who can read the secrets of the heart
Will judge with righteousness!
This is no doubtful path,
The voice of God within me cannot lie—
I will not harm the innocent.»

XXX.

He said, and from above,
As though it were the Voice of Night,
The startling answer came.
« Son of Hodeirah, think again!
One must depart from hence,
Laila, or Thalaba;
She dies for thee, or thou for her,
It must be life for life!
Son of Hodeirah, weigh it well,
While yet the choice is thine!»

XXXI.

He hesitated not,
But, looking upward, spread his hands to Heaven,
« Oneiza, in thy bower of Paradise,
Receive me, still unstain'd!»

XXXII.

« What!» exclaim'd Okba, « darest thou disobey,
Abandoning all claim
To Allah's longer aid?»

XXXIII.

The eager exultation of his speech
Earthward recall'd the thoughts of Thalaba.
« And dost thou triumph, Murderer? dost thou deem
Because I perish, that the unsleeping lids
Of Justice shall be closed upon thy crime?
Poor, miserable man! that thou canst live
With such beast-blindness in the present joy,
When o'er thy head the sword of God
Hangs for the certain stroke!»

XXXIV.

« Servant of Allah, thou hast disobey'd,
God hath abandon'd thee,
This hour is mine!» cried Okba;
And shook his daughter off,
And drew the dagger from his vest,
And aim'd the deadly blow.

XXXV.

All was accomplish'd. Laila rush'd between
To save the saviour Youth.
She met the blow, and sunk into his arms,
And Azrael, from the hands of Thalaba,[12]
Receiv'd her parting soul.

BOOK XI.

Those, Sir, that traffick in these seas,
Fraught not their bark with fears.
SIR ROBERT HOWARD, *Blind Lady.*

I.

O FOOL, to think thy human hand
Could check the chariot-wheels of Destiny!
To dream of weakness in the all-knowing Mind,
That his decrees should change!
To hope that the united Powers
Of Earth, and Air, and Hell,
Might blot one letter from the Book of Fate,
Might break one link of the eternal chain!
Thou miserable, wicked, poor old man,
Fall now upon the body of thy child,
Beat now thy breast, and pluck the bleeding hairs
From thy grey beard, and lay
Thine ineffectual hand to close her wound,
And call on Hell to aid,
And call on Heaven to send
Its merciful thunderbolt!

II.

The young Arabian silently
Beheld his frantic grief.
The presence of the hated youth
To raging anguish stung
The wretched Sorcerer.
« Aye! look and triumph!» he exclaim'd,
This is the justice of thy God!
A righteous God is he, to let
His vengeance fall upon the innocent head!—
Curse thee, curse thee, Thalaba!»

III.

All feelings of revenge
Had left Hodeirah's son,
Pitying and silently he heard
The victim of his own iniquities;
Not with the busy hand
Of Consolation, fretting the sore wound
He could not hope to heal.

IV.

So as the Servant of the Prophet stood,
With sudden motion the night air
Gently fann'd his cheek.
T was a green Bird, whose wings
Had waved the quiet air.
On the hand of Thalaba
The Green Bird perch'd, and turn'd
A mild eye up, as if to win
The Adventurer's confidence.
Then, springing on, flew forward,
And now again returns
To court him to the way;
And now his hand perceives
Her rosy feet press firmer, as she leaps
Upon the wing again.

V.

Obedient to the call,
By the pale moonlight, Thalaba pursued,
O'er trackless snows, his way;
Unknowing he what blessed messenger
Had come to guide his steps,
That Laila's Spirit went before his path.
Brought up in darkness, and the child of sin,
Yet, as the meed of spotless innocence,
Just Heaven permitted her by one good deed
To work her own redemption, after death;
So, till the judgment day,
She might abide in bliss,
Green warbler of the Bowers of Paradise. 1

VI.

The morning sun came forth,
Wakening no eye to life
In this wide solitude;
His radiance, with a saffron hue, like heat,
Suffus'd the desert snow.
The Green Bird guided Thalaba;
Now oaring with slow wing her upward way;
Descending now in slant descent
On out-spread pinions motionless;
Floating now, with rise and fall alternate,
As if the billows of the air
Heav'd her with their sink and swell.
And when, beneath the noon,
The icy glitter of the snow
Dazzled his aching sight,
Then, on his arm alighted the Green Bird,
And spread before his eyes
Her plumage of refreshing hue.

VII.

Evening came on; the glowing clouds
Tinged with a purple ray the mountain ridge
That lay before the Traveller.
Ah! whither art thou gone,
Guide and companion of the youth, whose eye
Has lost thee in the depth of Heaven?
Why hast thou left alone
The weary wanderer in the wilderness?
And now the western clouds grow pale,
And night descends upon his solitude.

VIII.

The Arabian youth knelt down,
And bow'd his forehead to the ground,
And made his evening prayer.
When he arose, the stars were bright in heaven,
The sky was blue, and the cold Moon
Shone over the cold snow.
A speck in the air!
Is it his guide that approaches?
For it moves with the motion of life!
Lo! she returns, and scatters from her pinions
Odours diviner than the gales of morning
Waft from Sabea.

IX.

Hovering before the youth she hung,
Till, from her rosy feet, that at his touch
Uncurl'd their grasp, he took
The fruitful bough they bore.
He took and tasted, a new life
Flow'd through his renovated frame;
His limbs, that late were sore and stiff,

Felt all the freshness of repose;
His dizzy brain was calm'd,
The heavy aching of his lids
At once was taken off;
For Laila, from the Bowers of Paradise,
Had borne the healing fruit.[2]

X.
So up the mountain steep,
With untir'd foot he past,
The Green Bird guiding him,
Mid crags, and ice, and rocks,
A difficult way, winding the long ascent.
How then the heart of Thalaba rejoiced,
When, bosom'd in the mountain depths,
A shelter'd Valley open'd on his view!
It was the Simorg's vale,
The dwelling of the ancient Bird.

XI.
On a green and mossy bank,
Beside a rivulet,
The Bird of Ages stood.
No sound intruded on his solitude,
Only the rivulet was heard,
Whose everlasting flow,
From the birth-day of the world,[3] had made
The same unvaried murmuring.
Here dwelt the all-knowing Bird
In deep tranquillity,
His eye-lids ever clos'd
In full enjoyment of profound repose.

XII.
Reverently the youth approach'd
That old and only Bird,[4]
And crost his arms upon his breast,
And bow'd his head, and spake.
« Earliest of existing things,
Earliest thou, and wisest thou,
Guide me, guide me, on my way!
I am bound to seek the caverns
Underneath the roots of Ocean,
Where the Sorcerer brood are nurst.
Thou the eldest, thou the wisest,
Guide me, guide me, on my way! »

XIII.
The ancient Simorg on the youth
Unclos'd his thoughtful eyes,
And answer'd to his prayer.
« Northward by the stream proceed,
In the fountain of the rock
Wash away thy worldly stains,
Kneel thou there, and seek the Lord,
And fortify thy soul with prayer.
Thus prepar'd, ascend the Sledge,
Be bold, be wary, seek and find!
God hath appointed all. »
The ancient Simorg then let fall his lids,
Returning to repose.

XIV.
Northward, along the rivulet,
The adventurer went his way,
Tracing its waters upward to their source.

Green Bird of Paradise,
Thou hast not left the youth!—
With slow associate flight,
She companies his way,
And now they reach the fountain of the rock.

XV.
There, in the cold clear well,
Thalaba wash'd away his earthly stains,
And bow'd his face before the Lord,
And fortified his soul with prayer.
The while, upon the rock,
Stood the celestial Bird,
And, pondering all the perils he must pass,
With a mild melancholy eye,
Beheld the youth belov'd.

XVI.
And lo! beneath yon lonely pine, the sledge—
And there they stand, the harness'd Dogs,
Their wide eyes watching for the youth,
Their ears erected, turn'd towards his way.
They were lean, as lean might be,
Their furrowed ribs rose prominent,
And they were black from head to foot,
Save a white line on every breast,
Curv'd like the crescent moon.
And he is seated in the sledge,
His arms are folded on his breast,
The Bird is on his knees;
There is fear in the eyes of the Dogs,
There is fear in their pitiful moan,
And now they turn their heads,
And seeing him there, away!

XVII.
The Youth, with the start of their speed,
Falls back to the bar of the sledge;
His hair floats straight in the stream of the wind,
Like the weeds in the running brook.
They wind with speed the upward way,
An icy path through rocks of ice;
His eye is at the summit now,
And thus far all is dangerless;
And now upon the height
The black Dogs pause and pant;
They turn their eyes to Thalaba,
As if to plead for pity;
They moan, and moan with fear.

XVIII.
Once more away! and now
The long descent is seen,
A long, long, narrow path.
Ice-rocks aright, and hills of snow,
Aleft the giddy precipice.
Be firm, be firm, O Thalaba!
One motion now, one bend,
And on the crags below,
Thy shatter'd flesh will harden in the frost.
Why howl the Dogs so mournfully?
And wherefore does the blood flow fast
All purple o'er their sable hair?
His arms are folded on his breast,
Nor scourge nor goad hath he;
No hand appears to strike,

No sounding lash is heard :
But piteously they moan, and moan,
And track their way with blood.

XIX.

And lo! on yonder height,
A giant Fiend aloft,
Waits to thrust down the tottering avalanche!
If Thalaba looks back, he dies ;
The motion of fear is death.
On—on—with swift and steady pace,
Adown that dreadful way!
The Youth is firm, the Dogs are fleet,
The Sledge goes rapidly,
The thunder of the avalanche
Re-echoes far behind.
On—on—with swift and steady pace
Adown that dreadful way !
The Dogs are fleet, the way is steep,
The Sledge goes rapidly,
They reach the plain below.

XX.

A wide, wide plain, all desolate,
Nor tree, nor bush, nor herb !
On go the Dogs with rapid step,
The Sledge slides after rapidly,
And now the Sun went down.
They stopt and look'd at Thalaba,
The Youth perform'd his prayer ;
They knelt beside him as he pray'd,
They turn'd their heads to Mecca,
And tears ran down their cheeks.
Then down they laid them in the snow,
As close as they could lie,
They laid them down and slept,
And backward in the sledge
The Adventurer laid himself:
There peacefully slept Thalaba,
And the Green Bird of Paradise
Lay nestling in his breast.

XXI.

The Dogs awoke him at the dawn,
They knelt and wept again ;
Then rapidly they journey'd on,
And still the plain was desolate,
Nor tree, nor bush, nor herb !
And ever at the hour of prayer,
They stopt, and knelt, and wept ;
And still that green and graceful Bird
Was as a friend to him by day,
And ever, when at night he slept,
Lay nestling in his breast.

XXII.

In that most utter solitude,
It cheer'd his heart to hear
Her soft and soothing voice ;
Her voice was soft and sweet,
It swell'd not with the blackbird's thrill,
Nor warbled rich like the dear bird, that holds
The solitary man,
A loiterer in his thoughtful walk at eve ;
But if no overflowing joy
Spake in its tones of tenderness,

They sooth'd the soften'd soul.
Her bill was not the beak of blood :
There was a human meaning in her eye ;
Its mild affection fix'd on Thalaba,
Woke wonder while he gaz'd,
And made her dearer for the mystery.

XXIII.

Oh joy ! the signs of life appear,
The first and single Fir
That on the limits of the living world
Strikes in the ice its roots.
Another, and another now ;
And now the Larch, that flings its arms
Down-curving like the falling wave ;
And now the Aspin's scatter'd leaves
Grey glitter on the moveless twig ;
The Poplar's varying verdure now,
And now the Birch so beautiful,
Light as a lady's plumes.
Oh joy ! the signs of life ! the Deer
Hath left his slot beside the way ;
The little Ermine now is seen
White wanderer of the snow ;
And now, from yonder pines they hear
The clatter of the Grouse's wings :
And now the snowy Owl pursues
The Traveller's sledge, in hope of food ;
And hark ! the rosy-breasted bird,
The Throstle of sweet song !
Joy ! joy ! the winter-wilds are left !
Green bushes now, and greener grass,
Red thickets here, all berry-bright,
And here the lovely flowers !

XXIV.

When the last morning of their way arrived,
After the early prayer,
The Green Bird fix'd on Thalaba
A sad and supplicating eye,
And with a human voice she spake,
« Servant of God, I leave thee now.
If rightly I have guided thee,
Give me the boon I beg !»

XXV.

« O gentle Bird !» quoth Thalaba,
« Guide and companion of my dangerous way,
Friend and sole solace of my solitude,
How can I pay thee benefits like these?
Ask what thou wilt that I can give,
O gentle Bird, the poor return
Will leave me debtor still !»

XXVI.

« Son of Hodeirah !» she replied,
« When thou shalt see an Old Man crush'd beneath
The burthen of his earthly punishment,
Forgive him, Thalaba !
Yea, send a prayer to God in his behalf !»

XXVII.

A flush o'erspread the young Destroyer's cheek,
He turn'd his eye towards the Bird
As if in half repentance ; for he thought
Of Okba ; and his Father's dying groan
18

Came on his memory. The celestial Bird
Saw and renew'd her speech.
« O Thalaba, if she who in thine arms
Receiv'd the dagger-blow, and died for thee,
Deserve one kind remembrance,—save, O save,
The Father that she lov'd, from endless death!»

XXVIII.

« Laila! and is it thou?» the youth replied.
« What is there that I durst refuse to thee?
This is no time to harbour in my heart
One evil thought;—here I put off revenge,
The last rebellious feeling—Be it so!
God grant to me the pardon that I need,
    As I do pardon him!—
But who am I, that I should save
    The sinful soul alive?»

XXIX.

« Enough!» said Laila. « When the hour shall come,
Remember me! my task is done.
We meet again in Paradise!»
She said, and shook her wings, and up she soar'd
With arrow-swiftness through the heights of Heaven.

XXX.

His aching eye pursued her path,
When starting onward went the Dogs,
More rapidly they hurried on,
    In hope of near repose.
It was the early morning yet,
When, by the well-head of a brook
They stopt, their journey done.
The spring was clear, the water deep,[5]
A venturous man were he, and rash,
That should have probed its depths,
For all its loosen'd bed below
Heav'd strangely up and down,
And to and fro, from side to side,
It heav'd, and wav'd, and tost,
And yet the depths were clear,
And yet no ripple wrinkled o'er
The face of that fair Well.

XXXI.

And on that Well, so strange and fair,
    A little boat there lay,
Without an oar, without a sail;
One only seat it had, one seat,
    As if for only Thalaba.
And at the helm a Damsel stood,
A Damsel bright and bold of eye,
Yet did a maiden modesty
    Adorn her fearless brow.
Her face was sorrowful, but sure
    More beautiful for sorrow.
To her the Dogs look'd wistful up,
And then their tongues were loos'd,
« Have we done well, O Mistress dear!
And shall our sufferings end?»

XXXII.

The gentle Damsel made reply,
« Poor Servants of the God I serve,
When all this witchery is destroy'd,
Your woes will end with mine.

A hope, alas! how long unknown!
This new adventurer gives :
Now, God forbid, that he, like you,
    Should perish for his fears!
Poor Servants of the God I serve,
    Wait ye the event in peace.»
A deep and total slumber as she spake
Seiz'd them. Sleep on, poor sufferers! be at rest!
Ye wake no more to anguish;—ye have borne
The Chosen, the Destroyer!—soon his hand
    Shall strike the efficient blow;
Soon shaking off your penal forms, shall ye,
With songs of joy, amid the Eden groves,
    Hymn the Deliverer's praise !

XXXIII.

Then did the Damsel say to Thalaba,
« The morn is young, the Sun is fair,
And pleasantly, through pleasant banks,
    The quiet brook flows on —
Wilt thou embark with me?
Thou knowest not the water's way,
Think, Stranger, well! and night must come, —
    Wilt thou embark with me?
Through fearful perils thou must pass,—
Stranger, the wretched ask thine aid!
    Thou wilt embark with me!»
She smil'd in tears upon the youth!—
What heart were his, who could gainsay
    That melancholy smile?
« Sail on, sail on,» quoth Thalaba,
    «Sail on, in Allah's name!»

XXXIV.

He sate him on the single seat,
    The little boat mov'd on.
Through pleasant banks the quiet brook
    Went winding pleasantly;
By fragrant fir-groves now it past,
    And now, through alder-shores,
Through green and fertile meadows now
    It silently ran by.
The flag-flower blossom'd on its side,
    The willow tresses wav'd,
The flowing current furrow'd round
    The water-lily's floating leaf,
The fly of green and gauzy wing,
    Fell sporting down its course,
And grateful to the voyager
The freshness of the running stream,
    The murmur round the prow.
    The little boat falls rapidly
        Adown the rapid brook.

XXXV.

But many a silent spring meantime,
    And many a rivulet and rill
    Had swoln the growing brook;
And when the southern Sun began
To wind the downward way of heaven,[6]
    It ran a river deep and wide,
Through banks that widen'd still.
Then once again the Damsel spake,
« The stream is strong, the river broad,
    Wilt thou go on with me?
The day is fair, but night must come—

Wilt thou go on with me?
Far, far away, the sufferer's eye
For thee hath long been looking,—
Thou wilt go on with me!»
« Sail on, sail on,» quoth Thalaba,
« Sail on in Allah's name!»
The little boat falls rapidly
Adown the river-stream.

XXXVI.

A broader and a broader stream,
That rock'd the little boat!
The Cormorant stands upon its shoals,.
His black and dripping wings
Half open'd to the wind.
The Sun goes down, the crescent Moon
Is brightening in the firmament;
And what is yonder roar,
That sinking now, and swelling now,
But·roaring, roaring still,
Still louder, louder, grows?
The little boat falls rapidly·
Adown the rapid tide,
The Moon is bright above,
And the wide ocean opens on their way.

XXXVII.

Then did the Damsel speak again,
« Wilt thou go on with me?
The Moon is bright, the sea is calm,
And I know well the ocean-paths;
Wilt thou go on with me?—
Deliverer! yes! thou dost not fear!
Thou wilt go on with me!»
« Sail on, sail on!» quoth Thalaba,
« Sail on, in Allah's name!»

XXXVIII.

The Moon is bright, the sea is calm,
The little boat rides rapidly
Across the ocean waves;
The line of moonlight on the deep
Still follows as they voyage on;
The winds are motionless;
The gentle waters gently part
In murmurs round the prow.
He looks above, he looks around,
The boundless heaven, the boundless sea,
The crescent moon, the little boat,
Nought else above, below.

XXXIX.

The Moon is sunk, a dusky grey
Spreads o'er the Eastern sky,
The Stars grow pale and paler;—
Oh beautiful! the godlike Sun
Is rising o'er the sea!
Without an oar, without a sail,
The little boat rides rapidly;—
Is that a cloud that skirts the sea?
There is no cloud in heaven!
And nearer now, and darker now—
It is—it is—the Land!
For yonder are the rocks that rise
Dark in the reddening morn,

For loud around their hollow base
The surges rage and roar.

XL.

The little boat rides rapidly,
And now with shorter toss it heaves
Upon the heavier swell;
And now so near, they see
The shelves and shadows of the cliff,
And the low-lurking rocks,
O'er whose black summits, hidden half,
The shivering billows burst;—
And nearer now they feel the breaker's spray.
Then spake the Damsel, « Yonder is our path
Beneath the cavern arch.
Now is the ebb, and till the ocean-flow,.
We cannot over-ride the rocks.
Go thou, and on the shore
Perform thy last ablutions, and with prayer
Strengthen thy heart—I too have need to pray.»

XLI.

She held the helm with steady hand
Amid the stronger waves;
Through surge and surf she drove :
The adventurer leapt to land.

BOOK XII.

I.

Why should he that loves me, sorry be
For my deliverance, or at all complain
My good to bear, and toward joys to see ?
I go, and long desired have to go,
I go with gladness to my wished rest.
Spenser's Daphnaida.

I.

THEN Thalaba drew off Abdaldar's ring,
And cast it in the sea, and cried aloud,
« Thou art my shield, my trust, my hope, O God!
Behold and guard me now,
Thou who alone canst save.
If, from my childhood up, I have look'd on
With exultation to my destiny;
If, in the hour of anguish, I have felt,
The justice of the hand that chasten'd me;
If, of all selfish passions purified,
I go to work thy will, and from the world
Root up the ill-doing race,
Lord! let not thou the weakness of my arm
Make vain the enterprise!»

II.

The Sun was rising all magnificent,
Ocean and heaven rejoicing in his beams.
And now had Thalaba
Perform'd his last ablutions, and he stood
And gaz'd upon the little boat
Riding the billows near,
Where, like a sea-bird breasting the broad waves,
It rose and fell upon the surge:
Till, from the glitterance of the sunny main,
He turn'd his aching eyes,
And then upon the beach he laid him down,

And, watch'd the rising tide.
He did not pray, he was not calm for prayer ;
His spirit, troubled with tumultuous hope,
Toil'd with futurity ;
His brain, with busier workings, felt
The roar and raving of the restless sea,
The boundless waves that rose and roll'd and rock'd;
The everlasting sound
Opprest him, and the heaving infinite,
He clos'd his lids for rest.

III.

Meantime, with fuller reach, and stronger swell,
Wave after wave advanced ;
Each following billow lifted the last foam
That trembled on the sand with rainbow hues;
The living flower, that, rooted to the rock,
Late from the thinner element
Shrunk down within its purple stem to sleep,
Now feels the water, and again
Awakening, blossoms out
All its green anther-necks.

IV.

Was there a Spirit in the gale
That fluttered o'er his cheek ?
For it came on him like the gentle sun
Which plays and dallies o'er the night-clos'd flower,
And wooes it to unfold anew to joy ;
For it came on him as the dews of eve
Descend with healing and with life
Upon the summer mead ;
Or liker the first sound of seraph song
And Angel hail, to him
Whose latest sense had shuddered at the groan
Of anguish, kneeling by his death-bed side.

V.

He starts, and gazes round to seek
The certain presence. « Thalaba !» exclaim'd
The Voice of the Unseen ;—
« Father of my Oneiza !» he replied,
« And have thy years been numbered ? art thou too
Among the Angels ?»—« Thalaba !»
A second and a dearer voice repeats,
« Go in the favour of the Lord,
My Thalaba, go on !
My husband, I have drest our bower of bliss.
Go, and perform the work,
Let me not longer suffer hope in Heaven !»

VI.

He turn'd an eager glance toward the sea,
« Come !» quoth the Damsel, and she drove
Her little boat to land.
Impatient through the rising wave,
He rush'd to meet its way,
His eye was bright, his cheek was flush'd with joy.
« Hast thou had comfort in thy prayers ?» she cried.—
« Yea,» answer'd Thalaba,
« A heavenly visitation.» « God be prais'd !»
She uttered, « then I do not hope in vain !»
And her voice trembled, and her lips
Quivered, and tears ran down.

VII.

« Stranger,» quoth she, « in years long past
Was one who vow'd himself
The Champion of the Lord, like thee,
Against the race of Hell.
Young was he, as thyself,
Gentle, and yet so brave !
A lion-hearted man.
Shame on me, Stranger ! in the arms of love
I held him from his calling, till the hour
Was past ; and then the Angel who should else
Have crown'd him with his glory-wreath,
Smote him in anger—Years and years are gone—
And in his place of penance he awaits
Thee, the Deliverer,—surely thou art he !
It was my righteous punishment,
In the same youth unchanged,
And love unchangeable,
And grief for ever fresh,
And bitter penitence,
That gives no respite night nor day to woe,
To abide the written hour, when I should waft
The doom'd Destroyer and Deliverer here.
Remember thou, that thy success involves
No single fate, no common misery.»

VIII.

As thus she spake, the entrance of the cave
Darken'd the boat below.
Around them, from their nests,
The screaming sea-birds fled,
Wondering at that strange shape,
Yet, unalarm'd at sight of living man,
Unknowing of his sway and power misus'd :
The clamours of their young
Echoed in shriller yells,
Which rung in wild discordance round the rock.
And farther as they now advanced,
The dim reflection of the darken'd day
Grew fainter, and the dash
Of the out-breakers deaden'd ; farther yet,
And yet more faint the gleam,
And there the waters, at their utmost bound,
Silently rippled on the rising rock.
They landed and advanced, and deeper in,
Two adamantine doors
Clos'd up the cavern pass.

IX.

Reclining on the rock beside,
Sate a grey-headed man,
Watching an hour-glass by.
To him the Damsel spake,
« Is it the hour appointed ?» The old man
Nor answered her awhile,
Nor lifted he his downward eye,
For now the glass ran low,
And, like the days of age,
With speed perceivable,
The latter sands descend ;
And now the last are gone.
Then he look'd up, and rais'd his arm, and smote
The adamantine gates.

X.

The gates of adamant,
Unfolding at the stroke,

Open'd and gave the entrance.   Then she turn'd
To Thalaba and said,
« Go, in the name of God!
I cannot enter,—I must wait the end
In hope and agony.
God and Mahommed prosper thee,
For thy sake and for ours!»

XI.

He tarried not,—he past
The threshold, over which was no return.
All earthly thoughts, all human hopes
And passions now put off,
He cast no backward glance
Towards the gleam of day.
There was a light within,
A yellow light, as when the autumnal Sun,
Through travelling rain and mist
Shines on the evening hills.
Whether, from central fires effus'd,
Or if the sun-beams, day by day,
From earliest generations, there absorb'd,
Were gathering for the wrath-flame. Shade was none
In those portentous vaults ;
Crag overhanging, nor columnal rock
Cast its dark outline there;
For, with the hot and heavy atmosphere,
The light incorporate, permeating all,
Spread over all its equal yellowness.
There was no motion in the lifeless air,
He felt no stirring as he past
Adown the long descent;
He heard not his own footsteps on the rock,
That through the thick stagnation sent no sound.
How sweet it were, he thought,
To feel the flowing wind !
With what a thirst of joy
He should breathe in the open gales of heaven !

XII.

Downward, and downward still, and still the way,
The long, long, way is safe.
Is there no secret wile,
No lurking enemy ?
His watchful eye is on the wall of rock,—
And warily he marks the roof,
And warily survey'd
The path that lay before.
Downward, and downward still, and still the way,
The long, long way is safe ;
Rock only, the same light,
The same dead atmosphere,
And solitude, and silence like the grave.

XIII.

At length, the long descent
Ends on a precipice ;
No feeble ray entered its dreadful gulph,
For, in the pit profound,
Black Darkness, utter Night,
Repell'd the hostile gleam;
And, o'er the surface, the light atmosphere
Floated, and mingled not.
Above the depth, four over-awning wings,
Unplum'd, and huge and strong,
Bore up a little car ;

Four living pinions, headless, bodyless,
Sprung from one stem that branch'd below
In four down-arching limbs,
And clench'd the car-rings endlong and athwart
With claws of griffin grasp.

XIV.

But not on these, the depths so terrible,
The wonderous wings, fix'd Thalaba his eye ;
For there, upon the brink,
With fiery fetters fasten'd to the rock,
A man, a living man, tormented lay,
The young Othatha ; in the arms of love,
He who had lingered out the auspicious hour,
Forgetful of his call.
In shuddering pity, Thalaba exclaim'd,
« Servant of God, can I not succour thee ?»
He groan'd, and answered, « Son of Man,
I sinn'd, and am tormented ; I endure
In patience and in hope.
The hour that shall destroy the Race of Hell,
That hour shall set me free.»

XV.

« Is it not come ?» quoth Thalaba,
« Yea ! by this omen !»—and with fearless hand
He grasp'd the burning fetters, « in the name
Of God !»—and from the rock
Rooted the rivets, and adown the gulph
Hurl'd them.   The rush of flames roar'd up,
For they had kindled in their fall
The deadly vapours of the pit profound,
And Thalaba bent on, and look'd below.
But vainly he explor'd
The deep abyss of flame,
That sunk beyond the plunge of mortal eye,
Now all ablaze, as if infernal fires
Illum'd the world beneath.
Soon was the poison-fuel spent,
The flame grew pale and dim,
And dimmer now it fades, and now is quench'd,
And all again is dark,
Save where the yellow air
Enters a little in, and mingles slow.

XVI.

Meantime, the freed Othatha claspt his knees,
And cried, « Deliverer !» struggling then
With joyful hope. « and where is she,» he cried,
« Whose promis'd coming for so many a year—»
« Go !» answered Thalaba,
« She waits thee at the gates.»
« And in thy triumph,» he replied,
« There thou wilt join us ?»—The Deliverer's eye
Glanced on the abyss, way else was none—
The depth was unascendable.
« Await not me,» he cried,
« My path hath been appointed ! go—embark !
Return to life,—live happy !»

OTHATHA.
But thy name,—
That through the nations we may blazon it,—
That we may bless thee !

THALABA.
Bless the merciful !

XVII.

Then Thalaba pronounced the name of God,
And leapt into the car.
Down, down, it sunk,—down, down—
He neither breathes nor sees;
His eyes are clos'd for giddiness,
His breath is sinking with the fall.
The air that yields beneath the car,
Inflates the wings above.
Down—down—a mighty depth!—
Was then the Simorg, with the Powers of ill,
Associate to destroy?
And was that lovely Mariner
A fiend as false as fair?
For still he sinks down—down—
But ever the uprushing wind
Inflates the wings above,
And still the struggling wings
Repel the rushing wind.
Down—down—and now it strikes.

XVIII.

He stands and totters giddily,
All objects round, awhile
Float dizzy on his sight;
Collected soon, he gazes for the way.
There was a distant light that led his search;
The torch a broader blaze,
The unprun'd taper flares a longer flame,
But this was fierce, as is the noon-tide sun,
So, in the glory of its rays intense,
It quiver'd with green glow.
Beyond was all unseen,
No eye could penetrate
That unendurable excess of light.

XIX.

It veil'd no friendly form, thought Thalaba;
And wisely did he deem,
For, at the threshold of the rocky door,
Hugest and fiercest of his kind accurst,
Fit warden of the sorcery gate,
A rebel Afreet lay. [1]
He scented the approach of human food,
And hungry hope kindled his eye of fire.
Raising his hand to save the dazzled sense,
Onward held Thalaba,
And lifted still at times a rapid glance;
Till the due distance gain'd,
With head abas'd, he laid
The arrow in its rest.
With steady effort, and knit forehead then,
Full on the painful light,
He fix'd his aching eye, and loos'd the bow.

XX.

An anguish-yell ensued;
And sure, no human voice had scope or power
For that prodigious shriek,
Whose pealing echoes thundered up the rock.
Dim grew the dying light,
But Thalaba leapt onward to the doors
Now visible beyond.
And while the Afreet warden of the way
Was writhing with his death-pangs, over him

Sprung and smote the stony doors,
And bade them, in the name of God, give way!

XXI.

The dying Fiend, beneath him, at that name
Tossed in worse agony,
And the rocks shuddered, and the rocky doors
Rent at the voice asunder. Lo! within—
The Teraph and the Fire,
And Khawla, and in mail complete
Mohareb for the strife.
But Thalaba, with numbing force,
Smites his rais'd arm, and rushes by;
For now he sees the fire, amid whose flames,
On the white ashes of Hodeirah, lies
Hodeirah's holy Sword.

XXII.

He rushes to the fire;
Then Khawla met the youth,
And leapt upon him, and, with clinging arms,
Clasps him, and calls Mohareb now to aim
The effectual vengeance. O fool! fool! he sees
His Father's Sword, and who shall bar his way?
Who stand against the fury of that arm
That spurns her to the earth?—
She rises half, she twists around his knees,—
A moment—and he vainly strives
To shake her from her hold;
Impatient, then into her cursed breast
He stamps his crushing heel,
And from her body, heaving now in death,
Springs forward to the Sword.

XXIII.

The co-existent Flame
Knew the Destroyer; it encircled him,
Roll'd up his robe, and gathered round his head;
Condensing to intenser splendour there,
His Crown of Glory, and his Light of Life,
Hovered the irradiate wreath.

XXIV.

The moment Thalaba had laid his hand
Upon his Father's Sword,
The Living Image in the inner cave
Smote the Round Altar. The Domdaniel rock'd
Through all its thundering vaults;
Over the Surface of the reeling Earth,
The alarum shock was felt;
The Sorcerer brood, all, all, where'er dispersed,
Perforce obey'd the summons; all . . . they came
Compell'd by Hell and Heaven;
By Hell compell'd to keep
Their baptism-covenant,
And, with the union of their strength,
Oppose the common danger; forced by Heaven
To share the common doom.

XXV.

Vain are all spells! the Destroyer
Treads the Domdaniel floor!
They crowd with human arms, and human force,
To crush the single foe;
Vain is all human force!

He wields his Father's Sword,
The vengeance of awaken'd Deity!
But chief on Thalaba Mohareb prest.
The language of the inspired Witch
Announced one fatal blow for both,
And, desperate of self-safety, yet he hop'd
To serve the cause of Eblis, and uphold
His empire, true in death.

XXVI.

Who shall withstand the Destroyer?
Scattered before the sword of Thalaba
The sorcerer throng recede,
And leave him space for combat. Wretched man,
What shall the helmet or the shield avail
Against Almighty anger?.. wretched man,
Too late Mohareb finds that he hath chosen
The evil part!.. He rears his shield
To meet the Arabian's sword, ..
Under the edge of that fire-hardened steel,
The shield falls severed; his cold arm
Rings with the jarring blow : ..
He lifts his scymetar,
A second stroke, and lo! the broken hilt
Hangs from his palsied hand!
And now he bleeds! and now he flies!
And fain would hide himself amid the throng,
But they feel the sword of Hodeirah,
And they also fly from the ruin!
And hasten to the inner cave,
And fall all fearfully
Around the Giant Idol's feet,
Seeking salvation from the Power they serv'd.

XXVII.

It was a Living Image, by the art
Of magic hands, of flesh and bones compos'd,
And human blood, through veins and arteries
That flow'd with vital action. In the shape
Of Eblis it was made;
Its stature such, and such its strength,
As when among the sons of God
Pre-eminent, he rais'd his radiant head,
Prince of the Morning. On his brow
A coronet of meteor flames,
Flowing in points of light.
Self-pois'd in air before him,
Hung the Round Altar, rolling like the World
On its diurnal axis, like the World
Chequer'd with sea and shore,
The work of Demon art.
For where the sceptre in the Idol's hand
Touch'd the Round Altar, in its answering realm
Earth felt the stroke, and Ocean rose in storms,
And ruining Cities, shaken from their seat,
Crush'd all their habitants.
His other arm was rais'd, and its spread palm
Up-bore the ocean-weight,
Whose naked waters arch'd the sanctuary,
Sole prop and pillar he.

XXVIII.

Fallen on the ground, around his feet
The Sorcerers lay. Mohareb's quivering arms
Clung to the Idol's knees;
The Idol's face was pale,
And calm in terror he beheld
The approach of the Destroyer.

XXIX.

Sure of his stroke, and therefore in pursuit
Following, nor blind, nor hasty, on his foe,
Mov'd the Destroyer. Okba met his way,
Of all that brotherhood
He only fearless, miserable man,
The one that had no hope.
« On me, on me,» the childless Sorcerer cried,
« Let fall the weapon! I am he who stole
Upon the midnight of thy Father's tent;
This is the hand that pierced Hodeirah's heart,
That felt thy brethren's and thy sister's blood
Gush round the dagger-hilt. Let fall on me
The fated sword! the vengeance-hour is come!
Destroyer, do thy work!»

XXX.

Nor wile, nor weapon, had the desperate wretch :
He spread his bosom to the stroke.
« Old man, I strike thee not!» said Thalaba;
« The evil thou hast done to me and mine
Brought its own bitter punishment.
For thy dear Daughter's sake, I pardon thee,
As I do hope Heaven's pardon...For her sake,
Repent while time is yet!...thou hast my prayers
To aid thee; thou poor sinner, cast thyself
Upon the goodness of offended God!
I speak in Laila's name! and what if now
Thou canst not think to join in Paradise
Her spotless Spirit,..hath not Allah made
Al-Araf, in his wisdom? ² where the sight
Of heaven shall kindle in the penitent
The strong and purifying fire of hope.
Till, at the day of judgment, he shall see
The Mercy-Gates unfold.»

XXXI.

The astonish'd man stood gazing as he spake,
At length his heart was soften'd, and the tears
Gush'd, and he sobb'd aloud.
Then suddenly was heard
The all-beholding Prophet's divine voice,
« Thou hast done well, my Servant!
Ask and receive thy reward!»

XXXII.

A deep and awful joy
Seem'd to distend the heart of Thalaba;
With arms in reverence crost upon his breast,
Upseeking eyes suffused with transport-tears,
He answered to the Voice, « Prophet of God,
Holy, and good, and bountiful!
One only earthly wish have I, to work
Thy will, and thy protection grants me that.
Look on this Sorcerer! heavy are his crimes,
But infinite is mercy! if thy servant
Have now found favour in the sight of God,
Let him be touched with penitence, and save
His soul from utter death.»

XXXIII.

« The groans of penitence,» replied the Voice,
« Never arise unheard!

But, for thyself, prefer the prayer;
The treasure-house of Heaven
Is open to thy will.»

XXXIV.

« Prophet of God!» then answered Thalaba,
« I am alone on earth:
Thou knowest the secret wishes of my heart!
Do with me as thou wilt! thy will is best.»

XXXV.

There issued forth no Voice to answer him;
But, lo! Hodeirah's Spirit comes to see
His vengeance, and beside him, a pure form
Of roseate light, his Angel mother hung.
« My child, my dear, my glorious...blessed..Child,
My promise is perform'd..fulfil thy work!»

XXXVI.

Thalaba knew that his death hour was come,
And on he leapt, and springing up,
Into the Idol's heart
Hilt deep he drove the Sword.
The Ocean-Vault fell in, and all were crush'd.
In the same moment, at the gate
Of Paradise, Oneiza's Houri form
Welcom'd her Husband to eternal bliss.

NOTES.

BOOK I.

Note 1, page 89, col. 2.
Like the round ocean, girdled with the sky.

Henry More had a similar picture in his mind when he wrote of

Vast plains with lowly cottages forlorn,
Rounded about with the low-wavering sky.

Note 2, page 89, col. 2.
Saw Zeinab in her bliss.

It may be worth mentioning, that, according to Pietro della Valle, this is the name of which the Latins have made Zenobia.

Note 3, page 89, col. 2.
He gave, he takes away!

The Lord gave, and the Lord taketh away; blessed be the name of the Lord.—Job i, 21.

I have placed a scripture phrase in the mouth of a Mahommedan; but it is a saying of Job, and there can be no impropriety in making a modern Arab speak like an ancient one. Resignation is particularly inculcated by Mahommed, and of all his precepts it is that which his followers have best observed: it is even the vice of the East. It had been easy to have made Zeinab speak from the Koran, if the tame language of the Koran could be remembered by the few who have toiled through its dull tautology. I thought it better to express a feeling of religion in that language with which our religious ideas are connected.

Note 4, page 90, col. 1.
And rested like a dome.

La mer n'est plus qu'un cercle aux yeux des Matelots,
Ou le Ciel forme un dôme appuyé sur les flots.
Le Nouveau Monde, par M. Le Suire.

Note 5, page 90, col. 2.
Here studding azure tablatures.

The magnificent Mosque at Tauris is faced with varnished bricks, of various colours, *like most fine buildings in Persia*, says Tavernier. One of its domes is covered with white flower-work upon a green ground; the other has a black ground, spotted with white stars. Gilding is also common upon oriental buildings. At Boghar in Bactria our old traveller Jenkinson[1] saw « many houses, temples, and monuments of stone, sumptuously builded and gilt.»

In Pegu « they consume about their Varely or idol houses great store of leafe-gold, for that they overlay all the tops of the houses with gold, and some of them are covered with gold from the top to the foote; in covering whereof there is a great store of gold spent, for that every ten years they new overlay them with gold, from the top to the foote, so that with this vanitie they spend great aboundance of golde. For every ten years the rain doth consume the gold from these houses.»— *Cæsar Frederick, in Hakluyt.*

A waste of ornament and labour characterises all the works of the Orientalists. I have seen illuminated Persian manuscripts that must each have been the toil of many years, every page painted, not with representations of life and manners, but usually like the curves and lines of a turkey carpet, conveying no idea whatever, as absurd to the eye as nonsense-verses to the ear. The little of their literature that has reached us is equally worthless. Our *barbarian* scholars have called Ferdusi the Oriental Homer. We have a specimen of his poem; the translation is said to be bad, and certainly must be unfaithful, for it is in rhyme; but the vilest copy of a picture at least represents the subject and the composition. To make this Iliad of the East, as they have sacrilegiously styled it, a good poem, would be realizing the dreams of alchemy, and transmuting lead into gold.

The Arabian Tales certainly abound with genius; they have lost their metaphorical rubbish in passing through the filter of a French translation.

Note 6, page 90, col. 2.
Sennamar built at Hirah, etc.

The Arabians call this palace one of the wonders of the world. It was built for Nôman-al-Aôuar, one of those Arabian Kings who reigned at Hirah. A single stone fastened the whole structure; the colour of the walls varied frequently in a day. Nôman richly rewarded the architect Sennamar; but recollecting afterwards that he might build palaces equal, or superior in beauty, for his rival kings, ordered that he should be thrown from the highest tower of the edifice.—*D'Herbelot.*

An African colony had been settled in the north of Ireland long before the arrival of the Neimhedians. It is recorded, that Neimheidh had employed four of

[1] Hakluyt.

their artisans to erect for him two sumptuous palaces, which were so highly finished, that, jealous lest they might construct others on the same, or perhaps a grander plan, he had them privately made away with, the day after they had completed their work.—*O'Halloran's History of Ireland.*

Note 7, page 91, col. 1.
The paradise of Irem, etc.

The tribe of Ad were descended from Ad, the son of Aus or Uz, the son of Irem, the son of Shem, the son of Noah, who, after the confusion of tongues, settled in Al-Ahkâf, or the winding sands in the province of Hadramaut, where his posterity greatly multiplied. Their first King was Shedad, the son of Ad, of whom the eastern writers deliver many fabulous things, particularly that he finished the magnificent city his father had begun; wherein he built a fine palace, adorned with delicious gardens, to embellish which he spared neither cost nor labour, proposing thereby to create in his subjects a superstitious veneration of himself as a God. This garden or paradise was called the Garden of Irem, and is mentioned in the Koran, and often alluded to by the Oriental writers. The city, they tell us, is still standing in the deserts of Aden, being preserved by Providence as a monument of divine justice, though it be invisible, unless very rarely, when God permits it to be seen: a favour one Colabah pretended to have received in the reign of the Khalif Moâwiyah, who sending for him to know the truth of the matter, Colabah related his whole adventure: that, as he was seeking a camel he had lost, he found himself on a sudden at the gates of this city, and entering it, saw not one inhabitant; at which being terrified, he stayed no longer than to take with him some fine stones, which he showed the Khalif.—*Sale.*

The descendants of Ad in process of time falling from the worship of the true God into idolatry, God sent the prophet Houd (who is generally agreed to be Heber) to preach the unity of his essence, and reclaim them. Houd preached for many years to this people without effect, till God at last was weary of waiting for their repentance. The first punishment which he inflicted was a famine of three years' continuance, during all which time the heavens were closed upon them. This, with the evils which it caused, destroyed a great part of this people, who were then the richest and most powerful of all in Arabia.

The Adites seeing themselves reduced to this extremity, and receiving no succour from their false gods, resolved to make a pilgrimage to a place in the province of Hegiaz, where at present Mecca is situated. There was then a hillock of red saud there, around which a great concourse of different people might always be seen; and all these nations, the faithful as well as the unfaithful, believed that by visiting this spot with devotion, they should obtain from God whatever they petitioned for, respecting the wants and necessities of life.

The Adites having then resolved to undertake this religious journey, chose seventy men, at whose head they appointed Mortadh and Kail, the two most considerable personages of the country, to perform this duty in the name of the whole nation, and by this means procure rain from Heaven, without which their country must be ruined. The deputies departed, and were hospitably received by Moâwiyah, who at that time reigned in the province of Hegiaz. They explained to him the occasion of their journey, and demanded leave to proceed and perform their devotions at the Red Hillock, that they might procure rain.

Mortadh, who was the wisest of this company, and who had been converted by the Prophet Houd, often remonstrated with his associates, that it was useless to take this journey for the purpose of praying at this chosen spot, unless they had previously adopted the truths which the Prophet preached, and seriously repented of their unbelief. For how, said he, can you hope that God will shed upon us the abundant showers of his mercy, if we refuse to hear the voice of him whom he hath sent to instruct us?

Kail, who was one of the most obstinate in error, and consequently of the Prophet's worst enemies, hearing the discourses of his colleague, requested King Moâwiyah to detain Mortadh prisoner, whilst he and the remainder of his companions proceeded to make their prayers upon the Hillock. Moâwiyah consented, and, detaining Mortadh captive, permitted the others to pursue their journey, and accomplish their vow.

Kail, now the sole chief of the deputation, having arrived at the place, prayed thus, Lord, give to the people of Ad such rains as it shall please thee. And he had scarcely finished when there appeared three clouds in the sky, one white, one red, the third black. At the same time these words were heard to proceed from Heaven, Chuse which of the three thou wilt. Kail chose the black, which he imagined the fullest, and most abundant in water, of which they were in extreme want. After having chosen, he immediately quitted the place, and took the road to his own country, congratulating himself on the happy success of his pilgrimage.

As soon as Kail arrived in the valley of Magaith, a part of the territory of the Adites, he informed his countrymen of the favourable answer he had received, and of the cloud which was soon to water all their lauds. The senseless people all came out of their houses to receive it; but this cloud, which was big with the divine vengeance, produced only a wind, most cold and most violent, which the Arabs call Sarsar; it continued to blow for seven days and seven nights and exterminated all the unbelievers of the country, leaving only the Prophet Houd alive, and those who had heard him and turned to the faith.—*D'Herbelot.*

Note 8, page 91, col. 1.
O'er all the winding sands.

Al Ahkaf signifies the Winding Sands.

Note 9, page 91, col. 2.
Detects the ebony.

I have heard from a certain Cyprian botanist, that the Ebony does not produce either leaves or fruit, and that it is never seen exposed to the sun: that its roots are indeed under the earth, which the Æthiopians dig out, and that there are men among them skilled in finding the place of its concealment.—*Pausanias, translated by Taylor.*

Note 10, page 92, col. 1.
We to our Idols still applied for aid.

The Adites worshipped four Idols, Sakiah the dispenser of rain, Hafedah the protector of travellers, Razekah the giver of food, and Salemah the preserver in sickness.—*D'Herbelot.*

Note 11, page 92, col. 1.

Then to the place of concourse, etc.

Mecca was thus called. Mahommed destroyed the other superstitions of the Arabs, but he was obliged to adopt their old and rooted veneration for the Well and the Black Stone, and transfer to Mecca the respect and reverence which he had designed for Jerusalem.

Mecca is situated in a barren place (about one day's journey from the Red-Sea) in a valley, or rather in the midst of many little hills. The town is surrounded for several miles with many thousands of little hills, which are very near one to the other. I have been on the top of some of them near Mecca, where I could see some miles about, but yet was not able to see the farthest of the hills. They are all stony-rock, and blackish, and pretty near of a bigness, appearing at a distance like cocks of hay, but all pointing towards Mecca. Some of them are half a mile in circumference, etc., but all near of one height. The people here have an odd and foolish sort of *tradition* concerning them, viz. That when *Abraham* went about building the *Beat-Allah,* God by his wonderful providence did so order it, that every *mountain* in the world should contribute something to the building thereof; and accordingly every one did send its *proportion.* Though there is a *mountain* near *Algiers* which is called *Corra Dog,* i. e. *Black Mountain;* and the reason of its blackness, they say, is, because it did not send any part of itself towards building the Temple at Mecca. Between these hills is good and plain travelling, though they stand near one to another.—*A faithful Account of the Religion and Manners of the Mahomedans, etc. by Joseph Pitts of Exon.*

Adam after his fall was placed upon the mountain of *Vassem,* in the eastern region of the globe. *Eve* was banished to a place since called Djidda, which signifies the first of mothers (the celebrated port of *Gedda,* on the coast of *Arabia*). The Serpent was cast into the most horrid desert of the East, and the spiritual tempter, who seduced him, was exiled to the coasts of *Eblehh.* This fall of our first parent was followed by the infidelity and sedition of all the spirits, *Djinn,* who were spread over the surface of the earth. Then God sent against them the great *Azazil,* who with a legion of angels chased them from the continent, and dispersed them among the isles, and along the different coasts of the sea. Some time after, *Adam,* conducted by the spirit of God, travelled into Arabia, and advanced as far as *Mecca.* His footsteps diffused on all sides abundance and fertility. His figure was enchanting, his stature lofty, his complexion brown, his hair thick, long, and curled; and he then wore a beard and mustachios. After a separation of a hundred years, he rejoined *Eve* on Mount *Arafaith,* near *Mecca;* an event which gave that mount the name of *Arafaith,* or *Arefe,* that is, the Place of Remembrance. This favour of the Eternal Deity, was accompanied by another not less striking. By his orders the angels took a tent, *Khayme,* from paradise, and pitched it on the very spot where afterwards the *Keabe* was erected. This is the most sacred of the tabernacles, and the first temple which was consecrated to the worship of the Eternal Deity by the first of men, and by all his posterity. *Seth* was the founder of the sacred *Keabe :* in the same place where the angels had pitched the celestial tent, he erected a stone edifice, which he consecrated to the worship of the Eternal Deity.—*D'Ohsson.*

Bowed down by the weight of years, *Adam* had reached the limit of his earthly existence. At that moment he longed eagerly for the fruits of paradise. A legion of angels attended upon his latest sigh, and, by the command of the Eternal Being, received his soul. He died on Friday the 7th of April, *Nissan,* at the age of nine hundred and thirty years. The angels washed and purified his body; which was the origin of funeral ablutions. The archangel *Michael* wrapped it in a sheet, with perfumes and aromatics ; and the archangel *Gabriel,* discharging the duties of the Imameth, performed, at the head of the whole legion of angels, and of the whole family of this first of the patriarchs, the *Salath'ul Djenaze :* which gave birth to funeral prayers. The body of *Adam* was deposited at *Ghar'ul-Kenz* (the grotto of treasure), upon the mountain *Djebel-Eb'y Coubeyss,* which overlooks *Mecca.* His descendants, at his death, amounted to forty thousand souls.—*D'Ohsson.*

When Noah entered the ark, he took with him, by the command of the Eternal, the body of Adam, inclosed in a box-coffin. After the waters had abated, his first care was to deposit it in the same grotto from whence it had been removed.—*D'Ohsson.*

Note 12, page 92, col. 2.

So if the resurrection came.

Some of the Pagan Arabs, when they died, had their Camel tied by their Sepulchre, and so left without meat or drink to perish, and accompany them to the other world, lest they should be obliged at the Resurrection to go on foot, which was accounted very scandalous.

All affirmed that the pious, when they come forth from their sepulchres, shall find ready prepared for them white-winged Camels with saddles of gold. Here are some footsteps of the doctrine of the ancient Arabians.—*Sale.*

Note 13, page 92, col. 2.

She stared me in the face.

This line is in one of the most beautiful passages of our old Ballads, so full of beauty. I have never seen the ballad in print, and with some trouble have procured only an imperfect copy from memory. It is necessary to insert some of the preceding stanzas. The title is,

OLD POULTER'S MARE.

At length old age came on her,
    And she grew faint and poor ;
Her master he fell out with her,
    And turned her out of door,
Saying, if thou wilt not labour,
    I prithee go thy way,—
And never let me see thy face
    Until thy dying day.

These words she took unkind,
    And on her way she went,
For to fulfil her master's will
    Always was her intent ;
The hills were very high,
    The valleys very bare,
The summer it was hot and dry,—
    It starved Old Poulter's Mare.

Old Poulter he grew sorrowful,
    And said to his kinsman Will,
I'd have thee go and seek the Mare
    O'er valley and o'er hill ;

Go, go, go, go, says Poulter,
And make haste back again,
For until thou hast found the Mare,
In grief I shall remain.

Away went Will so willingly,
And all day long he sought;
Till when it grew towards the night,
He in his mind bethought
He would go home and rest him,
And come again to-morrow,
For if he could not find the Mare,
His heart would break with sorrow.

He went a little farther
And turned his head aside,
And just by goodman Whitfield's gate
Oh, there the Mare he spied.
He asked her how she did,
She stared him in the face,
Then down she laid her head again—
She was in wretched case.

Note 14, page 92, col. 2.

What, though unmov'd they bore the deluge weight.

Concerning the pyramids, « I shall put down,» says Greaves, « that which is confessed by the Arabian writers to be the most probable relation, as is reported by Ibn Abd Alhokm, whose words out of the Arabic are these: ' The greatest part of chronologers agree, that he which built the pyramids was Saurid Ibn Salhouk, King of Egypt, who lived three hundred years before the flood. The occasion of this was, because he saw, in his sleep, that the whole earth was turned over with the inhabitants of it, the men lying upon their faces, and the stars falling down and striking one another, with a terrible noise; and being troubled, he concealed it. After this he saw the fixed stars falling to the earth, in the similitude of white fowl, and they snatched up men, carrying them between two great mountains; and these mountains closed upon them, and the shining stars were made dark. Awaking with great fear, he assembles the chief priests of all the provinces of Egypt, an hundred and thirty priests; the chief of them was called Aclimum. Relating the whole matter to them, they took the altitude of the stars, and, making their prognostication, foretold of a deluge. The King said, Will it come to our country? they answered, Yea, and will destroy it. And there remained a certain number of years for to come, and he commanded in the mean space to build the Pyramids, and a vault to be made, into which the river Nilus entering, should run into the countries of the west, and into the land Al-Said. And he filled them with *telesmes,* [1] and with strange things, and with riches and treasures, and the like. He engraved in them all things that were told him by wise men, as also all profound sciences, the names of *alakakirs,* [2] the uses and hurts of them; the science of astrology and of arithmetic, and of geometry, and of physic. All this may be interpreted by him that knows their characters and language. After he had given order for this building, they cut out vast columns and wonderful stones. They fetch massy stones from the Æthiopians, and made with these the foundation of the three Pyramids, fastening them together with

[1] That which the Arabians commonly mean by *telesmes,* are certain *sigilla,* or *amuleta,* made under such and such an aspect, or configuration of the stars and planets, with several characters accordingly inscribed.

[2] *Alakakir,* amongst other significations, is the name of a precious stone; and therefore in Abulfeda 'it is joined with *yacut,* a ruby.— I imagine it here to signify some magical spell, which, it may be, was engraven on this stone.

lead and iron. They built the gates of them forty cubits under ground, and they made the height of the Pyramids one hundred royal cubits, which are fifty of ours in these times; he also made each side of them an hundred royal cubits. The beginning of this building was in a fortunate horoscope. After that he had finished it, he covered it with coloured sattin from the top to the bottom; and he appointed a solemn festival, at which were present all the inhabitants of his kingdom. Then he built in the western Pyramid thirty treasures, filled with store of riches, and utensils, and with signatures made of precious stones, and with instruments of iron, and vessels of earth, and with arms that rust not, and with glass which might be bended and yet not broken, and with several kinds of alakakirs, single and double, and with deadly poisons, and with other things besides. He made also in the east Pyramid divers celestial spheres and stars, and what they severally operate in their aspects, and the perfumes which are to be used to them, and the books which treat of these matters. He also put in the coloured Pyramid the commentaries of the Priests in chests of black marble, and with every Priest a book, in which were the wonders of his profession, and of his actions, and of his nature, and what was done in his time, and what is, and what shall be, from the beginning of time to the end of it. He placed in every Pyramid a treasurer. The treasurer of the westerly Pyramid was a statue of marble stone, standing upright with a lance, and upon his head a serpent, wreathed. He that came near it, and stood still, the serpent bit him of one side, and wreathing round about his throat and killing him, returned to his place. He made the treasurer of the east Pyramid, an idol of black agate, his eyes open and shining, sitting upon a throne with a lance; when any looked upon him, he heard of one side of him a voice, which took away his sense, so that he fell prostrate upon his face, and ceased not till he died. He made the treasurer of the coloured Pyramid a statue of stone, called *Albut,* sitting: he which looked towards it was drawn by the statue, till he stuck to it, and could not be separated from it, till such time as he died. The Coptites write in their books, that there is an inscription engraven upon them, the exposition of which, in Arabic, is this, ' I KING SAURID built the Pyramids in such and such a time, and finished them in six years: he that comes after me, and says that he is equal to me, let him destroy them in six hundred years; and yet it is known, that it is easier to pluck down, than to build up: I also covered them, when I had finished them, with sattin; and let him cover them with matts.' After that ALMAMON the Calif entered Ægypt, and saw the Pyramids, he desired to know what was within, and therefore would have them opened. They told him it could not possibly be done. He replied, I will have it certainly done. And that hole was opened for him, which stands open to this day, with fire and vinegar. Two smiths prepared and sharpened the iron and engines, which they forced in, and there was a great expense in the opening of it. The thickness of the walls was found to be twenty cubits; and when they came to the end of the wall, behind the place they had digged, there was an ewer of green emerald . in it were a thousand dinars very weighty, every dinar was an ounce of our ounces; they wondered at it, but knew not the meaning of it. Then ALMAMON said, cast up the account how much hath been spent in making the entrance;

they cast it up, and lo it was the same sum which they found; it neither exceeded nor was defective. Within they found a square well, in the square of it there were doors, every door opened into a house (or vault), in which there were dead bodies wrapped up in linen. They found towards the top of the Pyramid, a chamber, in which there was a hollow stone: in it was a statue of stone like a man, and within it a man, upon whom was a breast-plate of gold set with jewels; upon his breast was a sword of invaluable price, and at his head a carbuncle of the bigness of an egg, shining like the light of the day; and upon him were characters written with a pen, no man knows what they signify. After ALMAMON had opened it, men entered into it for many years, and descended by the slippery passage which is in it; and some of them came out safe, and others died.'»
—*Greaves's Pyramidographia.*

Note 15, page 92, col. 2.
The living carbuncle.

The Carbuncle is to be found in most of the subterranean palaces of Romance. I have no where seen so circumstantial an account of its wonderful properties as in a passage of Thuanus, quoted by Stephanius in his Notes to Saxo-Grammaticus.

«Whilst the King was at Bologna, a stone, wonderful in its species and nature, was brought to him from the East Indies, by a man unknown, who appeared by his manners to be a Barbarian. It sparkled as though all burning with an incredible splendour, flashing radiance, and shooting on every side its beams, it filled the surrounding air to a great distance, with a light scarcely by any eyes endurable. In this also it was wonderful, that being most impatient of the earth, if it was confined, it would force its way, and immediately fly aloft; neither could it be contained by any art of man, in a narrow place, but appeared only to love those of ample extent. It was of the utmost purity, stained by no soil nor spot. Certain shape it had none, for its figure was inconstant and momentarily changing, and though at a distance it was beautiful to the eye, it would not suffer itself to be handled with impunity, but hurt those who obstinately struggled with it, as many persons before many spectators experienced. If by chance any part of it was broken off, for it was not very hard, it became nothing less.'— *Thuanus,* lib. 8.

In the Mirror of Stones, Carbuncles are said to be male and female. The females throw out their brightness: the stars appear burning within the males.

Like many other jewels, the Carbuncle was supposed to be an animal substance, formed in the serpent. The serpent's ingenious method of preserving it from the song of the charmer, is related in an after-note.—*Book* 9.

Note 16, page 93, col. 1.
Yet innocent it grew.

Adam, says a Moorish author, after having eaten the forbidden fruit, sought to hide himself under the shade

¹ Since this note was written, I have found in Feyjoo the history of this story. It was invented as a riddle or allegory of *fire*, by a French physician, called Fernelio by the Spanish author, and published by him in a Dialogue, *De abditis rerum causis.* From hence it was extracted, and sent as a trick to Mizaldo, another physician, who had written a credulous work, *De Arcanis Naturæ*; and a copy of this letter came into the hands of Thuanus. He discovered the deception too late, for a second edition of his history had been previously published at Frankfort.

of the trees that form the bowers of Paradise: the Gold and Silver trees refused their shade to the father of the human race. God asked them why they did so? because, replied the Trees, Adam has transgressed against your commandment. Ye have done well, answered the Creator; and that your fidelity may be rewarded, 't is my decree that men shall hereafter become your slaves, and that in search of you they shall dig into the very bowels of the earth.—*Chenier.*

The black-lead of Borrodale is described as lying in the mine in the form of a tree; it hath a body or root, and veins or branches fly from it in different directions: the root or body is the finest black-lead, and the branches at the extremities the worst the farther they fly. The veins or branches sometimes shoot out to the surface of the ground.—*Hutchinson's Hist. of Cumberland.*

They have founde by experience, that the vein of golde is a living tree, and that the same by all waies that it spreadeth and springeth from the roote by the softe pores and passages of the earth, putteth forth branches, even unto the uppermost parts of the earth, and ceaseth not untill it discover itself unto the open aire: at which time it sheweth forthe certaine beautiful colours in the steede of floures, round stones of golden earth in the steede of fruites; and thinne plates insteede of leaves. They say that the roote of the golden tree extendeth to the center of the earth, and there taketh norishment of increase: for the deeper that they dig, they finde the trunkes thereof to be so much the greater, as farre as they maye followe it, for abundance of water springing in the mountains. Of the branches of this tree, they finde some as small as a thread, and others as bigge as a man's finger, according to the largeness or straightnesse of the riftes and cliftes. They have sometimes chanced upon whole caves, sustained and borne up as it were with golden pillers, and this in the waies by the which the branches ascende: the which being filled with the substance of the trunke creeping from beneath, the branche maketh itself waie by whiche it maie pass out. It is oftentimes divided, by encountring with some kind of harde stone; yet is it in other cliftes nourished by the exhalations and virtue of the roote.—*Pietro Martire.*

Metals, says Herrera, (5. 3. 15.) are like plants hidden in the bowels of the earth, with their trunk and boughs, which are the veins; for it appears in a certain manner, that like plants they go on growing, not because they have any inward life, but because they are produced in the entrails of the earth by the virtue of the sun and of the planets: and so they go on increasing. And as metals are thus, as it were, plants hidden in the earth; so plants are animals fixed to one place, sustained by the aliment which Nature has provided for them at their birth: And to animals, as they have a more perfect being, a sense and knowledge hath been given, to go about and seek their aliment. So that barren earth is the support of metal, and fertile earth of plants, and plants of animals: the less perfect serving the more perfect.

Note 17, page 93, col. 1.
The fine gold net-work, etc.

A great number of stringy fibres seem to stretch out from the boughs of the Palm, on each side, which cross one another in such a manner, that they take out from between the boughs a sort of bark like close net-work, and this they spin out with the hand, and with it make cords of all sizes, which are mostly used in Egypt. They also make of it a sort of brush for clothes.—*Pococke.*

Note 18, page 93, col. 1.
Crouch'd at this Nimrod's throne.

Shedad was the first King of the Adites. I have ornamented his palace less profusely than the Oriental writers who describe it. In the notes to the *Bahar-Danush* is the following account of its magnificence from the *Tafat al Mujalis.*

A pleasant and elevated spot being fixed upon, Shuddaud dispatched an hundred chiefs to collect skilful artists and workmen from all countries. He also commanded the monarchs of Syria and Ormus to send him all their jewels and precious stones. Forty camel-loads of gold, silver, and jewels, were daily used in the building, which contained a thousand spacious quadrangles of many thousand rooms. In the areas were artificial trees of gold and silver, whose leaves were emeralds, and fruit clusters of pearls and jewels. The ground was strowed with ambergris, musk, and saffron. Between every two of the artificial trees was planted one of delicious fruit. This romantic abode took up five hundred years in the completion. When finished, Shuddaud marched to view it; and, when arrived near, divided two hundred thousand youthful slaves, whom he had brought with him from Damascus, into four detachments, which were stationed in cantonments prepared for their reception on each side of the garden, towards which he proceeded with his favourite courtiers. Suddenly was heard in the air a voice like thunder, and Shuddaud, looking up, beheld a personage of majestic figure and stern aspect, who said, « I am the Angel of Death, commissioned to seize thy impure soul.» Shuddaud exclaimed, « Give me leisure to enter the garden,» and was descending from his horse, when the seizer of life snatched away his impure spirit, and he fell dead upon the ground. At the same time lightnings flashed, and destroyed the whole army of the infidel; and the rose-garden of Irim became concealed from the sight of man.

Note 19, page 93, col. 2.
O Shedad! only in the hour of death.

Lamai relates, that a great Monarch, whom he does not name, having erected a superb Palace, wished to show it to every man of talents and taste in the city; he therefore invited them to a banquet, and after the repast was finished, asked them if they knew any building more magnificent, and more perfect, in the architecture, in the ornaments, and in the furniture. All the guests contented themselves with expressing their admiration, and lavishing praise, except one, who led a retired and austere life, and was one of those persons whom the Arabians call Zahed.

This man spoke very freely to the Prince, and said to him, I find a great defect in this building; it is, that the foundation is not good, nor the walls sufficiently strong, so that Azrael can enter on every side, and the Sarsar can easily pass through. And when they showed him the walls of the Palace ornamented with azure and gold, of which the marvellous workmanship surpassed in costliness the richness of the materials, he replied, there is still a great inconvenience here; it is, that we

can never estimate these works well, till we are laid backwards. Signifying by these words, that we never understand these things rightly, till we are upon our death-bed, when we discover their vanity.—*D'Herbelot.*

Note 20, page 94, col. 1.
Breath'd through his moveless lips, etc,

Las horrendas palabras parecian
Salir por una trompa resonante,
Y que los yertos labios no movian.
Lupercio Leonardo.

Note 21, page 94, col. 1.
And err not from their aim!

Death is come up into our windows, and entered into our palaces, to cut off the children from without, and the young men from the streets.—*Jeremiah,* ix, 21.

The Trees shall give fruit, and who shall gather them? The Grapes shall ripen, and who shall tread them? for all places shall be desolate of men.—*2 Esdras,* xvi, 25.

For strong is his right hand that bendeth the Bow, his arrows that he shooteth are sharp, and shall not miss when they begin to be shot into the ends of the world.—*2 Esdras,* xvi, 13.

Note 22, page 94, col. 2.
Seems to partake of life.

There are several trees or shrubs of the genus Mimosa. One of these trees drops its branches whenever any person approaches it, seeming as if it saluted those who retire under its shade. This mute hospitality has so endeared this tree to the Arabians, that the injuring or cutting of it down is strictly prohibited.—*Niebuhr.*

Note 23, page 95, col. 1.
Let fall the drops of bitterness and death.

The Angel of Death, say the Rabbis, holdeth his sword in his hand at the bed's head, having on the end thereof three drops of gall; the sick man spying this deadly Angel, openeth his mouth with fear, and then those drops fall in, of which one killeth him, the second maketh him pale, the third rotteth and purifieth.—*Purchas.*

Possibly the expression—to taste the bitterness of death, may refer to this.

BOOK II.

Note 1, page 95, col. 2.
A Teraph stood against the cavern side.

The manner how the Teraphim were made is fondly conceited thus among the Rabbies. They killed a man that was a first-born son, and wrung off his head, and seasoned it with salt and spices, and wrote, upon a plate of gold, the name of an unclean spirit, and put it under the head upon a wall, and lighted candles before it, and worshipped it.—*Godwyn's Moses and Aaron.*

By *Rabbi Eleazar,* it is said to be the head of a child.

Note 2, page 96, col. 2.
But Eblis, etc.

The Devil, whom Mahommed names Eblis, from his despair, was once one of those angels who are nearest to God's presence, called Azazil; and fell (according to the doctrine of the Koran), for refusing to pay homage to Adam at the command of God.—*Koran*, ch. 2, 7, 15.

God created the body of Adam of *Salzal*, that is, of dry but unbaked clay; and left it forty nights, or, according to others, forty years, lying without a soul; and the Devil came to it, and kicked it, and it sounded. And God breathed into it a soul with his breath, sending it in at his eyes; and he himself saw his nose still dead clay, and the soul running through him, till it reached his feet, when he stood upright.—*Maracci*.

In the Nuremberg Chronicle is a print of the creation of Adam; the body is half made, growing out of a heap of clay under the Creator's hands. A still more absurd print represents Eve half-way out of his side.

The fullest Mahommedan Genesis is to be found in Rabadan the Morisco's Poems.

God, designing to make known to his whole choir of Angels, high and low, his scheme concerning the Creation, called the Archangel *Gabriel*, and delivering to him a pen and paper, commanded him to draw out an instrument of fealty and homage; in which, as God had dictated to his Secretary *Gabriel*, were specified the pleasures and delights he ordained to his creatures in this world; the term of years he would allot them; and how, and in what exercises, their time in this life was to be employed. This being done, *Gabriel* said, Lord, what more must I write? The pen resisteth, and refuseth to be guided forwards! God then took the deed, and, before he folded it, signed it with his sacred hand, and affixed thereunto his royal signet, as an indication of his incontestable and irrevocable promise and covenant. Then *Gabriel* was commanded to convey what he had written throughout the hosts of Angels; with orders that they all, without exception, should fall down and worship the same: and it was so abundantly replenished with glory, that the angelical potentates universally reverenced and paid homage thereunto. *Gabriel* returning, said, O Lord! I have obeyed thy commands: what else am I to do? God replied, Close up the writing in this crystal; for this is the inviolable covenant of the fealty the mortals I will hereafter create shall pay unto me, and by the which they shall acknowledge me. *El Hassan* tells us, that no sooner had the blessed Angel closed the said crystal, but so terrible and astonishing a voice issued out thereof, and it cast so unusual and glorious a light, that, with the surprise of so great and unexpected a mystery, the angel remained fixed and immoveable; and although he had a most ardent desire to be let into the secret *Arcanas* of that wonderful prodigy, yet all his innate courage, and heavenly magnanimity, were not sufficient to furnish him with assurance or power, to make the enquiry.

All being now completed, and put in order, God said to his Angels, « Which of you will descend to the Earth, and bring me up a handful thereof?» When immediately such infinite numbers of celestial spirits departed, that the universal surface was covered with them; where, consulting among themselves, they unanimously confirmed their loathing and abhorrence to touch it, saying, How dare we be so presumptuous as to expose, before the throne of the Lord, so glorious and sovereign as ours is, a thing so filthy, and of a form and composition so vile and despicable! and, in effect, they all returned, fully determined not to meddle with it. After these went others, and then more; but not one of them, either first or last, dared to defile the purity of their hands with it. Upon which *Azarael*, an Angel of an extraordinary stature, flew down, and, from the four corners of the Earth, brought up a handful of it which God had commanded. From the south and the north, from the west and from the east, took he it; of all which four different qualities, human bodies are composed.

The Almighty, perceiving in what manner *Azarael* had signalized himself in this affair, beyond the rest of the Angels, and taking particular notice of his goodly form and stature, said to him; « O *Azarael*, it is my pleasure to constitute thee to be Death itself; thou shalt be him who separateth the souls from the bodies of those creatures I am about to make; Thou henceforth shalt be called *Azarael Malec el Mout*, or *Azarael*, the Angel of Death.»

Then God caused the Earth, which *Azarael* had brought, to be washed and purified in the *fountains of Heaven*: and *El Hassan* tells us, that it became so resplendently clear, that it cast a more shining and beautiful light than the Sun in its utmost glory. Gabriel was then commanded to convey this lovely, though as yet inanimate, *lump of clay*, throughout the Heavens, the Earth, the Centres, and the Seas; to the intent, and with a positive injunction, that whatsoever had life might behold it, and pay honour and reverence thereunto.

When the Angels saw all these incomprehensible mysteries, and that so beautiful an image, they said, « Lord! if it will be pleasing in thy sight, we will, in thy most high and mighty name, prostrate ourselves before it: » To which voluntary proposal, God replied; I am content you pay adoration to it; and I command you so to do :—when instantly they all bowed, inclining their shining celestial countenances at his feet; only *Eblis* detained himself, obstinately refusing; proudly and arrogantly valuing himself upon his Heavenly composition. To whom God sternly said, « prostrate thyself to Adam.» He made a show of so doing, but remained only upon his knees, and then rose up, before he had performed what God had commanded him. When the Angels beheld his insolence and disobedience, they a second time prostrated themselves, to complete what the haughty and presumptuous Angel had left undone. From hence it is, that in all our prayers, at each inclination of the body, we make two prostrations, one immediately after the other. God being highly incensed against the rebellious Eblis, said unto him, « Why didst thou not reverence this statue which I have made, as the other Angels all have done?» To which Eblis replied, « I will never lessen or disparage my grandeur so much, as to humble myself to a piece of clay; I who am an immortal Seraphim, of so apparently a greater excellency than *that*; I, whom thou didst create out of the celestial fire, what an indignity would it be to my splendor, to pay homage to a thing composed of so vile a metal." The irritated Monarch, with a voice of thunder, then pronounced against him this direful anathema and malediction: «Begone, enemy; depart, Rebel, from my abode! Thou no longer shalt continue in my celestial dominions.—Go, thou accursed flaming thunderbolt of fire! My curse pursue thee! My condemnation overtake thee! My torments afflict thee! And my chastisement accompany thee! »—Thus fell this enemy of God and mankind, both he, and all his followers and abettors, who sided or were partakers with him in his pride and presumptuous disobedience.

God now was pleased to publish and make manifest his design of animating man, out of that beautiful and resplendent crystal; and accordingly commanded Gabriel to breathe into the body of clay, that it might become flesh and blood: But at the instant, as the immaculate Spirit was going to enter therein, it returned, and humbling itself before the Lord, said, " O Merciful King! for what reason is it that thou intendest to inclose me in this loathsome prison? I, who am thy servant, thou shuttest up within mine enemy, where my purity will be defiled, and where, against my will, I shall disobey thee, without being able to resist the instigation and power of this rebellious flesh; whereby I shall become liable to suffer thy rigorous punishment, insupportable and unequal to my strength, for having perpetrated the enormities obnoxious to the frailty of human flesh: Spare me, O Lord! spare me! suffer me not to taste of this bitter draught! To thee it belongs to command, and to me to supplicate thee.»

Thus spoke the pure and unspotted Spirit, when God, to give it some satisfaction to these complaints, and that it might contentedly resign itself to obey his commands, ordered it should be conducted near his throne, where, in innumerable and infinite parts thereof, it beheld certain letters decyphered up and down, importing, Mahomet the triumphant leader! And over all the seven heavens, on their gates, and in all their books, he saw those words stamped, exceedingly bright and resplendent. This was the blazon which all the Angels and other celestial beings carried between their beautiful eyes, and for their devices on their apparel.

The Spirit having seen all this, returned to the throne of glory, and being very desirous to understand the signification of those cyphers and characters, he asked, What name was that which shined so in every place? To which question, God answered; Know, that from thee, and from that flesh, shall proceed a chieftain, a leader, who shall bear that name, and use that language; by whom, and for whose sake, I the Lord, the heavens, the earths, and the seas, shall be honoured, as shall likewise all who believe in that name.

The Spirit, bearing these wonders, immediately conceived so mighty a love to the body, a love not to be expressed, nor even imagined, that it longed with impatience to enter into it; which it had no sooner done, but it miraculously and artificially was influenced and distilled into every individual part and member thereof whereby the body became animated.—*Rabadan.*

It is to be regretted, that the original of this very curious poem has not been published, and that it did not meet with a more respectable translator. How well would the erudition of Sale have been employed in elucidating it!

Note 3, page 97, col. 1.

Where art thou, Hodeirah, now?

These lines contain the various opinions of the Mahommedans respecting the intermediate state of the Blessed, till the Day of Judgment.

Note 4, page 97, col. 1.

Is thy soul in Zemzem-well?

Hagar being near time, and not able any longer to endure the ill-treatment she received from Sara, resolved to run away. Abraham coming to hear of her discontent, and fearing she might make away with the child, especially if she came to be delivered without the assistance of some other women, followed her, and found her already delivered of a son; who, dancing with his little feet upon the ground, had made way for a spring to break forth. But the water of the spring came forth in such abundance, as also with such violence, that Hagar could make no use of it to quench her thirst, which was then very great. Abraham coming to the place, commanded the spring to glide more gently, and to suffer that water might be drawn out of it to drink; and having thereupon stayed the course of it with a little bank of sand, he took of it, to make Hagar and her child drink. The said spring is to this day called *Semsem*, from Abraham making use of that word to stay it.—*Olearius.*

Note 5, page 97, col. 1.

And with the living reptile lash'd his neck.

Excepting in this line, I have avoided all resemblance to the powerful poetry of Lucan.

Aspicit astantem projecti corporis umbram,
Exanimes artus, invisaque claustra timentem
Carceris antiqui ; pavet ire in pectus apertum,
Visceraque, et raptas letali vulnere fibras.
Ab miser, extremum cui mortis munus iniquæ
Eripitur, non posse mori! miratur Erichtho
Has fatis licuisse moras, irataque morti
Verberat immotum vivo serpente cadaver.
* * * * * * * * *
Protinus astrictus caluit cruor, atraque fovit
Vulnera, et in venas extremaque membra cucurrit.
Percussæ gelido trepidant sub pectore fibræ ;
Et nova desuetis subrepens vita medullis,
Miscetur morti : tunc omnis palpitat artus ;
Tenduntur nervi ; nec se tellure cadaver
Paulatim per membra levat, terraque repulsum est,
Erectumque simul. Distento lumina rictu
Nudantur. Nondum facies viventis in illo,
Jam morientis erat ; remanet pallorque rigorque,
Et stupet illatus mundo.
Lucan.

A curious instance of French taste occurs in this part of Brebeuf's translation. The re-animated corpse is made the corpse of Burrhus, of whose wife, Octavia, Sextus is enamoured. Octavia hears that her husband has fallen in battle; she seeks his body, but in vain. A light at length leads her to the scene of Erichtho's incantations, and she beholds Burrhus, to all appearance, living. The witch humanely allows them time for a long conversation, which is very complimentary on the part of the husband.

Brebeuf was a man of genius. The Pharsalia is as well told in his version as it can be in the detestable French heroic couplet, which epigrammatizes every thing. He had courage enough, though a Frenchman, to admire Lucan,—and yet could not translate him without introducing a love-story.

Note 6, page 97, col. 2.

They mingle the arrows of Chance.

This was one of the superstitions of the Pagan Arabs forbidden by Mahommed.

The mode of divining by arrows was seen by Pietro Della Valle at Aleppo. The Mahommedan conjurer made two persons sit down, one facing the other, and gave each of them four arrows, which they were to hold perpendicularly, the point toward the ground. After questioning them concerning the business of which they wished to be informed, he muttered his invocations; and the eight arrows, by virtue of these charms, altered their posture, and placed themselves point to point. Whether those on the left, or those on the right, were above the others, decided the question.

Note 7, page 97, col. 2.
The powerful gem, etc.

Some imagine that the crystal is snow turned to ice, which has been hardening thirty years, and is turned to a rock by age.—*Mirror of Stones, by Camillus Leonardus, physician of Pisaro, dedicated to Cæsar Borgia.*

In the cabinet of the Prince of Monaco, among other rarities, are two pieces of crystal, each larger than both hands clenched together. In the middle of one is about a glass-full of water, and in the other is some moss, naturally inclosed there when the crystals congealed. These pieces are very curious.—*Tavernier.*

Crystal, precious stones, every stone that has a regular figure, and even flints in small masses, and consisting of concentric coats, whether found in the perpendicular fissures of rocks, or elsewhere, are only exudations, or the concreting juices of flint in large masses; they are, therefore, new and spurious productions, the genuine stalactites of flint or of granite.—*Buffon.*

Note 8, page 97, col. 2.
Gem of the gem, etc.

Burguillos, or Lope de Vega, makes an odd metaphor from such an illustration:

> El Verbo de Dios diamente
> En el anillo de cobre
> De nuestro circulo pobre.

Note 9, page 98, col. 1.
Before the tent they spread the skin.

With the Arabs either a round skin is laid on the ground for a small company, or large coarse woollen cloths for a great number spread all over the room, and about ten dishes repeated six or seven times over, laid round at a great feast, and whole sheep and lambs boiled and roasted in the middle. When one company has done, another sits round, even to the meanest, till all is consumed. And an Arab Prince will often dine in the street before his door, and call to all that pass, even beggars, in the usual expression, *Bisimillah*, that is, in the name of God; who come and sit down, and when they have done, give their *Hamdellilah*, that is, God be praised; for the Arabs, who are great levellers, put every body on a footing with them, and it is by such generosity and hospitality that they maintain their interest.—*Pococke.*

Note 10, page 98, col. 2.
With no false colours, etc.

'T is the custom of Persia to begin their feasts with fruits and preserves. We spent two hours in eating only those and drinking beer, hydromel, and aquavitæ. Then was brought up the meat in great silver dishes; they were full of rice of divers colours, and upon that, several sorts of meat, boiled and roasted, as beef, mutton, tame fowl, wild ducks, fish, and other things, all very well ordered, and very delicate.

The Persians use no knives at table, but the cooks send up the meat ready cut up into little bits, so that it was no trouble to us to accustom ourselves to their manner of eating. Rice serves them instead of bread. They take a mouthful of it, with the two fore-fingers and the thumb, and so put it into their mouths. Every table had a carver, whom they call Suffret-zi, who takes the meat brought up in the great dishes, to put it into lesser ones, which he fills with three or four sorts of meat, so as that every dish may serve two, or at most three persons. There was but little drunk till towards the end of the repast, and then the cups went about roundly, and the dinner was concluded with a vessel of porcelane, full of a hot blackish kind of drink, which they call Kahawa (*Coffee.*)—*Ambassador's Travels.*

They laid upon the floor of the Ambassador's room a fine silk cloth, on which there were set one-and-thirty dishes of silver, filled with several sorts of conserves, dry and liquid, and raw fruits, as Melons, Citrons, Quinces, Pears, and some others not known in Europe. Some time after, that cloth was taken away, that another might be laid in the room of it, and upon this was set rice of all sorts of colours, and all sorts of meat, boiled and roasted, in above fifty dishes of the same metal.—*Amb. Tra.*

There is not any thing more ordinary in Persia than rice soaked in water; they call it Plau, and eat of it at all their meals, and serve it up in all their dishes. They sometimes put thereto a little of the juice of pomegranates, or cherries and saffron, insomuch that commonly you have rice of several colours in the same dish.—*Amb. Tra.*

Note 11, page 98, col. 2.
And whoso drank of the cooling draught.

The Tamarind is equally useful and agreeable; it has a pulp of a vinous taste, of which a wholesome refreshing liquor is prepared; its shade shelters houses from the torrid heat of the sun, and its fine figure greatly adorns the scenery of the country.—*Niebuhr.*

Note 12, page 98, col. 2.
As out he pours its liquid, etc.

Of pumpkins and melons several sorts grow naturally in the woods, and serve for feeding Camels. But the proper melons are planted in the fields, where a great variety of them is to be found, and in such abundance, that the Arabians of all ranks use them, for some part of the year, as their principal article of food. They afford a very agreeable liquor. When its fruit is nearly ripe, a hole is pierced into the pulp; this hole is then stopped with wax, and the melon left upon the stalk. Within a few days the pulp is, in consequence of this process, converted into a delicious liquor.—*Niebuhr.*

Note 13, page 98, col. 2.
And listen'd with full hands.

> L'aspect imprévu de tant de Castillans,
> D'étonnement, d'effroi, peint ses regards brillans;
> Ses mains du choix des fruits se formant une etude,
> Demeurent un moment dans le même attitude.
> MADAME BOCCAGE. *La Colombiade.*

Note 14, page 99, col. 1.
It is the hour of prayer.

The Arabians divide their day into twenty-four hours, and reckon them from one setting sun to another. As very few among them know what a watch is, and as they conceive but imperfectly the duration of an hour, they usually determine time almost as when we say, it happened about noon, about evening, etc. The moment when the sun disappears is called *Maggrib*, about two hours afterwards they call it *El ascha*; two hours later, *El maerfa*; midnight, *Nus el lejl*; the dawn of morning, *El fedsjer*; sunrise, *Es subkh*. They eat about nine in the morning, and that meal is called *El ghadda*; noon, *Ed dukhr*; three hours after noon, *El asr*. Of all these divisions of time, only noon and midnight are well ascertained; they both fall upon the twelfth hour. The others are earlier or later, as the days are short or long. The five hours appointed for prayer are *Maggrib, Nus el lejl, El fedsjer, Duhhr,* and *El asr.—Niebuhr, Desc. de l' Arabie.*

The Turks say, in allusion to their canonical hours, that prayer is a tree which produces five sorts of fruit, two of which the sun sees, and three of which he never sees.—*Pietro della Valle.*

Note 15, page 99, col. 1.

After the law, etc.

The use of the bath was forbidden the Moriscoes in Spain, as being an *anti-christian* custom! I recollect no superstition but the Catholic in which nastiness is accounted a virtue; as if, says Jortin, piety and filth were synonymous, and religion, like the itch, could be caught by wearing foul clothes.

Note 16, page 99, col. 1.

Felt not the Simoom pass.

The effects of the Simoom are instant suffocation to every living creature that happens to be within the sphere of its activity, and immediate putrefaction of the carcasses of the dead. The Arabians discern its approach by an unusual redness in the air, and they say that they feel a smell of sulphur as it passes. The only means by which any person can preserve himself from suffering by these noxious blasts, is by throwing himself down with his face upon the earth, till this whirlwind of poisonous exhalations has blown over, which always moves at a certain height in the atmosphere. Instinct even teaches the brutes to incline their heads to the ground on these occasions.—*Niebuhr.*

The Arabs of the desert call these winds *Semoum,* or poison, and the Turks *Shamyela,* or wind of Syria, from which is formed the *Samiel.*

Their heat is sometimes so excessive, that it is difficult to form any idea of its violence without having experienced it; but it may be compared to the heat of a large oven at the moment of drawing out the bread. When these winds begin to blow, the atmosphere assumes an alarming aspect. The sky, at other times so clear in this climate, becomes dark and heavy: the sun loses his splendour, and appears of a violet colour. The air is not cloudy, but grey and thick, and is in fact filled with an extremely subtile dust, which penetrates every where. This wind, always light and rapid, is not at first remarkably hot, but it increases in heat in proportion as it continues. All animated bodies soon discover it, by the change it produces in them. The lungs, which a too rarefied air no longer expands, are contracted, and become painful. Respiration is short and difficult, the skin parched and dry, and the body consumed by an internal heat. In vain is recourse had to large draughts of water; nothing can restore perspiration. In vain is coolness sought for; all bodies in which it is usual to find it, deceive the hand that touches them. Marble, iron, water, notwith-

standing the sun no longer appears, are hot. The streets are deserted, and the dead silence of night reigns every where. The inhabitants of houses and villages shut themselves up in their houses, and those of the desert in their tents, or in pits they dig in the earth, where they wait the termination of this destructive heat. It usually lasts three days; but if it exceeds that time, it becomes insupportable. Woe to the traveller whom this wind surprises remote from shelter! he must suffer all its dreadful consequences, which sometimes are mortal. The danger is most imminent when it blows in squalls, for then the rapidity of the wind increases the heat to such a degree as to cause sudden death. This death is a real suffocation; the lungs, being empty, are convulsed, the circulation disordered, and the whole mass of blood driven by the heart towards the head and breast; whence that hæmorrhage at the nose and mouth which happens after death. This wind is especially fatal to persons of a plethoric habit, and those in whom fatigue has destroyed the tone of the muscles and the vessels. The corpse remains a long time warm, swells, turns blue, and is easily separated; all which are signs of that putrid fermentation which takes place in animal bodies when the humours become stagnant. These accidents are to be avoided by stopping the nose and mouth with handkerchiefs: an efficacious method likewise is that practised by the camels, who bury their noses in the sand, and keep them there till the squall is over.

Another quality of this wind is its extreme aridity; which is such, that water sprinkled on the floor evaporates in a few minutes. By this extreme dryness, it withers and strips all the plants; and by exhaling too suddenly the emanations from animal bodies, crisps the skin, closes the pores, and causes that feverish heat which is the invariable effect of suppressed perspiration.

Volney.

BOOK III.

Note 1, page 99, col. 2.

Every gem, etc.

From the *Mirror of Stones* I extract a few specimens of the absurd ideas once prevalent respecting precious stones.

The *Amethyst* drives away drunkenness; for, being bound on the navel, it restrains the vapour of the wine, and so dissolves the ebriety.

Alectoria is a stone of a chrystalline colour, a little darkish, somewhat resembling limpid water; and sometimes it has veins of the colour of flesh. Some call it *Gallinaceus*, from the place of its generation, the intestines of capons, which were castrated at three years old, and had lived seven; before which time the stone ought not to be taken out, for the older it is, so much the better. When the stone is become perfect in the capon, he don't drink. However, it is never found bigger than a large bean. The virtue of this stone is, to render him who carries it invisible. Being held in the mouth, it allays thirst, and therefore is proper for wrestlers; makes a woman agreeable to her husband; bestows honors, and preserves those already acquired; it frees such as are bewitched; it renders a man eloquent, constant, agreeable, and amiable; it helps to regain a lost kingdom, and acquire a foreign one.

Borax, Nosa, Crapondinus, are names of the same stone, which is extracted from a toad. There are two species; that which is the best is rarely found; the other is black or dun with a cerulean glow, having in the middle the similitude of an eye, and must be taken out while the dead toad is yet panting; and these are better than those which are extracted from it after a long continuance in the ground. They have a wonderful efficacy in poisons. For whoever has taken poison, let him swallow this; which being down, rolls about the bowels, and drives out every poisonous quality that is lodged in the intestines, and then passes through the fundament, and is preserved.

Corvia or *Corvina*, is a stone of a reddish colour, and accounted artificial. On the calends of April, boil the eggs, taken out of a Crow's nest, till they are hard; and, being cold, let them be placed in the nest as they were before. When the crow knows this, she flies a long way to find the stone; and, having found it, returns to the nest; and the eggs being touched with it, they become fresh and prolific. The stone must immediately be snatched out of the nest. Its virtue is to increase riches, to bestow honours, and to foretell many future events.

Kinocetus is a stone not wholly useless—since it will cast out devils.

Note 2, page 99, col 2.
Conscious of poison, etc.

Giafar, the founder of the Barmecides, being obliged to fly from Persia, his native country, took refuge at Damascus, and implored the protection of the Caliph Soliman. When he was presented to that Prince, the Caliph suddenly changed colour, and commanded him to retire, suspecting that he had poison about him. Soliman had discovered it by means of ten stones which he wore upon his arm. They were fastened there like a bracelet, and never failed to strike one against the other, and make a slight noise when any poison was near. Upon enquiry it was found, that Giafar carried poison in his ring, for the purpose of self-destruction, in case he had been taken by his enemies.—*Marigny.*

These foolish old superstitions have died away, and gems are now neither pounded as poison, nor worn as antidotes. But the old absurdities respecting poisons have been renewed in our days, by authors who have revived the calumnies alledged against the Knights-Templar, with the hope of exciting a more extensive persecution.

Note 3, page 99, col. 2.
From spells, or blunt the hostile weapon's edge.

In the country called Panten, or Tathalamasin, « there be canes called Cassan, which overspread the earth like grasse, and out of every knot of them spring foorth certaine branches, which are continued upon the ground almost for the space of a mile. In the sayd canes there are found certaine stones, one of which stones whosoever carryeth about with him, cannot be wounded with any yron; and therefore the men of that country for the most part carry such stones with them, whithersoever they goe. Many also cause one of the armes of their children, while they are young, to be launced, putting one of the said stones into the wound, healing also, and closing up the said wound with the powder of a certain fish (the name whereof I do not know), which powder doth immediately consolidate and cure the said wound. And by the vertue of these stones the people aforesaid doe for the most part triumph both on sea and land. Howbeit there is one kind of stratageme which the enemies of this nation, knowing the vertue of the sayd stones, doe practise against them: namely, they provide themselves armour of yron or steele against their arrowes, and weapons also poisoned with the poyson of trees; and they carry in their hands wooden stakes most sharp and hard-pointed, as if they were yron: likewise they shoot arrowes without yron heades, and so they confound and slay some of their unarmed foes, trusting too securely unto the vertue of their stones.—*Odoricus in Hakluyt.*

We are obliged to jewellers for our best accounts of the East. In Tavernier there is a passage curiously characteristic of his profession. A European at Delhi complained to him that he had polished and set a large diamond for Oreng-zehe, who had never paid him for his work. But he did not understand his trade, says Tavernier; for if he had been a skilful jeweller, he would have known how to take two or three pieces out of the stone, and pay himself better than the Mogul would have done.

Note 4, page 100, col. 1.
With a convulsive effort shakes it out.

And Elisha died, and they buried him. And the bands of the Moabites invaded the land at the coming in of the year.

And it came to pass as they were burying a man, that behold they spied a band of men; and they cast the man into the sepulchre of Elisha: and when the man was let down, and touched the bones of Elisha, he revived and stood up on his feet.—2 *Kings*, xiii, 20, 21.

I must remind my readers, that an allusion to the Old Testament is no ways improper in a Mahommedan.

It happened the dead corpse of a man was cast ashore at Chatham, and, being taken up, was buried decently in the church-yard. Now there was an image or rood in the church, called our Lady of Chatham. This Lady, say the Monks, went the next night and roused up the clerk, telling him that a sinful person was buried near the place where she was worshipped, who offended her eyes with his ghastly grinning; and unless he were removed, to the great grief of good people she must remove from thence, and could work no more miracles. Therefore she desired him to go with her to take him up, and throw him into the river again: which being done, soon after the body floated again, and was taken up and buried in the church-yard; but from that time all miracles ceased, and the place where he was buried did continually sink downwards. This tale is still remembered by some aged people, receiving it by tradition from the Popish times of darkness and idolatry.—*Admirable Curiosities, Rarities, and Wonders in England.*

When Alburquerque wintered at the Isle of Camaram, in the Red Sea, a man at arms, who died suddenly, was thrown into the sea. In the night the watch felt several shocks, as though the ship were striking on a sand bank. They put out the boat, and found the dead body clinging to the keel by the rudder. It was taken up and buried on shore; and, in the morning, it was seen lying on the grave. Frey Francisco was then consulted. He conjectured, that the deceased had died under excommunication, and therefore absolved him. They interred him again, and then he rested in the grave.—*Joan de Barros.* Dec. 2. 8. 3.

Note 5, page 100, col. 1.
That Earth, etc.

Matthew of Westminster says, the History of the Old Woman of Berkeley will not appear incredible, if we read the dialogue of St Gregory, in which he relates how the body of a man buried in the church was thrown out by the Devils. Charles Martel also, because he had appropriated great part of the tithes to pay his soldiers, was most miserably, by the wicked Spirits, taken bodily out of his grave.

The Turks report, as a certain truth, that the corpse of Heyradin Barbarossa was found, four or five times, out of the ground, lying by his sepulchre, after he had been there inhumed : nor could they possibly make him lie quiet in his grave, till a Greek wizard counselled them to bury a black dog together with the body ; which done, he lay still and gave them no farther trouble.—*Morgan's History of Algiers.*

In supernatural affairs, dogs seem to possess a sedative virtue. When peace was made, about the year 1170, between the Earls of Holland and Flanders, « it was concluded, that Count Floris should send unto Count Philip, a thousand men, expert in making of ditches, to stop the hole which had beene made neere unto Dam, or the Sluce, whereby the countrey was drowned round about at everie high sea ; the which the Flemings could by no means fill up, neither with wood, nor any other matter, for that all sunke as in a gulfe without any bottome ; whereby, in succession of time, Bruges, and all that jurisdiction, had been in daunger to have bin lost by inundation, and to become all sea, if it were not speedily repaired. Count Floris having taken possession of the isle of Walcharan, returned into Holland, from whence hee sent the best workmen he could find in all his countries, into Flanders, to make dikes and causeies, and to stop the hole neere unto this Dam, or Sluce, and to recover the drowned land. These diggers being come to the place, they found at the entrie of this bottomless hole a Sea-dog, the which for six dayes together, did nothing but crie out and howle very fearfully. They, not knowing what it might signifie, having consulted of this accident, they resolved to cast this dog into the hole. There was a mad-headed Hollander among the rest, who going into the bottome of the dike, tooke the dogge by the taile, and cast him into the middest of the gulfe ; then speedily they cast earth and torfe into it, so as they found a bottome, and by little and little filled it up. And for that many workmen came to the repairing of this dike, who, for that they would not be far from their worke, coucht in Cabines, which seemed to be a pretie towne, Count Philip gave unto all these Hollanders, Zeelanders, and others, that would inhabit there, as much land as they could recover from Dam to Ardenbourg, for them and their successors, for ever, with many other immunities and freedoms. By reason whereof many planted themselves there, and in succession of time, made a good towne there, the which by reason of this dog, which they cast into the hole, they named *Hondtsdam*, that is to say, *a dog's sluce; Dam* in Flemish signifying a sluce, and *Hondt* dog ; and therefore at this day, the said towne (which is simply called *Dam*) carrieth a dog

in their armes and blason.—*Grimestone's Historie of the Netherlands,* 1608.

Note 6, page 100, col. 1.
The Vulture hovers yonder, etc.

The Vulture is very serviceable in Arabia, clearing the earth of all carcases, which corrupt very rapidly in hot countries. He also destroys the field mice, which multiply so prodigiously in some provinces, that, were it not for this assistance, the peasant might cease from the culture of the fields as absolutely vain. Their performance of these important services induced the ancient Egyptians to pay those birds divine honours, and even at present it is held unlawful to kill them in all the countries which they frequent.—*Niebuhr.*

Note 7, page 101, col. 1.
His dog beside him, etc.

The Bedouins, who, at all points, are less superstitious than the Turks, have a breed of very tall greyhounds, which likewise mount guard around their tents ; but they take great care of these useful servants, and have such an affection for them, that to kill the dog of a Bedouin would be to endanger your own life.—*Sonnini.*

Note 8, page 101, col. 2.
Or comes the Father, etc.

The Arabs call the West and South-West winds which prevail from November to February, *the fathers of the rains.*—*Volney.*

Note 9, page 101, col. 2.
Entwines the strong palm-fibres, etc.

Of the Palm leaves they make mattresses, baskets, and brooms; and of the branches, all sorts of cage-work, square baskets for packing, that serve for many uses instead of boxes ; and the ends of the boughs that grow next to the trunk being beaten like flax, the fibres separate, and being tied together at the narrow end, they serve for brooms.—*Pococke.*

Note 10, page 101, col. 2.
Shapes the green basket, etc.

The Doum, or wild palm-tree, grows in abundance, from which these people, when necessity renders them industrious, find great advantage. The shepherds, mule-drivers, camel-drivers, and travellers, gather the leaves, of which they make mats, fringes, baskets, hats, *shooaris*, or large wallets to carry corn, twine, ropes, girths, and covers for their pack-saddles. This plant, with which also they heat their ovens, produces a mild and resinous fruit, that ripens in September and October. It is in form like the raisin, contains a kernel, and is astringent, and very proper to temper and counteract the effects of the watery and laxative fruits, of which these people in summer make an immoderate use. That Power which is ever provident to all, has spread this wild plant over their deserts to supply an infinity of wants that would otherwise heavily burthen a people so poor.—*Chenier.*

Note 11, page 101, col. 2.
. . . Or lingers it a vernal brook.

We passed two of those vallies so common in Arabia, which, when heavy rains fall, are filled with water, and are then called *wadi* or rivers, although perfectly dry at other times of the year.—We now drew nearer to the river, of which a branch was dry, and having its channel filled with reeds growing to the height of 20 feet, served as a line of road, which was agreeably shaded by the reeds.—*Niebuhr.*

My brethren have dealt deceitfully as a brook, and as the stream of brooks they pass away.

Which are blackish by reason of the ice, and wherein the snow is hid:

What time they wax warm they vanish; when it is hot they are consumed out of their place.

The paths of their way are turned aside; they go to nothing, and perish.—*Job.*, vi, 15.

Note 12, page 101, col. 2.
Nor rich, nor poor, etc.

The simplicity, or, perhaps, more properly, the poverty, of the lower class of the Bedouins, is proportionate to that of their chiefs. All the wealth of a family consists of moveables, of which the following is a pretty exact inventory. A few male and female camels, some goats and poultry, a mare and her bridle and saddle, a tent, a lance sixteen feet long, a crooked sabre, a rusty musket, with a flint or matchlock; a pipe, a portable mill, a pot for cooking, a leathern bucket, a small coffee roaster; a mat, some clothes, a mantle of black woollen, and a few glass or silver rings, which the women wear upon their legs and arms; if none of these are wanting, their furniture is complete. But what the poor man stands most in need of, and what he takes most pleasure in, is his mare; for this animal is his principal support. With his mare the Bedouin makes his excursions against hostile tribes, or seeks plunder in the country, and on the highways. The mare is preferred to the horse, because she does not neigh, is more docile, and yields milk, which, on occasion, satisfies the thirst and even the hunger of her master.—*Volney.*

The Sheik, says Volney, with whom I resided in the country of Gaza, about the end of 1784, passed for one of the most powerful of those districts; yet it did not appear to me that his expenditure was greater than that of an opulent farmer. His personal effects, consisting in a few pelisses, carpets, arms, horses, and camels, could not be estimated at more than fifty thousand livres (a little above two thousand pounds); and it must be observed, that in this calculation, four mares of the breed of racers are valued at six thousand livres, (two hundred and fifty pounds), and each camel at ten pounds sterling. We must not therefore, when we speak of the Bedouins, affix to the words Prince and Lord, the ideas they usually convey; we should come nearer the truth, by comparing them to substantial farmers, in mountainous countries, whose simplicity they resemble in their dress, as well as in their domestic life and manners. A Sheik, who has the command of five hundred horse, does not disdain to saddle and bridle his own, nor to give him his barley and chopped straw. In his tent, his wife makes the coffee, kneads the dough, and superintends the dressing of the victuals. His daughters and kinswomen wash the linen, and go with pitchers on their heads, and veils over their faces, to draw water from the fountain. These manners agree precisely with the descriptions in Homer, and the history of Abraham, in Genesis. But it must be owned, that it is difficult to form a just idea of them without having ourselves been eye-witnesses.—*Volney.*

Note 13, page 101, col. 2.
No hoarded gold, etc.

Thus confined to the most absolute necessaries of life,

the Arabs have as little industry as their wants are few; all their arts consist in weaving their clumsy tents, and in making mats and butter. Their whole commerce only extends to the exchanging camels, kids, stallions, and milk; for arms, clothing, a little rice or corn, and *money which they bury.*—*Volney.*

Note 14, page 101, col. 2.
Grow in Oneiza's loom.

The chief manufacture among the Arabs is the making of *Hykes,* as they call woollen blankets, and webs of goats, hair for their tents. The women alone are employed in this work, as Andromache and Penelope were of old; who make no use of a shuttle, but conduct every thread of the woof with their fingers.—*Shaw.*

Note 15, page 102, col. 1.
Or at the hand-mill, etc.

If mine heart have been deceived by a woman, or if I have laid wait at my neighbour's door,

Then let my wife grind unto another.—*Job xxxi. 9, 10.*

Note 16, page 102, col. 1.
With bare wet arm, etc.

I was much amused by observing the dexterity of the Arab women in baking their bread. They have a small place built with clay, between two and three feet high, having a hole at the bottom, for the convenience of drawing out the ashes, something similar to that of a lime-kiln. The oven (which I think is the most proper name for this place) is usually about fifteen inches wide at the top, and gradually grows wider to the bottom. It is heated with wood, and when sufficiently hot, and perfectly clear from smoke, having nothing but clear embers at bottom, (which continue to reflect great heat), they prepare the dough in a large bowl, and mould the cakes to the desired size on a board or stone placed near the oven. After they have kneaded the cake to a proper consistence, they pat it a little, then toss it about with great dexterity in one hand, till it is as thin as they choose to make it. They then wet one side of it with water, at the same time wetting the hand and arm, with which they put it into the oven. The wet side of the cake adheres fast to the side of the oven till it is sufficiently baked, when, if not paid sufficient attention to, it would fall down among the embers. If they were not exceedingly quick at this work, the heat of the oven would burn the skin from off their hands and arms; but with such amazing dexterity do they perform it, that one woman will continue keeping three or four cakes at a time in the oven till she has done baking. This mode, let me add, does not require half the fuel that is made use of in Europe.—*Jackson.*

Note 17, page 102, col. 1.
Sheaths its young fruit, yet green.

Tamarinds grow on great trees, full of branches whereof the leaves are not bigger than, nor unlike to, the leaves of pimpernel, only something longer. The flower at first is like the peaches, but at last turns white, and puts forth its fruit at the end of certain strings; as soon as the sun is set, the leaves close up the fruit, to preserve it from the dew, and open as soon as that luminary appears again. The fruit at first is green, but ripening it becomes of a dark grey, drawing towards a red, inclosed in husks, brown or tawny, of taste a little bitter, like our prunelloes. The tree is as big as a walnut-tree, full of leaves, bearing its fruit at the branches, like the sheath of a knife, but not so straight, rather bent like a bow.—*Mandelslo.*

Note 18, page 102, col. 1.
Intones the holy Book.

I have often, says Niebuhr, heard the Sheiks sing passages from the Koran. They never strain the voice by attempting to raise it too high, and this natural music pleased me very much.

The airs of the Orientals are all grave and simple. They chuse their singers to sing so distinctly, that every word may be comprehended. When several instruments are played at once, and accompanied by the voice, you hear them all render the same melody, unless some one mingles a running base, either singing or playing, always in the same key. If this music is not greatly to our taste, ours is as little to the taste of the Orientals.

Niebuhr. Description.

Note 19, page 102, col. 1.
Its marble walls. etc.

The Mosques, which they pronounce Mesg-jid, are built exactly in the fashion of our churches, where, instead of such seats and benches as we make use of, they only strew the floor with mats, upon which they perform the several sittings and prostrations that are enjoined in their religion. Near the middle, particularly, of the principal Mosque of each city, there is a large pulpit erected, which is ballustraded round, with about half-a-dozen steps leading up to it. Upon these (for I am told none are permitted to enter the pulpit), the Mufty, or one of the Im-ams, placeth himself every Friday, the day of the congregation, as they call it, and from thence either explaineth some part or other of the Koran, or else exhorteth the people to piety and good works. That end of these Mosques which regards Mecca, whither they direct themselves throughout the whole course of their devotions, is called the Kiblah, in which there is commonly a niche, representing, as a judicious writer conjectures, the presence, and at the same time the invisibility of the Deity. There is usually a square tower erected at the other end, with a flag-staff upon the top of it. Hither the crier ascends at the appointed times, and, displaying a small flag, advertiseth the people, with a loud voice, from each side of the battlements, of the hour of prayer. These places of the Mahometan worship, together with the Mufty, Im-ams, and other persons belonging to them, are maintained out of certain revenues arising from the rents of lands and houses, either left by will, or set apart by the public for that use.—*Shaw.*

All the Mosques are built nearly in the same style. They are of an oblong square form, and covered in the middle with a large dome, on the top of which is fixed a gilt crescent. In front there is a handsome portico covered with several small cupolas, and raised one step above the pavement of the court. The Turks sometimes, in the hot season, perform their devotions there; and between the columns, upon cross iron bars, are suspended a number of lamps, for illuminations on the Thursday nights, and on all festivals. The entrance into the Mosque is by one large door. All these edifices are solidly built of freestone, and in several the domes are covered with lead. The minarets stand on one side, ad-

joining to the body of the Mosque. They are sometimes square, but more commonly round, and taper. The gallery for the maazeen, or criers, projecting a little from the column near the top, has some resemblance to a rude capital; and from this the spire, tapering more in proportion than before, soon terminates in a point crowned with a crescent.—*Russel's Aleppo.*

Note 20, page 102, col. 1.
The Stars of Heaven their point of prayer.

The Keabê is the point of direction, and the centre of union for the prayers of the whole human race, as the Beïth-Màmour [1] is for those of all the celestial beings; the Kursy [2] for those of the four Arch-angels, and the Arsch [3] for those of the cherubims and seraphims who guard the throne of the Almighty. The inhabitants of Mecca, who enjoy the happiness of contemplating the Keabê, are obliged, when they pray, to fix their eyes upon the sanctuary; but they who are at a distance from this valuable privilege, are required only, during prayer, to direct their attention towards that hallowed edifice. The believer who is ignorant of the position of the Keabe must use every endeavour to gain a knowledge of it; and after he has shown great solicitude, whatever be his success, his prayer is valid.—*D'Ohsson·*

Note 21, page 102, col. 1.
Rest on the pillar of the Tent.

The Bedoweens live in tents, called *Hymas,* from the shade they afford the inhabitants, and *Beet el Shar,* Houses of Hair, from the matter they are made of. They are the same with what the antients called Mapalia, which being then, as they are to this day, secured from the heat and inclemency of the weather, by a covering only of such hair-cloth as our coal sacks are made of, might very justly be described by Virgil to have thin roofs. When we find any number of them together (and I have seen from three to three hundred), then they are usually placed in a circle, and constitute a Douwar. The fashion of each tent is the same, being of an oblong figure, not unlike the bottom of a ship turned upside down, as Sallust hath long ago described them. However, they differ in bigness, according to the number of people who live in them : and are accordingly supported, some with one pillar, others with two or three : whilst a curtain or carpet placed, upon occasion, at each of these divisions, separateth the whole into so many apartments. The pillar, which I have mentioned, is a straight pole, 8 or 10 feet high, and 3 or 4 inches in thickness, serving not only to support the tent, but being full of hooks fixed there for the purpose, the Arabs hang upon it their clothes, baskets, saddles, and accoutrements of war. Holofernes, as we read in Judith, 13. 16. made the like use of the pillar of his tent, by hanging his fauchin upon it: it is there called the *pillar of the bed,* from the custom, perhaps, that hath always prevailed, of having the upper end of the carpet, mattrass, or whatever else they lie upon, turned from the skirts of the tent that way. But the Κωνωπειον, Canopy, as we render it, (ver. 9.) should, I presume, be

[1] Beïth-màmour, which means the house of prosperity and felicity, is the ancient Keabe of Mecca; which, according to tradition, was taken up into Heaven by the Angels at the deluge, where it was placed perpendicularly over the present sanctuary.

[2] Kursy, which signifies a seat, is the eighth firmament.

[3] Arsch is the throne of the Almighty, which is thought to be placed on the ninth, which is the highest of the firmaments.

Father called the gnat or muskeeta net, which is a close curtain of gauze or fine linen, used all over the Levant, by people of better fashion, to keep out the flies. The Arabs have nothing of this kind; who, in taking their rest, lie horizontally upon the ground, without bed, mattrass, or pillow, wrapping themselves up only in their *Hykes*, and lying, as they find room, upon a mat or carpet, in the middle or corner of the tent. Those who are married, have each of them a corner of the tent, cantoned off with a curtain.—*Shaw.*

The tents of the Moors are somewhat of a conic form, are seldom more than 8 or 10 feet high in the centre, and from 20 to 25 in length. Like those of the remotest antiquity, their figure is that of a ship overset, the keel of which is only seen. These tents are made of twine, composed of goat's hair, camel's wool, and the leaves of the wild palm, so that they keep out water; but, being black, they produce a disagreeable effect at a distant view.—*Chenier.*

Note 22, page 102, col. 1.
Knitting light palm-leaves for her brother's brow.

In the kingdom of Imam, the men of all ranks shave their heads. In some other countries of Yemen, all the Arabs, even the Sheiks themselves, let their hair grow, and wear neither bonnet nor *Sasch*, but a handkerchief instead, in which they tie their hair behind. Some let it fall upon their shoulders, and bind a small chord round their heads instead of a turban. The Bedouins, upon the frontiers of Hedsjas and of Yemen, wear a bonnet of palm leaves, neatly platted.—*Niebuhr.*

Note 23, page 102, col. 1.
So listen they the reed, etc.

The music of the Bedoweens rarely consists of more than one strain, suitable to their homely instruments, and to their simple invention. The Arabebbah, as they call the bladder and string, is in the highest vogue, and doubtless of great antiquity; as is also the Gasaph, which is only a common reed, open at each end, having the side of it bored, with three or more holes, according to the ability of the person who is to touch it: though the compass of their tunes rarely or never exceeds an octave. Yet sometimes, even in this simplicity of harmony, they observe something of method and ceremony; for in their historical *Cantatas* especially, they have their preludes and symphonies; each stanza being introduced with a flourish from the Arabebbah, while the narration itself is accompanied with the softest touches they are able to make, upon the Gasaph. The Tarr, another of their instruments, is made like a Sive, consisting (as Isidore describeth the Tympanum) of a thin rim, or hoop of wood, with a skin of parchment stretched over the top of it. This serves for the bass in all their concerts, which they accordingly touch very artfully with their fingers, and the knuckles or palms of their hands, as the time and measure require, or as force and softness are to be communicated to the several parts of the performance. The Tarr is undoubtedly the Tympanum of the Antients, which appears as well from the general use of it all over Barbary, Egypt, and the Levant, as from the method of playing upon it, and the figure of the instrument itself, being exactly of the same fashion with what we find in the hands of Cybele and the Bacchanals among the Basso Relievos and Statues of the Antients.—*Shaw.*

The Arabs have the *Cussuba*, or cane, which is only a piece of large cane, or reed, with stops, or holes, like a flute, and somewhat longer, which they adorn with tossels of black silk, and play upon like the German flute.—*Morgan's Hist. of Algiers.*

The young fellows, in several towns, play prettily enough on pipes made, and sounding very much like our flagelet, of the thigh-bones of cranes, storks, or such large fowl.—*Morgan's Hist. of Algiers.*

How great soever may have been the reputation the Libyans once had, of being famous musicians, and of having invented the pipe or flute, called by Greek authors *Hippophorbos*, I fancy few of them would be now much liked at our Opera. As for this *tibicen*, flute, or pipe, it is certainly lost, except it be the *gayta*, somewhat like the hautbois, called *surna* in Turkish, a martial instrument. Julius Pollux, in a chapter entitled *De tibiarum specie*, says, *Hippophorbos quam quidem Libyes Scenetes invenerunt;* and again, shewing the use and quality thereof, *hæc verò apud equorum pascua utuntur ejusque materia decorticata laurus est, cor enim ligni extractum acutissimam dat sonum.* The sound of the *gayta* agrees well with this description, though not the make. Several poets mention the *tibicen Libycus* and *Arabicus:* and Athenæus quotes Duris, and says, *Libycas tibia Poetæ appellant, ut inquit Duris, libro secundo de rebus gestis Agathoclis, quod scirites, primus, ut credunt, tibicinum artis inventor, è gente Nomadum Libycorum fuerit, primusque tibia Cerealium hymnorum cantor.*
                  Morgan's Hist. of Algiers.

Note 24, page 102, col. 1.
Or if he strung the pearls of Poesy.

Persæ « pulcherrimâ usi translatione, pro *versûs facere* dicunt *margaritas nectere;* quemadmodum in illo Ferdusii versiculo 'Siquidem calami acumine adamantido margaritas nexi, *in scientiæ mare penitus me immersi.*'»—*Poeseos Asiaticæ Commentarii.*

This is a favourite Oriental figure. « After a little time, lifting his head from the collar of reflection, he removed the talisman of silence from the treasure of speech, and scattered skirts-full of brilliant gems and princely pearls before the company in his mirth-exciting deliveries.»—*Bahar Danush.*

Again, in the same work—« he began to weigh his stored pearls in the scales of delivery.»

Abu Temam, who was a celebrated poet himself, used to say, that « fine sentiments, delivered in prose, were like gems scattered at random; but that when they were confined in a poetical measure, they resembled bracelets and strings of pearls.»—*Sir W. Jones, Essay on the Poetry of the Eastern Nations.*

In Mr Carlyle's translations from the Arabic, a Poet says of his friends and himself,

> They are a row of Pearls, and I
> The silken thread on which they lie.

I quote from memory, and recollect not the Author's name. It is somewhat remarkable, that the same metaphor is among the quaintnesses of Fuller. « Benevolence is the silken thread, that should run through the pearl chain of our virtues.»—*Holy State.*

It seems the Arabs are still great rhymers, and their verses are sometimes rewarded; but I should not venture to say, that there are great Poets among them. Yet I was assured in Yemens that it is not uncommon to find them among the wandering Arabs in the country of

Dsjâf. It is some few years since a Sheik of these Arabs was in prison at Sana: seeing by chance a bird upon a roof opposite to him, he recollected that the devout Mahommedans believe they perform an action agreeable to God in giving liberty to a bird encaged. He thought therefore he had as much right to liberty as a bird, and made a poem upon the subject, which was first learnt by his guards, and then became so popular, that'at last it reached the Imam. He was so pleased with it, that he liberated the Sheik, whom he had arrested for his robberies.—*Niebuhr, Desc. de l'Arabie.*

Note 25, page 102, col. 1.
A tale of love and woe.

They are fond of singing with a forced voice in the high tones, and one must have lungs like theirs to support the effort for a quarter of an hour. Their airs, in point of character and execution, resemble nothing we have heard in Europe, except the Seguidillas of the Spaniards. They have divisions more laboured even than those of the Italians, and cadences and inflections of tone impossible to be imitated by European throats. Their performance is accompanied with sighs and gestures, which paint the passions in a more lively manner than we should venture to allow. They may be said to excel most in the melancholy strain. To behold an Arab with his head inclined, his hand applied to his ear, his eye-brows knit, his eyes languishing; to hear his plaintive tones, his lengthened notes, his sighs and sobs, it is almost impossible to refrain from tears, which, as their expression is, are far from bitter: and indeed they must certainly find a pleasure in shedding them, since among all their songs they constantly prefer that which excites them most, as among all accomplishments singing is that they most admire.—*Volney.*

All their literature consists in reciting tales and histories in the manner of the Arabian Nights Entertainments. They have a peculiar passion for such stories; and employ in them almost all their leisure, of which they have a great deal. In the evening they seat themselves on the ground at the door of their tents, or under cover if it be cold, and there, ranged in a circle, round a little fire of dung, their pipes in their mouths, and their legs crossed, they sit awhile in silent meditation, till, on a sudden, one of them breaks forth with, *Once upon a time,*—and continues to recite the adventures of some young Shaik and female Bedouin: he relates in what manner the youth first got a secret glimpse of his mistress, and how he became desperately enamoured of her: he minutely describes the lovely fair, extols her black eyes, as large and soft as those of the gazelle; her languid and impassioned looks; her arched eye-brows, resembling two bows of ebony; her waist, straight and supple as a lance; he forgets not her steps, light as those of the *young filly,* nor her eye-lashes blackened with *kohl,* nor her lips painted blue, nor her nails tinged with the golden-coloured *henna,* nor her breasts, resembling two pomegranates, nor her words, sweet as honey. He recounts the sufferings of the young lover, *so wasted with desire and passion, that his body no longer yields any shadow.* At length, after detailing his various attempts to see his mistress, the obstacles on the part of the parents, the invasions of the enemy, the captivity of the two lovers, etc., he terminates, to the satisfaction of the audience, by restoring them, united and happy, to the paternal tent, and by receiving the tribute paid to his eloquence,

in the *masha allah* [1] he has merited. The Bedouins have likewise their love-songs, which have more sentiment and nature in them than those of the Turks, and inhabitants of the towns; doubtless because the former, whose manners are chaste, know what love is; while the latter, abandoned to debauchery, are acquainted only with enjoyment.—*Volney.*

Note 26, page 102, col. 1.
The mother Ostrich fixes on her egg.

We read in an Old Arabian Manuscript, that when the Ostrich would hatch her eggs, she does not cover them as other fowls do, but both the male and female contribute to hatch them by the efficacy of their looks only; and therefore when one has occasion to go to look for food, it advertises its companion by its cry, and the other never stirs during its absence, but remains with its eyes fixed upon the eggs, till the return of its mate, and then goes in its turn to look for food; and this care of theirs is so necessary, that it cannot be suspended for a moment; for, if it should, their eggs would immediately become addle.—*Vanslebe. Harris's Collection.*

This is said to emblem the perpetual attention of the Creator to the Universe.

Note 27, page 102, col. 1.
Round her smooth ankles, and her tawny arms.

« She had laid aside the rings which used to grace her ankles, lest the sound of them should expose her to calamity.»—*Asiatic Researches.*

Most of the Indian women have on each arm, and also above the ankle, ten or twelve rings of gold, silver, ivory, or coral. They spring on the leg, and, when they walk, make a noise, with which they are much pleased. Their hands and toes are generally adorned with large rings.—*Sonnerat.*

« In that day the Lord will take away the bravery of *their tinkling ornaments about their feet,* and their cauls, and their round tires like the moon.»

« The chains, and the bracelets, and the mufflers, the bonnets, and *the ornaments of the legs,*» etc.—*Isaiah,* iii, 18.

Note 28, page 102, col. 1.
Were her long fingers tinged.

His fingers, in beauty and slenderness appearing as the *Yed Bieza,* [2] or the rays of the sun, being tinged with Hinna, seemed branches of transparent red coral.—*Bahar Danush.*

She dispenses gifts with small delicate fingers, sweetly glowing at their tips, like the white and crimson worm of Dabia, or dentifrices made of Esel wood.—*Moallakat. Poem of Amriolkais.*

The Hinna, says the translator of the Bahar-Danush, is esteemed not merely ornamental, but medicinal: and I have myself often experienced in India a most refreshing coolness through the whole habit, from an embrocation, or rather plaster of Hinna, applied to the soles of my feet, by prescription of a native physician. The effect lasted for some days. Bruce says it is used not only for ornament, but as an astringent to keep the hands and feet dry.

This unnatural fashion is extended to animals.

Departing from the town of Anna, we met, about five

[1] An exclamation of praise, equivalent to *admirably well!*
[2] The miraculously shining hand of Moses.

hundred paces from the gate, a young man of good family, followed by two servants, and mounted, in the fashion of the country, upon an ass, whose rump was painted red.—*Tavernier.*

In Persia, « they dye the tails of those horses which are of a light colour with red or orange.»—*Hanway.*

Ali, the Moor, to whose capricious cruelty Mungo Park was so long exposed, « always rode upon a milk-white horse, with its tail dyed red.»

When Pietro della Valle went to Jerusalem, all his camels were made orange-colour with henna. He says he had seen in Rome the manes and tails of certain horses which came from Poland and Hungary, coloured in like manner. He conceived it to be the same plant, which was sold in a dry or pulverized state, at Naples, to old women, to dye their gray hairs flaxen.

Alfenado, a word derived from Alfena, the Portuguese or Moorish name of this plant, is still used in Portugal as a phrase of contempt for a fop.

Note 29, page 102, col. 1.
The light shone rosy ? that the darkened lids, etc.

The blackened eye-lids and the reddened fingers were Eastern customs, in use among the Greeks. They are still among the tricks of the Grecian toilette. The females of the rest of Europe have never added them to their list of ornaments.

Note 30, page 102, col. 2.
Wreath'd the red flower-crown round, etc.

The Mimosa Selam produces splendid flowers of a beautiful red colour, with which the Arabians crown their heads on their days of festival.—*Niebuhr.*

Note 31, page 102, col. 2.
Their work was done, their path of ruin past.

The large locusts, which are near three inches long, are not the most destructive; as they fly, they yield to the current of the wind, which hurries them into the sea, or into sandy deserts, where they perish with hunger or fatigue. The young locusts, that cannot fly, are the most ruinous; they are about fifteen lines in length, and the thickness of a goose quill. They creep over the country in such multitudes, that they leave not a blade of grass behind; and the noise of their feeding announces their approach at some distance. The devastations of locusts increase the price of provisions, and often occasion famines; but the Moors find a kind of compensation in making food of these insects; prodigious quantities are brought to market salted and dried like red herrings. They have an oily and rancid taste, which habit only can render agreeable; they are eat here, however, with pleasure.—*Chenier.*

In 1778, the empire of Morocco was ravaged by these insects. In the summer of that year, such clouds of locusts came from the south, that they darkened the air, and devoured a part of the harvest. Their offspring, which they left on the ground, committed still much greater mischief. Locusts appeared, and bred anew in the following year, so that in the spring the country was wholly covered, and they crawled one over the other in search of their subsistence.

It has been remarked, in speaking of the climate of Morocco, that the young locusts are those which are the most mischievous; and that it seems almost impossible to rid the land of these insects and their ravages, when the country once becomes thus afflicted. In order to preserve the houses and gardens in the neighbourhood of cities, they dig a ditch two feet in depth, and as much in width. This they pallisade with reeds close to each other, and inclined inward toward the ditch; so that the insects, unable to climb up the slippery reed, fall back into the ditch, where they devour one another.

This was the means by which the gardens and vineyards of Rabat, and the city itself, were delivered from this scourge, in 1779. The intrenchment, which was, at least, a league in extent, formed a semicircle from the sea to the river, which separates Rabat from Sallee. The quantity of young locusts here assembled was so prodigious, that, on the third day, the ditch could not be approached because of the stench. The whole country was eaten up, the very bark of the fig, pomegranate, and orange tree, bitter, hard, and corrosive as it was, could not escape the voracity of these insects.

The lands, ravaged throughout all the western provinces, produced no harvest; and the Moors being obliged to live on their stores, which the exportation of corn (permitted till 1774) had drained, began to feel a dearth. Their cattle, for which they make no provision, and which, in these climates, have no other subsistence than that of daily grazing, died with hunger; nor could any be preserved but those which were in the neighbourhood of mountains, or in marshy grounds, where the re-growth of pasturage is more rapid.

In 1780, the distress was still farther increased. The dry winter had checked the products of the earth, and given birth to a new generation of locusts, who devoured whatever had escaped from the inclemency of the season. The husbandman did not reap even what he had sowed, and found himself destitute of food, cattle, or seed corn. In this time of extreme wretchedness, the poor felt all the horrors of famine. They were seen wandering over the country to devour roots, and, perhaps, abridged their days, by digging into the entrails of the earth in search of the crude means by which they might be preserved.

Vast numbers perished of indigestible food and want. I have beheld country people in the roads, and in the streets, who had died of hunger, and who were thrown across asses to be taken and buried. Fathers sold their children. The husband, with the consent of his wife, would take her into another province, there to bestow her in marriage, as if she were his sister, and afterwards come and reclaim her when his wants were no longer so great. I have seen women and children run after camels, and rake in their dung, to seek for some indigested grain of barley, which, if they found, they devoured with avidity.—*Chenier.*

Note 32, page 103, col. 1.
From far Khorassan ?

The Abmelec, or eater of locusts, or grasshoppers, is a bird which better deserves to be described, perhaps, than most others of which travellers have given us an account, because the facts relating to it are not only strange in themselves, but so well and distinctly attested, that however surprising they may seem, we cannot but afford them our belief. The food of this creature is the locust, or the grasshopper; it is of the size of an ordinary hen, its feathers black, its wings large, and its flesh of a greyish colour. They fly generally in great flocks, as the starlings are wont to do with us. But the thing which renders these birds wonderful is, that they are so fond of the water of a certain fountain in Corasson, or Bactria, that wherever that water is carried, they follow; on which account it is carefully preserved; for wherever the locusts fall, the Armenian priests, who are provided with this water, bring a quantity of it, and place in jars, or pour it into little channels in the fields: the next day whole troops of these birds arrive, and quickly deliver the people from the locusts.—*Universal History*.

Sir John Chardin has given us the following passage from an ancient traveller, in relation to this bird. In Cyprus, about the time that the corn was ripe for the sickle, the earth produced such a quantity of cavalettes, or locusts, that they obscured sometimes the splendour of the sun. Wherever these came, they burnt and eat up all. For this there was no remedy, since, as fast as they were destroyed, the earth produced more: God, however, raised them up a means for their deliverance, which happened thus. In Persia, near the city of Cuerch, there is a fountain of water, which has a wonderful property of destroying these insects; for a pitcher full of this being carried in the open air, without passing through house or vault, and being set on an high place, certain birds which follow it, and fly and cry after the men who carry it from the fountain, come to the place where it is fixed. These birds are red and black, and fly in great flocks together, like starlings; the Turks and Persians call them Musulmans. These birds no sooner came to Cyprus, but they destroyed the locusts with which the island was infested; but if the water be spilt or lost, these creatures immediately disappear; which accident fell out when the Turks took this island; for one of them going up into the steeple of Famagusta, and finding there a pitcher of this water, he, fancying that it contained gold or silver, or some precious thing, broke it, and spilt what was therein: since which the Cypriots have been as much tormented as ever by the locusts.

On the confines of the Medes and of Armenia, at certain times a great quantity of birds are seen who resemble our blackbirds, and they have a property sufficiently curious to make me mention it. When the corn in these parts begins to grow, it is astonishing to see the number of Locusts with which all the fields are covered. The Armenians have no other method of delivering themselves from these insects, than by going in procession round the fields, and sprinkling them with a particular water, which they take care to preserve in their houses: for this water comes from a great distance. They fetch it from a well belonging to one of their convents near the frontiers, and they say that the bodies of many Christian martyrs were formerly thrown into this well. These processions, and the sprinkling, continue three or four days; after which, the birds that I have mentioned come in great flights; and whether it be that they eat the Locusts, or drive them away, in two or three days the country is cleared of them.—*Tavernier*.

At Mosul and at Haleb, says Niebuhr, I heard much of the Locust bird, without seeing it. They there call it *Samarmqr*, or, as others pronounce it, *Samarmog*. It is said to be black, larger than a sparrow, and no ways pleasant to the palate. I am assured that it every day destroys an incredible number of Locusts; they pretend nevertheless, that the Locusts sometimes defend themselves, and devour the bird with its feathers, when they have overpowered it by numbers. When the children in the frontier towns of Arabia catch a live Locust, they place it before them, and cry *Samarmog*! And because it stoops down terrified at the noise, or at the motion of the child, or clings more closely to its place, the children believe that it fears the name of its enemy, that it hides itself, and attempts to throw stones. The *Samarmog* is not a native of Mosul or Haleb, but they go to seek it in Khorasan with much ceremony. When the Locusts multiply very greatly, the government sends persons worthy of trust to a spring near the village of *Samarun*, situated in a plain between four mountains, by *Mesched*, or *Musa er ridda*, in that province of Persia. The deputies, with the ceremonies prescribed, fill a chest with this water, and pitch the chest so that the water may neither evaporate nor be spilt before their return. From the spring to the town whence they were sent, the chest must always be between heaven and earth; they must neither place it on the ground, nor under any roof, lest it should lose all its virtue. Mosul being surrounded with a wall, the water must not pass under the gate-way, but it is received over the wall, and the chest placed upon the Mosque *Nebbi Gurgis*, a building which was formerly a church, and which, in preference to all the other buildings, has had from time immemorial the honour to possess this chest upon its roof. When this precious water has been brought from Khorasan with the requisite precautions, the common Mahommedans, Christians, and Jews of Mosul, believe that the *Samarmog* follows the water, and remains in the country as long as there is a single drop left in the chest of *Nebbi-Gurgis*. Seeing one day a large stork's nest upon this vessel, I told a Christian of some eminence in the town, how much I admired the quick smell of the *Samarmog*, who perceived the smell of the water through such a quantity of ordure; he did not answer me, but was very much scandalized that the government should have permitted the stork to make her nest upon so rare a treasure, and still more angry, that for more than nine years, the government had not sent to procure fresh water.—*Niebuhr, Desc. de l'Arabie*.

Dr Russel describes this bird as about the size of a starling; the body of a flesh colour, the rest of its plumage black, the bill and legs black also.

Note 33, page 103, col. 1.

For these mysterious lines were legible.

The Locusts are remarkable for the hieroglyphic that they bear upon the forehead; their colour is green throughout the whole body, excepting a little yellow rim that surrounds their head, which is lost at their eyes. This insect has two upper wings pretty solid; they are green like the rest of the body, except that there is in each a little white spot. The Locust keeps them extended like great sails of a ship going before the wind; it has besides two other wings underneath the former, and which resemble a light transparent stuff pretty much like a cobweb, and which it makes use of in the manner of smack sails that are along a vessel; but when the Locust reposes herself, she does like a vessel that lies at anchor, for she keeps the second sails furled under the first.—*Norden*.

The Mahommedans believe some mysterious meaning is contained in the lines upon the Locust's forehead.

I compared the description in the poem with a Locust which was caught in Leicestershire. It is remarkable that a single insect should have found its way so far inland.

21

Note 34, page 103, col. 2.

Flies the large-headed Screamer of the night.

An Arabian expression from the Moallakat:—« She turns her right side, as if she were in fear of some large-headed Screamer of the night.»—*Poem of Antara.*

Note 35, page 103, col. 2.

Glare in the darkness of that dreadful noon.

In the ninth volume of the Spectator is an account of the total Eclipse of the Sun, Friday, April 22, 1715. It is in a strain of vile bombast; yet some circumstances are so fine that even such a writer could not spoil them: « The different modifications of the light formed colours the eye of man has been five hundred years unacquainted with, and for which I can find no name, unless I may be allowed to call it a dark gloomy sort of light, that scattered about a more sensible and genuine horror, than the most consummate darkness. All the birds were struck dumb, and hung their wings in moody sorrow; some few pigeons, that were on the wing, were afraid of being benighted even in the morn, alighted, and took shelter in the houses. The heat went away by degrees with the light. But when the rays of the sun broke out afresh, the joy and the thanks that were in me, that God made to us these signs and marks of his power before he exercised it, were exquisite, and such as never worked upon me so sensibly before. With my own ears I heard a cock crow as at the dawn of day, and he welcomed with a strange gladness, which was plainly discoverable by the cheerful notes of his voice, the sun at its second rising, and the returning light.»

The Paper is signed B. and is perhaps by Sir Richard Blackmore.

BOOK IV.

Note 1, page 104, col. 1.

How great our fathers were, how little we.

The Mussulmans are immutably prepossessed, that as the Earth approaches its dissolution, its sons and daughters gradually decrease in their dimensions. As for Dagjial, they say, he will find the race of mankind dwindled into such diminutive pigmies, that their habitations in cities, and all the best towns, will be of no other fabric than the shoes and slippers made in these present ages, placed in rank and file, in seemly and regular order; allowing one pair for two round families.—*Morgan's Hist. of Algiers.*

The Cady then asked me, « If I knew when Hagiuge was to come?» « I have no wish to know any thing about him,» said I; « I hope those days are far off, and will not happen in my time.» « What do your books say concerning him?» says he, affecting a look of great wisdom. « Do they agree with ours?» « I don't know that,» said I, « till I hear what is written in your books.» « Hagiuge Magiuge,» says he, « are little people not so big as bees, or like the zimb, or fly of Sennaar, that came in great swarms out of the earth, aye, in multitudes that cannot be counted; two of their chiefs are to ride upon an ass, and every hair of that ass is to be a pipe, and every pipe is to play a different kind of music, and

all that hear and follow them are to be carried to hell.» « I know them not,» said I; « and, in the name of the Lord, I fear them not, were they twice as little as you say they are, and twice as numerous. I trust in God I shall never be so fond of music as to go to hell after an ass, for all the tunes that he or they can play.»—*Bruce.*

These very little people, according to Thevenot, are to be great drinkers, and will drink the sea dry.

Note 2, page 104, col. 2.

In the mild lustre, etc.

The story of Haruth and Maruth, as in the Poem, may be found in D'Herbelot, and in Sale's notes to the Koran. Of the different accounts, I have preferred that which makes Zohara originally a woman, and metamorphoses her into the planet Venus, to that which says the planet Venus descended as Zohara to tempt the Angels.

The Arabians have so childish a love of rhyme, that when two names are usually coupled, they make them jingle, as in the case of Haruth and Maruth. Thus they call Cain and Abel, Abel and Kabel. I am informed that the Koran is crowded with rhymes, more particularly at the conclusion of the chapters.

Note 3, page 104, col. 2.

A previous price, the knowledge of the name
Of God.———

The Ism-Ablah—The Science of the Name of God.

They pretend that God is the lock of this science, and Mahommed the key; that consequently none but Mahommedans can attain it; that it discovers what passes in distant countries; that it familiarises the possessors with the Genii, who are at the command of the initiated, and who instruct them; that it places the winds and the seasons at their disposal; that it heals the bite of serpents, the lame, the maimed, and the blind. They say, that some of their greatest Saints, such as *Abdulkadir, Cheilani* of Bagdad, and *Ibn Alwan,* who resided in the south of Yemen, were so far advanced in this science by their devotion, that they said their prayers every noon in the Kaba of Mecca, and were not absent from their own houses any other part of the day. A merchant of Mecca, who had learnt it in all its forms from Mahommed el Dsjanâdsjeni (at present so famous in that city), pretended that he himself being in danger of perishing at sea, had fastened a billet to the mast with the usual ceremonies, and that immediately the tempest ceased. He showed me, at Bombay, but at a distance, a book which contained all sorts of figures and mathematical tables, with instructions how to arrange the billets, and the appropriate prayers for every circumstance. But he would neither suffer me to touch the book, nor copy the title.

There are some Mahommedans who shut themselves up in a dark place without eating and drinking for a long time, and there with a loud voice repeat certain short prayers till they faint. When they recover, they pretend to have seen not only a crowd of spirits, but God himself, and even the Devil. But the true initiated in the Ism-Allah do not seek these visions. The secret of discovering hidden treasures belongs also, if I mistake not, to the Ism-Allah.—*Niebuhr.*

Note 4, page 105, col. 1.

Huge as the giant race of elder times.

One of the Arabs, whom we saw from afar, and who

was mounted upon a camel, seemed higher than a tower, and to be moving in the air; at first this was to me a strange appearance, however it was only the effect of refraction. The Camel which the Arab was upon touching the ground like all others. There was nothing then extraordinary in this phenomenon, and I afterwards saw many appearances exactly similar in the dry countries.—*Niebuhr.*

« They surprised you, not indeed by a sudden assault; but they advanced, and the sultry vapour of noon, through which you saw them, increased their magnitude.»—*Moallakat. Poem of Hareth.*

Note 5, page 105, col. 2.
So in his loosen'd cloak
The Old Man wrapt himself.

One of these *Hykes* is usually six yards long and five or six feet broad, serving the Arab for a complete dress in the day, and for his bed and covering in the night. It is a loose but troublesome kind of garment, being frequently disconcerted and falling upon the ground, so that the person who wears it is every moment obliged to tuck it up, and fold it anew about his body. This shews the great use there is for a girdle in attending any active employment; and in consequence thereof, the force of the Scripture injunction alluding thereunto, of *having our loyns girded*. The method of wearing these garments, with the use they are at other times put to, in serving for coverlets to their beds, should induce us to take the finer sort of them, at least, such as are worn by the ladies and persons of distinction, to be the *peplus* of the ancients. It is very probable likewise, that the loose folding garment (the *Toga* I take it to be) of the Romans, was of this kind; for if the drapery of their statues is to instruct us, this is actually no other than what the Arabs appear in, when they are folded up in their *Hykes*. Instead of the *fibula*, they join together, with thread or a wooden bodkin, the two upper corners of this garment, which, being first placed over one of their shoulders, they fold the rest of it afterwards round their bodies.—*Shaw.*

The employment of the women is to prepare their wool, spin, and weave in looms hung lengthways in their tents. Those looms are formed by a list of an ell and a half long, to which the threads of the warp are fixed at one end, and at the other on a roller of equal length; the weight of which, being suspended, keeps them stretched. The threads of the warp are so hung as to be readily intersected. Instead of shuttles, the women pass the thread of the woof through the warp with their fingers, and with an iron comb, having a handle, press the woof to give a body to their cloth. Each piece, of about five ells long, and an ell and a half wide, is called a *haick*; it receives neither dressing, milling, nor dyeing, but is immediately fit for use. It is the constant dress of the Moors of the country, is without seam, and incapable of varying, according to the caprices of fashion: when dirty, it is washed. The Moor is wrapt up in it day and night; and this *haick* is the living model of the drapery of the ancients.—*Chenier.*

If thou at all take thy neighbour's raiment to pledge, thou shalt deliver it unto him by that the Sun goeth down.

For that is his covering only, it is his raiment for his skin: wherein shall he sleep?—*Exodus, xxii, 26, 27.*

Note 6, page 106, col. 2.
Consuming still in flames, and still renew'd.

Fear the fire, whose fuel is men and stones, prepared for the unbelievers.—*Koran,* Chap. 2.

Verily, those who disbelieve our signs, we will surely cast to be broiled in hell fire; so often as their skins shall be well burned, we will give them other skins in exchange, that they may take the sharper torment. *Koran,* Chap. 4.

Note 7, page 106, col. 2.
Their waving wings his sun-shield.

The Arabians attribute to Solomon a perpetual enmity and warfare against wicked Genii and Giants; on the subject of his wonder-working Ring, their tales are innumerable. They have even invented a whole race of Pre-Adamite Solomons, who, according to them, governed the world successively, to the number of 40, or as others affirm, as many as 72. All these made the evil Genii their unwilling Drudges.—*D'Herbelot.*

Anchieta was going in a canoe to the mouth of the river Aldea, a delightful spot, surrounded with mango trees, and usually abounding with birds called goarazes, that breed there. These birds are about the size of a hen, their colour a rich purple inclining to red. They are white when hatched, and soon become black; but as they grow larger, lose that colour, and take this rich and beautiful purple. Our navigators had reached the place, but when they should have enjoyed the fine prospect which delights all who pass it, the sun was excessively hot; and this eye-pleasure was purchased dearly, when the whole body was in a profuse perspiration, and the rowers were in a fever. Their distress called upon Joseph, and the remedy was no new one to him. He saw three or four of these birds perched upon a mango, and calling to them in the Brazilian language, which the rowers understood, said, Go you, call your companions, and come to shade these hot servants of the Lord. The birds stretched out their necks as if in obedience, and away they went to seek for others, and in a short time they came flying in the shape of an elegant cloud, and they shadowed the canoe a good league out to sea, till the fresh sea-breeze sprung up. Then he told them they might go about their business; and they separated with a clamour of rude, but joyful sounds, which were only understood by the Author of Nature, who created them. This was a greater miracle than that of the cloud with which God defended his chosen people in the wilderness from the heat of the sun, inasmuch as it was a more elegant and fanciful parasol. « Acho que foy maior portento este que o da nuvem, com que deos defendeo no deserto a seu Povo mimoso do calor do sol, tanto quanto mais tem de gracioso et aprasivel este chapeo de sol, que aquelle.»

This was one of Anchieta's common miracles. Jacob Biderman had an epigram upon the subject, quoted in the Jesuit's Life.

Hesperii poterent cum barbara litto.a mystæ,
  Et sociis æger pluribus unus erat,
Ille suum extincto, Phœbi quia lampadis æstu
  Occultoque uri, questus ab igne caput;
Quæsiit in prora, si quam daret angulus umbram,
  Nulla sed in proræ partibus umbra fuit.
Quæsiit in puppi, nihil umbræ puppis habebat,
  Summa sed urebant solis, et ima faces.
His cupiens Anchieta malis succurrere, solam
  Aera per medium tendere vidit avem.

Vidit, et socias, ait, i, quære cohortes
Aliger atque redux cum legione veni.
Dicta probavit avis, celerique citatior Euro,
Cognatum properat, quærere jussa gregem.
Milloque mox sociis comitata revertitur alis,
Mille sequi visæ, mille præire ducem.
Mille supra, et totidem, juxtaque, infraque volabant,
Omnis ad Anchietæ turba vocata preces.
Et simul expansis facta testudine pennis,
Desuper in tostas incubuere rates.
Et procul inde diem, et lucem populere diei,
Debile dum mollis conderet umbra caput.
Scilicet hæc fierent, ut canopea repente
Anchieta artifices, esse coegit aves.

« Vida do Veneravel Padre Joseph de Anchieta, da companhia de Jesu, Taumaturgo do Novo Mundo, na Provincia do Brasil. composta pello P. Simam de Vasconcellos, da mesma companhia.»—*Lisboa.* 1672.

The Jesuits probably stole this miracle from the Arabian story of Solomon; not that they are by any means deficient in invention; but they cannot be suspected of ignorance.

In a very old book, the *Margarita Philosophica,* is an account of a parasol more convenient, though not in so *elegant a taste,* as that of the wonder-working Anchieta. There is said to be a nation of one-legged men; and one of these unipeds is represented in a print, lying on his back, under the shade of his own great foot. It is probably a classical lie.

The most quaint account of Solomon's wisdom is in Du Bartas.

Hee knowes. . . . .
Whether the Heavens sweet-sweating kisse appear
To be Pearls parent, and the Oysters pheer,
And whether, dusk, it makes them dim withall,
Cleer breeds the cleer, and stormy brings the pale;
Whether from sea the amber-greece be sent,
Or be some fishes pleasant excrement;
He knowes why the Earth 's immoveable and round,
The lees of Nature, centre of the mound;
Hee knows her mesure; and hee knows beside
How *Coloquintida* (duely apply'd),
Within the darknesse of the Conduit-pipes,
Amid the winding of our inward tripes,
Can so discreetly the *white humour* take.
SYLVESTER's *Du Bartas.*

Note 8, page 106, col. 2.
He rode the wind, etc.

« And we made the wind [1] subject unto Solomon; it blew in the morning for a month, and in the evening for a month. And we made a fountain of molten brass to flow for [2] him. And some of the Genii were obliged to work in his presence, by the will of his Lord; and whoever of them turned aside from our command, we will cause him to taste the pain of hell-fire. [3] They made for him whatever he pleased, of palaces and sta-

[1] They say that he had a carpet of green silk, on which his throne was placed, being of a prodigious length and breadth, and sufficient for all his forces to stand on, the men placing themselves on his right hand, and the spirits on his left; and that when all were in order, the wind, at his command, took up the carpet, and transported it, with all that were upon it, wheresoever he pleased; the army of birds at the same time flying over their heads, and forming a kind of canopy to shade them from the sun.

[2] A fountain of molten brass. This fountain, they say, was in Yeman, and flowed three days in a month.

[3] We will cause him to taste the pain of hell-fire; or, as some expound the words, we caused him to taste the pain of burning; by which they understand the correction the disobedient Genii received at the hands of the Angel set over them, who whipped them with a whip of fire,

tues, [1] and large dishes like fish-ponds, [2] and cauldrons standing firm on their trevets. [3] And we said, Work righteousness, O family of David, with thanksgiving; for few of my servants are thankful. And when we had decreed that Solomon should die, nothing discovered his death unto them, except the creeping thing of the earth, which gnawed his staff. [4]

And when his body fell down, the Genii plainly perceived, that if they had known that which is secret, they had not continued in a vile punishment.»

Note 9, page 107, col. 2.
Oh for the Plover's pleasant cry.

In places where there was water, we found a beautiful variety of the plover.—*Niebuhr.*

Note 10, page 107, col. 2.
Oh for the camel-driver's song,

The camels of the hot countries are not fastened one to the tail of the other as in cold climates, but suffered to go at their will like herds of cows. The camel-driver follows singing, and from time to time giving a sudden whistle. The louder he sings and whistles, the faster the camels go, and they stop as soon as he ceases to sing. The camel-drivers, to relieve each other, sing alternately; and when they wish their beasts to browse for half an hour on what they can find, they amuse themselves by smoking a pipe; after which, beginning again to sing, the camels immediately proceed.—*Tavernier.*

Note 11, page 108, col. 1.
Even frantic famine loath'd.

At four in the afternoon we had an unexpected entertainment, which filled our hearts with a very short-lived joy. The whole plain before us seemed thick covered with green grass and yellow daisies. We advanced to the place with as much speed as our lame condition would suffer us; but how terrible was our

[1] Statues. Some suppose these were images of the Angels and Prophets, and that the making of them was not forbidden, or else that they were not such images as were forbidden by the law. Some say these Spirits made him two lions, which were placed at the foot of his throne, and two eagles, which were set above it; and that when he mounted it, the lions stretched out their paws, and when he sat down, the eagles shaded him with their wings.

[2] Dishes like fish-ponds; being so monstrously large, that a thousand men might eat out of each of them at once.

[3] And cauldrons standing firm on their trevets.—These cauldrons, they say, were cut out of the mountains of Yeman, and were so vastly big, that they could not be moved; and people went up to them by steps.

[4] Nothing discovered his death but the creeping thing of the earth, which gnawed his staff.—The commentators, to explain this passage, tell us, that David, having laid the foundations of the temple of Jerusalem, which was to be in lieu of the tabernacle of Moses, when he died, left it to be finished by his son Solomon, who employed the Genii in the work: that Solomon, before the edifice was completed, perceiving his end drew nigh, begged of God, that his death might be concealed from the Genii, till they had entirely finished it: that God therefore so ordered it, that Solomon died as he stood at his prayers, leaning on his staff, which supported the body in that posture a full year; and the Genii, supposing him to be alive, continued their work during that term; at the expiration whereof, the temple being perfectly completed, a worm, which had gotten into the staff, eat it through, and the corpse fell to the ground, and discovered the king's death.

Possibly this fable of the temple being built by Genii, and not by men, might take its rise from what is mentioned in Scripture, that the house was built of stone, made ready before it was brought thither; so that there was neither hammer nor axe, nor tool of iron heard in the house, while it was building.

disappointment, when we found the whole of that ver-
dure to consist in senna and coloquintida, the most
nauseous of plants, and the most incapable of being
substituted as food for man or beast!—*Bruce.*

Note 12, page 108, col. 1.
Then from his girdle Thalaba took the knife.

The girdles of these people are usually of worsted
very artfully woven into a variety of figures, and made
to wrap several times about their bodies; one end of
them, by being doubled and sewn along the edges,
serves them for a purse, agreeable to the acceptation of
the word Ζωνη in the Holy Scriptures: the Turks and
Arabs make a further use of their girdles, by fixing
their knives and poniards in them; whilst the Hojias,
i. e. the writers and secretaries, are distinguished by
having an inkhorn, the badge of their office, suspended
in the like situation.—*Shaw.*

Note 13, page 108, col. 1.
Across the Camel's throat.

On the road we passed the skeleton of a camel, which
now and then happens in the desert. These are poor
creatures that have perished with fatigue: for those
which are killed for the sustenance of the Arabs, are
carried away, bones and altogether. Of the hides are
made the soles of the slippers which are worn in Egypt,
without any dressing, but what the sun can give them.
The circumstances of this animal's death, when his
strength fails him on the road, have something in them
affecting to humanity. Such are his patience and per-
severance, that he pursues his journey without flagging,
as long as he has power to support its weight; and such
are his fortitude and spirit, that he will never give out,
until nature sinks beneath the complicated ills which
press upon him. Then, and then only, will he resign
his burden and body to the ground. Nor stripes, nor
caresses, nor food, nor rest, will make him rise again!
His vigour is exhausted, and life ebbs out apace! This
the Arabs are very sensible of, and kindly plunge a
sword into the breast of the dying beast, to shorten his
pangs. Even the Arab feels remorse when he commits
this deed; his hardened heart is moved at the loss of a
faithful servant.—*Eyles Irwin.*

In the *Monthly Magazine* for January 1800, is a letter
from Professor Heering recommending the introduc-
tion of these animals at the Cape; but the camel is
made only for level countries. « The animal is very ill
qualified to travel upon the snow or wet ground; the
breadth in which they carry their legs, when they slip,
often occasions their splitting themselves; so that when
they fall with great burdens, they seldom rise again.»
—*Jonas Hanway.*

The African Arabs say, if one should put the ques-
tion, « which is best for you, O Camel, to go up hill or
down?» he will make answer, « God's curse light on 'em
both, wheresoever they are to be met with.»—*Morgan's
Hist. of Algiers.*

No creature seems so peculiarly fitted to the climate
in which it exists. We cannot doubt the nature of the
one has been adapted to that of the other by some *dis-
posing intelligence.* Designing the Camel to dwell in
a country where he can find little nourishment, nature
has been sparing of her materials in the whole of his
formation. She has not bestowed upon him the plump
fleshiness of the ox, horse, or elephant; but limiting

herself to what is strictly necessary, she has given him
a small head without ears, at the end of a long neck
without flesh. She has taken from his legs and thighs
every muscle not immediately requisite for motion: and,
in short, has bestowed on his withered body only the
vessels and tendons necessary to connect his frame to-
gether. She has furnished him with a strong jaw, that
he may grind the hardest aliments; but lest he should
consume too much, she has contracted his stomach,
and obliged him to chew the cud. She has lined his
foot with a lump of flesh, which, sliding in the mud,
and being no way adapted for climbing, fits him only
for a dry, level, and sandy soil, like that of Arabia.
She has evidently destined him likewise to slavery, by
refusing him every sort of defence against his enemies.
Destitute of the horns of the bull, the hoofs of the
horse, the tooth of the elephant, and the swiftness of
the stag, how can the Camel resist or avoid the attacks
of the lion, the tiger, or even the wolf? To preserve
the species, therefore, nature has concealed him in the
depths of the vast deserts, where the want of vegetables
can attract no game, and whence the want of game
repels every voracious animal. Tyranny must have ex-
pelled man from the habitable parts of the earth, be-
fore the Camel could have lost his liberty. Become
domestic, he has rendered habitable the most barren
soil the world contains. He alone supplies all his mas-
ter's wants. The milk of the Camel nourishes the
family of the Arab, under the various forms of curds,
cheese, and butter; and they often feed upon his flesh.
Slippers and harness are made of his skin, and tents
and clothing of his hair. Heavy burthens are trans-
ported by his means; and when the earth denies forage
to the horse, so valuable to the Bedouin, the she-camel
supplies that deficiency by her milk, at no other cost,
for so many advantages, than a few stalks of brambles
or wormwood, and pounded date kernels. So great is
the importance of the Camel to the desert, that were it
deprived of that useful animal, it must infallibly lose
every inhabitant.—*Volney.*

Note 14, page 108, col. 1.
Of distant waters, etc.

Where any part of these Deserts is sandy and level,
the horizon is as fit for astronomical observations as
the sea, and appears, at a small distance, to be no less
a collection of water. It was likewise equally surpris-
ing to observe, in what an extraordinary manner every
object appeared to be magnified within it; insomuch,
that a shrub seemed as big as a tree, and a flock of
Achbobbas might be mistaken for a caravan of Camels.
This seeming collection of water always advances about
a quarter of a mile before us, whilst the intermediate
space appears to be in one continued glow, occasioned
by the quivering undulating motion of that quick suc-
cession of vapours and exhalations, which are extracted
by the powerful influence of the sun.—*Shaw.*

In the Bahar Danush is a metaphor drawn from this
optical deception. « It is the ancient custom of For-
tune, and time has long established the habit, that she
at first bewilders the thirsty travellers in the path of
desire, by the misty vapour of disappointment; but
when their distress and misery has reached extremity,
suddenly relieving them from the dark windings of
confusion and error, she conducts them to the foun-
tains of enjoyment.»

«The burning heat of the sun was reflected with double violence from the hot sand, and the distant ridges of the hills, seen through the ascending vapour, seemed to wave and fluctuate like the unsettled sea.»— *Mungo Park.*

«I shake the lash over my Camel, and she quickens her pace, while the sultry vapour rolls in waves over the burning cliffs.»—*Moallakat. Poem of Tarafa.*

Note 15, page 108, col. 1.

His tongue was dry and rough.

Perhaps no traveller but Mr Park ever survived to relate similar sufferings.

«I pushed on as fast as possible, in hopes of reaching some watering-place in the course of the night. My thirst was by this time become insufferable; my mouth was parched and inflamed; a sudden dimness would frequently come over my eyes, with other symptoms of fainting; and my horse being very much fatigued, I began seriously to apprehend that I should perish of thirst. To relieve the burning pain in my mouth and throat, I chewed the leaves of different shrubs, but found them all bitter, and of no service to me.

«A little before sun-set, having reached the top of a gentle rising, I climbed a high tree, from the topmost branches of which I cast a melancholy look over the barren wilderness, but without discovering the most distant trace of a human dwelling. The same dismal uniformity of shrubs and sand every where presented itself, and the horizon was as level and uninterrupted as that of the sea.

«Descending from the tree, I found my horse devouring the stubble and brushwood with great avidity; and as I was now too faint to attempt walking, and my horse too much fatigued to carry me, I thought it but an act of humanity, and perhaps the last I should ever have it in my power to perform, to take off his bridle and let him shift for himself; in doing which I was suddenly affected with sickness and giddiness, and falling upon the sand, felt as if the hour of death was fast approaching. Here then, thought I, after a short but ineffectual struggle, terminate all my hopes of being useful in my day and generation; here must the short span of my life come to an end.—I cast (as I believed) a last look on the surrounding scene, and whilst I reflected on the awful change that was about to take place, this world, with its enjoyments, seemed to vanish from my recollection. Nature, however, at length, resumed its functions; and on recovering my senses, I found myself stretched upon the sand with the bridle still in my hand, and the sun just sinking behind the trees. I now summoned all my resolution, and determined to make another effort to prolong my existence. And as the evening was somewhat cool, I resolved to travel as far as my limbs would carry me, in hopes of reaching (my only resource) a watering-place. With this view I put the bridle on my horse, and driving him before me, went slowly along for about an hour, when I perceived some lightning from the north-east, a most delightful sight, for it promised rain. The darkness and lightning increased very rapidly; and in less than an hour I heard the wind roaring among the bushes. I had already opened my mouth to receive the refreshing drops which I expected, but I was instantly covered with a cloud of sand, driven with such force by the wind as to give a very disagreeable sensation to my face and arms, and I was obliged to mount my horse and stop under a bush, to prevent being suffocated. The sand continued to fly in amazing quantities for near an hour, after which I again set forward, and travelled with difficulty, until ten o'clock. About this time I was agreeably surprised by some very vivid flashes of lightning, followed by a few heavy drops of rain. In a little time the sand ceased to fly, and I alighted, and spread out all my clean clothes to collect the rain, which at length I saw would certainly fall.— For more than an hour it rained plentifully, and I quenched my thirst by wringing and sucking my clothes.»— *Park's Travels in the Interior of Africa.*

Note 16, page 108, col. 2.

ould they have back'd the Dromedary, etc.

All the time I was in Barbary I could never get sight of above three or four Dromedaries. These the Arabs call Mehera, the singular is Meheri. They are of several sorts and degrees of value, some worth many common Camels, others scarce worth two or three. To look on, they seem little different from the rest of that species, only I think the excrescence on a Dromedary's back is somewhat less than that of a Camel. What is reported of their sleeping or rather seeming scarce alive, for some time after coming into this world, is no fable. The longer they lie so, the more excellent they prove in their kind, and consequently of higher price and esteem. None lie in that trance more than ten days and nights. These that do, are pretty rare, and are called Aashari, from Aashara, which signifies ten, in Arabic. I saw one such, perfectly white all over, belonging to Lella Oumane, Princess of that noble Arab Neja, named Heyl ben Ali, I spoke of, and upon which she put a very great value, never sending it abroad but upon some extraordinary occasion, when the greatest expedition was required; having others, inferior in swiftness, for more ordinary messages. They say that one of these Aasharies will, in one night, and through a level country, traverse as much ground as any single horse can perform in ten, which is no exaggeration of the matter, since many have affirmed to me, that it makes nothing of holding its rapid pace, which is a most violent hard trot, for four-and-twenty hours upon a stretch, without shewing the least sign of weariness, or inclination to bait, and that having then swallowed a ball or two of a sort of paste, made up of barley-meal, and may be a little powder of dates among it, with a bowl of water, or Camel's milk, if to be had, and which the courier seldom forgets to be provided with, in skins, as well for the sustenance of himself as of his Pegasus, the indefatigable animal will seem as fresh as at first setting out, and ready to continue running at the same scarce credible rate, for as many hours longer, and so on from one extremity of the African Deserts to the other, provided its rider could hold out without sleep, and other refreshment. This has been averred to me, by, I believe, more than a thousand Arabs and Moors, all agreeing in every particular.

I happened to be, once in particular, at the tent of that Princess, with Ali ben Mahamoud the Bey, or Vice-Roy of the Algerine Eastern Province, when he went thither to celebrate his nuptials with Ambarca, her only daughter, if I mistake not. Among other entertainments she gave her guests, the favourite white

Dromedary was brought forth, ready saddled and bridled. I say bridled, because the thong, which serves instead of a bridle, was put through the hole purposely made in the gristle of the creature's nose. The Arab appointed to mount, was straitly laced, from the very loins quite to his throat, in a strong leathern jacket; they never riding these animals any otherwise accoutred; so impetuously violent are the concussions the rider undergoes, during that rapid motion, that were he to be loose, I much question whether a few hours' such unintermitting agitation would not endanger the bursting of some of his entrails; and this the Arabs scruple not to acknowledge. We were to be diverted with seeing this fine Aashari run against some of the swiftest barbs in the whole Neja, which is famed for having good ones, of the true Libyan breed, shaped like greyhounds, and which will sometimes run down an ostrich; which few of the very best can pretend to do, especially upon a hard ground, perfectly level. We all started like racers, and for the first spurt, most of the best mounted among us kept up pretty well, but our grass-fed horses soon flagged: several of the Libyian and Numidian runners held pace till we, who still followed upon a good round hand-gallop, could no longer discern them, and then gave out; as we were told after their return. When the Dromedary had been out of our sight about half an hour, we again espied it flying towards us with an amazing velocity, and in a very few moments was among us, and seemingly nothing concerned; while the horses and mares were all in a foam, and scarce able to breathe, as was, likewise, a fleet, tall greyhound bitch, of the young Prince's, who had followed and kept pace the whole time, and was no sooner got back to us, but lay down panting as if ready to expire. I cannot tell how many miles we went; but we were near three hours in coming leisurely back to the tents, yet made no stop in the way. The young Prince Hamet ben al Guydom ben Sakhari, and his younger brother Messoud, told their new brother in-law, that they defied all the potentates of Africa to show him such an Aashari; and the Arab who rode it, challenged the Bey to lay his lady a wager of 1000 ducats, that he did not bring him an answer to a letter from the Prince of Wargalla, in less than four days, though Leo Africanus, Marmol, and several others, assure us, that it is no less than forty Spanish leagues, of four miles each, south of Tuggurt, to which place, upon another occasion, as I shall observe, we made six tedious days march from the neighbourhood of Biscara, north of which we were then, at least thirty hours riding, if I remember rightly. However, the Bey, who was a native of Biscara, and consequently well acquainted with the Sahara, durst not take him up. By all circumstances, and the description given us, besides what I know of the matter myself, it could not be much less than 400 miles, and as many back again, the fellow offered to ride, in so short a time; nay, many other Arabs boldly proffered to venture all they were worth in the world, that he would perform it with all the ease imaginable.— *Morgan's History of Algiers.*

Chenier says « the Dromedary can travel 60 leagues in a day; his motion is so rapid, that the rider is obliged to be girthed to the saddle, and to have a handkerchief before his mouth to break the current of the wind.» These accounts are probably much exaggerated.

« The royal couriers in Persia wear a white sash girded from the shoulders to their waist many times around their bodies, by which means they are enabled to ride for many days without great fatigue.»—*Hanway.*

Note 17, page 108, col. 2.
The dreadful sand-spouts mov'd.

We were here at once surprised and terrified by a sight surely the most magnificent in the world. In that vast expanse of desert, from W. and to N. W. of us, we saw a number of prodigious pillars of sand at different distances, at times moving with great celerity, at others stalking with a majestic slowness : at intervals, we thought they were coming in a very few moments to overwhelm us, and small quantities of sand did actually, more than once, reach us. Again they would retreat so as to be almost out of sight, their tops reaching to the very clouds. There the tops often separated from the bodies, and these, once disjoined, dispersed in the air, and did not appear more. Sometimes they were broken near the middle, as if struck with a large cannon-shot. About noon, they began to advance with considerable swiftness upon us, the wind being very strong at north. Eleven of them ranged along side of us about the distance of three miles. The greatest diameter of the largest appeared to me at that distance, as if it would measure ten feet. They retired from us with a wind at S. E. leaving an impression upon my mind to which I can give no name ; though surely one ingredient in it was fear, with a considerable deal of wonder and astonishment. It was in vain to think of flying, the swiftest horse, or fastest sailing ship, could be of no use to carry us out of this danger, and the full persuasion of this rivetted me as if to the spot where I stood.

On the 15th, the same appearance of moving pillars of sand presented themselves to us, only they seemed to be more in number, and less in size. They came several times in a direction close upon us; that is, I believe, within less than two miles. They began immediately after sun-rise, like a thick wood, and almost darkened the sun. His rays shining through them for near an hour, gave them an appearance of pillars of fire. Our people now became desperate : the Greeks shrieked out, and said it was the day of judgment. Ismael pronounced it to be hell, and the Tucorories that the world was on fire.—*Bruce.*

BOOK V.

Note 1, page 109, col. 2.
Laps the cool wave, etc.

The Pelican makes choice of dry and desert places to lay her eggs; when her young are hatched, she is obliged to bring water to them from great distances. To enable her to perform this necessary office, Nature has provided her with a large sack, which extends from the tip of the under mandible of her bill to the throat, and holds as much water as will supply her brood for several days. This water she pours into the nest, to cool her young, to allay their thirst, and to teach them to swim. Lions, Tigers, and other rapacious animals, resort to these nests, and drink the water, and are said not to injure the young.—*Smellie's Philosophy of Natural History.*

It is perhaps from this power of carrying a supply of water that the pelican is called *Jimmel el Bahar,* the Camel of the River. Bruce notices a curious blunder upon this subject in the translation of Norden's Travels. On looking into Mr Norden's Voyage, says he, I was struck at first sight with this paragraph : " We saw, this day, abundance of camels ; but they did not come near enough for us to shoot them." I thought with myself, to shoot camels in Egypt, would be very little better than to shoot men, and that it was very lucky for him the camels did not come near, if that was the only thing that prevented him. Upon looking at the note, I see it is a small mistake of the translator, who says, that in the original it is *Chameaux d'eau,* Water Camels ; but whether they are a particular species of camels, or a different kind of animal, he does not know.

Note 2, page 109, col. 2.
Every where scatter'd, etc.

These prominent features of an Oriental city will be found in all the views of Sir John Chardin.

The mosques, the minarets, and numerous cupolas, form a splendid spectacle ; and the flat roofs of the houses, which are situated on the hills, rising one behind another, present a succession of hanging terraces, interspersed with cypress and poplar trees.

Russel's Nat. Hist. of Aleppo.

The circuit of Ispahan, taking in the suburbs, is not less than that of Paris ; but Paris contains ten times the number of its inhabitants. It is not, however, astonishing that this city is so extensive and so thinly peopled, because every family has its own house, and almost every house its garden ; so that there is much void ground. From whatever side you arrive, you first discover the towers of the mosques, and then the trees which surround the houses ; at a distance, Ispahan resembles a forest more than a town. — *Tavernier.*

Of Alexandria, Volney says, " the spreading palm-trees, the terraced houses, which seem to have no roof, the lofty slender minarets, all announce to the traveller that he is in another world."

Note 3, page 109, col. 2.
Thou too art fallen, Bagdad! City of Peace.

Almanzor riding one day with his courtiers along the banks of the Tigris, where Seleucia formerly stood, was so delighted with the beauty of the country, that he resolved there to build his new capital. Whilst he was conversing with his attendants upon this project, one of them, separating from the rest, met a hermit, whose cell was near, and entered into talk with him, and communicated the design of the Caliph. The Hermit replied he well knew, by a tradition of the country, that a city would one day be built in that plain, but that its founder would be a man called Moclas, a name very different from both those of the Caliph, Giafar and Almanzor.

The Officer rejoined Almanzor, and repeated his conversation with the Hermit. As soon as the Caliph heard the name of Moclas, he descended from his horse, prostrated himself, and returned thanks to God, for that he was chosen to execute his orders. His courtiers waited for an explanation of this conduct with eagerness, and the Caliph told them thus : During the Caliphate of the Ommiades, my brothers and myself being very young, and possessing very little, were obliged to live in the country, where each in rotation was to provide sustenance for the whole. On one of my days, as I was without money, and had no means of procuring food, I took a bracelet belonging to my nurse, and pawned it. This woman made a great outcry, and after much search,

discovered that I had been the thief. In her anger she abused me plentifully, and, among other terms of reproach, she called me Moclas, the name of a famous robber in those days ; and, during the rest of her life, she never called me by any other name. Therefore I know that God has destined me to perform this work.

Marigny.

Almanzor named his new city Dar-al-Salam, the City of Peace ; but it obtained the name of Bagdad, from that of this Hermit, who dwelt upon its site.

Note 4, page 110, col. 1.
Thy founder the Victorious, etc.

Almanzor signifies the Victorious.

Bagdad was founded in consequence of a singular superstition. A sect called Ravendiens conceived, that they ought to render those honours to the Caliphs which the Moslem hold should only be paid to the Deity. They therefore came in great numbers to Haschemia, where the Caliph Almanzor usually resided, and made around his palace the same processions and ceremonies which the Moslem make around the temple at Mecca. The Caliph prohibited this, commanding them not to profane a religious ceremony which ought to be reserved solely to the Temple at Mecca. The Ravendiens did not regard the prohibition, and continued to act as before.

Almanzor, seeing their obstinacy, resolved to conquer it, and began by arresting a hundred of these fanatics. This astonished them ; but they soon recovered their courage, took arms, marched to the prison, forced the doors, delivered their friends, and then returned to make their procession round the palace in reverence of the Caliph.

Enraged at this insolence, the Caliph put himself at the head of his guards, and advanced against the Ravendiens, expecting that his appearance would immediately disperse them. Instead of this, they resisted and repulsed him so vigorously, that he had nearly fallen a victim. But timely succours arrived, and after a great slaughter, these fanatics were expelled the town. This singular rebellion, arising from excess of loyalty, so disgusted Almanzor, that he determined to forsake the town which had witnessed it, and accordingly laid the foundation of Bagdad. — *Marigny.*

Note 5, page 110, col. 1.
Met in her arch'd Bazars.

The houses in Persia are not in the same place with their shops, which stand, for the most part, in long and large arched streets, forty or fifty feet high ; which streets are called Basar, or the Market, and make the heart of the city, the houses being in the outparts, and having almost all gardens belonging to them. — *Chardin.*

At Tauris, he says, " there are the fairest Basars that are in any place of Asia ; and it is a lovely sight to see their vast extent, their largeness, their beautiful Duomos, and the arches over them."

At Bagdad the Bazars are all vaulted, otherwise the merchants could not remain in them on account of the heat. They are also watered two or three times a-day, and a number of the poor are paid for rendering this service to the public. — *Tavernier.*

Exeter Change is a Bazar.

Note 6, page 110, col. 1.
And Tigris on his tameless current bore.

On the other side of the river, towards Arabia, over against the city, there is a faire place or towne, and in it a fair Bazarro for merchants, with very many lodgings, where the greatest part of the merchants strangers which come to Babylon do lie with their merchandize. The passing over Tygris from Babylon to this Borough is by a long bridge, made of boates, chained together with great chaines: provided, that when the river waxeth great with the abundance of raine that falleth, then they open the bridge in the middle, where the one-halfe of the bridge falleth to the walles of Babylon, and the other to the brinks of this Borough, on the other side of the river; and as long as the bridge is open, they passe the river in small boats, with great danger, because of the smallness of the boats, and the overlading of them, that with the fiercenesse of the stream they be overthrowen, or els the streame doth carry them away; so that by this meanes many people are lost and drowned.—*Cæsar Frederick in Hakluyt.*

Here are great store of victuals, which come from Armenia down the river of Tygris. They are brought upon raftes made of goate's skinnes blown full of wind, and bordes layde upon them; which being discharged, they open their skinnes, and carry them backe by Camels.—*Ralph Fitch in Hakluyt.*

Note 7, page 110, col. 1.
The many-colour'd domes.

In Tavernier's time there were five Mosques at Bagdad, two of them fine, their large domes covered with varnished tiles of different colours.

Note 8, page 110, col. 1.
Kept their night-clatter still.

At Bagdad are many cranes, who build their nests upon the tops of the minarets, and the loftiest houses.

At Adanaqui, cranes are so abundant, that there is scarcely a house which has not several nests upon it. They are very tame, and the inhabitants never molest them. When any thing disturbs these birds, they make a violent clatter with their long beaks, which is some time repeated by the others all over the town; and this noise will sometimes continue for several minutes. It is as loud as a watchman's rattle, and not much unlike it in sound.—*Jackson.*

The cranes were now arrived at their respective quarters, and a couple had made their nest, which is bigger in circumference than a bushel, on a dome close by our chamber. This pair stood, side by side, with great gravity, showing no concern at what was transacting beneath them, but at intervals twisting about their long necks, and clattering with their beaks, turned behind them upon their backs, as it were in concert. This was continued the whole night. An Owl, a bird also unmolested, was perched hard by, and as frequently hooted. The crane is tall, like a heron, but much larger: the body white, with black pinions, the neck and legs very long, the head small, and the bill thick. The Turks call it friend and brother, believing it has an affection for their nation, and will accompany them into the countries they shall conquer. In the course of our journey we saw one hopping on a wall with a single leg, the maimed stump wrapped in linen.—*Chandler's Travels in Asia Minor.*

Note 9, page 110, col. 1.
The Bittern's boom came far.

I will rise up against them, saith the Lord of Hosts, and cut off from Babylon the name and remnant, and son and nephew, saith the Lord. I will also make it a possession for the Bittern and pools of water.—*Isaiah*, xiv, 22, 23.

Note 10, page 110, col. 1.
Once from her lofty walls the Charioteer.

   ——— Walls within
Whose large inclosure the rude hind, or guides
His plough, or binds his sheaves, while shepherds guard
Their flocks, secure of ill : on the broad top
Six chariots rattle in extended front.
Each side in length, in height, in solid bulk,
Reflects its opposite a perfect square;
Scarce sixty thousand paces can mete out
The vast circumference. An hundred gates
Of polished brass lead to that central point,
Where through the midst, bridged o'er with wondrous art,
Euphrates leads a navigable stream,
Branch'd from the current of his roaring flood.
          Rozaxs's Judah Restored.

Note 11, page 110, col. 1.
Hath been the aërial Gardens, etc.

   ——— Within the walls
Of Babylon was rais'd a lofty mound,
Where flowers and aromatic shrubs adorn'd
The pensile garden. For Nebassar's queen,
Fatigued with Babylonia's level plains,
Sigh'd for her Median home, where nature's hand
Had scoop'd the vale, and cloth'd the mountain's side
With many a verdant wood; nor long she pin'd
Till that uxorious mon-rch called on art
To rival nature's sweet variety.
Forthwith two hundred thousand slaves uprear'd
This hill, egregious work; rich fruits o'erhung
The sloping walks, and odorous shrubs entwine
Their undulating branches.
          Rozaxs's Judah Restored.

Note 12, page 110, col. 2.
Of Belus? etc.

Our early Travellers have given us strange and circumstantial accounts of what they conceive to have been the Temple of Belus.

The tower of Nimrod, or Babel, is situate on that side of Tygris that Arabia is, and in a very great plaine distant from Babylon seven or eight miles: which tower is ruinated on every side; and with the falling of it there is made a great mountaine, so that it hath no forme at all; yet there is a great part of it standing, which is compassed, and almost covered, with the aforesayd fallings. This Tower was builded and made of foure-square brickes; which brickes were made of earth, and dried in the Sunne in maner and forme following: First they layed a lay of brickes, then a mat made of canes, square as the brickes, and, instead of lime they daubed it with earth. These mats of canes are at this time so strong, that it is a thing wonderfull to beholde, being of such great antiquity. I have gone round about it, and have not found any place where there hath bene any door or entrance. It may be, in my judgment, in circuit about a mile, and rather lesse than more.

This Tower, in effect, is contrary to all other things which are seene afar off; for they seeme small, and the more neere a man commeth to them, the bigger they be : but this tower, afar off, seemeth a very great thing, and the nerer you come to it the lesser. My judgment

22

and reason of this is, that because the Tower is set in a very great plaine, and hath nothing more about to make any shew saving the ruines of it, which it hath made round about; and for this respect, descrying it afarre off, that piece of the Tower which yet standeth with the mountaine that is made of the substance that hath fallen from it, maketh a greater shew than you shall finde coming neere to it.—*Cæsar Frederick.*

John Eldred mentions the same deception: «Being upon a plaine grounde, it seemeth afarre off very great; but the nerer you come to it, the lesser and lesser it appeareth. Sundry times I have gone thither to see it, and found the remnants yet standing, about a quarter of a mile in compasse, and almost as high as the stoneworke of St Paul's steeple in London, but it sheweth much bigger.»—*Hakluyt.*

In the middle of a vast and level plain, about a quarter of a league from Euphrates, which in that place runs westward, appears a heap of ruined buildings, like a huge mountain, the materials of which are so confounded together, that one knows not what to make of it. Its figure is square, and rises in form of a tower, or pyramid, with four fronts, which answer to the four quarters of the compass; but it seems longer from north to south than from east to west, and is, as far as I could judge by my pacing it, a large quarter of a league. Its situation and form correspond with that pyramid which Strabo calls the tower of Belus; and is, in all likelihood, the tower of Nimrod in Babylon, or Babel, as that place is still called. In that author's time it had nothing remaining of the stairs, and other ornaments mentioned by Herodotus, the greatest part of it having been ruined by Xerxes; and Alexander, who designed to have restored it to its former lustre, but was prevented by death. There appear no marks of ruins without the compass of that huge mass, to convince one that so great a city as Babylon had ever stood there; all one discovers within fifty or sixty paces of it, being only the remains, here and there, of some foundations of buildings; and the country round about it is so flat and level, that one can hardly believe it should be chosen for the situation of so great and noble a city as Babylon, or that there were ever any remarkable buildings on it: But, for my part, I am astonished there appears so much as there does, considering it is at least 4000 years since that city was built; and that Diodorus Siculus tells us, it was reduced almost to nothing in his time. The height of this mountain of ruins is not in every part equal, but exceeds the highest palace in Naples: it is a misshapen mass, wherein there is no appearance of regularity; in some places it rises in points, is craggy and inaccessible; in others it is smoother, and is of easier ascent; there are also tracks of torrents from the top to the bottom, caused by the rains; and both withinside, and upon it, one sees parts some higher and some lower. It is not to be discovered whether ever there were any steps to ascend it, or any doors to enter into it; whence one may easily judge that the stairs ran winding about on the outside; and that being the less solid parts, they were soonest demolished, so that not the least sign of any appears at present.

Withinside one finds some grottos, but so ruined that one can make nothing of them, whether they were built at the same time with that work, or made since by the peasants for shelter: which last seems to be the most likely. The Mahommedans believe that these caverns were appointed by God as places of punishment for Harut and Marut, two angels, who they suppose were sent from heaven to judge the crimes of men, but did not execute their commissions as they ought. It is evident from these ruins, that the tower of Nimrod was built with great and thick bricks, as I carefully observed, causing holes to be dug in several places for the purpose; but they do not appear to have been burnt, but dried in the sun, which is extreme hot in those parts. In laying these bricks, neither lime nor sand was employed, but only earth tempered and petrified; and in those parts which made the floors, there had been mingled with that earth, which served instead of lime, bruised reeds, or hard straw, such as large mats are made of, to strengthen the work. Afterwards one perceives at certain distances, in diverse places, especially where the strongest buttresses were to be, several other bricks of the same size, but more solid, and burnt in a kiln, and set in good lime, or bitumen; nevertheless, the greatest number consists of those which are only dried in the sun.

I make no doubt but this ruin was the ancient Babel, and the tower of Nimrod; for, besides the evidence of its situation, it is acknowledged to be such by the people of the country, being vulgarly called Babil by the Arabs. —*Pietro delle Valle. Universal Hist.*

> Eight towers arise,
> Each above each, immeasurable height
> A monument, at once, of Eastern pride
> And slavish superstition. Round, a scale
> Of circling steps entwines the conic pile;
> And at the bottom, on vast hinges grate
> Four brazen gates, towards the four winds of heaven,
> Placed in the solid square.
>
> *Roscoe's Judah Restored.*

Note 13, page 110, col. 2.

*The wandering Arab never sets his tent
Within her walls, etc.*

And Babylon, the glory of kingdoms, the beauty of the Chaldees' excellency, shall be as when God overthrew Sodom and Gomorrah.

It shall never be inhabited, neither shall it be dwelt in from generation to generation; neither shall the Arabian pitch tent there, neither shall the Shepherds make their fold there.—*Isaiah,* xiii, 19, 20.

Note 14, page 110, col. 2.

Disclose their secret wealth.

The stupid superstition of the Turks, with regard to hidden treasures, is well known: it is difficult, or even dangerous, for a traveller to copy an inscription in sight of those barbarians.

«On a rising ground, at a league's distance from the river Shelliff, is *Memoun-turroy*, as they call an old square tower, formerly a sepulchral monument of the Romans. This, like many more ancient edifices, is supposed by the Arabs to have been built over a treasure; agreeably to which account, they tell us, these mystical lines were inscribed upon it. Prince *Maimoun Tizai* wrote this upon his tower:

> My Treasure is in my Shade,
> And my Shade is in my Treasure.
> Search for it; despair not:
> Nay despair; do not search.
> *Shaw.*

So of the ruins of the ancient Tubuna.

The Treasure of Tubnah lyeth under the shade of what is shaded. Dig for it: alas! it is not there.—*Shaw.*

Note 15, page 111, col. 2.

From Ait's bitumen lake, etc.

The springs of bitumen called *Oyun Hit*, the *fountains of Hit*, are much celebrated by the *Arabs* and *Persians*; the latter call it *Cheshmeh kir*, the *fountain of pitch*. This liquid bitumen they call *Nafta*; and the *Turks*, to distinguish it from pitch, give it the name of *hara sakiz*, or *black mastich*. A *Persian* geographer says, that *Nafta* issues out of the springs of the earth, as amber-grise issues out of those of the sea. All the modern travellers, except *Rauwolf*, who went to *Persia* and the *Indies* by the way of the *Euphrates*, before the discovery of the *Cape of Good Hope*, mention this fountain of liquid bitumen as a strange thing. Some of them take notice of the river mentioned by *Herodotus*, and assure us, that the people of the country have a tradition, that, when the tower of *Babel* was building, they brought the bitumen from hence; which is confirmed by the *Arab* and *Persian* historians.

Hit, *Heit*, *Eit*, *Ait*, or *Idt*, as it is variously written by travellers, is a great *Turkish* town, situate upon the right or west side of the *Euphrates*, and has a castle; to the south-west of which, and three miles from the town, in a valley, are many springs of this black substance; each of which makes a noise like a smith's forge, incessantly puffing and blowing out the matter so loud, that it may be heard a mile off: wherefore the *Moors* and *Arabs* call it *Bab al Jehannam* that is, *hell gate*. It swallows up all heavy things; and many camels, from time to time, fall into the pits, and are irrecoverably lost. It issues from a certain lake, sending forth a filthy smoke, and continually boiling over with the pitch, which spreads itself over a great field, that is always full of it. It is free for every one to take: they use it to caulk or pitch their boats, laying it on two or three inches thick; which keeps out the water: with it also they pitch their houses, made of palm-tree branches. If it was not that the inundations of the *Euphrates* carry away the pitch, which covers all the sands from the place where it rises to the river, there would have been mountains of it long since. The very ground and stones thereabouts afford bitumen; and the fields abundance of salt-petre. —*Universal History*.

Note 16, page 111, col. 2.

And dropping their beads fast, etc.

The Mussulmauns use, like the Roman Catholics, a rosary of beads, called *Tushah*, or implement of praise. It consists, if I recollect aright, of ninety-nine beads; in dropping which through the fingers, they repeat the attributes of God, as «O Creator, O Merciful, O Forgiving, O Omnipotent, O Omniscient,» etc., etc. This act of devotion is called *Taleel*, from the repetition of the letter L, or Laum, which occurs in the word Allah, (God), always joined to the epithet or attribute, as Ya Allah Khalick, O God, the Creator; Ya Allak Kerreem, O God, the Merciful, etc., etc. The devotees may be seen muttering their beads as they walk the streets, and in the intervals of conversation in company. The rosaries of persons of fortune and rank have the beads of diamonds, pearls, rubies, and emeralds. Those of the humble are strung with berries, coral, or glass-beads.— *Note to the Bahar-Danush.*

The ninety-nine beads of the Mahommedan rosary are divided into three equal lengths by a little string, at the end of which hangs a long piece of coral, and a large

bead of the same. The more devout, or hypocritical Turks, like the Catholics, have usually their bead-string in their hands.—*Tavernier*.

Note 17, page 112, col. 1.

Young Arab! when she wrote upon thy brow, etc.

«The Mahummedans believe, that the decreed events of every man's life are impressed in divine characters on his forehead, though not to be seen by mortal eye. Hence they use the word Nusseeb, *anglicé* stamped, for destiny. Most probably the idea was taken up by Mahummed from the sealing of the Elect, mentioned in the revelations.»—*Note to the Bahar-Danush.*

«The scribe of decree chose to ornament the edicts on my forehead with these flourishes of disgrace.»—*Bahar-Danush.*

The Spanish Physiognomical phrase, *traérlo escrito en la frente*, to have it written on the forehead, is perhaps of Arabian origin.

Rajah Chunder of Cashmeer was blest with a Vizier, endowed with wisdom and fidelity; but the wicked, envying his virtues, propagated unfavourable reports regarding him. On these occasions the great are generally staggered in their opinions, and make no use of their reason; forgetting every thing which they have read in history on the direful effects of envy. Thus *Rajah Burjin* gave ear to the stories fabricated against his vizier, and dismissed him from his office. The faithful vizier bore his disgrace with the utmost submission; but his enemies, not satisfied with what they compassed against him, represented to the Rajah that he was plotting to raise himself to the throne; and the deluded prince ordered him to be crucified. A short time after the execution, the Vizier's peer (his spiritual guide) passed the corpse, and read it decreed in his forehead as follows: «That he should be dismissed from his office, be sent to prison, and then crucified; but that, after all, he should be restored to life, and obtain the kingdom.» Astonished at what he beheld, he took down the body from the cross, and carried it to a secret place. Here he was incessantly offering up prayers to heaven for the restoration of his life, till one night the aërial spirits assembled together, and restored the body to life by repeating incantations. He shortly after mounted the throne, but, despising worldly pomp, soon abdicated it.—*Ayeen Akbery.*

Note 18, page 112, col. 1.

—— Zohak keeps the cave, etc.

Zohak was the fifth King of the Pischadian dynasty, lineally descended from Shedâd, who perished with the tribe of Ad. Zohak murdered his predecessor, and invented the punishments of the cross, and of fleaing alive. The Devil, who had long served him, requested at last as a recompense, permission to kiss his shoulders; immediately two serpents grew there, who fed upon his flesh, and endeavoured to get at his brain. The Devil now suggested a remedy, which was to quiet them by giving them every day the brains of two men, killed for that purpose: this tyranny lasted long; till a blacksmith of Ispahan, whose children had been nearly all slain to feed the King's serpents, raised his leathern apron as the standard of revolt, and deposed Zohak. Zohak, say the Persians, is still living in the cave of his punishment; a sulphureous vapour issues from the place; and, if a stone be flung in, there comes out a voice and cries, Why dost thou fling stones at me? This cavern is in the mountain of Demawend, which reaches from that of Elwend, towards Teheran.—*D'Herbelot. Olearius.*

Note 19, page 112, col. 1.
The salutary spell, etc.

I shall transcribe, says Grose, a foreign piece of superstition, firmly believed in many parts of France, Germany, and Spain. The account of it, and the mode of preparation, appears to have been given by a judge: in the latter there is a striking resemblance to the charm in Macbeth:

Of the Hand of Glory, which is made use of by house breakers, to enter into houses at night, without fear of opposition.

I acknowledge that I never tried the secret of the Hand of Glory, but I have thrice assisted at the definitive judgment of certain criminals, who, under the torture, confessed having used it. Being asked what it was, how they procured it, and what were its uses and properties? they answered, first, that the use of the Hand of Glory was to stupify those to whom it was presented, and to render them motionless, insomuch that they could not stir, any more than if they were dead; secondly, that it was the hand of a hanged man; and, thirdly, that it must be prepared in the manner following:

Take the hand, left or right, of a person hanged, and exposed on the highway; wrap it up in a piece of a shroud, or winding-sheet, in which let it be well squeezed, to get out any small quantity of blood that may have remained in it; then put it into an earthen vessel with Zimat, salpetre, salt, and long pepper, the whole well powdered; leave it fifteen days in that vessel; afterwards take it out, and expose it to the noontide sun in the dog-days, till it is thoroughly dry; and if the sun is not sufficient, put it into an oven heated with fern and vervain. Then compose a kind of candle with the fat of a hanged man, virgin wax, and sisame of Lapland. The Hand of Glory is used as a candlestick to hold this candle when lighted. Its properties are, that wheresoever any one goes with this dreadful instrument, the persons to whom it is presented will be deprived of all power of motion. On being asked if there was no remedy, or antidote, to counteract this charm, they said, the Hand of Glory would cease to take effect, and thieves could not make use of it, if the threshold of the door of the house, and other places by which they might enter, were anointed with an unguent composed of the gall of a black cat, the fat of a white hen, and the blood of a screech-owl; which mixture must necessarily be prepared during the dog-days. — *Grose. Provincial Glossary and Popular Superstitions.*

Something similar is recorded by Torquemade of the Mexican thieves. They carried with them the left hand and arm of a woman who had died in her first childbed; with this they twice struck the ground before the house which they designed to rob, and the door twice, and the threshold twice; and the inhabitants, if asleep, were hindered from waking by this charm; and, if awake, stupified and deprived of speech and motion while the fatal arm was in the house.—*Lib.* 14, c. 22.

Note 20, page 113, col. 1.
Some camel-kneed prayer-monger through the cave!

I knew not, when I used this epithet in derision, that the likeness had been seriously applied to St James. His knees were, after the guise of a camel's knee, benumbed and bereft of the sense of feeling, by reason of his continual kneeling in supplication to God, and petition for the people.—*Hegesippus, as quoted by Eusebius.*

Note 21, page 113, col. 1.
By some Saint's grave beside the public way, etc.

The habitations of the Saints are always beside the sanctuary, or tomb, of their ancestors, which they take care to adorn. Some of them possess, close to their houses, gardens, trees, or cultivated grounds, and particularly some spring or well of water. I was once travelling in the south in the beginning of October, when the season happened to be exceedingly hot, and the wells and rivulets of the country were all dried up. We had neither water for ourselves, nor for our horses; and after having taken much fruitless trouble to obtain some, we went and paid homage to a Saint, who at first pretended a variety of scruples before he would suffer infidels to approach; but, on promising to give him ten or twelve shillings, he became exceedingly humane, and supplied us with as much water as we wanted; still however vaunting highly of his charity, and particularly of his disinterestedness.—*Chenier.*

Note 22, page 113, col. 1.
Retail thy Koran scraps.

No nation in the world is so much given to superstition as the Arabs, or even as the Mahometans in general. They hang about their children's necks the figure of an open hand, which the Turks and Moors paint upon their ships and houses, as an antidote and counter-charm to an evil eye; for five is with them an unlucky number; and five (fingers perhaps) in your eyes, is their proverb of cursing and defiance. Those who are grown up, carry always about with them some paragraph or other of their Koran, which, like as the Jews did their phylacteries, they place upon their breast, or sew under their caps, to prevent fascination and witchcraft, and to secure themselves from sickness and misfortunes. The virtue of these charms and scrolls is supposed likewise to be so far universal, that they suspend them upon the necks of their cattle, horses, and other beasts of burden.
Shaw.

The hand-spell is still common in Portugal; it is called the *figa;* and thus probably our vulgar phrase—" *a fig for him,*" is derived from a Moorish amulet.

Note 23, page 113, col. 2.
Their robe of glory, purified of stain, etc.

In the Vision of Thurcillus, Adam is described as beholding the events of the world with mingled grief and joy; his original garment of glory gradually recovering its lustre, as the number of the elect increases, till it be fulfilled.—*Matthew Paris.*

This is more beautifully conceived than what the Archbishop of Toledo describes in his account of Mahommed's journey to Heaven : " Also in the first heaven I found a venerable man sitting upon a seat, and to him were shewn the souls of the dead; and when he beheld souls that did not please him, he turned away his eyes, saying, O sinful soul, thou hast departed from an unhappy body; and when a soul appeared which pleased him, then he said with applause, O happy Spirit, thou art come from a good body. I asked the Angel concerning a man so excellent, and of such reverence, who he should be; and he said it was Adam, who rejoiced in the good of his generation, but turned away his face from the evil.»

Roder. Ximenes.

BOOK VI.

Note 1, page 114, col. 1.

Of Solomon came down.

THE Arabian horses are divided into two great branches; the *Kadischi*, whose descent is unknown, and the *Kochlani*, of whom a written genealogy has been kept for 2000 years. These last are reserved for riding solely; they are highly esteemed, and consequently very dear; they are said to derive their origin from King Solomon's studs; however this may be, they are fit to bear the greatest fatigues, and can pass whole days without food; they are also said to show uncommon courage against an enemy; it is even asserted, that when a horse of this race finds himself wounded, and unable to bear his rider much longer, he retires from the fray, and conveys him to a place of security. If the rider falls upon the ground, his horse remains beside him, and neighs till assistance is brought. The *Kochlani* are neither large nor handsome, but amazingly swift; the whole race is divided into several families, each of which has its proper name. Some of these have a higher reputation than others, on account of their more ancient and uncontaminated nobility.— *Niebuhr.*

Note 2, page 114, col. 2.

And now, emerging, etc.

In travelling by night through the valleys of Mount Ephraim, we were attended, for above the space of an hour, with an Ignis Fatuus, that displayed itself in a variety of extraordinary appearances. For it was sometimes globular, or like the flame of a candle; immediately after it would spread itself and involve our whole company in its pale inoffensive light; then at once contract itself and disappear. But, in less than a minute, it would again exert itself as at other times; or else, running along from one place to another with a swift progressive motion, would expand itself, at certain intervals, over more than two or three acres of the adjacent mountains. The atmosphere, from the beginning of the evening, had been remarkably thick and hazy, and the dew, as we felt it upon our bridles, was unusually clammy and unctuous. In the like disposition of the weather, I have observed those luminous bodies, which at sea skip about the mast and yards of ships, and are called Corpusanse [1] by the mariners.— *Shaw.*

Note 3, page 114, col. 2.

They in their endless flow, etc.

The *Hammam Meskouteen*, the Silent or Inchanted Baths, are situated on a low ground, surrounded with mountains. There are several fountains that furnish the water, which is of an intense heat, and falls afterwards into the Zenati. At a small distance from these hot fountains, we have others, which, upon com-

parison, are of as intense a coldness; and a little below them, somewhat nearer the banks of the Zenati, there are the ruins of a few houses, built perhaps for the conveniency of such persons who came hither for the benefit of the waters.

Besides the strong sulphureous steams of the Hammam [1] Meskouteen, we are to observe farther of them, that their water is of so intense a heat, that the rocky ground it runs over, to the distance sometimes of a hundred feet, is dissolved, or rather calcined by it. When the substance of these rocks is soft and uniform, then the water, by making every way equal impressions, leaveth them in the shape of cones or hemispheres; which being six feet high, and a little more or less of the same diameter, the Arabs maintain to be so many tents of their predecessors turned into stone. But when these rocks, besides their usual soft chalky substance, contain likewise some layers of harder matter, not so easy to be dissolved; then, in proportion to the resistance the water is thereby to meet with, we are entertained with a confusion of traces and channels, distinguished by the Arabs into sheep, camels, horses, nay into men, women, and children, whom they suppose to have undergone the like fate with their habitations. I observed that the fountains which afforded this water, had been frequently stopped up; or rather ceasing to run at one place, broke out immediately in another; which circumstance seems not only to account for the number of cones, but for that variety likewise of traces, that are continued from one or other of these cones or fountains, quite down to the river Zenati.

This place, in riding over it, giveth back such a hollow sound, that we were afraid every moment of sinking through it. It is probable, therefore, that the ground below us was hollow; and may not the air, then, which is pent up within these caverns, afford, as we may suppose, in escaping continually through these fountains, that mixture of shrill, murmuring, and deep sounds, which, according to the direction of the winds and the motion of the external air, issue out along with the water? The Arabs, to quote their strength of imagination once more, affirm these sounds to be the music of the *Jenoune*, Fairies, who are supposed, in a particular manner, to make their abodes at this place, and to be the grand agents in all these extraordinary appearances.

There are other natural curiosities likewise at this place. For the chalky stone being dissolved into a fine impalpable powder, and carried down afterwards with the stream, lodgeth itself upon the sides of the channel, nay, sometimes upon the lips of the fountains themselves; or else, embracing twigs, straws, and other bodies in its way, immediately hardeneth, and shoots into a bright fibrous substance, like the Asbestos, forming itself at the same time into a variety of glittering figures, and beautiful crystallizations.—*Shaw.*

Note 4, page 115, col. 1.

By Oton-tala, like a sea of stars.

In the place where the Whang-ho rises there are more than an hundred springs which sparkle like stars, whence it is called Hotun Nor, the Sea of Stars. These

---

[1] A corruption of Cuerpo Santo, as this meteor is called by the Spaniards.

[1] They call the *Therma* of this country Hammams, from whence our Hummums.

sources form two great lakes called Hala Nor, the black sea or lake. Afterwards there appear three or four little rivers, which joined, form the Whang-ho, which has eight or nine branches. These sources of the river are called also Oton-tala. It is in Thibet.—*Gaubil. Astley's Collect. of Voy. and Travels.*

The Whang-ho, or, as the Portuguese call it, Hoamho, *i. e.* the Yellow-River, rises not far from the source of the Ganges, in the Tartarian mountains west of China, and having run through it with a course of more than six hundred leagues, discharges itself into the eastern sea. It hath its name from a yellow mud which always stains its water, and which, after rains, composes a third part of its quantity. The watermen clear it for use by throwing in alum. The Chinese say its waters cannot become clear in a thousand years; whence it is a common proverb among them for any thing which is never likely to happen, when the Yellow River shall run clear.—*Note to the Chinese Tale Hou Kiou Choan.*

Note 5, page 115, col. 2.
Beyond the same ascending straits, etc.

Among the mountains of the *Beni Abbess,* four leagues to the S. E. of the *Welled Mansoure,* we pass through a narrow winding defile, which, for the space of near half a mile, lieth on each side under an exceeding high precipice. At every winding, the rock or stratum that originally went across it, and thereby separated one valley from another, is cut into the fashion of a door-case six or seven feet wide, giving thereby the Arabs an occasion to call them *Beeban,* the Gates; whilst the Turks, in consideration of their strength and ruggedness, know them by the additional appellation of *Dammer Cappy,* the Gates of Iron. Few persons pass them without horror, a handful of men being able to dispute the passage with a whole army. The rivulet of salt water which glides through this valley, might possibly first point out the way which art and necessity would afterwards improve.—*Shaw.*

Note 6, page 115, col. 2.
No rich pavilions, bright with woven gold.

In 1568 the Persian Sultan gave the Grand Seigneur two most stately pavilions made of one piece, the curtains being interlaced with gold, and the supporters imbroidered with the same; also nine fair canopies to hang over the ports of their pavilions, things not used among the Christians.—*Knolles.*

Note 7, page 116, col. 1.
And broad-leaved plane-trees in long colonnades.

The expences the Persians are at in their gardens is that wherein they make greatest ostentation of their wealth. Not that they much mind furnishing of them with delightful flowers, as we do in Europe; but these they slight as an excessive liberality of Nature, by whom their common fields are strewed with an infinite number of tulips and other flowers; but they are rather desirous to have their gardens full of all sorts of fruit-trees, and especially to dispose them into pleasant walks of a kind of plane or poplar, a tree not known in Europe, which the Persians call Tzinnar. These trees grow up to the height of the Pine, and have very broad leaves, not much unlike those of the vine. Their fruit has some resemblance to the chesnut, while the outer

coat is about it, but there is no kernel within it, so that it is not to be eaten. The wood thereof is very brown, and full of veins; and the Persians use it in doors and shutters for windows, which, being rubbed with oil, look incomparably better than any thing made of walnut tree, nay indeed than the root of it, which is now [1] so very much esteemed.—*Amb. Travels.*

Note 8, page 116, col. 1.
With tulips, like the ruddy evening streak'd.

Major Scott informs us, that scars and wounds, by Persian writers, are compared to the streaky tints of the tulip. The simile here employed is equally obvious, and more suited to its place.

Note 9, page 116, col. 1.
And here amid her sable cup.

« We pitched our tents among some little hills where there was a prodigious number of lilies of many colours, with which the ground was quite covered. None were white, they were mostly either of a rich violet, with a red spot in the midst of each leaf, or of a fine black, and these were the most esteemed. In form they were like our lilies, but much larger."—*Tavernier.*

Note 10, page 116, col. 1.
Her paradise of leaves.

This expression is borrowed from one of Ariosto's smaller poems.

> Tal é proprio a veder quell' amorosa
> Fiamma, che nel bel viso
> Si sparge, ond' ella con soave riso
> Si va di sue bellezze innamorando;
> Qual' é a vedere, qual hor vermiglia rosa
> Scuopra il bel Paradiso
> De le rue foglie albor che 'l sol divino
> De l' Oriente sorge il giorno alzando.

Note 11, page 116, col. 1.
—— Of Orpheus bear a sweeter melody.

The Thracians say, that the nightingales which build their nests about the sepulchre of Orpheus, sing sweeter and louder than other nightingales.—*Pausanias.*

Gongora has addressed this bird with somewhat more than his usual extravagance of absurdity.

> Con diferencia tal, con gracia tanta
> Aquel Ruisenor llora, que sospecho,
> Que tiene otros cien mil dentro del pecho,
> Que alternan su dolor por su garganta.

> With such a grace that nightingale bewails,
> That I suspect, so exquisite his note,
> An hundred thousand other nightingales
> Within him, warble sorrow through his throat.

Note 12, page 116, col. 1.
Inhales her fragrant food.

In the *Caherman Nameh,* the Dives having taken in war some of the Peris, imprisoned them in iron cages which they hung from the highest trees they could find. There, from time to time, their companions visited them with the most precious odours. These odours were the usual food of the Peris, and procured them also another advantage, for they prevented the Dives from approaching or molesting them. The Dives could not bear the perfumes, which rendered them gloomy and melancholy whenever they drew near the cage in which a Peri was suspended.—*D'Herbelot.*

[1] 1637.

Note 13, page 116, col. 2.

Of man, for once, partook one common joy.

Dum autem ad nuptias celebrandas solemnissimum convivium pararetur, concussus est Angelis admirantibus, thronus Dei; atque ipse Deus majestate plenus præcepit Custodi Paradisi, ut puellas, ut pueros ejus cum festivis ornamentis educeret, et calices ad bibendum ordinatim disponeret: grandiores item puellas, et jam sororiantibus mammis præditas, ut juvenes illis coævos, pretiosis vestibus indueret. Jussit præterea Gabrielem vexillum laudis supra Meccanum Templum explicare. Tunc vero valles omnes et montes præ lætitiam gestire cœperunt, et tota Mecca nocte illa velut olla super ignem imposita efferbuit. Eodem tempore præcepit Deus Gabrieli, ut super omnes mortales unguenta pretiosissima dispergeret, admirantibus omnibus subitum illum atque insolitum odorem, quem in gratiam novorum conjugum divinitus exhalasse universi cognovere. —*Maracci.*

Note 14, page 116, col. 2.

On silken carpets sate the festive train.

Solymus II received the ambassadors sitting upon a pallet which the Turks call *Mastabe*, used by them in their chambers to sleep and to feed upon, covered with carpets of silk, as was the whole floor of the chamber also.—*Knolles.*

Among the presents that were exchanged between the Persian and Ottoman sovereigns in 1568, were carpets of silk, of camel's hair, lesser ones of silk and gold, and some called *Teftich*; made of the finest lawn, and so large that seven men could scarcely carry one of them.—*Knolles.*

In the beautiful story of Ali Beg, it is said Cha Sefi when he examined the house of his father's favourite, was much surprised at seeing it so badly furnished with plain skins and coarse carpets, whereas the other nobles in their houses trod only upon carpets of silk and gold.—*Tavernier.*

Note 15, page 116, col. 2.

Of pearly shell, etc.

On the way from Macao to Canton, in the rivers and channels, there is taken a vast quantity of oysters, of whose shells they make glass for the windows.—*Gemelli Careri.*

In the Chinese novel *Hau Kion Choann*, we read, Shuey-ping-sin ordered her servants to hang up a curtain of mother-of-pearl across the hall. She commanded the first table to be set for her guest without the curtain, and two lighted tapers to be placed upon it. Afterwards she ordered a second table, but without any light, to be set for herself within the curtain, so that *she could see every thing through it*, unseen herself.

Master George Tubervile, in his letters from Muscovy, 1568, describes the Russian windows:

They have no English glasse; of slices of a rocke
Hight Slada they their windows make, that English glasse doth mocke.
They cut it very thinne, and sow it with a thred
In pretie order like to panes, to serve their present need.
No other glasse, good faith, doth give a better light,
And sure the rock is nothing rich, the cost is very slight.
Hakluyt.

The Indians of Malabar use mother-of-pearl for window panes.—*Fra. Paolino da San Bartolomeo.*

Note 16, page 116, col. 2.

Or where the wine-vase, etc.

The King and the great Lords have a sort of cellar for magnificence, where they sometimes drink with persons whom they wish to regale. These cellars are square rooms, to which you descend by only two or three steps. In the middle is a small cistern of water, and a rich carpet covers the ground from the walls to the cistern. At the four corners of the cistern are four large glass bottles, each containing about twenty quarts of wine, one white, another red. From one to the other of these, smaller bottles are ranged of the same material and form, that is, round, with a long neck, holding about four or five quarts, white and red alternately. Round the cellar are several rows of niches in the wall, and in each niche is a bottle also of red and white alternately. Some niches are made to hold two. Some windows give light to the apartment, and all these bottles, so well ranged with their various colours, have a very fine effect to the eye. They are always kept full, the wine preserving better, and therefore are replenished as fast as they are emptied.—*Tavernier.*

Note 17, page 116, col. 2.

From golden goblets there, etc.

The Cuptzi, or king of Persia's merchant, treated us with a collation, which was served in, in plate vermilion gilt.

The Persians having left us, the ambassadors sent to the Chief Weywode a present, which was a large drinking cup, vermilion gilt.—*Ambassador's Travels.*

At Ispahan, the King's horses were watered with silver pails, thus coloured.

The Turks and Persians seem wonderfully fond of gilding; we read of their gilt stirrups, gilt bridles, gilt maces, gilt scymitars, etc. etc.

Note 18, page 116, col. 2.

That beverage, the mother of sins.

Mohammedes vinum appellabat *Matrem peccatorum;* cui sententiæ Hafez, Anacreon ille Persarum, minime ascribit suam; dicit autem.

« Acre illud (vinum) quod vir religiosus *matrem peccatorum* vocitat,

« Optabilius nobis ac dulcius videtur, quam virginis suavium.»—*Poeseos Asiat. Com.*

Illide ignem illum nobis liquidum,
Hoc est, ignem illum aquæ similem affer.
Hafez.

Note 19, page 116, col. 2.

That fragrant from its dewy vase, etc.

They export from Com earthen ware both white and varnished; and this is peculiar to the white ware which is thence transported, that in the summer it cools the water wonderfully and very suddenly, by reason of continual transpiration. So that they who desire to drink cool and deliciously, never drink in the same pot above five or six days at most. They wash it with rose-water the first time, to take away the ill smell of the earth, and they hang it in the air full of water, wrapped up in a moist linen cloth. A fourth part of the water transpires in six hours the first time: after that, still less from day to day, till at last the pores are closed up by the thick matter contained in the water which stops in the pores. But so soon as the pores are stopt, the water stinks in the pots, and you must take new ones.—*Chardin.*

In Egypt people of fortune burn *Scio mastic* in their cups; the penetrating odour of which pervades the porous substance, which remains impregnated with it a long time, and imparts to the water a perfume which requires the aid of habit to render it pleasing.—*Sonnini.*

Note 20, page 116, col. 2.
And Casbin's luscious grapes of amber hue.

Casbin produces the fairest grape in Persia, which they call *Chahoni*, or the royal grape, being of a gold colour, transparent, and as big as a small olive. These grapes are dried and transported all over the kingdom. They also make the strongest wine in the world, and the most luscious, but very thick, as all strong and sweet wines usually are. This incomparable grape grows only upon the young branches, which they never water. So that, for five months together, they grow in the heat of summer, and under a scorching sun, without receiving a drop of water, either from the sky or otherwise. When the vintage is over, they let in their cattle to browze in the vineyards; afterwards they cut off all the great wood, and leave only the young stocks about three feet high, which need no propping up with poles as in other places, and therefore they never make use of any such supporters. —*Chardin.*

Note 21, page 116, col. 2.
Here cased in ice, the apricot, etc.

Dr Fryer received a present from the Caun of Bunder-Abassæ, of apples candied in snow.

When Tavernier made his first visit to the Kan at Erivan, he found him with several of his officers regaling in the *Chambers of the Bridge.* They had wine which they cooled with ice, and all kinds of fruit and melons in large plates, under each of which was a plate of ice.

A great number of camels were laden with snow to cool the liquors and fruit of the Caliph Mahadi, when he made the pilgrimage to Mecca.

Note 22, page 117, col. 1.
Their ancles bound with bracelet-bells, etc.

Of the Indian dancing women who danced before the ambassadors at Ispahan, « some were shod after a very strange manner. They had above the instep of the foot a string tied, with little bells fastened thereto, whereby they discovered the exactness of their cadence, and sometimes corrected the music itself; as they did also by the Tzarpanes or Castagnets, which they had in their hands, in the managing whereof they were very expert.»

At Koojar, Mungo Park saw a dance « in which many performers assisted, all of whom were provided with little bells, which were fastened to their legs and arms.»

Note 23, page 117, col. 1.
Transparent garments to the greedy eye, etc.

At Seronge, a sort of cloth is made so fine, that the skin may be seen through it, as though it were naked. Merchants are not permitted to export this, the governor sending all that is made to the Seraglio of the Great Mogul, and the chief lords of his court. C'est de quoy les Sultanes et les femmes des Grands Seigneurs, se font des chemises, et des robes pour la chaleur, et le Roy et les Grands se plaisent à les voir au travers de ces chemises fines, et à les faire danser.—*Tavernier.*

Note 24, page 117, col. 1.
Loud from the chambers of the bridge below.

I came to a village called Cupri-Kent, or the Village of the Bridge, because there is a very fair bridge that stands not far from it, built upon a river called Tabadi. This bridge is placed between two mountains, separated only by the river, and supported by four arches, unequal both in their height and breadth. They are built after an irregular form, in regard of two great heaps of a rock that stand in the river, upon which they laid so many arches. Those at the two ends are hollowed on both sides, and serve to lodge passengers, wherein they have made to that purpose little chambers and porticos, with every one a chimney. The arch in the middle of the river is hollowed quite through, from one part to the other, with two chambers at the ends, and two large balconies covered, where they take the cool air in the summer with great delight, and to which there is a descent of two pair of stairs hewn out of the rock. There is not a fairer bridge in all Georgia.—*Chardin.*

Over the river Isperuth « there is a very fair bridge, built on six arches, each whereof hath a spacious room, a kitchen, and several other conveniences, lying even with water. The going down into it is by a stone pair of stairs, so that this bridge is able to find entertainment for a whole caravanne.»—*Amb. Tr.*

The most magnificent of these bridges is the bridge of Zulpha at Ispahan.

BOOK VII.

Note 1, page 117, col. 2.
Within its door, the lizard's track is left, etc.

THE dust which overspreads these beds of sand is so fine, that the lightest animal, the smallest insect, leaves there, as on snow, the vestiges of its track. The varieties of these impressions produce a pleasing effect, in spots where the saddened soul expects to meet with nothing but symptoms of the proscriptions of nature.— *It is impossible to see any thing more beautiful* than the traces of the passage of a species of very small lizards, extremely common in these deserts. The extremity of their tail forms regular sinuosities, in the middle of two rows of delineations, also regularly imprinted by their four feet, with their five slender toes. These traces are multiplied and interwoven near the subterranean retreats of these little animals, and present a singular assemblage which is *not void of beauty.*—*Sonnini.*

Note 2, page 118, col. 1.
In the world's foundations, etc.

These lines are feebly adapted from a passage in Burnet's Theory of the Earth.

Hæc autem dicta vellem de genuinis et majoribus terræ montibus; non gratos *Bacchi* colles hic intelligimus, aut amœnos illos monticulos, qui viridi herba et vicino fonte et arboribus, vim æstivi solis repellunt :

hisce non deest sua qualiscunque elegantia et jucunditas. Sed longe aliud hic respicimus, nempe longæva illa, tristia et squalentia corpora, telluris pondera, quæ duro capite rigent inter nubes, infixisque in terram saxeis pedibus, ab innumeris seculis steterunt immobilia, atque nudo pectore pertulerunt tot annorum ardentes soles, fulmina et procellas. Hi sunt primævi et immortales illi montes, qui non aliunde, quam ex fracta mundi compage ortum suum ducere potuerunt, nec nisi cum eadem perituri sunt.

The whole chapter *de montibus* is written with the eloquence of a poet. Indeed, Gibbon bestowed no exaggerated praise on Burnet in saying, that he had « blended scripture, history, and tradition, into one magnificent system, with a sublimity of imagination scarcely inferior to Milton himself.» This work should be read in Latin, the author's own translation is miserably inferior. He lived in the worst age of English prose.

Note 3, page 119, col. 1.
Of Zaccoum, cursed Tree.

The Zaccoum is a tree which issueth from the bottom of Hell; the fruit thereof resembleth the heads of devils; and the damned shall eat of the same, and shall fill their bellies therewith; and there shall be given them thereon a mixture of boiling water to drink; afterwards shall they return to Hell.—*Koran*, Chap. 37.

This Hellish Zaccoum has its name from a thorny tree in Tehama, which bears fruit like an almond, but extremely bitter; therefore the same name is given to the infernal tree.—*Sale.*

Note 4, page 119, col. 1.
Some daughter of the Homerites.

When the sister of the famous Derar was made prisoner before Damascus with many other Arabian women, she excited them to mutiny, they seized the poles of the tents, and attacked their captors. This bold resolution, says Marigny, was not inspired by impotent anger. Most of these women had military inclinations already; particularly those who were of the tribe of Himiar, or of the Homerites, where they are early exercised in riding the horse, and in using the bow, the lance, and the javelin. The revolt was successful, for, during the engagement, Derar came up to their assistance.—*Marigny.*

Note 5, page 119, col. 2.
The Paradise of Sin.

In the N. E. parts of Persia there was an old man named Aloadin, a Mahumetan, which had inclosed a goodly valley, situate between two hilles, and furnished it with all variety which nature and art could yield; as fruits, pictures, rilles of milk, wine, honey, water, pallaces, and beautiful damosells, richly attired, and called it Paradise. To this was no passage but by an impregnable castle; and daily preaching the pleasures of this Paradise to the youth which he kept in his court, sometimes would minister a sleepy drinke to some of them, and then conveigh them thither, where, being entertained with these pleasures four or five days, they supposed themselves rapt into Paradise, and then being again cast into a trance by the said drink, he caused them to be carried forth, and then would examine them of what they had scene, and by this delusion would make them resolute for any enterprize which he should

appoint them; as to murther any prince his enemy, for they feared not death in hope of their Mahumetical Paradise. But Haslor or Ulan, after three years siege, destroyed him, and this his fool's Paradise.—*Purchas.*

In another place, Purchas tells the same tale, but calls the impostor Aladeules, and says that Selim the Ottoman Emperor destroyed his Paradise.

The story is told by many writers, but with such difference of time and place, as wholly to invalidate its truth, even were the circumstances more probable.

Travelling on further towards the south, I arrived at a certaine countrey called Melistorte, which is a very pleasant and fertile place. And in this countrey there was a certeine aged man called Senex de Monte, who, round about two mountaines, had built a wall to inclose the sayd mountaines. Within this wall there were the fairest and most chrystall fountaines in the whole world; and about the sayd fountaines there were most beautiful virgins in great number, and goodly horses also; and, in a word, every thing that could be devised for bodily solace and delight, and therefore the inhabitants of the countrey call the same place by the name of Paradise.

The sayd olde Senex, when he saw any proper and valiant young man, he would admit him into his paradise. Moreover by certaine conducts, he makes wine and milk to flow abundantly. This Senex, when he hath a minde to revenge himselfe, or to slay any king or baron, commandeth him that is governor of the sayd Paradise to bring thereunto some of the acquaintance of the sayd king or baron, permitting him a while to take his pleasure therein, and then to give him a certeine potion, being of force to cast him into such a slumber as should make him quite void of all sense, and so being in a profounde sleepe, to convey him out of his paradise: who being awaked, and seeing himselfe thrust out of the paradise, would become so sorrowfull, that he could not in the world devise what to do, or whither to turne him. Then would he go unto the forsaide old man, beseeching him that he might be admitted againe into his paradise: who saith unto him, you cannot be admitted thither, unlesse you will slay such or such a man for my sake, and if you will give the attempt onely, whether you kill him or no, I will place you againe in paradise, that there you may remaine alwayes. Then would the party, without faile, put the same in execution, indeavouring to murther all those against whom the sayd olde man had conceived any hatred. And therefore all the kings of the East stood in awe of the sayd olde man, and gave unto him great tribute.

And when the Tartars had subdued a great part of the world, they came unto the sayd olde man, and tooke from him the custody of his paradise; who being incensed thereat, sent abroad divers desperate and resolute persons out of his forenamed paradise, and caused many of the Tartarian nobles to be slain. The Tartars, seeing this, went and besieged the city wherein the sayd olde man was, tooke him, and put him to a most cruell and ignominious death.—*Odoricus.*

The most particular account is given by that undaunted liar, Sir John Maundeville.

« Beside the Yle of Pentexoire, that is, the Lond of Prestre John, is a gret Yle, long and brode, that men clepen Milsterak; and it is in the Lordschipe of Prestre John. In that Yle is gret plentee of godes. There was

23

dwellinge sometyme a riche man ; and it is not long sithen, and men clept him Gatholonabes; and he was full of cauteles, and of sotyle disceytes; and had a fulle fair castelle, and a strong, in a mountayne, so strong and so noble, that no man cowde devise a fairere, ne a strengere.   And he had let muren all the mountayne aboute with a stronge walle and a fair. And withinne the walles he had the fairest gardyn that ony man might behold ; and therein were trees berynge all manner of frutes that ony man cowde devyse, and therein were also alle maner vertuous herbes of gode smelle, and all other herbes also that beren fair floures, and he had also in that gardyn many faire welles, and beside the welles he had lete make faire halles and faire chambres, depeynted alle with gold and azure. And there weren in that place many diverse thinges, and many diverse stories ; and of bestes and of bryddes that songen fulle delectabely, and moveden be craft that it semede that thei weren quike. And he had also in his gardyn all maner of fowles and of bestes, that ony man might thinke on, for to have pley or desport to beholde hem. And he had also in that place, the faireste damyseles that mighte ben founde under the age of 15 zere, and the fairest songe striplynges that men mighte gete of that same age ; and all thei weren clothed in clothes of gold fully rychely, and he seyde that tho weren angeles. And he had also let make three welles faire and noble, and all envyrouud with ston of jaspre, of cristalle, diapred with gold, and sett with precious stones, and grete orient perles. And he had made a conduyt under erthe, so that the three welles, at his list, on scholde renne milk, another wyn, and another hony, and that place he clept paradys. And whan that ony godd knyght, that was hardy and noble, came to see this Rialtee, he would lede him into his paradys, and schewen him theise wondirfulle thinges to his desport, and the marveyllous and delicious song of dyverse bryddes, and the faire damyseles and the faire welles of milk, wyn, and honey plenteyous rennynge. And he woulde let make dyverse instruments of musick to sownen in an high tour, so merily, that it was joye for to here, and no man scholde see the craft thereof : and tho, he sayde, weren Aungeles of God, and that place was paradys, that God had behyghte to his friendes, saying, *Dabo vobis terram fluentem lacte et melle.* And thanne wolde he maken hem to drynken of certeyn drink, whereof anon thei sholden be drouken, and thanne wolde hem thinken gretter delyt than thei hadden before. And then wolde he seye to hem, that zif thei wolde dyen for him and for his love, that after hire dethe thei scholde come to his paradys, and their scholde ben of the age of the damyseles, and thei scholde pleyen with hem and zit ben maydenes. And after that zit scholde he putten hem in a fayrere paradys, where that thei scholde see God of nature visibely in his magestee and in his blisse. And than wolde he schewe hem his entent and seye hem, that zif thei wolde go sle such a lord, or such a man, that was his enemye, or contrarious to his list, that thei scholde not drede to don it, and for to be sleyn therefore hemselfe ; for aftir hire dethe he wolde putten hem into another paradys, that was an hundred fold fairere than ony of the tothere : and there scholde thei dwellen with the most fairest damyseles that mighte be, and pley with hem ever more. And thus wenten many dyverse lusty bacheleres for to sle grete lords, in dyverse countrees, that weren his enemyes, and maden hemself to ben slayn in hope to have that paradys. And thus often tyme he

was revenged of his enemyes by his sotyle disceytes and false cauteles. And whan the worthe men of the contree hadden perceived this sotyle falshod of this Gatholonabes, thei assembled hem with force, and assayleden his castelle, and slowen him, and destroyden all the faire places, and alle the nobletees of that paradys. The place of the welles, and of the walles, and of many other thinges, bene zit apertly sene ; but the richesse is voyded clene. And it is not long gon sithen that place was destroyed.»
                                 Sir John Maundeville.

Note 6, page 120, col. 2.
« The man who serves him well !»

Let the royal apparel be brought which the king useth to wear, and the horse that the king rideth upon, and the crown royal which is set upon his head.

And let this apparel and horse be delivered to the hand of one of the king's most noble princes, that they may array the man withal whom the king delighteth to honour, and bring him on horseback through the street of the city, and proclaim before him, Thus shall it be done to the man whom the king delighteth to honour. —*Esther*, vi, 8, 9.

Note 7, page 121, col. 1.
Take me then to Mecca !

The Sheik Kotheddin discusses the question, whether it be, upon the whole, an advantage or disadvantage to live at Mecca ? for all doctors agree, that good works performed there have double the merit which they would have any where else. He therefore inquires, Whether the guilt of sins must not be augmented in a like proportion ?—*Notices des MSS. de la Bibl. Nat. t.* 4. 541.

BOOK VIII.

Note 1, page 122, col. 1.
« But when the Cryer from the Minaret,» etc.

As the celestial Apostle, at his retreat from *Medina*, did not perform always the five canonical prayers at the precise time, his disciples, who often neglected to join with him in the *Namaz*, assembled one day to fix upon some method of announcing to the public those moments of the day and night when their master discharged this first of religious duties. Flags, bells, trumpets, and fire, were successively proposed as signals. None of these, however, were admitted. The flags were rejected as unsuited to the sanctity of the object; the bells, on account of their being used by Christians; the trumpets, as appropriated to the Hebrew worship ; the fires, as having too near an analogy to the religion of the pyrolators. From this contrariety of opinions, the disciples separated without any determination. But one of them, *Abdullah ibn Zeid Abderyê*, saw the night following, in a dream, a celestial being clothed in green; he immediately requested his advice, with the most zealous earnestness, respecting the object in dispute. I am come to inform you, replied the heavenly visitor, how to discharge this important duty of your religion. He then ascended to the roof of the house, and declared the *Ezann* with a loud voice, and in the same words which have been ever since used to declare the canonical periods. When he awoke, *Abdullah* ran to declare his vision to the prophet, who loaded him with blessings.

and authorized that moment *Bilal Habeschy*, another of his disciples, to discharge, on the top of his house, that august office, by the title of *Muezzinn*.

These are the words of the Ezann: « Most high God! most high God! most high God! I acknowledge that there is no other except God; I acknowledge that there is no other except God! I acknowledge that *Mohammed* is the Prophet of God! Come to prayer! come to prayer! come to the temple of salvation? Great God! great God! there is no God except God.»

This declaration must be the same for each of the five canonical periods, except that of the morning, when the *Muezzinn* ought to add, after the words, *come to the temple of salvation*, the following: *prayer is to be preferred to sleep, prayer is to be preferred to sleep.*

This addition was produced by the zeal and piety of *Bilal Habeschy:* as he announced one day the Ezann of the dawn in the prophet's antichamber, Aische, in a whisper, informed him, that the celestial envoy was still asleep; this first of *Muezzinns* then added these words, *prayer is to be preferred to sleep;* when he awoke, the prophet applauded him, and commanded *Bilal* to insert them in all the morning Ezanns.

The words must be chanted, but with deliberation and gravity, those particularly which constitute the profession of the faith. The *Muezzinn* must pronounce them distinctly; he must pay more attention to the articulation of the words than to the melody of his voice; he must make proper intervals and pauses, and not precipitate his words, but let them be clearly understood by the people. He must be interrupted by no other object whatever. During the whole Ezann, he must stand with a finger in each ear, and his face turned, as in prayer, towards the *Keabe* of *Mecca*. As he utters these words, *come to prayer, come to the temple of salvation*, he must turn his face to the right and left, because he is supposed to address all the nations of the world, the whole expanded universe. At this time the auditors must recite, with a low voice, the *Tehhlil.* . . There is no strength, there is no power, but what is in God, in that supreme Being, in that powerful Being.—*D'Ohsson.*

Note 2, page 122, col. 1.

In the Meidan now, etc.

In the Meidan, or Great Place of the city of Tauris, there are people appointed every evening when the sun sets, and every morning when he rises, to make during half an hour a terrible concert of trumpets and drums. They are placed on one side of the square, in a gallery somewhat elevated; and the same practice is established in every city in Persia.—*Tavernier.*

Note 3, page 122, col. 2.

Into the Chamber of the Tomb, etc.

If we except a few persons, who are buried within the precincts of some sanctuary, the rest are carried out at a distance from their cities and villages, where a great extent of ground is allotted for that purpose. Each family hath a particular portion of it, walled in like a garden, where the bones of their ancestors have remained undisturbed for many generations. For in these enclosures[1] the graves are all distinct and separate; having each of them a stone, placed upright, both at the head and feet, inscribed with the name of the person who lieth there interred; whilst the intermediate space is either planted with flowers, bordered round with stone, or paved all over with tiles. The graves of the principal citizens are further distinguished by some square chambers or cupolas[1] that are built over them.

Now, as all these different sorts of tombs and sepulchres, with the very walls likewise of the enclosures, are constantly kept clean, white-washed, and beautified, they continue, to this day, to be an excellent comment upon that expression of our Saviour's, where he mentions the *garnishing of the sepulchres*, and again where he compares the scribes, pharisees, and hypocrites, to *whited sepulchres, which indeed appear beautiful outward, but are within full of dead men's bones and all uncleanness.* For the space of two or three months after any person is interred, the female relations go once a week to weep over the grave, and perform their parentalia upon it.—*Shaw.*

About a quarter of a mile from the town of Mylasa, is a sepulchre of the species called by the ancients, *Distæya*, or *Double-roofed.* It consisted of two square rooms. In the lower, which has a door-way, were deposited the urns, with the ashes of the deceased. In the upper, the relations and friends solemnized the anniversary of the funeral, and performed stated rites. A hole made through the floor was designed for pouring libations of honey, milk, or wine, with which it was usual to gratify the manes or spirits.—*Chandler's Travels in Asia Minor.*

St Anthony the Great once retired to the sepulchres; a brother shut him in one of the tombs, and regularly brought him food. One day he found the doors of the tomb broken, and Anthony lying upon the ground as dead, the devil had so mauled him. Once a whole army of devils attacked him; the place was shaken from its foundation, the walls were thrown down, and the crowd of multiform fiends rushed in. They filled the place with the shapes of lions, and bulls, and wolves, asps, serpents, scorpions, pards, and bears, yelling, and howling, and threatening, and flogging and wounding him. The brave saint defied them, and upbraided them for their cowardice in not attacking him one to one, and defended himself with the sign of the cross. And lo, a light fell from above, which at once put the hellish rabble to flight, and healed his wounds, and strengthened him; and the walls of the sepulchre rose from their ruins. Then knew Anthony the presence of the Lord, and the voice of Christ proceeded from the light, to comfort and applaud him.

Acta Sanctorum, tom. 2. *Jan.* 17. P. 123.
Vita S. Ant. auctore S. Athanasio.

The Egyptian saints frequently inhabited sepulchres. St James the hermit found an old sepulchre, made in the form of a cave, wherein many bones of the dead had been deposited, which, by length of time, were now become as dust. Entering there, he collected the bones into a heap, and laid them in a corner of the monument, and closed upon himself the old door of the cave.

Acta Sanct. tom. 2. *Jan.* 28. P. 872.
Vita S. Jacobi Eremitæ, apud Metaphrasten.

[1] They seem to be the same with the Περιϐολοι of the Ancients. Thus Euripides. Troad. 1, 4141.

Αλλ' αντι κεδρου περιϐολων τελαινων
Εν τηδε Θαψαι παιδα.

[1] Such places probably as these are to be understood, when the Demoniac is said to have *his dwelling among the tombs.*

Note 4, page 122, col. 2.
———— the vampire corpse, etc.

In the *Lettres Juives*, is the following extract from the *Mercure Historique et Politique*, Octob. 1736.

We have had in this country a new scene of Vampirism, which is duly attested by two officers of the Tribunal of *Belgrade*, who took cognizance of the affair on the spot, and by an officer in his Imperial Majesty's troops at *Gradisch* (in *Sclavonia*) who was an eye-witness of the proceedings.

In the beginning of September, there died at the village of *Kisilova*, three leagues from *Gradisch*, an old man of above threescore and two: three days after he was buried, he appeared in the night to his son, and desired he would give him somewhat to eat, and then disappeared. The next day the son told his neighbours these particulars. That night the father did not come, but the next evening he made him another visit, and desired something to eat. It is not known whether his son gave him any thing or not, but the next morning the young man was found dead in his bed. The magistrate or bailiff of the place had notice of this; as also that the same day five or six persons fell sick in the village, and died one after the other. He sent an exact account of this to the tribunal of *Belgrade*, and thereupon two commissioners were dispatched to the village, attended by an executioner, with instructions to examine closely into the affair. An officer in the Imperial service, from whom we have this relation, went also from *Gradisch*, in order to examine personally an affair of which he had heard so much. They opened in the first place the graves of all who had been buried in six weeks. When they came to that of the old man, they found his eyes open, his colour fresh, his respiration quick and strong, yet he appeared to be stiff and insensible. From these signs, they concluded him to be a notorious *Vampire*. The executioner thereupon, by the command of the commissioners, struck a stake through his heart; and when he had so done, they made a bonfire, and therein consumed the carcase to ashes. There was no marks of Vampirism found on his son, or on the bodies of the other persons who died so suddenly.

Thanks be to God, we are as far as any people can be from giving into credulity; we acknowledge that all the lights of physic do not enable us to give any account of this fact, nor do we pretend to enter into its causes. However, we cannot avoid giving credit to a matter of fact juridically attested by competent and unsuspected witnesses, especially since it is far from being the only one of the kind. We shall here annex an instance of the same sort in 1732, already inserted in the Gleaner, No. 18.

In a certain town of *Hungary*, which is called in Latin *Oppida Reidonum*, on the other side *Tibiscus*, vulgarly called the *Teysse*, that is to say, the river which washes the celebrated territory of *Tokay*, as also a part of *Transylvania*, the people known by the name of *Heydukes* believe that certain dead persons, whom they call Vampires, suck the blood of the living, insomuch that these people appear like skeletons, while the dead bodies of the suckers are so full of blood, that it runs out at all the passages of their bodies, and even at their very pores. This old opinion of theirs they support by a multitude of facts, attested in such a manner, that they leave no room for doubt. We shall here mention some of the most considerable.

It is now about five years ago, that a certain *Heyduke*, an inhabitant of the village of *Medreiga*, whose name was Arnold Paul, was bruised to death by a hay-cart which ran over him. Thirty days after his death, no less than four persons died suddenly in that manner, wherein, according to the tradition of the country, those people generally die who are sucked by Vampires. Upon this a story was called to mind that this *Arnold Paul* had told in his life-time, viz. that at *Cossova*, on the frontiers of the *Turkish Servia*, he had been tormented by a Vampire; (now the established opinion is, that a person sucked by a Vampire becomes a Vampire himself, and sucks in his turn.) But that he had found a way to rid himself of this evil, by eating some of the earth out of the Vampire's grave, and rubbing himself with his blood. This precaution, however, did not hinder his becoming a Vampire; insomuch, that his body being taken up forty days after his death, all the marks of a notorious Vampire were found thereon. His complexion was fresh, his hair, nails, and beard were grown; he was full of fluid blood, which ran from all parts of his body upon his shroud. The *Hadnagy* or *Bailiff* of the place, who was a person well acquainted with Vampirism, caused a sharp stake to be thrust, as the custom is, through the heart of *Arnold Paul*, and also quite through his body; whereupon he cried out dreadfully as if he had been alive. This done, they cut off his head, burnt his body, and threw the ashes thereof into the *Saave*. They took the same measures with the bodies of those persons who had died of Vampirism, for fear that they should fall to sucking in their turns.

All these prudent steps did not hinder the same mischief from breaking out again about five years afterwards, when several people in the same village died in a very odd manner. In the space of three months, seventeen persons of all ages and sexes died of Vampirism, some suddenly, and some after two or three days suffering. Amongst others, there was one *Stanoska*, the daughter of a *Heyduke*, whose name was *Jovitzo*, who, going to bed in perfect health, waked in the middle of the night, and making a terrible outcry, affirmed, that the son of a certain *Heyduke*, whose name was *Millo*, and who had been dead about three weeks, had attempted to strangle her in her sleep. She continued from that time in a languishing condition, and in the space of three days died. What this girl had said, discovered the son of *Millo* to be a Vampire. They took up the body, and found him so in effect. The principal persons of the place, particularly the physician and surgeons, began to examine very narrowly, how, in spite of all their precautions, Vampirism had again broke out in so terrible a manner. After a strict inquisition, they found that the deceased *Arnold Paul* had not only sucked the four persons before mentioned, but likewise several beasts, of whom the new Vampires had eaten, particularly the son of *Millo*. Induced by these circumstances, they took a resolution of digging up the bodies of all persons who had died within a certain time. They did so, and amongst forty bodies, there were found seventeen evidently Vampires. Through the hearts of these they drove stakes, cut off their heads, burnt their bodies, and threw the ashes into the river. All the informations we have been speaking of, were taken in a legal way, and all the executions were so performed, as appears by certificates drawn up in full form, attested by several officers in the neighbouring garrisons, by the surgeons of several regiments, and the principal inhabitants of the place. The verbal process was sent towards the latter end of last January, to the council of war at *Vienna*, who thereupon established a special commission to examine into these facts. Those just now mentioned were attested by the *Hadnagi Barriarer*, the principal *Heyduke* of the village, as also by *Battuer*, first lieutenant of Prince *Alexander of Wirtemberg*, *Flickstenger*, surgeon major of the regiment of *Fürstemberg*, three other surgeons of the same regiment, and several other persons.

This superstition extends to Greece.

The man, whose story we are going to relate, was a peasant of Mycone, naturally ill-natured and quarrelsome; this is a circumstance to be taken notice of in such cases. He was murdered in the fields, nobody knew how, or by whom. Two days after his being buried in a chapel in the town, it was noised about that he was seen to walk in the night with great haste, that he tumbled about people's goods, put out their lamps, griped them behind, and a thousand other monkey tricks. At first the story was received with laughter; but the thing was looked upon to be serious when the better sort of people began to complain of it; the Papas themselves gave credit to the fact, and no doubt had their reasons for so doing: masses must be said, to be sure: but for all this, the peasant drove his old trade, and heeded nothing they could do. After divers meetings of the chief people of the city, of priests, and monks, it was gravely concluded, that it was necessary, in consequence of some musty ceremonial, to wait till nine days after the interment should be expired.

On the tenth day, they said one mass in the chapel where the body was laid, in order to drive out the Demon which they imagined was got into it. After mass, they took up the body, and got every thing ready for pulling out its heart. The butcher of the town, an old clumsy fellow, first opens the belly instead of the breast; he groped a long while among the entrails, but could not find what he looked for; at last, somebody told him he should cut up the diaphragm. The heart was then pulled out, to the admiration of all the spectators. In the mean time, the corpse stunk so abominably, that they were obliged to burn frankincense; but the smoke mixing with the exhalations from the carcase, increased the stink, and began to muddle the poor people's pericranies. Their imagination, struck with the spectacle before them, grew full of visions. It came into their noddles that a thick smoke came out of the body; we durst not say it was the smoke of the incense. They were incessantly bawling out Vroucolacas, in the chapel and place before it; this is the name they give to these pretended Redivivi. The noise bellowed through the streets, and it seemed to be a name invented on purpose to rend the roof of the chapel. Several there present averred, that the wretch's blood was extremely red; the butcher swore the body was still warm; whence they concluded that the deceased was a very ill man for not being thoroughly dead, or, in plain terms, for suffering himself to be re-animated by Old Nick; which is the notion they have of Vroucolacas.

They then roared out that name in a stupendous manner. Just at this time came in a flock of people, loudly protesting, they plainly perceived the body was not grown stiff, when it was carried from the fields to church to be buried, and that consequently it was a true Vroucolacas; which word was still the burden of the song.

I don't doubt they would have sworn it did not stink, had not we been there; so mazed were the poor people with this disaster, and so infatuated with their notion of the dead being re-animated. As for us, who were got as close to the corpse as we could, that we might be more exact in our observations, we were almost poisoned with the intolerable stink that issued from it. When they asked us what we thought of this body, we told them we believed it to be very thoroughly dead: but as we were willing to cure, or at least not to exasperate their prejudiced imaginations, we represented to them, that it was no wonder the butcher should feel a little warmth when he groped among entrails that were then rotting, that it was no extraordinary thing for it to emit fumes, since dung turned up will do the same; that as for the pretended redness of the blood, it still appeared by the butcher's hands to be nothing but a very stinking nasty smear.

After all our reasons, they were of opinion it would be their wisest course to burn the dead man's heart on the sea-shore: but this execution did not make him a bit more tractable; he went on with his racket more furiously than ever; he was accused of beating folks in the night, breaking down doors, and even roofs of houses, clattering windows, tearing clothes, emptying bottles and vessels. It was the most thirsty devil! I believe he did not spare any body but the Consul in whose house we lodged. Nothing could be more miserable than the condition of this island; all the inhabitants seemed frighted out of their senses: the wisest among them were stricken like the rest; it was an epidemical disease of the brain, as dangerous and infectious as the madness of dogs. Whole families quitted their houses, and brought their tent beds from the farthest parts of the town into the public place, there to spend the night. They were every instant complaining of some new insult; nothing was to be heard but sighs and groans at the approach of night: the better sort of people retired into the country.

When the prepossession was so general, we thought it our best way to hold our tongues. Had we opposed it, we had not only been accounted ridiculous blockheads, but Atheists and Infidels; how was it possible to stand against the madness of a whole people? Those that believed that we doubted the truth of the fact, came and upbraided us with our incredulity, and strove to prove that there were such things as Vroucolacasses, by citations out of the Buckler of Faith, written by F. Richard, a Jesuit Missionary. He was a Latin, say they, and consequently you ought to give him credit. We should have got nothing by denying the justness of the consequence: it was as good as a comedy to us every morning to hear the new follies committed by this night bird; they charged him with being guilty of the most abominable sins.

Some citizens, that were most zealous for the good of the public, fancied they had been deficient in the most material part of the ceremony. They were of opinion that they had been wrong in saying mass be-

Note 5, page 128, col. 1.

Waste on the wind his baffled witchery.

A serpent which that aspidis
Is cleped, of his kinde hath this,
That he the stone, noblest of all,
The whiche that men carbuncle call,
Bereth in his head above on hight.
For whiche, whan that a man by slight
The stone to wynne, and him to dante,
With his carecte him wolde enchante,
Anone as he perceiveth that
He leyth downe his one ear all plat
Unto the ground, and halt it fast,
And eke that other eare als faste
He stoppeth with his taille so sore,
That he the wordes, lasse or more
Of his enchantement ne hereth.
And in this wise himself he skiereth,
So that he hath the wordes wayved,
And thus his eare is nought deceived.

Gower.

Does not « the deaf adder, that heareth not the voice of the charmer, charm he never so wisely,» allude to some snake that cannot be enticed by music, as they catch them in Egypt?

Note 6, page 128, col. 2.

That, from the perforated tree forced out.

As for the wax, it is the finest and whitest that may be had, though of bees : and there is such plenty as serves the whole empire. Several provinces produce it, but that of Huquam exceeds all the others, as well in quantity as whiteness. It is gathered in the province of Xantung, upon little trees ; but in that of Huquam, upon large ones, as big as those of the Indian pagods, or chesnut trees in Europe. The way nature has found to produce it, to us appears strange enough. There is in this province, a creature or insect, of the bigness of a flea, so sharp at stinging that it not only pierces the skins of men and beasts, but the boughs and bodies of the trees. Those of the province of Xantung are much valued, where the inhabitants gather their eggs from the trees, and carry them to sell in the province of Huquam. In the spring, there come from these eggs certain worms, which, about the beginning of the summer, they place at the foot of the tree, whence they creep up, spreading themselves wonderfully over all the branches. Having placed themselves there, they gnaw, pierce, and bore to the very pith, and their nourishment they convert into wax, as white as snow, which they drive out of the mouth of the hole they have made, where it remains congealed in drops by the wind and cold. Then the owners of the trees gather it, and make it into cakes as we do, which are sold about China.—*Gemelli Careri.*

Du Halde's account is somewhat different from this; the worms, he says, fasten on the leaves of the tree, and in a short time form combs of wax, much smaller than the honey-combs.

Note 7, page 128, col. 2.

A fire to kindle that strange fuel meet.

It being notorious that fire enters into the composition of a devil, because he breathes smoke and flames, there is an obvious propriety in supposing every witch her own tinder-box, as they approximate to diabolic nature. I am sorry that I have not the Hierarchie of the Blessed Angels to refer to; otherwise, by the best authorities, I could show that is the trick of Beelzebub to parody the costume of religion. The inflammability of saints may be abundantly exampled.

It happened upon a tyme, before St Elfled was chosen Abbesse, that being in the church at mattins, before day, with the rest of her sisters, and going into the middest, according to the costume, to read a lesson, the candle wherewith she saw to read, chanced to be put out, and thereupon wanting light, there came from the fingers of her right hand such an exceeding brightness upon the suddaine, that not only herselfe, but all the rest of the quire also, might read by it.—*English Martyrologe,* 1608.

Dead saints have frequently possessed this phosphoric quality, like rotten wood or dead fish. « St Bridget was interred at the towne of Dunne, in the province of Ulster, in the tombe togeather with the venerable bodyes of St Patricke and St. Columbe, which was afterward miraculously reveyled to the bishop of that place, as he was praying one night late in the church, about the yeare of Christ 1176, over which there shined a great light.»—*English Martyrologe.*

So, when the nurse of Mohammed first entered the chamber of Amena, his mother, she saw a coruscating splendour, which was the light of the infant prophet, so that Amena never kindled her lamp at night.—*Maracci.*

Another Mohammedan miracle of the same genus, is no ways improbable. When the head of Hosein was brought to Couffah, the governor's gates were closed, and Haula, the bearer, took it to his own house. He awoke his wife, and told her what had so speedily brought him home. I bring with me, said he, the most valuable present that could possibly be made to the Caliph. And the woman asking eagerly what it could be? the head of Hosein ; here it is ; I am sent with it to the governor. Immediately she sprung from the bed, not that she was shocked or terrified at the sight, for the Arabian women were accustomed to follow the army, and habituated to the sight of blood and massacre. But Hosein, by Fatima, his mother, was grandson of the prophet, and this produced an astonishing effect upon the mind of the woman. By the apostle of God, she exclaimed, I will never again lie down with a man who has brought me the head of his grandson. The Moslem who, according to the custom of his nation, had many wives, sent for another, who was not so conscientious. Yet the presence of the head, which was placed upon a table, prevented her from sleeping, *because,* she said, *she saw a great glory playing around it all night.*—*Marigny.*

After Affonso de Castro had been martyred in one of the Molucca islands, his body was thrown into the sea. But it was in a few days brought back by Providence to the spot where he had suffered, the wounds fresh as if just opened, and so strange and beautiful a splendour flowing from them, that it was evident the fountain of such a light must be that body, whose spirit was in the enjoyment of eternal happiness.

The Moors interpreted one of these *phosphoric* miracles, with equal ingenuity, to favour their own creed. A light was seen every night over the tomb of a Maronite whom they had martyred ; and they said the priest was not only tortured with fire in hell, but his very body burnt in the grave.—*Vasconcellos.*

Note 8, page 128, col. 2.
« There, waste away !» the Enchantress cried.

A well-known ceremony of witchcraft, old as classical superstition, and probably not yet wholly disbelieved.

Note 9, page 128, col. 2.
It lay amid the flames, etc.

Beautifully hath Milton painted this legend. « The fire, when it came to proof, would not do his work; but, *starting off like a full sail from the mast,* did but reflect a golden light upon his unviolated limbs, exhaling such a sweet odour, as if all the incense of Arabia had been burning.»—*Of Prelatical Episcopacy.*

Note 10, page 129, col. 1.
« The fore-world's wood to build the magic pile.»

On Mount Ararat, which is called *Lubar,* or the descending place, is an abbey of St Gregorie's Monks. These Monks, if any list to believe them, say that there remaineth yet some part of the arke, kept by angels, which if any seeke to ascend, carrie them backe as farre in the night, as they have climbed in the day.—*Purchas.*

Note 11, page 129, col. 1.
« Wreathes the Cerastes round her playful child.»

A thicket of balm trees is said to have sprung up from the blood of the Moslem slain at Beder.

Ælianus avoucheth, that those vipers which breed in the provinces of Arabia, although they do bite, yet their biting is not venomous, because they doe feede on the baulme tree, and sleepe under the shadow thereof. —*Treasury of Ancient and Modern Times.*

The balsam tree is nearly of the same size as a sprig of myrtle, and its leaves are like those of the herb sweet marjoram. Vipers take up their residence about these plants, and are in some places more numerous than in others; for the juice of the balsam tree is their sweetest food, and they are delighted with the shade produced by its leaves. When the time therefore arrives for gathering the juice of this tree, the Arabians come into the sacred grove, each of them holding two twigs. By shaking these, they put to flight the vipers; for they are unwilling to kill them, because they consider them as the sacred inhabitants of the balsam. And if it happens that any one is wounded by a viper, the wound resembles that which is made by iron, but is not attended with any dangerous consequences; for these animals being fed with the juice of the balsam tree, which is the most odoriferous of all trees, their poison becomes changed from a deadly quality into one which produces a milder effect.—*Pausanias.*

The inhabitants of Helicon say, that none of the herbs or roots which are produced in this mountain, are destructive to mankind. They add, that the pastures here even debilitate the venom of serpents; so that those who are frequently bit by serpents in this part, escape the danger with greater ease than if they were of the nation of the Psylli, or had discovered an antidote against poison.—*Pausanias.*

Note 12, page 129, col. 1.
« There is a Grave-wax, . . I have seen the Gouls,» etc.

The common people of England have long been acquainted with this change which muscular fibre undergoes. Before the circumstance was known to philoso-phers, I have heard them express a dislike and loathing to spermaceti, because it was dead men's fat.

Note 13, page 129, col. 2.
Feel feet unho'y trampling over them.

The Persians are strangely superstitious about the burial of their kings. For, fearing lest by some magical art, any enchantments should be practised upon their bodies to the prejudice of their children, they conceal, as much as in them lies, the real place of interment.

To this end, they send to several places several coffins of lead, with others of wood, which they call Taboat, and bury all alike with the same magnificence. In this manner they delude the curiosity of the people, who cannot discern by the outside, in which of the coffins the real body should be. Not but it might be discovered by such as would put themselves to the expense and trouble of doing it. And thus it shall be related in the life of Habas the Great, that twelve of these coffins were conveyed to twelve of the principal Mosques, not for the sake of their riches, but of the person which they enclosed; and yet nobody knew in which of the twelve the King's body was laid, though the common belief is, that it was deposited at Ardevil.

It is also said in the life of Sefie I, that there were three coffins carried to three several places, as if there had been a triple production from one body, though it were a thing almost certainly known, that the coffin where the body was laid, was carried to the same city of Kom, and to the same place where the deceased king commanded the body of his deceased father to be carried.—*Chardin.*

They imagine the dead are capable of pain. A Portuguese gentleman had one day ignorantly strayed among the tombs, and a Moor, after much wrangling, obliged him to go before the Cadi. The gentleman complained of violence, and asserted he had committed no crime; but the judge informed him he was mistaken, for that the poor dead suffered when trodden on by Christian feet. Muley Ishmael once had occasion to bring one of his wives through a burial-ground, and the people removed the bones of their relations, and murmuring, said, he would neither suffer the living nor the dead to rest in peace.—*Chenier. Additional Chap. by the Translator.*

Were the Moorish superstition true, there would have been some monkish merit in the last request of St Swithin, « when he was ready to depart out of this world, he commanded (for humilityes sake) his body to be buried in the church-yard, whereon every one might tread with their feet.»—*English Martyrologe.*

There is a story recorded, how that St Frithstane was wont every day to say masse and office for the dead; and one evening as he walked in the church-yard, reciting the said office, when he came to *requiescant in pace,* the voyces in the graves round about made answere aloud, and said, *Amen.*—*English Martyrologe.*

I observed at Damascus, says Thevenot, that the Turks leave a hole, of three fingers breadth in diameter, on the top of their tombs (where there is a channel of earth over the dead body), that serves to cool the dead; for the women, going thither on Thursday to pray, which they never fail to do every week, they pour in water by that hole, to refresh them, and quench their thirst; and at the end of the grave, they stick in a large branch of

24

box, and leave it there, to keep the dead cool. They have another no less pleasant custom, and that is, when a woman hath lost her husband, she still asks his counsel about her affairs. For instance, she will go to his grave, and tell him that such a person hath wronged her, or that such a man would marry her, and thereupon asks his counsel what she should do ; having done so, she returns home, expecting the answer, which her late husband fails not to come and give her the night following.

Note 14, page 129, col. 2.

« The gnawing of his hundred poison-mouths! »

The Mohammedan tradition is even more horrible than this. The corpse of the wicked is gnawed and stung till the resurrection by ninety-nine dragons, with seven heads each ; or, as others say, their sins will become venomous beasts, the grievous ones stinging like dragons, the smaller like scorpions, and the others like serpents ; circumstances which some understand in a figurative sense.—*Sale's Preliminary Discourse.*

This Mohammedan tale may be traced to the Scripture ; « whose worm dieth not. »

They also believe, that after a man is buried, the soul returns to the body ; and that two very terrible angels come into the grave, the one called *Munkir*, and the other *Guanequir*, who take him by the head, and make him kneel, and that, for that reason, they leave a tuft of hair on the crown of their head, that the angels who make them kneel may take hold of it. After that, the angels examine him in this manner : « Who is thy God, thy religion, and prophet ? » and he answers thus : « My God is the true God : my religion is the true religion ; and my prophet is Mahomet. » But if that man find himself to be guilty, and being afraid of their tortures, shall say—« You are my God and my prophet, and it is in you that I believe, » at such an answer, these angels smite him with a mace of fire, and depart ; and the earth squeezes the poor wretch so hard, that his mother's milk comes running out of his nose. After that come two other angels, bringing an ugly creature with them, that represents his sins and bad deeds, changed into that form ; then, opening a window, they depart into hell, and the man remains there with that ugly creature, being continually tormented with the sight of it, and the common miseries of the damned, until the day of judgment, when both go to hell together. But if he hath lived well, and made the first answer above-mentioned, they bring him a lovely creature, which represents his good actions, changed into that form ; then, the angels opening a window, go away to paradise, and the lovely creature remains, which gives him a great deal of content, and stays with him until the day of judgment, when both are received into paradise.—*Thevenot.*

Monkish ingenuity has invented something not unlike the Mohammedan article of faith.

St Elpheg, saith William of Malmsbury, in his tender years took the monastic habit at Dirherst, then a small monastery, and now only an empty monument of antiquity. There, after he had continued awhile, aspiring to greater perfection, he went to bathe, where, enclosing himself in a secret cell, he employed his mind in contemplation of celestial things. To him there, after a short time, were congregated a great number of religious persons, desiring his instructions and directions ;

and among them, being many, there were some who gave themselves to licentious feasting and drinking in the night time, their spiritual father, St Elpheg, not knowing of it. But Almighty God did not a long time suffer this their licence, but, at midnight, struck with a sudden death one who was the ringleader in this licentiousness, in the chamber where they practised such excesses. In the mean time, the holy man being at his prayers, was interrupted by a great noise, proceeding out of the same chamber, and wondering at a thing so unaccustomed, he went softly to the dore, looking in through certain clefts, he saw two devils of a vast stature, which, with frequent strokes, as of hammers, tormented the liveles carkeys ; from whence notwithstanding, proceeded loud clamours, as desiring help. But his tormentours answered, Thou didst not obey God, neither will we thee. This, the next morning, the holy man related to the rest ; and no wonder if his companions became afterward more abstemious.—*Cresoy.*

There is another ceremony to be undergone at the time of death, which is described in a most barbarous mixture of Arabic and Spanish. The original is given for its singularity.

« Sepa todo *Moslim* que quando viene a la muerte, que lenvia *Allah* cinco *Almalaques*. El pirimero viene quando *lurruh* (la alma) esta en la garganta, y dize le, *ye* fijo de Adam que es de tu cuerpo el forçudo, que tan falaco es oy ! y que es de tu lengua la fablante, como se enmudercido el dia de oy ? y que es de tu conpania y parientes ? oy te desaran solo. Y viene *lalmalac* segundo, quando le meten la mortaja, y dize le, *ye* fijo de Adam, que es de lo que tenias de la requeza para la povreza ? y que es de lo que alçaste del poblado para el yermo ? y que es de lo que alçaste del solaço para la soledad ? Y viene *lalmalac* tercero quando lo ponen en *lanaas,* (las andas) y dize le. Ye fijo de Adam, oy caminaras camino que nunca lo camines mas luente qu'el ; el dia de oy veras jente que nunca la veyerte nunca jamas ; el dia de oy entararas en casa que nunca entaraste en mas esterecha qu' ella jamas ni mas escura. Y viene *lalmalac* quarto, quando lo meten en la fuessa y *quirida* y dize. Ye fijo de Adam, ayer eras sobre la carra de la tierra alegre y goyoso, oy seras en su vientre ; y buen dia te vino si tu eres en la garacia de *Allah*, y mal dia te vino si tu cres en la ira de *Allah.* Y viene *lalmalac* cinqueno quando esta soterrado y *quirida*, y dize. Ye fijo de Adam oy quedaras solo y aunque quedaremos con tu no aporovejariamos ninguna cosa ; a *spelegado ellalgo* y desas lo para otri ; el dia de oy seras en *taljenna* (parayso) vicyuso, o en el fuego penoso. Aquestos cinco *Almalaques* vienen por mandamiento de *Allah* a todo peresono en el pasa de la muerte. Rogemos de *Allah* nos ponga por la rogarye y *alfadhila* (merecimiento) de nuestoro *alnabi* (profete) Mohammad (*salla allaho alayhi vasallam*) nos ponga de los siervos obidientes, que merescamos ser *seguros* del espanto de la fuessa y destos cincos *almalaques* por su santo *alrahma* (misericordia) y peadad. Amen. »—*Notices des Manuscrits de la Bibl. Nationale,* t. 4. 636.

Let every Moslem know, that when he comes to die, Allah sends five Almalaques.[1] The first comes when the soul is in the throat, and says to him, Now, son of Adam, what is become of thy body, the strong, which is to-day so feeble ? And what is become of thy tongue, the talker,

---

[1] I suppose this means angels, from the Hebrew word for king.

that is thus made dumb to-day? And where are thy companions and thy kin? To-day they have left thee alone. And the second Almalac comes when they put on the winding-sheet, and says, Now, son of Adam, what is become of the riches which thou hadst, in this poverty? And where are the peopled lands which were thine, in this desolation? And where are the pleasures which were thine, in this solitariness? And the third Almalac comes when they place him upon the bier, and says, Now, son of Adam, to-day thou shalt travel a journey, than which, thou hast never travelled longer; to-day thou shalt see a people, such as thou hast never seen before; to-day thou shalt enter a house, than which, thou hast never entered a narrower nor a darker. And the fourth Almalac comes when they put him in the grave, and says, Now, son of Adam, yesterday thou wert upon the face of the earth, blithe and joyous, to-day thou art in its bowels; a good day is to betide thee, if thou art in the grace of Allah, and an ill day will betide thee if thou art in the wrath of Allah. And the fifth Almalac comes when he is interred, and says, Now, son of Adam, to-day thou wilt be left alone, and though we were to remain with thee, we should profit thee nothing, as to the wealth which thou hast gathered together, and must now leave to another. To-day thou wilt be rejoicing in paradise, or tormented in the fire. These five Almalaques come by the command of Allah, to every person in the pass of death. Let us pray to Allah, that, through the mediation and merits of our prophet Mahommed, he may place us among his obedient servants, that we may be worthy to be safe from the terror of the grave, and of these five Almalaques, through his holy compassion and mercy. Amen.

Note 15, page 129, col. 2.
For this was that most holy night, etc.

The night, Leileth-ul-cadr, is considered as being particularly consecrated to ineffable mysteries. There is a prevailing opinion, that a thousand secret and invisible prodigies are performed on this night; that all the inanimate beings then pay their adoration to God; that all the waters of the sea lose their saltness, and become fresh at these mysterious moments; that such, in fine, is its sanctity, that prayers said during this night, are equal in value to all those which can be said in a thousand successive months. It has not however pleased God, says the author of the celebrated theological work entitled Ferkann, to reveal it to the faithful: no prophet, no saint has been able to discover it; hence this night, so august, so mysterious, so favoured by Heaven, has hitherto remained undiscovered.—D'Ohsson.

They all hold, that some time on this night, the firmament opens for a moment or two, and the glory of God appears visible to the eyes of those who are so happy as to behold it; at which juncture, whatever is asked of God by the fortunate beholder of the mysteries of that critical minute, is infallibly granted. This sets many credulous and superstitious people upon the watch all night long, till the morning begins to dawn. It is my opinion, that they go on full as wise as they come off; I mean, from standing sentinel for so many hours. Though many stories are told of people who have enjoyed the privilege of seeing that miraculous opening of the Heavens; of all which, few have had power to speak their mind, till it was too late, so great was their ecstacy. But one passage, pleasant enough, was once told me by a grave elderly gentlewoman at Costantina, in Barbary. There was, not many years before my time, said she, in this town, a Mulatta wench, belonging to such a great family, (naming one of the best in the town,) who being quite out of love with her woolly locks, and imagining that she wanted nothing to make her thought a pretty girl but a good head of hair, took her supper in her hand presently after sun-set, and without letting any body into her secret, stole away, and shut herself up in the uppermost apartment in the house, and went upon the watch. She had the good fortune to direct her optics towards the right quarter, the patience to look so long and so steadfastly, till she plainly beheld the beams of celestial glory darting through the amazing chasm in the divided firmament, and the resolution to cry out, with all her might, Ya Rabbi Kubbar Rassi; i. e. O Lord, make my head big! This expression is, figuratively, not improper to pray for a good head of hair. But, unhappily for the poor girl, it seems God was pleased to take her words in the literal sense; for, early in the morning, the neighbours were disturbed by the terrible noise and bawling she made; and they were forced to hasten to her assistance with tools proper to break down the walls about her ears, in order to get her head in at the window, it being grown to a monstrous magnitude, bigger in circumference than several bushels; I don't remember exactly how many; nor am I certain whether she survived her misfortune or not.—Morgan. Note to Rabadan.

According to Francklin, it is believed, that whatever Moslem die during the month of Ramadan, will most assuredly enter into paradise, because the gates of Heaven then stand open, by command of God.—Tour from Bengal to Persia, p. 136.

During the Asciur, the ten days of festive ceremony for Hosein, the Persians believe that the gates of paradise are thrown open, and that all the Moslem who die find immediate admittance.—Pietro delle Valle.

Note 16, page 130, col. 1.
And the Good Angel that abandoned her, etc.

The Turks also acknowledge guardian angels, but in far greater number than we do; for they say, that God hath appointed threescore and ten angels, though they be invisible, for the guard of every Musulman, and nothing befals any body but what they attribute to them. They have all their several offices, one to guard one member, and another another; one to serve him in such an affair, and another in another. There are, among all these angels, two who are the dictators over the rest; they sit one on the right side, and the other on the left; these they call Kerim Kiatib, that is to say, the merciful scribes. He on the right side, writes down the good actions of the man whom he has in tuition, and the other on the left hand, the bad. They are so merciful, that they spare him if he commit a sin before he goes to sleep, hoping he'll repent; and if he does not repent, they mark it down; if he does repent, they write down, Estig fourillah, that is to say, God pardons. They wait upon him in all places, except when he does his needs, where they let him go alone, staying for him at the door till he come out, and then they take him into possession again; wherefore, when the Turks go to the house-of-office, they put the left foot foremost, to the end the angel who registers their sius, may leave them first; and when they come out, they set the right foot before, that the angel who writes down their good works, may have them first under his protection.—*Thevenot.*

BOOK X.

Note 1, page 130, col. 2.
No faithful crowded round her bier.

When any person is to be buried, it is usual to bring the corpse at mid-day, or afternoon prayers, to one or other of these Mosques, from whence it is accompanied by the greatest part of the congregation to the grave. Their processions, at these times, are not so slow and solemn as in most parts of Christendom; for the whole company make what haste they can, singing, as they go along, some select verses of their Koran. That absolute submission which they pay to the will of God, allows them not to use any consolatory words upon these occasions; no loss or misfortune is to be hereupon regretted or complained of: instead likewise of such expressions of sorrow and condolence, as may regard the deceased, the compliments turn upon the person who is the nearest concerned, a blessing (say his friends) be upon your head.—*Shaw.*

All Mahometans inter the dead at the hour set apart for prayer; the defunct is not kept in the house, except he expires after sun-set; but the body is transported to the Mosque, whither it is carried by those who are going to prayer; each, from a spirit of devotion, is desirous to carry in his turn. Women regularly go on Friday to weep over, and pray at the sepulchres of the dead, whose memory they hold dear.—*Chenier.*

This custom of crowding about a funeral contributes to spread the plague in Turkey. It is not many years since, in some parts of Worcestershire, the mourners were accustomed to kneel with their heads upon the coffin during the burial service.

The fullest account of a Mahommedan funeral is in the *Lettres sur la Grèce,* of M. Guys. Chance made him the spectator of a ceremony which the Moslem will not suffer an infidel to profane by his presence.

About ten in the morning I saw the grave-digger at work; the slaves and the women of the family were seated in the burial-ground, many other women arrived, and then they all began to lament. After this prelude, they, one after the other, embraced one of the little pillars which are placed upon the graves, crying out *Ogloun ogloum, sæna Mussaphir gueldi,* My Son, my Son, a guest is coming to see thee. At these words their tears and sobs began anew; but the storm did not continue long; they all seated themselves, and entered into conversation.

At noon I heard a confused noise, and cries of lamentation; it was the funeral which arrived. A Turk preceded it, bearing upon his head a small chest; four other Turks carried the bier upon their shoulders, then came the father, the relations, and the friends of the dead, in great numbers. Their cries ceased at the entrance of the burial-ground, but then they quarrelled—and for this: The man who bore the chest opened it, it was filled with copies of the Koran: a crowd of Turks, young and old, threw themselves upon the books, and scrambled for them. Those who succeeded

ranged themselves around the Iman, and all at once began to recite the Koran, almost as boys say their lesson. Each of the readers received ten parats, about fifteen sols, wrapt in paper. It was then for these fifteen pence, that these pious assistants had quarrelled, and in our own country you might have seen them fight for less.

The bier was placed by the grave, in which the grave-digger was still working, and perfumes were burnt by it. After the reading of the Koran, the Iman chanted some Arabic prayers, and his full chant would, no doubt, have appeared to you, as it did to me, very ridiculous. All the Turks were standing; they held their hands open over the grave, and answered *Amen* to all the prayers which the Iman addressed to God for the deceased.

The prayers finished, a large chest was brought, about six feet long, and three broad; its boards were very thick. The coffin is usually made of cypress; thus, literally, is verified the phrase of Horace, that the cypress is our last possession:

> Neque harum, quas colis, arborum,
> Te, præter invisas cupresses,
> Ulla brevem dominum sequetur.

The cemeteries of the Turks are usually planted with these trees, to which they have a religious attachment. The chest, which was in loose pieces, having been placed in the grave, the coffin was laid in it, and above, planks, with other pieces of wood. Then all the Turks, taking spades, cast earth upon the grave to cover it. This is a part of the ceremony at which all the by-standers assisted in their turn.

Before the corpse is buried it is carried to the Mosque. Then, after having recited the *Fatka,* (a prayer very similar to our Lord's prayer, which is repeated by all present), the Iman asks the congregation what they have to testify concerning the life and morals of the deceased? Each then, in his turn, relates those good actions with which he was acquainted. The body is then washed, and wrapped up like a mummy, so that it cannot be seen. Drugs and spices are placed in the bier with it, and it is carried to interment. Before it is lowered into the grave, the Iman commands silence, saying, « Cease your lamentations for a moment, and let me instruct this Moslem how to act, when he arrives in the other world." Then, in the ear of the corpse, he directs him how to answer the Evil Spirit, who will not fail to question him respecting his religion, etc. This lesson finished, he repeats the *Fatka,* with all the assistants, and the body is let down into the grave. After they have thrown earth three times into the grave, as the Romans used, they retire. The Iman only remains, he approaches the grave, stoops down, inclines his ear, and listens to hear if the dead disputes when the Angel of Death comes to take him: then he bids him farewell; and in order to be well paid, never fails to report to the family the best news of the dead.

As soon as the ceremony of interment is concluded, the Imaum, seated with his legs bent under his thighs, repeats a short prayer; he then calls the deceased three times by his name, mentioning also that of his mother, but without the smallest allusion to that of his father. What will be considered as infinitely more extraordinary is, that should the Imaum be ignorant of the name of the mother, it is usual for him to substitute that of Mary, in honour of the Virgin, provided the deceased be a male, and that of Eve, in case the deceased be a female, in honour of the common mother of mankind. This custom is so invariable, that even at the interment of the Sultans, it is not neglected; the Imaum calling out, Oh Mustapha! Son of Mary! or, Oh Fatimah! Daughter of Eve!

Immediately afterwards he repeats a prayer, called *Telkeen*, which consists of the following words: "Remember the moment of thy leaving the world, in making this profession of faith. Certainly there is no God but God. He is one, and there is no association in Him. Certainly Mohammed is the prophet of God. Certainly Paradise is real. Certainly the resurrection is real, it is indisputable. Certainly God will bring to life the dead, and make them leave their graves. Certainly thou hast acknowledged God for thy God; Islamism for thy religion; Mohammed for thy prophet; the Koran for thy priest; the sanctuary of Mecca for thy Kibla; and the faithful for thy brethren. God is my God; there is no other God but he. He is the master of the august and sacred throne of Heaven. Oh Mustaphah! (or any other name) say that God is thy God (which the Imaum repeats thrice.) Say there is no other God but God (also repeated thrice). Say that Mohammed is the prophet of God; that thy religion is Islam, and that thy prophet is Mohammed, upon whom be the blessing of salvation, and the mercy of the Lord. O God, do not abandon us." After this ejaculation, the ceremony is concluded by a chapter of the Koran, and the party returns home.

As soon as the grave was filled up, each friend planted a sprig of cypress on the right, and another on the left hand of the deceased, and then took his leave. This was to ascertain, by their growth, whether the deceased would enjoy the happiness promised by Mohammed to all true believers, or whether he would for ever be denied the bliss of the Houris. The former would occur should the sprigs on the right hand take root, and the latter would be ascertained if the left only should flourish. If both succeeded, he would be greatly favoured in the next world; or, if both failed, he would be tormented by black angels, until, through the mediation of the prophet, he should be rescued from their persecutions.

The graves are not dug deep, but separated from each other carefully, that two bodies may not be placed together. The earth is raised, to prevent an unhallowed foot from treading upon it; and, instead of a plain flat stone being placed over it, one which is perforated in the centre is most commonly used, to allow of cypress trees, or odoriferous herbs, being planted immediately over the corpse. Occasionally a square stone, hollowed out, and without a cover, is preferred; which being filled with mould, the trees or herbs are cultivated in it.—*Griffiths.*

Note 2, page 130, col. 2.

No column raised by the way-side, etc.

The Turks bury not at all within the walls of the city, but the great Turkish Emperors themselves, with their wives and children about them, and some few other of their great Bassaes, and those only in chapels by themselves, built for that purpose. All the rest of the Turks are buried in the fields; some of the better sort, in tombs of marble; but the rest, with tomb-stones

laid upon them, or with two great stones, one set up at the head, and the other at the foot of every grave; the greatest part of them being of white marble, brought from the Isle of Matmora.

They will not bury any man where another hath been buried, accounting it impiety to dig up another man's bones: by reason whereof, they cover all the best ground about the city with such great white stones; which, for the infinite number of them, are thought sufficient to make another wall about the city.—*Knolles.*

The Turks bury by the way-side, believing that the passengers will pray for the souls of the dead.—*Tavernier.*

Note 3, page 131, col. 1.

His eyes are aching with the snow.

All that day we travelled over plains all covered with snow, as the day before; and indeed it is not only troublesome, but very dangerous, to travel through these deep snows. The mischief is, that the beams of the sun, which lie all day long upon it, molest the eyes and face with such a scorching heat, as very much weakens the sight, whatever remedy a man can apply, by wearing, as the people of the country do, a thin handkerchief of green or black silk, which no way abates the annoyance.—*Chardin.*

When they have to travel many days through a country covered with snow, travellers, to preserve their sight, cover the face with a silk kerchief, made on purpose, like a sort of black crape. Others have large furred bonnets, bordered with goat-skin, and the long goat-hair hanging over the face, is as serviceable as the crape.—*Tavernier.*

An Abyssinian historian says, that the village called Zinzenam, *rain upon rain,* has its name from an extraordinary circumstance that once happened in these parts; for a shower of rain fell, which was not properly of the nature of rain, as it did not run upon the ground, but remained very light, having scarce the weight of feathers, of a beautiful white colour, like flour; it fell in showers, and occasioned a darkness in the air more than rain, and liker to mist. It covered the face of the whole country for several days, retaining its whiteness the whole time, then went away like dew, without leaving any smell, or unwholesome effect behind it.—*Bruce.*

So the Dutch were formerly expelled from an East Indian settlement, because their Consul, in narrating to the Prince of the country the wonders of Europe, chanced to say, that in his own country, water became a solid body once a-year, for some time; when men, or even horses, might pass over it without sinking. The Prince, in a rage, said, that he had hitherto listened to his tales with patience, but this was so palpable a lie, that he would never more be connected with Europeans, who only could assert such monstrous falsehoods.

Note 4, page 131, col. 1.

Its broad, round-spreading branches, when they felt, etc.

A strange account of the cedars of Lebanon is given by De la Roque. — *Voyage de Syrie et du Mont Liban.* 1772.

"This little forest is composed of twenty cedars, of a prodigious size; so large indeed, that the finest planes, sycamores, and other large trees which we had seen, could not be compared with them. Besides these principal cedars, there were a great number of lesser ones, and some very small, mingled with the large trees, or in little clumps near them. They differed not in their foliage, which resembles the juniper, and is green throughout the year; but the great cedars spread at their summit, and form a perfect round, whereas the small ones rise in a pyramidal form like the cypress. Both diffuse the same pleasant odour; the large ones only yield fruit, a large cone, in shape almost like that of the pine, but of a browner colour, and compacter shell. It gives a very pleasant odour, and contains a sort of thick and transparent balm, which oozes out through small apertures, and falls drop by drop. This fruit, which it is difficult to separate from the stalk, contains a nut like that of the cypress; it grows at the end of the boughs, and turns its point upwards.

The nature of this tree is not to elevate its trunk, or the part between the root and the first branches; for the largest cedars which we saw, did not, in the height of their trunks, exceed six or seven feet. From this low, but enormously thick body, prodigious branches rise, spreading as they rise, and forming, by the disposition of their boughs and leaves, which point upward, a sort of wheel, which appears to be the work of art. The bark of the cedar, except at the trunk, is smooth and shining, of a brown colour. Its wood white and soft, immediately under the bark, but hard and red within, and very bitter, which renders it incorruptible, and almost immortal. A fragrant gum issues from the tree.

The largest cedar which we measured, was seven feet in circumference, wanting two inches; and the whole extent of its branches, which it was easy to measure, from their perfect roundness, formed a circumference of about 120 feet.

The Patriarch of the Maronites, fully persuaded of the rarity of these trees, and wishing, by the preservation of those that remain, to show his respect for a forest so celebrated in Scripture, has pronounced canonical pains, and even excommunication, against any Christians who shall dare to cut them; scarcely will he permit a little to be sometimes taken for crucifixes and little tabernacles in the chapels of our missionaries.

The Maronites themselves have such a veneration for these cedars, that on the day of transfiguration, they celebrate the festival under them with great solemnity; the Patriarch officiates, and says mass pontifically; and, among other exercises of devotion, they particularly honour the Virgin Mary there, and sing her praises, because she is compared to the cedars of Lebanon, and Lebanon itself used as a metaphor for the mother of Christ.

. . . .

The Maronites say, that the snows have no sooner begun to fall, than these cedars, whose boughs, in their infinite number, are all so equal in height, that they appear to have been shorn, and form, as we have said, a sort of wheel or parasol; than these cedars, I say, never fail at that time to change their figure. The branches, which before spread themselves, rise insensibly, gathering together, it may be said, and turn their points upward towards Heaven, forming altogether a pyramid. It is Nature, they say, who inspires this movement, and makes them assume a new shape, without which these trees never could sustain the immense weight of snow remaining for so long a time.

I have procured more particular information of this fact, and it has been confirmed by the testimony of many persons, who have often witnessed it. This is what the secretary of the Maronite Patriarch wrote to me in one of his letters, which I think it right to give in his own words. « Cedri Libani quos plantavit Deus, ut Psalmista loquitur, sitæ sunt in planitie quâdam, aliquantulum infra altissimum Montis Libani cacumen, ubi tempore hyemali maxima nivium quantitas descendit, tribusque et ultra mensibus mordaciter dominatur. Cedri in altum ascendunt extensis tamen ramis in gyrum solo parallelis, conficientibus suo gyro fere umbellam solarem. Sed superveniente nive, quia coacervaretur in magnâ quantitate eos desuper, neque possent pati tantum pondus tanto tempore premens, sine certo fractionis discrimine, Natura, rerum omnium provida mater, ipsis concessit, ut adveniente hyeme et descendente nive, statim rami in altum assurgant, et secum invicem uniti constituant quasi conum, ut melius sese ab adveniente hoste tueantur. Naturâ enim ipsâ verum est, virtutem quamlibet unitam simul reddi fortiorem.»

« The cedars of Lebanon, which, as the Psalmist says, God himself planted, are situated in a little plain, somewhat below the loftiest summit of Mount Lebanon, where, in the winter, a great quantity of snow falls, and continues for three months, or longer. The cedars are high, but their boughs spread out parallel with the ground into a circle, forming almost a shield against the sun. But when the snow falls, which would be heaped upon them in so great a quantity, that they could not endure such a weight so long a time, without the certain danger of breaking; Nature, the provident mother of all, has endued them with power, that when the winter comes, and the snow descends, their boughs immediately rise, and, uniting together, form a cone, that they may be the better defended from the coming enemy. For in Nature itself, it is true that virtue, as it is united, becomes stronger.»

Note 5, page 131, col. 1.

Passing in summer o'er the coffee-groves, etc.

The coffee plant is about the size of the orange tree. The flower, in colour, size, and smell, resembles the white jessamine. The berry is first green, then red, in which ripe state it is gathered.

Olearius's description of coffee is amusing. « They drink a certain black water, which they call cahwa, made of a fruit brought out of Egypt, and which is in colour like ordinary wheat, and in taste like Turkish wheat, and is of the bigness of a little bean. They fry, or rather burn it in an iron pan, without any liquor, beat it to powder, and boiling it with fair water, they make this drink thereof, which hath as it were the taste of a burnt crust, and is not pleasant to the palate.» — Amb. Travels.

Pietro della Valle liked it better, and says he should introduce it into Italy. If, said he, it were drank with wine instead of water, I should think it is the Nepenthe, which, according to Homer, Helen brought from Egypt, for it is certain that coffee comes from that country; and as Nepenthe was said to assuage trouble and disquietude, so does this serve the Turks as an ordinary pastime, making them pass their hours in conversation, and occasioning pleasant discourse, which induces forgetfulness of care.

Note 6, page 132, col. 2.

Fatherly fear and love. He read the stars, etc.

It is well known how much the Orientalists are addicted to this pretended science. There is a curious instance of public folly in Sir John Chardin's Travels.

« Sephie Mirza was born in the year of the *Egire* 1057. For the superstition of the Persians will not let us know the month or the day. Their addiction to astrology is such, that they carefully conceal the moments of their princes' birth, to prevent the casting their nativities, where they might meet perhaps with something which they should be unwilling to know.»

At the coronation of this prince, two astrologers were to be present, with an astrolabe in their hands, to take the fortunate hour, as they term it, and observe the lucky moments that a happy constellation should point out for proceedings of that importance.

Sephie-Mirza having by debauchery materially injured his health, the chief physician was greatly alarmed, « in regard his life depended upon the king's; or if his life were spared, yet he was sure to lose his estate and his liberty, as happens to all those who attend the Asiatic Sovereigns, when they die under their care. The queen-mother too accused him of treason or ignorance, believing that since he was her son's physician, he was obliged to cure him. This made the physician at his wit's end, so that all his receipts failing him, he bethought himself of one that was peculiarly his own invention, and which few physicians would ever have found out, as not being to be met with neither in Galen nor Hippocrates. What does he then do, but out of an extraordinary fetch of his wit, he begins to lay the fault upon the stars and the king's astrologers, crying out, that they were altogether in the wrong. That if the king lay in a languishing condition, and could not recover his health, it was because they had failed to observe the happy hour, or the aspect of a fortunate constellation at the time of his coronation.» The stratagem succeeded, the king was re-crowned, and by the new name of Solyman!—*Chardin.*

Note 7, page 133, col. 1.

It was a brazen Image, every limb, etc.

We have now to refute their error, who are persuaded that brazen heads, made under certain constellations, may give answers, and be as it were guides and counsellors, upon all occasions, to those that had them in their possession. Among these is one Yepes, who affirms, that Henry de Villena made such a one at Madrid, broken to pieces afterwards by order of John II, king of Castile. The same thing is affirmed by Bartholomew Sibillus, and the author of the *Image of the World*, of Virgil; by William of Malmsbury, of Sylvester; by John Gower, of Robert of Lincoln; by the common people of England, of Roger Bacon; and by Tostatus, bishop of Avila, George of Venice, Delrio, Sibillus, Raguseus, Delancre, and others, too many to mention, of Albertus Magnus; who, as the most expert, had made an entire man of the same metal, and had spent thirty years without any interruption in forming him under several aspects and constellations. For example, he formed the eyes, according to the said Tostatus, in his Commentaries upon Exodus, when the sun was in a sign of the Zodiac, correspondent to that part, casting them out of divers metals mixt together, and marked with the characters of the same signs and pla-

nets, and their several and necessary aspects. The same method he observed in the head, neck, shoulders, thighs, and legs, all which were fashioned at several times, and being put and fastened together in the form of a man, had the faculty to reveal to the said Albertus the solutions of all his principal difficulties. To which they add (that nothing be lost of the story of the Statue,) that it was battered to pieces by St Thomas, merely because he could not endure its excess of prating.

But, to give a more rational account of this Androides of Albertus, as also of all these miraculous heads, I conceive the original of this fable may well be deduced from the Teraph of the Hebrews, by which, as Mr Selden affirms, many are of opinion, that we must understand what is said in Genesis concerning Laban's Gods, and in the first book of Kings, concerning the image which Michol put into the bed in David's place. For R. Eleazar holds that it was made of the head of a male child, the first-born, and that dead-born, under whose tongue they applied a lamen of gold, whereon were engraved the characters and inscriptions of certain planets, which the Jews superstitiously wandered up and down with, instead of the Urim and Thummim, or the Ephod of the high-priest. And that this original is true and well deduced, there is a manifest indicium, in that Henry D'Assia, and Bartholomæus Sibillus affirm, that the Androides of Albertus, and the head made by Virgil, were composed of flesh and bone, yet not by nature, but by art. But this being judged impossible by modern authors, and the virtue of images, annulets, and planetary Sigills, being in great reputation, men have thought ever since, (taking their opinion from Trismegistus affirming in his Asclepion, that of the gods, some were made by the Sovereign God, and others by men, who, by some art, had the power to unite the invisible spirits to things visible and corporeal, as is explained at large by St Augustine,) that such figures were made of copper or some other metal, whereon men had wrought under some favourable aspects of Heaven and the planets.

My design is not absolutely to deny that he might compose some head or statue of man, like that of Memnon, from which proceeded a small sound and pleasant noise, when the rising sun came, by his heat to rarify and force out, by certain small conduits, the air which, in the cold of the night, was condensed within it. Or haply, they might be like those statues of Boetius, whereof Cassiodorus speaking, said, *Metalla mugiunt Diomedis in ære grues buccinant, æneus anguis insibilat, aves simulatæ fritinniunt, et quæ propriam vocem nesciunt, ab æra dulcedinem probantur emittere cantilenæ;* for such I doubt not but may be made by the help of that part of natural magic which depends on the mathematics.—*Davies's History of Magic.*

Note 8, page 134, col. 1.

And, on the everlasting Table there, etc.

This table is suspended in the Seventh Heaven, and guarded from the Demons, lest they should change or corrupt any thing thereon. Its length is so great as is the space between heaven and earth, its breadth equal to the distance from the east to the west, and it is made of one pearl. The divine pen was created by the finger of God; that also is of pearls, and of such length and breadth, that a swift horse could scarcely gallop round it in five hundred years. It is so endowed, that, self-moved, it writes all things, past, present, and to come. Light is its ink, and the language which it uses, only the Angel Seraphael understands.—*Maracci.*

Note 9, page 134, col. 1.
The yearly scroll of fate, etc.

They celebrate the night Leileth-ul-beraeth, on the 15th of the month of Schabann, with great apprehension and terror, because they consider it as the tremendous night on which the angels Kiramenn-keatibinn, placed on each side of mankind, to write down their good and bad actions, deliver up their books, and receive fresh ones for the continuance of the same employment. It is believed also, that on that night, the archangel Azrail, the angel of death, gives up also his records, and receives another book, in which are written the names of all those destined to die in the following year.—*D'Ohsson.*

Note 10, page 134, col. 1.
Her leaf hath withered on the Tree of Life.

Here, in the Fourth Heaven, I beheld a most prodigious angel, of an admirable presence and aspect, in whose awful countenance there appeared neither mirth nor sorrow, but an undescribable mixture of both. He neither smiled in my face, nor did he, indeed, scarce turn his eyes towards me to look upon me, as all the rest did, yet he returned my salutation after a very courteous, obliging manner, and said, « Welcome to these mansions, O Mahomet; thou art the person whom the Almighty hath endowed with all the united perfections of nature ; and upon whom he, of his immense goodness, hath been pleased to bestow the utmost of his divine graces.»

There stood before him a most beautiful table, of a vast magnitude and extent, written all over, almost from the top to the bottom, in a very close, and scarce distinguishable character, upon which written table his eyes were continually fixed ; and so exceedingly intent he was upon that his occupation, that, though I stood steadfastly observing his countenance, I could not perceive his eye-lids once to move. Casting my eyes towards the left side of him, I beheld a prodigious large shady tree, the leaves whereof were as innumerable as the sands of the ocean, and upon every one of which were certain characters inscribed. Being extremely desirous of knowing the secret of this wonderful mystery, I enquired of Gabriel the meaning of what I was examining with my eyes with so anxious a curiosity. The obliging angel, to satisfy my longing, said, That person, concerning whom thou art so very inquisitive, is the redoubtable *Azarael,* the Angel of Death, who was never yet known either to laugh, smile, or be merry; for, depend upon it, my beloved Mahomet, had he been capable of smiling, or looking pleasant upon any creature in nature, it would assuredly have been upon thee alone. This table, upon which thou beholdest him so attentively fixing his looks, is called *Et Lough Et Mahofoud,* and is the register upon which are engraven the names of every individual soul breathing; and, notwithstanding the inspection of that register taketh up the greatest part of his time, yet he more particularly looketh it all over five times a-day, which are at those very same instants wherein the true believers are obliged to offer up their adorations to our Omnipotent Lord. The means whereby he understandeth when the thread of each individual life is run out and expired, is to look upon the branches of that vast tree thou there beholdest, upon the leaves whereof are written the names of all mortals, every one having his peculiar leaf; there, forty days before the time of any person's life is expired, his respective leaf beginning to fade, wither, and grow dry, and the letters of his name to disappear; at the end of the fortieth day they are quite blotted out, and the leaf falleth to the ground, by which *Azarael* certainly knoweth that the breath of its owner is ready to leave the body, and hasteneth away to take possession of the departing soul.

The size or stature of this formidable angel was so incomprehensibly stupendous, so unmeasurably great, that if this earthly globe of ours, with all that is thereon contained, were to be placed in the palm of his hand, it would seem no more than one single grain of mustard-seed (though the smallest of all seeds) would do if laid upon the surface of the earth.—*Rabadan.*

Note 11, page 134, col. 2.
In the balance of thy trial must be weigh'd !

The balance of the dead is an article in almost every creed. Mahommed borrowed it from the Persians. I know not from whence the Monks introduced it; probably they were ignorant enough to have invented the obvious fiction.

In the Vision of Thurcillus, the ceremony is accurately described. « At the end of the north wall, within the church, sate St Paul, and opposite him, without, was the devil and his angels. At the feet of the devil, a burning pit flamed up, which was the mouth of the pit of hell. A balance, equally poised, was fixed upon the wall, between the devil and the apostle, one scale hanging before each. The apostle had two weights, a greater and a less, all shining, and like gold, and the devil also had two smoky and black ones. Therefore, the souls that were all black, came one after another, with great fear and trembling, to behold the weighing of their good and evil works ; for these weights weighed the works of all the souls, according to the good or evil which they had done. When the scale inclined to the apostle, he took the soul, and introduced it through the eastern gate, into the fire of Purgatory, that there it might expiate its crimes. But when the scale inclined and sunk towards the devil, then he and his angels snatched the soul, miserably howling and cursing he father and mother that begot it to eternal torments, and cast it with laughter and grinning into the deep and fiery pit which was at the feet of the devil. Of this balance of good and evil, much may be found in the writings of the Holy Fathers.»—*Matthew Paris.*

«Concerning the salvation of Charlemagne, Archbishop Turpin, a man of holy life, wrote thus : 'I, Turpin, Archbishop of Rheims, being in my chamber, in the city of Vienna, saying my prayers, saw a legion of devils in the air, who were making a great noise. I adjured one of them to tell me from whence they came, and wherefore they made so great an uproar. And he replied that they came from Aix la Chapelle, where a great lord had died, and that they were returning in anger, because they had not been able to carry away his soul. I asked him who the great lord was, and why they had not been able to carry away his soul? He replied, That it was Charlemagne, and that Santiago had been greatly against them. And I asked him how Santiago had been against them ; and he replied, We were weighing the good and the evil which he had done in this world, and Santiago brought so much timber, and so many stones from the churches which he had founded in his name, that they greatly over-balanced all his evil works; and so we had no power over his soul. And having said this, the devil disappeared.»

We must understand from this vision of Archbishop Turpin, that they who build or repair churches in this world, erect resting-places and inns for their salvation.
Historia do Imperador Carlos Magno, et dos Doze Pares de França.

Two other corollaries follow from the vision. The devil's way home from Aix la Chapelle lay through Vienna; and as churches go by weight, an architect of Sir John Vanbrugh's school should always be employed.

This balance of the dead was an easy and apt metaphor, but clumsily imagined as an actual mode of trial.

> For take thy ballaunce, if thou be so wise,
> And weigh the winde that under heaven doth blow;
> Or weigh the light that in the east doth rise:
> Or weigh the thought that from man's mind doth flow:
> But if the weight of these thou canst not show,
> Weigh but one word which from thy lips doth fall.—*Spenser.*

Note 12, page 134, col. 2.
And Azrael, from the hands of Thalaba, etc.

This double meaning is in the spirit of oracular prediction. The classical reader will remember the equivocations of Apollo. The fable of the Young Man and Lion in the Tapestry will be more generally recollected. We have many buildings in England to which this story has been applied. Cooke's Folly, near Bristol, derives its name from a similar tradition.

The History of the Buccaneers affords a remarkable instance of prophecy occasioning its own accomplishment.

«Before my first going over into the *South-Seas* with Captain *Sharp* (and indeed before any privateers, at least since *Drake* and *Oxengham*) had gone that way which we afterwards went, except *La Sound*, a *French* captain, who, by captain *Wright's* instructions, had ventured as far as *Cheapo* town with a body of men, but was driven back again; I being then on board Captain *Coxon*, in company with three or four more privateers, about four leagues to the east of *Portobel*, we took the packets bound thither from *Carthagena*. We opened a great quantity of the merchants' letters, and found the contents of many of them to be very surprising; the merchants of several parts of *Old-Spain* thereby informing their correspondents of *Panama*, and elsewhere, of a certain prophecy that went about *Spain* that year, the tenor of which was, *that there would be* English *privateers that year in the* West-Indies, *who would make such great discoveries, as to open a door into the* South-Seas, which they supposed was fastest shut; and the letters were accordingly full of cautions to their friends to be very watchful and careful of their coasts.

«This door they spake of, we all concluded must be the passage over-land through the country of the *Indians* of *Darien*, who were a little before this become our friends, and had lately fallen out with the *Spaniards*, breaking off the intercourse which for some time they had with them. And upon calling also to mind the frequent invitations we had from those Indians a little before this time to pass through their country, and fall upon the *Spaniards* in the *South-Seas*, we from henceforward began to entertain such thoughts in earnest, and soon came to a resolution to make those attempts which we afterwards did with Captains *Sharp*, *Coxon*, etc. So that the taking these letters gave the first life to those bold undertakings; and we took the advantage of the fears the *Spaniards* were in from that prophecy, or probable conjecture, or whatever it were; for we sealed up most of the letters again, and sent them ashore to *Portobel.*»—*Dampier.*

BOOK XI.

Note 1, page 135, col. 2.
Green Warbler of the Bowers of Paradise.

The souls of the blessed are supposed by some of the Mahommedans to animate green birds in the groves of paradise. Was this opinion invented to conciliate the Pagan Arabs, who believed, that of the blood near the dead person's brain was formed a bird named Hamah, which once in a hundred years visited the sepulchre?

To this there is an allusion in the Moallakat. «Then I knew with certainty, that, in so fierce a contest with them, many a heavy blow would make the perched birds of the brain fly quickly from every skull.»
Poem of Antara.

In the Bahar-Danush, parrots are called the green-vested resemblers of Heaven's dwellers. The following passages in the same work may, perhaps, allude to the same superstition, or perhaps are merely metaphorical, in the usual style of its true oriental bombast. «The bird of understanding fled from the nest of my brain.» «My joints and members seemed as if they would separate from each other, and the bird of life would quit the nest of my body.» «The bird of my soul became a captive in the net of her glossy ringlets.»

I remember in a *European Magazine* two similar lines by the author of the Lives of the Admirals:

> My beating Bosom is a well-wrought cage,
> Whence that sweet Gold-finch Hope shall ne'er elope!

The grave of Francisco Jorge, the Maronite martyr, was visited by two strange birds of unusual size. No one knew whence they came. They emblemed, says Vasconcellos, the purity and the indefatigable activity of his soul.

The inhabitants of Otaheite have assigned a less respectable part of the body as the seat of the soul.

The disembowelling of the body there, is always performed in great secrecy, and with much religious superstition. The bowels are, by these people, considered as the immediate organs of sensation, where the first impressions are received, and by which all the operations of the mind are carried on: it is therefore natural to conclude, that they may esteem and venerate the intestines, as bearing the greatest affinity to the immortal part. I have frequently held conversations on this subject, with a view to convince them that all intellectual operations were carried on in the head; at which they would generally smile and intimate, that they had frequently seen men recover whose skulls had been fractured, and whose heads had otherways been much injured; but that, in all cases in which the intestines had been wounded, the persons on a certainty died. Other arguments they would also advance in favour of their belief; such as the effect of fear, and other passions, which caused great agitation and uneasiness, and would sometimes produce sickness at the stomach, which they attributed entirely to the action of the bowels.—*Vancouver.*

Note 2, page 136, col. 1.
Had borne the healing fruit.

When Hosein, the son of Ali, was sick of a grievous disorder, he longed for a pomegranate, though that fruit was not then in season. Ali went out, and diligently enquiring, found a single one in the possession of a Jew. As he returned with it, a sick man met him, and begged half the pomegranate, saying it would restore his health. Ali gave him half, and when he had eaten it, the man requested he would give him the other half, the sooner to complete his recovery. Ali benignantly complied, returned to his son, and told him what had happened, and Hosein approved what his father had done.

Immediately behold a miracle! as they were talking together, the door was gently knocked at. He ordered the woman servant to go there, and she found a man, of all men the most beautiful, who had a plate in his hand, covered with green silk, in which were ten pomegranates. The woman was astonished at the beauty of the man and of the pomegranates, and she took one of them and hid it, and carried the other nine to Ali, who kissed the present. When he had counted them, he found that one was wanting, and said so to the servant; she confessed that she had taken it on account of its excellence, and Ali gave her her liberty. The pomegranates were from paradise; Hosein was cured of his disease only by their odour, and rose up immediately, recovered, and in full strength.—*Maracci.*

I suspect, says Maracci, that this is a true miracle, wrought by some Christian saint, and falsely attributed to Ali. However this may be, it does not appear absurd that God should, by some especial favour, reward an act of remarkable charity even in an infidel, as he has sometimes, by a striking chastisement, punished enormous crimes. But the assertion, that the pomegranates were sent from paradise, exposes the fable.

Maracci, after detailing and ridiculing the Mahommedan miracles, contrasts with them, in an appendix, a few of the real and permanent miracles of Christianity, which are proved by the testimony of the whole world. He selects five as examples. 1. The chapel of Loretto, brought by Angels from Nazareth to Illyricum, and from Illyricum to Italy; faithful messengers having been sent to both places, and finding in both its old foundations, in dimensions and materials exactly corresponding.

2. The cross of St Thomas at Meliapor. A Bramin, as the saint was extended upon his cross in prayer, slew him. On the anniversary of his martyrdom, during the celebration of mass, the cross gradually becomes luminous, till it shines one white glory. At elevating the host, it resumes its natural colour, and sweats blood profusely; in which the faithful dip their clothes, by which many miracles are wrought.

3. *Certissimum qui evidentissimum.*—At Bari, on the Adriatic, a liquor flows from the bones of St. Nicholas; they call it St Nicholas's manna, which, being preserved in bottles, never corrupts or breeds worms, except the possessor be corrupt himself, and daily it works miracles.

4. At Tolentino in the March of Anconia, the arms of St Nicholas swell with blood, and pour out copious streams, when any great calamity impends over Christendom.

5. The blood of St Januarius at Naples.

These, says Maracci, are *miracula perseverantia,* permanent miracles; and it cannot be said, as of the Mahommedan ones, that they are tricks of the devil.

Note 3, page 136, col. 1.
From the birth-day of the world, etc.

The birth-day of the world was logically ascertained in a provincial council held at Jerusalem, against the Quartodecimans, by command of Pope Victor, about the year 200. Venerable Bede (*Comm. de Æquinoct. Vern.*) supplies the mode of proof. « When the multitude of priests were assembled together, then Theophylus, the bishop, produced the authority sent unto him by Pope Victor, and explained what had been enjoined him. Then all the bishops made answer, Unless it be first examined how the world was at the beginning, nothing salutary can be ordained respecting the observations of Easter. And they said, What day can we believe to have been the first, except Sunday? And Theophylus said, Prove this which ye say. Then the bishop said, According to the authority of the Scriptures, the evening and the morning were the first day; and, in like manner, they were the second and the third, and the fourth and the fifth, and the sixth and the seventh; and on the seventh day, which was called the Sabbath, the Lord rested from all his works: therefore, since Saturday, which is the Sabbath, was the last day, which but Sunday can have been the first? Then said Theophylus, Lo, ye have proved that Sunday was the first day; what say ye now concerning the seasons—for there are four times or seasons in the year, Spring, Summer, Autumn, and Winter; which of these was the first? The bishops answered, Spring. And Theophylus said, Prove this which ye say. Then the bishods said, It is written, the earth brought forth grass and herb yielding seed after his kind, and the tree yielding fruit, whose seed was in itself, after his kind; but this is in the spring. Then said Theophylus, When do you believe the beginning of the world to have been, in the beginning of the season, or in the middle, or in the end? And the bishops answered, at the Equinox, on the eighth of the kalends of April. And Theophylus said, Prove this which ye say. Then they answered, It is written, God made the light, and called the light day, and he made the darkness, and called the darkness night, and he divided the light and the darkness into equal parts. Then said Theophylus, Lo ye have proved the day and the season.—What think ye now concerning the Moon; was it created when increasing, or when full, or on the wane? And the bishops answered, At the full. And he said, Prove this which ye say. Then they answered, God made two great luminaries, and placed them in the firmament of the Heavens, that they might give light upon the earth; the greater luminary in the beginning of the day, the lesser one in the beginning of the night. It could not have been thus unless the moon were at the full. Now, therefore, let us see when the world was created: it was made upon the Sunday, in the spring, at the Equinox, which is on the eighth of the kalends of April, and at the full of the moon.»

According to the form of a border-oath, the work of creation began by night. « You shall swear by Heaven above you, Hell beneath you, by your part of Paradise, *by all that God made in six days and seven nights,* and by God himself, you are whart out sackless

of art, part, way, witting, ridd, kenuing, having or re-
cetting of any of the goods and chattells named in this
bill. So help you God.»[:] (*Nicolson and Burn,* l. xxv.)
This, however, is assertion without proof, and would
not have been admitted by Theophylus and his bishops.

Note 4, page 136, col. 1.
That old and only Bird.

Simorg Anka, says my friend Mr Fox, in a note to his
Achmed Ardebeili, is a bird or griffon of extraordinary
strength and size, (as its name imports, signifying as
large as thirty eagles,) which, according to the Eastern
writers, was sent by the Supreme Being to subdue and
chastise the rebellious Dives. It was supposed to pos-
sess rational faculties and the gift of speech. The *Ca-
herman Nameh* relates, that Simorg Anka being asked
his age, replied, this world is very ancient, for it has
already been seven times replenished with beings dif-
ferent from man, and as often depopulated. That the
age of Adam, in which we now are, is to endure seven
thousand years, making a great cycle; that himself had
seen twelve of these revolutions, and knew not how
many more he had to see.

I am afraid that Mr Fox and myself have fallen into
a grievous heresy, both respecting the unity and the sex
of the Simorg. For this great bird is a hen; there is
indeed a cock also, but he seems to be of some inferior
species, a sort of Prince George of Denmark, the Si-
morg's consort, not the cock Simorg.

In that portion of the *Shah-Nameh* which has been
put into English rhyme by Mr Champion, some anec-
dotes may be found concerning this all-knowing bird,
who is there represented as possessing one species of
knowledge, of which she would not be readily suspect-
ed. Zalzer, the father of Rustam, is exposed in his in-
fancy by his own father, Saum, who takes him for a
young deviling, because his body is black, and his hair
white. The infant is laid at the foot of Mount Elburs,
where the Simorg has her nest, and she takes him up,
and breeds him with her young, who are very desirous
of eating him, but she preserves him. When Zalzer is
grown up, and leaves the nest, the Simorg gives him
one of her feathers, telling him, whenever he is in great
distress, to burn it, and she will immediately come to
his assistance. Zalzer marries Rodahver, who is likely
to die in childing; he then burns the feather, and the
Simorg appears and orders the Cæsarean operation to
be performed. As these stories are not Ferdusi's inven-
tion, but the old traditions of the Persians, collected
and arranged by him, this is, perhaps, the earliest fact
concerning that operation which is to be met with,
earlier probably than the fable of Semele. Zalzer was
ordered first to give her wine, which acts as a powerful
opiate, and after sewing up the incision, to anoint it
with a mixture of milk, musk, and grass, pounded to-
gether, and dried in the shade, and then to rub it with
a Simorg's feather.

In Mr Fox's collection of Persic books, is an illumi-
nated copy of Ferdusi, containing a picture of the Si-
morg, who is there represented as an ugly dragon-look-
ing sort of bird. I should be loth to believe that she
has so bad a physiognomy; and as, in the same vo-
lume, there are blue and yellow horses, there is good
reason to conclude that this is not a genuine portrait.

When the Genius of the Lamp is ordered by Aladdin
to bring a roc's egg, and hang it up in the hall, he is
violently enraged, and exclaims, Wretch, wouldst thou
have me hang up my master! From the manner in
which rocs are usually mentioned in the Arabian Tales,
the reader feels as much surprised at this indignation
as Aladdin was himself. Perhaps the original may have
Simorg instead of roc. To think, indeed, of robbing
the Simorg's nest, either for the sake of drilling the
eggs, or of poaching them, would, in a believer, whether
Shiah or Sunni, be the height of human impiety.

Since this note was written, the eighth volume of
the Asiatic Researches has appeared, in which Captain
Wilford identifies the roc with the Simorg. « Sindbad,»
he says, « was exposed to many dangers from the birds
called Rocs or Simorgs, the Garudas of the Paurnnics,
whom Persian Romancers represent as living in Mada-
gascar, according to Marco Polo.» But the Roc of the
Arabian Tales has none of the characteristics of the
Simorg; and it is only in the instance which I have
noticed, that any mistake of one for the other can be
suspected.

Note 5, page 138, col. 1.
The spring was clear, the water deep.

Some travellers may perhaps be glad to know, that
the spring from which this description was taken, is
near Bristol, about a mile from Stokes-Croft turnpike,
and known by the name of the Boiling-Well. Other,
and larger springs, of the same kind, called the Lady
Pools, are near Shobdon, in Herefordshire.

Note 6, page 138, col. 2.
It ran a river deep and wide.

A similar picture occurs in Miss Baillie's Comedy,
« The Second Marriage.» « By Heaven, there is nothing
so interesting to me as to trace the course of a pros-
perous man through this varied world. First, he is seen
like a little stream, wearing its shallow bed through the
grass, circling and winding, and gleaning up its trea-
sures from every twinkling rill, as it passes; further
on, the brown sand fences its margin, the dark rushes
thicken on its side; further on still, the broad flags
shake their green ranks, the willows bend their wide
boughs o'er its course; and yonder, at last, the fair
river appears, spreading his bright waves to the light.»

BOOK XII.

Note 1, page 142, col. 1.
A rebel Afreet lay.

One of these evil Genii is thus described in the Bahar
Danush : On his entrance, he beheld a black demon
heaped on the ground like a mountain, with two large
horns upon his head, and a long proboscis, fast asleep.
In his head the Divine Creator had joined the likenesses
of the elephant and the wild bull. His teeth grew out
as the tusks of a boar, and all over his monstrous car-
cass hung shaggy hairs, like those of the bear. The
eye of mortal born was dimmed at his appearance, and
the mind, at his horrible form and frightful figure,
was confounded.

*He was an Afreet, created from mouth to foot by
the wrath of God.*

*His hair like a bear's, his teeth like a boar's. No one
ever beheld such a monster.*

*Crook-backed, and crabbed-faced ; he might be scent-
ed at the distance of a thousand fersungs.*

His nostrils were like the ovens of brick-burners, and his mouth resembled the vat of a dyer.

When his breath came forth, from its vehemence the dust rose up as in a whirlwind, so as to leave a chasm in the earth; and when he drew it in, chaff, sand, and pebbles, from the distance of some yards, were attracted to his nostrils. — *Bahar Danush.*

Note 2, page 143, col. 2.

Al-Araf, in his wisdom ? etc.

Araf is a place between the Paradise and the Hell of the Mahommedans; some deem it a veil of separation, some a strong wall. Others hold it to be a Purgatory, in which those believers will remain, whose good and evil works have been so equal, that they were neither virtuous enough to enter Paradise, nor guilty enough to be condemned to the fire of Hell. From whence they see the glory of the blessed, and are near enough to congratulate them; but their ardent desire to partake the same happiness becomes a great pain. At length, at the day of judgment, when all men, before they are judged, shall be cited to render homage to their Creator, those who are here confined, shall prostrate themselves before the face of the Lord, in adoration; and by this act of religion, which shall be accounted a merit, the number of their good works will exceed their evil ones, and they will enter into glory.

Saadi says, that Araf appears a Hell to the happy, and a Paradise to the damned. — *D'Herbelot.*

Madoc.

Omne solum forti Patria.

TO CHARLES WATKIN WILLIAMS WYNN,

This Poem is inscribed,

AS A TOKEN OF SIXTEEN YEARS OF UNINTERRUPTED FRIENDSHIP.

PREFACE.

THE historical facts on which this Poem is founded may be related in few words. On the death of Owen Gwyneth, king of North Wales, A.D. 1169, his children disputed the succession. Yorwerth, the elder, was set aside without a struggle, as being incapacitated by a blemish in his face. Hoel, though illegitimate, and born of an Irish mother, obtained possession of the throne for a while, till he was defeated and slain by David, the eldest son of the late king by a second wife. The conqueror, who then succeeded without opposition, slew Yorwerth, imprisoned Rodri, and hunted others of his brethren into exile. But Madoc, meantime, abandoned his barbarous country, and sailed away to the West in search of some better resting-place. The land which he discovered pleased him: he left there part of his people, and went back to Wales for a fresh supply of adventurers, with whom he again set sail, and was heard of no more. Strong evidence has been adduced that he reached America, and that his posterity exist there to this day, on the southern branches of the Missouri, retaining their complexion, their language and, in some degree, [1] their arts.

About the same time, the Aztecas, an American tribe, in consequence of certain calamities, and of a particular omen, forsook Aztlan, their own country, under the guidance of Yuhidthiton. They became a mighty people, and founded the Mexican empire, taking the name of Mexicans, in honour of Mexitli, their tutelary god. Their emigration is here connected with the adventures of Madoc, and their superstition is represented as the same which their descendants practised, when discovered by the Spaniards. The manners of the Poem, in both its parts, will be found historically true. It assumes not the degraded title of Epic; and the question, therefore, is not whether the story is formed upon the rules of Aristotle, but whether it be adapted to the purposes of poetry.   1805.

Three things must be avoided in Poetry; the frivolous, the obscure, and the superfluous.

The three excellencies of Poetry; simplicity of language, simplicity of subject, and simplicity of invention.

The three indispensable purities of Poetry; pure truth, pure language, and pure manners.

Three things should all Poetry be; thoroughly erudite, thoroughly animated, and thoroughly natural.
                                                TRIADS.

COME, LISTEN TO A TALE OF TIMES OF OLD !
COME, FOR YE KNOW ME. I AM HE WHO SUNG
THE MAID OF ARC, AND I AM HE WHO FRAMED
OF THALABA THE WILD AND WONDROUS SONG.
COME, LISTEN TO MY LAY, AND YE SHALL HEAR
HOW MADOC FROM THE SHORES OF BRITAIN SPREAD
THE ADVENTUROUS SAIL, EXPLORED THE OCEAN PATHS,
AND QUELLED BARBARIAN POWER, AND OVERTHREW
THE BLOODY ALTARS OF IDOLATRY,
AND PLANTED IN ITS FANES TRIUMPHANTLY
THE CROSS OF CHRIST. COME LISTEN TO MY LAY !

[1] That country has now been fully explored, and wherever Madoc may have settled, it is now certain that no Welsh Indians are to be found upon any branches of the Missouri.—1815.

PART I.

MADOC IN WALES.

I.

The Return to Wales.

FAIR blows the wind,—the vessel drives along,
Her streamers fluttering at their length, her sails
All full,—she drives along, and round her prow
Scatters the ocean spray.   What feelings then
Filled every bosom, when the mariners,
After the peril of that weary way,
Beheld their own dear country! Here stands one
Stretching his sight toward the distant shore,
And as to well-known forms his busy joy
Shapes the dim outline, eagerly he points
The fancied headland and the cape and bay,
Till his eyes ache o'erstraining.   This man shakes
His comrade's hand, and bids him welcome home,
And blesses God, and then he weeps aloud :
Here stands another, who in secret prayer
Calls on the Virgin and his patron Saint,
Renewing his old vows of gifts and alms
And pilgrimage, so he may find all well.
Silent and thoughtful and apart from all
Stood Madoc; [1] now his noble enterprise
Proudly remembering, now in dreams of hope,
Anon of bodings full and doubt and fear.
Fair smiled the evening, and the favouring gale
Sung in the shrouds, and swift the steady bark
Rushed roaring through the waves.
                         The sun goes down.
Far off his light is on the naked crags
Of Penmanmawr, and Arven's ancient hills ;
And the last glory lingers yet awhile,
Crowning old Snowdon's venerable head,
That rose amid his mountains.   Now the ship
Drew nigh where Mona, the dark island, [2] stretched
Her shore along the ocean's lighter line.
There through the mist and twilight, many a fire
Up-flaming streamed upon the level sea
Red lines of lengthening light, which, far away
Rising and falling, flashed athwart the waves.
Thereat did many a thought of ill disturb
Prince Madoc's mind ;—did some new conqueror seize
The throne of David? had the tyrant's guilt
Awakened vengeance to the deed of death?
Or blazed they for a brother's obsequies,
The sport and mirth of murder?—Like the lights
Which there upon Aberfraw's [3] royal walls
Are waving with the wind, the painful doubt
Fluctuates within him.—Onward drives the gale,—
On flies the bark ;—and she hath reached at length
Her haven, safe from her unequalled way!
And now in louder and yet louder joy
Clamorous the happy mariners all-hail
Their native shore, and now they leap to land.

There stood an old man on the beach to wait
The comers from the ocean ; and he asked,
Is it the Prince? And Madoc knew his voice,
And turned to him and fell upon his neck ;
For it was Urien who had fostered him,
Had loved him like a child ; and Madoc loved,
Even as a father loved he that old man.
My sister? quoth the prince.—Oh, she and I
Have wept together, Madoc, for thy loss,—
That long and cruel absence !—She and I,
Hour after hour and day by day, have looked
Toward the waters, and with aching eyes
And aching heart sate watching every sail.

And David and our brethren? cried the prince,
As they moved on.—But then old Urien's lips
Were slow at answer ; and he spake, and paused
In the first breath of utterance, as to chuse
Fit words for uttering some unhappy tale.
More blood, quoth Madoc, yet ! Hath David's fear
Forced him to still more cruelty? Alas,—
Woe for the house of Owen !
                    Evil stars,
Replied the old man, ruled o'er thy brethren's birth.
From Dolwyddelan driven, his peaceful home,
Poor Yorwerth sought the church's sanctuary ;
The murderer followed !—Madoc, need I say
Who sent the sword?—Llewellyn, his brave boy,
Where wanders he? in this his rightful realm,
Houseless and hunted! richly would the king
Gift the red hand that rid him of that fear! [4]
Ririd, an outlawed fugitive, as yet
Eludes his brother's fury ; Rodri lives,
A prisoner he,—I know not in what fit
Of natural mercy from the slaughter spared.
Oh, if my dear old master saw the wreck
And scattering of his house !—that princely race!
The beautiful band of brethren that they were!

Madoc made no reply,—he closed his lids,
Groaning.   But Urien, for his soul was full,
Loving to linger on the woe, pursued :
I did not think to live to such an hour
Of joy as this! and often, when my eyes
Turned dizzy from the ocean, overcome
With heavy anguish, Madoc, I have prayed
That God would please to take me to his rest.

So as he ceased his speech, a sudden shout
Of popular joy awakened Madoc's ear :
And calling then to mind the festal fires,
He asked their import.   The old man replied,
It is the giddy people merry-making
To welcome their new queen: unheeding they
The shame and the reproach to the long line
Of our old royalty!—Thy brother weds
The Saxon's sister.
                    What !—in loud reply
Madoc exclaimed, hath he forgotten all!
David! King Owen's son,—my father's son,—
He wed the Saxon.—Plantagenet ! [5]

Quoth Urien, He so doats, as she had dropt
Some philtre in his cup, to lethargize
The British blood that came from Owen's veins.
Three days his halls have echoed to the song
Of joyaunce.
            Shame! foul shame! that they should hear
Songs of such joyaunce! cried the indignant prince ;

Oh that my father's hall, where I have heard
The song of Corwen and of Keiriog's day,
Should echo this pollution! Will the chiefs
Brook this alliance, this unnatural tie?

There is no face but wears a courtly smile,
Urien replied: Aberfraw's ancient towers
Beheld no pride of festival like this,
No like solemnities, when Owen came
In conquest, and Gowalchmai struck the harp.
Only Goervyl, careless of the pomp,
Sits in her solitude, lamenting thee.

Saw ye not then my banner? quoth the Lord
Of Ocean; on the topmast-head it stood
To tell the tale of triumph;—or did night
Hide the glad signal, and the joy hath yet
To reach her?
                Now had they almost attained
The palace portal. Urien stopt and said,
The child should know your coming; it is long
Since she hath heard a voice that to her heart
Spake gladness:—none but I must tell her this!
So Urien sought Goervyl! whom he found
Alone and gazing on the moonlight sea.

Oh you are welcome, Urien! cried the maid.
There was a ship came sailing hitherward—
I could not see his banner, for the night
Closed in so fast around her; but my heart
Indulged a foolish hope!
                    The old man replied,
With difficult effort keeping his heart down,
God in his goodness may reserve for us
That blessing yet! I have yet life enow
To trust that I shall live to see the day,
Albeit the number of my years well nigh
Be full.
            Ill-judging kindness! said the maid.
Have I not nursed for two long wretched years
That miserable hope, which every day
Grew weaker, like a baby sick to death,
Yet dearer for its weakness day by day!
No, never shall we see his daring bark!
I knew and felt it in the evil hour
When forth she fared! I felt it then! that kiss
Was our death-parting!—And she paused to curb
The agony: anon,—But thou hast been
To learn their tidings, Urien? He replied,
In half-articulate voice,—They said, my child,
That Madoc lived—that soon he would be here.

She had received the shock of happiness:
Urien! she cried—thou art not mocking me!
Nothing the old man spake, but spread his arms
Sobbing aloud. Goervyl from their hold
Started, and sunk upon her brother's breast.
Recovering first, the aged Urien said,
Enough of this,—there will be time for this,
My children! better it behoves ye now
To seek the king. And, Madoc, I beseech thee.
Bear with thy brother! gently bear with him,
My gentle prince! he is the headstrong slave
Of passions unsubdued; [6] he feels no tie
Of kindly love, or blood;—provoke him not,
Madoc!—It is his nature's malady.

Thou good old man! replied the prince, be sure
I shall remember what to him is due,
What to myself; for I was in my youth
Wisely and well trained up; nor yet hath time
Effaced the lore my foster-father taught.

Haste, haste! exclaimed Goervyl;—for her heart
Smote her in sudden terror at the thought
Of Yorwerth, and of Owen's broken house;—
I dread his dark suspicions!
                            Not for me
Suffer that fear, my sister! quoth the prince.
Safe is the straight and open way I tread!
Nor hath God made the human heart so bad
That thou or I should have a danger there.
So saying, they toward the palace gate
Went on, ere yet Aberfraw had received
The tidings of her wanderer's glad return.

II.

The Marriage Feast.

THE guests were seated at the festal board,[7]
Green rushes strewed the floor; high in the hall
Was David; Emma, in her bridal robe,
In youth, in beauty, by her husband's side
Sate at the marriage feast. The monarch raised
His eyes, he saw the mariner approach;
Madoc! he cried; strong nature's impulses
Prevailed, and with a holy joy he met
His brother's warm embrace.
                        With that what peals
Of exultation shook Aberfraw's tower!
How then re-echoing rang the home of kings,
When from subdued Ocean, from the World
That he had first foreseen, he first had found,
Came her triumphant child! The mariners,
A happy band, enter the clamorous hall;
Friend greets with friend, and all are friends; one joy
Fills with one common feeling every heart,
And strangers give and take the welcoming
Of hand and voice and eye. That boisterous joy
At length allayed, the board was spread anew,
Anew the horn was brimmed, the central hearth
Built up anew for later revelries.
Now to the ready feast! the seneschal
Duly below the pillars ranged the crew;
Toward the guest's most honourable seat
The king himself led his brave brother;—then,
Eyeing the lovely Saxon as he spake,
Here, Madoc, see thy sister! thou hast been
Long absent, and our house hath felt the while
Sad diminution; but my arm at last
Hath rooted out rebellion from the land;
And I have stablished now our ancient house,
Grafting a scion from the royal tree
Of England on the sceptre; so shall peace
Bless our dear country.
                    Long and happy years
Await my sovereigns! thus the chief replied,
And long may our dear country rest in peace!
Enough of sorrow hath our royal house
Known in the field of battles,—yet we reaped
The harvest of renown.

Aye,—many a day,
David replied, together have we led
The onset!—Dost thou not remember, brother,
How, in that hot and unexpected charge
On Keiriog's bank, we gave the enemy
Their welcoming?

And Berwyn's after-strife! [8]
Quoth Madoc, as the memory kindled him:
The fool that day, who in his masque attire
Sported before King Henry, [9] wished in vain
Fitlier habiliments of javelin proof!
And yet not more precipitate that fool
Dropt his mock weapons, than the archers cast
Desperate their bows and quivers full away,
When we leapt on, and in the mire and blood
Trampled their banner!

That, exclaimed the king,
That was a day indeed, which I may still
Proudly remember, proved as I have been
In conflicts of such perilous assay,
That Saxon combat seemed like woman's war.
When with the traitor Hoel I did wage
The deadly battle, then was I in truth
Put to the proof; no vantage-ground was there,
Nor famine, nor disease, nor storms to aid,
But equal, hard, close battle, man to man,
Briton to Briton! By my soul, pursued
The tyrant, heedless how from Madoc's eye
Flashed the quick wrath like lightning,—though I
    knew
The rebel's worth, [10] his prowess then excited
Unwelcome wonder! even at the last,
When stiff with toil and faint with wounds, he raised
Feebly his broken sword,—

Then Madoc's grief
Found utterance: Wherefore, David, dost thou rouse
The memory now of that unhappy day,
That thou shouldst wish to hide from earth and
    heaven?
Not in Aberfraw,—not to me this tale!
Tell it the Saxon!—he will join thy triumph,—
He hates the race of Owen!—but I loved
My brother Hoel—loved him?—that ye knew!
I was to him the dearest of his kin,
And he my own heart's brother.

David's cheek
Grew pale and dark; he bent his broad black brow
Full upon Madoc's crimson countenance;
Art thou returned to brave me? to my teeth
To praise the rebel bastard? to insult
The royal Saxon, my affianced friend?
I hate the Saxon! [11] Madoc cried; not yet
Have I forgotten, how from Keiriog's shame
Flying the coward wreaked his cruelty
On my poor brethren !—David, seest thou never
Those eyeless spectres by thy bridal bed? [12]
Forget that horror?—may the fire of God
Blast my right hand, or ever it be linked
With that accursed Plantagenet!

The while,
Impatience struggled in the heaving breast
Of David; every agitated limb
Shook with ungovernable wrath; the page,
Who chafed his feet, [13] in fear suspends his task;
In fear the guests gaze on him silently;
His eyeballs flashed, strong anger choked his voice,

He started up.—Him Emma, by the hand
Gently retaining, held, with gentle words
Calming his rage. Goervyl too in tears
Besought her generous brother: he had met
Emma's approaching glance, and self-reproved
While the warm blood flushed deeper o'er his cheek,
Thus he replied; I pray you pardon me,
My sister-queen! nay, you will learn to love
This high affection for the race of Owen,
Yourself the daughter of his royal house,
By better ties than blood.

Grateful the queen
Replied, by winning smile and eloquent eye
Thanking the gentle prince: a moment's pause
Ensued; Goervyl then with timely speech
Thus to the wanderer of the waters spake:
Madoc, thou hast not told us of the world
Beyond the ocean and the paths of man.
A lovely land it needs must be, my brother,
Or sure you had not sojourned there so long,
Of me forgetful, and my heavy hours
Of grief and solitude and wretched hope.
Where is Cadwallon? for one bark alone
I saw come sailing here.

The tale you ask
Is long, Goervyl, said the mariner,
And I in truth am weary. Many moons
Have waxed and waned, since from the distant world,
The country of my dreams and hope and faith,
We spread the homeward sail: a lovely world,
My sister! thou shalt see its goodliness,
And greet Cadwallon there—but this shall be
To-morrow's tale:—indulge we now the feast!—
You know not with what joy we mariners
Behold a sight like this.

Smiling he spake,
And turning, from the sewer's hand he took
The flowing mead. David, the while, relieved
From rising jealousies, with better eye
Regards his venturous brother. Let the bard,
Exclaimed the king, give his accustomed lay;
For sweet, I know, to Madoc is the song
He loved in earlier years.

Then, strong of voice,
The officer proclaimed the sovereign will, [14]
Bidding the hall be silent; loud he spake,
And smote the sounding pillar with his wand,
And hushed the banqueters. The chief of Bards
Then raised the ancient lay. [15]

Thee, Lord! he sung,
Father! the eternal One! whose wisdom, power,
And love,—all love, all power, all wisdom, Thou!
Nor tongue can utter, nor can heart conceive.
He in the lowest depth of Being framed
The imperishable mind; in every change,
Through the great circle of progressive life,
He guides and guards, till evil shall be known,
And being known as evil, cease to be; [16]
And the pure soul, emancipate by Death,
The Enlarger, [17] shall attain its end predoomed,
The eternal newness of eternal joy. [18]

He left this lofty theme; he struck the harp
To Owen's praise, [19] swift in the course of wrath,
Father of Heroes. That proud day he sung,
When from green Erin came the insulting host,

Lochlin's long burthens of the flood, and they
Who left their distant homes in evil hour,
The death-doomed Normen. There was heaviest toil,
There deeper tumult, where the dragon race
Of Mona trampled down the humbled head
Of haughty power; the sword of slaughter carved
Food for the yellow-footed fowl of heaven,
And Menai's waters, burst with plunge on plunge,
Curling above their banks with tempest-swell
Their bloody billows heaved.
                             The long-past days
Came on the mind of Madoc, as he heard
The song of triumph: on his sun-burnt brow
Sate exultation :—other thoughts arose,
As on the fate of all his gallant house
Mournful he mused; oppressive memory swelled
His bosom, over his fixed eye-balls swam
The tear's dim lustre, and the loud-toned harp
Rung on his ear in vain ;—its silence first
Roused him from dreams of days that were no more.

III.

Cadwallon.

Then on the morrow, at the banquet board,
The Lord of Ocean thus began his tale.

My heart beat high when with the favouring wind
We sailed away, Aberfraw! when thy towers,
And the huge headland of my mother isle,
Shrunk and were gone.
                      But, Madoc, I would learn,
Quoth David, how this enterprise arose,
And the wild hope of worlds beyond the sea;
For at thine outset being in the war,
I did not hear from vague and common fame
The moving cause. Sprung it from bardic lore,
The hidden wisdom of the years of old,
Forgotten long? or did it visit thee
In dreams that come from heaven?
                                 The prince replied,
Thou shalt hear all ;—but if, amid the tale,
Strictly sincere, I haply should rehearse
Aught to the king ungrateful, let my brother
Be patient with the involuntary fault.

I was the guest of Rhys at Dinevawr, [20]
And there the tidings found me, that our sire
Was gathered to his fathers :—not alone
The sorrow came; the same ill messenger
Told of the strife that shook our royal house,
When Hoel, proud of prowess, seized the throne [21]
Which you, for elder claim and lawful birth,
Challenged in arms. With all a brother's love,
I on the instant hurried to prevent
The impious battle :—all the day I sped,
Night did not stay me on my eager way—
Where'er I passed, new rumour raised new fear—
Midnight, and morn, and noon, I hurried on,
And the late eve was darkening when I reached
Arvon, the fatal field.--The sight, the sounds,
Live in my memory now,—for all was done!
For horse and horseman side by side in death,
Lay on the bloody plain ;—a host of men,

And not one living soul,—and not one sound,
One human sound,—only the raven's wing,
Which rose before my coming, and the neigh
Of wounded horses, wandering o'er the plain.

Night now was coming on; a man approached,
And bade me to his dwelling nigh at hand.
Thither I turned, too weak to travel on ;
For I was overspent with weariness,
And having now no hope to bear me up,
Trouble and bodily labour mastered me.
I asked him of the battle :—who had fallen
He knew not, nor to whom the lot of war
Had given my father's sceptre. Here, said he,
I came to seek if haply I might find
Some wounded wretch, abandoned else to death.
My search was vain, the sword of civil war
Had bit too deeply.
                    Soon we reached his home,
A lone and lowly dwelling in the hills,
By a grey mountain stream. Beside the hearth
There sate an old blind man; his head was raised
As he were listening to the coming sounds,
And in the fire-light shone his silver locks.
Father, said he who guided me, I bring
A guest to our poor hospitality!
And then he brought me water from the brook,
And homely fare, and I was satisfied :
That done, he piled the hearth, and spread around
The rushes of repose. I laid me down;
But worn with toil, and full of many fears,
Sleep did not visit me : the quiet sounds
Of nature troubled my distempered sense ;
My ear was busy with the stirring gale,
The moving leaves, the brook's perpetual flow.

So on the morrow languidly I rose,
And faint with fever : but a restless wish
Was working in me, and I said, My host,
Wilt thou go with me to the battle-field,
That I may search the slain? for in the fray
My brethren fought; and though with all my speed
I strove to reach them ere the strife began,
Alas, I sped too slow!
                       Grievest thou for that?
He answered, grievest thou that thou art spared
The shame and guilt of that unhappy strife,
Briton with Briton in unnatural war?
Nay, I replied, mistake me not! I came
To reconcile the chiefs; they might have heard
Their brother's voice.
                       Their brother's voice? said he;
Was it not so?—And thou, too, art the son
Of Owen!—Yesternight I did not know
The cause there is to pity thee. Alas,
Two brethren thou wilt lose when one shall fall!—
Lament not him whom death may save from guilt ;
For in the conqueror thou art doomed to find
A foe, whom his own fears make perilous!

I felt as though he wronged my father's sons,
And raised an angry eye, and answered him,—
My brethren love me.
                      Then the old man cried,
Oh! what is princes' love? what are the ties
Of blood, the affections growing as we grow,

If but ambition come?—Thou deemëst sure
Thy brethren love thee;—ye have played together
In childhood, shared your riper hopes and fears,
Fought side by side in battle:—they may be
Brave, generous, all that once their father was,
Whom ye, I ween, call virtuous.

        At the name,
With pious warmth I cried, Yes, he was good,
And great, and glorious! Gwyneth's ancient annals
Boast not a name more noble: in the war
Fearless he was,—the Saxon proved him so;
Wise was his counsel, and no supplicant
For justice ever from his palace-gate
Unrighted turned away. King Owen's name
Shall live in the after-world without a blot!

There were two brethren once, of kingly line.
The old man replied; they loved each other well,
And when the one was at his dying hour,
It then was comfort to him that he left
So dear a brother, who would duly pay
A father's duties to his orphan boy.
And sure he loved the orphan, and the boy
With all a child's sincerity loved him,
And learnt to call him father: so the years
Went on, till, when the orphan gained the age
Of manhood, to the throne his uncle came.
The young man claimed a fair inheritance,
His father's lands, and—mark what follows, prince;
At midnight he was seized, and to his eyes
The brazen plate was held—He looked around
His prison-room for help,—he only saw
The ruffian forms, who to the red-hot brass
Forced his poor eyes, and held the open lids,
Till the long agony consumed the sense;
And when their hold relaxed, it had been worth
The wealth of worlds if he could then have seen
Their ruffian faces!—I am blind, young prince,
And I can tell how sweet a thing it is
To see the blessèd light!

        Must more be told?
What farther agonies he yet endured?
Or hast thou known the consummated crime,
And heard Cynetha's fate? [22]

        A painful glow
Inflamed my cheek, and for my father's crime
I felt the shame of guilt. The dark-browed man
Beheld the burning flush, the uneasy eye,
That knew not where to rest. Come! we will search
The slain! arising from his seat, he said.
I followed; to the field of fight we went,
And over steeds and arms and men we held
Our way in silence. Here it was, quoth he,
The fiercest war was waged; lo! in what heaps
Man upon man fell slaughtered! Then my heart
Smote me, and my knees shook; for I beheld
Where, on his conquered foeman, Hoel lay.

He paused, his heart was full, and on his tongue
The imperfect utterance died; a general gloom
Saddened the hall, and David's cheek grew pale.
Commanding first his nature, Madoc broke
The oppressive silence.

        Then Cadwallon took
My hand, and, pointing to his dwelling, cried,
Prince, go and rest thee there, for thou hast need

Of rest;—the care of sepulture be mine.
Nor did I then comply, refusing rest,
Till I had seen in holy ground inearthed
My poor lost brother. Wherefore, he exclaimed,
(And I was awed by his severer eye)
Wouldst thou be pampering thy distempered mind?
Affliction is not sent in vain, young man,
From that good God, who chastens whom he loves!
Oh! there is healing in the bitter cup!
Go yonder, and before the unerring will
Bow, and have comfort! To the hut I went,
And there beside the lonely mountain-stream,
I veiled my head, and brooded on the past.
He tarried long; I felt the hours pass by,
As in a dream of morning, when the mind,
Half to reality awakened, blends
With airy visions and vague fantasies
Her dim perception; till at length his step
Aroused me, and he came. I questioned him,
Where is the body? hast thou bade the priests
Perform due masses for his soul's repose?

He answered me, The rain and dew of heaven
Will fall upon the turf that covers him,
And greener grass shall flourish on his grave.
But rouse thee, prince! there will be hours enough
For mournful memory;—it befits thee now
Take counsel for thyself:—the son of Owen
Lives not in safety here.

        I bowed my head
Oppressed by heavy thoughts: all wretchedness
The present; darkness on the future lay;
Fearful and gloomy both. I answered not.

Hath power seduced thy wishes? he pursued,
And wouldst thou seize upon thy father's throne?
Now God forbid! quoth I. Now God forbid!
Quoth he;—but thou art dangerous, prince! and what
Shall shield thee from the jealous arm of power?
Think of Cynetha!—the unsleeping eye
Of justice hath not closed upon his wrongs;—
At length the avenging arm is gone abroad,—
One woe is past,—woe after woe comes on,—
There is no safety here,—here thou must be
The victim or the murderer! Does thy heart
Shrink from the alternative!—look round!—behold
What shelter,—whither wouldst thou fly for peace?
What if the asylum of the church were safe,—
Were there no better purposes ordained
For that young arm, that heart of noble hopes?
Son of our kings,—of old Cassibelan,
Great Caratach, immortal Arthur's line—
Oh, shall the blood of that heroic race
Stagnate in cloister sloth?—Or wouldst thou leave
Thy native isle, and beg in awkward phrase
Some foreign sovereign's charitable grace,—
The Saxon or the Frank,—and earn his gold,—.
The hireling in a war whose cause thou knowest not,
Whose end concerns not thee?

        I sate and gazed,
Following his eye with wonder, as he paced
Before me to and fro, and listening still,
Though now he paced in silence. But anon,
The old man's voice and step awakened us,
Each from his thought; I will come out, said he,
That I may sit beside the brook, and feel

26

The comfortable sun. As forth he came,
I could not chuse but look upon his face :
Gently on him had gentle nature laid
The weight of years! all passions that disturb
Were past away; the stronger lines of grief
Softened and settled, till they told of grief
By patient hope and piety subdued.
His eyes, which had their hue and brightness left,
Fixed lifelessly, or objectless they rolled,
Nor moved by sense, nor animate with thought.
On a smooth stone beside the stream he took
His wonted seat in the sunshine. Thou hast lost
A brother, prince, he cried,—or the dim ear
Of age deceived me. Peace be with his soul!
And may the curse that lies upon the house
Of Owen turn away! wilt thou come hither,
And let me feel thy face?—I wondered at him;
Yet while his hand perused my lineaments,
Deep awe and reverence filled me. O my God,
Bless this young man! he cried; a perilous state
Is his;—but let not thou his father's sins
Be visited on him!

                    I raised my eyes,
Inquiring, to Cadwallon : Nay, young prince,
Despise not thou the blind man's prayer! he cried;
It might have given thy father's dying hour
A hope, that sure he needed!—for, know thou,
It is the victim of thy father's crime,
Who asks a blessing on thee!

                            At his feet
I fell, and claspt his knees : he raised me up;—
Blind as I was, a mutilated wretch,
A thing that nature owns not, I survived,
Loathing existence, and with impious voice
Accused the will of heaven, and groaned for death.
Years past away; this universal blank
Became familiar, and my soul reposed
On God, and I had comfort in my prayers.
But there were blessings for me yet in store .
Thy father knew not, when his bloody fear
All hope of an avenger had cut off,
How there existed then an unborn babe,
Child of my lawless love. Year after year
I lived a lonely and forgotten wretch,
Before Cadwallon knew his father's fate,
Long years and years before I knew my son;
For never, till his mother's dying hour,
Learnt he his dangerous birth. He sought me then ;
He woke my soul once more to human ties :—
I hope he hath not weaned my heart from heaven,
Life is so precious now!—
                        Dear good old man;
And lives he still? Goervyl cried, in tears.
Madoc replied, I scarce can hope to find
A father's welcome at my distant home.
I left him full of days, and ripe for death;
And the last prayer Cynetha breathed upon me
Went like a death-bed blessing to my heart !

When evening came, toward the echoing shore
I and Cadwallon walked together forth :
Bright with dilated glory shone the west;
But brighter lay the ocean-flood below,
The burnished silver sea, that heaved and flashed
Its restless rays, intolerably bright.
Prince, quoth Cadwallon, thou hast rode the waves

In triumph, when the invaders felt thine arm.
Oh! what a nobler conquest might be won,
There,—upon that wide field!—What meanëst thou?
I cried—That yonder waters are not spread
A boundless waste, a bourn impassable!—
That man should rule the Elements!—that there
Might manly courage, manly wisdom find
Some happy isle, some undiscovered shore,
Some resting place for peace.—Oh that my soul
Could seize the wings of Morning! soon would I
Behold that other world, where yonder sun
Speeds now, to dawn in glory!

                            As he spake,
Conviction came upon my startled mind,
Like lightning on the midnight traveller.
I caught his hand;—Kinsman and guide and friend,
Yea, let us go together!—Down we sate,
Full of the vision on the echoing shore.
One only object filled ear, eye, and thought :
We gazed upon the awful world of waves,
And talked and dreamt of years that were to come.

IV.

The Voyage.

Not with a heart unmoved I left thy shores,
Dear native isle! oh—not without a pang,
As thy fair uplands lessened on the view, [23]
Cast back the long involuntary look!
The morning cheered our outset; gentle airs
Curled the blue deep, and bright the summer sun
Played o'er the summer ocean, when our barks
Began their way.
                And they were gallant barks,
As ever through the raging billows rode!
And many a tempest's buffeting they bore.
Their sails all swelling with the eastern breeze,
Their tightened cordage clattering to the mast,
Steady they rode the main ; the gale aloft
Sung in the shrouds, the sparkling waters hissed
Before, and frothed, and whitened far behind.
Day after day, with one auspicious wind,
Right to the setting sun we held our course.
My hope had kindled every heart; they blest
The unvarying breeze, whose unabating strength
Still sped us onward; and they said that Heaven
Favoured the bold emprize.
                        How many a time,
Mounting the mast-tower-top, with eager ken
They gazed, and fancied in the distant sky
Their promised shore, beneath the evening cloud,
Or seen, low lying, through the haze of morn! [24]
I too with eyes as anxious watched the waves,
Though patient, and prepared for long delay;
For not on wild adventure had I rushed
With giddy speed, in some delirious fit
Of fancy; but in many a tranquil hour
Weighed well the attempt, till hope matured to faith.
Day after day, day after day the same,—
A weary waste of waters! still the breeze
Hung heavy in our sails, and we held on
One even course; a second week was gone,
And now another past, and still the same,
Waves beyond waves, the interminable sea!

What marvel, if at length the mariners
Grew sick with long expectance? I beheld
Dark looks of growing restlessness, I heard
Distrust's low murmuring; nor availed it long
To see and not perceive. Shame had awhile
Represt their fear, till like a smothered fire
It burst, and spread with quick contagion round,
And strengthened as it spread. They spake in tones
Which might not be mistaken,—they had done
What men dared do, ventured where never keel
Had cut the deep before; still all was sea,
The same unbounded ocean!—to proceed
Were tempting heaven.

    I heard with feigned surprise,
And, pointing then to where our fellow bark,
Gay with her fluttering streamers and full sails,
Rode, as in triumph, o'er the element,
I asked them what their comrades there would deem
Of those so bold ashore, who, when a day,
Perchance an hour, might crown their glorious toil,
Shrunk then, and coward-like returned to meet
Mockery and shame! true, they had ventured on
In seas unknown, beyond where ever man
Had ploughed the billows yet: more reason so
Why they should now, like him whose happy speed
Well nigh had run the race, with higher hope
Press onward to the prize. But late they said,
Marking the favour of the steady gale,
That Heaven was with us; Heaven vouchsafed us still
Fair seas and favouring skies; nor need we pray
For other aid, the rest was in ourselves;
Nature had given it, when she gave to man
Courage and constancy.

    They answered not,
Awhile obedient; but I saw with dread
The silent sullenness of cold assent.
Then, with what fearful eagerness I gazed,
At earliest daybreak, o'er the distant deep!
How sick at heart with hope, when evening closed,
Gazed through the gathering shadows!—but I saw
The sun still sink below the endless waves;
And still at morn, beneath the farthest sky,
Unbounded ocean heaved. Day after day,
Before the steady gale we drove along,—
Day after day! The fourth week now had past;
Still all around was sea,—the eternal sea!
So long that we had voyaged on so fast,
And still at morning where we were at night,
And where we were at morn, at nightfall still,
The centre of that drear circumference,
Progressive, yet no change!—almost it seemed
That we had past the mortal bounds of space,
And speed was toiling in infinity.
My days were days of fear, my hours of rest
Were like a tyrant's slumber. Sullen looks,
Eyes turned on me, and whispers meant to meet
My ear, and loud despondency, and talk
Of home, now never to be seen again,—
I suffered these, dissembling as I could, ·
Till that availed no longer. Resolute
The men came round me: They had shown enough
Of courage now, enough of constancy;
Still to pursue the desperate enterprise
Were impious madness! they had deemed, indeed,
That Heaven in favour gave the unchanging gale;—
More reason now to think offended God,

When man's presumptuous folly strove to pass
The fated limits of the world, had sent
The winds, to waft us to the death we sought.
Their lives were dear, they bade me know, and they
Many, and I the obstinate but one.
With that, attending no reply, they hailed
Our fellow bark, and told our fixed resolve:
A shout of joy approved. Thus, desperate now,
I sought my solitary cabin; there,
Confused with vague tumultuous feelings, lay,
And to remembrance and reflection lost,
Knew only I was wretched.

    Thus entranced
Cadwallon found me; shame, and grief, and pride,
And baffled hope, and fruitless anger swelled
Within me. All is over! I exclaimed;
Yet not in me, my friend, hath time produced
These tardy doubts and shameful fickleness;
I have not failed, Cadwallon! Nay, he cried,
The coward fears which persecuted me
Have shown what thou hast suffered. We have yet
One hope—I prayed them to proceed a day,—
But one day more;—this little have I gained,
And here will wait the issue; in yon bark
I am not needed,—they are masters there.

One only day!—The gale blew strong, the bark
'Sped through the waters; but the silent hours,
Who make no pause, went by; and centered still,
We saw the dreary vacancy of heaven
Close round our narrow view, when that brief term,
The last poor respite of our hopes expired.
They shortened sail, and called with coward prayer
For homeward winds. Why, what poor slaves are we!
In bitterness I cried; the sport of chance;
Left to the mercy of the elements,
Or the more wayward will of such as these,
Blind tools and victims of their destiny!
Yea, Madoc! he replied, the elements
Master indeed the feeble powers of man!
Not to the shores of Cambria will thy ships
Win back their shameful way!—or He, whose will
Unchains the winds, hath bade them minister
To aid us, when all human hope was gone,
Or we shall soon eternally repose
From life's long voyage.

    As he spake, I saw
The clouds hang thick and heavy o'er the deep;
And heavily, upon the long slow swell,
The vessel laboured on the labouring sea.
The reef points rattled on the shivering sail;
At fits the sudden gust howled ominous,
Anon with unremitting fury raged;
High rolled the mighty billows, and the blast
Swept from their sheeted sides the showery foam,
Vain, now, were all the seamen's homeward hopes,
Vain all their skill!—we drove before the storm.

'T is pleasant, by the chearful hearth, to hear
Of tempests, and the dangers of the deep,
And pause at times, and feel that we are safe;
Then listen to the perilous tale again,
And with an eager and suspended soul,
Woo terror to delight us—But to hear
The roaring of the raging elements,—
To know all human skill, all human strength,

Avail not,—to look round, and only see
The mountain wave incumbent with its weight
Of bursting waters, o'er the reeling bark,—
O God, this is indeed a dreadful thing!
And he who hath endured the horror once
Of such an hour, doth never hear the storm
Howl round his home, but he remembers it,
And thinks upon the suffering mariner!

Onward we drove: with unabating force
The tempest raged; night added to the storm
New horrors, and the morn arose, o'erspread
With heavier clouds. The weary mariners
Called on Saint Cyric's [25] aid; and I too placed
My hope on heaven, relaxing not the while
Our human efforts. Ye who dwell at home,
Ye do not know the terrors of the main!
When the winds blow, ye walk along the shore,
And, as the curling billows leap and toss,
Fable that Ocean's mermaid Shepherdess
Drives her white flocks afield, and warns in time
The wary fisherman. Gwenhidwy [26] warned us
When we had no retreat! My secret heart
Almost had failed me.—Were the Elements
Confounded in perpetual conflict here,
Sea, Air, and Heaven? Or were we perishing
Where at their source the Floods, for ever thus,
Beneath the nearer influence of the Moon,
Laboured in these mad workings? [27] Did the Waters
Here on their outmost circle meet the Void, [28]
The verge and brink of Chaos? or this Earth,—
Was it indeed a living thing, [29]—its breath
The ebb and flow of Ocean? and had we
Reached the storm rampart of its Sanctuary,
The insuperable boundary, raised to guard
Its mysteries from the eye of man profane?
Three dreadful nights and days we drove along;
The fourth, the welcome rain came rattling down:
The wind had fallen, and through the broken cloud
Appeared the bright dilating blue of heaven.
Emboldened now, I called the mariners:—
Vain were it should we bend a homeward course,
Driven by the storm so far: they saw our barks,
For service of that long and perilous way,
Disabled, and our food belike to fail.
Silent they heard, reluctant in assent;
Anon, they shouted joyfully,—I looked
And saw a bird slow sailing overhead,
His long white pinions by the sunbeam edged
As though with burnished silver;—never yet
Heard I so sweet a music as his cry!

Yet three days more, and hope more eager now,
Sure of the signs of land,'—weed-shoals, and birds
Who flocked the main, and gentle airs which breathed,
Or seemed to breathe, fresh fragrance from the shore. [30]
On the last evening, a long shadowy line
Skirted the sea;—how fast the night closed in!
I stood upon the deck, and watched till dawn.
But who can tell what feelings filled my heart,
When like a cloud the distant land arose
Grey from the ocean,—when we left the ship,
And cleft, with rapid oars, the shallow wave,
And stood triumphant on another world!

V.

Lincoya.

MADOC had paused a while; but every eye
Still watched his lips, and every voice was hushed.
Soon as I leapt ashore, pursues the Lord
Of Ocean, prostrate on my face I fell,
Kissed the dear earth, and prayed with thankful tears.
Hard by a brook was flowing;—never yet,
Even from the gold-tipt horn of victory
With harp and song amid my father's hall,
Pledged I so sweet a draught, as lying there,
Beside that streamlet's brink!—to feel the ground,
To quaff the cool clear water, to inhale
The breeze of land, while fears and dangers past
Recurred and heightened joy, as summer storms
Make the fresh evening lovelier!
                               To the shore
The natives thronged; astonished, they beheld
Our wingèd barks, and gazed in wonderment
On the strange garb and bearded countenance
And skin so white, in all unlike themselves.
I see with what inquiring eyes you ask
What men were they? Of dark-brown colour, tinged
With sunny redness; wild of eye; their brows
So smooth, as never yet anxiety
Nor busy thought had made a furrow there;
Beardless, and each to each of lineaments
So like, they seemed but one great family.
Their loins were loosely cinctured, all beside
Bare to the sun and wind; and thus their limbs
Unmanacled displayed the truest forms
Of strength and beauty: fearless sure they were,
And while they eyed us grasped their spears, as if,
Like Britain's injured but unconquered sons,
They too had known how perilous it was
To see an armèd stranger set his foot
In their free country.
                        Soon the courteous guise
Of men nor purporting nor fearing ill,
Won confidence; their wild distrustful looks
Assumed a milder meaning; over one
I cast my mantle, on another's head
The velvet bonnet placed, and all was joy.
We now besought for food; at once they read
Our gestures, but I cast a hopeless eye
On mountains, thickets, woods, and marshy plains,
A waste of rank luxuriance all around.
Thus musing to a lake I followed them,
Left when the rivers to their summer course
Withdrew; they scattered on its water drugs
Of such strange potency, that soon the shoals
Cooped there by Nature prodigally kind,
Floated inebriate. As I gazed, a deer
Sprung from the bordering thicket; the true shaft
Scarce with the distant victim's blood had stained
Its point, when instantly he dropt and died,
Such deadly juice imbued it; yet on this
We made our meal unharmed, and I perceived
The wisest leech that ever in our world
Culled herbs of hidden virtue, was to these
Even as an infant.
                     Sorrowing we beheld
The night come on; but soon did night display

More wonders than it veiled : innumerous tribes
From the wood-cover swarmed, and darkness made
Their beauties visible ; one while they streamed
A bright blue radiance upon flowers which closed
Their gorgeous colours from the eye of day ;
Now motionless and dark eluded search,
Self-shrouded ; and anon starring the sky
Rose like a shower of fire.

     Our friendly hosts
Now led us to the hut, our that night's home,
A rude and spacious dwelling : twisted boughs,
And canes and withies formed the walls and roof ;
And from the unhewn trunks which pillared it,
Low nets of interwoven reeds [31] were hung.
With shouts of honour here they gathered round me,
Ungarmented my limbs, and in a net
With softest feathers lined, a pleasant couch,
They laid and left me.

     To our ships returned,
After soft sojourn here we coasted on,
Insatiate of the wonders and the charms
Of earth and air and sea. Thy summer woods
Are lovely, O my mother isle ! the birch
Light bending on thy banks, thy elmy vales,
Thy venerable oaks !—but there, what forms
Of beauty clothed the inlands and the shore !
All these in stateliest growth, and mixt with these
Dark spreading cedar, and the cypress tall,
Its pointed summit waving to the wind
Like a long beacon flame ; and loveliest
Amid a thousand strange and lovely shapes,
The lofty palm, that with its nuts supplied
Beverage and food ; they edged the shore and crowned
The far-off mountain summits, their straight stems
Bare without leaf or bough erect and smooth,
Their tresses nodding like a crested helm,
The plumage of the grove.

     Will ye believe
The wonders of the ocean ? how its shoals
Sprung from the wave, [32] like flashing light,—took wing,
And twinkling with a silver glitterance,
Flew through the air and sunshine ? yet were these
To sight less wondrous than the tribe who swam,
Following like fowlers with uplifted eye
Their falling quarry :—language cannot paint
Their splendid tints ! [33] though in blue ocean seen,
Blue, darkly, deeply, beautifully blue,
In all its rich variety of shades,
Suffused with glowing gold.

     Heaven too had there
Its wonders :—from a deep, black, heavy cloud,
What shall I say ?—a shoot,—a trunk,—an arm
Came down ;—yea ! like a demon's arm, it seized
The waters : Ocean smoked beneath its touch,
And rose like dust before the whirlwind's force.
But we sailed onward over tranquil seas,
Wafted by airs so exquisitely mild,
That even to breathe became an act of will,
And sense and pleasure ! Not a cloud by day
With purple islanded the dark-blue deep :
By night the quiet billows heaved and glanced
Under the moon,—that heavenly moon ! so bright,
That many a midnight have I paced the deck,
Forgetful of the hours of due repose ;
Yea till the Sun in his full majesty
Went forth, like God beholding his own works.

Once when a chief was feasting us on shore,
A captive served the food : I marked the youth,
For he had features of a gentler race ;
And oftentimes his eye was fixed on me,
With looks of more than wonder. We returned
At evening to our ships ; at night a voice
Came from the sea, the intelligible voice
Of earnest supplication : he had swam
To trust our mercy ; up the side he sprung,
And looked among the crew, and singling me,
Fell at my feet. Such friendly tokenings
As our short commerce with the native tribes
Had taught, I proffered, and sincerity
Gave force and meaning to the half-learnt forms ;
For one we needed who might speak for us,
And well I liked the youth, the open lines
Which charactered his face, the fearless heart,
Which gave at once and won full confidence :
So that night at my feet Lincoya slept.

When I displayed whate'er might gratify,
Whate'er surprise, with most delight he viewed
Our arms, the iron helm, the pliant mail,
The buckler strong to save ; and then he shook
The lance, and grasped the sword, and turned to me
With vehement words and gestures, every limb
Working with one strong passion ; and he placed
The falchion in my hand, and gave the shield,
And pointed south and west, that I should go
To conquer and protect ; anon he wept
Aloud, and clasped my knees, and falling, fain
He would have kissed my feet. Went we to shore ?
Then would he labour restlessly to show
A better place lay onward ; and in the sand,
To south and west he drew the line of coast,
And figured how a mighty river there
Ran to the sea. The land bent westward soon,
And thus confirmed we voyaged on to seek
The river inlet, following at the will
Of our new friend : and we learnt after him,
Well pleased and proud to teach, what this was called,
What that, with no unprofitable toil.
Nor light the joy I felt at hearing first
The pleasant accents of my native tongue,
Albeit in broken words and tones uncouth,
Come from these foreign lips.

     At length we came
Where the great river, amid shoals and banks
And islands, growth of its own gathering spoils,
Through many a branching channel, wide and full,
Rushed to the main. The gale was strong ; and safe,
Amid the uproar of conflicting tides,
Our gallant vessels rode. A stream as broad,
As turbid, when it leaves the Land of Hills,
Old Severn rolls ; but banks so fair as these
Old Severn views not in his Land of Hills,
Nor even where his turbid waters swell
And sully the salt sea.

     So we sailed on
By shores now covered with impervious woods,
Now stretching wide and low, a reedy waste ;
And now through vales where earth profusely poured
Her treasures, gathered from the first of days.
Sometimes a savage tribe would welcome us,
By wonder from their lethargy of life
Awakened ; then again we voyaged on

Through tracts all desolate, for days and days,
League after league, one green and fertile mead,
That fed a thousand herds.
                              A different scene
Rose on our view, of mount on mountain piled,
Which when I see again in memory,
The giant Cader Idris by their bulk
Is dwarfed, and Snowdon with its eagle haunts
Shrinks, and seems dwindled like a Saxon hill.

Here with Cadwallon and a chosen band,
I left the ships.   Lincoya guided us
A toilsome way among the heights ; at dusk
We reached the village skirts ; he bade us halt,
And raised his voice ; the elders of the land
Came forth, and led us to an ample hut,
Which in the centre of their dwelling stood,
The Stranger's House. [34]   They eyed us wondering,
Yet not for wonder ceased they to observe
Their hospitable rites ; from hut to hut
They spread the tale that strangers were arrived,
Fatigued and hungry and athirst ; anon,
Each from his means supplying us, came food
And beverage such as cheers the weary man.

VI.

Erillyab.

At morning their high-priest Ayayaca
Came with our guide : the venerable man
With reverential awe accosted us,
For we, he weened, were children of a race
Mightier than they, and wiser, and by heaven
Beloved and favoured more : [35] he came to give
Fit welcome, and he led us to the Queen.
The fate of war had reft her of her realm ;
Yet with affection and habitual awe,
And old remembrances, which gave their love
A deeper and religious character,
Fallen as she was, and humbled as they were,
Her faithful people still in all they could
Obeyed Erillyab. She too in her mind
Those recollections cherished, and such thoughts,
As, though no hope allayed their bitterness,
Gave to her eye a spirit, and a strength
And pride to features, which perchance had borne,
Had they been fashioned to a happier fate,
Meaning more gentle and more womanly,
Yet not more worthy of esteem and love.
She sate upon the threshold of her hut ;
For in the palace where her sires had reigned
The conqueror dwelt.   Her son was at her side,
A boy now near to manhood ; by the door,
Bare of its bark, the head and branches shorn,
Stood a young tree with many a weapon hung,
Her husband's war-pole, [36] and his monument.
There had his quiver mouldered, his stone axe
Had there grown green with moss, his bow-string there
Sung as it cut the wind.
                           She welcomed us
With a proud sorrow in her mien ; fresh fruits
Were spread before us, and her gestures said
That when he lived whose hand was wont to wield
Those weapons,—that in better days,—that ere

She let the tresses of her widowhood
Grow wild, she could have given to guests like us
A worthier welcome.   Soon a man approached,
Hooded with sable, his half-naked limbs
Smeared black ; the people at his sight drew round,
The women wailed and wept, the children turned
And hid their faces on their mothers' knees.
He to the Queen addrest his speech, then looked
Around the children, and laid hands on two,
Of different sexes but of age alike,
Some six years each, who at his touch shrieked out ;
But then Lincoya rose, and to my feet
Led them, and told me that the conquerors claimed
These innocents for tribute ; that the Priest
Would lay them on the altar of his god,
Tear out their little hearts in sacrifice,
Yea with more cursed wickedness himself
Feast on their flesh !—I shuddered, and my hand
Instinctively unsheathed the holy sword.
He with most passionate and eloquent signs,
Eye-speaking earnestness and quivering lips,
Besought me to preserve himself, and those
Who now fell suppliant round me,—youths and maids,
Grey-headed men, and mothers with their babes.

I caught the little victims up, I kissed
Their innocent cheeks, I raised my eyes to heaven,
I called upon Almighty God, to hear
And bless the vow I made : in our own tongue
Was that sworn promise of protection pledged—
Impetuous feeling made no pause for thought.
Heaven heard the vow ; the suppliant multitude
Saw what was stirring in my soul ; the Priest,
With eye inflamed and rapid answer, raised
His menacing hand ; the tone, the bitter smile,
Interpreting his threat.
                          Meanwhile the Queen,
With watchful eye and steady countenance,
Had listened ; now she rose and to the Priest
Addressed her speech. Low was her voice and calm,
As one who spake with effort to subdue
Sorrow that struggled still ; but while she spake,
Her features kindled to more majesty,
Her eye became more animate, her voice
Rose to the height of feeling ; on her son
She called, and from her husband's monument
His battle-axe she took ; and I could see,
That when she gave the boy his father's arms,
She called his father's spirit to look on
And bless them to his vengeance.
                                  Silently
The tribe stood listening as Erillyab spake ;
The very priest was awed : once he essayed
To answer ; his tongue failed him, and his lip
Grew pale and fell. He to his countrymen
Of rage and shame and wonder full, returned,
Bearing no victims for their shrines accurst,
But tidings that the Hoamen had cast off
Their vassalage, roused to desperate revolt
By men in hue and speech and garment strange,
Who in their folly dared defy the power
Of Aztlan.
            When the king of Aztlan heard
The unlooked-for tale, ere yet he roused his strength,
Or pitying our rash valour, or belike
Curious to see the man so bravely rash,

He sent to bid me to his court.   Surprised,
I should have given to him no credulous faith,
But fearlessly Erillyab bade me trust
Her honourable foe.   Unarmed I went,
Lincoya with me to exchange our speech
So as he could, of safety first assured;
For to their damned idols he had been
A victim doomed, and from the bloody rites
Flying been carried captive far away.

From early morning till the midnoon hour
We travelled in the mountains; then a plain
Opened below, and rose upon the sight,
Like boundless ocean from a hill-top seen.
A beautiful and populous plain it was;
Fair woods were there and fertilizing streams,
And pastures spreading wide, and villages
In fruitful groves embowered, and stately towns,
And many a single dwelling specking it,
As though for many a year the land had been
The land of peace.   Below us, where the base
Of the great mountain to the level sloped,
A broad blue lake extended far and wide
Its waters, dark beneath the light of noon.
There Aztlan stood upon the farther shore;
Amid the shade of trees its dwellings rose,
Their level roofs with turrets set around,
And battlements all burnished white, which shone
Like silver in the sunshine. 37   I beheld
The imperial city, her far-circling walls,
Her garden groves and stately palaces,
Her temples mountain size, her thousand roofs;
And when I saw her might and majesty
My mind misgave me then.
                        We reached the shore:
A floating islet 38 waited for me there,
The beautiful work of man.   I set my foot
Upon green-growing herbs and flowers, and sate
Embowered in odorous shrubs: four long light boats
Yoked to the garden, with accordant song,
And dip and dash of oar in harmony,
Bore me across the lake.
                        Then in a car
Aloft by human bearers was I borne;
And through the city gate, and through long lines
Of marshalled multitudes who thronged the way,
We reached the palace court.   Four priests were there;
Each held a burning censer in his hand, 39
And strewed the precious gum as I drew nigh,
And held the steaming fragrance forth to me,
Honouring me like a god.   They led me in,
Where on his throne the royal Azteca
Coanocotzin sate.   Stranger, said he,
Welcome; and be this coming to thy weal!
A desperate warfare doth thy courage court;
But thou shalt see the people and the power
Whom thy deluded zeal would call to arms;
So may the knowledge make thee timely wise!
The valiant love the valiant—Come with me!
So saying he rose; we went together forth
To the great Temple.   'T was a huge square hill, 40
Or rather like a rock it seemed, hewn out
And squared by patient labour.   Never yet
Did our forefathers o'er beloved chief
Fallen in his glory, heap a monument
Of that prodigious bulk, though every shield

Was laden for his grave, and every hand
Toiled unremitting at the willing work
From morn till eve, all the long summer day.

The ascent was lengthened with provoking art,
By steps which led but to a wearying path
Round the whole structure; then another flight,
Another road around, and thus a third,
And yet a fourth, before we reached the height.
Lo, now, Coanocotzin cried, thou seest
The cities of this widely peopled plain;
And, wert thou on yon farthest temple-top,
Yet as far onward wouldst thou see the land
Well husbanded like this, and full of men.
They tell me that two floating palaces
Brought thee and all thy people;—when I sound
The Tambour of the God, 41 ten Cities hear
Its voice, 42 and answer to the call in arms.

In truth I felt my weakness, and the view
Had wakened no unreasonable fear,
But that a nearer sight had stirred my blood;
For on the summit where we stood, four Towers
Were piled with human skulls, 43 and all around
Long files of human heads were strung to parch
And whiten in the sun.   What then I felt
Was more than natural courage—'t was a trust
In more than mortal strength—a faith in God,—
Yea, inspiration from him! I exclaimed,
Not though ten Cities ten times told obeyed
The king of Aztlan's bidding, should I fear
The power of man!
                Art thou then more than man?
He answered; and I saw his tawny cheek
Lose its life-colour as the fear arose;
Nor did I undeceive him from that fear,
For sooth I knew not how to answer him,
And therefore let it work.   So not a word
Spake he, till we again had reached the court;
And I too went in silent thoughtfulness:
But then when, save Lincoya, there was none
To hear our speech, again did he renew
The query,—Stranger! art thou more than man,
That thou shouldst set the power of man at nought?

Then I replied, Two floating Palaces
Bore me and all my people o'er the seas.
When we departed from our mother land,
The Moon was newly born; we saw her wax
And wane, and witnessed her new birth again;
And all that while alike by day and night,
We travelled through the sea, and caught the winds,
And made them bear us forward.   We must meet
In battle, if the Hoamen are not freed
From your accursèd tribute,—thou and I,
My people and thy countless multitudes,
Your arrows shall fall from us as the hail
Leaps on a rock,—and when ye smite with swords,
Not blood but fire shall follow from the stroke.
Yet think not thou that we are more than men!
Our knowledge is our power, and God our strength,
God, whose almighty will created thee,
And me, and all that hath the breath of life.
He is our strength;—for in His name I speak,—
And when I tell thee that thou shalt not shed
The life of man in bloody sacrifice,

It is His holy bidding which I speak:
And if thou wilt not listen and obey,
When I shall meet thee in the battle-field
It is His holy cause for which I fight,
And I shall have His power to conquer thee!

And thinkëst thou our Gods are feeble? cried
The king of Aztlan; dost thou deem they lack
Power to defend their altars, and to keep
The kingdom which they gave us strength to win?
The Gods of thirty nations have opposed
Their irresistible might, and they lie now
Conquered and caged and fettered at their feet.
That they who serve them are no coward race
Let prove the ample realm they won in arms:—
And I their leader am not of the sons
Of the feeble! As he spake, he reached a mace,
The trunk and knotted root of some young tree,
Such as Old Albion and his monster-brood
From the oak-forest for their weapons plucked,
When father Brute and Corineus set foot
On the White Island first. Lo this, quoth he,
My club! and he threw back his robe; and this
The arm that wields it!—'T was my father's once:
Erillyab's husband, King Tepollomi,
He felt its weight—did I not show thee him?
He lights me at my evening banquet. " There,
In very deed, the dead Tepollomi
Stood up against the wall, by devilish art
Preserved; and from his black and shrivelled hand
The steady lamp hung down.
                              My spirit rose
At that abomination; I exclaimed,
Thou art of noble nature, and full fain
Would I in friendship plight my hand with thine;
But till that body in the grave be laid,
Till thy polluted altars be made pure,
There is no peace between us. May my God,
Who, though thou knowest him not, is also thine,
And after death, will be thy dreadful Judge,
May it please him to visit thee, and shed
His mercy on thy soul!—But if thy heart
Be hardened to the proof, come when thou wilt!
I know thy power, and thou shalt then know mine.

VII.

The Battle.

Now then to meet the war! Erillyab's call
Roused all her people to revenge their wrongs;
And, at Lincoya's voice, the mountain tribes
Arose and broke their bondage. I, meantime,
Took council with Cadwallon and his sire,
And told them of the numbers we must meet,
And what advantage from the mountain straits
I thought, as in the Saxon wars, to win.
Thou sawest their weapons then, Cadwallon said;
Are they like these rude works of ignorance,
Bone-headed shafts, and spears of wood, and shields
Strong only for such strife?
                              We had to cope
With wiser enemies, and abler armed.
What for the sword they wielded was a staff
Set thick with stones across; you would have judged

The uncouth shape was cumbrous; but a hand
Expert, and practised to its use, could drive
Its heavy edge with deadly impulse down.
Their mail, if mail it may be called, was woven
Of vegetable down, like finest flax,
Bleached to the whiteness of the new-fallen snow;
To every bend and motion flexible,
Light as the warrior's summer-garb in peace;
Yet, in that lightest, softest, habergeon,
Harmless the sharp stone arrow-head would hang.
Others, of higher office, were arrayed
In feathery breast-plates of more gorgeous hue
Than the gay plumage of the mountain-cock,
Than the pheasant's glittering pride. But what were these,
Or what the thin gold hauberk, when opposed
To arms like ours in battle? What the mail
Of wood fire-hardened, or the wooden helm,
Against the iron arrows of the South,
Against our northern spears, or battle-axe,
Or good sword, wielded by a British hand?

Then, quoth Cadwallon, at the wooden helm
Of these weak arms the weakest, let the sword
Hew, and the spear be thrust. The mountaineers,
So long inured to crouch beneath their yoke,
We will not trust in battle; from the heights
They, with their arrows, may annoy the foe;
And, when our closer strife has won the fray,
Then let them loose for havoc.
                              O, my son!
Exclaimed the blind old man, thou counsellest ill!
Blood will have blood, revenge beget revenge,
Evil must come of evil. We shall win,
Certes, a cheap and easy victory
In the first field; their arrows from our arms
Will fall, and on the hauberk and the helm
The stone-edge blunt and break; while through their
     limbs,
Naked, or vainly fenced, the griding steel
Shall sheer its mortal way. But what are we
Against a nation? Other hosts will rise
In endless warfare, with perpetual fights
Dwindling our all-too-few; or multitudes
Will wear and weary us, till we sink subdued
By the very toil of conquest. Ye are strong;
But he who puts his trust in mortal strength
Leans on a broken reed! First prove your power;
Be in the battle terrible, but spare
The fallen, and follow not the flying foe;
Then may ye win a nobler victory,
So dealing with the captives as to fill
Their hearts with wonder, gratitude, and awe,
That love shall mingle with their fear, and fear
Stablish the love, else wavering. Let them see,
That as more pure and gentle is your faith,
Yourselves are gentler, purer. Ye shall be
As gods among them, if ye thus obey
God's precepts.
                              Soon the mountain-tribes, in arms,
Rose at Lincoya's call: a numerous host,
More than in numbers, in the memory
Of long oppression, and revengeful hope,
A formidable foe. I stationed them
Where, at the entrance of the rocky straits,
Secure themselves, their arrows might command
The coming army. On the plain below

We took our stand, between the mountain-base
And the green margin of the waters. Soon
Their long array came on. Oh what a pomp
And pride and pageantry of war [45] was there!
Not half so gorgeous, for their May-day mirth
All wreathed and ribanded, our youths and maids,
As these stern Aztecas in war attire!
The golden glitterance, and the feather-mail,
More gay than glittering gold; and round the helm,
A coronal of high upstanding plumes
Green as the spring grass in a sunny shower;
Or scarlet bright, as in the wintry wood
The clustered holly; or of purple tint,—
Whereto shall that be likened? to what gem
Indiademed,—what flower,—what insect's wing?
With war-songs and wild music they came on,
We the while kneeling, raised with one accord
The hymn of supplication.
                                  Front to front,
And now the embattled armies stood: a band
Of priests, all sable-garmented, advanced;
They piled a heap of sedge before our host,[46]
And warned us,—Sons of Ocean! from the land
Of Aztlan, while ye may, depart in peace!
Before the fire shall be extinguished, hence!
Or, even as yon dry sedge amid the flame,
So ye shall be consumed.—The arid heap
They kindled, and the rapid flame ran up,
And blazed, and died away. Then from his bow,
With steady hand, their chosen archer loosed
The Arrow of the Omen.[47] To its mark
The shaft of divination fled; it smote
Cadwallon's plated breast; the brittle point
Rebounded. He, contemptuous of their faith,
Stoopt for the shaft, and while with zealous speed
To the rescue they rushed onward, snapping it
Asunder, cast the fragments back in scorn.
Fierce was their onset; never in the field
Encountered I with braver enemies.
Nor marvel ye, nor think it to their shame,
If soon they staggered, and gave way, and fled,
So many from so few; they saw their darts
Recoil, their lances shiver, and their swords
Fall ineffectual, blunted with the blow.
Think ye no shame of Aztlan that they fled,
When the bowmen of Deheubarth plied so well
Their shafts with fatal aim; through the thin gold,
Or feather-mail, while Gwyneth's deep-driven spears[48]
Pierced to the bone and vitals; when they saw
The falchion, flashing late so lightning-like,
Quenched in their own life-blood. Our mountaineers
Showered from the heights, meantime, an arrowy storm,
Themselves secure; and we who bore the brunt
Of battle, iron men, impassable,
Stood in our strength unbroken. Marvel not
If then the brave felt fear, already impressed
That day by ominous thoughts, to fear akin;
For so it chanced, high heaven ordaining so,
The king, who should have led his people forth,
At the army head as they began their march,
Was with sore sickness stricken; and the stroke
Came like the act and arm of very God,
So suddenly, and in that point of time.

A gallant man was he, who, in his stead,
That day commanded Aztlan; his long hair,

Tufted with many a cotton lock, proclaimed
Of princely prowess many a feat achieved,
In many a field of fame. Oft had he led
The Aztecas, with happy fortune, forth;
Yet could not now Yuhidthiton inspire
His host with hope: he, not the less, that day,
True to his old renown, and in the hour
Of rout and ruin with collected mind,
Sounded his signals shrill, and in the voice
Of loud reproach and anger, and brave shame,
Called on the people.—But when nought availed,
Seizing the standard from the timid hand
Which held it in dismay, alone he turned,
For honourable death resolved, and praise
That would not die. Thereat the braver chiefs
Rallied, anew their signals rung around,
And Aztlan, seeing how we spared her flight,
Took heart, and rolled the tide of battle back.
But when Cadwallon from the chieftain's grasp
Had cut the standard staff away, and stunned
And stretched him at his mercy on the field;
Then fled the enemy in utter rout,
Broken and quelled at heart. One chief alone
Bestrode the body of Yuhidthiton;
Bareheaded did young Malinal bestride
His brother's body, wiping from his brow
With the shield-hand the blinding blood away,
And dealing franticly, with broken sword,
Obstinate wrath, the last resisting foe.
Him, in his own despite, we seized and saved.
Then, in the moment of our victory,
We purified our hands from blood, and knelt,
And poured to heaven the grateful prayer of praise,
And raised the choral psalm. Triumphant thus
To the hills we went our way; the mountaineers
With joy, and dissonant song, and antic dance;
The captives sullenly, deeming that they went
To meet the certain death of sacrifice,
Yet stern and undismayed. We bade them know,
Ours was a law of mercy and of love;
We healed their wounds, and set the prisoners free.
Bear ye, quoth I, my bidding to your king;
Say to him, Did the Stranger speak to thee
The words of truth, and hath he proved his power?
Thus saith the Lord of Ocean, in the name
Of God, Almighty, Universal God,
Thy Judge and mine, whose battles I have fought,
Whose bidding I obey, whose will I speak;
Shed thou no more, in impious sacrifice,
The life of man; restore into the grave
The dead Tepollomi; set this people free,
And peace shall be between us.
                                  On the morrow
Came messengers from Aztlan, in reply.
Coanocotzin with sore malady
Hath, by the Gods, been stricken: will the Lord
Of Ocean visit his sick-bed?—He told
Of wrath, and as he said, the vengeance came:
Let him bring healing now, and stablish peace.

VIII.

The Peace.

Again, and now with better hope, I sought
The city of the King: there went with me

27

Iolo, old Iolo, he who knows
The virtue of all herbs of mount or vale,
Or greenwood shade, or quiet brooklet's bed;
Whatever lore of science, or of song,
Sages and Bards of old have handed down.
Aztlan that day poured forth her swarming sons,
To wait my coming.   Will he ask his God
To stay the hand of anger? was the cry,
The general cry,—and will he save the King?
Coanocotzin too had nurst that thought,
And the strong hope upheld him: he put forth
His hand, and raised a quick and anxious eye,—
Is it not peace and mercy?—thou art come
To pardon and to save!
                    I answered him,
That power, O King of Aztlan, is not mine!
Such help as human cunning can bestow,
Such human help I bring; but health and life
Are in the hand of God, who at his will
Gives or withdraws; and what he wills is best.
Then old Iolo took his arm, and felt
The symptom, and he bade him have good hope,
For life was strong within him.   So it proved;
The drugs of subtle virtue did their work;
They quelled the venom of the malady,
And from the frame expelled it,—that a sleep
Fell on the king, a sweet and natural sleep,
And from its healing he awoke refreshed,
Though weak, and joyful like a man who felt
The peril past away.
                    Ere long we spake
Of concord, and how best to knit the bonds
Of lasting friendship.   When we won this land,
Coanocotzin said, these fertile vales
Were not, as now, with fruitful groves embowered,
Nor rich with towns and populous villages,
Abounding, as thou seest, with life and joy:
Our fathers found bleak heath, and desert moor,
Wide woodland, and savannahs wide and waste,
Rude country of rude dwellers.   From our arms
They to the mountain fastnesses retired,
And long with obstinate and harassing war
Provoked us, hoping not for victory,
Yet mad for vengeance: till Tepollomi
Fell by my father's hand; and with their king,
The strength and flower of all their youth cut off,
All in one desolating day, they took
The yoke upon their necks.   What wouldest thou
That to these Hoamen I should now concede?
Lord of the Ocean, speak!
                    Let them be free!
Quoth I.   I come not from my native isle
To wage the war of conquest, and cast out
Your people from the land which time and toil
Have rightly made their own.   The world is wide:
There is enough for all.   So they be freed
From that accursed tribute, and ye shed
The life of man no more in sacrifice,
In the most holy name of God I say,
Let there be peace between us!
                    Thou hast won
Their liberty, the King replied: henceforth,
Free as they are, if they provoke the war,
Reluctantly will Aztlan raise her arm.
Be thou the peace-preserver.   To what else
Thou sayest, instructed by calamity,

I lend a humble ear; but to destroy
The worship of my fathers, or abate
Or change one point, lies not within the reach
And scope of kingly power.   Speak thou hereon
With those whom we hold holy, with the sons
Of the Temple, they who commune with the Gods;
Awe them, for they awe me.   So we resolved
That when the bones of King Tepollomi
Had had their funeral honours, they and I
Should by the green lake-side, before the King,
And in the presence of the people, hold
A solemn talk.
                    Then to the mountain huts,
The bearer of good tidings, I returned,
Leading the honourable train who bore
The relics of the King; not parched and black,
As I had seen the unnatural corpse stand up,
In ghastly mockery of the attitude
And act of life;—his bones had now been blanched
With decent reverence.   Soon the mountaineers
Saw the white deer-skin shroud;[49] the rumour spread,
They gathered round, and followed in our train.
Before Erillyab's hut the bearers laid
Their burthen down.   She, calm of countenance,
And with dry eye, albeit her hand the while
Shook like an agueish limb, unrolled the shroud.
The multitude stood gazing silently,
The young and old alike all awed and hushed
Under the holy feeling,—and the hush
Was awful; that huge multitude so still,
That we could hear distinct the mountain stream
Roll down its rocky channel far away.
And this was all; sole ceremony this,
The sight of death and silence,—till at length,
In the ready grave his bones were laid to rest.
'T was in her hut and home, yea, underneath
The marriage bed, the bed of widowhood,
Her husband's grave was dug;[50] on softest fur
The bones were laid,[51] with fur were covered o'er,
Then heapt with bark and boughs, and, last of all,
Earth was to earth trod down.
                    And now the day
Appointed for our talk of peace was come.
On the green margin of the lake we met,
Elders, and Priests, and Chiefs; the multitude
Around the circle of the council stood.
Then, in the midst, Coanocotzin rose,
And thus the King began; Pabas,[52] and Chiefs
Of Aztlan, hither ye are come to learn
The law of peace.   The Lord of Ocean saith,
The Tribes whom he hath gathered underneath
The wings of his protection, shall be free;
And, in the name of his great God, he saith,
That ye shall never shed in sacrifice
The blood of man.   Are ye content? that so
We may together here, in happy hour,
Bury the sword!
                    Hereat a Paba rose,
And answered for his brethren:—He hath won
The Hoamen's freedom, that their blood no more
Shall on our altars flow; for this the Lord
Of Ocean fought, and Aztlan yielded it
In battle: but if we forego the rites
Of our forefathers, if we wrong the Gods,
Who give us timely sun and timely showers,
Their wrath will be upon us; they will shut

Their ears to prayer, and turn away the eyes
Which watch for our well-doing, and withhold
The hands that scatter our prosperity.

Cynetha then arose; between his son
And me supported, rose the blind old man.
Ye wrong us, men of Aztlan, if ye deem
We bid ye wrong the Gods; accurst were he
Who would obey such bidding,—more accurst
The wretch who should enjoin impiety!'
It is the will of God which we make known,
Your God and ours. Know ye not him, who laid
The deep foundations of the earth, and built
The arch of heaven, and kindled yonder sun,
And breathed into the woods and waves and sky
The power of life?
                We know Him, they replied,
The great For-Ever One, the God of Gods,
Ipalnemoani, He by whom we live![53]
And we too, quoth Ayayaca, we know
And worship the Great Spirit, who in clouds
And storms, in mountain caves, and by the fall
Of waters, in the woodland solitude,
And in the night and silence of the sky,
Doth make his being felt. [54] We also know,
And fear, and worship the Beloved One.

Our God, replied Cynetha, is the same,
The Universal Father. He to the first
Made his will known; but when men multiplied,
The Evil Spirits darkened them, and sin
And misery came into the world, and men
Forsook the way of truth, and gave to stocks
And stones the incommunicable name.
Yet with one chosen, one peculiar Race,
The knowledge of their Father and their God
Remained, from sire to son transmitted down.
While the bewildered Nations of the earth
Wandered in fogs, and were in darkness lost,
The light abode with them; and when at times
They sinned and went astray, the Lord hath put
A voice into the mouths of holy men,
Raising up witnesses unto himself,
That so the saving knowledge of his name
Might never fail; nor the glad promise, given
To our first parent, that at length his sons,
From error, sin, and wretchedness redeemed,
Should form one happy family of love.
Nor ever hath that light, howe'er bedimmed,
Wholly been quenched; still in the heart of man
A feeling and an instinct it exists,
His very nature's stamp and privilege,
Yea, of his life the life. I tell ye not,
O Aztecas! of things unknown before;
I do but waken up a living sense
Which sleeps within ye! Do ye love the Gods
Who call for blood? Doth the poor sacrifice
Go with a willing step, to lay his life
Upon their altars?—Good must come of good,
Evil of evil; if the fruit be death,
The poison springeth from the sap and root,
And the whole tree is deadly; if the rites
Be evil, they who claim them are not good,
Not to be worshipped then; for to obey
The evil will is evil. Aztecas!
From the For-Ever, the beloved One,

The Universal Only God I speak,
Your God and mine, our Father and our Judge.
Hear ye his law,—hear ye the perfect law
Of love, « Do ye to others, as ye would
That they should do to you!» He bids us meet
To praise his name, in thankfulness and joy;
He bids us, in our sorrow, pray to him,
The Comforter, love him, for he is good!
Fear him, for he is just! obey his will,
For who can bear his anger!
                    While he spake,
They stood with open mouth, and motionless sight,
Watching his countenance, as though the voice
Were of a God; for sure it seemed that less
Than inspiration could not have infused
That eloquent passion in a blind man's face.
And when he ceased, all eyes at once were turned
Upon the Pabas, waiting their reply,
If that to that acknowledged argument
Reply could be devised; but they themselves,
Stricken by the truth, were silent; and they looked
Toward their chief and mouth-piece, the High Priest
Tezozomoc; he too was pale and mute,
And when he gathered up his strength to speak,
Speech failed him, his lip faltered, and his eye
Fell utterly abashed, and put to shame.
But in the Chiefs, and in the multitude,
And in the King of Aztlan, better thoughts
Were working; for the Spirit of the Lord
That day was moving in the heart of man.[55]
Coanocotzin rose : Pabas, and Chiefs,
And men of Aztlan, ye have heard a talk
Of peace and love, and there is no reply.
Are ye content with what the Wise Man saith
And will ye worship God in that good way
Which God himself ordains? If it be so,
Together here will we in happy hour
Bury the sword.
                Tezozomoc replied,
This thing is new, and in the land till now
Unheard :—what marvel, therefore, if we find
No ready answer? Let our Lord the King
Do that which seemeth best.
                        Yuhidthiton,
Chief of the Chiefs of Aztlan, next arose.
Of all her numerous sons, could Aztlan boast.
No mightier arm in battle, nor whose voice
To more attentive silence hushed the hall
Of council. When the Wise Man spake, quoth he,
I asked of mine own heart if it were so,
And, as he said, the living instinct there
Answered, and owned the truth. In happy hour,
O King of Aztlan, did the Ocean Lord
Through the great waters hither wend his way;
For sure he is the friend of God and man!

With that an uproar of assent arose
From the whole people, a tumultuous shout
Of universal joy and glad acclaim.
But when Coanocotzin raised his hand,
That he might speak, the clamour and the buzz
Ceased, and the multitude, in tiptoe hope,
Attent and still, await the final voice.
Then said the Sovereign, Hear, O Aztecas,
Your own united will! From this day forth
No life upon the altar shall be shed,

No blood shall flow in sacrifice; the rites
Shall all be pure, such as the blind old man,
Whom God hath taught, will teach.   This ye have
    willed;
And therefore it shall be!
                The King hath said!
Like thunder the collected voice replied:
Let it be so!
            Lord of the Ocean, then
Pursued the King of Aztlan, we will now
Lay the war-weapon in the grave, and join
In right-hand friendship.   By our custom, blood
Should sanctify and bind the solemn act;
But by what oath and ceremony thou
Shalt proffer, by the same will Aztlan swear.

Nor oath, nor ceremony, I replied,
O King, is needful.   To his own good word
The good and honourable man will act:
Oaths will not curb the wicked.   Here we stand
In the broad day-light; the For-Ever one,
The Every-Where beholds us.   In his sight
We join our hands in peace: if e'er again
Should these right hands be raised in enmity,
Upon the offender will His judgment fall.

The grave was dug; Coanocotzin laid
His weapon in the earth; Erillyab's son,
Young Amalahta, for the Hoamen, laid
His hatchet there; and there I laid the sword.

Here let me end.   What followed was the work
Of peace, no theme of story; how we fixed
Our sojourn in the hills, and sowed our fields,
And, day by day, saw all things prospering.
Thence have I sailed, Goervyl, to announce
The tidings of my happy enterprise;
There I return, to take thee to our home.
I love my native land; with as true love
As ever yet did warm a British heart,
Love I the green fields of the beautiful Isle,
My father's heritage! but far away,
Where nature's boonier hand has blest the earth,
My heritage hath fallen; beyond the seas
Madoc hath found his home; beyond the seas
A country for his children hath he chosen,
A land wherein their portions may be peace.

IX.

Emma.

But while Aberfraw echoed to the sounds
Of merriment and music, Madoc's heart
Mourned for his brethren. Therefore, when no ear
Was nigh, he sought the King, and said to him,
To-morrow, I set forth for Mathraval;
For long I must not linger here, to pass
The easy hours in feast and revelry,
Forgetful of my people far away.
I go to tell the tidings of success,
And seek new comrades. What if it should chance
That, for this enterprise, our brethren,
Foregoing all their hopes and fortunes here,
Would join my banner?—Let me send abroad

Their summons, O my brother! so secure,
You may forgive the past, and once again
Will peace and concord bless our father's house.
Hereafter will be time enow for this,
The King replied; thy easy nature sees not,
How, if the traitors for thy banner send
Their bidding round, in open war against me,
Their own would soon be spread.   I charge thee,
    Madoc,
Neither to see nor aid these fugitives,
The shame of Owen's blood.
              Sullen he spake,
And turned away; nor farther commune now
Did Madoc seek, nor had he more endured;
For bitter thoughts were rising in his heart,
And anguish, kindling anger.   In such mood
He to his sister's chamber took his way.
She sate with Emma, with the gentle Queen;
For Emma had already learnt to love
The gentle maid.   Goervyl saw what thoughts
Troubled her brother's brow.   Madoc, she cried,
Thou hast been with the king, been rashly pleading
For Ririd and for Rodri!—He replied,
I did but ask him little,—did but say,
Belike our brethren would go forth with me,
To voluntary exile; then, methought,
His fear and jealousy might well have ceased,
And all be safe.
          And did the King refuse?
Quoth Emma.   I will plead for them, quoth she,
With dutiful warmth and zeal will plead for them;
And surely David will not say me nay.

O sister! cried Goervyl, tempt him not!
Sister, you know him not! alas, to touch
That perilous theme is, even in Madoc here,
A perilous folly—Sister, tempt him not!
You do not know the King!
             But then a fear
Fled to the cheek of Emma, and her eye,
Quickening with wonder, turned toward the Prince,
As if expecting that his manly mind
Would mould Goervyl's meaning to a shape
Less fearful, would interpret and amend
The words she hoped she did not hear aright.
Emma was young; she was the sacrifice
To that sad king-craft, which, in marriage-vows
Linking two hearts, unknowing each of each,
Perverts the ordinance of God, and makes
The holiest tie a mockery and curse.
Her eye was patient, and she spake in tones
So sweet and of so pensive gentleness,
That the heart felt them.   Madoc! she exclaimed,
Why dost thou hate the Saxons? O, my brother,
If I have heard aright the hour will come
When the Plantagenet shall wish herself
Among her nobler, happier countrymen,
From these unnatural enmities escaped,
And from the curse which they must call from heaven.

Shame then suffused the Prince's countenance,
Mindful how, drunk in anger, he had given
His hatred loose.   My sister Queen, quoth he,
Marvel not you that with my mother's milk
I sucked that hatred in.   Have they not been
The scourge and the devouring sword of God,

The curse and pestilence which he hath sent
To root us from the land? Alas, our crimes
Have drawn this fearful visitation down!
Our sun hath long been westering; and the night,
And darkness, and extinction are at hand.
We are a fallen people!—From ourselves
The desolation and the ruin come!
In our own vitals doth the poison work—
The House that is divided in itself,
How shall it stand?—A blessing on you, Lady!
But in this wretched family the strife
Is rooted all too deep; it is an old
And cankered wound,—an eating, killing sore,
For which there is no healing!—If the King
Should ever speak his fear,—and sure to you
All his most inward thoughts he will make known—
Counsel him then to let his brethren share
My enterprise, to send them forth with me
To everlasting exile.—She hath told you
Too rudely of the King; I know him well;
He hath a stormy nature; and what germs
Of virtue would have budded in his heart,
Cold winds have checked, and blighting seasons nipt,
Yet in his heart they live.—A blessing on you,
That you may see their blossom and their fruit!

X.

Mathraval.

And now went Madoc forth for Mathraval;
O'er Menai's ebbing tide, up mountain-paths,
Beside grey mountain-stream, and lonely lake,
And through old Snowdon's forest solitude,
He held right on his solitary way.
Nor paused he in that rocky vale, where oft
Up the familiar path, with gladder pace,
His steed had hastened to the well-known door,—
That valley, o'er whose crags, and sprinkled trees,
And winding stream, so oft his eye had loved
To linger, gazing, as the eve grew dim,
From Dolwyddelan's, [56] Tower;—alas! from thence
As from his brother's monument, he turned
A loathing eye, and through the rocky vale
Sped on. From morn till noon, from noon till eve,
He travelled on his way; and when at morn
Again the Ocean Chief bestrode his steed,
The heights of Snowdon on his backward glance
Hung like a cloud in heaven. O'er heath and hill
And barren height he rode; and darker now,
In loftier majesty thy mountain-seat,
Star-loving Idris, rose. Nor turned he now
Beside Kregennan, where his infant feet
Had trod Ednywain's hall; [57] nor loitered he
In the green vales of Powys, till he came
Where Warnway rolls his waters underneath
The walls of Mathraval, old Mathraval,
Cyveilioc's princely and paternal seat.

But Madoc rushed not forward now to greet
The chief he loved, for from the hall was heard
The voice of harp and song. It was, that day,
The feast of victory at Mathraval;
Around the Chieftain's board the warriors sate:
The sword, and shield, and helmet, on the wall,

And round the pillars, were in peace hung up;
And, as the flashes of the central fire
At fits arose, a dance of wavy light
Played o'er the reddening steel. The Chiefs, who late
So well had wielded, in the play of war,
Those weapons, sate around the board, to quaff
The beverage of the brave, and hear their fame.
Cyveilioc stood before them,—in his pride
Stood up the Poet-Prince of Mathraval;
His hands were on the harp, his eyes were closed,
His head, as if in reverence to receive
The inspiration, bent; anon, he raised
His glowing countenance, and brighter eye,
And swept, with passionate hand, the ringing harp.

Fill high the Hilas [58] Horn! to Grufydd bear
Its frothy beverage,—from his crimson lance
The invader fled;—fill high the gold-tipt Horn!
Heard ye in Maelor the step of war—
The hastening shout—the onset?—Did ye hear
The clash and clang of arms—the battle-din,
Loud as the roar of Ocean, when the winds
At midnight are abroad?—the yell of wounds—
The rage—the agony?—give to him the Horn
Whose spear was broken, and whose buckler pierced
With many a shaft, yet not the less he fought
And conquered;—therefore let Ednyved share
The generous draught; give him the long blue Horn!
Pour out again, and fill again the spoil
Of the wild bull, with silver wrought of yore;
Bear ye to Tudyr's hand the golden lip,
Eagle of battle! for Moreiddig fill
The honourable Hirlas!—where are They?
Where are the noble Brethren? Wolves of war,
They kept their border well, they did their part,
Their fame is full, their lot is praise and song—
A mournful song to me, a song of woe!—
Brave Brethren! for their honour brim the cup,
Which they shall quaff no more.

　　　　　　　　We drove away
The strangers from our land; profuse of life,
Our warriors rushed to battle, and the Sun
Saw, from his noontide fields, their manly strife.
Pour thou the flowing mead! Cup-bearer, fill
The Hirlas! for hadst thou beheld the day
Of Llidom, thou hadst known how well the Chiefs
Deserve this honour now. Cyveilioc's shield
Were they in danger, when the Invader came;
Be praise and liberty their lot on earth,
And joy be theirs in heaven!
　　　　　　　　Here ceased the song.
Then from the threshold on the rush-strewn floor
Madoc advanced. Cyveilioc's eye was now
To present forms awake, but, even as still
He felt his harp-chords throb with dying sounds,
The heat and stir and passion had not yet
Subsided in his soul. Again he struck
The loud-toned harp.—Pour from the silver vase,
And brim the honourable Horn, and bear
The draught of joy to Madoc,—he who first
Explored the desert ways of Ocean, first
Through the wide waste of sea and sky, held on
Undaunted, till upon another World,
The Lord and Conqueror of the Elements,
He set his foot triumphant! Fill for him
The Hirlas! fill the honourable Horn!

This is a happy hour, for Madoc treads
The hall of Mathraval; by every foe
Dreaded, by every friend beloved the best,
Madoc, the Briton Prince, the Ocean Lord,
Who never for injustice reared his arm.
Give him the Hirlas Horn, fill, till the draught
Of joy shall quiver o'er the golden brim!
In happy hour the hero hath returned!
In happy hour the friend, the brother treads
Cyveilioc's floor!

   He sprung to greet his guest;
The cordial grasp of fellowship was given;
They gave the seat of honour, and they filled
For him the Hirlas Horn.—So there was joy
In Mathraval. Cyveilioc and his Chiefs,
All eagerly, with wonder-waiting eyes,
Look to the Wanderer of the Waters' tale.
Nor mean the joy which kindled Madoc's brow,
When as he told of daring enterprise
Crowned with deserved success. Intent they heard
Of all the blessings of that happier clime;
And when the adventurer spake of soon return,
Each on the other gazed, as if to say,
Methinks it were a goodly lot to dwell
In that fair land in peace!

   Then said the Prince
Of Powys, Madoc, at a happy time
Thy feet have sought the house of Mathraval;
For on the morrow, in the eye of light,
Our bards will hold their congress. Seekest thou
Comrades to share success? proclaim abroad
Thine invitation there, and it shall spread
Far as our father's ancient tongue is known.
The mantling mead went round at Mathraval;—
That was a happy hour! Of other years
They talked, of common toils, and fields of war
Where they fought side by side; of Corwen's day
Of glory, and of comrades now no more:—
Themes of delight, and grief which brought its joy.
Thus they beguiled the pleasant hours, while night
Waned fast away; then late they laid them down,
Each on his bed of rushes, stretched around
The central fire.

   The Sun was newly risen
When Madoc joined his host, no longer now
Clad as the conquering chief of Maelor,
In princely arms, but in his nobler robe,
The sky blue mantle of the bard, arrayed.
So for the place of meeting they set forth;
And now they reached Melangall's lonely church.
Amid a grove of evergreens it stood,
A garden and a grove, where every grave
Was decked with flowers, or with unfading plants
O'ergrown, sad rue, and funeral rosemary.
Here Madoc paused. The morn is young, quoth he,
A little while to old remembrance given
Will not belate us—Many a year hath fled,
Cyveilioc, since you led me here, and told
The legend of the Saint. Come!—be not loth!
We will not loiter long.—So soon to mount
The bark, which will for ever bear me hence,
I would not willingly pass by one spot
Which thus recalls the thought of other times,
Without a pilgrim's visit.

   Thus he spake,
And drew Cyveilioc through the church-yard porch,

To the rude image of Saint Monacel. [59]
Dost thou remember, Owen, said the Prince,
When first I was thy guest in early youth,
That once, as we had wandered here at eve,
You told, how here a poor and hunted hare
Ran to the Virgin's feet, and looked to her
For life?—I thought, when listening to the tale,
She had a merciful heart, and that her face
Must with a saintly gentleness have beamed,
When beasts could read its virtue. Here we sate
Upon the jutting root of this old yeugh—
Dear friend! so pleasant didst thou make those days,
That in my heart, long as my heart shall beat,
Minutest recollections still will live,
Still be the source of joy.

   As Madoc spake,
His glancing eye fell on a monument,
Around whose base the rosemary drooped down,
As yet not rooted well. Sculptured above,
A warrior lay; the shield was on his arm;
Madoc approached, and saw the blazonry,—
A sudden chill ran through him, as he read,
Here Yorwerth lies—it was his brother's grave.
Cyveilioc took him by the hand : For this,
Madoc, was I so loth to enter here!
He sought the sanctuary, but close upon him
The murderers followed, and by yonder copse
The stroke of death was given. All I could
Was done;—I saw him here consigned to rest,
Daily due masses for his soul are sung,
And duly hath his grave been decked with flowers.

So saying, from the place of death he led
The silent prince. But lately, he pursued,
Llewelyn was my guest, thy favourite boy.
For thy sake and his own, it was my hope
That he would make his home at Mathraval :
He had not needed then a father's love.
But he, I know not on what enterprise,
Was brooding ever ; and these secret thoughts
Led him away. God prosper the brave boy!
It were a happier day for this poor land
If e'er Llewelyn mount his rightful throne.

     XI.

   The Gorsedd.

The place of meeting was a high hill-top, [60]
Nor bowered with trees nor broken by the plough,
Remote from human dwellings and the stir
Of human life, and open to the breath
And to the eye of Heaven. In days of yore,
There had the circling stones been planted ; there,
From earliest ages, the primeval lore,
Through Bard to Bard with reverence handed down.
They whom to wonder, or the love of song,
Or reverence of their father's ancient rites
Led thither, stood without the ring of stones.
Cyveilioc entered to the initiate Bards,
Himself, albeit his hands were stained with war,
Initiate; for the Order, in the lapse
Of years and in their nation's long decline,
From the first rigour of their purity
Somewhat had fallen. [61] The Masters of the Song

In azure robes were robed,—that one bright hue
To emblem unity, and peace, and truth,
Like Heaven, which o'er a world of wickedness
Spreads its eternal canopy serene.

Within the Stones of Federation there,
On the green turf, and under the blue sky,
A noble band, the Bards of Britain stood,
Their heads in reverence bare, and bare of foot.
A deathless brotherhood! Cyveilioc there,
Lord of the Hirlas; Llywarc there was seen,
And old Cynddelow, to whose lofty song,
So many a time amid his father's hall,
Resigning all his soul, had Madoc given
The flow of feeling loose. But Madoc's heart
Was full; old feelings and remembrances,
And thoughts from which was no escape, arose :
He was not there to whose sweet lay, so oft,
With all a brother's fond delight, he loved
To listen,—Hoel was not there!—the hand
That once so well, amid the triple chords,
Moved in the rapid maze of harmony,
It had no motion now; the lips were dumb
Which knew all tones of passion; and that heart,
That warm, ebullient heart, was cold and still,
Upon its bed of clay. He looked around,
And there was no familiar countenance,
None but Cynddelow's face, which he had learnt
In childhood, and old age had set his mark,
Making unsightly alteration there.
Another generation had sprung up,
And made him feel how fast the days of man
Flow by, how soon their number is told out.
He knew not then that Llywarc's lay should give
His future fame; his spirit on the past
Brooding, beheld, with no forefeeling joy,
The rising sons of song, who there essayed
Their eaglet flight. But there among the youth
In the green vesture of their earliest rank,
Or with the aspirants clad in motley garb,
Young Benvras stood; and, one whose favoured race
Heaven with the hereditary power had blest,
The old Gowalchmai's not degenerate child;
And there another Einion; gifted youths,
The heirs of immortality on earth,
Whose after-strains, through many a distant age
Cambria shall boast, and love the songs that tell
The fame of Owen's house.
                              There, in the eye
Of light and in the face of day, the rites
Began. Upon the Stone of Covenant
The sheathed sword was laid; the Master then
Upraised his voice, and cried, Let them who seek
The high degree and sacred privilege
Of Bardic science, and of Cimbric lore,
Here to the Bards of Britain make their claim!
Thus having said, the Master bade the youths
Approach the place of peace, and merit there
The Bard's most honourable name : [62] With that,
Heirs and transmitters of the ancient light,
The youths advanced; they heard the Cimbric lore, [63]
From earliest days preserved; they struck their harps,
And each in due succession raised the song.

Last of the aspirants, as of greener years,
Young Caradoc advanced; his lip as yet

Scarce darkened with its down, his flaxen locks
Wreathed in contracting ringlets waving low;
Brightened his large blue eyes, and kindled now
With that same passion that inflamed his cheek ;
Yet in his cheek there was the sickliness
Which thought and feeling leave, wearing away
The hue of youth. Inclining on his harp,
He, while his comrades in probation song
Approved their claim, stood hearkening, as it seemed,
And yet like unintelligible sounds
He heard the symphony and voice attuned ;
Even in such feelings as, all undefined.
Come with the flow of waters to the soul,
Or with the motions of the moonlight sky.
But when his bidding came, he at the call
Arising from that dreamy mood, advanced,
Threw back his mantle, and began the lay.

Where are the sons of Gavran? where his tribe,
The faithful? [64] following their belovéd Chief,
They the Green Islands of the Ocean sought;
Nor human tongue hath told, nor human ear,
Since from the silver shores they went their way,
Hath heard their fortunes. In his crystal Ark,
Whither sailed Merlin with his band of Bards,
Old Merlin, master of the mystic lore? [65]
Belike his crystal Ark, instinct with life,
Obedient to the mighty Master, reached
The Land of the Departed; there, belike,
They in the clime of immortality,
Themselves immortal, drink the gales of bliss,
Which o'er Flathinnis [66] breathe eternal spring,
Blending whatever odours make the gale
Of evening sweet, whatever melody
Charms the wood-traveller. In their high-roofed halls
There, with the Chiefs of other days, feel they
The mingled joy pervade them ?—Or beneath
The mid-sea waters, did that crystal Ark
Down to the secret depths of Ocean plunge
Its fated crew? Dwell they in coral bowers
With Mermaid loves, teaching their paramours
The songs that stir the sea, or make the winds
Hush, and the waves be still? In fields of joy
Have they their home, where central fires maintain
Perpetual summer, where one emerald light
Through the green element for ever flows? [67]

Twice have the sons of Britain left her shores,
As the fledged eaglets quit their native nest;
Twice over ocean have her fearless sons
For ever sailed away. Again they launch
Their vessels to the deep.—Who mounts the bark?
The son of Owen, the belovéd Prince,
Who never for injustice reared his arm.
Respect his enterprise, ye Ocean Waves!
Ye Winds of Heaven, waft Madoc on his way!
The Waves of Ocean, and the Winds of Heaven,
Became his ministers, and Madoc found
The world he sought.
                        Who seeks the better land?
Who mounts the vessel for the world of peace?
He who hath felt the throb of pride, to hear
Our old illustrious annals; who was taught
To lisp the fame of Arthur, to revere
Great Caratach's unconquered soul, and call
That gallant chief his countryman, who led

The wrath of Britain from her chalky shores
To drive the Roman robber. He who loves
His country, and who feels his country's shame,
Whose bones amid a land of servitude
Could never rest in peace; who, if he saw
His children slaves, would feel a pang in heaven,—
He mounts the bark, to seek for liberty.

Who seeks the better land? The wretched one,
Whose joys are blasted all, whose heart is sick,
Who hath no hope, to whom all change is gain,
To whom remembered pleasures strike a pang
Which only guilt should know;—he mounts the bark!
The Bard will mount the bark of banishment;
The harp of Cambria shall, in other lands,
Remind the Cambrian of his father's fame;—
The Bard will seek the land of liberty,
The world of peace.—O Prince, receive the Bard!

He ceased the song. His cheek, now fever-flushed,
Was turned to Madoc, and his asking eye
Lingered on him in hope; nor lingered long
The look expectant; forward sprung the Prince,
And gave to Caradoc the right-hand pledge,
And for the comrade of his enterprise,
With joyful welcome, hailed the joyful Bard.

Nor needed now the Searcher of the Sea
Announce his enterprize, by Caradoc
In song announced so well; from man to man
The busy murmur spread, while from the Stone
Of Covenant the sword was taken up,
And from the Circle of the Ceremony
The Bards went forth, their meeting now fulfilled.
The multitude, unheeding all beside,
Of Madoc and his noble enterprise
Held stirring converse on their homeward way,
And spread abroad the tidings of the Land,
Where Plenty dwelt with Liberty and Peace.

XII.

Dinevawr.

So in the court of Powys pleasantly,
With hawk and hound afield, and harp in hall,
The days went by; till Madoc, for his heart
Was with Cadwallon, and in early spring
Must he set forth to join him over-sea,
Took his constrained farewell. To Dinevawr
He bent his way, whence many a time with Rhys
Had he gone forth to smite the Saxon foe.
The Son of Owen greets his father's friend
With reverential joy : nor did the Lord
Of Dinevawr with cold or deadened heart
Welcome the Prince he loved; though not with joy
Unmingled now, nor the proud consciousness
Which in the man of tried and approved worth
Could bid an equal hail. Henry had seen
The Lord of Dinevawr between his knees
Vow homage: yea, the Lord of Dinevawr
Had knelt in homage to that Saxon king,
Who set a price upon his father's head,
That Saxon, on whose soul his mother's blood
Cried out for vengeance. Madoc saw the shame

Which Rhys [68] would fain have hidden, and, in grief
For the degenerate land, rejoiced at heart
That now another country was his home.

Musing on thoughts like these, did Madoc roam
Alone along the Towy's winding shore.
The beavers [69] in its bank had hollowed out
Their social place of dwelling, and had dammed
The summer-current, with their perfect art
Of instinct, erring not in means nor end.
But as the floods of spring had broken down
Their barrier, so its breaches unrepaired
Were left, and round the piles, which, deeper driven,
Still held their place, the eddying waters whirled.
Now in those habitations desolate
One sole survivor dwelt: him Madoc saw,
Labouring alone, beside his hermit house;
And in that mood of melancholy thought,—
For in his boyhood he had loved to watch
Their social work, and for he knew that man
In bloody sport had well-nigh rooted out
The poor community,—the ominous sight
Became a grief and burthen. Eve came on;
The dry leaves rustled to the wind, and fell
And floated on the stream; there was no voice
Save of the mournful rooks, who overhead
Winged their long line; for fragrance of sweet flowers,
Only the odour of the autumnal leaves;—
All sights and sounds of sadness.—And the place
To that despondent mood was ministrant;—
Among the hills of Gwyneth and its wilds
And mountain glens, perforce he cherished still
The hope of mountain liberty; they braced
And knit the heart and arm of hardihood;—
But here, in these green meads, by these low slopes
And hanging groves, attempered to the scene,
His spirit yielded. As he loitered on,
There came toward him one in peasant garb,
And called his name;—he started at the sound,
For he had heeded not the man's approach;
And now that sudden and familiar voice
Came on him, like a vision. So he stood
Gazing, and knew him not in the dim light,
Till he again cried, Madoc!—then he woke,
And knew the voice of Ririd, and sprang on,
And fell upon his neck, and wept for joy
And sorrow.
              O my brother! Ririd cried,
Long, very long it is since I have heard
The voice of kindness!—Let me go with thee!
I am a wanderer in my father's land,—
Hoel he killed, and Yorwerth hath he slain;
Llewelyn hath not where to hide his head
In his own kingdom; Rodri is in chains;—
Let me go with thee, Madoc, to some land
Where I may look upon the sun, nor dread
The light that may betray me; where at night
I may not, like a hunted beast, rouse up,
If the leaves rustle over me.
                          The Lord
Of Ocean struggled with his swelling heart.
Let me go with thee?—but thou didst not doubt
Thy brother?—Let thee go?—with what a joy,
Ririd, would I collect the remnant left,
The wretched remnant now of Owen's house,
And mount the bark of willing banishment,

And leave the tyrant to his Saxon friends,
And to his Saxon yoke!—I urged him thus,
Curbed down my angry spirit, and besought
Only that I might bid our brethren come,
And share my exile;—and he spurned my prayer!—
Thou hast a gentle pleader at his court;
She may prevail; till then abide thou here;—
But not in this, the garb of fear and guilt.
Come thou to Dinevawr,—assume thyself;—
The good old Rhys will bid thee welcome there,
And the Great Palace, like a sanctuary,
Is safe. 70   If then Queen Emma's plea should fail,
My timely bidding hence shall summon thee,
When I shall spread the sail.—Nay, hast thou learnt
Suspicion?—Rhys is noble, and no deed
Of treachery ever sullied his fair fame!

Madoc then led his brother to the hall
Of Rhys.   I bring to thee a suppliant,
O King, he cried; thou wert my father's friend!
And till our barks be ready in the spring,
I know that here the persecuted son
Of Owen will be safe.
                    A welcome guest!
The old warrior cried; by his good father's soul,
He is a welcome guest at Dinevawr!
And rising as he spake, he pledged his hand
In hospitality—How now! quoth he,
This raiment ill beseems the princely son
Of Owen!—Ririd at his words was led
Apart; they washed his feet, they gave to him
Fine linen, as beseemed his royal race,
The tunic of soft texture woven well,
The broidered girdle, the broad mantle edged
With fur and flowing low, the bonnet last,
Formed of some forest martin's costly spoils.
The Lord of Dinevawr sat at the dice
With Madoc, when he saw him, thus arrayed,
Returning to the hall.   Aye! this is well!
The noble Chief exclaimed; 't is as of yore,
When in Aberfraw, at his father's board,
We sate together, after we had won
Peace and rejoicing, with our own right hands,
By Corwen, where, commixt with Saxon blood,
Along its rocky channel the dark Dee
Rolled darker waters·—Would that all his house
Had, in their day of trouble, thought of me,
And honoured me like this! David respects
Deheubarth's strength, nor would respect it less,
When such protection leagued its cause with Heaven.

I had forgot his Messenger! quoth he,
Arising from the dice.   Go, bid him here!
He came here this morning at an ill-starred hour,
To Madoc he pursued; my lazy grooms
Had let the hounds play havoc in my flock,
And my old blood was chafed.   I'faith, the King
Hath chosen well his messenger—he saw
That in such mood, I might have rendered him
A hot and hasty answer, and hath waited,
Belike to David's service and to mine,
My better leisure.
                    Now the Messenger
Entered the hall; Goagan of Powys-land, 71
He of Caer-Einion was it, who was charged
From Gwyneth to Dcheubarth; a brave man,

Of copious speech.   He told the royal son
Of Gryffidd, the descendant of the line
Of Rhys-ab-Tudyr mawr, that he came there
From David, son of Owen, of the stock
Of kingly Cynan.   I am sent, said he,
With friendly greeting; and as I receive
Welcome and honour so, in David's name,
Am I to thank the Lord of Dinevawr.

Tell on! quoth Rhys, the purport and the cause
Of this appeal!
                    Of late, some fugitives
Came from the South to Mona, whom the King
Received with generous welcome.   Some there were
Who blamed his royal goodness; for they said,
These were the subjects of a rival Prince,
Who, peradventure, would with no such bounty
Cherish a northern suppliant.   This they urged,
I know not if from memory of old feuds,
Better forgotten, or in envy.   Moved
Hereby, King David swore he would not rest
Till he had put the question to the proof,
Whether with liberal honour the Lord Rhys
Would greet his messenger; but none was found,
Of all who had instilled that evil doubt,
Ready to bear the embassy: I heard it,
And did my person tender,—for I knew
The nature of Lord Rhys of Dinevawr.
Well! quoth the Chief, Goagan of Powys-land,
This honourable welcome that thou seekèst,
Wherein may it consist?
                    In giving me,
Goagan of Powys-land replied, a horse,
Better than mine, to bear me home; a suit
Of seemly raiment, and ten marks in coin,
With raiment and two marks for him who leads
My horse's bridle.
                    For his sake, said Rhys,
Who sent thee, thou shalt have the noblest steed
In all my studs—I double thee the marks,
And give the raiment threefold.   More than this,—
Say thou to David, that the guests who sit
At board with me, and drink of my own cup,
Are Madoc and Lord Ririd.   Tell the King,
That thus it is Lord Rhys of Dinevawr
Delighteth to do honour to the sons
Of Owen, of his old and honoured friend.

XIII.

Llewelyn.

FAREWELL, my brother, cried the Ocean Chief;
A little while farewell! as through the gate
Of Dinetawr he past, to pass again
That hospitable threshold never more.
And thou, too, O thou good old man, true friend
Of Owen, and of Owen's house, farewell!
'T will not be told me, Rhys, when thy grey hairs
Are to the grave gone down; but oftentimes
In the distant world I shall remember thee,
And think that, come thy summons when it may,
Thou wilt not leave a braver man behind.—
Now God be with thee, Rhys!
                    The old Chief paused
28

A moment ere he answered, as for pain;
Then shaking his hoar head, I never yet
Gave thee this hand unwillingly before!
When for a guest I spread the board, my heart
Will think on him, whom ever with most joy
It leapt to welcome: should I ever lift
The spear against the Saxon,—for old Rhys
Hath that within him yet, that could uplift
The Cimbric spear,—I then shall wish his aid,
Who oft has conquered with me: when I kneel
In prayer to Heaven, an old man's prayer shall beg
A blessing on thee!

                     Madoc answered not,
But grasped his hand in silence, then sprang up
And spurred his courser on. A weary way,
Through forest and o'er fell, Prince Madoc rode;
And now he skirts the bay whose reckless waves
Roll o'er the plain of Gwaelod : 7² fair fields
And busy towns and happy villages,
They overwhelmed in one disastrous day;
For they by their eternal siege had sapped
The bulwark of the land, while Seithenyn
Took of his charge no thought, till, in his sloth
And riotous cups surprised, he saw the sea
Roll like an army o'er the levelled mound.
A supplicant in other courts, he mourned
His crime and ruin; in another's court
The kingly harp of Garanhir was heard,
Wailing his kingdom wrecked; and many a Prince,
Warned by the visitation, sought and gained
A saintly crown, Tyneio, Merini,
Boda and Brenda and Aëlgyvarch,
Gwynon and Celynin and Gwynodyl.

To Bardsey 7³ was the Lord of Ocean bound;
Bardsey, the holy Islet, in whose soil
Did many a Chief and many a Saint repose,
His great progenitors. He mounts the skiff;
Her canvass swells before the breeze, the sea
Sings round her sparkling keel, and soon the Lord
Of Ocean treads the venerable shore.

There was not, on that day, a speck to stain
The azure heaven; the blessèd Sun, alone,
In unapproachable divinity,
Careered, rejoicing in his fields of light.
How beautiful, beneath the bright blue sky,
The billows heave! one glowing green expanse,
Save where along the bending line of shore
Such hue is thrown, as when the peacock's neck
Assumes its proudest tint of amethyst,
Embathed in emerald glory. All the flocks
Of Ocean are abroad: like floating foam,
The sea-gulls rise and fall upon the waves;
With long protruded neck the cormorants
Wing their far flight aloft, and round and round
The plovers wheel, and give their note of joy.
It was a day that sent into the heart
A summer feeling: even the insect swarms
From their dark nooks and coverts issued forth,
To sport through one day of existence more;
The solitary primrose on the bank
Seemed now as though it had no cause to mourn
Its bleak autumnal birth; the Rocks, and Shores,
The Forest and the everlasting Hills,
Smiled in that joyful sunshine,—they partook

The universal blessing.
                     To this Isle,
Where his forefathers were consigned to dust,
Did Madoc come for natural piety,
Ordering a solemn service for their souls.
Therefore for this the Church that day was dressed;
For this the Abbot, in his alb arrayed,
At the high altar stood; for this infused,
Sweet incense from the waving thuribule
Rose like a mist, and the grey brotherhood
Chaunted the solemn mass. And now on high
The mighty Mystery had been elevate,
And now around the graves the brethren
In long array proceed: each in his hand,
Tall as the staff of some wayfaring man,
Bears the brown taper, with their daylight flames
Dimming the cheerful day. Before the train
The Cross is borne, where, fashioned to the life
In shape and size and ghastly colouring,
The awful image hangs. Next, in its shrine
Of gold and crystal, by the Abbot held,
The mighty Mystery came; on either hand
Three Priests uphold above, on silver wands,
The purple pall. With holy water next
A father went, therewith from hyssop branch
Sprinkling the graves; the while, with one accord,
The solemn psalm of mercy all entoned.

Pure was the faith of Madoc, though his mind
To all this pomp and solemn circumstance
Yielded a willing homage. But the place
Was holy;—the dead air, which underneath
Those arches never felt the healthy sun,
Nor the free motion of the elements,
Chilly and damp, infused associate awe:
The sacred odours of the incense still
Floated; the daylight and the taper-flames
Commingled, dimming each, and each bedimmed;
And as the slow procession paced along,
Still to their hymn, as if in symphony,
The regular foot-fall sounded: swelling now,
Their voices in one chorus, loud and deep,
Rung o'er the echoing aisle; and when it ceased,
The silence of that huge and sacred pile
Came on the heart. What wonder if the Prince
Yielded his homage now? the influences
Of that sweet autumn day made every sense
Alive to every impulse,—and beneath
The stones whereon he stood, his ancestors
Were mouldering, dust to dust. Father! quoth he,
When now the rites were ended,—far away
It hath been Madoc's lot to pitch his tent
On other shores; there, in a foreign land,
Far from my father's burial-place, must I
Be laid to rest; yet would I have my name
Be held with theirs in memory. I beseech you,
Have this a yearly rite for evermore,
As I will leave endowment for the same,
And let me be remembered in the prayer.
The day shall be a holy day with me,
While I do live; they who come after me,
Will hold it holy; it will be a bond
Of love and brotherhood, when all beside
Hath been dissolved; and though wide ocean rolls
Between my people and their mother Isle,
This shall be their communion : They shall send,

Linked in one sacred feeling at one hour,
In the same language, the same prayer to Heaven,
And each remembering each in piety,
Pray for the other's welfare.

           The old man
Partook that feeling, and some pious tears
Fell down his aged cheek. Kinsman and son,
It shall be so! said he; and thou shalt be
Remembered in the prayer : nor then alone ;
But till my sinking sands be quite run out,
This feeble voice shall, from its solitude,
Go up for thee to Heaven !

           And now the bell
Rung out its cheerful summons; to the hall,
In seemly order, pass the brotherhood :
The serving-men wait with the ready ewer;
The place of honour to the Prince is given,
The Abbot's right-hand guest; the viands smoke,
The horn of ale goes round; and now, the cates
Removed, for days of festival reserved,
Comes choicer beverage, clary, hippocras,
And mead mature, that to the goblet's brim
Sparkles and sings and smiles. It was a day
Of that allowable and temperate mirth
Which leaves a joy for memory. Madoc told
His tale; and thus, with question and reply
And cheerful intercourse, from noon till nones
The Brethren sate; and when the quire was done,
Renewed their converse till the vesper bell.

And now the Porter called Prince Madoc out,
To speak with one, he said, who from the land
Had sought him and required his private ear.
Madoc in the moonlight met him : in his hand
The stripling held an oar, and on his back,
Like a broad shield, the coracle was hung. 74
Uncle ! he cried, and, with a gush of tears,
Sprung to the glad embrace.

           O my brave boy!
Llewelyn ! my dear boy! with stifled voice,
And interrupted utterance, Madoc cried;
And many times he claspt him to his breast,
And many times drew back and gazed upon him,
Wiping the tears away which dimmed the sight,
And told him how his heart had yearned for him
As with a father's love, and bade him now
Forsake his lonely haunts and come with him,
And sail beyond the seas and share his fate.

No! by my God! the high-hearted youth replied,
It never shall be said Llewelyn left
His father's murderer on his father's throne !
I am the rightful king of this poor land—
Go thou, and wisely go; but I must stay,
That I may save my people. Tell me, Uncle,
The story of thy fortunes ; I can hear it
Here in this lonely Isle, and at this hour,
Securely

           Nay, quoth Madoc, tell me first
Where are thy haunts and coverts, and what hope
Thou hast to bear thee up? Why goest thou not
To Mathraval? there would Cyveilioc give
A kinsman's welcome : or at Dinevawr,
The guest of honour shouldst thou be with Rhys;
And he, belike, from David might obtain
Some recompense, though poor.

           What recompense ?
Exclaimed Llewelyn; what hath he to give,
But life for life? and what have I to claim
But vengeance, and my father Yorwerth's throne?
If with aught short of that my soul could rest,
Would I not through the wide world follow thee,
Dear Uncle! and fare with thee, well or ill,
And show to thine old age the tenderness
My childhood found from thee!—What hopes I have
Let time display. Have thou no fear for me!
My bed is made within the ocean caves,
Of sea-weeds, bleached by many a sun and shower;
I know the mountain dens, and every hold
And fastness of the forest; and I know,—
What troubles him by day and in his dreams,—
There 's many an honest heart in Gwyneth yet!
But tell me thine adventure ; that will be
A joy to think of in long winter nights,
When stormy billows make my lullaby.
So, as they walked along the moonlight shore,
Did Madoc tell him all; and still he strove,
By dwelling on that noble end and aim,
That of his actions was the heart and life,
To win him to his wish. It touched the youth;
And when the Prince had ceased, he heaved a sigh,
Long-drawn and deep, as if regret were there.
No, no ! he cried, it must not be ! lo yonder
My native mountains, and how beautiful
They rest in the moonlight! I was nurst among them;
They saw my sports in childhood, they have seen
My sorrows, they have saved me in the hour
Of danger;.. I have vowed, that as they were
My cradle, they shall be my monument !—
But we shall meet again, and thou wilt find me
When next thou visitest thy native Isle,
King in Aberfraw!

           Never more, Llewelyn,
Madoc replied, shall I behold the shores
Of Britain, nor will ever tale of me
Reach the Green Isle again. With fearful care
I chuse my little company, and leave
No traces of our path, where Violence,
And bloody Zeal, and bloodier Avarice,
Might find their blasting way.

           If it be so,—
And rightly thou hast judged, the youth replied,
Thou wilt not know my fate ;—but this be sure,
It shall not be inglorious. I have in me
A hope from Heaven—Give me thy blessing, Uncle!

Llewelyn, kneeling on the sand, embraced
His knees, with lifted head and streaming eyes
Listening. He rose, and fell on Madoc's neck,
And clasped him, with a silent agony,—
Then launched his coracle, and took his way,
A lonely traveller on the moonlight sea.

XIV.

Llaian.

Now hath Prince Madoc left the holy Isle,
And homeward to Aberfraw, through the wilds
Of Arvon, bent his course. A little way
He turned aside, by natural impulses

Moved, to behold Cadwallon's lonely hut.

That lonely dwelling stood among the hills,
By a grey mountain-stream: just elevate
Above the winter torrents did it stand,
Upon a craggy bank; an orchard slope
Arose behind, and joyous was the scene
In early summer, when those antic trees
Shone with their blushing blossoms, and the flax
Twinkled beneath the breeze its liveliest green.
But, save the flax-field and that orchard slope,
All else was desolate, and now all wore
One sober hue; the narrow vale which wound
Among the hills, was grey with rocks, that peered
Above its shallow soil; the mountain side
Was loose with stones bestrewn, which oftentimes
Clattered adown the steep, beneath the foot
Of straggling goat dislodged, or towered with crags,
One day when winter's work hath loosened them,
To thunder down. All things assorted well
With that grey mountain hue; the low stone lines,
Which scarcely seemed to be the work of man,
The dwelling rudely reared with stones unhewn,
The stubble flax, the crooked apple-trees
Grey with their fleecy moss and misseltoe.
The white-barked birch now leafless, and the ash
Whose knotted roots were like the rifted rock,
Through which they forced their way. Adown the vale,
Broken by stones and o'er a stony bed,
Rolled the loud mountain-stream.
                            When Madoc came.
A little child was sporting by the brook,
Floating the fallen leaves, that he might see them
Whirl in the eddy now, and now be driven
Down the descent, now on the smoother stream
Sail onward far away. But when he heard
The horse's tramp, he raised his head and watched
The Prince, who now dismounted and drew nigh.
The little boy still fixed his eyes on him,
His bright blue eyes; the wind just moved the curls
That clustered round his brow; and so he stood,
His rosy cheeks still lifted up to gaze
In innocent wonder. Madoc took his hand,
And now had asked his name, and if he dwelt
There in the hut, when from that cottage-door
A woman came, who seeing Madoc stopt
With such a fear,—for she had cause for fear,—
As when a bird returning to her nest,
Turns to a tree beside, if she behold
Some prying boy too near the dear retreat.
Howbeit advancing soon she now approached
The approaching Prince, and timidly inquired,
If on his wayfare he had lost the track,
That thither he had strayed. Not so, replied
The gentle Prince; but having known this place,
And its old habitants, I came once more
To view the lonely hut among the hills.
Hath it been long your dwelling?
                            Some few years,
Here we have dwelt, quoth she, my child and I.
Will it please you enter, and partake such fare
As we can give? Still timidly she spake,
But gathering courage from the gentle mien
Of him with whom she conversed. Madoc thanked
Her friendly proffer, and toward the hut
They went, and in his arms he took the boy.
Who is his father? said the prince, but wished

The word unuttered; for thereat her cheek
Was flushed with sudden heat and manifest pain;
And she replied, He perished in the war.

They entered now her home; she spread the board,
Bringing fresh curds and cheese-like curd so white,
The orchard fruits, and what sweet beverage
Her bees, who now were slumbering in the hive,
Had toiled to purvey all the summer long.
Three years, said Madoc, have gone by, since here
I found a timely welcome, overworn
With toil and sorrow and sickness:—three long years
'T was when the battle had been waged hard by,
Upon the plain of Arvon.
                            She grew pale,
Suddenly pale; and seeing that he marked
The change, she told him, with a feeble voice,
That was the fatal fight which widowed her.

O Christ! cried Madoc, 't is a grief to think
How many a gallant Briton died that day,
In that accursèd strife! I trod the field
When all was over,—I beheld them heaped—
Aye like ripe corn within the reaper's reach,
Strewn round the bloody spot where Hoel lay;
Brave as he was, himself cut down at last,
Oppressed by numbers, gashed with wounds, yet still
Clenching in his dead hand the broken sword!—
But you are moved,—you weep at what I tell.
Forgive me, that renewing my own grief,
I should have awakened yours! Did you then know
Prince Hoel?
                            She replied, Oh no! my lot
Was humble, and my loss a humble one;
Yet was it all to me! They say, quoth she,—
And, as she spake, she struggled to bring forth
With painful voice the interrupted words,—
They say Prince Hoel's body was not found;
But you who saw him dead perchance can tell
Where he was laid, and by what friendly hand.
Even where he fell, said Madoc, is his grave;
For he who buried him was one whose faith
Recked not of boughten prayers, nor passing bell.
There is a hawthorn grows beside the place,
A solitary tree, nipt by the winds,
That it doth seem a fitting monument
For one untimely slain.—But wherefore dwell we
On this ungrateful theme?
                            He took a harp
Which stood beside, and passing o'er its chords,
Made music. At the touch the child drew nigh,
Pleased by the sounds, and leant on Madoc's knee,
And bade him play again: So Madoc played,
For he had skill in minstrelsy, and raised
His voice, and sung Prince Hoel's lay of love. 75

I have harnessed thee, my Steed of shining grey,
And thou shalt bear me to the dear white walls.
I love the white walls by the verdant bank,
That glitter in the sun, where Bashfulness
Watches the silver sea-mew sail along.
I love that glittering dwelling, where we hear
The ever-sounding billows; for there dwells
The shapely Maiden, fair as the sea-spray,
Her cheek as lovely as the apple flower,
Or summer evening's glow. I pine for her;

In crowded halls my spirit is with her;
Through the long sleepless night I think on her;
And happiness is gone, and health is lost,
And fled the flush of youth, and I am pale
As the pale ocean on the sunless morn.
I pine away for her, yet pity her
That she should spurn a love so true as mine.

He ceased, and laid his hand upon the child,—
And didst thou like the song? The child replied,—
Oh yes! it is a song my mother loves,
And so I love it too. He stoopt and kissed
The boy, who still was leaning on his knee,
Already grown familiar. I should like
To take thee with me, quoth the Ocean Lord,
Over the seas.

        Thou art Prince Madoc, then!—
The mother cried, . . . thou art indeed the Prince!
That song—that look—and at his feet she fell,
Crying—Oh take him, Madoc! save the child!
Thy brother Hoel's orphan!

        Long it was
Ere that in either agitated heart
The tumult could subside. One while the Prince
Gazed on the child, tracing intently there
His brother's lines; and now he caught him up,
And kissed his cheek, and gazed again till all
Was dim and dizzy,—then blest God, and vowed
That he should never need a father's love.

At length when copious tears had now relieved
Her burthened heart, and many a broken speech
In tears had died away, O Prince, she cried,
Long hath it been my dearest prayer to heaven,
That I might see thee once, and to thy love
Commit this friendless boy! For many a time,
In phrase so fond did Hoel tell thy worth,
That it hath wakened misery in me
To think I could not as a sister claim
Thy love! and therefore was it that till now
Thou knewëst me not; for I entreated him
That he would never let thy virtuous eye
Look on my guilt, and make me feel my shame.
Madoc, I did not dare to see thee then,
Thou wilt not scorn me now,—for I have now
Forgiven myself; and, while I here performed
A mother's duty in this solitude,
Have felt myself forgiven.

        With that she clasped
His hand, and bent her face on it and wept.
Anon collecting she pursued,—My name
Is Llaian: by the chance of war I fell
Into his power, when all my family
Had been cut off, all in one hour of blood.
He saved me from the ruffian's hand, he soothed
With tenderest care my sorrow.—You can tell
How gentle he could be, and how his eyes,
So full of life and kindliness, could win
All hearts to love him. Madoc, I was young;
I had no living friend;—and when I gave
This infant to his arms, when with such joy
He viewed it o'er and o'er again, and pressed
A father's kiss upon its cheek, and turned
To me, and made me feel more deeply yet
A mother's deep delight,—oh! I was proud
To think my child in after years should say,

Prince Hoel was his father!

        Thus I dwelt
In the white dwelling by the verdant bank,—
Though not without my melancholy hours,
Happy. The joy it was when I beheld
His steed of shining grey come hastening on,
Across the yellow sand! . . Alas! ere long,
King Owen died. I need not tell thee, Madoc,
With what a deadly and forefeeling fear
I heard how Hoel seized his father's throne,
Nor with what ominous woe I welcomed him,
In that last little miserable hour
Ambition gave to love. I think his heart,
Brave as it was, misgave him. When I spake
Of David and my fears, he smiled upon me;
But 't was a smile that came not from the heart,—
A most ill-boding smile!—O Madoc! Madoc!
You know not with what misery I saw
His parting steps,—with what a dreadful hope
I watched for tidings!—And at length it came,—
Came like a thunderbolt!—I sought the field!
O Madoc, there were many widows there,
But none with grief like mine! I looked around;
I dragged aside the bodies of the dead,
To search for him, in vain;—and then a hope
Seized me, which it was agony to lose!

Night came. I did not heed the storm of night!
But for the sake of this dear babe, I sought
Shelter in this lone hut : 't was desolate;
And when my reason had returned, I thought
That here the child of Hoel might be safe,
Till we could claim thy care. But thou, meantime,
Didst go to roam the ocean; so I learnt
To bound my wishes here. The carkanet,
The embroidered girdle, and what other gauds
Were once my vain adornments, soon were changed
For things of profit, goats and bees, and this,
The tuneful solace of my solitude.
Madoc the harp is as a friend to me;
I sing to it the songs which Hoel loved,
And Hoel's own sweet lays; it comforts me,
And gives me joy in grief.

        Often I grieved,
To think the son of Hoel should grow up
In this unworthy state of poverty;
Till Time, who softens all regrets, had worn
That vain regret away, and I became
Humbly resigned to God's unerring will.
To him I looked for healing, and he poured
His balm into my wounds. I never formed
A prayer for more,—and lo! the happiness
Which he hath, of his mercy, sent me now!

XV.

The Excommunication.

On Madoc's docile courser Llaian sits,
Holding her joyful boy; the Chief beside
Paces afoot, and like a gentle Squire
Leads her loose bridle; from the saddle-bow
His shield and helmet hang, and with the lance,
Staff-like, he stayed his steps.. Before the sun

Had climbed his southern eminence, they left
The mountain-feet; and hard by Bangor now,
Travelling the plain before them they espy
A princely cavalcade, for so it seemed,
Of knights, with hawk in hand and hounds in leash,
Squires, pages, serving-men, and armed grooms,
And many a sumpter-beast and laden wain,
Far following in their rear.   The bravery
Of glittering bauldricks and of plumed crests,
Embroidered surcoats and emblazoned shields,
And lances whose long streamers played aloft,
Made a rare pageant, as with sound of trump,
Tambour, and cittern, proudly they went on;
And ever, at the foot-fall of their steeds,
The tinkling horse-bells, in rude symphony,
Accorded with the joy.

                          What have we here?
Quoth Madoc then to one who stood beside
The threshold of his osier-woven hut.
'T is the great Saxon Prelate, he returned,
Come hither for some end, I wis not what,
Only be sure no good!—How stands the tide?
Said Madoc; can we pass?—'T is even at flood,
The man made answer, and the Monastery
Will have no hospitality to spare
For one of Wales to-day.   Be ye content
To guest with us.

                    He took the Prince's sword:
The daughter of the house brought water then,
And washed the stranger's feet; the board was spread,
And o'er the bowl they communed of the days
Ere ever Saxon set his hateful foot
Upon the beautiful Isle. 76

                            As so they sate,
The bells of the Cathedral rung abroad
Unusual summons.   What is this? exclaimed
Prince Madoc; let us see!—Forthwith they went,
He and his host, their way.   They found the rites
Begun; the mitred Baldwin, in his hand
Holding a taper, at the altar stood.
Let him be cursed!—were his words which first
Assailed their ears,—living and dead, in limb
And life, in soul and body, be he curst
Here and hereafter! Let him feel the curse
At every moment, and in every act,
By night and day, in waking and in sleep!
We cut him off from Christian fellowship;
Of Christian sacraments we deprive his soul;
Of Christian burial we deprive his corpse;
And when that carrion to the Fiends is left
In unprotected earth, thus let his soul
Be quenched in hell!

                      He dashed upon the floor
His taper down, and all the ministring Priests
Extinguished each his light, to consummate
The imprecation.

                  Whom is it ye curse,
Cried Madoc, with these horrors? They replied,
The Contumacious Prince of Mathraval, 77
Cyveilioc.

              What! quoth Madoc, and his eye
Grew terrible,—Who is he that sets his foot
In Gwyneth here, and with this hellish hate
Insults the blameless Lord of Mathraval?—
We wage no war with women nor with Priests;
But if there be a knight amid your train,

Who dare come boldly forth, and to my face
Say that Cyveilioc hath deserved this curse,
Lo! here stand I, Prince Madoc, who will make
That wretched man cry craven in the dust,
And eat his lying words!

                          Be temperate!
Quoth one of Baldwin's Priests, who, Briton born,
Had known Prince Madoc in his father's court;
It is our charge, throughout this Christian land
To call upon all Christian men to join
The armies of the Lord, and take the cross;
That so, in battle with the Infidels,
The palm of victory or of martyrdom,
Glorious alike, may be their recompense.
This holy badge, whether in godless scorn,
Or for the natural blindness of his heart,
Cyveilioc hath refused; thereby incurring
The pain, which, not of our own impulse, we
Inflict upon his soul, but at the will
Of our most holy Father, from whose word
Lies no appeal on earth.

                          'T is well for thee,
Intemperate Prince! said Baldwin, that our blood
Flows with a calmer action than thine own!
Thy brother David hath put on the cross,
To our most pious warfare piously
Pledging his kingly sword.   Do thou the like,
And for this better object lay aside
Thine other enterprise, which, lest it rob
Judea of one single Christian arm,
We do condemn as sinful.   Follow thou
The banner of the church to Palestine;
So shalt thou expiate this rash offence,
Against the which we else should fulminate
Our ire, did we not see in charity,
And therefore rather pity than resent
The rudeness of this barbarous land.

                                      At that,
Scorn tempering wrath, yet anger sharpening scorn,
Madoc replied, Barbarians as we are,
Lord Prelate, we received the law of Christ
Many a long age before your pirate sires
Had left their forest dens: nor are we now
To learn that law from Norman or from Dane,
Saxon, Jute, Angle, or whatever name
Suit best your mongrel race! Ye think, perchance,
That like your own poor woman-hearted King,
We too in Gwyneth are to take the yoke
Of Rome upon our necks;—but you may tell
Your Pope, that when I sail upon the seas,
I shall not strike a topsail for the breath
Of all his maledictions!

                          Saying thus,
He turned away, lest farther speech might call
Farther reply, and kindle farther wrath,
More easy to avoid than to allay.
Therefore he left the church; and soon his mind
To gentler mood was won, by social talk
And the sweet prattle of that blue-eyed boy,
Whom in his arms he fondled.

                              But when now
Evening had settled, to the door there came
One of the brethren of the Monastery,
Who called Prince Madoc forth.   Apart they went,
And in the low suspicious voice of fear,
Though none was nigh, the Monk began.   Be calm,

Prince Madoc, while I speak, and patiently
Hear to the end! Thou knowest that, in his life,
Becket did excommunicate thy sire
For his unlawful marriage; but the King,
Feeling no sin in conscience, heeded not
The inefficient censure. Now, when Baldwin
Beheld his monument to-day, impelled,
As we do think, by anger against thee,
He swore that, even as Owen in his deeds
Disowned the Church when living, even so
The Church disowned him dead, 78 and that his corpse
No longer should be suffered to pollute
The sanctuary—Be patient, I beseech,
And hear me out. Gerald at this, who felt
A natural horror, sought,—as best he knew
The haughty Primate's temper,—to dissuade
By politic argument, and chiefly urged
The quick and fiery nature of our nation,—
How at the sight of such indignity,
They would arise in arms, and limb from limb
Tear piecemeal him and all his company.
So far did this prevail, that he will now
Commit the deed in secret; and, this night,
Thy father's body from its resting-place,
O Madoc! shall be torn, and cast aside
In some unhallowed pit, with foul disgrace
And contumelious wrong.
                    Sayest thou to-night?
Quoth Madoc.—Aye, at midnight, he replied,
Shall this impiety be perpetrated.
Therefore hath Gerald, for the reverence
He bears to Owen's royal memory,
Sent thee the tidings. Now be temperate
In thy just anger, Prince! and shed no blood.
Thou knowest how dearly the Plantagenet
Atones for Becket's death; and be thou sure,
Though thou thyself shouldst sail beyond the storm,
That it would fall on Britain.
                    While he spake,
Madoc was still; the feeling worked too deep
For speech, or visible sign. At length he cried,
What if amid their midnight sacrilege
I should appear among them?
                    It were well;
The Monk replied, if, at a sight like that,
Thou canst withhold thy hand.
                    Oh, fear me not!
Good and true friend, said Madoc. I am calm,
And calm as thou beholdest me will prove
In word and action. Quick I am to feel
Light ills,—perhaps o'er-hasty: summer gnats,
Finding my cheek unguarded, may infix
Their skin-deep stings, to vex and irritate;
But if the wolf, or forest boar, be nigh,
I am awake to danger. Even so
Bear I a mind of steel and adamant
Against all greater wrongs. My heart hath now
Received its impulse; and thou shalt behold
How in this strange and hideous circumstance
I shall find profit.—Only, my true friend,
Let me have entrance.
                    At the western porch,
Between the complines and the matin-bell,—
The Monk replied: there thou shalt find the door
Ready. Thy single person will suffice;
For Baldwin knows his danger, and the hour

Of guilt or fear convicts him, both alike
Opprobrious. Now, farewell!
                    Then Madoc took
His host aside, and in his private ear
Told him the purport, and wherein his help
Was needed. Night came on; the hearth was heapt,
The women went to rest. They twain, the while,
Sate at the board, and while the untasted bowl
Stood by them, watched the glass whose falling sands
Told out the weary hours. The hour is come;
Prince Madoc helmed his head, and from his neck
He slung the bugle-horn; they took their shields,
And lance in hand went out. And now arrived,
The bolts give back before them, and the gate
Rolls on its heavy hinge.
                    Beside the grave
Stood Baldwin and the Prior, who, albeit
Cambrian himself, in fear and awe obeyed
The lordly Primate's will. They stood and watched
The ministers perform the irreverent work.
And now with spade and mattock have they broken
Into the house of death, and now have they
From the stone coffin wrenched the iron cramps,
When sudden interruption startled them,
And clad in complete mail from head to foot,
They saw the Prince come on. Their tapers gleamed
Upon his visage, as he wore his helm
Open; and when in that pale countenance,—
For the strong feeling blanched his cheek,—they saw
His father's living lineaments, a fear
Like ague shook them. But anon that fit
Of scared imagination to the sense
Of other peril yielded, when they heard
Prince Madoc's dreadful voice. Stay! he exclaimed,
For now they would have fled;—stir not a man,—
Or if I once put breath into this horn,
All Wales will hear, as if dead Owen called
For vengeance from that grave. Stir not a man,
Or not a man shall live! The doors are watched,
And ye are at my mercy!
                    But at that,
Baldwin from the altar seized the crucifix,
And held it forth to Madoc, and cried out,
He who strikes me, strikes Him; forbear, on pain
Of endless———
                    Peace! quoth Madoc, and profane not
The holy Cross, with those polluted hands
Of midnight sacrilege!—Peace! I harm thee not,—
Be wise, and thou art safe.—For thee, thou knowest,
Prior, that if thy treason were divulged,
David would hang thee on thy steeple top,
To feed the steeple daws: Obey and live!
Go, bring fine linen and a coffer meet
To bear these relics; and do ye, meanwhile,
Proceed upon your work.
                    They at his word
Raised the stone cover, and displayed the dead,
In royal grave-clothes habited, his arms
Crossed on the breast, with precious gums and spice
Fragrant, and incorruptibly preserved.
At Madoc's bidding, round the corpse they wrap
The linen web, fold within fold involved;
They laid it in the coffer, and with cloth
At head and foot filled every interval
And prest it down compact; they closed the lid,
And Madoc with his signet sealed it thrice.

Then said he to his host, Bear thou at dawn
This treasure to the ships. My father's bones
Shall have their resting-place, where mine one day
May moulder by their side. He shall be free
In death, who living did so well maintain
His and his country's freedom. As for ye,
For your own safety, ye I ween will keep
My secret safe. So saying he went his way.

XVI.

David.

Now hath the Lord of Ocean once again
Set feet in Mona. Llaian there receives
Sisterly greeting from the royal maid,
Who, while she tempers to the public eye
Her welcome, safely to the boy indulged
In fond endearments of instinctive love.
When the first flow of joy was overpast,
How went the equipment on, the Prince inquired.
Nay, brother, quoth Goervyl, ask thou that
Of Urien;—it hath been his sole employ
Daily from cock-crow until even-song,
That he hath laid aside all other thoughts,
Forgetful even of me! she said and smiled
Playful reproach upon the good old man,
Who in such chiding as affection loves,
Dallying with terms of wrong, returned rebuke.
There, Madoc, pointing to the shore, he cried,
There are they moored; six gallant barks, as trim
And worthy of the sea as ever yet
Gave canvass to the gale. The mariners
Flock to thy banner, and the call hath roused
Many a brave spirit. Soon as Spring shall serve,
There need be no delay. I should depart
Without one wish that lingers, could we bear
Ririd from hence, and break poor Rodri's chains,
Thy lion-hearted brother;—and that boy,
If he were with us, Madoc! that dear boy
Llewelyn!
          Sister, said the Prince at that.
How sped the Queen?
                   Oh Madoc! she replied,
A hard and unrelenting heart hath he.
The gentle Emma told me she had failed,
And that was all she told; but in her eye
I could see sorrow struggling. She complains not,
And yet, I know, in bitterness laments
The hour which brought her as a victim here.

Then I will seek the Monarch, Madoc cried;
And forth he went. Cold welcome David gave,
Such as might chill a suppliant; but the Prince
Fearless began. I found at Dinevawr
Our brother Ririd, and he made his suit
That he might follow me, a banished man.
He waits thy answer at the court of Rhys.
Now I beseech thee, David, say to him
His father's hall is open!
                          Then the king
Replied, I told thee, Madoc, thy request
Displeased me heretofore; I warned thee, too,
To shun the rebel; yet my messenger
Tells me, the guests at Dinevawr who sate

At board with Rhys and drank of his own cup,
Were Madoc and Lord Ririd—Was this well,
This open disobedience to my will,
And my express command?
                        Madoc subdued
His rising wrath. If I should tell thee, Sire,
He answered, by what chance it so fell out,
I should of disobedience stand excused,
Even were it here a crime. Yet think again,
David, and let thy better mind prevail!
I am his surety here; he comes alone;
The strength of yonder armament is mine;
And when did I deceive thee?—I did hope,
For natural love and public decency,
That ye would part in friendship—let that pass!
He may remain, and join me in the hour
Of embarkation. But for thine own sake,
Cast off these vile suspicions, and the fear
That makes its danger! Call to mind, my brother,
The rampart that we were to Owen's throne!
Are there no moments when the thoughts and loves
Of other days return?—Let Rodri loose!
Restore him to his birth-right!—Why wouldst thou
Hold him in chains, when benefits would bind
His noble spirit?
                 Leave me! cried the King;
Thou knowest the theme is hateful to my ear.
I have the mastery now, and idle words,
Madoc, shall never thrust me from the throne,
Which this right arm in battle hardly won.
There must he lie till Nature set him free,
And so deliver both. Trespass no more!

A little yet bear with me, Madoc cried.
I leave this land for ever; let me first
Behold my brother Rodri, lest he think
My summer love be withered, and in wrath
Remember me hereafter.
                       Leave me, Madoc!
Speedily, ere indulgence grow a fault,
Exclaimed the Monarch. Do not tempt my wrath;
Thou knowest me!
                Aye! the Ocean Prince replied,
I know thee, David, and I pity thee,
Thou poor, suspicious, miserable man!
Friend hast thou none, except thy country's foe,
That hateful Saxon, he whose bloody hand
Plucked out thy brethren's eyes; and for thy kin,
Them hast thou made thy perilous enemies.
What if the Lion Rodri were abroad?
What if Llewelyn's banner were displayed?
The sword of England could not save thee then.
Frown not, and menace not! for what am I,
That I should fear thine anger?—And with that
He turned indignant from the wrathful king.

XVII.

The Departure.

WINTER hath passed away; the vernal storms
Have spent their rage, the ships are stored, and now
To-morrow they depart. That day a Boy,
Weary and foot-sore, to Aberfraw came,
Who to Goervyl's chamber made his way,

And caught the hem of her garment, and exclaimed,
A boon,—a boon,—dear Lady! Nor did he
Wait more reply than that encouragement
Which her sweet eye and lovely smile bestowed;
I am a poor, unhappy, orphan boy,
Born to fair promises and better hopes,
But now forlorn. Take me to be your page!—
For blessëd Mary's sake, refuse me not!
I have no friend on earth, nor hope but this.

The boy was fair; and though his eyes were swoln,
And cheek defiled with tears, and though his voice
Came choaked by grief; yet to that earnest eye
And supplicating voice so musical,
It had not sure been easy to refuse
The boon he begged. I cannot grant thy suit,
Goervyl cried, but I can aid it, boy!—
Go ask of Madoc!—and herself arose,
And led him where her brother on the shore
That day the last embarkment oversaw.
Mervyn then took his mantle by the skirt,
And knelt and made his suit; she too began
To sue, but Madoc smiling on the Maid,
Won by the virtue of the countenance
Which looked for favour, lightly gave the yes.

Where wert thou, Caradoc, when that fair boy
Told his false tale? for hadst thou heard the voice,
The gentle voice so musically sweet,
And seen that earnest eye, it would have healed
Thy wounded heart, and thou hadst voyaged on
The happiest man that ever yet forsook
His native country! He, on board the bark,
Leant o'er the vessel-side, and there he stood
And gazed, almost unconscious that he gazed,
Toward yon distant mountains where she dwelt,
Senena, his belovëd. Caradoc,
Senena, thy belovëd, is at hand!
Her golden locks are clipt, and her blue eye
Is wandering through the throng in search of thee,
For whose dear sake she hath forsaken all.
You deem her false, that her frail constancy
Shrunk from her father's anger, that she lives
Another's victim bride; but she hath fled
From that unnatural anger; hath escaped
The unnatural union; she is on the shore,
Senena, blue-eyed Maid, a seemly boy,
To share thy fortunes, to reward thy love,
And to the land of peace to follow thee,
Over the ocean waves.
                    Now all is done.
Stores, beeves and flocks and water all aboard;
The dry East blows, and not a sign of change
Stains the clear firmament. The Sea-Lord sate
At the last banquet in his brother's court,
And heard the song: It told of Owen's fame;
When with his Normen and assembled force
Of Guienne and Gascony, and Anjou's strength,
The Fleming's aid and England's chosen troops,
Along the ascent of Berwyn, many a day
The Saxon vainly on his mountain foes
Denounced his wrath; for Mona's dragon sons,
By wary patience baffled long his force,
Winning slow Famine to their aid, 79 and helped
By the angry elements, and sickness sent
From Heaven, and Fear that of its vigour robbed

The healthy arm;—then in quick enterprise
Fell on his weary and disheartened host,
Till with defeat and loss and obloquy
He fled with all his nations. Madoc gave
His spirit to the song; he felt the theme
In every pulse; the recollection came,
Revived and heightened to intenser pain,
That in Aberfraw, in his father's hall,
He never more should share the feast, nor hear
The echoing harp again! His heart was full;
And, yielding to its yearnings, in that mood
Of aweful feeling, he called forth the King,
And led him from the palace-porch, and stretched
His hand toward the ocean, and exclaimed,
To-morrow over yon wide waves I go;
To-morrow, never to return, I leave
My native land! O David, O my brother,
Turn not impatiently a reckless ear
To that affectionate and natural voice
Which thou wilt hear no more! Release our brethren,
Recall the wanderers home, and link them to thee
By cordial confidence, by benefits
Which bless the benefactor. Be not thou
As is the black and melancholy yeugh,
That strikes into the grave its baleful roots,
And prospers on the dead! 80—The Saxon King—
Think not I hate him now;—an hour like this
Hath softened all my harsher feelings down;
Nor will I hate him for his sister's sake,
Thy gentle Queen,—whom that great God may bless,
And, blessing her, bless thee and our dear country,
Shall never be forgotten in my prayers;
But he is far away; and should there come
The evil hour upon thee,—if thy kin,
Wearied by suffering, and driven desperate,
Should lift the sword, or young Llewelyn raise
His banner and demand his father's throne,—
Were it not trusting to a broken reed,
To lean on England's aid?—I urge thee not
For answer now; but sometimes, O my brother!
Sometimes recall to mind my parting words,
As 't were the death-bed counsel of the friend
Who loved thee best!

            The affection of his voice,
So mild and solemn, softened David's heart;
He saw his brother's eyes, suffused with tears,
Shine in the moon-beam as he spake; the King
Remembered his departure, and he felt
Feelings, which long from his disnatured breast
Ambition had expelled: he could almost
Have followed their strong impulse. From the shore,
Madoc with quick and agitated step
Had sought his home; the monarch slow returned,
Serious and slow, and laid him down that night
With painful recollections, and such thoughts
As might, if heaven had willed it, have matured
To penitence and peace.

            The day is come:
The adventurers in Saint Cybi's holy fane
Hear the last mass, and all assoiled of sin
Partake the bread of Christian fellowship.
Then, as the Priest his benediction gave,
They knelt, in such an awful stillness hushed,
As with yet more oppression seemed to load
The oppressed heart. At times and half supprest,
Womanly sobs were heard, and manly cheeks

Were wet with silent tears. Now forth they go,
And at the portal of the Church unfurl
Prince Madoc's banner: at that sight a shout
Burst from his followers, and the hills and rocks
Thrice echoed their acclaim.
                              There lie the ships,
Their sails all loose, their streamers rolling out
With sinuous flow and swell, like water-snakes,
Curling aloft; the waves are gay with boats,
Pinnace and barge and coracle,—the sea
Swarms like the shore with life. Oh what a sight
Of beauty for the spirit unconcern'd,
If heart there be which unconcern'd could view
A sight like this! how yet more beautiful
For him, whose soul can feel and understand
The solemn import! Yonder they embark,
Youth, beauty, valour, virtue, reverend age;
Some led by love of noble enterprise,
Others, who, desperate of their country's weal,
Fly from the impending yoke; all warm alike
With confidence and high heroic hope,
And all in one fraternal bond conjoin'd
By reverence to their Chief, the best beloved
That ever yet on hopeful enterprise
Led gallant army forth. He, even now
Lord of himself, by faith in God and love
To man subdues the feeling of this hour,
The bitterest of his being.
                            At this time,
Pale, and with feverish eye, the King came up,
And led him somewhat from the throng apart,
Saying, " I sent at day-break to release
Rodri from prison, meaning that with thee
He should depart in peace; but he was gone.
This very night he had escaped!—Perchance,
As I do hope,—it was thy doing, Madoc?
Is he aboard the fleet?»
                         « I would he were! »
Madoc replied; «with what a lightened heart
Then should I sail away! Ririd is there
Alone—alas! that this was done so late!»
« Reproach me not!» half sullenly the King,
Answering, exclaim'd; « Madoc, reproach me not!
Thou know'st how hardly I attain'd the throne:
And is it strange that I should guard with fear
The precious prize?—Now,—when I would have taken
Thy counsel,—be the evil on his head!
Blame me not now, my brother, lest sometimes
I call again to mind thy parting words
In sorrow!»
            God be with thee! Madoc cried;
And if at times the harshness of a heart,
Too prone to wrath, have wrong'd thee, let these tears
Efface all faults. I leave thee, O my brother,
With all a brother's feelings!
                               So he said,
And grasp'd, with trembling tenderness, his hand,
Then calm'd himself, and moved toward the boat.
Emma, though tears would have their way and sighs
Would swell, suppressing still all words of woe,
Follow'd Goervyl to the extremest shore.
But then as on the plank the maid set foot,
Did Emma, staying her by the hand, pluck out
The crucifix, which next her heart she wore
In reverence to its relic, and she cried,
Yet ere we part, change with me! dear Goervyl,—

Dear sister, loved too well, or lost too soon,—
I shall betake me often to my prayers,
Never in them, Goervyl, of thy name
Unmindful;—thou too wilt remember me
Still in thine orisons;—but God forefend
That ever misery should make thee find
This Cross thy only comforter!
                               She said,
And kiss'd the holy pledge, as each to each
Transferr'd the mutual gift. Nor could the Maid
Answer for agony, to that farewell;
She held Queen Emma to her breast, and close
She clasp'd her with a strong convulsive sob,
Silently. Madoc too in silence went,
But prest a kiss on Emma's lips, and left
His tears upon her cheek. With dizzy eyes
Gazing she stood, nor saw the boat push off,—
The dashing of the oars awaken'd her;
She wipes her tears away to view once more
Those dear familiar faces;—they are dim
In the distance; never shall her waking eye
Behold them, till the hour of happiness,
When death hath made her pure for perfect bliss![8]

Two hearts alone of all that company,
Of all the thousands who beheld the scene,
Partook unmingled joy. Dumb with delight,
Young Hoel views the ships and feels the boat
Rock on the heaving waves; and Llaian felt
Comfort,—though sad, yet comfort,—that for her
No eye was left to weep, nor heart to mourn.
Hark! 't is the mariners with voice attuned
Timing their toil! and now with gentle gales,
Slow from the holy haven they depart!

XVIII.

Rodri.

Now hath the evening settled; the broad Moon
Rolls through the rifted clouds. With gentle gales
Slowly they glide along, when they behold
A boat with press of sail and stress of oar
Speed forward to the fleet; and now, arrived
Beside the Chieftain's vessel, one enquires
If Madoc be aboard? the answer given,
Swift he ascended up the lofty side.
With joyful wonder did the Ocean Lord
Again behold Llewelyn; but he gazed
Doubtfully on his comrade's countenance,—
A meagre man, severe of brow, his eye
Stern. Thou dost view me, Madoc, he exclaim'd,
As 't were a stranger's face. I marvel not!
The long afflictions of my prison house
Have changed me.
                 Rodri! cried the Prince, and fell
Upon his neck;—last night, subdued at length
By my solicitations, did the King
Send to deliver thee, that thou shouldst share
My happy enterprise;—and thou art come,
Even to my wish!
                 Nay, Madoc, nay, not so!
He answer'd with a stern and bitter smile;
This gallant boy had given me liberty,
And I will pay him with his father's throne: ·

Ay, by my father's soul!—Last night we fled
The house of bondage, and in the sea-caves
By day we lurk'd securely. Here I come,
Only to see thee once before I die,
And say farewell,—dear brother!'
                            Would to God
This purpose could be changed! the Sea Lord cried;
But thou art roused by wrongs, and who shall tame
That lion heart?—This only, if your lot
Fall favourable, will I beseech of ye,
That to his Queen, the fair Plantagenet,
All honourable humanity ye show
For her own virtue, and in gratitude,
As she hath pleaded for you, and hath urged
Her husband on your part, till it hath turn'd
His wrath upon herself. Oh! deal ye by her
As by your dearest sister in distress!
For even so dear is she to Madoc's heart:
And now I know she from Aberfraw's tower
Watcheth these spots upon the moonlight sea,
And weeps for my departure, and for me
Sends up her prayers to Heaven, nor thinks that now
I must make mine to man in her behalf!

Quoth Rodri, Rest assured for her. I swear,
By our dead mother, so to deal with her
As thou thyself wouldst dictate, as herself
Shall wish.
            The tears fell fast from Madoc's eyes:
O Britain! O my country! he exclaim'd,
For ever thus by civil strife convulsed,
Thy children's blood flowing to satisfy
Thy children's rage, how wilt thou still support
The struggle with the Saxon?
                            Rodri cried,
Our strife shall not be long. Mona will rise
With joy to welcome me her rightful Lord;
And woe be to the king who rules by fear,
When danger comes against him!
                            Fear not thou
For Britain! quoth Llewelyn; for not yet
The country of our fathers shall resign
Her name among the nations. Though her Sun
Slope from his eminence, the voice of man
May yet arrest him on his downward way.
My dreams by day, my visions in the night,
Are of her welfare. I shall mount the throne,—
Yes, Madoc! and the Bard of years to come,
Who harps of Arthur's and of Owen's deeds,
Shall with the Worthies of his country rank
Llewelyn's name. Dear uncle, fare thee well!—
And I almost could wish I had been born
Of humbler lot, that I might follow thee,
Companion of this noble enterprise.
Think of Llewelyn often, who will oft
Remember thee in love!
                        For the last time
He grasp'd his Uncle's hand, and Rodri gave
The last farewell; then went the twain their way.
So over ocean through the moonlight waves,
Prince Madoc sailed with all his company.
No nobler crew fill'd that heroic bark,
Which bore the first adventurers of the deep
To seek the Golden Fleece on barbarous shores:
Nor richlier fraught did that illustrious fleet
Home to the Happy Island hold its way,

When Amadis with his prime chivalry,
He of all chivalry himself the flower,
Came from the rescue, proud of Roman spoils,
And Oriana, freed from Roman thrall.

PART II.

MADOC IN AZTLAN.

I.

The Return to Aztlan.

Now go your way, ye gallant company!
God and good Angels guard ye as ye go!
Blow fairly, Winds of Heaven! ye Ocean Waves,
Swell not in anger to that fated fleet!
For not of conquest greedy nor of gold;
Seek they the distant world.—Blow fairly, Winds!
Waft, Waves of Ocean, well your blessed load!

Fair blew the Winds, and safely did the Waves
Bear that beloved charge. It were a tale
Would rouse adventurous courage in a boy,
Making him long to be a mariner
That he might rove the main, if I should tell
How pleasantly for many a summer-day,
Over the sunny sea with wind at will,
Prince Madoc sailed; and of those happy Isles,
Which had he seen ere that ordained storm
Drove southward his slope course, there he had pitched
His tent, and blest his lot that it had fallen
In land so fair; and human blood had reeked
Daily on Aztlan's cursed altars still.
But other doom was his, more arduous toil
Yet to achieve, worse danger to endure,
Worse evil to be quelled, and higher good
Which passeth not away educed from ill;
Whereof all unforeseeing, yet for all
Of ready heart, he over ocean sails,
Wafted by gentle winds o'er gentle waves,
As if the elements combined to serve
The perfect Prince, by God and man beloved:
And now how joyfully he views the land;
Skirting like morning clouds the dusky sea;
With what a searching eye recals to mind
Foreland and creek and cape; how happy now
Up the great river bends at last his way!
No watchman had been stationed on the height
To seek his sails,—for with Cadwallon's hope
Too much of doubt was blended and of fear:
Yet thitherward whene'er he walked abroad
His face, as if instinctively, was turned;
And duly morn and eve Lincoya there,
As though religion led his duteous feet,
Went up to gaze. He on a staff had scored
The promised moons and days; and many a time
Counting again its often-told account,
So to beguile impatience, day by day
Smoothed off with more delight the daily notch.
But now that the appointed time was nigh,
Did that perpetual presence of his hope
Haunt him, and mingle with his sleep and mar

The natural rest and trouble him by day,
That all his pleasure was at earliest light
To take his station, and at latest eve,
If he might see the sails where far away
Through wide savannahs rolled the silver stream.
Oh then with what a sudden start his blood
Flowed from its quickened spring, when far away
He spied the glittering topsails! for a while
Distrustful of that happy sight, till now
Slowly he sees them rise, and wind along
Through wide savannahs up the silver stream.
Then with a breathless speed he flies to spread
The joy; and with Cadwallon now descends,
And drives adown the tide the light canoe,
And mounts the vessel-side, and once again
Falls at the Ocean Lord's beloved feet.

First of the general weal did Madoc ask;
Cadwallon answered, All as yet is well,
And by this seasonable aid secured,
Will well remain.—Thy father? quoth the Prince.
Even so, replied Cadwallon, as that eye
Of hesitation augurs,—fallen asleep.
The good old man remembered thee in death,
And blest thee ere he died.
                              By this the shores
And heights were thronged; from hill to hill, from rock
To rock, the shouts of welcome rung around.
Forward they press to view the man beloved,
Britons and Hoamen with one common joy
Hailing their common friend. Happy that day
Was he who heard his name from Madoc's voice;
Happy who met the greeting of his eye;
Yea happy he who shared his general smile,
Amid the unacknowledged multitude.
Caermadoc,—by that name Cadwallon's love
Called it in memory of the absent Prince,—
Stood in a mountain vale, by rocks and heights
A natural bulwark girt. A rocky stream
Which from the fells came down there spread itself
Into a quiet lake, to compass which
Had been a two hours' pleasurable toil;
And he who from a well-strung bow could send
His shaft across, had needs a sinewy arm,
And might from many an archer far and near
Have borne away the bell. Here had the Chief
Chosen his abiding-place, for strength preferred,
Where vainly might an host in equal arms
Attempt the difficult entrance; and for all
Which could delight the eye and heart of man;
Whate'er of beauty or of usefulness
Heart could desire, or eye behold, being here.
What he had found an idle wilderness
Now gave rich increase to the husbandman,
For Heaven had blest their labour. Flourishing
He left the happy vale; and now he saw
More fields reclaimed, more habitations reared,
More harvests rising round. The reptile race,
And every beast of rapine, had retired
From man's asserted empire; and the sound
Of axe and dashing oar, and fisher's net,
And song beguiling toil, and pastoral pipe,
Were heard, where late the solitary hills
Gave only to the mountain-cataract
Their wild response.
                        Here, Urien, cried the Prince,

These craggy heights and overhanging groves
Will make thee think of Gwyneth. And this hut,
Rejoined Cadwallon, with its roof of reeds,
Goervyl, is our palace: it was reared
With lighter labour than Aberfraw's towers;
Yet, Lady, safer are its wattled sides
Than Mona's kingly walls.—Like Gwyneth, said he?
Oh no! we neighbour nearer to the Sun,[1]
And with a more benignant eye the Lord
Of Light beholds us here.
                              So thus did they
Cheerfully welcome to their new abode
These, who albeit aweary of their way,
And glad to reach at length the place of rest,
Felt their hearts overburdened, and their eyes
Ready to overflow. Yet not the less,
The buzz of busy joy was heard around,
Where every dwelling had its guest, and all
Gave the long eve to hospitable mirth.

II.

The Tidings.

BUT when the Lord of Ocean from the stir
And tumult was retired, Cadwallon then
Thus rendered his account.
                              When we had quelled
The strength of Aztlan, we should have thrown down
Her altars, cast her Idols to the fire,
And on the ruins of her fanes accurst
Planted the Cross triumphant. Vain it is
To sow the seed, where noxious weeds and briers
Must choke it in the growth.
                              Yet I had hope
The purer influence of exampled good
Might to the saving knowledge of the truth
Lead this bedarkened race; and when thy ship
Fell down the stream to distant Britain bound,
All promised well. The Strangers' God had proved
Mightier in war, and Aztlan could not chuse
But see, nor seeing could she fail to love,
The freedom of his service. Few were now
The offerings at her altars, few the youths
And virgins to the temple-toils devote.
Therefore the Priests combined to save their craft;
And soon the rumour ran of evil signs
And tokens; in the temple had been heard
Wailings and loud lament; the eternal fire
Gave dismally a dim and doubtful flame;
And from the censer which at morn should steam
Sweet odours to the sun, a fetid cloud
Black and portentous rose. And now no Priest
Approached our dwelling. Even the friendly Prince
Yuhidthiton was at Caermadoc now
Rarely a guest; and if that tried good-will
Which once he bore us did at times appear,
A sullen gloom and silence like remorse
Followed the imagined crime.
                              But I the while
Recked not the brooding of the storm; for now
My father to the grave was hastening down.
Patiently did the pious man endure,
In faith anticipating blessedness,
Already more than man in those sad hours

When man is meanest. I sate by his side,
And prayed with him and talked with him of death
And life to come. O Madoc! those were hours
Which even in anguish gave my soul a joy :
I think of them in solitude, and feel
The comfort of my faith.

                But when that time
Of bitterness was past, and I returned
To daily duties, no suspicious sign
Betokened ill; the Priests among us came
As heretofore, and I their intercourse
Encouraged as I could, suspecting nought,
Nor conscious of the subtle-minded men
I dealt with, how inveterate in revenge,
How patient in deceit. Lincoya first
Forewarned me of the danger. He, thou knowest,
Had from the death of sacrifice escaped,
And lived a slave among a distant tribe,
When seeing us he felt a hope, that we,
Lords as he deemed us of the Elements,
Might pity his oppressèd countrymen,
And free them from their bondage. Didst thou hear
How from yon devilish altars he was saved?
For in the eternal chain his fate and ours
Were linked together then.

              The Prince replied,
I did but hear a broken tale. Tell on!

Among the Gods of yon unhappy race,
Tezcalipoca [2] as the chief they rank,
Or with the chief co-equal; maker he,
And master of created things esteemed.
He sits upon a throne of trophied skulls,
Hideous and huge ; a shield is on his arm,
And with his black right hand he lifts, as though
In wrath, the menacing spear. His festival,
Of all this wicked nation's wicked rites,
With most solemnity and circumstance,
And pomp of hellish piety, is held.
From all whom evil fortune hath subdued
To their inhuman thraldom, they select
Him whom they judge, for comely countenance
And shapely form and all good natural gifts,
Worthiest to be the victim; and for this
Was young Lincoya chosen, being in truth
The flower of all his nation. For twelve months,
Their custom is, that this appointed youth
Be as the Idol's living image held.
Garbed therefore like the Demon Deity,
Whene'er he goes abroad, an antic train
With music and with dance attend his way;
The crowd before him fall and worship him;
And those infernal Priests who guard him then
To be their victim and their feast at last,
At morning and at evening incense him,
And mock him with knee-reverence. Twenty days
Before the bloody festival arrive,
As 't were to make the wretch in love with life,
Four maids the loveliest of the land are given
In spousals. With Lincoya all these rites
Duly were kept; and at the stated time,
Four maids the loveliest of the land were his.
Of these was one, whom even at that hour
He learnt to love, so excellently good
Was she ; and she loved him and pitied him.
She is the daughter of an aged Priest ;

I oftentimes have seen her ; and in truth,
Compared with Britain's maids so beautiful,
Or with the dark-eyed daughters of the South,
She would be lovely still. Her cotton vest
Falls to the knee, and leaves her olive arms
Bare in their beauty ; loose, luxuriant, long,
Flow the black tresses of her glossy hair;
Mild is her eye's jet lustre; and her voice!—
A soul which harboured evil never breathed
Such winning tones.

            Thou knowest how manfully
These tribes, as if insensible to pain,
Welcome their death in battle, or in bonds
Defy their torturers. To Lincoya's mind
Long preparation now had made his fate
Familiar; and he says the thought of death
Broke not his sleep, nor mingled with his dreams,
Till Coatel was his. But then it woke;—
It hung,—it prest upon him like a weight
On one who scarce can struggle with the waves ;
And when her soul was full of tenderness,
That thought recurring to her, she would rest
Her cheek on his and weep.

              The day drew nigh;
And now the eve of sacrifice was come.—
What will not woman, gentle woman, dare,
When strong affection stirs her spirit up!—
She gathered herbs, which, like our poppy, bear
The seed of sleep, [3] and with the temple food
Mingled their power ; herself partook the food,
So best to lull suspicion; and the youth,
Instructed well, when all were laid asleep,
Fled far away.

            After our conquering arms
Had freed the Hoamen from their wretched yoke,
Lincoya needed but his Coatel
To fill his sum of earthly happiness.
Her to the temple had her father's vow
Awhile devoted, and some moons were still
To pass away, ere yet she might become
A sojourner with us, Lincoya's wife,
When from the Paba's wiles his watchful mind
Foreboded ill. He bade me take good heed,
And fear the sudden kindness of a foe.
I started at his words ;—these artful men,
Hostile at heart, as well we knew they were,
These were lip-lavish of their friendship now,
And courted confidence, while our tried friend
Yuhidthiton, estranged, a seldom guest,
Sullen and joyless, seemed to bear at heart
Something that rankled there. These things are strange;
The omens, too, had ceased ;—we heard no more
Of twilight voices, nor the unholy cloud
Steamed from the morning incense. Why was this?

Young Malinal had from the hour of peace
Been our indweller, studious to attain
Our language and our arts. To him I told
These doubts, assured of his true love and truth;
For he had learnt to understand and feel
Our holy faith, and tended like a son
Cynetha's drooping age, and shared with me
His dying benediction. He thus long
Intent on better things, had been estranged
From Aztlan and her councils ; but at this
He judged it for her welfare and for ours,

Now to resume his rank;—belike his voice
Might yet be heard, or if the worst befell,
His timely warning save us from the snare.

But in their secret councils Malinal
No longer bore a part; the Chiefs and King
Yielding blind reverence to the Pabas now,
Deluded or dismayed. He sent to say
Some treachery was designed, and bade me charge
His brother with the crime. On that same day,
Lincoya came from Aztlan; he had found
Coatel labouring with a wretchedness
She did not seek to hide; and when the youth
Revealed his fear, he saw her tawny cheek
Whiten, and round his neck she clung and wept.
She told him something dreadful was at hand,
She knew not what: That in the dead of night,
Coanocotzin at Mexitli's shrine
Had stood with all his nobles; human blood
Had then been offered up, and secret vows
Vowed with mysterious horror: That but late,
When to her father of the days to come
She spake, and of Lincoya and her lot
Among the strangers, he had frowned, and strove
Beneath dissembled anger to conceal
Oppressive grief. She knew not what to fear,
But something dreadful surely was at hand,
And she was wretched.
           When I heard these things,
Yuhidthiton and the Priest Heluha
Were in our dwellings. Them I called apart.—
There should be peace between us, I began;
Why is it otherwise?
           The Priest replied,
Is there not peace, Cadwallon? seek we not
More frequent and more friendly intercourse,
Even we, the servants of our Country-Gods,
Whose worship ye have changed, and for whose sake
We were and would have been your enemies?
But as those Gods have otherwise ordained,
Do we obey. Why, therefore, is this doubt?
The Power who led us hither, I replied,
Over the world of waters, who hath saved,
And who will save his people, warns me now.
Then on Yuhidthiton I fixed my eye.
Danger is near! I cried; I know it near!
It comes from Aztlan.
           His disordered cheek,
And the forced and steady boldness of his eye,
Which in defiance met the look it feared,
Confessed the crime. I saw his inward shame;
Yet with a pride like angry innocence
Did he make answer, I am in your hands,
And you believe me treacherous!—Kill me now!

Not so, Yuhidthiton! not so! quoth I;
You were the Strangers' friend, and yet again
That wisdom may return. We are not changed;—
Lovers of peace, we know, when danger comes,
To make the evil on the guilty head
Fall heavily and sure! with our good arms,
And our good cause, and that Almighty One,
We are enough, had we no other aid,
We of Caermadoc here, to put to shame
Aztlan, with all her strength and all her wiles.
But even now is Madoc on the seas;

He leads our brethren here; and should he find
That Aztlan hath been false,—oh! hope not then,
By force or fraud, to baffle or elude
Inevitable vengeance! While ye may,
Look to your choice; for we are friends or foes,
Even to your own desert.
           So saying, I left
The astonished men, whose unprovided minds
Failed them; nor did they aim at answer more,
But homeward went their way. Nor knew I then,—
For this was but a thing of yesterday,—
How near the help I boasted. Now, I trust,
Thy coming shall discomfit all their wiles.

III.

Neolin.

Nor yet at rest, my Sister! quoth the Prince,
As at her dwelling-door he saw the Maid
Sit gazing on that lovely moonlight scene :—
To bed, Goervyl Dearest, what hast thou
To keep thee wakeful here at this late hour,
When even I shall bid a truce to thought,
And lay me down in peace?—Good night, Goervyl!
Dear sister mine,—my own dear mother's child!

She rose and bending on with lifted arms,
Met the fond kiss, obedient then withdrew.
Yet could not he so lightly as he weened
Lay wakeful thoughts aside; for he foresaw
Long strife and hard adventure to achieve,
And forms of danger vague disturbed his dreams.
Early at morn the colonists arose;
Some pitch the tent-pole, and pin down the lines
That stretch the o'er-awning canvass; to the wood
Others with saw and axe and bill for stakes
And undergrowth to weave the wicker walls;
These to the ships, with whom Cadwallon sends
The Elk and Bison, broken to the yoke.

Ere noon Erillyab and her son arrived,
To greet the Chief. She wore no longer now
The lank loose locks of careless widowhood;
Her braided tresses round her brow were bound,
Bedecked with tufts of grey and silvery plumes
Plucked from the eagle's pennons. She with eye
And countenance which spake no feigned delight,
Welcomed her great deliverer. But her son
Had Nature charactered so legibly,
That when his tongue told fair, his face bewrayed
The lurking falsehood; sullen, slow of speech,
Savage, down-looking, dark, that at his words
Of welcome, Madoc in his heart conceived
Instinctive enmity.
           In a happy hour
Did the Great Spirit, said Erillyab,
Give bidding to the Winds to speed thee here!
For this I made my prayer; and when He sent
For the Belovèd Teacher, to restore him
Eyesight and youth, of him I then besought,
As he had been thy friend and ours on earth,
That he would intercede.—Brother, we know,
That the Great Spirit loves thee; He hath blest
Thy going and thy coming, and thy friends

Have prospered for thy sake; and now when first
The Powers of Evil do begin to work,
Lo! thou art here!—Brother, we have obeyed
Thy will, and the Belovëd Teacher's words
Have been our law; but now the Evil Ones
Cry out for blood, and say they are athirst,
And threaten vengeance. I have brought the Priest,
To whom they spake in darkness;—thou art wise,
And the Great Spirit will enlighten thee;—
We know not what to answer.—Tell thy tale,
Neolin!

      Hereat did Madoc fix upon him
A searching eye; but he, no whit abashed,
Began with firm effrontery his speech.
The Feast of the departed is at hand,
And I, in preparation, on the Field
Of the Spirit [4] past the night. It came to me
In darkness, after midnight, when the moon
Was gone, and all the stars were blotted out;
It gathered round me, with a noise of storms,
And entered into me, and I could feel
It was the Snake-God rolled and writhed within;
And I, too, with the inward agony,
Rolled like a snake and writhed. Give! give! he cried:
I thirst!—His voice was in me, and it burnt
Like fire, and all my flesh and bones were shaken;
Till, with a throe which seemed to rend my joints
Asunder, he past forth, and I was left
Speechless and motionless, gasping for breath.

Then Madoc, turning to Ayayaca,
Inquired, who is the man?—The good old Priest
Replied, he hath attended from his youth
The Snake-God's temple, and received for him
All offerings, and performed all sacrifice,
Till the Belovëd Teacher made us leave
The wicked way.

      Hear me! quoth Neolin,
With antic gesture and loud vehemence;
Before this generation, and before
These ancient forests,—yea, before yon lake
Was hollowed out, or one snow-feather fell
On yonder mountain-top, now never bare,—
Before these things I was, [5]—where, or from whence,
I know not,—who can tell? But then I was,
And in the shadow of the Spirit stood;
And I beheld the Spirit, and in him
Saw all things, even as they were to be;
And I held commune with him, not of words,
But thought with thought. Then was it given me
That I should chuse my station when my hour
Of mortal birth was come,—hunter, or chief,
Or to be mightiest in the work of war,
Or in the shadow of the Spirit live,
And he in me. According to my choice,
For ever overshadowed by his power,
I walk among mankind. At times I feel not
The burden of his presence; then am I
Like other men; but when the season comes,
Or if I seek the visitation, then
He fills me, and my soul is carried on,
And then do I foreflive the race of men,
So that the things that will be, are to me
Past.

      Amalahta lifted then his eyes
A moment.—It is true, he cried; we know

He is a gifted man, and wise beyond
The reach of mortal powers. Ayayaca
Hath also heard the warning.

           As I slept,
Replied the aged Priest, upon the Field
Of the Spirit, a loud voice awakened me,
Crying, I thirst! Give,—give! or I will take!
And then I heard a hiss, as if a snake
Were threatening at my side.—But saw you nothing?
Quoth Madoc.—Nothing; for the night was dark.
And felt you nothing? said the Ocean Prince.
He answered, Nothing; only sudden fear.—
No inward struggle, like possession?—None.
I thought of the Belovëd Teacher's words,
And crost myself, and then he had no power.

Thou hast slept heretofore upon the Field,
Said Madoc; didst thou never witness voice,
Or ominous sound! Ayayaca replied,
Certes the Field is holy! it receives,
All the year long, the operative power
Which falleth from the sky, or from below
Pervades the earth; no harvest groweth there,
Nor tree, nor bush, nor herb is left to spring.
But there the virtue of the elements
Is gathered, till the circle of the months
Be full; then, when the Priest, by mystic rites,
Long vigils and long abstinence prepared,
Goeth there to pass the appointed night alone,
The whole collected influence enters him.
Doubt not but I have felt strange impulses
On that mysterious Field, and in my dreams
Been visited; and have heard sounds in the air,
I knew not what;—but words articulate
Never till now. It was the Wicked One!
He wanted blood.

         Who says the Wicked One?
It was our Fathers' God! cried Neolin.
Son of the Ocean, why should we forsake
The worship of our fathers? [6] Ye obey
The White-Man's Maker; but to us was given
A different skin and speech and land and law.
The Snake-God understands the Red-Man's prayer,
And knows his wants and loves him. Shame be to us,
That since the Stranger here set foot among us,
We have let his lips be dry!

             Enough! replied
Madoc, who at Cadwallon's look represt
His answering anger. We will hold a talk
Of this hereafter. Be ye sure, mean time,
That the Great Sprit will from Evil Powers
Protect his people. This, too, be ye sure,
That every deed of darkness shall be brought
To light,—and woe be to the lying lips!

IV.

Amalahta.

Soon as the coming of the fleet was known,
Had Queen Erillyab sent her hunters forth.
They from the forest now arrive, with store
Of venison; fires are built before the tents,
Where Llaian and Goervyl for their guests
Prepare the feast; and now the ready board
With grateful odour steams. But while they sate

At meat, did Amalahta many a time
Lift his slow eye askance, and eagerly
Gaze on Goervyl's beauty; for whate'er
In man he might have thought deformed or strange
Seemed beautiful in her,—her golden curls,
Bright eyes of heavenly blue, and that clear skin,7
Blooming with health and youth and happiness.
He, lightly yielding to the impulse, bent
His head aside, and to Erillyab spake.
Mother, said he, tell them to give to me
That woman for my wife, that we may be
Brethren and friends. She, in the same low tone
Rebuked him, in her heart too well aware
How far unworthy he. Abashed thereby,
As he not yet had wholly shaken off
Habitual reverence, he sate sullenly,
Brooding in silence his imagined wiles,
By sight of beauty made more apt for ill;
For he himself being evil, good in him
Worked evil.

        And now Madoc, pouring forth
The ripe metheglin, to Erillyab gave
The horn of silver brim. Taste, Queen and friend,
Said he, what from our father-land we bring,
The old belovèd beverage. Sparingly
Drink, for it hath a strength to stir the brain,
And trouble reason, if intemperate lips
Abuse its potency. She took the horn,
And sipt with wary wisdom—Canst thou teach us
The art of this rare beverage? quoth the Queen;
Or is the gift reserved for ye alone,
By the Great Spirit, who hath favoured ye
In all things above us?—The Chief replied,
All that we know of useful and of good
Ye also shall be taught, that we may be
One people. While he spake, Erillyab passed
The horn to Amalahta. Sparingly!
Madoc exclaimed; but when the savage felt
The luscious flavour, and the poignant life,
He heeded nought beyond the immediate joy.
Deep did he drink, and still with clinching hands
Struggled, when from his lips unsatisfied,
Erillyab plucked the cup with sharp reproof,
Chiding his stubborn wilfulness. Ere long
The generous liquor flushed him : he could feel
His blood play faster, and the joyful dance
Of animal life within him. Bolder grown,
He at Goervyl lifts no longer now
The secret glance, but gloats with greedy eye;
Till, at the long and loathsome look abashed,
She rose, and nearer to her brother drew,
On light pretence of speech, being half in fear.
But he, regardless of Erillyab now,
To Madoc cried aloud, Thou art a King,
And I a King!—Give me thy sister there
To be my wife, and then we will be friends,
And reign together.

        Let me answer him,
Madoc! Cadwallon cried. I better know
Their language, and will set aside all hope,
Yet not incense the savage—A great thing,
Prince Amalahta, hast thou asked! said he,
Nor is it in Lord Madoc's power to give
Or to withhold; for marriage is with us
The holiest ordinance of God, whereon
The bliss or bale of human life depends.

Love must be won by love, and heart to heart
Linked in mysterious sympathy, before
We pledge the marriage-vow; and some there are,
Who hold, that, e'er we enter into life,
Soul hath with soul been mated, each for each
Especially ordained. Prince Madoc's will
Avails not, therefore, where this secret bond
Hath not been framed in heaven.

          The skilful speech
Which, with wild faith and reason, thus confirmed,
Yet tempered the denial, for a while
Silenced him, and he sate in moody dreams
Of snares and violence. Soon a drunken thirst,
And longing for the luscious beverage,
Drove those dark thoughts aside. More drink!
        quoth he.
Give me the drink!—Madoc again repeats
His warning, and again with look and voice
Erillyab chides; but he of all restraint
Impatient, cries aloud, Am I a child?
Give! give! or I will take!—Perchance ye think
I and my God alike cry out in vain!
But ye shall find us true!

          Give him the horn!
Cadwallon answered; there will come upon him
Folly and sleep, and then an after pain,
Which may bring wisdom with it, if he learn
Therefrom to heed our warning.—As thou sayest,
No child art thou!—the choice is in thy hand ;—
Drink, if thou wilt, and suffer, and in pain
Remember us.

        He clenched the horn, and swilled
The sweet intoxication copious down.
So bad grew worse. The potent draught provoked
Fierce pride and savage insolence. Aye! now
It seems that I have taught ye who I am!
The inebriate wretch exclaimed. This land is mine,
Not hers; the kingdom and the power are mine!
I am the master!

        Hath it made thee mad?
Erillyab cried.—Ask thou the Snake-God that!
Quoth he ; ask Neolin and Aztlan that!
Hear me, thou Son of the Waters! wilt thou have me
For friend or foe?—Give me that woman there,
And store me with this blessèd beverage,
And thou shalt dwell in my domains,—or else,
Blood, blood! the Snake-God calls for blood; the
        Gods
Of Aztlan and the people call for blood;
They call on me, and I will give them blood,
Till they have had their fill.

        Meanwhile the Queen,
In wonder and amazement heard and grief;
Watching the fiendish workings of his face,
And turning to the Prince at times, as if
She looked to him for comfort. Give him drink,
To be at peace! quoth Madoc. The good mead
Did its good office soon ; his dizzy eyes
Rolled with a sleepy swim; the joyous thrill
Died away; and as every limb relaxed,
Down sunk his heavy head and down he fell.
Then said the Prince, We must rejoice in this,
O Queen and friend, that, evil though it be,
Evil is brought to light; he hath divulged,
In this mad mood, what else had been concealed
By guilty cunning. Set a watch upon him

And on Priest Neolin; they plot against us;
Your fall and mine alike do they conspire,
Being leagued with Aztlan to destroy us both.
Thy son will not remember that his lips
Have let the treason pass. Be wary, then,
And we shall catch the crafty in the pit
Which they have dug for us.
　　　　　　　　　　Erillyab cast
A look of anger, made intense by grief,
On Amalahta—Cursëd be the hour
Wherein I gave thee birth! she cried; that pain
Was light to what thy base and brutal nature
Hath sent into my soul—But take thou heed!
I have borne many a woe and many a loss,—
My father's realm, the husband of my youth,
My hope in thee!—all motherly love is gone,—
Sufferance well nigh worn out.
　　　　　　　　　　When she had ceased,
Still the deep feeling filled her, and her eye
Dwelt on him, still in thought. Brother! she cried,
As Madoc would have soothed her, doubt not me!
Mine is no feeble heart. Abundantly
Did the Great Spirit overpay all woes,
And this the heaviest, when he sent thee here,
The friend and the deliverer. Evil tongues
May scatter lies; bad spirits and bad men
May league against thy life; but go thou on,
Brother! He loves thee and will be thy shield.

V.

War Denounced.

This is the day, when, in a foreign grave,
King Owen's relics shall be laid to rest.
No bright emblazonries bedecked his bier,
No tapers blazed, no prelate sung the mass,
No choristers the funeral dirge intoned,
No mitred abbots, and no tonsured train,
Lengthened the pomp of ceremonious woe.
His decent bier was with white linen spread
And canopied; two elks and bisons yoked,
Drew on the car; foremost Cadwallon bore
The Crucifix, with single voice, distinct,
The good priest Llorien chaunted loud and deep
The solemn service; Madoc next the bier
Followed his father's corpse; bareheaded then
Came all the people, silently and slow.

The burial-place was in a grassy plat,
A little level field of sunny green,
Between the river and a rocky bank,
Which, like a buttress, from the precipice
Of naked rock sloped out. On either side
'T was skirted by the woodlands. A stone cross
Stood on Cynetha's grave, sole monument.
Beneath a single cocoa, whose straight trunk
Rose like an obelisk, and waved on high
Its palmy plumage, green and never sere.
Here by Cynetha's side, with Christian prayers,
All wrongs forgotten now, was Owen laid.
Rest, King of Gwyneth, in a foreign grave!
From foul Indignity of Romish pride
And bigot priesthood, from a falling land
Thus timely snatched; and from the impending yoke,—
Rest in the kingdom of thy noble son!

Ambassadors from Aztlan in the vale
Awaited their return ;—Yuhidthiton,
Chief of the Chiefs, and Helhua the priest:
With these came Malinal. They met the Prince,
And with a sullen stateliness returned
His salutation, then the Chief began;
Lord of the Strangers, hear me! by my voice
The People and the Pabas and the King
Of Aztlan speak. Our injured Gods have claimed
Their wonted worship, and made manifest
Their wrath; we dare not impiously provoke
The Dreadful! Worship ye in your own way;
But we must keep the path our fathers kept.

We parted, O Yuhidthiton! as friends
And brethren, said the Christian Prince;—alas,
That this should be our meeting! When we pledged,
In the broad daylight and the eye of Heaven,
Our hands in peace, ye heard the will of God,
And felt and understood. This calm assent
Ye would belie, by midnight miracles
Scared, and such signs of darkness as beseem
The demons whom ye dread! or likelier
Duped by the craft of those accursed men,
Whose trade is blood. Ask thou of thine own heart,
Yuhidthiton.—
　　　　　　　But Helhua broke his speech;
Our bidding is to tell thee, quoth the Priest,
That Aztlan hath restored, and will maintain,
Her ancient faith. If it offendeth thee,
Move thou thy dwelling place!
　　　　　　　　　　Madoc replied,
This day have I deposited in earth
My father's bones, and where his bones are laid,
There mine shall moulder.
　　　　　　　　　　Malinal at that
Advanced ;—Prince Madoc, said the youth, I come,
True to thy faith and thee, and to the weal
Of Aztlan true, and bearing, for that truth,
Reproach and shame and scorn and obloquy.
In sorrow come I here, a banished man;
Here take, in sorrow, my abiding-place,
Cut off from all my kin, from all old ties
Divorced; all dear familiar countenances
No longer to be present to my sight;
The very mother-language which I learnt,
A lisping baby on my mother's knees,
No more with its sweet sounds to comfort me.
So be it !—To his brother then he turned;
Yuhidthiton, said he, when thou shalt find,—
As find thou wilt,—that those accursed men
Have played the juggler with thee, and deceived
Thine honest heart,—when Aztlan groans in blood,—
Bid her remember then, that Malinal
Is in the dwellings of her enemy :
Where all his hope in banishment hath been
To intercede for her, and heal her wounds,
And mitigate her righteous punishment.

Sternly and sullenly his brother heard ;
Yet hearkened he as one whose heart perforce
Suppress its instinct, and there might be seen
A sorrow in his silent stubbornness.
And now his ministers on either hand
A water-vessel fill, and heap dry sedge
And straw before his face, and fire the pile.

30

He, looking upward, spread his arms and cried,
Hear me, ye Gods of Aztlan, as we were,
And are, and will be yours! behold your foes!
He stoopt, and lifted up one ample urn,—
Thus let their blood be shed!8—and far away
He whirled the scattering water. Then again
Raised the full vase, — Thus let their lives be
    quenched!
And out he poured it on the flaming pile.
The steam-cloud, hissing from the extinguished heap,
Spread like a mist, and, ere it melted off,
Homeward the heralds of the war had turned.

VI.

The Festival of the Dead.9

THE Hoamen in their Council-hall10 are met
To hold the Feast of Souls: seat above seat,
Ranged round the circling theatre they sit.
No light but from the central fire, whose smoke,
Slow passing through the over aperture,
Excludes the day, and fills the conic roof,
And hangs above them like a cloud. Around,
The ghastly bodies of their chiefs are hung,
Shrivelled and parched, by heat; the humbler dead
Lie on the floor,—white bones, exposed to view,
On deer, or elk-skin laid, or softer fur,
Or web, the work of many a mournful hour;
The loathlier forms of fresh mortality
Swathed, and in decent tenderness concealed.
Beside each body pious gifts are laid,
Mantle and belt and feathery coronal,
The bow he used in war, his drinking-shell,
His arrows for the chase, the sarbacan,11
Through whose long tube the slender shaft, breath-
    driven,
Might pierce the wingëd game. Husbands and wives,
Parents and children, there in death they lie;
The widowed and the parent and the child
Look on in silence. Not a sound is heard
But of the crackling brand, or mouldering fire,
Or when, amid yon pendant string of shells,12
The slow wind wakes a shrill and feeble sound,—
A sound of sorrow to the mind attuned
By sights of woe.
            Ayayaca at length
Came forward.—Spirits, is it well with ye?
Is it well, Brethren? said the aged Priest;
Have ye received your mourning, and the rites
Of righteous grief? or round your dwelling-place
Still do your shadows roam dissatisfied,
And to the cries of wailing woe return
A voice of lamentation?13 Teach us now,
If we in aught have failed, that I, your Priest,
When I shall join ye soon, as soon I must,
May unimpeded pass the perilous floods,
And, in the Country of the Dead, be hailed
By you, with song and dance and grateful joy.
So saying, to the Oracle he turned,
Awaiting there the silence which implied
Peaceful assent. Against the eastern wall,
Fronting the narrow portal's winding way,
An Image stood: a cloak of fur disguised
The rude proportion of its uncouth limbs;

The skull of some old seer14 of days of old
Topped it, and with a visor this was masked,
Honouring the oracular Spirit, who at times
There took his resting-place. Ayayaca
Repeated, Brethren, is it well with ye?
And raised the visor. But he started back,
Appalled and shuddering; for a moony light
Lay in its eyeless sockets, and there came
From its immoveable and bony jaws
A long deep groan, thrice uttered, and thrice felt
In every heart of all the hearers round.
The good old Priest stood tottering, like a man
Stricken with palsy; and he gazed with eyes
Of asking horror round, as if he looked
For counsel in that fear. But Neolin
Sprung boldly to the oracle, and cried,
Speak, Spirit! tell us of our sin, and teach
The atonement! A sepulchral voice replied,
Ye have for other Gods forsaken us,
And we abandon you!—and crash with that,
The Image fell.
            A loud and hideous shriek,
As of a demon, Neolin set up;
So wild a yell, as, even in that hour,
Came with fresh terror to the startled ear.
While yet they sate, pale and irresolute,
Helhua the Azteca came in. He bore
A shield and arrow, tokens these of war,
Yet now beheld with hope, so great relief
They felt his human presence.
                    Hoamen, hear me!
The messenger began; Erillyab hear,
Priests, Elders, People! but hear chiefly thou
Prince Amalahta, as of these by birth,
So now of years mature, the rightful Lord!—
Shall it be peace or war?—Thus Aztlan saith;
She, in her anger, from the land will root
The Children of the Sea; but viewing you
In mercy, to your former vassalage
Invites ye, and remits the tribute lives,
And for rebellion claimeth no revenge.
Oh praise your Gods! cried Neolin, and hail
This day spring of new hope! Aztlan remits
The tribute lives,—what more could Madoc give?
She claimeth no revenge, and, if she claimed,
He could not save. O Hoamen, bless your Gods;
Appease them! Thou, Prince Amalahta, speak,
And seize the mercy.
                    Amalahta stood
In act of speech; but then Erillyab rose—
Who gives thee, Boy, this Elder's privilege?
The Queen exclaimed;—and thou, Priest Neolin,
Curb thou thy traitorous tongue! The reign is mine;
I hold it from my father, he from his;
Age before age, beyond the memory
Of man it hath been thus. My father fell
In battle for his people, and his sons
Fell by his side; they perished, but their names
Are with the names we love,—their happy souls
Pursue, in fields of bliss, the shadowy deer;15
The spirit of that noble blood which ran
From their death-wounds, is in the ruddy clouds
Which go before the Sun, when he comes forth
In glory. 16 Last of that illustrious race
Was I, Erillyab. Ye remember well,
Elders, that day when I assembled here

The people, and demanded at their choice
The worthiest, to perpetuate our old line
Of Kings and Warriors.—To the wind he spread
His black and blood-red banner. Even now
I hear his war-drum's tripled sound, that called
The youth to battle; even now behold
The hope which lit his dark and fiery eye,
And kindled with a sunnier glow his cheek,
As he from yonder war-pole, in his pride,
Took the death-doers down.—Lo here the bones
Of King Tepollomi!—my husband's bones !—
There should be some among ye who beheld,
When, all with arrows quilled, and clothed with blood,
As with a purple garment, he sustained
The unequal conflict, till the Aztecas
Took him at vantage, and their monarch's club
Let loose his struggling soul. Look, Hoamen, here,
See through how wide a wound his spirit fled!
Twenty long years of mournful widowhood
Have past away; so long have I maintained
The little empire left us, loving well
My people, and by them as well beloved.
Say, Hoamen, am I still your Queen?

　　　　　　　　　　At once
The whole assembly rose with one acclaim,—
Still, O Erillyab, O Belovëd, rule
Thy own belovëd people!

　　　　　　　　　But the Gods!
Cried Amalahta,—but the Oracle!
The Oracle! quoth she; what hath it said
That forty years of suffering hath not taught
This wretched people?—They abandon us?—
So let them go! Where were they at that hour,
When, like a blasting night-wind in the spring,
The multitudes of Aztlan came upon us?
Where were they when my father went to war?
Where were they when my father's stiffened corpse,
Even after death a slave, held up the lamp
To light his conqueror's revels?—Think not, Boy,
To palter with me thus! a fire may tremble
Within the sockets of a skull, and groans
May issue from a dead mean's fleshless jaws,
And images may fall, and yet no God
Be there !—If it had walked abroad with life,
That had indeed been something!

　　　　　　　　Then she turned
Her voice toward the people.—Ye have heard
This Priest of Aztlan, whose insidious tongue
Bids ye desert the Children of the Sea,
And vow again your former vassalage. .
Speaks Aztlan of the former? O my people,
I too could tell ye of the former days,[17]
When yonder plain was ours, with all its woods
And waters and savannahs!—of those days,
When, following where her husband's stronger arm
Had opened the light glebe, the willing wife
Dropt in the yellow maize; ere long to bear
Its increase to the general store, and toss
Her flowing tresses in the dance of joy.
And I could tell ye how these summer stores
Were hoarded for the invader's winter feasts;
And how the widows clipt those flowing locks
To strew them,—not upon their husband's graves,—
Their husbands had no graves!—but on the rocks
And mountains in their flight. And even these rocks
And mountains could not save us! year by year

Our babes, like firstlings of the flock, were culled
To be the banquet of these Aztecas!
This very wretch, who tells us of the past,
Hath chosen them for the butchery.—Oh, I thank you
For this brave anger!—in your name I take
The war-gift!

　　　　　　Gods of Aztlan, Helhua cried,
As to Erillyab's ready hand he gave
The deadly token, in your name I give
The war-gift! Ye have thirsted over long;
Take now your fill of blood!—He turned away;
And Queen Erillyab bade the tribe fulfil
Their customary rites.

　　　　　　　Each family
Bore its own dead, and to the general grave,
With melancholy song and sob of woe,
The slow procession moves. The general grave
Was delved within a deep and shady dell,
Fronting a cavern in the rock,—the scene
Of many a bloody rite, ere Madoc came,—
A temple, as they deemed, by Nature made,
Where the Snake-Idol[18] stood. On fur and cloth
Of woven grass, they lay their burthens down,
Within the ample pit; their offerings range
Beside, and piously a portion take
Of that cold earth, to which for ever now
Consigned, they leave their fathers, dust to dust;[19]
Sad relic that, and wise remembrancer.
But as with bark and resinous boughs they pile
The sepulchre, suddenly Neolin
Sprung up aloft, and shrieked, as one who treads
Upon a viper in his heedless path.
The God! the very God! he cried, and howled
One long, shrill, piercing, modulated cry;
Whereat from that dark temple issued forth
A Serpent, huge and hideous. On he came,
Straight to the sound, and curled around the Priest
His mighty folds innocuous, overtopping
His human height, and, arching down his head,
Sought in the hands of Neolin for food;
Then questing, reared and stretched and waved his neck,
And glanced his forky tongue. Who then had seen
The man, with what triumphant fearlessness,
Arms, thighs, and neck, and body, wreathed and ringed
In those tremendous folds, he stood secure,
Played with the reptile's jaws, and called for food,
Food for the present God!—who then had seen
The fiendish joy which fired his countenance,
Might well have weened that he had summoned up
The dreadful monster from its native Hell,
By devilish power, himself a fiend infleshed.
Blood for the God! he cried; Lincoya's blood!
Friend of the Serpent's foe!—Lincoya's blood!
Cried Amalahta, and the people turned
Their eyes to seek the victim, as if each
Sought his own safety in that sacrifice.
Alone Erillyab raised her voice, confused
But not confounded; she alone exclaimed,
Madoc shall answer this! unheard her voice
By the bewildered people, by the Priest
Unheeded; and Lincoya sure had fallen
The victim of their fear, had he been found
In that wild hour; but when his watchful eye
Beheld the monster from his den come forth,
He fled to bear the tidings.—Neolin
Repeats the accursëd call, Food for the God!

Ayayaca, his unbelieving Priest!
At once all eager eyes were fixed on him,
But he came forward calmly at the call;
Lo! here am I! quoth he; and from his head
Plucking the thin grey hairs, he dealt them round[20]—
Countrymen, kinsmen, brethren, children, take
These in remembrance of me! there will be
No relic of your aged Priest but this.
From manhood to old age, full threescore years,
Have I been your true servant: fit it is
That I, who witnessed Aztlan's first assault,
Should perish her last victim!—and he moved
Towards the death. But then Erillyab
Seized him, and by the garment drew him back!—
By the Great Spirit, but he shall not die!
The Queen exclaimed; nor shalt thou triumph thus,
Liar and traitor! Hoamen, to your homes!
Madoc shall answer this!

Irresolute
They heard, and inobedient; to obey
Fearing, yet fearful to remain. Anon,
The Queen repeats her bidding, To your homes,
My people!—But when Neolin perceived
The growing stir and motion of the crowd,
As from the outward ring they moved away,
He uttered a new cry, and disentangling
The passive reptile's folds, rushed out among them,
With outstretched hands, like one possessed, to seize
His victim. Then they fled; for who could tell
On whom the madman, in that hellish fit,
Might cast the lot? An eight-years' boy he seized
And held him by the leg, and, whirling him
In ritual dance, till breath and sense were gone,
Set up the death-song of the sacrifice.
Amalahta, and what others rooted love
Of evil leagued with him, accomplices
In treason, joined the death-song and the dance.
Some too there were, believing what they feared,
Who yielded to their old idolatry,
And mingled in the worship. Round and round
The accursèd minister of murder whirled
His senseless victim; they, too, round and round
In maddening motion, and with maddening cries
Revolving, whirled and wheeled. At length, when now,
According to old rites he should have dashed
On the stone Idol's head the wretch's brains,
Neolin stopt, and once again began
The long, shrill, piercing, modulated cry.
The Serpent knew the call, and, rolling on,
Wave above wave, his rising length, advanced
His open jaws; then, with the expected prey,
Glides to the dark recesses of his den.

VII.

The Snake-God.

MEANTIME Erillyab's messenger had girt
His loins, and, like a roebuck, o'er the hills
He sped. He met Cadwallon and the Prince
In arms, so quickly Madoc had obeyed
Lincoya's call; at noon he heard the call,
And still the sun was riding high in heaven,
When up the valley where the Hoamen dwelt
He led his twenty spears. O welcome, friend

And brother! cried the Queen. Even as thou saidst
So hath it proved: and those accursèd schemes
Of treachery, which that wretched boy revealed
Under the influence of thy potent drink,
Have ripened to effect. From what a snare
The timely warning saved me! for, be sure,
What I had seen I else should have believed,
In utter fear confounded. The Great Spirit,
Who taught thee to foresee the evil thing,
Will give thee power to quell it.

On they went
Towards the dell, where now the Idolaters
Had built their dedicated fire, and still
With feast, and fits of song, and violent dance,
Pursued their rites. When Neolin perceived
The Prince approach, fearlessly he came forth,
And raised his arm, and cried, Strangers, away!
Away, profane! hence to your mother-land!
Hence to your waters! for the God is here;—
He came for blood, and he shall have his fill!
Impious, away!

Seize him, exclaimed the Prince:
Nor had he time for motion nor for flight,
So instantly was that command obeyed.
Hoamen, said Madoc, hear me!—I came here,
Stranger alike to Aztlan and to you;
I found ye an oppressèd, wretched race,
Groaning beneath your chains; at your request,
For your deliverance, I unsheathed the sword,
Redeemed ye from your bondage, and preserved
Your children from the slaughter. With those foes
Whose burden ye for forty years endured,
This traitor hath conspired, against yourselves,
Your Queen, and me your friend; the solemn faith
Which in the face of yonder sun we pledged,
Each to the other, this accursèd man
Hath broken, and hath stained his hands this day
With innocent blood. Life must atone for life:
Ere I destroy the Serpent, whom his wiles
Have trained so well, last victim, he shall glut
The monster's maw.

Strike, man! quoth Neolin.
This is my consummation! the reward
Of my true faith! the best that I could ask,
The best the God could give:—to rest in him,
Body with body be incorporate,
Soul into soul absorbed, and I and he
One life, inseparable, for evermore.
Strike, I am weary of this mortal part;
Unite me to the God!

Triumphantly
He spake; the assembled people, at his words,
With rising awe gazed on the miscreant;
Madoc himself, when now he would have given
The sign for death, in admiration paused,
Such power hath fortitude. And he perceived
The auspicious moment, and set up his cry.
Forth, from the dark recesses of the cave,
The serpent came: [21] the Hoamen at the sight
Shouted, and they who held the Priest, appalled
Relaxed their hold. On came the mighty Snake,
And twined, in many a wreath, round Neolin,
Darting aright, aleft, his sinuous neck,
With searching eye, and lifted jaw and tongue
Quivering, and hiss as of a heavy shower
Upon the summer woods. The Britons stood

Astounded at the powerful reptile's bulk,
And that strange sight. His girth was as of man,
But easily could he have overtopped
Goliath's helmëd head, or that huge King
Of Basan, hugest of the Anakim: [20]
What then was human strength, if once involved
Within those dreadful coils?—The multitude
Fell prone, and worshipped; pale Erillyab grew,
And turned upon the Prince a doubtful eye;
The Britons, too, were pale, albeit they held
Their spears protended; and they also looked
On Madoc, who the while stood silently,
Contemplating how wiseliest he might cope
With that surpassing strength.
                            But Neolin,
Well hoping now success, when he had awed
The general feeling thus, exclaimed aloud,
Blood for the God! give him the Stranger's blood!
Avenge him on his foes! and then, perchance,
Terror had urged him to some desperate deed,
Had Madoc pondered more, or paused in act
One moment. From the sacrificial flames
He snatched a fire-brand, and, with fire and sword,
Rushed at the monster: back the monster drew
His head, upraised recoiling, and the Prince
Smote Neolin; all circled as he was,
And clipt in his false Deity's embrace,
Smote he the accursëd Priest; the avenging sword
Fell on his neck; through flesh and bone it drove
Deep in the chest: the wretched criminal,
Tottered, and those huge rings a moment held
His bloody corpse upright, while Madoc struck
The Serpent: twice he struck him, and the sword
Glanced from the impenetrable scales; nor more
Availed its thrust, though driven by that strong arm;
For on the unyielding skin the tempered blade
Bent. He sprung upward then, and in the eyes
Of the huge monster flashed the fiery brand.
Impatient of the smoke and burning, back
The reptile wreathed, and from his loosening clasp
Dropt the dead Neolin, and turned, and fled
To his dark den.
                    The Hoamen, at that sight
Raised a loud wonder-cry, with one accord,
Great is the Son of Ocean, and his God
Is mightiest! But Erillyab silently
Approached the great Deliverer; her whole frame
Trembled with strong emotion, and she took
His hand, and gazed a moment earnestly,
Having no power of speech, till with a gush
Of tears her utterance came, and she exclaimed,
Blessed art thou, my brother! for the power
Of God is in thee!—and she would have kissed
His hand in adoration; but he cried,
God is indeed with us, and in his name
Will we fulfil the work!—then to the cave
Advanced and called for fire. Bring fire! quoth he;
By his own element this spawn of hell
Shall perish! and he entered, to explore
The cavern depths. Cadwallon followed him,
Bearing in either hand a flaming brand,
For sword or spear availed not.
                        Far in the hill,
Cave within cave, the ample grotto pierced,
Three chambers in the rock. Fit vestibule
The first to that wild temple, long and low,

Shut out the outward day. The second vault
Had its own daylight from a central chasm
High in the hollow; here the Image stood,
Their rude idolatry,—a sculptured snake,—
If term of art may such mis-shapen form
Beseem,—around a human figure coiled,
And all begrimed with blood. The inmost cell
Dark; and far up within its blackest depth
They saw the Serpent's still small eye of fire.
Not if they thinned the forest for their pile,
Could they, with flame or suffocating smoke,
Destroy him there; for through the open roof
The clouds would pass away. They paused not long:
Drive him beneath the chasm, Cadwallon cried,
And hem him in with fire, and from above
We crush him.
                Forth they went and climbed the hill,
With all their people. Their united strength
Loosened the rocks, and ranged them round the brink,
Impending. With Cadwallon on the height
Ten Britons wait; ten with the Prince descend,
And with a firebrand each in either hand,
Enter the outer cave. Madoc advanced,
And at the entrance of the inner den,
He took his stand alone. A bow he bore,
And arrows, round whose heads dry tow was twined,
In pine-gum dipt; [23] he kindled these, and shot
The fiery shafts. Upon his scaly skin,
As on a rock, the bone-tipt arrows fell;
But, at their bright and blazing light effrayed,
Out rushed the reptile. Madoc from his path
Retired against the side, and called his men,
And in they came and circled round the Snake,
And, shaking all their flames, as with a wheel
Of fire, they ringed him in. From side to side
The monster turns;—where'er he turns, the flame
Flares in his nostrils and his blinking eyes;
Nor aught against the dreaded element
Did that brute force avail, which could have crushed
Milo's young limbs, or Theban Hercules,
Or old Manoah's mightier son, ere yet
Shorn of his strength. They press him now, and now
Give back, here urging, and here yielding way,
Till right beneath the chasm they centre him.
At once the crags are loosed, and down they fall,
Thundering. They fell like thunder, but the crash
Of scale and bone was heard. In agony
The Serpent writhed beneath the blow; in vain,
From under the incumbent load essayed
To drag his mangled folds. One heavier stone
Fastened and flattened him; yet still, with tail
Ten cubits long, he lashed the air, and foined
From side to side, and raised his raging head
Above the height of man, though half his length
Lay mutilate. Who then had felt the force
Of that wild fury, little had to him
Buckler or corselet profited, or mail,
Or might of human arm. The Britons shrunk
Beyond its arc of motion; but the Prince
Took a long spear, and springing on the stone
Which fixed the monster down, provoked his rage.
Uplifts the Snake his head retorted, high
He lifts it over Madoc, then darts down
To seize his prey. The Prince, with foot advanced,
Inclines his body back, and points the spear,
With sure and certain aim, then drives it up,

Into his open jaws; two cubits deep
It pierced, the monster forcing on the wound.
He closed his teeth for anguish, and bit short
The ashen hilt. But not the rage which now
Clangs all his scales, can from its seat dislodge
The barbëd shaft; nor those contortions wild,
Nor those convulsive shudderings, nor the throes
Which shake his inmost entrails, as with the air
In suffocating gulps the monster now
Inhales his own life-blood. The Prince descends;
He lifts another lance; and now the Snake,
Gasping, as if exhausted, on the ground
Reclines his head one moment. Madoc seized
That moment, planted in his eye the spear,
Then, setting foot upon his neck, drove down
Through bone and brain and throat, and to the earth
Infixed the mortal weapon. Yet once more
The Snake essayed to rise; his dying strength
Failed him, nor longer did those mighty folds
Obey the moving impulse; crushed and scotched,
In every ring, through all his mangled length,
The shrinking muscles quivered, then collapsed
In death.
        Cadwallon and his comrades now
Enter the den; they roll away the crag
Which fixed him down, pluck out the mortal spear,
Then drag him forth to day; the force conjoined
Of all the Britons difficultly drag
His lifeless bulk. But when the Hoamen saw
That form portentous trailing in its gore,
The jaws which, in the morning, they had seen
Purpled with human blood, now in their own
Blackening,—aknee they fell before the Prince,
And in adoring admiration raised
Their hands with one accord, and all in fear
Worshipped the mighty Deicide. But he,
Recoiling from those sinful honours, cried,
Drag out the Idol now, and heap the fire,
That all may be consumed!
        Forthwith they heaped
The sacrificial fire, and on the pile
The Serpent and the Image and the corpse
Of Neolin were laid; with prompt supply
They feed the raging flames, hour after hour,
Till now the black and nauseous smoke is spent,
And mingled with the ruins of the pile,
The undistinguishable ashes lay.
Go! cried Prince Madoc, cast them in the stream,
And scatter them upon the winds, that so
No relic of this foul idolatry
Pollute the land. To-morrow meet me here,
Hoamen, and I will purify yon den
Of your abominations. Come ye here
With humble hearts; for ye, too, in the sight
Of the Great Spirit, the Belovëd One,
Must be made pure, and cleansed from your offence,
And take upon yourselves his holy law.

VIII.

The Conversion of the Hoamen.

How beautiful, O Sun, is thine uprise,
And on how fair a scene! Before the Cave
The Elders of the Hoamen wait the will

Of their Deliverer; ranged without their ring
The tribe look on, thronging the narrow vale,
And what of gradual rise the shelving combe
Displayed, or steeper eminence of wood,
Broken with crags and sunny slope of green,
And grassy platform. With the elders sate
The Queen and Prince, their rank's prerogative,
Excluded else for sex unfit, and youth
For counsel immature. Before the arch,
To that rude fane, rude portal, stands the Cross,
By Madoc's hand victorious planted there.
And lo, Prince Madoc comes! no longer mailed
In arms of mortal might; the spear and sword,
The hauberk and the helmet laid aside,
Gorget and gauntlet, greaves and shield,—he comes
In peaceful tunic clad, and mantle long;
His hyacinthine locks now shadowing
That face, which late, with iron overbrowed,
Struck from within the aventayle such awe
And terror to the heart. Bareheaded he,
Following the servant of the altar, leads
The reverential train. Before them, raised
On high, the sacred images are borne.
There, in faint semblance, holiest Mary bends
In virgin beauty o'er her babe divine,—
A sight which almost to idolatry
Might win the soul by love. But who can gaze
Upon that other form, which on the rood
In agony is stretched?—his hands transfixed,
And lacerate with the body's pendent weight;[24]
The black and deadly paleness of his face,
Streaked with the blood which from that crown of
   scorn
Hath ceased to flow; the side wound streaming still;
And open still those eyes, from which the look
Not yet hath past away, that went to Heaven,
When, in that hour, the Son of Man exclaimed,
Forgive them, for they know not what they do!
And now arrived before the cave, the train
Halt: to the assembled elders, where they sate
Ranged in half circle, Madoc then advanced,
And raised, as if in act to speak, his hand.
Thereat was every human sound suppressed;
And every quickened ear and eager eye
Were centered on his lips.
        The Prince began,—
Hoamen, friends, brethren,—friends we have been long,
And brethren shall be, ere the day go down,—
I come not here propounding doubtful things,
For counsel, and deliberate resolve
Of searching thought; but with authority
From Heaven, to give the law, and to enforce
Obedience. Ye shall worship God alone,
The One Eternal. That Belovëd One
Ye shall not serve with offered fruits, or smoke
Of sacrificial fire, or blood, or life;
Far other sacrifice he claims,—a soul
Resigned, a will subdued, a heart made clean
From all offence. Not for your lots on earth,
Menial or mighty, slave or highly-born,
For cunning in the chase, or strength in war,
Shall ye be judged hereafter;[25]—as ye keep
The law of love, as ye shall tame your wrath,
Forego revenge, forgive your enemies,
Do good to them that wrong ye, ye will find
Your bliss or bale. This law came down from Heaven.

Lo, ye behold him there by whom it came;
The Spirit was in Him, and for the sins
Of man He suffered thus, and by His death
Must all mankind be blest. Not knowing Him,
Ye wandered on in error; knowing now,
And not obeying, what was error once
Is guilt and wilful wrong. If ever more
Ye bow to your false deities the knee;
If ever more ye worship them with feast,
Or sacrifice or dance; whoso offends
Shall from among the people be cut off,
Like a corrupted member, lest he taint
The whole with death. With what appointed rites
Your homage must be paid, ye shall be taught;
Your children, in the way that they shall go,
Be trained from childhood up. Make ye, mean time,
Your prayer to that Belovëd One, who sees
The secrets of all hearts; and set ye up
This, the memorial of his chosen Son,
And Her, who, blessëd among women, fed
The Appointed at Her breast, and by His cross
Endured intenser anguish; therefore sharing
His glory now, with sunbeams roamed, the Moon
Her footstool, and a wreath of stars her crown.

Hoamen, ye deem us children of a race
Mightier than ye, and wiser, and by heaven
Beloved and favoured more. From this pure law
Hath all proceeded,—wisdom, power, whate'er
Here elevates the soul, and makes it ripe
For higher powers, and more exalted bliss.
Share then our law, and be with us, on earth,
Partakers of these blessings, and, in Heaven,
Co-heritors with us of endless joy.

Ere yet one breath or motion had disturbed
The reverential hush, Erillyab rose.
My people, said the Queen, their God is best
And mightiest. Him, to whom we offered up
Blood of our blood, and of our flesh the flesh,
Vainly we deemed divine; no spirit he
Of good or evil, by the conquering arm
Of Madoc mortal proved. What then remains
But that the blessing proffered thus in love,
In love we take?—Deliverer, Teacher, Friend,
First in the fellowship of faith I claim
The initiatory rite.
                    I also, cried
The venerable Priest Ayayaca,
Old as I am, I also, like a child,
Would learn this wisdom yet before I die.
The Elders rose and answered, We and all!
And from the congregated tribe burst forth
One universal shout,—Great is the God
Of Madoc,—worthy to be served is He!

Then to the mountain rivulet, which rolled
Like amber over its dark bed of rock,
Did Madoc lead Erillyab, in the name
Of Jesus, to his Christian family
Accepted now. On her and on her son,
The Elders and the People, Llorien
Sprinkled the sanctifying waters. Day
Was scarcely two hours old when he began
His work, and when he ceased, the sun had past
The heights of noon. Ye saw that blessëd work,

Sons of the Cymry, Cadog, Deiniol,
Padarn, and Teilo![26] ye whose sainted names
Your monumental temples still record;
Thou, David,[27] still revered, who in the vale,
Where, by old Hatteril's wintry torrents swoln,
Rude Hodney rolls his raging stream, didst chuse
Thy hermit home; and ye who by the sword
Of the fierce Saxon, when the bloodier Monk
Urged on the work of murder, for your faith
And freedom fell,—Martyrs and Saints, ye saw
This triumph of the Cymry and the Cross,
And struck your golden harps to hymns of joy.

IX.

Tlalala.

As now the rites were ended, Caradoc
Came from the ships, leading an Azteca
Guarded and bound. Prince Madoc, said the Bard,
Lo! the first captive of our arms I bring.
Alone, beside the river I had strayed,
When, from his lurking place, the savage hurled
A javelin. At the rustle of the reeds,
From whence the blow was aimed, I turned in time,
And heard it whiz beside me. Well it was,
That from the ships they saw and succoured me;
For, subtle as a serpent in my grasp,
He seemed all joint and flexure; nor had I
Armour to ward, nor weapon to offend,
To battle all unused and unprepared;
But I too, here, upon this barbarous land,
Like Elmur and like Aronan of old,
Must lift the ruddy spear.[28]
                    This is no day
For vengeance, answered Madoc, else his deed
Had met no mercy. Freely let him go!
Perchance the tidings of our triumph here
May yet reclaim his country.—Azteca,
Go, let your Pabas know that we have crushed
Their complots here; beneath our righteous sword
The Priest and his false Deity have fallen,
The Idols been consumed, and in their stead
The emblems of our holy faith set up,
Whereof the Hoamen have this day been made
Partakers. Say to Aztlan, when she too
Will make her temples clean, and put away
Her foul abominations, and accept
The Christian Cross, that Madoc then accords
Forgiveness for the past, and peace to come.
This better part let her, of her free will
And wisdom, chuse in time.
                    Till Madoc spake,
The captive reckless of his peril stood,
Gazing with resolute and careless eye,
As one in whom the lot of life or death
Moved neither fear nor feeling; but that eye
Now glowing with defiance.—Seek ye peace?
He cried: O weak and woman-hearted man!
Already wouldst thou lay the sword to rest?
Not with the burial of the sword this strife
Must end, for never doth the Tree of Peace
Strike root and flourish till the strong man's hand
Upon his enemy's grave hath planted it.
Come ye to Aztlan then in quest of peace?

Ye feeble souls, if that be what ye seek
Fly hence! our Aztlan suffers on her soil
No living stranger.
             Do thy bidding, Chief!
Calmly Cadwallon answered. To her choice
Let Aztlan look, lest what she now reject
In insolence of strength, she take upon her,
In sorrow and in suffering and in shame,
By strong compulsion, penitent too late.
Thou hast beheld our ships with gallant men
Freighted, a numerous force—and for our arms—
Surely thy nation hath acquired of them
Disastrous knowledge.
             Curse upon your arms!
Exclaimed the Savage:—Is there one among you
Dare lay that cowardly advantage by,
And meet me, man to man, in honest strife?
That I might grapple with him, weaponless,
On yonder rock, breast against breast, fair force
Of limb and breath and blood,—till one, or both,
Dash'd down the shattering precipice, should feed
The mountain eagle!—Give me, I beseech you,
That joy!
        As wisely, said Cynetha's son,
Thy foe might challenge thee, and bid thee let
Thy strong right hand hang idle in the fray;
That so his weakness with thy strength might cope
In equal battle!—Not in wrongful war,
The tyrants of our weaker bröthèren,
Wield we these dreadful arms,—but when assailed
By fraud and force, when called upon to aid
The feeble and oppressèd, shall we not
Then put our terrors forth, and thunder-strike
The guilty?
        Silently the Savage heard;
Joy brightened in his eyes, as they unloosed
His bonds; he stretched his arms at length, to feel
His liberty, and, like a greyhound then
Slipt from the leash, he bounded o'er the hills.
What was from early morning till noon day
The steady travel of a well-girt man,
He, with fleet feet and unfatiguable,
In three short hours hath traversed; in the lake
He dashed, now shooting forth his pointed arms,
Arrow-like darting on; recumbent now,
Forces, with springing feet, his easier way;
Then, with new speed, as freshened by repose,
Again he breasts the waters. On the shore
Of Aztlan now he stands, and breathes at will,
And wrings his dripping locks; then through the gate
Pursued his way.
        Green garlands deck the gate;
Gay are the temples with green boughs affixed;
The door-posts and the lintels hung with wreaths;
The fire of sacrifice, with flames bedimmed,
Burns in the sun-light, pale; the victims wait
Around, impatient of their death delayed.
The Priest, before Tezcalipoca's shrine,
Watches the maize-strewn threshold, to announce
The footsteps of the God; for this the day,
When to his favoured city he vouchsafes
His annual presence, [29] and, with unseen feet,
Imprints the maize-strewn threshold; followed soon
By all whose altars with eternal fires
Aztlan illumed, and fed with human blood;—
Mexitli, woman-born, [30] who from the womb,

Child of no mortal sire, leapt terrible,
The armed avenger of his mother's fame;
And he whose will the subject winds obey,
Quetzalcoal; [31] and Tlaloc, [32] Water-God,
And all the host of Deities, whose power
Requites with bounty Aztlan's pious zeal,
Health and rich increase giving to her sons,
And withering in the war her enemies.
So taught the Priests, and therefore were the gates
Green-garlanded, the temples green with boughs,
The door-posts and the lintels hung with wreaths;
And yonder victims, ranged around the fire,
Are destined, with the steam of sacrifice,
To greet their cursèd coming.
             With the train
Of warrior Chiefs Coanacotzin stood,
That when the Priest proclaimed the entered God,
His lips before the present Deity
Might pour effectual prayer. The assembled Chiefs
Saw Tlalala [33] approach, more welcome now,
As one whose absence from the appointed rites
Had wakened fear and wonder.—Think not ye,
The youth exclaimed, careless impiety
Could this day lead me wandering. I went forth
To dip my javelin in the Strangers' blood,—
A sacrifice, methought, our Gods had loved
To scent, and sooner hastened to enjoy.
I failed, and fell a prisoner; but their fear
Released me,—coward fear, or idiot hope,
That, like Yuhidthiton, I might become
Their friend, and merit chastisement from Heaven,
Pleading the Strangers' cause. They bade me go
And proffer peace.—Chiefs, were it possible
That tongue of mine could win you to that shame,
Up would I pluck the member, though my soul
Followed its bloody roots. The Stranger finds
No peace in Aztlan, but the peace of death!

'T is bravely said! Yuhidthiton replied,
And fairly mayest thou boast, young Tlalala,
For thou art brave in battle. Yet 't were well
If that same fearless tongue were taught to check
Its boyish license now. No law forbade
Our friendship with the Stranger, when my voice
Pleaded for proffered peace; that fault I shared
In common with the King, and with the Chiefs,
The Pabas and the People, none foreseeing
Danger or guilt: but when at length the Gods
Made evident their wrath in prodigies,
I yielded to their manifested will
My prompt obedience.—Bravely hast thou said,
And brave thou art, young Tiger of the War! [34]
But thou hast dealt with other enemies
Than these impenetrable men,—with foes,
Whose conquered Gods lie idle in their chains,
And with tame weakness brook captivity. [35]
When thou hast met the Strangers in the fight,
And in the doings of that fight outdone
Yuhidthiton, revile him then for one
Slow to defend his country and his faith:
Till then, with reverence, as beseems thy youth,
Respect thou his full fame!
             I wrong it not!
I wrong it not! cried the young Azteca;
But truly, as I hope to equal it,
Honour thy well-earned glory.—But this peace!—

Renounce it!—say that it shall never be!—
Never,—as long as there are Gods in Heaven,
Or men in Aztlan!

    That, the King replied,
The Gods themselves have answered. Never yet
By holier ardour were our countrymen
Possessed: peace-offerings of repentance fill
The temple courts; [26] from every voice ascends
The contrite prayer; daily the victim's heart
Sends its propitiatory steam to Heaven;
And if the aid divine may be procured
By the most dread solemnities of faith,
And rigour of severest penitence,
Soon shall the present influence strengthen us,
And Aztlan be triumphant.

      While they spake,
The ceaseless sound of song and instrument
Rung through the air, now rising like the voice
Of angry ocean, now subsiding soft,
As when the breeze of evening dies away.
The horn, and shrill-toned pipe, and drum, that gave
Its music to the hand, and hollowed wood,
Drum-like, whose thunders, ever and anon,
Commingling with the sea-shell's spiral roar,
Closed the full harmony. And now the eve
Past on, and, through the twilight visible,
The frequent fire-flies' brightening beauties shone.
Anxious and often now the Priest surveyed
The maize-strewn threshold; for the wonted hour
Was come, and yet no footstep of the God!
More radiant now the fire of sacrifice,
Fed to full fury, blazed, and its red smoke
Imparted to the darker atmosphere
Such obscure light, as, o'er Vesuvio seen,
Or pillared upon Etna's mountain-head,
Makes darkness dreadful. In the captives' cheeks
Then might a livid paleness have been seen,
And wilder terror in their ghastly eyes,
Expecting momently the pang of death.
Soon in the multitude a doubt arose,
Which none durst mention, lest his neighbour's fears,
Divulged, should strengthen his—the hour was past,
And yet no foot had marked the sprinkled maize!

X.

The Arrival of the Gods.

Now every moment gave their doubts new force,
And each alarmëd eye disclosed the fear
Which on the tongue was trembling, when to the King,
Emaciate like some bare anatomy,
And deadly pale, Tezozomoc was led,
By two supporting Priests. Ten painful months,
Immured amid the forest, had he dwelt,
In abstinence and solitary prayer
Passing his nights and days: [27] thus did the Gods
From their High Priest exact, when they enforced,
By danger or distress, the penance due
For public sins; and he had dwelt ten months
Praying and fasting and in solitude
Till now might every bone of his lean limbs
Be told, and in his starved and bony face
The living eye appeared unnatural,
A ghostly sight.

    In breathless eagerness
The multitude drew round as he began,—
O King, the Gods of Aztlan are not come;
They will not come before the Strangers' blood
Smoke on their altars: but they have beheld
My days of prayer, and nights of watchfulness,
And fasts austere, and bloody disciplines,
And have revealed their pleasure.—Who is here,
Who to the White King's dwelling-place dare go,
And execute their will?

     Scarce had he said,
When Tlalala exclaimed, I am the man.

Hear then! Tezozomoc replied—Ye know
That self-denial and long penance purge
The film and foulness of mortality,
For more immediate intercourse with Heaven
Preparing the pure spirit; and all eyes
May witness that with no relaxing zeal
I have performed my duty. Much I feared
For Aztlan's sins, and oft, in bitterness,
Have groaned and bled for her iniquity;
But chiefly for this solemn day the fear
Was strong upon me, lest her Deities,
Estranged, should turn away, and we be left
A spiritless and God-abandoned race,
A warning to the earth. Ten weary months
Have the raw maize and running water been
My only food; but not a grain of maize
Hath stayed the gnawing appetite, nor drop
Of water cooled my parched and painful tongue,
Since yester morn arose. Fasting I prayed,
And, praying, gashed myself; and all night long,
I watched and wept and supplicated Heaven,
Till the weak flesh, its life-blood almost drained,
Sunk with the long austerity: a dread
Of death came over me; a deathy chill
Ran through my veins, and loosened every limb;
Dim grew mine eyes; and I could feel my heart
Dying away within me, intermit
Its slow and feeble throbs, then suddenly
Start, as it seemed exerting all its force
In one last effort. On the ground I fell,
I know not if entranced, or dead indeed,
But without motion, hearing, sight, or sense,
Feeling, or breath, or life. From that strange state,
Even in such blessed freedom from all pain,
That sure I thought myself in very Heaven,
I woke, and raised my eyelids, and beheld
A light which seemed to penetrate my bones
With life and health. Before me, visible,
Stood Coatlantona; [28] a wreath of flowers
Circled her hair, and from their odorous leaves
Arose a lambent flame; not fitfully,
Nor with faint flash or spark of earthly flowers;
From these, for ever flowing forth, there played,
In one perpetual dance of pointed light,
The azure radiance of innocuous fire.
She spake—Hear, Aztlan! and give ear, O King!
She said, Not yet the offended Gods relax
Their anger; they require the Strangers' blood,
The foretaste of their banquet. Let their will
Be known to Aztlan, and the brave perform
Their bidding; I, meantime, will seek to soothe,
With all a mother's power, Mexitli's wrath.
So let the Maidens daily with fresh flowers

31

Garland my temple!—Daily with fresh flowers
Garland her temple, Aztlan! and revere
The gentle mother of thy guardian God!

And let the brave, exclaimed young Tlalala,
Perform her bidding! Servant of the Gods,
Declare their will!—Is it, that I should seek
The Strangers, in the first who meets my way
To plunge the holy weapon? Say thou to me
Do this;—and I depart to do the deed,
Though my life-blood should mingle with the foe's.

O brave young Chief! Tezozomoc replied,
With better fortune may the grateful Gods
Reward thy valour! deed so hazardous
They ask not. Couldst thou from the mountain holds
Tempt one of these accursèd to pursue
Thine artful flight, an ambushed band might rise
Upon the unsuspecting enemy,
And intercept return; then hitherward
The captive should be led, and Aztlan's Gods
On their own altars see the sacrifice,
Well pleased, and Aztlan's sons, inspirited,
Behold the omen of assured success.
Thou knowest that Tlaloc's annual festival
Is close at hand. A Stranger's child would prove
A victim, whose rare value would deserve
His certain favour. More I need not say.
Chuse thou the force for ambush; and thyself
Alone, or with a chosen comrade, seek
The mountain dwellers.
                        Instant as he ceased,
Ocellopan exclaimed, I go with thee,
O Tlalala! My friend!—If one alone
Could have the honour of this enterprise,
My love might yield it thee;—but thou wilt need
A comrade—Tlalala, I go with thee!

The Chief replied, Whom should my heart select,
Its tried companion else, but thee, so oft
My brother in the battle? We will go,
Shedder of blood! together will we go,
Now, ere the midnight!
                        Nay! the Priest exclaimed,
A little while delay; and, ere ye go,
Devote yourselves to Heaven! Feebly he spake,
Like one exhausted; gathering then new force,
As with laborious effort, he pursued,—
Bedew Mexitli's altar with your blood,
And go beneath his guidance. I have yet
Strength to officiate, and to bless your zeal.
So saying, to the Temple of the God
He led the way. The warriors followed him:
And, with his chiefs, Coanocotzin went,
To grace with all solemnity the rite.
They pass the Wall of Serpents, and ascend
The massive fabric; four times they surround
Its ample square, the fifth they reach the height.
There, on the level top, two temple-towers
Were reared; the one Tezcalipoca's fane,
Supreme of Heaven, where now the wily Priest
Stood, watchful for his presence, and observed
The maize-strewn threshold. His the other pile,
By whose peculiar power and patronage
Aztlan was blest, Mexitli, woman-born.

Before the entrance, the eternal fire
Was burning; bare of foot they entered there.

On a blue throne, with four huge silver snakes,
As if the keepers of the sanctuary,
Circled with stretching neck and fangs displayed,
Mexitli sate; another graven snake
Belted with scales of gold his monster bulk.
Around the neck a loathsome collar hung,
Of human hearts; the face was masked with gold;
His specular eyes seemed fire; one hand upreared
A club, the other, as in battle, held
The shield; and over all, suspended, hung
The banner of the nation. They beheld
In awe, and knelt before the Terrible God.

Guardian of Aztlan! cried Tezozomoc,
Who to thy mortal mother hast assigned
The kingdom o'er all trees and arborets
And herbs and flowers, giving her endless life,
A Deity among the Deities;
While Coatlantona implores thy love
To thine own people, they in fear approach
Thy awful fane, who know no fear beside,
And offer up the worthiest sacrifice,
The blood of heroes!
                        To the ready Chiefs
He turned, and said, Now stretch your arms, and make
The offering to the God. They their bare arms
Stretched forth, and stabbed them with the aloe-point.
Then, in a golden vase, Tezozomoc
Received the mingled streams, and held it up
Toward the giant Idol, and exclaimed,
Terrible God! Protector of our realm!
Receive thine incense! Let the steam of blood
Ascend to thee, delightful! So mayest thou
Still to thy chosen people lend thine aid;
And these blaspheming strangers from the earth
Be swept away; as erst the monster race
Of Mammuth, [39] Heaven's fierce ministers of wrath,
Who drained the lakes in thirst, and for their food
Exterminated nations. And as when,
Their dreadful ministry of death fulfilled,
Ipalnemoani, by whom we live,
Bade thee go forth, and with thy lightnings fill
The vault of Heaven, and with thy thunders rock
The rooted earth, till of the monster race
Only their monumental bones remained,—
So arm thy favoured people with thy might,
Terrible God! and purify the land
From these blaspheming foes!
                        He said, and gave
Ocellopan the vase—Chiefs, ye have poured
Your strength and courage to the Terrible God,
Devoted to his service; take ye now
The beverage he hath hallowed. In your youth
Ye have quaffed manly blood, that manly thoughts
Might ripen in your hearts; [40] so now with this,
Which, mingling, from such noble veins hath flowed,
Increase of valour drink, and added force.
Ocellopan received the bloody vase,
And drank, and gave in silence to his friend
The consecrated draught; then Tlalala
Drained off the offering. Braver blood than this
My lips can never taste! quoth he; but soon
Grant me, Mexitli, a more grateful cup,—

The Stranger's life!

    Are all the rites performed?
Ocellopan enquired. Yea, all is done,
Answered the Priest. Go! and the guardian God
Of Aztlan be your guide!

       They left the fane.
Lo! as Tezozomoc was passing by
The eternal fire, the eternal fire shot up
A long blue flame. He started; he exclaimed,
The God! the God! Tezcalipoca's Priest
Echoed the welcome cry, The God! the God!
For lo! his footsteps mark the maize-strewn floor!
A mighty shout from all the multitude
Of Aztlan rose; they cast into the fire
The victims, whose last shrieks of agony
Mingled unheeded with the cries of joy.
Then louder from the spiral sea-shell's depth
Swelled the full roar, and from the hollow wood
Pealed deeper thunders. Round the choral band,
The circling nobles, gay with gorgeous plumes,
And gems which sparkled to the midnight fire,
Moved in the solemn dance; each in his hand,
In measured movements, lifts the feathery shield,
And shakes a rattling ball to measured sounds.
With quicker steps, the inferior chiefs without,
Equal in number, but in just array,
The spreading radii of the mystic wheel,[41]
Revolve; and, outermost, the youths roll round,
In motions rapid as their quickened blood.
So thus, with song and harmony, the night
Past on in Aztlan, and all hearts rejoiced:

<h3 style="text-align:center">XI.</h3>

<h3 style="text-align:center">The Capture.</h3>

MEANTIME from Aztlan, on their enterprize,
Shedder of Blood and Tyger of the War,
Ocellopan and Tlalala set forth.
With chosen followers, through the silent night;
Silent they travelled on. After a way
Circuitous and far through lonely tracks,
They reached the mountains, and amid the shade
Of thickets covering the uncultured slope,
Their patient ambush placed. The chiefs alone
Held on, till winding in ascent they reached
The heights which o'er the Briton's mountain hold
Impended; there they stood, and by the moon
Who yet, with undiminished lustre, hung
High in the dark blue firmament, from thence
Explored the steep descent. Precipitous
The rock beneath them lay, a sudden cliff
Bare and unbroken; in its midway holes,
Where never hand could reach, nor eye intrude,
The eagle built her eyrie. Farther on,
Its interrupted crags and ancient woods
Offered a difficult way. From crag to crag,
By rocky shelf, by trunk, or root, or bough,
A painful toil and perilous, they past.
And now, stretched out amid the matted shrubs,
Which, at the entrance of the valley, clothed
The rugged bank, they crouched.

      By this the stars
Grew dim; the glow-worm hath put out her lamp;
The owls have ceased their night-song. On the top

Of yon magnolia the loud turkey's voice
Is heralding the dawn;[42] from tree to tree
Extends the wakening watch-note, far and wide,
Till the whole woodlands echo with the cry.
Now breaks the morning; but as yet no foot
Hath marked the dews, nor sound of man is heard.
Then first Ocellopan beheld, where near,
Beneath the shelter of a half-roofed hut,
A sleeping stranger lay. He pointed him
To Tlalala. The Tyger looked around:
None else was nigh—Shall I descend, he said,
And strike him? here is none to see the deed.
We offered to the Gods our mingled blood
Last night; and now, I deem it, they present
An offering which shall more propitiate them,
And omen sure success. I will go down
And kill!

    He said, and, gliding like a snake,
Where Caradoc lay sleeping made his way.
Sweetly slept he, and pleasant were his dreams
Of Britain, and the blue-eyed maid he loved.
The Azteca stood over him; he knew
His victim, and the power of vengeance gave
Malignant joy. Once hast thou 'scaped my arm:
But what shall save thee now? the Tyger thought,
Exulting; and he raised his spear to strike.
That instant, o'er the Briton's unseen harp
The gale of morning past, and swept its strings
Into so sweet a harmony, that sure
It semed no earthly tone. The savage man
Suspends his stroke; he looks astonished round;
No human hand is near;.. and hark! again
The aërial music swells and dies away.
Then first the heart of Tlalala felt fear:
He thought that some protecting spirit lived
Beside the Stranger, and, abashed, withdrew.

A God protects him! to Ocellopan,
Whispering, he said. Didst thou not hear the sound
Which entered into me, and fixed my arm
Powerless above him?

      Was it not a voice
From thine own Gods, to strengthen thee, replied
His sterner comrade, and make evident
Their pleasure in the deed?

      Nay! Tlalala
Rejoined; they speak in darkness and in storms:
The thunder is their voice, that peals through Heaven,
Or, rolling underneath us, makes earth rock
In tempest, and destroys the sons of men.
It was no sound of theirs, Ocellopan!
No voice to hearten,—for I felt it pass
Unmanning every limb; yea, it relaxed
The sinews of my soul. Shedder of Blood,
I cannot lift my hand against the man.
Go, if thy heart be stronger!

      But meantime
Young Caradoc arose, of his escape
Unconscious; and by this the stirring sounds
Of day began, increasing now, as all
Now to their toil betake them. Some go fell
The stately wood; some from the tree low-laid
Hew the huge boughs; here round the fire they char
The stake-points; here they level with a line
The ground-plot, and infix the ready piles,
Or, interknitting them with osiers, weave

The wicker wall; others along the lake,
From its shoal waters gather reeds and canes,—
Light roofing, suited to the genial sky.
The woodman's measured stroke, the regular saw,
The wain slow-creaking, and the voice of man
Answering his fellow, or, in single toil,
Cheering his labour with a cheerful song,
Strange concert made to those fierce Aztecas,
Who, beast-like, in their silent lurking-place
Couched close and still, observant for their prey.

All overseeing, and directing all,
From place to place moved Madoc, and beheld
The dwellings rise. Young Hoel at his side
Ran on, best pleased when at his Uncle's side
Courting indulgent love. And now they came
Beside the half-roofed hut of Caradoc;
Of all the mountain-dwellings that the last.
The little boy, in boyish wantonness,
Would quit his Uncle's hold, and haste away,
With childhood's frolic speed, then laugh aloud,
To tempt pursuit, now running to the huts,
Now toward the entrance of the valley straits.
But wheresoe'er he turned, Ocellopan
With hunter-eye pursued his heedless course,
In breath-suspending vigilance. Ah me!
The little wretch toward his lurking place
Draws near, and calls on Madoc; and the Prince
Thinks of no danger nigh, and follows not
The childish lure! nearer the covert now
Young Hoel runs, and stops, and calls again;
Then like a lion, from his couching place
Ocellopan leapt forth, and seized his prey.

Loud shrieked the affrighted child, as in his arms
The savage graspt him; startled at the cry,
Madoc beheld him hastening through the pass.
Quick as instinctive love can urge his feet
He follows, and he now almost hath reached
The incumbered ravisher, and hope inspires
New speed,—yet nearer now, and nearer still,
And lo! the child holds out his little arms!
That instant, as the Prince almost had laid
His hand upon the boy, young Tlalala
Leapt on his neck, and soon, though Madoc's strength,
With frantic fury, shook him from his hold,
Far down the steep Ocellopan had fled.
Ah! what avails it now, that they, by whom
Madoc was standing to survey their toil,
Have missed their Chief, and spread the quick alarm?
What now avails it, that, with distant aid,
His gallant men come down? Regarding nought
But Hoel, but the wretched Llaian's grief,
He rushes on; and ever as he draws
Near to the child, the Tiger Tlalala
Impedes his way; and now they reach the place
Of ambush, and the ambushed band arise,
And Madoc is their prisoner.
                              Caradoc,
In vain thou leadest on the late pursuit!
In vain, Cadwallon, thy alarmèd love
Caught the first sound of evil! They pour out
Tumultuous, from the vale, a half-armed troop;
Each with such weapons as his hasty hand
Can seize, they rush to battle. Gallant men,
Your valour boots not! It avails not now,

With such fierce onset that ye charge the foe,
And drive with such full force the weapon home!
They, while ye slaughter them, impede pursuit,
And far away, meantime, their comrades bear
The prisoner Prince. In vain his noble heart
Swells now with wild and suffocating rage;
In vain he struggles:—they have bound his limbs
With the tough osier, and his struggles now
But bind more close and cuttingly the band.
They hasten on; and while they bear the prize,
Leaving their ill-doomed fellows in the fight
To check pursuit, foremost afar of all,
With unabating strength by joy inspired,
Ocellopan to Aztlan bears the child.

XII.

Hoel.

GOOD tidings travel fast.—The chief is seen;
He hastens on; he holds the child on high;
He shouts aloud. Through Aztlan spreads the news;
Each to his neighbour tells the happy tale.—
Joy,—joy to Aztlan! the Blood-shedder comes!
Tlaloc hath given his victim.
                              Ah, poor child!
They from the gate swarm out to welcome thee,
Warriors, and men grown grey, and youths and maids,
Exulting, forth they crowd. The mothers throng
To view thee, and, while, thinking of thy doom,
They clasp their own dear infants to the breast
With deeper love, delighted think that thou
Shalt suffer for them. He, poor child, admires
The strange array; with wonder he beholds
Their olive limbs, half bare, their plumy crowns,
And gazes round and round, where all was new,
Forgetful of his fears. But when the Priest
Approached to take him from the Warrior's arms,
Then Hoel screamed, and from that hideous man
Averting, to Ocellopan he turned,
And would have clung to him, so dreadful late,
Stern as he was, and terrible of eye,
Less dreadful than the Priest, whose dark aspect
Which nature with her harshest characters
Had featured, art made worse. His cowl was white; [43]
His untrimmed hair, a long and loathsome mass,
With cotton cords intwisted, clung with gum,
And matted with the blood, which, every morn,
He from his temples drew before the God,
In sacrifice: bare were his arms, and smeared
Black: but his countenance a stronger dread
Than all the horrors of that outward garb,
Struck with quick instinct to young Hoel's heart;
It was a face, whose settled sullenness
No gentle feeling ever had disturbed;
Which, when he probed a victim's living breast,
Retained its hard composure.
                              Such was he
Who took the son of Llaian, heeding not
His cries and screams, and arms in suppliant guise,
Stretched out to all around, and strugglings vain.
He to the Temple of the Water-God
Conveyed his victim. By the threshold, there
The ministering Virgins stood, a comely band
Of high-born damsels, to the temple rites

By pious parents vowed. Gladly to them
The little Hoel leapt; their gentle looks
No fear excited; and he gazed around,
Pleased and surprised, unconscious to what end
These things were tending. O'er the rush-strewn floor
They to the azure Idol led the boy,
Now not reluctant, and they raised the hymn.

God of the Waters! at whose will the streams
Flow in their wonted channel, and diffuse
Their plenty round, the blood and life of earth;
At whose command they swell, and o'er their banks
Burst with resistless ruin, making vain
The toils and hopes of man,—behold this child!
O, strong to bless, and mighty to destroy,
Tlaloc! behold thy victim! so mayest thou
Restrain the peaceful streams within their banks,
And bless the labours of the husbandman.
God of the Mountains! at whose will the clouds
Cluster around the heights; who sendest them
To shed their fertilizing showers, and raise
The drooping herb, and o'er the thirsty vale
Spread their green freshness; at whose voice the hills
Grow black with storms; whose wrath the thunder speaks,
Whose bow of anger shoots the lightning shafts,
To blast the works of man;—behold this child!
O, strong to bless, and mighty to destroy,
Tlaloc! behold thy victim! so mayest thou
Lay by the fiery arrows of thy rage,
And bid the genial rains and dews descend.

O thou, Companion of the powerful God!
Companion and Beloved!—when he treads
The mountain-top, whose breath diffuses round
The sweets of summer; when he rides the waves,
Whose presence is the sunshine and the calm,—
Aiauh, O green-robed Goddess, see this child!
Behold thy victim! so mayest thou appease
The sterner mind of Tlaloc when he frowns,
And Aztlan flourish in thy fostering smile.

Young Spirits! ye whom Aztlan's piety
Hath given to Tlaloc, to enjoy with him,
For aye, the cool delights of Tlalocan,[44]—
Young Spirits of the happy; who have left
Your Heaven to-day, unseen assistants here,—
Behold your comrade! see the chosen child,
Who through the lonely cave of death must pass,
Like you, to join you in eternal joy.

Now from the rush-strewn temple they depart.
They place their smiling victim in a car,
Upon whose sides of pearly shell there played,
Fading and shifting still, the rainbow light.
On virgin shoulders is he borne aloft,
With dance before, and song and music round:
And thus they seek, in festival array,
The water-side. There lies the sacred bark,
All gay with gold, and garlanded with flowers:
The virgins with the joyous boy embark;
Then boatmen urge them on; the Priests behind
Follow, and all the long solemnity.
The lake is overspread with boats; the sun
Shines on the gilded prows, the feathery crowns,
The sparkling waves. Green islets float along,[45]
Where high-born damsels, under jasmin bowers,

Raise the sweet voice, to which the echoing oars,
In modulated motion rise and fall.
The moving multitude along the shore
Flows like a stream; bright shines the unclouded sky;
Heaven, earth, and waters wear one face of joy.
Young Hoel with delight beholds the pomp;
His heart throbs joyfully; and if he thinks
Upon his mother now, 't is but to think
How beautiful a tale for her glad ear
He hath when he returns. Meantime the maids
Weave garlands for his head, and pour the song.

Oh, happy thou, whom early from the world
The gods require! not by the wasting worm
Of sorrow canker'd, nor condemn'd to feel
The pang of sickness, nor the wound of war,
Nor the long miseries of protracted age;
But called in youth, the chosen of the God,
To share his joys! Soon shall thy rescued soul,
Child of the Stranger! in his blissful world,
Mix with the blessed spirits: for not thine,
Amid the central darkness of the earth,
To endure the eternal void;—not thine to live,
Dead to all objects of eye, ear, or sense,
In the long horrors of one endless night,
With endless being curst. For thee the bowers
Of Tlalocan have blossom'd with new sweets;
For thee have its immortal trees matured
The fruits of Heaven; thy comrades even now
Wait thee, impatient, in their fields of bliss;
The God will welcome thee, his chosen child,
And Aiauh love thee with a mother's love.
Child of the Stranger! dreary is thy way!
Darkness and Famine through the cave of Death
Must guide thee. Happy thou, when on that night
The morning of the eternal day shall dawn.

So as they sung young Hoel's song of death,
With rapid strength the boatmen plied their oars,
And through the water swift they glided on.
And now to shore they drew. The stately bank
Rose, with the majesty of woods o'erhung,
And rocks, or peering through the forest shade,
Or rising from the lake, and with their bulk
Glassing its dark, deep waters. Half-way up,
A cavern pierced the rock; no human foot
Had trod its depths, nor ever sunbeam reach'd
Its long recesses and mysterious gloom.
To Tlaloc it was hallow'd; and the stone,
Which closed its entrance, never was removed,
Save when the yearly festival returned,
And in its womb a child was sepulchred,
The living victim.[46] Up the winding path
That to the entrance of the cavern led,
With many a painful step, the train ascend:
But many a time, upon that long ascent,
Young Hoel would have paused, with weariness
Exhausted now. They urge him on,—poor child!
They urge him on.—Where is Cadwallon's aid?
Where is the sword of Ririd? where the arm
Of Madoc now?—Oh! better had he lived,
Unknowing and unknown, on Arvon's plain,
And trod upon his noble father's grave,
With peasant feet, unconscious!—They have reach'd
The cavern now, and from its mouth the Priests
Roll the huge portal. Thitherward they force

The son of Llaian. A cold air comes out;—
It chills him, and his feet recoil;—in vain
His feet recoil;—in vain he turns to fly,
Affrighted at the sudden gloom that spreads
Around;—the den is closed, and he is left
In solitude and darkness,—left to die!

XIII.

Coatel.

THAT morn from Aztlan Coatel had gone,
In search of flowers amid the woods and crags,
To deck the shrine of Coatlantona;
Such flowers as in the solitary wilds
Hiding their modest beauty, made their worth
More valued for its rareness. 'T was to her
A grateful task; not only for she fled
Those cruel rites, to which nor reverent use
Nor frequent custom could familiarize
Her gentle heart, and teach it to put off
All womanly feeling;—but that from all eyes
Escaped, and all obtrusive fellowship,
She, in that solitude, might send her soul
To where Lincoya with the Strangers dwelt.
She, from the summit of the woodland heights,
Gazed on the lake below. The sound of song
And instrument, in soften'd harmony,
Had reach'd her where she stray'd; and she beheld
The pomp, and listen'd to the floating sounds,
A moment, with delight: but then a fear
Came on her, for she knew with what design
The Tyger and Ocellopan had sought
The dwellings of the Cymry—Now the boats
Drew nearer, and she knew the Stranger's child.
She watch'd them land below; she saw them wind
The ascent:—and now from that abhorred cave
The stone is roll'd away,—and now the child
From light and life is cavern'd. Coatel
Thought of his mother then, of all the ills
Her fear would augur, and how worse than all
Which even a mother's maddening fear could feign,
His dreadful fate. She thought of this, and bow'd
Her face upon her knees, and closed her eyes,
Shuddering. Suddenly in the brake beside,
A rustling startled her, and from the shrubs,
A vulture rose.

                    She moved toward the spot,
Led by an idle impulse, as it seem'd,
To view from whence the carrion bird had fled.
The bushes overhung a narrow chasm
Which pierced the hill: upon its mossy sides
Shade-loving herbs and flowers luxuriant grew:
And jutting crags made easy the descent.
A little way descending, Coatel
Stoop'd for the flowers, and heard, or thought she heard,
A feeble sound below. She raised her head,
And anxiously she listened for the sound,
Not without fear—Feebly again, and like
A distant cry, it came; and then she thought,
Perhaps it was the voice of that poor child,
By the slow pain of hunger doom'd to die.
She shudder'd at the thought, and breathed a groan
Of unavailing pity;—but the sound
Came nearer, and her trembling heart conceived

A dangerous hope. The Vulture from that chasm
Had fled, perchance accustom'd in the cave
To seek his banquet, and by living feet
Alarm'd:—there was an entrance then below;
And were it possible that she could save
The Stranger's child,—Oh what a joy it were
To tell Lincoya that!

                    It was a thought
Which made her heart with terror and delight
Throb audibly. From crag to crag she past
Descending, and beheld a narrow cave
Enter the hill. A little way the light
Fell,—but its feeble glimmering she herself
Obstructed half, as stooping in she went.
The arch grew loftier, and the increasing gloom
Filled her with more affright; and now she paused;
For at a sudden and abrupt descent
She stood, and feared its unseen depth; her heart
Failed, and she back had hastened; but the cry
Reached her again, the near and certain cry
Of that most pitiable innocent.
Again adown the dark descent she looked,
Straining her eyes; by this the strengthened sight
Had grown adapted to the gloom around,
And her dilated pupils now received
Dim sense of objects near. Something below,
White, in the darkness lay : it marked the depth.
Still Coatel stood dubious; but she heard
The wailing of the child, and his loud sobs;—
Then, clinging to the rock, with fearful hands,
Her feet explored below, and twice she felt
Firm footing, ere her fearful hold relaxed.
The sound she made, along the hollow rock
Ran echoing. Hoel heard it, and he came
Groping along the side. A dim, dim light
Broke on the darkness of his sepulchre;
A human form drew near him ;—he sprung on,
Screaming with joy, and clung to Coatel,
And cried, O take me from this dismal place!
She answered not ; she understood him not;
But clasped the little victim to her breast,
And shed delightful tears.

                    But from that den
Of darkness and of horror, Coatel
Durst not convey the child, though in her heart
There was a female tenderness which yearned,
Even with maternal love, to cherish him.
She hushed his clamours, fearful lest the sound
Might reach some other ear ; she kissed away
The tears that streamed adown his little cheeks;
She gave him food which in the morn she brought,
For her own wants from Aztlan. Some few words
Of Britain's ancient language she had learnt
From her Lincoya, in those happy days
Of peace, when Aztlan was the Stranger's friend :
Aptly she learnt, what willingly he taught,
Terms of endearment, and the parting words
Which promised quick return. She on the child
The endearing phrase bestowed ; and if it chanced
Imperfect knowledge, or some difficult sound
Checked her heart's utterance, then the gentle tone,
The fond caress, intelligibly spake
Affection's language.

                    But when she arose,
And would have climbed the ascent, the affrighted boy
Close clasped her, and his tears interpreted

he prayer to leave him not. Again she kissed
his tears away; again of soon return
assured and soothed him; till reluctantly
and weeping, but in silence, he unloosed
His grasp; and up the difficult ascent
Coatel climbed, and to the light of day
Returning, with her flowers she hastened home.

XIV.

The Stone of Sacrifice.

Who comes to Aztlan, bounding like a deer
Along the plain?—The herald of success;
For lo! his locks are braided, and his loins
Cinctured with white; and see, he lifts the shield,
And brandishes the sword. The populace
Flock round, impatient for the tale of joy,
And follow to the palace in his path.
Joy! joy! the Tiger hath achieved his quest!
They bring a captive home!—Triumphantly
Coanocotzin and his Chiefs go forth
To greet the youth triumphant, and receive
The victim whom the gracious gods have given,
Sure omen and first fruits of victory.
A woman leads the train, young, beautiful,—
More beautiful for that translucent joy
Flushing her cheek, and sparkling in her eye;—
Her hair is twined with festal flowers, her robe
With flowing wreaths adorned; she holds a child,
He, too, bedecked and garlanded with flowers,
And, lifting him, with agile force of arm,
In graceful action, to harmonious step
Accordant, leads the dance. It is the wife
Of Tlalala, who, with his child, goes forth
To meet her hero husband.

And behold
The Tiger comes! and ere the shouts and sounds
Of gratulation cease, his followers bear
The captive Prince. At that so welcome sight
Loud rose the glad acclaim; nor knew they yet
That he who there lay patient in his bonds,
Expecting the inevitable lot,
Was Madoc. Patient in his bonds he lay,
Exhausted with vain efforts, desperate now,
And silently resigned. But when the King
Approached the prisoner, and beheld his face,
And knew the Chief of Strangers, at that sound
Electric joy shot through the multitude,
And, like the raging of the hurricane,
Their thundering transports pealed. A deeper joy,
A nobler triumph kindled Tlalala,
As, limb by limb, his eye surveyed the Prince,
With a calm fierceness. And by this the Priests
Approached their victim, clad in vestments white
Of sacrifice, which from the shoulders fell,
As from the breast unbending, broad and straight
Leaving their black arms bare. The blood-red robe,
The turquoise pendant from his down-drawn lip,
The crown of glossy plumage, whose green hue
Vied with his emerald ear-drops, marked their Chief,
Tezozomoc: his thin and ghastly cheek,
Which,—save the temple serpents,[47] when he brought
Their human banquet,—never living eye
Rejoiced to see, became more ghastly now,

As, in Mexitli's name, upon the Prince
He laid his murtherous hand. But as he spake,
Updarted Tlalala his eagle glance—
Away! away! he shall not perish so!
The warrior cried—Not tamely, by the knife,
Nor on the jasper-stone, his blood shall flow!
The Gods of Aztlan love a Warrior Priest!
I am their Priest to-day!

A murmuring
Ran through the train; nor waited he to hear
Denial thence; but on the multitude
Aloud he called—When first our fathers seized
This land, there was a savage Chief who stopt
Their progress. He had gained the rank he bore,
By long probation: stripes, which laid his flesh
All bleeding bare, had forced not one complaint;
Not, when the working bowels might be seen;
One movement: hand-bound, he had been confined
Where myriad insects on his nakedness
Infixed their venomous anger, and no start,
No shudder, shook his frame: [48] last, in a net
Suspended, he had felt the agony
Of fire, which to his bones and marrow pierced,
And breathed the suffocating smoke which filled
His lungs with fire, without a groan, a breath,
A look betokening sense; so gallantly
Had he subdued his nature. This brave man
Met Aztlan in the war, and put her Chiefs
To shame. Our Elders have not yet forgot
How from the slaughtered brother of their King
He stript the skin, and formed of it a drum,
Whose sound affrighted armies.[49] With this man
My father coped in battle; here he led him,
An offering to the God; and, man to man,
He slew him here in fight. I was a child,
Just old enough to lift my father's shield;
But I remember, on that glorious day,
When from the sacred combat he returned,
His red hands reeking with the hot heart's blood,
How in his arms he took me, and besought
The God whom he had served, to bless his boy,
And make me like my father. Men of Aztlan!
Mexitli heard his prayer!—Here I have brought
The Stranger-Chief, the noblest sacrifice
That ever graced the altar of the God;
Let then his death be noble! so my boy
Shall, in the day of battle, think of me;
And as I followed my brave father's steps,
Pursue my path of glory.

Ere the Priest
Could frame denial, had the Monarch's look
Bespake assent.—Refuse not this, he cried,
O servant of the Gods! He hath not here
His arms to save him; and the Tiger's strength
Yields to no mortal might. Then for his sword
He called, and bade Yuhidthiton address
The Stranger-Chief.

Yuhidthiton began:
The Gods of Aztlan triumph, and thy blood
Must wet their altars. Prince, thou shalt not die
The coward's death; but, sworded, and in fight,
Fall as becomes the valiant. Should thine arm
Subdue in battle six successive foes,
Life, liberty, and glory, will repay
The noble conquest. [50] Madoc, hope not this!
Strong are the brave of Aztlan!

Then they loosed
The Ocean Chieftain's bonds; they rent away
His garments; and, with songs and shouts of joy,
They led him to the Stone of Sacrifice.
Round was that Stone of blood! the half-raised arm
Of one of manly growth, who stood below,
Might rest upon its height; the circle small,
An active boy might almost bound across.
Nor needed, for the combat, ampler space;
For in the centre was the prisoner's foot
Fast fettered down.   Thus fettered Madoc stood.
He held a buckler, light and small, of cane
O'erlaid with beaten gold; his sword the King,
Honouring a noble enemy, had given,
A weapon tried in war,—to Madoc's grasp
Strange and unwieldy: 't was a broad strong staff,
Set thick with transverse stones, on either side
Keen-edged as Syrian steel. But when he felt
The weapon, Madoc called to mind his deeds
Done on the Saxon in his father's land,
And hope arose within him.   Nor though now
Naked he stood, did fear, for that, assail
His steady heart; for often had he seen
His gallant countrymen, with naked breasts,
Rush on their iron-coated enemy, [51]
And win the conquest.

Now hath Tlalala
Arrayed himself for battle. First he donned
A gipion, quilted close of gossampine;
O'er that a jointed mail of plates of gold,
Bespotted like the tyger's speckled pride,
To speak his rank; it clad his arms half-way,
Half-way his thighs; but cuishes had he none,
Nor gauntlets, nor feet-armour. On his helm
There yawned the semblance of a tiger's head,
The long white teeth extended, as for prey;
Proud crest, to blazon his proud title forth.
And now toward the fatal stage, equipped
For war, he went; when, from the press behind,
A warrior's voice was heard, and clad in arms,
And shaking in his angry grasp the sword,
Ocellopan rushed on, and called aloud
On Tlalala, and claimed the holy fight.
The Tiger, heedless of his clamour, sprung
Upon the stone, and turned him to the war.
Fierce leaping forward came Ocellopan,
And bounded up the ascent, and seized his arm :—
Why wouldst thou rob me of a deed like this?
Equal our peril in the enterprise,
Equal our merit;—thou wouldst reap alone
The guerdon! Never shall my children lift
Their little hands at thee, and say, Lo! there
The Chief who slew the White King!—Tlalala,
Trust to the lot, or turn on me, and prove,
By the best chance to which the brave appeal,
Who best deserves this glory!

Stung by wrath,
The Tiger answered not; he raised his sword,
And they had rushed to battle; but the Priests
Came hastening up, and by their common Gods,
And by their common country, bade them cease
Their impious strife, and let the lot decide
From whom Mexitli should that day receive
His noble victim. Both unsatisfied,
But both obedient, heard. Two equal shafts,
As outwardly they seemed, the Paba brought;

His mantle hid their points; and Tlalala
Drew forth the broken stave. A bitter smile
Darkened his cheek, as angrily he cast
To earth the hostile lot.—Shedder of Blood,
Thine is the first adventure! he exclaimed;
But thou mayest perish here!—and in his heart,
The Tiger hoped Ocellopan might fall,
As sullenly retiring from the stage,
He mingled with the crowd.

And now opposed
In battle, on the Stone of Sacrifice,
Prince Madoc and the Life-Destroyer stood.
This clad in arms complete, free to advance
In quick assault, or shun the threatened blow,
Wielding his wonted sword; the other, stript,
Save of that fragile shield, of all defence;
His weapon strange and cumbrous; and pinned down,
Disabled from all onset, all retreat.

With looks of greedy joy, Ocellopan
Surveyed his foe, and wondered to behold
The breast so broad, the bare and brawny limbs,
Of matchless strength. The eye of Madoc, too,
Dwelt on his foe; his countenance was calm,
Something more pale than wonted; like a man
Prepared to meet his death. The Azteca
Fiercely began the fight; now here, now there,
Aright, aleft, above, below, he wheeled
The rapid sword: still Madoc's rapid eye
Pursued the motion, and his ready shield,
In prompt interposition, caught the blow,
Or turned its edge aside.   Nor did the Prince
Yet aim the sword to wound, but held it forth,
Another shield, to save him, till his hand,
Familiar with its weight and shape uncouth,
Might wield it well to vengeance. Thus he stood,
Baffling the impatient enemy, who now
Waxed wrathful, thus to waste in idle strokes,
Reiterate so oft his bootless strength.
And now yet more exasperate he grew;
For, from the eager multitude, was heard,
Amid the din of undistinguished sounds,
The Tiger's murmured name, as though they thought.
Had he been on the stone, ere this, be sure,
The Gods had tasted of their sacrifice,
Now all too long delayed. Then fiercelier,
And yet more rapidly, he drove the sword;
But still the wary Prince or met its fall,
And broke the force, or bent him from the blow;
And now retiring, and advancing now,
As one free foot permitted, still provoked,
And baffled still the savage; and sometimes,
With cautious strength did Madoc aim attack,
Mastering each moment now with abler sway
The acquainted sword. But, though as yet unharmed
In life or limb, more perilous the strife
Grew momently; for, with repeated strokes,
Battered and broken now, the shield hung loose;
And shouts of triumph from the multitude
Arose, as, piece-meal, they beheld it fall,
And saw the Prince exposed.

That welcome sight,
Those welcome sounds, inspired Ocellopan;
He felt each limb new-strung. Impatient now
Of conquest long delayed, with wilder rage
He drives the weapon; Madoc's lifted sword

leceived its edge, and shivered with the blow.
A shriek of transport burst from all around;
For lo! the White King, shieldless, weaponless,
Naked before his foe! That savage foe,
Dallying with the delight of victory,
Drew back a moment to enjoy the sight,
Then yelled in triumph, and sprang on to give
The consummating blow. Madoc beheld
The coming death; he darted up his hand
Instinctively to save, and caught the wrist
In its mid fall, and drove with desperate force
The splintered truncheon of his broken sword
Full in the enemy's face. Beneath his eye
It broke its way, and where the nasal nerves
Branch in fine fibrils o'er their mazy seat,
Burst through, and slanting upward in the brain
Buried its jagged point.

Madoc himself

Stood at his fall astonished, at escape
Unhoped, and strange success. The multitude
Beheld, and they were silent, and they stood
Gazing in terror. But far other thoughts
Rose in the Tiger's heart; it was a joy
To Tlalala; and forth he sprang, and up
The Stone of Sacrifice, and called aloud
To bring the Prince another sword and shield,
For his last strife. Then in that interval,
Upon Ocellopan he fixed his eyes,
Contemplating the dead, as though thereby
To kindle in his heart a fiercer thirst
For vengeance. Nor to Madoc was the sting
Of anger wanting, when, in Tlalala,
He knew the captive whom his mercy freed,
The man whose ambush had that day destroyed
Young Hoel and himself;—for, sure, he deemed
Young Hoel was with God, and he himself
At his death-day arrived. And now he graspt
A second sword, and held again the shield;
And from the Stone of Blood Ocellopan
Was borne away; and, fresh in arms, and fierce
With all that makes a savage thirst for war,
Hope, vengeance, courage, superstitious hate,
A second foe came on. By this the Prince
Could wield his weapon well; and dreading now
Lest, in protracted combat, he should stand
Again defenceless, he put forth his strength,
As oft assailing as assailed, and watched
So well the Tiger's motions, and received
The Tiger's blows so warily, and aimed
His own so fierce and fast, that in the crowd
Doubt and alarm prevailed. Ilanquel grew
Pale at her husband's danger; and she clasped
The infant to her breast, whom late she held
On high, to see his victory. The throng
Of the beholders silently looked on;
And in their silence might at times be heard
An indrawn breath of terror; and the Priests
Angrily murmured, that in evil hour,
Coanocotzin had indulged the pride
Of vaunting valour, and from certain death
Reprieved the foe.

But now a murmur rose

Amid the multitude; and they who stood
So thickly thronged, and with such eager eyes
Late watched the fight, hastily now broke up,
And with disordered speed and sudden arms,

Ran to the city gates. More eager now,
Conscious of what had chanced, fought Tlalala;
And hope invigorated Madoc's heart;
For well he weened Cadwallon was at hand,
Leading his gallant friends. Aright he weened;
At hand Cadwallon was! His gallant friends
Came from the mountains with impetuous speed,
To save or to revenge. Nor long endured
The combat now: the Priests ascend the stone,
And bid the Tiger hasten to defend
His country and his Gods; and, hand and foot,
Binding the captive Prince, they bear him thence
And lay him in the temple. Then his heart
Resigned itself to death, and Madoc thought
Of Llaian and Goervyl; and he felt
That death was dreadful. But not so the King
Permitted; but not so had Heaven decreed;
For noble was the King of Aztlan's heart,
And pure his tongue from falsehood: he had said,
That by the warrior's death should Madoc die;
Nor dared the Pabas violently break
The irrevocable word. There Madoc lay
In solitude; the distant battle reached
His ear; inactive and in bonds he lay,
Expecting the dread issue, and almost
Wished for the perils of the fight again.

XV.

The Battle.

Not unprepared Cadwallon found the sons
Of Aztlan, nor defenceless were her walls;
But when the Britons' distant march was seen,
A ready army issued from her gates,
And dight themselves to battle: these the King
Coanocotzin had, with timely care,
And provident for danger, thus arrayed.
Forth issuing from the gates, they met the foe,
And with the sound of sonorous instruments,
And with their shouts and screams and yells, drove back
The Britons' fainter war-cry, [52] as the swell
Of ocean, flowing onward, up its course
Forces the river-stream. Their darts and stones
Fell like the rain-drops of the summer-shower,
So fast; and on the helmet and the shield,
On the strong corselet and the netted mail,
So innocent they fell. But not in vain
The bowmen of Deheubarth sent, that day,
Their iron bolts abroad; those winged deaths
Descended on the naked multitude,
And through the chieftain's quilted gossampine,
Through feathery breastplate and effulgent gold,
They reached the life.

But soon no interval

For archer's art was left, nor scope for flight
Of stone from whirling sling: both hosts, alike
Impatient for the proof of war, press on;
The Aztecas, to shun the arrowy storm,
The Cymry, to release their Lord, or heap
Aztlan in ruins, for his monument.
Spear against spear, and shield to shield, and breast
To breast they met; equal in force of limb
And strength of heart, in resolute resolve,
And stubborn effort of determined wrath:

3 z

The few, advantaged by their iron mail;
The weaklier armed, of near retreat assured
And succour close at hand, in tenfold troops
Their foemen overnumbering.   And of all
That mighty multitude, did every man
Of either host, alike inspired by all
That stings to will and strengthens to perform,
Then put forth all his power; for well they knew
Aztlan that day must triumph or must fall.
Then sword and mace on helm and buckler rang,
And hurtling javelins whirred along the sky.
Nor when they hurled the javelin, did the sons
Of Aztlan, prodigal of weapons, loose
The lance, to serve them for no second stroke;
A line of ample measure still retained
The missile shaft; [53] and when its blow was spent,
Swiftly the dexterous spearman coiled the string,
And sped again the artificer of death.
Rattling, like summer hailstones, they descend,
But from the Britons' iron panoply,
Baffled and blunted, fell; nor more availed
The stony falchion there, whose broken edge
Inflicts no second wound; nor profited,
On the strong buckler or the crested helm,
The knotty club; though fast, in blinding showers,
Those javelins fly, those heavy weapons fall
With stunning weight. Meantime, with wonted strength
The men of Gwyneth through their fenceless foes
Those lances thrust, whose terrors had so oft
Affrayed the Saxons, and whose home-driven points
So oft had pierced the Normen's knightly arms.
Little did then his pomp of plumes bestead
The Azteca, or glittering pride of gold,
Against the tempered sword; little his casque,
Gay with its feathery coronal, or drest
In graven terrors, when the Briton's hand
Drove in through helm and head the spiked mace;
Or swung its iron weights with shattering sway,
Which, where they fell, destroyed. Beneath those arms
The men of Aztlan sunk; and whoso dropt
Dead or disabled, him his comrades bore
Away with instant caution, lest the sight
Of those whom they had slaughtered might inspire
The foe with hope and courage.   Fast they fell,
And fast were resupplied, man after man
Succeeding to the death.   Nor in the town
Did now the sight of their slain countrymen,
Momently carried in and piled in heaps,
Create one thought of fear.   Hark! through the streets
Of Aztlan, how from house to house, and tower
To tower, reiterate, Paynalton's [54] name
Calls all her sons to battle! at whose name
All must go forth, and follow to the field
The Leader of the Armies of the Gods,
Whom, in his unseen power, Mexitli now
Sends out to lead his people.   They, in crowds,
Throng for their weapons to the House of Arms, [55]
Beneath their guardian Deity preserved,
Through years of peace; and there the Pabas stood
Within the temple-court, and dealt around
The ablution of the Stone of Sacrifice, [56]
Bidding them, with the holy beverage,
Imbibe diviner valour, strength of arm
Not to be wearied, hope of victory,
And certain faith of endless joy in Heaven,
Their sure reward.—Oh! happy, cried the Priests,

Your brethren who have fallen! already they
Have joined the company of blessëd souls;
Already they, with song and harmony,
And in the dance of beauty, are gone forth,
To follow down his western path of light
Yon Sun, the Prince of Glory, from the world
Retiring, to the palace of his rest.
Oh, happy they, who for their country's cause,
And for their Gods, shall die the brave man's death!
Them will their country consecrate with praise!
Them will the Gods reward!—They heard the Priests,
Intoxicate, and from the gate swarmed out,
Tumultuous to the fight of martyrdom.
But when Cadwallon every moment saw
The enemies increase, and with what rage
Of drunken valour to the fight they rushed,
He, against that impetuous attack,
As best he could, providing, formed the troops
Of Britain into one collected mass:
Three equal sides it offered to the foe,
Close and compact; no multitude could break
The condensed strength: its narrow point prest on,
Entering the throng's resistance, like a wedge,
Still from behind impelled.   So thought the Chief
Likeliest the gates of Aztlan might be gained,
And Hoel and the Prince preserved, if yet
They were among mankind.   Nor could the force
Of hostile thousands break that strength condensed,
Against whose iron sides the stream of war
Rolled unavailing, as the ocean waves,
Which idly round some insulated rock
Foam furious, warring with their silvery smoke
The mariner far off.   Nor could the point
Of that compacted body, though it bore
Right on the foe, and with united force
Pressed on to enter, through the multitude
Win now its difficult way; as where the sea
Pours through some strait its violent waters, swoln,
By inland fresh, vainly the oarmen there
With all their weight and strength essay to drive
Their galley through the pass, the stress and strain
Availing scarce to stem the impetuous stream.

And hark! above the deafening din of fight
Another shout, heard like the thunder-peal
Amid the war of winds! Lincoya comes,
Leading the mountain-dwellers.   From the shock
Aztlan recoiled.   And now a second troop
Of Britons to the town advanced, for war
Impatient and revenge.   Cadwallon these,
With tidings of their gallant Prince enthralled,
Had summoned from the ships.   That dreadful tale
Roused them to fury.   Not a man was left
To guard the fleet; for who could have endured
That idle duty? who could have endured
The long, inactive, miserable hours,
And hope and expectation and the rage
Of maddening anguish? Ririd led them on;
In whom a brother's love had called not up
More spirit-stirring pain, than trembled now
In every British heart; so dear to all
Was Madoc.   On they came; and Aztlan then
Had fled appalled; but in that dangerous hour
Her faith preserved her.   From the gate her Priests
Rushed desperate out, and to the foremost rank
Forced their wild way, and fought with martyr zeal.

Through all the host contagious fury spread :
Nor had the sight that hour enabled them
To mightier efforts, had Mexitli, clad
In all his imaged terrors, gone before
Their way, and driven upon his enemies
His giant club destroying.   Then more fierce
The conflict grew; the din of arms, the yell
Of savage rage, the shriek of agony,
The groan of death commingled in one sound
Of undistinguished horrors; while the Sun,
Retiring slow beneath the plain's far verge,
Shed o'er the quiet hills his fading light.

XVI.

The Women.

Silent and solitary is thy vale,
Caermadoc! and how melancholy now
That solitude and silence!—broad noon-day,
And not a sound of human life is there!
The fisher's net, abandoned in his haste,
Sways idly in the waters; in the tree,
Which its last stroke had pierced, the hatchet hangs;
The birds, beside the mattock and the spade,
Hunt in the new-turned mould, and fearlessly
Fly through the cage-work of the imperfect wall;
Or through the vacant dwelling's open door,
Pass and repass secure.

         In Madoc's house,
And on his bed of reeds, Goervyl lies,
Her face toward the ground. She neither weeps,
Nor sighs, nor groans; too strong her agony
For outward sign of anguish, and for prayer
Too hopeless was the ill; and though, at times,
The pious exclamation past her lips,
Thy will be done! yet was that utterance
Rather the breathing of a broken heart,
Than of a soul resigned. Mervyn beside,
Hangs over his dear mistress silently,
Having no hope or comfort to bestow,
Nor aught but sobs and unavailing tears.
The women of Caermadoc, like a flock
Collected in their panic, stand around
The house of their lost leader; and they too
Are mute in their despair. Llaian alone
Is absent; wildly hath she wandered forth
To seek her child, and such the general woe,
That none hath marked her absence. Yet have they,
Though unprotected thus, no selfish fear;
The sudden evil had destroyed all thought,
All sense of present danger to themselves,
All foresight.

        Yet new terrors! Malinal,
Panting with speed, bursts in, and take sthe arms
Of Madoc down. Goervyl, at that sound,
Started in sudden hope; but when she saw
The Azteca, she uttered a faint scream
Of wrongful fear, remembering not the proofs
Of his tried truth, nor recognizing aught
In those known features, save their hostile hue.
But he, by worser fear abating soon
Her vain alarm, exclaimed, I saw a band
Of Hoamen coming up the straits, for ill
Be sure, for Amalahta leads them on.

Buckle this harness on, that, being armed,
I may defend the entrance.
        Scarce had she
Fastened the breast-plate with her trembling hands,
When, flying from the sight of men in arms,
The women crowded in.   Hastily he seized
The shield and spear, and on the threshold took
His stand; but, wakened now to provident thought,
Goervyl, following, helmed him.   There was now
No time to gird the bauldric on; she held
Her brother's sword, and bade him look to her
For prompt supply of weapons; in herself
Being resolved not idly to abide,
Nor unprepared of hand or heart to meet
The issue of the danger, nor to die
Reluctant now.

        Rightly had they divined
The Hoaman's felon purpose. When he heard
The fate of Madoc, from his mother's eye
He masked his secret joy, and took his arms,
And to the rescue, with the foremost band,
Set forth.   But soon, upon the way, he told
The associates of his crime, that now their hour
Of triumph was arrived; Caermadoc, left
Defenceless, would become, with all its wealth,
The spoiler's easy prey, raiment and arms
And iron; skins of that sweet beverage,
Which to a sense of its own life could stir
The joyful blood; the women above all,
Whom to the forest they might bear away,
To be their slaves; if so their pleasure was;
Or, yielding them to Aztlan, for such prize
Receive a royal guerdon.   Twelve there were,
Long leagued with him in guilt, who turned aside:
And they have reached Caermadoc now, and now
Rush onward, where they see the women fly;
When, on the threshold, clad in Cimbric arms,
And with long lance protended, Malinal
Rebuffs them from the entrance.   At that sight
Suddenly quailed they stood, as midnight thieves
Who find the master waking; but ere long,
Gathering assured courage, as they saw
No other guard, pressed forward, and essayed
To turn his spear aside. Its steady point,
True to the impelling strength, held on, and thrust
The foremost through the breast, and breath and blood
Followed the re-drawn shaft.   Nor seemed the strife
Unequal now, though, with their numbers, they
Beleaguered in half-ring the door, where he,
The sole defender, stood.   From side to side,
So well and swiftly did he veer the lance,
That every enemy beheld its point
Aimed at himself direct.   But chief on one
Had Malinal his deadly purpose fixed,
On Amalahta; by his death to quell
The present danger, and cut off the root
Of many an evil, certain else to spring
From that accursed stock.   On him his eye
Turned with more eager wilfulness, and dwelt
With keener ken; and now, with sudden step
Bending his body on, at him he drives
The meditated blow: but that ill Prince,
As chiefly sought, so chiefly fearing, swerved
Timely aside; and ere the Azteca
Recovered from the frustrate aim, the spear
Was seized, and from his hold, by stress and weight

Of numbers wrenched.   He, facing still the foe,
And holding at arm's length the targe, put back
His hand, and called Goervyl, and from her
Received the sword;—in time, for the enemy
Prest on so near, that having now no scope
To raise his arm, he drove the blade straight on.
It entered at the mouth of one who stood
With face aslant, and glanced along the teeth
Through to the ear, then, slivering downward, left,
The cheek-flap dangling.   He, in that same point
Of time, as if a single impulse gave
Birth to the double action, dashed his shield
Against another's head, with so fierce swing
And sway of strength, that this third enemy
Fell at his feet.   Astounded by such proof
Of prowess, and by unexpected loss
Dismayed, the foe gave back, beyond the reach
Of his strong arm ; and there awhile they stood,
Beholding him at bay, and counselling
How best to work their vengeance upon him,
Their sole opponent.   Soon did they behold
The vantage, overlooked by hasty hope,
How vulnerable he stood, his arms and thighs
Bare for their butt.   At once they bent their bows ;
At once ten arrows fled : seven, shot in vain,
Rung on his shield ; but, with unhappier mark,
Two shafts hung quivering in his leg ; a third
Below the shoulder pierced.   Then Malinal
Groaned, not for anguish of his wounds, but grief
And agony of spirit ; yet resolved
To his last gasp to guard that precious post,
Nor longer able to endure afoot,
He, falling on his knees, received unharmed
Upon the shield, now ample for defence,
Their second shower, and still defied the foe.
But they, now sure of conquest, hasten on
To thrust him down, and he too felt his strength
Ebbing away.   Goervyl, in that hour
Of horror and despair, collected still,
Caught him, and by the shoulders drew him in ;
And, calling on her comrades, with their help
Shut to the door in time, and with their weight
Secured it, not their strength ; for she alone,
Found worthy of her noble ancestry,
In this emergence, felt her faculties
All present, and heroic strength of heart,
To cope with danger and contempt of death.
Shame on ye, British women ! shame ! exclaimed
The daughter of King Owen, as she saw
The trembling hands and bloodless countenance
Pale as sepulchral marble ; silent some ;
Others with womanish cries lamenting now
That ever, in unhappy hour, they left
Their native land ;—a pardonable fear ;
For hark, the war-hoop ! sound, whereto the howl
Of tigers or hyenas, heard at night
By captive from barbarian foes escaped,
And wandering in the pathless wilderness,
Were music.   Shame on ye ! Goervyl cried ;
Think what your fathers were, your husbands what,
And what your sons should be !   These savages
Seek not to wreak on ye immediate death ;
So are ye safe, if safety such as this
Be worth a thought ; and in the interval
We yet may gain, by keeping to the last
This entrance, easily to be maintained

By us, though women, against foes so few,—
Who knows what succour chance, or timely thought
Of our own friends may send, or Providence,
Who slumbereth not ?—While thus she spake, a hand
In at the window came, of one who sought
That way to win the entrance.   She drew out
The arrow through the arm of Malinal,
With gentle care,—the readiest weapon that,—
And held it short above the bony barb,
And, adding deeds to words, with all her might
She stabbed it through the hand.   The sudden pain
Provoked a cry, and back the savage fell,
Loosening his hold, and maimed for farther war.
Nay ! leave that entrance open ! she exclaimed
To one who would have closed it,—who comes next
Shall not go thence so cheaply !—for she now
Had taken up a spear to guard that way,
Easily guarded, even by female might.
O heart of proof ! what now avails thy worth
And excellent courage ? for the savage foe,
With mattock and with spade, for other use
Designed, hew now upon the door, and rend
The wattled sides ; and they within shrink back,
For now it splinters through,—and lo, the way
Is open to the spoiler !
                    Then once more,
Collecting his last strength, did Malinal
Rise on his knees, and over him the maid
Stands with the ready spear, she guarding him
Who guarded her so well.   Roused to new force
By that exampled valour, and with will
To achieve one service yet before he died,—
If death indeed, as sure he thought, were nigh,—
Malinal gathered up his fainting powers ;
And, reaching forward, with a blow that threw
His body on, upon the knee he smote
One Hoaman more, and brought him to the ground.
The foe fell over him ; but he, prepared,
Threw him with sudden jerk aside, and rose
Upon one hand, and with the other plunged
Between his ribs the mortal blade.   Meantime
Amalahta, rushing in blind eagerness
To seize Goervyl, set at nought the power
Of female hand, and, stooping as he came,
Beneath her spear-point, thought with lifted arm
To turn the thrust aside.   But she drew back,
And lowered at once the spear, with aim so sure,
That on the front it met him, and ploughed up
The whole scalp-length.   He, blinded by the blood,
Staggered aside, escaping by that chance
A second push, else mortal.   And by this,
The women, learning courage from despair,
And by Goervyl's bold example fired,
Took heart, and rushing on with one accord,
Drove out the foe.   Then took they hope ; for then
They saw but seven remain in plight for war ;
And, knowing their own number, in the pride
Of strength, caught up stones, staves, or axe, or spear,
To hostile use converting whatsoe'er
The hasty hand could seize.   Such fierce attack
Confused the ruffian band ; nor had they room
To aim the arrow, nor to speed the spear,
Each now beset by many.   But their Prince,
Still mindful of his purport, called to them,—
Secure my passage while I bear away
The White King's Sister ; having her, the law

Of peace is in our power.—And on he went
Toward Goervil, and, with sudden turn,
While on another foe her eye was fixed,
Ran in upon her, and stoopt down, and claspt
The maid above the knees, and throwing her
Over his shoulder, to the valley straits
Set off:—ill seconded in ill attempt;
For now his comrades are too close beset
To aid their Chief, and Mervyn hath beheld
His Lady's peril. At the sight, inspired
With force, as if indeed that manly garb
Had clothed a manly heart, the Page ran on,
And with a bill-hook striking at his ham,
Cut the back sinews. Amalahta fell;
The Maid fell with him: and she first hath risen,
While, grovelling on the earth, he gnashed his teeth
For agony. Yet, even in those pangs,
Remembering still revenge, he turned and seized
Goervyl's skirt, and plucked her to the ground,
And rolled himself upon her, and essayed
To kneel upon her breast; but she clenched fast
His bloody locks, and drew him down aside,
Faint now with anguish, and with loss of blood;
And Mervyn, coming to her help again,
As once again he rose, around the neck
Seized him, with throttling grasp, and held him down—
Strange strife and horrible!—till Malinal
Crawled to the spot, and thrust into his groin
The mortal sword of Madoc; he himself,
At the same moment, fainting, now no more
By his strong will upheld, the service done.
The few surviving traitors, at the sight
Of their fallen Prince and Leader, now, too late
Believed that some diviner power had given
These female arms strength for their overthrow,
Themselves proved weak before them, as, of late,
Their God, by Madoc crushed.

       Away they fled
Toward the valley straits; but in the gorge
Erillyab met their flight; and then her heart,
Boding the evil, smote her, and she bade
Her people seize, and bring them on in bonds,
For judgment. She herself, with quickened pace,
Advanced, to know the worst; and o'er the dead
She cast a rapid glance, and knew her son.
She knew him by his garments, by the work
Of her own hands; for now his face, besmeared
And black with gore, and stiffened in its pangs,
Bore of the life no semblance—God is good!
She cried, and closed her eyelids, and her lips
Shook, and her countenance changed. But in her heart
She quelled the natural feeling—Bear away
These wretches!—to her followers she exclaimed;
And root them from the earth. Then she approached
Goervyl, who was pale and trembling now,
Exhausted with past effort; and she took
Gently the maiden's tremulous hand, and said,
God comfort thee, my Sister! At that voice
Of consolation, from her dreamy state,
Goervyl to a sense of all her woe
Awoke, and burst into a gush of tears.
God comfort thee, my Sister! cried the Queen,
Even as He strengthens me. I would not raise
Deceitful hope,—but in His Hand, even yet,
The issue hangs; and He is merciful.

Yea, daughter of Aberfraw, take thou hope!
For Madoc lives!—he lives to wield the sword
Of righteous vengeance, and accomplish all.

XVII

The Deliverance.

Madoc, meantime, in bonds and solitude,
Lay listening to the tumult. How his heart
Panted! how, then, with fruitless strength, he strove
And struggled for enlargement, as the sound
Of battle from without the city came;
While all things near were still, nor foot of man
Nor voice, in that deserted part, were heard,
At length one light and solitary step
Approached the place; a woman crossed the door:
From Madoc's busy mind her image passed,
Quick as the form that caused it; but not so
Did the remembrance fly from Coatel,
That Madoc lay in bonds. That thought possessed
Her soul, and made her, as she garlanded
The fane of Coatlantona with flowers,
Tremble in strong emotion.

       It was now
The hour of dusk; the Pabas all were gone,
Gone to the battle;—none could see her steps;
The gate was nigh. A momentary thought
Shot through her; she delayed not to reflect,
But hastened to the Prince, and took the knife
Of sacrifice, which by the altar hung,
And cut his bonds, and, with an eager eye,
Motioning haste and silence, to the gate
She led him. Fast along the forest way,
And fearfully, he followed to the chasm.
She beckoned, and descended, and drew out
From underneath her vest, a cage, or net
It rather might be called, so fine the twigs
Which knit it, where confined two fire-flies gave
Their lustre. [57] By that light did Madoc first
Behold the features of his lovely guide;
And through the entrance of the cavern gloom,
He followed in full trust.

       Now have they reached
The abrupt descent; there Coatel held forth
Her living lamp, and turning, with a smile
Sweet as good Angels wear when they present
Their mortal charge before the throne of Heaven,
She showed where little Hoel slept below.
Poor child! he lay upon that very spot,
The last whereto his feet had followed her;
And, as he slept, his hand was on the bones
Of one, who years agone had perished there;
There, on the place where last his wretched eyes
Could catch the gleam of day. But when the voice,
The well-known voice of Madoc wakened him—
His Uncle's voice—he started, with a scream
Which echoed through the cavern's winding length,
And stretched his arms to reach him. Madoc hushed
The dangerous transport, raised him up the ascent,
And followed Coatel again, whose face,
Though tears of pleasure still were coursing down,
Betokened fear and haste. Adown the wood
They went; and, coasting now the lake, her eye

First what they sought beheld, a light canoe,
Moored to the bank.   Then in her arms she took
The child, and kissed him with maternal love,
And placed him in the boat; but when the Prince,
With looks and gestures and imperfect words
Such as the look, the gesture, well explained,
Urged her to follow, doubtfully she stood:
A dread of danger, for the thing she had done,
Came on her, and Lincoya rose to mind.
Almost she had resolved; but then she thought
Of her dear father, whom that flight would leave
Alone in age; how he would weep for her,
As one among the dead, and to the grave
Go sorrowing; or, if ever it were known
What she had dared, that on his head the weight
Of punishment would fall.   That dreadful fear
Resolved her, and she waved her head, and raised
Her hand, to bid the Prince depart in haste,
With looks whose painful seriousness forbade
All farther effort.   Yet unwillingly,
And boding evil, Madoc from the shore
Pushed off his little boat.   She on its way
Stood gazing for a moment, lost in thought,
Then struck into the woods.

           Swift through the lake
Madoc's strong arm impelled the light canoe.
Fainter and fainter to his distant ear
The sound of battle came; and now the Moon
Arose in heaven, and poured o'er lake and land
A soft and mellowing ray.   Along the shore
Llaian was wandering with distracted steps,
And groaning for her child. · She saw the boat
Approach; and as on Madoc's naked limbs,
And on his countenance, the moonbeam fell,
And as she saw the boy in that dim light,
It seemed as though the Spirits of the dead
Were moving on the waters; and she stood
With open lips that breathed not, and fixed eyes,
Watching the unreal shapes: but when the boat
Drew nigh, and Madoc landed, and she saw
His step substantial, and the child came near,
Unable then to move, or speak, or breathe,
Down on the sand she sunk.

           But who can tell,
Who comprehend, her agony of joy,
When, by the Prince's care restored to sense,
She recognized her child, she heard the name
Of mother from that voice, which, sure, she thought
Had poured upon some Priest's remorseless ear
Its last vain prayer for life! No tear relieved
The insupportable feeling that convulsed
Her swelling breast.   She looked, and looked, and felt
The child, lest some delusion should have mocked
Her soul to madness; then the gushing joy
Burst forth, and with caresses and with tears
She mingled broken prayers of thanks to heaven.

And now the Prince, when joy had had its course,
Said to her, Knowest thou the mountain path?
For I would to the battle.   But at that,
A sudden damp of dread came over her,—
O leave us not! she cried; lest haply ill
Should have befallen! for I remember now,
How in the woods I saw a savage band
Making toward Caermadoc, and I hid,
Lest they should stop my going.   God forefend

The evil that I fear!—What! Madoc cried,
Were ye then left defenceless!—She replied,
All fled to arms: there was no time for thought,
Nor counsel, in that sudden ill; nor one
Of all thy people, who could, in that hour,
Have brooked home-duty, when thy life or death
Hung on the chance.   •

           Now God be merciful!
Cried he;—for of Goervyl did he think,
And the cold sweat started at every pore—
Give me the boy!—he travels all too slow.
Then in his arms he took him, and sped on,
Suffering more painful terrors, than of late
His own near death provoked.   They held their way
In silence up the heights; and, when at length
They reached the entrance of the vale, the Prince
Bade her remain, while he went on, to spy
The footsteps of the spoiler.   Soon he saw
Men, in the moonlight, stretched upon the ground;
And quickening then his pace, in worse alarm,
Along the shade, with cautious step, he moved
Toward one, to seize his weapons; 't was a corpse;
Nor whether, at the sight, to hope or fear
Yet knew he.   But anon, a steady light,
As of a taper, seen in his own home,
Comforted him; and, drawing nearer now,
He saw his sister on her knees, beside
The rushes, ministering to a wounded man.
Safe that the dear one lived, then back he sped
With joyful haste, and summoned Llaian on,
And in loud talk advanced.   Erillyab first
Came forward at the sound; for she had faith
To trust the voice.—They live! they live! she cried;
God hath redeemed them!—Nor the maiden yet
Believed the actual joy: like one astound,
Or as if struggling with a dream, she stood,
Till he came close, and spread his arms, and called
Goervyl!—and she fell in his embrace.

But Madoc lingered not; his eager soul
Was in the war; in haste he donned his arms; ·
And, as he felt his own good sword again,
Exulting played his heart.—Boy, he exclaimed
To Mervyn, arm thyself, and follow me!
For, in this conquest, we shall break the power
Of our blood-thirsty foe: and in thine age,
Wouldst thou not wish, when young men crowd around,
To hear thee chronicle their fathers' deeds,
Wouldst thou not wish to add,—And I, too, fought
In that day's conflict!

           Mervyn's cheek turned pale
A moment, then, with terror all suffused,
Grew fever-red.   Nay, nay! Goervyl cried,
He is too young for battles.—But the Prince,
With erring judgment, in that fear-flushed cheek
Beheld the glow of enterprising hope,
And youthful courage.   I was such a boy,
Sister! he cried, at Counsylit; and that day,
In my first field, with stripling arm, smote down
Many a tall Saxon.   Saidst thou not but now,
How bravely, in the fight of yesterday,
He fleshed his sword,—and wouldst thou keep him here
And rob him of his glory? See his cheek!
How it hath crimsoned at the unworthy thought!
Arm !arm! and to the battle!

           How her heart

Then panted! how, with late regret, and vain,
Senena wished Goervyl then had heard
The secret, trembling on her lips so oft,
So oft by shame withheld. She thought that now
She could have fallen upon her Lady's neck,
And told her all; but when she saw the Prince,
Imperious shame forbade her, and she felt
It were an easier thing to die than speak.
Availed not now regret or female fear!
She mailed her delicate limbs; beneath the plate
Compressed her bosom; on her golden locks
The helmet's overheavy load she placed;
Hung from her neck the shield; and, though the sword
Which swung beside her lightest she had chosen,
Though in her hand she held the slenderest spear,
Alike unwieldy, for the maiden's grasp,
The sword and ashen lance. But as she touched
The murderous point, an icy shudder ran
Through every fibre of her trembling frame;
And, overcome by womanly terror then,
The damsel to Goervyl turned, and let
Her breastplate fall, and on her bosom placed
The Lady's hand, and hid her face, and cried
Save me! The warrior, who beheld the act,
And heard not the low voice, with angry eye
Glowed on the seemly boy of feeble heart.
But, in Goervyl, joy had overpowered
The wonder; joy, to find the boy she loved
Was one, to whom her heart with closer love
Might cling; and to her brother she exclaimed,
She must not go! We women in the war
Have done our parts.

        A moment Madoc dwelt
On the false Mervyn, with an eye from whence
Displeasure did not wholly pass away,
Nor loitering to resolve Love's riddle now,
To Malinal he turned, where, on his couch,
The wounded youth was laid.—True friend, said he,
And brother mine,—for truly, by that name
I trust to greet thee,—if, in this near fight,
My hour should overtake me,—as who knows
The lot of war?—Goervyl hath my charge
To 'quite thee for thy service with herself;
That so thou mayëst raise up seed to me
Of mine own blood, who may inherit here
The obedience of thy people and of mine—
Malinal took his hand, and to his lips
Feebly he prest it, saying, One boon more,
Father and friend, I ask!—if thou shouldst meet
Yuhidthiton in battle, think of me.

XVIII.

The Victory.

Merciful God! how horrible is night
Upon the plain of Aztlan! there the shout
Of battle, the barbarian yell, the bray
Of dissonant instruments, the clang of arms,
The shriek of agony, the groan of death,
In one wild uproar and continuous din,
Shake the still air; while, overhead, the Moon,
Regardless of the stir of this low world,
Holds on her heavenly way. Still unallayed
By slaughter raged the battle, unrelaxed

By lengthened toil; anger supplying still
Strength undiminished for the desperate strife.
And lo! where yonder, on the temple top,
Blazing aloft, the sacrificial fire
Scene more accurst and hideous than the war
Displays to all the vale; for whosoe'er
That night the Aztecas could bear away,
Hoaman or Briton, thither was he borne;
And, as they stretched him on the stone of blood,
Did the huge tambour of the God, with voice
Loud as the thunder-peal, and heard as far,
Proclaim the act of death, more visible
Than in broad day-light, by those midnight fires
Distinctlier seen. Sight, that with horror filled
The Cymry, and to mightier efforts roused.
Howbeit, this abhorred idolatry
Worked for their safety; the deluded foes,
Obstinate in their faith, forbearing still
The mortal stroke, that they might to the God
Present the living victim, and to him
Let the life flow.

        And now the orient sky
Glowed with the ruddy morning, when the Prince
Came to the field. He lifted up his voice,
And shouted Madoc! Madoc! They who heard
The cry, astonished, turned; and when they saw
The countenance his open helm disclosed,
They echoed, Madoc! Madoc! Through the host
Spread the miraculous joy,—He lives! he lives!
He comes himself in arms!—Lincoya heard,
As he had raised his arm to strike a foe,
And stayed the stroke, and thrust him off, and cried,
Go, tell the tidings to thy countrymen,
Madoc is in the war! Tell them his God
Hath set the White King free? Astonishment
Seized on the Azteca; on all who heard,
Amazement and dismay; and Madoc now
Stood in the foremost battle, and his sword,—
His own good sword,—flashed, like the sudden death
Of lightning in their eyes.

        The King of Aztlan
Heard and beheld, and in his noble heart
Heroic hope arose. Forward he moved,
And, in the shock of battle, front to front,
Encountered Madoc. A strong-statured man
Coanocotzin stood, one well who knew
The ways of war, and never yet in fight
Had found an equal foe. Adown his back
Hung the long robe of feathered royalty;
Gold fenced his arms and legs; upon his helm
A sculptured snake protends the arrowy tongue;
Around a coronet of plumes arose, .
Brighter than beam the rainbow hues of light,
Or than the evening glories which the sun
Slants o'er the moving many-coloured sea,
Such their surpassing beauty; bells of gold
Embossed his glittering helmet, [58] and where'er
Their sound was heard, there lay the press of war,
And death was busiest there. Over the breast,
And o'er the golden breastplate of the King,
A feathery cuirass, beautiful to eye,
Light as the robe of peace, yet strong to save;
For the sharp faulchion's baffled edge would glide
From its smooth softness. On his arm he held
A buckler overlaid with beaten gold;
And so he stood, guarding his thighs and legs,

His breast and shoulders also, with the length
Of his broad shield.•
            Opposed, in mail complete,
Stood Madoc in his strength. The flexile chains
Gave play to his full muscles, and displayed
How broad his shoulders, and his ample breast.
Small was his shield, there broadest where it fenced
The well of life, and gradual to a point
Lessening ; steel-strong, and wieldy in his grasp.
It bore those blazoned eaglets, at whose sight,
Along the Marches, or where holy Dee
Through Cestrian pastures rolls his tamer stream,
So oft the yeoman had, in days of yore,
Cursing his perilous tenure, wound the horn, 59
And warden from the castle-tower rung out
The loud alarum-bell, heard far and wide.
Upon his helm no sculptured dragon sate,
Sate no fantastic terrors ; a white plume
Nodded above, far-seen, floating like foam .
On the war-tempest. 60 Man to man they stood,
The King of Aztlan and the Ocean Chief.

Fast, on the intervening buckler, fell
The Azteca's stone faulchion. Who hath watched
The midnight lightnings of the summer storm,
That, with their awful blaze, irradiate heaven,
Then leave a blacker night ? so quick, so fierce,
Flashed Madoc's sword, which, like the serpent's tongue,
Seemed double, in its rapid whirl of light.
Unequal arms ! for on the British shield
Availed not the stone faulchion's brittle edge,
And, in the golden buckler, Madoc's sword
Bit deep. Coanocotzin saw, and dropt
The unprofitable weapon, and received
His ponderous club,—that club, beneath whose force,
Driven by his father's arm, Tepollomi
Had fallen subdued,—and fast and fierce he drove
The massy weight on Madoc. From his shield,
The deadening force, communicated, ran
Up his stunned arm ; anon, upon his helm,
Crashing, it came ;—his eyes shot fire, his brain
Swam dizzy,—he recoils,—he reels,—again
The club descends.
           That danger to himself
Recalled the Lord of Ocean. On he sprung,
Within the falling weapon's curve of death,
Shunning its frustrate aim, and breast to breast
He grappled with the King. The pliant mail
Bent to his straining limbs, while plates of gold,
The feathery robe, the buckler's amplitude,
Cumbered the Azteca, and from his arm,
Clenched in the Briton's mighty grasp, at once
He dropt the impeding buckler, and let fall
The unfastened club ; which when the Prince beheld,
He thrust him off, and drawing back resumed
The sword that from his wrist suspended hung,
And twice he smote the King ; twice from the quilt
Of plumes the iron glides ; and lo ! the King,
So well his soldiers watch their monarch's need,
Shakes in his hand a spear.
              But now a cry
Burst on the ear of Madoc, and he saw
Through opening ranks, where Urien was conveyed
A captive, to his death. Grief then and shame
And rage inspired him. With a mighty blow
He cleft Coanocotzin's helm ; exposed

The monarch stood ;—again the thunder-stroke
Came on him, and he fell.—The multitude,
Forgetful of their country and themselves,
Crowd round their dying King. Madoc, whose eye
Still followed Urien, called upon his men,
And, through the broken army of the foe,
Prest to his rescue.
           But far off the old man
Was borne with furious speed. Ririd alone
Pursued his path, and through the thick of war
Close on the captors, with avenging sword,
Followed right on, and through the multitude,
And through the gate of Aztlan, made his way,
And through the streets, till, from the temple-mound,
The press of Pabas and the populace
Repelled him, while the old man was hurried up.
Hark ! that infernal tambour ! o'er the lake
Its long loud thunders roll, and through the hills,
Awakening all their echoes. Ye accurst,
Ye blow the fall too soon ! Ye Dogs of Hell,
The Hart is yet at bay !—Thus long the old man,
As one exhausted or resigned, had lain,
Resisting not ; but, at that knell of death,
Springing with unexpected force, he freed
His feet, and shook the Pabas from their hold,
And, with his armed hand, between the eyes
Smote one so sternly, that to earth he fell,
Bleeding, and all astound. A man of proof
Was Urien in his day ; thought worthiest,
In martial thewes and manly discipline,
To train the sons of Owen. He had lost
Youth's supple sleight ; yet still the skill remained,
And in his stiffened limbs a strength, which yet
Might put the young to shame. And now he set
His back against the altar, resolute
Not as a victim by the knife to die,
But in the act of battle, as became
A man grown grey in arms : and in his heart
There was a living hope ; for now he knew
That Madoc lived, nor could the struggle long
Endure against that arm.
             Soon was the way
Laid open by the sword ; for, side by side,
The brethren of Aberfraw mowed their path ;
And, following close, the Cymry drive along,
Till on the summit of the mound, the cry
Of victory rings aloud. The temple floor,
So often which had reeked with innocent blood,
Steams now with righteous slaughter. Franticly,
In the wild fury of their desperate zeal,
The Priests crowd round the God, and with their knives
Hack at the foe, and call on him to save,—
At the altar, at the Idol's foot they fall.
Nor with less frenzy did the multitude
Flock to defend their God. Fast as they fell,
New victims rushed upon the British sword ;
And sure that day had rooted from the earth
The Aztecas, and on their conquerors drawn
Promiscuous ruin, had not Madoc now
Beheld from whence the fearless ardour sprang ;—
They saw Mexitli ; momently they hoped
That he would rise in vengeance. Madoc seized
A massy club, and from his azure throne
Shattered the giant idol.
             At that sight
The men of Aztlan pause ; so was their pause

Dreadful, as when a multitude expect
The Earthquake's second shock.   But when they saw
Earth did not open, nor the temple fall
To crush their impious enemies, dismayed,
They felt themselves forsaken by their Gods ;
Then from their temples and their homes they fled,
And, leaving Aztlan to the conqueror,
Sought the near city, whither they had sent
Their women, timely saved.
              But Tlalala,
With growing fury as the danger grew,
Raged in the battle ; but Yuhidthiton
Still with calm courage, till no hope remained,
Fronted the rushing foe.   When all was vain,
When back within the gate Cadwallon's force,
Resistless, had compelled them, then the Chief
Called on the Tiger,—Let us bear from hence
The dead Ocellopan, the slaughtered King ;
Not to the Strangers should their bones be left,
O Tlalala !—The Tiger wept with rage,
With generous anger.   To the place of death,
Where, side by side, the noble dead were stretched,
They fought their way. Eight warriors joined their
       shields ;
On these, a bier which well beseemed the dead,
The lifeless Chiefs were laid.   Yuhidthiton
Called on the people,—Men of Aztlan ! yet
One effort more ! Bear hence Ocellopan,
And save the body of your noble King !
Not to the Strangers should their bones be left !—
That whoso heard, with wailing and loud cries,
Prest round the body-bearers ; few indeed,
For few were they, who, in that fearful hour,
Had ears to hear,—but with a holy zeal,
Careless of death, around the bier they ranged
Their bulwark breasts.   So toward the farther gate
They held their steady way, while outermost,
In unabated valour, Tlalala
Faced, with Yuhidthiton, the foe's pursuit.
Vain valour then, and fatal piety,
As the fierce conquerors bore on their retreat,
If Madoc had not seen their perilous strife :
Remembering Malinal, and in his heart
Honouring a gallant foe, he called aloud,
And bade his people cease the hot pursuit.
So, through the city gate, they bore away
The dead ; and, last of all their countrymen,
Leaving their homes and temples to the foe,
Yuhidthiton and Tlalala retired.

XIX.
The Funeral.

SOUTHWARD of Aztlan stood, beside the Lake,
A city of the Aztecas, by name
Patamba.   Thither, from the first alarm,
The women and infirm old men were sent,
And children : thither they who from the fight,
And from the fall of Aztlan, had escaped,
In scattered bands repaired.   Their City lost,
Their Monarch slain, their Idols overthrown,—
These tidings spread dismay : but to dismay
Succeeded horror soon, and kindling rage,
Horror, by each new circumstance increased,
By numbers, rage emboldened.   Lo ! to the town,

Lamenting loud, a numerous train approach,
Like mountain torrents, swelling as they go.
Borne in the midst, upon the bier of shields,
The noble dead were seen.   To tenfold grief
That spectacle provoked, to tenfold wrath
That anguish stung them.   With their yells and groans
Curses are mixed, and threats, and bitter vows
Of vengeance full and speedy.   From the wreck
Of Aztlan who is saved ? Tezozomoc,
Chief servant of the Gods, their favoured Priest,
The voice by whom they speak ; young Tlalala,
Whom even defeat with fresher glory crowns ;
And, full of fame, their country's rock of strength,
Yuhidthiton : him to their sovereign slain
Allied in blood, mature in wisdom, him
Of valour unsurpassable, by all
Beloved and honoured, him the general voice
Acclaims their King ; him they demand, to lead
Their gathered force to battle, to revenge
Their Lord, their Gods, their kinsmen, to redeem
Their altars and their country.
             But the dead
First from the nation's gratitude require
The rites of death.   On mats of mountain palm,
Wrought of rare texture and of richest hues,
The slaughtered warriors, side by side, were laid ;
Their bodies wrapt in many-coloured robes
Of gossampine, bedecked with gems and gold.
The livid paleness of the countenance
A mask concealed, and hid their ghastly wounds.
The Pabas stood around, and one by one,
Placed in their hands the sacred aloe leaves,
With mystic forms and characters inscribed ;
And as each leaf was given, Tezozomoc
Addressed the dead,—So may ye safely pass
Between the mountains, which, in endless war,
Hurtle, with horrible uproar, and crush
Of rocks that meet in battle.[61] Armed with this,
In safety shall ye walk along the road,
Where the Great Serpent from his lurid eyes
Shoots lightning, and across the guarded way
Vibrates his tongue of fire.   Receive the third,
And cross the waters where the Crocodile
In vain expects his prey.   Your passport this
Through the Eight Deserts ; through the Eight Hills, this ;
And this be your defence against the Wind,
Whose fury sweeps, like dust, the uprooted rocks,
Whose keenness cuts the soul.   Ye noble Dead,
Protected with these potent amulets,
Soon shall your Spirits reach triumphantly
The Palace of the Sun !
            The funeral train
Moved to Mexitli's temple.   First on high
The noble dead were borne : in loud lament
Then follow'd all by blood allied to them,
Or by affection's voluntary ties
Attach'd more closely, brethren, kinsmen, wives.
The Peers of Aztlan, all who from the sword
Of Britain had escaped, honouring the rites,
Came clad in rich array, and bore the arms
And ensigns of the dead.   The slaves went last,
And dwarfs, the pastime of the living chiefs,
In life their sport and mockery, and in death
Their victims.   Wailing and with funeral hymns,
The long procession moved.   Mexitli's Priest,
With all his servants, from the temple-gate

33

Advanced to meet the train. Two piles were built
Within the sacred court, of odorous wood,
And rich with gums ; on these, with all their robes,
Their ensigns and their arms, they laid the dead:
Then lit the pile. The rapid light ran up,
Up flamed the fire, and o'er the darken'd sky
Sweet clouds of incense curl'd.
                        The Pabas then
Perform'd their bloody office. First they slew
The women whom the slaughter'd most had loved,
Who most had loved the dead. Silent they went
Toward the fatal stone, resisting not,
Nor sorrowing, nor dismay'd, but as it seem'd,
Stunn'd, senseless. One alone there was, whose cheek
Was flush'd, whose eye was animate with fire;
Her most in life Coanocotzin prized,
By ten years' love endear'd, his counsellor,
His friend, the partner of his secret thoughts;
Such had she been, such merited to be.
She, as she bared her bosom to the knife,
Called on Yuhidthiton—Take heed, O king!
Aloud she cried, and pointed to the Priests ;
Beware these wicked men! they to the war
Forced my dead Lord—Thou knowest, and I know,
He loved the Strangers; that his noble mind,
Enlighten'd by their lore, had willingly
Put down these cursed altars!—As she spake,
They dragg'd her to the stone—Nay! nay! she cried,
There needs not force! I go to join my Lord!
His blood and mine be on you!—Ere she ceased,
The knife was in her breast. Tezozomoc,
Trembling with wrath, held up toward the Sun
Her reeking heart.
                        The dwarfs and slaves died last.
That bloody office done, they gather'd up
The ashes of the dead, and coffer'd them
Apart; the teeth with them, which unconsumed
Among the ashes lay, a single lock
Shorn from the corpse, and his lip-emerald
Now held to be the Spirit's flawless heart,
In better worlds. The Priest then held on high
The little ark which shrined his last remains,
And call'd upon the people ;—Lo! behold!
This was your King, the bountiful, the brave,
Coanocotzin! Men of Aztlan, hold
His memory holy! learn from him to love
Your country and your Gods; for them to live
Like him, like him to die. So from yon Heaven,
Where in the Spring of Light his Spirit bathes,
Often shall he descend; hover above
On evening clouds, or plumed with rainbow wings,
Sip honey from the flowers, and warble joy.
Honour his memory! emulate his worth!
So saying, in the temple-tower he laid
The relics of the King.
                        These duties done,
The living claim their care. His birth, his deeds,
The general love, the general voice, have mark'd
Yuhidthiton for King. Bare-headed, bare
Of foot, of limb, scarf'd only round the loins,
The Chieftain to Mexitli's temple moved,
And knelt before the God. Tezozomoc
King over Aztlan there anointed him,
And over him, from hallow'd cedar-branch,
Sprinkled the holy water. Then the Priest
In a black garment robed him, figured white

With skulls and bones, a garb to emblem war,
Slaughter, and ruin, his imperial tasks.
Next in his hand the Priest a censer placed ;
And while he knelt, directing to the God
The steaming incense, thus address'd the King:
Chosen by the people, by the Gods approved,
Swear to protect thy subjects, to maintain
The worship of thy fathers, to observe
Their laws, to make the sun pursue his course,
The clouds descend in rain, the rivers hold
Their wonted channels, and the fruits of earth
To ripen in their season: Swear, O King!
And prosper as thou holdest good thine oath.[62]
He raised his voice, and swore. Then on his brow
Tezozomoc the crown of Aztlan placed;
And in the robe of emblem'd royalty,
Preceded by the golden wands of state,
Yuhidthiton went forth, anointed King.

XX.

The Death of Coatel.

WHEN now the multitude beheld their King,
In gratulations of reiterate joy
They shout his name, and bid him lead them on
To vengeance. But to answer that appeal,
Tezozomoc advanced—Oh! go not forth,
Cried the Chief Paba, till the land be purged
From her offence! No God will lead ye on,
While there is guilt in Aztlan. Let the Priests
Who from the ruin'd city have escaped,
And all who in her temples have perform'd
The ennobling service of her injured Gods,
Gather together now.
                        He spake; the train
Assembled, priests and matrons, youths and maids.
Servants of Heaven! aloud the Archpriest began,
The Gods had favour'd Aztlan; bound for death
The White King lay: our countrymen were strong
In battle, and the conquest had been ours,—
I speak not from myself, but as the Powers,
Whose voice on earth I am, impel the truth,—
The conquest had been ours; but treason lurk'd
In Aztlan, treason and foul sacrilege;
And therefore were her children in the hour
Of need abandon'd; therefore were her youth
Cut down, her altars therefore overthrown.
The White King, whom ye saw upon the Stone
Of Sacrifice, and whom ye held in bonds,
Stood in the foremost fight and slew your Lord.
Not by a God, O Aztecas, enlarged,
Broke he his bondage! by a mortal hand,
An impious, sacrilegious, traitorous hand,
Your city was betray'd, your King was slain,
Your shrines polluted. The insulted Power,
He who is terrible, beheld the deed,
And now he calls for vengeance.
                        Stern he spake,
And from Mexitli's altar bade the Priest
Bring forth the sacred water. In his hand
He took the vase, and held it up, and cried,
Cursed be he who did this deed! Accursed
The father who begat him, and the breast
At which he fed! Death be his portion now,
Eternal infamy his lot on earth,

His doom eternal horrors! Let his name,
From sire to son, be in the people's mouth,
Through every generation! Let a curse
Of deep and pious and effectual hate,
For ever follow the abhorred name;
And every curse inflict upon his soul
A stab of mortal anguish.

      Then he gave
The vase—Drink one by one! the innocent
Boldly; on them the water hath no power.
But let the guilty tremble! it shall flow
A draught of agony and death to him,
A stream of fiery poison.[63]
      Coatel!
What were thy horrors when the fatal vase
Pass'd to thy trial,—when Tezozomoc
Fix'd his keen eye on thee! A deathiness
Came over her,—her blood ran back,—her joints
Shook like the palsy, and the dreadful cup
Dropp'd from her conscious hold. The Priest exclaim'd,
The hand of God! the avenger manifest!
Drag her to the altar!—At that sound of death
The life forsook her limbs, and down she fell,
Senseless. They dragg'd her to the Stone of Blood,
All senseless as she lay;—in that dread hour
Nature was kind.
     Tezozomoc then cried,
Bring forth the kindred of this wretch accurst,
That none pollute the earth. An aged Priest
Came forth and answer'd, There is none but I,
The father of the dead.
     To death with him!
Exclaim'd Tezozomoc; to death with him;
And purify the nation!—But the King
Permitted not that crime—Chief of the Priests,
If he be guilty, let the guilty bleed,
Said he; but never, while I live and reign,
The innocent shall suffer. Hear him speak!

Hear me! the old man replied. That fatal day
I never saw my child. At morn she left
The city, seeking flowers to dress the shrine
Of Coatlantona; and that at eve
I stood among the Pabas in the gate,
Blessing our soldiers, as they issued out,
Let them who saw bear witness—Two came forth,
And testified Aculhua spake the words
Of truth.
    Full well I know, the old man pursued,
My daughter loved the Strangers,—that her heart
Was not with Aztlan: but not I the cause!
Ye all remember how the Maid was given,—
She being, in truth, of all our Maids the flower,—
In spousals to Lincoya, him who fled
From sacrifice. It was a misery
To me to see my only child condemn'd
In early widowhood to waste her youth,—
My only and my beautifullest girl!
Chief of the Priests, you order'd, I obey'd.
Not mine the fault, if, when Lincoya fled,
And fought among the enemies, her heart
Was with her husband.
     He is innocent!
He shall not die! Yuhidthiton exclaim'd.
Nay, King Yuhidthiton! Aculhua cried,
I merit death. My country overthrown,

My daughter slain, alike demand on me
That justice. When her years of ministry
Vow'd to the temple had expired, my love,
My selfish love, still suffer'd her to give
Her youth to me, by filial piety
In widowhood detain'd. That selfish crime
Heavily,—heavily,—do I expiate!
But I am old; and she was all to me.
O King Yuhidthiton, I ask for death;
In mercy, let me die; cruel it were
To bid me waste away alone in age,
By the slow pain of grief—Give me the knife
Which pierced my daughter's bosom!
      The old man
Moved to the altar; none opposed his way;
With a firm hand he buried in his heart
The reeking blade, and fell upon his child.

XXI.

The Sports.[64]

A TRANSITORY gloom that sight of death
Impress'd upon the assembled multitude;
But soon the brute and unreflecting crew
Turn'd to their sports. Some bare their olive limbs,
And in the race contend; with hopes and fears,
Which rouse to rage, some urge the mimic war.
Here one upon his ample shoulders bears
A comrade's weight, upon whose head a third
Stands poised, like Mercury in act to fly.
There other twain upon their shoulders prop
A forked beam, while on its height the third
To nimble cadence shifts his glancing feet,
And shakes a plume aloft, and wheels around
A wreath of bells with modulating sway.
Here round a lofty mast the dancers move
Quick, to quick music; from its top affix'd,
Each holds a coloured cord, and, as they weave
The complex crossings of the mazy dance,
The chequered network twists around the tree,
Its intertexture of harmonious hues.
But now a shout went forth, the Flyers mount,
And from all meaner sports the multitude
Flock to their favourite pastime. In the ground,
Branchless and barked, the trunk of some tall pine
Is planted; near its summit a square frame;
Four cords pass through the perforated square,
And fifty times and twice around the tree,
A mystic number, are entwined above.
Four Aztecas, equipped with wings, ascend,
And round them bind the ropes; anon they wave
Their pinions, and upborne on spreading plumes
Launch on the air, and wheel in circling flight,
The lengthened cords untwisting as they fly.
A fifth above, upon the perilous point
Dances, and shakes a flag; and on the frame,
Others the while maintain their giddy stand,
Till now, with many a round, the wheeling cords
Draw near their utmost length, and toward the ground
The aërial circlers speed; then down the ropes
They spring, and on their way from line to line
Pass, while the shouting multitude endure
A shuddering admiration.
     On such sports,

Their feelings centered in the joy of sight,
The multitude stood gazing, when a man,
Breathless, and with broad eyes, came running on,
His pale lips trembling, and his bloodless cheek
Like one who meets a lion in his path.
The fire! the fire! the temple! he exclaimed;
Mexitli!—They, astonished at his words,
Hasten toward the wonder,—and behold!
The inner fane is sheeted white with fire.
Dumb with affright they stood; the inquiring King
Looked to Tezozomoc; the Priest replied,
I go! the Gods protect me;—and therewith
He entered boldly in the house of flame.
But instant bounding with inebriate joy,
He issues forth—The God! the God! he cries.
Joy!—joy!—the God!—the visible hand of Heaven!
Repressing then his transport,—Ye all know
How that in Aztlan Madoc's impious hand
Destroyed Mexitli's Image;—it is here,
Unbroken and the same!—Toward the gate
They press; they see the Giant Idol there,
The serpent girding him, his neck with hearts
Beaded, and in his hand the club,—even such
As oft in Aztlan, on his azure throne,
They had adored the God, they see him now,
Unbroken and the same!—Again the Priest
Entered; again a second joy inspired
To frenzy all around;—for forth he came,
Shouting with new delight,—for in his hand
The banner of the nation he upheld,
That banner to their fathers sent from Heaven,
By them abandoned to the conqueror.

He motioned silence, and the crowd were still.
People of Aztlan! he began, when first
Your fathers from their native land went forth,
In search of better seats, this banner came
From Heaven. The Famine and the Pestilence
Had been among them; in their hearts the spring
Of courage was dried up: with midnight fires
Radiate, by midnight thunders heralded,
This banner came from Heaven; and with it came
Health, valour, victory. Aztecas! again
The God restores the blessing. To the God
Move now in solemn dance of grateful joy;
Exalt for him the song.
                    They formed the dance,
They raised the hymn, and sung Mexitli's praise.
Glory to thee, the Great, the Terrible,
Mexitli, guardian God!—From whence art thou,
O Son of Mystery?—From whence art thou,
Whose sire thy mother knew not? She at eve
Walked in the temple-court, and saw from Heaven
A plume descend, as bright and beautiful,
As if some spirit had embodied there
The rainbow hues, or dipt it in the light
Of setting suns. To her it floated down;
She placed it in her bosom, to bedeck
The altar of the God; she sought it there;
Amazed she found it not; amazed she felt
Another life infused.—From whence art thou,
O Son of Mystery? From whence art thou,
Whose sire thy mother knew not?
                        Grief was hers,
Wonder and grief, for life was in her womb,
And her stern children with revengeful eyes

Beheld their mother's shame. She saw their frowns,
She knew their plots of blood. Where shall she look
For succour, when her sons conspire her death?
Where hope for comfort, when her daughter whets
The impious knife of murder?—From her womb
The voice of comfort came, the timely aid;
Already at her breast the blow was aim'd,
When forth Mexitli leapt, and in his hand
The angry spear, to punish and to save.
Glory to thee, the Great, the Terrible,
Mexitli, guardian God!
                    Arise and save,
Mexitli, save thy people! Dreadful one,
Arise, redeem thy city, and revenge!
An impious, an impenetrable foe,
Hath blackened thine own altars, with the blood
Of thine own priests; hath dashed thine Image down.
In vain did valour's naked breast oppose
Their mighty arms; in vain the feeble sword
On their impenetrable mail was driven.
Not against thee, Avenger, shall those arms
Avail, nor that impenetrable mail
Resist the fiery arrows of thy wrath.
Arise, go forth in anger, and destroy!

XXII.

The Death of Lincoya.

AZTLAN, meantime, presents a hideous scene
Of slaughter. The hot sunbeam, in her streets,
Parched the bloodpools; the slain were heaped in hills;
The victors, stretched in every little shade,
With unhelmed heads, reclining on their shields,
Slept the deep sleep of weariness. Ere long,
To needful labour rising, from the gates
They drag the dead; and with united toil,
They dig upon the plain the general grave,
The grave of thousands, deep and wide and long.
Ten such they delved, and o'er the multitudes
Who levelled with the plain the deep-dug pits,
Ten monumental hills they heaped on high.
Next, horror heightening joy, they overthrew
The skull-built towers, the files of human heads,
And earth to earth consigned them. To the flames
They cast the idols, and upon the wind
Scattered their ashes; then the temples fell,
Whose black and putrid walls were scaled with blood, 65
And not one stone of those accursèd piles
Was on another left.
                    Victorious thus
In Aztlan, it behoved the Cymry now
There to collect their strength, and there await,
Or thence with centred numbers urge, the war.
For this was Ririd missioned to the ships,
For this Lincoya from the hills invites
Erillyab and her tribe. There did not breathe,
On this wide world, a happier man that day
Than young Lincoya, when from their retreat
He bade his countrymen come repossess
The land of their forefathers; proud at heart
To think how great a part himself had borne
In their revenge, and that belovèd one,
The gentle saviour of the Prince, whom well
He knew his own dear love, and for the deed

Still dearer loved the dearest.   Round the youth,
Women and children, the infirm and old,
Gather to hear his tale ; and as they stood
With eyes of steady wonder, outstretched necks,
And open lips of listening eagerness,
Fast played the tide of triumph in his veins,
Flushed his brown cheek, and kindled his dark eye.
And now, reposing from his toil awhile,
Lincoya, on a crag above the straits,
Sate underneath a tree, whose twinkling leaves
Sung to the gale at noon.   Ayayaca
Sate by him in the shade : The old man had loved
The youth beside him from his boyhood up,
And still would call him boy.   They sate and watched
The laden bisons winding down the way,
The multitude who now with joy forsook
Their desolated dwellings ; and their talk
Was of the days of sorrow, when they groaned
Beneath the intolerable yoke, till sent
By the Great Spirit o'er the pathless deep,
Prince Madoc the Deliverer came to save.
As thus they communed, came a woman up,
Seeking Lincoya ; 't was Aculhua's slave,
The nurse of Coatel.   Her wretched eye,
Her pale and livid countenance, foretold
Some tale of misery, that his life-blood ebbed
In ominous fear.   But when he heard her words
Of death, he seized the lance, and raised his arm
To strike the blow of comfort.
                              The old man
Caught his uplifted hand.—O'erhasty boy,
Quoth he, regain her yet, if she was dear !
Seek thy beloved in the Land of Souls,
And beg her from the Gods.   The Gods will hear,
And in just recompense of fearless faith,
Restore their charge.
                        The miserable youth
Turned at his words a hesitating eye.
  knew a prisoner,—so the old man pursued,
Or hoping to beguile the youth's despair
With tales that suited the despair of youth,
Or credulous himself of what he told,—
  knew a prisoner once who welcomed death
With merriment and songs and joy of heart,
Because, he said, the friends whom he loved best
Were gone before him to the Land of Souls ;
Nor would they to resume their mortal state,
Even when the keeper of the Land allowed,
Forsake its pleasures ; therefore he rejoiced
To die and join them there.   I questioned him,
How of these hidden things unknowable
So certainly he spake.   The man replied,
One of our nation lost the maid he loved, [66]
Nor would he bear his sorrow,—being one
Into whose heart fear never found a way,—
But to the Country of the Dead pursued
Her spirit.   Many toils he underwent,
And many dangers gallantly surpassed,
Till to the Country of the Dead he came.
Gently the Guardian of the Land received
The living suppliant ; listened to his prayer,
And gave him back the Spirit of the Maid.
But from that happy country, from the songs
Of joyance, from the splendour-sparkling dance,
Unwillingly compelled, the Maiden's Soul
Loathed to return ; and he was warned to guard

The subtle captive well and warily,
Till in her mortal tenement relodged,
Earthly delights might win her to remain
A sojourner on earth.   Such lessoning
The Ruler of the Souls departed gave ;
And mindful of his charge the adventurer brought
His subtle captive home.   There underneath
The shelter of a hut, his friends had watched
The Maiden's corpse, secured it from the sun,
And fanned away the insect swarms of heaven.
A busy hand marred all the enterprise :
Curious to see the Spirit, he unloosed
The knotted bag which held her, and she fled.
Lincoya, thou art brave ; where man has gone
Thou wouldst not fear to follow ?
                              Silently
Lincoya listened, and with unmoved eyes ;
At length he answered, Is the journey long ?
The old man replied, A way of many moons.
I know a shorter path ! exclaimed the youth.
And up he sprung, and from the precipice
Darted : A moment,—and Ayayaca heard
His body dash upon the rocks below.

XXIII.

Caradoc and Senena.

MAID of the golden locks, far other lot
May gentle Heaven assign thy happier love,
Blue-eyed Senena !—She, though not as yet
Had she put off her boy-habiliments,
Had told Goervyl all the history
Of her sad flight, and easy pardon gained
From that sweet heart, for guile which meant no ill,
And secrecy, in shame too long maintained.
With her dear Lady now, at this still hour
Of evening, is the seeming page gone forth,
Beside Caermadoc mere.   They loitered on,
Along the windings of its grassy shore,
In such free interchange of inward thought
As the calm hour invited ; or at times,
Willingly silent, listening to the bird
Whose one repeated melancholy note,
By oft repeating melancholy made,
Solicited the ear ; or gladlier now
Hearkening that cheerful one, who knoweth all
The songs of all the wingèd choristers, [67]
And in one sequence of melodious sounds
Pours all their music.   But a wilder strain
At fits came o'er the water ; rising now,
Now with a dying fall, in sink and swell
More exquisitely sweet than ever art
Of man evoked from instrument of touch,
Or beat, or breath. [68]   It was the evening gale,
Which, passing o'er the harp of Caradoc,
Swept all its chords at once, and blended all
Their music into one continuous flow.
The solitary Bard beside his harp
Leant underneath a tree, whose spreading boughs,
With broken shade that shifted to the breeze,
Played on the waving waters.   Overhead
There was the leafy murmur, at his foot
The lake's perpetual ripple ; and from far,
Borne on the modulating gale, was heard

The roaring of the mountain-cataract.—
A blind man would have loved the lovely spot.
Here was Senena by her Lady led,
Trembling, but not reluctant.   They drew nigh,
Their steps unheard upon the elastic moss,
Till playfully Goervyl, with quick touch,
Ran o'er the harp-strings.   At the sudden sound
He rose.—Hath then thy hand, quoth she, O Bard,
Forgot its cunning, that the wind should be
Thine harper?—Come! one strain for Britain's sake;
And let the theme be Woman!—He replied,
But if the strain offend, O Lady fair,
Blame thou the theme, not me!—Then to the harp
He sung,—Three things a wise man will not trust,
The Wind, the Sunshine of an April day,
And Woman's plighted faith.   I have beheld
The Weathercock upon the steeple-point
Steady from morn till eve; and I have seen
The bees go forth upon an April morn,
Secure the sunshine will not end in showers;
But when was Woman true?
                                    False Bard! thereat,
With smile of playful anger, she exclaimed,
False Bard! and slanderous song! Were such thy thoughts
Of woman, when thy youthful lays were heard
In Heilyn's hall?—But at that name his heart
Leaped, and his cheek with sudden flush was fired;
In Heilyn's hall, quoth he, I learned the song.
There was a Maid, who dwelt among the hills
Of Arvon, and to one of humbler birth
Had pledged her troth;—nor rashly, nor beguiled,—
They had been playmates in their infancy,
And she in all his thoughts had borne a part,
And all his joys.   The Moon and all the Stars
Witnessed their mutual vows; and for her sake
The song was framed; for in the face of day
She broke them.—But her name! Goervyl cried.
Quoth he, The poet loved her still too well,
To couple it with shame.
                              O fate unjust
Of womankind! she cried; our virtues bloom,
Like violets, in shade and solitude,
While evil eyes hunt all our failings out,
For evil tongues to bruit abroad in jest,
And song of obloquy!—I knew a Maid,
And she too dwelt in Arvon, and she too
Loved one of lowly birth, who ill repaid
Her spotless faith; for he to ill reports,
And tales of falsehood cunningly devised,
Lent a light ear, and to his rival left
The loathing Maid.   The wedding-day arrived,
The harpers and the gleemen, far and near,
Came to the wedding-feast; the wedding-guests
Were come, the altar dressed, the bridemaids met,
The father, and the bridegroom, and the priest
Wait for the bride.   But she the while did off
Her bridal robes, and clipt her golden locks,
And put on boy's attire, through wood and wild
To seek her own true love; and over sea,
Forsaking all for him, she followed him,
Nor hoping nor deserving fate so fair;
And at his side she stood, and heard him wrong
Her faith with slanderous tales; and his dull eye,
As it had learnt his heart's forgetfulness,
Knows not the trembling one, who even now

Yearns to forgive him all!
                              He turned, he knew
The blue-eyed Maid, who fell upon his breast.

XXIV.

The Embassy.

HARK! from the towers of Aztlan how the shouts
Of clamorous joy re-ring! the rocks and hills
Take up the joyful sound, and o'er the lake
Roll their slow echoes.—Thou art beautiful,
Queen of the Valley! thou art beautiful,
Thy walls, like silver, sparkle to the sun.
Melodious wave thy groves, thy garden-sweets
Enrich the pleasant air, upon the lake
Lie the long shadows of thy towers, and high
In heaven thy temple-pyramids arise,
Upon whose summit now, far visible
Against the clear blue sky, the Cross of Christ
Proclaims unto the nations round the news
Of thy redemption.   Thou art beautiful,
Aztlan! O City of the Cymbric Prince!
Long mayest thou flourish in thy beauty, long
Prosper beneath the righteous conqueror,
Who conquers to redeem! Long years of peace
And happiness await thy Lord and thee,
Queen of the Valley!
                              Hither joyfully
The Hoamen came to repossess the land
Of their forefathers.   Joyfully the youth
Come shouting, with acclaim of grateful praise,
Their great Deliverer's name; the old, in talk
Of other days, which mingled with their joy
Memory of many a hard calamity, 69
And thoughts of time and change, and human life
How changeful and how brief.   Prince Madoc met
Erillyab at the gate.—Sister and Queen,
Said he, here let us hold united reign,
O'er our united people; by one faith,
One interest bound, and closer to be linked
By laws and language and domestic ties,
Till both become one race, for ever more
Indissolubly knit.
                              O friend, she cried,
The last of all my family am I;
Yet sure, though last, the happiest, and by Heaven
Favoured abundantly above them all.
Dear friend, and brother dear! enough for me
Beneath the shadow of thy shield to dwell,
And see my people, by thy fostering care,
Made worthy of their fortune.   Graciously
Hath the Beloved One ordained all,
Educing good from ill, himself being good.
Then to the royal palace of the Kings
Of Aztlan, Madoc led Erillyab,
There, where her sires had held their ruder reign,
To pass the happy remnant of her years,
Honoured and loved by all.
                              Now had the Prince
Provided for defence, disposing all
As though a ready enemy approached.
But from Patamba yet no army moved;
Four Heralds only, by the King dispatched,

Drew nigh the town. The Hoamen, as they came,
Knew the green mantle of their privilege,
The symbols which they bore, an arrow-point
Depressed, a shield, a net, which, from the arm
Suspended, held their food. They through the gate
Pass with permitted entrance, and demand
To see the Ocean Prince. The Conqueror
Received them, and the elder thus began :
Thus to the White King, King Yuhidthiton
His bidding sends; such greeting as from foe
Foe may receive, where individual hate
Is none, but honour and assured esteem,
And what were friendship did the Gods permit,
The King of Aztlan sends. Oh dream not thou
That Aztlan is subdued; nor in the pride
Of conquest tempt thy fortune! Unprepared
For battle, at an hour of festival,
Her children were surprised; and thou canst tell
How perilously they maintained the long
And doubtful strife. From yonder temple-mount
Look round the plain, and count her towns, and mark
Her countless villages, whose habitants
All are in arms against thee! Thinkëst thou
To root them from the land? or wouldst thou live,
Harassed by night and day with endless war,
War at thy gates; and to thy children leave
That curse for their inheritance?—The land
Is all before thee : Go in peace, and chuse
Thy dwelling-place, North, South, or East, or West;
Or mount again thy houses of the sea
And search the waters. Whatsoe'er thy wants
Demand, will Aztlan willingly supply,
Prepared with friendly succour, to assist
Thy soon departure. Thus Yuhidthiton,
Remembering his old friendship, counsels thee;
Thus, as the King of Aztlan, for himself
And people, he commands. If obstinate,
If blind to your own welfare, ye persist,
Woe to ye, wretches! to the armëd man,
Who in the fight must perish; to the wife,
Who vainly on her husband's aid will call;
Woe to the babe that hangs upon the breast!
For Aztlan comes in anger, and her Gods
Spare none. 7°

       The Conqueror calmly answered him,—
By force we won your city, Azteca;
By force we will maintain it :—to the King
Repeat my saying.—To this goodly land
Your fathers came for an abiding-place.
Strangers as we, but not like us, in peace.
They conquered and destroyed. A tyrant race,
Bloody and faithless, to the hills they drove
The unoffending children of the vale,
And, day by day, in cruel sacrifice
Consumed them. God hath sent the Avengers here!
Powerful to save we come, and to destroy,
When Mercy on Destruction calls for aid.
Go tell your nation, that we know their force,
That they know ours! that their Patamba soon
Shall fall like Aztlan; and what other towns
They seek in flight shall like Patamba fall;
Till broken in their strength and spirit-crushed,
They bow the knee, or leave the land to us,
As worthier Lords.

         If this be thy reply,
Son of the Ocean! said the messenger,
I bid thee, in the King of Aztlan's name,
Mortal defiance. In the field of blood,
Before our multitudes shall trample down
Thy mad and miserable countrymen,
Yuhidthiton invites thee to the strife
Of equal danger. So may he avenge
Coanocotzin, or like him in death
Discharge his duty.

         Tell Yuhidthiton,
Madoc replied, that in the field of blood
I never shunned a foe. But say thou to him,
I will not seek him there, against his life
To raise the hand which hath been joined with his
In peace.—With that the Heralds went their way;
Nor to the right nor to the left they turn,
But to Patamba straight they journey back.

XXV.

The Lake Fight.

The mariners, meantime, at Ririd's will,
Unreeve the rigging, and the masts they strike;
And now ashore they haul the lightened hulks,
Tear up the deck, the severed planks bear off,
Disjoin the well-scarfed timbers, and the keel
Loosen asunder; then to the lake-side
Bear the materials, where the Ocean Lord
Himself directs their work. Twelve vessels there,
Fitted alike to catch the wind, or sweep
With oars the moveless surface, they prepare ;
Lay down the keel, the stern-post rear, and fix
The strong-curved timbers. Others from the wood
Bring the tall pines, and from their hissing trunks
Force, by the aid of fire, the needful gum;
Beneath the close-caulked planks its odorous stream
They pour; then, last, the round-projecting prows
With iron arm, and launch, in uproar loud
Of joy anticipating victory,
The galleys long and sharp. The masts are reared,
The sails are bent, and lo! the ready barks
Lie on the lake.

        It chanced, the Hoamen found
A spy of Aztlan, and before the Prince
They led him. But when Madoc bade him tell,
As his life-ransom, what his nation's force,
And what their plans; the savage answered him,
With dark and sullen eye and smile of wrath,
If aught the knowledge of my country's force
Could profit thee, be sure, ere I would let
My tongue play traitor, thou shouldst limb from limb
Hew me, and make each separate member feel
A separate agony of death. O Prince!
But I will tell ye of my nation's force,
That ye may know and tremble at your doom;
That fear may half subdue ye to the sword
Of vengeance—Can ye count the stars of Heaven?
The waves which ruffle o'er the lake? the leaves
Swept from the autumnal forest? Can ye look
Upon the eternal snows of yonder height,
And number each particular flake that formed
The mountain-mass?—so numberless they come,
Whoe'er can wield the sword, or hurl the lance,
Or aim the arrow; from the growing boy,
Ambitious of the battle, to the old man,

Who to revenge his country and his Gods
Hastens, and then to die. By land they come;
And years must pass away ere on their path
The grass again will grow : they come by lake;
And ye shall see the shoals of their canoes
Darken the waters. Strangers! when our Gods
Have conquered, when ye lie upon the Stone
Of Sacrifice extended one by one,
Half of our armies cannot taste your flesh,
Though given in equal shares, and every share
Minced like a nestling's food !
                              Madoc replied,
Azteca, we are few; but through the woods
The Lion walks alone. The lesser fowls
Flock multitudinous in heaven, and fly
Before the Eagle's coming. We are few;
And yet thy nation hath experienced us
Enough for conquest. Tell thy countrymen,
We can maintain the city which we won.
So saying he turned away, rejoiced at heart
To know himself alike by lake or land
Prepared to meet their power. The fateful day
Draws on; by night the Aztecas embark.
At day-break from Patamba they set forth,
From every creek and inlet of the lake,
All moving toward Aztlan; safely thus
Weening to reach the plain before her walls,
And fresh for battle. Shine thou forth, O Sun!
Shine fairly forth upon the scene so fair!
Their thousand boats, and the ten thousand oars
From whose broad bowls the waters fall and flash,
And twice ten thousand feathered helms, and shields,
Glittering with gold and scarlet plumery. ·
Onward they come with song and swelling horn;
While, louder than all voice and instrument,
The dash of their ten thousand oars, from shore
To shore and hill to hill, re-echoing rolls,
In undistinguishable peals of sound
And endless echo. On the other side
Advance the British barks; the freshening breeze
Fills the broad sail; around the rushing keel
The waters sing, while proudly they sail on
Lords of the water. Shine thou forth, O Sun!
Shine forth upon their hour of victory!
Onward the Cymry speed. The Aztecas,
Though wondering at that unexpected sight,
Bravely made on to meet them, seized their bows,
And showered, like rain, upon the pavaised barks,
The rattling shafts. Strong blows the auspicious gale;
Madoc, the Lord of Ocean, leads the way;
He holds the helm; the galley where he guides
Flies on, and full upon the first canoe
Drives shattering; midway its long length it struck,
And o'er the wreck with unimpeded force
Dashes among the fleet. The astonished men
Gaze in inactive terror. They behold
Their splintered vessels floating all around,
Their warriors struggling in the lake, with arms
Experienced in the battle vainly now.
Dismayed they drop their bows, and cast away
Their unavailing spears, and take to flight,
Before the Masters of the Elements,
· Who rode the waters, and who made the winds
Wing them to vengeance! Forward now they bend,
And backward then, with strenuous strain of arm,
Press the broad paddle.—Hope of victory

Was none, nor of defence, nor of revenge,
To sweeten death. Toward the shore they speed,
Toward the shore they lift their longing eyes:—
O fools, to meet on their own element
The Sons of Ocean !—Could they but aland
Set foot, the strife were equal, or to die
Less dreadful. But, as if with wings of wind,
On fly the British barks!—the favouring breeze
Blows strong;—far, far behind their roaring keels
Lies the long line of foam; the helm directs
Their force; they move, as with the limbs of life,
Obedient to the will that governs them.
Where'er they pass, the crashing shock is heard,
The dash of broken waters, and the cry
Of sinking multitudes. Here one plies fast
The practised limbs of youth, but o'er his head
The galley drives; one follows a canoe
With skill availing only to prolong
Suffering; another, as with wiser aim
He swims across, to meet his coming friends,
Stunned by the hasty and unheeding oar,
Sinks senseless to the depths. Lo! yonder boat
Graspt by the thronging strugglers; its light length
Yields to the overbearing weight, and all
Share the same ruin. Here, another shows
Crueller contest, where the crew hack off ·
The hands that hang for life upon its side,
Lest altogether perish; then in vain
The voice of friend or kinsman prays for mercy;
Imperious self controls all other thoughts;
And still they deal around unnatural wounds,
When the strong bark of Britain over all
Sails in the path of death.—God of the Lake,
Tlaloc! and thou, O Aiauh, green-robed Queen!
How many a wretch, in dying agonies,
Invoked ye in the misery of that day!
Long after, on the tainted lake, the dead
Weltered; there, perched upon his floating prey,
The vulture fed in daylight; and the wolves,
Assembled at their banquet round its banks,
Disturbed the midnight with their howl of joy.

XXVI.

The Close of the Century.

THERE was mourning in Patamba; the north wind
Blew o'er the lake, and drifted to the shore
The floating wreck and bodies of the dead.
Then on the shore the mother might be seen,
Seeking her child; the father to the tomb,
With limbs too weak for that unhappy weight,
Bearing the bloated body of his son;
The wife, who, in expectant agony,
Watched the black carcass on the coming wave.

On every brow terror was legible;
Anguish in every eye. There was not one,
Who in the general ruin did not share
Peculiar grief, and in his country's loss
Lament some dear one dead. Along the lake
The frequent funeral-piles, for many a day,
With the noonlight their melancholy flames
Dimly commingled; while the mourners stood,

Watching the pile, to feed the lingering fire,
As slowly it consumed the watery corpse.

Thou didst not fear, young Tlalala! thy soul,
Unconquered and unconquerable, rose
Superior to its fortune.   When the Chiefs
Hung their dejected heads, as men subdued
In spirit, then didst thou, Yuhidthiton,
Calm in the hour of evil, still maintain
Thy even courage.   They from man to man
Go, with the mourners mourning, and by grief
Rousing their rage, till, at the promised fight,
The hope of vengeance, a ferocious joy
Flashed in the eye which still retained the tear
Of tender memory.   To the brave they spake
Of Aztlan's strength,—for Aztlan still was strong :—
The late defeat,—not there by manly might,
By honourable valour, by the force
Of arms subdued, shame aggravated loss;
The White Men from the waters came, perchance
Sons of the Ocean, by their parent Gods
Aided, and conquerors not by human skill.
When man met man, when in the field of fight
The soldier on firm earth should plant his foot,
Then would the trial be, the struggle then,
The glory, the revenge.

Tezozomoc,
Alike unbroken by defeat, endured
The evil day ; but in his sullen mind
Worked thoughts of other vengeance. He the King
Summoned apart from all, with Tlalala,
And thus advised them : We have vainly tried
The war; these mighty Strangers will not yield
To mortal strength : yet shall they be cut off
So ye will heed my counsel, and to force
Add wisdom's aid. Put on a friendly front ;
Send to their Prince the messenger of peace ;
He will believe his words ; he will forgive
The past;—the offender may.   So days and months,
Yea, years, if needful, will we wear a face
Of friendliness, till some fit hour arrive,
When we may fire their dwellings in the night,
Or mingle poison in their cups of mirth.
The warrior, from whose force the Lion flies,
Falls by the Serpent's tooth.

Thou speakest well,
Tlalala answered; but my spirit ill
Can brook revenge delayed.

The Priest then turned
His small and glittering eye toward the King;
But on the Monarch's mild and manly brow
A meaning sate, which made his crafty eye
Bend, quickly abashed.   While yet I was a child,
Replied the King of Aztlan, on my heart
My father laid two precepts. Boy, be brave!
So, in the midnight battle, shalt thou meet,
Fearless, the sudden foe : Boy, let thy lips
Be clean from falsehood ! in the mid-day sun,
So never shalt thou need from mortal man
To turn thy guilty face.   Tezozomoc,
Holy I keep the lessons of my sire.

But if the enemy, with their dreadful arms,
Again, said Tlalala.—If again the Gods
Will our defeat, Yuhidthiton replied,
Vain is it for the feeble power of man

To strive against their will.   I omen not
Of ill, young Tyger ! but if ill betide,
The land is all before us.   Let me hear
Of perfidy and serpent-wiles no more!
In the noon-day war, and in the face of Heaven,
I meet my foes.   Let Aztlan follow me;
And if one man of all her multitudes
Shall better play the warrior in that hour,
Be his the sceptre! But if the people fear
The perilous strife, and own themselves subdued,
Let us depart! the universal Sun
Confines not to one land his partial beams;
Nor is man rooted, like a tree, whose seed
The winds on some ungenial soil have cast,
There where he cannot prosper.

The dark Priest
Concealed revengeful anger, and replied,
Let the King's will be done! An awful day
Draws on ; the Circle of the Years is full; 7¹
We tremble for the event. The times are strange;
There are portentous changes in the world;
Perchance its end is come.

Be it thy care,
Priest of the Gods, to see the needful rites
Duly performed, Yuhidthiton replied.
On the third day, if yonder God of Light
Begin the Circle of the Years anew,
Again we march to war.

One day is past;
Another day comes on.   At earliest dawn
Then was there heard through all Patamba's streets,
The warning voice,—Woe ! woe ! the Sun hath reached
The limits of his course; he hath fulfilled
The appointed cycle!—Fast, and weep, and pray,—
Four Suns have perished,—fast, and weep, and pray,
Lest the fifth perish also. On the first
The floods arose; the waters of the heavens,
Bursting their everlasting boundaries,
Whelmed in one deluge earth and sea and sky,
And quenched its orb of fire.   The second Sun
Then had its birth, and ran its round of years;
Till having reached its date, it fell from heaven,
And crushed the race of men. Another life
The Gods assigned to Nature; the third Sun
Formed the celestial circle; then its flames
Burst forth, and overspread earth, sea, and sky,
Deluging the wide universe with fire,
Till all things were consumed, and its own flames
Fed on itself, and spent themselves, and all
Was vacancy and darkness.   Yet again
The world had being, and another Sun
Rolled round the path of Heaven. That perished too :
The mighty Whirlwinds rose, and far away
Scattered its dying flames.   The fifth was born ;
The fifth to-day completes its destined course,
Perchance to rise no more.   O Aztlan, fast
And pray! the Cycle of the Years is full!

Thus, through Patamba, did the ominous voice
Exhort the people.   Fervent vows all day
Were made, with loud lament ; in every fane,
In every dwelling-place of man, were prayers,
The supplications of the affrighted heart,
Earnestly offered up with tears and groans.
So passed the forenoon ; and when now the Sun
Sloped, from his southern height, the downward way

34

Of Heaven, again the ominous warner cried,
Woe! woe! the Cycle of the Years is full!
Quench every fire! Extinguish every light!
And every fire was quenched, and every light
Extinguished at the voice.
      Meantime the Priests
Began the rites. They gashed themselves, and plunged
Into the sacred pond of Ezapan,
Till the clear water, on whose bed of sand
The sunbeams sparkled late, opaque with blood,
On its black surface mirrored all things round.
The children of the temple, in long search
Had gathered, for the service of this day,
All venomous things that fly, or wind their path
With sinuous trail, or crawl on reptile feet.
These, in one cauldron, o'er the sacred fire
They scorch, till of the loathsome living tribes,
Who, writhing in their burning agonies,
Fix on each other ill-directed wounds,
Ashes alone are left. In infants' blood
They mix the infernal unction, and the Priests
Anoint themselves therewith.
      Lo! from the South
The Orb of Glory his regardless way
Holds on. Again Patamba's streets receive
The ominous voice,—Woe! woe! the Sun pursues
His journey to the limits of his course!
Let every man in darkness veil his wife,
Veil every maiden's face; let every child
Be hid in darkness, there to weep and pray,
That they may see again the birth of light!
They heard, and every husband veiled his wife
In darkness; every maiden's face was veiled:
The children were in darkness led to pray,
That they might see the birth of light once more.

Westward the Sun proceeds; the tall tree casts
A longer shade; the night-eyed insect tribes
Wake to their portion of the circling hours;
The water-fowl, retiring to the shore,
Sweep in long files the surface of the lake.
Then from Patamba to the sacred mount
The Priests go forth; but with no songs of joy,
Nor cheerful instruments they go, nor train,
Of festive followers; silent and alone,
Leading one victim to his dreadful death,
They to the mountain-summit wend their way.

On the south shore, and level with the lake,
Patamba stood; westward were seen the walls
Of Aztlan rising on a gentle slope;
Southward the plain extended far and wide;
To the east the mountain-boundary began,
And there the sacred mountain reared its head,
Above the neighbouring heights, its lofty peak
Was visible far off. In the vale below,
Along the level borders of the lake,
The assembled Aztecas, with wistful eye,
Gaze on the sacred summit, hoping there
Soon to behold the fire of sacrifice
Arise, sure omen of continued light.
The Pabas to the sacred peak begin
Their way, and as they go, with ancient songs
Hymn the departing Sun.
      O, Light of Life,
Yet once again arise! yet once again

Commence thy course of glory! Time hath seen
Four generations of mankind destroyed,
When the four Suns expired; Oh, let not thou,
Human thyself of yore, the human race
Languish and die in darkness!
      The fourth Sun
Had perished; for the mighty Whirlwinds rose,
And swept it, with the dust of the shattered world,
Into the great abyss. The eternal Gods
Built a new World, and to a Hero race
Assigned it for their goodly dwelling-place;
And shedding on the bones of the destroyed
A quickening dew, from them, as from a seed,
Made a new race of humankind spring up,
The menials of the Heroes born of Heaven.
But in the firmament no orb of day
Performed its course; Nature was blind; the fount
Of light had ceased to flow; the eye of Heaven
Was quenched in darkness. In the sad obscure,
The earth-possessors to their parent Gods
Prayed for another Sun, their bidding heard,
And, in obedience, raised a flaming pile.
Hopeful they circled it, when from above
The voice of the Invisible proclaimed,
That he who bravely plunged amid the fire
Should live again in Heaven, and there shine forth
The Sun of the young World. The Hero race
Grew pale, and from the fiery trial shrunk.
Thou, O Nahuaztin, thou, O mortal born,
Heardëst! thy heart was strong, the flames received
Their victim, and the humbled Heroes saw
The orient sky, with smiles of rosy joy,
Welcome the coming of the new-born God.
O, human once, now let not humankind
Languish, and die in darkness!
      In the East
Then didst thou pause to see the Hero race
Perish. In vain, with impious arms, they strove
Against thy will; in vain against thine orb
They shot their shafts; the arrows of their pride
Fell on themselves; they perished, to thy praise.
So perish still thine impious enemies,
O Lord of Day! But to the race devout,
Who offer up their morning sacrifice,
Honouring thy godhead, and with morning hymns,
And with the joy of music and of dance,
Welcome thy glad uprise,—to them, O Sun,
Still let the fountain-streams of splendour flow!
Still smile on them propitious, thou whose smile
Is light and life and joyance! Once again,
Parent of Being, Prince of Glory, rise!
Begin thy course of beauty once again!

Such was their ancient song, as up the height
Slowly they wound their way. The multitude
Beneath repeat the strain; with fearful eyes
They watch the spreading glories of the west;
And when at length the hastening orb hath sunk
Below the plain, such sinking at the heart
They feel, as he who hopeless of return
From his dear home departs. Still on the light,
The last green light that lingers in the west,
Their looks are fastened, till the clouds of night
Roll on, and close in darkness the whole heaven.
Then ceased their songs; then o'er the crowded vale
No voice of man is heard. Silent and still

They stood, all turned toward the east, in hope
There on the holy mountain to behold
The sacred fire, and know that once again
The Sun begins his stated round of years.

The Moon arose; she shone upon the lake,
Which lay one smooth expanse of silver light;
She shone upon the hills and rocks, and cast
Upon their hollows and their hidden glens
A blacker depth of shade. Who then looked round,
Beholding all that mighty multitude,
Felt yet severer awe; so solemnly still
The thronging thousands stood. The breeze was heard
That rustled in the reeds; the little wave,
Which rippled to the shore and left no foam,
Sent its low murmurs far.
                          Meantime the Priests
Have stretched their victim on the mountain-top;
A miserable man: his breast is bare,
Bare for the death that waits him; but no hand
May there inflict the blow of mercy. Piled
On his bare breast, the cedar boughs are laid;
On his bare breast, dry sedge and odorous gums
Laid ready to receive the sacred spark,
And blaze, to herald the ascending Sun,
Upon his living altar. Round the wretch
The inhuman ministers of rites accurst
Stand, and expect the signal when to strike,
The seed of fire. Their Chief, Tezozomoc,
Apart from all, upon the pinnacle
Of that high mountain, eastward turns his eyes;
For now the hour draws nigh, and speedily
He looks to see the first faint dawn of day
Break through the orient sky.
                          Impatiently
The multitude await the happy sign.
Long hath the midnight past, and every hour,
Yea every moment, to their torturing fears
Seemed lengthened out, insufferably long.
Silent they stood, and breathless in suspense.
The breeze had fallen; no stirring breath of wind
Rustled the reeds. Oppressive, motionless,
It was a labour and a pain to breathe
The close, hot, heavy air.—Hark! from the woods
The howl of their wild tenants! and the birds,—
The day-birds, in blind darkness fluttering,
Fearful to rest, uttering portentous cries!
Anon, the sound of distant thunders came;
They peal beneath their feet. Earth shakes and yawns,—
And lo! upon the sacred mountain's top,
The light—the mighty flame! A cataract
Of fire bursts upward from the mountain-head,—
High,—high,—it shoots! the liquid fire boils out;
It streams,—it torrents down! Tezozomoc
Beholds the judgment: wretched,—wretched man!
On the upmost pinnacle he stands, and sees
The lava floods beneath him: and his hour
Is come. The fiery shower, descending, heaps
Red ashes round; they fall like drifted snows,
And bury and consume the accursed Priest.

The Tempest is abroad. Fierce from the North
The wind uptears the lake, whose lowest depths
Rock, while convulsions shake the solid earth.
Where is Patamba? where the multitudes

Who thronged her level shores? The mighty Lake
Hath burst its bounds, and yon wide valley roars,
A troubled sea, before the rolling storm.

XXVII.

The Migration of the Aztecas.

THE storm hath ceased; but still the lava-tides
Roll down the mountain-side in streams of fire;
Down to the lake they roll, and yet roll on,
All burning, through the waters. Heaven above
Glows round the burning mount, and fiery clouds
Scour through the black and starless firmament.
Far off, the Eagle, in her mountain-nest,
Lies watching in alarm, with steady eye,
The midnight radiance.
                        But the storm hath ceased;
The earth is still;—and lo! while yet the dawn
Is struggling through the eastern cloud, the barks
Of Madoc on the waters!
                        Who is he
On yonder crag, all dripping from the lake,
Who hath escaped its depths? He lies along,
Now near exhaust with self-preserving toil,
And still his eye dwells on the spreading waves,
Where late the multitudes of Aztlan stood,
Collected in their strength. It is the King
Of Aztlan, who, extended on the rock,
Looks vainly for his people. He beholds
The barks of Madoc plying to preserve
The strugglers!—but how few! upon the crags
Which verge the northern shore, upon the heights
Eastward, how few have refuged! Then the King
Almost repented him of life preserved,
And wished the waves had whelmed him, or the sword
Fallen on him, ere this ill, this wretchedness,
This desolation. Spirit-troubled thus,
He called to mind how, from the first, his heart
Inclined to peace, and how reluctantly,
Obedient to the Pabas and their Gods,
Had he to this unhappy war been driven.
All now was ended: it remained to yield,
To obey the inevitable will of Heaven,
From Aztlan to depart. As thus he mused,
A bird, upon a bough which overhung
The rock, as though in echo to his thought,
Cried out,—Depart! depart! for so the note,
Articulately in his native tongue,
Spake to the Azteca.[72] The King looked up:
The hour, the horrors round him, had impressed
Feelings and fears well fitted to receive
All superstition; and the voice which cried,
Depart! depart! seemed like the voice of fate.
He thought, perhaps Coanocotzin's soul,
Descending from his blissful halls in the hour
Of evil thus to comfort and advise,
Hovered above him.
                    Lo! toward the rock,
Oaring with feeble arms his difficult way,
A struggler hastens: he hath reached the rock,
Hath graspt it, but his strength, exhausted, fails
To lift him from the depth. The King descends
Timely in aid; he holds the feeble one

By his long locks, and on the safety-place
Lands him. He, panting, from his clotted hair
Shook the thick waters, from his forehead wiped
The blinding drops; on his preserver's face
Then looked, and knew the King. Then Tlalala
Fell on his neck, and groaned. They laid them down
In silence, for their hearts were full of woe.
The sun came forth, and shone upon the rock;
They felt the kindly beams; their strengthened blood
Flowed with a freer action. They arose,
And looked around, if aught of hope might meet
Their prospect. On the lake the galleys plied
Their toil successfully, ever to the shore
Bearing their rescued charge: the eastern heights,
Rightward and leftward of the fiery mount,
Were thronged with fugitives, whose growing crowds
Speckled the ascent. Then Tlalala took hope,
And his young heart, reviving, re-assumed
Its wonted vigour. Let us to the heights,
He cried;—all is not lost! Yuhidthiton!
When they behold thy countenance, the sight
Will cheer them in their woe, and they will bless
The Gods of Aztlan.

    To the heights they went
And when the remnant of the people saw
Yuhidthiton preserved, such comfort then
They felt, as utter wretchedness can feel,
That only gives grief utterance, only speaks
In groans and recollections of the past.
He looked around; a multitude was there,—
But where the strength of Aztlan? where her hosts?
Her marshalled myriads where, whom yester Sun
Had seen in arms arrayed, in spirit high,
Mighty in youth and courage?—What were these,
This remnant of the people? Women most,
Who from Patamba when the shock began
Ran with their infants; widowed now, yet each
Among the few who from the lake escaped,
Wandering, with eager eyes and wretched hope.
The King beheld and groaned; against a tree
He leant, and bowed his head, subdued of soul.

Meantime, amid the crowd, doth Tlalala
Seek for his wife and boy. In vain he seeks
Ilanquel there; in vain for her he asks:
A troubled look, a melancholy eye,
A silent motion of the hopeless head,
These answer him. But Tlalala represt
His anguish, and he called upon the King,—
Yuhidthiton! thou seest thy people left;
Their fate must be determined; they are here
Houseless, and wanting food.

    The King looked up,—
It is determined, Tlalala! the Gods
Have crushed us. Who can stand against their wrath?
Have we not life and strength? the Tiger cried.
Disperse these women to the towns which stand
Beyond the ruinous waters; against them
The White Men will not war. Ourselves are few,
Too few to root the invaders from our land,
Or meet them with the hope of equal fight:
Yet may we shelter in the woods, and share
The Lion's liberty; and man by man
Destroy them, till they shall not dare to walk
Beyond their city walls, to sow their fields,
Or bring the harvest in. We may steal forth

In the dark midnight, go and burn and kill,
Till all their dreams shall be of fire and death,
Their sleep be fear and misery.

    Then the King
Stretched forth his hand, and pointed to the lake
Where Madoc's galleys still to those who clung
To the tree-tops for life, or faintly still
Were floating on the waters, gave their aid.—
O think not, Tlalala, that ever more
Will I against those noble enemies
Raise my right hand in war, lest righteous Heaven
Should blast the impious hand and thankless heart!
The Gods are leagued with them; the Elements
Banded against us! for our overthrow
Were yonder mountain-springs of fire ordained
For our destruction the earth-thunders loosed,
And the everlasting boundaries of the lake
Gave way, that these destroying floods might roll
Over the brave of Aztlan!—We must leave
The country which our fathers won in arms;
We must depart.

    The word yet vibrated
Fresh on their hearing, when the Bird above,
Flapping his heavy wings, repeats the sound,
Depart! depart!—Ye hear! the King exclaimed;
It is an omen sent to me from Heaven;
I heard it late in solitude, the voice
Of fate.—It is Coanocotzin's soul,
Who counsels our departure.—And the Bird
Still flew around, and in his wheeling flight
Pronounced the articulate note. The people heard
In faith, and Tlalala made no reply;
But dark his brow, and gloomy was his frown.

Then spake the King, and called a messenger,
And bade him speed to Aztlan.—Seek the Lord
Of Ocean; tell him that Yuhidthiton
Yields to the will of Heaven, and leaves the land
His fathers won in war. Only one boon,
In memory of our former friendship, ask,
The Ashes of my Fathers,—if indeed
The conqueror have not cast them to the winds!

The herald went his way, circuitous,
Along the mountains,—for the flooded vale
Barred the near passage: but before his feet
Could traverse half their track, the fugitives
Beheld canoes from Aztlan, to the foot
Of that protecting eminence, whereon
They had their stand, draw nigh. The doubtful sight
Disturbed them, lest perchance with hostile strength
They came upon their weakness. Wrongful fear:—
For now Cadwallon, from his bark, unarmed,
Set foot ashore, and for Yuhidthiton
Enquired, if yet he lived. The King receives
His former friend.—From Madoc come I here,
The Briton said: Raiment and food he sends,
And peace; so shall this visitation prove
A blessing, if it knit the bonds of peace,
And make us as one people.

    Tlalala!
Hearest thou him? Yuhidthiton exclaimed.
Do thou thy bidding, King! the Tiger cried:
My path is plain.—Thereat Yuhidthiton,
Answering, replied, Thus humbled as thou seest,
Beneath the visitation of the Gods,

We bow before their will! To them we yield;
To you, their favourites, we resign the land
Our fathers conquered. Never more may Fate,
In your days or your children's, to the end
Of time, afflict it thus!

             He said, and called
The Heralds of his pleasure.—Go ye forth
Throughout the land: North, south, and east, and west,
Proclaim the ruin. Say to all who bear
The name of Azteca, that Heaven hath crushed
Their country: Say, the voice of Heaven was heard,—
Heard ye it not?—bidding us leave the land,
Who shakes us from her bosom. Ye will find
Women, old men, and babes; the many, weak
Of body and of spirit ill prepared,
With painful toil, through long and dangerous ways
To seek another country. Say to them,
The White Men will not lift the arm of power
Against the feeble; here they may remain
In peace, and to the grave in peace go down.
But they who would not have their children lose
The name their fathers bore, will join our march,
Ere ye set forth, behold the destined way!

He bade a pile be raised upon the top
Of that high eminence, to all the winds
Exposed. They raised the pile, and left it free
To all the winds of Heaven; Yuhidthiton
Alone approached it, and applied the torch.
The day was calm, and o'er the flaming pile
The wavy smoke hung lingering, like a mist
That in the morning tracks the valley-stream.
Swell over swell it rose, erect above,
On all sides spreading like a stately palm,
So moveless were the winds. Upward it rolled,
Still upward, when a stream of upper air,
Crossed it, and bent its top, and drove it on,
Straight over Aztlan. An acclaiming shout
Welcomed the will of Heaven; for lo, the smoke
Fast travelling on, while not a breath of air
Is felt below. Ye see the appointed course!
Exclaimed the King. Proclaim it where ye go!
On the third morning we begin our march.

Soon o'er the lake a wingèd galley sped,
Wafting the Ocean Prince. He bore, preserved,
When Aztlan's bloody temples were cast down,
The Ashes of the Dead. The King received
The relics, and his heart was full; his eye
Dwelt on his father's urn. At length he said,
One more request, O Madoc!—If the lake
Should ever to its ancient bounds return,
Shrined in the highest of Patamba's towers
Coanocotzin rests.—But wherefore this?
Thou wilt respect the ashes of the King.

Then said the Prince, Abide not here, O King,
Thus open to the changeful elements;
But till the day of your departure come,
Sojourn with me.—Madoc, that must not be!
Yuhidthiton replied. Shall I behold
A stranger dwelling in my father's house?
Shall I become a guest, where I was wont
To give the guest his welcome?—He pursued,
After short pause of speech,—For our old men,
And helpless babes and women; for all those

Whom wisely fear and feebleness deter
To tempt strange paths, through swamp and wilderness
And hostile tribes, for these Yuhidthiton
Asks thy protection. Under thy mild sway,
They will remember me without regret,
Yet not without affection.—They shall be
My people, Madoc answered.—And the rites
Of holiness transmitted from their sires,—
Pursued the King,—will these be suffered them?—
Blood must not flow, the Christian Prince replied;
No Priest must dwell among us; that hath been
The cause of all this misery!—Enough,
Yuhidthiton replied; I ask no more.
It is not for the conquered to impose
Their law upon the conqueror.

                Then he turned,
And lifted up his voice, and called upon
The people:—All whom fear or feebleness
Withhold from following my adventurous path,
Prince Madoc will receive. No blood must flow,
No Paba dwell among them. Take upon ye,
Ye who are weak of body or of heart,
The strangers' easy yoke: beneath their sway
Ye will remember me without regret.
Soon take your choice, and speedily depart,
Lest ye impede the adventurers.—As he spake
Tears flowed, and groans were heard. The line was
   drawn,
Which whoso would accept the Strangers' yoke
Should pass. A multitude o'erpast the line;
But all the youth of Aztlan crowded round
Yuhidthiton, their own belovèd King.

So two days long, with unremitting toil,
The barks of Britain to the adventurers
Bore due supply; and to new habitants
The city of the Cymry spread her gates;
And in the vale around, and on the heights,
Their numerous tents were pitched. Meantime the tale
Of ruin went abroad, and how the Gods
Had driven her sons from Aztlan. To the King,
Companions of his venturous enterprise,
The bold repaired; the timid and the weak,
All whom, averse from perilous wanderings,
A gentler nature had disposed to peace,
Beneath the Strangers' easy rule remained.
Now the third morning came. At break of day
The mountain echoes to the busy sound
Of multitudes. Before the moving tribe
The Pabas bear, enclosed from public sight,
Mexitli; and the ashes of the Kings
Follow the Chair of God.[73] Yuhidthiton
Then leads the marshalled ranks, and by his side,
Silent and thoughtfully, went Tlalala.

At the north gate of Aztlan, Malinal,
Borne in a litter, waited their approach;
And now alighting, as the train drew nigh,
Propt by a friendly arm, with feeble step
Advanced to meet the King. Yuhidthiton,
With eye severe and darkening countenance,
Met his advance. I did not think, quoth he,
Thou wouldst have ventured this! and liefer far
Should I have borne away with me the thought
That Malinal had shunned his brother's sight,
Because their common blood yet raised in him

A sense of his own shame!—Comest thou to show
Those wounds, the marks of thine unnatural war
Against thy country? or to boast the meed
Of thy dishonour? that thou tarriest here,
Sharing the bounty of the Conqueror,
While, with the remnant of his countrymen,
Saving the Gods of Aztlan and the name,
Thy brother and thy King goes forth to seek
His fortune!

    Calm and low the youth replied,
Ill dost thou judge of me, Yuhidthiton!
And foully, O my brother, wrong the heart
Thou better shouldst have known! Howbeit, I come
Prepared for grief. These honourable wounds
Were gained when, singly, at Caermadoc, I
Opposed the ruffian Hoamen; and even now,
Thus feeble as thou seest me, come I thence,
For this farewell. Brother,—Yuhidthiton,—
By the true love which thou didst bear my youth,
Which ever, with a love as true, my heart
Hath answered,—by the memory of that hour
When at our mother's funeral pile we stood,
Go not away in wrath, but call to mind
What thou hast ever known me! Side by side
We fought against the Strangers, side by side
We fell; together in the counsel-hall
We counselled peace, together in the field
Of the assembly pledged the word of peace.
When plots of secret slaughter were devised,
I raised my voice alone, alone I kept
My plighted faith, alone I prophesied
The judgment of just Heaven; for this I bore
Reproach and shame and wrongful banishment,
In the action self-approved, and justified
By this unhappy issue!

    As he spake,
Did natural feeling strive within the King,
And thoughts of other days, and brotherly love,
And inward consciousness that had he too
Stood forth, obedient to his better mind,
Nor weakly yielded to the wily priests,
Wilfully blind, perchance even now in peace
The kingdom of his fathers had preserved
Her name and empire.—Malinal, he cried
Thy brother's heart is sore; in better times
I may with kindlier thoughts remember thee,
And honour thy true virtue. Now fare well!

So saying, to his heart he held the youth,
Then turned away. But then cried Tlalala,
Farewell, Yuhidthiton! the Tiger cried;
For I too will not leave my native land,—
Thou who wert King of Aztlan! go thy way,
And be it prosperous. Through the gate thou seest
Yon tree that overhangs my father's house;
My father lies beneath it. Call to mind
Sometimes that tree; for at its foot in peace
Shall Tlalala be laid, who will not live
Survivor of his country.

    Thus he cried,
And through the gate, regardless of the King,
Turned to his native door. Yuhidthiton
Followed, and Madoc; but in vain their words
Essayed to move the Tiger's steady heart;
When from the door a tottering boy came forth
And clung around his knees with joyful cries,

And called him father. At the joyful sound
Out ran Ilanquel; and the astonished man
Beheld his wife and boy, whom sure he deemed
Whelmed in the floods; but them the British barks,
Returning homeward from their merciful quest,
Found floating on the waters—For a while,
Abandoned by all desperate thoughts he stood:
Soon he collected, and to Madoc turned,
And said, O Prince, this woman and her boy
I leave to thee. As thou hast ever found
In me a fearless unrelenting foe,
Fighting with ceaseless zeal my country's cause,
Respect them!—Nay, Ilanquel! hast thou yet
To learn with what unshakeable resolve
My soul maintains its purposes! I leave thee
To a brave foe's protection.—Lay me, Madoc,
Here, in my father's grave.

    With that he took
His mantle off, and veiled Ilanquel's face;—
Woman, thou canst not look upon the Sun,
Who sets to rise no more!—That done, he placed
His javelin-hilt against the ground; the point
He fitted to his heart; and, holding firm
The shaft, fell forward, still with steady hand
Guiding the death-blow on.

    So in the land
Madoc was left sole Lord; and far away
Yuhidthiton led forth the Aztecas,
To spread in other lands Mexitli's name,[74]
And rear a mightier empire, and set up
Again their foul idolatry; till Heaven,
Making blind Zeal and Bloody Avarice
Its ministers of vengeance, sent among them
The heroic Spaniard's unrelenting sword.

NOTES.

PART I.

Note 1, page 197, col. 1.

*Silent and thoughtful, and apart from all,
Stood Madoc.*

Long after these lines had been written, I was pleased at finding the same feeling expressed in a very singular specimen of metrical auto-biography:

A Nao, despregando as velas
Ja se aproveita do vento;
E de evidente alegria
 Os Portuguezes ja cheios
 Sobre o conves estam todos;
 Na terra se vam revendo
Igrejas, Palacios, Quintas,
 De que tem conhecimento,
 Daqui, dalli apontando
 Vam ledamente co dedo.
Todos fallando demostram
 Seus jubilos manifestos;
 Mas o Vieira occupado
 Vai de hum notavel silencio.
Seu excessivo alvoroço
 Tumultuante, que dentro
 No peito sente, lhe causa
 De sobresalto os effeitos.
Quanto mais elle chegando
 Vai ao suspirado termo,
 Mais se lhe augmenta o gostoso
 Susto no doce projecto.
    Vieira Lusitano.

Note 2, page 197, col. 1.

Mona, the dark Island.

Ynys Dowyll, the dark island.

Note 3, page 197, col. 1.

Aberfraw.

The palace of Gwynedd, or North Wales. Rhodri Mawr, about the year 873, fixed the seat of government here, which had formerly been at Dyganwy, but latterly at Caer Seiont in Arvon, near the present town of Caernarvon. «It is strange,» says Warrington, «that he should desert a country where every mountain was a natural fortress, and in times of such difficulty and danger, should make choice of a residence so exposed and defenceless.» But this very danger may have been his motive. The Danes, who could make no impression upon England against the great Alfred, had turned their arms upon Wales; Mona was the part most open to their ravages, and it may have been an act as well of policy as of courage in the king to fix his abode there. He fell there, at length, in battle against the Saxons. A barn now stands upon the site of the palace, in which there are stones, that by their better workmanship, appear to have belonged to the original building.

Note 4, page 197, col. 2.

Richly would the king
Gift the red hand that rid him of that fear.

It was the manner of those days, that the murtherer only, and he that gave the death's wound, should fly, which was called in Welsh *Llawrudd*, which is a red hand, because he had blouded his hands. The accessories and abettors to the murtherers were never hearkened after.— *Gwydir History*.

Note 5, page 197, col. 2.

David't King Owen's son—my father's son—
He wed the Saxon—the Plantagenet!

This marriage was in fact one of the means whereby Henry succeeded for a time in breaking the independent spirit of the Welsh. David immediately sent a thousand men to serve under his brother-in-law and liege lord in Normandy, and shortly after attended the parliament at Oxford upon his summons.

Note 6, page 198, col. 1.

He is the headstrong slave
Of passions unsubdued.

Caradoc represents Davydd as a prince greatly disliked on account of his cruelty and untractable spirit, killing and putting out the eyes of those who were not subservient to his will, *after the manner of the English!* —*Cambrian Biography*.

Note 7, page 198, col. 2.

The guests were seated at the festal board.

The order of the royal hall was established by law. The men to whom the right of a seat in the hall belongs are fourteen, of whom four shall sit in the lower, and ten in the upper part of the hall. The king is the first, he shall sit at the pillar, and next him the chancellor; and after him the guest, and then the heir apparent, and then the master of the hawks. The foot-bearer shall sit by the dish opposite the king, and the mead-maker at the pillar behind him. The priest of the household shall be at another pillar, who shall bless the meat, and chaunt the pater noster. The crier shall strike the pillar above the king's head. Next him shall be the judge of the palace, and next to him the musician, to whom the right of the seat belongs. The smith of the palace shall be at the bottom before the knees of the priest. The master of the palace shall sit in the lower hall with his left hand towards the door, with the serving men whom he shall chuse, and the rest shall be at the other side of the door, and at his other hand the musician of the household. The master of the horse shall sit at the pillar opposite the king, and the master of the hounds at the pillar opposite the priest of the household.— *Laws of Hoel Dha'*.

Note 8, page 199, col. 1.

Keirlog—and Berwyn's after-strife.

1165. The king gather'd another armie of chosen men, through all his dominions, as England, Normandy, Anjow, Gascoine, and Gwyen, sending for succours from Flanders and Brytain, and then returned towards North Wales, minding utterlie to destroy all that had life in the land; and coming to Croes Oswalt, called Oswald's-tree, incamped there. On the contrarie side, Prince Owen and his brother Cadwallader, with all the power of North Wales; and the Lord Rees, with the power of South Wales; and Owen Cyveilioc and the sonnes of Madoc ap Meredyth, with the power of Powyss, and the two sonnes of Madoc ap Ednerth, with the people betwixt Wye and Seavern, gathered themselves togither and came to Corwen in Edeyrneon, purposing to defend their country. But the king understanding that they were nigh, being wonderfull desirous of battel, came to the river Ceireoc, and caused the woods to be hewn down. Whereupon a number of the Welshmen understanding the passage, unknown to their captains met with the king's ward, where were placed the picked men of all the armie, and there began a hote skirmish, where diverse worthie men were slaine on either side; but in the end the king wanne the passage, and came to the mountain of Berwyn, where he laid in campe certaine days, and so both the armies stood in awe of each other; for the king kept the open plains, and was afraid to be intrapped in straits; but the Welshmen watched for the advantage of the place, and kept the king so straitlie, that neither forage nor victuall might come to his camp, neither durst anie souldiour stir abroad. And to augment their miseries there fell such raine, that the king's men could scant stand upon their feete upon those slipperie hilles. In the end, the king was compelled to return home without his purpose, and that with great loss of men and munition, besides his charges. Therefore in a great choler he caused the pledges eies, whom he had received long before that, to be put out; which were Rees and Cawdwalhon the sonnes of Owen, and Cynwric and Meredith the sonnes of Rees, and other.— *Powell*.

Note 9, page 199, col. 1.

The fool that day, who, in his masque attire,
Sported before King Henry.

Brienston in Dorsetshire was held in grand serjeantry by a pretty odd jocular tenure; viz. by finding a man to go before the king's army for forty days, when he should make war in Scotland, (some records say in Wales), bareheaded and barefooted, in his shirt and linen drawers, holding in one hand a bow without a string, in another an arrow without feathers.—*Gibson's Camden.*

Note 10, page 199, col. 1.
Though I knew
The rebel's worth.

There is a good testimony to Hoel's military talents in the old history of Cambria, by Powell. « At this time Cadel, Meredyth, and Rees, the sons of Gruffyth ap Rees, ap Theodor, did lead their powers against the castle of Gwys; which, after they saw they could not win, they sent for Howel the sonne of Owen, prince of North Wales, to their succour, who for his prowesse in the field, and his discretion in consultation, was counted the flowre of chivalrie; whose presence also was thought only sufficient to overthrow anie hold.»

Note 11, page 199, col. 1.
I hate the Saxon.

Of this name Saxon, which the Welsh still use, Higden gives an odd etymology. « Men of that cowntree ben more lyghter and stronger on the see than other scommers or theeves of the see, and pursue theyr enemyes full harde, both by water and by londe, and ben called Saxones, of Saxum, that is, a stone, for they ben as hard as stones, and uneasy to fare with.»—*Polycronycon,* 1. 26.

Note 12, page 199, col. 1.
Seest thou never
Those eyeless spectres by thy bridal-bed?

Henry in his attempt upon Wales, 1165, « did justice on the sons of Rhys, and also on the sons and daughters of other noblemen that were his accomplices, very rigorously; causing the eyes of the young striplings to be pecked out of their heads, and their noses to be cut off or slit; and the eares of the young gentlewomen to be stuffed. But yet I find in other authors that in this journey King Henry did not greatly prevail against his enemies, but rather lost many of his men of war, both horsemen and footmen; for by his severe proceeding against them, he rather made them more eager to seek revenge, than quieted them in any tumult.»—*Holinshed.* Among these unhappy hostages were some sons of Owen Gwynedh.

Note 13, page 199, col. 1.
The page who chafed his feet.

« The foot-bearer shall hold the feet of the king in his lap from the time when he reclines[1] at the board till he goes to rest, and he shall chafe them with a towel; and during all that time he shall watch that no hurt happen to the king. He shall eat of the same dish from which the king takes his meat, having his back turned toward the fire. He shall light the first candle before the king at his meal.»—*Laws of Hoel Dha'.*

Note 14, page 199, col. 2.
The officer proclaimed the sovereign will.

The crier to command silence was one of the royal household; first he performed this service by his voice, then by striking with the rod of his office the pillars above the king's head. A fine was due to him for every disturbance in the court.

[1] *Accubuerit* is the word in Wotton's version. It is evident that the king must have lain at his meal, after the Roman fashion, or this pedifer could not have chafed his feet.

Note 15, page 199, col. 2.
The chief of Bards
Then raised the ancient lay.

The lines which follow represent the Bardic [system, as laid down in the *Triads of Bardism.*

12. There are three Circles of Existence; the Circle of Infinity, where there is nothing but God, of living or dead, and none but God can traverse it; the Circle of Inchoation, where all things are by nature derived from Death,—this Circle hath been traversed by man; and the Circle of Happiness, where all things spring from Life,—this man shall traverse in Heaven.

13. Animated Beings have three States of Existence: that of Inchoation in the Great Deep, or Lowest point of Existence; that of Liberty in the State of Humanity; and that of Love, which is Happiness in Heaven.

14. All animated Beings are subject to three Necessities: Beginning in the Great Deep; Progression in the Circle of Inchoation; and Plenitude in the Circle of Happiness. Without these things nothing can possibly exist but God.

« 15. Three things are necessary in the circle of Inchoation; the least of all animation, and thence Beginning; the matterials of all things, and thence Increase, which cannot take place in any other state; the formation of all things out of the dead mass, and thence Discriminate Individuality.

« 16. Three things cannot but exist towards all animated Beings from the nature of Divine Justice: Cosufferance in the Circle of Inchoation, because without that none could attain to the perfect knowledge of any thing; Co-participation in the Divine love; and Co-ultimity from the nature of God's Power, and its attributes of Justice and Mercy.

« 17. There are three necessary occasions of Inchoation: to collect the materials and properties of every nature; to collect the knowledge of every thing; and to collect power towards subduing the Adverse and the Devastative, and for the divestation of Evil. Without this traversing every mode of animated existence, no state of animation, or of any thing in nature, can attain to Plenitude.»

Note 16, page 199, col. 2.
Till evil shall be known,
And being known as evil, cease to be.

« By the knowledge of three things will all Evil and Death be diminished and subdued; their nature, their cause, and their operation. This knowledge will be obtained in the Circle of Happiness.»—*Triads of Bardism,* Tr. 35.

Note 17, page 199, col. 2.
Death, the Enlarger.

Angau, the Welsh word for Death, signifies Enlargement.

Note 18, page 199, col. 2.
The eternal newness of eternal joy.

Nefoedd, the Welsh word for Heaven, signifies Renovation.

« The three Excellencies of changing the mode of Existence in the Circle of Happiness: Acquisition of Knowledge; beautiful Variety; and Repose, from not being able to endure uniform Infinity and uninterrupted Eternity.

« Three things none but God can do: endure the

Eternities of the Circle of Infinity; participate of every state of Existence without changing; and reform and renovate every thing without the loss of it.

« The three Plenitudes of Happiness: Participation of every nature, with a plenitude of One predominant; conformity to every cast of genius and character, possessing superior excellence in One; the Love of all Beings and Existences, but chiefly concentered in One object, which is God: and in the predominant One of each of these will the Plenitude of Happiness consist. »—*Triads of Bardism*, 40, 38, 45.

Note 19, page 199, col. 2.
———— he struck the harp
To Owen's praise.

« I will extol the generous Hero, descended from the race of Roderic, the bulwark of his country, a Prince eminent for his good qualities, the glory of Britain: Owen, the brave and expert in arms, that neither hoardeth nor coveteth riches.

« Three fleets arrived, vessels of the main, three powerful fleets of the first rate, furiously to attack him on the sudden : one from Iwerddon,* the other full of well-armed Lochlynians, making a grand appearance on the floods; the third from the transmarine Normans, which was attended with an immense though successless toil.

« The dragons of Mona's sons were so brave in action, that there was a great tumult on their furious attack; and before the prince himself there was vast confusion, havoc, conflict, honourable death, bloody battle, horrible consternation, and upon Tal Mavra, a thousand banners: there was an outrageous carnage, and the rage of spears and hasty signs of violent indignation. Blood raised the tide of the Menai, and the crimson of human gore stained the brine. There were glittering cuirasses, and the agony of gashing wounds, and the mangled warriors prostrate before the chief, distinguished by his crimson lance. Loegria was put into confusion; the contest and confusion was great, and the glory of our Prince's wide-wasting sword shall be celebrated in an hundred languages to give him his merited praise. »—*Panegyric upon Owen Gwynedd, Prince of North Wales*, by GWALCHMAI *the son of Melir, in the year* 1157. EVANS's *Specimens of Welsh Poetry.*

Note 20, page 200, col. 1.
Dinevawr.

Dinas Vawr, the Great Palace, the residence of the Princes of Deheubarth, or South Wales. This also was erected by Rhodri Mawr.

Note 21, page 200, col. 1.
Hoel seized the throne.

I have taken some liberties here with the history. Hoel kept possession of the throne nearly two years; he then went to Ireland to claim the property of his mother Pyvog, the daughter of an Irish chieftain; in the mean time David seized the government. Hoel raised all the force he could to recover the crown, but after a severe conflict was wounded and defeated. He returned to Ireland with the remains of his army, which probably consisted chiefly of Irishmen, and there died of his wounds.—*Cambrian Biography.*

¹ Ireland.

Note 22, page 201, col. 1.
———— hast thou known the consummated crime.
And heard Cynetha's fate?

The history of Cynetha and his brothers is very honestly related in the *Pentarchia.*

Cadwallonis erat primævus jure Cynetha ;
Proh pudor ! hunc oculis patruus privavit Oenus
Testiculisque simul, fundum dum rapiat avitum.
Houel ab irato suspensus rege Johanne,
Et Leolinus, eum privarunt lumine fratres.

This curious summary of Welsh history still remains unprinted.

Note 23, page 202, col. 2.
As thy fair uplands lessened on the view.

« Two of the names of Britain were derived from its hills: *Clas Merddin*, the high lands in the sea, and *Clas Meiddin*, the hilly lands or fields. »—E. WILLIAMS's *Poems.*

Note 24, page 202, col. 2.
Seen, low lying, in the haze of morn.

What sailors call cape Fly-away.

Note 25, page 204, col. 1.
Saint Cyric.

The saint to whom sailors addrest themselves. The St Elmo of the Welsh.

It was usual for all, even females, who went from North Wales in pilgrimage to St David's, to pass the dangerous strands and sail over the rough bays in slight coracles, without any one to guide or assist them ; so firmly were they convinced that that Saint and St Cyric, the ruler of the waves, would protect them. »—E. WILLIAMS's *Poems.*

Note 26, page 204, col. 1.
Gwenhidwy.

« A Mermaid. The white foamy waves are called her sheep ; the ninth wave her ram. The Welsh have two proverbs concerning her : Take the Mermaid's advice and save thyself ; Take shelter when you see the Mermaid driving her flocks ashore. »—E. WILLIAMS.

Note 27, page 204, col. 1.
Where at their source the floods, for ever thus,
Beneath the nearer influence of the Moon,
Laboured in these mad workings?

« Everyche flood aryseth more in Oecean than in the grete see, that is for the hole togyder is myghtyer and stronger than ony partye by hymself. Or for the hole Oecean is grete and large, and receyved more workynge of the mone than ony partye by hymselfe that is smaller and lasse. »—*Polycronicon*, l. 1, c. 9.

Note 28, page 204, col. 1.
Did the Waters
Here on their outmost circle meet the Void?

« The see of Oecean beclyppeth all the erthe abowte as a garlonde, and by tymes cometh and goth, ebbying and flowynge, and flodeth in sees and casteth them up, and wyndes blowen therein. »—*Polycronicon*, l. 1, c. 9.

Note 29, page 204, col. 1.
Or this Earth—
Was it indeed a living thing?

« Physici autumant mundum animal esse, eumque ex variis elementorum corporibus conglobatum, moveri

35

spiritu, regi mente. Quæ utraque diffusa per membra omnia, æternæ molis vigorem exerceant. Sicut ergo in corporibus nostris commertia sunt spiritalia, ita in profundis Oceani nares quasdam mundi constitutas, per quas emissi anhelitus, vel reducti, modo effient maria quomodo revocent.»—*Solinus*, cap. 36.

« I suppose the waters,» says Pietro Martire, « to be driven about the globe of the earth by the incessant moving and impulsion of the heavens, and not to be swallowed up and cast out again by the breathing of Demogorgon, as some have imagined, because they see the seas by increase and decrease, to flow and reflow.» *Dec.* 3, c. 6.

Note 30, page 204, col. 1.

—— gentle airs which breathed,
Or seemed to breathe, fresh fragrance from the shore.

« Our first notice of the approach of land was the fragrant and aromatic smell of the continent of South America, or of the islands in its vicinity, which we sensibly perceived as a squall came from that quarter.»— M'KINNEN's *Tour through the British West Indies.*

Dogs always are sensible when land is near, before it can be seen.

Note 31, page 205, col. 1.

Low nets of interwoven reeds.

« And for as much as I have made mention of their houses, it shall not be greatly from my purpose to describe in what manner they are builded : they are made round, like bells or round pavilions. Their frame is raysed of exceeding high trees, set close together, and fast rampaired in the ground, so standing aslope, and bending inward, that the toppes of the trees joyne together, and bear one against another, having also within the house certain strong and short proppes or posts, which susteyne the trees from falling. They cover them with the leaves of date trees and other trees strongly compact and hardened, wherewith they make them close from winde and weather. At the short posts, or proppes, within the house, they tie ropes of the cotton of gossampine trees, or other ropes made of certain long and rough roots, much like unto the shrubbe called *Spartum*, whereof in old time they used to make bands for vines, and gables and ropes for shippes. These they tie overthwart the house from post to post; on these they lay as it were certain mattresses made of the cotton of gossampine trees, which grow plentifully in these islandes. This cotton the Spanyards call *Algodon*, and the Italians *Bombasine*, and thus they sleepe in hanging beddes.»—PIETRO MARTIRE.

Note 32, page 205, col. 1.

Will ye believe
The wonders of the ocean ? how its shoals
Sprung from the wave.

I have somewhere seen an anecdote of a sailor's mother, who believed all the strange lies which he told her for his amusement, but never could be persuaded to believe there could be in existence such a thing as a flying fish. A Spanish author, who wrote before the voyage of Columbus, describes these fish as having been seen on the coast of Flanders. « Hay alli unos pescados que vuelan sobre el agua ; algunos dellos atravesaban volando por encima de las galeras, e aun algunos dellos caian dentro.» *Coronica de D. Pero Nino.*

A still earlier author mentions such a sight in the Straits as a miracle. « As they sailed from Algesiras, a fish came flying through the air, and fell upon the deck of the Infantes Galley, with which they had some fresh food that day ; and because I, who write this history, have never heard or seen of any like thing, I here recount it, because it appears to me a thing marvellous, and in my judgement out of the course of nature.»— GOMES EANNES.

« At Barbadoes the negroes, after the example of the Charaibs, take the flying fish very successfully in the dark ; they spread their nets before a light, and disturb the water at a small distance ; the fish, rising eagerly, fly towards the light, and are intercepted by the nets.» —M'KINNEN.—These flying fishes, says the writer of Sir Thomas Roe's Voyage, are like men professing two trades, and thrive at neither.

Note 33, page 205, col. 1.

Language cannot paint
Their splendid tints !

Atkins, with some feeling describes the Dolphin as *a glorious coloured* fish. A laboured description of its beauty would not have conveyed so lively a sense of admiration. He adds, quite naturally, that it is of dry taste, but makes good broth.—*Voyage to Guinea in his Majesty's Ships the Swallow and Weymouth.*

Herbert has given this fish a very extraordinary character, upon the authority of the ancients.

« The dolphin is no bigger than a salmon, it glitters in the ocean with a variety of beautiful colours ; has few scales ; from its swiftness and spirit metonymically sirnamed the Prince and Arrow of the sea ; celebrated by many learned Pens in sundry Epithets ; *Philanthropoi,* for affecting men, and *Monogamoi,* for their turtle constancy ; generated they be of sperme, nourish like men, imbrace, join, and go 10 months great. *In faciem versi dulces celebrant hymenæos Delphines, similes hominis complexibus hærent* : A careful husband over his gravid associate, detesting incest, abhorring bigamy, tenderly affecting Parents, whom, when 300 years old, they feed and defend against hungry fishes ; and, when dead, (to avoid the Shark and like marine Tyrants) carry them ashore, and there (if *Aristotle, Ælyan,* and *Pliny,* erre not) inhume and bedew their Sepulchres ; they were glad of our company, as it were affecting the sight and society of men, many hundred miles in an eager and unwearied pursuit, frisking about us ; and as a Poet observed,

Undique dans saltus, multaque aspergine rorant,
Emurguntque iterum, redeuntque sub æquora rursus,
Inque chori ludunt speciem lascivaque jactant
Corpore, et acceptum patulis mare naribus effiant.»
                                   HERBERT's *Travels.*

Note 34, page 206, col. 1.

The Stranger's House.

« There is in every village of the Susquehannah Indians, a vacant dwelling called the Stranger's House. When a traveller arrives within hearing of a village, he stops and halloos, for it is deemed uncivil to enter abruptly. Two old men lead him to the house, and then go round to the inhabitants, telling them a stranger is arrived fatigued and hungry. They send them all they can spare, bring tobacco after they are refreshed, and then ask questions whence they come and whither they go.»—FRANKLIN.

Note 35, page 206, col. 1.

——— a race
Mightier than they, and wiser, and by Heaven
Beloved and favoured more.

« They are easily persuaded that the God that made Englishmen is a greater God than theirs, because he hath so richly endowed the English above themselves. But when they hear that about 1600 years ago, England and the inhabitants thereof were like unto themselves, and since have received from God clothes, books, etc. they are greatly affected with a secret hope concerning themselves.» *A Key into the language of America*, by ROGER WILLIAMS, 1643.

Note 36, page 206, col. 1.

Her husband's war-pole.

« The war-pole is a small peeled tree painted red, the top and boughs cut off short. It is fixed in the ground opposite the door of the dead warrior, and all his implements of war are hung on the short boughs of it till they rot.»—ADAIR.

This author, who knew the manners of the North American Indians well, though he formed a most wild theory to account for them, describes the rites of mourning. « The widow, through the long term of her weeds, is compelled to refrain from all public company and diversions, at the penalty of an adultress, and likewise to go with flowing hair, without the privilege of oil to anoint it. The nearest kinsmen of the deceased husband keep a very watchful eye over her conduct in this respect. The place of interment is also calculated to wake the widow's grief, for he is entombed in the house under her bed; and if he was a war-leader, she is obliged, for the first moon, to sit in the day-time under his mourning war-pole, which is decked with all his martial trophies, and must be heard to cry with bewailing notes. But none of them are fond of that month's supposed religious duty, it chills, or sweats and wastes them so exceedingly, for they are allowed no shade or shelter.»

Note 37, page 207, col. 1.

——— Battlements—which shone
Like silver in the sunshine.

So dazzlingly white were the houses at Zempoalla, that one of the Spaniards galloped back to Cortes to tell him the walls were of silver.—BERNAL DIAZ, 30.

Torquemada also says, « that the temple and palace courts at Mexico were so highly polished, that they actually shone like burnished gold or silver in the sun.» —T. 1, p. 251.

I have described Aztlan like the cities which the Spaniards found in New Spain. How large and how magnificent they were may be learnt from the True History of the Conquest of Mexico, by Bernal Diaz. This delightful work has been rendered into English by Mr Keating, and if the reader has not seen it, he may thank me for recommending it to his notice.

Gomera's description of Zempoallan will show, that cities as splendid in their appearance as Aztlan did exist among the native Americans.

« They descried Zempoallan, which stoode a myle distant from them, all beset with fayre Orchardes and Gardens, verye plesaunte to beholde : they used alwayes to water them with sluices when they pleased. There proceeded out of the Towne many persons to behold and receyve so strange a people unto them. They came with smiling countenance, and presented unto them divers kinde of floures and sundry fruites which none of our menne had heretofore seene. These people came without feare among the ordinance; with this pompe, triumphe, and joy, they were received into the Citie, which seemed a beautiful Garden : for the trees were so greene and high that scarcely the houses appeared.

« Sixe horsemen, which hadde gone before the army to discover, returned backe as Cortes was entering into the Citie, saying, that they had seene a great house and court, and that the walles were garnished with silver. Cortes commanded them to proceed on, willing them not to shew any token of wonder of any thing that they should see. All the streetes were replenished with people, whiche stoode gapping and wondering at the horses and straungers. And passing through a great market place, they saw, on their right hand a great walled house made of lyme and stone, with loupe holes and towers, whited with playster that shined like silver, being so well burnished and the sunne glistering upon it, and that was the thing that the Spaniards thought had beene walles of silver. I doe believe that with the imagination and great desire which they had of golde and silver, all that shined they deemed to be of the same metall.»—*Conquest of the Weast India.*

Cortes himself says of Cholulla, that he counted above four hundred temple towers in that city; and the city of Iztapalapa, he says, contained from 12,000 to 15,000 inhabitants.—*Carta de Relacion*, 16, 20.

Note 38, page 207, col. 1.

A floating islet.

Islets of this kind, with dwelling huts upon them, were common upon the Lake of Mexico. They were moved at pleasure from bay to bay, as the inhabitants wanted sunshine or shelter.—CLAVIGERO.

Note 39, page 207, col. 1.

Each held a burning censer in his hand.

Tendilli, says the old translator of Gomara, according to their usance, did his reverence to the Captaine, burning frankincense, and little strawes touched in bloud of his own bodie. And at Chiauiztlan, the Lord toke a little chafyng-dishe in his hande, and cast into it a certaine gum, whyche savoured in sweete smel much like unto frankincense; and with a censer he smoked Cortes, with the ceremonye they use in theyr salutations to theyr Gods and nobilitie. So also the Tlascallan Embassadors burnt copal before Cortes, having thrice made obeicence, and they touched the ground with their hands, and kissed the earth.

The nexte day in the morning, the Spaniards came to Chololla, and there came out near ten thousand Indians to receyve him, with their Captaines in good order. Many of them presented unto him bread, foules, and roses : and every Captayne, as he approached, welcomed Cortes, and then stood aside, that the rest, in order, mighte come unto him; and when he came entering into the citie, all the other citizens receyved him, marvelling to see such men and horses.

After all this came out all the religious menne, as, Priests and Ministers to the idols, who were many and straunge to behold, and all were clothed in white, like unto surplices, and hemmed with common threede; some brought instruments of musicke like unto Cornettes, others brought instruments made of bones; others an instrument like a ketel covered with skin; some brought chafing-dishes of coals, with perfumes; others brought idols covered; and, finally, they al came singing in their language, which was a terrible noyse, and drew neere Cortes and his company, sensing them with sweete smelles in their sensers. With this pomp and solemnitie, which truely was great, they brought him unto the cittie.—*Conquest of the Weast India.*

Gage's account of Mexico is copied verbatim from this old translation, even, in some places, to the literal error of using the hard c instead of z, which the ç with the cedilla represents.

Note 40, page 207, col. 1.
The Great Temple. 'T was a huge square hill.

The great Cu of Mexico, for thus these mounds were called, had 114 steps to the summit : that of Tezcuco, 115; of Cholula, 120. Gold and jewels, and the different seeds of the country, and human blood, were thrown in the foundations. The Spaniards found great treasures when they raised the Cu at Mexico, to make room for a church to Santiago.—BERNAL DIAZ.

The lines which follow describe its structure, as related by Clavigero and by the Spanish Conquerors. The Tower of Babel is usually painted with the same kind of circuitous ascent.

Note 41, page 207, col. 2.
The Tambour of the God.

Gumilla (c. 36.) describes a prodigious drum used as a signal to assemble the people in time of danger, by some of the Orinoco tribes, especially by the Caverres, to whom the invention is ascribed. It is a hollowed piece of wood, in thickness about an inch, in girth as much as two men can clasp, in length about eleven or twelve feet. This is suspended by a withe at each end from a sort of gallows. On the upper surface are three apertures like those in a fiddle, and in the bottom of the instrument, immediately under the middle of the middle aperture, which is shaped like a half-moon, a flint about two pounds in weight is fastened with gum. This is said to be necessary to the sound. Both ends of this long tube are carefully closed, and it is beaten on the middle aperture with a pellet which is covered with a sort of gum called Currucay. Gumilla positively affirms, and on his own knowledge, that its sound may be heard four leagues round. This is scarcely possible. I doubt whether the loudest gong can be heard four miles, and it is not possible that wood can be made as sonorous as metal.

Note 42, page 207, col. 2.
Ten Cities hear its voice.

« There, in the great Cu, they had an exceeding large drum; and when they beat it, the sound was such and so dismal, that it was like an instrument of hell, and was heard for more than two leagues round. They said that the cover of that drum was made of the skin of huge serpents.»—BERNAL DIAZ.

After Cortes had been defeated, he always heard this drum when they were offering up the recking hearts of his men. The account in Bernal Diaz, of their midnight sacrifice, performed by torch-light, and in the sight of the Spanish army, is truly terrific.

Note 43, page 207, col. 2.
Four Towers
Were piled with human skulls.

These skull-built temples are delineated in Picart's great work; I suppose he copied them from De Bry. They are described by all the historians of Mexico. Human heads have often been thus employed. Tavernier and Hanway had seen pyramids of them in Persia erected as trophies. The *Casa dos Ossos* at Evora gave me an idea of what these Mexican temples must have been. It is built of skulls and thigh-bones in alternate layers, and two whole bodies, dried and shrivelled, are hung up against the walls, like armour in an old baron's hall.

Note 44, page 208, col. 1.
He lights me at my evening banquet.

The King of Chalco having treacherously taken and slain two sons of the King of Tetzcuco, had their bodies dried, and placed as candelabras in his palace, to hold the lights.—TORQUEMADA, i, 151.

This same king wore round his neck a chain of human hearts set in gold — the hearts of the bravest men whom he had slain, or taken and sacrificed.—*Ditto,* 152.

The more usual custom was to stuff the skin of the royal or noble prisoner, and suspend it as a trophy in the palace, or the house of the priest. Gomara's account of this custom is a dreadful picture of the most barbarous superstition which ever yet disgraced mankind. « On the last day of the first month, a hundred slaves were sacrificed : this done, they pluckt off the skinnes of a certaine number of them, the which skinnes so many ancient persons put, incontinent, upon their naked bodies, all fresh and bloudy as they were fleane from the dead carcases. And being open in the backe parte and shoulders, they used to lace them, in such sort that they came fitte upon the bodies of those that ware them; and being in this order attired, they came to daunce among many others. In Mexico the King himself did put on one of these skinnes, being of a principall captive, and daunced among the other disguised persons, to exalte and honour the feast; and an infinite number followed him, to behold his terrible gesture; although some hold opinion, that they followed him to contemplate his greate devotion. After the sacrifice ended, the owner of the slaves did carry their bodies home to their houses, to make of their fleshe a solemne feaste to all their friendes, leaving their heads and hartes to the Priests, as their dutie and offering : and the skinnes were filled with cotton wool, or strawe, to be hung in the temple and kyng's palayce for a memorie.»—*Conquest of the Weast India.*

After the Inga Yupangui had successfully defended Cuzco against the Chancas, he had all of them who were slain skinned, and their skins stuffed and placed in various attitudes, some beating tambours, others blowing flutes, etc. in a large building which he erected as a monument for those who had fallen in defending the city.—HERRERA, 5. 3. 12.

Note 45, page 209, col. 1.
Oh, what a pomp,
And pride, and pageantry of war!

Gomara thus describes the Tlascallan army : « They were trimme felowes, and wel armed, according to their

use, although they were painted so, that their faces
shewed like divals, with great tuffes of feathers and tri-
umphed gallantry. They had also slinges, staves, speares,
swordes, bowes, and arrowes, skulles, splintes, gantlettes
all of wood, gilte, or else covered with feathers, or lea-
ther; their corslets were made of cotton woole, their
targettes and bucklers, gallant and strong, made of
woode covered with leather, and trimmed with laton
and feathers; theyr swordes were staves, with an edge
of flint stone cunningly joyned into the staffe, which
would cutte very well, and make a sore wounde. Their
instruments of warre were hunters' hornes, and drum-
mes, called attabals, made like a caldron, and covered
with vellum.»—*Conquest of the Weast India.*

In the inventory of the treasure which Grijalva brought
from his expedition are, a whole harness of furniture for
an armed man, of gold thin beaten; another whole ar-
mour of wood, with leaves of gold, garnished with little
black stones; four pieces of armour of wood, made for
the knees, and covered with golden leaf. And among
presents designed for the king, where five targets of
feathers and silver, and 24 of feathers and gold, set with
pearls, both curious and gallant to behold.

Note 46, page 209, col. 1.

They piled a heap of sedge before our host.

When the Spaniards discovered Campeche, the In-
dians heaped up a pile of dry sedge, and ranged them-
selves in troops. Ten Priests then came from a temple
with censers and copal, wherewith they incensed the
strangers; and then told them by signs to depart, before
that pile, which they were about to kindle, should be
burnt out. The pile was immediately lighted; the Priest
withdrew without another word or motion, and the
people began to whistle and sound their shells. The
Spaniards were weak, and many of them wounded, and
they prudently retired in peace.—*Bernal Diaz, 3.*

At the sacring of the Popes, when the new-elected
Pope passeth (as the manner is) before St Gregory's
chapel, the Master of the Ceremonies goeth before him,
bearing two dry reeds, at the end of the one a burning
wax candle tied, and at the end of the other a handfull
of flax, the which he setteth on fire, saying, with a loud
voice, *Pater Sancte, sic transit gloria mundi.*—*Came-
rarius.*

Note 47, page 209, col. 1.

The Arrow of the Omen.

The Tlaxcaltecas had two arrows, which they regard-
ed with great reverence, and used to augur the event of
a battle. Two of their bravest Chiefs were to shoot them
at the enemy, and recover them or die. If the arrow
struck and wounded, it was held an omen that the fight
would be prosperous; but if they neither struck, nor
drew blood, the army retired.—*Torquemada, i. 34.*

This is more particularly noticed by Gomara. «In the
warres the Tlascallans use their standerde to be carried
behynde the army: but when the battyle is to be fought,
they place the standerde where all the hoste may see it;
and he that commeth not incontinent to hys ancient,
payeth a penaltie. Their standerde hath two crosse bow
arrowes set thereon, whiche they esteeme as the relikes
of their ancestors. This standerde two olde soldiers,
and valiant menne, being of the chiefest Captaynes, have
the charge to carrie; in the which standerde, an abusion
of southsaying, eyther of losse or victory, is noted. In

this order they shote one of these arrowes against the
first enemies that they meete; and if with that arrowe
they do eyther kill or hurte, it is a token that they shall
have the victorie; and if it neyther kill nor hurte then,
they assuredly believe that they shall lose the field.»—
Conquest of the Weast India.

Note 48, page 209, col. 1.

The bowmen of Dheubarth—Gwyneth's spears.

«Sunt autem his in partibus (Ardudwy) lanceæ lon-
gissimæ: sicut enim arcu prevalet Sudwallia, sic lanceis
prævalet Venedotia, adeo ut ictum hic lancea cominus
datum ferrea loricæ tricatura minime sustineat.»—*Gi-
raldus Cambrensis.*

Thus also Trevisa, in his lame rhymes:

The south bete Demecia,
And the other Venedocia;
The first shoteth and arrowes beres,
That other dealeth all with spere.

Polycronicon.

Note 49, page 210, col. 2.

The white deer-skin shroud.

« The Indians use the same ceremonies to the bones
of their dead, as if they were covered with their former
skin, flesh, and ligaments. It is but a few days since I
saw some return with the bones of nine of their people,
who had been two months before killed by the enemy.
They were tied in white deer-skins separately, and when
carried by the door of one of the houses of their fa-
mily, they were laid down opposite to it, till the female
relations convened, with flowing hair, and wept over
them about half an hour. Then they carried them
home to their friendly magazines of mortality, wept
over them again, and then buried them with the usual
solemnities. The chieftains carried twelve short sticks,
tied together in the form of a quadrangle, so that each
square consisted of three. The sticks were only peeled,
without any painting; but there were swan feathers
tied to each corner. They called that frame the White
Circle, and placed it over the door while the women
were weeping over the bones.»—*Adair.*

Note 50, page 210, col. 2.

'T was in her hut and home, yea, underneath The marriage-bed, the bed of widowhood, Her husband's grave was dug.

« The Mosqueto Indians, when they die, are buried
in their houses, and the very spot they lay over when
alive, and have their hatchet, harpoon lances, with
mushelaw, and other necessaries, buried with them;
but if the defunct leaves behind him a gun, some friend
preserves that from the earth, that would soon dam-
nify the powder, and so render it unserviceable in that
strange journey. His boat, or *dorea,* they cut in pieces,
and lay over his grave, with all the rest of his house-
hold goods, if he hath any more. If the deceased leave
behind him no children, brothers, or parents, the cou-
sins, or other his relations, cut up, or destroy his plant-
ations, least any living should, as they esteem it, rob
the dead.»—*The Mosqueto Indian and his Golden Ri-
ver, by M. W. Lintot, and Osborn's Collection.*

Note 51, page 210, col. 2.

On softest fur the bones were laid.

When the body is in the grave, they take care to
cover it in such a manner, that the earth does not

touch it. It lies as in a little cave, lined with skins, much neater, and better adorned, than their cabins.—CHARLEVOIX.

Adair was present at one of their funerals. « They laid the corpse in his tomb in a sitting posture, with his feet towards the east, his head anointed with bear's oil, and his face painted red; but not streaked with black, because that is a constant emblem of war and death. He was drest in his finest apparel, having his gun and pouch, and trusty hiccory bow, with a young panther's skin full of arrows, along side of him, and every other useful thing he had been possessed of, that when he rises again they may serve him in that track of land which pleased him best before he went to take his long sleep. His tomb was firm and clean inside; they covered it with thick logs so as to bear several tiers of cypress bark, and such a quantity of clay, as would confine the putrid smell, and be on a levesd with the rest of the floor. They often sleep over these tombs; which, with the loud wailing of the women at the dusk of the evening, and dawn of the day, on benches close by the tombs, must awake the memory of their relations very often; and if they were killed by an enemy, it helps to irritate, and set on such revengeful tempers to retaliate blood for blood. »

Note 52, page 210, col. 2.

Pabas.

Papa is the word which Bernal Diaz uses when he speaks of the Mexican priests; and in this he is followed by Purchas. The appellation in Torquemada is Quaquil. I am not certain that Bernal Diaz did not mean to call them *Popes*, and that Purchas has not mistaken his meaning. An easy alteration made it more suitable for English verse, than the more accurate word would have been.

I perceive by Herrera (3. 2. 15.) that the word is Mexican, and that the Devil was the author of it, in imitation of the Church.

Note 53, page 211, col. 1.

Ipalnemoani, by whom we live.

The Mexicans had some idea, though a very imperfect one, of a supreme, absolute, and independent being. They represented him in no external form, because they believed him to be invisible; and they named him only by the common appellation of God, or in their language *Teotl*; a word resembling still more in its meaning than its pronunciation, the Θεος of the Greeks. But they applied to him certain epithets, which were highly expressive of the grandeur and power which they conceived him to possess; *Ipalnemoani*, « He by whom we live:» and *Tloque Nahuaque*, « He who has all in himself.»—CLAVIGERO.

Torquemada has a very characteristic remark upon these appellations: «Although,» says he, « these blinded men went astray in the knowledge of God, and adored the Devil in his stead, they did not err in the names which they gave him, those being truly and properly his own: the Devil using this cunning with them, that they should apply to him these, which, by nature and divine right, are God's; his most holy Majesty permitting this on account of the enormity and shamefulness of their depraved customs, and the multitude of their iniquities».—L. vi, c. 8.

Note 54, page 211, col. 1.

The Great Spirit, who in mountain caves,
And by the fall of waters,
Doth make his being felt.

« About thirty miles below the falls of St Anthony, is a remarkable cave, of an amazing depth. The Indians term it Wakon-teebe; that is, the dwelling of the Great Spirit. The entrance into it is about ten feet wide; the arch within is near fifteen feet high, and about thirty feet broad. The bottom of it consists of fine clean sand. About twenty feet from the entrance begins a lake, the water of which is transparent, and extends to an unsearchable distance; for the darkness of the cave prevents all attempts to acquire a knowledge of it. I threw a small pebble towards the interior parts of it, with my utmost strength; I could hear that it fell into the water, and, notwithstanding it was of so small a size, it caused an astonishing and horrible noise, that reverberated through all those gloomy regions. I found in this cave many Indian hieroglyphics, which appeared very ancient, for time had nearly covered them with moss. They were cut in a rude manner upon the inside of the walls, which were composed of a stone so extremely soft, that it might easily be penetrated with a knife: a stone every where to be found near the Mississipi. The cave is only accessible by ascending a narrow steep passage that lies near the brink of the river.»—CARVER.

« The Prince had no sooner gained the point that overlooks this wonderful cascade (the falls of St Anthony) than he began with an audible voice to address the Great Spirit, one of whose places of residence he supposed this to be. He told him he had come a long way to pay his adorations to him, and now would make him the best offerings in his power. He accordingly first threw his pipe into the stream; then the roll that contained his tobacco; after these, the bracelets he wore on his arms and wrists; next, an ornament that encircled his neck, composed of beads and wires; and at last, the ear-rings from his ears; in short, he presented to his God every part of his dress that was valuable; during this he frequently smote his breast with great violence, threw his arms about, and appeared to be much agitated.

« All this while he continued his adorations, and at length concluded them with fervent petitions that the Great Spirit would constantly afford us his protection on our travels, giving us a bright sun, a blue sky, and clear untroubled waters; nor would he leave the place till we had smoked together with my pipe in honour of the Great Spirit.»—CARVER.

Note 55, page 211, col. 2.

The Spirit of the Lord
That day was moving in the heart of man.

There is a passage in Bede which well illustrates the different feelings whereby barbarians are induced to accept a new religion.

« Edwin of Northumbria had summoned his chiefs and counsellors to advise with him concerning his intended conversion. The first person who delivered his opinion was Coifi, the Chief Priest of the Idols. ‘For this which is preached to us,’ said he, ‘do you, O King, see to it, what it may be. I will freely confess to you what I have learnt, that the religion which we have held till now has no virtue in it. No one of your subjects has devoted himself to the worship of our Gods more earnestly than I, and yet many there are who have received greater bounties and greater favours from your hand, and have prospered better in all their undertakings and desires. Now, if our Gods could have done any thing, they would rather have assisted me than them.' To this another of the nobles added, 'The present life of man upon earth, when compared with the future, has appeared to me, O King, like as when you and your Chiefs and servants have been seated at your supper, in winter time, the hearth blazing in the centre, and the viands smoking, while without it is storm, or rain, or snow, and a sparrow flies through the hall, entering at one door and passing out at another; while he is within, in that little minute he does not feel the weather, but after that instant of calm, he returns again to winter as from winter he came, and is gone. Such and so transitory is the life of man, and of what follows it or what preceded it we are altogether ignorant. Wherefore, if this new doctrine should bring any thing more certain, it well deserves to be followed.»—*Lib.* 2, c. 13.

John Wesley has preserved a very interesting dialogue between himself and the Chicasaws.

« Q. Do you believe there is One above who is over all things? Paustoobee answered, We believe there are four Beloved Things above, the Clouds, the Sun, the Clear Sky, and He that lives in the Clear Sky.

« Q. Do you believe there is but one that lives in the Clear Sky?

« A. We believe there are Two with him; Three in all.

« Q. Do you think He made the Sun and the other Beloved Things?

« A. We cannot tell. Who hath seen?

« Q. Do you think He made you?

« A. We think He made all men at first.

« Q. How did He make them at first?

« A. Out of the ground.

« Q. Do you believe He loves you?

« A. I do not know. I cannot see Him.

« Q. But has He not often saved your life?

« A. He has. Many bullets have gone on this side, and many on that side, but He would never let them hurt me. And many bullets have gone into these young men, and yet they are alive.

« Q. Then cannot he save you from your enemies now?

« A. Yes, but we know not if he will. We have now so many enemies round about us, that I think of nothing but death; and if I am to die, I shall die, and I will die like a man. But if He will have me to live, I shall live. Though I had ever so many enemies He can destroy them all.

« Q. How do you know that?

« A. From what I have seen. When our enemies came against us before, then the Beloved Clouds came for us; and often much rain and sometimes hail has come upon them, and that in a very hot day. And I saw when many French and Choctaws and other nations came against one of our towns, and the ground made a noise under them, and the Beloved Ones in the air behind them, and they were afraid, and went away,

and left their meat and their drink, and their guns. I tell no lie, all these saw it too.

« Q. Have you heard such noises at other times?

« A. Yes, often; before and after almost every battle.

« Q. What sort of noises were they?

« A. Like the noise of drums and guns and shouting.

« Q. Have you heard any such lately?

« A. Yes; four days after our last battle with the French.

« Q. Then you heard nothing before it?

« A. The night before I dreamed I heard many drums up there, and many trumpets there, and much stamping of feet and shouting. Till then I thought we should all die; but then I thought the Beloved Ones were come to help us. And the next day I heard above a hundred guns go off before the fight began, and I said when the Sun is there the Beloved Ones will help us, and we shall conquer our enemies; and we did so.

« Q. Do you often think and talk of the Beloved Ones?

« A. We think of them always wherever we are. We talk of them and to them, at home and abroad, in peace and in war, before and after we fight, and indeed whenever and wherever we meet together.

« Q. Where do you think your souls go after death?

« A. We believe the souls of red men walk up and down near the place where they died, or where their bodies lie, for we have often heard cries and noises near the place where any prisoners had been burnt.

« Q. Where do the souls of white men go after death?

« A. We cannot tell; we have not seen.

« Q. Our belief is that the souls of bad men only walk up and down; but the souls of good men go up.

« A. I believe so too; but I told you the talk of the nation.

« Mr Andrews. They said at the burying they knew what you was doing. You was speaking to the Beloved Ones above to take up the soul of the young woman.

« Q. We have a book that tells us many things of the Beloved Ones above; would you be glad to know them?

« A. We have no time now but to fight. If we should ever be at peace, we should be glad to know.

« Q. Do you expect ever to know what the white men know?

« Mr Andrews. They told Mr O. they believe the time will come when the red and white men will be one.

« Q. What do the French teach you?

« A. The French Black Kings (the Priests) never go out. We see you go about: we like that; that is good.

« Q. How came your nation by the knowledge they have?

« A. As soon as ever the ground was sound and fit to stand upon, it came to us, and has been with us ever since. But we are young men, our old men know more; but all of them do not know. There are but a few whom the Beloved One chuses from a child, and is in them, and takes care of them, and teaches them. They know these things, and our old men practise, therefore they know: but I do not practise, therefore I know little.»—WESLEY'S *Journal*, No. I, 39.

Note 56, page 213, col. 1.
Dolwyddelan.

« Dolwyddelan is situated in a rocky valley which is sprinkled with stunted trees, and watered by the Lleder. The boundaries are rude and barren mountains, and among others, the great bending mountain Seabod, often conspicuous from most distant places. The castle is placed on a high rock precipitous on one side, and insulated: it consists of two square towers, one 40 feet by 25, the other 32 by 20: each had formerly three floors. The materials of this fortress are the shattery stone of the country; yet well squared, the masonry good, and the mortar hard; the castle yard lay between the towers.»—PENNANT's *Snowdon*.

The rudeness and barrenness of the surrounding mountains I can well testify, having been bewildered and benighted upon them.

« In the beginning of Edward the Fourth his reign, Dolwyddelan was inhabited by Howell ap Evan ap Rheys Gethin, a base son, captain of the country, and an outlaw. Against this man David ap Jenkin rose and contended with him for the sovereignty of the country, and being superior to him in the end, he drew a draught for him, and took him in his bed at Penanonen with his concubine, performing by craft what he could not by force; for after many bickerings betweeen Howell and David, David being too weak was fayne to fly the country and to goe to Ireland, where he was a year or thereabouts; in the end he returned, in a summer time, having himself and all his followers clad in greene; which being come into the country, he dispersed here and there among his friends, lurking by day and walking by night, for fear of his adversaries; and such of the country as happened to have a sight of him and of his followers, said they were fayries, and so ran away.»—GWYDIR's *History*.

Note 57, page 213, col. 1.
Nor turned he now
Beside Kregennan, where his infant feet
Had trod Ednywain's hall.

At some distance beyond the two pools called Llynian Cragenan, in the neighbourhood of Cader Idris near the river Kregennan, I saw the remains of Llys Bradwen, the Court or Palace of Ednowain, chief of one of the fifteen tribes of North Wales, either in the reign of Gruffydd ap Cynan, or soon after. The relics are about thirty yards square: the entrance above seven feet wide, with a large upright stone on each side, by way of doorcase; the walls with large stones, uncemented by any mortar: in short, the structure of this palace shows the very low state of architecture in those times; it may be paralleled only by the artless fabric of a cattle house.—PENNANT's *Snowdon*.

Note 58, page 213, col. 2.
The Hirlas.

Mr Owen, to whose indefatigable industry Cymbric literature is so much indebted, has favoured me with a literal version of this remarkable poem.

When the dawn uprose a shout was given;
Foes were sending a luckless destiny.
Mangled with ruddy wounds our men, after heavy toil,
were seen scattered about the wall of the Vale of Maelor.
I chased away the strangers inured to contention,
dauntless in the conflict, with red-stained weapons.
Who insults the brave let him beware his presence!
the result of molesting him is a source of affliction.

Pour out, thou Cup-bearer, thus yielding pleasure,
the Horn in the hand of Rhys, in the hall of the director of bounty,
the hall of Owen, that has ever been maintained on spoil,
the feasting of a thousand thou ma est hear; open are the gates.
Cup-bearer! I am sad and silent: bas he not left me?
Reach thou the horn for mutual drinking;
Full of sorrow am I for the leader of the hue of the ninth wave;[1]
long and blue its characteristic, gold its cover:
so bring it forth with *Bragod*, a liquor of exalted pledge,
into the hand of the froward Gwgan, to requite his deed.
The whelps of Goronwy are mighty in the path of wrath,
aptly springing whelps, confident their feet,
men who claim a reward in every difficulty;
men in the shout greatly valued, of mighty deliverance.
The shepherd of Havern (*Severn*) it elates the soul to hear them
sounding the Horns of mead that greatly rouse desire.

Pour out thou the Horn covered with a yellow top,
honourably drunk with over-frothing mead;
and if thou seekest life to one year's close,
diminish not its respect, since it is not meet;
And bear to Grafydd, the crimson-lanced foe,
wine with pellucid glass around it;
the dragon of Arwstli, safeguard of the borders,
the dragon of Owen, the generous, of the race of Cynvyn,
a dragon from his beginning, and never scared by a conflict
of triumphant slaughter, or afflicting chase.
Men of combat departed for the acquirement of fame,
armed sons of the banquet with gleaming weapons;
they requited well their mead, like Belyn's men of yore;
fairly did they toil while a single man was left.

Pour out thou the Horn, for it is my purpose
that its potent sway may incite a sprightly conversation,
in the right hand of our leader of devastation,
gleaming beneath the broad light shield;
in the hand of Ednyved, the lion of his land irreproachable;
all dexterous in the push of spears, shivered away his shield.
The tumult hurries on the two fearless of nature;
they would break as a whirlwind over a fair retreat,
with opposing fronts in the combat of battle,
where the face of the gold-bespangled shield they would quickly break.
Thoroughly stained their shafts after head-cleaving blows,
Thoroughly active in defending the glory-bounded Garthran,
and there was heard in Maelor a great and sudden outcry,
with horrid scream of men in agony of wounds,
and thronging round the carnage they interwove their paths.
As it was in Bangor round the fire of spears,
when two sovereigns over horns made discord,
when there was the banquet of Morac Morvran.

Pour thou out the Horn, for I am contemplating
where they defend both their mead and their country.
Selyc the undaunted, of the station of Gwygyr,
look to it, who insults him of eagle heart!
And Madoc's only son, the generous Tudyr of high renown,
and the claim of the wolf, a slayer with gleaming shafts.
Two heroic ones, two lions in their onset,
two of cruel energy, the two sons of Ynyr;
two unrestrained in the day of battle their onward course,
of irresistible progress and of matchless feat.
The stroke of the fierce lions fiercely cut through warriors
of battle-leading forms, red their ashen thrusters
of violence, bending in pursuit with ruthless glory.
The shivering of their two shields may be likened
to the loud-voiced wind, over the green-sea brink
checking the incessant waves; so seemed the scene of Talgarth.

Pour out, thou Cup-bearer, seek not death,
the Horn with honour in festivals,
the long blue bugle of high privilege, with ancient silver
that covers it, with opposite lips,
and bear to Tudyr, eagle of conflicts,
a prime beverage of the blushing wine.
If there come not in of mead the best of all
the liquor from the bowl, thy head is forfeit,
to the hand of Moreiddig the encourager of songs;

[1] The ninth wave is an expression much used by the Welsh Poets. It occurs in the Hoianau of Myrddin. « I will prophesy before the ninth wave.»—*Arch.* p. 135. So in the eulogy on Eva: « Eva, of the hue of the spraying foam before the ninth wave.»—*Arch.* p. 217.

may they become old in fame before their cold depositure!
Brothers blameless! of highly soaring minds,
of dauntless vigour earning your deserts,
warriors who for me have achieved services,
not old with unsightliness, but old in dexterity,
toilers, impellers, leaders that are wolves
of the cruel foremost rank, with gory limbs.
Brave captains of the men of Mocnant, a Powysian l. nd,
both possess the prowess of the brave;
the deliverers in every need, ruddy are their weapons,
securely they would keep their bounds from tumult,
praise is their meed, they who are so blest.—
Cry of death was it? be the two to me then changed!
Oh my Christ! how sad am I from these wounds!
By the loss of Morefddig greatly is his absence felt.
Pour thou out the Horn, for they do not sigh for me!
the Hirlas, cheeringly in the hand of Morgant,
a man who deserves the homage of peculiar praise.
Like poison to the happy is the track of his spear,
a matter accursed is the abiding his blade,
smooth its two sid s, keen its edges.
Pour out, thou Cup-bearer, from a silver vessel
the solemn festive boon with due respect.
On the plain of great Gwestun I saw the raw throbbing.
To baffle Goronwy were a task for a hundred men;
the warriors a mutual purpose did accomplish there,
supporters of the battle, heedless of life.
The exalted chief did meet the dispersed ones of slaughter.
a governor was slain, burnt was a fort on the flood mark of the
      sea;
a magnanimous prisoner they fetched away,
Mairyc son of Grufydd, the theme of prophetic song:
Were they not all bathed in sweat when they returned,
for full of sunshine were the extended hill and dale?

Pour thou out the Horn to the mutually toiling ones,
the whelps of Owen with connected spears in united leap;
they would pour abroad in a noted spot
a store where the glittering irons go rebounding;
Madoc and Meller, men nurtured in depredation,
for iniquity the stemming opponents,
the instructors for tumult of a shield-bearing host,
and froward conductors of subjects trained for conflicts.
It is heard how from the feast of mead went the chief of Catraeth;
upright their purpose with keen-edged weapons;
the train of Mynyddo., for their being consigned to sleep,
obtained their recording, leaders of a wretched fray!
None achieved what my warriors did in the hard toil of Maelor.—
the release of a prisoner belongs to the harmonious eulogy.

Pour out, thou Cup-bearer, sweet mead distilled
of spear-impelling spirit in the sweating toil,
from bugle horns proudly overlaid with gold
to requite the pledge of their lives.
Of the various distresses that chieftains endure
no one knows but God and he who speaks.
A man who will not pay, will not pledge, will abide no law,
Daniel the auxiliary chief, so fair of loyalty.
Cup-bearer, great the deed that claims to be honoured,
of men refraining not from death if they find not hospitality.
Cup-bearer, a choicest tread of mead must be served us together,
an ardent fire bright, a light of ardently bright tapers.
Cup-bearer, thou mightest have seen a house of wrath in Lledwn
      land,
a sullenly subjected prey that shall be highly praised.
Cup-bearer, I cannot be continued here: nor avoid a separation;
Be it in Paradise that we be received;
with the Supreme of Kings long be our abode,
where there is to be seen the secure course of truth.

The passage in the poem would have stood very differently had I seen this literal version before it was printed. I had written from the faithless paraphrase of Evans, in which every thing characteristic or beautiful is lost.

Few persons who read this song can possibly doubt its authenticity. Those who chose to consider the Welsh poems as spurious had never examined them. Their groundless and impudent incredulity, however, has been of service to literature, as it occasioned Mr Turner to write his Vindication, which settled the question for ever.

Note 59, page 214, col. 2.
Saint Monacel.

« In Pennant-Melangle church was the tomb of St. Monacella, who, protecting a hare from the pursuit of Brocwell Yscythbrog, Prince of Powis, he gave her land to found a religious house, of which she became first Abbess. Her hard bed is shewn in the cleft of a neighbouring rock, her tomb was in a little chapel, now the vestry, and her image is still to be seen in the churchyard, where is also that of Edward, eldest son of Owen Gwynedh, who was set aside from the succession on account of a broken nose, and flying here for safety, was slain not far off, at a place called *Bwlch Croes Iorwerth*. On his shield is inscribed, *Hic jacet Etward*.»—Gough's *Camden*.

I had procured drawings of these monuments, designing to have had them engraved in this place; but on examination it appears that Mr. Gough has certainly been mistaken concerning one, if not concerning both. What he supposed to be the Image of St Monacel is evidently only the monumental stone of some female of distinction, the figure being recumbent, with the hands joined, and the feet resting upon some animal.

Note 60, page 214, col. 2.
The place of meeting was a high hill top.

The Bardic meetings, or *Gorseddau*, were held in the open air, on a conspicuous place, while the sun was above the horizon; for they were to perform every thing *in the eye of light, and in the face of the sun.* The place was set apart by forming a Circle of Stones, with a large stone in the middle, beside which the presiding Bard stood. This was termed *Cylç Cyngrair*, or the Circle of Federation, and the middle stone *Maen Llog*, the Stone of Covenant.

Mr Owen's very curious introduction to his translation of Llywarc Hen has supplied me with materials for the account of the *Gorsedd*, introduced in the poem. That it might be as accurate as possible, he himself and Edward Williams the Bard did me the favour of examining it. To their knowledge, and to that of Mr Turner, the historian of the Anglo-Saxons, and to the liberality and friendliness with which they have ever been willing to assist me therewith, I am greatly and variously indebted.

The Bard at these meetings wore the distinguishing dress of his order: a robe of sky blue, as an emblem of truth, being unicoloured, and also as a type, that, amid the storms of the moral world, he must assume the serenity of the unclouded sky. The dress of the *Ovydd*, the third order, or first into which the candidate could be admitted, was green. The *Awenyddion*, the Disciples, wore a variegated dress of blue, green, and white, the three Bardic colours, white being the dress of the Druids, who were the second order. The bards stood within the circle, bareheaded and barefooted, and the ceremony opened by sheathing a sword and laying it on the Stone of Covenant. The Bardic traditions were then recited.

Note 61, page 214, col. 2.
Himself, albeit his hands were stained with war,
Initiate; for the Order, in the lapse \
Of years, and in their nation's long decline,

36

From the first rigour of their purity
Somewhat had fallen.

« By the principles of the Order a Bard was never to
bear arms, nor in any other manner to become a party
in any dispute, either political or religious; nor was a
naked weapon ever to be held in his presence, for under
the title of *Bardd Ynyss Prydain*, Bard of the Isle of
Britain, he was recognised as the sacred Herald of
Peace. He could pass unmolested from one country
to another, where his character was known; and when-
ever he appeared in his unicoloured robe, attention was
given to him on all occasions; if it was even between
armies in the heat of action, both parties would in-
stantly desist.»—OWEN's *Llywarc Hen*.

Six of the elder Bards are enumerated in the Triads
as having borne arms in violation of their Order; but
in these latter days the perversion was become more
frequent. Meiler, the Bard of Grufydd ab Cynan, dis-
tinguished himself in war; Cynddelw, *Brydydd Mawr*,
the Great Bard, was eminent for his valour; and Gwal-
chmai boasts in one of his poems that he had defended
the Marches against the Saxons.—WARRINGTON.

Note 62, page 215, col. 1.

The Bard's most honourable name.

No people seem to have understood the poetical cha-
racter so well as the Welsh; witness their Triads.

« The three primary requisites of poetical Genius; an
eye that can see Nature, a heart that can feel Nature,
and a resolution that dares follow Nature.

« The three foundations of Genius; the gift of God,
man's exertion, and the events of life.

« The three indispensables of Genius; understanding,
feeling, and perseverance.

« The three things which constitute a poet; genius,
knowledge, and impulse.

« The three things that enrich Genius; contentment
of mind, the cherishing of good thoughts, and exercis-
ing the memory.»—E. WILLIAMS's *Poems*. OWEN's
Llywarc Hen.

Note 63, page 215, col. 1.

Cimbric lore.

« The Welsh have always called themselves *Cymry*,
of which the strictly literal meaning is Aborigines.
There can be no doubt that it is the same word as the
Cimbri of the ancients; they call their language *Cym-
raeg*, the Primitive Tongue.»—E. WILLIAMS's *Poems*.

Note 64, page 215, col. 2.

Where are the sons of Gavran; where his tribe,
The faithful?

« Gavran, the son of Aeddan Vradog ab Dyvnwall Hen,
a chieftain of distinguished celebrity in the latter part of
the fifth century. Gavran, Cadwallon, and Gwenddolau
were the heads of the three faithful tribes of Britain.
The family of Gavran obtained that title by accom-
panying him to sea to discover some islands, which, by
a traditionary memorial, were known by the name of
Gwerdonnan Llion, or the green Islands of the Ocean.
This expedition was not heard of afterwards, and the si-
tuation of those islands became lost to the Britons.
This event the voyage of Merddin Emrys with the
twelve Bards, and the expedition of Madoc, were called
the three losses by disappearance »—*Cambrian Bio-
graphy*.

Of these Islands, or green Spots of the Floods, there
are some singular superstitions. They are the abode of
the *Tylwyth Teg*, or the Fair family, the souls of the
virtuous Druids, who, not having been Christians, cannot
enter the Christian heaven, but enjoy this heaven of
their own. They however discover a love of mischief,
neither becoming happy Spirits, nor consistent with
their original character; for they love to visit the
earth, and, seizing a man, enquire whether he will travel
above wind, mid wind, or below wind; above wind is
a giddy and terrible passage, below wind is through
bush and break; the middle is a safe course. But the
spell of security is, to catch hold of the grass, for these
beings have not power to destroy a blade of grass. In
their better moods they come over and carry the Welsh
in their boats. He who visits these islands imagines
on his return that he has been absent only a few hours,
when, in truth, whole centuries have passed away.

If you take a turf from St David's church-yard, and
stand upon it on the sea-shore, you behold these islands.
A man once, who had thus obtained sight of them,
immediately put to sea to find them; but they disap-
peared, and his search was in vain. He returned, look-
ed at them again from the enchanted turf, again set
sail, and failed again. The third time he took the
turf into his vessel, and stood upon it till he reached
them.

« The inhabitants of Arran More, the largest of the
south isles of Arran, on the coast of Galway, are per-
suaded that in a clear day they can see *Hy Brasail*, the
Enchanted Island, from the coast, the Paradise of the
Pagan Irish.»—*Collectanea de rebus Hibernicis*. BEAU-
FORD's *Ancient Topography of Ireland*.

General Vallancey relates a different history of this
superstition. « The old Irish,» he says, « say, that great
part of Ireland was swallowed up by the sea, and that
the sunken part often rises, and is frequently to be seen
on the horizon from the Northern coast. On the North-
west of the island they call this enchanted country *Tir
Hudi*, or the city of Hud, believing that the city stands
there which once possessed all the riches of the world,
and that its key lies buried under some druidical monu-
ment. When Mr Burton, in 1765, went in search of
the Ogham monument, called Conane's Tomb, on Cal-
lan mountain, the people could not be convinced that
the search was made after an inscription, but insisted
that he was seeking after an Enchanted Key that lay
buried with the Hero, and which, when found, would
restore the Enchanted City to its former splendour, and
convert the moory heights of Callan mountain into rich
and fruitful plains. They expect great riches whenever
this city is discovered.»

This enchanted country is called *O Breasil*, or *O Bra-
zil*, which, according to General Vallancey's interpret-
ation, signifies the Royal Island. He says it is evidently
the lost city of Arabian story, visited by their fabulous
prophet Houd,—the City and Paradise of Irem! He
compares this tradition with the remarks of White-
hurst on the Giant's Causeway, and suspects that it
refers to the lost Atlantis, which Whitehurst thinks
perhaps existed there.

Is that very extraordinary phenomenon, known in
Sicily by the name of Morgaine le Fay's works, ever
witnessed on the coast of Ireland? If so, the super-
stition is explained by an actual apparition.—I had
not, when this note was written, seen Mr Latham's ac-
count of a similar phenomenon at Hastings, (Phil.

Trans. 1798), which completely establishes what I had here conjectured. Mr Nicholson, in his remarks on it, says the same thing has been seen from Broadstairs, and that these appearances are much more frequent and general than has usually been supposed.

Note 65, page 215, col. 2.

In his crystal Ark,
Whither sailed Merlin with his band of Bards,
Old Merlin, master of the mystic lore?

The name of Merlin has been so canonised by Ariosto and our diviner Spenser, that it would have been a heresy in poetry to have altered it to its genuine orthography.

Merddin was the bard of Emrys Wledig, the Ambrosius of Saxon history, by whose command he erected Stonehenge, in memory of the Plot of the Long Knives, when, by the treachery of Gwrytheyrn, or Vortigern and the Saxons, three hundred British chiefs were massacred. He built it on the side of a former Circle. The structure itself affords proof that it cannot have been raised much earlier, inasmuch as it deviates from the original principle of Bardic circles, where no appearauce of art was to be admitted. Those of Avebury, Stanton, Drew, Keswick, etc. exemplify this. It is called by the Welsh *Gwaith Emrys*, the work of Ambrosius. Drayton's reproach, therefore, is ill founded,—

Ill did those mighty men to trust thee with their story,
Thou hast forgot their names, who reared thee for their glory.

The Welsh traditions say that Merddin made a House of Glass, in which he went to sea, accompanied by the Nine Cylveirdd Bards, and was never heard of more. This was one of the three disappearances from the isle of Britain. Merddin is also one of the Three principal Christian Bards of Britain; Merddin Wyllt and Taliesin are the other two.—*Cambrian Biography*.

A diving House of Glass is also introduced in the Spanish Romance of Alexander, written about the middle of the 13th century, by Joan Lorenzo Segura de Astorga.

Unas facianas suelen las gentes retraer,
Non yaz en escrito, è es grave de creer ;
Si es verdat o non, yo non he y que veer,
Pero no lo quiero en olvido poner.

Dicen que por saber que facen los pescados,
Como viven los chicos entre los mas granados,
Fizo cuba de vidrio con pantos bien cerrados,
Metios en elia dentro con dos de sus criados.

Estos furon catados de todos los meiores,
Por tal que non oviessen dona los traedores,
Ca que el o que ellos avrien aguardadores,
Non farien à sus guisas los malos revoltores.

Fu de bona betume la cuba aguisada,
Fu con bonas cadenas bien presa è calzada,
Fu con priegos firmes à las naves pregada,
Que fonder non se podiesse è estodiesse colgada.

Mando que quinze dias lo dexassen by durar,
Las naves con todesto pensassen de tost andar,
Assaz podrie en esto saber e messurar.
Metria en escrito los secretos del mar.

La cuba fue fecha en quel fecha el Rey acia,
A los unos pesaba, à los otros placia :
Bien cuidaban algunos que nunca ende saldria,
Mas destaiado era que en mar non moriria.

Andabal bon Rey en su casa cerrada,
Sela grant corazon en angosta dosada ;
Vela toda la mai de pescados poblada,
No es bestia nel sieglo que non fes y trobada.

Non vive en el mundo nenguna creatura
Que non cria la mar semojante figura ;
Traen enemizades entre si por natura,
Los fuertes a los flacos danles mala ventura.

Estonce vio el Rey en aquellas andadas
Como echan los unos a los otros celadas ;
Dicen que ende furon presas è sossacadas,
Furon desent aca por el sieglo usadas.

Tanto se acogien al Rey los pescados
Como si los ovies el Rey por sublugados,
Venien fasta la cuba todos cabezcolgados,
Tremian todos antel como mosos moiades.

Juraba Alexandre per lo su diestro llado,
Que nunca fura domes meior acompannado ;
De los pueblos del mar tovose por pagado,
Contaba que avie grant emperio ganado.

Otra faciana vio en essos pobladores,
Vio que los maiores comien à los menores,
Los chicos à los grandes tenienos por sennores,
Maltraen los mas fuertes à los que son menores.

Diz el Rey, soberbia es en todolos lugares,
Forcia es enna tierra è dentro ennos mares :
Las aves esso mismo no se caton por pares,
Dios confunda tal vicio que tien tantos lugares.

Nacio entre los angelos è fizo muchos caer,
Arromólos Dios per la tierra, e dioles grant poder,
La mesnada non puede su derecho aver,
Ascondio la cabeza, non osaba parecer.

Quien mas puede mas face, non de bien, mas de mal,
Quien mas à aver mas quier, è morre por ganal ;
Non veerla de su grado nenguno so igual :
Mal peccado, nenguno no es à Dios leal.

Las aves e las bestias, los omes, los pescados,
Todos son ent e si a bandos derramados ;
De vicio è de soberbia son todos entregados.
Los flacos de los fuertes andan desafiados.

Se como sabel Rey bien todesto osmar,
Quisiesse assimismo à dere has iulgar,
Bien debie un poet su lengua refrenar,
Que en tant fieras grandias non quisiesse andar.

De su gradol Rey mas oviera estado,
Mas a sus criazones faciesles pesado,
Temiendo la ocasion que suel venir privado,
Sacaronlo bien ante dul termino passado.

The sweet flow of language and metre in so early a poem is very remarkable; but no modern language can boast of monuments so early and so valuable as the Spanish. To attempt to versify this passage would be laborious and unprofitable. Its import is, that Alexander being desirous to see how the Fish lived, and in what manner the great Fish behaved to the little ones, ordered a vessel of glass to be made, and fastened with long chains to his ships, that it might not sink too deep. He entered it with two chosen servants, leaving orders that the ships should continue their course, and draw him up at the end of fifteen days. The vessel had been made perfectly water-tight. He descended, and found the fish as curious to see him as he had been to see the fish. They crowded round his machine, and trembled before him as if he had been their conqueror, so that he thought he had acquired another empire. But Alexander perceived the same system of tyranny in the water as on the land, the great eat the little, and the little eat the less; upon which tyranny he made sundry moral observations, which would have come with more propriety from any other person than from himself. However, he observed the various devices which were used for catching fish, and which, in consequence of this discovery, have been used in the world ever since. His people were afraid some accident might happen, and drew him up long before the fifteen days were expired.

The Poet himself does not believe this story. «People say so,» he says, « but it is not in writing, and it is a thing difficult to believe. It is not my business to examine whether it be true or not, but I do not choose to pass it over unnoticed.» The same story was pointed out to me by Mr Coleridge in one of the oldest German poems; and what is more remarkable, it is mentioned by one of the old Welsh Bards. DAVIES's *Celtic Researches,* p. 196.   Jests, and the fictions of romance and superstition, seem to have travelled every where.

Note 66, page 215, col. 2.

Flathinnis.

Flath-innis, the Noble Island, lies surrounded with tempests in the Western Ocean. I fear the account of this Paradise is but apocryphal, as it rests upon the evidence of Macpherson, and has every internal mark of a modern fiction.

In former days there lived in Skerr [1] a magician [2] of high renown. The blast of wind waited for his commands at the gate; he rode the tempest, and the troubled wave offered itself as a pillow for his repose. His eye followed the sun by day; his thoughts travelled from star to star in the season of night; he thirsted after things unseen; he sighed over the narrow circle which surrounded his days; he often sat in silence beneath the sound of his groves; and he blamed the careless billows that rolled between him and the Green Isle of the West.

One day, as the Magician of Skerr sat thoughtful upon a rock, a storm arose on the sea: a cloud, under whose squally skirts the foaming waters complained, rushed suddenly into the bay. and from its dark womb at once issued forth a boat, with its white sails bent to the wind, and hung around with a hundred moving oars. But it was destitute of mariners, itself seeming to live and move. An unusual terror seized the aged Magician; he heard a voice: though he saw no human form, « Arise! behold the boat of the heroes! arise, and see the Green Isle of those who have passed away!»

He felt a strange force on his limbs; he saw no person; but he moved to the boat; immediately the wind changed; in the bosom of the cloud he sailed away. Seven days gleamed faintly round him, seven nights added their gloom to his darkness: his ears were stunned with shrill voices; the dull murmurs of winds passed him on either side; he slept not, but his eyes were not heavy; he ate not, but he was not hungry: on the eighth day the waves swelled into mountains; the boat was rocked violently from side to side; the darkness thickened around him, when a thousand voices at once cried aloud, The Isle! the Isle! The billows opened wide before him; the calm land of the departed rushed in light on his eyes.

It was not a light that dazzled, but a pure, distinguishing, and placid light, which called forth every object to view in their most perfect form. The isle spread large before him like a pleasing dream of the soul, where distance fades not on the sight, where nearness fatigues not the eye. It had its gently-slop-

[1] Skerr signifies, in general, a rock in the Ocean.
[2] A magician is called Druidh in the Gaelic.

ing hills of green, nor did they wholly want their clouds; but the clouds were bright and transparent, and each involved in its bosom the source of a stream, —a beauteous stream, which, wandering down the steep, was like the faint notes of the half-touched harp to the distant ear.   The valleys were open and free to the ocean; trees loaded with leaves, which scarcely waved to the light breeze, were scattered on the green declivities and rising grounds; the rude winds walked not on the mountain; no storm took its course through the sky. All was calm and bright; the pure sun of Autumn shone from his blue sky on the fields; he hastened not to the West for repose, nor was he seen to rise from the East: he sits in his mid-day height, and looks obliquely on the Noble Isle.

In each valley is its slow moving stream; the pure waters swell over the bank, yet abstain from the fields; the showers disturb them not, nor are they lessened by the heat of the sun. On the rising hill are the halls of the departed,—the high-roofed dwellings of the heroes of old.

The departed, according to the Tale, retained, in the midst of their happiness, a warm affection for their country and living friends. They sometimes visited the first; and by the latter, as the Bard expresses it, they were transiently seen in the hour of peril, and especially on the near approach of death; it was then that at midnight the death-devoted, to use the words of the Tale, were suddenly awakened by a strange knocking at their gates; it was then that they heard the indistinct voice of their departed friends calling them away to the Noble Isle; « a sudden joy rushed in upon their minds, and that pleasing melancholy which looks forward to happiness in a distant land.»—MACPHERSON'S *Introduction to the History of Great Britain.*

« The softer sex, among the Celtæ,» he adds, «passed with their friends to the fortunate isles; their beauty increased with the change, and, to use the words of the Bard, they were ruddy lights in the Island of Joy.»

Note 67, page 215, col. 2.

Where one emerald light
Through the green element for ever flows?

I have supplied Merlin with light when he arrived at his world of Mermankind, but not for his submarine voyage; let Paracelsus do this.

« Urim and Thummim were the Philosopher's Stone, and it was this which gave light in the Ark.

« For God commanded Noah to make a clear light in the Ark, which some take for a window. But since the Text saith, *Day and night shall no more cease;* it seems *it did then cease,* and therefore there could be no exterior light.

« The Rabbis say, that the Hebrew word Zohar, which the Chaldees translate Neher, is only to be found in this place. Other Hebrew doctors believe it to have been a precious stone hung up in the Ark, which gave light to all living creatures therein. This the greatest carbuncle could not do, nor any precious stone which is only natural. But the Universal Spirit, fixed in a transparent body, shines like the sun in glory, and this was the light which God commanded Noah to make. » —PARACELSUS' *Urim and Thummim.*

Note 68, page 216, col. 2.

Rhys ab Grufydd ab Rhys.

Was one of the bravest, wisest, most liberal, and most

celebrated of the princes of South Wales. He is thus praised in the Pentarchia :

Quis queat heroem calamo describere tantum,
Quantus ut ipse fult, modo civibus Hectoris instar,
Fortes in hostiles modo turmas instar Achillis.
Ultus avos patriæ fere sexaginta per annos,
Quot fusas acies, quot castra recepta, quot arbes,
Spes patriæ, columen pacis, lux urbis et orbis,
Gentis bonos, decus armorum, falmenque duelli,
Quæ neque pace prior, neque fortior alter in armis.

In Hearne's Collection of Curious Discourses, are these funeral verses upon Lord Rhys, as preserved by Camden :

Nobile Cambrensis cecidit diadema decoris,
Hoc est Rhesus obiit, Cambria tota gemit.
Subtrahitur, sed non moritur, quia semper habetur
Ipsius egregium nomen in orbe novum.
Hic tegitur, sed detegitur, quia fama perennis
Non sinit illustrem voce latere ducem.
Excessit probitate modum, sensu probitatem,
Eloquio sensum, moribus eloquium.

Rhys ap Gryffith, say the Chronicles, was no less remarkable in courage, than in the stature and lineaments of his body, wherein he exceeded most men.—*Royal Tribes.*

Note 69, page 216, col. 2.

Beavers.

When Giraldus Cambrensis wrote, that is, at the time whereof the poem treats, the only Beavers remaining in Wales or England were in the Towy. *Inter universos Cambriæ, seu etiam Loegriæ fluvios, solus hic (Teivi) castores habet.*

The Beaver is mentioned also in the laws of Hoel Dha, and one of those dark deep resting-places or pits of the river Conway, which the Spaniards call the *remansos del rio*, is called the Beavers' pool.

Note 70, page 217, col. 1.

The Great Palace, like a sanctuary, Is safe.

Dinas Vawr, the Great Palace. It was regarded as an asylum.

Note 71, page 217, col. 1.

Goagan of Powys-land.

Properly Gwgan; but I have adapted the orthography to an English eye. This very characteristic story is to be found, as narrated in the poem, in Mr Yorke's curious work upon the Royal Tribes of Wales. Gwgan's demand was for five pounds, instead of ten marks; this is the only liberty I have taken with the fact, except that of fitting it to the business of the poem, by the last part of Rhys's reply. The ill humour in which the Lord of Dinvawr confesses the messenger had surprised him, is mentioned more bluntly by the historian. « Gwgan found him in a furious temper, beating his servants and hanging his dogs.» I have not lost the character of the anecdote, by relating the cause of his anger, instead of the effects.

Note 72, page 218, col. 1.

The Bay whose reckless waves Roll o'er the plain of Gwaelod.

A large tract of fenny country, called Cantrev y Gwaelod, the Lowland Canton, was, about the year 500, inundated by the sea, for Seithenyn, in a fit of drunkenness, let the sea through the dams which se-

cured it. He is therefore distinguished with Geraint and Gwrtheyrn, under the appellation of the Three arrant Drunkards. This district, which forms the present Cardigan Bay, contained sixteen principal towns of the Cymry, the inhabitants of which, who survived the inundation, fled into the mountainous parts of Meirion and Arvon, which were till then nearly uncultivated. Gwyddno Garanhir, one of the petty Princes whose territories were thus destroyed, was a poet. There were lately (and I believe, says Edmund Williams, are still) to be seen in the sands of this bay large stones with inscriptions on them, the characters Roman, but the language unknown. E. WILLIAMS's *Poems.—Cambrian Biography.*

The two other arrant Drunkards were both Princes; the one set fire to the standing corn in his country, and so occasioned a famine ; Gwrtheyrn, the other, is the Vortigern of Saxon history, thus distinguished for ceding the Isle of Thanet, in his drunkenness, as the price of Rowena. This worthless King is also recorded as one of the Three disgraceful men of the Island, and one of the Three treacherous conspirators, whose families were for ever divested of privilege.—*Cambrian Biography.*

Note 73, page 218, col. 1.

Bardsey.

« This little island,» says Giraldus, « is inhabited by certain monks of exceeding piety, whom they call Culdees (*Calibes vel Colideos*). This wonderful property it hath, either from the salubrity of its air, which it partakes with the shores of Ireland, or rather from some miracle by reason of the merits of the Saints, that diseases are rarely known there, and seldom or never does any one die till worn out by old age. Infinite numbers of Saints are buried there.»

Note 74, page 219, col. 1.

On his back, Like a broad shield, the coracle was hung.

« The Coracles are generally five feet and a half long and four broad, their bottom is a little rounded, and their shape nearly oval. These boats are ribbed with light laths, or split twigs, in the manner of basket-work, and are covered with a raw hide or strong canvass, pitched in such a mode as to prevent their leaking ; a seat crosses just above the centre, towards the broader end ; they seldom weigh more than between 20 and 30 pounds. The men paddle them with one hand while they fish with the other, and when their work is completed, they throw the coracles over their shoulders, and without difficulty return with them home.

« Riding through Abergwilly we saw several of these phænomena resting with their bottoms upwards against the houses, and resembling the shells of so many enormous turtles ; and indeed a traveller, at the first view of a coracle on the shoulders of a fisherman, might fancy he saw a tortoise walking on his hinder legs.»—WINDHAM.

The Saxon pirates ventured to sea in vessels of basket-work covered with skins : they were used also by the ancient Spaniards ; perhaps the coracle succeeded the canoe, implying more skill than is necessary to scoop out a tree, or hollow it with fire, and less than is required to build a boat. The boats of bark which the savages of Canada use are equally ingenious, and possess the same advantages.

Note 75, page 220, col. 2.

Prince Hoel's lay of love.

Eight poems by Prince Hoel are preserved: they are here given in Mr Owen's translation.

1.

My choice is a lady, elegant, slender, and fair, whose lengthened white form is seen through the thin blue veil; and my choicest faculty is to muse on superior female excellence, when she with diffidence utters the becoming sentiment; and my choicest participation is to become united with the maid, and to share mutual confidence as to thoughts and fortune. I chuse the bright hue of the spreading wave, thou who art the most discreet in thy country, with thy pure Welsh speech, chosen by me art thou; what am I with thee? how! dost thou refrain from speaking? ah! thy silence even is fair! I have chosen a maid, so that with me there should be no hesitation; it is right to chuse the choicest fair one; chuse, fair maid!

2.

I love the white glittering walls on the side of the bank, clothed in fresh verdancy, where bashfulness loves to observe the modest sea-mew's course; it would be my delight, though I have met with no great return of love in my much-desired visit on the sleek white steed, to behold my sister of flippant smile; to talk of love since it has come to my lot; to restore my ease of mind, and to renew her slighted troth with the nymph as fair as the hue of the shore-beating wave.

From her country, who is bright as the coldly-drifted snow upon the lofty hill, a censure has come to us, that I should be so treated with disdain in the Hall of Ogyrvan.

Playful, from her promise was new-born expectation;—she is gone with my soul away: I am made wretched!—Am I not become for love like Garwy Hir to the fair one of whom I am debarred in the Hall of Ogyrvan!

3.

I love the castle of proud workmanship in the Cyvylci, where my own assuming form is wont to intrude; the high of renown, in full bustle, seek admittance there, and by it speaks the mad resounding wave.

It is the chosen place of a luminary of splendid qualities and fair; glorious her rising from the verge of the torrent, and the fair one shines upon the now progressive year in the wild of Arvon, in the Snowdonian hills.

The tent does not attract; the glossy silk is not looked on by her I love, with passing tenderness: if her conquest could be wrought by the muse's aid, ere the night that comes, I should next to her be found.

4.

I have harnessed thee to-day, my steed of shining grey; I will traverse on thee the fair region of Cynlas; and I will hold a hard dispute before death shall cut me off in obstructing sleep, and thus obstructing health; and on me it has been a sign, no longer being the honoured youth, the complexion is like the pale blue waves.

Oppressed with longing is my memory in society; regret for her by whom I am hated; whilst I confer on the maid the honoured eulogy; she, to prosper pain, deigns not to return the consolation of the slightest grace.

Broken is my heart! my portion is regret, caused by the form of a slender lady, with a girdle of ruddy gold; my treatment is not deserved, she is not this day where my appointed place was fixed. Son of the God of Heaven! if before a promise of forbearance she goes away, woe to me that I am not slain.

5.

When the ravens rejoice, when blood is hastening, when the gore runs bubbling, when the war doth rage, when the houses redden in Ruzlan, when the red hall is burning, when we glow with wrath; the ruddy flame it blazes up to heaven; our abode affords no shelter; and plainly is the bright conflagration seen from the white walls upon the shore of Menai.

They perished on the third day of May, three hundred ships of a fleet roving the ocean; and ten hundred times the number the sword would put to flight, leaving not a single beard on Menai.

6.

Five evening tides were celebrated when France was saved, when barbarian chiefs were made to fly, when there was pressure round the steel-clad bodies; should a weapon yet be brandished round the beard, a public triumph would my wrath procure, scouring the bounds of Loegyr, and on her habitation hurling ruin; there should be the hand of the hastening host upon the cross, the keen edge slaughtering, the blade reeking with blood, the blood hue over the abject throng, a blood veil hiding its place of falling, and a plain of blood, and a cheek suffused with gore.

7.

I love the time of summer; then the gladly-exulting steed of the warrior prances before a gallant chief; the wave is crowned with foam; the limb of the active more quickly moves; the apple tree has arrayed itself in another livery; bordered with white is my shield on my shoulder, prepared for violence. I have loved with ardency of desire, the object which I have not obtained.

Ceridwen, fair and tall, of slowly languid gait, her complexion vies with the warm dawn in the evening hour, of a splendid delicate form, beautifully mild and white-hued presence! in stepping over a rush nearly falling seems the little tiny fair one; gentle in her air, she appears but scarcely older than a tenth year infant. Young, shapely, and full of gracefulness, it were a congenial virtue that she should freely give; but the youthful female does more embarrass good fortune by a smile, than an expression from her lips checks impertinence.

A worshipping pilgrim she will send me to the celestial presence; how long shall I worship thee? stop and think of thine office! If I am unskilful through the dotage of love, Jesus, the well-informed, will not rebuke me.

8.

Fair foam-crowned wave, spraying over the sacred tomb of Ruvon the brave, the chief of princes, behold this day I love the utmost hate of England, a flat and unenergetic land, with a race involved in every wile. I love the spot that gave me the much-desired gift of mead, where the seas extend a tedious conflict. I love the society and thick inhabitants therein, and which, obedient to its lord, directs its view to peace. I love its sea-coasts and its mountains, its city bordering on its forest, its fair landscape, its dales, its water, and its vales, its white sea-mews, and its beauteous women. I love its warriors and its well-trained steeds, its woods, its strong-holds, and its social domicil. I love its fields clothed with tender trefoil, where I had the glory of a mighty triumph. I love its cultivated regions, the prerogative of heroism, and its far-extended wild, and its sports of the chase, which, Son of God! have been great and wonderful: how sleek the melodious deer, and in what plenty found! I achieved by the push of a spear an excellent deed between the chief Powys and happy Gwynez, and upon the pale-hued element of ever-struggling motion may I accomplish a liberation from exile. I will not take breath until my party comes; a dream declares it, and God wills it to be so, fair foam-crowned wave spraying over the grave.

Fair foam-crowned wave, impetuous in thy course, like in colour to the hoar when it accumulates; I love the sea-coast in Meirionyz, where I have had a white-arm for a pillow. I love the nightingale upon the privet-brake in Cymmer Denzur, a celebrated vale. Lord of heaven and earth, the glory of the blest, though so far it is from Ceri to Caerliwelyz, I mounted the yellow steed, and from Maelienyz reached the land of Reged between the night and day. Before I am in the grave, may I enjoy a new blessing from the land of Tegyngyl of fairest aspect! Since I am a lovewight, one inured to wander, may God direct my fate! fair foam-crowned wave of impetuous course.

I will implore the Divine Supreme, the wonderful in subjugating to his will, as king, to create an excelling muse for a song of praise to the women, such as Merzin sung, who have claimed my bardic lore so long, who are so tardy in dispensing grace. The most eminent in all the west I name, from the gates of Chester to the port of Ysgewin : The first is the nymph who will be the subject of universal praise, Gwenliant, whose complexion is like the summer's day. The second is another of high state, far from my embrace, adorned with golden necklace, fair Gweirvyl, from whom nor token nor confidence have I obtained, nor has any of my race; though I might be slain by two-edged blades, she whose foster-brother was a king, should be my theme; and next for the handsome Gwladys, the young and modest virgin, the idol of the multitude, I utter the secret sigh; I will worship her with the yellow blossoms of the furze. Soon may I see my vigour rouse to combat, and in my hand my blade, bright Leucu, my companion, laughing, and whose husband laughs not from anxiety. Great anxiety oppresses me, makes me sad; and longing, alas! is habitual for fair Nêst, for her who is like the apple-tree blossom; and for Perwewr, the centre of my desire; for Generys the chaste, who grants not a smile for me : may continence not overcome her! for Hunyz, whose fame will last till the day of doom; for Hawis, who claims my choicest eulogy. On a memorable day I had a nymph; I had a second, more be their praise; I had a third and a fourth with prosperity; I had a fifth of those with a skin white and delicate; I had a sixth bright and fair, avoiding not the temptation, above the white walls did she arrest me; I had a seventh, and this was satiety of love; I had eight in

recompense for a little of the praise which I sung; but the teeth most opportunely bar the tongue.

Note 76, page 222, col. 1.

Ere ever Saxon set his hateful foot
Upon the beautiful Isle.

« The three names of this Island ; the first, before it was inhabited it was called the Water-guarded Green Spot ; after it was inhabited it was called the Honey-Island ; and after its subjection to Prydain, the son of Aedd Mawr, he gave it the name of the Isle of Prydain.»—*Cambrian Register.*

This name was appropriately given to it, for Ynis Prydain signifies the Beautiful Isle.—*Cambrian Biography*, E. WILLIAMS.

Note 77, page 222, col. 1.

The contumacious Prince of Mathraval.

« Oenum de Cevelioc, quia solus inter Walliæ principes Archipræsuli cum populo suo non occurrerat, excommunicavimus. Oenus iste præ aliis Cambriæ principibus, et linguæ dicacis extiterat, et in terræ suæ moderamine ingenii perspicacis.»—GIRALDUS CAMBRENSIS.

Note 78, page 223, col. 1.

Even as Owen in his deeds
Disowned the Church when living, even so
The Church disowns him dead.

Owen Gwyneth was buried at Bangor. When Baldwin, Archbishop of Canterbury, coming to preach the crusade against the Saracens, saw his tomb, he charged the Bishop to remove the body out of the Cathedral, when he could find a fit opportunity so to do; in regard that Archbishop Becket had excommunicated him heretofore, because he had married his first cousin, the daughter of Grono ab Edwyn, and that notwithstanding he had continued to live with her till she died. The Bishop, in obedience to the charge, made a passage from the vault through the south wall of the church, under ground, and so secretly shoved the body into the churchyard.—*Royal Tribes, from the* HENGWRT MS.

Note 79, page 225, col. 1.

Winning slow famine to their aid.

« I am much affected,» says old Fuller, « with the ingenuity of an English nobleman, who, following the camp of King Henry III in these parts (Caernarvonshire), wrote home to his friends, about the end of September 1243, the naked truth indeed as followeth : ' We lie in our tents, watching, fasting, praying, and freezing ; we watch for fear of the Welchmen, who are wont to invade us in the night; we fast for want of meat, for the half-penny loaf is worth five-pence ; we pray to God to send us home speedily; we freeze for want of winter garments, having nothing but thin linen betwixt us and the wind.'»

Note 80, page 225, col. 2.

Be not thou
As is the black and melancholy yew,
That strikes into the grave its baleful roots,
And prospers on the dead.

Borrowed from an old play by John Webster:

Like the black and melancholic yew-tree,
Dost think to root thyself in dead men's graves,
And yet to prosper?
The White Devil, or Vittoria Corombona.

Note 81, page 226, col. 2.

Never shall her waking eye
Behold them, till the hour of happiness
When Death hath made her pure for perfect bliss.

« The three Restorations in the Circle of Happiness; Restoration of original genius and character; *Restoration of all that was beloved*; and the Restoration of remembrance from the origin of all things : without these perfect happiness cannot exist.»—*Triads of Bardism*, 32.

I have thought it unnecessary to give a connected account of the Bardic system in these Notes, as it has been so well done by my friend, Mr Turner, in his Vindication of the Ancient British Poems.

PART II.

Note 1, page 228, col. 1.

We neighbour nearer to the Sun!

Columbus inferred this from the elevation of the Pole at Paria. « How it cometh to pass,» says Pietro Martire, « that at the beginning of the evening twilight it is elevate in that region only five degrees in the month of June, and in the morning twilight to be elevate fifteen degrees by the same quadrant, I do not understand, nor yet do the reasons which he bringeth in any point satisfy me. For he sayeth that he hereby conjectured that the Earth is not perfectly round, but that, when it was created, there was a certain heap raised thereon, much higher than the other parts of the same. So that, as he sayth, it is not round after the form of an apple or a ball, as others think, but rather like a pear as it hangeth on the tree, and that Paria is the region which possesseth the supereminent or highest part thereof, nearest unto heaven. In so much, that he earnestly contendeth the earthly Paradise to be situate in the tops of those three hills which the Watchmen saw out of the top castle of the ship; and that the outrageous streams of the fresh waters which so violently issue out of the red gulfs, and strive so with the salt water, fall headlong from the tops of the said mountains.»—PIETRO MARTIRE, *Dec. 1, Book 6.*

Note 2, page 229, col. 1.

Te-calipoca.

A devout worshipper of this Deity once set out to see if he could find him; he reached the sea-coast, and there the God appeared to him, and bade him call the Whale, and the Mermaid, and the Tortoise, to make a bridge for him, over which he might pass to the House of the Sun, and bring back from thence instruments of music and singers to celebrate his festivals. The Whale, the Mermaid, and the Tortoise accordingly made the bridge, and the man went over it, singing, as he went, a song which the God taught him. As soon as the Sun heard him, he cautioned all his servants and people not to answer to the song, for they who answered would be obliged to abandon his House and follow the Singer. Some there were, however, who could not resist the voice of the charmer, and these he brought back with him to earth, together with the drums called *Huahuneth Tepunaztli.*—TORQUEMADA, *L. vi, c. 43.*

The particular sacrifice related in the poem is described by this author, *L. 10, c. 14.* It is sufficient merely to refer to my authorities in such instances as these, where no other liberty has been taken than that of omission.

Note 3, page 229, col. 2.

She gather'd herbs which, like our poppy, bear
The seed of sleep.

The expression is Gower's :

Poppy, which beareth the sede of sleepe.

The Spanish name for the poppy is *adormidera*.

Note 4, page 231, col. 1.

The field of the Spirit.

Every Spring the Akanceas go in a body to some retired place, and there turn up a large space of land, which they do with the drums beating all the while. After this they take care to call it the Desart, or the field of the Spirit. And thither they go in good earnest when they are in their enthusiastic fits, and there wait for inspiration from their pretended Deity. In the meanwhile, as they do this every year, it proves of no small advantage to them, for by this means they turn up all their land insensibly, and it becomes abundantly more fruitful.—TONTI.

Note 5, page 231, col. 1.

Before these things I was.

« The manner in which, he says, he obtained the spirit of divination was this: He was admitted into the presence of a Great Man, who informed him that he loved, pitied, and desired to do him good. It was not in this world that he saw the Great Man, but in a world above, at a vast distance from this. The Great Man, he says, was clothed with the Day, yea with the brightest Day, he ever saw; a Day of many years, yea of everlasting continuance! This whole world, he says, was drawn upon him, so that *in* him the Earth and all things in it might be seen. I asked him if rocks, mountains, and seas were drawn *upon* or appeared *in* him? he replied, that every thing that was beautiful and lovely in the earth was upon him, and might be seen by looking on him, as well as if one was on the earth to take a view of them there. By the side of the Great Man, he says, stood his Shadow or Spirit, for he used *chichung,* the word they commonly make use of to express that of the man which survives the body, which word properly signifies a shadow. This shadow, he says, was as lovely as the Man himself, and *filled all places,* and was most agreeable as well as wonderful to him. Here, he says, he tarried some time, and was unspeakably entertained and delighted with a view of the Great Man, of his Shadow, and of all things in him. And what is most of all astonishing, he imagines all this to have passed before he was born; he never had been, he says, in this world at that time, and what confirms him in the belief of this is, that the Great Man told him, that he must come down to earth, be born of such a woman, meet with such and such things, and in particular that he should once in his life be guilty of murder; at this he was displeased, and told the Great Man he would never murder. But the Great Man replied, I have said it, and it shall be so; which has accordingly happened. At this time, he says, the Great Man asked him what he would chuse in life; he replied, first to be a Hunter, and afterwards to be a *Powwow,* or Divine; whereupon the Great Man told him, he should have what he desired, and that his Shadow should go along with him down to earth, and be with him for ever. There was, he says, all this time no words spoken between them; the conference was not carried on by any human language, but they had a kind of mental intelligence of each other's thoughts, dispositions, and proposals. After this, he says, he saw the Great Man no more, but supposes he now came down to earth to be born; but the Shadow of the Great Man still attended him, and ever after continued to appear to him in dreams and other ways. This shadow used sometimes to direct him in dreams to go to such a place and hunt, assuring him he should there meet with success, which accordingly proved so; and when he had been there some time the Spirit would order him to another place, so that he had success in hunting, according to the Great Man's promise, made to him at the time of his chusing this employment.

« There were some times when this Spirit came upon him in a special manner, and he was full of what he saw in the Great Man, and then, he says, he was *all light,* and not only *light himself,* but it was *light all around him,* so that he could see through men, and knew the thoughts of their hearts. These depths of Satan I leave to others to fathom or to dive into as they please, and do not pretend, for my own part, to know what ideas to affix to such terms, and cannot well guess what conceptions of things these creatures have at these times when they call themselves *all light.*» —DAVID BRAINERD's *Journal.*

Had Brainerd been a Jesuit, his superiors would certainly have thought him a fit candidate for the crown of martyrdom, and very worthy to be made a Saint.

He found one of the Indian conjurers who seemed to have something like grace in him, only he would not believe in the Devil. « Of all the sights,» says he, « I ever saw among them, or indeed any where else, none appeared so frightful, or so near a kin to what is usually imagined of infernal powers! none ever excited such images of terror in my mind as the appearance of one, who was a devout and zealous reformer, or rather restorer, of what he supposed was the ancient religion of the Indians. He made his appearance in his pontifical garb, which was a coat of bears' skins, dressed with the hair on, and hanging down to his toes, a pair of bear-skin stockings, and a great wooden face, painted the one half black, and the other tawny, about the colour of an Indian's skin, with an extravagant mouth, cut very much awry; the face fastened to a bear-skin cap, which was drawn over his head. He advanced toward me with the instrument in his hand that he used for music in his idolatrous worship, which was a dry Tortoise-shell, with some corn in it, and the neck of it drawn on to a piece of wood, which made a very convenient handle. As he came forward, he beat his tune with the rattle, and danced with all his might, but did n't suffer any part of his body, not so much as his fingers, to be seen; and no man would have guessed by his appearance and actions that he could have been a human creature, if they had not had some intimation of it otherwise. When he came near me, I could no: but shrink away from him, although it was then noon day, and I knew who it was, his appearance and gestures were so prodigiously frightful. He had a house consecrated to religious uses, with divers images cut

out upon the several parts of it; I went in, and found the ground beat almost as hard as a rock, with their frequent dancing in it. I discoursed with him about Christianity, and some of my discourse he seemed to like, but some of it he disliked entirely. He told me, that God had taught him his religion, and that he never would turn from it, but wanted to find some that would join heartily with him in it; for the Indians, he said, were grown very degenerate and corrupt. He had thought, he said, of leaving all his friends, and travelling abroad, in order to find some that would join with him; for he believed God had some good people somewhere that felt as he did. He had not always, he said, felt as he now did, but had formerly been like the rest of the Indians, until about four or five years before that time; then, he said, his heart was very much distressed, so that he could not live among the Indians, but got away into the woods, and lived alone for some months. At length, he said, God comforted his heart, and showed him what he should do, and since that time he had known God, and tried to serve him; and loved all men, be they who they would, so as he never did before. He treated me with uncommon courtesy, and seemed to be hearty in it; and I was told by the Indians, that he opposed their drinking strong liquor with all his power; and if at any time he could not dissuade them from it by all he could say, he would leave them, and go crying into the woods. It was manifest he had a set of religious notions that he had looked into for himself, and not taken for granted upon bare tradition; and he relished or disrelished whatever was spoken of a religious nature, according as it either agreed with or disagreed with his standard. And while I was discoursing he would sometimes say, 'Now that I like; so God has taught me;' and some of his sentiments seemed very just. Yet he utterly denied the being of a Devil, and declared there was no such creature known among the Indians of old times, whose religion, he supposes, he was attempting to revive. He likewise told me that departed souls all went southward, and that the difference between the good and bad was this, that the former were admitted into a beautiful town with spiritual walls, or walls agreeable to the nature of souls; and that the latter would for ever hover round those walls, and in vain attempt to get in. He seemed to be sincere, honest, and conscientious in his own way, and according to his own religious notions, which was more than I ever saw in any other Pagan: and I perceived he was looked upon and derided by most of the Indians as a precise zealot, who made a needless noise about religious matters. But I must say, there was something in his temper and disposition, that looked more like true religion than any thing I ever observed amongst other Heathens.»—BRAINERD.

Note 6, page 231, col. 2.

**Why should we forsake
The worship of our fathers?**

Olearius mentions a very disinterested instance of that hatred of innovation which is to be found in all ignorant persons, and in some wise ones.

« An old country fellow in Livonia being condemned, for faults enormous enough, to lie along upon the ground to receive his punishment, and Madame de la Barre, pitying his almost decrepit age, having so far interceded for him, as that his corporal punishment

should be changed into a pecuniary mulct of about
fifteen or sixteen pence; he thanked her for her kind-
ness, and said, that, for his part, being an old man, he
would not introduce any novelty, nor suffer the cus-
toms of the country to be altered, but was ready to
receive the chastisement which his predecessors had
not thought much to undergo; put off his clothes,
laid himself upon the ground, and received the blows
according to his condemnation.»—*Ambassador's Tra-
vels.*

Note 7, page 232, col. 1.
—— her flaxen hair,
Bright eyes of heavenly hue, and that clear skin.

A good description of Welsh beauty is given by Mr
Yorke, from one of their original chronicles, in the ac-
count of Grufydd ab Cynan and his Queen.

« Grufydd in his person was of moderate stature,
having yellow hair, a round face, and a fair and agree-
able complexion; eyes rather large, light eye-brows, a
comely beard, a round neck, white skin, strong limbs,
long fingers, straight legs, and handsome feet. He was,
moreover, skilful in divers languages, courteous and
civil to his friends, fierce to his enemies, and resolute
in battle; of a passionate temper, and fertile imagin-
ation.—Angharad, his wife, was an accomplished
person: her hair was long and of a flaxen colour; her
eyes large and rolling; and her features brilliant and
beautiful. She was tall and well-proportioned; her
leg and foot handsome; her fingers long, and her nails
thin and transparent. She was good-tempered, cheer-
ful, discreet, witty, and gave good advice as well as
alms to her needy dependants, and never transgressed
the laws of duty.»

Note 8, page 234, col. 1.
Thus let their blood be shed.

This ceremony of declaring war with fire and water
is presented by De Bry, in the eleventh print of the
description of Florida, by Le Moyne de Morgues.

Note 9, page 234, col. 1.
The Festival of the Dead.

Lafitau.   Charlevoix.

Note 10, page 234, col. 1.
The Council Hall.

« The town house, in which are transacted all public
business and diversions, is raised with wood and covered
over with earth, and has all the appearance of a small
mountain at a little distance. It is built in the form of
a sugar loaf, and large enough to contain 500 persons,
but extremely dark, having (besides the door, which is
so narrow that but one at a time can pass, and that
after much winding and turning) but one small aperture
to let the smoke out, which is so ill contrived that
most of it settles in the roof of the house. Within it
has the appearance of an ancient amphitheatre, the
seats being raised one above another, leaving an area
in the middle, in the centre of which stands the fire:
the seats of the head warriors are nearest it.»—*Me-
moirs of Lieutenant* HENRY TIMBERLAKE, *who accom-
panied the Cherokee Indians to England in* 1762.

Note 11, page 234, col. 1.
The Sarbacan.

« The children at eight or ten years old are very ex-
pert at killing birds and smaller game with a sarbacan,
or hollow cane, through which they blow a small dart,
whose weakness obliges them to shoot at the eye of the
larger sort of prey, which they seldom miss.»—TIMBER-
LAKE.

Note 12, page 234, col. 1.
Yon pendent string of shells.

« The doors of their houses and chambers were full
of diverse kindes of shells, hanging loose by small
cordes, that being shaken by the wind they make a
certaine ratteling, and also a whisteling noise, by ga-
thering their wind in their hollowe places; for herein
they have great delight, and impute this for a goodly
ornament.»—PIETRO MARTIRE.

Note 13, page 234, col. 1.
Still do your shadows roam dissatisfied,
And to the cries of wailing woe return
A voice of lamentation.

« They firmly believe that the Spirits of those who
are killed by the enemy, without equal revenge of
blood, find no rest, and at night haunt the houses of
the tribe to which they belonged; but when that kin-
dred duty of retaliation is justly executed, they imme-
diately get ease and power to fly away.»—ADAIR.

« The answering voices heard from caves and hollow
holes, which the Latines call Echo, they suppose to be
the Soules wandering through those places.»—PIETRO
MARTIRE. This superstition prevailed in Cumana—
they believed the Echo to be the voice of the Soul,
thus answering when it was called.—HERRERA, 3, 4. 11.

The word by which they express the funeral wailing
in one of the Indian languages is very characteristic,—
Mauo; which bewailing, says Roger Williams, is very
solemn amongst them morning and evening, and some-
times in the night, they bewail their lost husbands,
wives, children, etc.; sometimes a quarter, half, yea a
whole year and longer, if it be for a great Prince.

Note 14, page 234, col. 2.
The skull of some old Seer.

On the coast of Paria oracles were thus delivered.—
TORQUEMADA, l. 6. c. 26.

Note 15, page 234, col. 2.
Their happy souls
Pursue, in fields of bliss, the shadowy deer.

This opinion of the American Indians may be illus-
trated by a very beautiful story from Carver's Travels:

« Whilst I remained among them, a couple, whose
tent was adjacent to mine, lost a son of about four
years of age. The parents were so much affected at
the death of their favourite child, that they pursued
the usual testimonies of grief with such uncommon
rigour, as through the weight of sorrow and loss of
blood to occasion the death of the father. The woman,
who had hitherto been inconsolable, no sooner saw
her husband expire, than she dried up her tears, and
appeared cheerful and resigned. As I knew not how
to account for so extraordinary a transition, I took an
opportunity to ask her the reason of it; telling her at
the same time, that I should have imagined the loss of
her husband would rather have occasioned an increase
of grief than such a sudden diminution of it.

« She informed me, that as the child was so young
when it died, and unable to support itself in the country

of spirits, both she and her husband had been apprehensive that its situation would be far from being happy; but no sooner did she behold its father depart for the same place, who not only loved the child with the tenderest affection, but was a good hunter, and would be able to provide plentifully for its support, than she ceased to mourn. She added, that she now saw no reason to continue her tears, as the child on whom she doated, was under the care and protection of a fond father, and she had only one wish that remained ungratified, which was that of being herself with them.

« Expressions so replete with unaffected tenderness, and sentiments that would have done honour to a Roman matron, made an impression on my mind greatly in favour of the people to whom she belonged, and tended not a little to counteract the prejudices I had hitherto entertained, in common with every other traveller, of Indian insensibility and want of parental tenderness. Her subsequent conduct confirmed the favourable opinion I had just imbibed, and convinced me that, notwithstanding the apparent suspension of her grief, some particles of that reluctance to be separated from a beloved relation, which is implanted by nature or custom in every human heart, still lurked in hers. I observed that she went almost every evening to the foot of the tree, on a branch of which the bodies of her husband and child were laid, and after cutting off a lock of her hair, and throwing it on the ground, in a plaintive melancholy song bemoaned its fate. A recapitulation of the actions he might have performed, had his life been spared, appeared to be her favourite theme; and whilst she foretold the fame that would have attended an imitation of his father's virtues, her grief seemed to be suspended. 'If thou hadst continued with us, my dear Son,' would she cry, 'how well would the bow have become thy hand, and how fatal would thy arrows have proved to the enemies of our bands! thou wouldst often have drunk their blood and eaten their flesh, and numerous slaves would have rewarded thy toils. With a nervous arm wouldest thou have seized the wounded buffalo, or have combated the fury of the enraged bear. Thou wouldst have overtaken the flying elk, and have kept pace on the mountain's brow with the fleetest deer. What feats mightest thou not have performed, hadst thou staid among us till age had given thee strength, and thy father had instructed thee in every Indian accomplishment!' In terms like these did this untutored savage bewail the loss of her son, and frequently would she pass the greatest part of the night in the affectionate employ.»

Note 16, page 234, col. 2.

The spirit of that noble blood which ran
From their death-wounds, is in the ruddy clouds
Which go before the Sun when he comes forth
In glory.

Among the last comers, one Avila, a cacique, had great authority, who understanding that Valdivia affirmed the God of the Christians was the only Creator of all things, in a great rage cried out, he would never allow Pillan, the God of the Chilenians, to be denied the power of creating. Valdivia inquired of him concerning this imaginary deity. Avila told him that his God did, after death, translate the chief men of the nation and soldiers of known bravery to places where there was dancing and drinking, there to live happy for ever; that the blood of noble men slain in battle was placed about the Sun, and changed into red clouds, which sometimes adorn his rising.—*Hist. of Paraguay, etc. by F. A. del Techo.*

Note 17, page 235, col. 1.

O my people,
I too could tell ye of the former days.

The mode of sowing is from the 21st plate of De Bry to J. Le Moyne de Morgues; the common store-houses are mentioned by the same author; and the ceremony of the widows strewing their hair upon their husband's graves is represented in the 19th plate.

Note 18, page 235, col. 2.

The Snake Idol.

Snake worship was common in America. *Bernal Dios, p. 3. 7. 125.* The idol described VII. p. 25, some what resembles what the Spaniards found at Campeche, which is thus described by the oldest historian of the Discoveries. « Our men were conducted to a broade crosse-way, standing on the side of the towne. Here they shew them a square stage or pulpit foure steppes high, partly of clammy bitumen, and partly of small stones, whereto the image of a man cut in marble was joyned, two foure-footed unknown beastes fastening upon him, which, like madde dogges, seemed they would tear the marble man's guts out of his belly. And by the Image stood a Serpent, besmeared all with goare bloud, devouring a marble lion, which Serpent, compacted of bitumen and small stones incorporated together, was seven and fortie feete in length, and as thicke as a great oxe. Next unto it were three rafters or stakes fastened to the grounde, which three others crossed underpropped with stones; in which place they punish malefactors condemned, for proof whereof they saw innumerable broken arrowes, all bloudie, scattered on the grounde, and the bones of the dead cast into an inclosed courte neere unto it.»—PIETRO MARTIRE.

It can scarcely be necessary to remark, that I have attributed to the Hoamen such manners and superstitions as, really existing among the savage tribes of America, best suited to the plan of the poem.

Note 19, page 235, col. 2.

—— piously a portion take
Of that cold earth, to which for ever now
Consigned, they leave their fathers, dust to dust.

Charlevoix assigns an unworthy motive for this remarkable custom, which may surely be more naturally explained; he says they fancy it procures luck at play.

Note 20, page 236, col. 1.

—— from his head
Plucking the thin grey hairs, he dealt them round.

Some passages in Mr Mackenzie's Travels, suggested this to me.

« Our guide called aloud to the fugitives, and entreated them to stay, but without effect; the old man, however, did not hesitate to approach us, and represented himself as too far advanced in life, and too indifferent about the short time he had to remain in the world, to be very anxious about escaping from any danger that threatened him; at the same time he pulled the grey hairs from his head by handfulls to distribute among us, and implored our favour for himself and his relations.

« As we were ready to embark, our new recruit was

desired to prepare himself for his departure, which he would have declined; but as none of his friends would take his place, we may be said, after the delay of an hour, to have compelled him to embark. Previous to his departure, a ceremony took place, of which I could not learn the meaning; he cut off a lock of his hair, and having divided·it into three parts, he fastened one of them to the hair on the upper parts of his wife's head, blowing on it three times with all the violence in his power, and uttering certain words. The other two he fastened, with the same formalities, on the heads of his two children.»—*Mackenzie.*

Note 21, page 236, col. 2.

Forth from the dark recesses of the cave
The Serpent came.

Of the wonderful docility of the snake one instance may suffice.

«An Indian belonging to the Menomonie, having taken a Rattle Snake, found means to tame it; and when he had done this treated it as a Deity; calling it his great Father, and carrying it with him in a box wherever he went. This he had done for several summers, when Mons. Pinnizance accidentally met with him at this carrying-place, just as he was setting off for a winter's hunt. The French gentleman was surprised one day to see the Indian place the box which contained his God on the ground, and opening the door, give him his liberty: telling him, whilst he did it, to be sure and return by the time he himself should come back, which was to be in the month of May following. As this was but October, Monsieur told the Indian, whose simplicity astonished him, that he fancied he might wait long enough, when May arrived, for the arrival of his great Father. The Indian was so confident of his creature's obedience, that he offered to lay the Frenchman a wager of two gallons of rum, that at the time appointed he would come and crawl into his box. This was agreed on, and the second week in May following fixed for the determination of the wager. At that period they both met there again; when the Indian set down his box, and called for his great Father. The Snake heard him not; and the time being now expired, he acknowledged that he had lost. However, without seeming to be discouraged, he offered to double the bet if his father came not within two days more. This was farther agreed on; when behold on the second day, about one o'clock, the Snake arrived, and, of his own accord, crawled into the box, which was placed ready for him. The French gentleman vouched for the truth of this story, and, from the accounts I have often received of the docility of those creatures, I see no reason to doubt its veracity.»—*Carver's Travels.*

We have not taken animals enough into alliance with us. In one of the most interesting families which it was ever my good fortune to visit, I saw a child suckled by a goat. The gull should be taught to catch fish for us in the sea, the otter in fresh water. The more spiders there were in the stable, the less would the horses suffer from the flies. The great American fire-fly should be imported into Spain to catch musquitos. Snakes would make good mousers; but one favourite mouse should be kept to rid the house of cock-roaches. The toad is an excellent fly-catcher, and in hot countries a reward should be offered to the man who could discover what insect feeds upon fleas; for, say the Spaniards, *no ay criatura tan li bre, a quien falta su Alguacil.*

Note 22, page 237, col. 1.

——— that huge King
Of Basan, hugest of the Anakim.

Og, the King of Basan, was the largest man that ever lived: all Giants, Titans, and Ogers are but dwarfs to him; Garagantua himself is no more compared to Og, than Tom Thumb is to Garagantua. For thus say the Rabbis; Moses chose out twelve Chiefs, and advanced with them till they approached the land of Canaan, where Jericho was, and there he sent those Chiefs that they might spy out the land for him. One of the Giants met them; he was called Og the son of Anak, and the height of his stature was twenty-three thousand and thirty-three cubits. Now Og used to catch the clouds and draw them towards him and drink their waters; and he used to take the fishes out of the depths of the sea, and toast them against the orb of the Sun and eat them. It is related of him, by tradition, that in the time of the deluge he went to Noah and said to him, Take me with thee in the Ark; but Noah made answer, Depart from me, O thou enemy of God! And when the water covered the highest mountains of the earth, it did not reach to Og's knees. Og lived three thousand years, and then God destroyed him by the hand of Moses. For when the army of Moses covered a space of nine miles, Og came and looked at it, and reached out his hand to a mountain, and cut from it a stone so wide, that it could have covered the whole army, and he put it upon his head, that he might throw it upon them. But God sent a lapwing, who made a hole through the stone with his bill, so that it slipt over his head, and hung round his neck like a necklace, and he was borne down to the ground by its weight. Then Moses ran to him; Moses was himself ten cubits in stature, and he took a spear ten cubits long, and threw it up ten cubits high, and yet it only reached the heel of Og, who was lying prostrate, and thus he slew him. And then came a great multitude with scythes, and cut off his head, and when he was dead his body lay for a whole year, reaching as far as the River Nile in Egypt. His mother's name was Enac, one of the daughters of Adam, and she was the first harlot; her fingers were two cubits long, and upon every finger she had two sharp nails, like two sickles. But because she was a harlot, God sent against her lions as big as elephants, and wolves as big as camels, and eagles as big as asses, and they killed her and eat her.

When Og met the spies who were sent by Moses, he took them all twelve in his hand and put them in his wallet; and carried them to his wife and said to her, Look, I beseech you, at these men who want to fight with us! and he emptied them out before her, and asked her if he should tread upon them? but she said, Let them go and tell their people what they have seen. When they were got out they said to each other, If we should tell these things to the Children of Israel, they would forsake Moses; let us therefore relate what we have seen only to Moses and Aaron. And they took with them one grape stone from the grapes of that country, and it was as much as a camel could carry. And they began to advise the people that they should not go to war, saying what they had seen; but two of them, namely, Caleb the son of Jepho, and Joshua the son of Nun, concealed it.—*Maracci.*

Even if the grapes had not been proportioned to Og's capacious mouth, the Rabbi's would not have let him starve. There were Behemoths for him to roast whole, and Bar-Chana saw a fish to which Whales are but sprats, and Leviathan but a herring. «We saw a fish,» says he, «into whose nostrils the worm called Tinna had got and killed it; and it was cast upon the shore with such force by the sea, that it overthrew sixty maritime cities : sixty other cities fed upon its flesh, and what they left was salted for the food of sixty cities more.»

From one of the pupils of his eyes they filled thirty barrels of oil. A year or two afterwards, as we past by the same place, we saw men cutting up his bones, with which the same cities were built up again.—MARACCI.

Note 23, page 237, col. 2.

Arrows, around whose heads dry tow was twined,
In pine-gum dipt.

This mode of offence has been adopted wherever bows and arrows were in use. De Bry represents it in the 31st plate to Le Moyne de Morgues.

« The Medes poisoned their arrows with a bituminous liquor called naphta, whereof there was great plenty in Media, Persia, and Assyria. The arrow, being steeped in it, and shot from a slack bow (for swift and violent motion took off from its virtue), burnt the flesh with such violence, that water rather increased than extinguished the malignant flame : dust alone could put a stop to it, and, in some degree, allay the unspeakable pain it occasioned.»—*Universal History.*

Note 24, page 238, col. 2.

His hands transfixed
And lacerate with the body's pendent weight.

Laceras toto membrorum pondere palmas.
MANSRUNT Constantinus, sive Idololatria Debellata.

Note 25, page 238, col. 2.

Not for your lots on earth,
Menial or mighty, slave, or highly-born,
Shall ye be judged hereafter.

They are informed in some places that the Kings and Noblemen have immortal souls, and believe that the souls of the rest perish together with their bodies, except the familiar friends of the Princes themselves, and those only who suffer themselves to be buried alive together with their masters' funerals : for their ancestors have left them so persuaded, that the souls of Kings, deprived of their corporeal clothing, joyfully walk to perpetual delights, through pleasant places always green, eating, drinking, and giving themselves to sports, and dancing with women after their old manner while they were living, and this they hold for a certain truth. Thereupon many, striving with a kind of emulation, cast themselves headlong into the sepulchres of their Lords, which, if his familiar friends defer to do, they think their souls become temporary of eternal.—PIETRO MARTIRE.

When I was upon the Sierras of Guaturo, says Oviedo, and had taken prisoner the Cacique of the Province who had rebelled, I asked him whose graves were those which were in a house of his; and he told me, of some Indians who had killed themselves when the Cacique his father died. But because they often used to bury a quantity of wrought gold with them, I had two of the graves opened, and found in them a small quantity of maize, and a small instrument. When I inquired the reason of this, the Cacique and his Indians replied, that they who were buried there were labourers, who had been well skilled in sowing corn and in gathering it in, and were his and his father's servants, who, that their souls might not die with their bodies, had slain themselves upon his father's death, and that maize with the tools was laid there with them that they might sow it in heaven. In reply to this, I bade them see how the Tuyra had deceived them, and that all he had told them was a lie : for, though they had long been dead, they had never fetched the maize, which was now rotten and good for nothing, so that they had sown nothing in heaven. But the Cacique answered, that was because they found plenty there, and did not want it.—*Relacion sumaria de la Historia Natural de las Indias, par el Capitan* GONZALO FERNANDEZ DE OVIEDO.

The Tlascallans believed that the souls of Chiefs and Princes became clouds, or beautiful birds, or precious stones; whereas those of the common people would pass into beetles, rats, mice, weasels, and all vile and stinking animals.—TORQUEMADA, L. 6. c. 47.

Note 26, page 239, col. 2.

Cadog, Deiniol,
Padarn, and Teilo.

The two first of these Saints with Madog Morvyn, are called the three holy bachelors of the Isle of Britain. Cadog the Wise was a Bard who flourished in the sixth century. He is one of the three protectors of innocence; his protection was through the church law : Blas's by the common law ; and Pedrogyl's by the law of arms; these three were also called the just Knights of the Court of Arthur. Cadog was the first of whom there is any account, who collected the British Proverbs. There is a church dedicated to him in Caermarthenshire, and two in Monmouthshire. Deiniol has churches dedicated to him in Monmouth, Cardigan, and Pembroke shires. In the year 525 he founded a college at Bangor, where he was Abbot, and when it was raised to the dignity of Bishopric he was the first Bishop. Padarn and Teilo rank with Dewi or David, as the three blessed Visitors, for they went about preaching the faith to all degrees of people, not only without reward, but themselves alleviating the distresses of the poor as far as their means extended. Padarn founded a congregation at a place called from him Llanbadarn Vaar, where he had the title of Archbishop. Teilo established the college at Llandaff; the many places called Llandeilo were so named in honour of him. He and Cadog and David were the three canonical Saints of Britain.—*Cambrian Biography.*

Teilo, or Teliau, as he is called by David Williams, took an active part against the heresy of Pelagius, the great Welshman. « Such was the lustre of his zeal, that by something like a pun on his name, he was compared to the sun and called Ηλιου; and when slain at the altar, devotees contended with so much virulence for the reputation of possessing his body, that the Priests, to avoid scandalous divisions, found three miraculous bodies of the Saint, as similar, according to the phrase used on the occasion, as one egg to another; and miracles were equally performed at the tombs of all the three.»—D. WILLIAMS's *Hist. of Monmouthshire*.

This Miracle is claimed by some Agiologists for St Baldred, Confessour ; « whose memory in ancient tymes hath byn very famous in the kingdome of Scotland. For that he having sometymes preached to the people of three villages neere adjoyning one to the other in Scotland, called Aldham, Tiuingham, and Preston, was so holy a man of life, that when he was dead, the people of ech village contended one with another which of them should have his body ; in so much, that at last, they not agreeing therabout, took earmes, and each of them sought by force to enjoy the same. And when the matter came to issue, the said sacred body was found all whole in three distinct places of the house where he died; so as the people of each village coming thither, and carrying the same away, placed it in their churches, and kept it with great honour and veneration for the miracles that at each place it pleased God to worke.»—*English Martyrology*.

The story may be as true of the one Saint as of the other, a solution in which Catholicks and Protestants will agree. Godwin (*in Catal. Ep. Landao*) says that the Churches which contended for the Welsh Saint, were Pennalum, the burial place of his family, Llandeilo Vaar, where he died, and Llandaff, where he had been Bishop ; and he adds, in honour of his own church, that by frequent miracles at his tomb it was certain Llandaff possessed the true body.—Yet in such a case as this the fac-simile might have been not unreasonably deemed more curious than the original.

The polypus's power of producing as many heads, legs, and arms as were wanted, has been possessed by all the great Saints. This miracle of triplification would have been more appropriate had it been worked upon some zealous Homoousian.

St Teilo left his own country for a time because it was infested by an infectious disorder. called the *Yellow Plague*, which attacked both men and beasts.—*Capgrave, quoted in Cressy's Church History of Brittany*.

Note 27, page 239, col. 2.

David.

'Mongst Hatterill's lofty hills, that with the clouds are crown'd,
The valley Ewias lies, immured so deep and round,
As they below who see the mountains rise so high,
Might think the straggling herds were grazing in the sky :
Which in it such a shape of solitude doth bear,
As Nature at the first appointed it for prayer.
Where in an aged cell, with moss and ivy grown,
In which not to this day the Sun hath ever shone,
That reverend British Saint, in zealous ages past,
To contemplation lived ; and did so truly fast,
As he did only drink what crystal Hodney yields,
And fed upon the leeks he gathered in the fields ;
In memory of whom, in each revolving year,
The Welshmen on his day that sacred herb do wear.

* * * * * *

Of all the holy men whose fame so fresh remains,
To whom the Britons built so many sumptuous fanes,
This Saint before the rest their patron still they hold,
Whose birth their ancient bards to Cambria long foretold ;
And seated here a see, his bishopric of yore,
Upon the farthest point of this unfruitful shore,
Selected by himself, that far from all resort
With contemplation seemed most fitly to comport,
That void of all delight, cold, barren, bleak, and dry,
No pleasure might allure, nor steal the wandering eye.

DRAYTON.

« A. D. 462. It happened on a day, as Gildas was in sermon, (Reader, whether smiling or frowning, forgive the digression) a Nunne big with child came into the congregation, whereat the preacher presently was struck dumb (would not a maid's child amaze any man ?) and could proceed no farther. Afterwards he gave this reason for his silence, because that Virgin bare in her body an infant of such signal sanctity as far transcended him. Thus, as lesser load stones are reported to lose their virtue in the presence of those that are bigger, so Gildas was silenced at the approach of the Welsh St David (being then but Hanse in Kelder) though afterwards, like Zachary, he recovered, his speech again.»—FULLER's *Church History of Great Britain*.

« David one day was preaching in an open field to the multitude, and could not be well seen because of the concourse, (though they make him four cubits high, a man and half in stature), when behold the Earth whereon he stood, officiously heaving itself up, mounted him up to a competent visibility above all his audience. Whereas our Saviour himself, when he taught the people, was pleased to chuse a mountain, making use of the advantage of Nature without improving his miraculous power.»—FULLER.

David is indebted to the Romancers for his fame as a Champion of Christendom : how he came by his leek is a question which the Antiquarians have not determined. I am bound to make grateful mention of St David, having in my younger days been benefited by his merits at Westminster, where the first of March is an *early play*.

Note 28, page 239, col. 2.

But I too here upon this barbarous land,
Like Elmur and like Aronan of old,
Must lift the ruddy spear.

Elmur, Cynhaval, and Avaon the son of Taliesin, all deserted the Bardic principles to bear arms, and were called the three Chiefs like Bulls in conflict. Avaon, Aronan, and Dygynelw are the three Bards of the ruddy spear.

Note 29, page 240, col. 1.

———— for this the day
When to his favoured city he vouchsafes
His annual presence.

The feast of the Arrival of the Gods is minutely described by Torquemada, *L. 10. c. 24*. Tezcalipoca was believed to arrive first, because he was the youngest of the Gods, and never waxed old : Telpuctli, the Youth, was one of his titles. On the night of his arrival a general carousal took place, in which it was the custom, particularly for old people, men and women alike, to drink immoderately; for they said the liquor which they drank would go to wash the feet of the God, after his journey. And I, says the Franciscan provincial,—who, if he had been a philosopher, would perhaps have not written a book at all, or certainly not so interesting a one,—I say, that this is a great mistake, and the truth is, that they washed their own stripes and filled them with liquor, which made them merry, and the fumes got up into their heads and overset them; with which fall it is not to be wondered at that they fell into such errors and foolishness.

It was thought that this God often visited the Mexicans, but except on this occasion, he always came incognito. A stone seat was placed at every crossing, or division, of a street, called *Momoztli* or *Ichialoca, where he is expected;* and this was continually hung with fresh garlands and green boughs, that he might rest there.—TORQUEMADA, *L.* 6. *c.* 20.

Note 30, page 240, col. 1.
Mexitli, woman-born.

The history of Mexitli's birth is related in the Poem, Part 2. Sect. XXI. Though the Mexicans took their name from him, he is more usually called Huitzilupuchtli, or corruptly Vitzliputzli. In consequence of the vengeance, which he exercised as soon as born, he was stiled Tetzahuitl, Terror, and Tetzauhteotl, the Terrible God.—CLAVIGERO. TORQUEMADA, *L.* 6. *c.* 21.

Note 31, page 240, col. 2.
Quetzalcoal.

God of the Winds: his temple was circular, « for even as the ayre goeth rounde about the heavens, even for that consideration they made his temple round. The entrance of that temple had a dore made lyke unto the mouth of a serpent, and was paynted with foule and divilish gestures, with great teeth and gummes wrought, which was a thing to feare those that should enter thereat, and especially the Christians, unto whom it represented very Hell with that ougly face and monsterous teeth.»—GOMORA.

Some history is blended with fable in the legend of Quetzalcohuatl, for such is the *uglyography* of his name. He was chief of a band of strangers who landed at Panuco, coming from the North: their dress was black, long, and loose, like the Turkish dress, or the Cassock, says Torquemada, open before, without hood or cape, the sleeves full, but not reaching quite to the elbow : such dresses were, even in his time, used by the natives in some of their dances, in memory of this event. Their leader was a white man, florid, and having a large beard. At first he settled in Tullan, but left that province in consequence of the vices of its Lords, Huemac and Tezcalipoca, and removed to Cholullan. He taught the natives to cut the green stones, called chalchihuites, which were so highly valued, and to work silver and gold. Every thing flourished in his reign; the head of maize was a man's load, and the cotton grew of all colours; he had one palace of emeralds, another of silver, another of shells, one of all kinds of wood, one of turquoises, and one of feathers; his commands were proclaimed by a crier from the Sierra of Tzatzitepec, near the city of Tulla, and were heard as far as the sea-coast, and for more than a hundred leagues round. Fr. Berdardino de Sahagun heard such a voice once in the dead of the night, far exceeding the power of any human voice: he was told that it was to summon the labourer to the maize fields; but both he and Torquemada believe it was the Devil's doing. Notwithstanding his power, Quetzalcoal was driven out by Tezcalipoca and Huemac: before he departed he burnt or buried all his treasures, converted the cocoa trees into others of less worth, and sent off all the sweet singing birds, who had before abounded, to go before him to Tlapallan, the land of the Sun, whither he himself had been summoned. The Indians always thought he would return, and when first they saw the Spanish ships, thought he was come in these moving temples. They worshipped him for the useful

arts which he had taught, for the tranquillity they had enjoyed under his government, and because he never suffered blood to be shed in sacrifice, but ordered bread and flowers, and incense to be offered up instead.—TORQUEMADA, *L.* 3. *c.* 7. *L.* 6. *c.* 24.

Some authors have supposed that these strangers came from Ireland, because they scarred their faces and eat human flesh : this is no compliment to the Irish, and certainly does not accord with the legend. Others that they were Carthaginians, because New Spain was called Anahuace, and the Phenicians were children of Anak. That the Carthaginians peopled America, is the more likely, say they, because they bored their ears, and so did the Incas of Peru. One of these princes, in process of time, says Garcillasso, being willing to enlarge the privileges of his people, gave them permission to bore their ears also, but not so wide as the Incas.

This much may legitimately be deduced from the legend, that New Spain, as well as Peru, was civilized by a foreign adventurer, who, it seems, attempted to destroy the sanguinary superstition of the country, but was himself driven out by the Priests.

Note 32, page 240, col. 2.
Tlaloc.

God of the Waters : he is mentioned more particularly in Section XII. Tlalocatecuhtli, the Lord of Paradise as he is also called, was the oldest of the country Gods. His image was that of a man sitting on a square seat, with a vessel before him, in which a specimen of all the different grains and fruit seeds in the country was to be offered; it was a sort of pumice-stone, and according to tradition, had been found upon the mountains. One of the Kings of Tetzcuco ordered a better Idol to be made, which was destroyed by lightning, and the original one in consequence replaced with fear and trembling. As one of the arms had been broken in removing, it was fastened with three large golden nails; but in the time of the first Bishop Tumarraga, the golden nails were taken away and the idol destroyed.

Tlaloc dwelt among the mountains, where he collected the vapours and dispensed them in rain and dew. A number of inferior Deities were under his command.

Note 33, page 240, col. 2.
Tlalala.

Some of my readers will stumble at this name : but to those who would accuse me of designing to *Hottentotify* the language by introducing one of the barbarous clacks, I must reply, that the sound is Grecian. The writers who have supposed that America was peopled from Plato's Island, observe that the *tl*, a combination so remarkably frequent in the Mexican tongue, has probably a reference to At*lantis* and the At*lantic*, At*l* being the Mexican word for water, and *Tlaloc* the God of the waters. An argument quite worthy of the hypothesis.—FR. GREGORIO GARCIA. *Origen de los Indios,* Lib. 4. *c.* 8. sect. 2.

The quaintest opinion ever started upon this obscure subject is that of Fr. Pedro Simon, who argued, that the Indians were of the tribe of Issachar, because he was «a strong ass in a pleasant land, who bowed his shoulder to bear, and became a servant unto tribute.» If the Hebrew word, which is rendered tribute, may

mean taxes as well, I humbly submit it to considera-
tion, whether Issachar doth not typify John Bull.

Note 34, page 240, col. 2.
Tiger of the War.

This was one of the four most honourable titles
among the Mexicans: the others were Shedder of
Blood, Destroyer of Men, and Lord of the Dark House.
Great Slayer of Men was also a title among the Natchez;
but to obtain this it was necessary that the warrior
should have made ten prisoners, or brought home twenty
scalps.

The Chinese have certain soldiers whom they call
Tygers of War. On their large round shields of basket
work are painted monstrous faces of some imaginary
animal, intended to frighten the enemy.—BARROW's
Travels in China.

Note 35, page 240, col. 2.
Whose conquered Gods lie idle in their chains,
And with tame weakness brook captivity.

The Gods of the conquered nations were kept fast-
ened and caged in the Mexican temples. They who
argued for the Phænician origin of the Indians, might
have compared this with the triumph of the Philistines
over the Ark, when they placed it in the temple of
Dagon.

Note 36, page 241, col. 1.
——peace offerings of repentance fill
The temple courts.

Before the Mexican temples were large courts, kept
well cleansed, and planted with the trees which they call
Ahuchuetl, which are green throughout the year, and
give a pleasant shade, wherefore they are much esteemed
by the Indians: they are our savin (*sabines de Espana*).
In the comfort of their shade the Priests sit, and await
those who come to make offerings or sacrifice to the
idol.—*Historia de la Fundacion y Discurso de la Pro-
vincia de Santiago de Mexico de la orden Predicadores;
por el Maestro* FRAY AUGUSTIN DAVILA PADILLA. *Brus-
seles,* 1625.

Note 37, page 241, col. 1.
Ten painful months
Immured amid the forest had he dwelt,
In abstinence and solitary prayer
Passing his nights and days.

Torquemada, *L. 9. c.* 25. Clavigero.

The most painful penance to which any of these
Priests were subjected, was that which the Chololtecas
performed every four years in honour of Quetzalcoal.
All the Priests sat round the walls in the temple, hold-
ing a censer in their hands: from this posture they
were not permitted to move, except when they went
out for the necessary calls of nature; two hours they
might sleep at the beginning of the night, and one after
the sunrise; at midnight they bathed, smeared them-
selves with a black unction, and pricked their ears to
offer the blood: the twenty-one remaining hours they
sate in the same posture incensing the Idol, and in that
same posture took the little sleep permitted them; this
continued sixty days; if any one slept out of his time,
his companions pricked him: the ceremony continued
twenty days longer, but they were then permitted more
rest.—TORQUEMADA, *L.* 10. *c.* 32.

Folly and madness have had as much to do as kna-
very in priestcraft. The knaves in general, have made

the fools their instruments, but they not unfrequently
have suffered in their turn.

Note 38, page 241, col. 2.
Coatlantona.

The mother of Mexitli, who being a mortal woman,
was made immortal for her son's sake, and appointed
Goddess of all herbs, flowers, and trees.—CLAVIGERO.

Note 39, page 242, col. 2.
Mammoth.

Mr Jefferson informs us that a late governor of Vir-
ginia, having asked some delegates of the Delawares
what they knew or had heard respecting this animal,
the chief speaker immediately put himself into an ora-
torical attitude, and, with a pomp suited to the eleva-
tion of his subject, informed him, that it was a tradition
handed down from their fathers, that in ancient times
a herd of them came to the Big-bone-licks, and began
an universal destruction of the bears, deer, elks, buffa-
loes, and other animals which had been created for the
use of the Indians; that the Great Man above, looking
down and seeing this, was so enraged, that he seized his
lightning, descended to the earth, and seated himself
upon a neighbouring mountain on a rock, on which
his seat and the print of his feet are still to be seen,
and hurled his bolts among them till the whole were
slaughtered, except the Big Bull, who, presenting his
forehead to the shafts, shook them off as they fell; but
at length missing one, it wounded him on the side,
whereon springing around, he bounded over the Ohio,
the Wabash, the Illinois, and, finally, over the great
lakes, where he is living at this day.

Colonel G. Morgan, in a note to Mr Morse, says,
« these bones are found only at the Salt Licks on the
Ohio; some few scattered grinders have, indeed, been
found in other places; but it has been supposed these
have been brought from the above-mentioned deposit
by Indian warriors and others who have passed it, as
we know many have been spread in this manner.
When I first visited the Salt Licks,» says the Colonel,
« in 1766, I met here a large party of the Iroquois and
Wyandot Indians, who were then on a war-expedition
against the Chicasaw tribe. The head chief was a very
old man to be engaged in war; he told me he was
eighty-four years old; he was probably as much as
eighty. I fixed on this venerable Chief, as a person
from whom some knowledge might be obtained.
After making him some acceptable presents of to-
bacco, paint, ammunition, etc. and complimenting
him upon the wisdom of his nation, their prowess
in war, and prudence in peace, I intimated my igno-
rance respecting the great bones before us which
nothing but his superior knowledge could remove, and
accordingly requested him to inform me what he knew
concerning them. Agreeably to the customs of his na-
tion, he informed me in substance as follows:

« Whilst I was yet a boy, I passed this road several
times to war against the Catawbas; and the wise old
chiefs, among whom was my grandfather, then gave me
the tradition, handed down to us, respecting these
bones, the like to which are found in no other part of
the country; it is as follows: After the Great Spirit
first formed the world, he made the various birds and
beasts which now inhabit it. He also made man; but
having formed him white, and very imperfect and ill-

tempered, he placed him on one side of it where he now inhabits, and from whence he has lately found a passage across the great water, to be a plague to us. As the Great Spirit was not pleased with this his work, he took a black clay, and made what *you* call a negro, with a woolly head. This black man was much better than the white man: but still he did not answer the wish of the Great Spirit; that is, he was imperfect. At last the Great Spirit having procured a piece of pure, fine red clay, formed from it the red man, perfectly to his mind; and he was so well pleased with him, that he placed him on this great island, separate from the white and black men, and gave him rules for his conduct, promising happiness in proportion as they should be observed. He increased exceedingly, and was perfectly happy for ages; but the foolish young people, at length forgetting his rules, became exceedingly ill-tempered and wicked. In consequence of this the Great Spirit created the Great Buffalo, the bones of which you now see before us; these made war upon the human species alone, and destroyed all but a few, who repented and promised the Great Spirit to live according to his laws, if he would restrain the devouring enemy: whereupon he sent lightning and thunder, and destroyed the whole race, in this spot, two excepted, a male and a female, which he shut up in yonder mountain, ready to let loose again, should occasion require.»

The following tradition, existing among the natives, we give in the very terms of a Shawanee Indian, to shew that the impression made on their minds by it must have been forcible. «Ten thousand moons ago, when nought but gloomy forests covered this land of the sleeping sun, long before the pale men, with thunder and fire at their command, rushed on the wings of the wind to ruin this garden of nature; when nought but the untamed wanderers of the woods, and men as unrestrained as they were the lords of the soil; a race of animals were in being, huge as the frowning precipice, cruel as the bloody panther, swift as the descending eagle, and terrible as the angel of night. The pines crashed beneath their feet, and the lake shrunk when they slaked their thirst; the forceful javelin in vain was hurled, and the barbed arrow fell harmless from their side. Forests were laid waste at a meal; the groans of expiring animals were every where heard; and whole villages inhabited by men were destroyed in a moment. The cry of universal distress extended even to the region of peace in the west, and the Good Spirit interposed to save the unhappy. The forked lightnings gleamed all around, and loudest thunder rocked the globe. The bolts of heaven were hurled upon the cruel destroyers alone, and the mountains echoed with the bellowings of death. All were killed except one male, the fiercest of the race, and him even the artillery of the skies assailed in vain. He ascended the bluest summit which shades the source of the Monongahela, and, roaring aloud, bid defiance to every vengeance. The red lightning scorched the lofty firs, and rived the knotty oaks, but only glanced upon the enraged monster. At length, maddened with fury, he leaped over the waves of the west at a bound, and this moment reigns the uncontrolled monarch of the wilderness, in despite of even Omnipotence itself.»—WINTERBOTHAM. The tradition probably is Indian, but certainly not the bombast.

Note 40, page 242, col. 2.

In your youth
Ye have quaffed manly blood, that manly thoughts
Might ripen in your hearts.

In Florida when a sick man was bled, women who were suckling a man-child drank the blood, if the patient were a brave or strong man, that it might strengthen their milk and make the boys braver. Pregnant women also drank it.—LE MOYNE DE MORGUES.

There is a more remarkable tale of kindred barbarity in Irish history. The royal family had been all cut off except one girl, and the wise men of the country fed her upon children's flesh to make her the sooner marriageable. I have not the book to refer to, and cannot therefore give the names; but the story is in Keating's history.

Note 41, page 243, col. 1.

The spreading radii of the mystic wheel.

This dance is described from Clavigero; from whom also the account of their musical instruments is taken.

Note 42, page 243, col. 2.

On the top
Of yon magnolia the loud turkey's voice
Is heralding the dawn.

«I was awakened in the morning early, by the cheering converse of the wild turkey-cock (*Meleagris occidentalis*) saluting each other, from the sun-brightened tops of the lofty *Cupressus disticha* and *Magnolia grandiflora*. They begin at early dawn, and continue till sun-rise, from March to the last of April. The high forests ring with the noise, like the crowing of the domestic cock, of these social centinels, the watch-word being caught and repeated, from one to another, for hundreds of miles around; insomuch, that the whole country is, for an hour or more, in an universal shout. A little after sunrise, their crowing gradually ceases, they quit their high lodging-places and alight on the earth, where, expanding their silver-bordered train, they strut and dance round about the coy female, while the deep forests seem to tremble with their shrill noise.»—BARTRAM.

Note 43, page 244, col. 2.

His cowl was white.

«They wore large garments like surplices, which were white, and had hoods such as the Canons wear; their hair long and matted, so that it could not be parted, and now full of fresh blood from their ears, which they had that day sacrificed; and their nails very long.»—B. DIAZ. Such is the description of the Mexican priests by one who had seen them.

Note 44, page 245, col. 1.

Tlalocan.

The Paradise of Tlaloc.

«They distinguished three places for the souls when separated from the body: Those of soldiers who died in battle or in captivity among their enemies, and those of women who died in labour, went to the House of the Sun, whom they considered as the Prince of Glory, where they led a life of endless delight; where, every day, at the first appearance of the sun's rays, they hailed his birth with rejoicings; and with dancing, and the music of instruments and of voices; attended him

38

to his meridian; there they met the souls of the women, and with the same festivity accompanied him to his setting: they next supposed, that these spirits, after four years of that glorious life, went to animate clouds, and birds of beautiful feathers and of sweet song, but always at liberty to rise again to heaven, or to descend upon the earth, to warble and suck the flowers.— The souls of those that were drowned or struck by lightning, of those who died of dropsy, tumours, wounds, and other such diseases, went along with the souls of children, at least of those which were sacrificed to Tlaloc the God of Water, to a cool and delightful place called Tlalocan, where that God resided, and where they were to enjoy the most delicious repasts, with every other kind of pleasure.— Lastly, the third place allotted to the souls of those who suffered any other kind of death, was the Mictlan, or Hell, which they conceived to be a place of utter darkness, in which reigned a God, called Mictlanteuctli, Lord of Hell, and a Goddess, named Miclancihuatl. I am of opinion that they believed Hell to be a place in the centre of the earth, but they did not imagine that the souls underwent any other punishment there than what they suffered by the darkness of their abode. Siguenza thought the Mexicans placed Hell in the northern part of the earth, as the word Mictlampa signified towards both.»—CLAVIGERO.

When any person whose manner of death entitled him to a place in Tlalocan was buried (for they were never burnt), a rod or bough was laid in the grave with him, that it might bud out again and flourish in that Paradise.—TORQUEMADA, l. 13, c. 48.

The souls of all the children, who had been offered to Tlaloc, were believed to be present at all after sacrifices, under the care of a large and beautiful serpent, called Xiuhcoatl.—TORQUEMADA, l. 8, c. 14,

Note 45, page 245, col. 1.
Green islets float along.

Artificial islands are common in China as well as in Mexico.

« The Chinese fishermen, having no houses on shore, nor stationary abode, but moving about in their vessels upon the extensive lakes and rivers, have no inducement to cultivate patches of ground, which the pursuits of their profession might require them to leave for the profit of another; they prefer, therefore, to plant their onions on rafts of bamboo, well interwoven with reeds and long grass, and covered with earth : and these floating gardens are towed after their boats.»—BARROW's *China*.

Note 46, page 245, col. 2.
To Tlaloc it was hallowed, and the stone
Which closed its entrance, never was removed,
Save when the yearly festival returned,
And in its womb a child was sepulchred,
The living victim.

There were three yearly sacrifices to Tlaloc: At the first, two children were drowned in the Lake of Mexico; but in all the provinces they were sacrificed on the mountains; they were a boy and girl, from three to four years old: in this last case the bodies were preserved in a stone chest, as relics, I suppose, says Torquemada, of persons whose hands were clean from actual sin; though their souls were foul with the original stain, of which they were neither cleansed nor purged, and

therefore they went to the place appointed for all, like them who perish unbaptized.— At the second, four children, from six to seven years of age, who were bought for the purpose, the price being contributed by the chiefs, were shut up in a cavern, and left to die with hunger; the cavern was not opened again till the next year's sacrifice.— The third continued during the three rainy months, during all which time children were offered up on the mountains; these also were bought; the heart and blood were given in sacrifice, the bodies were feasted on by the chiefs and priests.—TORQUEMADA, L. 7. c. 21.

« In the country of the Mistecas was a cave sacred to the Water God. Its entrance was concealed, for, though this Idol was generally reverenced, this his temple was known to few; it was necessary to crawl the length of a musket-shot, and then the way, sometimes open and sometimes narrow, extended for a mile, before it reached the great dome, a place 70 feet long, and 40 wide, where were the Idol and the altar; the Idol was a rude column of stalactydes, or incrustation, formed by a spring of petrifying water, and other fantastic figures had thus grown around it. The ways of the cave were so intricate, that sometimes those who had unwarily bewildered themselves there perished. The Friar who discovered this Idol destroyed it, and filled up the entrance.»—PADILLA, p. 643.

Note 47, page 247, col. 1.
The temple serpents.

« The head of a sacrificed person was strung up; the limbs eaten at the feast; the body given to the wild beasts which were kept within the temple circuits; moreover, in that accursed house they kept vipers and venomous snakes, who had something at their tails which sounded like morris-bells, and they are the worst of all vipers; these were kept in cradles, and barrels, and earthen vessels upon feathers, and there they laid their eggs, and nursed up their snakelings, and they were fed with the bodies of the sacrificed and with dogs' flesh. We learnt for certain, that, after they had driven us from Mexico, and slain above 850 of our soldiers and of the men of Narvaez, these beasts and snakes, who had been offered to their cruel Idol to be in his company, were supported upon their flesh for many days. When these lions and tigers roared, and the jackals and foxes howled, and the snakes hissed, it was a grim thing to hear them, and it seemed like hell.»—BERNAL DIAZ.

Note 48, page 247, col. 2.
He had been confined
Where myriad insects on his nakedness
Infixed their venomous anger, and no start,
No shudder, shook his frame.

Some of the Orinoco Tribes required these severe probations, which are described by Gumilla, C. 35; the principle upon which they acted is strikingly stated by the Abbé Marigny in an Arabian anecdote.

« Ali having been chosen by Nasser for Emir, or general of his army against Makan, being one day before this prince, whose orders he was receiving, made a convulsive motion with his whole body on feeling an acute bite : Nasser perceived it not. After receiving his orders, the Emir returned home, and taking off his clothes to examine the bite, found the scorpion that had bitten him. Nasser, learning this adventure, when next he saw the Emir, reproved him, for having sustained the evil, without complaining at the moment, that it might have been remedied. « How, Sir,» replied the Emir, « should I be capable of braving the arrow's point, and the sabre's edge, at the head of your armies and far from you, if in your presence I could not bear the bite of a scorpion!»

Rank in war among savages can only be procured by superior skill or strength.

> Y desde niñez al ejercicio..
>   Los apremian por fuerza y los incitan,
> Y en el bélico estudio y duro oficio
>   Entrando en mas edad los ejercitan;
> Si alguno de flaqueza da un indicio
>   Del uso militar lo inhabilitan,
> Y el que sale en las armas señalado
> Conforme á su valor le dan el grado.
>
> Los cargos de la guerra y preeminencia
>   No son por flacos medios proveidos,
> Ni van por calidad, ni por herencia
>   Ni por hacienda, y ser mejor nacidos;
> Mas la virtud del brazo y la excelencia,
>   Esta hace los hombres preferidos,
> Esta ilustra, habilita, perficiona,
> Y quilata el valor de la persona.
>
> *Araucana*, I.

Note 49, page 247, col. 2.

> ——from the slaughtered brother of their king
> He stript the skin, and formed of it a drum,
> Whose sound affrighted armies.

In some provincés they flead the captives taken in war, and with their skins covered their drums, thinking with the sound of them to affright their enemies: for their opinion was, that when the kindred of the slain heard the sound of these drums, they would immediately be seized with fear and put to flight.—*Garcilaso de la Vega.*

« In the Palazzo Caprea at Bologna are several Turkish bucklers lined with human skin, dressed like leather; they told us it was that of the backs of Christian prisoners taken in battle; and the Turks esteem a buckler lined with it to be a particular security against the impression of an arrow, or the stroke of a sabre.»— LADY MILLER's *Letters from Italy.*

Note 50, page 247, col. 2.

> Should thine arm
> Subdue in battle six successive foes,
> Life, liberty, and glory will repay
> The noble conquest.

Clavigero. One instance occurred, in which, after the captive had been victorious in all the actions, he was put to death, because they durst not venture to set at liberty so brave an enemy. But this is mentioned as a very dishonourable thing. I cannot turn to the authority, but can trust my memory for the fact.

Note 51, page 247, col. 2.

> Often had he seen
> His gallant countrymen with naked breast
> Rush on their iron-coated enemy.

> Schyr Mawrice alsua the Berclay
> Fra the gret battaill held hys way,
> With a great rout off Wallis men;
> Quharenir yeid men mycht them ken,
> For that weie ner all nakyt war,
> Or lynnya clayths had but mar.
>
> *The Bruce.* B. 13. p. 147.

Note 52, page 249, col. 2.

> And with the sound of sonorous instruments,
> And with their shouts and screams and yells drove back
> The Britons' fainter war-cry.

Music seems to have been as soon applied to military as to religious uses.

> Con flautus, cuernos,.roncos instrumentos,
>   Alto estruendo, alaridos desdeñosos,
> Salen los fieros barbaros sangrientos
>   Contra los Espanoles valerosos.
>
> *Araucana,* C. 4.

« James Reid, who had acted as Piper to a rebel regiment in the Rebellion, suffered death at York on Nov. 15, 1746, as a rebel. On his trial it was alleged in his defence, that he had not carried arms. But the Court observed, that a Highland Regiment never marched without a Piper, and therefore his bagpipe, in the eye of the law, was an instrument of war.»—WALKER's *Irish Bards.*

The construction was too much in the spirit of military law. Esop's trumpeter should not have served as a precedent. Croxall's Fables have been made of much practical consequence: this poor Piper was hung for not remembering one, and Gilbert Wakefield imprisoned for quoting another.

Note 53, page 250, col. 1.

> A line of ample measure still retained
> The missile shaft.

A retractile weapon of tremendous effect was used by the Gothic tribes. Its use is thus described in a very interesting poem of the sixth century.

> At nonus pugnæ Helmnod successit, et ipse
> Incertam triplici, gestabat fune tridentem,
> Quem post terga quidem stantes socii tenuerunt;
> Consiliumque fuit, dum cuspes missa sederet
> In clypeo, cuncti pariter traxisse studerent,
> Ut vel sic hominem dejecissent furibundum,
> Atque sub hac certam sibi spe posuere triumphum.
> Nec mora; Dux, totas fundens in brachia vires,
> Misit in adversum magna cum voce tridentem,
> Et dicens, finis ferro tibi, calve, sub isto.
> Qui, ventos penetrans, jaculorum more coruscat;
> Quod genus aspidis, ex alta sese arbore, tanto
> Turbine demittit, quo cuncta obstantia vincat.
> Quid moror? umbonem scindit, peltaque resultat.
> Clamorem Franci tollunt, saltusque resultant;
> Obnixique trahunt restim simul atque vicissim;
> Nec dubitat princeps tali se aptare labori;
> Manarunt cunctis sudoris flumina membris;
> Sed tamen hic intra velut escilus astitit heros,
> Qui non plus petit astra comis, quam tartara fibris,
> Contemnens omnes ventorum, immota, fragores.
>
> *De prima Expeditione Attilæ, Regis Hunnorum, in Gallias, ac de Rebus Gestis Waltharii Aquitanorum Principis. Carmen Epicum.*

This weapon, which is described by Suidas, Eustatius, and Agathias, was called Ango, and was a barbed trident; if it entered the body it could not be extracted without certain death, and if it only pierced the shield, the shield became unmanageable, and the enemy was left exposed.

The *Cataia*, which Virgil mentions as a Teutonic weapon, was also retractile. This was a club of about a yard long, with a heavy end worked into four sharp points; to the thin end, or handle, a cord was fixed, which enabled a person, well trained, to throw it with great force and exactness, and then by a jerk to bring it back to his hand, either to renew his throw, or to use it in close combat. This weapon. was called *Cat* and *Catai.—Cambrian Register.*

The Irish horsemen were attended by servants on foot commonly called Daltini, armed only with darts or javelins, to which thongs of leather were fastened, wherewith to draw them back after they were cast.— Sir JAMES WARE's *Antiquities of Ireland.*

Note 54, page 250, col. 1.

Paynalton.

When this name was pronounced it was equivalent to a Proclamation for rising in mass.—TORQUEMADA, *L.* 6. *c.* 22.

Note 55, page 250, col. 1.

The House of Arms.

The name of this arsenal is a tolerable specimen of Mexican sesquipedalianism; Tlacochcalcoatlyacapan.— TORQUEMADA, *L.* 8. *c.* 13.

Cortes consumed all the weapons of this arsenal in the infamous execution of Qualpopoca and his companions.—HERRERA, 2. 8. 9.

Note 56, page 250, col. 1.

The ablution of the Stone of Sacrifice.

An old Priest of the Tlatelucas, when they were at war with the Mexicans, advised them to drink the holy beverage before they went to battle : this was made by washing the Stone of Sacrifice ; the. King drank first, and then all his chiefs and soldiers in order ; it made them eager and impatient for the fight.—TORQUEMADA, *L.* 2. *c.* 58.

To physic soldiers before a campaign seems an odd way of raising their courage, yet this was done by one of the fiercest American tribes.

« When the warriors among the Natchez had assembled in sufficient numbers for their expedition, the Medicine of War was prepared in the Chief's cabin. This was an emetic, composed of a root boiled in water. The warriors, sometimes to the number of three hundred, seated themselves round the kettles or cauldrons ; about a gallon was served to each : the ceremony was to swallow it at one draught, and then discharge it again with such loud eructations and efforts as might be heard at a great distance.»—HERIOT's *History of Canada.*

Odd as this method of administering medicine may appear, some tribes have a still more extraordinary mode of dispensing it.

« As I was informed there was to be a physic dance at night, curiosity led me to the town-house to see the preparation. A vessel of their own make, that might contain twenty gallons (there being a great many to take the medicine), was set on the fire, round which stood several gourds filled with river water, which was poured into the pot. This done, there arose one of the beloved Women, who, opening a deer-skin filled with various roots and herbs, took out a small handful of something like fine salt, part of which she threw on the head man's seat, and part on the fire close to the pot; she then took out the wing of a swan, and, after flourishing it over the pot, stood fixed for near a minute muttering something to herself ; then taking a shrub like laurel, which I supposed was the physic, she threw it into the pot and returned to her seat. As no more ceremony seemed to be going on, I took a walk till the Indians assembled to take it. At my return I found the house quite full ; they danced near an hour round the pot, till one of them, with a small gourd that might hold about a gill, took some of the physic, and drank it, after which all the rest took in turn. One of their head men presented me with some, and in a manner compelled me to drink, though I would willingly have declined. It was, however, much more palatable than I expected, having a strong taste of sassafras ; the Indian who presented it told me it was taken to wash away their sins, so that this is a spiritual medicine, and might be ranked among their religious ceremonies. They are very solicitous about its success; the conjuror for several mornings before it is drank, makes a dreadful howling, yelling, and hollowing from the top of the town-house, to frighten away apparitions and evil spirits. »—TIMBERLAKE.

Note 57, page 253, col. 2.

—— two fire-flies gave
Their lustre.

It is well known that Madame Merian painted one of these insects by its own light.

« In Hispaniola and the rest of the Ocean Islandes, there are plashy and marshy places, very fitt for the feeding of heardes of cattel. Gnattes of divers kindes, ingendered of that moyste heate, grievously afflict the colonies seated on the brinke thereof, and that not only in the night, as in other countries ; therefore the inhabitants build low houses, and make little doores therein, scarce able to receive the master, and without holes, that the gnatts may have no entrance. And for that cause also, they forbeare to light torches or candels, for that the gnatts by natural instinct follow the light ; yet nevertheless they often finde a way in. Nature hath given that pestilent mischiefe, and hath also given a remedy ; as she hath given us cattes to destroy the filthy progeny of mise, so hath she given them pretty and commodious hunters, which they call *Cucuij.* These be harmless winged worms, somewhat less than battes or reere mise, I should rather call them a kind of beetles, because they have other wings after the same order under their hard-winged sheath, which they close within the sheath when they leave flying. To this little creature (as we see flyes shine by night, and certaine sluggish worms lying in thick hedges) provident nature hath given some very cleere looking-glasses ; two in the seate of the eyes, and two lying hid in the flank, under the sheath, which he then sheweth, when, after the manner of the beetle, unsheathing his thin wings, he taketh his flight into the ayre ; whereupon every *Cucuius* bringeth four lights or candels with him. But how they are a remedy for so great a mischiefe, as is the stinging of these gnatts, which in some places are little less than bees, it is a pleasant thing to hear. Hee who understandeth he hath those troublesome guestes (the gnattes) at home, or feareth lest they may get in, diligently hunteth after the *Cucuij,* which he deceiveth by this means and industry, which necessity (effecting wonders) hath sought out : whoso wanteth *Cucuij,* goeth out of the house in the first twilight of the night carrying a burning fire-brande in his hande, and ascendeth the next hillock, that the *Cucuij* may see it, and hee swingeth the fire-brande about calling *Cucuius* aloud, and beateth the ayre with, often calling and crying out *Cucuie, Cucuie.* Many simple people suppose that the *Cucuij,* delighted with that noise, come flying and flocking together to the bellowing sound of him that calleth them, for they come with a speedy and headlong course : but I rather thinke the *Cucuij* make haste to the brightness of the fire-brande, because swarmes of gnatts fly unto every light, which the *Cucuij* eate in the very ayre, as the martlets and swallowes doe. Behold the desired number of *Cucuij,* at what time the hunter casteth the fire-brande out of his hand. Some *Cucuius* sometimes followeth the fire-brande, and lighteth on the grounde ; then is he easily taken, as travellers may take a beetle if they have need thereof, walking with his wings shutt. Others denie that the *Cucuij* are woont to be taken after this manner, but say, that the hunters especially have boughs full of leaves ready prepared, or broad linnen cloaths, wherewith they smite the *Cucuius* flying about on high, and strike him to the ground, where he lyeth as it were astonished, and suffereth himself to bee taken ; or, as they say, following the fall of the fly, they take the preye, by casting the same bushie bough of linen cloath upon him : howsoever it bee, the hunter havinge the hunting *Cucuij,* returneth home, and shutting the doore of the house, letteth the preye goe. The *Cucuij* loosed, swiftly flyeth about the whole house seeking gnatts, under their hanging bedds, and about the faces of them that sleepe, whiche the gnatts used to assayle : they seem to execute the office of watchmen, that such as are shut in may quietly rest. Another pleasant and profitable commodity proceedeth from the *Cucuij.* As many eyes as every *Cucuius* openeth, the hoste enjoyeth the light of so many candels ; so that the inhabitants spinne, sewe, weave, and dance by the light of the flying *Cucuij.* The inhabitants thinke that the *Cucuius* is delighted with the harmony and melody of their singing, and that hee also exerciseth his motion in the ayre according to the action of their dancing ; but hee, by reason of the divers circuit of the gnatts, of necessity swiftly flyeth about divers ways to seek his food. Our men also reade and write by that light, which alwayes continueth until he have gotten enough whereby he may be well and fedd. The gnatts being cleansed, or driven out of doors, the *Cucuius* beginning to famish, the light beginneth to faile ; therefore when they see his light to waxe dim, opening the little doore, they set him at libertie, that he may seeke his foode.

« In sport and merriment, or to the intent to terrifie such as are afrayd of every shadow, they say, that many wanton wild fellowes sometimes rubbed their faces by night with the flesh of a *Cucuius,* being killed, with purpose to meet their neighbours with a flaming countenance, as with us sometimes wanton young men, putting a gaping toothed wizard over their face, endeavour to terrifie children, or women, who are easily frighted ; for the face being anointed with the lump or fleshy part of the *Cucuius,* shineth like a flame of fire ; yet in short space that fiery virtue waxeth feeble and is extinguished, seeing it is a certain bright humour received in a thin substance. There is also another wonderful commodity proceeding from the *Cucuius;* the islanders, appointed by our menn, goe with their good will by night, with two *Cucuij* tied to the great toes of their feet ; for the traveller goeth better by the direction of these lights, than if he brought so many candels with him as their open eyes ; he also carryeth another in his hand to seek

the *Utiæ* by night, a certain kind of cony, a little exceeding a mouse in bignesse and bulke of bodie : which four-footed beast they onely knewe before our coming thither, and did eate the same. They also go a fishing by the light of the *Cucuij.»*—PIETRO MARTIRE.

Note 58, page 255, col. 2.
Bells of gold
Embossed his glittering helmet.

Among the presents which Cortes sent to Spain were « two helmets covered with blue precious stones ; one edged with golden belles and many plates of gold, two golden knobbes sustaining the belles. The other covered with the same stones, but edged with 25 golden belles, crested with a greene foule sitting on the top of the helmet, whose feet, bill, and eyes were all of gold ; and several golden knobbes sustained every bell.»—PIETRO MARTIRE.

Note 59, page 256, col. 1.
So oft the yeoman had, in days of yore,
Cursing his perilous tenure, wound the horn.

Cornage Tenure.

Note 6o, page 256, col. 1.
A white plume
Nodded above, far seen, floating like foam
On the war tempest.

His tall white plume, which, like a high-wrought foam,
Floated on the tempestuous stream of fight,
Shewed where he swept the field.
Young's *Busiris.*

Note 61, page 257, col. 2.
The Journey of the Dead.
Clavigero. Torquemada, *L.* 13. *c.* 47.

The fighting mountains of the Mexicans are less absurd than the moving rocks of the Greeks, as they are placed, not in this world, but in the road to the next.

« L. Martio et Sex. Julio consulibus, in agro Mutinensi duo montes inter se concurrerunt, crepitu maximo assultantes et recedentes, et inter eos flammâ fumoque exeunte. Quo concursu villæ omnes elisæ sunt ; animalia permulta quæ intra fuerant, exanimata sunt.» J. RAVISII TEXTORIS *Officina,* f. 210.

A fiery mountain is a bad neighbour, but a quarrelsome one must be infinitely worse, and a dancing one would not be much better. It is a happy thing for us, who live among the mountains, that they are now-a-days very peaceable, and have left off « skipping like rams.»

Note 62, page 258, col. 2.
Funeral and Coronation.
Clavigero. Torquemada.

This coronation oath resembles in absurdity the language of the Chinese, who, in speaking of a propitious event occurring, either in their own or any other country, generally attribute it to the joint will of Heaven and the Emperor of China.—BARROW.

I once heard a methodist street-preacher exhort his auditors to praise God as the first cause of all good things, and the King as the second.

Note 63, page 259, col. 1.
Let the guilty tremble ! it shall flow
A draught of agony and death to him,
A stream of fiery poison.

I have no other authority for attributing this artifice

to 'Tezozomoc, than that it has been practised very often and very successfully.

"A Chief of Dsedjedda," says Niebuhr, "informed me that two hundred ducats had been stolen from him, and wanted me to discover the thief. I excused myself, saying, that I left that sublime science to the Mahommedan sages; and very soon afterwards a celebrated schech shewed, indeed, that he knew more than I did. He placed all the servants in a row, made a long prayer, then put into the mouth of each a bit of paper, and ordered them all to swallow it, after having assured them that it would not harm the innocent, but that the punishment of Heaven would fall on the guilty; after which he examined the mouth of every one, and one of them, who had not swallowed the paper, confessed that he had stolen the money."

A similar anecdote occurs in the old Legend of Pierre Faifeu.

Comment la Dame de une grosse Maison ou il hantoit, perdit ung Dyamant en sa maison, qu'il luy fist subtillement recouvrer.—Chap. 22. p. 58.

Ung certain jour, la Dame de l'hostel
Eut ung ennuy, le quel pour vray fut tel,
Car elle avoit en sa main gauche ou dextre
Ung Dyamant, que l'on renommoit de estre
De la valeur de bien cinq cens ducatz ;
Or, pour soubdain vous advertir du cas,
Ou en dormant, ou en faisant la veille,
Du doy luy cheut, dont cres font s'esmerveille,
Qu'el' ne le treuve est son cueur très marry,
Et n'ose aussi le dire a son mary ;
Mais a Faifeu allee est s'en complaindre,
Qui respondit, sans grandement la plaindre,
Que bien failloit que le Seigneur le sceust,
Et qu'elle luy dist ains qu'il s'en apperçeust.
En ce faisant le vaillant Pierre Maistre
La recouvrer luy est allé promettre,
Ce moyennant qu'il eust cinquante escuz,
Qu'elle luy promist, sans en fair refuz,
Pareillement qu' aucban de la maison
L'eust point trouvé, il en rendroit raison.
Leurs propos tins, s'en alla seure et ferme
La dicte Dame, et au Seigneur afferme
Du Dyamant le susdict interest,
Dont il ne fist pas grant conte ou arrest,
Ce nonobstant que fust le don de nopces,
Qu'avoit donne par sur autres negoces :
Car courrouceur sa femme assez en veoit
L'avoit perdu, mais grand deuil en avoit :
Or toutes fois a Faifeu il ordonne
Faire son vueil, et puissance il luy donne
A son plaisir faire ainsi qu'il entend.
Incontinent Faifeu fist tout content
Tost assembler serviteurs et servantes,
Grans et petitz, et les portes-fermantes,
Les fist rengu en une chambre a part.
Ou de grant pour chascun d'eulx avoit part.
Quant il eust fait, appella Sieur et Dame,
Desquelz amé estoit de corps et de ame,
Et devant eulx au servans fist sermon
Du Dyamant, leur disant ; nous chermon,
Et scavons bien par l'art de nicromance
Celuy qui le a et tout en evidance
Feignoit chermer la chambre en tous endroitz,
Se pourmenant devant boytteu ou droitz.
Il apperceut parmy une verriere,
Emmy la court, ung garsonnet arriere,
Qui n'estoit point o les autres venu,
Dont vous orrez qu'il en est advenu.
Ce nonobstant qu'il y en eust grant nombre,
Cinquante ou plus, soubdain faignit soube umbre
De diviner, que tout n'y estoit point,
Les serviteurs ne congnoissans le point
Dirent que nul ne restoit de la bende
Fors le berger ; donc, dist-il, qu'on le mande,
Bien le scavois et autres choses scay,
Qu'il vienne tost, et vous verrez l'essay.

Quant fut venu, demande une arballeste
Que bender fist o grand peine et moleste,
Car forte estoit ce meilleures qui soient.
Les assistens tresfort s'esbabyssoient
Que faire il veult, car dessus il fait mettre
Ung font raillon, puis ainsi la remettre
Dessus la table, et couchee a travers
Tout droit tendue, et atournee envers,
Par ou passer on doit devant la table.
Tout ce cas fait, comme resolu et stable,
Dist à la Dame, et aussi au Seigneur,
Que nul d'eulx ne beut tant fiance en son heur.
De demander la bague dessus dicte,
Par nul barat ou cautelle maudicte ;
Car il convient, sans faire nul destour,
Que chascun d'eulx passe et face son tour
Devant le trect, arc, arballeste ou flesche,
Sans que le cueur d'aucun se plye ou flesche ;
Et puis apres les servans passeront,
Mais bien croyez que ne repasseront,
Ceulx ou celuy qui la bague retiennent,
Mais estre mortz tous asseurez se tiennent.
Son dit finy, chacun y a passé,
Sans que nul fust ne blecé ne cassé ;
Mais quant ce fut a cil qui a la bague,
A ce ne veult user de mine ou brague,
Car pour certain se trouva si vain cueur,
Que s'excuser ne sceut est vaincquer ;
Mais tout soubdain son esprit se tendit
Cryer mercy, et la bague rendit,
En offermant qu'il eu l'avoit robee,
Mais sans Faifeu eust este absorbée.
Asquel on quist s'il estoit bien certain
Du laronneau, mais jura que incertain
Il en estoit, et sans science telle
Qu'on estimoit, avoit quis la cautelle
Espoventer par subtille Leçon
Ceulx qui la bague avoient, en la façon
Vous pouvez voir que, par subtile prouve,
Tel se dit bon, qui meschant on approuve.

The trial by ordeal more probably originated in cunning than in susperstition. The Water of Jealousy is the oldest example. This seems to have been a device to enable women, when unjustly suspected, fully to exculpate themselves ; for no one who was guilty would have ventured upon the trial.

I remember an anecdote of John Henderson, which is characteristic of the man. The maid-servant one evening at a house where he was visiting, begged that she might be excused from bringing in the tea, for he was a conjurer, she said. When this was told him, he desired the mistress would insist upon her coming in ; this was done : he fixed his eye upon her, and after she had left the room said, Take care of her ; she is not honest. It was soon found that he had rightly understood the cause of her alarm.

Note 64, page 259, col. 2.
The Sports.

These are described from Clavigero, who gives a print of the Flyers ; the tradition of the banner is from the same author ; the legend of Mexitli from Torquemada, L. 6. c. 21.

Note 65, page 260, col. 2.
Then the Temples fell
Whose black and putrid walls were scaled with blood.

I have not exaggerated. Bernal Diaz was an eye-witness, and he expressly says, that the walls and the floor of Mexitli's temple were black and flaked with blood, and stenching.—*Historia Verdadera*, p. 71.

Note 66, page 261, col. 1.
One of our nation lost the maid he loved.

There was a young man in despair for the death of

his sister, whom he loved with extreme affection. The idea of the departed recurred to him incessantly. He resolved to seek her in the Land of Souls, and flattered himself with the hope of bringing her back with him. His voyage was long and laborious, but he surmounted all the obstacles, and overcame every difficulty. At length he found a solitary old man, or rather genius, who, having questioned him concerning his enterprise, encouraged him to pursue it, and taught him the means of success. He gave him a little empty calabash to contain the soul of his sister, and promised on his return to give him the brain, which he had in his possession, being placed there, by virtue of his office, to keep the brains of the dead. The young man profited by his instructions, finished his course successfully, and arrived in the Land of Souls, the inhabitants of which were much astonished to see him, and fled at his presence. Tharonhiaouagon received him well, and protected him by his counsel from the old woman his grandmother, who, under the appearance of a feigned regard, wished to destroy him by making him eat the flesh of serpents and vipers, which were to her delicacies. The souls being assembled to dance, as was their custom, he recognized that of his sister; Tharonhiaouagon assisted him to take it by surprise, without which help he never would have succeeded, for when he advanced to seize it, it vanished as a dream of the night, and left him as confounded as was Æneas when he attempted to embrace the shade of his father Anchises. Nevertheless he took it, confined it, and, in spite of the attempts and stratagems of this captive soul, which sought but to deliver itself from its prison, he brought it back the same road by which he came, to his own village. I know not if he recollected to take the brain, or judged it unnecessary; but as soon as he arrived he dug up the body, and prepared it according to the instructions he had received, to render it fit for the reception of the soul, which was to reanimate it. Every thing was ready for this resurrection, when the impertinent curiosity of one of those who were present prevented its success. The captive soul, finding itself free, fled away, and the whole journey was rendered useless. The young man derived no other advantage than that of having been at the Land of Souls, and the power of giving certain tidings of it, which were transmitted to posterity.–. LAFITAU *sur les moeurs de Sauvages Ameriquains*, Tom. I. p. 4o1.

« One, I remember, affirmed to me that himself had been dead four days; that most of his friends in that time were gathered together to his funeral; and that he should have been buried, but that some of his relations at a great distance, who were sent for upon that occasion, were not arrived, before whose coming he came to life again. In this time he says he went to the place where the sun rises (imagining the earth to be plain), and directly over that place, at a great height in the air, he was admitted, he says, into a great house, which he supposes was several miles in length, and saw many wonderful things, too tedious as well as ridiculous to mention. Another person, a woman, whom I have not seen, but been credibly informed of by the Indians, declares she was dead several days; that her soul went southward, and feasted and danced with the happy spirits; and that she found all things exactly agreeable to the Indian notions of a future state.»—BRAINERD.

—— that sweeter one that knoweth all
The songs of all the winged choristers.

The Mocking Bird is often mentioned, and with much feeling, in Mr Davis's Travels in America, a very singular and interesting volume. He describes himself in one place as listening by moonlight to one that usually perched within a few yards of his log hut. A negress was sitting on the threshold of the next door, smoking the stump of an old pipe. *Please God Almighty*, exclaimed the old woman, *how sweet that Mocking Bird sing! he never tire*. By day and by night it sings alike; when weary of mocking others, the bird takes up its own natural strain, and so joyous a creature is it, that it will jump and dance to its own music. The bird is perfectly domestic, for the Americans hold it sacred. Would that we had more of these humane prejudices in England!—if that word may be applied to a feeling so good in itself and in its tendency.

A good old protestant missionary mentions another of the American singing-birds very technically.

« Of black birds there be millions, which are great devourers of the Indian corn as soon as it appears out of the ground: unto this sort of birds, especially, may the mystical fowls, the Divells, be well resembled (and so it pleaseth the Lord Jesus himself to observe, *Matt. 13*), which mystical fowl follow the sowing of the word, pick it up from loose and careless hearers, as these black birds follow the material seed: against these they are very careful, both to set their corn deep enough, that it may have a strong root, not so apt to be pluckt up, as also they put up little watch-houses in the middle of their fields, in which they or their biggest children lodge.»—ROGER WILLIAMS.

But of all the songsters in America who warble their wood-notes wild, the frogs are the most extraordinary.

« Prepared as I was,» says a traveller, « to hear something extraordinary from these animals, I confess the first frog concert I heard in America was so much beyond any thing I could conceive of the powers of these musicians, that I was truly astonished. This performance was *al fresco*, and took place on the 18t (April) instant, in a large swamp, where there were at least ten thousand performers, and, I really believe not two exactly in the same pitch, if the octave can possibly admit of so many divisions, or shades, of semitones. An Hibernian musician, who, like myself, was present for the first time at this concert of *antimusic* exclaimed, 'By Jasus, but they stop out of tune to a nicety!'

« I have been since informed by an *amateur* who resided many years in this country, and made this species of music his peculiar study, that on these occasions the treble is performed by the Tree Frogs, the smallest and most beautiful species; they are always of the same colour as the bark of the tree they inhabit, and their note is not unlike the chirp of a cricket: the next in size are our counter-tenors, they have a note resembling the setting of a saw. A still larger species sing tenor, and the under part is supported by the Bull Frogs, which are as large as a man's foot, and bellow out the bass in a tone as loud and sonorous as that of the animal from which they take their name.»—*Travel in America*, by W. PRIEST, Musician.

« I have often thought,» says this lively traveller

« if an enthusiastic cockney of weak nerves, who had never been out of the sound of Bow-bell, could suddenly be conveyed from his bed in the middle of the night, and laid fast asleep in an American swamp, he would, on waking, fancy himself in the infernal regions: his first sensations would be from the stings of a myriad of musquitoes; waking with the smart, his ears would be assailed with the horrid noises of the frogs; on lifting up his eyes he would have a faint view of the night-hawks, flapping their ominous wings over his devoted head, visible only from the glimmering light of the fire-flies, which he would naturally conclude were sparks from the bottomless pit. Nothing would be wanting at this moment to complete the illusion, but one of those dreadful explosions of thunder and lightning, so extravagantly described by Lee in Oedipus. ' Call you these peals of thunder but the yawn of bellowing clouds? by Jove, they seem to me the world's last groans, and those large sheets of flame its last blaze!' »

Note 68, page 261, col. 2.

In sink and swell
More exquisitely sweet than ever
Of man evoked from instrument of touch,
Or beat, or breath.

The expression is from an old Spanish writer; « Tanian instrumentos de diversas maneras de la musica, de pulso, e flato, e tato, e voz.»—*Cronica de* PERO NINO.

Note 69, page 262, col. 2.

———— The old in talk
Of other days, that mingled with their joy
Memory of many a hard calamity.

And when the builders laid the foundation of the Temple of the Lord, they set the Priests in their apparel with trumpets, and the Levites the sons of Asaph with cymbals, to praise the Lord, after the ordinance of David King of Israel.

« And they sang together by course in praising and giving thanks unto the Lord, because he is good, for his mercy endureth for ever toward Israel. And all the people shouted with a great shout when they praised the Lord, because the foundation of the house of the Lord was laid.

« But many of the Priests and Levites and chief of the fathers, who were ancient men, that had seen the first house, when the foundation of this house was laid before their eyes wept with a loud voice; and many shouted aloud with joy :

« So that the people could not discern the noise of the shout of joy from the noise of the weeping of the people; for the people shouted with a loud shout, and the noise was heard afar off.»—EZRA, iii, 10. 13.

Note 70, page 263, col. 1.

For Aztlan comes in anger, and her Gods
Spare none.

Kill all that you can, said the Tlascallans to Cortes;
the young that they may not bear arms, the old that they may not give counsel.—BERNAL DIAZ, p. 56.

Note 71, page 265, col. 2.
The Circle of the Years is full.

Torquemada, L. 10, c. 33. The tradition of the Five Suns is related by Clavigero: the origin of the present by the same author and by Torquemada, L. 6. c. 42; the whole of the ceremonies is accurately stated.

Note 72, page 267, col. 2.
Depart! depart! for so the note
Articulately in his native tongue
Spake to the Azteca.

My excuse for this insignificant agency, as I fear it will be thought, must be, that the fact itself is historically true; by means of this omen the Aztecas were induced to quit their country, after a series of calamities. The leader who had address enough to influence them was Huitziton, a name which I have altered to Yuhidthiton for the sake of euphony; the note of the bird is expressed in Spanish and Italian thus, *tihui*; the cry of the *peewhit* cannot be better expressed.—TORQUEMADA, L. 2. c. 1. CLAVIGERO.

Note 73, page 269, col. 2.
The Chair of God.

Mexitli, they said, appeared to them during their emigration, and ordered them to carry him before them in a chair; Teoycpalli it was called. — TORQUEMADA, L. 2. c. 1.

The hideous figures of their idols are easily accounted for by the Historian of the Dominicans in Mexico.

« As often as the Devil appeared to the Mexicans, they made immediately an idol of the figure in which they had seen him, sometimes as a lion, othertimes as a dog, othertimes as a serpent; and as the ambitious Devil took advantage of this weakness, he assumed a new form every time to gain a new image in which he might be worshipped. The natural timidity of the Indians aided the design of the Devil, and he appeared to them in horrible and affrighting figures that he might have them the more submissive to his will; for this reason it is that the idols which we still see in Mexico, placed in the corners of the streets as spoils of the Gospel, are so deformed and ugly.» — AUGUSTIN DAVILA PADILLA.

Note 74, page 270, col. 2.
To spread in other lands Mexitli's name.

It will scarcely be believed that the resemblance between Mexico and Messiah should have been adduced as a proof that America was peopled by the ten tribes. Fr. Estevan de Salazar discovered this wise argument, which is noticed in Gregorio Garcia's very credulous and very learned work on the Origin of the Indians, L. 3. c. 7. sect. 2.

The Curse of Kehama.

Καταραι, ως και τα αλεκτρυονονεοττα, οικον αει, οψε κεν επανηξαν εγκαθισομεναι.

Αποφθ. Ανεκ. του Γυδιελ. του Μητ.

Curses are like young chickens, they always come home to roost.

TO THE AUTHOR OF GEBIR,

WALTER SAVAGE LANDOR,

This Poem is Inscribed,

BY ROBERT SOUTHEY.

Ετησατε μοι πρωτη πολυτροπον, οφρα φανειη
Ποικιλον ειδος εχων, οτι ποικιλον υμνον αρασσω.

Νον Διον.

FOR I WILL FOR NO MAN'S PLEASURE
CHANGE A SYLLABLE OR MEASURE;
PEDANTS SHALL NOT TIE MY STRAINS
TO OUR ANTIQUE POETS' VEINS;
BEING BORN AS FREE AS THESE,
I WILL SING AS I SHALL PLEASE.

GEORGE WITHER.

PREFACE.

IN the religion of the Hindoos, which of all false religions is the most monstrous in its fables, and the most fatal in its effects, there is one remarkable peculiarity. Prayers, penances, and sacrifices, are supposed to possess an inherent and actual value, in no degree depending upon the disposition or motive of the person who performs them. They are drafts upon Heaven, for which the Gods cannot refuse payment. The worst men, bent upon the worst designs, have in this manner obtained power which has made them formidable to the Supreme Deities themselves, and rendered an *Avatar*, or Incarnation of Veeshnoo the Preserver, necessary. This belief is the foundation of the following Poem. The story is original; but, in all its parts, consistent with the superstition upon which it is built; and however startling the fictions may appear, they might almost be called credible when compared with the genuine tales of Hindoo mythology.

No figures can be imagined more anti-picturesque, and less poetical, than the mythological personages of the Bramins. This deformity was easily kept out of sight :—their hundred hands are but a clumsy personification of power; their numerous heads only a gross image of divinity, « whose countenance, » as the Bhagvat-Geeta expresses it, « is turned on every side. » To the other obvious objection, that the religion of Hindostan is not generally known enough to supply fit machinery for an English poem, I can only answer, that, if every allusion to it throughout the work is not sufficiently self-explained to render the passage intelligible, there is

a want of skill in the poet. Even those readers who should be wholly unacquainted with the writings of our learned Orientalists, will find all the preliminary knowledge that can be needful, in the following brief explanation of mythological names :

BRAMA, ... the Creator.

VEESHNOO, the Preserver.

SEEVA, ... the Destroyer.

These form the Trimourtee, or Trinity, as it has been called, of the Bramins. The allegory is obvious, but has been made for the Trimourtee, not the Trimourtee for the allegory; and these Deities are regarded by the people as three distinct and personal Gods. The two latter have at this day their hostile sects of worshippers; that of Seeva is the most numerous; and in this Poem, Seeva is represented as Supreme among the Gods. This is the same God whose name is variously written Seeb, Sieven and Siva, Chiven by the French, Xiven by the Portuguese, and whom European writers sometimes denominate Eswara, Iswaren, Mahadeo, Mahadeva, Rutren,—according to which of his thousand and eight names prevailed in the country where they obtained their information.

INDRA, ... God of the Elements.

The SWERGA, .. his Paradise, — one of the Hindoo heavens.

YAMEN, ... Lord of Hell, and Judge of the Dead.

PADALON, ... Hell,—under the Earth, and, like the Earth, of an octagon shape; its eight gates are guarded by as many Gods.

MARRIATALY, .. the Goddess who is chiefly worshipped by the lower casts.

POLLEAR, ... or Ganesa,—the Protector of Travellers. His statues are placed in the highways, and sometimes in a small lonely sanctuary, in the streets and in the fields.

CASYAPA, ... the Father of the Immortals.

DEVETAS, ... The Inferior Deities.

SURAS, ... Good Spirits.

ASURAS, ... Evil Spirits, or Devils.

GLENDOVEERS, . the most beautiful of the Good Spirits, the Grindouvers of Sonnerat.

39

I.

THE FUNERAL.

MIDNIGHT, and yet no eye
Through all the Imperial City closed in sleep!
Behold her streets a-blaze
With light that seems to kindle the red sky,
Her myriads swarming thro' the crowded ways!
Master and slave, old age and infancy,
All, all abroad to gaze;
House-top and balcony
Clustered with women, who throw back their veils
With unimpeded and insatiate sight
To view the funeral pomp which passes by,
As if the mournful rite
Were but to them a scene of joyaunce and delight.

Vainly, ye blessed twinklers of the night,
Your feeble beams ye shed,
Quench'd in the unnatural light which might out-stare
Even the broad eye of day;
And thou from thy celestial way
Pourest, O Moon, an ineffectual ray!
For lo! ten thousand torches flame and flare
Upon the midnight air,
Blotting the lights of heaven
With one portentous glare.
Behold the fragrant smoke in many a fold,
Ascending floats along the fiery sky,
And hangeth visible on high,
A dark and waving canopy.

Hark! 't is the funeral trumpet's breath!
'T is the dirge of death!
At once ten thousand drums begin,
With one long thunder-peal the ear assailing;
Ten thousand voices then join in,
And with one deep and general din
Pour their wild wailing.
The song of praise is drown'd
Amid that deafening sound;
You hear no more the trumpet's tone,
You hear no more the mourner's moan,
Though the trumpet's breath, and the dirge of death,
Mingle and swell the funeral yell.
But rising over all in one acclaim
Is heard the echoed and re-echoed name,
From all that countless rout:
Arvalan! Arvalan!
Arvalan! Arvalan!
Ten times ten thousand voices in one shout
Call Arvalan! The overpowering sound,
From house to house repeated rings about,
From tower to tower rolls round.

The death-procession moves along,
Their bald heads shining to the torches' ray;
The Bramins lead the way,
Chaunting the funeral song.
And now at once they shout,
Arvalan! Arvalan!
With quick rebound of sound,
All in accordant cry,
Arvalan! Arvalan!
The universal multitude reply.
In vain ye thunder on his ear the name!

Would ye awake the dead?
Borne upright in his palankeen,
There Arvalan is seen!
A glow is on his face,—a lively red;
It is the crimson canopy
Which o'er his cheek the reddening shade hath shed.
He moves,—he nods his head,—
But the motion comes from the bearers' tread,
As the body, borne aloft in state,
Sways with the impulse of its own dead weight.
Close following his dead son, Kehama came,
Nor joining in the ritual song,
Nor calling the dear name;
With head deprest and funeral vest,
And arms enfolded on his breast,
Silent and lost in thought he moves along.
King of the world, his slaves unenvying now
Behold their wretched Lord; rejoiced they see
The mighty Rajah's misery;
For Nature in his pride hath dealt the blow,
And taught the Master of Mankind to know
Even he himself is man, and not exempt from woe.

O sight of grief! the wives of Arvalan,
Young Azla, young Nealliny, are seen!
Their widow-robes of white,
With gold and jewels bright,
Each like an Eastern queen.
Woe! woe! around their palankeen,
As on a bridal day,
With symphony, and dance, and song,
Their kindred and their friends come on.
The dance of sacrifice! the funeral song!
And next the victim slaves in long array,
Richly bedight to grace the fatal day,
Move onward to their death;
The clarions' stirring breath
Lifts their thin robes in every flowing fold,
And swells the woven gold,
That on the agitated air
Trembles, and glitters to the torches' glare.

A man and maid of aspect wan and wild,
Then, side by side, by bowmen guarded, came.
O wretched father! O unhappy child!
Them were all eyes of all the throng exploring—
Is this the daring man
Who raised his fatal hand at Arvalan?
Is this the wretch condemn'd to feel
Kehama's dreadful wrath?
Then were all hearts of all the throng deploring,
For not in that innumerable throng
Was one who lov'd the dead; for who could know
What aggravated wrong
Provoked the desperate blow!
Far, far behind, beyond all reach of sight,
In ordered files the torches flow along,
One ever-lengthening line of gliding light:
Far—far behind,
Rolls on the undistinguishable clamour
Of horn, and trump, and tambour;
Incessant as the roar
Of streams which down the wintry mountain pour,
And louder than the dread commotion
Of stormy billows on a rocky shore,
When the winds rage over the waves,
And Ocean to the Tempest raves.

And now toward the bank they go
Where, winding on their way below,
Deep and strong the waters flow.
Here doth the funeral pile appear
With myrrh and ambergris bestrew'd,
And built of precious sandal-wood.
They cease their music and their outcry here;
Gently they rest the bier:
They wet the face of Arvalan,
No sign of life the sprinkled drops excite;
They feel his breast,—no motion there;
They feel his lips,—no breath;
For not with feeble, nor with erring hand,
The stern avenger dealt the blow of death.
Then with a doubting peal and deeper blast,
The tambours and the trumpets sound on high,
And with a last and loudest cry
They call on Arvalan.

Woe! woe! for Azla takes her seat
Upon the funeral pile!
Calmly she took her seat, ¹
Calmly the whole terrific pomp survey'd
As on her lap the while
The lifeless head of Arvalan was laid.
The young Nealliny!
Woe! woe! Nealliny,
They strip her ornaments away, ²
Bracelet and anklet, ring, and chain, and zone;
Around her neck they leave
The marriage knot alone, ³—
That marriage band, which when
Yon waning moon was young,
Around her virgin neck
With bridal joy was hung.
Then with white flowers, the coronal of death,
Her jetty locks they crown.
O sight of misery!
You cannot hear her cries,—all other sound
In that wild dissonance is drown'd;—
But in her face you see
The supplication and the agony,—
See in her swelling throat the desperate strength
That with vain effort struggles yet for life;
Her arms contracted now in fruitless strife,
Now wildly at full length
Towards the crowd in vain for pity spread,—
They force her on, they bind her to the dead. ⁴

Then all around retire:
Circling the Pile, the ministring Bramins stand,
Each lifting in his hand a torch on fire.
Alone the Father of the dead advanced
And lit the funeral pyre.

At once on every side
The circling torches drop,
At once on every side
The fragrant oil is pour'd,
At once on every side
The rapid flames rush up.
Then hand in hand the victim band
Roll in the dance around the funeral pyre;
Their garments' flying folds
Float inward to the fire.
In drunken whirl they wheel around;
One drops,—another plunges in? ⁵

And still with overwhelming din
The tambours and the trumpets sound;
And clap of hand, and shouts, and cries,
From all the multitude arise:
While round and round, in giddy wheel,
Intoxicate they roll and reel,
Till one by one whirl'd in they fall,
And the devouring flames have swallow'd all.

Then all was still; the drums and clarions ceas'd;
The multitude were hush'd in silent awe;
Only the roaring of the flames was heard.

II.

THE CURSE.

ALONE towards the Table of the dead,
Kehama mov'd; there on the altar-stone
Honey and rice he spread.
There with collected voice and painful tone
He call'd upon his son.
Lo! Arvalan appears. ⁶
Only Kehama's powerful eye beheld
The thin etherial spirit hovering nigh;
Only the Rajah's ear
Receiv'd his feeble breath.
And is this all? the mournful Spirit said,
This all that thou canst give me after death?
This unavailing pomp,
These empty pageantries that mock the dead!
In bitterness the Rajah heard,
And groan'd, and smote his breast, and o'er his face
Cowl'd the white mourning vest.

ARVALAN.

Art thou not powerful,—even like a God?
And must I, through my years of wandering,
Shivering and naked to the elements,
In wretchedness await
¡The hour of Yamen's wrath?
I thought thou wouldst embody me anew,
Undying as I am, ⁷—
Yea, re-create me!—Father, is this all!
This all! and thou Almighty!

But in that wrongful and upbraiding tone,
Kehama found relief,
For rising anger half supprest his grief.
Reproach not me! he cried,
Had I not spell-secur'd thee from disease,
Fire, sword,—all common accidents of man,—
And thou!—fool, fool—to perish by a stake!
And by a peasant's arm!—
Even now, when from reluctant Heaven,
Forcing new gifts and mightier attributes,
So soon I should have quell'd the Death-God's power.

Waste not thy wrath on me, quoth Arvalan,
It was my hour of folly! ⁸ Fate prevail'd,
Nor boots it to reproach me that I fell.
I am in misery, Father! Other souls
Predoom'd to Indra's Heaven, enjoy the dawn
Of bliss,—to them the tempered elements
Minister joy: genial delight the sun

Sheds on their happy being, and the stars
Effuse on them benignant influences;
And thus o'er earth and air they roam at will,
And when the number of their days is full,
Go fearlessly before the awful throne.
But I,—all naked feeling and raw life, 9—
What worse than this hath Yamen's hell in store?
If ever thou didst love me, mercy, Father!
Save me, for thou canst save:—the Elements
Know and obey thy voice.

KEHAMA.

        The Elements
Shall torture thee no more; even while I speak
Already dost thou feel their power is gone.
Fear not! I cannot call again the past,
Fate hath made that its own; but Fate shall yield
To me the future; and thy doom be fix'd
By mine, not Yamen's will. Meantime all power
Whereof thy feeble spirit can be made
Participant, I give. Is there aught else
        To mitigate thy lot?

ARVALAN.

Only the sight of vengeance. Give me that!
Vengeance, full worthy vengeance!—not the stroke
Of sudden punishment,—no agony
That spends itself and leaves the wretch at rest,
    But lasting long revenge.

KEHAMA.

What, boy? is that cup sweet? then take thy fill!
So as he spake, a glow of dreadful pride
Inflam'd his cheek: with quick and angry stride
    He mov'd toward the pile,
And rais'd his hand to hush the crowd, and cried,
Bring forth the murderer! At the Rajah's voice,
Calmly, and like a man whom fear had stunn'd,
Ladurlad came, obedient to the call.
    But Kailyal started at the sound,
And gave a womanly shriek, and back she drew,
    And eagerly she roll'd her eyes around,
As if to seek for aid, albeit she knew
    No aid could there be found.

It chanced that near her on the river-brink,
The sculptur'd form of Marriataly 10 stood;
It was an idol roughly hewn of wood,
    Artless, and poor, and rude.
    The Goddess of the poor was she;
None else regarded her with piety.
But when that holy image Kailyal view'd,
To that she sprung, to that she clung,
On her own goddess with close clasping arms,
    For life the maiden hung.
They seiz'd the maid; with unrelenting grasp
    They bruis'd her tender limbs;
She, nothing yielding, to this only hope
Clings with the strength of frenzy and despair.
She screams not now, she breathes not now,
    She sends not up one vow,
She forms not in her soul one secret prayer,
All thought, all feeling, and all powers of life
In the one effort centering. Wrathful they
With tug and strain would force the maid away;—
    Didst thou, O Marriataly, see their strife?

In pity didst thou see the suffering maid?
Or was thine anger kindled, that rude hands
Assail'd thy holy image?—for behold
    The holy image shakes!
Irreverently bold, they deem the maid
Relax'd her stubborn hold,
And now with force redoubled drag their prey;
And now the rooted idol to their sway
Bends,—yields,—and now it falls. But then they scream,
For lo! they feel the crumbling bank give way,
    And all are plunged into the stream.
She hath escap'd my will, Kehama cried,
She hath escap'd,—but thou art here,
    I have thee still,
    The worser criminal!
And on Ladurlad, while he spake, severe
    He fix'd his dreadful frown.
    The strong reflection of the pile
    Lit his dark lineaments,
Lit the protruded brow, the gathered front,
    The steady eye of wrath.

But while the fearful silence yet endur'd,
    Ladurlad rous'd his soul;
    Ere yet the voice of destiny
Which trembled on the Rajah's lips was loos'd,
    Eager he interpos'd,
As if despair had waken'd him to hope;
    Mercy! oh mercy! only in defence—
    Only instinctively,—
Only to save my child, I smote the Prince.
    King of the world, be merciful!
Crush me,—but torture not!
The Man-Almighty deign'd him no reply,
Still he stood silent; in no human mood
Of mercy, in no hesitating thought
Of right and justice. At the length he rais'd
His brow yet unrelax'd,—his lips unclos'd,
    And utter'd from the heart,
With the whole feeling of his soul enforced,
    The gather'd vengeance came.

    I charm thy life
    From the weapons of strife,
    From stone and from wood,
    From fire and from flood,
    From the serpent's tooth,
    And the beasts of blood:
    From Sickness I charm thee,
    And Time shall not harm thee,
    But Earth which is mine,
    Its fruits shall deny thee;
    And Water shall hear me,
    And know thee and fly thee;
    And the Winds shall not touch thee
    When they pass by thee,
    And the Dews shall not wet thee,
    When they fall nigh thee,
    And thou shalt seek Death
    To release thee, in vain;
    Thou shalt live in thy pain,
    While Kehama shall reign,
    With a fire in thy heart,
    And a fire in thy brain;
    And sleep shall obey me,
    And visit thee never,

And the curse shall be on thee
For ever and ever.

There where the Curse had stricken him,
There stood the miserable man,
There stood Ladurlad, with loose-hanging arms,
And eyes of idiot wandering.
Was it a dream? alas,
He heard the river flow,
He heard the crumbling of the pile,
He heard the wind which shower'd
The thin white ashes round.
There motionless he stood,
As if he hop'd it were a dream,
And fear'd to move, lest he should prove
The actual misery;
And still at times he met Kehama's eye,
Kehama's eye that fasten'd on him still.

III.

THE RECOVERY.

The Rajah turn'd toward the pile again,
Loud rose the song of death from all the crowd;
Their din the instruments begin,
At once again join in
With overwhelming sound.
Ladurlad starts,—he looks around.
What hast thou here in view,
O wretched man! in this disastrous scene?
The soldier train, the Bramins who renew
Their ministry around the funeral pyre,
The empty palankeens,
The dimly-fading fire.
Where too is she whom most his heart held dear,
His best-beloved Kailyal, where is she,
The solace and the joy of many a year
Of widowhood! is she then gone,
And is he left all-utterly alone,
To bear his blasting curse, and none
To succour or deplore him?
He staggers from the dreadful spot; the throng
Give way in fear before him;
Like one who carries pestilence about,
Shuddering they shun him, where he moves along.
And now he wanders on
Beyond the noisy rout;
He cannot fly and leave his curse behind,
Yet doth he seem to find
A comfort in the change of circumstance.
Adown the shore he strays,
Unknowing where his wretched feet shall rest,
But farthest from the fatal place is best.

By this in the orient sky appears the gleam
Of day. Lo! what is yonder in the stream,
Down the slow river floating slow,
In distance indistinct and dimly seen?
The childless one with idle eye
Followed its motion thoughtlessly;
Idly he gaz'd, unknowing why,
And half unconscious that he watch'd its way.
Belike it is a tree
Which some rude tempest, in its sudden sway,

Tore from the rock, or from the hollow shore
The undermining stream hath swept away.

But when anon outswelling by its side,
A woman's robe he spied,
Oh then Ladurlad started,
As one, who in his grave
Had heard an angel's call.
Yea, Marriataly, thou hast deign'd to save!
Yea, Goddess! it is she,
Kailyal, still clinging senselessly
To thy dear image, and in happy hour
Upborne amid the wave
By that preserving power.

Headlong in hope and in joy
Ladurlad dash'd in the water.
The water knew Kehama's spell,
The water shrunk before him.
Blind to the miracle,
He rushes to his daughter,
And treads the river-depths in transport wild,
And clasps and saves his child.

Upon the farther side a level shore
Of sand was spread: thither Ladurlad bore
His daughter, holding still with senseless hand
The saving Goddess; there upon the sand
He laid the livid maid,
Rais'd up against his knees her drooping head;
Bent to her lips,—her lips as pale as death,—
If he might feel her breath,
His own the while in hope and dread suspended;
Chaf'd her cold breast, and ever and anon
Let his hand rest, upon her heart extended.

Soon did his touch perceive, or fancy there,
The first faint motion of returning life.
He chafes her feet, and lays them bare
In the sun; and now again upon her breast
Lays his hot hand; and now her lips he prest,
For now the stronger throb of life he knew:
And her lips tremble too!
The breath comes palpably,
Her quivering lids unclose,
Feebly and feebly fall,
Relapsing as it seem'd to dead repose.

So in her father's arms thus languidly,
While over her with earnest gaze he hung,
Silent and motionless she lay,
And painfully and slowly writh'd at fits,
At fits to short convulsive starts was stung.
Till when the struggle and strong agony
Had left her, quietly she lay repos'd:
Her eyes now resting on Ladurlad's face,
Relapsing now, and now again unclos'd.
The look she fix'd upon his face, implies
Nor thought nor feeling, senselessly she lies,
Compos'd like one who sleeps with open eyes.
Long he leant over her,
In silence and in fear.
Kailyal!—at length he cried in such a tone
As a poor mother ventures who draws near,
With silent footstep, to her child's sick bed.
My Father! cried the maid, and rais'd her head,

Awakening then to life and thought,—thou here?
For when his voice she heard,
The dreadful past recurr'd,
Which dimly, like a dream of pain,
Till now with troubled sense confus'd her brain.

And hath he spar'd us then? she cried,
Half rising as she spake,
For hope and joy the sudden strength supplied;
In mercy hath he curb'd his cruel will,
That still thou livest? But as thus she said,
Impatient of that look of hope, her sire
Shook hastily his head;
Oh! he hath laid a Curse upon my life,
A clinging curse, quoth he;
Hath sent a fire into my heart and brain,
A burning fire, for ever there to be!
The winds of Heaven must never breathe on me;
The rains and dews must never fall on me;
Water must mock my thirst and shrink from me;
The common earth must yield no fruit to me;
Sleep, blessed Sleep! must never light on me;
And Death, who comes to all, must fly from me;
And never, never set Ladurlad free.

This is a dream! exclaim'd the incredulous maid,
Yet in her voice the while a fear exprest,
Which in her larger eye was manifest.
This is a dream! she rose and laid her hand
Upon her father's brow, to try the charm;
He could not bear the pressure there;—he shrunk,—
He warded off her arm,
As though it were an enemy's blow, he smote
His daughter's arm aside.
Her eye glanced down, his mantle she espied
And caught it up; Oh misery! Kailyal cried,
He bore me from the river-depths, and yet
His garment is not wet!

IV.

THE DEPARTURE.

RECLIN'D beneath a Cocoa's feathery shade
Ladurlad lies,
And Kailyal on his lap her head hath laid,
To hide her streaming eyes.
The boatman, sailing on his easy way,
With envious eye beheld them where they lay;
For every herb and flower
Was fresh and fragrant with the early dew,
Sweet sung the birds in that delicious hour,
And the cool gale of morning as it blew,
Not yet subdued by day's increasing power,
Ruffling the surface of the silvery stream,
Swept o'er the moisten'd sand, and rais'd no shower.
Telling their tale of love,
The boatman thought they lay
At that lone hour, and who so blest as they!

But now the Sun in heaven is high,
The little songsters of the sky
Sit silent in the sultry hour,[11]
They pant and palpitate with heat;
Their bills are open languidly

To catch the passing air;
They hear it not, they feel it not,
It murmurs not, it moves not.
The boatman, as he looks to land,
Admires what men so mad to linger there,
For yonder Cocoa's shade behind them falls,
A single spot upon the burning sand.

There all the morning was Ladurlad laid,
Silent and motionless, like one at ease;
There motionless upon her father's knees,
Reclin'd the silent maid.
The man was still, pondering with steady mind,
As if it were another's Curse,
His own portentous lot;
Scanning it o'er and o'er in busy thought,
As though it were a last night's tale of woe,
Before the cottage door
By some old beldame sung,
While young and old, assembled round,
Listened, as if by witchery bound,
In fearful pleasure to her wonderous tongue.

Musing so long he lay, that all things seem
Unreal to his sense, even like a dream,
A monstrous dream of things which could not be.
That beating, burning brow,—why it was now
The height of noon, and he was lying there
In the broad sun, all bare!
What if he felt no wind? the air was still,
That was the general will
Of nature, not his own peculiar doom;
Yon rows of rice erect and silent stand,
The shadow of the Cocoa's lightest plume
Is steady on the sand.
Is it indeed a dream? he rose to try,
Impatient to the water-side he went,
And down he bent,
And in the stream he plung'd his hasty arm
To break the visionary charm.
With fearful eye and fearful ear,
His daughter watch'd the event;
She saw the start and shudder,
She heard the in-drawn groan,
For the Water knew Kehama's charm,
The Water shrunk before his arm.
His dry hand mov'd about unmoisten'd there;
As easily might that dry hand avail
To stop the passing gale,
Or grasp the impassive air.
He is Almighty then!
Exclaim'd the wretched man in his despair;
Air knows him, Water knows him; Sleep
His dreadful word will keep;
Even in the grave there is no rest for me,
Cut off from that last hope,—the wretch's joy;
And Veeshnoo hath no power to save,
Nor Seeva to destroy.

Oh! wrong not them! quoth Kailyal,
Wrong not the Heavenly Powers!
Our hope is all in them: They are not blind!
And lighter wrongs than ours,
And lighter crimes than his,
Have drawn the Incarnate down among mankind.
Already have the Immortals heard our cries,

And in the mercy of their righteousness
Beheld us in the hour of our distress!
She spake with streaming eyes,
Where pious love and ardent feeling beam.
And turning to the Image, threw
Her grateful arms around it.—It was thou
Who saved'st me from the stream!
My Marriataly, it was thou!
I had not else been here
To share my Father's Curse,
To suffer now,—and yet to thank thee thus!

Here then, the maiden cried, dear Father, here
Raise our own Goddess, our divine Preserver!
The mighty of the earth despise her rites,
She loves the poor who serve her.
Set up her Image here,
With heart and voice the guardian Goddess bless,
For jealously would she resent
Neglect and thanklessness;—
Set up her Image here,
And bless her for her aid with tongue and soul sincere.

So saying, on her knees the maid
Began the pious toil.
Soon their joint labour scoops the easy soil;
They raise the Image up with reverent hand,
And round its rooted base they heap the sand.
O Thou whom we adore,
O Marriataly, thee do I implore,
The virgin cried; my Goddess, pardon thou
The unwilling wrong, that I no more,
With dance and song,
Can do thy daily service, as of yore!
The flowers which last I wreath'd around thy brow,
Are withering there; and never now
Shall I at eve adore thee,
And swimming round with arms outspread,
Poise the full pitcher on my head,
In dextrous dance before thee,
While underneath the reedy shed, at rest
My father sat the evening rites to view,
And blest thy name, and blest
His daughter too.

Then heaving from her heart a heavy sigh,
O Goddess! from that happy home, cried she,
The Almighty Man hath forced us!
And homeward with the thought unconsciously
She turn'd her dizzy eye—But there on high,
With many a dome, and pinnacle, and spire,
The summits of the Golden Palaces
Blaz'd in the dark blue sky, aloft, like fire.
Father, away! she cried, away!
Why linger we so nigh?
For not to him hath Nature given
The thousand eyes of Deity,
Always and every where with open sight,
To persecute our flight!
Away—away! she said,
And took her father's hand, and like a child
He followed where she led.

V.

THE SEPARATION.

Evening comes on : arising from the stream,
Homeward the tall flamingo wings his flight;
And where he sails athwart the setting beam,
His scarlet plumage glows with deeper light.
The watchman,[12] at the wish'd approach of night,
Gladly forsakes the field, where he all day,
To scare the winged plunderers from their prey,
With shout and sling, on yonder clay-built height,
Hath borne the sultry ray.
Hark! at the Golden Palaces,[13]
The Bramin strikes the hour.
For leagues and leagues around, the brazen sound
Rolls through the stillness of departing day,
Like thunder far away.

Behold them wandering on their hopeless way,
Unknowing where they stray,
Yet sure where'er they stop to find no rest.
The evening gale is blowing,
It plays among the trees;
Like plumes upon a warrior's crest
They see yon cocoas tossing to the breeze.
Ladurlad views them with impatient mind,
Impatiently he hears
The gale of evening blowing,
The sound of waters flowing,
As if all sights and sounds combin'd,
To mock his irremediable woe:
For not for him the blessed waters flow,
For not for him the gales of evening blow;
A fire is in his heart and brain,
And Nature hath no healing for his pain.

The Moon is up, still pale
Amid the lingering light.
A cloud ascending in the eastern sky,
Sails slowly o'er the vale,
And darkens round and closes-in the night.[14]
No hospitable house is nigh
No traveller's home the wanderers to invite.
Forlorn, and with long watching overworn,
The wretched father and the wretched child
Lie down amid the wild.

Before them full in sight,
A white flag flapping to the winds of night,
Marks where the tiger seiz'd his human prey.[15]
Far, far away with natural dread,
Shunning the perilous spot,
At other times abhorrent had they fled;
But now they heed it not.
Nothing they care; the boding death-flag now
In vain for them may gleam and flutter there.
Despair and agony in him,
Prevent all other thought;
And Kailyal hath no heart or sense for ought,
Save her dear father's strange and miserable lot.
There in the woodland shade,
Upon the lap of that unhappy maid,
His head Ladurlad laid,
And never word he spake;

Nor heav'd he one complaining sigh,
Nor groan'd he with his misery,
But silently for her dear sake
Endur'd the raging pain.
And now the moon was hid on high,
No stars were glimmering in the sky;
She could not see her father's eye,
How red with burning agony.
Perhaps he may be cooler now;
She hoped, and long'd to touch his brow
With gentle hand, yet did not dare
To lay the painful pressure there.
Now forward from the tree she bent,
And anxiously her head she leant,
And listened to his breath.
Ladurlad's breath was short and quick,
Yet regular it came,
And like the slumber of the sick,
In pantings still the same.
Oh if he sleeps!—her lips unclose,
Intently listening to the sound,
That equal sound so like repose.
Still quietly the sufferer lies,
Bearing his torment now with resolute will;
He neither moves, nor groans, nor sighs.
Doth satiate cruelty bestow
This little respite to his woe,
She thought, or are there Gods who look below!

Perchance, thought Kailyal, willingly deceiv'd,
Our Marriataly hath his pain reliev'd,
And she hath bade the blessed sleep assuage
His agony, despite the Rajah's rage.
That was a hope which fill'd her gushing eyes,
And made her heart in silent yearnings rise,
To bless the power divine in thankfulness.
And yielding to that joyful thought her mind,
Backward the maid her aching head reclin'd
Against the tree, and to her father's breath
In fear she hearken'd still with earnest ear.
But soon forgetful fits the effort broke:
In starts of recollection then she woke,
Till now benignant Nature overcame
The Virgin's weary and exhausted frame,
Nor able more her painful watch to keep,
She clos'd her heavy lids, and sunk to sleep.
Vain was her hope! he did not rest from pain,
The Curse was burning in his brain.
Alas! the innocent maiden thought he slept,
But sleep the Rajah's dread commandment kept,
Sleep knew Kehama's Curse.
The dews of night fell round them now,
They never bath'd Ladurlad's brow,
They knew Kehama's Curse.
The night-wind is abroad,
Aloft it moves among the stirring trees.
He only heard the breeze,—
No healing aid to him it brought,
It play'd around his head and touch'd him not,
It knew Kehama's Curse.

Listening, Ladurlad lay in his despair,
If Kailyal slept, for wherefore should she share
Her father's wretchedness which none could cure?
Better alone to suffer; he must bear
The burthen of his Curse, but why endure

The unavailing presence of her grief?
She too, apart from him, might find relief;
For dead the Rajah deem'd her, and as thus
Already she his dread revenge had fled,
So might she still escape and live secure.

Gently he lifts his head,
And Kailyal does not feel;
Gently he rises up,—she slumbers still;
Gently he steals away with silent tread.
Anon she started, for she felt him gone;
She call'd, and through the stillness of the night,
His step was heard in flight.
Mistrustful for a moment of the sound,
She listens! till the step is heard no more;
But then she knows that he indeed is gone,
And with a thrilling shriek she rushes on.
The darkness and the wood impede her speed;
She lifts her voice again,
Ladurlad!—and again, alike in vain,
And with a louder cry
Straining its tone to hoarseness;—far away,
Selfish in misery,
He heard the call and faster did he fly.

She leans against that tree whose jutting bough
Smote her so rudely. Her poor heart
How audibly it panted,
With sudden stop and start;
Her breath how short and painfully it came!
Hark! all is still around her,—
And the night so utterly dark,
She opened her eyes and she closed them,
And the blackness and blank were the same.

'T was like a dream of horror, and she stood
Half doubting whether all indeed were true.
A Tiger's howl loud echoing through the wood,
Rous'd her; the dreadful sound she knew,
And turn'd instinctively to what she fear'd.
Far off the Tiger's hungry howl was heard;
A nearer horror met the maiden's view,
For right before her a dim form appear'd,
A human form in that black night,
Distinctly shaped by its own lurid light,
Such light as the sickly moon is seen to shed,
Through spell-rais'd fogs, a bloody baleful red.

That Spectre fix'd his eyes upon her full;
The light which shone in their accursed orbs
Was like a light from Hell,
And it grew deeper, kindling with the view.
She could not turn her sight
From that infernal gaze, which like a spell
Bound her, and held her rooted to the ground.
It palsied every power;
Her limbs avail'd her not in that dread hour.
There was no moving thence,
Thought, memory, sense were gone:
She heard not now the Tiger's nearer cry,
She thought not on her father now,
Her cold heart's blood ran back,
Her hand lay senseless on the bough it clasp'd,
Her feet were motionless;
Her fascinated eyes
Like the stone eye-balls of a statue fix'd,
Yet conscious of the sight that blasted them.

The wind is abroad,
It opens the clouds;
Scattered before the gale,
They skurry through the sky,
And the darkness retiring rolls over the vale.
The stars in their beauty come forth on high,
And through the dark blue night
The moon rides on triumphant, broad and bright.
Distinct and darkening in her light
Appears that Spectre foul.
The moon-beam gives his face and form to sight,
The shape of man,
The living form and face of Arvalan!—
His hands are spread to clasp her.

But at that sight of dread the maid awoke;
As if a lightning-stroke
Had burst the spell of fear.
Away she broke all franticly, and fled.
There stood a temple near beside the way,
An open fane of Pollear, [16] gentle God,
To whom the travellers for protection pray.
With elephantine head and eye severe,
Here stood his image, such as when he seiz'd
And tore the rebel giant from the ground,
With mighty trunk wreath'd round
His impotent bulk, and on his tusks, on high
Impal'd upheld him between earth and sky.

Thither the affrighted maiden sped her flight,
And she hath reach'd the place of sanctuary;
And now within the temple in despite,
Yea, even before the altar, in his sight,
Hath Arvalan with fleshly arm of might
Seiz'd her. That instant the insulted God
Caught him aloft, and from his sinuous grasp,
As if from some tort catapult let loose,
Over the forest hurl'd him all abroad.

O'ercome with dread,
She tarried not to see what heavenly power
Had saved her in that hour.
Breathless and faint she fled.
And now her foot struck on the knotted root
Of a broad manchineil, and there the maid
Fell senselessly beneath the deadly shade.

VI.

CASYAPA.

SHALL this then be thy fate, O lovely Maid,
Thus, Kailyal, must thy sorrows then be ended?
Her face upon the ground,
Her arms at length extended,
There like a corpse behold her laid,
Beneath the deadly shade.
What if the hungry Tiger, prowling by,
Should snuff his banquet nigh?
Alas, Death needs not now his ministry;
The baleful boughs hang o'er her,
The poison-dews descend.
What power will now restore her,
What God will be her friend?
Bright and so beautiful was that fair night,

It might have calm'd the gay amid their mirth,
And given the wretched a delight in tears.
One of the Glendoveers, [17]
The loveliest race of all of heavenly birth,
Hovering with gentle motion o'er the earth,
Amid the moonlight air,
In sportive flight was floating round and round,
Unknowing where his joyous way was tending.
He saw the maid where motionless she lay,
And stoopt his flight descending,
And rais'd her from the ground.
Her heavy eye-lids are half clos'd,
Her cheeks are pale and livid like the dead,
Down hang her loose arms lifelessly,
Down hangs her languid head.

With timely pity touch'd for one so fair,
The gentle Glendoveer
Prest her thus pale and senseless to his breast,
And springs aloft in air with sinewy wings,
And bears the Maiden there,
Where Himakoot, [18] the holy Mount, on high
From mid-earth rising in mid-Heaven,
Shines in its glory like the throne of Even.
Soaring with strenuous flight above,
He bears her to the blessed Grove,
Where in his ancient and august abodes,
There dwells old Casyapa, the Sire of Gods.

The Father of the Immortals sate,
Where underneath the Tree of Life,
The fountain of the Sacred River sprung:
The Father of the Immortals smil'd
Benignant on his son.
Know'st thou, he said, my child,
Ereenia, know'st thou whom thou bringest here,
A mortal to the holy atmosphere?

EREENIA.

I found her in the Groves of Earth,
Beneath a poison-tree,
Thus lifeless as thou seest her.
In pity have I brought her to these bowers,
Not erring, Father! by that smile—
By that benignant eye!

CASYAPA.

What if the maid be sinful? if her ways
Were ways of darkness, and her death predoom'd
To that black hour of midnight, when the Moon
Hath turn'd her face away,
Unwilling to behold
The unhappy end of guilt? [19]

EREENIA.

Then what a lie, my Sire, were written here,
In these fair characters! and she had died,
Sure proof of purer life and happier doom,
Now in the moonlight, in the eye of Heaven
If I had left so fair a flower to fade.
But thou,—all knowing as thou art
Why askest thou of me?
O Father, oldest, holiest, wisest, best
To whom all things are plain,
Why askest thou of me?

40

CASYAPA.
Knowest thou Kehama?

EREENIA.
The Almighty Man!
Who knows not him and his tremendous power?
The Tyrant of the Earth,
The Enemy of Heaven!

CASYAPA.
Fearest thou the Rajah?

EREENIA.
He is terrible!

CASYAPA.
Yea, he is terrible! such power hath he
That hope hath entered Hell.
The Asuras and the spirits of the damn'd
Acclaim their Hero; Yamen, with the might
Of Godhead, scarce can quell
The rebel race accurst:
Half from their beds of torture they uprise,
And half uproot their chains.
Is there not fear in Heaven?
The souls that are in bliss suspend their joy;
The danger hath disturb'd
The calm of Deity,
And Brama fears, and Veeshnoo turns his face
In doubt toward Seeva's throne.

EREENIA.
I have seen Indra[20] tremble at his prayers,
And at his dreadful penances[21] turn pale.
They claim and wrest from Seeva power so vast,
That even Seeva's self,[22]
The Highest, cannot grant and be secure.

CASYAPA.
And darest thou, Ereenia, brave
The Almighty Tyrant's power?

EREENIA.
I brave him, Father! I?

CASYAPA.
Darest thou brave his vengeance?—for if not,
Take her again to earth,
Cast her before the tiger in his path,
Or where the death-dew-dropping tree
May work Kehama's will.

EREENIA.
Never!

CASYAPA.
Then meet his wrath! for he, even he,
Hath set upon this worm his wanton foot.

EREENIA.
I knew her not, how wretched and how fair,
When here I wafted her—poor Child of Earth,
Shall I forsake thee, seeing thee so fair,
So wretched? O my Father, let the maid
Dwell in the Sacred Grove!

CASYAPA.
That must not be,
For Force and Evil then would enter here;
Ganges, the holy stream which cleanseth sin,
Would flow from hence polluted in its springs,
And they who gasp upon its banks in death,
Feel no salvation.   Piety, and Peace,
And Wisdom, these are mine; but not the power
Which could protect her from the Almighty Man;
Nor when the spirit of dead Arvalan
Should persecute her here to glut his rage,
To heap upon her yet more agony,
And ripen more damnation for himself.

EREENIA.
Dead! Arvalan?

CASYAPA.
All power to him, whereof
The disembodied spirit in its state
Of weakness could be made participant,
Kehama hath assign'd, until his days
Of wandering shall be numbered.

EREENIA.
Look! she drinks
The gale of healing from the blessed Groves.
She stirs, and lo! her hand
Hath touch'd the Holy River in its source,
Who would have shrunk if aught impure were nigh.

CASYAPA.
The Maiden, of a truth, is pure from sin.
The waters of the Holy Spring
About the hand of Kailyal play;
They rise, they sparkle, and they sing,
Leaping where languidly she lay,
As if with that rejoicing stir
The Holy Spring would welcome her.
The Tree of Life which o'er her spread,
Benignant bow'd its sacred head,
And dropt its dews of healing;
And her heart-blood at every breath,
Recovering from the strife of death,
Drew in new strength and feeling.
Behold her beautiful in her repose,
A life-bloom reddening now her dark-brown cheek;
And lo! her eyes unclose,
Dark as the depth of Ganges' spring profound
When night hangs over it,
Bright as the moon's refulgent beam,
That quivers on its clear up-sparkling stream.

Soon she let fall her lids,
As one who, from a blissful dream
Waking to thoughts of pain,
Fain would return to sleep, and dream again.
Distrustful of the sight,
She moves not, fearing to disturb
The deep and full delight.
In wonder fix'd, opening again her eye
She gazes silently,
Thinking her mortal pilgrimage was past,
That she had reach'd her heavenly home of rest,
And these were Gods before her,
Or spirits of the blest.

Lo! at Ereenia's voice,
A Ship of Heaven[23] comes sailing down the skies.
Where wouldst thou bear her? cries
    The ancient Sire of Gods.
Straight to the Swerga, to my bower of bliss,
    The Glendoveer replies,
        To Indra's own abodes.
Foe of her foe, were it alone for this
Indra should guard her from his vengeance there;
    But if the God forbear,
Unwilling yet the perilous strife to try,
Or shrinking from the dreadful Rajah's might,—
    Weak as I am, O Father, even I
    Stand forth in Seeva's sight.

    Trust thou in him whate'er betide,
    And stand forth fearlessly!
    The Sire of Gods replied:
All that he wills is right, and doubt not thou,
Howe'er our feeble scope of sight
    May fail us now,
His righteous will in all things must be done.
My blessing be upon thee, O my son!

VII.

THE SWERGA.

Then in the Ship of Heaven, Ereenia laid
    The waking, wondering Maid;
The Ship of Heaven, instinct with thought, display'd
Its living sail, and glides along the sky.
    On either side in wavy tide,
The clouds of morn along its path divide;
The Winds who swept in wild career on high,
Before its presence check their charmed force;
The Winds that loitering lagg'd along their course,
    Around the living Bark enamour'd play,
Swell underneath the sail, and sing before its way.
That Bark, in shape, was like the furrow'd shell
Wherein the Sea-Nymphs to their parent-king,
On festal day, their duteous offerings bring.
    Its hue?—Go watch the last green light
Ere Evening yields the western sky to Night;
Or fix upon the Sun thy strenuous sight
·Till thou hast reach'd its orb of chrysolite.
    The sail from end to end display'd
    Bent, like a rainbow, o'er the Maid.
        An Angel's head, with visual eye,
Through trackless space, directs its chosen way;
    Nor aid of wing, nor foot, nor fin,
Requires to voyage o'er the obedient sky.
    Smooth as the swan when not a breeze at even
    Disturbs the surface of the silver stream,
Through air and sunshine sails the Ship of Heaven.

    Recumbent there the Maiden glides along
        On her aerial way,
How swift she feels not, though the swiftest wind
    Had flagg'd in flight behind.
    Motionless as a sleeping babe she lay,
    And all serene in mind,
    Feeling no fear; for that etherial air
With such new life and joyance fill'd her heart,
    Fear could not enter there;
For sure she deem'd her mortal part was o'er,

And she was sailing to the heavenly shore;
And that angelic form, who moved beside,
Was some good spirit sent to be her guide.

Daughter of Earth; therein thou deem'st aright,
    And never yet did form more beautiful,
In dreams of night descending from on high,
Bless the religious Virgin's gifted sight,
    Nor, like a vision of delight,
Rise on the raptured Poet's inward eye.
Of human form divine was he,
The immortal Youth of Heaven who floated by,
Even such as that divinest form shall be
In those blest stages of our onward race
        When no infirmity,
Low thought, nor base desire, nor wasting care,
Deface the semblance of our heavenly sire.
The wings of Eagle or of Cherubim
    Had seem'd unworthy him:
Angelic power and dignity and grace
Were in his glorious pennons; from the neck
Down to the ankle reach'd their swelling web
Richer than robes of Tyrian dye, that deck
        Imperial majesty:
Their colour like the winter's moonless sky,
When all the stars of midnight's canopy
Shine forth; or like the azure deep at noon,
Reflecting back to heaven a brighter blue.
Such was their tint when closed, but when outspread,
        The permeating light
Shed through their substance thin a varying hue;
        Now bright as when the Rose,
Beauteous as fragrant, gives to scent and sight
A like delight; now like the juice that flows
        From Douro's generous vine,
Or ruby when with deepest red it glows;
Or as the morning clouds refulgent shine,
When, at forthcoming of the Lord of Day,
        The Orient, like a shrine,
Kindles as it receives the rising ray,
        And heralding his way,
Proclaims the presence of the power divine.
    Thus glorious were the wings
Of that celestial Spirit, as he went
Disporting through his native element.
        Nor these alone
The gorgeous beauties that they gave to view:
Through the broad membrane branch'd a pliant bone,
Spreading like fibres from their parent stem;
    Its veins like interwoven silver shone,
        Or as the chaster hue
Of pearls that grace some Sultan's diadem.
Now with slow stroke and strong, behold him smite
    The buoyant air, and now in gentler flight,
On motionless wing expanded, shoot along.

Through air and sunshine sails the Ship of Heaven.
        Far, far beneath them lies
    The gross and heavy atmosphere of earth;
        And with the Swerga gales,
        The Maid of mortal birth
At every breath a new delight inhales.
And now towards its port the Ship of Heaven,
Swift as a falling meteor, shapes its flight,
Yet gently as the dews of night that gem,
And do not bend the hare-bell's slenderest stem.

Daughter of Earth, Ereenia cried, alight,
This is thy place of rest, the Swerga this,
Lo here my bower of bliss!

He furl'd his azure wings, which round him fold
Graceful as robes of Grecian chief of old.
The happy Kailyal knew not where to gaze,
Her eyes around in joyful wonder roam.
Now turn'd upon the lovely Glendoveer,
Now on his heavenly home.

EREENIA.

Here, Maiden, rest in peace,
And I will guard thee, feeble as I am.
The Almighty Rajah shall not harm thee here,
While Indra keeps his throne.

KAILYAL.

Alas, thou fearest him!
Immortal as thou art, thou fearest him!
I thought that death had saved me from his power:
Not even the dead are safe.

EREENIA.

Long years of life and happiness,
O Child of Earth, be thine!
From death I saved thee, and from all thy foes
Will save thee, while the Swerga is secure.

KAILYAL.

Not me alone, O gentle Deveta!
I have a father suffering upon earth,
A persecuted, wretched, poor good man,
For whose strange misery
There is no human help,
And none but I dare comfort him
Beneath Kehama's curse.
O gentle Deveta, protect him too!

EREENIA.

Come, plead thyself to Indra! words like thine
May win their purpose, rouse his slumbering heart,
And make him yet put forth his arm to wield
The thunder, while the thunder is his own.

Then to the Garden of the Deity
Ereenia led the Maid.
In the mid garden tower'd a giant Tree;
Rock-rooted on a mountain-top, it grew,
Rear'd its unrivall'd head on high,
And stretch'd a thousand branches o'er the sky,
Drinking with all its leaves celestial dew.
Lo! where from thence as from a living well
A thousand torrents flow! 24
For still in one perpetual shower,
Like diamond drops, etherial waters fell
From every leaf of all its ample bower.
Rolling adown the steep
From that aerial height,
Through the deep shade of aromatic trees,
Half-seen, the cataracts shoot their gleams of light,
And pour upon the breeze
Their thousand voices; far away the roar
In modulations of delightful sound,
Half-heard and ever varying, floats around.
Below an ample lake expanded lies,

Blue as the o'er-arching skies;
Forth issuing from that lovely Lake,
A thousand rivers water Paradise.
Full to the brink, yet never overflowing,
They cool the amorous gales, which, ever blowing,
O'er their melodious surface love to stray;
Then winging back their way,
Their vapours to the parent tree repay;
And ending thus where they began,
And feeding thus the source from whence they came,
The eternal rivers of the Swerga ran,
For ever renovate, yet still the same.
On that etherial lake whose waters lie
Blue and transpicuous, like another sky,
The Elements had rear'd their King's abode.
A strong controlling power their strife suspended,
And there their hostile essences they blended,
To form a Palace worthy of the God.
Built on the Lake the waters were its floor;
And here its walls were water arch'd with fire,
And here were fire with water vaulted o'er;
And spires and pinnacles of fire
Round watery cupolas aspire,
And domes of rainbow rest on fiery towers,
And roofs of flame are turreted around
With cloud, and shafts of cloud with flame are bound.
Here, too, the elements for ever veer,
Ranging around with endless interchanging;
Pursued in love, and so in love pursuing,
In endless revolutions here they roll;
For ever their mysterious work renewing;
The parts all shifting, still unchanged the whole.
Even we on earth, at intervals, descry
Gleams of the glory, streaks of flowing light,
Openings of heaven, and streams that flash at night
In fitful splendour, through the northern sky.

Impatient of delay, Ereenia caught
The Maid aloft, and spread his wings abroad,
And bore her to the presence of the God.
There Indra sate upon his throne reclined,
Where Devetas adore him;
The lute of Nared, 25 warbling on the wind,
All tones of magic harmony combined
To soothe his troubled mind,
While the dark-eyed Asparas danced before him.
In vain the God-musician play'd,
In vain the dark-eyed Nymphs of Heaven essay'd
To charm him with their beauties in the dance;
And when he saw the mortal Maid appear,
Led by the heroic Glendoveer,
A deeper trouble fill'd his countenance.
What hast thou done, Ereenia, said the God,
Bringing a mortal here?
And while he spake his eye was on the Maid.
The look he gave was solemn, not severe;
No hope to Kailyal it convey'd,
And yet it struck no fear;
There was a sad displeasure in his air,
But pity, too, was there.

EREENIA.

Hear me, O Indra! On the lower earth
I found this child of man, by what mishap
I know not, lying in the lap of death.
Aloft I bore her to our Father's grove,

Not having other thought, than when the gales
Of bliss had heal'd her, upon earth again
To leave its lovely daughter. Other thoughts
Arose, when Casyapa declar'd her fate ;
For she is one who groans beneath the power
Of the dread Rajah, terrible alike
To men and Gods. His son, dead Arvalan,
Arm'd with a portion, Indra, of thy power,
Already wrested from thee, persecutes
The Maid, the helpless one, the innocent.
What then behov'd me but to waft her here
To my own Bower of Bliss ? what other choice ?
The spirit of foul Arvalan, not yet
Hath power to enter here ; here thou art yet
Supreme, and yet the Swerga is thine own.

INDRA.

No child of man, Ereenia, in the Bowers
Of Bliss may sojourn, till he hath put off
His mortal part ; for on mortality
Time and Infirmity and Death attend,
Close followers they, and in their mournful train
Sorrow and Pain and Mutability :
Did they find entrance here, we should behold
Our joys, like earthly summers, pass away.
Those joys perchance may pass ; a stronger hand
May wrest my sceptre, and unparadise
The Swerga ;—but, Ereenia, if we fall,
Let it be Fate's own arm that casts us down,
We will not rashly hasten and provoke
The blow, nor bring ourselves the ruin on.

EREENIA.

Fear courts the blow, Fear brings the ruin on.
Needs must the chariot-wheels of Destiny
Crush him who throws himself before their track,
Patient and prostrate.

INDRA.

All may yet be well.
Who knows but Veeshnoo will descend, and save,
Once more incarnate ?

EREENIA.

Look not there for help,
Nor build on unsubstantial hope thy trust.
Our Father Casyapa hath said he turns
His doubtful eye to Seeva, even as thou
Dost look to him for aid. But thine own strength
Should for thine own salvation be put forth ;
Then might the higher powers approving see
And bless the brave resolve—Oh, that my arm
Could wield yon lightnings which play idly there,
In inoffensive radiance, round thy head !
The Swerga should not need a champion now,
Nor Earth implore deliverance still in vain !

INDRA.

Think'st thou I want the will ? rash Son of Heaven,
What if my arm be feeble as thine own
Against the dread Kehama ? He went on
Conquering in irresistible career,
Till his triumphant car had measured o'er
The insufficient earth, and all the kings
Of men received his yoke ; then had he won
His will, to ride upon their necks elate,

And crown his conquests with the sacrifice
That should, to men and gods, proclaim him Lord
And Sovereign Master of the vassal World, [26]
Sole Rajah, the Omnipotent below. [27]
The steam of that portentous sacrifice
Arose to Heaven. Then was the hour to strike,
Then in the consummation of his pride,
His height of glory, then the thunder-bolt
Should have gone forth, and hurl'd him from his throne
Down to the fiery floor of Padalon,
To everlasting burnings, agony
Eternal, and remorse which knows no end.
That hour went by : grown impious in success
By prayer and penances he wrested now
Such power from Fate, that soon, if Seeva turn not
His eyes on earth, and no Avatar save,
Soon will he seize the Swerga for his own,
Roll on through Padalon his chariot wheels,
Tear up the adamantine bolts which lock
The accurst Asuras to its burning floor,
And force the drink of Immortality
From Yamen's charge—Vain were it now to strive ;
My thunder cannot pierce the sphere of power
Wherewith, as with a girdle, he is bound.

KAILYAL.

Take me to earth, O gentle Deveta !
Take me again to earth ! This is no place
Of hope for me !—my Father still must bear
His curse—he shall not bear it all alone ;
Take me to earth, that I may follow him !—
I do not fear the Almighty Man ! the Gods
Are feeble here ; but there are higher powers
Who will not turn their eyes from wrongs like ours ;
Take me to earth, O gentle Deveta !—

Saying thus she knelt, and to his knees she clung
And bow'd her head, in tears and silence praying.
Rising anon, around his neck she flung
Her arms, and there with folded hands she hung,
And fixing on the guardian Glendoveer
Her eyes, more eloquent than Angel's tongue,
Again she cried, There is no comfort here !
I must be with my Father in his pain—
Take me to earth, O Deveta, again !
Indra with admiration heard the Maid.
O Child of Earth. he cried,
Already in thy spirit thus divine,
Whatever weal or woe betide,
Be that high sense of duty still thy guide,
And all good Powers will aid a soul like thine.
Then turning to Ereenia, thus he said,
Take her where Ganges hath its second birth,
Below our sphere, and yet above the earth :
There may Ladurlad rest beyond the power
Of the dread Rajah, till the fated hour.

VIII.

THE SACRIFICE. [28]

Dost thou tremble, O Indra, O God of the Sky,
Why slumber those Thunders of thine ?
Dost thou tremble on high,—
Wilt thou tamely the Swerga resign,

Art thou smitten, O Indra, with dread?
Or seest thou not, seest thou not, Monarch divine,
　　How many a day to Seeva's shrine
　　Kehama his victim hath led?
　　Nine and ninety days are fled,
　　Nine and ninety steeds have bled;
　　One more, the rite will be complete,
One victim more, and this the dreadful day.
Then will the impious Rajah seize thy seat,
And wrest the thunder-sceptre from thy sway.
　　Along the mead the hallowed Steed
　　Yet bends at liberty his way;
' At noon his consummating blood will flow.
　　O day of woe! above, below,
That blood confirms the Almighty Tyrant's reign!
　　Thou tremblest, O Indra, O God of the Sky,
　　　　Thy thunder is vain!
　　Thou tremblest on high for thy power!
　　But where is Veeshnoo at this hour,
　　　　But where is Seeva's eye?
　　　　Is the Destroyer blind?
　　Is the Preserver careless for mankind?

　　Along the mead the hallowed Steed
　　Still wanders wheresoe'er he will,
　　O'er hill, or dale, or plain;
No human hand hath trick'd that mane
From which he shakes the morning dew;
　His mouth has never felt the rein,
　His lips have never froth'd the chain;
　For pure of blemish and of stain,
　His neck unbroke to mortal yoke,
Like Nature free the Steed must be,
Fit offering for the Immortals he.
A year and day the Steed must stray
Wherever chance may guide his way,
　Before he fall at Seeva's shrine;
　The year and day have pass'd away,
Nor touch of man hath marr'd the right divine.
And now at noon the Steed must bleed,
The perfect rite to-day must force the meed
Which Fate reluctant shudders to bestow;
　　Then must the Swerga-God
Yield to the Tyrant of the World below;
　Then must the Devetas obey
The Rajah's rod, and groan beneath his hateful sway.

　The Sun rides high; the hour is nigh;
　　The multitude who long,
　　Lest aught should mar the rite,
　　In circle wide on every side,
　　Have kept the Steed in sight,
Contract their circle now, and drive him on.
Drawn in long files before the Temple-court,
The Rajah's archers flank an ample space;
Here, moving onward still, they drive him near,
Then, opening, give him way to enter here.

Behold him, how he starts and flings his head!
On either side, in glittering order spread,
The archers ranged in narrowing lines appear;
　The multitude behind close up the rear
　With moon-like bend, and silently await
　　　The awful end,
The rite that shall from Indra wrest his power.
In front, with far-stretch'd walls, and many a tower,

Turret and dome and pinnacle elate,
The huge Pagoda seems to load the land:
　　And there before the gate
　　The Bramin band expectant stand,
　The axe is ready for Kehama's hand.
　　Hark! at the Golden Palaces
　　The Bramin strikes the time!
One, two, three, four, a thrice-told chime,
　　And then again, one, two.
The bowl that in its vessel floats, [29] anew
　　Must fill and sink again,
　Then will the final stroke be due.
The Sun rides high, the noon is nigh;
　　And silently, as if spell-bound,
　　The multitude expect the sound.

Lo! how the Steed, with sudden start,
　Turns his quick head to every part;
Long files of men on every side appear.
The sight might well his heart affright,
　And yet the silence that is here
　　Inspires a stranger fear;
For not a murmur, not a sound
Of breath or motion rises round,
No stir is heard in all that mighty crowd;
He neighs, and from the temple-wall
　The voice re-echoes loud,
Loud and distinct, as from a hill
Across a lonely vale, when all is still.

Within the temple, on his golden throne
　　Reclin'd, Kehama lies,
　　Watching with steady eyes
The perfum'd light that, burning bright,
　　Metes out the passing hours.
On either hand his eunuchs stand,
Freshening with fans of peacock-plumes the air,
Which, redolent of all rich gums and flowers,
Seems, overcharged with sweets, to stagnate there.
　Lo! the time-taper's flame ascending slow
　Creeps up its coil [30] toward the fated line;
　Kehama rises and goes forth,
And from the altar, ready where it lies,
　He takes the axe of sacrifice.

That instant from the crowd, with sudden shout,
　　　A Man sprang out
To lay upon the Steed his hand profane.
A thousand archers, with unerring eye,
　　　At once let fly,
And with their hurtling arrows fill the sky.
In vain they fall upon him fast as rain;
He bears a charmed life, which may defy
All weapons,—and the darts that whizz around,
　　As from an adamantine panoply
　　Repell'd, fall idly to the ground.
Kehama clasp'd his hands in agony,
And saw him grasp the hallowed courser's mane,
　　Spring up with sudden bound,
　　　And with a frantic cry,
And madman's gesture, gallop round and round.

They seize, they drag him to the Rajah's feet.
What doom will now be his,—what vengeance meet
　Will he, who knows no mercy, now require?
The obsequious guards around, with blood-hound eye,

Look for the word, in slow-consuming fire,
By piece-meal death, to make the wretch expire,
Or hoist his living carcass, hooked on high,
To feed the fowls and insects of the sky;
Or if aught worse inventive cruelty
To that remorseless heart of royalty
Might prompt, accursed instruments they stand
To work the wicked will with wicked hand.
Far other thoughts were in the multitude;
Pity, and human feelings, held them still;
And stifled sighs and groans supprest were there,
And many a secret curse and inward prayer
Call'd on the insulted Gods to save mankind.
Expecting some new crime, in fear they stood,
Some horror which would make the natural blood
Start, with cold shudderings thrill the sinking heart,
Whiten the lip, and make the abhorrent eye
Roll back and close, prest in for agony.

How then fared he for whom the mighty crowd
Suffered in spirit thus,—how then fared he?
A ghastly smile was on his lip, his eye
Glared with a ghastly hope, as he drew nigh,
And cried aloud, Yes, Rajah! it is I!
And wilt thou kill me now?
The countenance of the Almighty Man
Fell when he knew Ladurlad, and his brow
Was clouded with despite, as one asham'd.
That wretch again! indignant he exclaim'd,
And smote his forehead, and stood silently
Awhile in wrath: then, with ferocious smile,
And eyes which seem'd to darken his dark cheek,
Let him go free! he cried; he hath his curse,
And vengeance upon him can wreak no worse—
But ye who did not stop him—tremble ye!

He bade the archers pile their weapons there:
No manly courage fill'd the slavish band,
No sweetening vengeance rous'd a brave despair.
He call'd his horsemen then, and gave command
To hem the offenders in, and hew them down.
Ten thousand scymitars at once uprear'd,
Flash up, like waters sparkling to the sun;
A second time the fatal brands appear'd
Lifted aloft,—they glitter'd then no more,
Their light was gone, their splendour quench'd in gore.
At noon the massacre begun,
And night clos'd in before the work of death was done.[31]

IX.

THE HOME-SCENE.

The steam of slaughter from that place of blood
Spread o'er the tainted sky.
Vultures, for whom the Rajah's tyranny
So oft had furnish'd food, from far and nigh
Sped to the lure: aloft with joyful cry,
Wheeling around, they hover'd over head;
Or, on the temple perch'd, with greedy eye,
Impatient watch'd the dead.
Far off the tigers, in the inmost wood,
Heard the death-shriek, and snuff'd the scent of blood.
They rose, and through the covert went their way,

Couch'd at the forest edge, and waited for their prey.
He who had sought for death went wandering on,
The hope which had inspir'd his heart was gone,
Yet a wild joyance still inflam'd his face,
A smile of vengeance, a triumphant glow.
Where goes he?—Whither should Ladurlad go!
Unwittingly the wretch's footsteps trace
Their wonted path toward his dwelling-place;
And wandering on, unknowing where,
He starts at finding he is there.

Behold his lowly home,
By yonder broad-bough'd plane o'ershaded:[32]
There Marriataly's Image stands,
And there the garland twin'd by Kailyal's hands
Around its brow hath faded.
The peacocks, at their master's sight,
Quick from the leafy thatch alight,
And hurry round, and search the ground,
And veer their glancing necks from side to side,
Expecting from his hand
Their daily dole, which erst the Maid supplied,
Now all too long denied.
But as he gaz'd around,
How strange did all accustom'd sights appear!
How differently did each familiar sound
Assail his alter'd ear!
Here stood the marriage bower,[33]
Rear'd in that happy hour
When he, with festal joy and youthful pride,
Brought his Yedillian home, his beauteous bride.
Leaves not its own, and many a borrow'd flower,
Had then bedeck'd it, withering ere the night;
But he who look'd, from that auspicious day,
For years of long delight,
And would not see the marriage bower decay,
There planted and nurst up, with daily care,
The sweetest herbs that scent the ambient air,
And train'd them round to live and flourish there.
Nor when dread Yamen's will
Had call'd Yedillian from his arms away,
Ceas'd he to tend the marriage bower, but still,
Sorrowing, had drest it like a pious rite
Due to the monument of past delight.
He took his wonted seat before the door,—
Even as of yore,
When he was wont to view, with placid eyes,
His daughter at her evening sacrifice.
Here were the flowers which she so carefully
Did love to rear for Marriataly's brow;
Neglected now,
Their heavy heads were drooping, over-blown:
All else appeared the same as heretofore,
All—save himself alone;
How happy then,—and now a wretch for evermore!

The market-flag,[34] which, hoisted high,
From far and nigh,
Above yon cocoa grove is seen,
Hangs motionless amid the sultry sky.
Loud sounds the village drum; a happy crowd
Is there; Ladurlad hears their distant voices
But with their joy no more his heart rejoices;
And how their old companion now may fare,
Little they know, and less they care.
The torment he is doom'd to bear

Was but to them the wonder of a day,
A burden of sad thoughts soon put away.

They knew not that the wretched man was near,
And yet it seem'd, to his distemper'd ear,
As if they wrong'd him with their merriment.
Resentfully he turn'd away his eyes,
Yet turn'd them but to find
Sights that enraged his mind
With envious grief more wild and overpowering.
The tank which fed his fields was there, and there
The large-leav'd lotus on the waters flowering.
There, from the intolerable heat,
The buffaloes retreat;[35]
Only their nostrils rais'd to meet the air,
Amid the sheltering element they rest.
Impatient of the sight, he clos'd his eyes,
And bow'd his burning head, and in despair
Calling on Indra,—Thunder-God! he said,
Thou owest to me alone this day thy throne,
Be grateful, and in mercy strike me dead!

Despair had rous'd him to that hopeless prayer,
Yet thinking on the heavenly Powers, his mind
Drew comfort; and he rose and gather'd flowers,
And twin'd a crown for Marriataly's brow;
And taking then her wither'd garland down,
Replac'd it with the blooming coronal.
Not for myself, the unhappy father cried,
Not for myself, O mighty one! I pray,
Accursed as I am beyond thy aid!
But, oh! be gracious still to that dear Maid
Who crown'd thee with these garlands day by day.
And danced before thee aye at even-tide
In beauty and in pride.
O Marriataly, whereso'er she stray
Forlorn and wretched, still be thou her guide!

A loud and fiendish laugh replied,
Scoffing his prayer.   Aloft, as from the air,
The sound of insult came: he look'd, and there
The visage of dead Arvalan came forth,
Only his face amid the clear blue sky,
With long-drawn lips of insolent mockery,
And eyes whose lurid glare
Was like a sulphur fire
Mingling with darkness ere its flames expire.

Ladurlad knew him well: enraged to see
The cause of all his misery,
He stoop'd and lifted from the ground
A stake, whose fatal point was black with blood;
The same wherewith his hand had dealt the wound,
When Arvalan, in hour with evil fraught,
For violation seiz'd the shrieking Maid.
Thus arm'd, in act again to strike he stood,
And twice with inefficient wrath essay'd
To smite the impassive shade.
The lips of scorn their mockery-laugh renew'd,
And Arvalan put forth a hand and caught
The sun-beam, and condensing there its light,
Upon Ladurlad turn'd the burning stream.
Vain cruelty! the stake
Fell in white ashes from his hold, but he
Endur'd no added pain; his agony
Was full, and at the height;

The burning stream of radiance nothing harm'd him:
A fire was in his heart and brain,
And from all other flame,
Kehama's Curse had charm'd him.

Anon the Spirit wav'd a second hand;
Down rush'd the obedient whirlwind from the sky,
Scoop'd up the sand like smoke, and from on high
Shed the hot shower upon Ladurlad's head.
Where'er he turns, the accursed Hand is there;
East, West, and North, and South, on every Side
The Hand accursed waves in air to guide
The dizzying storm; ears, nostrils, eyes, and mouth
It fills and chokes, and, clogging every pore,
Taught him new torments might be yet in store.
Where shall he turn to fly? behold his house
In flames! uprooted lies the marriage-bower,
The Goddess buried by the sandy shower.
Blindly, with staggering step, he reels about,
And still the accursed Hand pursued,
And still the lips of scorn their mockery-laugh renew'd.

What, Arvalan! hast thou so soon forgot
The grasp of Pollear? Wilt thou still defy
The righteous Powers of Heaven? or know'st thou not
That there are yet superior Powers on high,
Son of the Wicked?—Lo, in rapid flight,
Ereenia hastens from the etherial height;
Bright is the sword celestial in his hand,
Like lightning in its path athwart the sky.
He comes and drives, with angel-arm, the blow.
Oft have the Asuras, in the wars of Heaven,
Felt that keen sword by arm angelic driven,
And fled before it from the fields of light.
Thrice through the vulnerable shade
The Glendoveer impels the griding blade.
The wicked Shade flies howling from his foe.
So let that Spirit foul
Fly, and for impotence of anger, howl,
Writhing with pain, and o'er his wounds deplore;
Worse punishment hath Arvalan deserv'd,
And righteous fate hath heavier doom in store.

Not now the Glendoveer pursues his flight.
He bade the Ship of Heaven alight,
And gently there he laid
The astonish'd father by the happy Maid,
The Maid now shedding tears of deep delight.
Beholding all things with incredulous eyes,
Still dizzy with the sand-storm, there he lay,
While sailing up the skies, the living Bark,
Through air and sunshine, held its heavenly way.

X.

MOUNT MERU. [36]

Swift through the sky the vessel of the Suras
Sails up the fields of ether like an Angel.
Rich is the freight, O Vessel, that thou bearest!
Beauty and Virtue,
Fatherly cares and filial veneration,
Hearts which are prov'd and strengthen'd by affliction,
Manly resentment, fortitude and action,
Womanly goodness;

All with which Nature halloweth her daughters,
Tenderness, truth and purity and meekness,
Piety, patience, faith and resignation,
Love and devotement.
Ship of the Gods! how richly art thou laden!
Proud of the charge, thou voyagest rejoicing.
Clouds float around to honour thee, and Evening
Lingers in heaven.

A Stream descends on Meru mountain;[37]
None hath seen its secret fountain;
It had its birth, so Sages say,
Upon the memorable day
When Parvati[38] presumed to lay,
In wanton play,
Her hands, too venturous Goddess, in her mirth,
On Seeva's eyes, the light and life of Earth.
Thereat the heart of the Universe stood still;[39]
The Elements ceas'd their influences; the Hours
Stopt on the Eternal round; Motion and Breath,
Time, Change, and Life and Death,
In sudden trance opprest, forgot their powers.
A moment, and the dread eclipse was ended;
But, at the thought of nature thus suspended,
The sweat on Seeva's forehead stood,
And Ganges thence upon the World descended,
The Holy River, the Redeeming Flood.

None hath seen its secret fountain;
But on the top of Meru mountain
Which rises o'er the hills of earth,
In light and clouds, it hath its mortal birth.
Earth seems that pinnacle to rear
Sublime above this worldly sphere,
Its cradle, and its altar and its throne,
And there the new-born River lies
Outspread beneath its native skies,
As if it there would love to dwell
Alone and unapproachable.
Soon flowing forward, and resign'd
To the will of the Creating Mind,
It springs at once, with sudden leap,
Down from the immeasurable steep.
From rock to rock, with shivering force rebounding,
The mighty cataract rushes; Heaven around,
Like thunder, with the incessant roar resounding,
And Meru's summit shaking with the sound.
Wide spreads the snowy foam, the sparkling spray
Dances aloft; and ever there, at morning,
The earliest sun-beams haste to wing their way,
With rainbow-wreaths the holy flood adorning;
And duly the adoring Moon at night
Sheds her white glory there,
And in the watery air
Suspends her halo-crowns of silver light.

A mountain-valley in its blessed breast
Receives the stream, which there delights to lie,
Untroubled and at rest,
Beneath the untainted sky.
There in a lovely lake it seems to sleep,
And thence through many a channel dark and deep,
Their secret way the holy Waters wind,
Till, rising underneath the root
Of the Tree of Life on Hemakoot,
Majestic forth they flow to purify mankind.

Towards this Lake, above the nether sphere,
The living Bark, with angel eye,
Directs its course along the obedient sky.
Kehama hath not yet dominion here;
And till the dreaded hour,
When Indra by the Rajah shall be driven
Dethron'd from Heaven,
Here may Ladurlad rest beyond his power.
The living Bark alights; the Glendoveer
Then lays Ladurlad by the blessed Lake;—
O happy Sire, and yet more happy Daughter!
The etherial gales his agony aslake,
His daughter's tears are on his cheek,
His hand is in the water;
The innocent man, the man opprest,
Oh joy!—hath found a place of rest
Beyond Kehama's sway,
His curse extends not here; his pains have past away.

O happy Sire, and happy Daughter!
Ye on the banks of that celestial water
Your resting-place and sanctuary have found.
What! hath not then their mortal taint defil'd
The sacred solitary ground?
Vain thought! the Holy Valley smil'd
Receiving such a Sire and Child;
Ganges, who seem'd asleep to lie,
Beheld them with benignant eye,
And rippled round melodiously,
And roll'd her little waves, to meet
And welcome their beloved feet.
The gales of Swerga thither fled,
And heavenly odours there were shed
About, below, and overhead;
And Earth rejoicing in their tread,
Hath built them up a blooming Bower,
Where every amaranthine flower
Its deathless blossom interweaves
With bright and undecaying leaves.

Three happy beings are there here,
The Sire, the Maid, the Glendoveer;
A fourth approaches,—who is this
That enters in the Bower of Bliss?
No form so fair might painter find
Among the daughters of mankind;
For death her beauties hath refin'd,
And unto her a form hath given
Fram'd of the elements of Heaven;
Pure dwelling-place for perfect mind.
She stood and gaz'd on Sire and Child;
Her tongue not yet had power to speak,
The tears were streaming down her cheek;
And when those tears her sight beguil'd,
And still her faultering accents fail'd,
The Spirit, mute and motionless,
Spread out her arms for the caress,
Made still and silent with excess
Of love and painful happiness.
The Maid that lovely form survey'd;
Wistful she gaz'd; and knew her not;
But Nature to her heart convey'd
A sudden thrill, a startling thought,
A feeling many a year forgot,
Now like a dream anew recurring,
As if again in every vein

41

Her mother's milk was stirring.
With straining neck and earnest eye
She stretch'd her hands imploringly,
As if she fain would have her nigh,
Yet fear'd to meet the wish'd embrace,
At once with love and awe opprest.
Not so Ladurlad; he could trace,
Though brighten'd with angelic grace,
His own Yedillian's earthly face;
He ran and held her to his breast!
Oh joy above all joys of Heaven,
By Death alone to others given,
This moment hath to him restor'd
The early-lost, the long-deplor'd.

They sin who tell us Love can die.
With life all other passions fly,
All others are but vanity;
In Heaven Ambition cannot dwell,
Nor Avarice in the vaults of Hell:
Earthly these passions of the Earth,
They perish where they have their birth;
But Love is indestructible:
Its holy flame for ever burneth,
From Heaven it came, to Heaven returneth.
Too oft on Earth a troubled guest,
At times deceiv'd, at times opprest,
It here is tried and purified,
Then hath in Heaven its perfect rest:
It soweth here with toil and care,
But the harvest-time of love is there.
Oh! when a Mother meets on high
The Babe she lost in infancy,
Hath she not then, for pains and fears,
The day of woe, the watchful night,
For all her sorrow, all her tears,
An over-payment of delight?
A blessed family is this
Assembled in the Bower of Bliss!
Strange woe, Ladurlad, hath been thine,
And pangs beyond all human measure,
And thy reward is now divine,
A foretaste of eternal pleasure.
He knew indeed there was a day
When all these joys would pass away,
And he must quit this blest abode;
And, taking up again the spell,
Groan underneath the baleful load,
And wander o'er the world again,
Most wretched of the sons of men:
Yet was this brief repose, as when
A traveller in the Arabian sands,
Half-fainting on his sultry road,
Hath reach'd the water-place at last;
And resting there beside the Well,
Thinks of the perils he has past,
And gazes o'er the unbounded plain,
The plain which must be travers'd still,
And drinks,—yet cannot drink his fill;
Then girds his patient loins again.
So to Ladurlad now was given
New strength, and confidence in Heaven,
And hope, and faith invincible.
For often would Ereenia tell
Of what in elder days befell,
When other Tyrants, in their might,

Usurp'd dominion o'er the earth;
And Veeshnoo took a human birth,
Deliverer of the Sons of men;
And slew the huge Ermaccasen,
And piece-meal rent, with lion force,
Errenen's accursed corse,
And humbled Baly in his pride;
And when the Giant Ravanen
Had borne triumphant, from his side,
Sita, the earth-born God's beloved bride,
Then, from his island-kingdom, laugh'd to scorn
The insulted husband, and his power defied;
How to revenge the wrong in wrath he hied,
Bridging the sea before his dreadful way,
And met the hundred-headed foe,
And dealt him the unerring blow:
By Brama's hand the righteous lance was given,
And by that arm immortal driven,
It laid the mighty Tyrant low;
And Earth and Ocean, and high Heaven,
Rejoiced to see his overthrow.
Oh! doubt not thou, Yedillian cried,
Such fate Kehama will betide;
For there are Gods who look below,—
Seeva, the Avenger, is not blind,
Nor Veeshnoo careless for mankind.

Thus was Ladurlad's soul imbued
With hope and holy fortitude;
And Child and Sire, with pious mind
Alike resolv'd, alike resign'd,
Look'd onward to the evil day:
Faith was their comfort, Faith their stay;
They trusted woe would pass away,
And Tyranny would sink subdued,
And Evil yield to Good.

Lovely wert thou, O Flower of Earth!
Above all flowers of mortal birth;
But foster'd in this blissful bower,
From day to day, and hour to hour,
Lovelier grew the lovely flower.
O blessed, blessed company!
When men and heavenly spirits greet,
And they whom Death had severed meet,
And hold again communion sweet;—
O blessed, blessed company!
The Sun, careering round the sky,
Beheld them with rejoicing eye,
And bade his willing Charioteer
Relax his speed as they drew near;
Aurounin check'd the rainbow reins,
The seven green coursers shook their manes,
And brighter rays around them threw;
The Car of Glory in their view
More radiant, more resplendent grew;
And Surya, ⁴⁰ through his veil of light,
Beheld the Bower, and blest the sight.
The Lord of Night, as he sail'd by,
Stay'd his pearly boat on high;
And, while around the blissful Bower,
He bade the softest moonlight flow,
Linger'd to see that earthly flower,
Forgetful of his Dragon foe, ⁴¹
Who, mindful of their ancient feud,
With open jaws of rage pursued.

There all good Spirits of the air,
Suras [42] and Devetas repair,
Aloft they love to hover there,
And view the flower of mortal birth
Here, for her innocence and worth,
Transplanted from the fields of earth ;—
And him, who on the dreadful day
When Heaven was fill'd with consternation,
And Indra trembled with dismay,
And, for the sounds of joy and mirth,
Woe was heard and lamentation,
Defied the Rajah in his pride,
Though all in Heaven and Earth beside
Stood mute in dolorous expectation ;
And, rushing forward in that hour,
Saved the Swerga from his power.
Grateful for this they hover nigh,
And bless the blessed Company.

One God alone, with wanton eye,
Beheld them in their Bower;
O ye, he cried, who have defied
The Rajah, will ye mock my power?
'T was Camdeo [43] riding on his lory,
'T was the immortal Youth of Love ;
If man below and Gods above,
Subject alike, quoth he, have felt these darts,
Shall ye alone, of all in story,
Boast impenetrable hearts ?
Hover here, my gentle lory,
Gently hover, while I see
To whom hath Fate decreed the glory,
To the Glendoveer or me.

Then, in the dewy evening sky,
The bird of gorgeous plumery
Pois'd his wings and hover'd nigh.
It chanced at that delightful hour
Kailyal sate before the Bower,
On the green bank with amaranth sweet,
Where Gauges warbled at her feet.
Ereenia there, before the Maid,
His sails of ocean blue displayed ;
And sportive in her sight,
Mov'd slowly o'er the lake with gliding flight ;
Anon, with sudden stroke and strong,
In rapid course careering, swept along ;
Now shooting downward from his heavenly height,
Plunged in the deep below,
Then rising, soar'd again,
And shook the sparkling waters off like rain,
And hovering o'er the silver surface hung.
At him young Camdeo bent the bow ;
With living bees the bow was strung,
The fatal bow of sugar-cane,
And flowers which would inflame the heart
With their petals barb'd the dart.

The shaft, unerringly addrest,
Unerring flew, and smote Ereenia's breast,
Ah, Wanton ! cried the Glendoveer,
Go aim at idler hearts,
Thy skill is baffled here !
A deeper love I bear that Maid divine,
Sprung from a higher will,
A holier power than thine !

A second shaft, while thus Ereenia cried,
Had Camdeo aim'd at Kailyal's side,
But, lo ! the Bees which strung his bow
Broke off, and took their flight.
To that sweet Flower of earth they wing their way,
Around her raven tresses play,
And buzz about her with delight,
As if with that melodious sound,
They strove to pay their willing duty
To mortal purity and beauty.
Ah ! Wanton ! cried the Glendoveer,
No power hast thou for mischief here !
Chuse thou some idler breast,
For these are proof, by nobler thoughts possest.
Go, to thy plains of Matra go,
And string again thy broken bow !
Rightly Ereenia spake ; and ill had thoughts
Of earthly love beseem'd the sanctuary
Where Kailyal had been wafted, that the Soul
Of her dead Mother there might strengthen her,
Feeding her with the milk of heavenly lore,
And influxes of Heaven imbue her heart
With hope and faith, and holy fortitude,
Against the evil day. Here rest a while
In peace, O Father ! mark'd for misery
Above all sons of men ; O daughter ! doom'd
For sufferings and for trials above all
Of women ;—yet both favour'd, both beloved
By all good Powers, here rest a while in peace.

XI.

THE ENCHANTRESS.

WHEN from the sword, by arm angelic driven,
Foul Arvalan fled howling, wild in pain,
His thin essential spirit, rent and riven
With wounds, united soon and heal'd again ;
Backward the accursed turn'd his eye in flight,
Remindful of revengeful thoughts even then,
And saw where, gliding through the evening light,
The Ship of Heaven sail'd upward through the sky,
Then, like a meteor, vanish'd from his sight.
Where should he follow ? vainly might he try
To trace through trackless air its rapid course,
Nor dar'd he that angelic arm defy,
Still sore and writhing from its dreaded force.

Should he the lust of vengeance lay aside?
Too long had Arvalan in ill been train'd ;
Nurst up in power and tyranny and pride,
His soul the ignominious thought disdain'd.
Or to his mighty Father should he go,
Complaining of defeature twice sustain'd,
And ask new powers to meet the immortal foe ?—
Repulse he fear'd not, but he fear'd rebuke,
And sham'd to tell him of his overthrow.
There dwelt a dread Enchantress in a nook
Obscure; old help-mate she to him had been,
Lending her aid in many a secret sin ;
And there, for counsel, now his way he took.

She was a woman whose unlovely youth,
Even like a canker'd rose, which none will cull,
Had wither'd on the stalk; her heart was full

Of passions which had found no natural scope,
Feelings which there had grown but ripen'd not;
    Desires unsatisfied, abortive hope,
Repinings which provoked vindictive thought,
These restless elements for ever wrought,
    Fermenting in her with perpetual stir,
    And thus her spirit to all evil mov'd;
She hated men because they lov'd not her,
And hated women because they were lov'd.
And thus, in wrath and hatred and despair,
She tempted Hell to tempt her; and resign'd
    Her body to the Demons of the Air,
Wicked and wanton fiends, who, where they will,
    Wander abroad, still seeking to do ill,
And take whatever vacant form they find,
Carcase of man or beast, that life hath left;
Foul instrument for them of fouler mind.
To these the Witch her wretched body gave,
So they would wreak her vengeance on mankind,
She thus at once their mistress and their slave;
    And they to do such service nothing loth,
Obey'd her bidding, slaves and masters both.

So from this cursed intercourse she caught
Contagious power of mischief, and was taught
    Such secrets as are damnable to guess.
    Is there a child whose little lovely ways
Might win all hearts,—on whom his parents gaze
    Till they shed tears of joy and tenderness?
Oh! hide him from that Witch's withering sight!
    Oh! hide him from the eye of Lorrinite!
    Her look hath crippling in it, and her curse
All plagues which on mortality can light;
Death is his doom if she behold,—or worse,—
    Diseases loathsome and incurable,
And inward sufferings that no tongue can tell.
Woe was to him, on whom that eye of hate
Was bent; for, certain as the stroke of Fate,
It did its mortal work; nor human arts
Could save the unhappy wretch, her chosen prey
For gazing, she consum'd his vital parts,
    Eating his very core of life away.[44]
The wine which from yon wounded palm on high
    Fills yonder gourd, as slowly it distills,
Grows sour at once if Lorrinite pass by.
The deadliest worm, from which all creatures fly,
    Fled from the deadlier venom of her eye;
The babe unborn, within its mother's womb,
Started and trembled when the Witch came nigh;
    And in the silent chambers of the tomb,
Death shudder'd her unholy tread to hear,
And from the dry and mouldering bones did fear
Force a cold sweat, when Lorrinite was near.

Power made her haughty: by ambition fired,
Ere long to mightier mischiefs she aspired.
    The Calis,[45] who o'er Cities rule unseen,
    Each in her own domain a Demon Queen,
And there ador'd with blood and human life,
They knew her, and in their accurst employ
She stirr'd up neighbouring states to mortal strife.
Sani, the dreadful God, who rides abroad
    Upon the King of the Ravens,[46] to destroy
The offending sons of men, when his four hands
Were weary with their toil, would let her do
His work of vengeance upon guilty lands;

And Lorrinite, at his commandment, knew
When the ripe earthquake should be loos'd, and where
    To point its course.   And in the baneful air
The pregnant seeds of death he bade her strew,
All deadly plagues and pestilence to brew.
The Locusts were her army, and their bands,
Where'er she turn'd her skinny finger, flew;
    The floods in ruin roll'd at her commands;
And when, in time of drought, the husbandman
    Beheld the gather'd rain about to fall,
Her breath would drive it to the desert sands.
While in the marshes parch'd and gaping soil,
The rice-roots by the searching Sun were dried;
    And in lean groupes, assembled at the side
Of the empty tank, the cattle dropt and died,
    And Famine, at her bidding, wasted wide
The wretched land, till, in the public way,
Promiscuous where the dead and dying lay,
Dogs fed on human bones in the open light of day.

    Her secret cell the accursed Arvalan,
In quest of vengeance, sought, and thus began.
        Mighty mother! mother wise!
        Revenge me on my enemies.

LORRINITE.

Com'st thou, son, for aid to me?
Tell me who have injur'd thee,
Where they are, and who they be;
    Of the Earth, or of the Sea,
    Or of the aerial company?
Earth, nor Sea, nor Air is free
From the powers who wait on me,
And my tremendous witchery.

ARVALAN.

She for whom so ill I sped,
Whom my Father deemeth dead,
Lives, for Marriataly's aid
From the water sav'd the maid.
In hatred I desire her still,
And in revenge would have my will.
A Deveta with wings of blue,
And sword whose edge even now I rue,
In a Ship of Heaven on high,
    Pilots her along the sky.
Where they voyage thou canst tell,
Mistress of the mighty spell.

At this the Witch, through shrivell'd lips and thin,
Sent forth a sound half-whistle and half-hiss.
        Two winged Hands came in,
        Armless and bodyless,
Bearing a globe of liquid crystal, set
In frame as diamond bright, yet black as jet.
A thousand eyes were quench'd in endless night,
    To form that magic globe; for Lorrinite
Had, from their sockets, drawn the liquid sight,
    And kneaded it, with re-creating skill,
Into this organ of her mighty will.
        Look in yonder orb, she cried,
        Tell me what is there descried.

ARVALAN.

A mountain top, in clouds of light
Envelop'd, rises on my sight;

Thence a cataract rushes down,
Hung with many a rainbow crown;
Light and clouds conceal its head,
Below, a silver Lake is spread;
Upon its shores a Bower I see,
Fit home for blessed company.
See they come forward,—one, two, three,—
The last a Maiden,—it is she!
The foremost shakes his wings of blue,
'T is he whose sword even yet I rue;
And in that other one I know
The visage of my deadliest foe.
Mother, let thy magic might
Arm me for the mortal fight;
Helm and shield and mail afford
Proof against his dreaded sword.
Then will I invade their seat,
Then shall vengeance be compltee.

LORRINITE.

Spirits, who obey my will,
Hear him, and his wish fulfill.

So spake the mighty one, nor farther spell
Needed; anon a sound, like smother'd thunder,
Was heard, slow rolling under;
The solid pavement of the cell
Quak'd, heav'd, and cleft asunder,
And at the feet of Arvalan display'd,
Helmet and mail, and shield and scymitar, were laid.

The Asuras, often put to flight,
And scatter'd in the fields of light,
By their foes' celestial might,
Forged this enchanted armour for the fight.
'Mid fires intense did they anneal,
In mountain furnaces, the quivering steel,
Till, trembling through each deepening hue,
It settled in a midnight blue;
Last they cast it, to aslake,
In the penal icy lake.
Then, they consign'd it to the Giant brood;
And, while they forged the impenetrable arms,
The Evil Powers, to oversee them, stood,
And there imbued
The work of Giant strength with magic charms.
Foul Arvalan, with joy, survey'd
The crescent sabre's cloudy blade,
With deeper joy the impervious mail,
The shield and helmet of avail.
Soon did he himself array,
And bade her speed him on his way.

Then she led him to the den,
Were her chariot, night and day,
Stood harness'd, ready for the way.
Two Dragons, yok'd in adamant, convey
The magic car; from either collar sprung
An adamantine rib, which met in air,
O'er-arch'd, and crost and bent diverging there,
And firmly in its arc upbore,
Upon their brazen necks, the seat of power.
Arvalan mounts the car, and in his hand
Receives the magic reins from Lorrinite;
The dragons, long obedient to command,
Their ample sails expand;

Like steeds well-broken to fair lady's hand,
They feel the reins of might,
And up the northern sky begin their flight.

Son of the Wicked, doth thy soul delight
To think its hour of vengeance now is nigh?
Lo! where the far-off light
Of Indra's palace flashes on his sight,
And Meru's heavenly summit shines on high,
With clouds of glory bright,
Amid the dark-blue sky.
Already, in his hope, doth he espy,
Himself secure in mail of tenfold charms,
Ereenia writhing from the magic blade,
The Father sent to bear his Curse,—the Maid
Resisting vainly in his impious arms.

Ah, Sinner! whose anticipating soul
Incurs the guilt even when the crime is spar'd!
Joyous toward Meru's summit on he far'd,
While the twin Dragons, rising as he guides,
With steady flight, steer northward for the pole.
Anon, with irresistible controul,
Force mightier far than his arrests their course;
It wrought as though a Power unseen had caught
Their adamantine yokes to drag them on.
Straight on they bend their way, and now, in vain,
Upward doth Arvalan direct the rein;
The rein of magic might avails no more,
Bootless its strength against that unseen Power
That, in their mid career,
Hath seiz'd the Chariot and the Charioteer.
With hands resisting, and down-pressing feet
Upon their hold insisting,
He struggles to maintain his difficult seat.
Seeking in vain with that strange Power to vie,
Their doubled speed the affrighted Dragons try.
Forced in a stream from whence was no retreat,
Strong as they are, behold them whirled along,
Headlong, with useless pennons, through the sky.

What Power was that, which; with resistless might,
Foil'd the dread magic thus of Lorrinite?
'T was all-commanding Nature.—They were here
Within the sphere of the adamantine rocks
Which gird Mount Meru round, as far below
That heavenly height where Ganges hath its birth
Involv'd in clouds and light,
So far above its roots of ice and snow.
On—on they roll,—rapt headlong they roll on;—
The lost canoe, less rapidly than this,
Down the precipitous stream is whirl'd along
To the brink of Niagara's dread abyss.
On—on they roll, and now, with shivering shock,
Are dash'd against the rock that girds the Pole.
Down from his shatter'd mail the unhappy Soul
Is dropt,—ten thousand thousand fathoms down,—
Till in an ice-rift, 'mid the eternal snow,
Foul Arvalan is stopt. There let him howl,
Groan there,—and there, with unavailing moan,
For aid on his Almighty Father call.
All human sounds are lost
Amid those deserts of perpetual frost,
Old Winter's drear domain,
Beyond the limits of the living World,
Beyond Kehama's reign.

Of utterance and of motion soon bereft,
Frozen to the ice-rock, there behold him lie,
Only the painful sense of Being left,
A Spirit who must feel, and cannot die,
Bleaching and bare beneath the polar sky.

XII.

THE SACRIFICE COMPLETED.

O Ye who, by the Lake
On Meru Mount, partake
The joys which Heaven hath destin'd for the blest,
Swift, swift, the moments fly,
The silent hours go by,
And ye must leave your dear abode of rest.
O wretched Man, prepare
Again thy Curse to bear!
Prepare, O wretched Maid, for farther woe!
The fatal hour draws near,
When Indra's heavenly sphere
Must own the Tyrant of the World below.
To-day the hundredth Steed,
At Seeva's shrine, must bleed,
The dreadful sacrifice is full to-day;
Nor man nor God hath power,
At this momentous hour,
Again to save the Swerga from his sway.
Fresh woes, O Maid divine,
Fresh trials must be thine;
And what must thou, Ladurlad, yet endure!
But let your hearts be strong,
And bear ye bravely on,
For Providence is good, and virtue is secure.

They, little deeming that the fatal day
Was come, beheld where, through the morning sky,
A Ship of Heaven drew nigh.
Onward they watch it steer its steady flight
Till, wondering, they espy
Old Casyapa, the Sire of Gods, alight.
But, when Ereenia saw the Sire appear,
At that unwonted and unwelcome sight
His heart receiv'd a sudden shock of fear:
Thy presence doth its doleful tidings tell,
O Father! cried the startled Glendoveer,
The dreadful hour is near! I know it well!
Not for less import would the Sire of Gods
Forsake his ancient and august abodes.

Even so, serene the immortal Sire replies;
Soon like an earthquake will ye feel the blow
Which consummates the mighty sacrifice:
And this world, and its Heaven, and all therein
Are then Kehama's. To the second ring
Of these seven Spheres, the Swerga-King,
Even now, prepares for flight
Beyond the circle of the conquer'd world,
Beyond the Rajah's might.
Ocean, that clips this inmost of the Spheres,
And girds it round with everlasting roar,
Set like a gem appears
Within that bending shore.
Thither fly all the Sons of heavenly race:
I, too, forsake mine ancient dwelling-place.

And now, O Child and Father, ye must go,
Take up the burthen of your woe,
And wander once again below.
With patient heart hold onward to the end,—
Be true unto yourselves, [47] and bear in mind
That every God is still the good Man's friend;
And they, who suffer bravely, save mankind.

Oh tell me, cried Ereenia, for from thee
Naught can be hidden, when the end will be!

Seek not to know, old Casyapa replied,
What pleaseth Heaven to hide.
Dark is the abyss of Time,
But light enough to guide your steps is given;
Whatever weal or woe betide,
Turn never from the way of truth aside,
And leave the event, in holy hope, to Heaven.
The moment is at hand, no more delay,
Ascend the etherial bark, and go your way;
And Ye, of heavenly nature, follow me.

The will of Heaven be done, Ladurlad cried,
Nor more the man replied;
But placed his daughter in the ethereal Bark,
Then took his seat beside.
There was no word at parting, no adieu.
Down from that empyreal height they flew:
One groan Ladurlad breath'd, yet utter'd not,
When, to his heart and brain,
The fiery Curse again like lightning shot.
And now on earth the Sire and Child alight,
Up soar'd the Ship of Heaven, and sail'd away from sight.

O ye immortal Bowers,
Where hitherto the Hours
Have led their dance of happiness for aye,
With what a sense of woe
Do ye expect the blow,
And see your heavenly dwellers driven away!
Lo! where the aunnay-birds [48] of graceful mien,
Whose milk-white forms were seen,
Lovely as Nymphs, your ancient trees between,
And by your silent springs,
With melancholy cry
Now spread unwilling wings;
Their stately necks reluctant they protend,
And through the sullen sky,
To other worlds, their mournful progress bend.
The affrighted gales to-day
O'er their beloved streams no longer play,
The streams of Paradise have ceas'd to flow;
The Fountain-Tree withholds its diamond shower,
In this portentous hour,—
This dolorous hour,—this universal woe.
Where is the Palace, whose far-flashing beams,
With streaks and streams of ever-varying light,
Brighten'd the polar night
Around the frozen North's extremest shore?
Gone like a morning rainbow,—like a dream,—
A star that shoots and falls, and then is seen no more.

Now! now!—Before the Golden Palaces,
The Bramin strikes the inevitable hour.
The fatal blow is given,
That over Earth and Heaven

Confirms the Almighty Rajah in his power.
All evil Spirits then,
That roam the World about,
Or wander through the sky,
Set up a joyful shout.
The Asuras and the Giants join the cry,
The damn'd in Padalon acclaim
Their hop'd Deliverer's name;
Heaven trembles with the thunder-drowning sound;
Back starts affrighted Ocean from the shore,
And the adamantine vaults, and brazen floor
Of Hell, are shaken with the roar.
Up rose the Rajah through the conquer'd sky,
To seize the Swerga for his proud abode;
Myriads of evil Genii round him fly,
As royally, on wings of winds, he rode,
And scaled high Heaven, triumphant like a God.

XIII.

THE RETREAT.

Around her Father's neck the Maiden lock'd
Her arms, when that portentous blow was given;
Clinging to him she heard the dread uproar,
And felt the shuddering shock which ran through
    Heaven;
Earth underneath them rock'd,
Her strong foundations heaving in commotion,
Such as wild winds upraise in raving Ocean,
As though the solid base were rent asunder.
And lo! where, storming the astonish'd sky,
Kehama and his evil host ascend!
Before them rolls the thunder,
Ten thousand thousand lightnings round them fly,
Upward the lengthening pageantries aspire,
Leaving from Earth to Heaven a widening wake of fire.

When the wild uproar was at length allay'd,
And Earth, recovering from the shock, was still,
Thus to her father spake the imploring Maid.
Oh! by the love which we so long have borne
Each other, and we ne'er shall cease to bear,—
    Oh! by the sufferings we have shar'd,
    And must not cease to share,—
One boon I supplicate in this dread hour,
One consolation in this hour of woe!
Thou hast it in thy power, refuse not thou
    The only comfort now
    That my poor heart can know.

O dearest, dearest Kailyal! with a smile
Of tenderness and sorrow, he replied,
O best belov'd, and to be lov'd the best
Best worthy,—set thy duteous heart at rest.
I know thy wish, and let what will betide,
Ne'er will I leave thee wilfully again.
My soul is strengthen'd to endure its pain;
Be thou, in all my wanderings, still my guide;
Be thou, in all my sufferings, at my side.

The Maiden, at those welcome words, imprest
A passionate kiss upon her father's cheek:
They look'd around them, then, as if to seek
Where they should turn, North, South, or East or West,

Wherever to their vagrant feet seem'd best,
But, turning from the view her mournful eyes,
Oh, whether should we wander, Kailyal cries,
Or wherefore seek in vain a place of rest?
Have we not here the Earth beneath our tread,
    Heaven overhead,
A brook that winds through this sequester'd glade,
    And yonder woods, to yield us fruit and shade!
    The little all our wants require is nigh;
Hope we have none,—why travel on in fear?
We cannot fly from Fate, and Fate will find us here.

'T was a fair scene wherein they stood,
A green and sunny glade amid the wood,
And in the midst an aged 49 Banian grew.
    It was a goodly sight to see
    That venerable tree.
For o'er the lawn, irregularly spread,
Fifty straight columns propt its lofty head;
    And many a long depending shoot,
    Seeking to strike its root,
Straight like a plummet, grew towards the ground.
Some on the lower boughs, which crost their way,
    Fixing their bearded fibres, round and round, .
    With many a ring and wild contortion wound;
    Some to the passing wind at times, with sway
        Of gentle motion swung;
Others of younger growth, unmov'd, were hung
Like stone-drops from the cavern's fretted height.
    Beneath was smooth and fair to sight,
Nor weeds nor briars deform'd the natural floor,
And through the leafy cope which bower'd it o'er
    Came gleams of checquer'd light.
So like a temple did it seem, that there
A pious heart's first impulse would be prayer.

A brook, with easy current, murmur'd near;
    Water so cool and clear
The peasants drink not from the humble well,
    Which they, with sacrifice of rural pride,
Have wedded to the cocoa-grove beside;50
Nor tanks51 of costliest masonry dispense
    To those in towns who dwell,
The work of Kings, in their beneficence.
Fed by perpetual springs, a small lagoon,
Pellucid, deep, and still, in silence join'd
And swell'd the passing stream.   Like burnish'd steel
Glowing, it lay beneath the eye of noon;
    And when the breezes, in their play,
    Ruffled the darkening surface, then, with gleam
    Of sudden light, around the lotus52 stem
It rippled, and the sacred flowers that crown
    The lakelet with their roseate beauty, ride,
    In gentlest waving rock'd, from side to side;
        And as the wind upheaves
Their broad and buoyant weight, the glossy leaves
Flap on the twinkling waters, up and down.

They built them here a bower53 of jointed cane,
Strong for the needful use, and light and long
Was the slight frame-work rear'd, with little pain;
Lithe creepers, then, the wicker-sides supply,
And the tall jungle-grass54 fit roofing gave
        Beneath the genial sky.
And here did Kailyal, each returning day,
Pour forth libations from the brook, to pay

The Spirits of her Sires their grateful rite;
In such libations pour'd in open glades,
Beside clear streams and solitary shades,
The Spirits of the virtuous dead delight.[55]
And duly here, to Marriataly's praise,
The Maid, as with an angel's voice of song,
Pour'd her melodious lays
Upon the gales of even,
And gliding in religious dance along,
Mov'd, graceful as the dark-eyed Nymphs of Heaven,
Such harmony to all her steps was given.

Thus ever, in her Father's doting eye,
Kailyal perform'd the customary rite;
He, patient of his burning pain the while,
Beheld her, and approv'd her pious toil:
And sometimes, at the sight,
A melancholy smile
Would gleam upon his awful countenance.
He, too, by day and night, and every hour,
Paid to a higher Power his sacrifice;
An offering, not of ghee, or fruit, or rice,
Flower-crown, or blood; but of a heart subdued,
A resolute, unconquer'd fortitude,
An agony represt, a will resign'd,
To her, who, on her secret throne reclin'd,
Amid the milky Sea, by Veeshnoo's side,
Looks with an eye of mercy on mankind.
By the Preserver, with his power endued,
There Woomdavee [56] beholds this lower clime,
And marks the silent sufferings of the good,
To recompense them in her own good time.

O force of faith! O strength of virtuous will!
Behold him, in his endless martyrdom,
Triumphant still!
The Curse still burning in his heart and brain,
And yet doth he remain
Patient the while, and tranquil, and content!
The pious soul hath fram'd unto itself
A second nature, to exist in pain
As in its own allotted element.

Such strength the will reveal'd had given
This holy pair, such influxes of grace,
That to their solitary resting-place
They brought the peace of Heaven.
Yea all around was hallow'd! Danger, Fear,
Nor thought of evil ever enter'd here.
A charm was on the Leopard when he came
Within the circle of that mystic glade;
Submiss he crouch'd before the heavenly Maid,
And offer'd to her touch his speckled side;
Or with arch'd back erect, and bending head,
And eyes half-clos'd for pleasure, would he stand,
Courting the pressure of her gentle hand.

Trampling his path through wood and brake,
And canes which crackling fall before his way,
And tassel-grass, [57] whose silvery feathers play
O'ertopping the young trees,
On comes the Elephant, to slake
His thirst at noon in yon pellucid springs.
Lo! from his trunk upturn'd, aloft he flings
The grateful shower; and now
Plucking the broad-leav'd bough

Of yonder plane, with waving motion slow,
Fanning the languid air,
He moves it to and fro. [58]
But when that form of beauty meets his sight,
The trunk its undulating motion stops,
From his forgetful hold the plane-branch drops,
Reverent he kneels, and lifts his rational eyes
To her as if in prayer;
And when she pours her angel voice in song,
Entranced he listens to the thrilling notes,
Till his strong temples, bath'd with sudden dews,
Their fragrance of delight and love diffuse. [59]

Lo! as the voice melodious floats around,
The Antelope draws near,
The Tigress leaves her toothless cubs to hear,
The Snake comes gliding from the secret brake,
Himself in fascination forced along
By that enchanting song;
The antic Monkeys, whose wild gambols late,
When not a breeze wav'd the tall jungle grass,
Shook the whole wood, [60] are hush'd, and silently
Hang on the cluster'd trees.
All things in wonder and delight are still;
Only at times the Nightingale is heard,
Not that in emulous skill that sweetest bird
Her rival strain would try, [61]
A mighty songster, with the Maid to vie;
She only bore her part in powerful sympathy.

Well might they thus adore that heavenly Maid!
For never Nymph of Mountain,
Or Grove, or Lake, or Fountain,
With a diviner presence fill'd the shade.
No idle ornaments deface
Her natural grace, [62]
Musk-spot, nor sandal-streak, [63] nor scarlet stain,
Ear-drop nor chain, nor arm nor ankle-ring, [64]
Nor trinketry on front, or neck, or breast,
Marring the perfect form: she seem'd a thing
Of Heaven's prime uncorrupted work, a child
Of early nature undefil'd,
A daughter of the years of innocence.
And therefore all things lov'd her. When she stood
Beside the glassy pool, the fish, that flies
Quick as an arrow from all other eyes,
Hover'd to gaze on her. The mother bird,
When Kailyal's step she heard,
Sought not to tempt her from her secret nest,
But, hastening to the dear retreat,[65] would fly
To meet and welcome her benignant eye.

Hope we have none, said Kailyal to her Sire.
Said she aright? and had the mortal Maid
No thoughts of heavenly aid,—
No secret hopes her inmost heart to move
With longings of such deep and pure desire,
As vestal Maids, whose piety is love,
Feel in their ecstasies, when, rapt above,
Their souls unto their heavenly Spouse aspire?
Why else so often doth that searching eye
Roam through the scope of sky?
Why, if she sees a distant speck on high,
Starts there that quick suffusion to her cheek?
'T is but the Eagle, in his heavenly height;
Reluctant to believe, she hears his cry,

And marks his wheeling flight,
Then languidly averts her mournful sight.
Why ever else, at morn, that waking sigh,
Because the lovely form no more is nigh
Which hath been present to her soul all night;
And that injurious fear
Which ever, as it riseth, is represt,
Yet riseth still within her troubled breast,
That she no more shall see the Glendoveer!

Hath he forgotten me? The wrongful thought
Would stir within her, and, though still repell'd
With shame and self-reproaches, would recur.
Days after days unvarying come and go,
And neither friend nor foe
Approaches them in their sequester'd bower.
Maid of strange destiny! but think not thou
Thou art forgotten now,
And hast no cause for farther hope or fear.
High-fated Maid, thou dost not know
What eyes watch over thee for weal and woe!
Even at this hour,
Searching the dark decrees divine,
Kehama, in the fulness of his power,
Perceives his thread of fate entwin'd with thine.
The Glendoveer, from his far sphere,
With love that never sleeps, beholds thee here,
And, in the hour permitted, will be near.
Dark Lorrinite on thee hath fix'd her sight,
And laid her wiles, to aid
Foul Arvalan when he shall next appear;
For well she ween'd his Spirit would renew
Old vengeance now, with unremitting hate;
The Enchantress well that evil nature knew,
The accursed Spirit hath his prey in view;
And thus, while all their separate hopes pursue,
All work, unconsciously, the will of Fate.

Fate work'd its own the while. A band
Of Yoguees, as they roam'd the land
Seeking a spouse for Jaga-Naut their God,
Stray'd to this solitary glade,
And reach'd the bower wherein the Maid abode.
Wondering at form so fair, they deem'd the Power
Divine had led them to his chosen bride,
And seiz'd and bore her from her Father's side.

XIV.

JAGA-NAUT.66

Joy in the City of great Jaga-Naut!
Joy in the seven-headed Idol's67 shrine!
A virgin-bride his ministers have brought,
A mortal maid, in form and face divine,
Peerless among all daughters of mankind;
Search'd they the world again from East to West,
In endless quest,
Seeking the fairest and the best,
No maid so lovely might they hope to find;—
For she hath breath'd celestial air,
And heavenly food hath been her fare,
And heavenly thoughts and feelings give her face
That heavenly grace.
Joy in the City of great Jaga-Naut,

Joy in the seven-headed Idol's shrine!
The fairest Maid his Yoguees sought,
A fairer than the fairest have they brought,
A maid of charms surpassing human thought,
A maid divine.

Now bring ye forth the Chariot of the God!68
Bring him abroad,
That through the swarming City he may ride;
And by his side
Place ye the Maid of more than mortal grace,
The Maid of perfect form and heavenly face!
Set her aloft in triumph, like a bride
Upon the bridal car,
And spread the joyful tidings wide and far,—
Spread it with trump and voice,
That all may hear, and all who hear rejoice;—
The Mighty One hath found his mate! the God
Will ride abroad!
To-night will he go forth from his abode!
Ye myriads who adore him,
Prepare the way before him!

Uprear'd on twenty wheels elate,
Huge as a Ship, the bridal car appear'd;
Loud creak its ponderous wheels, as through the gate
A thousand Bramins drag the enormous load.
There, throned aloft in state,
The Image of the seven-headed God
Came forth from his abode; and at his side
Sate Kailyal like a bride;
A bridal statue rather might she seem,
For she regarded all things like a dream,
Having no thought, nor fear, nor will, nor aught
Save hope and faith, that liv'd within her still.

O silent Night, how have they startled thee
With the brazen trumpet's blare!
And thou, O Moon! whose quiet light serene
Filleth wide heaven, and bathing hill and wood,
Spreads o'er the peaceful valley like a flood,
How have they dimm'd thee with the torches' glare,
Which round yon moving pageant flame and flare,
As the wild rout, with deafening song and shout,
Fling their long flashes out,
That, like infernal lightnings, fire the air.

A thousand pilgrims strain
Arm, shoulder, breast and thigh, with might and main,
To drag that sacred wain,
And scarce can draw along the enormous load.
Prone fall the frantic votaries in its road,
And, calling on the God,
Their self-devoted bodies there they lay
To pave his chariot-way.
On Jaga-Naut they call,
The ponderous Car rolls on, and crushes all.
Through blood and bones it ploughs its dreadful path.
Groans rise unheard; the dying cry,
And death and agony
Are trodden under foot by yon mad throng,
Who follow close, and thrust the deadly wheels along.

Pale grows the Maid at this accursed sight;
The yells which round her rise
Have roused her with affright,

42

And fear hath given to her dilated eyes
A wilder light.
Where shall those eyes be turn'd? she knows not where!
Downward they dare not look, for there
Is death, and horror, and despair;
Nor can her patient looks to Heaven repair,
For the huge Idol over her, in air,
Spreads his seven hideous heads, and wide
Extends their snaky necks on every side;
And all around, behind, before,
The bridal Car, is the raging rout,
With frantic shout, and deafening roar,
Tossing the torches' flames about.
And the double double peals of the drum are there,
And the startling burst of the trumpet's blare;
And the gong, that seems, with its thunders dread,
To stun the living, and waken the dead.
The ear-strings throb as if they were broke,
And the eye-lids drop at the weight of its stroke.
Fain would the Maid have kept them fast,
But open they start at the crack of the blast.

Where art thou, Son of Heaven, Ereenia! where
In this dread hour of horror and despair?
Thinking on him, she strove her fear to quell,
If he be near me, then will all be well;
And, if he reck not for my misery,
Let come the worst, it matters not to me.
Repel that wrongful thought,
O Maid! thou feelest, but believ'st it not;
It is thine own imperfect nature's fault
That lets one doubt of him arise within.
And this the Virgin knew; and, like a sin,
Repell'd the thought, and still believ'd him true;
And summon'd up her spirit to endure
All forms of fear, in that firm trust secure.
She needs that faith, she needs that consolation,
For now the Car hath measured back its track
Of death, and hath re-entered now its station.
There, in the Temple-court, with song and dance,
A harlot-band,[69] to meet the Maid, advance.
The drum hath ceas'd its peals; the trump and gong
Are still; the frantic crowd forbear their yells;
And sweet it was to hear the voice of song,
And the sweet music of their girdle-bells,
Armlets and anklets, that, with cheerful sound,
Symphonious tinkled as they wheel'd around.
They sung a bridal measure,
A song of pleasure,
A hymn of joyaunce and of gratulation.
Go, chosen One, they cried,
Go, happy bride!
For thee the God descends in expectation;
For thy dear sake
He leaves his heaven, O Maid of matchless charms!
Go, happy One, the bed divine partake,
And fill his longing arms!
Thus to the inner fane,
With circling dance and hymeneal strain,
The astonish'd Maid they led,
And there they laid her on the bridal bed.
Then forth they went, and clos'd the Temple-gate,
And left the wretched Kailyal to her fate.

Where art thou, Son of Heaven, Ereenia, where?
From the loathed bed she starts, and in the air

Looks up, as if she thought to find him there!
Then, in despair,
Anguish and agony, and hopeless prayer,
Prostrate she laid herself upon the floor.
There, trembling as she lay,
The Bramin of the fane advanced
And came to seize the prey.
But as the Priest drew nigh,
A power invisible opposed his way;
Starting, he utter'd wildly a death-cry,
And fell. At that the Maid all eagerly
Lifted in hope her head;
She thought her own deliverer had been near;
When lo! with other life re-animate,
She saw the dead arise,
And in the fiendish joy within his eyes,
She knew the hateful Spirit who look'd through
Their specular orbs,—cloth'd in the flesh of man,
She knew the accursed soul of Arvalan.

But not in vain, with the sudden shriek of fear,
She calls Ereenia now; the Glendoveer
Is here! Upon the guilty sight he burst
Like lightning from a cloud, and caught the accurst,
Bore him to the roof aloft, and on the floor
With vengeance dash'd him, quivering there in gore.
Lo! from the pregnant air,—heart-withering sight!
There issued forth the dreadful Lorrinite:
Seize him! the Enchantress cried;
A host of Demons at her word appear,
And like tornado winds, from every side
At once, they rush upon the Glendoveer.
Alone against a legion, little here
Avails his single might,
Nor that celestial faulchion, which in fight
So oft had put the rebel race to flight.
There are no Gods on earth to give him aid;
Hemm'd round, he is overpower'd, beat down, and bound,
And at the feet of Lorrinite is laid.

Meantime the scattered members of the slain,
Obedient to her mighty voice, assum'd
Their vital form again,
And that foul Spirit, upon vengeance bent,
Fled to the fleshly tenement.
Lo! here, quoth Lorrinite, thou seest thy foe!
Him in the Ancient Sepulchres, below
The billows of the Ocean, will I lay;
Gods are there none to help him now, and there
For Man there is no way.
To that dread scene of durance and despair,
Asuras, bear your enemy! I go
To chain him in the Tombs. Meantime do thou,
Freed from thy foe, and now secure from fear,
Son of Kehama, take thy pleasure here.

Her words the accursed race obey'd;
Forth with a sound like rushing winds they fled,
And of all aid from Earth or Heaven bereft,
Alone with Arvalan the Maid was left.
But in that hour of agony, the Maid
Deserted not herself; her very dread
Had calm'd her; and her heart
Knew the whole horror, and its only part.
Yamen, receive me undefil'd! she said,
And seiz'd a torch, and fir'd the bridal bed.

Up ran the rapid flames; on every side
They find their fuel wheresoe'er they spread,
Thin hangings, fragrant gums, and odorous wood,
That pil'd like sacrificial altars stood.
Around they run, and upward they aspire,
And, lo! the huge Pagoda lin'd with fire.

The wicked Soul, who had assum'd again
A form of sensible flesh, for his foul will,
Still bent on base revenge, and baffled still,
Felt that corporeal shape alike to pain
Obnoxious as to pleasure : forth he flew,
Howling and scorch'd by the devouring flame;
Accursed Spirit! still condemn'd to rue,
The act of sin and punishment the same.
Freed from his loathsome touch, a natural dread
Came on the self-devoted, and she drew
Back from the flames, which now toward her spread,
And, like a living monster, seem'd to dart
Their hungry tongues toward their shrinking prey.
Soon she subdued her heart;
O Father! she exclaim'd, there was no way
But this! and thou, Ereenia, who for me
Sufferest, my soul shall bear thee company.

So having said, she knit
Her body up to work her soul's desire,
And rush at once amid the thickest fire.
A sudden cry withheld her,—Kailyal, stay!
Child! Daughter! I am here! the voice exclaims,
And from the gate, unharm'd, through smoke and flames
Like as a God, Ladurlad made his way;
Wrapt his preserving arms around, and bore
His Child, uninjur'd, o'er the burning floor.

XV.

THE CITY OF BALY.⁷⁰

KAILYAL.
Ereenia!

LADURLAD.
Nay, let no reproachful thought
Wrong his heroic heart! The Evil Powers
Have the dominion o'er this wretched World,
And no good Spirit now can venture here.

KAILYAL.
Alas, my Father! he hath ventur'd here,
And sav'd me from one horror. But the Powers
Of Evil beat him down, and bore away
To some dread scene of durance and despair,
The Ancient Tombs, methought their Mistress said,
Beneath the ocean-waves; no way for Man
Is there; and Gods, she boasted, there are none
On Earth to help him now.

LADURLAD.
Is that her boast?
And hath she laid him in the Ancient Tombs,
Relying that the Waves will guard him there?
Short-sighted are the eyes of Wickedness,
And all its craft but folly. O, my child!
The Curses of the Wicked are upon me,

And the immortal Deities, who see
And suffer all things for their own wise end,
Have made them blessings to us!

KAILYAL.
Then thou knowest
Where they have borne him?

LADURLAD.
To the Sepulchres
Of the Ancient Kings, which Baly, in his power,
Made in primeval times; and built above them
A City, like the Cities of the Gods,
Being like a God himself. For many an age
Hath Ocean warr'd against his Palaces,
Till overwhelm'd, they lie beneath the waves,
Not overthrown, so well the Mighty One
Had laid their deep foundations. Rightly said
The Accursed, that no way for Man was there,
But not like Man am I!

Up from the ground the Maid exultant sprung,
And clapp'd her happy hands, in attitude
Of thanks to Heaven, and flung
Her arms around her Father's neck, and stood
Struggling awhile for utterance, with excess
Of hope and pious thankfulness.
Come—come! she cried, O let us not delay,
He is in torments there,—away!—away!

Long time they travell'd on; at dawn of day,
Still setting forward with the earliest light,
Nor ceasing from their way
Till darkness clos'd the night.
Short refuge from the noontide heat,
Reluctantly compell'd, the Maiden took;
And ill her indefatigable feet
Could that brief respite brook.
Hope kept her up, and her intense desire
Supports that heart which ne'er at danger quails,
Those feet which never tire,
That frame which never fails.

Their talk was of the City of the days
Of old, Earth's wonder once; and of the fame
Of Baly its great founder,—he whose name
In ancient story, and in poets' praise,
Liveth and flourisheth for endless glory,
Because his might
Put down the wrong, and aye upheld the right.
Till for ambition, as old sages tell,
The mighty Monarch fell :
For he too, having made the World his own,
Then, in his pride, had driven
The Devetas from Heaven,
And seiz'd triumphantly the Swerga throne.
The Incarnate came before the Mighty One,
In dwarfish stature, and in mien obscure;
The sacred cord ⁷¹ he bore,
And ask'd, for Brama's sake, a little boon,
Three steps of Baly's ample reign, no more.
Poor was the boon requir'd, and poor was he
Who begg'd,—a little wretch it seem'd to be;
But Baly ne'er refus'd a suppliant's prayer.
A glance of pity, in contemptuous mood,
He on the Dwarf cast down,

And bade him take the boon,
And measure where he would.

Lo, Son of giant birth,
I take my grant! the Incarnate power replies.
With his first step he measur'd o'er the Earth,
The second spann'd the skies.
Three paces thou hast granted,
Twice have I set my footstep, Veeshnoo cries,
Where shall the third be planted?

Then Baly knew the God, and at his feet,
In homage due, he laid his humbled head.
Mighty art thou, O Lord of Earth and Heaven,
Mighty art thou! he said,
Be merciful, and let me be forgiven.
He ask'd for mercy of the merciful,
And mercy for his virtue's sake was shown.
For though he was cast down to Padalon,
Yet there, by Yamen's throne,
Doth Baly sit in majesty and might,
To judge the dead, and sentence them aright.
And forasmuch as he was still the friend
Of righteousness, it is permitted him,
Yearly, from those drear regions to ascend
And walk the Earth, that he may hear his name
Still hymn'd and honour'd, by the grateful voice
Of humankind, and in his fame rejoice.

Such was the talk they held upon their way,
Of him to whose old City they were bound;
And now, upon their journey, many a day
Had risen and clos'd, and many a week gone round,
And many a realm and region had they past,
When now the Ancient Towers appear'd at last. 72
Their golden summits, in the noon-day light,
Shone o'er the dark green deep that roll'd between;
For domes, and pinnacles, and spires were seen
Peering above the sea,—a mournful sight!
Well might the sad beholder ween from thence
What works of wonder the devouring wave
Had swallowed there, when monuments so brave
Bore record of their old magnificence.
And on the sandy shore, beside the verge
Of Ocean, here and there, a rock-hewn fane
Resisted in its strength the surf and surge
That on their deep foundations beat in vain.
In solitude the Ancient temples stood,
Once resonant with instrument and song,
And solemn dance of festive multitude;
Now as the weary ages pass along,
Hearing no voice save of the Ocean flood,
Which roars for ever on the restless ores;
Or, visiting their solitary caves,
The lonely sound of Winds, that moan around
Accordant to the melancholy waves.

With reverence did the travellers see
The works of ancient days, and silently
Approach the shore. Now on the yellow sand,
Where round their feet the rising surges part,
They stand. Ladurlad's heart
Exulted in his wonderous destiny.
To Heaven he rais'd his hand
In attitude of stern heroic pride;
Oh what a power, he cried,

Thou dreadful Rajah, doth thy Curse impart!
I thank thee now!—Then turning to the Maid,
Thou see'st how far and wide
Yon Towers extend, he said,
My search must needs be long.   Meantime the flood
Will cast thee up thy food,—
And in the Chambers of the Rock by night,
Take thou thy safe abode.
No prowling beast to harm thee, or affright,
Can enter there; but wrap thyself with care
From the foul Bird obscene that thirsts for blood;
For in such caverns doth the Bat delight
To have its haunts.   Do thou with stone and shout,
Ere thou liest down at evening, scare them out,
And in this robe of mine involve thy feet.
Duly commend us both to Heaven in prayer,
Be of good heart, and let thy sleep be sweet.

So saying, he put back his arm, and gave
The cloth which girt his loins, and prest her hand
With fervent love, then from the sand
Advanced into the sea; the coming Wave,
Which knew Kehama's Curse, before his way
Started, and on he went as on dry land,
And still around his path the waters parted.
She stands upon the shore, where sea-weeds play
Lashing her polish'd ankles, and the spray
Which off her Father, like a rainbow, fled,
Falls on her like a shower; there Kailyal stands,
And sees the billows rise above his head.
She, at the startling sight, forgot the power
The Curse had given him, and held forth her hands
Imploringly,—her voice was on the wind,
And the deaf Ocean o'er Ladurlad clos'd.
Soon she recall'd his destiny to mind,
And shaking off that natural fear, compos'd
Her soul with prayer, to wait the event resign'd.

Alone, upon the solitary strand,
The lovely one is left; behold her go,
Pacing with patient footsteps, to and fro,
Along the bending sand.
Save her, ye Gods! from Evil Powers, and here
From Man she need not fear:
For never Traveller comes near
These awful ruins of the days of yore,
Nor fisher's bark, nor ventureus mariner,
Approach the sacred shore.
All day she walk'd the beach, at night she sought
The Chamber of the Rock; with stone and shout
Assail'd the Bats obscene, and scar'd them out;
Then in her Father's robe involv'd her feet,
And wrapt her mantle round to guard her head,
And laid her down: the rock was Kailyal's bed,
Her chamber-lamps were in the starry sky,
The winds and waters were her lullaby.

Be of good heart, and let thy sleep be sweet,
Ladurlad said,—Alas! that cannot be
To one whose days are days of misery.
How often did she stretch her hands to greet
Ereenia, rescued in the dreams of night!
How oft amid the vision of delight
Fear in her heart all is not as it seems;
Then from unsettled slumber start, and hear
The Winds that moan above, the Waves below!

Thou hast been call'd, O Sleep! the friend of Woe,
But 't is the happy who have call'd thee so.[73]

Another day, another night are gone,
A second passes, and a third wanes on.
So long she paced the shore,
So often on the beach she took her stand,
That the wild Sea-Birds knew her, and no more
Fled, when she past beside them on the strand.
Bright shine the golden summits in the light
Of the noon-sun, and lovelier far by night
Their moonlight glories o'er the sea they shed:
Fair is the dark-green deep : by night and day
Unvex'd with storms, the peaceful billows play,
As when they clos'd upon Ladurlad's head :
The firmament above is bright and clear;
The sea-fowl, lords of water, air, and land,
Joyous alike upon the wing appear,
Or when they ride the waves, or walk the sand ;
Beauty and light and joy are every-where;
There is no sadness and no sorrow here,
Save what that single human breast contains,
But oh ! what hopes, and fears, and pains are there !

Seven miserable days the expectant Maid,
From earliest dawn till evening, watch'd the shore;
Hope left her then; and in her heart she said,
Never should she behold her Father more.

XVI.

THE ANCIENT SEPULCHRES.

When the broad Ocean on Ladurlad's head
Had clos'd and arch'd him o'er,
With steady tread he held his way
Adown the sloping shore.
The dark green waves, with emerald hue,
Imbue the beams of day,
And on the wrinkled sand below,
Rolling their mazy network to and fro,
Light shadows shift and play.
The hungry Shark, at scent of prey,
Toward Ladurlad darted ;
Beholding then that human form erect,
How like a God the depths he trod,
Appall'd the monster started,
And in his fear departed.
Onward Ladurlad went with heart elate,
And now hath reach'd the Ancient City's gate.

Wondering, he stood awhile to gaze
Upon the works of elder days.
The brazen portals open stood,
Even as the fearful multitude
Had left them, when they fled
Before the rising flood.
High over-head, sublime,
The mighty gateway's storied roof was spread,
Dwarfing the puny piles of younger time.
With the deeds of days of yore
That ample roof was sculptur'd o'er;
And many a godlike form there met his eye,
And many an emblem dark of mystery.
Through these wide portals oft had Baly rode

Triumphant from his proud abode,
When, in his greatness, he bestrode
The Aullay,[74] hugest of four-footed kind,
The Aullay-Horse, that in his force,
With elephantine trunk, could bind
And lift the elephant, and on the wind
Whirl him away, with sway and swing,
Even like a pebble from the practis'd sling.

Those streets which never, since the days of yore,
By human footstep had been visited;
Those streets which never more
A human foot shall tread,
Ladurlad trod. In sun-light, and sea-green,
The thousand palaces were seen
Of that proud city, whose superb abodes
Seem'd rear'd by Giants for the immortal Gods,
How silent and how beautiful they stand,
Like things of Nature ! the eternal rocks
Themselves not firmer.   Neither hath the sand
Drifted within their gates, and choak'd their doors,
Nor slime defil'd their pavements and their floors.
Did then the Ocean wage
His war for love and envy, not in rage,
O thou fair City, that he spares thee thus?[75]
Art thou Varounin's capital and court,
Where all the Sea-Gods for delight resort,
A place too godlike to be held by us,
The poor degenerate children of the Earth?
So thought Ladurlad, as he look'd around,
Weening to hear the sound
Of Mermaid's shell, and song
Of choral throng from some imperial hall,
Wherein the Immortal Powers, at festival,
Their high carousals keep.
But all is silence dread,
Silence profound and dead,
The everlasting stillness of the Deep.

Through many a solitary street,
And silent market-place, and lonely square,
Arm'd with the mighty Curse, behold him fare.
And now his feet attain that royal fane
Where Baly held of old his awful reign.
What once had been the Garden spread around,
Fair Garden, once which wore perpetual green,
Where all sweet flowers through all the year were found,
And all fair fruits were through all seasons seen ;
A place of Paradise, where each device
Of emulous Art with Nature strove to vie;
And Nature, on her part,
Call'd forth new powers wherewith to vanquish Art.
The Swerga-God himself, with envious eye,
Survey'd those peerless gardens in their prime ;
Nor ever did the Lord of Light,
Who circles Earth and Heaven upon his way,
Behold from eldest time a goodlier sight
Than were the groves which Baly, in his might,
Made for his chosen place of solace and delight.

It was a Garden still beyond all price,
Even yet it was a place of Paradise;
For where the mighty Ocean could not spare,
There had he, with his own creation,
Sought to repair his work of devastation.
And here were coral bowers,

And grots of madrepores,
And banks of spunge, as soft and fair to eye
As e'er was mossy bed
Whereon the Wood Nymphs lie
Their languid limbs in summer's sultry hours.
Here, too, were living flowers
Which, like a bud compacted,
Their purple cups contracted,
And now in open blossom spread,
Stretch'd like green anthers many a seeking head.
And arborets of jointed stone were there,
And plants of fibres fine, as silkworm's thread;
Yea, beautiful as Mermaid's golden hair
Upon the waves dispread:
Others that, like the broad banana growing,
Rais'd their long wrinkled leaves of purple hue,
Like streamers wide out-flowing.
And whatsoe'er the depths of Ocean hide
From human eyes, Ladurlad there espied,
Trees of the deep, and shrubs and fruits and flowers,
As fair as ours,
Wherewith the Sea-Nymphs love their locks to braid,
When to their father's hall, at festival
Repairing, they in emulous array,
Their charms display,
To grace the banquet, and the solemn day.

The golden fountains had not ceas'd to flow,
And, where they mingled with the briny Sea,
There was a sight of wonder and delight,
To see the fish, like birds in air,
Above Ladurlad flying.
Round those strange waters they repair,76
Their scarlet fins outspread and plying,
They float with gentle hovering there;
And now upon those little wings,
As if to dare forbidden things,
With wilful purpose bent,
Swift as an arrow from a bow
They dash across, and to and fro,
In rapid glance, like lightning go
Through that unwonted element.
Almost in scenes so wonderous fair,
Ladurlad had forgot
The mighty cause which led him there;
His busy eye was every where,
His mind had lost all thought;
His heart, surrendered to the joys
Of sight, was happy as a boy's.
But soon the awakening thought recurs
Of him who, in the Sepulchres,
Hopeless of human aid, in chains is laid;
And her who, on the solitary shore,
By night and day her weary watch will keep,
Till she shall see them issuing from the deep.

Now hath Ladurlad reach'd the Court
Of the great Palace of the King; its floor
Was of the marble rock; and there before
The imperial door,
A mighty Image on the steps was seen,
Of stature huge, of countenance serene.
A crown and sceptre at his feet were laid;
One hand a scroll display'd,
The other pointed there, that all might see;
My name is Death, it said,

In mercy have the Gods appointed me.
Two brazen gates beneath him, night and day
Stood open; and within them you behold
Descending steps, which in the living stone
Were hewn, a spacious way
Down to the Chambers of the Kings of old.

Trembling with hope, the adventurous man descended.
The sea-green light of day
Not far along the vault extended:
But where the slant reflection ended,
Another light was seen
Of red and fiery hue,
That with the water blended,
And gave the secrets of the Tombs to view.

Deep in the marble rock, the Hall
Of Death was hollowed out, a chamber wide,
Low-roof'd, and long; on either side,
Each in his own alcove, and on his throne,
The Kings of old were seated: in his hand
Each held the sceptre of command,
From whence, across that scene of endless night,
A carbuncle diffused its everlasting light.

So well had the embalmers done their part
With spice and precious unguents, to imbue
The perfect corpse, that each had still the hue
Of living man, and every limb was still
Supple and firm and full, as when of yore
Its motion answered to the moving will.
The robes of royalty which once they wore,
Long since had mouldered off and left them bare:
Naked upon their thrones behold them there,
Statues of actual flesh,—a fearful sight!
Their large and rayless eyes
Dimly reflecting to that gem-born light,
Glaz'd, fix'd, and meaningless,—yet, open wide,
Their ghastly balls belied
The mockery of life in all beside.

But if, amid these Chambers drear,
Death were a sight of shuddering and of fear,
Life was a thing of stranger horror here.
For at the farther end, in yon alcove,
Where Baly should have lain, had he obey'd
Man's common lot, behold Ereenia laid.
Strong fetters link him to the rock; his eye
Now rolls and widens, as with effort vain
He strives to break the chain,
Now seems to brood upon his misery.
Before him couch'd there lay
One of the mighty monsters of the deep,
Whom Lorrinite encountering on the way,
There station'd, his perpetual guard to keep;
In the sport of wanton power, she charm'd him there,
As if to mock the Glendoveer's despair.
Upward his form was human, save that here
The skin was cover'd o'er with scale on scale
Compact, a panoply of natural mail.
His mouth, from ear to ear,
Weapon'd with triple teeth, extended wide,
And tusks on either side;
A double snake below, he roll'd
His supple length behind in many a sinuous fold.

With red and kindling eye, the Beast beholds
A living man draw nigh,
And, rising on his folds,
In hungry joy awaits the expected feast,
His mouth half-open, and his teeth unsheath'd.
Then on he sprung, and in his scaly arms
Seiz'd him, and fasten'd on his neck, to suck,
With greedy lips, the warm life-blood : and sure
But for the mighty power of magic charms,
As easily as, in the blithesome hour
Of spring, a child doth crop the meadow-flower,
Piecemeal those claws
Had rent their victim, and those armed jaws
Snapt him in twain.   Naked Ladurlad stood,
Yet fearless and unharm'd in this dread strife,
So well Kehama's Curse had charm'd his fated life.

He too,—for anger, rising at the sight
Of him he sought, in such strange thrall confin'd,
With desperate courage fir'd Ladurlad's mind,—
He, too, unto the fight himself addrest,
And, grappling breast to breast,
With foot firm-planted stands,
And seiz'd the monster's throat with both his hands.
Vainly, with throttling grasp, he prest
The impenetrable scales ;
And lo ! the Guard rose up, and round his foe,
With gliding motion, wreath'd his lengthening coils,
Then tighten'd all their folds with stress and strain.
Nought would the raging Tiger's strength avail
If once involv'd within those mighty toils ;
The arm'd Rhinoceros, so clasp'd, in vain
Had trusted to his hide of rugged mail,
His bones all broken, and the breath of life
Crush'd from the lungs, in that unequal strife.
Again, and yet again, he sought to break
The impassive limbs ; but when the Monster found
His utmost power was vain,
A moment he relax'd in every round,
Then knit his coils again with closer strain,
And, bearing forward, forced him to the ground.

Ereenia groan'd in anguish at the sight
Of this dread fight : once more the Glendoveer
Essay'd to break his bonds, and fear
For that brave spirit who had sought him here,
Stung him to wilder strugglings.   From the rock
He rais'd himself half up, with might and main
Pluck'd at the adamantine chain ;
And now, with long and unrelaxing strain,
In obstinate effort of indignant strength,
Labour'd and strove in vain ;
Till his immortal sinews fail'd at length ;
And yielding, with an inward groan, to fate,
Despairingly, he let himself again
Fall prostrate on his prison-bed of stone,
Body and chain alike with lifeless weight.

Struggling they lay in mortal fray
All day, while day was in our upper sphere,
For light of day,
And natural darkness never entered here ;
All night, with unabated might,
They waged the unremitting fight.
A second day, a second night,
With furious will they wrestled still.

The third came on, the fourth is gone ;
Another comes, another goes,
And yet no respite, no repose !
But day and night, and night and day,
Involv'd in mortal strife they lay ;
Six days and nights have past away,
And still they wage, with mutual rage,
The unremitting fray.
With mutual rage their war they wage,
But not with mutual will ;
For when the seventh morning came,
The monster's worn and wearied frame
In this strange contest fails ;
And weaker, weaker, every hour,
He yields beneath strong Nature's power,
For now the Curse prevails.

Sometimes the Beast sprung up to bear
His foe aloft ; and, trusting there
To shake him from his hold,
Relax'd the rings that wreath'd him round ;
But on his throat Ladurlad hung
And weigh'd him to the ground ;
And if they sink, or if they float,
Alike with stubborn clasp he clung,
Tenacious of his grasp ;
For well he knew with what a power,
Exempt from Nature's laws,
The Curse had arm'd him for this hour ;
And in the monster's gasping jaws,
And in his hollow eye,
Well could Ladurlad now descry
The certain signs of victory.

And now the Guard no more can keep
His painful watch ; his eyes, opprest,
Are fainting for their natural sleep ;
His living flesh and blood must rest,
The Beast must sleep or die.
Then he, full faint and languidly,
Unwreathes his rings and strives to fly,
And still retreating, slowly trails
His stiff and heavy length of scales.
But that unweariable foe,
With will relentless, follows still ;
No breathing-time, no pause of fight
He gives, but presses on his flight ;
Along the vaulted chambers, and the ascent
Up to the emerald-tinted light of day,
He harasses his way,
Till lifeless, underneath his grasp,
The huge Sea-Monster lay.

That obstinate work is done ! Ladurlad cried,
One labour yet remains !
And thoughtfully he eyed
Ereenia's ponderous chains ;
And with faint effort, half-despairing, tried
The rivets deep in-driven.   Instinctively,
As if in search of aid, he look'd around :
Oh, then, how gladly, in the near alcove,
Fallen on the ground its lifeless Lord beside,
The crescent scymitar he spied,
Whose cloudy blade, with potent spells imbued,
Had lain so many an age unhurt in solitude.

Joyfully springing there
He seiz'd the weapon, and with eager stroke
Hew'd at the chain; the force was dealt in vain,
For not as if through yielding air
Past the descending scymitar,
Its deaden'd way the heavy water broke;
Yet it bit deep. Again, with both his hands,
He wields the blade, and dealt a surer blow.
The baser metal yields
To that fine edge, and lo! the Glendoveer
Rises and snaps the half-sever'd links, and stands
Freed from his broken bands.

XVII.

BALY.

This is the appointed night,
The night of joy and consecrated mirth,
When, from his judgment-seat in Padalon,
By Yamen's throne,
Baly goes forth, that he may walk the Earth
Unseen, and hear his name
Still hymn'd and honour'd by the grateful voice
Of humankind, and in his fame rejoice.
Therefore from door to door, and street to street,
With willing feet,
Shaking their firebrands, the glad children run;
Baly! great Baly! they acclaim,
Where'er they run they bear the mighty name,
Where'er they meet,
Baly! great Baly! still their choral tongues repeat.
Therefore at every door the votive flame
Through pendant lanterns sheds its painted light,
And rockets hissing upward through the sky,
Fall like a shower of stars
From Heaven's black canopy.
Therefore, on yonder mountain's templed height,
The brazen cauldron blazes through the night.
Huge as a Ship that travels the main sea
Is that capacious brass; its wick as tall
As is the mast of some great admiral.
Ten thousand votaries bring
Camphor and ghee to feed the sacred flame;
And while, through regions round, the nations see
Its fiery pillar curling high in heaven,
Baly! great Baly! they exclaim,
For ever hallowed be his blessed name!
Honour and praise to him for ever more be given!

Why art not thou among the festive throng,
Baly, O Mighty One! to hear thy fame?
Still, as of yore, with pageantry and song,
The glowing streets along,
They celebrate thy name;
Baly! great Baly! still
The grateful habitants of Earth acclaim,
Baly! great Baly! still
The ringing walls and echoing towers proclaim.
From yonder mountain the portentous flame
Still blazes to the nations as before;
All things appear to human eyes the same,
As perfect as of yore;
To human eyes,—but how unlike to thine!
Thine which were wont to see

The Company divine,
That with their presence came to honour thee!
For all the blessed ones of mortal birth
Who have been cloth'd with immortality,
From the eight corners of the Earth,
From the Seven Worlds assembling, all
Wont to attend thy solemn festival.
Then did thine eyes behold
The wide air peopled with that glorious train;
Now mayst thou seek the blessed ones in vain,
For Earth and Air are now beneath the Rajah's reign.

Therefore the Mighty One hath walk'd the Earth
In sorrow and in solitude to-night.
The sound of human mirth
To him is no delight;
He turns away from that ungrateful sight,
Hallowed not now by visitants divine,
And there he bends his melancholy way
Where in yon full-orbed Moon's refulgent light,
The Golden Towers of his old City shine
Above the silver sea. The mighty Chief
There bent his way in grief,
As if sad thoughts indulged would work their own re-
lief.
There he beholds upon the sand
A lovely Maiden in the moonlight stand.
The land-breeze lifts her locks of jet,
The waves around her polish'd ancles play,
Her bosom with the salt sea-spray is wet:
Her arms are crost, unconsciously, to fold
That bosom from the cold,
While statue-like she seems her watch to keep,
Gazing intently on the restless deep.

Seven miserable days had Kailyal there,
From earliest dawn till evening, watch'd the deep;
Six nights within the chamber of the rock,
Had laid her down, and found in prayer
That comfort which she sought in vain from sleep.
But when the seventh night came,
Never should she behold her father more,
The wretched Maiden said in her despair;
Yet would not quit the shore,
Nor turn her eyes one moment from the sea:
Never before
Had Kailyal watch'd it so impatiently,
Never so eagerly had hoped before,
As now when she believed, and said, all hope was o'er.

Beholding her, how beautiful she stood,
In that wild solitude,
Baly from his invisibility
Had issued then, to know her cause of woe;
But that in the air beside her, he espied
Two Powers of Evil for her hurt allied,
Foul Arvalan and dreadful Lorrinite.
The Mighty One they could not see,
And marking with what demon-like delight
They kept their innocent prey in sight,
He waits, expecting what the end may be.

She starts; for lo! where floating many a rood,
A Monster, hugest of the Ocean brood,
Weltering and lifeless, drifts toward the shore.
Backward she starts in fear before the flood,

And, when the waves retreat,
They leave their hideous burthen at her feet.

She ventures to approach with timid tread,
She starts, and half draws back in fear,
Then stops, and stretches on her head,
To see if that huge Beast indeed be dead.
Now growing bold, the Maid advances near,
Even to the margin of the ocean-flood.
Rightly she reads her Father's victory,
And lifts her joyous hands, exultingly,
To Heaven in gratitude.
Then spreading them toward the Sea,
While pious tears bedim her streaming eyes,
Come! come! my Father, come to me,
Ereenia, come! she cries.
Lo! from the opening deep they rise,
And to Ladurlad's arms the happy Kailyal flies.

She turn'd from him, to meet, with beating heart,
The Glendoveer's embrace.
Now turn to me, for mine thou art!
Foul Arvalan exclaim'd; his loathsome face
Came forth, and from the air,
In fleshly form, he burst.
Always in horror and despair,
Had Kailyal seen that form and face accurst,
But yet so sharp a pang had ne'er
Shot with a thrill like death through all her frame,
As now when on her hour of joy the Spectre came.

Vain is resistance now,
The fiendish laugh of Lorrinite is heard;
And, at her dreadful word,
The Asuras once again appear,
And seize Ladurlad and the Glendoveer.
Hold your accursed hands!
A voice exclaim'd, whose dread commands
Were fear'd through all the vaults of Padalon;
And there among them, in the midnight air,
The presence of the mighty Baly shone.
He, making manifest his mightiness,
Put forth on every side an hundred arms,
And seiz'd the Sorceress; maugre all her charms,
Her and her fiendish ministers he caught
With force as uncontrollable as fate;
And that unhappy Soul, to whom
The Almighty Rajah's power availeth not
Living to avert, nor dead to mitigate
His righteous doom.

Help, help, Kehama! Father, help! he cried,
But Baly tarried not to abide
That mightier One; with irresistible feet
He stampt and cleft the Earth; it opened wide,
And gave him way to his own judgment-seat.
Down, like a plummet, to the World below
He sunk, and bore his prey
To righteous punishment, and endless woe.

XVIII.

KEHAMA'S DESCENT.

THE Earth, by Baly's feet divided,
Clos'd o'er his way as to the judgement-seat

He plunged and bore his prey.
Scarce had the shock subsided,
When, darting from the Swerga's heavenly heights,
Kehama, like a thunderbolt, alights.
In wrath he came, a bickering flame
Flash'd from his eyes which made the moonlight dim;
And passion forcing way from every limb,
Like furnace-smoke, with terrors wrapt him round.
Furious he smote the ground;
Earth trembled underneath the dreadful stroke,
Again in sunder riven;
He hurl'd in rage his whirling weapon down.
But lo! the fiery sheckra77 to his feet
Return'd, as if by equal force re-driven,
And from the abyss the voice of Baly came:
Not yet, O Rajah, hast thou won
The realms of Padalon!
Earth and the Swerga are thine own,
But, till Kehama shall subdue the throne
Of Hell, in torments Yamen holds his son.

Fool that he is!—in torments let him lie!
Kehama, wrathful at his son, replied.
But what am I,
That thou shouldst brave me?—kindling in his pride
The dreadful Rajah cried.
Ho! Yamen! hear me. God of Padalon,
Prepare thy throne,
And let the Amreeta cup
Be ready for my lips, when I anon
Triumphantly shall take my seat thereon,
And plant upon thy neck my royal feet.
In voice like thunder thus the Rajah cried,
Impending o'er the abyss, with menacing hand
Put forth, as in the action of command,
And eyes that darted their red anger down.
Then drawing back he let the earth subside,
And, as his wrath relax'd, survey'd,
Thoughtful and silently, the mortal Maid.
Her eye the while was on the farthest sky,
Where up the ethereal height
Ereenia rose and past away from sight.
Never had she so joyfully
Beheld the coming of the Glendoveer,
Dear as he was and he deserv'd to be,
As now she saw him rise and disappear.
Come now what will, within her heart, said she,
For thou art safe, and what have I to fear?

Meantime the Almighty Rajah, late
In power and majesty and wrath array'd,
Had laid his terrors by,
And gazed upon the Maid.
Pride could not quit his eye,
Nor that remorseless nature from his front
Depart; yet whoso had beheld him then
Had felt some admiration mix'd with dread,
And might have said,
That sure he seem'd to be the King of Men;
Less than the greatest that he could not be,
Who carried in his port such might and majesty.

In fear no longer for the Glendoveer,
Now toward the Rajah Kailyal turn'd her eyes
As if to ask what doom awaited her.
But then surprise,

Even as with fascination held them there,
So strange a thing it seem'd to see the change
Of purport in that all-commanding brow,
That thoughtfully was bent upon her now.
Wondering she gazed, the while her Father's eye
Was fix'd upon Kehama haughtily;
It spake defiance to him, high disdain,
Stern patience, unsubduable by pain,
And pride triumphant over agony.

Ladurlad, said the Rajah, thou and I
Alike have done the work of Destiny,
Unknowing each to what the impulse tended;
But now that over Earth and Heaven my reign
Is stablish'd, and the ways of Fate are plain
Before me, here our enmity is ended.
I take away thy Curse—As thus he said,
The fire which in Ladurlad's heart and brain
Was burning, fled, and left him free from pain.
So rapidly his torments were departed,
That at the sudden ease he started,
As with a shock, and to his head
His hands upfled,
As if he felt through every failing limb
The power and sense of life forsaking him.
Then turning to the Maid, the Rajah cried,
O Virgin, above all of mortal birth
Favour'd alike in beauty and in worth,
And in the glories of thy destiny,
Now let thy happy heart exult with pride,
For Fate hath chosen thee
To be Kehama's bride,
To be the Queen of Heaven and Earth,
And of whatever Worlds beside
Infinity may hide—For I can see
The writing which at thy nativity,
All-knowing Nature wrought upon thy brain,[78]
In branching veins, which to the gifted eye
Map out the mazes of futurity.
There is it written, Maid, that thou and I,
Alone of human kind a deathless pair,
Are doom'd to share
The Amreeta-drink divine
Of immortality.   Come, Maiden mine!
High fated One, ascend the subject sky,
And by Kehama's side
Sit on the Swerga throne, his equal bride.

Oh never,—never—Father! Kailyal cried;
It is not as he saith,—it cannot be!
I!—I his bride!
Nature is never false; he wrongeth her!
My heart belies such lines of destiny,
There is no other true interpreter!

At that reply Kehama's darkening brow
Bewray'd the anger which he yet suppress'd.
Counsel thy daughter; tell her thou art now
Free from thy Curse, he said, and bid her bow
In thankfulness to Fate's benign behest.
Bid her her stubborn will restrain,
For Destiny at last must be obey'd,
And tell her, while obedience is delay'd,
Thy Curse will burn again.

She needeth not my counsel, he replied,
And idly, Rajah, dost thou reason thus

Of Destiny! for though all other things
Were subject to the starry influencings,
And bow'd submissive to thy tyranny,
The virtuous heart, and resolute will are free.
Thus in their wisdom did the Gods decree
When they created man.   Let come what will,
This is our rock of strength; in every ill,
Sorrow, oppression, pain, and agony,
The spirit of the good is unsubdued,
And, suffer as they may, they triumph still.

Obstinate fools! exclaim'd the Mighty One,
Fate and my pleasure must be done,
And ye resist in vain!
Take your fit guerdon till we meet again!
So saying, his vindictive hand he flung
Towards them, fill'd with curses; then on high
Aloft he sprung, and vanish'd through the Sky.

XIX.

MOUNT CALASAY.

THE Rajah, scattering curses as he rose,
Soar'd to the Swerga, and resumed his throne.
Not for his own redoubled agony,
Which now through heart and brain,
With renovated pain,
Rush'd to its seat, Ladurlad breathes that groan,
That groan is for his child; he groan'd to see
The lovely one defiled with leprosy,
Which, as the enemy vindictive fled,
O'er all her frame with quick contagion spread.
She, wondering at events so passing strange,
And fill'd with hope and fear,
And joy to see the Tyrant disappear,
And glad expectance of her Glendoveer,
Perceived not in herself the hideous change.
His burning pain, she thought, had forced the groan
Her father breathed; his agonies alone
Were present to her mind; she clasp'd his knees,
Wept for his Curse, and did not feel her own.

Nor when she saw her plague, did her good heart,
True to itself, even for a moment fail.
Ha, Rajah! with disdainful smile she cries,
Mighty and wise and wicked as thou art,
Still thy blind vengeance acts a friendly part,
Shall I not thank thee for this scurf and scale
Of dire deformity, whose loathsomeness,
Surer than panoply of strongest mail,
Arms me against all foes! Oh, better so,
Better such foul disgrace,
Than that this innocent face
Should tempt thy wooing! That I need not dread;
Nor ever impious foe
Will offer outrage now, nor farther woe
Will beauty draw on my unhappy head,
Safe through the unholy world may Kailyal go.
Her face in virtuous pride
Was lifted to the skies,
As him and his poor vengeance she defied;
But earthward, when she ceased, she turn'd her eyes,
As if she sought to hide
The tear which in her own despite would rise.

Did then the thought of her own Glendoveer
Call forth that natural tear?
Was it a woman's fear,
A thought of earthly love which troubled her?
Like yon thin cloud amid the moonlight sky
That flits before the wind
And leaves no trace behind,
The womanly pang pass'd over Kailyal's mind.
This is a loathsome sight to human eye,
Half-shrinking at herself, the Maiden thought,
Will it be so to him?   Oh surely not!
The immortal Powers, who see
Through the poor wrappings of mortality,
Behold the soul, the beautiful soul, within,
Exempt from age and wasting malady,
And undeform'd, while pure and free from sin.
This is a loathsome sight to human eye,
But not to eyes divine,
Ereenia, Son of Heaven, oh not to thine!

The wrongful thought of fear, the womanly pain
Had pass'd away, her heart was calm again.
She raised her head, expecting now to see
The Glendoveer appear;
Where hath he fled, quoth she,
That he should tarry now?   Oh had she known
Whither the adventurous Son of Heaven was flown,
Strong as her spirit was, it had not borne
The awful thought, nor dared to hope for his return.

For he in search of Seeva's throne was gone,
To tell his tale of wrong;
In search of Seeva's own abode
The daring one began his heavenly road.
O wild emprise! above the farthest skies
He hoped to rise!
Him who is throned beyond the reach of thought,
The Alone, the Inaccessible, he sought.
O wild emprize! for when in days of yore,
For proud pre-eminence of power,
Brama and Veeshnoo, wild with rage, contended,
And Seeva, in his might,
Their dread contention ended;
Before their sight
In form a fiery column did he tower,
Whose head above the highest height extended,
Whose base below the deepest depth descended.
Downward, its depth to sound,
Veeshnoo a thousand years explored
The fathomless profound,
And yet no base he found:
Upward, to reach its head,
Ten myriad years the aspiring Brama soar'd,
And still, as up he fled,
Above him still the Immeasurable spread.
The rivals own'd their Lord,
And trembled and adored.
How shall the Glendoveer attain
What Brama and what Veeshno sought in vain?

Ne'er did such thought of lofty daring enter
Celestial Spirit's mind.   O wild adventure
That throne to find, for he must leave behind
This World, that in the centre,
Within its salt-sea girdle, lies confined ;
Yea, the Seven Earths,[79] that, each with its own ocean,

Ring clasping ring, compose the mighty round.
What power of motion,
In less than endless years, shall bear him there,
Along the limitless extent,
To the utmost bound of the remotest spheres?
What strength of wing
Suffice to pierce the Golden Firmament
That closes all within?
Yet he hath pass'd the measureless extent,
And pierced the Golden Firmament;
For Faith hath given him power, and Space and Time
Vanish before that energy sublime.
Nor doth eternal Night,
And outer Darkness, check his resolute flight;
By strong desire through all he makes his way,
Till Seeva's seat appears,—behold Mount Calasay!

Behold the Silver Mountain! round about
Seven ladders stand, so high, the aching eye,
Seeking their tops in vain amid the sky,
Might deem they led from earth to highest heaven.
Ages would pass away,
And Worlds with age decay,
Ere one whose patient feet, from ring to ring
Must win their upward way,
Could reach the summit of Mount Calasay.[80]
But that strong power that nerv'd his wing,
That all-surmounting will,
Intensity of faith and holiest love,
Sustain'd Ereenia still,
And he hath gain'd the plain, the sanctuary above.

Lo, there the Silver Bell,
That, self-sustain'd, hangs buoyant in the air!
Lo! the broad Table there, too bright
For mortal sight,
From whose four sides the bordering gems unite
Their harmonizing rays,
In one mid fount of many-colour'd light.
The stream of splendour, flashing as it flows,
Plays round, and feeds the stem of yon celestial Rose!
Where is the Sage whose wisdom can declare
The hidden things of that mysterious flower,
That flower which serves all mysteries to bear?
The sacred Triangle is there,
Holding the Emblem which no tongue may tell.
Is this the Heaven of Heavens, where Seeva's self doth
dwell?

Here first the Glendoveer
Felt his wing flag, and paused upon his flight.
Was it that fear came over him, when here
He saw the imagin'd throne appear?
Not so, for his immortal sight
Endur'd the Table's light;
Distinctly he beheld all things around,
And doubt and wonder rose within his mind
That this was all he found.
Howbeit he lifted up his voice and spake.
There is oppression in the World below;
Earth groans beneath the yoke; yea, in her woe,
She asks if the Avenger's eye is blind?
Awake, O Lord, awake!
Too long thy vengeance sleepeth.   Holy One!
Put thou thy terrors on for mercy's sake,
And strike the blow, in justice to mankind!

So as he prayed, intenser faith he felt,
His spirit seem'd to melt
With ardent yearnings of increasing love;
Upward he turned his eyes
As if there should be something yet above;
Let me not, Seeva! seek in vain! he cries;
Thou art not here,—for how should these contain thee?
Thou art not here,—for how should I sustain thee?
But thou, where'er thou art,
Canst hear the voice of prayer,
Canst hear the humble heart.
Thy dwelling who can tell,
Or who, O Lord, hath seen thy secret throne?
But thou art not alone,
Not unapproachable!
O all-embracing Mind,
Thou who art every where,[81]
Whom all who seek shall find,
Hear me, O Seeva! hear the suppliant's prayer!

So saying, up he sprung,
And struck the Bell, which self-suspended hung
Before the mystic Rose.
From side to side the silver tongue
Melodious swung, and far and wide
Soul-thrilling tones of heavenly music rung.
Abash'd, confounded,
It left the Glendoveer—yea all astounded
In overpowering fear and deep dismay;
For when that Bell had sounded,
The Rose, with all the mysteries it surrounded,
The Bell, the Table, and Mount Calasay,
The holy Hill itself, with all thereon,
Even as a morning dream before the day
Dissolves away, they faded and were gone.

Where shall he rest his wing, where turn for flight,
For all around is Light,
Primal, essential, all-pervading Light!
Heart cannot think, nor tongue declare,
Nor eyes of Angel bear
That Glory unimaginably bright;[82]
The Sun himself had seem'd
A speck of darkness there,[83]
Amid that Light of Light!
Down fell the Glendoveer,
Down through all regions, to our mundane sphere
He fell; but in his ear
A voice, which from within him came, was heard,
The indubitable word
Of Him to whom all secret things are known;
Go, ye who suffer, go to Yamen's throne.
He hath the remedy for every woe;
He setteth right whate'er is wrong below.

XX.

THE EMBARKATION.

Down from the Heaven of Heavens Ereenia fell
Precipitate, yet imperceptible
His fall, nor had he cause nor thought of fear;
And when he came within this mundane sphere,
And felt that Earth was near,
The Glendoveer his azure wings expanded,

And, sloping down the sky
Toward the spot from whence he sprung on high,
There on the shore he landed.
Kailyal advanced to meet him,
Not moving now as she was wont to greet him,
Joy in her eye and in her eager pace;
With a calm smile of melancholy pride
She met him now, and, turning half aside,
Her warning hand repell'd the dear embrace.
Strange things, Ereenia, have befall'n us here,
The Virgin said; the Almighty Man hath read
The lines which, traced by Nature on my brain,
There to the gifted eye
Make all my fortunes plain,
Mapping the mazes of futurity.
He sued for peace, for it is written there
That I with him the Amreeta cup must share;
Wherefore he bade me come, and by his side
Sit on the Swerga-throne, his equal bride.
I need not tell thee what reply was given;
My heart, the sure interpreter of Heaven,
His impious words belied.
Thou seest his poor revenge! So having said,
One look she glanced upon her leprous stain
Indignantly, and shook
Her head in calm disdain.

O Maid of soul divine!
O more than ever dear,
And more than ever mine,
Replied the Glendoveer;
He hath not read, be sure, the mystic ways
Of Fate; almighty as he is, that maze
Hath mock'd his fallible sight.
Said he the Amreeta-cup? So far aright
The Evil One may see; for Fate displays
Her hidden things in part, and part conceals,
Baffling the wicked eye
Alike with what she hides, and what reveals,
When with unholy purpose it would pry
Into the secrets of futurity.
So may it be permitted him to see
Dimly the inscrutable decree;
For to the World below,
Where Yamen guards the Amreeta, we must go;
Thus Seeva hath exprest his will, even he
The Holiest hath ordained it; there, he saith,
All wrongs shall be redrest
By Yamen, by the righteous Power of Death.

Forthwith the Father and the fated Maid,
And that heroic Spirit, who for them
Such flight had late essay'd,
The will of Heaven obey'd.
They went their way along the road
That leads to Yamen's dread abode.

Many a day hath past away
Since they began their arduous way,
Their way of toil and pain;
And now their weary feet attain
The Earth's remotest bound,
Where outer Ocean girds it round.
But not like other Oceans this,
Rather it seem'd a drear abyss,
Upon whose brink they stood.

Oh, scene of fear! the travellers hear
The raging of the flood;
They hear how fearfully it roars,
But clouds of darker shade than night
For ever hovering round those shores,
Hide all things from their sight;
The Sun upon that darkness pours
His unavailing light,
Nor ever Moon nor Stars display,
Through the thick shade, one guiding ray
To shew the perils of the way.

There, in a creek, a vessel lay.
Just on the confines of the day,
It rode at anchor in its bay,
These venturous pilgrims to convey
Across that outer Sea.
Strange vessel sure it seem'd to be,
And all unfit for such wild sea!
For through its yawning side the wave
Was oozing in; the mast was frail,
And old and torn its only sail.
How shall that crazy vessel brave
The billows, that in wild commotion
For ever roar and rave?
How hope to cross the dreadful Ocean,
O'er which eternal shadows dwell,
Whose secrets none return to tell?

Well might the travellers fear to enter!
But summon'd once on that adventure,
For them was no retreat.
Nor boots it with reluctant feet
To linger on the strand;
Aboard! aboard!
An awful voice, that left no choice,
Sent forth its stern command,
Aboard! aboard!
The travellers hear that voice in fear,
And breathe to Heaven an inward prayer,
And take their seats in silence there.
Self-hoisted then, behold the sail
Expands itself before the gale;
Hands, which they cannot see, let slip
The cable of that fated ship;
The land breeze sends her on her way,
And lo! they leave the living light of day!

XXI.

THE WORLD'S END.

SWIFT as an arrow in its flight
The Ship shot through the incumbent night;
And they have left behind
The raging billows and the roaring wind,
The storm, the darkness, and all mortal fears;
And lo! another light
To guide their way appears,
The light of other spheres.

That instant, from Ladurlad's heart and brain
The Curse was gone; he feels again
Fresh as in Youth's fair morning, and the Maid
Hath lost her leprous stain.

The Mighty One hath no dominion here,
Starting she cried; O happy, happy hour!
We are beyond his power!
Then raising to the Glendoveer,
With heavenly beauty bright, her angel face,
Turn'd not reluctant now, and met his dear embrace.

Swift glides the Ship, with gentle motion,
Across that calm and quiet ocean;
That glassy sea, which seem'd to be
The mirror of tranquillity.
Their pleasant passage soon was o'er,
The Ship hath reach'd its destin'd shore;
A level belt of ice which bound,
As with an adamantine mound,
The waters of the sleeping Ocean round.
Strange forms were on the strand
Of earth-born spirits slain before their time;
Who, wandering over sea and sky and land,
Had so fulfill'd their term; and now were met
Upon this icy belt, a motley band,
Waiting their summons, at the appointed hour,
When each before the judgment-seat must stand,
And hear his doom from Baly's righteous power.

Foul with habitual crimes, a hideous crew
Were there, the race of rapine and of blood.
Now, having overpast the mortal flood,
Their own deformity they knew,
And knew the meed that to their deeds was due.
Therefore in fear and agony they stood,
Expecting when the Evil Messenger
Among them should appear. But with their fear
A hope was mingled now;
O'er the dark shade of guilt a deeper hue
It threw, and gave a fiercer character
To the wild eye and lip and sinful brow.
They hop'd that soon Kehama would subdue
The inexorable God, and seize his throne,
Reduce the infernal World to his command,
And, with his irresistible right hand,
Redeem them from the vaults of Padalon.

Apart from these a milder company,
The victims of offences not their own,
Look'd when the appointed Messenger should come;
Gather'd together some, and some alone
Brooding in silence on their future doom.
Widows whom, to their husbands' funeral fire,
Force or strong error led, to share the pyre,
As to their everlasting marriage-bed:
And babes, by sin unstain'd,
Whom erring parents vow'd
To Ganges, and the holy stream profan'd
With that strange sacrifice, rite unordain'd
By Law, by sacred Nature unallow'd:
Others more hapless in their destiny,
Scarce having first inhaled this vital breath,
Whose cradles from some tree
Unnatural hands suspended, 84
Then left, till gentle Death,
Coming like Sleep, their feeble moanings ended;
Or for his prey the ravenous Kite descended;
Or, marching like an army from their caves,
The Pismires blacken'd o'er, then bleach'd and bare
Left their unharden'd bones to fall asunder there.

Innocent Souls! thus set so early free
From sin and sorrow and mortality,
Their spotless spirits all-creating Love
Receiv'd into its universal breast.
    Yon blue serene above
Was their domain; clouds pillow'd them to rest;
The Elements on them like nurses tended,
And with their growth etherial substance blended.
Less pure than these is that strange Indian bird,[85]
Who never dips in earthly streams her bill,
But, when the sound of coming showers is heard,
Looks up, and from the clouds receives her fill.
Less pure the footless fowl of Heaven, that never
Rest upon earth, but on the wing for ever
Hovering o'er flowers, their fragrant food inhale,
Drink the descending dew upon its way,
And sleep aloft while floating on the gale.
And thus these innocents in yonder sky
Grow and are strengthen'd, while the allotted years
Perform their course, then hitherward they fly,
Being free from moral taint, so free from fears,
    A joyous band, expecting soon to soar
        To Indra's happy spheres,
And mingle with the blessed company
Of heavenly spirits there for evermore.
    A Gulf profound surrounded
    This icy belt; the opposite side
    With highest rocks was bounded;
    But where their heads they hide,
    Or where their base is founded,
None could espy. Above all reach of sight
They rose, the second Earth was on their height,
Their feet were fix'd on everlasting night.

        So deep the Gulf, no eye
        Could plumb its dark profundity,
Yet all its depth must try; for this the road
To Padalon, and Yamen's dread abode.
        And from below continually
        Ministrant Demons rose and caught
        The Souls whose hour was come;
        Then, with their burthen fraught,
Plunged down, and bore them to receive their doom.

Then might be seen who went in hope, and who
        Trembled to meet the meed
Of many a foul misdeed, as wild they threw
Their arms retorted from the Demons' grasp,
    And look'd around, all eagerly, to seek
For help, where help was none; and strove for aid
        To clasp the nearest shade;
Yea, with imploring looks and horrent shriek,
    Even from one Demon to another bending,
        With hands extending,
        Their mercy they essay'd.
    Still from the verge they strain,
And from the dreadful gulph avert their eyes,
In vain; down plunge the Demons, and their cries
Feebly, as down they sink, from that profound arise.

What heart of living man could, undisturb'd,
Bear sight so sad as this! What wonder there
If Kailyal's lip were blanch'd with inmost dread!
    The chill which from that icy belt
Struck through her, was less keen than what she felt
With her heart's-blood through every limb dispread.

Close to the Glendoveer she clung,
And clasping round his neck her trembling hands,
She clos'd her eyes, and there in silence hung.

    Then to Ladurlad said the Glendoveer,
These Demons, whom thou seest, the ministers
        Of Yamen, wonder to behold us here;
But for the dead they come, and not for us:
Therefore, albeit they gaze upon thee thus,
        Have thou no fear.
    A little while thou must be left alone,
    Till I have borne thy daughter down,
    And placed her safely by the throne
Of him who keeps the Gate of Padalon.

Then taking Kailyal in his arms, he said,
    Be of good heart, Beloved! it is I
Who bear thee. Saying this, his wings he spread,
Sprung upward in the sky, and pois'd his flight,
Then plunged into the Gulf, and sought the World of
        Night.

XXII.

THE GATE OF PADALON.

The strong foundations of this inmost Earth
Rest upon Padalon. That icy Mound
Which girt the mortal Ocean round,
        Reach'd the profound,—
    Ice in the regions of the upper air,
    Crystal midway, and adamant below,
    Whose strength sufficed to bear
The weight of all this upper World of ours,
And with its rampart clos'd the Realm of Woe.
Eight gates hath Padalon; eight heavenly Powers
Have them in charge, each alway at his post,
Lest, from their penal caves, the accursed host,
    Maugre the might of Baly and the God,
    Should break, and carry ruin all abroad.

Those gates stand ever open, night and day,
        And Souls of mortal men
        For ever throng the way.
    Some from the dolorous den,
Children of sin and wrath, return no more:
They, fit companions of the Spirits accurst,
Are doom'd, like them in baths of fire immerst,
Or weltering upon beds of molten ore,
    Or, stretch'd upon the brazen floor,
Are fasten'd down with adamantine chains;
    While on their substance inconsumable,
    Leeches of fire for ever hang and pull,
And worms of fire for ever gnaw their food,
        That, still renew'd,
    Freshens for ever their perpetual pains.
Others there were whom Baly's voice condemn'd,
    By long and painful penance, to atone
Their fleshly deeds. Them, from the judgment-Throne,
    Dread Azyoruca, where she sat involv'd
In darkness as a tent, receiv'd, and dealt
To each the measure of his punishment;
Till, in the central springs of fire, the Will
Impure is purged away; and the freed soul,
    Thus fitted to receive its second birth,
    Embodied once again, revisits Earth.

But they whom Baly's righteous voice absolv'd,
And Yamen, [86] viewing with benignant eye,
Dismiss'd to seek their heritage on high,
How joyfully they leave this gloomy bourne,
　　The dread sojourn
Of Guilt and twin-born Punishment and Woe,
And wild Remorse, here link'd with worse Despair!
They to the eastern Gate rejoicing go :
The Ship of Heaven awaits their coming there,
And on they sail, greeting the blessed light
　　Through realms of upper air,
Bound for the Swerga once ; but now no more
　　Their voyage rests upon that happy shore.
Since Indra, by the dreadful Rajah's might
　　Compell'd, hath taken flight,
On to the second World their way they wend,
And there, in trembling hope, await the doubtful end.

For still in them doth hope predominate,
Faith's precious privilege, when higher Powers
Give way to fear in these portentous hours.
　　Behold the Wardens eight,
　　Each silent at his gate
Expectant stands ; they turn their anxious eyes
Within, and, listening to the dizzy din
Of mutinous uproar, each in all his hands
Holds all his weapons, ready for the fight.
　　For, hark ! what clamorous cries
　　Upon Kehama, for deliverance, call !
Come, Rajah ! they exclaim, too long we groan
In torments.　Come, Deliverer ! yonder throne
Awaits thee—Now, Kehama ! Rajah, now !
Earthly Almighty, wherefore tarriest thou ?—
Such were the sounds that rung, in wild uproar,
O'er all the echoing vaults of Padalon ;
And as the Asuras from the Brazen floor,
Struggling against their fetters, strove to rise,
Their clashing chains were heard, and shrieks and cries,
With curses mix'd, against the Fiends who urge,
Fierce on their rebel limbs, the avenging scourge.

These were the sounds which, at the southern gate,
Assail'd Ereenia's ear ; alighting here,
He laid before Neroodi's feet the Maid,
　　Who, pale and cold with fear,
Hung on his neck, well-nigh a lifeless weight.

Who and what art thou ? cried the Guardian Power,
Sight so unwonted wondering to behold,—
　　O Son of Light !
Who comest here at this portentous hour,
　　When Yamen's throne
Trembles, and all our might can scarce keep down
The rebel race from seizing Padalon :
Who and what art thou, and what wild despair,
Or wilder hope, from realms of upper air,
　　Tempts thee to bear
This mortal Maid to our forlorn abodes ?
Fitter for her, I ween, the Swerga bowers,
And sweet society of heavenly Powers,
　　Than this,—a doleful scene,
　　Even in securest hours.
　　And whither would ye go ?
Alas ! can human or celestial ear,
　　Unmadden'd, hear
The shrieks and yellings of infernal woe ?

Can living flesh and blood
Endure the passage of the fiery flood ?

Lord of the Gate, replied the Glendoveer,
We come obedient to the will of Fate ;
　　And haply doom'd to bring
Hope and salvation to the Infernal King,
　　For Seeva sends us here,
Even He to whom futurity is known,
The Holiest, bade us go to Yamen's throne.
Thou seest my precious charge ;
Under thy care, secure from harm, I leave her,
While I ascend to bear her father down.
Beneath the shelter of thine arm receive her !

　　Then, quoth he to the Maid,
Be of good cheer, my Kailyal ! dearest dear,
　　In faith subdue thy dread,
Anon I shall be here.　So having said,
Aloft, with vigorous bound, the Glendoveer
　　Sprung in celestial might,
And soaring up, in spiral circles, wound
　　His indefatigable flight.

　　But, as he thus departed,
The Maid, who at Neroodi's feet was lying,
　　Like one entranced or dying,
Recovering strength from sudden terror, started ;
And gazing after him with straining sight,
　　And straining arms, she stood,
　　As if in attitude
　　To win him back from flight.
Yea, she had shap'd his name
For utterance, to recal and bid him stay,
Nor leave her thus alone ; but virtuous shame
Represt the unbidden sounds upon their way ;
　　And calling faith to aid,
Even in this fearful hour, the pious Maid
Collected courage, till she seem'd to be
Calm and in hope, such power hath piety.
Before the Giant Keeper of the Gate
She crost her patient arms, and at his feet,
　　Prepar'd to meet
The awful will of Fate with equal mind,
　　She took her seat resign'd.

Even the stern trouble of Neroodi's brow
Relax'd as he beheld the valiant Maid.
　　Hope, long unfelt till now,
Rose in his heart reviving, and a smile
Dawn'd in his brightening countenance, the while
He gaz'd on her with wonder and delight.
The blessing of the Powers of Padalon,
Virgin, be on thee ! cried the admiring God ;
And blessed be the hour that gave thee birth,
　　Daughter of Earth,
For thou to this forlorn abode hast brought
Hope, who too long hath been a stranger here.
And surely for no lamentable lot,
　　Nature, who erreth not,
To thee that heart of fortitude hath given,
Those eyes of purity, that face of love :—
If thou beest not the inheritrix of Heaven,
There is no truth above.

Thus as Neroodi spake, his brow severe

Shone with an inward joy; for sure he thought
When Seeva sent so fair a creature here,
In this momentous hour,
Ere long the World's deliverance would be wrought,
And Padalon escape the Rajah's power.
With pious mind the Maid, in humble guise
Inclin'd, receiv'd his blessing silently,
And rais'd her grateful eyes
A moment, then again
Abas'd them at his presence.   Hark! on high
The sound of coming wings!—her anxious ears
Have caught the distant sound.   Ereenia brings
His burthen down!   Upstarting from her seat,
How joyfully she rears
Her eager head! and scarce upon the ground
Ladurlad's giddy feet their footing found,
When, with her trembling arms, she claspt him round.
No word of greeting,
Nor other sign of joy at that strange meeting.
Expectant of their fate,
Silent, and hand in hand,
Before the Infernal Gate,
The Father and his heavenly Daughter stand.

Then to Neroodi said the Glendoveer,
No Heaven-born Spirit e'er hath visited
This region drear and dread; but I, the first
Who tread your World accurst.
Lord of the Gate, to whom these realms are known,
Direct our fated way to Yamen's throne.

Bring forth my Chariot, Carmala! quoth then
The Keeper of the way.
It was the Car wherein
On Yamen's festal day,
When all the Powers of Hell attend their King,
Yearly to Yamenpur did he repair
To pay his homage there.
Pois'd on a single wheel, it mov'd along,
Instinct with motion; by what wondrous skill
Compact, no human tongue could tell,
Nor human wit devise; but on that wheel
Moving or still,
As if an inward life sustain'd its weight,
Supported, stood the Car of miracle.
Then Carmala brought forth two mantles, white
As the swan's breast, and bright as mountain snow,
When from the wintry sky
The sun, late-rising, shines upon the height,
And rolling vapours fill the vale below.
Not without pain the unaccustom'd sight
That brightness could sustain;
For neither mortal stain,
Nor parts corruptible, remain,
Nor aught that time could touch, or force destroy,
In that pure web whereof the robes were wrought;
So long had it in ten-fold fires been tried,
And blanch'd, and to that brightness purified.
Apparell'd thus, alone,
Children of Earth, Neroodi cried,
In safety may ye pass to Yamen's throne.
Thus only can your living flesh and blood
Endure the passage of the fiery flood.

Of other frame, O son of Heaven, art thou!
Yet hast thou now to go

Through regions which thy heavenly mould will try.
Glories unutterably bright, I know,
And beams intense of empyrean light,
Thine eye divine can bear: but fires of woe,
The sight of torments, and the cry
Of absolute despair,
Might not these things dismay thee on thy flight,
And thy strong pennons flag and fail thee there?
Trust not thy wings, celestial though thou art,
Nor thy good heart, which horror might assail
And pity quail,
Pity in these abodes of no avail;
But take thy seat this mortal pair beside,
And Carmala the infernal Car will guide.
Go, and may happy end your way betide!
So, as he spake, the self-moved Car roll'd on,
And lo! they pass the Gate of Padalon.

XXIII.

PADALON.

Whoe'er hath lov'd with venturous step to tread
The chambers dread
Of some deep cave, and seen his taper's beam
Lost in the arch of darkness overhead,
And mark'd its gleam,
Playing afar upon the sunless stream,
Where, from their secret bed,
And course unknown and inaccessible,
The silent waters well;
Whoe'er hath trod such caves of endless night,
He knows, when measuring back the gloomy way,
With what delight refreshed, his eye
Perceives the shadow of the light of day,
Through the far portal slanting, where it falls
Dimly reflected on the wat'ry walls;
How heavenly seems the sky,
And how, with quicken'd feet, he hastens up,
Eager again to greet
The living World, and blessed sunshine there,
And drink, as from a cup
Of joy, with thirsty lips, the open air.

Far other light than that of day there shone
Upon the travellers, entering Padalon.
They, too, in darkness enter'd on their way,
But, far before the Car,
A glow, as of a fiery furnace light,
Fill'd all before them.   'Twas a light which made
Darkness itself appear
A thing of comfort, and the sight, dismay'd,
Shrunk inward from the molten atmosphere.
Their way was through the adamantine rock
Which girt the World of Woe; on either side
Its massive walls arose, and overhead
Arch'd the long passage; onward as they ride,
With stronger glare the light around them spread,
And lo! the regions dread,
The World of Woe before them, opening wide.

There rolls the fiery flood,
Girding the realms of Padalon around.
A sea of flame it seem'd to be,
Sea without bound;
For neither mortal, nor immortal sight,

Could pierce across through that intensest light.
A single rib of steel,
Keen as the edge of keenest scymitar,
Spann'd this wide gulph of fire.   The infernal Car
Roll'd to the Gulf, and on its single wheel
Self-balanced, rose upon that edge of steel.
Red-quivering float the vapours overhead,
The fiery gulf beneath them spread,
Tosses its billowing blaze with rush and roar;
Steady and swift the self-mov'd Chariot went,
Winning the long ascent,
Then, downward rolling, gains the farther shore.

But, oh! what sounds and sights of woe,
What sights and sounds of fear,
Assail the mortal travellers here!
Their way was on a causey straight and wide,
Where penal vaults on either side were seen,
Ranged like the cells wherein
Those wonderous winged alchemists infold
Their stores of liquid gold.
Thick walls of adamant divide
The dungeons; and from yonder circling flood,
Off-streams of fire through secret channels glide,
And wind among them, and in each provide
An everlasting food
Of righteous torments for the accursed brood.

These were the rebel race, who, in their might
Confiding impiously, would fain have driven
The Deities supreme from highest Heaven;
But by the Suras, in celestial fight,
Oppos'd and put to flight,
Here, in their penal dens, the accursed crew,
Not for its crime, but for its failure, rue
Their wild ambition.   Yet again they long
The contest to renew,
And wield their arms again in happier hour;
And with united power,
Following Kehama's triumph, to press on
From World to World, and Heaven to Heaven, and Sphere
To Sphere, till Hemakoot shall be their own,
And Meru Mount, and Indra's Swerga-Bowers,
And Brama's region, where the heavenly Hours
Weave the vast circle of his age-long day. [87]
Even over Veeshnoo's empyreal seat
They trust the Rajah shall extend their sway,
And that the seven-headed Snake, whereon
The strong Preserver sets his conquering feet,
Will rise and shake him headlong from his throne,
When, in their irresistible array,
Amid the Milky Sea, they force their way.
Even higher yet their frantic thoughts aspire,
Yea, on their beds of torment as they lie,
The highest, holiest Seeva, they defy,
And tell him they shall have anon their day,
When they will storm his realm, and seize Mount Calasay.

Such impious hopes torment
Their raging hearts, impious and impotent;
And now, with unendurable desire
And lust of vengeance, that, like inward fire,
Doth aggravate their punishment, they rave
Upon Kehama; him the accursed rout
Acclaim; with furious cries and maddening shout
They call on him to save;

Kehama! they exclaim;
Thundering, the dreadful echo rolls about,
And Hell's whole vault repeats Kehama's name.

Over these dens of punishment, the host
Of Padalon maintain eternal guard,
Keeping upon the walls their vigilant ward.
At every angle stood
A watch-tower, the decurion Demon's post,
Where, rais'd on high, he view'd with sleepless eye
His trust, that all was well.   And over these,
Such was the perfect discipline of Hell,
Captains of fifties and of hundreds held
Authority, each in his loftier tower;
And chiefs of legions over them had power;
And thus all Hell with towers was girt around.
Aloft the brazen turrets shone
In the red light of Padalon,
And on the walls between
Dark moving, the infernal Guards were seen,
Gigantic Demons pacing to and fro;
Who ever and anon,
Spreading their crimson pennons, plunged below,
Faster to rivet down the Asuras' chains;
And with the snaky scourge and fiercer pains,
Repress their rage rebellious.   Loud around,
In mingled sound, the echoing lash, the clash
Of chains, the ponderous hammer's iron stroke,
With execrations, groans, and shrieks and cries
Combin'd, in one wild dissonance, arise;
And through the din there broke,
Like thunder heard through all the warring winds,
The dreadful name.   Kehama, still they rave,
Hasten and save!
Now, now, Deliverer! now, Kehama, now!
Earthly Almighty, wherefore tarriest thou!

Oh, if that name abhorr'd,
Thus utter'd, could well nigh
Dismay the Powers of Hell, and daunt their Lord,
How fearfully to Kailyal's ear it came!
She, as the Car roll'd on its rapid way,
Bent down her head, and clos'd her eyes for dread;
And deafening, with strong effort from within,
Her ears against the din,
Cover'd and prest them close with both her hands.
Sure if the mortal Maiden had not fed
On heavenly food, and long been strengthened
With heavenly converse for such end vouchsaf'd,
Her human heart had fail'd, and she had died
Beneath the horrors of this awful hour.
But Heaven supplied a power
Beyond her earthly nature, to the measure
Of need infusing strength;
And Fate, whose secret and unerring pleasure
Appointed all, decreed
An ample meed and recompense at length.
High-fated Maid, the righteous hour is nigh!
The all-embracing Eye
Of Retribution still beholdeth thee;
Bear onward to the end, O Maid, courageously!

On roll'd the Car, and lo! afar
Upon its height the Towers of Yamenpur
Rise on the astonish'd sight.
Behold the infernal City, Yamen's seat
44

Of empire, in the midst of Padalon,
Where the eight causeys meet.
There on a rock of adamant it stood,
Resplendent far and wide,
Itself of solid diamond edified,
And all around it roll'd the fiery flood.
Eight bridges arch'd the stream; huge piles of brass
Magnificent, such structures as beseem
The Seat and Capital of such great God,
Worthy of Yamen's own august abode.
A brazen tower and gateway at each end
Of each was rais'd, where Giant Wardens stood,
Station'd in arms the passage to defend,
That never foe might cross the fiery flood.

Oh what a gorgeous sight it was to see
The Diamond City blazing on its height
With more than mid-sun splendour, by the light
Of its own fiery river!
Its towers and domes and pinnacles and spires,
Turrets and battlements, that flash and quiver
Through the red restless atmosphere for ever;
And hovering over head,
The smoke and vapours of all Padalon,
Fit firmament for such a world, were spread,
With surge and swell, and everlasting motion,
Heaving and opening like tumultuous ocean.

Nor were there wanting there
Such glories as beseem'd such region well;
For though with our blue heaven and genial air
The firmament of Hell might not compare,
As little might our earthly tempests vie
With the dread storms of that infernal sky,
Whose clouds of all metallic elements
Sublim'd were full. For, when its thunder broke,
Not all the united World's artillery,
In one discharge, could equal that loud stroke;
And though the Diamond Towers and Battlements
Stood firm upon their adamantine rock,
Yet, while it volleyed round the vault of Hell,
Earth's solid arch was shaken with the shock,
And Cities in one mighty ruin fell.
Through the red sky terrific meteors scour;
Huge stones come hailing down; or sulphur-shower,
Floating amid the lurid air like snow,
Kindles in its descent,
And with blue fire-drops rains on all below.
At times the whole supernal element
Igniting, burst in one vast sheet of flame,
And roar'd as with the sound
Of rushing winds, above, below, around;
Anon the flame was spent, and overhead
A heavy cloud of moving darkness spread.

Straight to the brazen bridge and gate
The self-mov'd Chariot bears its mortal load.
At sight of Carmala,
On either side the Giant guards divide,
And give the chariot way.
Up yonder winding road it rolls along,
Swift as the bittern soars on spiral wing,
And lo! the Palace of the Infernal King!

Two forms inseparable in unity
Hath Yamen;[88] even as with hope or fear

The Soul regardeth him doth he appear,
For hope and fear,
At that dread hour, from ominous conscience spring,
And err not in their bodings. Therefore some,
They who polluted with offences come,
Behold him as the King
Of Terrors, black of aspect, red of eye,[89]
Reflecting back upon the sinful mind,
Heighten'd with vengeance, and with wrath divine,
Its own inborn deformity.
But to the righteous Spirit how benign
His awful countenance,
Where, tempering justice with parental love,
Goodness and heavenly grace
And sweetest mercy shine! Yet is he still
Himself the same, one form, one face, one will;
And these his twofold aspects are but one;
And change is none
In him, for change in Yamen could not be,
The Immutable is he.
He sate upon a marble sepulchre
Massive and huge, where at the Monarch's feet,
The righteous Baly had his judgment-seat.
A golden throne before them vacant stood;
Three human forms sustain'd its ponderous weight,
With lifted hands outspread, and shoulders bow'd
Bending beneath the load.
A fourth was wanting. They were of the hue
Of coals of fire; yet were they flesh and blood,
And living breath they drew;
And their red eye-balls roll'd with ghastly stare,
As thus, for their misdeeds, they stood tormented there.

On steps of gold those fiery Statues stood,
Who bore the Golden Throne. A cloud behind
Immoveable was spread; not all the light
Of all the flames and fires of Padalon
Could pierce its depth of night.
There Azyoruca[90] veil'd her awful form
In those eternal shadows: there she sate,
And as the trembling Souls, who crowd around
The Judgment-Seat, receiv'd the doom of fate,
Her giant arms, extending from the cloud,
Drew them within the darkness. Moving out,
To grasp and bear away the innumerous rout,
For ever and for ever, thus were seen
The thousand mighty arms of that dread Queen.

Here, issuing from the car, the Glendoveer
Did homage to the God, then rais'd his head.
Suppliants we come, he said,
I need not tell thee by what wrongs opprest,
For nought can pass on earth to thee unknown;
Sufferers from tyranny we seek for rest,
And Seeva bade us go to Yamen's throne;
Here, he hath said, all wrongs shall be redrest.
Yamen replied, Even now the hour draws near,
When Fate its hidden ways will manifest.
Not for light purpose would The Wisest send
His suppliants here, when we, in doubt and fear,
The awful issue of the hour attend.
Wait ye in patience and in faith the end!

XXIV.

THE AMREETA.

So spake the King of Padalon, when, lo!
The voice of lamentation ceas'd in Hell,
And sudden silence all around them fell,
Silence more wild and terrible
Than all the infernal dissonance before.
Through that portentous stillness, far away,
Unwonted sounds were heard, advancing on
And deepening on their way;
For now the inexorable hour
Was come, and, in the fulness of his power,
Now that the dreadful rites had all been done,
Kehama from the Swerga hastened down,
To seize upon the throne of Padalon.

He came in all his might and majesty,[91]
With all his terrors clad, and all his pride;
And, by the attribute of Deity,
Which he had won from Heaven, self-multiplied,
The dreadful One appear'd on every side.[92]
In the same indivisible point of time,
At the eight Gates he stood at once, and beat
The Warden-Gods of Hell beneath his feet;
Then, in his brazen Cars of triumph, straight,
At the same moment, drove through every gate.
By Aullays, hugest of created kind,
Fiercest, and fleeter than the viewless wind,
His Cars were drawn, ten yokes of ten abreast,—
What less sufficed for such almighty weight?
Eight bridges from the fiery flood arose
Growing before his way; and on he goes,
And drives the thundering Chariot-wheels along,
At once o'er all the roads of Padalon.

Silent and motionless remain
The Azuras on their bed of pain,
Waiting, with breathless hope, the great event.
All Hell was hush'd in dread,
Such awe that Omnipresent coming spread;
Nor had its voice been heard, though all its rout
Innumerable had lifted up one shout;
Nor if the infernal firmament
Had, in one unimaginable burst,
Spent its collected thunders, had the sound
Been audible, such louder terrors went
Before his forms substantial. Round about
The presence scattered lightnings far and wide,
That quench'd on every side,
With their intensest blaze, the feebler fire
Of Padalon, even as the stars go out,
When, with prodigious light,
Some blazing meteor fills the astonish'd night.
The Diamond City shakes!
The adamantine Rock
Is loosen'd with the shock!
From its foundation mov'd, it heaves and quakes;
The brazen portals crumbling fall to dust;
Prone fall the Giant Guards
Beneath the Aullays crush'd;
On, on, through Yamenpur, their thundering feet
Speed from all points to Yamen's judgment-seat.
And lo! where multiplied,

Behind, before him, and on every side,
Wielding all weapons in his countless hands,
Around the Lord of Hell Kehama stands!
Then, too, the Lord of Hell put forth his might:
Thick darkness, blacker than the blackest night,
Rose from their wrath, and veil'd
The unutterable fight.
The power of Fate and Sacrifice prevail'd,
And soon the strife was done.
Then did the Man-God re-assume
His unity, absorbing into one
The consubstantiate shapes; and as the gloom
Opened, fallen Yamen on the ground was seen,
His neck beneath the conquering Rajah's feet,
Who on the marble tomb
Had his triumphal seat.

Silent the Man-Almighty sate; a smile
Gleam'd on his dreadful lips, the while
Dallying with power, he paused from following up
His conquest, as a man in social hour
Sips of the grateful cup,
Again and yet again, with curious taste,
Searching its subtle flavour ere he drink:
Even so Kehama now forbore his haste:
Having within his reach whate'er he sought,
On his own haughty power he seem'd to muse,
Pampering his arrogant heart with silent thought
Before him stood the Golden throne in sight,
Right opposite; he could not chuse but see,
Nor seeing chuse but wonder. Who are ye
Who bear the Golden Throne, tormented there?
He cried; for whom doth Destiny prepare
The imperial seat, and why are ye but Three?

FIRST STATUE.

I of the Children of Mankind was first,
Me miserable! who, adding store to store,
Heapt up superfluous wealth; and now accurst,
For ever I the frantic crime deplore.

SECOND STATUE.

I o'er my Brethren of Mankind the first
Usurping power, set up a throne sublime,
A King and Conqueror: therefore thus accurst,
For ever I in vain repent the crime.

THIRD STATUE.

I on the Children of Mankind the first,
In God's most holy name, impos'd a tale
Of impious falsehood; therefore thus accurst,
For ever I in vain the crime bewail.
Even as thou here beholdest us,
Here we have stood, tormented thus,
Such countless ages, that they seem to be
Long as eternity,
And still we are but Three.
A Fourth will come to share
Our pain, at yonder vacant corner bear
His portion of the burthen, and complete
The golden Throne for Yamen's judgment-seat.
Thus hath it been appointed: he must be
Equal in guilt to us, the guilty Three.
Kehama, come! too long we wait for thee!

Thereat, with one accord,

The Three took up the word, like choral song,
Come, Rajah! Man-God! Earth's Almighty Lord!
Kehama, come! we wait for thee too long.

A short and sudden laugh of wondering pride
Burst from him in his triumph: to reply
Scornful he deign'd not; but with alter'd eye
Wherein some doubtful meaning seem'd to lie,
He turn'd to Kailyal. Maiden, thus he cried,
I need not bid thee see
How vain it is to strive with Fate's decree,
When hither thou hast fled to fly from me,
And lo! even here thou find'st me at thy side.
Mine thou must be, being doom'd with me to share
The Amreeta-cup of immortality; 93
Yea, by Myself I swear
It hath been thus appointed. Joyfully
Join then thy hand and heart and will with mine,
Nor at such glorious destiny repine,
Nor in thy folly more provoke my wrath divine.
She answer'd; I have said. It must not be!
Almighty as thou art,
Thou hast put all things underneath thy feet,
But still the resolute heart
And virtuous will are free.
Never, oh! never,—never—can there be
Communion, Rajah, between thee and me.
Once more, quoth he, I urge, and once alone.
Thou seest yon Golden Throne,
Where I anon shall set thee by my side;
Take thou thy seat thereon,
Kehama's willing bride,
And I will place the Kingdoms of the World
Beneath thy Father's feet,
Appointing him the King of mortal men:
Else underneath that Throne,
The Fourth supporter, he shall stand and groan;
Prayers will be vain to move my mercy then.

Again the Virgin answer'd, I have said!
Ladurlad caught her in his proud embrace,
While on his neck she hid
In agony her face.

Bring forth the Amreeta-cup! Kehama cried
To Yamen, rising sternly in his pride.
It is within the Marble Sepulchre,
The vanquish'd Lord of Padalon replied;
Bid it be opened. Give thy treasure up!
Exclaim'd the Man-Almighty to the Tomb.
And at his voice and look
The massy fabric shook, and opened wide.
A huge Anatomy was seen reclin'd
Within its marble womb. Give me the Cup!
Again Kehama cried; no other charm
Was needed than that voice of stern command.
From his repose the ghastly form arose,
Put forth his bony and gigantic arm,
And gave the Amreeta to the Rajah's hand.
Take! drink! with accents dread the Spectre said,
For thee and Kailyal hath it been assign'd,
Ye only of the Children of Mankind.

Then was the Man-Almighty's heart elate;
This is the consummation! he exclaim'd;
Thus have I triumphed over Death and Fate.

Now, Seeva! look to thine abode!
Henceforth, on equal footing we engage,
Alike immortal now, and we shall wage
Our warfare, God to God!
Joy fill'd his impious soul,
And to his lips he rais'd the fatal bowl.

Thus long the Glendoveer had stood
Watching the wonders of the eventful hour,
Amaz'd but undismay'd; for in his heart
Faith, overcoming fear, maintain'd its power.
Nor had that faith abated, when the God
Of Padalon was beaten down in fight;
For then he look'd to see the heavenly might
Of Seeva break upon them. But when now
He saw the Amreeta in Kehama's hand,
An impulse which defied all self-command
In that extremity
Stung him, and he resolved to seize the cup,
And dare the Rajah's force in Seeva's sight.
Forward he sprung to tempt the unequal fray,
When lo! the Anatomy,
With warning arm, withstood his desperate way,
And from the Golden Throne the fiery Three
Again, in one accord, renew'd their song,
Kehama, come! we wait for thee too long.

O fool of drunken hope and frantic vice!
Madman! to seek for power beyond thy scope
Of knowledge, and to deem
Less than omniscience could suffice
To wield omnipotence! O fool, to dream
That immortality could be
The meed of evil!—yea thou hast it now,
Victim of thine own wicked heart's device,
Thou hast thine object now, and now must pay the price.

He did not know the awful mystery
Of that divinest cup, that as the lips
Which touch it, even such its quality,
Good or malignant; Madman! and he thinks
The blessed prize is won, and joyfully he drinks.

Then Seeva opened on the Accursed One
His Eye of Anger: upon him alone
The wrath-beam fell. He shudders—but too late;
The deed is done,
The dreadful liquor works the will of Fate.
Immortal he would be,
Immortal he remains; but through his veins
Torture at once, and immortality,
A stream of poison doth the Amreeta run,
Infinite everlasting agony.
And while within the burning anguish flows,
His outward body glows
Like molten ore, beneath the avenging eye,
Doom'd thus to live and burn eternally.
The fiery Three,
Beholding him, set up a fiendish cry,
A song of jubilee:
Come, Brother, come! they sung; too long
Have we expected thee,
Henceforth we bear no more
The unequal weight; Come, Brother, we are Four!

Vain his almightiness, for mightier pain

Subdued all power; pain ruled supreme alone.
And yielding to the bony hand
The unemptied cup, he mov'd toward the throne,
And at the vacant corner took his stand.
Behold the Golden Throne at length complete,
And Yamen silently ascends the Judgment-Seat.

For two alone, of all mankind, to me
The Amreeta-Cup was given,
Exclaim'd the Anatomy;
The Man hath drunk, the Woman's turn is next.
Come, Kailyal, come, receive thy doom,
And do the Will of Heaven!—
Wonder, and Fear, and Awe at once perplext
The mortal Maiden's heart, but over all
Hope rose triumphant. With a trembling hand,
Obedient to his call,
She took the fated Cup; and, lifting up
Her eyes, where holy tears began to swell,
Is it not your command,
Ye heavenly Powers? as on her knees she fell,
The pious Virgin cried:
Ye know my innocent will, my heart sincere,
Ye govern all things still,
And wherefore should I fear!
She said, and drank. The Eye of Mercy beam'd
Upon the Maid: a cloud of fragrance steam'd
Like incense-smoke, as all her mortal frame
Dissolved beneath the potent agency
Of that mysterious draught; such quality,
From her pure touch, the fated Cup partook.
Like one entranced she knelt,
Feeling her body melt
Till all but what was heavenly past away:
Yet still she felt
Her Spirit strong within her, the same heart,
With the same loves, and all her heavenly part,
Unchang'd, and ripen'd to such perfect state,
In this miraculous birth, as here on Earth
Dimly our holiest hopes anticipate.

Mine! mine! with rapturous joy Ereenia cried,
Immortal now, and yet not more divine;
Mine, mine,—for ever mine!
The immortal Maid replied,
For ever, ever, thine!

Then Yamen said, O thou to whom, by Fate,
Alone of all mankind, this lot is given,
Daughter of Earth, but now the Child of Heaven!
Go with thy heavenly Mate,
Partaker now of his immortal bliss;
Go to the Swerga Bowers,
And there recall the hours
Of endless happiness.

But that sweet Angel, for she still retain'd
Her human loves and human piety,
As if reluctant at the Gods commands,
Linger'd, with anxious eye
Upon her father fix'd and spread her hands
Toward him wistfully.
Go! Yamen cried, nor cast that look behind
Upon Ladurlad at this parting hour,
For thou shalt find him in thy Mother's Bower.
The Car, for Carmala his word obey'd,

Mov'd on, and bore away the Maid,
While from the Golden Throne the Lord of Death
With love benignant, on Ladurlad smil'd,
And gently on his head his blessing laid.
As sweetly as a Child,
Whom neither thought disturbs nor care encumbers,
Tir'd with long play, at close of summer day,
Lies down and slumbers,
Even thus as sweet a boon of sleep partaking
By Yamen blest, Ladurlad sunk to rest.
Blessed that sleep! more blessed was the waking!
For on that night a heavenly morning broke,
The light of heaven was round him when he woke,
And in the Swerga, in Yedillian's Bower,
All whom he lov'd he met, to part no more.

NOTES.

Note 1, page 307, col. 1.
Calmly she took her seat.

SHE, says Bernier, whom I saw burn herself, when I parted from *Surat* to travel into *Persia*, in the presence of Monsieur *Chardin* of *Paris*, and of many *English* and *Dutch*, was of a middle age, and not unhandsome. To represent unto you the undaunted cheerfulness that appeared in her countenance, the resolution with which she marched, washed herself, spoke to the people; the confidence with which she looked upon us, viewed her little cabin, made up of very dry millet-straw and small wood, went into this cabin, and sat down upon the pile, and took her husband's head into her lap, and a torch into her own hand, and kindled the cabin, whilst I know not how many *Brahmans* were busy in kindling the fire round about: to represent to you, I say, all this as it ought, is not possible for me; I can at present scarce believe it myself, though it be but a few days since I saw it.

Note 2, page 307, col. 1.
They strip her ornaments away.

She went out again to the river, and taking up some water in her hands, muttered some prayers, and offered it to the sun. All her ornaments were then taken from her; and her armlets were broken, and chaplets of white flowers were put upon her neck and hands. Her hair was tucked up with five combs; and her forehead was marked with clay in the same manner as that of her husband.—STAVORINUS.

Note 3, page 307, col. 1.
Around her neck they leave
The marriage-knot alone.

When the time for consummating the marriage is come, they light the fire Homan with the wood of Ravasiton. The Bramin blesses the former, which, being done, the bridegroom takes three handfuls of rice, and throws it on the bride's head, who does the same to him. Afterwards the bride's father clothes her in a dress according to his condition, and washes the bridegroom's feet; the bride's mother observing to pour out the water. This being done, the father puts his daughter's hand in his own, puts water into it, some pieces of money, and, giving it to the bridegroom, says, at the same time, I have no longer any thing to do with you, and I give you up to the power of another. The *Tali*, which is a ribbon with a golden head hanging at it, is held ready; and, being shown to the company, some prayers and blessings are pronounced; after which the bridegroom takes it, and hangs it about the bride's neck. This knot is what particularly secures his possession of her; for, before he had had the *Tali* on, all the rest of the ceremonies might have been made to no purpose; for it has sometimes happened, that, when the bridegroom was going to fix it on, the bride's father has discovered his not being satisfied with the bridegroom's gift, when another, offering more, has carried off the bride with her father's consent. But, when once the *Tali* is put on, the marriage is indissoluble; and, whenever the husband dies, the *Tali* is burnt along with him, to shew that the marriage bands are broke. Besides these particular ceremonies, the people have notice of the wedding by a *Pandal*, which is raised before the bride's door some days before. The whole concludes with an entertainment which the bride's father gives to the common friends; and during this festivity, which continues five days, alms are given to the poor, and the fire Homan is kept in. The seventh day, the new-married couple set out for the bridegroom's house, whither they frequently go by torch-light. The bride and bridegroom are carried in a sedan, pass through the chief streets of the city, and are accompanied by their friends, who are either on horseback or mounted on elephants.—A. ROGER.

Note 4, page 307, col. 1.
They force her on, they bind her to the dead.

'T is true, says Bernier, that I have seen some of them, which, at the sight of the pile and the fire, appeared to have some apprehension, and that, perhaps, would have gone back. Those demons, the Bramins, that are there with their great sticks, astonish them, and hearten them up, or even thrust them in; as I have seen it done to a young woman that retreated five or six paces from the pile, and to another, that was much disturbed when she saw the fire take hold of her clothes, these executioners thrusting her in with their long poles.

At Lahor, I saw a very handsome and a very young woman burnt; I believe she was not above twelve years of age. This poor unhappy creature appeared rather dead than alive when she came near the pile; she shook and wept bitterly. Meanwhile, three or four of these executioners, the Bramins, together with an old hag that held her under the arm, thrust her on, and made her sit down upon the wood; and, lest she should run away, they tied her legs and hands; and so they burnt her alive. I had enough to do to contain myself for indignation.—BERNIER.

Pietro Della Valle conversed with a widow, who was about to burn herself by her own choice. She told him, that, generally speaking, women were not forced to burn themselves; but sometimes, among people of rank, when a young woman, who was handsome, was left a widow, and in danger of marrying again, (which is never practised among them, because of the confusion and disgrace which are inseparable from such a thing) or of falling into other irregularities, then, indeed, the relations of the husband, if they are at all tenacious of the honour of the family, compel her to burn herself, whether she likes it or no, merely to prevent the inconveniencies which might take place.

Dellon also, whom I consider as one of the best travellers in the East, expressly asserts, that widows are burnt there « de gré, ou de force. L'on n'en voit que trop qui après avoir désiré et demandé la mort avec un courage intrepide, et après avoir obtenu et acheté la permission de se brûler, ont tremblé à la vue du bucher, se sont repenties, mais trop tard, de leur imprudence, et ont fait d'inutiles efforts pour se retracter. Mais lorsque cela arrive, bien loin que les Bramenes soient touchés d'aucune pitié, ils lient cruellement ces malheureuses, et les brûlent par force, sans avoir aucun égard a leurs plaintes, ni à leurs cris.»—Tom. i, p. 138.

It would be easy to multiply authorities upon this point. Let it suffice to mention one important historical fact: When the great Albuquerque had established himself at Goa, he forbade these accursed sacrifices, the women extolled him for it as their benefactor and deliverer, (*Commentarios de Alb.* ii. 20,) and no European in India was ever so popular, or so revered by the natives. Yet, if we are to believe the anti-missionaries, none but fools, fanatics, and pretenders to humanity, would wish to deprive the Hindoo women of the right of burning themselves! « It may be useful (says Colonel Mark Wilks) to examine the reasonableness of interfering with the most exceptionable of all their institutions. It has been thought an abomination not to be tolerated, that a widow should immolate herself on the funeral pile of her deceased husband. But what judgment should we form of the Hindoo, who (if any of our institutions admitted the parallel) should *forcibly* pretend to stand between a Christian and the hope of eternal salvation? And shall we not hold him to be a driveller in politics and morals, a fanatic in religion, and a pretender in humanity, who would forcibly wrest this hope from the Hindoo widow?»—*Historical Sketches of the South of India*, vol. i, p. 499.

Such opinions, and such language, may safely be left to the indignation and pity which they cannot fail to excite. I shall only express my astonishment, that any thing so monstrous, and so miserably futile, should have proceeded from a man of learning, great good sense, and general good feelings, as Colonel Wilks evidently appears to be.

Note 5, page 307, col. 1.
One drops, another plunges in.

When Bernier was passing from Amad-Avad to Agra, there came news to him in a borough, where the caravan rested under the shade (staying for the cool of the evening to march on their journey), that a woman was then upon the point of burning herself with the body of her husband. I presently rose, says he, and ran to the place where it was to be done, which was a great pit, with a pile of wood raised in it, whereon I saw laid a dead corpse and a woman, which, at a distance, seemed to me pretty fair, sitting near it on the same pile, besides four or five Bramins, putting the fire to it from all sides; five women of a middle age, and well enough dressed, holding one another by the hand, and dancing about the pit, and a great crowd of people, men and women, looking on. The pile of wood was presently all on fire, because store of oil and butter had been thrown upon it: and I saw, at the same time, through the flames, that the fire took hold of the clothes of the woman, that were imbued with well-scented oils, mingled with powder of sandal and saffron. All this I saw, but observed not that the woman was at all disturbed; yea, it was said, that she had been heard to pronounce, with great force, these two words, *five, two*, to signify, according to the opinion of those that hold the soul's transmigration, that this was the fifth time she had burnt herself with the same husband, and that there remained but two more for perfection; as if she had that time this remembrance, or some prophetical spirit. But here ended not this infernal tragedy: I thought it was only by way of ceremony that these five women sung and danced about the pit; but I was altogether surprised when I saw that the flame, having taken hold of the clothes of one of them, she cast herself, with her head foremost, into the pit; and that after her, another, being overcome by the flame and the smoke, did the like; and my astonishment redoubled afterwards, when I saw that the remaining three took one another again by the hand, continued their dance without any apparent fear; and that at length they precipitated themselves, one after another, into the fire, as their companions had done. I learnt that these had been five slaves, who, having seen their mistress extremely afflicted at the sickness of her husband, and heard her promise him, that she would not survive him, but burn herself with him, were so touched with compassion and tenderness towards this their mistress, that they engaged themselves in a promise to follow her in her resolution, and to burn themselves with her.—*Bernier*.

This excellent traveller relates an extraordinary circumstance which occurred at one of these sacrifices. A woman was engaged in some love-intrigues with a young Mahommedan, her neighbour, who was a tailor, and could play finely upon the tabor. This woman, in the hopes she had of marrying this young man, poisoned her husband, and presently came away to tell the tailor, that it was time to be gone together, as they had projected, or else she should be obliged to burn herself. The young man, fearing lest he might be entangled in a mischievous business, flatly refused her. The woman, not at all surprised at it, went to her relations, and advertised them of the sudden death of her husband, and openly protested that she would not survive him, but burn herself with him. Her kindred, well satisfied with so generous a resolution, and the great honour she did to the whole family, presently had a pit made and filled with wood, exposing the corpse upon it, and kindling the fire. All being prepared, the woman goes to embrace and bid farewell to all her kindred that were there about the pit, among whom was also the tailor, who had been invited to play upon the tabor that day, with many others of that sort of men, according to the custom of the country. This fury of a woman being also come to this young man, made sign as if she would bid him farewell with the rest; but, instead of gently embracing him, she taketh him with all her force about his collar, pulls him to the pit, and tumbleth him, together with herself, into the ditch, where they both were soon dispatched.—*Bernier*.

The Hindoos sometimes erect a chapel on the spot where one of these sacrifices has been performed, both on account of the soul of the deceased, and as a trophy of her virtue. I remember to have seen one of these places, where the spot on which the funeral pile had been erected was inclosed and covered with bamboos, formed into a kind of bower, planted with flowering creepers. The inside was set round with flowers, and at one end there was an image.—*Crawfurd*.

Some of the Yogees, who smear themselves with ashes, use none but what they collect from funeral piles,—human ashes!—*Pietro Della Valle*.

From a late investigation, it appears, that the number of women who sacrifice themselves within thirty miles round Calcutta every year, is, on an average, upwards of two hundred. The Pundits have already been called on to produce the sanction of their Shasters for this custom. The passages exhibited are vague and general in their meaning, and differently interpreted by the same casts. Some sacred verses commend the practice, but none command it; and the Pundits refer once more to *custom*. They have, however, intimated, that if government will pass a regulation, amercing by fine every Brahmin who attends a burning, or every Zemindar who permits him to attend it, the practice cannot possibly long continue; for that the ceremony, unsanctified by the presence of the priests, will lose its dignity and consequence in the eyes of the people.

The civilized world may expect soon to hear of the abolition of this opprobrium of a Christian administration, the female sacrifice; which has subsisted, to our certain knowledge, since the time of Alexander the Great.—*Claudius Buchanan*.

This practice, however, was manifestly unknown when the Institutes of Menu were written. Instructions are there given for the conduct of a widow : « Let her,» it is said, « emaciate her body, by living voluntarily on pure flowers, roots, and fruit; but let her not, when her lord is deceased, even pronounce the name of another man. Let her continue till death forgiving all injuries, performing harsh duties, avoiding every sensual pleasure, and cheerfully practising the incomparable rules of virtue, which have been followed by such women as were devoted to one only husband. Many thousands of Brahmins, having avoided sensuality from their early youth, and having left no issue in their families, have ascended nevertheless to heaven; and, like those abstemious men, a virtuous wife ascends to heaven, though she have no child, if, after the decease of her lord, she devote herself to pious austerity : but a widow, who, from a wish to bear children, slights her deceased husband by marrying again, brings disgrace on herself here below, and shall be excluded from the seat of her lord.»— *Inst. of Menu*, ch. 5. 157-161.

Second marriages were permitted to men.—*Ibid.* 167, 8-9.

Note 6, page 307, col. 2.

Lo ! Arvalan appears.

Many believe that some souls are sent back to the spot where their bodies were burnt, or where their ashes are preserved, to wait there until the new bodies they are destined to occupy be ready for their reception. This appears to correspond with an opinion of Plato, which, with many other tenets of that philosopher, was adopted by the early Christians; and an ordinance of the Romish church is still extant, prohibiting having lights or making merriment in church-yards at night, lest they should disturb the souls that might come thither.—*Crawfurd*.

According to the Danish missionaries, the souls of those who are untimely slain wander about as diabolical spectres, doing evil to mankind, and possessing those whom they persecute.—NIECAMP. i, 10, sect. 14.

The inhabitants of the hills near Rajamahall believe that when God sends a messenger to summon a person to his presence, if the messenger should mistake his object, and carry off another, he is desired by the Deity to take him away; but as the earthly mansion of this soul must be decayed, it is destined to remain midway between heaven and earth, and never can return to the presence of God. Whoever commits homicide without a divine order, and whoever is killed by a snake, as a punishment for some concealed crime, will be doomed to the same state of wandering; and whoever hangs himself will wander eternally with a rope about his neck.—*Asiat. Researches.*

Pope Benedict XII drew up a list of 117 heretical opinions held by the Armenian Christians, which he sent to the king of Armenia,—instead of any other assistance, when that prince applied to him for aid against the Mahomedans. This paper was first published by Bernino, and exhibits a curious mixture of mythologies. One of their opinions was, that the souls of the adult wander about in the air till the day of judgment; neither hell, nor the heavenly, nor the terrestrial paradise, being open to them till that day shall have past.

Davenant, in one of his plays, speculates upon such a state of wandering as the lot of the soul after death:—

> I must to darkness go, hover in clouds,
> Or in remote untroubled air, silent
> As thoughts, or what is uncreated yet;
> Or I must rest in some cold shade, and shall
> Perhaps ne'er see that everlasting spring
> Of which philosophy so long has dreamt,
> And seems rather to wish than understand.
> *Love and Honour.*

I know no other author who has so often expressed to those who could understand him, his doubts respecting a future state, and how burthensome he felt them.

Note 7, page 307, col. 2.
Undying as I am!

The Soul is not a thing of which a man may say, it hath been, it is about to be, or is to be hereafter; for it is a thing without birth; it is ancient, constant, and eternal, and is not to be destroyed in this its mortal frame. How can the man who believeth that this thing is incorruptible, eternal, inexhaustible, and without birth, think that he can either kill or cause it to be killed! As a man throweth away old garments, and putteth on new, even so the Soul, having quitted its old mortal frames, entereth into others which are new. The weapon divideth it not, the fire burneth it not, the water corrupteth it not, the wind drieth it not away;—for it is indivisible, inconsumable, incorruptible, and is not to be dried away;—it is eternal, universal, permanent, immoveable; it is invisible, inconceivable, and unalterable.—BHAGVAT GEETA.

Note 8, page 307, col. 2.
It was my hour of folly.

Among the qualities required for the proper execution of public business, mention is made, « That a man must be able to keep in subjection his lust, his anger, his avarice, his *folly*, and his pride.» The folly there specified is not to be understood in the usual sense of the word in an European idiom, as a negative quality, or the mere want of sense, but as a kind of obstinately stupid lethargy, or perverse absence of mind, in which the will is not altogether passive: It seems to be a weakness peculiar to Asia, for we cannot find a term by which to express the precise idea in the European languages. It operates somewhat like the violent impulse of fear, under which men will utter falsehoods totally incompatible with each other, and utterly contrary to their own opinion, knowledge, and conviction; and, it may be added also, their inclination and intention.

A very remarkable instance of this temporary frenzy happened lately in the supreme Court of Judicature at Calcutta, where a man (not an idiot) swore, upon a trial, that he was no kind of relation to his brother, who was then in Court, and who had constantly supported him from his infancy; and that he lived in a house by himself, for which he paid the rent from his own pocket, when it was proved that he was not worth a rupee, and when the person in whose house he had always resided stood at the bar close to him.

Another conjecture, and that exceedingly acute and ingenious, has been started upon this *folly*, that it may mean the deception which a man permits to be imposed upon his judgment by his passions, as acts of rapacity and avarice are often committed by men who ascribe them to prudence and a just assertion of their own right: malice and rancour pass for justice, and brutality for spirit. This opinion, when thoroughly examined, will very nearly tally with the former; for all the passions, as well as fear, have an equal efficacy to disturb and distort the mind: But to account for the *folly* here spoken of as being the offspring of the passions, instead of drawing a parallel between it and the impulses of those passions, we must suppose the impulses to act with infinitely more violence upon an Asiatic mind than we can ever have seen exemplified in Europe. It is, however, something like the madness so inimitably delineated in the Hero of Cervantes, sensible enough upon some occasions, and at the same time completely wild, and unconscious of itself upon others; and that, too, originally produced by an effort of the will, though, in the end, overpowering and superseding its functions.—HALHED.

Note 9, page 308, col. 1.
But I, all naked feeling and raw life.

By the vital souls of those men who have committed sins in the body, another body, composed of *nerves*, *with* five sensations, in order to be susceptible of torment, shall certainly be assumed after death; and being intimately united with those minute nervous particles, according to their distribution, they shall feel in that new body the pangs inflicted in each case by the sentence of Yama.—*Inst. of Menu.*

Henry More, the Platonist, has two applicable stanzas in his Song of the Soul:—

> Like to a light fast lock'd in lanthorn dark,
> Whereby by night our wary steps we guide
> In slabby streets, and dirty channels mark,
> Some weaker rays through the black top do glide,
> And flusher streams, perhaps, from horny side;
> But when we 've past the peril of the way,
> Arrived at home, and laid that case aside,—
> The naked light how clearly doth it ray,
> And spread its joyful beams as bright as summer's day.

Even so the soul, in this contracted state,
Confined to these straight instruments of sense,
More dull and narrowly doth operate ;
At this hole hears,—the sight must ray from thence,—
Here tastes, there smells ;—but when she 's gone from hence,
Like naked lamp she is one shining sphere,
And round about has perfect cognoscence,
Whate'er in her horizon doth appear.
She is one orb of sense, all eye, all airy ear.

Amid the uncouth allegory, and more uncouth language, of this strange series of poems, a few passages are to be found of exceeding beauty. Milton, who was the author's friend, had evidently read them.

Note 10, page 308, col. 1.

Mariataly.

Mariatale, as Sonnerat spells the name, was wife of the penitent Chamadaguini, and mother of Parassouaramа, who was, in part, an incarnation of Veeshno. This goddess, says Sonnerat, commanded the elements, but could not preserve that empire longer than her heart was pure. One day, while she was collecting water out of a tank, and, according to her custom, was making a bowl of earth to carry it to the house, she saw on the surface of the water some figures of Grindovers (Glendoveers) which were flying over her head. Struck with their beauty, her heart admitted an impure thought, and the earth of the bowl dissolved. From that time she was obliged to make use of an ordinary vessel. This discovered to Chamadaguini that his wife had deviated from purity ; and in the excess of his rage, he ordered his son to drag her to the place where criminals were executed, and to behead her. The order was executed ; but Parassouramа was so much afflicted for the loss of his mother, that Chamadaguini told him to take up the body, and fasten the head upon it, and repeat a prayer (which he taught him for that purpose) in her ear, and then his mother would come to life again. The son ran eagerly to perform what he was ordered, but, by a very singular blunder, he joined the head of his mother to the body of a Parichi, who had been executed for her crimes ; a monstrous union, which gave to this woman the virtues of a goddess, and the vices of a criminal. The goddess, becoming impure by such a mixture, was driven from her house, and committed all kinds of cruelties. The Deverkels, perceiving the destruction she made, appeased her by giving her power to cure the small-pox, and promising that she should be implored for that disorder. Mariatale is the great goddess of the Parias ;—to honour her, they have a custom of dancing with several pots of water on their heads, placed one above the other : These pots are adorned with the leaves of the Margosies, a tree consecrated to her.

Note 11, page 310, col. 1.

The little songsters of the sky
Sit silent in the sultry hour.

The tufted lark, fixed to this fruitful land, says Sonnini, speaking of Egypt, never forsakes it ; it seems, however, that the excessive heat annoys him. You may see these birds, as well as sparrows, in the middle of the day, with their bills half open, and the muscles of their breasts agitated, breathing with difficulty, and as if they panted for respiration. The instinct, which induces them to prefer those means of subsistence which are easily obtained, and in abundance, although attended with some suffering, resembles the mind of man, whom a thirst for riches engages to brave calamities and dangers without number.

Note 12, page 311, col. 2.

The watchman.

The watchmen are provided with no offensive weapons excepting a sling ; on the contrary, they continue the whole day standing in one single position, upon a pillar of clay raised about ten feet, where they remain bellowing continually, that they may terrify, without hurting, the birds who feed upon the crop. Every considerable field contains several such sentinels, stationed at different corners, who repeat the call from one to another so incessantly, that the invaders have hardly any opportunity of making good a livelihood in the field.

These watchmen are forced, during the rains, to erect, instead of a clay pillar, a scaffolding of wood as high as the crop, over which they suspend a roof of straw, to shelter their naked bodies from the rain.—TENNANT.

Note 13, page 311, col. 2.

The Golden Palaces.

Every thing belonging to the Sovereign of Ava has the addition of shoe, or golden, annexed to it ; even his majesty's person is never mentioned but in conjunction with this precious metal. When a subject means to affirm that the king has heard any thing, he says, « it has reached the golden ears ;» he who obtained admission to the royal presence has been at the « golden feet.» The perfume of otta of roses, a nobleman observed one day, « was an odour grateful to the golden nose.» —SYMES.

Note 14, page 311, col. 2.

A cloud ascending in the eastern sky
Sails slowly o'er the vale,
And darkens round, and closes in the night.

At this season of the year, it is not uncommon, towards the evening, to see a small black cloud rising in the eastern part of the horizon, and afterwards spreading itself to the north-west. This phenomenon is always attended with a violent storm of wind, and flashes of the strongest and most vivid lightning and heavy thunder, which is followed by rain. These storms sometimes last for half an hour or more ; and, when they disperse, they leave the air greatly freshened, and the sky of a deep, clear, and transparent blue. When they occur near the full moon, the whole atmosphere is illuminated by a soft but brilliant silver light, attended with gentle airs. —HODGES.

Note 15, page 311, col. 2.

A white flag, flapping to the winds of night,
Marks where the tiger seiz'd his human prey.

It is usual to place a small white triangular flag, fixed to a bamboo staff, of ten or twelve feet long, at the place where a tiger has destroyed a man. It is common for the passengers, also, each to throw a stone, or brick, near the spot, so that, in the course of a little time, a pile equal to a good waggon-load is collected. This custom, as well as the fixing a rag on any particular thorn-bush, near the fatal spot, is in use likewise on various accounts. Many brambles may be seen in a day's journey, completely covered with this motley assemblage of remnants. The sight of the flags and piles of stones imparts a certain melancholy, not perhaps altogether devoid of apprehension. They may

45

be said to be of service, in pointing out the places most frequented by tigers.—*Oriental Sports*, vol. ii, p. 22.

Note 16, page 313, col. 1.

Pollear.

The first and greatest of the sons of Sevee is Pollear: he presides over marriages: The Indians build no house without having first carried a Pollear on the ground, which they sprinkle with oil, and throw flowers on it every day. If they do not invoke it before they undertake any enterprise, they believe that God will make them forget what they wanted to undertake, and that their labour will be in vain. He is represented with an elephant's head, and mounted on a rat; but in the pagodas they place him on a pedestal, with his legs almost crossed. A rat is always put before the door of his chapel. This rat was a giant, called Gudja-mouga-chourin, on whom the gods had bestowed immortality, as well as great powers, which he abused, and did much harm to mankind. Pollear, entreated by the sages and penitents to deliver them, pulled out one of his tusks, and threw it against Gudja-mouga-chourin; the tooth entered the giant's stomach, and overthrew him, who immediately changed himself into a rat as large as a mountain, and came to attack Pollear; who sprung on his back, telling him, that hereafter he should ever be his carrier.

The Indians, in their adoration of this god, cross their arms, shut the fist, and in this manner give themselves several blows on the temples; then, but always with the arms crossed, they take hold of their ears, and make three inclinations, bending the knee; after which, with their hands joined, they address their prayers to him, and strike their forehead. They have a great veneration for this deity, whose image they place in all temples, streets, highways, and, in the country at the foot of some tree; that all the world may have an opportunity of invoking him before they undertake any concern; and that travellers may make their adorations and offerings to him before they pursue their journey.—SONNERAT.

Note 17, page 313, col. 2.

The Glendoveers.

This word is altered from the *Grindouvers* of Sonnerat, who describes these celestial children of Casyapa as famous for their beauty; they have wings, he adds, and fly in the air with their wives. I do not know whether they are the *Gandharvas* of the English orientalists. The wings with which they are attired in the poem are borrowed from the neglected story of Peter Wilkins, a work of great genius. Whoever the author was, his winged people are the most beautiful creatures of imagination that ever were devised. I copy his minute description of the *graundee*, as he calls it;—Stothard has made some delightful drawings of it in the Novelist's Magazine.

« She first threw up two long branches, or ribs, of the whale-bone, as I called it before, (and indeed for several of its properties, as toughness, elasticity, and pliableness, nothing I have ever seen can so justly be compared to it,) which were jointed behind to the upper-bone of the spine, and which, when not extended, lie bent over the shoulders on each side of the neck forwards, from whence, by nearer and nearer approaches, they just meet at the lower rim of the belly in a sort of point; but, when extended, they stand their whole length above the shoulders, not perpendicularly, but spreading outwards, with a web of the softest and most pliable and spungy membrane that can be imagined in the interstices between them, reaching from their root or joint on the back up above the hinder part of the head, and near half way their own length; but, when closed, the membrane falls down in the middle upon the neck, like an handkerchief. There are also two other ribs, rising, as it were, from the same root, which, when open, run horizontally, but not so long as the others. These are filled up in the interstice between them and the upper ones with the same membrane; and on the lower side of this is also a deep flap of the membrane, so that the arms can be either above or below it in flight, and are always above it when closed. This last rib, when shut, flaps under the upper one, and also falls down with it before to the waist; but it is not joined to the ribs below. Along the whole spine-bone runs a strong, flat, broad, grisly cartilage, to which are joined several other of these ribs, all which open horizontally, and are filled in the interstices with the above membrane, and are jointed to the ribs of the person just where the plane of the back begins to turn towards the breast and belly; and, when shut, wrap the body round to the joints on the contrary side, folding neatly one side over the other.

« At the lower spine are two more ribs extended horizontally when open, jointed again to the hips, and long enough to meet the joint on the contrary side cross the belly: and from the hip-joint, which is on the outermost edge of the hip-bone, runs a pliable cartilage quite down the outside of the thigh and leg to the ancle; from which there branch out divers other ribs, horizontally also when open, but, when closed, they encompass the whole thigh and leg, rolling inwards cross the back of the leg and thigh, till they reach and just cover the cartilage. The interstices of these are filled up with the same membrane. From the two ribs which join to the lower spine-bone, there hangs down a sort of short apron, very full of plaits, from hip-joint to hip-joint, and reaches below the buttocks, half way or more to the hams. This has also several small limber ribs in it. Just upon the lower spine-joint, and above the apron, as I call it, there are two other long branches, which, when close, extend upon the back from the point they join at below to the shoulders, where each rib has a clasper, which reaching over the shoulders, just under the fold of the uppermost branch or ribs, hold up the two ribs flat to the back, like a V, the interstices, of which are filled up with the aforesaid membrane. This last piece, in flight, falls down almost to the ancles, where the two claspers, lapping under each leg within side, hold it very fast; and then, also, the short apron is drawn up, by the strength of the ribs in it, between the thighs forward, and covers as far as the rim of the belly. The whole arms are covered also from the shoulders to the wrist with the same delicate membrane, fastened to ribs of proportionable dimensions, and jointed to a cartilage on the outside in the same manner as on the legs. It is very surprising to feel the difference of these ribs when open and when closed: for closed they are as pliable as the finest whale-bone, or more so; but when extended, are as strong and stiff as a bone. They are tapering from the roots,

and are broader or narrower, as best suits the places
they occupy, and the stress they are put to, up to their
points, which are almost as small as a hair. The
membrane between them is the most elastic thing I
ever met with, occupying no more space, when the ribs
are closed, than just from rib to rib, as flat and smooth
as possible; but, when extended in some postures, will
dilate itself surprisingly.

« It is the most amazing thing in the world to observe
the large expansion of this graundee when open, and,
when closed (as it all is in a moment, upon the party's
descent), to see it fit so close and compact to the body
as no tailor can come up to it; and then the several
ribs lie so justly disposed in the several parts, that
instead of being, as one would imagine, a disadvantage
to the shape, they make the body and limbs look ex-
tremely elegant; and by the different adjustment of
their lines on the body and limbs, the whole, to my
fancy, somewhat resembles the dress of the old Roman
warriors in their buskins; and, to appearance, seems
much more noble than any fictitious garb I ever saw,
or can frame a notion of to myself.»

Note 18, page 313, col. 2.

Mount Himakoot.

Dushmanta. Say, Matali, what mountain is that which,
like an evening cloud, pours exhilarating streams, and
forms a golden zone between the western and eastern
seas?

Matali. That, O king! is the mountain of Gandharvas, named Hémacúta: The universe contains not a
more excellent place for the successful devotion of the
pious. There Casyapa, father of the immortals, ruler
of men, son of Marichi, who sprang from the self-
existent, resides with his consort Aditi, blessed in holy
retirement.—We now enter the sanctuary of him who
rules the world, and the groves which are watered by
streams from celestial sources.

Dushmanta. I see with equal amazement both the
pious and their awful retreat. It becomes, indeed, pure
spirits to feed on balmy air in a forest blooming with
trees of life; to bathe in rills dyed yellow with the gol-
den dust of the lotus, and to fortify their virtue in the
mysterious bath; to meditate in caves, the pebbles of
which are unblemished gems; and to restrain their
passions, even though nymphs of exquisite beauty fro-
lick around them. In this grove alone is attained the
summit of true piety, to which other hermits in vain
aspire.—SACONTALA.

Note 19, page 313, col. 2.

Her death predoom'd
To that black hour of midnight, when the Moon
Hath turn'd her face away,
Unwilling to behold
The unhappy end of guilt?

I will now speak to thee of that time in which, should
a devout man die, he will never return; and of that
time in which, dying, he shall return again to earth.

Those holy men who are acquainted with Brahm,
departing this life in the fiery light of day, in the bright
season of the moon, within the six months of the sun's
northern course, go unto him: but those who depart
in the gloomy night of the Moon's dark season, and
whilst the Sun is yet within the southern path of his
journey, ascend for a while into the regions of the
Moon, and again return to mortal birth. These two,

Light and Darkness, are esteemed the World's eternal
ways: he who walketh in the former path returneth
not; whilst he who walketh in the latter, cometh back
again upon the earth.—KREESHNA,—in the Bhagvat
Geeta.

Note 20, page 314, col. 1.

Indra.

The Indian God of the visible Heavens is called
Indra, or the King; and Divespetir, Lord of the Sky.
He has the character of the Roman Genius, or chief of
the Good Spirits. His consort is named Sachi; his
celestial city, Amaravati; his palace, Vaijayanta; his
garden, Nandana; his chief elephant, Airevat; his
charioteer, Matali; and his weapon, Vajra, or the
thunder-bolt. He is the regent of winds and showers,
and though the East is peculiarly under his care, yet his
Olympus is Meru, or the North Pole, allegorically re-
presented as a mountain of gold and gems. He is the
Prince of the Beneficent Genii.—Sir W. JONES.

A distinct idea of Indra, the King of Immortals, may
be collected from a passage in the ninth section of the
Geeta.

« These having, through virtue, reached the mansion
of the king of Suras, feast on the exquisite heavenly
food of the Gods; they, who have enjoyed this lofty
region of SWERGA, but whose virtue is exhausted, revisit
the habitation of mortals.»

He is the God of thunder and the five elements, with
inferior Genii under his command; and is conceived to
govern the eastern quarter of the world, but to preside,
like the Genius or Agathodæmon of the ancients, over
the celestial bands, which are stationed on the summit
of MERU, or the North Pole, where he solaces the Gods
with nectar and heavenly music.

The Cinnaras are the male dancers in SWERGA, or
the Heaven of Indra, and the Apsaras are his dancing
girls, answering to the fairies of the Persians, and to
the damsels called in the Koran hhúru lúyùn, or, with
antelopes' eyes.—Sir W. JONES.

Note 21, page 314, col. 1.

I have seen Indra tremble at his prayer,
And at his dreadful penances turn pale.

Of such penances Mr Halhed has produced a curious
specimen.

In the wood Midhoo, which is on the confines of
the kingdoms of Brege, Tarakee selected a pleasant and
beautiful spot, adorned with verdure and blossoms, and
there exerted himself in penance and mortification, ex-
ternally, with the sincerest piety, but, in reality, the
most malignant intention, and with the determined
purpose of oppressing the Devetas; penances such as
credulity itself was astonished to hear; and they are
here recounted:—

1. For a hundred years, he held up his arms and one
foot towards heaven, and fixed his eyes upon the sun
the whole time.

2. For a hundred years, he remained standing on
tiptoe.

3. For a hundred years more, he nourished himself
with nothing but water.

4. For a hundred years more he lived upon nothing
but air.

5. For a hundred years more he stood and made his
adorations in the river.

6. For a hundred years more, he made those adorations buried up to his neck in the earth.

7. For a hundred years more, enveloped with fire.

8. For a hundred years more, he stood upon his head with his feet towards heaven.

9. For a hundred years more, he stood upon the palm of one hand resting on the ground.

10. For a hundred years more, he hung by his hand from the branch of a tree.

11. For a hundred years more, he hung from a tree with his head downwards.

When he at length came to a respite from these severe mortifications, a radiant glory encircled the devotee, and a flame of fire, arising from his head, began to consume the whole world.»—*From the Seeva Pooraun,* MAURICE's *History of Hindostan.*

You see a pious Yogi, motionless as a pollard, holding his thick bushy hair, and fixing his eyes on the solar orb. Mark—his body is half covered with a white ant's edifice made of raised clay, the skin of a snake supplies the place of his sacerdotal thread, and part of it girds his loins; a number of knotty plants encircle and wound his neck, and surrounding birds'-nests almost conceal his shoulders.

Dushmanta. I bow to a man of his austere devotion. —SACONTALA.

Note 22, page 214, col. 1.

That even Seeva's self,
The Highest, cannot grant, and be secure.

It will be seen from the following fable, that Seeva had once been reduced to a very humiliating employment by one of Kehama's predecessors:

Ravana, by his power and infernal arts, had subjugated all the gods and demigods, and forced them to perform menial offices about his person and household. *Indra* made garlands of flowers to adorn him withal; *Agni* was his cook; *Surya* supplied light by day, and *Chandra* by night; *Varuna* purveyed water for the palace; *Kuvera* furnished cash. The whole *nava-graha* (the *nine planetary* spheres) sometimes arranged themselves into a ladder, by which, they serving as steps, the tyrant ascended his throne: *Brahma* (for the great gods were there also; and I give this anecdote as I find it in my memoranda, without any improved arrangement)—*Brahma* was a herald, proclaiming the giant's titles, the day of the week, month, etc. daily in the palace,—a sort of speaking almanack: *Mahadeva* (i. e. Seeva) in his Avatara of *Kandeh-roo,* performed the office of barber, and trimmed the giants' beards: *Vishnu* had the honourable occupation of instructing and drilling the dancing and singing girls, and selecting the fairest for the royal bed: *Ganesa* had the care of the cows, goats, and herds; *Vayu* swept the house; *Yama* washed the linen;—and in this manner were all the gods employed in the menial offices of *Ravana,* who rebuked and flogged them in default of industry and attention. Nor were the female divinities exempted; for *Bhavani,* in her name and form of *Satni,* was head Aya, or nurse, to Ravana's children; *Laksmi* and *Saraswati* were also among them, but it does not appear in what capacity.—MOORE's *Hindu Pantheon,* p. 333.

Seeva was once in danger even of annihilation: «In passing from the town of Silgut to Deonhully,» says Colonel Wilks, « I became accidentally informed of a sect peculiar, as I since understand, to the north-eastern parts of Mysoor, the women of which universally undergo the amputation of the first joints of the third and fourth fingers of their right hands. On my arrival at Deonhully, after ascertaining that the request would not give offence, I desired to see some of these women; and, the same afternoon, seven of them attended at my tent. The sect is a sub-division of the *Murresoo Wokul,*[1] and belongs to the fourth great class of the Hindoos, viz. the Souder. Every woman of the sect, previously to piercing the ears of her eldest daughter, preparatory to her being betrothed in marriage, must necessarily undergo this mutilation, which is performed by the blacksmith of the village, for a regulated fee, by a surgical process sufficiently rude. The finger to be amputated is placed on a block; the blacksmith places a chisel over the articulation of the joint, and chops it off at a single blow. If the girl to be betrothed is motherless, and the mother of the boy have not before been subject to the operation, it is incumbent on her to perform the sacrifice. After satisfying myself with regard to the facts of the case, I inquired into the origin of so strange a practice, and one of the women related, with great fluency, the following traditionary tale, which has since been repeated to me, with no material deviation, by several others of the sect:

«A Rachas (or giant) named *Vrica,* and in after times *Busmaa-soor,* or the giant of the ashes, had, by a course of austere devotion to *Mahadeo* (Seeva) obtained from him the promise of whatever boon he should ask. The Rachas accordingly demanded, that every person on whose head he should place his right hand, might instantly be reduced to ashes; and Mahadeo conferred the boon, without suspicion of the purpose for which it was designed.

« The Rachas no sooner found himself possessed of this formidable power, than he attempted to use it for the destruction of his benefactor. Mahadeo fled, the Rachas pursued, and followed the fugitive so closely as to chase him into a thick grove; where Mahadeo, changing his form and bulk, concealed himself in the centre of a fruit, then called *tunda pundoo,* but since named *linga tunda,* from the resemblance which its kernel thenceforward assumed to the *ling,* the appropriate emblem of Mahadeo.

«The Rachas, having lost sight of Mahadeo, inquired of a husbandman, who was working in the adjoining field, whether he had seen the fugitive, and what direction he had taken. The husbandman, who had attentively observed the whole transaction, fearful of the future resentment of Mahadeo, and equally alarmed for the present vengeance of the giant, answered aloud, that he had seen no fugitive, but pointed at the same time, with the little finger of his right hand, to the place of Mahadeo's concealment.

« In this extremity,[2] Vishnou descended, in the form of a beautiful damsel, to the rescue of Mahadeo. The Rachas became instantly enamoured;—the damsel was a *pure* Brahmin, and might not be approached by the *unclean* Rachas. By degrees she appeared to relent; and, as a previous condition to farther advances, enjoined the performance of his ablutions in a neighbour-

[1] Murresoo, or Mursoo, in the Hala Canara, signifies *rude, uncivilized;*—*Wokul,* a *husbandman.*

[2] Dignus vindice nodus.

ing pool. After these were finished, she prescribed, as a farther purification, the performance of the *Sundia*,—a ceremony in which the right hand is successively applied to the breast, to the crown of the head, and to other parts of the body. The Rachas, thinking only of love, and forgetful of the powers of his right hand, performed the *Sundia*, and was himself reduced to ashes.

« Mahadeo now issued from the *linga tunda*, and, after the proper acknowledgments for his deliverance, proceeded to discuss the guilt of the treacherous husbandman, and determined on the loss of the finger with which he had offended, as the proper punishment of his crime.

« The wife of the husbandman, who had just arrived at the field with food for her husband, hearing this dreadful sentence, threw herself at the feet of Mahadeo. She represented the certain ruin of her family, if her husband should be disabled for some months from performing the labours of the farm, and besought the Deity to accept two of her fingers, instead of one from her husband. Mahadeo, pleased with so sincere a proof of conjugal affection, accepted the exchange, and ordained, that her female posterity, in all future generations, should sacrifice two fingers at his temple, as a memorial of the transaction, and of their exclusive devotion to the God of the Ling.

« The practice is, accordingly, confined to the supposed posterity of this single woman, and is not common to the whole sect of Murresoo-Wokul. I ascertained the actual number of families who observed this practice in three successive districts through which I afterwards passed, and I conjecture that, within the limits of Mysoor, they may amount to about two thousand houses.

« The Hill of *Sectee*, in the talook of Colar, where the giant was destroyed, is (according to this tradition) formed of the ashes of Busmaa-soor: It is held in particular veneration by this sect, as the chief seat of their appropriate sacrifice; and the fact of its containing little or no moisture, is held to be a miraculous proof that the ashes of the giant continue to absorb the most violent and continued rain. This is a remarkable example of easy credulity. I have examined the mountain, which is of a sloping form, and composed of coarse granite.»—*Hist. Sketches of the South of India*, vol. i, p. 442, note.

Note 23, page 314, col. 1.
A Ship of Heaven.

I have converted the *Vimana*, or self-moving Car of the Gods, into a Ship. Captain Wilford has given the history of its invention,—and, what is more curious, has attempted to settle the geography of the story:

« A most pious and venerable sage, named RISHI'CE'-SA, being very far advanced in years, had resolved to visit, before he died, all the famed places of pilgrimage; and, having performed his resolution, he bathed at last in the sacred water of the *Ca'li*, wher ehe observed some fishes engaged in amorous play, and reflecting on their numerous progeny, which would sport like them in the stream, he lamented the improbability of leaving any children : but, since he might possibly be a father, even at his great age, he went immediately to the king of that country, HIRANYAVERNA, who had fifty daughters, and demanded one of them in marriage. So strange a demand gave the prince great uneasiness: yet he was unwilling to incur the displeasure of a saint, whose imprecations he dreaded; he, therefore, invoked *Heri*, or *Vishnu*, to inspire him with a wise answer, and told the hoar philosopher, that he should marry any one of his daughters, who, of her own accord, should fix on him as her bridegroom. The sage, rather disconcerted, left the palace; but, calling to mind the two sons of ASWINI, he hastened to their terrestrial abode, and requested that they would bestow on him both youth and beauty: they immediately conducted him to *Abhimatada*, which we suppose to be *Abydus* in Upper Egypt; and when he had bathed in the pool of *Rupayauvana*, he was restored to the flower of his age, with the graces and charms of CA'MA'DE'VA. On his return to the palace, he entered the secret apartments, called *antahpura*, where the fifty princesses were assembled; and they were all so transported with the vision of more than human beauty, that they fell into an ecstacy, whence the place was afterwards named *Mohast-han*, or *Mohana*, and is, possibly, the same with *Mohannan*. They no sooner had recovered from their trance, than each of them exclaimed, that she would be his bride; and their altercation having brought HIRANYAVERNA into their apartment, he terminated the contest by giving them all in marriage to RISHI'CE'SA, who became the father of a hundred sons; and when he succeeded to the throne, built the city of *Suc-haverdhana*, framed *vimánas*, or celestial, self-moving cars, in which he visited the gods, and made gardens abounding in delights, which rivalled the bowers of INDRA; but, having granted the desire which he formed at *Matoyasangama*, or the place where the fish were assembled, he resigned the kingdom to his eldest son HIRANYAVRIDDAH, and returned, in his former shape, to the banks of the *Ca'li*, where he closed his days in devotion.—WILFORD. *Asiatic Researches.*

Dushmanta. In what path of the winds are we now journeying?

Matali. This is the way which leads along the triple river, heaven's brightest ornament, and causes yon luminaries to roll in a circle with diffused beams: it is the course of a gentle breeze which supports the floating forms of the gods; and this path was the second step of Vishnu when he confounded the proud Bali.

* * * *

Dushmanta. The car itself instructs me that we are moving over clouds pregnant with showers; for the circumference of its wheels disperses pellucid water.

* * * *

Dushmanta. These chariot wheels yield no sound; no dust arises from them, and the descent of the car gave me no shock.

Matali. Such is the difference, O King! between thy car and that of Indra.—SACONTALA.

Note 24, page 316, col. 1.
The Raining Tree.

The island of *Fierro* is one of the most considerable of the Canaries, and I conceive that name to be given it upon this account, that its soil, not affording so much as a drop of fresh water, seems to be of *iron*; and, indeed, there is in this island neither river, nor rivulet, nor well, nor spring, save that only, towards the sea-side, there are some wells; but they lie at such a distance from the city, that the inhabitants can make no use thereof. But the great Preserver and Sustainer of all, remedies this inconvenience by a way so extraordinary, that a man will be forced to sit down and acknowledge that he gives in this an undeniable demonstration of his goodness and infinite providence.

For, in the midst of the island, there is a tree, which is the only one of its kind, inasmuch as it hath no resemblance to those mentioned by us in this relation, nor to any other known to us in Europe. The leaves of it are long and narrow, and continue in a constant verdure, winter and summer; and its branches are covered with a cloud, which is never dispelled, but resolved into a moisture, which causes to fall from its leaves a very clear water, and that in such abundance, that the cisterns, which are placed at the foot of the tree to receive it, are never empty, but contain enough to supply both men and beasts.—MANDELSLO.

Feyjoo denies the existence of any such tree, upon the authority of P. Tallandier, a French jesuit, (quoted in Mém. de Trevoux, 2715, art. 97.) who visited the island. « Assi no dudo,» he adds, « que este Fenix de las plantas es ten fingedo como el de las aves.»—Theat. Crit. Tom. ii, Disc. 2. sect 65. What authority is due to the testimony of this French jesuit I do not know, never having seen his book; but it appears, from the undoubted evidence of Glas, that its existence is believed in the Canaries, and positively affirmed by the inhabitants of Fierro itself.

« There are,» says this excellent author, « only three fountains of water in the whole island. one of them is called Acof,[1] which, in the language of the ancient inhabitants, signifies river; a name, however, which does not seem to have been given it on account of its yielding much water, for in that respect it hardly deserves the name of a fountain. More to the northward is another called Hapio; and in the middle of the island is a spring, yielding a stream about the thickness of a man's finger. This last was discovered in the year 1565, and is called the Fountain of Anton Hernandez. On account of the scarcity of water, the sheep, goats, and swine here do not drink in the summer, but are taught to dig up the roots of fern, and chew them, to quench their thirst. The great cattle are watered at those fountains, and at a place where water distils from the leaves of a tree. Many writers have made mention of this famous tree; some in such a manner as to make it appear miraculous; others again deny the existence of any such tree, among whom is Father Feyjoo, a modern Spanish author, in his Theatro Critico. But he, and those who agree with him in this matter, are as much mistaken as they who would make it appear miraculous. This is the only island of all the Canaries which I have not been in; but I have sailed with natives of Hierro, who, when questioned about the existence of this tree, answered in the affirmative.

« The author of the History of the Discovery and Conquest has given us a particular account of it, which I shall relate here at large. ' The district in which this tree stands is called Tigulahe; near to which, and in the cliff, or steep rocky ascent that surrounds the whole island, is a narrow gutter or gulley, which commences at the sea, and continues to the summit of the cliff, where it joins or coincides with a valley, which is terminated by the steep front of a rock. On the top of this rock grows a tree, called, in the language of the ancient inhabitants, Garse, i. e. Sacred or Holy Tree, which, for many years, has been preserved sound, entire, and fresh. Its leaves constantly distil such a quantity of water as is sufficient to furnish drink to every living creature in Hierro; nature having provided this remedy for the drought of the island. It is situated about a league and a half from the sea. Nobody knows of what species it is, only that it is called Til. It is distinct from other trees, and stands by itself; the circumference of the trunk is about twelve spans, the diameter four, and in height, from the ground to the top of the highest branch, forty spans: The circumference of all the branches together, is one hundred and twenty feet. The branches are thick and extended; the lowest commence about the height of an ell from the ground. Its fruit resembles the acorn, and tastes something like the kernel of a pine-nut, but is softer and more aromatic. The leaves of this tree resemble those of the laurel, but are larger, wider, and more curved; they come forth in a perpetual succession, so that the tree always remains green. Near to it grows a thorn, which fastens on many of its branches, and interweaves with them; and, at a small distance from the Garse, are some beech-trees, bresos, and thorns. On the north side of the trunk are two large tanks, or cisterns, of rough stone, or rather one cistern divided, each half being twenty feet square, and sixteen spans in depth. One of these contains water for the drinking of the inhabitants, and the other that which they use for their cattle, washing, and such like purposes. Every morning, near this part of the island, a cloud or mist arises from the sea, which the south and easterly winds force against the fore-mentioned steep cliff; so that the cloud, having no vent but by the gutter, gradually ascends it, and from thence advances slowly to the extremity of the valley, where it is stopped and checked by the front of the rock which terminates the valley, and then rests upon the thick leaves and wide-spreading branches of the tree; from whence it distils in drops during the remainder of the day, until it is at length exhausted, in the same manner that we see water drip from the leaves of trees after a heavy shower of rain. This distillation is not peculiar to the Garse, or Til, for the bresos which grow near it likewise drop water; but their leaves being but few and narrow, the quantity is so trifling, that, though the natives save some of it, yet they make little or no account of any but what distils from the Til; which, together with the water of some fountains, and what is saved in the winter season, is sufficient to serve them and their flocks. This tree yields most water in those years when the Levant, or easterly winds, have prevailed for a continuance; for by these winds only, the clouds or mists are drawn hither from the sea. A person lives on the spot near which this tree grows, who is appointed by the Council to take care of it and its water, and is allowed a house to live in, with a certain salary. He every day distributes to each family of the district seven pots or vessels full of water, besides what he gives to the principal people of the island.'

« Whether the tree which yields water at this present time be the same as that mentioned in the above description, I cannot pretend to determine, but it is probable there has been a succession of them; for Pliny, describing the Fortunate Islands, says, « In the mountains of Ombrion are trees resembling the plant Ferula, from which water may be procured by pressure: What comes

[1] In the Azanaga dialect of the Lybian tongue, Ascif signifies a river.

from the black kind is bitter, but that which the white yields is sweet and palatable.»—GLAS's *History of the Canary Islands.*

Cordeyro (*Historia Insulana*, lib. ii. c. 5.) says, that this tree resembles what in other places is called the *Til*, (*Tilia*) the Linden Tree; and he proceeds, from these three letters, to make it an emblem of the Trinity. The water, he says, was called the *Agua Santa,* and the tree itself the *Santa Arvore,*—appellations not ill bestowed. According to his account the water was delivered out in stated portions.

There is an account of a similar tree in Cockburne's Travels; but this I believe to be a work of fiction. Bernal Diaz, however, mentions one as growing at Naco, in Honduras, « Que en mitad de la siesta, por recio sol que hiziesse, parecia que la sombra del arbol refrescava el corazon, caia del uno como rozio muy delgada que confortava las cabezas.»—206.

There may be some exaggeration in the accounts of the Fierro Tree, but that the story has some foundation I have no doubt. The islanders of St Thomas say, that they have a sort of trees whose leaves continually are distilling water. (*Barbot. in Churckle.* 405.) It is certain that a dew falls in hot weather from the lime,—a fact of which any person may easily convince himself. The same property has been observed in other English trees, as appears by the following extract from the Monthly Magazine:

« In the beginning of August, after a sun-shine day, the air became suddenly misty about six o'clock; I walked, however, by the road-side from seven to eight, and observed, in many places, that a shower of big drops of water was falling under the large trees, although no rain fell elsewhere. The road and path continued dusty, and the field-gates showed no signs of being wetted by the mist. I have often noticed the like fact, but have not met with a satisfactory explanation of this power in trees to condense mist.»

I am not the only poet who was availed himself of the Fierro Tree. It is thus introduced in the Columbus of Carrara,—a singular work, containing, amid many extravagancies, some passages of rare merit:

Ecce autem inspector miri dum devius ignis
Fertur, in occursum miræ magis incidit undæ.
Æquoris in medio diffusi largiter arbor
Stabat, opaca, ingens, ævoque intecta priori,
Grata quies Nymphis, et grata colentibus umbram
Alitibus sedes, quarum vox blanda nec ullâ
Musicus arte canor sylvam resonare docebat.
Auditor primum rari modulaminis, atque
Cominus admovit gressum, spectator et hæsit;
Namque videbat, uti de cortice, deque supernis
Crinibus, argentum guttatim mitteret humens
Truncus, et ignaro plueret Jove; morque serenus
In concham caderet subjecti marmoris imber.
Donec ibi in fontem collectis undique rivis
Cresceret, atque ipso jam non ingratus ab ortu
Redderet humorem matri, quæ commodat umbram.

Dum stat, et quærit, cur internodia possit
Unda; per et fibras, virides et serpere rugas,
Et ferri sursum, genio ducente deorsum;
Adstitit en Nympha; dubitat decernere, Nais,
Anne Dryas, custos num fontis, an arboris esset;
Verius ut credam, Genius sub imagine Nymphæ
Ille loci fuerat. Quam præstantiss.mus Heros
Protinus ut vidit, Parce, o pulcherrima, dixit,
Si miser, et vestras ejectus nuper ad oras
Naufragus, idem audax videor fortasse rogando.
Dic age, quas labi video de stipite, lymphæ
Montibus anne cadant, per operta foramina ductæ,

Mox trabis irriguæ saliant in frondea sursum
Brachia, ramalesque tubos; genitalia an alvus
Umbrosæ genitricis alat; ceu sæpe videmus
Balsama de truncis, stillare electra racemis.
Pandere ne grave sit cupienti noscere causam
Vilia quæ vobis usus miracula fecit.

Hæc ubi dicta, silet. Tum Virgo ita reddidit, Hospes
Quisquis es (eximium certe præsentia prodit),
Deciperis, si forte putas, quas aspicis undas
Esse satas terra; procul omni a sede remota
Mira arbos, uni debet sua munera Cœlo.
Quâ ratione tamen capiat, quia noscere gestis
Edicam; sed dicendis ne tædia repant,
Hic locus, hæc eadem, de quâ cantabitur, arbor
Dat tempestivam blandis affatibus umbram:
Hic una sedeamus;—et ambo fontis ad undam
Consedere; dehinc intermittente parumper
Concentu volucrum, placido sic incipit ore.

Nomine Canariæ, de quâ tenet Insula nomen
Virgo fuit, non ore minus, quam prædita rarê
Laude pudicitiæ, mirum quæ pectore votum
Clausit, ut esse eadem genitrix et Virgo cuperet.
At quia in Urbe satam fuerat sortita parentem
Ortum rure Patrem, diversis moribus hausit
Hinc sylvæ austeros, teneros hinc Urbis amores
Sæpe ubi visendi studio convenerat Urbes,
Et dare blanditias natis et sumere matres
Viderat ante fores, ut mater amavit amari.
Sæpe ubi rure fuit de nymphis una Dianæ,
Viderat atque Deam thalami consorte carentem,
Esse Deæ similis, nec amari ut mater amavit.
Sed quid agat? cernit fieri non posse quod optat;
Non optare tamen, crudelius urit amantem.
Noctis erat medium : quo nos sumus, hoc erat illa
Forte loco, Cœloque videns splendescere Lunam,
O Dea, cui triplicis concessa potentia regni,
Parce precor, dixit, si quæ nunc profero, non sum
Ausa prius; quod non posses audire Diana,
Cum sis Luna potes; tenebræ minuere pudorem.
Est mihi Virginitas, fateor, re charior omni,
Attamen, hâc salvâ, fœcundæ si quoque Matris
Nomina miscerem, duplici de nomine quantam
Ambitiosa forem; certe non parva voluptas
Me caperet, coram si quis me luderet infans
Si mecum gestu, mecum loqueretur ocellis,
Cumque potest, quacumque potest, me voce vocaret,
Cujus et in vultu multum de matre viderem.
Ni sinat hoc humana tamen natura licere,
Fiat quâ ratione potest; mutare figuram
Nil refert, voti compos si denique fiam.
Annuit oranti facilis Dea; Virgine digna
Et quia vota tulit, Virgo probat. Eligit ergo
De grege Plantarum ligni quæ cœlibis esset.
Visa fuit Platanus: placet hæc; si veritat in istam
Canariæ corpus, sibi tempus in omne futuram
Tam caram esse videt, quam sit sua laurea Phœbo.
Nec mora, poscenti munus, ne signa decessent
Certa dati, movit falcatæ cornua frontis.
Virginis extemplo cœpere rigere crura
Tenvia vestiri duro præcordia libro,
Ipsaque miratur, cervix quod eburnea, quantum
It Cœlo, tantum tendant in Tartara plantæ;
Et jam formosâ de Virgine stabat et Arbos
Non formosa minus; qui toto in corpore pridem
Par ebori fuerat, candor quoque cortice mansit.
Sed deerat conjux uxoris moribus æque
Integer et cœlebs, et Virginitatis amator,
Quo fœcunda foret; verum tellure petendus
Non hic, ab axe fuit. Quare incorruptus et idem
Purior e cunctis stellatæ noctis alumnis
Poscitur Hersophorus, sic Graii nomine dicunt,
Rorem Itali. Quocumque die (quis credere posset?)
Tamquam ex condito cum Sol altissimus extat,
Sydereus conjux nebulæ velatus amicta
Labitur huc, niveisque maritam amplectitur alis:
Quodque fidem superat, parvo post tempora fœtum
Concipit, et parvo post tempore parturit arbor.
Molle puerperium vis noscere? consule fontem,
Qui nos propter adest, in quo mixtura duorum
Agnosci possit, splendet materque paterque.
Læta fovet genitrix, compos jam facta cupiti;

The Walking-Leaf would have been better than the Canary Bird.

Note 25, page 316, col. 2.

Nared.

A very distinguished son of Brahma, named Nared, bears a strong resemblance to Hermes or Mercury: he was a wise legislator, great in arts and in arms, an eloquent messenger of the Gods either to one another, or to favoured mortals, and a musician of exquisite skill. His invention of the *Vina*, or Indian lute, is thus described in the poem entitled *Magha* : « Nared sat watching from time to time his large *Vina*, which by the impulse of the breeze, yielded notes that pierced successively the regions of his ear, and proceeded by musical intervals."—*Asiatic Researches*, Sir W. JONES.

The *Vina* is an Æolian harp. The people of Amboyna have a different kind of Æolian instrument, which is thus described in the first account of D'Entrecasteaux's Voyage : « Being on the sea-shore, I heard some wind-instruments, the harmony of which, though sometimes very correct, was intermixed with discordant notes that were by no means unpleasing. These sounds, which were very musical, and formed fine cadences, seemed to come from such a distance, that I for some time imagined the natives were having a concert beyond the road-stead, near a myriameter from the spot where I stood. My ear was greatly deceived respecting the distance, for I was not an hundred meters from the instrument. It was a bamboo at least twenty meters in height, which had been fixed in a vertical situation by the sea-side. I remarked between each knot a slit about three centimeters long by a centimeter and a half wide; these slits formed so many holes, which, when the wind introduced itself into them, gave agreeable and diversified sounds. As the knots of this long bamboo were very numerous, care had been taken to make holes in different directions, in order that, on whatever side the wind blew, it might always meet with some of them. I cannot convey a better idea of the sound of this instrument, than by comparing them to those of the Harmonica."—LABILLARDIERE. *Voyage in Search of La Perouse.*

Nareda, the mythological offspring of *Saraswati*, pa-troness of music, is famed for his talents in that science. So great were they, that he became presumptuous; and, emulating the divine strains of *Krishna*, he was punished by having his *Vina* placed in the paws of a bear, whence it emitted sounds far sweeter than the minstrelsy of the mortified musician. I have a picture of this joke, in which *Krishna* is forcing his reluctant friend to attend to his rough-visaged rival, who is ridiculously touching the chords of poor *Nareda's Vina*, accompanied by a brother bruin on the cymbals. Krishna passed several practical jokes on his humble and affectionate friend: he metamorphosed him once into a woman, at another time into a bear.—MOORE's *Hindu Pantheon*, p. 204.

Note 26, page 317, col. 2.

------ The sacrifice
That should, to men and gods, proclaim him Lord
And Sovereign Master of the vassal World.

The Raisoo Yug, or Feast of Rajahs, could only be performed by a monarch who had conquered all the other sovereigns of the world.—HALHED. *Note to the Life of Creeshna.*

Note 27, page 317, col. 2.

Sole Rajah, the Omnipotent below.

No person has given so complete a sample of the absurdity of oriental titles as the Dutch traveller Struys, in his enumeration of "the proud and blasphemous titles of the King of Siam,—they will hardly bear sense," says the translator, in what he calls, by a happy blunder, "the idiotism of our tongue."

The Alliance, written with letters of fine gold, being full of godlike glory. The most Excellent, containing all wise sciences. The most Happy, which is not in the world among men. The Best and most Certain that is in Heaven, Earth, and Hell. The greatest Sweet, and friendly Royal Word: whose powerful sounding properties and glorious fame range through the world, as if the dead were raised by a godlike power, and wonderfully purged from ghostly and corporal corruption. At this both spiritual and secular men admire with a special joy, whereas no dignity may be herewith compared. Proceeding from a friendly illustrious, inconquerable, most mighty and most high Lord; and a royal Crown of Gold, adorned with nine sorts of precious stones. The greatest, clearest, and most godlike Lord of unblameable Souls. The most Holy, seeing every where, and protecting Sovereign of the city JUDIA, whose many streets and open gates are thronged by troops of men, which is the chief metropolis of the whole world, the royal throne of the earth, that is adorned with nine sorts of stones and most pleasant valleys. He who guides the reins of the world, and has a house more than the Gods of fine gold and of precious stones; they the godlike Lords of thrones and of fine gold; the White, Red, and Round-tayl'd Elephants,—which excellent creatures are the chiefest of the nine sorts of Gods. To none hath the divine Lord given, in whose hand is the victorious sword; who is like the fiery-armed God of Battails, to the most illustrious.

The second is as blasphemous as the first, though hardly swells so far out of sense.

The highest PADUCCO SYRY SULTAN, NELMONAM WELGACA, NELMOCHADIM MAGIVIITHA, JOUKEN DER

EAUTEN ALLAULA FYLAN, King of the whole world; who makes the water rise and flow. A King that is like a God, and shines like the Sun at noon-day. A King that gives a glance like the Moon when it is at full. Elected of God to be worthy as the North Star, being of the race and offspring of the great Alexander; with a great understanding, as a round orb, that tumbles hither and thither, able to guess at the depth of the great sea. A King that hath amended all the funerals of the departed Saints, and is as righteous as God, and of such power that all the world may come and shelter under his wings. A King that doth right in all things, as the Kings of old have done. A King more liberal than all Kings. A King that hath many mines of gold that God hath lent him; who hath built temples half gold and half brass; sitting upon a throne of pure gold, and of all sorts of precious stones. A King of the white Elephant, which Elephant is the King of all Elephants, before whom many thousands of other Elephants must bow and fall upon their knees. He whose eyes shine like the morning-star. A King that hath Elephants with four teeth, red, purple, and pied. Elephants, ay, and a BYYTENAQUES Elephant; for which God has given him many and divers sorts of apparel wrought with most fine gold, ennobled with many precious stones: and, besides these, so many Elephants used in battel, having harnesses of iron, their teeth tipt with steel, and their harnesses laid over with shining brass. A King that has many hundred horses, whose trappings are wrought with fine gold, and adorned with precious stones of every sort that are found in the universal world where the Sun shines, and these shod with fine gold: besides so many hundred horses that are used in war of every kind. A King who has all Emperours, Kings, Princes, and Sovereigns in the whole world, from the rising to the going down of the sun, under subjection;—and such as can obtain his favour are by him promoted to great honour; but on the contrary, such as revolt, he burns with fire. A King who can show the power of God, and whatever God has made.

And so, by this time, I hope you have heard enough of a King of Elephants and Horses, though not a word of his Asses.—STRUYS.

Note 28, page 317, col. 2.

The Sacrifice.

The *Aswamedha*, or sacrifice of a horse. Considerable difficulties usually attended that ceremony; for the consecrated horse was to be set a liberty for a certain time, and followed at a distance by the owner, or his champion, who was usually one of his near kinsmen; and, if any person should attempt to stop it in its rambles, a battle must inevitably ensue; besides, as the performer of a hundred *Aswamedhas* became equal to the God of the firmament, *Indra* was perpetually on the watch, and generally carried off the sacred animal by force or by fraud. —WILFORD. *Asiat. Res.*

Mr Halhed gives a very curious account of this remarkable sacrifice:

« The Ashum-meed-Jugg does not merely consist in the performance of that ceremony which is open to the inspection of the world, namely, in bringing a horse and sacrificing him; but Ashum-meed is to be taken in a mystic signification, as implying that the sacrificer must look upon himself to be typified in that horse, such as he shall be described, because the religious duty of the Ashum-meed-Jugg comprehends all those other religious duties, to the performance of which all the wise and holy direct all their actions, and by which all the sincere professors of every different faith aim at perfection: The mystic signification thereof is as follows:

« The head of that unblemished horse is the symbol of the morning; his eyes are the sun; his breath the wind; his wide-opening mouth is the Bishwaner, or that innate warmth which invigorates all the world: His body typifies one entire year; his back paradise; his belly the plains; his hoof this earth; his sides the four quarters of the heavens; the bones thereof the intermediate spaces between the four quarters; the rest of his limbs represent all distinct matter; the places where those limbs meet, or his joints, imply the months and halves of the months, which are called *peche* (or fortnights): His feet signify night and day; and night and day are of four kinds, 1. The night and day of Birhma, 2. The night and day of angels, 3. The night and day of the world of the spirits of deceased ancestors, 4. The night and day of mortals; these four kinds are typified in his four feet. The rest of his bones are the constellations of the fixed stars, which are the twenty-eight stages of the moon's course, called the Lunar year; his flesh is the clouds; his food the sand; his tendons the rivers; his spleen and his liver the mountains; the hair of his body the vegetables, and his long hair the trees; the fore part of his body typifies the first half of the day, and the hinder part the latter half; his yawning is the flash of the lightning, and his turning himself is the thunder of the cloud: His urine represents the rain, and his mental reflection is his only speech. The golden vessels, which are prepared before the horse is let loose, are the light of the day, and the place where those vessels are kept is a type of the Ocean of the East; the silver vessels, which are prepared after the horse is let loose, are the light of the night; and the place where those vessels are kept is a type of the Ocean of the West: these two sorts of vessels are always before and after the horse. The Arabian horse, which, on account of his swiftness, is called Hy, is the performer of the journies of angels; the Tajee, which is of the race of Persian horses, is the performer of the journies of the Kundherps (or good spirits); the Wazba, which is of the race of the deformed Tazee horses, is the performer of the journies of the Jins, (or demons;) and the Ashoo, which is of the race of Turkish horses, is the performer of the journies of mankind. This one horse, which performs these several services, on account of his four different sorts of riders, obtains the four different appellations. The place where this horse remains is the great ocean, which signifies the great spirit of Perm-Atma, or the Universal Soul, which proceeds also from that Perm-Atma, and is comprehended in the same Perm-Atma. The intent of this sacrifice is, that a man should consider himself to be in the place of that horse, and look upon all these articles as typified in himself; and, conceiving the Atma (or divine soul) to be an ocean, should let all thought of self be absorbed in that Atma.»—HALHED, *from Darul Shekuh.*

Compare this specimen of eastern sublimity with the description of the horse in Job! Compare it also with the account of the Bengal horses, in the very amusing work of Captain Williamson,—« which said horses,» he says, « have generally Roman noses, and sharp narrow foreheads, much white in their eyes, ill-shaped ears, square

46

heads, thin necks, narrow chests, shallow girths, lank bellies, cat hams, goose rumps, and switch tails.»—*Oriental Sports*, vol. ii, p. 206.

Note 29, page 318, col. 2.
The Bowl that in its vessel floats.

The day and night are here divided into four quarters, each of six hours, and these again into fifteen parts, of twenty-four minutes each. For a chronometer they use a kind of dish of thin brass, at the bottom of which there is a little hole, this is put into a vessel with water, and it runs full in a certain time. They begin their first quarter at six in the morning. They strike the quarters and subdivisions of time with a wooden hammer, upon a flat piece of iron or steel, of about ten inches in diameter, which is called a *garnial,* and gives a pretty smart sound, which can be heard at some distance. The quarters are first struck, and then as many times as the brass dish has run full in that quarter. None but the chief men of a district are allowed to have a *garnial,* and still they may not strike the first division of the first quarter, which is a privilege reserved to the nabob alone. Those who attend at these clocks must be of the Bramin cast.—STAVORINUS.

Note 30, page 318, col. 2.
Lo, the time-taper's flame, ascending slow, Creeps up its coil.

They make a sort of paste of the dust of a certain sort of wood, (the learned and rich men of sandal, eagle-wood, and others that are odoriferous,) and of this paste they make sticks of several sorts, drawing them through a hole, that they may be of an equal thickness. They commonly make them one, two, or three yards long, about the thickness of a goose-quill, to burn in the pagods before their idols, or to use like a match to convey fire from one thing to another. These sticks or ropes they coil, beginning at the centre, and so form a spiral conical figure, like a fisherman's wheel, so that the last circle shall be one, two or three spans diameter, and will last one, two, or three days, or more, according as it is in thickness. There are of them in the temples that last ten, twenty, and thirty days. This thing is hung up by the centre, and is lighted at the lower end, whence the fire gently and insensibly runs round all the coil, on which there are generally five marks, to distinguish the five parts of the night. This method of measuring time is so exact and true, that they scarce ever find any considerable mistake in it. The learned travellers, and all others, who will rise at a certain hour to follow their business, hang a little weight at the mark that shews the hour they have a mind to rise at, which, when the fire comes thither, drops into a brass bason set under it: and so the noise of it falling awakes them, as our alarum-clocks do.—GEMELLI CARERI.

Note 31, page 319, col. 1.
At noon the massacre begun, And night clos'd in before the work of death was done.

Of such massacres the ancient and modern history of the East supply but too many examples. One may suffice:

After the surrender of the Ilbars Khan, Nadir prohibited his soldiers from molesting the inhabitants; but their rapacity was more powerful than their habits of obedience, or even their dread of his displeasure, and they accordingly began to plunder. The instant Nadir heard of their disobedience, he ordered the offenders to be brought before him, and the officers were beheaded in his presence, and the private soldiers dismissed with the loss of their ears and noses. The executioners toiled till sun-set, when he commanded the headless trunks with their arms to be carried to the main-guard, and there to be exposed for two days, as an example to others. I was present the whole time, and saw the wonderful hand of God, which employs such instruments for the execution of his divine vengeance; although not one of the executioners was satisfied with Nadir Shah, yet nobody dared to disobey his commands:—a father beheaded his son, and a brother a brother, and yet presumed not to complain.—ABDUL KURREEM.

Note 32, page 319, col. 2.
Behold his lowly home, By yonder broad-bough'd plane o'ershaded.

The plane-tree, that species termed the *Platanus Orientalis,* is commonly cultivated in Kashmire, where it is said to arrive at a greater perfection than in other countries. This tree, which in most parts of Asia is called the *Chinar,* grows to the size of an oak, and has a taper straight trunk, with a silver-coloured bark; and its leaf, not unlike an expanded hand, is of a pale green. When in full foliage, it has a grand and beautiful appearance; and, in the hot weather, it affords a refreshing shade.—FORSTER.

Note 33, page 319, col. 2.
The marriage-bower.

The Pandal is a kind of arbour or bower raised before the doors of young married women. They set up two or three poles, seven or eight foot in length, round which the leaves of the Pisan-tree, the symbol of joy, are entwined. These poles support others that are laid cross-ways, which are covered with leaves in order to form a shade. The Siriperes are allowed to set up no more than three pillars, and the infringing of this custom would be sufficient to cause an insurrection.—A. ROGER, *in Picart.*

Note 34, page 319, col. 2.
The market-flag.

Many villages have markets on particular days, when not only fruits, grain, and the common necessaries of life are sold, but occasionally manufactures of various descriptions. These markets are well known to all the neighbouring country, being on appointed days of the week, or of the lunar month; but, to remind those who may be travelling of their vicinity to the means of supply, a *naugaurah,* or large kettle-drum, is beat during the forenoon, and a small flag, usually of white linen, with some symbolic figure in colours, or with a coloured border, is hoisted on a very long bamboo, kept upright by means of ropes fastened to pins driven into the ground. The flags of Hindoo villages are generally square and plain; those of the Mussulmans towns are ordinarily triangular, and bear the type of their religion, viz. a double-bladed scymitar.—*Oriental Sports,* vol. i, p. 100.

Note 35, page 320, col. 1.
There, from the intolerable heat, The buffaloes retreat.

About noon, in hot weather, the buffalo throws herself into the water or mud of a tank, if there be one accessible at a convenient distance; and leaving nothing above water but her nose, continues there for five or six hours, or until the heat abates.—BUCHANAN.

In the hot season, when water becomes very scarce, the buffaloes avail themselves of any puddle they may find among the covers, wherein they roll and rub themselves, so as in a short time to change what was at first a shallow flat, into a deep pit, sufficient to conceal their own bulk. The humidity of the soil, even when the water may have been evaporated, is particularly gratifying to these animals, which cannot bear heat, and which, if not indulged in a free access to the water, never thrive.—*Oriental Sports*, vol. i, p. 259.

The buffalo not only delights in the water, but will not thrive unless it have a swamp to wallow in. There rolling themselves, they speedily work deep hollows, wherein they lay immersed. No place seems to delight the buffalo more than the deep verdure on the confines of jiels and marshes, especially if surrounded by tall grass, so as to afford concealment and shade, while the body is covered by the water. In such situations they seem to enjoy a perfect ecstacy, having in general nothing above the surface but their eyes and nostrils, the horns being kept low down, and consequently entirely hidden from view.—*Oriental Sports*, vol. ii, p. 49.

Captain Beaver describes these animals as to be found during the heat of the day in the creeks and on the shores of the island of Bulama, almost totally immerged in water, little more than their heads appearing above it.

Note 36, page 320, col. 2.
Mount Meru.

According to the orthodox Hindus, the globe is divided into two hemispheres, both called *Meru;* but the superior hemisphere is distinguished by the name of *Sumeru*, which implies beauty and excellence, in opposition to the lower hemisphere, or *Cumeru*, which signifies the reverse: By *Meru*, without any adjunct, they generally mean the higher or northern hemisphere, which they describe with a profusion of poetic imagery as the seat of delights: while they represent *Cumeru* as the dreary habitation of demons, in some parts intensely cold, and in others so hot that the waters are continually boiling. In strict propriety, Meru denotes the pole and the polar regions; but it is the celestial north pole round which they place the gardens and metropolis of *Indra*, while *Yama* holds his court in the opposite polar circle, or the station of *Asuras*, who warred with the *Suras*, or gods of the firmament.—WILFORD. *Asiatic Researches*.

In the *Vaya Purana*, we are told, that the water, or *Ogha* of the ocean, coming down from heaven like a stream of *Amrita* upon *Meru*, encircles it through seven channels, for the space of 84,000 *Yojanas*, and then divides into four streams, which, falling from the immense height of Meru, rest themselves in four lakes, from which they spring over the mountains through the air, just brushing the summits. This wild account was not unknown in the west; for this passage is translated almost verbally, by Pliny and Q. Curtius, in speaking of the Ganges. *Cum magno fragore ipsius statim fontis Ganges erumpit, et magnorum montium juga recto alveo stringit, et ubi primum mollis planities contingat, in quodam lacu hospitatur.* The words in Italics are from Pliny (vi, c. 18.) the others from Cur-

tius (viii, c. 9.)—Capt. WILFORD. *As. Res.* vol. viii, p. 322. Calcutta edition.

The Swarganga, or Mandacini, rises from under the feet of Veeshno, at the polar star, and, passing through the circle of the moon, it falls upon the summit of Meru; where it divides into four streams, flowing toward the four cardinal points. These four branches pass through four rocks, carved into the shape of four heads of different animals. The Ganges running towards the south passes through a cow's head: to the west is a horse's head, from which flows the Chaashu or Oxus; towards the east is the head of an elephant, from which flows the river Sita; and to the north is a lion's head, from which flows the Bhadrasama.—WILFORD. *As. Res.* v. viii, p. 317. Calcutta edition.

The mountains through which the Ganges flows at Hurdwar, present the spectator with the view of a grand natural amphitheatre; their appearance is rugged and destitute of verdure; they run in ridges and bluff points, in a direction east and west: At the back of the largest range, rise, towering to the clouds, the lofty mountains of Himmalayah, whose tops are covered with perpetual snow, which, on clear days, present a most sublime prospect. Their large jagged masses, broken into a variety of irregular shapes, added to their stupendous height, impress the mind with an idea of antiquity and grandeur coeval with the creation; and the eternal frost with which they are encrusted appears to preclude the possibility of mortals ever attaining their summit.

In viewing this grand spectacle of nature, the traveller may easily yield his assent to, and pardon the superstitious veneration of the Hindoo votary, who, in the fervour of his imagination, assigns the summit of these icy regions as the abode of the great Mahadeo, or First Cause, where, seated on his throne of ice, he is supposed to receive the homage of the surrounding universe.—FRANKLIN's *Life of George Thomas*, p. 41.

At Gangottara, three small streams fall down from impassable snowy precipices, and unite into a small bason below, which is considered by the Hindus as the source of the Ganges, over which, at that place, a man can step. This is one of the five *Tirthas*, or stations, more eminently sacred than the rest upon this sacred river. Narayana Shastri, who gave this account, had visited it.—BUCHANAN.

The mountain, called Cailasa Cungri, is exceedingly lofty. On its summit there is a Bhowjputr tree, from the root of which sprouts or gushes a small stream, which the people say is the source of the Ganges, and that it comes from Vaicont'ha, or Heaven, as is also related in the Puranas; although this source appears to the sight to flow from the spot where grows this Bhowjputr tree, which is at an ascent of some miles; and yet above this there is a still loftier summit, where no one goes: But I have heard that, on that uppermost pinnacle, there is a fountain or cavity, to which a Jogui somehow penetrated, who, having immersed his little finger in it, it became petrified.—PURANA POORI. *Asiatic Researches*.

Respecting the true source of the Ganges much uncertainty still prevails. In vain one of the most powerful sovereigns of Indostan, the emperor Acbar, at the close of the sixteenth century, sent a number of men, an army of discoverers, provided with every necessary, and the most potent recommendations, to explore the course of the mighty river which adorned and fertilized the vast extent of his dominions. They were not able to penetrate beyond the famous *Mouth of the Cow.* This is an immense aperture, in a ridge of the mountains of Thibet, to which the natives of India have given this appellation, from the fancied or real resemblance of the rocks which form the stupendous chasm, to the mouth of an animal esteemed sacred throughout Indostan from the remotest antiquity. From this opening the Ganges, precipitating itself into a large and deep bason at the foot of the mountains, forms a cataract, which is called Gangotri. The impracticability of scaling these precipitous rocks, and advancing beyond this formidable pass, has prevented the tracing whence this rushing mass of water takes its primary rise.—WILCOCKE, *Note to Stavorinus.*

Note 37, page 321, col. 1.
The birth of Ganges.

I am indebted to Sir William Jones's Hymn to Ganga for this fable:

Above the stretch of mortal ken,
On bless'd *Cailasu's* top, where every stem
Glow'd with a vegetable gem,
Mahe'sa stood, the dread and joy of men ;
While Párvati, to gain a boon,
Fix'd on his locks a beamy moon,
And hid his frontal eye in jocund play,
With reluctant sweet delay.
All nature straight was lock'd in dim eclipse,
Till *Brahmans* pure, with hallow'd lips,
And warbled prayers, restored the day ;
When Ganga from his brow, by heavenly fingers press'd,
Sprang radiant, and, descending, graced the caverns of the west.

The descent of the Ganges is related in the Ramayuna, one of the most celebrated of the sacred books of the Bramins. This work the excellent and learned Baptist missionaries at Serampore are at this time employed in printing and translating; one volume has arrived in Europe, and from it I am tempted here to insert an extract of considerable length. The reader will be less disposed to condemn the fictions of Kehama as extravagant, when he compares them with this genuine specimen of Hindoo fable. He will perceive, too, that no undue importance has been attributed to the Horse of the Sacrifice in the Poem.

" The son of Kooshika having, in mellifluous accents, related these things to Rama, again addressed the descendant of Kakootitha. Formerly, O hero! there was a king of Hyoodhya, named Sugura, the Sovereign of Men, virtuous, desirous of children, but childless; O Rama! the daughter of Vidurbhakeshinee, virtuous, attached to truth, was his chief consort, and the daughter of Urishtunemi, Soomuti, unequalled in beauty, his second spouse. With these two consorts, the great king, going to Himuvat, engaged in sacred austerities on the mountain in whose sacred stream Bhrigoo constantly bathed. A hundred years being completed, the sage Bhrigoo, clothed with truth, rendered propitious by his austerities, granted him this blessing: O sinless One! thou shalt obtain a most numerous progeny; thy fame, O chief of men! will be unparalleled in the universe. From one of thy consorts, O sire! shall spring the founder of thy race, and, from the other, sixty thousand sons.

" The queens, pleased, approached the chief of men who was thus speaking, and, with hands respectfully joined, asked, O Brahman! whose shall be the one son, and who shall produce the multitude? We, O Brahman! desire to hear. May thy words be verified. Hearing their request, the most virtuous Bhrigoo replied in these admirable words : Freely say which of these favours ye desire, whether the one, founder of the family, or the multitude of valiant, renowned, energetic sons. O Rama! son of Rughoo, Keshinee hearing the words of the sage, in the presence of the king accepted the one son, the founder of the family ; and Soomuti, sister of Soopurna, accepted the sixty thousand sons, active and renowned. The king, O son of Rughoo! having respectfully circumambulated the sage, bowing the head, returned with his spouses to his own city.

" After some time had elapsed, his eldest spouse Keshinee bore to Sugura a son, named Usumunja; and Soomuti, O chief of men ! brought forth a gourd, from which, on its being opened, came forth sixty thousand sons. These, carefully brought up by their nurses, in jars filled with clarified butter, in process of time attained the state of youth; [1] and, after a long period, the sixty thousand sons of Sugura, possessed of youth and beauty, became men. The eldest son, the offspring of Sugura, O son of Rughoo! chief of men, seizing children, would throw them into the waters of the Suruyoo, and sport himself with their drowning pangs. This evil person, the distresser of good men, devoted to the injury of the citizens, was by his father expelled from the city. The son of Usumunja, the heroic Ungshooman, in conversation courteous and affectionate, was esteemed by all.

" After a long time, O chief of men! Sugura formed the steady resolve, (I will perform a sacrifice.) Versed in the Veda, the king, attended by his instructors, having determined the things relating to the sacrificial work, began to prepare the sacrifice.

" Hearing the words of Vishwa-mitra, the son of Rughoo, highly gratified in the midst of the story, addressed the sage, bright as the ardent flame, Peace be to Thee : I desire, O Brahman ! to hear this story at large, how my predecessors performed the sacrifice. Hearing his words, Vishwa-mitra, smiling, pleasantly replied to Rama : " Attend, then, O Rama ! to the story of Sugura, repeated at full length. Where the great mountain Himuvat, the happy father-in-law of Shunkura, and the mountain Bindhyo, overlooking the country around, proudly vie with each other, there was the sacrifice of the great Sugura performed. That land, sacred and renowned, is the habitation of Rakshuses. At the command of Sugura, the hero Ungshooman, O Rama ! eminent in archery, a mighty charioteer, was the attendant (of the horse.)[2] While the king was performing the sacrifice, a serpent, assuming the form of Ununta, rose from the earth, and seized the sacrificial horse. The sacrificial victim being stolen, all the priests, O son of Rughoo! going to the king, said, Thy consecrated horse has been stolen by some one in the form of a serpent. Kill the thief, and bring back the sacred horse. This interruption in the sacrifice portends evil to us all. Take those steps, O king! which may

---

[1] The Hindoos call a child *Bala,* till it attains the age of fifteen years old. From the sixteenth year to the fiftieth, *Youvuna,* or a state of youth, is supposed to continue. Each of these has several subdivisions; and in certain cases the period admits of variation, as appears to have been the case here.

[2] The horse intended for the sacrifice.

lead to the completion of the sacrifice. Having heard the advice of his instructors, the king, calling his sixty thousand sons into the assembly, said, I perceive that the Rakshuses have not been to this great sacrifice. A sacrifice of the Nagas is now performing by the sages, and some god, in the form of a serpent, has stolen the devoted horse. Whoever he be, who, at the time of the Deeksha, has been the cause of this afflictive circumstance, this unhappy event, whether he be gone to Patala, or whether he remain in the waters, kill him, O sons! and bring back my victim. May success attend you, O my sons! At my command traverse the sea-girt earth, digging with mighty labour, till you obtain a sight of the horse; each one piercing the earth to the depth of a yojuna, go you in search of him who stole the sacred horse. Being consecrated by the Deeksha, I, with my grandson and my teachers, will remain with the sacrifice unfinished, till I again behold my devoted horse.

« Thus instructed by their father Sugura, they, in obedience to him, went with cheerful mind, O Rama! to the bottom of the earth. The strong ones, having gone over the earth without obtaining a sight of the horse, each of these mighty men pierced the earth, to the depth of a yojuna, with their mighty arm, the stroke of which resembled the thunder-bolt. Pierced by Kooddalas,[1] by Purighas,[2] by Shoolas,[3] by Mooshulas,[4] and Shuktis,[5] the earth cried out as in darkness. Then arose, O Raghuva! a dreadful cry of the serpents, the Usooras, the Rakshuses, and other creatures, as of beings suffering death. These angry youths, O son of Rughoo! dug the earth even to Patala, to the extent of sixty thousand yojunas. Thus, O prince! the sons of the sovereign of men traversed Jumboodweepa, inclosed with mountains, digging wherever they came. The gods now, with the Gundhurwas and the great serpents, struck with astonishment, went all of them to Bruhma, and, bowing even to the foot of the great spirit, they, full of terror, with dejected countenance, addressed him, thus: ' O Deva! O divine One! the whole earth, covered with mountains and woods, with rivers and continents, the sons of Sugura are now digging up. By these digging, O Bruhma! the mightiest beings are killed. This is the stealer of our consecrated victims; by this (fellow) our horse was taken away.' Thus saying, these sons of Sugura destroy all creatures. O most Powerful! having heard this, it becomes thee to interpose, before these horse-seekers destroy all thy creatures endued with life.»

Thus far the thirty-second Section, describing the digging of earth.

SECTION XXXIII.—« Hearing the words of the gods, the divine Bruhma replied to these affrighted ones, stupified with the Yumalike power of these youths: The wise Vasoo-deva, the great Madhuva, who claims the earth for his spouse, that divine one, residing in the form of Kupila, supports the earth. By the fire of his wrath he will destroy the sons of the king. This piercing of the earth must, I suppose, be perceived by him, and he will (effect) the destruction of the long-sighted sons of Sugura. The thirty-three gods,[6] enemy-subduing,

having heard the words of Bruhma, returned home full of joy. The sons of Sugura highly renowned, thus digging the earth, a sound was produced resembling that of conflicting elements. Having encompassed and penetrated the whole earth, the sons of Sugura, returning to their father, said, The whole earth has been traversed by us; and all the powerful gods, the Danuvas, the Ruckshuses, the Pishachas, the serpents, and hydras, are[1] killed; but we have not seen thy horse, nor the thief. What shall we do? Success be to thee: be pleased to determine what more is proper. The virtuous king, having heard the words of his sons, O son of Rughoo! angrily replied, Again commence digging. Having penetrated the earth, and found the stealer of the horse, having accomplished your intention, return again. Attentive to the words of their father, the great Sugura, the sixty thousand descended to Patala, and there renewed their digging. There, O chief of men! they saw the elephant of that quarter of the globe, in size resembling a mountain, with distorted eyes, supporting with his head this earth, with its mountains and forests, covered with various countries, and adorned with numerous cities. When, for the sake of rest, O Kakootstha! the great elephant, through distress, refreshes himself by moving his head, an earthquake is produced.

« Having respectfully circumambulated this mighty elephant, guardian of the quarter, they, O Rama! praising him, penetrated into Patala. After they had thus penetrated the east quarter, they opened their way to the south. Here they saw that great elephant Muhapudma, equal to a huge mountain, sustaining the earth with his head. Beholding him, they were filled with surprise; and, after the usual circumambulation, the sixty thousand sons of the great Sugura perforated the west quarter. In this these mighty ones saw the elephant Soumunusa, of equal size. Having respectfully saluted him, and inquired respecting his health, these valiant ones digging, arrived at the north. In this quarter, O chief of Rughoo! they saw the snow-white elephant Bhudra, supporting this earth with his beautiful body. Circumambulating him, they again penetrated the earth, and proceeded north-east to that renowned quarter; all the sons of Sugura, through anger, pierced the earth again. There all those magnanimous ones, terrible in swiftness, and of mighty prowess, saw Kupila, Vasodeva the eternal,[2] and near him the horse feeding. Filled, O son of Rughoo! with unparalleled joy, they all knowing him to be the stealer of the horse, with eyes starting with rage, seizing their spades and their *langulas*, and even trees and stones, ran towards him full of wrath, calling out, Stop, stop! thou art the stealer of our sacrificial horse: Thou stupid one, know that we who have found thee are the sons of Rughoo. Kupila, filled with excessive anger, uttered from his nostrils a loud sound, and instantly, O Kakoostha! by Kupila of immeasurable power, were all the sons of Sugura turned to a heap of ashes.»

Thus far the thirty-third Section, describing the interview with Kupila.

SECTION XXXIV.—« O son of Rughoo! Sugura, per-

---

[1] The Indian spade, formed like a hoe, with a short handle.
[2] An instrument said to be formed like an ox's yoke.
[3] A dart, or spear.
[4] A club, or crow.
[5] A weapon, now unknown.
[6] The eight Vusoos, the eleven Roodras, the twelve Adityas, and Ushwinee and Koomara.

[1] This seems to have been spoken by these youths in the warmth of their imagination.
[2] The Hindoos say, that Kupila, or Vasoo-deva, is an incarnation of Vishnoo, whom they describe as having been thus partially incarnate twenty-four times.

ceiving that his sons had been absent a long time, thus addressed his grandson, illustrious by his own might : Thou art a hero, possessed of science, in prowess equal to thy predecessors. Search out the fate of thy paternal relatives, and the person by whom the horse was stolen, that we may avenge ourselves on these subterraneous beings, powerful and great. Take thy scymitar and bow, O beloved one! and finding out thy deceased paternal relatives, destroy my adversary. The proposed end being thus accomplished, return. Bring me happily through this sacrifice.

"Thus particularly addressed by the great Sugura, Ungshooman, swift and powerful, taking his bow and scymitar, departed. Urged by the king, the chief of men traversed the subterraneous road dug by his great ancestors. There the mighty one saw the elephant of the quarter, adored by the gods, the Danuvas and Rukshuses, the Pishachas, the birds and the serpents. Having circumambulated him, and asked concerning his welfare, Ungshooman inquired for his paternal relatives, and the stealer of the sacred victim. The mighty elephant of the quarter hearing, replied, O son of Usumunja! thou wilt accomplish thine intention, and speedily return with the horse. Having heard this, he, with due respect, inquired, in regular succession, of all the elephants of the quarters. Honoured by all these guardians of the eight sides of the earth, acquainted with speech, and eminent in eloquence, he was told, Thou wilt return with the horse. Upon this encouraging declaration, he swiftly went to the place where lay his paternal relatives, the sons of Sugura, reduced to a heap of ashes. (At this sight) the son of Usumunja, overwhelmed with sorrow on account of their death, cried out with excess of grief. In this state of grief, the chief of men beheld, grazing near, the sacrificial horse. The illustrious one, desirous of performing the funeral obsequies of these sons of the king, looked around for a receptacle of water, but in vain. Extending his eager view, he saw, O Rama! the sovereign of birds, the uncle of his paternal relatives, Soopurna, in size resembling a mountain. Vinuteya, of mighty prowess, addressed him thus: Grieve not, O chief of men! this slaughter is approved by the universe. These great ones were reduced to ashes by Kupila of unmeasurable might. It is not proper for thee, O wise one! to pour common water upon these ashes. Gunga, O chief of men! is the eldest daughter of Himuvut. With her sacred stream, O valiant one! perform the funeral ceremonies for thine ancestors. If the purifier of the world flow on them, reduced to a heap of ashes, these ashes, being wetted by Gunga, the illuminator of the world, the sixty thousand sons of thy grandfather will be received into heaven. May success attend thee! Bring Gunga to the earth from the residence of the gods. If thou art able, O chief of men! possessor of the ample share, let the descent of Gunga be accomplished by thee. Take the horse, and go forth. It is thine, O hero! for to complete the great paternal sacrifice.

"Having heard these words of Soopurna, Ungshooman, the heroic, speedily seizing the horse, returned. Then, O son of Rughoo! being come to the king, who was still performing the initiatory ceremonies, he related to him the whole affair, and the advice of Soopurna.

"After hearing the terror-inspiring relation of Ung-

shooman, the king finished the sacrifice, in exact conformity to the tenor and spirit of the ordinance : Having finished his sacrifice, the sovereign of the earth returned to his palace. The king, however, was unable to devise any way for the descent of Gunga from heaven : after a long time, unable to fix upon any method, he departed to heaven, having reigned thirty thousand years.

"Sugura having, O Rama! paid the debt of nature, the people chose Ungshooman, the pious, for their sovereign. Ungshooman, O son of Rughoo! was a very great monarch. His son was called Dwileepa. Having placed him on the throne, he, O Raguva! retiring to the pleasant top of Mount Himuvut, performed the most severe austerities. This excellent sovereign of men, illustrious as the immortals, was exceedingly desirous of the descent of Gunga: but not obtaining his wish, the renowned monarch, rich in sacred austerities, departed to heaven, after having abode in the forest sacred to austerities thirty-two thousand years. Dwileepa, the highly energetic, being made acquainted with the slaughter of his paternal great-uncles, was overwhelmed with grief; but was still unable to fix upon a way of deliverance. How shall I accomplish the descent of Gunga? How shall I perform the funeral ablutions of these relatives? How shall I deliver them? In such cogitations was his mind constantly engaged. While these ideas filled the mind of the king, thoroughly acquainted with sacred duties, there was born to him a most virtuous son, called Bhugee-rutha. The illustrious king Dwileepa performed many sacrifices, and governed the kingdom for thirty thousand years; but, O chief of men! no way of obtaining the deliverance of his ancestors appearing, he, by a disease, discharged the debt of nature. Having installed his own son Bhugee-rutha in the kingdom, the lord of men departed to the paradise of Indra, through the merits of his own virtuous deeds.

"The pious, the royal sage, Bhugee-Rutha, O son of Rughoo! was childless. Desirous of offspring, yet childless, the great monarch entrusted the kingdom to the care of his counsellors; and, having his heart set on obtaining the descent of Gunga, engaged in a long course of sacred austerities upon the mountain Gokurna. With hands erected, he, O son of Rughoo! surrounded in the hot season with five fires,[1] according to the prescribed ordinance in the cold season lying in water; and in the rainy season exposed to the descending clouds, feeding on fallen leaves, with his mind restrained, and his sensual feelings subdued, this valiant and great king continued a thousand years in the practice of the most severe austerities. The magnanimous monarch of mighty arm having finished this period, the divine Bruhma, the lord of creatures, the supreme governor, was highly pleased; and with the gods, going near to the great Bughee-rutha, employed in sacred austerities, said to him, I am propitious. O performer of sacred vows! ask a blessing. The mighty, the illustrious Bhugee-rutha, with hands respectfully joined, replied to the sire of all, O divine one! if thou art pleased with me, if the fruit of my austerities may be granted, let all the sons of Sugura obtain water for their funeral rites. The ashes of the great ones being wetted by the water of Gunga, let all

[1] One towards each of the cardinal points, and the sun over his head, towards which he was constantly looking.

my ancestors ascend to the eternal heaven.[1] Let a child, O divine one! be granted to us, that our family become not extinct. O God! let this great blessing be granted to the family of Ikshwakoo. The venerable sire of all replied to the king thus requesting in the sweetest and most pleasing accents: Bhugee-rutha, thou mighty charioteer, be this great wish of thine heart accomplished. Let prosperity attend thee, thou increaser of the family of Ikshwakoo? Engage Hura, O king! to receive (in her descent) Gunga, the eldest daughter of the mountain Ilimuvut. The earth, O king! cannot sustain the descent of Gunga, nor beside Shoolee[2] do I behold any one, O king! able to receive her. The creator having thus replied to the king, and spoken to Gunga, returned to heaven with Macroots and all the gods."

Thus far the thirty-fourth Section, describing the gift of the blessing to Bhugee-rutha.

Section XXXV.—"Pruja-puti being gone, Bhugee-rutha, O Rama! with uplifted arm, without support, without a helper, immoveable as a dry tree, and feeding on air, remained day and night on the tip of his great toe upon the afflicted earth. A full year having now elapsed, the husband of Ooma, and the lord of animals, who is reverenced by all worlds, said to the king, I am propitious to thee, O chief of men! I will accomplish thy utmost desire. To him the sovereign replied, O Hura, receive Gunga! Bhurga,[3] thus addressed, replied, I will perform thy desire; I will receive her on my head, the daughter of the mountain. Muheshwura then, mounting on the summit of Himuvut, addressed Gunga, the river flowing in the ether, saying, Descend, O Gunga! The eldest daughter of Himuvut, adored by the universe, having heard the words of the lord of Ooma, was filled with anger, and assuming, O Rama! a form of amazing size, with insupportable celerity, fell from the air upon the auspicious head of Shiva. The goddess Gunga, irresistible, thought within herself, I will bear down Shunkura with my stream, and enter Patala. The divine Hura, the three-eyed God, was aware of her proud resolution, and, being angry, determined to prevent her design. The purifier, fallen upon the sacred head of Roodra, was detained, O Rama! in the recesses of the orb of his Juta, resembling Aimuvut, and was unable, by the greatest efforts, to descend to the earth. From the borders of the orb of his Juta, the goddess could not obtain regress, but wandered there for many series of years. Thus situated, Bhugee-rutha beheld her wandering there, and again engaged in severe austerities.

With these austerities, O son of Rughoo! Hura being greatly pleased, discharged Gunga towards the lake Vindoo. In her flowing forth seven streams were produced. Three of these streams[4] beautiful, filled with water conveying happiness, Hladinee,[5] Pavunee,[6] and Nulinee,[7] directed their course eastward; while Soochukohoo,[8] Seeta,[9] and Sindhoo,[10] three pellucid mighty rivers, flowed to the west. The seventh of these streams

[1] The heaven from which there can be no fall.
[2] Shiva, from Shoola, the spear which he held.
[3] Shiva.
[4] Literally, three Gungas. Wherever a part of Gunga flows it is dignified with her name: Thus the Hindoos say, the Gunga of Pouyaga, etc.
[5] The river of joy.   [6] The purifier.
[7] Abounding with water.   [8] Beautiful-eyed.
[9] White.   [10] Probably the Indus.

followed king Bhugee-rutha. The royal sage, the illustrious Bhugee-rutha, seated on a resplendent car, led the way, while Gunga followed. Pouring down from the sky upon the head of Shunkura, and afterwards upon the earth, her streams rolled along with a shrill sound. The earth was willingly chosen by the fallen fishes, the turtles, the porpoises, and the birds. The royal sages, the Gundhurvas, the Yukshas, and the Siddhas, beheld her falling from the ether to the earth; yea, the gods, immeasurable in power, filled with surprise, came thither with chariots resembling a city, horses, and elephants, and litters, desirous of seeing the wonderful and unparalleled descent of Gunga into the world. Irradiated by the descending gods, and the splendour of their ornaments, the cloudless atmosphere shone with the splendour of an hundred suns, while, by the uneasy porpoises, the serpents, and the fishes, the air was coruscated as with lightning. Through the white foam of the waters, spreading in a thousand directions, and the flights of water-fowl, the atmosphere appeared filled with autumnal clouds. The water, pure from defilement, falling from the head of Shunkura, and thence to the earth, ran in some places with a rapid stream, in others in a tortuous current; here widely spreading, there descending into caverns, and again spouting upward; in some places it moved slowly, stream uniting with stream; while, repelled in others, it rose upwards, and again fell to the earth. Knowing its purity, the sages, the Gundhurvas, and the inhabitants of the earth, touched the water fallen from the body of Bhuva.[1] Those who, through a curse, had fallen from heaven to earth, having performed ablution in this stream, became free from sin: cleansed from sin by this water, and restored to happiness, they entered the sky, and returned again to heaven. By this illustrious stream was the world rejoiced, and by performing ablution in Gunga, became free from impurity.

"The royal sage, Bhugee-rutha, full of energy, went before, seated on his resplendent car, while Gunga followed after. The gods, O Rama! with the sages, the Dityas, the Danuvas, the Rakshuses, the chief Gundhurvas, and Yukshas, with the Kinnuras, the chief serpents, and all the Upsuras, together with aquatic animals, following the chariot of Bhugee-rutha, attended Gunga. Whither king Bhugee-rutha went, thither went the renowned Gunga, the chief of streams, the destroyer of all sin.

"After this, Gunga, in her course, inundated this sacrificial ground of the great Juhnoo of astonishing deeds, who was then offering sacrifice. Juhnoo, O Raghuva! perceiving her pride enraged, drank up the whole of the water of Gunga:—a most astonishing deed! At this the gods, the Gundhurvas, and the sages, exceedingly surprised, adored the great Juhnoo, the most excellent of men, and named Gunga the daughter of this great sage.

"The illustrious chief of men, pleased, discharged Gunga from his ears. Having liberated her, he, recognizing the great Bhugee-rutha, the chief of kings, then present, duly honoured him, and returned to the place of sacrifice. From this deed Gunga, the daughter of Jahnoo, obtained the name Jahnuvee.

"Gunga now went forward again, following the chariot of Bhugee-rutha. Having reached the sea, the chief of streams proceeded to Patala, to accomplish the work

[1] Shiva, the existant.

of Bhagee-rutha. The wise and royal sage, having with great labour conducted Gunga thither, there beheld his ancestors reduced to ashes. Then, O chief of Rughoo's race, that heap of ashes, bathed by the excellent waters of Gunga, and purified from sin, the sons of the king obtained heaven. Having arrived at the sea, the king, followed by Gunga, entered the subterraneous regions, where lay the sacred ashes. After these, O Rama! had been laved by the water of Gunga, Bruhma, the lord of all, thus addressed the king; O chief of men! thy predecessors, the sixty thousand sons of the great Sugura, are all delivered by thee: and the great and perennial receptacle of water, called by Sugura's name, shall henceforth be universally known by the appellation of Sagura.[1] As long, O king! as the waters of the sea continue in the earth, so long shall the sons of Sugura remain in heaven, in all the splendour of gods.

« This Gunga, O king! shall be thy eldest daughter, known throughout the three worlds (by the name) Bhagee-ruthee; and because she passed through the earth, the chief of rivers shall be called Gunga[2] throughout the universe. (She shall also be) called Triputhaga, on account of her proceeding forward in three different directions, watering the three worlds. Thus is she named by the gods and sages. She is called Gunga, O sovereign of the Vashyas! on account of her flowing through Gang;[3] and her third name, O thou observer of vows! is Bhagee-ruthee. O, accomplished one! through affection to thee, and regard to me, these names will remain: as long as Gunga, the great river, shall remain in the world, so long shall thy deathless fame live throughout the universe. O lord of men! O king! perform here the funeral rites of all thine ancestors. Relinquish thy vows,[4] O king! this devout wish of theirs was not obtained by thine ancestors highly renowned, chief among the pious; not by Ungsnooman, unparalleled in the universe, so earnestly desiring the descent of Gunga, O beloved one! was this object of desire obtained. Nor, O possessor of prosperity! O sinless one! could she be (obtained) by thine illustrious father Dwileepa, the Rajurshi eminently accomplished, whose energy was equal to that of a Muhurshi, and who, established in all the virtues of the Kshutras, in sacred austerities equalled myself. This great design has been fully accomplished by thee, O chief of men! Thy fame, the blessing so much desired, will spread throughout the world. O subduer of enemies! this descent of Gunga has been effected by thee. This Gunga is the great abode of virtue: by this deed thou art become possessed of the divinity itself. In this stream constantly bathe thyself, O chief of men! Purified, O most excellent of mortals! be a partaker of the fruit of holiness; perform the funeral ceremonies of all thy ancestors. May blessings attend thee, O chief of men! I return to heaven.

« The renowned one, the sovereign of the gods, the sire of the universe, having thus spoken, returned to heaven.

« King Bhagee-rutha, the royal sage, having performed the funeral ceremonies of the descendants of Segura, in

proper order of succession, according to the ordinance; the renowned one having also, O chief of men! performed the customary ceremonies, and purified himself, returned to his own city, where he governed the kingdom. Having (again), O Raghura! possessed of abundant wealth, obtained their king, his people rejoiced; their sorrow was completely removed; they increased in wealth and prosperity, and were freed from disease.

« Thus, O Rama! has the story of Gunga been related at large by me. May prosperity attend thee : May every good be thine. The evening is fast receding. He who causes this relation, securing wealth, fame, longevity, posterity, and heaven, to be heard among the Brahmans, the Kshutriyas, or the other tribes of men, his ancestors rejoice, and to him are the gods propitious: and he who hears this admirable story of the descent of Gunga, ensuring long life, shall obtain, O Kacootstha! all the wishes of his heart. All his sins shall be destroyed, and his life and fame be abundantly prolonged. »

End of the thirty-fifth section, describing the descent of Gunga.

Note 38, page 321, col. 1.
Parvati.

All the Devatas, and other inhabitants of the celestial regions, being collected, at the summons of Bhagavat, to arrange the ceremonials of the marriage of Seeva and Parvati, first came Brahma, mounted on his goose, with the Reyshees at his stirrup; next Veeshnu, riding on Garoor his eagle, with the chank, the chakra, the club, and the pedive in his hands; Eendra also, and Yama, and Cuvera, and Varuna, and the rivers Ganga and Jumna, and the seven Seas. The Gandarvas also, and Apsaras, and Vasookee, and other serpents, in obedience to the commands of Seeva, all dressed in superb chains and habits of ceremony, were to be seen in order amidst the crowded and glittering cavalcade.

And now, Seeva, after the arrival of all the Devatas, and the completion of the preparations for the procession, set out, in the utmost pomp and splendour, from the mountain Kilas. His third eye flamed like the sun, and the crescent on his forehead assumed the form of a radiated diadem; his snakes were exchanged for chains and necklaces of pearls and rubies, his ashes for sandal and perfume, and his elephant's skin for a silken robe, so that none of the Devatas in brilliance came near his figure. The bridal attendants now spread wide abroad the carpet of congratulation, and arranged in order the banquet of bliss. Nature herself assumed the appearance of renovated youth, and the sorrowing universe recalled its long-forgotten happiness. The Gandarvas and Apsaras began their melodious songs, and the Genes and Keenners displayed the magic of their various musical instruments. The earth and its inhabitants exulted with tongues of glorification and triumph; fresh moisture invigorated the withered victims of time; a thousand happy and animating conceptions inspired the hearts of the intelligent, and enlightened the wisdom of the thoughtful : The kingdom of external forms obtained gladness, the world of intellect acquired brightness. The dwellers upon earth stocked the casket of their ideas with the jewels of delight, and reverend pilgrims exchanged their beads for pearls. The joy of those on earth ascended up to Heaven, and the Tree of the bliss of those in Heaven extended its auspicious branches downwards to the earth. The eyes of the Devatas flamed like torches on behold-

[1] Sagura is one of the most common names for the seas which the Hindoos have.
[2] From the root gum, signifying motion.
[3] The earth.
[4] The end of thy vows is accomplished, therefore now relinquish thy vows of being an ascetic.

ing these scenes of rapture, and the hearts of the just kindled like touchwood on hearing these ravishing symphonies. Thus Seeva set off like a garden in full blow, and Paradise was eclipsed by his motion. — MAURICE, *from the Seeva-Pooraun.*

Note 39, page 321, col. 1.
Thereat the heart of the Universe stood still.

After these lines were written, I was amused at finding a parallel passage in a sermon:

«Quando o Sol parou às vozes de Josuè, aconteceram no mundo todas aquellas consequencias, que parando o movimento celeste, consideram os Filosofos. As plantas por todo aquelle tempo nam creceram; as calidades dos elementos, e dos mixtos, nam se alteraram; a geraçam e corrupçam com que se conservo o mundo, cessou; as artes e os exercicios de hum e outro Emisferio estiveram suspensos; os Antipodas nam trabalhavam, porque lhes faltava a luz, os de cima cançados de tam comprido dia deixavam o trabalho; estes pasmados de verem o Sol que se nam movia; aquelles tambem pasmados de esperarem pelo Sol, que nam chegava; cuidavam que se acabarà para elles a luz; imaginavam que se acabava o mundo: tudo era lagrimas, tudo assombros, tudo horrores, tudo confusoens.» —VIEYRA, *Sermoens,* tom. ix, p. 505.

Note 40, page 322, col 2.
Surya.

Surya, the Sun. The poets and painters describe his car as drawn by seven green horses, preceded by *Arun,* or the Dawn, who acts as his charioteer, and followed by thousands of genii, worshipping him, and modulating his praises. Surya is believed to have descended frequently from his car in a human shape, and to have left a race on earth, who are equally renowned in the Indian stories with the Heliadai of Greece. It is very singular that his two sons, called *Aswinau,* or *Aswinicumarau,* in the Dual, should be considered as twin brothers, and painted like Castor and Pollux; but they have each the character of Æsculapius among the gods, and are believed to have been born of a nymph, who, in the form of a mare, was impregnated with sun-beams. — Sir W. JONES.

That sun, O daughter of Ganga! than which nothing is higher, to which nothing is equal, enlightens the summit of the sky—with the sky enlightens the earth—with the earth enlightens the lower worlds;—enlightens the higher worlds, enlightens other worlds; —it enlightens the breast, — enlightens all besides the breast. — Sir W. JONES, *from the Veda.*

Note 41, page 322, col. 2.
Forgetful of his Dragon foe.

Ra'hu was the son of *Cas'yapa* and *Dity,* according to some authorities; but others represent *Sinhica'* (perhaps the sphinx) as his natural mother. He had four arms; his lower parts ended in a tail like that of a dragon; and his aspect was grim and gloomy, like the *darkness* of the chaos, whence he had also the name of *Tamas.* He was the adviser of all mischief among the *Daityas,* who had a regard for him: but among the *De'vatas* it was his chief delight to sow dissension; and when the gods had produced the *amrit,* by churning the ocean, he disguised himself like one of them, and received a portion of it; but the Sun and Moon having discovered his fraud, *Vishnu* severed his

head and two of his arms from the rest of his monstrous body. That part of the nectareous fluid which he had time to swallow secured his immortality: his trunk and dragon-like tail fell on the mountain of *Malaya,* where *Mini,* a *Brahman,* carefully preserved them by the name of *Ce'tu;* and, as if a complete body had been formed from them, like a dismembered *polype,* he is even said to have adopted *Ce'tu* as his own child. The head, with two arms, fell on the sands of *Barbara,* where *Pi'the'na's* was then walking with *Sinhica',* by some called his wife: They carried the *Daitya* to their palace, and adopted him as their son; whence he acquired the name of *Paite he'nasi.* This extravagant fable is, no doubt, astronomical; *Ra'hu* and *Ce'tu* being clearly the *nodes,* or what astrologers call the *head* and *tail* of the dragon. It is added, that they appeased *Vishnu,* and obtained re-admission to the firmament but were no longer visible from the earth, their enlightened sides being turned from it; that *Ra'hu* strives, during eclipses, to wreak vengeance on the Sun and Moon, who detected him; and that *Ce'tu* often appears as a comet, a whirlwind, a fiery meteor, a water-spout, or a column of sand.—WILFORD. *Asiatic Researches.*

Note 42, page 323, col. 1.
Suras.

The word *Sura* in Sanscrit signifies both wine and true wealth; hence, in the first *C'hand* of the *Ramayan* of VALMIC, it is expressly said that the *Devatas,* having received the *Sura,* acquired the title of *Suras,* and the *Daityas* that of *Asura,* from not having received it. The *Veda* is represented as that wine and true wealth. —PATERSON. *Asiat. Researches.*

Note 43, page 323, col. 1.
Camdeo.

Eternal CAMA! or doth SMARA bright,
Or proud ANANGA, give thee more delight?
Sir W. Jones.

He was the son of MAYA, or the general *attracting* power, and married to RETTY, or *Affection,* and his bosom friend is BESSENT, or *Spring.* He is represented as a beautiful youth, sometimes conversing with his mother and consort in the midst of his gardens and temples; sometimes riding by moonlight on a parrot or lory, and attended by dancing girls or nymphs, the foremost of whom bears his colours, which are a *fish* on a red ground. His favourite place of resort is a large tract of country round *Agra,* and principally the plains of *Matra,* where KRISHEN also, and the nine GOPIA, who are clearly the *Apollo* and *Muses* of the Greeks, usually spend the night with music and dance. His bow of sugar-cane or flowers, with a string of bees, and his *five* arrows, each pointed with an Indian blossom of a heating quality, are allegories equally new and beautiful.

It is possible that the words *Dipuc* and *Cupid,* which have the same signification, may have the same origin; since we know that the old Hetrurians, from whom great part of the Roman language and religion was derived, and whose system had a near affinity with that of the Persians and Indians, used to write their lines alternately forwards and backwards, as furrows are made by the plough.—Sir W. JONES.

Mahadeva and Parvati were playing with dice at the ancient game of Chaturanga, when they disputed, and parted in wrath; the goddess retiring to the forest of

47

Gauri, and the god repairing to Cushadwip. They seve-rally performed rigid acts of devotion to the Supreme Being; but the fires which they kindled blazed so vehe-mently as to threaten a general conflagration. The De-vas, in great alarm, hastened to Brahma, who led them to Mahadeva, and supplicated him to recall his consort; but the wrathful deity only answered, That she must come by her own free choice. They accordingly dis-patched Ganga, the river goddess, who prevailed on Parvati to return to him, on condition that his love for her should be restored. The celestial mediators then employed Cama-Deva, who wounded Mahadeva with one of his flowery arrows; but the angry divinity re-duced him to ashes with a flame from his eye. Parvati soon after presented herself before him in the form of a Ciraty, or daughter of a mountaineer, and, seeing him enamoured of her, resumed her own shape. In the place where they were reconciled, a grove sprang up, which was named Camavana; and the relenting god, in the character of Cameswara, consoled the afflicted Reti, the widow of Cama, by assuring her that she should rejoin her husband when he should be born again in the form of Pradyumna, son of Crishna, and should put Sambara to death. This favourable prediction was in due time accomplished, and Pradyumna having sprung to life, he was instantly seized by the demon Sambara, who placed him in a chest, which he threw into the ocean; but a large fish, which had swallowed the chest, was caught in a net, and carried to the palace of a tyrant, where the unfortunate Reti had been compelled to do menial service. It was her lot to open the fish, and seeing an infant in the chest, she nursed him in private, and educated him, till he had suffi-cient strength to destroy the malignant Sambara. He had before considered Reti as his mother; but the minds of them both being irradiated, the prophecy of Maha-deva was remembered, and the God of Love was again united with the Goddess of Pleasure.—WILFORD. *Asiatic Researches.*

Note 44, page 324, col. 1.

Eating his very core of life away.

One of the wonders of this country is the *Jiggerkhar*, (or liver-eater.) One of this class can steal away the liver of another by looks and incantations. Other ac-counts say, that, by looking at a person, he deprives him of his senses, and then steals from him something re-sembling the seed of a pomegranate, which he hides in the calf of his leg. The *Jiggerkhar* throws on the fire the grain before described, which thereupon spreads to the size of a dish, and he distributes it amongst his fel-lows, to be eaten; which ceremony concludes the life of the fascinated person. A *Jiggerkhar* is able to com-municate his art to another, which he does by learning him the incantations, and by making him eat a bit of the liver-cake. If any one cut open the calf of the magician's leg, extract the grain, and give it to the af-flicted person to eat, he immediately recovers. Those *Jiggerkhars* are mostly women. It is said, moreover, that they can bring intelligence from a great distance in a short space of time; and if they are thrown into a river, with a stone tied to them, they nevertheless will not sink. In order to deprive any one of this wicked power, they brand his temples, and every joint in his body, cram his eyes with salt, suspend him for forty days in a subterraneous cavern, and repeat over him

certain incantations. In this state he is called *Detche-reh.* Although, after having undergone this discipline, he is not able to destroy the liver of any one, yet he retains the power of being able to discover another *Jiggerkhar*, and is used for detecting those disturbers of mankind. They can also cure many diseases, by administering a potion, or by repeating an incantation. Many other marvellous stories are told of these people. —AYEEN ACBERY.

An Arabian old woman, by name Meluk, was thrown in prison, on a charge of having bewitched, or, as they call it, eaten the heart of a young native of Ormuz, who had lately, from being a Christian, turned Mahomme-dan. The cause of offence was, that the young man, after keeping company some time with one of her daugh-ters, had forsaken her: He himself, who was in a pitia-ble condition, and in danger of his life, was one of her accusers. This sort of witchcraft, which the Indians call eating the heart, and which is what we call bewitching, as sorcerers do by their venomous and deadly looks, is not a new thing, nor unheard of elsewhere; for many persons practised it formerly in Sclavonia, and the coun-try of the Triballes, as we learn from Ortelius, who took the account from Pliny, who, upon the report of Isi-gones, testifies, that this species of enchantment was much in use among these people, and many others whom he mentions, as it is at present here, especially among the Arabians who inhabit the western coast of the Per-sian gulph, where this art is common. The way in which they do it is only by the eyes and the mouth, keeping the eyes fixed steadily upon the person whose heart they design to eat, and pronouncing, between their teeth, I know not what diabolical words, by virtue of which, and by the operation of the devil, the person, how hale and strong soever, falls immediately into an unknown and incurable disease, which makes him appear phthy-sical, consumes him little by little, and at last destroys him. And this takes place faster or slower as the heart is eaten, as they say; for these sorcerers can either eat the whole or a part only; that is, can consume it entirely and at once, or bit by bit, as they please. The vulgar give it this name, because they believe that the devil, acting upon the imagination of the witch when she mutters her wicked words, represents invisi-bly to her the heart and entrails of the patient, taken out of his body, and makes her devour them. In which these wretches find so delightful a task, that very often, to satisfy their appetite, without any impulse of resent-ment or enmity, they will destroy innocent persons, and even their nearest relatives, as there is a report that our prisoner killed one of her own daughters in this manner.

This was confirmed to me by a similar story, which I heard at Ispahan, from the mouth of P. Sebastian de Jesus, a Portugueze Augustinian, a man to be believed, and of singular virtue, who was prior of their convent when I departed. He assured me, that, in one of the places dependant upon Portugal, on the confines of Ara-bia Felix, I know not whether it was at Mascate or at Ormuz, an Arab having been taken up for a similar crime, and convicted of it, for he confessed the fact, the captain, or governor of the place, who was a Portugueze, that he might better understand the truth of these black and de-vilish actions, of which there is no doubt in this country, made the sorcerer be brought before him before he was led to his punishment, and asked him, if he could eat the inside of a cucumber without opening it, as well as the heart of a man? The sorcerer said yes; and, in order to prove it, a cucumber was brought: he looked at it, never touching it, steadily for some time, with his usual enchantments, and then told the captain he had eaten the whole inside; and accordingly, when it was opened, nothing was found but the rind. This is not impossible; for the devil, of whom they make use in these operations, having, in the order of nature, greater power than all inferior creatures, can, with God's permission, produce these effects, and others more marvellous.

The same father told me, that one of these sorcerers, whether it was the same or not I do not know, having been taken for a similar offence, was asked if he could eat the heart of the Portugueze captain? and he replied no; for the Franks had a certain thing upon the breast, which covered them like a cuirass, and was so impenetrable, that it was proof against all his charms. This can be nothing else than the virtue of baptism, the armour of the faith, and the privileges of the sons of the church, against which the gates of hell cannot prevail.

To return, however, to my first subject:—This witch of Combru made some difficulty at first to confess her guilt; but seeing herself pressed with threats of death, and being led, in fact, to the public square, where I saw her with the sick young man, she said, that though she had not been the cause of his complaint, perhaps she could cure it, if they would let her remain alone with him, in his house, without interruption; by which she tacitly confessed her witchcraft: For it is held certain in these countries, that these wicked women can remove the malady which they have caused, if it be not come to the last extremity. And of many remedies which they use to restore health to the sufferers, there is one very extraordinary, which is, that the witch casts something out of her mouth, like the grain of a pomegranate, which is believed to be a part of the heart that she had eaten. The patient picks it up immediately, as part of his own intestines, and greedily swallows it; and by this means, as if his heart was replaced in his body, he recovers by degrees his health. I dare not assure you of these things as certainly true, not having myself seen them, surpassing as they do the course of nature. If they are as is said, it can be only in appearance, by the illusions of the devil; and if the afflicted recover actually their health, it is because the same devil ceases to torment them. Without dwelling longer upon these curious speculations,—the witch having given hopes that she would cure the patient, the officers promised that she should receive no injury, and they were both sent home; but an archer was set over her as a guard, that she might not escape.—PIETRO DELLA VALLE.

Note 45, page 324, col. 1.
The Calis.

The Calis and Pandaris are the protectresses of cities; each city has its own. They address prayers to these tutelary divinities, and build temples to them, offering to them blood in sacrifice, and sometimes human victims. These objects of worship are not immortal, and they take their name from the city over which they preside, or from the form in which they are represented. They are commonly framed of a gigantic stature, having several arms, and the head surrounded with flames; several fierce animals are also placed under their feet.—SONNERAT.

Note 46, page 324, col. 1.
Sani, the dreadful God, who rides abroad Upon the King of the Ravens.

Mr Moor has a curious remark upon this subject:

«Sani being among the astrologers of India, as well as with their sapient brethren of Europe, a planet of malignant aspects, the ill-omened raven may be deemed a fit *Vahan* for such a dreaded being. But this is not, I think, a sufficient reason for the conspicuous introduction of the raven into the mythological machinery of the Hindu system, so accurate, so connected, and so complete in all its parts; although the investigations that it hath hitherto undergone have not fully developed or reached such points of perfection. Now let me ask the reason, why, both in England and in India, the raven is so rare a bird? It breeds every year, like the crow, and is much longer lived; and while the latter bird abounds every where, to a degree bordering on nuisance, a pair of ravens, for they are seldom seen singly or in trios, are scarcely found duplicated in any place. Perhaps, take England or India over, two pair of ravens will not be found, on an average, in the extent of five hundred or a thousand acres. I know not, for I write where I have no access to books, if our naturalists have sought the theory of this; or whether it may have first occurred to me, which it did while contemplating the character and attributes of Sani, that the raven destroys its young; and if this notion be well founded, and on no other can I account for the rareness of the annual-breeding long-lived raven, we shall at once see the propriety of symbolizing it with Saturn, or Kronos, or Time, devouring or destroying his own offspring.—MOOR's *Hindu Pantheon*, p. 311.

Note 47, page 326, col. 2.
Be true unto yourselves.

The passage in which Menu exhorts a witness to speak the truth is one of the few sublime ones in his Institutes. «The soul itself is its own witness; the soul itself is its own refuge; offend not thy conscious soul, the supreme internal witness of men!—The sinful have said in their hearts, none see us. Yes, the gods distinctly see them, and so does the spirit within their breasts. The guardian deities of the firmament, of the earth, of the waters, of the human heart, of the moon, of the sun, and of fire, of punishment after death, of the winds, of night, of both twilights, and of justice, perfectly know the state of all spirits clothed with bodies.—O friend to virtue! that supreme Spirit, *which thou believest one and the same with thyself*, resides in thy bosom perpetually, and is an all-knowing inspector of thy goodness or of thy wickedness. If thou beest not at variance, by speaking falsely, with Yama, the subduer of all, with Vaivaswata the punisher, with that great Divinity who dwells in thy breast,—go not on a pilgrimage to the river Ganga, nor to the plains of Curu, for thou hast no need of expiation.—Ch. viii, p. 84, 85, 86, 91, 92.

Note 48, page 326, col. 2.
The Aunnay Birds.

The Aunnays act a considerable part in the history of the Nella Rajah, an amusing romance, for a translation of which we are indebted to Mr Kindersley. They are milk-white, and remarkable for the gracefulness of their walk.

Note 49, page 327, col. 2.
The Banian Tree.

THE *Burghut*, or Banian, often measures from twenty-four to thirty feet in girth. It is distinguished from every other tree hitherto known, by the very peculiar circumstance of throwing out roots from all its branches. These, being pendent, and perfectly lax, in time reach the ground, which they penetrate, and ultimately become substantial props to the very massy horizontal boughs, which, but for such a support, must either be stopt in their growth, or give way, from their own weight. Many of these *quondam* roots, changing their outward appearance from a brown rough rind to a regular bark, not unlike that of the beech, increase to a great diameter. They may be often seen from four to five feet in circumference, and in a true perpendicular line. An observer, ignorant of their nature, might think them artificial, and that they had been placed for the purpose of sustaining the boughs from which they originated. They proceed from all the branches indiscriminately, whether near or far removed from the ground. They appear like new swabs, such as are in use on board ships: however, few reach sufficiently low to take a hold of the soil, except those of the lower branches. I have seen some do so from a great height, but they were thin, and did not promise well. Many of the ramifications pendent from the higher boughs are seen to turn round the lower branches, but without any obvious effect on either; possibly, however, they may derive sustenance, even from that partial mode of communication. The height of a full-grown Banian may be from sixty to eighty feet; and many of them, I am fully confident, cover at least two acres. Their leaves are similar to, but rather larger than those of the laurel. The wood of the trunk is used only for fuel; it is light and brittle; but the pillars formed by the roots are valuable, being extremely elastic and light, working with ease, and possessing great toughness: it resembles a good kind of ash.—*Oriental Field Sports*, vol. ii, p. 113.

Note 50, page 327, col. 2.
—————— The Well
Which they, with sacrifice of rural pride,
Have wedded to the Cocoa-Grove beside.

It is a general practice, that, when a plantation is made, a well should be dug at one of its sides. The well and the topè are married; a ceremony at which all the village attends, and in which often much money is expended. The well is considered as the husband, as its waters, which are copiously furnished to the young trees during the first hot season, are supposed to cherish and impregnate them. Though vanity and superstition are evidently the basis of these institutions, yet we cannot help admiring their effects, so beautifully ornamenting a torrid country, and affording such general convenience.—*Oriental Sports*, p. 10.

Note 51, page 327, col. 2.
Tanks.

Some of these tanks are of very great extent, often covering eight or ten acres; and, besides having steps of masonry, perhaps fifty or sixty feet in breadth, are faced with brick-work, plaistered in the most substantial manner. The corners are generally ornamented with round or polygon pavilions of a neat appearance. *Oriental Sports*, vol. ii, p. 116.

There are two kinds of tanks, which we confound under one common name, though nothing can be more different. The first is the *Eray*, which is formed by throwing a mound or bank across a valley or hollow ground, so that the rain water collects in the upper part of the valley, and is let out on the lower part by sluices, for the purposes of cultivation. The other kind is the *Culam*, which is formed by digging out the earth, and is destined for supplying the inhabitants with water for domestic purposes. The *Culams* are very frequently lined on all the four sides with cut stone, and are the most elegant works of the natives.—BUCHANAN.

Where there are no springs or rivers to furnish them with water, as it is in the northern parts, where there are but two or three springs, they supply this defect by saving of rain water; which they do by casting up great banks in convenient places, to stop and contain the rains that fall, and so save it till they have occasion to let it out into the fields: They are made rounding like a (, or half-moon. Every town has one of these ponds, which, if they can but get filled with water, they count their corn is as good as in the barn. It was no small work to the ancient inhabitants to make all these banks, of which there is a great number, being some two, some three fathoms in height, and in length some above a mile, some less, not all of a size. They are now grown over with great trees, and so seem natural hills. When they would use the water, they cut a gap in one end of the bank, and so draw the water by little and little, as they have occasion, for the watering their corn.

These ponds, in dry weather, dry up quite. If they should dig these ponds deep, it would not be so convenient for them. It would, indeed, contain the water well, but would not so well, nor in such plenty, empty out itself into their grounds. In these ponds are alligators, which when the water is dried up, depart into the woods and down to the rivers, and in the time of rains, come up again into the ponds. They are but small, nor do use to catch people, nevertheless they stand in some fear of them.

The corn they sow in these parts is of that sort that is soonest ripe, fearing lest their waters should fail. As the water dries out of these ponds, they make use of them for fields, treading the mud with buffaloes, and then sowing rice thereon, and frequently casting up water with scoops on it.—KNOX, p. 9.

Note 52, page 327, col. 2.
The Lotus.

The lotus abounds in the numerous lakes and ponds of the province of Garah; and we had the pleasure of comparing several varieties; single and full, white, and tinged with deep or with faint tints of red. To a near view, the simple elegance of the white lotus gains no accession of beauty from the multiplication of its petals, nor from the tinge of gaudy hue; but the richest tint is most pleasing, when a lake, covered with full-blown lotus, is contemplated. — *Journey from Mirzapur to Nagpur*. Asiatic Annual Register, 1806.

Note 53, page 327, col. 2.
They built them here a Bower, etc.

The materials of which these houses are made are always easy to be procured, and the structure is so simple, that a spacious, and by no means uncomfortable dwelling, suited to the climate, may be erected in one day. Our habitation, consisting of three small rooms, and a hall open to the north, in little more than four hours was in readiness for our reception; fifty or sixty labourers completed it in that time, and on emergency could perform the work in much less. Bamboos, grass for thatching, and the ground rattan, are all the materials requisite: not a nail is used in the whole edifice: a row of strong bamboos, from eight to ten feet high, are fixed firm in the ground, which describe the outline, and are the supporters of the building: smaller bamboos are then tied horizontally, by strips of the ground rattan, to these upright posts: The walls, composed of bamboo mats, are fastened to the sides with similar ligatures: bamboo rafters are quickly raised, and a roof formed, over which thatch is spread in regular layers, and bound to the roof by filaments of rattan. A floor of bamboo grating is next laid in the inside, elevated two or three feet above the ground; this grating is supported on bamboos, and covered with mats and carpets. Thus ends the process, which is not more simple than effectual. When the workmen take pains, a house of this sort is proof against very inclement weather. We experienced, during our stay at Meeaday, a severe storm of wind and rain, but no water penetrated, nor thatch escaped: and if the tempest should blow down the house, the inhabitants would run no risk of having their brains knocked out, or their bones broken; the fall of the whole fabric would not crush a lady's lap-dog.—SYMES's *Embassy to Ava*.

Note 54, page 327, col. 2.
Jungle-grass.

In this district the long grass called jungle is more prevalent than I ever yet noticed. It rises to the height of seven or eight feet, and is topped with a beautiful white down, resembling a swan's feather. It is the mantle with which nature here covers all the uncultivated ground, and at once veils the indolence of the people and the nakedness of their land. It has a fine shewy appearance, as it undulates in the wind, like the waves of the sea. Nothing but the want of greater variety to its colour prevents it from being one of the finest and most beautiful objects in that rich store of productions with which nature spontaneously supplies the improvident natives.—TENNANT.

Note 55, page 328, col. 1.
In such libations, pour'd in open glades,
Beside clear streams and solitary shades,
The Spirits of the virtuous dead delight.

The Hindoos are enjoined by the *Veds* to offer a cake, which is called *Peenda*, to the ghosts of their ancestors, as far back as the third generation. This ceremony is performed on the day of the new moon in every month. The offering of water is in like manner commanded to be performed daily; and this ceremony is called *Tarpan*, to satisfy, to appease. The souls of such men as have left children to continue their generation, are supposed to be transported, immediately upon quitting their bodies, into a certain region called the *Petree Log*, where they may continue in proportion to their former virtues, provided these ceremonies be not neglected; otherwise they are precipitated into *Nark*, and doomed

to be born again in the bodies of unclean beasts; and until, by repeated regenerations, all their sins are done away, and they attain such a degree of perfection as will entitle them to what is called *Mooktee*, eternal salvation, by which is understood a release from future transmigration, and an absorption in the nature of the godhead, who is called Brahm.—WILKINS. *Note to the Bhagvat Geeta*.

The divine manes are always pleased with an oblation in empty glades, naturally clean, on the banks of rivers, and in solitary spots.—*Inst. of Menu*.

Note 56, page 328, col. 1.
Voomdavee.

This wife of Veeshnoo is the Goddess of the Earth and of Patience. No direct adoration is paid her; but she is held to be a silent and attentive spectator of all that passes in the world.—KINDERSLEY.

Note 57, page 328, col. 1.
Tassel Grass.

The *Surput*, or tassel-grass, which is much the same as the guinea grass, grows to the height of twelve or fourteen feet. Its stem becomes so thick as to resemble in some measure a reed. It is very strong, and grows very luxuriantly: it is even used as a fence against cattle; for which purpose it is often planted on banks, excavated from ditches, to enclose fields of corn, etc. It grows wild in all the uncultivated parts of India, but especially in the lower provinces, in which it occupies immense tracts; sometimes mixing with, and rising above coppices; affording an asylum for elephants, rhinoceroses, tigers, etc. It frequently is laid by high winds, of which breeding sows fail not to take advantage, by forming their nests, and concealing their young under the prostrate grass.—*Oriental Sports*, vol. i, p. 32.

Note 58, page 328, col. 2.
Lo, from his trunk, upturn'd, aloft he flings
The grateful shower, and now
Plucking the broad-leav'd bough
Of yonder plane,—he moves it to and fro.

Nature has provided the elephant with means to cool its heated surface, by enabling it to draw from its throat, by the aid of its trunk, a copious supply of saliva, which the animal spurts with force very frequently all over its skin. It also sucks up dust, and blows it over its back and sides, to keep off the flies, and may often be seen fanning itself with a large bough, which it uses with great ease and dexterity.—*Oriental Sports*, vol. i, p. 100.

Note 59, page 328, col. 2.
Till his strong temples, bath'd with sudden dews,
Their fragrance of delight and love diffuse.

The Hindoo poets frequently allude to the fragrant juice which oozes, at certain seasons, from small ducts in the temples of the male elephant, and is useful in relieving him from the redundant moisture, with which he is then oppressed; and they even describe the bees as allured by the scent, and mistaking it for that of the sweetest flowers. When Crishna visited Sanc'ha-dwip, and had destroyed the demon who infested that delightful country, he passed along the bank of a river, and was charmed with a delicious odour, which its waters diffused in their course: He was eager to view the source of so fragrant a stream, but was informed by the natives that it flowed from the temples of an elephant, immensely large, milk-white, and beautifully formed; that he governed a numerous race of elephants; and that the odoriferous fluid which exuded from his temples in the season of love had formed the river; that the Devas, or inferior gods, and the Apsarases, or nymphs, bathed and sported in its waters, impassioned and intoxicated with the liquid perfume.—WILFORD. *Asiatic Researches.*

Note 60, page 328, col. 2.

The antic monkeys, whose wild gambols late
Shook the whole wood.

They are so numerous on the island of Bulama, says Captain Beaver in his excellent book, that I have seen, on a calm evening, when there was not an air sufficiently strong to agitate a leaf, the whole surrounding wood in as much motion, from their playful gambols among its branches, as if it had blown a strong wind.

Note 61, page 328, col. 2.

Not that in emulous skill that sweetest bird
Her rival strain would try.

I have been assured, by a credible eye-witness, that two wild antelopes used often to come from their woods to the place where a more savage beast, Sirajuddaulah, entertained himself with concerts, and that they listened to the strains with an appearance of pleasure, till the monster, in whose soul there was no music, shot one of them, to display his archery. A learned native of this country told me that he had frequently seen the most venomous and malignant snakes leave their holes, upon hearing tunes on a flute, which, as he supposed, gave them peculiar delight. An intelligent Persian, who repeated his story again and again, and permitted me to write it down from his lips, declared, he had more than once been present when a celebrated lutanist, *Mirza Mohammed*, surnamed *Bulbul*, was playing to a large company, in a grove near *Shiraz*, where he distinctly saw the nightingales trying to vie with the musician; sometimes warbling on the trees, sometimes fluttering from branch to branch, as if they wished to approach the instrument whence the melody proceeded, and at length dropping on the ground, in a kind of ecstacy, from which they were soon raised, he assured me, by a change of the mode. I hardly know, says Sir William Jones, how to disbelieve the testimony of men who had no system of their own to support, and could have no interest in deceiving me.—*Asiatic Researches.*

Note 62, page 328, col. 2.

No idle ornaments deface
Her natural grace.

The Hindoo Wife, in Sir William Jones's poem, describes her own toilet-tasks:—

Nor were my night thoughts, I confess,
Free from solicitude for dress;
How best to bind my flowing hair
With art, yet with an artless air,—
My hair, like musk in scent and hue,
Oh! blacker far, and sweeter too!
In what nice braid, or glossy curl,
To fix a diamond or a pearl,
And where to smooth the love-spread toils
With nard or jasmin's fragrant oils;
How to adjust the golden *Teic*,[1]
And most adorn my forehead sleek;

[1] Properly *Tsica*, an ornament of gold placed above the nose.

What *Condals*[1] should emblaze my ears,
Like *Seita's*[2] waves, or *Seita's* tears;[3]
How elegantly to dispose
Bright circlets for my well-form'd nose:
With strings of rubies how to deck,
Or emerald rows, my stately neck;
While some that ebon tower embraced,
Some pendent sought my slender waist;
How next my purfled veil to chuse
From silken stores of varied hues,
Which would attract the roving view,
Pink, violet, purple, orange, blue;
The loveliest mantle to select,
Or unembellish'd or bedeck'd;
And how my twisted scarf to place
With most inimitable grace,
(Too thin its warp, too fine its woof,
For eyes of males not beauty-proof;)
What skirts the mantle best would suit,
Ornate, with stars, or tissued fruit,
The flower-embroider'd or the plain,
With silver or with golden vein,
The *Chury*[4] bright, which gayly shows
Fair objects aptly to compose;
How each smooth arm, and each soft wrist,
By richest *Cosees*[5] might be kiss'd,
While some my taper ankles round,
With sunny radiance tinged the ground.

See how he kisses the lip of my rival, and imprints on her forehead an ornament of pure musk, black as the young antelope on the lunar orb! Now, like the husband of *Reti*, he fixes white blossoms on her dark locks, where they gleam like flashes of lightning among the curled clouds. On her breasts, like two firmaments, he places a string of gems like a radiant constellation; he binds on her arms, graceful as the stalks of the water-lily, and adorned with hands glowing like the petals of its flower, a bracelet of sapphires, which resemble a cluster of bees. Ah! see how he ties round her waist a rich girdle illumined with golden bells, which seem to laugh as they tinkle, at the inferior brightness of the leafy garlands which lovers hang on their bowers, to propitiate the god of desire. He places her soft foot, as he reclines by her side, on his ardent bosom, and stains it with the ruddy hue of Yavaca.—*Songs of Jayadeva.*

Note 63, page 328, col. 2.

Sandal-streak.

The Hindoos, especially after bathing, paint their faces with ochre and sandal-wood ground very fine into a pulp.

The custom is principally confined to the male sex, though the women occasionally wear a round spot, either of sandal, which is of a light dun colour, or of *singuiff*, that is, a preparation of vermilion, between the eye-brows, and a stripe of the same running up the front of the head, in the furrow made according to the general practice of dividing all the frontal hair equally to the right and left, where it is rendered smooth, and glazed by a thick mucilage, made by steeping lintseed for a while in water. When dry, the hair is all firmly matted together, and will retain its form for many days together.—*Oriental Sports*, vol. i, p. 271.

[1] Pendents.
[2] *Seita Cund*, or the *Pool of Seita*, the wife of Rani, is the name given to the wonderful spring at Mungeir, with boiling water, of exquisite clearness and purity.
[3] Her tears, when she was made captive by the giant *Rawan.*
[4] A small mirror worn in a ring.
[5] Bracelets.

Note 64, page 328, col. 2.

Nor arm nor ankle-ring.

Glass rings are universally worn by the women of the Decan, as an ornament on the wrists; and their applying closely to the arm is considered as a mark of delicacy and beauty, for they must of course be past over the hand. In doing this a girl seldom escapes without drawing blood, and rubbing part of the skin from her hand; and as every well-dressed girl has a number of rings on each arm, and as these are frequently breaking, the poor creatures suffer much from their love of admiration.—*Buchanan.*

Note 65, page 328, col. 2.

The dear retreat.

There is a beautiful passage in Statius, which may be quoted here: It is in that poet's best manner:

Qualis vicino volucris jam sedula partu,
Jamque timens quâ fronde domum suspendat inanem,
Providet hinc ventos, hinc anxia cogitat angues,
Hinc homines; tandem dubiæ placet umbra, novisque
Vix stetit in ramis, et protinus arbor amatur.
Achil. II, 212.

Note 66, page 329, col. 1.

Jaga-Naut.

This temple is to the Hindoos what Mecca is to the Mahommedans. It is resorted to by pilgrims from every quarter of India. It is the chief seat of Brahminical power, and a strong-hold of their superstition. At the annual festival of the Butt Jattra, seven hundred thousand persons (as has been computed by the Pundits in College) assemble at this place. The number of deaths in a single year, caused by voluntary devotement, by imprisonment for non-payment of the demands of the Brahmins, or by the scarcity of provisions for such a multitude, is incredible. The precincts of the place are covered with bones.—*Claudius Buchanan.*

Many thousands of people are employed in carrying water from Hurdwar to Juggernat, for the uses of that temple. It is there supposed to be peculiarly holy, as it issues from what is called the Cow's Mouth. This superstitious notion is the cause of as much lost labour as would long since have converted the largest province of Asia into a garden. The numbers thus employed are immense; they travel with two flasks of the water slung over the shoulder by means of an elastic piece of bamboo. The same quantity which employs, perhaps, fifteen thousand persons, might easily be carried down the Ganges in a few boats annually. Princes and families of distinction have this water carried to them in all parts of Hindostan; it is drunk at feasts, as well as upon religious occasions.—*Tennant.*

A small river near Kinouge is held by some as even more efficacious in washing away moral defilement than the Ganges itself. Dr Tennant says, that a person in Ceylon drinks daily of this water, though at the distance of, perhaps, three thousand miles, and at the expense of five thousand rupees per month!

No distinction of casts is made at this temple, but all, like a nation descended from one common stock, eat, drink, and make merry together.—*Stavorinus.*

Note 67, page 329, col. 1.

The seven-headed Idol.

The idol of *Jaggernat* is in shape like a serpent, with seven heads; and on the cheeks of each head it hath the form of a wing upon each cheek, which wings open and shut and flap as it is carried in a stately chariot, and the idol in the midst of it; and one of the *moguls* sitting behind it in the chariot, upon a convenient place, with a canopy, to keep the sun from injuring of it.

When I, with horror, beheld these strange things, I called to mind the eighteenth chapter of the *Revelations*, and the first verse, and likewise the sixteenth and seventeenth verses of the said chapter, in which places there is a beast, and such idolatrous worship, mentioned; and those sayings in that text are herein truly accomplished in the sixteenth verse; for the *Bramins* are all marked in the forehead, and likewise all that come to worship the idol are marked also in their foreheads.—*Bruton. Churchill's Collection.*

Note 68, page 329, col. 2.

The Chariot of the God.

The size of the chariot is not exaggerated. Speaking of other such, Niecamp says, *Currus tam horrendæ magnitudinis sunt, ut vel mille homines uni trahendo vix sufficiant.*—I. 10. sec. 18.

They have built a great chariot, that goeth on sixteen wheels of a side, and every wheel is five feet in height, and the chariot itself is about thirty feet high. In this chariot, on their great festival days, at night, they place their wicked god *Jaggarnat;* and all the *Bramins,* being in number nine thousand, then attend this great idol, besides of *ashmen* and *fackeires* some thousands, or more than a good many.

The chariot is most richly adorned with most rich and costly ornaments; and the aforesaid wheels are placed very complete in a round circle, so artificially, that every wheel doth its proper office without any impediment; for the chariot is aloft, and in the centre betwixt the wheels: they have also more than two thousand lights with them: And this chariot, with the idol, is also drawn with the greatest and best men of the town; and they are so eager and greedy to draw it, that whosoever, by shouldering, crowding, shoving, heaving, thrusting, or any violent way, can but come to lay a hand upon the ropes, they think themselves blessed and happy: and, when it is going along the city, there are many that will offer themselves as a sacrifice to this idol, and desperately lie down on the ground, that the chariot-wheels may run over them, whereby they are killed outright; some get broken arms, some broken legs; so that many of them are so destroyed, and by this means they think to merit heaven.—*Bruton. Churchill's Collection.*

They sometimes lie down in the track of this machine a few hours before its arrival, and, taking a soporiferous draught, hope to meet death asleep.—CLAUDIUS BUCHANAN.

Note 69, page 330, col. 1.

A harlot-band.

There are in India common women, called Wives of the Idol. When a woman has made a vow to obtain children, if she brings into the world a beautiful daughter, she carries her to *Bod,* so their idol is called, with whom she leaves her. This girl, when she is arrived at a proper age, takes an apartment in the public place, hangs a curtain before the door, and waits for those who are passing, as well Indians as those of other sects among whom this debauchery is permitted. She prostitutes herself for a certain price, and all that she can thus acquire she carries to the priest of the idol, that he may apply it to the service of the temple. Let us, says the Mohammedan relater, bless the almighty and glorious God, that he has chosen us, to exempt us from all the crimes into which men are led by their unbelief.—*Anciennes Relations.*

Incited, unquestionably, says Mr Maurice, by the hieroglyphic emblem of vice so conspicuously elevated, and so strikingly painted in the temples of Mahadeo, the priests of that deity industriously selected the most beautiful females that could be found, and, in their tenderest years, with great pomp and solemnity, consecrated them (as it is impiously called) to the service of the presiding divinity of the pagoda. They were trained up in every art to delude and to delight; and, to the fascination of external beauty, their artful betrayers added the attractions arising from mental accomplishments. Thus was an invariable rule of the Hindoos, *that women have no concern with literature,* dispensed with upon this infamous occasion. The moment these hapless victims reached maturity, they fell victims to the lust of the Brahmins. They were early taught to practise the most alluring blandishments, to roll the expressive eye of wanton pleasure, and to invite to criminal indulgence, by stealing upon the beholder the tender look of voluptuous languishing. They were instructed to mould their elegant and airy forms into the most enticing attitudes and the most lascivious gestures, while the rapid and graceful motion of their feet, adorned with golden bells, and glittering with jewels, kept unison with the exquisite melody of their voices. Every pagoda has a band of these young syrens, whose business, on great festivals, is to dance in public before the idol, to sing hymns in his honour, and in private to enrich the treasury of that pagoda with the wages of prostitution. These women are not, however, regarded in a dishonourable light; they are considered as *wedded to the idol,* and they partake of the veneration paid to him. They are forbidden ever to desert the pagoda where they are educated, and are never permitted to marry; but the offspring, if any, of their criminal embraces are considered as sacred to the idol: the boys are taught to play on the sacred instruments used at the festivals, and the daughters are devoted to the abandoned occupations of their mothers.—*Indian Antiquities.*

These impostors take a young maid, of the fairest they can meet with, to be the bride (as they speak and bear the besotted people in hand) of *Jagannat,* and they leave her all night in the temple (whither they have carried her) with the idol, making her believe that *Jagannat* himself will come and embrace her, and appointing her to ask him, whether it will be a fruitful year, what kind of processions, feasts, prayers, and alms he demands to be made for it. In the mean time one of these lustful priest enters at night by a little back-door into the temple, deflowereth this young maid, and maketh her believe any thing he pleaseth; and the next day, being transported from this temple into another with the same magnificence, she was carried before upon the chariot of triumph, on the side of *Jagannat* her bridegroom: these *Brahmans* make her say aloud, before all the people, whatsoever she hath been taught of these cheats, as if she had learnt it from the very mouth of *Jagannat*—BERNIER.

Note 70, page 331, col. 1.
Baly.

The fifth incarnation was in a Bramin dwarf, under the name of Vamen; it was wrought to restrain the pride of the giant Baly. The latter, after having conquered the gods, expelled them from Sorgon; he was generous, true to his word, compassionate, and charitable. Vichenou, under the form of a very little Bramin, presented himself before him while he was sacrificing, and asked him for three paces of land to build a hut. Baly ridiculed the apparent imbecility of the dwarf, in telling him, that he ought not to limit his demand to a bequest so trifling; that his generosity could bestow a much larger donation of land. Vamen answered, That, being of so small a stature, what he asked was more than sufficient. The prince immediately granted his request, and, to ratify his donation, poured water into his right hand; which was no sooner done than the dwarf grew so prodigiously, that his body filled the universe! He measured the earth with one pace, and the heavens with another, and then summoned Baly to give him his word for the third. The prince then recognised Vichenou, adored him, and presented his head to him; but the god, satisfied with his submission, sent him to govern the Padalon, and permitted him to return every year to the earth, the day of the full moon, in the month of November.—SONNERAT's *Voyages,* vol. i, p. 24.

Note 71, page 331, col. 2.
The sacred cord.

The Brahmans who officiate at the temples generally go with their heads uncovered, and the upper part of the body naked. The *Zennar,* or sacred string, is hung round the body from the left shoulder; a piece of white cotton cloth is wrapped round the loins, which descends under the knee, but lower on the left side than on the other; and in cold weather they sometimes cover their bodies with a shawl, and their heads with a red cap.—The *Zennar* is made of a particular kind of perennial cotton, called *Verma:* it is composed of a certain number of threads of a fixed length: the *Zennar* worn by the Khatries has fewer threads than that worn by the Brahmans, and that worn by the Bhyse fewer than that worn by the Khatries; but those of the Soodra cast are excluded from this distinction, none of them being permitted to wear it.—CRAUFURD.

Note 72, page 332, col. 1.
The City of Baly.

Ruins of Mahàbalipûr, the City of the great Baly.

A rock, or rather hill of stone, is that which first engrosses the attention on approaching the place; for as it rises abruptly out of a level plain of great extent, consists chiefly of one single stone, and is situated very near to the sea-beach, it is such a kind of object as an inquisitive traveller would naturally turn aside to examine. Its shape is also singular and romantic, and, from a distant view, has an appearance like some antique and lofty edifice. On coming near to the foot of the rock from the north, works of imagery and sculpture crowd so thick upon the eye, as might seem to favour the idea of a petrified town, like those that have been fabled in different parts of the world, by too credulous travellers. Proceeding on by the foot of the hill, on the side facing the sea, there is a pagoda rising out of the ground, of one solid stone, about sixteen or eighteen feet high, which seems to have been cut upon the spot, out of a detached rock, that has been found of a proper size for that purpose. The top is arched, and the style of architecture according to which it is formed different from any now used in those parts. A little further on, there appears, upon a huge surface of stone, that juts out a little from the side of the hill, a numerous group of human figures, in bass-relief, considerably larger than life, representing the most remarkable persons whose actions are celebrated in the Mahábharit, each of them in an attitude, or with weapons, or other insignia, expressive of his character; or of some one of his most famous exploits. All these figures are doubtless much less distinct than they were at first; for upon comparing these and the rest of the sculptures that are exposed to the sea-air, with others at the same place, whose situation has afforded them protection from that element, the difference is striking; the former being every where much defaced, while the others are fresh as recently finished. An excavation in another part of the east side of the great rock appears to have been made on the same plan, and for the same purpose, that Chowltries are usually built in that country, that is to say, for the accommodation of travellers. The rock is hollowed out to the size of a spacious room, and two or three rows of pillars are left, as a seeming support to the mountainous mass of stone which forms the roof.

The ascent of the hill on the north is, from its natural shape, gradual and easy at first, and is in other parts rendered more so, by very excellent steps, cut out in several places where the communication would be difficult or impracticable without them. A winding stair of this sort leads to a kind of temple cut out of the solid rock, with some figures of idols in high relief upon the walls, very well finished. From this temple there are flights of steps, that seem to have led to some edifice formerly standing upon the hill; nor does it seem absurd to suppose that this may have been a palace, to which this temple may have appertained; for, besides the small detached ranges of stairs that are here and there cut in the rock, and seem as if they had once led to different parts of one great building, there appear in many places small water channels cut also in the rock, as if for drains to an house; and the whole top of the hill is strewed with small round pieces of brick, which may be supposed, from their appearance, to have been worn down to their present form during the lapse of many ages. On a plain surface of the rock, which may once have served as the floor of some apartment, there is a platform of stone, about 8 or 9 feet long, by 3 or 4 wide, in a situation rather elevated, with two or three steps leading up to it, perfectly resembling a couch or bed, and a lion very well executed at the upper end of it, by way of pillow: the whole of one piece, being part of the hill itself. This the Bramins, inhabitants of the place, call the bed of Dhermarájah, or Judishter, the eldest of the five brothers, whose exploits are the leading subject in the Mahabhárit. And at a considerable distance from this, at such a distance, indeed, as the apartments of the women might be supposed to be from that of the men, is a bath, excavated also from the rock, with steps on the inside, which the Bramins call the Bath of Dropedy, the wife of Judishter and his brothers. How much credit is due to this tradition, and whether this stone couch may not have been anciently used as a kind of throne, rather

than a bed, is matter for future enquiry. A circumstance, however, which may seem to favour this idea is, that a throne, in the Shanscrit and other Hindoo languages, is called Singhásen, which is compounded of Sing, a lion, and ásen, a seat.

But though these works may be deemed stupendous, they are surpassed by others that are to be seen at the distance of about a mile or mile and half, to the south of the hill. They consist of two pagodas, of about 30 feet long, by 20 feet wide, and about as many in height, cut out of the solid rock, and each consisting originally of one single stone. Their form is different from the style of architecture according to which idol temples are now built in that country. These sculptures approach nearer to the Gothic taste, being surmounted by arched roofs, or domes, not semicircular, but composed of two segments of circles meeting in a point at top. Near these also stand an elephant full as big as life, and a lion much larger than the natural size, both hewn also out of one stone.

The great rock is about 50 or 100 yards from the sea; but close to the sea are the remains of a pagoda built of brick, and dedicated to Sib, the greatest part of which has evidently been swallowed up by that element; for the door of the innermost apartment, in which the idol is placed, and before which there are always two or three spacious courts surrounded with walls, is now washed by the waves, and the pillar used to discover the meridian at the time of founding the pagoda, is seen standing at some distance in the sea. In the neighbourhood of this building there are some detached rocks, washed also by the waves, on which there appear sculptures, though now much worn and defaced: And the natives of the place declared to the writer of this account, that the more aged people among them remembered to have seen the tops of several pagodas far out in the sea, which, being covered with copper, (probably gilt,) were particularly visible at sun-rise, as their shining surface used then to reflect the sun's rays, but that now that effect was no longer produced, as the copper had since become incrusted with mould and verdigrease.—CHAMBERS. *Asiatic Researches.*

Note 73, page 333, col. 1.

Thou hast been called, O Sleep! the friend of Woe,
But 't is the happy who have call'd thee so.

Daniel has a beautiful passage concerning Richard II —sufficiently resembling this part of the poem to be inserted here:

To Flint, from thence, into a restless bed,
That miserable night he comes convey'd;
Poorly provided, poorly followed,
Uncourted, unrespected, unobey'd;
Where, if uncertain Sleep but hovered
Over the drooping cares that heavy weigh'd,
Millions of figures Fantasy presents
Unto that sorrow waken'd grief augments.

His new misfortune makes deluded Sleep
Say 't was not so:—false dreams the truth deny:
Wherewith he starts; feels waking cares do creep
Upon his soul, and give his dreams the lie,
Then sleeps again:—and then again as deep
Doubts of darkness mock his misery.
Civil War, Book ii, st. 51, 53.

Note 74, page 333, col. 2.
The Aullay.

This monster of Hindoo imagination is a horse with the trunk of an elephant, but bearing about the same

48

378 SOUTHEY'S POETICAL WORKS.

proportion to the elephant in size, that the elephant itself does to a common sheep. In one of the prints to Mr Kindersley's « Specimens of Hindoo Literature,» an aullay is represented taking-up an elephant with his trunk.

Note 75, page 333, col. 2.
—— Did then the Ocean wage
His war for love and envy, not in rage,
O thou fair City, that he spares thee thus?

Malecheren, (which is probably another name for Baly), in an excursion which he made one day alone, and in disguise, came to a garden in the environs of his city Mahábalipoor, where was a fountain so inviting, that two celestial nymphs had come down to bathe there. The Rajah became enamoured of one of them, who condescended to allow of his attachment to her; and she and her sister nymph used thenceforward to have frequent interviews with him in that garden. On one of those occasions they brought with them a male inhabitant of the heavenly regions, to whom they introduced the Rajah; and between him and Malecheren a strict friendship ensued; in consequence of which he agreed, at the Rajah's earnest request, to carry him in disguise to see the court of the divine Inder,—a favour never before granted to any mortal. The Rajah returned from thence with new ideas of splendour and magnificence, which he immediately adopted in regulating his court and his retinue, and in beautifying his seat of government. By this means Mahábalipoor became soon celebrated beyond all the cities of the earth; and an account of its magnificence having been brought to the gods assembled at the court of Inder, their jealousy was so much excited at it, that they sent orders to the God of the Sea to let loose his billows, and overflow a place which impiously pretended to vie in splendour with their celestial mansions. This command he obeyed, and the city was at once overflowed by that furious element, nor has it ever since been able to rear its head.
—CHAMBERS. Asiat. Res.

Note 76, page 334, col. 1.
Round those strange waters they repair.

In the Bahia dos Artifices, which is between the river Jagoarive and S. Miguel, there are many springs of fresh water, which may be seen at low tide, and these springs are frequented by fish and by the sea-cow, which they say comes to drink there.—Noticias do Brazil. MSS. i, 8.

The inhabitants of the Feroe Islands seek for cod in places where there is a fresh-water spring at the bottom.—LANDT.

Note 77, page 337, col. 2.
The sheckra.

This weapon, which is often to be seen in one of the wheel-spoke hands of a Hindoo god, resembles a quoit: the external edge is sharp: it is held in the middle, and, being whirled along, cuts wherever it strikes.

Note 78, page 338, col. 1.
The writing which, at thy nativity,
All-knowing Nature wrought upon thy brain.

Brahma is considered as the immediate creator of all things, and particularly as the disposer of each person's fate, which he inscribes within the skull of every created being, and which the gods themselves cannot avert.
—KINDERSLEY, p. 21. NIECAMP. vol. i, p. 10. sect. 7.

It is by the sutures of the skull that these lines of destiny are formed. See also a note to Thalaba upon a like superstition of the Mahommedans.

« Quand on leur reproche quelque vice, ou qu'on les reprend d'une mauvaise action, ils répondent froidement, que cela est écrit sur leur tête, et qu'ils n'ont pu faire autrement. Si vous paroissez étonné de ce langage nouveau, et que vous demandiez à voir où cela est écrit, ils vous montrent les diverses jointures du crâne de leur tête, prétendant que les sutures même sont les caractères de cette écriture mysterieuse. Si vous les pressez de dechiffrer ces caractères, et de vous faire connoitre ce qu'ils signifient, ils avouent qu'ils ne le sçavent pas. Mais puisque vous ne sçavez pas lire cette écriture, disois-je quelquefois à ces gens entêtés, qui est-ce donc qui vous la lit? qui est-ce qui vous en explique le sens, et qui vous fait connoître ce qu'elle contient? D'ailleurs ces pretendus caractères étant les memes sur la tête de tous les hommes, d'où vient qu'ils agissent si différemment, et qu'ils sont si contraires les uns aux autres dans leurs vues, dans leurs desseins, et dans leurs projets?»

« Les Brames m'écoutoient de sang froid, et sans s'inquiéter ni des contradictions où ils tomboient, ni des consequences ridicules qu'ils étoient obligés d'avouer. Enfin, lorsqu'ils se sentoient vivement pressés, toute leur ressource étoit de se retirer sans rien dire.»—P. MAUDUIT, Lettres Edifiantes, t. x, p. 248.

Note 79, page 339, col. 1.
The Seven Earths.

The seas which surround these earths are, 1. of salt water, inclosing our inmost earth; 2. of fresh water; 3. of tyre, curdled milk; 4. of ghee, clarified butter; 5. of cauloo, a liquor drawn from the pullum tree; 6. of liquid sugar; 7. of milk. The whole system is inclosed in one broad circumference of pure gold, beyond which reigns impenetrable darkness.—KINDERSLEY.

I know not whether the following fable was invented to account for the saltness of our sea:

« Agastya is recorded to have been very low in stature; and one day, previously to the rectifying the too oblique posture of the earth, walking with Veeshnu on the shore of the ocean, the insolent Deep asked the god, who that dwarf was strutting by his side? Veeshnu replied, it was the patriarch Agastya going to restore the earth to its true balance. The sea, in utter contempt of his pigmy form, dashed him with his spray as he passed along; on which the sage, greatly incensed at the designed affront, scooped up some of the water in the hollow of his hand, and drank it off: he again and again repeated the draught, nor desisted till he had drained the bed of the ocean of the entire volume of its waters. Alarmed at this effect of his holy indignation, and dreading an universal drought, the Devatas made intercession with Agastya to relent from his anger, and again restore an element so necessary to the existence of nature, both animate and inanimate. Agastya, pacified, granted their request, and discharged the imbibed fluid in a way becoming the histories of a gross physical people to relate, but by no means proper for this page; a way, however, that evinced his sovereign power, while it marked his ineffable contempt for the vain fury of an element, contending with a being armed with the delegated power of the Creator of all things. After this miracle, the earth being, by the same power, restored to its just balance, Agastya and Veeshnu separated: when the latter, to prevent any similar accident occurring, commanded the *great serpent* (that is, of the sphere) to wind its enormous folds round the seven continents, of which, according to Sanscreet geography, the earth consists, and appointed, as perpetual guardians, to watch over and protect it, the eight powerful genii, so renowned in the Hindoo system of mythology, as presiding over the eight points of the world.»—MAURICE.

The Pauranics (said Ramachandra to Sir William Jones) will tell you that our earth is a plane figure studded with eight mountains, and sorrounded by seven seas of milk, nectar, and other fluids; that the part which we inhabit is one of seven islands, to which eleven smaller isles are subordinate; that a god, riding on a huge elephant, guards each of the eight regions; and that a mountain of gold rises and gleams in the centre.—*Asiatic Researches.*

«Eight original mountains and seven seas, BRAHMA, INDRA, the SUN, and RUDRA, *these are permanent;* not thou, not I, not this or that people. Wherefore then should anxiety be raised in our minds?»—*Asiatic Res.*

Note 80, page 339, col. 2.

Mount Calasay.

The residence of *Ixora* is upon the silver mount *Calaja,* to the south of the famous mountain *Mahameru,* being a most delicious place, planted with all sorts of trees, that bear fruit all the year round. The roses and other flowers send forth a most odoriferous scent; and the pond at the foot of the mount is inclosed with pleasant walks of trees, that afford an agreeable shade, whilst the peacocks and divers other birds entertain the ear with their harmonious noise, as the beautiful women do the eyes. The circumjacent woods are inhabited by a certain people called *Munis,* or *Rixis,* who, avoiding the conversation of others, spend their time in offering daily sacrifices to their god.

It is observable, that though these pagans are generally black themselves, they do represent these *Rixis* to be of a fair complexion, with long white beards, and long garments hanging cross-ways, from about the neck down over the breast. They are in such high esteem among them, they believe that whom they bless are blessed, and whom they curse are cursed.

Within the mountain lives another generation, called *Jexaquinnera* and *Quendra,* who are free from all trouble, spend their days in continual contemplations, praises, and prayers to God. Round about the mountain stand seven ladders, by which you ascend to a spacious plain, in the middle whereof is a bell of silver, and a square table, surrounded with nine precious stones, of divers colours. Upon this table lies a silver rose, called *Tamara Pua,* which contains two women as bright and fair as a pearl: one is called *Brigasiri,* i. e. *the Lady of the Mouth;* the other *Tarasiri,* i. e. *the Lady of the Tongue,*—because they praise God with the mouth and tongue. In the centre of this rose is the *triangle of Quivelinga,* which they say is the permanent residence of God.—BALDÆUS.

Note 81, page 340, col. 1.

O All-embracing Mind,
Thou who art every-where.

Perhaps it would have been better if I had written *all-containing* mind.

«Even I was even at first, not any other thing; that which exists, unperceived, supreme: afterwards I am that which is; and he who must remain, am I.

«Except the First Cause, whatever may appear, and may not appear, in the mind, know that to be the mind's *Màyà,* or *delusion,* as light, as darkness.

«As the great elements are in various beings, entering, yet not entering, (that is, pervading, not destroying,) thus am I in them, yet not in them.

«Even thus far may inquiry be made by him who seeks to know the principle of mind in union and separation, which must be *everywhere, always.»—Asiat. Researches.* Sir W. JONES, *from the Bhagavat.*

I am the creation and the dissolution of the whole universe. There is not any thing greater than I, and all things hang on me, even as precious gems upon a string. I am moisture in the water, light in the sun and moon, invocation in the *Veds,* sound in the firmament, human nature in mankind, sweet-smelling savour in the earth, glory in the source of light: In all things I am life; and I am zeal in the zealous: and know, O Arjoon! that I am the eternal seed of all nature. I am the understanding of the wise, the glory of the proud, the strength of the strong, free from lust and anger; and in animals I am desire regulated by moral fitness.—KREESHNA, *in the Bhagavat-Geeta.*

Note 82, page 340, col. 1.

Heart cannot think, nor tongue declare,
Nor eyes of angel bear
That glory, unimaginably bright.

Being now in the splendorous lustre of the divine bliss and glory, I there saw in spirit the choir of the holy angels, the choir of the prophets and apostles, who, with heavenly tongues and music, sing and play around the throne of God; yet not in just such corporeal forms or shapes as are those we *now* bear and walk about in; no, but in shapes all spiritual; the holy angels in the shape of a multitude of flames of fire, the souls of believers in the shape of a multitude of glittering or luminous sparkles; God's throne in the shape, or under the appearance of a great splendour.—HANS ENGELBRECHT.

Something analogous to this unendurable presence of Seeva is found amid the nonsense of Joanna Southcott. Apollyon is there made to say of the Lord, «thou knowest it is written, he is a consuming fire, and who can dwell in everlasting burnings? who could abide in devouring flames? Our backs are not brass, nor our sinews iron, to dwell with God in heaven.»—*Dispute between the Woman and the Powers of Darkness.*

Note 83, page 340, col. 1.

The Sun himself had seem'd
A speck of darkness there.

«There the sun shines not, nor the moon and stars: these lightnings flash not in that place: how should even fire blaze there? God irradiates all this bright substance, and by its effulgence the universe is enlightened.»—*From the Yajurveda. Asiat. Res.*

Hæc alt, et sese radiorum nocte suorum
Claudit inaccessum.——CARRARA.

Note 84, page 341, col. 2.

Whose cradles from some tree
Unnatural hands suspended.

I heard a voice crying out under my window; I

looked out, and saw a poor young girl lamenting the unhappy case of her sister. On asking what was the matter, the reply was, *Boot Laggeosa*, a demon has seized her. These unhappy people say *Boot Laggeosa*, if a child newly born will not such; and they expose it to death in a basket, hung on the branch of a tree. One day, as Mr Thomas and I were riding out, we saw a basket hung in a tree, in which an infant had been exposed, the skull of which remained, the rest having been devoured by ants.—*Periodical Accounts of the Baptist Missionaries.*

Note 85, page 342, col. 1.
That strange Indian Bird.

The Chatookee. They say it never drinks at the streams below, but, opening its bill when it rains, it catches the drops as they fall from the clouds.—*Periodical Accounts of the Baptist Missionaries*, vol. ii, p. 309.

Note 86, page 343, col. 1.
Yamen.

Yamá was a child of the Sun, and thence named *Vaivaswata;* another of his titles was *Dhermaraja*, or King of Justice; and a third *Pitripeti*, or Lord of the Patriarchs : but he is chiefly distinguished as Judge of departed souls ; for the Hindus believe, that, when a soul leaves its body, it immediately repairs to *Yamapur*, or the city of *Yama*, where it receives a just sentence from him, and thence either ascends to *Swerga*, or the first Heaven ; or is driven down to *Narac*, the region of serpents ; or assumes on earth the form of some animal, unless its offence has been such, that it ought to be condemned to a vegetable, or even to a mineral prison.—Sir W. JONES.

There is a story concerning Yamen which will remind the reader, in its purport, of the fable of Love and Death. « A famous penitent, *Morrugandumagarexi* by name, had, during a long series of years, served the gods with uncommon and most exemplary piety. This very virtuous man having no children, was extremely desirous of having one, and therefore daily besought the god Xiven (or Seeva) to grant him one. At length the god heard his desire, but, before he indulged it him, he asked him, whether he would have several children, who should be long-lived and wicked, or one virtuous and prudent, who should die in his sixteenth year? The penitent chose the latter : his wife conceived, and was happily delivered of the promised son, whom they named Marcandem. The boy, like his father, zealously devoted himself to the worship of Xiven, but as soon as he had attained his sixteenth year, the officers of Yhamen, god of death, were sent on the earth, to remove him from thence.

« Young Marcandem being informed on what errand they were come, told them, with a resolute air, that he was resolved not to die, and that they might go back, if they pleased. They returned to their master, and told him the whole affair. Yhamen immediately mounted his great buffle, and set out. Being come, he told the youth that he acted very rashly in refusing to leave the world, and it was unjust in him, for Xiven had promised him a life only of sixteen years, and the term was expired. But this reason did not satisfy Marcandem, who persisted in his resolution not to die ; and, fearing lest the god of death should attempt to take him away by force, he ran to his oratory, and taking the Lingam, clasped it to his breast. Mean time Yhamen came down from his buffle, threw a rope about the youth's neck, and held him fast therewith, as also the Lingam, which Marcandem grasp'd with all his strength, and was going to drag them both into hell, when Xiven issued out of the Lingam, drove back the king of the dead, and gave him so furious a blow, that he killed him on the spot.

« The god of death being thus slain, mankind multiplied so that the earth was no longer able to contain them. The gods represented this to Xiven, and he, at their entreaty, restored Yhamen to life, and to all the power he had before enjoyed. Yhamen immediately dispatched a herald to all parts of the world, to summon all the old men. The herald got drunk before he set out, and, without staying till the fumes of the wine were dispelled, mounted an elephant, and rode up and down the world, pursuant to his commission ; and, instead of publishing this order, he declared, that it was the will and pleasure of Yhamen, that, from this day forward, all the leaves, fruits, and flowers, whether ripe or green, should fall to the ground. This proclamation was no sooner issued than men began to yield to death : But before Yhamen was killed, only the old were deprived of life, and now people of all ages are summoned indiscriminately.»—PICART.

Note 87, page 345, col. 1.
And Brama's region. where the heavenly Hours
Weave the vast circle of his age-long day.

They who are acquainted with day and night know that the day of Brahma is as a thousand revolutions of the *Yoogs*, and that his night extendeth for a thousand more. On the coming of that day all things proceed from invisibility to visibility ; so, on the approach of night, they are all dissolved away in that which is called invisible. The universe, even, having existed, is again dissolved ; and now again, on the approach of day, by divine necessity, it is reproduced. That which, upon the dissolution of all things else, is not destroyed, is superior and of another nature from that visibility : it is invisible and eternal. He who is thus called invisible and incorruptible is even he who is called the Supreme Abode ; which men having once obtained, they never more return to earth : that is my mansion.—KREESHNA, *in the Bhagavat-Geeta.*

The guess, that Brama and his wife Saraswadi may be Abraham and Sarah, has more letters in its favour than are usually to be found in such guesses.—NIECAMP, p. i, c. 10. sect. 2.

The true cause why there is no idol of Brama (except the head, which is his share in the Trimourter,) is probably to be found in the conquest of his sect. A different reason, however, is implied in the Veeda : « Of Him, it says, whose glory is so great, there is no image :—He is the incomprehensible Being which illumines all, delights all, whence all proceeded !—that by which they live when born, and that to which all must return.»—MOOR's *Hindu Pantheon*, p. 4.

Note 88, page 346, col. 1.
Two forms inseparable in unity,
Hath Yamen.

The *Dharma-Raja*, or king of justice, has two countenances ; one is mild and full of benevolence ; those alone who abound with virtue see it. He holds a court of justice, where are many assistants, among whom are many just and pious kings: *Chitragupta* acts as chief secretary. These holy men determine what is *dharma* and *adharma*, just and unjust. His (*Dharma-Raja's*) servant is called *Carmala*: he brings the righteous on celestial cars, which go of themselves, whenever holy men are to be brought in, according to the directions of the *Dharma-Raja*, who is the sovereign of the *Pitris*. This is called his *divine countenance*, and the righteous alone do see it. His other *countenance*, or *form*, is called *Yama*; this the wicked alone can see: It has large teeth and a monstrous body. *Yama* is the lord of *Patala*; there he orders some to be beaten, some to be cut to pieces, some to be devoured by monsters, etc. His servant is called *Cashmala*, who, with ropes round their necks, drags the wicked over rugged paths, and throws them headlong into hell. He is unmerciful, and hard is his heart; every body trembles at the sight of him.—WILFORD. *Asiatic Researches.*

Note 89, page 346, col. 2.
Black of aspect, red of eye.

Punishment is the Magistrate; Punishment is the inspirer of Terror; Punishment is the Defender from Calamity; Punishment is the Guardian of those that sleep; Punishment, with a black aspect and a red eye, tempts the guilty.—HALHED's *Gentoo Code*, ch. xxi, sect. 8.

Note 90, page 346, col. 2.
Asyoruca.

In Patala (or the infernal regions) resides the sovereign Queen of the Nagas, (large snakes, or dragons:) she is beautiful, and her name is Asyoruca. There, in cave, she performed Taparya with such rigorous austerity, that fire sprang from her body, and formed numerous agnitiraths (places of sacred fire) in Patala. These fires, forcing their way through the earth, waters, and mountains, formed various openings or mouths, called from thence the flaming mouths, or juala muihi. By Samudr, (Oceanus,) a daughter was born unto her, called Rama-Devi. She is most beautiful; she is Lacshmi, and her name is Asyotcarsha, or Asyoterishta. Like a jewel she remains concealed in the Ocean.—WILFORD. *Asiat. Res.*

Note 91, page 347, col. 1.
He came in all his might and majesty.

What is this to the coming of Seeva, as given us by Sir Maurice, from the Seeva Paurana?

« In the place of the right wheel blazed the Sun, in the place of the left was the Moon; instead of the brazen nails and bolts, which firmly held the ponderous wheels, were distributed Bramins on the right hand, and Reyshees on the left; in lieu of the canopy on the top of the chariot was overspread the vault of Heaven; the counterpoise of the wheels was on the east and west, and the four Semordres were instead of the cushions and bolsters; the four Vedas were placed as the horses of the chariot, and Saraswaty was for the bell; the piece of wood by which the horses are driven as the three-lettered Mantra, while Brama himself as the charioteer, and the Naeshatras and stars were distributed about it by way of ornaments. Sumaru as in the place of a bow, the serpent Seschanaga was stationed as the string, Veeshnu instead of an arrow, and fire was constituted its point. Ganges and other rivers were appointed its precursors; and the setting

out of the chariot, with its appendages and furniture, one would affirm to be the year of twelve months gracefully moving forwards.

« When Seeva, with his numerous troops and prodigious army, was mounted, Brama drove so furiously, that thought itself, which, in its rapid career, compasses Heaven and Earth, could not keep pace with it. By the motion of the chariot Heaven and Earth were put into a tremor; and, as the Earth was not able to bear up under this burthen, the Cow of the Earth, Kam-deva, took upon itself to support the weight. Seeva went with intention to destroy Treepoor: and the multitude of Devatas and Reyshees and Apsaras who waited on his stirrup, opening their mouths, in transports of joy and praise, exclaimed, Jaya! Jaya! so that Parvati, not being able to bear his absence, set out to accompany Seeva, and, in an instant, was up with him; while the light which brightened on his countenance, on the arrival of Parvati, surpassed all imagination and description. The Genii of the eight regions, armed with all kinds of weapons, but particularly with *agnyastra*, or fire-darts, like moving mountains, advanced in front of the army; and Eendra and other Devatas, some of them mounted on elephants, some on horses, others on chariots, or on camels or buffaloes, were stationed on each side; while all the other order of Devatas, to the amount of some lacs, formed the centre. The Munietuvaras, with long hair on their heads, like Saniassis, holding their staves in their hands, danced as they went along; the Syddyhas, who revolve about the heavens, opening their mouths in praise of Seeva, rained flowers upon his head; and the vaulted heaven, which is like an inverted goblet, being appointed in the place of a drum, exalted his dignity by its majestic resounding.»

Throughout the Hindoo fables there is the constant mistake of bulk for sublimity.

Note 92, page 347, col. 1.
By the attribute of Deity
——self-multiplied
The dreadful One appear'd on every side.

This more than polypus power was once exerted by Krishna, on a curious occasion.

It happened in *Dwarka*, a splendid city built by *Viswakarma*, by command of *Krishna*, on the sea-shore, in the province of *Gazerat*, that his musical associate, *Nareda*, had no wife or substitute; and he hinted to his friend the decency of sparing him one from his long catalogue of ladies. *Krishna* generously told him to win and wear any one he chose, not immediately in requisition for himself. *Nareda* accordingly went wooing to one house, but found his master there; to a second—he was again forestalled; a third, the same; to a fourth, fifth, the same: in fine, after the round of sixteen thousand of these domiciliary visits, he was still forced to sigh and keep single; for *Krishna* was in every house, variously employed, and so domesticated, that each lady congratulated herself on her exclusive and uninterrupted possession of the ardent deity.—MOOR's *Hindu Pantheon*, p. 204.

Eight of the chief gods have each their *sacti*, or energy, proceeding from them, differing from them in sex, but in every other respect exactly like them, with the same form, the same decorations, the same weapons, and same vehicle.—*Asiat. Res.* 8vo edit. vol. viii, p. 68, 82.

The manner in which this divine power is displayed by Kehama, in his combat with Yamen, will remind some readers of the Irishman, who brought in four prisoners, and being asked how he had taken them, replied, he had surrounded them.

Note 93, page 348, col. 1.

The Amreeta, or Drink of Immortality.

Mr Wilkins has given the genuine history of this liquor, which was produced by churning the sea with a mountain.

"There is a fair and stately mountain, and its name is Meroo, a most exalted mass of glory, reflecting the sunny rays from the splendid surface of its gilded horns. It is clothed in gold, and is the respected haunt of Dews and Gandarvas. It is inconceivable, and not to be encompassed by sinful man; and it is guarded by dreadful serpents. Many celestial medicinal plants adorn its sides; and it stands, piercing the heaven with its aspiring summit, a mighty hill, inaccessible even by the human mind. It is adorned with trees and pleasant streams, and resoundeth with the delightful songs of various birds.

"The Soors, and all the glorious hosts of heaven, having ascended to the summit of this lofty mountain, sparkling with precious gems, and for eternal ages raised, were sitting in solemn synod, meditating the discovery of the Amreeta, the Water of Immortality. The Dew Narayan being also there, spoke unto Brahma, whilst the Soors were thus consulting together, and said, 'Let the Ocean, as a pot of milk, be churned by the united labour of the Soors and Asoors; and when the mighty waters have been stirred up, the Amreeta shall be found. Let them collect together every medicinal herb, and every precious thing, and let them stir the Ocean, and they shall discover the Amreeta.'

"There is also another mighty mountain, whose name is Mandar, and its rocky summits are like towering clouds. It is clothed in a net of the entangled tendrils of the twining creeper, and resoundeth with the harmony of various birds. Innumerable savage beasts infest its borders; and it is the respected haunt of Kennars, Dews, and Apsars. It standeth eleven thousand Yojan above the earth, and eleven thousand more below its surface.

"As the united bands of Dews were unable to remove this mountain, they went before Veeshnoo, who was sitting with Brahma, and addressed them in these words; 'Exert, O masters! your most superior wisdom to remove the mountain Mandar, and employ your utmost power for our good.'

"Veeshnoo and Brahma having said, 'it shall be according to your wish,' he with the lotus eye directed the King of Serpents to appear; and Ananta arose, and was instructed in that work by Brahma, and commanded by Narayan to perform it. Then Ananta, by his power, took up that king of mountains, together with all its forests and every inhabitant thereof; and the Soors accompanied him into the presence of the Ocean, whom they addressed, saying, 'We will stir up thy waters to obtain the Amreeta.' And the Lord of the Waters replied, 'Let me also have a share, seeing I am to bear the violent agitation that will be caused by the whirling of the mountain!' Then the Soors and Asoors spoke unto Koorma-raj, the King of the Tortoises, upon the strand of the Ocean, and said, 'My lord is able to be the supporter of this mountain.' The Tortoise replied, 'Be it so;' and it was placed upon his back.

"So the mountain being set upon the back of the Tortoise, Eendra began to whirl it about as it were a machine. The mountain Mandar served as a churn, and the serpent Vasoakee for the rope; and thus in former days did the Dews, and Asoors, and the Danoos, begin to stir up the waters of the ocean for the discovery of the Amreeta.

"The mighty Asoors were employed on the side of the serpent's head, whilst all the Soors assembled about his tail. Ananta, that sovereign Dew, stood near Narayan.

"They now pull forth the serpent's head repeatedly, and as often let it go; whilst there issued from his mouth, thus violently drawing to and fro by the Soors and Asoors, a continual stream of fire and smoke and wind, which ascending in thick clouds, replete with lightning, it began to rain down upon the heavenly bands, who were already fatigued with their labour; whilst a shower of flowers was shaken from the top of the mountain, covering the heads of all, both Soors and Asoors. In the mean time the roaring of the ocean, whilst violently agitated with the whirling of the mountain Mandar by the Soors and Asoors, was like the bellowing of a mighty cloud. Thousands of the various productions of the waters were torn to pieces by the mountain, and confounded with the briny flood; and every specific being of the deep, and all the inhabitants of the great abyss which is below the earth, were annihilated; whilst, from the violent agitation of the mountain, the forest trees were dashed against each other, and precipitated from its utmost height, with all the birds thereon; from whose violent confrication a raging fire was produced, involving the whole mountain with smoke and flame, as with a dark blue cloud, and the lightning's vivid flash. The lion and the retreating elephant are overtaken by the devouring flames, and every vital being and every specific thing, are consumed in the general conflagration.

"The raging flames, thus spreading destruction on all sides, were at length quenched by a shower of cloud-borne water, poured down by the immortal Eendra. And now a heterogeneous stream of the concocted juices of various trees and plants ran down into the briny flood.

"It was from this milk-like stream of juices, produced from those trees and plants and a mixture of melted gold, that the Soors obtained their immortality.

"The waters of the Ocean now being assimilated with those juices, were converted into milk, and from that milk a kind of butter was presently produced; when the heavenly bands went again into the presence of Brahma, the granter of boons, and addressed him, saying, 'Except Narayan, every other Soor and Asoor is fatigued with his labour, and still the Amreeta doth not appear; wherefore the churning of the Ocean is at a stand.' Then Brahma said unto Narayan, 'Endue them with recruited strength, for thou art their support. And Narayan answered and said, 'I will give fresh vigour to such as co-operate in the work. Let Mandar be whirled about, and the bed of the ocean be kept steady.'

"When they heard the words of Narayan, they all returned again to the work, and began to stir about with great force that butter of the ocean, when there presently arose from out the troubled deep, first the Moon, with a pleasing countenance, shining with ten thousand beams of gentle light; next followed Sree, the goddess of fortune, whose seat is the white lily of the waters; then *Soora-Devee*, the goddess of wine, and the white horse called *Oohisrava*. And after these there was produced from the unctuous mass the jewell *Kowstoobh*, that glorious sparkling gem worn by Narayan on his breast; also *Pareejat*, the tree of plenty, and *Soorabhee*, the cow that granted every heart's desire.

« The moon, *Soora-Devee*, the goddess of *Sree*, and the Horse, as swift as thought, instantly marched away towards the *Dews*, keeping in the path of the Sun.

« Then the *Dew Dhanwantaree*, in human shape, came forth, holding in his hand a white vessel filled with the immortal juice *Amreeta*. When the *Asoors* beheld these wondrous things appear, they raised their tumultuous voices for the *Amreeta*, and each of them clamorously exclaimed, 'This of right is mine.'

« In the mean time *Travat*, a mighty elephant, arose, now kept by the god of thunder; and as they continued to churn the ocean more than enough, that deadly poison issued from its bed, burning like a raging fire, whose dreadful fumes in a moment spread throughout the world, confounding the three regions of the universe with the mortal stench, until *Seev*, at the word of *Brahma*, swallowed the fatal drug, to save mankind; which, remaining in the throat of that Sovereign *Dew* of magic form, from that time he hath been called *Neel-Kant*, because his throat was stained blue.

« When the *Asoors* beheld this miraculous deed, they became desperate, and the *Amreeta* and the goddess *Sree* became the source of endless hatred.

« Then *Narayan* assumed the character and person of *Moheenee Maya*, the power of enchantment, in a female form of wonderful beauty, and stood before the *Asoors*, whose minds being fascinated by her presence, and deprived of reason, they seized the *Amreeta*, and gave it unto her.

« The *Asoors* now clothe themselves in costly armour, and, seizing their various weapons, rush on together to attack the *Soors*. In the mean time *Narayan*, in the female form, having obtained the *Amreeta* from the hands of their leader, the hosts of *Soors*, during the tumult and confusion of the *Asoors*, drank of the living water.

« And it so fell out, that whilst the *Soors* were quenching their thirst for immortality, *Rahoo*, an *Asoor*, assumed the form of a *Soor*, and began to drink also: And the water had but reached his throat, when the Sun and Moon, in friendship to the *Soors*, discovered the deceit; and instantly *Narayan* cut off his head as he was drinking, with his splendid weapon *Chakra*. And the gigantic head of the *Asoor*, emblem of a mountain's summit, being thus separated from his body by the *Chakra's* edge, bounded into the heavens with a dreadful cry, whilst his ponderous trunk fell, cleaving the ground asunder, and shaking the whole earth unto its foundation, with all its islands, rocks, and forests: And from that time the head of Rahoo resolved an eternal enmity, and continueth, even unto this day, at times to seize upon the Sun and Moon.

« Now Narayan, having quitted the female figure he had assumed, began to disturb the *Asoors* with sundry celestial weapons; and from that instant a dreadful battle was commenced, on the ocean's briny strand, between the *Asoors* and the *Soors*. Innumerable sharp and missile weapons were hurled, and thousands of piercing darts and battle-axes fell on all sides. The

Asoors vomit blood from the wounds of the *Chakra*, and fall upon the ground pierced by the sword, the spear, and spiked club. Heads, glittering with polished gold, divided by the *Pattees'* blade, drop incessantly; and mangled bodies, wallowing in their gore, lay like fragments of mighty rocks, sparkling with gems and precious ores. Millions of sighs and groans arise on every side; and the sun is overcast with blood, as they clash their arms, and wound each other with their dreadful instruments of destruction.

« Now the battle is fought with the iron-spike club, and, as they close, with clenched fist; and the din of war ascendeth to the heavens. They cry 'Pursue! strike! fell to the ground!' so that a horrid and tumultuous noise is heard on all sides.

« In the midst of this dreadful hurry and confusion of the fight, *Nar* and *Narayan* entered the field together. *Narayan*, beholding a celestial bow in the hand of *Nar*, it reminded him of his *Chakra*, the destroyer of the *Asoors*. The faithful weapon, by name *Soodarsan*, ready at the mind's call, flew down from heaven with direct and refulgent speed, beautiful, yet terrible to behold: And being arrived, glowing like the sacrificial flame, and spreading terror around, *Narayan*, with his right arm formed like the elephantine trunk, hurled forth the ponderous orb, the speedy messenger and glorious ruin of hostile towns; who, raging like the final all-destroying fire, shot bounding with desolating force, killing thousands of the *Asoors* in his rapid flight, burning and involving, like the lambent flame, and cutting down all that would oppose him. Anon he climbeth the heavens, and now again darteth into the field like a *Peesach*, to feast in blood.

« Now the dauntless *Asoors* strive, with repeated strength, to crush the *Soors* with rocks and mountains, which, hurled in vast numbers into the heavens, appeared like scattered clouds, and fell, with all the trees thereon, in millions of fear-exciting torrents, striking violently against each other with a mighty noise; and in their fall the earth, with all its fields and forests, is driven from its foundation: they thunder furiously at each other as they roll along the field, and spend their strength in mutual conflict.

« Now *Nar*, seeing the *Soors* overwhelmed with fear, filled up the path to Heaven with showers of golden-headed arrows, and split the mountain summits with his unerring shafts; and the *Asoors* finding themselves again sore pressed by the *Soors*, precipitately flee; some rush headlong into the briny waters of the ocean, and others hide themselves within the bowels of the earth.

« The rage of the glorious *Chakra*, *Soodarsan*, which for a while burnt like the oil-fed fire, now grew cool, and he retired into the heavens from whence he came. And the *Soors* having obtained the victory, the mountain *Mandar* was carried back to its former station with great respect, whilst the waters also retired, filling the firmament and the heavens with their dreadful roarings.

« The *Soors* guarded the *Amreeta* with great care, and rejoiced exceedingly because of their success. And *Eendra*, with all his immortal bands, gave the water of life unto *Narayan*, to keep it for their use.»—MAHABBARAT.

Amrita, or Immortal, is, according to Sir William Jones, the name which the mythologists of Tibet apply to a celestial tree, bearing ambrosial fruit, and adjoining to four vast rocks, from which as many sacred rivers derive their several streams.

Roderick, the Last of the Goths.

Tanto acrior apud majores, sicut virtutibus gloria, ita flagitiis pœnitentia, fuit.
Sed hæc aliaque, ex veteri memoriâ petita, quoties res locusque exempla
recti, aut solatia mali, poscet, haud absurdè memorabimus.

TACITI, *Hist. lib.* 3, *c.* 51.

As the ample Moon
In the deep stillness of a summer even
Rising behind a thick and lofty Grove,
Burns like an unconsuming fire of light
In the green trees; and kindling on all sides
Their leafy umbrage, turns the dusky veil
Into a substance glorious as her own,
Yea, with her own incorporated, by power
Capacious and serene: Like power abides
In man's celestial Spirit, Virtue thus
Sets forth and magnifies herself; thus feeds
A calm, a beautiful and silent fire,
From the incumbrances of mortal life,
From error, disappointment,—nay from guilt;
And sometimes, so relenting Justice wills,
From palpable oppressions of Despair.

WORDSWORTH.

TO GROSVENOR CHARLES BEDFORD,

This Poem is inscribed,

IN LASTING MEMORIAL OF A LONG AND UNINTERRUPTED FRIENDSHIP,

BY HIS OLD SCHOOL-FELLOW,

THE AUTHOR.

PREFACE.

The history of the Wisi-Goths for some years before their overthrow is very imperfectly known. It is however apparent, that the enmity between the royal families of Chindasuintho and Wamba was one main cause of the destruction of the kingdom, the latter party having assisted in betraying their country to the Moors for the gratification of their own revenge. Theodofred and Favila were younger sons of King Chindasuintho; King Witiza, who was of Wamba's family, put out the eyes of Theodofred, and murdered Favila, at the instigation of that Chieftain's wife, with whom he lived in adultery. Pelayo, the son of Favila, and afterwards the founder of the Spanish monarchy, was driven into exile. Roderick, the son of Theodofred, recovered the throne, and put out Witiza's eyes in vengeance for his father; but he spared Orpas, the brother of the tyrant, as being a Priest, and Ebba and Sisibert, the two sons of Witiza, by Pelayo's mother. It may be convenient thus briefly to premise these circumstances of an obscure portion of history, with which few readers can be supposed to be familiar; and a list of the principal persons who are introduced, or spoken of, may as properly be prefixed to a Poem as to a Play.

WITIZA, ... King of the Wisi-Goths; dethroned and blinded by Roderick.

THEODOFRED, . . son of King Chindasuintho, blinded by King Witiza.

FAVILA, ... his brother; put to death by Witiza.

The Wife of Favila, Witiza's adulterous mistress.

(These four persons are dead before the action of the poem commences.)

RODERICK, ... the last King of the Wisi-Goths: son of Theodofred.

PELAYO, ... the founder of the Spanish Monarchy: son of Favila.

GAUDIOSA, ... his wife.

GUISLA, ... his sister.

FAVILA, ... his son.

HERMESIND, ... his daughter.

RUSILLA, ... widow of Theodofred, and mother of Roderick.

COUNT PEDRO, . . . }
COUNT EUDON, . . . } powerful Lords of Cantabria.

ALPHONSO, ... Count Pedro's son, afterwards King.

URBAN, ... Archbishop of Toledo.

ROMANO, ... a Monk of the Caulian Schools, near Merida.

ABDALAZIS, ... the Moorish Governor of Spain.

EGILONA,......formerly the wife of Roderick, now of Abdalaziz.

ABULCACEM,....
ALCAHMAN,.....
AYUB,........ } Moorish Chiefs.
IBRAHIM,.......
MAGUED,......

ORPAS,........brother to Witiza, and formerly Arch-bishop of Seville, now a renegade.

SISIBERT,...... } sons of Witiza and of Pelayo's mo-
EBBA,......... } ther.

NUMACIAN,.....a renegade, governor of Gegio.

COUNT JULIAN,..a powerful Lord among the Wisi-Goths, now a renegade.

FLORINDA,......his daughter, violated by King Rode-rick.

* * * * *

ADOSINDA,......daughter of the Governor of Auria.

ODOAR,........Abbot of St Felix.

SIVERIAN,.....Roderick's foster-father.

FAVINIA,......Count Pedro's wife.

The four latter persons are imaginary. All the others are mentioned in history. I ought, however, to observe, that Romano is a creature of monkish legends; that the name of Pelayo's sister has not been preserved; and that that of Roderick's mother, Ruscilo, has been alter-ed to Rusilla, for the sake of euphony.

I.

RODERICK AND ROMANO.

LONG had the crimes of Spain cried out to Heaven;
At length the measure of offence was full.
Count Julian called the invaders: [1] not because
Inhuman priests with unoffending blood
Had stained their country; [2] not because a yoke
Of iron servitude oppressed and galled
The children of the soil; [3] a private wrong
Roused the remorseless Baron. Mad to wreak
His vengeance for his violated child
On Roderick's head, in evil hour for Spain,
For that unhappy daughter and himself,
Desperate apostate,—on the Moors he called;
And like a cloud of locusts, whom the South
Wafts from the plains of wasted Africa,
The Mussulmen upon Iberia's shore
Descend. A countless multitude they came;
Syrian, Moor, Saracen, Greek renegade,
Persian and Copt and Tatar, in one bond
Of erring faith conjoin'd,—strong in the youth
And heat of zeal,—a dreadful brotherhood,
In whom all turbulent vices were let loose;
While Conscience, with their impious creed accurst,
Drunk, as with wine, had sanctified to them
All bloody, all abominable things.

Thou, Calpë, sawest their coming: ancient Rock
Renowned, no longer now shalt thou be called
From Gods and Heroes of the years of yore,
Kronos, or hundred-handed Briareus,
Bacchus or Hercules; but doomed to bear
The name of thy new conqueror, [4] and thenceforth

To stand his everlasting monument.
Thou sawest the dark-blue waters flash before
Their ominous way, and whiten round their keels;
Their swarthy myriads darkening o'er thy sands.
There on the beach the misbelievers spread
Their banners, flaunting to the sun and breeze:
Fair shone the sun upon their proud array,
White turbans, glittering armour, shields engrailed
With gold, and scymitars of Syrian steel;
And gently did the breezes, as in sport,
Curl their long flags outrolling, and display
The blazoned scrolls of blasphemy. Too soon
The gales of Spain from that unhappy land
Wafted, as from an open charnel-house,
The taint of death; and that bright Sun, from fields
Of slaughter, with the morning dew drew up
Corruption through the infected atmosphere.

Then fell the kingdom of the Goths; their hour
Was come, and Vengeance, long withheld, went loose.
Famine and Pestilence had wasted them, [5]
And Treason, like an old and eating sore,
Consumed the bones and sinews of their strength;
And, worst of enemies, their sins were armed
Against them. [6] Yet the sceptre from their hands
Past not away inglorious; nor was shame
Left for their children's lasting heritage.
Eight summer days, from morn till latest eve,
The fatal fight endured, till perfidy
Prevailing to their overthrow, they sunk
Defeated, not dishonoured. On the banks
Of Chrysus, Roderick's royal car [7] was found;
His battle-horse Orelio, and that helm
Whose horns, amid the thickest of the fray
Eminent, had marked his presence. [8] Did the stream
Receive him with the undistinguished dead,
Christian and Moor, who clogged its course that day?
So thought the Conqueror, and from that day forth,
Memorial of his perfect victory,
He bade the river bear the name of joy. [9]
So thought the Goths; they said no prayer for him,
For him no service sung, nor mourning made,
But charged their crimes upon his head, and curst
His memory.

Bravely in that eight-days' fight
The King had striven,—for victory first, while hop
Remained, then desperately in search of death.
The arrows past him by to right and left,
The spear-point pierced him not, the scymitar
Glanced from his helmet. Is the shield of Heaven,
Wretch that I am, extended over me?
Cried Roderick; and he dropt Orelio's reins,
And threw his hands aloft in frantic pray'r,—
Death is the only mercy that I crave,
Death soon and short, death and forgetfulness!
Aloud he cried; but in his inmost heart
There answered him a secret voice, that spake
Of righteousness and judgment after death,
And God's redeeming love, which fain would save
The guilty soul alive. 'T was agony,
And yet 't was hope;—a momentary light,
That flashed through utter darkness on the Cross
To point salvation, then left all within
Dark as before. Fear, never felt till then,
Sudden and irresistible as stroke
Of lightning, smote him. From his horse he dropt,

Whether with human impulse, or by Heaven
Struck down, he knew not; loosened from his wrist
The sword-chain, and let fall the sword, whose hilt
Clung to his palm a moment ere it fell,
Glued there with Moorish gore. His royal robe,
His horned belmet and enamelled mail,
He cast aside, and taking from the dead
A peasant's garment, in those weeds involved,
Stole, like a thief in darkness, from the field.

Evening closed round to favour him.—All night
He fled, the sound of battle in his ear
Ringing, and sights of death before his eyes,
With dreams more horrible of eager fiends
That seemed to hover round, and gulphs of fire
Opening beneath his feet. At times the groan
Of some poor fugitive, who, bearing with him
His mortal hurt, had fallen beside the way,
Roused him from these dread visions, and he called
In answering groans on his Redeemer's name,
That word the only prayer that past his lips
Or rose within his heart. Then would he see
The Cross whereon a bleeding Saviour hung,
Who called on him to come and cleanse his soul
In those all-healing streams, which from his wounds,
As from perpetual springs, for ever flowed.
No hart e'er panted for the water-brooks
As Roderick thirsted there to drink and live:
But Hell was interposed; and worse than Hell,
Yea to his eyes more dreadful than the fiends
Who flocked like hungry ravens round his head,—
Florinda stood between, and warned him off
With her abhorrent hands,—that agony
Still in her face, which, when the deed was done,
Inflicted on her ravisher the curse
That it invoked from Heaven——Oh what a night
Of waking horrors! Nor when morning came
Did the realities of light and day
Bring aught of comfort; wheresoe'er he went
The tidings of defeat had gone before;
And leaving their defenceless homes to seek
What shelter walls and battlements might yield,
Old men with feeble feet, and tottering babes,
And widows with their infants in their arms,
Hurried along. Nor royal festival,
Nor sacred pageant, with like multitudes
E'er filled the public way. All whom the sword
Had spared were here; bed-rid infirmity
Alone was left behind: the cripple plied
His crutches, with her child of yesterday
The mother fled, and she whose hour was come
Fell by the road.
　　　　　Less dreadful than this view
Of outward suffering which the day disclosed,
Had night and darkness seemed to Roderick's heart,
With all their dread creations. From the throng
He turned aside, unable to endure
This burthen of the general woe: nor walls,
Nor towers, nor mountain fastnesses he sought;
A firmer hold his spirit yearned to find,
A rock of surer strength. Unknowing where,
Straight through the wild he hastened on all day,
And with unslackened speed was travelling still
When evening gathered round. Seven days from morn
Till night he travelled thus; the forest oaks,
The fig-grove by the fearful husbandman

Forsaken to the spoiler, and the vines,
Where fox and household dog together now
Fed on the vintage, gave him food: the hand
Of heaven was on him, and the agony
Which wrought within, supplied a strength, beyond
All natural force of man.
　　　　　　　　When the eighth eve
Was come, he found himself on Ana's banks,
Fast by the Caulian Schools. [10] It was the hour
Of vespers, but no vesper bell was heard,
Nor other sound, than of the passing stream,
Or stork, who, flapping with wide wing the air,
Sought her broad nest upon the silent tower.
Brethren and pupils thence alike had fled
To save themselves within the embattled walls
Of neighbouring Merida. One aged Monk
Alone was left behind; he would not leave
The sacred spot beloved, for having served
There from his childhood up to ripe old age
God's holy altar, it became him now,
He thought, before that altar to await
The merciless misbelievers, and lay down
His life, a willing martyr. So he staid
When all were gone, and duly fed the lamps,
And kept devotedly the altar drest,
And duly offered up the sacrifice.
Four days and nights he thus had past alone,
In such high mood of saintly fortitude,
That hope of Heaven became a heavenly joy;
And now at evening to the gate he went
If he might spy the Moors,—for it seemed long
To tarry for his crown.
　　　　　　　　Before the Cross
Roderick had thrown himself: his body raised,
Half kneeling, half at length he lay; his arms
Embraced its foot, and from his lifted face
Tears streaming down bedewed the senseless stone.
He had not wept till now, and at the gush
Of these first tears, it seemed as if his heart,
From a long winter's icy thrall let loose,
Had opened to the genial influences
Of Heaven. In attitude, but not in act
Of prayer he lay; an agony of tears
Was all his soul could offer. When the Monk
Beheld him suffering thus, he raised him up,
And took him by the arm, and led him in;
And there before the altar, in the name
Of Him whose bleeding image there was hung,
Spake comfort, and adjured him in that name
There to lay down the burthen of his sins.
Lo! said Romano, I am waiting here
The coming of the Moors, that from their hands
My spirit may receive the purple robe
Of martyrdom, and rise to claim its crown.
That God who willeth not the sinner's death
Hath led thee hither. Threescore years and five,
Even from the hour when I, a five-years' child,
Entered the schools, have I continued here
And served the altar: not in all those years
Hath such a contrite and a broken heart
Appeared before me. O my brother, Heaven
Hath sent thee for thy comfort, and for mine,
That my last earthly act may reconcile
A sinner to his God.
　　　　　　　　Then Roderick knelt
Before the holy man, and strove to speak.

Thou seest, he cried,—thou seest,—but memory
And suffocating thoughts repress the word,
And shudderings, like an ague fit, from head
To foot convulsed him; till at length, subduing
His nature to the effort, he exclaimed,
Spreading his hands and lifting up his face, [11]
As if resolved in penitence to bear
A human eye upon his shame,—Thou seest
Roderick the Goth! That name would have sufficed
To tell the whole abhorred history:
He not the less pursued,—the ravisher,
The cause of all this ruin! Having said,
In the same posture motionless he knelt,
Arms straightened down, and hands outspread, and eyes
Raised to the Monk, like one who from his voice
Expected life or death.

     All night the old man
Prayed with his penitent, and ministered
Unto the wounded soul, till he infused
A healing hope of mercy, that allayed
Its heat of anguish. But Romano saw
What strong temptations of despair beset,
And how he needed in this second birth,
Even like a yearling child, a fosterer's care.
Father in heaven, he cried, thy will be done!
Surely I hoped that I this day should sing
Hosannahs at thy throne; but thou hast yet
Work for thy servant here. He girt his loins,
And from her altar took with reverent hands
Our lady's image down: In this, quoth he,
We have our guide and guard and comforter,
The best provision for our perilous way.
Fear not but we shall find a resting place—
The Almighty's hand is on us.

      They went forth,
They crost the stream, and when Romano turned
For his last look toward the Caulian towers,
Far off the Moorish standards in the light
Of morn were glittering, where the miscreant host
Toward the Lusitanian capital
To lay their siege advanced: the eastern breeze
Bore to the fearful travellers far away
The sound of horn and tambour o'er the plain.
All day they hastened, and when evening fell
Sped toward the setting sun, as if its line
Of glory came from Heaven to point their course.
But feeble were the feet of that old man
For such a weary length of way; and now
Being past the danger (for in Merida
Sacaru long in resolute defence
Withstood the tide of war), with easier pace
The wanderers journeyed on; till having crost
Old Tagus, and the rapid Zezere,
They from Albardos' hoary height beheld
Pine-forest, fruitful vale, and that fair lake
Where Alcoa, mingled there with Basa's stream,
Rests on its passage to the western sea,
That sea the aim and boundary of their toil.

The fourth week of their painful pilgrimage [12]
Was full, when they arrived where from the land
A rocky hill, rising with steep ascent,
O'erhung the glittering beach; there on the top
A little lowly hermitage they found,
And a rude Cross, and at its foot a grave,
Bearing no name, nor other monument.

Where better could they rest than here, where faith
And secret penitence and happiest death
Had blest the spot, and brought good angels down,
And opened, as it were, a way to Heaven?
Behind them was the desert, offering fruit
And water for their need: on either side
The white sand sparkling to the sun; in front,
Great Ocean with its everlasting voice,
As in perpetual jubilee, proclaimed
The wonders of the Almighty, filling thus
The pauses of their fervent orisons.
Where better could the wanderers rest than here?

II.

RODERICK IN SOLITUDE.

TWELVE months they sojourned in their solitude,
And then beneath the burthen of old age
Romano sunk. No brethren were there here
To spread the sackcloth, and with ashes strew
That penitential bed, and gather round
To sing his requiem, and with prayer and psalm
Assist him in his hour of agony.
He lay on the bare earth, which long had been
His only couch; beside him Roderick knelt,
Moistened from time to time his blackened lips,
Received a blessing with his latest breath,
Then closed his eyes, and by the nameless grave
Of the fore-tenant of that holy place
Consigned him earth to earth.

     Two graves are here,
And Roderick transverse at their feet began
To break the third. In all his intervals
Of prayer, save only when he searched the woods
And filled the water-cruise, he laboured there;
And when the work was done, and he had laid
Himself at length within its narrow sides
And measured it, he shook his head to think
There was no other business now for him.
Poor wretch, thy bed is ready, he exclaimed,
And would that night were come!—It was a task,
All gloomy as it was, which had beguiled
The sense of solitude; but now he felt
The burthen of the solitary hours:
The silence of that lonely hermitage
Lay on him like a spell; and at the voice
Of his own prayers, he started, half aghast.
Then too, as on Romano's grave he sate
And pored upon his own, a natural thought
Arose within him,—well might he have spared
That useless toil: the sepulchre would be
No hiding-place for him; no Christian hands
Were here who should compose his decent corpse
And cover it with earth. There he might drag
His wretched body at its passing hour,
And there the Sea-Birds of her heritage
Would rob the worm, or peradventure seize,
Ere death had done its work, their helpless prey.
Even now they did not fear him: when he walked
Beside them on the beach, regardlessly
They saw his coming; and their whirring wings
Upon the height had sometimes fanned his cheek,
As if, being thus alone, humanity
Had lost its rank, and the prerogative
Of man was done away.

For his lost crown
And sceptre never had he felt a thought
Of pain: repentance had no pangs to spare
For trifles such as these,—the loss of these
Was a cheap penalty:—that he had fallen
Down to the lowest depth of wretchedness,
His hope and consolation.　But to lose
His human station in the scale of things,—
To see brute Nature scorn him, and renounce
Its homage to the human form divine;—
Had then almighty vengeance thus revealed
His punishment, and was he fallen indeed
Below fallen man,—below redemption's reach,—
Made lower than the beasts, and like the beasts
To perish!—Such temptations troubled him
By day, and in the visions of the night;
And even in sleep he struggled with the thought,
And waking with the effort of his prayers
The dream assailed him still.
　　　　　　　　A wilder form
Sometimes his poignant penitence assumed,
Starting with force revived from intervals
Of calmer passion, or exhausted rest;
When floating back upon the tide of thought
Remembrance to a self-excusing strain
Beguiled him, and recalled in long array
The sorrows and the secret impulses
Which to the abyss of wretchedness and guilt
Led their unwary victim.　The evil hour
Returned upon him, when reluctantly
Yielding to worldly counsel his assent,
In wedlock to an ill-assorted mate
He gave his cold unwilling hand: then came
The disappointment of the barren bed,
The hope deceived, the soul dissatisfied.
Home without love, and privacy from which
Delight was banished first, and peace too soon
Departed.　Was it strange that when he met
A heart attuned,—a spirit like his own,
Of lofty pitch, yet in affection mild,
And tender as a youthful mother's joy,—
Oh was it strange if at such sympathy
The feelings which within his breast repelled
And chilled had shrunk, should open forth like flowers
After cold winds of night, when gentle gales
Restore the genial sun!　If all were known,
Would it indeed be not to be forgiven?—
(Thus would he lay the unction to his soul,)
If all were truly known, as Heaven knows all,
Heaven that is merciful as well as just,—
A passion slow and mutual in its growth,
Pure as fraternal love, long self-concealed,
And when confessed in silence, long controlled;
Treacherous occasion, human frailty, fear
Of endless separation, worse than death,—
The purpose and the hope with which the Fiend
Tempted, deceived, and maddened him;—but then
As at a new temptation would he start,
Shuddering beneath the intolerable shame,
And clench in agony his matted hair;
While in his soul the perilous thought arose,
How easy 't were to plunge where yonder waves
Invited him to rest.
　　　　　　Oh for a voice
Of comfort,—for a ray of hope from Heaven!
A hand that from these billows of despair

May reach and snatch him ere he sink engulphed!
At length, as life when it hath lain long time
Opprest beneath some grievous malady,
Seems to rouse up with re-collected strength,
And the sick man doth feel within himself
A second spring; so Roderick's better mind
Arose to save him.　Lo! the western sun
Flames o'er the broad Atlantic; on the verge
Of glowing ocean rests; retiring then
Draws with it all its rays, and sudden night
Fills the whole cope of Heaven.　The penitent
Knelt by Romano's grave, and, falling prone,
Claspt with extended arms the funeral mould.
Father! he cried; Companion! only friend,
When all beside was lost! thou too art gone,
And the poor sinner whom from utter death
Thy providential hand preserved, once more
Totters upon the gulph.　I am too weak
For solitude,—too vile a wretch to bear
This everlasting commune with myself.
The Tempter hath assailed me; my own heart
Is leagued with him; Despair hath laid the nets
To take my soul, and Memory, like a ghost,
Haunts me, and drives me to the toils.　O Saint,
While I was blest with thee, the hermitage
Was my sure haven! Look upon me still,
For from thy heavenly mansion thou canst see
The suppliant; look upon thy child in Christ.
Is there no other way for penitence?
I ask not martyrdom; for what am I
That I should pray for triumphs, the fit meed
Of a long life of holy works like thine;
Or how should I presumptuously aspire
To wear the heavenly crown resigned by thee,
For my poor sinful sake? Oh point me thou
Some humblest, painfullest, severest path,—
Some new austerity, unheard of yet
In Syrian fields of glory, or the sands
Of holiest Egypt.[13] Let me bind my brow
With thorns, and barefoot seek Jerusalem,
Tracking the way with blood; there day by day
Inflict upon this guilty flesh the scourge,
Drink vinegar and gall, and for my bed
Hang with extended limbs upon the Cross,
A nightly crucifixion!—any thing
Of action, difficulty, bodily pain,
Labour, and outward suffering,—any thing
But stillness and this dreadful solitude!
Romano! Father! let me hear thy voice
In dreams, O sainted Soul! or from the grave
Speak to thy penitent; even from the grave
Thine were a voice of comfort.
　　　　　　　　Thus he cried,
Easing the pressure of his burthened heart
With passionate prayer; thus poured his spirit forth,
Till the long effort had exhausted him,
His spirit failed, and laying on the grave
His weary head, as on a pillow, sleep
Fell on him.　He had prayed to hear a voice
Of consolation, and in dreams a voice
Of consolation came.　Roderick, it said,—
Roderick, my poor, unhappy, sinful child,
Jesus have mercy on thee!—Not if Heaven
Had opened, and Romano, visible
In his beatitude, had breathed that prayer;—
Not if the grave had spoken, had it pierced

So deeply in his soul, nor wrung his heart
With such compunctious visitings, nor given
So quick, so keen a pang. It was that voice
Which sung his fretful infancy to sleep
So patiently; which soothed his childish griefs;
Counselled, with anguish and prophetic tears,
His headstrong youth. And lo! his Mother stood
Before him in the vision: in those weeds
Which never from the hour when to the grave
She followed her dear lord Theodofred
Rusilla laid aside;[14] but in her face
A sorrow that bespake a heavier load
At heart, and more unmitigated woe,—
Yea a more mortal wretchedness than when
Witiza's ruffians and the red-hot brass
Had done their work, and in her arms she held
Her eyeless husband;[15] wiped away the sweat
Which still his tortures forced from every pore;
Cooled his scorched lids with medicinal herbs,
And prayed the while for patience for herself
And him, and prayed for vengeance too, and found
Best comfort in her curses. In his dream,
Groaning he knelt before her to beseech
Her blessing, and she raised her hands to lay
A benediction on him. But those hands
Were chained, and casting a wild look around,
With thrilling voice she cried, Will no one break
These shameful fetters? Pedro, Theudemir,
Athanagild, where are ye? Roderick's arm
Is wither'd,—Chiefs of Spain, but where are ye?
And thou, Pelayo, thou our surest hope,
Dost thou too sleep?—Awake, Pelayo!—up!—
Why tarriest thou, Deliverer?—But with that
She broke her bonds, and lo! her form was changed!
Radiant in arms she stood! a bloody Cross
Gleamed on her breast-plate, in her shield displayed
Erect a lion ramped; her helmèd head
Rose like the Berecynthian Goddess crowned
With towers, and in her dreadful hand the sword
Red as a fire-brand blazed. Anon the tramp
Of horsemen, and the din of multitudes
Moving to mortal conflict, rang around:
The battle-song, the clang of sword and shield,
War-cries and tumult, strife and hate and rage,
Blasphemous prayers, confusion, agony,
Rout and pursuit and death; and over all
The shout of victory—Spain and Victory!
Roderick, as the strong vision mastered him,
Rushed to the fight rejoicing: starting then,
As his own effort burst the charm of sleep,
He found himself upon that lonely grave
In moonlight and in silence. But the dream
Wrought in him still; for still he felt his heart
Pant, and his withered arm was trembling still:
And still that voice was in his ear which called
On Jesus for his sake.
                            O might he hear
That actual voice! and if Rusilla lived,—
If shame and anguish for his crimes not yet
Had brought her to the grave,—sure she would bless
Her penitent child, and pour into his heart
Prayers and forgiveness, which, like precious balm,
Would heal the wounded soul. Nor to herself
Less precious, or less healing, would the voice
That spake forgiveness flow. She wept her son
For ever lost, cut off with all the weight

Of unrepented sin upon his head,
Sin which had weighed a nation down:—what joy
To know that righteous Heaven had in its wrath
Remembered mercy; and she yet might meet
The child whom she had born, redeemed, in bliss?
The sudden impulse of such thoughts confirmed
That unacknowledged purpose, which till now
Vainly had sought its end. He girt his loins,
Laid blessèd Mary's image in a cleft
Of the rock, where, sheltered from the elements,
It might abide till happier days came on,
From all defilement safe; poured his last prayer
Upon Romano's grave, and kissed the earth
Which covered his remains, and wept as if
At long leave-taking, then began his way.

III.

ADOSINDA.

'T was now the earliest morning; soon the Sun,
Rising above Albardos, poured his light
Amid the forest, and with ray aslant
Entering its depth, illumed the branchless pines,
Brightened their bark, tinged with a redder hue
Its rusty stains, and cast along the floor
Long lines of shadow, where they rose erect
Like pillars of the temple. With slow foot
Roderick pursued his way; for penitence,
Remorse which gave no respite, and the long
And painful conflict of his troubled soul,
Had worn him down. Now brighter thoughts arose,
And that triumphant Vision floated still
Before his sight with all her blazonry,
Her castled helm, and the victorious sword
That flashed like lightning o'er the field of blood.
Sustained by thoughts like these, from morn till eve
He journeyed, and drew near Leyria's walls.
'T was even-song time, but not a bell was heard:
Instead thereof, on her polluted towers,
Bidding the Moors to their unhallowed prayer,
The cryer stood, and with his sonorous voice
Filled the delicious vale where Lena winds
Through groves and pastoral meads. The sound, the sight
Of turban, girdle, robe, and scymitar,
And tawny skins, awoke contending thoughts
Of anger, shame, and anguish in the Goth;
The unaccustomed face of human-kind
Confused him now, and through the streets he went
With haggèd mien, and countenance like one
Crazed or bewildered. All who met him turned,
And wondered as he past. One stopt him short,
Put alms into his hand, and then desired,
In broken Gothic speech, the moon-struck man
To bless him. With a look of vacancy
Roderick received the alms; his wandering eye
Fell on the money, and the fallen King,
Seeing his own royal impress on the piece,
Broke out into a quick convulsive voice,
That seemed like laughter first, but ended soon
In hollow groans supprest: the Musselman
Shrunk at the ghastly sound, and magnified
The name of Allah as he hastened on.
A Christian woman spinning at her door

Beheld him, and, with sudden pity touched,
She laid her spindle by, and running in
Took bread, and following after called him back,
And placing in his passive hands the loaf,
She said, Christ Jesus for his mother's sake
Have mercy on thee! With a look that seemed
Like idiotcy he heard her, and stood still,
Staring awhile; then bursting into tears
Wept like a child, and thus relieved his heart,
Full even to bursting else with swelling thoughts.
So through the streets, and through the northern gate
Did Roderick, reckless of a resting-place,
With feeble yet with hurried step, pursue
His agitated way; and when he reached
The open fields, and found himself alone
Beneath the starry canopy of Heaven,
The sense of solitude, so dreadful late,
Was then repose and comfort. There he stopt
Beside a little rill, and brake the loaf;
And shedding o'er that unaccustomed food
Painful but quiet tears, with grateful soul
He breathed thanksgiving forth, then made his bed
On heath and myrtle.

　　　　　　　But when he arose
At day-break and pursued his way, his heart
Felt lightened that the shock of mingling first
Among his fellow-kind was overpast;
And journeying on, he greeted whom he met
With such short interchange of benison
As each to other gentle travellers give,
Recovering thus the power of social speech
Which he had long disused. When hunger prest
He asked for alms : slight supplication served;
A countenance so pale and woe-begone
Moved all to pity; and the marks it bore
Of rigorous penance and austerest life,
With something too of majesty that still
Appeared amid the wreck, inspired a sense
Of reverence too. The goat-herd on the hills
Opened his scrip for him; the babe in arms,
Affrighted at his visage, turned away,
And clinging to its mother's neck in tears
Would yet again look up, and then again,
With cry renewed, shrink back. The bolder imps
Who played beside the way, at his approach
Brake off their sport for wonder, and stood still
In silence; some among them cried, A Saint!
The village matron when she gave him food
Besought his prayers; and one entreated him
To lay his healing hands upon her child,
For with a sore and hopeless malady
Wasting, it long had lain,—and sure, she said,
He was a man of God.

　　　　　　　Thus travelling on
He past the vale where wild Arunca pours
Its wintry torrents; and the happier site
Of old Conimbrica, whose ruined towers
Bore record of the fierce Alani's wrath. [16]
Mondego too he crost, not yet renowned
In poets' amorous lay; and left behind
The walls at whose foundation pious hands
Of Priest and Monk and Bishop meekly toiled,—
So had the insulting Arian given command.
Those stately palaces and rich domains
Were now the Moor's, and many a weary age
Must Coimbra wear the misbeliever's yoke,

Before Fernando's banner through her gate
Shall pass triumphant, and her hallowed Mosque
Behold the hero of Bivar receive
The knighthood which he glorified so oft
In his victorious fields. Oh if the years
To come might then have risen on Roderick's soul,
How had they kindled and consoled his heart!—
What joy might Douro's haven then have given,
Whence Portugal, the faithful and the brave,
Shall take her name illustrious!—what, those walls
Where Mumadona [17] one day will erect
Convent and town and towers, which shall become
The cradle of that famous monarchy!
What joy might these prophetic scenes have given,—
What ample vengeance on the Musselman,
Driven out with foul defeat, and made to feel
In Africa the wrongs he wrought to Spain;
And still pursued by that relentless sword,
Even to the farthest Orient, where his power
Received its mortal wound.

　　　　　　　O years of pride!
In undiscoverable futurity,
Yet unevolved, your destined glories lay;
And all that Roderick in these fated scenes
Beheld, was grief and wretchedness,—the waste
Of recent war, and that more mournful calm
Of joyless, helpless, hopeless servitude.
'T was not the ruined walls of church or tower,
Cottage or hall or convent, black with smoke;
'T was not the unburied bones, which, where the dogs
And crows had strewn them, lay amid the field
Bleaching in sun or shower, that wrung his heart
With keenest anguish : 't was when he beheld
The turban'd traitor shew his shameless front
In the open eye of Heaven,—the renegade,
On whose base brutal nature unredeemed
Even black apostacy itself could stamp
No deeper reprobation, at the hour
Assigned fall prostrate, and unite the names
Of God and the Blasphemer,—impious prayer,—
Most impious, when from unbelieving lips
The accursèd utterance came. Then Roderick's heart
With indignation burnt, and then he longed
To be a King again, that so, for Spain
Betrayed and his Redeemer thus renounced,
He might inflict due punishment, and make
These wretches feel his wrath. But when he saw
The daughters of the land,—who, as they went
With cheerful step to church, were wont to shew
Their innocent faces to all passers' eyes,
Freely, and free from sin as when they looked
In adoration and in praise to Heaven,—
Now masked in Moorish mufflers, to the Mosque
Holding uncompanied their jealous way,
His spirit seemed at that unhappy sight
To die away within him, and he too
Would fain have died, so death could bring with it
Entire oblivion.

　　　　　　　Rent with thoughts like these,
He reached that city, once the seat renowned
Of Suevi kings, where, in contempt of Rome
Degenerate long, the North's heroic race
Raised first a rival throne; now from its state
Of proud regality debased and fallen.
Still bounteous Nature o'er the lovely vale,
Where like a Queen rose Bracara august,

Poured forth her gifts profuse; perennial springs
Flowed for her habitants, and genial suns,
With kindly showers to bless the happy clime,
Combined in vain their gentle influences:
For patient servitude was there, who bowed
His neck beneath the Moor, and silent grief
That eats into the soul. The walls and stones
Seemed to reproach their dwellers; stately piles
Yet undecayed, the mighty monuments
Of Roman pomp, Barbaric palaces,
And Gothic halls, where haughty Barons late
Gladdened their faithful vassals with the feast
And flowing bowl, alike the spoiler's now.

Leaving these captive scenes behind, he crost
Cavado's silver current, and the banks
Of Lima, through whose groves in after years,
Mournful yet sweet, Diogo's amorous lute
Prolonged its tuneful echoes. [18] But when now
Beyond Arnoya's tributary tide,
He came where Minho rolled its ampler stream
By Auria's ancient walls, fresh horrors met
His startled view; for prostrate in the dust
Those walls were laid, and towers and temples stood
Tottering in frightful ruins, as the flame
Had left them black and bare; and through the streets,
All with the recent wreck of war bestrewn,
Helmet and turban, scymitar and sword,
Christian and Moor in death promiscuous lay,
Each where they fell; and blood-flakes, parched and
    cracked
Like the dry slime of some receding flood;
And half-burnt bodies, which allured from far
The wolf and raven, and to impious food
Tempted the houseless dog. A thrilling pang,
A sweat like death, a sickness of the soul,
Came over Roderick. Soon they past away,
And admiration in their stead arose,
Stern joy, and inextinguishable hope,
With wrath, and hate, and sacred vengeance now
Indissolubly linked. O valiant race,
O people excellently brave, he cried,
True Goths ye fell, and faithful to the last;
Though overpowered triumphant, and in death
Unconquered! Holy be your memory!
Blessèd and glorious now and evermore
Be your heroic names!—Led by the sound,
As thus he cried aloud, a woman came
Toward him from the ruins. For the love
Of Christ, she said, lend me a little while
Thy charitable help!—Her words, her voice,
Her look, more horror to his heart conveyed
Than all the havoc round : for though she spake
With the calm utterance of despair, in tones
Deep-breathed and low, yet never sweeter voice
Poured forth its hymns in ecstacy to Heaven.
Her hands were bloody, and her garments stained
With blood, her face with blood and dust defiled.
Beauty and youth, and grace and majesty,
Had every charm of form and feature given:
But now upon her rigid countenance
Severest anguish set a fixedness
Ghastlier than death.
                She led him through the streets
A little way along, where four low walls,

Heapt rudely from the ruins round, enclosed
A narrow space : and there upon the ground
Four bodies, decently composed, were laid,
Though horrid all with wounds and clotted gore;
A venerable ancient, by his side
A comely matron, for whose middle age,
(If ruthless slaughter had not intervened,)
Nature it seemed, and gentle Time, might well
Have many a calm declining year in store;
The third an armèd warrior, on his breast
An infant, over whom his arms were crost.
There,—with firm eye and steady countenance,
Unfaltering, she addrest him,—there they lie,
Child, Husband, Parents,—Adosinda's all!
I could not break the earth with these poor hands,
Nor other tomb provide,—but let that pass!
Auria itself is now but one wide tomb
For all its habitants : [19]—What better grave?
What worthier monument?—Oh cover not
Their blood, thou Earth! and ye, ye blessed Souls
Of Heroes and of murdered Innocents,
Oh never let your everlasting cries
Cease round the eternal throne, till the Most High
For all these unexampled wrongs hath given
Full,—overflowing vengeance!
                While she spake
She raised her lofty hands to Heaven, as if
Calling for justice on the Judgment-seat;
Then laid them on her eyes, and leaning on
Bent o'er the open sepulchre.
                But soon
With quiet mien collectedly, like one
Who from intense devotion, and the act
Of ardent prayer, arising, girds himself
For this world's daily business,—she arose,
And said to Roderick, Help me now to raise
The covering of the tomb.
                With half-burnt planks,
Which she had gathered for this funeral use,
They roofed the vault : then laying stones above
They closed it down : last, rendering all secure,
Stones upon stones they piled, till all appeared
A huge and shapeless heap. Enough, she cried;
And taking Roderick's hands in both her own,
And wringing them with fervent thankfulness,
May God shew mercy to thee, she exclaimed,
When most thou needèst mercy! Who thou art
I know not; not of Auria, for of all
Her sons and daughters, save the one who stands
Before thee, not a soul is left alive.
But thou hast rendered to me, in my hour
Of need, the only help which man could give.
What else of consolation may be found
For one so utterly bereft, from Heaven
And from myself must come. For deem not thou
That I shall sink beneath calamity.
This visitation, like a lightning-stroke,
Hath scathed the fruit and blossom of my youth;
One hour hath orphaned me, and widowed me,
And made me childless. In this sepulchre
Lie buried all my earthward hopes and fears,
All human loves and natural charities;—
All womanly tenderness, all gentle thoughts,
All female weakness too, I bury here,
Yea, all my former nature. There remain
Revenge and death :—the bitterness of death

Is past, and Heaven already hath vouchsafed
A foretaste of revenge.
     Look here ! she cried,
And drawing back, held forth her bloody hands,—
'T is Moorish !—In the day of massacre,
A captain of Alcahman's murderous host
Reserved me from the slaughter. Not because
My rank and station tempted him with thoughts
Of ransom, for amid the general waste
Of ruin all was lost :—Nor yet, be sure,
That pity moved him,—they who from this race
Accurst for pity look, such pity find
As ravenous wolves shew the defenceless flock.
My husband at my feet had fallen ; my babe,—
Spare me that thought, O God !—and then—even then
Amid the maddening throes of agony
Which rent my soul,—when if this solid Earth
Had opened and let out the central fire,
Before whose all-involving flames wide Heaven
Shall shrivel like a scroll and be consumed,
The universal wreck had been to me
Relief and comfort ;—even then this Moor
Turned on me his libidinous eyes, and bade
His men reserve me safely for an hour
Of dalliance,—me !—me in my agonies !
But when I found for what this miscreant child
Of Hell had snatched me from the butchery,
The very horror of that monstrous thought
Saved me from madness ; I was calm at once,—
Yea comforted and reconciled to life :
Hatred became to me the life of life,
Its purpose and its power.
     The glutted Moors
At length broke up. This hell-dog turned aside
Toward his home : We travelled fast and far,
Till by a forest edge at eve he pitched
His tents. I washed and ate at his command,
Forcing revolted nature ; I composed
My garments and bound up my scattered hair :
And when he took my hand, and to his couch
Would fain have drawn me, gently I retired
From that abominable touch, and said,
Forbear to-night I pray thee, for this day
A widow, as thou seest me, am I made ;
Therefore, according to our law, must watch
And pray to-night. The loathsome villain paused
Ere he assented, then laid down to rest ;
While at the door of the pavilion, I
Knelt on the ground, and bowed my face to earth ;
But when the neighbouring tents had ceased their stir,
The fires were out, and all were fast asleep,
Then I arose. The blessed Moon from Heaven
Lent me her holy light. I did not pray
For strength, for strength was given me as I drew
The scymitar, and, standing o'er his couch,
Raised it in both my hands with steady aim,
And smote his neck. Upward, as from a spring
When newly opened by the husbandman,
The villain's life-blood spouted. Twice I struck,
So making vengeance sure ; then, praising God,
Retired amid the wood, and measured back
My patient way to Auria, to perform
This duty which thou seest.
     As thus she spake,
Roderick intently listening had forgot
His crown, his kingdom, his calamities,

His crimes,—so like a spell upon the Goth
Her powerful words prevailed. With open lips,
And eager ear, and eyes which, while they watched
Her features, caught the spirit that she breathed,
Mute and enrapt he stood, and motionless ;
The vision rose before him ; and that shout,
Which, like a thunder-peal, victorious Spain
Sent through the welkin, rung within his soul
Its deep prophetic echoes. On his brow
The pride and power of former majesty
Dawned once again, but changed and purified :
Duty and high heroic purposes,
Now hallowed it, and, as with inward light,
Illumed his meagre countenance austere.

Awhile in silence Adosinda stood,
Reading his altered visage, and the thoughts
Which thus transfigured him. Aye, she exclaimed,
The tale hath moved thee : it might move the dead,
Quicken captivity's dead soul, and rouse
This prostrate country from her mortal trance :
Therefore I live to tell it. And for this
Hath the Lord God Almighty given to me
A spirit not mine own, and strength from Heaven ;
Dealing with me as in the days of old
With that Bethulian Matron, when she saved
His people from the spoiler. What remains
But that the life which he hath thus preserved
I consecrate to him ? Not veiled and vowed
To pass my days in holiness and peace ;
Nor yet between sepulchral walls immured,
Alive to penitence alone ; my rule
He hath himself prescribed, and hath infused
A passion in this woman's breast, wherein
All passions and all virtues are combined :
Love, hatred, joy, and anguish, and despair,
And hope, and natural piety, and faith,.
Make up the mighty feeling. Call it not
Revenge : thus sanctified and thus sublimed,
'T is duty, 't is devotion. Like the grace
Of God, it came and saved me ; and in it
Spain must have her salvation. In thy hands
Here, on the grave of all my family,
I make my vow.
     She said, and kneeling down,
Placed within Roderick's palms her folded hands.
This life, she cried, I dedicate to God,
Therewith to do him service in the way
Which he hath shown. To rouse the land against
This impious, this intolerable yoke,—
To offer up the invader's hateful blood,—
This shall be my employ, my rule and rite,
Observances and sacrifice of faith ;
For this I hold the life which he hath given,
A sacred trust ; for this, when it shall suit
His service, joyfully will lay it down.
So deal with me as I fulfil the pledge,
O Lord my God, my Saviour and my Judge !

Then rising from the earth, she spread her arms,
And looking round with sweeping eyes, exclaimed,
Auria, and Spain, and Heaven receive the vow !

IV.

THE MONASTERY OF ST FELIX.

'Hus long had Roderick heard her powerful words
In silence, awed before her; but his soul
Was filled the while with swelling sympathy,
And now with impulse not to be restrained
The feeling overpowered him. Hear me too,
Auria, and Spain, and Heaven! he cried; and thou
Who risest thus above mortality,
Sufferer and patriot, saint and heroine,
The servant and the chosen of the Lord,
For surely such thou art,—receive in me
The first-fruits of thy calling. Kneeling then,
And placing as he spake his hands in hers,
As thou hast sworn, the royal Goth pursued,
Even so I swear; my soul hath found at length
Her rest and refuge; in the invader's blood
She must efface her stains of mortal sin,
And in redeeming this lost land, work out
Redemption for herself. Herein I place
My penance for the past, my hope to come,
My faith and my good works; here offer up
All thoughts and passions of mine inmost heart,
My days and nights,—this flesh, this blood, this life,
Yea this whole being, I devote it here
For Spain. Receive the vow, all Saints in Heaven,
And prosper its good end!—Clap now your wings,
The Goth with louder utterance as he rose
Exclaimed,—clap now your wings exultingly,
Ye ravenous fowl of Heaven; and in your dens
Set up, ye wolves of Spain, a yell of joy;
For lo! a nation hath this day been sworn
To furnish forth your banquet; for a strife
Hath been commenced, the which from this day forth
Permits no breathing-time, and knows no end
Till in this land the last invader bow
His neck beneath the exterminating sword.

Said I not rightly? Adosinda cried;
The will which goads me on is not mine own,
'T is from on high,—yea, verily of Heaven!
But who art thou who hast professed with me,
My first sworn brother in the appointed rule?
Tell me thy name.
                    Ask any thing but that!
The fallen King replied. My name was lost
When from the Goths the sceptre past away.
The nation will arise regenerate;
Strong in her second youth, and beautiful,
And like a spirit which hath shaken off
The clog of dull mortality, shall Spain
Arise in glory. But for my good name
No resurrection is appointed here.
Let it be blotted out on earth : in Heaven
There shall be written with it penitence,
And grace and saving faith, and such good deeds
Wrought in atonement as my soul this day
Hath sworn to offer up.
                    Then be thy name,
She answered, Maccabee, from this day forth :
For this day art thou born again; and like
Those brethren of old times, whose holy names
Live in the memory of all noble hearts

For love and admiration, ever young,—
So for our native country, for her hearths
And altars, for her cradles and her graves,
Hast thou thyself devoted. Let us now
Each to our work. Among the neighbouring hills,
I to the vassals of my father's house ;
Thou to Visonia. Tell the Abbot there
What thou hast seen at Auria; and with him
Take counsel who of all our Baronage
Is worthiest to lead on the sons of Spain,
And wear upon his brow the Spanish crown.
Now, brother, fare thee well! we part in hope,
And we shall meet again, be sure, in joy.

So saying, Adosinda left the King
Alone amid the ruins. There he stood,
As when Elisha, on the farther bank
Of Jordan, saw that elder prophet mount
The fiery chariot, and the steeds of fire,
Trampling the whirlwind, bear him up the sky:
Thus gazing after her did Roderick stand;
And as the immortal Tishbite left behind
His mantle and prophetic power, even so
Had her inspiring presence left infused
The spirit which she breathed. Gazing he stood,
As at a heavenly visitation there
Vouchsafed in mercy to himself and Spain ;
And when the heroic mourner from his sight
Had past away, still reverential awe
Held him suspended there and motionless.
Then turning from the ghastly scene of death
Up murmuring Lona, he began toward
The holy Bierzo his obedient way.
Sil's ample stream he crost, where through the vale
Of Orras, from that sacred land it bears
The whole collected waters : northward then,
Skirting the heights of Aguiar, he reached
That consecrated pile, amid the wild,
Which sainted Fructuoso in his zeal
Reared to St Felix, on Visonia's banks. [20]

In commune with a priest of age mature,
Whose thoughtful visage and majestic mien
Bespake authority and weight of care,
Odoar, the venerable Abbot, sate;
When ushering Roderick in, the Porter said,
A stranger came from Auria, and required
His private ear. From Auria? said the old man,
Comest thou from Auria, brother? I can spare
Thy painful errand then,—we know the worst.

Nay, answered Roderick, but thou hast not heard
My tale. Where that devoted city lies
In ashes, mid the ruins and the dead
I found a woman, whom the Moors had borne
Captive away; but she, by Heaven inspired
And her good heart, with her own arm had wrought
Her own deliverance, smiting in his tent
A lustful Moorish miscreant, as of yore
By Judith's holy deed the Assyrian fell.
And that same spirit which had strengthened her
Worked in her still. Four walls with patient toil
She reared, wherein, as in a sepulchre,
With her own hands she laid her murdered babe,
Her husband and her parents, side by side;
And when we covered in this shapeless tomb,

50

There on the grave of all her family,
Did this courageous mourner dedicate
All thoughts and actions of her future life
To her poor country. For she said, that Heaven
Supporting her, in mercy had vouchsafed
A foretaste of revenge; that, like the grace
Of God, revenge had saved her; that in it
Spain must have her salvation; and henceforth
That passion, thus sublimed and sanctified,
Must be to all the loyal sons of Spain
The pole-star of their faith, their rule and rite,
Observances and worthiest sacrifice.
I took the vow, unworthy as I am,
Her first sworn follower in the appointed rule;
And then we parted: She among the hills
To rouse the vassals of her father's house:
I at her bidding hitherward, to ask
Thy counsel, who of our old Baronage
Shall place upon his brow the Spanish crown.

The Lady Adosinda? Odoar cried.
Roderick made answer, So she called herself.

Oh none but she! exclaimed the good old man,
Clasping his hands, which trembled as he spake,
In act of pious passion raised to Heaven,—
Oh none but Adosinda!—none but she,—
None but that noble heart, which was the heart
Of Auria while it stood, its life and strength,
More than her father's presence, or the arm
Of her brave Lord, all valiant as he was.
Hers was the spirit which inspired old age,
Ambitious boyhood, girls in timid youth,
And virgins in the beauty of their spring,
And youthful mothers, doting like herself
With ever-anxious love: She breathed through all
That zeal and that devoted faithfulness,
Which to the invader's threats and promises
Turned a deaf ear alike; which in the head
And flood of prosperous fortune checked his course,
Repelled him from the walls; and when at length
His overpowering numbers forced their way,
Even in that uttermost extremity
Unyielding, still from street to street, from house
To house, from floor to floor, maintained the fight:
Till by their altars falling, in their doors,
And on their household hearths, and by their beds
And cradles, and their fathers' sepulchres,
This noble army, gloriously revenged,
Embraced their martyrdom. Heroic souls!
Well have ye done, and righteously discharged
Your arduous part! Your service is performed,
Your earthly warfare done! Ye have put on
The purple robe of everlasting peace!
Ye have received your crown! Ye bear the palm
Before the throne of Grace!
                    With that he paused,
Checking the strong emotions of his soul.
Then with a solemn tone addressing him
Who shared his secret thoughts, Thou knowest, he said,
O Urban, that they have not fallen in vain;
For by this virtuous sacrifice they thinned
Alcahman's thousands; and his broken force,
Exhausted by their dear-bought victory,
Turned back from Auria, leaving us to breathe
Among our mountains yet. We lack not here

Good hearts, nor valiant hands. What walls or towers
Or battlements are like these fastnesses,
These rocks and glens and everlasting hills?
Give but that Aurian spirit, and the Moors
Will spend their force as idly on these holds,
As round the rocky girdle of the land
The wild Cantabrian billows waste their rage.
Give but that spirit!—Heaven hath given it us.
If Adosinda thus, as from the dead,
Be granted to our prayers!
                    And who art thou,
Said Urban, who hast taken on thyself
This rule of warlike faith? Thy countenance
And those poor weeds bespeak a life ere this
Devoted to austere observances.

Roderick replied, I am a sinful man,
One who in solitude hath long deplored
A life mis-spent; but never bound by vows,
Till Adosinda taught me where to find
Comfort, and how to work forgiveness out.
When that exalted woman took my vow,
She called me Maccabee; from this day forth
Be that my earthly name. But tell me now,
Whom shall we rouse to take upon his head
The crown of Spain? Where are the Gothic Chiefs,
Sacaru, Theudemir, Athanagild,
All who survived that eight days' obstinate fight,
When clogged with bodies Chrysus scarce could force
Its bloody stream along? Witiza's sons,
Bad offspring of a stock accurst, I know,
Have put the turban on their recreant heads.
Where are your own Cantabrian Lords? I ween,
Eudon, and Pedro, and Pelayo now
Have ceased their rivalry. If Pelayo live,
His were the worthy heart and rightful hand
To wield the sceptre and the sword of Spain.

Odoar and Urban eyed him while he spake,
As if they wondered whose the tongue might be
Familiar thus with Chiefs and thoughts of state.
They scanned his countenance, but not a trace
Betrayed the royal Goth: sunk was that eye
Of sovereignty; and on the emaciate cheek
Had penitence and anguish deeply drawn
Their furrows premature,—forestalling time,
And shedding upon thirty's brows more snows
Than threescore winters in their natural course
Might else have sprinkled there. It seems indeed
That thou hast past thy days in solitude,
Replied the Abbot, or thou wouldst not ask
Of things so long gone by. Athanagild
And Theudemir have taken on their necks
The yoke. Sacaru played a nobler part.
Long within Merida did he withstand
The invader's hot assault; and when at length,
Hopeless of all relief, he yielded up
The gates, disdaining in his father's land
To breathe the air of bondage, with a few
Found faithful to the last, indignantly
Did he toward the ocean bend his way,
And shaking from his feet the dust of Spain,
Took ship, and hoisted sail through seas unknown
To seek for freedom.[21] Our Cantabrian Chiefs
All have submitted, but the wary Moor
Trusteth not all alike: At his own Court

He holds Pelayo, as suspecting most
That calm and manly spirit; Pedro's son
There too is held as hostage, and secures
His father's faith; Count Eudon is despised,
And so lives unmolested. When he pays
His tribute, an uncomfortable thought
May then perhaps disturb him :—or more like
He meditates how profitable 't were
To be a Moor; and if apostacy
Were all, and to be unbaptized might serve,—
But I waste breath upon a wretch like this;
Pelayo is the only hope of Spain,
Only Pelayo.

        If, as we believe,
Said Urban then, the hand of Heaven is here,
And dreadful though they be, yet for wise end
Of good, these visitations do its work;
All dimly as our mortal sight may scan
The future, yet methinks my soul descries
How in Pelayo should the purposes
Of Heaven be best accomplished. All too long,
Here in their own inheritance, the sons
Of Spain have groaned beneath a foreign yoke,[22]
Punic and Roman, Kelt, and Goth, and Greek:
This latter tempest comes to sweep away
All proud distinctions which commingling blood
And time's long course have failed to efface; and now
Perchance it is the will of Fate to rear
Upon the soil of Spain a Spanish throne,
Restoring in Pelayo's native line
The sceptre to the Spaniard.

        Go thou, then,
And seek Pelayo at the Conqueror's court.
Tell him the mountaineers are unsubdued;
The precious time they needed hath been gained
By Auria's sacrifice, and all they ask
Is him to guide them on. In Odoar's name
And Urban's, tell him that the hour is come.

Then pausing for a moment, he pursued.
The rule which thou hast taken on thyself
Toledo ratifies: 'tis meet for Spain,
And as the will divine, to be received,
Observed, and spread abroad. Come hither thou,
Who for thyself hast chosen the good part;
Let me lay hands on thee, and consecrate
Thy life unto the Lord.

        Me! Roderick cried;
Me? sinner that I am!—and while he spake
His withered cheek grew paler, and his limbs
Shook. As thou goest among the infidels,
Pursued the Primate, many thou wilt find
Fallen from the faith; by weakness some betrayed,
Some led astray by baser hope of gain,
And haply too by ill example led
Of those in whom they trusted. Yet have these
Their lonely hours, when sorrow, or the touch
Of sickness, and that awful power divine
Which hath its dwelling in the heart of man,
Life of his soul, his monitor and judge,
Move them with silent impulse; but they look
For help, and finding none to succour them,
The irrevocable moment passeth by.
Therefore, my brother, in the name of Christ
Thus I lay hands on thee, that in His name
Thou with His gracious promises mayst raise

The fallen, and comfort those that are in need,
And bring salvation to the penitent.
Now, brother, go thy way: the peace of God
Be with thee, and his blessing prosper us!

V.

RODERICK AND SIVERIAN.

BETWEEN St Felix and the regal seat
Of Abdalazis, ancient Cordoba,
Lay many a long day's journey interposed;
And many a mountain range hath Roderick crost,
And many a lovely vale, ere he beheld
Where Betis, winding through the unbounded plain,
Rolled his majestic waters. There at eve
Entering an inn, he took his humble seat
With other travellers round the crackling hearth,
Where heath and cistus gave their fragrant flame.
That flame no longer, as in other times,
Lit up the countenance of easy mirth
And light discourse: the talk which now went round
Was of the grief that prest on every heart;
Of Spain subdued; the sceptre of the Goths
Broken; their nation and their name effaced;
Slaughter and mourning, which had left no house
Unvisited; and shame, which set its mark
On every Spaniard's face. One who had seen
His sons fall bravely at his side, bewailed
The unhappy chance which, rescuing him from death,
Left him the last of all his family;
Yet he rejoiced to think that none who drew
Their blood from him remained to wear the yoke,
Be at the miscreant's beck, and propagate
A breed of slaves to serve them. Here sate one
Who told of fair possessions lost, and babes
To goodly fortunes born, of all bereft.
Another for a virgin daughter mourned,
The lewd barbarian's spoil. A fourth had seen
His only child forsake him in his age,
And for a Moor renounce her hope in Christ.
His was the heaviest grief of all, he said;
And clenching as he spake his hoary locks,
He cursed King Roderick's soul.

        Oh curse him not!
Roderick exclaimed, all shuddering as he spake,
Oh, for the love of Jesus, curse him not!
Sufficient is the dreadful load of guilt
Which lies upon his miserable soul!
O brother, do not curse that sinful soul,
Which Jesus suffered on the cross to save!

But then an old man, who had sate thus long
A silent listener, from his seat arose,
And moving round to Roderick took his hand;
Christ bless thee, brother, for that Christian speech!
He said; and shame on me that any tongue
Readier than mine was found to utter it!
His own emotion filled him while he spake,
So that he did not feel how Roderick's hand
Shook like a palsied limb; and none could see
How, at his well-known voice, the countenance
Of that poor traveller suddenly was changed,
And sunk with deadlier paleness; for the flame
Was spent, and from behind him, on the wall
High hung, the lamp with feeble glimmering played.

Oh it is ever thus! the old man pursued,
The crimes and woes of universal Spain
Are charged on him; and curses which should aim
At living heads, pursue beyond the grave
His poor unhappy soul! As if his sin
Had wrought the fall of our old monarchy!
As if the Musselmen in their career
Would ne'er have overleapt the gulf which parts
Iberia from the Mauritanian shore,
If Julian had not beckoned them!—Alas!
The evils which drew on our overthrow,
Would soon by other means have wrought their end,
Though Julian's daughter should have lived and died
A virgin vowed and veiled.
                    Touch not on that,
Shrinking with inward shiverings at the thought,
The penitent exclaimed. Oh, if thou lovest
The soul of Roderick, touch not on that deed!
God in his mercy may forgive it him,
But human tongue must never speak his name
Without reproach and utter infamy,
For that abhorrèd act. Even thou—But here
Siverian taking up the word, broke off
Unwittingly the incautious speech. Even I,
Quoth he, who nursed him in his father's hall,—
Even I can only for that deed of shame
Offer in agony my secret prayers.
But Spain hath witnessed other crimes as foul:
Have we not seen Favila's [23] shameless wife,
Thron'd in Witiza's ivory car, parade
Our towns with regal pageantry, and bid
The murderous tyrant in her husband's blood
Dip his adulterous hand? Did we not see
Pelayo, by that bloody king's pursuit,
And that unnatural mother, from the land
With open outcry, like an outlawed thief,
Hunted? And saw ye not Theodofred,
As through the streets I guided his dark steps,
Roll mournfully toward the noon-day sun
His blank and senseless eye-balls? Spain saw this,
And suffered it—I seek not to excuse
The sin of Roderick. Jesu, who beholds
The burning tears I shed in solitude,
Knows how I plead for him in midnight prayer.
But if, when he victoriously revenged
The wrongs of Chindasuintho's house, his sword
Had not for mercy turned aside its edge,
Oh what a day of glory had there been
Upon the banks of Chrysus! Curse not him,
Who in that fatal conflict to the last
So valiantly maintained his country's cause;
But if your sorrow needs must have its vent
In curses, let your imprecations strike
The caitiffs, who, when Roderick's hornèd helm
Rose eminent amid the thickest fight,
Betraying him who spared and trusted them,
Forsook their King, their Country, and their God,
And gave the Moor his conquest.
                    Aye! they said,
These were Witiza's hateful progeny;
And in an evil hour the unhappy King
Had spared the viperous brood. With that they talked
How Sisibert and Ebba through the land
Guided the foe: and Orpas, who had cast
The mitre from his renegado brow,
Went with the armies of the infidels;

And how in Hispalis, even where his hands
Had minister'd so oft the bread of life,
The circumcised apostate did not shame
To shew in open day his turban'd head—
The Queen too, Egilona, one exclaimed;
Was she not married to the enemy,
The Moor, the Misbeliever? [24] What a soul
Were hers that she could pride and plume herself
To rank among his herd of concubines,
Having been what she had been! And who could say
How far domestic wrongs and discontent
Had wrought upon the King!—At this the old man
Raising beneath the knit and curly brow
His mournful eyes, replied, This I can tell,
That that unquiet spirit and unblest,
Though Roderick never told his sorrows, drove
Rusilla from the palace of her son.
She could not bear to see his generous mind
Wither beneath the unwholesome influence,
And cankering at the core. And I know well,
That oft when she deplored his barren bed,
The thought of Egilona's qualities
Came like a bitter medicine to her grief,
And to the extinction of her husband's line,
Sad consolation, reconciled her heart.

But Roderick, while they communed thus, had ceased
To hear, such painfullest anxiety
The sight of that old venerable man
Awoke. A sickening fear came over him:
The hope which led him from his hermitage
Now seemed for ever gone: for well he knew
Nothing but death could break the ties which bound
That faithful servant to his father's house.
She, then, for whose forgiveness he had yearned,
Who in her blessing would have given and found
The peace of Heaven,—she, then, was to the grave
Gone down disconsolate at last: in this
Of all the woes of her unhappy life,
Unhappiest that she did not live to see
God had vouchsafed repentance to her child.
But then a hope arose that yet she lived;
The weighty cause which led Siverian here
Might draw him from her side: better to know
The worst than fear it. And with that he bent
Over the embers, and with head half-raised
Aslant, and shadowed by his hand, he said,
Where is King Roderick's mother? lives she still?

God hath upheld her, the old man replied;
She bears this last and heaviest of her griefs,
Not as she bore her husband's wrongs, when hope
And her indignant heart supported her:
But patiently, like one who finds from Heaven
A comfort which the world can neither give
Nor take away.—Roderick inquired no more;
He breathed a silent prayer in gratitude,
Then wrapt his cloak around him, and lay down
Where he might weep unseen.
                    When morning came,
Earliest of all the travellers he went forth,
And lingered for Siverian by the way,
Beside a fountain, where the constant fall
Of water its perpetual gurgling made,
To the wayfaring or the musing man
Sweetest of all sweet sounds. The Christian band,

Whose general charity for man and beast
Built it in better times, had with a cross
Of well-hewn stone crested the pious work,
Which now the misbelievers had cast down,
And broken in the dust it lay defiled.
Roderick beheld it lying at his feet,
And gathering reverently the fragments up
Placed them within the cistern, and restored
With careful collocation its dear form,—
So might the waters, like a crystal shrine,
Preserve it from pollution. Kneeling then,
O'er the memorial of redeeming love
He bent, and mingled with the fount his tears;
And poured his spirit to the Crucified.

A Moor came by, and seeing him, exclaimed,
Ah, Kaffer! worshipper of wood and stone,
God's curse confound thee! And as Roderick turned
His face, the miscreant spurned him with his foot
Between the eyes. The indignant King arose,
And felled him to the earth. But then the Moor
Drew forth his dagger, rising as he cried,
What! darest thou, thou infidel and slave,
Strike a believer? and he aimed a blow
At Roderick's breast. But Roderick caught his arm,
And closed, and wrenched the dagger from his hold,—
Such timely strength did those emaciate limbs
From indignation draw,—and in his neck
With mortal stroke he drove the avenging steel
Hilt deep. Then, as the thirsty sand drank in
The expiring miscreant's blood, he looked around
In sudden apprehension, lest the Moors
Had seen them; but Siverian was in sight,
The only traveller, and he smote his mule
And hastened up. Ah, brother! said the old man,
Thine is a spirit of the ancient mould!
And would to God a thousand men like thee
Had fought at Roderick's side on that last day
When treason overpowered him! Now, alas!
A manly Gothic heart doth ill accord
With these unhappy times. Come, let us hide
This carrion, while the favouring hour permits.

So saying he alighted. Soon they scooped
Amid loose-lying sand a hasty grave,
And levelled over it the easy soil.
Father, said Roderick, as they journeyed on,
Let this thing be a seal and sacrament
Of truth between us: Wherefore should there be
Concealment between two right Gothic hearts
In evil days like these? What thou hast seen
Is but the first fruit of the sacrifice,
Which on this injured and polluted soil,
As on a bloody altar, I have sworn
To offer to insulted Heaven for Spain,
Her vengeance and her expiation. This
Was but a hasty act, by sudden wrong
Provoked: but I am bound for Cordoba,
On weighty mission from Visonia sent,
To breathe into Pelayo's ear a voice
Of spirit-stirring power, which, like the trump
Of the Archangel, shall awake dead Spain.
The northern mountaineers are unsubdued;
They call upon Pelayo for their chief;
Odoar and Urban tell him that the hour
Is come. Thou too, I ween, old man, art charged

With no light errand, or thou wouldst not now
Have left the ruins of thy master's house.

Who art thou? cried Siverian, as he searched
The wan and withered features of the King.
The face is of a stranger, but thy voice
Disturbs me like a dream.
                            Roderick replied,
Thou seest me as I am,—a stranger; one
Whose fortunes in the general wreck were lost,
His name and lineage utterly extinct,
Himself in mercy spared, surviving all;—
In mercy, that the bitter cup might heal
A soul diseased. Now, having cast the slough
Of old offences, thou beholdest me
A man new-born; in second baptism named,
Like those who in Judea bravely raised
Against the Heathen's impious tyranny
The banner of Jehovah, Maccabee:
So call me. In that name hath Urban laid
His consecrating hands upon my head;
And in that name have I myself for Spain
Devoted. Tell me now why thou art sent
To Cordoba; for sure thou goëst not
An idle gazer to the Conqueror's court.

Thou judgest well, the old man replied. I too
Seek the Cantabrian Prince, the hope of Spain.
With other tidings charged, for other end
Designed, yet such as well may work with thine.
My noble Mistress sends me to avert
The shame that threats his house. The renegade
Numacian, he who for the infidels
Oppresses Gegio, insolently woos
His sister. Moulded in a wicked womb,
The unworthy Guisla hath inherited
Her mother's leprous taint; and willingly
She to the circumcised and upstart slave,
Disdaining all admonishment, gives ear.
The Lady Gaudiosa sees in this,
With the quick foresight of maternal care,
The impending danger to her husband's house,
Knowing his generous spirit ne'er will brook
The base alliance. Guisla lewdly sets
His will at nought; but that vile renegade,
From hatred, and from avarice, and from fear,
Will seek the extinction of Pelayo's line.
This too my venerable Mistress sees;
Wherefore these valiant and high-minded dames
Send me to Cordoba; that if the Prince
Cannot by timely interdiction stop
The irrevocable act of infamy,
He may at least to his own safety look,
Being timely warned.
                      Thy Mistress sojourns then
With Gaudiosa, in Pelayo's hall?
Said Roderick. 'T is her natural home, rejoined
Siverian: Chindasuintho's royal race
Have ever shared one lot of weal or woe:
And she who hath beheld her own fair shoot,
The goodly summit of that ancient tree,
Struck by Heaven's bolt, seeks shelter now beneath
The only branch of its majestic stem
That still survives the storm.
                               Thus they pursued
Their journey, each from other gathering store

For thought, with many a silent interval
Of mournful meditation, till they saw
The temples and the towers of Cordoba
Shining majestic in the light of eve.
Before them Betis rolled his glittering stream,
In many a silvery winding traced afar
Amid the ample plain.   Behind the walls
And stately piles which crowned its margin, rich
With olives, and with sunny slope of vines,
And many a lovely hamlet interspersed,
Whose citron bowers were once the abode of peace,
Height above height, receding hills were seen
Imbued with evening hues; and o'er all
The summits of the dark sierra rose,
Lifting their heads amid the silent sky.
The traveller who with a heart at ease
Had seen the goodly vision, would have loved
To linger, seeking with insatiate sight
To treasure up its image, deep impressed,
A joy for years to come.   O Cordoba,
Exclaimed the old man, how princely are thy towers,
How fair thy vales, thy hills how beautiful!
The sun who sheds on thee his parting smiles
Sees not in all his wide career a scene
Lovelier, nor more exuberantly blest
By bounteous earth and heaven.   The very gales
Of Eden waft not from the immortal bowers
Odours to sense more exquisite, than these
Which, breathing from thy groves and gardens, now
Recall in me such thoughts of bitterness.
The time has been when happy was their lot
Who had their birthright here; but happy now
Are they who to thy bosom are gone home,
Because they feel not in their graves the feet
That trample upon Spain.   'T is well that age
Hath made me like a child, that I can weep:
My heart would else have broken, overcharged,
And I, false servant, should lie down to rest
Before my work is done.
                          Hard by their path,
A little way without the walls, there stood
An edifice, whereto, as by a spell,
Siverian's heart was drawn.   Brother, quoth he,
'T is like the urgency of our return
Will brook of no retardment; and this spot
It were a sin if I should pass, and leave
Unvisited.   Beseech you turn with me,
Just while I offer up one duteous prayer.

Roderick made no reply.   He had not dared
To turn his face toward those walls; but now
He followed where the old man led the way.
Lord! in his heart the silent sufferer said,
Forgive my feeble soul, which would have shrunk
From this,—for what am I that I should put
The bitter cup aside! O let my shame
And anguish be accepted in thy sight!

VI.

RODERICK IN TIMES PAST.

The mansion whitherward they went, was one
Which in his youth Theodofred had built:
Thither had he brought home in happy hour
His blooming bride; there fondled on his knee

The lovely boy she bore him.   Close beside,
A temple to that Saint he reared, who first,
As old tradition tells, proclaimed to Spain
The gospel-tidings; and in health and youth,
There mindful of mortality, he saw
His sepulchre prepared.   Witiza seized
For his adulterous leman and himself
The stately pile: but to that sepulchre,
When from captivity and darkness death
Enlarged him, was Theodofred consigned;
For that unhappy woman, wasting then
Beneath a mortal malady, at heart
Was smitten, and the tyrant at her prayer
This poor and tardy restitution made.
Soon the repentant sinner followed him;
And calling on Pelayo ere she died,
For his own wrongs, and for his father's death,
Implored forgiveness of her absent child,—
If it were possible he could forgive
Crimes black as hers, she said.   And by the pangs
Of her remorse,—by her last agonies,—
The unutterable horrors of her death,—
And by the blood of Jesus on the cross
For sinners given, did she beseech his prayers
In aid of her most miserable soul.
Thus mingling sudden shrieks with hopeless vows,
And uttering franticly Pelayo's name,
And crying out for mercy in despair,
Here had she made her dreadful end, and here
Her wretched body was deposited.
That presence seemed to desecrate the place:
Thenceforth the usurper shunned it with the heart
Of conscious guilt; nor could Rusilla bear
These groves and bowers, which, like funereal shades,
Opprest her with their monumental forms:
One day of bitter and severe delight, 25
When Roderick came for vengeance, she endured,
And then for ever left her bridal halls.

Oh when I last beheld yon princely pile,
Exclaimed Siverian, with what other thoughts
Full, and elate of spirit, did I pass
Its joyous gates! The weedery which through
The interstices of those neglected courts
Unchecked had flourished long, and seeded there,
Was trampled now and bruised beneath the feet
Of thronging crowds.   Here drawn in fair array,
The faithful vassals of my master's house,
Their javelins sparkling to the morning sun,
Spread their triumphant banners; high-plumed helms
Rose o'er the martial ranks, and prancing steeds
Made answer to the trumpet's stirring voice;
While yonder towers shook the dull silence off
Which long to their deserted walls had clung,
And with redoubling echoes swelled the shout
That hailed victorious Roderick.   Louder rose
The acclamation, when the dust was seen
Rising beneath his chariot-wheels far off;
But nearer as the youthful hero came,
All sounds of all the multitude were hushed,
And from the thousands and ten thousands here,
Whom Cordoba and Hispalis sent forth,—
Yea whom all Bætica, all Spain poured out
To greet his triumph,—not a whisper rose
To Heaven, such awe and reverence mastered them:
Such expectation held them motionless.

Conqueror and King he came; but with no joy
Or conquest, and no pride of sovereignty
That day displayed; for at his father's grave
Did Roderick come to offer up his vow
Of vengeance well performed. Three coal-black steeds
Drew on his ivory chariot: by his side,
Still wrapt in mourning for the long-deceased,
Rusilla sate; a deeper paleness blanched
Her faded countenance, but in her eye
The light of her majestic nature shone.
Bound, and expecting at their hands the death
So well deserved, the Tyrant followed them;
Aghast and trembling, first he gazed around,
Wildly from side to side; then from the face
Of universal execration shrunk,
Hanging his wretched head abased; and poor
Of spirit, with unmanly tears deplored
His fortune, not his crimes. With bolder front,
Confiding in his priestly character,
Came Orpas next; and then the spurious race
Whom in unhappy hour Favila's wife
Brought forth for Spain. O mercy ill bestowed,
When Roderick, in compassion for their youth,
And for Pelayo's sake, forbore to crush
The brood of vipers!
        Err perchance he might,
Replied the Goth, suppressing as he spake
All outward signs of pain, though every word
Went like a dagger to his bleeding heart;—
But sure, I ween, that error is not placed
Among his sins. Old man, thou mayest regret
The mercy ill deserved, and worse returned,
But not for this wouldst thou reproach the King!

Reproach him? cried Siverian;—I reproach
My child,—my noble boy,—whom every tongue
Blest at that hour,—whose love filled every heart
With joy, and every eye with joyful tears!
My brave, my beautiful, my generous boy!
Brave, beautiful, and generous as he was,
Never so brave, so beautiful, so great
As then,—not even on that glorious day,
When on the field of victory, elevate
Amid the thousands who acclaimed him King,
Firm on the shield above their heads upraised,
Erect he stood, and waved his bloody sword—
Why dost thou shake thy head as if in doubt?
I do not dream, nor fable! Ten short years
Have scarcely past away, since all within
The Pyrenean hills, and the three seas
Which girdle Spain, echoed in one response
The acclamation from that field of fight.—
Or doth aught ail thee, that thy body quakes
And shudders thus?
      'T is but a chill, replied
The King, in passing from the open air
Under the shadow of this thick-set grove.

Of! if this scene awoke in thee such thoughts
As swell my bosom here, the old man pursued,
Sunshine, or shade, and all things from without,
Would be alike indifferent. Gracious God,
Only but ten short years,—and all so changed!
Ten little years since in yon court he checked
His fiery steeds. The steeds obeyed his hand,
The whirling wheels stood still, and when he leapt

Upon the pavement, the whole people heard,
In their deep silence, open-eared, the sound.
With slower movement from the ivory seat
Rusilla rose, her arm, as down she stept,
Extended to her son's supporting hand;
Not for default of firm or agile strength,
But that the feeling of that solemn hour
Subdued her then, and tears bedimmed her sight.
Howbeit when to her husband's grave she came,
On the sepulchral stone she bowed her head
Awhile; then rose collectedly, and fixed
Upon the scene her calm and steady eye.
Roderick,—oh when did valour wear a form
So beautiful, so noble, so august?
Or vengeance, when did it put on before
A character so awful, so divine?
Roderick stood up, and reaching to the tomb
His hands, my hero cried, Theodofred!
Father! I stand before thee once again,
According to thy prayer, when kneeling down
Between thy knees I took my last farewell;
And vowed by all thy sufferings, all thy wrongs,
And by my mother's days and nights of woe,
Her silent anguish, and the grief which then
Even from thee she did not seek to hide,
That if our cruel parting should avail
To save me from the Tyrant's jealous guilt,
Surely should my avenging sword fulfil
Whate'er he omened. Oh that time, I cried,
Would give the strength of manhood to this arm,
Already would it find a manly heart
To guide it to its purpose! And I swore
Never again to see my father's face,
Nor ask my mother's blessing, till I brought,
Dead or in chains, the Tyrant to thy feet.
Boy as I was, before all saints in Heaven,
And highest God, whose justice slumbereth not,
I made the vow. According to thy prayer,
In all things, O my father, is that vow
Performed, alas too well! for thou didst pray,
While looking up I felt the burning tears
Which from thy sightless sockets streamed, drop down,—
That to thy grave, and not thy living feet,
The oppressor might be led. Behold him there,—
Father! Theodofred! no longer now
In darkness, from thy heavenly seat look down,
And see before thy grave thine enemy
In bonds, awaiting judgment at my hand!

Thus while the hero spake, Witiza stood
Listening in agony, with open mouth,
And head, half-raised toward his sentence turned;
His eye-lids stiffened and pursed up,—his eyes
Rigid, and wild, and wide; and when the King
Had ceased, amid the silence which ensued,
The dastard's chains were heard, link against link
Clinking. At length upon his knees he fell,
And lifting up his trembling hands, outstretched
In supplication,—Mercy! he exclaimed,—
Chains, dungeons, darkness,—any thing but death!—
I did not touch his life.
      Roderick replied,
His hour, whenever it had come, had found
A soul prepared: he lived in peace with Heaven,
And life prolonged for him, was bliss delayed.
But life, in pain and darkness and despair,

For thee, all leprous as thou art with crimes,
Is mercy.—Take him hence, and let him see
The light of day no more!

        Such Roderick was
When last I saw these courts,—his theatre
Of glory;—such when last I visited
My master's grave! Ten years have hardly held
Their course,—ten little years—break, break, old heart—
Oh why art thou so tough!

        As thus he spake
They reached the church. The door before his hand
Gave way; both blinded with their tears, they went
Straight to the tomb; and there Siverian knelt,
And bowed his face upon the sepulchre,
Weeping aloud; while Roderick, overpowered,
And calling upon earth to cover him,
Threw himself prostrate on his father's grave.
Thus as they lay, an awful voice in tones
Severe addressed them. Who are ye, it said,
That with your passion thus, and on this night,
Disturb my prayers? Starting they rose : there stood
A man before them of majestic form
And stature, clad in sackcloth, bare of foot,
Pale, and in tears, with ashes on his head.

VII.

RODERICK AND PELAYO.

'T was not in vain that on her absent son,
Pelayo's mother, from the bed of death,
Call'd for forgiveness, and in agony
Besought his prayers; all guilty as she was,
Sure he had not been human, if that cry
Had failed to pierce him. When he heard the tale
He blest the messenger, even while his speech
Was faltering,—while from head to foot he shook
With icy feelings from his inmost heart
Effused. It changed the nature of his woe,
Making the burthen more endurable:
The life-long sorrow that remained, became
A healing and a chastening grief, and brought
His soul, in close communion, nearer Heaven.
For he had been her first-born, and the love
Which at her breast he drew, and from her smiles,
And from her voice of tenderness imbibed,
Gave such unnatural horror to her crimes,
That when the thought came over him, it seemed
As if the milk which with his infant life
Had blended, thrilled like poison through his frame.
It was a woe beyond all reach of hope,
Till with the dreadful tale of her remorse
Faith touched his heart; and ever from that day
Did he for her who bore him, night and morn,
Pour out the anguish of his soul in prayer:
But chiefly as the night returned, which heard
Her last expiring groans of penitence,
Then through the long and painful hours, before
The altar, like a penitent himself,
He kept his vigils; and when Roderick's sword
Subdued Witiza, and the land was free,
Duly upon her grave he offered up
His yearly sacrifice of agony
And prayer. This was the night, and he it was
Who now before Siverian and the King

Stood up in sackcloth.

        The old man, from fear
Recovering, and from wonder, knew him first.
It is the Prince! he cried, and bending down
Embraced his knees. The action and the word
Awakened Roderick; he shook off the load
Of struggling thoughts, which, pressing on his heart,
Held him like one entranced ; yet, all untaught
To bend before the face of man, confused
Awhile he stood, forgetful of his part.
But when Siverian cried, My Lord, my Lord,
Now God be praised that I have found thee thus,
My Lord and Prince, Spain's only hope and mine!
Then Roderick, echoing him, exclaimed, My Lord
And Prince, Pelayo!—and approaching near,
He bent his knee obeisant : but his head
Earthward inclined ; while the old man, looking up,
From his low gesture to Pelayo's face,
Wept at beholding him for grief and joy.

Siverian! cried the Chief,—of whom hath Death
Bereaved me, that thou comest to Cordoba?—
Children, or wife?—Or hath the merciless scythe
Of this abhorred and jealous tyranny
Made my house desolate at one wide sweep?
They are as thou couldst wish, the old man replied,
Wert thou but lord of thine own house again,
And Spain were Spain once more. A tale of ill
I bear, but one which touches not the heart
Like what thy fears forebode. The renegade
Numacian woos thy sister, and she lends
To the vile slave, unworthily, her ear:
The lady Gaudiosa hath in vain
Warned her of all the evils which await
A union thus accurst ; she sets at nought
Her faith, her lineage, and thy certain wrath.

Pelayo hearing him, remained awhile
Silent ; then turning to his mother's grave,—
O thou poor dust, hath then the infectious taint
Survived thy dread remorse, that it should run
In Guisla's veins? he cried;—I should have heard
This shameful sorrow any where but here!—
Humble thyself, proud heart;—thou, gracious Heaven,
Be merciful!—it is the original flaw,—
And what are we?—a weak unhappy race,
Born to our sad inheritance of sin
And death!—He smote his forehead as he spake,
And from his head the ashes fell, like snow
Shaken from some dry beech-leaves, when a bird
Lights on the bending spray. A little while
In silence, rather than in thought, he stood
Passive beneath the sorrow : turning then,
And what doth Gaudiosa counsel me?
He asked the old man ; for she hath ever been
My wise and faithful counsellor—He replied,
The Lady Gaudiosa bade me say
She sees the danger which on every part
Besets her husband's house—Here she had ceased :
But when my noble Mistress gave in charge,
How I should tell thee that in evil times
The bravest counsels ever are the best ;
Then that high-minded Lady thus rejoined,
Whatever be my Lord's resolve, he knows
I bear a mind prepared.

        Brave spirits! cried

Pelayo, worthy to remove all stain
Of weakness from their sex! I should be less
Than man, if, drawing strength where others find
Their hearts most open to assault of fear,
I quailed at danger.   Never be it said
Of Spain, that in the hour of her distress
Her women were as heroes, but her men
Performed the woman's part!
                              Roderick at that
Looked up, and taking up the word, exclaimed,
O Prince, in better days the pride of Spain,
And, prostrate as she lies, her surest hope,
Hear now my tale.   The fire which seemed extinct
Hath risen revigorate : a living spark
From Auria's ashes, by a woman's hand
Preserved and quickened, kindles far and wide
The beacon-flame o'er all the Asturian hills.
There hath a vow been offered up, which binds
Us and our children's children to the work
Of holy hatred.   In the name of Spain
That vow hath been pronounced, and registered
Above, to be the bond whereby we stand
For condemnation or acceptance.   Heaven
Received the irrevocable vow, and Earth
Must witness its fulfilment; Earth and Heaven
Call upon thee, Pelayo! Upon thee
The spirits of thy royal ancestors
Look down expectant; unto thee, from fields
Laid waste, and hamlets burnt, and cities sacked,
The blood of infancy and helpless age
Cries out; thy native mountains call for thee,
Echoing from all their armed sons thy name.
And deem not thou that hot impatience goads
Thy countrymen to counsels immature:
Odoar and Urban from Visonia's banks
Send me, their sworn and trusted messenger,
To summon thee, and tell thee in their name
That now the hour is come? For sure it seems,
Thus saith the primate, Heaven's high will to rear
Upon the soil of Spain a Spanish throne,
Restoring in thy native line, O Prince,
The sceptre to the Spaniard.[26] Worthy son
Of that most ancient and heroic race.
Which with unweariable endurance still
Hath striven against its mightier enemies,
Roman or Carthaginian, Greek or Goth;
So often by superior arms opprest,
More often by superior arts beguiled;
Yet amid all its sufferings, all the waste
Of sword and fire remorselessly employed,
Unconquered and unconquerable still;—
Son of that injured and illustrious stock,
Stand forward thou; draw forth the sword of Spain,
Restore them to their rights too long withheld,
And place upon thy brow the Spanish crown.

When Roderick ceased, the princely Mountaineer
Gazed on the passionate orator awhile,
With eyes intently fixed, and thoughtful brow ;
Then turning to the altar, he let fall
The sackcloth robe, which late with folded arms
Against his heart was prest ; and, stretching forth
His hands toward the crucifix, exclaimed,
My God and my Redeemer! where but here,
Before thy awful presence, in this garb,
With penitential ashes thus bestrewn,

Could I so fitly answer to the call
Of Spain; and for her sake, and in thy name,
Accept the Crown of Thorns she proffers me![27]
And where but here, said Roderick in his heart,
Could I so properly, with humbled knee
And willing soul, confirm my forfeiture?—
The action followed on that secret thought :
He knelt, and took Pelayo's hand, and cried,
First of the Spaniards, let me with this kiss
Do homage to thee here, my Lord and King!—
With voice unchanged and steady countenance
He spake; but when Siverian followed him,
The old man trembled as his lips pronounced
The faltering vow; and rising he exclaimed,
God grant thee, O my Prince, a better fate
Than thy poor kinsman's, who in happier days
Received thy homage here!—Grief choked his speech,
And, bursting into tears, he sobbed aloud.
Tears too adown Pelayo's manly cheek
Rolled silently.   Roderick alone appeared
Unmoved and calm; for now the Royal Goth
Had offered his accepted sacrifice,
And therefore in his soul he felt that peace
Which follows painful duty well performed,—
Perfect and heavenly peace,—the peace of God.

VIII.

ALPHONSO.

Fain would Pelayo have that hour obeyed
The call, commencing his adventurous flight,
As one whose soul impatiently endured
His country's thraldom, and in daily prayer
Imploring her deliverance, cried to Heaven,
How long, O Lord, how long!—But other thoughts
Curbing his spirit, made him yet awhile
Sustain the weight of bondage.   Him alone,
Of all the Gothic baronage, the Moors
Watched with regard of wary policy,—
Knowing his powerful name, his noble mind,
And how in him the old Iberian blood,
Of royal and remotest ancestry,
From undisputed source flowed undefiled ;
His mother's after-guilt attainting not
The claim legitimate he derived from her,
Her first-born in her time of innocence.
He too of Chindasuintho's regal line
Sole remnant now, drew after him the love
Of all true Goths, uniting in himself
Thus by this double right, the general heart
Of Spain.   For this the renegado crew,
Wretches in whom their conscious guilt and fear
Engendered cruellest hatred, still advised
The extinction of Pelayo's house; but most
The apostate Prelate, in iniquity
Witiza's genuine brother as in blood,
Orpas, pursued his life.   He never ceased
With busy zeal, true traitor, to infuse
His deadly rancour in the Moorish chief:
Their only danger, ever he observed,
Was from Pelayo; root his lineage out,
The Caliph's empire then would be secure,
And universal Spain, all hope of change
Being lost, receive the Prophet's conquering law

51

Then did the Arch-villain urge the Moor at once
To cut off future peril, telling him
Death was a trusty keeper, and that none
E'er broke the prison of the grave.   But here
Keen malice overshot its mark: The Moor,
Who from the plunder of their native land
Had bought the recreant crew that joined his arms,
Or cheaplier with their own possessions bribed
Their sordid souls, saw through the flimsy show
Of policy wherewith they sought to cloak
Old enmity, and selfish aims: he scorned
To let their private purposes incline
His counsels, and believing Spain subdued,
Smiled, in the pride of power and victory,
Disdainful at the thought of farther strife.
Howbeit he held Pelayo at his court,
And told him that until his countrymen
Submissively should lay their weapons down,
He from his children and paternal hearth
Apart must dwell, nor hope to see again
His native mountains and their vales beloved,
Till all the Asturian and Cantabrian hills
Had bowed before the Caliph; Cordóba
Must be his nightly prison till that hour.
This night, by special favour from the Moor
Asked and vouchsafed, he past without the walls,
Keeping his yearly vigil; on this night
Therefore the princely Spaniard could not fly,
Being thus in strongest bonds by honour held.
Nor would he by his own escape expose
To stricter bondage, or belike to death,
Count Pedro's son.   The ancient enmity
Of rival houses from Pelayo's heart
Had, like a thing forgotten, past away;
He pitied child and parent, separated
By the stern mandate of unfeeling power;
And almost with a father's eyes beheld
The boy, his fellow in captivity.
For young Alphonso was in truth an heir
Of nature's largest patrimony; rich
In form and feature, growing strength of limb,
A gentle heart, a soul affectionate,
A joyous spirit filled with generous thoughts,
And genius heightening and ennobling all.
The blossom of all manly virtues made
His boyhood beautiful.   Shield, gracious Heaven,
In this ungenial season perilous,—
Thus would Pelayo sometimes breathe in prayer
The aspirations of prophetic hope,—
Shield, gracious Heaven, the blooming tree! and let
This goodly promise, for thy people's sake,
Yield its abundant fruitage.
                        When the Prince,
With hope and fear and grief and shame disturbed,
And sad remembrance, and the shadowy light
Of days before him, thronging as in dreams,
Whose quick succession filled and overpowered
Awhile the unresisting faculty,
Could in the calm of troubled thoughts subdued
Seek in his heart for counsel, his first care
Was for the boy : how best they might evade
The Moor, and renegade's more watchful eye;
And leaving in some unsuspicious guise
The city, through what unfrequented track
Safeliest pursue with speed their dangerous way.
Consumed in cares like these, the fleeting hours

Went by.   The lamps and tapers now grew pale,
And through the eastern window slanting fell
The roseate ray of morn.   Within those walls
Returning day restored no cheerful sounds,
Or joyous motions of awakening life;
But in the stream of light the speckled motes,
As if in mimickry of insect play,
Floated with mazy movement.   Sloping down
Over the altar passed the pillared beam,
And rested on the sinful woman's grave
As if it entered there, a light from Heaven.
So be it! cried Pelayo, even so!
As, in a momentary interval, ᶜ
When thought expelling thought, had left his mind
Open and passive to the influxes
Of outward sense, his vacant eye was there,—
So be it, heavenly Father, even so!
Thus may thy vivifying goodness shed
Forgiveness there; for let not thou the groans
Of dying penitence, nor my bitter prayers
Before thy mercy-seat, be heard in vain!
And thou, poor soul, who from the dolorous house
Of weeping and of pain, dost look to me
To shorten and assuage thy penal term,
Pardon me that these hours in other thoughts
And other duties than this garb, this night,
Enjoin, should thus have past!   Our mother-land
Exacted of my heart the sacrifice;
And many a vigil must thy son perform
Henceforth in woods and mountain fastnesses,
And tented fields, outwatching for her sake
The starry host, and ready for the work
Of day, before the sun begins his course.[28]

The noble Mountaineer, concluding then
With silent prayer the service of the night,
Went forth.   Without the porch awaiting him
He saw Alphonso, pacing to and fro
With patient step, and eye reverted oft.
He, springing forward when he heard the door
Move on its heavy hinges, ran to him,
And welcomed him with smiles of youthful love.
I have been watching yonder moon, quoth he,
How it grew pale and paler as the sun
Scattered the flying shades : but woe is me,
For on the towers of Cordoba the while
That baleful crescent glittered in the morn,
And with its insolent triumph seemed to mock
The omen I had found—Last night I dreamt
That thou wert in the field in arms for Spain,
And I was at thy side: the infidels
Beset us round, but we with our good swords
Hewed out a way.   Methought I stabbed a Moor
Who would have slain thee; but with that I woke
For joy, and wept to find it but a dream.

Thus as he spake a livelier glow o'erspread
His cheek, and starting tears again suffused
The brightening lustre of his eyes.   The Prince
Regarded him a moment stedfastly,
As if in quick resolve; then looking round
On every side with keen and rapid glance,
Drew him within the church.   Alphonso's heart
Throbbed with a joyful boding as he marked
The calmness of Pelayo's countenance
Kindle with solemn thoughts, expressing now

High purposes of resolute hope. He gazed
All eagerly to hear what most he wished.
If, said the Prince, thy dream were verified,
And I indeed were in the field in arms
For Spain,—wouldst thou be at Pelayo's side?
If I should break these bonds, and fly to rear
Our country's banner on our native hills,
Wouldst thou, Alphonso, share my dangerous flight,.
Dear boy,—and wilt thou take thy lot with me
For death, or for deliverance ?
                              Shall I swear?
Replied the impatient boy ; and laying hand
Upon the altar, on his knee he bent,
Looking toward Pelayo with such joy
Of reverential love, as if a God
Were present to receive the eager vow.
Nay, quoth Pelayo ; what hast thou to do
With oaths?—Bright emanation as thou art,
It were a wrong to thy unsullied soul,
A sin to nature, were I to require
Promise or vow from thee! Enough for me
That thy heart answers to the stirring call.
Alphonso, follow thou, in happy faith,
Alway the indwelling voice that counsels thee;
And then, let fall the issue as it may,
Shall all thy paths be in the light of Heaven,
The peace of Heaven be with thee in all hours.

How then, exclaimed the boy, shall I discharge
The burthen of this happiness,—how ease
My overflowing soul!—Oh gracious God,
Shall I behold my mother's face again,—
My father's hall,—my native hills and vales,
And hear the voices of their streams again,—
And free as I was born amid those scenes
Beloved, maintain my country's freedom there,—
Or, failing in the sacred enterprise,
Die as becomes a Spaniard!—Saying thus,
He lifted up his hands and eyes toward
The image of the Crucified, and cried,.
O thou who didst with thy most precious blood
Redeem us, Jesu! help us while we seek
Earthly redemption from this yoke of shame
And misbelief and death.
                    The noble boy
Then rose, and would have knelt again to clasp
Pelayo's knees, and kiss his hand in act
Of homage; but the Prince, preventing this,
Bent over him in fatherly embrace,
And breathed a fervent blessing on his head.

IX.

FLORINDA.

There sate a woman like a supplicant,
Muffled and cloaked, before Pelayo's gate,
Awaiting when he should return that morn.
She rose at his approach, and bowed her head,
And, with a low and trembling utterance,
Besought him to vouchsafe her speech within
In privacy. And when they were alone,
And the doors closed, she knelt and claspt his knees,
Saying, a boon! a boon! This night, O Prince,
Hast thou kept vigil for thy mother's soul:

For her soul's sake, and for the soul of him
Whom once, in happier days, of all mankind
Thou heldëst for thy chosen bosom.friend,
Oh for the sake of his poor suffering soul,.
Refuse me not!
                    How should I dare refuse,
Being thus abjured! he answered. Thy request
Is granted, woman,—be it what it may,
So it be lawful, and within the bounds
Of possible achievement :—aught unfit
Thou wouldst not with these adjurations seek.
But who thou art, I marvel, that dost touch
Upon that string, and ask in Roderick's name !—
She bared her face, and, looking up, replied,
Florinda!—Shrinking then, with both her hands
She hid herself, and bowed her head abased
Upon her knee,—as one who, if the grave
Had oped beneath.her, would have thrown herself,
Even like a lover, in the arms of Death.

Pelayo stood confused: he had not seen
Count Julian's daughter since in Roderick's court,
Glittering in beauty and in innocence,
A radiant vision, in her joy she moved :
More like a poet's dream, or form divine,
Heaven's prototype of perfect womanhood,
So lovely was the presence,—than a thing
Of earth and perishable elements.
Now had he seen her in her winding-sheet,
Less painful would that spectacle have proved ;
For peace is with.the dead, and piety
Bringeth a patient hope to those who mourn
O'er the departed : but this altered face,
Bearing its deadly sorrow charactered,
Came to him like a ghost, which in the grave
Could find no rest. He, taking her cold hand,
Raised her, and would have spoken; but his tongue
Failed in its office, and could only speak
In under tones compassionate her name.

The voice of pity soothed and melted her;
And when the Prince bade her be comforted,
Proffering his zealous aid in whatsoe'er
Might please her to appoint, a feeble smile
Past slowly over her pale countenance,
Like moonlight on a marble statue. Heaven
Requite thee, Prince! she answered. All I ask
Is but a quiet resting-place, wherein
A broken heart, in prayer and humble hope,
May wait for its deliverance. Even this
My most unhappy fate denies me here.
Griefs which are known too widely and too well
I need not now remember. I could bear
Privation of all Christian ordinances;
The woe which kills hath saved me too, and made
A temple of this ruined tabernacle,
Wherein redeeming God doth not disdain
To let his presence shine. And I could bear
To see the turban on my father's brow,—
Sorrow beyond all sorrows,—shame of shames,.
Yet to be borne, while I with tears of blood,.
And throes of agony, in his behalf
Implore, and wrestle with offended Heaven.
This I have borne resigned: but other ills
And worse assail me now; the which to bear,
If to avoid be possible, would draw

Damnation down. Orpas, the perjured Priest,
The apostate Orpas, claims me for his bride.
Obdurate as he is, the wretch profanes
My sacred woe, and woos me to his bed,
The thing I am,—the living death thou seest!

Miscreant! exclaimed Pelayo. Might I meet
That renegado sword to scymitar
In open field, never did man approach
The altar for the sacrifice in faith
More sure, than I should hew the villain down!
But how should Julian favour his demand?—
Julian, who hath so passionately loved
His child, so dreadfully revenged her wrongs!

Count Julian, she replied, hath none but me,
And it hath therefore been his heart's desire
To see his ancient line by me preserved.
This was their covenant when in fatal hour
For Spain, and for themselves, in traitorous bond
Of union they combined. My father, stung
To madness, only thought of how to make
His veangeance sure: the Prelate, calm and cool,
When he renounced his outward faith in Christ,
Indulged at once his hatred of the King,
His inbred wickedness, and a haughty hope,
Versed as he was in treasons, to direct
The invaders by his secret policy,
And at their head, aided by Julian's power,
Reign as a Moor upon that throne to which
The priestly order else had barred his way.
The African hath conquered for himself;
But Orpas coveteth Count Julian's lands,
And claims to have the covenant performed.
Friendless, and worse than fatherless, I come
To thee for succour. Send me secretly,—
For well I know all faithful hearts must be
At thy devotion,—with a trusty guide
To guard me on the way, that I may reach
Some Christian land, where Christian rites are free,
And there discharge a vow, alas! too long,
Too fatally delayed. Aid me in this
For Roderick's sake, Pelayo! and thy name
Shall be remembered in my latest prayer.

Be comforted! the Prince replied; but when
He spake of comfort, twice did he break off
The idle words, feeling that earth had none
For grief so irremediable as her's.
At length he took her hand, and pressing it,
And forcing through involuntary tears
A mournful smile affectionate, he said,
Say not that thou art friendless while I live!
Thou couldst not to a readier ear have told
Thy sorrows, nor have asked in fitter hour
What for my country's honour, for my rank,
My faith, and sacred knighthood, I am bound
In duty to perform; which not to do
Would show me undeserving of the names
Of Goth, Prince, Christian, even of Man. This day,
Lady, prepare to take thy lot with me,
And soon as evening closes meet me here.
Duties bring blessings with them, and I hold
Thy coming for a happy augury,
In this most awful crisis of my fate.

X.

RODERICK AND FLORINDA.

WITH sword and breast-plate under rustic weeds
Concealed, at dusk Pelayo past the gate,
Florinda following near, disguised alike.
Two peasants on their mules they seemed, at eve
Returning from the town. Not distant far,
Alphonso by the appointed orange-grove,
With anxious eye and agitated heart,
Watched for the Prince's coming. Eagerly
At every foot-fall through the gloom he strained
His sight, nor did he recognize him when
The Chieftain thus accompanied drew nigh;
And when the expected signal called him on,
Doubting this female presence, half in fear
Obeyed the call. Pelayo too perceived
The boy was not alone; he not for that
Delayed the summons, but lest need should be,
Laying hand upon his sword, toward him bent
In act soliciting speech, and low of voice
Inquired if friend or foe. Forgive me, cried
Alphonso, that I did not tell thee this,
Full as I was of happiness, before.
'T is Hoya, servant of my father's house,
Unto whose dutiful care and love, when sent
To this vile bondage, I was given in charge.
How could I look upon my father's face,
If I had in my joy deserted him,
Who was to me found faithful?—Right! replied
The Prince; and viewing him with silent joy,
Blessèd the Mother, in his heart he said,
Who gave thee birth! but sure of womankind
Most blessèd she whose hand her happy stars
Shall link with thine! and with that thought the form
Of Hermesind,[29] his daughter, to his soul
Came in her beauty.
     Soon by devious tracks
They turned aside. The favouring moon arose,
To guide them on their flight through upland paths
Remote from frequentage, and dales retired,
Forest and mountain glen. Before their feet
The fire-flies, swarming in the woodland shade,
Sprung up like sparks, and twinkled round their way;
The timorous blackbird, starting at their step,
Fled from the thicket, with shrill note of fear;
And far below them in the peopled dell,
When all the soothing sounds of eve had ceased,
The distant watch-dog's voice at times was heard,
Answering the nearer wolf. All through the night
Among the hills they travelled silently;
Till when the stars were setting, at what hour
The breath of Heaven is coldest, they beheld
Within a lonely grove the expected fire,
Where Roderick and his comrade anxiously
Looked for the appointed meeting. Halting there,
They from the burthen and the bit relieved
Their patient bearers, and around the fire
Partook of needful food and grateful rest.

Bright rose the flame replenished; it illumed
The cork-tree's furrowed rind, its rifts and swells
And redder scars,—and where its aged boughs

O'erbowered the travellers, cast upon the leaves
A floating, grey, unrealizing gleam.
Alphonso, light of heart, upon the heath
Lay carelessly dispread, in happy dreams
Of home: his faithful Hoya slept beside.
Years and fatigue to old Siverian brought
Easy oblivion; and the Prince himself,
Yielding to weary nature's gentle will,
Forgot his cares awhile. Florinda sate
Beholding Roderick with fixed eyes intent,
Yet unregardant of the countenance
Whereon they dwelt; in other thoughts absorbed,
Collecting fortitude for what she yearned,
Yet trembled to perform. Her steady look
Disturbed the Goth, albeit he little weened
What agony awaited him that hour.
Her face, well nigh as changed as his, was now
Half-hidden, and the lustre of her eye
Extinct; nor did her voice awaken in him
One startling recollection when she spake,
So altered were its tones.
                          Father, she said,
All thankful as I am to leave behind
The unhappy walls of Cordoba, not less
Of consolation doth my heart receive
At sight of one to whom I may disclose
The sins which trouble me, and at his feet
Lay down repentantly, in Jesus' name,
The burthen of my spirit. In his name
Hear me, and pour into a wounded soul
The balm of pious counsel—Saying thus,
She drew toward the minister ordained,
And kneeling by him, Father, dost thou know
The wretch who kneels beside thee? she inquired.
He answered, Surely we are each to each
Equally unknown.
                 Then said she, Here thou seest
One who is known too fatally for all,—
The daughter of Count Julian. Well it was
For Roderick that no eye beheld him now:
From head to foot a sharper pang than death
Thrilled him; his heart, as at a mortal stroke,
Ceased from its functions; his breath failed, and when
The power of life recovering set its springs
Again in action, cold and clammy sweat
Starting at every pore suffused his frame.
Their presence helped him to subdue himself;
For else, had none been nigh, he would have fallen
Before Florinda prostrate on the earth,
And in that mutual agony belike
Both souls had taken flight. She marked him not:
For having told her name, she bowed her head;
Breathing a short and silent prayer to Heaven,
While, as the penitent, she wrought herself
To open to his eye her hidden wounds.

Father, at length she said, all tongues amid
This general ruin shed their bitterness
On Roderick, load his memory with reproach,
And with their curses persecute his soul—
Why shouldst thou tell me this? exclaimed the Goth,
From his cold forehead wiping as he spake
The death-like moisture:—Why of Roderick's guilt
Tell me? Or thinkëst thou I know it not?
Alas! who hath not heard the hideous tale
Of Roderick's shame! Babes learn it from their nurses,

And children, by their mothers unreproved,
Link their first execrations to his name.
Oh, it hath caught a taint of infamy,
That, like Iscariot's, through all time shall last,
Reeking and fresh for ever!
                            There! she cried,
Drawing her body backward where she knelt,
And stretching forth her arms with head upraised,—
There! it pursues me still!—I came to thee,
Father, for comfort, and thou heapëst fire
Upon my head. But hear me patiently,
And let me undeceive thee! self-abased,
Not to arraign another, do I come ;—
I come a self-accuser, self-condemned,
To take upon myself the pain deserved;
For I have drank the cup of bitterness,
And having drank therein of heavenly grace,
I must not put away the cup of shame.

Thus as she spake she faltered at the close,
And in that dying fall her voice sent forth
Somewhat of its original sweetness. Thou!—
Thou self-abased! exclaimed the astonished King;—
Thou self-condemned!—The cup of shame for thee!—
Thee—thee, Florinda!—But the very excess
Of passion checked his speech, restraining thus
From farther transport, which had haply else
Mastered him; and he sate like one entranced,
Gazing upon that countenance so fallen,
So changed : her face, raised from its muffler now,
Was turned toward him, and the fire-light shone
Full on its mortal paleness; but the shade
Concealed the King.
                    She roused him from the spell
Which held him like a statue motionless.
Thou too, quoth she, dost join the general curse,
Like one who when he sees a felon's grave,
Casting a stone there as he passes by,
Adds to the heap of shame. Oh what are we,
Frail creatures as we are, that we should sit
In judgment man on man ! and what were we,
If the All-merciful should mete to us
With the same rigorous measure wherewithal
Sinner to sinner metes! But God beholds
The secrets of the heart,—therefore his name
Is Merciful. Servant of God, see thou
The hidden things of mine, and judge thou then
In charity thy brother who hath fallen—
Nay, hear me to the end! I loved the King,—
Tenderly, passionately, madly loved him.
Sinful it was to love a child of earth
With such entire devotion as I loved
Roderick, the heroic Prince, the glorious Goth!
And yet methought this was its only crime,
The imaginative passion seemed so pure:
Quiet and calm like duty, hope nor fear
Disturb the deep contentment of that love :
He was the sunshine of my soul, and like
A flower, I lived and flourished in his light.
Oh bear not with me thus impatiently!
No tale of weakness this, that in the act
Of penitence, indulgent to itself,
With garrulous palliation half repeats
The sin it ill repents. I will be brief,
And shrink not from confessing how the love
Which thus began in innocence, betrayed

My unsuspecting heart ; nor me alone,
But him, before whom, shining as he shone
With whatsoe'er is noble, whatsoe'er
Is lovely, whatsoever good and great,
I was as dust and ashes,—but him, alas!
This glorious being, this exalted Prince,
Even him, with all his royalty of soul,
Did this ill-omened, this accursèd love,
To his most lamentable fall betray
And utter ruin. Thus it was: The King,
By counsels of cold statesmen ill-advised,
To an unworthy mate had bound himself
In politic wedlock. Wherefore should I tell
How Nature upon Egilona's form,
Profuse of beauty, lavishing her gifts,
Left, like a statue from the graver's hands,
Deformity and hollowness beneath
The rich external? For the love of pomp
And emptiest vanity, hath she not incurred
The grief and wonder of good men, the gibes
Of vulgar ribaldry, the reproach of all;
Profaning the most holy sacrament
Of marriage, to become chief of the wives
Of Abdalaziz, of the Infidel,
The Moor, the tyrant-enemy of Spain!
All know her now; but they alone who knew
What Roderick was can judge his wretchedness,
To that light spirit and unfeeling heart
In hopeless bondage bound. No children rose
From this unhapy union, towards whom
The springs of love within his soul confined
Might flow in joy and fulness; nor was he
One, like Witiza, of the vulgar crew,
Who in promiscuous appetite can find
All their vile nature seeks. Alas for man!
Exuberant health diseases him, frail worm!
And the slight bias of untoward chance
Makes his best virtues from the even line,
With fatal declination, swerve aside.
Aye, thou mayest groan for poor mortality,—
Well, Father, mayest thou groan.
                                My evil fate
Made me an inmate of the royal house,
And Roderick found in me, if not a heart
Like his,—for who was like the heroic Goth?—
One which at least felt his surpassing worth,
And loved him for himself.—A little yet
Bear with me, reverend Father, for I touch
Upon the point, and this long prologue goes,
As justice bids, to palliate his offence,
Not mine. The passion, which I fondly thought
Such as fond sisters for a brother feel,
Grew day by day, and strengthened in its growth,
Till the beloved presence was become
Needful as food or necessary sleep,
My hope, light, sunshine, life, and every thing.
Thus lapt in dreams of bliss, I might have lived
Contented with this pure idolatry,
Had he been happy : but I saw and knew
The inward discontent and household griefs
Which he subdued in silence; and, alas!
Pity with admiration mingling then,
Alloyed and lowered and humanized my love,
Till to the level of my lowliness
It brought him down; and in this treacherous heart
Too often the repining thought arose,

That if Florinda had been Roderick's Queen,
Then might domestic peace and happiness
Have blest his home and crowned our wedded loves.
Too often did that sinful thought recur,
Too feebly the temptation was repelled.

See, Father, I have probed my inmost soul;
Have searched to its remotest source the sin;
And tracing it through all its specious forms
Of fair disguisement, I present it now,
Even as it lies before the eye of God,
Bare and exposed, convicted and condemned.
One eve, as in the bowers which overhang
The glen where Tagus rolls between his rocks ³⁰
I roamed alone, alone I met the King.
His countenance was troubled, and his speech
Like that of one whose tongue to light discourse
At fits constrained, betrays a heart disturbed :
I too, albeit unconscious of his thoughts,
With anxious looks revealed what wandering words
In vain essayed to hide. A little while
Did this oppressive intercourse endure,
Till our eyes met in silence, each to each
Telling their mutual tale, then consciously
Together fell abashed. He took my hand
And said, Florinda, would that thou and I
Earlier had met; oh what a blissful lot
Had then been mine, who might have found in thee
The sweet companion and the friend endeared,
A fruitful wife and crown of earthly joys!
Thou too shouldst then have been of womankind
Happiest, as now the loveliest—And with that,
First giving way to passion first disclosed,
He prest upon my lips a guilty kiss,—
Alas! more guilty received than given.
Passive and yielding, and yet self-reproached,
Trembling I stood, upheld in his embrace;
When coming steps were heard, and Roderick said,
Meet me to-morrow, I beseech thee, here,
Queen of my heart! Oh meet me here again,
My own Florinda, meet me here again!—
Tongue, eye, and pressure of the impassioned hand
Solicited and urged the ardent suit,
And from my hesitating hurried lips
The word of promise fatally was drawn.
O Roderick, Roderick! hadst thou told me all
Thy purpose at that hour, from what a world
Of woe had thou and I—The bitterness
Of that reflection overcame her then,
And choked her speech.   But Roderick sate the while
Covering his face with both his hands close prest,
His head bowed down, his spirit to such point
Of sufferance knit, as one who patiently
Awaits the uplifted sword.
                            Till now, said she,
Resuming her confession, I had lived,
If not in innocence, yet self-deceived,
And of my perilous and sinful state
Unconscious. But this fatal hour revealed
To my awakening soul her guilt and shame;
And in those agonies with which remorse,
Wrestling with weakness and with cherished sin,
Doth triumph o'er the lacerated heart,
That night—that miserable night—I vowed,
A virgin dedicate, to pass my life
Immured; and, like redeemèd Magdalen, ³¹

Or that Egyptian penitent, [32] whose tears
Fretted the rock and moistened round her cave
The thirsty desert, so to mourn my fall.
The struggle ending thus, the victory
Thus, as I thought, accomplished, I believed
My soul was calm, and that the peace of Heaven
Descended to accept and bless my vow;
And in this faith, prepared to consummate
The sacrifice, I went to meet the King.
See, Father, what a snare had Satan laid!
For Roderick came to tell me that the Church
From his unfruitful bed would set him free,
And I should be his Queen.

            O let me close
The dreadful tale! [33] I told him of my vow;
And from sincere and scrupulous piety,
But more, I fear me, in that desperate mood
Of obstinate will perverse, the which, with pride
And shame and self reproach, doth sometimes make
A woman's tongue, her own worst enemy,
Run counter to her dearest heart's desire,—
In that unhappy mood did I resist
All his most earnest prayers to let the power
Of holy Church, never more rightfully
Invoked, he said, than now in our behalf,
Release us from our fatal bonds. He urged
With kindly warmth his suit, like one whose life
Hung on the issue: I dissembled not
My cruel self-reproaches, nor my grief,
Yet desperately maintained the rash resolve;
Till in the passionate argument he grew
Incensed, inflamed, and maddened or possessed,—
For Hell too surely at that hour prevailed,
And with such subtile toils enveloped him,
That even in the extremity of guilt
No guilt he purported, but rather meant
An amplest recompense of life-long love
For transitory wrong, which fate perverse,
Thus madly he deceived himself, compelled,
And therefore stern necessity excused.
Here then, O Father, at thy feet I own
Myself the guiltier; for full well I knew
These were his thoughts, but vengeance mastered me,
And in my agony I curst the man
Whom I loved best.

            Dost thou recall that curse?
Cried Roderick, in a deep and inward voice,
Still with his head depressed, and covering still
His countenance. Recall it? she exclaimed;
Father, I come to thee because I gave
The reins to wrath too long,—because I wrought
His ruin, death, and infamy.—O God,
Forgive the wicked vengeance thus indulged,
As I forgive the King!—But teach me thou
What reparation more than tears and prayers
May now be made;—how shall I vindicate
His injured name, and take upon myself—
Daughter of Julian, firmly he replied,
Speak not of that, I charge the! On his fame
The Ethiop dye, fixed ineffaceably,
For ever will abide; so it must be,
So should be; 'tis his rightful punishment;
And if to the full measure of his fault
The punishment hath fallen, the more our hope
That through the blood of Jesus he may find
His sins forgiven him.

            Pausing then, he raised
His hand, and pointed where Siverian lay
Stretched on the heath. To that old man, said he,
And to the mother of the unhappy Goth,
Tell, if it please thee, not what thou hast poured
Into my secret ear, but that the child
For whom they mourn with anguish unallayed,
Sinned not from vicious will, or heart corrupt,
But fell by fatal circumstance betrayed.
And if in charity to them thou sayest
Something to palliate, something to excuse
An act of sudden frenzy when the fiend
O'ercame him, thou wilt do for Roderick
All he could ask thee, all that can be done
On earth, and all his spirit could endure.

Venturing towards her an imploring look,
Wilt thou join with me for his soul in prayer?
He said, and trembled as he spake. That voice
Of sympathy was like Heaven's influence,
Wounding at once and comforting the soul.
O Father, Christ requite thee! she exclaimed;
Thou hast set free the springs which withering griefs
Have closed too long. Forgive me, for I thought
Thou wert a rigid and unpitying judge;
One whose stern virtue, feeling in itself
No flaw of frailty, heard impatiently
Of weakness and of guilt. I wronged thee, Father!—
With that she took his hand, and kissing it,
Bathed it with tears. Then in a firmer speech,
For Roderick, for Count Julian and myself,
Three wretchedest of all the human race,
Who have destroyed each other and ourselves,
Mutually wronged and wronging, let us pray!

XI.

COUNT PEDRO'S CASTLE.

Twelve weary days with unremitting speed,
Shunning frequented tracks, the travellers
Pursued their way; the mountain-path they chose,
The forest or the lonely heath wide-spread,
Where cistus shrubs sole-seen exhaled at noon
Their fine balsamic odour all around:
Strew'd with their blossoms, frail as beautiful,
The thirsty soil at eve; and when the sun
Relumed the gladden'd earth, opening anew
Their stores exuberant, prodigal as frail,
Whiten'd again the wilderness. They left
The dark Sierra's skirts behind, and cross'd
The wilds where Ana in her native hills
Collects her sister springs, and hurries on
Her course melodious, amid loveliest glens,
With forest and with fruitage overbower'd.
These scenes profusely blest by Heaven they left,
Where o'er the hazel and the quince the vine
Wide-mantling spreads; and, clinging round the cork
And ilex, hangs amid their dusky leaves
Garlands of brightest hue, with reddening fruit
Pendant, or clusters cool of glassy green.
So holding on o'er mountain and o'er vale,
Tagus they cross'd where midland on his way
The King of Rivers rolls his stately stream;
And rude Alverches' wild and stony bed;

And Duero distant far; and many a stream
And many a field obscure, in future war
For bloody theatre of famous deeds
Foredoom'd: and deserts, where in years to come
Shall populous towns arise, and crested towers
And stately temples rear their heads on high.

Cautious with course circuitous they shunn'd
The embattled city, which in eldest time
Thrice greatest Hermes built, so fables say,
Now subjugate, but fated to behold
Ere long the heroic Prince (who passing now
Unknown and silently the dangerous track,
Turns thither his regardant eye) come down
Victorious from the heights, and bear abroad
Her banner'd Lion, symbol to the Moor
Of rout and death through many an age of blood.
Lo, there the Asturian hills! Far in the west,
Huge Rabanal and Foncebadon huge,
Pre-eminent, their giant bulk display,
Darkening with earliest shade the distant vales
Of Leon, and with evening premature.
Far in Cantabria eastward, the long line
Extends beyond the reach of eagle's eye,
When buoyant in mid-heaven the bird of Jove
Soars at his loftiest pitch. In the north, before
The travellers the Erbasian mountains rise,
Bounding the land beloved, their native land.

How then, Alphonso, did thy eager soul
Chide the slow hours and painful way, which seem'd
Lengthening to grow before their lagging pace!
Youth of heroic thought and high desire,
'T is not the spur of lofty enterprise
That with unequal throbbing hurries now
The unquiet heart, now makes it sink dismay'd:
'T is not impatient joy which thus disturbs
In that young breast the healthful spring of life:
Joy and ambition have forsaken him,
His soul is sick with hope. So near his home,
So near his mother's arms:—alas! perchance
The longed-for meeting may be yet far off
As earth from heaven. Sorrow in these long months
Of separation may have laid her low;
Or what if at his flight the bloody Moor
Hath sent his ministers of slaughter forth,
And he himself should thus have brought the sword
Upon his father's head?—Sure Hoya too
The same dark presage feels, the fearful boy
Said in himself; or wherefore is his brow
Thus overcast with heaviness, and why
Looks he thus anxiously in silence round?

Just then that faithful servant raised his hand,
And turning to Alphonso with a smile,
He pointed where Count Pedro's towers far off
Peer'd in the dell below: faint was the smile,
And while it sate upon his lips, his eye
Retain'd its troubled speculation still.
For long had he look'd wistfully in vain,
Seeking where far or near he might espy
From whom to learn if time or chance had wrought
Change in his master's house: but on the hills
Nor goat-herd could he see, nor traveller,
Nor huntsman early at his sports afield,
Nor angler following up the mountain glen

His lonely pastime; neither could he hear
Carol, or pipe, or shout of shepherd's boy,
Nor woodman's axe, for not a human sound
Disturb'd the silence of the solitude.

Is it the spoiler's work? At yonder door
Behold the favourite kidling bleats unheard;
The next stands open, and the sparrows there
Boldly pass in and out. Thither he turn'd
To seek what indications were within:
The chesnut bread was on the shelf; the churn,
As if in haste forsaken, full and fresh;
The recent fire had moulder'd on the hearth;
And broken cobwebs marked the whiter space
Where from the wall the buckler and the sword
Had late been taken down. Wonder at first
Had mitigated fear, but Hoya now
Returned to tell the symbols of good hope,
And they pricked forward joyfully. Ere long,
Perceptible above the ceaseless sound
Of yonder stream, a voice of multitudes,
As if in loud acclaim, was heard far off;
And nearer as they drew, distincter shouts
Came from the dell, and at Count Pedro's gate
The human swarm were seen,—a motley group,
Maids, mothers, helpless infancy, weak age,
And wondering children and tumultuous boys,
Hot youth and resolute manhood gather'd there
In uproar all. Anon the moving mass
Falls in half circle back; a general cry
Bursts forth, exultant arms are lifted up,
And caps are thrown aloft, as through the gate
Count Pedro's banner came. Alphonso shriek'd
For joy, and smote his steed and galloped on.

Fronting the gate the standard-bearer holds
His precious charge. Behind the men divide
In order'd files; green boyhood presses there,
And waning eld, pleading a youthful soul,
Entreats admission. All is ardour here,
Hope and brave purposes, and minds resolved.
Nor where the weaker sex is left apart
Doth aught of fear find utterance, though perchance
Some paler cheeks might there be seen, some eyes
Big with sad bodings, and some natural tears.
Count Pedro's war-horse in the vacant space
Strikes with impatient hoof the trodden turf,
And gazing round upon the martial show,
Proud of his stately trappings, flings his head,
And snorts and champs the bit, and neighing shrill
Wakes the near echo with his voice of joy.
The page beside him holds his master's spear,
And shield and helmet. In the castle gate
Count Pedro stands, his countenance resolved
But mournful, for Favinia on his arm
Hung, passionate with her fears, and drew him back.
Go not, she cried, with this deluded crew!
She hath not, Pedro, with her frantic words
Bereft thy faculty,—she is crazed with grief,
And her delirium hath infected these:
But, Pedro, thou art calm; thou dost not share
The madness of the crowd; thy sober mind
Surveys the danger in its whole extent;
And sees the certain ruin,—for thou know'st
I know thou hast no hope. Unhappy man,
Why then for this most desperate enterprise

Wilt thou devote thy son, thine only child?
Not for myself I plead, nor even for thee;
Thou art a soldier, and thou canst not fear
The face of death; and I should welcome it
As the best visitant whom Heaven could send.
Not for our lives I speak then,—were they worth
The thought of preservation;—Nature soon
Must call for them; the sword that should cut short
Sorrow's slow work were merciful to us.
But spare Alphonso! there is time and hope
In store for him. O thou who gavest him life,
Seal not his death, his death and mine at once!

Peace! he replied; thou know'st there is no choice.
I did not raise the storm; I cannot turn
Its course aside; but where yon banner goes
Thy Lord must not be absent! Spare me then,
Favinia, lest I hear thy honour'd name
Now first attainted with deserved reproach.
The boy is in God's hands. He who of yore
Walked with the sons of Judah in the fire,
And from the lion's den drew Daniel forth
Unhurt, will save him,—if it be his will.

Just as he spake the astonished troop set up
A shout of joy which rung through all the hills.
Alphonso heeds not how they break their ranks
And gather round to greet him; from his horse
Precipitate and panting off he springs.
Pedro grew pale, and trembled at his sight;
Favinia claspt her hands, and looking up
To heaven as she embraced the boy, exclaimed,
Lord God, forgive me for my sinful fears!
Unworthy that I am,—my son, my son!

XII.

THE VOW.

ALWAYS I knew thee for a generous foe,
Pelayo! said the Count; and in our time
Of enmity, thou too, I know, didst feel
The feud between us was but of the house,
Not of the heart. Brethren in arms henceforth
We stand or fall together: nor will I
Look to the event with one misgiving thought,—
That were to prove myself unworthy now
Of Heaven's benignant providence, this hour,
Scarcely by less than miracle, vouchsafed.
I will believe that we have days in store
Of hope, now risen again as from the dead,—
Of vengeance,—of portentous victory,—
Yea, maugre all unlikelihoods, of peace.
Let us then here indissolubly knit
Our ancient houses, that those happy days,
When they arrive, may find us more than friends,
And bound by closer than fraternal ties.
Thou hast a daughter, Prince, to whom my heart
Yearns now, as if in winning infancy
Her smiles had been its daily food of love.
I need not tell thee what Alphonso is,—
Thou knowest the boy!
                            Already had that hope,
Replied Pelayo, risen within my soul.
O Thou, who in thy mercy from the house

Of Moorish bondage hast delivered us,
Fulfil the pious purposes for which
Here, in thy presence, thus we pledge our hands!

Strange hour to plight espousals! yielding half
To superstitious thoughts, Favinia cried,
And these strange witnesses!—The times are strange,
With thoughtful speech composed her Lord replies,
And what thou seest accords with them. This day
Is wonderful; nor could auspicious Heaven
With fairer or with fitter omen gild
Our enterprise, when strong in heart and hope
We take the field, preparing thus for works
Of piety and love. Unwillingly
I yielded to my people's general voice,
Thinking that she who with her powerful words
To this excess had roused and kindled them,
Spake from the spirit of her griefs alone,
Not with prophetic impulse. Be that sin
Forgiven me! and the calm and quiet faith
Which, in the place of incredulity,
Hath filled me, now that seeing I believe,
Doth give of happy end to righteous cause
A presage, not presumptuous, but assured.

Then Pedro told Pelayo how from vale
To vale the exalted Adosinda went,
Exciting sire and son, in holy war
Conquering or dying, to secure their place
In Paradise: and how reluctantly,
And mourning for his child by his own act
Thus doomed to death, he bade with heavy heart
His banner be brought forth. Devoid alike
Of purpose and of hope himself, he meant
To march toward the western Mountaineers,
Where Odoar by his counsel might direct
Their force conjoined. Now, said he, we must haste
To Cangas, there, Pelayo, to secure,
With timely speed, I trust in God, thy house.

Then looking to his men, he cried, Bring forth
The armour which in Wamba's wars [34] I wore—
Alphonso's heart leapt at the auspicious words.
Count Pedro marked the rising glow of joy:—
Doubly to thee, Alphonso, he pursued,
This day above all other days is blest,
From whence as from a birth-day thou wilt date
Thy life in arms!
                        Rejoicing in their task,
The servants of the house with emulous love
Dispute the charge. One brings the cuirass, one
The buckler; this exultingly displays
The sword, his comrade lifts the helm on high:
The greaves, the gauntlets they divide; a spur
Seems now to dignify the officious hand
Which for such service bears it to his Lord.
Greek artists in the imperial city forged
That splendid armour, perfect in their craft;
With curious skill they wrought it, framed alike
To shine amid the pageantry of war,
And for the proof of battle. Many a time
Alphonso from his nurse's lap had stretched
His infant hands toward it eagerly,
Where gleaming to the central fire it hung
High in the hall; and many a time had wished
With boyish ardour, that the day were come

52

When Pedro to his prayers would grant the boon,
His dearest heart's desire. Count Pedro then
Would smile, and in his heart rejoice to see
The noble instinct manifest itself.
Then too Favinia with maternal pride
Would turn her eyes exulting to her Lord,
And in that silent language bid him mark
His spirit in his boy: all danger then
Was distant, and if secret forethought faint
Of manhood's perils, and the chance of war,
Hateful to mothers, past across her mind,
The ill remote gave to the present hour
A heightened feeling of secure delight.

No season this for old solemnities,
For wassailry and sport;—the bath, the bed, [35]
The vigil,—all preparatory rites
Omitted now,—here in the face of Heaven,
Before the vassals of his father's house,
With them in instant peril to partake
The chance of life or death, the heroic boy
Dons his first arms; the coated scales of steel
Which o'er the tunic to his knees depend, [36]
The hose, the sleeves of mail: bareheaded then
He stood. But when Count Pedro took the spurs,
And bent his knee in service to his son,
Alphonso from that gesture half drew back,
Starting in reverence, and a deeper hue
Spread o'er the glow of joy which flushed his cheeks.
Do thou the rest, Pelayo! said the Count;
So shall the ceremony of this hour
Exceed in honour what in form it lacks.
The Prince from Hoya's faithful hand received
The sword; he girt it round the youth, and drew
And placed it in his hand; unsheathing then
His own good falchion, with its burnished blade
He touched Alphonso's neck, and with a kiss
Gave him his rank in arms.
                          Thus long the crowd
Had looked intently on, in silence hushed;
Loud and continuous now with one accord,
Shout following shout, their acclamations rose:
Blessings were breathed from every heart, and joy,
Powerful alike in all, which as with force
Of an inebriating cup inspired
The youthful, from the eye of age drew tears.
The uproar died away, when, standing forth,
Roderick with lifted hand besought a pause
For speech, and moved toward the youth. I too,
Young Baron, he began, must do my part;
Not with prerogative of earthly power,
But as the servant of the living God,
The God of Hosts. This day thou promisest
To die when honour calls thee, for thy faith,
For thy liege Lord, and for thy native land:
The duties which at birth we all contract,
Are by the high profession of this hour
Made thine especially. Thy noble blood,
The thoughts with which thy childhood hath been fed,
And thine own noble nature more than all,
Are sureties for thee. But these dreadful times
Demand a farther pledge; for it hath pleased
The Highest, as he tried his saints of old,
So in the fiery furnace of his wrath
To prove and purify the sons of Spain;
And they must knit their spirits to the proof,

Or sink, for ever lost. Hold forth thy sword,
Young Baron, and before thy people take
The vow which, in Toledo's sacred name,
Poor as these weeds bespeak me, I am here
To minister with delegated power.

With reverential awe was Roderick heard
By all, so well authority became
That mien and voice and countenance austere.
Pelayo with complacent eye beheld
The unlooked-for interposal, and the Count
Bends toward Alphonso his approving head.
The youth obedient loosened from his belt
The sword, and looking, while his heart beat fast,
To Roderick, reverently expectant stood.

O noble youth, the Royal Goth pursued,
Thy country is in bonds: an impious foe
Oppresses her: he brings with him strange laws,
Strange language, evil customs, and false faith,
And forces them on Spain. Swear that thy soul
Will make no covenant with these accurst,
But that the sword shall be from this day forth
Thy children's portion, to be handed down
From sire to son, a sacred heritage,
Through every generation, till the work
Be done, and this insulted land hath drunk,
In sacrifice, the last invader's blood!

Bear witness, ancient mountains! cried the youth,
And ye, my native streams, who hold your course,
For ever;—this dear earth, and yonder sky,
Be witness! for myself I make the vow,
And for my children's children. Here I stand
Their sponsor, binding them in sight of Heaven,
As by a new baptismal sacrament,
To wage hereditary, holy war,
Perpetual, patient, persevering war,
Till not one living enemy pollute
The sacred soil of Spain.
                          So as he ceased,
While yet toward the clear blue firmament
His eyes were raised, he lifted to his lips
The sword, with reverent gesture bending then
Devoutly kissed its cross.
                          And ye! exclaimed
Roderick, as turning to the assembled troop
He motioned with authoritative hand,—
Ye children of the hills and sons of Spain!

Through every heart the rapid feeling ran,—
For us! they answered all with one accord,
And at the word they knelt. People and Prince,
The young and old, the father and the son,
At once they knelt; with one accord they cried,
For us, and for our seed! with one accord
They crost their fervent arms, and with bent head
Inclined toward that awful voice from whence
The inspiring impulse came. The Royal Goth
Made answer, I receive your vow for Spain
And for the Lord of Hosts: your cause is good,
Go forward in his spirit and his strength.
Ne'er in his happiest hours had Roderick
With such commanding majesty dispensed
His princely gifts, as dignified him now,
When with slow movement, solemnly upraised,

Toward the kneeling troop he spread his arms,
As if the expanded soul diffused itself.
And carried to all spirits with the act
Its effluent inspiration. Silently
The people knelt, and when they rose, such awe
Held them in silence, that the eagle's cry,
Who far above them, at her highest flight
A speck scarce visible, wheeled round and round,
Was heard distinctly; and the mountain stream,
Which from the distant glen sent forth its sound
Wafted upon the wind, was audible
In that deep hush of feeling, like the voice
Of waters in the stillness of the night.

XIII.

COUNT EUDON.

That awful silence still endured, when one,
Who to the northern entrance of the vale
Had turned his casual eye, exclaimed, The Moors!—
For from the forest verge a troop were seen
Hastening toward Pedro's hall. Their forward speed
Was checked when they beheld his banner spread,
And saw his ordered spears in prompt array
Marshalled to meet their coming. But the pride
Of power and insolence of long command
Pricked on their Chief presumptuous : We are come
Late for prevention, cried the haughty Moor,
But never time more fit for punishment!
These unbelieving slaves must feel and know
Their master's arm!—on, faithful Musselmen,
On—on,—and hew down the rebellious dogs!—
Then as he spurred his steed, Allah is great!
Mahommed is his prophet! he exclaimed,
And led the charge.
                    Count Pedro met the Chief
In full career; he bore him from his horse
A full spear's length upon the lance transfixed;
Then leaving in his breast the mortal shaft,
Past on, and breaking through the turban'd files
Opened a path. Pelayo,,who that day
Fought in the ranks afoot, for other war
Yet unequipped, pursued and smote the foe,
But ever on Alphonso at his side
Retained a watchful eye. The gallant boy
Gave his good sword that hour its earliest taste
Of Moorish blood,—that sword whose hungry edge,
Through the fair course of all his glorious life
From that auspicious day, was fed so well.
Cheap was the victory now for Spain achieved;
For the first fervour of their zeal inspired
The Mountaineers,—the presence of their Chiefs,
The sight of all dear objects, all dear ties,
The air they breathed, the soil whereon they trod,
Duty, devotion, faith, and hope and joy.
And little had the misbelievers weened
In such impetuous onset to receive
A greeting deadly as their own intent;
Victims they thought to find, not men prepared
And eager for the fight; their confidence
Therefore gave way to wonder, and dismay
Effected what astonishment began.
Scattered before the impetuous Mountaineers,
Buckler and spear and scymitar they dropt,

As in precipitate rout they fled before
The Asturian sword : the vales and hills and rocks
Received their blood, and where they fell the wolves
At evening found them.
                    From the fight apart
Two Africans had stood, who held in charge
Count Eudon. When they saw their countrymen
Falter, give way, and fly before the foe,
One turned toward him with malignant rage,
And saying, Infidel ! thou shalt not live
To join their triumph ! aimed against his neck
The moony falchion's point. His comrade raised
A hasty hand and turned its edge aside,
Yet so that o'er the shoulder glancing down
It scarred him as it past. The murderous Moor,
Not tarrying to secure his vengeance, fled ;
While he of milder mood, at Eudon's feet
Fell and embraced his knees. The conqueror
Who found them thus, withheld at Eudon's voice
His wrathful hand, and led them to his Lord.

Count Pedro and Alphonso and the Prince
Stood on a little rocky eminence
Which overlooked the vale. Pedro had put
His helmet off, and with sonorous horn
Blew the recall ; for well he knew what thoughts,
Calm as the Prince appeared and undisturbed,
Lay underneath his silent fortitude ;
And how at this eventful juncture speed
Imported more than vengeance. Thrice he sent
The long-resounding signal forth, which rung
From hill to hill, re-echoing far and wide.
Slow and unwillingly his men obeyed
The swelling horn's reiterated call ;
Repining that a single foe escaped
The retribution of that righteous hour.
With lingering step reluctant from the chase
They turned,—their veins full-swoln, their sinews strung
For battle still, their hearts unsatisfied ;
Their swords were dropping still with Moorish gore,
And where they wiped their reeking brows, the stain
Of Moorish blood was left. But when they came
Where Pedro, with Alphonso at his side,
Stood to behold their coming, then they prest,
All emulous, with gratulation round,
Extolling for his deeds that day displayed
The noble boy. Oh! when had Heaven, they said,
With such especial favour manifest
Illustrated a first essay in arms!
They blest the father from whose loins he sprung,
The mother at whose happy breast he fed ;
And prayed that their young hero's fields might be
Many, and all like this.
                    Thus they indulged
The honest heart, exuberant of love,—
When that loquacious joy at once was checked,
For Eudon and the Moor were led before
Count Pedro. Both came fearfully and pale,
But with a different fear : the African
Felt at this crisis of his destiny
Such apprehension as without reproach
Might blanch a soldier's cheek, when life and death
Hang on another's will, and helplessly
He must abide the issue. But the thoughts
Which quailed Count Eudon's heart, and made his limbs
Quiver, were of his own unworthiness,

Old enmity, and that he stood in power
Of hated and hereditary foes.
I came not with them willingly! he cried,
Addressing Pedro and the Prince at once,
Rolling from each to each his restless eyes
Aghast,—the Moor can tell I had no choice;
They forced me from my castle:—in the fight
They would have slain me:—see I bleed! The Moor
Can witness that a Moorish scymitar
Inflicted this:—he saved me from worse hurt:
I did not come in arms:—he knows it all;—
Speak, man, and let the truth be known to clear
My innocence!

    Thus as he ceased, with fear
And rapid utterance panting open-mouthed,
Count Pedro half represt a mournful smile,
Wherein compassion seemed to mitigate
His deep contempt. Methinks, said he, the Moor
Might with more reason look himself to find
An intercessor, than be called upon
To play the pleader's part. Didst thou then save
The Baron from thy comrades?

    Let my Lord
Show mercy to me, said the Musselman,
As I am free from falsehood. We were left,
I and another, holding him in charge;
My fellow would have slain him when he saw
How the fight fared: I turned the scymitar
Aside, and trust that life will be the meed
For life by me preserved.

    Nor shall thy trust,
Rejoined the Count, be vain. Say farther now,
From whence ye came,—your orders what:—what
  force
In Gegio, and if others like yourselves
Are in the field!

    The African replied,
We came from Gegio, ordered to secure
This Baron on the way, and seek thee here
To bear thee hence in bonds. A messenger
From Cordoba, whose speed denoted well
He came with urgent tidings, was the cause
Of this our sudden movement. We went forth
Three hundred men; and equal force was sent
For Cangas, on like errand as I ween.
Four hundred in the city then were left.
If other force be moving from the south,
I know not, save that all appearances
Denote alarm and vigilance.

    The Prince
Fixed upon Eudon then his eye severe;
Baron, he said, the die of war is cast;
What part art thou prepared to take? against,
Or with the oppressor?

    Not against my friends,—
Not against you!—the irresolute wretch replied,
Hasty, yet faltering in his fearful speech:
But—have ye weighed it well?—It is not yet
Too late,—their numbers,—their victorious force,
Which hath already trodden in the dust
The sceptre of the Goths;—the throne destroyed,—
Our towns subdued,—our country overrun,—
The people to the yoke of their new Lords
Resigned in peace—Can I not mediate?—
Were it not better through my agency

To gain such terms,—such honourable terms—
Terms! cried Pelayo, cutting short at once
That dastard speech, and checking, ere it grew
Too powerful for restraint, the incipient rage,
Which in indignant murmurs breathing round,
Rose like a gathering storm. Learn thou what terms
Asturias, this day speaking by my voice,
Doth constitute to be the law between
Thee and thy country. Our portentous age,
As with an earthquake's desolating force,
Hath loosened and disjointed the whole frame
Of social order, and she calls not now
For service with the voice of sovereign will.
That which was common duty in old times,
Becomes an arduous, glorious virtue now;
And every one, as between Hell and Heaven,
In free election must be left to chuse.
Asturias asks not of thee to partake
The cup which we have pledged; she claims from none
The dauntless fortitude, the mind resolved,
Which only God can give;—therefore such peace
As thou canst find where all around is war,
She leaves thee to enjoy. But think not, Count,
That because thou art weak, one valiant arm,
One generous spirit must be lost to Spain!
The vassal owes no service to the Lord
Who to his country doth acknowledge none.
The summons which thou hast not heart to give,
I and Count Pedro over thy domains
Will send abroad; the vassals who were thine
Will fight beneath our banners, and our wants
Shall from thy lands, as from a patrimony
Which hath reverted to the common stock,
Be fed: such tribute, too, as to the Moors
Thou renderest, we will take: It is the price
Which in this land for weakness must be paid
While evil stars prevail. And mark me, Chief!
Fear is a treacherous counsellor! I know
Thou thinkest that beneath his horses' hoofs
The Moor will trample our poor numbers down.
But join not, in contempt of us and Heaven,
His multitudes! for if thou shouldst be found
Against thy country, on the nearest tree
Thy recreant bones shall rattle in the wind,
When the crows have left them bare.

    As thus he spake,
Count Eudon heard and trembled: every joint
Was loosened, every fibre of his flesh
Thrilled, and from every pore effused, cold sweat
Clung on his quivering limbs. Shame forced it forth,
Envy and inward consciousness, and fear
Predominant, which stifled in his heart
Hatred and rage. Before his livid lips
Could shape to utterance their essayed reply,
Compassionately Pedro interposed.
Go, Baron, to the castle, said the Count;
There let thy wound be looked to, and consult
Thy better mind at leisure. Let this Moor
Attend upon thee there, and, when thou wilt,
Follow thy fortunes.—To Pelayo then
He turned, and saying, All-too-long, O Prince,
Hath this unlooked-for conflict held thee here,—
He bade his gallant men begin their march.

Flushed with success, and in auspicious hour,

The Mountaineers set forth. Blessings and prayers
Pursued them at their parting, and the tears
Which fell were tears of fervour, not of grief.
The sun was verging to the western slope
Of Heaven, but they till midnight travelled on;
Renewing then at early dawn their way,
They held their unremitting course from morn
Till latest eve, such urgent cause impelled ;
And night had closed around, when to the vale
Where Sella in her ampler bed receives
Pionia's stream they came. Massive and black
Pelayo's castle there was seen ; its lines
And battlements against the deep blue sky
Distinct in solid darkness visible.
No light is in the tower. Eager to know
The worst, and with that fatal certainty
To terminate intolerable dread,
He spurred his courser forward. All his fears
Too surely are fulfilled,—for open stand
The doors, and mournfully at times a dog
Fills with his howling the deserted hall.
A moment overcome with wretchedness,
Silent Pelayo stood ! recovering then,
Lord God, resigned he cried, thy will be done !

XIV.

THE RESCUE.

COUNT, said Pelayo, Nature hath assigned
Two sovereign remedies for human grief ;
Religion, surest, firmest, first and best,
Strength to the weak and to the wounded balm ;
And strenuous action next. Think not I came
With unprovided heart. My noble wife,
In the last solemn words, the last farewell
With which she charged her secret messenger,
Told me that whatsoe'er was my resolve,
She bore a mind prepared. And well I know
The evil, be it what it may, hath found
In her a courage equal to the hour.
Captivity, or death, or what worse pangs,
She in her children may be doomed to feel,
Will never make that steady soul repent
Its virtuous purpose. I too did not cast
My single life into the lot, but knew
These dearer pledges on the die were set ;
And if the worst have fall'n, I shall but bear
That in my breast, which, with transfiguring power
Of piety, makes chastening sorrow take
The form of hope, and sees, in Death, the friend
And the restoring Angel. We must rest
Perforce, and wait what tidings night may bring,
Haply of comfort. Ho there ! kindle fires,
And see if aught of hospitality
Can yet within these mournful walls be found !

Thus while he spake, lights were descried far off
Moving among the trees, and coming sounds
Were heard as of a distant multitude.
Anon a company of horse and foot,
Advancing in disorderly array,
Came up the vale : before them and beside
Their torches flashed on Sella's rippling stream ;
Now gleamed through chesnut groves, emerging now,
O'er their huge boughs and radiated leaves

Cast broad and bright a transitory glare.
That sight inspired with strength the mountaineers ;
All sense of weariness ; all wish for rest
At once were gone : impatient in desire
Of second victory alert they stood ;
And when the hostile symbols, which from far
Imagination to their wish had shaped,
Vanished in nearer vision, high-wrought hope
Departing, left the spirit palled and blank.
No turban'd race, no sons of Africa
Were they who now came winding up the vale,
As waving wide before their horses' feet
The torch-light floated, with its hovering glare
Blackening the incumbent and surrounding night.
Helmet and breast-plate glittered as they came,
And spears erect ; and nearer as they drew
Were the loose folds of female garments seen
On those who led the company. Who then
Had stood beside Pelayo, might have heard
The beating of his heart.
                        But vainly there
Sought he with wistful eye the well-known forms
Beloved ; and plainly might it now be seen
That from some bloody conflict they returned
Victorious,—for at every saddle-bow
A gory head was hung. ³⁷ Anon they stopt,
Levelling in quick alarm their ready spears.
Hold! who goes there ? cried one. A hundred tongues
Sent forth with one accord the glad reply,
Friends and Asturians. Onward moved the lights,—
The people knew their Lord.
                        Then what a shout
Rung through the valley ! From their clay-built nests,
Beneath the overbrowing battlements,
Now first disturbed, the affrighted martins flew,
And uttering notes of terror short and shrill,
Amid the yellow glare and lurid smoke
Wheeled giddily. Then plainly was it shown
How well the vassals loved their generous Lord,
How like a father the Asturian Prince
Was dear. They crowded round ; they claspt his knees ;
They snatched his hand ; they fell upon his neck,—
They wept ;—they blest Almighty Providence,
Which had restored him thus from bondage free ;
God was with them and their good cause, they said ;
His hand was here,—His shield was over them,—
His spirit was abroad,—His power displayed :
And pointing to their bloody trophies then,
They told Pelayo there he might behold
The first-fruits of the harvest they should soon
Reap in the field of war ! Benignantly,
With voice and look and gesture, did the Prince
To these warm greetings of tumultuous joy
Respond ; and sure if at that moment aught
Could for awhile have overpowered those fears
Which from the inmost heart o'er all his frame
Diffused their chilling influence, worthy pride,
And sympathy of love and joy and hope,
Had then possessed him wholly. Even now
His spirit rose ; the sense of power, the sight
Of his brave people, ready where he led
To fight their country's battles, and the thought
Of instant action, and deliverance,—
If Heaven, which thus far had protected him,
Should favour still,—revived his heart, and gave
Fresh impulse to its spring. In vain he sought

Amid that turbulent greeting to inquire
Where Gaudiosa was, his children where,
Who called them to the field, who captained them;
And how these women, thus with arms and death
Environed, came amid their company;
For yet, amid the fluctuating light
And tumult of the crowd, he knew them not.

Guisla was one. The Moors had found in her
A willing and concerted prisoner.
Gladly to Gegio, to the renegade
On whom her loose and shameless love was bent,
Had she set forth; and in her heart she cursed
The busy spirit, who, with powerful call
Rousing Pelayo's people, led them on
In quick pursual, and victoriously
Achieved the rescue, to her mind perverse
Unwelcome as unlooked for. With dismay
She recognized her brother, dreaded now
More than he once was dear; her countenance
Was turned toward him,—not with eager joy
To court his sight, and meeting its first glance,
Exchange delightful welcome, soul with soul;
Hers was the conscious eye, that cannot chuse
But look to what it fears. She could not shun
His presence, and the rigid smile constrained,
With which she coldly drest her features, ill
Concealed her inward thoughts, and the despite
Of obstinate guilt and unrepentant shame.
Sullenly thus upon her mule she sate,
Waiting the greeting which she did not dare
Bring on. But who is she that at her side,
Upon a stately war-horse eminent,
Holds the loose rein with careless hand? A helm
Presses the clusters of her flaxen hair;
The shield is on her arm; her breast is mailed;
A sword-belt is her girdle, and right well
It may be seen that sword hath done its work
To-day, for upward from the wrist or sleeve
Is stiff with blood. An unregardant eye,
As one whose thoughts were not of earth, she cast
Upon the turmoil round. One countenance
So strongly marked, so passion-worn was there,
That it recalled her mind. Ha! Maccabee!
Lifting her arm, exultingly she cried,
Did I not tell thee we should meet in joy?
Well, Brother, hast thou done thy part,—I too
Have not been wanting! Now be His the praise,
From whom the impulse came!

                    That startling call,
That voice so well remembered, touched the Goth
With timely impulse now; for he had seen
His mother's face,—and at her sight, the past
And present mingled like a frightful dream,
Which from some dread reality derives
Its deepest horror. Adosinda's voice
Dispersed the waking vision. Little deemed
Rusilla at that moment that the child,
For whom her supplications day and night
Were offered, breathed the living air. Her heart
Was calm; her placid countenance, though grief
Deeper than time had left its traces there,
Retained its dignity serene; yet when
Siverian, pressing through the people, kissed
Her reverend hand, some quiet tears ran down.
As she approached the Prince, the crowd made way

Respectful. The maternal smile which bore
Her greeting, from Pelayo's heart almost
Dispelled its boding. What he would have asked
She knew, and bending from her palfrey down,
Told him that they for whom he looked were safe,
And that in secret he should hear the rest.

XV.

RODERICK AT CANGAS.

How calmly gliding through the dark-blue sky
The midnight Moon ascends! Her placid beams
Through thinly scattered leaves and boughs grotesque,
Mottle with mazy shades the orchard slope;
Here, o'er the chesnut's fretted foliage grey
And massy, motionless they spread; here shine
Upon the crags, deepening with blacker night
Their chasms; and there the glittering argentry
Ripples and glances on the confluent streams.
A lovelier, purer light than that of day
Rests on the hills; and oh how awfully
Into that deep and tranquil firmament
The summits of Auseva rise serene!
The watchman on the battlements partakes
The stillness of the solemn hour; he feels
The silence of the earth, the endless sound
Of flowing water soothes him, and the stars,
Which in that brightest moon-light well-nigh quenched,
Scarce visible, as in the utmost depth
Of yonder sapphire infinite, are seen,
Draw on with elevating influence
Toward eternity the attempered mind.
Musing on worlds beyond the grave he stands,
And to the Virgin Mother silently
Breathes forth her hymn of praise.
                    The mountaineers
Before the castle, round their mouldering fires,
Lie on the hearth outstretched. Pelayo's hall
Is full, and he upon his careful couch
Hears all around the deep and long-drawn breath
Of sleep; for gentle night hath brought to these
Perfect and undisturbed repose, alike
Of corporal powers and inward faculty.
Wakeful the while he lay, yet more by hope
Than grief or anxious thoughts possessed,—though grief
For Guisla's guilt, which freshened in his heart
The memory of their wretched mother's crime,
Still made its presence felt, like the dull sense
Of some perpetual inward malady;
And the whole peril of the future lay
Before him clearly seen. He had heard all:
How that unworthy sister, obstinate
In wrong and shameless, rather seemed to woo
The upstart renegado than to wait
His wooing; how, as guilt to guilt led on,
Spurning at gentle admonition first,
When Gaudiosa hopelessly forebore
From farther counsel, then in sullen mood
Resentful, Guisla soon began to hate
The virtuous presence before which she felt
Her nature how inferior, and her fault
How foul! Despiteful thus she grew, because
Humbled yet unrepentant. Who could say
To what excess bad passions might impel

A woman thus possessed? She could not fail
To mark Siverian's absence, for what end
Her conscience but too surely had divined;
And Gaudiosa, well aware that all
To the vile paramour was thus made known,
Had to safe hiding-place with timely fear
Removed her children. Well the event had proved
How needful was that caution; for at night
She sought the mountain solitudes, and morn
Beheld Numacian's soldiers at the gate.
Yet did not sorrow in Pelayo's heart
For this domestic shame prevail that hour,
Nor gathering danger weigh his spirit down.
The anticipated meeting put to flight
These painful thoughts: to-morrow will restore
All whom his heart holds dear; his wife beloved,
No longer now remembered for regret,
Is present to his soul with hope and joy;
His inward eye beholds Favila's form
In opening youth robust, and Hermesind,
His daughter, lovely as a budding rose:
Their images beguile the hours of night,
Till with the earliest morning he may seek
Their secret hold.

        The nightingale not yet
Had ceased her song, nor had the early lark
Her dewy nest forsaken, when the Prince
Upward beside Pionia took his way
Toward Auseva. Heavily to him,
Impatient for the morrow's happiness,
Long night had lingered, but it seemed more long
To Roderick's aching heart. He too had watched
For dawn, and seen the earliest break of day,
And heard its earliest sounds; and when the Prince
Went forth, the melancholy man was seen
With pensive pace upon Pionia's side
Wandering alone and slow. For he had left
The wearying place of his unrest, that morn
With its cold dews might bathe his throbbing brow,
And with its breath allay the feverish heat
That burnt within. Alas! the gales of morn
Reach not the fever of a wounded heart!
How shall he meet his Mother's eye, how make
His secret known, and from that voice revered
Obtain forgiveness,—all that he has now
To ask, ere on the lap of earth in peace
He lay his head resigned! In silent prayer
He supplicated Heaven to strengthen him
Against that trying hour, there seeking aid
Where all who seek shall find; and thus his soul
Received support, and gathered fortitude,
Never than now more needful, for the hour
Was nigh. He saw Siverian drawing near,
And with a dim but quick foreboding met
The good old man: yet when he heard him say,
My Lady sends to seek thee, like a knell
To one expecting and prepared for death,
But fearing the dread point that hastens on,
It smote his heart. He followed silently,
And knit his suffering spirit to the proof.

He went resolved to tell his Mother all,
Fall at her feet, and drinking the last dregs
Of bitterness, receive the only good
Earth had in store for him. Resolved for this
He went; yet was it a relief to find

That painful resolution must await
A fitter season, when no eye but Heaven's
Might witness to their mutual agony.
Count Julian's daughter with Rusilla sate;
Both had been weeping, both were pale, but calm.
With head as for humility abased
Roderick approached, and bending, on his breast
He crossed his humble arms. Rusilla rose
In reverence to the priestly character,[38]
And with a mournful eye regarding him,
Thus she began. Good Father, I have heard
From my old faithful servant and true friend,
Thou didst reprove the inconsiderate tongue,
That in the anguish of its spirit poured
A curse upon my poor unhappy child.
O Father Maccabee, this is a hard world,
And hasty in its judgments! Time has been,
When not a tongue within the Pyrenees
Dared whisper in dispraise of Roderick's name,
Lest, if the conscious air had caught the sound,
The vengeance of the honest multitude
Should fall upon the traitrous head, or brand
For life-long infamy the lying lips.
Now if a voice be raised in his behalf,
'T is noted for a wonder, and the man
Who utters the strange speech shall be admired
For such excess of Christian charity.
Thy Christian charity hath not been lost;—
Father, I feel its virtue:—it hath been
Balm to my heart:—with words and grateful tears,—
All that is left me now for gratitude,—
I thank thee, and beseech thee in thy prayers
That thou wilt still remember Roderick's name.
Roderick so long had to this hour looked on,
That when the actual point of trial came,
Torpid and numbed it found him: cold he grew,
And as the vital spirits to the heart
Retreated, o'er his withered countenance,
Deathy and damp, a whiter paleness spread.
Unmoved the while the inward feeling seemed,
Even in such dull insensibility
As gradual age brings on, or slow disease,
Beneath whose progress lingering life survives
The power of suffering. Wondering at himself,
Yet gathering confidence, he raised his eyes,
Then slowly shaking as he bent his head,
O venerable Lady, he replied,
If aught may comfort that unhappy soul,
It must be thy compassion, and thy prayers.
She whom he most hath wronged, she who alone
On earth can grant forgiveness for his crime,
She hath forgiven him; and thy blessing now
Were all that he could ask,—all that could bring
Profit or consolation to his soul,
If he hath been, as sure we may believe,
A penitent sincere.

        Oh had he lived,
Replied Rusilla, never penitence
Had equalled his! full well I know his heart,
Vehement in all things. He would on himself
Have wreaked such penance as had reached the height
Of fleshly suffering,—yea, which being told
With its portentous rigour should have made
The memory of his fault, o'erpowered and lost
In shuddering pity and astonishment,
Fade like a feebler horror. Otherwise

Seemed good to Heaven. I murmur not, nor doubt
The boundless mercy of redeeming love.
For sure I trust that not in his offence
Hardened and reprobate was my lost son,
A child of wrath, cut off!—that dreadful thought,
Not even amid the first fresh wretchedness,
When the ruin burst around me like a flood,
Assailed my soul. I ever deemed his fall
An act of sudden madness; and this day
Hath in unlooked-for confirmation given
A livelier hope, a more assured faith.
Smiling benignant then amid her tears,
She took Florinda by the hand, and said,
I little thought that I should live to bless
Count Julian's daughter! She hath brought to me
The last, the best, the only comfort earth
Could minister to this afflicted heart.
And my grey hairs may now unto the grave
Go down in peace.

          Happy, Florinda cried,
Are they for whom the grave hath peace in store!
The wrongs they have sustained, the woes they bear,
Pass not that holy threshold, where Death heals
The broken heart. O Lady, thou mayst trust
In humble hope, through Him who on the cross
Gave his atoning blood for lost mankind,
To meet beyond the grave thy child forgiven.
I too with Roderick there may interchange
Forgiveness. But the grief which wastes away
This mortal frame, hastening the happy hour
Of my enlargement, is but a light part
Of what my soul endures!—that grief hath lost
Its sting:—I have a keener sorrow here,—
One which,—but God forefend that dire event,—
May pass with me the portals of the grave,
And with a thought, like sin which cannot die,
Embitter Heaven. My father has renounced
His hope in Christ! It was his love for me
Which drove him to perdition.—I was born
To ruin all who loved me,—all I loved!
Perhaps I sinned in leaving him;—that fear
Rises within me to disturb the peace
Which I should else have found.

          To Roderick then
The pious mourner turned her suppliant eyes:
O Father, there is virtue in thy prayers!—
I do beseech thee offer them to Heaven
In his behalf! For Roderick's sake, for mine,
Wrestle with Him whose name is Merciful,
That Julian may with penitence be touched,
And clinging to the Cross, implore that grace
Which ne'er was sought in vain. For Roderick's sake
And mine, pray for him! We have been the cause
Of his offence! What other miseries
May from that same unhappy source have risen,
Are earthly, temporal, reparable all;—
But if a soul be lost through our misdeeds,
That were eternal evil! Pray for him,
Good Father Maccabee, and be thy prayers
More fervent, as the deeper is the crime.

While thus Florinda spake, the dog who lay
Before Rusilla's feet, eyeing him long
And wistfully, had recognised at length,
Changed as he was and in those sordid weeds,
His royal master. And he rose and licked

His withered hand, and earnestly looked up
With eyes whose human meaning did not need
The aid of speech; and moaned, as if at once
To court and chide the long-withheld caress.
A feeling uncommixed with sense of guilt
Or shame, yet painfullest, thrilled through the King;
But he, to self-control now long inured,
Represt his rising heart, nor other tears,
Full as his struggling bosom was, let fall
Than seemed to follow on Florinda's words.
Looking toward her then, yet so that still
He shunned the meeting of her eye, he said,
Virtuous and pious as thou art, and ripe
For Heaven, O Lady, I will think the man
Hath not by his good Angel been cast off
For whom thy supplications rise. The Power
Whose justice doth in its unerring course
Visit the children for the sire's offence,
Shall He not in his boundless mercy hear
The daughter's prayer, and for her sake restore
The guilty parent? My soul shall with thine
In earnest and continual duty join—
How deeply, how devoutly, He will know
To whom the cry is raised!

          Thus having said,
Deliberately, in self-possession still,
Himself from that most painful interview
Dispeeding, he withdrew. The watchful dog
Followed his footsteps close. But he retired
Into the thickest grove; there yielding way
To his o'erburthened nature, from all eyes
Apart, he cast himself upon the ground,
And threw his arms around the dog, and cried,
While tears streamed down, Thou, Theron, then hast
    known
Thy poor lost master,—Theron, none but thou!

XVI.

COVADONGA.

MEANTIME Pelayo up the vale pursued
Eastward his way, before the sun had climbed
Auseva's brow, or shed his silvering beams
Upon Europa's summit, where the snows
Through all revolving seasons hold their seat.
A happy man he went, his heart at rest,
Of hope and virtue and affection full,
To all exhilarating influences
Of earth and heaven alive. With kindred joy
He heard the lark, who from her airy height,
On twinkling pinions poised, poured forth profuse,
In thrilling sequence of exuberant song,
As one whose joyous nature overflowed
With life and power, her rich and rapturous strain.
The early bee, buzzing along the way,
From flower to flower, bore gladness on her wing
To his rejoicing sense; and he pursued,
With quickened eye alert, the frolic hare,
Where from the green herb in her wanton path
She brushed away the dews. For he long time,
Far from his home and from his native hills,
Had dwelt in bondage; and the mountain breeze,
Which he had with the breath of infancy
Inhaled, such impulse to his heart restored,

As if the seasons had rolled back, and life
Enjoyed a second spring.

               Through fertile fields
He went, by cots with pear-trees overbowered,
Or spreading to the sun their trelliced vines;
Through orchards now, and now by thymy banks,
Where wooden hives in some warm nook were hid
From wind and shower; and now thro' shadowy paths,
Where hazels fringed Pionia's vocal stream;
Till where the loftier hills to narrower bound
Confine the vale, he reached those huts remote
Which should hereafter to the noble line
Of Soto origin and name impart:
A gallant lineage, long in fields of war
And faithful chronicler's enduring page
Blazoned; but most by him illustratëd,
Avid of gold, yet greedier of renown,
Whom not the spoils of Atabalipa
Could satisfy insatiate, [39] nor the fame
Of that wide empire overthrown appease;
But he to Florida's disastrous shores
In evil hour his gallant comrades led,
Through savage woods and swamps, and hostile tribes,
The Apalachian arrows, and the snares
Of wilier foes, hunger, and thirst, and toil;
Till from ambition's feverish dream the touch
Of Death awoke him; and when he had seen
The fruit of all his treasures, all his toil,
Foresight, and long endurance, fade away,
Earth to the restless one refusing rest,
In the great river's midland bed he left
His honoured bones.

              A mountain rivulet,
Now calm and lovely in its summer course,
Held by those huts its everlasting way
Toward Pionia. They whose flocks and herds
Drink of its water call it Deva. Here
Pelayo southward up the ruder vale
Traced it, his guide unerring. Amid heaps
Of mountain wreck, on either side thrown high,
The wide-spread traces of its wintry might,
The tortuous channel wound; o'er beds of sand
Here silently it flows; here from the rock
Rebutted, curls and eddies; plunges here
Precipitate; here, roaring among crags,
It leaps and foams and whirls and hurries on.
Grey alders here and bushy hazels hid
The mossy side; their wreath'd and knotted feet
Bared by the current, now against its force
Repaying the support they found, upheld
The bank secure. Here, bending to the stream,
The birch fantastic stretch'd its rugged trunk,
Tall and erect, from whence, as from their base
Each like a tree, its silver branches grew.
The cherry here hung for the birds of heaven
Its rosy fruit on high. The elder there
Its purple berries o'er the water bent,
Heavily hanging. Here, amid the brook,
Grey as the stone to which it clung, half root,
Half trunk, the young ash rises from the rock;
And there its parent lifts a lofty head,
And spreads its graceful boughs; the passing wind
With twinkling motion lifts the silent leaves,
And shakes its rattling tufts.

              Soon had the Prince
Behind him left the farthest dwelling-place

Of man; no fields of waving corn were here,
Nor wicker storehouse for the autumnal grain,[40]
Vineyard, nor bowery fig, nor fruitful grove;
Only the rocky vale, the mountain stream,
Incumbent crags, and hills that over hills
Arose on either hand, here hung with woods,
Here rich with heath, that o'er some smooth ascent
Its purple glory spread, or golden gorse;
Bare here, and striated with many a hue,
Scored by the wintry rain; by torrents here
Riven, and with overhanging rocks abrupt.
Pelayo, upward as he cast his eyes
Where crags loose-hanging o'er the narrow pass
Impended, there beheld his country's strength
Insuperable, and in his heart rejoiced.
Oh that the Musselman were here, he cried,
With all his myriads! While thy day endures,
Moor! thou mayst lord it in the plains; but here
Hath Nature for the free and brave prepared
A sanctuary, where no oppressor's power,
No might of human tyranny can pierce.

The tears which started then sprang not alone
From lofty thoughts of elevating joy;
For love and admiration had their part,
And virtuous pride. Here then thou hast retired,
My Gaudiosa! in his heart he said;
Excellent woman! ne'er was richer boon
By fate benign to favour'd man indulged,
Than when thou wert before the face of Heaven
Given me to be my children's mother, brave
And virtuous as thou art! here thou hast fled,
Thou who wert nursed in palaces, to dwell
In rocks and mountain caves!—The thought was proud,
Yet not without a sense of inmost pain;
For never had Pelayo till that hour
So deeply felt the force of solitude.
High over head the eagle soar'd serene,
And the gray lizard on the rocks below
Basked in the sun: no living creature else
In this remotest wilderness was seen;
Nor living voice was there,—only the flow
Of Deva, and the rushing of its springs
Long in the distance heard, which nearer now,
With endless repercussion deep and loud,
Throbb'd on the dizzy sense.

              The ascending vale,
Long straiten'd by the narrowing mountains, here
Was closed. In front a rock, abrupt and bare,
Stood eminent, in height exceeding far
All edifice of human power, by king
Or caliph, or barbaric sultan rear'd,
Or mightier tyrants of the world of old,
Assyrian or Egyptian, in their pride:
Yet far above, beyond the reach of sight,
Swell after swell, the heathery mountain rose.
Here, in two sources, from the living rock
The everlasting springs of Deva gushed.
Upon a smooth and grassy plat below,
By nature there as for an altar drest,
They joined their sister stream, which from the earth
Welled silently. In such a scene rude man
With pardonable error might have knelt,
Feeling a present Deity, and made
His offering to the fountain Nymph devout.
The arching rock disclosed above the springs

A cave, where hugest son of giant birth,
That e'er of old in forest of romance
'Gainst knights and ladies waged discourteous war,
Erect within the portal might have stood.
The broken stone allow'd for hand and foot
No difficult ascent, above the base
In height a tall man's stature, measured thrice.
No holier spot than Covadonga Spain
Boasts in her wide extent, though all her realms
Be with the noblest blood of martyrdom
In elder or in later days enrich'd,
And glorified with tales of heavenly aid
By many a miracle made manifest;
Nor in the heroic annals of her fame
Doth she show forth a scene of more renown.
Then, save the hunter, drawn in keen pursuit
Beyond his wonted haunts, or shepherd's boy,
Following the pleasure of his straggling flock,
None knew the place.
         Pelayo, when he saw
Those glittering sources and their sacred cave,
Took from his side the bugle silver-tipt,
And with a breath long drawn and slow expired
Sent forth that strain, which, echoing from the walls
Of Cangas, wont to tell his glad return
When from the chace he came.   At the first sound
Favila started in the cave, and cried,
My father's horn!—A sudden flame suffused
Hermesind's cheek, and she with quicken'd eye
Look'd eager to her mother silently;
But Gaudiosa trembled and grew pale,
Doubting her sense deceived.   A second time
The bugle breathed its well-known notes abroad;
And Hermesind around her mother's neck
Threw her white arms, and earnestly exclaim'd,
'T is he!—But when a third and broader blast
Rung in the echoing archway, ne'er did wand,
With magic power endued, call up a sight
So strange, as sure in that wild solitude
It seem'd, when from the bowels of the rock
The mother and her children hasten'd forth.
She in the sober charms and dignity
Of womanhood mature, nor verging yet
Upon decay; in gesture like a queen,
Such inborn and habitual majesty
Ennobled all her steps,—or priestess, chosen
Because within such faultless work of Heaven
Inspiring Deity might seem to make
Its habitation known—Favila such
In form and stature as the Sea-Nymph's son,
When that wise Centaur from his cave well-pleased
Beheld the boy divine his growing strength
Against some shaggy lionet essay,
And fixing in the half-grown mane his hands,
Roll with him in fierce dalliance intertwined.
But like a creature of some higher sphere
His sister came; she scarcely touched the rock,
So light was Hermesind's aerial speed.
Beauty and grace and innocence in her
In heavenly union shone.   One who had held
The faith of elder Greece, would sure have thought
She was some glorious nymph of seed divine,
Oread or Dryad, of Diana's train
The youngest and the loveliest: yea she seem'd
Angel, or soul beatified, from realms
Of bliss, on errand of parental love

To earth re-sent,—if tears and trembling limbs
With such celestial natures might consist.

Embraced by all, in turn embracing each,
The husband and the father for a while
Forgot his country and all things beside:
Life hath few moments of such pure delight,
Such foretaste of the perfect joy of Heaven.
And when the thought recurr'd of sufferings past,
Perils which threaten'd still, and arduous toil
Yet to be undergone, remember'd griefs
Heighten'd the present happiness; 'and hope
Upon the shadows of futurity
Shone like the sun upon the morning mists,
When driven before his rising rays they roll,
And melt and leave the prospect bright and clear.

When now Pelayo's eyes had drank their fill
Of love from those dear faces, he went up
To view the hiding-place.   Spacious it was
As that Sicilian cavern in the hill
Wherein earth-shaking Neptune's giant son
Duly at eve was wont to fold his flock,
Ere the wise Ithacan, o'er that brute force
By wiles prevailing, for a life-long night
Seeled his broad eye.   The healthful air had here
Free entrance, and the cheerful light of heaven;
But at the end, an opening in the floor
Of rock disclosed a wider vault below,
Which never sun-beam visited, nor breath
Of vivifying morning came to cheer.
No light was there but that which from above
In dim reflection fell, or found its way,
Broken and quivering, through the glassy stream,
Where through the rock it gushed. That shadowy light
Sufficed to show, where from their secret bed
The waters issued; with whose rapid course,
And with whose everlasting cataracts
Such motion to the chill damp atmosphere
Was given, as if the solid walls of rock
Were shaken with the sound.
         Glad to respire
The upper air, Pelayo hastened back
From that drear den.   Look! Hermesind exclaimed,
Taking her father's hand, thou hast not seen
My chamber:—See! did ever ring-dove chuse
In so secure a nook her hiding-place,
Or build a warmer nest?   T is fragrant too,
As warm, and not more sweet than soft; for thyme
And myrtle with the elastic heath are laid,
And, over all, this dry and pillowy moss.—
Smiling she spake.   Pelayo kissed the child,
And, sighing, said within himself, I trust
In Heaven, whene'er thy May of life is come,
Sweet bird, that thou shalt have a blither bower!
Fitlier, he thought, such chamber might beseem
Some hermit of Hilarion's school austere,
Or old Antonius, he who from the hell
Of his bewildered fantasy saw fiends
In actual vision, a foul throng grotesque
Of all horrific shapes and forms obscene,
Crowd in broad day before his open eyes.
That feeling cast a momentary shade
Of sadness o'er his soul.   But deeper thoughts,
If he might have foreseen the things to come,
Would there have filled him; for within that cave

His own remains were one day doomed to find
Their final place of rest; and in that spot,
Where that dear child with innocent delight
Had spread her mossy couch, the sepulchre
Shall in the consecrated rock be hewn,
Where with Alphonso, her beloved lord,
Laid side by side, must Hermesind partake
The everlasting marriage-bed, when he,
Leaving a name perdurable on earth,
Hath changed his earthly for a heavenly crown.
Dear child, upon that fated spot she stood,
In all the beauty of her opening youth,
In health's rich bloom, in virgin innocence,
While her eyes sparkled and her heart o'erflowed
With pure and perfect joy of filial love.

Many a slow century since that day hath filled
Its course, and countless multitudes have trod
With pilgrim feet that consecrated cave;
Yet not in all those ages, amid all
The untold concourse, hath one breast been swoln
With such emotions as Pelayo felt
That hour.   O Gaudioso, he exclaimed,
And thou couldst seek for shelter here, amid
This awful solitude, in mountain caves!
Thou noble spirit! Oh when hearts like thine
Grow on this sacred soil, would it not be
In me, thy husband, double infamy,
And tenfold guilt, if I despaired of Spain?
In all her visitations, favouring Heaven
Hath left her still the unconquerable mind;
And thus being worthy of redemption, sure
Is she to be redeemed.
                    Beholding her
Through tears he spake, and prest upon her lips
A kiss of deepest love. Think ever thus,
She answered, and that faith will give the power
In which it trusts. When to this mountain hold
These children, thy dear images, I brought,
I said within myself, where should they fly
But to the bosom of their native hills?
I brought them here as to a sanctuary,
Where, for the temple's sake, the indwelling God
Would guard his supplicants. O my dear Lord,
Proud as I was to know that they were thine,
Was it a sin if I almost believed,
That Spain, her destiny being linked with theirs,
Would save the precious charge?
                         So let us think,
The chief replied, so feel and teach and act.
Spain is our common parent : let the sons
Be to the parent true, and in her strength
And Heaven, their sure deliverance they will find.

XVII

RODERICK AND SIVERIAN.

O noliest Mary, Maid and Mother! thou
In Covadonga, *⁴ at thy rocky shrine,
Hast witnessed whatsoe'er of human bliss
Heart can conceive most perfect! Faithful love,
Long crost by envious stars, hath there attained
Its crown, in endless matrimony given;
The youthful mother there hath to the font

Her first-born borne, and there, with deeper sense
Of gratitude for that dear babe redeemed
From threatening death, returned to pay her vows.
But ne'er on nuptial, nor baptismal day,
Nor from their grateful pilgrimage discharged,
Did happier group their way down Deva's vale
Rejoicing hold, than this blest family,
O'er whom the mighty Spirit of the Land
Spread his protecting wings. The children, free
In youthhead's happy season from all cares
That might disturb the hour, yet capable
Of that intense and unalloyed delight
Which childhood feels when it enjoys again
The dear parental presence long deprived;
Nor were the parents now less blest than they,
Even to the height of human happiness;
For Gaudiosa and her Lord that hour
Let no misgiving thoughts intrude : she fixed
Her hopes on him, and his were fixed on Heaven;
And hope in that courageous heart derived
Such rooted strength and confidence assured
In righteousness, that 't was to him like faith—
An everlasting sunshine of the soul,
Illumining and quickening all its powers.

But on Pionia's side meantime a heart
As generous, and as full of noble thoughts,
Lay stricken with the deadliest bolts of grief.
Upon a smooth grey stone sate Roderick there;
The wind above him stirred the hazel boughs,
And murmuring at his feet the river ran.
He sate with folded arms and head declined
Upon his breast, feeding on bitter thoughts,
Till nature gave him in the exhausted sense
Of woe a respite something like repose;
And then the quiet sound of gentle winds
And waters with their lulling consonance
Beguiled him of himself. Of all within
Oblivious there he sate, sentient alone
Of outward nature,—of the whispering leaves
That soothed his ear,—the genial breath of heaven
That fanned his cheek,—the stream's perpetual flow,
That, with its shadows and its glancing lights,
Dimples and thread-like motions infinite,
For ever varying and yet still the same,
Like time toward eternity, ran by.
Resting his head upon his master's knees,
Upon the bank beside him Theron lay.
What matters change of state and circumstance,
Or lapse of years, with all their dread events,
To him? What matters it that Roderick wears
The crown no longer, nor the sceptre wields?—
It is the dear-loved hand, whose friendly touch
Had flattered him so oft : it is the voice,
At whose glad summons to the field so oft
From slumber he had started, shaking off
Dreams of the chase, to share the actual joy;
The eye, whose recognition he was wont
To watch and welcome with exultant tongue.

A coming step, unheard by Roderick, roused
His watchful ear, and turning he beheld
Siverian. Father, said the good old man,
As Theron rose and fawn'd about his knees,
Hast thou some charm, which draws about thee thus
The hearts of all our house,—even to the beast

That lacks discourse of reason, but too oft,
With uncorrupted feeling and dumb faith,
Puts lordly man to shame?—The king replied,
'T is that mysterious sense by which mankind
To fix their friendships and their loves are led,
And which with fainter influence doth extend
To such poor things as this.   As we put off
The cares and passions of this fretful world,
It may be too that we thus far approach
To elder nature, and regain in part
The privilege through sin in Eden lost.
The timid hare soon learns that she may trust
The solitary penitent, and birds
Will light upon the hermit's harmless hand. 42

Thus Roderick answered in excursive speech,
Thinking to draw the old man's mind from what
Might touch him else too nearly, and himself
Disposed to follow on the lure he threw,
As one whom such imaginations led
Out of the world of his own miseries.
But to regardless ears his words were given,
For on the dog Siverian gazed the while,
Pursuing his own thoughts.   Thou hast not felt,
Exclaimed the old man, the earthquake and the storm;
The kingdom's overthrow, the wreck of Spain,
The ruin of thy royal master's house,
Have reached not thee!—Then turning to the King,
When the destroying enemy drew nigh
Toledo, he continued, and we fled
Before their fury, even while her grief
Was fresh, my Mistress would not leave behind
This faithful creature.   Well we knew she thought
Of Roderick then, although she named him not;
For never since the fatal certainty
Fell on us all, hath that unhappy name,
Save in her prayers, been known to pass her lips
Before this day.   She names him now, and weeps :
But now her tears are tears of thankfulness,
For blessed hath thy coming been to her
And all who loved the King.

                              His faultering voice
Here failed him, and he paused : recovering soon,
When that poor injured Lady, he pursued,
Did in my presence to the Prince absolve
The unhappy King—

                    Absolve him! Roderick cried,
And in that strong emotion turned his face
Sternly toward Siverian, for the sense
Of shame and self-reproach drove from his mind
All other thoughts.   The good old man replied.
Of human judgments humanly I speak.
Who knows not what Pelayo's life hath been ?
Not happier in all dear domestic ties,
Than worthy for his virtue of the bliss
Which is that virtue's fruit; and yet did he
Absolve, upon Florinda's tale, the King.
Siverian, thus he said, what most I hoped,
And still within my secret heart believed,
Is now made certain.   Roderick hath been
More sinned against than sinning.   And with that
He claspt his hands, and, lifting them to Heaven,
Cried, Would to God that he were yet alive !
For not more gladly did I draw my sword
Against Vitiza in our common cause,
Than I would fight beneath his banners now,

And vindicate his name!

                         Did he say this?
The Prince? Pelayo? in astonishment
Roderick exclaimed.—He said it, quoth the old man.
None better knew his kinsman's noble heart,
None loved him better, none bewailed him more :
And as he felt, like me, for his reproach
A deeper grief than for his death, even so
He cherished in his heart the constant thought
Something was yet untold, which, being known,
Would palliate his offence, and make the fall
Of one till then so excellently good,
Less monstrous, less revolting to belief,
More to be pitied, more to be forgiven.
While thus he spake, the fallen King felt his face
Burn, and his blood flow fast.   Down, guilty thoughts!
Firmly he said within his soul; lie still,
Thou heart of flesh ! I thought thou hadst been quelled,
And quelled thou shalt be ! Help me, O my God,
That I may crucify this inward foe!
Yea, thou hast helped me, Father! I am strong,
O Saviour, in thy strength.

                         As he breathed thus
His inward supplications, the old man
Eyed him with frequent and unsteady looks.
He had a secret trembling on his lips,
And hesitated, still irresolute
In utterance to embody the dear hope :
Fain would he have it strengthened and assured
By this concording judgment, yet he feared
To have it chilled in cold accoil.   At length
Venturing, he brake with interrupted speech
The troubled silence.   Father Maccabee,
I cannot rest till I have laid my heart
Open before thee.   When Pelayo wished
That his poor kinsman were alive to rear
His banner once again, a sudden thought—
A hope—a fancy—what shall it be called ?
Possessed me, that perhaps the wish might see
Its glad accomplishment,—that Roderick lived,
And might in glory take the field once more
For Spain.—I see thou startest at the thought;
Yet spurn it not with hasty unbelief,
As though 't were utterly beyond the scope
Of possible contingency.   I think
That I have calmly satisfied myself
How this is more than idle fancy, more
Than mere imaginations of a mind
Which from its wishes builds a baseless faith.
His horse, his royal robe, his hornèd helm,
His mail and sword were found upon the field;
But if King Roderick had in battle fall'n,
That sword, I know, would only have been found
Clenched in the hand which, living, knew so well
To wield the dreadful steel ! Not in the throng
Confounded, nor amid the torpid stream,
Opening with ignominious arms a way
For flight, would he have perished ! Where the strife
Was hottest, ringed about with slaughtered foes,
Should Roderick have been found: by this sure mark
Ye should have known him, if nought else remained,
That his whole body had been gored with wounds,
And quilled with spears, as if the Moors had felt
That in his single life the victory lay,
More than in all the host !

                         Siverian's eyes

Shone with a youthful ardour while he spake,
His gathering brow grew stern, and as he raised
His arm, a warrior's impulse charactered
The impassioned gesture. But the King was calm,
And heard him with unchanging countenance;
For he had taken his resolve, and felt
Once more the peace of God within his soul,
As in that hour when by his father's grave
He knelt before Pelayo.
                                Soon the old man
Pursued in calmer tones,—Thus much I dare
Believe, that Roderick fell not on that day
When treason brought about his overthrow.
If yet he live, for sure I think I know
His noble mind, 't is in some wilderness,
Where, in some savage den inhumed, he drags
The weary load of life, and on his flesh
As on a mortal enemy, inflicts
Fierce vengeance with immitigable hand.
O that I knew but where to bend my way
In his dear search! my voice perhaps might reach
His heart, might reconcile him to himself,
Restore him to his mother ere she dies,
His people and his country; with the sword,
Them and his own good name should be redeem.
O might I but behold him once again
Leading to battle these intrepid bands,
Such as he was,—yea rising from his fall
More glorious, more beloved! Soon I believe
Joy would accomplish then what grief hath failed
To do with this old heart, and I should die
Clasping his knees with such intense delight,
That when I woke in Heaven, even Heaven itself
Could have no higher happiness in store.

Thus fervently he spake, and copious tears
Ran down his cheeks. Full oft the Royal Goth,
Since he came forth again among mankind,
Had trembled lest some curious eye should read
His lineaments too closely; now he longed
To fall upon the neck of that old man,
And give his full heart utterance. But the sense
Of duty, by the pride of self-controul
Corroborate, made him steadily repress
His yearning nature. Whether Roderick live,
Paying in penitence the bitter price
Of sin, he answered, or if earth hath given
Rest to his earthly part, is only known
To him and Heaven. Dead is he to the world;
And let not these imaginations rob
His soul of thy continual prayers, whose aid
Too surely, in whatever world, he needs.
The faithful love that mitigates his fault,
Heavenward addrest, may mitigate his doom.
Living or dead, old man, be sure his soul,—
It were unworthy else,—doth hold with thine
Entire communion! Doubt not he relies
Firmly on thee, as on a father's love,
Counts on thy offices, and joins with thee
In sympathy and fervent act of faith,
Though regions, or though worlds, should intervene.
Lost as he is, to Roderick this must be
Thy first, best, dearest duty; next must be
To hold right onward in that noble path,
Which he would counsel, could his voice be heard.
Now therefore aid me, while I call upon

The Leaders and the People, that this day
We may acclaim Pelayo for our King.

XVIII.

THE ACCLAMATION.

Now when from Covadonga down the vale
Holding his way, the princely mountaineer
Came with that happy family in sight
Of Cangas and his native towers, far off
He saw before the gate, in fair array,
The assembled land. Broad banners were displayed,
And spears were sparkling to the sun, shields shone,
And helmets glittered, and the blairing horn,
With frequent sally of impatient joy,
Provoked the echoes round. Well he areeds,
From yonder ensigns and augmented force,
That Odoar and the Primate from the west
Have brought their aid; but wherefore all were thus
Instructed, as for some great festival,
He found not, till Favila's quicker eye
Catching the ready buckler, the glad boy
Leapt up, and clapping his exultant hands,
Shouted, King! King! my father shall be King
This day! Pelayo started at the word,
And the first thought which smote him brought a sigh
For Roderick's fall; the second was of hope,
Deliverance for his country, for himself
Enduring fame, and glory for his line.
That high prophetic forethought gathered strength,
As looking to his honoured mate, he read
Her soul's accordant augury; her eyes
Brightened; the quickened action of the blood
Tinged with a deeper hue her glowing cheek,
And on her lips there sate a smile which spake
The honourable pride of perfect love,
Rejoicing, for her husband's sake, to share
The lot he chose, the perils he defied,
The lofty fortune which their faith foresaw.

Roderick, in front of all the assembled troops,
Held the broad buckler, following to the end
That steady purpose to the which his zeal
Had this day wrought the Chiefs. Tall as himself,
Erect it stood beside him, and his hands
Hung resting on the rim. This was an hour
That sweetened life, repaid and recompensed
All losses; and although it could not heal
All griefs, yet laid them for awhile to rest.
The active agitating joy that filled
The vale, that with contagious influence spread
Through all the exulting mountaineers, that gave
New ardour to all spirits, to all breasts
Inspired fresh impulse of excited hope,
Moved every tongue, and strengthened every limb,—
That joy which every man reflected saw
From every face of all the multitude,
And heard in every voice, in every sound,
Reached not the King. Aloof from sympathy,
He from the solitude of his own soul
Beheld the busy scene. None shared or knew
His deep and incommunicable joy;
None but that Heavenly Father, who alone

Beholds the struggles of the heart, alone
Knows and rewards the secret sacrifice. 43

Among the chiefs conspicuous Urban stood,
He whom, with well-weighed choice, in arduous time,
To arduous office the consenting Church
Had called when Sindered 44 fear-smitten fled ;
Unfaithful shepherd, who for life alone
Solicitous, forsook his flock, when most
In peril and in suffering they required
A pastor's care. Far off at Rome he dwells
In ignominious safety, while the Church
Keeps in her annals the deserter's name ;
But from the service which with daily zeal
Devout her ancient prelacy recalls,
Blots it, unworthy to partake her prayers. 45
Urban, to that high station thus being called,
From whence disanimating fear had driven
The former primate, for the general weal
Consulting first, removed with timely care
The relics and the written works of saints,
Toledo's choicest treasure, prized beyond
All wealth, their living and their dead remains ;
These to the mountain fastnesses he bore
Of unsubdued Cantabria, there deposed,
One day to be the boast of yet unbuilt
Oviedo, and the dear idolatry
Of multitudes unborn. 46 To things of state
Then giving thought mature, he held advice
With Odoar, whom of counsel competent
And firm of heart he knew. What then they planned,
Time and the course of over-ruled events
To earlier act had ripened, than their hope
Had ever in its gladdest dream proposed ;
And here by agents unforeseen, and means
Beyond the scope of foresight brought about,
This day they saw their dearest heart's desire
Accorded them: All-able Providence
Thus having ordered all, that Spain this hour
With happiest omens, and on surest base,
Should from its ruins rear again her throne.

For acclamation and for sacring now
One form must serve, more solemn for the breach
Of old observances, whose absence here
Deeplier imprest the heart, than all display
Of regal pomp and wealth pontifical,
Of vestments radiant with their gems, and stiff
With ornature of gold ; the glittering train,
The long procession, and the full-voiced choir.
This day the forms of piety and war,
In strange but fitting union must combine.
Not in his alb and cope and orary 47
Came Urban now, nor wore he mitre here,
Precious or auriphrygiate ; 48 bare of head
He stood, all else in arms complete, and o'er
His gorget's iron rings the pall was thrown
Of wool undyed, which on the Apostle's tomb
Gregory had laid, 49 and sanctified with prayer ;
That from the living Pontiff and the dead
Replete with holiness, it might impart
Doubly derived its grace. One Page beside
Bore his broad-shadowed helm; another's hand
Held the long spear, more suited in these times
For Urban, than the crosier richly wrought
With silver foliature, the elaborate work

Of Grecian or Italian artist, trained
In the eastern capital, or sacred Rome,
Still o'er the West predominant, though fallen.
Better the spear befits the shepherd's hand
When robbers break the fold. Now he had laid
The weapon by, and held a natural cross
Of rudest form, unpeeled, even as it grew
On the near oak that morn.
                        Mutilate alike
Of royal rites was this solemnity.
Where was the rubied crown, the sceptre where,
And where the golden pome, the proud array
Of ermines, aureate vests, and jewelry,
With all which Leuvigild for after kings
Left, ostentatious of his power ? 50 The Moor
Had made his spoil of these, and on the field
Of Xeres, where contending multitudes
Had trampled it beneath their bloody feet,
The standard of the Goths forgotten lay
Defiled, and rotting there in sun and rain.
Utterly is it lost ; nor ever more
Herald or antiquary's patient search
Shall from forgetfulness avail to save
Those blazoned arms, so fatally of old
Renowned through all the affrighted Occident.
That banner, before which imperial Rome
First to a conqueror bowed her head abased ;
Which when the dreadful Hun with all his powers
Came like a deluge rolling o'er the world,
Made head, and in the front of battle broke
His force, till then resistless ; which so oft
Had with alternate fortune braved the Frank ;
Driven the Byzantine from the farthest shores
Of Spain, long lingering there, to final flight ;
And of their kingdoms and their name despoiled
The Vandal, and the Alan, and the Sueve ; 51
Blotted from human records is it now
As it had never been. So let it rest
With things forgotten ! But Oblivion ne'er
Shall cancel from the historic roll, nor Time,
Who changeth all obscure that fated sign,
Which brighter now than mountain snows at noon
To the bright sun displays its argent field.

Rose not the vision then upon thy soul,
O Roderick, when within that argent field
Thou saw'st the rampant Lion, red as if
Upon some noblest quarry he had rolled,
Rejoicing in his satiate rage, and drunk
With blood and fury? Did the auguries
Which opened on thy spirit bring with them
A perilous consolation, deadening heart
And soul, yet worse than death,—that thou through all
Thy chequered way of life, evil and good,
Thy errors and thy virtues, hadst but been
The poor mere instrument of things ordained,—
Doing or suffering, impotent alike
To will or act,—perpetually bemocked
With semblance of volition, yet in all
Blind worker of the ways of destiny !
That thought intolerable, which in the hour
Of woe indignant conscience had repelled,
As little might it find reception now,
When the regenerate spirit self-approved
Beheld its sacrifice complete. With faith
Elate, he saw the bannered Lion float

Refulgent, and recalled that thrilling shout
Which he had heard when on Romano's grave
The joy of victory woke him from his dream,
And sent him with prophetic hope to work
Fulfilment of the great events ordained,
There in imagination's inner world
Prefigured to his soul.   Alone advanced
Before the ranks, the Goth in silence stood,
While from all voices round, loquacious joy
Mingling its buzz continuous with the blast
Of horn, shrill pipe, and tinkling cymbals' clash,
And sound of deafening drum. But when the Prince
Drew nigh, and Urban with the cross upheld
Stept forth to meet him, all at once were stilled
With instantaneous hush; as when the wind,
Before whose violent gusts the forest oaks,
Tossing like billows their tempestuous heads,
Roar like a raging sea, suspends its force,
And leaves so dead a calm that not a leaf
Moves on the silent spray.   The passing air
Bore with it from the woodland undisturbed
The ringdove's wooing, and the quiet voice
Of waters warbling near.   Son of a race
Of Heroes and of Kings! the Primate thus
Addressed him, Thou in whom the Gothic blood,
Mingling with old Iberia's, has restored
To Spain a ruler of her native line,
Stand forth, and in the face of God and man
Swear to uphold the right, abate the wrong,
With equitable hand, protect the cross
Whereon thy lips this day shall seal their vow,
And underneath that hallowed symbol, wage
Holy and inextinguishable war
Against the accursed nation that usurps
Thy country's sacred soil!   So speak of me
Now and for ever, O my countrymen!
Replied Pelayo; and so deal with me
Here and hereafter, thou, Almighty God,
In whom I put my trust!   Lord God of Hosts, [52]
Urban pursued, of Angels and of Men
Creator and Disposer, King of Kings,
Ruler of Earth and Heaven,—look down this day,
And multiply thy blessings on the head
Of this thy servant, chosen in thy sight!
Be thou his counsellor, his comforter,
His hope, his joy, his refuge, and his strength!
Crown him with justice, and with fortitude!
Defend him with thy all-sufficient shield!
Surround him every where with the right hand
Of thine all-present power! and with the might
Of thine omnipotence, send in his aid
Thy unseen angels forth, that potently
And royally against all enemies
He may endure and triumph! Bless the land
O'er which he is appointed; bless it with
The waters of the firmament, the springs
Of the low-lying deep, the fruits which sun
And moon mature for man, the precious stores
Of the eternal hills, and all the gifts
Of earth, its wealth and fulness!
                              Then he took
Pelayo's hand, and on his finger placed

The mystic circlet.—With this ring, O Prince,
To our dear Spain, who like a widow now
Mourneth in desolation, I thee wed:
For weal or woe thou takest her, till death
Dispart the union: Be it blest to her,
To thee, and to thy seed!
                    Thus when he ceased,
He gave the awaited signal.   Roderick brought
The buckler: [53] Eight for strength and stature chosen
Came to their honoured office: Round the shield
Standing, they lower it for the Chieftain's feet,
Then slowly raised upon their shoulders lift
The steady weight.   Erect Pelayo stands,
And thrice he brandishes the shining sword,
While Urban to the assembled people cries,
Spaniards, behold your King!   The multitude
Then sent forth all their voice with glad acclaim,
Raising the loud *Real;* thrice did the word
Ring through the air, and echo from the walls
Of Cangas.   Far and wide the thundering shout,
Rolling among reduplicating rocks,
Pealed o'er the hills, and up the mountain vales.
The wild ass starting in the forest glade
Ran to the covert; the affrighted wolf
Skulked through the thicket, to a closer brake;
The sluggish bear, awakened in his den,
Roused up, and answered with a sullen growl,
Low-breathed and long; and at the uproar scared,
The brooding eagle from her nest took wing.

Heroes and Chiefs of old! and ye who bore
Firm to the last your part in that dread strife,
When Julian and Witiza's viler race
Betrayed their country, hear ye from yon heaven
The joyful acclamation which proclaims
That Spain is born again! O ye who died
In that disastrous field, and ye who fell
Embracing with a martyr's love your death
Amid the flames of Auria; and all ye
Victims innumerable, whose cries unheard
On earth, but heard in heaven, from all the land
Went up for vengeance; not in vain ye cry
Before the eternal throne!—Rest, innocent blood!
Vengeance is due, and vengeance will be given!
Rest, innocent blood! The appointed age is come!
The star that harbingers a glorious day
Hath risen! Lo there the avenger stands! Lo there
He brandishes the avenging sword! Lo there
The avenging banner spreads its argent field
Refulgent with auspicious light!—Rejoice,
O Leon, for thy banner is displayed, [54]
Rejoice with all thy mountains, and thy vales
And streams! And thou, O Spain, through all thy realms,
For thy deliverance cometh! Even now,
As from all sides the miscreant hosts move on;—
From southern Betis; from the western lands
Where through redundant vales smooth Minho flows,
And Douro pours through vine-clad hills the wealth
Of Leon's gathered waters; from the plains
Burgensian, in old time Vardulia called,
But in their castellated strength ere long
To be designed Castille, a deathless name;
From midland regions where Toledo reigns
Proud city on her royal eminence,
And Tagus bends his sickle round the scene
Of Roderick's fall; [55] from rich Rioja's fields;

Dark Ebro's shores; the walls of Salduba,
Seat of the Sedetanians old, by Rome
Cæsarian and August denominate,
Now Zaragoza, in his later time
Above all cities of the earth renowned
For duty perfectly performed;—East, West,
And South, where'er their gathered multitudes
Urged by the speed of vigorous tyranny,
With more than with commeasurable strength
Haste to prevent the danger, crush the hopes
Of rising Spain, and rivet round her neck
The eternal yoke,—the ravenous fowls of heaven
Flock there presentient of their food obscene,
Following the accursëd armies, whom too well
They know their purveyors long. Pursue their march,
Ominous attendants! Ere the moon hath filled
Her horns, these purveyors shall become the prey,
And ye on Moorish not on Christian flesh
Wearying your beaks, shall clog your scaly feet
With foreign gore.   Soon will ye learn to know,
Followers and harbingers of blood, the flag
Of Leon where it bids you to your feast!
Terror and flight shall with that flag go forth,
And Havoc and the Dogs of War and Death.
Thou Covadonga with the tainted stream
Of Deva, and this now rejoicing vale,
Soon its primitial triumphs wilt behold!
Nor shall the glories of the noon be less
Than such miraculous promise of the dawn:
Witness Calvijo, where the dreadful cry
Of Santiago, then first heard, o'erpowered
The Akbar, and that holier name blasphemed
By misbelieving lips! Simancas, thou
Be witness! And do ye your record bear,
Tolosan mountains, where the Almohade
Beheld his myriads scattered and destroyed,
Like locusts swept before the stormy North!
Thou too, Salado, on that later day
When Africa received her final foil,
And thy swoln stream incarnadined, rolled back
The invaders to the deep,—there shall they toss
Till on their native Mauritanian shore
The waves shall cast their bones to whiten there.

XIX.

RODERICK AND RUSILLA.

WHEN all had been performed, the royal Goth
Looked up toward the chamber in the tower,
Where, gazing on the multitude below,
Alone Rusilla stood.   He met her eye,
For it was singling him amid the crowd;
Obeying then the hand which beckoned him,
He went with heart prepared, nor shrinking now,
But arm'd with self-approving thoughts that hour.
Entering in tremulous haste, he closed the door,
And turned to clasp her knees; but lo, she spread
Her arms, and catching him in close embrace,
Fell on his neck, and cried, My Son, my Son!—
Ere long, controlling that first agony,
With effort of strong will, backward she bent,
And gazing on his head now shorn and grey,
And on his furrowed countenance, exclaimed,
Still, still, my Roderick! the same noble mind!

The same heroic heart! Still, still, my Son!—
Changed,—yet not wholly fall'n,—not wholly lost,
He cried,—not wholly in the sight of Heaven
Unworthy, O my Mother, nor in thine!
She locked her arms again around his neck,
Saying, Lord let me now depart in peace!
And bowed her head again, and silently
Gave way to tears.
                    When that first force was past,
And passion in exhaustment found relief,—
I knew thee, said Rusilla, when the dog
Rose from my feet, and licked his master's hand.
All flashed upon me then; the instinctive sense
That goes unerringly where reason fails,—
The voice, the eye,—a mother's thoughts are quick;—
Miraculous as it seemed,—Siverian's tale,—
Florinda's,—every action,—every word,—
Each strengthening each, and all confirming all,
Revealed thee, O my son! but I restrained
My heart, and yielded to thy holier will
The thoughts which rose to tempt a soul not yet
Weaned wholly from the world.
                            What thoughts? replied
Roderick.   That I might see thee yet again
Such as thou wert, she answered; not alone
To Heaven and me restored, but to thyself,—
Thy Crown,—thy Country,—all within thy reach;
Heaven so disposing all things, that the means
Which wrought the ill, might work the remedy.
Methought I saw thee once again the hope,—
The strength,—the pride of Spain! The miracle
Which I beheld made all things possible.
I know the inconstant people, how their mind,
With every breath of good or ill report,
Fluctuates, like summer corn before the breeze:
Quick in their hatred, quicker in their love,
Generous and hasty, soon would they redress
All wrongs of former obloquy.—I thought
Of happiness restored,—the broken heart
Healed,—and Count Julian, for his daughter's sake,
Turning in thy behalf against the Moors
His powerful sword:—all possibilities
That could be found or fancied, built a dream
Before me; such as easiest might illude
A lofty spirit trained in palaces,
And not alone amid the flatteries
Of youth with thoughts of high ambition fed
When all is sunshine, but through years of woe,
When sorrow sanctified their use, upheld
By honourable pride and earthly hopes.
I thought I yet might nurse upon my knee
Some young Theodofred, and see in him
Thy father's image and thine own renewed,
And love to think the little hand which there
Played with the bauble, should in after days
Wield the transmitted sceptre;—that through him
The ancient seed should be perpetuate,
That precious seed revered so long, desired
So dearly, and so wonderously preserved.

Nay, he replied, Heaven hath not with its bolts
Scathed the proud summit of the tree, and left
The trunk unflawed; ne'er shall it clothe its boughs
Again, nor push again its scyons forth,
Head, root, and branch, all mortified alike!—
Long ere these locks were shorn had I cut off

The thoughts of royalty! Time might renew
Their length, as for Manoah's captive son,
And I too on the miscreant race, like him,
Might prove my strength regenerate; but the hour
When in its second best nativity,
My soul was born again through grace, this heart
Died to the world. Dreams such as thine pass now
Like evening clouds before me; if I think
How beautiful they seem, 't is but to feel
How soon they fade, how fast the night shuts in.
But in that World to which my hopes look on,
Time enters not, nor Mutability:
Beauty and Goodness are unfading there;
Whatever there is given us to enjoy,
That we enjoy for ever, still the same—
Much might Count Julian's sword achieve for Spain
And me; but more will his dear daughter's soul
Effect in Heaven; and soon will she be there
An Angel at the Throne of Grace, to plead
In his behalf and mine.
                                I knew thy heart,
She answered, and subdued the vain desire.
It was the World's last effort. Thou hast chosen
The better part. Yea, Roderick, even on earth
There is a praise above the monarch's fame,
A higher, holier, more enduring praise,
And this will yet be thine!
                                O tempt me not,
Mother! he cried, nor let ambition take
That specious form to cheat us! What but this,
Fallen as I am, have I to offer Heaven?
The ancestral sceptre, public fame, content
Of private life, the general good report,
Power, reputation, happiness,—whate'er
The heart of man desires to constitute
His earthly weal,—unerring Justice claimed
In forfeiture. I with submitted soul
Bow to the righteous law and kiss the rod.
Only while thus submitted, suffering thus,—
Only while offering up that name on earth,
Perhaps in trial offered to my choice,
Could I present myself before thy sight;
Thus only could endure myself, or fix
My thoughts upon that fearful pass, where Death
Stands in the Gate of Heaven!—Time passes on,
The healing work of sorrow is complete;
All vain desires have long been weeded out,
All vain regrets subdued; the heart is dead,
The soul is ripe and eager for her birth.
Bless me, my Mother! and come when it will
The inevitable hour, we die in peace.

So saying, on her knees he bowed his head;
She raised her hands to Heaven and blest her child;
Then bending forward, as he rose, embraced
And claspt him to her heart, and cried, Once more,
Theodofred, with pride behold thy son!

XX.

THE MOORISH CAMP.

The times are big with tidings; every hour,
From east and west and south the breathless scouts
Bring swift alarums in; the gathering foe,

Advancing from all quarters to one point,
Close their wide crescent. Nor was aid of fear
To magnify their numbers needed now:
They came in myriads. Africa had poured
Fresh shoals upon the coast of wretched Spain;
Lured from their hungry deserts to the scene
Of spoil, like vultures to the battle-field,
Fierce, unrelenting, habited in crimes,
Like bidden guests the mirthful ruffians flock
To that free feast which in their Prophet's name
Rapine and Lust proclaimed. Nor were the chiefs
Of victory less assured, by long success
Elate, and proud of that o'erwhelming strength,
Which, surely they believed, as it had rolled
Thus far uncheck'd, would roll victorious on,
Till, like the Orient, the subjected West
Should bow in reverence at Mahommed's name;
And pilgrims, from remotest Arctic shores,
Tread with religious feet the burning sands
Of Araby and Mecca's stony soil.
Proud of his part in Roderick's overthrow,
Their leader Abulcacem came, a man
Immitigable, long in war renowned.
Here Magued comes, who on the conquered walls
Of Cordoba by treacherous fear betrayed,
Planted the moony standard; Ibrahim here,
He, who by Genil and in Darro's vales,
Had for the Moors the fairest portion won
Of all their spoils, fairest and best maintained,
And to the Alpuxarras given in trust
His other name, through them preserved in song.
Here too Alcahman, vaunting his late deeds
At Auria, all her children by the sword
Cut off, her bulwarks rased, her towers laid low,
Her dwellings by devouring flames consumed.
Bloody and hard of heart, he little weened,
Vain boastful chief! that from those fatal flames
The fire of retribution had gone forth
Which soon should wrap him round.
                                The renegades
Here too were seen, Ebba and Sisibert;
A spurious brood, but of their parents' crimes
True heirs in guilt begotten, and in ill
Trained up. The same unnatural rage that turned
Their swords against their country, made them seek,
Unmindful of their wretched mother's end,
Pelayo's life. No enmity is like
Domestic hatred! For his blood they thirst,
As if that sacrifice might satisfy
Witiza's guilty ghost, efface the shame
Of their adulterous birth, and, one crime more
Crowning a hideous course, emancipate
Thenceforth their spirits from all earthly fear.
This was their only care; but other thoughts
Were rankling in that elder villain's mind,
Their kinsman Orpas, he of all the crew,
Who in this fatal visitation fell,
The foulest and the falsest wretch that e'er
Renounced his baptism. From his cherished views
Of royalty cut off, he coveted
Count Julian's wide domains, and hopeless now
To gain them through the daughter, laid his toils
Against the father's life,—the instrument
Of his ambition first, and now designed
Its victim. To this end with cautious hints,
At favouring season ventured, he possessed

The leader's mind; then, subtly fostering
The doubts himself had sown, with bolder charge
He bade him warily regard the Count,
Lest underneath an outward show of faith
The heart uncircumcised were Christian still:
Else, wherefore had Florinda not obeyed
Her dear-loved sire's example, and embraced
The saving truth! Else, wherefore was her hand,
Plighted to him so long, so long withheld,
Till she had found a fitting hour to fly
With that audacious Prince, who now in arms
Defied the Caliph's power;—for who could doubt
That in his company she fled, perhaps
The mover of his flight? What if the Count
Himself had planned the evasion which he feigned
In sorrow to condemn? What if she went
A pledge assured, to tell the mountaineers
That when they met the Musselmen in the heat
Of fight, her father passing to their side
Would draw the victory with him?—Thus he breathed
Fiend-like in Abulcacem's ear his schemes
Of murderous malice; and the course of things,
Ere long, in part approving his discourse,
Aided his aim, and gave his wishes weight.
For scarce on the Asturian territory
Had they set foot, when, with the speed of fear,
Count Eudon, nothing doubting that their force
Would like a flood sweep all resistance down,
Hastened to plead his merits;—he alone,
Found faithful in obedience through reproach
And danger, when the maddened multitude
Hurried their chiefs along, and high and low
With one infectious frenzy seized, provoked
The invincible in arms.   Pelayo led
The raging crew,—he doubtless the prime spring
Of all these perilous movements; and 't was said
He brought the assurance of a strong support,
Count Julian's aid, for in his company
From Cordoba, Count Julian's daughter came.
Thus Eudon spake before the assembled chiefs,
When instantly a stern and wrathful voice
Replied, I know Pelayo never made
That senseless promise! He who raised the tale
Lies foully; but the bitterest enemy
That ever hunted for Pelayo's life
Hath never with the charge of falsehood touched
His name.
   The Baron had not recognised
Till then, beneath the turban's shadowing folds,
Julian's swart visage, where the fiery suns
Of Africa, through many a year's long course,
Had set their hue inburnt.   Something he sought
In quick excuse to say of common fame,
Lightly believed and busily diffused,
And that no enmity had moved his speech
Repeating rumour's tale.   Julian replied,
Count Eudon, neither for thyself nor me
Excuse is needed here.   The path I tread
Is one wherein there can be no return,
No pause, no looking back!   A choice like mine
For time and for eternity is made,
Once and for ever! and as easily
The breath of vain report might build again
The throne which my just vengeance overthrew,
As in the Caliph and his captain's mind
Affect the opinion of my well-tried truth.

The tidings which thou givest me of my child
Touch me more vitally; bad though they be,
A secret apprehension of aught worse
Makes me with joy receive them.
     Then the Count
To Abulcacem turned his speech, and said,
I pray thee, Chief, give me a messenger
By whom I may to this unhappy child
Dispatch a father's bidding, such as yet
May win her back.   What I would say requires
No veil of privacy: before ye all
The errand shall be given.
     Boldly he spake,
Yet wary in that show of open truth,
For well he knew what dangers girt him round
Amid the faithless race.   Blind with revenge,
For them in madness had he sacrificed
His name, his baptism, and his native land,
To feel, still powerful as he was, that life
Hung on their jealous favour.   But his heart
Approved him now, where love, too long restrained,
Resumed its healing influence, leading him
Right on with no misgiving.   Chiefs, he said,
Hear me, and let your wisdom judge between
Me and Prince Orpas!—Known it is to all,
Too well, what mortal injury provoked
My spirit to that vengeance which your aid
So signally hath given.   A covenant
We made when first our purpose we combined,
That he should have Florinda for his wife,
My only child, so should she be, I thought,
Revenged and honoured best.   My word was given
Truly, nor did I cease to use all means
Of counsel or command, entreating her
Sometimes with tears, and oft with menaces
Of direst anger and a father's curse,
To lead her to obey.   The Christian law,
She said, forbade, and she had vowed herself
A servant to the Lord.   In vain I strove
To win her to the Prophet's saving faith,
Using, perhaps, a rigour to that end
Beyond permitted means, and to my heart,
Which loved her dearer than its own life-blood,
Abhorrent.   Silently she suffered all,
Or when I urged her with most vehemence,
Only replied, I knew her fixed resolve,
And craved my patience but a little while
Till death should set her free.   Touched as I was,
I yet persisted, till at length to escape
The ceaseless importunity, she fled;
And verily I feared until this hour,
My rigour to some fearfuller resolve
Than flight had driven my child.   Chiefs, I appeal
To each and all, and, Orpas, to thyself
Especially, if, having thus essayed
All means that law and nature have allowed
To bend her will, I may not rightfully
Hold myself free, that promise being void
Which cannot be fulfilled.
     Thou sayest then,
Orpas replied, that from her false belief
Her stubborn opposition drew its force.
I should have thought that from the ways corrupt
Of these idolatrous Christians, little care
Might have sufficed to wean a duteous child,
The example of a parent so beloved

Leading the way; and yet I will not doubt
Thou didst enforce with all sincerity
And holy zeal upon thy daughter's mind
The truths of Islam.

     Julian knit his brow,
And scowling on the insidious renegade,
He answered, By what reasoning my poor mind
Was from the old idolatry reclaimed,
None better knows than Seville's mitred chief,
Who first renouncing errors which he taught,
Led me his follower to the Prophet's pale.
Thy lessons I repeated as I could,
Of graven images, unnatural vows,
False records, fabling creeds, and juggling priests,
Who making sanctity the cloak of sin,
Laughed at the fools on whose credulity
They fattened. To these arguments, whose worth
Prince Orpas, least of all men, should impeach,
I added, like a soldier bred in arms,
And to the subtleties of schools unused,
The flagrant fact, that Heaven with victory,
Where'er they turned, attested and approved
The chosen Prophet's arms. If thou wert still
The mitred metropolitan, and I
Some wretch of Arian or of Hebrew race,
Thy proper business then might be to pry,
And question me for lurking flaws of faith,
We Musselmen, Prince Orpas, live beneath
A wiser law, which with the iniquities
Of thine old craft, hath abrogated this
Its foulest practice!

    As Count Julian ceased,
From underneath his black and gathered brow
There went a look, which with these wary words
Bore to the heart of that false renegade
Their whole envenomed meaning. Haughtily
Withdrawing then his altered eyes, he said,
Too much of this! return we to the sum
Of my discourse. Let Abulcacem say,
In whom the Caliph speaks, if with all faith
Having essayed in vain all means to win
My child's consent, I may not hold henceforth
The covenant discharged.

     The Moor replied,
Well hast thou said, and rightly mayst assure
Thy daughter that the Prophet's holy law
Forbids compulsion. Give thine errand now;
The messenger is here.

     Then Julian said,
Go to Pelayo, and from him entreat
Admittance to my child, where'er she be.
Say to her, that her father solemnly
Annuls the covenant with Orpas pledged,
Nor with solicitations, nor with threats,
Will urge her more, nor from that liberty
Of faith restrain her, which the Prophet's law,
Liberal as Heaven from whence it came, to all
Indulges. Tell her that her father says
His days are numbered, and beseeches her
By that dear love, which from her infancy
Still he hath borne her, growing as she grew,
Nursed in our weal and strengthened in our woe,
She will not in the evening of his life
Leave him forsaken and alone. Enough
Of sorrow, tell her, have her injuries
Brought on her father's head; let not her act

Thus aggravate the burden. Tell her too,
That when he prayed her to return, he wept
Profusely as a child; but bitterer tears
Than ever fell from childhood's eyes, were those
Which traced his hardy cheeks.

     With faultering voice
He spake, and after he had ceased from speech
His lip was quivering still. The Moorish chief
Then to the messenger his bidding gave.
Say, cried he, to these rebel infidels,
Thus Abulcacem in the Caliph's name
Exhorteth them: Repent and be forgiven!
Nor think to stop the dreadful storm of war,
Which conquering and to conquer must fulfil
Its destined circle, rolling eastward now
Back from the subjugated west, to sweep
Thrones and dominions down, till in the bond
Of unity all nations join, and Earth
Acknowledge, as she sees one sun in heaven,
One God, one Chief, one Prophet, and one Law.
Jerusalem, the holy City, bows
To holier Mecca's creed ; the crescent shines
Triumphant o'er the eternal pyramids :
On the cold altars of the worshippers
Of fire moss grows, and reptiles leave their slime ;
The African idolatries are fallen,
And Europe's senseless gods of stone and wood
Have had their day. Tell these misguided men,
A moment for repentance yet is left,
And mercy the submitted neck will spare
Before the sword is drawn ; but once unsheathed,
Let Auria witness how that dreadful sword
Accomplishes its work! They little know
The Moors who hope in battle to withstand
Their valour, or in flight escape their rage!
Amid our deserts we hunt down the birds
Of heaven,—wings do not save them ![56] Nor shall rocks,
And holds, and fastnesses, avail to save
These mountaineers. Is not the Earth the Lord's?
And we, his chosen people, whom he sends
To conquer and possess it in his name?

XXI.

THE FOUNTAIN IN THE FOREST.

The second eve had closed upon their march
Within the Asturian border, and the Moors
Had pitched their tents amid an open wood
Upon the mountain side. As day grew dim,
Their scattered fires shone with distincter light
Among the trees, above whose top the smoke
Diffused itself, and stained the evening sky.
Ere long the stir of occupation ceased,
And all the murmur of the busy host
Subsiding died away, as through the camp
The crier from a knoll proclaimed the hour
For prayer appointed, and with sonorous voice,
Thrice in melodious modulation full,
Pronounced the highest name. There is no God
But God, he cried ; there is no God but God!
Mahommed is the Prophet of the Lord!
Come ye to prayer! to prayer! The Lord is great!
There is no God but God!—Thus he pronounced
His ritual form, mingling with holiest truth

The audacious name accurst. The multitude
Made their ablutions in the mountain stream.
Obedient, then their faces to the earth
Bent in formality of easy prayer.

An arrow's flight above that mountain stream
There was a little glade, where underneath
A long smooth mossy stone a fountain rose.
An oak grew near, and with its ample boughs
O'ercanopied the spring ; its fretted roots
Embossed the bank, and on their tufted bark
Grew plants which love the moisture and the shade—
Short ferns, and longer leaves of wrinkled green
Which bent toward the spring, and when the wind
Made itself felt, just touched with gentle dip
The glassy surface, ruffled ne'er but then,
Save when a bubble rising from the depth
Burst, and with faintest circles marked its place,
Or if an insect skimmed it with its wing,
Or when in heavier drops the gathered rain
Fell from the oak's high bower. The mountain roe,
When, having drunk there, he would bound across,
Drew up upon the bank his meeting feet,
And put forth half his force. With silent lapse
From thence through mossy banks the water stole,
Then murmuring hastened to the glen below.
Diana might have loved in that sweet spot
To take her noontide rest ! and when she stoopt
Hot from the chase to drink, well pleased had seen
Her own bright crescent, and the brighter face
It crowned, reflected there.
               Beside that spring
Count Julian's tent was pitched upon the green;
There his ablutions Moor-like he had made,
And Moor-like knelt in prayer, bowing his head.
Upon the mossy bank. There was a sound
Of voices at the tent when he arose;
And lo! with hurried step a woman came
Toward him ; rightly then his heart presaged,
And ere he could behold her countenance,
Florinda knelt, and with uplifted arms
Embraced her sire. He raised her from the ground,
Kissed her, and claspt her to his heart, and said,
Thou hast not then forsaken me, my child ;
Howe'er the inexorable will of Fate
May in the world which is to come divide
Our everlasting destinies, in this
Thou wilt not, O my child, abandon me!
And then with deep and interrupted voice,
Nor seeking to restrain his copious tears,
My blessing be upon thy head, he cried,
A father's blessing! Though all faiths were false,
It should not lose its worth!—She locked her hands
Around his neck, and gazing in his face
Through streaming tears, exclaimed, Oh never more,
Here or hereafter, never let us part!
And breathing then a prayer in silence forth,
The name of Jesus trembled on her tongue.

Whom hast thou there? cried Julian, and drew back,
Seeing that near them stood a meagre man
In humble garb, who rested with raised hands
On a long staff, bending his head, like one
Who, when he hears the distant vesper-bell,
Halts by the way, and, all unseen of men,
Offers his homage in the eye of Heaven.

She answered, Let not my dear father frown
In anger on his child! Thy messenger
Told me that I should be restrained no more
From liberty of faith, which the new law
Indulged to all : how soon my hour might come
I knew not, and although that hour will bring
Few terrors, yet methinks I would not be
Without a Christian comforter in death.

A Priest! exclaimed the Count, and drawing back,
Stoopt for his turban, that he might not lack
Some outward symbol of apostacy;
For still in war his wonted arms he wore,
Nor for the scymitar had changed the sword
Accustomed to his hand. He covered now
His short grey hair, and under the white folds
His swarthy brow, which gathered as he rose,
Darkened. O frown not thus! Florinda cried,
A kind and gentle counsellor is this,
One who pours balm into a wounded soul,
And mitigates the griefs he cannot heal.
I told him I had vowed to pass my days
A servant of the Lord, yet that my heart,
Hearing the message of thy love, was drawn
With powerful yearnings back. Follow thy heart—
It answers to the call of duty here,
He said, nor canst thou better serve the Lord
Than at thy father's side.
                  Count Julian's brow,
While thus she spake, insensibly relaxed.
A Priest, cried he, and thus with even hand
Weigh vows and natural duty in the scale !
In what old heresy hath he been trained?
Or in what wilderness hath he escaped
The domineering Prelate's fire and sword?
Come hither, man, and tell me who thou art !

A sinner, Roderick, drawing nigh, replied,
Brought to repentance by the grace of God,
And trusting for forgiveness through the blood
Of Christ in humble hope.
                 A smile of scorn
Julian assumed, but merely from the lips
It came; for he was troubled while he gazed
On the strong countenance and thoughtful eye
Before him. A new law hath been proclaimed,
Said he, which overthrows in its career
The Christian altars of idolatry.
What think'st thou of the Prophet?—Roderick
Made answer, I am in the Moorish camp,
And he who asketh is a Musselman:
How then should I reply?—Safely, rejoined
The renegade, and freely mayst thou speak
To all that Julian asks. Is not the yoke
Of Mecca easy, and its burthen light?—
Spain hath not found it so, the Goth replied,
And groaning, turned away his countenance.

Count Julian knit his brow, and stood awhile
Regarding him with meditative eye
In silence. Thou art honest too! he cried;
Why 't was in quest of such a man as this
That the old Grecian searched by lanthorn light
In open day the city's crowded streets,
So rare he deemed the virtue. Honesty
And sense of natural duty in a Priest !

Now for a miracle, ye Saints of Spain!
  shall not pry too closely for the wires,
For, seeing what I see, ye have me now
  In the believing mood!

                    O blessed Saints,
Florinda cried, 't is from the bitterness,
Not from the hardness of the heart, he speaks!
Fear him! and in your goodness give the scoff
The virtue of a prayer! So saying, she raised
Her hands in fervent action claspt to Heaven;
Then as, still claspt, they fell, toward her sire
She turned her eyes, beholding him through tears.
The look, the gesture, and that silent woe,
Softened her father's heart, which in this hour
Was open to the influences of love.
Priest, thy vocation were a blessed one,
Said Julian, if its mighty power were used
To lessen human misery, not to swell
The mournful sum, already all too great.
If, as thy former counsel should imply,
Thou art not one who would for his craft's sake
Fret with corrosives and inflame the wound,
Which the poor sufferer brings to thee in trust,
That thou with virtuous balm wilt bind it up,—
If, as I think, thou art not one of those
Whose villany makes honest men turn Moors,
Thou then wilt answer with unbiassed mind
What I shall ask thee, and exorcise thus
The sick and feverish conscience of my child,
From inbred phantoms, fiend-like, which possess
Her innocent spirit. Children we are all
Of one great Father, in whatever clime
Nature or chance hath cast the seeds of life,
All tongues, all colours : neither after death
Shall we be sorted into languages
And tints,—white, black, and tawny, Greek and Goth,
Northmen and offspring of hot Africa ;
The All-Father, he in whom we live and move,
Be the indifferent Judge of all, regards
Nations, and hues, and dialects alike.
According to their works shall they be judged,
When even-handed Justice in the scale
Their good and evil weighs. All creeds, I ween,
Agree in this, and hold it orthodox.

Roderick, perceiving here that Julian paused,
As if he waited for acknowledgment
Of that plain truth, in motion of assent
Inclined his brow complacently, and said,
Even so. What follows?—This, resumed the Count,
That creeds like colours being but accident,
Are therefore in the scale imponderable ;—
Thou seest my meaning ;—that from every faith
As every clime, there is a way to Heaven,
And thou and I may meet in Paradise.

Oh grant it, God! cried Roderick fervently,
And smote his breast. Oh grant it, gracious God!
Through the dear blood of Jesus, grant that he
And I may meet before the Mercy-throne!
That were a triumph of Redeeming Love,
For which admiring Angels would renew
Their hallelujahs through the choir of Heaven!

Man! quoth Count Julian, wherefore art thou moved
To this strange passion? I require of thee

Thy judgment, not thy prayers!

                    Be not displeased!
In gentle voice subdued the Goth replies;
A prayer, from whatsoever lips it flow,
By thy own rule should find the way to Heaven,
So that the heart in its sincerity
Straight forward breathe it forth. I, like thyself,
Am all untrained to subtleties of speech,
Nor competent of this great argument
Thou openest; and perhaps shall answer thee
Wide of the words, but to the purport home.
There are to whom the light of gospel truth
Hath never reached ; of such I needs must deem
As of the sons of men who had their day
Before the light was given. But, Count, for those
Who, born amid the light, to darkness turn,
Wilful in error,—I dare only say,
God doth not leave the unhappy soul without
An inward monitor, and till the grave
Open, the gate of mercy is not closed.

Priest-like! the renegade replied, and shook
His head in scorn. What is not in the craft
Is error, and for error there shall be
No mercy found in him whom yet ye name
The merciful!

                    Now God forbid, rejoined
The fallen King, that one who stands in need
Of mercy for his sins should argue thus
Of error! Thou hast said that thou and I,
Thou dying in name a Musselman, and I
A servant of the Cross, may meet in Heaven.
Time was when in our fathers' ways we walked
Regardlessly alike; faith being to each,—
For so far thou hast reasoned rightly,—like
Our country's fashion and our mother-tongue,
Of mere inheritance,—no thing of choice
In judgment fixed, nor rooted in the heart.
Me have the arrows of calamity
Sore stricken ; sinking underneath the weight
Of sorrow, yet more heavily opprest
Beneath the burthen of my sins, I turned
In that dread hour to Him who from the Cross
Calls to the heavy-laden. There I found
Relief and comfort; there I have my hope,
My strength and my salvation; there, the grave
Ready beneath my feet, and Heaven in view,
I to the King of Terrors say, Come, Death,—
Come quickly! Thou too wert a stricken deer,
Julian,—God pardon the unhappy hand
That wounded thee !—but whither didst thou go
For healing? Thou hast turned away from Him,
Who saith, Forgive, as ye would be forgiven;
And that the Moorish sword might do thy work,
Received the creed of Mecca : with what fruit
For Spain, let tell her cities sacked, her sons
Slaughtered, her daughters than thine own dear child
More foully wronged, more wretched! For thyself,
Thou hast had thy fill of vengeance, and perhaps
The cup was sweet : but it hath left behind
A bitter relish! Gladly would thy soul
Forget the past; as little canst thou bear
To send into futurity thy thoughts :
And for this Now, what is it, Count, but fear,—
However bravely thou mayst bear thy front,—
Danger, remorse, and stinging obloquy ?

One only hope, one only remedy,
One only refuge yet remains—My life
Is at thy mercy, Count! Call, if thou wilt,
Thy men, and to the Moors deliver me!
Or strike thyself! Death were from any hand
A welcome gift; from thine, and in this cause,
A boon indeed! My latest words on earth
Should tell thee that all sins may be effaced,
Bid thee repent, have faith, and be forgiven!
Strike, Julian, if thou wilt, and send my soul
To intercede for thine, that we may meet,
Thou and thy child and I, beyond the grave.

Thus Roderick spake, and spread his arms as if
He offered to the sword his willing breast,
With looks of passionate persuasion fixed
Upon the Count: who in his first access
Of anger, seemed as though he would have called
His guards to seize the Priest. The attitude
Disarmed him, and that fervent zeal sincere,
And, more than both, the look and voice, which like
A mystery troubled him. Florinda too
Hung on his arm with both her hands, and cried,
O father, wrong him not! he speaks from God!
Life and Salvation are upon his tongue!
Judge thou the value of that faith whereby,
Reflecting on the past, I murmur not,
And to the end of all look on with joy
Of hope assured!
        Peace, innocent! replied
The Count, and from her hold withdrew his arm.
Then, with a gathered brow of mournfulness
Rather than wrath, regarding Roderick, said,
Thou preachest that all sins may be effaced:
Is there forgiveness, Christian, in thy creed
For Roderick's crime?—For Roderick and for thee,
Count Julian, said the Goth, and as he spake
Trembled through every fibre of his frame,
The gate of Heaven is open. Julian threw
His wrathful hand aloft, and cried, Away!
Earth could not hold us both, nor can one Heaven
Contain my deadliest enemy and me!

My father, say not thus! Florinda cried;
I have forgiven him! I have prayed for him!
For him, for thee, and for myself I pour
One constant prayer to Heaven! In passion then
She knelt, and bending back, with arms and face
Raised toward the sky, the supplicant exclaimed,
Redeemer, heal his heart! It is the grief
Which festers there that hath bewildered him!
Save him, Redeemer! by thy precious death
Save, save him, O my God! Then on her face
She fell, and thus with bitterness pursued
In silent throes her agonizing prayer.

Afflict not thus thyself, my child, the Count
Exclaimed; O dearest, be thou comforted:
Set but thy heart at rest, I ask no more!
Peace, dearest, peace!—and weeping as he spake,
He knelt to raise her. Roderick also knelt;
Be comforted, he cried, and rest in faith
That God will hear thy prayers! they must be heard.
He who could doubt the worth of prayers like thine
May doubt of all things! Sainted as thou art
In sufferings here this miracle will be

Thy work and thy reward!
        Then raising her,
They seated her upon the fountain's brink,
And there beside her sate. The moon had risen,
And that fair spring lay blackened half in shade,
Half like a burnished mirror in her light.
By that reflected light Count Julian saw
That Roderick's face was bathed with tears, and pale
As monumental marble. Friend, said he,
Whether thy faith be fabulous, or sent
Indeed from Heaven, its dearest gift to man,
Thy heart is true: and had the mitred Priest
Of Seville been like thee, or hadst thou held
The place he filled;—but this is idle talk,—
Things are as they will be; and we, poor slaves,
Fret in the harness as we may, must drag
The car of Destiny where'er she drives,
Inexorable and blind!
        Oh wretched man!
Cried Roderick, if thou seekëst to assuage
Thy wounded spirit with that deadly drug,
Hell's subtlest venom! look to thine own heart,
Where thou hast Will and Conscience to belie
This juggling sophistry, and lead thee yet
Through penitence to Heaven!
        Whate'er it be
That governs us, in mournful tone the Count
Replied, Fate, Providence, or Allah's will,
Or reckless fortune, still the effect the same,
A World of evil and of misery!
Look where we will we meet it; wheresoe'er
We go we bear it with us. Here we sit
Upon the margin of this peaceful spring,
And oh what volumes of calamity
Would be unfolded here, if either heart
Laid open its sad records! Tell me not
Of goodness! Either in some freak of power
This frame of things was fashioned, then cast off
To take its own wild course, the sport of chance;
Or the Bad Spirit o'er the Good prevails,
And in the eternal conflict hath arisen
Lord of the ascendant!
        Rightly wouldst thou say
Were there no world but this! the Goth replied.
The happiest child of earth that e'er was marked
To be the minion of prosperity,
Richest in corporal gifts and wealth of mind,
Honour and fame attending him abroad,
Peace and all dear domestic joys at home,
And sunshine till the evening of his days
Closed in without a cloud,—even such a man
Would from the gloom and horror of his heart
Confirm thy fatal thought, were this world all!
Oh who could bear the haunting mystery,
If death and retribution did not solve
The riddle, and to heavenliest harmony
Reduce the seeming chaos!—Here we see
The water at its well-head; clear it is,
Not more transpicuous the invisible air;
Pure as an infant's thoughts; and here to life
And good directed all its uses serve.
The herb grows greener on its brink; sweet flowers
Bend o'er the stream that feeds their freshen'd roots;
The red-breast loves it for its wintry haunts;
And when the buds begin to open forth,
Builds near it with his mate their brooding nest;

The thirsty stag with widening nostrils there
Invigorated draws his copious draught;
And there amid its flags the wild-boar stands,
Nor suffering wrong nor meditating hurt.
Through woodlands wild and solitary fields
Unsullied thus it holds its bounteous course;
But when it reaches the resorts of men,
The service of the city there defiles
The tainted stream; corrupt and foul it flows
Through loathsome banks and o'er a bed impure,
Till in the sea, the appointed end to which
Through all its way it hastens, 't is received,
And, losing all pollution, mingles there
In the wide world of waters. So is it
With the great stream of things, if all were seen;
Good the beginning, good the end shall be,
And transitory evil only make
The good end happier. Ages pass away,
Thrones fall, and nations disappear, and worlds
Grow old and go to wreck; the soul alone
Endures, and what she chuseth for herself,
The arbiter of her own destiny,
That only shall be permanent.
                              But guilt,
And all our suffering? said the Count. The Goth
Replied, Repentance taketh sin away,
Death remedies the rest.—Soothed by the strain
Of such discourse, Julian was silent then,
And sate contemplating. Florinda too
Was calm'd: If sore experience may be thought
To teach the uses of adversity,
She said, alas! who better learn'd than I
In that sad school! Methinks if ye would know
How visitations of calamity
Affect the pious soul, 't is shown ye there!
Look yonder at that cloud, which through the sky
Sailing alone, doth cross in her career
The rolling moon! I watched it as it came,
And deem'd the deep opake would blot her beams;
But, melting like a wreath of snow, it hangs
In folds of wavy silver round, and clothes
The orb with richer beauties than her own,
Then passing, leaves her in her light serene.

Thus having said, the pious sufferer sate,
Beholding with fix'd eyes that lovely orb,
Till quiet tears confused in dizzy light
The broken moonbeams. They too by the toil
Of spirit, as by travail of the day
Subdued, were silent, yielding to the hour.
The silver cloud diffusing slowly past,
And now into its airy elements
Resolved is gone; while through the azure depth
Alone in heaven the glorious moon pursues
Her course appointed, with indifferent beams
Shining upon the silent hills around,
And the dark tents of that unholy host,
Who, all unconscious of impending fate,
Take their last slumber there. The camp is still;
The fires have moulder'd, and the breeze which stirs
The soft and snowy embers, just lays bare
At times a red and evanescent light,
Or for a moment wakes a feeble flame.
They by the fountain hear the stream below,
Whose murmurs as the wind arose or fell,
Fuller or fainter reach the ear attuned.

And now the nightingale, not distant far,
Began her solitary song; and pour'd
To the cold moon a richer, stronger strain
Than that with which the lyric lark salutes
The new-born day. Her deep and thrilling song
Seem'd with its piercing melody to reach
The soul, and in mysterious unison
Blend with all thoughts of gentleness and love
Their hearts were open to the healing power
Of nature; and the splendour of the night,
The flow of waters and that sweetest lay
Came to them like a copious evening dew
Falling on vernal herbs which thirst for rain.

XXII.

THE MOORISH COUNCIL.

Thus they beside the fountain sate, of food
And rest forgetful, when a messenger
Summon'd Count Julian to the Leader's tent.
In council there at that late hour he found
The assembled Chiefs, on sudden tidings call'd
Of unexpected weight from Cordoba.
Jealous that Abdalazis had assumed
A regal state, affecting in his court
The forms of Gothic sovereignty, the Moors,
Whom artful spirits of ambitious mould
Stirr'd up, had risen against him in revolt:
And he who late had in the Caliph's name
Ruled from the Ocean to the Pyrenees,
A mutilate and headless carcass now,
From pitying hands received beside the road
A hasty grave scarce hidden there from dogs
And ravens, nor from wintry rains secure.[57]
She, too, who in the wreck of Spain preserved
Her queenly rank, the wife of Roderick first,
Of Abdalazis after, and to both
Alike unhappy, shared the ruin now
Her counsels had brought on; for she had led
The infatuate Moor, in dangerous vauntery,
To these aspiring forms,—so should he gain
Respect and honour from the Musselmen,
She said, and that the obedience of the Goths
Follow'd the sceptre. In an evil hour
She gave the counsel, and in evil hour
He lent a willing ear; the popular rage
Fell on them both; and they to whom her name
Had been a mark for mockery and reproach,
Shudder'd with human horror at her fate.
Ayub was heading the wild anarchy;
But where the cement of authority
Is wanting, all things there are dislocate:
The mutinous soldiery, by every cry
Of rumour set in wild career, were driven
By every gust of passion, setting up
One hour, what in the impulse of the next,
Equally unreasoning, they destroy'd: thus all
Was in misrule where uproar gave the law,
And ere from far Damascus they could learn
The Caliph's pleasure, many a moon must pass.
What should be done? should Abulcacem march
To Cordoba, and in the Caliph's name
Assume the power which to his rank in arms
Rightly devolved, restoring thus the reign

Of order? or pursue with quicken'd speed
The end of this great armament, and crush
Rebellion first, then to domestic ills
Apply his undivided mind and force
Victorious? What in this emergency
Was Julian's counsel, Abulcacem asked;
Should they accomplish soon their enterprise?
Or would the insurgent infidels prolong
The contest, seeking by protracted war
To weary them, and trusting in the strength
Of these wild hills?
     Julian replied, The Chief
Of this revolt is wary, resolute,
Of approved worth in war: a desperate part
He for himself deliberately hath chosen,
Confiding in the hereditary love
Borne to him by these hardy mountaineers,
A love which his own noble qualities
Have strengthen'd, so that every heart is his.
When ye can bring them to the open proof
Of battle, ye will find them in his cause
Lavish of life; but well they know the strength
Of their own fastnesses, the mountain paths
Impervious to pursuit, the vantages
Of rock, and pass, and woodland, and ravine;
And hardly will ye tempt them to forego
These natural aids wherein they put their trust
As in their stubborn spirit, each alike
Deem'd by themselves invincible, and so
By Roman found and Goth,—beneath whose sway,
Slowly persuaded rather than subdued
They came, and still through every change retain'd
Their manners obstinate and barbarous speech.
My counsel, therefore, is, that we secure
With strong increase of force the adjacent posts,
And chiefly Gegio, leaving them so manned
As may abate the hope of enterprise,
Their strength being told. Time in a strife like this
Becomes the ally of those who trust in him :
Make then with Time your covenant. Old feuds
May disunite the chiefs : some may be gained
By fair entreaty, others by the stroke
Of nature, or of policy, cut off.
This was the counsel which in Cordoba
I offered Abdalazis : in ill hour
Rejecting it, he sent upon this war
His father's faithful friend ! Dark are the ways
Of Destiny ! had I been at his side
Old Muza would not now have mourned his age
Left childless, nor had Ayub dared defy
The Caliph's represented power. The case
Calls for thy instant presence, with the weight
Of thy legitimate authority.

Julian, said Orpas, turning from beneath
His turban to the Count a crafty eye,
Thy daughter is returned : doth she not bring
Some tidings of the movements of the foe?
The Count replied, When child and parent meet
First reconciled from discontents which wrung
The hearts of both, ill should their converse be
Of warlike matters ! There hath been no time
For such inquiries, neither should I think
To ask her touching that for which I know
She hath neither eye nor thought.
     There was a time,

Orpas with smile malignant thus replied,
When in the progress of the Caliph's arms
Count Julian's daughter had an interest
Which touched her nearly! But her turn is served,
And hatred of Prince Orpas may beget
Indifference to the cause. Yet Destiny
Still guideth to the service of the faith
The wayward heart of woman; for as one
Delivered Roderick to the avenging sword,
So hath another at this hour betrayed
Pelayo to his fall. His sister came
At nightfall to my tent, a fugitive.
She tells me that on learning our approach,
The rebel to a cavern in the hills
Had sent his wife and children, and with them
Those of his followers, thinking there concealed
They might be safe. She, moved by injuries
Which stung her spirit, on the way escaped,
And for revenge will guide us. In reward
She asks her brother's forfeiture of lands
In marriage with Numacian : something too
Touching his life, that for her services
It might be spared, she said :—an after-thought
To salve decorum, and if conscience wake
Serve as a sop : but when the sword shall smite
Pelayo and his dangerous race, I ween
That a thin kerchief will dry all the tears
The Lady Guisla sheds!
     'T is the old taint!
Said Julian mournfully : from her mother's womb
She brought the inbred wickedness which now
In ripe infection blossoms. Woman, woman,
Still to the Goths art thou the instrument
Of overthrow; thy virtue and thy vice
Fatal alike to them!
     Say rather, cried
The insidious renegade, that Allah thus
By woman punisheth the idolatry
Of those who raise a woman to the rank
Of godhead, calling on their Mary's name
With senseless prayers. In vain shall they invoke
Her trusted succour now! like silly birds
By fear betrayed, they fly into the toils!
And this Pelayo, who in lengthened war,
Baffling our force, has thought perhaps to reign
Prince of the Mountains, when we hold his wife
And offspring at our mercy, must himself
Come to the lure.
     Enough, the Leader cried:
This unexpected work of favouring Fate
Opens an easy way to our desires,
And renders farther counsel needless now.
Great is the Prophet whose protecting power
Goes with the faithful forth! the rebels' days
Are numbered! Allah hath delivered them
Into our hands!
     So saying he arose;
The Chiefs withdrew : Orpas alone remained
Obedient to his indicated will.
The event, said Abulcacem, hath approved
Thy judgment in all points; his daughter comes
At the first summons even as thou saidst;
Her errand with the insurgents done, she brings
Their well-concerted project back, a safe
And unsuspected messenger;—the Moor,—
The shallow Moor,—must see and not perceive;

Must hear and understand not; yea must bear,
Poor easy fool, to serve their after mirth,
A part in his own undoing! But just Heaven
With this unlooked-for incident hath marred
Their complots, and the sword shall cut their web
Of treason.

      Well, the renegade replied,
Thou knowest Count Julian's spirit, quick in wiles,
In act audacious. Baffled now, he thinks
Either by instant warning to apprise
The rebels of their danger, or preserve
The hostages when fallen into our power,
Till secret craft contrive, or open force
Win their enlargement. Haply too he dreams
Of Cordoba, the avenger and the friend
Of Abdalazis, in that cause to arm
Moor against Moor, preparing for himself
The victory o'er the enfeebled conquerors.
Success in treason hath emboldened him,
And power but serves him for fresh treachery, false
To Roderick first, and to the Caliph now.
The guilt, said Abulcacem, is confirmed,
The sentence past; all that is now required
Is to strike sure and safely. He hath with him
A veteran force devoted to his will,
Whom to provoke were perilous; nor less
Of peril lies there in delay: what course
Between these equal dangers should we steer?

They have been trained beneath him in the wars
Of Africa, the renegade replied;
Men are they who, from their youth up, have found
Their occupation and their joy in arms;
Indifferent to the cause for which they fight,
But faithful to their leader, who hath won
By licence largely given, yet tempered still
With exercise of firm authority,
Their whole devotion. Vainly should we seek
By proof of Julian's guilt to pacify
Such martial spirits, unto whom all creeds
And countries are alike; but take away
Their head, and forthwith their fidelity
Goes at the market price. The act must be
Sudden and secret; poison is too slow.
Thus it may best be done; the Mountaineers,
Doubtless, ere long will rouse us with some spur
Of sudden enterprise: at such a time
A trusty minister approaching him
May smite him, so that all shall think the spear
Comes from the hostile troops.

      Right, counsellor!
Cried Abulcacem, thou shalt have his lauds,
The proper meed of thy fidelity:
His daughter thou mayest take or leave. Go now
And find a faithful instrument to put
Our purpose in effect!—And when 't is done,
The Moor, as Orpas from the tent withdrew,
Muttering pursued,—look for a like reward
Thyself! that restless head of wickedness
In the grave will brood no treasons. Other babes
Scream when the Devil, as they spring to life,
Infects them with his touch; but thou didst stretch
Thy arms to meet him, and like mother's milk
Suck the congenial evil! Thou hast tried
Both laws, and, were there aught to gain, would prove
A third as readily; but when thy sins

Are weighed, 't will be against an empty scale,
And neither Prophet will avail thee then!

XXIII.

THE VALE OF COVADONGA.

THE camp is stirring, and ere day hath dawned
The tents are struck. Early they rise whom hope
Awakens, and they travel fast with whom
She goes companion of the way. By noon
Hath Abulcacem in his speed attained
The vale of Cangas. Well the trusty scouts
Observe his march, and fleet as mountain roes,
From post to post with instantaneous speed
The warning bear: none else is nigh; the vale
Hath been deserted, and Pelayo's hall
Is open to the foe, who on the tower
Hoist their white signal-flag. [58] In Sella's stream
The misbelieving multitude perform,
With hot and hasty hand, their noontide rite,
Then hurryingly repeat the Impostor's prayer.
Here they divide; the Chieftain halts with half
The host, retaining Julian and his men,
Whom where the valley widened he disposed,
Liable to first attack, that so the deed
Of murder planned with Orpas might be done.
The other force the Moor Alcahman led,
Whom Guisla guided up Pionia's stream
Eastward to Soto. Ibrahim went with him,
Proud of Granada's snowy heights subdued,
And boasting of his skill in mountain war;
Yet sure he deemed an easier victory
Awaited him this day. Little, quoth he,
Weens the vain Mountaineer who puts his trust
In dens and rocky fastnesses, how close
Destruction is at hand! Belike he thinks
The Humma's happy wings have shadowed him, [59]
And therefore Fate with royalty must crown
His chosen head! Pity the scymitar
With its rude edge so soon should interrupt
The pleasant dream!

      There can be no escape
For those who in the cave seek shelter, cried
Alcahman; yield they must, or from their holes
Like bees we smoke them out. The Chief perhaps
May reign awhile King of the wolves and bears,
Till his own subjects hunt him down, or kites
And crows divide what hunger may have left
Upon his ghastly limbs. Happier for him
That destiny should this day to our hands
Deliver him; short would be his sufferings then;
And we right joyfully should in one hour
Behold our work accomplished, and his race
Extinct.

      Thus these in mockery and in thoughts
Of bloody triumph, to the future blind,
Indulged the scornful vein; nor deemed that they
Whom to the sword's unsparing edge they doomed,
Even then in joyful expectation prayed
To Heaven for their approach, and, at their post
Prepared, were trembling with excess of hope.
Here in these mountain straits the Mountaineer
Had felt his country's strength insuperable;
Here he had prayed to see the Musselman

55

With all his myriads ; therefore had he looked
To Covadonga as a sanctuary
Apt for concealment, easy of defence ;
And Guisla's flight, though to his heart it sent
A pang more poignant for their mother's sake,
Yet did it further in its consequence
His hope and project, surer than decoy
Well-laid, or best-concerted stratagem.
That sullen and revengeful mind, he knew,
Would follow to the extremity of guilt
Its long fore-purposed shame : the toils were laid,
And she who by the Musselmen full sure
Thought on her kindred her revenge to wreak,
Led the Moors in.
          Count Pedro and his son
Were hovering with the main Asturian force
In the wider vale to watch occasion there,
And with hot onset when the alarm began
Pursue the vantage. In the fated straits
Of Deva had the King disposed the rest :
Amid the hanging woods, and on the cliffs,
A long mile's length on either side its bed,
They lay. The lever and the axe and saw
Had skilfully been plied ; and trees and stones,
A dread artillery, ranged on crag and shelf
And steep descent, were ready at the word
Precipitate to roll resistless down.
The faithful maiden not more wistfully
Looks for the day that brings her lover home ;—
Scarce more impatiently the horse endures
The rein, when loud and shrill the hunter's horn
Rings in his joyous ears, than at their post
The Mountaineers await their certain prey.
Yet mindful of their Prince's order, oft
And solemnly enforced, with eagerness
Subdued by minds well-mastered, they expect
The appointed signal.
               Hand must not be raised,
Foot stirred, nor voice be uttered, said the Chief.
Till the word pass : impatience would mar all.
God hath delivered over to your hands
His enemies and ours, so we but use
The occasion wisely. Not till the word pass
From man to man transmitted, « In the name
« Of God, for Spain and vengeance,» let a hand
Be lifted ; on obedience all depends.
Their march below with noise of horse and foot,
And haply with the clang of instruments,
Might drown all other signal : this is sure.
But wait it calmly ; it will not be given
Till the whole line hath entered in the toils.
Comrades, be patient, so shall none escape
Who once set foot within these straits of death.
Thus had Pelayo on the Mountaineers
With frequent and impressive charge enforced
The needful exhortation. This alone
He doubted, that the Musselmen might see
The perils of the vale, and warily
Forbear to enter. But they thought to find,
As Guisla told, the main Asturian force
Seeking concealment there, no other aid
Soliciting from these their native hills ;
And that the babes and women having fallen
In thraldom, they would lay their weapons down,
And supplicate forgiveness for their sake.
Nor did the Moors perceive in what a strait

They entered ; for the morn had risen o'ercast,
And when the Sun had reached the height of heaven,
Dimly his pale and beamless orb was seen
Moving through mist. A soft and gentle rain,
Scarce heavier than the summer's evening dew,
Descended,—through so still an atmosphere,
That every leaf upon the moveless trees
Was studded o'er with rain-drops, bright and full,
None falling till from its own weight o'erswoln
The motion came.
          Low on the mountain side
The fleecy vapour hung, and in its veil
With all their dreadful preparations wrapt
The Mountaineers :—in breathless hope they lay,
Some blessing God in silence for the power
This day vouchsafed ; others with fervency
Of prayer and vow invoked the Mother-Maid,
Beseeching her that in this favouring hour
She would be strongly with them. From below
Meantime distinct they heard the passing tramp
Of horse and foot, continuous as the sound
Of Deva's stream, and barbarous tongues commixt
With laughter, and with frequent shouts,—for all
Exultant came, expecting sure success ;
Blind wretches, over whom the ruin hung !

They say, quoth one, that though the Prophet's soul
Doth with the black-eyed Houris bathe in bliss,
Life hath not left his body, [60] which bears up
By its miraculous power the holy tomb,
And holds it at Medina in the air
Buoyant between the temple's floor and roof :
And there the Angels fly to him with news
From East, West, North, and South, of what befalls
His faithful people. If when he shall hear
The tale of this day's work, he should for joy
Forget that he is dead, and walk abroad,—
It were as good a miracle as when
He sliced the moon! Sir Angel hear me now,
Whoe'er thou be'st who art about to speed
From Spain to Araby! when thou hast got
The Prophet's ear, be sure thou tellëst him
How bravely Ghauleb did his part to-day,
And with what special reverence he alone
Desired thee to commend him to his grace!—
Fie on thee, scoffer that thou art! replied
His comrade ; thou wilt never leave these gibes
Till some commissioned arrow through the teeth
Shall nail the offending tongue. Hast thou not heard
How when our clay is leavened first with life,
The ministering Angel brings it from that spot
Whereon 't is written in the eternal book
That soul and body must their parting take,
And earth to earth return? [61] How knowëst thou
But that the spirit who compounded thee,
To distant Syria from this very vale
Bore thy component dust, and Azrael here
Awaits thee at this hour?—Little thought he
Who spake, that in that valley at that hour
One death awaited both!
                    Thus they pursued
Toward the cave their inauspicious way.
Weak childhood there and ineffective age
In the chambers of the rock were placed secure ;
But of the women, all whom with the babes
Maternal care detained not, were aloft

To aid in the destruction; by the side
Of fathers, brethren, husbands, stationed there
They watch and pray. Pelayo in the cave
With the venerable primate took his post.
Ranged on the rising cliffs on either hand,
Vigilant sentinels with eye intent
Observe his movements, when to take the word
And pass it forward. He in arms complete
Stands in the portal : a stern majesty
Reigned in his countenance severe that hour,
And in his eye a deep and dreadful joy
Shone, as advancing up the vale he saw
The Moorish banners. God hath blinded them!
He cried; the measure of their crimes is full!
O Vale of Deva, famous shalt thou be
From this day forth for ever; and to these
Thy springs shall unborn generations come
In pilgrimage, and hallow with their prayers
The cradle of their native monarchy!

There was a stirring in the air, the sun
Prevailed, and gradually the brightening mist
Began to rise and melt. A jutting crag
Upon the right projected o'er the stream,
Not farther from the cave than a strong hand
Expert, with deadly aim, might cast the spear,
Or a strong voice, pitched to full compass, make
Its clear articulation heard distinct.
A venturous dalesman, once ascending there
To rob the eagle's nest, had fallen, and hung
Among the heather, wondrously preserved :
Therefore had he with pious gratitude
Placed on that overhanging brow a Cross,
Tall as the mast of some light fisher's skiff,
And from the vale conspicuous. As the Moors
Advanced, the Chieftain in the van was seen
Known by his arms, and from the crag a voice
Pronounced his name,—Alcahman, hoa! look up
Alcahman! As the floating mist drew up,
It had divided there, and opened round
The Cross; part clinging to the rock beneath,
Hovering and waving part in fleecy folds,
A canopy of silver light condensed
To shape and substance. In the midst there stood
A female form, one hand upon the Cross,
The other raised in menacing act: below
Loose flowed her raiment, but her breast was armed,
And helmeted her head. The Moor turned pale,
For on the walls of Auria he had seen
That well-known figure, and had well believed
She rested with the dead. What, hoa, she cried,
Alcahman! In the name of all who fell
At Auria in the massacre, this hour
I summon thee before the throne of God
To answer for the innocent blood! This hour,
Moor, Miscreant, Murderer, Child of Hell, this hour
I summon thee to judgment!—In the name
Of God! for Spain and Vengeance!
                    Thus she closed
Her speech; for taking from the Primate's hand
That oaken cross which at the sacring rites
Had served for crosier, at the cavern's mouth
Pelayo lifted it and gave the word.
From voice to voice on either side it past
With rapid repetition,—In the name
Of God! for Spain and Vengeance! and forthwith

On either side along the whole defile
The Asturians shouting in the name of God,
Set the whole ruin loose! huge trunks and stones,
And loosened crags, down down they rolled with rush
And bound, and thundering force. Such was the fall
As when some city by the labouring earth
Heaved from its strong foundations is cast down,
And all its dwellings, towers, and palaces
In one wide desolation prostrated.
From end to end of that long strait, the crash
Was heard continuous, and commixt with sounds
More dreadful, shrieks of horror and despair,
And death,—the wild and agonizing cry
Of that whole host in one destruction whelmed.
Vain was all valour there, all martial skill;
The valiant arm is helpless now; the feet
Swift in the race avail not now to save;
They perish, all their thousands perish there,—62
Horsemen and infantry they perish all,—
The outward armour and the bones within
Broken and bruised and crushed. Echo prolonged
The long uproar : a silence then ensued,
Through which the sound of Deva's stream was heard,
A lonely voice of waters, wild and sweet :
The lingering groan, the faintly-uttered prayer,
The louder curses of despairing death,
Ascended not so high. Down from the cave
Pelayo hastes, the Asturians hasten down,
Fierce and immitigable down they speed
On all sides, and along the vale of blood
The avenging sword did mercy's work that hour.

XXIV.

RODERICK AND COUNT JULIAN.

THOU hast been busy, Death, this day, and yet
But half thy work is done! The Gates of Hell
Are thronged, yet twice ten thousand spirits more,
Who from their warm and healthful tenements
Fear no divorce, must ere the sun go down
Enter the world of woe! the Gate of Heaven
Is open too, and Angels round the throne
Of Mercy on their golden harps this day
Shall sing the triumphs of Redeeming Love.

There was a Church at Cangas dedicate
To that Apostle unto whom his Lord
Had given the keys: a humble edifice,
Whose rude and time-worn structure suited well.
That vale among the mountains. Its low roof
With stone plants and with moss was overgrown,
Short fern, and richer weeds which from the eaves
Hung their long tresses down. White lichens clothed
The sides, save where the ivy spread, which bowered
The porch, and clustering round the pointed wall,
Wherein two bells, each open to the wind,
Hung side by side, threaded with hairy shoots
The double niche; and climbing to the cross,
Wreathed it and half concealed its sacred form
With bushy tufts luxuriant. Here in the font,—
Borne thither with rejoicings and with prayers
Of all the happy land, who saw in him
The lineage of their ancient Chiefs renewed,—
The Prince had been immersed : and here within

An oaken galilee, now black with age,
His old Iberian ancestors were laid.

Two stately oaks stood near, in the full growth
Of many a century.   They had flourished there
Before the Gothic sword was felt in Spain,
And when the ancient sceptre of the Goths
Was broken, there they flourished still.   Their boughs
Mingled on high, and stretching wide around,
Formed a deep shade, beneath which canopy
Upon the ground Count Julian's board was spread,
For to his daughter he had left his tent
Pitched for her use hard by.   He at the board
Sate with his trusted Captains, Gunderick,
Felix, and Miro, Theudered and Paul,
Basil and Cottila, and Virimar,
Men through all fortunes faithful to their Lord,
And to that old and tried fidelity,
By personal love and honour held in ties
Strong as religious bonds.   As there they sate,
In the distant vale a rising dust was seen,
And frequent flash of steel,—the flying fight
Of men who, by a fiery foe pursued,
Put forth their coursers at full speed, to reach
The aid in which they trust.   Up sprung the Chiefs,
And hastily taking helm and shield, and spear,
Sped to their post.

> Amid the chesnut groves
On Sella's side, Alphonso had in charge
To watch the foe; a prowling band came nigh,
Whom with the ardour of impetuous youth
He charged and followed them in close pursuit:
Quick succours joined them; and the strife grew hot,
Ere Pedro hastening to bring off his son,
Or Julian and his Captains,—bent alike
That hour to abstain from combat, (for by this
Full sure they deemed Alcahman had secured
The easy means of certain victory,)—
Could reach the spot.   Both thus in their intent
According, somewhat had they now allayed
The fury of the fight, though still spears flew,
And strokes of sword and mace were interchanged,
When passing through the troop a Moor came up
On errand from the Chief, to Julian sent;
A fatal errand fatally performed
For Julian, for the Chief, and for himself,
And all that host of Musselmen he brought;
For while with well-dissembled words he lured
The warrior's ear, the dexterous ruffian marked
The favouring moment and unguarded place,
And plunged a javelin in his side.   The Count
Fell, but in falling called to Cottila,
Treachery! the Moor! the Moor!—He too on whom
He called had seen the blow from whence it came,
And seized the murderer.   Miscreant! he exclaimed,
Who set thee on?   The Musselman, who saw
His secret purpose baffled, undismayed,
Replies, What I have done is authorized;
To punish treachery and prevent worse ill
Orpas and Abulcacem sent me here;
The service of the Caliph and the Faith
Required the blow.

> The Prophet and the Fiend
Reward thee then! cried Cottila; meantime
Take thou from me thy proper earthly meed;
Villain!—and lifting, as he spake, the sword,

He smote him on the neck: the trenchant blade
Through vein and artery passed and yielding bone;
And on the shoulder, as the assassin dropt,
His head half-severed fell.   The curse of God
Fall on the Caliph and the Faith and thee!
Stamping for anguish, Cottila pursued;
African dogs! thus is it ye requite
Our services?—But dearly shall ye pay
For this day's work!—O fellow-soldiers, here,
Stretching his hands toward the host, he cried,
Behold your noble leader basely slain!
He who for twenty years hath led us forth
To war, and brought us home with victory,
Here he lies foully murdered,—by the Moors,—
Those whom he trusted, whom he served so well!
Our turn is next! but neither will we wait
Idly, nor tamely fall!

> Amid the grief,
Tumult, and rage, of those who gathered round,
When Julian could be heard, I have yet life,
He said, for vengeance.   Virimar, speed thou
To yonder Mountaineers, and tell their Chiefs
That Julian's veteran army joins this day
Pelayo's standard!   The command devolves
On Gunderick.   Fellow-soldiers, who so well
Redressed the wrongs of your old General,
Ye will not let his death go unrevenged!—
Tears then were seen on many an iron cheek,
And groans were heard from many a resolute heart,
And vows with imprecations mixt went forth,
And curses checked by sobs.   Bear me apart,
Said Julian, with a faint and painful voice,
And let me see my daughter ere I die.

Scarce had he spoken when the pitying throng
Divide before her.   Eagerly she came;
A deep and fearful lustre in her eye,
A look of settled woe,—pale, deadly pale,
Yet to no lamentations giving way,
Nor tears nor groans;—within her breaking heart
She bore the grief, and kneeling solemnly
Beside him, raised her awful hands to heaven,
And cried, Lord God! be with him in this hour.—
Two things have I to think of, O my child,
Vengeance and thee, said Julian.   For the first
I have provided: what remains of life
As best may comfort thee may so be best
Employed; let me be borne within the church,
And thou, with that good man who follows thee,
Attend me there.

> Thus when Florinda heard
Her father speak, a gleam of heavenly joy
Shone through the anguish of her countenance.
O gracious God, she cried, my prayers are heard;
Now let me die!—They raised him from the earth;
He, knitting as they lifted him his brow,
Drew in through open lips and teeth firm-closed
His painful breath, and on the lance laid hand,
Lest its long shaft should shake the mortal wound.
Gently his men with slow and steady step
Their suffering burthen bore, and in the Church
Before the altar laid him down, his head
Upon Florinda's knees.—Now, friends, said he,
Farewell.   I ever hoped to meet my death
Among ye, like a soldier,—but not thus!
Go join the Asturians; and in after years,

When of your old commander ye shall talk,
How well he loved his followers, what he was
In battle, and how basely he was slain,
Let not the tale its fit completion lack,
But say how bravely was his death revenged.
Vengeance! in that good word doth Julian make
His testament; your faithful swords must give
The will its full performance.   Leave me now;
I have done with worldly things.   Comrades, farewell,
And love my memory!

          They with copious tears
Of burning anger, grief exasperating
Their rage, and fury giving force to grief,
Hastened to form their ranks against the Moors.
Julian meantime toward the altar turned
His languid eyes: That Image, is it not
St Peter, he inquired, he who denied
His Lord and was forgiven?—Roderick rejoined,
It is the Apostle; and may that same Lord,
O Julian, to thy soul's salvation bless
The seasonable thought!

              The dying Count
Then fixed upon the Goth his earnest eyes.
No time, said he, is this for bravery,
As little for dissemblance.   I would fain
Die in the faith wherein my fathers died,
Whereto they pledged me in mine infancy:—
A soldier's habits, he pursued, have steeled
My spirit, and perhaps I do not fear
This passage as I ought.   But if to feel
That I have sinned, and from my soul renounce
The Impostor's faith, which never in that soul
Obtained a place,—if at the Saviour's feet,
Laden with guilt, to cast myself and cry,
Lord, I believe! help thou my unbelief!—
If this in the sincerity of death
Sufficeth,—father, let me from thy lips
Receive the assurances with which the Church
Doth bless the dying Christian.

               Roderick raised
His eyes to Heaven, and crossing on his breast
His open palms, Mysterious are thy ways
And merciful, O gracious Lord! he cried,
Who to this end hast thus been pleased to lead
My wandering steps! O Father, this thy son
Hath sinned and gone astray: but hast not Thou
Said, when the sinner from his evil ways
Turneth, that he shall save his soul alive,
And Angels at the sight rejoice in Heaven!
Therefore do I, in thy most holy name,
Into thy family receive again
Him who was lost, and in that name absolve
The Penitent.—So saying, on the head
Of Julian solemnly he laid his hands.
Then to the altar tremblingly he turned,
And took the bread, and breaking it, pursued,
Julian! receive from me the Bread of Life! [63]
In silence reverently the Count partook
The reconciling rite, and to his lips
Roderick then held the consecrated cup.

Me too! exclaimed Florinda, who till then
Had listened speechlessly: Thou Man of God,
I also must partake! The Lord hath heard
My prayers! one sacrament,—one hour,—one grave,—
One resurrection!

          That dread office done,
Count Julian with amazement saw the Priest
Kneel down before him.   By the sacrament
Which we have here partaken, Roderick cried,
In this most awful moment; by that hope,—
That holy faith which comforts thee in death,
Grant thy forgiveness, Julian, ere thou diest!
Behold the man who most hath injured thee!
Roderick, the wretched Goth, the guilty cause
Of all thy guilt,—the unworthy instrument
Of thy redemption,—kneels before thee here,
And prays to be forgiven!

             Roderick! exclaimed
The dying Count,—Roderick!—and from the floor
With violent effort half he raised himself;
The spear hung heavy in his side, and pain
And weakness overcame him, that he fell
Back on his daughter's lap.   O Death, cried he,—
Passing his hand across his cold damp brow,—
Thou tamëst the strong limb, and conquerëst
The stubborn heart!   But yesterday I said
One Heaven could not contain mine enemy
And me; and now I lift my dying voice
To say, Forgive me, Lord, as I forgive
Him who hath done the wrong!—He closed his eyes
A moment; then with sudden impulse cried,—
Roderick, thy wife is dead,—the Church hath power
To free thee from thy vows,—the broken heart
Might yet be healed, the wrong redressed, the throne
Rebuilt by that same hand which pulled it down,
And these curst Africans—Oh for a month
Of that waste life which millions misbestow!—
His voice was passionate, and in his eye
With glowing animation while he spake
The vehement spirit shone: its effort soon
Was past, and painfully with feeble breath
In slow and difficult utterance he pursued,—
Vain hope, if all the evil was ordained,
And this wide wreck the will and work of Heaven,
We but the poor occasion! Death will make
All clear, and joining us in better worlds,
Complete our union there! Do for me now
One friendly office more :—draw forth the spear,
And free me from this pain!—Receive his soul,
Saviour! exclaimed the Goth, as he performed
The fatal service.   Julian cried, O friend!—
True friend!—and gave to him his dying hand.
Then said he to Florinda, I go first,
Thou followest!—kiss me, child!—and now good
     night!

When from her father's body she arose,
Her cheek was flushed, and in her eyes there beamed
A wilder brightness.   On the Goth she gazed,
While underneath the emotions of that hour
Exhausted life gave way.   O God! she said,
Lifting her hands, thou hast restored me all,—
All—in one hour!—and round his neck she threw
Her arms and cried, My Roderick! mine in Heaven!
Groaning, he claspt her close, and in that act
And agony her happy spirit fled.

XXV.

RODERICK IN BATTLE.

EIGHT thousand men had to Asturias marched
Beneath Count Julian's banner; the remains
Of that brave army which in Africa
So well against the Musselman made head,
Till sense of injuries insupportable,
And raging thirst of vengeance, overthrew
Their leader's noble spirit.   To revenge
His quarrel, twice that number left their bones,
Slain in unnatural battle, on the field
Of Xeres, where the sceptre from the Goths
By righteous Heaven was reft.   Others had fallen
Consumed in sieges, alway by the Moor
To the front of war opposed.   The policy,
With whatsoever show of honour cloaked,
Was gross, and this surviving band had oft
At their carousals of the flagrant wrong
Held such discourse as stirs the mounting blood,
The common danger with one discontent
Affecting chiefs and men.   Nor had the bonds
Of rooted discipline and faith attached,
Thus long restrained them, had they not known well
That Julian in their just resentment shared,
And fixed their hopes on him.   Slight impulse now
Sufficed to make these fiery martialists
Break forth in open fury; and though first
Count Pedro listened with suspicious ear
To Julian's dying errand, deeming it
Some new decoy of treason,—when he found
A second legate followed Virimar,
And then a third, and saw the turbulence
Of the camp, and how against the Moors in haste
They formed their lines, he knew that Providence
This hour had for his country interposed,
And in such faith advanced to use the aid
Thus wonderously ordained.   The eager Chiefs
Hasten to greet him, Cottila and Paul,
Basil and Miro, Theudered, Gunderick,
Felix, and all who held authority;
The zealous services of their brave host
They proffered, and besought him instantly
To lead against the African their force
Combined, and in good hour assail a foe
Divided, not for such attack prepared.

While thus they communed, Roderick from the church
Came forth, and seeing Pedro, bent his way
Toward them.   Sirs, said he, the Count is dead:
He died a Christian, reconciled to Heaven,
In faith; and when his daughter had received
His dying breath, her spirit too took flight.
One sacrament, one death, united them;
And I beseech ye, ye who from the work
Of blood which lies before us may return,—
If, as I think, it should not be my fate—
That in one grave with Christian ceremonies
Ye lay them side by side.   In Heaven I ween
They are met through mercy:—ill befall the man
Who should in death divide them!—Then he turned
His speech to Pedro in an under voice;
The King, said he, I know with noble mind
Will judge of the departed; christian-like

He died, and with a manly penitence:
They who condemn him most should call to mind
How grievous was the wrong which maddened him;
Be that remembered in his history,
And let no shame be offered his remains. 64

As Pedro would have answered, a loud cry
Of menacing imprecation from the troops
Arose; for Orpas, by the Moorish Chief
Sent to allay the storm his villany
Had stirred, came hastening on a milk-white steed,
And at safe distance having checked the rein,
Beckoned for parley.   'T was Orelio
On which he rode, Roderick's own battle-horse,
Who from his master's hand had wont to feed,
And with a glad docility obey
His voice familiar.   At the sight the Goth
Started, and indignation to his soul
Brought back the thoughts and feelings of old time.
Suffer me, Count, he cried, to answer him,
And hold these back the while! Thus having said,
He waited no reply, but as he was,
Bareheaded, in his weeds, and all unarmed,
Advanced toward the renegade.   Sir Priest,
Quoth Orpas as he came, I hold no talk
With thee; my errand is with Gunderick
And the Captains of the host, to whom I bring
Such liberal offers and clear proof—
                                    The Goth,
Breaking with scornful voice his speech, exclaimed,
What, could no steed but Roderick's serve thy turn?
I should have thought some sleek and sober mule
Long trained in shackles to procession pace,
More suited to my lord of Seville's use
Than this good war-horse,—he who never bore
A villain, until Orpas crost his back!—
Wretch! cried the astonished renegade, and stoopt,
Foaming with anger, from the saddle-bow
To reach his weapon.   Ere the hasty hand
Trembling in passion could perform its will,
Roderick had seized the reins.   How now, he cried,
Orelio! old companion,—my good horse,—
Off with this recreant burthen !—And with that
He raised his hand, and reared and backed the steed,
To that remembered voice and arm of power
Obedient.   Down the helpless traitor fell
Violently thrown, and Roderick over him
Thrice led with just and unrelenting hand
The trampling hoofs.   Go, join Witiza now,
Where he lies howling, the avenger cried,
And tell him Roderick sent thee!
                                    At that sight,
Count Julian's soldiers and the Asturian host
Set up a shout, a joyful shout, which rung
Wide through the welkin.   Their exulting cry
With louder acclamation was renewed,
When from the expiring miscreant's neck they saw
That Roderick took the shield, and round his own
Hung it, and vaulted in the seat.   My horse!
My noble horse! he cried, with flattering hand
Patting his high-arched neck! the renegade,
I thank him for 't, hath kept thee daintily!
Orelio, thou art in thy beauty still,
Thy pride and strength! Orelio, my good horse,
Once more thou bearest to the field thy Lord,
He who so oft hath fed and cherished thee,

He for whose sake, wherever thou wert seen,
Thou wert by all men honoured.   Once again
Thou hast thy proper master! Do thy part
As thou wert wont; and bear him gloriously,
My beautiful Orelio,—to the last—
The happiest of his fields!—Then he drew forth
The scymitar, and waving it aloft,
Rode toward the troops; its unaccustomed shape
Disliked him: Renegade in all things! cried
The Goth, and cast it from him ; to the Chiefs
Then said, If I have done ye service here,
Help me, I pray you, to a Spanish sword!
The trustiest blade that e'er in Bilbilis
Was dipt, would not to-day be misbestowed
On this right hand!—Go, some one, Gunderick cried,
And bring Count Julian's sword. Whoe'er thou art,
The worth which thou hast shown avenging him
Entitles thee to wear it. But thou goest
For battle unequipped;—haste there and strip
Yon villain of his armour!

                    Late he spake,
So fast the Moors came on. It matters not,
Replied the Goth; there's many a mountaineer,
Who in no better armour cased this day
Than his wonted leathern gipion,[65] will be found
In the hottest battle, yet bring off untouched
The unguarded life he ventures—Taking then
Count Julian's sword, he fitted round his wrist
The chain, and eying the elaborate steel
With stern regard of joy, The African
Under unhappy stars was born, he cried,
Who tastes thy edge!—Make ready for the charge!
They come—they come!—On, brethren, to the field,—
The word is Vengeance!

                    Vengeance was the word;
From man to man, and rank to rank it past,
By every heart enforced, by every voice
Sent forth in loud defiance of the foe.
The enemy in shriller sounds returned
Their Akbar, and the Prophet's trusted name.
The horsemen lowered their spears, the infantry
Deliberately with slow and steady step
Advanced ; the bow-strings twang'd, and arrows hissed,
And javelins hurtled by. Anon the hosts
Met in the shock of battle, horse and man
Conflicting : shield struck shield, and sword and mace
And curtle-axe on helm and buckler rung;
Armour was riven, and wounds were interchanged,
And many a spirit from its mortal hold
Hurried to bliss or bale. Well did the Chiefs
Of Julian's army in that hour support
Their old esteem; and well Count Pedro there
Enhanced his former praise; and by his side,
Rejoicing like a bridegroom in the strife,
Alphonso through the host of infidels
Bore on his bloody lance dismay and death.
But there was worst confusion and uproar,
There widest slaughter and dismay, where, proud
Of his recovered Lord, Orelio plunged
Through thickest ranks, trampling beneath his feet
The living and the dead. Where'er he turns
The Moors divide and fly. What man is this,
Appalled they say, who to the front of war
Bareheaded offers thus his naked life?
Replete with power he is, and terrible,
Like some destroying Angel! Sure his lips

Have drank of Kaf's dark fountain, and he comes
Strong in his immortality! Fly! fly!
They said, this is no human foe!—Nor less
Of wonder filled the Spaniards when they saw
How flight and terror went before his way,
And slaughter in his path. Behold, cries one,
With what command and knightly ease he sits
The intrepid steed, and deals from side to side
His dreadful blows! Not Roderick in his power
Bestrode with such command and majesty
That noble war-horse. His loose robe this day
Is death's black banner, shaking from its folds
Dismay and ruin. Of no mortal mould
Is he who in that garb of peace affronts
Whole hosts, and sees them scatter where he turns!
Auspicious Heaven beholds us, and some Saint
Revisits earth!

                    Aye, cries another, Heaven
Hath ever with especial bounty blest
Above all other lands its favoured Spain;
Chusing her children forth from all mankind
For its peculiar people, as of yore
Abraham's ungrateful race beneath the Law.
Who knows not how on that most holy night
When Peace on Earth by Angels was proclaimed,
The light which o'er the fields of Bethlehem shone,
Irradiated whole Spain?[66] not just displayed,
As to the Shepherds, and again withdrawn;
All the long winter hours from eve till morn
Her forests and her mountains and her plains,
Her hills and valleys were embathed in light,
A light which came not from the sun or moon
Or stars, by secondary powers dispensed,
But from the fountain-springs, the Light of Light
Effluent.   And wherefore should we not believe
That this may be some Saint or Angel, charged
To lead us to miraculous victory?
Hath not the Virgin Mother oftentimes
Descending, clothed in glory, sanctified
With feet adorable our happy soil?—
Marked ye not, said another, how he cast
In wrath the unhallowed scymitar away,
And called for Christian weapon? Oh be sure
This is the aid of Heaven! On, comrades, on!
A miracle to-day is wrought for Spain!
Victory and Vengeance! Hew the miscreants down,
And spare not! hew them down in sacrifice!
God is with us! his Saints are in the field!
Victory! miraculous Victory!

                    Thus they
Inflamed with wild belief the keen desire
Of vengeance on their enemies abhorred.
The Moorish chief, meantime, o'erlooked the fight
From an eminence, and cursed the renegade
Whose counsels sorting to such ill effect
Had brought this danger on. Lo, from the East
Comes fresh alarm! a few poor fugitives
Well-nigh with fear exanimate came up,
From Covadonga flying, and the rear
Of that destruction, scarce with breath to tell
Their dreadful tale. When Abulcacem heard,
Stricken with horror, like a man bereft
Of sense, he stood. O Prophet, he exclaimed,
A hard and cruel fortune hast thou brought
This day upon thy servant! Must I then
Here with disgrace and ruin close a life

Of glorious deeds? But how should man resist
Fate's irreversible decrees, or why
Murmur at what must be! They who survive
May mourn the evil which this day begins:
My part will soon be done!—Grief then gave way
To rage, and cursing Guisla, he pursued,
Oh that that treacherous woman were but here!
It were a consolation to give her
The evil death she merits!.

           That reward
She hath had, a Moor replied. For when we reached
The entrance of the vale, it was her choice
There in the farthest dwellings to be left
Lest she should see her brother's face; but thence
We found her, flying at the overthrow,
And, visiting the treason on her head,
Pierced her with wounds.—Poor vengeance for a host
Destroyed! said Abulcacem in his soul.
Howbeit, resolving to the last to do
His office, he roused up his spirit. Go,
Strike off Count Eudon's head! he cried; the fear
Which brought him to our camp will bring him else
In arms against us now! For Sisibert
And Ebba, he continued thus in thought,
Their uncle's fate for ever bars all plots
Of treason on their part; no hope have they
Of safety but with us. He called them then
With chosen troops to join him in the front
Of battle, that by bravely making head,
Retreat might now be won. Then fiercer raged
The conflict, and more frequent cries of death,
Mingling with imprecations and with prayers,
Rose through the din of war.

           By this the blood
Which Deva down her fatal channel poured,
Purpling Pionia's course, had reached and stained
The wider stream of Sella. Soon far off
The frequent glance of spears and gleam of arms
Were seen, which sparkled to the westering orb,
Where down the vale impatient to complete
The glorious work so well that day begun,
Pelayo led his troops. On foot they came,
Chieftains and men alike; the Oaken Cross [67]
Triumphant borne on high precedes their march,
And broad and bright the argent banner shone.
Roderick, who, dealing death from side to side,
Had through the Moorish army now made way,
Beheld it flash, and judging well what aid
Approached, with sudden impulse that way rode,
To tell of what had passed,—lest in the strife
They should engage with Julian's men, and mar
The mighty consummation. One ran on
To meet him fleet of foot, and having given
His tale to this swift messenger, the Goth
Halted awhile to let Orelio breathe.
Siverian, quoth Pelayo, if mine eyes
Deceive me not, yon horse, whose reeking sides
Are red with slaughter, is the same on whom
The apostate Orpas in his vauntery
Wont to parade the streets of Cordoba.
But thou shouldst know him best; regard him well:
Is 't not Orelio?

           Either it is he,
The old man replied, or one so like to him,
Whom all thought matchless, that similitude
Would be the greater wonder. But behold.

What man is he who in that disarray
Doth with such power and majesty bestride
The noble steed, as if he felt himself
In his own proper seat? Look how he leans
To cherish him; and how the gallant horse
Curves up his stately neck, and bends his head,
As if again to court that gentle touch,
And answer to the voice which praises him.
Can it be Maccabee? rejoined the King,
Or are the secret wishes of my soul
Indeed fulfilled, and hath the grave given up
Its dead!—So saying, on the old man he turned
Eyes full of wide astonishment, which told
The incipient thought that for incredible
He spake no farther. But enough had past,
For old Siverian started at the words
Like one who sees a spectre and exclaimed,
Blind that I was to know him not till now!
My Master, O my Master!

           He meantime
With easy pace moved on to meet their march.
King, to Pelayo he began, this day
By means scarce less than miracle, thy throne
Is stablished, and the wrongs of Spain revenged.
Orpas the accursed, upon yonder field
Lies ready for the ravens. By the Moors
Treacherously slain, Count Julian will be found
Before Saint Peter's altar; unto him
Grace was vouchsafed; and by that holy power
Which at Visonia by the Primate's hand
Of his own proper act to me was given,
Unworthy as I am,—yet sure I think
Not without mystery, as the event hath shown,—
Did I accept Count Julian's penitence,
And reconcile the dying man to heaven.
Beside him hath his daughter gone to rest.
Deal honourably with his remains, and let
One grave with Christian rites receive them both.
Is it not written that as the Tree falls,
So it shall lie?

           In this and all things else,
Pelayo answered, looking wistfully
Upon the Goth, thy pleasure shall be done.
Then Roderick saw that he was known, and turned
His head away in silence. But the old man
Laid hold upon his bridle, and looked up
In his master's face, weeping and silently.
Thereat the Goth with fervent pressure took
His hand, and bending down toward him, said,
My good Siverian, go not thou this day
To war! I charge thee keep thyself from harm!
Thou art past the age for combats, and with whom
Hereafter should thy mistress talk of me
If thou wert gone?—Thou seest I am unarmed:
Thus disarrayed as thou beholdest me,
Clean through yon miscreant army have I cut
My way unhurt; but being once by Heaven
Preserved, I would not perish with the guilt
Of having wilfully provoked my death.
Give me thy helmet and thy cuirass!—nay—
Thou wert not wont to let me ask in vain,
Nor to oppose me when my will was known!
To thee methinks I should be still the King.
Thus saying they withdrew a little way
Within the trees. Roderick alighted there,
And in the old man's armour dight himself.

Dost thou not marvel by what wonderous chance,
Said he, Orelio to his master's hand
Hath been restored? I found the renegade
Of Seville on his back, and hurled him down
Headlong to the earth. The noble animal
Rejoicingly obeyed my hand to shake
His recreant burthen off, and trample out
The life which once I spared in evil hour.
Now let me meet Witiza's viperous sons
In yonder field, and then I may go rest
In peace,—my work is done!

               And nobly done!
Exclaimed the old man. Oh! thou art greater now
Than in that glorious hour of victory
When grovelling in the dust Witiza lay,
The prisoner of thy hand!—Roderick replied,
O good Siverian, happier victory
Thy son hath now achieved,—the victory
Over the world, his sins, and his despair.
If on the field my body should be found,
See it, I charge thee, laid in Julian's grave,
And let no idle ear be told for whom .
Thou mournest. Thou wilt use Orelio
As doth beseem the steed which hath so oft
Carried a king to battle:—he hath done
Good service for his rightful Lord to-day,
And better yet must do. Siverian, now
Farewell! I think we shall not meet again
Till it be in that world where never change
Is known, and they who love shall part no more.
Commend me to my mother's prayers, and say
That never man enjoyed a heavenlier peace
Than Roderick at this hour. O faithful friend,
How dear thou art to me these tears may tell!

With that he fell upon the old man's neck;
Then vaulted in the saddle, gave the reins,
And soon rejoined the host. On, comrades, on!
Victory and Vengeance! he exclaimed, and took
The lead on that good charger, he alone
Horsed for the onset. They with one consent
Gave all their voices to the inspiring cry,
Victory and Vengeance! and the hills and rocks
Caught the prophetic shout and rolled it round.
Count Pedro's people heard amid the heat
Of battle, and returned the glad acclaim.
The astonished Musselmen, on all sides charged,
Hear that tremendous cry; yet manfully
They stood, and every where with gallant front
Opposed in fair array the shock of war.
Desperately they fought, like men expert in arms,
And knowing that no safety could be found,
Save from their own right hands. No former day
Of all his long career had seen their chief
Approved so well; nor had Witiza's sons
Ever before this hour atchieved in fight
Such feats of resolute valour. Sisibert
Beheld Pelayo in the field afoot,
And twice essayed beneath his horse's feet
To thrust him down. Twice did the Prince evade
The shock, and twice upon his shield received
The fratricidal sword. Tempt me no more,
Son of Witiza, cried the indignant chief,
Lest I forget what mother gave thee birth!
Go meet thy death from any hand but mine!
He said, and turned aside. Fitliest from me!

Exclaimed a dreadful voice, as through the throng
Orelio forced his way: fitliest from me
Receive the rightful death too long withheld!
'Tis Roderick strikes the blow! And as he spake,
Upon the traitor's shoulder fierce he drove
The weapon, well-bestowed. He in the seat
Tottered and fell. The Avenger hastened on
In search of Ebba; and in the heat of fight
Rejoicing and forgetful of all else,
Set up his cry as he was wont in youth,
Roderick the Goth!—his war-cry known so well.
Pelayo eagerly took up the word,
And shouted out his kinsman's name beloved,
Roderick the Goth! Roderick and Victory!
Roderick and Vengeance! Odoar gave it forth!
Urban repeated it, and through his ranks
Count Pedro sent the cry. Not from the field
Of his great victory, when Witiza fell,
With louder acclamations had that name
Been borne abroad upon the winds of heaven.
The unreflecting throng, who yesterday,
If it had past their lips, would with a curse
Have clogged it, echoed it as if it came
From some celestial voice in the air, reveal'd
To be the certain pledge of all their hopes.
Roderick the Goth! Roderick and Victory!
Roderick and Vengeance! O'er the field it spread,
All hearts and tongues uniting in the cry;
Mountains and rocks and vales re-echoed round;
And he rejoicing in his strength rode on,
Laying on the Moors with that good sword, and smote,
And overthrew, and scatter'd, and destroy'd,
And trampled down; and still at every blow
Exultingly he sent the war-cry forth,
Roderick the Goth! Roderick and Victory!
Roderick and Vengeance!

            Thus he made his way,
Smiting and slaying through the astonish'd ranks,
Till he beheld where on a fiery barb,
Ebba, performing well a soldier's part,
Dealt to the right and left his deadly blows.
With mutual rage they met. The renegade
Displays a scymitar, the splendid gift
Of Walid from Damascus sent; its hilt
Embossed with gems, its blade of perfect steel,
Which like a mirror sparkling to the sun [68]
With dazzling splendour flashed. The Goth objects
His shield, and on its rim received the edge
Driven from its aim aside, and of its force
Diminished. Many a frustrate stroke was dealt
On either part, and many a foin and thrust
Aimed and rebated; many a deadly blow
Straight, or reverse, delivered and repelled.
Roderick at length with better speed hath reached
The apostate's turban, and through all its folds
The true Cantabrian weapon making way
Attained his forehead. Wretch! the avenger cried,
It comes from Roderick's hand! Roderick the Goth,
Who spared, who trusted thee, and was betrayed!
Go tell thy father now how thou hast sped
With all thy treasons! Saying thus, he seized
The miserable, who, blinded now with blood,
Reeled in the saddle; and with sidelong step
Backing Orelio, drew him to the ground.
He shrieking, as beneath the horse's feet
He fell, forgot his late-learnt creed, and called

56

On Mary's name. The dreadful Goth past on,
Still plunging through the thickest war, and still
Scattering, where'er he turn'd, the affrighted ranks.

Oh who could tell what deeds were wrought that day;
Or who endure to hear [69] the tale of rage,
Hatred, and madness, and despair, and fear,
Horror, and wounds, and agony, and death,
The cries, the blasphemies, the shrieks, and groans,
And prayers, which mingled with the din of arms
In one wild uproar of terrific sounds;
While over all predominant was heard
Reiterate from the conquerors o'er the field,
Roderick the Goth! Roderick and Victory!
Roderick and Vengeance!—Woe for Africa!
Woe for the circumcised! Woe for the faith
Of the lying Ishmaelite that hour! The Chiefs
Have fallen; the Moors, confused and captainless,
And panic-stricken, vainly seek to escape
The inevitable fate. Turn where they will,
Strong in his cause, rejoicing in success,
Insatiate at the banquet of revenge,
The enemy is there; look where they will,
Death hath environed their devoted ranks;
Fly where they will, the avenger and the sword
Await them,—wretches! whom the righteous arm
Hath overtaken!—Joined in bonds of faith
Accurst, the most flagitious of mankind
From all parts met are here; the apostate Greek,
The vicious Syrian, and the sullen Copt,
The Persian cruel and corrupt of soul,
The Arabian robber, and the prowling sons
Of Africa, who from their thirsty sands
Pray that the locusts on the peopled plain
May settle and prepare their way. [70] Conjoined
Beneath an impious faith, which sanctifies
To them all deeds of wickedness and blood,—
Yea and halloos them on,—here are they met
To be conjoined in punishment this hour.
For plunder, violation, massacre,
All hideous, all unutterable things,
The righteous, the immitigable sword
Exacts due vengeance now! the cry of blood
Is heard: the measure of their crimes is full:
Such mercy as the Moor at Auria gave,
Such mercy hath he found this dreadful hour!

The evening darkened, but the avenging sword
Turned not away its edge till night had closed
Upon the field of blood. The Chieftains then
Blew the recall, and from their perfect work
Returned rejoicing, all but he for whom
All looked with most expectance. He full sure
Had thought upon that field to find his end
Desired, and with Florinda in the grave
Rest, in indissoluble union joined.
But still where through the press of war he went
Half-armed, and like a lover seeking death,
The arrows past him by to right and left,
The spear-point pierced him not, the scymitar
Glanced from his helmet: he, when he beheld
The rout complete, saw that the shield of Heaven
Had been extended over him once more,
And bowed before its will. Upon the banks
Of Sella was Orelio found, his legs
And flanks incarnadined, his poitral smeared

With froth and foam and gore, his silver mane
Sprinkled with blood, which hung on every hair,
Aspersed like dew-drops; trembling there he stood
From the toil of battle, and at times sent forth
His tremulous voice far echoing loud and shrill,
A frequent, anxious cry, with which he seemed
To call the master whom he loved so well,
And who had thus again forsaken him.
Siverian's helm and cuirass on the grass
Lay near; and Julian's sword, its hilt and chain
Clotted with blood; but where was he whose hand
Had wielded it so well that glorious day?—[71]

Days, months, and years, and generations past,
And centuries held their course, before, far off
Within a hermitage near Viseu's walls
A humble tomb was found, [72] which bore inscribed
In ancient characters King Roderick's name.

NOTES.

Note 1, page 385, col. 1.

Count Julian called the invaders.

The story of Count Julian and his daughter has been
treated as a fable by some authors, because it is not men-
tioned by the three writers who lived nearest the time
But those writers state the mere fact of the conquest of
Spain as briefly as possible, without entering into parti-
culars of any kind; and the best Spanish historians and
antiquaries are persuaded that there is no cause for dis-
believing the uniform and concurrent tradition of both
Moors and Christians.

For the purposes of poetry, it is immaterial whether
the story be true or false. I have represented the Count
as a man both sinned against and sinning, and equally
to be commiserated and condemned. The author of
the Tragedy of Count Julian has contemplated his
character in a grander point of view, and represented
him as a man self-justified in bringing an army of
foreign auxiliaries to assist him in delivering his country
from a tyrant, and foreseeing, when it is too late to
recede, the evils which he is thus bringing upon her.

> Not victory that o'ershadows him, sees he!
> No airy and light passion stirs abroad
> To ruffle or to sooth him; all are quell'd
> Beneath a mightier, sterner stress of mind:
> Wakeful he sits, and lonely and unmoved,
> Beyond the arrows, views, or shouts of men:
> As oftentimes an eagle, when the sun
> Throws o'er the varying earth his early ray,
> Stands solitary, stands immoveable
> Upon some highest cliff, and rolls his eye,
> Clear, constant, unobservant, unabased,
> In the cold light, above the dews of morn.
> Act V, Scene 2.

Parts of this tragedy are as fine in their kind as any
thing which can be found in the whole compass of
English poetry.

Juan de Mena places Count Julian with Orpas, the re-
negado Archbishop of Seville, in the deepest pit of hell

> No buenamente te puedo callar
> Orpas maldito ni a ti Julian,
> Pues soys en el valle mas hondo de afan,
> Que no se redime jamas por llorar;

Qual ya crueza vos pudo indignar
A vender en um dia las tierras y leyes
De España, las quales pujança de reyes
En años é tantos no pudo cobrar.

Copla 91.

A Portugueze poet, Andre da Sylva Mascarenhas, is more indulgent to the Count, and seems to consider it as a mark of degeneracy in his own times, that the same crime would no longer provoke the same vengeance. His catalogue of women who have become famous by the evil of which they have been the occasion, begins with Eve, and ends with Anne Boleyn.

Louvar se pode ao Conde o sentimento
Da offensa da sua honestidade,
Se o nam vituperara co cruento
Disbarate da Hispana Christandade ;
Se hoje ouvera stupros cento e cento
Nesta nossa infeliz lasciva idade,
Nam se perdera nam a forte Espanha.
Que o crime frequentado nam se estranha.
Por mulheres porem se tem perdido
Muitos reynos da outra e desta vida ;
Por Eva se perdeo o Ceo sobido,
Por Helena a Asia esclarecida ;
Por Cleopatra o Egypto foi vencido,
Assiria por Semiramis perdida,
Por Cava se perdeo a forte Espanha
E por Anna Bolona a Gram Bretanha.

Destruicam de Espanha, p. 9.

Note 2, page 385, col. 1.

Inhuman priests with unoffending blood
Had stained their country.

Never has any country been so cursed by the spirit of persecution as Spain. Under the Heathen Emperors it had its full share of suffering, and the first fatal precedent of appealing to the secular power to punish heresy with death, occurred in Spain. Then came the Arian controversy. There was as much bigotry, as much rancour, as little of the spirit of Christianity, and probably as much intolerance, on one part as on the other; but the successful party were better politicians, and more expert in the management of miracles.

Near to the city of Osen, or Ossel, there was a famous Athanasian church, and a more famous baptistery, which was in the form of a cross. On Holy Thursday in every year, the bishop, the clergy, and the people assembled there, saw that the baptistery was empty, and enjoyed a marvellous fragrance which differed from that of any, or all, flowers and spices, for it was an odour which came as the vesper of the divine virtue that was about to manifest itself : Then they fastened the doors of the church and sealed them. On Easter Eve the doors were opened, the baptistery was found full of water, and all the children born within the preceding twelve months were baptized. Theudisclo, an Arian king, set his seal also upon the doors for two successive years, and set a guard there. Still the miraculous baptistery was filled. The third year he suspected pipes, and ordered a trench to be dug round the building; but before the day of trial arrived, he was murdered, as opportunely as Arius himself. The trench was dry, but the workmen did not dig deep enough, and the miracle was continued. When the victory of the catholic party was complete, it was no longer necessary to keep it up. The same baptistery was employed to convince the Spaniards of their error in keeping Easter. In Brito's time, a few ruins called Oscla, were shewn near the river Cambria; the broken baptistery

was then called the Bath, and some wild superstitions which the peasantry related bore traces of the original legend. The trick was not uncommon; it was practised in Sicily and in other places. The story, however, is of some value, as showing that baptism was [1] administered only once a year, (except in cases of danger,) that immersion was the manner, and that infants were baptised.

Arianism seems to have lingered in Spain long after its defeat. The name Pelayo (Pelagius), and Arius, certainly appear to indicate a cherished heresy, and Brito [2] must have felt this when he deduced the former name from Saint Pelayo of the tenth century; for how came the saint by it, and how could Brito have forgotten the founder of the Spanish monarchy?

In the latter half of the eleventh century, the Count of Barcelona, Ramon Berenguer, *Cap de estopa*, as he was called, for his bushy head, made war upon some Christians who are said to have turned Arians, and took the castles into which they retired. [3] By the number of their castles, which he gave to those chiefs who assisted him in conquering them, they appear to have been numerous. It is not improbable that those people were really what they are called; for Arian has ever been, like Manichæan, a term ignorantly and indiscriminately given to heretics of all descriptions; and there is no heresy which would be so well understood in Spain, and so likely to have revived there.

The feelings of the triumphant party toward their opponents, are well marked by the manner in which St Isidore speaks of the death of the Emperor Valens. « Thraciam ferro incendiisque depopulantur, deletoque Romanorum exercitu ipsum Valentem jaculo vulneratum, in quadam villa fugientem succenderunt, ut merito ipse ab eis vivus temporali cremaretur incendio, qui tam pulchras animas ignibus æternis tradiderat.» [4] If the truth of this opinion should be doubted, there is a good Athanasian miracle in the Chronicon [5] of S. Isidore and of Melitus, to prove it. A certain Arian, by name Olympius, being in the bath, blasphemed the Holy Trinity, and behold! being struck by an angel with three fiery darts, he was visibly consumed.

With regard to the Arians, the Catholics only did to the others as the others would have done with them ; but the persecution of the Jews was equally unprovoked and inhuman. They are said to have betrayed many towns to the Moors; and it would be strange indeed if they had not, by every means in their power, assisted in overthrowing a government under which they were miserably oppressed. St Isidore has a memorable passage relating to their cruel persecution and compulsory conversion under Sisebut. « Qui initio regni Judæos ad Fidem Christianam permovens æmulationem quidem habuit, sed non secundum scientiam : potestate enim compulit, quos provocare fidei ratione oportuit. Sed sicut est scriptum sive per occasionem sive per verita-

[1] In the seventeenth, and last council of Toledo, it was decreed that the baptistery should be shut up, and sealed with the episcopal seal, during the whole year, till Good Friday ; on that day the bishop, in his pontificals, was to open it with great solemnity, in token that Christ, by his passion and resurrection, had opened the way to heaven for mankind, as on that day the hope was opened of obtaining redemption through the holy sacrament of baptism.— *Morales*, 12, 62, 3.

[2] Monarchia Lusitana, 2, 7, 19.

[3] Pere Tomich. c. 34, ff. 26.

[4] Hist. Goth. apud Florez. Espana Sagrada, T. 6, 486.

[5] Espana Sagrada, T. 6, 474.

tem, Christus annuntiatur, in hoc gaudeo et gaudebo.»
—*S. Isidor. Christ. Goth. Espana Sagrada*, 6. 5o2.

The Moorish conquest procured for them an interval of repose, till the Inquisition was established, and by its damnable acts put all former horrors out of remembrance.

When Toledo was recovered from the Moors by Alonzo VI, the Jews of that city waited upon the conqueror, and assured him that they were part of the ten tribes whom Nebuchadnezzar had transported into Spain; not the descendants of the Jerusalem Jews who had crucified Christ. Their ancestors, they said, were entirely innocent of the crucifixion; for when Caiaphas the high-priest had written to the Toledan synagogues to ask their advice respecting the person who called himself the Messiah, and whether he should be slain, the Toledan Jews returned for answer, that in their judgment the prophecies seemed to be fulfilled in this person, and therefore he ought not by any means to be put to death. This reply they produced in the original Hebrew, and in Arabic, as it had been translated by command of King Galifre. Alonzo gave ear to the story, had the letter rendered into Latin and Castilian, and deposited it among the archives of Toledo. The latter version is thus printed by Sandoval:

« Levi Archisinagogo, et Samuel, et Joseph, homes bonos del Aljama de Toledo, a Eleazar Muyd gran Sacerdote, e a Samuel Canud, y Anas, y Cayphas, homes bonos de la Aljama de la Terra Santa, Salud en el Dios de Israel.

« Azarias voso home, Maeso en ley nos aduxo las cartas que vos nos embiavades, por las quales nos faziades saber cuemo passava la facienda del Propheta Nazaret, que diz que facie muchas sennas. Colo por esta vila non ha mucho, un cierto Samuel, fil de Amacias, et fablo nusco, et reconto muchas bondades deste home, que ye, que es home homildoso et manso, que fabla con los laçeriados, que faz a todos bien, e que faciendole a el mal, el non faz mal a ninguem; et que es home fuerte con superbos et homes malos, et que vos malamente teniades enemiga con ele, por quanto en faz el descubria vosos pecados, ca por quanto facia esto, le aviades mala voluntad. Et perquirimos deste home, en que anno, o mes o dia, avia nacido: et que nos lo dixesse: falamos que el dia de la sua Natividade foron vistos en estas partes tres soles muelle a muelle, fizieron soldemente un sol; et cuemo nosos padres cataron esta senna, asmados dixeron que cedo el Messias naceria, et que por aventura era ja nacido. Catad hermanos si por aventura ha ja venido et non le ayades acatado. Relataba tambien el susodicho home, que el suo pay le recontava, que ciertos Magos, homes de mucha sapiencia, en la sua Natividade legaron a tierra santa, perquiriendo logar donde e ninno sancto era nacido; y que Herodes voso Rey se asmo, et disposito junto a homes sabios de sua vila, e perquirio donde nasceria el Infante, por quien perquirian Magos, et le respondieron, en Betlem de Juda, segun que Micheas depergino profeto. Et que dixeron aqueles Magos, que una estrella de gran craredad, de luenne aduxo a tierra santa: catad non sea esta quela profezia, cataran Reyes, et andaran en craridad de la sua Natividade. Otro si, catad non persigades al que forades tenudos mucho honrar et recibir de bon talante. Mais fazed lo que tuvieres por bien aguisada; nos vos dezimos que nin por consejo, nin

por noso alvedrio veniremos en consentimiento de la sua morte. Ca, si nos esto fiziessemos, logo seria nuesco, que la profezia que diz, congregaronse de consuno contra el Sennor, et contra el suo Messias. E damos vos este consejo, maguera sodes homes de muyta sapença, que tengades grande aficamento sobre tamana fazienda, porque el Dios de Israel enojado con vusco, non destruya casa segunda de voso segundo templo. Ca sepades cierto, cedo ha de ser destruyda; et por esta razon nosos antepassados, que salieron de captiverio de Babylonia, siendo suo Capitane Pyrro, que embio Rey Cyro, et aduxo nusco muytas requeças que tollo de Babylonia el anno de sesenta et nueve de captividade, et foron recebidos en Toledo de Gentiles que y moravan, et edificaron una grande Aljama, et non quisieron bolver a Jerusalem otra vegada a edificar Temple, aviendo ser destruido otra vegada. De Toledo catorze dias del mes Nisan. Era de Cesar diez y ocho, y de Augusto Octaviano setenta y uno.»—*Sandoval*, 71.

Had Alonzo been as zealous as some of his Gothic predecessors, or his Most Catholic successors, he might have found a fair pretext in this letter for ordering all the Jews of Toledo to the font, unless they would show cause why they should adhere to the opinion of Caiaphas and the Jerusalem Jews, rather than to that of their own ancestors.

General Vallancy believes that the Spanish Jews were brought into the Peninsula by Nebuchadnezzar, and admits these Toledans as authority. He quotes Count Gebelin, and refers to Strabo and Ezekiel. The proof from Ezekiel rests upon the word Orb, Earb, Warb, or Gharb; which is made into Algarve!

A Jew in Tirante el Blanco (p. 2. c. 74. f. 243.) explains the difference between the different races of Jews. They are three, he says. One the progeny of those who took counsel for the death of Christ; and they were known by this, that they were in continual motion, hands and feet, and never could rest; neither could their spirit ever be still, and they had very little shame. The second were the descendants of those who put in execution and assisted at the various parts of the sufferings and death of Christ, and they never could look any man in the face, nor could they, without great difficulty, ever look up to heaven. The third were the children of David, who did all they could to prevent the death of Christ, and shut themselves up in the temple that they might not witness it. These are affable, good men, who love their neighbours; a quiet peaceable race, who can look any where.

Thomas Tomaio de Vargas, the editor of the spurious Luitprand, says, that not only many Hebrew words are mixed with the old Spanish, but that, *prô dolor!* the black and stinking Jewish blood had been mingled with the most pure blood of the Spaniards, (p. 96). They were very anxious, he says, to intermarry, and spoil the pure blood. And he adds, that the Spaniards call them *putos*, quia *putant*. « But,» says Sir Thomas Brown, « that an unsavoury odour is gentilitious, or national to the Jews, we cannot well concede. And if, (according to good relations), where they may freely speak it, they forbear not to boast that there are at present many thousand Jews in Spain, France, and England; and some dispensed withal even to the degree of priesthood, it is a matter very considerable, and could they be smelled out, would much advantage not only the church of Christ but also the coffers of princes.—The ground that begat or propagated this assertion might be the distasteful averseness of the Christian from the Jew upon the villainy of that fact, which made them abominable, and 'stink in the nostrils of all men.' Which real practice and metaphorical expression did after proceed into a literal construction; but was a fraudulent illation; for such an evil savour their father Jacob acknowledged in himself, when he said his sons had made him stink in the land, that is, to be abominable unto the inhabitants thereof.—Another cause is urged by Campegius, and much received by Christians; that this ill savour is a curse derived upon them by Christ, and stands as a badge or brand of a generation that crucified their *Salvator*. But this is a conceit without all warrant, and an easy way to take off dispute in what point of obscurity soever.»—*Vulgar Errors*, Book iv, ch. 10.

The Mahommedans also hold a like opinion of the unsavouriness of the Jews, and account for it by this legend, which is given by Sale. « Some of the children of Israel abandoned their dwellings because of a pestilence, or, as others say, to avoid serving in a religious war; but as they fled, God struck them all dead in a certain valley. About eight days or more after, when their bodies were corrupted, the Prophet Ezekiel happening to pass that way, at the sight wept; whereupon God said to him, 'Call to them, O Ezekiel, and I will restore them to life.' And accordingly, on the prophet's call, they all arose, and lived several years after; but they retained the colour and stench of dead corpses as long as they lived, and the clothes they wore were changed as black as pitch, which qualities they transmitted to their posterity.»

One of our own travellers [1] tells us of a curious practical application of this belief in Barbary. «The Moors of Tangier,» he says, « when they want rain, and have prayed in vain for it, set the Jews to work, saying, that though God would not grant it to the prayers of the faithful, he would to the Jews, in order to be rid of their stink.» Ludicrous as this is, South has a passage concerning the Jews, which is little more reasonable, in one of his sermons. « The truth is,» he says, « they were all along a cross, odd, untoward sort of people, and such as God seems to have chosen, and (as the Prophets sometimes phrase it) to have espoused to himself, upon the very same account that Socrates espoused Xantippe, only for her extreme ill conditions, above all that he could possibly find or pick out of that sex: and so the fittest argument both to exercise and declare his admirable patience to the world.»—Vol. i, 421.

Note 3, page 385, col. 1.

A yoke
Of iron servitude oppressed and galled
The children of the soil.

Of the condition of slaves under the Spanish Wisigoths, I have given an account in the Introduction to the Chronicle of the Cid. This also, like the persecution of the Jews, must greatly have facilitated the Moorish conquest. Another facilitating cause was, that notwithstanding their frequent civil disturbances, they had in great measure ceased to be a warlike people. The many laws in the Fuero Iuzgo, for compelling men to military service, prove this. These laws are full of complaints that the people would avoid the service if they could. Habits of settled life seem throughout Europe to have effeminated the northern conquerors, till the Normans renovated the race, and the institutions of chivalry and the crusades produced a new era.

Note 4, page 385, col. 1.

Thou, Calpé, sawest their coming : ancient Rock
Renowned, no longer now shalt thou be called,
From Gods and Heroes of the years of yore,
Kronos, or hundred-handed Briareus,
Bacchus or Hercules ; but doomed to bear
The name of thy new conqueror.

Gibel-al-Tarif, the mountain of Tarif, is the received etymology of Gibraltar: Ben Hazel, a Granadan Moor, says expressly, that the mountain derived its name from this general. Its former appellations may be seen in the Historia de Gibraltar, by Don Ignacio Lopez de Ayala. The derivation of the word Calpe is not known: Florian de Ocampo identifies it with the English word *galloping*, in a passage which will amuse the Spanish scholar. «La segunda nombradía fue llamarle Calpe, cuya razon, segun dicen algunos, procedió de que los Andaluces ancianos en su lengua vieja solian llamar Calepas y Calpes á qualesquier cosas enhiestas y levantadas, agora fuesen peñascos, ó pizarras, ó maderos, ó piedras menores, como lo significamos en los diez y ocho capítulos precedentes: y dicen que con estar alli junto de Gibraltar sobre sus marinas el risco, que ya dixe muy encumbrado y enhiesto, qual hoy dia parece, lo llamaban Calpes aquellos Andaluces pasados: y por su respecto la mesma poblacion vino tambien á tener despues aquel proprio nombre. No faltan otras personas que siguiendo las Escrituras Griegas pongan esta razon del nombre Calpes mucho diversamente, diciendo, que quando los cosarios Argonautas desembarcaron en España, cerca del estrecho, segun ya lo declaramos, el tiempo que hacian sus exercicios arriba dichos, de saltos y luchas, y musicas acordadas, bien asi como los pastores espanoles comarcanos recibian contentamiento grande, mirando las tales desenvolturas y ligerezas, no menos aquellos Griegos recien venidos notaban algunos juegos, dado que trabajosos y dificiles, que los mesmos pastores obraban entre sí para su recreacion y deporte; particularmente consideraban un regocijo de caballos, donde ciertos dias aplazados venian todos á se juntar como para cosa de gran pundonor.

«El qual regocijo hacian desta manera. Tomaban yeguas en pelo, quanto mas corredoras y ligeras podian haber, y puestos ellos encima desnudos sin alguna ropa, ataban en las quixadas barbicachos de rama, torcidos y majados á manera de freno, con que salian del puesto dos á dos á la par corriendo lo mas que sus yeguas podian, para llegar á cierta senal de pizarras enhiestas ó de maderos hincados y levantados en fin de la carrera. Venidos al medio trecho de su corrida saltaban de las yeguas en tierra, no las parando ni deteniendo : y asi trabados por el barbicacho, corrian tambien ellos á pie, sin las dexar, puesto que mas furia llevasen : porque si las dexaban ó se desprendian dellas, y no sustentaban el freno continuamente, hasta ser pasada la carrera, perdian la reputacion y las apuestas, quedando tan amenguados y vencidos, quanto quedaria triunfante quien primero llegase con su yegua para tomar la presa que tenian en el fin de la carrera sobre las pizarras ó maderos hincados. Quando saltaban de sus yeguas, dicen que les iban hablando porque no se detuviesen,

[1] Hist. of the Captivity of Thomas Pellow, p. 257.

voceándoles y diciéndoles á menudo palabras animosas y dulces : llamábanles pies hermosos, generosas en el correr, casta real, hembras preciosas, acrecentadoras de sus honras, y mas otras razones muchas con que las tenian vezadas, á no se parar ni perder el ímpetu comenzado : de manera que los tropeles en este punto, los pundonores y regocijos de correr, y de no mostrar floxedad era cosa mucho de notar, asi por la parte de los hombres, como por parte de las yeguas. A los Griegos Argonautas les pareció juego tan varonil que muchas veces lo probaron tambien ellos á revuelta de los Españoles, como quiera que jamas pudieron tener aquella vigilancia ni ligereza, ni reciura que tenian estos otros para durar con sus yeguas. Y dado que las tales yeguas corriesen harto furiosas, y les enseñasen muchos dias antes á seguir estas parejas, quanto mejor entendian á la verdad, ni las de los unos, ni las de los otros corrian tanto despues que saltaban dellas, como quando los traian encima : y asi las palabras que los Griegos en aquella sazon puestos á pie hablaban eran tambien al mesmo propósito conformes á las de los Andaluces Españoles en su lengua provincial, nombrándolas Calopes, Calopes, Calopes á la continua, que fue palabra Griega, compuesta de dos vocablos : uno Calos, que significa cosa hermosa, ligera y agraciada : otro Pus, que quiere decir pie, como que las llamasen pies agraciados, ó pies desenvueltos y ligeros : y por abreviar mas el vocablo, para que sus yeguas lo pudiesen mas presto sentir, acortábanlo con una letra menos en el medio, y en lugar de nombrarlas Calopes, les decian Calpes, que significa lo mesmo Calopes : la qual palabra me parece dura todavía hasta nuestro siglo presente, donde pocas letras mudadas, por decir Calopes ó Calpes, lo pronunciamos Galopes, quando los caballos y yeguas, ó qualesquier otros animales, no corren á todo poder sino trote largo seguido. Vino desto que las mesmas fiestas y manera del juego se nombraron Calpes : dado que para conmigo bastara saber la victoria deste juego consistir en ligereza de pies, y por eso solo deberse llamar Calopes á Calpe, sin anadir lo que hablaban á las yeguas, pues aquello primero comprehende bastantemente la razon deste vocablo. Pero si todavía fue cierto que les decian aquellas palabras quando corrian sus parejas, ninguna cosa daña dexarlas aqui puestas.»—Coronica General de España, c. 38.

Note 5, page 385, col. 2.

Famine and pestilence had wasted them.

In the reign of Egica, Witiza's father,—« plaga inguinalis immisericorditer illabitur.» (Isid. Pacensis.) And for two years before the Moorish invasion,—« habia habido continua hambre y pestilencia en España, con que se habian debilitado mucho los cuerpos, sin lo que el ocio las habia enflaquecido.»—Morales, 12. 69. 5.

St Isidore, in his History of the Goths, distinctly describes the Northern Lights among the signs that announced the wars of Attila. « Multa eodem tempore cœli et terræ signa præcesserunt, quorum prodigiis tam crudele bellum significaretur. Nam, assiduis terræ motibus factis, a parte Orientis Luna fuscata est, a solis occasu stella cometes apparuit, atque ingenti magnitudine aliquandiu fulsit. *Ab Aquilonis plaga cælum rubens, sicut ignis aut sanguis, effectus est, permistis perigneum ruborem lineis clarioribus in speciem hastarum rutilantium deformatis.* Nec mirum, ut in tam ingenti

cæsorum strage, divinitus tam multa signorum demonstraretur ostensio.»—España Sagrada, t. vi, 491.

Note 6, page 385, col. 2.

And, worst of enemies, their Sins were armed
Against them.

The following description of the state of the Christian world when the Saracens began their conquests, is taken from a singular manuscript, « wherein the history of the Cruisades and of all the Mahommedan emperors from A.D. 558, to A.D. 1588, is gathered out of the Chronikes of William Archbishop of Tyreus, the protoscribe of Palestine, of Basilius Jhohannes Heraldus, and sundry others, and reduced into a poem epike by Robert Barret, 1610.» The author was an old soldier, whose language is a compound of Josuah Sylvester and King Cambyses, with a strong relish of Ancient Pistol.

Now in this sin-flood age not only in East
Did the impious imps the faithful persecute,
But like affliction them pursued in West,
And in all parts the good trod under foot,
For Faith in some was cold, from others fled ;
And fear of God dislodged out human hearts ;
Astrea flown to skies, and in her stead
Iniquity enthronized ; in all parts
Violence had vogue, and on sathanized earth
Fraud, Mischief, Murder martialled the camp ;
Sweet Virtue fled the field : Hope, out of breath ;
And Vice, all-stainer, every soul did stamp ;
So that it seem'd World drew to 's evening tide,
Nought else expecting but Christ's second coming ;
For Charity was cold on every side,
And Truth and Trust were gone from earth a-mumming.
All things confused ran, so that it seemed
The World return would to his chaos old :
Princes the path of justice not esteemed,
Headlong with prince ran people young and old.
All sainct confederations infringed,
And for light cause would prince with prince enquarrel ;
Countries bestreamed with blood, with fire besinged,
All set to each, all murders sorts unbarrelled.
No wight his own could own ; 't was current coin
Each man to strip, provided he were rich.
The church sacriledged, choir made cot for swine,
And zealous ministers were made to scritche.
Robbing was made fair purchase, murder manhood,
And none secure by land ne sea could pass ;
The humble heartless, ireful hearts ran wood,
Esteemed most who mischief most could dress ;
All lubrick lusts shameless without comptroll
Ran full career ; each would a rider be ;
And Heaven's friend, all sainct Continency,
Was banished quite ; Lasciviousness did roll,
Frugality, healthful Sobriety
No place could find : all parts enquartered were
With Bacchus-brutes and Satyres-luxury.
All lawless games bore sway, with blasphemes roare,
'Twixt Clerk and Laick difference was none,
Disguized all, phantastick out of norme ;
But as the Prophet says, as Priests do run,
So run the people, peevish in disform.
The Bishops graded once, dumb dogs become,
Their heads sin vncting, flocks abandon soon
Princes applauders, person-acceptors,
The good's debarrers and the bad's abetters ;
Fleshly all, all filthy simonized,
Preferring profit 'fore the Eternal's praise.
The church enchismed, court all atheized,
The commons kankred, all all in distrayes,
The plotting politician's pate admired,
Their skill consisting in preventions scull,
Pathicks preferred, Cyprin ware desired,
Ocean of mischiefs flowing moon-tide full :
So that it seem'd that all flesh desperately
Like wolf-scared sheep were plunged headlong down
In pit of hell : puddled all pestfully
The court, church, commons, province, city, town ;

All haggards; none reclaimed once could be,
Ne by the word, word 'bused by organs bad,
Ne yet by signs that spotted chrystal sky,
Ne other prodigies, presages sad,
Neither gust shakings of this settled globe ;
Neither sharpe pencil of war, famine, pest,
Could once one ray engrave in steeled breast,
Or Christians cause their sin-jagged robe disrobe.

Thus stood the sad state of that sin-stain'd time,
And Christians of this our all-zeal cold time,
Let us now par'llel that time with our time:
Our parallel'd time will parallel that time,
Then triple-sainct, thou just geometer true,
Our time not parallel by thy justice line,
But with thy mercy's paralleling brow,
Reform our crimeful Angels by grace thine.

Note 7, page 385, col. 2.

Roderick's royal car.

« Roderike, the first day after the battayle, observing the auncient guise of his countrey, came into the fielde apparailled in a gowne of beaten golde, having also on his head a crown of gold, and golden shoes, and all his other apparaile set with rich pearles and precious stones, rydiug in a horse-litter of ivorie, drawne by two goodly horses ; which order the Goths used alwayes in battailes for this consideration, that the souldiours, well knowing their king could not escape away by flight from them, should be assured that there was none other way but either to die togither in that place, or else to winne the victorie ; for it had bene a thing most shamefull and reproachful to forsake their prince and anoynted sove- raigne. Which custome and maner many free confe- derate cities of Italie folowing, trimmed and adorned for the warres a certain chayre of estate, called *Carocio*, wherein were set the penons and ensigns of all the con- federates ; this chayre, in battaile, was drawn by many oxen, wherby the whole hoast was given to understand that they could not with any honesty flie, by reason of the slow pace and unweldiness of those heavie beasts.» —*A notable Historie of the Saracens, drawen out of Augustine Curio, and sundry other good Authours. By Thomas Newton*, 1575.

En ruedas de marfil, envuelto en sedas, .
De oro la frente orlada, y mas dispuesto
Al triunfo y al festin que á la pelea,
El sucesor indigno de Alarico
Llevó tras si la maldicion eterna.
Ah! yo la vi : la lid por siete dias
Duró, mas no fue lid, fue una sangrienta
Carniceria :Huyeron los cobardes
Los traidores vendieron sus banderas,
Los fuertes, los leales perecieron.

QUINTANA.

The author of the chivalrous Chronicle of King Don Rodrigo gives a singular description of this car, upon the anthority of his pretended original Eleastras; for he, « seeing that calamities went on increasing, and that the destruction of the Goths was at hand, thought that if things were to end as they had begun, it would be a marvel if there should be in Spain any king or lord of the lineage of the Goths after the death of King Don Rodrigo ; and therefore it imported much that he should leave behind him a remembrance of the customs of the Gothic kings, and of the manner in which they were wont to enter into battle and how they went to war. And he says, that the king used to go in a car made after a strange fashion. The wheels of this car were made of the bones of elephants, and the axle-tree was of fine silver, and the perch was of fine gold. It was drawn by two horses, who were of great size, and gentle ; and upon the car there was pitched a tent, so large that it covered the whole car, and it was of fine cloth of gold, upon which were wrought all the great feats in arms which had been atchieved until that time ; and the pillar of the tent was of gold, and many stones of great value were set in it, which sent forth such splen- dour, that by night there was no need of any other light therein. And the car and the horses bore the same adornments as the king, and these were full of pearls the largest which could be found. And in the middle of the car there was a seat placed against the pillar of the tent ; and this seat was of great price, insomuch that the value of it cannot be summed up, so many and so great were the stones which were set in it ; and it was wrought so subtly, and of such rare workmanship, that they who saw it marvelled thereat. And upon this seat the king was seated, being lifted up so high that all in the host, little or great, might behold him. And in this manner it was appointed that the king should go to war. And round about the car there were to go a thousand knights, who had all been knighted by the hand of the king, all armed ; and in the day of battle they were to be on foot round about the car ; and all plighted homage to the king not to depart from it in any manner whatsoever, and that they would rather receive their death there, than go from their place beside the car. And the king had his crown upon his head. And in this guise all the kings of the Goths, who had been lords of Spain, were to go to battle ; and this cus- tom they had all observed till the King Don Rodrigo ; but he, because of the great grief which he had in his heart, would never ascend the car, neither did he go in it into the battle.»—Part i, c. 215.

Entró Rodrigo en la batalla fiera,
Armado en blanco de un arnes dorado,
El yelmo coronado de una esfera
Que en luzes vence al circulo estrellado :
En unas ricas andas, ó litera
Que al hijo de Climene despeñado
Engañaran mejor que el carro de oro
De igual peligro, y de mayor tesoro.

La púrpura real las armas cubre,
El grave rostro en magestad le baña,
El ceptro por quien era le descubre
Rodrigo último Godo Rey de España :
Mas de la suerte que en lluvioso Otubre
Lo verde que le veste y acompaña
Desnuda al olmo blanco, rompe y quita
Vulturno ayrado que al invierno incita ;

Caen las hojes sobre el agua clara
Que le bañava el pie, y el ornamento
Del tronco imita nuestra edad que para
En su primero humilde fundamento:
Desierta queda la frondosa vara,
Sigue la rama, en remolino, al viento,
Que la aparta del árbol, que saltea
Su blanca, verde, y palida librea.

Asi Rodrigo el miserable dia
Ultimo de esta guerra desdichada
Quedó en el campo, donde ya tenia
La magestad del ombro derribada:
Alli la rota púrpura yacia
Teñida en sangre, y en sudor sañada,
Alli el verde laurel, y el ceptro de oro,
Siendo el arbol su cuerpo, el viento el Moro.

LOPE DE VEGA. *Jerusalen Conquistada*, l. vi, f. 136.

Note 8, page 385, col. 2.

That helm,
Whose horns amid the thickest of the fray
Eminent, had mark'd his presence.

Morales describes this horned helmet from a coin. « Tiene de la una parte su rostro, harto diferente de los que en las otras Monedas de estos Reyes parecen. Tiene manera de estar armado, y salenle por cima de la celada unas puntas como cuernos pequeños y derechos por ambos lados, que lo hacen estraño y espantable.» Florez has given this coin in his Medallas de España, from the only one which was known to be in existence, and which was then in the collection of the Infante D. Gabriel. It was struck at Egitania, the present Idana, and, like all the coins of the Visigoth kings, is of the rudest kind. The lines which Morales describes are sufficiently apparent, and if they are not intended for horns, it is impossible to guess what else they may have been meant to represent.

« These Gothic coins,» says P. D. Jeronymo Contador de Argote, « have a thousand barbarisms, as well in their letters as in other circumstances. They mingle Greek characters with Latin ones ; and in what regards the relief or figure, nothing can be more dissimilar than the representation to the thing which it is intended to represent. I will relate what happened to me with one, however much D. Egidio de Albornos de Macedo may reprehend me for it in his Parecer Anathomico. Valerio Pinto de Sa, an honourable citizen of Braga, of whom, in various parts of these Memoirs, I have made well-deserved mention, and of whose friendship I have been proud ever since I have been in that city, gave me, some six or seven years ago, a gold coin of King Leovigildo, who was the first of the Gothic kings of Spain that coined money, for till then both Goths and Sueves used the Roman. I examined leisurely, and what I clearly saw was a cross on the one side upon some steps, and some ill-shaped letters around it ; and on the reverse something, I knew not what : It seemed to me like a tree, or a stake which shot out some branches : Round about were some letters, more distinct : I could not, however, ascertain what they signified. It happened about that time that I had the honour of a visit from the most illustrious Sr. D. Francisco de Almeida, then a most worthy academician of the Royal academy, and at present a most deserving and eminent principal of the Holy Patriarchal Church. He saw this coin, and he also was puzzled by the side which represented what I called a tree. He asked me to lend it him, that he might examine it more at leisure. He took it away, and after some days returned it, saying, that he had examined it with a microscope, and that what I had taken for a stake was without question the portrait of King Leovigildo. I confess that I was not yet entirely satisfied : however, I showed it afterwards to divers persons, all of whom said they knew not what the said figure could be ; but when I desired them to see if it could be this portrait, they all agreed that it was. This undeceived me, and by looking at the coin in every possible light, at last I came to see it also, and acknowledge the truth with the rest. And afterwards I found in the Dialogues of Antonio Agostinho, treating of these Gothic coins, that there are some of such rude workmanship, that where a face should be represented, some represent a pitcher, and others an urn.»—*Memorias de Braga,* t. iii, p. lix.

Note 9, page 385, col. 2.

He bade the river bear the name of joy.

Guadalete had been thus interpreted to Florez (España Sagrada, t. 9, p. 53.) Earlier writers had asserted, (but without proof,) that the Ancients called it Lethe, and the Moors added to these names their word for river. Lope de Vega alludes to this opinion :

Siempre lamentable Guadalete
Que llevó tanta sangre al mar de España,
Si por olvido se llamaba el Lete
Trueque este nombre la vitoria estraña,
Y llámase memoria deste día
En que España perdio la que tenia.
Que por donde á la mar entraba apenas
Diferenciando el agua, ya se via
Con roxo humor de las sangrientas venas
Por donde le cortaba y dividia :
Gran tiempo conservaron sus arenas
(Y pienso que ha llegado á la edad mia)
Reliquias del estrago y piedras hechas
Armas, hierros de lanza y de flechas.

Jerusalem Conquistada, l. vi, ff. 136.

The date of the battle is given with grandiloquous circumstantiality by Miguel de Barrios.

Salió la tercer alva del tonante
Noviembre, con vestido nebuloso,
sobre el alado bruto que al brillante
carro, saca del piélago espumoso ;
y en el frio Escorpion casa rotante
del fiero Marte, el Astro luminoso
al son que compasó sus plantas sueltas
dió setecientas y catorze bueltas.

Coro de las Musas, p. 100.

He states the chronology of Pelayo's accession in the same taste.

Era el Pontificado del Segundo
Gregorio ; Emperador Leon Tercero
del docto Griego ; y del Persiano inmundo,
Zuleyman Miramamolin guerrero ;
y de Daphne el amante rubicundo
surcava el mar del fulgido Carnero
setecientas y diez y ocho vezes,
dexando el puerto de los aureos Pesces.

Ditto, p. 102.

Note 10, page 386, col. 2.

He found himself on Ana's banks,
Fast by the Caulian schools.

The site of this monastery, which was one of the most flourishing seminaries of that age, is believed to have been two leagues from Merida, upon the Guadiana, where the Ermida, or Chapel of Cubillana, stands at present, or was standing a few years ago. The legend, from which I have taken such circumstances as might easily have happened, and as suited my plan, was invented by a race of men who, in the talent of inventing, have left all poets and romancers far behind them. Florez refers to Brito for it, and excuses himself from relating it, because it is not necessary to his[1] subject ; — in reality he neither believed the story, nor chose to express his objections to it. His disbelief was probably founded upon the suspicious character of Brito, who was not at that time so decidedly condemned by his countrymen as he is at present. I give the legend from this veracious Cistercian. Most of his other fabrications have been exploded, but this has given rise to a popular and fashionable idolatry, which still maintains its ground.

« The monk did not venture to leave him alone in that

[1] España Sagrada, t. xiii, p. 242.

disconsolate state, and taking him apart, besought him by the passion of Jesus Christ to consent that they twain should go together, and save a venerable image of the Virgin Mary our Lady, which in that convent flourished with great miracles, and had been brought from the city of Nazareth by a Greek monk, called Cyriac, at such time as a heresy in the parts of the East arose against the use and veneration of images; and with it a relic of the Apostle St Bartholomew, and another of St Bras, which were kept in an ivory coffer, for it would be a great sacrilege to leave them exposed to the ill-treatment of barbarians, who according to public fame, left neither temple nor sacred place which they did not profane, casting the images into the fire, and dragging them at their horses' tails for a greater opprobrium to the baptised people. The King, seeing himself thus conjured by the passion of our Redeemer Jesus Christ, in whom alone he had consolation and hope of remedy, and considering the piety of the thing in which he was chosen for companion, let himself be overcome by his entreaties; and taking in his arms the little image of our Lady, and Romano the coffer with the relics, and some provision for the journey, they struck into the middle of Portugal, having their faces alway towards the west, and seeking the coast of the ocean sea, because in those times it was a land more solitary, and less frequented by people, where they thought the Moors would not reach so soon, because, as there were no countries to conquer in those parts, there was no occasion which should lead them thither. Twenty-and-six days the two companions travelled without touching at any inhabited place, and after enduring many difficulties in crossing mountains and fording rivers, they had sight of the ocean sea on the 22d of November, being the day of the Virgin Martyr St Cecilia; and as if in that place they should have an end of their labours, they took some comfort, and gave thanks to God, for that he had saved them from the hand of their enemies. The place which they reached is in the *Coutos* of Alcobaça, near to where we now see the town of Pederneira, on the eastern side of which there rises, in the midst of certain sands, a hill of rock and firm land, somewhat prolonged from north to south, so lofty and well proportioned that it seemeth miraculously placed in that site, being surrounded on all sides with plains covered with sand, without height or rock to which it appears connected. And forasmuch as the manner thereof draws to it the eyes of whosoever beholds this work of nature, the king and the monk desired to ascend the height of it, to see whether it would afford a place for them in which to pass their lives. They found there a little hermitage with a holy crucifix, and no other signs of man, save only a plain tomb, without writing or epitaph to declare whose it might be. The situation of the place, which, ascending to a notable height, gives a prospect by sea and by land as far as the eyes can reach, and the sudden sight of the crucifix, caused in the mind of the king such excitement and so great consolation, that, embracing the foot of the cross, he lay there melting away in rivers of tears, not now of grief for the kingdoms and dominions which he had lost, but of consolation in seeing that in exchange the crucified Jesus himself had in this solitary mountain offered himself to him, in whose company he resolved to pass the remainder of his life; and this he declared to the monk, who, to content him, and also because he saw that the place was convenient for contemplation, approved the king's re-

solve, and abode there with him some days; during which perceiving some inconvenience in living upon the summit of the mountain, from whence it was necessary to descend with much labour, whenever they would drink, or seek for herbs and fruits for their food; and moreover understanding that it was the king's desire to remain there alone, that he might vent himself in tears and exclamations, which he made oftentimes before the image of Christ, he went with his consent to a place little more than a mile from the mountain, which being on the one side smooth and of easy approach, hangs on the other over the sea with so huge a precipice that it is two hundred fathoms in perpendicular height, from the top of the rock to the water. There, between two great rocks, each of which projects over the sea, hanging suspended from the height in such a form, that they seem to threaten destruction to him who sees them from the beach, Romano found a little cave, made naturally in the cliff, which he enlarged with some walls of loose stone, built up with his own hands, and having thus made a sort of hermitage, he placed therein the image of the Virgin Mary of Nazareth, which he had brought from the Caulinean convent, and which being small, and of a dark colour, with the infant Jesus in its arms, hath in the countenance a certain perfection, with a modesty so remarkable, that at first sight it presents something miraculous; and having been known and venerated so great a number of years, during many of which it was in a place which did not protect it from the injuries of weather, it hath never been painted, neither hath it been found necessary to renew it. The situation of this hermitage was, and is now, within sight of the mountain where the king dwelt; and though the memorials from whence I am deriving the circumstances of these events do not specify it, it is to be believed that they often saw each other, and held such divine communion as their mode of life and the holiness of the place required; especially considering the great temptations of the Devil which the king suffered at the beginning of his penitence, for which the counsels and instructions of the monk would be necessary, and the aid of his prayers, and the presence of the relics of St Bartholomew, which miraculously saved him many times from various illusions of the enemy. And in these our days there are seen upon the top of the mountain, in the living rock, certain human footsteps, and others of a different form, which the common people, without knowing the person, affirm to be the footsteps of St Bartholomew and the Devil, who was there defeated and his illusions confounded by the saint, coming in aid of a devout man who called upon him in the force of his tribulation. This must have been the king, (though the common people know it not,) whom the saint thus visibly aided; and he chose that for a memorial of this aid, and of the power which God has given him over the evil spirits, these marks should remain impressed upon the living rock. And the ancient name of the mountain being Seano, it was changed into that of the Apostle, and is called at present St Bartholomew's; and the hermitage which remains upon the top of it is under the invocation of the same saint and of St Bras, which must have arisen from the relics of these two saints that Romano brought with him, and left with the king for his consolation, when he withdrew with the image of Our Lady to the place of which we have spoken, where he lived little more than a year; and then knowing the time of his

57

death, he communicated it to the king, beseeching him that, in requital for the love with which he had accompanied him, he would remember to pray to God for his soul, and would give his body to the earth, from which it had sprung; and that having to depart from that land, he would leave there the image and the relics, in such manner as he should dispose them before he died. With that Romano departed to enjoy the reward deserved by his labours, leaving the king with fresh occasion of grief for want of so good a companion. Of what more passed in this place, and of the temptations and tribulations which he endured till the end of his life, there is no authentic historian, nor memorial which should certify them, more than some relations mingled with fabulous tales in the ancient Chronicle of King Don Rodrigo, where, among the truths which are taken from the Moor Rasis, there are many things notoriously impossible; such as the journey which the king took, being guided by a white cloud till he came near Viseo; and the penance in which he ended his life there, inclosing himself alive in a certain tomb with a serpent which he had bred for that purpose. But as these are things difficult to believe, we will pass them over in silence, leaving to the judgment of the curious the credit which an ancient picture deserves, still existing near Viseo, in the church of St Michael, over the tomb of the said King Don Roderick, in which is seen a serpent painted with two heads; and in the tomb itself, which is of wrought stone, a round hole, through which they say that the snake entered. That which is certain of all this is, as our historians relate, that the king came to this place, and in the hermitage of St Michael, which we now see near Viseo, ended his days in great penance, no man knowing the manner thereof; neither was there any other memorial clearer than that in process of time a writing was found upon a certain tomb in this church with these words; HIC REQVIESCIT RUDERICUS ULTIMUS REX GOTHORUM, Here rests Roderick, the last King of the Goths. I remember to have seen these very words written in black upon an arch of the wall, which is over the tomb of the king, although the Archbishop Don Rodrigo, and they who follow him, give a longer inscription, not observing that all which he has added are his own curses and imprecations upon Count Don Julian, (as Ambrosio de Morales has properly remarked, following the Bishop of Salamanca and others,) and not parts of the same inscription, as they make them. The church in which is the tomb of the king is at present very small, and of great antiquity, especially the first chapel, joined to which on either side is a cell of the same length, but narrow, and dark also, having no more light than what enters through a little window opening to the east. In one of these cells (that which is on the south side) it is said that a certain hermit dwelt, by whose advice the king governed himself in the course of his penance; and at this time his grave is shown close to the walls of the chapel, on the Epistle side. In the other cell (which is on the north) the king past his life, paying now, in the straitness of that place, for the largeness of his palaces and the liberties of his former life, whereby he had offended his Creator. And in the wall of the chapel which answers to the Gospel side, there remains a sort of arch, in which the tomb is seen, wherein are his bones; and it is devoutly visited by the natives, who believe that through his means the Lord does miracles there upon persons afflicted with

agues and other like maladies. Under the said arch, in the part answering to it in the inside of the cell, I saw painted on the wall the hermit and the king, with the serpent with two heads, and I read the letters which are given above, all defaced by time, and bearing marks of great antiquity, yet so that they could distinctly be seen. The tomb is flat and made of a single stone, in which a man's body can scarcely find room. When I saw it it was open, the stone which had served to cover it not being there, neither the bones of the king, which they told me had been carried into Castille some years before, but in what manner they knew not, nor by whose order; neither could I discover, by all the enquiries which I made among the old people of that city, who had reason to be acquainted with a thing of so much importance, if it were as certain as some of them affirmed it to be.»— BRITO, Monarchia Lusitania, P. ii, l. 7, c. 3.

« The great venerableness of the Image of Our Lady of Nazareth which the king left hidden in the very place where Romano in his lifetime had placed it, and the continual miracle which she shewed formerly, and still shews,» induced F. Bernardo de Brito to continue the history of this Image, which, no doubt, he did the more willingly because he bears a part in it himself. In the days of Affonso Henriquez, the first king of Portugal, this part of the country was governed by D. Fuas Roupinho, a knight famous in the Portugueze chronicles, who resided in the castle at Porto de Mos. This Dom Fuas, « when he saw the land secure from enemies, used often to go out hunting among the sands and thickets between the town and the sea, where, in those days, there used to be great store of game, and even now, though the land is so populous, there is still some; and as he followed this exercise, the proper pastime of noble and spirited men, and came sometimes to the sea-shore, he came upon that remarkable rock, which being level on the side of the north, and on a line with the flat country, ends towards the south in a precipice over the waves of the sea, of a prodigious height, causing the greater admiration to him who, going over the plain country without finding any irregularity, finds himself, when least expecting it, suddenly on the summit of such a height. And as he was curiously regarding this natural wonder, he perceived between the two biggest cliffs which stand out from the ground and project over the sea, a sort of house built of loose stones, which, from its form and antiquity, made him go himself to examine it; and descending by the chasm between the two rocks, he entered into a low cavern, where, upon a little altar, he saw the venerable Image of the Virgin Mary of Nazareth, being of such perfection and modesty as are found in very few images of that size. The catholic knight venerated it with all submission, and would have removed it to his castle of Porto de Mos, to have it held in more veneration, but that he feared to offend it if he should move it from a habitation where it had abode for so many years. This consideration made him leave it for the present in the same place and manner in which he found it; and although he visited it afterwards when in course of the chase he came to those parts, nevertheless he never took in hand to improve the poor hermitage in which it was, nor would he have done it, if the Virgin had not saved him from a notorious danger of death, which, peradventure, God permitted, as a punishment for his negligence, and in this manner to make the virtue of the Holy Image manifest to the world. It was thus, that going to his ordinary exercise of the chase, in the month of September, in the year of Christ 1182, and on the 14th of the month, being the day on which the church celebrates the festival of the Exaltation of the Cross, upon the which Christ redeemed the human race, as the day rose thick with clouds, which ordinarily arise from the sea, and the country round about could not be seen by reason of the clouds, save for a little space, it befell that the dogs put up a stag (if indeed it were one), and Dom Fuas pressing his horse in pursuit, without fear of any danger, because he thought it was all plain ground, and the mist hindered him from seeing where he was, found himself upon the very edge of the rock on the precipice, two hundred fathoms above the sea, at a moment when it was no longer in his power to turn the reins, nor could he do any thing more than invoke the succours of the Virgin Mary, whose image was in that place; and she succoured him in such a manner, that less than two palms from the edge of the rock, on a long and narrow point thereof, the horse stopt as if it had been made of stone, the marks of his hoofs remaining in proof of the miracle imprinted in the living rock, such as at this day they are seen by all strangers and persons on pilgrimages, who go to visit the Image of Our Lady; and it is a notable thing, and deserving of serious consideration, to see that in the midst of this rock, upon which the miracle happened, and on the side towards the east, and in a part where, because it is suspended in the air, it is not possible that any human being could reach, Nature herself has impressed a cross as if nailed to the hardness of the rock, as though she had sanctified that cliff therewith, and marked it with that holy sign, to be the theatre in which the miraculous circumstance was to be celebrated; which, by reason that it took place on the day of the Exaltation of the Cross, seemed as if it showed the honour and glory which should from thence redound to the Lord who redeemed us thereon. Dom Fuas seeing himself delivered from so great danger, and knowing from whence the grace had come to him, went to the little hermitage, where, with the great devotion which the presence of the miracle occasioned, he gave infinite thanks to the Lady, accusing himself before her of having neglected to repair the house, and promising all the amends which his possibility permitted. His huntsmen afterwards arrived, following the track of the horse, and knowing the marvel which had occurred, they prostrated themselves before the Image of the Lady, adding with their astonishment to the devotion of Dom Fuas, who hearing that the stag had not been seen, and that the dogs had found no track of him in any part, though one had been represented before him to draw him on, understood that it was an illusion of the devil, seeking by that means to make him perish miserably. All these considerations enhanced the greatness of the miracle, and the obligations of Dom Fuas, who, tarrying there some days, made workmen come from Leyria and Porto de Mos, to make another hermitage, in which the Lady should be more venerated; and as they were demolishing the first, they found placed between the stones of the altar a little box of ivory, and within it relicks of St Bras, St Bartholomew, and other saints, with a parchment, wherein a relation was given of how, and at what time those relicks and the image were brought there, according as has been aforesaid. A vaulted chapel was soon made,

after a good form for times so ancient, over the very place where the Lady had been; and to the end that it might be seen from all sides, they left it open with four arches, which in process of time were closed, to prevent the damage which the rains and storms did within the chapel, and in this manner it remains in our days. The Lady remained in her place, being soon known and visited by the faithful, who flocked there upon the fame of her appearance: the valiant and holy king D. Affonso Henriquez, being one of the first whom Dom Fuas advised of what had happened, and he, accompanied with the great persons of his court, and with his son, D. Sancho, came to visit the Image of the Lady, and see with his own eyes the marks of so rare a miracle as that which had taken place; and with his consent, D. Fuas made a donation to the Lady of a certain quantity of land round about, which was at that time a wild thicket, and for the greater part is so still, being well nigh all wild sands incapable of giving fruit, and would produce nothing more than heath and some wild pine-trees. And because it establishes the truth of all that I have said, and relates in its own manner the history of the Image of The Lady, I will place it here in the form in which I saw it in the Record-Room at Alcobaça, preserving throughout the Latin and the barbarism of its composition; which is as follows:

«Sub nomine Patris, nec non et ejus prolis, in unius potentia Deitatis, incipit carta donationis, necnon et devotionis, quam ego Fuas Ropinho tenens Porto de Mos, et terram de Albardos usque Leirenam, et Turres Veteres, facio Ecclesiæ Sanctæ Mariæ de Nazareth, quæ de pauco tempore surgit fundata super mare, ubi de sæculis antiquis jacebat, inter lapides et spinas multas, de tota illa terra quæ jacet inter flumina quæ venit per Alcaubaz, et aquam nuncupatam de furaturio, et dividitur de isto modo: de illa foz de flumine Alcobaz, quomodo vadit per aquas bellas, deinde inter mare et mata de Patayas usque; finir in ipso furaturio, quam ego obtinui de rege Alfonso, et per suum consensum facio præsentem seriem ad prædictam Ecclesiam Beatæ Mariæ Virginis, quam feci supra mare, ut in sæculis perpetuis memorentur mirabilia Dei, et sit notum omnibus hominibus, quomodo a morte fuerim salvatus per pietatem Dei et Beatæ Mariæ quam vocant de Nazaret, tali sucesu. Cum manerem in castro Porto de Mos, et inde veniebam ad ocidendos venatos, per Melvam et matam de Patayas usque ad mare, supra quam inveni furnam, et parvam domunculam inter arbustas et vepres, in qua erat una Imago Virginis Mariæ, et veneravimus illam, et abivimus inde; veni deinde xviii kal. Octobris, circa dictum locum, cum magna obscuratione nebulæ sparsa super totam terram, et invenimus venatum, tres quem fui in meo equo, usque venirem ad esbarrondadeiro supra mare, quod cadit ajuso sine mensura hominis et pavet visus si cernit furnam cadentem ad aquas. Pavi ego miser peccator, et venit ad remembrancam de imagine ibi posita, et magna voce dixi, SANCTA MARIA VAL. Benedicta sit illa in mulieribus, quia meum equum sicut si esset lapis fecit stare, pedibus fixis in lapide, et erat jam vazatus extra terram in punta de saxo super mare. Descendi de equo, et veni ad locum ubi erat imago, et ploravi et gratias feci, et venerunt monteiros et viderunt, et laudaverunt Deum et Beatam Mariam; Misi homines per Leirenam et Porto de Mos, et per loca vicina, ut venirent Alvanires, et facerent ecclesiam bono opere operatam de fornice et lapide, et jam laudatur Deus finita est. Nos vero non sciebamus unde esset, et unde venisset ista imago; sed ecce cum destruebatur altare per Alvanires, inventa est arcula de ebore antiquo, et in illa uno envoltorio, in quo erant ossa aliquorum sanctorum, et cartula cum hac inscriptione : Hic sunt reliquiæ Sanctorum Blasii et Bartholomei Apostoli, quas detulit a Monasterio Cauliniana Romanus monachus, simul cum venerabili Imagine Virginis Mariæ de Nazareth, quæ olim in Nazareth Civitate Gallileæ multis miraculis claruerat, et inde asportata per Græcum monachum nomine Cyriacum, Gothorum Regum tempore, in prædicto monasterio per multum temporis manserat, quo usque Hispania à Mauris debelata, et Rex Rodericus superatus in prælio solus, lacrymabilis, abjectus, et pene defficiens pervenit ad præfatum monasterium Cauliniana, ibique a prædicto Romano pœnitentiæ et Eucharistiæ Sacramentis susceptis, pariter cum illo, cum imagine, et reliquiis ad Seanum montem pervenerunt 10 kal. Decemb. in quo rex solus per annum integrum permansit, in Ecclesia ibi inventa cum Christi crucifixi imagine, et ignoto sepulchro. Romanus vero cum hac Sacra Virginis effigie inter duo ista saxa, usque ad extremum vitæ permansit; et ne futuris temporibus aliquem ignorantia teneat, hæc cum reliquiis sacris in hac extremæ orbis parte recondimus. Deus ista omnia a Maurorum manibus servet. Amen. De his lectis et a Presbyteris apertis satis multum sumus gavisi, quia nomen de sanctis reliquiis, et de Virgine scivimus, et ut memorentur per semper in ista serie testamenti scribere fecimus. Do igitur prædictam hæreditatem pro reparatione prefatæ Ecclesiæ cum pascuis, et aquis, de monte in fonte, ingressibus et regressibus, quantum a prestitum hominis est, et illam in melliorate foro aliquis potest habere per se. Ne igitur aliquis homo de nostris vel de estraneis hoc factum nostrum ad irrumpendum veniat, quod si tentaverit peche ad dominum terræ trecentos marabitinos, et carta nihilominus in suo robore permaneat, et insuper sedeat excommunicatus et cum Juda proditore pœnas luat damnatorum. Facta series testamenti vi Idus Decemb. era M,CLXX, Alfonsus Portugaliæ Rex confirm. Sancius Rex confirm. Regina Dona Tarasia confirm. Petrus Fernandez, regis Sancii dapifer confirm. Menendus Gunsalui, ejusdem signifer confirm. Donus Joannes Fernandez curiæ regis maiordomus confirm. Donus Julianus Cancellarius regis confirm. Martiniis Gonsalui Pretor Colimbriæ confirm. Petrus Omariz Capellanus regis confirm. Menendus Abbas confirm. Theotonius conf. Fernandus Nuniz, testis. Egeas Nuniz, testis. Dn Telo, testis. Petrus Nuniz, testis. Fernandus Vermundi, testis. Lucianus Præsbyter Notavit.»

This deed, which establishes all the principal facts that I have related, did not take effect, because the lands of which it disposed were already part of the *Coutos* of Alcobaça, which King Don Affonso had given some years before to our father St Bernard, and Dom Fuas compensated for them with certain properties near Pombal, as is proved by another writing annexed to the former, but which I forbear to insert, as appertaining little to the thread of my history : and resuming the course thereof, you must know, that the image of the Virgin Mary of Nazareth remained in the chapel which Dom Fuas made for it, till the year of Christ 1377, in the which, King Dom Fernando of Portugal founded for it the house in which it now is, having been enlarged and beautified by Queen Dona Lianor, wife of King Dom Joam II, and surrounded with porticoes by King Dom Manoel. And now in our times a chapel (*Capela mor*) of good fabric has been built, with voluntary contributions, and the rents of the brotherhood; and in the old hermitage founded by Dom Fuas I., with the help of some devout persons had another chapel opened under ground, in order to discover the very rock and cavern in which the Holy Image had been hidden so great a number of years; there is a descent to it by eight or ten steps, and a notable consolation it is to those who consider the great antiquity of that sanctuary. And for that the memory of things so remarkable ought not to be lost, I composed an inscription briefly recounting the whole : and Dr Ruy Lourenço, who was then Provedor of the Comarca of Leyria, and visitor of the said church for the king, ordered it to be engraven in marble. It is as follows :

« Sacra Virginis Mariæ veneranda Imago, a Monasterio Cauliniana prope Emeritam, quo Gothorum tempore, a Nazareth translata, miraculis claruerat, in generali Hispaniæ clade, Ann. Dni DCCXIIII. a Romano monacho, comite, ut fertur, Roderico Rege, ad hanc extremam orbis partem adducitur, in qua dum unus moritur, alter proficiscitur, per CCCCLXIX. annos inter duo hæc prærupta saxa sub parvo delituit tugurio : deinde a Fua Ropinio, Portus Molarum duce, anno Domini MCLXXXII (ut ipse in donatione testatur), inventa, dum incaute agitato equo fugacem, fictumque forte, insequitur cervum, ad ultimumque immanis hujus præcipitii cuneum, jam jam ruiturus accedit, nomine Virginis invocato, a ruina, et mortis faucibus ereptus, hoc ei prius dedicat sacellum; tandem a Ferdinando Portugaliæ Rege, ad majus aliud templum, quod ipse a fundamentis erexerat transfertur, Ann. Domini MCCCLXXVII. Virgini et perpetuitati D.D.F.B.D.B. ex voto.»

From these things, taken as faithfully as I possibly could from the deed of gift and from history, we see clearly the great antiquity of this sanctuary, since it is 893 years since the Image of The Lady was brought to the place where it now is; and although we do not know the exact year in which it was brought from Nazareth, it is certain at least that it was before King Recaredo, who began to reign in the year of Christ 586; so that it is 1021 years, a little more or less, since it came to Spain; and as it came then, as one well known, and celebrated for miracles in the parts of the East, it may well be understood that this is one of the most famous and ancient Images, and nearest to the times of the apostles, that the world at present possesses.—*Brito Monarchia Lusitana*, p. 2. L. 7. C. 4.

This legend cannot have been invented before Emanuel's reign, for Duarte Galvam says nothing of it in his Chronicle of Affonso Henriquez, though he relates the exploits and death of D. Fuas Roupinho. I believe there is no earlier authority for it than Bernardo de Brito himself. It is one of many articles of the same kind from the great manufactory at Alcobaça, and is at this day as firmly believed by the people of Portugal as any article of the Christian faith. How indeed should they fail to believe it? I have a print, it is one of the most popular devotional prints in Portugal, which represents the miracle. The diabolical stag is flying down the precipice, and looking back with a wicked turn of the head, in hopes of seeing Dom Fuas follow him; the horse is rearing up with his hind feet upon the brink of the precipice; the knight has dropt his hunting-spear, his cocked hat is falling behind him, and an exclamation to the Virgin is coming out of his mouth. The Virgin with a crown upon her head, and the Babe with a crown upon his, at her breast, appear in the sky amidst clouds of glory. *N. S. de Nazareé*, is written above this precious print, and this more precious information below it,—*O. Emo. Snr. Cardeal Patriarcha concede* 50 *dias de Indulga. a qm. rezar huma have ma. diante desta Image.* His Eminency the Cardinal Patriarch grants fifty days indulgence to whosoever shall say an Ave-Maria before this Image. The print is included, and plenty of Ave-Marias are said before it in full faith, for this *nossa senhora* is in high vogue. Before the French invasion, this famous Image used annually to be escorted by the court to Cape Espichel. In 1796 I happened to be upon the Tagus at the time of her embarkation at Belem. She was carried in a sort of sedan-chair, of which the fashion resembled that of the Lord Mayor's coach; a processional gunboat preceded the Image and the Court, and I was literally caught in a shower of rockets; if any of which had fallen upon the heretical heads of me and my companion, it would not improbably have been considered as a new miracle wrought by the wonderworking Senhora.

In July 1808, the French, under General Thomieres, robbed the church of this Lady of Nazareth; their booty, in jewels and plate, was estimated at more than 200,000 crusados. Jose Accursio das Neves, the Portugueze historian of those disastrous times, expresses his surprise that no means should have been taken by those who had the care of these treasures, for securing them in time. Care, however, seems to have been taken of the Great Diana of the Temple, for though it is stated that they destroyed or injured several images, no mention is made of any insult or damage having been offered to this. They sacked the town and set fire to it, but it escaped with the loss of only thirteen or fourteen houses; the suburb or village, on the beach, was less fortunate: there only four houses of more than 300 remain unconsumed, and all the boats and nets were destroyed.—*Historia de Invasam, etc.* t. 4, p. 85.

Note 11, page 387, col. 1.
Spreading his hands and lifting up his face, etc.

The *Vision of Don Roderick* supplies a singular contrast to the picture which is represented in this passage. I have great pleasure in quoting the stanzas; if the contrast had been intentional, it could not have been more complete.

> But, far within, Toledo's Prelate lent
> An ear of fearful wonder to the King;
> The silver lamp a fitful lustre sent,
> So long that sad confession witnessing:
> For Roderick told of many a hidden thing,
> Such as are lothly uttered to the air,
> When Fear, Remorse, and Shame, the bosom wring,
> And Guilt his secret burthen cannot bear,
> And Conscience seeks in speech a respite from Despair.
>
> Full on the Prelate's face, and silver hair,
> The stream of failing light was feebly roll'd;
> But Roderick's visage, though his head was bare,
> Was shadow'd by his hand and mantle's fold.

> While of his hidden soul the sins he told,
> Proud Alaric's descendant could not brook
> That mortal man his bearing should behold,
> Or boast that he had seen, when conscience shook,
> Fear tame a monarch's brow, remorse a warrior's look.

This part of the story is thus nakedly stated by Dr Andre da Sylva Mascarenhas, in a long narrative poem with this title,—*A destruiçam de Espanha, Restauraçam Summaria da mesma.*

> Achouse o pobre Rey em Cauliniana
> Mosteiro junto ao rio Guadiana.

> Eram os frades fugidos do Mosteiro
> Com receos dos Barbaros malvados,
> De bruços esteve el Rey hum dia inteiro
> Na Igreja, chorando seus peccados:
> Hum Monge veo alli por derradeiro
> A conhecer quem era, ouvindo os brados
> Que o disfarçado Rey aos ares dava,
> Este Monge Romano se chamava.

> Perguntoulhe quem era, e donde vinha,
> Por ver no pobre traje gram portento,
> El Rey lho respondeo como convinha
> Sem declarar seu posto, ou seu intento;
> Pediulhe confissam, e o Monge asinha
> Lha concedeo e o Santo Sacram.nto
> Era força que el Rey na confissam
> Lhe declarasse o posto e a tençam.

> Como entendeo o bom Religioso
> Que aquelle era seu Rey que por estranhas
> Terras andava roto e lacrimoso,
> Mil ays tirou das intimas entranhas:
> Lançouselhe aos pes, e com piedoso
> Affecto o induziu e varias manhas,
> O quizesse tambem levar consigo
> Por socio no desterro e no perigo.——P. 278.

Note 12, page 387, col. 1.
The fourth week of their painful pilgrimage.

> Dias vinte e sete na passagem
> Gastaram, desviandosse do humano
> Trato, e maos encontros que este mundo
> Traz sempre a quem busca o bem profundo.
> *Destruiçam de Espanha.*

Note 13, page 388, col. 2.
> Some new austerity unheard of yet
> In Syrian fields of glory, or the sands
> Of holiest Egypt.

Egypt has been, from the earliest ages, the theatre of the most abject and absurd superstitions, and very little benefit was produced by a conversion which exchanged crocodiles and monkeys for monks and mountebanks. The first monastery is said to have been established in that country by St Anthony the Great, towards the close of the third century. He who rests in solitude, said the saint, is saved from three conflicts, —from the war of hearing, and of speech, and of sight; and he has only to maintain the struggle against his own heart. (*Acta Sanctorum*, T. ii, p. 143.) Indolence was not the only virtue which he and his disciples introduced into the catalogue of Christian perfections. S. Eufraxia entered a convent consisting of an hundred and thirty nuns, not one of whom had ever washed her feet; the very mention of the bath was an abomination to them.—(*Acta Sanctorum, March* 13.) St Macarius had renounced most of the decencies of life; but he returned one day to his convent, humbled and mortified, exclaiming,—I am not yet a monk, but I have seen monks! for he had met two of these wretches stark naked.—*Acta Sanctorum*, i, p. 107.

The principles which these madmen established were, that every indulgence is sinful; that whatever is gratifying to the body, must be injurious to the soul; that in proportion as man inflicts torments upon himself, he pleases his Creator; that the ties of natural affection wean the heart from God; and that every social duty must be abandoned by him who would be perfect The doctrine of two principles has never produced such practical evils in any system as in the catholic. Manes, indeed, attributes all evil to the equal power of the Evil Principle, (that power being only for a time,) but some of the corrupted forms of Christianity actually exclude a good one!

There is a curious passage in the Bibliotheca Orientalis of Assemanus, in which the deserts are supposed to have been originally intended for the use of these saints, compensating for their sterility by the abundant crop of virtues which they were to produce! «In illâ vero soli vastitate, quæ procul a Nili ripis quaquaversus latissime protenditur, non urbes, non domicilia, non agri, non arbores, sed desertum, arena, feræ; Non tamen hanc terræ partem (ut Eucherii verbis utar) inutilem, et inhonoratam dimisit Deus, quum in primordiis rerum omnia in sapientiâ faceret, et singula quæque futuris usibus apta distingueret; sed cuncta non magis præsentis magnificentiâ, quam futuri præscientiâ creans, venturis, ut arbitror, Sanctis Eremum paravit. Credo, his illam locupletem fructibus voluit, et pro indulgentioris naturæ vice, hanc Sanctorum dare fœcundiam, ut sic pinguescerent fines deserti: Et quum irrigaret de superioribus suis montes, abundaret quoque multiplicata fruge convaless locorumque damna supplicet, quum habitationem sterilem habitatore ditaret.»

«If the ways of religion,» says South, «are ways of pleasantness, such as are not ways of pleasantness are not truly and properly ways of religion. Upon which ground it is easy to see what judgment is to be passed upon all those affected, uncommanded, absurd austerities, so much prized and exercised by some of the Romish profession. Pilgrimages, going barefoot, hair-shirts and whips, with other such gospel-artillery, are their only helps to devotion: things never enjoined, either by the prophets under the Jewish, or by the apostles under the Christian economy, who yet surely understood the proper and the most efficacious instruments of piety, as well as any confessor or friar of all the order of St Francis, or any casuist whatsoever.

«It seems that with them a man sometimes cannot be a penitent unless he also turns vagabond, and foots it to Jerusalem, or wanders over this or that part of the world, to visit the shrines of such or such a pretended saint, though perhaps in his life ten times more ridiculous than themselves. Thus, that which was Cain's error, is become their religion. He that thinks to expiate a sin by going bare-foot, only makes one folly the atonement for another. Paul, indeed, was scourged and beaten by the Jews, but we never read that he beat or scourged himself; and if they think that his *keeping under of his body* imports so much, they must first prove that the body cannot be kept under by a virtuous mind, and that the mind cannot be made virtuous but by a scourge, and consequently that thongs and whip-cord are means of grace, and things necessary to salvation. The truth is, if men's religion lies no deeper than their skin, it is possible that they may scourge themselves into very great improvements.

«But they will find that bodily exercise touches not the soul, and that neither pride, nor lust, nor covetousness, was ever mortified by corporal discipline; 't is not the back, but the heart that must bleed for sin; and, consequently, that in their whole course they are like men out of their way; let them lash on never so fast, they are not at all the nearer to their journey's end; and howsoever they deceive themselves and others, they may as well expect to bring a cart as a soul to heaven by such means.»—*Sermons*, vol. i, p. 34.

Note 14, page 389, col. 1.

In those weeds
Which never from the hour when to the grave
She followed her dear Lord Theodofred,
Rusilla laid aside.

«Vide nuper ipse in Hispaniis constitutus et admiratus sum antiquum hunc morem, ab Hispanis adhuc omnibus observari; mortuâ quippe uxore maritus, mortuo marito conjux, mortuis filiis patres, mortuis patribus filii, defunctis quibuslibet cognatis cognati, extinctis, quolibet casu amicis amici, statim arma deponunt, sericas vestes, peregrinarum pellium tegmina abjiciunt, totumque penitus multi colorem, ac pretiosum habitum, abdicantes, nigris tantum vilibusque indumentis se contegunt. Sic crinibus propriis sic jumentorum suorum caudis decurtatis, seque et ipsa atro prorsus colore denigrant. Talibus luctui dolorisve insignibus, subtractos charissimos deflent, et integri ad minus spatium anni, in tali mærore publica lege consumant.»—*Petri Venerabilis Epist. quoted in Yepes, t. vii, ff. 21.*»

Note 15, page 389, col. 1.

Her eyeless husband.

Witiza put out the eyes of Theodofred, *inhabilitandole para la monarchia*, says Ferreras. This was the common mode of incapacitating a rival for the throne.

Un Conde de Gallicia que fuera valido,
Pelayo avie nombre, ome fo desforzado,
Perdio la vision, andaba embargado,
Ca ome que non vede, non de' is seer nado.
Gonzalo de Berceo. S. Dom. 388.

The history of Europe during the dark ages abounds with examples of *exoculation*, as it was called by those writers who endeavoured, towards the middle of the 17th century, to introduce the style ornate into our prose after it had been banished from poetry. In the East, the practice is still continued. When Alboquerque took possession of Ormuz, he sent to Portugal fifteen of its former kings, whom he found there, each of whom, in his turn, had been deposed and blinded!

In the semi-barbarous stage of society, any kind of personal blemish seems to have been considered as disqualifying a prince from the succession, like the law of the Nazarenes. Yorwerth, the son of Owen Gynedh, was set aside in Wales because of his broken nose; Count Oliba, in Barcelona, because he could never speak till he had stamped with his foot three times like a goat. «Aquest Oliba frare del Conte en Grifa no era a dret de sos mem bras. Car lo dit Oliba james no podia parlar, si primer, no donas colps ab lo peu en terra quart o sinc vegades, axi comsi fos cabra; e per aquesta raho li fou imposat lo nom, dient li Oliba Cabreta, e per aquest accident lo dit Oliba perde la

successio del frare en lo Comtat de Barcelona, e fou
donat lo dit Comtat o en Borrell, Comte de Urgell, qui
era sou cosin germa.»—*Pere Tomich*, c. xxviii, ff. 20.

In the treaty between our Henry V, and Charles VI
of France, by which Henry was appointed King of
France after Charles's decease, it was decreed that the
French should « swear to become liege men and vassals
to our said son King Henry, and obey him as the true
King of France, and without any opposition or dispute
shall receive him as such, and never pay obedience to
any other as king or regent of France, but to our said
son King Henry, unless our said son should lose life or
limb, or be attacked by a *mortal disease*, or suffer dimi-
nution in person, state, honour, [1] or goods.»

Lope de Vega alludes to the blindness of Theodofred
in his Jerusalen Conquistada :

> Criavase con ostras bellas damas
> Florinda bella,——
> Esta miro Rodrigo desdichado,
>   Ay si como su padre fuera ciego !
> Sacó sus ojos Witisa ayrado,
>   Fuera mejor los de Rodrigo luego :
> Gozara España el timbre coronado
>   De sus castillos en mayor sossiego
> Que le dió Leovigildo, y no se viera
> Estampa de Africano en su ribera.
>   L. vi, ß. 131.

A remarkable instance of the inconvenient manner in
which the *b* and the *v* are indiscriminately used by the
Spaniards, occurs here in the original edition. The *w*
not being used in that language, it would naturally be
represented by *vv*; and here, the printer, using most un-
luckily his typographical licence, has made the word
Vbitisa.

« The Spaniards,» says that late worthy Jo. Sanford,
some time fellow of Magdalane college, in Oxford, (in
his Spanish Grammar, 1632) «do with a kind of wanton-
ness so confound the sound of *b* with *v*, that it is hard
to determine when and in what words it should retain
its own power of a labial letter, which gave just cause
of laughter at that Spaniard who, being in conversation
with a French lady, and minding to commend her
children for fair, said unto her, using the Spanish liberty
in pronouncing the French,—*Madame vous avez des
veaux enfans,* telling her that she had calves to her
children, instead of saying, *beaux enfans,* fair children.
Neither can I well justify him who wrote *veneficio* for
beneficio.»

Note 16, page 390, col. 1.

> Conimbrica, whose ruined towers
> Bear record of the fierce Alani's wrath.

The Roman Conimbrica stood about two leagues
from the present Coimbra, on the site of Condeyxa Velha.
Ataces, king of the Alanes, won it from the Sueves, and,
in revenge for its obstinate resistance, dispeopled it,
making all its inhabitants, without distinction of per-
sons, work at the foundation of Coimbra where it now
stands. Hermenerico, the king of the Sueves, attacked
him while thus employed, but was defeated and pursued
to the Douro; peace was then made, and Sindasunda,
daughter of the conquered, given in marriage to the
conqueror. In memory of the pacification thus effect-
ed, Ataces bore upon his banners a damsel in a tower,
with a dragon vert on one side, and a lion rouge on the

other, the bearings of himself and his marriage-father
and this device being sculptured upon the towers of
Coimbra, still remains as the city arms. Two letters of
Arisbert, bishop of Porto, to Samerius, archdeacon of
Braga, which are preserved at Alcobaça, relate these
events as the news of the day,—that is, if the authority
of Alcobaçan records and of Bernardo de Brito can be
admitted.—*Mon. Lus.* 26. 3.

Ataces was an Arian, and therefore made the Catho-
lic bishops and priests work at his new city, but his
queen converted him.

Note 17, page 390, col. 2.

Mumadona.

Casper Estaco has shown that this is the name of the
foundress of Guimaraens, and that it is not, as some
writers had supposed, erroneously thus written, because
the words Muma and Dona followed each other in the
deeds of gift wherein it is preserved ; the name being
frequently found with its title affixed thus, Dma Mu-
madna.

Note 18, page 391, col. 1.

> —— the banks
> Of Lima, through whose groves in after years
> Mournful, yet sweet, Diogo's amorous lute
> Prolong'd its tuneful echoes.

Diogo Bernardes, one of the best of the Portugueze
poets, was born on the banks of the Lima, and passion-
ately fond of its scenery. Some of his sonnets will
bear comparison with the best poems of their kind.
There is a charge of plagiarism against him for having
printed several of Camoens's sonnets as his own : to
obtain any proofs upon this subject would be very dif-
ficult; this, however, is certain, that his own undisputed
productions resemble them so closely in unaffected
tenderness, and in sweetness of diction, that the whole
appear like the works of one author.

Note 19, page 391, col. 2.

> Auria itself is now but one wide tomb
> For all its habitants.

The present Orense. The Moors entirely destroyed it;
depopulavit usque ad solum, are the words of one of
the old brief chronicles. In 832, Alonzo el Casto found
it too completely ruined to be restored.—*Espagna Sa-
grada,* xvii, p. 48.

Note 20, page 393, col. 2.

> That consecrated pile amid the wild
> Which sainted Fructuoso in his zeal
> Reared to St Felix, on Visonia's banks.

Of this saint, and the curious institutions which he
formed, and the beautiful track of country in which
they were placed, I have given an account in the third
edition of Letters from Spain and Portugal, vol. i,
p. 103.

Note 21, page 394, col. 2.

> Sacaru——indignantly
> Did he toward the ocean bend his way.
> And shaking from his feet the dust of Spain,
> Took ship and hoisted sail, through seas unknown,
> To seek for freedom.

This tale, which is repeated by Bleda, rests on no bet-
ter authority than that of Abulcacim, [1] which may,
however, be admitted, so far as to show that it was a
prevalent opinion in his time.

---

[1] Johnes's Monstrellet, vol. i, p. 190.

[1] C. 13.

Antonio Galvam, in his *Tratado dos Descobrementos Antigos e Modernos*, relates a current and manifestly fabulous story, which has been supposed to refer to Sacaru, and the companions of his emigration. They say, he says, that at this time, A. D. 1447, a Portugueze ship sailing out of the Straits of Gibraltar, was carried by a storm much farther to the west than she had intended, and came to an island where there were seven cities, and where our language was spoken; and the people asked whether the Moors still occupied Spain, from whence they had fled after the loss of King Don Rodrigo. The contramaster of the ship said, that he brought away a little sand from the island, and sold it to a goldsmith in Lisbon, who extracted from it a good quantity of gold. It is said that the Infante D. Pedro, who governed at that time, ordered these things to be written in the Casa de Tombo. And some will have it that these lands and islands at which the Portugueze touched, were those which are now called the Antillas and New Spain (p. 24).

This Antilia, or Island of the Seven Cities, is laid down in Martin Behaim's map; the story was soon improved by giving seven bishops to the seven cities; and Galvam has been accused by Hornius of having invented it to give his countrymen the honour of having discovered the West Indies! Now it is evident that Antonio Galvam relates the story as if he did not believe it, — *contam* — they relate, — and, *diz*, it is said, — never affirming the fact, nor making any inference from it, but merely stating it as a report; and it is certain, which perhaps Hornius did not know, that there never lived a man of purer integrity than Antonio Galvam; a man whose history is disgraceful, not to his country but to the government under which he lived, and whose uniform and unsullied virtue entitles him to rank among the best men that have ever done honour to human nature.

The writers who repeat this story of the Seven Islands and their bishops, have also been pleased to find traces of Sacaru in the new world, for which the imaginary resemblances to Christianity which were found in Yucatan and other places, serve them as proofs.— *Gregorio Garcia, Origen de los Indios*, l. iv, c. 20.

The work of Abulcacim, in which the story first appears, has been roundly asserted to be the forgery of the translator, Miguel de Luna.

The Portugueze academician, Contador de Argote, speaking of this romantic history, acquits him of the fraud, which has with little reflection been laid to his charge. Pedraça, he says, in the Grandezas de Granada, and Rodrigo Caro, in the Grandezas de Sevilla, both affirm that the original Arabic exists in the Escurial, and Escolano asserts the same, although Nicholas Antonio says that the catalogues of that library do not make mention of any such book. If Luna had forged it, it would not have had many of those blunders which are observed in it; nor is there any reason for imputing such a fraud to Luna, a man well skilled in Arabic, and of good reputation. What I suspect is, that the book was composed by a Granadan Moor, and the reason which induces me to form this opinion is, the minuteness with which he describes the conquest which Tarif made of those parts of the kingdom of Granada, of the Alpuxarras and the Serra Neveda, pointing out the etymologies of the names of places, and other circumstances, which any one who reads with attention will observe. As to the time in which the composer of this amusing romance flourished, it was certainly after the reign of Bedeci Aben Abuz, who governed, and was Lord of Granada about the year 1013, as Marmol relates, after the Arabian writers; and the reason which I have for this assertion is, that in the romance of Abulcacim the story is told which gave occasion to the said Bedeci Aben Habuz to set up in Granada that famous vane, which represents a knight upon horseback in bronze, with a spear in the right hand, and a club in the left, and these words in Arabic,—Bedeci Aben Habuz says that in this manner Andalusia must be kept! the figure moves with every wind, and veers about from one end to another.— *Memorias de Braga*, T. iii. p. 120.

In the fabulous Chronicle of D. Rodrigo, Sacarus, as he is there called, is a conspicuous personage; but the tale of his emigration was not then current, and the author kills him before the Moors appear upon the stage. He seems to have designed him as a representation of perfect generosity.

Note 22, page 395, col. 1.

All too long,
Here in their own inheritance, the sons
Of Spain have groaned beneath a foreign yoke.

There had been a law to prohibit intermarriages between the Goths and Romans; this law Recesuintho annulled,[1] observing in his edict, that the people ought in no slight degree to rejoice at the repeal. It is curious that the distinction should have existed so long; but it is found also in a law of Wamba's, and doubtless must have continued till both names were lost together in the general wreck. The vile principle was laid down in the laws of the Wisigoths, that such as the root is, such ought the branch to be, —*gran confusion es de linage, quando el fiyo non semeya al padre, que aquelo ques de la raiz, deba ser en a cima,* and upon this principle a law was made to keep the children of slaves, slaves also.

« Many men well versed in history,» says Contador de Argote, (Memorias de Braga, 3. 273.) « think, and think rightly, that this was a civil war, and that the monarchy was divided into two factions, of which the least powerful availed itself of the Arabs as auxiliaries; and that these auxiliaries made themselves masters, and easily effected their intent by means of the divisions in the country.»

« The natives of Spain,» says Joam de Barros, « never bore much love to the Goths, who were strangers and comelings, and when they came had no right there, for the whole belonged to the Roman empire. It is believed that the greater part of those whom the Moors slew were Goths, and it is said that, on one side and on the other, in the course of two years there were slain by the sword seven hundred thousand men. The Christians who escaped chose that the name of Goths should be lost: and though some Castillians complain that the race should be extinguished, saying with Don Jorge Manrique,

Pues la sangre de los Godos
y el linage y la nobleza
tan crecida,
por quantas vias y modos
se sume su grande alteza
en esta vida,

I must say that I see no good foundation for this; for

[1] Fuero Juzgo, l. 3, tit. 1, leg. 1.

they were a proud nation and barbarous, and were a long time heretics of the sects of Arius and Eutychius and Pelagius, and can be praised as nothing except as warriors, who were so greedy for dominion, that wherever they reached they laid every thing bare like locusts, and therefore the empéror ceded to them this country. The people who dwelt in it before were a better race, always praised and feared and respected by the Romans, loyal and faithful and true and reasonable; and if the Goths afterwards were worthy of any estimation they became so here: for as plants lose their bitterness and improve by being planted and translated into a good soil (as is said of peaches), so does a good land change its inhabitants, and of rustic and barbarous make them polished and virtuous.

« The Moors did not say that they came against the Christians, but against the Goths, who had usurped Spain; and it appears that to the people of the land it mattered little whether they were under Goths or Moors; or indeed it might not be too much to say that they preferred the Moors, not only because all new things and changes would be pleasing, but because they were exasperated against the Goths for what they had done against the Christians, (i. e. the Catholicks,) and for the bad government of King Witiza.»

« You are not to think,» says the chronicler, « that Count Don Julian and the Bishop Don Orpas came of the lineage of the Goths, but of the lineage of the Cæsars, and therefore they were not grieved that the good lineage should be destroyed.»—*Chr. del K. D. Rodrigo,* p. i, c. 248.

Note 23, page 396, col. 1.

Favila.

Barrios, taking a punster's licence in orthography, plays upon the name of Pelayo's father:—

—— del gran Favila (que centella significa) Pelayo, marcial llama, restauro el Leones reyno con aquella lez que alcanço la victoriosa rama.
Coro de las Musas, p. 102.

Note 24, page 396, col. 2.

The Queen too, Egilona,—
Was she not married to the enemy,
The Moor, the Misbeliever?

For this fact there is the unquestionable testimony of Isidorus Pacensis. «Per idem tempus in Æra 735, anno imperii ejus 9. Arabum 97. Abdalaziz omnem Hispaniam per tres annos sub censuario jugo pacificans, cum Hispali divitiis et honorum fascibus cum Regina Hispani in conjugio copulata, filias Regum ac Principum pellicatas, et imprudenter distractas æstuaret, seditione suorum facta, orationi instans, consilio Ajub, occiditur; atque eo Hispaniam retinente, mense impleto, Alahor in regno Hesperiæ per principalia jussa succedit, cui de morte Abdalaziz ita edicitur, ut quasi consilio Egilonis Regiæ conjugis quondam Ruderici regis, quam sibi sociaberat, jugum Arabicum a sua cervice conaretur avertere, et regnum invasum Hiberiæ sibimet retemptare.»—*Espana Sagrada,* t. 8, p. 302.

Florez relates the story in the words of the old translation of an Arabic original imputed to Rasis. «When Belazin, the son of Muza, remained for Lord of Spain, and had ordered his affairs right well, they told him tidings of Ulaca, who had been the wife of King D. Rodrigo, that she was a right worthy dame, and right beautiful, and of a great lineage, and that she was a native of Africa; whereupon he sent for her, and ordered that beasts should be given her, and much property, and men-servants and maid-servants, and all things that she could require, till she could come to him. And they brought her unto him, and when he saw her, he was well pleased with her, and said, Ulaca, tell me of thy affairs, and conceal nothing from me; for thou knowest I may do with thee according to my will, being my captive. And when she heard this, it increased the grief which she had in her heart, and her sorrow was such, that she had well nigh fallen dead to the ground, and she replied weeping and said, Baron, what wouldst thou know more of my affairs? For doth not all the world know, that I, a young damsel, being married with King D. Rodrigo, was with him Lady of Spain, and dwelt in honour and in all pleasure, more than I deserved; and therefore it was God's will that they should endure no longer. And now I am in dishonour greater than ever was dame of such high state: For I am plundered, and have not a single palm of inheritance; and I am a captive, and brought into bondage. I also have been mistress of all the land that I behold. Therefore, Sir, have pity upon my misfortunes; and in respect of the great lineage which you know to be mine, suffer not that wrong or violence be offered me by any one; and, Sir, if it be your grace you will sell me. There are men I know who would take compassion on me, and give you for me a great sum. And Belazin said to her, Be certain that so long as I live, you shall never go from my house. And Ulaca said, What then, Sir, would you do with me? and Belazin said, I will that you should remain in my house, and there you shall be free from all wretchedness, with my other wives. And she said, In an evil day was I born, if it is to be true that I have been wife of the honoured king of Spain, and now have to live in a stranger's house as the concubine and captive of another! And I swear unto God, whose pleasure it is to dismay me thus, that I will rather seek my own death as soon as I can; for I will endure no more misery, seeing that by death I can escape it. And when Belazin saw that she thus lamented, he said to her, Good dame, think not that we have concubines, but by our law we may have seven wives, if we can maintain them, and therefore you shall be my wife, like each of the others; and all things which your law requires that a man should do for his wife, will I do for you; and therefore you have no cause to lament; and be sure that I will do you much honour, and will make all who love me serve and honour you, and you shall be mistress of all my wives. To this she made answer and said, Sir, offer me no violence concerning my law, but let me live as a Christian: And to this Belazin was nothing loth; and he granted it, and his marriage was performed with her according to the law of the Moors: and every day he liked her more, and did her such honour that greater could not be. And it befell that Belazin being one day with Ulaca, she said to him, Sir, do not think it ill if I tell you of a thing in which you do not act as if you knew the custom. And he said, Wherein is it that I err? Sir, said she, because you have no crown, for no one was ever confirmed in Spain, except he had a crown upon his head. He said, This which you say is nothing, for we have it not of our lineage, neither is it our custom to wear a crown. She said, many good

58

reasons are there why a crown is of use, and it would injure you nothing, but be well for you, and when you should wear your crown upon your head, God would know you and others also by it: And she said, You would look full comely with it, and it would be great nobleness to you, and be right fitting, and you should wear in it certain stones, which will be good for you, and avail you. And in a short time afterwards Belazin went to dwell at Seville, and he carried Ulaca with him, and she took of her gold, and of her pearls, and of her precious stones, which she had many and good, and made him the noblest crown that ever was seen by man, and gave it him, and bade him take it, and place it where it should be well kept; and Ulaca, as she was a woman of understanding and prudence, ordered her affairs as well as Belazin, so that he loved her much, and did great honour to her, and did many of those things which she desired; so that he was well pleased with the Christians, and did them much good, and showed favour unto them.»—*Memorias da las Reynas Catholicas*, i, p. 28.

The issue of this was fatal to Abdalaziz. In Abulcacim's history, it is said that he was converted by this Christian wife, and for that reason put to death by his father. Others have supposed that by means of her influence he was endeavouring to make himself King of Spain, independent of the Caliph. A characteristic circumstance is added. Egilona was very desirous to convert her husband, and that she might at least obtain from him some mark of outward respect for her images, made the door of the apartment in which she kept them, so low, that he could not enter without bowing. —*Bleda*, p. 214.

> Deixam a Abdalaziz, que de Bellona
>   Mamara o leite, por Rector da Hesperia;
> Este caza co a inclyta Egilona,
>   Mulher de Dom Rodrigo, (o gram miseria!)
> Tomou Coroa de ouro, e a Matrona
>   Lhe deu para a tomar larga materia,
> Foi notado à misera raynha
> Cazarse com hum Mouro tam asinha.
>   *Destruicam de Espanha*, p. 237.

The Character of this Queen is beautifully conceived by the author of Count Julian:—

> Beaming with virtue inaccessible
> Stood Egilona; for her lord she lived,
> And for the heavens that raised her sphere so high:
> All thoughts were on her—all beside her own
> Negligent as the blossoms of the field,
> Arrayed in candour and simplicity,
> Before her path she heard the streams of joy
> Murmur her name in all their cadences,
> Saw them in every scene, in light, in shade,
> Reflect her image; but acknowledged them
> Hers most complete when flowing from her most.
> All things in want of her, herself of none,
> Pomp and dominion lay beneath her feet
> Unfelt and unregarded: now behold
> The earthly passions war against the heavenly!
> Pride against love; ambition and revenge
> Against devotion and compliancy—
> Her glorious beams adversity hath blunted,
> And coming nearer to our quiet view,
> The original clay of coarse mortality
> Hardens and flaws around her.

Note 25, page 398, col. 2.

One day of bitter and severe delight.

I have ventured to borrow this expression from the tragedy of Count Julian. Nothing can be finer than the passage in which it occurs.

Abdalaziz. Thou lovest still thy country.
Julian. Abdalazis,

> All men with human feelings love their country.
> Not the high-born or wealthy man alone,
> Who looks upon his children, each one led
> By its gay hand-maid, from the high alcove,
> And hears them once a-day; not only he
> Who hath forgotten, when his guest inquires
> The name of some far village all his own;
> Whose rivers bound the province, and whose hills
> Touch the last cloud upon the level sky:
> No; better men still better love their country.
> 'T is the old mansion of their earliest friends,
> The chapel of their first and best devotions;
> When violence, or perfidy, invades,
> Or when unworthy lords hold wassail there,
> And wiser heads are drooping round its moats,
> At last they fix their steady and stiff eye
> There, there alone—stand while the trumpet blows,
> And view the hostile flames above its towers
> Spire, with a bitter and severe delight.

Note 26, page 401, col. 1.

Restoring in thy native line, O Prince,
The Sceptre to the Spaniard.

This was a favourite opinion of Garibays, himself a Biscayan, but he has little better proof for it than the fact, that Gothic names disappeared with Roderick, and that Pelayo and his successors drew their nomenclature from a different stock. He says, indeed, that ancient writings are not wanting to support his opinion. Some rude commentator has written against this assertion in the margin of my copy, *miente Garibay*; and I am afraid the commentator is the truer man of the two.

There is a fabulous tale of Pelayo's birth, which, like many other tales of no better authority, has legends and relics to support it. The story, according to Dr D. Christoval Lozano, in his history of Los Reyes Nuevos de Toledo, is this. Luz, niece to Egilona, and sister of Roderick, dwelt at Toledo, in the palace of King Egica. Duke Favila, her father's brother, fell in love with her, and came from his residence in Cantabria to ask her in marriage, expecting to find no other obstacle than the dispensable one of consanguinity. But it so happened, that the King was wooing Luz to become his concubine; her refusal made him jealous, as he could not conceive that it proceeded from any cause except love for another, and as his temper and power were not to be provoked without danger, Favila dared not openly make his suit. He and his mistress therefore met in private, and plighted their vows before an image of the Virgin. The consequences soon became apparent,—the more so, because, as Dr Lozano assures us, there were at that time no fashions to conceal such things,—*Y mas que en aquella era no se avian inventado los guarda-infantes*. The king observed the alteration in her shape, and placed spies upon her, meaning to destroy the child and punish the mother with the rigour of the law, death by fire being the punishment for such an offence. Luz was well aware of the danger. She trusted her *Camarera* and one servant: they made an ark: She herself, as soon as the infant was born, threw water in his face, and baptised him by the name of Pelayo: a writing was placed with him in the ark, requesting that whoever should find it would breed up the boy with care, for he was of good lineage. Money enough was added to support him for eight years, and the ark was then launched upon the Tagus, where it floated down the stream all night, all day, and all the following night. On the second morning it grounded near Alcantara, and was found by Grafeses, who happened to be Luz's uncle. The king's suspicion being confirmed by the sudden alteration in the lady's appearance, he used every means to detect her, but without avail; he even ordered all children to be examined who had been born in or around Toledo within three months, and full enquiry to be made into the circumstances of their births: To the astonishment of later historians, 35,000 of that age were found, and not one among them of suspicious extraction. The tale proceeds in the ordinary form of romance. The lady is accused of incontinence, and to be burnt, unless a champion defeats her accuser. Favila of course undertakes her defence, and of course is victorious. A second battle follows with the same success, and fresh combats would have followed, if a hermit had not brought the king to repentance. Grafeses in due time discovers the secret, and restores the child to his parents.

This fabulous chronicle seems to be the oldest written source of this story, but some such tradition had probably long been current. The ark was shewn at Alcantara, in the convent of St Benito; and a description of it, with reasons why its authenticity should be admitted, may be found in Francisco de Pisa's Description de Toledo, L. iii. c. i.

Note 27, page 401, col. 2.

——— And in thy name
Accept the crown of thorns she proffers me.

Godfrey was actually crowned with thorns in Jerusalem,—a circumstance which has given rise to a curious question in heraldry,—thus curiously stated and commented by Robert Barret, in that part of his long poem which relates to this Prince:

A Prince religious, if ever any,
Considering the age wherein he lived,
Vice-hater great, endued with virtues many,
True humilized, void of mundane pride;
For though he now created were great king,
Yet would he not as royal pomp requires,
Encrowned be with crownet glistering
Of gold and gems to mundains vain desires:
But with a pricking, pricking crown of thorn,
Bearing thereto a Christian reverence,
Sith Heaven's-King, man's-Redeemer, did scorn
To wear such crown within that city's fence,
When us, cross-laden, humblely he went,
All cowring under burden of that wood,
To free man To pay the pain of man's due punishment.
from Hell. And free from Pluto's bands Prometheus brood.

By reas'n of Godfrey's great humility
Refusing golden-crownets dignity,
Some blundering in world-witted heraldry,
The foolish- Not knowing how t' distinguish vertues trye,
ness of He- Do question make this Christian king to set
ralds. In catalogue of gold-diademed kings;
Regarding glitter of the external jet,
And not true garnish of th' internal things;
Th' internal virtues, soul's sweet ornaments,
So pleasing to th' Eternal's sacred eyes,
In angels chore consorting sweet concents
Of heavenly harmony 'bove christal skies.
But we, *à contra*, him not only deem
A Christian king, but perfect Christian king,
A christal fanal, lamping light divine
To after-comer kings, world emp'rizing.
For he, religious prince, did not despise
The Heaven-sent gift to be anointed king,
But disesteem'd the mundane pompous guize
Tickling the hearts of princes monarching.

Annotacion. Potentates regard this heaven-aspiring Prince,
Not priding, as up proves his dignity;

High-throned kings aspect the starred fence
Of this true map of true kings royalty;
Not Nembrothizing in cloud-kissing towers,
Not Semiramizing in prides palaces,
Not Neronizing in all sanguine hours,
Not Heliogabalizing in lusts lees;
But Joshuadizing in his Christian camp,
And Judithizing in his Salem's seat,
And Davidizing in his Sion's stamp,
And Solomonizing in all sacred heat.

Note 28, page 402, col. 2.

Outwatching for her sake
The starry host, and ready for the work
Of war before the sun begins his course.

Garci Fernandez Manrique surprised the Moors so often during the night, that he was called Garci Madrugi,—an appellation of the same import as Peep-of-day-boy. He founded the convent of St Salvador de Palacios de Benagel for Benedictine nuns, and when he called up his merry men, used to say, Up, sirs, and fight, for my nuns are up and praying; *Levantaos Senores à pelear, que mis monjas son levantedas a rezar.*
Pruebas de la Hist. de la Casa de Lara, p. 42.

Note 29, page 404, col. 2.

Hermesind.

Mariana derives the name of Hermesinda from the reverence in which Hermenegild was held in Spain,—a prince who has been sainted for having renounced the Homooisian creed, and raised a civil war against his father in favour of the Homoousian one. It is not a little curious when the fate of D. Carlos is remembered, that his name should have been inserted in the Kalendar, at the solicitation of Philip II! From the same source Mariana derives the names Hermenisinda, Armengol, Ermengaud, Hermegildez, and Hermildez. But here, as Brito has done with Pelayo, he seems to forget that the name was current before it was borne by the Saint, and the derivations from it as numerous. Its root may be found in Hermann, whose German name will prevail over the latinized Arminius.

Note 30, page 406, col. 2.

The glen where Tagus rolls between his rocks.

The story of the Enchanted Tower at Toledo is well known to every English reader. It neither accorded with the character of my poem to introduce the fiction, nor would it have been prudent to have touched upon it after Walter Scott. The account of the Archbishop Rodrego, and of Abulcacim, may be found in his notes. What follows here is translated from the fabulous chronicle of King Don Rodrigo.

« And there came to him the keepers of the house which was in Toledo, which they called Pleasure with Pain, the Perfect Guard, the secret of that which is to come; and it was called also by another name, the Honour of God. And these keepers came before the king, and said unto him, Sire, since God hath done thee such good, and such favour as that thou shouldest be king of all Spain, we come to require of thee that thou wouldst go to Toledo, and put thy lock upon the house which we are appointed to keep. And the king demanded of them what house was that, and wherefore he should put upon it his lock. And they said unto him, Sire, we will willingly tell thee that thou mayest know. Sire, true it is, that when Hercules the Strong came into Spain he made in it many marvellous things in those places where he understood that they might best remain; and thus when he was in Toledo he understood well that that city would be one of the best in Spain; and saw that the kings who should be Lords of Spain, would have more pleasure to continue dwelling therein than in any other part; and seeing that things would come after many ways, some contrariwise to others, it pleased him to leave many enchantments made, to the end that after his death his power and wisdom might by them be known. And he made in Toledo a house, after the manner which we shall now describe, with great mastership, so that we have not heard tell of any other such: The which is made after this guise. There are four lions of metal under the foundation of this house: and so large are they that a man sitting upon a great horse on the one side, and another in like manner upon the other, cannot see each other, so large are the lions. And the house is upon them, and it is entirely round, and so lofty that there is not a man in the world who can throw a stone to the top: And many have attempted this, but they never could. And there is not a man of this age who can tell you by what manner this house was made, neither whose understanding can reach to say in what manner it is worked within. But of that which we have seen without, we have to tell thee. Certes in the whole house there is no stone bigger than the hand of a man, and the most of them are off jasper and marble, so clear and shining that they seem to be crystal. They are of so many colours that we do not think there are two stones in it of the same colour; and so cunningly are they joined one with another, that if it were not for the many colours, you would not believe but that the whole house was made of one entire stone. And the stones are placed in such manner one by another, that seeing them you may know all the things of the battles aforepast, and of great feats. And this is not by pictures, but the colour of the stones, and the great art of joining one with the other, make it appear thus. And sans doubt he who should wish to know the truth of the great deeds of arms which have been wrought in the world, might by means of that house know it. See now in what manner Hercules was wise and fortunate, and right valiant, and acquainted with the things which were to come. And when he was Lord of Spain, he made it after this guise, which we have related unto you. And he commanded that neither King nor Lord of Spain who might come after him, should seek to know that which was within; but that every one instead should put a lock upon the doors thereof, even as he himself did, for he first put on a lock, and fastened it with his key. And after him there has been no King nor Lord in Spain, who has thought it good to go from his bidding; but every one as he came put on each his lock, according to that which Hercules appointed. And now that we have told thee the manner of the house, and that which we know concerning it, we require of thee that thou shouldest go thither, and put on thy lock on the gates thereof, even as all the kings have done who have reigned in Spain until this time. And the King Don Rodrigo hearing the marvellous things of this house, and desiring to know what there was within, and moreover being a man of a great heart, wished to know of all things how they were and for what guise. He made answer, that no such lock would he put upon that house, and that by all means he would know what there was within. And they said unto him, Sire, you will not do that which has never

been done in Spain; be pleased therefore to observe that which the other kings have observed. And the king said unto them, Leave off now, and I will appoint the soonest that may be how I may go to see this house, and then I will do that which shall seem good. And he would give them no other reply. And when they saw that he would give them no other reply, they dared not persist farther, and they dispeeded themselves of him, and went their way.

«Now it came to pass that the King Don Rodrigo called to mind how he had been required to put a lock upon the doors of the house which was in Toledo, and he resolved to carry into effect that unto which his heart inclined him. And one day he gathered together all the greatest knights of Spain, who were there with him, and went to see this house, and he saw that it was more marvellous than those who were its keepers had told him, and as he was thus beholding it, he said, Friends, I will by all means see what there is in this house which Hercules made. And when the great Lords who were with him heard this, they began to say unto him that he ought not to do this; for there was no reason why he should do that which never king nor Cæsar, that had been Lord of Spain since Hercules, had done until that time. And the king said unto them, Friends, in this house there is nothing but what may be seen. I am well sure that the enchantments cannot hinder me, and this being so, I have nothing to fear. And the knights said, Do that, sir, which you think good, but this is not done by our counsel. And when he saw that they were all of a different accord from that which he wished to do, he said, Now gainsay me as you will, for let what will happen, I shall not forbear to do my pleasure. And forthwith he went to the doors, and ordered all the locks to be opened; and this was a great labour, for so many were the keys and the locks, that if they had not seen it, it would have been a great thing to believe. And after they were unlocked, the king pushed the door with his hand, and he went in, and the chief persons who were there with him, as many as he pleased, and they found a hall made in a square, being as wide on one part as on the other, and in it there was a bed richly furnished, and there was laid in that bed the statue of a man, exceeding great, and armed at all points, and he had the one arm stretched out, and a writing in his hand. And when the king and those who were with him saw this bed, and the man who was laid in it, they marvelled what it might be, and they said, Certes, that bed was one of the wonders of Hercules and of his enchantments. And when they saw the writing which he held in his hand, they showed it to the king, and the king went to him, and took it from his hand, and opened it and read it, and it said thus, Audacious one, thou who shalt read this writing, mark well what thou art, and how great evil through thee shall come to pass, for even as Spain was peopled and conquered by me, so by thee shall it be depopulated and lost. And I say unto thee, that I was Hercules the strong, he who conquered the greater part of the world, and all Spain; and I slew Geryon the Great, who was Lord thereof; and I alone subdued all these lands of Spain, and conquered many nations and brave knights, and never any one could conquer me, save only Death. Look well to what thou doest, for from this world thou wilt carry with thee nothing but the good which thou hast done.

«And when the king had read the writing he was

troubled, and he wished then that he had not begun this thing. Howbeit he made semblance as if it touched him not, and said that no man was powerful enough to know that which is to come, except the true God. And all the knights who were present were much troubled because of what the writing said; and having seen this they went to behold another apartment, which was so marvellous, that no man can relate how marvellous it was. The colours which were therein were four. The one part of the apartment was white as snow: and the other, which was over-against it, was more black than pitch; and another part was green as a fine emerald, and that which was over-against it was redder than fresh blood; and the whole apartment was bright and more lucid than crystal, and it was so beautiful, and the colour thereof so fine, that it seemed as if each of the sides were made of a single stone, and all who were there present said that there was not more than a single stone in each, and that there was no joining of one stone with another, for every side of the whole four appeared to be one solid slab; and they all said that never in the world had such a work as this elsewhere been made, and that it must be held for a remarkable thing, and for one of the wonders of the world. And in all the apartments there was no beam, nor any work of wood, neither within nor without; and as the floor thereof was flat, so also was the ceiling. Above these were windows, and so many, that they gave a great light, so that all which was within might be seen as clearly as that which was without. And when they had seen the apartment how it was made, they found in it nothing but one pillar, and that not very large, and round, and of the height of a man of mean stature: and there was a door in it right cunningly made, and upon it was a little writing in Greek letters, which said, Hercules made this house in the year of Adam three hundred and six. And when the king had read these letters, and understood that which they said, he opened the door, and when it was opened they found Hebrew letters which said, This house is one of the wonders of Hercules; and when they had read these letters they saw a nich made in that pillar, in which was a coffer of silver, right subtly wrought, and after a strange manner, and it was gilded, and covered with many precious stones, and of great price, and it was fastened with a lock of mother-of-pearl. And this was made in such a manner that it was a strange thing, and there were cut upon it Greek letters which said, It cannot be but that the king, in whose time this coffer shall be opened, shall see wonders before his death; thus said Hercules, the Lord of Greece and of Spain, who knew some of those things which are to come. And when the king understood this, he said, Within this coffer lies that which I seek to know, and which Hercules has so strongly forbidden to be known. And he took the lock and broke it with his hands, for there was no other who durst break it; and when the lock was broken, and the coffer open, they found nothing within, except a white cloth folded between two pieces of copper; and he took it and opened it, and found Moors pourtrayed therein with turbans, and banners in their hands, and with their swords round their necks, and their bows behind them at the saddle-bow, and over these figures were letters which said, When this cloth shall be opened, and these figures seen, men apparelled like them shall conquer Spain and shall be Lords thereof.

«When the King Don Rodrigo saw this he was troubled at heart, and all the knights who were with him. And they said unto him, Now, sir, you may see what has befallen you, because you would not listen to those who counselled you not to pry into so great a thing, and because you despised the kings who were before you, who all observed the commands of Hercules, and ordered them to be observed, but you would not do this. And he had greater trouble in his heart than he had ever before felt; howbeit he began to comfort them all, and said to them, God forbid that all this which we have seen should come to pass. Nevertheless, I say, that if things must be according as they are here declared, I could not set aside that which hath been ordained, and therefore it appears that I am he by whom this house was to be opened, and that for me it was reserved. And seeing it is done, there is no reason that we should grieve for that which cannot be prevented, if it must needs come. And let come what may, with all my power I will strive against that which Hercules has foretold, even till I take my death in resisting it: and if you will all do in like manner, I doubt whether the whole world can take from us our power. But if by God it hath been appointed, no strength and no art can avail against his Almighty power, but that all things must be fulfilled even as to him seemeth good. In this guise they went out of the house, and he charged them all that they should tell no man of what they had seen there, and ordered the doors to be fastened in the same manner as before. And they had hardly finished fastening them, when they beheld an eagle fall right down from the sky, as if it had descended from Heaven, carrying a burning fire-brand, which it laid upon the top of the house, and began to fan it with its wings; and the fire-brand with the motion of the air began to blaze, and the house was kindled and burnt as if it had been made of rosin; so strong and mighty were the flames and so high did they blaze up, that it was a great marvel, and it burnt so long that there did not remain the sign of a single stone, and all was burnt into ashes. And after a while there came a great flight of birds small and black, who hovered over the ashes, and they were so many, that with the fanning of their wings, all the ashes were stirred up, and rose into the air, and were scattered over the whole of Spain; and many of those persons upon whom the ashes fell, appeared as if they had been besmeared with blood. All this happened in a day, and many said afterwards, that all those persons upon whom those ashes fell, died in battle when Spain was conquered and lost; and this was the first sign of the destruction of Spain.»—*Chronica del Rey D. Rodrigo,* Part I, c. 28, 30.

«Y siendo verdad lo que escriven nuestros Chronistas, y el Alcayde Tarif, las letras que en este Palacio fueron halladas, no se ha de entender que fueron puestas por Hercules en su fundacion, ni por algun nigromantico, como algunos piensan, pues solo Dios sabe las cosas por venir, y aquellos aquien el es servido revelarlas : bien puede ser que fuessen puestas por alguna santa persona aquien nuestro Señor lo oviesse revelado y mandado ; como reveló el castigo que avia de suceder del deluvio general en tiempo de Noe, que fue pregonero de la justicia de Dios ; y el de las ciudades de Sodoma y Gomorra á Abraham.»—*Fran. de Pisa, Descr. de Toledo.* l. 2, c. 31.

The Spanish ballad upon the subject, fine as the subject is, is flat as a flounder :—

De los nobilissimos Godos
que en Castilla avian reynado
Rodrigo reynó el postrero
de los reyes que han passado;
en cuyo tiempo los Moros
todo España avian ganado,
sino fuera las Asturias
que defendió Don Pelayo.
En Toledo está Rodrigo
al comienço del reynado,
vínole gran voluntad
de ver lo que esta cerrado
en la torre que esta alli,
antigua de muchos años.
En esta torre los reyes
cada uno hechó un canado
porque lo ordenara ansi
Hercules el afamado
que ganó primero á España
de Gerion gran tirano.
Creyó el rey que avia en la torre
gran thesoro alli guardado;
la torre fue luego abierta
y quitados los canados;
no ay en ella cosa alguna,
sola una caxa han hallado,
El rey la mandara abrir;
un paño dentro se ha hallado,
con unas letras latinas
que dicen en Castellano,
Quando aquestas cerraduras
que cierran estos canados,
fueran abiertas y visto
lo en el paño debuxado,
España sera perdida,
y toda ella asolada;
ganaranla gente estraña
como aqui estan figurados
los rostros muy denegridos,
los braços arremangados,
muchas colores vestidas,
en las cabeças tocados,
alçadas traeran sus señas
en cavallos cavalgando,
largas lanças en sus manos,
con espadas en su lado.
Alarabes se diran
y de aquesta tierra estraños;
perderse toda España,
que nada no aura fincado.
El rey con sus ricos hombres
todos se avian espantado
quando vieron las figuras
y letras que hemos contado,
buelven á cerrar la torre,
quedó el rey muy angustiado,

Juan Yague de Salas relates a singular part of this miracle, which I have not seen recorded any where but in his curious poem:—

Cantó como rompidos los candados
De la lobrega cueva, y despedidas
De sus senos obscuros vozes tristes
No bien articuladas, si á remiendos,
Repetidas adentro por el ayre,
Y una mas bronca se escuchó que dize,
Desdichado Rey Ro (y acaba digo,
Quedando la R submersa entre piçarras)
La Coro perderas, y el Man, y el Ce,
No dixo el na, ni el do, ni el tro, no dixo;
Almenos no se oyó, si bien oyose
Por lascivo tirano, y por sobervio,
Que ya permita el cielo que el de Meca
Castigue por tu causa el Reyno Godo.
Por solo que lo riges con mal modo.
                              Los Amantes de Teruel, p. 29.

The Chronica General del Rey Don Alfonso gives a singular account of the first inhabitant of this fatal spot:—

« There was a king who had to name Rocas; he was of the east country from Edom, wherein was Paradise, and for the love of wisdom he forsook his kingdom, and went about the world seeking knowledge. And in a country between the east and the north he found seventy pillars; thirty were of brass, thirty of marble, and they lay upon the ground, and upon them was written all knowledge and the nature of things. These Rocas translated, and carried with him the book in which he had translated them, by which he did marvels. He came to Troy when the people under Laomedon were building the city, and seeing them he laughed. They asked him why, and he replied, that if they knew what was to happen, they would cease from their work. Then they took him and led him before Laomedon, and Laomedon asked him for why he had spoken these words, and Rocas answered, that he had spoken truth, for the people should be put to the sword, and the city be destroyed by fire. Wherefore the Trojans would have slain him, but Laomedon, judging that he spake from folly, put him in prison to see if he would repent. He, fearful of death, by his art sent a sleep upon the guards, and filed off his irons; and went his way. And he came to the seven hills by the Tyber, and there upon a stone he wrote the letters Roma, and Romulus found them, and gave them as a name to his city, because they bore a resemblance to his own.

« Then went King Rocas westward, and he entered Spain, and went round it and through it, till coming to the spot where Toledo stands, he discovered that it was the central place of the country, and that one day a city should there be built, and there he found a cave into which he entered. There lay in it a huge dragon, and Rocas in fear besought the dragon not to hurt him, for they were both creatures of God. And the dragon took such love towards him, that he always brought him part of his food from the chase, and they dwelt together in the cave. One day an honourable man of that land, by name Tartus, was hunting in that mountain, and he found a bear, and the bear fled into the cave, and Rocas in fear addressed him as he had done the dragon, and the bear quietly lay down, and Rocas fondled his head, and Tartus following, saw Rocas how his beard was long, and his body covered with hair, and he thought it was a wild man, and fitted an arrow to his bow, and drew the string. Then Rocas besought him in the name of God not to slay him, and obtained security for himself and the bear under his protection. And when Tartus heard how he was a king, he invited him to leave that den and return with him, and he would give him his only daughter in marriage, and leave him all that he had. By this the dragon returned. Tartus was alarmed, and would have fled, but Rocas interfered, and the dragon threw down half an ox, for he had devoured the rest, and asked the stranger to stop and eat. Tartus declined the invitation, for he must be gone. Then said Rocas to the dragon, My friend, I must now leave you, for we have sojourned together long enough. So he departed, and married, and had two sons, and for love of the dragon he built a tower over the cave, and dwelt there. After his death, one of his sons built another, and King Pirros added more buildings, and this was the beginning of Toledo. »

Note 31, page 406, col. 2.
Redeemed Magdalen.

Lardner published a letter to Jonas Hanway, showing

why houses for the reception of penitent harlots ought not to be called Magdalen Houses : Mary Magdalen not being the sinner recorded in the 7th chapter of Luke, but a woman of distinction and excellent character, who laboured under some bodily infirmity, which our Lord miraculously healed.

In the Shebboleth of Jean Despagne, is an article thus entitled, « De Marie Magdelaine, laquelle faussement on dit avoir esté femme de mauvaise vie : Le tort que luy font les Theologiens pour la plut part en leurs sermons, en leurs livres; et specialement la Bible Angloise en l'Argument du 7e chap. de S. Luc.»

« The injury,» says this Hugonot divine, « which the Romish church does to another Mary, the sister of Lazarus, has been sufficiently confuted by the orthodox. It has been ignorantly believed that this Mary, and another who was of Magdala, and the sinner who is spoken of in the 7th of Luke, are the same person, confounding the three in one. We have justified one of the three, to wit, her of Bethany, the sister of Lazarus; but her of Magdala we still defame, as if that Magdalen were the sinner of whom St Luke speaks.

« Nothing is more common in the mouth of the vulgar than the wicked life of the Magdalene. The preachers who wish to confess souls that are afflicted with horror at their sins, represent to them this woman as one of the most immodest and dissolute that ever existed, to whom, however, God has shewn mercy. And, upon this same prejudice, which is altogether imaginary, has been founded a reason why the Son of God having been raised from the dead appeared to Mary Magdalene before any other person; for, say they, it is because she had greater need of consolation, having been a greater sinner than the others. — He who wrote the Practice of Piety places her with the greatest offenders, even with Manasses, one of the wickedest of men : and to authorise this error the more, it has been inserted in the Bible itself. For the argument to the 7th of Luke in the English version says, that the woman whose sins were in greater number than those of others,—the woman, who till then had lived a wicked and infamous life, was Mary Magdalen. But, 1st, The text gives no name to this sinner : Where then has it been found? Which of the Evangelists, or what other authentic writing, has taught us the proper name or surname of the woman? For she who poured an ointment upon Christ (Matth. xxvi, John, xii,) was not this sinner, nor Mary Magdalene, but a sister of Lazarus. All these circumstances show that they are two different stories, two divers actions, performed at divers times, in divers places, and by divers persons. 2dly, Where do we find that Mary Magdalene ever anointed the feet of our Saviour? 3dly, Where do we find that Mary Magdalene had been a woman of evil life? The gospel tells us that she had been tormented with seven devils or evil spirits, an affliction which might happen to the holiest person in the world : but we do not see even the shadow of a word there which marks her with infamy. Why then do we still adhere to an invention not only fabulous, but injurious to the memory of a woman illustrious in piety? We ought in all to beware of bearing false witness against the dead as against the living.

« It is remarkable that neither the sinner (Luke, vii), nor the adultress who is spoken of in the 8th of John, are named in the sacred history, any more than the thief who was converted on the cross. There are particular reasons, beyond a doubt, and we may in part conjecture them, why the Holy Spirit has abstained from relating the names of these great sinners, although converted. It is not then for us to impose them ; still less to appropriate them to persons whom the Scripture does not accuse of any enormous sins.»

Note 32, page 407, col. 1.
The Egyptian penitent.

St Mary the Egyptian. This is one of those religious romances which may probably have been written to edify the people without any intention of deceiving them. Some parts of the legend are beautifully conceived. An English catholic has versified it in eight books, under the title of the Triumph of the Cross, or Penitent of Egypt, Birmingham, 1776. He had the advantage of believing his story,—which ought to have acted like inspiration.

Note 33, page 407, col. 1.
The dreadful tale.

Amava el Rey la desigual Florinda
    En ser gentil, y desdeñosa dama,
Que quiere amor, que quando un Rey se rinda
    Desdenes puedan resistir su llama :
No fue de Grecia mas hermosa y linda
    La que le dió por su desdicha fama,
Ni desde el Sagitario a Cynosura
Se vió en tanto rigor tanta hermosura.

Creció el amor como el desden crecia ;
    Enojose el poder ; la resistencia
Se fue aumentando, pero no podia
    Sufrir un Rey sujeta competencia :
Estendiose á furor la cortesia,
    Los términos passó de la paciencia,
Haziendo los mayores desengaños
Las horas meses, y los meses años.

Cansado ya Rodrigo de que fuesse
    Teórica el amor, y intentos vanos,
Sin que demostracion alguna huviesse,
    Puso su gusto en pratica de manos :
Pues quien de tanto amor no le tuviesse
    Con los medios mas fáciles y humanos,
Como tendria entonces sufrimiento
De injusta fuerça en el rigor violento?

Ansias, congojas, lágrimas y vozes,
    Amenazas, amores, fuerça, injuria,
Pruevan, pelean, llegan, dan ferozes
    Al que ama, rabia, al que abhorrece, furia :
Discurren los pronósticos velozes, .
    Que ofrece el pensamiento á quien injuria ;
Rodrigo temo, y ama, y fuerça, y ella
Quanto mas se resiste, está mas bella.

Ya viste de jazmines el desmayo
    Las eladas mexillas siempre hermosas,
Ya la vergüença del clavel de Mayo,
    Alexandrinas, y purpúreas rosas :
Rodrigo ya como encendido rayo,
    Que no respeta las sagradas cosas,
Ni se ahoga en sus lágrimas, ni mueve
Porque se abrase, ó se convierta en nieve.

Rindiose al fin la femenil flaqueza
    Al varonil valor y atrevimiento ;
Quedó sin lustre la mayor belleza
    Que es de una casta Virgen ornamento :
Siguió á la injusta furia la tibieza.
    Apareciose el arrepentimiento,
Que viene como sombra pecado,
Principios del castigo del culpado.

Fue con Rodrigo este mortal disgusto,
    Y quedó con Florinda la vengança,
Que le propuso el hecho mas injusto
    Que de muger nuestra memoria alcança :

464 SOUTHEY'S POETICAL WORKS.

Dizese que no ver en ol Rey gusto,
Sino de tanto amor tanta mudança
Fue la ocasion, que la muger gozada
Mas siente aborrecida que forçada.
Jerusalen Conquistada, t. 6, ff. 132.

Lope de Vega quotes scripture in proof of the opinion exprest in this last couplet. 2 Kings, ch. xiii.

Old Barret tells the story as Ancient Pistol would have done.

In Ulit's time there regalized in Spain
One Roderick, king from the Gothians race't;
Into whose secret heart with silent strain
Instretcht the 'sturber of hart pudike chast,
Him enamourizing of a piece,
A piece by Nature quaintly symmetrized,
Enfayred with beauty as Helen fair of Greece:
Count Julian's daughter of bed-wedlo kized,
Ycleaped Caba; who in court surshrined
The rest, as Hesperus the dimmed stars.
This piece the king in his Love's-closet shrined,
Surviciting her by wile, gold, gems, or forced jars.

It is thus related in the fabulous Chronicle. « Despues que el Rey ovo descubierto su coraçon á la Cava, no era dia que la no requiriesse una vez o dos, y ella se defendia con buena razon: empero al cabo como el Rey no pensava cosa como en esto, un dia en la fiesta embió con un donzel suyo por la Cava; y ella vino á su mandado; y como en essa hora no avia en toda su camara otro ninguno sino ellos todos tres, el cumplió con ella todo lo que puso. Empero tanto sabed que si ella quisiera dar bozes que bien fuera oyda de la reyna, mas callose con lo que el Rey quiso fazer.»—P. i, c. 172.

In this fabulous Chronicle Roderick's fall is represented as the work of his stars. — « Y aunque a las vezes pensava el gran yerro en que tocava, y en la maldad que su coraçon avia cometido, tanto era el ardor que tenia que lo olvidava todo, y esto acarreava la malandança que le avia de venir, y la destruycion de España que avia de aver comienço para se fazer; y quiero vos dezir que su constelacion no podia escusar que esto no passasse assi; y ya Dios lo avia dexado en su discrecion; y el por cosa que fuesse no se podia arredrar que no topase en ello.»—P. i, c. 164.

« Certes,» says the fabulous Chronicler, « he was a Lord of greater bounty than ever had been seen before his time.—He used to say, that if all the world were his, he would rather lose it than one friend; for the world was a thing, which if it were lost, might be recovered; but a friend once lost could never be recovered for all the treasure in the world. And because he was thus bountiful, all those of Spain were likewise; and they had the fame of being the most liberal men in the world, especially those of the lineage of the Goths. Never a thing was asked at his hands, whether great or small, to which he could say no; and never king nor other great Lord asked aid of him that he denied, but gave them of his treasures and of his people as much as they needed. And doubt not, but that if fortune had not ordered that in his time the lineage of the Goths should be cut off, and Spain destroyed, there was no king or emperor whom he would not have brought into subjection; and if the whole world ought to be placed in the power of one man, (speaking of worldly things,) there never was, nor will he, a man deserving to possess it, save he alone. But as envy is the beginning of all evil, and saw how great was the goodness of this king, she never rested till she had brought about that things should be utterly reversed, even till she had destroyed him. Oh what

great damage to the world will it be when God shall consent that so much bounty, and courage, and frankness, and loyalty should be destroyed for ever! All nations ought to clad themselves in wretched weeds one day in the week to mourn for the flower of the world, and especially ought the people of Spain to make such mourning.»—*Chronica del Rey Don Rodrigo*, p. 1, c. 55.

And again, when the last battle is approaching, he praises the king,—« Y el Rey era el mas esforçado hombre de coraçon que nunca se oyo dezir: y el mas franco de todo lo que podia aver; y preciava mas cobrar amigos que no quanto tesoro pudiesse estar en su reyno, hasta el dia que creyó el consejo del traydor del conde Don Julian; y á maravilla era buen cavallero, que al tiempo que el no era rey, no se fallava cavallero que á la su bondad se ygualasse, y tanto sabed que sino por estas malandanças que le vinieron, nunca cavallero al mundo de tales condiciones fue; que nunca á el vino chico ni grande que del se partiesse despagado á culpa suya.»— P. 1, c. 213.

The manner in which Florinda calls upon her father to revenge her is curiously expressed by Lope de Vega.

Al escrivirle tiemblan pluma y mano,
Llega el agravio, la piedad retira,
Pues quanto escrive la venгança, tanto
Quiero borrar de la verg̃ença el llanto.

No son menos las letras que soldados,
Los ringlones yleras y esquadrones,
Que al son de los suspiros van formados
Haciendo las distancias las diciones:
Los mayores caracteres, armados
Navios, tiendas, máquinas, pendones:
Los puntos, los incisos, los acentos
Capitanes, Alferez y Sargentos.

Breve processo escrive, aunque el sucesso
Significar quexosa determina,
Pero en tan breve causa, en tal processo
La perdicion de España se fulmina.
Jerusalen Conquistada, l. 6, ff. 138.

I remember but one of the old poets who has spoken with compassion of Florinda: It is the Portugueze Bras Garcia Mascarenhas, a writer who, with many odd things in his poem, has some fine ones.

Refresca em Covilham a gente afita,
Nam se sabe que nome entam a honrava;
Muyto deposis foy Cava Julia dita,
Por nascer nella a desditada Cava.
Nam a deslustra, antes a acredita
Filha que a honra mais que hum Rey presava;
Hespenha culpe a força sem desculpa,
Nam culpe a bella, que nam teve culpa.
Viriato Tragico, canto ii, st. 118.

Note 34, page 409, col. 2.

Wamba's wars.

In the valuable history of this king by a contemporary writer, the following character of the French is given:—
« Hujus igitur gloriosis temporibus, Galliarum terra altrix perfidiæ infami denotatur elogio, quæ utique inæstimabili infidelitatis febre vexata, genita a se infidelium depasceret membra. Quid enim non in illa crudele vel lubricum? ubi conjuratorum conciliabulum, perfidiæ signum, obscœnitas operum, fraus negotiorum, vænale judicium, et quod pejus his omnibus est, contra ipsum Salvatorem nostrum et Dominum, Judæorum blasphemantium prostibulum habebatur. Hæc enim terra suo, ut ita dixerim, partu, perditionis suæ sibimet

præparavit excidium, et ex ventris sui generatione viperea eversionis suæ nutrivit decipulam. Etenim dum multo jam tempore his febrium diversitatibus ageretur, subito in ea unius nefandi capitis prolapsione turbo infidelitatis adsurgit, et conscensio perfidiæ per unum ad plurimos transit.»—*St Julian, Hist. Wambæ,* sect. 5.—*Espana Sagrada,* 6. 544.

Note 35, page 410, col. 1.

**The bath, the bed,
The vigil.**

The Partidas have some curious matter upon this subject.

« Cleanliness makes things appear well to those who behold them, even as propriety makes them seemly, each in its way. And therefore the ancients held it good that knights should be made cleanly. For even as they ought to have cleanliness within them in their manners and customs, so ought they to have it without in their garments, and in the arms which they wear. For albeit their business is hard and cruel, being to strike and to slay; yet notwithstanding they may not so far forego their natural inclinations, as not to be pleased with fair and goodly things, especially when they wear them. For on one part they give joy and delight, and on the other make them fearlessly perform feats of arms, because they are aware that by them they are known, and that because of them men take more heed to what they do. Therefore, for this reason, cleanliness and propriety do not diminish the hardihood and cruelty which they ought to have. Moreover, as is aforesaid, that which appears without is the signification of what they have in their inclinations within. And therefore the ancients ordained that the squire, who is of noble lineage, should keep vigil the day before he receives knighthood. And after mid-day the squires shall bathe him, and wash his head with their hands, and lay him in the goodliest bed that may be. And there the knights shall draw on his hose, and clothe him with the best garments that can be had. And when the cleansing of the body has been performed, they shall do as much to the soul, taking him to the church, where he is to labour in watching and beseeching mercy of God, that he will forgive him his sins, and guide him so that he may demean himself well in that order which he is about to receive; to the end that he may defend his law, and do all other things according as it behoveth him, and that he would be his defender and keeper in all danger and in all difficulties. And he ought to bear in mind how God is powerful above all things, and can show his power in them when he listeth, and especially in affairs of arms. For in his hand are life and death, to give and to take away, and to make the weak strong, and the strong weak. And when he is making this prayer, he must be with his knees bent, and all the rest of the time on foot, as long as he can bear it. For the vigil of knights was not ordained to be a sport, nor for any thing else, except that they, and those who go there should pray to God to protect them, and direct them in the right way, and support them, as men who are entering upon the way of death.»—*Part.* ii, *Tit.* 21. *Ley* 13.

« When the vigil is over, as soon as it is day, he ought first to hear mass, and pray God to direct all his feats to his service. And afterwards he who is to knight him shall come and ask him, if he would receive the order of knighthood; and if he answereth yea, then shall it be asked him, if he will maintain it as it ought to be maintained; and when he shall have promised to do this, that knight shall fasten on his spurs, or order some other knight to fasten them on, according to what manner of man he may be, and the rank which he holdeth. And this they do to signify, that as a knight putteth spurs on the right and on the left, to make his horse gallop straight forward, even so he ought to let his actions be straight forward, swerving on neither side. And then shall his sword be girt on over his *brial.*—— Formerly it was ordained that when noble men were made knights, they should be armed at all points, as if they were about to do battle. But it was not held good that their heads should be covered, for they who cover their heads do so for two reasons: the one to hide something there which hath an ill look, and for that reason they may well cover them with any fair and becoming covering. The other reason is, when a man hath done some unseemly thing of which he is ashamed. And this in no wise becometh noble knights. For when they are about to receive so noble and so honourable a thing as knighthood, it is not fitting that they should enter into it with any evil shame, neither with fear. And when they shall have girded on his sword, they shall draw it from out the scabbard, and place it in his right hand, and make him swear these three things: first, That he shall not fear to die for his faith, if need be; secondly, For his natural Lord; thirdly, For his country.; and when he hath sworn this, then shall the blow on the neck be given him, in order that these things aforesaid may come into his mind, saying God guard him to his service, and let him perform all that he hath promised; and after this, he who hath conferred the order upon him, shall kiss him, in token of the faith and peace and brotherhood which ought to be observed among knights. And the same ought all the knights to do who are in that place, not only at that time, but whenever they shall meet with him during that whole year.»—*Part.* ii, *Tit.* 21, *Ley* 14.

« The gilt spurs which the knights put on have many significations; for the gold, which is so greatly esteemed, he puts upon his feet, denoting thereby, that the knight shall not for gold commit any malignity or treason, or like deed, that would detract from the honour of knighthood. The spurs are sharp, that they may quicken the speed of the horse; and this signifies that the knight ought to spur and prick on the people, and make them virtuous; for one knight with his virtues is sufficient to make many people virtuous, and on the other hand, he ought to prick a perverse people to make them fearful.»—*Tirante il Blanco,* p. 1, c. 19, ff. 44.

The hermit reads to Tirante a chapter from the *Arbor de batteglie,* explaining the origin of knighthood. The world, it is there said, was corrupted, when God, to the intent that he might be loved, honoured, served, and feared once more, chose out from every thousand men who was more amiable, more affable, more wise, more loyal, more strong, more noble-minded, more virtuous, and of better customs than all the others: And then he sought among all beasts for that which was the goodliest, and the swiftest, and which could bear the greatest fatigue, and might be convenient for the service of man; and he chose the horse, and gave him to this man who was chosen from the thousand; and for this reason he was called *cavallerio,* because the best animal was thus joined to the most noble man. And when Romulus founded Rome, he chose out a thousand young men to be knights, and *furno nominati militi porche mille furono fatti in un tempo cavalleri.*—P. 1, c. 14, ff. 40.

The custom which some kings had of knighting themselves is censured by the Partidas.—P. ii, T. 21, L. 11. It is there said, that there must be one to give, and another to receive the order. And a knight can no more knight, than a priest ordain himself.

When the Infante Hernando of Castile was chosen king of Aragon, he knighted himself on his coronation day :—« de que tots los Barons nobles ho tengeren una gran maravella com el matex se feu cavaller, qui segons los dessus dits deyen nenguno pot esser cavaller sino dones nos fa cavaller de ma de cavaller qui hage lorde de cavalleria.»—*Tomich.* C. 47, ff. 68.

« The qualifications for a knight, cavallerio, or horse-soldier, in the barbarous stage of society, were three : 1st, That he should be able to endure fatigue, hardship, and privations. 2dly, That he should have been used to strike, that his blows might be the more deadly. 3dly, That he should be bloody-minded, and rob, hack, and destroy the enemy without compunction. The persons, therefore, who were preferred, were mountaineers, accustomed to hunting,—carpenters, blacksmiths, stone-cutters, and butchers. But it being found that such persons would sometimes run away, it was then discovered that they who were chosen for cavaliers ought to have a natural sense of shame. And for this reason it was appointed that they should be men of family.»—*Partida*, ii, T. 21, L. 2. *Vegetius*, L. 1, c. 7.

The privileges of knighthood were at one time so great, that if the goods of a knight were liable to seizure, they could not be seized where he or his wife were present, nor even where his cloak or shield was to be found.—*Part.* ii, *Tit.* 21, *Ley* 23.

Note 36, page 410, col. 1.

The coated scales of mail
Which o'er the tunic to his knees depend.

Canciani (T. 3 p. 34,) gives a representation of Roland from the porch of the Cathedral at Verona, which is supposed to have been built about the beginning of the ninth century. The figure is identified by the inscription on the sword,—*Du-rin-dar-da.* The *lorica*, which Canciani explains, *Vestica bellica maculis ferreis contexta*, is illustrated by this figure. It is a coat or frock of *scale*-mail reaching to the knees, and with half sleeves. The only hand which appears is unarmed, as far as the elbow. The right leg also is unarmed, the other leg and foot are in the same sort of armour as the coat. The end of a loose garment appears under the mail. The shield reaches from the chin to the middle of the leg, it is broad enough at the top to cover the breast and shoulder, and slopes gradually off to the form of a long oval.

Note 37, page 413, col. 2.

At every saddle-bow
A gory head was hung.

This picture frequently occurs in the Spanish Chronicles. Sigurd the elder, Earl of Orkney, owed his death to a like custom. « Suddenly clapping spurs to his horse, as he was returning home in triumph, bearing, like each of his followers, one of these bloody spoils, a large front tooth in the mouth of the head which hung dangling by his side, struck the calf of his leg,—the wound mortified, and he died.—The Earl must have been bare-legged. »—*Torfæus, quoted in Edmonston's View of the Zetland Islands,* vol. i. p. 33.

Note 38, page 415, col. 2.

In reverence to the priestly character.

« At the synod of Mascou, laymen were enjoined to do honour to the honourable clergy by humbly bowing the head, and uncovering it, if they were both on horseback, and by alighting also if the clergyman were a-foot.»—*Pierre de Marca. Hist. de Bearn,* l. 1, ch. 18, sect. 2.

Note 39, page 417, col. 1.

Whom not the spoils of Atabalipa
Could satisfy insatiate.

Hernando de Soto,—the history of whose expedition to Florida by the Inca Garcilaso, is one of the most delightful books in the Spanish language.

Note 40, page 417, col. 2.

Nor wicker storehouse for the autumnal grain.

« Morales (8. 23. 3.), speaking of the Asturians, mentions with wonder their chairs, furniture, and granaries of basket-work,—las sillas y otras cosas de servicio recias y firmas que hacen entretexidas de mimbres y varas de avellano. Y aun a mé no me espantaba en aquella tierra tanto esto, como ver los graneros, que ellos llaman los horreos, fabricados desta misma obra de varas entretexidas, y tan tupidas y de tanta firmeza, que sufren gran carga como buenas paredes.»

Note 41, page 419, col. 1.

Covadonga.

The valley of Covadonga is thus described by the Conde de Salduena ;—and the description is a fair specimen of his poem :

Yace de Asturias, donde el Sol Infante
Sus montes con primeras luces baña,
De Covadonga el sitio, que triunfante
Cuna fue en que nació la insigne España
Vierte en el Sela liquidos cristales
Con Buena y Deba, que de la montaña
Deben la vida á la fragosa copa,
A quien la antigüedad llamó de Europa.

Aqui la juventud de un bello llano
Compite á flores, luces de la esphera ;
Y burlando el Invierno y el Verano
Eterna vive en el la Primavera :
Sobre sus glebas de derrama ufano
El prodigioso cuerno de la Fiera
De Amaltea, y aromas, y colores
Confunden los matices con olores.

Robustos troncos, con pobladas ramas
Vuelven el sitio rústica Alameda,
Y del Sol no permiten á las llamas
Lo espeso penetrar de la Arboleda :
Pierden sus rayos las ardientes famas,
Pues la frondosidad opuesta veda
La luz al dia, y denso verde muro
Crepúsculo le viste al ayre puro.

Siguiendo la ribera de Peonia
Al Oriente Estival, y algo inclinado
A la parte que mira al medio dia,
Otro valle se ve mas dilatado :
A la derecha de esta selva umbria
Reynazo corre, que precipitado
Va á dar á Buena en liquidos abrazos
Su pobre vena en cristalinos lazos.

Sin passar de Reynazo el successivo
Curso, dexando presto su torrente,

Con el cristal se encuentra fugitivo
  De Deba, á quien la Cueba dió la fuente:
La admiracion aqui raro motivo
  Ve, formando la senda su corriente,
Pues lo estrecho del sitio peñascoso
Hace camino del licor undoso.

Hecho serpiente Deva del camino
  En circulo se enrosca tortuoso,
Vomitando veneno cristalino
  En el liquido aljofar proceloso:
En las orillas con vivaz destino,
  En tosigo se vuelve, que espumoso
Inficiona lethal al pie ligero,
Quando le pisa incanto el passagero.

Ya de este valle cierran las campañas,
  Creciendo de sus riscos la estatura,
Desmesuradas tanto las montañas
  Que ofuscan ya del Sol la lumbre pura
Son rústicos los lados, las entrañas
  Del valle visten siempre la hermosura
Frondidad el ayre, y de colores
El suelo texe alfombra de primores.

Aunque los montes con espesas breñas
  El lado al sitio forman horroroso,
Y contra su verdor desnudas peñas
  Compiten de lo llano lo frondoso;
Pintados pajarillos dulces señas
  Al son del agua en trino sonoroso
De ignorados idiomas en su canto
Dan con arpados picos dulce encanto.

Lo último de este valle la alta sierra
  De Covadonga ocupa, donde fuerte
Se expone el Heroe al juego de la guerra,
  Sin temor negro acaso de la suerte:
Los que animosos este sitio encierra
  El ceno despreciando de la muerte,
Su pecho encienden en la altiva llama
Que no cabrá en las trompas de la Fama.

De Diba e della la preciosa fuente
  Al llano brota arroyos de cristales,
Donde en pequeña balsa su corriente
  Se detiene en suspensos manantiales:
Despues se precipita su torrente
  Quanto sus ondas enfreno neutrales,
Con sonoroso ruido de la peña
El curso de sus aguas se despeña.

Cierra todo este valle esta robusta
  Peña, donde la Cueva está divina,
Que amenaza tajada á ser injusta
  Del breve llano formidable ruina:
Parece quiere ser con sana adusta
  Seco padron, y fiera se destina
A erigirse epitafio peñascoso,
Sepultando su horror el sitio hermoso.

De piedra viva tan tremenda altura
  Que la vista al mirarla se extremece;
Vasta greña se viste, y la hermosura
  De la fertilidad seca aborrece:
Es tan desmesurada su estatura
  Que estrecha el ayre, y bárbara parece
Que quiere que la sirvan de Cimera
Las fulminantes luces de la Esphera.

Como á dos picas en la peña dura
  Construye en circo una abertura rara,
De una pica de alto, y dos de anchura,
  Rica de sombras su mansion avara:
Ventana, ó boca de la cueva obscura
  Donde el Sol no dispensa su luz clara,
Tan corta, que su centro tenebroso
Aun no admite crepúsculo dudoso.

En este sitio pues, donde compite
  La rustiquez con las pintadas flores,
Pues la pelada sierra no permite
  A la vista, sino es yertos horrores:

Por el contrario el llano que en si admito
  De los bellos matices los primores,
Efecto siendo de naturaleza
  La union en lo fealdad, y la belleza.

A tiorba de cristal las dulces aves
  Corresponden en trinos amorosos,
Vertiendo en blando son tonos suaves
  Ecos los ayres beben harmoniosos:
Enmudecen su canto quando graves
  Bemoles gorgeando mas preciosos,
Es maestro á la bárbara Capilla
El Ruysenor, plumada maravilla.

Elige este distrito la Divina
  Providencia á lo grave de la hazana,
Pues aqui su justicia determina
  La monarquia fabricar de España:
A las cortas reliquias, que á la ruina
  Reservó su piedad, enciende en sana
Religiosa, que á Imperio sin segunda
Abra futura llave Nuevo Mundo.

El Pelayo, cant. ix.

Christoval de Mesa also describes the scene.

—— Acercándose mas, oye el sonido
  Del agua, con un manso y sordo ruydo.

El qual era de quatro claras fuentes
  Que estavan de la ermita en las esquinas,
Cuyas puras de plata aguas corrientes
  Mostró la blanca Luna cristalinas;
Y corriendo por partes diferentes
  Eran de grande maravilla dignas,
Y en qualquiera de todas por su parte
Naturaleza se esmeró con arte.

La una mana de una viva peña,
  Y qual si tambien fuera el agua viva,
Parte la baña, y parte se despeña,
  Con rápida corriente fugitiva:
Despues distinto un largo arroyo enseña
  Que por diversas partes se derriba,
Con diferente curso en vario modo
Hasta que á donde nace buelve todo.

Otra, que alta descubre ancho Orizonte,
  Como agraviada del lugar segundo,
Sustenta un monstruo que parece un monte,
  Qual Atlante que tiene en peso el mundo
Y como suele el caudaloso Oronte
  Dar el ancho tributo al mar profundo
Assi se arroja con furiosas ondas,
Por las partes mas baxas y mas hondas.

Sale bramando la tercera fuente,
  Como un mar, y despues por el arena
Va con tan mansa y plácida corriente
  Tan grata y sossegada, y tan serena,
Que á las fieras, ganados, peces, gente,
  Puede aplacar la sed, menguar la pena,
Y da despues la buelta, y forma el cuerno
De la Luna, imitando el curso eterno.

Nace la quarta de una gran caverna,
  Y siguiendo su próspera derrota
Parece que por arte se govierna,
  Segun va destilando gota a gota:
No vido antigua edad, edad moderna
  En region muy propinqua, ó muy remota,
Fuente tan peregrina, obra tan nueva,
En gruta artificiosa, o tosca cueva.

Restauracion de Espana. lib. 2, ff. 27.

Morales has given a minute description both of the scenery and antiquities of this memorable place. The Conde de Saldueña evidently had it before him. I also am greatly indebted to this faithful and excellent author.

Note 42, page 420 , col. 1.

The timid hare soon learns that she may trust
The solitary penitent, and birds
Will light upon the hermit's harmless hand.

Con mil mortificaciones
  Sus passiones crucifican,
  Porque ellas de todo mueran
  Porque el alma solo viva.
Hazen por huyr al ocio
  Cestos, y espuertas texidas
  De las hojas de las palmas
  Que alli crecen sin medida.
Los árboles, y las plantas
  Porque á su gusto los sirvan
  Para esto verjas offrecen,
  De las mas tiernas que crian.
Tambien de corcho hazen vasos
  Cuentas, Cruzes, y basillas,
  Cuyo modô artificioso.
  El oro, y la plata embidian.
Este los cilicios texe,
  Aquel hazo disciplinas,
  El otro las calaveras
  En tosco palo esculpidas.
Uno á sombra del aliso,
  Con la escritura divina
  Misticos sentidos saca
  De sus literales minas.
Otro junto de la fuente
  Que murmura en dulce risa
  Mira en los libros las obras
  De los santos Eremitas.
Qual cerca del arroyuelo
  Que sultando corre aprissa,
  Discurre como á la muerte
  Corre sin parar la vida.
Qual con un Christo abraçado
  Besándole las heridas,
  Herido de sus dolores
  A sus pies llora, y suspira.
Qual en las flores que al campo
  Entre esmeraldas matizan,
  Las grandezas soberanas
  Del immenso autor medita.
Qual subida en las piçarras
  Que plata, y perlas distilan,
  Con lagrimas acrecienta
  Su corriente cristalina.
Qual á las fieras convoca,
  Las aves llama, y combida
  A que al criador de todo
  Alaben agradecidas.
Qual immoble todo el cuerpo,
  Con las acciones perdidas,
  Tiene arrebatada el alma
  Allá donde amando anima.
Y de aquel extasi quando
  Parece que resuscita,
  Dize con razon que muere
  Porque no perdió la vida.
La fuerça de amor á vezes
  Sueño, y reposo los quita,
  Y saliendo de su estancia
  Buscan del Cielo la vista.
Quando serena la noche
  Clara se descubre Cynthia,
  Borlando de azul, y plata
  El postrer mobil que pisa ;
Quando el oro de su hermano
  No puede tener embidia,
  Que llena del que le presta
  Haze de la noche dia ;
Del báculo acompañado
  El amante Anachorita
  Solo por las soledades
  Solitarios pasos guia.
Y parando entre el silencio
  Las claras estrellas mira
  Que le deleitan por obra
  De la potencia divina.
En altas bozes alaba
  Sin tener quien se lo impida

Al amador soberano
  Cuya gracia solicita.
Contempla sus perfeciones,
  Sus grandezas soleniza,
  Sus misericordias canta,
  Sus eccelencias publica.
La noche atenta entre tanto
  Callando porque él prosiga.
  Cruxen los vezinos ramos,
  Y blando el viento respira.
Gimen las aves nocturnas
  Por bazerle compania,
  Suenan las fuentes, y arroyos,
  Retumban las peñas frias.
Todo ayuda al solitario,
  Mientras con el alma fixa
  En sus queridos amores
  Contemplandolos se alivia.
              Soledades de Busaco.

Fuller the Worthy has a beautiful passage in his Church History concerning « Primitive Monks with their Piety and Painfulness.»—« When the furnace of persecution in the infancy of Christianity was grown so hot, that most cities, towns, and populous places were visited with that epidemical disease, many pious men fled into desarts, there to live with more safety, and serve God with less disturbance. No wild humour to make themselves miserable, and to chuse and court their own calamity, put them on this project, much less any superstitious opinion of transcendent sanctity in a solitary life, made them willingly to leave their former habitations. For whereas all men by their birth are indebted to their country, there to stay and discharge all civil relations, it had been dishonesty in them like bankrupts to run away into the wilderness to defraud their country, their creditor, except some violent occasion (such as persecution was) forced them thereunto ; and this was the first original of monks in the world, so called from μόνος, because living alone by themselves.

« Here they in the desarts hoped to find rocks and stocks, yea beasts themselves, more kind than men had been to them. What would hide and heat, cover and keep warm, served them for clothes, not placing (as their successors in after ages) any holiness in their habit, folded up in the affected fashion thereof. As for their food, the grass was their cloth, the ground their table, herbs and roots their diet, wild fruits and berries their dainties, hunger their sauce, their nails their knives, their hands their cups, the next well their wine-cellar; but what their bill of fare wanted in cheer it had in grace, their life being constantly spent in prayer, reading, musing, and such like pious employments. They turned solitariness itself into society; and cleaving themselves asunder by the divine art of meditation, did make of one, two, or more, opposing, answering, moderating in their own bosoms, and busy in themselves with variety of heavenly recreations. It would do one good even but to think of their goodness, and at the rebound and second hand to meditate upon their meditations. For if ever poverty was to be envied it was here. And I appeal to the moderate men of these times, whether in the height of these woeful wars, they have not sometimes wisht (not out of passionate distemper, but serious recollection of themselves) some such private place to retire unto, where, out of the noise of this clamorous world, they might have reposed themselves, and served God with more quiet.»

Note 43, page 422, col. 1.

None but that heavenly Father, who alone
Beholds the struggles of the heart, alone
Knows and rewards the secret sacrifice.

Men amor faça em Deos seu fundamento
Em Deos, que so conhece e so estima
A nobreza e o valor de hum pensamento.
Fernam Alvares do Oriente.

Note 44, page 422, col. 1.

Sindered.

« Per idem tempus divinæ memoriæ Sinderebus urbis Regiæ Metropolitanus Episcopus sanctimoniæ studio claret ; atque longævos et merito honorabiles viros quos in suprafata sibi commissa Ecclesia repetit, non secundum scientiam zelo sanctitatis stimulat, atque instinctu jam dicti Witizæ Principis eos sub ejus tempore convexare non cessat ; qui et post medium incursus Arabum expavescens, non ut pastor, sed ut mercenarius, Christi oves contra decreta majorum deserens, Romanæ patriæ sese adventat.»—*Isid. Pacensis, Espana Sagrada*, T. 8, p. 298.

« E assi como el Arçobispo fue cierto de la mala andança partió de Córdova ; y nunca cessó de andar dia ni noche fasta que llegó á Toledo ; y no embargante que él era hombre de buena vida, no se quisso mostrar por tal como deviera ser, y sufrir antes martyrio por amor de Jesu Christo y esforçar los suyos, porque se defendiessen, y que las gentes no desamparassen la tierra ; ca su intencion fue de ser confessor antes que martyr.»—*Cor del K. D. Rodriga*, p. 2, c. 48.

Note 45, page 422, col. 1.

While the Church

Keeps in her annals the deserter's name ;
But from the service which with daily zeal
Devout her ancient prelacy recalls,
Blots it, unworthy to partake her prayers.

« Je ne serois pas en grande peine, *says Pierre de Marca*, de rechercher les noms des Evesques des Bearn, si la saincte et louable pratique des anciens Peres d'inserer dans les Diptyches, et cayers sacrés de chascune Eglise, les noms des Evesques orthodoxes, et qui estoient decedés dans la communion de l' Eglise Catholique, eust este continuée jusqu' aux derniers siecles. Et je pourrois me servir en cette rencontre du moyen que l' Empereur Justinian et le cinquiesme Concile General employerent, pour sçavoir si Theodore Evesque de Mopsuestie estoit reconnu apres sa mort pour Evesque de l' Eglise qu'il avoit possedée durant sa vie. Car ils ordonnerent a l' Evesque et au Clergé de cette ville , de revoir les Diptyches de leur Eglise, et de rapporter fidellement ce qu'ils y trouveroient. Ce qu' ayant executé diligemment, ils firent rapport qu' apres avoir feuilleté quatre divers cayers en parchemin, qui estoient leurs Diptyches, ils y avoient trouvé le nom de touts les Evesques de ce siege ; horsmis qu' en la place de Theodore, avoit esté substitué le nom de Cyrille, qui estoit le Patriarche d' Alexandrie ; lequel presidant au Concile d' Ephese avoit condamné l' heresie de Nestorius et de Theodore de Mopsuestie. D'ou il apert que les noms de tous les Evesques depuis l'origine et l'establissement de chascune des Eglises estoient enregistrés dans les cayers que l'on appelloit Diptyches, et que l'on les recitoit nom par nom en leur tieu, pendant la celebration de la Liturgie, tant pour tesmoigner la continuation de la communion avec les Evesques decedés, que l'on avoit eüe avec euxmesmes vivans, qu' afin de procurer par les

prieres publiques, et par l'efficace du sacrifice non sanglant, en la celebration du quel ils estoient recommendés à Dieu, suivant l'ordonnance des apostres, un grand profit, soulagement, et rafraichissement pour leurs ames, comme enseignent Cyrille de Hierusalem, Chrysostome, et Epiphane.»—*Histoire de Bearn*, l. 4, c. 9, sec. 1.

« Some time before they made oblation for the dead, it was usual in some ages to recite the names of such eminent bishops, or saints, or martyrs, as were particularly to be mentioned in this part of the service. To this purpose they had certain books, which they called their Holy Books, and commonly their *Diptychs*, from their being folded together, wherein the names of such persons were written, that the deacon might rehearse them as occasion required in the time of divine service. Cardinal Bona and Schelstrade make three sorts of these *Diptychs* ; one wherein the names of bishops only were written, and more particularly such bishops as had been governors of that particular church : a second, wherein the names of the living were written, who were eminent and conspicuous either for any office and dignity, or some benefaction and good work, whereby they had deserved well of the church ; in this rank were the patriarchs and bishops of great sees, and the bishop and clergy of that particular church : together with the emperors and magistrates, and others most conspicuous among the people : the third was the book containing the names of such as were deceased in catholic communion.—These therefore were of use, partly to preserve the memory of such eminent men as were dead in the communion of the church, and partly to make honourable mention of such general councils as had established the chief articles of the faith : and to erase the names either of men or councils out of these *Diptychs*, was the same thing as to declare that they were heterodox, and such as they thought unworthy to hold communion with, as criminals, or some way, deviating from the faith. Upon this account St Cyprian ordered the name of Geminius Victor to be left out among those that were commemorated at the holy table, because he had broken the rules of the church. And Evagrius observes of Theodorus bishop of Mopsuestia, that his name was struck out of the Holy Books, that is, the *Diptychs*, upon the account of his heretical opinions after death. And St Austin, speaking of Cæcilian, Bishop of Carthage, whom the Donatists falsely accused of being ordained by *Traditores*, or men who had delivered up the Bible to be burned in the times of persecution, tells them that if they could make good any real charge against him, they would no longer name him among the rest of the bishops, whom they believed to be faithful and innocent, at the altar.»—*Bingham*, b. 15, ch. 3, sect. 17.

Note 46, page 422, col. 1.

The relics, and the written works of Saints,
Toledo's choicest treasure, prized beyond
All wealth, their living and their dead remains ;
These to the mountain fastnesses he bore
Of unsubdued Cantabria, there deposed
One day to be the boast of yet unbuilt
Oviedo, and the dear idolatry
Of multitudes unborn.

« Among those, says Morales, who then passed from Toledo to Asturias, was the archbishop of Toledo, named Urban.—He, with a holy foresight, collected the sacred relics which he could, and the most precious books of his own church and of others, determining to carry them all to the Asturias, in order that the holy relics might not be profaned or treated with little reverence by the infidels; and that the books of the Holy Scriptures, and of the ecclesiastical offices, and the works of our holy doctors, might not be lost.—And although many relics are mentioned which the archbishop then carried from Toledo, especial mention is made of a holy ark full of many and most remarkable relics, which, through divers chances and dangers, had been brought from Jerusalem to Toledo, and of which all that is fitting shall be related in its place, if it please God that this history should proceed. It is also expressly said, that the cope which Our Lady gave to St Ildefonso, was then carried to the Asturias with the other relics; and being so capital a relic, it was a worthy thing to write of it thus particularly. Of the sacred books which were saved at that time, there are specified the Holy Scriptures, the Councils, the works of St Isidore, and St Ildefonso, and of St Julian the archbishop of Toledo. And as there is at this day in the church of Oviedo that holy ark, together with many others of the relics which were then removed, so do I verily believe that there are in the library of that church three or four books of those which were then brought from Toledo. I am led to this belief by seeing that they are written in a form of Gothic letters which, being compared with writings six hundred years old, are without doubt much older, and of characters so different, that they may well be attributed to the times of the Goths. One is the volume of the Councils, another is a *Santoral*, another contains the books of St Isidore *de Naturis Rerum*, with other works of other authors. And there are also some leaves of a Bible.—To put these sacred relics in greater security, and avoid the danger of the Moors, they hid them in a cave, and in a sort of deep pit therein, two leagues from the city of Oviedo, (which was not at that time built,) in a mountain, which was for this reason called Montesacro. It is now by a slight corruption called Mousagro; and the people of that country hold the cave in great veneration, and a great romery, or pilgrimage, is made on St Magdalen's day.»—*Morales*, l. 12, c. 71.

The place where the relics were deposited is curiously described in the Romantic Chronicle. « He found that in this land of Asturias there was a sierra, full great, and high, the which had only two entrances, after this manner. On the one entrance there was a great river, which was to be passed seven times, and in none of those seven places was it fordable at any time, except in the month of July. And after the river had been crost seven times, there was an ascent of a long league up a high mountain, which is full of many great trees, and great thickets, wherein are many wild beasts, such as bears and boars and wolves, and there is a pass there between two rocks, which ten men might defend against the whole world, and this is the one entrance. The other is, that you must ascend this great mountain, by a path of two full leagues in length, on the one side having always the river, and the way so narrow, that one man must go before another, and one man can defend the path in such manner, that no arbalist, nor engine of other kind, nor any other thing, can hurt him, not if the whole world were to come against him. And if any one were to stumble upon this path, he

would fall more than two thousand bracas, down over rocks into the river, which lies at such a depth that the water appears blacker than pitch. And upon that mountain there is a good spring, and a plain where there are good meadows, and room enough to raise grain for eight or ten persons for a year; and the snow is always there for company, enduring from one year to another. And upon that mountain the archbishop made two churches, one to the honour of St Mary Magdalene, and the other to the honour of St Michael, and there he placed all these reliques, where he had no fear that any should take them; and for the honour of these relics, the archbishop consecrated the whole mountain, and appointed good guard over the sacred relics, and left there three men of good life, who were willing to remain there, serving God and doing penance for their sins.»—P. 2, c. 48.

Of the *Camara Santa*, Morales has given a curious account in his Journal: the substance, with other remarkable circumstances, he afterwards thus inserted in his great history :—

« The other church (or chapel) which King Alonso el Casto ordered to be built on the south side of the Iglesia Mayor (or cathedral), was with the advocation of the Glorious Archangel St Michael. And in order that he might elevate it, he placed under it another church of the Virgin and Martyr St Leocadia, somewhat low, and vaulted with a strong arch, to support the great weight which was to be laid upon it. The king's motive for thus elevating this church of St Michael, I believe certainly to have been because of the great humidity of that land. He had determined to place in this church the famous relics of which we shall presently speak, and the humidity of the region is so great, that even in summer the furniture of the houses on high ground is covered with mold. This religious prince therefore elevated the church with becoming foresight for reverence and better preservation of the precious treasure which was therein to be deposited. For this reason they call it Camara, (the chamber,) and for the many and great relics which it contains, it has most deservedly the appellation of Holy. You ascend to it by a flight of twenty-two steps, which begin in the cross of the Iglesia Mayor, (or cathedral,) and lead to a vaulted apartment twenty feet square, where there is an altar upon which mass is said; for within there is no altar, neither is mass said there by reason of the reverence shewn to so great a sanctuary; and it may be seen that K. D. Alonso intended in his plan that there should be no altar within. In this apartment or outer chapel is a great arched door, with a very strong fastening; it leads to another smaller square chamber, vaulted also, with a square door, which also is fastened with another strong fastening, and these are the fastenings and keys which the Bishop Sampyro admires for their strength and security.

« The square door is the door of the Holy Chamber, which is in the form of a complete church, and you descend to it by twelve steps. The body of this church is twenty-four feet in length, and sixteen in width. Its arched roof is of the same dimensions. The roof is most richly wrought, and supported upon six columns of divers kinds of marbles, all precious and right beautiful, upon which the twelve apostles are sculptured, two and two. The ground is laid with Mosaic work, with variety of columns, representing jasper ware. The

Bishop Sampyro had good reason to complain of the darkness of this church, which has only one small window in the upper part of the chapel; and, therefore, in this which we call the body of the church, there are commonly three silver lamps burning, the one in the middle larger than the other two, and many other lights are kindled when the relics are shown. These are kept within a grating, which divides the chapel from the church. The chapel has two rich marbles at the entrance; it is eighteen feet in length, and its width somewhat less; the floor and the roof are after the same fashion as those of the church, but it is one *estado* lower, which in those times seems to have been customary in Asturias and in Gallicia, the Capillas Mayores, or principal chapels, being much lower than the body of the church. The roof of the chapel is plain, and has painted in the middle our Saviour in the midst of the four evangelists; and this performance is so ancient, that it is manifestly of the age of the founder. At this iron grating strangers are usually detained; there is a lower one within of wood, to which persons are admitted who deserve this privilege for their dignity; and few there be who enter farther. This church the king built to remove to it, as accordingly he forthwith removed the holy ark, the holy bodies, and the other great relics which, at the destruction of Spain, were hidden in the cave and well of Monsagro, and for this cause he had it built with so much care, and so richly, and with such security.

« I have described the Camara Santa thus particularly, that what I may say of the most precious relics which it contains may be the better enjoyed. I will particularize the most principal of them, beginning with the Holy Ark, which with great reason has deserved this name. It is in the midst of the chapel, close to the wooden grate, so that you can only go round it on three sides, and it is placed upon a stone pedestal, wrought with mouldings of a palm in height. It is a varo and a half (about five feet) in length; little less than a varo wide, and about as deep, that part, which is of silver, not including the height which the pedestal gives it. The cover is flat, and it is covered in all parts with silver plates of some thickness, and gilt on some places. In the front, or that side which fronts the body of the church, it has the twelve apostles in more than half relief, and on the sides there are histories of Our Lady in the same silver-work. On the flat part of the cover there is a large crucifix engraved, with many other images round about it. The sides are elaborately wrought with foliage, and the whole displays great antiquity. The cover has round about it four lines in the silver, which, however, are imperfect, the silver being wanting in some places. What they contain is this, as I have copied it faithfully, with its bad Latin and other faults:—

« Omnis conventus populi Deo dignus catholici cognoscat, quorum inclytas veneratur reliquias, intra preiosissima præsentis archælatera. Hoc est de ligno plurimum, sive de cruce Domini. De vestimentis illius, quod per sortem divisum est. De pane delectabili unde in cena usus est. De sindone Dominico ejus adque sudario et cruore sanctissimo. De terra sancta quam piis calcavit tunc vestigiis. De vestimentis matris jus Virginis Mariæ. De lacte quoque ejus, quod multum est mirabile. His pariter conjunctæ sunt quædam sanctorum maxime prestantes reliquiæ, quorum prout

potuimus, hæc nomina subscripsimus. Hoc est de Sancto Petro, de Sancto Thoma, Sancti Bartolmei. De ossibus Prophetarum, de omnibus Apostolis, et de aliis quam plurimus sanctis, quorum nomina sola Dei scientia colligit. His omnibus egregius Rex Adefonsus humili devotione perditus fecit hoc receptaculum, sanctorum pignoribus insignitum argento deauratum, exterius adornatum non vilibus operibus: per quod post ejus vitam mereatur consortium illorum in cælestibus sanctorum jubari precibus. Hæc quidem saluti et re ——*Here a large piece of the silver is gone.*—Novit omnis provintia in terra sine dubio.——*Here there is another great chasm.*—Manus et industria clericorum et præsulum, qui propter hoc convenimus cum dicto Adefonso Principe, et cum germana lætissima Urraca nomina dicta: quibus Redemptor omnium concedit indulgentiam et suorum peccatorum veniam, per hoc sanctorum pignora Apostolorum et Sanci Justi et Pastoris, Cosmæ et Damiani, Eulaliæ Virginis, et Maximi, Germani, Baudili, Pantaleonis, Cypriani et Justinæ, Sebastiani, Facundi et Primitivi, Christophori, Cucufati, Felicis, Sulpicii.

« This inscription, with its bad Latin and other defects, and by reason of the parts that are lost, can ill be translated. Nevertheless I shall render it, in order that it may be enjoyed by all. It says thus: Know all the congregation of Catholic people, worthy of God, whose the famous relics are, which they venerate within the most precious sides of this ark. Know then that herein is great part of the wood or cross of our Lords Of his garment for which they cast lots. Of the blessed bread whereof he ate at the Supper. Of his linen, of the holy handkerchief (the Sudario), and of his most holy blood. Of the holy ground which he then trod with his holy feet. Of the garments of his mother the Virgin Mary, and also of her milk, which is a great wonder. With these also there are many capital relics of saints, whose names we shall write here as we can. Saint Peter, St Thomas, St Bartholomew. Bones of the Prophets, and of all the Apostles, and of many other Saints whose names are known only to the wisdom of God. The noble King Don Alonso, being full of humble devotion for all these holy relics, made this repository, adorned and ennobled with pledges of the Saints, and on the outside covered with silver, and gilded with no little cunning. For the which may he deserve after this life the company of these Saints in Heaven, being aided by their intercession.—These holy relics were placed here by the care and by the hands of many Clergy and Prelates, who were here assembled with the said King D. Alonso, and with his chosen sister called Donna Urraca. To whom may the Redeemer of all grant remission and pardon of their sins, for the reverence and rich reliquary which they made for the said relics of the Apostles, and for those of the Saints, St Justus and Pastor, St Cosme and St Damian, St Eulalia the Virgin, and of the Saints Maximus, Germanus, Baudilus, Pantaleon, Cyprianus and Justina, Sebastian, Facundus and Primitivus, Christopher, Cucufatus, Felix and Sulpicius.——

« The sum of the manner in which this Holy Ark came into Spain is this, conformably to what is written by all our grave authors. When Cosroes, the King of Persia, in the time of the Emperor Heraclius, came upon the Holy Land, and took the city of Jerusalem, the bishop of that city, who was called Philip, and his clergy, with pious foresight, secreted the Holy Ark, which from the time of the Apostles had been kept there, and its stores augmented with new relics, which were deposited therein. After the victory of Cosroes, the Bishop Philip, with many of his clergy, passed into Africa, carrying with them the Holy Ark: and there it remained some years, till the Saracens entered into that province also, and then Fulgentius the Bishop of Ruspina, with providence like that which had made Philip bring it to Africa, removed it into Spain. Thus it came to the Holy Church of Toledo, and was from thence removed to Asturias, and hidden in the cave of Monsagro: finally, King D. Alonso el Casto removed it to the Camara Santa; and afterwards K. D. Alonso the Great enriched it. Thus our histories write, and the same is read in the lessons on the festival which the Church of Oviedo celebrates of the coming there of this Holy Ark, with a sermon proper for the day, and much solemnity, the service being said on the 13th of March after vespers, above in the church of the Camara Santa. This is a most weighty testimony which the Holy Ark possesses of its own authenticity, and on the genuineness of the most great treasure which it contains.—There also are strong testimonies, that K. D. Alonso the Great should not only have made the Ark so rich, but that this king should also have fortified the city of Oviedo, surrounding it with walls, and making for it a castle, and building also the castle of Gauzon upon the shore, for the defence and security of this holy treasure, and for another end, as he left written upon the stone of which we have elsewhere spoken. Another testimony of great authority, is the great reverence which has been shown to this Holy Ark, from the time which is spoken of by Alonso the Great in the inscription, to these our days. This is so great that no one has dared to open it, melancholy examples being related of some daring attempts which have been made. That which occurred in our days is not mournful, but rather of much devotion and holy joy. The most illustrious Sir D. Christoval de Rojas y Sandoval, who is now the most worthy Archbishop of Seville, when he was Bishop of Oviedo, determined to open the Holy Ark. For this, as the singular devotion and most holy zeal for the glory of God which he has in all things admonished him, he made such pious preparations as the fame of so celestial a treasure showed to be necessary. He proclaimed solemnly a fast of forty days in his church and through all his diocese, commanding that prayers should be made to our Lord, beseeching him that he would be pleased with what was intended, his Most-Illustriousness giving the example, which is very common and very edifying in his church, in himself, and in the ministers thereof. Three days before the Sunday on which the Ark was to be opened, he ordered all persons to fast, and to make greater prayers with processions. When the day arrived, he said pontifical mass, and preached, infusing with his holy exhortations, much of his own devout desires, into the hearts of the hearers. The mass being finished, clad as he was, he ascended to the Camera Santa, with much outward solemnity, and with much fervour of devotion internally in his heart: and having there again renewed his humble prayers to our Lord, and quickened the ardour of that sacred desire which had influenced him; on his knees as he was before the Holy Ark, he took the key to open it. At the moment

when he stretched out his hand to put the key in the lock, suddenly he felt such horror and dismay, and found himself so bereft of all power (tan impossibilitudo) to move it in any way, that it was impossible for him to proceed, or do any thing but remain in that holy consternation, without having strength or ability for more, and as if he had come there to oppose and prevent that which purposely, and with so much desire and preparation he had intended to do, he desisted from his intent, and gave it up, his whole desire being turned into a chill of humble shrinking and fear. Among other things which his most Illustrious Lordship relates of what he then felt, he says, that his hair stood up in such a manner and with such force, that it seemed to him, as if it lifted the mitre a considerable way from his head. Now, we all know that this famous prelate has vigour and persevering courage for all the great things which he undertakes in the service of our Lord; but in this manner the Holy Ark remained unopened then, and thus I believe it will always remain, fastened more surely with veneration and reverence, and with respect of these examples, than with the strong bolt of its lock.

« In the inscription of this Holy Ark, mention is made of the relics of St Baudilus, and by reason that he is a Saint very little known, it will be proper to say something of him. This Saint is much reverenced in Salamanca and in Zamora, and in both cities he has a parochial church, and in Zamora they have a good part of his relics. They have so much corrupted the name, calling him St Boal, that the Saint is now scarcely known by his own.

« They of the church say, that the cope of St Ildefonso, which Our Lady gave him, is in the Ark. This may well be believed, since our good authors particularly relate that it was carried to Oviedo with the Holy Ark, and with the other relics, and it does not now appear among it, and there is much more reason to think that it has been very carefully put away, than that it has been lost. Also they say, that when the celestial cope was put into the Holy Ark, they took out of it the piece of the holy Sudario, in which the head of our Redeemer was wrapt up for his interment, as is said in the inscription of the Ark. This is one of the most famous relics in all Christendom, and therefore it is most richly adorned, and reverently preserved, being shown only three times in the year with the greatest solemnity. The box in which it is kept is wrought without of gold and azure, with beautiful mouldings and pictures, and other ornaments of much authority. Within this there is a square piece of wood, covered entirely with black velvet, with silver handles, and other decorations of silver round about; in the hollow of this square, the holy Sudario is stretched and fastened upon the velvet; it is a thin linen cloth, three quarters long and half a varo wide, and in many places full of the divine blood from the head of our Redeemer, in divers forms and stains of various sizes; wherein some persons observe marks of the divine countenance and other particularities. I did not perceive this; but the feeling which came upon me when I looked at it is sufficient to make me believe any thing of it; and if a wretch like me was thus affected, what must it do to those who deserve of our Lord greater regalements on such an occasion? It is exhibited to the people three times in the year; on Good Friday, and on the two festivals of the Cross in May and in September, and there is then a great concourse from all the country, and from distant parts. This part of the cross of the church where the Camara Santa is, is richly hung, and in the first apartment of the Camara, a corridor is erected for this exhibition; the which is closed that day with curtains of black velvet, and a canopy that extends over the varandas. The Bishop in his pontificals, with his assistants and other grave persons, places himself behind the curtains with the Holy Sudario, holding it by the silver handles, covered with a veil. The curtains are undrawn, and the quiristers below immediately begin the *miserere*. The Bishop lifts the veil, and at the sight of the Holy Sudario, another music begins of the voices of the people, deeply affected with devotion, which verily penetrates all hearts. The Bishop stands some time, turning the Sacred Relic to all sides, and afterwards the veil being replaced, and the curtains redrawn, he replaces the Holy Sudario in its box. With all these solemnities, the very Illustrious and most Reverend Sennor, M. D. Gonzalo de Solorzano, Bishop of Oviedo, exhibited this Holy Relic on the day of Santiago, in the year of our Redeemer 1572, in order that I might bear a more complete relation of the whole to the King our Lord; I having at that time undertaken the sacred journey by his command.

« Another chest, with a covering of crimson and brocade, contains a good quantity of bones, and some pieces of a head; which although they are very damp, have a most sweet odour, and this all we who were present perceived, when they were shown me, and we spoke of it as of a notable and marvellous thing. The account which they of the church give of this holy body is, that it is that of St Serrano, without knowing any thing more of it. I, considering the great dampness of the sacred bones, believe certainly that it was brought up to the Camara Santa from the church of Leocadia, which, as it has been seen, is underneath it. And there, in the altar, the great stone-chest is empty, in which King Alonso el Casto enclosed many relics, as the Bishop Sampyro writes. For myself I have always held for certain, that the body of St Leocadia is that which is in this rich chest. And in this opinion I am the more confirmed since the year 1580, when such exquisite diligence has been used by our Spaniards in the monastery of St Gisleno, near Mons de Henao in Flanders, to verify whether the body of St Leocadia, which they have there, is that of our Saint. The result has been, that it was ascertained beyond all doubt to be the same; since an authentic writing was found of the person who carried it thither by favour of one of our earliest kings, and he carried it from Oviedo without dispute; because, according to my researches, it is certain that it was there. Now I affirm, that the king who gave part left part also; and neither is that which is there so much, that what we saw at Oviedo might not well have been left, neither is this so much but that which is at Mons might well have been given.

« In the church below, in a hollow made for this purpose, with grates, and a gate well ornamented, is one of the vessels which our Redeemer Jesus Christ filled with miraculous wine at the marriage in Galilee. It is of white marble, of an ancient fashion, more than three feet high, and two wide at the mouth, and contains more than six *arrobas*. And forasmuch as it is in the wall of the church of K. Alonso el Casto, and all the

work about it is very ancient, it may be believed that the said king ordered it to be placed there.»—*Cronica General de Espana*, L. 13, c. 40.

Morales gives an outline of this vessel in his Journal, and observes, that if the Christians transported it by land, particular strength and the aid of God would have been necessary to carry it so many leagues, and move it over the rugged mountains of Europa;—but, he adds, it might have come by water from Andalusia or Portugal, and in that case this would have been a land journey of only four or five leagues.—In his Journal, Morales mentions certain other relics of which the church of Oviedo boasted, but for which he required better evidence than could be adduced for them. Such were a portion of Tobit's fish, and of Sampson's honey-comb, with other such things, which, he says, would lessen the credit of the Ark, where, according to the Bishop of Oviedo, D. Pelayo, and Sebastian, Bishop of Salamanca, they were deposited. Of these precious relics he says nothing in his history, neither does he mention a piece of Moses's rod, a large piece of St Bartholomew's skin, and the sole of St Peter's shoe, all which he enumerates in his Journal, implying rather than expressing his doubts of their authenticity. As a scrupulous and faithful antiquary, Morales was accustomed to require evidence, and to investigate it; and for these he could find no other testimony than tradition and antiquity, which, as presumptive proofs, were strong corroborants of faith, but did not suffice of themselves. The Holy Ark has all the evidence which he required, and the reverence with which he regarded it, is curiously expressed in his Journal. «I have now,» he says, «described the material part of the Camara Santa. The spiritual and devout character which it derives from the sacred treasures which it contains, and the feeling which is experienced upon entering it, cannot be described without giving infinite thanks to our Lord, that he has been pleased to suffer a wretch like me to enjoy it. I write this in the church before the grating, and God knows I am as it were beside myself with fear and reverence, and I can only beseech God to give me strength to proceed with that for which I have no power myself.»—T. 10. *Viage*, p. 91.

Morales, like Origen, had given in his youth a decisive proof of the sincerity of his religious feelings, and it sometimes seems as if he had emasculated his mind as well as his body. But with all this abject superstition, he was a thoroughly pious and good man. His life is deeply interesting; and his writings, besides their great historical and antiquarian value, derive additional interest from the picture of the author's mind which they so frequently display. The portrait prefixed to the last edition of his work is singularly characteristic.

Note 47, page 422, col. 1.
Orary.

« The Council of Laodicea has two canons concerning the little habit called the *Orarium*, which was a scarf or tippet to be worn upon the shoulders; and might be used by bishops, presbyters, and deacons, but not by subdeacons, singers, or readers, who are expressly debarred the use of it in that council.—The first council of Braga speaks of the *tunica* and the *orarium* as both belonging to deacons. And the third council of Braga orders priests to wear the *orarium* on both shoulders when they ministered at the altar. By which we learn that the *tunica* or *surplice* was common to all the clergy, the *orarium* on the left shoulder proper to deacons, and on both shoulders the distinguishing badge of priests.—The fourth council of Toledo is most particular in these distinctions. For in one canon it says, that if a bishop, presbyter, or deacon, be unjustly degraded, and be found innocent by a synod, yet they shall not be what they were before, unless they receive the degrees they had lost from the hands of the bishops before the altar. If he be a bishop, he must receive his *orarium*, his ring, and his staff: if a presbyter, his *orarium,* and *planeta*: if a deacon, his *orarium* and *alba.* And in another canon, that the deacon shall wear but one *orarium*, and that upon his left shoulder, wherewith he is to give the signal of prayers to the people. Where we may observe also the reason of the name *orarium* in the ecclesiastical sense *ab orando*, from praying, though in common acceptation it signifies no more than an handkerchief to wipe the face, and so comes *ab ore*, in which signification it is sometimes used by St Ambrose and St Austin, as well as by the old Roman authors. But here we take it in the ecclesiastical sense for a sacred habit appropriated to bishops, priests, and deacons, in the solemnities of divine service, in, which sense it appears to have been a habit distinct from that of civil and common use, by all the authorities that have been mentioned.»—*Bingham*, b. 13, ch. 8, sect. 2.

Note 48, page 422, col. 1.

Nor wore he mitre here,
Precious, or auriphrygiate.

« Mitræ usus antiquissimus est, et ejus triplex est species: una quæ pretiosa dicitur, quia gemmis et lapidibus pretiosis, vel laminis aureis, vel argenteis contexta esse solet; altera auriphrygiata sine gemmis, et sine laminis aureis vel argenteis; sed vel aliquibus parvis margaritis composita, vel ex serico albo auro intermisto, vel ex tela aurea simplici sine laminis et margaritis; tertia, quæ simplex vocatur, sine auro, ex simplici sirico Damasceno, vel alio, aut etiam linea, ex tela alba confecta, rubeis laciniis seu frangiis et vittis pendentibus. Pretiosa utitur Episcopus in solemnioribus festis et generaliter quandocumque in officio dicitur hymnus *Te Deum laudamus, etc.* et in missa *Gloria in excelsis Deo.* Nihilominus in eisdem festis etiam auriphrygiata uti poterit, sed potius ad commoditatem quam ex necessitate; ne scilicet Episcopus nimis gravetur, si in toto officio pretiosa utatur: propterea usu receptum est, tam in Vesperis, quam in Missis, ut pretiosa utatur Episcopus in principio et in fine Vesperarum et Missarum solemnium, ac eundo ad Ecclesiam et redeundo ab ea; et quando lavat manus et dat benedictionem solemnem. Intermedio autem spatio loco pretiosæ accipit auriphrygiatam.— Auriphrygiata mitra utitur Episcopus ab Adventu Domini usque ad festum Nativitatis, excepta Dominica tertia Adventus, in qua dicitur Introitus *Gaudete, etc.* ideoque in signum lætitiæ utitur tunc pretiosa. Item a Septuagesima usque ad feriam quartam majoris hebdomadæ inclusivè, excepta Dominica quarta Quadragesimæ, in qua dicitur Introitus *Lætare, etc.* Item in omnibus vigiliis, quæ jejunantur, et in omnibus quatuor temporibus; in Rogationibus, Litaniis et processionibus, quæ ex causa penitentiæ fiunt; in festo Innocentium, nisi veniat in Dominica; et benedictionibus, et consecrationibus, quæ private aguntur. Quibus quidem temporibus abstinet, Episcopus a mitra pretiosa. Poterit tamen Episcopus dum utitur auriphrygiata, uti etiam simplici eodem modo et forma, prout de pretiosa et auriphrygiatà dictum est. Simplici vero mitra utitur Episcopus feria sexta in Parasceve, et in officiis et Missis defunctorum.»—*Cæremoniale Episcoporum*, l. 1, c. 17.

Note 49, page 422, col. 1.

The pall
Of wool undyed, which on the Apostle's tomb
Gregory had laid.

« By the way, the pall is a pontifical vestment, considerable for the matter, making, and mysteries thereof. For the matter, it is made of lamb's wooll and superstition. I say of lamb's wooll, as it comes from the sheep's back, without any other artificiall colour, spun, say some, by a peculiar order of nunnes, first cast into the tombe of St Peter, taken from his body, say others, surely most sacred if from both; and superstitiously adorned with little black crosses. For the form thereof; the breadth exceeded not three fingers, one of our bachelours lambskin hoods in Cambridge would make three of them, having two labells hanging down before and behind, which the archbishops onely, when going to the altar, put about their necks, above their other pontificall ornaments. Three mysteries were couched therein. *First,* Humility, which beautifies the clergy above all their costly copes. *Secondly,* Innocency, to imitate lamb-like simplicitie. And, *Thirdly,* Industry, to follow him who fetched his wandering sheep home on his shoulders. But to speak plainly, the mystery of mysteries in the pall was, that the archbishops receiving it shewed therein their dependence on Rome; and a mote in this manner ceremoniously taken was a sufficient acknowledgement of their subjection. And as it owned Rome's power, so in after ages it increased their profit. For, though now such palls were freely given to archbishops, whose places in Britain for the present were rather cumbersome than commodious, having little more than their paines for their labour; yet in after ages the archbishop of Canterburie's pall was sold for five thousand florenes, so that the pope might well have the golden fleece if he could sell all his lamb's wooll at that rate. Onely let me add, that the author of Canterbury-book stiles this pall *Tanquam grande Christi Sacramentum.* It is well *tanquam* came in to help it, or else we should have had eight sacraments.» —*Fuller's Church History*, page 71.

Note 50, page 422, col. 2.

The proud array,
—Which Leuvigild for after kings
Left, ostentatious of his power?

« Postremum bellum Suevis intulit, regnumque eorum in jura gentis suæ mirà celeritate transmisit. Hispania magna ex parte potitus, nam antea gens Gothorum angustis finibus arctabatur.—Fiscum quoque primus iste locupletavit, primusque ærarium de rapinis civium, hostiumque manubiis auxit. Primusque etiam inter suos regali veste opertus in solio resedit. Nam ante cum et habitus et consessus communis, ut populo, ita et regibus erat.»—*S. Isidor. Hist. Goth.*—*Espana Sagrada*, 6, 498-9.

Note 51, page 422, col. 2.

The Sueve.

As late as the age of the Philips, the Portugueze were

called Sevosos by the Castillians, as an opprobrious name. Brito says, It was the old word Suevos continued and corrupted, and used contemptuously, because its origin was forgotten.—*Monarchia Lusitana*, 2, 6, 4.

When the Suevi and Alani over-ran Spain they laid siege to Lisbon, and the Saints Maxima, Julia, and Verissimus (a most undoubted personage) being Lisbonians, were applied to by their town's people to deliver them. Accordingly, a sickness broke out in the besieger's camp, and they agreed to depart upon payment of a sum of money. Bernardo de Brito complains that Blondus and Sabellicus, in their account of this transaction, have been so careless as to mention the money, and omit the invocation of the Saints.—*M. Lus.* 2, 5, 23.

Note 52, page 423, col. 1.
Lord of Hosts, etc.

The substance of these prayers will be found in the forms of coronation observed by the Anglo-Saxons, and in the early ages of the French monarchy. I am indebted for them to Turner's most valuable History of the Anglo-Saxons, and to Mr Lingard's Antiquities of the Anglo-Saxon Church, a work not more full of erudition than it is of Catholic sophistry and misrepresentation.

Note 53, page 423, col. 2.
Roderick brought
The buckler.

Toman, diziendo aquesto, un ancho escudo
El Duque y Conde y hombres principales,
De pies encima el Principe membrudo
Lo levantan assi del suelo iguales :
Y alçarlo en peso, quanto alçar se pudo
De alçarlo por su Rey fueron señales,
Real, Real, Real, diziendo todos,
Segun costumbre antigua de los Godos.
Ch. de Messa. Restauracion de Espana, l. 4. ff. 34.

Note 54, page 423, col. 2.
Rejoice,
O Leon, for thy banner is display'd.

« La primera ciudad que ganó dizen fue Leon, y desde alli se llamó Rey de Leon, y tomó por armas un Leon roxo en campo blanco, dexando las antiguas armas de los Godos, que eran un Leon bermejo rapante, en campo azul, buelta la cara atras, sobre tres ondas blancas y azules.»—*Fran. de Pisa. Desc. de Toledo*, l. 3, c. 2.

Fue la del quinto globo roxa estrella
rayo de su valor, voz de su fama,
y Leon de su escudo y luzimiento,
heredado blason, Signo sangriento.
Coro de las Musas, p. 102.

« Les anciennes armes estoient parlantes, comme l'on void en celles des Comtes de Castille et des Rois de Leon, qui prindrent des Chateaux et des Lions, pour signifier les noms vulgaires des Provinces, par le blason de leurs armes ; qui ne se reportent pas a l'ancienne denomination de Castulo et de Legio, chés Pline.»—*Pierre de Marca. Hist. de Bearn*, l. 1, c. 12, § 11.

The Lion's grinders are, « relevées de trois pointes un peu creusées dans leur centre, dans lesquelles les speculatifs croyent voir la figure d'une fleur de lys. Je n'ay garde de dire le contraire,» says P. Labat, « il est permis a bien des gens de voir dans les nues et dans les charbons ardens tout ce qu'il plait à leur imagination de s'y représenter ; pourquoy ne sera-t-il pas libre de voir sur les dents du Lion la figure des fleurs de lys ? Je doute que les Espagnols en conviennent, eux qui prennent le Lion pour les armes et le symbole de leur monarchie ; car on pourroit leur dire que c'est une marque que sans le secours de la France, leur Lion ne seroit pas fort a craindre.»—*Afrique Occidentale*, t. 2, p. 14.

Note 55, page 423, col. 2.
And Tagus bends his sickle round the scene
Of Roderick's fall.

There is a place at Toledo called la Alcurnia. « E nombre de Alcurnia es Arabigo, que es dezir cosa de cuerno, ó en forma de cuerno, lo que Christianos llamavan foz, ó hoz de Tago. Llámase assi porque desde que este rio passa por debaxo de la puente de Alcántara, va haziendo una buelta y torcedura, que en una escritura antigua se llama hoz de Tajo. Lo mesmo aconteció á Arlauça cerca de Lara, de donde se llamó la hoz de Lara, como lo nota Ambrosio de Morales ; y en el Reyno de Toledo ay la hoz de Jucar.»—*Francisco de Pisa. Desc. de Toledo*, l. 1, c. 14.

Note 56, page 427, col. 2.
Amid our deserts we hunt down the birds
Of heaven,—wings do not save them !

The Moors have a peculiar manner of *hunting* the partridge. In the plains of Akkermute and Jibbel Hidded in Shedma, they take various kinds of dogs with them, from the greyhound to the shepherd's dog, and following the birds on horseback, and allowing them no time to rest, they soon fatigue them, when they are taken by the dogs. But as the Mooselmin eats nothing but what has had its throat cut, he takes out his knife, and exclaiming *Bismillah*, in the name of God, cuts the throat of the game.—*Jackson's Marocco*, p. 121.

Note 57, page 431, col. 2.
A hasty grave, scarce hidden there from dogs
And ravens, nor from wintry rains secure.

In composing these lines I remembered a far more beautiful passage in one of the Eclogues of the Jesuit Bussieres :—

Artesius ruit ecce furens, finesque propinquos
Insultans, stragem agricolis fugientibus infert.
Quid facerem ? matrem, ut potui, tenerumque puellum
Raptabam, et mediis abdebam corpora silvis.
Aspera jam frigebat hyems, frondosaque quercus
Pro tecto et latebris ramos prædebat opacos ;
Algentem fovi matrem ; fovet illa rigentem
Infantem gremio. Sub prima crepuscula lucis
Progredior, tectum miseris si forte pateret ;
Silvam fusus eques telis infensus habebat ;
Bona fugio, et capio compendia tuta viarum.
Conditur atra dies ; cœlo nox horrida surgit.
Quam longis mihi nox misero producitur horis !
Quos gemitus fletusque dedi : quam proxima votum
Lux fuit ! heu tristi lux infensissima clade !
Currebam ad notam quercum per devia tesqua,
Dux amor est. Annam video, puerumque jacentem
Afflxum uberibus, duræ succumbere morti.
Ipsa parens, postquam ad vocem conversa vocantis
In me amplexantem morientia lumina fixit,
Eluctantem animam glaciato e corpore mittit.
Obrigui, friguaque novum penetravit in ossa :
Felix, si simili potuissem occumbere letho ;
Sors infesta vetat. Restabat cura sepulchri
Quo foderem ferrum deerat ; miserabile corpus
Frondibus obtexi, puerum nec ab ubere vulsi
Sicut erat foliis tegitur ; funusque paratur,
Heu nimis incertum, et primis violabile ventis.

Note 58, page 433, col. 2.

— their white signal-flag.

A white flag, called *El Alem*, the signal, is hoisted every day at twelve o'clock, to warn the people out of hearing, or at a great distance, to prepare, by the necessary preliminary ablutions, to prostrate themselves before God at the service of prayer.—*Jackson's Marocco*, p. 149.

Note 59, page 433, col. 2.

The Humma's happy wings have shadowed him.

The humma is a fabulous bird: The head over which its shadow once passes will assuredly be encircled with a crown.—*Wilkes, S. of India*, v. i, p. 423.

Note 60, page 434, col. 2.

Life hath not left his body.

Among the *Prérogatives et Propriétés singulières du Prophète*, Gagnier states that, « Il est vivant dans son Tombeau. Il fait la prière dans ce Tombeau à chaque fois que le Crieur en fait la proclamation, et au même tems qu'on la recite. Il y a un Ange posté sur son Tombeau qui a le soin de lui donner avis des Prières que les Fidèles font pour lui. »—*Vie de Mahomet*, l. 7, c. 18.

The common notion, that the Impostor's tomb is suspended by means of a loadstone is well known. Labat, in his *Afrique Occidentale* (t. 3, p. 143), mentions the lie of a Marabout, who, on his return from a pilgrimage to Mecca and Medina, affirmed « que le tombeau de Mahomet étoit porté en l'air par le moyen de certains Anges qui se relayent d'heure en heures pour soutenir ce fardeau. » These fables, however, are modest in comparison with those which the Franciscans have invented to magnify their founder.

Note 61, page 434, col. 2.

Hast thou not heard
How when our clay is leaven'd first with life,
The ministering Angel brings it from the spot
Whereon 't is written in the eternal book,
That soul and body must their parting take,
And earth to earth return?

The Persians in their creed have a pleasant imagination concerning the death of men. They say, that every one must come and die in the place where the Angel took the earth of which he hath been made, thinking that one of these spirits has the care of forming the human creature, which he doth by mingling a little earth with the seed.—*Thevenot.*

Note 62, page 435, col. 2.

They perish, all their thousands perish there.

The battle of Covadonga is one of the great miracles of Spanish history. It was asserted for many centuries without contradiction, and is still believed by the people, that when the Moors attacked Pelayo in the cave, their weapons were turned back upon themselves; that the Virgin Mary appeared in the clouds, and that part of a mountain fell upon the Infidels, and crushed those who were flying from the destruction. In what manner that destruction might have been effected, was exemplified upon a smaller scale in the Tyrol in the memorable war of 1809.

Barret sums up the story briefly, and in the true strain of Mine Ancient:

The Sarr'cen hearing that th' Asturianites
Had king created, and stood on their guard,
Sends multitudes of Mahometized knights
To rouse them out their rocks, and force their ward.
Paligias, bearing of this enterprize,
Prepares his petty power on Auseve mount;
Alchameb comes with Zarzen multiplies,
Meaning Pelagius' forces to dismount.
To blows they come: but lo ! a stroke divine.
The Iber, few, beats numbrous Sarracone,
Two myriads with Mahome went to dine
In Parca's park.

Note 63, page 437, col. 1.

The Bread of Life.

It is now admitted by the best informed of the Romish writers themselves, that, for a thousand years, no other but common or leavened bread was used in the Eucharist. The wafer was introduced about the eleventh century. And as far down as the twelfth century the people were admitted to communicate in both kinds.

Note 64, page 438, col. 2.

And let no shame be offered his remains.

According to the Comendador Fernan Nunez, in his Commentary upon the *Trezientas*, the tomb of Count Julian was shown in his days about four leagues from Huesca at a castle called Loarri, on the outside of a church which was in the castle.

Note 65, page 439, col. 1.

His wonted leathern gipion.

The Musical Pilgrim in Purchas thus describes the Leonese:—

Wymmen in that land use no vullen,
But alle in lether be the wounden :
And her hevedez wonderly ben trust,
Standing in her forheved as a crest,
In rould clouthez lappet alle be forn
Like to the prikke of a N' unicorn.
And men have doubelettez full schert,
Bare legget and light to stert.—P. 1231.

Purchas supposes this very curious poem to have been written about 200 years before he published it, *i. e.* about 1425. It is probably much older. In entering Castille from Elvas, the author says,

Now into Casteil schall we faire
Over the river, the land is bare.
Full of heath and hunger also,
And Sarasynez Governourlz thereto.

Now Badajoz and that part of the country was finally recovered from the Moors in the early part of the thirteenth century. Purchas perhaps judged from the age of the manuscript, which may have been written about the time on which he fixes, and the language modernised by the transcriber.

Note 66, page 439, col. 2.

The light which o'er the fields of Bethlehem shone,
Irradiated whole Spain.

« Fallamos en las estorias que aquella ora que nuestro Señor Jesu Christo nasció, seyendo media noche, aparesció una nuve sobre España que dió tan gran claridad, e tan gran resplandor, e tan gran calor, como el sol en medio del dia quando va mas apoderado sobre la tierra. E departen los sabios e dizen que se entiende por aquella que despues de Jesu Christo vernie su mandadero a España a predicar a los gentiles la çeguedad en que estavan, e que los alumbrarie con la fee de Jesu

Chrysto, e aquesto fue San Pablo. Otros departen que en España avia de nasçer un prinçipe chrystiano que serie señor de todo el mundo, e valdrie mas por el todo el linaje de los omes, bien como esclaresçió toda la tierra por la claridad de aquella nuve en quanto ella duró.»—*Coronica General. ff.* 71.

A more extraordinary example of the divine favour towards Spain is triumphantly brought forward by Francisco de Pisa. «Our Lord God,» says he, «has been pleased to preserve these kingdoms in the purity of the Faith, like a terrestrial Paradise, by means of the Cherubim of the Holy Ofûce, which with its sword of fire has defended the entrance, through the merits and patronage of the serenest Virgin Mary the Mother of God.» «Ha sido servido nuestro Señor Dios conservar estos reynos de España en la entereza de la Fe, como a un Parayso terrenal, mediante el Cherubin del Santo Officio, que con su espada de fuego les ha defendido la entrada por los meritos y patrocinio de la serenissima Virgen Maria Madre de Dios.»—*Desc. de Toledo, L.* 1. *C.* 25.

This passage is truly and lamentably characteristic.

Note 67, page 440, col. 1.
The Oaken Cross.

The oaken cross, which Pelayo bore in battle, is said to have been preserved at Oviedo in the Camara Santa in company with that which the angels made for Alfonso the Great, concerning which Morales delivers a careful opinion, how much of it was made by the Angels, and how much has been human workmanship. The people of Cangas, not willing that Pelayo's cross should be in any thing inferior to his successor's, insist that it fell from Heaven. Morales, however, says, it is more certain that the king had it made to go out with it to battle at Covadonga. It was covered with gold and enamel in the year 908; when Morales wrote, it was in fine preservation, and doubtless so continued till the present generation. Upon the top branch of the cross there was this inscription : « Susceptum placide maneat hoc in honore Dei, quod offerunt famuli Christi Adefonsus Princeps et Scemena Regina.» On the right arm, « Quisquis auferre hæc donaria nostra presumpserit, fulmine divino intereat ipse.» On the left, « Hoc opus perfectum est, concessum est Sancto Salvatori Ovetensis Sedis. Hoc signo tuetur pius, hoc signo vincitur inimicus.» On the foot, « Et operatum est in Castello Gauzon anno Regni nostri XVII discurrente Era DCCCCXLVI.»

« There is no other testimony,» says Morales, « that this is the cross of King Don Pelayo, than tradition handed down from one age to another. I wish the king had stated that it was so in his inscription, and I even think he would not have been silent upon this point, unless he had wished to imitate Alonso el Casto, who, in like manner, says nothing concerning the Angels upon his cross.» This passage is very characteristic of good old Ambrosio.

Note 68, page 441, col. 2.
Like a mirror sparkling to the sun.

The Damascus blades are so highly polished, that when any one wants to arrange his turban, he uses his scymetar for a looking-glass.—*Le Brocquiere,* p. 138.

Note 69, page 442, col. 1.
Oh who could tell what deeds were wrought that day,
Or who endure to hear!

I have nowhere seen a more curious description of a battle between Christians and Saracens than in Barret's manuscript :

The forlorn Christian troops Moon'd troops encharge,
The Mooned troops requite them with the like;
Whilst Grecian lance cracks (thundering) Parthian targe,
Parth's flame-flash arrow Grecian through doth prick :
And whilst that Median scymetar unlimbs
The Christian knight, doth Christian curtle-axe
Unhead the Median horsemen ; whilst hero dims
The Pagan's goggling-eyes by Greekish axe,
The Greek unhorsed lies by Persian push,
And both all rageful grapple on the ground.
And whilst the Saracen with furious rush
The Syrian shocks, the Syrian as round
Down shouldreth Saracen : whilst Babel blade
Sends soul Byzantine to the starred cell,
Byzantine pike with like-employed trade,
Packs Babel's spirit posting down to hell.

Note 70, page 442, col. 1.
Who from their thirsty sands,
Pray that the locusts on the peopled plain
May settle and prepare their way.

The Saharawans, or Arabs of the Desert, rejoice to see the clouds of locusts proceeding towards the north, anticipating therefrom a general mortality, which they call *elkhere*, the good, or the benediction; for, after depopulating the rich plains of Barbary, it affords to them an opportunity of emanating from their arid recesses in the desert, to pitch their tents in the desolated plains, or along the banks of some river.—*Jackson's Marocco,* p. 106.

Note 71, page 442, col. 2.
But where was he whose hand
Had wielded it so well that glorious day?

The account which the Fabulous Chronicle gives of Roderick after his disappearance, is in so singular a strain of fiction that I have been tempted to translate it. It strikingly exemplifies the doctrine of penance, of which monastic history supplies many instances almost as extraordinary as this fable.

Chap. 238.—*How the King Don Rodrigo left the battle and arrived at a hermitage, and of that which befell him.*

«Now when the King Don Rodrigo had escaped from the battle, he began to go as fast as he could upon his horse along the banks of the Guadalete, and night came on, and the horse began to fail by reason of the many wounds which he had received; and as he went thus by the river side deploring the great ruin which had come upon him, he knew not where he was, and the horse got into a quagmire, and when he was in he could not get out. And when the king saw this he alighted, and stript off all his rich arms and the furniture thereof, and took off his crown from his head, and threw them all into the quagmire, saying, Of earth was I made, and even so are all my deeds like unto mud and mire. Therefore my pomp and vanity shall be buried in this mud till it has all returned again to earth, as I myself must do. And the vile end which I have deserved will beseem me well, seeing that I have been the principal cause of this great cruelty. And as he thus stript off all his rich apparel, he cast the shoes from his feet, and went his way, and wandered on towards Portugal; and he travelled so far that night and the day following, that he came to a hermitage near the sea, where there was a good man who had dwelt there serving God for full forty years; and now he was of great age, for he was well nigh a hundred years old. And he entered into the hermitage, and found a crucifix therein, being the image of our Lord Jesus Christ, even as he was crucified; and for the remembrance of Him, he bent both his knees to the ground, and claspt his hands, weeping and confessing his sins before God, for he weened not that any man in the world saw or heard him. And he said thus, O true Lord, who by thy word hast made all the world from nothing which it was, and hast created all things, those which are visible to men, and those which are invisible, the heavenly as well as the earthly, and who didst incarnate thyself that thou mightest undergo thy passion and death, to save those who firmly put their trust in thee, giving up thy holy ghost from thy glorified body upon the tree of the true cross,— and who didst descend into Hell, and deliveredst thy friends from thence, and didst regale them with the glory of Heaven: And afterward thy holy spirit came again into that most holy body, which thou wast pleased to take upon thee in this world; and, manifesting thyself for the true God which thou wert, thou didst deign to abide in this dark world forty days with their nights, and then thou didst ascend into thy heavenly glory, and didst enlighten with the grace of the Holy Ghost thy beloved disciples. I beseech thee, O Lord, that thou wouldst enlighten me, a king in tribulation, wretched and full of many sins, and deserving all evils; let not the soul which is thine, and which cost thee so dear, receive the evil and the desert of this abominable flesh; and may it please thee, O Lord, after the downfall, destruction, perdition, and desolation, which I, a miserable king, have suffered in this world, that my disconsolate soul may not be forgotten by thee, and that all this misery may be in satisfaction for my errors. And I earnestly beseech thee, O Lord, that thy grace may breathe upon me, that in this world I may make satisfaction for my sins, so that at the Great Day of Judgment I may not be condemned to the torments of hell.

« Having said these words, weeping as though he would burst, he remained there a long hour. And when the hermit heard him say all this, he was greatly astonished, and he went unto him. And when the king saw him he was little pleased; howbeit after he had talked with him, he would rather have found him there than have been restored again to the great honour which he had lost; for the Hermit comforted him in such wise in this his tribulation, that he was right well contented; and he confessed unto him, and told him all that concerned him. And the Hermit said to him, King, thou shalt remain in this hermitage, which is a remote place, and where thou mayest lead thy life as long as it shall please God. And for me, on the third day from hence, I shall pass away out of this world; and thou shalt bury me, and thou shalt take my garments, and fulfil the time of a year in this hermitage. Take no thought as to provision for thy support, for every Friday thou shalt have it after the same manner as I, and thou shalt so husband it, that it may suffice thee for the whole week: That flesh which hath been fostered in great delight shall suffer abstinence, lest it should grow proud; and thou shalt endure hunger and cold and thirst in the love of our Lord, that he may have compassion upon thee. Thy station till the hour of sleep must always be upon that rock, where there is an oratory facing the east: and thou shalt continue the service of God in such manner as God will direct thee to do. And take heed that thy soul fall not into temptation. And since thou hast spoken this day of penitence, to-morrow thou shalt communicate and receive the true body of our Lord Jesus Christ, who will be thy protection and support against the enemy and the persecutor. And put thou thy firm trust in the sign of the Cross; and thus shalt thou please thy Saviour.

« Many other things the holy Hermit said, which made the King right joyful to hear them; and there they continued till it was the hour for sleep. And the holy Hermit shewed him his bed, and said, When I shall have left thy company, thou wilt follow the ways which I have followed, for which our Lord will have mercy upon thee, and will extend his hand over thee, that thou mayest persevere in good, and in his holy service. And then they laid down and slept till it was the hour of matins, when they should both arise. And the Hermit awoke him, for as the King had not slept for a long time, and was moreover full weary, he would not have awaked so soon, if the Hermit had not roused him; and they said their hours. And when it was time the Hermit said mass, and the King heard it with great devotion, and communicated with great contrition, and remained in prayer for the space of two hours. And the hour for taking food came, and the Hermit took a loaf which was made of pannick and of rye, and gave half thereof to the King, and took for himself the other half: And they ate little of it, as men who could not eat more, the one by reason of age, and the other because he was not used to such fare. And thus they continued till the third day, when the holy Hermit departed this life.

Ch. 239.—*How the Hermit died, and the King found a writing in his hand.*

« On the third day, the pious Hermit expired at the same hour which he had said to the King, whereat the King was full sorrowful, as one who took great consolation in the lessons which he gave. And when he had thus deceased, the King by himself, with his hands, and with an oaken stick which was there, made his grave. And when he was about to bury him, he found a writing in his hand; and he took it and opened it, and found that it contained these words.

Ch. 240.—*Of the rule of life which the Hermit left written for King Don Rodrigo.*

« O King, who through thy sins has lost the great honour in which thou wert placed, take heed that thy soul also come not into the same judgment which hath fallen upon thy flesh. And receive into thy heart the instructions that I shall give thee now, and see that thou swerve not from them, nor abatest them a jot; for if thou observest them not, or departest in ought from them, thou wilt bring damnation upon thy soul; for all that thou shalt find in this writing is given thee for penance, and thou must learn with great contrition of repentance, and with humbleness of patience, to be content with that which God hath given thee to suffer in this world. And that thou mayest not be deceived in case any company should come unto thee, mark and observe this and pass it in thy life. Thou shalt arise two hours after midnight, and say thy matins within the hermitage. When the day breaks thou shalt go to the oratory, and kneeling upon the ground, say the whole hours by the breviary, and when thou hast finished them thou shalt say certain prayers of our Lord, which thou wilt find there. And when thou hast done this, contemplate then upon the great power of our Lord, and upon his mercy, and also upon the most holy passion which he suffered for mankind upon the cross, being himself very God, and maker of all things; and how with great humility he chose to be incarnate in a poor virgin, and not to come as a king, but as a mediator among the nations. And contemplate also upon the poor life which he always led in this world, to give us an example; and that he will come at the day of judgment to judge the quick and the dead, and give to every one the meed which he hath deserved. Then shalt thou give sustenance to thy flesh of that bread of pannick and rye, which shall be brought to thee every Friday in the manner that I have said; and of other food thou shalt not eat, although it should be given or sent thee; neither shalt thou change thy bread. And when thou hast eaten give thanks to God, because he has let thee come to repentance; and then thou shalt go to the oratory, and there give praise to the Virgin our Lady holy Mary, mother of God, in such manner as shall come to thee in devotion. If when thou hast finished, heaviness should come upon thee, thou mayest sleep, and when thou shalt have rested as long as is reasonable, return thou to thy oratory, and there remain, making thy prayers always upon thy knees, and for nothing which may befall thee depart thou from thence, till thou hast made an end of thy prayers, whether it rain or snow, or if a tempest should blow. And forasmuch as the flesh could sustain so many mundane pleasures, so must it suffer also celestial abstinences; two masses thou hast heard in this hermitage, and in it it is God's will that thou shalt hear no more, for more would not be to his service. And if thou observest these things, God will have compassion upon thy deserts. And when the King had read this, he laid it upon the altar, in a place where it would be well preserved.

Ch. 241.—*How the Devil came in the form of a Hermit to deceive the King Don Rodrigo.*

« Now when the King had made a grave in which to bury the Hermit, the Devil was troubled at the good course which the King had taken, and he cast about for means how he might deceive him; and he found none so certain as to come to him in the figure of a hermit, and keep company with him, to turn him aside from those doctrines which the Hermit had given him, that he might not fulfil his penitence. And the King being in great haste to bury the body, the Devil came to him with a long white beard, and a great hood over the eyes, and some paternosters hanging from his girdle, and supporting himself upon a staff as though he were lame, and could not go. And when he came where the King was he humbled himself, and said unto him, Peace be with thee! And the King turned toward that side from which he came, and when he saw him of so great age, he thought that it was some holy man who knew of the death of the Hermit, and was come to bury him; and he humbled himself, and went to him to kiss his hand, and the Devil would not, saying, It is not fitting that a King should kiss the hand of a poor servant of God. And the King was astonished at hearing himself named, and believed that this must needs be a man of holy life, and that he spake by some revelation; nevertheless he said, I am not a king, but a miserable sinner, for whom it had been better never to have been born, than that so much evil should have happened through me. And the false Hermit said to him, Think not that thou hast so much fault as thou imaginest in what has now been done, for even if thou hadst had no part in it, this destruction would have fallen at this time. And since it was ordained that it should be so, the fault is not thine; some fault thou hadst, but it was very little. And think not that I speak this of myself; for my words are those of a spirit made and created by the will of God, who speaks through me this and many other things, which hereafter thou shalt know, that thou mayest see how God has given me power that I should know all thy concerns, and counsel thee in what manner thou shouldst live. And albeit I have more need of rest than of labour, by reason of my age, which is far greater than my countenance shows, yet I have disposed myself to labour for the love of thee, to console thee in this thy persecution, knowing that this good man was about to die. Of a truth you may believe that on this day month I was in Rome, being there in the church of St John de Lateran, out of which I had never gone for thirty years, till I came now to keep thee company according as I am commanded. Marvel not that a man of so great age and crippled as I am, should have been able to traverse so much land in so short time, for certes I tell thee that he who speaks in this form which thou seest hast given me strength to go through so great a journey; and sans doubt I feel myself as strong now as on the day when I set forth. And the King said to him, Friend of God, I rejoice much in thy coming, for that in my misfortunes I shall be by thee consoled and instructed in that which must be done to fulfil my penitence; I rejoice also that this holy Hermit here shall receive burial from the hands of a man much more righteous than I. And the false Hermit said, Think not, King, that it is for the service of God to give to any person a name not appertaining to him. And this I say because I well know the life of this person, what it was; and as thou knowest nothing of celestials, thou thinkest that as the tongue speaketh, even such is the heart. But I tell thee the habit doth not make the monk, and it is from such persons as these that the saying arose which is common in the world, I would have justice, but not for my own house. This I say to thee, because he commanded thee to perform a penance such as never man did, the which is, that thou shouldst eat only once a day, and that of such bread that even the shepherds' dogs would not eat it: and of this that thou shouldst not eat as much as thou couldst; and appointed thee the term of a year that thou shouldst continue in this diet. Also he commanded thee that thou shouldst not hear mass during the time that thou abidest here, for that the two masses which thou hast heard should suffice; look now if that doctrine be good, which bids a man forget the holy sacrament! Certes I tell that only for that which he commanded thee to observe, his soul is consigned to a place where I would not that thine should go for all the world, if it were in my power, with all its riches. Nevertheless, to be rid of the ill smell which he would give, it is fit that you should bury him, and while you do this I will go for food. And the King said, Friend of God, do not take this trouble, but remain still, and before noon there will come food, which will suffice for you and for me; help me now to give burial to this good man, which will be much for the service of God, although he may have been a sinner. And the false hermit answered, King, it would be less evil to roll him over these rocks into the sea; but if not, let him lie thus upon the earth till the birds and the beasts devour his flesh. And the King marvelled at this: nevertheless, though he believed that this false hermit was a servant of God, he left not for that to bury the good Hermit who there lay without life, and he began by himself to carry him to the grave which he had made. And as he was employed in burying him, he saw that the false Hermit went away over the mountains at a great rate not as one who was a cripple, but like a stout man and a young; and he marvelled what this might mean.

Ch. 242.—*How King Don Rodrigo informed himself concerning the penance which he was to perform, from the writing which the holy Hermit left him.*

« When the King had finished burying the good servant of God, he went to the altar, and took the writing in his hand, and read it to inform himself well of it. And when he had read it, he saw that of a certainty all that was said therein was for the service of God, and was of good doctrine for his soul; and he said, that, according to the greatness of his sins, it behoved that his penitence must be severe, if he wished to save his soul. And then he called to mind the life which St Mary Magdalene endured, for which God had mercy on her. And forthwith he went to his oratory, and began his prayers; and he remained there till it was near noon; and he knew that he had nothing to eat, and awaited till it should be brought him.

Ch. 243.—*How the Devil brought meat to King Don Rodrigo that he should eat it; and he would only eat of the Hermit's bread.*

« After it was mid-day the false hermit came with a basket upon his shoulders, and went straight to where the King was, and he came sweating and weary. And the King had compassion on him, howbeit he said nothing, neither did he leave his prayer. And the false Hermit said to him, King, make an end of thy prayers, for it is time to eat; and here I bring food. And the King lifted up his eyes and looked toward him, and he saw that there came into the hermitage a shepherd with a wallet upon his back, and he thought this must be he who brought him that which he was to eat. And so in truth it was, that that shepherd brought every Friday four loaves of pannick and rye for the holy Hermit, upon which he lived during the week. And as this shepherd knew not that the good man was dead, he did no more than put his bread upon the altar, and go his way. And the King, when he had ceased praying, rose up from the oratory, and went to the false Hermit. And he found the four loaves, and he took one, and brake it in the middle, and laid by the rest carefully, and he went out of the hermitage into the Portal, where there was a table full small, and he laid a cloth upon it, and the bread which he was to eat, and the water; and he began to bless the table, and then seated himself. And the false Hermit noted well how he blest the table, and arose from where he was, and went to the King, and said, King, take of this poor fare which I have brought, and which has been given me in alms. And he took out two loaves which were full white, and a roasted partridge, and a fowl, of which the legs were wanting; and he placed it upon the table. And when the King saw it, his eyes were filled with tears, for he could not but call to mind his great honour in former times, and how it was now fallen, and that his table had never before been served like this. And he said, addressing himself to the Lord, Praised be thy name, thou who canst make the high low, and the low nothing. And he turned to his bread and did eat thereof. And though he had great hunger, yet could he scarcely eat thereof, for he had never used it till in that hermitage, and now it seemed worse by reason of the white bread which that false Hermit had brought. And the false Hermit, who saw that he gave no regard neither to the bread, nor the meat which he had brought, said to the King, Why eatest thou not of this which God has sent thee? And the King said, I came not to this hermitage to serve God, but to do penance for my sins, that my soul may not be lost. And the penance which is given me in this life, I must observe for a year and not depart from it, lest it should prove to my great hurt. And the false Hermit said, How, King, hath it been given thee for penance, that thou shouldst let thyself die for despair? The Gospel commands not so; contrariwise it forbids man to do any such penance through which the body might be brought to death; for if in killing another, he who causes the death is held for a murderer, much more is he who killeth himself; and such thou wouldst be. And now through despair thou wouldst let thyself die of hunger, that thou mightest no longer live in this world, wherefore I say eat of this food that I have brought thee some little, that thou mayest not die. And with that he began to eat right heartily. And the King, when he beheld him, was seized with affection to do the like, howbeit he was withheld, and would eat nothing thereof. And as it was time when he would drink of the water, the false Hermit said to him, that he should drink of the wine; and the King would only taste of that water; and as he went to take of it, the false Hermit struggled with him, but he could not prevail, and the King did according to his rule, and departed not from it. And when he had eaten, he began to give thanks to God. And the false Hermit, who saw that he would have to cross himself at arising from the table, rose up before him, as one who was about to do something; and the King heeded it not. And when he had thus eaten, he went to the oratory, and began to give praises to the Virgin Mary, according as the good man had commanded him; when that traitor went to him and said, Certes this doctrine which thou holdest is no way to serve God, for sans doubt when the stomach is heated with food the will shall have no power to pray as it ought; and although the tongue may say the prayers, the heart confirms them not, being hindered by the force which nature derives from the food. Therefore I say to thee that thou oughtest to sleep first; for whilst thou art sleeping the food will settle, and the will will then be more able for contemplation. Moreover, God is not pleased with prayers without contrition, as with one who speaketh of one thing, and hath his heart placed on another, so that he can give no faith to the words which he beginneth. If thou wouldest be saved, O King, it behoves thee to listen to me; and if thou wilt not believe me, I will depart and leave thee, as one who will take no counsel, except from himself. And the King replied, If I should see that thou confirmedst the good manner of life whereof my soul hath need, according as it was appointed by the good man whom I have buried, then would I follow thy way. But I see that thy life is not that of a man of abstinence, nor of one who forsakes worldly enjoyments for the love of God; rather it seemeth by what I see in thee that thy life is a strengthening of worldly glory; for thou satisfiest thy flesh with good viands as I was wont to do, when I was puffed up with the vanities of the world. Wherefore I will in no wise follow thy way, for I see that thou art a worldly man, who deceivest God and the world, and when it comes to the end thou thyself wilt be deceived.

Ch. 244.—*Of what the Devil said to King Don Rodrigo to dispart him from his penance.*

« The false Hermit said to him, For what reason art thou certain that the rule which this deceiver whom thou hast buried appointed for thee, will be salvation for thy soul, and that what I say to thee is not of a truth? Thou understandest me not well : I never forbade thee that thou shouldst hear mass, as he has done; for this is one of the good things that man may every day see his Saviour and adore him. And seeing that he forbade thee to do this, thou mayest be certain that as he deceived his own soul, he would deceive thine also. For at the hour when man passeth away out of the world, he would fain that that same hour should be the end of all the world; and thus that enemy did, for where he went, thither he would draw thee also. Now since God hath given thee sense and reason, thou mayest clearly understand that his counsel and doctrine are deceitful, and what thou oughtest to do.

Ch. 245.—*Of the Reply which the King made to the Devil.*

« Sans doubt, said the King, he forbade me not that I should hear mass; but because he commanded me that I should fulfil my penance here for the term of a year, as he knew the hour of his own death, so also he knew that no other person who could say mass would come to this hermitage within the year; and therefore he said to me, that in this hermitage I should not hear mass, but he never forbade me from hearing it.

Ch. 246.—*Of the Reasoning which the false Hermit made to King Don Rodrigo.*

« The false Hermit said, Now thou thyself manifestest that thou wast not so worthy as a man ought to be who knows that which is to come. For according to thy words, he knew not that I should come here, who can say mass if I please; and if there be good judgment in thee, thou wilt understand that I must needs be nearer

to God, because I know all which he had commanded thee to do, and also how he was to die. And I can know better in what place he is, than he who has commanded thee to observe this rule, knew concerning himself while he was here. But this I tell thee, that as I came to teach thee the way in which thou shouldst live, and thou wilt not follow my directions, I will return as I came. And now I marvel not at any thing which has befallen thee, for thou hast a right stubborn heart; hard and painful wilt thou find the way of thy salvation, and in vain wilt thou do all this, for it is a thing which profiteth nothing.

Ch. 247.—*Of the Reply which King Don Rodrigo made to the false Hermit.*

« Good man, said the King, all that thou shalt command me to do beyond the rule which the holy Hermit appointed me, that will I do; that in which my penance may be more severe, willingly will I do it. But in other manner I will not take thy counsel; and as thou hast talked enough of this, leave me therefore to my prayers. And then the King bent his knees, and began to go on with his rule. And the false Hermit, when he saw this, departed, and returned not again for a month; and all that time the King maintained his penance, in the manner which had been appointed him. And by reason that he ate only of that black bread, and drank only water, his flesh fell away, and he became such that there was not a man in the world who would have known him. Thus he remained in the hermitage, thinking of no other thing than to implore the mercy of God that he would pardon him.

Ch. 248.—*Of what the false Hermit said to King Don Rodrigo to dispart him from his Rule.*

« King Don Rodrigo living thus, one day, between midnight and dawn, the false Hermit came to the hermitage; and not in the same figure as before, but appearing more youthful, so· that he would not be known. And he called at the door, and the King looked who it might be, and saw that he was habited like a servant of God, and he opened the door forthwith. And they saluted each other. And when they saw each other, the false Hermit greeted the King, and demanded of him where the father was; and the King answered, that for more than a month there had been no person dwelling there save himself. And the false Hermit, when he heard this, made semblance as if he were afflicted with exceeding grief, and said, How came this to be, for it is not yet six weeks since I came here and confessed my sins to the father who abode here, and then departed from this hermitage to my own, which is a league from hence? And King Don Rodrigo said, Friend, know that this hermit is now in Paradise, as I believe, and I buried him with my own hands : and he shewed him the place where he lay. And when he went there he began to kiss the earth of the grave, and to make great dole and lamentation over him. And when some half hour had past, he withdrew, making semblance as if he wished to say his hours. And before the King had finished to say his, he came to him, and said, Good man, will you say mass? And the King answered, that he never said it. Then, said the false Hermit, Hear me then in penitence, for I would confess. And the King seeing that it was for the service of God to hear him in penitence, they seated themselves both at the foot of the altar. And when the false Hermit spake, it appeared that he had no sin to confess : for he began to relate many great services which he had done to God, as well in the life which he led as in other things. And before the King could absolve him he rose up, and asked if things were ready for the mass. And the King said that he knew not, and bade him look. It was now time that he should go to his oratory. And the false Hermit asked him that he should assist him in saying mass, and then he should hear it. And the King said, that for nothing in the world would he leave to fulfil his penance, according as it had been appointed him : and he went to his oratory. And the false Hermit made as if he put on the vestments and all the ornaments, and began to say mass, to the end that he might deceive the King, and make him cease to observe his penance, and come to adore the mass. And he made a watery cloud arise, so that it rained heavily where the King was. And when he saw that he could in no ways entice him, then he went to him, and said, Good man, for that you may be placed out of danger in cases which at all times will happen, seeing that you are alone, I have consecrated the body of Jesus Christ, that you may adore it every day, since you may not hear mass ; and thus may you fulfil your penance as a faithful Christian. And with that he dispeeded himself, saying, In the coffer upon the altar you will find the Corpus Christi : when you rise from hence go and adore it. When he had said this, he went his way. And the King believed that what he said was true, and held that he was a good man, and of holy life.

Ch. 249.—*How the Holy Ghost visited King Don Rodrigo.*

« Now when the King had ended his prayers, which he used to say every day before he took his food, he saw a good man come towards him, clad in white garments, and with a fresh countenance and a cheerful, and a cross upon his breast. And as he arrived where the King was, he blest him ; and when the King saw him he perceived that it was a revelation of God, and he joined his hands and placed himself on his knees upon the ground, weeping plentifully. And the holy man said, King, who art desirous of heavenly glory, continue the service which thou art performing for the love of my holy name; and take heed lest the enemy overcome thee, as he who many times hath overcome thee, whereby thou hast come to what thou now art. And believe none of all those who may come to thee here, for they come for no other cause but only to deceive thee, and withdraw thee from the service which thou dost me. And always observe the rule given thee by the holy man whom thou buriedst; for I am content with it, and thy soul shall receive refreshment if thou observest it. Come here, and I will show thee how the Devil thought to deceive thee, that thou mightest adore him. Then the King arose and went, alway upon his knees, following the Holy Spirit of God; and when he was within the hermitage, our Lord spake and said, Depart from hence, thou cursed one, and go thy way, for thou hast no power to deceive him who continues in my service. Get thee to the infernal pains which are suffered by those who are in the ninth torment!

And at that hour the King plainly saw how from the ark, which was upon the altar, there went out a foul and filthy devil, with more than fifty tails and as many eyes, who, uttering great yells, departed from the place. And the King was greately dismayed at the manner in which the false Hermit had deceived him. And the Holy Spirit of God said to him, King, let thy hope be in my name, and I will alway be with thee, so thou wilt not let thyself be vanquished by the enemy. Then the Holy Spirit of God departed, and the King remained full joyful and greatly comforted, as if he had been in celestial glory. And thus he continued his life for nearly two months.

Ch. 250.—*How the Devil would have deceived King Don Rodrigo in the figure of Count Don Julian.*

« The King was in his oratory one Sunday toward night-fall, just as the sun was setting, when he saw a man coming toward him, clad in such guise as is fitting for one who follows arms. And as he looked at him, he saw that it was the Count Don Julian who approached; and he saw that behind him there came a great power of armed people. And the false Count, when he drew nigh, made obeisance to him : and the King was amazed at seeing him, for he knew him well : nevertheless he remained still. And the false Count came to him, and would have kissed his hand, but the King would not give it, neither would he rise up from the oratory : and the false Count knelt upon the ground before him, and said, Sir, forasmuch as I am he who sinned against thee like a man who is a traitor to his Lord, and as I did it with great wrath and fury, which possessed my heart through the strength of the Devil, our Lord God hath had compassion upon me, and would not that I should be utterly lost, nor that Spain should be destroyed, nor that thou, sir, shouldst be put down from thy great honour and state, and the great lordship which thou hadst in Spain. And he has shewn me, in a revelation, how thou wert here in this hermitage doing this great penance for thy sins. Wherefore I say to thee, that thou shouldst do justice upon me, and take vengeance according to thy will, as upon one who deserves it, for I acknowledge that thou wert my lord, and also the great treason into which I have fallen. Wherefore, sir, I pray and beseech thee by the one only God, that thou wilt take the power of Spain, which is there awaiting thee, and that thou wilt go forth to defend the faith of our Lord Jesus Christ, and suffer not that poor Spain should be utterly destroyed, seeing that thou canst defend it and protect it. And then Count Julian drew his sword, and gave it to the King, saying, Sir, take this my sword, and with thine own hand do justice upon me, and take such vengeance as thou pleasest; for I will suffer it with much patience, seeing I have sinned against thee. And the King was greatly troubled at his sight, and at his words also, and knew not what he should do, neither what he should say. Howbeit, presently he called to mind what the Holy Spirit of God had said to him, how he should take heed lest the Devil should subdue him; and so he said nothing, but continued in his prayer. And the false Count Don Julian said to him, Sir, wilt thou not turn for the Holy Faith of Jesus Christ, which is utterly going to destruction? rise up and defend it, for I bring thee a full great power; and thus thou wilt serve God and recover the honour which thou hadst lost. Rise then and go forth, and have pity upon miserable Spain, which is about to be lost : and have compassion also upon so many people as are perishing for want of a Lord who should defend them. Now all these words were only meant to deceive him, for it was the Devil who had taken the form of Count Don Julian, and not the Count himself. But the King could no longer restrain himself from replying, and he said, Go you, Count, and defend the land with this force which you have assembled, even as you went to destroy it by the great treason which you committed against me and against God. And even as you brought the men, who are enemies of God and of his Holy Faith, and led them into Spain, so now thrust them out and defend it; for I will neither slay you, nor assist you in it. Leave me to myself; I am no longer for the world, for here I will do penance for my sins. Urge me, therefore, no more with these reasons. And the false Count Don Julian rose, and went to the great company which he had brought there, and brought them all before the King. And the King, when he beheld that great company of knights, saw some among them whom he surely thought had been slain in battle. And they all said to him with loud voices, Sir, whom wilt thou send us, that we may take him for our King and lord to protect and defend us, seeing that thou wilt not defend the land, neither go with us? Wouldst thou give us thy nephew the Infant Don Sancho? He is dead. What then wouldst thou command us that we should do? Look to it well, sir; it is no service of God that thou shouldst let perish so great a Christianity as is every day perishing, because thou art here dwelling in this solitude. Look to it, for God will require an account at thy hands : thou hadst the charge of defending them, and thou lettest them die. And tell us what course shall we take. And when the King heard these words he was moved to compassion : and the tears came into his eyes, so that he could not restrain them : and he was in such state that his thoughts failed him, and he was silent, and made no reply to any thing that they could say. And all these companies who saw him complained so much the more, and sent forth great cries, and made a great tumult and uproar, and said, O miserable King, why wilt thou not rouse thyself for thy own sake, and for that of all thy people whom thou seest without a Lord? and thou wilt not even speak a word to comfort them, and tell them what they shall do. And all this while the King did nothing but weep, and answered them never a word. And when this vile race saw that they could not take him from thence, and that he answered them nothing, and that they could not overcome him by whatever they might do, they went forthwith from the mountain down into a plain, which was then made to appear before the King, and there they drew up their battles in such guise as the King Don Rodrigo was used to darrain them. And eft-soon he saw great multitudes of strange people, who came from the other side, and they began a battle so fierce and so cruel, that the King thought he had never seen one like it. And the one party put the other to the worst, and followed after them in pursuit. And then there came messengers to the King, telling him that his people had conquered, and had slain many of the enemy; but the King was confounded, and as it were beside himself, and heeded not, neither did he know what they said, and he answered nothing. And then they all went away, and seemed to the King that the one were pursuing the others, and this continued till the first crowing of the cock. And the King recovered his senses : howbeit he knew not whether it was a vision, or if it had indeed happened; but he called to mind that he had not completed the prayers which he made every day; and he began them again and finished them. And when he had finished, great part of the night was past, and he laid himself down to sleep. And then for three months he had no other temptation.

Ch. 251.—*How the Devil, in the Figure of La Cava, the Daughter of Count Don Julian, sought to deceive King Don Rodrigo.*

« The King was saying his prayers at the hour of vespers on a Tuesday, when he saw people on horseback coming toward him : and as they were about the reach of a cross-bow from him, he saw that they alighted, and that there came toward him a woman, who was full nobly clad; and when she came near, he knew her that she was La Cava, the daughter of Count Don Julian, and she seemed to him more beautiful than he had ever before seen her in his life. And when she drew nigh she humbled herself, and said, Sir, what fortune has brought you to this wretched life in which you have so long continued? And the King held his peace and said nothing. And that false Cava said, Sir, it is a month since a holy man, clad in white garments, and having a red cross upon his breast, appeared to me when I was with my father Count Don Julian in Toledo; where he now holds the seat of the lordship of Spain, as he who, by force of arms, has subdued the Moors, and killed or made captives of them all. At the hour when this holy man appeared to me I was alone in my chamber, having great sorrow in my heart, because I had no certain news where you was, and whether your soul continued to live in this world, or in another. And, moreover, I was full sorrowful, because of the death of my Lady the Queen Eliaca, your wife, who is now deceased. And for these things my heart was full sorrowful, and in great trouble with griefs and thoughts, which came to me I know not from whence, and I was like one bereft of his judgment. And while I was contemplating in this state, the holy man appeared to me in such wise as I have said, and said to me, Of what art thou taking thought? Cease to lament, for without me thou canst do nothing certain of that which thou desirest. But that the dominion of Spain may not pass away from the power of the Goths, and that he who shall have it may descend from thy seed, and be of the generation of King Don Rodrigo, it is my will that thou shouldst know where he is, and that thou shouldst go to him, and that he should go in unto thee, and that thou shouldst conceive of him a son, and shalt call his name Felbersan, the which shall be such a one that he shall reduce under his forces all the earth which is below the firmament. Depart, therefore, from hence, and go to the place where he is, and make no tarriance; for thus it behoveth for the service of God, and for the weal and protection and defence of the land. And I said to him, Sir, how can this be which you tell me, seeing that King Don Rodrigo is dead ; for his enemies slew him when they won the battle in which the great chivalry of Spain perished. And he said to me, Cava, think not he is dead, for he liveth, and passeth his life alone in a hermitage; of the which thy father Count Don Julian will certify thee, for he went to seek him there, and found him there when he overcame the Moors. He will tell thee that he is alive, and in what place is the hermitage wherein he abideth. And I said to him, But if King Don Rodrigo passeth his life after this manner in the service of God, he will not approach me that I may conceive of him this son who should prove so good. And since it thus pleases you, give me a sign by which I may shew him that this is pleasing to God, and that he may do this which you say, seeing so great good is to follow from it. And, moreover, he will be brought to such weakness that he will not be able to obey, by reason of the great abstinence to which his body has been subjected during his continuance there. And the holy man said to me, Care not for this, for God will give him strength; and thou shalt say to him for a sign that he may believe thee, how I told him that he should take heed lest the enemy deceive him, and how I bade the Devil depart from the altar where he was in the ark instead of the Corpus Christi, for that he should adore him. When thou tellest him this he will believe thee, and will understand that it is by the command of God. And when he had said these words he disappeared, so that I saw him no more; and I remained for a full hour, being greatly comforted, because I knew of your life, so that it seemed to me there were no other glory in this world. And when I came to myself, I went incontinently to my father Count Don Julian, and told him all that had befallen me with the holy man who came in that holy vision; and I asked him if he knew aught concerning you. And he told me how he had gone to you with all his chivalry to bid you come out from thence to defend your country, which the enemies had taken from you, and that you would not; but rather commended it to him that he should undertake it, and defend the land and govern it; and that it grieved him to think that you would not be alive, because of the great abstinence which you imposed every day upon your flesh: nevertheless, since it pleases our Lord that I should have a son by you, who should be so good a man that he should recover all Spain, he would have me go to this place, where I should find you if you were alive; and right content would he be that there should remain of you so great good. And I, sir King, seeing how it pleased God that this should be accomplished, according as I have said, am come here in secret, for neither man nor woman knoweth of this, save my father Count Don Julian; for I have told my people who came with me to remain yonder, because I would go and confess to a holy man who had made his abode here more than fifty years. Now, since God is the author of this, recover yourself, and remember the time when you told me that there was nothing in the world which you loved so much as me, nor which you desired so greatly as to obtain a promise of me; the which I could not give at that hour, by reason that the Queen was living, and I knew it to be great sin. And if I come to you now, it is by command of God, for it pleases him to send me here; and, also, because the Queen is no longer in this present life. And because you are so fallen away of your strength, let us go into the hermitage, or I will order a tent to be placed here, and let us sup together, that your heart may revive and you may fulfil the command of God.

Ch. 252.—How the Devil would have deceive King Don Rodrigo, if the Holy Spirit had not visited and protected him.

« As the King heard all this his whole body began to tremble, and his soul within him also; and all sense and power past away from him, so that he was in a trance, and then it was revealed to him that he should take heed against that temptation. And the false Cava, who saw him thus entranced, made many burning torches of wax come there, by reason that it was cold, and because that the King should derive heat; also there was a pavilion pitched there, and a table set within it with many viands thereon, and all the people who came with her were seen to lodge themselves far away upon the mountain. And when he had recovered himself, he saw that the false Cava was drest in a close-fitting kirtle, which came half way below the knee, and she seemed to him the fairest woman that he had ever seen in his life, and it appeared to the King that she said to him, Here, sir, come and take your supper. And the King began again to tremble and lose his judgment, and fell into such a state that he knew not where he was, and it was revealed to him in that hour that he should guard against the temptation. And when he came to himself he saw that the pavilion was spread over his head; and seeing himself in that place, he looked for the oratory, and perceived that it was where it used to be; and within the pavilion he saw the false Cava, who was there with him, and that she was standing beside a bed, which was a full rich one, and that she began to take off her kirtle, and remained in her shift only, and with her long hair, which reached to her feet; and she said to him, See, sir, here in your power, that which you most desired, and which is now awaiting you. Rejoice, then, and take heart, and do that which God has appointed, which will recover Spain, and recompense the losses, and sorrows, and wrongs which you have endured. And then she turned toward the King, for the Devil thought thus to tempt him, and make him break the penance which he had begun; and certes I ween there was no living man who would not right gladly have approached her. And then before him, in his sight, she began to comb and to plait her golden locks. And the King, seeing how beautiful she was, began to tremble all over, as if he had been struck with palsy; and he lost his judgment again, and became entranced, and remained thus a long while before he came again to himself. And it was revealed to him again that he should take heed how the Devil tempted him, and that he should have firm hope in God, and not break the penance which the holy Hermit had appointed him. But ever when he recovered from these trances, he forgot all which had been revealed to him while he was entranced; and now he found that there was a large *estrado* placed by him, and that La Cava was lying there beside him on some pillows, which were richly wrought in gold, undrest, as he had seen her, and that she said to him, Come. sir, for you tarry long, and it will soon be day-break. And the King seeing her so near him, then he was greatly troubled, yet could he not withdraw his eyes from her: but he called to mind how the Holy Spirit of God had bade him that he should always confide in his name, and place his true hope in the sign of the Cross. And he claspt his hands, and lifted them towards Heaven, and weeping bitterly, and in great contrition, he said, O Lord and very Jesus Christ, deliver me from all temptation, and preserve my soul, that it fall not into perdition. And while he was praying thus, he saw how there came from the hermitage a great brightness, and he said, Deliver me, Lord, from the power of the Devil, that I may not be deceived, nor withdrawn from thy holy service. And at that hour he made the sign of the cross upon his forehead, and blest himself; and at that hour the false Cava fell down the rock into the sea, with such a sound as if the whole world were falling to pieces; and with the plunge which she made the sea dashed up so high, that where the oratory was the King was wetted with the spray. And he remained in such astonishment that he could not for an hour recover himself. And when he came to himself he began to pray with great repentance, as if he had been on the point of falling into temptation. And the Holy Spirit of God came to him in that same manner in which he had seen it the former time. And he fell on his face upon the ground, and began to lament full bitterly, and to say, Lord, have mercy upon my soul, and forsake me not among mine enemies, who would withdraw me from thee. And the Holy Spirit said to him, O King, of little faith, how hast thou been on the point of perishing! And the King made no reply, for he did nothing but weep. And the Holy Spirit of God said to him, Take heed, King, lest the Devil deceive thee, and have power over thee, that thou shouldst not fulfil the penance which thou hast commenced, neither save thy soul. And the King lifted up his countenance, and had great shame to behold him. Howbeit he took courage, and said, Lord, have mercy upon me, and let me not be tempted by the enemy, for my heart is weak, and hath no power to defend itself against the false one: for my judgment is clean confounded, as one who hath no virtue if he be not aided by thy grace. Deliver me, Lord, for thy holy mercy and compassion: my salvation cannot come through the strength of my heart, for it is wholly full of fear, like a thing which is overcome. And the Holy Spirit of God said to him, Take courage and fear not, for thou shalt depart from this place sooner than thou thinkest. And when it is time I will guide thee to the place where thou shalt do thy penance, that thy soul may receive salvation. When thou shalt see a little white cloud appear above thee, and that there is no other in the sky, follow after it: and in the place where it shall stop shalt thou fulfil thy penance, according as the chief priest in that place shall appoint it thee. And take heart, and alway call to mind my holy name, and have true faith and constant hope in thy Saviour. And when he had said this he departed. And the King was greatly comforted and full of grace, as one with whom God was present in his mercy. And he abode in the hermitage a whole year, according to his reckoning, and twelve days more. And one day, when it was full clear, the King looked up and saw above him the cloud of which the Holy Spirit of God had told him; and when he saw it he was full joyful, and gave many thanks to God. Nevertheless the King did not rise from his prayers, neither did the cloud move from above him. And when he had finished his prayers he looked at the cloud, and saw that it moved forward.»

Ch. 253.—*How King Don Rodrigo departed from the Hermitage, and arrived where he was to do penance.*

« The King arose from the oratory and followed the cloud; and so great was the pleasure which he had, that he cared not for food, neither remembered it, but went after that his holy guide. And at night he saw how the cloud, when the sun was about to set, turned to the right of the road toward the mountains; and it went on so far, that before night had closed it came to a hermitage, in which there was a good man for a Hermit, who was more than ninety years of age, and there it stopt. And the King perceived that he was to rest there, and the good man welcomed the King, and they spake together of many things. And the King was well contented with his speech, and saw that certes he was a servant of God. And all that day the King had not eaten, and he was barefoot, and his raiment tattered: and as he had not been used to travel a-foot, and with his feet bare, his feet were swoln with blisters. And when it was an hour after night, the Hermit gave him a loaf, full small, which was made of rye, and there were ashes kneaded with it, and the king ate it: and when he had eaten they said prayers. And when they had said their hours, they lay down to sleep. And when it was midnight they arose and said their hours: and when they had said them, the King went out of the hermitage, and saw that the cloud did not move: and then the King understood that he had to tarry here, or that he was to hear mass before he departed, and he asked the Hermit to hear his confession, and the Hermit confessed him. And when he had confessed, he said that he would communicate, and the good Hermit saw that it was good, and he put on his vestments and said mass; and the King heard the mass, and received the very body of our Lord Jesus Christ. And when the King had done this, he went out to look at the cloud. And as he went out of the hermitage he saw that the cloud began to move, and then he dispeeded himself from the Hermit, and they embraced each other weeping, and each entreated the other, that he would bear him in mind, and remember him in his prayers. And when the King had dispeeded himself, he followed after his holy guide, and the holy Hermit returned to his hermitage. And the King Don Rodrigo, notwithstanding his feet were swoln and full of blisters, and that in many places they were broken and bleeding, such and so great was the joy which he felt at going on in the course which he now held, that he endured it all as though he felt nothing. And he went, according as it seemed to him, full six leagues, and arrived at a convent of Black Monks, and there the cloud stopt, and would proceed no farther. And at that convent there was an Abbot who led an extraordinarily good and holy life; and they were not there like other monks; and he was a great friend of God and of our Lady the Virgin St Mary: and this Abbot took the King to his cell, and asked if he would eat as he was wont to do, or like the other monks; and the King said, that he would do as he should direct him. And the Abbot ordered that a loaf should be brought of pannick and maize mixed together, and a jar of water, and on the other side he had food placed such as the monks used; and the King would eat only of the pannick bread, as he had been wont to do, and he drank of the water. And when he had eaten, the Abbot asked of him if he would remain that night or not, and the King said that he knew not, but that he would go out and see whether he were to go or to remain. And the Abbot said that it was the hour of vespers, and that he ought to remain; and the

King went out and saw that the cloud moved, and that it behoved him to go, and he dispeeded himself from the Abbot, and they commended themselves each to the other in his prayers. And the Abbot saw plainly how that cloud guided him, and how there was no other in the sky, and he marvelled greatly, and said, Certes this is some holy man, and he gave thanks to God. And the King went on that evening till he came to a church which was solitary and remote from peopled places: and there the cloud stopt, and he abode there that night. And the King went into the church, and found in it a lamp burning, and it rejoiced him much, for by the light of it he said his hours as well before he should sleep as after. And on the morrow when he had made his prayer, he went out of the church and beheld the cloud, and saw that it moved: and he went after it, and after two days' journey he came to a place which where it is, or what it is called, is not said, save that it is the place of his burial, for such it is. And there the cloud stopt and proceeded no farther; and it rested without the town over an ancient hermitage. And the elder of that place incontinently knew by the Holy Spirit how King Don Rodrigo was come there; but he knew not his name, neither who he was; and he asked him if he meant to lead his life there, and he answered that it was to be as God should please. And the Elder said to him, Friend, I am the Elder of this place, for all the others, when they knew that King Don Rodrigo and his chivalry were slain and vanquished, fled from hence for fear of the Moors, and of the traitor Count Don Julian, and they all went to the mountains to escape. And I remained, putting my trust in our Lord God, and in his holy hands: for that I would rather abide that which may befall and take my adventure here, than utterly forsake our mother holy church; while I am able I will remain here and not forsake it, but rather receive my death. And therefore I say, that if you are to abide here you must provide yourself of that whereof you have need. And the King said, Friend of God, concerning my tarriance I cannot certify you; though surely I think that I shall abide; and if for the the service of God you will be pleased to send me every day that I remain a loaf of pannick and water, I shall be contented therewith. And the Elder promised this, and departed forthwith and went to his home, and sent him a loaf of pannick and water. And the cloud remained there three days over that hermitage, and when the three days were at an end, it was seen no more. And the King, when he could no longer see it, understood that there he must perform his penance, and gave many thanks to God, and was full joyful thereat. And on the morrow the Elder came to see him, and they communed with each other in such manner, that the King confessed to him all the sins which he had committed during his whole life till that time, all which he called to mind with great contrition, weeping full bitterly and groaning for his errors and sins. And the Elder was greatly astonished, and said, That on the third day from thence he would appoint him his penance. And he went to his church and confessed, and addrest himself to prayer in such guise that he neither ate nor drank, nor raised himself from one place, weeping bitterly, and beseeching God that he would shew him what penance he should appoint the King; for after no other manner did he think to appoint it, than such as his holy mercy and compassion should

direct. And on the third day he heard a voice which said thus, Command King Don Rodrigo that he go to a fountain which is below his hermitage, and he shall find there a smooth stone; and bid him lift it up, and under it he shall find three little serpents, the one having two heads. And bid him take that which hath two heads, and carry it away, and place it in a jar, and nurse it secretly, so that no person in the world shall know thereof, save only he and thou; and let him keep it till it wax so great that it hath made three turns within the jar, and puts its head out; and when it is of that greatness, then let him take it out, and lay it in a tomb which is there, and lie down himself with it, naked; and close the tomb well, that the serpent may not be able to go out; and in this manner God is pleased that King Don Rodrigo should do penance.

Ch. 254.—*Of the Penance which was appointed King Don Rodrigo.*

«The Elder when he heard the voice was greatly amazed at so rigorous a penance as this, and gave many thanks to God, and he went to King Don Rodrigo, and told him the manner how he had heard the voice; and the King was full joyful and content and pleased therewith, and gave many thanks to our Lord, for that he should now complete his penance and save his soul. And therewith in great joy, and shedding many tears for pleasure, he went to the fountain as he had been directed, and found the smooth stone. And when he had lifted it up, he found the three serpents according as the Elder had said, and he took that which had two heads, and he took it and put it in a great jar, such as would be a large wine vessel, and nurst it there till it was of such bigness as the voice had said. And when King Don Rodrigo saw that it was of this bigness he confessed to the Elder, weeping full bitterly, demanding favour of God that he would give him grace and strength with patience to fulfil that penance without any temptation or trouble of soul; to the end that, the penance being completed, it might please our Lord God to receive his soul into his glory. And before the fifth day after the serpent was thus big, the King and the Elder went to the tomb, and they cleansed it well within; and the King placed himself in it naked as he was born, and the serpent with him, and the Elder with a great lever laid the stone upon the top. And the King besought the Elder that he would pray to our Lord to give him grace that he might patiently endure that penance, and the Elder promised him, and thus the King remained in his tomb, and the serpent with him. And the Elder consoled him, saying to him many things to the end that he might not be dismayed, neither fall into despair, whereby he should lose the service of God. And all this was so secret that no man knew it, save only the King and the Elder. And when it was daybreak the Elder went to the church and said mass, with many tears and with great devotion beseeching God that he would have mercy and compassion upon King Don Rodrigo, that with true devotion and repentance he might complete his penance in this manner, which was for his service. And when he had said mass, he went to the place where King Don Rodrigo lay, and asked him how he fared, and the King answered, Well, thanks to God, and better than he deserved, but that as yet he was just as when he went in. And the Elder strengthened him as much as he could, telling him that he should call to mind how he had been a sinner, and that he should give thanks to our Lord God, for that he had visited him in this world, and delivered him from many temptations, and had himself appointed for him this penance; the which he should suffer and take with patience, for soon he would be in heavenly glory. And the King said to him, that he well knew how according to his great sins he merited a stronger penance: but that he gave many thanks to our Lord Jesus, for that he himself had given him this penance, which he did receive and take with great patience; and he besought the Elder that he would continue to pray our Lord God that he would let him fulfil it. And the Elder said to him many good things concerning our Lord God. And the King lay there three days, during all which time the serpent would not seize on him. And when the third day, after that he had gone into the tomb, was completed, the serpent rose from his side, and crept upon his belly and his breast, and began with the one head to eat at his nature, and with the other straight toward his heart. And at this time the Elder came to the tomb, and asked him how he fared, and he said, Well, thanks to God, for now the serpent had begun to eat. And the Elder asked him at what place, and he answered at two, one right against the heart with which he had conceived all the ills that he had done, and the other at his nature, the which had been the cause of the great destruction of Spain. And the Elder said that God was with him, and exhorted him that he should be of good courage, for now all his persecutions both of the body and of the soul would have an end. And the King ceased not always to demand help of our Lord, and to entreat that of his holy mercy he would be pleased to forgive him. And the Elder went to his home, and would not seat himself to eat, but retired into his chamber, and weeping, prayed full devoutly to our Lord that he would give strength to the King that he might complete his penance. And the serpent, as he was dying for hunger, and moreover was large, had in one minute eaten the nature, and began to eat at the bowels; nevertheless he did not eat so fast, but that the King endured in that torment from an hour before night till it was past the middle of the day. And when the serpent broke through the web of the heart, he staid there and ate no further. And incontinently the King gave up his spirit to our Lord, who by his holy mercy took him into his glory. And at that hour when he expired all the bells of the place rang of themselves as if men had rung them. Then the elder knew that the King was dead, and that his soul was saved.»

Thomas Newton, in his « Notable History of the Saracens,» seems to imagine that this story is allegorical. « Nowe,» he says, « wheras it is reported, and written, that he folowed a starre or a messenger of God, which conducted and guided him in his way; it may be so, and the same hath also happened to others; but it may as well also be understoode of a certaine secrete starre moving and directing his will.

« And wheras they say he was put by that holy man into a cave or hole, and a serpent with him that had two heads, which in two days space gnawed all the flesh of his body from the bones; this, beyng simplie taken and understanded, hath no likelihood of any truth. For what sanctity, what religion, or what pietie, commandeth to kyll a penitent person, and one that seeketh comfort of hys afflicted mind by amendment of life, with such horrible torments and straunge punishment? Wherefore I woulde rather think it to be spoken mysticallye, and that the serpent with two heads signifieth his sinful and gylty conscience.»

Note 72, page 442, col. 2.
A humble tomb was found.

How Carestes found the grave of King Don Rodrigo at Viseo in Portugal.

« I, Carestes, vassal of King Don Alfonso of Leon, son-in-law of the Knight of God, King Don Pelayo when the said King Don Alfonso won Viseo from the Moors who held it, found a grave in a field, upon the which were written in Gothic letters, the words which you shall here read. This grave was in front of a little church, without the town of Viseo, and the superscription of the writing was thus:—

Of the writing which was upon the grave of King Don Rodrigo.

« Here lies King Don Rodrigo, the last of the Goths. Cursed be the wrath of the traitor Julian, for it was of long endurance, and cursed be his anger, for it was obdurate and evil, for he was mad with rage, and stomachful with pride, and puffed up with folly, and void of loyalty, and unmindful of the laws, and a despiser thereof; cruel in himself, a slayer of his Lord, a destroyer of his country, as traitor to his countrymen; bitter is his name; and it is a grief and sorrow in the mouth of him who pronounces it; and it shall always be cursed by all that speak of him.»

That veracious chronicler Carestes then concludes his true history in these words: « And by this which I found written upon this grave, I am of mind that King Don Rodrigo lies there, and because of the life which he led in his penitence, according as ye have heard, which also was in the same tomb written in a book of parchment, I believe without doubt that it is true, and because of the great penance which he did, that God was pleased to make it known in such manner as it past, for those who hereafter shall have to rule and govern, to the end that all men may see how soon pride is abased and humility exalted. This Chronicle is composed in memory of the noble King Don Rodrigo; that God pardon his sins, and that son of the Virgin without stain, Jesus Christ, bring us to true repentance, who liveth and reigneth for ever, and ever. Amen. Thanks be to God!»

I believe the Archbishop Roderick of Toledo is the earliest writer who mentioned this discovery. He died in 1247. The fact may very possibly have been true, for there seems to have been no intention of setting up a shrine connected with it. The Archbishop's words are as follow:—

« Quid de Rege Roderico acciderit ignoratur; tamen corona, vestes et insignia et calciamenta auro et lapidibus adornata, et equus qui Orelia dicebatur, in loco tremulo juxta fluvium sine corpore sunt inventa. Quid autem de corpore fuerit factum penitus ignoratur, nisi

quod modernis temporibus apud Viseum civitatem Por-
tugalliæ inscriptus tumulus invenitur, Hic jacet Rode-
ricus ultimus Rex Gothorum.   Maledictus furor impius
Juliani quia pertinax, et indignatio, quia dura; animo-
sus indignatione, impetuosus furore, oblitus fidelitatis,
immemor religionis, contemptor divinitatis, crudelis in
se, homicida in dominum, hostis in domesticos, vastator
in patriam, reus in omnes, memoria ejus in omni ore
amarescet, et nomen ejus in æternum putrescet.»—
Rod. Tol. l, 3, c. 19.

Lope de Vega has made this epitaph, with its accom-
panying reflections, into two stanzas of Latin rhymes,
which occur in the midst of one of his long poems.

Hoc jacet in sarcophago Rex ille
   Penultimus Gothorum in Hispania,
Infelix Rodericus; viator sile,
   Ne forte pereat tota Lusitania;
Provocatus Cupidinis missile
   Telo, tam magna affectus fuit insania
Quam tota Hiberia vinculis astricta
Testatur mœsta, lachrimatur victa.

Execrabilem Comitem Julianum
   Abhorreant omnes, nomine et remoto
Patrio, appellent Erostratum Hispanum,
   Nec tantum nostri, sed in orbe toto:
Dum current cæli sidera, vesanum
   Vociferant, testante Mauro et Gotho,
Cesset Florindæ nomen insuave,
Cava viator est, a Cava cave.
       Jerusalem Conquistada, l. 6. ff. 137.

Wat Tyler;

A DRAMATIC POEM.

DRAMATIS PERSONÆ.

KING RICHARD.
ARCHBISHOP OF CANTERBURY.
SIR JOHN TRESILIAN.
WALWORTH, *Lord Mayor.*
PHILPOT.
WAT TYLER.
JOHN BALL.
PIERS.
HOB CARTER.
JACK STRAW.
TOM MILLER.

ALICE, *Daughter to Wat Tyler.*

Tax-gatherers, Heralds, Soldiers, Mob, etc.

ACT I.

Scene—A Blacksmith's Shop.

Wat Tyler at work within. A May-pole before the Door.

ALICE, PIERS, ETC.

SONG.

CHEERFUL on this holiday,
Welcome we the merry May.

On every sunny hillock spread,
The pale primrose rears her head;
Rich with sweets the western gale
Sweeps along the cowslip'd dale.
Every bank, with violets gay,
Smiles to welcome in the May.

The linnet from the budding grove,
Chirps her vernal song of love.
The copse resounds the throstle's notes
On each wild gale sweet music floats;

And melody from every spray
Welcomes in the merry May.
Cheerful on this holiday,
Welcome we the merry May.
                        [Dance.

During the Dance, TYLER *lays down his hammer, and
sits mournfully down before his door.*
                        [To him

HOB CARTER.

Why so sad, neighbour?—do not these gay sports,
This revelry of youth, recall the days
When we too mingled in the revelry;
And, lightly tripping in the morris dance,
Welcom'd the merry month?

TYLER.
                   We were young;
No cares had quell'd the hey-day of the blood:
We sported deftly in the April morning,
Nor mark'd the black clouds gathering o'er our noon;
Nor fear'd the storm of night.

HOB.
                   Beshrew me, Tyler,
But my heart joys to see the imps so cheerful!
Young, hale, and happy, why should they destroy
These blessings by reflection?

TYLER.
                 Look ye, neighbour—
You have known me long.

HOB.
              Since we were boys together,
And play'd at barley-brake, and danced the morris :—
Some five-and-twenty years!

TYLER.
              Was not I young,
And hale, and happy?

HOB.
         Cheerful as the best.

TYLER.
Have not I been a staid, hard-working man?
Up with the lark at labour—sober—honest—
Of an unblemish'd character?

HOB.
                    Who doubts it?
There's never a man in Essex bears a better.
                    TYLER.
And shall not these, though young, and hale, and happy,
Look on with sorrow to the future hour?
Shall not reflection poison all their pleasures?
When I—the honest, staid, hard-working Tyler,
Toil through the long course of the summer's day,
Still toiling, yet still poor! when with hard labour
Scarce can I furnish out my daily food—
And age comes on to steal away my strength,
And leave me poor and wretched! why should this be?
My youth was regular—my labour constant—
I married an industrious, virtuous woman;
Nor while I toiled and sweated at the anvil,
Sat she neglectful of her spinning-wheel.—
Hob—I have only six groats in the world,
And they must soon by law be taken from me.
                    HOB.
Curse on these taxes—one succeeds another—
Our ministers—panders of a king's will—
Drain all our wealth away—waste it in revels—
And lure, or force away our boys, who should be
The props of our old age—to fill their armies,
And feed the crows of France! Year follows year,
And still we madly prosecute the war;—
Draining our wealth—distressing our poor peasants—
Slaughtering our youths—and all to crown our chiefs
With glory!—I detest the hell-sprung name.
                    TYLER.
What matters me who wears the crown of France?
Whether a Richard or a Charles possess it?
They reap the glory—they enjoy the spoil—
We pay—we bleed!—The sun would shine as cheerly,
The rains of heaven as seasonably fall,
Though neither of these royal pests existed.
                    HOB.
Nay—as for that, we poor men should fare better;
No legal robbers then should force away
The hard-earn'd wages of our honest toil.
The Parliament for ever cries, *More money,*
The service of the state demands more money.
Just heaven! of what service is the state?
                    TYLER.
Oh! 't is of vast importance! who should pay for
The luxuries and riots of the court?
Who should support the flaunting courtier's pride,
Pay for their midnight revels, their rich garments,
Did not the state enforce?—Think ye, my friend,
That I—a humble blacksmith, here at Deptford,
Would part with these six groats—earn'd by hard toil,
All that I have! to massacre the Frenchmen,
Murder as enemies men I never saw!
Did not the state compel me?
(*Tax-gatherers pass by.*)   There they go,
Privileg'd r——s!—
                    [PIERS *and* ALICE *advance to him.*
                    ALICE.
Did we not dance it well to-day, my father?
You know I always lov'd these village sports,
Even from my infancy, and yet methinks
I never tript along the mead so gaily.
You know they chose me queen, and your friend Piers
Wreath'd me this cowslip garland for my head—
Is it not simple?—you are sad, my father!

You should have rested from your work to-day,
And given a few hours up to merriment—
But you are so serious!
                    TYLER.
                    Serious, my good girl!
I may well be so: when I look at thee
It makes me sad! thou art too fair a flower
To bear the wintry wind of poverty!
                    PIERS.
Yet I have often heard you speak of riches
Even with contempt: they cannot purchase peace,
Or innocence, or virtue:—sounder sleep
Waits on the weary ploughman's lowly bed,
Than on the downy couch of luxury
Lulls the rich slave of pride and indolence.
I never wish for wealth! my arm is strong,
And I can purchase by it a coarse meal,
And hunger savours it.
                    TYLER.
                    Young man, thy mind
Has yet to bear the hard lesson of experience.
Thou art yet young, the blasting breath of want
Has not yet froze the current of thy blood.
                    PIERS.
Fare not the birds well, as from spray to spray
Blithesome they bound—yet find their simple food
Scatter'd abundantly?
                    TYLER.
No fancied boundaries of mine and thine
Restrain their wanderings: Nature gives enough
For all; but Man, with arrogant selfishness,
Proud of his heaps, hoards up superfluous stores,
Robb'd from his weaker fellows, starves the poor,
Or gives to pity what he owes to justice!
                    PIERS.
So I have heard our good friend John Ball preach.
                    ALICE.
My father, wherefore was John Ball imprison'd?
Was he not charitable, good, and pious?
I have heard him say that all mankind are brethren,
And that like brethren they should love each other;—
Was not that doctrine pious?
                    TYLER.
                    Rank sedition—
High treason, every syllable, my child!
The priests cry out on him for heresy,
The nobles all detest him as a rebel;
And this good man, this minister of Christ,
This man, the friend and brother of mankind,
Lingers in the dark dungeon!—My dear Alice,
Retire awhile.
                    [*Exit* ALICE.
                    Piers, I would speak to thee
Even with a father's love! you are much with me,
And I believe do court my conversation;
Thou couldst not chuse thee forth a truer friend;
I would fain see thee happy, but I fear
Thy very virtues will destroy thy peace.
My daughter—she is young—not yet fifteen—
Piers, thou art generous, and thy youthful heart
Warm with affection; this close intimacy
Will ere long grow to love.
                    PIERS.
                    Suppose it so;
Were that an evil, Walter? She is mild,
And cheerful, and industrious—now methinks

With such a partner life would be most happy.
Why would you warn me then of wretchedness?
Is there an evil that can harm our lot?
I have been told the virtuous must be happy,
And have believed it true; tell me, my friend,
What shall disturb the virtuous?

TYLER.
                              Poverty—
A bitter foe!

PIERS.
              Nay, you have often told me
That happiness does not consist in riches.

TYLER.
It is most true: but tell me, my dear boy,
Couldst thou be happy to behold thy wife
Pining with want?—the children of your loves
Clad in the squalid rags of wretchedness?
And when thy hard and unremitting toil
Had earn'd with pain a scanty recompense,
Couldst thou be patient when the law should rob thee,
And leave thee without bread, and pennyless?

PIERS.
It is a dreadful picture.

TYLER.
                          'T is a true one.

PIERS.
But yet, methinks, our sober industry
Might drive away the danger; 't is but little
That I could wish—food for our frugal meals,
Raiment, however homely, and a bed
To shield us from the night.

TYLER.
                            Thy honest reason
Could wish no more: but were it not most wretched
To want the coarse food for the frugal meal?
And, by the orders of your merciless lord,
If you by chance were guilty of being poor,
To be turn'd out adrift to the bleak world,
Unhous'd, unfriended?—Piers, I have not been idle,
I never ate the bread of indolence—
Could Alice be more thrifty than her mother?
Yet but with one child, and that one, how good
Thou knowest, I scarcely can provide the wants
Of nature: look at these wolves of the law,
They come to drain me of my heard-earn'd wages.
I have already paid the heavy tax
Laid on the wool that clothes me—on my leather,
On all the needful articles of life!
And now three groats (and I work'd hard to earn them)
The Parliament demands—and I must pay them,
Forsooth for liberty to wear my head.—

Enter Tax-gatherers.

COLLECTOR.
Three groats a head for all your family.

PIERS.
Why is this money gathered?—'t is a hard tax
On the poor labourer!—it can never be
That government should thus distress the people.
Go to the rich for money—honest labour
Ought to enjoy its fruits.

COLLECTOR.
                          The state wants money.
War is expensive—'t is a glorious war,
A war of honour, and must be supported.—
Three groats a head.

TYLER.
There, three for my own head,
Three for my wife's!—what will the state tax next?

COLLECTOR.
You have a daughter.

TYLER.
                     She is below the age—not yet fifteen.

COLLECTOR.
You would evade the tax.—

TYLER.
                          Sir Officer,
I have paid you fairly what the law demands.

[ALICE *and her Mother enter the Shop. The Tax-*
gatherers go to her. One of them lays hold of
her. She screams. TYLER goes in.

COLLECTOR.
You say she 's under age.

[ALICE *screams again. TYLER knocks out the*
Tax-gatherer's Brains. His Companions fly.

PIERS.
A just revenge.

TYLER.
Most just indeed; but in the eye of the law
'T is murder—and the murderer's lot is mine.
                              [PIERS *goes out.*
(TYLER *sits down mournfully.*)

ALICE.
Fly, my dear father! let us leave this place
Before they raise pursuit.

TYLER.
                           Nay, nay, my child,
Flight would be useless—I have done my duty,
I have punish'd the brute insolence of lust,
And here will wait my doom.

WIFE.
                            Oh, let us fly!
My husband, my dear husband!

ALICE.
                             Quit but this place,
And we may yet be safe, and happy too.

TYLER.
It would be useless, Alice—'t would but lengthen
A wretched life in fear.
                              [*Cry without.*
Liberty! Liberty!

(*Enter Mob,* HOB CARTER, *etc.*)

(*Cry*) Liberty! liberty!—No Poll-tax!—No War!

HOB.
We have broke our chains—we will arise in anger—
The mighty multitude shall trample down
The handful that oppress them.

TYLER.
                               Have ye heard
So soon then of my murder?

HOB.
                           Of your vengeance.
Piers ran throughout the village—told the news—
Cried out, To arms!—arm, arm for Liberty!
For Liberty and Justice!

TYLER.
                         My good friends,
Heed well your danger, or be resolute;
Learn to laugh menaces and force to scorn,

Or leave me. I dare answer the bold deed—
Death must come once; return you to your homes,
Protect my wife and child, and on my grave
Write why I died; perhaps the time may come,
When honest Justice shall applaud the deed.

HOB.

Nay, nay,—we are oppressed, and have too long
Knelt at our proud lords' feet—we have too long
Obey'd their orders—bow'd to their caprices—
Sweated for them the wearying summer's day,
Wasted for them the wages of our toil;
Fought for them, conquer'd for them, bled for them,
Still to be trampled on, and still despis'd;
But we have broke our chains.

TOM MILLER.

Piers is gone on
Through all the neighbouring villages, to spread
The glorious tidings.

HOB.

He is hurried on
To Maidstone, to deliver good John Ball,
Our friend, our shepherd.

[*Mob increases.*

TYLER.

Friends and Countrymen,
Will ye then rise to save an honest man
From the fierce clutches of the bloody law?—
Oh do not call to mind my private wrongs,
That the state drain'd my hard-earn'd pittance from me;
That, of his office proud, the foul Collector
Durst with lewd hand seize on my darling child,
Insult her maiden modesty and force
A father's hand to vengeance; heed not this:
Think not, my countrymen, on private wrongs;
Remember what yourselves have long endur'd.
Think of the insults, wrongs, and contumelies,
Ye bear from your proud lords—that your hard toil
Manures their fertile fields—you plough the earth,
You sow the corn, you reap the ripen'd harvest,—
They riot on the produce!—That, like beasts,
They sell you with their land—claim all the fruits
Which the kindly earth produces as their own.
The privilege, forsooth, of noble birth!
On, on to Freedom; feel but your own strength,
Be but resolved, and these destructive tyrants
Shall shrink before your vengeance.

HOB.

On to London—
The tidings fly before us—the court trembles—
Liberty!—Vengeance—Justice!

ACT II.

Scene—Blackheath.

TYLER, HOB, *etc.*

SONG.

' WHEN Adam delv'd, and Eve span,
' Who was then the gentleman?,

Wretched is the infant's lot,
Born within the straw-roof'd cot!
Be he generous, wise, or brave,
He must only be a slave.

Long, long labour, little rest,
Still to toil to be oppress'd;
Drain'd by taxes of his store,
Punish'd next for being poor:
This is the poor wretch's lot,
Born within the straw-roof'd cot.

While the peasant works—to sleep;
What the peasant sows—to reap;
On the couch of ease to lie,
Rioting in revelry;
Be he villain, be he fool,
Still to hold despotic rule,
Trampling on his slaves with scorn;
This is to be nobly born.

' When Adam delv'd, and Eve span,
' Who was then the gentleman?,

JACK STRAW.

The mob are up in London—the proud courtiers
Begin to tremble.

TOM MILLER.

Aye, aye, 't is time to tremble;
Who 'll plow their fields, who 'll do their drudgery now?
And work like horses, to give them the harvest?

JACK STRAW.

I only wonder we lay quiet so long.
We had always the same strength, and we deserv'd
The ills we met with for not using it.

HOB.

Why do we fear those animals call'd lords?
What is there in the name to frighten us?
Is not my arm as mighty as a Baron's?

Enter PIERS *and* JOHN BALL.

PIERS (*to* TYLER).
Have I done well, my father?—I remember'd
This good man lay in prison.

TYLER.

My dear child,
Most well; the people rise for liberty,
And their first deed should be to break the chains
That bind the virtuous :—O thou honest priest—
How much hast thou endur'd!

JOHN BALL.

Why, aye, my friend!
These squalid rags bespeak what I have suffer'd.
I was revil'd—insulted—left to languish
In a damp dungeon; but I bore it cheerily—
My heart was glad—for I have done my duty.
I pitied my oppressors, and I sorrow'd
For the poor men of England.

TYLER.

They have felt
Their strength—look round this heath! 'tis throng'd with men
Ardent for freedom; mighty is the event
That waits their fortune.

JOHN BALL.

I would fain address them.

TYLER.

Do so, my friend, and teach to them their duty;
Remind them of their long-withholden rights.
What, ho there! silence!

PIERS.

               Silence there, my friends ;
This good man would address you.

MOB.

                   Aye, aye, hear him—
He is no mealy-mouth'd court orator,
To flatter vice, and pamper lordly pride.

JOHN BALL.

Friends ! Brethren ! for ye are my brethren all ;
Englishmen met in arms to advocate
The cause of freedom ! hear me ! pause awhile
In the career of vengeance : it is true
I am a priest ; but, as these rags may speak,
Not one who riots in the poor man's spoil,
Or trades with his religion. I am one
Who preach the law of Christ, and in my life
Would practise what he taught. The Son of God
Came not to you in power :—humble in mien,
Lowly in heart, the man of Nazareth
Preach'd mercy, justice, love : « Woe unto ye,
Ye that are rich :—if that ye would be sav'd,
Sell that ye have, and give unto the poor.»
So taught the Saviour : oh, my honest friends !
Have ye not felt the strong indignant throb
Of justice in your bosoms, to behold
The lordly baron feasting on your spoils?
Have you not in your hearts arraign'd the lot
That gave him on the couch of luxury
To pillow his head, and pass the festive day
In sportive feasts, and ease, and revelry?
Have you not often in your conscience ask'd
Why is the difference, wherefore should that man,
No worthier than myself, thus lord it over me,
And bid me labour, and enjoy the fruits?
The God within your breasts has argued thus !
The voice of truth has murmur'd ; came ye not
As helpless to the world?—shines not the sun
With equal ray on both?—do ye not feel
The self-same winds of heaven as keenly parch ye?
Abundant is the earth—the Sire of all
Saw and pronounc'd that it was very good.
Look round : the vernal fields smile with new flowers,
The budding orchard perfumes the soft breeze,
And the green corn waves to the passing gale.
There is enough for all ; but your proud baron
Stands up, and, arrogant of strength, exclaims,
« I am a lord—by nature I am noble :
These fields are mine, for I was born to them,
I was born in the castle—you, poor wretches,
Whelp'd in the cottage, are by birth my slaves.»
Almighty God ! such blasphemies are utter'd !
Almighty God ! such blasphemies believ'd !

TOM MILLER.

This is something like a sermon.

JACK STRAW.

                  Where 's the bishop
Would tell you truths like these ?

HOB.

There was never a bishop among all the apostles.

JOHN BALL.

My brethren !

PIERS.

           Silence, the good priest speaks.

JOHN BALL.

My brethren, these are truths, and weighty ones :
Ye are all equal ; nature made ye so.

Equality is your birth-right ;—when I gaze
On the proud palace, and behold one man
In the blood-purpled robes of royalty,
Feasting at ease, and lording over millions ;
Then turn me to the hut of poverty,
And see the wretched labourer, worn with toil,
Divide his scanty morsel with his infants ;
I sicken, and, indignant at the sight,
« Blush for the patience of humanity.»

JACK STRAW.

We will assert our rights.

TOM MILLER.

               We 'll trample down
These insolent oppressors.

JOHN BALL.

              In good truth
Ye have cause for anger : but, my honest friends,
Is it revenge or justice that ye seek ?

MOB.

Justice, justice!

JOHN BALL.

            Oh then remember mercy ;
And though your proud oppressors spar'd not you,
Show you excel them in humanity.
They will use every art to disunite you,
To conquer separately, by stratagem,
Whom in a mass they fear—but be ye firm—
Boldly demand your long-forgotten rights,
Your sacred, your inalienable freedom—
Be bold—be resolute—be merciful!
And while you spurn the hated name of slaves,
Show you are men !

MOB.

           Long live our honest priest !

JACK STRAW.

He shall be made archbishop.

JOHN BALL.

             My brethren, I am plain John Ball, your friend,
Your equal ; by the law of Christ enjoin'd
To serve you, not command.

JACK STRAW.

               March we for London.

TYLER.

Mark me, my friends—we rise for liberty—
Justice shall be our guide : let no man dare
To plunder in the tumult.

MOB.

              Lead us on—
Liberty ! Justice !

[*Exeunt, with cries of «Liberty»—«No Poll-Tax»—«No War.»*]

Scene changes to the Tower.

KING RICHARD, ARCHBISHOP OF CANTERBURY, SIR
JOHN TRESILIAN, WALWORTH, PHILPOT.

KING.

What must we do? the danger grows more imminent—
The mob increases.

PHILPOT.

             Every moment brings
Fresh tidings of our peril.

KING.

              It were well
To yield them what they ask.

ARCHBISHOP.

Aye, that, my liege,
Were politic. Go boldly forth to meet them,
Grant all they ask—however wild and ruinous—
Meantime the troops you have already summon'd
Will gather round them.   Then my Christian power
Absolves you of your promise.

WALWORTH.

Were but their ringleaders cut off—the rabble
Would soon disperse.

PHILPOT.

United in a mass,
There's nothing can resist them—once divide them,
And they will fall an easy sacrifice.

ARCHBISHOP.

Lull them by promises—bespeak them fair—
Go forth, my liege—spare not, if need requires,
A solemn oath, to ratify the treaty.

KING.

I dread their fury.

ARCHBISHOP.

'Tis a needless dread,
There is divinity about your person;
It is the sacred privilege of Kings,
Howe'er they act, to render no account
To man.   The people have been taught this lesson,
Nor can they soon forget it.

KING.

I will go—
I will submit to every thing they ask;
My day of triumph will arrive at last.

[Shouts without.

Enter Messenger.

MESSENGER.

The mob are at the city gates.

ARCHBISHOP.

Haste, haste,
Address them ere too late.   I'll remain here,
For they detest me much.

[Shouts again.

Enter another Messenger.

MESSENGER.

The Londoners have opened the city gates,
The rebels are admitted.

KING.

Fear then must give me courage: my Lord Mayor,
Come you with me.

[Exeunt. Shouts without.

Scene—Smithfield.

WAT TYLER, JOHN BALL, PIERS, etc. Mob.

PIERS.

So far triumphant are we: how these nobles,
These petty tyrants, who so long oppress'd us,
Shrink at the first resistance!

MOB.

They were powerful
Only because we fondly thought them so!
Where is Jack Straw?

TYLER.

Jack Straw is gone to the Tower
To seize the king, and so to end resistance.

JOHN BALL.

It was well judg'd: fain would I spare the shedding
Of human blood: gain we that royal puppet,
And all will follow fairly: depriv'd of him,
The nobles lose their pretext, nor will dare
Rebel against the people's majesty.

Enter Herald.

HERALD.

Richard the Second, by the grace of God,
Of England, Ireland, France, and Scotland, King,
And of the town of Berwick-upon-Tweed,
Would parley with Wat Tyler.

TYLER.

Let him know
Wat Tyler is in Smithfield.

[Exit Herald.

I will parley
With this young monarch; as he comes to me
Trusting my honour, on your lives I charge you,
Let none attempt to harm him.

JOHN BALL.

The faith of courts
Is but a weak dependence! You are honest—
And better is it even to die the victim
Of credulous honesty, than live preserv'd
By the cold policy that still suspects.

Enter KING, WALWORTH, PHILPOT, etc.

KING.

I would speak to thee, Wat Tyler: bid the mob
Retire awhile.

PIERS.

Nay, do not go alone—
Let me attend you.

TYLER.

Wherefore should I fear?
Am I not arm'd with a just cause?—retire,
And I will boldly plead the cause of Freedom.

[Advances.

KING.

Tyler, why have you killed my officer?
And led my honest subjects from their homes,
Thus to rebel against the Lord's anointed?

TYLER.

Because they were oppress'd.

KING.

Was this the way
To remedy the ill?—you should have tried
By milder means—petitioned at the throne—
The throne will always listen to petitions.

TYLER.

King of England,
Petitioning for pity is most weak,
The sovereign people ought to demand justice.
I kill'd your officer, for his lewd hand
Insulted a maid's modesty: your subjects
I lead to rebel against the Lord's anointed,
Because his ministers have made him odious:
His yoke is heavy, and his burden grievous.
Why do we carry on this fatal war,
To force upon the French a king they hate;
Tearing our young men from their peaceful homes;
Forcing his hard-earned fruits from the honest peasant;
Distressing us to desolate our neighbours?
Why is this ruinous poll-tax impos'd,

But to support your court's extravagance,
And your mad title to the crown of France?
Shall we sit tamely down beneath these evils,
Petitioning for pity?

    King of England!
Why are we sold like cattle in your markets—
Depriv'd of ev'ry privilege of man?
Must we lie tamely at our tyrant's feet,
And, like your Spaniels, lick the hand that beats us?
You sit at ease in your gay palaces,
The costly banquet courts your appetite,
Sweet music soothes your slumbers; we, the while,
Scarce by hard toil can earn a little food,
And sleep scarce shelter'd from the cold night wind:
Whilst your wild projects wrest the little from us
Which might have cheer'd the wintry hour of age:
The Parliament for ever asks more money:
We toil and sweat for money for your taxes:
Where is the benefit, what food reap we
From all the councils of your government?
Think you that we should quarrel with the French?
What boots to us your victories, your glory?
We pay, we fight, you profit at your ease.
Do you not claim the country as you own?
Do you not call the venison of the forest,
The birds of heaven, your own?—prohibiting us,
Even though in want of food, to seize the prey
Which nature offers?—King! is all this just?
Think you we do not feel the wrongs we suffer?
The hour of retribution is at hand,
And tyrants tremble—mark me, King of England.

    WALWORTH.
  (Comes behind him and stabs him.)
Insolent rebel, threatening the King.

    PIERS.
Vengeance! vengeance!

    BOB.
    Seize the King.

    KING.
I must be bold.   [Advancing.
  My friends and loving subjects,
I will grant all you ask: you shall be free—
The tax shall be repeal'd—all, all you wish.
Your leader menac'd me, he deserv'd his fate.
Quiet your angers; on my royal word
Your grievances shall all be done away,
Your vassalage abolish'd—a free pardon
Allow'd to all: so help me God, it shall be.

    JOHN BALL.
Revenge, my brethren, beseems not Christians.
Send us these terms sign'd with your seal of state.
We will await in peace: deceive us not—
Act justly, so to excuse your late foul deed.

    KING.
The charter shall be drawn out: on mine honour,
All shall be justly done.

ACT III.

Scene—Smithfield.

PIERS (meeting JOHN BALL).
You look disturb'd, my father?

    JOHN BALL.
    Piers, I am so.

Jack Straw has forc'd the Tower; seiz'd the Archbishop,
And beheaded him.

    PIERS.
  The curse of insurrection!

    JOHN BALL.
Aye, Piers! our nobles level down their vassals—
Keep them at endless labour like their brutes,
Degrading ev'ry faculty by servitude,
Repressing all the energy of mind.
We must not wonder then, that, like wild beasts,
When they have burst their chains, with brutal rage
They revenge them on their tyrants.

    PIERS.
    This Archbishop!
He was oppressive to his humble vassals:
Proud, haughty, avaricious.—

    JOHN BALL.
    A true high-priest!
Preaching humility with his mitre on!
Praising up alms and Christian charity,
Even whilst his unforgiving hand distress'd
His honest tenants.

    PIERS.
  He deserv'd his fate then.

    JOHN BALL.
Justice can never link with cruelty.
Is there among the catalogue of crimes
A sin so black that only Death can expiate?
Will Reason never rouse her from her slumbers,
And darting through the veil her eagle eye,
See in the sable garment of the law
Revenge conceal'd? — This high-priest has been
  haughty—
He has oppress'd his vassals: tell me, Piers,
Does his Death remedy the ills he caus'd?
Were it not better to repress his power
Of doing wrong—that so his future life
Might expiate the evils of the past,
And benefit mankind?

    PIERS.
    But must not vice
Be punished?

    JOHN BALL.
  Is not punishment revenge?
The momentary violence of anger
May be excus'd: the indignant heart will throb
Against oppression, and the outstretch'd arm
Resent its injur'd feelings: the Collector
Insulted Alice, and rous'd the keen emotions
Of a fond father. Tyler murder'd him.

    PIERS.
Murder'd!—a most harsh word.

    JOHN BALL.
    Yes, murder'd him:
His mangled feelings prompted the bad act,
And Nature will almost commend the deed
That Justice blames; but will the awaken'd feelings
Plead with their heart-emoving eloquence
For the cool deliberate murder of Revenge?
Would you, Piers, in your calmer hour of reason,
Condemn an erring brother to be slain?
Cut him at once from all the joys of life,
All hopes of reformation! to revenge
The deed his punishment cannot recall?
My blood boil'd in me at the fate of Tyler,
Yet I revenged it not.

PIERS.
Oh my Christian father!
They would not argue thus humanely on us,
Were we within their power.

JOHN BALL.
I know they would not:
But we must pity them that they are vicious,
Not imitate their vice.

PIERS.
Alas, poor Tyler!
I do repent me much that I stood back,
When he advanced fearless in rectitude
To meet these royal assassins.

JOHN BALL.
Not for myself,
Though I have lost an honest virtuous friend,
Mourn I the death of Tyler: he was one
Gifted with the strong energy of mind,
Quick to perceive the right, and prompt to act
When Justice needed: he would listen to me
With due attention, yet not yielding lightly
What had to him seem'd good: severe in virtue,
He aw'd the ruder people whom he led
By his stern rectitude.

PIERS.
Witness that day
When they destroy'd the palace of the Gaunt;
And hurl'd the wealth his avarice had amass'd,
Amid the fire: the people, fierce in zeal,
Threw in the flames the wretch whose selfish hand
Purloin'd amid the tumult.

JOHN BALL.
I lament
The death of Tyler, for my country's sake.
I shudder lest posterity enslav'd
Should rue his murder!—who shall now control
The giddy multitude, blind to their own good,
And listening with avidity to the tale
Of courtly falsehood?

PIERS.
The King must perform
His plighted promise.
(Cry without)—The Charter!—the Charter!

Enter Mob and Herald.

TOM MILLER.
Read it out—read it out.

HOB.
Aye, aye, let's hear the Charter.

HERALD.
Richard Plantagenet, by the grace of God, King of England, Ireland, France, Scotland, and the town of Berwick upon Tweed, to all whom it may concern, these presents: Whereas our loving subjects have complained to us of the heavy burdens they endure, particularly from our late enacted poll-tax; and whereas they have risen in arms against our officers, and demanded the abolition of personal slavery, vassalage, and manorial rights; we, ever ready in our sovereign mercy to listen to the petitions of our loving subjects, do annul all these grievances.

MOB.
Huzza! long live the King!

HERALD.
And do, of our royal mercy, grant a free pardon to all who may have been any ways concerned in the late insurrections. All this shall be faithfully performed on our royal word. So help us God.
God save the King!
(Loud and repeated shouts.)

HERALD.
Now then depart in quiet to your homes.

JOHN BALL.
Nay, my good friend—the people will remain
Embodied peaceably, till Parliament
Confirm the royal charter: tell your King so:
We will await the Charter's confirmation,
Meanwhile comporting ourselves orderly,
As peaceful citizens, not risen in tumult,
But to redress their evils.
(Exit Herald, etc. HOB, PIERS, and JOHN BALL remain.)

HOB.
'T was well order'd;
I place but little trust in courtly faith.

JOHN BALL.
We must remain embodied; else the King
Will plunge again in royal luxury;
And when the storm of danger is pass'd over,
Forget his promises.

HOB.
Aye, like an aguish sinner,
He'll promise to repent when the fit's on him;
When well recover'd, laugh at his own terrors.

PIERS.
Oh! I am grieved that we must gain so little!
Why are not all these empty ranks abolish'd,
King, slave, and lord, « ennobled into MAN?»
Are we not equal all?—have you not told me,
Equality is the sacred right of man,
Inalienable, though by force withheld?

JOHN BALL.
Even so: but, Piers, my frail and fallible judgment
Knows hardly to decide, if it be right
Peaceably to return, content with little,
With this half restitution of our rights,
Or boldly to proceed through blood and slaughter,
Till we should all be equal, and all happy.
I chose the milder way:—perhaps I err'd.

PIERS.
I fear me—by the mass, the unsteady people
Are flocking homewards! how the multitude
Diminishes!

JOHN BALL.
Go thou, my son, and stay them.
Carter, do you exert your influence,
All depends on their stay: my mind is troubled,
And I would fain compose my thoughts for action.
(Exeunt HOB and PIERS.)
Father of mercies! I do fear me much
That I have err'd: thou gavest my ardent mind
To pierce the mists of superstitious falsehood;—
Gavest me to know the truth. I should have urged it
Through every opposition: now, perhaps,
The seemly voice of pity has deceived me,
And all this mighty movement ends in ruin!
I fear me, I have been like the weak leech,
Who, sparing to cut deep, with cruel mercy
Mangles his patient without curing him.
(Great tumult.)
What means this tumult? hark! the clang of arms!

God of eternal justice! the false monarch
Has broke his plighted vow!

Enter PIERS *wounded.*

PIERS.

Fly, fly, my father—the perjured King—fly! fly!

JOHN BALL.

Nay, nay, my child—I dare abide my fate,
Let me bind up thy wounds.

PIERS.

'T is useless succour:
They seek thy life; fly, fly, my honour'd father.
Fain would I die in peace to hope thee safe.
I shall soon join thee, Tyler!—they are murdering
Our unsuspecting brethren: half unarm'd,
Trusting too fondly to the tyrant's vows,
They were dispersing:—the streets swim with blood.
Oh! save thyself.

Enter Soldiers.

SOLDIER.

This is that old seditious heretic.
(*Seizes* JOHN BALL.)

SECOND SOLDIER.

And here the young spawn of rebellion;
My orders are n't to spare him.
(*Stabs* PIERS.)

Come you old stirrer up of insurrection,
You bell-wether of the mob—you are n't to die
So easily.

(*They lead off* JOHN BALL—*the tumult increases
—Mob fly across the stage—the Troops pursue
them—loud cries and shouts.*)

Scene—Westminster Hall.

KING, WALWORTH, PHILPOT, SIR JOHN TRESILIAN, etc.

WALWORTH.

My liege, 't was wisely order'd to destroy
The dunghill rabble, but take prisoner
That old seditious priest: his strange wild notions
Of this equality, when well exposed,
Will create ridicule, and shame the people,
Of their late tumults.

SIR JOHN TRESILIAN.

Aye, there's nothing like
A fair free open trial, where the King
Can chuse his jury and appoint his judges.

KING.

Walworth, I must thank you for my deliverance:
'T was a bold deed to stab him in the parley!
Kneel down, and rise a knight, Sir William Walworth.

Enter Messenger.

MESSENGER.

I left them hotly at it. Smithfield smoked
With the rebels' blood: your troops fought loyally,
There 's not a man of them will lend an ear
To pity.

SIR WILLIAM WALWORTH.

Is John Ball secured?

MESSENGER.

They 've seized him.

Enter Guards with JOHN BALL.

GUARD.

We 've brought the old villain.

SECOND GUARD.

An old mischief-maker—
Why there 's fifteen hundred of the mob are kill'd,
All through his preaching!

SIR JOHN TRESILIAN.

Prisoner! are you the arch-rebel, John Ball?

JOHN BALL.

I am John Ball; but I am not a rebel.
Take ye the name, who, arrogant in strength,
Rebel against the people's sovereignty.

SIR JOHN TRESILIAN.

John Ball, you are accused of stirring up
The poor deluded people to rebellion;
Not having the fear of God and of the King
Before your eyes; of preaching up strange notions,
Heretical and treasonous; such as saying
That kings have not a right from heaven to govern;
That all mankind are equal; and that ranks,
And the distinctions of society,
Ay, and the sacred rights of property,
Are evil and oppressive:—plead you guilty
To this most heavy charge?

JOHN BALL.

If it be guilt—
To preach what you are pleased to call strange notions:—
That all mankind as brethren must be equal;
That privileged orders of society
Are evil and oppressive; that the right
Of property is a juggle to deceive
The poor whom you oppress—I plead me guilty.

SIR JOHN TRESILIAN.

It is against the custom of this court
That the prisoner should plead guilty.

JOHN BALL.

Why then put you
The needless question?—Sir Judge, let me save
The vain and empty insult of a trial.
What I have done, that I dare justify.

SIR JOHN TRESILIAN.

Did you not tell the mob they were oppress'd,
And preach upon the equality of man;
With evil intent thereby to stir them up
To tumult and rebellion?

JOHN BALL.

That I told them
That all mankind are equal, is most true:
Ye came as helpless infants to the world;
Ye feel alike the infirmities of nature;
And at last moulder into common clay.
Why then these vain distinctions?—Bears not the earth
Food in abundance?—must your granaries
O'erflow with plenty, while the poor man starves?
Sir Judge, why sit you there clad in your furs?
Why are your cellars stored with choicest wines?
Your larders hung with dainties; while your vassal,
As virtuous, and as able too by nature,
Though by your selfish tyranny deprived
Of mind's improvement, shivers in his rags,
And starves amid the plenty he creates.
I have said this is wrong, and I repeat it—
And there will be a time when this great truth
Shall be confess'd—be felt by all mankind.

The electric truth shall run from man to man,
And the blood-cemented pyramid of greatness
Shall fall before the flash!

SIR JOHN TRESILIAN.

Audacious rebel!
How darest thou insult this sacred court,
Blaspheming all the dignities of rank?
How could the government be carried on,
Without the sacred orders of the king
And the nobility?

JOHN BALL.

Tell me, Sir Judge,
What does the government avail the peasant?
Would not he plough his field, and sow the corn,
Aye, and in peace enjoy the harvest too:
Would not the sunshine and the dews descend,
Though neither King nor Parliament existed?
Do your court politics aught matter him?
Would he be warring even unto the death
With his French neighbours?—Charles and Richard
         contend;
The people fight and suffer:—think ye, Sirs,
If neither country had been cursed with a chief,
The peasants would have quarrell'd?

KING.

This is treason!
The patience of the court has been insulted—
Condemn the foul-mouth'd, contumacious rebel.

SIR JOHN TRESILIAN.

John Ball, whereas you are accused before us
Of stirring up the people to rebellion,
And preaching to them strange and dangerous doctrines;

And whereas your behaviour to the court
Has been most insolent and contumacious;
Insulting Majesty—and since you have pleaded
Guilty to all these charges; I condemn you
To death: you shall be hanged by the neck,
But not till you are dead—your bowels open'd—
Your heart torn out and burnt before your face—
Your traitorous head be sever'd from your body—
Your body quarter'd, and expos'd upon
The city gates—a terrible example—
And the Lord God have mercy on your soul!

JOHN BALL.

Why, be it so. I can smile at your vengeance,
For I am arm'd with rectitude of soul.
The truth, which all my life I have divulg'd,
And am now doom'd in torment to expire for,
Shall still survive—the destin'd hour must come,
When it shall blaze with sun-surpassing splendour,
And the dark mists of prejudice and falsehood
Fade in its strong effulgence. Flattery's incense
No more shall shadow round the gore-dyed throne;
That altar of oppression, fed with rites
More savage than the Priests of Moloch taught,
Shall be consum'd amid the fire of Justice;
The ray of truth shall emanate around,
And the whole world be lighted!

KING.

Drag him hence—
Away with him to death! order the troops
Now to give quarter, and make prisoners—
Let the blood-reeking sword of war be sheath'd,
That the law may take vengeance on the rebels.

Carmen Triumphale,

FOR THE COMMENCEMENT OF THE YEAR 1814.

Illi justitiam confirmavere triumphi,
Præsentes docuere Deos.

CLAUDIAN.

I.

In happy hour doth he receive
The Laurel, meed of famous Bards of yore,
Which Dryden and diviner Spenser wore,—
In happy hour, and well may he rejoice,
Whose earliest task must be
To raise the exultant hymn for victory,
And join a nation's joy with harp and voice,
Pouring the strain of triumph on the wind,
Glory to God, his song, Deliverance for Mankind!

II.

Wake, lute and harp! My Soul take up the strain!
Glory to God! Deliverance for Mankind!
Joy,—for all Nations joy! but most for thee
Who hast so nobly fill'd thy part assign'd,
O England! O my glorious native land!
For thou in evil days didst stand
Against leagued Europe all in arms array'd,
Single and undismay'd,

Thy hope in Heaven and in thine own right hand.
Now are thy virtuous efforts overpaid,
Thy generous counsels now their guerdon find,—
Glory to God! Deliverance for Mankind!

III.

Dread was the strife, for mighty was the foe
Who sought with his whole strength thy overthrow.
The Nations bow'd before him; some in war
Subdued, some yielding to superior art;
Submiss, they follow'd his victorious car.
Their Kings, like Satraps, waited round his throne;
For Britain's ruin and their own,
By force or fraud in monstrous league combined.
Alone in that disastrous hour
Britain stood firm and braved his power!
Alone she fought the battles of mankind.

IV.

O virtue which above all former fame,
Exalts her venerable name!

63

O joy of joys for every British breast!
That with that mighty peril full in view,
The Queen of Ocean to herself was true!
That no weak heart, no abject mind possess'd
Her counsels,[1] to abase her lofty crest,—
(Then had she sunk in everlasting shame,)
But ready still to succour the oppress'd,
Her Red-Cross floated on the waves unfurl'd,
Offering Redemption to the groaning world.

V.

First from his trance the heroic Spaniard woke;
His chains he broke,
And casting off his neck the treacherous yoke,
He call'd on England, on his generous foe:
For well he knew that wheresoe'er
Wise policy prevailed, or brave despair,
Thither would Britain's liberal succours flow,
Her arm be present there.
Then, too, regenerate Portugal display'd
Her ancient virtue, dormant all too long.
Rising against intolerable wrong,
On England, on her old ally for aid
The faithful nation call'd in her distress:
And well that old ally the call obey'd,
Well was that faithful friendship then repaid.

VI.

Say from thy trophied field how well,
Vimeiro! rocky Douro tell!
And thou, Busaco, on whose sacred height
The astonish'd Carmelite,
While those unwonted thunders shook his cell,
Join'd with his prayers the fervour of the fight![2]
Bear witness those Old Towers,[3] where many a day
Waiting with foresight calm the fitting hour,
The Wellesley, gathering strength in wise delay,
Defied the Tyrant's undivided power.
Swore not the boastful Frenchman in his might,
Into the sea to drive his Island-foe?
Tagus and Zezere, in the secret night,
Ye saw that host of ruffians take their flight![4]
And in the Sun's broad light
Onoro's Springs[5] beheld their overthrow!

VII.

Patient of loss, profuse of life,
Meantime had Spain endured the strife;
And tho' she saw her cities yield,
Her armies scatter'd in the field,
Her strongest bulwarks fall,
The danger undismay'd she view'd,
Knowing that nought could e'er appal
The Spaniards' fortitude.[6]
What though the Tyrant, drunk with power,
Might vaunt himself, in impious hour,
Lord and Disposer of this earthly ball?[7]
Her cause is just, and Heaven is over all.

VIII.

Therefore no thought of fear debased
Her judgment, nor her acts disgraced.
To every ill, but not to shame resign'd,
All sufferings, all calamities she bore.
She bade the people call to mind
Their heroes of the days of yore,

Pelayo and the Campeador,[8]
With all who, once in battle strong,
Lived still in story and in song.
Against the Moor, age after age,
Their stubborn warfare did they wage;
Age after age, from sire to son,
The hallowed sword was handed down;
Nor did they from that warfare cease,
And sheathe that hallowed sword in peace,
Until the work was done.

IX.

Thus in the famous days of yore,
Their fathers triumph'd o'er the Moor,
They gloried in his overthrow,
But touch'd not with reproach his gallant name;
For fairly, and with hostile aim profest,
The Moor had rear'd his haughty crest;
An open, honourable foe;
But as a friend the treacherous Frenchman came,
And Spain receiv'd him as a guest.
Think what your fathers were! she cried!
Think what ye are, in sufferings tried,
And think of what your sons must be—
Even as ye make them—slaves or free!

X.

Strains such as these from Spain's three seas,
And from the farthest Pyrenees,
Rung through the region. Vengeance was the word;[9]
One impulse to all hearts at once was given;
From every voice the sacred cry was heard,
And borne abroad by all the Winds of Heaven.
Heaven too, to whom the Spaniards look'd for aid,
A spirit equal to the hour bestow'd;
And gloriously the debt they paid,
Which to their valiant ancestors they ow'd,
And gloriously against the power of France,
Maintain'd their children's proud inheritance.
Their steady purpose no defeat could move,
No horrors could abate their constant mind;
Hope had its source and resting-place above,
And they, to loss of all on earth resign'd,
Suffered, to save their country, and mankind.
What strain heroic might suffice to tell,
How Zaragoza stood, and how she fell?
Ne'er since yon sun began his daily round,
Was higher virtue, holier valour found,
Than on that consecrated ground.

XI.

Alone the noble Nation stood,
When from Corunna in the main,
The star of England set in blood.
Ere long on Talavera's plain,
That star resplendent rose again;
And though that day was doom'd to be
A day of frustrate victory,
Not vainly bled the brave!
For French and Spaniard there might see
That England's arm was strong to save;
Fair promise there the Wellesley gave,
And well in sight of Earth and Heaven,
Did he redeem the pledge which there was given.

XII.

Lord of Conquest, heir of Fame,
From rescued Portugal he came.
Rodrigo's walls in vain oppose;
In vain thy bulwarks, Badajoz;
And Salamanca's heights proclaim
The Conqueror's praise, the Wellesley's name.
Oh, had the sun stood still that hour,
When Marmont and his broken power
Fled from their field of shame!
Spain felt through all her realms the electric blow;
Cadiz in peace expands her gates again;
And Betis, who to bondage long resign'd,
Flow'd mournfully along the silent plain,
Into her joyful bosom unconfin'd,
Receives once more the treasures of the main.

XIII.

What now shall check the Wellesley, when at length
Onward he goes, rejoicing in his strength?
From Douro, from Castille's extended plain,
The foe, a numerous band,
Retire; amid the heights which overhang
Dark Ebro's bed, they think to make their stand.
He reads their purpose, and prevents their speed;
And still as they recede,
Impetuously he presses on their way;
Till by Vittoria's walls they stood at bay,
And drew their battle up in fair array.

XIV.

Vain their array, their valour vain:
There did the practised Frenchman find
A master arm, a master mind!
Behold the veteran army driven
Like dust before the breath of Heaven,
Like leaves before the autumnal wind!
Now, Britain, now thy brow with laurels bind;
Raise now the song of joy for rescued Spain!
And Europe, take thou up the awakening strain—
Glory to God! Deliverance for Mankind!

XV.

From Spain the living spark went forth:
The flame hath caught, the flame is spread!
It warms,—it fires the farthest North.
Behold! the awaken'd Moscovite
Meets the Tyrant in his might; [10]
The Brandenburg, at Freedom's call,
Rises more glorious from his fall;
And Frederic, best and greatest of the name,
Treads in the path of duty and of fame.
See Austria from her painful trance awake!
The breath of God goes forth,—the dry bones shake!
Up Germany!—with all thy nations rise!
Land of the virtuous and the wise,
No longer let that free, that mighty mind,
Endure its shame! She rose as from the dead,
She broke her chains upon the oppressor's head—[11]
Glory to God! Deliverance for Mankind!

XVI.

Open thy gates, O Hanover! display
Thy loyal banners to the day;
Receive thy old illustrious line once more!
Beneath an Upstart's yoke oppress'd,
Long hath it been thy fortune to deplore

That line, whose fostering and paternal sway
So ma● an age thy grateful children blest.
The yoke is broken now!—A mightier hand
Hath dash'd,—in pieces dash'd,—the iron rod.
To meet her Princes, the delivered land
Pours her rejoicing multitudes abroad;
The happy bells from every town and tower,
Roll their glad peals upon the joyful wind;
And from all hearts and tongues, with one consent,
The high thanksgiving strain to Heaven is sent,—
Glory to God! Deliverance for Mankind!

XVII

Egmont and Horn, heard ye that holy cry,
Martyrs of Freedom, from your seats in Heaven?
And William the Deliverer, doth thine eye
Regard from you empyreal realm the land
For which thy blood was given!
What ills hath that poor Country suffered long!
Deceived, despised, and plunder'd, and oppress'd,
Mockery and insult aggravating wrong!
Severely she her errors hath atoned,
And long in anguish groan'd,
Wearing the patient semblance of despair,
While fervent curses rose with every prayer!
In mercy Heaven at length its ear inclined;
The avenging armies of the North draw nigh,
Joy for the injured Hollander,—the cry
Of Orange rends the sky!
All hearts are now in one good cause combined,—
Once more that flag triumphant floats on high,—
Glory to God! Deliverance for Mankind!

XVIII.

When shall the Dove go forth? Oh when
Shall Peace return among the Sons of Men?
Hasten, benignant Heaven, the blessed day!
Justice must go before,
And Retribution must make plain the way;
Force must be crushed by Force,
The power of Evil by the power of Good,
Ere Order bless the suffering world once more
Or Peace return again.
Hold then right on in your auspicious course,
Ye Princes, and ye People, hold right on!
Your task not yet is done:
Pursue the blow,—ye know your foe,—
Complete the happy work so well begun:
Hold on and be your aim with all your strength
Loudly proclaim'd and steadily pursued!
So shall this fatal Tyranny at length
Before the arms of Freedom fall subdued.
Then when the waters of the flood abate,
The Dove her resting-place secure may find:
And France restored, and shaking off her chain,
Shall join the Avengers in the joyful strain,
Glory to God! Deliverance for Mankind!

NOTES.

Note 1, page 498, col. 1.

That no weak heart, no abject mind possessed
Her counsels.

«Can any man of sense,» said the *Edinburgh Review*

«does any plain, unaffected man, above the level of a dri-
velling courtier or a feeble fanatic, dare ● say he can
look at this impending contest, without trembling every
inch of him, for the result?»—*No. XXIV*, p. 441.

With all proper deference to so eminent a critic, I
would venture to observe, that trembling has been
usually supposed to be a symptom of feebleness, and
that the case in point has certainly not belied the re-
ceived opinion.

Note 2 , page 498, col. 1.

And thou, Busaco, on whose sacred height
     The astonish'd Carmelite,
While those unwonted thunders shook his cell,
Join'd with his prayers the fervour of the fight.

Of Busaco, which is now as memorable in the mili-
tary, as it has long been in the monastic history of
Portugal, I have given an account in the second volume
of Omhiana. Dona Bernarda Ferreira's poem upon this
venerable place, contains much interesting and some
beautiful description.   The first intelligence of the
battle which reached England was in a letter written
from this Convent by a Portuguese Commissary.   « I
have the happiness to acquaint you,» said the writer,
« that this night the French lost nine thousand men
near the Convent of Busaco.—I beg you not to consider
this news as a fiction,—for I, from where I am, saw
them fall.   This place appears like the ante-chamber of
Hell.»——What a contrast to the images which the
following extracts present !

Es pequeña aquella Iglesia,
     Mas para pobres bastante ;
     Pobre de todo aderezo
     Con que el rico suele ornarse.
No ay alli plata, ni oro,
     Telas y sedas no valen
     Donde reyna la pobreza,
     Que no para en bienes tales ;
Asperando á los del Cielo
     Los demas tiene por males,
     Y rica de altos deseos
     Menosprecia vanidades.
En el retablo se mira
     El soberano estandarte,
     Lecho donde con la Iglesia
     Quiso Cristo desposarse ;
La tabla donde se salva
     El misero naufragante
     Del piélago de la culpa,
     Y á puerto glorioso sale.
Con perfecion y concierto
     Se aderezan los altares
     (por manos de aquellos santos)
     De bellas flores suaves.
En toscos vasos de corcho
     Lustran texidos con arte
     Los variados ramilletes
     Mas que en el oro el esmalte.
La florida rama verde
     Que en aquellos bosques nace,
     Da colgaduras al templo,
     Y los brocados abate.
En dias de mayor fiesta
     Esto con excesos hacen,
     Y al suelo por alcatifas
     Diversas flores reparten.
Huele el divino aposento
     Hurtando sutil el ayre
     A las rosas y boninas
     Mil olores que derrame.
Humildes estan las celdas
     De aquellos humildes padres,
     Cercando al sacro edificio
     Do tienen su caro amante.

Cada celda muy pequeña
     Encierra probreza grande,
     Que en competencia sus dueño;
     Gustan de mortificarse.
Despues que alli entró el silencio
     No quiso que mas sonase
     Ruido que aquel que forma
     Entre los ramos el ayre ;
El de las fuentes y arroyos,
     Y de las parleras aves,
     Porque si ellos por Dios lloran,
     Ellas sus lágrimas canten.
De corcho tosco las puertas,
     Tambien de pobreza imágen,
     Son mas bellas en sus ojos
     Que los Toscanos portales.
Es su cama estrecha tabla
     Do apenas tendidos caben,
     Porque hasta en ella durmiendo.
     Crucificados descansen.
Una Cruz, y calavera
     Que tienen siempre delante,
     Con ásperas disciplinas
     Teñidas de propria sangre,
Son alhajas de su casa.
     Y en aquellas soledades
     Hablando con sabios mudos
     Suelen tal vez aliviarse ;
Que á los hijos de Theresa
     Tanto los libros aplacen,
     Que en los yermos mas remotos
     Les dan del dia una parte.
Tiene cada qual su huerto
     (porque en él pueda ocuparse)
     De árboles de espino, y flores
     Siempre de olor liberales.
Libres ansi del tumulto
     Que embaraza los mortales,
     Ferverosas oraciones
     Mandan á Dios cada instante.
Sus devotos exercicios
     No se los perturba nadie,
     Ni sus penitencias hallan
     Testigos que las estrañen.
Qual con cadenas de puas
     Tan duras como diamantes,
     Agudas y rigurosas
     Ciñe su afligida carne ;
Qual con cilicios y sogas
     Aspérrimas, intractables,
     De que jamas se les quitan
     Las cavernosas senales.

* * * * * *

Aquel divino desierto
     Que Busaco denomina,
     Y es tambien denominado
     Del árbol de nuestra vida,
Se muestra sembrado á trechos
     De solitarias Ermitas,
     Que en espacios desiguales
     Unas de las otras distan.
Parece tocan las nubes,
     Para servirles de sillas,
     Las que coronando peñas
     Apenas toca la vista.
Yacen otras por los valles
     En las entrañas benignas
     De nuestra madre comun
     Que humilde se les inclina.
Qual en las concavidades
     De las rocas escondida,
     Que labró naturaleza
     Con perfecion infinita.
Qual entre las arboledas
     De verde rama vestida,
     Informándoles de gracias
     Sus formas vegetativas.
Qual del cristalino arroyo
     Las bellas márgenes pisa,
     Por lavar los pies descalzos
     Entre sus cándidas guijas.

Qual en el tronco del árbol
  Dentro en sus cortezas mismas,
  Por vencer en gracia al arte
  Naturaleza fabrica.
Unas aprieta con lazos
  Aquella planta lasciva
  Que hasta las piedras abraza
  Con ser tan duras y frias.
Otras de amarillos musgos
  Por el techo se matizan,
  Verdes, obscuros, y negros,
  Y de color de ceniza.
Toscos alli los portales
  De yerva y moho se pintan,
  Y de salitre se labran
  Que en gotas al agua imita.
Cada Ermitaño á la puerta
  Tiene una pequeña esquila,
  En el ramo de algun árbol
  Donde pendiente se arrima ;
O en el resquicio gracioso
  De alguna piedra metida,
  Y quando toca la Iglesia
  Todas a tocar se aplican.

Note 3, page 498, col. 1.

Bear witness those Old Towers.

Torres Vedras. *Turres Veteres*,—a name so old as to have been given when the Latin tongue was the language of Portugal. This town is said to have been founded by the Turduly, a short time before the commencement of the Christian Æra.

In remembering the lines of Torres Vedras, the opinion of the wise men of the North ought not to be forgotten, « If they (the French) do not make an effort to drive us out of Portugal, it is because we are better there than any where else. We fear they will not leave us on the Tagus many days longer than suits their own purposes.»—*Edinburgh Rev. No. XXVII*, p. 263.

The opinion is delivered with happy precision of language :—Our troops were indeed, to use the same neat, and felicitous expression, *better there than any where else.*

Note 4, page 498, col. 1.

Tagus and Zezere, in the secret night,
Ye saw that host of ruffians take their flight!

Beacons of infamy, they light the way
  Where cowardice and cruelty unite,
To damn with double shame their ignominious flight.

O triumph for the Fiends of lust and wrath !
  Ne'er to be told, yet ne'er to be forgot,
What wanton horrors mark their wrackful path!
  The peasant butcher'd in his ruined cot,
The hoary priest even at the altar shot,
  Childhood and age given o'er to sword and flame,
Woman to infamy ; no crime forgot,
  By which inventive demons might proclaim
Immortal hate to Man, and scorn of God's great name.

The rudest sentinel, in Britain born,
  With horror paused to view the havoc done,
Gave his ; oor crust to feed some wretch forlorn,
  Wiped his stern eye, then fiercer grasp'd his gun.
                Scott's *Vision of Don Roderick.*

No cruelties recorded in history exceed those which were systematically committed by the French during their retreat from Portugal. « Their conduct, (says Lord Wellington in his dispatch of the 14th of March, 1811,) throughout this retreat, has been marked by a barbarity seldom equalled, and never surpassed.

« Even in the towns of Torres Novas, Thomar, and Pernes, in which the head-quarters of some of the corps had been for four months, and in which the inhabitants had been induced by promises of good treatment to remain, they were plundered, and many of their houses destroyed on the night the enemy withdrew from their position ; and they have since burnt every town and village through which they have passed. The Convent of Alcobaça was burnt by order from the French head-quarters. The Bishop's Palace, and the whole town of Leyria, in which General Drouet had had his head-quarters, shared the same fate ; and there is not an inhabitant of the country, of any class or description, who has had any dealing or communication with the French army who has not had reason to repent of it, or to complain of them. This is the mode in which the promises have been performed, and the assurances have been fulfilled, which were held out in the proclamation of the French commander in chief, in which he told the inhabitants of Portugal, that he was not come to make war upon them, but with a powerful army of one hundred and ten thousand men to drive the English into the sea. It is to be hoped, that the example of what has occurred in this country will teach the people of this and other nations what value they ought to place on such promises and assurances, and that there is no security for life or for any thing that renders life valuable, except in decided resistance to the enemy.»

As exact an account of these atrocities was collected as it was possible to obtain,—and that record will for ever make the French name detested in Portugal. In the single diocese of Coimbra, 2969 persons, men, women, and children, were murdered,—every one with some shocking circumstance of aggravated cruelty.— *Nem huma so das 2969 mortes commettidas pelo inimigo, deixou de ser atroz e dolorosissima.* (Breve Memoria dos Estragos Causados no Bispado de Coimbra pelo Exercito Francez, commandado pelo General Massena. Extrahida das Enformaçoens que deram os Reverendos Parocos, e remettida a Junta dos Socorros da Subscripsam Britannica, pelo Reverendo Provisor Governador do mesmo Bispado. p. 12.) Some details are given in this brief Memorial. « A de tels forfaits, » says J. J. Rousseau, « celui qui détourne ses regards est un lâche, un déserteur de la justice: la véritable humanité les envisage pour les connoître, pour les juger, pour les détester.» (*Le Levite d'Ephraim.*) I will not, however, in this place repeat abominations which at once outrage humanity and disgrace human nature.

When the French, in 1792, entered Spire, some of them began to commit excesses which would soon have led to a general sack. Custine immediately ordered a captain, two officers, and a whole company to be shot. This dreadful example, he told the National Convention, he considered as the only means of saving the honour of the French Nation,—and it met with the approbation of the whole army. But the French armies had not then been systematically brutalized. It was reserved for Buonaparte to render them infamous, as well as to lead them to destruction.

The French soldier, says Capmany, is executioner and robber at the same time: he leaves the unhappy wretch who is delivered over to his mercy, naked to the skin,— stripping off the clothes that they may not be torn by the musket-shot !—The pen falls from my hand, and I cannot proceed!

« Para que se junte á esta crueldad la mayor infamia, el soldado Frances es verdugo y ladron en una pieza; deja en cueros vivos al malaventurado que entregan á su discrecion, quitándole la ropa antes que los fusilazos se la destrozen. La pluma se cae de la mano, y no puede proseguir.»—*Centinela contra Franceses, P. 2, p. 35.*

Yet the *Edinburgh Review* says, « the hatred of the name of a Frenchman in Spain has been such as the reality will by no means justify ; and the detestation of the French government has, among the inferior orders, been carried to a pitch wholly unauthorized by its proceedings towards them.» *No XXVII. p. 262.* This passage might be read with astonishment, if any thing absurd, any thing mischievous, or any thing false, could excite surprise when it comes from that quarter.

Note 5, page 498, col. 1.
Onoro's Springs.

Fuentes d'Onoro. This name has sometimes been rendered Fountains of Honour, by an easy mistake, or a pardonable licence.

Note 6, page 498, col. 1.
Knowing that nought could e'er appal
The Spaniards' fortitude.

« The fate of Spain, we think, *is decided,* and that fine and *misguided* country has probably yielded, by this time, to the fate which has fallen on the greater part of continental Europe. *Her European dominions have yielded already to the unrelaxing grasp of the insatiable conqueror.*»—*Edinburgh Review, No XXVI, p. 298.*

« The fundamental position which we ventured to lay down respecting the Spanish question was this ;—that the spirit of the people, however enthusiastic and universal, was in its nature more uncertain and short-lived, more likely to be extinguished by reverses, or to go out of itself amidst the delays of a protracted contest, than the steady, regular, moderate feeling which calls out disciplined troops, and marshals them under known leaders, and supplies them by systematic arrangements:—a proposition so plain and obvious, that if it escaped ridicule as a truism, it might have been reasonably expected to avoid the penalties of heresy and paradox. The event has indeed wofully proved its truth.» —*Edinburgh Rev. No XXVII, p. 246.*

These gentlemen could see no principle of permanence in the character of the Spaniards, and no proof of it in their history ;—and they could discover no principle of dissolution in the system of Buonaparte ;—a system founded upon force and falsehood, in direct opposition to the interest of his own subjects and to the feelings of human nature !

Note 7, page 498, col. 1.
What though the Tyrant, drunk with power,
Might vaunt himself, in impious hour,
Lord and Disposer of this earthly ball?

« Lo he dicho varias veces, y lo repito ahora, que las tres épocas terribles en los anales del mundo son, el diluvio universal, Mahoma, y Buonaparte. Aquel pretendia convertir todas las religiones en una, y este todas las naciones, para ser él su cabeza. Aquel predicaba la unidad de Dios con la cimitarra ; y este no le nombra uno ni trino, pues solo predica, ó hace predicar su propia divinidad, dejándose dar de sus infames y sacrílegos adoradores, los periodistas franceses, el dictado de Todopoderoso. Él mismo se ha llegado á creer tal, y se ha hecho creer la cobardía y vileza de las naciones que se

han dejado subyugar. Solo la España le ha obligado á reconocerse, que no era antes, ni es ahora, sino un hombre, y hombre muy pequeño, á quien la fortuna ciega ha hecho grande á los ojos de los pueblos espantados del terror de su nombre, que miden la grandeza del poder por la de las atrocidades.»—*Centinela contra Franceses, p 48.*

« I have sometimes said, and I repeat it now, that the three terrible epochs in the annals of the World are the General Deluge, Mahommed, and Buonaparte. Mahommed pretended to convert all religions into one, and this man all nations into one, in order to make himself their head. Mahommed preached the unity of God with the scimitar ; and this man neither his Unity nor his Trinity, for he neither preaches, nor causes to be preached, any thing except his own Divinity, letting his infamous and sacrilegious adorers, the French journalists, give him the appellation of Almighty. He has gone so far as to believe himself such, and the cowardice and baseness of the nations who have suffered themselves to be subdued, have made him believe it. Spain alone has compelled him to know himself, that he neither was formerly nor is now any thing more than a mere man, and a very little one, whom blind Fortune has made appear great in the eyes of people astonished at the terror of his name, and measuring the greatness of his power by that of his atrocities.

Note 8, page 498, col. 2.
The Campeador.

The Cid, Rodrigo Diaz de Bivar. The word has been variously explained, but its origin seems to be satisfactorily traced by Verstegan, in his explanation of some of our English surnames.

« Cemp or Kemp, properly one that fighteth hand to hand, whereunto the name in Teutonic of Kemp-fight accordeth, and in French of Combat.

« Certain among the ancient Germans made profession of being Camp-fighters or Kemp-fighters, for all is one ; and among the Danes and Swedes were the like, as Scarcater, Arngrim, Arnerod, Haldan, and sundry others. They were also called Kempanas, whereof is derived our name of Campion, which after the French orthography some pronounce Champion.»

« Dene or Den is the termination of sundry of our surnames, as for example of Camden, which I take anciently to have been Campden, and signifieth the Dene or Dale belonging to some Cemp or Camp-fighter (for both is one) in our now used language called a Champion, but in the Teutonic a Campion. A Campden may also have been some place appointed for Campions, Combat-fighters, or men of arms to encounter each other. And so the place became afterward to be the surname of him and his family that owned it, as others in like sort have done.»

« Kemp, — of his profession of being a Kemper or Combat-fighter, as divers in old time among our ancestors were.»

Note 9, page 498, col. 2.
Vengeance was the word.

This feeling is forcibly expressed by Capmany. « O Vísperas Sicilianas tan famosas en la historia, quando os podremos acompanar con completas, para que los Angeles canten laudes en el Cielo.»—*Centinela, contra Franceses, p. 96.*

O Sicilian Vespers! so famous in history, when shall we be able to accompany you with Complines, that the Angels may sing Lauds in Heaven?

Note 10, page 499, col. 1.

Behold! the awaken'd Moscovite
Meets the tyrant in his might.

Ecce iterum Crispinus! What says the *Edinburgh Review* concerning Russia? « Considering how little that power has shown itself capable of effecting for the salvation of Europe,—how wretched the state of its subjects is under the present government,—how trifling an acquisition of strength the common enemy could expect to obtain from the entire possession of its resources, we acknowledge that we should contemplate with great composure any change which might lay the foundation of future improvement, and scatter the forces of France over the dominion of the Czars.»— *No. XXVIII*, p. 460.

This is a choice passage. The reasoning is worthy of the writer's judgment, the feeling perfectly consistent with his *liberality*, and the conclusion as consistent with his politics.

Note 11, page 499, col. 1.

Up Germany———
——— She rose as from the dead;
She broke her chains upon the oppressor's head.

Hear the Edinburgh Reviewer! « It would be as chimerical to expect a mutiny amongst the vassal states of France who are the most impatient of her yoke, as amongst the inhabitants of Bordeaux, or the conscripts of the years 1808 and 1809. In making this comparison, we are indeed putting the case much more strongly against France than the facts warrant, for with the exception of Holland, and the States into which the conscription has been introduced, either immediately. or by means of large requisitions of men made to their Government,[1] the changes effected by the French invasion have been favourable to the individual happiness of the inhabitants,[2] so that the hatred of France is liable to considerable diminution, inasmuch as the national antipathy and spirit of independence are gradually undermined by the solid benefits which the change of masters has conferred.»—*No. XXVIII*, p. 458.

Great as a statesman, profound as a philosopher, amiable as an optimist of the Pangloss school,—but not altogether fortunate as a Prophet!

POSTSCRIPT.

As a proper accompaniment to the preceding Notes, upon their republication, I subjoin an extract from a *William-Smithic* epistle, begun a few years ago upon sufficient provocation, but left unfinished, because better employments delayed its completion till the offence, gross as it was, seemed no longer deserving of a thought.

. . . .

My fortune has been somewhat remarkable in this respect, that, bestowing less attention than most men upon contemporary literature, I am supposed to concern myself with it in a degree which would leave me

[1] N.B. These little exceptions include all the countries which were annexed to the French Empire, all Italy, and all the States of the Confederation of the Rhine.
[2] Particularly the commercial part of them.

no time for any worthier occupation. Half the persons who are wounded in the *Quarterly Review* fix upon me as the object of their resentment; some, because they are conscious of having deserved chastisement at my hands; others, because they give credit to an empty report, a lying assertion, or their own conceited sagacity in discovering a writer by his style. As for the former, they flatter themselves egregriously in supposing that I should throw away my anger upon such subjects. But by the latter I would willingly have it understood, that I heartily disapprove the present fashion of criticism, and sincerely wish that you, Sir, and your friend, had taken out an exclusive patent for it, when you brought it into vogue.

With regard to literary assailants, I should as little think of resenting their attacks in anger, as of making war upon midges and mosquitos. I have therefore never noticed your amiable colleague in his critical capacity. Let him blunder and misquote, and misrepresent, and contradict himself in the same page, or in the same sentence, with as much ingenuity as he will: "'T is his vocation, Hal!" and some allowances must be made for habit. I remember what Lord Anson's linguist said to him at Canton, upon the detection of some notable act of dishonesty: "*Chinaman very great rogue truly: but have fashion: no can help.*" Concerning *me*, and any composition of mine, it is impossible that this gentleman can write wisely unless his nature should undergo a radical change; for it is written in the wisest book which ever proceeded from mere humanity, that « into a malicious soul, wisdom shall not enter.»

You may have seen a mastiff of the right English breed assailed by a little, impertinent, noisy, meddling cur, who runs behind him, snapping and barking at his heels, and sometimes gets staggered by a chance whisk of his tail. The mastiff continues his way peaceably; or if he condescends to notice the yelper, it is only by stopping half a minute, and lifting his leg over him. Just such, Sir, is the notice which I bestow upon your colleague in his critical character.

But for F. J., *Philomath, and Professor of the Occult Sciences*, he is a grave personage, whose political and prophetical pretensions entitle him to high consideration in these days. He is as great a man as Lilly in the time of the Commonwealth, or as Partridge after him. It is well known what infinite pains he bestowed in casting the nativities of Lord Wellington, Buonaparte, and the Emperor of Russia; all for the good of mankind! and it is also notorious that he mistook the aspects, and made some very unfortunate errors in his predictions. At a time when he was considerably indisposed in consequence of this mortification, I took the liberty of administering to him a dose of his own words, mixed, perhaps, Sir, with a few of yours, for you were his fellow-student in astrology, and are known to have assisted him in these his calculations. The medicine was given in the form of extract; but the patient could not have used more wry faces had it been extract of coloquintida. And indeed it produced a most un pleasant effect. Ever since that time his paroxysms have been more violent, and he has been troubled with occasional ravings, accompanied with periodical discharges of bile in its most offensive state. Nevertheless, dreadfully bilious as he is, and tormented with acrid humours, it is hoped that by a cool diet, by the proper use of refrigerants, above all, by paying due attention to the state of the *primæ viæ*, and observing a strict abstinence from the *Quarterly Review*, the danger of a *cholera morbus* may be averted.

I have not been travelling out of the record while thus incidentally noticing a personage with whom you, Sir, are more naturally and properly associated than I have been with Mr Wordsworth, this your colleague and you being the Gog and Magog of the Edinburgh Review. Had it not been for a difference of opinion upon political points between myself and certain writers in that journal who laid claim to the faculty of the second sight, I suspect that I should never have incurred your hostility. What those points of difference were I must here be permitted to set forth for the satisfaction of those readers who may not be so well acquainted with them as you are: they related to the possibility of carrying on the late war to an honourable and successful termination.

It was in our state of feeling, Sir, as well as in our state of knowledge that we differed, in our desires as much as in our judgment. They predicted for us nothing but disgrace and defeat; *predicted* is the word; for they themselves assured us that they were *« seriously occupied with the destinies of Europe and of mankind;»—*

As who should say I am Sir Oracle!

They ridiculed « *the romantic hopes of the English nation*,» and imputed the spirit by which the glory of that nation has been raised to its highest point, and the deliverance of Europe accomplished, to « *the tricks of a paltry and interested party.*» They said that events had « *verified their predictions*,» had « *more than justified their worst forebodings.*» They told us in 1810 that the fate of Spain was *decided*, and that that «*misguided*» country (misguided in having ventured to resist the most insolent usurpation that ever was attempted) « *had yielded to the Conqueror.*» This manner of speaking of an event in the preter-pluperfect tense, before it has come to pass, may be either a slight grammatical slip, or a prophetical figure of speech: but as old Dr Eachard says, « I hate all small ambiguous surmises, all quivering and mincing conjectures: give me the lusty and bold thinker, who when he undertakes to prophecy, does it punctually.»« *It would be blood-thirsty and cruel*,» they said, « *to foment petty insurrections*, (meaning the war in Spain and Portugal,) *after the only contest is over from which any good can spring in the present unfortunate state of affairs.*» *France has conquered Europe. This is the melancholy truth. Shut our eyes to it as we may, there can be no doubt about the matter. For the present, peace and submission must be the lot of the vanquished.*» « *Let us hear no more of objections to a Buonaparte ruling in Spain.*»

Harry, the wish was father to that thought!

They told us that if Lord Wellington was not driven out of Portugal, it was because the French government thought him « *better there than any where else.*» They told us they were prepared to « *contemplate with great composure*» the conquest of Russia, by Buonaparte, as a « change which would lay the foundation of future improvement in the dominions of the Czars.»—

Si mens sit læta tibi crederis esse propheta,

says an old Leonine rhymester.—And as for expecting

« a MUTINY (hear, Germany! for so they qualified it!) *amongst the vassal states of France, it would be as chimerical*,» they said, « *as to expect one amongst the inhabitants of Bordeaux.*» And here these lucky prophets were peculiarly felicitous; the inhabitants of Bordeaux having been the first people in France who threw off the yoke of Buonaparte's tyranny, and mounted the white cockade.

Omnia jam fiunt, fieri quæ posse negabam.

Poor Oracle! the face is double-bronzed; and yet it is but a wooden head!

I stood upon firm ground, while they were sticking in the Slough of Despond. *Hinc illæ lachrymæ!* I charged them at the time with ignorance, presumption, and pusillanimity. And now, Sir, I ask of you, were they or were they not ignorant? Here are their assertions!—Were they or were they not presumptuous? Here are their predictions!—Were they or were they not pusillanimous? Have they or have they not been confuted and confounded, and exposed, and shamed, and stultified by the event?

They who know me will bear witness, that before a rumour of war was heard from the Peninsula, I had looked toward that quarter as the point where we might hope first to see the horizon open; and that from the hour in which the struggle commenced, I never doubted of its final success, provided England should do its duty: this confidence was founded upon a knowledge of the country and the people, and upon the principles which were then and there first brought into action against the enemy. At the time when every effort was made (as you, Sir, well know) to vilify and disgust our allies, to discourage the public, to impede the measures of government, to derange its finances, and thereby cut off its means, to paralyse the arm and deaden the heart of England;—when we were told of the irresistible power and perfect policy of Buonaparte, the consummate skill of his Generals, and the invincibility of his armies, my language was this: «The one business of England is to abate the power of France: that power she must beat down or fall herself; that power she will beat down, if she do but strenuously put forth her own mighty means.» And again,—« For our soldiers to equal our seamen, it is only necessary for them to be equally well commanded. They have the same heart and soul, as well as the same flesh and blood. Too much, indeed, may be exacted from them in a retreat: but set their face toward a foe, and there is nothing within the reach of human achievement which they cannot perform.» And again; «Carry on the war with all the heart, and with all the soul, and with all the strength of this mighty empire, and you will beat down the power of France.» Was I wrong, Sir? Or has the event corresponded to this confidence?

Ἀμέραι ἐπίλοιποι
Μάρτυρες σοφώτατοι.

Bear witness Torres Vedras, Salamanca, and Vittoria! Bear witness Orthes and Thoulouse! Bear witness Waterloo, and that miserable tyrant, who was then making and unmaking kings with a breath, and now frets upon the rock of St Helena, like a tiger in his cage!

. . . . .

Carmina Aulica,

WRITTEN IN 1814, ON THE ARRIVAL OF THE ALLIED SOVEREIGNS
IN ENGLAND.

Εχω χαλά τε φράσαι, τόλμα τέ μοι
Εὐθεῖα γλῶσσαν ὀρνύει λέγειν.
PINDAR. *Olymp.* XIII.

ODE

TO HIS

ROYAL HIGHNESS THE PRINCE REGENT

OF THE UNITED KINGDOM OF GREAT BRITAIN
AND IRELAND.

I.

PRINCE of the mighty Isle!
Proud day for thee and for thy kingdoms this,
When Britain round her spear
The olive garland twines, by Victory won.

II.

Rightly mayst thou rejoice,
For in a day of darkness and of storms,
An evil day, a day of woe,
To thee the sceptre fell.
The Continent was leagued,
Its numbers wielded by one will,
Against the mighty Isle;
All shores were hostile to the Red-Cross flag,
All ports against it closed;
Save where, behind their ramparts driven,
The Spaniard, and the faithful Portugal,
Each on the utmost limits of his land,
Invincible of heart,
Stood firm, and put their trust
In their good cause and thee.

III.

Such perils menaced from abroad,
At home worse dangers compassed thee,
Where shallow counsellors,
A weak but clamorous crew,
Pester'd the land, and with their withering breath
Poison'd the public ear.
For peace, the feeble raised their factious cry:
Oh, madness, to resist
The Invincible in arms!
Seek the peace-garland from his dreadful hand!
And at the Tyrant's feet
They would have knelt, to take
The wreath of aconite for Britain's brow.
Prince of the mighty Isle!
Rightly mayst thou rejoice,
For in the day of danger thou didst turn
From their vile counsels thine indignant heart;
Rightly mayst thou rejoice,

When Britain round her spear
The olive-garland twines, by Victory won.

IV.

Rejoice, thou mighty Isle,
Queen of the Seas, rejoice!
Ring round, ye merry bells,
Till every steeple rock,
And the wide air grow giddy with your joy!
Flow, streamers, to the breeze:
And ye victorious banners, to the sun
Unroll the proud Red-Cross!
Now let the anvil rest;
Shut up the loom; and open the school-doors,
That young and old may with festivities
Hallow for memory through all after years
This memorable time:
This memorable time,
When Peace, long absent, long deplored, returns!
Not as vile Faction would have brought her home,
Her countenance for shame abased,
In servile weeds array'd,
Submission leading her,
Fear, Sorrow, and Repentance following close;
And War, scarce deigning to conceal
Beneath the mantle's folds his armed plight,
Dogging her steps with deadly eye intent,
Sure of his victim, and in devilish joy
Laughing behind the mask.

V.

Not thus doth Peace return!—
A blessed visitant she comes :—
Honour in his right hand
Doth lead her like a bride,
And Victory goes before;
Hope, Safety, and Prosperity, and Strength,
Come in her joyful train.
Now let the churches ring
With high thanksgiving songs,
And the full organ pour
Its swelling peals to Heaven,
The while the grateful nation bless in prayer
Their Warriors and their Statesmen and their Prince,
Whose will, whose mind, whose arm
Have thus with happy end their efforts crown'd.
Prince of the mighty Isle,
Rightly mayst thou rejoice,
When Britain round her spear
The olive garland twines, by Victory won.

VI.

Enjoy thy triumph now,
Prince of the mighty Isle!
Enjoy the rich reward, so rightly due,
When rescued nations, with one heart and voice,
Thy counsels bless and thee.
Thou on thine own Firm-Island seest the while,
As if the tales of old Romance
Were but to typify these splendid days,
Princes and Potentates,
And Chiefs renown'd in arms,
From their great enterprise achieved,
In friendship and in joy collected here.

VII.

Rejoice, thou mighty Isle!
Queen of the Seas, rejoice!
For ne'er in elder nor in later times
Have such illustrious guests
Honour'd thy silver shores.
No such assemblage shone in Edward's hall,
Nor brighter triumphs graced his glorious reign.
Prince of the mighty Isle,
Proud day for thee and for thy kingdoms this!
Rightly mayst thou rejoice,
When Britain round her spear
The olive garland twines, by Victory won.

VIII.

Yet in the pomp of these festivities,
One mournful thought will rise within thy mind—
The thought of Him who sits
In mental as in visual darkness lost.
How had his heart been fill'd
With deepest gratitude to Heaven,
Had he beheld this day!
O King of kings, and Lord of lords,
Thou who hast visited thus heavily
The anointed head,
Oh! for one little interval,
One precious hour,
Remove the blindness from his soul,
That he may know it all,
And bless thee ere he die!

IX.

Thou also shouldst have seen
This harvest of thy hopes,
Thou whom the guilty act
Of a great spirit overthrown,
Sent to thine early grave in evil hour!
Forget not him, my country, in thy joy!
But let thy grateful hand
With laurel garlands hang
The tomb of Perceval.
Virtuous, and firm, and wise,
The Ark of Britain in her darkest day
He steer'd through stormy seas;
And long shall Britain hold his memory dear,
And faithful History give
His meed of lasting praise.

X.

That earthly meed shall his compeers enjoy,
Britain's true counsellors,
Who see with just success their counsels crown'd.

They have their triumph now, to him denied.
Proud day for them is this!
Prince of the mighty Isle!
Proud day for them and thee,
When Britain round her spear
The olive garland twines, by Victory won.

ODE

TO HIS IMPERIAL MAJESTY

ALEXANDER THE FIRST, EMPEROR OF ALL THE RUSSIAS.

I.

CONQUEROR, Deliverer, Friend of human-kind,
The free, the happy Island welcomes thee!
Thee from thy wasted realms,
So signally revenged;
From Prussia's rescued plains;
From Dresden's field of slaughter, where the ball
Which struck Moreau's dear life,
Was turn'd from thy more precious head aside;
From Leipsic's dreadful day,
From Elbe, and Rhine, and Seine,
In thy career of conquest overpast:
From the proud Capital
Of haughty France subdued,
Then to her rightful line of Kings restored;
Thee, Alexander! thee, the Great, the Good,
The Glorious, the Beneficent, the Just,
Thee to her honour'd shores
The mighty Island welcomes in her joy.

II.

Six-score full years have past,
Since to these friendly shores
Thy famous ancestor,
Illustrious PETER came.
Wise traveller, He, who over Europe went,
Marking the ways of men;
That so to his dear country, which then rose
Among the nations in uncultured strength,
He might bear back the stores
Of elder polity,
Its sciences and arts.
Little did then the industrious German think,—
The soft Italian, lapt in luxury,—
Helvetia's mountain sons, of freedom proud,—
The patient Hollander,
Prosperous and warlike then,—
Little thought they that in that farthest North,
From PETER's race should the Deliverer spring,
Destined by Heaven to save
Art, Learning, Industry,
Beneath the bestial hoof of Godless might
All trampled in the dust.
As little did the French,
Vaunting the power of their Great Monarch then,
(His schemes of wide ambition yet uncheck'd),
As little did they think,
That from rude Moscovy the stone should come,
To smite their huge Colossus, which bestrode
The subject Continent;
And from its feet of clay,

Breaking the iron limbs and front of brass,
Strew the rejoicing Nations with the wreck.

III.

Rous'd as thou wert with insult and with wrong,
Who should have blamed thee if, in high-wrought
mood
Of vengeance and the sense of injured power,
Thou from the flames which laid
The City of thy Fathers in the dust,
Hadst bid a spark be brought,
And borne it in thy tent,
Religiously by night and day preserved,
Till on Montmartre's height
When open to thine arms,
Her last defence o'erthrown,
The guilty city lay,
Thou hadst call'd every Russian of thine host
To light his flambeau at the sacred flame,
And sent them through her streets,
And wrapt her roofs and towers,
Temples and palaces,
Her wealth and boasted spoils,
In one wide flood of fire,
Making the hated Nation feel herself
The miseries she had spread.

IV.

Who should have blamed the Conqueror for that deed?
Yea, rather would not one exulting cry
Have risen from Elbe to Nile,
How is the Oppressor fallen!
Moscow's re-rising walls
Had rung with glad acclaim;
Thanksgiving hymns had fill'd
Tyrol's rejoicing vales;
How is the Oppressor fallen!
The Germans in their grass-grown marts had met
To celebrate the deed;
Holland's still waters had been starr'd
With festive lights, reflected there
From every house and hut,
From every town and tower;
The Iberian and the Lusian's injured realms,
From all their mountain-holds,
From all their ravaged fields,
From cities sack'd, from violated fanes,
And from the sanctuary of every heart,
Had pour'd that pious strain,
How is the Oppressor fallen!
Righteous art thou, O Lord!
Thou Zaragoza, from thy sepulchres
Hadst join'd the hymn; and from thine ashes thou,
Manresa, faithful still!
The blood that calls for vengeance in thy streets
Madrid, and Porto thine,
And that which from the beach
Of Tarragona sent its cry to Heaven,
Had rested then appeased.
Orphans had clapt their hands,
And widows would have wept exulting tears,
And childless parents with a bitter joy
Have blest the avenging deed.

V.

But thou hadst seen enough
Of horrors,—amply hadst avenged mankind.

Witness that dread retreat,
When God and nature smote
The Tyrant in his pride,
No wider ruin overtook
Sennacherib's impious host;
Nor when the frantic Persian led
His veterans to the Lybian sands;
Nor when united Greece
O'er the barbaric power that victory won
Which Europe yet may bless,
A fouler Tyrant cursed the groaning earth,—
A fearfuller destruction was dispensed.
Victorious armies followed on his flight;
On every side he met
The Cossacks' dreadful spear;
On every side he saw
The injured nation rise,
Invincible in arms.
What myriads, victims of one wicked will,
Spent their last breath in curses on his head,
There where the soldiers' blood
Froze in the festering wound;
And nightly the cold moon
Saw sinking thousands in the snow lie down,
Whom there the morning found
Stiff, as their icy bed.

VI.

Rear high the monument!
In Moscow and in proud Petropolis,
The brazen trophy build;
Cannon on cannon piled,.
Till the huge column overtop your towers!
From France the Tyrant brought
These instruments of death
To work your overthrow!
He left them in his flight
To form the eternal record of his own.
Raise, Russia, with thy spoils,
A nobler monument
Than e'er imperial Rome
Built in her plenitude of pride and power!
Still Alexander on the banks of Seine,
Thy noblest monument
For future ages stands—
Paris subdued and spared.

VII.

Conqueror, Deliverer, Friend of human-kind,
The free, the happy Island welcomes thee!
Thee, Alexander! thee, the Great, the Good,
The Glorious, the Beneficent, the Just!
Thee to her honour'd shores
The mighty Island welcomes in her joy.

ODE

TO HIS MAJESTY,

FREDERICK WILLIAM THE FOURTH, KING OF PRUSSIA.

I.

Welcome to England, to the happy Isle,
Brave Prince of gallant people! Welcome Thou,
In adverse as in prosperous fortunes tried!

Frederick, the well-beloved!
Greatest and best of that illustrious name,
Welcome to these free shores!
In glory art thou come,
Thy victory perfect, thy revenge complete.

II.

Enough of sorrow hast thou known,
Enough of evil hath thy realm endured,
Oppress'd but not debased,
When thine indignant soul,
Long suffering, bore its weight of heaviest woe.
But still, through that dark day
Unsullied Honour was thy counsellor;
And Hope, that had its trust in Heaven,
And in the heart of man
Its strength, forsook thee not.
Thou hadst thy faithful people's love,
The sympathy of noble minds;
And wistfully, as one
Who through the weary night has long'd for day
Looks eastward for the dawn,
So Germany to thee
Turn'd in her bondage her imploring eyes.

III.

Oh, grief of griefs, that Germany,
The wise, the virtuous land,
The land of mighty minds,
Should bend beneath the frothy Frenchman's yoke!
Oh, grief of griefs, to think
That she should groan in bonds,
She who had blest all nations with her gifts!
There had the light of Reformation risen,
The light of Knowledge there was burning clear.
Oh, grief, that her unhappy sons
Should toil and bleed and die,
To quench that sacred light,
The wretched agents of a tyrant's will!
How often hath their blood
In his accursed cause
Reek'd on the Spaniard's blade!
Their mangled bodies fed
The wolves and eagles of the Pyrenees;
Or stiffening in the snows of Moscovy,
Amid the ashes of the watch-fire lay,
Where dragging painfully their frozen limbs,
With life's last effort in the flames they fell.

IV.

Long, Frederick, didst thou bear
Her sorrows and thine own;
Seven miserable years
In patience didst thou feed thy heart with hope;
Till, when the arm of God
Smote the blaspheming Tyrant in his pride,
And Alexander with the voice of power
Raised the glad cry, Deliverance for Mankind,
First of the Germans, Prussia broke her chains.

V.

Joy, joy for Germany,
For Europe, for the World,
When Prussia rose in arms!
Oh, what a spectacle
For present and for future times was there,

When for the public need
Wives gave their marriage rings,
And mothers, when their sons
The Band of Vengeance join'd,
Bade them return victorious from the field,
Or with their country fall.

VI.

Twice o'er the field of death
The trembling scales of Fate hung equipoised:
For France, obsequious to her Tyrant still,
Mighty for evil, put forth all her power;
And still beneath his hateful banners driven,
Against their father-land
Unwilling Germans bore unnatural arms.
What though the Boaster made his temples ring
With vain thanksgivings for each doubtful day,—
What though with false pretence of peace
His old insidious arts he tried,—
The spell was broken! Austria threw her sword
Into the inclining scale,
And Leipsic saw the wrongs
Of Germany avenged.

VII.

Ne'er till that awful time had Europe seen
Such multitudes in arms;
Nor ever had the rising Sun beheld
Such mighty interests of mankind at stake;
Nor o'er so wide a scene
Of slaughter e'er had Night her curtain closed.
There, on the battle-field,
With one accord the grateful monarchs knelt,
And raised their voice to Heaven;
« The cause was thine, O Lord!
O Lord! thy hand was here!»
What Conquerors e'er deserved
So proud, so pure a joy!
It was a moment when the exalted soul
Might almost wish to burst its mortal bounds,
Lest all of life to come
Vapid and void should seem
After that high-wrought hour.

VIII.

But thou hadst yet more toils,
More duties and more triumphs yet in store.
Elbe must not bound thine arms!
Nor on the banks of Rhine
Thine eagles check their flight;
When o'er that barrier stream,
Awakened Germany
Drove her invaders with such rout and wreck
As overtook the impious Gaul of old,
Laden with plunder, and from Delphi driven.

IX.

Long had insulting France
Boasted her arms invincible,
Her soil inviolate:
At length the hour of retribution comes!
Avenging nations on all sides move on;
In Gascony the flag of England flies,
Triumphant, as of yore,
When sable Edward led his peerless host.
Behold the Spaniard and the Portugal,

For cities burnt, for violated fanes,
For murders, massacres,
All monstrous, all unutterable crimes,
Demanding vengeance with victorious cries,
Pour from the Pyrenees.
The Russian comes, his eye on Paris fix'd,
The flames of Moscow present to his heart;
The Austrian to efface
Ulm, Austerlitz, and Wagram's later shame;
Rejoicing Germany
With all her nations swells the avenging train;
And in the field and in the triumph first,
Thy banner, Frederick, floats.

X.

Six weeks in daily strife
The veteran Blucher bore the brunt of war.
Glorious old man,
The last and greatest of his master's school,
Long may he live to hear
The people bless his name!
Late be it ere the wreath
That crowns his silver hair
Adorn his monument!
Glorious old man,
How oft hath he discomfited
The boasted chiefs of France,
And foil'd her vaunting Tyrant's desperate rage!

Glorious old man,
Who from Silesia's fields,
O'er Elbe, and Rhine, and Seine,
From victory to victory marching on,
Made his heroic way; till at the gates
Of Páris, open'd by his arms, he saw
His King triumphant stand.

XI.

Bear back the sword of Frederick now!
The sword which France amid her spoils display'd,
Proud trophy of a day ignobly won.
With laurels wreathe the sword;
Bear it in triumph back,
Thus gloriously regain'd!
And when thou lay'st it in its honour'd place,
O Frederick, well-beloved,
Greatest and best of that illustrious name,
Lay by its side thine own,
A holier relic there!

XII.

Frederick, the well-beloved!
Welcome to these free shores,
To England welcome, to the happy Isle!
In glory art thou come,
Thy victory perfect, thy revenge complete.

The Lay of the Laureate.

CARMEN NUPTIALE.

TO HER ROYAL HIGHNESS THE PRINCESS CHARLOTTE

The following Poem is Dedicated

WITH PROFOUND RESPECT BY, HER ROYAL HIGHNESS'S MOST DUTIFUL
AND MOST DEVOTED SERVANT,

ROBERT SOUTHEY.

PROEM.

I.

THERE was a time when all my youthful thought
Was of the Muse; and of the Poet's fame,
How fair it flourisheth and fadeth not,—
Alone enduring, when the Monarch's name
Is but an empty sound, the Conqueror's bust
Moulders and is forgotten in the dust.

II.

How best to build the imperishable lay
Was then my daily care, my dream by night;
And early in adventurous essay
My spirit imped her wings for stronger flight;
Fair regions Fancy opened to my view,—
« There lies thy path, she said; do thou that path pursue!

III.

« For what hast thou to do with wealth or power,
Thou whom rich Nature at thy happy birth
Blest in her bounty with the largest dower
That Heaven indulges to a child of Earth,—
Then when the sacred Sisters for their own
Baptized thee in the springs of Helicon!

IV.

« They promised for thee that thou shouldst eschew
All low desires, all empty vanities;
That thou shouldst, still to Truth and Freedom true,
The applause or censure of the herd despise;
And in obedience to their impulse given,
Walk in the light of Nature and of Heaven.

V.

« Along the World's high-way let others crowd,
  Jostling and moiling on through dust and heat;
Far from the vain, the vicious, and the proud,
  Take thou content in solitude thy seat;
To noble ends devote thy sacred art,
And nurse for better worlds thine own immortal part! »

VI.

Praise to that Power who from my earliest days,
  Thus taught me what to seek and what to shun;
Who turned my footsteps from the crowded ways,
  Appointing me my better course to run
In solitude, with studious leisure blest,
The mind unfettered, and the heart at rest.

VII.

For therefore have my days been days of joy,
  And all my paths are paths of pleasantness:
And still my heart, as when I was a boy,
  Doth never know an ebb of cheerfulness;
Time, which matures the intellectual part,
Hath tinged my hairs with grey, but left untouched my
                                                     heart.

VIII.

Sometimes I soar where Fancy guides the rein,
  Beyond this visible diurnal sphere;
But most with long and self-approving pain,
  Patient pursue the historian's task severe;
Thus in the ages which are past I live,
And those which are to come my sure reward will give.

IX.

Yea in this now, while Malice frets her hour,
  Is foretaste given me of that meed divine;
Here undisturbed in this sequestered bower,
  The friendship of the good and wise is mine;
And that green wreath which decks the Bard when dead,
That laureate garland crowns my living head.

X.

That wreath which in Eliza's golden days
  My master dear, divinest Spenser wore,
That which rewarded Drayton's learned lays,
  Which thoughtful Ben and gentle Daniel bore,—
Grin Envy, through thy ragged mask of scorn!
In honour it was given, with honour it is worn!

XI.

Proudly I raised the high thanksgiving strain
  Of victory in a rightful cause achieved;
For which I long had looked and not in vain,
  As one who with firm faith and undeceived,
In history and the heart of man could find
Sure presage of deliverance for mankind.

XII.

Proudly I offered to the royal ear
  My song of joy when war's dread work was done,
And glorious Britain round her satiate spear
  The olive garland twined by Victory won;
Exulting as became me in such cause,
I offered to the Prince his People's just applause.

XIII.

And when, as if the tales of old Romance
  Were but to typify his splendid reign,
Princes and Potentates from conquered France,
  And chiefs in arms approved, a peerless train,
Assembled at his Court,—my duteous lays
Preferred a welcome of enduring praise.

XIV.

And when that last and most momentous hour,
  Beheld the re-risen cause of evil yield
To the Red Cross and England's arm of power,
  I sung of Waterloo's unequalled field,
Paying the tribute of a soul embued
With deepest joy devout and awful gratitude.

XV.

Such strains beseemed me well. But how shall I
  To hymeneal numbers tune the string,
Who to the trumpet's martial symphony,
  And to the mountain gales am wont to sing?
How may these unaccustomed accents suit
To the sweet dulcimer and courtly lute?

XVI.

Fitter for me the lofty strain severe,
  That calls for vengeance for mankind opprest;
Fitter the songs that youth may love to hear,
  Which warm and elevate the throbbing breast;
Fitter for me with meed of solemn verse,
In reverence to adorn the hero's hearse.

XVII.

But then my Master dear arose to mind,
  He on whose song while yet I was a boy,
My spirit fed, attracted to its kind,
  And still insatiate of the growing joy;—
He on whose tomb these eyes were wont to dwell,
With inward yearnings which I may not tell;

XVIII.

He whose green bays shall bloom for ever young,
  And whose dear name whenever I repeat,
Reverence and love are trembling on my tongue;
  Sweet Spenser,—sweetest Bard; yet not more sweet
Than pure was he, and not more pure than wise,
High Priest of all the Muses' mysteries.

XIX.

I called to mind that mighty Master's song,
  When he brought home his beautifullest bride,
And Mulla murmured her sweet undersong,
  And Mole with all his mountain woods replied;
Never to mortal lips a strain was given,
More rich with love, more redolent of Heaven.

XX.

His cup of joy was mantling to the brim,
  Yet solemn thoughts enhanced his deep delight;
A holy feeling filled his marriage-hymn,
  And Love aspired with Faith a heavenward flight.
And hast not thou, my Soul, a solemn theme?
I said, and mused until I fell into a dream.

THE DREAM.

I.

METHOUGHT I heard a stir of hasty feet,
  And horses tramped and coaches rolled along,
And there were busy voices in the street,
  As if a multitude were hurrying on;
A stir it was which only could befall
Upon some great and solemn festival.

II.

Such crowds I saw, and in such glad array,
  It seemed some general joy had filled the land;
Age had a sunshine on its cheek that day,
  And children, tottering by the mother's hand,
Too young to ask why all this joy should be,
Partook it, and rejoiced for sympathy.

III.

The shops, that no dull care might intervene,
  Were closed; the doors within were lined with heads;
Glad faces were at every window seen,
  And from the clustered house-tops and the leads,
Others who took their stand in patient row,
Looked down upon the crowds that swarmed below.

IV.

And every one of all that numerous throng
  On head or breast a marriage symbol bore;
The war-horse proudly as he paced along
  Those joyous colours in his forelock wore,
And arched his stately neck as for delight,
To show his mane thus pompously bedight.

V.

From every church the merry bells rung round
  With gladdening harmony heard far and wide;
In many a mingled peal of swelling sound,
  The hurrying music came on every side;
And banners from the steeples waved on high,
And streamers fluttered in the sun and sky.

VI.

Anon the cannon's voice in thunder spake,
  Westward it came, the East returned the sound;
Burst after burst the innocuous thunders brake,
  And rolled from side to side with quick rebound.
O happy land, where that terrific voice
Speaks but to bid all habitants rejoice!

VII.

Thereat the crowd rushed forward one and all,
  And I too in my dream was borne along.
Eftsoon, methought, I reached a festal hall,
  Where guards in order ranged repelled the throng,
But I had entrance through that guarded door,
In honour to the laureate crown I wore.

VIII.

That spacious hall was hung with trophies round,
  Memorials proud of many a well-won day:
The flag of France there trailed toward the ground;
  There in captivity her Eagles lay,
And under each in aye-enduring gold,
One well-known word its fatal story told.

IX.

There read I Nile conspicuous from afar,
  And Egypt and Maida there were found;
And Copenhagen there and Trafalgar;
  Vimeiro and Busaco's day renowned;
There too was seen Barrosa's bloody name,
And Albuhera, dear-bought field of fame.

X.

Yon spoils from boastful Massena were won;
  Those Marmont left in that illustrious fight
By Salamanca, when too soon the sun
  Went down, and darkness hid the Frenchman's flight.
These from Vittoria's plain the Wellesley bore,
When from the Intruder's head Spain's stolen crown he tore.

XI.

These on Pyrene's aweful heights were gained,
  The trophies of that memorable day,
When deep with blood her mountain springs were stained.
  Above the clouds and lightnings of that fray,
Wheeling afar the affrighted eagles fled;
At eve the wolves came forth and preyed upon the dead.

XII.

And blood stained flags were here from Orthies borne,
  Trampled by France beneath her flying feet;
And what before Thoulouse from Soult were torn
  When the stern Marshal met his last defeat,
Yielding once more to Britain's arm of might,
And Wellington in mercy spared his flight.

XIII.

There hung the Eagles which with victory flushed,
  From Fleurus and from Ligny proudly flew,
To see the Usurper's high-swoln fortune crushed
  For ever on the field of Waterloo,—
Day of all days, surpassing in its fame
  All fields of elder or of later name!

XIV.

There too the painter's universal art,
  Each story told to all beholders' eyes;
And Sculpture there had done her fitting part,
  Bidding the forms perdurable arise
Of those great Chiefs, who in the field of fight
Had best upheld their country's sacred right.

XV.

There stood our peerless Edward, gentle-souled,
  The Sable Prince, of chivalry the flower;
And that Plantagenet of sterner mould,
  He who the conquered crown of Gallia wore;
And Blake, and Nelson, Glory's favourite son,
And Marlborough there, and Wolfe and Wellington.

XVI.

But from the statues and the storied wall,
  The living scene withdrew my wondering sense;
For with accordant pomp that gorgeous hall
  Was filled; and I beheld the opulence
Of Britain's Court,—a proud assemblage there,
Her Statesmen, and her Warriors, and her Fair.

XVII.

Amid that Hall of Victory side by side,
  Conspicuous o'er the splendid company,
There sate a royal Bridegroom and his Bride;
  In her fair cheek, and in her bright blue eye,
Her flaxen locks and her benignant mien,
The marks of Brunswick's Royal Line were seen.

XVIII.

Of princely lineage and of princely heart,
  The Bridegroom seemed,—a man approved in fight,
Who in the great deliverance bore his part,
  And had pursued the recreant Tyrant's flight
When driven from injured Germany he fled,
Bearing the curse of God and Man upon his head.

XIX.

Guerdant before his feet a Lion lay,
  The Saxon Lion, terrible of yore,
Who in his withered limbs and lean decay,
  The marks of long and cruel bondage bore,
But broken now beside him lay the chain,
Which galled and fretted late his neck and mane.

XX.

A Lion too was couched before the Bride;
  That noble Beast had never felt the chain;
Strong were his sinewy limbs and smooth his hide,
  And o'er his shoulders broad the affluent mane
Dishevelled hung; beneath his feet were laid
Torn flags of France, whereon his bed he made.

XXI.

Full different were those Lions twain in plight,
  Yet were they of one brood; and side by side
Of old, the Gallic Tiger in his might
  They many a time had met, and quelled his pride,
And made the treacherous spoiler from their ire
Cowering and crippled to his den retire.

XXII.

Two Forms divine on either side the throne,
  Its heavenly guardians, male and female stood.
His eye was bold, and on his brow there shone
  Contempt of all base things, and pride subdued
To wisdom's will: a warrior's garb he wore,
And HONOUR was the name the Genius bore.

XXIII.

That other form was in a snow-white vest,
  As well her virgin loveliness became;
Erect her port, and on her spotless breast
  A blood-red cross was hung: FAITH was her name,
As by that sacred emblem might be seen,
And by her eagle eye, and by her dove-like mien.

XXIV.

Her likeness such to that robuster power,
  That sure his sister she might have been deemed,
Child of one womb at one auspicious hour.
  Akin they were, yet not as thus it seemed,
For he of VALOUR was the eldest son,
From Areté in happy union sprung.

XXV.

But her to Phronis Eusebeia bore,
  She whom her mother Dicé sent to earth;
What marvel then if thus their features wore
  Resemblant lineaments of kindred birth,
Dicé being child of Him who rules above,
VALOUR his earth-born son; so both derived from Jove.

XXVI.

While I stood gazing, suddenly the air
  Was filled with solemn music breathing round;
And yet no mortal instruments were there,
  Nor seemed that melody an earthly sound,
So wonderously it came, so passing sweet,
For some strange pageant sure a prelude meet.

XXVII.

In every breast methought there seemed to be
  A hush of reverence mingled with dismay;
For now appeared a heavenly company
  Toward the royal seat who held their way;
A female Form majestic led them on,—
With awful port she came, and stood before the Throne.

XXVIII.

Gentle her mien and void of all offence;
  But if aught wronged her she could strike such fear,
As when Minerva in her Sire's defence
  Shook in Phlegræan fields her dreadful spear.
Yet her benignant aspect told that ne'er
Would she refuse to heed a suppliant's prayer.

XXIX.

The Trident of the Seas in her right hand,
  The sceptre which that Bride was born to wield,
She bore, in symbol of her just command,
  And in her left displayed the Red-Cross shield.
A plume of milk-white feathers overspread
The laurelled helm which graced her lofty head.

XXX.

Daughter of Brunswick's fated line, she said,
  While joyful realms their gratulations pay,
And ask for blessings on thy bridal bed,
  We too descend upon this happy day,—
Receive with willing ear what we impart,
And treasure up our counsels in thy heart!

XXXI.

Long may it be ere thou art called to bear
  The weight of empire in a day of woe!
Be it thy favoured lot meantime to share
  The joys which from domestic virtue flow,
And may the lessons which are now imprest
In years of leisure, sink into thy breast.

XXXII.

Look to thy Sire, and in his steady way,
  As in his Father's he, learn thou to tread;
That thus, when comes the inevitable day,
  No other change be felt than of the head
Which wears the crown; thy name will then be blest
Like theirs, when thou too shalt be called to rest.

XXXIII.

Love peace and cherish peace; but use it so
  That war may find thee ready at all hours;
And ever when thou strikest, let the blow
  Be swift and sure : then put forth all the powers
Which God hath given thee to redress thy wrong,
And, powerful as thou art, the strife will not be long.

XXXIV.

Let not the sacred Trident from thy hand
  Depart, nor lay the falchion from thy side!
Queen of the Seas, and mighty on the land,
  Thy power shall then be dreaded far and wide:
And, trusting still in God and in the Right,
Thou mayest again defy the World's collected might.

XXXV.

Thus as she ceased a comely Sage came on,
  His temples and capacious forehead spread
With locks of venerable eld, which shone
  As when in wintry morns on Skiddaw's head
The cloud, the sunshine, and the snow unite,
So silvery, so unsullied, and so white.

XXXVI.

Of Kronos and the Nymph Mnemosyné
  He sprung,—on either side a birth divine;
Thus to the Olympian Gods allied was he,
  And brother to the sacred Sisters nine,
With whom he dwelt in interchange of lore,
Each thus instructing each for evermore.

XXXVII.

They called him Praxis in the Olympian tongue,
  But here on earth EXPERIENCE was his name.
Whatever things have past to him were known,
  And he could see the future ere it came;
Such foresight was his patient wisdom's meed,—
Alas for those who his wise counsels will not heed!

XXXVIII.

He bore a goodly volume, which he laid
  Between that princely couple on the throne.
Lo there my work for this great realm, he said,
  My work, which with the kingdom's growth has grown,
The rights, the usages, the laws wherein
Blessed above all nations she hath been.

XXXIX.

Such as the sacred trust to thee is given,
  So unimpaired transmit it to thy line :
Preserve it as the choicest gift of Heaven,
  Alway to make the bliss of thee and thine :
The talisman of England's strength is there,—
With reverence guard it, and with jealous care!

XL.

The next who stood before that royal pair
  Came gliding like a vision o'er the ground;
A glory went before him through the air,
  Ambrosial odours floated all around,
His purple wings a heavenly lustre shed,
A silvery halo hover'd round his head.

XLI.

The Angel of the English Church was this,
  With whose divinest presence there appear'd
A glorious train, inheritors of bliss,
  Saints in the memory of the good revered,
Who having render'd back their vital breath
To Him from whom it came, were perfected by Death.

XLII.

Edward, the spotless Tudor, there I knew,
  In whose pure breast, with pious nurture fed,
All generous hopes and gentle virtues grew ;
  A heavenly diadem adorn'd his head,—
Most blessed Prince, whose saintly name might move
The understanding heart to tears of reverent love.

XLIII.

Less radiant than King Edward, Cranmer came,
  But purged from persecution's sable spot;
For he had given his body to the flame,
  And now in that right hand, which flinching not
He proffer'd to the fire's atoning doom,
Bore he the unfading palm of martyrdom.

XLIV.

There too came Latimer, in worth allied,
  Who to the stake when brought by Romish rage,
As if with prison weeds he cast aside
  The infirmity of flesh and weight of age,
Bow-bent till then with weakness, in his shroud
Stood up erect and firm before the admiring crowd.

XLV.

With these, partakers in beatitude,
  Bearing like them the palm, their emblem meet,
The Noble Army came, who had subdued
  All frailty, putting death beneath their feet:
Their robes were like the mountain snow, and bright
As though they had been dipp'd in the fountain springs
      of light.

XLVI.

For these were they who valiantly endured
  The fierce extremity of mortal pain,
By no weak tenderness to life allured,
  The victims of that hateful Henry's reign,
And of the bloody Queen, beneath whose sway
Rome lit her fires, and Fiends kept holiday.

XLVII.

O pardon me, thrice holy Spirits dear,
  That hastily I now must pass ye by !
No want of duteous reverence is there here;
  None better knows nor deeplier feels than I
What to your sufferings and your faith we owe,
Ye valiant champions for the truth below!

XLVIII.

Hereafter haply with maturer care,
  (So Heaven permit) that reverence shall be shown.
Now of my vision I must needs declare,
  And how the Angel stood before the throne,
And fixing on that Princess as he spake
His eye benign, the awful silence brake.

65

XLIX.

Thus said the Angel, Thou to whom one day
  There shall in earthly guardianship be given
The English Church, preserve it from decay!
  Ere now for that most sacred charge hath Heaven
In perilous times provided female means,
Blessing it beneath the rule of pious Queens.

L.

Bear thou that great Eliza in thy mind,
  Who from a wreck this fabric edified;
And Her who to a nation's voice resign'd,
  When Rome in hope its wiliest engines plied,
By her own heart and righteous Heaven approved,
Stood up against the Father whom she loved.

LI.

Laying all mean regards aside, fill Thou
  Her seats with wisdom and with learned worth;
That so whene'er attacked, with fearless brow
  Her champions may defend her rights on earth:
Link'd is her welfare closely with thine own,
One fate attends the Altar and the Throne!

LII.

Think not that lapse of ages shall abate
  The inveterate malice of that Harlot old;
Fall'n though thou deem'st her from her high estate,
  She proffers still the envenom'd cup of gold,
And her fierce Beast, whose names are Blasphemy,
The same that was, is still, and still must be.

LIII.

The stern Sectarian in unnatural league
  Joins her to war against their hated foe;
Error and Faction aid the bold intrigue,
  And the dark Atheist seeks her overthrow,
While giant Zeal in arms against her stands,
Barks with an hundred mouths, and lifts an hundred
    hands.

LIV.

Built on a rock, the fabric may repel
  Their utmost rage, if all within be sound:
But if within the gates Indifference dwell,
  Woe to her then! there needs no outward wound!
Through her whole frame benumb'd, a lethal sleep,
Like the cold poison of the asp will creep.

LV.

In thee, as in a cresset set on high,
  The light of piety should shine far seen,
A guiding beacon fixed for every eye:
  Thus from the influence of an honour'd Queen,
As from its spring, should public good proceed,—
The peace of Heaven will be thy proper meed.

LVI.

So should return that happy state of yore
  When piety and joy went hand in hand;
The love which to his flock the shepherd bore,
  The old observances which cheer'd the land,
The household prayers, which, honouring God's high
    name,
Kept the lamp trimm'd and fed the sacred flame.

LVII.

Thus having spoke, away the Angel past
  With all his train, dissolving from the sight:
A transitory shadow overcast
  The sudden void they left; all meaner light
Seeming like darkness to the eye which lost
The full effulgence of that heavenly host.

LVIII.

Eftsoon, in reappearing light confess'd,
  There stood another minister of bliss,
With his own radiance clothed as with a vest.
  One of the angelic company was this,
Who, guardians of the rising human race,
Alway in Heaven behold the Father's face.

LIX.

Somewhile he fix'd upon the royal Bride
  A contemplative eye of thoughtful grief;
The trouble of that look benign implied
  A sense of wrongs for which he sought relief,
And that Earth's evils which go unredrest
May waken sorrow in an Angel's breast.

LX.

I plead for babes and sucklings, he began,
  Those who are now, and who are yet to be;
I plead for all the surest hopes of man,
  The vital welfare of humanity:
Oh! let not bestial Ignorance maintain
Longer within the land her brutalizing reign.

LXI.

O Lady, if some new-born babe should bless,
  In answer to a nation's prayers, thy love,
When thou, beholding it in tenderness,
  The deepest, holiest joy of earth shalt prove,
In that the likeness of all infants see,
And call to mind that hour what now thou hear'st from
    me.

LXII.

Then seeing infant man, that Lord of Earth,
  Most weak and helpless of all breathing things,
Remember that as Nature makes at birth
  No different law for Peasants or for Kings,
And at the end no difference may befall,
The « short parenthesis of life » is all.[1]

LXIII.

But in that space, how wide may be their doom
  Of honour or dishonour, good or ill!
From Nature's hand like plastic clay they come,
  To take from circumstance their woe or weal;
And as the form and pressure may be given,
They wither upon earth, or ripen there for Heaven.

LXIV.

Is it then fitting that one soul should pine
  For lack of culture in this favour'd land ?—
That spirits of capacity divine
  Perish, like seeds upon the desert sand ?—
That needful knowledge in this age of light
Should not by birth be every Briton's right ?

LXV.

Little can private zeal effect alone;
  The State must this state-malady redress!
For as of all the ways of life, but one—
  The path of duty, leads to happiness,
So in their duty States must find at length
Their welfare, and their safety, and their strength.

LXVI.

This the first duty, carefully to train
  The children in the way that they should go.
Then of the family of guilt and pain
  How large a part were banish'd from below!
How should the people love with surest cause
Their country, and revere her venerable laws!

LXVII.

Is there, alas! within the human soul
  An in-bred taint disposing it for ill?
More need that early culture should controul
  And discipline by love the pliant will!
The heart of man is rich in all good seeds;
Neglected, it is choked with tares and noxious weeds.

LXVIII.

He ceased, and sudden from some unseen throng
  A choral peal arose and shook the hall;
As when ten thousand children with their song
  Fill the resounding temple of Saint Paul;—
Scarce can the heart their powerful tones sustain;—
« Save, or we perish!» was the thrilling strain.

LXIX.

« Save, or we perish!» thrice the strain was sung
  By unseen Souls innumerous hovering round,
And whilst the hall with their deep chorus rung,
  The inmost heart was shaken with the sound:
I felt the refluent blood forsake my face,
And my knees trembled in that awful place.

LXX.

Anon two female forms before our view
  Came side by side, a beauteous couplement;
The first a virgin clad in skyey blue;
  Upward to Heaven her stedfast eyes were bent;
Her countenance an anxious meaning bore,
Yet such as might have made her loved the more.

LXXI.

This was that maiden, « sober, chaste, and wise,»
  Who bringeth to all hearts their best delight:
« Though spoused, yet wanting wedlock's solemnize;
  Daughter of Cœlia, and Speranza hight,»²
I knew her well as one whose portraiture
In my dear Master's verse for ever will endure.³

LXXII.

Her sister too the same divinest page,
  Taught me to know⁴ for that Charissa fair,
« Of goodly grace and comely personage,
  Of wonderous beauty and of bounty rare,
Full of great love,» in whose most gentle mien
The charms of perfect womanhood were seen.

LXXIII.

This lovely pair unrolled before the throne
  « Earth's melancholy map,»⁵ whereon to sight
Two broad divisions at a glance were shown,—
  The empires these of Darkness and of Light.
Well might the thoughtful bosom sigh to mark
How wide a portion of the map was dark.

LXXIV.

Behold, Charissa cried, how large a space
  Of Earth lies unredeemed! Oh grief to think
That countless myriads of immortal race,
  In error born, in ignorance must sink,
Trained up in customs which corrupt the heart,
And following miserably the evil part?

LXXV.

Regard the expanded Orient, from the shores
  Of scorched Arabia and the Persian sea,
To where the inhospitable Ocean roars
  Against the rocks of frozen Tartary;
Look next at those Australian isles, which lie
Thick as the stars that stud the wintry sky;

LXXVI.

Then let thy mind contemplative survey
  That spacious region where in elder time
Earth's unremembered conquerors held the sway;
  And Science, trusting in her skill sublime,
With lore abstruse the sculptured walls o'erspread,
Its import now forgotten with the dead.

LXXVII.

From Nile and Congo's undiscovered springs
  To the four seas which gird the unhappy land,
Behold it left a prey to barbarous Kings,
  The Robber, or the Trader's ruthless hand;
Sinning and suffering, every where unblest,
Behold her wretched sons, oppressing and opprest!

LXXVIII.

To England is the Eastern empire given,
  And hers the sceptre of the circling main;
Shall she not then diffuse the word of Heaven
  Through all the regions of her trusted reign,—
Wage against evil things the hallowed strife,
And sow with liberal hand the seeds of life!

LXXIX.

By strenuous efforts in a rightful cause
  Gloriously hath she surpassed her ancient fame,
And won in arms the astonished World's applause.
  Yet may she win in peace a nobler name,
And Nations, which now lie in error blind,
Hail her the Friend and Teacher of Mankind!

LXXX.

Oh! what a part were that, Speranza then
  Exclaimed, to act upon Earth's ample stage!
Oh! what a name among the sons of men
  To leave, which should endure from age to age!
And what a strength that ministry of good
Should find in love and human gratitude!

LXXXI.

Speed thou the work, Redeemer of the World!
    That the long miseries of mankind may cease !
Where'er the Red Cross banner is unfurled
    There let it carry truth, and light, and peace !
Did not the Angels who announced thy birth,
Proclaim it with the sound of Peace on Earth?

LXXXII.

Bless thou this happy Island, that the stream
    Of blessing far and wide from hence may flow!
Bless it that so thy saving Mercy's beam
    Reflected hence may shine on all below !
Thy kingdom come ! thy will be done, O Lord!
And be Thy Holy Name through all the world
    adored !

LXXXIII.

Thus as Speranza cried she clasped her hands,
    And heavenward lifted them in ardent prayer.
Lo! at the act the vaulted roof expands,—
    Heaven opens,—and in empyreal air
Pouring its splendours through the inferior sky,
More bright than noon-day suns the Cross appears on
    high.

LXXXIV.

A strain of heavenly harmony ensued,
    Such as but once to mortal ears was known,—
The voice of that Angelic Multitude
    Who in their Orders stand around the Throne;
Peace upon Earth, Good will to Men ! they sung,
And Heaven and Earth with that prophetic anthem
    rung.

LXXXV.

In holy fear I fell upon the ground,
    And hid my face, unable to endure
The glory, or sustain the piercing sound :
    In fear and yet in trembling joy, for sure
My soul that hour yearned strongly to be free,
That it might spread its wings in immortality.

LXXXVI.

Gone was the glory when I raised my head,
    But in the air appeared a form half-seen,
Below with shadows dimly garmented,
    And indistinct and dreadful was his mien :
Yet when I gazed intentlier, I could trace
Divinest beauty in that awful face.

LXXXVII.

Hear me, O Princess! said the shadowy form,
    As in administering this mighty land
Thou with thy best endeavour shalt perform
    The will of Heaven, so shall my faithful hand
Thy great and endless recompense supply ;—
My name is DEATH : the last best friend am I !

EPILOGUE.

I.

Is this the Nuptial Song? with brow severe
    Perchance the votaries of the world will say :
Are these fit strains for Royal ears to hear?
    What man is he who thus assorts his lay,
And dares pronounce with inauspicious breath,
In Hymeneal verse, the name of Death !

II.

Remote from cheerful intercourse of men,
    Hath he indulged his melancholy mood,
And like the hermit in some sullen den,
    Fed his distempered mind in solitude?
Or have fanatic dreams distraught his sense,
That thus he should presume with bold irreverence?

III.

O Royal Lady, ill they judge the heart
    That reverently approaches thee to-day,
And anxious to perform its fitting part,
    Prefers the tribute of this duteous lay !
Not with displeasure should his song be read
Who prays for Heaven's best blessings on thy head.

IV.

He prays that many a year may pass away
    Ere the State call thee from a life of love ;
Vexed by no public cares, that day by day
    Thy heart the dear domestic joys may prove,
And gracious Heaven thy chosen nuptials bless
With all a Wife's and all a Mother's happiness.

V.

He prays, that for thine own and England's sake,
    The Virtues and the Household Charities
Their favoured seat beside thy hearth may take ;
    That when the Nation thither turn their eyes,
There the conspicuous model they may find
Of all which makes the bliss of human-kind.

VI.

He prays, that when the sceptre to thy hand
    In due succession shall descend at length,
Prosperity and Peace may bless the Land,
    Truth be thy counsellor, and Heaven thy strength ;
That every tongue thy praises may proclaim,
And every heart in secret bless thy name.

VII.

He prays, that thou mayest strenuously maintain
    The wise laws handed down from sire to son :
He prays, that under thy auspicious reign
    All may be added which is left undone,
To make the realm, its polity complete,
In all things happy as in all things great :

VIII.

That through the will of thy enlightened mind,
    Brute man may be to social life reclaimed :
That in compassion for forlorn mankind,
    The saving Faith may widely be proclaimed
Through erring lands, beneath thy fostering care ;—
This is his ardent hope, his loyal prayer.

IX.

In every cottage may thy power be blest,
    For blessings which should every-where abound ;
Thy will beneficent from East to West
    May bring forth good where'er the sun goes round ;
And thus through future times should Charlotte's fame
Surpass our great Eliza's golden name.

X.

Of awful subjects have I dared to sing,
　　Yet surely are they such as, viewed aright,
Contentment to thy better mind may bring :
　　A strain which haply may thy heart invite
To ponder well, how to thy choice is given
A glorious name on Earth, a high reward in Heaven.

XI.

Light strains, though cheerful as the hues of spring,
　　Would wither like a wreath of vernal flowers ;
The amaranthine garland which I bring
　　Shall keep its verdure through all after hours ;—
Yea, while the Poet's name is doomed to live,
So long this garland shall its fragrance give.

XII.

« Uneasy lies the head that wears a crown ;»
　　Thus said the Bard who spake of kingly cares :
But calmly may the Sovereign then lie down
　　When grateful Nations guard him with their prayers :
How sweet a sleep awaits the Royal head,
When these keep watch and ward around the bed !

L'ENVOY.

Go, little Book, from this my solitude,
　　I cast thee on the waters :—go thy ways !
And if, as I believe, thy vein be good,
　　The world will find thee after many days.
Be it with thee according to thy worth :—
Go, little Book! in faith I send thee forth.

NOTES.

Note 1, page 514, col. 2.

The « short parenthesis of life» is all.

I have borrowed this striking expression from
Storer.

> All as my chrysom, so my winding sheet ;
> None joy'd my birth, none mourn'd my death to see ;
> The short parenthesis of life was sweet,
> But short ;—what was before, unknown to me,
> And what must follow is the Lord's decree.
> 　　　　　STORER's *Life and Death of Wolsey.*

Let me insert here a beautiful passage from this
forgotten poet, whose work has been retrieved from
oblivion in the Heliconia.　Wolsey is speaking.

> More fit the dirige of a mournful quire
> In dull sad notes all sorrows to exceed,
> For him in whom the Prince's love is dead.
>
> I am the tomb where that affection lies,
> 　　That was the closet where it living kept :
> Yet wise men say affection never dies,—
> 　　No, but it turns, and when it long hath slept,
> *Looks heavy, like the eye that long hath wept.*
> O could it die,—that were a restful state !
> But living, it converts to deadly hate.

Note 2, page 515, col. 1.

Daughter of Cœlia and Speranza hight.

4.

> Dame Cœlia men did her call as thought
> From Heaven to come, or thither to arise.

> The mother of three daughters well up-brought
> In goodly thews or godly exercise :
> The eldest two, most sober chaste and wise,
> Fidelia and Speranza virgins were,
> Tho' spoused yet wanting wedlock's solemnize ;
> But fair Charissa to a lovely fere
> Was linked, and by him had many pledges dear.
> 　　　　　*Faery Queen, Book* I, c. 10.

Note 3, page 515, col. 1.

I knew her well, as one whose portraiture
In my dear Master's verse for ever will endure.

12.

> Thus as they gan of sundry things devise,
> Lo two most goodly virgins came in place,
> Ylinked arm in arm in lovely wise,
> With countenance demure, and modest grace,
> They numbred equal steps and even pace :
> Of which the eldest, that Fidelia hight,
> Like sunny beams threw from her chrystal face,
> That could have dazed the rash beholder's sight,
> And round about her head did shine like Heaven's light.

13.

> She was arrayed all in lilly white,
> And in her right hand bore a cup of gold,
> With wine and water filled up to the height,
> In which a serpent did himself enfold,
> That horror made to all that did behold ;
> But she no whit did change her constant mood ;
> And in her other hand she fast did hold
> A book, that was both signed and sealed with blood,
> Wherein dark things were writ, hard to be understood.

14.

> Her younger sister, that Speranza hight,
> Was clad in blue that her beseemed well ;
> Not all so chearful seemed she of sight
> As was her sister ; whether dread did dwell,
> Or anguish in her heart, is hard to tell.
> Upon her arm a silver anchor lay,
> Whereon she leaned ever, as befell ;
> And ever up to Heaven as she did pray,
> Her stedfast eyes were bent, ne swarved other way.
> 　　　　　*Faery Queen, Book* I, c. 10.

Note 4, page 515, col. 1.

Her sister too the same divinest page
Taught me to know.

30.

> She was a woman in her freshest age,
> Of wondrous beauty, and of bounty rare,
> With goodly grace and comely personage,
> That was on earth not easy to compare,
> Full of great love.
> 　　　　　*Faery Queen, Book* I, c. 10.

Note 5, page 515, col. 2.

«Earth's melancholy map.»

> A part how small of the terraqueous globe
> Is tenanted by man ! the rest a waste ;
> Rocks, deserts, frozen seas, and burning sands,
> Wild haunts of monsters, poisons, stings, and death !
> Such is Earth's melancholy map ! but far
> More sad ! this earth is a true map of man.
> 　　　　　YOUNG, *Night* I, l. 285.

It is the moral rather than the physical map which
ought to excite this mournful feeling,—but such con-
templations ought to excite our hope and our zeal also,
for how large a part of all existing evil, physical as well
as moral, is remediable by human means !

The Poet's Pilgrimage to Waterloo.

Εὐανθεα δ' ἀναβάσομαι
Στόλον ἀμφ' ἀρετᾷ
Κελαδέων.
PIND. *Pyth.* II.

TO JOHN MAY,

AFTER A FRIENDSHIP OF TWENTY YEARS,

This Poem is Inscribed,

IN TESTIMONY OF THE HIGHEST ESTEEM AND AFFECTION,

BY ROBERT SOUTHEY.

ARGUMENT.

THE first part of this Poem describes a journey to the scene of war. The second is in an allegorical form; it exposes the gross material philosophy which has been the guiding principle of the French politicians, from Mirabeau to Buonaparte; and it states the opinions of those persons who lament the restoration of the Bourbons, because the hopes which they entertained from the French Revolution have not been realized; and of those who see only evil, or blind chance, in the course of human events.

To the Christian philosopher all things are consistent and clear. Our first parents brought with them the light of natural religion and the moral law: as men departed from these, they tended toward barbarous and savage life; large portions of the world are in this degenerated state; still, upon the great scale, the human race, from the beginning, has been progressive. But the direct object of Buonaparte was to establish a military despotism wherever his power extended; and the immediate and inevitable consequence of such a system is to brutalize and degrade mankind. The contest in which this country was engaged against that Tyrant, was a struggle between good and evil principles, and never was there a victory so important to the best hopes of human nature as that which was won by British valour at Waterloo,—its effects extending over the whole civilized world, and involving the vital interests of all mankind.

That victory leaves England in security and peace. In no age and in no country has man ever existed under circumstances so favourable to the full development of his moral and intellectual faculties, as in England at this time. The peace which she has won by the battle of Waterloo, leaves her at leisure to pursue the great objects and duties of bettering her own condition, and diffusing the blessings of civilization and Christianity.

PROEM.

I.

ONCE more I see thee, Skiddaw! once again
  Behold thee in thy majesty serene,
Where like the bulwark of this favoured plain,
  Alone thou standest, monarch of the scene—
Thou glorious Mountain, on whose ample breast
The sunbeams love to play, the vapours love to rest!

II.

Once more, O Derwent, to thy awful shores
  I come, insatiate of the accustomed sight;
And listening as the eternal torrent roars,
  Drink in with eye and ear a fresh delight:
For I have wandered far by land and sea,
In all my wanderings still remembering thee.

III.

Twelve years, (how large a part of man's brief day!)
  Nor idly, nor ingloriously spent,
Of evil and of good have held their way,
  Since first upon thy banks I pitched my tent.
Hither I came in manhood's active prime,
And here my head hath felt the touch of time.

IV.

Heaven hath with goodly increase blest me here,
  Where childless and opprest with grief I came;
With voice of fervent thankfulness sincere
  Let me the blessings which are mine proclaim:
Here I possess,—what more should I require?
Books, children, leisure,—all my heart's desire.

V.

O joyful hour, when to our longing home
  The long-expected wheels at length drew nigh!
When the first sound went forth, « they come! they
      come !»
And hope's impatience quickened every eye!
« Never had man whom Heaven would heap with bliss
More glad return, more happy hour than this.»

VI.

Aloft on yonder bench, with arms dispread,
  My boy stood, shouting there his father's name,
Waving his hat around his happy head;
  And there, a younger group, his sisters came:
Smiling they stood with looks of pleased surprise,
While tears of joy were seen in elder eyes.

VII.

Soon each and all came crowding round to share
  The cordial greeting, the beloved sight;
What welcomings of hand and lip were there!
  And when those overflowings of delight
Subsided to a sense of quiet bliss,
Life hath no purer, deeper happiness.

VIII.

The young companion of our weary way
  Found here the end desired of all her ills;
She who in sickness pining many a day
  Hungered and thirsted for her native hills,
Forgetful now of sufferings past and pain,
Rejoiced to see her own dear home again.

IX.

Recovered now, the homesick mountaineer
  Sate by the playmate of her infancy,
Her twin-like comrade,—rendered doubly dear
  For that long absence: full of life was she,
With voluble discourse and eager mien
Telling of all the wonders she had seen.

X.

Here silently between her parents stood
  My dark-eyed Bertha, timid as a dove;
And gently oft from time to time she wooed
  Pressure of hand, or word, or look of love,
With impulse shy of bashful tenderness,
Soliciting again the wished caress.

XI.

The younger twain in wonder lost were they,
  My gentle Kate, and my sweet Isabel:
Long of our promised coming, day by day
  It had been their delight to hear and tell;
And now when that long-promised hour was come,
Surprise and wakening memory held them dumb.

XII.

For in the infant mind, as in the old,
  When to its second childhood life declines,
A dim and troubled power doth Memory hold:
  But soon the light of young Remembrance shines
Renewed, and influences of dormant love
Wakened within, with quickening influence move.

XIII.

O happy season theirs, when absence brings
  Small feeling of privation, none of pain,
Yet at the present object love re-springs,
  As night-closed flowers at morn expand again!
Nor deem our second infancy unblest,
When gradually composed we sink to rest.

XIV.

Soon they grew blithe as they were wont to be;
  Her old endearments each began to seek:
And Isabel drew near to climb my kneee,
  And pat with fondling hand her father's cheek;
With voice and touch and look reviving thus
The feelings which had slept in long disuse.

XV.

But there stood one whose heart could entertain
  And comprehend the fullness of the joy;
The father, teacher, playmate, was again
  Come to his only and his studious boy:
And he beheld again that mother's eye,
  Which with such ceaseless care had watched his
                    infancy.

XVI.

Bring forth the treasures now,—a proud display,—
  For rich as Eastern merchants we return!
Behold the black Beguine, the Sister grey,
  The Friars whose heads with sober motion turn,
The Ark well-filled with all its numerous hives,
Noah and Shem and Ham and Japhet, and their wives.

XVII.

The tumbler, loose of limb; the wrestlers twain,
  And many a toy beside of quaint device,
Which, when his fleecy troops no more can gain
  Their pasture on the mountains hoar with ice,
The German shepherd carves with curious knife,
Earning in easy toil the food of frugal life.

XVIII.

It was a group which Richter, had he viewed,
  Might have deemed worthy of his perfect skill;
The keen impatience of the younger brood,
  Their eager eyes and fingers never still;
The hope, the wonder, and the restless joy
Of those glad girls, and that vociferous boy!

XIX.

The aged friend serene with quiet smile,
  Who in their pleasure finds her own delight;
The mother's heart-felt happiness the while;
  The aunts, rejoicing in the joyful sight;
And he who in his gaiety of heart,
With glib and noisy tongue performed the showman's
                    part.

XX.

Scoff ye who will! but let me, gracious Heaven,
  Preserve this boyish heart till life's last day!
For so that inward light by Nature given
  Shall still direct, and cheer me on my way,
And brightening as the shades of age descend,
Shine forth with heavenly radiance at the end.

XXI.

This was the morning light vouchsafed, which led
  My favoured footsteps to the Muses' hill,
Whose arduous paths I have not ceased to tread,
  From good to better persevering still;
And if but self-approved, to praise or blame
Indifferent, while I toil for lasting fame.

XXII.

And O ye Nymphs of Castaly divine!
   Whom I have dutifully served so long,
Benignant to your votary now incline,
   That I may win your ear with gentle song,
Such as, I ween, is ne'er disowned by you,—
A low prelusive strain, to nature true.

XXIII.

But when I reach at themes of loftier thought,
   And tell of things surpassing earthly sense,
(Which by yourselves, O Muses, I am taught,)
   Then aid me with your fuller influence,
And to the height of that great argument
Support my spirit in her strong ascent!

XXIV.

So may I boldly round my temples bind
   The laurel which my master Spenser wore;
And free in spirit as the mountain wind
   That makes my symphony in this lone hour,
No perishable song of triumph raise,
But sing in worthy strains my country's praise.

PART I.

—————

THE JOURNEY.

Τῶν πολυκτόνων γὰρ
'Ουκ' ἄσκοποι Θεοί.—ÆSCHYLUS.

I.

FLANDERS.

I.

Our world hath seen the work of war's debate
   Consummated in one momentous day
Twice in the course of time; and twice the fate
   Of unborn ages hung upon the fray:
First at Platæa, in that awful hour
When Greece united smote the Persian's power.

II.

For had the Persian triumphed, then the spring
   Of knowledge from that living source had ceast;
All would have fallen before the barbarous King,
   Art, Science, Freedom; the despotic East,
Setting her mark upon the race subdued,
Had stamped them in the mould of sensual servitude.

III.

The second day was that when Martel broke
   The Musselmen, [1] delivering France opprest,
And in one mighty conflict, from the yoke
   Of misbelieving Mecca saved the West;
Else had the Impostor's law destroyed the ties
Of public weal and private charities.

IV.

Such was the danger when that Man of Blood
   Burst from the iron Isle, and brought again,
Like Satan rising from the sulphurous flood,
   His impious legions to the battle plain:
Such too was our deliverance when the field
Of Waterloo beheld his fortunes yield.

V.

I, who with faith unshaken from the first,
   Even when the Tyrant seemed to touch the skies,
Had looked to see the high-blown bubble burst,
   And for a fall conspicuous as his rise,
Even in that faith had looked not for defeat
So swift, so overwhelming, so complete.

VI.

Me most of all men it behoved to raise
   The strain of triumph for this foe subdued,
To give a voice to joy, and in my lays
   Exalt a nation's hymn of gratitude,
And blazon forth in song that day's renown,—
For I was graced with England's laurel crown.

VII.

But as I once had journeyed to behold
   Far off, Ourique's consecrated field,
Where Portugal the faithful and the bold
   Assumed the symbols of her sacred shield,
More reason now that I should bend my way
The field of British glory to survey.

VIII.

So forth I set upon this pilgrimage,
   And took the partner of my life with me,
And one dear girl, just ripe enough of age
   Retentively to see what I should see;
That thus with mutual recollections fraught,
We might bring home a store for after-thought.

IX.

We left our pleasant Land of Lakes, and went
   Throughout whole England's length, a weary way,
Even to the farthest shores of eastern Kent:
   Embarking there, upon an autumn day,
Toward Ostend we held our course all night,
And anchored by its quay at morning's earliest light.

X.

Small vestige there of that old siege [2] appears,
   And little of remembrance would be found,
When for the space of three long painful years
   The persevering Spaniard girt it round,
And gallant youths of many a realm from far
Went students to that busy school of war.

XI.

Yet still those wars of obstinate defence
   Their lessons offer to the soldier's hand;
Large knowledge may the statesman draw from thence:
   And still from underneath the drifted sand,
Sometimes the storm, or passing foot lays bare
Part of the harvest Death has gathered there.

XII.

Peace be within thy walls, thou famous town,
   For thy brave bearing in those times of old ;
May plenty thy industrious children crown,
   And prosperous merchants day by day behold
Many a rich vessel from the injurious sea,
Enter the bosom of thy quiet quay. [3]

XIII.

Embarking there, we glided on between
   Strait banks raised high above the level land,
With many a cheerful dwelling white and green
   In goodly neighbourhood on either hand.
Huge-timbered bridges o'er the passage lay,
Which wheeled aside and gave us easy way.

XIV.

Four horses, aided by the favouring breeze,
   Drew our gay vessel, slow and sleek and large ;
Crack goes the whip, the steersman at his ease
   Directs the way, and steady went the barge.
Ere evening closed to Bruges [4] thus we came,—
Fair city, worthy of her ancient fame.

XV.

The season of her splendour is gone by,
   Yet every where its monuments remain ;
Temples which rear their stately heads on high,
   Canals that intersect the fertile plain,
Wide streets and squares, with many a court and hall
Spacious and undefaced, but ancient all.

XVI.

Time hath not wronged her, nor hath Ruin sought
   Rudely her splendid structures to destroy,
Save in those recent days with evil fraught,
   When Mutability, in drunken joy
Triumphant, and from all restraint released,
Let loose the fierce and many-headed beast.

XVII.

But for the scars in that unhappy rage
   Inflicted, firm she stands and undecayed ;
Like our first sires', a beautiful old age
   Is hers, in venerable years arrayed ;
And yet to her benignant stars may bring,
What fate denies to man,—a second spring.

XVIII.

When I may read of tilts in days of old,
   And tourneys graced by chieftains of renown,
Fair dames, grave citizens, and warriors bold,
   If Fancy would pourtray some stately town,
Which for such pomp fit theatre should be,
Fair Bruges, I shall then remember thee.

XIX.

Nor did thy landscape yield me less delight,
   Seen from the deck as slow it glided by,
Or when beneath us, from thy Belfroy's height,
   Its boundless circle met the bending sky ;
The waters smooth and straight, thy proper boast,
And lines of road-side trees in long perspective lost.

XX.

No happier landscape may on earth be seen,
   Rich gardens all around and fruitful groves,
White dwellings trim relieved with lively green,
   The pollard that the Flemish painter loves,
With aspins tall and poplars fair to view,
Casting o'er all the land a grey and willowy hue.

XXI.

My lot hath lain in scenes sublime and rude,
   Where still devoutly I have served and sought
The Power divine which dwells in solitude.
   In boyhood was I wont, with rapture fraught,
Amid those rocks and woods to wander free,
Where Avon hastens to the Severn sea.

XXII.

In Cintra also have I dwelt erewhile,
   That earthly Eden, and have seen at eve
The sea-mists, gathering round its mountain pile,
   Whelm with their billows all below, but leave
One pinnacle sole seen, whereon it stood
Like the Ark on Ararat, above the flood.

XXIII.

And now am I a Cumbrian mountaineer;
   Their wintry garment of unsullied snow
The mountains have put on, the heavens are clear,
   And yon dark lake spreads silently below;
Who sees them only in their summer hour
Sees but their beauties half, and knows not half their
    power.

XXIV.

Yet hath the Flemish scene a charm for me
   That soothes and wins upon the willing heart;
Though all is level as the sleeping sea,
   A natural beauty springs from perfect art,
And something more than pleasure fills the breast,
To see how well-directed toil is blest.

XXV.

Two nights have past; the morning opens well,
   Fair are the aspects of the opening sky;
Soon yon sweet chimes the appointed hour will tell,
   For here to music Time moves merrily :
Aboard! aboard! no more must we delay,—
Farewell, good people of the *Fleur de Bled!*

XXVI.

Beside the busy wharf the Trekschuit rides,
   With painted plumes and tent-like awning gay;
Carts, barrows, coaches, hurry from all sides,
   And passengers and porters throng the way,
Contending all at once in clamorous speech,
French, Flemish, English, each confusing each.

XXVII.

All disregardant of the Babel sound,
   A swan kept oaring near with upraised eye,—
A beauteous pensioner, who daily found
   The bounty of such casual company;
Nor did she leave us till the bell was rung,
And slowly we our watery way begun.

XXVIII.

Europe can boast no richer, goodlier scene,
  Than that through which our pleasant passage lay,
By fertile fields and fruitful gardens green,
  The journey of a short autumnal day;
Sleek well-fed steeds our steady vessel drew,
The heavens were fair, and Mirth was of our crew.

XXIX.

Along the smooth canal's unbending line,
  Beguiling time with light discourse, we went,
Nor wanting savoury food nor generous wine.
  Ashore too there was feast and merriment;
The jovial peasants at some village fair
Were dancing, drinking, smoking, gambling there.

XXX.

Of these, or of the ancient towers of Ghent
  Renowned, I must not tarry now to tell;
Of picture, or of church, or monument;
  Nor how we mounted to that ponderous bell,
The Belfroy's boast, which bears old Roland's name,
Nor yields to Oxford Tom, or Tom of Lincoln's fame.

XXXI.

Nor of that sisterhood whom to their rule
  Of holy life no hasty vows restrain, 5
Who, meek disciples of the Christian school,
  Watch by the bed of sickness and of pain :
Oh what a strength divine doth Faith impart
To inborn goodness in the female heart!

XXXII.

A gentle party from the shores of Kent
  Thus far had been our comrades as befell;
Fortune had linked us first, and now Consent,—
  For why should Choice divide whom Chance so well
Had joined, seeing they to view the famous ground,
Like us, were to the Field of Battle bound.

XXXIII.

Farther as yet they looked not than that quest,—
  The land was all before them where to chuse.
So we consorted here as seemed best;
  Who would such pleasant fellowship refuse
Of ladies fair and gentle comrades free?—
Certes we were a joyous company.

XXXIV.

Yet lacked we not discourse for graver times,
  Such as might suit sage auditors, I ween;
For some among us, in far distant climes
  The cities and the ways of men had seen;
No unobservant travellers they, but well
Of what they there had learnt they knew to tell.

XXXV.

The one of frozen Moscovy could speak,
  And well his willing listeners entertain
With tales of that inclement region bleak,
  The pageantry and pomp of Catherine's reign,
And that proud city, which with wise intent
The mighty founder raised, his own great monument.

XXXVI.

And one had dwelt with Malabars and Moors,
  Where fertile earth and genial heaven dispense
Profuse their bounty upon Indian shores;
  Whate'er delights the eye, or charms the sense,
The valleys with perpetual fruitage blest,
The mountains with unfading foliage drest.

XXXVII.

He those barbaric palaces had seen,
  The work of Eastern potentates of old;
And in the Temples of the Rock had been,
  Awe-struck their dread recesses to behold;
A gifted hand was his, which by its skill
Could to the eye pourtray such wonderous scenes
        at will.

XXXVIII.

A third, who from the Land of Lakes with me
  Went out upon this pleasant pilgrimage,
Had sojourned long beyond the Atlantic sea;
  Adventurous was his spirit as his age,
For he in far Brazil, through wood and waste,
Had travelled many a day, and there his heart was
        placed.

XXXIX.

Wild region,—happy if at night he found
  The shelter of some rude Tapuya's shed;
Else would he take his lodgement on the ground,
  Or from the tree suspend his hardy bed;
And sometimes starting at the jaguar's cries,
See through the murky night the prowler's fiery eyes.

XL.

And sometimes over thirsty deserts drear,
  And sometimes over flooded plains he went;—
A joy it was his fire-side tales to hear,
  And he a comrade to my heart's content :
For he of what I most desired could tell,
And loved the Portugals because he knew them well.

XLI.

Here to the easy barge we bade adieu;
  Land travellers now along the well-paved way,
Where road-side trees still lengthening on the view,
  Before us and behind unvarying lay:
Through lands well-laboured to Alost we came,
Where whilome treachery stained the English name. 6

XLII.

Then saw we Afflighem, by ruin rent, 7
  Whose venerable fragments strew the land;
Grown wise too late, the multitude lament
  The ravage of their own unhappy hand;
Its records in their frenzy torn and tost,
Its precious stores of learning wrecked and lost.

XLIII.

Whatever else we saw was cheerful all,
  The signs of steady labour well repaid;
The grapes were ripe on every cottage wall,
  And merry peasants seated in the shade
Of garner, or within the open door,
From gathered hop-vines plucked the plenteous store.

XLIV.

Through Assche for water and for cakes renowned, [8]
  We past, pursuing still our way, though late;
And when the shades of night were closing round,
  Brussels received us through her friendly gate,—
Proud city, fated many a change to see,
And now the seat of new-made monarchy.

II.

BRUSSELS.

I.

WHERE might a gayer spectacle be found
  Than Brussels offered on that festive night,
Her squares and palaces irradiate round
  To welcome the imperial Moscovite,
Who now, the wrongs of Europe twice redressed,
Came there, a welcome and a glorious guest?

II.

Her mile-long avenue with lamps was hung,
  Innumerous, which diffused a light like day;
Where through the line of splendour, old and young
  Paraded all in festival array;
While fiery barges, plying to and fro,
Illumined as they moved the liquid glass below.

III.

By day with hurrying crowds the streets were thronged,
  To gain of this great Czar a passing sight;
And music, dance, and banquetings prolonged
  The various work of pleasure through the night.
You might have deemed, to see that joyous town,
That wretchedness and pain were there unknown.

IV.

Yet three short months had scarcely passed away,
  Since, shaken with the approaching battle's breath,
Her inmost chambers trembled with dismay;
  And now within her walls, insatiate Death,
Devourer whom no harvest e'er can fill,
The gleanings of that field was gathering still.

V.

Within those walls there lingered at that hour
  Many a brave soldier on the bed of pain,
Whom aid of human art should ne'er restore
  To see his country and his friends again;
And many a victim of that fell debate
Whose life yet wavered in the scales of fate.

VI.

Some I beheld, for whom the doubtful scale
  Had to the side of life inclined at length;
Emaciate was their form, their features pale,
  The limbs, so vigorous late, bereft of strength;
And for their gay habiliments of yore,
The habit of the House of Pain they wore.

VII.

Some in the courts of that great hospital,
  . That they might taste the sun and open air,
Crawled out; or sate beneath the southern wall;
  Or leaning in the gate, stood gazing there
In listless guise upon the passers by,
Whiling away the hours of slow recovery.

VIII.

Others in waggons borne abroad I saw,
  Albeit recovering, still a mournful sight:
Languid and helpless some were stretched on straw,
  Some more advanced sustained themselves upright;
And with bold eye and careless front, methought,
Seemed to set wounds and death again at nought.

IX.

Well had it fared with these; nor went it ill
  With those whom war had of a limb bereft,
Leaving the life untouched, that they had still
  Enough for health as for existence left;
But some there were who lived to draw the breath
Of pain through hopeless years of lingering death.

X.

Here might the hideous face of war be seen,
  Stript of all pomp, adornment, and disguise;
It was a dismal spectacle, I ween,
  Such as might well to the beholders' eyes
Bring sudden tears, and make the pious mind
Grieve for the crimes and follies of mankind.

XI.

What had it been then in the recent days
  Of that great triumph, when the open wound
Was festering, and along the crowded ways,
  Hour after hour was heard the incessant sound
Of wheels, which o'er the rough and stony road
Conveyed their living agonizing load!

XII.

Hearts little to the melting mood inclined
  Grew sick to see their sufferings; and the thought
Still comes with horror to the shuddering mind,
  Of those sad days when Belgian ears were taught
The British soldier's cry, half groan, half prayer,
Breathed when his pain is more than he can bear. [9]

XIII.

Brave spirits, nobly had their part been done!
  Brussels could show, where Senne's slow waters glide,
The cannon which their matchless valour won,
  Proud trophies of the field, ranged side by side ; .
Where, as they stood in inoffensive row,
The solitary guard paced to and fro.

XIV.

Unconscious instruments of human woe,
  Some for their mark the royal lilies bore,
Fixed there when Britain was the Bourbon's foe;
  And some embossed in brazen letters wore
The sign of that abhorred misrule, which broke
The guilty nation for a Tyrant's yoke.

XV.

Others were stampt with that Usurper's name,—
  Recorders thus of many a change were they,
Their deadly work through every change the same;
  Nor ever had they seen a bloodier day
Than when, as their late thunders rolled around,
Brabant in all her cities felt the sound. [10]

XVI.

Then ceased their occupation. From the field
  Of battle here in triumph were they brought;
Ribands and flowers and laurels half concealed
  Their brazen mouths, so late with ruin fraught;
Women beheld them pass with joyful eyes,
And children clapt their hands, and rent the air with cries.

XVII.

Now idly on the banks of Senne they lay,
  Like toys with which a child is pleased no more:
Only the British traveller bends his way
  To see them on that unfrequented shore,
And as a mournful feeling blends with pride,
Remembers those who fought, and those who died.

III.

THE FIELD OF BATTLE.

I.

SOUTHWARD from Brussels lies the field of blood,
  Some three hours' journey for a well-girt man;
A horseman who in haste pursued his road
  Would reach it as the second hour began.
The way is through a forest deep and wide,
Extending many a mile on either side.

II.

No cheerful woodland this of antic trees,
  With thickets varied and with sunny glade;
Look where he will, the weary traveller sees
  One gloomy, thick, impenetrable shade
Of tall straight trunks, which move before his sight,
With interchange of lines of long green light.

III.

Here, where the woods receding from the road
  Have left on either hand an open space
For fields and gardens, and for man's abode,
  Stands Waterloo; a little lowly place,
Obscure till now, when it hath risen to fame,
And given the victory its English name.

IV.

What time the second Carlos ruled in Spain,
  Last of the Austrian line by Fate decreed,
Here Castanaza reared a votive fane, [11]
  Praying the Patron Saints to bless with seed
His childless sovereign; Heaven denied an heir,
And Europe mourned in blood the frustrate prayer.

V.

That temple to our hearts was hallowed now:
  For many a wounded Briton there was laid,
With such poor help as time might then allow
  From the fresh carnage of the field conveyed;
And they whom human succours could not save,
Here in its precincts found a hasty grave.

VI.

And here on marble tablets set on high,
  In English lines by foreign workmen traced,
Are names familiar to an English eye;
  Their brethren here the fit memorials placed,
Whose unadorned inscriptions briefly tell
Their gallant comrades' rank, and where they fell.

VII.

The stateliest monument of public pride,
  Enriched with all magnificence of art,
To honour Chieftains who in victory died,
  Would wake no stronger feeling in the heart
Than these plain tablets, by the soldier's hand
Raised to his comrades in a foreign land. [12]

VIII.

Not far removed you find the burial-ground,
  Yet so that skirts of woodland intervene;
A small enclosure, rudely fenced around;
  Three grave-stones only for the dead are seen:
One bears the name of some rich villager,
The first for whom a stone was planted there.

IX.

Beneath the second is a German laid,
  Whom Bremen, shaking off the Frenchman's yoke,
Sent with her sons the general cause to aid;
  He in the fight received his mortal stroke,
Yet for his country's aggravated woes
Lived to see vengeance on her hated foes.

X.

A son of Erin sleeps below the third;
  By friendly hands his body where it lay
Upon the field of blood had been interred,
  And thence by those who mourned him borne away
In pious reverence for departed worth,
Laid here with holy rites in consecrated earth.

XI.

Repose in peace, brave soldiers, who have found
  In Waterloo and Soigny's shade your rest!
Ere this hath British valour made that ground
  Sacred to you, and for your foes unblest,
When Marlborough here, victorious in his might
Surprised the French, and smote them in their flight. [13]

XII.

Those wars are as a tale of times gone by,
  For so doth perishable fame decay,—
Here on the ground wherein the slaughtered lie,
  The memory of that fight is past away;—
And even our glorious Blenheim to the field
Of Waterloo and Wellington must yield.

XIII.

Soon shall we reach that scene of mighty deeds,
  In one unbending line a short league hence;
Aright the forest from the road recedes,
  With wide sweep trending south and westward thence;
Aleft along the line it keeps its place
Some half-hour's distance at a traveller's pace.

XIV.

The country here expands, a wide spread scene;
  No Flemish gardens fringed with willows these,
Nor rich Brabantine pastures ever green,
  With trenches lined and rows of aspin trees;
In tillage here the unwooded open land
Returns its increase to the farmer's hand.

XV.

Behold the scene where Slaughter had full sway!
  A mile before us lieth Mount St John,
The hamlet which the Highlanders that day
  Preserved from spoil; [14] yet as much farther on
The single farm is placed, now known to fame,
Which from the sacred hedge derives its name.

XVI.

Straight onward yet for one like distance more,
  And there the house of Belle Alliance stands,
So named, I guess, by some in days of yore,
  In friendship or in wedlock joining hands:
Little did they who called it thus foresee
The place that name should hold in history!

XVII.

Beyond these points the fight extended not,—
  Small theatre for such a tragedy! [15]
Its breadth scarce more, from eastern Papelot
  To where the groves of Hougoumont on high
Rear in the west their venerable head,
And cover with their shade the countless dead.

XVIII.

But wouldst thou tread this celebrated ground,
  And trace with understanding eyes a scene
Above all other fields of war renowned,
  From western Hougoumont thy way begin;
There was our strength on that side, and there first,
In all its force, the storm of battle burst.

XIX.

Strike eastward then across toward La Haye,
  The single farm: with dead the fields between
Are lined, and thou wilt see upon the way
  Long wave-like dips and swells which intervene,
Such as would breathe the war-horse, and impede,
When that deep soil was wet, his martial speed.

XX.

This is the ground whereon the young Nassau,
  Emuling that day his ancestors' renown,
Received his hurt; admiring Belgium saw
  The youth proved worthy of his destined crown: [16]
All tongues his prowess on that day proclaim,
And children lisp his praise and bless their Prince's name.

XXI.

When thou hast reached La Haye, survey it well,
  Here was the heat and centre of the strife,
This point must Britain hold whate'er befell,
  And here both armies were profuse of life:
Once it was lost,—and then a stander by
Belike had trembled for the victory.

XXII.

Not so the leader, on whose equal mind
  Such interests hung in that momentous day;
So well had he his motley troops assigned,
  That where the vital points of action lay,
There had he placed those soldiers whom he knew
No fears could quail, no dangers could subdue.

XXIII.

Small was his British force, nor had he here
  The Portugals, in heart so near allied,
The worthy comrades of his late career,
  Who fought so oft and conquered at his side,
When with the Red Cross joined in brave advance,
The glorious Quinas mocked the air of France.

XXIV.

Now of the troops with whom he took the field,
  Some were of doubtful faith, and others raw;
He stationed these where they might stand or yield;
  But where the stress of battle he foresaw,
There were his links (his own strong words I speak)
And rivets which no human force could break.

XXV.

O my brave countrymen, ye answered well
  To that heroic trust! Nor less did ye,
Whose worth your grateful country aye shall tell,
  True children of our sister Germany,
Who while she groaned beneath the oppressor's chain,
Fought for her freedom in the fields of Spain.

XXVI.

La Haye, bear witness! sacred is it hight,
  And sacred is it truly from that day;
For never braver blood was spent in fight
  Than Britain here hath mingled with the clay.
Set where thou wilt thy foot, thou scarce canst tread
Here on a spot unhallowed by the dead.

XXVII.

Here was it that the Highlanders withstood
  The tide of hostile power, received its weight
With resolute strength, and stemmed and turned the flood;
  And fitly here, as in that Grecian strait,
The funeral stone might say, Go traveller, tell
Scotland, that in our duty here we fell.

XXVIII.

Still eastward from this point thy way pursue.
  There grows a single hedge along the lane,—
No other is there far or near in view:
  The raging enemy essayed in vain
To pass that line,—a braver foe withstood,
And this whole ground was moistened with their blood.

XXIX.

Leading his gallant men as he was wont,
  The hot assailant's onset to repel,
Advancing hat in hand, here in the front
  Of battle and of danger, Picton fell ;
Lamented Chief! than whom no braver name
His country's annals shall consign to fame.

XXX.

Scheldt had not seen us, had his voice been heard,
  Return with shame from her disastrous coast :
But Fortune soon to fairer fields preferred
  His worth approved, which Cambria long may boast:
France felt him then, and Portugal and Spain
His honoured memory will for aye retain.

XXXI.

Hence to the high-walled house of Papelot,
  The battle's boundary on the left, incline ;
Here thou seest Frischermont not far remote,
  From whence, like ministers of wrath divine,
The Prussians issuing on the yielding foe,
Consummated their great and total overthrow.

XXXII.

Deem not that I the martial skill should boast
  Where horse and foot were stationed, here to tell,
What points were occupied by either host,
  And how the battle raged, and what befell,
And how our great Commander's eagle eye
Which comprehended all. secured the victory.

XXXIII.

This were the historian's, not the poet's part ;
  Such task would ill the gentle Muse beseem,
Who to the thoughtful mind and pious heart
  Comes with her offering from this awful theme ;
Content if what she saw and gathered there
She may in unambitious song declare.

XXXIV.

Look how upon the Ocean's treacherous face
  The breeze and summer sunshine softly play,
And the green-heaving billows bear no trace
  Of all the wrath and wreck of yesterday ;—
So from the field which here we looked upon,
The vestiges of dreadful war were gone.

XXXV.

Earth had received into her silent womb
  Her slaughtered creatures : horse and man they lay,
And friend and foe, within the general tomb.
  Equal had been their lot ; one fatal day
For all,—one labour,—and one place of rest
They found within their common parent's breast.

XXXVI.

The passing seasons had not yet effaced
  The stamp of numerous hoofs impressed by force
Of cavalry, whose path might still be traced.
  Yet nature every where resumed her course ;
Low pansies to the sun their purple gave,
And the soft poppy blossomed on the grave.

XXXVII.

In parts the careful farmer had renewed
  His labours, late by battle frustrated ;
And where the unconscious soil had been imbued
  With blood, profusely there like water shed,
There had his plough-share turned the guilty ground,
And the green corn was springing all around.

XXXVIII.

The graves he left for natural thought humane
  Untouched ; and here and there, where in the strife
Contending feet had trampled down the grain,
  Some hardier roots were found, which, of their life
Tenacious, had put forth a second head,
And sprung, and eared, and ripened on the dead.

XXXIX.

Some marks of wreck were scattered all around,
  As shoe, and belt, and broken bandoleer,
And hats which bore the mark of mortal wound ;
  Gun-flints and balls for those who closelier peer ;
And sometimes did the breeze upon its breath
Bear from ill-covered graves a taint of death.

XL.

More vestige of destructive man was seen
  Where man in works of peace had laboured more ;
At Hougoumont the hottest strife had been,
  Where trees and walls the mournful record bore
Of war's wild rage, trunks pierced with many a wound,
And roofs and half-burnt rafters on the ground.

XLI.

A goodly mansion this, with gardens fair,
  And ancient groves and fruitful orchard wide,
Its dovecot and its decent house of prayer,
  Its ample stalls and garners well supplied,
And spacious bartons clean, well walled around,
Where all the wealth of rural life was found.

XLII.

That goodly mansion on the ground was laid,
  Save here and there a blackened broken wall ;
The wounded who were borne beneath its shade
  Had there been crushed and buried by the fall ;
And there they lie where they received their doom,—
Oh let no hand disturb that honourable tomb !

XLIII.

Contiguous to this wreck the little fane
  For worship hallowed, still uninjured stands,
Save that its Crucifix displays too plain
  The marks of outrage from irreverent hands.
Alas, to think such irreligious deed
Of wrong from British soldiers should proceed !

XLIV.

The dovecot too remains ; scared at the fight,
  The birds sought shelter in the forest shade ;
But still they kept their native haunts in sight,
  And when few days their terror had allayed,
Forsook again the solitary wood,
For their old home and human neighbourhood.

XLV.

The gardener's dwelling was untouched; his wife
  Fled with her children to some near retreat,
And there lay trembling for her husband's life:
  He stood the issue, saw the foe's retreat,
And lives unhurt where thousands fell around,
To tell the story of that famous ground.

XLVI.

His generous dog was well approved that hour,
  By courage as by love to man allied;
He through the fiery storm and iron shower
  Kept the ground bravely by his master's side:
And now when to the stranger's hand he draws,
The noble beast seems conscious of applause.

XLVII.

Toward the grove the wall with musket holes
  Is pierced; our soldiers here their station held
Against the foe, and many were the souls
  Then from their fleshly tenements expelled.
Six hundred Frenchmen have been burnt close by,
And underneath one mound their bones and ashes lie.

XLVIII.

One streak of blood upon the wall was traced,
  In length a man's just stature from the head;
There where it gushed you saw it uneffaced:
  Of all the blood which on that day was shed
This mortal stain alone remained impressed,—
The all-devouring earth had drunk the rest.

XLIX.

Here from the heaps who strewed the fatal plain
  Was Howard's corse by faithful hands conveyed,
And not to be confounded with the slain,
  Here in a grave apart with reverence laid,
Till hence his honoured relics o'er the seas
Were borne to England, where they rest in peace.

L.

Another grave had yielded up its dead,
  From whence to bear his son a father came,
That he might lay him where his own grey head
  Ere long must needs be laid. That soldier's name
Was not remembered there, yet may the verse
Present this reverent tribute to his hearse.

LI.

Was it a soothing or a mournful thought
  Amid this scene of slaughter as we stood,
Where armies had with recent fury fought,
  To mark how gentle Nature still pursued
Her quiet course, as if she took no care
For what her noblest work had suffered there?

LII.

The pears had ripened on the garden wall;
  Those leaves which on the autumnal earth were spread,
The trees, though pierced and scarred with many a ball,
  Had only in their natural season shed:
Flowers were in seed whose buds to swell began
When such wild havoc here was made of man!

LIII.

Throughout the garden, fruits and herbs and flowers
  You saw in growth, or ripeness, or decay!
The green and well-trimmed dial marked the hours
  With gliding shadow as they past away;
Who would have thought, to see this garden fair,
Such horrors had so late been acted there!

LIV.

Now, Hougoumont, farewell to thy domain!
  Might I dispose of thee, no woodman's hand
Should e'er thy venerable groves profane;
  Untouched, and like a temple should they stand,
And, consecrate by general feeling, wave
Their branches o'er the ground where sleep the brave.

LV.

Thy ruins as they fell should aye remain,—
  What monument so fit for those below?
Thy garden through all ages should retain
  The form and fashion which it weareth now,
That future pilgrims here might all things see
Such as they were at this great victory.

IV.

THE SCENE OF WAR.

I.

No cloud the azure vault of heaven distained
  That day when we the field of war surveyed;
The leaves were falling, but the groves retained
  Foliage enough for beauty and for shade;
Soft airs prevailed, and through the sunny hours
The bees were busy on the year's last flowers.

II.

Well was the season with the scene combined.
  The autumnal sunshine suited well the mood
Which here possessed the meditative mind,—
  A human sense upon the field of blood,
A Christian thankfulness, a British pride,
Tempered by solemn thought, yet still to joy allied.

III.

What British heart that would not feel a flow
  Upon that ground, of elevating pride?
What British cheek is there that would not glow
  To hear our country blest and magnified?—
For Britain here was blest by old and young,
Admired by every heart and praised by every tongue.

IV.

Not for brave bearing in the field alone
  Doth grateful Belgium bless the British name;
The order and the perfect honour shown
  In all things, have enhanced the soldier's fame:
For this we heard the admiring people raise
One universal voice sincere of praise.

V.

Yet with indignant feeling they inquired
  Wherefore we spared the author of this strife?
Why had we not, as highest law required,
  With ignominy closed the culprit's life?
For him alone had all this blood been shed,—
Why had not vengeance struck the guilty head?

VI.

O God! they said, it was a piteous thing
  To see the after-horrors of the fight,
The lingering death, the hopeless suffering,—
  What heart of flesh unmoved could bear the sight!
One man was cause of all this world of woe,—
Ye had him,—and ye did not strike the blow!

VII.

How will ye answer to all after time
  For that great lesson which ye failed to give?
As if excess of guilt excused the crime.
  Black as he is with blood, ye let him live!
Children of evil, take your course henceforth,
For what is Justice but a name on earth!

VIII.

Vain had it been with these in glosing speech
  Of precedents to use the specious tongue:
This might perplex the ear, but fail to reach
  The heart, from whence that honest feeling sprung:
And had I dared my inner sense belie,
The voice of blood was there to join them in their cry.

IX.

We left the field of battle in such mood
  As human hearts from thence should bear away,
And musing thus our purposed route pursued,
  Which still through scenes of recent bloodshed lay,
Where Prussia late with strong and stern delight
Hung on her hated foes to persecute their flight.

X.

No hour for tarriance that, or for remorse!
  Vengeance, who long had hungered, took her fill,
And Retribution held its righteous course:
  As when in elder time, the Sun stood still
On Gibeon, and the Moon above the vale
Of Ajalon hung motionless and pale.

XI.

And what though no portentous day was given
  To render here the work of wrath complete,
The Sun, I ween, seemed standing still in heaven
  To those who hurried from that dire defeat;
And when they prayed for darkness in their flight,
The Moon arose upon them broad and bright.

XII.

No covert might they find; the open land,
  O'er which so late exultingly they past,
Lay all before them and on either hand;
  Close on their flight the avengers followed fast,
And when they reached Genappe [7] and there drew
    breath,
Short respite found they there from fear and death.

XIII.

That fatal town betrayed them to more loss;
  Through one long street the only passage lay,
And then the narrow bridge they needs must cross
  Where Dyle, a shallow streamlet, crossed the way:
For life they fled,—no thought had they but fear,
And their own baggage choked the outlet here.

XIV.

He who had bridged the Danube's affluent stream,
  With all the unbroken Austrian power in sight,
(So had his empire vanished like a dream)
  Was by this brook impeded in his flight;—
And then what passions did he witness there—
Rage, terror, execrations, and despair!

XV.

Ere through the wreck his passage could be made,
  Three miserable hours, which seemed like years,
Was he in that ignoble strait delayed;
  The dreadful Prussians' cry was in his ears,
Fear in his heart, and in his soul that hell
Whose due rewards he merited so well.

XVI.

Foremost again as he was wont to be
  In flight, though not the foremost in the strife,
The Tyrant hurried on, of infamy
  Regardless, nor regarding aught but life;—
Oh wretch! without the courage or the faith
To die with those whom he had led to death!

XVII.

Meantime his guilty followers in disgrace,
  Whose pride for ever now was beaten down,
Some in the houses sought a hiding-place;
  While at the entrance of that fatal town
Others, who yet some show of heart displayed,
A short vain effort of resistance made:

XVIII.

Feeble and ill-sustained! The foe burst through;
  With unabating heat they searched around;
The wretches from their lurking-holes they drew,—
  Such mercy as the French had given they found.
Death had more victims there in that one hour
Than fifty years might else have rendered to his power.

XIX.

Here did we inn upon our pilgrimage,
  After such day an unfit resting-place:
For who from ghastly thoughts could disengage
  The haunted mind, when every where the trace
Of death was seen,—the blood-stain on the wall,
And musket-marks in chamber and in hall!

XX.

All talk too was of death. They showed us here
  The room where Brunswick's body had been laid,
Where his brave followers, bending o'er the bier,
  In bitterness their vows of vengeance made;
Where Wellington beheld the slaughtered Chief,
And for awhile gave way to manly grief.

XXI.

Duhesme, whose crimes the Catalans may tell,
 Died here;—with sabre strokes the posts are scored,
Hewn down upon the threshold where he fell,
 Himself then tasting of the ruthless sword;
A Brunswicker discharged the debt of Spain,
And where he dropt the stone preserves the stain.

XXII.

Too much of life hath on thy plains been shed,
 Brabant! so oft the scene of war's debate;
But ne'er with blood were they so largely fed
 As in this rout and wreck; when righteous Fate
Brought on the French, in warning to all times,
A vengeance wide and sweeping as their crimes:

XXIII.

Vengeance for Egypt and for Syria's wrong;
 For Portugal's unutterable woes;
For Germany, who suffered all too long
 Beneath these lawless, faithless, godless foes;
For blood which on the Lord so long had cried,
For Earth opprest, and Heaven insulted and defied.

XXIV.

We followed from Genappe their line of flight
 To the Cross Roads,[18] where Britain's sons sustained
Against such perilous force the desperate fight:
 Deserving for that field so well maintained,
Such fame as for a like devotion's meed
The world hath to the Spartan band decreed.

XXV.

Upon this ground the noble Brunswick died,
 Led on too rashly by his ardent heart;
Long shall his grateful country tell with pride
 How manfully he chose the better part;
When groaning Germany in chains was bound,
He only of her Princes faithful found.

XXVI.

And here right bravely did the German band
 Once more sustain their well-deserved applause;
As when, revenging there their native land,
 In Spain they laboured for the general cause.
In this most arduous strife none more than they
Endured the heat and burthen of the day.

XXVII.

Here too we heard the praise of British worth,
 Still best approved when most severely tried;
Here were broad patches of loose-lying earth,
 Sufficing scarce the mingled bones to hide,—
And half-uncovered graves, where one might see
The loathliest features of mortality.

XXVIII.

Eastward from hence we struck, and reached the field
Of Ligny, where the Prussian, on that day
By far-outnumbering force constrained to yield,
 Fronted the foe, and held them still at bay;
And in that brave defeat acquired fresh claim
To glory, and enhanced his country's fame.

XXIX.

Here was a scene which fancy might delight
 To treasure up among her cherished stores,
And bring again before the inward sight
 Often when she recalls the long-past hours;—
Well-cultured hill and dale extending wide,
Hamlets and village spires on every side;

XXX.

The autumnal-tinted groves; the upland mill
 Which oft was won and lost amid the fray;
Green pastures watered by the silent rill;
 The lordly Castle yielding to decay,
With bridge and barbican and moat and tower,
A fairer sight perchance than when it frowned in power:

XXXI.

The avenue before its ruined gate,
 Which when the Castle, suffering less from time
Than havoc, hath foregone its strength and state,
 Uninjured flourisheth in nature's prime;
To us a grateful shade did it supply,
Glad of that shelter from the noontide sky:

XXXII.

The quarries deep, where many a massive block
 For some Parisian monument of pride,
Hewn with long labour from the granite rock,
 Lay in the change of fortune cast aside;
But rightly with those stones should Prussia build
Her monumental pile on Ligny's bloody field!

XXXIII.

The wealthy village, bearing but too plain
 The dismal marks of recent fire and spoil;
Its decent habitants, an active train,
 And many a one at work with needful toil
On roof or thatch, the ruin to repair,—
May never War repeat such devastation there!

XXXIV.

Ill had we done if we had hurried by
 A scene in faithful history to be famed
Through long succeeding ages; nor may I
 The hospitality let pass unnamed,
And courteous kindness on that distant ground,
Which, strangers as we were, for England's sake we
 found.

XXXV.

And dear to England should be Ligny's name:
 Prussia and England both were proved that day;
Each generous nation to the other's fame
 Her ample tribute of applause will pay;
Long as the memory of those labours past,
Unbroken may their Fair Alliance last!

XXXVI.

The tales which of that field I could unfold,
 Better it is that silence should conceal.
They who had seen them shuddered while they told
 Of things so hideous; and they cried with zeal,
One man hath caused all this, of men the worst,—
O wherefore have ye spared his head accurst![19]

67

XXXVII.

It fits not now to tell our farther way
  Through many a scene by bounteous nature blest;
Nor how we found, where'er our journey lay,
  An Englishman was still an honoured guest;
But still upon this point, where'er we went,
The indignant voice was heard of discontent.

XXXVIII.

And hence there lay, too plainly might we see,
  An ominous feeling upon every heart:
What hope of lasting order could there be,
  They said, where Justice had not had her part?
Wisdom doth rule with Justice by her side;
Justice from Wisdom none may e'er divide.

XXXIX.

The shaken mind felt all things insecure:
  Accustomed long to see successful crimes,
And helplessly the heavy yoke endure,
  They now looked back upon their fathers' times,
Ere the wild rule of Anarchy began,
As to some happier world, or golden age of man.

XL.

As they who in the vale of years advance,
  And the dark eve is closing on their way,
When on their mind the recollections glance
  Of early joy, and Hope's delightful day,
Behold, in brighter hues than those of truth,
The light of morning on the fields of youth;—

XLI.

Those who amid these troubles had grown grey,
  Recurred with mournful feeling to the past:
Blest had we known our blessings! they would say,
  We were not worthy that our bliss should last!
Peaceful we were, and flourishing and free,
But madly we required more liberty!

XLII.

Remorseless France had long oppressed the land,
  And for her frantic projects drained its blood;
And now they felt the Prussian's heavy hand: [20]
  He came to aid them; bravely had he stood
In their defence;—but oh! in peace how ill
The soldier's deeds, how insolent his will!

XLIII.

One general wish prevailed,—if they might see
  The happy order of old times restored!
Give them their former laws and liberty,
  This their desires and secret prayers implored;—
Forgetful, as the stream of time flows on,
That that which passes is for ever gone.

PART II.

THE VISION.

Ἔπεχε νῶν σκοπῷ τόξον,
Ἄγε θυμέ.   PINDAR.

I.

THE TOWER.

I.

I THOUGHT upon these things in solitude,
  And mused upon them in the silent night;
The open graves, the recent scene of blood,
  Were present to the soul's creative sight;
These mournful images my mind possest,
And mingled with the visions of my rest.

II.

Methought that I was travelling o'er a plain
  Whose limits, far beyond all reach of sense,
The aching anxious sight explored in vain.
  How I came there I could not tell, nor whence;
Nor where my melancholy journey lay;
Only that soon the night would close upon my way.

III.

Behind me was a dolorous, dreary scene,
  With huge and mouldering ruins widely spread;
Wastes which had whilome fertile regions been,
  Tombs which had lost all record of the dead;
And where the dim horizon seemed to close,
Far off the gloomy Pyramids arose.

IV.

Full fain would I have known what lay before,
  But lifted there in vain my mortal eye;
That point with cloud and mist was covered o'er,
  As though the earth were mingled with the sky.
Yet thither, as some power unseen impelled,
My blind involuntary way I held.

V.

Across the plain innumerable crowds
  Like me were on their destined journey bent,
Toward the land of shadows and of clouds:
  One pace they travelled, to one point they went;—
A motley multitude of old and young,
Men of all climes and hues, and every tongue.

VI.

Ere long I came upon a field of dead,
  Where heaps of recent carnage filled the way;
A ghastly sight,—nor was there where to tread,
  So thickly slaughtered, horse and man, they lay.
Methought that in that place of death I knew
Again the late-seen field of Waterloo.

VII.

Troubled I stood, and doubtful where to go,—
  A cold damp shuddering ran through all my frame :
Fain would I fly from that dread scene, when lo!
  A voice as from above pronounced my name;
And looking to the sound, by the way-side
I saw a lofty structure edified.

VIII.

Most like it seemed to that aspiring Tower
  Which old Ambition reared on Babel's plain,
As if he weened in his presumptuous power
  To scale high Heaven with daring pride profane;
Such was its giddy height : and round and round
The spiral steps in long ascension wound.

IX.

Its frail foundations upon sand were placed,
  And round about it mouldering rubbish lay;
For easily by time and storms defaced,
  The loose materials crumbled in decay :
Rising so high, and built so insecure,
Ill might such perishable work endure.

X.

I not the less went up, and as I drew
  Toward the top, more firm the structure seemed,
With nicer art composed, and fair to view :
  Strong and well-built perchance I might have deemed
The pile, had I not seen and understood
Of what frail matter formed, and on what base it stood.

XI.

There on the summit a grave personage
  Received and welcomed me in courteous guise;
On his grey temples were the marks of age,
  As one whom years methought should render wise.
I saw that thou wert filled with doubt and fear,
He said, and therefore have I called thee here.

XII.

Hence from this eminence sublime I see
  The wanderings of the erring crowd below,
And pitying thee in thy perplexity,
  Will tell thee all that thou canst need to know
To guide thy steps aright. I bent my head
As if in thanks,—And who art thou? I said.

XIII.

He answered, I am Wisdom. Mother Earth
  Me, in her vigour self-conceiving, bore;
And as from eldest time I date my birth,
  Eternally with her shall I endure;
Her noblest offspring I, to whom alone
The course of sublunary things is known.

XIV.

Master! quoth I, regarding him, I thought
  That Wisdom was the child divine of Heaven.
So, he replied, have fabling preachers taught,
  And the dull world a light belief hath given;
But vainly would these fools my claim decry,—
Wisdom I am, and of the Earth am I.

XV.

Thus while he spake I scanned his features well :
  Small but audacious was the Old Man's eye;
His countenance was hard, and seemed to tell
  Of knowledge less than of effrontery.
Instruct me then, I said, for thou shouldst know,
From whence I came, and whither I must go.

XVI.

Art thou then one who would his mind perplex
  With knowledge bootless, even if attained?
Fond man! he answered;—wherefore shouldst thou vex
  Thy heart with seeking what may not be gained?
Regard not what has been, nor what may be,
O Child of Earth, this Now is all that toucheth thee!

XVII.

He who performs the journey of to-day
  Cares not if yesterday were shower or sun:
To-morrow let the heavens be what they may,
  And what recks he?—his wayfare will be done.
Heedless of what hereafter may befall,
Live whilst thou livest, for this life is all!

XVIII.

I kept my rising indignation down,
  That I might hear what farther he would teach;
Yet on my darkened brow the instinctive frown,
  Gathering at that abominable speech,
Maintained its place : he marked it and pursued,
Tuning his practised tongue to subtle flattery's mood:

XIX.

Do I not know thee,—that from earliest youth
  Knowledge hath been thy only heart's-desire?
Here seeing all things as they are in truth,
  I show thee all to which thy thoughts aspire:
No vapours here impede the exalted sense,
Nor mists of earth attain this eminence!

XX.

Whither thy way, thou askest me, and what
  The region dark whereto thy footsteps tend,
And where by one inevitable lot
  The course of all yon multitude must end.
Take thou this glass, whose perfect power shall aid
Thy faulty vision, and therewith explore the shade.

XXI.

Eager I looked; but seeing with surprise
  That the same darkness still the view o'erspread,
Half angrily I turned away mine eyes.
  Complacent then the Old Man smiled and said,
Darkness is all! what more wouldst thou descry?
Rest now content, for farther none can spy.

XXII.

Now mark me, Child of Earth! he thus pursued;
  Let not the hypocrites thy reason blind,
And to the quest of some unreal good
  Divert with dogmas vain thine erring mind:
Learn thou, whate'er the motive they may call,
That Pleasure is the aim, and Self the spring of all.

XXIII.

This is the root of knowledge.   Wise are they
  Who to this guiding principle attend:
They, as they press along the world's high-way,
  With single aim pursue their steady end:
No vain compunction checks their sure career;
No idle dreams deceive; their heart is here.

XXIV.

They from the nature and the fate of man,
  Thus clearly understood, derive their strength;
Knowing that as from nothing they began,
  To nothing they must needs return at length;
This knowledge steels the heart and clears the mind,
And they create on earth the Heaven they find.

XXV.

Such, I made answer, was the Tyrant's creed
  Who bruised the nations with his iron rod,
Till on yon field the wretch received his meed
  From Britain, and the outstretched arm of God!
Behold him now,—Death ever in his view,
The only change for him,—and Judgment to ensue!

XXVI.

Behold him when the unbidden thoughts arise
  Of his old passions and unbridled power;
As the fierce tiger in confinement lies,
  And dreams of blood that he must taste no more,—
Then waking in that appetite of rage,
Frets to and fro within his narrow cage.

XXVII.

Hath he not chosen well? the Old Man replied;
  Bravely he aimed at universal sway,
And never earthly Chief was glorified
  Like this Napoleon in his prosperous day.
All-ruling Fate itself hath not the power
To alter what has been: and he has had his hour!

XXVIII.

Take him, I answered, at his fortune's flood;
  Russia his friend, the Austrian wars surceased;
When Kings, his creatures some, and some subdued,
  Like vassals waited at his marriage feast;
And Europe like a map before him lay,
Of which he gave at will, or took away.

XXIX.

Call then to mind Navarre's heroic chief,
  Wandering by night and day through wood and glen,
His country's sufferings like a private grief
  Wringing his heart: would Mina even then
Those perils and that sorrow have foregone
To be that Tyrant on his prosperous throne?

XXX.

But wherefore name I him whose arm was free?
  A living hope his noble heart sustained,
A faith which bade him through all dangers see
  The triumph his enduring country gained.
See Hofer with no earthly hope to aid,—
His country lost,—himself to chains and death betrayed!

XXXI.

By those he served deserted in his need;
  Given to the unrelenting Tyrant's power,
And by his mean revenge condemned to bleed,—
  Would he have bartered in that awful hour
His heart, his conscience, and his sure renown,
For the malignant murderer's crimes and crown?

XXXII.

Him too, I know, a worthy thought of fame
  In that dread trance upheld;—the foresight sure
That in his own dear country his good name
  Long as the streams and mountains should endure;
The shepherds on the hills should sing his praise,
And children learn his deeds through all succeeding days.

XXXIII.

Turn we to those in whom no glorious thought
  Lent its strong succour to the passive mind;
Nor stirring enterprise within them wrought;—
  Who, to their lot of bitterness resigned,
Endured their sorrows by the world unknown,
And looked for their reward to Death alone:

XXXIV.

Mothers within Gerona's leaguered wall,
  Who saw their famished children pine and die;—
Widows surviving Zaragoza's fall
  To linger in abhorred captivity;—
Yet would not have exchanged their sacred woe
For all the empire of their miscreant foe!

XXXV.

Serene the Old Man replied, and smiled with scorn,
  Behold the effect of error! thus to wear
The days of miserable life forlorn,
  Struggling with evil and consumed with care;—
Poor fools, whom vain and empty hopes mislead!
They reap their sufferings for their only meed.

XXXVI.

O false one! I exclaimed, whom canst thou fool
  With such gross sophisms, but the wicked heart!
The pupils of thine own unhappy school
  Are they who chuse the vain and empty part;
How oft in age, in sickness, and in woe,
Have they complained that all was vanity below!

XXXVII.

Look at that mighty Gaznevide Mahmood,
  When pining in his Palace of Delight,
He bade the gathered spoils of realms subdued
  Be spread before him to regale his sight,
Whate'er the Orient boasts of rich and rare,—
And then he wept to think what toys they were!

XXXVIII.

Look at the Russian minion when he played
  With pearls and jewels which surpassed all price;
And now apart their various hues arrayed,
  Blended their colours now in union nice,
Then weary of the baubles, with a sigh,
Swept them aside, and thought that all was vanity!

XXXIX.

Weaned by the fatal messenger from pride,
　The Syrian through the streets exposed his shroud;
And one that ravaged kingdoms far and wide
　Upon the bed of sickness cried aloud,
What boots my empire in this mortal throe,
For the Grave calls me now, and I must go!

XL.

Thus felt these wretched men, because decay
　Had touched them in their vitals, Death stood by;
And Reason, when the props of flesh gave way,
　Purged as with euphrasy the mortal eye.
Who seeks for worldly honours, wealth or power,
Will find them vain indeed at that dread hour!

XLI.

These things are vain; but all things are not so,
　The virtues and the hopes of human kind!—
Yea, by the God who, ordering all below,
　In his own image made the immortal mind,
Desires there are which draw from Him their birth,
And bring forth lasting fruits for Heaven and Earth.

XLII.

Therefore, through evil and through good content,
　The righteous man performs his part assigned;
In bondage lingering, or with sufferings spent,
　Therefore doth peace support the heroic mind;
And from the dreadful sacrifice of all,
Meek woman doth not shrink at Duty's call.

XLIII.

Therefore the Martyr [21] clasps the stake in faith,
　And sings thanksgiving while the flames aspire;
Victorious over agony and death,
　Sublime he stands and triumphs in the fire,
As though to him Elijah's lot were given,
And that the Chariot and the steeds of Heaven.

II.

THE EVIL PROPHET.

I.

WITH that my passionate discourse I brake;
　Too fast the thought, too strong the feeling came.
Composed the Old Man listened while I spake,
　Nor moved to wrath, nor capable of shame;
And when I ceased, unaltered was his mien,
His hard eye unabashed, his front serene.

II.

Hard is it error from the mind to weed,
　He answered, where it strikes so deep a root:
Let us to other argument proceed,
　And, if we may, discover what the fruit
Of this long strife,—what harvest of great good
The World shall reap for all this cost of blood!

III.

Assuming then a frown as thus he said,
　He stretched his hand from that commanding height,
Behold, quoth he, where thrice ten thousand dead
　Are laid, the victims of a single fight!
And thrice ten thousand more at'Ligny lie,
Slain for the prelude to this tragedy!

IV.

This but a page of the great book of war,—
　A drop amid the scene of human woes!—
Thou canst remember when the Morning Star
　Of Freedom on rejoicing France arose,
Over her vine-clad hills and regions gay,
Fair even as Phosphor who foreruns the day.

V.

Such and so beautiful that Star's uprise;
　But soon the glorious dawn was overcast:
A baleful track it held across the skies,
　Till now, through all its fatal changes past,
Its course fulfilled, its aspects understood,
On Waterloo it hath gone down in blood.

VI.

Where now the hopes with which thine ardent youth
　Rejoicingly to run its race began?
Where now the reign of Liberty and Truth,
　The Rights Omnipotent of Equal Man,
The principles should make all discord cease,
And bid poor humankind repose at length in peace?

VII.

Behold the Bourbon to that throne by force
　Restored, from whence by fury he was cast:
Thus to the point where it began its course,
　The melancholy cycle comes at last;
And what are all the intermediate years?—
What, but a bootless waste of blood and tears!

VIII.

The peace which thus at Waterloo ye won,
　Shall it endure with this exasperate foe?
In gratitude for all that ye have done,
　Will France her ancient enmity forego?
Her wounded spirit, her envenomed will
Ye know,—and ample means are left her still.

IX.

What though the tresses of her strength be shorn,
　The roots remain untouched; and as of old
The bondsman Sampson felt his power return
　To his knit sinews, so shall ye behold
France, like a giant fresh from sleep, arise
And rush upon her slumbering enemies.

X.

Woe then for Belgium! for this ill-doomed land,
　The theatre of strife through every age!
Look from this eminence whereon we stand,—
　What is the region round us but a stage,
For the mad pastime of Ambition made,
Whereon War's dreadful drama may be played'

XI.

Thus hath it been from history's earliest light,
  When yonder by the Sabis Cæsar stood,
And saw his legions, raging from the fight,
  Root out the noble nation they subdued:
Even at this day the peasant findeth there
The relics of that ruthless massacre.

XII.

Need I recall the long religious strife?
  Or William's hard-fought fields? or Marlborough's fame
Here purchased at such lavish price of life,—
  Or Fontenoy, or Fleurus' later name?
Wherever here the foot of man may tread,
The blood of man hath on that spot been shed.

XIII.

Shall then Futurity a happier train
  Unfold, than this dark picture of the past?
Dreamest thou again of some Saturnian reign,
  Or that this ill-compacted realm should last?
Its wealth and weakness to the foe are known,
And the first shock subverts its baseless throne.

XIV.

O wretched country, better should thy soil
  Be laid again beneath the invading seas,
Thou goodliest masterpiece of human toil,
  If still thou must be doomed to scenes like these!
O Destiny inexorable and blind!
O miserable lot of poor mankind!

XV.

Saying thus, he fixed on me a searching eye
  Of stern regard, as if my heart to reach:
Yet gave he now no leisure to reply;
  For ere I might dispose my thoughts for speech,
The Old Man, as one who felt and understood
His strength, the theme of his discourse pursued.

XVI.

If we look farther, what shall we behold
  But every where the swelling seeds of ill,
Half-smothered fires, and causes manifold
  Of strife to come; the powerful watching still
For fresh occasion to enlarge his power,
The weak and injured waiting for their hour!

XVII.

Will the rude Cossack with his spoils bear back
  The love of peace and humanising art?
Think ye the mighty Moscovite shall lack
  Some specious business for the ambitious heart;
Or the black Eagle, when she moults her plume,
The form and temper of the Dove assume?

XVIII.

From the old Germanic chaos hath there risen
  A happier order of established things?
And is the Italian Mind from papal prison
  Set free to soar upon its native wings?
Or look to Spain, and let her Despot tell
If there thy high-raised hopes are answered well!

XIX.

At that appeal my spirit breathed a groan,
  But he triumphantly pursued his speech:
O Child of Earth, he cried with loftier tone,
  The present and the past one lesson teach!
Look where thou wilt, the history of man
Is but a thorny maze, without a plan!

XX.

The winds which have in viewless heaven their birth,
  The waves which in their fury meet the clouds,
The central storms which shake the solid earth,
  And from volcanoes burst in fiery floods,
Are not more vague and purportless and blind,
Than is the course of things among mankind!

XXI.

Rash hands unravel what the wise have spun;
  Realms which in story fill so large a part,
Reared by the strong are by the weak undone;
  Barbarians overthrow the work of art,
And what force spares is sapped by sure decay,—
So earthly things are changed and pass away.

XXII.

And think not thou thy England hath a spell,
  That she this general fortune should elude;
Easier to crush the foreign foe, than quell
  The malice which misleads the multitude,
And that dread malady of erring zeal,
Which like a cancer eats into the commonweal.

XXIII.

The fabric of her power is undermined;
  The earthquake underneath it will have way,
And all that glorious structure, as the wind
  Scatters a summer cloud, be swept away:
For Destiny on this terrestrial ball
Drives on her iron car, and crushes all.

XXIV.

Thus as he ended, his mysterious form
  Enlarged, grew dim, and vanished from my view.
At once on all sides rushed the gathered storm,
  The thunders rolled around, the wild winds blew,
And as the tempest round the summit beat,
The whole frail fabric shook beneath my feet.

III.

THE SACRED MOUNTAIN.

I.

But then methought I heard a voice exclaim,
  Hither my Son, Oh hither take thy flight!
A heavenly voice which called me by my name,
  And bade me hasten from that treacherous height:
The voice it was which I was wont to hear,
Sweet as a Mother's to her infant's ear.

II.

I hesitated not, but at the call
  Sprung from the summit of that tottering tower.
There is a motion known in dreams to all,
  When buoyant by some self-sustaining power,
Through air we seem to glide, as if set free
From all incumbrance of mortality.

III.

Thus borne aloft I reached the Sacred Hill,
  And left the scene of tempests far behind:
But that old tempter's parting language still
  Prest like a painful burthen on my mind;
The troubled soul had lost her inward light,
And all within was black as Erebus and Night.

IV.

The Thoughts which I had known in youth returned,
  But oh how changed! a sad and spectral train:
And while for all the miseries past I mourned,
  And for the lives which had been given in vain,
In sorrow and in fear I turned mine eye
From the dark aspects of futurity.

V.

I sought the thickest woodland's shade profound,
  As suited best my melancholy mood,
And cast myself upon the gloomy ground.
  When lo! a gradual radiance filled the wood;
A heavenly presence rose upon my view,
And in that form divine the awful Muse I knew.

VI.

Hath then that Spirit false perplexed thy heart,
  O thou of little faith! severe she cried.
Bear with me, Goddess, heavenly as thou art,
  Bear with my earthly nature! I replied,
And let me pour into thine ear my grief:
Thou canst enlighten, thou canst give relief.

VII.

The ploughshare had gone deep, the sower's hand
  Had scattered in the open soil the grain;
The harrow too had well prepared the land;
  I looked to see the fruit of all this pain!—
Alas! the thorns and old inveterate weed
Have sprung again, and stifled the good seed.

VIII.

I hoped that Italy should break her chains,
  Foreign and papal, with the world's applause,
Knit in firm union her divided reigns,
  And rear a well-built pile of equal laws:
Then might the wrongs of Venice be forgiven,
And joy should reach Petrarca's soul in Heaven.

IX.

I hoped that that abhorred Idolatry
  Had in the strife received its mortal wound:
The Souls which from beneath the Altar cry,
  At length, I thought, had their just vengeance found;—
In purple and in scarlet clad, behold
The Harlot sits, adorned with gems and gold! [22]

X.

The golden cup she bears full to the brim
  Of her abominations as of yore!
Her eyeballs with inebriate triumph swim;
  Though drunk with righteous blood, she thirsts for more,
Eager to reassert her influence fell,
And once again let loose the Dogs of Hell.

XI.

Woe for that people too who by their path
  For these late triumphs first made plain the way;
Whom in the Valley of the Shade of Death
  No fears nor fiery sufferings could dismay:
Art could not tempt, nor violence enthrall
Their firm devotion, faithful found through all.

XII.

Strange race of haughty heart and stubborn will,
  Slavery they love and chains with pride they wear;
Inflexible alike in good or ill,
  The inveterate stamp of servitude they bear.
Oh fate perverse, to see all change withstood,
There only where all change must needs be good!

XIII.

But them nor foe can force, nor friend persuade;
  Impassive souls in iron forms inclosed,
As though of human mould they were not made,
  But of some sterner elements composed,
Against offending nations to be sent,
The ruthless ministers of punishment.

XIV.

Where are those Minas after that career
  Wherewith all Europe rang from side to side?
In exile wandering! Where the Mountaineer,—
  Late, like Pelayo, the Asturian's pride?
Had Ferdinand no mercy for that life,
Exposed so long for him in daily,—hourly strife!

XV.

From her Athenian orator of old
  Greece never listened to sublimer strain
That that with which, for truth and freedom bold,
  Quintana moved the inmost soul of Spain.
What meed is his let Ferdinand declare—
Chains, and the silent dungeon, and despair!

XVI.

For this hath England borne so brave a part!
  Spent with endurance, or in battle slain,
Is it for this so many an English heart
  Lies mingled with the insensate soil of Spain?
Is this the issue, this the happy birth
In those long throes and that strong agony brought forth?

XVII.

And oh! if England's fatal hour draw nigh,—
  If that most glorious edifice should fall
By the wild hands of bestial Anarchy,—
  Then might it seem that He who ordereth all
Doth take for sublunary things no care:—
The burthen of that thought is more than I can bear.

XVIII.

Even as a mother listens to her child,
  My plaint the Muse divine benignant heard,
Then answer'd in reproving accents mild:
  What if thou seest the fruit of hope deferr'd;
Dost thou for this in faltering faith repine?
A manlier, wiser virtue should be thine!

XIX.

Ere the good seed can give its fruit in Spain,
  The light must shine on that bedarken'd land,
And Italy must break her papal chain,
  Ere the soil answer to the sower's hand;
For till the sons their fathers' fault repent,
The old error brings its direful punishment.[23]

XX.

Hath not experience bid the wise man see
  Poor hope from innovations premature?
All sudden change is ill: slow grows the tree,
  Which in its strength through ages shall endure.
In that ungrateful earth it long may lie
Dormant, but fear not that the seed should die.

XXI.

Falsely that Tempter taught thee that the past
  Was but a blind inextricable maze:
Falsely he taught that evil overcast
  With gathering tempests these propitious days,
That he in subtle snares thy soul might bind,
And rob thee of thy hopes for human kind.

XXII.

He told thee the beginning and the end
  Were indistinguishable all, and dark;
And when from his vain Tower he bade thee bend
  Thy curious eye, well knew he that no spark
Of heavenly light would reach the baffled sense,
The mists of earth lay round him all too dense.

XXIII.

Must I, as thou hadst chosen the evil part,
  Tell thee that Man is free and God is good?
These primal truths are rooted in thy heart:
  But these being rightly felt and understood,
Should bring with them a hope, calm, constant, sure,
Patient, and on the rock of faith secure.

XXIV.

The Monitress Divine, as thus she spake,
  Induced me gently on, ascending still,
And thus emerging from that mournful brake
  We drew toward the summit of the hill,
And reach'd a green and sunny place, so fair,
As well with long-lost Eden might compare.

XXV.

Broad cedars grew around that lovely glade,
  Exempted from decay, and never sere,
Their wide spread boughs diffused a fragrant shade;
  The cypress incorruptible was here,
With fluted stem, and head aspiring high,
Nature's proud column, pointing to the sky.

XXVI.

There too the vigorous olive in its pride,
  As in its own Apulian soil uncheck'd,
Tower'd high, and spread its willowy foliage wide:
  With liveliest hues the mead beneath was deck'd,
Gift of that grateful tree, that with its root
Repays the earth from whence it feeds its fruit.

XXVII.

There too the sacred bay, of brighter green,
  Exalted its rejoicing head on high:
And there the martyr's holier palm was seen
  Waving its plumage as the breeze went by.
All fruits which ripen under genial skies
Grew there as in another Paradise.

XXVIII.

And over all that lovely glade there grew
  All wholesome roots and plants of healing power;
The herb of grace, the medicinal rue,
  The poppy rich in worth as gay in flower:
The heart's-ease that delighteth every eye,
And sage divine and virtuous euphrasy.

XXIX.

Unwounded here Judæa's balm distill'd
  Its precious juice; the snowy jasmine here
Spread its luxuriant tresses wide, and fill'd
  With fragrance the delicious atmosphere;
More piercing still did orange-flowers dispense
From golden groves the purest joy of sense.

XXX.

As low it lurk'd the tufted moss between,
  The violet there its modest perfume shed,
Like humble virtue, rather felt than seen:
  And here the Rose of Sharon rear'd its head,
The glory of all flowers, to sense and sight
Yielding their full contentment of delight.

XXXI.

A gentle river wound its quiet way
  Through this sequestered glade, meandering wide;
Smooth as a mirror here the surface lay;
  Where the pure lotus, floating in its pride,
Enjoy'd the breath of heaven, the sun's warm beam,
And the cool freshness of its native stream.

XXXII.

Here o'er green weeds whose tresses waved outspread,
  With silent lapse the glassy waters run:
Here in fleet motion o'er a pebbly bed
  Gliding they glance and ripple to the sun:
The stirring breeze that swept them in its flight,
Raised on the stream a shower of sparkling light.

XXXIII.

And all sweet birds sung there their lays of love;
  The mellow thrush, the black-bird loud and shrill;
The rapturous nightingale that shook the grove,
  Made the ears vibrate and the heart-strings thrill;
The ambitious lark, that soaring in the sky,
Pour'd forth her lyric strain of ecstacy.[24]

XXXIV.

Sometimes when that wild chorus intermits,
  The linnet's song was heard amid the trees,
A low sweet voice: and sweeter still, at fits
  The ring-dove's wooing came upon the breeze;
While with the wind which moved the leaves among,
The murmuring waters joined in undersong.

XXXV.

The hare disported here, and fear'd no ill,
  For never evil thing that glade came nigh;
The sheep were free to wander at their will,
  As needing there no earthly shepherd's eye;
The bird sought no concealment for her nest,
So perfect was the peace wherewith those bowers were
      blest.

XXXVI.

All blending thus with all in one delight,
  The soul was soothed and satisfied and fill'd:
This mingled bliss of sense and sound and sight,
  The flow of boisterous mirth might there have still'd,
And sinking in the gentle spirit deep,
Have touched those strings of joy which make us weep.

XXXVII.

Even thus in earthly gardens had it been,
  If earthly gardens might with these compare;
But more than all such influences I ween
  There was a heavenly virtue in the air,
Which laid all vain perplexing thoughts to rest,
And healed and calmed and purified the breast.

XXXVIII.

Then said I to that guide divine, My soul
  When here we entered, was o'ercharged with grief,
For evil doubts which I could not controul ·
  Beset my troubled spirit.   This relief,—
This change,—whence are they? Almost it might seem
I never lived till now; all else had been a dream.

XXXIX.

My heavenly teacher answered, Say not *seem*;—
  In this place all things *are* what they appear;
And they who feel the past a feverish dream,
  Wake to reality on entering here.
These waters are the Well of Life, and lo!
The Rock of Ages there, from whence they flow.

XL.

Saying thus we came upon an inner glade,
  The holiest place that human eyes might see;
For all that vale was like a temple made
  By Nature's hand, and this the sanctuary;
Where in its bed of living rock, the Rood
Of man's redemption, firmly-planted stood,

XLI.

And at its foot the never-failing Well
  Of Life profusely flowed that all might drink.
Most blessed water! Neither tongue can tell.
  The blessedness thereof, nor heart can think,
Save only those to whom it hath been given
To taste of that divinest gift of Heaven.

XLII.

There grew a goodly Tree this Well beside,—
  Behold a branch from Eden planted here,
Plucked from the Tree of Knowledge, said my guide.
  O Child of Adam, put away thy fear,—
In thy first father's grave it hath its root;
Taste thou the bitter, but the wholesome fruit.

XLIII.

In awe I heard, and trembled, and obeyed ﹀
  The bitterness was even as of death;
I felt a cold and piercing thrill pervade.
  My loosened limbs, and losing sight and breath,
To earth I should have fallen in my despair,
Had I not clasped the Cross and been supported there.

XLIV.

My heart, I thought, was bursting with the force
  Of that most fatal fruit; soul-sick I felt,
And tears ran down in such continuous course,
  As if the very eyes themselves should melt.
But then I heard my heavenly teacher say,
Drink, and this mortal stound will pass away.

XLV.

I stooped and drank of that divinest Well,
  Fresh from the Rock of Ages where it ran;
It had a heavenly quality to quell
  My pain :—I rose a renovated man,
And would not now, when that relief was known,
For worlds the needful suffering have foregone.

XLVI.

Even as the Eagle (ancient storyers say)
  When faint with years she feels her flagging wing,
Soars up toward the mid-sun's piercing ray,
  Then filled with fire into some living spring
Plunges, and casting there her aged plumes,
The vigorous strength of primal youth resumes:

XLVII.

Such change in me that blessed Water wrought:
  The bitterness which from its fatal root,
The tree derived with painful healing fraught,
  Passed clean away; and in its place the fruit
Produced by virtue of that wondrous wave,
The savour which in paradise it gave.

XLVIII.

Now, said the heavenly Muse, thou mayst advance,
  Fitly prepared toward the mountain's height.
O Child of Man, this necessary trance
  Hath purified from flaw thy mortal sight,
That with scope unconfined of vision free,
Thou the beginning and the end mayst see.

XLIX.

She took me by the hand and on we went;
  Hope urged me forward and my soul was strong.
With winged speed we scaled the steep ascent,
  Nor seemed the labour difficult or long,
Ere on the summit of the sacred hill
Upraised I stood, where I might gaze my fill.

L.

Below me lay, unfolded like a scroll,
    The boundless region where I wandered late,
Where I might see realms spread and oceans roll,
    And mountains from their cloud-surmounting state
Dwarfed like a map beneath the excursive sight—
So ample was the range from that commanding height.

LI.

Eastward with darkness round on every side,
    An eye of light was in the farthest sky.
Lo, the beginning!—said my heavenly Guide;
    The steady ray which there thou canst descry,
Comes from lost Eden, from the primal land
Of man, « waved over by the fiery brand.»

LII.

Look now toward the end ! no mists obscure,
    Nor clouds will there impede the strengthened sight:
Unblenched thine eye the vision may endure.
    I looked,—surrounded with effulgent light
More glorious than all glorious hues of even,
The Angel Death stood there in the open Gate of Heaven.

IV.

THE HOPES OF MAN.

I.

Now, said my heavenly Teacher, all is clear !—
    Bear the Beginning and the End in mind,
The course of human things will then appear
    Beneath its proper laws; and thou wilt find,
Through all their seeming labyrinth, the plan
Which « vindicates the ways of God to Man.»

II.

Free choice doth man possess of good or ill,—
    All were but mockery else. From Wisdom's way
Too oft perverted by the tainted will
    Is his rebellious nature drawn astray ;
Therefore an inward monitor is given,
A voice that answers to the law of Heaven.

III.

Frail as he is, and as an infant weak,
    The knowledge of his weakness is his strength ;
For succour is vouchsafed to those who seek
    In humble faith sincere ; and when at length
Death sets the disembodied spirit free,
According to their deeds their lot shall be.

IV.

Thus, should the chance of private fortune raise
    A transitory doubt, Death answers all.
And in the scale of nations, if the ways
    Of Providence mysterious we may call,
Yet rightly viewed, all history doth impart
Comfort and hope and strength to the believing heart.

V.

For through the lapse of ages may the course
    Of moral good progressive still be seen,
Though mournful dynasties of Fraud and Force,
    Dark Vice and purblind Ignorance intervene ;
Empires and nations rise, decay and fall,
But still the Good survives and perseveres through all.

VI.

Yea even in those most lamentable times,
    When every-where to wars and woes a prey,
Earth seemed but one wide theatre of crimes,
    Good unperceived hath worked its silent way,
And all those dread convulsions did but clear
The obstructed path to give it free career.

VII.

But deem not thou some over-ruling Fate,
    Directing all things with benign decree,
Through all the turmoil of this mortal state,
    Appoints that what is best shall therefore be :
Even as from man his future doom proceeds,
So nations rise or fall according to their deeds.

VIII.

Light at the first was given to humankind,
    And Law was written in the human heart :
If they forsake the Light, perverse of mind,
    And wilfully prefer the evil part,
Then to their own devices are they left,
By their own choice of Heaven's support bereft.

IX.

The individual culprit may sometimes
    Unpunished to his after-reckoning go :
Not thus collective man,—for public crimes
    Draw on their proper punishment below ; [25]
When nations go astray, from age to age
The effects remain, a fatal heritage.

X.

Bear witness, Egypt, thy huge monuments
    Of priestly fraud and tyranny austere !
Bear witness thou whose only name presents
    All holy feelings to religion dear,—
In Earth's dark circlet once the precious gem
Of living light,—O fallen Jerusalem !

XI.

See barbarous Africa, on every side
    To error, wretchedness, and crimes resigned !
Behold the vicious Orient, far and wide
    Enthralled in slavery ! as the human mind
Corrupts and goes to wreck, Earth sickens there,
And the contagion taints the ambient air.

XII.

They had the Light, and from the Light they turned ; [26]
    What marvel if they grope in darkness lost ?
They had the Law ;—God's natural Law they scorned,
    And chusing error, thus they pay the cost !
Wherever Falsehood and Oppression reign,
There degradation follows in their train.

XIII.

What then in these late days had Europe been,—
 This moral, intellectual heart of earth,—
From which the nations who lie dead in sin
 Should one day yet receive their second birth,—
To what had she been sunk if brutal Force
Had taken unrestrained its impious course!

XIV.

The Light had been extinguished,—this be sure
 The first wise aim of conscious Tyranny,
Which knows it may not with the Light endure:
 But where Light is not, Freedom cannot be;
« Where Freedom is not, there no Virtue is;»
Where Virtue is not, there no Happiness.

XV.

If among hateful Tyrants of all times
 For endless execration handed down,
One may be found surpassing all in crimes,
 One that for infamy should bear the crown,
Napoleon [27] is that man, in guilt the first,
Pre-eminently bad among the worst.

XVI.

For not, like Scythian conquerors, did he tread
 From his youth up the common path of blood;
Nor like some Eastern Tyrant was he bred
 In sensual harems, ignorant of good;—
Their vices from the circumstance have grown,
His by deliberate purpose were his own.

XVII.

Not led away by circumstance he erred,
 But from the wicked heart his error came:
By Fortune to the highest place preferred,
 He sought through evil means an evil aim,
And all his ruthless measures were designed
To enslave, degrade, and brutalize mankind.

XVIII.

Some barbarous dream of empire to fulfil,
 Those iron ages he would have restored,
When Law was but the ruffian soldier's will,
 Might governed all, the sceptre was the sword,
And Peace, not elsewhere finding where to dwell,
Sought a sad refuge in the convent cell.

XIX.

Too far had he succeeded! In his mould
 An evil generation had been framed,
By no religion tempered or controlled,
 By foul examples of all crimes inflamed,
Of faith, of honour, of compassion void;—
Such were the fitting agents he employed.

XX.

Believing as yon lying spirit taught,
 They to that vain philosophy held fast,
And trusted that as they began from nought,
 To nothing they should needs return at last;
Hence no restraint of conscience, no remorse,
But every baleful passion took its course.

XXI.

And had they triumphed, Earth had once again,
 To Violence subdued, and impious Pride,
Verged to such state of wickedness, as when
 The Giantry of old their God defied,
And Heaven, impatient of a world like this,
Opened its flood-gates, and broke up the abyss.

XXII.

That danger is gone by. On Waterloo
 The Tyrant's fortune in the scale was weighed,—
His fortune and the World's,—and England threw
 Her sword into the balance—down it swayed:
And when in battle first he met that foe,
There he received his mortal overthrow.

XXIII.

O my brave countrymen, with that I said,
 For then my heart with transport overflowed,
O men of England! nobly have ye paid
 The debt which to your ancestors ye owed!
And gathered for your children's heritage
A glory that shall last from age to age!

XXIV.

And we did well when on our Mountain's height
 For Waterloo we raised the festal flame,
And in our triumph taught the startled night
 To ring with Wellington's victorious name,
Making the far-off mariner admire
To see the crest of Skiddaw plumed with fire.

XXV.

The Moon who had in silence visited
 His lonely summit from the birth of time,
That hour an unavailing splendour shed,
 Lost in the effulgence of the flame sublime,
In whose broad blaze rejoicingly we stood,
And all below a depth of blackest solitude.

XXVI.

Fit theatre for this great joy we chose:
 For never since above the abating Flood
Emerging, first that pinnacle arose,
 Had cause been given for deeper gratitude,
For prouder joy to every English heart,
When England had so well performed her arduous part.

XXVII.

The Muse replied with gentle smile benign,—
 Well mayst thou praise the land that gave thee birth,
And bless the Fate which made that country thine;
 For of all ages and all parts of earth,
To chuse thy time and place did Fate allow,
Wise choice would be this England and this Now.

XXVIII.

From bodily and mental bondage, there
 Hath Man his full emancipation gained;
The viewless and illimitable air
 Is not more free than Thought; all unrestrained,
Nor pined in want, nor sunk in sensual sloth,
There may the immortal Mind attain its growth.

XXIX.

There, under Freedom's tutelary wing,
  Deliberate Courage fears no human foe,
There undefiled, as in their native spring,
  The living waters of Religion flow;
There like a beacon the transmitted Light
Conspicuous to all nations burneth bright.

XXX.

The virtuous will she hath, which should aspire
  To spread the sphere of happiness and light:
She hath the power to answer her desire,
  The wisdom to direct her power aright;
The will, the power, the wisdom thus combined,
What glorious prospects open on mankind!

XXXI.

Behold! she cried, and lifting up her hand,
  The shaping elements obeyed her will;
A vapour gathered round our lofty stand,
  Rolled in thick volumes o'er the Sacred Hill;
Descending then, its surges far and near
Filled all the wide subjacent atmosphere.

XXXII.

As I have seen from Skiddaw's stony height
  The fleecy clouds scud round me on their way,
Condense beneath, and hide the vale from sight,
  Then opening, just disclose where Derwent lay
Burnished with sunshine like a silver shield,
Or old Enchanter's glass, for magic forms fit field;

XXXIII.

So at her will, in that receding sheet
  Of mist wherewith the world was overlaid,
A living picture moved beneath our feet:
  A spacious City first was there displayed,
The seat where England from her ancient reign
Doth rule the Ocean as her own domain.

XXXIV.

In splendour with those famous cities old,
  Whose power it hath surpassed, it now might vie;
Through many a bridge the wealthy river rolled;
  Aspiring columns reared their heads on high,
Triumphal arches spanned the roads, and gave
Due guerdon to the memory of the brave.

XXXV.

A landscape followed, such as might compare
  With Flemish fields for well-requited toil:
The wonder-working hand had every where
  Subdued all circumstance of stubborn soil;
In fen and moor reclaimed rich gardens smiled,
And populous hamlets rose amid the wild.

XXXVI.

There the old seaman on his native shore
  Enjoyed the competence deserved so well;
The soldier, his dread occupation o'er,
  Of well-rewarded service loved to tell;
The grey-haired labourer there whose work was done,
In comfort saw the day of life go down.

XXXVII.

Such was the lot of eld; for childhood there
  The duties which belong to life was taught:
The good seed early sown, and nurst with care,
  This bounteous harvest in its season brought:
Thus youth for manhood, manhood for old age
Prepared, and found their weal in every stage.

XXXVIII.

Enough of knowledge unto all was given
  In wisdom's way to guide their steps on earth,
And make the immortal spirit fit for heaven.
  This needful learning was their right of birth;
Further might each who chose it persevere;
No mind was lost for lack of culture here.

XXXIX.

And that whole happy region swarmed with life,—
  Village and town; as busy bees in spring
In sunny days when sweetest flowers are rife,
  Fill fields and gardens with their murmuring.
Oh joy to see the State in perfect health!
Her numbers were her pride and power and wealth.

XL.

Then saw I, as the magic picture moved,
  Her shores enriched with many a port and pier;
No gift of liberal Nature unimproved.
  The seas their never-failing harvest here
Supplied, as bounteous as the air which fed
Israel, when manna fell from heaven for bread.

XLI.

Many a tall vessel in her harbours lay,
  About to spread its canvas to the breeze,
Bound upon happy errand to convey
  The adventurous colonist beyond the seas,
Toward those distant lands where Britain blest
With her redundant life the East and West.

XLII.

The landscape changed; a region next was seen,
  Where sable swans on rivers yet unfound
Glided through broad savannahs ever-green;
  Innumerous flocks and herds were feeding round,
And scattered farms appeared and hamlets fair,
And rising towns which made another Britain there.

XLIII.

Then thick as stars which stud the moonless sky,
  Green islands in a peaceful sea were seen;
Darkened no more with blind idolatry,
  Nor cursed with hideous usages obscene,
But healed of leprous crimes, from butchering strife
Delivered, and reclaimed to moral life.

XLIV.

Around the rude Morai, the temple now
  Of truth, hosannahs to the Holiest rung:
There from the Christian's equal marriage-vow,
  In natural growth the household virtues sprung:
Children were taught the paths of heavenly peace,
And age in hope looked on to its release.

XLV.

The light those happy Islanders enjoyed,
  Good messengers from Britain had conveyed;
(Where might such bounty wiselier be employed?)
  One people with their teachers were they made,
Their arts, their language, and their faith the same,
And blest in all, for all they blest the British name.

XLVI.

Then rose a different land, where loftiest trees
  High o'er the grove their fan-like foliage rear;
Where spicy bowers upon the passing breeze
  Diffuse their precious fragrance far and near;
And yet untaught to bend his massive knee,
Wisest of brutes, the elephant roams free.

XLVII.

Ministrant there to health and public good,
  The busy axe was heard on every side,
Opening new channels, that the noxious wood
  With wind and sunshine might be purified,
And that wise Government, the general friend,
Might every where its eye and arm extend.

XLVIII.

The half-brutal Bedah came from his retreat,
  To human life by human kindness won;
The Cingalese beheld that work complete
  Which Holland in her day had well begun;
The Candian, prospering under Britain's reign,
Blest the redeeming hand which broke his chain.

XLIX.

Colours and castes were heeded there no more:
  Laws which depraved, degraded, and opprest,
Were laid aside, for on that happy shore
  All men with equal liberty were blest;
And through the land, the breeze upon its swells
Bore the sweet music of the sabbath bells.

L.

Again the picture changed; those Isles I saw
  With every crime through three long centuries curst,
While unrelenting Avarice gave the law;
  Scene of the injured Indians' sufferings first,
Then doomed, for Europe's lasting shame, to see
The wider-wasting guilt of Slavery.

LI.

That foulest blot had been at length effaced;
  Slavery was gone, and all the power it gave,
Whereby so long our nature was debased,
  Baleful alike to master and to slave.
O lovely Isles! ye were indeed a sight
To fill the spirit with intense delight!

LII.

For willing industry and cheerful toil
  Performed their easy task, with Hope to aid;
And the free children of that happy soil
  Dwelt each in peace beneath his cocoa's shade;—
A race, who with the European mind,
The adapted mould of Africa combined.

LIII.

Anon, methought that in a spacious Square
  Of some great town the goodly ornament,
Three statues I beheld, of sculpture fair:
  These, said the Muse, are they whom one consent
Shall there deem worthy of the purest fame,—
Knowest thou who best such gratitude may claim?

LIV.

Clarkson, I answered, first; whom to have seen
  And known in social hours may be my pride,
Such friendship being praise: and one, I ween,
  Is Wilberforce, placed rightly at his side,
Whose eloquent voice in that great cause was heard
So oft and well.   But who shall be the third?

LV.

Time, said my Teacher, will reveal the name
  Of him who with these worthies shall enjoy
The equal honour of enduring fame;—
  He who the root of evil shall destroy,
And from our Laws shall blot the accursed word
Of Slave, shall rightly stand with them preferred.

LVI.

Enough! the Goddess cried; with that the cloud
  Obeyed, and closed upon the magic scene:
Thus much, quoth she, is to thine hopes allowed;
  Ills may impede, delays may intervene,
But scenes like these the coming age will bless,
If England but pursue the course of righteousness.

LVII.

On she must go progressively in good,
  In wisdom and in weal,—or she must wane.
Like Ocean, she may have her ebb and flood,
  But stagnates not.   And now her path is plain:
Heaven's first command she may fulfil in peace,
Replenishing the earth with her increase.

LVIII.

Peace she hath won,—with her victorious hand
  Hath won through rightful war auspicious peace,
Nor this alone, but that in every land
  The withering rule of violence may cease.
Was ever War with such blest victory crowned!
Did ever Victory with such fruits abound!

LIX.

Rightly for this shall all good men rejoice,
  They most who most abhor all deeds of blood;
Rightly for this with reverential voice
  Exalt to Heaven their hymns of gratitude;
For ne'er till now did Heaven thy country bless
With such transcendant cause for joy and thankfulness.

LX.

If they in heart all tyranny abhor,
  This was the fall of Freedom's direst foe:
If they detest the impious lust of war,
  Here hath that passion had its overthrow;—
As the best prospects of mankind are dear,
Their joy should be complete, their prayers of praise sincere.

LXI.

And thou to whom in spirit at this hour
  The vision of thy Country's bliss is given,
Who feelest that she holds her trusted power
  To do the will and spread the word of Heaven,—
Hold fast the faith which animates thy mind,
And in thy songs proclaim the hopes of humankind.

NOTES.

Note 1, page 520, col. 1.

The second day was that when Martel broke
The Mussulmen.

Upon this subject Miss Plumptre relates a remarkable anecdote, in the words of one of the sufferers at Lyons.

« At my entrance into the prison of the Recluse I found about twelve hundred of my fellow-citizens already immured there, distributed in different apartments. The doom of four-fifths of them at least was considered as inevitable: it was less a prison than a fold, where the innocent sheep patiently waited the hour that was to carry them to the revolutionary shambles. In this dreary abode, how long, how tedious did the days appear! they seemed to have many more than twenty-four hours. Yet we were allowed to read and write, and were composed enough to avail ourselves of this privilege; nay we could sometimes even so far forget our situation as to sport and gambol together. The continued images of destruction and devastation which we had before our eyes, the little hope that appeared to any of us of escaping our menaced fate, so familiarized us with the idea of death, that a stoical serenity had taken possession of our minds: we had been kept in a state of fear till the sentiment of fear was lost. All our conversation bore the character of this disposition: it was reflective, but not complaining; it was serious without being melancholy; and often presented novel and striking ideas. One day, when we were conversing on the inevitable chain of events, and the irrevocable order of things, on a sudden one of our party exclaimed that we owed all our misfortunes to Charles Martel. We thought him raving; but thus he reasoned to prove his hypothesis. 'Had not Charles Martel,' said he, ' conquered the Saracens, these latter, already masters of Guienne, of Saintonge, of Perigord, and of Poitou, would soon have extended their dominion over all France, and from that time we should have had no more religious quarrels, no more state disputes; we should not now have assemblies of the people, clubs, committees of public safety, sieges, imprisonments, bloody executions.' To this man the Turkish system of government appeared preferable to the revolutionary regime; and, all chances calculated, he preferred the bow-string of the Bashaw, rarely drawn, to the axe of the guillotine, incessantly at work.»

Note 2, page 520, col. 2.

That old siege.

« It is uncertain what numbers were slain during the siege of Ostend, yet it is said that there was found in a commissary's pocket, who was slain before Ostend the 7th of August, before the yielding thereof, divers remarkable notes and observations, and among the rest what number died without in the archduke's camp, of every degree.

Masters of the camp.	7
Colonels	15
Sergeants Maiors.	29
Captaines.	565
Lieutenants	1116
Ensignes	322
Sergeants.	1911
Corporals.	1166
Lanspisadoes.	600
Soldiers.	34663
Marriners.	614
Women and children.	119

All which amount to 41,124 persons; which number is not so great, considering the long siege, sickness, and the cold winters upon the sea coast, in so cold a climate, fighting against the elements. It is unknown what number died in the town, the which is thought much less, for that there were not so many in the town, who were better lodged, had more ease, and were better victualled. »—GRIMESTONE'S Hist. of the Netherlands, p. 1317.

« The besieged in Ostend had certain adventuring soldiers whom they called Lopers, of the which among other captains, were the young captain Grenu, and captain Adam Van Leest. Their arms which they bore were a long and a great pike, with a flat head at the neather end thereof; to the end that it should not sink too deep into the mud, a barquebuse hung in a scarf, as we have said of Frebuters, a coutelas at his side, and his dagger about his neck, who would usually leap over a ditch four and twenty foot broad, skirmishing often with his enemy so as no horseman could overtake them before they had leapt over the ditches againe.» Ib. 1299.

« In remembrance of the long siege of Ostend, and the winning of Sluce, there were certaine counters made in the United Provinces, both of silver and copper, the one having on the one side the picture of Ostend, and on the other the towns of Rhinberk, Grave, Sluce, Ardenbourg, and the forts of Isendyke and Cadsant, with this inscription round about, ' Plus triennio obsessa, hosti rudera, patriæ quatuor ex me urbes dedi. Anno 1604. Ostend being more than three years besieged, gave the enemie a heap of stones, and to her native country four townes.

«The town of Utrecht did also make a triumphant peace of Coyne both of gold and silver, where on the one side stood the siege of Ostend, and on the other the siege of Sluce, and all the forts and havens, and on both sides round about was graven,

' Jehovah prius dederat plus quam perdidimus.'»

Ibidem, 1318.

Note 3, page 521, col. 1.

Many a rich vessel from the injurious sea
Enter the bosom of thy quiet quay.

These lines are borrowed from Quarles;—the passage in which they occur would be very pleasing if he had not disfigured it in a most extraordinary manner.

Saile gentle Pinnace! now the heavens are clear,
The winds blow fair: behold the harbor's neer.
Tridented Neptune hath forgot to frowne,
The rocks are past; the storme is overblowne.
Up weather-beaten voyagers and rouze ye,
Forsake your loathbed Cabbins; up and louze ye

Upon the open decks, and smell the land:
Cheare up, the welcome shoare is nigh at hand.
Saile gentle Pinnace with a prosperous gale
To the Isle of Peace: saile, gentle Pinnace, saile!
Fortune conduct thee; let thy keele divide
The silver streams, that thou maist safely slide
Into the bosome of thy quiet Key,
And quite thee fairly of the injurious Sea.

QUARLES's *Argalus and Parthenia.*

Note 4, page 521, col. 1.

Bruges.

Urbs est ad miraculum pulchra, potens, amœna, says Luigi Guicciardini. Its power is gone by, but its beauty is perhaps more impressive now than in the days of its splendour and prosperity.

M. Paquet Syphorien, and many writers after him, mention the preservation of the monuments of Charles the Bold, and his daughter Mary of Burgundy, wife to the Archduke Maximilian; but they do not mention the name of the Beadle who preserved them at the imminent risk of his own life. Pierre Dezutter is this person's name. During the revolutionary frenzy, when the mob seemed to take most pleasure in destroying whatever was most venerable, he took these splendid tombs to pieces and buried them during the night, for which he was proscribed and a reward of 2000 francs set upon his head. Buonaparte, after his marriage into the Austrian family, rewarded him with 1000 francs, and gave 10,000 for ornamenting the chapel in which the tombs were replaced. This has been done with little taste.

Note 5, page 522, col. 1.

That sisterhood whom to their rule Of holy life no hasty vows restrain.

The Beguines. Helyot is mistaken when he says (*t. 8. p. 6,*) that the Beguinage at Mechlin is the finest in all Flanders; it is not comparable to that at Ghent, which for extent and beauty may be called the Capital of the community.

Note 6, page 522, col. 2.

Alost— Where whilome treachery stained the English name.

In 1583, « the English garrison of Alost being mutinied for their pay, the Ganthois did not only refuse to give it them, but did threaten to force them out, or else to famish them. In the mean time the Prince of Parma did not let slip this opportunity to make his profit thereby, but did solicit them by fair words and promises to pay them; and these English companies, not accustomed to endure hunger and want, began to give ear unto him, for that their Colonel Sir John Norris and the States were somewhat slow to provide for their pay, for the which they intended to give order, but it was too late. For after that the English had chased away the rest of the garrison which were of the country, then did Captain Pigot, Vincent, Tailor, and others, agree to deliver up the town unto the Spaniard, giving them for their pay, which they received, thirty thousand pistolets. And so the said town was delivered unto the Spaniard in the beginning of December, and filled with Wallons. Most of these English went to serve the Prince of Parma in his camp before Eckloo, but finding that he trusted them not, they ran in a manner all away.»

GRIMESTONE, 833.

It is one proof of the improved state of general feeling in the more civilized states of Europe, that instances of this kind of treachery have long since ceased even to be suspected. During the long wars in the Netherlands, nothing was more common than for officers to change their party,—considering war as a mere profession, in which their services, like those of a lawyer, were for the best bidder.

Note 7, page 522, col. 2.

Then saw we Affligbem, by ruin rent.

This magnificent Abbey was destroyed during the Revolution,—an act of popular madness which the people in its vicinity now spoke of with unavailing regret. The library was at one time the richest in Brabant; «*celeberrima,*» Luigi Guicciardini calls it, « adeo quidem, ut quod ad libros antiquos habeatur pro locupletissima simul et laudatissima universa istius tractus.» The destruction of books during the Revolution was deplorably great. A bookseller at Brussels told me he had himself at one time sent off five-and-twenty waggon-loads for waste paper, and sold more than 100,000lb. weight for the same purpose! In this manner were the convent-libraries destroyed.

Note 8, page 523, col. 1.

Assche, for water and for cakes renowned.

The Flemish name of these said cakes has a marvellously uncouth appearance,—*suyker-koekxkens,*—nevertheless they are good cakes, and are sold by Judocus de Bisschop, at the sign of the Moor, next door to the Auberge *la Tête-de-Bœuf.* This information is for those whom it may concern.

Note 9, page 523, col. 2.

When Belgian ears were taught The British soldier's cry, half groan, half prayer, Breathed when his pain is more than he can bear.

One of our coachmen, who had been employed (like all his fraternity) in removing the wounded, asked us what was the meaning of the English word *O Lord!* for thus, he said, the wounded were continually crying out.

Note 10, page 524, col. 1.

Brabant in all her cities felt the sound.

The battle of the 18th was heard throughout the whole of Brabant, and in some directions far beyond it. It was distinctly perceived at Herve; and I have been assured, incredible as it may seem, that it was perceived at Amiens. The firing on the 16th was heard at Antwerp,—not that of the 18th, though the scene of action was nearer.

Note 11, page 524, col. 1.

Here Castanaza reared a votive fane.

The following dedicatory inscription is placed over the portico of Waterloo Church.

D. O. M.
Et D. D. Josepho et Annæ
Hoc Sacellum
Pro Desiderata Dominiis Catholicis
Caroll 2. Hisp. Ind. Regis Belg. Principis Prosapia
Fran. Ant. Agurto Marchio de Castanaca Belg. Gubernator.

The *a* in *Gubernator* has been left out, either by the mistake of the workmen, or for want of room.

Carlos II of Spain, one of the most wretched of men, married for his first wife Marie Louise, Lewis the Fourteenth's niece. A curious instance of the public anxiety that she should produce an heir to the throne is preserved by Florez in his *Memorias de las Reynas Catholicas*. When she had been married two years without issue, this strange epigram, if so it may be called, was circulated:

Parid bella Flor de Lis
En afflccion tan estraña:
Si Paris, Paris á España,
Si no Paris, á Paris.

Florez describes the dress of the bride at her espousals: it was a robe of murray velvet embroidered with fleur de lys of gold trimmed with ermine and jewels, and with a train of seven ells long;—the princesses of the blood had all long trains, but not so long, the length being according to their proximity to the throne. The description of a Queen's dress accorded well with the antiquarian pursuits of Florez; but it is amusing to observe some of the expressions of this laborious writer, a monk of the most rigid habits, whose life was spent in severe study and in practices of mortification. In her head-dress, he says, she wore porcelain pins which supported large diamonds,—*y convertian en cielo aquel poco de tierra*, and at the ball after the espousals, *el Christianissimo danzó con la Catholica*. These appellations sound almost as oddly as Messrs Bogue and Bennett's description of St Paul in a minuet, and Timothy at a card-table.

This poor Queen lived eight years with a husband whose mind and body were equally debilitated. Never were the miseries of a mere state-marriage more lamentably exemplified. In her last illness, when she was advised to implore the prayers of a personage who was living in the odour of sanctity for her recovery, she replied, Certainly I will not;—it would be folly to ask for a life which is worth so little. And when toward the last her Confessor inquired if any thing troubled her, her answer was, that she was in perfect peace, and rejoiced that she was dying,—« en paz me hallo Padre, y muy gustosa de morir.» She died on the 12th of February; and such was the solicitude for an heir to the monarchy, that on the 15th of May a second marriage was concluded for the King.

Note 12, page 524, col. 2.

Plain tablets by the soldier's hand
Raised to his comrades in a foreign land.

The inscriptions in the church are as follows.

Sacred
to the memory
of
Lt. Col. Edward Stables
——Sir Francis d'Oyley, K. C. B.
——Charles Thomas
——William Miller
——William Henry Milner
Capt. Robert Adair
——Edward Grose
——Newton Chambers
——Thomas Brown
Ensign Edward Pardoe
——James Lord Hay
——the Hon. S. S. P. Barrington
of
His Britannic Majesty's
First Regiment of Foot Guards
who fell gloriously in the battle
of Quatre Bras and Wateloo,* on
the 16th and 18th of June,
1815.
The Officers of the

* The word is thus mis-spelt.

Regiment have erected this
Monument in commemoration
of the fall of their
Gallant Companions.

———

To
the Memory
of
Major Edwin Griffith,
Lt. Isaac Sherwood, and
Lt. Henry Buckley
Officers in the XV King's Regiment of Hussars
(British)
who fell in the battle of
Waterloo,
June 18, 1815.
This stone was erected by the Officers
of that Regiment,
as a testimony of their respect.

———

Dulce et decorum est pro patria mori.

———

The two following are the epitaphs in the churchyard:

D. O. M.
Sacred to the Memory of Lieutenant-Colonel Fitz Gerald, of the Second Regiment of Life Guards of his Britannic Majesty, who fell gloriously at the battle of La Belle Alliance, near this town, on the 18th of June, 1815, in the 41st year of his life, deeply and deservedly regretted by his family and friends. To a manly loftiness of soul, he united all the virtues that could render him an ornament to his profession, and to private and social life.

Aux mânes du plus vertueux des hommes, généralement estimé et regretté de sa famille et de ses amis, le Lieutenant-Colonel Richard Fitz Gerald, de la Garde du Corps de sa Majesté Britannique, tué glorieusement à la bataille de la Belle Alliance, le 18 Juin, 1815.

R. I. P.

D. O. M.
Ici repose le Colonel
De Langrebr, Commandant
le premier Bataillon de
Bremen, blessé à mort à
la bataille de Waterloo,
le 18 Juin, 1815, et enterré
le lendemain, âgé de
40 ans.
R. I. P.

Lord Uxbridge's leg is buried in a garden opposite to the inn, or rather public-house, at Waterloo. The owner of the house in which the amputation was performed considers it as a relic which has fallen to his share. He had deposited it at first behind the house, but as he intended to plant a tree upon the spot, he considered, that as the ground there was not his own property, the boys might injure or destroy the tree, and therefore he removed the leg into his own garden, where it lies in a proper sort of coffin, under a mound of earth about three or four feet in diameter. A tuft of Michaelmas daisies was in blossom upon this mound when we were at Waterloo; but this was a temporary ornament: in November the owner meant to plant a weeping willow there. He was obliging enough to give me a copy of an epitaph which he had prepared, and which, he said, was then in the stone-cutter's hands. It is as follows:

Ci est enterrée la Jambe de l'illustre, brave, et vaillant Comte Uxbridge, Lieutenant Général, Commandant en Chef la Cavalerie Angloise, Belge, et Hollandoise; blessé le 18 Juin, 1815, à la memorable bataille de Waterloo; qui par son heroïsme a concouru au triomphe de la cause du Genre humain, glorieusement décidée par l'eclatante victoire du dit jour.

Note 13, page 524, col. 2.

When Marlborough here, victorious in his might,
Surprised the French, and smote them in their flight.

A detachment of the French was entrenched at Waterloo Chapel, August 1705, when the Duke of Marlborough advanced to attack the French army at Over Ysche, and this detachment was destroyed with great slaughter. (*Echard's Gazetteer.*) The Sieur La Lande says, « *on donne la chasse à un parti François qui etoit à Waterloo.*» Marlborough was prevented by the Deputies of the States from pursuing his advantage, and attacking the enemy, at a time when he made sure of victory.—*Hist. de l'Empereur Charles VI,* t. 2, p. 80.

Note 14, page 525, col. 1.

Mount St John,
The hamlet which the Highlanders that day
Preserved from spoil.

The peasant who led us over the field resided at this hamlet. Mont St Jean was every thing to him, and his frequent exclamations of admiration for the courage of the Highlanders in particular, and indeed of the whole army, always ended with a reference to his own dwelling-place: « if they had not fought so well, Oh *mon Dieu,* Mont St Jean would have been burnt.»

This was an intelligent man, of very impressive countenance and manners. Like all the peasantry with whom we conversed, he spoke with the bitterest hatred of Buonaparte, as the cause of all the slaughter and misery he had witnessed, and repeatedly expressed his astonishment that he had not been put to death. My house, said he, was full of the wounded:—it was nothing but sawing off legs and sawing off arms. Oh my God, and all for one man! Why did you not put him to death? I myself would have put him to death with my own hand.

Note 15, page 525, col. 1.

Small theatre for such a tragedy.

So important a battle perhaps was never before fought within so small an extent of ground. I computed the distance between Hougoumont and Papelot at three miles; in a straight line it might probably not exceed two and a half.

Our guide was very much displeased at the name which the battle had obtained in England. Why call it the battle of Waterloo? he said,—call it Mont St Jean, call it La Belle Alliance, call it Hougoumont, call it La Haye Sainte, call it Papelot,—any thing but Waterloo.

Note 16, page 525, col. 1.

Admiring Belgium saw
The youth proved worthy of his destined crown.

A man at Les Quatre Bras, who spoke with the usual enthusiasm of the Prince of Orange's conduct in the campaign, declared that he fought « like a devil on horseback.» Looking at a portrait of the Queen of the Netherlands, a lady observed that there was a resemblance to the Prince; a young Fleming was quite angry at this,—he could not bear that his hero should not be thought beautiful as well as brave.

Note 17, page 528, col. 2.

Genappe.

At the Roy d'Espagne, where we were lodged, Wellington had his head-quarters on the 17th, Buonaparte on the 18th, and Blucher on the 19th. The coachmen had told us that it was an *assez bonne auberge;* but when one of them in the morning asked how we had passed the night, he observed that no one ever *slept* at Genappe,—it was impossible, because of the continual passing of posts and coal-carts.

Note 18, page 529, col. 1.

The Cross Roads.

It is odd that the inscription upon the directing-post at Les Quatre Bras, (or rather boards, for they are fastened against a house,) should be given wrongly in the account of the campaign printed at Frankfort. The real directions are,

$\frac{3}{4}$ de p^{te} ver St Douler
$\frac{3}{4}$ de p^{te} ver Genappe
$\frac{2}{4}$ de p^{te} ver Marbais
$\frac{3}{4}$ de p^{te} ver Frasne

spelt in this manner, and ill cut. I happened to copy it in a mood of superfluous minuteness.

A fat and jolly Walloon, who inhabited this corner house, ate his dinner in peace at twelve o'clock on the 16th, and was driven out by the balls flying about his ears at four the same day. This man described that part of the action which took place in his sight with great animation. He was particularly impressed by the rage,—the absolute fury which the French displayed; they cursed the English while they were fighting, and cursed the precision with which the English grape-shot was fired, which, said the man, was neither too high nor too low, but struck right in the middle. The last time that a British army had been in this place, the Duke of York slept in this man's bed,—an event which the Walloon remembered with gratitude as well as pride, the Duke having given him a louis d'or.

Note 19, page 529, col. 2.

Oh wherefore have ye spared his head accurst.

Among the peasantry with whom we conversed this feeling was universal. We met with many persons who disliked the union with Holland, and who hated the Prussians, but none who spoke in favour or even in palliation of Buonaparte. The manner in which this ferocious beast, as they call him, has been treated, has given a great shock to the moral feelings of mankind. The almost general mode of accounting for it on the Continent, is by a supposition that England purposely let him loose from Elba in order to have a pretext for again attacking France, and crippling a country which she had left too strong, and which would soon have outstripped her in prosperity. I found it impossible to dispossess even men of sound judgment and great ability of this belief, preposterous as it is; and when they read the account of the luxuries which have been sent to St Helena for the accommodation of this great criminal, they will consider it as the fullest proof of their opinion.

Note 20, page 530, col. 1.

And now they felt the Prussian's heavy hand.

Wherever we went we heard one cry of complaint against the Prussians,—except at Ligny, where the people had witnessed only their courage and their sufferings. This is the effect of making the military spirit predominate in a nation. The conduct of our own

69

men was universally extolled; but it required years of exertion and severity before Lord Wellington brought the British army to its present state of discipline. The moral discipline of an army has never perhaps been understood by any General except the great Gustavus. Even in its best state, with all the alleviations of courtesy and religion, war is so great an evil, that to engage in it without a clear necessity is a crime of the blackest dye. When the necessity is clear, (and such, assuredly, I hold it to have been in our struggle with Buonaparte,) it then becomes a crime to shrink from it.

What I have said of the Prussians relates solely to their conduct in an allied country; and I must also say that the Prussian officers with whom I had the good fortune to associate, were men who in every respect did honour to their profession and to their country. But that the general conduct of their troops in Belgium had excited a strong feeling of disgust and indignation we had abundant and indisputable testimony. In France they had old wrongs to revenge,—and forgiveness of injuries is not among the virtues which are taught in camps. The annexed anecdotes are reprinted from one of our newspapers, and ought to be preserved.

A Prussian Officer, on his arrival at Paris, particularly requested to be billetted on the house of a lady inhabiting the Faubourg St Germain. His request was complied with, and on his arriving at the lady's hotel he was shewn into a small but comfortable sitting-room, with a handsome bedchamber adjoining it. With these rooms he appeared greatly dissatisfied, and desired that the lady should give up to him her apartment, (on the first floor) which was very spacious, and very elegantly furnished. To this the lady made the strongest objections; but the Officer insisted, and she was under the necessity of retiring to the second floor. He afterwards sent a message to her by one of her servants, saying that he destined the second floor for his Aide-de-Camp, etc. etc. This occasioned more violent remonstrances from the lady, but they were totally unavailing, and unattended to by the Officer, whose only answer was, « obéissez à mes ordres.» He then called for the cook, and told him he must prepare a handsome dinner for six persons, and desired the lady's butler to take care that the best wines the cellar contained should be forthcoming. After dinner he desired the hostess should be sent for;—she obeyed the summons. The Officer then addressed her, and said, « No doubt, Madam, but you consider my conduct as indecorous and brutal in the extreme.» « I must confess,» replied she, « that I did not expect such treatment from an officer; as, in general, military men are ever disposed to show every degree of deference and respect to our sex.» « You think me then a most perfect barbarian? answer me frankly.» « If you really, then, desire my undisguised opinion of the subject, I must say, that I think your conduct truly barbarous.» « Madam, I am entirely of your opinion; but I only wished to give you a specimen of the behaviour and conduct of your son, during six months that he resided in my house, after the entry of the French army into the Prussian capital. I do not, however, mean to follow a bad example. You will resume, therefore, your apartment to-morrow, and I will seek lodgings at some public hotel.» The lady then retired, extolling the generous conduct of the Prussian officer, and deprecating that of her son.

Another Prussian officer was lodged at the house of Marshal Ney, in whose stables and coach house he found a great number of horses and carriages. He immediately ordered some Prussian soldiers, who accompanied him, to take away *nine* of the horses and *three* of the carriages. Ney's servants violently remonstrated against this proceeding, on which the Prussian Officer observed, « they are my property, inasmuch as your master took the same number of horses and carriages from me when he entered Berlin with the French army.» I think you will agree with me, that the *lex talionis* was never more properly nor more justly resorted to.

Note 21, page 533, col. 1.
The Martyr.

Sir Thomas Brown writes upon this subject with his usual feeling.

« We applaud not,» says he, « the judgment of Machiavel, that Christianity makes men cowards, or that, with the confidence of but half dying, the despised virtues of patience and humility have abased the spirits of men, which Pagan principles exalted; but rather regulated the wildness of audacities in the attempts, grounds, and eternal sequels of death, wherein men of the boldest spirit are often prodigiously temerarious. Nor can we extenuate the valour of ancient martyrs, who contemned death in the uncomfortable scene of their lives, and in their decrepit martyrdoms did probably lose not many months of their days, or parted with life when it was scarce worth living. For (beside that long time past holds no consideration unto a slender time to come) they had no small disadvantage from the constitution of old age, which naturally makes men fearful, and complexionally superannuated from the bold and courageous thoughts of youth and fervent years. But the contempt of death from corporal animosity promoteth not our felicity. They may sit in the Orchestra and noblest seats of Heaven, who have held up shaking hands in the fire, and humanly contended for glory.» *Hydriotaphia,* 17.

Note 22, page 535, col. 1.
In purple and in scarlet clad, behold
The Harlot sits, adorned with gems and gold.

The homely but scriptural appellation by which our fathers were wont to designate the Church of Rome has been delicately softened down by later writers. I have seen her some where called the Scarlet Woman,—and Helen Maria Williams names her *the Dissolute* of Babylon.

Let me here offer a suggestion in defence of Voltaire. Is it not probable, or rather can any person doubt, that the *écrasez l'infame,* upon which so horrible a charge against him has been raised, refers to the Church of Rome, under this well-known designation? No man can hold the principles of Voltaire in stronger abhorrence than I do,—but it is an act of justice to exculpate him from this monstrous accusation.

Note 23, page 536, col. 1.
For till the sons their fathers' crimes repent,
The old error brings its direful punishment.

« Political chimeras,» says Count Stolberg, « are innumerable; but the most chimerical of all is the project of imagining that a people deeply sunk in degeneracy are capable of recovering the ancient grandeur of freedom. Who tosses the bird into the air after his wings are clipped? So far from restoring it to the power of flight, it will but disable it more.»—*Travels*, 3, 139.

Note 24, page 536, col. 2.
The lark
Poured forth her lyric strain.

The epithet *lyric*, as applied to the lark, is borrowed from one of Donne's poems. I mention this more particularly for the purpose of repairing an accidental omission in the notes to Roderick;—it is the duty of every poet to acknowledge all his obligations of this kind to his predecessors.

Note 25, page 538, col. 2.
Public crimes
Draw on their proper punishment below.

I will insert here a passage from one of Lord Brooke's poems. Few writers have ever given proofs of profounder thought than this friend of Sir Philip Sidney. Had his powers of language been equal to his strength of intellect, I scarcely know the author whom he would not have surpassed.

21.

Some love no equals, some superiors scorn,
  One seeks more worlds, and this will Helen have;
This covets gold, with divers faces borne,
  These humours reign, and lead men to their grave;
Whereby for bayes and little wages, we
Ruin ourselves to raise up tyranny.

22.

And as when winds among themselves do jar,
  Seas there are tost, and wave with wave must fight;
So when power's restless humours bring forth War,
  There people bear the faults and wounds of Might;
The error and diseases of the head
Descending still until the limbs be dead.

23.

Yet are not people's errors ever free
  From guilt of wounds they suffer by the war;
Never did any public misery
  Rise of itself: God's plagues still grounded are
On common stains of our humanity;
And to the flame which ruineth mankind
Man gives the matter, or at least gives wind.

A Treatise of Warres.

The extract which follows, from the same author, bears as directly upon the effects of the military system as if it had been written with a reference to Buonaparte's government. The thoughtful reader will perceive its intrinsic value, through its difficult language and uncouth versification:—the fool and the coxcomb may scoff if they like.

59.

Let us then thus conclude, that only they
  Whose end in this world is the world to come.
Whose hearts' desire is that their desires may
  Measure themselves by Truth's eternal doom,
Can in the *War* find nothing that they prize,
Who in the world would not be great or wise.

60.

With these, I say, War, Conquest, Honour, Fame,
  Stand (as the world) neglected or forsaken,
Like Error's cobwebs, in whose curious frame
  She only joys and mourns, takes and is taken;
In which these dying, that to God live thus,
Endure our conquests, would not conquer us.

61.

Where all states else that stand on power, not grace,
  And gage desire by no such spiritual measure,
Make it their end to reign in every place,
  To war for honour, for revenge, and pleasure;

Thinking the strong should keep the weak in awe,
And every inequality give law.

62.

These serve the world to rule her by her arts,
  Raise mortal trophies upon mortal passion;
Their wealth, strength, glory, growing from those hearts
  Which to their ends they ruin and disfashion;
The more remote from God the less remorse;
Which still gives Honour power, Occasion force.

63.

These make the Sword their judge of wrong and right,
  Their story Fame, their laws but Power and Wit;
Their endless mine all vanities of Might,
  Rewards and Pains the mystery of it;
And in this sphere, this wilderness of evils,
None prosper highly but the perfect Devils.

A Treatise of Warres.

Note 26, page 538, col. 2.
They had the light, and from the light they turned.

« Let no ignorance,» says Lord Brooke, « seem to excuse mankind; since the light of truth is still near us, the tempter and accuser at such continual war within us, the laws that guide so good for them that obey, and the first shape of every sin so ugly, as whosoever does but what he knows, or forbears what he doubts, shall easily follow nature unto grace.»

« God left not the world without information from the beginning; so that wherever we find ignorance, it must be charged to the account of man, as having rejected, and not to that of his Maker, as having denied, the necessary means of instruction.»—HORNE's *Considerations on the Life of St John the Baptist.*

Note 27, page 539, col. 1.
Napoleon.

It is amusing to look back upon the flattery which was offered to Buonaparte. Some poems of Mme Fanny de Beauharnois exhibit rich specimens of this kind: she praises him for

la douce humanité
Qui le dévore de sa flamme.

Of the battle of Austerlitz she says,

Dans ce jour mémorable on dut finir la guerre,
  Et que nommeront maints auteurs
La Trinité des Empereurs,
  Vous seul en êtes le mystère.

Subsequent events give to some of these adulatory strains an interest which they would else have wanted.

Napoléon, objet de nos hommages,
Et Joséphine, objet non moins aimé,
Couple que l'Eternel l'un pour l'autre a formé,
  Vous êtes ses plus beaux ouvrages.

In some stanzas called *Les Trois Bateaux,* upon the vessels in which Alexander and Buonaparte held their conferences before the Peace of Tilsit, the following prophecy is introduced, with a felicity worthy of the *Edinburgh Review:*

Tremble, tremble, fière Albion!
  Guidé par d'heureuses étoiles,
Ces généreux bateaux, exempts d'ambition,
Vont triompher par tout de tes cent mille voiles.

The *Grand Napoleon* is the

Enfant chéri de Mars et d'Apollon,
Qu'aucun revers ne peut abattre.

Here follows part of an Arabic poem by Michael Sabbag, addressed to Buonaparte on his marriage with Marie Louise, and printed with translations in French prose and German verse, in the first volume of the *Fundgruben des Orients.*

« August Prince, whom Heaven has given us for Sovereign, and who holdest among the greatest monarchs of thy age the same rank which the diadem holds upon the head of Kings,

« Thou hast reached the summit of happiness, and by thine invincible courage hast attained a glory which the mind of man can scarcely comprehend.

« Thou hast imprinted upon the front of time the remembrance of thine innumerable exploits in characters of light, one of which alone suffices with its brilliant rays to enlighten the whole universe.

« Who can resist him who is never abandoned by the assistance of Heaven, who has Victory for his guide, and whose course is directed by God himself?

« In every age Fortune produces a hero who is the pearl of his time; amidst all these extraordinary men thou shinest like an inestimable diamond in a necklace of precious stones.

« The least of thy subjects, in whatever country he may be, is the object of universal homage, and enjoys thy glory, the splendour of which is reflected upon him.

« All virtues are united in thee, but the justice which regulates all thy actions would alone suffice to immortalize thy name.

. . . . . .

« Perhaps the English will now understand at last that it is folly to oppose themselves to the wisdom of thy designs, and to strive against thy fortune.»

« A figure of Liberty, which during the days of Jacobinism was erected at Aix in Provence, was demolished during the night about the time when Buonaparte assumed the empire. Among the squibs to which this gave occasion, was the following question and answer between Pasquin and Marforio. Pasquin inquires, *Mais qu'est ce qui est devenu donc de la Liberté?*—Heyday, what is become of Liberty then?— To which Marforio replies, *Bête! elle est morte en s'accouchant d'un Empereur.*—Blockhead! she is dead in bringing forth an Emperor.»—Miss PLUMPTRE's *Narrative,* 2, 382.

Well may the lines of Pindar respecting Tantalus be applied to Buonaparte.

> Εἰ δὲ δή τιν' ἄν-
> δρα θνατὸν 'Ολύμπου σκοποὶ ἐτίμα-
> σαν, ἦν Τάνταλος οὗτος. 'Αλλὰ γὰρ κατα-
> πέψαι μέγαν ὄλβον οὐκ ἐδυ-
> νάσθη· κόρῳ δ' ἔλεν
> Ἄταν ὑπέροπλον.

PINDAR, *Ol.* 1.

« Nam se deve accusar a Fortuna de cega, mas sô aos que della se deixam cegar.» It is not Fortune, says D. Luiz da Cunha, who ought to be accused of blindness,— but they who let themselves be blinded by her.—*Memorias desde* 1659 *athé* 1706. MSS.

Lieutenant Bowerbank, in his Journal of what passed on board the Bellerophon, has applied a passage from Horace to the same effect, with humorous felicity.

> I, Bonx, quo virtus tua te vocat,
> Grandia laturus meritorum præmia.
>
> *Epist.* II, lib. ii, v. 37.

One bead more in this string of quotations : « Un Roi philosophe,» says the Comte de Puissaye, speaking of Frederic of Prussia, « dans le sens de nos jours, est selon moi le plus terrible fléau que le ciel puisse envoyer aux habitans de la terre. Mais l'idée d'un Roi philosophe et despote, est un injure au sens commun, un outrage à la raison.»—*Mémoires, tome* 3, 125.

A Tale of Paraguay.

> Go forth, my little book !
> Go forth and please the gentle and the good.
> WORDSWORTH.

DEDICATION.

TO EDITH MAY SOUTHEY.

I.

EDITH! ten years are number'd, since the day,
Which ushers in the cheerful month of May,
To us by thy dear birth, my daughter dear,
Was blest. Thou therefore didst the name partake
Of that sweet month, the sweetest of the year;
But fitlier was it given thee for the sake
Of a good man, thy father's friend sincere,
Who at the font made answer in thy name.
Thy love and reverence rightly may he claim,
For closely hath he been with me allied
In friendship's holy bonds, from that first hour
When in our youth we met on Tejo's side;
Bonds which, defying now all Fortune's power,
Time hath not loosen'd, nor will Death divide.

II.

A child more welcome, by indulgent Heaven
Never to parents' tears and prayers was given!
For scarcely eight months at thy happy birth
Had pass'd, since of thy sister we were left,—
Our first-born and our only babe, bereft.
Too fair a flower was she for this rude earth!
The features of her beauteous infancy
Have faded from me, like a passing cloud,
Or like the glories of an evening sky :
And seldom hath my tongue pronounced her name
Since she was summon'd to a happier sphere.
But that dear love, so deeply wounded then,
I in my soul with silent faith sincere
Devoutly cherish till we meet again.

III.

I saw thee first with trembling thankfulness,
O daughter of my hopes and of my fears!
Press'd on thy senseless cheek a troubled kiss,
And breathed my blessing over thee with tears.
But memory did not long our bliss alloy;
For gentle nature, who had given relief,
Wean'd with new love the chasten'd heart from grief,
And the sweet season minister'd to joy.

IV.

It was a season when their leaves and flowers
The trees as to an Arctic summer spread:
When chilling wintry winds and snowy showers,
Which had too long usurp'd the vernal hours,
Like spectres from the sight of morning, fled
Before the presence of that joyous May;
And groves and gardens all the live-long day
Rung with the birds' loud love-songs. Over all,
One thrush was heard from morn till even-fall:
Thy Mother well remembers when she lay
The happy prisoner of the genial bed,
How from yon lofty poplar's topmost spray
At earliest dawn his thrilling pipe was heard;
And when the light of evening died away,
That blithe and indefatigable bird
Still his redundant song of joy and love preferr'd.

V.

How I have doted on thine infant smiles
At morning when thine eyes unclos'd on mine;
How, as the months in swift succession roll'd,
I mark'd thy human faculties unfold,
And watch'd the dawning of the light divine;
And with what artifice of playful guiles
Won from thy lips with still-repeated wiles
Kiss after kiss, a reckoning often told,—
Something I ween thou know'st; for thou hast seen
Thy sisters in their turn such fondness prove,
And felt how childhood in its winning years
The attempered soul to tenderness can move.
This thou canst tell; but not the hopes and fears
With which a parent's heart doth overflow,—
The thoughts and cares inwoven with that love,—
Its nature and its depth, thou dost not, canst not know.

VI.

The years which since thy birth have pass'd away
May well to thy young retrospect appear
A measureless extent:—like yesterday
To me, so soon they fill'd their short career.
To thee discourse of reason have they brought,
With sense of time and change; and something too
Of this precarious state of things have taught,
Where Man abideth never in one stay;
And of mortality a mournful thought.
And I have seen thine eyes suffused in grief,
When I have said that with autumnal grey
The touch of eld hath mark'd thy father's head;
That even the longest day of life is brief,
And mine is falling fast into the yellow leaf.

VII.

Thy happy nature from the painful thought
With instinct turns, and scarcely canst thou bear
To hear me name the Grave: Thou knowest not
How large a portion of my heart is there!
The faces which I loved in infancy
Are gone; and bosom-friends of riper age,
With whom I fondly talk'd of years to come,
Summon'd before me to their heritage,
Are in the better world beyond the tomb.
And I have brethren there, and sisters dear,
And dearer babes. I therefore needs must dwell
Often in thought with those whom still I love so well.

VIII.

Thus wilt thou feel in thy maturer mind:
When grief shall be thy portion, thou wilt find
Safe consolation in such thoughts as these,—
A present refuge in affliction's hour.
And if indulgent Heaven thy lot should bless
With all imaginable happiness,
Here shalt thou have, my child, beyond all power
Of chance, thy holiest, surest, best delight.
Take therefore now thy Father's latest lay,—
Perhaps his last;—and treasure in thine heart
The feelings that its musing strains convey.
A song it is of life's declining day,
Yet meet for youth. Vain passions to excite,
No strains of morbid sentiment I sing,
Nor tell of idle loves with ill-spent breath;
A reverent offering to the Grave I bring,
And twine a garland for the brow of Death.

PREFACE

One of my friends observed to me in a letter, that many stories which are said to be *founded* on fact, have in reality been *foundered* on it. This is the case if there be any gross violation committed, or ignorance betrayed, of historical manners in the prominent parts of a narrative wherein the writer affects to observe them: or when the ground-work is taken from some part of history so popular and well known that any mixture of fiction disturbs the sense of truth. Still more so, if the subject be in itself so momentous that any alloy of invention must of necessity debase it: but most of all in themes drawn from scripture, whether from the more familiar, or the more awful portions; for when what is true is sacred, whatever may be added to it is so surely felt to be false, that it appears profane.

Founded on fact the Poem is, which is here committed to the world: but whatever may be its defects, it is liable to none of these objections. The story is so singular, so simple, and withal so complete, that it must have been injured by any alteration. How faithfully is has been followed, the reader may perceive if he chuses to consult the abridged translation of Dobrizhoffer's History of the Abipones; and for those who may be gratified with what Pinkerton has well called the lively singularity of the old man's Latin, the passage from the original is here subjoined:

« Ad Australes fluvii Empalado ripas Hispanorum turma Herbæ Paraquaricæ conficiendæ operam dabat. Deficientibus jam arboribus, è quibus illa folia rescinduntur, exploratores tres emiserant, qui trans illud flumen arbores desideratas investigarent. Forte in tugurium, agrumque frumento Turcico consitum incidere, ex quo hanc sylvam barbarorum contuberniis scatere perperam arguebant. Hæc notitia tanto omnes perculit metu, ut suspenso, ad quem conducti fuerant, labore suis aliquamdiu in tuguriis laterent, ut limax intra concham. Diu noctuque hostilis aggressio formidabatur. Ad liberandos se hoc terrore cursor ad S. Joachimi oppidum missus, qui, ut barbaros istic habitantes perquiramus, inventosque ad nostram transferamus coloniam flagitavit. Sine tergiversatione operam addixi meam. Licet trium hebdomadum itinere defunctus Nato servatori sacra die ex Mbaebera domum redierim, S. Joannis apostoli festo iter mox aggressus sum cum quadraginta Indorum meorum comitatu. Fluviis ob continuatum dies complures imbrem turgentibus profectio perardua nobis exstitit. Accepto ex Hispanorum tugurio viarum duce, trajectoque flumine Empalado sylvas omnes ad fluvii Mondag miri ripas usque attentis oculis pervagati, tertio demum die, humano, quod deteximus, vestigio nos ducente ædiculam attigimus, ubi mater vetula, cum filio vicesimum, filiaque quintum decimum annum agente annis abhinc multis degebat. Quibus in latebris Indi alii versarentur, à me rogata mater, neminem mortalium præter se, binasque proles, his in sylvis superesse, omnes, qui per hanc viciniam habitaverant, variolarum dira peste dudum extinctos fuisse, respondit. De dicti veritate ancipitem me dum observaret filius: tutò, ait, fidem adhibueris matri meæ ista affirmanti : namque ipsus ego uxorem mihi quæsiturus remotissimas etiam sylvas identidem percursavi, quin tamen vel hominis umbram reperirem uspiam. En! uteræ instinctu adolescens barbarus, conjugium cum sorore sibi neutiquam licere, intellexit. Is multis post mensibus meo in oppido, nullos præter se homines illis in sylvis degere, iterum, iterumque ingenue mihi asseveravit. Idem confirmarunt Hispani, à quibus evocatus sum, ultra biennium in conquirenda herba dein per illas sylvas occupati, non mediocri cum quæstu.

« Vetulam matrem congruis argumentis hortatus sum ad meum ut oppidum, siquidem luberet, commigraret ocyus, se, suosque meliori fortuna illic usuros, pollicitus. Lubenter invitationi meæ obtemperaturam se, respondit; rem unicam migrationi suæ obstare. Sunt mihi, ait, tres, quos coram vides, apri à prima ætate mansuefacti; nos quoquo euntes caniculi more sequuntur. Hi, si campum aridum videant, vel extra sylvarum umbram à sole ardenti videantur, peribunt confestim, timeo. Hanc solicitudinem, quæso, animo ejicias tuo, reposui; cordi mihi fore chara animalcula, nil dubites. Sole æstuante umbram, ubi ubi demum, captabimus. Neque lacunæ, amnes, paludes, ubi refrigerentur tua hæc corcula, usquam deerunt. Talibus delinita promissis se nobiscum ituram, spopondit. Et vero postridie iter ingressi, calendis Januarii incolumes oppidum attigimus, licet per viam binæ fulminibus, imbribusque horrendis fœtæ tempestates nobis incubuerint, ac tigris rugitu assiduo totam per noctem minitans nobis iterum, iterumque propinquàrit. Hispanos, queis matrem duabus cum prolibus per transennam exhibui, nihilque omnino Indorum sylvestrium in tota late vicinia superesse, significavi, timoris sui et puduit, et pœnituit. Autumaverant equidem sylvas Empalado, et Mondag fluminibus interjectas barbarorum habitationibus, per-

inde ut formicis, undique scatere. Jam de forma, habitudine, vivendi ratione, quam in matre, ejusque prolibus observaveram, dicendum obiter aliquid. Ab ineunte ætate in Mondag litoribus, culicum, serpentum, aliorumque animalculorum noxiorum frequentia oppido infectis consedere. Palmarum ramis tuguriolum definiebatur. Aqua semper lutulenta potum; arborum fructus, alces, damulæ, cuniculi, aves variæ, frumentum turcicum, radices arboris mandio dapem; tela ex foliis caraquatà contexta vestitum, lectumque præbuere. Mel, quod exesis in arboribus passim prostat, inter cupedias numerabatur. Tabacæ, quam *peti* vocant Quaranii, fumum ex arundine, cui ligneum vasculum cacabi instar præfixum, diu noctuque hauserat vetula; filius tabacæ folia in pulverem redacta ore mandere nunquam desiit. Concha ad lapidem exacuta pro cultro utebantur, interdum arundine fissa. Adolescens matris, sororisque nutricius bina ferri frustilla, cultri olim confracti reliquias, pollicem lata, et pollice nil longiora, ligno, ceu manubrio inserta, cera, filoque circumligata cingulo gestabat suo. Hoc instrumento sagittas scitissime elaborare, decipulas è ligno ad capiendas alces facere, arbores, ubi mellis indicium viderat, perfodere, aliaque id genus præstare solebat. Cum argilla, è qua ollæ conficiuntur, nusquam esset, carnibus assis, non coctis vescebantur per omnem vitam. Herbæ Paraquaricæ folia non nisi frigida perfudere, cum vas, quo aquam recepto more calefacerent, non haberent. Ignem per affrictum celerem duorum ligneellorum nôrunt promptissime elicere, omnium Americanorum more, quod alio loco exponam uberius. Ad restinguendam sitim aqua palustri, semperque, ni ab Austro frigido refrigeretur tantisper, tepida utebantur, cui adferendæ, asservandæque ingentes cucurbitæ pro cantharis serviunt. Ut, quam curta illis domi fuerit suppellex, porro videas, de eorum vestitu facienda est mentio.

« Juveni lacerna è caraquatà filis concinnata è scapulis ad genua utrinque defluebat; ventre funiculis præcincto, se, suosque cucurbitam tabacæ pulveribus, quos mandit, plenam suspendit. Rete crassioribus è filis matri lectus noctu, interdiu vestis fuit unica.

« Puellæ pariter breve reticulum, in quo noctibus cubabat, per diem vestitus instar fuerat. Cum nimis diaphana mihi videretur, ut verecundiæ consultum irem in Indorum, Hispanorumque præsentia, linteum gossipinum, quo lotas manus tergimus, illius nuditati tegendæ destinavi. Puella linteum, quod illi Indi mei porrexerant, iterum, iterumque complicatum papyri instar, capiti imposuit suo, ceu clypeum contra solis æstus; verum admonita ab Indis illo se involvit. Juveni quoque, ne verecundos offenderet oculos, perizomata linea, quibus in itineribus contra culicum morsus caput obvolveram meum, invito obtrusi. Prius celsissimas arbores simii velocitate scandebat, ut fructus ab apris tribus devorandos, inde decerperet. Caligis, veluti compedibus impeditus vix gressum figere potuit. Tanta rerum penuria, frugalitate tanta cum in solitudine victitarent semper, ac anachoretarum veterum rigores, asperitatesque experirentur, sorte sua contentissimos, tranquillo animo, corporeque morborum nescios illos suspexi. Ex quo palam fit, naturam paucis contentam esse; erubescant illi, quibus saturandis, ornandisque totus orbis vix sufficit. Ex ultimis terræ finibus, ex oceani, sylvarum, camporum, montium, tellurisque gremio, ex elementis omnibus, et unde non? avide petuntur subsidia, quæ ad comendum corpus, ad oblectandum palatum faciunt. Verum dum oblectare se, ornareque putant, se onerant, opprimuntque. Dum delicias multiplicant suas, opes, viresque imminuunt quotidie, formæ venustatem labefactant, morbos adsciscunt sibi, mortemque accelerant eo infeliciores, quo fuerint delicatiores.

« Tres mei sylvicolæ, de quibus sermo, rituum Quaraniis barbaris propriorum vel immemores, vel contemptores fuerunt. Crinibus passis sine ulla incisione, vel ligamine incedebant. Juveni nec labium pertusum, nec vertex psittacorum plumis coronatus. Matri, filiæque inaures nullæ, quamvis illa collo circumdederit monilis loco funiculum, è quo frustilla ligni pyramidati, sat multi ponderis pendebant; è mutuo illorum collisu ad quemvis gressum strepitus edebatur. Primo conspectu interrogavi vetulam: num ad terrendos culices strepitans hoc monile è collo suspenderit! moxque globulorum vitreorum exquisiti coloris fascem ligneis his ponderibus substitui. Mater, filiusque corpore erant procero, forma honesta; filia vultu tam candido, tamque eleganti, ut à Poetis Driadas inter Nymphas, Hamadriadasque numerari, ab Europæo quovis pulchra dici tutò posset. Hilaritatem decoram affabilitati conjunctam præ se ferebat. Nostro adventu repentino minime terreri, recreari potius videbatur. Quaranica lingua loquentes nos liberales inter cachinnos risit, nos illam eâdem respondentem. Cum enim extra aliorum Indorum societatem fratri, matrique duntaxat colloqueretur, verbis Quaranicis retentis quidem, ridicula quædam dialectus irrepsit. Sic *quaraçi* sol: *yaçi* luna: *cheraçi* ægroto dicimus reliqui, et illud *c* cum subjecta notula veluti *s* pronunciamus, *quarassi, yassi, cherassi*; illi *quaratschi, yatschi, cheratschi* dicebant. Juvenis præter matrem, sororemque nullam unquam vidit fœminam; neque præter patrem suum virum aliquem. Puella matrem duntaxat novit, nullam præterea fœminam. Virum præter fratrem suum ne eminus quidem conspexit, dum enim utero à matre gestabatur, pater ejus à tigride fuerat discerptus. Ad fructus seu humi, seu in arboribus natos conquirendos, ad ligua, foco necessaria, colligenda sylvam dumetis, arundinibus, spinisque horrentem solers puella peragravit quotidie, quibus pedes misere pertusos habebat. Ne incomitata esset, psittacum exilem humero, simiolum brachio insidentem circumtulit plerumque, nullo tigridum metu, queis omnis illa vicinia abundat, vel me ipso teste oculato. Pridie ejus diei, quo in istorum contubernium incurrimus, parum abfuit, quin dormiens à propinqua jam tigride devoraret. Indi mei ejus rugitu expergefacti et hastis et admotis celeriter ignibus vitam servarunt meam. His in nemoribus, cum minor sit ferarum copia, tigrides fame stimulante ferociunt atrocius, avidiusque in obvios assiliunt homines, quam in campis, ubi, cum infinita vis pecorum omnis generis oberret, præda, famisque remedium, quoties lubet, illis in promptu est. Novi proselyti in oppido mox vestiti reliquorum more, et præ reliquis quotidiano cibo liberaliter refecti sunt. Curatum quoque à me diligenter, ad sylvas vicinas cum aliis ut excurrant frequentius, umbra, amœnaque arborum, queis assueverant, viriditate fruituri. Experientia equidem novimus, ut pisces extra aquam cito intereunt, sic barbaros è sylvis ad oppida translatos sæpe contabescere, victus, aerisque mutatione, ac solis potissimum æstu corporum habitudinem perturbante, quippe quæ à pueritia humidis, frigidiusculis, opacisque nemoribus assueverunt. Idem fuit matris, filii, filiæque nostro in

oppido fatum. Paucis ab adventu suo hebdomadibus gravedine, rheumateque totum corpus pervadente tentabantur omnes. His oculorum, auriumque dolor, ac haud multo post surditas successit. Mœrore animi, cibique omnis fastidium vires absumpsit adeo, ut extrema demum macies, tabesque nullis remediis proficientibus consequeretur. Aliquot mensibus languescens mater senicula, Christianæ disciplinæ rudimentis rite imbuta, sacroque tincta latice prima occubuit, animo tam sereno, Divinisque voluntatibus acquiescente, ut illam ad superos transisse nil dubitaverim. Puella, quæ plena vigoris, venustatisque oppidum ingrediebatur, viribus exhausta, sui omnino jam dissimilis, floris instar paulatim marcescens vix ossibus hæsit, ac denique matrem ad tumulum secuta est, et nisi vehementissime fallor, ad Cœlum. Quid si cum regum sapientissimo dicamus : illam post sacrum, quo expiata est, baptisma consummatum in brevi explevisse tempora multa : placitam Deo fuisse animam illius : raptam esse, ne malitia mutaret intellectum ejus. Illud certissimum : qui innocentissimæ puellæ integritatem laudibus, funus præproperum lacrymis non prosequeretur, neminem in oppido fuisse. Frater illius tum superstes eandem, quâ mater, sororque extinctæ sunt, invaletudinem sensit, sed, quia robustior, superavit. Quin et ex morbillis, qui multas in oppido edebant strages, subinde convaluit adeo, ut confirmata penitus valetudine nihil illi porro metuendum esse videretur. Hilari erat animo, statis horis sacram adivit ædem, Christiana dogmata condidicit perdiligenter, morigerum, placidumque se præbuit omnibus, ac frugis optimæ indicia passim dedit. Ad periclitandam tamen illius in oppido perseverantiam tantisper differendum ejus baptismum existimavi. Hæc inter adest forte Indus Christianus, qui hunc catechumenum me jubente suis dudum habebat in ædibus, vir probus, et agri dives. Hic : mi Pater, ajebat, sylvicola noster equidem optime valet, verum mihi videtur ad delirandum propendere. Nil sibi jam dolere, sed noctes sibi insomnes abire, inquit, spectabilem sibi matrem cum sorore adesse quot noctibus, et amica voce sibi dicere : *Ndecaray, ndecaray ânga, nderemimõ a eÿrupi orõ yu yebi ndererahabone*. Sine te, quæso, baptizari. Præter tuam expectationem veniemus iterum te abducturæ. Hoc alloquio, hoc aspectu sibi somnum impediri, ait. Jubeas illum meo nomine, respondi, bono esse animo. Tristem matris, sororisque, quibuscum, per omnem ætatem versatus est, recordationem somniorum ejusmodi causam esse. Illas cœlo, ut quidem mihi verisimile, receptas nihil jam negoti his in terris habere. Hæc ego. Verum paucos post dies idem redit Indus, eadem, quæ nuper, refert, suamque de timenda catechumeni deliratione suspicionem confirmat. Aliquid rei subesse, suspicatus actutum ejus in domum propero, sedentem deprehendo. Rogatus à me : qui se habeat? incolumem, doloris omnis expertem se esse ridens reponit, addit tamen : vigilando semper se noctem agere, quod mater, sororque identidem præsentes sibi offerantur, de baptismo accelerando moneant, et inopinate se abducendum, minentur; idcirco nullam se quietis partem capere posse, iterum, iterumque mihi affirmat candore, ut semper alias, summo. Somniari ab illo talia, atque adeo contemni posse, autumaveram; memor tamen, somnia monitiones cœlestes, Dei oracula non raro exstitisse, uti divinis ex literis patet, in negotio tanti momenti visum mihi est catechumeni et securitati et tranquillitati consulere. De illius perseverantia, de religio-

nis capitum scientia sat certus præmissis interrogatio-
nibusque necessariis eum sacris undis mox ablui, Lu-
dovici nomine insignivi. Hoc a me præstitum 23 Junii,
S. Joannis Baptistæ vigilia circa horam decimam ante-
meridianam. Eodem die circa vesperum nullo morbo,
aut apoplexiæ indicio accedente placidissime expiravit.

« Hic eventus, universo oppido compertus, quemque
juratus testari possum, in admirationem rapuit omnes.
Lectoris arbitrio, quid de hoc sentiendum sit, relinquo.
Nunquam tamen in animum inducere meum, potui, ut
factum hoc fortuitum putarem. Eximiæ Dei clementiæ
tribuo, quod hi tres sylvicolæ à me sint reperti in ignotis
sylvarum latebris, quod mihi ad oppidum meum, ad
amplectendam religionem se hortanti morem promptis-
sime gesserint, quod sacro latice expiati vitam clause-
rint. Optimum Numen in Cœlo consociatos voluit, qui
tot annos in sylva contubernales fuere incredibili mo-
rum integritate. Fateor, dulcissimam mihi etiamnum
accidere expeditionis ad flumen Empalado memoriam,
quæ licet multis molestiis, periculisque mihi constiterit,
ternis illis sylvicolis felicissima fuit; Hispanis utilissima:
hi equidem à me facti certiores, quod per immensos
illos nemorum tractus nulla porro Barbarorum vestigia
extent, istic per triennium quæstu maximo multa cen-
tenariorum millia herbæ Paraquaricæ collegerunt. Ne-
que id rarum, missionariorum, qui sylvas herbæ feraces
barbaris liberant, sudore, ac periculo Hispanos ditescere
mercatores. His tamen nunquam in mentem venit ad
alendos, vestiendosque catechumenos vel micam, filumve
contribuere. Illorum corpora, ut animi missionariorum
sæpissime inopum curæ relinquuntur.»—*Dobrizhoffer
de Abiponibus, Lib. Prodromus*, pp. 97—106.

PROEM.

THAT was a memorable day for Spain,
When on Pamplona's towers, so basely won,
 The Frenchmen stood, and saw upon the plain
Their long-expected succours hastening on:
Exultingly they mark'd the brave array,
And deem'd their leader should his purpose gain,
Though Wellington and England barr'd the way.
Anon the bayonets glitter'd in the sun,
And frequent cannon flash'd, whose lurid light
Redden'd through sulphurous smoke: fast vollying
 round
Roll'd the war-thunders, and with long rebound
Backward from many a rock and cloud-capt height
In answering peals Pyrene sent the sound.
Impatient for relief, toward the fight
The hungry garrison their eye-balls strain:
Vain was the Frenchman's skill, his valour vain;
And even then, when eager hope almost
Had moved their irreligious lips to prayer,
Averting from the fatal scene their sight,
They breathed the imprecations of despair.
For Wellesley's star hath risen ascendant there;
Once more he drove the host of France to flight,
And triumphed once again for God and for the right.

That was a day, whose influence far and wide
The struggling nations felt; it was a joy
Wherewith all Europe rung from side to side.
Yet hath Pamplona seen in former time
A moment big with mightier consequence,
Affecting many an age and distant clime.
That day it was which saw in her defence,
Contending with the French before her wall,
A noble soldier of Guipuzcoa fall,
Sore hurt, but not to death. For when long care
Restored his shatter'd leg and set him free,
He would not brook a slight deformity,
As one who being gay and debonnair,
In courts conspicuous, as in camps must be :
So he forsooth a shapely boot must wear ; [1]
And the vain man, with peril of his life,
Laid the recovered limb again beneath the knife.

Long time upon the bed of pain he lay
Whiling with books the weary hours away ; [2]
And from that circumstance and this vain man
A train of long events their course began,
Whose term it is not given us yet to see.
Who hath not heard Loyola's sainted name,
Before whom Kings and Nations bow'd the knee?
Thy annals, Ethiopia, might proclaim
What deeds arose from that prolific day ;
And of dark plots might shuddering Europe tell.
But Science too her trophies would display ;
Faith give the martyrs of Japan their fame ;
And Charity on works of love would dwell
In California's dolorous regions drear;
And where, amid a pathless world of wood,
Gathering a thousand rivers on his way,
Huge Orellana rolls his affluent flood ;
And where the happier sons of Paraguay,
By gentleness and pious art subdued,
Bow'd their meek heads beneath the Jesuit's sway,
And lived and died in filial servitude.
I love thus uncontroll'd, as in a dream,
To muse upon the course of human things ;
Exploring sometimes the remotest springs,
Far as tradition lends one guiding gleam ;
Or following, upon Thought's audacious wings,
Into Futurity, the endless stream.
But now in quest of no ambitious height,
I go where truth and nature lead my way,
And ceasing here from desultory flight,
In measured strains I tell a Tale of Paraguay.

CANTO I.

I.

JENNER! for ever shall thy honour'd name
Among the children of mankind be blest,
Who by thy skill hast taught us how to tame
One dire disease [3]—the lamentable pest
Which Africa sent forth to scourge the West,
As if in vengeance for her sable brood
So many an age remorselessly opprest.
For that most fearful malady subdued
Receive a poet's praise, a father's gratitude.

II.

Fair promise be this triumph of an age
When Man, with vain desires no longer blind,
And wise though late, his only war shall wage
Against the miseries which afflict mankind,
Striving with virtuous heart and strenuous mind
Till evil from the earth shall pass away.
Lo, this his glorious destiny assign'd!
For that blest consummation let us pray,
And trust in fervent faith, and labour as we may.

III.

The hideous malady which lost its power
When Jenner's art the dire contagion stay'd,
Among Columbia's sons, in fatal hour,
Across the wide Atlantic wave convey'd,
Its fiercest form of pestilence display'd :
Where'er its deadly course the plague began
Vainly the wretched sufferer look'd for aid;
Parent from child, and child from parent ran,
For tyrannous fear dissolved all natural bonds of man. 4

IV.

A feeble nation of Guarani race,
Thinn'd by perpetual wars, but unsubdued,
Had taken up at length a resting place
Among those tracts of lake and swamp and wood,
Where Mondai issuing from its solitude
Flows with slow stream to Empalado's bed.
It was a region desolate and rude;
But thither had the horde for safety fled,
And being there conceal'd in peace their lives they led.

V.

There had the tribe a safe asylum found
Amid those marshes wide and woodlands dense,
With pathless wilds and waters spread around,
And labyrinthine swamps, a sure defence
From human foes,—but not from pestilence.
The spotted plague appear'd, that direst ill,—
How brought among them none could tell, or whence;
The mortal seed had lain among them still,
And quicken'd now to work the Lord's mysterious will.

VI.

Alas, it was no medicable grief
Which herbs might reach! Nor could the juggler's power
With all his antic mummeries bring relief.
Faith might not aid him in that ruling hour,
Himself a victim now. The dreadful stour
None could escape, nor aught its force assuage.
The marriageable maiden had her dower
From death; the strong man sunk beneath its rage,
And death cut short the thread of childhood and of age.

VII.

No time for customary mourning now ;
With hand close-clench'd to pluck the rooted hair,
To beat the bosom, on the swelling brow
Inflict redoubled blows, and blindly tear
The cheeks, indenting bloody furrows there,
The deep-traced signs indelible of woe;
Then to some crag, or bank abrupt, repair,
And giving grief its scope infuriate, throw
The impatient body thence upon the earth below.

VIII.

Devices these by poor weak nature taught,
Which thus a change of suffering would obtain ;
And flying from intolerable thought
And piercing recollections, would full fain
Distract itself by sense of fleshly pain
From anguish that the soul must else endure.
Easier all outward torments to sustain,
Than those heart-wounds which only time can cure,
And He in whom alone the hopes of man are sure.

IX.

None sorrow'd here; the sense of woe was sear'd,
When every one endured his own sore ill.
The prostrate sufferers neither hoped nor fear'd
The body labour'd, but the heart was still;—
So let the conquering malady fulfil
Its fatal course, rest cometh at the end!
Passive they lay with neither wish nor will
For aught but this; nor did they long attend
That welcome boon from death, the never-failing friend.

X.

Who is there to make ready now the pit,
The house that will content from this day forth
Its easy tenant? Who in vestments fit
Shall swathe the sleeper for his bed of earth,
Now tractable as when a babe at birth ?
Who now the ample funeral urn shall knead,
And burying it beneath his proper hearth
Deposit there with careful hands the dead,
And lightly then relay the floor above his head?

XI.

Unwept, unshrouded, and unsepulchred,
The hammock where they hang, for winding-sheet
And grave suffices the deserted dead :
There from the armadillo's searching feet
Safer than if within the tomb's retreat.
The carrion birds obscene in vain essay
To find that quarry : round and round they beat
The air, but fear to enter for their prey,
And from the silent door the jaguar turns away. 5

XII.

But nature for her universal law
Hath other surer instruments in store,
Whom from the haunts of men no wonted awe
Withholds as with a spell. In swarms they pour
From wood and swamp : and when their work is o'er
On the white bones the mouldering roof will fall;
Seeds will take root, and spring in sun and shower;
And Mother Earth ere long with her green pall,
Resuming to herself the wreck, will cover all.

XIII.

Oh! better thus with earth to have their part,
Than in Egyptian catacombs to lie,
Age after age preserved by horrid art,
In ghastly image of humanity! 6
Strange pride that with corruption thus would vie!
And strange delusion that would thus maintain
The fleshly form, till cycles shall pass by,
And in the series of the eternal chain,
The spirit come to seek its old abode again.

70

XIV.

One pair alone survived the general fate ;
Left in such drear and mournful solitude,
That death might seem a preferable state.
Not more deprest the Arkite patriarch stood,
When landing first on Ararat he view'd,
Where all around the mountain summits lay,
Like islands seen amid the boundless flood!
Nor our first parents more forlorn than they,
Through Eden when they took their solitary way.

XV.

Alike to them, it seem'd in their despair,
Whither they wander'd from the infected spot.
Chance might direct their steps : they took no care ;
Come well or ill to them, it matter'd not!
Left as they were in that unhappy lot,
The sole survivors they of all their race,
They reck'd not when their fate, nor where, nor what,
In this resignment to their hopeless case,
Indifferent to all choice or circumstance of place.

XVI.

That palsying stupor past away ere long,
And as the spring of health resumed its power,
They felt that life was dear, and hope was strong.
What marvel! 'T was with them the morning hour,
When bliss appears to be the natural dower
Of all the creatures of this joyous earth ;
And sorrow fleeting like a vernal shower
Scarce interrupts the current of our mirth ;
Such is the happy heart we bring with us at birth.

XVII.

Though of his nature and his boundless love
Erring, yet tutor'd by instinctive sense,
They rightly deem'd the Power who rules above
Had saved them from the wasting pestilence.
That favouring power would still be their defence :
Thus were they by their late deliverance taught
To place a child-like trust in Providence,
And in their state forlorn they found this thought
Of natural faith with hope and consolation fraught.

XVIII.

And now they built themselves a leafy bower,
Amid a glade, slow Mondai's stream beside,
Screen'd from the southern blast of piercing power :
Not like their native dwelling, long and wide,
By skilful toil of numbers edified,
The common home of all, their human nest,
Where threescore hammocks pendant side by side
Were ranged, and on the ground the fires were drest ;
Alas that populous hive hath now no living guest!

XIX.

A few firm stakes they planted in the ground,
Circling a narrow space, yet large enow ;
These strongly interknit they closed around
With basket-work of many a pliant bough.
The roof was like the sides ; the door was low,
And rude the hut, and trimm'd with little care,
For little heart had they to dress it now ;
Yet was the humble structure fresh and fair,
And soon its inmates found that Love might sojourn
        there.

XX.

Quiara could recall to mind the course
Of twenty summers ; perfectly he knew
Whate'er his fathers taught of skill or force.
Right to the mark his whizzing lance he threw,
And from his bow the unerring arrow flew
With fatal aim : and when the laden bee
Buzz'd by him in its flight, he could pursue
Its path with certain ken,[7] and follow free
Until he traced the hive in hidden bank or tree.

XXI.

Of answering years was Monnema, nor less
Expert in all her sex's household ways.
The Indian weed she skilfully could dress ;
And in what depth to drop the yellow maize
She knew, and when around its stem to raise
The lighten'd soil ; and well could she prepare
Its ripen'd seed for food, her proper praise ;
Or in the embers turn with frequent care
Its succulent head yet green, sometimes for daintier fare.

XXII.

And how to macerate the bark she knew,
And draw apart its beaten fibres fine,
And bleaching them in sun, and air, and dew ;
From dry and glossy filaments entwine
With rapid twirl of hand the lengthening line ;
Next interknitting well the twisted thread,
In many an even mesh its knots combine,
And shape in tapering length the pensile bed,
Light hammock there to hang beneath the leafy shed.

XXIII.

Time had been when expert in works of clay
She lent her hands the swelling urn to mould,
And fill'd it for the appointed festal day
With the beloved beverage which the bold
Quaff'd in their triumph and their joy of old ;
The fruitful cause of many an uproar rude,
When in their drunken bravery uncontroll'd,
Some bitter jest awoke the dormant feud,
And wrath and rage and strife and wounds and death
        ensued.

XXIV.

These occupations were gone by : the skill
Was useless now, which once had been her pride.
Content were they, when thirst impell'd, to fill
The dry and hollow gourd from Mondai's side ;
The river from its sluggish bed supplied
A draught for repetition all unmeet ;
Howbeit the bodily want was satisfied ;
No feverish pulse ensued, nor ireful heat,
Their days were undisturb'd, their natural sleep was
        sweet.

XXV.

She too had learnt in youth how best to trim
The honoured Chief for his triumphal day,
And covering with soft gums the obedient limb
And body, then with feathers overlay,
In regular hues disposed,[8] a rich display.
Well-pleased the glorious savage stood and eyed
The growing work ; then vain of his array
Look'd with complacent frown from side to side,
Stalk'd with elater step, and swell'd with statelier pride.

XXVI.

Feasts and carousals,9 vanity and strife,
Could have no place with them in solitude
To break the tenor of their even life.
Quiara day by day his game pursued,
Searching the air, the water, and the wood,
With hawk-like eye, and arrow sure as fate;
And Monnema prepared the hunter's food :
Cast with him here in this forlorn estate,
In all things for the man was she a fitting mate.

XXVII.

The Moon had gather'd oft her monthly store
Of light, and oft in darkness left the sky,
Since Monnema a growing burthen bore
Of life and hope.   The appointed weeks go by;
And now her hour is come, and none is nigh
To help : but human help she needed none.
A few short throes endured with scarce a cry,
Upon the bank she laid her new-born son,
Then slid into the stream, and bathed, and all was done.

XXVIII.

Might old observances have there been kept,
Then should the husband to that pensile bed,
Like one exhausted with the birth have crept,
And laying down in feeble guise his head,
For many a day been nursed and dieted
With tender care, to childing mothers due.
Certes a custom strange, and yet far spread
Through many a savage tribe, howe'er it grew,
And once in the old world known as widely as the new.10

XXIX.

This could not then be done; he might not lay
The bow and those unerring shafts aside;
Nor through the appointed weeks forego the prey,
Still to be sought amid those regions wide,
None being there who should the while provide
That lonely household with their needful food :
So still Quiara through the forest plied
His daily task, and in the thickest wood
Still laid his snares for birds, and still the chase pursued.

XXX.

But seldom may such thoughts of mingled joy
A father's agitated breast dilate,
As when he first beheld that infant boy.
Who hath not prov'd it, ill can estimate
The feeling of that stirring hour,—the weight
Of that new sense, the thoughtful, pensive bliss.
In all the changes of our changeful state,
Even from the cradle to the grave, I wis,
The heart doth undergo no change so great as this.

XXXI.

A deeper and unwonted feeling fill'd
These parents, gazing on their new-born son.
Already in their busy hopes they build
On this frail sand.   Now let the seasons run,
And let the natural work of time be done
With them,—for unto them a child is born :
And when the hand of Death may reach the one,
The other will not now be left to mourn
A solitary wretch, all utterly forlorn.

XXXII.

Thus Monnema and thus Quiara thought,
Though each the melancholy thought represt;
They could not chuse but feel, yet uttered not
The human feeling, which in hours of rest
Often would rise, and fill the boding breast
With a dread foretaste of that mournful day,
When, at the inexorable Power's behest,
The unwilling spirit, called perforce away,
Must leave, for ever leave, its dear connatural clay.

XXXIII.

Link'd as they were, where each to each was all,
How might the poor survivor hope to bear
That heaviest loss which one day must befall,
Nor sink beneath the weight of his despair.
Scarce could the heart even for a moment dare
That miserable time to contemplate,
When the dread Messenger should find them there,
From whom is no escape,—and reckless Fate,
Whom it had bound so close, for ever separate.

XXXIV.

Lighter that burthen lay upon the heart
When this dear babe was born to share their lot;
They could endure to think that they must part.
Then too a glad consolatory thought
Arose, while gazing on the child they sought
With hope their dreary prospect to delude,
Till they almost believed, as fancy taught,
How that from them a tribe should spring renew'd,
To people and possess that ample solitude.

XXXV.

Such hope they felt, but felt that whatsoe'er
The undiscoverable to come might prove,
Unwise it were to let that bootless care
Disturb the present hours of peace and love.
For they had gain'd a happiness above
The state which in their native horde was known :
No outward causes were there here to move
Discord and alien thoughts; being thus alone
From all mankind, their hearts and their desires were one.

XXXVI.

Different their love in kind and in degree
From what their poor depraved forefathers knew,
With whom degenerate instincts were left free
To take their course, and blindly to pursue,
Unheeding they the ills that must ensue,
The bent of brute desire.   No moral tie
Bound the hard husband to his servile crew
Of wives; and they the chance of change might try,
All love destroy'd by such preposterous liberty.

XXXVII.

Far other tie this solitary pair
Indissolubly bound; true helpmates they,
In joy or grief, in weal or woe to share,
In sickness or in health, through life's long day;
And reassuming in their hearts her sway
Benignant Nature made the burthen light.
It was the Woman's pleasure to obey,
The Man's to ease her toil in all he might,
So each in serving each obtain'd the best delight.

XXXVIII.

And as connubial, so parental love
Obey'd unerring Nature's order here,
For now no force of impious custom strove
Against her law;—such as was wont to sear
The unhappy heart with usages severe,
Till harden'd mothers in the grave could lay
Their living babes with no compunctious tear, [11]
So monstrous men become, when from the way
Of primal light they turn thro' heathen paths astray.

XXXIX.

Deliver'd from this yoke, in them henceforth
The springs of natural love may freely flow:
New joys, new virtues with that happy birth
Are born, and with the growing infant grow.
Source of our purest happiness below
Is that benignant law which hath entwined
Dearest delight with strongest duty, so
That in the healthy heart and righteous mind
Ever they co-exist, inseparably combined.

XL.

Oh! bliss for them when in that infant face
They now the unfolding faculties descry,
And fondly gazing, trace—or think they trace
The first faint speculation in that eye,
Which hitherto hath roll'd in vacancy!
Oh! bliss in that soft countenance to seek
Some mark of recognition, and espy
The quiet smile which in the innocent cheek
Of kindness and of kind its consciousness doth speak!

XLI.

For him, if born among their native tribe,
Some haughty name his parents had thought good,
As weening that therewith they should ascribe
The strength of some fierce tenant of the wood,
The water, or the aërial solitude,
Jaguar or vulture, water wolf or snake,
The beast that prowls abroad in search of blood,
Or reptile that within the treacherous brake
Waits for the prey, upcoil'd, its hunger to aslake.

XLII.

Now soften'd as their spirits were by love,
Abhorrent from such thoughts they turn'd away;
And with a happier feeling, from the dove,
They named the child Yeruti. [12]   On a day
When smiling at his mother's breast in play,
They in his tones of murmuring pleasure heard
A sweet resemblance of the stock-dove's lay,
Fondly they named him from that gentle bird,
And soon such happy use endear'd the fitting word.

XLIII.

Days pass, and moons have wax'd and waned, and still
This dovelet nestled in their leafy bower
Obtains increase of sense, and strength and will,
As in due order many a latent power
Expands,—humanity's exalted dower:
And they while thus the days serenely fled
Beheld him flourish like a vigorous flower
Which lifting from a genial soil its head
By seasonable suns and kindly showers is fed.

XLIV.

Ere long the cares of helpless babyhood
To the next stage of infancy give place,
That age with sense of conscious growth endued,
When every gesture hath its proper grace:
Then come the unsteady step, the tottering pace;
And watchful hopes and emulous thoughts appear;
The imitative lips essay to trace
Their words, observant both with eye and ear,
In mutilated sounds which parents love to hear.

XLV.

Serenely thus the seasons pass away;
And, oh! how rapidly they seem to fly
With those for whom to-morrow like to-day
Glides on in peaceful uniformity!
Five years have since Yeruti's birth gone by,
Five happy years;—and ere the Moon which then
Hung like a Sylphid's light canoe on high
Should fill its circle, Monnema again
Laying her burthen down must bear a mother's pain.

XLVI.

Alas, a keener pang before that day,
Must by the wretched Monnema be borne!
In quest of game Quiara went his way
To roam the wilds as he was wont, one morn;
She look'd in vain at eve for his return.
By moonlight thro' the midnight solitude
She sought him; and she found his garment torn,
His bow and useless arrows in the wood,
Marks of a jaguar's feet, a broken spear, and blood.

CANTO II.

I.

O THOU who listening to the Poet's song
Dost yield thy willing spirit to his sway,
Look not that I should painfully prolong
The sad narration of that fatal day
With tragic details: all too true the lay!
Nor is my purpose e'er to entertain
The heart with useless grief; but as I may,
Blend in my calm and meditative strain
Consolatory thoughts, the balm for real pain.

II.

O Youth or Maiden, whosoe'er thou art,
Safe in my guidance may thy spirit be!
I wound not wantonly the tender heart:
And if sometimes a tear of sympathy
Should rise, it will from bitterness be free,—
Yea, with a healing virtue be endued,
As thou in this true tale shalt hear from me
Of evils overcome, and grief subdued,
And virtues springing up like flowers in solitude.

III.

The unhappy Monnema when thus bereft
Sunk not beneath the desolating blow,
Widow'd she was : but still her child was left;
For him must she sustain the weight of woe,
Which else would in that hour have laid her low.
Nor wish'd she now the work of death complete :
Then only doth the soul of woman know
Its proper strength, when love and duty meet;
Invincible the heart wherein they have their seat.

IV.

The seamen who upon some coral reef
Are cast amid the interminable main,
Still cling to life, and hoping for relief
Drag on their days of wretchedness and pain.
In turtle shells they hoard the scanty rain,
And eat its flesh, sun-dried for lack of fire,
Till the weak body can no more sustain
Its wants, but sinks beneath its sufferings dire;
Most miserable man who sees the rest expire!

V.

He lingers there while months and years go by :
And holds his hope tho' months and years have past.
And still at morning round the farthest sky,
And still at eve his eagle glance is cast,
If there he may behold the far-off mast
Arise, for which he hath not ceased to pray.
And if perchance a ship should come at last,
And bear him from that dismal bank away,
He blesses God that he hath lived to see that day.

VI.

So strong a hold hath life upon the soul,
Which sees no dawning of eternal light,
But subject to this mortal frame's controul,
Forgetful of its origin and right,
Content in bondage dwells and utter night.
By worthier ties was this poor mother bound
To life; even while her grief was at the height,
Then in maternal love support she found
And in maternal cares a healing for her wound.

VII.

For now her hour is come : a girl is born,
Poor infant, all unconscious of its fate,
How passing strange, how utterly forlorn !
The genial season served to mitigate
In all it might their sorrowful estate,
Supplying to the mother at her door
From neighbouring trees which bent beneath their
weight,
A full supply of fruitage now mature,
So in that time of need their sustenance was sure.

VIII.

Nor then alone, but alway did the Eye
Of Mercy look upon that lonely bower.
Days past, and weeks; and months and years went by,
And never evil thing the while had power
To enter there. The boy in sun and shower
Rejoicing in his strength to youthhead grew ; .
And Mooma, that beloved girl, a dower
Of gentleness from bounteous nature drew,
With all that should the heart of womankind imbue.

IX.

The tears which o'er her infancy were shed
Profuse, resented not of grief alone :
Maternal love their bitterness allay'd,
And with a strength and virtue all its own
Sustain'd the breaking heart.   A look, a tone,
A gesture of that innocent babe, in eyes
With saddest recollections overflown,
Would sometimes make a tender smile arise,
Like sunshine breaking thro' a shower in vernal skies.

X.

No looks but those of tenderness were found
To turn upon that helpless infant dear ;
And as her sense unfolded, never sound
Of wrath or discord brake upon her ear.
Her soul its native purity sincere
Possess'd, by no example here defiled ;
From envious passions free, exempt from fear,
Unknowing of all ill, amid the wild
Beloving and beloved she grew, a happy child.

XI.

Yea, where that solitary bower was placed,
Though all unlike to Paradise the scene,
(A wide circumference of woodlands waste,)
Something of what in Eden might have been
Was shadowed there imperfectly, I ween,
In this fair creature : safe from all offence,
Expanding like a shelter'd plant serene,
Evils that fret and stain being far from thence,
Her heart in peace and joy retain'd its innocence.

XII.

At first the infant to Yeruti proved
A cause of wonder and disturbing joy.
A stronger tie than that of kindred moved
His inmost being, as the happy boy
Felt in his heart of hearts without alloy
The sense of kind : a fellow creature she,
In whom when now she ceased to be a toy
For tender sport, his soul rejoiced to see
Connatural powers expand, and growing sympathy.

XIII.

For her he cull'd the fairest flowers, and sought
Throughout the woods the earliest fruits for her.
The cayman's eggs, the honeycomb he brought
To this beloved sister,—whatsoe'er,
To his poor thought, of delicate or rare
The wilds might yield, solicitous to find.
They who affirm all natural acts declare
Self-love to be the ruler of the mind,
Judge from their own mean hearts, and foully wrong
mankind.

XIV.

Three souls in whom no selfishness had place
Were here : three happy souls, which undefiled,
Albeit in darkness, still retain'd a trace
Of their celestial origin.   The wild
Was as a sanctuary where Nature smiled
Upon these simple children of her own,
And cherishing whate'er was meek and mild,
Call'd forth the gentle virtues, such alone,
The evils which evoke the stronger being unknown.

XV.

What though at birth we bring with us the seed
Of sin a mortal taint,—in heart and will
Too surely felt, too plainly shown in deed,—
Our fatal heritage ; yet are we still
The children of the All Merciful : and ill
They teach, who tell us that from hence must flow
God's wrath, and then his justice to fulfil,
Death everlasting, never-ending woe :
O miserable lot of man if it were so!

XVI.

Falsely and impiously teach they who thus
Our heavenly Father's holy will misread!
In bounty hath the Lord created us,
In love redeem'd. From this authentic creed
Let no bewildering sophistry impede
The heart's entire assent, for God is good.
Hold firm this faith, and, in whatever need,
Doubt not but thou wilt find thy soul endued
With all-sufficing strength of heavenly fortitude!

XVII.

By nature peccable and frail are we,
Easily beguiled ; to vice, to error prone ;
But apt for virtue too. Humanity
Is not a field where tares and thorns alone
Are left to spring ; good seed hath there been sown
With no unsparing hand. Sometimes the shoot
Is choked with weeds, or withers on a stone ;
But in a kindly soil it strikes its root,
And flourisheth, and bringeth forth abundant fruit.

XVIII.

Love, duty, generous feeling, tenderness,
Spring in the uncontaminated mind ;
And these were Mooma's natural dower. Nor less
Had liberal Nature to the boy assign'd.
Happier herein than if among mankind
Their lot had fallen,—oh, certes happier here !
That all things tended still more close to bind
Their earliest ties, and they from year to year
Retain'd a childish heart, fond, simple, and sincere.

XIX.

They had no sad reflection to alloy
The calm contentment of the passing day,
No foresight to disturb the present joy.
Not so with Monnema ; albeit the sway
Of time had reach'd her heart, and worn away,
At length, the grief so deeply seated there,
The future often, like a burthen, lay
Upon that heart, a cause of secret care
And melancholy thought ; yet did she not despair.

XX.

Chance from the fellowship of human kind
Had cut them off, and chance might reunite.
On this poor possibility her mind
Reposed ; she did not for herself invite
The unlikely thought, and cherish with delight
The dream of what such change might haply bring ;
Gladness with hope long since had taken flight
From her ; she felt that life was on the wing,
And happiness like youth has here no second spring.

XXI.

So were her feelings to her lot composed
That to herself all change had now been pain,
For Time upon her own desires had closed ;
But in her children as she lived again,
For their dear sake she learnt to entertain
A wish for human intercourse renew'd ;
And oftentimes, while they devour'd the strain,
Would she beguile their evening solitude
With stories strangely told and strangely understood.

XXII.

Little she knew, for little had she seen,
And little of traditionary lore
Had reach'd her ear ; and yet to them I ween
Their mother's knowledge seem'd a boundless store.
A world it opened to their thoughts, yea more,—
Another world beyond this mortal state.
Bereft of her they had indeed been poor,
Being left to animal sense, degenerate,
Mere creatures, they had sunk below the beasts' estate.

XXIII.

The human race, from her they understood,
Was not within that lonely hut confined,
But distant far beyond their world of wood
Were tribes and powerful nations of their kind ;
And of the old observances which bind
People and chiefs, the ties of man and wife,
The laws of kin religiously assign'd,
Rites, customs, scenes of riotry and strife,
And all the strange vicissitudes of savage life.

XXIV.

Wondering they listen to the wonderous tale,
But no repining thought such tales excite :
Only a wish, if wishes might avail,
Was haply felt, with juvenile delight,
To mingle in the social dance at night,
Where the broad moonshine, level as a flood,
O'erspread the plain, and in the silver light,
Well-pleased, the placid elders sate and view'd
The sport, and seem'd therein to feel their youth renew'd.

XXV.

But when the darker scenes their mother drew,
What crimes were wrought when drunken fury raged,
What miseries from their fatal discord grew
When horde with horde in deadly strife engaged :
The rancorous hate with which their wars they waged,
The more unnatural horrors which ensued,
When, with inveterate vengeance unassuaged,
The victors round their slaughtered captives stood,
And babes were brought to dip their little hands in blood :

XXVI.

Horrent they heard ; and with her hands the Maid
Prest her eyes close as if she strove to blot
The hateful image which her mind pourtray'd.
The Boy sate silently, intent in thought ;
Then with a deep-drawn sigh, as if he sought
To heave the oppressive feeling from his breast,
Complacently compared their harmless lot
With such wild life, outrageous and unblest :
Securely thus to live, he said, was surely best.

XXVII.

On tales of blood they could not bear to dwell,
From such their hearts abhorrent shrunk in fear.
Better they liked that Monnema should tell
Of things unseen; what power had placed them
    here, 13
And whence the living spirit came, and where
It past, when parted from this mortal mold;
Of such mysterious themes with willing ear
They heard, devoutly listening while she told
Strangely-disfigured truths, and fables feign'd of old.

XXVIII.

By the Great Spirit man was made, she said;
His voice it was which peal'd along the sky,
And shook the heavens and fill'd the earth with dread.
Alone and inaccessible, on high
He had his dwelling-place eternally,
And Father was his name. 14 This all knew well;
But none had seen his face: and if his eye
Regarded what upon the earth befell,
Or if he cared for man, she knew not:—who could tell?

XXIX.

But this, she said, was sure, that after death
There was reward and there was punishment:
And that the evil doers, when the breath
Of their injurious lives at length was spent,
Into all noxious forms abhorr'd were sent,
Of beasts and reptiles; so retaining still
Their old propensities, on evil bent,
They work'd where'er they might their wicked will,
The natural foes of men, whom we pursue and kill.

XXX.

Of better spirits, some there were who said
That in the grave they had their place of rest.
Lightly they laid the earth upon the dead,
Lest in its narrow tenement the guest
Should suffer underneath such load opprest.
But that death surely set the spirit free,
Sad proof to them poor Monnema addrest,
Drawn from their father's fate; no grave had he
Wherein his soul might dwell. This therefore could
    not be.

XXXI.

Likelier they taught who said that to the Land
Of Souls the happy spirit took its flight,
A region underneath the sole command
Of the Good Power; by him for the upright
Appointed and replenish'd with delight;
A land where nothing evil ever came,
Sorrow, nor pain, nor peril, nor affright,
Nor change, nor death; but there the human frame,
Untouch'd by age or ill, continued still the same.

XXXII.

Winds would not pierce it there, nor heat and cold
Grieve, nor thirst parch and hunger pine; but there
The sun by day its even influence hold
With genial warmth, and through the unclouded air
The moon upon her nightly journey fare:
The lakes and fish-full streams are never dry;
Trees ever green perpetual fruitage bear;
And, wheresoe'er the hunter turns his eye,
Water and earth and heaven to him their stores supply.

XXXIII.

And once there was a way to that good land,
For in mid-earth a wondrous Tree there grew, 15
By which the adventurer might with foot and hand
From branch to branch his upward course pursue;
An easy path, if what were said be true,
Albeit the ascent was long: and when the height
Was gain'd, that blissful region was in view,
Wherein the traveller safely might alight,
And roam abroad at will, and take his free delight.

XXXIV.

O happy time, when ingress thus was given
To the upper world, and at their pleasure they
Whose hearts were strong might pass from earth to
    heaven
By their own act and choice! In evil day
Mishap had fatally cut off that way,
And none may now the Land of Spirits gain,
Till from its dear-loved tenement of clay,
Violence or age, infirmity and pain
Divorce the soul which there full gladly would remain.

XXXV.

Such grievous loss had by their own misdeed
Upon the unworthy race of men been brought.
An aged woman there who could not speed
In fishing, earnestly one day besought
Her countrymen, that they of what they caught
A portion would upon her, wants bestow.
They set her hunger and her age at nought,
And still to her entreaties answered no,
And mock'd her, till they made her heart with rage
    o'erflow.

XXXVI.

But that old woman by such wanton wrong
Inflamed, went hurrying down; and in the pride
Of magic power wherein the crone was strong,
Her human form infirm she laid aside.
Better the Capiguara's limbs supplied
A strength accordant to her fierce intent:
These she assumed, and, burrowing deep and wide
Beneath the Tree, with vicious will, she went,
To inflict upon mankind a lasting punishment.

XXXVII.

Downward she wrought her way, and all around
Labouring, the solid earth she undermined
And loosen'd all the roots; then from the ground
Emerging, in her hatred of her kind,
Resumed her proper form, and breathed a wind
Which gather'd like a tempest round its head:
Eftsoon the lofty Tree its top inclined
Uptorn with horrible convulsion dread,
And over half the world its mighty wreck lay spread.

XXXVIII.

But never scion sprouted from that Tree,
Nor seed sprang up; and thus the easy way,
Which had till then for young and old been free,
Was closed upon the sons of men for aye.
The mighty ruin moulder'd where it lay
Till not a trace was left; and now in sooth
Almost had all remembrance past away.
This from the elders she had heard in youth;
Some said it was a tale, and some a very truth.

XXXIX.

Nathless departed spirits at their will
Could from the land of souls [16] pass to and fro;
They come to us in sleep when all is still,
Sometimes to warn against the impending blow,
Alas! more oft to visit us in woe:
Though in their presence there was poor relief!
And this had sad experience made her know,
For when Quiara came, his stay was brief,
And waking then, she felt a freshen'd sense of grief.

XL.

Yet to behold his face again, and hear
His voice, though painful was a deep delight:
It was a joy to think that he was near,
To see him in the visions of the night,—
To know that the departed still requite
The love which to their memory still will cling:
And though he might not bless her waking sight
With his dear presence, 't was a blessed thing
That sleep would thus sometimes his actual image
bring.

XLI.

Why comes he not to me? Yeruti cries:
And Mooma echoing with a sigh the thought,
Ask'd why it was that to her longing eyes
No dream the image of her father brought?
Nor Monnema to solve that question sought
In vain, content in ignorance to dwell;
Perhaps it was because they knew him not;
Perhaps—but sooth she could not answer well;
What the departed did, themselves alone could tell.

XLII.

What one tribe held another disbelieved,
For all concerning this was dark, she said;
Uncertain all, and hard to be received.
The dreadful race, from whom their fathers fled,
Boasted that even the Country of the Dead
Was theirs, and where their Spirits chose to go,
The ghosts of other men retired in dread
Before the face of that victorious foe;
No better, then, the world above, than this below!

XLIII.

What, then, alas! if this were true, was death?
Only a mournful change from ill to ill!
And some there were who said the living breath
Would ne'er be taken from us by the will
Of the Good Father, but continue still
To feed with life the mortal frame he gave,
Did not mischance or wicked witchcraft kill;—
Evils from which no care avail'd to save,
And whereby all were sent to fill the greedy grave.

XLIV.

In vain to counterwork the baleful charm
By spells of rival witchcraft was it sought,
Less potent was that art to help than harm.
No means of safety old experience brought:
Nor better fortune did they find who thought
From Death, as from some living foe, to fly: [17]
For speed or subterfuge avail'd them nought,
But wheresoe'er they fled they found him nigh:
None ever could elude that unseen enemy.

XLV.

Bootless the boast, and vain the proud intent
Of those who hoped, with arrogant display
Of arms and force, to scare him from their tent,
As if their threatful shouts and fierce array
Of war could drive the Invisible away!
Sometimes, regardless of the sufferer's groan,
They dragg'd the dying out [18] and as a prey
Exposed him, that content with him alone
Death might depart, and thus his fate avert their own.

XLVI.

Depart he might,—but only to return
In quest of other victims, soon or late;
When they who held this fond belief, would learn,
Each by his own inevitable fate,
That in the course of man's uncertain state
Death is the one and only certain thing.
Oh folly then to fly or deprecate
That which at last Time, ever on the wing,
Certain as day and night, to weary age must bring!

XLVII.

While thus the Matron spake, the youthful twain
Listen'd in deep attention, wistfully;
Whether with more of wonder or of pain
Uneath it were to tell. With steady eye
Intent they heard; and when she paused, a sigh
Their sorrowful foreboding seem'd to speak:
Questions to which she could not give reply
Yeruti ask'd; and for that Maiden meek,—
Involuntary tears ran down her quiet cheek.

XLVIII.

A different sentiment within them stirr'd,
When Monnema recall'd to mind one day,
Imperfectly, what she had sometimes heard
In childhood, long ago, the Elders say:
Almost from memory had it past away,—
How there appear'd amid the woodlands men
Whom the Great Spirit sent there to convey
His gracious will; but little heed she then
Had given, and like a dream it now recurr'd again.

XLIX.

But these young questioners from time to time
Call'd up the long-forgotten theme anew.
Strange men they were, from some remotest clime
She said, of different speech, uncouth to view,
Having hair upon their face, and white in hue:
Across the world of waters wide they came
Devoutly the Father's work to do,
And seek the Red Men out, and in his name
His merciful laws, and love, and promises proclaim.

L.

They served a Maid more beautiful than tongue
Could tell, or heart conceive. Of human race,
All heavenly as that Virgin was, she sprung ;
But for her beauty and celestial grace,
Being one in whose pure elements no trace
Had e'er inhered of sin or mortal stain,
The highest Heaven was now her dwelling-place;
There as a Queen divine she held her reign,
And there in endless joy for ever would remain.

LI.

Her feet upon the crescent Moon were set,[19]
And, moving in their order round her head,
The stars compose her sparkling coronet.
There at her breast the Virgin Mother fed
A Babe divine, who was to judge the dead,
Such power the Spirit gave this awful Child;
Severe he was, and in his anger dread,
Yet always at his Mother's will grew mild,
So well did he obey that Maiden undefiled.[20]

LII.

Sometimes she had descended from above
To visit her true votaries, and requite
Such as had served her well. And for her love,
These bearded men, forsaking all delight,
With labour long and dangers infinite,
Across the great blue waters came, and sought
The Red-Men here, to win them, if they might,
From bloody ways, rejoiced to profit aught
Even when with their own lives the benefit was bought.

LIII.

For trusting in this heavenly Maiden's grace,
It was for them a joyful thing to die,
As men who went to have their happy place
With her, and with that Holy Child, on high,
In fields of bliss above the starry sky,
In glory, at the Virgin Mother's feet:
And all who kept their lessons faithfully
An everlasting guerdon there would meet,
When Death had led their souls to that celestial seat.

LIV.

On earth they offered, too, an easy life
To those who their mild lessons would obey,
Exempt from want, from danger, and from strife;
And from the forest leading them away,
They placed them underneath this Virgin's sway,
A numerous fellowship, in peace to dwell;
Their high and happy office there to pay
Devotions due, which she requited well,
Their heavenly Guardian she in whatsoe'er befell.

LV.

Thus, Monnema remember'd, it was told
By one who in his hot and headstrong youth
Had left her happy service; but when old
Lamented oft with unavailing ruth,
And thoughts which sharper than a serpent's tooth
Pierced him, that he had changed that peaceful place
For the fierce freedom and the ways uncouth
Of their wild life, and lost that Lady's grace,
Wherefore he had no hope to see in Heaven her face.

LVI.

And she remember'd too when first they fled
For safety to the farthest solitude
Before their cruel foes, and lived in dread
That thither too their steps might be pursued
By those old enemies athirst for blood,
How some among them hoped to see the day
When these beloved messengers of good
To that lone hiding-place might find the way,
And them to their abode of blessedness convey.

LVII.

Such tales excited in Yeruti's heart
A stirring hope that haply he might meet
Some minister of Heaven; and many a part
Untrod before of that wild wood retreat,
Did he with indefatigable feet
Explore; yet ever from the fruitless quest
Return'd at evening to his native seat
By daily disappointment undeprest,—
So buoyant was the hope that fill'd his youthful breast.

LVIII.

At length the hour approach'd that should fulfil
His harmless heart's desire, when they shall see
Their fellow-kind, and take for good or ill
The fearful chance, for such it needs must be,
Of change from that entire simplicity.
Yet wherefore should the thought of change appal!
Grief it perhaps might bring, and injury,
And death;—but evil never can befall
The virtuous, for the Eye of Heaven is over all.

CANTO III.

I.

AMID those marshy woodlands far and wide
Which spread beyond the soaring vulture's eye,
There grew on Empalado's southern side
Groves of that tree whose leaves adust supply
The Spaniards with their daily luxury;
A beverage whose salubrious use obtains
Through many a land of mines and slavery,
Even over all La Plata's sea-like plains,
And Chili's mountain realm, and proud Peru's domains.

II.

But better for the injured Indian race
Had woods of manchineel the land o'erspread:
Yea in that tree so blest by Nature's grace
A direr curse had they inherited,
Than if the Upas there had rear'd its head,
And sent its baleful scyons all around,
Blasting where'er its effluent force was shed,
In air and water, and the infected ground,
All things wherein the breath or sap of life is found.

III.

The poor Guaranies dreamt of no such ill,
When for themselves in miserable hour,
The virtues of that leaf, with pure good will
They taught their unsuspected visitor,
New in the land as yet. They learnt his power
Too soon, which law nor conscience could restrain,
A fearless but inhuman conqueror,
Heart-hardened by the accursed lust of gain.
O fatal thirst of gold! O foul reproach for Spain!

71

IV.

For gold and silver had the Spaniards sought
Exploring Paraguay with desperate pains,
Their way through forests axe in hand they wrought;
Drench'd from above by unremitting rains
They waded over inundated plains,
Forward by hope of plunder still allured;
So they might one day count their golden gains,
They cared not at what cost of sin procured,
All dangers they defied, all sufferings they endured.

V.

Barren alike of glory and of gold
That region proved to them; nor would the soil
Unto their unindustrious hands unfold
Harvests, the fruit of peace,—and wine and oil,
The treasures that repay contented toil
With health and weal; treasures that with them bring
No guilt for priest and penance to assoil,
Nor with their venom arm the awaken'd sting
Of conscience at that hour when life is vanishing.

VI.

But keen of eye in their pursuit of gain
The conquerors look'd for lucre in this tree:
An annual harvest there might they attain,
Without the cost of annual industry.
'T was but to gather in what there grew free,
And share Potosi's wealth.   Nor thence alone,
But gold in glad exchange they soon should see
From all that once the Incas called their own,
Or where the Zippa's power or Zaque's laws were known.

VII.

For this, in fact though not in name a slave,
The Indian from his family was torn;
And droves on droves were sent to find a grave
In woods and swamps, by toil severe outworn,
No friend at hand to succour or to mourn,
In death unpitied, as in life unblest.
O miserable race, to slavery born!
Yet when we look beyond this world's unrest,
More miserable then the oppressors than the opprest.

VIII.

Often had Kings essay'd to check the ill
By edicts not so well enforced as meant;
A present power was wanting to fulfil
Remote authority's sincere intent.
To Avarice, on its present purpose bent,
The voice of distant Justice spake in vain;
False magistrates and priests their influence lent
The accursed thing for lucre to maintain:
O fatal thirst of gold! O foul reproach for Spain![21]

IX.

O foul reproach! but not for Spain alone,
But for all lands that bear the Christian name!
Where'er commercial slavery is known,
O shall not Justice trumpet-tongued proclaim
The foul reproach, the black offence the same?
Hear, guilty France! and thou, O England, hear!
Thou who hast half redeem'd thyself from shame,
When slavery from thy realms shall disappear,
Then from this guilt, and not till then, wilt thou be
clear.

X.

Uncheck'd in Paraguay it ran its course,
Till all the gentler children of the land
Well nigh had been consumed without remorse.
The bolder tribes meantime, whose skilful hand
Had tamed the horse, in many a warlike band
Kept the field well with bow and dreadful spear.
And now the Spaniards dared no more withstand
Their force, but in their towns grew pale with fear
If the Mocobio, or the Abipon drew near.

XI.

Bear witness, Chaco, thou, from thy domain
With Spanish blood, as erst with Indian, fed!
And Corrientes, by whose church the slain
Were piled in heaps, till for the gather'd dead
One common grave was dug, one service said!
Thou too, Parana, thy sad witness bear
From shores with many a mournful vestige spread,
And monumental crosses here and there
And monumental names that tell where dwellings were!

XII.

Nor would with all their power the Kings of Spain,
Austrian or Bourbon, have at last avail'd
This torrent of destruction to restrain,
And save a people every where assail'd
By men before whose face their courage quail'd,
But for the virtuous agency of those
Who with the Cross alone, when arms had fail'd,
Achiev'd a peaceful triumph o'er the foes,
And gave that weary land the blessings of repose.

XIII.

For whensoe'er the Spaniards felt or fear'd
An Indian enemy, they call'd for aid
Upon Loyola's sons, now long endear'd
To many a happy tribe, by them convey'd
From the open wilderness or woodland shade,
In towns of happiest polity to dwell.
Freely these faithful ministers essay'd
The arduous enterprise, contented well
If with success they sped, or if as martyrs fell.

XIV.

And now it chanced some traders who had fell'd
The trees of precious foliage far and wide
On Empalado's shore, when they beheld
The inviting woodlands on its northern side,
Crost thither in their quest, and there espied
Yeruti's footsteps: searching then the shade
At length a lonely dwelling they descried,
And at the thought of hostile hordes dismay'd
To the nearest mission sped, and ask'd the Jesuits' aid.

XV.

That was a call which ne'er was made in vain
Upon Loyola's sons.   In Paraguay
Much of injustice had they to complain,
Much of neglect; but faithful labourers they
In the Lord's vineyard, there was no delay
When summon'd to his work.   A little band
Of converts made them ready for the way;
Their spiritual father took a cross in hand
To be his staff, and forth they went to search the land.

XVI.

He was a man of rarest qualities,
Who to this barbarous region had confined
A spirit with the learned and the wise
Worthy to take its place, and from mankind
Receive their homage, to the immortal mind
Paid in its just inheritance of fame.
But he to humbler thoughts his heart inclined;
From Gratz amid the Styrian hills he came,
And Dobrizhoffer was the good man's honour'd name.

XVII.

It was his evil fortune to behold
The labours of his painful life destroy'd;
His flock which he had brought within the fold
Dispersed; the work of ages render'd void,
And all of good that Paraguay enjoy'd
By blind and suicidal power o'erthrown.
So he the years of his old age employ'd,
A faithful chronicler in handing down
Names which he loved, and things well worthy to be
    known.

XVIII.

And thus when exiled from the dear-loved scene,
In Proud Vienna he beguiled the pain
Of sad remembrance: and the Empress Queen,
That great Teresa, she did not disdain
In gracious mood sometimes to entertain
Discourse with him both pleasurable and sage;
And sure a willing ear she well might deign
To one whose tales may equally engage
The wondering mind of youth, the thoughtful heart of
    age.

XIX.

But of his native speech because well nigh
Disuse in him forgetfulness had wrought,
In Latin he composed his history;
A garrulous, but a lively tale, and fraught
With matter of delight and food for thought.
And if he could in Merlin's glass have seen
By whom his tomes to speak our tongue were taught,
The old man would have felt as pleased, I ween,
As when he won the ear of that great Empress Queen.

XX.

Little he deem'd when with his Indian band
He through the wilds set forth upon his way,
A Poet then unborn, and in a land
Which had proscribed his order, should one day
Take up from thence his moralizing lay,
And shape a song that, with no fiction drest,
Should to his worth its grateful tribute pay,
And sinking deep in many an English breast,
Foster that faith divine that keeps the heart at rest.

XXI.

Behold him on his way! the breviary,
Which from his girdle hangs, his only shield;
That well-known habit is his panoply,
That cross, the only weapon he will wield:
By day he bears it for his staff afield,
By night it is the pillar of his bed;
No other lodging these wild woods can yield
Than earth's hard lap, and rustling overhead
A canopy of deep and tangled boughs far spread.

XXII.

Yet may they not without some cautious care
Take up their inn content upon the ground.
First it behoves to clear a circle there,
And trample down the grass and plantage round,
Where many a deadly reptile might be found,
Whom with its bright and comfortable heat
The flame would else allure: such plagues abound
In these thick woods, and therefore must they beat
The earth, and trample well the herbs beneath their feet.

XXIII.

And now they heap dry reeds and broken wood;
The spark is struck, the crackling faggots blaze,
And cheer that unaccustomed solitude.
Soon have they made their frugal meal of maize:
In grateful adoration then they raise
The evening hymn. How solemn in the wild
That sweet accordant strain wherewith they praise
The Queen of Angels, merciful and mild:
Hail, holiest Mary! Maid, and Mother undefiled.

XXIV.

Blame as thou mayest the Papist's erring creed,
But not their salutary rite of even!
The prayers that from a pious soul proceed,
Though misdirected, reach the ear of Heaven.
Us unto whom a purer faith is given,
As our best birthright it behoves to hold
The precious charge. But, oh, beware the leaven
Which makes the heart of charity grow cold!
We own one Shepherd, we shall be at last one fold.

XXV.

Thinkest thou the little company who here
Pour forth their hymn devout at close of day,
Feel it no aid that those who hold them dear,
At the same hour the self-same homage pay,
Commending them to Heaven when far away?
That the sweet bells are heard in solemn chime
Through all the happy towns of Paraguay,
Where now their brethren in one point of time
Join in the general prayer, with sympathy sublime?

XXVI.

That to the glorious Mother of their Lord
Whole Christendom that hour its homage pays?
From court and cottage that with one accord
Ascends the universal strain of praise?
Amid the crowded city's restless ways,
One reverential thought pervades the throng;
The traveller on his lonely road obeys
The sacred hour, and as he fares along,
In spirit hears and joins his household's even-song.

XXVII.

What if they think that every prayer enroll'd
Shall one day in their good account appear;
That guardian Angels hover round and fold
Their wings in adoration while they hear;
Ministrant Spirits through the ethereal sphere
Waft it with joy, and to the grateful theme
Well pleased, the Mighty Mother bends her ear?
A vain delusion this we rightly deem:
Yet what they feel is not a mere illusive dream.

XXVIII.

That prayer perform'd, around the fire reclin'd
Beneath the leafy canopy they lay
Their limbs: the Indians soon to sleep resign'd ;
And the good Father with that toilsome day
Fatigued, full fain to sleep,—if sleep he may,
Whom all tormenting insects there assail;
More to be dreaded these than beasts of prey
Against whom strength may cope, or skill prevail,
But art of man against these enemies must fail.

XXIX.

Patience itself, that should be sovereign cure
For ills that touch ourselves alone, supply,
Lends little aid to one who must endure
This plague: the small tormentors fill the sky,
And swarm about their prey; there he must lie
And suffer while the hours of darkness wear;
At time he utters with a deep drawn sigh
Some name adored, in accents of despair
Breathed sorrowfully forth, half murmur and half prayer.

XXX.

Welcome to him the earliest gleam of light;
Welcome to him the earliest sound of day;
That from the sufferings of that weary night
Released, he may resume his willing way,
Well pleased again the perils to essay
Of that drear wilderness, with hope renew'd:
Success will all his labours overpay:
A quest like his is cheerfully pursued;
The heart is happy still that is intent on good.

XXXI.

And now where Empalado's waters creep
Through low and level shores of woodland wide,
They come; prepared to cross the sluggish deep,
An ill-shaped coracle of hardest hide,
Ruder than ever Cambrian fisher plied
Where Towey and the salt sea-waters meet,
The Indian's launch; they steady it and guide,
Winning their way with arms and practised feet,
While in the tottering boat the Father keeps his seat.

XXXII.

For three long summer days on every side
They search in vain the sylvan solitude.
The fourth a human footstep is espied,
And through the mazes of the pathless wood
With hound-like skill and hawk-like eye pursued ;
For keen upon their pious quest are they,
As e'er were hunters on the track of blood.
Where softer ground or trodden herbs betray
The slightest mark of man, they there explore the way.

XXXIII.

More cautious when more certain of the trace
In silence they proceed; not like a crew
Of jovial hunters, who the joyous chase
With hound and horn in open field pursue,
Cheering their way with jubilant halloo,
And hurrying forward to their spoil desired,
The panting game before them, full in view:
Humaner thoughts this little band inspired,
Yet with a hope as high their gentle hearts were fired.

XXXIV.

Nor is their virtuous hope devoid of fear ;
The perils of that enterprise they know ;
Some savage horde may have its fastness here,
A race to whom a stranger is a foe ;
Who not for friendly words, nor proffer'd show
Of gifts, will peace or parley entertain.
If by such hands their blameless blood should flow
To serve the Lamb who for their sins was slain,
Blessed indeed their lot, for so to die is gain !

XXXV.

Them thus pursuing where the track may lead,
A human voice arrests upon their way.
They stop, and thither whence the sounds proceed,
All eyes are turned in wonder,—not dismay,
For sure such sounds might charm all fear away.
No nightingale whose brooding mate is nigh,
From some sequestered bower at close of day,
No lark rejoicing in the orient sky
Ever pour'd forth so wild a strain of melody.

XXXVI.

The voice which through the ringing forest floats
Is one which having ne'er been taught the skill
Of marshalling sweet words to sweeter notes,
Utters all unpremeditate, at will,
A modulated sequence loud and shrill
Of inarticulate and long-breathed sound,
Varying its tones with rise and fall and trill,
Till all the solitary woods around
With that far-piercing power of melody resound.

XXXVII.

In mute astonishment attent to hear,
As if by some enchantment held, they stood,
With bending head, fix'd eye, and eager ear,
And hand upraised in warning attitude
To check all speech or step that might intrude
On that sweet strain. Them leaving thus spell-bound,
A little way alone into the wood
The Father gently moved toward the sound,
Treading with quiet feet upon the grassy ground.

XXXVIII.

Anon advancing thus the trees between,
He saw beside her bower the songstress wild,
Not distant far, himself the while unseen.
Mooma it was, that happy maiden mild,
Who in the sunshine, like a careless child
Of nature, in her joy was caroling.
A heavier heart than his it had beguiled
So to have heard so fair a creature sing
The strains which she had learnt from all sweet birds
of spring.

XXXIX.

For these had been her teachers, these alone ;
And she in many an emulous essay,
At length into a descant of her own
Had blended all their notes,[22] a wild display
Of sounds in rich irregular array ;
And now as blithe as bird in vernal bower,
Pour'd in full flow the unexpressive lay,
Rejoicing in her consciousness of power,
But in the inborn sense of harmony yet more.

XL.

In joy had she begun the ambitious song,
With rapid interchange of sink and swell;
And sometimes high the note was raised, and long
Produced, with shake and effort sensible,
As if the voice exulted there to dwell;
But when she could no more that pitch sustain,
So thrillingly attuned the cadence fell,
That with the music of its dying strain
She moved herself to tears of pleasurable pain.

XLI.

It may be deem'd some dim presage[23] possess'd
The virgin's soul; that some mysterious sense
Of change to come, upon her mind impress'd,
Had then call'd forth, ere she departed thence,
A requiem to their days of innocence.
For what thou losest in thy native shade
There is one change alone that may compense,
O Mooma, innocent and simple maid,
Only one change, and it will not be long delay'd!

XLII.

When now the Father issued from the wood
Into that little glade in open sight,
Like one entranced, beholding him, she stood;
Yet had she more of wonder than affright,
Yet less of wonder than of dread delight,
When thus the actual vision came in view;
For instantly the maiden read aright
Wherefore he came; his garb and beard she knew;
All that her mother heard had then indeed been true.

XLIII.

Nor was the Father filled with less surprise;
He too strange fancies well might entertain,
When this so fair a creature met his eyes.
He might have thought her not of mortal strain;
Rather, as bards of yore were wont to feign,
A nymph divine of Monday's secret stream,
Or haply of Diana's woodland train:
For in her beauty Mooma such might seem,
Being less a child of earth than like a poet's dream.

XLIV.

No art of barbarous ornament had scarr'd
And stain'd her virgin limbs, or 'filed her face;
Nor ever yet had evil passion marr'd
In her sweet countenance the natural grace
Of innocence and youth; nor was there trace
Of sorrow, or of hardening want and care.
Strange was it in this wild and savage place,
Which seem'd to be for beasts a fitting lair,
Thus to behold a maid so gentle and so fair.

XLV.

Across her shoulders was a hammock flung,[24]
By night it was the maiden's bed, by day
Her only garment. Round her as it hung,
In short unequal folds of loose array,
The open meshes, when she moves, display
Her form. She stood with fix'd and wondering eyes,
And trembling like a leaf upon the spray,
Even for excess of joy, with eager cries
She call'd her mother forth to share that glad surprise.

XLVI.

At that unwonted call with quickened pace
The matron hurried thither, half in fear.
How strange to Monnema a stranger's face!
How strange it was a stranger's voice to hear,
How strangely to her disaccustomed ear
Came even the accents of her native tongue!
But when she saw her countrymen appear,
Tears for that unexpected blessing sprung,
And once again she felt as if her heart were young.

XLVII.

Soon was her melancholy story told,
And glad consent unto that Father good
Was given, that they to join his happy fold
Would leave with him their forest solitude.
Why comes not now Yeruti from the wood?
Why tarrieth he so late this blessed day?
They long to see their joy in his renew'd,
And look impatiently toward his way,
And think they hear his step, and chide his long delay.

XLVIII.

He comes at length, a happy man, to find
His only dream of hope fulfill'd at last.
The sunshine of his all-believing mind
There is no doubt or fear to overcast;
No chilling forethought checks his bliss; the past
Leaves no regret for him, and all to come
Is change and wonder and delight. How fast
Hath busy fancy conjured up a sum
Of joys unknown, whereof the expectance makes him
    dumb!

XLIX.

O happy day, the Messenger of Heaven
Hath found them in their lonely dwelling-place!
O happy day, to them it would be given
To share in that Eternal Mother's grace,
And one day see in heaven her glorious face
Where Angels round her mercy-throne adore!
Now shall they mingle with the human race,
Sequester'd from their fellow kind no more;
O joy of joys supreme! O bliss for them in store!

L.

Full of such hopes this night they lie them down,
But not as they were wont, this night to rest.
Their old tranquillity of heart is gone;
The peace wherewith till now they have been blest
Hath taken its departure. In the breast
Fast following thoughts and busy fancies throng;
Their sleep itself is feverish, and possest
With dreams that to the wakeful mind belong;
To Mooma and the youth then first the night seem'd
    long.

LI.

Day comes, and now a first and last farewell
To that fair bower within their native wood,
Their quiet nest till now. The bird may dwell
Henceforth in safety there, and rear her brood,
And beasts and reptiles undisturb'd intrude.
Reckless of this, the simple tenants go,
Emerging from their peaceful solitude,
To mingle with the world,—but not to know
Its crimes, nor to partake its cares, nor feel its woe.

CANTO IV.

I.

The bells rung blithely from St Mary's tower
When in St Joachin's the news was told
That Dobrizhoffer from his quest that hour
Drew nigh: the glad Guaranies young and old
Throng through the gate, rejoicing to behold
His face again; and all with heartfelt glee
Welcome the Pastor to his peaceful fold,
Where so beloved amid his flock was he
That this return was like a day of jubilee.

II.

How more than strange, how marvellous a sight
To the new-comers was this multitude!
Something like fear was mingled with affright
When they the busy scene of turmoil view'd.
Wonder itself the sense of joy subdued,
And with its all-unwonted weight opprest
These children of the quiet solitude;
And now and then a sigh that heaved the breast
Unconsciously bewray'd their feeling of unrest.

III.

Not more prodigious than that little town
Seem'd to these comers, were the pomp and power
To us, of ancient Rome in her renown;
Nor the elder Babylon, or ere that hour
When her high gardens, and her cloud-capt tower,
And her broad walls before the Persian fell;
Nor those dread fanes on Nile's forsaken shore
Whose ruins yet their pristine grandeur tell,
Wherein the demon gods themselves might deign to
    dwell.

IV.

But if, all humble as it was, that scene
Possess'd a poor and uninstructed mind
With awe, the thoughtful spirit, well I ween,
Something to move its wonder there might find,
Something of consolation for its kind,
Some hope and earnest of a happier age,
When vain pursuits no more the heart shall blind,
But Faith the evils of this earth assuage,
And to all souls assure their heavenly heritage.

V.

Yes; for in history's mournful map, the eye
On Paraguay, as on a sunny spot,
May rest complacent: to humanity,
There, and there only, hath a peaceful lot
Been granted, by Ambition troubled not,
By Avarice undebased, exempt from care,
By perilous passions undisturb'd. And what
If Glory never rear'd her standard there,
Nor with her clarion's blast awoke the slumbering air?

VI.

Content, and cheerful Piety were found
Within those humble walls. From youth to age
The simple dwellers paced their even round
Of duty, not desiring to engage
Upon the busy world's contentious stage,
Whose ways they wisely had been train'd to dread:
Their inoffensive lives in pupilage
Perpetually, but peacefully they led,
From all temptation saved, and sure of daily bread.

VII.

They on the Jesuit, who was nothing loth,
Reposed alike their conscience and their cares;
And he, with equal faith, the trust of both
Accepted and discharged. The bliss is theirs
Of that entire dependence that prepares
Entire submission, let what may befall:
And his whole careful course of life declares
That for their good he holds them thus in thrall,
Their Father and their Friend, Priest, Ruler, all in all.

VIII.

Food, raiment, shelter, safety, he provides;
No forecast, no anxieties have they;
The Jesuit governs, and instructs and guides;
Their part it is to honour and obey,
Like children under wise parental sway.
All thoughts and wishes are to him confest;
And when at length in life's last weary day
In sure and certain hope they sink to rest,
By him their eyes are closed, by him their burial blest.[24]

IX.

Deem not their lives of happiness devoid,
Though thus the years their course obscurely fill;
In rural and in household arts employ'd,
And many a pleasing task of pliant skill,
For emulation here unmix'd with ill,
Sufficient scope was given. Each had assign'd
His proper part, which yet left free the will;
So well they knew to mould the ductile mind
By whom the scheme of that wise order was combined.

X.

It was a land of priestcraft, but the priest
Believed himself the fables that he taught:
Corrupt their forms, and yet those forms at least
Preserved a salutary faith that wrought,
Maugre the alloy, the saving end it sought.
Benevolence had gain'd such empire there,
That even superstition had been brought
An aspect of humanity to wear,
And make the weal of man its first and only care.

XI.

Nor lack'd they store of innocent delight,
Music and song and dance and proud array,
Whate'er might win the ear, or charm the sight;
Banners and pageantry in rich display
Brought forth upon some Saint's high holiday,
The altar drest, the church with garlands hung,
Arches and floral bowers beside the way,
And festal tables spread for old and young,
Gladness in every heart, and mirth on every tongue.

XII.

Thou who despisest so debased a fate,
As in the pride of wisdom thou mayst call
These meek submissive Indians' low estate,
Look round the world, and see where over all
Injurious passions hold mankind in thrall!
How barbarous Force asserts a ruthless reign,
Or Mammon, o'er his portion of the ball,
Hath learn'd a baser empire to maintain,
Mammon, the god of all who give their souls to gain.

XIII.

Behold the fraudful arts, the covert strife,
The jarring interests that engross mankind;
The low pursuits, the selfish aims of life;
Studies that weary and contract the mind,
That bring no joy, and leave no peace behind;
And Death approaching to dissolve the spell!
The immortal soul, which hath so long been blind,
Recovers then clear sight, and sees too well
The error of its ways, when irretrievable.

XIV.

Far happier the Guaranies' humble race,
With whom in dutiful contentment wise,
The gentle virtues had their dwelling place.
With them the dear domestic charities
Sustain'd no blight from fortune; natural ties
There suffer'd no divorcement, save alone
That which in course of nature might arise:
No artificial wants and ills were known;
But there they dwelt as if the world were all their own.

XV.

Obedience in its laws that takes delight
Was theirs; simplicity that knows no art;
Love, friendship, grateful duty in its height;
Meekness and truth, that keep all strife apart,
And faith and hope which elevate the heart
Upon its heavenly heritage intent.
Poor, erring, self-tormentor that thou art;
O Man! and on thine own undoing bent,
Wherewith canst thou be blest, if not with these content?

XVI.

Mild pupils, in submission's perfect school,
Two thousand souls were gather'd here, and here
Beneath the Jesuit's all embracing rule
They dwelt, obeying him with love sincere,
That never knew distrust, nor felt a fear,
Nor anxious thought, which wears the heart away.
Sacred to them their laws, their Ruler dear;
Humbler or happier none could be than they
Who knew it for their good in all things to obey.

XVII.

The Patron Saint, from whom their town was named,
Was that St Joachin,[25] who, legends say,
Unto the Saints in Limbo first proclaim'd
The Advent. Being permitted, on the day
That Death enlarged him from this mortal clay,
His daughter's high election to behold,
Thither his soul, glad herald, wing'd its way,
And to the Prophets and the Patriarchs old
The tidings of great joy and near deliverance told.

XVIII.

There on the altar was his image set,
The lamp before it burning night and day,
And there was incensed, when his votaries met
Before the sacred shrine, their beads to say,
And for his fancied intercession pray,
Devoutly as in faith they bent the knee.
Such adoration they were taught to pay.
Good man, how little had he ween'd that he
Should thus obtain a place in Rome's idolatry!

XIX.

But chiefly there the Mother of our Lord,
His blessed daughter, by the multitude
Was for their special patroness adored.
Amid the square on high her image stood,
Clasping the Babe in her beatitude,
The Babe divine on whom she fix'd her sight;
And in their hearts, albe the work was rude,
It raised the thought of all-commanding might,
Combined with boundless love and mercy infinite.

XX.

To this great family the Jesuit brought
His new-found children now; for young and old
He deem'd alike his children while he wrought
For their salvation,—seeking to unfold
The saving mysteries in the creed enroll'd,
To their slow minds, that could but ill conceive
The import of the mighty truths he told.
But errors they have none to which they cleave,
And whatsoe'er he tells they willingly believe.

XXI.

Safe from that pride of ignorance were they
That with small knowledge thinks itself full wise.
How at believing aught should these delay,
When every where new objects meet their eyes
To fill the soul with wonder and surprise?
Not of itself, but by temptation bred,
In man doth impious unbelief arise;
It is our instinct to believe and dread,
God bids us love, and then our faith is perfected.

XXII.

Quick to believe, and slow to comprehend,
Like children, unto all the teacher taught
Submissively an easy ear they lend:
And to the font at once he might have brought
These converts, if the Father had not thought
Theirs was a case for wise and safe delay,
Lest lightly learnt might lightly be forgot;
And meanwhile due instruction day by day
Would to their opening minds the sense of truth convey.

XXIII.

Of this they reck'd not whether soon or late;
For overpowering wonderment possest
Their faculties; and in this new estate
Strange sights and sounds and thoughts well nigh opprest
Their sense, and raised a turmoil in the breast
Resenting less of pleasure than of pain;
And sleep afforded them no natural rest,
But in their dreams, a mix'd disorder'd train,
The busy scenes of day disturb'd their hearts again.

XXIV.

Even when the spirit to that secret wood
Return'd, slow Mondai's silent stream beside,
No longer there it found the solitude
Which late it left: strange faces were descried,
Voices, and sounds of music far and wide,
And buildings seem'd to tower amid the trees,
And forms of men and beasts on every side,
As ever-wakeful fancy hears and sees,
All things that it had heard, and seen, and more than
　　　these.

XXV.

For in their sleep strange forms deform'd they saw
Of frightful fiends, their ghostly enemies :
And souls who must abide the rigorous law
Weltering in fire, and there, with dolorous cries
Blaspheming roll around their hopeless eyes;
And those who, doom'd a shorter term to bear
In penal flames, look upward to the skies,
Seeking and finding consolation there,
And feel, like dew from Heaven, the precious aid of
　　　prayer.

XXVI.

And Angels who around their glorious Queen
In adoration bent their heads abased ;
And infant faces in their dreams were seen
Hovering on cherub wings; and Spirits placed
To be their guards invisible, who chased
With fiery arms their fiendish foes away :
Such visions overheated fancy traced,
Peopling the night with a confused array
That made its hours of rest more restless than the day.

XXVII.

To all who from an old erratic course
Of life, within the Jesuit's fold were led,
The change was perilous.　They felt the force
Of habit, when, till then in forests bred,
A thick perpetual umbrage overhead,
They came to dwell in open light and air.
This ill the Fathers long had learnt to dread,
And still devised such means as might prepare
The new-reclaim'd unhurt this total change to bear.

XXVIII.

All thoughts and occupations to commute,
To change their air, their water, and their food,
And those old habits suddenly uproot
Conform'd to which the vital powers pursued
Their functions, such mutation is too rude
For man's fine frame unshaken to sustain.
And these poor children of the solitude
Began ere long to pay the bitter pain
That their new way of life brought with it in its train.

XXIX.

On Monnema the apprehended ill
Came first ; the matron sunk beneath the weight
Of a strong malady, whose force no skill
In healing might avert or mitigate.
Yet happy in her children's safe estate
Her thankfulness for them she still exprest;
And yielding then complacently to fate,
With Christian rites her passing hour was blest,
And with a Christian's hope she was consign'd to rest.

XXX.

They laid her in the Garden of the Dead.
Such as a Christian burial-place should be
Was that fair spot, where every grave was spread
With flowers, and not a weed to spring was free ;
But the pure blossoms of the orange tree
Dropt, like a shower of fragrance, on the bier;
And palms, the type of immortality,
Planted in stately colonnades, appear,
That all was verdant there throughout the unvarying
　　　year.

XXXI.

Nor ever did irreverent feet intrude
Within that sacred spot; nor sound of mirth,
Unseemly there profane the solitude,
Where solemnly committed earth to earth,
Waiting the summons for their second birth,
Whole generations in Death's peaceful fold
Collected lay, green innocence, ripe worth,
Youth full of hope, and age whose days were told,
Compress'd alike into that mass of mortal mould.

XXXII.

Mortal, and yet at the Archangel's voice
To put on immortality.　That call
Shall one day make the sentient dust rejoice;
These bodies then shall rise and cast off all
Corruption, with whate'er of earthly thrall
Had clogg'd the heavenly image, then set free.
How then should Death a Christian's heart appal?
Lo, Heaven for you is open ;—enter, ye
Children of God, and heirs of his eternity!

XXXIII.

This hope supported Mooma, hand in hand
When with Yeruti at the grave she stood.
Less even now of death they understand
Than of the joys eternal that ensued ;
The bliss of infinite beatitude
To them had been their teacher's favourite theme,
Wherewith their hearts so fully were imbued,
That it the sole reality might seem,
Life, death, and all things else, a shadow or a dream.

XXXIV.

Yea, so possest with that best hope were they,
That if the heavens had opened overhead,
And the Archangel with his trump that day
To judgment had convoked the quick and dead,
They would have heard the summons not with dread,
But in the joy of faith that knows no fear :
Come Lord! come quickly! would this pair have said,
And thou, O Queen of men and Angels dear,
Lift us whom thou hast loved into thy happy sphere!

XXXV.

They wept not at the grave, though overwrought
With feelings there as if the heart would break.
Some haply might have deem'd they suffered not :
Yet they who look'd upon that Maiden meek
Might see what deep emotion blanched her cheek.
An inward light there was which fill'd her eyes,
And told, more forcibly than words could speak,
That this disruption of her earliest ties
Had shaken mind and frame in all their faculties.

XXXVI.

It was not passion only that disturb'd
Her gentle nature thus; it was not grief;
Nor human feeling by the effort curb'd
Of some misdeeming duty, when relief
Were surely to be found, albeit brief,
If sorrow at its springs might freely flow;
Nor yet repining, stronger than belief
In its first force, that shook the Maiden so,
Though these alone might that frail fabric overthrow.

XXXVII.

The seeds of death were in her at that hour.
Soon was their quickening and their growth display'd:
Thenceforth she droop'd and withered like a flower,
Which when it flourished in its native shade
Some child to his own garden hath convey'd,
And planted in the sun, to pine away.
Thus was the gentle Mooma seen to fade,
Not under sharp disease, but day by day
Losing the powers of life in visible decay.

XXXVIII.

The sunny hue that tinged her cheek was gone,
A deathly paleness settled in its stead;
The light of joy which in her eyes had shone,
Now like a lamp that is no longer fed
Grew dim: but when she raised her heavy head
Some proffered help of kindness to partake,
Those feeble eyes a languid lustre shed,
And her sad smile of thankfulness would wake
Grief even in callous hearts for that sweet sufferer's sake.

XXXIX.

How had Yeruti borne to see her fade?
But he was spared the lamentable sight,
Himself upon the bed of sickness laid.
Joy of his heart, and of his eyes the light
Had Mooma been to him, his soul's delight,
On whom his mind for ever was intent,
His darling thought by day, his dream by night,
The playmate of his youth in mercy sent,
With whom his life had past in peacefullest content.

XL.

Well was it for the youth, and well for her,
As there in placid helplessness she lay,
He was not present with his love to stir
Emotions that might shake her feeble clay,
And rouse up in her heart a strong array
Of feelings, hurtful only when they bind
To earth the soul that soon must pass away.
But this was spared them; and no pain of mind
To trouble her had she, instinctively resigned.

XLI.

Nor was there wanting to the sufferers aught
Of careful kindness to alleviate
The affliction; for the universal thought
In that poor town was of their sad estate,
And what might best relieve or mitigate
Their case, what help of nature or of art:
And many were the prayers compassionate
That the good Saints their healing would impart,
Breathed in that maid's behalf from many a tender heart.

XLII.

And vows were made for her, if vows might save;
She for herself the while preferr'd no prayer;
For when she stood beside her Mother's grave,
Her earthly hopes and thoughts had ended there.
Her only longing now was, free as air
From this obstructive flesh to take her flight
For Paradise, and seek her Mother there,
And then regaining her beloved sight,
Rest in the eternal sense of undisturb'd delight.

XLIII.

Her heart was there, and there she felt and knew
That soon full surely should her spirit be.
And who can tell what foretastes might ensue
To one, whose soul, from all earth's thraldom free,
Was waiting thus for immortality?
Sometimes she spake with short and hurried breath
As if some happy sight she seem'd to see,
While in the fulness of a perfect faith
Even with a lover's hope she lay and look'd for death.

XLIV.

I said that for herself the patient maid
Preferr'd no prayer; but oft her feeble tongue
And feebler breath a voice of praise essay'd;
And duly when the vesper bell was rung,
Her evening hymn in faint accord she sung
So piously, that they who gathered round
Awe-stricken on her heavenly accents hung,
As though they thought it were no mortal sound,
But that the place whereon they stood was holy ground.

XLV.

At such an hour when Dobrizhoffer stood
Beside her bed, oh how unlike, he thought
This voice to that which ringing through the wood
Had led him to the secret bower he sought!
And was it then for this that he had brought
That harmless household from their native shade?
Death had already been the mother's lot;
And this fair Mooma, was she form'd to fade
So soon,—so soon must she in earth's cold lap be laid?

XLVI.

Yet he had no misgiving at the sight;
And wherefore should he? he had acted well,
And deeming of the ways of God aright,
Knew that to such as these, whate'er befell
Must needs for them be best. But who could dwell
Unmoved upon the fate of one so young,
So blithesome late? What marvel if tears fell,
From that good man as over her he hung,
And that the prayers he said came faltering from his
tongue!

XLVII.

She saw him weep, and she could understand
The cause thus tremulously that made him speak.
By his emotion moved she took his hand;
A gleam of pleasure o'er her pallid cheek
Past, while she look'd at him with meaning meek,
And for a little while, as loth to part,
Detaining him, her fingers lank and weak,
Play'd with their hold; then letting him depart
She gave him a slow smile that touch'd him to the heart.

XLVIII.

Mourn not for her! for what hath life to give
That should detain her ready spirit here?
Thinkest thou that it were worth a wish to live,
Could wishes hold her from her proper sphere?
That simple heart, that innocence sincere
The world would stain. Fitter she ne'er could be
For the great change; and now that change is near,
Oh who would keep her soul from being free?
Maiden beloved of Heaven, to die is best for thee!

XLIX.

She hath past away, and on her lips a smile
Hath settled, fix'd in death. Judged they aright,
Or suffered they their fancy to beguile
The reason, who believed that she had sight
Of Heaven before her spirit took its flight;
That Angels waited round her lowly bed;
And that in that last effort of delight,
When lifting up her dying arms, she said,
I come! a ray from Heaven upon her face was shed?

L.

St Joachin's had never seen a day
Of such profuse and general grief before,
As when with tapers, dirge, and long array
The Maiden's body to the grave they bore.
All eyes, all hearts, her early death deplore;
Yet wondering at the fortune they lament,
They the wise ways of Providence adore,
By whom the Pastor surely had been sent
When to the Mondai woods upon his quest he went.

LI.

This was, indeed, a chosen family,
For Heaven's especial favour mark'd, they said;
Shut out from all mankind they seem'd to be,
Yet mercifully there were visited,
That so within the fold they might be led,
Then call'd away to bliss. Already two
In their baptismal innocence were dead;
The third was on the bed of death they knew,
And in the appointed course must presently ensue.

LII.

They marvell'd, therefore, when the youth once more
Rose from his bed and walk'd abroad again;
Severe had been the malady, and sore
The trial, while life struggled to maintain
Its seat against the sharp assaults of pain:
But life in him was vigorous; long he lay
Ere it could its ascendancy regain:
Then when the natural powers resumed their sway
All trace of late disease past rapidly away.

LIII.

The first inquiry when his mind was free,
Was for his sister. She was gone, they said,
Gone to her Mother, evermore to be
With her in Heaven. At this no tears he shed
Nor was he seen to sorrow for the dead;
But took the fatal tidings in such part
As if a dull unfeeling nature bred
His unconcern; for hard would seem the heart
To which a loss like his no suffering could impart.

LIV.

How little do they see what is, who frame
Their hasty judgment upon that which seems;
Waters that babble on their way proclaim
A shallowness: but in their strength deep streams
Flow silently. Of death Yeruti deems
Not as an ill, but as the last great good,
Compared with which all other he esteems
Transient and void: how then should thought intrude
Of sorrow in his heart for their beatitude?

LV.

While dwelling in their sylvan solitude
Less had Yeruti learnt to entertain
A sense of age than death. He understood
Something of death from creatures he had slain;
But here the ills which follow in the train
Of age, had first to him been manifest,—
The shrunken form, the limbs that move with pain,
The failing sense, infirmity, unrest,—
That in his heart he said to die betimes was best.

LVI.

Nor had he lost the dead: they were but gone
Before him, whither he should shortly go.
Their robes of glory they had first put on;
He, cumbered with mortality, below
Must yet abide awhile, content to know
He should not wait in long expectance here.
What cause then for repining, or for woe?
Soon shall he join them in their heavenly sphere,
And often, even now, he knew that they were near.

LVII.

'T was but in open day to close his eyes,
And shut out the unprofitable view
Of all this weary world's realities,
And forthwith, even as if they lived anew,
The dead were with him: features, form and hue,
And looks and gestures were restored again:
Their actual presence in his heart he knew;
And when their converse was disturbed, Oh then
How flat and stale it was to mix with living men!

LVIII.

But not the less, whate'er was to be done,
With living men he took his part content,
At loom, in garden, or afield, as one
Whose spirit wholly on obedience bent,
To every task its prompt attention lent.
Alert in labour he among the best;
And when to church the congregation went,
None more exact than he to cross his breast,
And kneel, or rise, and do in all things like the rest.

LIX.

Cheerful he was, almost like one elate
With wine, before it hath disturb'd his power
Of reason. Yet he seem'd to feel the weight
Of time; for alway when from yonder tower
He heard the clock tell out the passing hour,
The sound appeared to give him some delight:
And when the evening shades began to lower,
Then was he seen to watch the fading light
As if his heart rejoiced at the return of night.

LX.

The old man to whom he had been given in care,
To Dobrizhoffer came one day and said,
The trouble which our youth was thought to bear
With such indifference, hath deranged his head.
He says that he is nightly visited.
His Mother and his Sister come and say
That he must give this message from the dead
Not to defer his baptism, and delay
A soul upon the earth which should no longer stay.

LXI.

A dream the Jesuit deem'd it; a deceit
Upon itself by feverish fancy wrought;
A mere delusion which it were not meet
To censure, lest the youth's distempered thought
Might thereby be to farther error brought;
But he himself its vanity would find,—
They argued thus,—if it were noticed not.
His baptism was in fitting time design'd,
The Father said, and then dismiss'd it from his mind.

LXII.

But the old Indian came again ere long
With the same tale, and freely then confest
His doubt that he had done Yeruti wrong;
For something more than common seem'd imprest;
And now he thought that certes it were best
From the youth's lips his own account to hear,
Haply the Father then to his request
Might yield, regarding his desire sincere,
Nor wait for farther time if there were aught to fear.

LXIII.

Considerately the Jesuit heard and bade
The youth be called. Yeruti told his tale.
Nightly these blessed spirits came, he said,
To warn him he must come within the pale
Of Christ without delay; nor must he fail
This warning to their Pastor to repeat,
Till the renewed intreaty should prevail.
Life's business then for him would be complete,
And 't was to tell him this they left their starry seat.

LXIV.

Came they to him in dreams?—He could not tell.
Sleeping or waking now small difference made;
For even while he slept he knew full well
That his dear Mother and that darling Maid
Both in the Garden of the Dead were laid:
And yet he saw them as in life, the same,
Save only that in radiant robes arrayed,
And round about their presence when they came
There shone an effluent light as of a harmless flame.

LXV.

And where he was he knew, the time, the place,—
All circumstantial things to him were clear.
His own heart undisturb'd. His Mother's face
How could he chuse but know; or knowing, fear
Her presence and that Maid's, to him more dear
Than all that had been left him now below?
Their love had drawn them from their happy sphere;
That dearest love unchanged they came to show;
And he must be baptized, and then he too might go.

LXVI.

With searching ken the Jesuit while he spake
Perused him, if in countenance or tone
Aught might be found appearing to partake
Of madness. Mark of passion there was none;
None of derangement: in his eye alone,
As from a hidden fountain emanate,
Something of an unusual brightness shone:
But neither word nor look betrayed a state
Of wandering, and his speech, though earnest, was se
date.

LXVII.

Regular his pulse, from all disorder free;
The vital powers perform'd their part assign'd;
And to whate'er was ask'd, collectedly
He answer'd. Nothing troubled him in mind;
Why should it? Were not all around him kind?
Did not all love him with a love sincere,
And seem in serving him a joy to find?
He had no want, no pain, no grief, no fear:
But he must be baptized; he could not tarry here. [26]

LXVIII.

Thy will be done, Father in heaven who art!
The Pastor said, nor longer now denied;
But with a weight of awe upon his heart
Entered the Church, and there the font beside,
With holy water, chrism and salt applied,
Perform'd in all solemnity the rite.
His feeling was that hour with fear allied;
Yeruti's was a sense of pure delight,
And while he knelt his eyes seem'd larger and more
bright.

LXIX.

His wish hath been obtain'd, and this being done
His soul was to its full desire content.
The day in its accustomed course past on:
The Indian mark'd him ere to rest he went,
How o'er his beads, as he was wont, he bent,
And then, like one who casts all care aside,
Lay down. The old man fear'd no ill event,
When, « Ye are come for me!» Yeruti cried;
« Yes, I am ready now!» and instantly he died.

NOTES.

Note 1, page 552, col. 2.

So he forsooth a shapely boot must wear.

His leg had been set by the French after their conquest of Pamplona, and re-set after his removal to his father's house. The latter operation is described as having been most severe, but borne by him in his wonted manner without any manifestation of suffering. For some time his life was despaired of. «When the danger of death was past, and the bones were knit and becoming firm, two inconveniences remained: one occasioned by a portion of bone below the knee, which projected so as to occasion some deformity; the other was a contraction of the leg, which prevented him from walking erect or standing firmly on his feet. Now as he was very solicitous about his appearance, and intended at that time to follow the course of a military life which he had begun, he enquired of his medical attendants in the first place whether the bone could be removed which stood out in so unsightly a manner. They answered that it was possible to remove it, but the operation would be exceedingly painful, much more so than any which he had before undergone. He nevertheless directed them to cut it out, that he might have his will, and (as he himself related in my hearing, says Ribadeneira), that he might wear fashionable and well-fitting boots. Nor could he be dissuaded from this determination. He would not consent to be bound during the operation, and went through it with the same firmness of mind which he had manifested in the former operations. By this means the deformity of the bone was removed. The contraction of the leg was in some degree relieved by other applications, and especially by certain machines, with which during many days, and with great and continual pain, it was stretched; nevertheless it could not be so extended, but that it always remained something shorter than the other.»—*Ribadeneira, Vita S. Ignatii Loyolæ, Acta SS. Jul.* t. 7, p. 659.

A close-fitting boot seems to have been as fashionable at one time as close fitting *innominables* of buckskin were about the year 1790: and perhaps it was as severe an operation to get into them for the first time. «The greasy shoemaker,» says Tom Nash, «with his squirrel's skin, and a whole stall of ware upon his arm enters, and wrencheth his legs for an hour together, and after shows his tally. By St Loy that draws deep.»—*Nash's Lenten Stuff. Hart. Miscel.* vol. ii, p. 289, 8vo edition.

The operation of fitting a Spanish dandy with short laced quarter boots is thus minutely described by Juan de Zavaleta, who was historiographer at the commencement of Carlos the Second's reign.

«Entra el zapatero oliendo á cansado. Saca de las hormas los zapatos, con tanta dificultad como si desollara las hormas. Siéntase en una silla el galan; hincase el zapatero de rodillas, apóderase de una pierna con tantos tirones y desagrados, como si le enviaran á que le diera tormento. Mete un calzador en el talon del zapato, encapíllale otro en la punta del pie, y luego empieza á guiar el zapato por encima del calzador. Apenas ha caminado poco mas que los dedos del pie, quando es menester arrastrarle con unas tenazas, y aun arrastrado se resiste. Pónese en pie el paciente fatigado, pero contento de que los zapatos le vengan angostos; y de órden del zapatero da tres ó quatro patadas en el suelo, con tanta fuerza, que pues no se quiebra, debe de ser de bronce.

«Acozeados dan de sí el cordoban y la suela; pellejos en fin de animales, que obedecen á golpes. Vuélvese á sentar el tal señor, dobla ácia fuera el copete del zapato, cógele con la boca de las tenazas, hinca el oficial junto á él entrambas rodillas, afirmase en el suelo con la mano izquierda, y puesto de bruzas sobre el pie, hecho arco los dos dedos de la mano derecha que forman el jeme, va con ellos ayudando á llevar por el empeine arriba el cordoban, de quien tira con las tenazas su dueño. Vuelve á ponerse en una rodilla, como primero estaba; empuña con la una mano la punta del pie, y con la palma de la otra da sobre su mano tan grandes golpes como si los diera con una pala de jugar á la pelota; que es la necesidad tan discreta, que se hace el pobre el mal á sí mismo, por no hacersele a aquel de quien necesita.

«Ajustada ya la punta del pie, acude al talon, humedece con la lengua los remates de las costuras, porque no falseen las costuras de secas por los remates. Tremenda vanidad, sufrir en sus pies un hombre la boca de otro hombre, solo por tener aliñados los pies! Desdobla el zapatero el talon, dase uno vuelta con el calzador á la mano, y empieza á encaxar en el pie la segunda porcion del zapato. Manda que se baxe la punta, y hácese lo que manda. Llama ácia á sí el zapato con tal fuerza, que entre su cuerpo y el espaldar de la silla abrevia torpe y desaliñadamente al que calza. Dicele luego que haga talon, y el hombre obedece como un esclavo. Ordénale despues que dé en el suelo una patada, y el da la patada, como se le ordena. Vuelve á sentarse; saca el cruel ministro el calzador del empeine, y por donde salió el calzador mete un palo, que llaman costa, y contra el vuelve y revuelve el sacabocados, que saca los bocados del cordoban, para que entren las cintas; y dexa en el empeine del pie un dolor, y unas señales, como si hubiera sacado de allí los bocados. Agujerea las orejas, passa la cinta con una aguja, lleva las orejas á que cierren el zapato, ajústalos, y da luego con tanta fuerza el nudo, que si pudieran ahogar á un hombre por la garganta del pie, le ahogara. Hace la rosa despues con mas cuydado que gracia. Vuelve á devanarse á la mano el calzador, que está colgando del talon; tira dél como quien retoca, da con la otra mano palmadas en la planta, como quien asienta, y saca el calzador, echándose todo ácia atras. Pone el galan el pie en el suelo, y quédase mirándole. Levántase el zapatero, arrasa con el dedo el sudor de la frente, y queda respirando como si hubiera corrido. Todo esto se ahorraba con hacerse el zapato un poco mayor que el pie. Padecen luego entrambos otro tanto con el pie segundo. Llega el último y fiero trance de darle el dinero. Recoge el oficial sus baratijas. Recibe su estipendio, sale por la puerta de la sala mirando si es buena la plata que le han dado, dexando á su dueño de movimientos tan torpes como si le hubiera echado unos grillos.

«Si pensaran los que se calzan apretado que se achican el pie. Si lo piensan se engañan. Los huesos no se pueden meter unos en otros: con esto es fuerza que si le quitan de lo largo al zapato, se doble el pie por las coyunturas, y crezca ácia arriba lo que le menguan de adelante. Si le estrechan lo ancho, es preciso que se alargue aquella carne oprimida. Con la misma cantidad de pie que se tenian, se quedan los que calzan sisado. Lo que hacen es atormentarse, y dexar los pies de peor hechura. El animal á quien mas largos pies dió la naturaleza segun su cantidad, es el hombre; porque, como ha de andar todo el cuerpo sobre ellos, y no son mas de dos, quiso que anduviesse seguro. El que se los quiere abreviar, gana parece que tiene de caer, y de caer en los vicios, donde se hará mayor mal, que en las piedras. La parte que le puso Dios ad hombre en la fábrica de su cuerpo mas cerca de la tierra, son los pies: quiso sin duda que fuera la parte mas humilde de su fábrica, pero los galanes viciosos les quitan la humildad con los aliños, y los ensoberecen con el cuydado. Enfada esto á Dios tanto, que abiendo de hacer al hombre animal que pisasse la tierra, hizo la tierra de tal calidad, que se pudiesse imprimir en ella la huella del hombre. Abierta dexa su sepultura el pie que se levanta, y parece que se levanta de la sepultura. Tremenda crueldad es enloquecer con el adorno al que se quiere tragar la tierra á cada passo.»—*El dia de Fiesta. Obras de D. Juan de Zavaleta,* p. 179—180.

«In comes the shoemaker in the odour of haste and fatigue. He takes the shoes off the last with as much difficulty as if he were skinning the lasts. The gallant seats himself upon a chair; the shoemaker kneels down, and takes possession of one foot, which he handles as if he were sent there to administer the torture. He puts one shoeing skin [1] in the heel of the shoe, fits the other upon the point of the foot, and then begins to guide the shoe over the shoeing skin. Scarcely has it got farther than the toes when it is found necessary to draw it on with pincers, and even then it is hard work. The patient stands up, fatigued with the operation, but well pleased that the shoes are tight; and by the shoemaker's directions he stamps three or four times on the floor, with such force that it must be of iron if it does not give way.

« The cordovan and the soles being thus beaten, submit; they are the skins of animals who obey blows. Our gallant returns to his seat, he turns up the upper-leather of the shoe, and lays hold on it with the pincers: the tradesman kneels close by him on both knees, rests on the ground with his left hand, and bending in this all-four's position over the foot, making an arch with those fingers of the right hand which form the span, assists in drawing on the upper part of the cordovan, the gallant pulling the while with the pincers. He then puts himself on one knee, lays hold of the end of the foot with one hand, and with the palm of the other strikes his own hand, as hard as if he were striking a ball with a racket. For necessity is so discreet that the poor man inflicts this pain upon himself that he may give none to the person of whose custom he stands in need.

« The end of the foot being thus adjusted he repairs to the heel, and with his tongue moistens the end of the seams, that they may not give way for being dry. Tremendous vanity, that one man should allow the mouth of another to be applied to his feet that he may have them trimly set out! The shoemaker unfolds the heel, turns round with the shoeing skin in his hand, and begins to fit the second part of the shoe upon the foot. He desires the gallant to put the end of the foot down, and the gallant does as he is desired. He draws the shoe towards him with such force that the person who is thus being shoed is compressed in an unseemly manner between the shoemaker's body and the back of the chair. Presently he tells him to put his heel down, and the man is as obedient as a slave. He orders him then to stamp upon the ground, and the man stamps as he is ordered. The gallant then seats himself again ; the cruel operator draws the shoeing skin from the instep, and in its place drives in a stick which they call *costa.* [2] He then turns upon it the punch, which makes the holes in the leather, through which the ribbons are to pass; he again twists round his hand the strip of hare-skin which hangs from the heel, and pulls it as if he were ringing a bell, and leaves upon the upper part of the top a pain and marks as if he had punched the holes in it. He bores the ears, passes the string through with

---

[1] A piece of hare-skin is used in Spain for this purpose, as it appears by the former extract from Tom Nash that squirrel-skin was in England.

[2] Which is used to drive it upon the last to raise a shoe higher in the instep.

a bodkin, brings the ears together that they may fasten the shoe, fits them to their intended place, and ties the knot with such force, that if it were possible to strangle a man by the neck of his foot, strangled the gallant would be. Then he makes the rose, with more care than grace. He goes then to take out the shoeing skin which is still hanging from the heel ; he lays hold of this, strikes the sole of the foot with his other hand as if settling it, and draws out the skin, bringing out all with it. The gallant puts his foot to the ground, and remains looking at it. The shoemaker rises, wipes the sweat from his forehead with his fingers, and draws his breath like one who has been running. All this trouble might have been saved by making the shoe a little larger than the foot. Presently both have to go through the same pains with the other foot. Now comes the last and terrible act of payment. The tradesman collects his tools, receives his money, and goes out at the door, looking at the silver to see if it is good, and leaving the gallant walking as much at his ease as if he had been put in fetters.

« If they who wear tight shoes think that thereby they can lessen the size of their feet, they are mistaken. The bones cannot be squeezed one into another ; if therefore the shoe is made short, the foot must be crooked at the joints, and grow upward if it is not allowed to grow forward. If it is pinched in the breadth, the flesh which is thus constrained must extend itself in length. They who are shod thus miserably remain with just the same quantity of foot.

« Of all animals, man is the one to which, in proportion to its size, nature has given the largest feet ; because as his whole body is to be supported upon them, and he has only two, she chose that he should walk in safety. He who wishes to abbreviate them acts as if he were inclined to fall, and to fall into vices which will do him more injury than if he fell upon stones. The feet are the part which in the fabric of the human body are placed nearest to the earth ; they are meant therefore to be the humblest part of his frame, but gallants take away all humility by adorning and setting them forth in bravery. This so displeases the Creator, that having to make man an animal who should walk upon the earth, he made the earth of such properties, that the footsteps should sink into it. The foot which is lifted from the ground, leaves its own grave open, and seems as if it rose from the grave. What a tremendous thing is it then to set off with adornments that which the earth wishes to devour at every step!»

Note 2, page 552, col. 2.
Whiling with books the weary hours away.

«Vede quanto importa a lição de bons livros! Se o livro fora de cavallerias, sahiria Ignacio hum grande cavalleyro ; foy hum livro de vidas de Santos, sahio hum grande Santo. Se lera cavallerias, sahiria Ignacio hum Cavelleyro da ardente espada; leo vidas de Santos sahio hum Santo da ardente tocha.»—*Vieyra, Serman de St Ignacio,* t. i, p. 368.

See, says Vieyra, the importance of reading good books. If it had been a book of knight errantry, Ignacio would have become a great knight errant; it was the Lives of the Saints, and Ignatius became a great saint. If he had read about knights, he might have proved a Knight of the Burning Sword : he read about saints, and proved a saint of the burning torch.

Nothing could seem more probable than that Cervantes had this part of Loyola's history in his mind when he described the rise of Don Quixote's madness, if Cervantes had not shown himself in one of his dramas to be thoroughly imbued with the pestilent superstition of his country. *El dichoso Rufian* is one of those monstrous compositions which nothing but the anti-christian fables of the Romish church could have produced.

Landor, however, supposes that Cervantes intended to satirize a favourite dogma of the Spaniards. The passage occurs in his thirteenth conversation.

« The most dexterous attack ever made against the worship among catholics, which opens so many side chapels to pilfering and imposture, is that of Cervantes.

« *Leopold.* I do not remember in what part.

« *President.* Throughout Don Quixote. Dulcinea was the peerless, the immaculate, and death was denounced against all who hesitated to admit the assertion of her perfections. Surely your highness never could have imagined that Cervantes was such a knight errant as to attack knight errantry, a folly that had ceased more than a century, if indeed it was any folly at all; and the idea that he ridiculed the poems and romances founded on it, is not less improbable, for they contained all the literature of the nation, excepting the garniture of chapterhouses, theology, and pervaded, as with a thread of gold, the beautiful histories of this illustrious people. He delighted the idlers of romance by the jokes he scattered amongst them on the false taste of his predecessors and of his rivals; and he delighted his own heart by this solitary archery; well knowing what amusement those who came another day would find in picking up his arrows and discovering the bull's-eye hits.

« Charles V was the knight of La Mancha, devoting his labours and vigils, his wars and treaties, to the chimerical idea of making all minds, like watches, turn their indexes, by a simultaneous movement to one point. Sancho Panza was the symbol of the people, possessing sound sense in all other matters, but ready to follow the most extravagant visionary in this, and combining implicit belief in it, with the grossest sensuality. For religion, when it is hot enough to produce enthusiasm, burns up and kills every seed entrusted to its bosom.»—*Imaginary Conversations,* vol. i, 187.

Benedetto di Virgilio, the Italian ploughman, thus describes the course of Loyola's reading, in his heroic poem upon that Saint's life.

> Mentre le vote indebolite vene
> Stass' egli rinforzando a poco a poco
> Dentro i paterni tetti, e si trattiene
> Or sù la ricca zimbra, or presso al foco,
> Fuor' del costume suo, pensier gli viene,
> Di legger libri più che d'altro gioco;
> Quant' era dianzi innamorato, e d'armi
> Tant' or, mutando stile, inchina a i carmi.
>
> Quinci comanda, che i volumi ornati
> D'alti concetti, e di leggiadra rima,
> Dentro la stanza sua vengan portati,
> Che passar con lor versi il tempo stima:
> Cercan ben tosto i paggi in tutti i lati
> Ove posar solean tai libri prima,
> Ma nè per questa parte, nè per quella
> Ponno istoria trovar vecchia, o novella.
>
> I volumi vergati in dolci canti
> S'ascondon sì, che nulla il cercar giova.
> Ma pur cercando i più secreti canti
> Per gran fortuna un tomo ecco si trova,

> Tomo divin, che le vite de' Santi
> Conserva, e de la etade prisca e nova,
> Onde per far la brama sua contenta
> Tal opra un fido servo à lui presenta.
>
> Il volume, che spiega in ogni parte
> De' guerrieri del ciel l'opre famose,
> Fa ch' Ignazio s'accenda a seguir l'arte
> Che à soffrir tanto i sacri Eroi dispose,
> Egli già sprezza di Bellona e Marte
> Gli studi, che a seguir prima si pose,
> E s' accinge a troncar maggior d'Alcide,
> L'Hidra del vizio, e le sue teste infide.
>
> Tutto giocondo a contemplar s'appiglia
> Si-degni fogli, e da principio al fine;
> Qui ritrova di Dio l'ampia famiglia,
> Spirti beati ed alme peregrine:
> Tra gli altri osserva con sua meraviglia.
> Il pio Gusman, che colse da le spine
> Rose celesti de la terra santa,
> Onde del buon Giesù nacque la pianta.
>
> Contempla dopo il Serafico Magno
> Fondator de le bigge immense squadre;
> La divina virtù, l'alto guadagno
> De l'opre lor mirabili e leggiadre:
> Rimira il Padoan di lui compagno,
> Che liberò da indegna morte il padre,
> E per provar di quella causa il torto,
> Vivo fè da la tomba uscire il morto.
>
> Quinci ritrova il Celestin, che spande
> Trionfante bandiera alla campagna,
> De l'egregie virtù sue memorande
> Con Italia s'ingemma e Francia e Spagna:
> Ornati i figli suoi d'opre ammirande
> Son per l'Africa sparti, e per Lamagna,
> E in parti infide al Ciel per lor si vede
> Nascer la Chiesa, e pullular la fede.
>
> Quivi s'avvisa, come il buon Norcino
> Inclito Capitan del Rè superno,
> Un giorno guerreggiando sù 'l Casino
> Gl' Idoli fracassò, vinse l'Inferno,
> E con aita del motor divino
> Guastò tempio sacrato al cieco Averno,
> Por di novo l'eresse à l'alta prole
> Divino essempio de l'eterno Sole.
>
> Legge come Brunone al divin Regge
> Accolse al Rè del Ciel cigni felici,
> E dando ordine lor, regola e legge
> Gl' imparò calpestare aspre pendici;
> E quelle de le donne anco vi legge;
> Che qui di ricche dotar mendici
> Per trovar poi sù le sedi superne
> Lor doti incorruttibili ed eterne.
>
> Chiara tra l'altre nota è Caterina,
> Che per esser di Dio fedele amante,
> Fù intrepida a i tormenti: e la Regina
> Di Siena, e seco le compagne tante:
> Orsola con la schiera peregrina,
> Monache sacre, verginelle sante,
> Che sprezzando del mondo il vano rito,
> Elessero Giesù lor gran marito.
>
> E tra i Romiti mira Ilarione,
> E di Vienna quel sì franco e forte
> Che debellò la furia, e 'l gran Campione
> Ch' appo il Natal di Christo hebbe la morte;
> Risguarda quel del primo Gonfalone,
> Che del Ciel guarda le superne porte;
> E gli undici compagni, e come luce
> Il divo Agnello di lor capo e Duce.
>
> Mentre in questo penetra e meglio intende
> D'Eroi si gloriosi il nobil vanto,
> Aura immortal del Ciel sovra lui scende,
> Aura immortal di spirto divo e santo:

Gia gli sgombra gli errori e già gli accende
In guisa il cor, che distilla in pianto ;
Lagrime versa, e le lagrime sparte
Bagnan del libro le vergate carte.

Qual duro ghiaccio sovra i monti alpini
Da la virtù del sole intenerito,
Suol liquefarsi, e di bei cristallini
Rivi l'herbe insffiar del suol fiorito ;
Tal da la forza degli ardor divini
Del Giovanetto molle il cor ferito,
Hor si discioglie in tepidi liquori,
E rigan del bel volto i vaghi fiori

Com' altri nel cristallo, o nel diamante
Specchiarsi suol, tal ei si specchia, e mira
Nel specchio di sua mente, indi l'errante
Vita discerne, onde con duol sospira :
Quinci risolve intrepido e costante
Depor gli orgogli giovanili e l'ira,
Per imitar ne l'opra e ne gli effetti
I celesti guerrier del libro letti.

Ignatio Loiola, Canto 2. 1647.

The Jesuits, however, assure us, that Loyola is *not* the author of their society, and that it is not allowable either to think or say so. « Societas Jesu ut à S. Ignatio de Loiolà non ducit nomen, ita neque originem primam, et aliud sentire aut loqui, nefas.» (Imago primi Sæculi Soc. Jesu, p. 64.) « Jesus primus ac præcipuus auctor Societatis,» is the title of a chapter in this their secular volume, which is a curious and very beautiful book. Then follows « Beata Virgo nutrix, patrona, imò altera velut auctor Societatis.» *Lastly,* « Post Christum et Mariam Societatis Auctor et Parens sanctus Ignatius.»

« On the 26th August 1794, the French plundered the rich church of Loyola, at Azpeitia, and proceeding to Elgoibas, loaded five carts with the spoils of the church of that place. This party of marauders consisted of 200. The peasants collected, fell upon them, and after an obstinate conflict of three hours, recovered the whole booty, which they conveyed to Vittoria in triumph. Among other things, a relic of Loyola was recovered, which was carried in procession to the church, the victorious peasants accompanying it.»—*Marcillac, Hist. de la Guerre de l'Espagne,* p. 86.

Note 3, page 552, col. 2.

Vaccination.

It is odd that in Hindostan, where it might have been supposed superstition would have facilitated the introduction of this practice, a pious fraud was found necessary for removing the prejudice against it.

Mooperal Streenivaschary, a Brahmin, thus writes to Dr Anderson at Madras, on vaccine inoculation.

« It might be useful to remove a prejudice in the minds of the people, arising from the term cow-pock, being taken literally in our Tamul tongue; whereas there can be no doubt that it has been a drop of nectar from the exuberant udders of the cows in England, and no way similar to the humour discharged from the tongue and feet of diseased cattle in this country.»— FORBES's *Oriental Memoirs,* vol. iii, p. 423.

Note 4, page 553, col. 1.

For tyrannous fear dissolved all natural bonds of man.

Mackenzie gives a dreadful picture of the effect of small-pox among the North American Indians.

« The small-pox spread its destructive and desolating power, as the fire consumes the dry grass of the field. The fatal infection spread around with a baneful rapi-dity, which no flight could escape, and with a fatal effect that nothing could resist. It destroyed with its pestilential breath whole families and tribes; and the horrid scene presented to those who had the melancholy and afflicting opportunity of beholding it, a combination of the dead, the dying, and such as, to avoid the horrid fate of their friends around them, prepared to disappoint the plague of its prey, by terminating their own existence.

« The habits and lives of these devoted people, which provided not to-day for the wants of to-morrow, must have heightened the pains of such an affliction, by leaving them not only without remedy, but even without alleviation. Nought was left them but to submit in agony and despair.

« To aggravate the picture, if aggravation were possible, may be added the putrid carcasses which the wolves, with a furious voracity, dragged forth from the huts, or which were mangled within them by the dogs, whose hunger was satisfied with the disfigured remains of their masters. Nor was it uncommon for the father of a family, whom the infection had not reached, to call them around him, to represent the cruel sufferings and horrid fate of their relations, from the influence of some evil spirit, who was preparing to extirpate their race; and to incite them to baffle death, with all its horrors, by their own poniards. At the same time, if their hearts failed them in this necessary act, he was himself ready to perform the deed of mercy with his own hand, as the last act of his affection, and instantly to follow them to the common place of rest and refuge from human evil.»

Note 5, page 553, col. 2.

And from the silent door the jaguar turns away.

I may be forgiven for not having strictly adhered to natural history in this instance. The liberty which I have taken is mentioned, that it may not be supposed to have arisen from ignorance of this animal's habits.

The jaguar will not attack a living horse if a dead one be near, and when it kills its prey it drags it to its den, but is said not to eat the body till it becomes putrid. They are caught in large traps of the cage kind, baited with stinking meat, and then speared or shot through the bars. The Chalcaquines had a braver way of killing them: they provoked the animal, fronted it, received its attack upon a thick truncheon, which they held by the two ends, threw it down while its teeth were fixed in the wood, and ripped the creature up before it could recover. (*Techo,* p. 29.) A great profit is made by their skins. The jaguar which has once tasted human flesh becomes a most formidable animal; such a beast is called a *tigre cevado,* a fleshed tiger. There was one who infested the road between Santa Fé and Santiago, and killed ten men; after which a party of soldiers were sent to destroy it. The same thing is said of the lion and other beasts of prey, probably with truth ; not as is vulgarly supposed, because they have a particular appetite for this kind of food, but because having once fed upon man, they from that time regard him like any animal of inferior strength, as their natural prey. « It is a constant observation in Numidia,» says Bruce, « that the lion avoids and flies from the face of men, till by some accident they have been brought to engage, and the beast has prevailed against him ; then that feeling of superiority, imprinted by the

Creator in the heart of all animals, for man's preservation, seems to forsake him. The lion having once tasted human blood, relinquishes the pursuit after the flock. He repairs to some highway or frequented path, and has been known, in the kingdom of Tunis, to interrupt the road to a market for several weeks; and in this he persists, till hunters or soldiers are sent out to destroy him." Dobrizhoffer saw the skin of a jaguar which was as long as the standard hide. He says, also, that he saw one attack two horses which were coupled with a thong, kill one, and drag the other away after it.

A most unpleasant habit of the beast is, that in cold or wet weather he chuses to lodge within doors, and will steal into the house. A girl at Corrientes, who slept with her mother, saw one lying under the bed when she rose in the morning: she had presence of mind to bid her mother lie still, went for help, and soon rid the house of its perilous visitor. Cat-like, the jaguar is a good climber; but Dobrizhoffer tells us how a traveller who takes to one for shelter may profit by the position: *In promptu consilium; urina pro armis est: hæc si tigridis ad arboris pedem minitantis oculos consperseris, salva res est. Quâ datâ portu fuget illico.* (i. 280.) He who first did this must have been a good marksman as well as a cool fellow, and it was well for him that he reserved his fire till the jaguar was within shot.

Dobrizhoffer seems to credit an opinion (which is held in India of the tiger also) that the jaguar's claws are in a certain degree venomous; the scar which they leave is said to be always liable to a very painful and burning sense of heat. But that author, in his usual amusing manner, repeats many credulous notions concerning the animal: as that its burnt claws are a remedy for the tooth-ache; and that it has a mode of decoying fish, by standing neck deep in the water, and spitting out a white foam, which allures them within reach. Techo (30.) says the same thing of a large snake.

An opinion that wounds inflicted by the stroke of animals of this kind are envenomed is found in the East also. Captain Williamson says, " However trivial the scratches made by the claws of tigers may appear, yet, whether it be owing to any noxious quality in the claw itself, to the manner in which the tiger strikes, or any other matter, I have no hesitation in saying, that at least a majority of such as have been under my notice died; and I have generally remarked, that those whose cases appeared the least alarming were most suddenly carried off. I have ever thought the perturbation arising from the nature of the attack to have a considerable share in the fatality alluded to, especially as I never knew any one wounded by a tiger to die without suffering for some days under that most dreadful symptom, a locked jaw! Such as have been wounded to appearance severely, but accompanied with a moderate hæmorrhage, I have commonly found to recover, excepting in the rainy season: at that period I should expect serious consequences from either a bite or a scratch." —*Oriental Sports*, v. i, p. 52.

Wild beasts were so numerous and fierce in one part of Mexico, among the Otomites, that Fr. Juan de Grijalva says in his time, in one year, more than 250 Indians were devoured by them. " There then prevailed an opinion," he proceeds, " and still it prevails among many, that those tigers and lions were certain Indian sorcerers, whom they call Nahuales, who by diabolical art transform themselves into beasts, and tear the Indians in pieces, either to revenge themselves for some offences which they have received, or to do them evil, which is the proper condition of the Devil, and an effect of his fierceness. Some traces of these diabolical acts have been seen in our time, for in the year 1579, the deaths of this kind being many, and the suspicion vehement, some Indians were put to the question, and they confessed the crime, and were executed for it.— With all this experience and proof, there are many persons who doubt these transformations, and say that the land being mountainous produces wild beasts, and the beasts being once fleshed commit these great ravages. And it was through the weak understandings of the Indians that they were persuaded to believe their conjurors could thus metamorphose themselves; and if these poor wretches confessed themselves guilty of such a crime, it was owing to their weakness under the torture; and so they suffered for an offence which they had never committed."

Father Grijalva, however, holds with his Father S. Augustine, who has said concerning such things, *hæc ad nos non quibuscunque qualibus credere putaremus indignum, sed eis referentibus pervenerunt, quos nobis non existimaremus fuisse mentitos.* " In the days of my father S. Augustine," he says, " wonderful things were related of certain innkeepers in Italy, who transformed passengers into beasts of burthen, to bring to their inns straw, barley, and whatever was wanted from the towns, and then metamorphosed them into their own persons, that they might purchase, as customers, the very commodities they had carried. And in our times the witches of Logrono make so many of these transformations, that now no one can doubt them.— This matter of the Nahuales, or sorcerers of Tututepec, has been confessed by so many, that that alone suffices to make it credible. The best proof which can be had is, that they were condemned to death by course of justice; and it is temerity to condemn the judges, for it is to be believed that they made all due enquiry. Our brethren who have been ministers there, and are also judges of the interior court (that is of the conscience) have all held these transformations to be certain: so that there ought to be no doubt concerning it. On the contrary, it is useful to understand it, that if at any time in heathen lands the devil should work any of these metamorphoses, the Indians may see we are not surprised at them, and do not hold them as miraculous, but can explain to them the reason and cause of these effects, which astonish and terrify them so greatly."

He proceeds to show that the devil can only exercise this power as far as he is permitted by God, in punishment for sin, and that the metamorphosis is not real, but only apparent; the sorcerer not being actually transformed into a lion, but seeming as if he were both to himself and others. In what manner he can tear a man really to pieces with imaginary claws, and devour him in earnest with an imaginary mouth, the good friar has not condescended to explain.—*Historia de la Orden de S. Augustin en la Provincia de N. España*, pp. 34, 35.

Note 6, page 553, col. 2.

Preserved with horrid art
In ghastly image of humanity.

The more ghastly in proportion as more of the appearance of life is preserved in the revolting practice. Such, however, it was not to the feelings of the Egyptians, who had as much pride in a collection of their ancestors, as one of the strongest family feeling could have in a collection of family pictures. The body, Diodorus says, is delivered to the kindred with every member so whole and entire that no part of the body seems to be altered, even to the very hairs of the eyelids and the eyebrows, so that the beauty and shape of the face seems just as before. By which means many of the Egyptians laying up the bodies of their ancestors in stately monuments, perfectly see the true visage and countenance of those who were buried many ages before they themselves were born: so that in regarding the proportion of every one of these bodies, and the lineaments of their faces, they take exceeding great delight, even as if they were still living among them. —(Book i.)

They believe, says Herodotus (*Euterpe*, sect. 123), that on the dissolution of the body the soul immediately enters into some other animal; and that after using as vehicles every species of terrestrial, aquatic, and winged creatures, it finally enters a second time into a human body. They affirm that it undergoes all these changes in the space of three thousand years. This opinion some among the Greeks have at different periods of time adopted as their own, but I shall not, though I could, specify their names.

How little did the Egyptians apprehend that the bodies which they preserved with such care to be ready again for use when the cycle should be fulfilled, would one day be regarded as an article of trade, broken up, exported piecemeal, and administered in grains and scruples as a costly medicine to rich patients. A preference was even given to virgin mummy!

The bodies of the Incas from the founder of the empire were preserved in the Temple of the Sun; they were seated each on his litter, and in such excellent preservation that they seemed to be alive; according to the testimony of P. Acosta and Garcilaso, who saw them and touched them. It is not known in what manner they were prepared, so as to resist the injuries of time. Gomara (c. 195) says they were embalmed by the juice of certain fragrant trees, which was poured down their throats, and by unguents of gum. Acosta says that a certain bitumen was used, and that plates of gold were placed instead of eyes, so well fitted that the want of the real eye was not perceived. Garcilaso thought the chief preparation consisted in freezing them with snow. They were buried in one of the courts of the hospital of St Andres.—*Merc. Peruano*, No. 221.

Hideous exhibitions of this kind are sometimes made in monasteries, where they are in perfect accord with monastic superstition. I remember seeing two human bodies dry and shrivelled, suspended in the *Casa dos Ossos*, at Evora, in a chapel, the walls of which are lined with skulls and bones.

« Among the remarkable objects in the vicinity of Palermo pointed out to strangers, they fail not to singularise a convent of Capuchins at a small distance from town, the beautiful gardens of which serve as a public walk. You are shown, under the fabric, a vault divided into four great galleries, into which the light is admitted by windows cut out at the top of each extremity. In this vault are preserved, not in flesh, but in skin and bone, all the Capuchins who have died in the convent since its foundation, as well as the bodies of several persons from the city. There are here private tombs belonging to opulent families, who, even after annihilation, disdain to be confounded with the vulgar part of mankind. It is said, that in order to secure the preservation of these bodies, they are prepared by being gradually dried before a slow fire, so as to consume the flesh without greatly injuring the skin; when perfectly dry, they are invested with the Capuchin habit, and placed upright, on tablets, disposed step above step along the sides of the vault; the head, the arms, and the feet are left naked. A preservation like this is horrid. The skin discoloured, dry, and as if it had been tanned, nay, torn in some places, glued close to the bones. It is easy to imagine, from the different grimaces of this numerous assemblage of fleshless figures, rendered still more frightful by a long beard on the chin, what a hideous spectacle this must exhibit; and whoever has seen a Capuchin alive, may form an idea of this singular repository of dead friars. »—*Sonnini.*

It is not surprising that such practices arise from superstition; but it is strange, indeed, that they should afford any gratification to pride. That excellent man, Fletcher of Madeley, has a striking remark upon this subject. « The murderer, » says he, « is dissected in the surgeon's hall, gratis; and the rich sinner is embowelled in his own apartment at great expence. The robber, exposed to open air, wastes away in hoops of iron; and the gentleman, confined to a damp vault, moulders away in sheets of lead; and while the fowls of the air greedily prey upon the one, the vermin of the earth eagerly devour the other. »

How different is the feeling of the Hindoos upon this subject from that of the Egyptians! « A mansion with bones for its rafters and beams; with nerves and tendons for cords; with muscles and blood for mortar; with skin for its outward covering; filled with no sweet perfume, but loaded with feces and urine; a mansion infested by age and by sorrow, the seat of malady, harassed with pains, haunted with the quality of darkness, and incapable of standing long—Such a mansion of the vital soul lets its occupier always cheerfully quit. »—*Inst. of Menu.*

Note 7, page 554, col. 2.

When the laden bee
Buzzed by him in its flight, he could pursue
Its path with certain ken.

It is difficult to explain the superior quickness of sight which savages appear to possess. The Brazilian tribes used to eradicate the eyelashes and eyebrows, as impeding it. « Some Indians, » P. Andres Perez de Ribas says, « were so quicksighted that they could ward off the coming arrow with their own bow. »—L. ii, c. 3, p. 41.

Note 8, page 554, col. 2.

Covering with soft gums the obedient limb
And body, then with feathers overlay,
In regular hues disposed.

Inconvenient as this may seem, it was the full-dress of the Tupi and Guarani tribes. A fashion less gorgeous and elaborate, but more refined, is described by one of the best old travellers to the East, François Pyrard.

« The inhabitants of the Maldives use on feast days this kind of gallantry. They bruise sanders (sandalwood) and camphire, on very slicke and smooth stones, (which they bring from the firm land,) and sometimes other sorts of odoriferous woods. After they compound it with water distilled of flowers, and overspread their bodies with this paste, from the girdle upwards; adding many forms with their finger, such as they imagine. It is somewhat like cut and pinked doublets, and of an excellent savour. They dress their wives or lemans in this sort, and make upon their backs works and shadows as they please.» Skin-prints Purchas calls this.—*Pyrard de Laval. Purchas,* p. 1655.

The abominable practice of tarring and feathering was but too well known during the American war. It even found its way to England. I remember, when a child, to have seen a man in this condition in the streets of Bristol.

The costume of the savages who figured so frequently in the pageants of the sixteenth century, seems to have been designed to imitate the Brazilian tribes, best known to the French and English at that time. Indeed, this is expressed by Vincent Carloix, when in describing an entertainment given to Marechal de Vieilleville by the captains of the galley at Marseilles, he says, « Ayant lié six galères ensemble de front, et faict dresser les tables dessus, et tapissées en façon de grandes salles; ayant accoustrés les forcats en Bressiliens pour servir, ils firent une infinité de gambades et de tourbions à la façon des sauvages, que personne n'avoit encore veues; dont tout le monde, avec une extresme allaigresse, s'esbahissoit merveilleusement.»—*Mémoires,* l. x, ch. 18.

Note 9, page 555, col. 1.
Drinking feasts.

The point of honour in drinking is not the same among the savages of Guiana, as among the English potators; they account him that is drunk first the bravest fellow.—*Harcourt's Voyage.*

Note 10, page 555, col. 1.

A custom strange, and yet far spread
Through many a savage tribe, howe'er it grew,
And once in the old world known as widely as the new.

« Je la trouve chez les Iberiens, ou les premiers peuples d'Espagne; je la trouve chez les anciens habitants de l'Isle de Corse; elle étoit chez les Tibareniens en Asie; elle est aujourd'hui dans quelques-unes de nos provinces voisines d'Espagne, ou cela s'appele faire couvade; elle est encore vers le Japon, et dans l'Amerique chez les Caraibes et les Galibis.»—*Lafitau, Mœurs des Sauvages,* t. i. p. 50.

Strabo says, this strange custom existed in Cantabria, (L. iii, p. 174, ed. 1571.) so that its Gascon extraction has been direct. Diodorus Siculus is the authority for its existence in Corsica. (Book iii, ch. 1, English translation, 1814. vol. i. p. 305.) Apollonius Rhodius describes it among the Tibareni (L. ii. 1012.) ὡς ἱστορεῖ Νυμφόδωρος ἔν τισιν νόμοις, says the scholiast.

« Voicy la brutalité de nos sauvages dans leur réjouissance pour l'accroissement de leur famille. C'est qu'au même temps que la femme est delivrée le mary se met au lit, pour s'y plaindre et y faire l'accouchée; coutume qui, bien que sauvage et ridicule, se trouve neantmoins,

à ce que l'on dit, parmy les paysans d'une certaine province de France; et ils appellent cela *faire la couvade.* Mais ce qui est de fâcheuse pour le pauvre Caraibe qui s'est mis au lit au lieu de l'accouchée, c'est qu'on luy fait faire diete dix ou douze jours de suite, ne lui donnant rien par jour qu'un petit morceau de cassave, et un peu d'eau dans laquelle on a aussi fait bouillir un peu de ce pain de racine. Après il mange un peu plus; mais il n'entame la cassave qui luy est presentée que par le milieu durant quelques quarante jours, en laissant les bords entiers qu'il pend à sa case, pour servir à un festin qu'il fait ordinairement en suite à tous ses amis. Et même il s'abstient après cela, quelquefois dix mois ou un an entier de plusieurs viandes, comme de lamantin, de tortuë, de pourceau, de poules, de poisson, et de choses délicates, craignant par une pitoyable folie que cela ne nuise à l'enfant. Mais il ne font ce grand jusne qu'à la naissance de leur premier enfant.»—*Rochefort. Hist. Morale,* c. 23. p. 495.

Marco Polo (L. ii, c. 41), the other authority to which Lafitau refers, speaks of the custom as existing in the great Khan's province of Cardandan. « Hanno un' usanza che subito ch'una donna ha partorito, si leva del letto, e lavato il fanciullo e ravolto ne' panni, il marito si mette a giacere in letto in sua vece, e tiene il figliuolo appresso di se, havendo la cura di quello per quaranta giorni, che non si parte mai. Et gli amici e parenti vanno a visitarlo per rallegrarlo e consolarlo; e le donne che sono da parto fanno quel che bisogna per casa, portando da mangiare e bere al marito, ch' e nel letto, e dando il latte al fanciullo, che gli è appresso. » —*Ramusio,* t. ii, p. 36, ed. 1583.

Yet this custom, preposterous as it is, is not more strange than an opinion which was once so prevalent in this country that Primerose made it the subject of a chapter in his work *de Vulgi Erroribus in Medicina,* and thought it necessary to prove, by physical reasons, *maritum loco uxoris gravidæ non ægrotare,* for such is the title of one of his chapters. He says, « Inter errores quamplurimos maximè ridendus hic esse videtur, quod vir credatur ægrotare, iisque affici symptomatis, quibus ipsa mulier prægnans solet, illudque experientiâ confirmatum plurimi esse volunt. Habebam ægrum febre laborantem cum urinâ valde accensâ et turbidâ, qui ægrotationis suæ nullam causam agnoscebat quam uxoris suæ graviditatem. Nullibi terrarum quam in Angliâ id observatum memini me audivisse, aut legisse unquam.—Nec si quis maritus cum uxor gravida est, ægrotat, ab uxore infectus fuit, sed potest ex peculiari proprii corporis vitio id pati. Sicut dum hæc scribo, pluit; non est tamen pluvia aut causa scriptionis, aut scriptura pluviæ. Res nova non est, viros et mulieres etiam simul ægrotare. At mirum est hactenusque ignotum, graviditatem affectum esse contagiosum, et non alias mulieres sed viros, quos natura immunes ab hoc labore fecit, solos infici. Præterea observatum est non omnibus mulieribus ejusmodi symptomata, aut saltem non omnia singulis contingere; et tamen accidit sæpe ut cum mulier bene valet, ægrotet maritus, etiam absens per aliquot milliaria. Sed quoniam ex solâ relatione absurditas hujus erroris patet, plura non addam. Jupiter Bacchum in femore. Palladem in cerebro gestavit. Sed hoc illi esto proprium.» Lib. ii, c. 13.

This notion, however, is probably not yet extinct, for I know that it existed in full force some thirty years ago, and that not in the lowest rank of life.

Note 11, page 556, col. 1.

Till hardened mothers in the grave could lay
Their living babes with no compunctious tear.

This dreadful practice is carried to such an extent in the heart of South America that whole tribes have become extinct in consequence of it, and of another practice hardly less nefarious.

Those bloody African savages, the Giagas, reared no children whatsoever; « for as soon,» says Battell, « as the woman is delivered of her child, it is presently buried quick; so that there is not one child brought up in all this generation. But when they take any town they keep the boys and girls of thirteen or fourteen years of age as their own children, but the men and women they kill and eat. These little boys they train up in the wars, and hang a collar about their necks for a disgrace, which is never taken off till he proveth himself a man, and brings his enemy's head to the general; and then it is taken off, and he is a free man, and is called ' gonso' or ' soldier.' This maketh them all desperate and forward to be free, and counted men, and so they do increase.» A generation without generation, says Purchas, p. 977.

Among the causes for which the Knisteneaux women procure abortion, Mackenzie (p. 98) assigns that of hatred for the father. No other traveller has ever suspected the existence of this motive. They sometimes kill their female children to save them from the miseries which they themselves have suffered.

The practice among the Panches of Bogota was, that if the first-born proved a girl, it was destroyed, and every girl in succession till the mother bore a boy, after which girls were allowed to live; but if the first-born were a boy, all the children then were reared.— *Piedrahita*, p. 11.

Perhaps the most flagitious motive for which this crime has ever become a practice, is that which the Guana women assign for it; they destroy the greater number of their female infants in order to keep up the value of the sex. (*Azara*, t. ii, 85—100. See *Hist. of Brazil*, vol. ii, 379.) A knowledge of the evils which polygamy brings upon some of their neighbours may have led to this mode of preventing it.

Father Gumilla one day bitterly reproved a Betoya woman (whom he describes as having more capacity than any other of the Indians in those parts) for killing her new-born daughter. She listened to him without lifting her eyes from the ground, and when he had done, and thought that she was convinced of her guilt and heartily repented of it, she said, « Father, if you will not be angry, I will tell you what is in my heart.» He promised that he would not, and bade her speak freely. This she said to me, he says, as follows, literally translated from the Betoya tongue. « Would to God, Father, would to God my mother when she brought me forth had loved me so well and pitied me so much as to have saved me from all those troubles which I have endured till this day, and am to endure till death! If my mother had buried me as soon as I was born, I should have died, but should not have felt death, and should have been spared from that death which must come, and should have escaped so many things bitterer than death: who knows how many more such I must endure before I die! Consider well, Father, the hardships that a poor Indian woman endures among these Indians! They go with us to the plantation, but they have a bow and arrow in their hands, nothing more; we go with a basket full of things on the back, one child at the breast, another upon the basket. Their business is to shoot a bird or a fish, ours is to dig and work in the field; at evening they go home without any burthen; we, besides our children, have to carry roots for their food, and maize to make their drink. They, when they reach the house, go to converse with their friends, we have to seek wood, fetch water, and prepare their supper. Having supped, they go to sleep; but we almost all the night are pounding maize to make their *chicha*. And what is the end of this our watching and labour! They drink the *chicha*, they get drunk, and being out of their senses, beat us with sticks, take us by the hair, drag us about and trample on [us. Would to God, Father, that my mother had buried me when she brought me forth! You know that I complain with cause, for all that I have said you witness every day. But our greatest pain you do not know, because you never can suffer it. You do not know, Father, the death it is for the poor Indian woman, when having served her husband as a slave, sweating in the field, and in the house without sleep, at the end of twenty years she sees him take a girl for another wife. Her he loves, and though she ill uses our children, we cannot interfere, for he neither loves us nor cares for us now. A girl is to command over us, and treat us as her servants, and if we speak, they silence us with sticks. Can any Indian woman do better for the daughter which she brings forth than to save it from all these troubles, and deliver it from this slavery, worse than death? I say again, Father, would to God my mother had made me feel her kindness by burying me as soon as I was born! Then would not this heart have had now so much to feel, nor these eyes so much to weep for.»

Here, says Gumilla, tears put an end to her speech: and the worst is, that all which she said, and all she would have said, if grief had allowed her to proceed, is true.—*Orinoco Illustrado*, t. ii, p. 65, ed. 1791.

Note 12, page 556, col. 1.

From the dove
They named the child Yeruti.

This is the Guarani name for the species described by Azara, t. iv, p. 130, No cccxx.

Note 13, page 559, col. 1.

What power had placed them here.

Some of the Orinoco tribes believe that their first forefathers grew upon trees.—*Gumilla*, t. i, c. 6.

The Othomacas, one of the rudest of the Orinoco tribes, suppose themselves descended from a pile of stones upon the top of a rock called Barraguan, and that they all return to stone as they came from it; so that this mass of rock is composed of their forefathers. Therefore, though they bury their dead, within the year they take off their heads and carry them to the holes in the rock.—*Gumilla*, t. i. c. 6.

These are the odd people who always for a first marriage give a girl to an old man, and a youth to an old woman. Polygamy is not in use among them; and they say, that if the young people came together there could be no good household management.—*Gumilla*, t. i, c. 12.

P. Labbé (*Lett. Edif.* t. viii, p. 180, edit. 1781) speaks

of a tribe on the N. bank of the Plata who put their women to death when they were thirty years old, thinking they had then lived long enough. I have not seen this custom mentioned by any other writer, nor do I believe that it can possibly have existed.

Note 14, page 559, col. 1.
And Father was his name.

Tupa. It is the Tupi and Guarini name for Father, for Thunder, and for the Supreme Being.

The Patagones call the Supreme Being *Soychu,* a word which is said to express that which cannot be seen, which is worthy of all veneration, and which is out of the world. They may thus explain the word; but it cannot contain this meaning; it is a definition of what they mean, and apparently not such as a savage would give. The dead they call *Soychuhet;* they who are with God, and out of the world.

The Puelches, Picunches, and Moluches have no name for God. Their prayers are made to the sun, whom they regard as the giver of all good. A Jesuit once admonished them to worship that God who created all things, and this orb among the rest; but they replied, they had never known any thing greater or better than the sun.—*Dobrizhoffer,* t. ii, p. 100.

The most remarkable mode of superstition I remember to have met with, is one which is mentioned by the Bishop of Santa Marta, in his History of the Nuevo Reyno de Granada. He tells us, that « the Pijaos of the Nuevo Reyno worshipped nothing visible or invisible, except the spirits of those whom they killed for the purpose of deifying them. For they thought that if an innocent person were put to death he became a god, and in that capacity would be grateful to those who were the authors of his apotheosis. For this reason they used to catch strangers and kill them; not thinking one of their own horde, or of their enemies, could be esteemed innocent, and therefore fitting. A woman or a child would do. But after a few months they held it necessary to make a new god, the old one either having lost his power, or changed his place, or perhaps by that time discharged himself of his debt of gratitude.—*Piedrahita,* p. 12.

Note 15, page 559, col. 2.
And once there was a way to that good land,
For in mid earth a wonderous tree there grew.

« Los Mocobis fingian un Arbol, que en su idioma llamaban Nalliagdigua, de altura tan desmedida que llegaba desde la tierra al cielo. Por él de rama en rama ganando siempre mayor elevacion subian las almas á pescar de un rio y lagunas muy grandes, que abundaban de pescado regaladísimo. Pero un dia que el alma de una vieja no pudo pescar cosa alguna, y los pescadores la negaron el socorro de una limosna para su mantenimiento, se irritó tanto contra la nacion Mocobi que, transfigurada en Capiguara tomó el exercicio de roer el Arbol por donde subian al cielo, y no desistió hasta derribarlo en tierra con increible sentimiento y daño irreparable de toda la nacion.»

This legend is contained in a manuscript history of Paraguay, the Rio de la Plata, and Tucuman. For the use of the first volume (a transcript of which is in my possession), I am beholden, as for other civilities of the same kind, to Mr Thomas Kinder. This portion of the work contains a good account of the native tribes;

the second volume contains the historical part; but when Mr Kinder purchased the one at Buenos Ayres, the other was on its way to the United States, having been borrowed from the owner by an American, and not returned. Fortunately the subjects of the two volumes are so distinct that each may be considered as a complete work; and I have referred to that which I possess, in the history of Brazil, by the title of *Noticias del Paraguay, etc.*

Note 16, page 560, col. 1.
The land of souls.

Many of the Indian speculations respecting the condition of souls in a future state are given in the History of Brazil. A description of a Keltic Island of the Blessed, as drest up by Ossian Macpherson, may be found in the notes to Madoc. A Tonga one is thus described in the very curious and valuable work of Mr Mariner.

« The Tonga people universally and positively believe in the existence of a large island lying at a considerable distance to the N. W. of their own islands, which they consider to be the place of residence of their gods, and of the souls of their nobles and mataboohes. This island is supposed to be much larger than all their own islands put together; to be well stocked with all kinds of useful and ornamental plants always in a state of high perfection, and always bearing the richest fruits and the most beautiful flowers, according to their respective natures; that when these fruits or flowers are plucked others immediately occupy their place, and that the whole atmosphere is filled with the most delightful fragrance that the imagination can conceive, proceeding from these immortal plants. The island is also well stocked with the most beautiful birds of all imaginable kinds, as well as with abundance of hogs, all of which are immortal, unless they are killed to provide food for the hotooas or gods; but the moment a hog or bird is killed, another living hog or bird immediately comes into existence to supply its place, the same as with the fruits and flowers; and this, as far as they know or suppose, is the only mode of propagation of plants and animals. The island of Bolotoo is supposed to be so far off as to render it dangerous for their canoes to attempt going there; and it is supposed moreover that even if they were to succeed in reaching so far, unless it happened to be the particular will of the gods, they would be sure to miss it. They give, however, an account of a Tonga canoe, which, in her return from the Feejee islands a long time ago, was driven by stress of wheater to Bolotoo : ignorant of the place where they were, and being much in want of provisions, and seeing the country abound in all sorts of fruit, the crew landed, and proceeded to pluck some bread-fruit, but to their unspeakable astonishment they could no more lay hold of it than if it were a shadow. They walked through the trunks of the trees, and passed through the substance of the houses (which were built like those of Tonga), without feeling any resistance. They at length saw some of the Hotooas, who passed through the substance of their bodies as if there was nothing there. The Hotooas recommended them to go away immediately, as they had no proper food for them, and promised them a fair wind and a speedy passage. They accordingly put directly to sea, and in two days, sailing with the utmost velocity, they arrived at Hamoa, (the Navigator's Island,) at which place they wanted to touch before they got to Tonga. Having remained at Hamoa two or three days, they sailed for Tonga, where they arrived with great speed; but in the course of a few days they all died, not as a punishment for having been at Bolotoo, but as a natural consequence, the air of Bolotoo, as it were, infecting mortal bodies with speedy death.»

In Yucatan their notion of the happy after death was, that they rested in a delightful land, under the shade of a great tree, where there was plenty of food and drink.—*Herrera*, iv, 10, n.

The Austral tribes believe that the dead live in some region under the earth, where they have their tents, and hunt the souls of ostriches.—*Dobrizh.* ii, 295.

The Persians have a great reverence for large old trees, thinking that the souls of the happy delight to dwell in them; and for this reason they call them *pir*, which signifies an old man, by which name they also designate the supposed inhabitant. Pietro Della Valle describes a prodigious tree of this character, in the hollow of which tapers were always kept burning to the honour of the *Pir*. He pitched his tent under its boughs twice; once with his wife when on his way to embark for Europe, and again when returning with her corpse. The passage wherein he speaks of this last night's lodging is very affecting. We soon forgive this excellent traveller for his coxcombry, take an interest in his domestic affairs, and part with him at last as with an old friend.

Note 17, page 560, col. 1.

Who thought
From death, as from living foe, to fly.

An opinion of this kind has extended to people in a much higher grade of society than the American Indians.

« After this DEATH appeared in Dwaraka in a human shape, the colour of his skin being black and yellow, his head close shorn, and all his limbs distorted. He placed himself at men's doors, so that all those who saw him shuddered with apprehension, and became even as dead men from mere affright. Every person to whose door he came shot an arrow at him, and the moment the arrow quitted the bow-string they saw the spectre no more, nor knew which way he was gone.»—*Life of Creeshna.*

This is a poetical invention; but such an invention as formed a popular belief in Greece, if M. Pouqueville may be trusted.

« The *Evil Eye*, the *Cacodæmon*, has been seen wandering over the roofs of the houses. Who can dare to doubt this? It was in the form of a withered old woman, covered with funeral rags: she was heard to call by their names those who are to be cut off from the number of the living. Nocturnal concerts, voices murmuring amid the silence of the darkest nights, have been heard in the air; phantoms have been seen wandering about in solitary places, in the streets, in the markets; dogs have howled with the most dismal and melancholy tone, and their cries have been repeated by the echoes along the desert streets. It is when such things happen, as I was told very seriously by an inhabitant of Nauplia di Romania, that great care must be taken not to answer if you should be called during the night, if you hear symphonies bury yourself in the bed clothes, and do not listen to them; it is the *old woman*, it is the plague itself that knocks at your door.»—*Pouqueville*, 189.

The Patagones and other Austral tribes attribute all diseases to an evil spirit. Their conjurors therefore beat drums by the patient, which have hideous figures painted upon them, thinking thus to frighten away the cause. If he dies, his relations endeavour to take vengeance upon those who pretended to cure him; but if one of the chiefs dies, all the conjurors are slain, unless they can save themselves by flight.—*Dobrizhoffer*, t. ii. 286.

Note 18, page 560, col. 2.

They dragged the dying out.

The Austral tribes sometimes bury the dying, thinking it an act of mercy thus to shorten their sufferings. (*Dobrizh.* t. ii, 286.) But in general this practice, which extends widely among savages, arises from the selfish feeling assigned in the text. Superstition, without this selfishness, produces a practice of the same kind, though not absolutely as brutal, in the East. « The *moorda* or *chultries* are small huts in which a Hindoo, when given over by his physicians, is deposited, and left alone to expire, and be carried off by the sacred flood.»—*Cruso, in Forbes*, iv, 99.

« When there is no hope of recovery, the patient is generally removed from the bed, and laid on a platform of fresh earth, either out of doors, or prepared purposely in some adjoining room or viranda, that he may there breathe his last. In a physical sense, this removal at so critical a period must be often attended with fatal consequences; though perhaps not quite so decisive as that of exposing an aged parent or a dying friend on the banks of the Ganges. I now only mention the circumstances as forming part of the Hindoo religious system. After having expired upon the earth, the body is carried to the water-side, and washed with many ceremonies. It is then laid upon the funeral pile, that the fire may have a share of the victim: the ashes are finally scattered in the air, and fall upon the water.

« During the funeral ceremony, which is solemn and affecting, the Brahmins address the respective elements in words to the following purport; although there may be a different mode of performing these religious rites in other parts of Hindostan.

« O Earth! to thee we commend our brother; of thee he was formed; by thee he was sustained; and unto thee he now returns!

« O Fire! thou hadst a claim in our brother; during his life he subsisted by thy influence in nature; to thee we commit his body; thou emblem of purity, may his spirit be purified on entering a new state of existence.

« O Air! while the breath of life continued our brother respired by thee; his last breath is now departed; to thee we yield him.

« O Water! thou didst contribute to the life of our brother; thou wert one of his sustaining elements. His remains are now dispersed; receive thy share of him, who has now taken an everlasting flight!»—*Forbes's Oriental Memoirs*, iii, 12.

Note 19, page 561, col. 1.

Her feet upon the crescent moon were set.

This is a common representation of the Virgin, from the Revelation.

Virgem de Sol vestida, e dos seus raios
Claros envolta toda, e das Estrellas
Coroada, e debaixo os pés a Lua.

Francisco de Sa de Miranda.

These lines are highly esteemed by the Portuguese critics.

Note 20, page 561, col. 1.

Severe he was, and in his anger dread,
Yet alway at his Mother's will grew mild,
So well did he obey that Maiden undefiled.—

« How hath the conceit of Christ's humiliation here on earth, of his dependance on his *mother* during the time of his formation and birth, and of his subjection to her in his infancy, brought forth preposterous and more than heathenish transformations of his glory in the superstitious daughters of the idolatrous church! They cannot conceive Christ as king, unless they acknowledge her as queen dowager of heaven: her title of Lady is æquiparant to his title of Lord: her authority for some purposes held as great, her bowels of compunction (towards the weaker sex especially) more tender. And as the heathens frame gods suitable to their own desire, soliciting them most (though otherwise less potent) whom they conceive to be most favourable to their present suits: so hath the blessed Virgin throughout the *Romish Church* obtained (what she never sought) the entire monopoly of women's prayers in their travails; as if her presence at other's distressful labours (for she herself, by their doctrine, brought forth her first born and only son without pain,) had wrought in her a truer feeling or tenderer touch, than the high priest of their souls can have of their infirmities; or as if she would use more faithful and effectual intercession with her son, than he can or will do with his Father. Some in our times, out of the weakness of their sex, matching with the impetuousness of their adulterous and disloyal zeal, have in this kind been so impotently outrageous as to intercept others' supplications directed to Christ, and *superscribe* them in this form unto his mother; *Blessed Lady,* command thy son to hear this woman's prayers, and send her deliverance! These, and the like speeches, have moved some good women, in other points tainted rather with superstition than preciseness, to dispense with the law of secrecy, seldom violated in their parliaments; and I know not whether I should attribute it to their courage or stupidity, not to be more affrighted at such blasphemies, than at some monstrous and prodigious birth. This and the like inbred inclinations unto superstition, in the rude and uninstructed people, are more artificially set forward by the fabulous *Roman Legendary* and his *Limner,* than the like were in the heathen, by heathen poets and painters. »—*Dr Thomas Jackson's Works,* vol. i, 1007.

Note 21, page 562, col. 1.
Tyranny of the Spaniards.

The consumption of the Indians in the Paraguay tea-trade, and the means taken by the Jesuits for cultivating the Caa tree, are described by Dobrizhoffer.

The Encomenderos compelled the unhappy people whom they found living where they liked, to settle in such places as were most convenient for the work in which they were now to be compulsorily employed. All their work was task-work, imposed with little moderation, and exacted without mercy. This tyranny extended to the women and children, and as all the Spa-

niards, the officer of justice as well as the Encomenderos were implicated in it, the Indians had none to whom they could look for protection. Even the Institutions of Christianity, by which the Spanish government hoped to better the temporal condition of its new subjects, were made the occasion of new grievances and more intolerable oppression. For as the Indians were legally free,—free, therefore, to marry where they pleased, and the wife was to follow the husband, every means was taken to prevent a marriage between two Indians who belonged to different *Repartimientos,* and the interest of the master counteracted all the efforts of the priest. The Spanish women are said to have exceeded their husbands in cruelty on such occasions, and to have instigated them to the most violent and iniquitous measures, that they might not lose their female attendants. The consequence was, that profligacy of manners among the Indians was rather encouraged than restrained, as it is now in the English sugar islands, where the planter is not a religious man.—*Lozano,* l. 1, sect. 3, 6, 7.

Note 22, page 564, col. 2.

And she in many an emulous essay,
At length into a descent of her own
Had blended all their notes.

An extract from a journal written in Switzerland will be the best comment upon the description in these stanzas, which indeed were probably suggested by my recollections of the Staubach.

« While we were at the waterfall, some half score peasants, chiefly women and girls, assembled just out of reach of the spray, and set up—surely the wildest chorus that ever was heard by human ears,—a song not of articulate sounds, but in which the voice was used as a mere instrument of music, more flexible than any which art could produce,—sweet, powerful, and thrilling beyond description. »

It will be seen by the subjoined sonnet of Mr Wordsworth's, who visited this spot three years after me, that he was not less impressed than *I* had been by this wild concert of voices.

On approaching the Staub-bach, Lauterbrunnen.

Tracks let me follow far from human kind
Which these illusive greetings may not reach;
Where only Nature tunes her voice to teach
Careless pursuits, and raptures unconfined.
No Mermaid warbles (to allay the wind
That drives some vessel towards a dangerous beach,)
More thrilling melodies! no caverned Witch
Chaunting a love-spell, ever intertwined
Notes shrill and wild with art more musical!
Alas! that from the lips of abject Want
And Idleness in tatters mendicant
They should proceed—enjoyment to enthral,
And with regret and useless pity haunt
This bold, this pure, this sky-born Waterfall!

« The vocal powers of these musical beggars (says Mr Wordsworth) may seem to be exaggerated; but this wild and savage air was utterly unlike any sounds I had ever heard; the notes reached me from a distance, and on what occasion they were sung I could not guess, only they seemed to belong in some way or other to the waterfall; and reminded me of religious services chaunted to streams and fountains in Pagan times. »

Note 23, page 565, col. 1.
Some dim presage.

Upon this subject an old Spanish romancer speaks

thus:—« Aunque hombre no sabe lo de adelante como ha de venir, el espíritu lo siente, y ante que venga se duele dello: y de aqui se levantaron los grandes sospiros que hombres dan á sobrevienta no pensando en ningun cosa, como á muchos acaesce, que aquel que el sospiro echa de sí, el espíritu es que siente el mal que ha de ser.»—*Chronica del Rey D. Rodrigo*, p. ii c. 171.

Note 24, page 566, col. 2.

Across her shoulders was a hammock flung.

Pinkerton, in his Geography (vol. ii. p. 535. n. 3d edit.) says, that nets are sometimes worn among the Guaranis instead of clothes, and refers to this very story in proof of his assertion. I believe he had no other ground for it. He adds that « perhaps they were worn only to keep off the flies ;" as if those blood-suckers were to be kept off by open net-work!

We owe something, however, to the person who introduces us to a good and valuable book, and I am indebted originally to Mr Pinkerton for my knowledge of Dobrizhoffer. He says of him, when referring to the *Historia de Abiponibus*, « the lively singularity of the old man's Latin is itself an amusement ; and though sometimes garrulous, he is redundant in authentic and curious information. His work, though bearing a restricted title, is the best account yet published of the whole viceroyalty of La Plata.»

Note 25, page 567, col. 1.

St Joachin.

The legend of his visit to Limbo is given here in a translated extract from that very curious work, the Life of the Virgin Mary, as related by herself to Sister Maria de Jesus, Abbess of the Franciscan Convent de la Inmaculada Conception at Agreda, and published with the sanction of all the ecclesiastical authorities in Spain.

After some conversation between the Almighty and the Virgin, at that time three years and a half old, the Franciscan confessor, who was the accomplice of the abbess in this blasphemous imposture, proceeds thus :—

« The Most High received this morning sacrifice from his tender spouse, Mary the most holy, and with a pleased countenance said to her, 'Thou art beautiful in thy thoughts, O Prince's daughter, my dove, and my beloved ! I admit thy desires, which are agreeable to my eyes; and it is my will, in fulfilment of them, that thou shouldest understand the time draws nigh, when by my divine appointment, thy father Joachin must pass from this mortal life to the life immortal and eternal. His death shall be short, and he will soon rest in peace, and be placed with the Saints in Limbo, awaiting the redemption of the whole human race.' This information from the Lord neither disturbed nor troubled the regal breast of Mary, the Princess of Heaven ; yet as the love of children to their parents is a debt due by nature, and that love in all its perfection existed in this most holy child, a natural grief at losing her most holy father, Joachin, whom as a daughter she devoutly loved, could not fail to be resented. The tender and sweet child, Mary, felt a movement of grief compatible with the serenity of her magnanimous heart: and acting with greatness in every thing, following both grace and nature, she made a fervent prayer for her father Joachin ; she besought the Lord, that, as the mighty and true God, he would look upon him in the

hour of his happy death, and defend him from the Devil, especially in that hour, and preserve him, and appoint him in the number of his elect, as one who in his life had confessed and magnified his holy and adorable name. And the more to oblige his Majesty, the most faithful daughter offered to endure for her father, the most holy Joachin, all that the Lord might ordain.

« His Majesty accepted this petition, and consoled the divine child, assuring her that he would be with her father as a merciful and compassionate remunerator of those who love and serve him, and that he would place him with the Patriarchs, Abraham, Isaac, and Jacob ; and he prepared her again to receive and suffer other troubles. Eight days before the death of the holy Patriarch Joachin, Mary the most holy had other advices from the Lord, declaring the day and hour in which he was to die, as in fact it occurred, only six months after our Queen went to reside in the temple. When her Highness had received this information from the Lord, she besought the twelve angels, (who, I have before said, were those whom St John names in the Revelation,) that they would be with her father Joachin in his sickness, and comfort him, and console him in it; and thus they did. And for the last hour of his transit she sent all those of her guard, and besought the Lord that he would make them manifest to her father for his greater consolation. The Most High granted this, and in every thing fulfilled the desire of his elect, unique, and perfect one : and the great Patriarch and happy Joachin saw the thousand holy angels who guarded his daughter Maria, at whose petition and desire the grace of the Almighty superabounded, and by his command the Angels said to Joachin these things :—

« ' Man of God, the Most High and Mighty is thy eternal salvation, and he sends thee from his holy place the necessary and timely assistance for thy soul ! Mary, thy daughter, sends us to be with thee at this hour, in which thou hast to pay to thy Creator the debt of natural death. She is thy most faithful and powerful intercessor with the Most High, in whose name and peace depart thou from this world with consolation and joy, that he hath made thee parent of so blessed a daughter. And although his incomprehensible Majesty in his serene wisdom hath not till now manifested to thee the sacrament and dignity in which he will constitute thy daughter, it is his pleasure that thou shouldest know it now, to the intent that thou mayest magnify him and praise him, and that at such news the jubilee of thy spirit may be joined with the grief and natural sadness of death. Mary thy daughter and our Queen, is the one chosen by the arm of the Omnipotent, that the Divine Word may in her clothe himself with flesh and with the human form. She is to be the happy mother of the Messiah, blessed among women, superior to all creatures, and inferior only to God himself. Thy most happy daughter is to be the repairer of what the human race lost by the first fall; and the high mountain whereon the new law of grace is to be formed and established. Therefore, as thou leavest now in the world its restauratrix and daughter, by whom God prepares for it the fitting remedy, depart thou in joy, and the Lord will bless thee from Zion, and will give thee a place among the Saints, that thou mayest attain to the sight and possession of the happy Jerusalem.'

« While the holy Angels spake these words to Joachin, St Anna his wife was present, standing by the pillow of his bed; and she heard, and by divine permission understood them. At the same time the holy Patriarch Joachin lost his speech, and entering upon the common way of all flesh, began to die, with a marvellous struggle between the delight of such joyful tidings and the pain of death. During this conflict with his interior powers, many and fervent acts of divine love, of faith, and adoration, and praise, and thanksgiving, and humiliation, and other virtues, did he heroically perform: and thus absorbed in the new knowledge of so divine a mystery, he came to the end of his natural life, dying the precious death of the Saints. His most holy spirit was carried by the Angels to the Limbo of the Holy Fathers and of the Just: and for a new consolation and light in the long night wherein they dwelt, the Most High ordered that the soul of the holy Patriarch Joachin should be the new Paranymph and Ambassador of his Great Majesty, for announcing to all that congregation of the Just, how the day of eternal light had now dawned, and the day-break was born, Mary, the most holy daughter of Joachin and of Anna, from whom should be born the Sun of Divinity, Christ, Restorer of the whole human race. The Holy Fathers and the Just in Limbo heard these tidings, and in their jubilee composed new hymns of thanksgiving to the Most High.

«This happy death of the Patriarch St Joachin occurred (as I have before said), half a year after his daughter Mary the most holy entered the Temple; and when she was at the tender age of three and a half, she was thus left in the world without a natural father. The age of the patriarch was sixty and nine years, distributed and divided thus: at the age of forty-six years he took St Anna to wife; twenty years after this marriage Mary the most holy was born; and the three years and a half of her Highness's age make sixty-nine and a half, a few days more or less.

«The holy Patriarch and father of our Queen being dead, the holy Angels of her guard returned incontinently to her presence, and gave her notice of all that had occurred in her father's transit. Forthwith the most prudent child solicited with prayers for the consolation of her mother St Anna, intreating that the Lord would, as a father, direct and govern her in the solitude wherein, by the loss of her husband Joachin, she was left. St Anna herself sent also news of his death, which was first communicated to the Mistress of our divine Princess, that in imparting it she might console her. The Mistress did this, and the most wise child heard her, with all composure and dissimulation, but with the patience and the modesty of a Queen; but she was not ignorant of the event which her Mistress related to her as news.»—*Mistica Ciudad de Dios*, par. 1, l. 2, c. 16, § 664—669. Madrid, 1744.

It was in the middle of the seventeenth century that the work from which this extract is translated was palmed upon the Spaniards as a new revelation. Gross and blasphemous as the imposture is, the work was still current when I procured my copy, about twenty years ago; and it is not included in the Spanish Index Expurgatorius of 1790, the last, (I believe), which was published, and which is now before me.

Note 26, page 571, col. 2.

He could not tarry here.

A case precisely of the same kind is mentioned by Mr Mariner. «A young Chief at Tonga, a very handsome man, was inspired by the ghost of a woman in Bolotoo, who had fallen in love with him. On a sudden he felt himself low-spirited, and shortly afterwards fainted away. When he came to himself he was very ill, and was taken accordingly to the house of a priest. As yet he did not know who it was that inspired him, but the priest informed him that it was a woman of Bolotoo, mentioning her name, who had died some years before, and who wished him now to die, that he might be near her. He accordingly died in two days. The Chief said he suspected this from the dreams he had had at different times, when the figure of a woman came to him in the night. Mr Mariner was with the sick Chief three or four times during his illness, and heard the priest foretell his death, and the occasion of it.»—*Mariner.*

A Vision of Judgment.

TO THE KING.

SIR,

ONLY to Your Majesty can the present publication with propriety be addressed. As a tribute to the sacred memory of our late revered Sovereign, it is my duty to present it to Your Majesty's notice; and to whom could an experiment, which, perhaps, may be considered hereafter as of some importance in English Poetry, be so fitly inscribed, as to the Royal and munificent Patron of science, art, and literature?

We owe much to the House of Brunswick; but to none of that illustrious House more than to Your Majesty, under whose government the military renown of Great Britain has been carried to the highest point of glory. From that pure glory there has been nothing to detract; the success was not more splendid than the cause was good; and the event was deserved by the generosity, the justice, the wisdom, and the magnanimity of the counsels which prepared it. The same perfect integrity has been manifested in the whole administration of public affairs. More has been done than was ever before attempted, for mitigating the evils incident to our stage of society; for imbuing the rising race with those sound principles of religion on which the welfare of states has its only secure foundation; and for opening new regions to the redundant enterprise and industry of the people. Under Your Majesty's government, the Metropolis is rivalling in beauty those cities which it has long surpassed in greatness: sciences, arts, and letters are flourishing beyond all former example; and the last triumph of nautical discovery and of the British flag, which had so often been essayed in vain, has been accomplished. The brightest portion of British history will be that which records the improvements, the works, and the achievements of the Georgian Age.

That Your Majesty may long continue to reign over a free and prosperous people, and that the blessings of the happiest form of government which has ever been raised by human wisdom under the favour of Divine Providence may, under Your Majesty's protection, be transmitted unimpaired to posterity, is the prayer of

Your MAJESTY'S

Most dutiful Subject and Servant,

ROBERT SOUTHEY.

PREFACE.

I.

HAVING long been of opinion that an English metre might be constructed in imitation of the ancient hexameter, which would be perfectly consistent with the character of our language, and capable of great richness, variety, and strength, I have now made the experiment. It will have some disadvantages to contend with, both among learned and unlearned readers; among the former especially, because, though they may divest themselves of all prejudice against an innovation, which has generally been thought impracticable, and may even be disposed to regard the attempt favourably, nevertheless they will, from inveterate association, be continually reminded of rules which are inapplicable to our tongue; and looking for quantity where emphasis only ought to be expected, will perhaps less easily be reconciled to the measure, than those persons who consider it simply as it is. To the one class it is necessary that I should explain the nature of the verse; to the other, the principle of adaption which has been followed.

First, then, to the former, who, in glancing over these long lines, will perceive that they have none of the customary characteristics of English versification, being neither marked by rhyme, nor by any certain number of syllables, nor by any regular recurrence of emphasis throughout the verse. Upon closer observation, they will find that (with a very few exceptions), there is a regular recurrence of emphasis in the last five syllables of every line, the first and the fourth of those syllables being accented, the others not. These five syllables form two of the feet by which the verse is measured, and which are called dactyls and trochees, the dactyl consisting of one long syllable and two short ones, as exemplified in the name of Wellington; the trochee, of one long and one short, as exemplified in the name of Nelson. Of such feet, there are six in every verse. The four first are disposed according to the judgment and convenience of the writer; that is, they may be all dactyls or all trochees, or any mixture of both in any arrangement: but the fifth is always a dactyl, and the sixth always a trochee, except in some rare instances, when, for the sake of variety, or of some particular effect, a trochee is admitted in the fifth place. One more remark will suffice for this prelimi-

nary explanation. These feet are not constituted each by a separate word, but are made up of one or more, or of parts of words, the end of one and the beginning of another, as may happen. A verse of the Psalms, originally pointed out by Harris of Salisbury, as a natural and perfect hexameter, will exemplify what has been said :

Why do the | heathen | rage, and the | people I– | –magine a | vain thing?

This, I think, will make the general construction of the metre perfectly intelligible to those persons who may be unacquainted with the rules of Latin versification; those especially who are still to be called gentle readers, in this ungentle age. But it is not necessary to understand the principle upon which the verse is constructed, in order to feel the harmony and power of a metrical composition;—if it were, how few would be capable of enjoying poetry! In the present case, any one who reads a page of these hexameters aloud, with just that natural regard to emphasis which the sense of the passage indicates, and the usual pronunciation of the words requires, will perceive the rhythm, and find no more difficulty in giving it its proper effect, than in reading blank verse. This has often been tried, and with invariable success. If, indeed, it were not so, the fault would be in the composition, not in the measure.

The learned reader will have perceived by what has already been said, that in forming this English measure in imitation, rather than upon the model of the ancient hexameter, the trochee has been substituted for the spondee, as by the Germans. This substitution is rendered necessary by the nature of our pronunciation, which is so rapid, that I believe the whole vocabulary of the language does not afford a single instance of a genuine native[1] spondee. The spondee, of course, is not excluded from the verse; and where it occurs, the effect, in general, is good. This alteration was necessary; but it is not the only one which, upon mature consideration and fair trial, it has been deemed expedient to make. If every line were to begin with a long syllable, the measure would presently appear exotic and forced, as being directly opposite to the general character of all our dignified metres, and indeed to the genius of the English language. Therefore the license has been taken of using any foot of two or three syllables at the beginning of a line; and sometimes, though less frequently, in the second, third, or fourth place. The metre, thus constructed, bears the same analogy to the ancient hexameter that our ten-syllable or heroic line does to iambic verse: iambic it is called, and it is so in its general movement; but it admits of many other feet, and would, in fact, soon become insupportably monotonous without their frequent intermixture.

II.

Twenty years ago, when the rhythmical romance of Thalaba was sent from Portugal to the press, I requested, in the preface to that poem, that the author

[1] And only one of foreign derivation, which is the word Egypt. Some readers, who have never practised metrical composition in their own language, may perhaps doubt this, and suppose that such words as *twilight* and *evening*, are spondaic; but they only appear so when they are pronounced singly, the last syllable then hanging upon the tongue, and dwelling on the ear, like the last stroke of the clock. Used in combination, they become pure trochees.

might not be supposed to prefer the rhythm in which it was written, abstractedly considered, to the regular blank verse, the noblest measure, in his judgment, of which our admirable language is capable : it was added, that the measure which was there used, had, in that instance, been preferred, because it suited the character of the poem, being, as it were, the Arabesque ornament of an Arabian tale. Notwithstanding this explicit declaration, the duncery of that day attacked me as if I had considered the measure of Thalaba to be in itself essentially and absolutely better than blank verse. The duncery of this day may probably pursue the same course on the present occasion. With that body I wage no war, and enter into no explanations. But to the great majority of my readers, who will take up the book without malevolence, and having a proper sense of honour in themselves, will believe the declarations of a writer whose veracity they have no reason to doubt, I will state what are the defects, and what the advantages, of the metre which is here submitted to their judgment, as they appear to me after this fair experiment of its powers.

It is not a legitimate inference, that because the hexameter has been successfully introduced in the German language, it can be naturalized as well in English. The English is not so well adapted for it, because it does not abound in like manner with polysyllabic words. The feet, therefore, must too frequently be made up of monosyllables, and of distinct words, whereby the verse is resolved and decomposed into its component feet, and the feet into their component syllables, instead of being articulated and inosculated throughout, as in the German, still more in the Greek, and most in the Latin measure. This is certainly a great defect. [1] From the same cause the *cæsura* generally coincides with a pause in the sentence; but, though this breaks the continuity of the verse, it ought perhaps rather to be considered as an advantage : for the measure, like blank verse, thus acquires greater variety. It may possibly be objected, that the four first feet are not metrical enough in their effect, and the two last too much so. I do not feel the objection; but it has been advanced by one, whose opinion upon any question, and especially upon a question of poetry, would make me distrust my own, where it happened to be different. Lastly, the double-ending may be censured as double rhymes used to be; but that objection belongs to the duncery.

On the other hand, the range of the verse being from thirteen syllables to seventeen, it derives from that range an advantage in the union of variety with regularity, which is peculiar to itself. The capability which is thus gained, may perhaps be better appreciated by a few readers from their own sense of power, than it is exemplified in this experiment.

[1] It leads also to this inconvenience, that the English line greatly exceeds the ancient one in literal length, so that it is actually too long for any page, if printed in types of the ordinary proportion to the size of the book, whatever that may be. The same inconvenience was formerly felt in that fine measure of the Elizabethan age, the seven-footed couplet; which, to the diminution of its powers, was, for that reason, divided into quatrains (the pause generally falling upon the eighth syllable), and then converted into the common ballad stanza. The hexameter cannot be thus divided, and therefore must generally look neither like prose nor poetry. This is noticed as merely a dissight, and of no moment, our poetry not being like that of the Chinese, addressed to the eye instead of the ear.

I do not, however, present the English hexameter as something better than our established metres, but as something different, and which therefore, for that reason, may sometimes advantageously be used. Take our blank verse, for all in all, in all its gradations, from the elaborate rhythm of Milton, down to its loosest structure in the early dramatists, and I believe that there is no measure comparable to it, either in our own or in any other language, for might and majesty, and flexibility and compass. And this is affirmed, not as the predilection of a young writer, or the preference of one inexperienced in the difficulties of composition, but as an opinion formed and confirmed during the long and diligent study, and the long and laborious practice of the art. But I am satisfied also that the English hexameter is a legitimate and good measure, with which our literature ought to be enriched. « I first adventure ; follow me who list! »

III.

I am well aware that the public are peculiarly intolerant of such innovations; not less so than the populace are of any foreign fashion, whether of foppery or convenience. Would that this literary intolerance were under the influence of a saner judgment, and regarded the morals more than the manner of a composition ; the spirit rather than the form ! Would that it were directed against those monstrous combinations of horrors and mockery, lewdness and impiety, with which English poetry has, in our days, first been polluted! For more than half a century English literature had been distinguished by its moral purity, the effect, and in its turn the cause, of an improvement in national manners. A father might, without apprehension of evil, have put into the hands of his children any book which issued from the press, if it did not bear, either in its title-page or frontispiece, manifest signs that it was intended as furniture for the brothel. There was no danger in any work which bore the name of a respectable publisher, or was to be procured at any respectable bookseller's. This was particularly the case with regard to our poetry. It is now no longer so; and woe to those by whom the offence cometh! The greater the talents of the offender, the greater is his guilt, and the more enduring will be his shame. Whether it be that the laws are in themselves unable to abate an evil of this magnitude, or whether it be that they are remissly administered, and with such injustice that the celebrity of an offender serves as a privilege whereby he obtains impunity, individuals are bound to consider that such pernicious works would neither be published nor written, if they were discouraged as they might, and ought to be, by public feeling ; every person, therefore, who purchases such books, or admits them into his house, promotes the mischief, and thereby, as far as in him lies, becomes an aider and abettor of the crime.

The publication of a lascivious book is one of the worst offences which can be committed against the well-being of society. It is a sin, to the consequences of which no limits can be assigned, and those consequences no after repentance in the writer can counteract. Whatever remorse of conscience he may feel when his hour comes (and come it must!) will be of no avail. The poignancy of a death-bed repentance cannot cancel one copy of the thousands which are sent abroad;

and as long as it continues to be read, so long is he the pander of posterity, and so long is he heaping up guilt upon his soul in perpetual accumulation.

These remarks are not more severe than the offence deserves, even when applied to those immoral writers who have not been conscious of any evil intention in their writings, who would acknowledge a little levity, a little warmth of colouring, and so forth, in that sort of language with which men gloss over their favourite vices, and deceive themselves. What then should be said of those for whom the thoughtlessness and inebriety of wanton youth can no longer be pleaded, but who have written in sober manhood and with deliberate purpose? —Men of diseased hearts and depraved imaginations,[1] who, forming a system of opinions to suit their own unhappy course of conduct, have rebelled against the holiest ordinances of human society, and hating that revealed religion which, with all their efforts and bravadoes, they are unable entirely to disbelieve, labour to make others as miserable as themselves, by infecting them with a moral virus that eats into the soul! The school which they have set up may properly be called the Satanic school; for though their productions breathe the spirit of Belial in their lascivious parts, and the spirit of Moloch in those loathsome images of atrocities and horrors which they delight to represent, they are more especially characterized by a Satanic spirit of pride and audacious impiety, which still betrays the wretched feeling of hopelessness wherewith it is allied.

This evil is political as well as moral, for indeed moral and political evils are inseparably connected. Truly has it been affirmed by one of our ablest and clearest reasoners,[2] that «the destruction of governments may be proved and deduced from the general corruption of the subjects' manners, as a direct and natural cause thereof, by a demonstration as certain as any in the mathematics.» There is no maxim more frequently enforced by Machiavelli, than that where the manners of a people are generally corrupted, there the government cannot long subsist,—a truth which all history exemplifies; and there is no means whereby that corruption can be so surely and rapidly diffused, as by poisoning the waters of literature.

Let rulers of the state look to this, in time! But, to use the words of South, if « our physicians think the best way of *curing* a disease is to *pamper* it,—the Lord

[1] Summi poetæ in omni poetarum sæculo viri fuerunt probi : in nostris id vidimus et videmus; neque alius est error a veritate longiùs quàm magna ingenia magnis necessario corrumpi vitiis. Secundo plerique posthabeant primum, hi malignitate, illi ignorantiâ : et quum aliquem inveniunt styli morumque vitiis notatum, nec inficetum tamen nec in libris edendis parcum, eum stipant, prædicant, occupant, amplectuntur. Si mores aliquantulùm vellet corrigere, si stylum curare paululùm, si fervido ingenio temperare, si morem tantillum interponere, tàm ingens nescio quid et verè ac epicum, quadraginta annos natus, procuderat. Ignorant verò febriculis non indicari vires, impatientiam ab imbecillitate non differre; ignorant a levi homine et inconstante multa fortassè scribi posse plus quàm mediocria, nihil compositum, arduum, æternum.

SAVAGIUS LANDOR, *De Cultu atque Usu Latini Sermonis.*

This essay, which is full of fine critical remarks and striking thoughts felicitously expressed, reached me from Pisa, while the proof of the present sheet was before me. Of its author (the author of Gebir and Count Julian), I will only say in this place, that, to have obtained his approbation as a poet, and possessed his friendship as a man, will be remembered among the honours of my life, when the petty enmities of this generation will be forgotten, and its ephemeral reputations will have past away.

[2] South.

in mercy prepare the kingdom to suffer, what He by miracle only can prevent!»

No apology is offered for these remarks. The subject led to them; and the occasion of introducing them was willingly taken, because it is the duty of every one, whose opinion may have any influence, to expose the drift and aim of those writers who are labouring to subvert the foundations of human virtue, and of human happiness.

IV.

Returning to the point from whence I digressed, I am aware not only that any metrical innovation which meets the eye of the reader generally provokes his displeasure, but that there prevails a particular prejudice against the introduction of hexameters in our language. The experiment, it is alleged, was tried in the Elizabethan age, and failed, though made under the greatest possible advantages of favour, being encouraged by the great patron of literature, Sir Philip Sidney, (in letters, as well as in all other accomplishments and all virtues, the most illustrious ornament of that illustrious court,) and by the Queen herself.

That attempt failed, because it was made upon a scheme which inevitably prevented its success. No principle of adaption was tried. Sidney and his followers wished to subject the English pronunciation to the rules of Latin prosody: but if it be difficult to reconcile the public to a new tune in verse, it is plainly impossible to reconcile them to a new pronunciation.[1] There was the farther obstacle of unusual and violent elisions; and, moreover, the easy and natural order of our speech was distorted by the frequent use of forced inversions, which are utterly improper in an uninflected language. Even if the subjects for the experiment had been judiciously chosen, and well composed in all other respects, these errors must have been fatal; but Sidney, whose prose is so full of imagery and felicitous expressions that he is one of our greatest poets in prose, and whose other poems contain beauties of a high order, seems to have lost all ear for rhythm, and all feeling of poetry,[2] when he was engaged in metrical experiments.

What in Sidney's hands was uncouth and difficult, was made ridiculous by Stanihurst, whose translation of the four first books of the Æneid into hexameters is one of the most portentous compositions in any language. No satire could so effectually have exposed the measure to derision. The specimens which Abraham Fraunce produced were free from Stanihurst's eccentricities, and were much less awkward and constrained than Sidney's. But the mistaken principle upon which the metre was constructed was fatal, and would have proved so even if Fraunce had possessed greater powers of thought and of diction. The failure therefore was complete,[3] and for some generations it seems to have prevented any thought of repeating the experiment.

[1] For example :
Neither be bears reverènce to a prince, nor pity to a beggar.
That to my àdvancement their wisdoms have me abased.
Well may a pastor plain ; but, alas! his plaints he not èsteemed.
òpprest with ruinoùs conceits by the help of an outcry.
Dèspair most tragicàl clause to a deadly request.
Hard like a rich marblè ; hard but a fair diamond.

[2] That the reader may not suppose I have depreciated Sidney and his followers, by imputing to the faults of their execution a failure which the nature of the metre itself might explain, I have added a few fair samples at the end of the Notes.

[3] A writer in the *Censura Literaria* (vol. iv, 386) has said, that

Goldsmith,[1] in later days, delivered an opinion in its favour, observing, that all the feet of the ancient poetry are still found in the versification of living languages, and that it is impossible the same measure, composed of the same times, should have a good effect upon the ear in one language, and a bad effect in another. He had seen, he says, several late specimens of English hexameters and sapphics, so happily composed, that they were, in all respects, as melodious and agreeable to the ear as the works of Virgil and Horace. What these specimens were I have not discovered:[2]—the sapphics may possibly have been those by Dr Watts. Proofs of the practicability of the hexameter were given about twenty years ago, by some translations from the Messiah of Klopstock, which appeared in the Monthly Magazine; and by an eclogue, entitled The Showman, printed in the second volume of the Annual Anthology. These were written by my old friend Mr William Taylor of Norwich, the translator of Bürger's Lenora:—of whom it would be difficult to say, whether he is more deservedly admired by all who know him for the variety of his talents, the richness and ingenuity of his discourse, and the liveliness of his fancy, or loved and esteemed by them for the goodness of his heart. In repeating the experiment upon a more adequate scale, and upon a subject suited to the movement, I have fulfilled one of the hopes and intentions of my early life.

hexameters were « much in vogue, owing to the pernicious example of Spenser and Gabriel Harvey.» They were never in vogue. There is no reason to believe, that Spenser ever wrote an English hexameter;—and Gabriel Harvey's example only incurred ridicule. With so little knowledge of facts, and so little regard to accuracy, are confident assertions sometimes made!

Gabriel Harvey was one of the great promoters of the attempt; and Spenser, who was his intimate friend, is believed to have sanctioned it by his opinion—certainly not by his example. That great master of versification has left only one piece which is not written in rhyme. It was printed in Davison's *Poetical Rhapsodie*, and is inserted in Warton's *Observations on the Faery Queen*, vol. ii, p. 245.—The author has called it an Iambic Elegy, but neither by any rule of quantity, or violence of accentuation, can it be reduced to iambics.

[1] « It is generally supposed,» says Goldsmith, « that the genius of the English language will not admit of Greek or Latin measure; but this, we apprehend, is a mistake owing to the prejudice of education. It is impossible that the same measure, composed of the same times, should have a good effect upon the ear in one language, and a bad effect in another. The truth is, we have been accustomed from our infancy to the numbers of English poetry, and the very sound and signification of the words dispose the ear to receive them in a similar manner; so that its disappointment must be attended with a disagreeable sensation. In imbibing the first rudiments of education, we acquire, as it were, another ear for the numbers of Greek and Latin poetry; and this being reserved entirely for the sounds and significations of the words that constitute those dead languages, will not easily accommodate itself to the sounds of our vernacular tongue, though conveyed in the same time and measure. In a word, Latin and Greek have annexed to them the ideas of the ancient measure, from which they are not easily disjoined. But we will venture to say, this difficulty might be surmounted by an effort of attention and a little practice; and, in that case, we should in time be as well pleased with English, as with Latin hexameters.»—Goldsmith's *Essays*, vol. ii, p. 265.

[2] Mr Park (*Censura Literaria*, vol. iv, 233) mentions an attempt to revive what he calls « this obsolete whimsey, by an anonymous writer in 1737, who translated the first and fourth Eclogues of Virgil, etc. into hexametrical verse; and prefixed a vindication of his attempt, with directions for the reader's pronunciation.»

I venture to hope that this excellent English scholar will no longer think the scheme of writing English hexameters a mere whimsey. Glad, indeed, should I be, if my old acquaintance were to be as well pleased with the present attempt, as I have been with some of his Morning Thoughts and Midnight Musings.

I.

THE TRANCE.

'T was at that sober hour when the light of day is receding,

And from surrounding things the hues wherewith day has adorn'd them

Fade, like the hopes of youth, [1] till the beauty of earth is departed:

Pensive, though not in thought, I stood at the window, beholding

Mountain and lake and vale; the valley disrobed of its verdure;

Derwent retaining yet from eve a glassy reflection

Where his expanded breast, then still and smooth as a mirror,

Under the woods reposed: the hills that, calm and majestic,

Lifted their heads in the silent sky, from far Glaramar,

Bleacrag, and Maidenmawr, to Grizedal and westermost Withop.

Dark and distinct they rose. The clouds had gather'd above them

High in the middle air, huge, purple, pillowy masses,

While in the west beyond was the last pale tint of the twilight;

Green as a stream in the glen whose pure and chrysolite waters

Flow o'er a schistous bed, [2] and serene as the age of the righteous.

Earth was hushed and still; all motion and sound were suspended:

Neither man was heard, bird, beast, nor humming of insect,

Only the voice of the Greta, heard only when all is in stillness.

Pensive I stood and alone, the hour and the scene had subdued me,

And as I gazed in the west, where Infinity seem'd to be open,

Yearn'd to be free from time, and felt that this life is a thraldom.

Thus as I stood, the bell which awhile from its warning had rested,

Sent forth its note again, toll, toll, through the silence of evening.

'T is a deep dull sound that is heavy and mournful at all times,

For it tells of mortality always. But heavier this day

Fell on the conscious ear its deeper and mournfuller import,

Yea, in the heart it sunk; for this was the day when the herald

Breaking his wand should proclaim, that George our King was departed.

Thou art released! I cried: thy soul is deliver'd from bondage!

Thou who hast lain so long in mental and visual darkness,

Thou art in yonder heaven! thy place is in light and in glory.

Come, and behold!—methought a startling Voice from the twilight

Answered; and therewithal I felt a stroke as of light-
ning,
With a sound like the rushing of winds, or the roaring
of waters.
If from without it came, I knew not, so sudden the
seizure;
Or if the brain itself in that strong flash had expended
All its electric stores. Of strength and of thought it
bereft me;
Hearing, and sight, and sense, were gone; and when I
awaken'd,
'T was from a dream of death, in silence and uttermost
darkness;
Knowing not where or how, nor if I was rapt in the body,
Nor if entranced, or dead, but all around me was black-
ness,
Utterly blank and void, as if this ample creation
Had been blotted out, and I were alone in the chaos.
Yet had I even then a living hope to sustain me
Under that awful thought, and I strengthen'd my spirit
with prayer.

Comfort I sought and support, and both were found
in retiring
Into that inner world, the soul's stronghold and her
kingdom.
Then came again the Voice, but then no longer appalling,
Like the voice of a friend it came : O son of the Muses!
Be of good heart, it said, and think not that thou art
abandon'd;
For to thy mortal sight shall the Grave unshadow its
secrets;
Such as of yore the Florentine saw, Hell's perilous cham-
bers
He who trod in his strength; and the arduous Mountain
of Penance,
And the regions of Paradise, sphere within sphere inter-
circled.
Child of Earth, look up! and behold what passes before
thee.

II.

THE VAULT.

So by the unseen comforted, raised I my head in obe-
dience,
And in a vault I found myself placed, arch'd over on all
sides.
Narrow and low was that house of the dead. Around it
were coffins,
Each in its niche, and palls, and urns, and funeral hatch-
ments;
Velvets of Tyrian dye, retaining their hues unfaded;
Blazonry vivid still, as if fresh from the touch of the
limner;
Nor was the golden fringe, nor the golden broidery tar-
nish'd.

Whence came the light whereby that place of death
was discover'd?
For there was there no lamp, whose wonderous flame
inextinguish'd,
As with a vital power endued, renewing its substance,
Age after age unchanged, endureth in self-subsistence:
Nor did the cheerful beam of day, direct or reflected,

Penetrate there. That low and subterranean chamber
Saw not the living ray, nor felt the breeze; but for ever
Closely immured, was seal'd in perpetual silence and
darkness.
Whence then this lovely light, calm, pure, and soft, and
cerulean,
Such as the sapphire sheds? And whence this air that
infuses
Strength while I breathe it in, and a sense of life, and a
stillness,
Filling the heart with peace, and giving a joy that con-
tents it?
Not of the Earth that light; and these paradisiacal breath-
ings,
Not of the Earth are they!
                    These thoughts were passing within me,
When there arose around a strain of heavenly music,
Such as the hermit hears when Angels visit his slumbers.
Faintly it first began, scarce heard; and gentle its rising,
Low as the softest breath that passes in summer at
evening
O'er the Eolian strings, felt there when nothing is moving,
Save the thistle-down, lighter than air, and the leaf of the
aspin.
Then as it swell'd and rose, the thrilling melody
deepen'd;
Such, methought, should the music be, which is heard
in the cloister,
By the sisterhood standing around the beatified Virgin,
When with her dying eyes she sees the firmament open,
Lifts from the bed of dust her arms towards her
beloved,
Utters his name adored, and breathes out her soul in a
rapture.

Well could I then believe such legends, and well
could I credit
All that the poets old relate of Amphion and Orpheus;
How to melodious sounds wild beasts their strength
have surrender'd,
Men were reclaim'd from the woods, and stones in har-
monious order
Mov'd, as their atoms obey'd the mysterious attraction
of concord.
This was a higher strain; a mightier, holier virtue
Came with its powerful tones. O'ercome by the pierc-
ing emotion,
Dizzy I grew, and it seem'd as though my soul were
dissolving.
How might I bear unmov'd such sounds? For, like as
the vapours
Melt on the mountain side, when the sun comes forth
in his splendour,
Even so the vaulted roof and whatever was earthly
Faded away; the Grave was gone, and the dead was
awaken'd.

III.

THE AWAKENING.

Then I beheld the King. From a cloud which cover'd
the pavement
His reverend form uprose: heavenward his face was
directed,

Heavenward his eyes were rais'd, and heavenward his arms were extended.

Lord, it is past! he cried; the mist, and the weight and the darkness;—

That long and weary night that long drear dream of desertion.

Father, to Thee I come! My days have been many and evil,

Heavy my burthen of care, and grievous hath been my affliction.

Thou hast releas'd me at length. O Lord, in Thee have I trusted,

Thou art my hope and my strength!—And then in profound adoration,

Crossing his arms on his breast, he bent and worshipp'd in silence.

Presently one approach'd to greet him with joyful obeisance;

He of whom in an hour of woe, the assassin bereav'd us

When his counsels most, and his resolute virtue were needed.

Thou, said the Monarch, here?—Thou, Perceval, summon'd before me?—

Then as his waken'd mind to the weal of his country reverted,

What of his son, he ask'd, what course by the Prince had been follow'd.

Right in his Father's steps hath the Regent trod, was the answer:

Firm hath he proved and wise, at a time when weakness or error

Would have sunk us in shame, and to ruin have hurried us headlong.

True to himself hath he been, and Heaven has rewarded his counsels.

Peace is obtain'd then at last, with safety and honour! the Monarch

Cried, and he clasp'd his hands;—I thank Thee, O merciful Father!

Now is my heart's desire fulfill'd.

With honour surpassing
All that in elder time had adorn'd the annals of England,

Peace hath been won by the sword, the faithful minister answer'd.

Paris hath seen once more the banners of England in triumph

Wave within her walls, and the ancient line is establish'd.

While that man of blood, the tyrant, faithless and godless,

Render'd at length the sport, as long the minion of Fortune,

Far away, confined in a rocky isle of the ocean,

Fights his battles again, and pleas'd to win in the chamber

What he lost in the field, in fancy conquers his conqueror.

There he reviles his foes, and there the ungrateful accuses

For his own defaults the men who too faithfully serv'd him;

Frets and complains and intrigues, and abuses the mercy that spared him.

Oh that my King could have known these things! could have witness'd how England

Check'd in its full career the force of her enemy's empire,

Singly defied his arms and his arts, and baffled them singly,

Rous'd from their lethal sleep with the stirring example the nations,

And the refluent tide swept him and his fortune before it.

Oh that my King, ere he died, might have seen the fruit of his counsels!

Nay, it is better thus, the Monarch piously answer'd:
Here I can bear the joy; it comes as an earnest of Heaven.

Righteous art Thou, O Lord! long-suffering, but sure are thy judgments.

Then having paused awhile, like one in devotion abstracted,

Earthward his thoughts recurred, so deeply the care of his country

Lay in that royal soul reposed: and he said, Is the spirit

Quell'd which hath troubled the land? and the multitude freed from delusion,

Know they their blessings at last, and are they contented and thankful?

Still is that fierce and restless spirit at work, was the answer;

Still it deceiveth the weak, and inflameth the rash and the desperate.

Even now, I ween, some dreadful deed is preparing;

For the Souls of the Wicked are loose, and the Powers of Evil

Move on the wing alert. Some nascent horror they look for,

Be sure! some accursed conception of filth and of darkness

Ripe for its monstrous birth. Whether France or Britain be threaten'd,

Soon will the issue show; or if both at once are endanger'd:[3]

For with the ghosts obscene of Robespierre, Danton, and Hebert,

Faux and Despard I saw, and the band of rabid fanatics,

They whom Venner led, who rising in frantic rebellion
Made the Redeemer's name their cry of slaughter and treason.

IV.

THE GATE OF HEAVEN.

Thus as he spake, methought the surrounding space dilated.

Over head I beheld the infinite ether; beneath us

Lay the solid expanse of the firmament spread like a pavement:

Wheresoever I look'd there was light and glory around me.

Brightest it seem'd in the East, where the New Jerusalem glitter'd.

Eminent on a hill, there stood the Celestial City;

Beaming afar it shone; its towers and cupolas rising

High in the air serene, with the brightness of gold in the furnace,
Where on their breadth the splendour lay intense and quiescent:
Part with a fiercer glow, and a short quick tremulous motion,
Like the burning pyropus; and turrets and pinnacles sparkled,
Playing in jets of light, with a diamond-like glory coruscant.
Groves of all hues of green their foliage intermingled,
Tempering with grateful shade the else unendurable lustre.
Drawing near, I beheld what over the portal was written:
This is the Gate of Bliss,[4] it said; through me is the passage
To the City of God, the abode of beatified Spirits.
Weariness is not there, nor change, nor sorrow, nor parting;
Time hath no place therein; nor evil. Ye who would enter,
Drink of the Well of Life, and put away all that is earthly.

O'er the adamantine gates an Angel stood at the summit.
Ho! he exclaim'd, King George of England cometh to judgement!
Hear Heaven! Ye Angels hear! Souls of the Good and the Wicked
Whom it concerns, attend! Thou, Hell, bring forth his accusers!
As the sonorous summons was utter'd, the Winds, who were waiting,
Bore it abroad through Heaven; and Hell, in her nethermost caverns,
Heard, and obey'd in dismay.
Anon a body of splendour
Gather'd before the gate, and veil'd the Ineffable Presence,
Which, with a rushing of wings, came down. The sentient ether
Shook with that dread descent, and the solid firmament trembled.
Round the cloud were the Orders of Heaven—Archangel and Angel,
Principality, Cherub and Seraph, Thrones, Dominations,
Virtues, and Powers. The Souls of the Good, whom Death had made perfect,
Flocking on either hand, a multitudinous army,
Came at the awful call. In semicircle inclining,
Tier over tier they took their place: aloft in the distance,
Far as the sight could pierce, that glorious company glisten'd.
From the skirts of the shining assembly, a silvery vapour
Rose in the blue serene, and moving onward it deepen'd,
Taking a denser form; the while from the opposite region
Heavy and sulphurous clouds roll'd on, and completed the circle.
There with the Spirits accurst, in congenial darkness enveloped,

Were the Souls of the Wicked, who wilful in guilt and in error,
Chose the service of sin, and now were abiding its wages.
Change of place to them brought no reprieval from anguish;
They in their evil thoughts and desires of impotent malice,
Envy and hate, and blasphemous rage, and remorse unavailing,
Carried a Hell within, to which all outer affliction,
So it abstracted the sense, might be deem'd a remission of torment.
At the edge of the cloud, the Princes of Darkness were marshall'd:
Dimly descried within were wings and truculent faces;
And in the thick obscure there struggled a mutinous uproar,
Railing, and fury, and strife, that the whole deep body of darkness
Roll'd like a troubled sea, with a wide and a manifold motion.

V.

THE ACCUSERS.

On the cerulean floor by that dread circle surrounded,
Stood the soul of the King alone. In front was the Presence
Veil'd with excess of light; and behind was the blackness of darkness.
Then might be seen the strength of holiness, then was its triumph,
Calm in his faith he stood, and his own clear conscience upheld him.

When the trumpet was blown, and the Angel made proclamation—
Lo, where the King appears! Come forward ye who arraign him!
Forth from the lurid cloud a Demon came at the summons.
It was the Spirit by whom his righteous reign had been troubled;
Likest in form uncouth to the hideous Idols whom India
(Long by guilty neglect to hellish delusions abandon'd),
Worships with horrible rites of self-destruction and torture.
Many-headed and monstrous the Fiend; with numberless faces,
Numberless bestial ears erect to all rumours and restless,
And with numberless mouths which were fill'd with lies as with arrows.
Clamours arose as he came, a confusion of turbulent voices,
Maledictions, and blatant tongues, and viperous hisses;
And in the hubbub of senseless sounds the watchwords of faction,
Freedom, Invaded Rights, Corruption, and War, and Oppression,
Loudly enounced were heard.
But when he stood in the Presence,

Then was the Fiend dismay'd, though with impudence
     clothed as a garment;
And the lying tongues were mute, and the lips which
     had scatter'd
Accusation and slander, were still. No time for evasion
This, in the Presence he stood: no place for flight; for
     dissembling
No possibility there. From the souls on the edge of
     the darkness,
Two he produced, prime movers and agents of mis-
     chief, and bade them
Show themselves faithful now to the cause for which
     they had labour'd.
Wretched and guilty souls, where now their audacity?
     Where now
Are the insolent tongues so ready of old at rejoinder?
Where the lofty pretences of public virtue and freedom?
Where the gibe, and the jeer, and the threat, the enve-
     nom'd invective,
Calumny, falsehood, fraud, and the whole ammunition
     of malice?
Wretched and guilty souls, they stood in the face of
     their Sovereign,
Conscious and self-condemn'd; confronted with him
     they had injured,
At the Judgement-seat they stood.
              Beholding the foremost,
Him by the cast of his eye oblique, I knew as the fire-
     brand
Whom the unthinking populace held for their idol and
     hero,
Lord of Misrule in his day. But how was that coun-
     tenance alter'd
Where emotion of fear or of shame had never been wit-
     ness'd;
That invincible forehead abash'd; and those eyes where-
     in malice
Once had been wont to shine with wit and hilarity tem-
     per'd,
Into how deep a gloom their mournful expression had
     settled!
Little avail'd it now that not from a purpose malignant,
Not with evil intent he had chosen the service of evil;
But of his own desires the slave, with profligate im-
     pulse,
Solely by selfishness moved, and reckless of aught that
     might follow.
Could he plead in only excuse a confession of baseness?
Could he hide the extent of his guilt; or hope to atone for
Faction excited at home, when all old feuds were aba-
     ted,
Insurrection abroad, and the train of woes that had fol-
     low'd?
Discontent and disloyalty, like the teeth of the dragon,
He had sown on the winds; they had ripen'd beyond
     the Atlantic;[5]
Thence in natural birth sedition, revolt, revolution;
France had received the seeds, and reap'd the harvest
     of horrors;—
Where—where should the plague be stay'd? Oh, most
     to be pitied
They of all souls in bale, who see no term to the evil
They by their guilt have raised, no end to their inner
     upbraidings!
    Him I could not choose but know, nor knowing but
     grieve for.

Who might the other be, his comrade in guilt and in
     suffering,
Brought to the proof like him, and shrinking like him
     from the trial?
Nameless the libeller lived, and shot his arrows in dark-
     ness;
Undetected he pass'd to the grave, and leaving behind
     him
Noxious works on earth, and the pest of an evil example,
Went to the world beyond, where no offences are hid-
     den.
Mask'd had he been in his life, and now a visor of iron
Riveted round his head, had abolish'd his features for
     ever.
Speechless the slanderer stood, and turn'd his face from
     the Monarch
Iron bound as it was,—so insupportably dreadful
Soon or late to conscious guilt is the eye of the injured.

    Caitiffs, are ye dumb? cried the multifaced Demon
     in anger;
Think ye then by shame to shorten the term of your
     penance?
Back to your penal dens!—And with horrible grasp
     gigantic
Seizing the guilty pair, he swung them aloft, and in ven-
     geance
Hurl'd them all abroad, far into the sulphurous dark-
     ness.
Sons of Faction, be warn'd! And ye, ye Slanderers!
     learn ye
Justice, and bear in mind that after death there is
     judgment.[6]
Whirling, away they flew. Nor long himself did he
     tarry,
Ere from the ground where he stood, caught up by a
     vehement whirlwind,
He too was hurried away; and the blast with lightning
     and thunder
Volleying aright and aleft amid the accumulate black-
     ness,
Scatter'd its inmates accurst, and beyond the limits of
     ether
Drove the hircine host obscene: they howling and groan-
     ing
Fell precipitate, down to their dolorous place of endur-
     ance.
Then was the region clear; the arrowy flashes which
     redden'd
Thro' the foul thick throng, like sheeted argentry floating
Now o'er the blue serene, diffused an innocuous
     splendour,
In the infinite dying away. The roll of the thunder
Ceased, and all sounds were hush'd, till again from the
     gate adamantine
Was the voice of the Angel heard through the silence
     of Heaven.

VI.

THE ABSOLVERS.

Ho! he exclaim'd, King George of England standeth in
     judgment!
Hell hath been dumb in his presence. Ye who on earth
     arraign'd him,

Come ye before him now, and here accuse or absolve
him!
For injustice hath here no place.

             From the Souls of the Blessed
Some were there then who advanced; and more from
the skirts of the meeting,
Spirits who had not yet accomplish'd their purifica-
tion,
Yet being cleansed from pride, from faction and error
deliver'd,
Purged of the film wherewith the eye of the mind is
clouded,
They, in their better state, saw all things clear; and
discerning
Now in the light of truth what tortuous views had
deceived them,
They acknowledged their fault, and own'd the wrong
they had offer'd;
Not without ingenuous shame, and a sense of com-
punction,
More or less, as each had more or less to atone for.
One alone remain'd, when the rest had retired to their
station:
Silently he had stood, and still unmoved and in silence,
With a steady mien, regarded the face of the Monarch.
Thoughtful awhile he gazed; severe, but serene, was his
aspect;
Calm, but stern; like one whom no compassion could
weaken,
Neither could doubt deter, nor violent impulses alter:
Lord of his own resolves,—of his own heart absolute
master.
Awful Spirit! his place was with ancient sages and
heroes:
Fabius, Aristides, and Solon, and Epaminondas.

   Here then at the Gate of Heaven we are met! said
the Spirit;
King of England! albeit in life opposed to each other,
Here we meet at last. Not unprepared for the meeting
Ween I; for we had both outlived all enmity, rendering
Each to each that justice which each from each had
withholden.
In the course of events, to thee I seem'd as a Rebel,
Thou a Tyrant to me;—so strongly doth circumstance
rule men
During evil days, when right and wrong are confounded,
Left to our hearts we were just. For me, my actions have
spoken,
That not for lawless desires, nor goaded by desperate
fortunes,
Nor for ambition, I chose my part; but observant of
duty,
Self-approved. And here, this witness I willingly bear
thee,—
Here, before Angels and Men, in the awful hour of
judgment,—
Thou too didst act with upright heart, as befitted a
Sovereign,
True to his sacred trust, to his crown, his kingdom,
and people.
Heaven in these things fulfill'd its wise, though inscru-
table purpose,
While we work'd its will, doing each in his place as
became him.

Washington! said the Monarch, well hast thou spoken
and truly,
Just to thyself and to me. On them is the guilt of the
contest,
Who, for wicked ends, with foul arts of faction and
falsehood,
Kindled and fed the flame: but verily they have their
guerdon.
Thou and I are free from offence. And would that the
nations,
Learning of us, would lay aside all wrongful resent-
ment,
All injurious thought, and honouring each in the other
Kindred courage and virtue, and cognate knowledge and
freedom,
Live in brotherhood wisely conjoined. We set the
example⑦
They who stir up strife, and would break that natural
concord,
Evil they sow, and sorrow will they reap for their
harvest.

VII.

THE BEATIFICATION.

WHEN that Spirit withdrew, the Monarch around the
assembly
Look'd, but none else came forth; and he heard the voice
of the Angel,—
King of England, speak for thyself! here is none to ar-
raign thee.
Father, he replied, from whom no secrets are hidden,
What should I say? Thou knowest that mine was an
arduous station,
Full of cares, and with perils beset. How heavy the
burthen
Thou alone canst tell! Short-sighted and frail hast
Thou made us,
And Thy judgments who can abide? But as surely
Thou knowest
The desire of my heart hath been alway the good of my
people,
Pardon my errors, O Lord, and in mercy accept the in-
tention!
As in Thee I have trusted, so let me not now be con-
founded!

   Bending forward he spake with earnest humility.
Well done,
Good and faithful servant! then said a Voice from the
Brightness,
Enter thou into the joy of thy Lord.—The ministring
Spirits
Clapt their pennons therewith, and from that whole
army of Angels
Songs of thanksgiving and joy resounded, and loud hal-
lelujahs;
While on the wings of Winds uprais'd, the pavilion of
splendour
Where inscrutable light enveloped the Holy of Holies,
Moved, and was borne away, through the empyrean as-
cending

75

Beautiful then on its hill appear'd the Celestial City,
Soften'd, like evening suns, to a mild and bearable
     lustre.
Beautiful was the ether above; and the sapphire beneath
     us,
Beautiful was its tone, to the dazzled sight as refreshing
As the fields with their loveliest green at the coming of
     summer,
When the mind is at ease, and the eye and the heart are
     contented.

Then methought we approach'd the gate. In front
     of the portal,
From a rock where the standard of man's Redemption
     was planted,
Issued the Well of Life, where whosoever would enter,
So it was written, must drink, and put away all that is
     earthly.
Earth among its gems, its creations of art and of nature,
Offers not aught whereto that marvellous Cross may be
     liken'd
Even in dim similitude, such was its wonderful sub-
     stance.
Pure it was and diaphanous. It had no visible lustre;
Yet from It alone whole Heaven was illuminate alway;
Day and Night being none in the upper firmament,
     neither
Sun, nor Moon, nor Stars; but from that Cross as a
     fountain
Flow'd the Light uncreated; light all-sufficing, eternal,
Light which was, and which is, and which will be, for
     ever and ever;
Light of light, which, if daringly gazed on, would blind
     an Archangel,
Yet the eye of weak man may behold, and beholding is
     strengthened.
Yea, while we wander below, opprest with our bodily
     burthen,
And in the shadow of death, this Light is in mercy
     vouchsafed us,
So we seek it with humble heart; and the soul that re-
     ceives it
Hath with it healing and strength, peace, love, and life
     everlasting.

Thither the King drew nigh, and kneeling he drank
     of the water.
Oh what a change was wrought! In the semblance of
     age he had risen,
Such as at last he appear'd, with the traces of time and
     affliction
Deep on his faded form, when the burthen of years was
     upon him.
Oh what a change was wrought! For now the cor-
     ruptible put on
Incorruption; the mortal put off mortality. Rising
Rejuvenescent he stood in a glorified body, obnoxious
Never again to change, nor to evil and trouble and
     sorrow,
But for eternity form'd, and to bliss everlasting ap-
     pointed.

VIII.

THE SOVEREIGNS.

Lift up your heads, ye Gates; and ye everlasting Por-
     tals,
Be ye lift up! For lo! a glorified Monarch approacheth,
One who in righteousness reign'd, and religiously go-
     vern'd his people.
Who are these that await him within? Nassau the
     Deliverer,
Him I knew: and the Stuart, he who, serene in his
     meekness,
Bow'd his anointed head beneath the axe of rebellion,
Calm in that insolent hour, and over his fortune tri-
     umphant. [8]

Queen of the eagle eye, thou too, O matchless Eliza,
Excellent Queen, wert there! and thy brother's beauti-
     ful spirit;
O'er whose innocent head there hover'd a silvery halo,
Such as crowns the Saint when his earthly warfare is
     ended.

There too was he of the sable mail, the hero of
     Cressy,
Flower of chivalry, he, in arms and in courtesy peer-
     less.
There too his royal sire I saw, magnificent Edward,
He who made the English renown, and the fame of his
     Windsor
In the Orient and Occident known, from Tagus to
     Tigris. [9]
Lion-hearted Richard was there, redoubtable warrior,
At whose irresistible presence the Saracen trembled;
At whose name the Caliph exclaim'd in dismay on Ma-
     hommed,
Syrian mothers grew pale, and their children were
     scared into silence.
Born in a bloody age, did he in his prowess exulting
Run like a meteor his course, and fulfil the service
     assign'd him,
Checking the Mussulman power in the height of its
     prosperous fortune;
But that leonine heart was with virtues humaner en-
     nobled,
(Otherwhere else, be sure, his doom had now been ap-
     pointed),
Friendship, disdain of wrong, and generous feeling
     redeem'd it,
Magnanimity there had its seat, and the love of the
     Muses.

There with the Saxon Kings who founded our laws
     and our temples,
(Gratefully still to be named while these endure in re-
     membrance,
They, for the pious work!) I saw the spirit of Alfred;
Alfred than whom no Prince with loftier intellect gifted,
Nor with a finer soul, nor in virtue more absolute, ever
Made a throne twice-hallow'd, and reign'd in the hearts
     of his people.
With him the Worthies were seen who in life partook of
     his labours,
Shared his thoughts, and with him for the weal of pos-
     terity travail'd:

Some who in cloisters immured, and to painful study
 devoted
Day and night, their patient and innocent lives ex-
 hausted,
And in meekness possess'd their souls: and some who
 in battle
Put the Raven to flight: and some who intrepid in duty
Reach'd the remotest East, or invading the kingdom of
 Winter,
Plough'd with audacious keel the Hyperborean Ocean.
I could perceive the joy which fill'd their beatified spirits
While of the Georgian age they thought, and the glory
 of England.

IX.

THE ELDER WORTHIES.

Lift up your heads, ye Gates! and ye everlasting
 Portals,
Be ye lift up! Behold the Worthies are there to re-
 ceive him,
They who in later days, or in elder ages, ennobled
Britain's dear name. Bede I beheld, who, humble and
 holy,
Shone like a single star, serene in a night of darkness.
Bacon also was there, the marvellous Friar; and he who
Struck the spark from which the Bohemian kindled his
 taper;
Thence the flame, long and hardly preserv'd, was to Lu-
 ther transmitted,
Mighty soul, and he lifted his torch, and enlighten'd the
 nations.

Thee too, Father Chaucer! I saw, and delighted to
 see thee,
At whose well undefiled I drank in my youth, and was
 strengthen'd;
With whose mind immortal so oft I have communed,
 partaking
All its manifold moods, and willingly moved at its plea-
 sure.
Bearing the palm of martyrdom, Cranmer was there in
 his meekness,
Holy name to be ever revered! And Cecil, whose
 wisdom
'Stablish'd the Church and State, Eliza's pillar of council.
And Shakespeare, who in our hearts for himself hath
 erected an empire
Not to be shaken by Time, nor e'er by another divided.
But with what love did I then behold the face of my
 master,—
Spenser, my master dear! with whom in boyhood I
 wander'd
Through the regions of Faery Land, in forest or garden
Spending delicious hours, or at tilt and tourney re-
 joicing;
Yea, by the magic of verse enlarged, and translated in
 spirit,
In the World of Romance free denizen I;—till awake-
 ning,
When the spell was dissolved, this real earth and its
 uses
Seem'd to me weary, and stale, and flat.
      With other emotion
Milton's severer shade I saw, and in reverence humbled

Gazed on that soul sublime: of passion now as of
 blindness
Heal'd, and no longer here to Kings and to Hierarchs
 hostile,
He was assoil'd from taint of the fatal fruit; and in
 Eden
Not again to be lost, consorted an equal with Angels.
Taylor too was there, from whose mind of its treasures
 redundant
Streams of eloquence flow'd, like an inexhaustible
 fountain:
And the victor of Blenheim, alike in all virtues accom-
 plish'd,
Public or private, he; the perfect soldier and states-
 man,
England's reproach and her pride, her pride for his
 noble achievements,
Her reproach for the wrongs he endur'd: And Newton,
 exalted
There above those orbs whose motions from earth he
 had measur'd,
Through infinity ranging in thought: And Berkeley,
 angelic
Now in substance as soul, that kingdom enjoying where
 all things
Are what they seem, and the good and the beautiful
 there are eternal.

X.

THE WORTHIES OF THE GEORGIAN AGE.

These with a kindred host of great and illustrious
 spirits
Stood apart, while a train whom nearer duty attracted
Through the Gate of Bliss came forth to welcome their
 Sovereign.
Many were they and glorious all. Conspicuous among
 them
Wolfe was seen: And the seaman who fell on the shores
 of Owhyhee,
Leaving a lasting name, to humanity dear as to science:
And the mighty musician of Germany, ours by adop-
 tion,
Who beheld in the King his munificent pupil and
 patron.
Reynolds, with whom began that school of art which
 hath equall'd
Richest Italy's works, and the masterly labours of Bel-
 gium,
Came in that famous array: and Hogarth, who followed
 no master,
Nor by pupil shall e'er be approach'd, alone in his
 greatness.
Reverend in comely mien, of aspect mild and be-
 nignant,
There, too, Wesley I saw and knew, whose zeal apos-
 tolic,
Though with error alloy'd, hath on earth its merited
 honour,
As in Heaven its reward. And Mansfield the just and
 intrepid;
Wise Judge, by the craft of the Law ne'er seduced from
 its purpose;
And when the misled multitude raged like the winds
 in their madness,

Not to be moved from his rightful resolves. And Burke
   I beheld there,
Eloquent statesman and sage, who, though late, broke
   loose from his trammels,
Giving then to mankind what party too long had
   diverted.
Here, where wrongs are forgiven, was the injured Has-
   tings beside him :
Strong in his high deserts, and in innocence happy,
   though injured,
He, in his good old age, outlived persecution and
   malice.
Even where he had stood a mark for the arrows of
   slander,
He had his triumph at last, when moved with one feel-
   ing, the Senate
Rose in respect at his sight, and atoned for the sin of
   their fathers.

Cowper, thy lovely spirit was there, by death disen-
   chanted
From that heavy spell which had bound it in sorrow
   and darkness,
Thou wert there, in the kingdom of peace and of light
   everlasting.
Nelson also was there in the kingdom of peace, though
   his calling
While upon earth he dwelt, was to war and the work
   of destruction.
Not in him had that awful ministry deaden'd, or
   weaken'd
Quick compassion, and feelings that raise while they
   soften our nature.
Wise in counsel, and steady in purpose, and rapid in
   action,
Never thought of self from the course of his duty se-
   duced him,
Never doubt of the issue unworthily warpt his in-
   tention.
Long shall his memory live, and while his example is
   cherish'd,
From the Queen of the Seas, the Sceptre shall never be
   wrested.

XI.

THE YOUNG SPIRITS.

Ye whom I leave unnamed, ye other Worthies of Britain,
Lights of the Georgian age,—for ye are many and noble,
How might I name ye all, whom I saw in this glorious
   vision ?—
Pardon ye the imperfect tale! Yet some I beheld there,
Whom should I pretermit, my heart might rightly up-
   braid me,
That its tribute of honour, poor though it be, was with-
   holden.
Somewhat apart they came in fellowship gather'd to-
   gether,
As in goodly array they follow'd the train of the wor-
   thies.
Chosen spirits were these, of the finest elements temper'd,
And embodied on earth in mortality's purest texture;
But in the morning of hope, in the blossom of virtue
   and genius,

They were cut down by death. What then,—were it
   wise to lament them,
Seeing the mind bears with it its wealth, and the soul
   its affections?
What we sow, we shall reap; and the seeds whereof
   earth is not worthy
Strike their roots in a kindlier soil, and ripen to har-
   vest.

Here were the gallant youths of high heroic aspiring,
Who, so fate had allow'd, with the martial renown of
   their country
Would have wedded their names, for perpetual honour
   united ;
Strong of heart and of mind, but in undistinguishing
   battle,
Or by pestilence stricken, they fell, unknown and con-
   founded
With the common dead. Oh! many are they who
   were worthy,
Under the Red Cross flag, to have wielded the thunders
   of Britain,
Making her justice felt, and her proper power upholding
Upon all seas and shores, wheresoever her rights were
   offended,
Followers of Nelson's path, and the glorious career of
   the Wellesley.
Many are they, whose bones beneath the billows have
   whiten'd,
Or in foreign earth they have moulder'd, hastily cover'd
In some wide and general grave.
               Here also were spirits
To have guided, like Cecil of old, the councils of Eng-
   land;
Or have silenced and charm'd a tumultuous Senate, like
   Canning,
When to the height of his theme, the consummate
   Orator rising,
Makes our Catalines pale, and rejoices the friends of
   their country.

Others came in that goodly band whom benigner
   fortune
Led into pleasanter ways on earth: children of Science
Some, whose unerring pursuit would, but for death, have
   extended
O'er the unknown and material, Man's intellectual em-
   pire,
Such their intuitive power; like Davy, disarming de-
   struction
When it moves on the vapour; or him, who discovering
   the secret
Of the dark and ebullient abyss, with the fire of Vesu-
   vius
Arm'd the chemist's hand:[10] well then might Eleusinian
   Ceres
Yield to him, from whom the seas and the mountains
   conceal'd not
Nature's mystery, hid in their depths.
             Here, lost in their promise
And prime, were the children of Art, who should else
   have deliver'd
Works and undying names to grateful posterity's keep-
   ing,
Such as Haydon will leave on earth; and he who, return-
   ing,

Rich in praise to his native shores, hath left a remembrance

Long to be honour'd and loved on the banks of Thames and of Tiber:

So may America, prizing in time the worth she possesses,

Give to that hand free scope, and boast hereafter of Allston.

Here too, early lost and deplored, were the youths whom the Muses

Mark'd for themselves at birth, and with dews from Castalia sprinkled:

Chatterton first (for not to his affectionate spirit

Could the act of madness innate for guilt be accounted): [11]

Marvellous boy, whose antique songs and unhappy story,

Shall, by gentle hearts, be in mournful memory cherish'd

Long as thy ancient towers endure, and the rocks of St Vincent,

Bristol! my birth-place dear.—What though I have chosen a dwelling

Far away, and my grave shall not be found by the stranger

Under thy sacred care, nathless in love and in duty

Still am I bound to thee, and by many a deep recollection!

City of elder days, I know how largely I owe thee;

Nor least for the hope and the strength that I gather'd in boyhood,

While on Chatterton musing, I fancied his spirit was with me

In the haunts which he loved upon earth. 'T was a joy in my vision

When I beheld his face—And here was the youth of Loch Leven,

Nipt, like an April flower, that opens its leaves to the sunshine,

While the breath of the East prevails. And Russell and Bampfylde,

Bright emanations they! And the Poet, whose songs of childhood

Trent and the groves of Clifton heard; not alone by the Muses

But by the Virtues loved, his soul in its youthful aspirings

Sought the Holy Hill, and his thirst was for Siloa's waters.

Was I deceived by desire, or, Henry, indeed did thy spirit

Know me, and meet my look, and smile like a friend at the meeting?

XII.

THE MEETING.

Lift up your heads, ye Gates; and ye everlasting Portals,

Be ye lift up! Behold the splendent train of the Worthies

Halt; and with quicker pace a happy company issues

Forth from the Gate of Bliss: the Parents, the Children, and Consort,

Come to welcome in Heaven the Son, the Father, and Husband!

Hour of perfect joy that o'erpays all earthly affliction;

Yea, and the thought whereof supporteth the soul in its anguish!

There came England's blossom of hope,—the beautiful Princess;

She in whose wedded bliss all hearts rejoiced, and whose death-bell,

Heard from tower to tower through the islands, carried a sorrow,

Felt by all like a private grief, which, sleeping or waking,

Will not be shaken away; but possesses the soul and disturbs it.

There was our late-lost Queen, the nation's example of virtue;

In whose presence vice was not seen, nor the face of dishonour,

Pure in heart, and spotless in life, and secret in bounty,

Queen, and Mother, and Wife unreproved.—The gentle Amelia [12]

Stretch'd her arms to her father there, in tenderness shedding

Tears, such as Angels weep. That hand was toward him extended

Whose last pressure he could not bear, when merciful Nature,

As o'er her dying bed he bent in severest anguish,

Laid on his senses a weight, and suspended the sorrow for ever.

He hath recover'd her now: all, all that was lost is restored him;—

Hour of perfect bliss that o'erpays all earthly affliction!

They are met where Change is not known, nor Sorrow, nor Parting.

Death is subdued, and the Grave, which conquers all, hath been conquer'd.

When I beheld them meet, the desire of my soul overcame me;

And when with harp and voice the loud hosannahs of welcome

Fill'd the rejoicing sky, as the happy company enter'd

Through the everlasting Gates; I, too, press'd forward to enter:—

But the weight of the body withheld me. I stoopt to the fountain,

Eager to drink thereof, and to put away all that was earthly.

Darkness came over me then at the chilling touch of the water,

And my feet methought sunk, and I fell precipitate. Starting,

Then I awoke, and beheld the mountains in twilight before me,

Dark and distinct; and instead of the rapturous sound of hosannahs,

Heard the bell from the tower, toll! toll! through the silence of evening.

NOTES.

Note 1, page 588, col. 2.

—— From surrounding things the hues with which day has adorn'd them

Fade, like the hopes of youth.

This effect of twilight, and in the very scene described, has been lately represented by Mr William Westall, in one of his Views of the Lakes, with the true feeling and power of genius. The range of mountains which is described in these introductory lines, may also be seen in his View of the Vale of Keswick from the Penrith road.

Note 2, page 588, col. 2.

— The last pale tint of the twilight,
Green as a stream in the glen whose pure and chrysolite waters
Flow o'er a schistous bed.

St Pierre, who is often a fanciful, generally a delightful, but always an animated and ingenious writer, has some characteristic speculations concerning this green light of evening. He says, « Je suis porté à attribuer à la couleur verte des végétaux qui couvrent en été une grande partie de notre hémisphère, cette belle teinte d'émeraude que l'on apperçoit quelquefois dans cette saison au firmament, vers le coucher du soleil. Elle est rare dans nos climats; mais elle est fréquente entre les tropiques, où l'été dure toute l'année. Je sais bien qu'on peut rendre raison de ce phénomène par la simple réfraction des rayons du soleil dans l'atmosphère, ce prisme sphérique de notre globe. Mais, outre qu'on peut objecter que la couleur verte ne se voit point en hiver dans notre ciel, c'est que je peux apporter à l'appui de mon opinion d'autres faits qui semblent prouver que la couleur même azurée de l'atmosphère n'est qu'une réflexion de celle de l'océan. En effet, les glaces flottantes qui descendent tous les ans du pôle nord, s'annoncent, devant de paraître sur l'horizon, par une lueur blanche qui éclaire le ciel jour et nuit, et qui n'est qu'un reflet des neiges cristallisées qui les composent. Cette lueur paraît semblable à celle de l'aurore boréale, dont le foyer est au milieu des glaces même du pôle nord, mais dont la couleur blanche est mélangée de jaune, de rouge, et de vert, parcequ'elle participe des couleurs du sol ferrugineux et de la verdure des forêts de sapins qui couvrent notre zone glaciale. La cause de cette variation de couleurs dans notre aurore boréale est d'autant plus vraisemblable, que l'aurore australe, comme l'a observé le Capitaine Cook, en diffère en ce que sa couleur blanche n'est jamais mélangée que de teintes bleues, qui n'ont lieu, selon moi, que parce que les glaces du pôle austral, sans continent et sans végétaux, sont entourées de toutes parts de l'océan, qui est bleu. Ne voyons-nous pas que la lune, que nous supposons couverte en grande partie de glaciers très élevés, nous renvoie en lumière d'un blanc bleuâtre les rayons du soleil, qui sont dorés dans notre atmosphère ferrugineuse? N'est-ce pas par la réverbération d'un sol composé de fer, que la planète de Mars nous réfléchit, en tout temps, une lumière rouge? N'est-il pas plus naturel d'attribuer ces couleurs constantes aux réverbérations du sol, des mers, et des végétaux de ces planètes, plutôt qu'aux réfractions variables des rayons du soleil dans leurs atmosphères, dont les couleurs devraient changer à toute heure, suivant leurs différens aspects avec cet astre? Comme Mars apparaît constamment rouge à la terre, il est possible que la terre apparoisse à Mars comme une pierrerie brillante des couleurs de l'opale au pôle nord, de celles de l'aigue-marine au pôle sud, et, tour-à-tour, de celles du saphir et de l'émeraude dans le reste de sa circonférence. Mais, sans sortir de notre atmosphère, je crois que la terre y renvoie la couleur bleue de son océan avec des reflets de la couleur verte de ses végétaux, en tout temps dans la zone torride, et en été seu-

lement dans nos climats, par la même raison que ces deux pôles y réfléchissent des aurores boréales différentes, qui participent des couleurs de la terre, ou des mers qui les avoisinent.

« Peut-être même notre atmosphère réfléchit-elle quelquefois les formes des paysages, qui annoncent les îles aux navigateurs bien long-temps avant qu'ils puissent y aborder. Il est remarquable qu'elles ne se montrent comme les reflets de verdure qu'à l'horizon et du côté du soleil couchant. Je citerai, à ce sujet, un homme de l'Ile de France qui apercevoit dans le ciel les images des vaisseaux qui étaient en pleine mer : le célèbre Vernet, qui m'a attesté avoir vu une fois dans les nuages les tours et les remparts d'une ville située à sept lieues de lui ; et le phénomène du détroit de Sicile, connu sous le nom de Fée-Morgane. Les nuages et les vapeurs de l'atmosphère peuvent fort bien réfléchir les formes et les couleurs des objets terrestres, puisqu'ils réfléchissent dans les parélies l'image du soleil au point de la rendre ardente comme le soleil lui-même. Enfin, les eaux de la terre répètent les couleurs et les formes des nuages de l'atmosphère, pourquoi les vapeurs de l'atmosphère, à leur tour, ne pourroient-elles pas réfléchir le bleu de la mer, la verdure et le jaune de la terre, ainsi que les couleurs chatoyantes des glaces polaires?

« Au reste, je ne donne mon opinion que comme mon opinion. L'histoire de la nature est un édifice à peine commencé ; ne craignons pas d'y poser quelques pierres d'attente : nos neveux s'en serviront pour l'agrandir, ou les supprimeront comme superflues. Si mon autorité est nulle dans l'avenir, peu importera que je me sois trompé sur ce point : mon ouvrage rentrera dans l'obscurité d'où il était sorti. Mais s'il est un jour de quelque considération, mon erreur en physique sera plus utile à la morale, qu'une vérité d'ailleurs indifférente au bonheur des hommes. On en concluera avec raison qu'il faut être en garde contre les écrivains même accrédités. »—*Harmonies de la Nature*, t. i, 129.

« I am inclined to attribute to the green colour of the vegetables with which, during the summer, a great part of our hemisphere is covered, that beautiful emerald tint which we sometimes perceive at that season in the firmament, towards the setting of the sun. It is rare in our climates, but is frequent between the tropics, where summer continues throughout the year. I know that this phenomenon may be explained by the simple refraction of the rays of the sun in the atmosphere, that spherical prism of our globe. But to this it may be objected, that the green colour is not seen during the winter in our sky; and moreover, I can support my opinion by other facts, which appear to prove that even the azure colour of the atmosphere is only a reflection of that of the ocean. In fact, the floating ice which descends every year from the North Pole, is announced before it appears upon the horizon, by a white blink, which enlightens the heaven day and night, and which is only a reflection of the crystallized snows, of which those masses are composed. This blink resembles the light of the *aurora borealis*, the centre of which is in the middle of the ice of our pole, but the white colour of which is mixed with yellow, with red, and with green, because it partakes of the colour of a ferruginous soil, and of the verdure of the pine forests which cover our icy zone. This explanation of these variations of colour in our *aurora borealis*, is so much the more probable, because that of the *aurora australis*, as Captain

Cook has observed, differs in that its white colour is mixed with blue tints alone, which can only be, according to my opinion, because the ice of the austral pole (where there is no continent and no vegetation), is surrounded on all parts with the ocean, which is blue. Do we not see that the moon, which we suppose to be covered in great part with very elevated glaciers, sends back to us, in a light of a bluish white, the rays of the sun, which are golden in our ferruginous atmosphere? Is it not by the reverberation of a soil composed of iron, that the planet Mars reflects upon us at all times a red light? Is it not more natural to attribute these constant colours to the reverberation of the soil, of the seas, and of the vegetables of these planets, rather than to the variable refractions of the rays of the sun in their atmospheres, the colours of which ought to change every hour, according to their different aspects with regard to that star. As Mars appears constantly red to the earth, it is possible that the earth might appear to Mars like a brilliant jewel, of the colour of the opal towards the North Pole, of the agoa marina at the South Pole, and alternately of the sapphire in the rest of its circumference. But without going out of our atmosphere, I believe that the earth reflects there the blue colour of its ocean with the green of its vegetation, at all times in the torrid zone, and in summer only in our climate, for the same reason that its two poles reflect their different *auroras*, which participate of the colours of the earth or the seas that are near them.

« Perhaps our atmosphere sometimes reflects landscapes, which announce islands to the sailors long before they reach them. It is remarkable that they show themselves, like the reflections of verdure, only in the horizon and on the side of the setting sun. I shall cite, on this subject, a man of the Isle of France, who used to perceive in the sky the images of vessels, which were out in full sea; the celebrated Vernet, who related to me that he had once seen in the clouds the ramparts of a town, situated seven leagues distant from him, and the phenomenon of the straits of Sicily, known under the name of the *Fata Morgana*. The clouds and the vapours of the atmosphere may very well reflect the forms and the colours of earthly objects, since they reflect in parhelions the image of the sun, so as to render it burning as the sun itself. In fine, if the waters of the earth repeat the colours and the forms of the clouds of the atmosphere, why then should not the vapours of the atmosphere, in their turn, reflect the blue of the sea, the verdure and the yellow of the earth, as well as the glancing colours of the polar ices?

« I advance my opinion, however, only as my opinion. The history of nature is an edifice which, as yet, is scarcely commenced; let us not fear to carry some stones towards the building; our grandchildren will use them, or lay them aside if they be useless. If my authority is of no weight hereafter, it will import little that I have deceived myself upon this point; my work will enter into obscurity, from whence it came; but if it should be, in future, of some consideration, my error, in physics, will be more useful to morals than a truth, otherwise indifferent to the happiness of mankind. For it will be inferred with reason, that it is necessary to regard even writers of credit with caution.»

In one point of fact, St Pierre is certainly mistaken. The green evening light is seen as often in winter as in summer. Having been led to look for it in consequence of suspecting the accuracy of his remarks, I noticed it on the very day when this extract was transcribed for the press, (late in December,) and twice in the course of the ensuing week, and I observed it, not in the evening alone, and in the west, (in which quarter, however, and at which time, it is most frequently seen,) but in different parts of the sky, and at different times of the day.

Note 3, page 590, col. 2.

Whether France or Britain be threaten'd,
Soon will the issue show, or if both at once are endanger'd.

The murder of the Duke of Berry, and the Cato-street conspiracy, were both planned at the time of the King's death.

Note 4, page 591, col. 2.
This is the Gate of Bliss.

The reader will so surely think of the admirable passage of Dante, which was in the writer's mind when these lines were composed, that I should not think it necessary to notice the imitation, were it not that we live in an age of plagiarism; when not our jackdaws only, but some of our swans also, trick themselves in borrowed plumage. I have never contracted an obligation of this kind, either to contemporary, or predecessor, without acknowledging it.

Note 5, page 592, col 1.

Discontent and disloyalty, like the teeth of the dragon,
He had sown on the winds; they had ripen'd beyond the Atlantic.

«Our New World,» says M. Simond, «has generally the credit of having first lighted the torch which was to illuminate, and soon set in a blaze, the finest part of Europe; yet I think the flint was struck, and the first spark elicited, by the patriot, John Wilkes, a few years before. In a time of profound peace, the restless spirits of men, deprived of other objects of public curiosity, seized, with avidity, on those questions which were then agitated with so much violence in England, touching the rights of the people, and of the government, and the nature of power. The end of the political drama was in favour of what was called, and in some respect was, the liberty of the people. Encouraged by the success of this great comedian, the curtain was no sooner dropt on the scene of Europe, than new actors hastened to raise it again in America, and to give the world a new play, infinitely more interesting, and more brilliant than the first.»

Dr Franklin describes the state of things during the reign of Wilkes and liberty. He says, «There have been amazing contests all over the kingdom, twenty or thirty thousand pounds of a side spent in several places, and inconceivable mischief done by drunken, mad mobs, to houses, windows, etc. The scenes have been horrible. London was illuminated two nights running, at the command of the mob, for the success of Wilkes in the Middlesex election; the second night exceeded any thing of the kind ever seen here on the greatest occasions of rejoicing, as even the small cross streets, lanes, courts, and other out-of-the-way places, were all in a blaze with lights, and the principal streets all night long, as the mobs went round again after two o'clock, and obliged people who had extinguished their candles, to light them again. Those who refused had all their windows destroyed. The damage done, and the expense of candles, has been computed at fifty thousand pounds. It must have been great, though probably not so much. The ferment is not yet over, for he has promised to surrender to the court next Wednesday, and another tumult is then expected; and what the upshot will be, no one can yet foresee. It is really an extraordinary event, to see an outlaw and exile, of bad personal character, not worth a farthing, come over from France, set himself up as a candidate for the capital of the kingdom, miss his election only by being too late in his application, and immediately carrying it for the principal county. The mob (spirited up by numbers of different ballads, sung or roared in every street), requiring gentlemen and ladies of all ranks, as they passed in their carriages, to shout for Wilkes and liberty, marking the same words on all their coaches with chalk, and No 45 on every door, which extends a vast way along the roads in the country. I went last week to Winchester, and observed that for fifteen miles out of town, there was scarce a door or window-shutter next the road unmarked: and this continued here and there quite to Winchester, which is sixty-four miles.

*　　*　　*　　*　　*

Even this capital, the residence of the king, is now a daily scene of lawless riot and confusion. Mobs patrolling the streets at noon-day, some knocking all down that will not roar for Wilkes and liberty; courts of justice afraid to give judgment against him; coal-heavers and porters pulling down the houses of coal-merchants that refuse to give them more wages; sawyers destroying saw-mills; sailors unrigging all the outward-bound ships, and suffering none to sail till merchants agree to raise their pay; watermen destroying private boats, and threatening bridges; soldiers firing among the mobs, and killing men, women, and children, which seems only to have produced an universal sullenness, that looks like a great black cloud coming on, ready to burst in a general tempest. What the event will be God only knows. But some punishment seems preparing for a people who are ungratefully abusing the best constitution, and the best king, any nation was ever blessed with; intent on nothing but luxury, licentiousness, power, places, pensions, and plunder; while the ministry, divided in their councils, with little regard for each other, wearied by perpetual oppositions, in continual apprehension of changes, intent on securing popularity, in case they should lose favour, have, for some years past, had little time or inclination to attend to our small affairs, whose remoteness makes them appear still smaller.

*　　*　　*　　*　　*

All respect to law and government seems to be lost among the common people, who are moreover continually inflamed by seditious scribblers to trample on authority, and every thing that used to keep them in order.»

Note 6, page 592, col. 2.

Sons of slander, be warn'd! and ye, ye Factionists, learn ye
Justice, and bear in mind, that after death there is judgment.

Discite justitiam moniti, et non temnere Divos.
VIRGIL.

Note 7, page 593, col. 2.

Would that the nations,
Learning of us, would lay aside all wrongful resentment,
All injurious thought, and honouring each in the other,
Kindred courage and virtue, and cognate knowledge and freedom,
Live in brotherhood wisely conjoined. We set the example.

The wise and dignified manner in which the late king received the first minister from the United States of America is well known. It is not so generally known that anxiety and sleeplessness, during the American war, are believed by those persons who had the best opportunity for forming an opinion upon the subject, to have laid the foundation of that malady by which the king was afflicted during the latter years of his life.

Upon the publication of Captain Cooke's Voyages, a copy of this national work was sent to Dr Franklin, by the King's desire, because he had given orders for the protection of that illustrious navigator, in case he should fall in with any American cruisers on his way home.

Note 8, page 594, col. 2.

Calm in that insolent hour, and over his fortune triumphant.

The behaviour of Charles in that insolent hour extorted admiration, even from the better part of the Commonwealth's-men. It is thus finely described by Andrew Marvell:—

While round the armed bands
Did clap their bloody hands,
He nothing common did, or mean,
Upon that memorable scene;
But with his keener eye
The axe's edge did try:
Nor call'd the Gods with vulgar spight
To vindicate his helpless right;
But bow'd his comely head
Down, as upon a bed.

Note 9, page 594, col. 2.

Magnificent Edward,
He who made the English renown, and the fame of his Windsor
In the Orient and Occident known from Tagus to Tigris.

The celebrity which Windsor had obtained, as being the most splendid court in Christendom, and the seat of chivalry, may be plainly seen in the romance of Amadis, which was written in Portugal, towards the latter end of Edward the Third's reign. The Portugueze in that age took their military terms from the English, and St George came into fashion among them at the same time as being the English Santiago.

A dispute arose between two knights, the one a Cypriot, the other a Frenchman, who were serving the King of Armenia against the Soldan of Babylon. The other Christian captains in the army determined that they should decide it by single combat before King Edward of England, as the most worthy and honourable prince in all Christendom; and the quarrel, which began in Armenia, was actually thus decided within the lists, at the palace of Westminster. It was won, not very honourably, by the Frenchman.

Note 10, page 596, col. 2.*

He who discovering the secret
Of the dark and ebullient abyss, with the fire of Vesuvius
Arm'd the Chemist's hand.

Though chemistry is one of the subjects of which I am contented to be ignorant, I can nevertheless perceive and appreciate the real genius indicated by Dr Clarke's discovery in the art of fusion. See his Treatise upon the Gas Blow-Pipe; or the account of it in the *Quarterly Review*, No 46, p. 466.

In referring to the Safety Lamp of Sir Humphrey Davy, I must not be understood as representing that to be the most important of his many and great discoveries. No praise can add to his deserved celebrity.

Note 11, page 597, col. 1.

Not to his affectionate spirit
Could the act of madness innate for guilt be accounted.

The act of suicide is very far from being so certain an indication of insanity as it is usually considered by our inquests. But in the case of Chatterton, it was the manifestation of an hereditary disease. There was a madness in his family. His only sister, during one part of her life, was under confinement.

The law respecting suicide is a most barbarous one; and of late years has never been carried into effect without exciting horror and disgust. It might be a salutary enactment, that all suicides should be given up for dissection. This would certainly prevent many women from committing self-murder, and possibly might in time be useful to physiology.

Note 12, page 597, col. 2.

The gentle Amelia.

In one of his few intervals of sanity, after the death of this beloved daughter, the late King gave orders, that a monument should be erected to the memory of one of her attendants, in St George's Chapel, with the following inscription:

KING GEORGE III
caused to be interred near this place
the body of MARY GASCOIGNE,
Servant to the Princess AMELIA;
and this stone
to be inscribed in testimony of his grateful
sense
of the faithful services and attachment
of an amiable Young Woman to his beloved
Daughter,
whom she survived only three months.
She died 19th of February 1811.

This may probably be considered as the last act of his life;—a very affecting one it is, and worthy of remembrance. Such a monument is more honourable to the King, by whom it was set up, than if he had erected a pyramid.

SPECIMENS, ETC.

THE annexed Specimens of Sir Philip Sidney's hexameters will sufficiently evince that the failure of the attempt to naturalize this fine measure in his days, was owing to the manner in which the attempt was made, not to the measure itself.

First shall fertile grounds not yield increase of a good seed.
First the rivers shall cease to repay their floods to the ocean:
First may a trusty greyhound transform himself to a tiger.
First shall vertue be vice, and beauty be counted a blemish;
Ere that I leave with song of praise her praise to solemnize,
Her praise, whence to the world all praise hath his only beginning:
But yet well I do find each man most wise in his own case.
None can speak of a wound with skill, if he have not a wound felt:
Great to thee my state seems, thy state is blest by my judgment:
And yet neither of us great or blest deemeth his own self,
For yet (weigh this, alas!) great is not great to the greater.
What judge you doth a hillock show, by the lofty Olympus?
Such my minute greatness doth seem compar'd to the greatest.
When Cedars to the ground fall down by the weight of an Emmet,
Or when a rich Rubie's price be the worth of a Walnut,
Or to the Sun for wonders seem small sparks of a candle:
Then by my high Cedar, rich Rubie, and only shining Sun,
Vertues, riches, beauties of mine shall great be reputed.
Oh, no, no, worthy Shepherd, worth can never enter a title,

Where proofs justly do teach, thus matcht, such worth to be nought, worth;
Let not a Puppet abuse thy sprite, Kings' Crowns do not help them
From the cruel headach, nor shoes of gold do the gout heal;
And precious Couches full oft are shak't with a feaver.
If then a bodily evil in a bodily gloze be not hidden,
Shall such morning dews be an ease to the heat of a love's fire?

Sidney's pentameters appear even more uncouth than his hexameters, as more unlike their model; for, in our pronunciation, the Latin pentameter reads as if it ended with two trochees.

Fortune, Nature, Love, long have contended about me,
Which should most miseries cast on a worm that I am.
Fortune thus 'gan say, misery and misfortune is all one,
And of misfortune, fortune hath only the gift.
With strong foes on land, on sea with contrary tempests,
Still do I cross this wretch what so he taketh in hand.
Tush, tush, said Nature, this is all but a trifle, a man's self,
Gives haps or mishaps, even as he ordereth his heart.
But so his humor I frame, in a mould of choler adusted,
That the delights of life shall be to him dolorous.
Love smiled, and thus said; What joyn'd to desire is unhappy:
But if he nought do desire, what can Heraclitus ail?
None but I work by desire: by desire have I kindled in his soul
Infernal agonies into a beauty divine:
Where thou poor Nature left'st all thy due glory, to Fortune
Her vertue is soveraign, Fortune a vassal of hers.
Nature abasht went back: Fortune blusht: yet she replied thus:
And even in that love shall I reserve him a spite.
Thus, thus, alas! woful by Nature, unhappy by Fortune;
But most wretched I am, now love awakes my desire.

Sidney has also given examples in his Arcadia of Anacreontic, Phaleucian, Sapphic, and Asclepiad verse, all written upon the same erroneous principle. Those persons who consider it ridiculous to write English verses upon any scheme of Latin versification, may perhaps be surprised to learn that they have read, as blank verse, many lines which are perfect Sapphics or Phaleucians. Rowe's tragedies are full of such lines.

The Censura Literaria supplies me with two choice samples of Stanihurst's Virgil.

Neere joynctlye brayeth with rufflerye [1] rumbled Ætna.
Soomtyme owt it bolcketh [2] from bulck clowds grimly bedimmed
Like fyerd pitcho skorching, or flash flame sulphurus heating:
Flownce to the stars towring thee fire like a pellet is hurled,
Ragd rocks, up raking, and guts of mounten yrented
From roote up he jogleth: stoans hudge slag [3] molten he rowseth,
With routo snort grumbling, in bottom flash furie kindling.
Men say that Enceladus, with bolt haulf blasted, here harbrought,
Ding'd [4] with this squising [5] and massive burthen of Ætna,
Which pres on him nailed, from broached chimneys stil heateth:
As oft as the giant his brold [6] syds croompeled altreth,
So oft Sicil [7] al shivereth, therewith flaks smoakye be sparckled.

T'ward Sicil is seated, to the welkin loftily peaking,
A soyl, ycleapt Liparon, from whence with flounce furye flinging,
Stoans and hurlye bulets, like tampounds, maynelye betowring.
Under is a kennel, wheare chymneys fyrye be scorching
Of Cyclopan tosters, with rent rocks chamferye sharded,
Lowd rub a dub tabering with frapping rip rap of Ætna.
In the den are drumming gads of steele, parchfulye sparckling,
And flam's fierclye glowing, from furnace flashye be whisking.
Vulcan his boate fordgharth, named oke thee Vulcian Island.
Doun from the hev'nlye palace travayled the firye God hither.
In this cave the rakehels yr'no bars, bigge bulcked ar hamring,
Brontes and Steropes, with baerlym swartie Pyracmon.
These thre nere upbotching, not shapte, but partlye wel onward,

[1] Ruffling seems to be turbulent noise. A ruffler was formerly a boisterous bully.
[2] To bolck or boke, is *ructare*.
[3] Slag is the dross of iron.
[4] Dash'd down.
[5] Squeezing.
[6] *i. e.* Broiled sides crumpled.
[7] Trinacria.

76

A clapping fier-bolt (such as oft with rounce rebel hobble,
Jove to the ground clattreth) but yeet not finnished holye.
Three showrs wringlye wrythen glimmering, and forciblye sowcing,
Thre watrye clowds shymring to the craft they rampired hizzing,
Three wheru's fierd glystring, with south winds rufflered huffling.
Now doe they rayse gastly lightnings, now grislye reboundings
Of ruffe raffe roaring, mens hurts with terror agrysing,
With peale meale ramping, with thwick thwack sturdilye than-
    dering.

Stanihurst's Virgil is certainly one of those curiosities
in our literature which ought to be reprinted. Yet
notwithstanding the almost incredible absurdity of this
version, Stanihurst is entitled to an honourable remem-
brance for the part which he contributed to Holinshed's
Collection of Chronicles. None of our chroniclers pos-
sessed a mind better stored, nor an intellect more per-
petually on the alert.

Sidney, who failed so entirely in writing hexameters,
has written concerning them, in his Defence of Poesie,
with the good sense and propriety of thought by which
that beautiful treatise is distinguished. Let me not be
thought to disparage this admirable man and delightful
writer, because it has been necessary for me to show
the cause of his failure in an attempt wherein I have
now followed him. I should not forgive myself, were
I ever to mention Sidney without an expression of re-
verence and love.

« Of versifying,» he says, « there are two sorts, the
one ancient, the other modern; the ancient marked
the quantity of each syllable, and, according to that,
framed his verse; the modern, observing only number,
with some regard of the accent; the chief life of it
standeth in that like sounding of the words, which we
call Rhyme. Whether of these be the more excellent,
would bear many speeches, the ancient, no doubt, more
fit for musick, both words and time observing quan-
tity, and more fit, lively to express divers passions by
the low or lofty sound of the well-weighed syllable.
The latter likewise with his Rhyme striketh a certain
musick to the ear; and, in fine, since it doth delight,
though by another way, it obtaineth the same purpose,
there being in either sweetness, and wanting in neither
majesty. Truly the English, before any vulgar lan-
guage I know, is fit for both sorts; for, for the ancient,
the Italian is so full of vowels, that it must ever be
cumbered with elisions: the Dutch so, of the other
side, with consonants, that they cannot yield the sweet
sliding, fit for a verse. The French, in his whole lan-
guage, hath not one word that hath his accent in the
last syllable, saving two, called Antepenultima; and
little more hath the Spanish, and therefore very grace-
lessly may they use Dactyls; the English is subject to
none of these defects. Now for Rhyme, though we do
not observe quantity, yet we observe the accent very
precisely, which other languages either cannot do, or
will not do so absolutely.

« That Cæsura, or breathing-place, in the midst of the
verse, neither Italian nor Spanish have; the French and
we never almost fail of. Lastly, the very Rhyme itself
the Italian cannot put in the last syllable, by the French
named the Masculine Rhyme, but still in the next to
the last, which the French call the Female, or the next
before that, which the Italian call Sdrucciola: the ex-
ample of the former, is Buono Suono: of the Sdruc-
ciola, is Femina Semina. The French, on the other

side, hath both the male, as Bon Son; and the Female,
as Plaise, Taise, but the Sdrucciola he hath not, where
the English hath all three, as Due, True, Father, Rather,
Motion, Potion, with much more, which might be said,
but that already I find the trifling of this discourse is
too much enlarged.»

The French attempted to introduce the ancient me-
tres some years before the trial was made in England.
Pasquier says, that Estienne Jodelle led the way in the
year 1553, by this distich upon the poems of Olivier de
Maigny, « lequel,» he adds, « est vrayement une petit
chef d'œuvre.»

    Phœbus, Amour, Cypris, veut sauver, nourrir et orner
      Ton vers et chef, d'umbre, de flamme, de fleurs.

Pasquier himself, three years afterwards, at the soli-
citation of a friend, produced the following « essay de
plus longue haleine.»

Rien ne me plaist sinon de te chanter, et servir et orner ;
  Rien ne te plaist mon bien, rien ne te plaist que ma mort.
Plus je roquiers, et plus je me tiens seur d'estre refusé,
  Et ce refus pourtant point ne me semble refus.
O trompeurs attraicts, desir ardent, prompte volonté,
  Espoir, non espoir, ains miserable pipeur.
Discours mensongers, trahistreux œil, aspre cruauté,
  Qui me ruine le corps, qui me ruine le cœur.
Pourquoy tant de faveurs t'ont les Cieux mis à l'abandon,
  Ou pourquoy dans moy si violente fureur ?
Si vaine est ma fureur, si vain est tout ce que des cieux
  Tu tiens, s'en toy gist cette cruelle rigeur :
Dieux patrons de l'amour bannissez d'elle la beauté,
  Ou bien l'accouple d'une amiable pitié ;
Ou si dans le miel vous meslez un venimeux fiel,
  Vueillez Dieux que l'amour r'entre dedans le Chaos :
Commandez que le froid, l'eau, l'Esté, l'humide, l'ardeur :
  Brief que ce tout par tout tende à l'abisme de tous,
Pour finir ma douleur, pour finir cette cruauté,
  Qui me ruine le corps, qui me ruine le cœur.
Non helas que ce rond soit tout un sans se rechanger,
  Mai que ma Sourde se change, ou de face, ou de façons :
Mais que ma Sourde se change, et plus douce escoute les voix,
  Voix que je seme criant, voix que je seme, riant.
Et que le feu du froid desormais puisse triompher,
  Et que le froid au feu perde sa lente vigeur :
Ainsi s'assopira mon tourment, et la cruauté
  Qui me ruine le corps, qui me ruine le cœur.

« Je ne dy pas,» says the author, « que ces vers soient
de quelque valeur, aussi ne les mets-je icy sur la mon-
stre en intention qu'on les trouve tels ; mais bien estime-
je qu'ils sont autant fluides que les Latins, et à tant
veux-je que l'on pense nostre vulgaire estre aucune-
ment capable de ce subject.» Pasquier's verses were
not published till many years after they were written;
and in the meantime Jean Antoine de Baif made the
attempt upon a larger scale,—« toutesfois,» says Pas-
quier, « en ce subject si mauvais parrain que non seule-
ment il ne fut suivy d'aucun, mais au contraire des-
couragea un chacun de s'y employer. D'autant que
tout ce qu'il en fit estoit tant despourveu de cette naif-
veté qui doit accompagner nos œuvres, qu'aussi tost que
cette sienne poësie voit la lumière, elle mourut comme
un avorton.» The Abbé Goujet, therefore, had no rea-
son to represent this attempt as a proof of the bad taste
of the age: the bad taste of an age is proved, when vi-
cious compositions are applauded, not when they are
unsuccessful. Jean Antoine de Baif is the writer of
whom the Cardinal du Perron said « qu'il étoit bon
homme, mais qu'il étoit méchant poète François.»

I subjoin a specimen of Spanish Hexameters, from an Eclogue by D. Esteban de Villegas, a poet of great and deserved estimation in his own country.

Licidas y Coridon, Coridon el amante de Filis,
Pastor el uno de cabras, el otro de blancas ovejas,
Ambos á dos tiernos, mozos ambos, Arcades ambos,
Viendo que los rayos del Sol fatigaban al Orbe,
Y que vibrando fuego feroz la Canicula ladra,
Al puro cristal, que cria la fuente sonora,
Llevados del son alegre de su blando susurro,
Las plantas veloces mueven, los pasos animan,
Y al tronco de un verde enebro se sientan amigos.

Tú, que los erguidos sobrepujas del hondo Timavo
Peñones, generoso Duque, con tu inclita frente,
Si acaso tocare el eco de mi rústica avena
Tus sienes, si acaso llega a tu fértil alcono,
Francisco, del acento mio la sonora Talia,
Oye pio, responde grato, censura severo :
No menos al caro hermano generoso retratas,
Que al tronco prudente sigues, generoso naciste
Héroe, que guarde el Cielo dilatando tus años ;
Licidas y Coridon, Coridon el amante de Filis,
Pastores, las Musas aman, recrearte desean :
Tu, cuerdo, perdona entretanto la bárbara Musa,

Que presto, inspirando Pean con amigo Coturno,
En trompa, que al Olimpo llegue por el ábrego suelta,
Tu fama llevarán los ecos del Gangos al Istro,
Y luego, torciendo el vuelo, del Aquilo al Austro?

It is admitted by the Spaniards, that the fitness of their language for the hexameter has been established by Villegas; his success, however, did not induce other poets to follow the example. I know not whom it was that he followed, for he was not the first to make the attempt. Neither do I know whether it was ever made in Portuguese, except in some verses upon St Ursula and the Eleven Thousand Virgins, which are Latin as well as Portuguese, and were written as a whimsical proof of the affinity of the two languages. I have found no specimens in Italian. The complete success of the metre in Germany is well known. The Bohemians have learnt the tune, and have, like their neighbours, a translation of the Iliad in the measure of the original. This I learn accidentally from a Bohemian grammar; which shows me also, that the Bohemians make a dactyl of Achilles, probably because they pronounce the χ with a strong aspirate.

Minor Poems.

Nos hæc novimus esse nihil.

TO EDITH SOUTHEY.

WITH way-worn feet, a traveller woe-begone,
Life's upward road I journey'd many a day,
And framing many a sad yet soothing lay,
Beguiled the solitary hours with song.
Lonely my heart and rugged was the way,
Yet often pluck'd I, as I past along,
The wild and simple flowers of poesy ;
And sometimes unreflecting as a child
Entwined the weeds which pleased a random eye.
Take thou the wreath, BELOVED ! it is wild
And rudely garlanded ; yet scorn not thou
The humble offering, where dark rosemary weaves
Amid gay flowers its melancholy leaves,
And myrtle gathered to adorn thy brow.
1796.

TO MARY WOLLSTONECRAFT.

THE lily cheek, the « purple light of love,»
The liquid lustre of the melting eye,—
MARY ! of these the Poet sung, for these
Did Woman triumph ;—Wilt thou with a frown
Regard the theme unworthy ?—At that age
No MAID of ARC had snatch'd from coward man
The avenging sword of freedom : woman-kind
Recorded then no ROLAND's martyrdom ;
No CORDE's angel and avenging arm
Had sanctified again the Murderer's name,
As erst when Cæsar perish'd : and some strains
Haply may hence be drawn, befitting me
To offer, nor unworthy thy regard.

THE TRIUMPH OF WOMAN.

The Subject of the following Poem may be found in the Third and Fourth Chapters of the First Book of Esdras.

GLAD as the weary traveller tempest-tost
To reach secure at length his native coast,
Who wandering long o'er distant lands has sped,
The night-blast wildly howling round his head,
Known all the woes of want, and felt the storm
Of the bleak winter parch his shivering form ;
The journey o'er and every peril past
Beholds his little cottage-home at last,
And as he sees afar the smoke curl slow,
Feels his full eyes with transport overflow;
So from the scene where Death and Anguish reign,
And Vice and Folly drench with blood the plain,
Joyful I turn, to sing the Woman's praise
Avail'd again Jerusalem to raise,
Call'd forth the sanction of the Despot's nod,
And freed the nation best beloved of God.

Darius gives the feast ; to Persia's court,
Awed by his will, the obedient throng resort :
Attending Satraps swell their prince's pride,
And vanquish'd Monarchs grace the Conqueror's side.
No more the Warrior wears the garb of war,
Girds on the sword, or mounts the scythed car ;
No more Judæa's sons dejected go,
And hang the head, and heave the sigh of woe.
From Persia's rugged hills descend the train,
From where Orontes foams along the plain,

From where Choaspes rolls his royal waves,
And India sends her sons, submissive slaves.
Thy daughters, Babylon, for this high feast
Weave the loose robe, and paint the flowery vest,
With roseate wreaths they braid the glossy hair,
They tinge the cheek which nature form'd so fair,
Learn the soft step, the soul-subduing glance,
Melt in the song, and swim adown the dance,
Exalted on the Monarch's golden throne,
In royal state the fair Apame shone;
Her form of majesty, her eyes of fire,
Chill with respect, or kindle with desire.
The admiring multitude her charms adore,
And own her worthy of the rank she bore.

Now on his couch reclined Darius lay,
Tired with the toilsome pleasures of the day;
Without Judæa's watchful sons await,
To guard the sleeping idol of the state.
Three youths were these of Judah's royal race,
Three youths whom Nature dower'd with every grace,
To each the form of symmetry she gave,
And haughty genius curs'd each favourite slave;
These fill'd the cup, around the Monarch kept,
Served when he spake, and guarded while he slept.

Yet oft for Salem's hallow'd towers laid low
The sigh would heave, the unbidden tear would flow;
And when the dull and wearying round of power
Allow'd Zorobabel one vacant hour,
He loved on Babylon's high wall to roam,
And lingering gaze toward his distant home;
Or on Euphrates's willowy banks reclined
Hear the sad Harp moan fitful to the wind.

As now the perfumed lamps stream wide their light,
And social converse cheers the livelong night,
Thus spake Zorobabel : « Too long in vain
For Zion desolate her sons complain ;
All hopelessly our years of sorrow flow,
And these proud heathen mock their captives' woe.
While Cyrus triumphed here in victor state
A brighter prospect cheer'd our exiled fate;
Our sacred walls again he bade us raise,
And to Jehovah rear the pile of praise.
Quickly these fond hopes faded from our eyes,
As the frail sun that gilds the wintry skies,
And spreads a moment's radiance o'er the plain,
Soon hid by clouds which dim the scene again.

Opprest by Artaxerxes' jealous reign,
We vainly pleaded here, and wept in vain.
Now when Darius, chief of mild command,
Bids joy and pleasure fill the festive land,
Still shall we droop the head in sullen grief,
And sternly silent shun to seek relief?
What if amid the Monarch's mirthful throng
Our harps should echo to the cheerful song?»

« Fair is the occasion,» thus the one replied,
« Now then let all our tuneful skill be tried.
While the gay courtiers quaff the smiling bowl,
And wine's strong fumes inspire the madden'd soul,
Where all around is merriment, be mine
To strike the lute, and praise the power of Wine.»

« And while,» his friend replied, « in state alone,
Lord of the earth, Darius fills the throne,
Be yours the mighty power of Wine to sing,
My lute shall sound the praise of Persia's King.»

To them Zorobabel : « On themes like these
Seek ye the Monarch of Mankind to please :
To Wine superior, or to Power's strong arms,
Be mine to sing resistless Woman's charms.
To him victorious in the rival lays
Shall just Darius give the meed of praise ;
The purple robe his honour'd frame shall fold,
The beverage sparkle in his cup of gold ;
A golden couch support his bed of rest,
The chain of honour grace his favour'd breast;
His the rich turban, his the car's array,
O'er Babylon's high wall to wheel its way,
And for his wisdom seated on the throne,
For the KING's COUSIN shall the Bard be known.»

Intent they meditate the future lay,
And watch impatient for the dawn of day.
The morn rose clear, and shrill were heard the flute,
The cornet, sackbut, dulcimer, and lute ;
To Babylon's gay streets the throng resort,
Swarm through the gates, and fill the festive court.
High on his throne Darius tower'd in pride,
The fair Apame graced the Sovereign's side :
And now she smiled, and now with mimic frown
Placed on her brow the Monarch's sacred crown.
In transport o'er her faultless form he bends,
Loves every look, and every act commends.

And now Darius bids the herald call
Judæa's Bards to grace the thronging hall.
Hush'd is each sound, the attending crowd are mute,
And then the Hebrew gently touch'd the lute:

When the Traveller on his way,
Who has toil'd the livelong day ;
Feels around on every side
The chilly mists of eventide,
Fatigued and faint his weary mind
Recurs to all he leaves behind ;
He thinks upon the well-trimm'd hearth,
The evening hour of social mirth.
And her who at departing day
Weeps for her husband far away.
Oh give to him the flowing bowl !
Bid it renovate his soul !
Then shall sorrow sink to sleep,
And he who wept no more shall weep ;
For his care-clouded brow shall clear,
And his glad eye will sparkle through the tear.

When the poor man heart-opprest
Betakes him to his evening rest,
And worn with labour thinks in sorrow
Of the labour of to-morrow :
When sadly musing on his lot
He hies him to his joyless cot,
And loathes to meet his children there,
The rivals for his scanty fare ;
Oh give to him the flowing bowl !
Bid it renovate his soul !

The generous juice with magic power
Shall cheat with happiness the hour,
And with each warm affection fill
The heart by want and wretchedness made chill.

When, at the dim close of day,
The Captive loves alone to stray
Along the haunts recluse and rude
Of sorrow and of solitude;
When he sits with mournful eye
To mark the lingering radiance die,
And lets distempered Fancy roam
Amid the ruins of his home;—
Oh give to him the flowing bowl!
Bid it renovate his soul!
The bowl shall better thoughts bestow,
And lull to rest his wakeful woe,
And joy shall bless the evening hour,
And make the Captive Fortune's conqueror.

When the wearying cares of state
Oppress the Monarch with their weight,
When from his pomp retired alone
He feels the duties of the throne,
Feels that the multitude below
Depend on him for weal or woe;
When his powerful will may bless
A realm with peace and happiness,
Or with desolating breath
Breathe ruin round, and woe, and death:
Oh give to him the flowing bowl!
Bid it humanize his soul!
He shall not feel the empire's weight,
He shall not feel the cares of state,
The bowl shall each dark thought beguile,
And Nations live and prosper from his smile.

Hush'd was the lute, the Hebrew ceased the song,
Long peals of plaudits echoed from the throng;
Each tongue the liberal words of praise repaid,
On every cheek a smile applauding play'd;
The rival Bard approach'd, he struck the string,
And pour'd the loftier song to Persia's King.
Why should the wearying cares of state
Oppress the Monarch with their weight?
Alike to him if peace shall bless
The multitude with happiness;
Alike to him if frenzied War
Careers triumphant on the embattled plain
And rolling on o'er myriads slain,
With gore and wounds shall clog his scythed car.
What though the tempest rage! no sound
Of the deep thunder shakes his distant throne,
And the red flash that spreads destruction round,
Reflects a glorious splendour on the crown.

Where is the Man who with ennobling pride
Beholds not his own nature? where is he
Who without awe can see
The mysteries of the human mind,
The miniature of Deity?
For Man the vernal clouds descending
Shower down their fertilizing rain;
For Man the ripen'd harvest bending
Waves with soft murmur o'er the plenteous plain.
He spreads the sail on high,

The rude gale wafts him o'er the main;
For him the winds of heaven subservient blow,
Earth teems for him, for him the waters flow,
He thinks, and wills, and acts, a Deity below!

Where is the King who with elating pride
Sees not this Man, this godlike Man his slave?
Mean are the mighty by the Monarch's side;
Alike the wise, alike the brave
With timid step and pale, advance,
And tremble at the royal glance;
Suspended millions watch his breath,
Whose smile is happiness, whose frown is death.

Why goes the Peasant from that little cot,
Where PEACE and LOVE have blest his humble life?
In vain his agonizing wife
With tears bedews her husband's face,
And clasps him in a long and last embrace;
In vain his children round his bosom creep,
And weep to see their mother weep,
Fettering their father with their little arms!
What are to him the war's alarms?
What are to him the distant foes?
He at the earliest dawn of day
To daily labour went his way;
And when he saw the sun decline,
He sate in peace beneath his vine—
The King commands, the peasant goes,
From all he loved on earth he flies,
And for his monarch toils, and fights, and bleeds,
and dies.

What though yon City's castled wall
Cast o'er the darken'd plain its crested shade?
What though her Priests in earnest terror call
On all their host of Gods to aid?
Vain is the bulwark, vain the tower!
In vain her gallant youths expose
Their breasts, a bulwark, to the foes!
In vain at that tremendous hour,
Clasp'd in the savage soldier's reeking arms,
Shrieks to tame Heaven the violated Maid!
By the rude hand of Ruin scatter'd round,
Their moss-grown towers shall spread the desert ground.
Low shall the mouldering palace lie,
Amid the princely halls the grass wave high,
And through the shatter'd roof descend the inclement
sky.

Gay o'er the embattled plain
Moves yonder warrior train,
Their banners wanton on the morning gale!
Full on their bucklers beams the rising ray,
Their glittering helms give glory to the day;
The shout of war rings echoing o'er the vale;
Far reaches as the aching eye can strain
The splendid horror of their wide array.
Ah! not in vain expectant, o'er
Their glorious pomp the vultures soar!
Amid the Conqueror's palace high
Shall sound the song of victory;
Long after journeying o'er the plain
The traveller shall with startled eye
See their white bones then blanched by many a winter
sky.

Lord of the earth! we will not raise
The temple to thy bounded praise.
For thee no victim need expire;
For thee no altar blaze with hallowed fire.
The burning City flames for thee,
Thine Altar is the field of victory!
Thy sacred Majesty to bless
Man a self-offer'd victim freely flies;
To thee he sacrifices Happiness
And Peace, and Love's endearing ties;
To thee a Slave he lives, for thee a Slave he dies.

Hush'd was the lute, the Hebrew ceased to sing;
The shout rush'd forth, For ever live the King!
Loud was the uproar, as when Rome's decree
Pronounced Achaia once again was free;
Assembled Greece enrapt with 'fond belief
Heard the false boon, and bless'd the treacherous Chief.
Each breast with freedom's holy ardour glows,
From every voice the cry of rapture rose;
Their thundering clamours rend the astonished sky,
And birds o'erpassing hear, and drop, and die.
Thus o'er the Persian dome their plaudits ring,
And the high hall re-echoed—Live the King!
The Mutes bow'd reverent down before their Lord,
The assembled Satraps envied and adored;
Joy sparkled in the Monarch's conscious eyes,
And his pleased pride already doom'd the prize.

Silent they saw Zorobabel advance:
Quick on Apame shot his timid glance;
With downward eye he paused a moment mute,
Then with light finger touch'd the softer lute.
Apame knew the Hebrew's grateful cause,
And bent her head, and sweetly smiled applause.

Why is the warrior's cheek so red?
Why downward droops his musing head?
Why that slow step, that faint advance,
That keen yet quick retreating glance;
That crested head in war tower'd high,
No backward glance disgraced that eye,
No flushing fear that cheek o'erspread,
When stern he strode o'er heaps of dead:
Strange tumult now his bosom moves,—
The Warrior fears because he loves.

Why does the Youth delight to rove
Amid the dark and lonely grove?
Why in the throng where all are gay,
With absent eyes from gaiety distraught,
Sits he alone in silent thought?
Silent he sits, for far away
His passion'd soul delights to stray;
Recluse he roves as if he fain would shun
All human-kind, because he loves but One!

Yes, King of Persia, thou art blest!
But not because the sparkling bowl
To rapture elevates thy waken'd soul;
But not because of Power possest;
Nor that the Nations dread thy nod,
And Princes reverence thee their earthly God!
Even on a Monarch's solitude
Will Care, dark visitant, intrude;

The bowl brief pleasure can bestow,
The purple cannot shield from woe!
But, King of Persia, thou art blest,
For Heaven who raised thee thus the world above,
Hath made the happy in Apame's love!

Oh! I have seen him fondly trace
The heavenly features of her face,
Rove o'er her form with eager eye,
And sigh and gaze, and gaze and sigh.
Lo! from his brow with mimic frown
Apame takes the sacred crown;
Those sparkling eyes, that radiant face,
Give to the diadem new grace:
And subject to a Woman's laws,
Darius sees, and smiles applause!

He ceased, and silent still remain'd the throng,
While rapt attention own'd the power of song.
Then, loud as when the wintry whirlwinds blow,
From every voice the thundering plaudits flow;
Darius smiled, Apame's sparkling eyes
Glanced on the King, and Woman won the prize.

Now silent sate the expectant crowd: Alone
The victor Hebrew gazed not on the throne;
With deeper hue his cheek distemper'd glows,
With statelier stature loftier now he rose;
Heavenward he gazed, regardless of the throng,
And pour'd with awful voice sublimer song.

Ancient of days! Eternal Truth! one hymn,
One holier strain the Bard shall raise to thee,
Thee Powerful! Thee Benevolent! Thee Just!
Friend! Father! All in All!—The Vine's rich blood,
The Monarch's might, and Woman's conquering charms,
These shall we praise alone?—O ye who sit
Beneath your vine, and quaff at evening hour
The healthful bowl, remember Him whose dews,
Whose rains, whose sun, matured the growing fruit,
Creator and Preserver!—Reverence Him,
O thou who from thy throne dispensest life
And death, for He hath delegated power,
And thou shalt one day at the throne of God
Render thy strict account!—O ye who gaze
Enrapt on Beauty's fascinating form,
Gaze on with love, and loving beauty, learn
To shun abhorrent all the mental eye
Beholds deform'd and foul; for so shall Love
Climb to the source of goodness. God of truth!
All-Just! All-Mighty! I should ill deserve
Thy noblest gift, the gift divine of song,
If, so content with ear-deep melodies,
To please all-profitless, I did not pour
Severer strains; of Truth—eternal Truth,
Unchanging Justice, universal Love.
Such strains awake the Soul to loftiest thoughts;
Such strains the blessed Spirits of the Good
Waft, grateful incense! to the Halls of Heaven.

The dying notes still murmur'd on the string,
When from his throne arose the raptured king.
About to speak he stood, and waved his hand,
And all-expectant sate the obedient band.

Then just and generous, thus the Monarch cries,
" Be thine, Zorobabel, the well-earn'd prize.

The purple robe of state thy form shall fold,
The beverage sparkle in thy cup of gold;
The golden couch, the car, and honour'd chain,
Requite the merits of thy favour'd strain,
And raised supreme the ennobled race among
Be call'd MY COUSIN for the victor song.
Nor these alone the victor song shall bless,
Ask what thou wilt, and what thou wilt possess.»

« Fallen is Jerusalem !» the Hebrew cries,
And patriot anguish fills his streaming eyes,
« Hurl'd to the earth by Rapine's vengeful rod,
Polluted lies the temple of our God;
Far in a foreign land her sons remain,
Hear the keen taunt, and drag the captive chain;
In fruitless woe they wear the wearying years,
And steep the bread of bitterness in tears.
O monarch, greatest, mildest, best of men,
Restore us to those ruined walls again!
Allow us to rebuild that sacred dome,
To live in liberty, and die at Home.»

So spake Zorobabel.—Thus Woman's praise
Availed again Jerusalem to raise,
Call'd forth the sanction of the Despot's nod,
And freed the Nation best beloved of God.

1793.

POEMS CONCERNING THE SLAVE TRADE. [1]

SONNET I.

HOLD your mad hands! for ever on your plain
Must the gorged vulture clog his beak with blood?
For ever must your Niger's tainted flood
Roll to the ravenous shark his banquet slain?
Hold your mad hands! what demon prompts to rear
The arm of Slaughter! on your savage shore
Can Hell-sprung Glory claim the feast of gore,
With laurels water'd by the widow's tear
Wreathing his helmet crown?—Lift high the spear!
And like the desolating whirlwind's sweep,
Plunge ye yon bark of anguish in the deep;

[1] When first the Abolition of the SLAVE-TRADE was agitated in England, the friends of humanity endeavoured by two means to accomplish it—to destroy the Trade immediately by the interference of Government; or by the disuse of West-Indian productions: *a slow but certain method.* For a while Government held the language of Justice, and individuals with enthusiasm banished sugar from their tables. This enthusiasm soon cooled; the majority of those who had made this *sacrifice* (I prostitute the word, but such they thought it), persuaded themselves that parliament would do all, and that individual efforts were no longer necessary. Thus ended the one attempt; it is not difficult to say why the other has failed,—it is not difficult, when the minister has once found himself in the minority, and on the side of Justice.— Would to God that the interests of those who dispose of us as they please, had been as closely connected with the preservation of Peace and Liberty, as with the continuance of this traffic in human flesh !

There are yet two other methods remaining, by which this traffic will probably be abolished—by the introduction of East-Indian or maple sugar, or by the just and general rebellion of the Negroes.

To these past and present prospects the following Poems occasionally allude: to the English custom of exciting wars upon the slave-coast that they may purchase prisoners, and to the punishment sometimes inflicted upon a Negro for Murder, of which Hector St John was an eye-witness.

For the pale fiend cold-hearted Commerce there
Hath spread his toils accursed wide and far,
And calls, to share the prey, his kindred Demon War.

SONNET II.

WHY dost thou beat thy breast and rend thine hair,
And to the deaf sea pour thy frantic cries?
Before the gale the laden vessel flies;
The Heavens all-favouring smile, the breeze is fair;
Hark to the clamours of the exulting crew!
Hark how their thunders mock the patient skies!
Why dost thou shriek, and strain thy red-swoln eyes,
As the white sail is lessening from thy view?
Go pine in want and anguish and despair,
There is no mercy found in human-kind!
Go, Widow, to thy grave and rest thee there!
But may the God of justice bid the wind
Whelm that curst bark beneath the mountain wave,
And bless with Liberty and Death the Slave !

SONNET III.

OH, he is worn with toil! the big drops run
Down his dark cheek; hold—hold thy merciless hand,
Pale tyrant! for beneath thy hard command
O'erwearied nature sinks. The scorching Sun,
As pitiless as proud Prosperity,
Darts on him his full beams: gasping he lies
Arraigning with his looks the patient skies,
While that inhuman trader lifts on high
The mangling scourge. O ye who at your ease
Sip the blood-sweeten'd beverage! thoughts like these
Haply ye scorn: I thank thee, Gracious God,
That I do feel upon my cheek the glow
Of indignation, when beneath the rod
A sable brother writhes in silent woe.

SONNET IV.

'T is night; the mercenary tyrants sleep
As undisturb'd as Justice! but no more
The wretched Slave, as on his native shore,
Rests on his reedy couch: he wakes to weep!
Though through the toil and anguish of the day
No tear escaped him, not one suffering groan
Beneath the twisted thong, he weeps alone
In bitterness; thinking that far away
Though the gay Negroes join the midnight song,
Though merriment resounds on Niger's shore,
She whom he loves far from the cheerful throng
Stands sad, and gazes from her lowly door
With dim-grown eye, silent and woe-begone,
And weeps for him who will return no more.

SONNET V.

DID then the Negro rear at last the Sword
Of Vengeance? drench'd he deep its thirsty blade
In the hard heart of his tyrannic lord?
Oh! who shall blame him? through the midnight shade
Still o'er his tortured memory rush'd the thought
Of every past delight; his native grove,
Friendship's best joys, and Liberty and Love,

All lost for ever! Then Remembrance wrought
His soul to madness : round his restless bed
Freedom's pale spectre stalk'd, with a stern smile
Pointing the wounds of Slavery, the while
She shook her chains and hung her sullen head:
No more on Heaven he calls with fruitless breath,
But sweetens with revenge the draught of death.

SONNET VI.

High in the air exposed the Slave is hung,
To all the birds of Heaven, their living food!
He groans not, though awaked by that fierce Sun
New tortures live to drink their parent blood!
He groans not, though the gorging Vulture tear
The quivering fibre! Hither gaze, O ye
Who tore this Man from Peace and Liberty!
Gaze hither, ye who weigh with scrupulous care
The right and prudent; for beyond the grave
There is another world!—And call to mind,
Ere your decrees proclaim to all mankind
Murder is legalized, that there the Slave,
Before the Eternal, « thunder-tongued shall plead
Against the deep damnation of your deed.»
                                   1794.

TO THE GENIUS OF AFRICA.

O thou, who from the mountain's height
Roll'st down thy clouds with all their weight
Of waters to old Nile's majestic tide ;
    Or o'er the dark sepulchral plain
    Recallest Carthage in her ancient pride,
        The Mistress of the Main;
Hear, Genius, hear thy children's cry!
Not always shouldst thou love to brood
    Stern o'er the desert solitude,
Where seas of Sand toss their hot surges high;
Nor, Genius, should the midnight song
    Detain thee in some milder mood
        The palmy plains among,
    Where Gambia to the torch's light
Flows radiant through the awaken'd night.

    Ah, linger not to hear the song!
    Genius, avenge thy children's wrong!
    The Demon Avarice on your shore
    Pours all the horrors of his train,
And hark! where from the field of gore
    Howls the hyena o'er the slain!
Lo! where the flaming village fires the skies!
    Avenging Power, awake! arise!

    Arise, thy children's wrongs redress!
    Ah, heed the mother's wretchedness!
        When in the hot infectious air
    O'er her sick babe she bows opprest,—
    Ah, hear her when the Traders tear
    The drooping infant from her breast!
    Whelm'd in the waters he shall rest!
    Hear thou the wretched mother's cries,
    Avenging Power! awake! arise!

By the rank infected air
That taints those dungeons of despair,

By the scourges blacken'd o'er
And stiff and hard with human gore,
By every groan of deep distress,
By every curse of wretchedness,
By all the train of Crimes that flow
From the hopelessness of Woe,
By every drop of blood bespilt,
By Afric's wrongs and Europe's guilt,
    Awake! arise! avenge!

And thou hast heard! and o'er their blood-fed plains
    Swept thine avenging hurricanes;
And bade thy storms with whirlwind roar
Dash their proud navies on the shore;
    And where their armies claim'd the fight
    Wither'd the warrior's might;
And o'er the unholy host with baneful breath,
There, Genius, thou hast breathed the gales of Death.[1]
                                   1795.

THE SAILOR,

WHO HAD SERVED IN THE SLAVE TRADE.

In September, 1798, a Dissenting Minister of Bristol discovered
a Sailor in the neighbourhood of that City, groaning and praying in
a cow-house. The circumstance which occasioned his agony of mind
is detailed in the annexed Ballad, without the slightest addition or
alteration. By presenting it as a Poem the story is made more pub-
lic, and such stories ought to be made as public as possible.

It was a Christian minister,
    Who, in the month of flowers,
Walk'd forth at eve amid the fields
    Near Bristol's ancient towers.

When from a lonely out-house breathed,
    He heard a voice of woe,
And groans which less might seem from pain,
    Than wretchedness to flow ·

Heart-rending groans they were, with words
    Of bitterest despair,
Yet with the holy name of Christ
    Pronounced in broken prayer.

The Christian minister went in,
    A sailor there he sees,
Whose hands were lifted up to Heaven,
    And he was on his knees.

Nor did the Sailor so intent
    His entering footsteps heed,
But now « Our Father» said, and now
    His half-forgotten creed;

And often on his Saviour call'd
    With many a bitter groan,
But in such anguish as may spring
    From deepest guilt alone.

The miserable man was ask'd
    Why he was kneeling there,
And what had been the crime that caused
    The anguish of his prayer.

[1] Alluding to the fatalities attending the British armament to and
in the West Indies.

I have done a cursed thing! he cried,
  It haunts me night and day,
And I have sought this lonely place
  Here undisturb'd to pray.

Aboard I have no place for prayer,
  So I came here alone,
That I might freely kneel and pray,
  And call on Christ, and groan.

If to the mainmast head I go,
  The Wicked One is there;
From place to place, from rope to rope,
  He follows every where.

I shut my eyes—it matters not—
  Still, still the same I see,—
And when I lie me down at night,
  'T is always day with me!

He follows, follows every where,
  And every place is Hell!
O God—and I must go with him
  In endless fire to dwell!

He follows, follows every where,
  He's still above—below!
Oh, tell me where to fly from him!
  Oh, tell me where to go!

But tell thou, quoth the Stranger then,
  What this thy crime hath been,
So haply I may comfort give
  To one who grieves for sin.

O cursed, cursed is the deed!
  The wretched man replies,
And night and day and every where
  'T is still before my eyes.

I sail'd on board a Guinea-man,
  And to the slave-coast went;—
Would that the sea had swallow'd me
  When I was innocent!

And we took in our cargo there,
  Three hundred negro slaves,
And we sail'd homeward merrily
  Over the ocean-waves.

But some were sulky of the slaves,
  And would not touch their meat,
So therefore we were forced by threats
  And blows to make them eat.

One woman, sulkier than the rest,
  Would still refuse her food,—
O Jesus God! I hear her cries!
  I see her in her blood!

The captain made me tie her up,
  And flog while he stood by,
And then he cursed me if I staid
  My hand to hear her cry.

She groan'd, she shriek'd,—I could not spare,
  For the Captain he stood by—
Dear God! that I might rest one night
  From that poor creature's cry!

What woman's child a sight like that
  Could bear to look upon!
And still the Captain would not spare—
  But bade me still flog on.

She could not be more glad than I
  When she was taken down:
A blessed minute!—'t was the last
  That I have ever known!

I did not close my eyes all night,
  Thinking what I had done;
I heard her groans and they grew faint
  Towards the rising sun.

She groan'd and moan'd, but her voice grew
  Fainter at morning tide,
Fainter and fainter still it came
  Until at noon she died.

They flung her overboard;—poor wretch!
  She rested from her pain,—
But when—O Christ! O blessed God!
  Shall I have rest again!

I saw the sea close over her,
  Yet she is still in sight;
I see her twisting every where;
  I see her day and night.

Go where I will, do what I can,
  The Wicked One I see:
Dear Christ; have mercy on my soul!
  O God, deliver me!

Oh give me comfort, if you can!
  Oh tell me where to fly!
Oh tell me if there can be hope
  For one so lost as I!

What said the Minister of Christ?
  He bade him trust in Heaven,
And call on Him for whose dear sake
  All sins shall be forgiven.

He told him of that precious blood
  Which should all sins efface;
Told him that none are lost, but they
  Who turn from proffer'd grace.

He bade him pray, and knelt with him,
  And join'd him in his prayers:—
And some who read the dreadful tale
  Perhaps will aid with theirs.

                                        1798.

VERSES

SPOKEN IN THE THEATRE AT OXFORD, UPON THE
INSTALLATION OF LORD GRENVILLE.

GRENVILLE, few years have had their course, since last
Exulting Oxford view'd a spectacle
Like this day's pomp; and yet to those who throng'd
These walls, which echoed then with Portland's praise,
What change hath intervened! The bloom of spring
Is fled from many a cheek, where roseate joy
And beauty bloom'd; the inexorable grave
Hath claim'd its portion; and the band of youths,
Who then, collected here as in the port
From whence to launch on life's adventurous sea,
Stood on the beach, ere this have found their lots
Of good or evil. Thus the lapse of years,
Evolving all things in its quiet course,
Hath wrought for them: and though those years have
                                                seen
Fearful vicissitudes, of wilder change
Than history yet had learnt, or old romance
In wildest mood imagined, yet these, too,
Portentous as they seem, not less have risen,
Each of its natural cause the sure effect,
All righteously ordain'd. Lo! kingdoms wreck'd,
Thrones overturn'd, built up, then swept away
Like fabrics in the summer clouds, dispersed
By the same breath that heap'd them; rightful kings,
Who, from a line of long-drawn ancestry
Held the transmitted sceptre, to the axe
Bowing the anointed head; or dragg'd away
To eat the bread of bondage; or escaped
Beneath the shadow of Britannia's shield,
There only safe. Such fate have vicious courts,
Statesmen corrupt, and fear-struck policy,
Upon themselves drawn down; till Europe, bound
In iron chains, lies bleeding in the dust,
Beneath the feet of upstart tyranny:
Only the heroic Spaniard, he alone
Yet unsubdued in these degenerate days,
With desperate virtue, such as in old time
Hallow'd Saguntum and Numantia's name,
Stands up against the oppressor undismay'd:
So may the Almighty bless the noble race,
And crown with happy end their holiest cause!

Deem not these dread events the monstrous birth
Of chance! And thou, O England, who dost ride
Serene amid the waters of the flood,
Preserving, even like the Ark of old,
Amid the general wreck, thy purer faith,
Domestic loves, and ancient liberty,
Look to thyself, O England! for be sure,
Even to the measure of thine own desert,
The cup of retribution to thy lips
Shall soon or late be dealt!—a thought that well
Might fill the stoutest heart of all thy sons
With awful apprehension! Therefore, they
Who fear the Eternal's justice, bless thy name,
Grenville, because the wrongs of Africa
Cry out no more to draw a curse from heaven
On England;—for if still the trooping sharks
Track by the scent of death the accursed ship
Freighted with human anguish, in her wake
Pursue the chase, crowd round her keel, and dart

Toward the sound contending, when they hear
The frequent carcass from her guilty deck
Dash in the opening deep, no longer now
The guilt shall rest on England; but if yet
There be among her children, hard of heart
And sear'd of conscience, men who set at nought
Her laws and God's own word, upon themselves
Their sin be visited!—the Red-cross flag,
Redeem'd from stain so foul, no longer now
Covereth the abomination.
                                This thy praise,
O Grenville, and while ages roll away
This shall be thy remembrance! Yea, when all
For which the tyrant of these abject times
Hath given his honourable name on earth,
His nights of innocent sleep, his hopes of heaven:
When all his triumphs and his deeds of blood,
The fretful changes of his feverish pride,
His midnight murders and perfidious plots,
Are but a tale of years so long gone by,
That they who read distrust the hideous truth,
Willing to let a charitable doubt
Abate their horror: Grenville, even then
Thy memory will be fresh among mankind!
Afric with all her tongues will speak of thee,
With Wilberforce and Clarkson, he whom Heaven,
To be the apostle of this holy work
Raised up and strengthen'd, and upheld through all
His arduous toil. To end the glorious task,
That blessed, that redeeming deed was thine:
Be it thy pride in life, thy thought in death,
Thy praise beyond the tomb. The statesman's fame
Will fade, the conqueror's laurel crown grow sere;
Fame's loudest trump upon the ear of Time
Leaves but a dying echo. They alone
Are held in everlasting memory,
Whose deeds partake of heaven. Long ages hence
Nations unborn, in cities that shall rise
Along the palmy coast, will bless thy name;
And Senegal and secret Niger's shore,
And Calabar, no longer startled then
With sounds of murder, will, like Isis now,
Ring with the songs that tell of Grenville's praise.
                                                    1810.

BOTANY-BAY ECLOGUES.

Where a sight shall shuddering Sorrow find,
Sad as the ruins of the human mind.
                                            BOWLES.

ELINOR.

Time, Morning. Scene, the Shore.

ONCE more to daily toil, once more to wear
The livery of shame, once more to search
With miserable task this savage shore!
O thou who mountest so triumphantly
In yonder Heaven, beginning thy career
Of glory, O thou blessed Sun! thy beams
Fall on me with the same benignant light
Here, at the furthest limits of the world,
And blasted as I am with infamy,
As when in better years poor ELINOR
Gazed on thy glad uprise with eye undimm'd

By guilt and sorrow, and the opening morn
Woke her from quiet sleep to days of peace.
In other occupation then I trod
The beach at eve; and then when I beheld
The billows as they roll'd before the storm
Burst on the rock and rage, my timid soul
Shrunk at the perils of the boundless deep,
And heaved a sigh for suffering mariners.
Ah! little thinking I myself was doom'd
To tempt the perils of the boundless deep,
An Outcast, unbeloved and unbewail'd.

Still wilt thou haunt me, Memory! still present
The fields of England to my exiled eyes,
The joys which once were mine! Even now I see
The lowly lovely dwelling! even now
Behold the woodbine clasping its white walls,
Where fearlessly the red-breasts chirp around
To ask their morning meal: and where at eve
I loved to sit and watch the rook sail by,
And hear his hollow tones, what time he sought
The church-yard elm, that with its ancient boughs
Full-foliaged half conceal'd the house of God;
That holy house, where I so oft have heard
My father's voice explain the wondrous works
Of heaven to sinful man. Ah! little deem'd
His virtuous bosom, that his shameless child
So soon should spurn the lesson! sink, the slave
Of Vice and Infamy! the hireling prey
Of brutal appetite! at length worn out
With famine, and the avenging scourge of guilt,
Should share dishonesty—Yet dread to die!

Welcome, ye savage lands, ye barbarous climes,
Where angry England sends her outcast sons,
I hail your joyless shores! My weary bark,
Long tempest-tost on Life's inclement sea,
Here hails her haven! welcomes the drear scene,
The marshy plain, the briar-entangled wood,
And all the perils of a world unknown.
For Elinor has nothing now to fear
From fickle Fortune! All her rankling shafts,
Barb'd with disgrace, and venom'd with disease,
Have pierced my bosom, and the dart of death
Has lost its terrors to a wretch like me.

Welcome, ye marshy heaths! ye pathless woods,
Where the rude native rests his wearied frame
Beneath the sheltering shade: where, when the storm,
As rough and bleak it rolls along the sky,
Benumbs his naked limbs, he flies to seek
The dripping shelter. Welcome, ye wild plains
Unbroken by the plough, undelved by hand
Of patient rustic; where for lowing herds,
And for the music of the bleating flocks,
Alone is heard the kangaroo's sad note
Deepening in distance. Welcome, ye rude climes,
The realm of Nature; for, as yet unknown
The crimes and comforts of luxurious life,
Nature benignly gives to all enough,
Denies to all a superfluity.
What though the garb of infamy I wear,
Though day by day along the echoing beach
I cull the wave-worn shells; yet day by day
I earn in honesty my frugal food,
And lay me down at night to calm repose,

No more condemn'd the mercenary tool
Of brutal lust, while heaves the indignant heart
With Virtue's stifled sigh, to fold my arms
Round the rank felon, and for daily bread
To hug contagion to my poison'd breast;
On these wild shores the saving hand of Grace
Shall probe my secret soul; shall cleanse its wounds,
And fit the faithful penitent for Heaven.

1794.

HUMPHREY AND WILLIAM.

Time, *Noon.*

HUMPHREY.

SEEST thou not, William, that the scorching Sun
By this time half his daily race has run?
The savage thrusts his light canoe to shore,
And hurries homeward with his fishy store.
Suppose we leave awhile this stubborn soil,
To eat our dinner and to rest from toil!

WILLIAM.

Agreed. Yon tree, whose purple gum bestows
A ready medicine for the sick man's woes,
Forms with its shadowy boughs a cool retreat
To shield us from the noontide's sultry heat.
Ah, Humphrey! now upon old England's shore
The weary labourer's morning work is o'er:
The woodman there rests from his measured stroke,
Flings down his axe, and sits beneath the oak;
Savour'd with hunger there he eats his food,
There drinks the cooling streamlet of the wood.
To us no cooling streamlet winds its way,
No joys domestic crown for us the day;
The felon's name, the outcast's garb we wear,
Toil all the day, and all the night despair.

HUMPHREY.

Aye, William! labouring up the furrow'd ground,
I used to love the village clock's dull sound,
Rejoice to hear my morning toil was done,
And trudge it homewards when the clock went one.
'T was ere I turn'd a soldier and a sinner!
Pshaw! curse this whining—let us fall to dinner.

WILLIAM.

I too have loved this hour, nor yet forgot
Each joy domestic of my little cot.
For at this hour my wife with watchful care
Was wont her humble dainties to prepare;
The keenest sauce by hunger was supplied,
And my poor children prattled at my side.
Methinks I see the old oak table spread,
The clean white trencher and the good brown bread,
The cheese my daily food which Mary made,
For Mary knew full well the housewife's trade:
The jug of cider,—cider I could make—
And then the knives,—I won 'em at the wake.
Another has them now! I toiling here
Look backward like a child, and drop a tear.

HUMPHREY.

I love a dismal story: tell me thine,
Meantime, good Will, I'll listen as I dine.
I too, my friend, can tell a piteous story,
When I turn'd hero, how I purchased glory.

WILLIAM.

But, Humphrey, sure thou never canst have known
The comforts of a little home thine own:
A home so snug, so cheerful too, as mine—
'T was always clean, and we could make it fine;
For there King Charles's Golden Rules were seen,
And there—God bless 'em both—the King and Queen.
The pewter plates, our garnish'd chimney's grace,
So bright that in them you might see your face;
And over all, to frighten thieves. was hung,
Well clean'd, although but seldom used, my gun.
Ah! that damn'd gun! I took it down one morn,—
A desperate deal of harm they did my corn!
Our testy Squire too lov'd to save the breed,
So covey upon covey ate my seed.
I marked the mischievous rogues, and took my aim;
I fired, they fell, and—up the keeper came.
That cursed morning brought on my undoing;
I went to prison, and my farm to ruin.
Poor Mary! for her grave the parish paid,
No tomb-stone tells where her poor corpse is laid!
My Children—my poor boys—

HUMPHREY.

     Come!—Grief is dry.—
You to your dinner—to my story I.
To you my friend who happier days have known,
And each calm comfort of a home your own,
This is bad living : I have spent my life
In hardest toil and unavailing strife,
And here (from forest ambush safe at least)
To me this scanty pittance seems a feast.
I was a plough-boy once; as free from woes
And blithesome as the lark with whom I rose.
Each evening at return a meal I found;
And, though my bed was hard, my sleep was sound.
One Whitsuntide, to go to Fair, I drest
Like a great bumpkin in my Sunday's best;
A primrose posey in my hat I stuck,
And to the revel went to try my luck.
From show to show, from booth to booth I stray,
See, stare, and wonder all the live-long day.
A Sergeant to the fair recruiting came,
Skilled in man-catching, to beat up for game;
Our booth he enter'd and sat down by me;—
Methinks even now the very scene I see!
The canvas roof, the hogshead's running store,
The old blind fiddler seated next the door,
The frothy tankard passing to and fro,
And the rude rabble round the puppet-show.
The Sergeant eyed me well; the punch-bowl comes,
And as we laugh'd and drank, up struck the drums.
And now he gives a bumper to his wench,
God save the King, and then, God damn the French!
Then tells the story of his last campaign,
How many wounded and how many slain,
Flags flying, cannons roaring, drums a-beating,
The English marching on, the French retreating.—
« Push on—push on, my lads! they fly before ye,
March on to riches, happiness, and glory !»
At first I wonder'd, by degrees grew bolder,
Then cried, « 'T is a fine thing to be a soldier !»
« Aye, Humphrey !» says the Sergeant,—« that's your name?
'T is a fine thing to fight the French for fame!
March to the field,—knock out a Mounseer's brains,
And pick the scoundrel's pocket for your pains.

Come, Humphrey, come! thou art a lad of spirit;
Rise to a halbert, as I did,—by merit!
Wouldst thou believe it? even I was once
As thou art now, a plough-boy and a dunce;
But courage raised me to my rank. How now, boy!
Shall Hero Humphrey still be Numps the plough-boy?
A proper-shaped young fellow! tall and straight!
Why, thou wert made for glory!—five feet eight!
The road to riches is the field of fight!
Didst ever see a guinea look so bright?
Why, regimentals, Numps, would give thee grace,
A hat and feather would become that face;
The girls would crowd around thee to be kist!
Dost love a girl ?»—«Od Zounds!» I cried, « I 'll list !»
So pass'd the night : anon the morning came,
And off I set a volunteer for fame.
« Back shoulders, turn out your toes, hold up your head,
Stand easy !» so I did—till almost dead.
O how I long'd to tend the plough again,
Trudge up the field, and whistle o'er the plain,
When tired and sore amid the piteous throng
Hungry and cold and wet I limp'd along,
And growing fainter as I pass'd and colder,
Cursed that ill hour when I became a soldier !
In town I found the hours more gaily pass,
And time fled swiftly with my girl and glass;
The girls were wond'rous kind and wond'rous fair,
They soon transferr'd me to the Doctor's care ;
The Doctor undertook to cure the evil,
And he almost transferr'd me to the Devil.
'T were tedious to relate the dismal story
Of fighting, fasting, wretchedness, and glory.
At last discharged, to England's shores I came,
Paid for my wounds with want instead of fame;
Found my fair friends, and plunder'd as they bade me
They kist me, coax'd me, robb'd me, and betray'd me.
Tried and condemn'd His Majesty transports me,
And here in peace, I thank him, he supports me.
So ends my dismal and heroic story,
And Humphrey gets more good from guilt than glory.

            1794.

JOHN, SAMUEL, AND RICHARD.

Time, Evening.

JOHN.

'T is a calm pleasant evening, the light fades away,
And the sun going down has done watch for the day.
To my mind we live wonderous well when transported;
It is but to work, and we must be supported.
Fill the cann, Dick! Success here to Botany-Bay!

RICHARD.

Success if you will,—but God send me away!

JOHN.

You lubberly landsmen don't know when you're well!
Hadst thou known half the hardships of which I can tell!
The sailor has no place of safety in store;
From the tempest at sea, to the press-gang on shore!
When Roguery rules all the rest of the earth,
God be thank'd in this corner I've got a good birth.

SAMUEL.

Talk of hardships! what these are the sailor don't know.
'T is the soldier, my friend, that's acquainted with woe,
Long journeys, short halting, hard work and small pay,

To be popt at like pigeons for sixpence a day!—
Thank God I'm safe quarter'd at Botany-Bay.

JOHN.

Ah! you know but little: I'll wager a pot
I have suffer'd more evils than fell to your lot.
Come, we'll have it all fairly and properly tried,
Tell story for story, and Dick shall decide.

SAMUEL.

Done.

JOHN.

Done. 'T is a wager, and I shall be winner;
Thou wilt go without grog, Sam, to-morrow at dinner.

SAMUEL.

I was trapp'd by the Sergeant's palav'ring pretences,
He listed me when I was out of my senses.
So I took leave to-day of all care and all sorrow,
And was drill'd to repentance and reason to-morrow.

JOHN.

I would be a sailor and plough the wide ocean,
But was soon sick and sad with the billows' commotion,
So the Captain he sent me aloft on the mast,
And cursed me, and bade me cry there,—and hold fast!

SAMUEL.

After marching all day, faint and hungry and sore,
I have lain down at night on the swamps of the moor,
Unshelter'd and forced by fatigue to remain,
All chill'd by the wind and benumb'd by the rain.

JOHN.

I have rode out the storm when the billows beat high,
And the red gleaming lightnings flash'd through the
    dark sky;
When the tempest of night the black sea overcast,
Wet and weary I labour'd, yet sung to the blast.

SAMUEL.

I have march'd, trumpets sounding, drums beating,
    flags flying,
Where the music of war drown'd the shrieks of the
    dying,
When the shots whizz'd around me all dangers defied,
Push'd on when my comrades fell dead at my side;
Drove the foe from the mouth of the cannon away,
Fought, conquer'd, and bled,—all for sixpence a day.

JOHN.

And I too, friend Samuel! have heard the shots rattle!
But we seamen rejoice in the play of the battle;
Though the chain and the grape-shot roll splintering
    round,
With the blood of our messmates though slippery the
    ground,
The fiercer the fight, still the fiercer we grow,
We heed not our loss so we conquer the foe;
And the hard battle won, if the prize be not sunk,
The Captain gets rich, and the Sailors get drunk.

SAMUEL.

God help the poor soldier when backward he goes
In disgraceful retreat through a country of foes!
No respite from danger by day or by night,
He is still forced to fly, still o'ertaken to fight;
Every step that he takes he must battle his way,
He must force his hard meal from the peasant away;
No rest, and no hope, from all succour afar,
God forgive the poor soldier for going to the war!

JOHN.

But what are these dangers to those I have past
When the dark billows roar'd to the roar of the blast!
When we work'd at the pumps worn with labour and
    weak,
And with dread still beheld the increase of the leak?
Sometimes as we rose on the wave could our sight
From the rocks of the shore catch the light-house's
    light;
In vain to the beach to assist us they press,
We fire faster and faster our guns of distress;
Still with rage unabating the wind and waves roar;
How the giddy wreck reels, as the billows burst o'er!
Leap, leap; for she yawns, for she sinks in the wave!
Call on God to preserve—for God only can save!

SAMUEL.

There 's an end of all troubles, however, at last!
And when I in the waggon of wounded was cast,
When my wounds with the chilly night-wind smarted
    sore,
And I thought of the friends I should never see more,
No hand to relieve, scarce a morsel of bread,
Sick at heart, I have envied the peace of the dead!
Left to rot in a jail till by treaty set free,
Old England's white cliffs with what joy did I see!
I had gain'd enough glory, some wounds, but no good,
And was turn'd on the public to shift how I could.
When I think what I 've suffer'd, and where I am now,
I curse him who snared me away from the plough.

JOHN.

When I was discharged I went home to my wife,
There in comfort to spend all the rest of my life.
My wife was industrious, we earn'd what we spent,
And though little we had, were with little content;
And whenever I listen'd and heard the wind roar,
I bless'd God for my little snug cabin on shore.
At midnight they seized me, they dragg'd me away,
They wounded me sore when I would not obey,
And because for my country I'd ventured my life,
I was dragg'd like a thief from my home and my wife.
Then the fair wind of fortune chopt round in my face,
And Want at length drove me to guilt and disgrace.
But all 's for the best;—on the world's wide sea cast,
I am haven'd in peace in this corner at last.

SAMUEL.

Come, Dick! we have done—and for judgment we call.

RICHARD.

And in faith I can give you no judgment at all:
But that as you 're now settled, and safe from foul
    weather,
You drink up your grog, and be merry together.

FREDERIC.

Time, *Night.* Scene, *The Woods.*

WHERE shall I turn me? whither shall I bend
My weary way? thus worn with toil and faint,
How through the thorny mazes of this wood
Attain my distant dwelling? That deep cry
That rings along the forest seems to sound
My parting knell: it is the midnight howl
Of hungry monsters prowling for their prey!
Again! O save me—save me, gracious Heaven!
I am not fit to die!
                    Thou coward wretch,
Why heaves thy trembling heart? why shake thy limbs
Beneath their palsied burden? Is there aught

So lovely in existence? wouldst thou drain
Even to its dregs the bitter draught of life?
Stamp'd with the brand of Vice and Infamy,
Why should the felon Frederic shrink from Death?

Death! Where the magic in that empty name
That chills my inmost heart? why at the thought
Starts the cold dew of fear on every limb?
There are no terrors to surround the Grave,
When the calm Mind collected in itself
Surveys that narrow house: the ghastly train
That haunt the midnight of delirious Guilt
Then vanish; in that home of endless rest
All sorrows cease!—Would I might slumber there!

Why then this panting of the fearful heart?
This miser love of life, that dreads to lose
Its cherish'd torment? Shall the man diseased
Yield up his members to the surgeon's knife,
Doubtful of succour, but to rid his frame
Of fleshly anguish; and the coward wretch,
Whose ulcerated soul can know no help,
Shrink from the best Physician's certain aid?
Oh, it were better far to lie me down
Here on this cold damp earth, till some wild beast
Seize on his willing victim!
                    If to die
Were all, 't were sweet indeed to rest my head
On the cold clod, and sleep the sleep of Death.
But if the Archangel's trump at the last hour
Startle the ear of Death, and wake the soul
To frenzy?—Dreams of infancy; fit tales
For garrulous beldames to affrighten babes!
What if I warr'd upon the world? the world
Had wrong'd me first: I had endur'd the ills
Of hard injustice; all this goodly earth
Was but to me one wide waste wilderness;
I had no share in nature's patrimony;
Blasted were all my morning hopes of youth,
Dark Disappointment followed on my ways,
Care was my bosom inmate, and keen Want
Gnawed at my heart. Eternal One, thou knowest
How that poor heart even in the bitter hour
Of lewdest revelry has inly yearn'd
For peace!
            My Father! I will call on thee,
Pour to thy mercy-seat my earnest prayer,
And wait thy righteous will, resign'd of soul.
O thoughts of comfort! how the afflicted heart,
Tired with the tempest of its passions, rests
On you with holy hope! The hollow howl
Of yonder harmless tenant of the woods
Comes with no terror to the sober'd sense.
If I have sinn'd against mankind, on them
Be that past sin; they made me what I was.
In these extremest climes can Want no more
Urge to the deeds of darkness, and at length
Here shall I rest. What though my hut be poor—
The rains descend not through its humble roof:—
Would I were there again! The night is cold;
And what if in my wanderings I should rouse
The savage from his thicket!
                    Hark! the gun!
And lo, the fire of safety! I shall reach
My little hut again! again by toil
Force from the stubborn earth my sustenance,

And quick-ear'd guilt will never start alarm'd
Amid the well-earn'd meal. This felon's garb—
Will it not shield me from the winds of Heaven?
And what could purple more? O strengthen me,
Eternal One, in this serener state!
Cleanse thou mine heart, so Penitence and Faith
Shall heal my soul, and my last days be peace.
                                        1794.

SONNETS.

Go, Valentine, and tell that lovely maid
    Whom fancy still will portray to my sight,
How here I linger in this sullen shade,
    This dreary gloom of dull monastic night.
Say, that from every joy of life remote
    At evening's closing hour I quit the throng,
Listening in solitude the ring-dove's note,
    Who pours like me her solitary song.
Say, that her absence calls the sorrowing sigh;
    Say, that of all her charms I love to speak,
In fancy feel the magic of her eye,
    In fancy view the smile illume her cheek,
Court the lone hour when silence stills the grove,
And heave the sigh of Memory and of Love.
                                        1794.

Think, Valentine, as speeding on thy way
    Homeward thou hastest light of heart along,
If heavily creep on one little day
    The medley crew of travellers among,
Think on thine absent friend: reflect that here
    On life's sad journey comfortless he roves,
Remote from every scene his heart holds dear,
    From him he values, and from her he loves.
And when, disgusted with the vain and dull
    Whom chance companions of thy way may doom,
Thy mind, of each domestic comfort full,
    Turns to itself and meditates on home,
Ah think what cares must ache within his breast
Who loathes the road, yet sees no home of rest!
                                        1794.

Not to thee, Bedford, mournful is the tale
    Of days departed. Time in his career
Arraigns not thee that the neglected year
Hath past unheeded onward. To the vale
Of years thou journeyest; may the future road
    Be pleasant as the past! and on my friend
    Friendship and Love, best blessings! still attend,
Till full of days he reach the calm abode
Where Nature slumbers. Lovely is the age
    Of Virtue: with such reverence we behold
    The silver hairs, as some grey oak grown old
That whilom mock'd the rushing tempest's rage,
Now like the monument of strength decay'd,
With rarely-sprinkled leaves casting a trembling shade.
                                        1794.

As thus I stand beside the murmuring stream
    And watch its current, Memory here portrays
    Scenes faintly form'd of half-forgotten days,
Like far-off woodlands by the moon's bright beam

Dimly descried, but lovely. I have worn
  Amid these haunts the heavy hours away,
  When Childhood idled through the Sabbath-day;
Risen to my tasks at winter's earliest morn;
  And when the twilight slowly darken'd, here,
Thinking of home, and all of heart forlorn,
  Have sigh'd and shed in silence many a tear.
  Dream-like and indistinct those days appear,
As the faint sounds of this low brooklet borne
  Upon the breeze, reach fitfully the ear. [1]

1794.

TO THE EVENING RAINBOW.

MILD arch of promise! on the evening sky
  Thou shinest fair with many a lovely ray
Each in the other melting. Much mine eye
  Delights to linger on thee; for the day,
Changeful and many-weather'd, seem'd to smile
Flashing brief splendour through the clouds awhile,
  Which deepen'd dark anon and fell in rain:
But pleasant is it now to pause, and view
Thy various tints of frail and watery hue,
  And think the storm shall not return again.
Such is the smile that Piety bestows
  On the good man's pale cheek, when he, in peace
Departing gently from a world of woes,
  Anticipates the realm where sorrows cease.

1794.

WITH many a weary step, at length I gain
  Thy summit, Lansdown; and the cool breeze plays
  Gratefully round my brow, as hence I gaze
Back on the fair expanse of yonder plain.
  'T was a long way and tedious! To the eye
Though fair the extended vale, and fair to view
The autumnal leaves of many a faded hue,
  That eddy in the wild gust moaning by.
Even so it fared with life! in discontent
Restless through Fortune's mingled scenes I went—
  Yet wept to think they would return no more!
But cease, fond heart, in such sad thoughts to roam;
For surely thou ere long shalt reach thy home,
  And pleasant is the way that lies before.

1794.

[1] This beautiful sonnet was originally addressed « To a Brook
near the Village of Corston;» but as the alterations which Mr Southey
afterwards thought fit to make on it are considerable, the reader
will not be displeased to see it such as it appeared when first given
to the public.—EDIT.

  As thus I bend me o'er thy babbling stream
    And watch thy current, Memory's hand portrays
    The faint form'd scenes of the departed days,
  Like the far forest by the moon's pale beam
  Dimly descried yet lovely. I have worn
    Upon thy banks the live-long hour away,
    When sportive childhood wantoned through the day,
  Joy'd at the opening splendour of the morn,
  Or as the twilight darken'd, heaved the sigh
    Thinking of distant home; as down my cheek
    At the fond thought slow stealing on, would speak
  The silent eloquence of the full eye.
  Dim are the long past days, yet still they please
  As thy soft sounds half heard, borne on the inconstant breeze.

FAIR is the rising morn when o'er the sky
  The orient sun expands his roseate ray,
And lovely to the bard's enthusiast eye
  Fades the soft radiance of departing day;
But fairer is the smile of one we love
  Than all the scenes in Nature's ample sway,
And sweeter than the music of the grove,
  The voice that bids us welcome. Such delight,
  EDITH! is mine, escaping to thy sight
From the hard durance of the empty throng.
  Too swiftly then towards the silent night,
Ye hours of happiness! ye speed along;
  Whilst I, from all the World's cold cares apart,
  Pour out the feelings of my burthen'd heart.

1794.

How darkly o'er yon far-off mountain frowns
  The gather'd tempest! from that lurid cloud
  The deep-voiced thunders roll, awful and loud
Though distant; while upon the misty downs
Fast falls in shadowy streaks the pelting rain.
  I never saw so terrible a storm!
Perhaps some way-worn traveller in vain
  Wraps his torn raiment round his shivering form,
Cold even as Hope within him! I the while
Pause me in sadness, though the sun-beams smile
  Cheerily round me. Ah that thus my lot
Might be with Peace and Solitude assigned,
  Where I might from some little quiet cot
Sigh for the crimes and miseries of mankind!

1794.

O THOU sweet Lark, that in the heaven so high
Twinkling thy wings dost sing so joyfully,
  I watch thee soaring with no mean delight;
And when at last I turn mine aching eye
  That lags, how far below that lofty flight,
Still silently receive thy melody.
O thou sweet Lark, that I had wings like thee!
  Not for the joy it were in yon blue light
  Upward to plunge, and from my heavenly height
Gaze on the creeping multitude below,
  But that I soon would wing my eager flight
To that loved home where Fancy even now
Hath fled, and Hope looks onward through a tear,
Counting the weary hours that keep her here.

1798.

THOU lingerest, Spring! still wintry is the scene,
  The fields their dead and sapless russet wear;
  Scarce does the glossy celandine appear
Starring the sunny bank, or early green
  The elder yet its circling tufts put forth.
The sparrow tenants still the eaves-built nest
Where we should see our martin's snowy breast
  Oft darting out. The blasts from the bleak north
And from the keener east still frequent blow.
Sweet Spring, thou lingerest! and it should be so,—
  Late let the fields and gardens blossom out!
Like man when most with smiles thy face is drest,
'T is to deceive, and he who knows ye best,
When most ye promise, ever most must doubt.

1799.

Beware a speedy friend, the Arabian said,
  And wisely was it he advised distrust:
  The flower that blossoms earliest fades the first.
Look at yon Oak that lifts its stately head,
And dallies with the autumnal storm, whose rage
  Tempests the ocean waves; slowly it rose,
Slowly its strength increased through many an age,
  And timidly did its light leaves disclose,
As doubtful of the spring, their palest green.
  They to the summer cautiously expand,
  And by the warmer sun and season bland
Matured, their foliage in the grove is seen,
  When the bare forest by the wintry blast
Is swept, still lingering on the boughs the last.
                                          1798.

TO A GOOSE.

If thou didst feed on western plains of yore;
  Or waddle wide with flat and flabby feet
Over some Cambrian mountain's plashy moor;
  Or find in farmer's yard a safe retreat
  From gypsey thieves, and foxes sly and fleet;
If thy grey quills, by lawyer guided, trace
Deeds big with ruin to some wretched race,
  Or love-sick poet's sonnet, sad and sweet,
  Wailing the rigour of his lady fair;
Or if, the drudge of housemaid's daily toil,
Cobwebs and dust thy pinions white besoil,
  Departed goose! I neither know nor care.
But this I know, that thou wert very fine,
Season'd with sage, and onions, and port wine.
                                          1797.

I marvel not, O sun! that unto thee
In adoration man should bow the knee,
  And pour his prayers of mingled awe and love;
For like a God thou art, and on thy way
Of glory sheddest with benignant ray,
  Beauty, and life, and joyance from above.
No longer let these mists thy radiance shroud,
These cold raw mists that chill the comfortless day;
But shed thy splendour through the opening cloud
  And cheer the earth once more. The languid flowers
Lie odourless, bent down with heavy rain,
  Earth asks thy presence, saturate with showers!
O Lord of Light! put forth thy beams again,
  For damp and cheerless are the gloomy hours.
                                          1798.

Fair be thy fortunes in the distant land,
  Companion of my earlier years and friend!
Go to the Eastern world, and may the hand
  Of Heaven its blessing on thy labour send.
And may I, if we ever more should meet,
  See thee with affluence to thy native shore
Return'd;—I need not pray that I may greet
  The same untainted goodness as before.
Long years must intervene before that day;
  And what the changes Heaven to each may send,
  It boots not now to bode! Oh early friend!
Assured, no distance e'er can wear away
  Esteem long rooted, and no change remove
The dear remembrance of the friend we love.
                                          1798.

Farewell my home, my home no longer now,
  Witness of many a calm and happy day;
And thou fair eminence, upon whose brow
  Dwells the last sunshine of the evening ray,
Farewell! Mine eyes no longer shall pursue
  The western sun beyond the utmost height,
  When slowly he forsakes the fields of light.
No more the freshness of the falling dew,
Cool and delightful, here shall bathe my head,
  As from this western window dear, I lean,
  Listening, the while I watch the placid scene,
The martins twittering underneath the shed.
Farewell, my home! where many a day has past
In joys whose loved remembrance long shall last.
                                          1799.

Porlock, thy verdant vale so fair to sight,
  Thy lofty hills with fern and furze so brown,
  The waters that so musical roll down
Thy woody glens, the traveller with delight
Recalls to memory, and the channel grey
  Circling its surges in thy level bay;—
Porlock, I also shall forget thee not,
  Here by the unwelcome summer rain confined;
  And often shall hereafter call to mind
How here, a patient prisoner, 't was my lot
To wear the lonely, lingering close of day,
  Making my Sonnet by the alehouse fire,
  Whilst Idleness and Solitude inspire
Dull rhymes to pass the duller hours away.
                                  August 9, 1799.

Stately yon vessel sails adown the tide,
  To some far distant land adventurous bound;
  The sailors' busy cries from side to side
Pealing among the echoing rocks resound:
A patient, thoughtless, much-enduring band,
  Joyful they enter on their ocean way,
With shouts exulting leave their native land,
  And know no care beyond the present day.
But is there no poor mourner left behind,
  Who sorrows for a child or husband there?
Who at the howling of the midnight wind
  Will wake and tremble in her boding prayer!
So may her voice be heard, and Heaven be kind!—
  Go, gallant ship, and be thy fortune fair!
                                          1799.

O God have mercy in this dreadful hour
  On the poor mariner! in comfort here
  Safe shelter'd as I am, I almost fear
The blast that rages with resistless power.
  What were it now to toss upon the waves,—
The madden'd waves, and know no succour near;
The howling of the storm alone to hear,
  And the wild sea that to the tempest raves,
To gaze amid the horrors of the night
And only see the billow's gleaming light;
  And in the dread of death to think of her
Who, as she listens sleepless to the gale,
Puts up a silent prayer and waxes pale?—
  O God! have mercy on the mariner!
                                          1799.

SHE comes majestic with her swelling sails,
   The gallant bark! along her watery way
Homeward she drives before the favouring gales;
   Now flirting at their length the streamers play,
And now they ripple with the ruffling breeze.
   Hark to the sailors' shouts! the rocks rebound,
   Thundering in echoes to the joyful sound.
Long have they voyaged o'er the distant seas,
   And what a heart-delight they feel at last,
   So many toils, so many dangers past,
To view the port desired, he only knows
   Who on the stormy deep for many a day
   Hath tost, aweary of his ocean way,
And watch'd, all anxious, every wind that blows.

1799.

A WRINKLED, crabbed man they picture thee,
   Old Winter, with a rugged beard as grey
As the long moss upon the apple-tree;
   Blue lipt, an ice-drop at thy sharp blue nose;
   Close muffled up, and on thy dreary way,
Plodding alone through sleet and drifting snows.
They should have drawn thee by the high-heapt hearth,
   Old Winter! seated in thy great-arm'd chair,
Watching the children at their Christmas mirth,
   Or circled by them as thy lips declare
Some merry jest or tale of murder dire,
   Or troubled spirit that disturbs the night,
Pausing at times to rouse the mouldering fire,
   Or taste the old October brown and bright.

1799.

THE AMATORY POEMS OF ABEL SHUFFLEBOTTOM.

DELIA AT PLAY.

SHE held a Cup and Ball of Ivory white,
   Less white the Ivory than her snowy hand!
   Enrapt I watch'd her from my secret stand,
As now, intent, in innocent delight,
   Her taper fingers twirl'd the giddy ball,
Now tost it, following still with EAGLE sight,
   Now on the pointed end infix'd its fall.
Marking her sport I mused, and musing sigh'd,
   Methought the BALL she play'd with was my HEART!
(Alas! that Sport like that should be her pride!)
   And the keen point which stedfast still she eyed
   Wherewith to pierce it, that was CUPID's dart;
Shall I not then the cruel Fair condemn
Who on that dart IMPALES my BOSOM's GEM?

TO A PAINTER ATTEMPTING DELIA'S PORTRAIT.

RASH Painter! canst thou give the ORB OF DAY
In all its noontide glory? or portray
   The DIAMOND, that athwart the taper'd hall
Flings the rich flashes of its dazzling light?
Even if thine art could boast such magic might,
   Yet if it strove to paint my Angel's EYE,
Here it perforce must fail. Cease! lest I call

Heaven's vengeance on thy sin: Must thou be told
   The CRIME it is to paint DIVINITY?
Rash Painter! should the world her charms behold,
   Dim and defiled, as there they needs must be,
They to their old idolatry would fall,
   And bend before her form the pagan knee.
   Fairer than VENUS, DAUGHTER OF THE SEA.

HE PROVES THE EXISTENCE OF A SOUL FROM HIS LOVE FOR DELIA.

SOME have denied a soul! THEY NEVER LOVED.
Far from my Delia now by fate removed,
   At home, abroad, I view her every where;
   Her ONLY in the FLOOD OF NOON I see.
   My Goddess-Maid, my OMNIPRESENT FAIR,
For Love annihilates the world to me!
And when the weary SOL around his bed
   Closes the SABLE CURTAINS of the night,
   SUN OF MY SLUMBERS, on my dazzled sight
SHE shines confest. When every sound is dead,
The SPIRIT OF HER VOICE comes then to roll
   The surge of music o'er my wavy brain.
   Far, far from her my Body drags its chain,
But sure with Delia I exist A SOUL!

THE POET EXPRESSES HIS FEELINGS RESPECTING A PORTRAIT IN DELIA'S PARLOUR.

I WOULD I were that Reverend Gentleman
With gold-laced hat and golden-headed cane,
   Who hangs in Delia's parlour! For whene'er
From book or needlework her looks arise,
On him converge the SUN-BEAMS of her eyes,
   And he unblamed may gaze upon MY FAIR,
And oft MY FAIR his favour'd form surveys.
O HAPPY PICTURE! still on HER to gaze!
   I envy him! and jealous fear alarms,
   Lest the STRONG glance of those divinest charms
WARM HIM TO LIFE, as in the ancient days,
   When MARBLE MELTED in Pygmalion's arms.
I would I were that Reverend Gentleman
With gold-laced hat and golden-headed cane.

THE POET RELATES HOW HE OBTAINED DELIA'S POCKET-HANDKERCHIEF.

'T IS mine! what accents can my joy declare?
   Blest be the pressure of the thronging rout!
Blest be the hand so hasty of my fair,
   That left the tempting corner hanging out!

I envy not the joy the pilgrim feels,
   After long travel to some distant shrine,
When at the relic of his saint he kneels,
   For Delia's POCKET-HANDKERCHIEF IS MINE.

When first with filching fingers I drew near,
   Keen hope shot tremulous through every vein,
And when the finish'd deed removed my fear,
   Scarce could my bounding heart its joy contain.

What though the Eighth Commandment rose to mind,
   It only serv'd a moment's qualm to move;
For thefts like this it could not be design'd,
   The Eighth Commandment WAS NOT MADE FOR LOVE!

78

Here when she took the macaroons from me,
  She wiped her mouth to clean the crumbs so sweet!
Dear napkin! yes, she wiped her lips in thee!
  Lips *sweeter* than the *macaroons* she eat.

And when she took that pinch of Mocabaw,
  That made my Love so *delicately* sneeze,
Thee to her Roman nose applied I saw,
  And thou art doubly dear for things like these.

No washerwoman's filthy hand shall e'er,
  SWEET POCKET-HANDKERCHIEF! thy worth profane;
For thou hast touch'd the *rubies* of my fair,
  And I will kiss thee o'er and o'er again.

THE POET INVOKES THE SPIRITS OF THE ELEMENTS TO APPROACH DEL'A. HE DESCRIBES HER SINGING.

YE SYLPHS, who *banquet* on my Delia's blush,
  Who on her locks of FLOATING GOLD repose,
Dip in her cheek your GOSSAMERY BRUSH,
  And with its bloom of beauty *tinge* THE ROSE.

Hover around her lips on *rainbow wing*,
  Load from her honeyed breath your *viewless* feet,
Bear thence a richer fragrance for the Spring,
  And make the lily and the violet sweet.

Ye GNOMES, whose toil through many a dateless year
  Its nurture to the infant gem supplies,
From central caverns bring your diamonds here,
  To *ripen in the* SUN OF DELIA'S EYES.

And ye who bathe in Etna's lava springs,
  Spirits of fire! to see my love advance;
Fly, SALAMANDERS, on ASBESTOS' wings,
  To wanton in my Delia's *fiery* glance.

She weeps, she weeps! her eye with anguish swells,
  Some tale of sorrow melts my FEELING GIRL!
NYMPHS! catch the tears, and in your lucid shells
  Enclose them, EMBRYOS OF THE ORIENT PEARL.

She sings! the Nightingale with envy hears,
  The CHERUBIM bends from his starry throne,
And motionless are stopt the attentive SPHERES,
  To hear *more heavenly music* than their own.

Cease, Delia, cease! for all the ANGEL THRONG,
  Listening to thee, let sleep their golden wires!
Cease, Delia, cease! that *too surpassing* song,
  Lest, *stung to envy*, they should break their lyres.

Cease, ere my senses are to madness driven
  By the strong joy! cease, Delia, lest my soul
Enrapt, already THINK ITSELF IN HEAVEN,
  And burst the feeble Body's frail controul.

THE POET EXPATIATES ON THE BEAUTY OF DELIA'S HAIR.

THE comb between whose ivory teeth she strains
  The straitening curls of gold so *beamy bright*,
Not spotless merely from the touch remains,
  But issues forth *more pure*, *more milky white*.

The rose-pomatum that the FRISEUR spreads
  Sometimes with honour'd fingers for my fair,
No added perfume on her tresses sheds,
  But borrows sweetness from her sweeter hair.

Happy the FRISEUR who in Delia's hair
  With licensed fingers uncontroul'd may rove!
And happy in his death the DANCING BEAR,
  Who died to make pomatum for my LOVE.

Oh could I hope that e'er my favour'd lays
  Might *curl those lovely locks* with conscious pride,
Nor Hammond, nor the Mantuan Shepherd's praise
  I'd envy then, nor wish reward beside.

Cupid has strung from you, O tresses fine,
  The bow that in my breast impell'd his dart;
From you, sweet locks! he wove the subtile line
  Wherewith the urchin *angled for* MY HEART.

Fine are my Delia's tresses as the threads
  That from the silk-worm, *self-interr'd*, proceed;
Fine as the GLEAMY GOSSAMER that spreads
  Its filmy web-work o'er the tangled mead.

Yet with these tresses Cupid's power elate
  My captive *heart* has *handcuff'd* in a chain,
Strong as the cables of some huge first-rate,
  THAT BEARS BRITANNIA'S THUNDERS O'ER THE MAIN.

The SYLPHS that round her radiant locks repair,
  In *flowing lustre* bathe their brightening wings:
And ELFIN MINSTRELS with assiduous care
  The ringlets rob for FAERY FIDDLE-STRINGS.

THE POET RELATES HOW HE STOLE A LOCK OF DELIA'S HAIR, AND HER ANGER.

OH! be the day accurst that gave me birth!
  Ye Seas, to swallow me in kindness rise!
Fall on me, Mountains! and thou merciful Earth,
  Open, and hide me from my Delia's eyes!

Let universal Chaos now return,
  Now let the central fires their prison burst,
And EARTH and HEAVEN and AIR and OCEAN burn—
  For Delia FROWNS—SHE FROWNS, *and I am curst!*

Oh! I could dare the fury of the fight,
  Where hostile MILLIONS sought my single life;
Would storm VOLCANO BATTERIES with delight,
  And grapple with GRIM DEATH in glorious strife.

Oh! I could brave the bolts of angry JOVE,
  When ceaseless lightnings fire the midnight skies;
What is *his wrath* to that of HER I love?
  What is *his* LIGHTNING to my DELIA'S EYES?

Go, fatal lock! I cast thee to the wind;
  Ye *serpent* CURLS, ye *poison-tendrils*, go—
Would I could tear thy memory from my mind,
  ACCURSED LOCK,—thou cause of all my woe!

Seize the CURST CURLS, ye Furies, as they fly!
  Demons of darkness, guard the infernal roll,
That thence your cruel vengeance when I die,
  May *knit the* KNOTS OF TORTURE *for my* SOUL.

Last night,—Oh hear me, Heaven, and grant my
    prayer!
The BOOK OF FATE before thy suppliant lay,
And let me from its ample records tear
    Only the single PAGE OF YESTERDAY!

Or let me meet OLD TIME upon his flight,
    And I will STOP HIM on his restless way;
Omnipotent in Love's resistless might,
    I'll force him back the ROAD OF YESTERDAY.

Last night, as o'er the page of Love's despair,
    My Delia bent *deliciously* to grieve,
I stood a *treacherous loiterer* by her chair,
    And drew the FATAL SCISSARS from my sleeve:

And would that at that instant o'er my thread
    The SHEARS OF ATROPOS had open'd then;
And when I reft the lock from Delia's head,
    Had cut me sudden from the sons of men!

She heard the scissars that fair lock divide,
    And whilst my heart with transport panted big,
She cast a fury frown on me, and cried,
    « You stupid puppy,—you have spoil'd my wig!»

SONGS OF THE AMERICAN INDIANS.

THE HURON'S ADDRESS TO THE DEAD.

BROTHER, thou wert strong in youth!
Brother, thou wert brave in war!
Unhappy man was he
For whom thou hadst sharpen'd the tomahawk's edge!
Unhappy man was he
On whom thine angry eye was fix'd in fight!
And he who from thy hand
Received the calumet
Blest Heaven, and slept in peace.

When the Evil Spirits seized thee,
Brother, we were sad at heart:
We bade the Jongler come
And bring his magic aid;
We circled thee in mystic dance,
With songs and shouts and cries,
To free thee from their power.
Brother, but in vain we strove,
The number of thy days was full.

Thou sittest amongst us on thy mat,
The bear-skin from thy shoulder hangs,.
Thy feet are sandal'd ready for the way.
Those are the unfatiguable feet
That traversed the forest track!
Those are the lips that late
Thunder'd the yell of war;
And that is the strong right arm
Which never was lifted in vain.
Those lips are silent now,
The limbs that were active are stiff,
Loose hangs the strong right arm!

And where is That which in thy voice
The language of friendship spake?
That gave the strength of thine arm?
That fill'd thy limbs with life?
It was not thou, for Thou art here,
Thou art amongst us still,
But the Life and the Feeling are gone.
The Iroquois will learn
That thou hast ceased from war;
'T will be a joy like victory,
For thou wert the scourge of their nation.

Brother, we sing thee the song of death;
In thy coffin of bark we lay thee to rest;
The bow shall be placed by thy side,
And the shafts that are pointed and feather'd for flight.
To the country of the Dead
Long and painful is thy way!
Over rivers wide and deep
Lies the road that must be past,
By bridges narrow-wall'd,
When scarce the Soul can force its way,
While the loose-fabric totters under it.

Safely may our Brother pass!
Safely may he reach the fields,
Where the sound of the drum and the shell
Shall be heard from the Country of Souls!
The Spirits of thy Sires
Shall come to welcome thee;
The God of the Dead in his Bower
Shall receive thee and bid thee join
The dance of eternal joy.

Brother, we pay thee the rites of death,
Rest in the Bower of Delight!
               1799.

THE PERUVIAN'S DIRGE OVER THE BODY
OF HIS FATHER.

REST in peace, my Father, rest!
With danger and toil have I borne thy corpse
From the Stranger's field of death.
I bless thee, O Wife of the Sun,
For veiling thy beams with a cloud,
While at the pious task
Thy votary toil'd in fear.
Thou badest the clouds of night
Enwrap thee, and hide thee from Man;
But didst thou not see my toil,
And put on the darkness to aid,
O Wife of the visible God?

Wretched, my Father, thy life!
Wretched the life of the Slave!
All day for another he toils;
Overwearied at night he lies down.
And dreams of the freedom that once he enjoy'd.
Thou wert blest in the days of thy youth,
My Father! for then thou wert free.
In the fields of the nation thy hand
Bore its part of the general task;
And when, with the song and the dance,
Ye brought the harvest home,

As all in the labour had shared,
So justly they shared in the fruits.

Thou visible Lord of the Earth,
Thou God of my Fathers, thou God of my heart,
O Giver of light and of life!
When the Strangers came to our shores,
Why didst thou not put forth thy power?
Thy thunders should then have been hurl'd;
Thy fires should in lightnings have flash'd!—
Visible God of the Earth,
The Strangers mock at thy might!
To idols and beams of wood
They force us to bow the knee!
They plunge us in caverns and dens,
Where never thy blessed light
Shines on our poisonous toil!
But not in the caverns and dens,
O Sun, are we mindless of thee!
We pine for the want of thy beams,
We adore thee with anguish and groans.

My Father, rest in peace!
Rest with the dust of thy Sires!
They placed their Cross in thy dying grasp;—
They bore thee to their burial-place,
And over thy breathless frame
Their bloody and merciless Priest
Mumbled his mystery words.
Oh! could thy bones be at peace
In the fields where the Strangers are laid?—
Alone, in danger and in pain,
My Father, I bring thee here:
So may our God, in reward,
Allow me one faithful friend
To lay me beside thee when I am released!
So may he release me soon,
That my Spirit may join thee there,
Where the Strangers never shall come!

                1799.

SONG OF THE ARAUCANS

DURING A THUNDER STORM.[1]

THE storm-cloud grows deeper above;
Araucans! the tempest is ripe in the sky;
Our forefathers come from their Islands of Bliss,
They come to the war of the winds.

The Souls of the Strangers are there,
In their garments of darkness they ride through the
     heaven;
Yon cloud that rolls luridly over the hill
Is red with their weapons of fire.

[1] Respecting storms, the people of Chili are of opinion that, the departed souls are returning from their abode beyond the sea to assist their relations and friends. Accordingly, when it thunders over the mountains, they think that the souls of their forefathers are taken in an engagement with those of the Spaniards. The roaring of the winds they take to be the noise of horsemen attacking one another, the howling of the tempest for the beating of drums, and the claps of thunder for the discharge of muskets and cannons.— When the wind drives the clouds towards the possessions of the Spaniards, they rejoice that the souls of their forefathers have repulsed those of their enemies, and call out aloud to them to give them no quarter. When the contrary happens, they are troubled and dejected, and encourage the yielding souls to rally their forces, and summon up the last remains of their strength.—MOLINA.

Hark! hark! in the howl of the wind
The shout of the battle, the clang of their drums,
The horsemen are met, and the shock of the fight
     Is the blast that disbranches the wood.

Behold from the clouds of their power
The lightning,—the lightning is lanced at our sires!
And the thunder that shakes the broad pavement of
         Heaven!
     And the darkness that quenches the day!

Ye Souls of our Fathers, be brave!
Ye shrunk not before the invaders on earth,
Ye trembled not then at their weapons of fire,
     Brave Spirits, ye tremble not now!

We gaze on your warfare in hope,
We send up our shouts to encourage your arms!
Lift the lance of your vengeance, O Fathers! with force,
     For the wrongs of your country strike home!

Remember the land was your own
When the Sons of Destruction came over the seas;
That the old fell asleep in the fullness of days,
     And their children wept over their graves,

Till the Strangers came into the land
With tongues of deceit and with weapons of fire:
Then the strength of the people in youth was cut off,
     And the father wept over his son.

It thickens—the tumult of fight!
Louder and louder the blast of the battle is heard!—
Remember the wrongs that your country endures!
     Remember the fields of your fame!

Joy! joy! for the Strangers recoil,—
They give way,—they retreat to the land of their life!
Pursue them! pursue them! remember your wrongs!
     Let your lances be drunk with their wounds.

The Souls of your wives shall rejoice
As they welcome you back to your Islands of Bliss;
And the breeze that refreshes the toil-throbbing brow
     Waft thither the song of your praise.

                1799.

SONG OF THE CHIKKASAH WIDOW.

'T was the voice of my husband that came on the gale.
The unappeased Spirit in anger complains!
     Rest, rest Ollanahta, be still!
     The day of revenge is at hand.

The stake is made ready, the captives shall die;
To-morrow the song of their death shalt thou hear,
     To-morrow thy widow shall wield
     The knife and the fire;—be at rest!

The vengeance of anguish shall soon have its course,—
The fountains of grief and of fury shall flow.—
     I will think, Ollanahta! of thee,
     Will remember the days of our love.

Ollanahta, all day by thy war-pole I sat,
Where idly thy hatchet of battle is hung;
     I gazed on the bow of thy strength
     As it waved on the stream of the wind.

The scalps that we number'd in triumph were there,
And the musket that never was levell'd in vain,—
　　What a leap has it given to my heart
　　To see thee suspend it in peace!

When the black and blood-banner was spread to the
　　gale,
When thrice the deep voice of the war-drum was heard,
　　I remember thy terrible eyes
　　How they flash'd the dark glance of thy joy.

I remember the hope that shone over thy cheek
As thy hand from the pole reach'd its doers of death;
　　Like the ominous gleam of the cloud
　　Ere the thunder and lightning are born.

He went, and ye came not to warn him in dreams,
Kindred Spirits of him who is holy and great!
　　And where was thy warning, O Bird,
　　The timely announcer of ill?

Alas! when thy brethren in conquest return'd;
When I saw the white plumes bending over their heads
　　And the pine-boughs of triumph before,
　　Where the scalps of their victory swung,—

The war-hymn they pour'd, and thy voice was not
　　there!
I call'd thee,—alas, the white deer-skin was brought;
　　And thy grave was prepared in the tent
　　Which I had made ready for joy!

Ollanahta, all day by thy war-pole I sit,—
Ollanahta, all night I weep over thy grave!
　　To-morrow the victims shall die,
　　And I shall have joy in revenge.

　　　　　　　　　　　　　　　　　　1799.

THE OLD CHIKKASAH TO HIS GRANDSON.

Now go to the battle, my Boy!
　　Dear child of my son,
　　There is strength in thine arm,
　　There is hope in thy heart,
Thou art ripe for the labours of war.
Thy Sire was a stripling like thee
When he went to the first of his fields.
He return'd, in the glory of conquest return'd;
　　Before him his trophies were borne,
These scalps that have hung till the Sun and the Rain
Have rusted their raven locks.
Here he stood when the morn of rejoicing arrived,
　　The day of the warrior's reward;
When the banners sun-beaming were spread,
　　And all hearts were dancing in joy
To the sound of the victory drum.
The Heroes were met to receive their reward;
But distinguish'd among the young Heroes that day,
The pride of his nation, thy Father was seen:
　　The swan-feathers hung from his neck,
　　His face like the rainbow was tinged,
　　And his eye,—how it sparkled in pride!
The Elders approach'd, and they placed on his brow
　　The crown that his valour had won,
And they gave him the old honour'd name.
They reported the deeds he had done in the war,

And the youth of the nation were told
　　To respect him and tread in his path.

My Boy! I have seen, and with hope,
　　The courage that rose in thine eye
When I told thee the tale of his death.
　　His war-pole now is grey with moss,
　　His tomahawk red with rust;
His bowstring whose twang was death
　　Now sings as it cuts the wind!
But his memory is fresh in the land,
And his name with the names that we love.

Go now and revenge him, my Boy!
That his Spirit no longer may hover by day
O'er the hut where his bones are at rest,
　　Nor trouble our dreams in the night.
My Boy, I shall watch for the warriors' return,
　　And my soul will be sad
　　Till the steps of thy coming I see.

　　　　　　　　　　　　　　　　　　1799.

INSCRIPTIONS.

The three utilities of Poetry: the praise of Virtue and Goodness, the memory of things remarkable, and to invigorate the Affections.
—*Welsh Triad.*

FOR A COLUMN AT NEWBURY.

ART thou a Patriot, Traveller?—On this field
Did FALKLAND fall, the blameless and the brave,
Beneath a Tyrant's banners—Dost thou boast
Of loyal ardour? HAMBDEN perished here,
The rebel HAMBDEN, at whose glorious name
The heart of every honest Englishman
Beats high with conscious pride. Both uncorrupt,
Friends to their common country both, they fought,
They died in adverse armies. Traveller!
If with thy neighbour thou shouldst not accord,
In charity remember these good men,
And quell all angry and injurious thoughts.

　　　　　　　　　　　　　　　　　　1796.

FOR A CAVERN THAT OVERLOOKS THE RIVER AVON.

ENTER this cavern, Stranger! the ascent
Is long and steep and toilsome; here awhile
Thou mayst repose thee, from the noontide heat
Shelter'd beneath this bending vault of rock.
Round the rude portal clasping with rough arms,
The antique ivy spreads a canopy,
From whose grey blossoms the wild bees collect
Their last autumnal stores. No common spot
Receives thee, for the power who prompts the song
Loves this secluded cell. The tide below
Scarce sends the sound of waters to thine ear;
And yon high-hanging forest to the wind
Varies its many hues. Gaze, Stranger, here!
And let thy soften'd heart intensely feel
How good, how lovely, Nature! When from hence
Departing to the city's crowded streets,
Thy sickening eye at every step revolts
From scenes of vice and wretchedness; reflect
That Man creates the evil he endures.

　　　　　　　　　　　　　　　　　　1796.

FOR A TABLET AT SILBURY-HILL.[1]

This mound in some remote and dateless day
Rear'd o'er a Chieftain of the Age of Hills,
May here detain thee, Traveller! from thy road
Not idly lingering. In his narrow house
Some Warrior sleeps below, whose gallant deeds
Haply at many a solemn festival
The Bard hath harp'd; but perish'd is the song
Of praise, as o'er these bleak and barren downs
The wind that passes and is heard no more.
Go, Traveller, and remember when the pomp
Of earthly Glory fades, that one good deed,
Unseen, unheard, unnoted by mankind,
Lives in the eternal register of Heaven.

1796.

FOR A MONUMENT IN THE NEW FOREST.

This is the place where William's kingly power
Did from their poor and peaceful homes expel,
Unfriended, desolate, and shelterless,
The habitants of all the fertile track
Far as these wilds extend. He levell'd down
Their little cottages, he bade their fields
Lie barren, so that o'er the forest waste
He might more royally pursue his sports!
If that thine heart be human, Passenger!
Sure it will swell within thee, and thy lips
Will mutter curses on him. Think thou then
What cities flame, what hosts unsepulchred
Pollute the passing wind, when raging Power
Drives on his blood-hounds to the chase of Man;
And as thy thoughts anticipate that day
When God shall judge aright, in charity
Pray for the wicked rulers of mankind.

FOR A TABLET ON THE BANKS OF A STREAM.

Stranger! awhile upon this mossy bank
Recline thee. If the Sun rides high, the breeze,
That loves to ripple o'er the rivulet,
Will play around thy brow, and the cool sound
Of running waters soothe thee. Mark how clear
It sparkles o'er the shallows, and behold
Where o'er its surface wheels with restless speed
Yon glossy insect, on the sand below
How the swift shadow flits. The stream is pure
In solitude, and many a healthful herb
Bends o'er its course and drinks the vital wave:
But passing on amid the haunts of man,
It finds pollution there, and rolls from thence
A tainted tide. Seek'st thou for Happiness?
Go, Stranger, sojourn in the woodland cot
Of Innocence, and thou shalt find her there.

1796.

FOR THE CENOTAPH AT ERMENONVILLE.

Stranger! the Man of Nature lies not here:
Enshrined far distant by the Scoffer's[2] side

<hr/>

[1] The northern nations distinguished the two periods when the
bodies of the dead were consumed by fire, and when they were bu-
ried beneath the tumuli so common in this country, by the Age of
Fire and the Age of Hills.
[2] Voltaire.

His relics rest, there by the giddy throng
With blind idolatry alike revered!
Wiselier directed have thy pilgrim feet
Explored the scenes of Ermenonville. Rousseau
Loved these calm haunts of Solitude and Peace;
Here he has heard the murmurs of the lake,
And the soft rustling of the poplar grove,
When o'er their bending boughs the passing wind
Swept a grey shade. Here, if thy breast be full,
If in thine eye the tear devout should gush,
His Spirit shall behold thee, to thine home
From hence returning, purified of heart.

1796.

FOR A MONUMENT AT OXFORD.

Here Latimer and Ridley in the flames
Bore witness to the truth. If thou hast walk'd
Uprightly through the world, proud thoughts of joy
Will fill thy breast in contemplating here
Congenial virtue. But if thou hast swerved
From the right path, if thou hast sold thy soul,
And served, with hireling and apostate zeal,
The cause thy heart disowns,—oh! cherish well
The honourable shame that sure this place
Will wake within thee, timely penitent,
And let the future expiate the past.

1797.

FOR A MONUMENT IN THE VALE OF EWIAS

Here was it, Stranger, that the patron Saint
Of Cambria past his age of penitence,
A solitary man; and here he made
His hermitage, the roots his food, his drink
Of Hodney's mountain stream. Perchance thy youth
Has read with eager wonder how the Knight
Of Wales in Ormandine's enchanted bower,
Slept the long sleep: and if that in thy veins
Flow the pure blood of Britain, sure that blood
Hath flow'd with quicker impulse at the tale
Of David's deeds, when through the press of war
His gallant comrades follow'd his green crest
To conquest. Stranger! Hatterill's mountain heights
And this fair vale of Ewias, and the stream
Of Hodney, to thine after-thoughts will rise
More grateful, thus associate with the name
Of David and the deeds of other days.

1798.

EPITAPH ON ALGERNON SIDNEY.

Here Sidney lies, he whom perverted law,
The pliant jury and the bloody judge,
Doom'd to the traitor's death. A tyrant King
Required, an abject country saw and shared
The crime. The noble cause of Liberty
He loved in life, and to that noble cause
In death bore witness. But his Country rose
Like Sampson from her sleep, and broke her chains,
And proudly with her worthies she enroll'd
Her murder'd Sidney's name. The voice of man
Gives honour or destroys; but earthly power
Gives not, nor takes away, the self-applause

Vhich on the scaffold suffering virtue feels,
'or that which God appointed its reward.

1799.

EPITAPH ON KING JOHN.

OHN rests below. A man more infamous
'ever hath held the sceptre of these realms,
nd bruised beneath the iron rod of Power
'he oppressed men of England. Englishman!
'urse not his memory. Murderer as he was,
'oward and slave, yet he it was who sign'd
'hat Charter which should make thee morn and night
'e thankful for thy birth-place:—Englishman!
'hat holy Charter, which, shouldst thou permit
'orce to destroy, or Fraud to undermine,
'hy children's groans will persecute thy soul,
'or they must bear the burthen of thy crime.

1798.

IN A FOREST.

STRANGER! whose steps have reach'd this solitude,
Know that this lonely spot was dear to one
Devoted with no unrequited zeal
To Nature. Here, delighted he has heard
The rustling of these woods, that now perchance
Melodious to the gale of summer move;
And underneath their shade on yon smooth rock,
With grey and yellow lichens overgrown,
Often reclined; watching the silent flow
Of this perspicuous rivulet, that steals
Along its verdant course,—till all around
Had fill'd his senses with tranquillity,
And ever sooth'd in spirit he return'd
A happier, better man. Stranger! perchance,
Therefore the stream more lovely to thine eye
Will glide along, and to the summer gale
The woods wave more melodious. Cleanse thou then
The weeds and mosses from this letter'd stone.

1798.

FOR A MONUMENT AT TORDESILLAS.

SPANIARD! if thou art one who bows the knee
Before a despot's footstool, hie thee hence!
This ground is holy: here Padilla died,
Martyr of Freedom. But if thou dost love
Her cause, stand then as at an altar here,
And thank the Almighty that thine honest heart,
Full of a brother's feelings for mankind,
Rebels against oppression. Not unheard
Nor unavailing shall the grateful prayer
Ascend; for loftiest impulses will rise
To elevate and strengthen thee, and prompt
To virtuous action. Relics silver-shrined,
And chaunted mass, would wake within the soul
Thoughts valueless and cold compared with these.

1796.

FOR A COLUMN AT TRUXILLO.

PIZARRO here was born; a greater name
The list of Glory boasts not. Toil and Pain,
Famine and hostile Elements, and Hosts
Embattled, fail'd to check him in his course,

Not to be wearied, not to be deterr'd,
Not to be overcome. A mighty realm
He overran, and with relentless arm
Slew or enslaved its unoffending sons,
And wealth, and power, and fame, were his rewards.
There is another world, beyond the Grave,
According to their deeds where men are judged.
O reader! if thy daily bread be earn'd
By daily labour,—yea, however low,
However wretched be thy lot assign'd,
Thank thou, with deepest gratitude, the God
Who made thee, that thou art not such as he.

1796.

FOR THE CELL OF HONORIUS, AT THE CORK CONVENT, NEAR CINTRA.

HERE cavern'd like a beast Honorius dwelt
In self-denial, solitude, and prayer,
Long years of penance. He had rooted out
All human feelings from his heart, and fled
With fear and loathing from all human joys
As from perdition. But the law of Christ
Enjoins not this. To aid the fatherless,
Comfort the sick, and be the poor man's friend,
And in the wounded heart pour gospel-balm;
These are the active duties of that law,
Which whoso keeps shall have a joy on earth,
Calm, constant, still increasing, preluding
The eternal bliss of Heaven. Yet mock not thou,
Stranger, the Anchorite's mistaken zeal!
He painfully his painful duties kept,
Sincere though erring: Stranger, do thou keep
Thy better and thine easier rule as well.

1798.

FOR A MONUMENT AT TAUNTON.

THEY suffer'd here whom Jefferies doom'd to death
In mockery of all justice, when the Judge
Unjust, subservient to a cruel King,
Perform'd his work of blood. They suffer'd here,
The victims of that Judge, and of that King,
In mockery of all justice here they bled,
Unheard! But not unpitied, nor of God
Unseen, the innocent suffered! not in vain
The innocent blood cried vengeance! for at length,
The indignant Nation in its power arose,
Resistless. Then that wicked Judge took flight,
Disguised in vain:—not always is the Lord
Slow to revenge! a miserable man
He fell beneath the people's rage, and still
The children curse his memory. From his throne
The lawless bigot who commission'd him,
Inhuman James, was driven. He lived to drag
Long years of frustrate hope, he lived to load
More blood upon his soul. Let tell the Boyne,
Let Londonderry tell his guilt and shame;
And that immortal day when on thy shores,
La Hogue, the purple ocean dash'd the dead!

1798.

FOR A TABLET AT PENSHURST.

ARE days of old familiar to thy mind,
O Reader? Hast thou let the midnight hour

Pass unperceived, whilst thou in fancy lived
With high-born beauties and enamour'd chiefs,
Sharing their hopes, and with a breathless joy
Whose expectation touch'd the verge of pain,
Following their dangerous fortunes? If such lore
Hath ever thrill'd thy bosom, thou wilt tread,
As with a pilgrim's reverential thoughts,
The groves of Penshurst. Sidney here was born,
Sidney, than whom no gentler, braver man
His own delightful genius ever feign'd,
Illustrating the vales of Arcady
With courteous courage and with royal loves.
Upon his natal day the acorn here
Was planted. It grew up a stately oak,
And in the beauty of its strength it stood
And flourish'd, when his perishable part
Had moulder'd dust to dust. That stately oak
Itself hath moulder'd now, but Sidney's fame
Endureth in his own immortal works.

1799.

EPITAPH.

This to a mother's sacred memory
Her son hath hallow'd. Absent many a year
Far over sea, his sweetest dreams were still
Of that dear voice which soothed his infancy:
And after many a fight against the Moor
And Malabar, or that fierce Cavalry
Which he had seen covering the boundless plain
Even to the utmost limits where the eye
Could pierce the far horizon,—his first thought
In safety was of her, who when she heard
The tale of that day's danger, would retire
And pour her pious gratitude to Heaven
In prayers and tears of joy. The lingering hour
Of his return, long-look'd-for, came at length,
And full of hope he reach'd his native shore.
Vain hope that puts its trust in human life!
For ere he came the number of her days
Was full. O Reader, what a world were this,
How unendurable its weight, if they
Whom Death hath sunder'd did not meet again!

1810.

EPITAPH.

Here in the fruitful vales of Somerset
Was Emma born, and here the Maiden grew
To the sweet season of her womanhood
Beloved and lovely, like a plant whose leaf
And bud and blossom all are beautiful.
In peacefulness her virgin years were past;
And when in prosperous wedlock she was given,
Amid the Cumbrian mountains far away
She had her summer bower. 'T was like a dream
Of old Romance to see her when she plied
Her little skiff on Derwent's glassy lake;
The roseate evening resting on the hills,
The lake returning back the hues of heaven,
Mountains and vales and waters all imbued
With beauty and in quietness; and she,
Nymph-like, amid that glorious solitude
A heavenly presence, gliding in her joy.
But soon a wasting malady began

To prey upon her, frequent in attack,
Yet with such flattering intervals as mock
The hopes of anxious love, and most of all
The sufferer, self-deceived. During those days
Of treacherous respite, many a time hath he,
Who leaves this record of his friend, drawn back
Into the shadow from her social board,
Because too surely in her cheek he saw
The insidious bloom of death; and then her smiles
And innocent mirth excited deeper grief
Than when long-look'd-for tidings came at last,
That, all her sufferings ended, she was laid
Amid Madeira's orange groves to rest.
O gentle Emma! o'er a lovelier form
Than thine, Earth never closed; nor e'er did Heaven
Receive a purer spirit from the world!

1810.

ENGLISH ECLOGUES.

The following Eclogues, I believe, bear no resemblance to any poems in our language. This species of composition has become popular in Germany, and I was induced to attempt it by an account of the German Idylls given me in conversation. They cannot properly be styled imitations, as I am ignorant of that language at present, and have never seen any translations or specimens in this kind.— With bad Eclogues I am sufficiently acquainted, from Tityrus and Corydon down to our English Strephons and Thirsisses. No kind of poetry can boast of more illustrious names, or is more distinguished by the servile dulness of imitated nonsense. Pastoral writers, « more silly than their sheep,» have, like their sheep, gone on in the same track one after another. Gay stumbled into a new path. His eclogues were the only ones which interested me when I was a boy, and did not know they were burlesque. The subject would furnish matter for an essay, but this is not the place for it.—1799.

THE OLD MANSION-HOUSE.

STRANGER.
Old friend! why you seem bent on parish duty,
Breaking the highway stones,—and 't is a task
Somewhat too hard methinks for age like yours!

OLD MAN.
Why yes! for one with such a weight of years
Upon his back—I 've lived here, man and boy,
In this same parish, well nigh the full age
Of man, being hard upon threescore and ten.
I can remember sixty years ago
The beautifying of this mansion here,
When my late Lady's father, the old Squire,
Came to the estate.

STRANGER.
      Why then you have outlasted
All his improvements, for you see they 're making
Great alterations here.

OLD MAN.
      Aye—great indeed!
And if my poor old Lady could rise up—
God rest her soul! 't would grieve her to behold
The wicked work is here.

STRANGER.
      They 've set about it
In right good earnest. All the front is gone;
Here 's to be turf, they tell me, and a road
Round to the door. There were some yew trees too
Stood in the court.—

OLD MAN.
      Aye, Master! fine old trees!

My grandfather could just remember back
When they were planted there.   It was my task
To keep them trimm'd, and 't was a pleasure to me;
All straight and smooth, and like a great green wall!
My poor old Lady many a time would come
And tell me where to shear, for she had play'd
In childhood under them, and 't was her pride
To keep them in their beauty.   Plague, I say,
On their new-fangled whimsies! we shall have
A modern shrubbery here stuck full of firs
And your pert poplar trees;—I could as soon
Have plough'd my father's grave as cut them down!

STRANGER.
But 't will be lighter and more cheerful now;
A fine smooth turf, and with a gravel road
Round for the carriage,—now it suits my taste.
I like a shrubbery too, it looks so fresh;
And then there 's some variety about it.
In spring the lilac and the snow-ball flower,
And the laburnum with its golden strings
Waving in the wind: And when the autumn comes
The bright red berries of the mountain-ash,
With pines enough in winter to look green,
And show that something lives.   Sure this is better
Than a great hedge of yew that makes it look
All the year round like winter, and for ever
Dropping its poisonous leaves from the under boughs
Wither'd and bare!

OLD MAN.
                    Ah! so the new Squire thinks,
And pretty work he makes of it! what 't is
To have a stranger come to an old house!

STRANGER.
It seems you know him not?

OLD MAN.
                    No, Sir, not I.
They tell me he's expected daily now;
But in my Lady's time he never came
But once, for they were very distant kin.
If he had play'd about here when a child
In that fore court, and eat the yew-berries,
And sate in the porch threading the jessamine flowers
Which fell so thick, he had not had the heart
To mar all thus!

STRANGER.
                    Come—come! all is not wrong;
Those old dark windows—

OLD MAN.
                    They 're demolish'd too,
As if he could not see through casement glass!
The very red-breasts, that so regular
Came to my Lady for her morning crumbs,
Wo'n't know the window now!

STRANGER.
                    Nay they were small,
And then so darken'd round with jessamine,
Harbouring the vermin;—yet I could have wish'd
That jessamine had been saved, which canopied
And bower'd and lined the porch.

OLD MAN.
                    It did one good
To pass within ten yards when 't was in blossom.
There was a sweet-briar too that grew beside;
My Lady loved at evening to sit there
And knit; and her old dog lay at her feet
And slept in the sun; 't was an old favourite dog,—

She did not love him less that he was old
And feeble, and he always had a place
By the fire-side: and when he died at last
She made me dig a grave in the garden for him.
Ah! she was good to all! a woeful day
'T was for the poor when to her grave she went!

STRANGER.
They lost a friend then?

OLD MAN.
                    You 're a stranger here,
Or you wouldn't ask that question.   Were they sick?
She had rare cordial waters, and for herbs
She could have taught the Doctors.   Then at winter,
When weekly she distributed the bread
In the poor old porch, to see her and to hear
The blessings on her! and I warrant them
They were a blessing to her when her wealth
Had been no comfort else.   At Christmas, Sir!
It would have warm'd your heart if you had seen
Her Christmas kitchen,—how the blazing fire
Made her fine pewter shine, and holly boughs
So cheerful red,—and as for miseltoe,—
The finest bough that grew in the country round
Was mark'd for Madam.   Then her old ale went
So bountiful about! a Christmas cask,
And 't was a noble one!—God help me, Sir!
But I shall never see such days again.

STRANGER.
Things may be better yet than you suppose,
And you should hope the best.

OLD MAN.
                    It don't look well,—
These alterations, Sir! I'm an old man,
And love the good old fashions; we don't find
Old bounty in new houses.   They 've destroy'd
All that my Lady loved; her favourite walk
Grubb'd up,—and they do say that the great row
Of elms behind the house, which meet a-top,
They must fall too.   Well! well! I did not think
To live to see all this, and 't is perhaps
A comfort I sha'n't live to see it long.

STRANGER.
But sure all changes are not needs for the worse,
My friend?

OLD MAN.
                    May-hap they mayn't, Sir;—for all that
I like what I 've been used to.   I remember
All this from a child up, and now to lose it,
'T is losing an old friend.   There 's nothing left
As 't was;—I go abroad and only meet
With men whose fathers I remember boys;
The brook that used to run before my door,
That 's gone to the great pond; the trees I learnt
To climb are down; and I see nothing now
That tells me of old times,—except the stones
In the church-yard.   You are young, Sir, and I hope
Have many years in store,—but pray to God
You mayn't be left the last of all your friends.

STRANGER.
Well! well! you 've one friend more than you 're aware of
If the Squire's taste don't suit with yours, I warrant
That's all you 'll quarrel with: walk in and taste
His beer, old friend! and see if your old Lady
E'er broach'd a better cask.   You did not know me,
But we 're acquainted now.   T would not be easy
To make you like the outside; but within,

79

That is not changed, my friend! you 'll always find
The same old bounty and old welcome there.

THE GRANDMOTHER'S TALE.

JANE.

HARRY! I'm tired of playing. We 'll draw round
The fire, and Grandmamma perhaps will tell us
One of her stories.

HARRY.

Aye—dear Grandmamma!
A pretty story! something dismal now;
A bloody murder.

JANE.

Or about a ghost.

GRANDMOTHER.

Nay, nay, I should but frighten ye. You know
The other night when I was telling ye
About the light in the churchyard, how you trembled
Because the screech-owl hooted at the window,
And would not go to bed.

JANE.

Why, Grandmamma,
You said yourself you did not like to hear him.
Pray now!—we wo'n't be frightened.

GRANDMOTHER.

Well, well, children!
But you 've heard all my stories—Let me see,—
Did I never tell you how the smuggler murder'd
The woman down at Pill?

HARRY.

No—never! never!

GRANDMOTHER.

Not how he cut her head off in the stable?

HARRY.

Oh—now!—do tell us that!

GRANDMOTHER.

You must have heard
Your mother, children! often tell of her.
She used to weed in the garden here, and worm
Your uncle's dogs,[1] and serve the house with coal;
And glad enough she was in winter time
To drive her asses here! it was cold work
To follow the slow beasts through sleet and snow;
And here she found a comfortable meal
And a brave fire to thaw her, for poor Moll
Was always welcome.

HARRY.

Oh! 't was blear-eyed Moll
The collier woman,—a great ugly woman;
I 've heard of her.

GRANDMOTHER.

Ugly enough, poor soul!
At ten yards distance you could hardly tell
If it were man or woman, for her voice
Was rough as our old mastiff's, and she wore
A man's old coat and hat:—and then her face!
There was a merry story told of her,
How when the press-gang came to take her husband
As they were both in bed, she heard them coming,
Drest John up in her night-cap, and herself
Put on his clothes and went before the captain.

---

[1] I know not whether this cruel and stupid custom is common in
other parts of England. It is supposed to prevent the dogs from
doing any mischief should they afterwards become mad.

JANE.

And so they prest a woman!

GRANDMOTHER.

T was a trick
She dearly loved to tell; and all the country
Soon knew the jest, for she was used to travel
For miles around. All weathers and all hours
She cross'd the hill, as hardy as her beasts,
Bearing the wind and rain and drifting snow.
And if she did not reach her home at night,
She laid her down in the stable with her asses,
And slept as sound as they did.

HARRY.

With her asses!

GRANDMOTHER.

Yes; and she loved her beasts. For though, poor wretch,
She was a terrible reprobate, and swore
Like any trooper, she was always good
To the dumb creatures; never loaded them
Beyond their strength; and rather, I believe,
Would stint herself than let the poor beasts want,
Because she said they could not ask for food.
I never saw her stick fall heavier on them
Than just with its own weight. She little thought
This tender-heartedness would cause her death!
There was a fellow who had oftentimes,
As if he took delight in cruelty,
Ill-used her beasts. He was a man who lived
By smuggling, and,—for she had often met him
Crossing the down at night,—she threaten'd him,
If ever he abused them more, to inform
Of his unlawful ways. Well—so it was—
T was what they both were born to! he provoked her:
She laid an information; and one morning
They found her in the stable, her throat cut
From ear to ear, till the head only hung
Just by a bit of skin.

JANE.

Oh dear! oh dear!

HARRY.

I hope they hung the man!

GRANDMOTHER.

They took him up;
There was no proof, no man had seen the deed,
And he was set at liberty. But God,
Whose eye beholdeth all things, he had seen
The murder; and the murderer knew that God
Was witness to his crime. He fled the place,—
But nowhere could he fly the avenging hand
Of Heaven,—but nowhere could the murderer rest;
A guilty conscience haunted him; by day,
By night, in company, in solitude,
Restless and wretched, did he bear upon him
The weight of blood! Her cries were in his ears;
Her stifled groans, as when he knelt upon her,
Always he heard; always he saw her stand
Before his eyes; even in the dead of night
Distinctly seen as though in the broad sun,
She stood beside the murderer's bed, and yawn'd
Her ghastly wound; till life itself became
A punishment at last he could not bear,
And he confess'd it all, and gave himself
To death; so terrible, he said, it was
To have a guilty conscience!

HARRY.

Was he hung, then?

GRANDMOTHER.

Hung and anatomized. Poor wretched man,
Your uncles went to see him on his trial;
He was so pale, so thin, so hollow-eyed,
And such a horror in his meagre face,
They said he look'd like one who never slept.
He begg'd the prayers of all who saw his end,
And met his death with fears that well might warn
From guilt, though not without a hope in Christ.

HANNAH.

PASSING across a green and lonely lane
A funeral met our view. It was not here
A sight of every day, as in the streets
Of some great city, and we stopt and ask'd
Whom they were bearing to the grave. A girl,
They answer'd, of the village, who had pined
Through the long course of eighteen painful months
With such slow wasting, that the hour of death
Came welcome to her. We pursued our way
To the house of mirth, and with that idle talk
Which passes o'er the mind and is forgot,
We wore away the time. But it was eve
When homewardly I went, and in the air
Was that cool freshness, that discolouring shade
Which makes the eye turn inward: hearing then
Over the vale the heavy toll of death
Sound slow, it made me think upon the dead;
I question'd more, and learnt her mournful tale.
She bore unhusbanded a mother's pains,
And he who should have cherish'd her, far off
Sail'd on the seas. Left thus, a wretched one,
Scorn made a mock of her, and evil tongues
Were busy with her name. She had to bear
The sharper sorrow of neglect from him
Whom she had loved so dearly. Once he wrote,
But only once that drop of comfort came
To mingle with her cup of wretchedness;
And when his parents had some tidings from him,
There was no mention of poor Hannah there,
Or 't was the cold inquiry, more unkind
Than silence. So she pined and pined away,
And for herself and baby toil'd and toil'd,
Nor did she, even on her death-bed, rest
From labour, knitting there with lifted arms,
Till she sunk with very weakness. Her old mother
Omitted no kind office, working for her,
Albeit her hardest labour barely earn'd
Enough to keep life struggling, and prolong
The pains of grief and sickness. Thus she lay
On the sick bed of poverty, worn out
With her long suffering and those painful thoughts
Which at her heart were rankling, and so weak,
That she could make no effort to express
Affection for her infant; and the child,
Whose lisping love perhaps had solaced her,'
Shunn'd her as one indifferent. But she too
Had grown indifferent to all things of earth,
Finding her only comfort in the thought
Of that cold bed wherein the wretched rest.
There had she now, in that last home, been laid,
And all was over now,—sickness and grief,
Her shame, her suffering, and her penitence:
Their work was done. The school-boys as they sport
In the churchyard, for awhile might turn away

From the fresh grave till grass should cover it;
Nature would do that office soon; and none
Who trod upon the senseless turf would think
Of what a world of woes lay buried there!

1797.

THE SAILOR'S MOTHER.

WOMAN.

SIR, for the love of God, some small relief
To a poor woman!

TRAVELLER.

Whither are you bound?
'T is a late hour to travel o'er these downs,
No house for miles around us, and the way
Dreary and wild. The evening wind already
Makes one's teeth chatter; and the very Sun,
Setting so pale behind those thin white clouds,
Looks cold. 'T will be a bitter night!

WOMAN.

Aye, Sir,
'T is cutting keen! I smart at every breath;
Heaven knows how I shall reach my journey's end,
For the way is long before me, and my feet,
God help me! sore with travelling. I would gladly,
If it pleased God, at once lie down and die.

TRAVELLER.

Nay, nay, cheer up! a little food and rest
Will comfort you; and then your journey's end
Will make amends for all. You shake your head,
And weep. Is it some evil business then
That leads you from your home?

WOMAN.

Sir, I am going
To see my son at Plymouth, sadly hurt
In the late action, and in the hospital
Dying, I fear me, now.

TRAVELLER.

Perhaps your fears
Make evil worse. Even if a limb be lost,
There may be still enough for comfort left;
An arm or leg shot off, there 's yet the heart
To keep life warm, and he may live to talk
With pleasure of the glorious fight that maim'd him,
Proud of his loss. Old England's gratitude
Makes the maim'd Sailor happy.

WOMAN.

'T is not that,—
An arm or leg,—I could have borne with that.
It was no ball, Sir, but some cursed thing
Which bursts ' and burns that hurt him. Something, Sir,
They do not use on board our English ships,
It is so wicked!

TRAVELLER.

Rascals ! a mean art
Of cruel cowardice, yet all in vain!

WOMAN.

Yes, Sir; and they should show no mercy to them
For making use of such unchristian arms.

' The stink-pots used on board the French ships. In the engage-
ment between the Mars and L'Hercule, some of our sailors were
shockingly mangled by them: one in particular, as described in the
Eclogue, lost both his eyes. It would be right and humane to em-
ploy means of destruction, could they be discovered, powerful
enough to destroy fleets and armies; but to use any thing that only
inflicts additional torture upon the sufferers in war, is cruel and
wicked.

I had a letter from the hospital,
He got some friend to write it, and he tells me
That my poor boy has lost his precious eyes,
Burnt out.   Alas! that I should ever live
To see this wretched day!—they tell me, Sir,
There is no cure for wounds like his.   Indeed
'T is a hard journey that I go upon
To such a dismal end!

TRAVELLER.
                      He yet may live.
But if the worst should chance, why you must bear
The will of Heaven with patience.   Were it not
Some comfort to reflect your son has fall'n
Fighting his country's cause? and for yourself
You will not in unpitied poverty
Be left to mourn his loss.   Your grateful country,
Amid the triumph of her victory,
Remembers those who paid its price of blood,
And with a noble charity relieves
The widow and the orphan.

WOMAN.
                      God reward them!
God bless them! it will help me in my age,—
But, Sir! it will not pay me for my child!

TRAVELLER.
Was he your only child?

WOMAN.
                      My only one,
The stay and comfort of my widowhood,
A dear good boy!—when first he went to sea
I felt what it would come to,—something told me
I should be childless soon.   But tell me, Sir,
If it be true that for a hurt like his
There is no cure?   Please God to spare his life
Though he be blind, yet I should be so thankful!
I can remember there was a blind man
Lived in our village, one from his youth up
Quite dark, and yet he was a merry man,
And he had none to tend on him so well
As I would tend my boy!

TRAVELLER.
                      Of this be sure,
His hurts are look'd to well, and the best help
The land affords, as rightly is his due,
Ever at hand.   How happen'd it he left you?
Was a seafaring life his early choice?

WOMAN.
No, Sir! poor fellow,—he was wise enough
To be content at home, and 't was a home
As comfortable, Sir! even though I say it,
As any in the country.   He was left
A little boy when his poor father died,
Just old enough to totter by himself,
And call his mother's name.   We two were all,
And as we were not left quite destitute,
We bore up well.   In the summer time I work'd
Sometimes a-field.   Then I was famed for knitting,
And in long winter nights my spinning-wheel
Seldom stood still.   We had kind neighbours too,
And never felt distress.   So he grew up
A comely lad, and wonderous well disposed;
I taught him well; there was not in the parish
A child who said his prayers more regular,
Or answer'd readier through his Catechism.
If I had foreseen this! but 't is a blessing
We don't know what we're born to!

TRAVELLER.
                      But how came it
He chose to be a Sailor?

WOMAN.
                      You shall hear, Sir;
As he grew up he used to watch the birds
In the corn, child's work you know, and easily done.
'T is an idle sort of task; so he built up
A little hut of wicker-work and clay
Under the hedge, to shelter him in rain:
And then he took, for very idleness,
To making traps to catch the plunderers;
All sorts of cunning traps that boys can make,—
Propping a stone to fall and shut them in,
Or crush them with its weight, or else a springe
Swung on a bough.   He made them cleverly,—
And I, poor foolish woman! I was pleased
To see the boy so handy.   You may guess
What follow'd, Sir, from this unlucky skill.
He did what he should not when he was older:
I warn'd him oft enough; but he was caught
In wiring hares at last, and had his choice,
The prison or the ship.

TRAVELLER.
                      The choice at least
Was kindly left him, and for broken laws
This was, methinks, no heavy punishment.

WOMAN.
So I was told, Sir.   And I tried to think so,
But 't was a sad blow to me! I was used
To sleep at nights as sweetly as a child,—
Now if the wind blew rough, it made me start,
And think of my poor boy tossing about
Upon the roaring seas.   And then I seem'd
To feel that it was hard to take him from me
For such a little fault.   But he was wrong,
Oh very wrong,—a murrain on his traps!
See what they 've brought him to!

TRAVELLER.
                      Well! well! take comfort
He will be taken care of if he lives;
And should you lose your child, this is a country
Where the brave Sailor never leaves a parent
To weep for him in want.

WOMAN.
                      Sir, I shall want
No succour long.   In the common course of years
I soon must be at rest, and 't is a comfort,
When grief is hard upon me, to reflect
It only leads me to that rest the sooner.

THE WITCH.

NATHANIEL.
FATHER! here, father! I have found a horse-shoe!
Faith it was just in time; for t' other night
I laid two straws across at Margery's door,
And ever since I fear'd that she might do me
A mischief for 't.   There was the Miller's boy
Who set his dog at that black cat of hers,—
I met him upon crutches, and he told me
'T was all her evil eye.

FATHER.
                      'T is rare good luck!
I would have gladly given a crown for one

If 't would have done as well.   But where didst find it?

NATHANIEL.

Down on the common; I was going a-field,
And neighbour Saunders pass'd me on his mare;
He had hardly said «Good day,» before I saw
The shoe drop off.   'T was just upon my tongue
To call him back;—it makes no difference, does it,
Because I know whose 't was?

FATHER.

Why no, it can't;
The shoe's the same, you know, and you did find it.

NATHANIEL.

That mare of his has got a plaguy road
To travel, father;—and if he should lame her,—
For she is but tender-footed—

FATHER.

Aye, indeed!—
I should not like to see her limping back,
Poor beast!—But charity begins at home,
And, Nat, there 's our own horse in such a way
This morning!

NATHANIEL.

Why he han't been rid again!
Last night I hung a pebble by the manger
With a hole through, and every body says
That 't is a special charm against the hags.

FATHER.

It could not be a proper natural hole then,
Or 't was not a right pebble;—for I found him
Smoking with sweat, quaking in every limb,
And panting so! Lord knows where he had been
When we were all asleep, through bush and brake,
Up-hill and down-hill all alike, full stretch
At such a deadly rate!—

NATHANIEL.

By land and water,
Over the sea, perhaps!—I have heard tell
'T is many thousand miles off at the end
Of the world, where witches go to meet the Devil.
They used to ride on broomsticks, and to smear
Some ointment over them, and then away
Out of the window! but 't is worse than all
To worry the poor beasts so.   Shame upon it
That in a Christian country they should let
Such creatures live!

FATHER.

And when there 's such plain proof!
I did but threaten her because she robb'd
Our hedge, and the next night there came a wind
That made me shake to hear it in my bed!
How came it that that storm unroof'd my barn,
And only mine in the parish?—Look at her,
And that 's enough; she has it in her face!—
A pair of large dead eyes, sunk in her head,
Just like a corpse, and pursed with wrinkles round;
A nose and chin that scarce leave room between
For her lean fingers to squeeze in the snuff;
And when she speaks! I 'd sooner hear a raven
Croak at my door!—She sits there, nose and knees
Smoke-dried and shrivell'd o'er a starved fire,
With that black cat beside her, whose great eyes
Shine like old Beelzebub's; and to be sure
It must be one of his imps!—Aye, nail it hard.

NATHANIEL.

I wish old Margery heard the hammer go!
She 'd curse the music!

FATHER.

Here 's the Curate coming,
He ought to rid the parish of such vermin!
In the old times they used to hunt them out,
And hang them without mercy; but, Lord bless us!
The world is grown so wicked!

CURATE.

Good day, Farmer!
Nathaniel, what art nailing to the threshold?

NATHANIEL.

A horse-shoe, Sir; 't is good to keep off witchcraft,
And we 're afraid of Margery.

CURATE.

Poor old woman!
What can you fear from her?

FATHER.

What can we fear!
Who lamèd the Miller's boy? who raised the wind
That blew my old barn's roof down? who d' ye think
Rides my poor horse a'nights? who mocks the hounds?
But let me catch her at that trick again,
And I 've a silver bullet ready for her,
One that shall lame her, double how she will.

NATHANIEL.

What makes her sit there moping by herself,
With no soul near her but that great black cat?
And do but look at her!

CURATE.

Poor wretch; half blind
And crooked with her years, without a child
Or friend in her old age, 't is hard indeed
To have her very miseries made her crimes!
I met her but last week in that hard frost
Which made my young limbs ache, and when I ask'd
What brought her out in the snow, the poor old woman
Told me that she was forced to crawl abroad
And pick the hedges, just to keep herself
From perishing with cold,—because no neighbour
Had pity on her age; and then she cried,
And said the children pelted her with snow-balls,
And wish'd that she were dead.

FATHER.

I wish she was!
She has plagued the parish long enough!

CURATE.

Shame, Farmer!
Is that the charity your Bible teaches?

FATHER.

My Bible does not teach me to love witches.
I know what 's charity; who pays his tithes
And poor-rates readier?

CURATE.

Who can better do it?
You 've been a prudent and industrious man,
And God has blest your labour.

FATHER.

Why, thank God, Sir,
I 've had no reason to complain of fortune.

CURATE.

Complain! why you are wealthy!   All the parish
Look up to you.

FATHER.

Perhaps, Sir, I could tell
Guinea for guinea with the warmest of them.

CURATE.

You can afford a little to the poor;

And then, what's better still, you have the heart
To give from your abundance.

FATHER.

God forbid
I should want charity!

CURATE.

Oh! 't is a comfort
To think at last of riches well employ'd!
I have been by a death-bed, and know the worth
Of a good deed at that most awful hour
When riches profit not.

Farmer, I 'm going
To visit Margery. She is sick, I hear;—
Old, poor, and sick! a miserable lot,
And death will be a blessing. You might send her
Some little matter, something comfortable,
That she may go down easier to the grave,
And bless you when she dies.

FATHER.

What! is she going?
Well God forgive her then, if she has dealt
In the black art! I'll tell my dame of it,
And she shall send her something.

CURATE.

So I 'll say;
And take my thanks for hers.   [Goes.]

FATHER.

That 's a good man
That Curate, Nat, of ours, to go and visit
The poor in sickness; but he do'nt believe
In witchcraft, and that is not like a Christian.

NATHANIEL.

And so old Margery 's dying!

FATHER.

But you know
She may recover; so drive t' other nail in.

THE RUINED COTTAGE.

AY, Charles! I knew that this would fix thine eye!—
This woodbine wreathing round the broken porch,
Its leaves just withering, yet one autumn flower
Still fresh and fragrant; and yon holly-hock
That through the creeping weeds and nettles tall
Peers taller, lifting, column-like, a stem
Bright with the broad rose-blossoms. I have seen
Many an old convent reverend in decay,
And many a time have trod the castle courts
And grass-green halls, yet never did they strike
Home to the heart such melancholy thoughts
As this poor cottage. Look! its little hatch
Fleeced with that grey and wintry moss; the roof
Part moulder'd in, the rest o'ergrown with weeds,
House-leek, and long thin grass, and greener moss;
So Nature steals on all the works of man,
Sure conqueror she, reclaiming to herself
His perishable piles.

I led thee here,
Charles, not without design; for this hath been
My favourite walk even since I was a boy;
And I remember, Charles, this ruin here,
The neatest comfortable dwelling-place!
That when I read in those dear books which first
Woke in my heart the love of poesy,
How with the villagers Erminia dwelt,

And Calidore for a fair shepherdess
Forgot his quest to learn the shepherd's lore,
My fancy drew from this the little hut
Where that poor princess wept her hopeless love,
Or where the gentle Calidore at eve
Led Pastorella home. There was not then
A weed where all these nettles overtop
The garden-wall; but sweet-briar, scenting sweet
The morning air; rosemary and marjoram,
All wholesome herbs; and then, that woodbine wreathed
So lavishly around the pillar'd porch
Its fragrant flowers, that when I past this way,
After a truant absence hastening home,
I could not choose but pass with slacken'd speed
By that delightful fragrance. Sadly changed
Is this poor cottage! and its dwellers, Charles!—
Theirs is a simple melancholy tale,—
There 's scarce a village but can fellow it:
And yet, methinks, it will not weary thee,
And should not be untold.

A widow here
Dwelt with an orphan grandchild: just removed
Above the reach of pinching poverty,
She lived on some small pittance which sufficed,
In better times, the needful calls of life,
Not without comfort. I remember her
Sitting at evening in that open door-way,
And spinning in the sun. Methinks I see her
Raising her eyes and dark-rimm'd spectacles
To see the passer-by, yet ceasing not
To twirl her lengthening thread: or in the garden,
On some dry summer evening, walking round
To view her flowers, and pointing as she lean'd
Upon the ivory handle of her stick,
To some carnation whose o'erheavy head
Needed support; while with the watering-pot
Joanna follow'd, and refresh'd and trimm'd
The drooping plant; Joanna, her dear child,
As lovely and as happy then as youth
And innocence could make her.

Charles, it seems
As though I were a boy again, and all
The mediate years with their vicissitudes
A half-forgotten dream. I see the Maid
So comely in her Sunday dress! her hair,
Her bright brown hair, wreathed in contracting curls,
And then her cheek! it was a red and white
That made the delicate hues of art look loathsome.
The countrymen who on their way to church
Were leaning o'er the bridge, loitering to hear
The bell's last summons, and in idleness
Watching the stream below, would all look up
When she pass'd by. And her old Mother, Charles,
When I have heard some erring infidel
Speak of our faith as of a gloomy creed,
Inspiring superstitious wretchedness,
Her figure has recurr'd; for she did love
The Sabbath-day; and many a time hath cross'd
These fields in rain and through the winter snows,
When I, a graceless boy, wishing myself
By the fire-side, have wonder'd why she came
Who might have sate at home.

One only care
Hung on her aged spirit. For herself,
Her path was plain before her, and the close
Of her long journey near. But then her child

Soon to be left alone in this bad world,—
That was a thought which many a winter night
Had kept her sleepless; and when prudent love
In something better than a servant's state
Had placed her well at last, it was a pang
Like parting life to part with her dear girl.

One summer, Charles, when at the holidays
Return'd from school, I visited again
My old accustom'd walks, and found in them
A joy almost like meeting an old friend,
I saw the cottage empty, and the weeds
Already crowding the neglected flowers.
Joanna, by a villain's wiles seduced,
Had play'd the wanton, and that blow had reach'd
Her mother's heart. She did not suffer long,
Her age was feeble, and the heavy blow
Brought her grey hairs with sorrow to the grave.

I pass this ruin'd dwelling oftentimes,
And think of other days. It wakes in me
A transient sadness; but the feelings, Charles,
Which ever with these recollections rise,
I trust in God they will not pass away.

THE LAST OF THE FAMILY.

JAMES.

WHAT, Gregory! you are come, I see, to join us
On this sad business.

GREGORY.

      Aye, James, I am come,
But with a heavy heart, God knows it, man!
Where shall we meet the corpse?

JAMES.

      Some hour from hence;
By noon, and near about the elms, I take it.
This is not as it should be, Gregory,
Old men to follow young ones to the grave!
This morning when I heard the bell strike out,
I thought that I had never heard it toll
So dismally before.

GREGORY.

      Well, well! my friend,
'T is what we all must come to, soon or late.
But when a young man dies, in the prime of life,
One born so well, who might have blest us all
Many long years!—

JAMES.

      And then the family
Extinguish'd in him, and the good old name
Only to be remember'd on a tomb-stone!
A name that has gone down from sire to son
So many generations!—Many a time
Poor Master Edward, who is now a corpse,
When but a child, would come to me and lead me
To the great family-tree, and beg of me
To tell him stories of his ancestors,
Of Eustace, he that went to the Holy Land
With Richard Lion-heart, and that Sir Henry
Who fought at Cressy in King Edward's wars;
And then his little eyes would kindle so
To hear of their brave deeds! I used to think
The bravest of them all would not out-do
My darling boy.

GREGORY.

      This comes of your great schools
And college-breeding. Plague upon his guardians,
That would have made him wiser than his fathers!

JAMES.

If his poor father, Gregory, had but lived,
Things would not have been so. He, poor good man,
Had little of book-learning, but there lived not
A kinder, nobler-hearted gentleman,
One better to his tenants: When he died
There was not a dry eye for miles around.
Gregory, I thought that I could never know
A sadder day than that: but what was that,
Compared with this day's sorrow?

GREGORY.

      I remember,
Eight months ago, when the young Squire began
To alter the old mansion, they destroy'd
The martin's nests, that had stood undisturb'd
Under that roof,—aye! long before my memory.
I shook my head at seeing it, and thought
No good could follow.

JAMES,

      Poor young man! I loved him
Like my own child. I loved the family!
Come Candlemas, and I have been their servant
For five-and-forty years. I lived with them
When his good father brought my Lady home:
And when the young Squire was born, it did me good
To hear the bells so merrily announce
An heir. This is indeed a heavy blow—
I feel it, Gregory, heavier than the weight
Of threescore years. He was a noble lad,
I loved him dearly.

GREGORY.

      Every body loved him.
Such a fine, generous, open-hearted Youth!
When he came home from school at holidays,
How I rejoiced to see him! he was sure
To come and ask of me what birds there were
About my fields; and when I found a covey,
There 's not a testy Squire preserves his game
More charily, than I have kept them safe
For Master Edward. And he look'd so well
Upon a fine sharp morning after them,
His brown hair frosted, and his cheek so flush'd
With such a wholesome ruddiness,—ah, James,
But he was sadly changed when he came down
To keep his birth-day.

JAMES.

      Changed! why, Gregory,
'T was like a palsy to me, when he stepp'd
Out of the carriage. He was grown so thin,
His cheek so delicate sallow, and his eyes
Had such a dim and rakish hollowness;
And when he came to shake me by the hand,
And spoke as kindly to me as he used,
I hardly knew the voice.

GREGORY.

      It struck a damp
On all our merriment. 'T was a noble Ox
That smoked before us, and the old October
Went merrily in everflowing cans;
But 't was a skin-deep merriment. My heart
Seem'd as it took no share. And when we drank
His health, the thought came over me what cause

We had for wishing that, and spoilt the draught.
Poor Gentleman! to think ten months ago
He came of age, and now!

JAMES.

                 I fear'd it then!
He look'd to me as one that was not long
For this world's business.

GREGORY.

                 When the Doctor sent him
Abroad to try the air, it made me certain
That all was over. There 's but little hope,
Methinks, that foreign parts can help a man
When his own mother-country will not do.
The last time he came down, these bells rung so
I thought they would have rock'd the old steeple down;
And now that dismal toll! I would have staid
Beyond its reach, but this was a last duty:
I am an old tenant of the family,
Born on the estate, and now that I 've outlived it,
Why 't is but right to see it to the grave.
Have you heard aught of the new Squire?

JAMES.

                 But little,
And that not well. But be he what he may
Matters not much to me. The love I bore
To the old family will not easily fix
Upon a stranger. What 's on the opposite hill?
Is it not the funeral?

GREGORY.

              'T is, I think, some horsemen.
Aye! they are the black cloaks; and now I see
The white plumes on the hearse.

JAMES.

                 Between the trees;—
'T is hid behind them now.

GREGORY.

                 Aye! now we see it,
And there 's the coaches following, we shall meet
About the bridge. Would that this day were over!
I wonder whose turn 's next.

JAMES.

              God above knows!
When youth is summon'd, what must age expect!
God make us ready, Gregory, when it comes!

THE WEDDING.

TRAVELLER.

I PRAY you, wherefore are the village bells
Ringing so merrily!

WOMAN.

           A wedding, Sir,—
Two of the village folk. And they are right
To make a merry time on 't while they may!
Come twelve-months hence, I warrant them they 'd go
To church again more willingly than now,
If all might be undone.

TRAVELLER.

           An ill-match'd pair,
So I conceive you. Youth perhaps and age?

WOMAN.

No,—both are young enough.

TRAVELLER.

           Perhaps the man then,

A lazy idler,—one who better likes
The alehouse than his work?

WOMAN.

               Why, Sir, for that
He always was a well-condition'd lad,
One who'd work hard and well; and as for drink,
Save now and then mayhap at Christmas time,
Sober as wife could wish.

TRAVELLER.

               Then is the girl
A shrew, or else untidy;—one to welcome
Her husband with a rude unruly tongue,
Or drive him from a foul and wretched home
To look elsewhere for comfort. Is it so?

WOMAN.

She 's notable enough; and as for temper
The best good-humour'd girl! You see yon house,
There by the aspen-tree, whose grey leaves shine
In the wind? she lived a servant at the farm,
And often, as I came to weeding here,
I 've heard her singing as she milk'd her cows
So cheerfully:—I did not like to hear her,
Because it made me think upon the days
When I had got as little on my mind,
And was as cheerful too. But she would marry,
And folks must reap as they have sown. God help her

TRAVELLER.

Why, Mistress, if they both are well inclined,
Why should not both be happy?

WOMAN.

               They 've no money.

TRAVELLER.

But both can work; and sure as cheerfully
She 'd labour for herself as at the farm.
And he wo'n't work the worse because he knows
That she will make his fire-side ready for him,
And watch for his return.

WOMAN.

               All very well,
A little while.

TRAVELLER.

            And what if they are poor?
Riches can't always purchase happiness;
And much we know will be expected there
Where much was given.

WOMAN.

            All this I have heard at church!
And when I walk in the church-yard, or have been
By a death-bed, 't is mighty comforting.
But when I hear my children cry for hunger,
And see them shiver in their rags,—God help me!
I pity those for whom these bells ring up
So merrily upon their wedding-day,
Because I think of mine.

TRAVELLER.

           You have known trouble;
These haply may be happier.

WOMAN.

            Why for that
I 've had my share; some sickness and some sorrow:
Well will it be for them to know no worse.
Yet had I rather hear a daughter's knell
Than her wedding-peal, Sir, if I thought her fate
Promised no better things.

TRAVELLER.

           Sure, sure, good woman,

You look upon the world with jaundiced eyes!
All have their cares; those who are poor want wealth,
They who have wealth want more; so are we all
Dissatisfied, yet all live on, and each
Has his own comforts.

WOMAN.
                    Sir! d'ye see that horse
Turn'd out to common here by the way-side?
He's high in bone, you may tell every rib
Even at this distance.   Mind him! how he turns
His head, to drive away the flies that feed
On his gall'd shoulder!   There's just grass enough
To disappoint his whetted appetite.
You see his *comforts*, Sir!

TRAVELLER.
                    A wretched beast!
Hard labour and worse usage he endures
From some bad master.   But the lot of the poor
Is not like his.

WOMAN.
                    In truth it is not, Sir!
For when the horse lies down at night, no cares
About to-morrow vex him in his dreams;
He knows no quarter-day, and when he gets
Some musty hay or patch of hedge-row grass,
He has no hungry children to claim part
Of his half meal!

TRAVELLER.
                    'T is idleness makes want,
And idle habits.   If the man will go,
And spend his evenings by the alehouse fire,
Whom can he blame if there be want at home?

WOMAN.
Aye! idleness! the rich folks never fail
To find some reason why the poor deserve
Their miseries!—Is it idleness, I pray you,
That brings the fever or the ague fit?
That makes the sick one's sickly appetite
Turn at the dry bread and potatoe meal?
Is it idleness that makes small wages fail
For growing wants?—Six years agone, these bells
Rung on my wedding-day, and I was told
What I might look for,—but I did not heed
Good counsel.   I had lived in service, Sir;
Knew never what it was to want a meal;
Laid down without one thought to keep me sleepless
Or trouble me in sleep; had for a Sunday
My linen gown, and when the pedlar came
Could buy me a new riband.—And my husband,—
A towardly young man and well to do,—
He had his silver buckles and his watch;
There was not in the village one who look'd
Sprucer on holidays.   We married, Sir,
And we had children, but as wants increased
Wages did not.   The silver buckles went,
So went the watch; and when the holiday coat
Was worn to work, no new one in its place.[1]
For me—you see my rags! but I deserve them,

---

[1] A farmer once told the author of *Malvern Hills*, « that he almost constantly remarked a gradation of changes in those men he had been in the habit of employing.   Young men, he said, were generally neat in their appearance, active and cheerful, till they became married and had a family, when he had observed that their silver buttons, buckles, and watches gradually disappeared, and their Sunday's clothes became common without any other to supply their place,—*but*, said he, *some good comes from this, for they will then work for whatever they can get.* »—Note to COTTLE's *Malvern Hills*.

For wilfully, like this new-married pair,
I went to my undoing.

TRAVELLER.
                    But the Parish—

WOMAN.
Aye, it falls heavy there; and yet their pittance
Just serves to keep life in.   A blessed prospect,
To slave while there is strength, in age the workhouse,
A parish shell at last, and the little bell
Toll'd hastily for a pauper's funeral!

TRAVELLER.
Is this your child?

WOMAN.
                    Aye, Sir; and were he drest
And clean'd, he'd be as fine a boy to look on
As the Squire's young master.   These thin rags of his
Let comfortably in the summer wind;
But when the winter comes, it pinches me
To see the little wretch!   I've three besides;
And,—God forgive me! but I often wish
To see them in their coffins.—God reward you!
God bless you for your charity!

TRAVELLER.
                    You have taught me
To give sad meaning to the village bells!
                                    .1800.

THE ALDERMAN'S FUNERAL.

STRANGER.
Whom are they ushering from the world, with all
This pageantry and long parade of death?

TOWNSMAN.
A long parade, indeed, Sir, and yet here
You see but half; round yonder bend it reaches
A furlong farther, carriage behind carriage.

STRANGER.
'T is but a mournful sight, and yet the pomp
Tempts me to stand a gazer.

TOWNSMAN.
                    Yonder schoolboy
Who plays the truant, says the proclamation
Of peace was nothing to the show; and even
The chairing of the members at election
Would not have been a finer sight than this;
Only that red and green are prettier colours
Than all this mourning.   There, Sir, you behold
One of the red-gown'd worthies of the city,
The envy and the boast of our exchange;—
Aye, what was worth, last week, a good half-million,
Screw'd down in yonder hearse!

STRANGER.
                    Then he was born
Under a lucky planet, who to-day
Puts mourning on for his inheritance.

TOWNSMAN.
When first I heard his death, that very wish
Leapt to my lips; but now the closing scene
Of the comedy hath waken'd wiser thoughts;
And I bless God, that, when I go to the grave,
There will not be the weight of wealth like his
To sink me down.

STRANGER.
                    The camel and the needle,—
Is that then in your mind?

8o

TOWNSMAN.

           Even so.   The text
Is Gospel-wisdom. I would ride the camel,—
Yea leap him flying, through the needle's eye,
As easily as such a pampered soul
Could pass the narrow gate.

STRANGER.

               Your pardon, Sir,
But sure this lack of Christian charity
Looks not like Christian truth.

TOWNSMAN.

              Your pardon too, Sir,
If, with this text before me, I should feel
In the preaching mood! But for these barren fig-trees,
With all their flourish and their leafiness,
We have been told their destiny and use,
When the axe is laid unto the root and they
Cumber the earth no longer.

STRANGER.

              Was his wealth
Stored fraudfully,—the spoil of orphans wrong'd,
And widows who had none to plead their right?

TOWNSMAN.

All honest, open, honourable gains,
Fair legal interest, bonds and mortgages,
Ships to the East and West.

STRANGER.

            Why judge you then
So hardly of the dead?

TOWNSMAN.

           For what he left
Undone;—for sins, not one of which is mentioned
In the Ten Commandments. He, I warrant him,
Believed no other Gods than those of the Creed:
Bow'd to no idols,—but his money-bags:
Swore no false oaths, except at the custom-house:
Kept the Sabbath idle: built a monument
To honour his dead father: did no murder:
Was too old-fashion'd for adultery:
Never pick'd pockets: never bore false witness:
And never, with that all-commanding wealth,
Coveted his neighbour's house, nor ox, nor ass!

STRANGER.

You knew him then, it seems?

TOWNSMAN.

            As all men know
The virtues of your hundred-thousanders;
They never hide their lights beneath a bushel.

STRANGER.

Nay, nay, uncharitable Sir! for often
Doth bounty like a streamlet flow unseen,
Freshening and giving life along its course.

TOWNSMAN.

We track the streamlet by the brighter green
And livelier growth it gives;—but as for this—
This was a pool that stagnated and stunk;
The rains of heaven engendered nothing in it
But slime and foul corruption.

STRANGER.

            Yet even these
Are reservoirs whence public charity
Still keeps her channels full.

TOWNSMAN.

           Now, Sir, you touch

Upon the point. This man of half a million
Had all these public virtues which you praise:
But the poor man rung never at his door;
And the old beggar, at the public gate,
Who, all the summer long, stands, hat in hand,
He knew how vain it was to lift an eye
To that hard face. Yet he was always found
Among your ten and twenty pound subscribers,
Your benefactors in the newspapers.
His alms were money put to interest
In the other world,—donations to keep open
A running charity-account with heaven :—
Retaining fees against the last assizes,
When, for the trusted talents, strict account
Shall be required from all, and the old Arch-Lawyer
Plead his own cause as plaintiff.

STRANGER.

              I must needs
Believe you, Sir :—these are your witnesses,
These mourners here, who from their carriages
Gape at the gaping crowd. A good March wind
Were to be pray'd for now, to lend their eyes
Some decent rheum. The very hireling mute
Bears not a face blanker of all emotion
Than the old servant of the family!
How can this man have lived, that thus his death
Costs not the soiling one white handkerchief!

TOWNSMAN.

Who should lament for him, Sir, in whose heart
Love had no place, nor natural charity?
The parlour spaniel, when she heard his step,
Rose slowly from the hearth, and stole aside
With creeping pace; she never raised her eyes
To woo kind words from him, nor laid her head
Upraised upon his knee, with fondling whine.
How could it be but thus! Arithmetic
Was the sole science he was ever taught;
The multiplication-table was his Creed,
His Pater-noster, and his Decalogue.
When yet he was a boy, and should have breathed
The open air and sunshine of the fields,
To give his blood its natural spring and play,
He in a close and dusky counting-house,
Smoke-dried and sear'd and shrivell'd up his heart.
So, from the way in which he was train'd up,
His feet departed not; he toil'd and moil'd,
Poor muck-worm! through his three-score years and
     ten ;
And when the earth shall now be shovell'd on him;
If that which served him for a soul were still
Within his husk, 't would still be dirt to dirt.

STRANGER.

Yet your next newspapers will blazon him
For industry and honourable wealth
A bright example.

TOWNSMAN.

           Even half a million
Gets him no other praise. But come this way
Some twelve months hence, and you will find his
     virtues
Trimly set forth in lapidary lines,
Faith, with her torch beside, and little Cupids
Dropping upon his urn their marble tears.

                         1803.

BALLADS AND METRICAL TALES.

MARY THE MAID OF THE INN.

The subject of the following Ballad was related to me, when a school-boy, as a fact which had happened in the north of England. Either Furnes or Kirkstall Abbey (I forget which) was named as the scene. It seems, however, to have been founded upon a story related in Dr Plot's *History of Staffordshire*.

« Amongst the unusual accidents, » says this amusing author, « that have attended the female sex in the course of their lives, I think I may also reckon the narrow escapes they have made from death. Whereof I met with one mentioned with admiration by every body at Leek, that happened not far off at the Black Meer of Morridge, which, though famous for nothing for which it is commonly reputed so (as that it is bottomless, no cattle will drink of it, or birds fly over or settle upon it, all which I found false), yet is so, for the signal deliverance of a poor woman, enticed thither in a dismal stormy night, by a bloody ruffian, who had first gotten her with child, and intended in this remote inhospitable place to have dispatched her by drowning. The same night (Providence so ordering it) there were several persons of inferior rank drinking in an ale-house at Leek, whereof one having been out, and observing the darkness and other ill circumstances of the weather, coming in again, said to the rest of his companions, that he were a stout man indeed that would venture to go to the black Meer of Morridge in such a night as that: to which one of them replying, that for a crown or some such sum he would undertake it, the rest joining their purses, said he should have his demand. The bargain being struck, away he went on his journey with a stick in his hand, which he was to leave there as a testimony of his performance. At length coming near the Meer, he heard the lamentable cries of this distressed woman, begging for mercy, which at first put him to a stand; but being a man of great resolution and some policy, he went boldly on, however, counterfeiting the presence of divers other persons, calling Jack, Dick, and Tom, and crying *Here are the rogues we look'd for*, etc.; which being heard by the murderer, he left the woman and fled; whom the other man found by the Meer side almost stript of her clothes, and brought her with him to Leek as an ample testimony of his having been at the Meer, and of God's providence too. »—P. 291.

The metre is Mr Lewis's invention; and metre is one of the few things concerning which popularity may be admitted as a proof of merit. The Ballad has become popular owing to the metre and the story: as for every thing else, *dum relego scripsisse pudet*. It has however been made the subject of a fine picture by Mr Barker.

WHO is yonder poor Maniac, whose wildly-fix'd eyes
    Seem a heart overcharged to express?
She weeps not, yet often and deeply she sighs;
She never complains, but her silence implies
    The composure of settled distress.

No pity she looks for, no alms does she seek;
    Nor for raiment nor food doth she care:
Through her rags do the winds of the winter blow bleak
On that wither'd breast, and her weather-worn cheek
    Hath the hue of a mortal despair.

Yet cheerful and happy, nor distant the day,
    Poor Mary the Maniac hath been;
The Traveller remembers who journey'd this way
No damsel so lovely, no damsel so gay,
    As Mary, the Maid of the Inn.

Her cheerful address fill'd the guests with delight
    As she welcomed them in with a smile;
Her heart was a stranger to childish affright,
And Mary would walk by the Abbey at night
    When the wind whistled down the dark aisle.

She loved, and young Richard had settled the day,
    And she hoped to be happy for life:
But Richard was idle and worthless, and they
Who knew him would pity poor Mary, and say
    That she was too good for his wife.

'T was in autumn, and stormy and dark was the night,
    And fast were the windows and door;
Two guests sat enjoying the fire that burnt bright,
And smoking in silence, with tranquil delight
    They listen'd to hear the wind roar.

« 'T is pleasant, » cried one, « seated by the fire-side,
    To hear the wind whistle without. »
« What a night for the Abbey ! » his comrade replied,
« Methinks a man's courage would now be well tried
    Who should wander the ruins about.

« I myself, like a school-boy, should tremble to hear
    The hoarse ivy shake over my head;
And could fancy I saw, half persuaded by fear,
Some ugly old Abbot's grim spirit appear,
    For this wind might awaken the dead ! »

« I 'll wager a dinner, » the other one cried,
    « That Mary would venture there now. »
« Then wager and lose ! » with a sneer he replied,
« I 'll warrant she 'd fancy a ghost by her side,
    And faint if she saw a white cow. »

« Will Mary this charge on her courage allow ! »
    His companion exclaim'd with a smile;
« I shall win,—for I know she will venture there now,
And earn a new bonnet by bringing a bough
    From the elder that grows in the aisle. »

With fearless good-humour did Mary comply,
    And her way to the Abbey she bent;
The night was dark, and the wind was high,
And as hollowly howling it swept through the sky,
    She shiver'd with cold as she went.

O'er the path so well known still proceeded the Maid
    Where the Abbey rose dim on the sight.
Through the gateway she enter'd, she felt not afraid,
Yet the ruins were lonely and wild, and their shade
    Seem'd to deepen the gloom of the night.

All around her was silent, save when the rude blast
    Howl'd dismally round the old pile;
Over weed-cover'd fragments she fearlessly past,
And arrived at the innermost ruin at last
    Where the elder-tree grew in the aisle.

Well pleased did she reach it, and quickly drew near,
    And hastily gather'd the bough;
When the sound of a voice seem'd to rise on her ear—
She paused, and she listen'd all eager to hear,
    And her heart panted fearfully now.

The wind blew, the hoarse ivy shook over her head,
    She listen'd—nought else could she hear;
The wind fell, her heart sunk in her bosom with dread,
For she heard in the ruins distinctly the tread
    Of footsteps approaching her near.

Behind a wide column half breathless with fear
  She crept to conceal herself there:
That instant the moon o'er a dark cloud shone clear,
And she saw in the moonlight two ruffians appear,
  And between them a corpse did they bear.

Then Mary could feel her heart-blood curdle cold!
  Again the rough wind hurried by,—
It blew off the hat of the one, and behold
Even close to the feet of poor Mary it roll'd,—
  She felt, and expected to die.

« Curse the hat ! » he exclaims; « nay, come on till we
    hide
  The dead body,» his comrade replies.
She beholds them in safety pass on by her side,
She seizes the hat, fear her courage supplied,
  And fast through the Abbey she flies.

She ran with wild speed, she rush'd in at the door,
  She gazed horribly eager around,
Then her limbs could support their faint burthen no
    more,
And exhausted and breathless she sunk on the floor,
  Unable to utter a sound.

Ere yet her pale lips could the story impart,
  For a moment the hat met her view ;—
Her eyes from that object convulsively start,
For—what a cold horror then thrill'd through her heart
  When the name of her Richard she knew!

Where the old Abbey stands, on the common hard by,
  His gibbet is now to be seen;
His irons you still from the road may espy,
The traveller beholds them, and thinks with a sigh
  Of poor Mary, the Maid of the Inn.

                      1796.

DONICA.

« In Finland there is a Castle which is called the New Rock, moated about with a river of unsounded depth, the water black, and the fish therein very distasteful to the palate. In this are spectres often seen, which foreshow either the death of the Governor, or of some prime officer belonging to the place ; and most commonly it appeareth in the shape of a harper, sweetly singing and dallying and playing under the water. »

« It is reported of one Donica, that after she was dead, the Devil walked in her body for the space of two years, so that none suspected but she was still alive; for she did both speak and eat, though very sparingly ; only she had a deep paleness on her countenance, which was the only sign of death. At length a Magician coming by where she was then in the company of many other virgins, as soon as he beheld her he said, 'Fair Maids, why keep you company with this dead Virgin, whom you suppose to be alive?'—when, taking away the magic charm which was tied under her arm, the body fell down lifeless and without motion. »

The following Ballad is founded on these stories. They are to be found in the notes to *The Hierarchies of the Blessed Angels*; a Poem by Thomas Heywood, printed in folio by Adam Islip, 1635.

High on a rock whose castled shade
  Darken'd the lake below,
In ancient strength majestic stood
  The towers of Arlinkow.

The fisher in the lake below
  Durst never cast his net,
Nor ever swallow in its waves
  Her passing wing would wet.

The cattle from its ominous banks
  In wild alarm would run,
Though parch'd with thirst, and faint beneath
  The summer's scorching sun.

For sometimes when no passing breeze
  The long lank sedges waved,
All white with foam and heaving high
  Its deafening billows raved;

And when the tempest from its base
  The rooted pine would shake,
The powerless storm unruffling swept
  Across the calm dead lake.

And ever then when death drew near
  The house of Arlinkow,
Its dark unfathom'd waters sent
  Strange music from below.

The Lord of Arlinkow was old,
  One only child had he,
Donica was the Maiden's name,
  As fair as fair might be.

A bloom as bright as opening morn
  Flush'd o'er her clear white cheek ;
The music of her voice was mild,
  Her full dark eyes were meek.

Far was her beauty known, for none
  So fair could Finland boast;
Her parents loved the Maiden much,
  Young Eberhard loved her most.

Together did they hope to tread
  The pleasant path of life,
For now the day drew near to make
  Donica Eberhard's wife.

The eve was fair and mild the air,
  Along the lake they stray;
The eastern hill reflected bright
  The tints of fading day.

And brightly o'er the water stream'd
  The liquid radiance wide ;
Donica's little dog ran on
  And gambol'd at her side.

Youth, health, and love bloom'd on her cheek ;
  Her full dark eyes express
In many a glance to Eberhard
  Her soul's meek tenderness.

Nor sound was heard, nor passing gale
  Sigh'd through the long lank sedge;
The air was hush'd, no little wave
  Dimpled the water's edge.

Sudden the unfathom'd lake sent forth
  Its music from beneath,
And slowly o'er the waters sail'd
  The solemn sounds of death.

As those deep sounds of death arose,
  Donica's cheek grew pale,
And in the arms of Eberhard
  The lifeless Maiden fell.

Loudly the Youth in terror shriek'd,
  And loud he call'd for aid,
And with a wild and eager look
  Gazed on the lifeless Maid.

But soon again did better thoughts
  In Eberhard arise,
And he with trembling hope beheld
  The Maiden raise her eyes.

And on his arm reclined she moved
  With feeble pace and slow,
And soon with strength recover'd reach'd
  The towers of Arlinkow.

Yet never to Donica's cheek
  Return'd the lively hue:
Her cheeks were deathy white and wan,
  Her lips a livid blue.

Her eyes so bright and black of yore
  Were now more black and bright,
And beam'd strange lustre in her face
  So deadly wan and white.

The dog that gambol'd by her side,
  And loved with her to stray,
Now at his alter'd mistress howl'd,
  And fled in fear away.

Yet did the faithful Eberhard
  Not love the Maid the less;
He gazed with sorrow, but he gazed
  With deeper tenderness.

And when he found her health unharm'd
  He would not brook delay,
But pressed the not unwilling Maid
  To fix the bridal day.

And when at length it came, with joy
  He hail'd the bridal day,
And onward to the house of God
  They went their willing way.

But when they at the altar stood,
  And heard the sacred rite,
The hallow'd tapers dimly stream'd
  A pale sulphureous light.

And when the Youth with holy warmth
  Her hand in his did hold,
Sudden he felt Donica's hand
  Grow deadly damp and cold.

And loudly did he shriek, for lo!
  A Spirit met his view,
And Eberhard in the angel form
  His own Donica knew.

That instant from her earthly frame
  Howling the Dæmon fled,
And at the side of Eberhard
  The livid form fell dead.

1796.

RUDIGER.

"Divers Princes and Noblemen being assembled in a beautiful and fair Palace, which was situate upon the river Rhine, they beheld a boat or small barge make toward the shore, drawn by a Swan in a silver chain, the one end fastened about her neck, the other to the vessel; and in it an unknown soldier, a man of a comely personage and graceful presence, who stept upon the shore; which done, the boat guided by the Swan left him, and floated down the river. This man fell afterward in league with a fair gentlewoman, married her and by her had many children. After some years, the same Swan came with the same barge unto the same place;—the soldier entering into it, was carried thence the way he came, left wife, children and family, and was never seen amongst them after."

"Now who can judge this to be other than one of those spirits that are named Incubi?" says Thomas Heywood. I have adopted his story, but not his solution, making the unknown soldier not an evil spirit, but one who had purchased happiness of a malevolent being, by the promised sacrifice of his first-born child.

BRIGHT on the mountain's heathy slope
  The day's last splendours shine,
And rich with many a radiant hue,
  Gleam gaily on the Rhine.

And many a one from Waldhurst's walls
  Along the river stroll'd,
As ruffling o'er the pleasant stream
  The evening gales came cold.

So as they stray'd a swan they saw
  Sail stately up and strong,
And by a silver chain he drew
  A little boat along,—

Whose streamer to the gentle breeze
  Long floating fluttered light,
Beneath whose crimson canopy
  There lay reclined a knight.

With arching crest and swelling breast
  On sail'd the stately swan,
And lightly up the parting tide
  The little boat came on.

And onward to the shore they drew,
  Where having left the knight,
The little boat adown the stream
  Fell soon beyond the sight.

Was never a knight in Waldhurst's walls
  Could with this stranger vie;
Was never a youth at aught esteem'd
  When Rudiger was by.

Was never a maid in Waldhurst's walls
  Might match with Margaret;
Her cheek was fair, her eyes were dark,
  Her silken locks like jet.

And many a rich and noble youth
  Had strove to win the fair;
But never a rich and noble youth
  Could rival Rudiger.

At every tilt and tourney he
  Still bore away the prize;
For knightly feats superior still,
  And knightly courtesies.

His gallant feats, his looks, his love,
  Soon won the willing fair;
And soon did Margaret become
  The wife of Rudiger.

Like morning dreams of happiness
  Fast roll'd the months away;
For he was kind and she was kind,
  And who so blest as they?

Yet Rudiger would sometimes sit
  Absorb'd in silent thought,
And his dark downward eye would seem
  With anxious meaning fraught:

But soon he raised his looks again,
  And smiled his cares away,
And mid the hall of gaiety
  Was none like him so gay.

And onward roll'd the waning months—
  The hour appointed came,
And Margaret her Rudiger
  Hail'd with a father's name,

But silently did Rudiger
  The little infant see;
And darkly on the babe he gazed,—
  A gloomy man was he.

And when to bless the little babe
  The holy Father came,
To cleanse the stains of sin away
  In Christ's redeeming name,

Then did the cheek of Rudiger
  Assume a death-pale hue,
And on his clammy forehead stood
  The cold convulsive dew;

And faltering in his speech he bade
  The Priest the rites delay,
Till he could, to right health restored,
  Enjoy the festive day.

When o'er the many-tinted sky
  He saw the day decline,
He called upon his Margaret
  To walk beside the Rhine;

« And we will take the little babe,
  For soft the breeze that blows,
And the mild murmurs of the stream
  Will lull him to repose. »

And so together forth they went,
  The evening breeze was mild,
And Rudiger upon his arm
  Pillow'd the little child.

And many a one from Waldhurst's walls
  Along the banks did roam,
But soon the evening wind came cold,
  And all betook them home.

Yet Rudiger in silent mood
  Along the banks would roam,
Nor aught could Margaret prevail
  To turn his footsteps home.

« Oh turn thee, turn thee, Rudiger!
  The rising mists behold,
The evening wind is damp and chill,
  The little babe is cold! »

« Now hush thee, hush thee, Margaret,
  The mists will do no harm,
And from the wind the little babe
  Lies shelter'd on my arm. »

« Oh turn thee, turn thee, Rudiger!
  Why onward wilt thou roam?
The moon is up, the night is cold,
  And we are far from home. »

He answered not, for now he saw
  A swan come sailing strong,
And by a silver chain he drew
  A little boat along.

To shore they came, and to the boat
  Fast leapt he with the child,
And in leapt Margaret—breathless now,
  And pale with fear and wild.

With arching crest and swelling breast
  On sail'd the stately swan,
And lightly down the rapid tide
  The little boat went on.

The full orb'd moon, that beam'd around
  Pale splendour through the night,
Cast through the crimson canopy
  A dim discolour'd light.

And swiftly down the hurrying stream
  In silence still they sail,
And the long streamer fluttering fast,
  Flapp'd to the heavy gale.

And he was mute in sullen thought,
  And she was mute with fear,
Nor sound but of the parting tide
  Broke on the listening ear.

The little babe began to cry,
  Then Margaret raised her head,
And with a quick and hollow voice
  « Give me the child! » she said.

« Now hush thee, hush thee, Margaret,
  Nor my poor heart distress!
I do but pay perforce the price
  Of former happiness.

« And hush thee too, my little babe!
  Thy cries so feeble cease:
Lie still, lie still;—a little while
  And thou shalt be at peace. »

So as he spake to land they drew,
  And swift he stept on shore,
And him behind did Margaret
  Close follow evermore.

It was a place all desolate,
  Nor house nor tree was there;
And there a rocky mountain rose,
  Barren, and bleak, and bare.

And at its base a cavern yawn'd,
  No eye its depth might view,
For in the moon-beam shining round
  That darkness darker grew.

Cold horror crept through Margaret's blood,
  Her heart it paused with fear,
When Rudiger approach'd the cave,
  And cried, « Lo I am here!»

A deep sepulchral sound the cave
  Return'd « Lo I am here!»
And black from out the cavern gloom
  Two giant arms appear.

And Rudiger approach'd, and held
  The little infant nigh:
Then Margaret shriek'd, and gather'd then
  New powers from agony.

And round the baby fast and close
  Her trembling arms she folds,
And with a strong convulsive grasp
  The little infant holds.

« Now help me, Jesus!» loud she cries,
  And loud on God she calls;
Then from the grasp of Rudiger
  The little infant falls.

And loud he shriek'd, for now his frame
  The huge black arms clasp'd round,
And dragg'd the wretched Rudiger
  Adown the dark profound.

              1796.

JASPAR.

The stories of this and the following ballad are wholly imaginary. I may say of each, as John Bunyan did of his Pilgrim's Progress,

> *It came from mine own heart, so to my head,*
> *And thence into my fingers trickled;*
> *Then to my pen, from whence immediately*
> *On paper I did dribble it daintily.*

JASPAR was poor, and vice and want
  Had made his heart like stone;
And Jaspar look'd with envious eyes
  On riches not his own.

On plunder bent abroad he went
  Toward the close of day,
And loiter'd on the lonely road
  Impatient for his prey.

No traveller came—he loiter'd long,
  And often look'd around,
And paused and listen'd eagerly
  To catch some coming sound.

He sate him down beside the stream
  That cross'd the lonely way,
So fair a scene might well have charm'd
  All evil thoughts away:

He sate beneath a willow tree
  Which cast a trembling shade,
The gentle river full in front
  A little island made;

Where pleasantly the moon-beam shone
  Upon the poplar trees,
Whose shadow on the stream below
  Play'd slowly to the breeze.

He listen'd—and he heard the wind
  That waved the willow tree;
He heard the waters flow along,
  And murmur quietly.

He listen'd for the traveller's tread,
  The nightingale sung sweet,—
He started up, for now he heard
  The sound of coming feet;

He started up and graspt a stake,
  And waited for his prey;
There came a lonely traveller,
  And Jaspar crost his way.

But Jaspar's threats and curses fail'd
  The traveller to appal,
He would not lightly yield the purse
  Which held his little all.

Awhile he struggled, but he strove
  With Jaspar's strength in vain;
Beneath his blows he fell and groan'd,
  And never spake again.

Jaspar raised up the murder'd man,
  And plunged him in the flood,
And in the running water then
  He cleansed his hands from blood.

The waters closed around the corpse,
  And cleansed his hands from gore,
The willow waved, the stream flow'd on,
  And murmur'd as before.

There was no human eye had seen
  The blood the murderer spilt,
And Jaspar's conscience never knew
  The avenging goad of guilt.

And soon the ruffian had consumed
  The gold he gain'd so ill,
And years of secret guilt pass'd on,
  And he was needy still.

One eve beside the alehouse fire
  He sate as it befell,
When in there came a labouring man
  Whom Jaspar knew full well.

He sate him down by Jaspar's side
  A melancholy man,
For spite of honest toil, the world
  Went hard with Jonathan.

His toil a little earn'd, and he
  With little was content;
But sickness on his wife had fallen,
  And all he had was spent.

Then with his wife and little ones
  He shared the scanty meal,
And saw their looks of wretchedness,
  And felt what wretches feel.

That very morn the Landlord's power
  Had seized the little left,
And now the sufferer found himself
  Of every thing bereft.

He leant his head upon his hand,
  His elbow on his knee,
And so by Jaspar's side he sate,
  And not a word said he.

« Nay—why so downcast!» Jaspar cried,
  « Come—cheer up, Jonathan!
Drink, neighbour, drink! 't will warm thy heart.—
  Come! come! take courage, man!»

He took the cup that Jaspar gave,
  And down he drain'd it quick;
« I have a wife,» said Jonathan,
  « And she is deadly sick.

« She has no bed to lie upon,
  I saw them take her bed—
And I have children—would to God
  That they and I were dead!

« Our Landlord he goes home to-night,
  And he will sleep in peace—
I would that I were in my grave,
  For there all troubles cease.

« In vain I pray'd him to forbear,
  Though wealth enough has he!
God be to him as merciless
  As he has been to me!»

When Jaspar saw the poor man's soul
  On all his ills intent,
He plied him with the heartening cup,
  And with him forth he went.

« This landlord on his homeward road
  'T were easy now to meet.
The road is lonesome, Jonathan!—
  And vengeance, man! is sweet.»

He listen'd to the tempter's voice,
  The thought it made him start;—
His head was hot, and wretchedness
  Had harden'd now his heart.

Along the lonely road they went
  And waited for their prey,
They sate them down beside the stream
  That cross'd the lonely way.

They sate them down beside the stream
  And never a word they said,
They sate and listen'd silently
  To hear the traveller's tread.

The night was calm, the night was dark,
  No star was in the sky,
The wind it waved the willow boughs,
  The stream flow'd quietly.

The night was calm, the air was still,
  Sweet sung the nightingale;
The soul of Jonathan was soothed,
  His heart began to fail.

« 'T is weary waiting here,» he cried,
  « And now the hour is late,—
Methinks he will not come to-night,
  No longer let us wait.»

« Have patience, man!» the ruffian said,
  « A little we may wait,
But longer shall his wife expect
  Her husband at the gate.»

Then Jonathan grew sick at heart,
  « My conscience yet is clear!
Jaspar—it is not yet too late—
  I will not linger here.»

« How now!» cried Jaspar, « why I thought
  Thy conscience was asleep.
No more such qualms, the night is dark,
  The river here is deep.»

« What matters that,» said Jonathan,
  Whose blood began to freeze,
« When there is One above whose eye
  The deeds of darkness sees!»

« We are safe enough,» said Jaspar then,
  « If that be all thy fear!
Nor eye below, nor eye above,
  Can pierce the darkness here.»

That instant as the murderer spake
  There came a sudden light;
Strong as the mid-day sun it shone,
  Though all around was night:

It hung upon the willow tree,
  It hung upon the flood,
It gave to view the poplar isle,
  And all the scene of blood.

The traveller who journeys there,
  He surely hath espied
A madman who has made his home
  Upon the river's side.

His cheek is pale, his eye is wild,
  His look bespeaks despair;
For Jaspar since that hour has made
  His home unshelter'd there.

And fearful are his dreams at night,
  And dread to him the day!
He thinks upon his untold crime,
  And never dares to pray.

The summer suns, the winter storms,
  O'er him unheeded roll,
For heavy is the weight of blood
  Upon the maniac's soul!

              1798.

LORD WILLIAM.

No eye beheld when William plunged
  Young Edmund in the stream,
No human ear but William's heard
  Young Edmund's drowning scream.

Submissive all the vassals own'd
  The murderer for their Lord,
And he as rightful heir possess'd
  The house of Erlingford.

The ancient house of Erlingford
  Stood in a fair domain,
And Severn's ample waters near
  Roll'd through the fertile plain.

And often the way-faring man
  Would love to linger there,
Forgetful of his onward road,
  To gaze on scenes so fair.

But never could Lord William dare
  To gaze on Severn's stream;
In every wind that swept its waves
  He heard young Edmund scream.

In vain at midnight's silent hour
  Sleep closed the murderer's eyes,
In every dream the murderer saw
  Young Edmund's form arise.

In vain by restless conscience driven
  Lord William left his home,
Far from the scenes that saw his guilt,
  In pilgrimage to roam.

To other climes the pilgrim fled,
  But could not fly despair;
He sought his home again, but peace
  Was still a stranger there.

Slow were all passing hours, yet swift
  The months appear'd to roll;
And now the day return'd that shook
  With terror William's soul.

A day that William never felt
  Return without dismay,
For well had conscience kalendar'd
  Young Edmund's dying day.

A fearful day was that! the rains
  Fell fast with tempest roar,
And the swoln tide of Severn spread
  Far on the level shore.

In vain Lord William sought the feast,
  In vain he quaff'd the bowl,
And strove with noisy mirth to drown
  The anguish of his soul;

The tempest, as its sudden swell
  In gusty howlings came,
With cold and death-like feelings seem'd
  To thrill his shuddering frame.

Reluctant now, as night came on,
  His lonely couch he prest;
And wearied out, he sunk to sleep,—
  To sleep—but not to rest.

Beside that couch his brother's form,
  Lord Edmund seem'd to stand,
Such and so pale as when in death
  He grasp'd his brother's hand;

Such and so pale his face as when,
  With faint and faultering tongue,
To William's care, a dying charge,
  He left his orphan son.

« I bade thee with a father's love
  My orphan Edmund guard—
Well, William, hast thou kept thy charge!
  Now take thy due reward.»

He started up, each limb convulsed
  With agonizing fear:
He only heard the storm of night,—
  T was music to his ear.

When lo! the voice of loud alarm
  His inmost soul appals;
« What ho! Lord William, rise in haste!
  The water saps thy walls !»

He rose in haste, beneath the walls
  He saw the flood appear;
It hemm'd him round, 't was midnight now,
  No human aid was near.

He heard the shout of joy, for now
  A boat approach'd the wall,
And eager to the welcome aid
  They crowd for safety all.

« My boat is small,» the boatman cried,
  « 'T will bear but one away;
Come in, Lord William, and do ye
  In God's protection stay.»

Strange feeling fill'd them at his voice,
  Even in that hour of woe,
That, save their Lord, there was not one
  Who wish'd with him to go.

But William leapt into the boat,
  His terror was so sore:
« Thou shalt have half my gold,» he cried,
  « Haste—haste to yonder shore.»

The boatman plied the oar, the boat
  Went light along the stream;
Sudden Lord William heard a cry
  Like Edmund's drowning scream.

The boatman paused, « Methought I heard
  A child's distressful cry!»
« 'T was but the howling wind of night,»
  Lord William made reply.

« Haste—haste—ply swift and strong the oar!
  Haste—haste across the stream!»
Again Lord William heard a cry
  Like Edmund's drowning scream.

81

« I heard a child's distressful voice,»
  The boatman cried again,
« Nay hasten on—the night is dark—
  And we should search in vain.»

« O God! Lord William, dost thou know
  How dreadful 't is to die?
And canst thou without pitying hear
  A child's expiring cry?

« How horrible it is to sink
  Beneath the closing stream,
To stretch the powerless arms in vain,
  In vain for help to scream!»

The shriek again was heard: It came
  More deep, more piercing loud;
That instant o'er the flood the moon
  Shone through a broken cloud;

And near them they beheld a child,
  Upon a crag he stood,
A little crag, and all around
  Was spread the rising flood.

The boatman plied the oar, the boat
  Approach'd his resting place;
The moon-beam shone upon the child,
  And show'd how pale his face.

« Now reach thine hand!» the boatman cried,
  « Lord William reach and save!»
The child stretch'd forth his little hands
  To grasp the hand he gave.

Then William shriek'd; the hand he touch'd
  Was cold and damp and dead!
He felt young Edmund in his arms
  A heavier weight than lead.

The boat sunk down, the murderer sunk
  Beneath the avenging stream;
He rose, he shriek'd, no human ear
  Heard William's drowning scream.

                              1798.

THE CROSS ROADS.

The circumstance related in the following Ballad happened about
the year 1760, in a village adjacent to Bristol. A person who was
present at the funeral told me the story and the particulars of the
interment, as I have versified them.

There was an old man breaking stones
  To mend the turnpike way;
He sate him down beside a brook,
And out his bread and cheese he took,
  For now it was mid-day.

He leant his back against a post,
  His feet the brook ran by,
And there were water-cresses growing,
And pleasant was the water's flowing,
  For he was hot and dry.

A soldier with his knapsack on
  Came travelling o'er the down;
The sun was strong and he was tired;
And he of the old man inquired
  « How far to Bristol town?»

« Half an hour's walk for a young man,
  By lanes and fields and stiles;
But you the foot-path do not know,
And if along the road you go
  Why then 't is three good miles.»

The soldier took his knapsack off,
  For he was hot and dry;
And out his bread and cheese he took,
And he sat down beside the brook
  To dine in company.

« Old friend! in faith,» the soldier says,
  I envy you almost;
My shoulders have been sorely prest,
And I should like to sit and rest
  My back against that post.

« In such a sweltering day as this
  A knapsack is the devil!
And if on t' other side I sat,
It would not only spoil our chat,
  But make me seem uncivil.»

The old man laugh'd and moved—« I wish
  It were a great-arm'd chair!
But this may help a man at need:—
And yet it was a cursed deed
  That ever brought it there.

« There's a poor girl lies buried here,
  Beneath this very place;
The earth upon her corpse is prest,
The stake is driven into her breast,
  And a stone is on her face.»

The soldier had but just leant back,
  And now he half rose up,
« There's sure no harm in dining here,
My friend? and yet, to be sincere,
  I should not like to sup.»

« God rest her! she is still enough
  Who sleeps beneath my feet!»
The old man cried. « No harm I trow
She ever did herself, though now
  She lies where four roads meet.

« I have past by about that hour
  When men are not most brave;
It did not make my courage fail,
And I have heard the nightingale
  Sing sweetly on her grave.

« I have past by about that hour
  When Ghosts their freedom have;
But there was here no ghastly sight,
And quietly the glow-worm's light
  Was shining on her grave.

« There's one who like a Christian lies
  Beneath the church-tree's shade ;
I'd rather go a long mile round
Than pass at evening through the ground
  Wherein that man is laid.

« There's one who in the church-yard lies
  For whom the bell did toll ;
He lies in consecrated ground,
But for all the wealth in Bristol town
  I would not be with his soul !

« Didst see a house below the hill
  Which the winds and the rains destroy ?
'T was then a farm where he did dwell,
And I remember it full well
  When I was a growing boy.

« And she was a poor parish girl
  Who came up from the west :
From service hard she ran away,
And at that house in evil day
  Was taken in to rest.

« The man he was a wicked man,
  And an evil life he led ;
Rage made his face grow deadly white,
And his grey eyes were large and light,
  And in anger they grew red !

« The man was bad, the mother worse,
  Bad fruit of evil stem ;
'T would make your hair to stand on end
If I should tell to you, my friend,
  The things that were told of them !

« Didst see an out-house standing by ?
  The walls alone remain ;
It was a stable then, but now
Its mossy roof has fallen through
  All rotted by the rain.

« The poor girl she had served with them
  Some half-a-year or more,
When she was found hung up one day,
Stiff as a corpse and cold as clay,
  Behind that stable door !

« It is a wild and lonesome place,
  No hut or house is near ;
Should one meet a murderer there alone
'T were vain to scream, and the dying groan
  Would never reach mortal ear.

« And there were strange reports about ;
  But still the Coroner found
That she by her own hand had died,
And should buried be by the way-side,
  And not in Christian ground.

« This was the very place he chose,
  Just where these four roads met ;
And I was one among the throng
That hither follow'd them along,
  I shall never the sight forget !

« They carried her upon a board
  In the clothes in which she died ;
I saw the cap blow off her head,
Her face was of a dark dark red,
  Her eyes were starting wide :

« I think they could not have been closed,
  So widely did they strain.
I never saw a ghastlier sight,
And it often made me wake at night,
  For I saw it in dreams again.

« They laid her here where four roads meet,
  Beneath this very place.
The earth upon her corpse was prest,
The stake is driven into her breast,
  And a stone is on her face. »

1798.

GOD'S JUDGMENT ON A BISHOP.

Here followeth the History of Hatto, Archbishop of Mentz.

It hapned in the year 914, that there was an exceeding great famine in Germany, at what time Otho surnamed the Great was Emperor, and one Hatto, once Abbot of Fulda, was Archbishop of Mentz, of the Bishops after Crescens and Crescentius the two and thirtieth, of the Archbishops after St Bonifacius the thirteenth.— This Hatto in the time of this great famine afore-mentioned, when he saw the poor people of the country exceedingly oppressed with famine, assembled a great company of them together into a Barne, and, like a most accursed and mercilesse caitiffe, burnt up those poor innocent souls, that were so far from doubting any such matter, that they rather hoped to receive some comfort and relief at his hands. The reason that moved the prelat to commit that execrable impiety was, because he thought the famine would the sooner cease, if those unprofitable beggars that consumed more bread than they were worthy to eat, were dispatched out of the world. For he said that those poor folks were like to Mice, that were good for nothing but to devour corne. But God Almighty, the just avenger of the poor folks quarrel, did not long suffer this hainous tyranny, this most detestable fact, unpunished. For he mustered up an army of Mice against the Archbishop, and sent them to persecute him as his furious Alastors, so that they afflicted him both day and night, and would not suffer him to take his rest in any place. Whereupon the Prelate thinking that he should be secure from the injury of Mice if he were in a certaine tower, that standeth in the Rhine near to the towne, betook himself unto the said tower as to a safe refuge and sanctuary from his enemies, and locked himself in. But the innumerable troupes of Mice chased him continually very eagerly, and swumme unto him upon the top of the water to execute the just judgment of God, and so at last he was most miserably devoured by those sillie creatures ; who pursued him with such bitter hostility, that it is recorded they scraped and knawed out his very name from the walls and tapistry wherein it was written, after they had so cruelly devoured his body. Wherefore the tower wherein he was eaten up by the Mice is shown to this day, for a perpetual monument to all succeeding ages of the barbarous and inhuman tyranny of this impious Prelate, being situate in a little green Island in the midst of the Rhine near to the towne of Bing,[1] and is commonly called in the German Tongue, the Mowse-turn.—Coryat's *Crudities* p. 571, 572.

Other Authors who record this tale say that the Bishop was eaten by Rats.

The summer and autumn had been so wet, [?]
That in winter the corn was growing yet,
'T was a piteous sight to see all around
The grain lie rotting on the ground.

Every day the starving poor
Crowded around Bishop Hatto's door,
For he had a plentiful last-year's store,
And all the neighbourhood could tell
His granaries were furnish'd well.

[1] Hodie Bingen.

At last Bishop Hatto appointed a day
To quiet the poor without delay,
He bade them to his great l'arn repair,
And they should have food for the winter there.

Rejoiced such tidings good to hear,
The poor folk flock'd from far and near ;
The great Barn was full as it could hold
Of women and children, and young and old.

Then when he saw it could hold no more,
Bishop Hatto he made fast the door ;
And while for mercy on Christ they call,
He set fire to the Barn and burnt them all.

« I'faith 't is an excellent bonfire !» quoth he,
« And the country is greatly obliged to me,
For ridding it in these times forlorn
Of Rats that only consume the corn.»

So then to his palace returned he,
And he sat down to supper merrily,
And he slept that night like an innocent man,
But Bishop Hatto never slept again.

In the morning as he enter'd the hall
Where his picture hung against the wall,
A sweat like death all over him came,
For the Rats had eaten it out of the frame.

As he look'd there came a man from his farm,
He had a countenance white with alarm.
« My Lord, I open'd your granaries this morn,
And the Rats had eaten all your corn.»

Another came running presently,
And he was pale as pale could be,
« Fly ! my Lord Bishop, fly,» quoth he,
« Ten thousand Rats are coming this way,—
The Lord forgive you for yesterday !»

« I'll go to my tower on the Rhine,» replied he,
« 'T is the safest place in Germany,
The walls are high and the shores are steep
And the stream is strong and the water deep.»

Bishop Hatto fearfully hasten'd away,
And he crost the Rhine without delay,
And reach'd his tower, and barr'd with care
All the windows, doors, and loop-holes there.

He laid him down and closed his eyes;—
But soon a scream made him arise,
He started and saw two eyes of flame
On his pillow from whence the screaming came.

He listen'd and look'd ;—it was only the Cat;
But the Bishop he grew more fearful for that,
For she sat screaming, mad with fear
At the Army of Rats that were drawing near.

For they have swam over the river so deep,
And they have climb'd the shores so steep,
And now by thousands up they crawl
To the holes and windows in the wall.

Down on his knees the Bishop fell,
And faster and faster his beads did he tell,
As louder and louder drawing near
The saw of their teeth without he could hear.

And in at the windows and in at the door,
And through the walls by thousands they pour,
And down from the ceiling and up through the floor,
From the right and the left, from behind and before.
From within and without, from above and below,
And all at once to the Bishop they go.

They have whetted their teeth against the stones,
And now they pick the Bishop's bones,
They gnaw'd the flesh from every limb,
For they were sent to do judgment on him !

1799.

THE PIOUS PAINTER.

The story of the Pious Painter is related in the Pia Hilaria of Gazæus, but the Catholic Poet has omitted the conclusion. This is to be found in the Fabliaux of Le Grand.

PART I.

THERE once was a painter in Catholic days,
  Like JOB who eschewed all evil ;
Still on his Madonnas the curious may gaze
With applause and with pleasure, but chiefly his praise
  And delight was in painting the Devil.

They were angels, compared to the Devils he drew,
  Who besieged poor St Anthony's cell ;
Such burning hot eyes, such a furnace-like hue !
And round them a sulphurous vapour he threw
  That their breath seem'd of brimstone to smell.

And now had the artist a picture begun,
  'T was over the Virgin's church door ;
She stood on the Dragon embracing her Son,
Many Devils already the artist had done,
  But this must out-do all before.

The Old Dragon's imps as they fled through the air,
  At seeing it paused on the wing ;
For he had the likeness so just to a hair,
That they came as Apollyon himself had been there,
  To pay their respects to their King.

Every child at beholding it shiver'd with dread,
  And scream'd as he turn'd away quick ;
Not an old woman saw it, but, raising her head,
Dropt a bead, made a cross on her wrinkles, and said,
  Lord keep me from ugly Old Nick !

What the Painter so earnestly thought on by day,
  He sometimes would dream of by night ;
But once he was startled as sleeping he lay ;
'T was no fancy, no dream, he could plainly survey
  That the Devil himself was in sight.

« You rascally dauber !» old Beelzebub cries,
  « Take heed how you wrong me again !
Though your caricatures for myself I despise,
Make me handsomer now in the multitude's eyes,
  Or see if I threaten in vain !»

Now the Painter was bold, and religious beside,
    And on faith he had certain reliance,
So carefully he the grim countenance eyed,
And thank'd him for sitting with Catholic pride,
    And sturdily bade him defiance.

Betimes in the morning the Painter arose,
    He is ready as soon as 't is light.
Every look, every line, every feature he knows,
'T is fresh in his eye, to his labour he goes,
    And he has the old Wicked One quite.

Happy man! he is sure the resemblance can't fail;
    The tip of the nose is red-hot,
There 's his grin and his fangs, his skin cover'd with
        scale,
And that the identical curl of his tail,—
    Not a mark, not a claw, is forgot.

He looks and retouches again with delight;
    'T is a portrait complete to his mind!
He touches again, and again gluts his sight;
He looks round for applause, and he sees with affright
    The Original standing behind.

« Fool! Idiot!» old Beelzebub grinn'd as he spoke,
    And stampt on the scaffold in ire;
The Painter grew pale, for he knew it no joke,
'T was a terrible height, and the scaffolding broke,
    The Devil could wish it no higher.

« Help—help me! O Mary!» he cried in alarm,
    As the scaffold sunk under his feet.
From the canvas the Virgin extended her arm,
She caught the good Painter, she saved him from harm,
    There were hundreds who saw in the street.

The Old Dragon fled when the wonder he spied,
    And cursed his own fruitless endeavour;
While the Painter call'd after his rage to deride,
Shook his pallet and brushes in triumph, and cried,
    « I'll paint thee more ugly than ever!»

PART II.

The Painter so pious all praise had acquired
    For defying the malice of Hell;
The monks the unerring resemblance admired;
Not a Lady lived near but her portrait desired
    From one who succeeded so well.

One there was to be painted the number among
    Of features most fair to behold;
The country around of fair Marguerite rung,
Marguerite she was lovely and lively and young,
    Her husband was ugly and old.

O Painter, avoid her! O Painter, take care!
    For Satan is watchful for you!
Take heed lest you fall in the Wicked One's snare,
The net is made ready, O Painter, beware
    Of Satan and Marguerite too.

She seats herself now, now she lifts up her head,
    On the artist she fixes her eyes;
The colours are ready, the canvas is spread,
He lays on the white, and he lays on the red,
    And the features of beauty arise.

He is come to her eyes, eyes so bright and so blue!
    There 's a look which he cannot express;—
His colours are dull to their quick-sparkling hue;
More and more on the lady he fixes his view,
    On the canvas he looks less and less.

In vain he retouches, her eyes sparkle more,
    And that look which fair Marguerite gave!
Many Devils the Artist had painted of yore,
But he never had tried a live Angel before,—
    St Anthony, help him and save!

He yielded, alas! for the truth must be told,
    To the Woman, the Tempter, and Fate.
It was settled the Lady so fair to behold,
Should elope from her husband so ugly and old,
    With the Painter so pious of late!

Now Satan exults in his vengeance complete,
    To the Husband he makes the scheme known;
Night comes and the lovers impatiently meet,
Together they fly, they are seized in the street,
    And in prison the Painter is thrown.

With Repentance, his only companion, he lies,
    And a dismal companion is she!
On a sudden he saw the Old Serpent arise,
« Now, you villanous dauber!» Sir Beelzebub cries,
    « You are paid for your insults to me!

« But my tender heart you may easily move
    If to what I propose you agree;
That picture,—be just! the resemblance improve,
Make a handsomer portrait, your chains I'll remove,
    And you shall this instant be free.»

Overjoy'd, the conditions so easy he hears,
    « I'll make you quite handsome!» he said.
He said, and his chain on the Devil appears;
Released from his prison, released from his fears,
    The Painter is snug in his bed.

At morn he arises, composes his look,
    And proceeds to his work as before;
The people beheld him, the culprit they took;
They thought that the Painter his prison had broke,
    And to prison they led him once more.

They open the dungeon;—behold in his place
    In the corner old Beelzebub lay.
He smirks and he smiles and he leers with a grace,
That the Painter might catch all the charms of his
        face,
    Then vanish'd in lightning away.

Quoth the Painter, «I trust you 'll suspect me no more,
    Since you find my assertions were true;
But I'll alter the picture above the Church-door,
For I never saw Satan so closely before,
    And I must give the Devil his due.»
                                    1798.

ST MICHAEL'S CHAIR.

Merrily, merrily rung the bells,
    The bells of St Michael's tower,
When Richard Penlake and Rebecca his wife
    Arrived at St Michael's door.

Richard Penlake was a cheerful man,
  Cheerful and frank and free,
But he led a sad life with Rebecca his wife,
  For a terrible shrew was she.

Richard Penlake a scolding would take,
  Till patience avail'd no longer,
Then Richard Penlake his crab-stick would take,
  And show her that he was the stronger.

Rebecca his wife had often wish'd
  To sit in St Michael's chair;
For she should be the mistress then
  If she had once sat there.

It chanced that Richard Penlake fell sick,
  They thought he would have died;
Rebecca his wife made a vow for his life
  As she knelt by his bed-side.

« Now hear my prayer, St Michael! and spare
  My husband's life, » quoth she;
« And to thine altar we will go,
  Six marks to give to thee. »

Richard Penlake repeated the vow,
  For woundily sick was he;
« Save me, St Michael, and we will go
  Six marks to give to thee. »

When Richard grew well, Rebecca his wife
  Teazed him by night and by day:
« O mine own dear! for you I fear,
  If we the vow delay. »

Merrily, merrily rung the bells,
  The bells of St Michael's tower,
When Richard Penlake and Rebecca his wife
  Arrived at St Michael's door.

Six marks they on the altar laid,
  And Richard knelt in prayer:
She left him to pray, and stole away
  To sit in St Michael's chair.

Up the tower Rebecca ran,
  Round and round and round;
'T was a giddy sight to stand a-top,
  And look upon the ground.

« A curse on the ringers for rocking
  The tower! » Rebecca cried,
As over the church battlements
  She strode with a long stride.

« A blessing on St Michael's chair! »
  She said as she sat down:
Merrily, merrily rung the bells,
  And out Rebecca was thrown.

Tidings to Richard Penlake were brought
  That his good wife was dead:
« Now shall we toll for her poor soul
  The great church bell? » they said.

« Toll at her burying, » quoth Richard Penlake,
  « Toll at her burying, » quoth he;
« But don't disturb the ringers now
  In compliment to me. »   1798.

KING HENRY V. AND THE HERMIT OF DREUX.

While Henry V lay at the siege of Dreux, an honest Hermit unknown to him, came and told him the great evils he brought on Christendom by his unjust ambition, who usurped the kingdom of France, against all manner of right, and contrary to the will of God; wherefore in his holy name he threatened him with a severe and sudden punishment if he desisted not from his enterprise.—Henry took this exhortation either as an idle whimsey, or a suggestion of the dauphin's, and was but the more confirmed in his design. But the blow soon followed the threatening; for within some few months after he was smitten with a strange and incurable disease.—MEZERAY.

He past unquestion'd through the camp,
  Their heads the soldiers bent
In silent reverence, or begg'd
  A blessing as he went;
And so the Hermit past along
  And reached the royal tent.

King Henry sate in his tent alone,
  The map before him lay,
Fresh conquests he was planning there
  To grace the future day.

King Henry lifted up his eyes
  The intruder to behold;
With reverence he the hermit saw,
  For the holy man was old,
His look was gentle as a Saint's,
  And yet his eye was bold.

« Repent thee, Henry, of the wrongs
  Which thou hast done this land!
O King, repent in time, for know
  The judgment is at hand.

« I have past forty years of peace
  Beside the river Blaise,
But what a weight of woe hast thou
  Laid on my latter days!

« I used to see along the stream
  The white sail sailing down,
That wafted food in better times
  To yonder peaceful town.

« Henry! I never now behold
  The white sail sailing down;
Famine, Disease, and Death, and Thou
  Destroy that wretched town.

« I used to hear the traveller's voice
  As here he past along,
Or maiden as she loiter'd home
  Singing her even song.

« No traveller's voice may now be heard,
  In fear he hastens by,
But I have heard the village maid
  In vain for succour cry.

« I used to see the youths row down
  And watch the dripping oar,
As pleasantly their viol's tones
  Came soften'd to the shore.

« King Henry, many a blacken'd corpse
I now see floating down!
Thou bloody man! repent in time
And leave this leaguer'd town.»

« I shall go on,» King Henry cried,
« And conquer this good land,
Seest thou not, Hermit, that the Lord
Hath given it to my hand ?»

The Hermit heard King Henry speak,
And angrily look'd down;—
His face was gentle, and for that
More solemn was his frown.

« What if no miracle from heaven
The murderer's arm controul,
Think you for that the weight of blood
Lies lighter on his soul?

• Thou conqueror King, repent in time
Or dread the coming woe!
For, Henry, thou hast heard the threat,
And soon shalt feel the blow!»

King Henry forced a careless smile,
As the Hermit went his way;
But Henry soon remember'd him
Upon his dying day.

1798.

A BALLAD,

OF A YOUNG MAN THAT WOULD READ UNLAWFUL BOOKS, AND HOW HE WAS PUNISHED.

VERY PITHY AND PROFITABLE.

CORNELIUS Agrippa went out one day,
His Study he lock'd ere he went away,
And he gave the key of the door to his wife,
And charged her to keep it lock'd on her life.

« And if any one ask my Study to see,
I charge you trust them not with the key;
Whoever may beg, and entreat, and implore,
On your life let nobody enter that door.»

There lived a young man in the house, who in vain
Access to that Study had sought to obtain;
And he begg'd and pray'd the books to see,
Till the foolish woman gave him the key.

On the Study-table a book there lay,
Which Agrippa himself had been reading that day,
The letters were written with blood within,
And the leaves were made of dead men's skin.

And these horrible leaves of magic between
Were the ugliest pictures that ever were seen,
The likeness of things so foul to behold,
That what they were is not fit to be told.

The young man, he began to read
He knew not what, but he would proceed,
When there was heard a sound at the door
Which as he read on grew more and more.

And more and more the knocking grew,
The young man knew not what to do;
But trembling in fear he sat within,
Till the door was broke, and the Devil came in.

Two hideous horns on his head he had got,
Like iron heated nine times red-hot;
The breath of his nostrils was brimstone blue,
And his tail like a fiery serpent grew.

« What wouldst thou with me?» the Wicked One cried,
But not a word the young man replied;
Every hair on his head was standing upright,
And his limbs like a palsy shook with affright.

« What wouldst thou with me?» cried the Author of ill,
But the wretched young man was silent still;
Not a word had his lips the power to say,
And his marrow seem'd to be melting away.

« What wouldst thou with me?» the third time he cries,
And a flash of lightning came from his eyes,
And he lifted his griffin claw in the air,
And the young man had not strength for a prayer.

His eyes red fire and fury dart
As out he tore the young man's heart;
He grinn'd a horrible grin at his prey,
And in a clap of thunder vanish'd away.

THE MORAL.
Henceforth let all young men take heed
How in a Conjuror's books they read.

1798.

KING CHARLEMAIN.

« François Petrarque, fort renommé entre les Poëtes Italiens, discourant en une epistre son voyage de France et d'Allemaigne, nous raconte que passant par la ville d'Aix, il apprit de quelques Prestres une histoire prodigieuse qu'ils tenoient de main en main pour tres veritable. Qui estoit que Charles le Grand, apres avoir conquesté plusieurs pays, s'esperdit de telle façon en l'amour d'une simple femme, que mettant tout honneur et reputation in arriere, il oublia non seulement les affaires de son royaume, mais aussi le soing de sa propre personne, au grand desplaisir de chacun ; estant seulement ententif à courtiser ceste dame: laquelle par bonheur commença à s'aliter d'une grosse maladie, qui lui apport à la mort. Dont les Princes et grands Seigneurs furent fort resjouis, esperans que par ceste mort, Charles reprendroit comme devant et ses esprits et les affaires du royaume en main : toutesfois il se trouva tellement infatué de ceste amour, qu'encores cherissoit-il ce cadaver, l'embrassant, baisant, accolant de la mesme façon que devant, et au lieu de prester l'oreille aux legations qui luy survenoient, il l'entretenoit de mille bayes, comme s'il eust esté plein de vie. Ce corps commençoit dejà non seulement à mal sentir, mais aussi se tournoit en putrefaction, et neantmoins n'y avoit aucun de ses favoris qui luy en osast parler; dont advint que l'Archevesque Turpin mieux advisé que les autres, pourpensa que telle chose ne pouvoit estre advenue sans quelque sorcellerie. Au moyen de quoy espiant un jour l'heure que le Roy s'estoit absenté de la chambre, commença de fouiller le corps de toutes parts, finalement trouva dans sa bouche au dessous de sa langue un anneau qu'il luy osta. De jour mesme Charlemaigne retournant sur ses premieres brisees, se trouva fort estonné de voir une carcaisse ainsi puante. Parquoy, comme s'il se fust resveillé d'un profond sommeil, commanda que l'on l'ensevelist promptement. Ce qui fut fait ; mais en contr' eschange de ceste folie, il tourna tous ses pensemens vers l'Archevesque porteur de cest anneau, ne pouvant estre de la en avant sans luy, et le suivant en tous les endroits. Quoy voyant ce sage Prelat, et craignant que cest anneau ne tombast en mains de quelque autre, le jetta dans un lac prochain de la ville. Depuis lequel temps on dit que ce Roy se trouve si espris de l'amour du lieu, qu'il ne se desempara la ville d'Aix, où il bastit un Palais, et

un Monastere, en l'un desquels il partit le reste de ses jours et en
l'autre voulut estre ensevely, ordonnant par son testament que
tous les Empereurs de Rome eussent à se faire sacrer premierement
en ce lieu.»—*Les Recherches de la France, d'Estienne Pasquier.* Pa-
ris. 1611.

It was strange that he loved her, for youth was gone by,
　　And the bloom of her beauty was fled;
'T was the glance of the harlot that gleam'd in her eye,
And all but the Monarch could plainly descry
　　From whence came her white and her red.

Yet he thought with Agatha none might compare,
　　And he gloried in wearing her chain;
The court was a desert if she were not there,
To him she alone among women seem'd fair,
　　Such dotage possess'd Charlemain.

The soldier, the statesman, the courtier, the maid,
　　Alike the proud leman detest;
And the good old Archbishop, who ceased to upbraid,
Shook his grey head in sorrow, and silently pray'd
　　That he soon might consign her to rest.

A joy ill-dissembled soon gladdens them all,
　　For Agatha sickens and dies.
And now they are ready with bier and with pall,
The tapers gleam gloomy amid the high hall,
　　And the strains of the requiem arise.

But Charlemain he sent them in anger away,
　　For she should not be buried, he said;
And despite of all counsel, for many a day,
Where array'd in her costly apparel she lay,
　　The Monarch would sit by the dead.

The cares of the Kingdom demand him in vain,
　　And the army cry out for their Lord;
The Lombards, the fierce misbelievers of Spain,
Now ravage the realms of the proud Charlemain,
　　And still he unsheathes not the sword.

The Soldiers they clamour, the Monks bend in prayer
　　In the quiet retreats of the cell;
The Physicians to counsel together repair,
They pause and they ponder, at last they declare
　　That his senses are bound by a spell.

With relics protected, and confident grown,
　　And telling devoutly his beads,
The Archbishop prepares him, and when it was known,
That the King for awhile left the body alone,
　　To look for the spell he proceeds.

Now careful he searches with tremulous haste
　　For the spell that bewitches the King;
And under the tongue for security placed,
Its margin with mystical characters traced,
　　At length he discovers a ring.

Rejoicing he seized it and hastened away,
　　The Monarch re-entered the room,
The enchantment was ended, and suddenly gay
He bade the attendants no longer delay,
　　But bear her with speed to the tomb.

Now merriment, joyaunce, and feasting again
　　Enlivened the palace of Aix;
And now by his heralds did King Charlemain
Invite to his palace the courtier train
　　To hold a high festival day.

And anxiously now for the festival day
　　The highly-born Maidens prepare;
And now, all apparell'd in costly array,
Exulting they come to the palace of Aix,
　　Young and aged, the brave and the fair.

Oh! happy the Damsel who 'mid her compeers
　　For a moment engaged the King's eye!
Now glowing with hopes and now fever'd with fears,
Each maid or triumphant, or jealous, appears,
　　As noticed by him, or past by.

And now as the evening approach'd, to the ball
　　In anxious suspense they advance,
Each hoped the King's choice on her beauties might fall,
When lo! to the utter confusion of all,
　　He ask'd the Archbishop to dance.

The damsels they laugh and the barons they stare,
　　'T was mirth and astonishment all;
And the Archbishop started and mutter'd a prayer,
And, wroth at receiving such mockery there,
　　Withdrew him in haste from the hall.

The moon dimpled over the water with light
　　As he wander'd along the lake side;
When lo! where beside him the King met his sight;
« Oh turn thee, Archbishop, my joy and delight,
　　Oh turn thee, my charmer,» he cried;

« Oh come where the feast and the dance and the song
　　Invite thee to mirth and to love;
Or at this happy moment away from the throng
To the shade of yon wood let us hasten along,—
　　The moon never pierces that grove.»

Amazement and anger the Prelate possest,
　　With terror his accents he heard,
Then Charlemain warmly and eagerly prest
The Archbishop's old wither'd hand to his breast,
　　And kiss'd his old grey grizzle beard.

« Let us well then these fortunate moments employ!»
　　Cried the Monarch with passionate tone :
« Come away then, dear charmer,—my angel,—my joy,
Nay struggle not now,—'t is in vain to be coy,—
　　And remember that we are alone.»

« Blessed Mary, protect me!» the Archbishop cried;
　　« What madness is come to the King!»
In vain to escape from the Monarch he tried,
When luckily he on his finger espied
　　The glitter of Agatha's ring.

Overjoy'd, the old Prelate remember'd the spell,
　　And far in the lake flung the ring;
The waters closed round it, and, wondrous to tell,
Released from the cursed enchantment of hell,
　　His reason return'd to the King.

But he built him a palace there close by the bay,
  And there did he 'stablish his reign;
And the traveller who will, may behold at this day
A monument still in the ruins of Aix
  Of the spell that possess'd Charlemain.

1797.

ST ROMUALD.

« Les Catalans ayant appris que S. Romuald vouloit quitter leurs pays, en furent très-affligés; ils délibérèrent sur les moyens de l'en empêcher, et le seul qu'ils imaginèrent comme le plus sûr, fut de le tuer, afin de profiter du moins de ses reliques et des guerisons et autres miracles qu'elles opéreroient après sa mort. La dévotion que les Catalans avoient pour lui, ne plut point du tout à S. Romuald; il usa de stratagème et leur échappa.»—St Foix, *Essais Historiques sur Paris*, t. v. p. 163.

St Foix, who is often more amusing than trustworthy, has fathered this story upon the Spaniards, though it belongs to his own countrymen, the circumstance having happened when Romuald was a monk of the Convent of St Michael's, in Aquitaine. It is thus related by Yepes. « En esta ocasion sucedió una cosa bien extraordinaria, porque los naturales de la tierra donde estava el monasterio de San Miguel, estimavan en tanto a San Romoaldo, que faltandoles la paciencia de que se quisiesse yr, dieron en un terrible disparate, a quien llama muy bien San Pedro Damiano *Impia Pietas*, piedad cruel: porque queriendose yr San Romoaldo, determinaron de matarle, para que ya que no le podian tener en su tierra vivo, alomenos gozassen de sus reliquias y cuerpo santo. Supo San Romoaldo la determinacion bestial y indiscreta de aquella gente: y tomó una prudente resolucion, porque imitando a David, que fingió que estava loco, por no caer en manos de sus enemigos, assi San Romoaldo se hizo raer la cabeça, y con algunos ademanes, y palabras mal concertadas que dezia, le tuvieron por hombre que le avia faltado el juyzio, con que se asseguraron los naturales de la tierra que ya perpetuamente le tendrian en ella: y con semejante estratagema y traça tuvo lugar San Romoaldo de hurtarse, y a cencerros tapados (como dizen) huyr de aquella tierra, y llegar a Italia a la ciudad de Ravena.»—*Coronica General de la Orden de San Benito*, t. v, ff. 274.

Villegas in his *Flos Sanctorum* (February 7th), records some of St Romuald's achievements against the Devil and his imps. He records also the other virtues of the Saint, as specified in the poem. They are more fully stated by Yepes. « Tenia tres cilicios, los quales mudava de treynta en treynta dias: no los lavava, sino ponialos al ayre, y à la agua que llovia, con que se matavan algunas inmundicias, que se criavan en ellos.»—ff. 298. « Quando alguna vez era tentado de la gula, y desseava comer de algun manjar, tomavale en las manos, miravale, oliale, y despues que estava despierto el apetito, dezia, O gula, gula, quan dulce y suave te parece este manjar! pero no te has de entrar en provecho! y entonces se mortificava, y le dexava, y le embiava entero, o al sillericico, o a los pobres.» —*Ibid*. More concerning St Romuald may be seen in the *Omniana*, vol. i.

One day, it matters not to know
  How many hundred years ago,
A Frenchman stopt at an inn door:
The Landlord came to welcome him, and chat
  Of this and that,
For he had seen the Traveller there before.

  « Doth holy Romuald dwell
    Still in his cell? »
The Traveller ask'd, «or is the old man dead? »
  « No; he has left his loving flock, and we
So good a Christian never more shall see,»
The Landlord answer'd, and he shook his head.

  « Ah, Sir! we knew his worth!
If ever there did live a Saint on earth!—
Why, Sir, he always used to wear a shirt
For thirty days, all seasons, day and night:
  Good man, he knew it was not right

For dust and ashes to fall out with dirt;
  And then he only hung it out in the rain,
    And put it on again.
  There has been perilous work
With him and the Devil there in yonder cell;
For Satan used to maul him like a Turk.
  There they would sometimes fight
  All through a winter's night,
    From sun-set until morn,
He with a cross, the Devil with his horn;
The Devil spitting fire with might and main
Enough to make St Michael half afraid;
  He splashing holy water till he made
    His red hide hiss again,
And the hot vapour fill'd the smoking cell.
This was so common that his face became
All black and yellow with the brimstone flame,
And then he smelt,—Oh Lord! how he did smell!

  « Then, Sir! to see how he would mortify
The flesh! If any one had dainty fare,
  Good man, he would come there,
And look at all the delicate things, and cry,
    ' O Belly, Belly!
You would be gormandizing now I know;
  But it shall not be so!—
Home to your bread and water—home, I tell ye!'»

  «But,» quoth the Traveller, «wherefore did he leave
A flock that knew his saintly worth so well?»
  «Why,» said the Landlord, «Sir, it so befell
He heard unluckily of our intent
  To do him a great honour: and, you know,
  He was not covetous of fame below,
And so by stealth one night away he went.»

  «What might this honour be?» the Traveller cried;
    «Why, Sir,» the Host replied,
«We thought perhaps that he might one day leave us;
  And then should strangers have
    The good man's grave;
A loss like that would naturally grieve us,
For he 'll be made a Saint of to be sure.
Therefore we thought it prudent to secure
  His relics while we might;
And so we meant to strangle him one night.»

THE KING OF THE CROCODILES.

The people at Isna, in Upper Egypt, have a superstition concerning Crocodiles similar to that entertained in the West Indies; they say there is a King of them who resides near Isna, and who has ears, but no tail; and he possesses an uncommon regal quality, that of doing no harm. Some are bold enough to assert that they have seen him.—Browne's *Travels*.[1]

  « Now, Woman, why without your veil?
And wherefore do you look so pale?
And, Woman, why do you groan so sadly,
And wherefore beat your bosom madly?»

[1] Mr Browne had probably forgotten one of our legal axioms, or he would not have conceived that the privilege of doing no wrong was peculiar to this long-ear'd Sovereign.

« Oh! I have lost my darling boy,
In whom my soul had all its joy;
And I for sorrow have torn my veil,
And sorrow hath made my very heart pale.

« Oh, I have lost my darling child,
And that's the loss that makes me wild;
He stoop'd to the river down to drink,
And there was a Crocodile by the brink.

«He did not venture in to swim,
He only stoop'd to drink at the brim;
But under the reeds the Crocodile lay,
And struck with his tail and swept him away.

«Now take me in your boat, I pray,
For down the river lies my way,
And me to the Reed-Island bring,
For I will go to the Crocodile King.

«The King of the crocodiles never does wrong,
He has no tail so stiff and strong,
He has no tail to strike and slay,
But he has ears to hear what I say.

«And to the King I will complain,
How my poor child was wickedly slain;
The King of the Crocodiles he is good,
And I shall have the murderer's blood.»

The man replied, «No, Woman, no,
To the Island of Reeds I will not go;
I would not for any worldly thing
See the face of the Crocodile King.»

«Then lend me now your little boat,
And I will down the river float.
I tell thee that no worldly thing
Shall keep me from the Crocodile King.»

The Woman she leapt into the boat,
And down the river alone did she float,
And fast with the stream the boat proceeds,
And now she is come to the Island of Reeds.

The King of the Crocodiles there was seen,
He sat upon the eggs of the Queen,
And all around a numerous rout
The young Prince Crocodiles crawl'd about.

The Woman shook every limb with fear,
As she to the Crocodile King came near,
For never man without fear and awe
The face of his Crocodile Majesty saw.

She fell upon her bended knee,
And said, «O King, have pity on me,
For I have lost my darling child,
And that's the loss that makes me wild.

«A Crocodile ate him for his food;
Now let me have the murderer's blood,
Let me have vengeance for my boy,
The only thing that can give me joy.

«I know that you, Sire! never do wrong,
You have no tail so stiff and strong,
You have no tail to strike and slay,
But you have ears to hear what I say.»

«You have done well,» the King replies,
And fix'd on her his little eyes;
«Good Woman, yes, you have done right,
But you have not described me quite.

«I have no tail to strike and slay,
And I have ears to hear what you say:
I have teeth moreover, as you may see,
And I will make a meal of thee.»

1798.

THE ROSE.

Betweene the Cytee and the Chirche of Bethlehem, is the felde Floridus, that is to seyne, the felde floriched. For als moche as a fayre Mayden was blamed with wrong and sclaundred, that sche hadd don fornicacioun, for whiche cause sche was demed to the dethe, and to be brent in that place, to the whiche sche was ladd. And as the fyre began to brenne about hire, she made her preyeres to oure Lord, that als wissely as sche was not gylty of that synne, that he wold help hire, and make it to be knowen to alle men of his mercyfulle grace; and whanne sche had thus seyd, sche entered into the fuyer, and anon was the fuyer quenched and oute, and the brondes that weren brennynge, becomen white Roseres, fulle of roses, and theise werein the first Roseres and roses, both white and rede, that every ony man saughe. And thus was this Maiden saved be the grace of God.—*The Voiage and Traivaile of Sir John Maundeville.*

NAY, EDITH! spare the Rose;—perhaps it lives,
And feels the noon-tide sun, and drinks refresh'd
The dews of night; let not thy gentle hand
Tear its life-strings asunder, and destroy
The sense of being!—Why that infidel smile?
Come, I will bribe thee to be merciful;
And thou shalt have a tale of other days,
For I am skill'd in legendary lore,
So thou wilt let it live.   There was a time
Ere this, the freshest, sweetest flower that blooms,
Bedeck'd the bowers of earth.   Thou hast not heard
How first by miracle its fragrant leaves
Spread to the sun their blushing loveliness.

There dwelt at Bethlehem a Jewish maid,
And Zillah was her name, so passing fair
That all Judea spake the virgin's praise.
He who had seen her eyes' dark radiance
How it reveal'd her soul, and what a soul
Beam'd in the mild effulgence, woe was he!
For not in solitude, for not in crowds,
Might he escape remembrance, nor avoid
Her imaged form which followed every where,
And fill'd the heart, and fix'd the absent eye.
Woe was he, for her bosom own'd no love
Save the strong ardours of religious zeal,
For Zillah on her God had center'd all
Her spirit's deep affections.   So for her
Her tribes-men sigh'd in vain, yet reverenced
The obdurate virtue that destroy'd their hopes.

One man there was, a vain and wretched man,
Who saw, desired, despair'd, and hated her.
His sensual eye had gloated on her cheek
Even till the flush of angry modesty
Gave it new charms, and made him gloat the more.
She loath'd the man, for Hamuel's eye was bold,
And the strong workings of brute selfishness
Had moulded his broad features; and she fear'd

The bitterness of wounded vanity
That with a fiendish hue would overcast
His faint and lying smile.   Nor vain her fear,
For Hamuel vow'd revenge, and laid a plot
Against her virgin fame.   He spread abroad
Whispers that travel fast, and ill reports,
Which soon obtain belief; how Zillah's eye,
When in the temple heaven-ward it was raised,
Did swim with rapturous zeal, but there were those
Who had beheld the enthusiast's melting glance
With other feelings fill'd;—that 't was a task
Of easy sort to play the saint by day
Before the public eye, but that all eyes
Were closed at night;—that Zillah's life was foul,
Yea forfeit to the law.

          Shame—shame to man,
That he should trust so easily the tongue
Which stabs another's fame!   The ill report
Was heard, repeated, and believed,—and soon,
For Hamuel by his damned artifice
Produced such semblances of guilt, the Maid
Was judged to shameful death.

          Without the walls,
There was a barren field; a place abhorr'd,
For it was there where wretched criminals
Received their death; and there they built the stake,
And piled the fuel round, which should consume
The injured Maid, abandon'd, as it seem'd,
By God and Man.   The assembled Bethlemites
Beheld the scene, and when they saw the Maid
Bound to the stake, with what calm holiness
She lifted up her patient looks to Heaven,
They doubted of her guilt.   With other thoughts
Stood Hamuel near the pile; him savage joy
Led thitherward, but now within his heart
Unwonted feelings stirr'd, and the first pangs
Of wakening guilt, anticipating Hell.
The eye of Zillah as it glanced around
Fell on the murderer once, and rested there
A moment; like a dagger did it pierce,
And struck into his soul a cureless wound.
Conscience! thou God within us! not in the hour
Of triumph dost thou spare the guilty wretch,
Not in the hour of infamy and death
Forsake the virtuous! They draw near the stake,—
And lo! the torch!—hold, hold your erring hands!
Yet quench the rising flames!—they rise! they spread!
They reach the suffering Maid! oh God protect
The innocent one!

          They rose, they spread, they raged;
The breath of God went forth; the ascending fire
Beneath its influence bent, and all its flames
In one long lightning-flash concentrating,
Darted and blasted Hamuel,—him alone.
Hark!—what a fearful scream the multitude
Pour forth!—and yet more miracles! the stake
Buds out, and spreads its light green leaves, and bowers
The innocent Maid, and Roses bloom around,
Now first beheld since Paradise was lost,
And fill with Eden odours all the air.
                    1798.

THE LOVER'S ROCK.

De la Pena de los Enamorados.

Un moço Christiano estava cautivo en Granada, sus partes y diligencia eran tales, su buen término y cortesía, que su amo hazia mucha confiança dél dentro y fuera de su casa. Una hija suya al tanto se le aficiona, y puso en él los ojos. Pero como quier que ella fuesse casadera, y el moço esclavo, no podían passar adelante como deseavan ; ca el amor mal sa puede encubrir, y temían si el padre della, y amo dél, lo sabia, pagarían con las cabeças. Acordaron de huir á tierra de Christianos, resolucion que al moço venia mejor, por bolver á los suyos, que á ella por desterrarse de su patria : si ya no la movia el deseo de hazerse Christiana, lo que yo no creo. Tomaron su camino con todo secreto, hasta llegar al peñasco ya dicho, en que la moça cansada se puso á reposar. En esto vieron assomar á su padre con gente de acavallo, que venia en su seguimiento. Que podían hazer, ó á que parte bolverse ? que consejo tomar ? mentirosas las esperanças de los hombres y miserables sus intentos. Acudieron á lo que solo les quedava de encumbrar aquel peñol, trepando por aquellos riscos, que era reparo assaz flaco. El padre con un semblante sañudo los mandó abaxar : amenaçavales sino obedecian de executar en ellos una muerte muy cruel. Los que acompanavan al padre los amonestaven lo mismo, pues solo les restava aquella esperança de alançar perdon de la misericordia de su padre, con hazer lo que les mandava, y echarseles á los pies. No quisieron venir en esto. Los Moros puestos á pie acometieron á subir el peñasco : pero el moço les defendió la subida con galgas, piedras y palos, y todo lo demas que le venia á la mano, y le servia de armas en aquella desesperacion. El padre visto esto, hizo venir de un pueblo alli cerca vallesteros para que de lexos los flechassen. Ellos vista su perdicion, acordaron con su muerte librarse de los denuestos y tormentos mayores que temian. Las palabras que en este trance se dixeron, no ay para que relatarlas. Finalmente abraçados entre si fuertemente, se echaron del peñol abaxo, por aquella parte en que los mirava su cruel y sañudo padre. Deste manera espiraron antes de llegar á lo baxo, con lastima de los presentes, y aun con lagrimas de algunos que se movian con aquel triste espectaculo de aquellos moços desgraciados, y á pesar del padre, como estavan, los enterraron en aquel mismo lugar. Constancia que se empleara mejor en otra hazana, y les fuera bien contada la muerte, si la padecieron por la virtud y en defensa de la verdadera religion, y no por satisfacer á sus apetitos desenfrenados.—MARIANA.

The Maiden through the favouring night
From Granada took her flight,
She bade her father's house farewell,
And fled away with Manuel.

No Moorish maid might hope to vie
With Laila's cheek or Laila's eye,
No maiden love with purer truth,
Or ever loved a lovelier youth.

In fear they fled across the plain,
The father's wrath, the captive's chain,
In hope to Murcia on they flee,
To Peace, and Love, and Liberty.

And now they reach the mountain's height,
And she was weary with her flight,
She laid her head on Manuel's breast,
And pleasant was the maiden's rest.

But while she slept, the passing gale
Waved the maiden's flowing veil,
Her father, as he crost the height,
Saw the veil so long and white.

Young Manuel started from his sleep,
He saw them hastening up the steep,
And Laila shriek'd, and desperate now
They climb'd the precipice's brow.

They saw him raise his angry hand,
And follow with his armed band,
They saw them climbing up the steep,
And heard his curses loud and deep.

Then Manuel's heart grew wild with woe,
He loosen'd stones and roll'd below,
He loosen'd crags, for Manuel strove
For Life, and Liberty, and Love.

The ascent was steep, the rock was high,
The Moors they durst not venture nigh;
The fugitives stood safely there,
They stood in safety and despair.

The Moorish chief unmoved could see
His daughter bend the suppliant knee;
He heard his child for pardon plead,
And swore the offenders both should bleed.

He bade the archers bend the bow,
And make the Christian fall below;
He bade the archers aim the dart,
And pierce the Maid's apostate heart.

The archers aim'd their arrows there,
She clasp'd young Manuel in despair,
« Death, Manuel, shall set us free!
Then leap below and die with me.»

He clasp'd her close and cried farewell,
In one another's arms they fell;
They leapt adown the craggy side,
In one another's arms they died.

And side by side they there are laid,
The Christian youth and Moorish maid,
But never Cross was planted there,
Because they perish'd for despair.

Yet every Murcian maid can tell
Where Laila lies who loved so well,
And every youth who passes there
Says for Manuel's soul a prayer.

1798.

GARCI FERRANDEZ.

This story, which later historians have taken some pains to disprove, may be found in the Coronica General de Espana.

I.

In an evil day and an hour of woe
Did Garci Ferrandez wed!
He wedded the Lady Argentine,
He loved the Lady Argentine,
The Lady Argentine hath fled;
In an evil day and an hour of woe
She hath left the husband who loved her so,
To go to Count Aymerique's bed.

Garci Ferrandez was brave and young,
The comeliest of the land;
There was never a knight of Leon in fight
Who could meet the force of his matchless might,

There was never a foe in the infidel band
Who against his dreadful sword could stand;
And yet Count Garci's strong right hand
Was shapely, and soft, and white;
As white and as soft as a lady's hand
Was the hand of the beautiful knight.

In an evil day and an hour of woe
To Garci's Hall did Count Aymerique go;
In an evil day and a luckless night
From Garci's Hall did he take his flight,
And bear with him that lady bright,
That lady false, his bale and bane.
There was feasting and joy in Count Aymerique's bower,
When he with triumph, and pomp, and pride,
Brought home the adult'ress like a bride:
His daughter only sate in her tower,
She sate her in lonely tower alone,
And for her dead mother she made her moan.
« Methinks,» said she, « my father for me
Might have brought a bridegroom home.
A stepmother he brings hither instead,
Count Aymerique will not his daughter should wed,
But he brings home a leman for his own bed.»
So thoughts of good and thoughts of ill
Were working thus in Abba's will;
And Argentine with evil intent
Ever to work her woe was bent;
That still she sate in her tower alone,
And in that melancholy gloom,
When for her mother she made her moan,
She wish'd her father too in the tomb.

She watches the pilgrims and poor who wait
For daily food at her father's gate.
« I would some knight were there,» thought she,
« Disguised in pilgrim-weeds for me!
For Aymerique's blessing I would not stay,
Nor he nor his leman should say me nay,
But I with him would wend away.»
She watches her handmaid the pittance deal,
They took their dole and went away;
But yonder is one who lingers still
As though he had something in his will,
Some secret which he fain would say;
And close to the portal she sees him go,
He talks with her handmaid in accents low;
Oh then she thought that time went slow,
And long were the minutes that she must wait
Till her handmaid came from the castle-gate.

From the castle-gate her handmaid came,
And told her that a Knight was there,
Who sought to speak with Abba the fair,
Count Aymerique's beautiful daughter and heir.
She bade the stranger to her bower;
His stature was tall, his features bold;
A goodlier form might never maid
At tilt or tourney hope to see;
And though in pilgrim-weeds arrayed,
Yet noble in his weeds was he,
And his arms in them enfold
As they were robes of royalty.

He told his name to the damsel fair,
He said that vengeance led him there;

« Now aid me, lady dear,» quoth he,
« To smite the adult'ress in her pride ;
Your wrongs and mine avenged shall be,
And I will take you for my pride.»
He pledged the word of a true knight,
From out the weeds his hand he drew ;
She took the hand that Garci gave,
And then she knew the tale was true,
For she saw the warrior's hand so white,
And she knew the fame of the beautiful Knight.

II.
'T is the hour of noon,
The bell of the convent hath done,
And the Sexts are begun ;
The Count and his leman are gone to their meat.
They look to their pages, and lo they see
Where Abba, a stranger so long before,
The ewer, and bason, and napkin bore ;
She came and knelt on her bended knee,
And first to her father minister'd she ;
Count Aymerique look'd on his daughter down,
He look'd on her then without a frown.

And next to the Lady Argentine
Humbly she went and knelt ;
The Lady Argentine the while
A haughty wonder felt ;
Her face put on an evil smile ;
« I little thought that I should see
The Lady Abba kneel to me
In service of love and courtesy !
Count Aymerique,» the leman cried,
« Is she weary of her solitude,
Or hath she quell'd her pride ?»
Abba no angry word replied,
She only raised her eyes and cried,
« Let not the Lady Argentine
Be wroth at ministry of mine !»
She look'd at Aymerique and sigh'd
« My father will not frown, I ween,
That Abba again at his board should be seen !»
Then Aymerique raised her from her knee,
And kiss'd her eyes, and bade her be
The daughter she was wont to be.

The wine hath warm'd Count Aymerique,
That mood his crafty daughter knew ;
She came and kiss'd her father's cheek,
And stroked his beard with gentle hand,
And winning eye and action bland,
As she in childhood used to do.
« A boon ! Count Aymerique,» quoth she ;
« If I have found favour in thy sight,
Let me sleep at my father's feet to-night.
Grant this,» quoth she, « so I shall see
That you will let your Abba be
The daughter she was wont to be.»
With asking eye did Abba speak,
Her voice was soft and sweet ;
The wine had warm'd Count Aymerique,
And when the hour of rest was come,
She lay at her father's feet.

In Aymerique's arms the leman lay,
Their talk was of the distant day,

How they from Garci fled away
In the silent hour of night ;
And then amid their wanton play
They mock'd the beautiful Knight.
Far, far away his castle lay,
The weary road of many a day ;
« And travel long,» they said, « to him,
It seem'd, was small delight,
And he belike was loth with blood
To stain his hands so white.»
They little thought that Garci then
Heard every scornful word !
They little thought the avenging hand
Was on the avenging sword !
Fearless, unpenitent, unblest,
Without a prayer they sunk to rest,
The adulterer on the leman's breast.

Then Abba, listening still in fear,
To hear the breathing long and slow,
At length the appointed signal gave
And Garci rose and struck the blow.
One blow sufficed for Aymerique,—
He made no moan, he utter'd no groan ;
But his death-start waken'd Argentine,
And by the chamber-lamp she saw
The bloody falchion shine !
She raised for help her in-drawn breath,
But her shriek of fear was her shriek of death.
In an evil day and an hour of woe
Did Garci Ferrandez wed !
One wicked wife has he sent to her grave,
He hath taken a worse to his bed.
                                        1801.

KING RAMIRO.

The story of the following Ballad is found in the Nobiliario of the Conde D. Pedro ; and also in the Livro Velho das Linhagens, a work of the 13th century.

GREEN grew the alder-trees, and close
To the water-side by St Joam da Foz.
From the castle of Gaya the warden sees
The water and the alder-trees ;
And only these the warden sees,
No danger near doth Gaya fear,
No danger nigh doth the warden spy ;
He sees not where the galleys lie
Under the alders silently.
For the galleys with green are cover'd o'er,
They have crept by night along the shore,
And they lie at anchor, now it is morn,
Awaiting the sound of Ramiro's horn.

In traveller's weeds Ramiro sate
By the fountain at the castle-gate ;
But under the weeds was his breast-plate,
And the sword he had tried in so many fights,
And the horn whose sound would ring around,
And be known so well by his knights.
From the gate Aldonza's damsel came
To fill her pitcher at the spring,
And she saw, but she knew not, her master the king.
In the Moorish tongue Ramiro spake,

And begg'd a draught for mercy's sake,
That he his burning thirst might slake;
For worn by a long malady,
Not strength enow, he said, had he
To lift it from the spring.
She gave her pitcher to the king,
And from his mouth he dropt a ring
Which he had with Aldonza broken;
So in the water from the spring
Queen Aldonza found the token.
With that she bade her damsel bring
Secretly the stranger in.
« What brings thee hither, Ramiro?» she cried :
« The love of you,» the king replied.
« Nay! nay! it is not so!» quoth she,
« Ramiro, say not this to me!
I know your Moorish concubine
Hath now the love which once was mine.
If you had loved me as you say,
You would never have stolen Ortiga away;
If you had never loved another,
I had not been here in Gaya to-day
The wife of Ortiga's brother!
But hide thee here,—a step I hear,—
King Alboazar draweth near.»

In her alcove she bade him hide :
« King Alboazar, my lord,» she cried,
« What wouldst thou do, if at this hour
King Ramiro were in thy power?»
« This I would do,» the Moor replied,
« I would hew him limb from limb,
As he, I know, would deal by me,
So I would deal by him.»
« Alboazar!» Queen Aldonza said,
« Lo! here I give him to thy will;
In yon alcove thou hast thy foe,
Now thy vengeance then fulfil!»

With that upspake the Christian king :
« O! Alboazar deal by me
As I would surely deal with thee,
If I were you, and you were me!
Like a friend you guested me many a day,
Like a foe I stole your sister away;
The sin was great, and I felt its weight,
All joy by day the thought opprest,
And all night long it troubled my rest;
Till I could not bear the burthen of care,
But told my confessor in despair.
And he, my sinful soul to save,
This penance for atonement gave;
That I before you should appear
And yield myself your prisoner here,
If my repentance was sincere,
That I might by a public death
Breathe shamefully out my latest breath.

« King Alboazar, this I would do,
If you were I, and I were you;
I would give you a roasted capon first,
And a skinful of wine to quench your thirst,
And after that I would grant you the thing
Which you came to me petitioning.
Now this, O King, is what I crave,
That I my sinful soul may save :

Let me be led to your bull-ring,
And call your sons and daughters all,
And assemble the people both great and small,
And let me be set upon a stone,
That by all the multitude I may be known,
And bid me then this horn to blow,
And I will blow a blast so strong,
And wind the horn so loud and long
That the breath in my body at last shall be gone,
And I shall drop dead in sight of the throng.
Thus your revenge, O King, will be brave,
Granting the boon which I come to crave,
And the people a holiday sport will have,
And I my precious soul shall save;
For this is the penance my confessor gave.
King Alboazar, this I would do,
If you were I, and I were you.»

« This man repents his sin, be sure !»
To Queen Aldonza said the Moor,
« He hath stolen my sister away from me,
I have taken from him his wife;
Shame then would it be when he comes to me,
And I his true repentance see,
If I for vengeance should take his life.»

« O Alboazar!» then quoth she,
« Weak of heart as weak can be!
Full of revenge and wiles is he;
Look at those eyes beneath that brow,
I know Ramiro better than thou!
Kill him, for thou hast him now,
He must die, be sure, or thou.
Hast thou not heard the history
How, to the throne that he might rise,
He pluck'd out his brother Ordono's eyes?
And dost not remember his prowess in fight,
How often he met thee and put thee to flight,
And plunder'd thy country for many a day;
And how many Moors he has slain in the strife,
And how many more he has carried away?
How he came to show friendship—and thou didst believe
        him?
How he ravish'd thy sister, and wouldst thou forgive
        him?
And hast thou forgotten that I am his wife,
And that now by thy side I lie like a bride,
The worst shame that can ever a Christian betide?
And cruel it were when you see his despair,
If vainly you thought in compassion to spare,
And refused him the boon he comes hither to crave;
For no other way his poor soul can he save,
Than by doing the Penance his confessor gave.»

As Queen Aldonza thus replies,
The Moor upon her fixed his eyes,
And he said in his heart, unhappy is he
Who putteth his trust in a woman!
Thou art King Ramiro's wedded wife,
And thus wouldst thou take away his life!
What cause have I to confide in thee?
I will put this woman away from me.
These were the thoughts that past in his breast,
But he call'd to mind Ramiro's might :
And he fear'd to meet him hereafter in fight,
And he granted the king's request.

So he gave him a roasted capon first,
And a skinful of wine to quench his thirst;
And he call'd for his sons and daughters all,
And assembled the people both great and small;
And to the bull-ring he led the king;
And he set him there upon a stone,
That by all the multitude he might be known,
And he bade him blow through his horn a blast,
As long as his breath and his life should last.

Oh then his horn Ramiro wound:
The walls rebound the pealing sound,
That far and wide rings echoing round;
Louder and louder Ramiro blows,
And farther the blast and farther goes;
Till it reaches the galleys where they lie close
Under the alders, by St Joam da Foz.
It roused his knights from their repose,
And they and their merry men arose.
Away to Gaya they speed them straight;
Like a torrent they burst through the city gate;
And they rush among the Moorish throng,
And slaughter their infidel foes.

Then his good sword Ramiro drew,
Upon the Moorish king he flew,
And he gave him one blow which cleft him through.
They killed his sons and his daughters too;
Every Moorish soul they slew;
Not one escaped of the infidel crew;
Neither old nor young, nor babe nor mother;
And they left not one stone upon another.

They carried the wicked Queen aboard,
And they took counsel what to do to her;
They tied a mill-stone round her neck,
And overboard in the sea they threw her.
She had water enow in the sea I trow!
But glad would Queen Aldonza be,
Of one drop of water from that salt sea,
To cool her where she is now.

1802.

THE INCHCAPE ROCK.

An old writer [1] mentions a curious tradition which may be worth
quoting. « By east the Isle of May, » says he, « twelve miles from
all land in the German seas, lyes a great hidden rock, called Inch-
cape, very dangerous for navigators, because it is overflowed everie
tide. It is reported in old times, upon the spide rocke there was a
bell, fixed upon a tree or timber, which rang continually, being
moved by the sea, giving notice to the saylers of the danger. This
bell or clocke was put there and maintained by the Abbot of Aber-
brothok, and being taken down by a sea pirate, a yeare thereafter
he perished upon the same rocke, with ship and goodes. In the righ-
teous judgement of God. »—STODDART's *Remarks on Scotland*.

No stir in the air, no stir in the sea;
The ship was still as she could be;
Her sails from heaven received no motion,
Her keel was steady in the ocean.

Without either sign or sound of their shock
The waves flow'd over the Inchcape Rock;
So little they rose so little they fell,
They did not move the Inchcape Bell.

[1] See a Brief Description of Scotland, etc. by J. M., 1633.

The Abbot of Aberbrothok
Had placed that bell on the Inchcape Rock;
On a buoy in the storm it floated and swung,
And over the waves its warning rung.

When the Rock was hid by the surge's swell,
The mariners heard the warning bell;
And then they knew the perilous rock,
And blest the Abbot of Aberbrothok.

The sun in heaven was shining gay,
All things were joyful on that day;
The sea-birds scream'd as they wheel'd round,
And there was joyaunce in their sound.

The buoy of the Inchcape Bell was seen
A darker speck on the ocean green;
Sir Ralph the Rover walk'd his deck,
And he fix'd his eye on the darker speck.

He felt the cheering power of spring,
It made him whistle, it made him sing;
His heart was mirthful to excess,
But the Rover's mirth was wickedness.

His eye was on the Inchcape Float;
Quoth he, « My men, put out the boat,
And row me to the Inchcape Rock,
And I 'll plague the Abbot of Aberbrothok. »

The boat is lower'd, the boatmen row,
And to the Inchcape Rock they go;
Sir Ralph bent over from the boat,
And he cut the Bell from the Inchcape Float.

Down sunk the Bell with a gurgling sound,
The bubbles rose and burst around;
Quoth Sir Ralph, « the next who comes to the Rock
Wo'n't bless the Abbot of Aberbrothok. »

Sir Ralph the Rover sail'd away,
He scour'd the seas for many a day;
And now grown rich with plunder'd store,
He steers his course for Scotland's shore.

So thick a haze o'erspreads the sky
They cannot see the sun on high;
The wind hath blown a gale all day,
At evening it hath died away.

On the deck the Rover takes his stand,
So dark it is they see no land.
Quoth Sir Ralph, « It will be lighter soon,
For there is the dawn of the rising Moon. »

« Canst hear, » said one, « the breakers roar?
For methinks we should be near the shore. »
« Now, where we are I cannot tell,
But I wish we could hear the Inchcape Bell. »

They hear no sound, the swell is strong;
Though the wind hath fallen they drift along,
Till the vessel strikes with a shivering shock,—
« Oh Christ! it is the Inchcape Rock! »

Sir Ralph the Rover tore his hair;
He curst himself in his despair;
The waves rush in on every side,
The ship is sinking beneath the tide.

But even in his dying fear
One dreadful sound could the Rover hear,
A sound as if, with the Inchcape Bell,
The Devil below was ringing his knell.

1802.

THE WELL OF ST KEYNE.

« I know not whether it be worth the reporting, that there is in
Cornwall, near the parish of St Neots, a Well, arched over with the
robes of four kinds of trees, withy, oak, elm, and ash, dedicated to
St Keyne. The reported virtue of the water is this, that whether
husband or wife come first to drink thereof, they get the mastery
thereby. »—*Fuller.*

This passage in one of the folios of the Worthy old Fuller, who,
as he says, knew not whether it were worth the reporting, suggest-
ed the following Ballad: and the Ballad has produced so many imi-
tations that it may be prudent here thus to assert its originality,
lest I should be accused hereafter of having committed the plagia-
rism which has been practised upon it.

Of St Keyne, whose death is placed in the year 490, and whose de-
position used to be celebrated in Brecknockshire, on October 8,
there is a brief account in the *English Martyrologe.* Father Cressy
the Benedictine gives her history more fully. « Illustrious, » says
he, « she was for her birth, being the daughter of Braganus, prince
of that province in Wales, which, from him, was afterwards called
Brecknockshire; but more illustrious for her zeal to preserve her
chastity, for which reason she was called in the British language
Keynevayra, that is, Keyna the Virgin. »

2. This Prince Braganus, or Brachanus, the father of St Keyna,
is said to have had twelve sons and twelve daughters by his lady,[1]
called Marcella, daughter of Theodoric son of Tethphalt, Prince of
Garthmatrin, the same region called afterward Brecknock. Their
first-born son was St Canoc: and their eldest daughter was Gladus,
who was mother of Cadocus by St Gunley, a holy king of the southern
Britons. The second daughter was Melaria, the mother of the holy
Archbishop St David. Thus writes Capgrave, neither doth he men-
tion any of their children besides St Keyna.

3. But in Giraldus Cambrensis[2] another daughter is commemo-
rated, called St Almedha. And David Powel[3] makes mention of a
fifth named Tydvail, who was the wife of Congea the son of Cadel,
Prince of Powisland : and mother of Brochmael, surnamed Scithrog,
who slew Ethelfred King of the Northumbers.

4. Concerning the Holy Virgin St Keyna, we find this narration
in the author of her life, extant in Capgrave :[4] « She was of royal
blood, being daughter of Braganus, Prince of Brecknockshire.—
When she came to ripe years many noble persons sought her in
marriage; but she utterly refused that state, having consecrated
her virginity to our Lord by a perpetual vow. For which cause she
was afterward by the Britons called Keyn-wiri, that is, Keyna the
Virgin. »

5. At length she determined to forsake her country and find out
some desert place, where she might attend to contemplation. There-
fore, directing her journey beyond Severn, and there meeting with
certain woody places, she made her request to the prince of that
country that she might be permitted to serve God in that solitude.
His answer was, that he was very willing to grant her request, but
that that place did so swarm with serpents that neither men nor beasts
could inhabit in it. But she constantly replied, that her firm trust
was in the name and assistance of Almighty God, to drive all that
poisonous brood out of that region.

6. Hereupon the place was granted to the Holy Virgin; who pre-
sently prostrating herself in fervent prayer to God, obtained of him
to change all the serpents and vipers there into stones. And to this
day the stones in that region do resemble the windings of serpents
through all the fields and villages, as if they had been framed so by
the hand of the engraver.

7. Our learned Cambden, in his diligent search after antiquities,
seems to have visited this country, being a part of Somersetshire,
though he is willing to disparage the miracle. His words are, « On
the western bank of Avon is seen the town of Cainsham. Some are
of opinion, that it was named so from Keyna, a most holy British

[1] Antiquit. Glaston.
[2] Girald. Cambr. l. i, c. 2.
[3] D. Powel in Annotat. ad. Girald.
[4] Capgrav. in S. Keyna.

Virgin, who, according to the credulous persuasion of former ages,
is believed to have turned serpents into stones; because such like
miracles of sporting nature are there sometimes found in the quar-
ries. I myself saw a stone brought from thence representing a ser-
pent rolled up into a spire: the head of it stuck out in the outward
surface, and the end of the tail terminated in the centre. »

8. But let us prosecute the life of this holy Virgin. Many years
being spent by her in this solitary place, and the fame of her sanc-
tity every where divulged, and many oratories built by her, her
nephew St Cadoc performing a pilgrimage to the Mount of St Mi-
chael, met there with his blessed aunt, St Keyna, at whose sight he
was replenished with great joy. And being desirous to bring her
back to her own country, the inhabitants of that region would not
permit him. But afterward, by the admonition of an angel, the
holy Maid returned to the place of her nativity, where, on the top
of a hillock seated at the foot of a high mountain, she made a little
habitation for herself; and by her prayers to God obtained a spring
there to flow out of the earth, which, by the merits of the Holy Vir-
gin, afforded health to divers infirmities.

9. But when the time of her consummation approached, one night
she, by the revelation of the Holy Ghost, saw in a vision, as it were,
a fiery pillar, the base whereof was fixed on her bed : now her bed
was the pavement strewed over with a few branches of trees. And
in this vision two angels appeared to her; one of which approach-
ing respectfully to her, seemed to take off the sackcloth with which
she was covered, and instead thereof to put on her a smock of fine
linen, and over that a tunic of purple, and last of all a mantle all
woven with gold. Which having done, be thus said to her, « Pre-
pare yourself to come with us, that we may lead you into your
heavenly Father's kingdom. » Hereupon she wept with excess
of joy, and endeavouring to follow the angels she awaked, and
found her body inflamed with a fever, so that she perceived her end
was near.

10. Therefore, sending for her nephew Cadocus, she said to him.
« This is the place above all others beloved by me: here my memory
shall be perpetuated. This place I will often visit in spirit if it
may be permitted me. And I am assured it shall be permitted me,
because our Lord has granted me this place as a certain inheritance.
The time will come when this place shall be inhabited by a sinful
people, which notwithstanding I will violently root out of this seate.
My tomb shall be a long while unknown, till the coming of other
people whom by my prayers I shall bring hither : them will I pro-
tect and defend; and in this place shall the name of our Lord be
blessed for ever. »

11. After this, her soul being ready to depart out of her body
she saw standing before her a troop of heavenly angels, ready joy-
fully to receive her soul, and to transport it without any fear or
danger from her spiritual enemies. Which, having told to those
who stood by, her blessed soul was freed from the prison of her
body on the eighth day before the Ides of October. In her dissolu-
tion her face smiled, and was all of a rosy colour; and so sweet a
fragrancy proceeded from her sacred virgin body, that those who
were present thought themselves in the joy of Paradise. St Ca-
docus buried her in her own oratory, where for many years she had
led a most holy mortified life, very acceptable to God.— *Church His-
tory of Brittany, Book X. Ch. 14.*

Such is the history of St Keyne as related by F. Serenus Cressy.
permissu superiorum, et approbatione Doctorum! There was evidently
a scheme of setting up a shrine connected with the legend. In one
part it was well conceived, for the Cornu Ammonis is no where so
frequently found as near Keynsham; fine specimens are to be seen
over the doors of many of the houses there, and I have often ob-
served fragments among the stones which were broken up to mend
the road. The Welsh seem nearly to have forgotten this saint.—
Mr Owen, in his Cambrian Biography, enumerates two daughters
of Brychan, Ceindrech and Ceinwen, both ranked among saints, and
the latter having two churches dedicated to her in Mona. One of
these is probably St Keyne.

A WELL there is in the west country,
　And a clearer one never was seen;
There is not a wife in the west country
　But has heard of the Well of St Keyne.

An oak and an elm-tree stand beside,
　And behind does an ash-tree grow,
And a willow from the bank above
　Droops to the water below.

A traveller came to the Well of St Keyne;
  Joyfully he drew nigh,
For from cock-crow he had been travelling,
  And there was not a cloud in the sky.

He drank of the water so cool and clear,
  For thirsty and hot was he,
And he sat down upon the bank
  Under the willow-tree.

There came a man from the neighbouring town
  At the Well to fill his pail;
On the well-side he rested it,
  And he bade the Stranger hail.

« Now art thou a bachelor, Stranger?» quoth he,
  « For an if thou hast a wife,
The happiest draught thou hast drunk this day
  That ever thou didst in thy life.

« Or has thy good woman, if one thou hast,
  Ever here in Cornwall been?
For an if she have, I 'll venture my life
  She has drunk of the Well of St Keyne.»

« I have left a good woman who never was here,»
  The Stranger he made reply,
« But that my draught should be the better for that,
  I pray you answer me why?»

« St Keyne,» quoth the Cornish-man, « many a time
  Drank of this crystal Well,
And before the Angel summon'd her,
  She laid on the water a spell.

« If the husband of this gifted Well
  Shall drink before his wife,
A happy man henceforth is he,
  For he shall be master for life.

« But if the wife should drink of it first,—
  God help the husband then!»
The Stranger stoopt to the Well of St Keyne,
  And drank of the water again.

« You drank of the Well I warrant betimes?»
  He to the Cornish-man said :
But the Cornish-man smiled as the stranger spake,
  And sheepishly shook his head.

« I hasten'd as soon as the wedding was done,
  And left my wife in the porch;
But i' faith she had been wiser than me,
  For she took a bottle to church.»

                1798.

BISHOP BRUNO.

« Bruno, the Bishop of Herbipolitanum, sailing in the river of Danubius, with Henry the Third, then Emperor, being not far from a place which the Germanes call *Ben Strudel*, or the devouring gulfe, which is neere unto Grinon, a castle in Austria, a spirit was heard clamouring aloud, ' Ho, ho, Bishop Bruno, whither art thou travelling? but dispose of thyselfe how thou pleasest, thou shalt be my prey and spoil.' At the hearing of these words they were all stupified, and the Bishop with the rest crost and blest themselves. The issue was, that within a short time after, the Bishop, feasting with the Emperor in a castle belonging to the Countesse of Esburch, a rafter fell from the roof of the chamber wherein they sate, and strooke him dead at the table.»—Harwood's *Hierarchie of the Blessed Angels.*

Bishop Bruno awoke in the dead midnight,
And he heard his heart beat loud with affright :
He dreamt he had rung the palace bell,
And the sound it gave was his passing knell.

Bishop Bruno smiled at his fears so vain,
He turned to sleep and he dreamt again;
He rang at the palace gate once more,
And Death was the porter that open'd the door.

He started up at the fearful dream,
And he heard at his window the screech-owl scream !
Bishop Bruno slept no more that night,—
Oh ! glad was he when he saw the day-light !

Now he goes forth in proud array,
For he with the Emperor dines to-day;
There was not a Baron in Germany
That went with a nobler train than he.

Before and behind his soldiers ride,
The people throng'd to see their pride;
They bow'd the head, and the knee they bent,
But nobody blest him as he went.

So he went on stately and proud,
When he heard a voice that cried aloud,
« Ho ! ho ! Bishop Bruno ! you travel with glee,—
But I would have you know, you travel to me !»

Behind and before and on either side,
He look'd, but nobody he espied;
And the Bishop at that grew cold with fear,
For he heard the words distinct and clear.

And when he rang at the palace bell,
He almost expected to hear his knell;
And when the porter turn'd the key,
He almost expected Death to see.

But soon the Bishop recover'd his glee,
For the Emperor welcomed him royally :
And now the tables were spread, and there
Were choicest wines and dainty fare.

And now the Bishop had blest the meat,
When a voice was heard as he sat in his seat,—
« With the Emperor now you are dining in glee,
But know, Bishop Bruno ! you sup with me !»

The Bishop then grew pale with affright,
And suddenly lost his appetite;
All the wine and dainty cheer
Could not comfort his heart so sick with fear.

But by little and little recovered he,
For the wine went flowing merrily,
And he forgot his former dread,
And his cheeks again grew rosy red.

When he sat down to the royal fare
Bishop Bruno was the saddest man there;
But when the masquers enter'd the hall,
He was the merriest man of all.

83

Then from amid the masquers' crowd
There went a voice hollow and loud,—
« You have past the day, Bishop Bruno, in glee!
But you must pass the night with me!»

His cheek grows pale, and his eye-balls glare,
And stiff round his tonsure bristles his hair;
With that there came one from the masquers' band,
And took the Bishop by the hand.

The bony hand suspended his breath,
His marrow grew cold at the touch of Death;
On saints in vain he attempted to call,
Bishop Bruno fell dead in the palace hall.

1798.

THE BATTLE OF BLENHEIM.

It was a summer evening,
    Old Kaspar's work was done,
And he before his cottage door
    Was sitting in the sun,
And by him sported on the green
His little grandchild Wilhelmine.

She saw her brother Peterkin
    Roll something large and round,
Which he beside the rivulet
    In playing there had found;
He came to ask what he had found,
That was so large, and smooth, and round.

Old Kaspar took it from the boy,
    Who stood expectant by;
And then the old man shook his head,
    And with a natural sigh,
« 'T is some poor fellow's scull,» said he,
« Who fell in the great victory.

« I find them in the garden,
    For there 's many here about;
And often when I go to plough,
    The ploughshare turns them out!
For many thousand men,» said he,
« Were slain in that great victory.»

« Now tell us what 't was all about,»
    Young Peterkin, he cries;
And little Wilhelmine looks up
    With wonder-waiting eyes;
« Now tell us all about the war,
And what they kill'd each other for.»

« It was the English,» Kaspar cried,
« Who put the French to rout;
But what they kill'd each other for,
    I could not well make out.
But every body said,» quoth he,
« That 't was a famous victory.

« My father lived at Blenheim then,
    Yon little stream hard by;
They burnt his dwelling to the ground,
    And he was forced to fly;
So with his wife and child he fled,
Nor had he where to rest his head.

« With fire and sword the country round
    Was wasted far and wide,
And many a childing mother then,
    And new-born baby, died,
But things like that, you know, must be
At every famous victory.

« They say it was a shocking sight
    After the field was won;
For many thousand bodies here
    Lay rotting in the sun;
But things like that, you know, must be
After a famous victory.

« Great praise the Duke of Marlbro' won,
    And our good Prince Eugene.»
« Why 't was a very wicked thing!»
    Said little Wilhelmine.
« Nay—nay—my little girl,» quoth he,
« It was a famous victory.

« And every body praised the Duke
    Who this great fight did win.»
« But what good came of it at last?»
    Quoth little Peterkin.
« Why that I cannot tell,» said he,
« But 't was a famous victory.»

1798.

A TRUE BALLAD

OF ST ANTIDIUS, THE POPE, AND THE DEVIL.

« Deste Atendio cuentan las estorias que le avino, que el martes despues de Ramos, passó por la puente de un rio que ha nombre Divino; e vió en un campo gran compaña de diablos que estavan contando a sus principes los males que fazien por las tierras; e entre todos los otros estava un negro a manera de Etyopiano: e alabavase que avie siete anos que andava lidiando con el Papa por le fazer pecar, e nunca pudiera sy non etonces que le fiziera fazer ya que pecado muy grave; e esto provavalo por la sandalia del apostoligo que traye. E Sant Atendio que vido aquello, llamó aquel diablo, e conjurol por la virtud de Dios e por la Santa Cruz que lo llevasse a Roma; e cavalgó en el; e llevol a Roma. El jueves de la cena a hora de missa, el Papa que queria revestirse para dezir missa; dexó Sant Atendio al diablo a la puerta e dixol que lo atendiese; e el entró dentro el sacó e Papa aparte, e dixol que fiziesse penitencia de aquel pecado; e el quiso lo negar, mas fizo gelo otorgar el santo obispo con a sandalia que le dio. E fizo el Papa penitencia; e dixo Sant Atendio la missa en su logar, e consagró la crisma; e tomó una partida della para sy; e despediosse del Papa, e salio fuera, e cavalgó en el diablo, e llevólo a su arçobispado el sabado de pascua a hora de missa.»—Coronica de España, ff. 139.

This Saint Atendio, according to the Chronica General, was Bishop of Vesytana in Gaul, and martyred by the Vandals in the year 411. The Spaniards have a tradition that he was bishop of Jaen; they say, « that as the devil was crossing the sea with this unwelcome load upon his back, he artfully endeavoured to make Atendio pronounce the name of Jesus, which, as it breaks all spells, would have enabled him to throw him off into the water; but the Bishop, understanding his intent, only replied, Arre Diablo, « Gee-up, Devil!» and they add, « that when he arrived at Rome, his hat was still covered with the snow which had fallen upon it while he was passing the Alps, and that the hat is still shown at Rome in confirmation of the story and the miracle.» Feyjoo has two letters upon this whimsical legend among his Cartas Eruditas. In the first (t. i, carta 24) he replies to a correspondent who had gravely inquired his opinion upon the story, « De buen humor,» says he, « estaba V. md. quando le ocurrió inquirir mi dictamen, sobre la Historieta de el Obispo de Jahen, de quien se cuenta, que fue a Roma en una noche, caballero sobre la espalda de un Diablo de alquiler : Triste de mi, si essa curiosidad se hace contagiosa, y dan muchos en seguir el exemplo de V. md. consultandome sobre cuentos de niños y viejas.» Nevertheless, though he thus treats the story as an old wife's tale, he bestows some reasoning upon it. « As he heard it,» he says, « it did not appear whether the use which the Bishop made of the

Devil were licit or illicit; that is, whether he made use of him as a wizard, by virtue of a compact, or by virtue of authority, having the permission of the Most High so to do. In either case there is a great incongruity. In the first, inasmuch as it is not credible that the Devil should voluntarily serve the Bishop for the purpose of preventing a great evil to the church:—I say *voluntarily*, because the notion that a compact is so binding upon the Devil that he can in no ways resist the pleasure of the person with whom he has contracted *es cosa de Theologos de Vade a la cinta*. In the second, because the journey being designed for a holy purpose, it is more conformable to reason that it should have been executed by the ministry of a good angel than of a bad one; as, for instance, Habakkuk was transported by the ministry of a good angel from Judæa to Babylon, that he might carry food to the imprisoned Daniel. If you should oppose to me the example of Christ, who was carried by the Devil to the pinnacle of the Temple, I reply, that there are two manifest disparities. The first, that Christ conducted himself in this case passively and permissively; the second, that the Devil placed him upon the pinnacle of the Temple, not for any good end, but with a most wicked intention. « But,» pursues the good Benedictine, « why should I fatigue myself with arguing? I hold the story unworthy of being critically examined till it be shown me written in some history, either ecclesiastical or profane, which is entitled to some credit.»

Soon after this letter was published, another correspondent informed Feyjoo, that the story in question was written in the General Chronicle of King D. Alphonso the Wise. This incited him to farther inquiry. He found the same legend in the Speculum Historiale of Vincentius Belovacensis, and there discovered that the saint was called Antidius, not Athendius, and that the scene lay upon the river Dunius instead of the river Divinus. Here too he found a reference to Sigebertus Gemblacensis: and in that author, the account which the Chronicler had followed and the explanation of his errors in the topography: his Vesytania proving to be Besançon, and the river the Doux, which the Romans called Dubius, Dubis, and Aduadubis. But he found also to his comfort, that though Jean Jacques Chiflet, a physician of Besançon, had endeavoured to prove the truth of the story for the honour of his nation or city, in a book entitled, *Vesontio Civitas Imperialis Libera Sequanorum*, and had cited certain ancient Acts and Breviaries, in support of it; the veracious Bollandists had decided that these Acts were apocryphal, the Breviaries not to be believed in this point, and the whole story a fable which had been equally related of St Maximus Taurinensis, and Pope Leo the Great. These Bollandists strain at a gnat, and swallow an Aullay with equal gravity. Fortified by their authority, Feyjoo, who was worthy to have belonged to a more enlightened church, triumphantly dismissed the legend, and observed, « that the contriver was a clumsy fabler to make the Devil spend two days upon the journey, which,» as he says, « is slow travelling for an infernal postilion.» *Cartas Eruditas*, t. ii, c. 21.—The discussion, however, reminded him of a curious story, which he thus relates: « There is in this city of Oviedo a poor Porter, called by name Pedro Moreno, of whom a tale is told similar in substance to this of the Bishop of Jaen. The circumstance is related in this manner. Some letters had been delivered to him which he was to carry to Madrid with more than ordinary diligence, because expedition was of importance. At a little distance from this city he met with a friar, who offered to join company with him for the journey: to this he objected, upon the ground, that he was going in great haste, and that the friar would not be able to keep pace with him; but in fine, the friar prevailed upon him to let it be so. and at the same time gave him a walking-stick for his use. So they began to travel together, and that so well, that Valladolid being forty leagues (160 miles) from Oviedo, they got beyond that city on the first day to dinner. The rest of the journey was performed with the same celerity. This story spread through the whole place, and was believed by all the vulgar (and by some also who were not of the vulgar) when it came to my ears: the authority referred to, was the man himself, who had related it to an infinite number of persons. I sent for him to my cell to examine him. He affirmed that the story was true, but by questioning and cross-questioning him concerning the particulars, I made him fall into many contradictions. Moreover, I found that he had told the story with many variations to different persons. What I clearly ascertained was, that he had heard the legend of the Bishop of Jaen, and thought to become a famous man by making a like fable believed of himself. I believe that many persons were undeceived when my inquiry was known. But before this examination was made, to how many places had the report of this miraculous journey extended, where the exposure of the falsehood will never reach! Perhaps, if this writing should not prevent it, the journey of Pedro Moreno, the porter, will one day be little less famous in Spain than that of the Bishop of Jaen.»—*Cartas Eruditas*, t. i, c. 24.

It is Antidius the Bishop
Who now at even tide,
Taking the air and saying a prayer,
Walks by the river side.
The Devil had business that evening,
And he upon earth would go;
For it was in the month of August,
And the weather was close below.

He had his books to settle,
And up to earth he hied,
To do it there in the evening air,
All by the river side.

His imps came flying around him,
Of his affairs to tell;
From the north, and the south, and the east, and
the west;
They brought him the news that he liked best,
Of the things they had done, and the souls they
had won,
And how they sped well in the service of Hell.

There came a devil posting in
Return'd from his employ,
Seven years had he been gone from Hell,
And now he came grinning for joy.

« Seven years,» quoth he, « of trouble and toil
Have I labour'd the Pope to win;
And I to-day have caught him,
He hath done the deadly sin.»
And then he took the Devil's book,
And wrote the deed therein.

Oh, then King Beelzebub for joy,
He drew his mouth so wide,
You might have seen his iron teeth,
Four and forty from side to side.

He wagg'd his ears, he twisted his tail,
He knew not for joy what to do,
In his hoofs and his horns, in his heels and his corns,
It tickled him all through.

The Bishop who beheld all this,
Straight how to act bethought him;
He leapt upon the Devil's back,
And by the horns he caught him.

And he said a Pater-noster
As fast as he could say,
And made a cross on the Devil's head,
And bade him to Rome away.

Without bridle, or saddle, or whip, or spur,
Away they go like the wind,
The beads of the Bishop are hanging before,
And the tail of the Devil behind.

They met a witch and she hail'd them
As soon as she came within call;
« Ave Maria!» the Bishop exclaimed,
It frightened her broomstick and she got a fall.

He ran against a shooting star,
So fast for fear did he sail,
And he singed the beard of the Bishop
Against a Comet's tail.

And he pass'd between the horns of the Moon,
With Antidius on his back ;
And there was an eclipse that night,
Which was not in the Almanack.

The Bishop just as they set out,
To tell his beads begun ;
And he was by the bed of the Pope
Before the string was done.

The Pope fell down upon his knees,
In terror and confusion,
And he confess'd the deadly sin,
And he had absolution.

And all the Popes in bliss that be,
Sung, O be joyful! then ;
And all the Popes in bale that be,
They howl'd for envy then ;
For they before kept jubilee,
Expecting his good company,
Down in the Devil's den.
But what was this the Pope had done
To bind his soul to hell?
Ah! that is the mystery of this wonderful history,
And I wish that I could tell.

But would you know to hell you must go,
You can easily find the way,
It is a broad and a well-known road
That is travell'd by night and by day.

And you must look in the Devil's book ;
You will find one debt that was never paid yet
If you search the leaves throughout ;
And that is the mystery of this wonderful history,
And the way to find it out.
1802.

QUEEN ORRACA, AND THE FIVE MARTYRS OF MOROCCO.

This Legend is related in the Chronicle of Affonso II, and in the Historia Serafica of Fr. Manoel da Esperança.

The friars five have girt their loins,
And taken staff in hand ;
And never shall those friars again
Hear mass in Christian land.

They went to Queen Orraca,
To thank her and bless her them ;
And Queen Orraca in tears
Knelt to the holy men.

« Three things, Queen Orraca,
We prophesy to you :
Hear us, in the name of God!
For time will prove them true.

« In Morocco we must martyr'd be ;
Christ hath vouchsafed it thus :
We shall shed our blood for him
Who shed his blood for us.

« To Coimbra shall our bodies be brought ;
For such is the will divine ;
That Christians may behold and feel
Blessings at our shrine.

« And when unto the place of rest
Our bodies shall draw nigh,
Who sees us first, the King or you,
That one that night must die.

« Fare thee well, Queen Orraca ;
For thy soul a mass we will say,
Every day while we do live,
And on thy dying day.»

The friars they blest her, one by one,
Where she knelt on her knee ;
And they departed to the land
Of the Moors beyond the sea

« What news, O King Affonso?
What news of the friars five?
Have they preach'd to the Miramamolin ;
And are they still alive?»

« They have fought the fight, O Queen !
They have run the race ;
In robes of white they hold the palm
Before the throne of grace.

« All naked in the sun and air
Their mangled bodies lie ;
What Christian dared to bury them,
By the bloody Moors would die.»

« What news, O King Affonso,
Of the Martyrs five what news?
Doth the bloody Miramamolin
Their burial still refuse?»

« That on a dunghill they should rot,
The bloody Moor decreed ;
That their dishonour'd bodies should
The dogs and vultures feed :

« But the thunder of God roll'd over them,
And the lightning of God flash'd round ;
Nor thing impure, nor man impure,
Could approach the holy ground.

« A thousand miracles appall'd
The cruel Pagan's mind.
Our brother Pedro brings them here,
In Coimbra to be shrined.»

Every altar in Coimbra
Is drest for the festival day ;
All the people in Coimbra
Are dight in their richest array.

Every bell in Coimbra
Doth merrily, merrily ring ;
The clergy and the knights await,
To go forth with the Queen and the King.

« Come forth, come forth, Queen Orraca !
We make the procession stay.»
« I beseech thee, King Affonso,
Go you alone to-day.

« I have pain in my head this morning,
I am ill at heart also :
Go without me, King Affonso,
For I am too sick to go.»

« The relics of the Martyrs five
   All maladies can cure;
They will requite the charity
   You show'd them once, be sure:

« Come forth then, Queen Orraca!
   You make the procession stay:
It were a scandal and a sin
   To abide at home to-day.»

Upon her palfrey she is set,
   And forward then they go;
And over the long bridge they pass,
   And up the long hill wind slow.

« Prick forward, King Affonso,
   And do not wait for me;
To meet them close by Coimbra,
   It were discourtesy.'

« A little while I needs must wait,
   Till this sore pain be gone:—
I will proceed the best I can,
   But do you and your knights prick on.»

The King and his knights prick'd up the hill
   Faster than before;
The King and his knights have topp'd the hill,
   And now they are seen no more.

As the King and his knights went down the hill,
   A wild boar crost the way;
« Follow him! follow him!» cried the King;
« We have time by the Queen's delay!»

A-hunting of the boar astray
   Is King Affonso gone:
Slowly, slowly, but straight the while,
   Queen Orraca is coming on.

And winding now the train appears
   Between the olive-trees:
Queen Orraca alighted then,
   And fell upon her knees.

The friars of Alanquer came first,
   And next the relics past;—
Queen Orraca look'd to see
   The King and his knights come last.

She heard the horses tramp behind;
   At that she turn'd her face:
King Affonso and his knights came up
   All panting from the chase.

« Have pity upon my poor soul,
   Holy martyrs five!» cried she:
« Holy Mary, Mother of God,
   Virgin, pray for me!»

That day in Coimbra,
   Many a heart was gay;
But the heaviest heart in Coimbra,
   Was that poor Queen's that day.

The festival is over,
   The sun hath sunk in the west;
All the people in Coimbra
   Have betaken themselves to rest.

Queen Orraca's father confessor
   At midnight is awake;
Kneeling at the Martyr's shrine,
   And praying for her sake.

Just at the midnight hour, when all
   Was still as still could be,
Into the church of Santa Cruz,
   Came a saintly company:

All in robes of russet grey
   Poorly were they dight;
Each one girdled with a cord,
   Like a friar minorite.

But from those robes of russet grey,
   There flow'd a heavenly light;
For each one was the blessed soul
   Of a friar minorite.

Brighter than their brethren
   Among the beautiful band,
Five there were who each did bear
   A palm branch in his hand.

He who led the brethren,
   A living man was he;
And yet he shone the brightest
   Of all the company.

Before the steps of the altar,
   Each one bow'd his head;
And then with solemn voice they sung
   The service of the dead.

« And who are ye, ye blessed saints?»
   The father confessor said;
« And for what happy souls sing ye
   The service of the dead?»

« These are the souls of our brethren in bliss,
   The Martyrs five are we:
And this is our father Francisco,
   Among us bodily.

« We are come hither to perform
   Our promise to the Queen;
Go thou to King Affonso,
   And say what thou hast seen.»

There was loud knocking at the door,
   As the heavenly vision fled;
And the porter called to the confessor,
   To tell him the Queen was dead.

1803.

A BALLAD,

SHEWING HOW AN OLD WOMAN RODE DOUBLE,
AND WHO RODE BEFORE HER.

A. D. 852. Circa dies istos, mulier quædam malefica, in villâ quæ Berkeleia dicitur degens, gulæ amatrix ac petulantiæ, flagitiis modum usque in senium et auguriis non ponens, usque ad mortem impudica permansit. Hæc die quadam cum sederet ad prandium, cornicula quam pro deliciis pascebat, nescio quid garrire cœpit; quo audito, mulieris cultellus de manu excidit, simul et facies pallescere cœpit, et emisso rugitu, hodie, inquit, accipiam grande incommodum, hodieque ad sulcum ultimum meum pervenit aratrum. Quo dicto, nuncius doloris intravit; muliere vero percunctata ad quid veniret, affero, inquit, tibi filii tui obitum et totius familiæ ejus ex subitâ ruinâ interitum. Hoc quoque dolore mulier permota, lecto protinus decubuit graviter infirmata; sentiensque morbum subrepere ad vitalia, liberos quos habuit superstites, monachum videlicet et monacham, per epistolam invitavit; advenientes autem voce singultiente alloquitur. Ego, inquit, o pueri, meo miserabili fato dæmoniacis semper artibus inservivi; ego omnium vitiorum sentina, ego illecebrarum omnium fui magistra. Erat tamen mihi inter hæc mala, spes vestræ religionis, quæ meam solidaret animam desperatam; vos expectabam propugnatores contra dæmones, tutores contra sævissimos hostes. Nunc igitur quoniam ad finem vitæ perveni, rogo vos per materna ubera, ut mea tentatis alleviare tormenta. Insuite me defunctam in corio cervino, ac deinde in sarcophago lapideo supponite, operculumque ferro et plumbo constringite, ac demum lapidem tribus cathenis ferreis et fortissimis circundantes, clericos quinquaginta psalmorum cantores, et tot per tres dies presbyteros missarum celebratores applicate, qui ferocas lenigent adversariorum incursus. Ita si tribus noctibus secura jacuero, quartâ die me infodite humo.

Factumque est ut præceperat illis. Sed, proh dolor! nil preces, nil lachrymæ, nil demum valuere catenæ. Primis enim duabus noctibus, cum chori psallentium corpori assistebant, advenientes Dæmones ostium ecclesiæ confregerunt ingenti obice clausum, extremasque cathenas negotio levi dirumpunt; media autem quæ fortior erat, illibata manebat. Tertiâ autem nocte, circa gallicinium, strepitu hostium adventantium, omne monasterium visum est a fundamento moveri. Unus ergo dæmonum, et vultu cæteris terribilior et staturâ eminentior, januas Ecclesiæ impetu violento concussas in fragmenta dejecit. Divexerunt clerici cum laicis, metu steterunt omnium capilli, et psalmorum concentus defecit. Dæmon ergo gestu ut videbatur arroganti ad sepulchrum accedens, et nomen mulieris modicum ingeminans, surgere imperavit. Quâ respondente, quod nequiret pro vinculis, jam malo tuo, inquit, solveris; et protinus cathenam quæ cæterorum ferociam dæmonum deluserat, velut stuppeum vinculum rumpebat. Operculum etiam sepulchri pede depellens, mulierem palam omnibus ab ecclesiâ extraxit, ubi præ foribus niger equus superbe hinniens videbatur, uncis ferreis et clavis undique confixus, super quem misera mulier projecta, ab oculis assistentium evanuit. Audiebantur tamen clamores per quatuor fere milliaria horribiles, auxilium postulantes.

Ista itaque quæ retuli incredibilia non erunt, si legatur beati Gregorii dialogus, in quo refert, hominem in ecclesiâ sepultum, a dæmonibus foras ejectum. Et apud Francos Carolus Martellus insignis vir fortitudinis, qui Saracenos Galliam ingressos, Hispaniam redire compulit, exactis vitæ suæ diebus, in Ecclesiâ beati Dionysii legitur fuisse sepultus. Sed quia patrimonia, cum decimis omnium fere ecclesiarum Galliæ, pro stipendio commilitonum suorum mutilaverat, miserabiliter a malignis spiritibus de sepulchro corporaliter avulsus, usque in hodiernum diem nusquam comparuit.—*Matthew of Westminster.*

This story is also related by Olaus Magnus, and in the Nuremberg Chronicle.

THE Raven croak'd as she sate at her meal,
  And the Old Woman knew what he said,
And she grew pale at the Raven's tale,
  And sicken'd and went to her bed.

« Now fetch me my children, and fetch them with
    speed, »
  The Old Woman of Berkeley said,
« The monk my son, and my daughter the nun,
  Bid them hasten or I shall be dead. »

The monk her son, and her daughter the nun,
  Their way to Berkeley went,
And they have brought with pious thought
  The holy sacrament.

The Old Woman shriek'd as they enter'd her door,
  'T was fearful her shrieks to hear,
« Now take the sacrament away,
  For mercy, my children dear! »

Her lip it trembled with agony,
  The sweat ran down her brow,
« I have tortures in store for evermore,
  Oh! spare me, my children, now! »

Away they sent the sacrament,
  The fit it left her weak,
She look'd at her children with ghastly eyes,
  And faintly struggled to speak.

« All kind of sin I have rioted in,
  And the judgment now must be,
But I secured my children's souls,
  Oh! pray, my children, for me!

« I have suck'd the breath of sleeping babes,
  The fiends have been my slaves,
I have 'nointed myself with infants' fat,
  And feasted on rifled graves.

« And the Devil will fetch me now in fire,
  My witchcrafts to atone;
And I who have rifled the dead man's grave
  Shall never have rest in my own.

« Bless, I entreat, my winding-sheet,
  My children, I beg of you;
And with holy water sprinkle my shroud,
  And sprinkle my coffin too.

« And let me be chain'd in my coffin of stone,
  And fasten it strong, I implore,
With iron bars, and with three chains,
  Chain it to the church floor.

« And bless the chains and sprinkle them,
  And let fifty priests stand round,
Who night and day the mass may say,
  Where I lie on the ground.

« And see that fifty choristers
  Beside the bier attend me,
And day and night by the taper's light,
  With holy hymns defend me.

« Let the church bells all both great and small,
  Be toll'd by night and day,
To drive from thence the fiends who come
  To bear my body away.

« And ever have the church door barr'd
  After the even song;
And I beseech you, children dear,
  Let the bars and bolts be strong.

« And let this be three days and nights
  My wretched corpse to save,
Keep me so long from the fiendish throng,
  And then I may rest in my grave. »

The Old Woman of Berkeley laid her down,
  And her eyes grew deadly dim,
Short came her breath and the struggle of death
  Did loosen every limb.

They blest the old woman's winding-sheet
  With rites and prayers due,
With holy water they sprinkled her shroud,
  And they sprinkled her coffin too.

And they chain'd her in her coffin of stone,
  And with iron barr'd it down,
And in the church with three strong chains
  They chain'd it to the ground.

And they blest the chains and sprinkled them,
  And fifty priests stood round,
By night and day the mass to say
  Where she lay on the ground.

And fifty sacred choristers
  Beside the bier attend her,
Who day and night by the taper's light
  Should with holy hymns defend her.

To see the priests and choristers
  It was a goodly sight,
Each holding, as it were a staff,
  A taper burning bright.

And the church bells all both great and small,
  Did toll so loud and long,
And they have barr'd the church door hard,
  After the even song.

And the first night the tapers' light
  Burnt steadily and clear,
But they without a hideous rout
  Of angry fiends could hear;

A hideous roar at the church door
  Like a long thunder peal,
And the priests they pray'd and the choristers sung
  Louder in fearful zeal.

Loud toll'd the bell, the priests pray'd well,
  The tapers they burnt bright,
The monk her son, and her daughter the nun,
  They told their beads all night.

The cock he crew, the fiends they flew
  From the voice of the morning away;
Then undisturb'd the choristers sing,
  And the fifty priests they pray;
As they had sung and pray'd all night
  They pray'd and sung all day.

The second night the tapers' light
  Burnt dismally and blue,
And every one saw his neighbour's face
  Like a dead man's face to view.

And yells and cries without arise
  That the stoutest heart might shock,
And a deafening roaring like a cataract pouring
  Over a mountain rock.

The monk and nun they told their beads
  As fast as they could tell,
And aye as louder grew the noise
  The faster went the bell.

Louder and louder the choristers sung
  As they trembled more and more,
And the priests as they pray'd to heaven for aid,
  They smote their breasts full sore.

The cock he crew, the fiends they flew
  From the voice of the morning away;
Then undisturb'd the choristers sing,
  And the fifty priests they pray;
As they had sung and pray'd all night
  They pray'd and sung all day.

The third night came, and the tapers' flame
  A hideous stench did make,
And they burnt as though they had been dipt
  In the burning brimstone lake.

And the loud commotion, like the rushing of ocean,
  Grew momently more and more,
And strokes as of a battering ram,
  Did shake the strong church door.

The bellmen they, for very fear,
  Could toll the bell no longer,
And still as louder grew the strokes,
  Their fear it grew the stronger.

The monk and nun forgot their beads,
  They fell on the ground in dismay,
There was not a single saint in heaven
  To whom they did not pray.

And the choristers' song which late was so strong,
  Falter'd with consternation,
For the church did rock as an earthquake shock
  Uplifted its foundation.

And a sound was heard like the trumpet's blast,
  That shall one day wake the dead,
The strong church door could bear no more,
  And the bolts and the bars they fled.

And the taper's light was extinguish'd quite,
  And the choristers faintly sung,
And the priests dismay'd, panted and pray'd,
And on all Saints in Heaven for aid
  They call'd with trembling tongue.

And in He came with eyes of flame,
  The Devil to fetch the dead,
And all the church with his presence glow'd
  Like a fiery furnace red.

He laid his hand on the iron chains,
  And like flax they moulder'd asunder,
And the coffin lid, which was barr'd so firm,
  He burst with his voice of thunder.

And he bade the Old Woman of Berkeley rise,
  And come with her master away,
And the cold sweat stood on the cold, cold corpse,
  At the voice she was forced to obey.

She rose on her feet in her winding-sheet,
  Her dead flesh quiver'd with fear,
And a groan like that which the Old Woman gave
  Never did mortal hear.

She follow'd the fiend to the church door,
  There stood a black horse there;
His breath was red like furnace smoke,
  His eyes like a meteor's glare.

The fiend he flung her on the horse,
  And he leapt up before,
And away like the lightning's speed they went,
  And she was seen no more.

They saw her no more, but her cries and shrieks
  For four miles round they could hear,
And children at rest at their mothers' breast,
  Started and screamed with fear.

                           1798.

THE SURGEON'S WARNING.

The subject of this parody was given me by a friend, to whom also
I am indebted for some of the stanzas.

Respecting the patent coffins herein mentioned, after the manner
of Catholic Poets, who confess the actions they attribute to their
Saints and Deity to be but fiction, I hereby declare that it is by no
means my design to depreciate that useful invention; and all per-
sons to whom this Ballad shall come, are requested to take notice,
that nothing here asserted concerning the aforesaid Coffins is true,
except that the maker and patentee lives by St Martin's Lane.

THE Doctor whisper'd to the Nurse,
　And the Surgeon knew what he said;
And he grew pale at the Doctor's tale,
　And trembled in his sick-bed.

« Now fetch me my brethren, and fetch them with
　　speed,»
　The Surgeon affrighted said;
« The Parson and the Undertaker,
　Let them hasten or I shall be dead.»

The Parson and the Undertaker
　They hastily came complying,
And the Surgeon's Prentices ran up stairs
　When they heard that their master was dying.

The Prentices all they enter'd the room,
　By one, by two, by three,
With a sly grin came Joseph in,
　First of the company.

The Surgeon swore as they enter'd his door,
　'T was fearful his oaths to hear,—
« Now send these scoundrels out of my sight,
　I beseech ye, my brethren dear.»

He foam'd at the mouth with the rage he felt,
　And he wrinkled his black eye-brow,
« That rascal Joe would be at me, I know,
　But zounds let him spare me now!»

Then out they sent the Prentices,
　The fit it left him weak,
He look'd at his brothers with ghastly eyes,
　And faintly struggled to speak.

« All kinds of carcasses I have cut up,
　And the judgment now must be;
But, brothers, I took care of you,
　So pray take care of me.

« I have made candles of infants' fat,
　The Sextons have been my slaves,
I have bottled babes unborn, and dried
　Hearts and livers from rifled graves.

« And my Prentices now will surely come
　And carve me bone from bone,
And I who have rifled the dead man's grave
　Shall never have rest in my own.

« Bury me in lead when I am dead,
　My brethren, I entreat,
And see the coffin weigh'd I beg
　Lest the Plumber should be a cheat.

« And let it be solder'd closely down,
　Strong as strong can be, I implore,
And put it in a patent coffin,
　That I may rise no more.

« If they carry me off in the patent coffin
　Their labour will be in vain,
Let the Undertaker see it bought of the maker,
　Who lives by St Martin's Lane.

« And bury me in my brother's church,
　For that will safer be;
And I implore, lock the church door,
　And pray take care of the key.

« And all night long let three stout men
　The vestry watch within,
To each man give a gallon of beer,
　And a keg of Holland's gin;

« Powder and ball and blunderbuss,
　To save me if he can,
And eke, five guineas if he shoot
　A resurrection-man.

« And let them watch me for three weeks,
　My wretched corpse to save,
For then I think that I may stink
　Enough to rest in my grave.»

The Surgeon laid him down in his bed,
　His eyes grew deadly dim,
Short came his breath and the struggle of death
　Did loosen every limb.

They put him in lead when he was dead,
　And shrouded up so neat,
And they the leaden coffin weigh,
　Lest the plumber should be a cheat.

They had it solder'd closely down,
　And examined it o'er and o'er,
And they put it in a patent coffin
　That he might rise no more.

For to carry him off in a patent coffin,
　Would, they thought, be but labour in vain,
So the Undertaker saw it bought of the maker,
　Who lives by St Martin's Lane.

In his brother's church they buried him,
　That safer he might be,
They lock'd the door, and would not trust
　The Sexton with the key.

And three men in the vestry watch
　To save him if they can,
And should he come there to shoot they swear
　A resurrection-man.

And the first night by lanthorn light
　Through the church-yard as they went,
A guinea of gold the Sexton show'd
　That Mister Joseph sent.

But conscience was tough, it was not enough,
　And their honesty never swerved,
And they bade him go with Mister Joe
　To the Devil as he deserved.

So all night long by the vestry fire
  They quaff'd their gin and ale,
And they did drink as you may think,
  And told full many a tale.

The second night by lanthorn light
  Through the church-yard as they went,
He whisper'd anew and show'd them two
  That Mister Joseph sent.

The guineas were bright and attracted their sight
  They look'd so heavy and new,
And their fingers itch'd as they were bewitch'd,
  And they knew not what to do.

But they waver'd not long, for conscience was strong,
  And they thought they might get more,
And they refused the gold, but not
  So rudely as before.

So all night long by the vestry fire
  They quaff'd their gin and ale,
And they did drink, as you may think,
  And told full many a tale.

The third night as by lanthorn light
  Through the church-yard they went,
He bade them see and show'd them three
  That Mister Joseph sent.

They look'd askance with greedy glance,
  The guineas they shone bright,
For the Sexton on the yellow gold
  Let fall his lanthorn light.

And he look'd sly with his roguish eye,
  And gave a well-timed wink,
And they could not stand the sound in his hand,
  For he made the guineas chink.

And conscience, late that had such weight,
  All in a moment fails,
For well they knew that it was true
  A dead man told no tales.

And they gave all their powder and ball,
  And took the gold so bright,
And they drank their beer and made good cheer,
  Till now it was midnight.

Then, though the key of the church-door
  Was left with the parson, his brother,
It open'd at the Sexton's touch,—
  Because he had another.

And in they go with that villain Joe,
  To fetch the body by night,
And all the church look'd dismally
  By his dark-lanthorn light.

They laid the pick-axe to the stones,
  And they moved them soon asunder;
They shovell'd away the hard-prest clay,
  And came to the coffin under.

They burst the patent coffin first,
  And they cut through the lead;
And they laugh'd aloud when they saw the shroud,
  Because they had got at the dead.

And they allow'd the Sexton the shroud,
  And they put the coffin back;
And nose and knees they then did squeeze
  The Surgeon in a sack.

The watchmen as they past along
  Full four yards off could smell,
And a curse bestow'd upon the load
  So disagreeable.

So they carried the sack a-pick-a-back,
  And they carved him from bone to bone,
But what became of the Surgeon's soul
  Was never to mortal known.

                                    1798.

HENRY THE HERMIT.

It was a little island where he dwelt,
A solitary islet, bleak and bare,
Short scanty herbage spotting with dark spots
Its grey stone surface.   Never mariner
Approach'd that rude and uninviting coast,
Nor ever fisherman his lonely bark
Anchor'd beside its shore.   It was a place
Befitting well a wretched anchoret,
Dead to the hopes and vanities and joys,
And purposes of life: and he had dwelt
Many long years upon that lonely isle;
For in ripe manhood he abandon'd arms,
Honours and friends and country and the world,
And had grown old in solitude.   That isle
Some solitary man in other times
Had made his dwelling-place; and Henry found
The little chapel which his toil had built
Now by the storms unroof'd, his bed of leaves
Wind-scatter'd; and his grave o'ergrown with grass,
And thistles, whose white seeds, there wing'd in vain,
Wither'd on rocks, or in the waves were lost.
So he repair'd the chapel's ruin'd roof,
Clear'd the grey lichens from the altar-stone,
And underneath a rock that shelter'd him
From the sea-blast, he built his hermitage.

The peasants from the shore would bring him food,
And beg his prayers; but human converse else
He knew not in that utter solitude;
Nor ever visited the haunts of men,
Save when some sinful wretch on a sick-bed
Implored his blessing and his aid in death.
That summons he delay'd not to obey,
Though the night-tempest or autumnal wind
Madden'd the waves; and though the mariner,
Albeit relying on his saintly load,
Grew pale to see the peril.   Thus he lived
A most austere and self-denying man,
Till abstinence and age and watchfulness
Had worn him down, and it was pain at last
To rise at midnight from his bed of leaves
And bend his knees in prayer.   Yet not the less,
Though with reluctance of infirmity,
Rose he at midnight from his bed of leaves
And bent his knees in prayer; but with more zeal,
More self-condemning fervour, raised his voice
Imploring pardon for the natural sin
Of that reluctance, till the atoning prayer

84

Had satisfied his heart, and given it peace,
And the repented fault became a joy.

One night upon the shore his chapel-bell
Was heard; the air was calm, and its far sounds
Over the water came, distinct and loud.
Alarm'd at that unusual hour to hear
Its toll irregular, a monk arose,
And crost to the island-chapel. On a stone
Henry was sitting there, dead, cold, and stiff,
The bell-rope in his hand, and at his feet
The lamp that stream'd a long unsteady light.[1]

                                        1799.

ST GUALBERTO.

ADDRESSED TO A FRIEND.

THE work is done, the fabric is complete;
  Distinct the Traveller sees its distant tower,
Yet ere his steps attain the sacred seat,
  Must toil for many a league and many an hour.
Elate the Abbot sees the pile and knows,
Stateliest of convents now, his new Moscera rose.

Long were the tale that told Moscera's pride,
  Its columns' cluster'd strength and lofty state,
How many a saint bedeck'd its sculptured side,
  What intersecting arches graced its gate;
Its towers how high, its massy walls how strong,
These fairly to describe were sure a tedious song.

Yet while the fane rose slowly from the ground,
  But little store of charity, I ween,
The passing pilgrim at Moscera found;
  And often there the mendicant was seen
Hopeless to turn him from the convent-door,
For this so costly work still kept the brethren poor.

Now all is perfect, and from every side
  They flock to view the fabric, young and old.
Who now can tell Rodulfo's secret pride,
  When on the Sabbath-day his eyes behold
The multitudes that crowd his chapel-floor,
Some sure to serve their God, to see Moscera more!

So chanced it that Gualberto pass'd that way,
  Since sainted for a life of holy deeds.
He paused the new-rear'd convent to survey,
  And, whilst o'er all its bulk his eye proceeds,
Sorrows, as one whose holier feelings deem
That ill so proud a pile did humble monks beseem.

Him, musing as he stood, Rodulfo saw,
  And forth he came to greet the holy guest;
For he was known as one who held the law
  Of Benedict, and each severe behest
So duly kept with such religious care,
That Heaven had oft vouchsafed its wonders to his
                                        prayer.

" Good brother, welcome!» thus Rodulfo cries,
  « In sooth it glads me to behold you here;
It is Gualberto! and mine aged eyes
  Did not deceive me: yet full many a year
Hath slipt away, since last you bade farewell
To me your host and my uncomfortable cell.

«'T was but a sorry welcome then you found,
  And such as suited ill a guest so dear.
The pile was ruinous old, the base unsound;
  It glads me more to bid you welcome here,
For you can call to mind our former state!
Come, brother, pass with me the new Moscera's gate.

So spake the cheerful Abbot, but no smile
  Of answering joy relaxed Gualberto's brow;
He raised his hand and pointed to the pile,
  « Moscera better pleased me then than now!
A palace this, befitting kingly pride!
Will holiness, my friend, in palace pomp abide?»

« Aye,» cries Rodulfo, « 't is a stately place!
  And pomp becomes the house of worship well.
Nay, scowl not round with so severe a face!
  When earthly kings in seats of grandeur dwell,
Where art exhausted decks the sumptuous hall,
Can poor and sordid huts beseem the Lord of all?»

« And ye have rear'd these stately towers on high
  To serve your God!» the monk severe replied.
« It rose from zeal and earnest piety,
  And prompted by no worldly thoughts beside?
Abbot, to him who prays with soul sincere
In humble hermit cell, God will incline his ear.

« Rodulfo! while this haughty building rose,
  Still was the pilgrim welcome at your door?
Did charity relieve the orphans' woes?
  Clothed ye the naked? did ye feed the poor?
He who with alms most succours the distrest,
Proud Abbot! know, he serves his heavenly Father best

« Did they in sumptuous palaces go dwell
  Who first abandon'd all to serve the Lord?
Their place of worship was the desert cell,
  Wild fruits and berries spread their frugal board,
And if a brook, like this, ran murmuring by,
They blest their gracious God, and 'thought it luxury.'»

Then anger darken'd in Rodulfo's face;
  « Enough of preaching,» sharply he replied,
« Thou art grown envious : 't is a common case,
  Humility is made the cloak of pride.
Proud of our home's magnificence are we,
But thou art far more proud in rags and beggary.»

With that Gualberto cried in fervent tone,
  « O, Father, hear me! if this splendid pile
Was for thine honour rear'd, and thine alone,
  Bless it, O Father, with thy fostering smile!
Still may it stand, and never evil know,
Long as beside its walls the eternal stream shall flow.

« But, Lord, if vain and worldly-minded men
  Have wasted here the wealth which thou hast lent,
To pamper worldly pride; frown on it then!
  Soon be thy vengeance manifestly sent!
Let yonder brook, that flows so calm beside,
Now from its base sweep down the unholy house of
                                        pride!»

He said,—and lo, the brook no longer flows!
  The waters pause, and now they swell on high;
High and more high the mass of water grows;
  The affrighted brethren from Moscera fly,
And on their Saints and on their God they call,
For now the mountain bulk o'ertops the convent wall.

It falls, the mountain bulk, with thundering sound!
  Full on Moscera's pile the vengeance falls!
Its lofty tower now rushes to the ground,
  Prone lie its columns now, its high arch'd walls,
Earth shakes beneath the onward-rolling tide,
That from its base swept down the unholy house [1] of
        pride.

.   .   .   .   .   .

Were old Gualberto's reasons built on truth,
  Dear George, or like Moscera's base unsound?
This sure I know, that glad am I, in sooth,
  He only play'd his pranks in foreign ground;
For had he turn'd the stream on England too,
The Vandal monk had spoilt full many a goodly view.

Then Malmesbury's arch had never met my sight,
  Nor Battle's vast and venerable pile;
I had not traversed then with such delight
  The hallowed ruins of our Alfred's isle,
Where many a pilgrim's curse is well bestow'd
On those who rob its walls to mend the turnpike-road.

Wells would have fallen, dear George, our country's
        pride;
  And Canning's stately church been rear'd in vain,
Nor had the traveller Ely's tower descried,
  Which when thou seest far o'er the fenny plain,
Dear George, I counsel thee to turn that way,
Its ancient beauties sure will well reward delay.

And we should never then have heard, I think,
  At evening hour, great Tom's tremendous knell.
The fountain streams that now in Christ-church stink,
  Had niagara'd o'er the quadrangle;
But, as 't was beauty that deserved the flood,
I ween, dear George, thy own old Pompey might have
        stood.

Then had not Westminster, the house of God,
  Served for a concert-room, or signal-post;
Old Thames, obedient to the father's nod,
  Had swept down Greenwich, England's noblest boast;
And, eager to destroy the unholy walls,
Fleet-ditch had roll'd up hill to overwhelm St Paul's.

George, dost thou deem the legendary deeds
  Of Romish saints a useless medley store
Of lies, that he flings time away who reads?
  And wouldst thou rather bid me puzzle o'er
Matter and Mind and all the eternal round,
Plunged headlong down the dark and fathomless pro-
        found?

Now do I bless the man who undertook
  These monks and martyrs to biographize;
And love to ponder o'er his ponderous book,
  The mingle-mangle mass of truth and lies,
Where Angels now, now Beelzebubs appear,
And blind and honest zeal, and holy faith sincere.

All is not very truth, and yet 't were hard
  The fabling Priests for fabling to abuse;
What if a monk, from better theme debarr'd,
  Some pious subject for a tale should chuse,
How some good man the flesh and fiend o'ercame,
His taste methinks, and not his conscience, were to
        blame.

In after years, what he, good Christian, wrote,
  As we write novels to instruct our youth,
Went travelling on, its origin forgot,
  Till at the length it past for gospel-truth.
A fair account! and shouldst thou like the plea,
Thank thou thy valued friend, dear George, who taught
        it me.

All is not false which seems at first a lie.
  Fernan Antolinez, [1] a Spanish knight,
Knelt at the mass, when lo! the troops hard by
  Before the expected hour began the fight.
Though courage, duty, honour, summon'd there,
He chose to forfeit all; not leave the unfinish'd prayer.

But while devoutly thus the unarm'd knight
  Waits till the holy service should be o'er,
Even then the foremost in the furious fight
  Was he beheld to bathe his sword in gore,
First in the van his plumes were seen to play,
And Spain to him decreed the glory of the day.

The truth is told, and all at once exclaim,
  His guardian angel Heaven had deign'd to send;
And thus the tale is handed down to fame.
  Now if our good Sir Fernan had a friend
Who in the hour of danger served him well,
Dear George, the tale is true, and yet no miracle.

I am not one who scan with scornful eyes
  The dreams which make the enthusiast's best de-
        light;
Nor thou the legendary lore despise
  If of Gualberto yet again I write,

---

[1] Era amigo de pobreza, en tanto grado, que sentia mucho, que los Monasterios se edificassen sumptuosamente; y assi visitando el de Moscera y viendo un edificio grande, y elegante, buelto à Rodulpho, que era alli Abad, con el rostro ayrado le dixo: Con lo que has gastado, siguiendo tu parecer, en este magnifico edificio, has quitado el sustento a muchos pobres. Puso los ojos en un pequeño arroyo, que corria alli cerca, y dixo, Dios Omnipotente, que sueles hacer grandes cosas de pequeñas criaturas, yo te ruego, que ven por medio de este pequeño arroyo venganza de este gran edificio. Dixo esto, y fuese de alli como abominando el lugar; y siendo oido, el arroyuelo comenzó a crecer, y fue de suerte, que recogiendo un monte de agua, y tomando de atràs la corriente, vino con tan grande impetu, que llevando piedras y arboles consigo, derribo el edificio. — Flos Sanctorum, por El Maestro Alonso de Villegas.

[1] Aconteció en aquella [*] batalla una cosa digna de memoria. — Fernan Antolinez, hombre noble y muy devoto, oia missa al tiempo que se dió señal de acometer, costumbre ordinaria suya antes de la pelea; por no dexarla començada, se quedó en el templo quando se tocó à la arma. Esta piedad quan agradable fuesse a Dios, se entendió por un milagro. Estávase primero en la Iglesia, despues escondido en su casa, temia no le afrentassen como a cobarde. En tanto, otro à él semejante, es à saber, su Angel bueno, pelea entre los primeros tan valientemente, que la vitoria de aquel dia se atribuyó en gran parte al valor de el dicho Antolinez. Confirmaron e milagro las señales de los golpes, y las manchas de la sangre que se [1] hallaron frescas en sus armas y cavallo. Assi publicado el caso, y sabido lo que passava, quedó mas conocida la inocencia y esfuerço de Autolinez. — Mariana.

Perhaps this miracle, and its obvious interpretation, may have suggested to Florian the circumstance by which his Gonsalvo is prevented from combating and killing the brother of his mistress. Florian was fond of Spanish literature,

[*] Cerca de Santistevan de Gormaz, a la ribera del rio Duero. — A. D. 982.

How first impell'd he sought the convent-cell;
A simple tale it is, ' but one that pleased me well.

*   *   *   *   *   *   *

Fortune had smiled upon Gualberto's birth,
    The heir of Valdespesa's rich domain.
An only child, he grew in years and worth,
    And well repaid a father's anxious pain.
Oft had his sire in battle forced success,
Well for his valour known, and known for haughtiness.

It chanced that one in kindred near allied
    Was slain by his hereditary foe;
Much by his sorrow moved and more by pride,
    The father vow'd that blood for blood should flow,
And from his youth Gualberto had been taught
That with unceasing hate should just revenge be sought.

Long did they wait; at length the tidings came
    That through a lone and unfrequented way,
Soon would Anselmo, such the murderer's name,
    Pass on his journey home, an easy prey.
« Go,» cried the father, « meet him in the wood!»
And young Gualberto went, and laid in wait for blood.

When now the youth was at the forest shade
    Arrived, it drew toward the close of day;
Anselmo haply might be long delay'd,
    And he, already wearied with his way,
Beneath an ancient oak his limbs reclined,
And thoughts of near revenge alone possess'd his mind.

Slow sunk the glorious sun, a roseate light
    Spread o'er the forest from his lingering rays;
The glowing clouds upon Gualberto's sight
    Soften'd in shade,—he could not chuse but gaze;
And now a placid greyness clad the heaven,
Save where the west retain'd the last green light of even.

Cool breathed the grateful air, and fresher now
    The fragrance of the autumnal leaves arose;
The passing gale scarce moved the o'erhanging bough,
    And not a sound disturb'd the deep repose,

Save when a falling leaf came fluttering by,
Save the near brooklet's stream that murmur'd quietly.

Is there who has not felt the deep delight,
    The hush of soul, that scenes like these impart?
The heart they will not soften is not right,
    And young Gualberto was not hard of heart.
Yet sure he thinks revenge becomes him well,
When from a neighbouring church he heard the vesper-bell.

The Catholic who hears that vesper-bell,
    Howe'er employed, must send a prayer to Heaven.
In foreign lands I liked the custom well,
    For with the calm and sober thoughts of even
It well accords; and wert thou journeying there,
It would not hurt thee, George, to join that vesper-prayer.

Gualberto had been duly taught to hold
    Each pious duty with religious care,
And,—for the young man's feelings were not cold,
    He never yet had mist his vesper-prayer.
But strange misgivings now his heart invade,
And when the vesper-bell had ceased he had not pray'd?

And wherefore was it that he had not pray'd?
    The sudden doubt arose within his mind,
And many a former precept then he weigh'd,
    The words of Him who died to save mankind;
How 't was the meek who should inherit heaven,
And man must man forgive, if he would be forgiven.

Troubled at heart, almost he felt a hope,
    That yet some chance his victim might delay,
So as he mused adown the neighbouring slope
    He saw a lonely traveller on his way;
And now he knows the man so much abhorr'd,—
His holier thoughts are gone, he bares the murderous sword.

« The house of Valdespesa gives the blow!
    Go, and our vengeance to our kinsman tell!»—
Despair and terror seized the unarm'd foe,
    And prostrate at the young man's knees he fell,
And stopt his hand and cried, « Oh, do not take
A wretched sinner's life! mercy, for Jesus' sake!»

At that most blessed name, as at a spell,
    Conscience, the God within him, smote his heart.
His hand, for murder raised, unharming fell;
    He felt cold sweat-drops on his forehead start;
A moment mute in holy horror stood,
Then cried, « Joy, joy, my God! I have not shed his blood!»

He raised Anselmo up, and bade him live,
    And bless, for both preserved, that holy name:
And pray'd the astonish'd foeman to forgive
    The bloody purpose led by which he came.
Then to the neighbouring church he sped away,
His over-burden'd soul before his God to lay.

He ran with breathless speed,—he reach'd the door,
    With rapid throbs his feverish pulses swell,—
He came to crave for pardon, to adore
    For grace vouchsafed; before the cross he fell,

' Llamóse el padre Gualberto, y era señor de Valdespesa, que está entre Sena, y Florencia: seguia la milicia; y como le matassen un su deudo cercano injustamente, indignados, assi el hijo, que era ya hombre, como el padre, con mucho cuydado buscavan ocasion, como vengar aquella muerte. Sucedió, que veniendo à Florencia el hijo, con un criado suyo, hombre valiente, y los dos bien armados, à cavallo, vió à su enemigo, y en lugar que era imposible írseles: lo qual considerado por el contrario, y que tenia cierta su muerte, descendió de un cavallo, en que venia, y puesto de rodillas le pidió, juntas las manos, por Jesu-Christo crucificado, le perdonasse la vida. Enternecióse Juan Gualberto, oyendo el nombre de Jesu-Christo crucificado; y dixole, que por amor de aquel Señor, que rogó en la Cruz por los que le pusieron en ella, él le perdonava. Pidióle, que se levantasse, y perdiesse el temer, que ya no por enemigo, sino por amigo le queria, y que de Dios, por quien hacia esto, esperava el premio. Passó adelante Gualberto; y viendo una Iglesia en un monte cerca de Florencia, llamada de San Miniato, que era de Monges negros, entró en ella para dar gracias à Jesu-Christo nuestro Señor por la merced, que le havia hecho en favorecerle, de que perdonasse, y no tomasse venganza de su enemigo: púsose de rodillas delante de un Crucifixo, el qual, viendolo él, y otros que estavan presentes, desde la Cruz inclinó la cabeza à Gualberto, como agradeciendo, y dándole gracias, de que por su amor huviesse perdonado la vida á su enemigo. Descubrióse el caso, y fue público, y muy celebrado, y el Crucifixo fue tenido en grande reverencia en aquella Iglesia de S. Miniato. Quedó Juan Gualberto de este acaecimiento, trocado en otro varon, y determinó dexar el mundo, y las cosas perecederas de él.—*Flos Sanctorum.*

And raised his swimming eyes, and thought that there
He saw the imaged Christ smile favouring on his prayer.

A blest illusion! from that very night
The monk's austerest life devout he led;
And still he felt the enthusiast's deep delight,
Seraphic visions floated round his head;
The joys of heaven foretasted fill'd his soul,
And still the good man's name adorns the sainted roll.
1799.

LYRIC POEMS.

TO CONTEMPLATION.

Καὶ παγὰς φιλέοιμι τὸν ἐγγύθεν ἦχον ἀκούειν
Ἁ τέρπει ψοφέοισα τὸν ἄγγιχον, οὐχὶ ταράσσει.
ΜΟΣΚΟΣ.

FAINT gleams the evening radiance through the sky,
The sober twilight dimly darkens round;
In short quick circles the shrill bat flits by,
And the slow vapour curls along the ground.

Now the pleased eye from yon lone cottage sees
On the green mead the smoke long-shadowing play;
The Red-breast on the blossom'd spray
Warbles wild her latest lay,
And lo! the Rooks to yon high-tufted trees
Wing, in long files vociferous, their way.
Calm CONTEMPLATION, 't is thy favourite hour!
Come, tranquillizing Power!

I view thee on the calmy shore
When Ocean stills his waves to rest;
Or when slow-moving on the surges hoar
Meet with deep hollow roar
And whiten o'er his breast;
And when the Moon with softer radiance gleams,
And lovelier heave the billows in her beams.

When the low gales of evening moan along
I love with thee to feel the calm cool breeze,
And roam the pathless forest wilds among,
Listening the mellow murmur of the trees
Full-foliaged, as they lift their arms on high,
And wave their shadowy heads in wildest melody.

Or lead me where amid the tranquil vale
The broken stream flows on in silver light;
And I will linger where the gale
O'er the bank of violets sighs,
Listening to hear its soften'd sounds arise;
And hearken the dull beetle's drowsy flight,
And watch the horn-eyed snail
Creep o'er his long moon-glittering trail,
And mark where radiant through the night
Shines in the grass-green hedge the glow-worm's
living light.

Thee, meekest Power! I love to meet,
As oft with solitary pace
The shatter'd Abbey's hallowed rounds I trace,
And listen to the echoings of my feet.

Or on some half-demolish'd tomb,
Whose warning texts anticipate my doom,
Mark the clear orb of night
Cast through the storying glass a faintly-varied light.

Nor will I not in some more gloomy hour
Invoke with fearless awe thine holier power,
Wandering beneath the sainted pile
When the blast moans along the darksome aisle,
And clattering patters all around
The midnight shower with dreary sound.

But sweeter 't is to wander wild
By melancholy dreams beguiled,
While the summer moon's pale ray
Faintly guides me on my way
To some lone romantic glen,
Far from all the haunts of men;
Where no noise of uproar rude
Breaks the calm of solitude;
But soothing Silence sleeps in all,
Save the neighbouring waterfall,
Whose hoarse waters falling near
Load with hollow sounds the ear,
And with down-dasht torrent white
Gleam hoary through the shades of night.
Thus wandering silent on and slow,
I'll nurse Reflection's sacred woe,
And muse upon the happier day
When Hope would weave her visions gay,
Ere FANCY, chill'd by adverse fate,
Left sad REALITY my mate.

O CONTEMPLATION! when to Memory's eyes
The visions of the long-past days arise,
Thy holy power imparts the best relief,
And the calm'd Spirit loves the joy of grief.
1792.

TO HORROR.

I extract the following picture of consummate horror from the notes to a poem, *written in twelve-syllable verse*, upon the campaign of 1794 and 1795; it was during the retreat to Deventer. « We could not proceed a hundred yards without perceiving the dead bodies of men, women, children, and horses in every direction. One scene made an impression upon my memory which time will never be able to efface. Near another cart we perceived a stout-looking man, and a beautiful young woman with an infant, about seven months old, at the breast, all three frozen and dead. The mother had most certainly expired in the act of suckling her child; as with one breast exposed, she lay upon the drifted snow, the milk to all appearance in a stream, drawn from the nipple by the babe, and instantly congealed. The infant seemed as if its lips had but just then been disengaged, and it reposed its little head upon the mother's bosom, with an overflow of milk, frozen as it trickled from the mouth; their countenances were perfectly composed and fresh, resembling those of persons in a sound and tranquil slumber.»
The following description of a field of battle is in the words of one who passed over the field of Jemappe, after Dumourier's victory.—« It was on the third day after the victory obtained by Gen. Dumourier over the Austrians, that I rode across the field of battle. The scene lies on a waste common, rendered then more dreary by the desertion of the miserable hovels before occupied by peasants. Every thing that resembled a human habitation was desolated, and for the most part they had been burnt or pulled down, to prevent their affording shelter to the posts of the contending armies. The ground was ploughed up by the wheels of the artillery and waggons; every thing like herbage was trodden into mire; broken carriages, arms, accoutrements, dead horses and men were strewed over the heath. *This was the third day after the*

battle: it was the beginning of November, and for three days a bleak wind and heavy rain had continued incessantly. There were still remaining alive several hundred of horses and of the human victims of that dreadful fight. I can speak with certainty of having seen more than four hundred men still living, unsheltered, without food, and without any human assistance, most of them confined to the spot where they had fallen by broken limbs. The two armies had proceeded, and abandoned these miserable wretches to their fate. Some of the dead persons appeared to have expired in the act of embracing each other. Two young French officers, who were brothers, had crawled under the side of a dead horse, where they had contrived a kind of shelter by means of a cloak; they were both mortally wounded, and groaning for each other. One very fine young man had just strength enough to drag himself out of a hollow partly filled with water, and was laid upon a little hillock groaning with agony; *a grape-shot had cut across the upper part of his belly, and he was keeping in his bowels with a handkerchief and hat.* He begged of me for God's sake to end his misery! he complained of dreadful thirst. I filled him the hat of a dead soldier with water, which he nearly drank off at once, and left him to that end of his wretchedness which could not be far distant.»

I hope I have always felt and expressed an honest and christian abhorrence of wars, and of the systems that produce them; but my ideas of their immediate horrors fell infinitely short of this authentic picture.

Τὶν γὰρ ποταείσομαι
τὰν καὶ σκύλικες τρομέοντι
Ἐρχομέναν νεκύων ἀνά τ' ἠρία, καὶ μέλαν αἷμα.
ΘΕΟΚΡΙΤΟΣ.

DARK Horror! hear my call!
Stern Genius, hear from thy retreat
On some old sepulchre's moss-canker'd seat
Beneath the Abbey's ivied wall
That trembles o'er its shade;
Where wrapt in midnight gloom, alone,
Thou lovest to lie and hear
The roar of waters near,
And listen to the deep dull groan
Of some perturbed sprite
Borne fitful on the heavy gales of night.

Or whether o'er some wide waste hill
Thou mark'st the traveller stray,
Bewilder'd on his lonely way,
When, loud and keen and chill,
The evening winds of winter blow,
Drifting deep the dismal snow.

Or if thou followest now on Greenland's shore,
With all thy terrors, on the lonely way
Of some wreck'd mariner, where to the roar
Of herded bears, the floating ice-hills round
Pour their deep echoing sound,
And by the dim drear Boreal light
Givest half his dangers to the wretch's sight.

Or if thy fury form,
When o'er the midnight deep
The dark-wing'd tempests sweep,
Watches from some high cliff the increasing storm,
Listening with strange delight,
As the black billows to the thunder rave,
When by the lightning's light
Thou seest the tall ship sink beneath the wave.

Dark HORROR! bear me where the field of fight
Scatters contagion on the tainted gale,
When, to the Moon's faint beam,

On many a carcase shine the dews of night,
And a dead silence stills the vale,
Save when at times is heard the glutted Raven's scream.

Where some wreck'd army from the Conqueror's might
Speed their disastrous flight,
With thee, fierce Genius! let me trace their way,
And hear at times the deep heart-groan
Of some poor sufferer left to die alone,
His sore wounds smarting with the winds of night;
And we will pause, where, on the wild,
The mother to her frozen breast,
On the heap'd snows reclining, clasps her child,
And with him sleeps, chill'd to eternal rest!

Black HORROR! speed we to the bed of Death,
Where he, whose murderous power afar
Blasts with the myriad plagues of war,
Struggles with his last breath;
Then to his wildly-starting eyes
The phantoms of the murder'd rise;
Then on his frensied ear
Their groans for vengeance and the Demon's yell
In one heart-maddening chorus swell;
Cold on his brow convulsing stands the dew,
And night eternal darkens on his view.

HORROR! I call thee yet once more!
Bear me to that accursed shore,
Where round the stake impaled the Negro writhes.
Assume thy sacred terrors then! dispense
The blasting gales of Pestilence!
Arouse the race of Afric, holy Power!
Lead them to vengeance! and in that dread hour
When ruin rages wide,
I will behold and smile by MERCY's side.

1791.

TO A FRIEND.

Oh my faithful Friend!
Oh early chosen, ever found the same,
And trusted and beloved! once more the verse
Long destined, always obvious to thine ear,
Attend indulgent,

AKENSIDE.

AND wouldst thou seek the low abode
Where PEACE delights to dwell!
Pause, Traveller, on thy way of life!
With many a snare and peril rife
Is that long labyrinth of road!
Dark is the vale of years before;
Pause, Traveller, on thy way!
Nor dare the dangerous path explore
Till old EXPERIENCE comes to lend his leading ray.

Not he who comes with lanthorn light
Shall guide thy groping pace aright
With faltering feet and slow;
No! let him rear the torch on high,
And every maze shall meet thine eye,
And every snare and every foe;
Then with steady step and strong,
Traveller, shalt thou march along.

Though POWER invite thee to her hall,
Regard not thou her tempting call,
Her splendour's meteor glare;
Though courteous Flattery there await,
And Wealth adorn the dome of State,
There stalks the midnight spectre CARE:
PEACE, Traveller, doth not sojourn there.

If FAME allure thee, climb not thou
To that steep mountain's craggy brow
Where stands her stately pile;
For far from thence doth PEACE abide,
And thou shalt find FAME's favouring smile
Cold as the feeble Sun on Hecla's snow-clad side.

And, Traveller! as thou hopest to find
That low and loved abode,
Retire thee from the thronging road,
And shun the mob of human-kind.
Ah! hear how old EXPERIENCE schools,
« Fly, fly the crowd of Knaves and Fools,
And thou shalt fly from woe!
The one thy heedless heart will greet
With Judas-smile, and thou wilt meet
In every Fool a Foe!»

So safely mayst thou pass from these,
And reach secure the home of PEACE,
And FRIENDSHIP find thee there.
No happier state can mortal know,
No happier lot can Earth bestow,
If LOVE thy lot shall share.
Yet still CONTENT with him may dwell
Whom HYMEN will not bless,
And VIRTUE sojourn in the cell
Of HERMIT HAPPINESS.
1793.

REMEMBRANCE.

The remembrance of Youth is a sigh.—ALI.

MAN hath a weary pilgrimage
As through the world he wends,
On every stage from youth to age
Still discontent attends;
With heaviness he casts his eye
Upon the road before,
And still remembers with a sigh
The days that are no more.
To school the little exile goes,
Torn from his mother's arms,—
What then shall soothe his earliest woes,
When novelty hath lost its charms,
Condem'd to suffer through the day
Restraints which no rewards repay,
And cares where love has no concern:
Hope lengthens as she counts the hours
Before his wish'd return.
From hard controul and tyrant rules,
The unfeeling discipline of schools,
In thought he loves to roam,
And tears will struggle in his eye

While he remembers with a sigh
The comforts of his home.

Youth comes; the toils and cares of life
Torment the restless mind;
Where shall the tired and harass'd heart
Its consolation find?
Then is not Youth, as Fancy tells,
Life's summer prime of joy?
Ah no! for hopes too long delay'd,
And feelings blasted or betray'd,
The fabled bliss destroy;
And Youth remembers with a sigh
The careless days of Infancy.

Maturer Manhood now arrives,
And other thoughts come on,
But with the baseless hopes of Youth
Its generous warmth is gone;
Cold calculating cares succeed,
The timid thought, the wary deed,
The dull realities of Truth;
Back on the past he turns his eye,
Remembering with an envious sigh
The happy dreams of Youth.

So reaches he the latter stage
Of this our mortal pilgrimage,
With feeble step and slow;
New ills that latter stage await,
And old Experience learns too late
That all is vanity below.
Life's vain delusions are gone by,
Its idle hopes are o'er,
Yet age remembers with a sigh
The days that are no more.
1798.

THE SOLDIER'S WIFE.
DACTYLICS.

WEARY way-wanderer, languid and sick at heart,
Travelling painfully over the rugged road,
Wild-visaged Wanderer! ah for thy heavy chance!

Sorely thy little one drags by thee bare-footed,
Cold is the baby that hangs at thy bending back,
Meagre and livid and screaming its wretchedness.

¹ Woe-begone mother, half anger, half agony,
As over thy shoulder thou lookest to hush the babe,
Bleakly the blinding snow beats in thy hagged face.

Thy husband will never return from the war again,
Cold is thy hopeless heart even as Charity!—
Cold are thy famish'd babes.—God help thee, widowed
One!
1795.

THE WIDOW.
SAPPHICS.

COLD was the night wind, drifting fast the snow fell,
Wide were the downs and shelterless and naked,
When a poor Wanderer struggled on her journey,
Weary and way-sore.
¹ This stanza was supplied by S. T. COLERIDGE.

Dreary were the downs, more dreary her reflections;
Cold was the night-wind, colder was her bosom:
She had no home, the world was all before her,
    She had no shelter.

Fast o'er the heath a chariot rattled by her,
« Pity me ! » feebly cried the lonely wanderer.
« Pity me, strangers ! lest with cold and hunger
    Here I should perish.

« Once I had friends,—but they have all forsook me !
Once I had parents,—they are now in Heaven !
I had a home once—I had once a husband—
    Pity me, strangers !

« I had a home once—I had once a husband—
I am a widow poor and broken-hearted ! »
Loud blew the wind, unheard was her complaining,
    On drove the chariot.

Then on the snow she laid her down to rest her;
She heard a horseman, « Pity me ! » she groaned out;
Loud was the wind, unheard was her complaining,
    On went the horseman.

Worn out with anguish, toil and cold and hunger,
Down sunk the Wanderer, sleep had seized her senses;
There did the traveller find her in the morning;
    God had released her.
                   1796.

THE CHAPEL BELL.

Lo I, the man who erst the Muse did ask
    Her deepest notes to swell the Patriot's meeds,
Am now enforced, a far unfitter task,
    For cap and gown to leave my minstrel weeds;
For yon dull tone that tinkles on the air
Bids me lay by the lyre and go to morning prayer.

Oh how I hate the sound ! it is the knell
    That still a requiem tolls to Comfort's hour;
And loth am I at Superstition's bell,
    To quit or Morpheus' or the Muse's bower :
Better to lie and doze, than gape amain,
Hearing still mumbled o'er the same eternal strain.

Thou tedious herald of more tedious prayers,
    Say, hast thou ever summoned from his rest
One being wakening to religious cares?
    Or roused one pious transport in the breast?
Or rather, do not all reluctant creep
To linger out the hour in listlessness or sleep?

I love the bell, that calls the poor to pray,
    Chiming from village church its cheerful sound,
When the sun smiles on Labour's holy-day,
    And all the rustic train are gather'd round,
Each deftly dizen'd in his Sunday's best,
And pleased to hail the day of piety and rest.

And when, dim shadowing o'er the face of day,
    The mantling mists of even-tide rise slow,
As through the forest gloom I wend my way,
    The minster curfew's sullen voice I know,
And pause, and love its solemn toll to hear,
As made by distance soft it dies upon the ear.

Nor with an idle nor unwilling ear
    Do I receive the early passing-bell;
For, sick at heart with many a secret care
    When I lie listening to the dead man's knell,
I think that in the grave all sorrows cease,
And would full fain recline my head and be at peace.

But thou, memorial of monastic gall !
    What fancy sad or lightsome hast thou given ?
Thy vision-scaring sounds alone recall
    The prayer that trembles on a yawn to heaven !
And this Dean's gape, and that Dean's nasal tone,
And Roman rites retain'd, though Roman faith be
    flown.
                   1793.

TO HYMEN.

God of the torch, whose soul-illuming flame
Beams brightest radiance o'er the human heart,
    Of many a woe the cure,
    Of many a joy the source;

To thee I sing, if haply may the Muse
Pour forth the song unblamed from these dull haunts,
    Where never beams thy torch
    To cheer the sullen scene.

I pour the song to thee, though haply doom'd
Alone and unbeloved to waste my days,
    Though doom'd perchance to die
    Alone and unbewail'd.

Yet will the lark albeit in cage enthrall'd
Send out her voice to greet the morning sun,
    As wide his cheerful beams
    Light up the landscape round;

When high in heaven she hears the caroling,
The prisoner too begins her morning hymn,
    And hails the beam of joy,
    Of joy to her denied.

Friend to each better feeling of the soul,
I sing to thee, for many a joy is thine,
    And many a Virtue comes
    To join thy happy train.

Lured by the splendour of thy sacred torch,
The beacon-light of bliss, young Love draws near,
    And leads his willing slaves
    To wear thy flowery chain.

And chasten'd Friendship comes, whose mildest sway
Shall cheer the hour of age, where fainter burn
    The fading flame of Love,
    The fading flame of Life.

Parent of every bliss, the busy hand
Of Fancy oft will paint in brightest hues
    How calm, how clear, thy torch
    Illumes the wintry hour:

Will paint the wearied labourer at that hour,
When friendly darkness yields a pause to toil,
    Returning blithely home
    To each domestic joy;

Will paint the well-trimm'd fire, the frugal meal
Prepared with fond solicitude to please;
  The ruddy children round
  Climbing the father's knee.

And oft will Fancy rise above the lot
Of honest Poverty, and dream how man
  Nor rich, nor poor, enjoys
  His best and happiest state;

When toil no longer irksome and constrain'd
By hard necessity, but comes to please,
  To vary the still hour
  Of tranquil happiness.

Why, Fancy, wilt thou, o'er the lovely scene
Pouring thy vivid hues, why, sorceress sweet!
  Soothe sad reality
  With visionary bliss!

Turn thou thine eyes to where the hallowed light
Of Learning shines! ah rather lead thy son
  Along her mystic paths
  To drink the sacred spring.

Lead calmly on along the unvaried path
To solitary Age's drear abode;—
  Is it not Happiness
  That gives the sting to Death?

Well then is he whose unembitter'd years
Are waning on in lonely listlessness.
  If Life hath little joy,
  Death hath for him no sting.

        1794.

WRITTEN ON THE FIRST OF DECEMBER, 1793.

  Though now no more the musing ear
  Delights to listen to the breeze,
  That lingers o'er the green-wood shade,
   I love thee, Winter! well.

  Sweet are the harmonies of Spring,
  Sweet is the Summer's evening gale,
  And sweet the Autumnal winds that shake
   The many-colour'd grove.

  And pleasant to the sober'd soul
  The silence of the wintry scene,
  When Nature shrouds herself, entranced
   In deep tranquillity.

  Not undelightful now to roam
  The wild heath sparkling on the sight;
  Not undelightful now to pace
   The forest's ample rounds,

  And see the spangled branches shine,
  And mark the moss of many a hue
  That varies the old tree's brown bark,
   Or o'er the grey stone spreads.

  And mark the cluster'd berries bright
  Amid the holly's gay green leaves;
  The ivy round the leafless oak
   That clasps its foliage close.

So Virtue, diffident of strength,
Clings to Religion's firmer aid,
And by Religion's aid upheld,
  Endures calamity.

Nor void of beauties now the spring,
Whose waters hid from summer-sun
Have soothed the thirsty pilgrim's ear
  With more than melody.

The green moss shines with icy glare;
The long grass bends its spear-like form;
And lovely is the silvery scene
  When faint the sun-beams smile.

Reflection too may love the hour
When Nature, hid in Winter's grave,
No more expands the bursting bud,
  Or bids the flowret bloom,

For Nature soon in Spring's best charms,
Shall rise revived from Winter's grave,
Expand the bursting bud again,
  And bid the flower re-bloom.

WRITTEN ON THE FIRST OF JANUARY, 1794.

  Come, melancholy Moralizer, come!
  Gather with me the dark and wintry wreath;
   With me engarland now
   The Sepulchre of Time!

  Come, Moralizer, to the funeral song!
  I pour the dirge of the Departed Days;
   For well the funeral song
   Befits this solemn hour.

  But hark! even now the merry bells ring round
  With clamorous joy to welcome in this day,
   This consecrated day,
   To Mirth and Indolence.

  Mortal! whilst Fortune with benignant hand,
  Fills to the brim thy cup of happiness,
   Whilst her unclouded sun
   Illumes thy summer day,

  Canst thou rejoice,—rejoice that Time flies fast?
  That night shall shadow soon thy summer-sun?
   That swift the stream of Years
   Rolls to Eternity?

  If thou hast wealth to gratify each wish,
  If power be thine, remember what thou art!
   Remember thou art Man,
   And Death thine heritage;

  Hast thou known Love! doth Beauty's better sun
  Cheer they fond heart with no capricious smile,
   Her eye all eloquence,
   All harmony her voice?

  Oh state of happiness!—hark! how the gale
  Moans deep and hollow o'er the leafless grove!
   Winter is dark and cold;
   Where now the charms of Spring!

85

Sayst thou that Fancy paints the future scene
In hues too sombrous? that the dark-stoled Maid
    With stern and frowning front
    Appals the shuddering soul?

And wouldst thou bid me court her fairy form,
When, as she sports her in some happier mood,
    Her many-coloured robes
    Float varying in the sun?

Ah! vainly does the Pilgrim, whose long road
Leads o'er the barren mountain's storm-vext height,
    With anxious gaze survey
    The quiet vale, far off.

Oh there are those who love the pensive song,
To whom all sounds of Mirth are dissonant!
    They at this solemn hour
    Will love to contemplate!

For hopeless Sorrow hails the lapse of Time,
Rejoicing when the fading orb of day
    Is sunk again in night,
    That one day more is gone.

And he who bears Affliction's heavy load
With patient piety, well pleased he knows
    The World a pilgrimage,
    The grave the inn of rest.

WRITTEN ON SUNDAY MORNING.

Go thou and seek the House of Prayer!
I to the Woodlands wend, and there
In lovely Nature see the GOD OF LOVE.
    The swelling organ's peal
    Wakes not my soul to zeal,
Like the wild music of the wind-swept grove.
The gorgeous altar and the mystic vest
Rouse not such ardour in my breast,
    As where the noon-tide beam
    Flash'd from the broken stream,
Quick vibrates on the dazzled sight;
    Or where the cloud-suspended rain
    Sweeps in shadows o'er the plain;
Or when reclining on the cliff's huge height
I mark the billows burst in silver light.
    Go thou and seek the House of Prayer!
    I to the woodlands shall repair,
    Feed with all Nature's charms mine eyes,
    And hear all Nature's melodies.
The primrose bank shall there dispense
Faint fragrance to the awaken'd sense;
The morning beams that life and joy impart,
Shall with their influence warm my heart,
And the full tear that down my cheek will steal,
Shall speak the prayer of praise I feel!

Go thou and seek the House of Prayer!
I to the Woodlands bend my way,
    And meet RELIGION there!
She needs not haunt the high-arch'd dome to pray,
Where storied windows dim the doubtful day:
    With LIBERTY she loves to rove,
    Wide o'er the heathy hill or cowslipt dale;
Or seek the shelter of the embowering grove,
    Or with the streamlet wind along the vale.

Sweet are these scenes to her; and when the Night
Pours in the north her silver streams of light,
She woos Reflection in the silent gloom,
And ponders on the world to come.

                      1795.

THE RACE OF BANQUO.

FLY, son of Banquo! Fleance, fly!
Leave thy guilty sire to die!
O'er the heath the stripling fled,
The wild storm howling round his head;
Fear mightier through the shades of night
Urged his feet, and wing'd his flight;
And still he heard his father's cry,
Fly, son of Banquo! Fleance, fly!

Fly, son of Banquo! Fleance! fly!
Leave thy guilty sire to die!
On every blast was heard the moan,
The anguish'd shriek, the death-fraught groan;
Loathly night-hags join the yell,
And see—the midnight rites of Hell!

Forms of magic! spare my life!
Shield me from the murderer's knife!
Before me dim in lurid light
Float the phantoms of the night—
Behind I hear my Father cry,
Fly, son of Banquo—Fleance, fly!

Parent of the sceptred race,
Boldly tread the circled space;
Boldly Fleance venture near—
Sire of monarchs—spurn at fear.

Sisters, with prophetic breath,
Pour we now the dirge of Death!
       * * * * * *

                      1793.

TO RECOVERY.

RECOVERY, where art thou?
Daughter of Heaven, where shall we seek thy help?
Upon what hallow'd fountain hast thou laid,
    O Nymph adored, thy spell?

By the grey ocean's verge,
Daughter of Heaven, we seek thee, but in vain;
We find no healing in the breeze that sweeps
    The thymy mountain's brow.

Where are the happy hours,
The sunshine where, that cheer'd the morn of life!
For HEALTH is fled, and with her fled the joys
    Which made existence dear.

I saw the distant hills
Smile in the radiance of the orient beam,
And gazed delighted that anon our feet
    Should visit scenes so fair.

I look'd abroad at noon,
The shadow and the storm were on the hills;
The crags, which like a faery fabric shone,
    Darkness had overwhelm'd.

On you, ye coming years,
So fairly shone the April gleam of Hope;
So darkly o'er the distance, late so bright,
Now settle the black clouds.

Come thou and chase away
Sorrow and Pain, the persecuting Powers
Who make the melancholy day so long,
So long the restless night.

Shall we not find thee here,
Recovery, on the ocean's breezy strand?
Is there no healing in the gales that sweep
The thymy mountain's brow?

I look for thy approach,
O life-preserving Power! as one who strays
Alone in darkness o'er the pathless marsh
Watches the dawn of day.

July, 1799.

YOUTH AND AGE.

With cheerful step the traveller
Pursues his early way,
When first the dimly-dawning east
Reveals the rising day.

He bounds along his craggy road,
He hastens up the height,
And all he sees and all he hears,
Administer delight.

And if the mist, retiring slow,
Roll round its wavy white,
He thinks the morning vapours hide
Some beauty from his sight.

But when behind the western clouds
Departs the fading day,
How wearily the traveller
Pursues his evening way!

Sorely along the craggy road
His painful footsteps creep;
And slow, with many a feeble pause,
He labours up the steep.

And if the mists of night close round,
They fill his soul with fear;
He dreads some unseen precipice,
Some hidden danger near.

So cheerfully does youth begin
Life's pleasant morning stage,
Alas! the evening traveller feels
The fears of weary age!

1798.

THE OAK OF OUR FATHERS.

Alas for the Oak of our Fathers, that stood
In its beauty, the glory and pride of the wood!

It grew and it flourish'd for many an age,
And many a tempest wreak'd on it its rage;
But when its strong branches were bent with the blast,
It struck its root deeper, and flourish'd more fast.

Its head tower'd on high, and its branches spread round.
For its roots were struck deep, and its heart was sound,
The bees o'er its honey-dew'd foliage play'd,
And the beasts of the forest fed under its shade.

The Oak of our Fathers to Freedom was dear,
Its leaves were her crown, and its wood was her spear:
Alas for the Oak of our Fathers, that stood
In its beauty, the glory and pride of the wood!

There crept up an ivy and clung round the trunk,
It struck in its mouth and the juices it drunk;
The branches grew sickly deprived of their food,
And the oak was no longer the pride of the wood

The foresters saw and they gather'd around,
The roots still were fast, and the heart still was sound;
They lopt off the boughs that so beautiful spread,
But the ivy they spared on its vitals that fed.

No longer the bees o'er its honey-dews play'd,
Nor the beasts of the forest fed under its shade;
Lopt and mangled the trunk in its ruin is seen,
A monument now what its beauty has been.

The Oak has received its incurable wound,
They have loosen'd the roots, though the heart may be sound;
What the travellers at distance green-flourishing see,
Are the leaves of the ivy that poison'd the tree.

Alas for the Oak of our Fathers, that stood
In its beauty, the glory and pride of the wood!

1798.

THE BATTLE OF PULTOWA.

On Vorska's glittering waves
The morning sun-beams play;
Pultowa's walls are throng'd
With eager multitudes;
Athwart the dusty vale
They strain their aching eyes,
Where to the fight moves on
The Conqueror Charles, the iron-hearted Swede.

Him Famine hath not tamed,
The tamer of the brave;
Him Winter hath not quell'd;
When man by man his veteran troops sunk down,
Frozen to their endless sleep,
He held undaunted on;
Him Pain hath not subdued.
What though he mounts not now
The fiery steed of war?
Borne on a litter to the fight he goes.

Go, iron-hearted King!
Full of thy former fame.
Think how the humbled Dane
Crouch'd to thy victor sword;
Think how the wretched Pole
Resign'd his conquer'd crown;
Go, iron-hearted King!
Let Narva's glory swell thy haughty breast,—
The death-day of thy glory, Charles, hath dawn'd

Proud Swede, the Sun hath risen
That on thy shame shall set!

Now bend thine head from heaven,
Now Patkul be revenged!
For o'er that bloody Swede
Ruin hath raised his arm;
For ere the night descends,
His veteran host subdued,
His laurels blasted to revive no more,
He flies before the foe!

Long years of hope deceived
That conquered Swede must prove;
Patkul, thou art avenged!
Long years of idleness
That restless soul must bear;
Patkul, thou art avenged!
The Despot's savage anger took thy life,
Thy death has stabb'd his fame.
1798.

THE TRAVELLER'S RETURN.

SWEET to the morning traveller
The song amid the sky,
Where twinkling in the dewy light
The skylark soars on high.

And cheering to the traveller
The gales that round him play,
When faint and heavily he drags
Along his noon-tide way.

And when beneath the unclouded sun
Full wearily toils he,
The flowing water makes to him
A soothing melody.

And when the evening light decays,
And all is calm around,
There is sweet music to his ear
In the distant sheep-bell's sound.

But oh! of all delightful sounds
Of evening or of morn
The sweetest is the voice of Love,
That welcomes his return.
1798

THE OLD MAN'S COMFORTS,

AND HOW HE GAINED THEM.

You are old, Father William, the young man cried,
The few locks which are left you are grey;
You are hale, Father William, a hearty old man,
Now tell me the reason, I pray.

In the days of my youth, Father William replied,
I remember'd that youth would fly fast,
And abused not my health and my vigour at first,
That I never might need them at last.

You are old, Father William, the young man cried,
And pleasures with youth pass away,
And yet you lament not the days that are gone,
Now tell me the reason, I pray.

In the days of my youth, Father William replied,
I remember'd that youth could not last;
I thought of the future whatever I did,
That I never might grieve for the past.

You are old, Father William, the young man cried,
And life must be hastening away;
You are cheerful, and love to converse upon death!
Now tell me the reason I pray.

I am cheerful, young man, Father William replied,
Let the cause thy attention engage;
In the days of my youth I remember'd my God!
And He hath not forgotten my age.
1799.

TRANSLATION OF A GREEK ODE ON ASTRONOMY,

WRITTEN BY S. T. COLERIDGE, FOR THE PRIZE AT CAMBRIDGE, 1793.

HAIL, venerable NIGHT!
O first-created, hail!
Thou who art doom'd in thy dark breast to veil
The dying beam of light.
The eldest and the latest thou,
Hail, venerable NIGHT!
Around thine ebon brow,
Glittering plays with lightning rays
A wreath of flowers of fire.
The varying clouds with many a hue attire
Thy many-tinted veil.
Holy are the blue graces of thy zone!
But who is he whose tongue can tell
The dewy lustres which thine eyes adorn?
Lovely to some the blushes of the Morn;
To some the glory of the Day,
When, blazing with meridian ray,
The gorgeous Sun ascends his highest throne;
But I with solemn and severe delight
Still watch thy constant car, immortal NIGHT!

For then to the celestial Palaces
Urania leads, Urania, she
The Goddess who alone
Stands by the blazing throne,
Effulgent with the light of Deity.
Whom Wisdom, the Creatrix, by her side
Placed on the heights of yonder sky,
And smiling with ambrosial love, unlock'd
The depths of Nature to her piercing eye.
Angelic myriads struck their harps around,
And with triumphant song
The host of Stars, a beauteous throng,
Around the ever-living Mind
In Jubilee their mystic dance begun;
When at thy leaping-forth, O Sun!
The Morning started in affright,
Astonish'd at thy birth, her Child of Light!

Hail, O Urania, hail!
Queen of the Muses! Mistress of the Song!
For thou didst deign to leave the heavenly throng.
As earthward thou thy steps wert bending,
A ray went forth and harbinger'd thy way:

All Ether laugh'd with thy descending.
Thou hadst wreath'd thy hair with roses,
The flower that in the immortal bower
Its deathless bloom discloses.
Before thine awful mien, compelled to shrink,
Fled Ignorance abash'd with all her brood;
Dragons, and Hags of baleful breath,
Fierce Dreams, that wont to drink
The Sepulchre's black blood;
Or on the wings of storms
Riding in fury forms,
Shriek'd to the mariner the shriek of Death.

I boast, O Goddess, to thy name
That I have raised the pile of fame!
Therefore to me be given
To roam the starry path of Heaven,
To charioteer with wings on high,
And to rein in the Tempests of the sky.

Chariots of happy Gods! Fountains of Light!
Ye Angel-Temples bright!
May I unblamed your flamy thresholds tread?
I leave Earth's lowly scene;
I leave the Moon serene,
The lovely Queen of Night;
I leave the wide domains,
Beyond where Mars his fiercer light can fling,
And Jupiter's vast plains,
(The many-belted King;)
Even to the solitude where Saturn reigns,
Like some stern tyrant to just exile driven;
Dim-seen the sullen power appears
In that cold solitude of Heaven,
And slow he drags along
The mighty circle of long-lingering years.

Nor shalt thou escape my sight,
Who at the threshold of the sun-trod domes
Art trembling,—youngest Daughter of the Night!
And you, ye fiery-tressed strangers! you,
Comets who wander wide,
Will I along your pathless way pursue,
Whence bending I may view
The Worlds whom elder Suns have vivified.

For Hope with loveliest visions soothes my mind,
That even in Man, Life's winged power,
When comes again the natal hour,
Shall on heaven-wandering feet,
In undecaying youth,
Spring to the blessed seat;
Where round the fields of Truth
The fiery Essences for ever feed;
And o'er the ambrosial mead,
The breezes of serenity
Silent and soothing glide for ever by.

There, Priest of Nature! dost thou shine,
NEWTON! a King among the Kings divine.
Whether with harmony's mild force,
He guides along its course
The axle of some beauteous star on high;
Or gazing in the spring
Ebullient with creative energy,
Feels his pure breast with rapturous joy possest,
Inebriate in the holy ecstasy!

I may not call thee mortal then, my soul!
Immortal longings lift thee to the skies:
Love of thy native home inflames thee now
With pious madness wise.
Know then thyself! expand thy wings divine!
Soon mingled with thy fathers thou shalt shine
A star amid the starry throng,
A God the Gods among.
1801.

GOOSEBERRY-PIE.

A PINDARIC ODE.

GOOSEBERRY-PIE is best.
Full of the theme, O Muse, begin the song!
What though the sunbeams of the West
Mature within the Turtle's breast
Blood glutinous and fat of verdant hue?
What though the Deer bound sportively along
O'er springey turf, the Park's elastic vest?
Give them their honours due,—
But Gooseberry-Pie is best.

Behind his oxen slow
The patient Ploughman plods,
And as the Sower followed by the clods
Earth's genial womb received the living seed.
The rains descend, the grains they grow;
Saw ye the vegetable ocean
Roll its green ripple to the April gale?
The golden waves with multitudinous motion
Swell o'er the summer vale?

It flows through Alder banks along
Beneath the copse that hides the hill;
The gentle stream you cannot see,
You only hear its melody,
The stream that turns the Mill.
Pass on a little way, pass on,
And you shall catch its gleam anon;
And hark! the loud and agonizing groan
That makes its anguish known,
Where tortured by the Tyrant Lord of Meal
The brook is broken on the Wheel!

Blow fair, blow fair, thou orient gale!
On the white bosom of the sail
Ye winds enamour'd, lingering lie!
Ye waves of ocean spare the bark,
Ye tempests of the sky!
From distant realms she comes to bring
The sugar for my Pie.
For this on Gambia's arid side
The Vulture's feet are scaled with blood,
And Beelzebub beholds with pride,
His darling planter brood.

First in the spring thy leaves were seen,
Thou beauteous bush, so early green!
Soon ceased thy blossoms little life of love.
O safer than Alcides-conquer'd tree
That grew the pride of that Hesperian grove,—
No Dragon does there need for thee
With quintessential sting to work alarms,
And guard thy fruit so fine,

Thou vegetable Porcupine!
And didst thou scratch thy tender arms,
O Jane! that I should dine!

The flour, the sugar, and the fruit,
Commingled well, how well they suit,
And they were well bestow'd.
O Jane, with truth I praise your Pie,
And will not you in just reply
Praise my Pindaric Ode?

TO A BEE.

THOU wert out betimes, thou busy, busy Bee!
As abroad I took my early way,
Before the Cow from her resting-place
Had risen up and left her trace
On the meadow, with dew so grey,
Saw I thee, thou busy, busy Bee.

Thou wert working late, thou busy, busy Bee!
After the fall of the Cistus flower,
When the Primrose of evening was ready to burst,
I heard thee last, as I saw thee first;
In the silence of the evening hour,
Heard I thee, thou busy, busy Bee.

Thou art a miser, thou busy, busy Bee!
Late and early at employ;
Still on thy golden stores intent,
Thy summer in heaping and hoarding is spent
What thy winter will never enjoy;
Wise lesson this for me, thou busy, busy Bee!

Little dost thou think, thou busy, busy Bee!
What is the end of thy toil.
When the latest flowers of the ivy are gone,
And all thy work for the year is done,
Thy master comes for the spoil.
Woe then for thee, thou busy, busy Bee!
1799.

TO A SPIDER.

SPIDER! thou needst not run in fear about
To shun my curious eyes;
I won't humanely crush thy bowels out
Lest thou shouldst eat the flies;
Nor will I roast thee with a damn'd delight
Thy strange instinctive fortitude to see,
For there is one who might
One day roast me.

Thou art welcome to a Rhymer sore-perplext,
The subject of his verse:
There 's many a one who on a better text
Perhaps might comment worse.
Then shrink not, old Free-Mason, from my view,
But quietly like me spin out the line;
Do thou thy work pursue
As I will mine.

Weaver of snares, thou emblemest the ways
Of Satan, Sire of lies;
Hell's huge black Spider, for mankind he lays
His toils, as thou for flies.

When Betty's busy eye runs round the room,
Woe to that nice geometry if seen!
But where is he whose broom
The earth shall clean?

Spider! of old thy flimsy webs were thought,
And 't was a likeness true,
To emblem laws in which the weak are caught,
But which the strong break through.
And if a victim in thy toils is ta'en,
Like some poor client is that wretched fly;
I 'll warrant thee thou 'lt drain
His life-blood dry.

And is not thy weak work like human schemes
And care on earth employ'd?
Such are young hopes and Love's delightful dreams
So easily destroyed!
So does the Statesman, whilst the Avengers sleep,
Self-deem'd secure, his wiles in secret lay,
Soon shall Destruction sweep
His work away.

Thou busy labourer! one resemblance more
Shall yet the verse prolong,
For, Spider, thou art, like the Poet, poor
Whom thou hast help'd in song.
Both busily our needful food to win,
We work, as Nature taught, with ceaseless pains,
Thy bowels thou dost spin,
I spin my brains.

THE DESTRUCTION OF JERUSALEM.

THE rage of Babylon is roused,
The King puts forth his strength;
And Judah bends the bow
And points her arrows for the coming war.

Her walls are firm, her gates are strong,
Her youth gird on the sword;
High are her chiefs in hope,
For Egypt soon will send the promised aid.

But who is he whose voice of woe
Is heard amid the streets?
Whose ominous voice proclaims
Her strength and arms and promised succours vain?

His meagre cheek is pale and sunk,
Wild is his hollow eye,
Yet fearful its strong glance;
And who could bear the anger of his frown?

PROPHET of GOD! in vain thy lips
Proclaim the woe to come!
In vain thy warning voice
Summon'd her rulers timely to repent!

The Ethiop changes not his skin.
Impious and idiot still
The rulers spurn thy voice,
And now the measure of their crimes is full.

And now around Jerusalem
The countless foes appear;
Far as the eye can reach
Spreads the wide horror of the circling siege.

Why is the warrior's cheek so pale?
    Why droops the gallant youth,
    Who late so high of heart
Made sharp his javelin for the welcome war?

'T is not for terror that his eye
    Swells with the struggling woe;
    Oh! he could bear his ills,
Or rush to death and in the grave have peace.

His parents do not ask for food,
    But they are weak with want;
    His wife has given her babes
Her wretched meal,—she utters no complaint.

The consummating hour is come!
    Alas for Solyma!
    How is she desolate,—
She that was great among the nations, fallen!

And thou—thou miserable King—
    Where is thy trusted flock,
    Thy flock so beautiful,
Thy father's throne, the temple of thy God?

Repentance calls not back the past;
    It will not awake again
    Thy murdered sons to life,
Or bring back vision to thy blasted sight!

Thou wretched, childless, blind, old man—
    Heavy thy punishment!
    Dreadful thy present woes—
Alas more dreadful thy remember'd guilt!

                                    1798.

———

THE DEATH OF WALLACE.

Joy, joy in London now!
He goes, the rebel Wallace goes to death:
At length the traitor meets the traitor's doom,
    Joy, joy in London now!

He on a sledge is drawn,
His strong right arm unweapon'd and in chains,
And garlanded around his helmless head
    The laurel wreath of scorn.

They throng to view him now
Who in the field had fled before his sword,
Who at the name of Wallace once grew pale
    And falter'd out a prayer.

Yes! they can meet his eye,
That only beams with patient courage now;
Yes! they can gaze upon those manly limbs,
    Defenceless now and bound.

And that eye did not shrink
As he beheld the pomp of infamy;
Nor did one rebel feeling shake those limbs
    When the last moment came.

What though suspended sense
Was by their damned cruelty revived?
What though ingenious vengeance lengthen'd life
    To feel protracted death?

What though the hangman's hand
Graspt in his living breast the heaving heart?—
In the last agony, the last sick pang,
    Wallace had comfort still.

He call'd to mind his deeds
Done for his country in the embattled field;
He thought of that good cause for which he died,
    And that was joy in death!

Go, Edward, triumph now!
Cambria is fallen, and Scotland's strength is crush'd;
On Wallace, on Llewellyn's mangled limbs
    The fowls of Heaven have fed.

Unrivalled, unopposed,
Go, Edward, full of glory to thy grave!
The weight of Patriot blood upon thy soul,
    Go, Edward, to thy God!

                                    1798.

———

THE SPANISH ARMADA.

CLEAR shone the morn, the gale was fair,
    When from Coruna's crowded port
With many a cheerful shout and loud acclaim
    The huge Armada past.

To England's shores their streamers point,
    To England's shores their sails are spread;
They go to triumph o'er the sea-girt land,
    And Rome hath blest their arms.

Along the ocean's echoing verge,
    Along the mountain range of rocks,
The clustering multitudes behold their pomp,
    And raise the votive prayer.

Commingling with the ocean's roar
    Ceaseless and hoarse their murmurs rise,
And soon they trust to see the winged bark
    That bears good tidings home.

The watch-tower now in distance sinks,
    And now Galicia's mountain rocks
Faint as the far-off clouds of evening lie,
    And now they fade away.

Each like some moving citadel,
    On through the waves they sail sublime;
And now the Spaniards see the silvery cliffs,
    Behold the sea-girt land!

O fools! to think that ever foe
    Should triumph o'er the sea-girt land!
O fools! to think that ever Britain's sons
    Should wear the stranger's yoke!

For not in vain hath Nature rear'd
    Around her coast those silvery cliffs;
For not in vain old Ocean spreads his waves
    To guard his favourite isle!

On come her gallant mariners!
    What now avail Rome's boasted charms?
Where are the Spaniard's vaunts of eager wrath?
    His hopes of conquest now?

And hark! the angry winds arise,
Old Ocean heaves his angry waves;
The winds and waves against the invaders fight
To guard the sea-girt land.

Howling around his palace-towers
The Spanish Despot hears the storm;
He thinks upon his navies far away,
And boding doubts arise.

Long, over Biscay's boisterous surge
The watchman's aching eye shall strain!
Long shall he gaze, but never winged bark
Shall bear good tidings home.

1798.

ST BARTHOLOMEW'S DAY.

THE night is come, no fears disturb
The dreams of innocence;
They trust in kingly faith and kingly oaths,
They sleep,—alas! they sleep!

Go to the palace, wouldst thou know
How hideous night can be;
Eye is not closed in those accursed walls,
Nor heart at quiet there.

The Monarch from the window leans,
He listens to the night,
And with a horrible and eager hope
Awaits the midnight bell.

Oh he has hell within him now!
God, always art thou just!
For innocence can never know such pangs
As pierce successful guilt.

He looks abroad, and all is still.
Hark!—now the midnight bell
Sounds through the silence of the night alone,—
And now the signal-gun!

Thy hand is on him, righteous God!
He hears the frantic shriek,
He hears the glorying yells of massacre,
And he repents too late.

He hears the murderer's savage shout,
He hears the groan of death;
'In vain they fly,—soldiers defenceless now,
Women, old men, and babes.

Righteous and just art thou, O God!
For at his dying hour
Those shrieks and groans re-echoed in his ear,
He heard that murderous yell!

They throng'd around his midnight couch,
The phantoms of the slain!—
It prey'd like poison on his powers of life!—
Righteous art thou, O God!

Spirits! who suffer'd at that hour
For freedom and for faith,
Ye saw your country bent beneath the yoke,
Her faith and freedom crush'd!

And like a giant from his sleep
Ye saw when France awoke;
Ye saw the people burst their double chain,
And ye had joy in Heaven!

1798.

THE HOLLY TREE.

O READER! hast thou ever stood to see
The Holly Tree?
The eye that contemplates it well perceives
Its glossy leaves
Order'd by an intelligence so wise,
As might confound the Atheist's sophistries.

Below, a circling fence, its leaves are seen
Wrinkled and keen;
No grazing cattle through their prickly round
Can reach to wound;
But as they grow where nothing is to fear,
Smooth and unarm'd the pointless leaves appear.

I love to view these things with curious eyes,
And moralize:
And in this wisdom of the Holly Tree
Can emblems see
Wherewith perchance to make a pleasant rhyme,
One which may profit in the after-time.

Thus, though abroad perchance I might appear
Harsh and austere,
To those who on my leisure would intrude
Reserved and rude,
Gentle at home amid my friends I 'd be
Like the high leaves upon the Holly Tree.

And should my youth, as youth is apt, I know,
Some harshness show,
All vain asperities I day by day
Would wear away,
Till the smooth temper of my age should be
Like the high leaves upon the Holly Tree.

And as when all the summer trees are seen
So bright and green,
The Holly leaves their fadeless hues display
Less bright than they;
But when the bare and wintry woods we see,
What then so cheerful as the Holly Tree?

So serious should my youth appear among
The thoughtless throng,
So would I seem amid the young and gay
More grave than they,
That in my age as cheerful I might be
As the green winter of the Holly Tree.

1798.

THE EBB TIDE.

SLOWLY thy flowing tide
Came in, Old Avon! scarcely did mine eyes,
As watchfully I roam'd thy green-wood side,
Behold the gentle rise.

With many a stroke and strong
The labouring boatmen upward plied their oars,
And yet the eye beheld them labouring long
Between thy winding shores.

Now down thine ebbing tide
The unlabour'd boat falls rapidly along;
The solitary helmsman sits to guide,
And sings an idle song.

Now o'er the rocks that lay
So silent late, the shallow current roars;
Fast flow thy waters on their sea-ward way
Through wider-spreading shores.

Avon! I gaze and know
The lesson emblem'd in thy varying way;
It speaks of human joys that rise so slow,
So rapidly decay.

Kingdoms which long have stood,
And slow to strength and power attain'd at last,
Thus from the summit of high fortune's flood
Ebb to their ruin fast.

Thus like thy flow appears
Time's tardy course to manhood's envied stage;
Alas! how hurryingly the ebbing years
Then hasten to old age!

1799.

THE COMPLAINTS OF THE POOR.

And wherefore do the Poor complain?
The rich man ask'd of me.—
Come walk abroad with me, I said,
And I will answer thee.

'T was evening, and the frozen streets
Were cheerless to behold,
And we were wrapt and coated well,
And yet we were a-cold.

We met an old bare-headed man,
His locks were few and white;
I ask'd him what he did abroad
In that cold winter's night;

'T was bitter keen indeed, he said,
But at home no fire had he,
And therefore he had come abroad
To ask for charity.

We met a young bare-footed child,
And she begg'd loud and bold;
I ask'd her what she did abroad
When the wind it blew so cold;

She said her father was at home,
And he lay sick a-bed,
And therefore was it she was sent
Abroad to beg for bread.

We saw a woman sitting down
Upon a stone to rest,
She had a baby at her back
And another at her breast;

I ask'd her why she loiter'd there
When the night-wind was so chill;
She turn'd her head and bade the child
That scream'd behind, be still.

She told us that her husband served,
A soldier, far away,
And therefore to her parish she
Was begging back her way.

We met a girl, her dress was loose
And sunken was her eye,
Who with a wanton's hollow voice
Address'd the passers-by;

I ask'd her what there was in guilt
That could her heart allure
To shame, disease, and late remorse;
She answer'd, she was poor.

I turn'd me to the rich man then,
For silently stood he,—
You ask'd me why the poor complain,
And these have answer'd thee!

1798.

TO MARY.

Mary! ten chequer'd years have past
Since we beheld each other last;
Yet, Mary, I remember thee,
Nor canst thou have forgotten me.

The bloom was then upon thy face,
Thy form had every youthful grace;
I too had then the warmth of youth,
And in our hearts was all its truth.

We conversed, were there others by,
With common mirth and random eye;
But when escaped the sight of men,
How serious was our converse then!

Our talk was then of years to come,
Of hopes which ask'd a humble doom,
Themes which to loving thoughts might move,
Although we never spake of love.

At our last meeting sure thy heart
Was even as loth as mine to part;
And yet we little thought that then
We parted—not to meet again.

Long, Mary! after that adieu,
My dearest day-dreams were of you!
In sleep I saw you still, and long
Made you the theme of secret song.

When manhood and its cares came on,
The humble hopes of youth were gone;
And other hopes and other fears
Effaced the thoughts of happier years.

Meantime through many a varied year
Of thee no tidings did I hear,
And thou hast never heard my name
Save from the vague reports of fame.

But then I trust detraction's lie
Hath kindled anger in thine eye;
And thou my praise wert proud to see,—
My name should still be dear to thee.

86

Ten years have held their course; thus late
I learn the tidings of thy fate;
A Husband and a Father now,
Of thee, a Wife and Mother thou.

And, Mary, as for thee I frame
A prayer which hath no selfish aim,
No happier lot can I wish thee
Than such as Heaven hath granted me.

1802.

TO A FRIEND,

ENQUIRING IF I WOULD LIVE OVER MY YOUTH AGAIN.

Do I regret the past?
Would I again live o'er
The morning hours of life?
Nay, William! nay, not so!
In the warm joyance of the summer sun
I do not wish again
The changeful April day.
Nay, William! nay, not so!
Safe haven'd from the sea
I would not tempt again
The uncertain ocean's wrath.
Praise be to Him who made me what I am,
Other I would not be.

Why is it pleasant then to sit and talk
Of days that are no more?
When in his own dear home
The traveller rests at last,
And tells how often in his wanderings
The thought of those far off
Hath made his eyes o'erflow
With no unmanly tears;
Delighted he recalls
Through what fair scenes his lingering feet have trod:
But ever when he tells of perils past,
And troubles now no more,
His eyes most sparkle, and a readier joy
Flows thankful from his heart.

No, William, no, I would not live again
The morning hours of life;
I would not be again
The slave of hope and fear;
I would not learn again
The wisdom by Experience hardly taught.
To me the past presents
No object for regret;
To me the present gives
All cause for full content.
The future,—it is now the cheerful noon,
And on the sunny-smiling fields I gaze
With eyes alive to joy;
When the dark night descends,
I willingly shall close my weary lids,
Secure to wake again.

1798.

THE DEAD FRIEND.

Not to the grave, not to the grave, my Soul,
Descend to contemplate
The form that once was dear!
Feed not on thoughts so loathly horrible!

The Spirit is not there
Which kindled that dead eye,
Which throbb'd in that cold heart,
Which in that motionless hand
Hath met thy friendly grasp.
The Spirit is not there!
It is but lifeless, perishable flesh
That moulders in the grave;
Earth, air, and water's ministering particles
Now to the elements
Resolved, their uses done.
Not to the grave, not to the grave, my Soul,
Follow thy friend beloved,
The Spirit is not there!

Often together have we talk'd of death;
How sweet it were to see
All doubtful things made clear;
How sweet it were with powers
Such as the Cherubim,
To view the depth of Heaven!
O Edmund! thou hast first
Begun the travel of Eternity!
I gaze amid the stars,
And think that thou art there,
Unfetter'd as the thought that follows thee.

And we have often said how sweet it were
With unseen ministry of angel power
To watch the friends we loved.
Edmund! we did not err!
Sure I have felt thy presence! Thou hast given
A birth to holy thought,
Has kept me from the world unstain'd and pure.
Edmund! we did not err!
Our best affections here
They are not like the toys of infancy;
The Soul outgrows them not;
We do not cast them off;
Oh if it could be so,
It were indeed a dreadful thing to die!

Not to the grave, not to the grave, my Soul,
Follow thy friend beloved!
But in the lonely hour,
But in the evening walk,
Think that he companies thy solitude;
Think that he holds with thee
Mysterious intercourse;
And though Remembrance wake a tear,
There will be joy in grief.

THE RETROSPECT.

As on I journey through the vale of years,
By hopes enliven'd, or deprest by fears,
Allow me, Memory, in thy treasured store,
To view the days that will return no more.
And yes! before thine intellectual ray,
The clouds of mental darkness melt away!
As when, at earliest day's awakening dawn
The hovering mists obscure the dewy lawn,
O'er all the landscape spread their influence chill,
Hang o'er the vale, and wood, and hide the hill;
Anon, slow-rising comes the orb of day,
Slow fade the shadowy mists and roll away,

The prospect opens on the traveller's sight,
And hills and vales and woods reflect the living light.

O thou, the mistress of my future days,
Accept thy minstrel's retrospective lays:
To whom the minstrel and the lyre belong,
Accept, my EDITH, Memory's pensive song.
Of long-past days I sing, ere yet I knew
Or thought and grief, or happiness and you;
Ere yet my infant heart had learnt to prove
The cares of life, the hopes and fears of love.

Corston, twelve years in various fortunes fled
Have past with restless progress o'er my head,
Since in thy vale beneath the master's rule
I dwelt an inmate of the village school.
Yet still will Memory's busy eye retrace
Each little vestige of the well-known place;
Each wonted haunt and scene of youthful joy,
Where merriment has cheer'd the careless boy;
Well-pleased will fancy still the spot survey
Where once he triumph'd in the childish play,
Without one care where every morn he rose,
Where every evening sunk to calm repose.
Large was the house, though fallen by varying fate
From its old grandeur and manorial state.
Lord of the manor, here the jovial Squire
Once call'd his tenants round the crackling fire;
Here while the glow of joy suffused his face,
He told his ancient exploits in the chase,
And, proud his rival sportsmen to surpass,
He lit again the pipe, and fill'd again the glass.

But now no more was heard at early morn
The echoing clangor of the huntsman's horn;
No more the eager hounds with deep'ning cry
Leapt round him as they knew their pastime nigh;
The Squire no more obey'd the morning call,
Nor favourite spaniels fill'd the sportsman's hall;
For he, the last descendant of his race,
Slept with his fathers, and forgot the chase.
There now in petty empire o'er the school
The mighty master held despotic rule;
Trembling in silence all his deeds we saw,
His look a mandate, and his word a law;
Severe his voice, severe and stern his mien,
And wonderous strict he was, and wonderous wise I ween.

Even now through many a long, long year I trace
The hour when first with awe I view'd his face;
Even now recall my entrance at the dome,—
'T was the first day I ever left my home!
Years intervening have not worn away
The deep remembrance of that wretched day,
Nor taught me to forget my earliest fears,
A mother's fondness, and a mother's tears;
When close she prest me to her sorrowing heart,
As loth as even I myself to part;
And I, as I beheld her sorrows flow,
With painful effort hid my inward woe.
But time to youthful troubles brings relief,
And each new object weans the child from grief.
Like April showers the tears of youth descend,
Sudden they fall, and suddenly they end;
A fresher pleasure cheers the following hour
As brighter shines the sun after the April shower.

Methinks even now the interview I see,
The Mistress's glad smile, the Master's glee;
Much of my future happiness they said,
Much of the easy life the scholars led,
Of spacious play-ground and of wholesome air,
The best instruction and the tenderest care;
And when I followed to the garden-door
My father, till through tears I saw no more,—
How civilly they soothed my parting pain,
And how they never spake so civilly again.

Why loves the soul on earlier years to dwell,
When memory spreads around her saddening spell,
When discontent, with sullen gloom o'ercast,
Turns from the present and prefers the past?
Why calls reflection to my pensive view
Each trifling act of infancy anew,
Each trifling act with pleasure pondering o'er,
Even at the time when trifles please no more?
Yet is remembrance sweet, though well I know
The days of childhood are but days of woe;
Some rude restraint, some petty tyrant sours
The tranquil calm of childhood's easy hours;
Yet is it sweet to call those hours to mind,—
Those easy hours for ever left behind;
Ere care began the spirit to oppress,
When ignorance itself was happiness.

Such was my state in those remember'd years
When one small acre bounded all my fears;
And therefore still with pleasure I recall
The tapestried school, the bright-brown boarded hall,
The murmuring brook, that every morning saw
The due observance of the cleanly law,
The walnuts, where, when favour would allow,
Full oft I wont to search each well-stript bough;
The crab-tree, whence we hid the secret hoard
With roasted crabs to deck the wintry board,
These trifling objects then my heart possest,
These trifling objects still remain imprest;
So when with unskill'd hand the idle hind
Carves his rude name within the sapling's rind,
In after years the peasant lives to see
The expanding letters grow as grows the tree;
Though every winter's desolating sway
Shake the hoarse grove and sweep the leaves away,
That rude inscription uneffaced will last,
Unalter'd by the storm or wintry blast.

Oh while well pleased the letter'd traveller roams
Among old temples, palaces, and domes,
Strays with the Arab o'er the wreck of time
Where erst Palmyra's towers arose sublime,
Or marks the lazy Turk's lethargic pride
And Grecian slavery on Ilyssus' side,
Oh be it mine aloof from public strife
To mark the changes of domestic life,
The alter'd scenes where once I bore a part,
Where every change of fortune strikes the heart.
As when the merry bells with echoing sound
Proclaim the news of victory around,
Rejoicing patriots run the news to spread
Of glorious conquest and of thousands dead,
All join the loud huzza with eager breath,
And triumph in the tale of blood and death;
But if extended on the battle-plain,
Cut off in conquest some dear friend be slain,

Affection then will fill the sorrowing eye,
And suffering Nature grieve that one should die.

Cold was the morn; and bleak the wintry blast
Blew o'er the meadow, when I saw thee last.
My bosom bounded as I wander'd round
With silent step the long-remember'd ground,
Where I had loiter'd out so many an hour,
Chased the gay butterfly, and cull'd the flower,
Sought the swift arrow's erring course to trace,
Or with mine equals vied amid the chase.
I saw the church where I had slept away
The tedious service of the summer day;
Or, listening sad to all the preacher told,
In winter waked and shiver'd with the cold.
Oft have my footsteps roam'd the sacred ground
Where heroes, kings, and poets sleep around,
Oft traced the mouldering castle's ivied wall,
Or aged convent tottering to its fall,
Yet never had my bosom felt such pain,
As, Corston, when I saw thy scenes again;
For many a long-lost pleasure came to view,
For many a long-past sorrow rose anew;
Where whilom all were friends I stood alone,
Unknowing all I saw, of all I saw unknown.

There, where my little hands were wont to rear
With pride the earliest sallad of the year;
Where never idle weed to spring was seen,
Rank thorns and nettles rear'd their heads obscene:
Still all around and sad, I saw no more
The playful group, nor heard the playful roar;
There echoed round no shout of mirth and glee,
It seem'd as though the world were changed like me!
Enough! it boots not on the past to dwell,—
Fair scene of other years, a long farewell!
Rouse up, my soul! it boots not to repine,
Rouse up! for worthier feelings should be thine;
Thy path is plain and straight,—that light is given,—
Onward in faith—and leave the rest to Heaven.
1794.

THE PAUPER'S FUNERAL.

WHAT! and not one to heave the pious sigh!
Not one whose sorrow-swoln and aching eye,
For social scenes, for life's endearments fled,
Shall drop a tear and dwell upon the dead!
Poor wretched Outcast! I will weep for thee,
And sorrow for forlorn humanity.
Yes, I will weep; but not that thou art come
To the stern sabbath of the silent tomb:
For squalid Want, and the black scorpion Care,
Heart-withering fiends! shall never enter there.
I sorrow for the ills thy life has known,
As through the world's long pilgrimage, alone,
Haunted by Poverty and woe-begone,
Unloved, unfriended, thou didst journey on:
Thy youth in ignorance and labour past,
And thine old age all barrenness and blast!
Hard was thy Fate, which, while it doom'd to woe
Denied thee wisdom to support the blow;
And robb'd of all its energy thy mind,
Ere yet it cast thee on thy fellow-kind,
Abject of thought, the victim of distress,
To wander in the world's wide wilderness.

Poor Outcast, sleep in peace! the wintry storm
Blows bleak no more on thine unshelter'd form;
Thy woes are past; thou restest in the tomb;—
I pause—and ponder on the days to come.
1795.

ON MY OWN

MINIATURE PICTURE,

Taken at Two Years of Age.

AND I was once like this? that glowing cheek
Was mine, those pleasure-sparkling eyes; that brow
Smooth as the level lake, when not a breeze
Dies o'er the sleeping surface!—Twenty years
Have wrought strange alteration! Of the friends
Who once so dearly prized this miniature,
And loved it for its likeness, some are gone
To their last home; and some, estranged in heart,
Beholding me, with quick-averted glance
Pass on the other side! But still these hues
Remain unalter'd, and these features wear
The look of Infancy and Innocence.
I search myself in vain, and find no trace
Of what I was: those lightly arching lines
Dark and o'erhanging now; and that sweet face
Settled in these strong lineaments!—There were
Who formed high hopes and flattering ones of thee,
Young Robert! for thine eye was quick to speak
Each opening feeling: should they not have known,
If the rich rainbow on the morning cloud
Reflects its radiant dyes, the husbandman
Beholds the ominous glory, and foresees
Impending storms!—They augur'd happily,
That thou didst love each wild and wond'rous tale
Of faery fiction, and thine infant tongue
Lisp'd with delight the godlike deeds of Greece
And rising Rome; therefore they deem'd forsooth,
That thou shouldst tread PREFERMENT's pleasant path.
Ill-judging ones! they let thy little feet
Stray in the pleasant paths of POESY,
And when thou shouldst have prest amid the crowd,
There didst thou love to linger out the day,
Loitering beneath the laurel's barren shade.
SPIRIT OF SPENSER! was the wanderer wrong?
1796.

ON THE DEATH OF

A FAVOURITE OLD SPANIEL.

AND they have drown'd thee then at last! poor Phillis!
The burden of old age was heavy on thee,
And yet thou shouldst have lived! What though thine
eye
Was dim, and watch'd no more with eager joy
The wonted call that on thy dull sense sunk
With fruitless repetition, the warm Sun
Might still have cheer'd thy slumber: thou didst love
To lick the hand that fed thee, and though past
Youth's active season, even Life itself
Was comfort. Poor old friend! how earnestly
Would I have pleaded for thee! thou hadst been
Still the companion of my childish sports;
And as I roam'd o'er Avon's woody cliffs,
From many a day-dream has thy short quick bark

Recall'd my wandering soul. I have beguiled
Often the melancholy hours at school,
Sour'd by some little tyrant, with the thought
Of distant home, and I remember'd then
Thy faithful fondness: for not mean the joy,
Returning at the pleasant holidays,
I felt from thy dumb welcome. Pensively
Sometimes have I remark'd thy slow decay,
Feeling myself changed too, and musing much
On many a sad vicissitude of Life!
Ah, poor companion! when thou followedst last
Thy master's parting footsteps to the gate
Which closed for ever on him, thou didst lose
Thy truest friend, and none was left to plead
For the old age of brute fidelity!
But fare thee well! Mine is no narrow creed;
And He who gave thee being did not frame
The mystery of life to be the sport
Of merciless Man! There is another world
For all that live and move—a better one!
Where the proud bipeds, who would fain confine
INFINITE GOODNESS to the little bounds
Of their own charity, may envy thee.

1796.

ON A LANDSCAPE OF

GASPAR POUSSIN.

Poussin! how pleasantly thy pictured scenes
Beguile the lonely hour! I sit and gaze
With lingering eye, till charmed FANCY Makes
The lovely landscape live, and the rapt soul
From the foul haunts of herded human-kind
Flies far away with spirit speed, and tastes
The untainted air, that with the lively hue
Of health and happiness illumes the cheek
Of mountain LIBERTY. My willing soul
All eager follows on thy faery flights,
FANCY! best friend; whose blessed witcheries
With loveliest prospects cheat the traveller
O'er the long wearying desert of the world.
Nor dost thou, FANCY! with such magic mock
My heart, as, demon born, old Merlin knew,
Or Alquif, or Zarzafiel's sister sage,
Whose vengeful anguish for so many a year
Held in the jacinth sepulchre entranced
Lisuart the Grecian, pride of chivalry.
Friend of my lonely hours! thou leadest me
To such calm joys as Nature, wise and good,
Proffers in vain to all her wretched sons;
Her wretched sons who pine with want amid
The abundant earth, and blindly bow them down
Before the Moloch shrines of WEALTH and POWER,
AUTHORS of EVIL. Oh, it is most sweet
To medicine with thy wiles the wearied heart,
Sick of reality. The little pile
That tops the summit of that craggy hill
Shall be my dwelling: craggy is the hill
And steep; yet through yon hazels upward leads
The easy path, along whose winding way
Now close embower'd I hear the unseen stream
Dash down, anon behold its sparkling foam
Gleam through the thicket: and ascending on
Now pause me to survey the goodly vale
That opens on my vision. Half way up

Pleasant it were upon some broad smooth rock
To sit and sun myself, and look below,
And watch the goatherd down yon high-bank'd path
Urging his flock grotesque; and bidding now
His lean rough dog from some near cliff go drive
The straggler; while his barkings loud and quick
Amid their trembling bleat arising oft,
Fainter and fainter from the hollow road
Send their far echoes, till the waterfall,
Hoarse bursting from the cavern'd cliff beneath,
Their dying murmurs drown. A little yet
Onward, and I have gain'd the upmost height.
Fair spreads the vale below: I see the stream
Stream radiant on beneath the noontide sky.
A passing cloud darkens the bordering steep,
Where the town-spires behind the castle towers
Rise graceful; brown the mountain in its shade,
Whose circling grandeur, part by mists conceal'd,
Part with white rocks resplendent in the sun
Should bound mine eyes,—aye, and my wishes too,
For I would have no hope or fear beyond.
The empty turmoil of the worthless world,
Its vanities and vices, would not vex
My quiet heart. The traveller, who beheld
The low tower of the little pile, might deem
It were the house of God; nor would he err
So deeming, for that home would be the home
Of PEACE and LOVE, and they would hallow it
To HIM. Oh, life of blessedness! to reap
The fruit of honourable toil, and bound
Our wishes with our wants! Delightful thoughts,
That soothe the solitude of maniac HOPE,
Ye leave her to reality awaked,
Like the poor captive, from some fleeting dream
Of friends and liberty and home restored,
Startled, and listening as the midnight storm
Beats hard and heavy through his dungeon bars.

1796.

AUTUMN.

NAY, William, nay, not so! the changeful year
In all its due successions to my sight
Presents but varied beauties, transient all,
All in their season good. These fading leaves,
That with their rich variety of hues
Make yonder forest in the slanting sun
So beautiful, in you awake the thought
Of winter,—cold, drear winter, when these trees
Each like a fleshless skeleton shall stretch
Its bare brown boughs; when not a flower shall spread
Its colours to the day, and not a bird
Carol its joyaunce,—but all nature wear
One sullen aspect, bleak and desolate,
To eye, ear, feeling, comfortless alike.
To me their many-colour'd beauties speak
Of times of merriment and festival,
The year's best holiday: I call to mind
The school-boy days, when in the falling leaves
I saw with eager hope the pleasant sign
Of coming Christmas; when at morn I took
My wooden kalendar, and counting up
Once more its often-told account, smooth'd off
Each day with more delight the daily notch.
To you the beauties of the autumnal year

Make mournful emblems, and you think of man
Doom'd to the grave's long winter, spirit-broken,
Bending beneath the burthen of his years,
Sense-dull'd and fretful, «full of aches and pains,»
Yet clinging still to life.   To me they show
The calm decay of nature when the mind
Retains its strength, and in the languid eye
Religion's holy hopes kindle a joy
That makes old age look lovely.   All to you
Is dark and cheerless; you in this fair world
See some destroying principle abroad,
Air, earth, and water full of living things,
Each on the other preying; and the ways
Of man, a strange perplexing labyrinth,
Where crimes and miseries, each producing each,
Render life loathsome, and destroy the hope
That should in death bring comfort.   Oh, my friend,
That thy faith were as mine! that thou couldst see
Death still producing life, and evil still
Working its own destruction; couldst behold
The strifes and troubles of this troubled world
With the strong eye that sees the promised day
Dawn through this night of tempest! All things then
Would minister to joy; then should thine heart
Be heal'd and harmonized, and thou wouldst feel
God, always, every where, and all in all.
                                   1798.

THE VICTORY.

HARK,—how the church-bells' thundering harmony
Stuns the glad ear! tidings of joy have come,
Good tidings of great joy! two gallant ships
Met on the element,—they met, they fought
A desperate fight!—good tidings of great joy!
Old England triumph'd! yet another day
Of glory for the ruler of the waves!
For those who fell, 't was in their country's cause,
They have their passing paragraphs of praise,
And are forgotten.
                    There was one who died
In that day's glory, whose obscurer name
No proud historian's page will chronicle.
Peace to his honest soul! I read his name,
'T was in the list of slaughter, and blest God
The sound was not familiar to mine ear.
But it was told me after that this man
Was one whom lawful violence[1] had forced
From his own home and wife and little ones,
Who by his labour lived; that he was one
Whose uncorrupted heart could keenly feel
A husband's love, a father's anxiousness;
That from the wages of his toil he fed
The distant dear ones, and would talk of them
At midnight when he trod the silent deck
With him he valued,—talk of them, of joys
Which he had known,—oh God! and of the hour
When they should meet again, till his full heart,
His manly heart, at last would overflow,
Even like a child's with very tenderness.
Peace to his honest spirit! suddenly
It came, and merciful the ball of death,
For it came suddenly and shattered him,
And left no moment's agonizing thought

[1] The person alluded to was pressed into the service.

On those he loved so well.
                         He ocean-deep
Now lies at rest.   Be Thou her comforter
Who art the widow's friend!   Man does not know
What a cold sickness made her blood run back
When first she heard the tidings of the fight;
Man does not know with what a dreadful hope
She listened to the names of those who died;
Man does not know, or knowing will not heed,
With what an agony of tenderness
She gazed upon her children, and beheld
His image who was gone.   O God! be Thou,
Who art the widow's friend, her comforter!
                                   1798.

HISTORY.

THOU chronicle of crimes! I read no more;
For I am one who willingly would love
His fellow-kind.   O gentle Poesy,
Receive me from the court's polluted scenes,
From dungeon horrors, from the fields of war,
Receive me to your haunts,—that I may nurse
My nature's better feelings, for my soul
Sickens at man's misdeeds!
                          I spake, when lo!
There stood before me, in her majesty,
Clio, the strong-eyed Muse.   Upon her brow
Sate a calm anger.   Go, young man, she cried,
Sigh among myrtle bowers, and let thy soul
Effuse itself in strains so sorrowful sweet,
That love-sick Maids may weep upon thy page,
Pleased with delicious sorrow.   Oh shame! shame!
Was it for this I waken'd thy young mind?
Was it for this I made thy swelling heart
Throb at the deeds of Greece, and thy boy's eye
So kindle when that glorious Spartan died?
Boy! boy! deceive me not!—What if the tale
Of murder'd millions strike a chilling pang;
What if Tiberius in his island stews,
And Philip at his beads, alike inspire
Strong anger and contempt: hast thou not risen
With nobler feelings,—with a deeper love
For Freedom? Yes, if righteously thy soul
Loathes the black history of human crimes
And human misery, let that spirit fill
Thy song, and it shall teach thee, boy! to raise
Strains such as Cato might have deign'd to hear,
As Sidney in his hall of bliss may love.
                                   1798.

THE SOLDIER'S FUNERAL.

IT is the funeral march.   I did not think
That there had been such magic in sweet sounds!
Hark! from the blacken'd cymbal that dead tone!—
It awes the very rabble multitude;
They follow silently, their earnest brows
Lifted in solemn thought.   'T is not the pomp
And pageantry of death that with such force
Arrests the sense:—the mute and mourning train,
The white plume nodding o'er the sable hearse,
Had past unheeded, or perchance awoke
A serious smile upon the poor man's cheek
At pride's last triumph.   Now these measured sounds,

This universal language, to the heart
Speak instant, and on all these various minds
Compel one feeling.
               But such better thoughts
Will pass away how soon! and these who here
Are following their dead comrade to the grave,
Ere the night fall will in their revelry
Quench all remembrance. From the ties of life
Unnaturally rent, a man who knew
No resting-place, no dear delights of home,
Belike who never saw his children's face,
Whose children knew no father; he is gone,—
Dropt from existence, like a blasted leaf
That from the summer tree is swept away,
Its loss unseen. She hears not of his death
Who bore him, and already for her son
Her tears of bitterness are shed: when first
He had put on the livery of blood,
She wept him dead to her.
               We are indeed
Clay in the potter's hand! one favour'd mind,
Scarce lower than the Angels, shall explore
The ways of Nature, whilst his fellow-man,
Framed with like miracle, the work of God,
Must as the unreasonable beast drag on
A life of labour; like this soldier here,
His wondrous faculties bestow'd in vain,
Be moulded by his fate till he becomes
A mere machine of murder.
               And there are
Who say that this is well! as God has made
All things for man's good pleasure, so of men
The many for the few! Court-moralists,
Reverend lip-comforters, that once a-week
Proclaim how blessed are the poor, for they
Shall have their wealth hereafter, and though now
Toiling and troubled, though they pick the crumbs
That from the rich man's table fall, at length
In Abraham's bosom rest with Lazarus;
Themselves meantime secure their good things here,
And feast with Dives. These are they, O Lord!
Who in thy plain and simple Gospel see
All mysteries, but who find no peace enjoin'd,
No brotherhood, no wrath denounced on them
Who shed their brethren's blood,—blind at noon-day
As owls, lynx-eyed in darkness!
               O my God!
I thank thee, with no Pharisaic pride
I thank thee, that I am not such as these;
I thank thee for the eye that sees, the heart
That feels, the voice that in these evil days,
Amid these evil tongues, exalts itself,
And cries aloud against iniquity.

                        1795.

SAPPHO.

Scene, The Promontory of Leucadia.

This is the spot:—'t is here Tradition says
That hopeless Love from this high towering rock
Leaps headlong to Oblivion or to Death.
Oh, 't is a giddy height! my dizzy head
Swims at the precipice!—'t is death to fall!

Lie still, thou coward heart! this is no time
To shake with thy strong throbs the frame convulsed.
To die,—to be at rest,—oh, pleasant thought!
Perchance to leap and live; the soul all still,
And the wild tempest of the passions hush'd'
In one deep calm; the heart, no more diseased
By the quick ague fits of hope and fear,
Quietly cold.
           Presiding Powers, look down!
In vain to you I pour'd my earnest prayers,
In vain I sung your praises : chiefly thou,
VENUS! ungrateful Goddess, whom my lyre
Hymn'd with such full devotion! Lesbian groves,
Witness how often, at the languid hour
Of Summer twilight, to the melting song
Ye gave your choral echoes! Grecian maids,
Who hear with downcast look and flushing cheek,
That lay of love, bear witness! and ye youths,
Who hang enraptured on the impassion'd strain,
Gazing with eloquent eye, even till the heart
Sinks in the deep delirium! and ye, too,
Ages unborn! bear witness ye, how hard
Her fate who hymn'd the votive hymn in vain!
Ungrateful Goddess! I have hung my lute
In yonder holy pile : my hand no more
Shall wake the melodies that fail'd to move
The heart of Phaon!—yet when Rumour tells
How from Leucadia Sappho cast herself,
A self-devoted victim,—he may melt
Too late in pity, obstinate to love.

O haunt his midnight dreams, black NEMESIS!
Whom, [1] self-conceiving in the inmost depths
Of CHAOS, blackest NIGHT long labouring bore,
When the stern DESTINIES, her elder brood,
And shapeless DEATH, from that more monstrous birth
Leapt shuddering! haunt his slumbers, Nemesis!
Scorch with the fires of Phlegethon his heart,
Till helpless, hopeless, heaven-abandon'd wretch,
He too shall seek beneath the unfathom'd deep
To hide him from thy fury.
               How the sea
Far distant glitters as the sun-beams smile,
And gaily wanton o'er its heaving breast!
Phœbus shines forth, nor wears one cloud to mourn
His votary's sorrows! God of Day shine on!—
By Men despised, forsaken by the Gods,
I supplicate no more.
              How many a day,
O pleasant Lesbos! in thy secret streams
Delighted have I plunged, from the hot sun
Screen'd by the o'er-arching grove's delightful shade,
And pillow'd on the waters! Now the waves
Shall chill me to repose.
              Tremendous height!
Scarce to the brink will these rebellious limbs
Support me. Hark! how the rude deep below
Roars round the rugged base, as if it called
Its long reluctant victim! I will come!—
One leap, and all is over! The deep rest
Of Death, or tranquil Apathy's dead calm,
Welcome alike to me. Away, vain fears!

[1] Ου τινι κοιμηθεισα θεα τεκε ΝΥΞ ερεβεννη.
                         ΗΣΙΟΔΟΣ.

Phaon is cold, and why should Sappho live?
Phaon is cold, or with some fairer one—
Thought worse than death!

[*She throws herself from the precipice.*
1793.

XIMALPOCA.

Scene, *The Temple of Mexitli.*

SUBJECTS! friends! children! I may call you children,
For I have ever borne a father's love
Towards you; it is thirteen years since first
You saw me in the robes of royalty,—
Since here the multitudes of Mexico
Hail'd me their King. I thank you, friends, that now
In equal numbers and with equal love,
You come to grace my death.
                        For thirteen years
What I have been, ye know: that with all care,
That with all justness and all gentleness,
Seeking your weal, I govern'd. Is there one
Whom I have injured? one whose just redress
I have denied, or baffled by delay?
Let him come forth, that so no evil tongue
Speak shame of me hereafter. O my people,
Not by my sins have I drawn down upon me
The wrath of Heaven.
                        The wrath is heavy on me!
Heavy; a burthen more than I can bear,
I have endured contempt, insult, and wrongs,
From that Acolhuan tyrant; should I seek
Revenge? alas, my people, we are few,—
Feeble our growing state, it hath not yet
Rooted itself to bear the hurricane;
It is the lion-cub that tempts not yet
The tiger's full-aged fury. Mexicans,
He sent to bid me wear a woman's robe;—
When was the day that ever I look'd back
In battle? Mexicans, the wife I loved,
To faith and friendship trusted, in despite
Of me, of heaven, he seized, and spurn'd her back
Polluted!—coward villain, and he lurks
Behind his armies and his multitudes,
And mocks my idle wrath!—It is not fit,—
It is not possible that I should live!—
Live! and deserve to be the finger-mark
Of slave-contempt!—His blood I cannot reach,
But in my own all stains may be effaced;
It shall blot out the marks of infamy,
And when the warriors of the days to come
Tell of Ximalpoca, it shall be said
He died the brave man's death!
                        Not of the God
Unworthy, do I seek his altar thus,
A voluntary victim. And perchance
The sacrifice of life may profit ye,
My people, though all living efforts fail'd
By fortune, not by fault.
                        Cease your lament!
And if your ill-doom'd King deserved your love,
Say of him to your children, he was one
Who bravely bore misfortune; who, when life
Became dishonour, shook his body off,
And join'd the spirits of the heroes dead.

Yes! not in Miclanteuctli's dark abode.
With cowards shall your King receive his **doom** :
Not in the icy caverns of the North
Suffer through endless ages! He shall join
The Spirits of the brave, with them at morn
Shall issue from the eastern gate of Heaven,
And follow through his fields of light the Sun ;
With them shall raise the song and weave the dance ;
Sport in the stream of splendour ; company
Down to the western palace of his rest
The Prince of Glory ; and with equal eye
Endure his center'd radiance. Not of you
Forgetful, O my people, even then ;
But often in the amber cloud of noon
Diffused, will I o'erspread your summer fields,
And on the freshen'd maize and brightning meads
Shower plenty.
                Spirits of my valiant Sires,
I come ; Mexitli, never at thy shrine
Flow'd braver blood ! never a nobler heart
Steam'd up to thee its life ! Priest of the God,
Perform your office!

THE WIFE OF FERGUS.

*Fergusius 3 periit veneno ab uxore dato. Alii scribant cum uxor sæpe exprobrasset ei matrimonii contemptum et pellicum greges, neque quicquam profecisset, tandem noctu dormientem ab ea strangulatum. Quæstione de morte ejus habitâ, cum amicorum plurimi insimularentur, nec quisquam ne in gravissimis quidem tormentis quicquam fateretur, mulier, alioqui ferox, tot innoxiorum capitum miserta, in medium processit ac e superiore loco cædem a se factam confessa, ne ad ludibrium superesset, pectus cultro transfodit : quod ejus factum varie pro cujusque ingenio est acceptum, ac perinde sermonibus celebratum.—*BUCHANAN.

SCENE,—*The Palace Court. The Queen speaking from the Battlements.*

CEASE—cease your torments! spare the sufferers!
Scotchmen, not theirs the deed;—the crime was mine,
Mine is the glory.
                Idle threats! I stand
Secure. All access to these battlements
Is barr'd beyond your sudden strength to force;
And lo! the dagger by which Fergus died!
Shame on ye, Scotchmen, that a woman's hand
Was left to do this deed! Shame on ye, Thanes,
Who with slave-patience have so long endured
The wrongs, and insolence of tyranny!
Ye coward race!—that not a husband's sword
Smote that adulterous King! that not a wife
Revenged her own pollution ; in his blood
Wash'd her soul pure, and for the sin compell'd
Atoned by virtuous murder!—O my God!
Of what beast matter hast thou moulded them
To bear with wrongs like these? There was a time
When if the Bard had feign'd you such a tale,
Your eyes had throbb'd with anger, and your hands
In honest instinct would have graspt the sword.
O miserable men, who have disgraced
Your fathers, whom your sons must blush to name!
Aye,—ye can threaten me! ye can be brave
In anger to a woman! one whose virtue
Upbraids your coward vice; whose name will live
Honour'd and praised in song, when not a hand

Shall root from your forgotten monuments
The cankering moss. Fools! fools! to think that death
Is not a thing familiar to my mind!
As if I knew not what must consummate
My glory! as if aught that earth can give
Could tempt me to endure the load of life!—
Scotchmen! ye saw when Fergus to the altar
Led me, his maiden Queen. Ye blest me then,—
I heard you bless me, and I thought that Heaven
Had heard you also, and that I was blest,
For I loved Fergus. Bear me witness, God!
With what a sacred heart-sincerity
My lips pronounced the unrecallable vow
That made me his, him mine; bear witness, Thou!
Before whose throne I this day must appear
Stain'd with his blood and mine! my heart was his,—
His in the strength of all its first affections.
In all obedience, in all love, I kept
Holy my marriage-vow. Behold me, Thanes!
Time hath not changed the face on which his eye
So often dwelt, when with assiduous care
He sought my love; with seeming truth, for one,
Sincere herself, impossible to doubt!
Time hath not changed that face;—I speak not now
With pride of beauties that will feed the worm
To-morrow! but with joyful pride I say,
That if the truest and most perfect love
Deserved requital, such was ever mine.
How often reeking from the adulterous bed
Have I received him! and with no complaint.
Neglect and insult, cruelty and scorn,
Long, long did I endure, and long curb down
The indignant nature.
                        Tell your countrymen,
Scotchmen, what I have spoken! say to them
Ye saw the Queen of Scotland lift the dagger
Red from her husband's heart; that in her own
She plunged it.
                        [*Stabs herself.*
            Tell them also, that she felt
No guilty fear in death.

LUCRETIA.

Scene, The House of Collatine.

Welcome, my father! good Valerius,
Welcome! and thou too, Brutus! ye were both
My wedding guests, and fitly ye are come.
My husband—Collatine—alas! no more
Lucretia's husband, for thou shalt not clasp
Pollution to thy bosom,—hear me on!
For I must tell thee all.
                        I sat at eve
Spinning amid my maidens as I wont,
When from the camp at Ardea Sextus came.
Curb down thy swelling feelings, Collatine!
I little liked the man! yet for he came
From Ardea, for he brought me news of thee,
I gladly gave him welcome; gladly listen'd,—
Thou canst not tell how gladly! to his tales
Of battles, and the long and perilous siege;
And when I laid me down at night to sleep,
'T was with a lighten'd heart,—I knew thee safe,

My visions were of thee.
                    Nay, hear me out!
And be thou wise in vengeance, so thy wife
Not vainly shall have suffer'd. I have wrought
My soul up to the business of this hour,
That it may stir your noble spirits, and prompt
Such glorious deeds that ages yet unborn
Shall bless my fate. At midnight I awoke,
The Tarquin was beside me! O my husband!
Where wert thou then! gone was my rebel strength,—
All power of utterance gone! astonish'd, stunn'd,
I saw the coward ruffian, heard him urge
His damned suit, and bid me tamely yield,—
Yield to dishonour. When he proffer'd death,—
Oh, I had leapt to meet the merciful sword!
But that with most accursed vows he vow'd
That he would lay a dead slave by my side,
Murdering my spotless honour—Collatine
From what an anguish have I rescued thee!
And thou, my father, wretched as thou art,
Thou miserable, childless, poor old man,—
Think, father, what that agony had been!
Now thou mayst sorrow for me, thou mayst bless
The memory of thy poor, polluted child.
Look if it have not kindled Brutus' eye!
Mysterious man! at last I know thee now,
I see thy dawning g'ories!—to the grave
Not unrevenged Lucretia shall descend;
Not always shall her wretched country wear
The Tarquins' yoke! ye will deliver Rome,
And I have comfort in this dreadful hour.
Think'st thou, my husband, that I dreaded death?
O Collatine! the weapon that had gored
My bosom had been ease, been happiness,—
Elysium, to the hell of his hot grasp.
Judge if Lucretia could have fear'd to die!
                        [*Stabs herself.*

HYMN TO THE PENATES.

Remove far from me vanity and lies; give me neither poverty nor riches; feed me with food convenient for me.—The words of Agur.

ΟΙΚΟΙ βελτερον ειναι επει βλαβερον το θυρηφι.
                        ΗΣΙΟΔΟΣ.

Yet one Song more! one high and solemn strain,
Ere, Phœbus! on thy temple's ruin'd wall
I hang the silent harp : there may its strings,
When the rude tempest shakes the aged pile,
Make melancholy music. One Song more!
Penates! hear me! for to you I hymn
The votive lay; whether, as sages deem,
Ye dwell in the inmost Heaven,[1] the Counsellors [2]
Of Jove; or if, Supreme of Deities,
All things are yours, and in your holy train
Jove proudly ranks, and Juno, white-arm'd Queen,
And wisest of Immortals, the dread Maid
Athenian Pallas. Venerable Powers!
Hearken your hymn of praise! Though from your rites
Estranged, and exiled from your altars long,

[1] Hence one explanation of the name Penates, because they were supposed to reign in the inmost heavens.
[2] This was the belief of the ancient Hetrusci, who called them Concertes and Complices.

I have not ceased to love you, HOUSEHOLD GODS!
In many a long and melancholy hour
Of solitude and sorrow, hath my heart
With earnest longings pray'd to rest at length
Beside your hallow'd hearth—for PEACE is there!

Yes, I have loved you long! I call on you
Yourselves to witness with what holy joy,
Shunning the common herd of human kind,
I have retired to watch your lonely fires
And commune with myself.   Delightful hours,
That gave mysterious pleasure, made me know
Mine inmost heart, its weakness and its strength,
Taught me to cherish with devoutest care
Its strange unworldly feelings, taught me too
The best of lessons—to respect myself.
Nor have I ever ceased to reverence you,
DOMESTIC DEITIES! from the first dawn
Of reason, through the adventurous paths of youth
Even to this better day, when on mine ear
The uproar of contending nations sounds
But like the passing wind, and wakes no pulse
To tumult.   When a child—(and still I love
To dwell with fondness on my childish years,)
When first a little one, I left my home,
I can remember the first grief I felt,
And the first painful smile that clothed my front
With feelings not its own : sadly at night
I sat me down beside a stranger's hearth;
And when the lingering hour of rest was come,
First wet with tears my pillow.   As I grew
In years and knowledge, and the course of Time
Develop'd the young feelings of my heart,
When most I loved in solitude to rove
Amid the woodland gloom ; or where the rocks
Darken'd old Avon's stream, in the ivied cave
Recluse to sit and brood the future song,—
Yet not the less, PENATES, loved I then
Your altars; not the less at evening hour
Delighted by the well-trimm'd fire to sit,
Absorb'd in many a dear deceitful dream
Of visionary joys : deceitful dreams,—
And yet not vain; for painting purest bliss,
They form'd to Fancy's mould her votary's heart.

By Cherwell's sedgy side, and in the meads
Where Isis in her calm clear stream reflects
The willow's bending boughs, at early dawn,
In the noon-tide hour, and when the night-mist rose,
I have remember'd you ; and when the noise
Of lewd Intemperance on my lonely ear
Burst with loud tumult, as recluse I sate,
Pondering on loftiest themes of man redeem'd
From servitude, and vice, and wretchedness,
I blest you, HOUSEHOLD GODS! because I loved
Your peaceful altars and serener rites.
Nor did I cease to reverence you, when driven
Amid the jarring crowd, an unfit man
To mingle with the world; still, still my heart
Sigh'd for your sanctuary, and inly pined;
And, loathing human converse, I have stray'd
Where o'er the sea-beach chilly howl'd the blast,
And gazed upon the world of waves, and wish'd
That I were far beyond the Atlantic deep,
In woodland haunts, a sojourner with PEACE.

Not idly did the poets dream of old,
Who peopled earth with Deities.   They trod
The wood with reverence where the DRYADS dwelt;
At day's dim dawn or evening's misty hour
They saw the OREADS on their mountain haunts,
And felt their holy influence; nor impure
Of thought, or ever with polluted hands [1]
Touch'd they without a prayer the NAIAD's spring :
Yet was their influence transient; such brief awe
Inspiring as the thunder's long loud peal
Strikes to the feeble spirit.   HOUSEHOLD GODS,
Not such your empire! in your votaries' breasts
No momentary impulse ye awake;
Nor fleeting, like their local energies,
The deep devotion that your fanes impart.
O ye whom YOUTH has wilder'd on your way,
Or VICE with fair-mask'd foulness, or the lure
Of FAME that calls ye to her crowded path
With FOLLY's rattle, to your HOUSEHOLD GODS
Return ; for not in VICE's gay abodes,
Not in the unquiet unsafe halls of Fame
Doth HAPPINESS abide!   O ye who weep
Much for the many miseries of Mankind,
More for their vices; ye whose honest eyes
Frown on OPPRESSION,—ye whose honest hearts
Beat high when FREEDOM sounds her dread alarm;
O ye who quit the path of peaceful life
Crusading for mankind—a spaniel race
That lick the hand that beats them, or tear all
Alike in frensy; to your HOUSEHOLD GODS
Return, for by their altars VIRTUE dwells,
And HAPPINESS with her; for by their fires
TRANQUILLITY, in no unsocial mood,
Sits silent, listening to the pattering shower ;
For, so SUSPICION [2] sleep not at the gate
Of WISDOM, Falsehood shall not enter there.

As on the height of some huge eminence,
Reach'd with long labour, the way-faring man
Pauses awhile, and gazing o'er the plain
With many a sore step travell'd. turns him then
Serious to contemplate the onward road,
And calls to mind the comforts of his home,
And sighs that he has left them, and resolves
To stray no more : I on my way of life
Muse thus, PENATES, and with firmest faith
Devote myself to you.   I will not quit,
To mingle with the crowd, your calm abodes,
Where by the evening hearth CONTENTMENT sits
And hears the cricket chirp; where Love delights
To dwell, and on your altars lays his torch
That burns with no extinguishable flame.

Hear me, ye POWERS benignant! there is one
Must be mine inmate,—for I may not chuse

[1] Μηδε ποτ' αεναων ποταμων καλλιρροον υδωρ
Ποσσι περαν, πριν γ' ευξη ιδων ες καλα ρεεθρα,
Χειρας νιψαμενος πολυηρατω υδατι λευκω
Ος ποταμον διαβη, κακοτητι δε χειρας ανιπτος,
Τωδ: θεοι νεμεσωσι, και αλγεα δωκαν οπισσω.
                                    'ΗΣΙΟΔΟΣ.

[2] Oft though Wisdom wake, Suspicion sleeps
    At Wisdom's gate, and to Simplicity
    Resigns her charge, while Goodness thinks no ill
    Where no ill seems.
                            MILTON.

But love him. He is one whom many wrongs
Have sicken'd of the world. There was a time
When he would weep to hear of wickedness,
And wonder at the tale; when for the opprest
He felt a brother's pity, to the oppressor
A good man's honest anger. His quick eye
Betray'd each rising feeling, every thought
Leapt to his tongue. When first among mankind
He mingled, by himself he judged of them,
And loved and trusted them, to Wisdom deaf,
And took them to his bosom. FALSEHOOD met
Her unsuspecting victim, fair of front,
And lovely as Apega's [1] sculptured form,
Like that false image caught his warm embrace,
And gored his open breast. The reptile race
Clung round his bosom, and with viper folds
Encircling, stung the fool who foster'd them.
His mother was SIMPLICITY, his sire
BENEVOLENCE; in earlier days he bore
His father's name; the world who injured him
Call him MISANTHROPY. I may not chuse
But love him, HOUSEHOLD GODS! for we were nurst
In the same school.

PENATES! some there are
Who say, that not in the inmost heaven ye dwell,
Gazing with eye remote on all the ways
Of man, his GUARDIAN GODS; wiselier they deem
A dearer interest to the human race
Links you, yourselves the SPIRITS OF THE DEAD.
No mortal eye may pierce the invisible world,
No light of human reason penetrate
The depth where Truth lies hid. Yet to this faith
My heart with instant sympathy assents;
And I would judge all systems and all faiths
By that best touchstone, from whose test DECEIT
Shrinks like the Arch-Fiend at Ithuriel's spear,
And SOPHISTRY's gay glittering bubble bursts,
As at the spousals of the Nereid's son,
When that false Florimel, [2] by her prototype
Display'd in rivalry, with all her charms
Dissolved away.

Nor can the halls of Heaven
Give to the human soul such kindred joy,
As hovering o'er its earthly haunts it feels,
When with the breeze it wantons round the brow
Of one beloved on earth; or when at night
In dreams it comes, and brings with it the DAYS
And JOYS that are no more. Or when, perchance
With power permitted to alleviate ill
And fit the sufferer for the coming woe,
Some strange presage the SPIRIT breathes, and fills
The breast with ominous fear, and disciplines
For sorrow, pours into the afflicted heart

The balm of resignation, and inspires
With heavenly hope. Even as a child delights
To visit day by day the favourite plant
His hand has sown, to mark its gradual growth,
And watch all-anxious for the promised flower;
Thus to the blessed spirit in innocence
And pure affections like a little child,
Sweet will it be to hover o'er the friends
Beloved; then sweetest, if, as Duty prompts,
With earthly care we in their breasts have sown
The seeds of Truth and Virtue, holy flowers,
Whose odour reacheth Heaven.

When my sick Heart
(Sick with hope long delay'd, [1] than which no care
Weighs on the spirit heavier,) from itself
Seeks the best comfort, often have I deem'd
That thou didst witness every inmost thought,
SEWARD! my dear, dead friend! For not in vain,
O early summon'd on thy heavenly course!
Was thy brief sojourn here : me didst thou leave
With strengthen'd step to follow the right path.
Till we shall meet again. Meantime I soothe
The deep regret of nature, with belief,
O EDMUND! that thine eye's celestial ken
Pervades me now, marking with no mean joy
The movements of the heart that loved thee well!

Such feelings Nature prompts, and hence your rites,
DOMESTIC GODS! arose. When for his son
With ceaseless grief Syrophanes bewail'd,
Mourning his age left childless, and his wealth
Heapt for an alien, he with obstinate eye
Still on the imaged marble of the dead
Dwelt, pampering sorrow. Thither from his wrath,
A safe asylum, fled the offending slave,
And garlanded the statue, and implored
His young lost lord to save : Remembrance then
Soften'd the father, and he loved to see
The votive wreath renew'd, and the rich smoke
Curl from the costly censer slow and sweet.
From Egypt soon the sorrow-soothing rites
Divulging spread; before your idol forms [2]
By every hearth the blinded Pagan knelt,
Pouring his prayers to these, and offering there
Vain sacrifice or impious, and sometimes
With human blood your sanctuary defiled :
Till the first Brutus, tyrant-conquering chief,
Arose; he first the impious rites put down,
He fitliest, who for FREEDOM lived and died,
The friend of humankind. Then did your feasts
Frequent recur and blameless; and when came
The solemn festival, [3] whose happiest rites
Emblem'd EQUALITY, the holiest truth !
Crown'd with gay garlands were your statues seen,
To you the fragrant censer smoked, to you
The rich libation flow'd : vain sacrifice !
For not the poppy wreath nor fruits nor wine
Ye ask, PENATES! nor the altar cleansed

---

[1] One of the ways and means of the tyrant Nabis. If one of his subjects refused to lend him money, he commanded him to embrace his Apega ; the statue of a beautiful Woman so formed as to clasp the victim to her breast, in which a pointed dagger was concealed.

[2] Then did he set her by that snowy one,
Like the true saint beside the image set,
Of both their beauties to make paragone
And trial whether should the honour get ;
Streightway so soone as both together met,
The enchaunted damsell vanish'd into nought;
Her snowy substance melted as with heat ;
Ne of that goodly hew remayned ought
But the empty girdle which about her wast was wrought.
SPENSER.

---

[1] Hope deferred maketh the heart sick.—*Proverbs.*

Qua non gravior mortalibus addita cura,
Sera ubi longa venit.
STATIUS.

[2] It is not certainly known under what form the Penates were worshipped. Some assert, as wooden or brazen rods shaped like trumpets ; others, that they were represented as young men.

[3] The Saturnalia.

With many a mystic form; ye ask the heart
Made pure, and by domestic Peace and Love
Hallow'd to you.

        Hearken your hymn of praise,
PENATES! to your shrines I come for rest,
There only to be found. Often at eve,
Amid my wanderings I have seen far off
The lonely light that spake of comfort there;
It told my heart of many a joy of home,
And my poor heart was sad. When I have gazed
From some high eminence on goodly vales
And cots and villages embower'd below,
The thought would rise that all to me was strange
Amid the scene so fair, nor one small spot
Where my tired mind might rest, and call it *home.*
There is a magic in that little word :
It is a mystic circle that surrounds
Comforts and virtues never known beyond
The hallowed limit. Often has my heart
Ached for that quiet haven !—haven'd now,
I think of those in this world's wilderness
Who wander on and find no home of rest
Till to the grave they go! them POVERTY,
Hollow-eyed fiend, the child of WEALTH and POWER,
Bad offspring of worse parents, aye afflicts,
Cankering with her foul mildews the chill'd heart;—
Them WANT with scorpion scourge drives to the den
Of GUILT ;—them SLAUGHTER for the price of death
Throws to her raven brood. Oh, not on them,
GOD OF ETERNAL JUSTICE! not on them
Let fall thy thunder!
        HOUSEHOLD DEITIES!
Then only shall be Happiness on earth
When man shall feel your sacred power, and love
Your tranquil joys; then shall the city stand
A huge void sepulchre, and rising fair
Amid the ruins of the palace pile
The olive grow, there shall the TREE OF PEACE
Strike its roots deep and flourish. This the state
Shall bless the race redeem'd of Man, when WEALTH
And POWER and all their hideous progeny
Shall sink annihilate, and all mankind
Live in the equal brotherhood of love.
Heart-calming hope, and sure! for hitherward
Tend all the tumults of the troubled world,
Its woes, its wisdom, and its wickedness
Alike : so He hath will'd, whose will is just.

Meantime, all hoping and expecting all
In patient faith, to you, DOMESTIC GODS!
I come, studious of other lore than song,
Of my past years the solace and support :
Yet shall my Heart remember the past years
With honest pride, trusting that not in vain
Lives the pure song of LIBERTY and TRUTH.
                        1796.

METRICAL LETTER.

WRITTEN FROM LONDON.

MARGARET! my Cousin,—nay, you must not smile;
I love the homely and familiar phrase:
And I will call thee Cousin Margaret,
However quaint amid the measured line

The good old term appears. Oh! it looks ill
When delicate tongues disclaim old terms of kin,
Sir-ing and Madam-ing as civilly
As if the road between the heart and lips
Were such a weary and Laplandish way,
That the poor travellers came to the red gates
Half frozen. Trust me, Cousin Margaret,
For many a day my Memory hath play'd
The creditor with me on your account,
And made me shame to think that I should owe
So long the debt of kindness. But in truth,
Like Christian on his pilgrimage, I bear
So heavy a pack of business, that albeit
I toil on mainly, in our twelve hours' race
Time leaves me distanced. Loth indeed were I
That for a moment you should lay to me
Unkind neglect ; mine, Margaret, is a heart
That smokes not, yet methinks there should be some
Who know how warm it beats. I am not one
Who can play off my smiles and courtesies
To every Lady of her lap-dog tired
Who wants a play-thing; I am no sworn friend
Of half-an-hour, as apt to leave as love;
Mine are no mushroom feelings, which spring up
At once without a seed and take no root,
Wiseliest distrusted. In a narrow sphere,
The little circle of domestic life,
I would be known and loved : the world beyond
Is not for me. But, Margaret, sure I think
That you should know me well, for you and I
Grew up together, and when we look back
Upon old times, our recollections paint
The same familiar faces. Did I wield
The wand of Merlin's magic, I would make
Brave witchcraft. We would have a faery ship,
Aye, a new Ark, as in that other flood
Which cleansed the sons of Anak from the earth ;
The Sylphs should waft us to some goodly isle
Like that where whilom old Appollidon
Built up his blameless spell ; and I would bid
The Sea-Nymphs pile around their coral bowers,
That we might stand upon the beach, and mark
The far-off breakers shower their silver spray,
And hear the eternal roar, whose pleasant sound
Told us that never mariner should reach
Our quiet coast. In such a blessed isle
We might renew the days of infancy,
And Life like a long childhood pass away,
Without one care. It may be, Margaret,
That I shall yet be gather'd to my friends;
For I am not of those who live estranged
Of choice, till at the last they join their race
In the family-vault. If so, if I should lose,
Like my old friend the Pilgrim, this huge pack
So heavy on my shoulders, I and mine
Right pleasantly will end our pilgrimage.
If not, if I should never get beyond
This Vanity town, there is another world
Where friends will meet. And often, Margaret,
I gaze at night into the boundless sky,
And think that I shall there be born again,
The exalted native of some better star;
And, like the rude American, I hope
To find in Heaven the things I loved on earth.
                        1798.

SNUFF.

A DELICATE pinch! oh how it tingles up
The titillated nose! and fills the eyes
And breast, till in one comfortable sneeze
The full collected pleasure bursts at last!
Most rare Columbus! thou shalt be for this
The only Christopher in my Kalendar.
Why but for thee the uses of the Nose
Were half unknown, and its capacity
Of joy. The summer gale that from the heath,
At midnoon glittering with the golden gorse,
Bears its balsamic odour, but provokes
Not satisfies the sense; and all the flowers,
That with their unsubstantial fragrance tempt
And disappoint, bloom for so short a space,
That half the year the Nostrils would keep Lent,
But that the kind Tobacconist admits
No winter in his work; when Nature sleeps
His wheels roll on, and still administer
A plenitude of joy, a tangible smell.

What is Peru and those Golcondan mines
To thee, Virginia? miserable realms,
They furnish gold for knaves and gems for fools;
But thine are *common* comforts!—To omit
Pipe-panegyric and tobacco-praise,
Think what the general joy the snuff-box gives,
Europe, and far above Pizarro's name
Write Raleigh in thy records of renown!
Him let the school-boy bless if he behold
His master's box produced, for when he sees
The thumb and finger of Authority
Stuft up the nostrils; when hat, head, and wig
Shake all; when on the waistcoat black the dust
Or drop falls brown; soon shall the brow severe
Relax; and from vituperative lips
Words that of birch remind not, sounds of praise,
And jokes that *must* be laugh'd at shall proceed.

1799.

COOL REFLECTIONS

DURING A MIDSUMMER WALK.

O SPARE me—spare me, Phœbus! if indeed
Thou hast not let another Phaëton
Drive earthward thy fierce steeds and fiery car;
Mercy! I melt! I melt! No tree, no bush,
No shelter! not a breath of stirring air
East, West, or North, or South! Dear God of day,
Put on thy nightcap! crop thy locks of light,
And be in the fashion! turn thy back upon us,
And let thy beams flow upward! make it night
Instead of noon! one little miracle,
In pity, gentle Phœbus!

What a joy,
Oh what a joy, to be a seal and flounder
On an ice island! or to have a den
With the white bear, cavern'd in polar snow!
It were a comfort to shake hands with death,—
He has a rare cold hand! to wrap one's self
In the gift-shirt Deianeira sent,
Dipt in the blood of Nessus, just to keep
The sun off, or toast cheese for Beelzebub,—
That were a cool employment to this journey

Along a road whose white intensity
Would now make platina uncongealable
Like quicksilver.

Were it midnight, I should walk
Self-lanthorn'd, saturate with sunbeams. Jove!
O gentle Jove! have mercy, and once more
Kick that obdurate Phœbus out of heaven!
Give Boreas the wind-cholic, till he roar
For cardamum, and drink down peppermint,
Making what's left as precious as Tokay.
Send Mercury, to salivate the sky
Till it dissolve in rain. O gentle Jove!
But some such little kindness to a wretch
Who feels his marrow spoiling his best coat,—
Who swells with caloric as if a Prester
Had leaven'd every limb with poison-yeast;—
Lend me thine eagle just to flap his wings,
And fan me, and I will build temples to thee,
And turn true Pagan.

Not a cloud nor breeze,—
O you most heathen Deities! if ever
My bones reach home (for, for the flesh upon them,
It hath resolved itself into a dew,)
I shall have learnt owl-wisdom. Thou vile Phœbus,
Set me a Persian sun-idolater
Upon this turnpike road, and I'll convert him
With no inquisitorial argument
But thy own fires. Now woe be to me wretch,
That I was in a heretic country born!
Else might some mass for the poor souls that bleach,
And burn away the calx of their offences
In that great Purgatory crucible,
Help me. O Jupiter! my poor complexion!
I am made a copper-Indian of already;
And if no kindly cloud will parasol me,
My very cellular membrane will be changed,—
I shall be negrotied.

A brook! a brook!
Oh what a sweet cool sound!

'T is very nectar!
It runs like life through every strengthen'd limb!
Nymph of the stream; now take a grateful prayer.

1799.

THE PIG.

A COLLOQUIAL POEM.

JACOB! I do not love to see thy nose
Turn'd up in scornful curve at yonder Pig:
It would be well, my friend, if we, like him,
Were perfect in our kind!—And why despise
The sow-born grunter?—He is obstinate,
Thou answerest; ugly; and the filthiest beast
That banquets upon offal. Now I pray you
Hear the Pig's Counsel.

Is he obstinate?
We must not, Jacob, be deceived by words,
By sophist sounds. A democratic beast,
He knows that his unmerciful drivers seek
Their profit, and not his. He hath not learnt
That Pigs were made for man.—born to be brawn'd
And baconized; that he must please to give
Just what his gracious masters please to take;
Perhaps his tusks, the weapons Nature gave
For self-defence, the general privilege;

Perhaps,—hark Jacob! dost thou hear that horn?
Woe to the young posterity of pork!
Their enemy is at hand.
　　　　　　　Again. Thou say'st
The Pig is ugly. Jacob, look at him!
Those eyes have taught the Lover flattery.
His face,—nay, Jacob, Jacob! were it fair
To judge a Lady in her dishabille?
Fancy it drest, and with saltpetre rouged.
Behold his tail, my friend; with curls like that
The wanton hop marries her stately spouse:
So crisp in beauty Amoretta's hair
Rings round her lover's soul the chains of love.
And what is beauty, but the aptitude
Of parts harmonious? give thy fancy scope,
And thou wilt find that no imagined change
Can beautify this beast. Place at his end
The starry glories of the Peacock's pride;
Give him the Swan's white breast; for his horn-hoofs
Shape such a foot and ankle as the waves
Crowded in eager rivalry to kiss,
When Venus from the enamour'd sea arose;—
Jacob, thou canst but make a monster of him!
All alteration man could think would mar
His Pig-perfection.
　　　　　　　The last charge,—he lives
A dirty life. Here I could shelter him
With noble and right-reverend precedents, .
And show by sanction of authority,
That 't is a very honourable thing
To thrive by dirty ways. But let me rest
On better ground the unanswerable defence:
The Pig is a philosopher, who knows
No prejudice. Dirt? Jacob, what is dirt?
If matter,—why the delicate dish that tempts .
An o'ergorged Epicure to the last morsel
That stuffs him to the throat-gates is no more.
If matter be not, but as Sages say,
Spirit is all, and all things visible
Are one, the infinitely modified,
Think, Jacob, what that Pig is, and the mire
Wherein he stands knee-deep.
　　　　　　　And there! that breeze
Pleads with me, and has won thee to the smile
That speaks conviction. O'er yon blossom'd field
Of beans it came, and thoughts of bacon rise.

THE DANCING BEAR.

RECOMMENDED TO THE ADVOCATES FOR THE SLAVE-
TRADE.

RARE music! I would rather hear cat-courtship
Under my bed-room window in the night,
Than this scraped catgut's screak. Rare dancing too!
Alas, poor Bruin! How he foots the pole,
And waddles round it with unwieldy steps,
Swaying from side to side!—The dancing-master
Hath had as profitless a pupil in him
As when he would have tortured my poor toes,
To minuet grace, and made them move like clockwork
In musical obedience. Bruin! Bruin!
Thou art but a clumsy biped!—and the mob
With noisy merriment mock his heavy pace,
And laugh to see him led by the nose!—themselves

Led by the nose, embruted, and in the eye
Of Reason from their Nature's purposes
As miserably perverted.
　　　　　　　Bruin-Bear
Now could I sonnetize thy piteous plight,
And prove how much my sympathetic heart
Even for the miseries of a beast can feel,
In fourteen lines of sensibility.
But we are told all things were made for man;
And I'll be sworn there's not a fellow here
Who would not swear 't were hanging blasphemy
To doubt that truth. Therefore as thou wert born,
Bruin! for man, and man makes nothing of thee
In any other way,—most logically
It follows, that thou must be born to dance;
That that great snout of thine was form'd on purpose
To hold a ring; and that thy fat was given thee
Only to make pomatum!
　　　　　　　To demur
Were heresy. And politicians say
(Wise men who in the scale of reason give
No foolish feelings weight), that thou art here
Far happier than thy brother bears who roam
O'er trackless snow for food; that being born
Inferior to thy leader, unto him
Rightly belongs dominion; that the compact
Was made between ye, when thy clumsy feet
First fell into the snare, and he gave up
His right to kill, conditioning thy life
Should thenceforth be his property;—besides,
'T is wholesome for thy morals to be brought
From savage climes into a civilized state,
Into the decencies of Christendom.—
Bear! Bear! it passes in the Parliament
For excellent logic this! what if we say
How barbarously man abuses power?
Talk of thy baiting, it will be replied,
Thy welfare is thy owner's interest,
But were thou baited it would injure thee,
Therefore thou art not baited. For seven years
Hear it, O Heaven, and give ear, O Earth!
For seven long years this precious Syllogism
Hath baffled justice and humanity!

THE FILBERT.

NAY, gather not that Filbert, Nicholas,
There is a maggot there,—it is his house,—
His castle,—oh commit not burglary!
Strip him not naked,—'t is his clothes, his shell,
His bones, the case and armour of his life,
And thou shalt do no murder, Nicholas!
It were an easy thing to crack that nut
Or with thy crackers or thy double teeth,
So easily may all things be destroy'd!
But 't is not in the power of mortal man
To mend the fracture of a filbert shell.
There were two great men once amused themselves
Watching two maggots run their wriggling race,
And wagering on their speed; but Nick, to us
It were no sport to see the pamper'd worm
Roll out and then draw in his folds of fat,
Like to some Barber's leathern powder-bag
Wherewith he feathers, frosts, or cauliflowers
Spruce Beau, or Lady fair, or Doctor grave.

Enough of dangers and of enemies
Hath Nature's wisdom for the worm ordain'd:
Increase not thou the number! Him the Mouse
Gnawing with nibbling tooth the shell's defence
May from his native tenement eject;
Him may the Nut-hatch piercing with strong bill
Unwittingly destroy; or to his hoard
The Squirrel bear, at leisure to be crack'd.
Man also hath his dangers and his foes
As this poor Maggot hath; and when I muse
Upon the aches, anxieties, and fears,
The Maggot knows not, Nicholas, methinks
It were a happy metamorphosis
To be enkernell'd thus: never to hear
Of wars, and of invasions, and of plots,
Kings, Jacobines, and Tax-commissioners;
To feel no motion but the wind that shook
The Filbert Tree, and rock'd us to our rest;
And in the middle of such exquisite food
To live luxurious! the perfection this
Of snugness! it were to unite at once
Hermit retirement, Aldermanic bliss,
And Stoic independence of mankind.

ODE

WRITTEN DURING THE NEGOCIATIONS WITH
BUONAPARTE IN JANUARY, 1814.

WHO counsels peace at this momentous hour,
When God hath given deliverance to the oppress'd,
And to the injured power?
Who counsels peace, when Vengeance like a flood
Rolls on, no longer now to be repress'd;
When innocent blood
From the four corners of the world cries out
For justice upon one accursed head;
When Freedom hath her holy banners spread
Over all nations, now in one just cause
United; when with one sublime accord
Europe throws off the yoke abhorr'd,
And Loyalty and Faith, and Ancient Laws
Follow the avenging sword!

Woe, woe to England! woe and endless shame
If this heroic land,
False to her feelings and unspotted fame,
Hold out the olive to the Tyrant's hand!
Woe to the world if Buonaparte's throne
Be suffer'd still to stand!
For by what names shall Right and Wrong be
known,—
What new and courtly phrases must we feign
For Falsehood, Murder, and all monstrous crimes,
If that perfidious Corsican maintain
Still his detested reign,
And France, who yearns even now to break her chain,
Beneath his iron rule be left to groan!
No! by the innumerable dead,
Whose blood hath for his lust of power been shed,
Death only can for his foul deeds atone!
That peace which Death and judgment can bestow,
That peace be Buonaparte's,—that alone!

For sooner shall the Ethiop change his skin,
Or from the Leopard shall her spots depart,

Than this man change his old flagitious heart.
Have ye not seen him in the balance weigh'd,
And there found wanting? On the stage of blood
Foremost the resolute adventurer stood;
And when by many a battle won,
He placed upon his brow the crown,
Curbing delirious France beneath his sway,
Then, like Octavius in old time,
Fair name might he have handed down,
Effacing many a stain of former crime.
Fool! should he cast away that bright renown!
Fool! the redemption proffer'd should he lose!
When Heaven such grace vouchsafed him that the way
To Good and Evil lay
Before him, which to chuse.

But Evil was his Good,
For all too long in blood had he been nurst,
And ne'er was earth with fouler tyrant curst
Bold man and bad,
Remorseless, godless, full of fraud and lies,
And black with murders and with perjuries,
Himself in Hell's whole panoply he clad;
No law but his own headstrong will he knew,
No counsellor but his own wicked heart!
From evil thus portentous strength he drew,
And trampled under foot all human ties,
All holy laws, all natural charities.

O France! beneath this fierce Barbarian's sway
Disgraced thou art to all succeeding times!
Rapine and blood and fire have mark'd thy way,
All loathsome, all unutterable crimes!
A curse is on thee, France! from far and wide
It hath gone up to Heaven! All lands have cried
For vengeance upon thy detested head!
All nations curse thee, France! for wheresoe'er
In peace or war thy banner hath been spread,
All forms of human woe have follow'd there.
The Living and the Dead
Cry out alike against thee! They who bear
Crouching beneath its weight thine iron yoke,
Join in the bitterness of secret prayer
The voice of that innumerable throng,
Whose slaughter'd spirits day and night invoke
The everlasting Judge of right and wrong,
How long, O Lord! Holy and just, how long!

A merciless oppressor hast thou been,
Thyself remorselessly oppress'd meantime;
Greedy of war, when all that thou couldst gain
Was but to dye thy soul with deeper crime,
And rivet faster round thyself the chain.
O blind to honour, and to interest blind,
When thus in abject servitude resign'd
To this barbarian upstart, thou couldst brave
God's justice, and the heart of humankind!
Madly thou thoughtest to enslave the world,
Thyself the while a miserable slave!
Behold the flag of vengeance is unfurl'd?
The dreadful armies of the North advance!
While England, Portugal, and Spain combined,
Give their triumphant banners to the wind,
And stand victorious in the fields of France!

One man hath been for ten long wretched years
The cause of all this blood and all these tears!

One man in this most awful point of time
Draws on thy danger, as he caused thy crime.
Wait not too long the event,
For now whole Europe comes against thee bent!
His wiles and their own strength the nations know:
Wise from past wrongs, on future peace intent,
The people and the princes with one mind
From all parts move against the general foe:
One act of justice, one atoning blow,
One execrable head laid low,
Even yet, O France! averts thy punishment.
Open thine eyes! too long hast thou been blind!
Take vengeance for thyself, and for mankind!

Oh if thou lovest thine ancient fame,
Revenge thy sufferings and thy shame!
By the bones which bleach on Jaffa's beach;
By the blood which on Domingo's shore
Hath clogg'd the carrion-birds with gore;
By the flesh which gorged the wolves of Spain,
Or stiffen'd on the snowy plain
Of frozen Moscovy;
By the bodies which lie all open to the sky,
Tracking from Elbe to Rhine the Tyrant's flight;
By the widow's and the orphan's cry;
By the childless parent's misery;
By the lives which he hath shed;
By the ruin he hath spread;
By the prayers which rise for curses on his head;
Redeem, O France! thine ancient fame!
Revenge thy sufferings and thy shame!
Open thine eyes!—too long hast thou been blind!
Take vengeance for thyself, and for mankind?

By those horrors which the night
Witness'd when the torches' light
To the assembled murderers show'd
Where the blood of Condé flow'd;
By thy murder'd Pichegru's fame;
By murder'd Wright,—an English name;
By murder'd Palm's atrocious doom;
By murder'd Hofer's martyrdom;
Oh by the virtuous blood thus vilely spilt,
The Villain's own peculiar private guilt,
Open thine eyes! too long hast thou been blind!
Take vengeance for thyself and for mankind!
Pluck from the Upstart's head thy sullied crown!
Down with the Tyrant, with the Murderer down!

ODE

WRITTEN IN DECEMBER, 1814.

When shall the Island Queen of Ocean lay
The thunderbolt aside,
And, twining olives with her laurel crown,
Rest in the Bower of Peace?

Not long may this unnatural strife endure
Beyond the Atlantic deep;
Not long may men, with vain ambition drunk
And insolent in wrong,
Afflict with their misrule the indignant land
Where Washington hath left
His awful memory

A light for after times!
Vile instruments of fallen Tyranny
In their own annals by their countrymen
For lasting shame shall they be written down!
Soon may the better Genius there prevail!
Then will the Island Queen of Ocean lay
The thunderbolt aside,
And, twining olives with her laurel crown,
Rest in the Bower of Peace.

But not in ignominious ease
Within the Bower of Peace supine
The Ocean Queen shall rest!
Her other toils await,—
A holier warfare,—nobler victories;
And amaranthine wreaths,
Which, when the laurel crown grows sere,
Will live for ever green.

Hear me, O England! rightly may I claim
Thy favourable audience, Queen of Isles,
My Mother-land revered!
For in the perilous hour,
When weaker spirits stood aghast,
And sophist tongues, to thy dishonour bold,
Spit their cold venom on the public ear,
My voice was heard,—a voice of hope,
Of confidence and joy,—
Yea of such prophecy
As wisdom to her sons doth aye vouchsafe,
When with pure heart and diligent desire
They seek the fountain springs,
And of the ages past
Take counsel reverently.

Nobly hast thou stood up
Against the foulest Tyranny that ere
In elder or in later times,
Hath outraged humankind!
O glorious England, thou hast borne thyself
Religiously and bravely in that strife!
And happier victory hath blest thine arms
Than in the days of yore,
Thine own Plantagenets achieved,
Or Marlborough, wise in council as in field,
Or Wolfe, heroic name!
Now gird thyself for other war!
Look round thee, and behold what ills
Remediable and yet unremedied
Afflict man's wretched race!
Put on the panoply of faith!
Bestir thyself against thine inward foes,
Ignorance and Want, with all their brood
Of miseries and of crimes.

Powerful thou art: imperial Rome,
When in the Augustan age she closed
The temple of the two-faced God,
Could boast no power like thine.
Less opulent was Spain
When Mexico her sumless riches sent
To that proud monarchy;
And Hayti's ransack'd caverns gave their gold;
And from Potosi's recent veins
The unabating stream of treasure flow'd.
And blest art thou, above all nations blest,

For thou art Freedom's own beloved Isle!
The light of Science shines
Conspicuous like a beacon on thy shores :
Thy martyrs purchased at the stake
Faith uncorrupt for thine inheritance;
And by thine hearths Domestic Purity,
Safe from the infection of a tainted age,
Hath kept her sanctuaries.
Yet, O dear England! powerful as thou art,
And rich and wise and blest,
Yet would I see thee, O my Mother-land,
Mightier and wealthier, wiser, happier still!

For still doth Ignorance
Maintain large empire here,
Dark and unblest amid surrounding lights;
Even as within this favour'd spot,
Earth's wonder and her pride,
The traveller on his way
Beholds with weary eye
Bleak moorland, noxious fen, and lonely heath,
In drear extension spread.
Oh grief, that spirits of celestial seed,
Whom ever-teeming Nature hath brought forth,
With all the human faculties divine
Of sense and soul endued,—
Disherited of knowledge and of bliss,
The creatures of brute life,
Should·grope in darkness lost!

Must this reproach endure?
Honour and praise to him
The universal friend,
The general benefactor of mankind;
He who from Coromandel's shores
His perfected discovery brought;
He by whose generous toils
This foul reproach ere long shall be effaced,
This root of evil be eradicate!
Yea, generations yet unborn
Shall owe their weal to him,
And future nations bless
The honour'd name of Bell.

Now may that blessed edifice
Of public good be rear'd
Which holy Edward trac'd,
The spotless Tudor, he whom Death
Too early summon'd to his heavenly throne!
For Brunswick's line was this great work reserved,
For Brunswick's fated line;
They who from papal darkness, and the thrall
Of that worst bondage which doth hold
The immortal spirit chain'd,
Saved us in happy hour.
Fitly for them was this great work reserved;
So, Britain, shall thine aged monarch's wish
Receive its due accomplishment,
That wish which with the good,
(Had he no other praise,)
Through all succeeding times would rank his name,
That all within his realms
Might learn the Book, which all
Who rightly learn, shall live !

From public fountains the perennial stream
Of public weal must flow.

O England, wheresoe'er thy churches stand,
There on that sacred ground
Where the rich harvest of mortality
Is laid, as in a garner, treasured up,
There plant the Tree of Knowledge! Water it
With thy perpetual bounty! It shall spread
Its branches o'er the venerable pile,
Shield it against the storm,
And bring forth fruits of life.

Train up thy children, England! in the ways
Of righteousness, and feed them with the bread
Of wholesome doctrine. Where hast thou thy mines
But in their industry?
Thy bulwarks where but in their breasts?
Thy might but in their arms?
Shall not their numbers therefore be thy wealth,
Thy strength, thy power, thy safety, and thy pride?
Oh grief then, grief and shame,
If in this flourishing land
There should be dwellings where the new-born babe
Doth bring unto its parent's soul no joy!
Where squalid Poverty
Receives it at its birth,
And on her wither'd knees
Gives it the scanty food of discontent!

Queen of the Seas, enlarge thyself!
Redundant as thou art of life and power,
Be thou the hive of nations,
And send thy swarms abroad!
Send them like Greece of old,
With arts and science to enrich
The uncultivated earth;
But with more precious gifts than Greece or Tyre,
Or elder Egypt, to the world bequeathed;
Just laws, and rightful polity,
And, crowning all, the dearest boon of Heaven,
Its word and will reveal'd.

Queen of the Seas enlarge thyself,
Send thou thy swarms abroad!
For in the years to come,
Though centuries or milleniums intervene,
Where'er thy progeny,
Thy language and thy spirit shall be found,—
If on Ontario's shores,
Or late explored Missouri's pastures wide,
Or in that Austral world long sought,
The many-isled Pacific,—yea where waves,
Now breaking over coral reefs, affright
The venturous mariner,
When islands shall have grown, and cities risen
In cocoa groves embower'd;—
Where'er thy language lives,
By whatsoever name the land be call'd,
That land is English still.
Thrones fall, and Dynasties are chang'd;
Empires decay and sink
Beneath their own unwieldy weight;
Dominion passeth like a cloud away:
The imperishable mind
Survives all meaner things.

Train up thy children, England, in the ways
Of righteousness, and feed them with the bread

Of wholesome doctrine. Send thy swarms abroad!
Send forth thy humanizing arts,
Thy stirring enterprise,
Thy liberal polity, thy Gospel light!
Illume the dark idolater,
Reclaim the savage! O thou Ocean Queen,

Be these thy toils when thou hast laid
The thunderbolt aside.
He who hath blest thine arms
Will bless thee in these holy works of Peace!
Father! thy kingdom come, and as in Heaven
Thy will be done on Earth!

Suppressed Poems.

[The following comprise the MINOR POEMS *which were expunged by the author in the last edition, with some which have subsequently appeared in the Annuals, and other miscellaneous collections ; and also a few which have never before been published.]*

TO THE EXILED PATRIOTS
MUIR AND PALMER.

MARTYRS of Freedom! ye who firmly good,
Stept forth the champions in her glorious cause;
Ye, who against Corruption nobly stood
For Justice, Liberty, and equal laws ;

Ye, who have urged the cause of man so well,
Firm when Corruption's torrent swept along;
Ye, who so firmly stood, so nobly fell,
Accept one honest Briton's grateful song.

Take from one honest heart the meed of praise;
Let Justice strike her high-toned harp for you;
Take from the minstrel's hand the garland bays
Who feels your energy and sorrows too.

But be it yours to triumph in disgrace,
Above the storms of Fate be yours to tower
Unchanged in Virtue or by Time or Place,
Unscared is Justice by the throne of Power.

No, by the tyrant's heart let fear be known,
Let the Judge tremble who perverts his trust,
Let proud Oppression totter on his throne;
Fear is a stranger to the good and just.

And is there aught amid the tyrant's state,
Or aught in mighty Nature's ample reign,
So excellently good, so grandly great,
As Freedom struggling with Oppression's chain?

Swells not the soul with ardour at the view?
Bounds not the breast at Freedom's sacred call?
Ye, noble Martyrs, then she feels for you,
Glows in your cause, and crimsons at your fall.

And shall Oppression vainly think by Fear
To quench the fearless energy of Mind,
And glorying in your fall, exult it here,
As though no free-born soul was left behind?

Thinks the proud tyrant, by the pliant law,
The hireling Jury and the Judge unjust,
To strike the soul of Liberty with awe,
And scare the friends of Freedom from their trust?

As easy might the Despot's empty pride
The onward course of rushing Ocean stay:
As easy might his jealous caution hide
From mortal eyes the Orb of general day.

For like that general Orb's eternal flame
Glows the mild force of Virtue's constant light;
Though clouded by Misfortune, still the same,
For ever constant and for ever bright.

Not till eternal Chaos shall that light
Before Oppression's fury fade away;
Not till the Sun himself be quenched in night,
Not till the frame of Nature shall decay.

Go then—secure in steady Virtue—go,
Nor heed the peril of the stormy seas;
Nor heed the felon's name—the felon's woe,
Contempt and pain and sorrow and disease.

Though cankering cares corrode the sinking frame,
Though Sickness rankle in the sallow breast,
Though Death himself should quench the vital flame,
Think but for what ye suffer, and be blest.

So shall your great examples fire each soul,
So in each free-born breast for ever dwell,
Till MAN shall rise above the unjust control,
Stand where ye stood, and triumph where ye fell.

Ages unborn shall glory in your shame,
And curse the ignoble spirit of the time,
And teach their lisping infants to exclaim—
He who allows Oppression, shares the crime.

The sixth day of the first decade of the fourth month of the third year of the French Republic, ONE AND INDIVISIBLE.

THE KNELL.

IN days of yore, when Superstition's sway
Bound blinded Europe in her sacred spell,
The wizard priest enjoined the parting knell,
To fright the hovering Devil from his prey.
If some poor rustic died who could not pay,
Still slept the priest and silent hung the bell.
Then if a yeoman died, his children paid
One bell, to save his parting soul from hell;
And if a Bishop Death's dread call obeyed,
Through all the diocese was heard the toll,
For much his pious brethren were afraid
Lest Satan should receive the good man's soul.
But when Death's levelling hand laid low the King,
Since Kings in both worlds very well are known,
Through all his kingdoms every bell must ring,
For Satan comes with legions for his own.

MUSINGS

ON THE WIG OF A SCARE-CROW.

ALAS for this world's changes and the lot
  Of sublunary things! Yon Wig that there
  Moves with each motion of the inconstant air,
Invites my pensive mind to serious thought.
Was it for this its curious cawl was wrought,
  Close as the tender tendrils of the vine,
With clustered curls? Perhaps the artist's care
Its borrowed beauties for some lady fair
  Arranged with nicest art and fingers fine;
  Or for the forehead framed of some Divine
Its graceful gravity of grizzled grey;
  Or whether on some stern schoolmaster's brow
  Sate its white terrors, who shall answer now?
On yonder rag-robed pole for many a day
  Have those dishonour'd locks endur'd the rains,
And winds, and summer sun, and winter snow,
Scaring with vain alarms the robber crow,
  Till of its former form no trace remains,
None of its ancient honours! I survey
  Its alter'd state with moralizing eye,
And journey sorrowing on my lonely way,
  And muse on Fortune's mutability.

THE IVY.

I STOOD beneath the castle wall,
  And mark'd the ivy bower
That, fragrant in its autumn bloom,
  Wreathed round the mouldering tower.

The plant insinuates its roots
  To rend the ruined wall,
And yet with close and treacherous arms
  Suspends awhile its fall

I mus'd upon its ancient strength,
  Its hastening dissolution,
And thought upon the ivy friends
  Who prop our Constitution.

TO THE RAINBOW.

LOVELIEST of the meteor-train,
Girdle of the summer rain,
Finger of the dews of air,
Glowing vision fleet as fair,
While the evening shower retires
Kindle thy unhurting fires,
And among the meadows near
Thy refulgent pillar rear:
Or amid the dark-blue cloud
High thine orbed glories shroud,
Or the moisten'd hills between
Bent in mighty arch be seen,
Through whose sparkling portals wide
Fiends of storm and darkness ride.

Like Cheerfulness, thou art wont to gaze
Always on the brightest blaze;
Canst from setting suns deduce
Varied gleams and sprightly hues;
And on louring gloom imprint
Smiling streaks of gayest tint.

THE MORNING MIST.

LOOK, William, how the morning mists
  Have covered all the scene,
Nor house nor hill canst thou behold,
  Grey wood, or meadow green.

The distant spire across the vale
  These floating vapours shroud,
Scarce are the neighbouring poplars seen,
  Pale shadowed in the cloud.

But seest thou, William, where the mists
  Sweep o'er the southern sky,
The dim effulgence of the Sun
  That lights them as they fly?

Soon shall that glorious orb of day
  In all his strength arise,
And roll along his azure way,
  Through clear and cloudless skies.

Then shall we see across the vale
  The village spire so white,
And the grey wood and meadow green
  Shall live again in light.

So, William, from the moral world
  The clouds shall pass away;
The light that struggles through them now
  Shall beam eternal day.

SONNET.

TO MR UNDERWOOD, ON HIS SETTING OUT FOR A GEOLOGICAL EXCURSION IN CORNWALL, JULY 1795.

SEARCHER of Wisdom! in the earth's dark womb
  Thou those drear caves shalt visit, where the day
Has never glimmer'd through the eternal gloom:
  Go there,—and journeying in thy distant way,
Sometimes remember me. I too would share
  Thy lot, and haply might beguile the road
  With converse, tedious else; but me the load
Wearying, and hard weighs down of anxious care.
Hence dark of mind, and hence my furrow'd brow
  Lowers stern and sullen. There was once a day
  When thou hast heard me pour a happier lay:
This boots not to remember; and know thou
That not without a sinking of the heart,
My Friend, I shall behold thee hence depart.

SONNET.

THAT gooseberry-bush attracts my wandering eyes,
  Whose vivid leaves, so beautifully green,
  First opening in the early spring are seen:
I sit and gaze, and cheerful thoughts arise
Of that delightful season drawing near,
  When those grey woods shall don their summer dress,
  And ring with warbled love and happiness.
I sit and think that soon the advancing year
With golden flowers shall star the verdant vale:

Then may the enthusiast youth at eve's lone hour,
Led by mild Melancholy's placid power,
Go listen to the soothing nightingale,
And feed on meditation; while that I
Remain at home, and feed on gooseberry-pie.

SONNET.

WHAT though no sculptured monument proclaim
Thy fate—yet, Albert, in my breast I bear
Inshrined the sad remembrance: yet thy name
Will fill my throbbing bosom. When DESPAIR,
The child of murdered HOPE, fed on thy heart,
Loved honoured friend, I saw thee sink forlorn,
Pierced to the soul by cold Neglect's keen dart,
And Penury's hard ills, and pitying Scorn,
And the dark spectre of departed Joy,
Inhuman MEMORY. Often on thy grave
Love I the solitary hour to employ,
Thinking on other days; and heave the sigh
Responsive, when I mark the high grass wave,
Sad sounding as the cold breeze rustles by.

SONNET.

HARD by the road, where on that little mound
The high grass rustles to the passing breeze,
The child of Misery rests her head in peace.
Pause there in sadness: that unhallowed ground
Inshrines what once was Isabel. Sleep on,
Sleep on, poor Outcast! lovely was thy cheek,
And thy mild eye was eloquent to speak
The soul of Pity. Pale and woe-begone,
Soon did thy fair cheek fade, and thine eye weep
The tear of anguish for the babe unborn,
The helpless heir of Poverty and Scorn.
She drank the draught that chill'd her soul to sleep.
I pause and wipe the big drop from mine eye,
Whilst the proud Levite scowls and passes by.

SONNET.

TO ARISTE.

ARISTE! soon to sojourn with the crowd,
In soul abstracted must thy minstrel go;
Mix in the giddy, fond, fantastic show,
Mix with the gay, the envious, and the proud.
I go: but still my soul remains with thee,
Still will the eye of fancy paint thy charms,
Still, lovely Maid, thy imaged form I see,
And every pulse will vibrate with alarms.
When scandal spreads abroad her odious tale,
When envy at a rival's beauty sighs,
When rancour prompts the female tongue to rail,
And rage and malice fire the gamester's eyes,
I turn my wearied soul to her for ease,
Who only names to praise, who only speaks to please.

SONNET.

BE his to court the Muse, whose humble breast
The glow of genius never could inspire;
Who never, by the future song possest,
Struck the bold strings, and waked the daring lyre.
Let him invoke the Muses from their grove,
Who never felt the inspiring touch of love.
If I would sing how beauty's beamy blaze
Thrills through the bosom at the lightning view,
Or harp the high-ton'd hymn to virtue's praise,
Where only from the minstrel praise is due,
I would not court the Muse to prompt my lays,
My Muse, ARISTE, would be found in you!
And need I court the goddess when I move
The warbling lute to sound the soul of love?

SONNET.

LET ancient stories sound the painter's art,
Who stole from many a maid his Venus' charms,
Till warm devotion fir'd each gazer's heart,
And every bosom bounded with alarms.
He cull'd the beauties of his native isle,
From some the blush of beauty's vermeil dyes,
From some the lovely look, the winning smile,
From some the languid lustre of the eyes.
Low to the finish'd form the nations round
In adoration bent the pious knee;
With myrtle wreaths the artist's brow they crown'd,
Whose skill, ARISTE, only imaged thee.
Ill-fated artist, doom'd so wide to seek
The charms that blossom on ARISTE's cheek!

SONNET.

I PRAISE thee not, ARISTE, that thine eye
Knows each emotion of the soul to speak;
That lilies with thy face might fear to vie,
And roses can but emulate thy cheek.
I praise thee not because thine auburn hair
In native tresses wantons on the wind;
Nor yet because that face, surpassing fair,
Bespeaks the inward excellence of mind:
'T is that soft charm thy minstrel's heart has won,
That mild meek goodness that perfects the rest;
Soothing and soft it steals upon the breast,
As the soft radiance of the setting sun,
When varying through the purple hues of light,
The fading orbit smiles serenely bright.

SONNET.

DUNNINGTON CASTLE.

THOU ruin'd relique of the ancient pile,
Rear'd by that hoary bard, whose tuneful lyre
First breath'd the voice of music on our isle;
Where, warn'd in life's calm evening to retire,
Old CHAUCER slowly sunk at last to night;
Still shall his forceful line, his varied strain,
A firmer, nobler monument remain,
When the high grass waves o'er thy lonely site.
And yet the cankering tooth of envious age
Has sapp'd the fabric of his lofty rhyme;
Though genius still shall ponder o'er the page,
And piercing through the shadowy mist of time,
The festive Bard of EDWARD's court recall,
As fancy paints the pomp that once adorn'd thy wall.

SONNET.

As slow and solemn yonder deepening knell
  Tolls through the sullen evening's shadowy gloom,
  Alone and pensive, in my silent room,
On man and on mortality I dwell.
And as the harbinger of death I hear
  Frequent and full, much do I love to muse
On life's distemper'd scenes of hope and fear;
  And passion varying her camelion hues,
And man pursuing pleasure's empty shade,
  Till death dissolves the vision. So the child
  In youth's gay morn with wondering pleasure smil'd,
As with the shining ice well-pleas'd he play'd;
Nor, as he grasps the crystal in his play,
Heeds how the faithless bauble melts away.

SONNET.

TO THE FIRE.

My friendly fire, thou blazest clear and bright,
  Nor smoke nor ashes soil thy grateful flame;
Thy temperate splendour cheers the gloom of night,
  Thy genial heat enlivens the chill'd frame.
I love to muse me o'er the evening hearth,
  I love to pause in meditation's sway;
And whilst each object gives reflection birth,
  Mark thy brisk rise, and see thy slow decay:
And I would wish, like thee, to shine serene,
  Like thee, within mine influence, all to cheer;
And wish at last, in life's declining scene,
  As I had beam'd as bright, to fade as clear:
So might my children ponder o'er my shrine,
And o'er my ashes muse, as I will muse over thine.

SONNET.

THE FADED FLOWER.

Ungrateful he who pluckt thee from thy stalk,
  Poor faded flow'ret! on his careless way,
Inhal'd awhile thine odours on his walk,
  Then past along, and left thee to decay.
Thou melancholy emblem! had I seen
  Thy modest beauties dew'd with evening's gem,
I had not rudely cropt thy parent stem,
  But left thy blossom still to grace the green,
And now I bend me o'er thy wither'd bloom,
  And drop the tear, as Fancy, at my side
Deep-sighing, points the fair frail Emma's tomb;
  « Like thine, sad flower! was that poor wanderer's
        pride!
O, lost to love and truth! whose selfish joy
Tasted her vernal sweets, but tasted to destroy.»

SONNET.

TO THE NIGHTINGALE.

Sad songstress of the night, no more I hear
Thy soften'd warblings meet my pensive ear,
  As by thy wonted haunts again I rove;
Why art thou silent? wherefore sleeps thy lay?
For faintly fades the sinking orb of day,
  And yet thy music charms no more the grove.

The shrill bat flutters by; from yon dark tower
The shrieking owlet hails the shadowy hour;
  Hoarse hums the beetle as he drones along,
The hour of love is flown! thy full-fledg'd brood
No longer need thy care to cull their food,
  And nothing now remains to prompt the song:
But drear and sullen seems the silent grove,
No more responsive to the lay of love.

SONNET.

TO REFLECTION.

Hence, busy torturer, wherefore should mine eye
  Revert again to many a sorrow past?
Hence, busy torturer, to the happy fly,
  Those who have never seen the sun o'ercast
By one dark cloud, thy retrospective beam,
  Serene and soft, may on their bosoms gleam,
As the last splendour of the summer sky.
  Let them look back on pleasure, ere they know
To mourn its absence; let them contemplate
The thorny windings of our mortal state,
  Ere unexpected bursts the cloud of woe;
  Stream not on me thy torch's baneful glow,
Like the sepulchral lamp's funereal gloom,
In darkness glimmering to disclose a tomb.

THE MAD WOMAN.

The circumstance on which the following Ballad is founded, happened not many years ago in Bristol.

The Traveller's hands were white with cold,
    The Traveller's lips were blue,
Oh! glad was he when the village church
    So near was seen in view!

He hasten'd to the village Inn,
    That stood the church-door nigh,—
There sat a woman on a grave,
    And he could not pass her by.

Her feet were bare, and on her breast
    Through rags did the winter blow,
She sate with her face towards the wind,
    And the grave was cover'd with snow.

Is there never a Christian in the place,
    To her the Traveller cried,
Who will let thee, this cold winter time,
    Sit by his fire-side?

I have fire in my head, she answered him,
    I have fire in my heart also;
And there will be no winter time
    In the place where I must go!

A curse upon thee, man,
    For mocking me! she said;
And he saw the woman's eyes, like one
    In a fever-fit, were red.

And when he to the inn-door came,
    And the host his greeting gave,
He ask'd who that mad woman was
    Who sate upon the grave.

God in his mercy, quoth the host,
　　Forgive her for her sin;
For heavy is her crime, and strange
　　Her punishment hath been.

She was so pale and meagre-ey'd,
　　As scarcely to be known,
When to her mother she return'd
　　From service in the town.

She seldom spoke, she never smil'd,
　　What ail'd her no one knew,
But every day more meagre-pale
　　And sullen sad she grew.

It was upon last Christmas eve,
　　As we sat round the hearth,
And every soul but Martha's
　　Was full of Christmas mirth.

She sat, and look'd upon the fire
　　That then so fiercely shone,
She look'd into it earnestly,
　　And we heard a stifled groan.

And she shook like a dying wretch
　　In a convulsive fit;
And up she rose, and in the snows,
　　Went out on a grave to sit.

We follow'd her, and to the room
　　Besought her to return;
She groan'd and said, that in the fire,
　　She saw her Baby burn.

And in her dreadful madness then
　　To light her murder came,
How secretly from every eye
　　Nine months she hid her shame;

And how she slew the wretched babe
　　Just as he sprung to light,
And in the midnight fire consum'd
　　His little body quite.

Would I could feel the winter wind,
　　Would I could feel the snow!
I have fire in my head, poor Martha cried,
　　I have fire in my heart also.

So there from morn till night she sits—
　　Now God forgive her sin!
For heavy is her crime, and strange
　　Her punishment hath been.

ODE

TO A PIG WHILE HIS NOSE WAS BEING BORED.

HARK! hark! that Pig—that Pig! the hideous note,
　　More loud, more dissonant, each moment grows—
Would one not think the knife was in his throat?
　　And yet they are only boring through his nose.

You foolish beast, so rudely to withstand
　　Your master's will, to feel such idle fears!
Why, Pig, there's not a Lady in the land
　　Who has not also bor'd and ring'd her ears.

Pig! 't is your master's pleasure—then be still,
　　And hold your nose to let the iron through!
Dare you resist your lawful Sovereign's will?
　　Rebellious Swine! you know not what you do!

To man o'er beast the power was given;
　　Pig, hear the truth, and never murmur more!
Would you rebel against the will of Heaven?
　　You impious beast, be still, and let them bore!

The social Pig resigns his natural rights
　　When first with man he covenants to live;
He barters them for safer stye delights,
　　For grains and wash, which man alone can give.

Sure is provision on the social plan,
　　Secure the comforts that to each belong:
Oh, happy Swine! the impartial sway of man
　　Alike protects the weak Pig and the strong.

And you resist! you struggle now because
　　Your master has thought fit to bore your nose!
You grunt in flat rebellion to the laws
　　Society finds needful to impose!

Go to the forest, Piggy, and deplore
　　The miserable lot of savage Swine!
See how the young Pigs fly from the great Boar,
　　And see how coarse and scantily they dine!

Behold their hourly danger, when who will
　　May hunt or snare or seize them for his food!
Oh, happy Pig! whom none presumes to kill
　　Till your protecting master thinks it good!

And when, at last, the closing hour of life
　　Arrives (for Pigs must die as well as Man),
When in your throat you feel the long sharp knife,
　　And the blood trickles to the pudding-pan;

And when, at last, the death wound yawning wide,
　　Fainter and fainter grows the expiring cry,
Is there no grateful joy, no loyal pride,
　　To think that for your master's good you die?

TO A COLLEGE CAT.

WRITTEN SOON AFTER THE INSTALLATION AT OXFORD, 1793.

TOLL on, toll on, old Bell! I'll neither pray
Nor sleep away the hour. The fire burns bright,
And, bless the maker of this great-arm'd chair,
This is the throne of comfort! I will sit
And study most devoutly: not my Euclid,
For God forbid that I should discompose
That spider's excellent geometry!
I'll study thee, Puss: not to make a picture—
I hate your canvas cats and dogs and fools,
Themes that pollute the pencil! let me see
The Patriot's actions start again to life,
And I will bless the artist who awakes
The throb of emulation. Thou shalt give,
A better lesson Puss! come look at me.
Lift up thine emerald eyes! aye, purr away,
For I am praising thee, I tell thee, Puss,

And Cats as well as Kings love flattery.
For three whole days I heard an old Fur Gown
Beprais'd, that made a Duke a Chancellor:
Trust me, though I can sing most pleasantly
Upon thy well-streak'd coat, to that said Fur
I was not guilty of a single rhyme!
'T was an old turncoat Fur, that would sit easy
And wrap round any man, so it were tied
With a blue riband.
              What a magic lies
In beauty! thou on this forbidden ground
Mayest range, and when the Fellow looks at thee
Straight he forgets the statute.[1] Swell thy tail
And stretch thy claws, most Democratic beast,
I like thine independence! Treat thee well,
Thou art as playful as young Innocence;
But if we play the Governor, and break
The social compact, God has given thee claws,
And thou hast sense to use them. Oh! that Man
Would copy this thy wisdom! spaniel fool,
He crouches down and licks his tyrant's hand,
And courts oppression. Wiser animal,
I gaze on thee, familiar not enslaved,
And thinking how affection's gentle hand
Leads by a hair the large limb'd Elephant,[2]
With mingled pity and contempt behold
His drivers goad the patient biped beast.

ROMANCE.

WHAT wildly-beauteous form,
High on the summit of yon bicrown'd hill,
Lovely in horror, takes her dauntless stand?
   Though speeds the thunder there its deep'ning way,
   Though round her head the lightnings play,
Undaunted she abides the storm;
     She waves her magic wand,
     The clouds retire, the storm is still;
Bright beams the sun unwonted light around,
And many a rising flower bedecks the enchanted ground.

     ROMANCE! I know thee now,
     I know the terrors of thy brow;
   I know thine aweful mien, thy beaming eye;
     And lo! whilst mists arise around
     Yon car that cleaves the pregnant ground,
   Two fiery dragons whirl her through the sky.
     Her milder sister loves to rove
     Amid Parnassus' laurell'd grove,
     On Helicon's harmonious side,
     To mark the gurgling streamlet glide;
Meantime, through wilder scenes and sterner skies,
From clime to clime the ardent genius flies.

     She speeds to yonder shore,[3]
     Where ruthless tempests roar,
Where sturdy winter holds his northern reign,
Nor vernal suns relax the ice-pil'd plain:

Dim shadows circle round her secret seat,
Where wandering, who approach shall hear
   The wild wolf rend the air;
   Through the cloudy-mantled sky ·
   Shall see the imps of darkness fly,
And hear the sad scream from the grim retreat:
     Around her throne
Ten thousand dangers lurk, most fearful, most unknown.

     Yet lovelier oft in milder sway,
     She wends abroad her magic way;
     The holy prelate owns her power;
      In soft'ning tale relates
     The snowy Ethiop's matchless charms,
     The outlaw's den, the clang of arms,
      And love's too-varying fates;
     The storms of persecution lower,
     Austere devotion gives the stern command,
     « Commit yon impious legend to the fires;»—
      Calm in his conscious worth, the sage retires,
And saves the invalu'd work, and quits the thankless
     land;
     High tow'rs his name the sacred list above,
And ev'n the priest [1] is prais'd who wrote of blameless
     love.

     Around the tower, whose wall infolds
     Young THORA's blooming charms,
     Romance's serpent winds his glittering folds;
     The warrior clasps his shaggy arms,
     The monster falls, the damsel is the spoil,
     Matchless reward of REGNER's [2] matchless toil.

     Around the patriot board,
     The knights [3] attend their lord;
     The martial sieges hov'ring o'er,
   Enrapt the genius views the dauntless band;
     Still prompt for innocence to fight,
     Or quell the pride of proud oppression's might,
They rush intrepid o'er the land;
     She gives them to the minstrel lore,
     Hands down her LAUNCELOT's peerless name,
     Repays her TRISTRAM's woes with fame;
     Borne on the breath of song,
To future times descends the memory of the throng.

     Foremost mid the peers of France [4]
     ORLANDO hurls the death-fraught lance;
     Where DURLINDANA aims the blow,
     To darkness sinks the faithless foe;
     The horn with magic sound
     Spreads deep dismay around;
     Unborn to bleed, the chieftain goes,
     And scatters wide his Paynim foes;
     The genius hovers o'er the purple plain
     Where OLIVERO tramples on the slain;
     BAYARDO speeds his furious course,
     High towers ROGERO in his matchless force.

Romance the heighten'd tale has caught,
     Forth from the sad monastic cell,

---

[1] The statute that excludes cats, dogs, and *all other singing-birds*, from the college precincts.

[2] « Always encounter petulance with gentleness, and perverseness with kindness: a gentle hand will lead the elephant itself by a hair. »—*From the Persian Rosary, by Eddin Sadi. Enfield's History of Philosophy.*

[3] Fictions of Romance, popular in Scandinavia at an early period.

[1] Heliodorus chose rather to be deprived of his see than burn his Ethiopics. The bishop's name would have slept with his fathers, the romancer is remembered.

[2] First exploit of the celebrated Regner Lodbrog.

[3] Knights of the round table.

[4] The Paladines of France.

Where fiction with devotion loves to dwell,
The sacred legend [1] flies with many a wonder fraught;
  Deep roll the papal thunders [2] round,
And everlasting wrath to rebel reason sound.

Hark! Superstition sounds to war's alarms,
  War stalks o'er Palestine with scorching breath,
  And triumphs in the feast of death;
  All Europe flies to arms :
Enthusiast courage spreads her piercing sound,
Devotion caught the cry, and woke the echo around.
  Romance [3] before the army flies,
  New scenes await her wondering eyes;
  Awhile she firms her GODFREY's throne,
And makes Arabia's magic lore her own.

And hark! resound, in mingled sound,
  The clang of arms, the shriek of death;
  Each streaming gash bedews the ground,
And deep and hollow groans load the last struggling
    breath :
  Wide through the air the arrows fly,
  Darts, shields, and swords, commix'd appear;
  Deep is the cry, when thousands die,
  When CŒUR DE LION's arm constrains to fear :
    Aloft the battle-axe in air
    Whirls around confus'd despair;
    Nor Acre's walls can check his course;
    Nor Sarzin millions stay his force.

  Indignant, firm the warrior stood,
  The hungry lion gapes for food;
  His fearless eye beheld him nigh,
Unarm'd, undaunted, saw the beast proceed :
  Romance, o'erhovering, saw the monster die,
And scarce herself believ'd the more than wond'rous deed.

  And now, with more terrific mien,
  She quits the sad degenerate scene;
With many a talisman of mightiest pow'r,
  Borne in a rubied car, sublime she flies,
  Fire-breathing griffins waft her through the skies;
Around her head the innocuous tempest lowers,
  To Gallia's favour'd realm she goes,
And quits her magic state, and plucks her lovely rose. [4]

  Imagination waves her wizard wand,
  Dark shadows mantle o'er the land;
  The lightnings flash, the thunders sound,
  Convulsive throbs the labouring ground;
What fiends, what monsters, circling round, arise! [5]
  High towers of fire aloft aspire,
  Deep yells resound amid the skies,
  Yclad in arms, to Fame's alarms
  Her magic warrior flies.

By Fiction's shield secure, for many a year
  O'er cooler reason held the genius rule;
But lo! CERVANTES waves his pointed spear,
  Nor Fiction's shield can stay the spear of ridicule.

[1] Instead of forging the life of a saint, Archbishop Turpin was better employed in falsifying the history of Charlemagne.
[2] A bull was issued, commanding all good citizens to believe Ariosto's poem, founded upon Turpin's history.
[3] Arabian fictions ingrafted on the Gothic romance.
[4] Romance of the Rose, written soon after the Crusades.
[5] Early prose Romances, originally Spanish.

The blameless warrior comes; he first to wield
His fateful weapon in the martial field;
  By him created on the view,
  ARCADIA's valleys bloom anew,
  And many a flock o'erspreads the plain,
And love, with innocence, assumes his reign :
  Protected by a warrior's name,
  The kindred warriors live to fame :
Sad is the scene, where oft from Pity's eye
  Descends the sorrowing tear,
  As high the unheeding chieftain lifts the spear,
And gives the deadly blow, and sees PARTHENIA die!
  Where, where such virtues can we see,
  Or where such valour, SIDNEY, but in thee ?
O, cold of heart, shall pride assail thy shade,
Whom all Romance could fancy nature made?

  Sound, Fame, thy loudest blast,
  For SPENSER pours the tender strain,
And shapes to glowing forms the motley train; [1]
  The elfin tribes around
  Await his potent sound,
And o'er his head Romance her brightest splendours cast.
  Deep through the air let sorrow's banner wave!
For penury o'er SPENSER's friendless head
  Her chilling mantle spread;
  For Genius cannot save!
Virtue bedews the blameless poet's dust;
But fame, exulting, clasps her favourite's laurel'd bust.

  Fain would the grateful Muse, to thee, ROUSSEAU,
  Pour forth the energic thanks of gratitude;
  Fain would the raptur'd lyre ecstatic glow,
  To whom Romance and Nature form'd all good :
  Guide of my life, too weak these lays,
  To pour the unutterable praise;
  Thine aid divine for ever lend,
  Still as my guardian sprite attend;
  Unmov'd by Fashion's flaunting throng,
Let my calm stream of life smooth its meek course along;
  Let no weak vanity dispense
  Her vapours o'er my better sense;
  But let my bosom glow with fire,
  Let me strike the soothing lyre,
Although by all unheard the melodies expire.

TO URBAN.

Lo! where the livid lightning flies
  With transient furious force,
A moment's splendour streaks the skies,
  Where ruin marks its course :
Then see how mild the font of day
  Expands the stream of light,
Whilst living by the genial ray,
  All nature smiles delight.

So boisterous riot, on his course
  Uncurb'd by reason, flies;
And lightning, like its fatal force,
  Soon lightning-like it dies :
Whilst sober Temperance, still the same,
  Shall shun the scene of strife;
And, like the sun's enlivening flame,
  Shall beam the lamp of life.

[1] Fictions of Romance, allegorized by Spenser.

Let noise and folly seek the reign
　Where senseless riot rules;
Let them enjoy the pleasures vain
　Enjoy'd alone by fools.
URBAN! those better joys be ours,
　Which virtuous science knows,
To pass in milder bliss the hours,
　Nor fear the future woes.

So when stern time their frames shall seize,
　When sorrow pays for sin;
When every nerve shall feel disease,
　And conscience shrink within;
Shall health's best blessings all be ours,
　The soul serene at ease,
Whilst science gilds the passing hours,
　And every hour shall please.

Even now from solitude they fly,
　To drown each thought in noise;
Even now they shun Reflection's eye,
　Depriv'd of man's best joys.
So, when Time's unrelenting doom
　Shall bring the seasons' course,
The busy monitor shall come
　With aggravated force.

Friendship is ours: best friend, who knows
　Each varied hour to employ;
To share the lighted load of woes,
　And double every joy:
And Science too shall lend her aid,
　The friend that never flies,
But shines amid misfortune's shade
　As stars in midnight skies.

Each joy domestic bliss can know
　Shall deck the future hour;
Or if we taste the cup of woe,
　The cup has lost its power.
Thus may we live, till death's keen spear,
　Unwish'd, unfear'd, shall come;
Then sink, without one guilty fear,
　To slumber in the tomb.

THE MISER'S MANSION.

THOU, mouldering mansion, whose embattled side
　Shakes as about to fall at every blast;
Once the gay pile of splendour, wealth, and pride,
　But now the monument of grandeur past.

Fall'n fabric! pondering o'er thy time-trac'd walls,
　Thy mouldering, mighty, melancholy state,
Each object, to the musing mind, recalls
　The sad vicissitudes of varying fate.

Thy tall towers tremble to the touch of time,
　The rank weeds rustle in thy spacious courts;
Fill'd are thy wide canals with loathly slime,
　Where battening, undisturb'd, the foul toad sports.

Deep from her dismal dwelling yells the owl,
　The shrill bat flits around her dark retreat;
And the hoarse daw, when loud the tempests howl,
　Screams as the wild winds shake her secret seat.

'T was here AVARO dwelt, who daily told
　His useless heaps of wealth in selfish joy;
Who lov'd to ruminate o'er hoarded gold,
　And hid those stores he dreaded to employ.

In vain to him benignant Heaven bestow'd
　The golden heaps to render thousands blest;
Smooth aged penury's laborious road,
　And heal the sorrows of affliction's breast.

For, like the serpent of romance, he lay
　Sleepless and stern to guard the golden sight;
With ceaseless care he watch'd his heaps by day,
　With causeless fears he agoniz'd by night.

Ye honest rustics, whose diurnal toil
　Enrich'd the ample fields this churl possest;
Say, ye who paid to him the annual spoil,
　With all his riches, was AVARO blest?

Rose he, like you, at morn devoid of fear,
　His anxious vigils o'er his gold to keep?
Or sunk he, when the noiseless night was near,
　As calmly on his couch of down to sleep?

Thou wretch! thus curst with poverty of soul,
　What boot to thee the blessings fortune gave?
What boots thy wealth above the world's control,
　If riches doom their churlish lord a slave!

Chill'd at thy presence grew the stately halls,
　Nor longer echo'd to the song of mirth;
The hand of art no more adorn'd thy walls,
　Nor blaz'd with hospitable fires the hearth.

On well-worn hinges turns the gate no more,
　Nor social friendship hastes the friend to meet;
Nor when the accustom'd guest draws near the door,
　Run the glad dogs, and gambol round his feet.

Sullen and stern AVARO sat alone
　In anxious wealth amid the joyless hall,
Nor heeds the chilly hearth with moss o'ergrown,
　Nor sees the green slime mark the mouldering wall.

For desolation o'er the fabric dwells,
　And time, on restless pinion, hurried by;
Loud from her chimney'd seat the night-bird yells,
　And through the shatter'd roof descends the sky.

Thou melancholy mansion! much mine eye
　Delights to wander o'er thy sullen gloom,
And mark the daw from yonder turret fly,
　And muse how man himself creates his doom.

For here had Justice reign'd, had Pity known
　With genial power to sway AVARO's breast,
These treasur'd heaps which Fortune made his own,
　By aiding misery might himself have blest.

And Charity had oped her golden store
　To work the gracious will of Heaven intent,
Fed from her superflux the craving poor,
　And paid adversity what heaven had lent.

Then had thy turrets stood in all their state,
　Then had the hand of art adorn'd thy wall,
Swift on its well-worn hinges turn'd the gate,
　And friendly converse cheer'd the echoing hall.

89

Then had the village youth at vernal hour
  Hung round with flowery wreaths thy friendly gate,
And blest in gratitude that sovereign power
  That made the man of mercy good as great.

The traveller then to view thy towers had stood,
  Whilst babes had lispt their benefactor's name,
And call'd on heaven to give thee every good,
  And told abroad thy hospitable fame.

In every joy of life the hours had fled,
  Whilst time on downy pinions hurried by,
Till age with silver hairs had grac'd thy head,
  Wean'd from the world, and taught thee how to die.

And, as thy liberal hand had shower'd around
  The ample wealth by lavish fortune given,
Thy parted spirit had that justice found,
  And angels hymn'd the rich man's soul to heaven.

HOSPITALITY.

« LAY low yon impious trappings on the ground,
Bend, superstition, bend thy haughty head,
  Be mine supremacy, and mine alone :»
    Thus from his firm-establish'd throne,
Replete with vengeful fury, HENRY said.
High Reformation lifts her iron rod,
  But lo! with stern and threatful mien,
  Fury and rancour desolate the scene,
Beneath their rage the Gothic structures nod.
  Ah! hold awhile your angry hands;
  Ah! here delay your king's commands;
For Hospitality will feel the wound!
  In vain the voice of reason cries,
Whilst uncontroul'd the regal mandate flies.

Thou, AVALON! in whose polluted womb
The patriot monarch found his narrow tomb;
Where now thy solemn pile, whose antique head
With niche-fraught turrets awe-inspiring spread,
Stood the memorial of the pious age?
  Where wont the hospitable fire
  In cheering volumes to aspire,
And with its genial warmth the pilgrim's woes assuage.
    Low lie thy turrets now,
The desert ivy clasps the joyless hearth;
  The dome which luxury yrear'd,
  Though Hospitality was there rever'd,
    Now, from its shatter'd brow,
With mouldering ruins loads the unfrequented earth.

    Ye minstrel throng,
In whose bold breasts once glow'd the tuneful fire,
No longer struck by you shall breathe the plaintive
    lyre:
  The walls, whose trophied sides along
  Once rung the harp's energic sound,
  Now damp and moss-ymantled load the ground;
  No more the bold romantic lore
  Shall spread from Thulé's distant shore;
  No more intrepid Cambria's hills among,
In hospitable hall, shall rest the child of song.
  Ah, Hospitality! soft Pity's child,
    Where shall we seek thee now?
    Genius! no more thy influence mild
    Shall gild Affliction's clouded brow;

    No more thy cheering smiles impart
    One ray of joy to Sorrow's heart;
    No more within the lordly pile
  Wilt thou bestow the bosom-warming smile.

  Whilst haughty pride his gallery displays,
    Where hangs the row in sullen show
  Of heroes and of chiefs of ancient days,
    The gaudy toil of Turkish loom
    Shall decorate the stately room;
  Yet there the traveller, with wistful eye,
Beholds the guarded door, and sighs, and passes by.

  Not so where o'er the desert waste of sand
    Speeds the rude Arab wild his wandering way;
  Leads on to rapine his intrepid band,
    And claims the wealth of India for his prey;
    There, when the wilder'd traveller distrest
  Holds to the robber forth the friendly hand,
  The generous Arab gives the tent of rest,
  Guards him as the fond mother guards her child,
Relieves his every want, and guides him o'er the wild.

  Not so amid those climes where rolls along
    The Oroonoko deep his mighty flood;
  Where rove amid their woods the savage throng,
    Nurs'd up in slaughter, and inur'd to blood;
    Fierce as their torrents, wily as the snake
    That sharps his venom'd tooth in every brake,
  Aloft the dreadful tomahawk they rear;
    Patient of hunger, and of pain,
    Close in their haunts the chiefs remain,
  And lift in secret stand the deadly spear.
  Yet, should the unarm'd traveller draw near,
    And proffering forth the friendly hand,
    Claim their protection from the warrior band,
  The savage Indians bid their anger cease,
Lay down the ponderous spear, and give the pipe of peace.

  Such virtue Nature gives: when man withdraws
  To fashion's circle, far from nature's laws,
    How chang'd, how fall'n the human breast!
  Cold Prudence comes, relentless foe!
  Forbids the pitying tear to flow,
    And steels the soul of apathy to rest;
  Mounts in relentless state her stubborn throne,
And deems of other bosoms by her own.

INSCRIPTION

FOR THE APARTMENT IN CHEPSTOW CASTLE, WHERE
  HENRY MARTEN THE REGICIDE WAS
    IMPRISONED THIRTY YEARS.[1]

For thirty years, secluded from mankind,
Here Marten linger'd. Often have these walls
Echo'd his footsteps, as with even tread
He paced around his prison: not to him
Did Nature's fair varieties exist:
He never saw the sun's delightful beams,
Save when through yon high bars it pour'd a sad

[1] An imitation of this by Mr Canning appeared in the first number of the *Anti-Jacobin*, Nov. 20. 1797. entitled :—*Inscription for the door of the cell in Newgate, where Mrs Brownrigg the Prentice-cide was confined previous to her execution.*—EDITOR.

And broken splendour. Dost thou ask his crime?
He had rebell'd against the king, and sat
In judgment on him; for his ardent mind
Shaped goodliest plans of happiness on earth,
And peace and liberty. Wild dreams! but such
As PLATO loved; such as, with holy zeal
Our MILTON worshipp'd. Blessed hopes! awhile
From man withheld, even to the latter days,
When Christ shall come and all things be fulfill'd.

INSCRIPTION

FOR THE BANKS OF THE HAMPSHIRE AVON.

A LITTLE while, O traveller, linger here,
And let thy leisure eye behold and feel
The beauties of the place; yon heathy hill
That rises sudden from the vale so green,
The vale far stretching as the view can reach
Under its long dark ridge; the river here,
That, like a serpent, through the grassy mead
Winds on, now hidden, glittering now in light.
Nor fraught with merchant wealth, nor famed in song,
This river rolls; an unobtrusive tide,
Its gentle charms may soothe and satisfy
Thy feelings. Look! how bright its pebbled bed
Gleams through the ruffled current; and that bank
With flag leaves border'd, as with two-edged swords!
See where the water wrinkles round the stem
Of yonder water-lily, whose broad leaf
Lies on the wave.—And art thou not refresh'd
By the fresh odour of the running stream?
Soon, traveller! does the river reach the end
Of all its windings: from the near ascent
Thou wilt behold the ocean where it pours
Its waters and is lost. Remember thou,
Traveller! that even so thy restless years
Flow to the ocean of eternity.

INSCRIPTION

UNDER AN OAK.

HERE, Traveller! pause awhile. This ancient Oak
Will parasol thee if the sun ride high,
Or should the sudden shower be falling fast,
Here mayst thou rest umbrella'd. All around
Is good and lovely: hard by yonder wall
The kennel stands; the horse-flesh hanging near
Perchance with scent unsavoury may offend
Thy delicate nostrils, but remember thou
How sweet a perfume to the hound it yields.
And sure its useful odours will regale
More gratefully thy philosophic nose,
Than what the unprofitable violet
Wastes on the wandering wind. Nor wilt thou want
Such music as benevolence will love,
For from these fruitful boughs the acorns fall
Abundant, and the swine that grub around,
Shaking with restless pleasure their brief tails
That like the tendrils of the vine curl up,
Will grunt their greedy joy. Dost thou not love
The sounds that speak enjoyment? Oh! if not,
If thou wouldst rather with inhuman ear

Hark to the warblings of some wretched bird
Bereft of freedom, sure thine heart is dead
To each good feeling, and thy spirit void
Of all that softens or ennobles man.

INSCRIPTION

FOR A MONUMENT AT OLD SARUM.

READER, if thou canst boast the noble name
Of Englishman, it is enough to know
Thou standest in Old Sarum. But if, chance,
'T was thy misfortune in some other land,
Inheritor of slavery, to be born,
Read and be envious! dost thou see yon hut,
Its old mud mossy walls with many a patch
Spotted? Know, foreigner! so wisely well
In England it is order'd, that the laws
Which bind the people, from themselves should spring;
Know that the dweller in that little hut,
That wretched hovel, to the senate sends
Two delegates. Think, foreigner, where such
An individual's rights, how happy all!

EPITAPH.

TIME and the world, whose magnitude and weight
Bear on us in this now, and hold us here
To earth inthrall'd,—what are they in the past?
And in the prospect of the immortal soul
How poor a speck! Not here her resting-place;
Her portion is not here: and happiest they
Who, gathering early all that earth can give,
Shake off its mortal coil, and speed for Heaven.
Such fate had he whose relics here repose.
Few were his days; but yet enough to teach
Love, duty, generous feelings, high desires,
Faith, hope, devotion: and what more could length
Of days have brought him? what but vanity?
Joys, frailer even than health or human life?
Temptation; sin and sorrow, both too sure;
Evils that wound, and cares that fret the heart!
Repine not, therefore, ye who love the dead.

TO LYCON.

On yon wild waste of ruin thron'd, what form
  Beats her swoln breast, and tears her unkempt hair?
Why seems the spectre thus to court the storm?
  Why glare her full-fix'd eyes in stern despair?
    The deep dull groan I hear,
I see her rigid eye refuse the soothing tear.

    Ah! fly her dreadful reign,
  For desolation rules o'er all the lifeless plain;
For deadliest nightshade forms her secret bower;
    For oft the ill-omen'd owl
    Yells loud the dreadful howl,
And the night spectres shrick amid the midnight hour.

  Pale spectre, Grief! thy dull abodes I know,
    I know the horrors of thy barren plain,
  I know the dreadful force of woe,
    I know the weight of thy soul binding chain;

But I have fled thy drear domains,
Have broke thy agonizing chains,
Drain'd deep the poison of thy bowl,
Yet wash'd in Science' stream the poison from my soul.

Fair smiles the morn along the azure sky,
Calm and serene the zephyrs whisper by,
And many a flow'ret gems the painted plain;
As down the dale, with perfumes sweet,
The cheerful pilgrim turns his feet,
His thirsty ear imbibes the throstle's strain;
And every bird that loves to sing
The choral song to coming spring,
Tunes the wild lay symphonious through the grove,
Heaven, earth, and nature, all incite to love.

Ah, pilgrim! stay thy heedless feet,
Distrust each soul-subduing sweet,
Dash down alluring Pleasure's deadly bowl,
For thro' thy frame the venom'd juice will creep;
Lull reason's powers to sombrous sleep,
And stain with sable hue the spotless soul;
For soon the valley's charms decay,
In haggard Grief's ill-omen'd sway,
And barren rocks shall hide the cheering light of day:
Then reason strives in vain,
Extinguish'd hope's enchanting beam for aye,
And virtue sinks beneath the galling chain,
And sorrow deeply drains her lethal bowl,
And sullen fix'd despair benumbs the nerveless soul.

Yet on the summit of yon craggy steep
Stands Hope, surrounded with a blaze of light;
She bids the wretch no more despondent weep,
Or linger in the loathly realms of night;
And Science comes, celestial maid!
As mild as good she comes to aid,
To smooth the rugged steep with magic power,
And fill with many a wile the longly-lingering hour.

Fair smiles the morn, in all the hues of day
Array'd, the wide horizon streams with light;
Anon the dull mists blot the living ray,
And darksome clouds presage the stormy night:
Yet may the sun anew extend his ray,
Anew the heavens may shine in splendour bright;
Anew the sunshine gild the lucid plain,
And nature's frame reviv'd, may thank the genial rain.

And what, my friend, is life?
What but the many weather'd April day!
Now darkly dimm'd by clouds of strife,
Now glowing in propitious fortune's ray;
Let the reed yielding bend its weakly form,
For, firm in rooted strength, the oak defies the storm.

If thou hast plann'd the morrow's dawn to roam
O'er distant hill or plain,
Wilt thou despond in sadness at thy home,
Whilst heaven drops down the rain?
Or will thy hope expect the coming day,
When bright the sun may shine with unremitted ray?

Wilt thou float careless down the stream of time,
In sadness borne to dull oblivion's shore,
Or shake off grief, and «build the lofty rhyme,»
And live till Time himself shall be no more?

If thy light bark have met the storm,
If threatening clouds the sky deform,
Let honest truth be vain; look back on me,
Have I been «sailing on a summer's sea?»
Have only zephyrs fill'd my swelling sails,
As smooth the gentle vessel glides along?
LYCON, I met unscar'd the wintry gales,
And sooth'd the dangers with the song:
So shall the vessel sail sublime,
And reach the port of fame adown the stream of time.

TO LYCON.

AND does my friend again demand the strain,
Still seek to list the sorrow-soothing lay?
Still would he hear the woe-worn heart complain,
When melancholy loads the lingering day?
Shall partial friendship turn the favouring eye
No fault behold, but every charm descry;
And shall the thankless bard his honour'd strain deny?

« No single pleasure shall your pen bestow;»
Ah, LYCON! 't is that thought affords delight;
T is that can soothe the wearying weight of woe,
When memory reigns amid the gloom of night
For fancy loves the distant scene to see,
Far from the gloom of solitude to flee,
And think that absent friends may sometimes think
of me.

Oft when my steps have trac'd the secret glade,
What time the pale moon glimmering on the plain
Just mark'd where deeper darkness dyed the shade,
Has contemplation lov'd the night-bird's strain:
Still have I stood, or silent mov'd and slow,
Whilst o'er the copse the thrilling accents flow,
Nor deem'd the pensive bird might pour the notes of woe.

Yet sweet and lovely is the night-bird's lay,
The passing pilgrim loves her notes to hear,
When mirth's rude reign is sunk with parted day,
And silence sleeps upon the vacant ear;
For staid reflection loves the doubtful light,
When sleep and stillness lull the noiseless night,
And breathes the pensive song a soothing sad delight.

Fearful the blast, and loud the torrent's roar,
And sharp and piercing drove the pelting rain,
When wildly wandering on the Volga's shore,
The exil'd OVID pour'd his plaintive strain;
He mourn'd for ever lost the joys of Rome,
He mourn'd his widow'd wife, his distant home,
And all the weight of woe that load the exile's doom.

Oh! could my lays, like SULMO's minstrel, flow,
Eternity might love her BION's name;
The muse might give a dignity to woe,
And grief's steep path should prove the path to
fame:
But I have pluck'd no bays from PHŒBUS' bower,
My fading garland, form'd of many a flower,
May haply smile and bloom to last one little hour.

To please that little hour is all I crave:
Lov'd by my friends, I spurn the love of fame;
High let the grass o'erspread my lonely grave,
Let cankering moss obscure the rough-hewn name:

There never may the pensive pilgrim go,
Nor future minstrel drop the tear of woe,
For all would fail to wake the slumbering earth below.

Be mine, whilst journeying life's rough road along
O'er hill and dale the wandering bard shall go,
To hail the hour of pleasure with the song,
Or soothe with sorrowing strains the hour of woe;
The song each passing moment shall beguile;
Perchance too, partial friendship deigns to smile:
Let fame reject the lay, I sleep secure the while.

Be mine to taste the humbler joys of life,
Lull'd in oblivion's lap to wear away,
And flee from grandeur's scenes of vice and strife,
And flee from fickle fashion's empty sway:
Be mine, in age's drooping hour, to see
The lisping children climb their grandsire's knee,
And train the future race to live and act like me.

Then, when the inexorable hour shall come
To tell my death, let no deep requiem toll,
No hireling sexton dig the venal tomb,
Nor priest be paid to hymn my parted soul;
But let my children, near their little cot,
Lay my old bones beneath the turfy spot:
So let me live unknown, so let me die forgot.

ROSAMUND TO HENRY.

WRITTEN AFTER SHE HAD TAKEN THE VEIL.

HENRY, 't is past! each painful effort o'er,
Thy love, thy ROSAMUND, exists no more:
She lives, but lives no longer now for you;
She writes, but writes to bid the last adieu.

Why bursts the big tear from my guilty eye?
Why heaves my love-lorn breast the impious sigh?
Down, bosom! down, and learn to heave in prayer;
Flow, flow, my tears, and wash away despair:
Ah, no! still, still the lurking sin I see,
My heart will heave, my tears will fall for thee.
Yes, HENRY! through the vestal's guilty veins,
With burning sway the furious passion reigns;
For thee, seducer, still the tear will fall,
And Love torment in Godstow's hallow'd wall.

Yet virtue from her deathlike sleep awakes,
Remorse comes on, and rears her whip of snakes.
Ah, HENRY! fled are all those fatal charms
That led their victim to the monarch's arms;
No more responsive to the evening air
In wanton ringlets waves my golden hair;
No more amid the dance my footsteps move,
No more the languid eye dissolves with love;
Fades on the cheek of ROSAMUND the rose,
And penitence awakes from sin's repose.

Harlot! adultress! HENRY! can I bear
Such aggravated guilt, such full despair!
By me the marriage-bed defil'd, by me
The laws of heaven forsook, defied for thee!
Dishonour fix'd on CLIFFORD's ancient name,
A father sinking to the grave with shame;

These are the crimes that harrow up my heart,
These are the crimes that poison memory's dart;
For these each pang of penitence I prove,
Yet these, and more than these, are lost in love.

Yes, even here amid the sacred pile,
The echoing cloister, and the long-drawn aisle;
Even here, when pausing on the silent air,
The midnight bell awakes and calls to prayer;
As on the stone I bend my clay-cold knee,
Love heaves the sigh, and drops the tear for thee:
All day the penitent but wakes to weep,
Till nature and the woman sink in sleep;
Nightly to thee the guilty dreams repair,
And morning wakes to sorrow and despair!
Lov'd of my heart, the conflict soon must cease,
Soon must this harrow'd bosom rest in peace;
Soon must it heave the last soul-rending breath,
And sink to slumber in the arms of death.

To slumber! oh, that I might slumber there!
Oh, that that dreadful thought might lull despair!
That death's chill dews might quench this vital flame,
And life lie mouldering with this lifeless frame!
Then would I strike with joy the friendly blow,
Then rush to mingle with the dead below.
Oh, agonizing hour! when round my head
Dark-brow'd despair his shadowing wings shall spread;
When conscience from herself shall seek to fly,
And, loathing life, still more shall loath to die!
Already vengeance lifts his iron rod,
Already conscience sees an angry God!
No virtue now to shield my soul I boast,
No hope protects, for innocence is lost!

Oh, I was cheerful as the lark, whose lay
Trills through the ether, and awakes the day!
Mine was the heartfelt smile, when earliest light
Shot through the fading curtain of the night;
Mine was the peaceful heart, the modest eye
That met the glance, or turn'd it knew not why.
At evening hour I struck the melting lyre,
Whilst partial wonder fill'd my doating sire,
Till he would press me to his aged breast,
And cry, « My child, in thee my age is blest!
Oh! may kind heaven protract my span of life
To see my lovely ROSAMUND a wife;
To view her children climb their grandsire's knee,
To see her husband love, and love like me!
Then, gracious heaven, decree old CLIFFORD's end,
Let his grey hairs in peace to death descend.»

The dreams of bliss are vanish'd from his view,
The buds of hope are blasted all by you;
Thy child, O CLIFFORD! bears a mother's name,
A mother's anguish, and a harlot's shame;
Even when her darling children climb her knee,
Feels the full force of guilt and infamy!
Wretch, most unhappy! thus condemn'd to know,
Even in her dearest bliss, her keenest woe—
Curst be this form, accurst these fatal charms
That buried virtue in seduction's arms;
Or rather curst that sad, that fatal hour,
When HENRY first beheld and felt their power;
When my too partial brother's doating tongue
On each perfection of a sister hung;

Told of the graceful form, the rose-red cheek,
The ruby lip, the eye that knew to speak,
The golden locks, that shadowing half the face
Display'd their charms, and gave and hid a grace:
'T was at that hour when night's englooming sway
Steals on the fiercer glories of the day;
Sad all around, as silence stills the whole,
And pensive fancy melts the softening soul;
These hands upon the pictur'd arras wove
The mournful tale of Edwy's hapless love;
When the fierce priest, inflam'd with savage pride,
From the young monarch tore his blushing bride:
Loud rung the horn, I heard the coursers' feet,
My brothers came, o'erjoy'd I ran to meet;
But when my sovereign met my wandering eye,
I blush'd, and gaz'd, and fear'd, yet knew not why;
O'er all his form with wistful glance I ran,
Nor knew the monarch, till I lov'd the man:
Pleas'd with attention, overjoy'd I saw
Each look obey'd, and every word a law;
Too soon I felt the secret flame advance,
Drank deep the poison of the mutual glance;
And still I plied my pleasing task, nor knew
In shadowing Edwy I had portray'd you.

Thine, Henry, is the crime! 't is mine to bear
The aggravated weight of full despair;
To wear the day in woe, the night in tears,
And pass in penitence the joyless years:
Guiltless in ignorance, my love-led eyes
Knew not the monarch in the knight's disguise;
Fraught with deceit th' insidious monarch came
To blast his faithful subject's spotless name;
To pay each service of old Clifford's race
With all the keenest anguish of disgrace!
Of love he talk'd; abash'd my down-cast eye
Nor seem'd to seek, nor yet had power to fly;
Still, as he urg'd his suit, his wily art
Told not his rank till victor o'er my heart:
Ah, known too late! in vain my reason strove,
Fame, honour, reason, all were lost in love.

How heav'd thine artful breast the deep-drawn sigh?
How spoke thy looks? how glow'd thine ardent eye?
When skill'd in guile, that soft seductive tongue
Talk'd of its truth, and Clifford was undone.
Oh, cursed hour of passion's maddening sway,
Guilt which a life of tears must wash away!
Gay as the morning lark no more I rose,
No more each evening sunk to calm repose;
No more in fearless innocence mine eye
Or met the glance, or turn'd it knew not why;
No more my fingers struck the trembling lyre,
No more I ran with joy to meet my sire;
But guilt's deep poison ran through every vein,
But stern reflection claim'd his ruthless reign;
Still vainly seeking from myself to fly,
In anxious guilt I shunn'd each friendly eye;
A thousand torments still my steps pursue,
And guilt, still lovely, haunts my soul with you.
Harlot, adultress, each detested name,
Stamps everlasting blots on Clifford's fame!
How can this wretch prefer the prayer to heaven?
How, self-condemn'd, expect to be forgiven?

And yet, fond Hope, with self-deluding art,
Still sheds her opiate poison o'er my heart;
Paints thee most wretched in domestic strife,
Curst with a kingdom, and a royal wife;
And vainly whispers comfort to my breast—
« I curst myself that Henry might be blest.»
Too fond deluder! impotent thy power
To whisper comfort in the mournful hour;
Weak, vain seducer, Hope! thy balmy breath
To soothe Reflection on the bed of death;
To calm stern Conscience' self-afflicting care,
Or ease the raging pangs of wild Despair.

Why, nature, didst thou give this fatal face?
Why heap with charms to load me with disgrace?
Why bid mine eyes two stars of beauty move?
Why form the melting soul too apt for love?
Thy last best blessing meant, the feeling breast,
Gave way to guilt, and poison'd all the rest:
Now bound in sin's indissoluble chains,
Fled are the charms, the guilt alone remains!

Oh! had fate plac'd amidst Earl Clifford's hall
Of menial vassals, me most mean of all;
Low in my hopes, and homely rude my face,
Nor form, nor wishes, rais'd above my place;
How happy, Rosamund, had been thy lot,
In peace to live unknown, and die forgot!
Guilt had not then infix'd her piercing sting,
Nor scorn revil'd the harlot of a king;
Contempt had not revil'd my fallen fame,
Nor infamy debas'd a Clifford's name.

Oh, Clifford! oh! my sire! thy honours now
Thy child has blasted on thine ancient brow;
Fallen is that darling child from virtue's name,
And thy grey hairs sink to the grave with shame?
Still busy fancy bids the scene arise,
Still paints the father to these wretched eyes.
Methinks I see him now, with folded arms,
Think of his child, and curse her fatal charms;
Those charms, her ruin! that in happier days,
With all a father's love, he lov'd to praise:
Unkempt his hoary locks, his head hung low
In all the silent energy of woe;
Yet still the same kind parent, still all mild,
He prays forgiveness for his sinful child.
And yet I live! if this be life, to know
The agonizing weight of hopeless woe:
Thus far, remote from every friendly eye,
To drop the tear, and heave the ceaseless sigh,
Each dreadful pang remorse inflicts to prove,
To weep and pray, yet still to weep and love:
Scorn'd by the virgins of this holy dome,
A living victim in the cloister'd tomb,
To pray, though hopeless, justice should forgive,
Scorn'd by myself:—if this be life—I live!

Oft will remembrance, in her painful hour,
Cast the keen glance to Woodstock's lovely bower;
Recal each sinful scene of bliss to view,
And give the soul again to guilt and you.
Oh! I have seen thee trace the bower around,
And heard the forest echo Rosamund;
Have seen thy frantic looks, thy wildering eye,
Heard the deep groan and bosom-rending sigh!

Vain are the searching glance, the love-lorn groan,
I live—but live to penitence alone;
Depriv'd of every joy which life can give,
Most vile, most wretched, most despis'd, I live.

Too well thy deep regret, thy grief, are known,
Too true I judge thy sorrows by my own!
Oh! thou hast lost the dearest charm of life,
The fondest, tenderest, loveliest, more than wife;
One who, with every virtue, only knew
The fault, if fault it be, of loving you;
One whose soft bosom seem'd as made to share
Thine every joy, and solace every care;
For crimes like these secluded, doom'd to know
The aggravated weight of guilt and woe.

Still dear, still lov'd, I learnt to sin of thee,
Learn, thou seducer, penitence from me!
Oh! that my soul this last pure joy may know,
Sometimes to soothe the dreadful hour of woe:
HENRY! by all the love my life has shown,
By all the sinful raptures we have known,
By all the parting pangs that rend my breast,
Hear, my lov'd lord, and grant my last request;
And, when the last tremendous hour shall come,
When all my woes are buried in the tomb,
Then grant the only boon this wretch shall crave—
Drop the sad tear to dew my humble grave;
Pause o'er the turf in fullness bent of woe,
And think who lies so cold and pale below!
Think from the grave she speaks the last decree,
« What I am now—soon, HENRY, thou must be!»
Then be this voice of wonted power possest,
To melt thy heart, and triumph in thy breast:
So should my prayers with just success be crown'd,
Should HENRY learn remorse from ROSAMUND;
Then shall thy sorrow and repentance prove,
That even death was weak to end our love.

THE RACE OF ODIN.

LOUD was the hostile clang of arms,
    And hoarse the hollow sound,
When POMPEY scatter'd wild alarms
    The ravag'd East around.
    The crimson deluge dreadful dy'd the ground:
An iron forest of destructive spears
    Rear'd their stern stems, where late
The bending harvest wav'd its rustling ears:
    Rome, through the swarming gate,
Pour'd her ambitious hosts to slaughter forth:
    Such was the will of fate!
From the cold regions of the North,
    At length, on raven wings, shall vengeance come,
And justice pour the urn of bitterness on Rome.

« Roman!» 't was thus the chief of ASGARD cried,
    « Ambitious Roman! triumph for a while;
Trample on freedom in thy victor pride;
    Yet, though now thy fortune smile,
    Though MITHRIDATES fly forlorn,
    Once thy dread, but now thy scorn,
ODIN will never live a shameful slave;
    Some region will he yet explore,
    Beyond the reach of Rome;

Where, upon some colder shore,
    Freedom yet thy force shall brave,
    Freedom yet shall find a home:
There, where the Eagle dares not soar,
Soon shall the Raven find a safe retreat.
ASGARD, farewell! farewell my native seat!
    Farewell for ever! yet, whilst life shall roll
Her warm tide through thine injur'd chieftain's breast,
Oft will he to thy memory drop the tear:
    Never more shall ODIN rest,
    Never quaff the sportive bowl,
    Or soothe in peace his slothful soul,
Whilst Rome triumphant lords it here.
    Triumph in thy victor might,
    Mock the chief of ASGARD's flight;
But soon the seeds of vengeance shall be sown,
And ODIN's race hurl down thy blood-cemented throne.»

Nurtur'd by Scandinavia's hardy soil,
    Strong grew the vigorous plant;
    Danger could ne'er the nation daunt,
For war, to other realms a toil,
    Was but the pastime here:
Skill'd the bold youth to hurl the unerring spear,
    To wield the falchion, to direct the dart,
Firm was each warrior's frame, yet gentle was his heart.

Freedom, with joy, beheld the noble race,
    And fill'd each bosom with her vivid fire;
Nor vice, nor luxury, debase
    The free-born offspring of the free-born sire;
There genuine Poesy, in freedom bright,
Diffus'd o'er all her clear, her all-enlivening light.

From Helicon's meandering rills
    The inspiring goddess fled;
    Amid the Scandinavian hills
    In clouds she hid her head;
There the bold, the daring muse,
Every daring warrior woos;
The sacred lust of deathless fame
Burnt in every warrior's soul:
« Whilst future ages hymn my name,»
The son of ODIN cries,
« I shall quaff the foaming bowl
With my forefathers in yon azure skies;
Methinks I see my foeman's skull
With the mantling beverage full;
I hear the shield-roof'd hall resound
To martial music's echoing sound;
I see the virgins, valour's meed,—
Death is bliss—I rush to bleed.»

See where the murderer EGILL stands,
He grasps the harp with skilful hands,
And pours the soul-emoving tide of song;
Mute admiration holds the listening throng:
    The royal sire forgets his murder'd son;
ERIC forgives; a thousand years
    Their swift revolving course have run,
Since thus the bard could check the father's tears,
    Could soothe his soul to peace,
    And never shall the fame of EGILL cease.

Dark was the dungeon, damp the ground,
    Beneath the reach of cheering day,

Where REGNER dying lay;
Poisonous adders all around
On the expiring warrior hung,
Yet the full stream of verse flow'd from his dauntless
    tongue:
« We fought with swords,» the warrior cry'd,
« We fought with swords,» he said—he died.

Jomsburg lifts her lofty walls,
Sparta revives on Scandinavia's shore;
Undismay'd each hero falls,
And scorns his death in terror to deplore.
  « Strike, THORCHILL, strike! drive deep the blow,
Jomsburg's sons shall not complain,
Never shall the brave appear
Bound in slavery's shameful chain:
  Freedom ev'n in death is dear.
Strike, THORCHILL, strike! drive deep the blow,
We joy to quit this world of woe;
We rush to seize the seats above,
And gain the warrior's meed of happiness and love.»

The destin'd hour at length is come,
And vengeful heaven decrees the queen of cities' doom;
  No longer heaven withholds the avenging blow
    From those proud domes whence BRUTUS fled;
    Where just CHEREA bow'd his head,
  And proud oppression laid the GRACCHI low:
    In vain the timid slaves oppose,
    For freedom led their sinewy foes,
    For valour fled with liberty:
      Rome bows her lofty walls,
      The imperial city falls,
« She falls—and lo, the world again is free!»

THE DEATH OF ODIN.

SOUL of my much-lov'd FREYA! yes, I come!
  No pale disease's slow-consuming power
  Has hasten'd on thy husband's hour;
  Nor pour'd by victor's thirsty hand
  Has ODIN's life bedew'd the land:
I rush to meet thee by a self-will'd doom.
  No more my clattering iron car
  Shall rush amid the throng of war;
No more, obedient to my heavenly cause,
Shall crimson conquest stamp his ODIN's laws.
  I go—I go;
Yet shall the nations own my sway
Far as yon orb shall dart his all-enlivening ray:
  Big is the death-fraught cloud of woe
That hangs, proud Rome, impending o'er thy wall,
For ODIN shall avenge his ASGARD's fall.
Thus burst from ODIN's lips the fated sound,
  As high in air he rear'd the gleaming blade;
His faithful friends around
  In silent wonder saw the scene, affray'd:
He, unappall'd, towards the skies
Uplifts his death-denouncing eyes;
« Ope wide VALHALLA's shield-roof'd hall,
Virgins of bliss! obey your master's call;
From these injurious realms below
The sire of nations hastes to go.»

Say, faulters now your chieftain's breath?
Or chills pale terror now his death-like face?
Then weep not, THOR, thy friend's approaching death,
  Let no unmanly tears disgrace
  The first of mortal's valiant race:
  Dauntless HEIMDAL, mourn not now,
  BALDER! clear thy cloudy brow;
  I go to happier realms above,
  To realms of friendship and of love.

This unmanly grief dispelling,
  List to glory's rapturous call;
So with ODIN ever dwelling,
  Meet him in the shield-roof'd hall:
Still shall ODIN's fateful lance
Before his daring friends advance;
When the bloody fight beginning,
Helms and shields, and hauberks ringing,
Streaming life each fatal wound
Pours its current on the ground;
Still in clouds portentous riding
O'er his comrade host presiding,
ODIN, from the stormy air,
O'er your affrighted foes shall scatter wild despair.

'Mid the mighty din of battle,
Whilst conflicting chariots rattle,
Floods of purple slaughter streaming,
Fate-fraught falchions widely gleaming;
When MISTA marks her destin'd prey,
When dread and death deform the day;
Happy he amid the strife,
Who pours the current of his life;
Every toil and trouble ending,
ODIN from his hall descending,
Shall bear him to his blest retreat,
Shall place him in the warrior's seat.

  Not such the destin'd joys that wait
The wretched dastard's future fate:
Wild shrieks shall yell in every breath,—
The agonizing shrieks of death.
Adown his wan and livid face
Big drops their painful way shall trace;
Each limb in that tremendous hour
Shall quiver in disease's power.
Grim HELA o'er his couch shall hang,
Scoff at his groans, and point each pang;
No Virgin Goddess him shall call
To join you in the shield-roof'd hall;
No Valkery for him prepare
The smiling mead with lovely care:
Sad and scorn'd the wretch shall lie,
Despairing shriek—despairing die!
No Scald in never-dying lays
Shall rear the temple of his praise;
No Virgin in her vernal bloom
Bedew with tears his high-rear'd tomb;
No Soldier sound his honour'd name;
No song shall hand him down to fame;
But rank weeds o'er the inglorious grave
Shall to the blast their high heads wave;
And swept by time's strong stream away,
He soon shall sink—oblivion's prey;
And deep in Niflehim—dreary cell,
Aye shall his sprite tormented dwell,

Where grim Remorse for ever wakes,
Where Anguish feeds her torturing snakes,
Where Disappointment and Delay
For ever guard the doleful way;
Amid the joyless land of woe
Keen and bleak the chill blasts blow;
Drives the tempest, pours the rain,
Showers the hail with force amain;
Yell the night-birds as they fly
Flitting in the misty sky;
Glows the adder, swells the toad,
For sad is HELA's cold abode.

Spread then the Gothic banners to the sky,
Lift your sable banners high;
Yoke your coursers to the car,
Strike the sounding shield of war;
Go, my lov'd companions, go,
Trample on the opposing foe;
Be like the raging torrent's force,
That, rushing from the hills, speeds on its foaming
        course.

Haste, my sons, to war's alarms,
Triumph in the clang of arms;
Joy amid the warlike toil,
Feed the raven with your spoil;
Go, prepare the eagle's food,
Go, and drench the wolf with blood,
Till ye shall hear dark HELA's call,
And virgins waft ye to my hall;
There, wrapt in clouds, the shadowy throng
To airy combat glide along;
'Till wearied with the friendly fight,
SERIMNER's flesh recruits their might;
There, whilst I grasp the Roman skull,
With hydromel sweet-smiling full,
The festive song shall echo round,
The Scald repeat the deathless sound:
Then, THOR, when thou from fight shall cease,
When death shall lay that arm in peace,
Still shall the nations fear thy nod,
The first of warriors now, and then their god;
But be each heart with rage possest,
Let vengeance glow in every breast;
Let conquest fell the Roman wall,
Revenge on Rome my ASGARD's fall.

The Druid throng shall fall away,
And sink beneath your victor sway;
No more shall nations bow the knee,
Vanquish'd TARANIS, to thee;
No more upon the sacred stone,
TENTATES, shall thy victims groan;
The vanquish'd ODIN, Rome, shall cause thy fall,
And his destruction shake thy proud imperial wall.

Yet, my faithful friends, beware
Luxury's enerving snare;
'T was this that shook our ASGARD's dome,
That drove us from our native home;
'T was this that smooth'd the way for victor Rome:
Gaul's fruitful plains invite your sway,
Conquest points the destin'd way;
Conquest shall attend your call,
And your success shall gild still more VALHALLA's hall.

So spake the dauntless chief, and pierc'd his breast,
Then rush'd to seize the seat of endless rest.

TO INDOLENCE.

I DO not woo thy presence, INDOLENCE!
        Goddess, I would not rank
        A votary in thy train.

I will not ask to wear thy fett'ring flowers,
        O thou on whose cold lips
        Faint plays the heartless smile!

Pale, sickly as the unkindly shaded fruit,
        Thy languid cheek displays
        No sunny hues of health;

There is no radiance in thy listless eye,
        No active joy that fires
        Its sudden glances with life.

I do not wish upon thy downy couch,
        As in a conscious dream
        To doze away the hours,

Dead to all noble purposes of man,
        Useless among mankind,
        To live, unworthy life.

But to thy sister LEISURE I would pour
        The supplicating prayer,
        And woo her aid benign:

Nymph, on whose sunny cheek the hue of health
        Blooms like the ruddy fruit
        Matur'd by southern rays,

Whose eye beam sparkles to the speaking heart,
        Like the reflected noon
        Quick glancing on the waves.

Her would I pray that not for ever thus
        The ungentle voice of toil
        Might claim my daily task,

So should my hand a votive temple rear,
        Through many a distant age
        That undestroy'd should stand.

Long should the stately monument proclaim
        That no ungrateful heart
        Goddess! received thy boon.

OLD CHRISTOVAL'S ADVICE,

AND THE REASON WHY HE GAVE IT.

Recibio un Cavallero, paraque cultivasse sus tierras, a un Quintero, y para pagarle algo adelantado le pidio fiador, y no teniendo quien le fiasse, le prometio delante del sepulcro de San Isidro, que cumpliria su palabra, y si no, que el santo le castigasse: con lo qual el Cavallero le pago toda su soldada, ya le fió. Mas desagradecido aquel hombre, no haciendo caso de su promessa, se huyo, sin acabar de servir el tiempo concertado. Passo de noche sin reparar en ella, por la Iglesia de San Andres, donde estaba el cuerpo del siervo de Dios. Fué cosa maravéjllosa, que andando corriendo toda la noche, no se aparto de la Iglesia, sino que toda se le fue en dar mil bueltas al rededor de ella, hasta que por la mañana, yendo el amo a quexarse de San Isidro, y pad.rle cumpliesse su fianza,

90

halló à su Quintero alli, dandomas y mas bueltas, sin poderse haver apartado de aquel sitio. Pidio perdon al santo, y a su amo, al qual satisfizo despues enteramente poc sù trabajo.—*Flos Sanctorum, por* ALONSO DE VILLEGAS.

IF thy debtor be poor, old Christoval cried,
 Exact not too hardly thy due,
For he who preserves a poor man from want
 May preserve him from wickedness too.

If thy neighbour should sin, old Christoval cried,
 Never never unmerciful be!
For remember it is by the mercy of God
 That thou art not as wicked as he.

At sixty and seven the hope of heaven
 Is my comfort, Old Christoval cried,
But if God had cut me off in my youth
 I might not have gone there when I died.

You shall have the farm, young Christoval,
 My good master Henrique said;
But a surety provide, in whom I can confide,
 That duly the rent shall be paid.

I was poor and I had not a friend on earth,
 And I knew not what to say,
We stood by the porch of St Andres' church,
 And it was on St Isidro's day.

Accept for my surety St Isidro,
 I ventured to make reply,
The Saint in Heaven may perhaps be my friend,
 But friendless on earth am I.

We enter'd the church and came to his grave,
 And I fell on my bended knee;
I am friendless, holy St Isidro,
 And I venture to call upon thee.

I call upon thee my surety to be,
 Thou knowest my honest intent,
And if ever I break my plighted word,
 Let thy vengeance make me repent!

I was idle, the day of payment came on,
 And I had not the money in store,
I fear'd the wrath of St Isidro
 But I fear'd Henrique more.

On a dark night I took my flight
 And hastily fled away,
It chanced by St Andres' church
 The road I had chosen lay.

As I pass'd the door I thought what I had swore
 Upon St Isidro's day,
And I seem'd to fear because he was near,
 And faster I hasten'd away.

So all night long I hurried on,
 Pacing full many a mile,
I knew not his avenging hand
 Was on me all the while.

Weary I was, and safe I thought,
 But when it was day-light,
I had, I found, been running round
 And round the church all night.

I shook like a palsy and fell on my knees,
 And for pardon devoutly I pray'd:
When my master came up—what! Christoval,
 You are here betimes, he said.

I have been idle good master! I cried,
 Good master and I have been wrong,
And I have been running round the church
 In penance all night long.

If thou hast been idle, Henrique said,
 Go home and thy fault amend;
I will not oppress thee, Christoval,
 May the Saint thy labour befriend.

Homeward I went a penitent,
 And I never was idle more;
St Isidro blest my industry,
 As he punish'd my fault before.

When my debtor was poor, Old Christoval said,
 I have never exacted my due,
I remember'd Henrique was good to me
 And copied his goodness too.

When my neighbour has sinn'd, Old Christoval said,
 I have ever forgiven his sin,
For I thought of the night by St Andres' church,
 And remember'd what I might have been.

VERSES

INTENDED TO HAVE BEEN ADDRESSED TO HIS GRACE
THE DUKE OF PORTLAND, CHANCELLOR OF THE
UNIVERSITY, ETC. ON HIS INSTALLATION, 1793.

IN evil hour, and with unhallowed voice
Profaning the pure gift of Poesy,
Did he begin to sing, he first who sung
Of arms, and combats, and the proud array
Of warriors on the embattled plain, and rais'd
The aspiring spirit to hopes of fair renown
By deeds of violence. For since that time
The imperious victor, oft, unsatisfied
With bloody spoil and tyrannous conquest, dares
To challenge fame and honour; and too oft
The Poet bending low to lawless power
Hath paid unseemly reverence, yea, and brought
Streams, clearest of the Aonian fount, to wash
Blood-stain'd ambition. If the stroke of war
Fell certain on the guilty head, none else;
If they that make the cause might taste the effect,
And drink themselves the bitter cup they mix,
Then might the Bard (though child of Peace) delight
To twine fresh wreaths around the conqueror's brow,
Or haply strike his high-toned harp to swell
The trumpet's martial sound, and bid them on,
Whom Justice arms for vengeance: but, alas!
That undistinguishing and deathful storm
Beats heaviest on the exposed innocent;
And they that stir its fury, while it raves,
Stand at safe distance; send their mandate forth
Unto the mortal ministers that wait
To do their bidding. Ah, who then regards
The widow's tears, the friendless orphan's cry,
And famine, and the ghastly train of woes
That follow at the dogged heels of war?
They in the pomp and pride of victory

Rejoicing, o'er the desolated earth,
As at an altar wet with human blood,
And flaming with the fire of cities burnt,
Sing their mad hymns of triumph, hymns to God
O'er the destruction of his gracious works,
Hymns to the Father o'er his slaughter'd sons.
Detested be their sword, abhorr'd their name,
And scorn'd the tongues that praise them ! Happier,
    Thou,
Of Peace and Science friend, hast held thy course
Blameless and pure, and such is thy renown.
And let that secret voice within thy breast
Approve thee; then shall those high sounds of praise
Which thou hast heard, be as sweet harmony,
Beyond this concave to the starry sphere
Ascending, where the spirits of the blest
Hear it well-pleas'd.   For Fame can enter heaven,
If Truth and Virtue lead her ; else forbid,
She rises not above this earthly spot ;
And then her voice, transient and valueless,
Speaks only to the herd.   With other praise,
And worthier duty may she tend on thee ;
Follow thee still with honour, such as Time
Shall never violate, and with just applause,
Such as the wise and good might love to share.

THE KILLCROP.

A SCENE BETWEEN BENEDICT, A GERMAN PEASANT,
AND FATHER KARL, AN OLD NEIGHBOUR.

Eight years since (said Luther), at Dessaw, I did see and touch a
changed childe, which was twelve years of age ; Hee had his eies and
all his members like another childe : Hee did nothing but feed, and
would eat as much as two clowns, or threshers, were able to eat.—
When one touched it, then it cried out : When any evil happened
in the Hous, then it laughed and was joiful ; but when all went
well, then it cried, and was very sad.   I told the Prince of Anhalt,
if I were Prince of that countrie, so would I venture *Homicidium*
thereon, and would throw it into the River Moldaw.   I admonished
the people dwelling in that place devoutly to praie to God to take
away the Divel ; the same was done accordingly, and the second year
after the Changeling died.
   In Saxonia, near unto Halberstad, was a man that also had a
Killcrop, who sucked the mother and five other women drie : and
besides, devoured very much.   This man was advised that hee
should in his pilgrimage at Halberstad make a promiss of the Kill-
crop to the Virgin Marie, and should caus him there to bee rocked.
This advice the man followed, and carried the changeling ;thither
in a basket.   But going over a river, beeing upon the bridg, another
Divel that was below in the river called and said Killcrop, Killcrop !
Then the childe in the basket (which never before spake one word)
answered, Ho, Ho.   The Divel in the water asked further, Whither
art thou going ? The childe in the basket said, I am going towards
Hocklestad to our loving Mother to be rocked.
   The man being much affrighed thereat, threw the childe, with
the basket, over the bridg into the water.   Whe.eupon the two Di-
vels flew away together, and cried, Ho, Ho, Ho, tumbling themselvs
one over another, and so vanished.
   Such Changelings and Killcrops (said Luther) *supponit Satan in
locum verorum filiorum ;* for the Devil hath this power, that hee
changeth children, and instead thereof laieth Divels in the cradles,
which prosper not, onely they feed and suck : but such Changelings
live not above eighteen or nineteen years.   It oftentimes falleth
out, that the children of women in childe-bed are changed, and
Divels are laid in their stead, the mothers in such sort are sucked
out, that afterwards they are able to give suck no more.   Such
Changelings (said Luther) are also baptized, in regard that they can-
not be known the first year ; but are known onely by sucking the
mothers drie.—LUTHER's *Divine Discourses,* folio, p. 387.
   In justice however to Luther, it should be remembered, that this
superstition was common to the age in which he lived.

BENEDICT.

You squalling imp, lie still ! Is n't it enough
To eat two pounds for a breakfast, but again,
Before the Sun's half risen, I must hear
This cry ?—as though your stomach was as empty
As old Karl's head, that yonder limps along
Mouthing his crust.   I 'll haste to Hocklestad !
A short mile only.
        Enter FATHER KARL.

KARL.

           Benedict, how now !
Earnest and out of breath, why in this haste ?
What have you in your basket ?

BENEDICT.

             Stand aside !
No moment this for converse.   Ask to-morrow,
And I will answer you, but I am now
About to punish Belzebub.   Take care !
My business is important.

KARL.

             What! about
To punish the Arch-Fiend old Belzebub ?
A thing most rare.—But can't I lend a hand
On this occasion ?

BENEDICT.

           Father, stand aside !
I hate this parley.   Stand aside, I say !

KARL.

Good Benedict, be not o'ercome by rage,
But listen to an old man.—What is 't there
Within your basket ?

BENEDICT.

       'T is the Devil's changeling:
A thumping Killcrop !
            [*Uncovers the basket.*
         Yes, 'tween you and I,
             [*Whispering.*
Our neighbour Balderic's changed for his son Will.

KARL.

An idle thought ! I say it is a child,—
A fine one too.

BENEDICT.

       A child ! you dreaming grey-beard !
Nothing will you believe like other people.
Did ever mortal man see child like this ?
Why, 't is a Killcrop, certain, manifest ;
Look there ! I'd rather see a dead pig snap
At the butcher's knife, than call this thing a child.
View how he stares ! I 'm no young cub, d' ye see.

KARL.

Why, Benedict, this is most wonderful
To my plain mind. I've often heard of Killcrops,
And laugh'd at the tale most heartily ; but now
I 'll mark him well, and see if there 's any truth
In these said creatures.
           [*Looks at the basket.*
      A finer child ne'er breath'd !
Thou art mistaken, Benedict ! thine eyes
See things confused ! But let me hear thee say
What are the signs by which thou know'st the dif-
      ference
Twixt Crop and Child.

BENEDICT.

       The diff'rence ! mercy on us !
That I should talk to such a Heretic—
D' ye know the difference 'twixt the Moon and Stars ?

KARL.

Most certainly.

BENEDICT.

Then these are things so near,
That I might pardon one who hesitates,
Doubting between them. But the Crop and Child!
They are so opposite, that I should look
Sooner to hear the Frog teach harmony,
Than meet a man, with hairs so grey as thine,
Who did not know the difference.

KARL.

Benedict!
The oldest, ere he die, something might learn;
And I shall hear, gladly, the certain marks
That show the Killcrop.

BENEDICT.

Father, listen then—
The Killcrop, mark me, for a true man's child
At first might be mistaken—has two eyes
And nose and mouth, but these are semblances
Deceitful, and, as Father Luther says,
There's something underneath.

KARL.

Good Benedict!
If Killcrops look like children, by what power
Know you they are not?

BENEDICT.

This from you, old Father!
Why when they are pinch'd they squeak.

KARL.

This is not strange;
All children cry when pinch'd.

BENEDICT.

But then their maws!
The veriest company of threshing clowns
Would think they had no appetite, compared
With this and the rest of 'em.—Gormandizing beast!
See how he yawns for food!

KARL.

But, Benedict!
When hunger stings you, don't you ope your mouth?
What other evidence?

BENEDICT.

Why, Devil-like,
When any evil happens, by his grin
'T will always tell ye, and when tidings good
Come near, the beasts of twins delivered, or
Corn sold at market, or the harvest in,
The raven never croak'd more dismally
Before the sick man's window, than this Crop,
With disappointment howls. And then, a mark
Infallible, that shows the Killcrop true,
Is this, old man, he sucks his mother dry!
'T was but the other day, in our village,
A Killcrop suck'd his mother and five more
Dry as a whet-stone. Do you now believe?

KARL.

Good Benedict, all children laugh and cry!
I have my doubts.

BENEDICT.

Doubts have you? Well-a-day!
In t' other world you 'll sink ten fathoms deeper,
I promise you, for this foul heresy.
But nothing will move you,—you won't be moved.
I 'll tell ye as true a story as ever man
Told to another. I had a Changeling once

Laid in my cradle, but I spied him out;
Thou 'st never seen a creature so foul-mouth'd
And body'd too. But, knowing Satan's drift,
I balk'd him: to the lofty Church that stands
Over yon river, I the Killcrop took,
To ask advice, how to dispose of him,
Of th' holy Pastor. When, by the moon on high,
('T is true I fear'd him,) as I pass'd the bridge,
Bearing him in my arms, he gave a leap,
And over the rails jump'd headlong, laughing loud
With a fellow-fiend, that, from the waves beneath,
Bawl'd—Killcrop! Killcrop!

KARL.

Are you sure he laugh'd,
Might it not be a cry?

BENEDICT.

Why! that it might;
I won't be certain, but that he jump'd over
And splash'd and dash'd into the water beneath,
Making fierce gestures and loud bellowings:
I could as soon a witch's innocence
Believe, as doubt it.

KARL.

Benedict, now say,
Didst thou not throw him over?

BENEDICT.

Throw him over!
Why, man, I could as easily have held
A struggling whale. It needed iron arms
To hold the monster. Doubt whate'er you will,
He surely laugh'd. And when he reach'd the water,
Grasping the fiend, I never shall forget
The cries, the yells, the shouts; it seem'd to me
That thunder was doves' cooing to the noise
These Killcrops made, as, splashing, roaring, laughing,
With their ha, ha, ha, so ominous! they rush'd
Down the broad stream.—That very night our cow
Sicken'd and died. Saints aid us! Whilst these Crops
Poison the air, they 'll have enough to do
To stay the pestilence.

KARL.

But, Benedict,
Be not outrageous! I am old, d' ye see;
Trust me, thou art mistaken; 't is no Killcrop:
See how he smiles! Poor infant! give him me.

BENEDICT.

Stand off! The Devil lent him, and again
I will return him honestly, and rid
Earth of one bane.

KARL.

Thou dost not mean to kill!
Poor infant, spare him! I have young and old,
The poor, a houseful, yet I 'll not refuse
To take one more, if thou wilt give him me.
Let me persuade.

BENEDICT.

Away! I say, away!
Even if an Angel came to beg him of me,
I should suspect imposture, for I know
He could not ask a Killcrop. 'T is a thing
Heaven hath no need of. Ere an hour be past,
From yon tall rock I 'll hurl him to perdition.

KARL.

Repeat it not! Oh, spare the infant! Spare
His innocent laughter! My cold creeping blood

Doth boil with indignation, at the thought
Most horrible. Thou must not do the deed!
                              BENEDICT.
Not punish Satan! I have learnt too well
From Father Luther. Once again, stand off!
I'll rocket him.
                                    [Exeunt.

DRAMATIC FRAGMENT.

SCENE.—*Holland.* TIME, *during the Government of
the Duke of Alva.*

                              ELLIS.
                              NOT complain!
Endure in silence! suffer with beast patience
Oppressions such as these!
                              KLAUS.
                              Nay—an it please you,
Rail on, rail on! and when the rod of power
Falls heavy, why, no doubt 't will comfort you
Amid your dungeon miseries, to reflect
How valiantly you talk'd! you know Count Roderick;—
He would be railing, too!
                              ELLIS.
                              And what has followed?
                              KLAUS.
I saw him in his dungeon: 't is a place
Where the hell-haunted Murderer might almost
Rejoice to hear the hangman summon him.
By day he may divert his solitude
With watching through the grate the snow-flakes fall,
Or counting the long icicles above him;
Or he may trace upon the ice-glazed wall
Lines of most brave sedition! and at night
The frosty moon-beam for his meditation
Lends light enough. He told me that his feet
Were ulcered with the biting cold.—I would
Thou hadst been with me, Ellis.
                              ELLIS.
                              But does Philip
Command these things, or knowingly permit
The punishment to go before the judgment?
                              KLAUS.
Knowest thou not with what confidence the King
Reposes upon Alva? we believe
That 't is with Philip a twin act to know
Injustice, and redress; this article
Of our state-creed, 't were heresy to doubt.
But the dead echo of the dungeon groan,
How should it pierce the palace? how intrude
Upon the delicate ear of royalty?
                              ELLIS.
But sure Count Roderick's service—
                              KLAUS.
                              Powerful plea!
He served his country, and his country paid him
The wages of his service. Why but late
A man that in ten several fields had fought
His country's battles, by the hangman's hand
Died like a dog; and for a venial crime—
A deed that could not trouble with one doubt
A dying man! At Lepanto he had shared
The danger of that day whose triumph broke
The Ottoman's power, and this was pleaded for him:

Six months they stretch'd him on the rack of hope,
Then took his life.
                              ELLIS.
                              I would I were in England!
                              KLAUS.
Aye, get thee home again! you islanders
Live under such good laws, so mild a sway,
That you are no more fit to dwell abroad
Than a doting mother's favourite to endure
His first school hardships. We in Holland here
Know 't is as idle to exclaim against
These state oppressions, as with childish tears
To weep in the stone, or any other curse
Wherewith God's wrath afflicts us. And for struggling,
Why 't would be like an idiot in the gout
Stamping for pain!

FUNERAL SONG

FOR THE PRINCESS CHARLOTTE OF WALES.

IN its summer pride arrayed,
Low our Tree of Hope is laid!
Low it lies:—in evil hour,
Visiting the bridal bower,
Death hath levelled root and flower.
Windsor, in thy sacred shade,
(This the end of pomp and power!)
Have the rites of death been paid:
Windsor, in thy sacred shade
Is the Flower of Brunswick laid!

  Ye whose relics rest around,
Tenants of this funeral ground!
Know ye, Spirits, who is come,
By immitigable doom
Summoned to the untimely tomb?
Late with youth and splendour crown'd,
Late in beauty's vernal bloom,
Late with love and joyaunce blest;
Never more lamented guest
Was in Windsor laid to rest.

  Henry, thou of saintly worth,
Thou, to whom thy Windsor gave
Nativity, and name, and grave;
Thou art in this hallowed earth
Cradled for the immortal birth.
Heavily upon his head
Ancestral crimes were visited.
He, in spirit like a child,
Meek of heart and undefiled,
Patiently his crown resigned,
And fixed on heaven his heavenly mind,
Blessing, while he kiss'd the rod,
His Redeemer and his God.
Now may he in realms of bliss
Greet a soul as pure as his.

  Passive as that humble spirit,
Lies his bold dethroner too;
A dreadful debt did he inherit
To his injured lineage due;
Ill-starred Prince, whose martial merit
His own England long might rue!

Mournful was that Edward's fame,
Won in fields contested well,
While he sought his rightful claim :
Witness Aire's unhappy water,
Where the ruthless Clifford fell ;
And when Wharfe ran red with slaughter,
On the day of Towcester's field,
Gathering, in its guilty flood,
The carnage and the ill-spilt blood,
That forty thousand lives could yield.
Cressy was to this but sport,
Poictiers but a pageant vain,
And the victory of Spain
Seem'd a strife for pastime meant,
And the work of Agincourt
Only like a tournament;
Half the blood which there was spent,
Had sufficed again to gain
Anjou and ill-yielded Maine :
Normandy and Aquitaine,
And our Lady's ancient towers,
Maugre all the Valois' powers,
Had a second time been ours.
A gentle daughter of thy line,
Edward, lays her dust with thine.

Thou, Elizabeth, art here :
Thou to whom all griefs were known :
Thou wert placed upon the bier
In happier hour than on the throne.
Fatal Daughter, fatal Mother,
Raised to that ill-omen'd station,
Father, uncle, sons, and brother,
Mourn'd in blood her elevation ;
Woodville, in the realms of bliss,
To thine offspring thou mayst say,
Early death is happiness ;
And favour'd in their lot are they
Who are not left to learn below
That length of life is length of woe.
Lightly let this ground be prest ;
A broken heart is here at rest.

But thou, Seymour, with a greeting,
Such as sisters use at meeting ;
Joy, and Sympathy, and love,
Wilt hail her in the seats above.
Like in loveliness were ye,
By a like lamented doom,
Hurried to an early tomb ;
While together spirits blest,
Here your earthly relics rest.
Fellow angels shall ye be
In the angelic company.

Henry, too, hath here his part ;
At the gentle Seymour's side,
With his best beloved bride,
Cold and quiet, here are laid
The ashes of that fiery heart.
Not with his tyrannic spirit,
Shall our Charlotte's soul inherit ;
No, by Fisher's hoary head,
By More, the learned and the good,
By Katharine's wrongs and Boleyn's blood,
By the life so basely shed

Of the pride of Norfolk's line,
By the axe so often red,
By the fire with martyrs fed,
Hateful Henry, not with thee
May her happy spirit be!

And here lies one, whose tragic name
A reverential thought may claim ;
The murdered monarch, whom the grave,
Revealing its long secret, gave
Again to sight, that we might spy
His comely face, and waking eye ;
There, thrice fifty years, it lay,
Exempt from natural decay,
Unclosed and bright, as if to say,
A plague, of bloodier, baser birth
Than that beneath whose rage he bled,
Was loose upon our guilty earth ;
Such awful warning from the dead
Was given by that portentous eye ;
Then it closed eternally.

Ye, whose relics rest around,
Tenants of this funeral ground ;
Even in your immortal spheres,
What fresh yearnings will ye feel,
When this earthly guest appears !
Us she leaves in grief and tears ;
But to you will she reveal
Tidings of old England's weal ;
Of a righteous war pursued,
Long, through evil and through good,
With unshaken fortitude ;
Of peace, in battle twice achiev'd ;
Of her fiercest foe subdued,
And Europe from the yoke relieved,
Upon that Brabantine plain :
Such the proud, the virtuous story,
Such the great, the endless glory
Of her father's splendid reign.
He, who wore the sable mail,
Might, at this heroic tale,
Wish himself on earth again.

One who reverently, for thee,
Raised the strain of bridal verse,
Flower of Brunswick! mournfully
Lays a garland on thy herse.

SCOTLAND.

AN ODE,

WRITTEN AFTER THE KING'S VISIT TO THAT COUNTRY.

At length hath Scotland seen
The presence long desired ;
The pomp of royalty
Her ancient palace desolate how long !
From all parts far and near,
Highland and lowland, glen and fertile carse,
The silent mountain lake, the busy port,
Her populous cities, and her pastoral hills,
In generous joy convened
By the free impulse of the loyal heart,
Her sons have gather'd, and beheld their king.

Land of the loyal, as in happy hour
Revisited, so was thy regal seat
In happy hour for thee
Forsaken, under favouring stars, when James
His valediction gave,
And great Eliza's throne
Received its rightful heir,
The Peaceful and the Just.

A more auspicious union never Earth
From eldest days had seen,
Than when, their mutual wrongs forgiven,
And gallant enmity renounced
With honour, as in honour foster'd long,
The ancient kingdoms form'd
Their everlasting league.

Slowly by time matured,
A happier order then for Scotland rose:
And where inhuman force
And rapine unrestrained
Had lorded o'er the land,
Peace came, and polity,
And quiet industry, and frugal wealth;
And there the household virtues fix'd
Their sojourn undisturb'd.

Such blessings for her dowry Scotland drew
From that benignant union; nor less large
The portion that she brought.
She brought security and strength,
True hearts, and strenuous hands, and noble minds.
Say Ocean, from the shores of Camperdown,
What Caledonia brought! Say thou,
Egypt! Let India tell!
And let tell Victory
From her Brabantine field,
The proudest field of fame!

Speak ye, too, works of peace;
For ye too have a voice
Which shall be heard by ages! The proud bridge,
Through whose broad arches, worthy of their name
And place, his rising and his refluent tide
Majestic Thames, the royal river, rolls!
And that which, high in air,
A bending line suspended, shall o'erhang
Menai's Straits, as if
By Merlin's mighty magic there sustain'd!
And Pont-Cyssylté, not less wondrous work;
Where on gigantic columns raised
Aloft, a dizzying height,
The laden barge pursues its even way,
While o'er his rocky channel the dark Dee
Hurries below, a raging stream, scarce heard!
And that huge mole, whose deep foundations, firm
As if by Nature laid,
Repel the assailing billows, and protect
The British fleet, securely riding there,
Though southern storms possess the sea and sky,
And from its depths commoved,
Infuriate ocean raves.
Ye stately monuments of Britain's power,
Bear record ye, what Scottish minds
Have plann'd and perfected!
With grateful wonder shall posterity

See the stupendous works, and Rennie's name
And Telford's shall survive, till time
Leave not a wreck of sublunary things.

Him too may I attest for Scotland's praise,
Who seized and wielded first
The mightiest element
That lies within the scope of man's control;
Of evil and of good
Prolific spring, and dimly yet discern'd
The immeasureable results.
The mariner no longer seeks
Wings from the wind; creating now the power
Wherewith he wins his way,
Right on across the ocean-flood, he steers
Against opposing skies;
And reaching now the inmost continent,
Up rapid streams, innavigable else,
Ascends with steady progress, self-propell'd.

Nor hath the sister kingdom borne,
In science, and in arms
Alone, her noble part;
There is an empire which survives
The wreck of thrones, the overthrow of realms,
The downfall, and decay, and death
Of nations. Such an empire in the mind
Of intellectual man
Rome yet maintains, and elder Greece; and such
By indefeasible right
Hath Britain made her own.
How fair a part doth Caledonia claim
In that fair conquest! Whereso'er
The British tongue may spread,
(A goodly tree, whose leaf
No winter e'er shall nip:)
Earthly immortals, there, her sons of fame,
Will have their heritage;
In eastern and in occidental Ind;
The new antarctic world, where sable swans
Glide upon waters, called by British names,
And plough'd by British keels;
In vast America, through all its length
And breadth, from Massachusett's populous coast
To western Oregan;
And from the southern gulf,
Where the great river with his turbid flood
Stains the green ocean, to the polar sea.

There nations yet unborn shall trace
In Hume's perspicuous page,
How Britain rose, and through what storms attain'd
Her eminence of power.
In other climates, youths and maidens there
Shall learn from Thomson's verse in what attire
The various seasons, bringing in their change
Variety of good,
Revisit their beloved English ground.
There Beattie! in thy sweet and soothing strain
Shall youthful poets read
Their own emotions. There too, old and young,
Gentle and simple, by Sir Walter's tales
Spell-bound, shall feel
Imaginary hopes and fears
Strong as realities,
And, waking from the dream, regret its close.

These Scotland are thy glories; and thy praise
Is England's, even as her power
And opulence of fame are thine;
So hath our happy union made
Each in the other's weal participant,
Enriching, strengthening, glorifying both.

O House of Stuart, to thy memory still
For this best benefit
Should British hearts in gratitude be bound!
A deeper tragedy
Than thine unhappy tale hath never fill'd
The historic page, nor given
Poet or moralist his mournful theme!
O House severely tried,
And in prosperity alone
Found wanting; Time hath closed
Thy tragic story now!
Errors and virtues fatally betrayed,
Magnanimous suffering, vice,
Weakness, and headstrong zeal, sincere though blind,
Wrongs, calumnies, heart wounds,
Religious resignation, earthly hopes,
Fears and affections, these have had their course,
And over them in peace
The all-engulfing stream of years hath closed,
But this good work endures,
'Stablish'd and perfected by length of days,
The indissoluble union stands.

Nor hath the sceptre from that line
Departed, though the name hath lost
Its regal honours. Trunk and root have failed:
A scion from the stock
Liveth and flourisheth. It is the Tree
Beneath whose sacred shade,
In majesty and peaceful power serene,
The Island Queen of Ocean hath her seat;
Whose branches far and near
Extend their sure protection; whose strong roots
Are with the isle's foundations interknit;
Whose stately summit when the storm careers
Below, abides unmoved,
Safe in the sunshine and the peace of Heaven!

A SOLDIER'S EPITAPH.

STEEP is the soldier's path; nor are the heights
Of Glory to be won without long toil
And arduous efforts of enduring hope,
Save when death takes the aspirant by the hand,
And cutting short the work of years, at once
Lifts him to that conspicuous eminence.

Such fate was mine.—The standard of the Buffs
I bore at Albuhera, on that day
When, covered by a shower, and fatally
For friends misdeemed, the Polish lancers fell
Upon our rear. Surrounding me, they claimed
My precious charge!—« Not but with life!» I cried,
And life was given for immortality!
The flag which to my heart I held, when wet
With that heart's blood, was soon victoriously
Regained on that great day. In former times,
Marlborough beheld it borne at Ramillies;

For Brunswick and for liberty it waved
Triumphant at Culloden; and hath seen
The lilies on the Caribbean shores
Abased before it; then too in the front
Of battle did it flap exultantly,
When Douro, with its wide stream interposed,
Saved not the French invaders from attack,
Discomfiture, and ignominious rout.
My name is Thomas: undisgraced have I
Transmitted it. He who in days to come
May bear the honoured banner to the field
Will think of Albuhera, and of me!

LINES

TO THE MEMORY OF A YOUNG OFFICER, WHO WAS
MORTALLY WOUNDED IN THE BATTLE OF CORUNA.

MYSTERIOUS are the ways of Providence;—
Old men who have grown grey in camps, and wished,
And prayed, and sought in battle to lay down
The burthen of their age, have seen the young
Fall round, themselves untouched; and balls beside
The graceless and the unblest head have past,
Harmless as hail, to reach some precious life,
For which clasped hands, and supplicating eyes,
Duly at morn and eve were raised to Heaven;
And, in the depth and loneness of the soul
(Then boding all too truly) midnight prayers
Breathed from an anxious pillow wet with tears.
But blessed, even amid their grief, are they
Who, in the hour of visitation, bow
Beneath the unerring will, and look toward
Their Heavenly Father, merciful as just!
They, while they own his goodness, feel that whom
He chastens them he loves. The cup He gives
Shall they not drink it? Therefore doth the draught
Resent of comfort in its bitterness,
And carry healing with it. What but this
Could have sustained the mourners who were left,
With life-long yearnings, to remember him
Whose early death this monumental verse
Records? For never more auspicious hopes
Were nipt in flower, nor finer qualities
From Goodliest fabric of mortality
Divorced, nor virtues worthier to adorn
The world transferred to heaven, than when ere time
Had measured him the space of nineteen years,
Paul Burrard on Coruna's fatal field
Received his mortal hurt. Not unprepared
The heroic youth was found: for in the ways
Of piety had he been trained; and what
The dutiful child upon his mother's knees
Had learnt the soldier faithfully observed.
In chamber or in tent, the book of God
Was his beloved manual: and his life
Beseemed the lessons which from thence he drew.
For gallant as he was and blithe of heart,
Expert of hand, and keen of eye, and prompt
In intellect, religion was the crown
Of all his noble properties. When Paul
Was by, the scoffer, self-abased, restrained
The licence of his speech: and ribaldry
Before his virtuous presence sate rebuked.
And yet so frank and affable a form
His virtue wore, that wheresoe'er he moved

A sunshine of good will and cheerfulness
Enlivened all around.   Oh! marvel not,
If, in the morning of his fair career,
Which promised all that honour could bestow
On high desert, the youth was summoned hence!
His soul required no farther discipline,
Pure as it was, and capable of heaven.—
Upon the spot from whence he just had seen
His General borne away, the appointed ball
Reached him.   But not in that Gallician ground
Was it his fate, like many a British heart,
To mingle with the soil; the sea received
His mortal relics,—to a watery grave
Consigned so near his native shore, so near
His father's house, that they who loved him best,
Unconscious of its import, heard the gun
Which fired his knell!—Alas! if it were known
When, in the strife of nations dreadful Death
Mows down, with indiscriminating sweep,
His thousands ten times told,—if it were known
What ties are severed then, what ripening hopes
Blasted, what virtues in their bloom cut off,
How far the desolating scourge extends,
How wide the misery spreads, what hearts beneath
Their grief are broken, or survive to feel
Always the irremediable loss,
Oh! who of woman born could bear the thought!
Who but would join with fervent piety
The prayer that asketh in our time for peace!—
Nor in our time alone!—Enable us,
Father which art in Heaven! but to receive
And keep thy word, thy kingdom then should come,
Thy will be done on earth, the victory
Accomplished over Sin as well as Death,
And the great scheme of Providence fulfilled!

LOVE.

They sin who tell us love can die;—
With life all other passions fly,
All others are but vanity.
In heaven ambition cannot dwell,
Nor avarice in the vaults of hell;
Earthly these passions as of earth,
They perish where they have their birth;
But love is indestructible,—
Its holy flame for ever burneth,—
From heaven it came, to heaven returneth;
Too oft on earth a troubled guest,
At times deceived, at times opprest;
It here is tried and purified,
And hath in heaven its perfect rest;
It soweth here with toil and care,
But the harvest time of Love is there.
Oh when a mother meets on high
The babe she lost in infancy,
Hath she not then, for pains and fears,
The day of woe, the anxious night,
For all her sorrow, all her tears,
An over-payment of delight!

HOPE.

Man hath a weary pilgrimage
As through the world he wends,

Yet gentle Hope on every stage,
The comforter, attends;
And if the toil-worn traveller droops,
With heaviness opprest,
She cheers his heart, and bids him see
The distant place of rest.

To school the little exile goes,
And quits his mother's arms;
What then shall soothe his earliest woes,
When novelty has lost its charms,
Condemned to suffer through the day
Restraints that no rewards repay,
And cares where love has no concern?
If memory still the present sours,
Hope lightens as she counts the hours
That hasten his return.

Youth comes, and eager fancy hails
The long-expected days:
Youth comes, and he is doom'd to prove
The fears and jealousies of love,
And all its long delays.
But when the passions with their might
Afflict the doubtful breast,
Hope bids him yet expect delight,
And happiness, and rest.

When manhood comes with troubles rife,
And all the toils and cares of life
Usurp the busy mind,
Where shall the tired and harass'd heart
Its consolation find?
Hope doubts not yet the meed to obtain
Of difficulties past,
And looks beyond the toils of gain
To wealth, enjoy'd at last.

So to his journey's latter stage
His pilgrim feet attain,
And then he finds in wiser age
That earthly cares are vain.
Yet Hope the constant friend remains
Who soothed his troubles past,
Though oft deceiving and deceived,
The truest friend at last.
By Faith and Hope in life's last hour
Are life's last pangs relieved;
They give the expectation then
That cannot be deceived.

ODE

ON THE DEATH OF QUEEN CHARLOTTE.

Death has gone up into our palaces!
The light of day once more
Hath visited the last abode
Of mortal royalty,
The dark and silent vault.

But not as when the silence of that vault
Was interrupted last
Doth England raise her loud lament,
Like one by sudden grief
Surprised and overcome.

Then with a passionate sorrow we bewailed
  Youth on the untimely bier;
And hopes which seemed like flower-buds full,
  Just opening to the sun,
  For ever swept away.

The heart then struggled with repining thoughts,
  With feelings that almost
Arraigned the inscrutable decree,
  Embittered by a sense
  Of that which might have been.

This grief hath no repining; all is well,
  What hath been, and what is!
The Angel of Deliverance came
  To one who, full of years,
  Awaited her release.

All that our fathers in their prayers desired,
  When first their chosen Queen
Set on our shores her happy feet,
  All by indulgent Heaven
  Had largely been vouchsafed.

At Court the household Virtues had their place;
  Domestic Purity
Maintained her proper influence there;
  The marriage-bed was blest,
  And length of days was given.

No cause for sorrow then, but thankfulness;
  Life's business well performed,
When weary age full willingly
  Resigns itself to sleep,
  In sure and certain hope!

Oh end to be desired! whene'er, as now,
  Good works have gone before,
The seasonable fruit of Faith;
  And good Report, and good
  Example have survived!

Her left hand knew not of the ample alms
  Which her right hand had done,
And therefore in the awful hour
  The promises were hers
  To secret bounty made.

With more than Royal honours to the tomb
  Her bier is borne; with more
Than Pomp can claim or Power bestow;
  With blessings and with prayers
  From many a grateful heart.

Long, long then shall Queen Charlotte's name be dear;
  And future Queens to her
As to their best exemplar look;
  Who imitates her best
  May best deserve our love.

LUCY AND HER BIRD.

The Sky-lark hath perceived his prison-door
  Unclosed; for liberty the captive tries:
Puss eagerly hath watch'd him from the floor,
  And in her grasp he flutters, pants, and dies.

Lucy's own Puss, and Lucy's own dear Bird,
  Her foster'd favourites both for many a day;
That which the tender-hearted girl preferr'd,
  She in her fondness knew not sooth to say.

For if the Sky-lark's pipe were shrill and strong,
  And its rich tones the thrilling ear might please;
Yet Pussybel could breathe a fireside song
  As winning, when she lay on Lucy's knees.

Both knew her voice, and each alike would seek
  Her eye, her smile, her fondling touch to gain:
How faintly then may words her sorrow speak,
  When by the one she sees the other slain!

The flowers fall scatter'd from her lifted hands;
  A cry of grief she utters in affright;
And self-condemn'd for negligence she stands
  Aghast and helpless at the cruel sight.

Come, Lucy, let me dry those tearful eyes;
  Take thou, dear child, a lesson not unholy,
From one whom Nature taught to moralize
  Both in his mirth and in his melancholy.

I will not warn thee not to set thy heart
  Too fondly upon perishable things;
In vain the earnest preacher spends his art
  Upon that theme, in vain the poet sings.

It is our nature's strong necessity,
  And this the soul's unerring instincts tell:
Therefore, I say, let us love worthily,
  Dear Child, and then we cannot love too well.

Better it is all losses to deplore,
  Which dutiful affection can sustain,
Than that the heart should, to its inmost core,
  Harden without it, and have lived in vain.

This love which thou hast lavish'd, and the woe
  Which makes thy lip now quiver with distress,
Are but a vent, an innocent overflow,
  From the deep springs of female tenderness.

And something I would teach thee from the grief
  That thus hath fill'd those gentle eyes with tears,
The which may be thy sober, sure relief,
  When sorrow visits thee in after years.

I ask not whither is the spirit flown
  That lit the eye which there in death is seal'd;
Our Father hath not made that mystery known;
  Needless the knowledge, therefore not reveal'd.

But didst thou know, in sure and sacred truth,
  It had a place assign'd in yonder skies;
There, through an endless life of joyous youth,
  To warble in the bowers of Paradise.

Lucy, if then the power to thee were given
  In that cold clay its life to re-engage,
Wouldst thou call back the warbler from its heaven,
  To be again the tenant of a cage?

Only that thou mightst cherish it again,
  Wouldst thou the object of thy love recall
To mortal life, and chance, and change, and pain,
  And death, which must be suffer'd once by all?

Oh no, thou sayst,—oh surely not, not so!
  I read the answer which those looks express:
For pure and true affection well I know
  Leaves in the heart no room for selfishness.

Such love of all our virtues is the gem;
  We bring with us the immortal seed at birth:
Of Heaven it is, and heavenly; woe to them
  Who make it wholly earthly and of earth!

What we love perfectly, for its own sake
  We love, and not our own; being ready thus
Whate'er self-sacrifice is asked to make,
  That which is best for it, is best for us.

O, Lucy! treasure up that pious thought;
  It hath a balm for sorrow's deadliest darts,
And with true comfort thou wilt find it fraught,
  If grief should reach thee in thy heart of hearts.

STANZAS

ADDRESSED TO J. M. W. TURNER, ESQ. R. A. ON HIS
VIEW OF THE LAGO MAGGIORE, FROM ARONA.

TURNER, thy pencil brings to mind a day,
  When from Laveno and the Beuscer hill,
I over Lake Verbanus held my way
  In pleasant fellowship, with wind at will;
Smooth were the waters wide, the skies serene,
And our hearts gladden'd with the joyful scene.

Joyful,—for all things minister'd delight,
  The lake and land, the mountains and the vales:
The Alps their snowy summits rear'd in light,
  Tempering with gelid breath the summer gales;
And verdant shores and woods refresh'd the eye
That else had ached beneath that brilliant sky.

To that elaborate island were we bound,
  Of yore the scene of Borromean pride,—
Folly's prodigious work; where all around,
  Under its coronet and self belied,
Look where you will you cannot chuse but see
The obtrusive motto's proud «HUMILITY!»

Far off the Borromean Saint was seen,
  Distinct though distant, o'er his native town,
Where his Colossus with benignant mien
  Looks from its station on Arona down:
To it the inland sailor lifts his eyes,
From the wide lake, when perilous storms arise.

But no storm threaten'd on that summer day;
  The whole rich scene appear'd for joyance made;
With many a gliding bark the Mere was gay—
  The fields and groves in all their wealth arrayed:
I could have thought the sun beheld with smiles
Those towns and palaces and populous isles.

From fair Arona even on such a day,
  When gladness was descending like a shower,
Great painter, did thy gifted eye survey
  The splendid scene; and, conscious of its power,
Well hath thine hand inimitable given
The glories of the lake, and land, and heaven.

THE DEVIL'S WALK.[1]

FROM his brimstone bed, at break of day,
  A walking the Devil is gone,
To visit his snug little farm of the Earth,
  And see how his stock goes on;
And over the hill and over the dale
  He walked, and over the plain,
And backwards and forwards he switched his long tail,
  As a gentleman switches his cane.

And pray how was the Devil drest?
  O! he was in his Sunday's best,
His coat was red, and his breeches were blue,
  With a hole behind that his tail went through.
He saw a Lawyer killing a viper,
  On a dunghill, beside his own stable;
And the Devil smiled, for it put him in mind
  Of Cain and his brother Abel.

An Apothecary on a white horse
  Rode by on his avocations,
« Oh!» says the Devil, «there's my old friend
  Death in the Revelations.»
He saw a cottage with a double coach-house,
  A cottage of gentility;
And the Devil was pleased, for his darling vice
  Is the pride that apes humility!

He stepp'd into a rich Bookseller's shop:
  Says he, « We are both of one college;
For I myself sat, like a cormorant, once,
  Hard by on the Tree of Knowledge.»
As he pass'd through Cold Bath Fields he saw
  A solitary cell;
And the Devil was charm'd, for it gave him a hint
  For improving the prisons in Hell.

He saw a Turnkey in a trice
  Fetter a troublesome jade;
« Ah! nimble,» quoth he, «do the fingers move
  When they're used to their trade.»
He saw the same Turnkey unfetter the same,
  But with little expedition:
And the Devil thought on the long debates
  On the Slave-Trade Abolition.

Down the river did glide, with wind and with tide,
  A pig with vast celerity,
And the Devil grinn'd, for he saw all the while
  How it cut its own throat, and he thought with a smile,
Of « England's commercial prosperity!»

He saw a certain Minister
  (A Minister to his mind)
Go up into a certain House
  With a majority behind;
The Devil quoted Genesis
  Like a very learned clerk,
How « Noah and his creeping things
  Went up into the Ark.»

General Gascoigne's burning face
  He saw with consternation,
And back to Hell his way did take;
  For the Devil thought, by a slight mistake,
'T was the General Conflagration!

[1] This has generally been attributed to Professor Porson; but as
in the last edition of Coleridge's Works, it is given as his joint
production with Mr Southey, we insert it here.

EPISTLE TO ALLAN CUNNINGHAM.

WELL, Heaven be thanked! friend Allan, here I am,
Once more, to that dear dwelling-place returned,
Where I have passed the whole mid stage of life,
Not idly, certes,—not unworthily—
So let me hope; where Time upon my head
Hath laid his frore and monitory hand;
And when this poor frail earthly tabernacle
Shall be dissolved—(it matters not how soon
Or late, in God's good time)—where I would fain
Be gathered to my children, earth to earth.

Needless it were to say how willingly
I bade the huge metropolis farewell;
Its dust and dirt and din and smoke and smut,
Thames' water, pavior's ground, and London sky!
Weary of hurried days and restless nights;
Watchmen, whose office is to murder sleep,
When sleep might else have « weighed one's eyelids
            down;»
Rattle of carriages, and roll of carts,
And tramp of iron hoofs; and worse than all,
(Confusion being worse confounded then
With coachmen's quarrels, and with footmen's shouts)
My next door neighbours, in a street not yet
Macadamized (me miserable!) at home!
For then had we, from midnight until morn,
House-quakes, street thunders, and door batteries.
(O Government, in thy wisdom and thy wants,
Tax knockers! in compassion to the sick
And those whose sober habits are not yet
Inverted, topsy-turvying night and day;
Tax them more heavily than thou hast charged
Armorial bearings and bepowdered pates!)
Escaping from all this, the very whirl
Of mail-coach wheels, bound outwards from Lad Lane,
Was peace and quietness; three hundred miles
Of homeward way, seemed to the body rest,
And to the mind repose.
                            Donne did not hate
More perfectly that city.   Not for all
Its social, all its intellectual joys,
(Which having touched, I may not condescend
To name aught else the demon of the place
Might as his lure hold forth); not even for these
Would I forego gardens and green fields, walks,
And hedgerow trees and stiles and shady lanes,
And orchards,—were such ordinary scenes
Alone to me accessible, as those
Wherein I learnt in infancy to love
The sights and sounds of nature; wholesome sights,
Gladdening the eye that they refresh; and sounds
Which, when from life and happiness they spring,
Bear with them to the yet unhardened heart
A sense that thrills its cords of sympathy;
Or, if proceeding from insensate things,
Give to tranquillity a voice wherewith
To woo the ear and win the soul attuned.
Oh not for all that London might bestow,
Would I renounce the genial influences
And thoughts and feelings, to be found where'er
We breathe beneath the open sky, and see
Earth's liberal bosom.   Judge then from thyself,
Allan, true child of Scotland; thou who art

So oft in spirit on thy native hills,
And yonder Solway shores; a poet thou,
Judge from thyself how strong the ties which bind
A poet to his home, when—making thus
Large recompense for all that, haply, else
Might seem perversely or unkindly done,—
Fortune hath set his happy habitacle
Among the ancient hills, near mountain streams
And lakes pellucid; in a land sublime
And lovely, as those regions of romance,
Where his young fancy in its day dreams roamed,
Expatiating in forests wild and wide,
Loegrian, or of dearest Faery land.

Yet, Allan, of the cup of social joy
No man drinks freelier; nor with heartier thirst,
Nor keener relish, where I see around
Faces which I have known and loved so long,
That, when he prints a dream upon my brain,
Dan Morpheus takes them for his readiest types:
And therefore in that loathed metropolis
Time measured out to me some golden hours.
They were not leaden-footed while the clay,
Beneath the patient touch of Chantrey's hand,
Grew to the semblance of my lineaments.
Lit up in memory's landscape, like green spots
Of sunshine, are the mornings, when in talk
With him and thee and Bedford (my true friend
Of forty years) I saw the work proceed,
Subject the while myself to no restraint,
But pleasurably in frank discourse engaged;
Pleased too, and with no unbecoming pride,
To think this countenance, such as it is,
So oft by rascally mislikeness wronged,
Should faithfully to those who in his works
Have seen the inner man portrayed, be shown;
And in enduring marble should partake
Of our great Sculptor's immortality.

I have been libelled, Allan, as thou knowest,
Through all degrees of calumny: but they
Who put one's name, for public sale, beneath
A set of features slanderously unlike,
Are our worst libellers.   Against the wrong
Which they inflict, Time hath no remedy.
Injuries there are which Time redresseth best,
Being more sure in judgment, though perhaps
Slower in his process even than the Court,
Where Justice, tortoise-footed and mole-eyed,
Sleeps undisturbed, fanned by the lulling wings
Of harpies at their prey.   We soon live down
Evil or good report, if undeserved.
Let then the dogs of faction bark and bay,—
Its bloodhounds savaged by a cross of wolf,—
Its full-bred kennel from the Blatant Beast,—
Its poodles by unlucky training marred,—
Mongrel and cur and bobtail;—let them yelp
Till weariness and hoarseness shall at length
Silence the noisy pack; meantime be sure
I shall not stoop for stones to cast among them!
So too its foumarts and its skunks may « stink
And be secure:» and its yet viler swarm,
The vermin of the press, both those that skip
And those that creep and crawl,—I do not catch
And pin them for exposure on the page;
Their filth is their defence.

But I appeal
Against the limner and the graver's wrong!
Their evil works survive them.   Bilderdyk
(Whom I am privileged to call my friend),
Suffering by graphic libels in like wise,
Gave his wrath vent in verse.   Would I could give
The life and spirit of his vigorous Dutch,
As his dear consort hath transfused my strains
Into her native speech, and made them known
On Rhine, and Yssel, and rich Amstel's banks,
And wheresoe'er the voice of Vondel still
Is heard; and still Hooft and Antonides
Are living agencies; and Father Cats,
The Household Poet, teacheth in his songs
The love of all things lovely, all things pure;
Best poet, who delights the happy mind
Of childhood, stores with moral strength the heart
Of youth, with wisdom maketh mid life rich,
And fills with quiet tears the eyes of age.

Hear then, in English rhyme, how Bilderdyk
Describes his wicked portraits, one by one.

« A madman, who from Bedlam hath broke loose;
   An honest fellow of the numskull race;
And, pappier-headed still, a very goose
   Staring with eyes aghast and vacant face;
A Frenchman, who would mirthfully display
   On some poor idiot his malicious wit;
And, lastly, one who, trained up in the way
   Of worldly craft, hath not forsaken it,
But hath served Mammon with his whole intent,
   (A thing of Nature's worst materials made),
Low minded, stupid, base, and insolent.
   I—I—a poet,—have been thus portrayed!
Can ye believe that my true effigy
   Among these vile varieties is found?
What thought, or line, or word hath fallen from me
   In all my numerous works, whereon to ground
The opprobrious notion? safely I may smile
   At these, acknowledging no likeness here.
But worse is yet to come, so—soft a while!—
   For now in potter's earth must I appear,
And in such workmanship, that sooth to say,
   Humanity disowns the imitation,
And the dolt image is not worth its clay.
   Then comes there one who will to admiration
In plastic wax the perfect face present ;
   And what of his performance comes at last?
Folly itself in every lineament!
   Its consequential features overcast
With the coxcombical and shallow laugh
   Of one who would, for condescension, hide,
Yet in his best behaviour can but half
   Suppress, the scornfulness of empty pride.»

« And who is Bilderdyk?» methinks thou sayest:
A ready question; yet which, trust me, Allan,
Would not be asked, had not the curse that came
From Babel, clipt the wings of Poetry.
Napoleon asked him once, with cold fixed look,
« Art thou then in the world of letters known?»
And meeting his imperial look with eye
As little wont to turn away before
The face of man, the Hollander replied,
« At least I have done that whereby I have

There to be known deserved.»
                       A man he is
Who hath received upon his constant breast
The sharpest arrows of adversity.
Whom not the clamours of the multitude,
Demanding, in their madness and their might,
Iniquitous things, could shake in his firm mind;
Nor the strong hand of instant tyranny
From the straight path of duty turn aside;
But who, in public troubles, in the wreck
Of his own fortunes, in proscription, exile,
Want, obloquy, ingrate neglect, and what
Of yet severer trials Providence
Sometimes inflicteth, chastening whom it loves,—
In all, through all, and over all, hath borne
An equal heart; as resolute toward
The world, as humbly and religiously
Beneath his heavenly Father's rod resigned.
Right-minded, happy-minded, righteous man!
True lover of his country and his kind;
In knowledge and in inexhaustive stores
Of native genius rich; philosopher,
Poet, and sage.   The language of a state
Inferior in illustrious deeds to none,
But circumscribed by narrow bounds, and now
Sinking in irrecoverable decline,
Hath pent within its sphere a name, with which
Europe should else have rung from side to side.

Such, Allan, is the Hollander to whom
Esteem and admiration have attached
My soul, not less than pre-consent of mind
And gratitude for benefits, when being
A stranger, sick, and in a foreign land,
He took me, like a brother, to his house,
And ministered to me, and made the weeks
Which had been wearisome and careful else,
So pleasurable, that in my kalendar
There are no whiter days.   'T will be a joy
For us to meet in heaven, though we should look
Upon each other's earthly face no more.
—Such is this world's complexion! « cheerful thoughts
Bring sad thoughts to the mind,» and these again
Give place to calm content, and stedfast hope,
And happy faith, assured.—Return we now,
With such transition as our daily life
Imposes in its wholesome discipline,
To a lighter strain; and from the Gallery
Of the Dutch poet's misresemblances,
Pass into mine; where I will show thee, Allan,
Such an array of villanous visages,
That if among them all there were but one
Which as a likeness could be proved upon me,
It were enough to make me in mere shame
Take up an alias and forswear myself.

Whom have we first? a dainty gentleman,
His sleepy eyes half closed, and countenance
To no expression stronger than might suit
A simper, capable of being moved;
Saucy and sentimental, with an air
So lack-thought and so lack-a-daisycal,
That one might guess the book which in his hand
He holds were Zimmerman on Solitude.

Then comes a jovial Landlord, who hath made it
Part of his trade to be the shoeing-horn

For his commercial customers.   God Bacchus
Hath not a thirstier votary.   Many a pipe
Of Porto's vintage hath contributed
To give his cheeks that deep carmine engrained;
And many a runlet of right Nantes, I ween,
Hath suffered percolation through that trunk,
Leaving behind it in the boozy eyes
A swoln and red suffusion, glazed and dim.
Our next is in the evangelical line,—
A leaden-visaged specimen,—demure,
Because he hath put on his Sunday's face;
Dull by formation, by complexion sad,
By bile, opinions, and dyspepsy sour.
One of the sons of Jack,—I know not which,
For Jack hath a most numerous progeny,
Made up for Mr Colburn's magazine
This pleasant composite.   A bust supplied
The features; look, expression, character,
Are of the artist's fancy, and free grace.
Such was that fellow's birth and parentage!
The rascal proved prolific! one of his breed
By Docteur Pichot introduced in France,
Passes for Monsieur Sooté, and another,—
An uglier miscreant too,—the brothers Schumann,
And their most cruel copper-scratcher, Zschoch,
From Zwickau sent abroad through Germany.
I wish the Schumann and the copper-scratcher
No worse misfortune for their recompense
Than to fall in with such a cut-throat face
In the Black Forest, or the Odenwald.

The Bust, which was the innocent grandfather,
I blame not, Allan.   'T was the work of Smith—
A modest, mild, ingenious man; and errs,
Where erring, only because over true,
Too close a likeness for similitude;
Fixing to every part and lineament
Its separate character, and missing thus
That which results from all.
                    Sir Smug comes next;
Allan, I own Sir Smug! I recognise
That visage with its dull sobriety:
I see it duly as the day returns,
When at the looking-glass, with lathered chin
And razor-weaponed hand, I sit, the face
Composed, and apprehensively intent
Upon the necessary operation
About to be performed, with touch, alas,
Not always confident of hair-breadth skill.
Even in such sober sadness and constrained
Composure cold, the faithful painter's eye
Had fixed me like a spell, and I could feel
My features stiffen as he glanced upon them.
And yet he was a man whom I loved dearly,
My fellow traveller, my familiar friend,
My household guest.   But when he looked upon me,
Anxious to exercise his excellent art,
The countenance he knew so thoroughly
Was gone, and in its stead there sate—Sir Smug.

Under the graver's hand, Sir Smug became
Sir Smouch,—a son of Abraham.   Now albeit
I would far rather trace my lineage thence
Than with the proudest line of peers or kings
Claim consanguinity, that cast of features
Would ill accord with me, who in all forms

Of pork,—baked, roasted, toasted, boiled or broiled,
Fresh, salted, pickled, seasoned, moist, or dry,
Whether ham, bacon, sausage, souse, or brawn,
Leg, blade-bone, bald-rib, griskin, chine, or chop,
Profess myself a genuine philopig.
It was, however, as a Jew whose portion
Had fallen unto him in a goodly land
Of loans, of omnium, and of three per cents,
That Messrs. Percy, of the Anecdote-firm,
Presented me unto their customers.
Poor Smouch endured a worse judaization
Under another hand: in this next stage
He is on trial at the Old Bailey, charged
With dealing in base coin.   That he is guilty,
No judge or jury could have half a doubt,
When they saw the culprit's face; and he himself,
As you may plainly see, is comforted
By thinking he has just contrived to keep
Out of rope's reach, and will come off this time
For transportation.
                Stand thou forth for trial
Now William Darton, of the society
Of friends called Quakers; thou who in the fourth month
Of the year twenty-four, on Holborn Hill,
At No 58, didst wilfully,
Falsely, and knowing it was falsely done,
Publish upon a card, as Robert Southey's,
A face which might be just as like Tom Fool's,
Or John, or Richard.   Any body else's!
What had I done to thee, thou William Darton,
That thou shouldst for the lucre of base gain,
Yea, for the sake of filthy fourpences,
Palm on my countrymen that face for mine?
O William Darton, let the yearly meeting
Deal with thee for that falseness!—All the rest
Are traceable: Smug's Hebrew family;
The German who might properly adorn
A gibbet or a wheel, and Monsieur Sooté,
Sons of Fitzbust the evangelical;
I recognise all these unlikenesses,
Spurious abominations though they be,
Each filiated on some original,
But thou, Friend Darton,—and observe me, man,
Only in courtesy and quasi Quaker,
I call thee Friend!—hadst no original,
No likeness, or unlikeness, silhouette,
Outline, or plaister, representing me,
Whereon to form this misrepresentation!
If I guess rightly at the pedigree
Of thy bad groat's-worth, thou didst get a barber
To personate my injured Laureateship:
An advertising barber, one who keeps
A bear, and when he puts to death poor Bruin,
Sells his grease fresh as from the carcase cut,
Pro bono publico, the price per pound
Twelve shillings and no more.   From such a barber,
O Unfriend Darton! was that portrait made,
I think, or peradventure, from his block.
Next comes a minion, worthy to be set
In a wooden frame; and here I might invoke
Avenging Nemesis, if I did not feel
Just now, God Cynthius pluck me by the ear.
But, Allan, in what shape God Cynthius comes,
And wherefore he admonisheth me thus,
Thou and I will not tell the world; hereafter
The commentators, my Malones and Reeds,

May, if they can. And in my gallery,
Though there remaineth undescribed good store,
Yet « of enough enough, and now no more,»
(As honest old George Gascoigne said of yore);
Save only a last couplet to express
That I am always truly yours,—R. S.
    Keswick, Sept. 1, 1828.

INSCRIPTIONS

FOR

THE CALEDONIAN CANAL.

1. AT CLACHNACHARRY.

ATHWART the island here, from sea to sea,
Between these mountain barriers, the great glen
Of Scotland offers to the traveller,
Through wilds impervious else, an easy path,
Along the shore of rivers and of lakes,
In line continuous, whence the waters flow
Dividing, east and west. Thus had they held
For untold centuries their perpetual course
Unprofited, till in the Georgian age
This mighty work was plann'd, which should unite
The lakes, control the innavigable streams,
And through the bowels of the land deduce
A way, where vessels which must else have braved
The formidable cape, and have essay'd
The perils of the Hyperborean sea,
Might from the Baltic to the Atlantic deep
Pass and repass at will. So when the storm
Careers abroad, may they securely here,
Through birchen groves, green fields, and pastoral hills,
Pursue their voyage home. Humanity
May boast this proud expenditure, begun
By Britain in a time of arduous war;
Through all the efforts and emergencies
Of that long strife continued; and achieved
After her triumph, even at the time
When national burdens bearing on the State
Were felt with heaviest pressure. Such expense
Is best economy. In growing wealth,
Comfort, and spreading industry, behold
The fruits immediate! And in days to come,
Fitly shall this great British work be named
With whatsoe'er of most magnificence
For public use, Rome in her plenitude
Of power effected, or all-glorious Greece,
Or Egypt, mother-land of all the arts.

2. AT FORT AUGUSTUS.

Thou who hast reach'd this level, where the glede,
Wheeling between the mountains in mid-air,
Eastward or westward as his gyre inclines,
Descries the German or the Atlantic Sea,
Pause here; and as thou seest the ship pursue
Her easy way serene, call thou to mind
By what exertions of victorious art
The way was opened. Fourteen times upheaved,
The vessel hath ascended since she changed
The salt sea-water for the Highland lymph:
As oft, in imperceptible descent
Must, step by step, be lower'd, before she woo
The ocean breeze again. Thou hast beheld

What basins most capacious of their kind
Enclose her, while the obedient element
Lifts or depones its burthen. Thou hast seen
The torrent, hurrying from its native hills,
Pass underneath the broad canal inhumed,
Then issue harmless thence; the rivulet,
Admitted by its intake peaceably,
Forthwith by gentle overfall discharged;
And haply too thou hast observed the herds
Frequent their vaulted path, unconscious they
That the wide waters on the long low arch
Above them, lie sustain'd. What other works
Science, audacious in emprize, hath wrought,
Meet not the eye, but well may fill the mind.
Not from the bowels of the land alone,
From lake and stream hath their diluvial wreck
Been scoop'd to form this navigable way;
Huge rivers were controll'd, or from their course
Shoulder'd aside; and, at the eastern mouth,
Where the salt ooze denied a resting-place,
There were the deep foundations laid, by weight
On weight immersed, and pile on pile down-driven,
Till stedfast as the everlasting rocks
The massive outwork stands. Contemplate now
What days and nights of thought, what years of toil,
What inexhaustive springs of public wealth
The vast design required; the immediate good,
The future benefit progressive still,
And thou wilt pay thy tribute of due praise
To those whose counsels, whose decrees, whose care
For after ages, formed the generous work.

3. AT BANAVIE.

Where these capacious basins, by the laws
Of the subjacent element receive
The ship, descending or upraised, eight times,
From stage to stage with unfelt agency
Translated, fitliest may the marble here
Record the architect's immortal name.
Telford it was by whose presiding mind
The whole great work was plann'd and perfected;
Telford, who o'er the vale of Cambrian Dee,
Aloft in air, at giddy height upborne,
Carried his navigable road, and hung
High o'er Menai's straits the bending bridge;
Structures of more ambitious enterprise
Than Minstrels in the age of old romance
To their own Merlin's magic lore ascribed.
Nor hath he for his native land performed
Less, in this proud design; and where his piers
Around her coast from many a fisher's creek,
Unsheltered else, and many an ample port,
Repel the assailing storm; and where his roads
In beautiful and sinuous line far seen,
Wind with the vale, and win the long ascent,
Now o'er the deep morass sustained, and now
Across ravine, or glen, or estuary,
Opening a passage through the wilds subdued.

IMITATION FROM THE PERSIAN.

LORD! who art merciful as well as just,
Incline thine ear to me, a child of dust!
Not what I would, O Lord! I offer thee,
    Alas! but what I can.

92

Father Almighty, who hast made me man,
And bade me look to heaven, for thou art there,
Accept my sacrifice and humble prayer.
Four things which are not in thy treasury,
I lay before thee, Lord, with this petition :—
    My nothingness, my wants,
    My sins, and my contrition!

LINES

WRITTEN UPON THE DEATH OF THE PRINCESS CHARLOTTE.

'T is not the public loss which hath imprest
This general grief upon the multitude,
And made its way at once to every breast,
The young, the old, the gentle, and the rude;
'T is not that in the hour which might have crown'd
The prayers preferr'd by every honest tongue;
The very hour which should have sent around
Tidings wherewith all steeples would have rung,
And all our cities blazed with festal fire,
And all our echoing streets have peal'd with gladness;
That then we saw the high-raised hope expire,
And England's expectation quench'd in sadness.
It is to think of what thou wert so late,
O thou who now liest cold upon thy bier!
So young, and so beloved : so richly blest
Beyond the common lot of royalty;

The object of thy worthy choice possest;
And in thy prime, and in thy wedded bliss,
And in the genial bed,—the cradle drest,
Hope standing by, and Joy, a bidden guest!
'T is this that from the heart of private life
Makes unsophisticated sorrow flow:
We mourn thee as a daughter and a wife,
And in our human nature feel the blow.

EPITAPH.

TIME and the world, whose magnitude and weight
Bear on us in this now, and hold us here
To earth inthralled, what are they in the past?
And in the prospect of the immortal soul
How poor a speck! Not here her resting-place;
Her portion is not here : and happiest they
Who, gathering early all that earth can give,
Shake off its mortal coil, and speed for Heaven.
Such fate had he whose relics here repose.
Few were his days; but yet enough to teach
Love, duty, generous feelings, high desires,
Faith, hope, devotion : and what more could length
Of days have brought him! What but vanity?
Joys, frailer even than health or human life;
Temptation; sin and sorrow, both too sure;
Evils that wound, and cares that fret, the heart!
Repine not, therefore, ye who love the dead.

All for Love,

OR A SINNER WELL SAVED.

TO CAROLINE BOWLES.

COULD I look forward to a distant day
With hope of building some elaborate lay,
Then would I wait till worthier strains of mine
Might bear inscribed thy name, O Caroline!
For I would, while my voice is heard on earth,
Bear witness to thy genius and thy worth.
But we have both been taught to feel with fear
How frail the tenure of existence here,
What unforeseen calamities prevent,
Alas, how oft! the best resolved intent;
And therefore this poor volume I address
To thee, dear friend, and sister Poetess.

            ROBERT SOUTHEY.

Keswick, 21 *Feb.* 1829.

THE story of the following Poem is taken from a Life of St Basil, ascribed to his contemporary St Amphilochius, Bishop of Iconium; a Latin version of which, made by Cardinal Ursus in the ninth century, is inserted by Rosweyde, among the Lives of the Fathers, in his compilation *Historiæ Eremiticæ.* The original had not then been printed, but Rosweyde obtained a copy of it from the Royal Library at Paris. He intimates no suspicion concerning the authenticity of the life, or the truth of this particular legend; observing only, that *hæc narratio apud solum invenitur Amphilochium.* It is, indeed, the flower of the work, and as such had been culled by some earlier translator than Ursus.

The very learned Dominican, P. François Combefis, published the original with a version of his own, and endeavoured to establish its authenticity in opposition to Baronius, who supposed the life to have been written by some other Amphilochius, not by the Bishop of Iconium. Had Combefis possessed powers of mind equal to his erudition, he might even then have been in some degree prejudiced upon this subject, for, according to Baillet, *il avoit un attachement tout particulier pour St Basile.* His version is inserted in the *Acta Sanctorum* (Jun. t. ii. pp. 937—957). But the Bollandist Baert brands the life there as apocryphal; and in his annotations treats Combefis more rudely, it may be suspected, than he would have done, had he not belonged to a rival and hostile order.

Should the reader be desirous of comparing the Poem with the Legend, he may find the story, as transcribed from Rosweyde, among the Notes.

ALL FOR LOVE.

I.

A Youth hath entered the Sorcerer's door,
But he dares not lift his eye,
For his knees fail and his flesh quakes,
And his heart beats audibly.

« Look up, young man!» the Sorcerer said,
« Lay open thy wishes to me!
Or art thou too modest to tell thy tale?
If so,—I can tell it thee.

« Thy name is Eleëmon ;
Proterius's freedman thou art ;
And on Cyra, thy Master's daughter,
Thou hast madly fix'd thy heart.

« But fearing (as thou well mayest fear!)
The high-born Maid to woo,
Thou hast tried what secret prayers and vows
And sacrifice might do.

« Thou hast prayed unto all Saints in Heaven,
And to Mary their vaunted Queen ;
And little furtherance hast thou found
From them, or from her, I ween!

« And thou, I know, the Ancient Gods,
In hope forlorn hast tried,
If haply Venus might obtain
The maiden for thy bride.

« On Jove and Phœbus thou hast call'd,
And on Astartè's name ;
And on her, who still at Ephesus
Retains a faded fame.

« Thy voice to Baal hath been raised ;
To Nile's old Deities ;
And to all Gods of elder time
Adored by men in every clime
When they ruled earth, seas and skies.

« Their Images are deaf!
Their Oracles are dumb!
And therefore thou, in thy despair,
To Abibas art come.

« Aye, because neither Saints nor Gods
Thy pleasure will fulfil,
Thou comest to me, Eleëmon,
To ask if Satan will!

« I answer thee, Yes.   But a faint heart
Can never accomplish its ends!
Put thy trust boldly in him, and be sure
He never forsakes his friends.»

While Eleëmon listened
He shuddered inwardly,
At the ugly voice of Abibas,
And the look in his wicked eye.

And he could then almost have given
His fatal purpose o'er ;
But his Good Angel had left him
When he entered the Sorcerer's door.

So in the strength of evil shame,
His mind the young man knit
Into a desperate resolve,
For his bad purpose fit.

« Let thy Master give me what I seek,
O Servant of Satan,» he said,
« As I ask firmly, and for his
Renounce all other aid!

« Time presses.   Cyra is content
To bid the world farewell,
And pass her days, a virgin vowed,
Among Emmelia's sisterhood,
The tenant of a cell.

« Thus hath her Father will'd, that so
A life of rigour here below
May fit her for the skies ;
And Heaven acceptably receive
His costliest sacrifice.

« The admiring people say of this
That Angels, or that Saints in bliss,
The holy thought inspire ;
And she is called a blessed Maid,
And he a happy Sire.

« Through Cappadocia far and wide
The news hath found its way,
And crowds to Cæsarea flock
To attend the solemn day.

« The robes are ready, rich with gold,
Even like a bridal dress,
Which at the altar she will wear
When self-devoted she stands there
In all her loveliness.

« And that coarse habit too, which she
Must then put on, is made,
Therein to be for life and death
Unchangeably array'd.

« This night,—this precious night is ours,—
Late, late, I come to you ;
But all that must be dared, or done,
Prepared to dare and do.»

« Thou hast hesitated long!» said Abibas,
« And thou hast done amiss,
In praying to Him whom I name not,
That it never might come to this!

« But thou hast chosen thy part, and here thou art;
And thou shalt have thy desire.
And though at the eleventh hour
Thou hast come to serve our Prince of Power,
He will give thee in full thine hire.

« These Tablets take (he wrote as he spake);
« My letters, which thou art to bear,

Wherein I shall commend thee
To the Prince of the Powers of the Air.

« Go from the North Gate out, and take
On a Pagan's Tomb thy stand;
And, looking to the North, hold up
The Tablets in thy hand:

« And call the Spirits of the Air,
That they my messenger may bear
To the place whither he would pass,
And there present him to their Prince
In the name of Abibas.

« The passage will be swift and safe,
No danger awaits thee beyond;
Thou wilt only have now to sign and seal,
And hereafter to pay the Bond.»

II.

SHUNNING human sight, like a thief in the night,
Eleëmon made no delay,
But went unto a Pagan's tomb
Beside the public way.

Inclosed with barren elms it stood,
There planted when the dead
Within the last abode of man
Had been deposited.

And thrice ten years those barren trees,
Enjoying light and air,
Had grown and flourished, while the dead
In darkness mouldered there.

Long had they overtopt the tomb:
And closed was now that upper room
Where friends were wont to pour,
Upon the honoured dust below,
Libations through the floor.

There on that unblest monument
The young man took his stand,
And northward he the tablets held
In his uplifted hand.

A courage not his own he felt,
A wicked fortitude,
Wherewith bad Influences unseen
That hour his heart endued.

The rising Moon grew pale in heaven
At that unhappy sight;
And all the blessed Stars seem'd then
To close their twinkling light;
And a shuddering in the elms was heard,
Though winds were still that night.

He call'd the Spirits of the Air,
He call'd them in the name
Of Abibas; and at the call
The attendant Spirits came.

A strong hand which he could not see
Took his uplifted hand;
He felt a strong arm circle him,
And lift him from his stand;

A whirr of unseen wings he heard
About him everywhere,
Which onward, with a mighty force,
Impell'd him through the air.

Fast through the middle sky and far
It hurried him along;
The Hurricane is not so swift,
The Torrent not so strong:

The Lightning travels not so fast,
The Sunbeams not so far:
And now behind him he hath left
The Moon and every Star.

And still erect as on the tomb
In impious act he stood,
Is he rapt onward—onward—still
In that fix'd attitude.

But as he from the living world
Approach'd where Spirits dwell,
His bearers there in thinner air
Were dimly visible;

Shapeless, and scarce to be descried
In darkness where they flew;
But still as they advanced, the more
And more distinct they grew:

And when their way fast-speeding they
Through their own region went,
Then were they in their substance seen,
The angelic form, the fiendish mien,
Face, look and lineament.

Behold where dawns before them now,
Far off, the boreal ray,
Sole daylight of that frozen zone,
The limit of their way.

In that drear realm of outer night,
Like the shadow, or the ghost of light,
It moved in the restless skies,
And went and came, like a feeble flame
That flickers before it dies.

There the Fall'en Seraph reign'd supreme
Amid the utter waste;
There on the everlasting ice
His dolorous throne was placed. (1)

Son of the Morning! is it then
For this that thou hast given
Thy seat, pre-eminent among
The hierarchies of Heaven?

As if dominion here could joy
To blasted pride impart;
Or this cold region slake the fire
Of Hell within the heart!

Thither the Evil Angels bear
The youth, and rendering homage there
Their service they evince.
And in the name of Abibas
Present him to their Prince:

Just as they seized him when he made
The Sorcerer's mandate known,
In that same act and attitude
They set him before the throne.

The Fallen Seraph cast on him
A dark disdainful look;
And from his raised hand scornfully
The proffer'd tablets took.

« Aye,—love!» he cried.   « It serves me well.
There was the Trojan boy,—
His love brought forth a ten years' war,
And fired the towers of Troy.

« And when my own Mark Anthony
Against young Cæsar strove,
And Rome's whole world was set in arms,
The cause was,—all for love!

« Some for ambition sell themselves,
By avarice some are driven;
Pride, envy, hatred, best will move
Some souls, and some for only love
Renounce their hopes of Heaven.

« Yes, of all human follies, love,
Methinks, hath served me best :
The Apple had done but little for me
If Eve had not done the rest.

« Well then, young Amorist, whom love
Hath brought into this pass,
I am willing to perform the word
Of my servant Abibas.

« Thy Master's daughter shall be thine,
And with her sire's consent;
And not more to thy heart's desire
Than to her own content.

« Yea, more,—I give thee with the girl,
Thine after days to bless,
Health, wealth, long life, and whatsoe'er
The world calls happiness.

« But, mark me!—on conditions, youth!
No paltering here we know!
Dost thou here, solemnly, this hour,
Thy hope of Heaven forego?

Dost thou renounce thy baptism,
And bind thyself to me,
My woeful portion to partake
Through all eternity?

« No lurking purpose shall avail,
When youth may fail and courage quail,
To cheat me by contrition!
I will have thee written down among
The Children of Perdition.

« Remember, I deceive thee not,
Nor have I tempted thee!
Thou comest of thine own accord,
And actest knowingly.

« Dost thou, who now to chuse art free,
For ever pledge thyself to me?
As I shall help thee, say!»—
« I do? so help me, Satan!» said
The wilful castaway.

« A resolute answer,» quoth the Fiend;
« And now then, Child of Dust,
In further proof of that firm heart,
Thou wilt sign a Bond before we part,
For I take thee not on trust!»

Swift as thought a scroll and a reed were brought,
And to Eleëmon's breast,
Just where the heart-stroke plays the point
Of the reed was gently prest.

It pierced not in, nor touch'd the skin;
But the sense that it caused was such,
As when an electric pellet of light
Comes forcibly out at a touch.

A sense no sooner felt than gone.
But with that short feeling then
A drop of his heart's-blood came forth
And fill'd the fatal pen.

And with that pen accurst, he sign'd
The execrable scroll,
Whereby he to perdition bound
His miserable soul.

« Eleëmon, Eleëmon!» then said the Demon,
« The girl shall be thine,
By the tie she holds divine,
Till time that tie shall sever;
And by this writing thou art mine,
For ever and ever and ever!»

III.

Look at yon silent dwelling now!
A heavenly sight is there,
Where Cyra in her chamber kneels
Before the Cross in prayer.

She is not loth to leave the world;
For she hath been taught with joy
To think that prayer and praise thenceforth
Will be her life's employ.

And thus her mind hath she inclined,
Her pleasure being still
(An only child and motherless)
To do her Father's will.

The moonlight falls upon her face,
Upraised in fervour meek
While peaceful tears of piety
Are stealing down her cheek.

That duty done, the harmless maid
Disposed herself to rest;
No sin, no sorrow in her soul,
No trouble in her breast.

But when upon the pillow then,
Composed, she laid her head,
She little thought what unseen Powers
Kept watch beside her bed.

A double ward had she that night,
When evil near her drew;
Her own Good Angel guarding her,
And Eleëmon's too.

Their charge it was to keep her safe
From all unholy things;
And o'er her while she slept, they spread
The shadow of their wings.

So when an Evil Dream drew nigh
They barr'd him from access,
Nor suffer'd him to reach her with
A breath of sinfulness.

But with his instigations they
A hallowing influence blent,
And made his fiendish ministry
Subserve to their intent.

Thus while in troubled sleep she lay,
Strange impulses were given,
Emotions earthly and of earth,
With heavenly ones of Heaven.

And now the nightingale hath ceased
Her strain, who all night long
Hath in the garden rosier trill'd
A rich and rapturous song.

The storks on roof and dome and tower
Forbear their clattering din,
As now the motions and the sounds
Of daily life begin.

Then as from dreams that seem'd no dreams
The wondering Maid awoke,
A low sweet voice was in her ear;
Such as we might expect to hear
If some Good Angel spoke.

According with her dreams, it said,
« So, Cyra, must it be;
The duties of a wedded life
Hath Heaven ordain'd for thee. »

This was no dream full well she knew;
For open-eyed she lay,
Conscious of thought and wakefulness
And in the light of day;
And twice it spake, if doubt had been,
To do all doubt away.

Alas! but how shall she make known
This late and sudden change?
Or how obtain belief for what
Even to herself is strange?

How will her Father brook a turn
That must to all seem shame?
How bear to think that vulgar tongues
Are busy with her name!

That she should for a voice,—a dream,—
Expose herself to be the theme
Of wonder and of scorn;—
Public as her intent had been,
And this the appointed morn!

The Nuns even now are all alert;
The altar hath been drest,
The scissars that should clip her hair
Provided, and the black hood there,
And there the sable vest.

And there the Priests are robing now;
The Singers in their station;
Hark! in the city she can hear
The stir of expectation!

Through every gate the people pour,
And guests on roof and porch and tower
Expectant take their place;
The streets are swarming, and the church
Already fills apace.

Speak, then, she must: her heart she felt
This night had changed its choice;
Nor dared the Maiden disobey,—
Nor did she wish to (sooth to say)—
That sweet and welcome voice.

Her Father comes: she studies not
For gloss, or for pretence;
The plain straight course will Cyra take
(Which none without remorse forsake)
Of truth and innocence.

« O Father, hear me patiently!»
The blushing Maiden said;
« I tremble, Father, while I speak;
But surely not for dread!

« If all my wishes have till now
Found favour in thy sight,
And ever to perform thy will
Hath been my best delight,
Why should I fear to tell thee now
The visions of this night?

« I stood in a dream at the altar,—
But it was as an earthly Bride;
And Eleëmon thy freedman
Was the Bridegroom at my side.

« Thou, Father, gavest me to him,
With thy free and full consent;
And,—why should I dissemble it?—
Methought I was content.

« Months then and years were crowded
In the course of that busy night;
I claspt a baby to my breast,
And, oh! with what delight!

« Yea, I was fruitful as a Vine;
Our heavenly Parent me and mine
In all things seem'd to bless;
Our ways were ways of peace, our paths
Were paths of pleasantness.

« When I taught lisping lips to pray,
      The joy it was to me,
O Father, thus to train these plants
      For immortality!

« I saw their little winning ways
      Their grandsire's love engage ;
Methought they were the pride, the joy,
      The crown of his old age.

« When from the vision I awoke,
      A voice was in my ear,—
A waking voice,—I heard it twice;
      No human tongue was near;

« No human utterance so could reach
The secret soul, no human speech
      So make the soul rejoice;
In hearing it I felt and knew
      It was an Angel's voice!

« And thus in words distinct it said,
      ' So, Cyra, must it be!
The duties of a wedded life
Hath Heaven ordain'd for thee.' »

Her cheek was like the new-blown rose,
      While thus she told her tale;
Proterius listened earnestly,
      And as he heard grew pale.

For he, too, in the dreams of night
At the altar had seem'd to stand,
And to Eleëmon his freedman
Had given his daughter's hand.

Their offspring, courting his caress,
      About his knees had throng'd ;
A lovely progeny, in whom,
When he was in the silent tomb,
      His line should be prolong'd.

And he had heard a waking voice,
      Which said it so must be,
Pronouncing upon Cyra's name
      A holiest eulogy:

« Her shall her husband praise, and her
      Her children blest shall call :
Many daughters have done virtuously,
      But thine excelleth them all! »

No marvel if his heart were moved ;
      The dream he saw was one :
He kiss'd his trembling child, and said,
      « The will of Heaven be done! »

Little did child or sire in this
      The work of sorcery fear!
As little did Eleëmon think
That the hand of Heaven was here.

· IV.

FROM house to house, from street to street
      The rapid rumour flies;
Incredulous ears it found, and hands
      Are lifted in surprise;

And tongues through all the astonished town
      Are busier now than eyes.

« So sudden and so strange a change!
      A Freedman, too, the choice !
The shame,—the scandal,—and for what?
      A vision and a voice !

« Had she not chosen the strait gate,—
The narrow way,—the holy state,—
      The Sanctuary's abode?
Would Heaven call back its votary
      To the broad and beaten road ?

« To carnal wishes would it turn
      The mortified intent ?
For this are miracles vouchsafed?
      For this are Angels sent ?

« A plain collusion! a device
Between the girl and youth !
Good easy man must the Father be,
      To take such tale for truth! »

So judged the acrid and the austere,
      And they whose evil heart
Inclines them, in whate'er betides,
      To take the evil part.

But others, whom a kindlier frame
      To better thoughts inclined,
Preserved, amid their wonderment
      An equitable mind.

They would not of Proterius thus
      Injuriously misdeem,—
A grave, good man, and with the wise
      For wisdom in esteem.

No easy ear, or vain belief,
      Would he to falsehood lend;
Nor ever might light motive him
      From well-weighed purpose bend.

And surely on his pious child,
The gentle Cyra, meek and mild,
      Could no suspicion rest ;
For in this daughter he had been
      Above all fathers blest.

As dutiful as beautiful,
      Her praise was widely known,
Being one who, as she grew in years,
      Had still in goodness grown.

And what though Eleëmon were
      A man of lowly birth !
Enough it was if Nature had
      Ennobled him with worth.

« This was no doubtful thing, » they said,
« For he had in the house been bred,
      Nor e'er from thence removed;
But there from childhood had been known,
      And trusted and approved.

« Such as he was his qualities
Might to the world excuse
The Maid and Father for their choice,
Without the vision and the voice,
Had they been free to chuse.

- But Heaven by miracle had made
Its pleasure manifest;
That manifested will must set
All doubtful thoughts to rest.
Mysterious though they be, the ways
Of Providence are best. •

The wondering City thus discoursed;
To Abibas alone
The secret truth, and even to him
But half the truth, was known.

Meantime the Church hath been prepared
For spousal celebration;
The Sisters to their cells retire,
Amazed at such mutation.

The habit and hood of camel's hair,
Which with the sacred scissars there
On the altar were display'd,
Are taken thence, and in their stead
The marriage rings are laid.

Behold, in garments gay with gold,
For other spousals wrought,
The Maiden from her Father's house
With bridal pomp is brought. (2)

And now before the Holy Door
In the Ante-nave (3) they stand;
The Bride and Bridegroom side by side,
The Paranymphs in festal pride
Arranged on either hand.

Then from the Sanctuary the Priests,
With incense burning sweet,
Advance, and at the Holy Door
The Bride and Bridegroom meet.

There to the Bride and Bridegroom they
The marriage tapers gave;
And to the altar as they go,
With cross-way movement to and fro,
The thuribule they wave.

For fruitfulness, and perfect love,
And constant peace, they prayed,
On Eleëmon, the Lord's Servant,
And Cyra, the Lord's Handmaid.

They call'd upon the Lord to bless
Their spousal celebration,
And sanctify the marriage tie
To both their souls' salvation.

A pause at every prayer they made,
Whereat with one accord
The Choristers took up their part,
And sung in tones that thrilled the heart,
Have mercy on us, Lord!

Then with the marriage rings the Priests
Betrothed them each to each,
And, as the sacred pledge was given,
Resumed his awful speech;

Pronouncing them before high Heaven
This hour espoused to be,
Now and for ever more, for time
And for eternity.

This did he in the presence
Of Angels and of men:
And at every pause the Choristers
Intoned their deep Amen!

Then to that gracious Lord, the Priest
His supplication made,
Who, as our sacred Scriptures tell,
Did bring Rebecca to the well
When Abraham's servant pray'd.

He call'd upon that gracious Lord
To stablish with his power
The espousals made between them,
In truth and love, this hour;

And with his mercy and his word
Their lot, now link'd, to bless,
And let his Angel guide them
In the way of righteousness.

With a Christian benediction,
The Priest dismist them then,
And the Choristers, with louder voice,
Intoned the last Amen!

The days of Espousals are over:
And on the Crowning-day,
To the sacred fane the bridal train,
A gay procession, take again
Through thronging streets their way.

Before them, by the Paranymphs,
The coronals are borne,
Composed of all sweet flowers (4) of spring
By virgin hands that morn.

With lighted tapers in array
They enter the Holy Door,
And the Priest with the waving thuribule
Perfumes the way before.

He raised his voice, and call'd aloud
On Him who from the side
Of our first Father, while he slept,
Form'd Eve to be his bride;

Creating Woman thus for Man
A helpmate meet to be,
For youth and age, for good and ill,
For weal and woe, united still
In strict society:

Flesh of his flesh, appointing them
One flesh to be, one heart;
Whom God hath joined together
Them let not man dispart!

And on our Lord he call'd, by whom
The marriage feast was blest,
When first by miracle he made
His glory manifest.

Then in the ever-blessed Name,
Almighty over all,
From the man's Paranymph he took
The marriage coronal;

And crowning him therewith, in that
Thrice holy Name, he said,
« Eleëmon, the Servant of God, is crown'd
For Cyra, the Lord's Handmaid !»

Next, with like action and like words,
Upon her brow he set
Her coronal, intwined wherein
The rose and lily met;
How beautifully they beseem'd,
Her locks of glossy jet!

Her he for Eleëmon crown'd
The Servant of the Lord,—
Alas, how little did that name
With his true state accord!

« Crown them with honour, Lord! he said,»
« With blessings crown the righteous head!
To them let peace be given,
A holy life, a hopeful end,
A heavenly crown in Heaven !»

Still as he made each separate prayer
For blessings that they in life might share,
And for their eternal bliss,
The echoing Choristers replied,
« O Lord, so grant thou this!»

How differently meantime, before
The altar as they knelt,
While they the sacred rites partake
Which endless matrimony make,
The Bride and Bridegroom felt!

She, who possest her soul in peace
And thoughtful happiness,
With her whole heart had inly join'd
In each devout address.

His lips the while had only moved
In hollow repetition;
For he had steel'd himself, like one
Bound over to perdition.

In present joy he wrapt his heart,
And resolutely cast
All other thoughts beside him,
Of the future, or the past.

V.

TWELVE years have held their quiet course
Since Cyra's nuptial day:
How happily, how rapidly,
Those years have past away!

Blest in her husband she hath been;
He loved her as sincerely,
(Most sinful and unhappy man!)
As he had bought her dearly.

She hath been fruitful as a vine,
And in her children blest;
Sorrow hath not come near her yet,
Nor fears to shake, nor cares to fret,
Nor grief to wound the breast.

And blest alike would her husband be,
Were all things as they seem;
Eleëmon hath every earthly good,
And with every man's esteem.

But where the accursed reed had drawn
The heart-blood from his breast,
A small red spot remain'd
Indelibly imprest.

Nor could he from his heart throw off
The consciousness of his state;
It was there with a dull, uneasy sense,
A coldness and a weight;

It was there when he lay down at night,
It was there when at morn he rose :
He feels it whatever he does,
It is with him wherever he goes.

No occupation from his mind
That constant sense can keep;
It is present in his waking hours,
It is present in his sleep;

But still he felt it most,
And with painfullest weight it prest,—
O miserable man!
When he was happiest.

O miserable man,
Who hath all the world to friend,
Yet dares not in prosperity
Remember his latter end!

But happy man, whate'er
His earthly lot may be,
Who looks on Death as the Angel
That shall set his spirit free,
And bear it to its heritage
Of immortality!

In such faith hath Proterius lived;
And strong is that faith and fresh,
As if obtaining then new power,
When he hath reach'd the awful hour
Appointed for all flesh.

Eleëmon and his daughter
With his latest breath he blest,
And saying to them, « we shall meet
Again before the Mercy-seat!»
Went peacefully to rest.

This is the balm which God
Hath given for every grief;
And Cyra, in her anguish,
Look'd heavenward for relief.

93

But her miserable husband
Heard a voice within him say,
« Eleëmon, Eleëmon,
Thou art sold to the Demon !»
And his heart seem'd dying away.

Whole Cæsarea is pour'd forth
To see the funeral state,
When Proterius is borne to his resting-place
Without the Northern Gate.

Not like a Pagan's is his bier
At doleful midnight borne
By ghastly torchlight, and with wail
Of women hired to mourn.

With tapers in the face of day,
These rites their faithful hope display;
In long procession slow,
With hymns that fortify the heart,
And prayers that soften woe.

In honour of the dead man's rank,
But of his virtues more,
The holy Bishop Basil
Was one the bier who bore.

And with the Bishop side by side,
As nearest to the dead allied,
Was Eleëmon seen :
All mark'd, but none could rede aright,
The trouble in his mien.

« His master's benefits on him
Were well bestow'd,» they said,
« Whose sorrow now full plainly show'd
How well he loved the dead.»

They little ween'd what thoughts in him
The solemn psalm awoke,
Which to all other hearts that hour
Its surest comfort spoke:

« Gather my Saints together :
In peace let them be laid,
They who with me,» thus saith the Lord,
« Their covenant have made!»

What pangs to Eleëmon then,
O wretchedest of wretched men,
That psalmody convey'd!
For conscience told him that he too
A covenant had made.

And when he would have closed his ears
Against the unwelcome word,
Then from some elms beside the way
A Raven's croak was heard.

To him it seem'd a hollow voice
That warn'd him of his doom;
For the tree whereon the Raven sate
Grew over the Pagan's tomb.

VI.

When weariness would let her
No longer pray and weep,
And midnight long was past,
Then Cyra fell asleep.

Into that wretched sleep she sunk
Which only sorrow knows,
Wherein the exhausted body rests,
But the heart hath no repose.

Of her Father she was dreaming,
Still aware that he was dead,
When, in the visions of the night,
He stood beside her bed.

Crown'd, and in robes of light he came ;
She saw he had found grace ;
And yet there seem'd to be
A trouble in his face.

The eye and look were still the same
That she from her cradle knew ;
And he put forth his hand, and blest her,
As he had been wont to do.

But then the smile benign
Of love forsook his face,
And a sorrowful displeasure
Came darkly in its place;

And he cast on Eleëmon
A melancholy eye,
And sternly said, « I bless thee not,—
Bondsman ? thou knowest why !»

Again to Cyra then he turn'd,
« Let not thy husband rest,
Till he hath wash'd away with tears
The red spot from his breast !

« Hold fast thy hope, and Heaven will not
Forsake thee in thine hour :
Good Angels will be near thee,
And Evil ones shall fear thee,
And Faith will give thee power.»

Perturb'd, yet comforted, she woke,
For in her waking ear
The words were heard which promised her
A strength above all fear.

An odour, that refresh'd no less
Her spirit with its blessedness
Than her corporeal frame,
Was breathed around, and she surely found
That from Paradise it came.

And, though the form revered was gone,
A clear unearthly light
Remain'd, encompassing the bed,
When all around was night.

It narrow'd as she gazed;
And soon she saw it rest,
Concentred, like an eye of light,
Upon her husband's breast.

Not doubting now the presence
Of some good presiding power,
Collectedness as well as strength
Was given her in this hour.

And rising half, the while in deep
But troubled sleep he lay,
She drew the covering from his breast
With cautious hand away.

The small round blood-red mark she saw;
Eleëmon felt her not;
But in his sleep he groan'd, and cried
« Out! out—accursed spot!»

The darkness of surrounding night
Closed then upon that eye of light.
She waited for the break
Of day, and lay the while in prayer
For that poor sinner's sake.—

In fearful, miserable prayer;
But while she pray'd, the load of care
Less heavily bore on her heart,
And light was given, enabling her
To chuse her difficult part.

And she drew, as comfortable texts
Unto her thoughts recurr'd,
Refreshment from the living well
Of God's unerring word.

But when the earliest dawn appear'd,
Herself in haste she array'd,
And watch'd his waking patiently,
And still as she watch'd she pray'd;
And when Eleëmon had risen,
She spake to him, and said :

« We have been visited this night!
My Father's Ghost I have seen ;
I heard his voice,—an awful voice!—
And so hast thou, I ween !

Eleëmon was pale when he awoke;
But paler then he grew,
And over his whole countenance
There came a death-like hue.

Still he controll'd himself, and sought
Her question to beguile;
And forcing, while he answer'd her,
A faint and hollow smile,—

« Cyra,» he said, « thy thoughts possess
With one too painful theme,
Their own imaginations
For reality misdeem;
Let not my dearest, best beloved,
Be troubled for a dream !»

« O Eleëmon,» she replied,
« Dissemble not with me thus!
Ill it becomes me to forget
What dreams have been to us!

« Thinkest thou there can be peace for me,
Near to me as thou art,
While some unknown and fearful sin
Is festering at thy heart?

« Eleëmon, Eleëmon,
I may not let thee rest,
Till thou hast wash'd away with tears
The red spot from thy breast !

« Thus to conceal thy crime from me,
It is no tenderness !
The worst is better known than fear'd.
Whatever it be, confess ;
And the Merciful will cleanse thee
From all unrighteousness!»

Like an aspen leaf he trembled;
And his imploring eye
Bespake compassion, ere his lips
Could utter their dreaded reply.

« O dearly loved, as dearly bought,
My sin and punishment I had thought
To bear through life alone :
Too much the Vision hath reveal'd,
And all must now be known!

« On thee, methinks, and only thee
Dare I for pity call:
Abhor me not—renounce me not,—
My life, my love, my all!

« And Cyra, sure if ever cause
Might be a sinner's plea,
'T would be for that lost wretch who sold
His hope of Heaven for thee!

« Thou seest a miserable man
Given over to despair,
Who has bound himself by his act and deed
To the Prince of the Powers of the Air.»

She seized him by the arm,
And hurrying him into the street,
« Come with me to the Church,» she cried,
« And to Basil the Bishop's feet!»

VII.

Public must be the sinner's shame
As heinous his offence ;
So Basil said, when he ordain'd
His form of penitence.

And never had such dismay been felt
Through that astonished town,
As when, at morn, the Cryer went
Proclaiming up and down,

« The miserable sinner, Eleëmon,
Who for love hath sold himself to the Demon,
His guilt before God and man declares;
And beseeches all good Christians
To aid him with their prayers.»

Many were the hearts compassionate
Whom that woeful petition moved;
For he had borne his fortune meekly,
And therefore was well beloved.

Open his hand had been,
And liberal of its store;
And the prayers of the needy arose
Who had daily been fed at his door.

They too whom Cyra's secret aid
Relieved from pressing cares,
In this, her day of wretchedness,
Repaid her with their prayers.

And from many a gentle bosom
Supplications for mercy were sent,
If haply they might aid
The wretched penitent.

Sorely such aid he needed then!
Basil himself, of living men
The powerfullest in prayer, (5)
For pity, rather than in hope,
Had bidden him not despair.

So hard a thing for him it seem'd
To wrest from Satan's hand
The fatal Bond, which, while retain'd,
Must against him in judgment stand.

« Dost thou believe,» he said, « that Grace
Itself can reach this grief?»
With a feeble voice, and a woeful eye,
« Lord, I believe!» was the sinner's reply,
« Help thou mine unbelief!»

The Bishop then crost him on the brow,
And crost him on the breast:
And told him if he did his part
With true remorse and faithful heart,
God's mercy might do the rest.

« Alone in the holy relic-room (6)
Must thou pass day and night,
And wage with thy ghostly enemies
A more than mortal fight.

« The trial may be long, and the struggle strong,
Yet be not thou dismay'd;
For thou mayest count on Saints in Heaven,
And on earthly prayers for aid.

« And in thy mind this scripture bear
With stedfast faithfulness, whate'er
To appal thee may arrive;
' When the wicked man turneth away from his sin
He shall save his soul alive!'

« Take courage as thou lookest around
On the relics of the blest;
And night and day continue to pray,
Until thy tears have wash'd away
The stigma from thy breast!»

« Let me be with him!» Cyra cried;
« If thou mayest not be there,
In this sore trial I at least
My faithful part may bear:

« My presence may some comfort prove,
Yea, haply some defence;
O Father, in myself I feel
The strength of innocence!»

« Nay Daughter, nay; it must not be!
Though dutiful this desire;
He may, by Heaven's good grace, be saved,
But only as if by fire!

« Sights which should never meet thine eye
Before him may appear:
And fiendish voices proffer words
Which should never assail thy ear.
Alone must he this trance sustain:
Keep thou thy vigils here!»

He led him to the relic-room;
Alone he left him there;
And Cyra with the Nuns remain'd
To pass her time in prayer.

Alone was Eleëmon left
For mercy on Heaven to call;
Deep and unceasing were his prayers,
But not a tear would fall.

His lips were parch'd, his head was hot,
His eyeballs throbb'd with heat;
And in that utter silence
He could hear his temples beat.

But cold his feet, and cold his hands;
And at his heart there lay
An icy coldness unrelieved,
While he prayed the livelong day:

A long, long day! It past away
In dreadful expectation;
Yet free throughout the day was he
From outward molestation.

Nor sight appear'd, nor voice was heard,
Though every moment both he fear'd;
The Spirits of the Air
Were busy the while in infusing
Suggestions of despair.

And he in strong endeavour still
Against them strove with earnest will;
Heart-piercing was his cry,
Heart-breathed his groaning; but it seem'd
That the source of tears was dry.

And now had evening closed;
The dim lamp light alone
On the stone cross, and the marble walls,
And the shrines of the Martyrs, shone.

Before the cross Eleëmon lay;
His knees were on the ground;
Courage enough to touch the Cross
Itself, he had not found.

But on the steps of the pedestal
His lifted hands were laid;
And in that lowliest attitude
The suffering sinner pray'd.

A strong temptation of the Fiend,
Which bade him despair and die,
He with the aid of Scripture

Had faithfully put by;
And then, as with a dawning hope,
He raised this contrite cry :

« Oh that mine eyes were fountains!
If the good grace of Heaven
Would give me tears, methinks I then
Might hope to be forgiven!»

To that meek prayer a short loud laugh
From fiendish lips replied:
Close at his ear he felt it,
And it sounded on every side.

From the four walls and the vaulted roof
A shout of mockery rung;
And the echoing ground repeated the sound,
Which peal'd above, and below, and around,
From many a fiendish tongue.

The lamps went out (7) at that hideous shout;
But darkness had there no place,
For the room was fill'd with a lurid light
That came from a Demon's face.

A dreadful face it was,—too well
By Eleëmon known!
Alas! he had seen it when he stood
Before the dolorous throne.

« Eleëmon! Eleëmon!»
Sternly said the Demon,
« How have I merited this?
I kept my covenant with thee,
And placed thee in worldly bliss.

« And still thou mightest have had,
Thine after days to bless,
Health, wealth, long life, and whatsoe'er
The World calls happiness.

« Fool, to forego thine earthly joys,
Who hast no hope beyond!
For judgment must be given for me,
When I sue thee upon the Bond.

« Remember I deceived thee not;
Nor had I tempted thee;
Thou camest of thine own accord,
And didst act knowingly!

« I told thee thou mightest vainly think
To cheat me by contrition,
When thou wert written down among
The Children of Perdition!

« ' So help me, Satan!' were thy words
When thou didst this allow;
I help'd thee, Eleëmon, then,—
And I will have thee now!»

At the words of the Fiend, from the floor
Eleëmon in agony sprung;
Up the steps of the pedestal he ran,
And to the Cross he clung.

And then it seem'd as if he drew,
While he claspt the senseless stone,
A strength he had not felt till then,
A hope he had not known.

So when the Demon ceased,
He answered him not a word;
But looking upward, he
His faithful prayer preferr'd:

« All, all, to Thee, my Lord
And Saviour, I confess!
And I know that Thou canst cleanse me
From all unrighteousness!

« I have turned away from my sin!
In Thee do I put my trust!
To such Thou hast promised forgiveness,
And Thou art faithful and just!»

With that the Demon disappear'd;
The lamps resumed their light;
Nor voice, nor vision more
Disturb'd him through the night.

He stirr'd not from his station,
But there stood fix'd in prayer;
And when Basil the Bishop enter'd
At morn, he found him there.

VIII.

WELL might the Bishop see what he
Had undergone that night;
Remorse and agony of mind
Had made his dark hair white.

So should the inner change, he ween'd,
With the outward sign accord;
And holy Basil crost himself,
And blest our gracious Lord.

« Well hast thou done,» said he, « my son,
And faithfully fought the fight;
So shall this day complete, I trust,
The victory of the night.

« I fear'd that forty days and nights
Too little all might be;
But great and strange hath been the change
One night hath wrought in thee.»

« O Father, Father!» he replied,
« And hath it been but one?
An endless time it seem'd to me!
I almost thought Eternity
With me had been begun.

« And surely this poor flesh and blood
Such terrors could not have withstood,
If grace had not been given;
But when I claspt the blessed Cross,
I then had help from Heaven.

« The coldness from my heart is gone;
But still the weight is there,
And thoughts which I abhor, will come
And tempt me to despair.

« Those thoughts I constantly repel;
And all, methinks, might yet be well,
Could I but weep once more,
And with true tears of penitence
My dreadful state deplore.

« Tears are denied; their source is dried!
And must it still be so?
O Thou, who from a rock didst make
The living waters flow,

« A broken and a bleeding heart
This hour I offer Thee;
And, when Thou seest good, my tears
Shall then again be free!»

A knocking at the door was heard
As he ended this reply;
Hearing that unexpected sound,
The Bishop turn'd his eye,
And his venerable Mother,
Emmelia the Abbess, drew nigh.

« We have not ceased this mournful night,»
Said she, « on Heaven to call:
And our afflicted Cyra
Hath edified us all.

« More fervent prayers from suffering heart,
I ween, have ne'er been sent;
And now she asks, as some relief,
In this, her overwhelming grief,
To see the penitent.

« So earnestly she ask'd, that I
Her wish would not defer;
And I have brought her to the door,
Forgive me, Son, if I err.»

« Hard were I did I not consent
To thy compassionate intent,
O Mother,» he replied;
And raising then his voice, « Come in,
Thou innocent!» he cried.

That welcome word when Cyra heard,
With a sad pace and slow,
Forward she came, like one whose heart
Was overcharged with woe,

Her face was pale,—long illness would
Have changed those features less:
And long-continued tears had dimm'd
Her eyes with heaviness.

Her husband's words had reach'd her ear
When at the door she stood;
« Thou hast prayed in vain for tears,» she said,
« While I have pour'd a flood!

« Mine flow, and they will flow; they must;
They cannot be represt!
And oh that they might wash away
The stigma from thy breast!

« Oh that these tears might cleanse that spot,—
Tears which I cannot check!»
Profusely weeping as she spake,
She fell upon his neck.

He claspt the mourner close, and in
That passionate embrace,
In grief for her, almost forgot
His own tremendous case.

Warm as they fell he felt her tears,
And in true sympathy,
So gracious Heaven permitted then,
His own to flow were free.

And then the weight was taken off,
Which at his heart had prest;—
O mercy! and the crimson spot
Hath vanish'd from his breast!

At that most happy sight,
The four with one accord
Fell on their knees, and blest
The mercy of the Lord.

« What then! before the strife is done
Would ye of victory boast?»
Said a Voice above: « they reckon too soon,
Who reckon without their host!»

« Mine is he by a Bond
Which holds him fast in law:
I drew it myself for certainty,
And sharper than me must the Lawyer be
Who in it can find a flaw!

« Before the Congregation,
And in the face of day,
Whoever may pray, and whoever gainsay,
I will challenge him for my Bondsman,
And carry him quick away!»

« Ha, Satan! dost thou in thy pride,»
With righteous anger Basil cried,
« Defy the force of prayer?
In the face of the Church wilt thou brave it?
Why then we will meet thee there!

« There mayest thou set forth thy right,
With all thy might before the sight
Of all the Congregation:
And they that hour shall see the power
Of the Lord unto salvation!»

« A challenge fair! We meet then there,»
Rejoined the Prince of the Powers of the Air;
« The Bondsman is mine by right.
Let the whole city come at thy call;
And great and small, in face of them all,
I will have him in thy despite!»

So having said, he tarried not
To hear the Saint's reply.
« Beneath the sign which Constantine,»
Said Basil, « beheld in the sky,
We strive, and have our strength therein,
Therein our victory!»

IX.

The Church is fill'd, so great the faith
That City in its Bishop hath;

And now the Congregation
Are waiting there in trembling prayer
And terrible expectation.

Emmelia and her Sisterhood
Have taken there their seat:
And Choristers and Monks and Priests,
And Psalmists there, and Exorcists,
Are stationed in order meet.

In sackcloth clad, with ashes strewn
Upon his whiter hair,
Before the steps of the altar,
His feet for penance bare,
Eleëmon stands, a spectacle
For men and Angels there.

Beside him Cyra stood, in weal
Or woe, in good or ill,
Not to be severed from his side,
His faithful helpmate still.

Dishevell'd were her raven locks,
As one in mourner's guise;
And pale she was, but faith and hope
Had now relumed her eyes.

At the altar Basil took his stand;
He held the Gospel in his hand,
And in his ardent eye
Sure trust was seen, and conscious power,
And strength for victory.

At his command the Chorister
Enounced the Prophet's song,
» To God our Saviour mercies
And forgivenesses belong.»

Ten thousand voices join'd to raise
The holy hymn on high,
And hearts were thrill'd and eyes were fill'd
By that full harmony.

And when they ceased, and Basil's hand
A warning signal gave,
The whole huge multitude was hush'd
In a stillness like that of the grave.

The Sun was high in a bright blue sky,
But a chill came over the crowd,
And the Church was suddenly darken'd,
As if by a passing cloud.

A sound as of a tempest rose,
Though the day was calm as clear;
Intrepid must the heart have been
Which did not then feel fear.

In the sound of the storm came the dreadful Form;
The church then darken'd more,
And He was seen erect on the screen
Over the Holy Door.

Day-light had sickened at his sight;
And the gloomy presence threw
A shade profound over all around,
Like a cheerless twilight hue.

« I come hither,» said the Demon,
» For my Bondsman Eleëmon!
Mine is he, body and soul.
See all men!» and with that on high
He held the open scroll.

The fatal signature appear'd
To all the multitude,
Distinct as when the accursed pen
Had traced it with fresh blood.
« See all men!» Satan cried again,
And then his claim pursued.

« I ask for justice! I prefer
An equitable suit!
I appeal to the Law, and the case
Admitteth of no dispute.

» If there be justice here,
If Law have place in Heaven,
Award upon this Bond
Must then for me be given.

» What to my rightful claim,
Basil, canst thou gainsay,
That I should not seize the bondsman,
And carry him quick away?

« The writing is confess'd;—
No plea against it shown;—
The forfeiture is mine,
And now I take my own!»

» Hold there!» cried Basil, with a voice
That arrested him on his way,
When from the screen he would have swoopt
To pounce upon his prey;

« Hold there, I say! Thou canst not sue
Upon this Bond by law!
A sorry legalist were he
Who could not in thy boasted plea
Detect its fatal flaw.

« The Deed is null, for it was framed
With fraudulent intent;
A thing unlawful in itself;
A wicked instrument,
Not to be pleaded in the Courts—
Sir Fiend thy cause is shent!

» This were enough; but, more than this,
A maxim, as thou knowest, it is
Whereof all Laws partake,
That no one may of his own wrong
His own advantage make.

» The man, thou sayest, thy Bondsman is:
Mark now, how stands the fact!
Thou hast allowed,—nay, aided him
As a Freeman to contract
A marriage with this Christian woman here,
And by a public act.

» That act being publicly perform'd
With thy full cognizance,
Claim to him as thy Bondsman thou
Canst never more advance.

« For when they solemnly were then
United, in sight of Angels and men,
The matrimonial band
Gave to the wife a right in him;
And we on this might stand.

« Thy claim upon the man was by
Thy silence then forsaken;
A marriage thus by thee procured
May not by thee be shaken;
And thou, O Satan, as thou seest,
In thine own snare art taken!»

So Basil said, and paused awhile;
The Arch-Fiend answered not,
But he heaved in vexation
A sulphurous sigh for the Bishop's vocation,
And thus to himself he thought:

« The Law thy calling ought to have been,
With thy wit so ready, and tongue so free!
To prove by reason in reason's despite,
That right is wrong, and wrong is right,
And white is black, and black is white,— (8)
What a loss have I had in thee!»

« I rest not here,» the Saint pursued;
« Though thou in this mayest see,
That in the meshes of thine own net
I could entangle thee!

« Fiend! thou thyself didst bring about
The spousal celebration,
Which link'd them by the nuptial tie
For both their souls' salvation.

« Thou sufferedst them before high Heaven
With solemn rights espoused to be,
Then and for evermore, for time
And for eternity.

« That tie holds good; those rites
Will reach their whole intent;
And thou of his salvation wert
Thyself the instrument.

« And now, methinks, thou seest in this
A higher power than thine;
And that thy ways were overruled,
To work the will divine!»

With rising energy he spake,
And more majestic look;
And with authoritative hand
Held forth the Sacred Book.

Then with a voice of power he said,
« The Bond is null and void!
It is nullified, as thou knowest well,
By a Covenant whose strength by Hell
Can never be destroyed!

« The Covenant of Grace,
That greatest work of Heaven,
Which whoso claims in perfect faith,
His sins shall be forgiven!

« Were they as scarlet red
They should be white as wool;
This is the All-mighty's Covenant,
Who is All-merciful!

« His Minister am I!
In his All-mighty name
To this repentant sinner
God's pardon I proclaim!

« In token that against his soul
The sin shall no longer stand,
The writing is effaced, which there
Thou holdest in thy hand!

« Angels that are in bliss above
This triumph of Redeeming Love
Will witness, and rejoice;
And ye shall now in thunder hear
Heaven's ratifying voice!»

A peal of thunder shook the pile;
The Church was fill'd with light,
And when the flash was past, the Fiend
Had vanished from their sight.

He fled as he came, but in anger and shame,
The pardon was complete,
And the impious scroll was dropt, a blank,
At Eleëmon's feet. (9)

NOTES AND ILLUSTRATIONS.

FROM THE LIFE OF S. BASIL THE GREAT, BY S. AMPHI-
LOCHIUS, BISHOP OF ICONIUM.
Rosweyde, Vitæ Patrum, pp. 156, 158.

« HELLADIUS autem sanctæ recordationis, qui inspec-
tor et minister fuit miraculorum quæ ab eo patrata sunt,
qvique post obitum ejusdem Apostolicæ memoriæ Basi-
lii sedem illius suscipere meruit, vir miraculis et clarus,
atque omni virtute ornatus, retulit mihi, quia cùm se-
nator quidam fidelis, nomine Proterius, pergeret ad
sancta et percolenda loca, et ibidem filiam suam ton-
dere, et in unum venerabilium monasteriorum mittere,
et sacrificium Deo offerre voluisset; diabolus, qui ab
initio homicida est, invidens ejus religioso proposito,
commovit unum ex servis ejus, et hunc ad puellæ suc-
cendit amorem. Hic itaque cùm tanto voto esset in-
dignus, et non auderet propositum saltem contingere,
alloquitur unum ex detestandis maleficis, repromittens
illi, ut si fortè arte suâ posset illam commovere, mul-
tam ei auri tribueret quantitatem. At verò veneficus
dixit ad eum: O homo, ego ad hoc impos existo: sed si
vis, mitto te ad provisorem meum diabolum, et ille fa-
ciet voluntatem tuam, si tu duntaxat feceris voluntatem
ejus. Qui dixit ad eum: Quæcunque dixerit mihi, fa-
ciam. Ait ille: Abrenuntias, inquit, Christo in scriptis!
Dicit ei: Etiam. Porrò iniquitatis operarius dicit ei:
Si ad hoc paratus es, cooperator tibi efficiar. Ille au-
tem ad ipsum: Paratus sum, tantùm ut consequar desi-
derium. Et factâ epistolâ, pessimæ operationis minister
ad diabolum destinavit eam, habentem dictatum huju-
modi: Quoniam domino et provisori meo oportet me

dare operam, quò à Christianorum religione discedant, et ad tuam societatem accedant, ut compleatur portio tua; misi tibi præsentem, meas deferentem litterulas, cupidine puellæ sauciatum. Et obsecro ut hujus voti compos existat, ut et in hoc glorier, et cum affluentiori alacritate colligam amatores tuos. Et datà ei epistolà, dixit: Vade tali horà noctis, et sta supra monumentum alicujus pagani, et erige chartam in aëra, et adstabunt tibi, qui te debent ducere ad diabolum. Qui hoc alacriter gesto, emisit miserrimam illam vocem, invocans diaboli adjutorium: et continuò adstiterunt ei principes potestatis tenebrarum, spiritus nequitiæ, et suscepto qui fuerat deceptus, cum gaudio magno duxerunt eum ubi erat diabolus, quem et monstraverunt ei super excelsum solium sedentem, et in gyro ejus nequitiæ spiritus circumstantes; et susceptis venefici litteris, dixit ad infelicem illum: Credis in me? Qui dixit: Credo. Dixit ei diabolus: Tergiversatores estis vos Christiani, et quidem quando me opus habetis, venitis ad me; cùm autem consecuti fueritis affectum, abnegatis me, et acceditis ad Christum vestrum, qui, cùm sit bonus atque misericors, suscipit vos. Sed fac mihi in scriptis tam Christi tui et sancti baptismatis voluntariam abrenuntiationem, quàm in me per sæcula spontaneam repromissionem, et quia mecum eris in die judicii simul perfruiturus æternis suppliciis, quæ mihi sunt præparata. At ille exposuit propriæ manûs scriptum, quemadmodum fuerat expetitus. Rursusque ille corruptor animarum draco destinat dæmones fornicationi præpositos, et exardescere faciunt puellam ad amorem pueri, quæ projecit se in pavimentum, et cœpit clamare ad patrem: Miserere meî, miserere, qua atrociter torqueor propter talem puerum nostrum! Compatere visceribus tuis; ostende in me unigenitam tuam paternum affectum, et junge me puero, quem elegi. Quòd si hæc agere nolueris, videbis me amarà morte post paululùm mortuam, et rationem dabis Deo pro me in die judicii. Pater autem cum lachrymis dicebat: Heu mihi peccatori! quid est quod contigit miseræ filiæ meæ? quis thesaurum meum furatus est? quis filiæ meæ injuriam intulit? quis dulce oculorum meorum lumen exstinxit? ego te semper supercœlesti sponso conciliatus sum desponsare Christo, et Angelorum contubernio sociam constituere, et in psalmis et hymnis et canticis spiritualibus canere Deo accelerabam; tu autem in lasciviam petulantiæ insanisti! Dimitte me, sicut volo, cum Deo contractum facere, ne deducas senectutem meam cum mœrore in infernum, neque confusione nobilitatem parentum tuorum operias. Quæ in nihilum reputans, quæ à patre sibi dicebantur, perseverabat clamans: Pater mi, aut fac desiderium meum, aut priùs pauxillùm mortuam me videbis. Pater itaque ejus in magnà dementatione constitutus, tam immensitate mœstitiæ absorptus, quàm amicorum consiliis acquiescens se admonentium, ac dicentium, expedire potiùs voluntatem puellæ fieri, quàm sese manibus interficere, consensit, et præcepit fieri desiderium puellæ potiùs, quàm eam exitiabili tradere morti. Et mox protulit puerum qui quærebatur, simul et propriam genitam, et dans eis omnia bona sua, dixit: Salve, nata verè misera; multùm lamentaberis te pœnitens in novissimis, quando nihil tibi proderit. Porrò nefandi matrimonii conjugio facto, et diabolicæ operationis completo facinore, et pauco tempore pretereunte, notatus est puer à quibusdam, quòd non ingrederetur ecclesiam, neque attrectaret immortalia et vivifica Sacramenta, et dicunt miserandæ uxori ejus: Noveris quia maritus tuus, quem

elegisti, non est Christianus, sed extraneus est à fide, et penitùs est alienus. Quæ tenebris et dirà plagà referta, projecit se in pavimentum, et cœpit ungulis semetipsam discerpere, et percutere pectus, atque clamare: Nemo unquam qui parentibus inobediens fuit, salvus factus est. Quis annuntiabit patri meo confusionem meam? Heu mihi infelici! in quod perditionis profundum descendi! quare nata sum? vel nata quare non statim indireptibilis facta sum? Hujusmodi ergo eam comploratem seductus vir ejus agnoscens, venit ad eam, asseverans non se ita rei veritatem habere: quæ ei refrigerium suasoriis ejus verbis deveniens, dixit ad eum: Si vis mihi satisfacere, et infelicem animam meam certificare, cras ego et tu pergemus unanimiter ad ecclesiam, et coram me sume intemerata mysteria, et taliter mihi poteris satisfacere. Tunc coactus dixit ei sententiam capituli. Protinus ergo puella feminea infirmitate depositâ, et consilio bono accepto, currit ad pastorem et discipulum Christi Basilium, adversùs tantam clamans impietatem: Misericordiam mihi miseræ præsta, sancte Dei, miserere meî, discipule Domini, quæ contractum cum dæmonibus feci. Miserere meî, quæ proprio patri facta sum inobediens. Et cognita illi fecit rei gestæ negotia. Porrò sanctus Dei convocato puero, sciscitabatur ab eo si hæc hujusmodi essent. Qui ad sanctum cum lachrymis ait: Etiam, sancte Dei. Nam, etsi ergo tacuero, opera mea clamabunt. Et enarravit ei et ipse malignam diaboli operationem, qualiter ab exordio usque ad finem fuerit subsecutus. Tunc dicit ei: Vis converti ad Dominum Deum nostrum? Qui dixit: Etiam volo, sed non possum. Dicit ei: Cur? Respondit: In scriptis abrenuntiavi Christo, et fœdus pepigi cum diabolo. Dicit ei sanctus: Non tibi sit curæ: benignus est Deus noster, et suscipiet te pœnitentiam agentem. Benignus enim est super malitiis nostris. Et projiciens se puella ad pedes ejus, evangelicè rogabat eum, dicens: Discipule Christi Dei nostri, si quid potes, adjuva nos? Dicit sanctus ad puerum: Credis posse salvari? At ille dixit: Credo, Domine; adjuva incredulitatem meam. Et confestim adprehensâ manu ejus, et facto super eum Christi signo simul et oratione, retrusit illum in uno loco intra quem sacri habebantur amictus, et datà ei regulà oravit et ipse pro illo per tres dies. Post quos visitavit eum, et dixit: Quomodo te habes, fili? Dicit ei puer: In magnâ sum, Domine, defectione. Sancte Dei, non suffero clamores, pavores, jacula, et lapidationes ipsorum. Tenentes enim propriæ manus meæ scripturam, objurgantur in me, dicentes: Tu venisti ad nos, non nos ad te. Et dicit ei sanctus: Noli timere, fili mi, tantummodò crede. Et datà ei modicà escâ, et facto super eum Christi denuò signo et oratione, inclusit eum; et post paucos dies visitavit illum, et dixit: Quomodo te habes, fili? Ait: Pater sancte, à longe clamores eorum audio simul et minas; nam non video illos. Et rursus dato ei cibo, et effusà oratione, clausit ostium, et discessit. Præterea quadragesimo die abiit ad eum, et dicit illi: Quomodo te habes, frater? Respondit et dicit ei: Benè, sancte Dei. Vidi enim te hodie in somnio pugnantem pro me, et vincentem diabolum. Mox ergo secundùm consuetudinem factà oratione eduxit illum, et duxit illum ad cubiculum suum. Mane autem facto, convocato tam venerabili clero, quàm monasteriis et omni Christo amabili populo, dixit eis: Filii mei dilecti, universi gratias agamus Domino. Ecce enim futurum est, ut ovem perditam pastor bonus super humeros suos imponat, et reducat Ecclesiæ: Et nos oportet pervigilem

94

ducere noctem, et deprecari voluntatem ipsius, ut non vincat corruptor animarum. Quo protinus acto, et promptissimè populo congregato, per totam noctem unà cum bono pastore deprecati sunt Deum, cum lacrymis pro ipso clamantes, Kyrie, eleison. Et diluculò unà cum omni multitudine populi assumit sanctus puerum, et tenens dexteram manum ejus, duxit eum in sanctam Deiecclesiam cum psalmis et hymnis. Et ecce diabolus, qui vitæ nostræ semper invidit, si hanc sine tristitiâ viderit, cum totâ perniciosâ virtute suâ venit, et puero invisibiliter comprehenso, voluit rapere illum de manu sancti: et cœpit puer clamans dicere : Sancte Dei, auxiliare mihi, et adeò contra illum impudenti instantiâ venit, ut ipsum egregium Basilium simul cùm illum impelleret et subverteret. Conversus ergo sanctus ad diabolum ait : Impudentissime, et animarum violator, pater tenebrarum et perditionis, non tibi sufficit tua perditio, quam tibimet ipsi et his, qui sub te sunt, acquisisti ; sed adhuc non quiescis, et Dei mei plasma tentando ? Diabolus verò dixit ad eum : Præjudicas mihi, Basili ; ita ut multi ex nobis audirent voces ejus. At verò sanctus Dei ad eum : Increpat, inquit, tibi Dominus, diabole. At ille : Basili, præjudicium mihi facis. Non ivi ego ad eum, sed ille venit ad me, abrenuntiando Christum, mecumque est sponsione pactuatus, et ecce scriptum habeo, et in die judicii coram communi judice deferam illud. Sanctus autem Domini dixit : Benedictus Dominus Deus meus, non deponet populus iste manus ab excelso cœli, nisi reddideris scriptum. Et conversus dixit plebi : Tollite manus vestras in cœlum, universi clamantes cum lacrymis, Kyrie, eleison. Cùmque staret populus horâ multâ extensas habentes manus in cœlum, ecce scriptum pueri in aërem deportatum, et ab omnibus visum venit, et positum est in manus egregii patris nostri pastoris Basilii. Suscepto autem illo, gratias egit Deo, gavisusque vehementer unà cum universâ plebe, dixit ad puerum : Recognoscis litterulas has, frater ? At ille dixit ad eum : Etiam, sancte Dei ; propriæ manûs meæ scriptura est. Et diruptâ scripturâ introduxit eum in ecclesiam, et dignus habitus est sacris interesse Missarum officiis, et participationi sacrorum mysteriorum, et muneribus Christi. Et factâ susceptione magnâ recreavit universum populum, et ducto puero et instructo, atque datâ ei decenti regulâ, tradidit eum uxori ejus, indesinenter glorificantem et laudantem Deum. Amen.»

Baert, though he pronounces the life in which this legend appears to be apocryphal, does not deliver a decided opinion upon the legend itself. He says, «Helladium Basilii in Episcopatu successorem fuisse, omnibus est indubitatum ; vitam decessoris ab illo conscriptam, credimus (ut par est) St Joanni Damasceno, qui utinam ad nos tantum transmisisset thesaurum ; eum enim videtur præ oculis habuisse, cùm locum inde unum descripsit in oratione pro sacris Imaginibus. An verò ea, quæ hic narrantur, ex Helladio sunt, lector judicet. Potuit enim fieri, ut eo quo Pseudo-Amphilochius scripsit tempore, fragmentâ quædam Helladii extarent, quæ ipse retulerit in Basilium suum. Quod attinet ad Proterii filiam, a dæmone in amorem juvenis concitatam, simile quid contigisse B. Mariæ Antiochenæ referimus tomo 7 Maji, die 29, pag. 52. Mihi tamen verosimilius est, eumdem qui Amphilochium mentitus est, mentiri etiam Helladium potuisse.»—p. 952—3. Jun. t. 2.

The story, to which Baert refers, resembles the legend of St Basil in one part, but it is utterly unlike it in the circumstances wherein he has supposed the resemblance to exist. It appears to have been one of those fictions which were composed honestly as works of imagination, not like the lives of St Benedict, St Francis, St Dominic, St Ignatius Loyola, and so many of their respective orders, with a fraudulent intent, to impose upon mankind. Like other such fictions, however, it has been adopted and legitimated, by credulity and fraud ; and the blessed Mary, the Virgin of Antioch, has her place accordingly in the Acta Sanctorum, on the 29th of May. But as the legend evidently was not written when Antioch was a Christian city, and moreover, as the legend itself contains nothing whatever by which its age could be determined, Papebroche presents it as « eo habendam esse loco, quo multa in Vitis Sanctorum Patrum, utilem quidem instructionem continentia ad formandos mores, sed ad historicam certitudinem parum aut nihil. Igitur istam quoque ut talem hic damus ; liberum lectori relinquentes, ut eam quo volet gradu credibilitatis collocet.»

In this legend one of the chief persons in Antioch, Anthemius by name, failing to win the affections of Maria, who was the daughter of a poor widow, and had resolved to lead a life of celibacy, applies to a Magician to assist him. The Magician sends two demons to influence mother and daughter in their sleep, so as to bring Maria to Anthemius's bed-chamber ; but the temptations of worldly wealth, which are offered, have only the effect of alarming them ; they rise in the middle of the night, and go toward the Church, there to pray for protection and deliverance : and on the way thither one Demon takes upon him Maria's form, while the other personates the mother, and thus decoys Maria into the apartment where Anthemius is expecting her. She is however allowed to depart uninjured, upon a promise to return at the end of fifteen days, and live with him as a servant, provided he will offer her no violence.—Nothing can be more unlike the story of Proterius's daughter.—Having extorted an oath from her that she would return according to this promise, Anthemius remains, wondering at the great power of the Magician. « Certes,» thought he, « one who can do what he hath done in this matter, is greater than all men ; why, then, should I not offer him all I am worth if he will make me equal to himself ?» And, being inflamed with this desire, he said within himself. « If I were such as he is, whatever I might wish for would be within my reach.» This thought came into his mind as if it were by Divine Providence, to the end that he might willingly let the Virgin depart, and that she might not be bound by the nefarious oath which she had taken, and that the Devil, who was the instigator of his evil desires, might be confounded in his designs both upon the Virgin herself, and upon him who was at this time the Virgin's enemy.

« As soon, therefore, as it was day, Anthemius went out to seek for the Sorcerer, and to give him thanks. Having found him and saluted him, he delivered to him, with many thanks, the gold which he had promised ; and then falling at his feet, earnestly intreated, that he might be made such as the Sorcerer himself was, promising that, if this could be effected through his means, he would requite him with whatever sum he might demand. But the Sorcerer replied, 'that it was not possible for him to be made a sorcerer also, because he was a Christian, having been made such by his baptism.' But Anthemius answered, 'then I renounce my baptism and Christian name, if I may be made a sorcerer.' Still the Sorcerer replied, 'thou canst not be made a sorcerer, neither canst thou keep the laws of the sorcerers, the which, if thou wert not to keep, thou wouldest then fall from a place which could never again be recovered.' But Anthemius, again embracing his feet, promised that he would perform whatever should be enjoined him: then the Sorcerer, seeing his perseverance, asked for paper, and having written therein what he thought good, gave it to Anthemius, and said, 'take this writing; and in the dead of the night go out of the city, supperless, and stand upon yonder little bridge. A huge multitude will pass over it about midnight, with a mighty uproar, and with their Prince seated in a chariot: yet fear not thou, for thou wilt not be hurt, having with thee this my writing; but hold up the writing, so that it may be perceived; and if thou shouldest be asked what thou doest there at that hour, or who thou art, say 'the Great Master sent me to my Lord the Prince, with this letter, that I might deliver it unto him.' But take heed neither to sign thyself as a Christian, nor to call upon Christ, for in either case thy desire would then be frustrated.'

« Anthemius therefore having received the letter, went his way, and when night came he went out of the city, and took his stand upon the little bridge, holding up the writing in his hand. About midnight a great multitude came there, and horsemen in great numbers, and the Prince himself sitting in a chariot; and they who went first surrounded him, saying, 'who is this that standeth here?' To whom Anthemius made answer, 'the Great Master hath sent me to my Lord the Prince with this letter.' And they took the letter from him, and delivered it to the Prince who sat in the chariot, and he, having received and read the same, wrote something in the same paper, and gave it to Anthemius, that he should carry it to the Sorcerer. So in the morning Anthemius, having returned, delivered it to the Sorcerer, who, having perused it, said, 'wouldest thou know what he hath written to us? even just as I before said to thee, to wit, 'knowest thou not that this man is a Christian? such a one I can in no wise admit, unless, according to our manner, he performeth all things, and renounceth and abhorreth his faith.' When Anthemius heard this, he replied, 'Master, now as elsewhile I abjure the name of Christian, and the faith, and the baptism.' Then the Sorcerer wrote again: and giving the writing to Anthemius, said, 'go again, and take thy stand at night at the same place, and when he shall come, give him this, and attend to what he shall say.' Accordingly he went his way, and took his stand at the time and place appointed. Behold at the same hour the same company appeared again, and they said unto him, 'wherefore hast thou returned hither?' Anthemius answered and said, 'Lord, the Great Master hath sent me back with this writing.' The Prince then received it, and read, and again wrote in it, and gave it again to be returned to the Sorcerer. To whom Anthemius went again in the morning, and he, having read the writing, said unto him, 'knowest thou what he hath written unto me in reply? I wrote to him, saying, 'all these things, Lord, he hath abjured before me; admit him, therefore, if it pleaseth thee.' But he hath written back, 'unless he abjureth

all this in writing, and in his own hand, I will not admit him.' Say now, then, what wilt thou that I should do for thee?'

« The wretched Anthemius answered and said, 'Master, I am ready to do this also.' And with that he seated himself, and wrote thus.—'I, Anthemius, abjure Christ and his faith. I abjure also his baptism, and the cross, and the Christian name, and promise that I will never again use them, or invoke them.' But, while he was thus writing, a copious sweat ran from him, from the top of his head to the soles of his feet, so that his whole inner garment was wet therewith, as he himself afterwards, with continual tears, confessed. He nevertheless went on writing, and, when it was finished, he gave the writing to the Sorcerer to read, who, when he had perused it, said, 'this is well; go thy way again, and he will now certainly receive thee. And when he shall have admitted thee, say to him reverently, I beseech thee, Lord, assign to me those who may be at my bidding; and he will assign unto thee as many as thou wilt have. But this I advise thee, not to take more than one or two familiars, inasmuch as more would perplex thee, and would be perpetually disturbing thee night and day, that thou mightest give them what to do.' Then Anthemius returned to the same place as before, and awaited there, and the same company came there again at midnight, and the leader of them, having incontinently recognised Anthemius, began to cry out, 'Lord, the Great Master hath again sent hither this man with his commands:' and the Prince made him draw nigh. And Anthemius, drawing nigh, gave unto him his profession of abjuration, full of calamity and woe. He having received and read it, raised it on high in his hand, and began to exclaim, 'Christ, behold Anthemius, who heretofore was thine, hath by this writing abjured and execrated thee! I am not the author of this his deed; but he, offering himself to my service with many intreaties, hath of his own accord written this his profession of abjuration, and delivered it to me. Have thou then therefore no care of him from this time forth!' And he repeated these words a second time, and again a third.

« But when Anthemius heard that dreadful voice, he trembled from head to foot, and began at the same time to cry aloud, and to say, 'give me back the writing! I am a Christian! I beseech thee, I adjure thee! I will be a Christian! give me back the profession which I have wickedly written!' But when the miserable man was proceeding thus to exclaim, the Prince said unto him, 'never again mayest thou have this thy profession, which I shall produce in the terrible day of judgment. From this moment thou art mine, and I have thee in my power at will, unless an outrage be done to justice.' With these words he departed, leaving Anthemius. But Anthemius lay prostrate on his face upon the bridge till it was dawn, weeping and lamenting his condition. As soon as it was daylight he rose and returned to his own house, where he remained weeping and lamenting, not knowing what he should do. Now there was another city, some eighteen miles off, where there was said to be a Bishop, who was a man of God. To him, therefore, he resolved to repair, that he might obtain his intercession, and having confessed the whole matter even as it had taken place, to be again by him baptized: for in his own city he was ashamed to confess what he had done. Having then cut off his hair, and clad him-

self in sackcloth, he departed, and came unto that
Bishop, and having made himself known, was admitted
to him, and threw himself at his feet, saying, 'I beseech
thee, baptize me!' But the Bishop replied, 'can I be-
lieve that thou hast not yet been baptized?' Then he,
taking the Bishop apart, told him the whole matter, say-
ing, 'I have indeed received baptism when I was a
child, but having now renounced in writing, behold I
am unbaptized!' To which the Bishop replied, 'how
camest thou persuaded that thou hast been unbaptized
of the baptism which thou hast received?' Anthemius
answered, 'In that unhappy hour when I wrote the
abjuration of my Lord and Saviour, and of his bap-
tism, incontinently a profuse sweat burst out even from
the top of my head to the soles of my feet, so that
my inner garments were wet therewith; and from
that time I have believed of a truth, that even as I then
abjured my baptism, so did it depart from me. Now
if thou canst, O venerable Father, help me, in compas-
sion upon one who has thus voluntarily undone him-
self.' He said this prostrate on the ground, and bedewed
with tears.

« When the man of God, the Bishop, heard this, he
threw himself upon the ground, and lay there beside
Anthemius, weeping and praying to the Lord. Then,
after a long while, rising, he roused Anthemius, and said
to him, 'verily, son, I dare not again purify by baptism
a man who hath been already baptized, for among
Christians there is no second baptism, except of tears.
Yet do not thou despair of thy salvation, nor of the
divine mercy, but rather commit thyself to God, praying
and humbly beseeching him for all the remainder of thy
life; and God, who is good and merciful, may render
back to thee the writing of thy abjuration, and moreover
forgive thee that impiety, as he forgave the ten thousand
talents to the debtor in the Gospel. Hope not to find a
better way than this, for there is no other to be found.'
He then being persuaded thus to do, and having obtained
the Bishop's prayers, went his way, weeping and groan-
ing for the sin which he had committed; and having
returned home, he sold all his goods, and set at liberty
all his people, both men-servants and maid-servants,
giving them also of his possessions, and the rest of his
goods he distributed to the churches, and to the poor,
secretly, by the hand of a faithful servant. Moreover,
he gave three pounds of gold to the mother of that
Virgin, with the love of whom the Demon, to his own
destruction, had inflamed him, having placed them in a
certain church, saying, 'I beseech ye pray to God for
me a sinner: I shall never again trouble you, nor any
other person; for I depart I know not whither to bewail
the wickedness of my deeds.' Thus this man did,—and
from that time he was seen no more, casting himself
wholly upon the mercy of God, to which none who hath
betaken himself can perish.

« But we, who have heard the relation of this dreadful
thing, praise the Almighty Lord our God, and adore the
greatness of his works, that he hath protected the virgin
Maria in her holy intention of leading a single life, and
hath taken her mother out of poverty, affording liberally
to them both for their support and maintenance, and
hath delivered her also from the fear of sin, avoiding the
transgression of the oath, which had passed between
Maria the virgin and her enemy Anthemius, by annull-
ing it. For the Lord brought these things to pass before
the fifteen days, which were the appointed time between

them, had elapsed. Wherefore we may say with the
Evangelist, Our Lord hath done all things well. Nor
hath he suffered the suppliant, who seeks him in peni-
tence, to perish; for he saith, I came not to call the
righteous, but sinners to repentance. Let us, therefore,
continue to intreat him, that we may be protected by his
Almighty hand, and may be delivered from all the de-
vices of the Devil, and that, being aided by the prayers of
the Saints, we may be worthy to attain the kingdom of
Heaven. To the Lord our God belong all honour and
glory and adoration, now and always, for ever and ever.
Amen.»

The Greeks appear to have delighted in fictions of this
peculiar kind. The most extravagant of such legends is
that of St Justina and St Cyprian, which Martene and
Durand present as a veritable history, censuring Bishop
Fell for treating it as fabulous! It is much too long for
insertion in this place, but it would be injured by
abridging it. The reader may find it in the *Thesaurus
Novus Anecdotorum*, t. iii, pp. 1618—1650.

Note 1, page 730, col. 2.
There on the everlasting ice
His dolorous throne was placed.

It was the north of Heaven that Lucifer, according
to grave authors, attempted to take by storm. « En aver
criado Dios con tanta hermosura el cielo y la tierra,
quedo ordenada su celestial Corte de divinas Hierarchias;
mas reynò tanto la ingratitud en uno de los Cortesanos,
viendose tan lindo y bello, y en mas eminente lugar que
los demas (segun Theodoreto) que quiso emparejar con el
Altissimo, y subir al Aquilon, formando para esto una
quadrilla de sus confidentes y parciales.»

With this sentence Fr. Marco de Guadalajara y
Xavierr begins his account of the *Memorable Expulsion,
y justissimo destierro de los Moriscos de Espana.*

Note 2, page 734, col. 1.
The marriage.

The description of the marriage service is taken from
Dr King's work upon « the Rites and Ceremonies of
the Greek Church in Russia.» « In all the offices of the
Greek Church,» he says, « there is not perhaps a more
curious service than this of matrimony, nor any which
carries more genuine marks of antiquity; as from the
bare perusal of it may be seen, at one view, most of the
ceremonies which antiquarians have taken great pains
to ascertain.» It agrees very closely with the ritual
given by Martene, *De Antiquis Ecclesiæ Ritibus*, t. ii,
pp. 390—8.

In these ceremonies,

« The which do endless matrimony make,»

the parties are betrothed to each other « for their salva-
tion,»—« now and for ever, even unto ages of ages.»

Note 3, page 734, col. 1.
The Ante-nave.

The Προναος.

Note 4, page 734, col. 2.
The coronals ·
Composed of all sweet flowers.

« Formerly these crowns were garlands made of
flowers or shrubs; but now there are generally in all
churches crowns of silver, or other metals, kept for that
purpose.»—Dr KING's *Rites*, etc. p. 232.

« A certain crown of flowers used in marriages,» says

the excellent Bishop Heber (writing from the Carnatic), « has been denounced to me as a device of Satan! And a gentleman has just written to complain that the Danish Government of Tranquebar will not allow him to ex-communicate some young persons for wearing masks, and acting, as it appears, in a Christmas mummery, or at least in some private rustic theatricals. If this be heathenish, Heaven help the wicked! But I hope you will not suspect that I shall lend any countenance to this kind of ecclesiastical tyranny, or consent to men's con-sciences being burdened with restrictions so foreign to the cheerful spirit of the Gospel. »—vol. iii. pp. 446.

Note 5, page 738, col 1.

Basil, of living men
The powerfullest in prayer.

The most remarkable instance of St Basil's power in prayer is to be found, not in either of his lives, the vera-cious or the apocryphal one, but in a very curious account of the opinions held by the Armenian Christians, as drawn up for the information of Pope Benedict XII, and inserted by Dominico Bernino in his *Historia di tutte l'Heresie* (Secolo xiv, cap. iv, t. iii, pp. 508—536). It is there related that on the sixth day of the Creation, when the rebellious angels fell from heaven through that opening in the firmament which the Armenians call Arocea, and we the Galaxy, one unlucky angel, who had no participation in their sin, but seems to have been caught in the crowd, fell with them; and many others would in like manner have fallen by no fault of their own, if the Lord had not said unto them *Pax vobis*. But this unfortunate angel was not restored till he obtained, it is not said how, the prayers of St Basil; his condition meantime, from the sixth day of the Creation to the fourth century of the Christian era, must have been even more uncomfortable than that of Klopstock's repentant Devil.—p. 512, sec. 16.

Note 6, page 738, col. 1.

Eleémon's penance.

In the legend the penitent is left forty days and nights to contend with the Powers of Darkness in the Relic Chamber.

Captain Hall relates an amusing example of the manner in which penance may be managed at this time in Mexico.

« I went, » he says, « to the Convent of la Cruz to visit a friend who was doing penance, not for a sin he had committed, but for one he was preparing to commit. The case was this:—Don N. had recently lost his wife, and, not chusing to live in solitude, looked about for another helpmate; and being of a disposition to take little trouble in such a research, or, probably thinking that no labour could procure for him any one so suitable as what his own house afforded, he proposed the matter to his lately lamented wife's sister, who had lived in his house several years; and who, as he told me himself, was not only a very good sort of person, but one well ac-quainted with all the details of his household, known and esteemed by his children, and accustomed to his society.

« The church, however, looked exceedingly grave upon the occasion; not, however, as I at first supposed, from the nearness of the connection, or the shortness of the interval since the first wife's death, but because the intended lady had stood godmother to four of Don N.'s children. This, the church said, was a serious bar to the new alliance, which nothing could surmount but protracted penances and extensive charity. Don N. was urgent; and a council was assembled to deliberate on the matter. The learned body declared, after some dis-cussion, the case to be a very knotty one; and that, as the lady had been four times godmother to Don N.'s children, it was impossible she could marry him. Nevertheless, the Fathers (compassionate persons)! wished to give the unhappy couple another chance; and agreed to refer the question to a learned doctor in the neighbourhood, skilled in all difficult questions of casu-istry. This sage person decided that, according to the canons of the church, the marriage might take place, on payment of a fine of four hundred dollars: two for the poor in pocket, and two for the poor in spirit; namely, the priests. But, to expiate the crime of marrying a quadruple godmother, a slight penance must also be submitted to in the following manner. Don N. was to place himself on his knees before the altar, with a long wax candle burning in his hand, while his intended lady stood by his side, holding another: this was to be repeated in the face of the congregation, for one hour, during every Sunday and fast-day throughout a whole year; after which purifying exposure, the parties were to be held eligible to proceed with the marriage. Don N., who chose rather to put his conscience than his knees to such discipline, took his own measures on the occasion. What these were, the idle public took the liberty of guessing broadly enough, but no one could say positively. At the end of a week, however, it was announced, that the case had undergone a careful re-ex-amination, and that it had been deemed proper to com-mute the penance into one week's retirement from the world; that is to say, Don N. was to shut himself up in the Convent of La Cruz, there to fast and pray in soli-tude and silence for seven days. The manner in which this penance was performed is an appropriate commen-tary on the whole transaction. The penitent, aided and assisted by two or three of the jovial friars of the con-vent, passed the evening in discussing some capital wine, sent out for the occasion by Don N. himself, after eating a dinner, prepared by the cook of the convent, the best in New Galicia. As for silence and solitude, his romping boys and girls were with him during all the morning; besides a score of visitors, who strolled daily out of town as far as the convent, to keep up the poor man's spirits, by relating all the gossip which was afloat about his marriage, his penitence, and the wonderful kindness of the church. »—*Capt. Hall's Journal*, vol. ii, pp. 210—214.

« I have read of a gentleman, » says Bishop Taylor, « who, being on his death-bed, and his confessor search-ing and dressing of his wounded soul, was found to be obliged to make restitution of a considerable sum of money, with the diminution of his estate. His confessor found him desirous to be saved, a lover of his religion, and yet to have a kindness for his estate, which he desired might be entirely transmitted to his beloved heir: he would serve God with all his heart, and repented him of his sin, of his rapine and injustice; he begged for pardon passionately, he humbly hoped for mercy, he resolved, in case he did recover, to live strictly, to love God, to reverence his priests, to be charitable to the poor; but to make restitution he found impossible to him, and he hoped the commandment would not require it of him, and desired to be relieved by an easy and a favourable interpretation; for it is ten thousand pities so many good actions and good purposes should be in vain, but it is worse, infinitely worse, if the man should perish. What should the confessor do in this case?—shall not the man be relieved, and his piety be accepted; or shall the rigour and severity of his confessor, and his scrupulous fears and impertinent niceness, cast away a soul either into future misery, or present discomfort? neither one nor other was to be done; and the good man was only to consider what God had made necessary, not what the vices of his penitent and his present follies should make so. Well: the priest insists upon his first resolution, '*Non dimittitur peccatum, nisi restituatur ablatum:*' the sick man could have no ease by the loss of a duty. The poor clinic desires the confessor to deal with his son, and try if he could be made willing that his father might go to heaven at the charge of his son, which when he had attempted, he was answered with extreme rudeness and injurious language; which caused great trouble to the priest and to the dying father. At last the religious man found out this device, telling his penitent, that unless by corporal penances there could be made satisfaction in exchange of restitution, he knew no hopes; but because the profit of the estate, which was obliged to restitution, was to descend upon the son, he thought something might be hoped, if, by way of commutation, the son would hold his finger in a burning candle for a quarter of an hour. The glad father being overjoyed at this loop-hole of eternity, this glimpse of heaven, and the certain retaining of the whole estate, called to his son, told him the condition and the advantages to them both, making no question but he would gladly undertake the penance. But the son with indignation replied, 'he would not endure so much torture to save the whole estate.' To which the priest, espying his advantage, made this quick return to the old man: 'Sir, if your son will not, for a quarter of an hour, endure the pains of a burning finger to save your soul, will you, to save a portion of the estate for him, endure the flames of hell to eternal ages?' The unreasonableness of the odds, and the ungratefulness of the son, and the importunity of the priest, and the fear of hell, and the indispensable necessity of restitution, awakened the old man from his lethargy, and he bowed himself to the rule, made restitution, and had hopes of pardon and present comfort.» — *Works of* JEREMY TAYLOR, vol. xiii, p. 38.

The penances which Indian fanatics voluntarily undertake and perform would be deemed impossible in Europe, if they had not been witnessed by so many persons of unquestionable authority. The penances which the Bramins enjoin are probably more severe than they would otherwise be, on this account, lest they should seem trifling in the eyes of a people accustomed to such exhibitions.

« If a Shoodru go to a Bramhunee of bad character, he must renounce life by casting himself into a large fire. If a Shoodru go to a Bramhunee of unsullied character, he must tie straw round the different parts of his body, and cast himself into the fire. The woman must be placed on an ass and led round the city, and then *go the Great Way:* the meaning of this is, she must wander to those sacred places of the Hindoos where the climate is exceedingly cold, and proceed till she actually perish with cold. This is a meritorious way of terminating life, and is mentioned as such in the Hindoo writings.» —WARD, vol. i, p. 427.

Sometimes the law is frustrated by its own severity. « It is a dogma of general notoriety, that if a Jungum has the mischance to lose his Lingum, he ought not to survive the misfortune. Poornia, the present minister of Mysoor, relates an incident of a Ling-ayet friend of his, who had unhappily lost his portable god, and came to take a last farewell. The Indians, like more enlightened nations, readily laugh at the absurdities of every sect but their own, and Poornia gave him better counsel. It is a part of the ceremonial, preceding the sacrifice of the individual, that the principal persons of the sect should assemble on the banks of some holy stream, and, placing in a basket the lingum images of the whole assembly, purify them in the sacred waters. The destined victim, in conformity to the advice of his friend, suddenly seized the basket, and overturned its contents into the rapid Cavery. ' Now, my friends,' said he, 'we are on equal terms: let us prepare to die together.' The discussion terminated according to expectation. The whole party took an oath of inviolable secrecy, and each privately provided himself with a new image of the lingum.» —WILKS, vol. i, p. 506.

In 1790, when the Mahrattas were to have co-operated with Lord Cornwallis at Seringapatam, their general, Parasu Ram Bhao, became unclean from eating with a Bramin who had—kissed a cobler's wife. There was no stream near holy enough to wash away the impurity, so he marched his whole immense army to the junction of the Tungha and the Badra. Major Moor, who was with him, says, « during this march, uncalled for in a military point of view, the army laid waste scores of towns and thousands of acres,—indeed, whole districts; we fought battles, stormed forts, destroyed a large army, and ran every military risk. Having reached the sacred place of junction, he washed, and having been made clean, was weighed against gold and silver; his weight was 16,000 pagodas, about 7000l, which was given to the Bramins. They who had eaten with the Bramin at the same time, in like manner washed away the defilement; but the weighing is a ceremony peculiar to the great.» —MOOR'S *Hindu Infanticide*, p. 234.

« The present king of Travancore has conquered, or carried war into all the countries which lay round his dominions, and lives in the continual exercise of his arms. To atone for the blood which he has spilt, the Brachmans persuaded him that it was necessary he should be born anew: this ceremony consisted in putting the prince into the body of a golden cow of immense value, where, after he had lain the time prescribed, he came out regenerated, and freed from all the crimes of his former life. The cow was afterwards cut up, and divided amongst the seers who had invented this extraordinary method for the remission of his sins.» —ORME'S *Fragments.*

A far less expensive form was observed among the ancient Greeks, in cases wherein a second birth was deemed indispensable, « for in Greece they thought not those pure and clean who had been carried forth for dead to be interred, or whose sepulchre and funerals had been solemnized or prepared; neither were such allowed to frequent the company of others, nor suffered to come near unto their sacrifices. And there goeth a report of a certain man named Aristinus, one of those who had been possessed with this superstition; how he sent unto the oracle of Apollo at Delphos, for to make supplication and prayer unto the god, for to be delivered out of this perplexed anxiety that troubled him by occasion of the said custom, or law. then in force, and that the prophetess Pythia returned this answer:

> « Look whatsoever women do,
> in childbed newly laid,
> Unto their babes which they brought forth,
> the very same, I say,
> See that be done to thee again;
> and after that, be sure,
> Unto the Blessed Gods with hands
> to sacrifice, most pure.

« Which oracle thus delivered, Aristinus, having well pondered and considered, committed himself as an infant new born unto women, for to be washed, to be wrapped in swaddling-clothes, and to be suckled with the breasthead; after which all such others, whom we call *Hysteropotmous*, that is to say, those whose graves were made as if they were dead, did the semblable. Howbeit some do say that, before Aristinus was born, these ceremonies were observed about those Hysteropotmoi, and that this was a right ancient custom kept in the semblable case.» —PLUTARCH's *Morals, tr. by* PHILEMON HOLLAND, p. 852.

Note 7, page 739, col. 1.
The lamps went out.

There is the authority of a Holy Man in the Romance of Merlin,—which is as good authority for such a fact as anything in the Acta Sanctorum,—that the Devil, like other wild beasts who prowl about seeking what they may devour, is afraid of a light. The Holy Man's advice to a pious damsel is never to lie down in the dark; «garde que la où tu coucheras il y ait tousjours clarté, car le Diable haït toutes cleres choses; ni ne vient pas voulentiers où il y a clarté.»—vol. i, ff. 4.

Note 8, page 742, col. 1.
And white is black, and black is white.

Satan might have been reconciled to St Basil's profession if he had understood, by his faculty of secondsight, that this, which it is sometimes the business of a lawyer to prove, would one day be the duty of the Roman Catholics to *believe*, if their church were to tell them so. No less a personage than St Ignatius Loyola has asserted this. In his *Exercitia Spiritualia*, the 13th of the Rules which are laid down *ad sentiendum cum Ecclesiâ*, is in these words:

« Denique, ut ipsi Ecclesiæ Catholicæ omnino unanimes, conformesque simus, *si quid, quod oculis nostris apparet album, nigrum illa esse definierit, debemus itidem, quod nigrum sit, pronuntiare*. Indubitate namque credendum est, eumdem esse Domini nostri Jesu Christi, et Ecclesiæ orthodoxæ, sponsæ ejus, spiritum, per quem gubernamur ac dirigimur ad salutem; neque alium esse Deum, qui olim tradidit Decalogi præcepta, et qui nunc temporis Ecclesiam hierarchicam instruit atque regit.»—p. 141, Antwerpiæ, 1635.

Such is the implicit obedience enjoined in those Spiritual Exercises, of which Pope Paul III said in his brief, *sub annulo Piscatoris*, «omnia et singula in eis contenta, ex certâ scientiâ nostrâ, approbamus, collaudamus, ac præsentis scripti patrocinio communimus.» The Roman Catholics are to believe that black is white if the Roman Church tells them so: morally and politically it has

often told them so, and *they have believed and acted accordingly.*

Note 9, page 742, col. 2.
The impious scroll was dropt, a blank,
At Eleëmon's feet.

This is not the only miracle of this kind recorded of St Basil.

« There was a certain woman of noble family, and born of rich parents, who was wholly made up of the vanities of this world, and beyond measure arrogant in all things; she, becoming a widow, wasted her substance shamelessly, living a loose and profligate life, doing none of those things which are enjoined by the Lord, but wallowing like a swine in the mire and filth of her iniquities. But being at length by the will of God brought to a consideration of her own estate, and her mind filled with consciousness of the immeasurable offences which she had committed, she called to remembrance the multitude of her sins, and bewailed them penitently, saying, 'Woe to me a sinner, how shall I render an account of the multitude of my sins! I have profaned a spiritual temple; I have defiled the soul which inhabiteth this body! Woe is me, woe is me! what have I done! what hath befallen me! Shall I say, like the Harlot or the Publican, that I have sinned? But no one has sinned like me! How, then, shall I be assured that God will receive my repentance?' While she meditated in herself upon these things, He, who would that all should be saved and brought back into the way of truth, and would have no one perish, was pleased to bring unto her remembrance all the sins which she had committed from her youth up. And she set down in writing all these offences, even all that she had committed from her youth to this her elder age; and, last of all, she set down one great and heinous sin, the worst of all; and having done this, she folded up the writing, and fastened it with lead. After this, having waited till a convenient season, when holy Basil was accustomed to go to the church that he might pray there, she ran before to meet him, and threw the writing at his feet, and prostrated herself before him, saying, 'O, holy man of God, have compassion upon me a sinner, yea, the vilest of sinners!' The most blessed man stopt thereat, and asked of her 'wherefore she thus groaned and lamented:' and she said unto him. 'Saint of God, see I have set down all my sins and iniquities in this writing, and I have folded it, and fastened it with lead; do not thou, I charge thee, open it, but by thy powerful prayers blot out all that is written therein.' Then the great and holy Basil held up the writing, and, looking toward Heaven, said, 'O Lord, to Thee alone all the deeds of this woman are manifest! Thou hast taken away the sins of the world, and more easily mayest thou blot out those of this single soul. Before thee, indeed, all our offences are numbered; but thy mercy is infinite.' Saying thus, he went into the church, holding the aforesaid writing in his hand; and prostrating himself before the altar, there he remained through the night, and on the morrow, during the performance of all the masses which were celebrated there, intreating God for this woman's sake. And when she came to him, he gave her the writing, and said to her, 'Woman, hast thou heard that the remission of sins can come from God alone?' She answered, 'Yea, father; and therefore have I supplicated thee that thou shouldst intercede with that most merciful God in my behalf.' And then she opened the writing, and found that it was all blotted out, save only that the one great, and most heinous sin, still remained written there. But she, seeing that this great sin was still legible as before, beat her breast, and began to bewail herself; and falling at his feet again, with many tears she said, 'have compassion upon me, O Servant of the Most High, and as thou hast once exerted thyself in prayer for all my sins, and hast prevailed, so now intercede, as thou canst, that this offence also may be blotted out.' Thereat holy Basil wept for pity; and he said unto her, 'Woman arise! I also am a sinner, and have myself need of forgiveness. He who hath blotted out thus much, hath granted thee remission of thy sins as far as hath to Him seemed good; and God, who hath taken away the sins of the world, is able to take from thee this remaining sin also; and if thou wilt keep his commandments, and walk in his ways, thou shalt not only have forgiveness, but wilt also become worthy of glory. But go thou into the desert, and there thou wilt find a holy man, who is well known to all the holy fathers, and who is called Ephræm. Give thou this writing to him, and he will intercede for thee, and will prevail with the Lord.'

« The woman then commended herself to the holy Bishop's prayers, and hastened away into the desert, and performed a long journey therein. She came to the great and wonderful Hermit, who was called Ephræm by name, and knocking at his door, she cried aloud, saying, 'have compassion on me, saint of God, have compassion on me!' But he having been forewarned in spirit concerning the errand on which she came, replied unto her, saying, 'Woman depart, for I also am a man and a sinner, standing myself in need of au intercessor.' But she held out the writing, and said, 'the holy Archbishop Basil sent me to thee, that thou mightest intercede for me, and that therethrough the sin which is written herein might be blotted out. The other many sins holy Basil hath blotted out by his prayers: Saint of God, do not thou think it much to intercede with the Lord for me for this one sin, seeing that I am sent unto thee to that end.' But that confessor made answer, 'No, daughter! Could he obtain from the Lord the remission of so many other sins, and cannot he intercede and prevail for this single one? Go thy way back, therefore, and tarry not, that thou mayest find him before his soul be departed from his body.' Then the woman commended herself to the holy Confessor Ephræm, and returned to Cæsarea.

« But, when she entered that city, she met the persons who were bearing the body of St Basil to burial; seeing which, she threw herself upon the ground, and began to cry aloud against the holy man, saying, 'Woe is me a sinner, woe is me a lost wretch, woe is me! O man of God, thou hast sent me into the desert, that thou mightest be rid of me, and not wearied more; and behold I am returned from my bootless journey, having gone over so great a way in vain! The Lord God see to this thing, and judge between me and thee, inasmuch as thou couldest have interceded with Him for me, and have prevailed, if thou hadst not sent me away to another.' Saying this, she threw the writing upon the bier whereon the body of holy Basil was borne, and related before the people all that past between them. One of the clergy then desiring to know what this one sin was, took up the writing, and opened it, and found that it was

clean blotted out: whereupon he cried with a loud voice unto the woman, and said, 'O woman, there is nothing written herein! Why dost thou consume thyself with so much labour and sorrow, not knowing the great things of God unto thee ward, and his inscrutable mercies?' Then the multitude of the people, seeing this glorious and great miracle, glorified God, who hath such power, that he remitteth the sins of all who are living, and giveth grace to his servants, that after their decease they should heal all sickness and all infirmity: and hath given unto them power for remitting all sins to those who preserve a right faith in the Lord, continuing in good works, and glorifying God and our Lord and Saviour.»—*Vitæ Patrum*, pp. 159, 160.

« In the days of the blessed Theodemir, Bishop of Compostella, there was a certain Italian, who had hardly dared confess to his own Priest and Bishop a certain enormous crime which he had formerly committed. His Bishop having heard the confession, and being struck with astonishment and horror at so great an offence, dared not appoint what penance he should perform. Nevertheless, being moved with compassion, he sent the sinner with a schedule, in which the offence was written, to the Church of Santiago at Compostella, enjoining him that he should, with his whole heart, implore the aid of the blessed Apostle, and submit himself to the sentence of the Bishop of that Apostolical Church. He therefore without delay went to Santiago in Galicia, and there placed the schedule, which contained the statement of his crime, upon the venerable altar, repenting that he had committed so great a sin, and intreating forgiveness, with tears and sobs, from God and the Apostle. This was on Santiago's Day, being the eighth of the Kalends of August, and at the first hour.

« When the blessed Theodemir, Bishop of the See of Compostella, came attired in his pontificals to sing mass at the altar that day at the third hour, he found the schedule under the covering of the altar, and demanded forthwith, wherefore, and by whom it had been placed there. The Penitent upon this came forward, and on his knees declared, with many tears, before all the people, the crime which he had committed, and the injunctions which had been laid on him by his own Bishop. The holy Bishop then opened the schedule, and found nothing written therein; it appeared as if no letters had ever been inscribed there. A marvellous thing, and an exceeding joy, for which great praise and glory were incontinently rendered to God and the Apostle, the people all singing, 'this is the Lord's doing, and it is marvellous in our eyes!' The holy Bishop then of a truth believing that the penitent had obtained forgiveness with God through the merits of the Apostle, would impose upon him no other penance for the crime which he had committed, except that of keeping Friday as a fast from that time forth, and, having absolved him from all his other sins, he dismissed him to his own country. Hence it may be inferred, that if any one shall truly repent, and, going from distant countries to Galicia, shall there, with his whole heart, intreat pardon from God, and pray for the aid of the blessed Santiago, the record of his misdeeds shall, without all doubt be blotted out for ever.»—*Acta SS.* Jul. t. vi, p. 48.

There is a miracle of the same kind related of St Antonio,—and probably many other examples might be found.

The Pilgrim to Compostella;

BEING

THE LEGEND OF A COCK AND A HEN,

TO THE HONOUR AND GLORY OF SANTIAGO.

A CHRISTMAS TALE.

Res similis fictæ; sed quid mihi fingere prodest?
Ovid. *Met.* xiii, v. 935.

Hear also ao lean story of theirs!
LIGHTFOOT.

Tʜᴇ Legend (for a genuine Legend it is) which has been made the subject of the ensuing Ballad, is related by Bishop Patrick in his Parable of the Pilgrim (ch. xxxv, pp. 430—434.) Udal ap Rys relates it in his Tour through Spain and Portugal (pp. 35—38). Both these writers refer to Lucius Marineus Siculus as their authority. And it is told also in the *Journal du Voyage d'Espagne* (Paris, 1669), by a *Conseiller* who was attached to the French Embassy in that country (p. 18).

The story may likewise be found in the *Acta Sanctorum*. A duplicate of the principal miracle occurs in the third volume, for the month of May (*die* 12ᵃ, p. 171); and is there ascribed to S. Domingo de la Calzada, the author, Luiz de la Vega, contending, that both relations are to be received as true, the Bollandist (Henschenius) contrariwise opining that they are distinct miracles, but leaving the reader nevertheless to determine freely for himself *utrum id malit, an vero credere velit, unicum dumtaxat esse quod sub quadam circumstantiarum varietate refertur ut geminum.*

In the sixth volume of the same work, for the month of July (*die* 25ᵃ), the legend of the Pilgrim is twice told, once (p. 45) as occurring to a native of Utrecht (Cæsarius Heisterbachensis is the authority), once as having befallen a German at Toulouse (p. 50); the latter story is in the collection of Santiago's miracles, which Pope Calixtus II is said to have compiled. The extract from Lucius Marineus Siculus may also be seen there. It is here annexed as it stands in the fifth book of that author's work *de Rebus Hispaniæ Memorabilibus.*

« In antiquissimâ civitate quam Sancti Dominici Calciatensis, vulgus appellat, gallum vidimus et gallinam, qui dum vixerunt, cujus coloris fuissent ignoramus: posteà verò cùm jugulati fuissent et assi, candidissimi revixerunt, magnam Dei potentiam summumque miraculum referentes. Cujus rei veritas et ratio sic se habet. Vir quidam probus et amicus Dei, et uxor ejus, optima mulier, cum filio adolescentulo magnæ probitatis, ad Sanctum Jacobum Compostellam proficiscentes, in hanc urbem itineris labore defessi ingrediuntur, et quiescendi gratiâ restiterunt in domo cujusdam qui adultam filiam habebat. Quæ cùm adolescentem pulchrâ facie vidisset, ejus amore capta est. Et cùm juvenis ab eâ requisitus atque vexatus, ejus voto repugnâsset, amorem convertit in odium, et ei nocere cupiens, tempore quo discedere volebant ejus cucullo crateram sui patris clam reposuit.

Cùmque peregrini manè discessissent, exclamavit puella coram parentibus crateram sibi fuisse subreptam. Quod audiens Prætor satellites confestim misit, ut peregrinos reducerent. Qui cùm venissent, puella conscia sui sceleris accessit ad juvenem et crateram eruit è cucullo. Quapropter comperto delicto, juvenis in campum productus iniquâ sententiâ et sine culpâ laqueo suspensus est : miserique parentes cùm filium deplorâssent, posteà discedentes Compostellam pervenerunt. Ubi solutis votis et Deo gratias agentes, subinde redeuntes, ad locum pervenerunt, ubi filius erat suspensus, et mater multis perfusa lacrymis ad filium accessit, multùm dissuadente marito. Cùmque filium suspiceret, dixit ei filius, Mater mea, noli flere super me : ego enim vivus sum, quoniam Virgo Dei genetrix, et Sanctus Jacobus me sustinent et servant incolumem. Vade, charissima mater, ad judicem qui me falsò condemnavit, et dic ei me vivere propter innocentiam meam, ut me liberari jubeat, tibique restituat. Properat sollicita mater, et præ nimio gaudio flens uberiùs, Prætorem convenit in mensâ sedentem, qui gallum et gallinam assos scindere volebat. ' Prætor,' inquit, filius meus vivit ; jube solvi, obsecro !' Quod cùm audisset Prætor, existimans eam quod dicebat propter amorem maternum somniâsse, respondit subridens, ' Quid hoc est, bona mulier? Ne fallaris ! sic enim vivit filius tuus, ut vivunt hæ aves!' Et vix hoc dixerat cùm gallus et gallina saltaverunt in mensâ, statimque gallus cantavit. Quod cùm Prætor vidisset attonitus continuò egreditur, vocat sacerdotes, et cives, proficiscuntur ad juvenem suspensum : et invenerunt incolumem valdèque lætantem, et parentibus restituunt ; domumque reversi gallum capiunt et gallinam, et in ecclesiam transferunt magnâ solemnitate. Quæ ibi clausæ res admirabiles et Dei potentiam testificantes observantur, ubi septennio vivunt; hunc enim terminum Deus illis instituit ; et in fine septennii antequàm moriantur, pullum relinquunt et pullam sui coloris et magnitudinis; et hoc fit in eâ ecclesiâ quolibet septennio. Magnæ quoque admirationis est, quòd omnes per hanc urbem transeuntes peregrini, qui sunt innumerabiles, galli hujus et gallinæ plumam capiunt, et nunquam illis plumæ deficiunt. Hoc ego testor, proptereà quòd vidi et interfui, plumamque mecum fero. » — *Rerum Hispanicarum Scriptores*, t. ii, p. 805.

Luiz de la Vega agrees with Marineus Siculus in all the particulars of this perpetual miracle except the latter : « Sed scriptorem illum fictionis arguit, quòd

asserat plumas galli et gallinæ, quæ quotidiè peregrinis
illàc transeuntibus distribuuntur, prodigiosè multiplica-
ri: affirmat autem tanquam testis oculatus, in eâ ecclesiâ
designatum esse quemdam clericum, qui plumas illas
conservat et peregrinis distribuit; at negat continuum
multiplicationis miraculum à Marineo Siculo tam confi-
denter assertum, in eâ urbe videri, aut patrari. Multis
tamen probare nititur, reliqua omnia prodigia esse vera,
testaturque 'ad perpetuam rei memoriam in superiori
ecclesiæ parte omnium oculis exponi idem patibulum,
in quo peregrinus suspensus fuit.—*Acta Sanctorum*,
Jul. t. vi, p. 46.

THE
PILGRIM TO COMPOSTELLA.

PRELUDE.

Tell us a story, old Robin Gray!
This merry Christmas time:
We are all in our glory, so tell us a story,
Either in prose, or in rhyme.

Open your budget, old Robin Gray!
We very well know it is full:
Come! out with a murder,—a Goblin,—a Ghost,
Or a tale of a Cock and a Bull!

I have no tale of a Cock and a Bull,
My good little women and men;
But 't will do as well, perhaps, if I tell
A tale of a Cock and a Hen.

INTRODUCTION.

You have all of you heard of St James for Spain,
As one of the Champions Seven,
Who, having been good Knights on Earth,
Became Hermits and Saints in Heaven.

Their history once was in good repute,
And so it ought to be still;
Little friends, I dare say you have read it:
And if not, why I hope you will.

Of this St James that book proclaims
Great actions manifold:
But more amazing are the things
Which of him in Spain are told.

How once a ship, of marble made, (1)
Came sailing o'er the sea,
Wherein his headless corpse (2) was laid,
Perfumed with sanctity.

And how, though then he had no head,
He afterwards had two; (3)
Which both worked miracles so well,
That it was not possible to tell
The false one from the true.

Whereby, my little friends, we see
That an original may sometimes be
No better than its fac-simile;

And how he used to fight the Moors (4)
Upon a milk-white charger:
Large tales of him the Spaniards tell,
Munchausen tells no larger.

But in their cause of latter years
He has not been so hearty:
For that he never struck a stroke is plain,
When our Duke, in many a hard campaign,
Beat the French armies out of Spain,
And conquered Buonaparte.

Yet still they worship him in Spain,
And believe in him with might and main: (5)
Santiago there they call him: (6)
And if any one there should doubt these tales,
They 've an Inquisition to maul him. (7)

At Compostella in his Church
His body and one head
Have been for some eight hundred years
By Pilgrims visited. (8)

Old scores might there be clean rubb'd off,
And tickets there were given
To clear all toll-gates on the way
Between the Churchyard and Heaven.

Some went for payment of a vow
In time of trouble made;
And some who found that pilgrimage
Was a pleasant sort of trade.

And some, I trow, because it was
Believed, as well as said,
That all, who in their mortal stage
Did not perform this pilgrimage,
Must make it when they were dead. (9)

Some upon penance for their sins,
In person, or by attorney:
And some who were, or had been sick;
And some who thought to cheat Old Nick;
And some who liked the journey:

Which well they might when ways were safe;
And therefore rich and poor
Went in that age on pilgrimage,
As folks now make a tour.

The poor with scrip, the rich with purse,
They took their chance for better for worse
From many a foreign land,
With a scallop-shell (10) in the hat for badge,
And a Pilgrim's staff in hand.

A useful truth, I trow,
Which picture buyers won't believe,
But which picture-dealers know.

Young Connoisseurs who will be!
Remember I say this,—
For your benefit hereafter,—
In a parenthesis.

And not to interrupt
The order of narration,
This warning shall be printed
By way of annotation.

Something there is, the which to leave
Untold would not be well,
Relating to the Pilgrim's staff,
And to the scallop-shell.

For the scallop shows in a coat of arms,
That of the bearer's line
Some one, in former days, hath been
To Santiago's shrine.

And the staff was bored and holed for those
Who on a flute could play, (11)
And thus the merry Pilgrim had
His music on the way.

THE LEGEND.
PART I.

Once on a time three Pilgrims true,
Being Father and Mother and Son,
For pure devotion to the Saint,
This pilgrimage begun.

Their names, little friends, I am sorry to say,
In none of my books can I find;
But the son, if you please, we 'll call Pierre,
What the parents were called, never mind.

From France they came, in which fair land
They were people of good renown;
And they took up their lodging one night on the way
In La Calzada town.

Now, if poor Pilgrims they had been,
And had lodged in the Hospice instead of the Inn,
My good little women and men,
Why then you never would have heard,
This tale of the Cock and the Hen!

For the Innkeepers they had a daughter,
Sad to say, who was just such another
As Potiphar's daughter, I think, would have been
If she followed the ways of her mother.

This wicked woman to our Pierre
Behaved like Potiphar's wife;
And, because she fail'd to win his love,
She resolved to take his life.

So she pack'd up a silver cup
In his wallet privily:
And then, as soon as they were gone,
She raised a hue and cry.

The Pilgrims were overtaken:
The people gathered round.
Their wallets were search'd, and in Pierre's
The silver cup was found.

They dragg'd him before the Alcayde;
A hasty Judge was he:
« The theft,» he said, « was plain and proved,
And hang'd the thief must be.»

So to the gallows our poor Pierre
Was hurried instantly.

If I should now relate
The piteous lamentation,
Which for their son these parents made,
My little friends, I am afraid
You 'd weep at the relation.

But Pierre in Santiago still
His constant faith profess'd;
When to the gallows he was led,
« 'T was a short way to Heaven,» he said,
« Though not the pleasantest.»

And from their pilgrimage he charged
His parents not to cease,
Saying that unless they promised this,
He could not be hang'd in peace.

They promised it with heavy hearts;
Pierre then, therewith content,
Was hang'd: and they upon their way
To Compostella went.

PART II.

Four weeks they travelled painfully,
They paid their vows, and then
To La Calzada's fatal town
Did they come back again.

The Mother would not be withheld,
But go she must to see
Where her poor Pierre was left to hang
Upon the gallows tree.

Oh tale most marvellous to hear,
Most marvellous to tell!
Eight weeks had he been hanging there,
And yet was alive and well!

« Mother,» said he, « I am glad you 're return'd,
It is time I should now be released:
Though I cannot complain that I 'm tired,
And my neck does not ache in the least.

« The Sun has not scorch'd me by day,
The Moon has not chilled me by night;
And the winds have but help'd me to swing,
As if in a dream of delight.

« Go you to the Alcayde,
That hasty Judge unjust:
Tell him Santiago has saved me,
And take me down he must!»

Now, you must know the Alcayde,
Not thinking himself a great sinner,
Just then at table had sate down,
About to begin his dinner.

His knife was raised to carve,
The dish before him then:
Two roasted fowls were laid therein;

That very morning they had been
A Cock and his faithful Hen.

In came the Mother wild with joy;
« A miracle!» she cried;
But that most hasty Judge unjust
Repell'd her in his pride.

« Think not,» quoth he, « to tales like this
That I should give belief!
Santiago never would bestow
His miracles, full well I know,
On a Frenchman and a thief.»

And pointing to the Fowls, o'er which
He held his ready knife,
« As easily might I believe
These birds should come to life!»

The good Saint would not let him thus
The Mother's true tale withstand;
So up rose the Fowls in the dish,
And down dropt the knife from his hand.

The Cock would have crowed if he could;
To cackle the Hen had a wish:
And they both slipt about in the gravy
Before they got out of the dish.

And when each would have open'd its eyes,
For the purpose of looking about them,
They saw they had no eyes to open,
And that there was no seeing without them.

All this was to them a great wonder;
They stagger'd and reel'd on the table;
And either to guess where they were,
Or what was their plight, or how they came there,
Alas! they were wholly unable:

Because, you must know, that that morning,
A thing which they thought very hard,
The Cook had cut off their heads,
And thrown them away in the yard.

The Hen would have prank'd up her feathers,
But plucking had sadly deformed her;
And for want of them she would have shivered with cold;
If the roasting she had had not warm'd her.

And the Cock felt exceedingly queer;
He thought it a very odd thing
That his head and his voice were he did not know where,
And his gizzard tuck'd under his wing.

The gizzard got into its place,
But how Santiago knows best:
And so, by the help of the Saint,
Did the liver and all the rest.

The heads saw their way to the bodies,
In they came from the yard without check,
And each took its own proper station,
To the very great joy of the neck.

And in flew the feathers, like snow in a shower,
For they all became white on the way;
And the Cock and the Hen in a trice were refledged,
And then who so happy as they!

Cluck! cluck! cried the Hen right merrily then,
The Cock his clarion blew,
Full glad was he to hear again
His own cock-a-doo-del-doo!

PART III.

« A Miracle! a miracle!»
The people shouted, as they might well,
When the news went through the town;
And every child and woman and man
Took up the cry, and away they ran
To see Pierre taken down.

They made a famous procession;
My good little women and men,
Such a sight was never seen before,
And I think will never again.

Santiago's Image, large as life,
Went first with banners and drum and fife,
And next, as was most meet,
The twice-born Cock and Hen (12) were borne
Along the thronging street.

Perch'd on a cross-pole hoisted high,
They were raised in sight of the crowd;
And, when the people set up a cry,
The Hen she cluck'd in sympathy,
And the Cock he crow'd aloud.

And because they very well knew for why
They were carried in such solemnity,
And saw the Saint and his banners before 'em,
They behaved with the greatest propriety,
And most correct decorum.

The Knife, which had cut off their heads that morn,
Still red with their innocent blood, was borne,
The scullion boy he carried it;
And the Skewers also made a part of the show,
With which they were trussed for the spit.

The Cook in triumph bore that Spit
As high as he was able;
And the Dish was display'd wherein they were laid
When they had been served at table.

With eager faith the crowd prest round;
There was a scramble of women and men
For who should dip a finger-tip
In the blessed Gravy then.

Next went the Alcayde, beating his breast,
Crying aloud like a man distrest,
And amazed at the loss of his dinner,
« Santiago! Santiago!
Have mercy on me a sinner!»

And lifting oftentimes his hands
Towards the Cock and Hen,
« Orate pro nobis!» devoutly he cried,
And as devoutly the people replied,
Whenever he said it, « Amen!»

The Father and Mother were last in the train;
Rejoicingly they came,
And extolled, with tears of gratitude,
Santiago's glorious name.

So, with all honours that might be,
They gently unhang'd Pierre;
No hurt or harm had he sustained,
But, to make the wonder clear,
A deep black halter-mark remained
Just under his left ear.

PART IV.

And now, my little listening dears,
With open mouths and open ears,
Like a rhymer whose only art is
That of telling a plain unvarnish'd tale,
To let you know, I must not fail,
What became of all the parties.

Pierre went on to Compostella
To finish his pilgrimage:
His Parents went back with him joyfully:
After which they returned to their own country;
And there, I believe, that all the three
Lived to a good old age.

For the gallows on which Pierre
So happily had swung,
It was resolved that never more
On it should man be hung.

To the Church it was transplanted,
As ancient books declare;
And the people in commotion,
With an uproar of devotion,
Set it up for a relic there.

What became of the halter I know not, (13)
Because the old books show not;
But we may suppose and hope,
That the City presented Pierre
With that interesting rope.

For in his family, and this
The Corporation knew,
It rightly would be valued more
Than any *cordon bleu*.

The Innkeeper's wicked daughter
Confess'd what she had done,
So they put her in a Convent,
And she was made a Nun.

The Alcayde had been so frighten'd,
That he never ate fowls again;
And he always pull'd off his hat
When he saw a Cock and Hen.
Wherever he sat at table
Not an egg might there be placed;
And he never even muster'd courage for a custard,
Though garlic tempted him to taste
Of an omlet now and then.

But always after such a transgression
He hasten'd away to make confession;
And not till he had confess'd,
And the Priest had absolved him, did he feel
His conscience and stomach at rest.

The twice-born Birds to the Pilgrim's Church,
As by miracle consecrated,
Were given; and there unto the Saint
They were publicly dedicated.

At their dedication the Corporation
A fund for their keep supplied,
And, after following the Saint and his banners
This Cock and Hen were so changed in their manners,
That the Priests were edified.

Gentle as any turtle-dove
Saint Cock became all meekness and love:
Most dutiful of wives,
Saint Hen she never peck'd again,
So they led happy lives.

The ways of ordinary fowls
You must know they had clean forsaken.
And if every cock and hen in Spain
Had their example taken,
Why then—the Spaniards would have had
No eggs to eat with bacon.

These blessed Fowls, at seven years' end,
In the odour of sanctity died:
They were carefully pluck'd, and then
They were buried, side by side.

And lest the fact should be forgotten
(Which would have been a pity),
'Twas decreed, in honour of their worth,
That a Cock and Hen should be borne thenceforth
In the arms of that ancient City.

Two eggs Saint Hen had laid, no more;
The chickens were her delight;
A Cock and Hen they proved,
And both, like their parents, were virtuous and white.

The last act of the holy Hen
Was to rear this precious brood; and, when
Saint Cock and she were dead,
This couple, as the lawful heirs,
Succeeded in their stead.

They also lived seven years,
And they laid eggs but two;
From which two milk-white chickens
To Cock and Henhood grew:
And always their posterity
The self-same course pursue.

Not one of these eggs ever addled,
(With wonder be it spoken!)
Not one of them ever was lost,
Not one of them ever was broken.

Sacred they are; neither magpie, nor rat,
Snake, weasel, nor martin approaching them:
And woe to the irreverent wretch
Who should even dream of poaching them!

Thus then is this great miracle
Continued to this day;
And to their Church all Pilgrims go,
When they are on the way;
And some of the feathers are given them;
For which they always pay.

No price is set upon them,
And this leaves all persons at ease;
The Poor give as much as they can,
The Rich as much as they please.

But that the more they give the better
Is very well understood,
Seeing whatever is thus disposed of
Is for their own souls' good;

For Santiago will always
Befriend his true believers;
And the money is for him, the Priests
Being only his receivers.

To make the miracle the more,
Of these feathers there is always store,
And all are genuine too;
All of the original Cock and Hen,
Which the Priests will swear is true.

Thousands a thousand times told have bought them,
And if myriads and tens of myriads sought them,
They would still find some to buy;
For however great were the demand,
So great would be the supply.

And if any of you, my small friends,
Should visit those parts, I dare say
You will bring away some of the feathers,
And think of Old Robin Gray.

NOTES AND ILLUSTRATIONS.

Note 1, page 752, col. 1.
A ship of marble made.

The marble ship I have not found any where except in Geddes: who must have found it in some version of the legend which has not fallen into my hands. But that the ship was made of marble I believe to be quite as true as any other part of the legend of Santiago.— Whether of marble or not, it was a miraculous ship which, without oars or sails, performed the voyage from Joppa to Iria Flava, now El Padron, in Galicia, in seven days.

Classical fables were still so passable when the Historia Compostelana was written, that the safe passage of this ship over the Syrtes, and between Scylla and Charybdis, is ascribed to the presiding hand of Providence.—*España Sagrada*, t. xx, p. 6.

Note 2, page 752, col. 1.
——his beadless corpse.

How the body came to leave its head behind is a circumstance which has not been accounted for: and yet it requires explanation, because we are assured that Santiago took particular care not to part with his head, when it was cut off.

« At the moment,» says the Annalist of Galicia, « when the cruel executioner severed from its neck the precious head of the sacred Apostle, the body miraculously raised its hands and caught it, and in that posture it continued till night. The astonished Jews attempted to separate it, but in vain; for upon touching the venerable corpse their arms became cold, as if frozen, and they remained without the use of them.»—*Añales de Galicia, por El Doctor D. Francisco Xavier Manuel de la Huerta y Vega.—Santiago*, 1733.

> Cortada la cabeza no dió en tierra,
> Que por virtud de Dios, él con las manos,
> Antes que cayga al suelo i si la asierra,
> Que no pueden quitársela tyranos.
> CHRISTOVAL DE MESA: *El Patron de España*, ff. 62.

Perhaps his companions dropt it on their way to the coast, for the poet tells us they travelled in the dark, and in a hurry:

> Cubiertos de la noche con el manto
> Sin que ningun contrario los impida,
> Mas presto que si fueran á galope,
> Llevan el cuerpo á la ciudad de Jope.
> *Ib.* ff. 65.

But according to the *Historia Compostelana* (España Sagrada, t. xx, p. 6), there is the testimony of Pope St Leo, that the original head came with the body.

Note 3, page 752, col. 2.
And how, though then he had no head,
He afterwards had two.

This is a small allowance, and must be understood with reference to the two most authentic ones in that part of the world,—that at Braga, and one of the two at Compostella.

It is a common thing for Saints to be polycephalous; and Santiago is almost as great a pluralist in heads as St John the Baptist has been made by the dealers in relics. There are some half dozen heads, and almost as many whole bodies ascribed to him,—all in good odour, all having worked miracles, and all, beyond a doubt, equally authentic.

Note 4, page 752, col. 2.
And how he used to fight the Moors.

Most appropriately therefore, according to P. Sautel, was he called Boanerges.

> Conspicitur medio cataphractus in aëre ductor,
> Qui dedit in trepidam barbara castra fugam.
> Tam cito tam validæ cur terga dedere phalanges?
> Nimirum Tonitru Filius ista patrat.
> *Annus Sacer Poeticus*, vol. ii, p. 32.

—« siendo acá en España nuestro amparo y defensa en las guerras, mereció con razon este nombre: pues mas feroz que trueno ni rayo espantaba, confundia y desbarataba los grandes exercitos de los Moros.»—*Morales, Coronica Gen. de España*, l. ix c. vii, sec. 4.

> Vitoria España, vitoria,
> que tienes en tu defensa,
> uno de los Doce Pares;
> mas no de nacion Francesa.
> Hijo es tuyo, y tantos mata,
> que parece que su fuerza
> excede á la de la muerte
> quando mas furiosa y presta.
> LEDESMA, *Conceptos Espirituales*, p. 242.

The Spanish Clergy had a powerful motive for propagating these fables; their *Privilegio de los votos* being one of the most gainful, as well as most impudent forgeries, that ever was committed.

« The two sons of Zebedee manifested, » says Morales, « their courage and great heart, and the faith which was strengthening in them, by their eagerness to revenge the injury done to their kinsman and master when the Samaritans would not receive him into their city. Then Santiago and St John distinguished themselves from the other Apostles, by coming forward, and saying to our Saviour, ' Lord, wilt thou that we command fire to come down from Heaven and consume them?' It seems as if (according to the Castilian proverb concerning kinsmen) their blood boiled in them to kill and to destroy, because of the part which they had in his. But be not in such haste, O glorious Apostle Santiago, to shed the blood of others for Christ your cousin-german! It will not be long before you will give it to him, and for him will give all your own. Let him first shed his for you, that, when yours shall be mingled with it by another new tie of spiritual relationship, and by a new friendship in martyrdom, it shall be more esteemed by him, and held in great account. Let the debt be well made out, that the payment may be the more due. Let the benefit be completed, that you may make the recompense under greater obligation, and with more will. Then will it be worth more, and manifest more gratitude. Learn meantime from your Master, that love is not shown in killing and destroying the souls of others, for the beloved, but in mortifying and offering your own to death. This, which is the height and perfection of love, your Master will teach you, and thenceforth you will not content yourself with anything less. And if you are desirous, for Christ's sake, to smite and slay his enemies, have patience awhile, fierce Saint! (*Santo feroz.*) There will come a time when you shall wage war for your Master, sword in hand, and in your person shall slaughter myriads and myriads of Moors, his wicked enemies!»—*Coronica General de España*, l. ix, c. vii, sec. 8.

An old hymn, which was formerly used in the service of his day, likens this Apostle to—a Lion's whelp!

Electus hic Apostolus,
Decorus et amabilis,
Velut Leonis catulus
Vicit bella certaminis.
Divi Tutelares, 229.

« Thirty-eight visible appearances, » says the Padre Maestro Fray Felipe de la Gandara, Chronicler General of the Kingdom of Galicia, — « thirty-eight visible appearances, in as many different battles, aiding and favouring the Spaniards, are recounted by the very learned Don Miguel Erce Gimenez in his most erudite and laborious work upon the Preaching of Santiago in Spain; from which work the *illustrissimous* Doctor Don Antonio Calderon has collected them in his book upon the Excellencies of this Apostle. And I hold it for certain that his appearances have been many more; and that in every victory, which the Spaniards have achieved over their enemies, this their Great Captain has been present with his favour and intercession.»—*Armas i Triunfos del Reino de Galicia*, p. 648.

The Chronista General proceeds to say that Galicia may be especially proud of its part in all these victories, the Saint having publicly prided himself upon his connection with that kingdom; for being asked in battle once, who and what he was, (being a stranger), he replied, « I am a Soldier, a Kinsman of the Eternal King, a Citizen and Inhabitant of Compostella, and my name is James.» For this fact the Chronicler assures us that a book of manuscript sermons, preached in Paris three centuries before his time by a Franciscan Friar, is sufficient authority: « *es valiente autoridad!* »—*Armas i Triunfos del Reino de Galicia*, p. 649.

Note 5, page 752, col. 2.

——Still they worship him in Spain,
And believe in him with might and main.

« —calamo describi vix potest, aut verbis exprimi, quanto in Jacobum Apostolum Hispani amore ferantur, quam tenero pietatis sensu festos illius dies, et memoriam celebrent; quam se, suaque omnia, illius fidei et clientelæ devoveant; ipsius auspiciis bellicas expeditiones suscipere, et conficere soliti, et Jacobi nomine quasi tesserâ se milites illius esse profiteri. Cum pugnam ineunt, ut sibi animos faciant et hostibus terrorem incutiant, in primâ, quæ vehementior esse solet, impressione, illam vocem intonant, *Sancte Jacobe, urge Hispania,* hoc est, *Santiago, cierra Hespanha;* militari se illi sacramento addicunt; et illustrissimo Equitum Ordine Jacobi nomine instituto, ejusque numini sacro, cujus Rex ipse Catholicus Magnus Magister et Rector est: ejus se obsequiis dedicant et legibus adstringunt, ut nullius erga quenquam alium Sanctum Patronum gentis clariora extent, quam Hispanicæ erga Jacobum amoris et religionis indicia. Quàm verò bene respondeat huic amori et pietati Apostolus curâ, et solicitudine Patris et Patroni, ex rebus à suis clientibus, ejus auxilio, præclarè gestis, satis constat, tum in ipsa Hispania, tum in utrâque, ad Orientem et Occidentem Solem Indiâ, Hispanorum et Lusitanorum armis subactâ, et illorum operâ et industriâ ubique locorum propagatâ Christianâ religione.»—P. ANT. MACEDO. *Divi Tutelares Orbis Christiani*, p. 228.

Note 6, page 752, col. 2.

Santiago there they call him.

« The true name of this Saint, » says Ambrosio de Morales, « was Jacobo (that is, according to the Spanish form), taken with little difference from that of the Patriarch Jacob. A greater is that which we Spaniards have made, corrupting the word little by little, till it has become the very different one which we now use. From Santo Jacobo we shortened it, as we commonly do with proper names, and said Santo Jaco. We clipt it again after this abbreviation, and by taking away one letter, and changing another, made it into Santiago. The alteration did not stop here; but because Yago or Tiago by itself did not sound distinctly and well, we began to call it Diago, as may be seen in Spanish writings of two or three hundred years old. At last, having past through all these mutations, we rested with Diego for the ordinary name, reserving that of Santiago when we speak of the Saint.»—*Coronica General de España*, l. ix, c. vii, sec. 2.

Florez pursues the corruption further: « *nombrandole par la voz latina Jacobus Apostolus, con abreviacion y vulgaridad Jacobo Apostolo, ò Giacomo Postolo, ò Jiac Apostol.* »—*España Sagrada*, t. xix, p. 71.

It has not been explained how *Jack* in this country was transferred from James to John.

The Prior Cayrasco de Figueroa assures us that St James was a gentleman, his father Zebedee being

Varon de ilustre sangre y Galileo,
Puesto que usaba el arte piscatoria,

Que entonces no era ilicito, ni feo,
Ni hora en muchas partes menos gloria,
La gente principal tener oficio,
O por su menester, ó su exercicio.

Templo Militante, p. lll, p. 83.

Morales also takes some pains to establish this point.
Zebedee, he assures us, « era hombre principal, señor de
un navio, con que seguia la pesca :» and it is clear, he
says, « como padre y hijos seguian este trato de la pes-
queria honradamente, mas como señores que como ofi-
ciales!»—*Coronica Gen. de España*, l. ix, c. vii, sec. 3.

Note 7, page 752, col. 2.

They've an Inquisition to maul him.

Under the dominion of that atrocious Tribunal Am-
brosio de Morales might truly say, « no one will dare
deny that the body of the glorious Apostle is in the city
which is named after him, and that it was brought
thither, and afterwards discovered there by the great
miracles, »—of which he proceeds to give an account.
« People have been burnt for less, »—as a fellow at Leeds
said the other day of a woman whom he suspected of
bewitching him.

There is nothing of which the Spanish and Portu-
guese authors have boasted with greater complacency
and pleasure than of the said inquisition. A notable
example of this is afforded in the following passage
from the *Templo Militante, Flos Santorum, y Trium-
phos de sus Virtudes*, by D. Bartolome Cayrasco de
Figueroa, Prior and Canon of the Cathedral Church of
Grand Canary. (Lisbon, 1613.)

————gloriosa España,
Aunque de mucho puedes gloriarte,
No está en eso el valor que te acompaña,
Sino en tener la Fé por estandarte :
Por esta la provincia mas estraña,
Y todo el orbe teme de enojarte ;
Por esta de tu nombre tiembla el mundo
Y el cavernoso Tártaro profundo.

Agradecelo á Dios de cuya mano
Procede toda gracia, toda gloria ;
Y despues del al Principe Cristiano,
Philipo digno de inmortal memoria :
Porque con su gobierno soberano,
Con su justicia, y su piedad notoria,
Estas asegurada, y defendida,
De todos los peligros desta vida.

Este gran Rey decora tu terreno
Con veynte y dos insignes fortalezas,
Cuyas fuertes Alcaydes ponen freno
A todas las tartáricas bravezas :
Y con temor del malo, honor del bueno,
Castigan las malicias, y simplezas
De heréticas palabras y opiniones,
Que son las veynte y dos Inquisiciones.

De la Imperial Toledo es la primera ;
De la Real Sevilla la segunda,
De Córdoba la Ilustre la tercera,
La quarta de Granada la fecunda :
Tambien en Calahorra la bandera
De la sagrada Inquisicion se funda,
Y Margaritas son desta corona,
Zaragoza, Valencia, Barcelona.

Tambien Valladolid aventajada
Despues del gran incendio, en edificio ;
Cuenca, Murcia, Llerena celebrada
En mucha antigüedad del Santo Oficio :
En Galicia asi mismo está fundada
Torre deste santisimo exercicio,
En Evora, en Coimbra, en Ulisipo,
Que ya la Lusitania es de Philipo.

Tambien Sicilia en esta viva peña
De la importante Inquisicion estriva ;
Y Gran Canaria en pública reseña
Los adversarios de la Fé derriba :
Las islas de Mallorca y de Cerdeña,
Y el gran Reyno que fue de Atabalipa,
Y la postrera desta heróyca suma
Es la ciudad que fue de Motezuma.

Sobre estas fortalezas de importancia
Esta la general torre suprema,
Fundada sobre altissima constancia,
Cubierta de Católica diadema :
De cuya soberana vigilancia,
Resplandeciente luz, virtud estrema,
Procede á las demas, la fuerza, el brio,
El Cristiano valor, el poderio.

Estos pues son los célebres Castillos,
De la Fé verdaderos defensores,
Que con hábitos roxos y amarillos,
Castigan los heréticos errores :
Y a los pechos Católicos sencillos,
De la verdad Cristiana zeladores,
Les dan el justo premio, honor debido,
De la virtud heróyca merecido.

The Poet proceeds to eulogize Santiago as having
been the founder in Spain of that faith for the defence
and promotion of which these two-and-twenty Castles
were erected.

Pues si en el mundo es digno de memoria
El fundador de una ciudad terrena ;
Y luego es celebrada en larga historia
El inventor de alguna cosa buena,
Qué premio le daras? qué honor? qué gloria?
Felice España, de virtudes llena,
Al que fue de la Fé que aqui refiero,
En tus Provincias fundador primero?

Razon será, que su memoria sea
En todo tu distrito eternizada,
Y que en aqueste Santoral se lea
(Aunque con debil pluma) celebrada :
Pues alto España, porque el mundo vea
Que puedes en la Fé mas que en la espada,
Da me atentos oidos eniretanto
Que de tu Caballero ilustre canto.

Oyganme los magnánimos guerreros
Que ponen freno al bárbaro despecho,
Y en especial aquellos Cavalleros
Que adornan de su insinia roxa el pecho :
Veran que los blasones verdaderos
Se alcanzan, imitando en dicho y hecho
Al Español caudillo *Santiago*
Gran zelador del Agareno estrago.

P. lll, p. 81.

Note 8, page 752, col. 2.

At Compostella in his Church
His body and one head
Have been, for some eight hundred years,
By Pilgrims visited.

————a visitar el cuerpo santo
Todo fiel Cristiano la via toma :
Adonde viene peregrino tanto
Como á Jerusalem, y como á Roma,
Que á él de tierra y mar por los caminos
Vienen de todo el mundo peregrinos.

Varia gente fiel, pueblo devoto,
El Santuario célebre frequenta,
Acude el casi naufrago piloto,
Libre de la maritima tormenta :
Que del mar combatido hizo voto,
Teniendo de salvar el alma cuenta,
Que de la tempestad casi sin habla,
Con la vida salió sobre una tabla.

El coxo del lugar propio se alexa
De una azemila ó carro hecho carga,
Y representa su piadosa quexa,
De aquella enfermedad prolixa y larga:
Vuelve en sus pies, y las muletas dexa,
Y de alguna piadosa obra se encarga,
Gratificando con palabras santas,
Poder volver sobre sus propias plantas.

El que ya tuvo vista, y no tiene ojos,
Al Templo viene del Apostol Diego,
Hace oracion, y póstrase de hinojos,
Vuelve con luz, abiendo entrado ciego:
Y ojos de cera dexa por despojos,
De que alcanzó salud su humilde ruego,
Y en recompensa de la nueva vista,
Es del raro milagro coronista.

El que hablar no puede, aunque con lengua
Que súbito accidente hizo mudo,
Pide remedio de su falta y mengua,
Con un sonido balbuciente y rudo:
Su devocion humilde su mal mengua,
Y pudiendo decir lo que no pudo,
Con nueva voz, y con palabras claras,
Hace gracias por dádivas tan raras.

Si aqueste viene de sus miembros manco,
Y aquel sordo del todo, otro contrecho,
Con todos el Apostol es tan franco,
Con su medio con Dios es de provecho:
Cada qual con alegre hábito blanco,
Vuelve de su demanda satisfecho,
Dando vuelta á su tierra los dolientes,
Sanos de enfermedades diferentes.

A quien de prision saca, ó cautiverio,
Remedia enfermos, muertos resuscita,
Da á los desconsolados refrigerio,
Y diferentes aflicciones quita:
Sobre toda dolencia tiene imperio,
La milagrosa fábrica bendita,
Libra de muerte en agua, en hierro, en fuego,
El cuerpo santo del Apostol Diego.

Da toda alma fiel gracias al cielo,
Que perdonado al pecador que yerra,
Para remedio suyo, y su consuelo,
Tal bien el Reyno de Galizia encierra:
Para que venga desde todo el suelo
A las postreras partes de la tierra,
Todo fiel Católico Cristiano,
A implorar el auxilio soberano.

CRISTOVAL DE MESA, *El Patron de España*, ff. lxxii, p. 3.

The high altar at Compostella is, as all the altars formerly were in Galicia and Asturias, not close to the wall, but a little detached from it. It is ten feet in length, and very wide, with a splendid frontispiece of silver. The altar itself is hollow, and at the Gospel end there is a small door, never opened except to royal visitors, and when a new Archbishop first comes to take possession. It was opened for Ambrosio de Morales, because he was commissioned to inspect the churches: nothing, however, was to be seen within, except two large flat stones, which formed the floor, and at the end of them a hole about the size of an orange, but filled with mortar. Below is the vault in which the body of Santiago is said to be deposited in the marble coffin wherein it was found. The vault extends under the altar and its steps, and some way back under the Capella Mayor: it is in fact a part of the Crypt walled off with a thick wall, *para dexar cerrado del todo el santo cuerpo.*

The Saint, whose real presence is thus carefully concealed, receives his pilgrims in effigy. The image is a sitting figure of stone, a little less than life, gilt and painted, holding in one hand a book, and as if giving

a blessing with the other. *Esta en cabello*, without either crown or glory on the head, but a large silver crown is suspended immediately above, almost so as to touch the head ; and the last ceremony which a pilgrim performs is to ascend to the image, which is over the altar, by a stair-case from the Epistle side, kiss it reverently on the head, embrace it, and place this crown upon it, and then go down on the Gospel side.—*Viage de Morales*, t. xx, p. 154.

Ingens sub templo fornix, et claustra per umbras
Magna jacent, cæcæque domus, queis magna Jacobi
Ossa sepulchrali fama est in sede latere.
Nulli fas hominum sacratum insistere limen ;
Est vidisse nefas, nec eundi pervius usus :
E longè veniam exorant atque oscula figunt
Liminibus, redeuntque domos ; variasque galeris
Jacobi effigies addunt, humerosque bacillis
Circumdant, conchisque super fulgentibus ornant.

Pociecidos, lib. vii, p. 117.

The sepulchre was thus closed by the first Archbishop D. Diego Gelmirez, « que ya de ninguna manera se puede ver, ni entenderse como está. Y esto hizo con prudentísimo consejo aquel gran Príncipe y valeroso Prelado, y con reverencia devota, porque cada uno no quisiese ver y tratar aquel precioso relicario comunmente, y sin el debido respeto; que se pierde sin duda quando los cuerpos santos y sus sepulturas pueden ser vistas vulgarmente de todos.»—*Morales*, l. ix, c. vii, sec 67.

A print of the sepulchre, from an illuminated drawing in the manuscript of the *Historia Compostelana*, is given in the 20th volume of the *España Sagrada*. And in that history (pp. 50, 51) is the following characteristic account of the enlargement of the altar by D. Diego Gelmirez.

« Among the other worthinesses, with the which the aforesaid Bishop in no inactive solicitude hastened to decorate his Church, we have been careful to defend from the death of oblivion whatsoever his restauratory hand did to the altar of the said Church. But, lest in bringing forward all singular circumstances we should wander into devious ways, we will direct our intention to the straight path, and commit to succeeding remembrance so far as our possibility may reveal those things which we beheld with our own eyes. For of how small dimensions the altar of Santiago formerly was, lest we should be supposed to diminish it in our relation, may better be collected from the measure of the altarlet itself. But as religion increased in the knowledge of the Christian faith, that another altarlet, a little larger than the other, was placed over it by those who were zealous for their holy faith, our ancient fathers have declared unto us as well by faithful words, as by the assured testimony of writings. But the aforesaid Bishop being vehemently desirous of increasing the beauty of his Church, and seeing that this little altar, though thus enlarged, was altogether unworthy of so great an Apostle, thought it worthy of pious consideration to aggrandize the Apostolical altar. Wherefore, being confirmed thereunto by the prudent counsel of religious men, although the Canons stoutly resisted him in this matter, he declared his determination to demolish the habitacle which was made in the likeness of the sepulchre below, in which sepulchre we learn, without all doubt, that the remains of the most holy Apostle are inclosed. They indeed repeatedly asserted that a work which, rude and deformed as it was, was nevertheless edified in honour to the remains of such holy personages, ought by no means to be destroyed, lest they themselves or their lord should be stricken with lightning from heaven, and suffer the immediate punishment of such audacity. But he, like a strenuous soldier, protected with the impenetrable shield of a good resolution, forasmuch as, with the eye of his penetration, he perceived that they regarded external things more than inner ones, trampled upon their fears with the foot of his right intention, and levelled to the ground their habitacle, and enlarged the altar, which had originally been so small a one, now for the third time, with marble placed over and about it on all sides, making it as it ought to be. Without delay also he marvellously began a silver frontispiece for this egregious and excellent work, and more marvellously completed it. »

There used to be interpreters at Compostella for all languages ; lenguageros they were called. They had a silver wand, with a hand and finger pointed at the top, to show the relics with. Among those relics is the head of St James the Less ; a grinder, in a splendid gold reliquary, of one St James, it has not been determined which ; one of St Christopher's arms, of modest dimensions ; and seven heads of the Eleven Thousand Virgins. These are from the list which Morales gives : but that good and learned man, who often swallowed the bull and stuck at the tail, omits some more curious ones, which are noticed in an authentic inventory. (*España Sagrada*, t. xix, p. 344.) Among these are part of our Lord's raiment, of the earth on which he stood, of the bread which he brake, of his blood, and of the Virgin's milk.

A late editor of Old Fortunatus is reminded in one of his notes of Martinus Scriblerus, by a passage in the play, which, as he should have seen, is evidently allusive to such relics as those at Compostella.

    —————— there can I show thee
The ball of gold that set all Troy on fire :
There shalt thou see the scarf of Cupid's mother,
Snatch'd from the soft moist ivory of her arm
To wrap about Adonis' wounded thigh :
There shalt thou see a wheel of Titan's car,
Which dropp'd from Heaven when Phæton fired the world.
I 'll give thee—the fan of Proserpine,
Which, in reward for a sweet Thracian song,
The black-brow'd Empress threw to Orpheus,
Being come to fetch Eurydice from hell.

Note 9, page 752, col. 2.

—All who in their mortal stage
Did not perform this pilgrimage,
Must make it when they were dead.

Huc Lysiæ properant urbes, huc gentes Iberæ
Turbæ adeunt, Gallique omnes, et Flandria cantu
Insignis, populique Itali, Rhenusque bicornis
Confluit, et donis altaria sacra frequentant ;
Namque ferant vivi qui non hæc templa patentes
Invisunt, post fata illuc, et faneris umbras
Venturos, munusque istud præstare beatis
Lacte viam stellisque albam, quæ nocte serenâ
Fulgurat, et longo designat tramite cœlum.
    P. Bartholome Pereira, *Paciecidos*, lib. vii, p. 117.

Fray Luys de Escobar has this among the five hundred proverbs of his Litany,

    —el camino á la muerte
    es como el de Santiago.
      Las quatrocientas, etc. ff. 140.

It seems to allude to this superstition, meaning, that it is a journey which all must take. The particular part

of the pilgrimage, which must be performed ei: ghost or in person, is that of crawling through a the rock at El Padron, which the Apostle is said t made with his staff. In allusion to this part of grimage, which is not deemed so indispensable at postella as at Padron, they have this proverb, *va á Santiago, y non va á Padron, ó faz Romeri* The pilgrim, indeed, must be incurious who w extend his journey thither ; a copious fountain, coldest and finest water which Morales tasted in G rises under the high altar, but on the outside church ; the pilgrims drink of it, and wash in its as the Apostle is said to have done : they ascend t! in the rock upon their knees, and finally perfo passage which must be made by all : « y cierto, derado el sitio, y la hermosa vista que de alli h ciudad, que estaba abaxo en lo llano, y á toda i: hoya llena de grandes arboledas y frescuras de ma: leguas en largo, lugar es aparejado para mucha placion.»—*Viage de Morales*, p. 174.

One of Pantagruel's *Questions Encyclopéd*. « Utrum le noir Scorpion pourroit souffrir so'u continuité en sa substance, et par l'effusion de obscurcir et embrunir la voye lactée, au grand et dommage des Lifrelofres Jacobipetes.»—Rab t ii, p. 417.

Note 10, page 752, col. 2.

The scallop-shell.

« The escallops, being denominated by an thors the *Shells of Gales*, or *Galicia*, plainly apply pilgrimage in particular.»—Fosbrooke, *British* chism, p. 423.

Fuller is therefore mistaken when speaking Dacres family (Church Hist. cent. xii, p. 42), wh their arms *gules*, three scallop-shells argent, he « which scallop-shells (I mean the nethermost of because most concave and capacious), smooth and artificially plated without, was oft times dish to the pilgrims in Palestine, and thereupo arms often charged therewith.»

That the scallop belonged exclusively to the C tella pilgrim is certain, as the following mir show.

« The ship, in which the body of the Apos embarked, passed swiftly by a village in Portuga Bouzas, wherein there dwelt a noble and powerfui who on that day married one of his daughters to th of another person as considerable as himself, lord land of Amaya. The nuptials were celebrated i village of Bouzas, and many noble knights of tha vince came to the solemnity. One of their spor that of throwing the cane, and in this the brid chose to bear a part, commanding a troop, that h display his dexterity. The place for the sport the coast of the ocean, and the bridegroom's hor coming ungovernable, plunged into the sea, an under the immensity of its waters, and, at the m when the ship was passing by, rose again close h There were several miracles in this case. The fi that the sea bore upon its waves the horse and man, as if it had been firm land, after not drowned them when they were so long a time water. The second was, that the wind, whic driving the ship full speed to its port, suddeni and left it motionless ; the third, and most rema

was, that both the garments of the knight, and the trap-
pings of the horse, came out of the sea covered with
scallop-shells.

« The knight, astonished at such an unexpected
adventure, and seeing the disciples of the Apostle, who
with equal astonishment were looking at him from the
ship, asked them what it was that had brought him
where he found himself. To which the disciples, being
inspired by heaven, replied, ' that certes Christ, through
the merit of a certain servant of his, whose body they
were transporting in that ship, had chosen to manifest
power upon him, for his good, by means of this
miracle.' The knight then humbly requested them to
tell him who Christ was, and who was that Servant of
of whom they spake, and what was the good which
was to derive. The disciples then briefly catechised
him; and the knight, having thus been instructed, said
them, ' Friends and Sirs, you, who have served Christ
his holy Apostle, which I as yet have not done, ask
of him to show you for what purpose he has put these
scallop-shells upon me, because so strange a marvel
must have been wrought without some great mystery.'
And that the disciples made their prayer accordingly,
and when they had prayed, they heard a voice from
heaven, which said thus unto the knight, ' Our Lord
God has thought good to show by this act all persons
at Rome, who may chuse to love and serve
his servant, and who shall go to visit him where he
is to be interred, that they take with them from thence
such scallop-shells as these with which thou art
adorned, as a seal of privilege, confirming that they are
and will be so from that time forward : and he pro-
that afterwards, in the Day of the Last Judgment,
shall be recognised of God for his; and that, because
honours which they have done to this his servant
and friend, in going to visit him and to venerate him,
receive them into his glory and his Paradise.'
When the knight heard these words, immediately
the disciples baptize him; and while they were
he noticed, with devotion and attention, the
ceremonies of the sacred ministry; and when it was done,
took his leave of them, commending himself to their
and intreating of them that they would commend
their prayers to Christ and his Apostle Santiago.
instant the wind, which till then had been still,
sails, and the ship began to cleave the wide
the knight then directed his course toward the
riding upon the water, in sight of the great mul-
which from the shore was watching him; and
he reached the shore, and was surrounded by
related to them what had happened. The
astonished at the sight of such stupendous
were converted, and the knight, with his own
baptized his bride. »

are thus related, to the letter, in the Sanctoral
from whence the Breviaries of Alcobaça and
copied it, and that of Oviedo in the Hymn
Apostle's Day,—from which authorities the mo-
taken it.—The Genealogists say that the
of Portugal are descended from this knight,
the scallop is called by that name in their
and that family bear it in their arms. The
make the same pretensions, and also bear
ps in their shield. The Ribadaneyras also
similar claim, and they bear a cross with five

« This is the origin of the shells with which the pilgrims,
who come to visit the body of our glorious Patron, adorn
themselves, the custom having, without doubt, been pre-
served by tradition from that time. The circumstances
are confirmed by pictures representing it, which from
ancient times have been preserved in various cities. In
the Church of St Maria de Araceli at Rome, on the
Gospel side, there is a spacious chapel, dedicated to our
glorious Patron ; it was painted in the year 1441, and in
one compartment this adventure is represented : there
is the ship, having the body of the Apostle on the poop,
and the seven Disciples on board : close to the ship,
upon the sea, is a Knight upon a black horse, with a red
saddle and trappings, both covered with scallop-shells.
The same story is painted in the parish church of San-
tiago at Madrid : and it is related in a very ancient
manuscript, which is preserved in the library of the
Monastery of St Juan de los Reyes, at Toledo. In the
Ancient Breviary of the Holy Church of Oviedo, mention
is made of this prodigy in these verses, upon the vesper
of the glorious Saint.

Cunctis mare cernentibus,
Sed a profundo ducitur,
Natus Regis submergitur
Totus plenus conchyllibus.

Finally, the fact is authenticated by their Holinesses
Alexander III, Gregory IX, and Clement V, who in
their Bulls grant a faculty to the Archbishop of Compos-
tella, that they may excommunicate those who sell these
shells to pilgrims anywhere except in the city of San-
tiago, and they assign this reason, because the shells are
the badge of the Apostle Santiago. And thus in the
Church of St Clement at Rome, which is enriched with
the body of St Clement, Pope and Martyr, is a picture of
the Apostle Santiago, apparently more than five hundred
years old, which is adorned with scallop-shells on the
garment and hat, as his proper badge. »—Añales de Ga-
licia, vol. i, pp. 95, 96.

Gwillim, in his account of this bearing, says nothing
of its origin. But he says « the Escallop (according to
Dioscorides) is engendered of the Dew and Air, and hath
no blood at all in itself, notwithstanding in man's
body of any other food it turneth soonest into blood.
The eating of this fish raw is said to cure a surfeit.
Such (he adds) is the beautiful shape that nature hath
bestowed upon this shell, as that the Collar of the Order
of St Michel in France, in the first institution thereof,
was richly garnished with certain pieces of gold artifi-
cially wrought, as near as the artificer could by imita-
tion express the stamp of nature. »—Display of Heraldry,
p. 171 (first edit.).

One of the three manners in which Santiago is com-
monly represented, is in the costume of a Compostellan
pilgrim, with a scallop-shell in his hat. All three, are
described in a book, as rare of occurrence as curious in
its subject, thus entitled, PICTOR CHRISTIANUS ERUDITUS:
« Sive, De Erroribus, qui passim admittuntur circa pin-
gendas atque effingendas Sacras Imagines. Libri Octo
cum Appendice. Opus Sacræ Scripturæ, atque Eccle-
siasticæ Historiæ studiosis non inutile. Authore R. P.
M. Fr. Joanne Interian de Ayala, Sacri, Regii ac Milita-
ris Ordinis Beatæ Mariæ de Mercede Redemptionis Cap-
tivorum, Salmanticensis Academiæ Doctore Theologo,
atque ibidem Sanctæ Theologiæ cum sacrarum Lingua-
rum interpretatione Professore jam pridem emerito.

Anno D. 1730, MATRITI: *Ex Typographia Conventus præfati Ordinis.* fol.»

One of the Censors of this book says, « Prodit in lucem *Pictor Christianus* eruditissimi pectoris eruditissimus fœtus, obstetricante N. RR. P. Mⁱ Fr. Josepho Campazano de la Vega.» The work was published by the Master's direction at the cost of the Order; the Master dedicated it to N. Señora de las Mercedes as *elaboratum excultumque quantum potuit,* by her assistance; and there is a *censura* prefixed by Ferreras the Historian, speaking forcibly of the importance of the undertaking, and of the great ability with which it is executed.

Instead of perceiving that Santiago is represented in the costume of his own pilgrims, this author supposed that the Saint is so attired because he had travelled over Spain! The whole passage is curious for its grave and cool credulity. « Sanctus Jacobus Zebedei filius, Hispaniæ primarius (quidquid alii commenti sint) Patronus atque Apostolus, bifariam sæpius a Pictoribus describitur. Pingitur enim peregrini habitu, oblongo innixus baculo, ex quo etiam bursa pendeat, et circa humeros amiculo, quod Hispani *Esclavinam* vocant; insuper et cum galero satis amplo, quem tamen ornant conchæ, quæ circa littus maris passim se offerunt : Totum id ex eo arbitror proficisci, quod Hispaniam celerrimè, et ut decebat Tonitru filium, peragraverat : ubi postmodum corpus ejus è Hierosolymis translatum condigno honore colitur. Sed ab aliis etiam cum gladio pingitur, cumque libro aperto. 'Quæ pictura (inquit frequens nobis auctor) etsi rarior sit, priori tamen est præferenda, quòd ex Sacrâ Scripturâ desumpta sit, et martyrium ejus explicet. Quod ita habetur, Occidit autem Jacobum fratrem Joannis gladio.'¹ Sæpè etiam pingitur equo insistens, armatusque gladio, acies Maurorum impigrè perrumpens, eosque ad internecionem usque cædens. Quod non exiguâ cum Hispani nominis gloriâ rectè fit ; cùm sæpè visus sit pro Hispanis in aëre pugnans ; *de cujus rei fide dubium esse non potest iis qui interfuerunt ejus Ecclesiastico officio,* ubi illud metricè habetur, .

    Tu bello càm nos cingerent,
    Es visus ipso in prælio,
    Equoque et ense acerrimus
    Mauros furentes sternere.

Atque idem alibi solutâ oratione describitur illis verbis :² ' Ipse etiam gloriosus Apostolus in difficillimis præliis palàm se conspiciendum præbens, Hispanos adversùs Infideles pugnantes mirificè juvit.'» — Lib. vii, c. 2, p. 320, 321.

Note 11, page 753, col. 1.
The Staff was bored and drill'd for those Who on a flute could play.

Sir John Hawkins says, « that the pilgrims to St James of Compostella excavated a staff, or walking stick, into a musical instrument for recreation on their journey.»—*History of Music*, vol. iv, p. 139, quoted in FOSBROOKE's *British Monachism*, p. 469. Mr Fosbrooke thinks that « this ascription of the invention of the *Bourdon* to these pilgrims in particular is very questionable.» Sir John probably supposed with Richelet that the *Bourdon* was peculiar to these pilgrims, and therefore that they had invented it.

Mr Fosbrooke more than doubts the Etymon from a musical use. « The barbarous Greek Βορδονια,» he ob-

serves, « signified a beast of burden, and the *L* was a staff of support. But the various meaning word, as given by Cotgrave, make out its histo factorily. *Bourdon,* a drone, or dorre-bee (Rich. grosse mouche, ennemie des abeilles), also the hu or buzzing of bees; also the drone of a bagpipe pilgrim's staff; also a walking-staff, having a sw within it.

« It was doubtless applied to the use of pitc note, or accompanying the songs with which : used to recreate themselves on their journeys, posed by Menestrier to be hymns and can FOSBROOKE, p. 422.

In Germany, « walking-sticks that serve as. pipes, with a compressing pump at one end t fire, and a machine at the other for impalir. without destroying their beauty, are commo. SKIN's *Travels,* vol. ii, p. 135.) I have seen a and a barometer in a walking-stick, if that n be applied to a staff of copper.

Note 12, page 754, col. 2.
The twice-born Cock and Hen.

There is another story of a bird among th of Santiago ; the poor subject of the miracle v fortunate as the Cock and Hen of the Alcayd story is true. It occurred in Italy ; *and* fable is not more characteristic of the frauduler tices carried on in the Romish Church, than the story is of the pitiable superstition which such fostered, and which was, and is to this day, enco by the dignitaries of that church.

At the request of St Atto, Bishop of Pistoja, tojans say that some relics, taken from Santiag precious head, were given to their church by th bishop of Compostella, Diego Gelmirez, a per known in Spanish history. « Nullus umquam mo hoc donum impetrare posset,» he affirmed v made the gift : and the historian of the transla « quod verè a Domino factum credimus et non mus, sicut manifestis et apertis indiciis manu apertè miracula declarabunt.» There is a good tion of these miracles, but this of the Bird is th remarkable.

« In those days,» says the writer, « another as pious as it is glorious, was wrought by the the which he who worthily perpends it will what may pertain to the edification of all those the shrine of Santiago, and of all faithful C. About three weeks after the consecration of San altar, a certain girl of the country near Pistoj plucking hemp in a garden, when she observed a flying through the air, which came near her. alighted : upon which she put up a prayer to th Santiago, saying, ' O Lord Santiago, if the thing are related of thee at Pistoja be true, and thou miracles as the Pistojans affirm, give me this that it may come into my hands!' Forthwith t geon rose from the spot where it had alighted, if it were a tame bird, came to her, and she to her hands, and held it there as if it had been li What then did the girl do? She carried it showed it to her father, and to him and the rest family related in what manner it had come to her ! Some of them said, ' let us kill it and eat it :' oth ' do not hurt it, but let it go.' So the girl open

---

¹ Molan. lib. iii, c. 26.
² In festo Translat. ejusdem. 30 Dec.

hand, to see what it would do. The pigeon, finding itself at liberty, flew to the ground, and joined the poultry which were then picking up their food, nor did it afterwards go from the house, but remained in their company as if it belonged to them.

« All therefore regarding, with no common wonder, the remarkable tameness of this pigeon, which indeed was not a tame bird but a wild one, they went to a priest in the adjacent city, and acquainted him with the circumstances. The priest, giving good counsel to the girl and her father, as he was bound to do, said, ' we will go together to our Lord the Bishop on Sunday, and act as he may think proper to direct us in this matter.' Accordingly on the Sunday they went to Pistoja, and presented the pigeon to the Bishop, who with his Canons was then devoutly celebrating mass in honour of Santiago, upon the holy altar which had been consecrated to his honour. The Prelate, when he had listened to their story, took the bird, and placed it upon the wall of the chancel, which is round about the altar of Santiago, and there it remained three weeks, never departing from thence, excepting that sometimes, and that very seldom, it flew about the church, but always returned without delay to its own station, and there mildly, gently, harmlessly, and tamely continued; and rarely did it take food.

« But people from Lucca, and other strangers, plucked feathers from its neck, that they might carry them away for devotion, and moreover, that they might exhibit them to those who had not seen the bird itself. From such injuries it never attempted to defend itself, though its neck was skinned by this plucking, and this the unthinking people continued to do, till at length the pigeon paid the debt of nature. And it was no wonder that it died; for how could any creature live that scarcely ever ate or slept? People came thither night and day from all parts, and one after another disturbed it; and every night vigils were kept there, the clergy and the people with loud voices singing praises to the Lord, and many lights were continually burning there : how, therefore, could it live, when it was never allowed to be at rest? The clergy and people grieving at its death, as indeed it was a thing to be lamented, took counsel, and hung up the skin and feathers to be seen there by all comers.

« In such and so great a matter what could be more gratifying, what more convenient than this wonderful sign which the Almighty was pleased to give us? There is no need to relate anything more concerning the aforesaid pigeon; it was seen there openly and publicly by all comers, so that not only the laity and clergy of that city, but many religious people from other parts, abbots, friars, clergy, and laity, are able to attest the truth. And I also add this my testimony as a true and faithful witness, for I saw the pigeon myself for a whole week, and actually touched it with my own hands. »

There is a postscript to this story, as melancholy as the tale itself. The sick, and the crippled, and the lame, had been brought to this church, in expectation of obtaining a miraculous cure by virtue of the new relics which had arrived. Among these was a poor woman in the last stage of disease, who had been brought upon her pallet into the church, and was laid in a corner, and left there ; nor was it observed that this poor creature was in *articulo mortis*, till the pigeon flew to the place, and alighted upon her, and so drew the attention of the people in the church to the dying woman, *quam quidem, prout credimus, nisi columba monstrasset, nemo morientem vidisset.* They removed her out of the church just before she breathed her last,—and in consequence of this miracle, as it was deemed, they gave her an honourable funeral.—*Acta Sanctorum,* Jul. t. vi, p. 64.

Note 13, page 755, col. 1.

What became of the halter I know not,
Because the old books show not.

Antiguedad sagrada, el que se arriedra
De te, sera su verso falto y manco.

So Christoval de Mesa observes when he proceeds to relate how the rude stone, upon which the disciples of Santiago laid his body when they landed with it in Spain, formed itself into a sepulchre of white marble.—*El Patron de España,* ff. 68.

THE END.

Lightning Source UK Ltd.
Milton Keynes UK
UKHW050923010422
400950UK00006B/369